ARCHITECTURAL GRAPHIC STANDARDS

JOHN WILEY & SONS: Project Direction: Wm. Dudley Hunt, Jr., FAIA, Architecture Editor.
Production Direction: Robert J. Fletcher, IV, General Manager of Production.
Illustration Reproduction Direction: Jeramiah McCarthy, Manager, Illustration Department.
Copy Editing: Valda Aldzeris, Editorial Manager.
Design Coordination: Aline Walton, Senior Designer.
Production Assistant: Lilian Brady.

THE AMERICAN INSTITUTE OF ARCHITECTS: John R. Hoke, Jr., AIA, Assistant Editor.
William G. Miner, AIA, Technical Editor.

JOHN WILEY & SONS

THE AMERICAN INSTITUTE OF ARCHITECTS

RAMSEY/SLEEPER

ARCHITECTURAL GRAPHIC STANDARDS

SEVENTH EDITION

ROBERT T. PACKARD, AIA

EDITOR

NEW YORK CHICHESTER BRISBANE TORONTO

The drawings, tables, data, and other information in this book have been obtained from many sources, including government organizations, trade associations, suppliers of building materials, and professional architects or architectural firms. The American Institute of Architects (AIA), the Architectural Graphic Standards Committee of the AIA, and the publisher have made every reasonable effort to make this reference work accurate and authoritative, but do not warrant, and assume no liability for, the accuracy or completeness of the text or its fitness for any particular purpose. It is the responsibility of users to apply their professional knowledge in the use of information contained in this book, to consult the original sources for additional information when appropriate, and, if they themselves are not professional architects, to consult an architect when appropriate.

Library of Congress Cataloging in Publication Data:

American Institute of Architects.
    Architectural graphic standards.

    "A Wiley-Interscience publication."
    First five editions by the late Charles G. Ramsey and Harold R. Sleeper.
    Includes index.
    1. Building—Details—Drawings. I. Packard, Robert T. II. Ramsey, Charles George, 1884-1963. Architectural graphic standards. III. Title.

TH2031.A48   1980   721'.022'3   80-18151
ISBN 0-471-04683-3

Printed in the United States of America

10 9 8 7 6 5 4 3 2

PUBLISHERS NOTE

In the fall of 1932, the lowest point of the Great Depression, I joined the House of Wiley and soon learned that there had been published in May a promising new book. Martin Matheson, then Manager of Marketing, had persuaded Charles George Ramsey, AIA, author of an earlier Wiley textbook, and his younger colleague, Harold Reeve Sleeper, FAIA, to develop their ideas and prepare the plates for what became *Architectural Graphic Standards*. Subsequently, Matheson directed the design and layout of the book and personally oversaw its production and manufacture.

The immediate acceptance and success of *Architectural Graphic Standards* extended far beyond its anticipated audience of architects, builders, draftsmen, engineers, and students. Interior designers, real estate agents and brokers, homeowners, insurance underwriters, and lovers of fine books are all among its known users and admirers.

Soon after the publication of *Architectural Graphic Standards* suggestions and requests came from many enthusiastic readers, which called for changes and additions. Inevitably, the decision was made to publish a second edition which was almost 25 percent larger. It appeared in 1936, a short time after the first. Recovery from the Great Depression had begun when the second edition came out, and the demand for *Architectural Graphic Standards* increased. To serve its users' growing needs work soon began on a third edition which, when published in 1941, was almost twice as large as the original edition.

World War II lengthened the interval between editions; the fourth edition prepared by Sleeper appeared in 1951 and had grown to 614 pages; the fifth edition, Sleeper's last revision with 758 pages, was issued in 1956. The co-authors' achievement for a decade, followed by that of Sleeper, provided untold thousands of users with an invaluable resource for almost 40 years.

Harold Sleeper's foresight led to his suggestion, heartily supported by John Wiley & Sons, that the American Institute of Architects sponsor the sixth and subsequent editions. The first AIA revision, which became the sixth edition, was successfully brought to publication in 1970 by the extraordinary leadership of Harold D. Hauf, FAIA, Chairman of the Editorial Advisory Committee, the skill of Joseph N. Boaz, AIA, Editor, and the guidance of Walker G. Stone, Vice President of John Wiley & Sons, as Project Director and Technical Editor.

The foreword to this seventh edition, by William Dudley Hunt, Jr., FAIA, and the preface by Robert T. Packard, AIA, are most informative and are commended to all users, new and old. John Wiley & Sons takes pride in the part its officers and staff have played in the enduring success of *Architectural Graphic Standards* and in the association with the American Institute of Architects. Architects and the construction industry will continue to be well served by the seventh edition.

W. BRADFORD WILEY
Chairman
John Wiley & Sons, Inc.

FOREWORD

In the nearly 50 years since its first edition *Architectural Graphic Standards* has become firmly established as the most essential single reference for the building industry. Generations of architects, engineers, landscape architects, interior designers, and contractors, as well as people engaged in design, drafting, specification writing, construction administration, and other phases of building, have kept copies of the book in almost continuous use in their offices and drafting rooms.

Great numbers of students, in these and other disciplines, acquired much of their knowledge from the pages of this book and have kept it close at hand after graduation. Others not so directly involved in the building industry have found its pages filled with information they can use.

This seventh edition carries on the traditions. It is organized, generally, according to the principles of the Uniform Construction Index. Within the pages of the new edition can be found the most basic, useful, current, and proved information required for the increasingly complex design and technology of architecture and building construction today. The fundamental emphasis remains on the graphic presentation of this information. In such characteristics, as well as in its format, the seventh edition resembles the sixth, but there are major differences.

It became evident to all who worked on the new edition that extensive changes have occurred since the sixth was published 10 years ago. Although the number of pages has increased only 13 percent, changing practices, technology, and concerns have led to approximately 70 percent new material in the seventh edition.

The new edition places increased emphasis on important current and future concerns, such as proper use and conservation of energy, design for the handicapped, environmental protection, engineering, anthropometric data, and the metric system (SI), which is the subject of a new chapter. In all, there are three new chapters, the two combined chapters of the preceding edition, Specialties and Equipment and Mechanical and Electrical, have been divided and expanded. Greatly enlarged lists of data sources and index are provided.

In a very real sense the new edition is the result not only of close collaboration of the American Institute of Architects with John Wiley & Sons, Inc. but of the entire architectural profession and the building industry. Hundreds of architects, engineers, and other professionals and experts, in practice and in governmental agencies, industry associations, and other organizations, contributed to the book. Their involvement has assured its relevance and reliability.

Of equal importance was the deep involvement and dedication of the members of the AIA *Architectural Graphic Standards* Committee, who devoted their time, knowledge, and talents to retaining or deleting data, adding the new and locating important new sources, attracting expert consultants, preparing drawings and other kinds of information, and reviewing the content at every step, from inception to final pages.

In the preparation of the seventh edition books, standards, regulations, catalogs, and other data were assembled into a sizable library. All information that went into the book was researched and verified by the use of these data, further researched and verified by the professionals and other experts consulted, and finally approved for inclusion in the book by the AIA Committee members, the AIA editorial staff, and the Wiley staff.

The person with overall responsibility for research, data gathering, page preparation, and reviews was Editor Robert T. Packard, AIA. And his was the basic overall plan and organization of the book and its individual pages. His total involvement, talent, perseverance, method, and attention to detail, as well those of his staff, were essential.

The seventh edition of *Architectural Graphic Standards* will continue to provide the value and usefulness the book had had for so many years for so many people.

WILLIAM DUDLEY HUNT, Jr., FAIA
Architecture Editor
John Wiley & Sons, Inc.

PREFACE

The seventh edition of *Architectural Graphic Standards* is the second edition prepared by the American Institute of Architects. Published 49 years after the first edition, it carries on the work of the originating authors, Charles George Ramsey, AIA, and Harold Reeve Sleeper, FAIA. Their major contribution to the architectural profession in the first five sequentially updated editions established the book as the most widely recognized handbook reference in the construction industry. Sleeper expressed the hope that on his death the American Institute of Architects would assume his editorial responsibilities for updating the book. In 1964 John Wiley & Sons and the Institute entered into an agreement for this purpose. The sixth edition, published in 1970, was the first result of this agreement, and the present edition represents further development of this essential reference book.

Wiley representation on this project is centered on the staff of the Professional Group, John Wiley & Sons, headed by Michael Harris, Vice President and General Manager, and Robert B. Polhemus, Vice President. As had been true for many years, Walker G. Stone represented John Wiley's interest in the project during the early planning of the seventh edition. After Stone's retirement in 1976, Wiley named William Dudley Hunt, Jr., FAIA, as Wiley's editor for the Architectural Graphic Standards project. During the development of the seventh edition an excellent working relationship has been enjoyed between the Wiley staff and the AIA. Dudley Hunt's encouragement, guidance, and counsel was continuously supportive of the AIA staff effort. The book could not have been completed without the full cooperation of the Wiley production staff. Robert J. Fletcher, Manager of Production, has ably steered the project to completion with the skilled assistance of Jeramiah McCarthy in the graphic production and Valda Aldzeris whose careful copy editing helped pull the book together.

When, in 1976, the AIA Board approved preparation of a new edition, the AIA undertook a search for an editor for the new edition. William L. Slayton, Hon. AIA, Executive Vice President of the AIA until 1978, assigned the project to the Practice Department then headed by Edward G. Petrazio,

FAIA. The Architectural Graphic Standards Task Force was named, and Robert T. Packard, AIA, named Editor by mid-1976. In the ensuing period the project was moved to the new AIA Department of Practice and Design administered by Michael B. Barker, AICP, reporting to the AIA Board Commission in this area and to Group Executive James A. Scheeler, FAIA. Continued enthusiastic support from David Olan Meeker, Jr., FAIA, Executive Vice President of the AIA since 1978, has provided excellent encouragement for completion of the project.

During the four-year preparation the AIA Presidents and Chairmen of the Commission on Practice and Design have monitored the development of the project. Listed below are those whose continued support has been essential to timely completion of the book:

Year	Presidents of AIA	Chairmen of Commission on Practice and Design
1976	Louis DeMoll, FAIA	Donald J. Stephens, FAIA
1977	John M. McGinty, FAIA	Adolph R. Scrimenti, FAIA
1978	Elmer E. Botsai, FAIA	Frank R. Mudano, FAIA
1979	Ehrman B. Mitchell, Jr., FAIA	Thomas H. Teasdale, FAIA
1980	Charles E. Schwing, FAIA	Donald L. Hardison, FAIA

The AIA Committee on Architectural Graphic Standards was reestablished to oversee the administration of the new edition, and its membership was constituted so as to combine the required continuity from previous editions, fresh insights of those not previously involved, and the interdisciplinary participation of representatives of other design professions. Elliott Carroll, FAIA, Assistant to the Architect of the Capitol who had, as AIA Deputy Executive Vice President, acted as Project Director for the sixth edition, has been its effective Chairman. The Committee organized an Editorial Review Board headed by Joseph A. Wilkes, FAIA, of Wilkes and Faulkner, Washington, D.C. Joseph A. Wilkes' long hours of voluntary service were a major contribution to the profession. Members included several persons who performed similar functions for the sixth edition, including Bernard B. Rothschild, FAIA, of FABRAP, Atlanta, Georgia, and Robert E. Walters, AIA, of CRS, Houston, Texas. Victor C. Gilbertson, FAIA, of Hills/Gilbertson/Fisher, Inc., Minneapolis, Minnesota, closely identified with the sixth edition, was also named to the new committee, as was William H. Scheick, FAIA, former AIA Executive Director who gave his good advice during 1976 and 1977.

Other members of the expanded committee include Jean Paul Carlhian, FAIA, of Shepley, Bulfinch, Richardson and Abbot, Boston, Massachusetts, Richard K. Dee, ASLA, Johnson and Dee of Avon, Connecticut, Porter Driscoll, AIA, of the National Bureau of Standards, Robert E. Fehlberg, FAIA, of CTA Architects-Engineers, Billings, Montana, Ian Grad, PE of Syska & Hennessey, New York, P. Richard Rittlemann, AIA of Burt, Hill, Kosar, Rittlemann Associates, Butler, Pennsylvania, and Adolph R. Scrimenti, FAIA of Scrimenti/Shriver/Spinelli/Peratoni Architects, Somerville, New Jersey.

Editorial offices were established at AIA Headquarters. To aid in the determination of the content of the new edition, Wiley conducted an extensive survey confirming the wide-ranging interests of the users of *Architectural Graphic Standards*. A detailed outline was developed and procedures established for acquiring drawings for what has become a 70 percent new edition. As work proceeded, AIA staff was enlarged with the joint support of Wiley and AIA. The editor, assistant editor John R. Hoke, Jr., AIA, and technical editor William G. Miner, AIA, have been augmented by a number of secretaries and draftspersons. Particular thanks should go to Lou Ellen Utermohle, who has worked on the project since its earliest days and has contributed so much to the smooth running of the project.

It has been the design professional offices that have prepared the bulk of material. The high quality contribution of the more than 140 professional firms (up from 100 firms participating in the sixth edition) involved indicates the scope of interest and involvement in this national cooperative venture. In addition, substantial contributions have been made by trade and professional associations and government agencies. The Center for Building Technology and the Solar Energy Research Institute have been particularly helpful. The increase in building technology and engineering, as well as renewed interest in energy efficient systems, has prompted some expansion of the book. Other areas of added material include more data on the design basis of regulations, as in seismic design, design for the handicapped, fire safety considerations, and energy conservation. A separate chapter has been added to introduce metric conversion concepts. The book has been expanded from 14 chapters to 17.

Firms that offered to assist in the work were provided with detailed instructions and were asked to submit rough pencil sketches for review before preparing final manuscript and pencil drawings. These in turn were processed and approved for preparation of inked drawings and typesetting by the publisher. This effort was supplemented by illustrators and the editorial staff in Washington. This time-consuming process is what gives *Architectural Graphic Standards* its far-reaching authoritative character.

Care has been taken to refer the readers of *Architectural Graphic Standards* to other sources for additional and current data. This book is a compilation of material available at the time of preparation and is a general guide to construction technology. Resources of the AIA Library have been most helpful to the editorial staff, as well as to the many publications generally available to the construction industry.

The members of the AIA editorial staff have enjoyed their part in the process. Our thanks to the architects, engineers, and other professionals who are the real authors of this book.

ROBERT T. PACKARD, AIA
Editor

CONTENTS

ARCHITECTURAL GRAPHIC STANDARDS

CHAPTER 1 GENERAL PLANNING AND DESIGN DATA

INTRODUCTION TO ANTHROPOMETRIC DATA

The following anthropometric drawings show three values for each measurement: the top figure is for the large person or 97.5 percentile; the middle figure, the average person or 50 percentile; and the lower figure, the small person or 2.5 percentile. The chosen extreme percentiles thus include 95%. The remaining 5% include some who learn to adapt and others, not adequately represented, who are excluded to keep designs for the majority from becoming too complex and expensive. Space and access charts are designed to accept the 97.5 percentile large man and will cover all adults except a few giants. Therefore, use the 97.5 percentile to determine space envelopes, the 2.5 percentile to determine the maximum "kinetospheres" or reach areas by hand or foot, and the 50 percentile to establish control and display heights. To accommodate both men and women, it is useful at times to add a dimension of the large man to the corresponding dimension of the small woman and divide by 2 to obtain data for the average adult. This is the way height standards evolve. Youth data are for combined sex. Although girls and boys do not grow at the same rate, differences are small when compared with size variations.

Pivot point and link systems make it easy to construct articulating templates and manikins. Links are simplified bones. The spine is shown as a single link; since it can flex, pivot points may be added. All human joints are not simple pivots, though it is convenient to assume so. Some move in complicated patterns like the roving shoulder. Reaches shown are easy and comfortable; additional reach is possible by bending and rotating the trunk and by extending the shoulder. Stooping to reach low is better than stretching to reach high. The dynamic body may need 10% more space than the static posture allows. Shoes have been included in all measurements; allowance may need to be made for heavy clothing. Sight lines and angles of vision given in one place or another apply to all persons.

The metric system of measurement has been included, since it is used in scientific work everywhere and is the most practical system of measurement ever devised. Millimeters have been chosen to avoid use of decimals. Rounding to 5 mm aids mental retention while being within the tolerance of most human measurements.

Disabilities are to be reckoned as follows: 3.5% of men and 0.2% of women are color blind; 4.5% of adults are hard of hearing; over 30% wear glasses; 15 to 20% are handicapped, and 1% are illiterate. Left-handed people have increased in number to more than 10%.

SAFETY INFORMATION

Maximum safe temperature of metal handles is 50°C (122°F) and of nonmetallic handles, 62°C (144°F); maximum air temperature for warm air hand dryers is 60°C (140°F); water temperatures over 46.1°C (115°F) are destructive to human tissue. Environmental temperature range is 17.2 to 23.9°C (63 to 75°F). Weights lifted without discomfort or excessive strain are 22.7 kg (50 lb) for 90% of men and 15.9 kg (35 lb) for women; limit weight to 9.07 kg (20 lb) if carried by one hand for long distances. Push and pull forces, like moving carts, are 258 N (58 lbf) and 236 N (53 lbf) initially, but 129 N (29.1 lbf) and 142 N (32 lbf) if sustained. Noise above the following values can cause permanent deafness: 90 dB for 8 hr, 95 dB for 4 hr, 100 dB for 2 hr, 105 dB for 1 hr, and 110 dB for 0.5 hr.

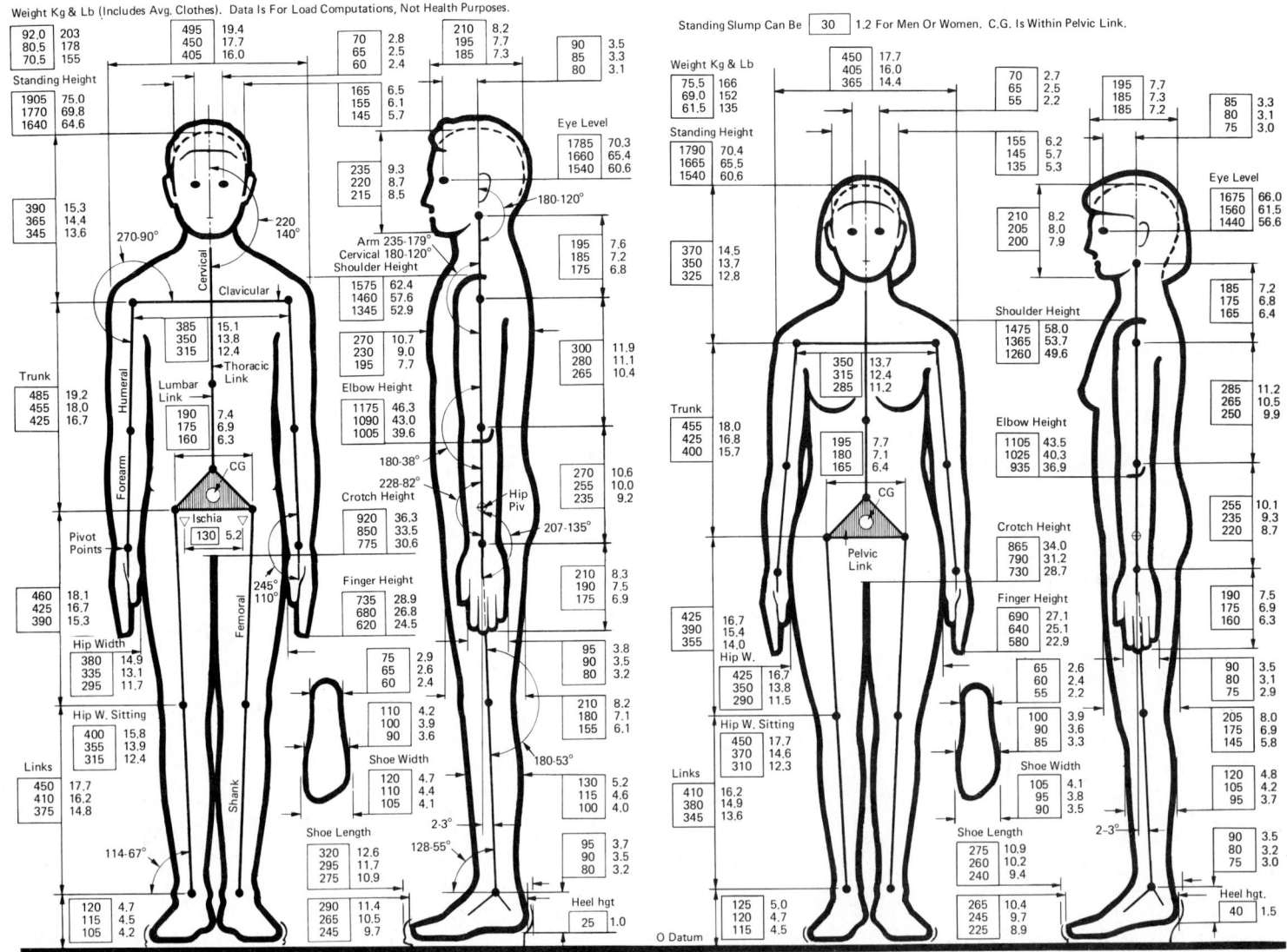

Weight Kg & Lb (Includes Avg. Clothes). Data Is For Load Computations, Not Health Purposes.

Standing Slump Can Be 30 1.2 For Men Or Women. C.G. Is Within Pelvic Link.

Male and	female standing heights (including shoes):		
1905 75.0	1790 70.4 large = 97.5 percentile	includes
1775 69.8	1665 65.5 average = 50 percentile	95% U.S.
1640 64.6	1540 60.6 small = 2.5 percentile	adults.

Niels Diffrient, Alvin R. Tilley; Henry Dreyfuss Associates; New York, New York

Dimensional notation system:

1000	39.3	Numbers appearing in boxes are measurements
100	3.9	in millimeters. Numbers outside boxes are
25.4	1.0	measurements in inches.

1

DESIGN ELEMENTS

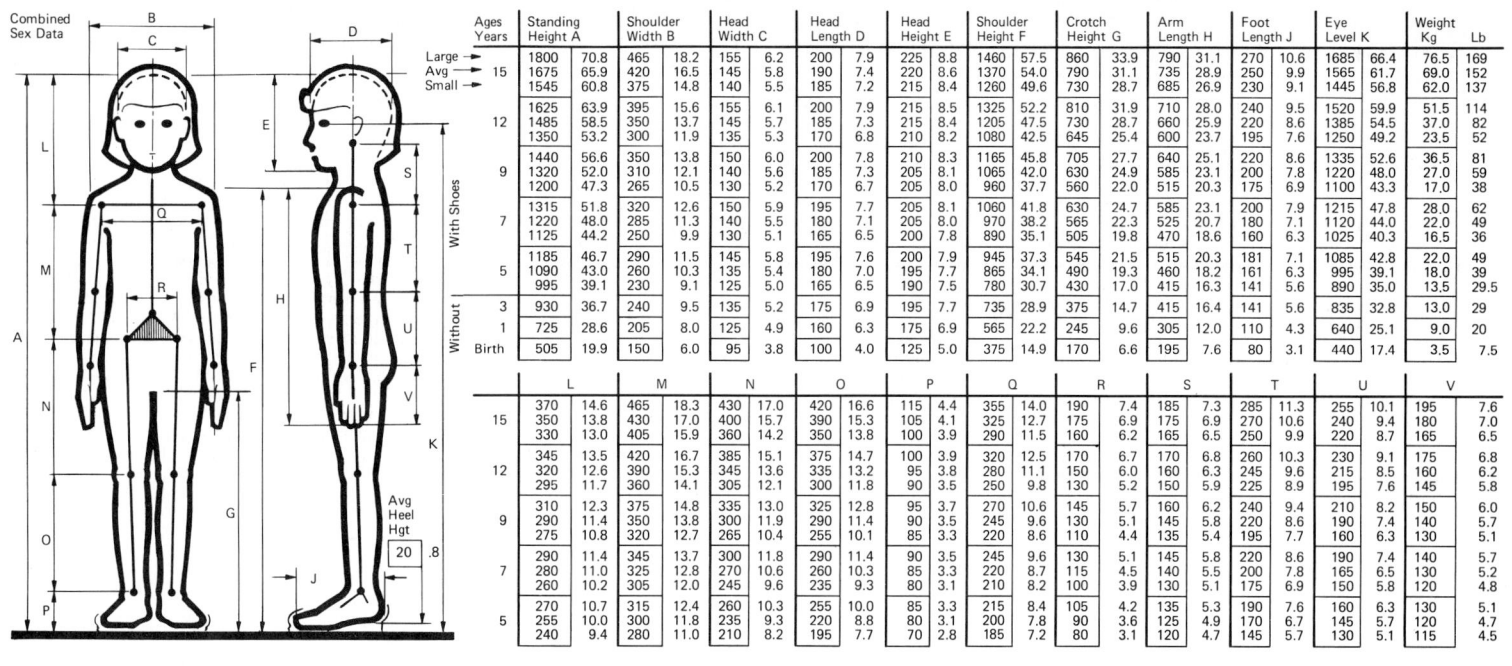

Combined Sex Data

Ages Years		Standing Height A		Shoulder Width B		Head Width C		Head Length D		Head Height E		Shoulder Height F		Crotch Height G		Arm Length H		Foot Length J		Eye Level K		Weight Kg	Lb
Large →	15	1800	70.8	465	18.2	155	6.2	200	7.9	225	8.8	1460	57.5	860	33.9	790	31.1	270	10.6	1685	66.4	76.5	169
Avg →		1675	65.9	420	16.5	145	5.8	190	7.4	220	8.6	1370	54.0	790	31.1	735	28.9	250	9.9	1565	61.7	69.0	152
Small →		1545	60.8	375	14.8	140	5.5	185	7.2	215	8.4	1260	49.6	730	28.7	685	26.9	230	9.1	1445	56.8	62.0	137
	12	1625	63.9	395	15.6	155	6.1	200	7.9	215	8.5	1325	52.2	810	31.9	710	28.0	240	9.5	1520	59.9	51.5	114
		1485	58.5	350	13.7	145	5.7	185	7.3	215	8.4	1205	47.5	730	28.7	660	25.9	220	8.6	1385	54.5	37.0	82
		1350	53.2	300	11.9	135	5.3	170	6.8	210	8.2	1080	42.5	645	25.4	600	23.7	195	7.6	1250	49.2	23.5	52
With Shoes	9	1440	56.6	350	13.8	150	6.0	200	7.8	210	8.3	1165	45.8	705	27.7	640	25.1	220	8.6	1335	52.6	36.5	81
		1320	52.0	310	12.1	140	5.6	185	7.3	205	8.1	1065	42.0	630	24.9	585	23.1	200	7.8	1220	48.0	27.0	59
		1200	47.3	265	10.5	130	5.2	170	6.7	205	8.0	960	37.7	560	22.0	515	20.3	175	6.9	1100	43.3	17.0	38
	7	1315	51.8	320	12.6	150	5.9	200	7.7	205	8.1	1060	41.8	630	24.7	585	23.1	200	7.9	1215	47.8	28.0	62
		1220	48.0	285	11.3	140	5.5	180	7.1	205	8.0	970	38.2	565	22.3	525	20.7	180	7.1	1120	44.0	22.0	49
		1125	44.2	250	9.9	130	5.1	165	6.5	200	7.8	890	35.1	505	19.8	470	18.6	160	6.3	1025	40.3	16.5	36
	5	1185	46.7	290	11.5	145	5.8	195	7.6	200	7.9	945	37.3	545	21.5	515	20.3	181	7.1	1085	42.8	22.0	49
		1090	43.0	260	10.3	135	5.4	180	7.0	195	7.7	865	34.1	490	19.3	460	18.2	161	6.3	995	39.1	18.0	39
Without		995	39.1	230	9.1	125	5.0	165	6.5	190	7.5	780	30.7	430	17.0	415	16.3	141	5.6	890	35.0	13.5	29.5
	3	930	36.7	240	9.5	135	5.2	175	6.9	195	7.7	735	28.9	375	14.7	415	16.4	141	5.6	835	32.8	13.0	29
	1	725	28.6	205	8.0	125	4.9	160	6.3	175	6.9	565	22.2	245	9.6	305	12.0	110	4.3	640	25.1	9.0	20
	Birth	505	19.9	150	6.0	95	3.8	100	4.0	125	5.0	375	14.9	170	6.6	195	7.6	80	3.1	440	17.4	3.5	7.5

	L		M		N		O		P		Q		R		S		T		U		V	
15	370	14.6	465	18.3	430	17.0	420	16.6	115	4.4	355	14.0	190	7.4	185	7.3	285	11.3	255	10.1	195	7.6
	350	13.8	430	17.0	400	15.7	390	15.3	105	4.1	325	12.7	175	6.9	175	6.9	270	10.6	240	9.4	180	7.0
	330	13.0	405	15.9	360	14.2	350	13.8	100	3.9	290	11.5	160	6.2	165	6.5	250	9.9	220	8.7	165	6.5
12	345	13.5	420	16.7	385	15.1	375	14.7	100	3.9	320	12.5	170	6.7	170	6.8	260	10.3	230	9.1	175	6.8
	320	12.6	390	15.3	345	13.6	335	13.2	95	3.8	280	11.1	150	6.0	160	6.3	245	9.6	215	8.5	160	6.2
	295	11.7	360	14.1	305	12.1	300	11.8	90	3.5	250	9.8	130	5.2	150	5.9	225	8.9	195	7.6	145	5.8
9	310	12.3	375	14.8	335	13.0	325	12.8	95	3.7	270	10.6	145	5.7	160	6.2	240	9.4	210	8.2	150	6.0
	290	11.4	350	13.8	300	11.9	290	11.4	90	3.5	245	9.6	130	5.1	145	5.8	220	8.6	190	7.4	140	5.7
	275	10.8	320	12.7	265	10.4	255	10.1	85	3.3	220	8.6	110	4.4	135	5.4	195	7.7	160	6.3	130	5.1
7	290	11.4	345	13.7	300	11.8	290	11.4	90	3.5	245	9.6	130	5.1	145	5.8	220	8.6	190	7.4	140	5.7
	280	11.0	325	12.8	270	10.6	260	10.3	85	3.3	220	8.7	115	4.5	140	5.5	200	7.8	165	6.5	130	5.2
	260	10.2	305	12.0	245	9.6	235	9.3	80	3.1	210	8.2	100	3.9	130	5.1	175	6.9	150	5.8	120	4.8
5	270	10.7	315	12.4	260	10.3	255	10.0	85	3.3	215	8.4	105	4.2	135	5.3	190	7.6	160	6.3	130	5.1
	255	10.0	300	11.8	235	9.3	220	8.8	80	3.1	200	7.8	90	3.6	125	4.9	170	6.7	145	5.7	120	4.7
	240	9.4	280	11.0	210	8.2	195	7.7	70	2.8	185	7.2	80	3.1	120	4.7	145	5.7	130	5.1	115	4.5

	Ages	High Reach A		Low Reach B		Reach Distance C		High Reach D		Reach Radius E		Eye Level F	
HS	15	2085	82.0	815	32.0	735	29.0	1440	56.7	660	25.9	1215	47.8
		1915	75.3	730	28.7	685	27.0	1375	54.1	610	24.1	1160	45.6
		1765	69.4	665	26.2	635	25.1	1315	51.7	570	22.4	1100	43.3
Jr. HS	12	1860	73.2	705	27.6	665	26.2	1320	52.0	600	23.6	1100	43.3
		1705	67.1	630	24.7	620	24.3	1250	49.2	555	21.9	1040	41.0
		1545	60.9	560	22.1	565	22.3	1185	46.6	510	20.1	990	38.9
4th.	9	1645	64.8	605	23.8	600	23.6	1175	46.3	540	21.2	975	38.4
		1510	59.4	555	21.8	550	21.7	1120	44.0	495	19.5	925	36.5
		1345	53.0	510	20.0	485	19.1	1040	40.9	435	17.1	880	34.6
2nd.	7	1505	59.3	545	21.5	550	21.7	1080	42.6	500	19.6	890	35.0
		1370	53.9	510	20.1	495	19.5	1015	40.0	445	17.5	850	33.5
		1245	49.0	485	19.0	445	17.5	960	37.7	395	15.6	815	32.0
KDG	5	1330	52.3	500	19.7	480	19.0	970	38.1	430	16.9	815	32.1
		1210	47.7	465	18.3	435	17.1	915	36.1	385	15.2	770	30.4
		1085	42.7	425	16.7	390	15.3	865	34.1	345	13.6	720	28.4

↑ Starting School Grades

Up To Ages	Hat Shelf Height G		Lavatory Height H		Work Top J		Work Depth K		Table Height L		Seat Length M	
15	1675	66.0	760	30.0	915	36.0	460	18.0	650	25.5	370	14.6
12	1485	58.5	685	27.0	795	31.3	420	16.5	590	23.3	340	13.3
9	1320	52.0	635	25.0	695	27.3	380	15.0	525	20.7	300	11.8
7	1220	48.0	585	23.0	635	25.0	355	14.0	480	18.9	275	10.8
5	1090	43.0	485	19.0	570	22.5	330	13.0	445	17.5	250	9.9

Ages	Seat Height N		Seat To Backrest O		Min Backrest Height P		Armrest Spacing Q		Seat Width R		Basic Table Width S	
15	405	15.9	150	6.0	175	6.8	445	17.5	380	15.0	760	30.0
12	370	14.6	145	5.7	160	6.2	420	16.5	370	14.5	710	28.0
9	325	12.8	135	5.4	140	5.6	355	14.0	330	13.0	610	24.0
7	290	11.4	130	5.1	130	5.1	330	13.0	305	12.0	610	24.0
5	265	10.4	120	4.8	125	5.0	305	12.0	280	11.0	535	21.0

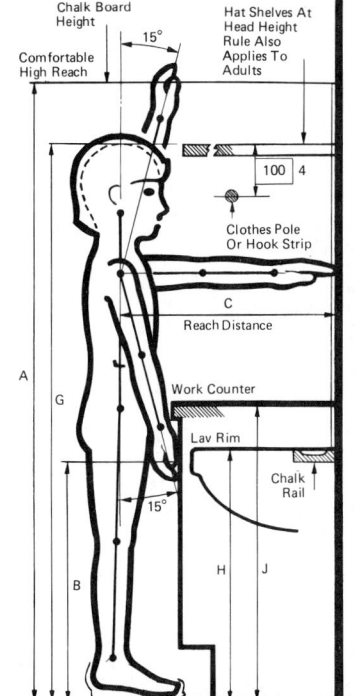

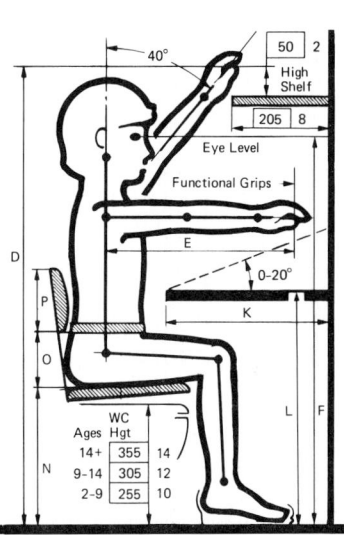

WC Ages	Hgt	
14+	355	14
9-14	305	12
2-9	255	10

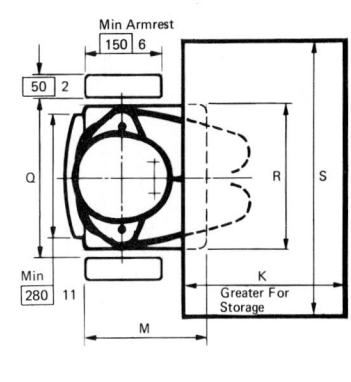

Standing heights (including shoes)—typical example:

1800	70.8 large 15 year youth = 97.5 percentile	} combined
1675	65.9 average 15 year youth = 50 percentile	} sex data
1545	60.8 small 15 year youth = 2.5 percentile	} U.S. youths

Niels Diffrient, Alvin R. Tilley; Henry Dreyfuss Associates; New York, New York

Dimensional notation system:

1000	39.3	Numbers appearing in boxes are measurements
100	3.9	in millimeters. Numbers outside boxes are
25.4	1.0	measurements in inches.

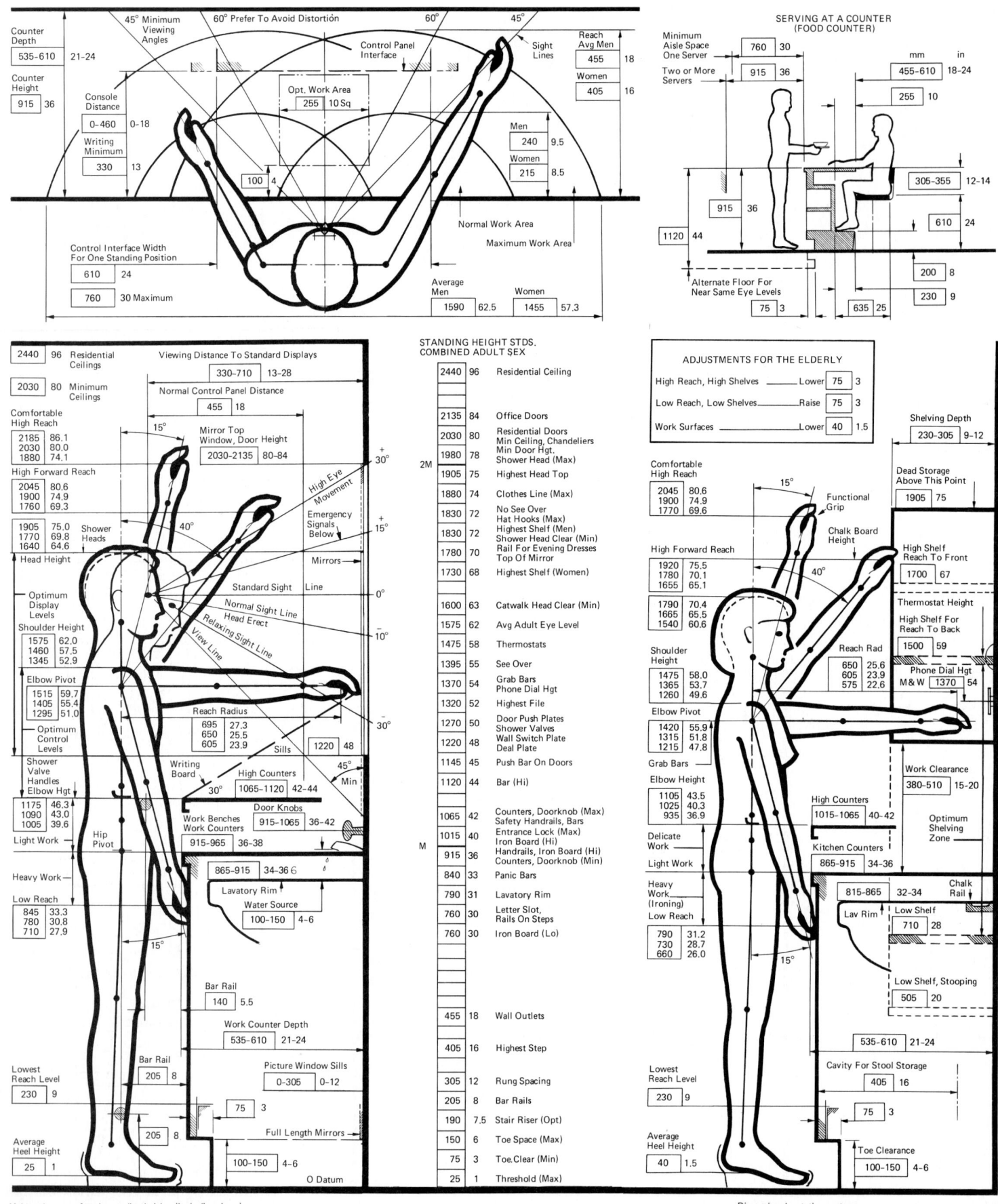

Niels Diffrient, Alvin R. Tilley; Henry Dreyfuss Associates; New York, New York

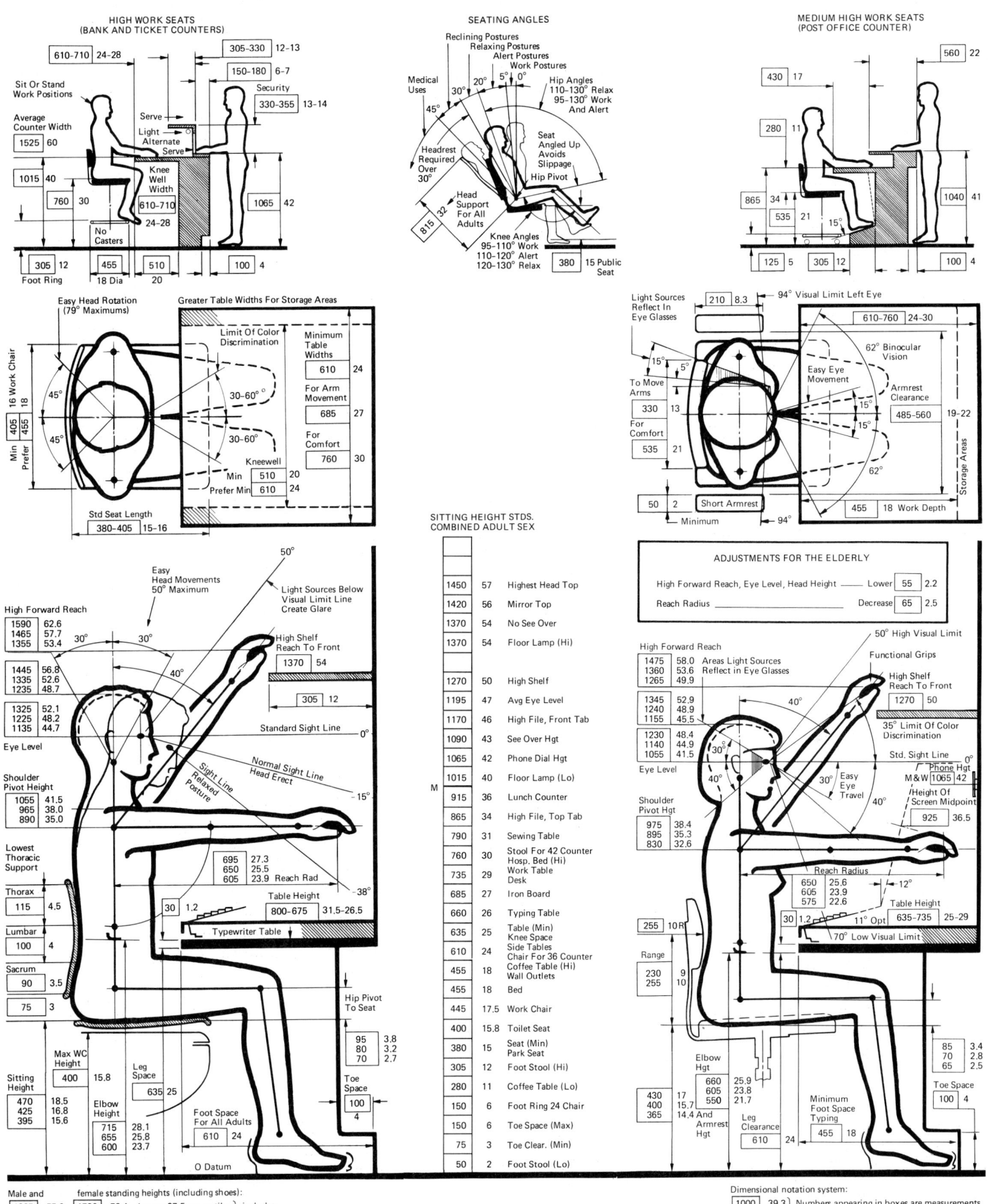

Niels Diffrient, Alvin R. Tilley; Henry Dreyfuss Associates; New York, New York

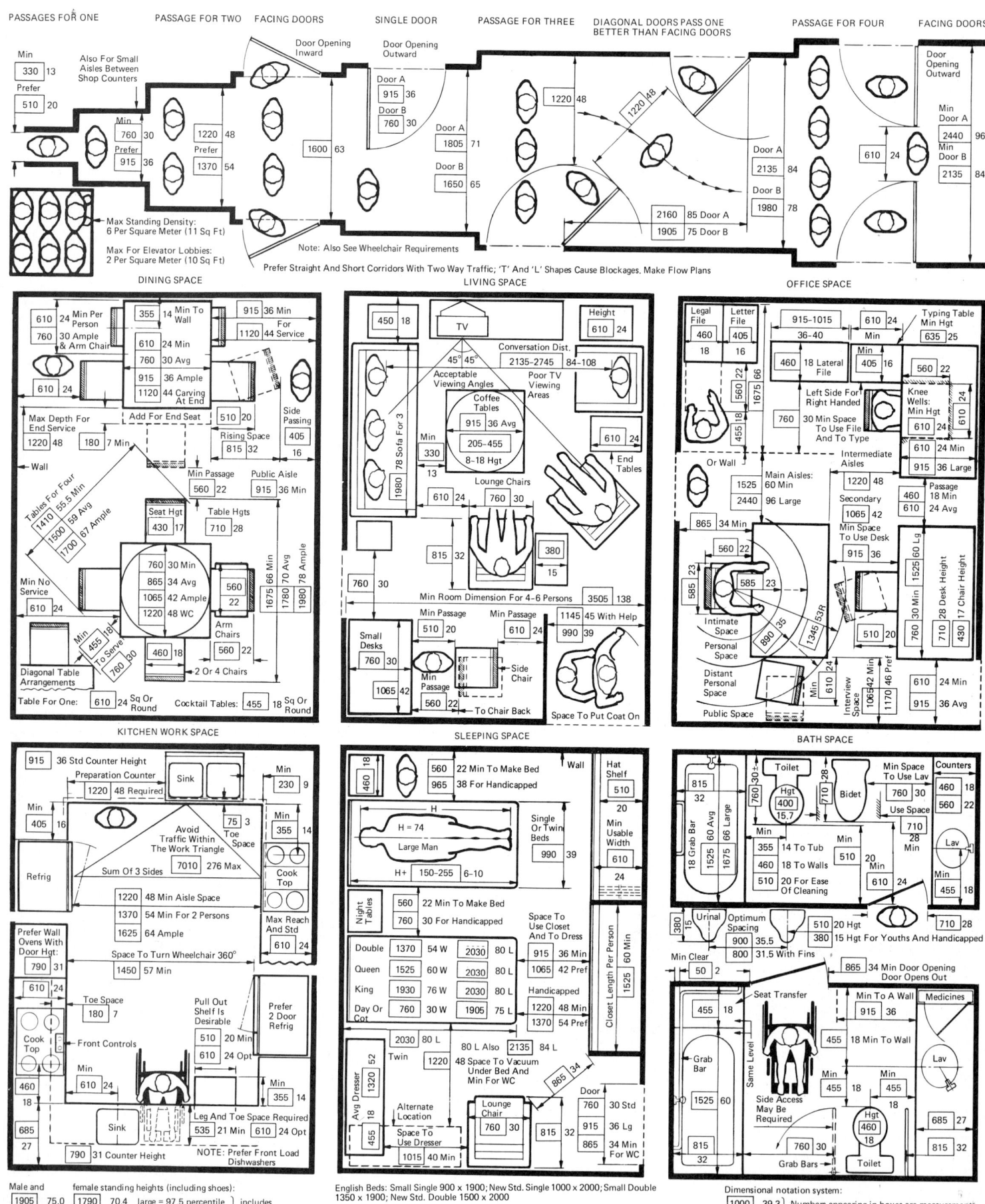

Niels Diffrient, Alvin R. Tilley; Henry Dreyfuss Associates; New York, New York

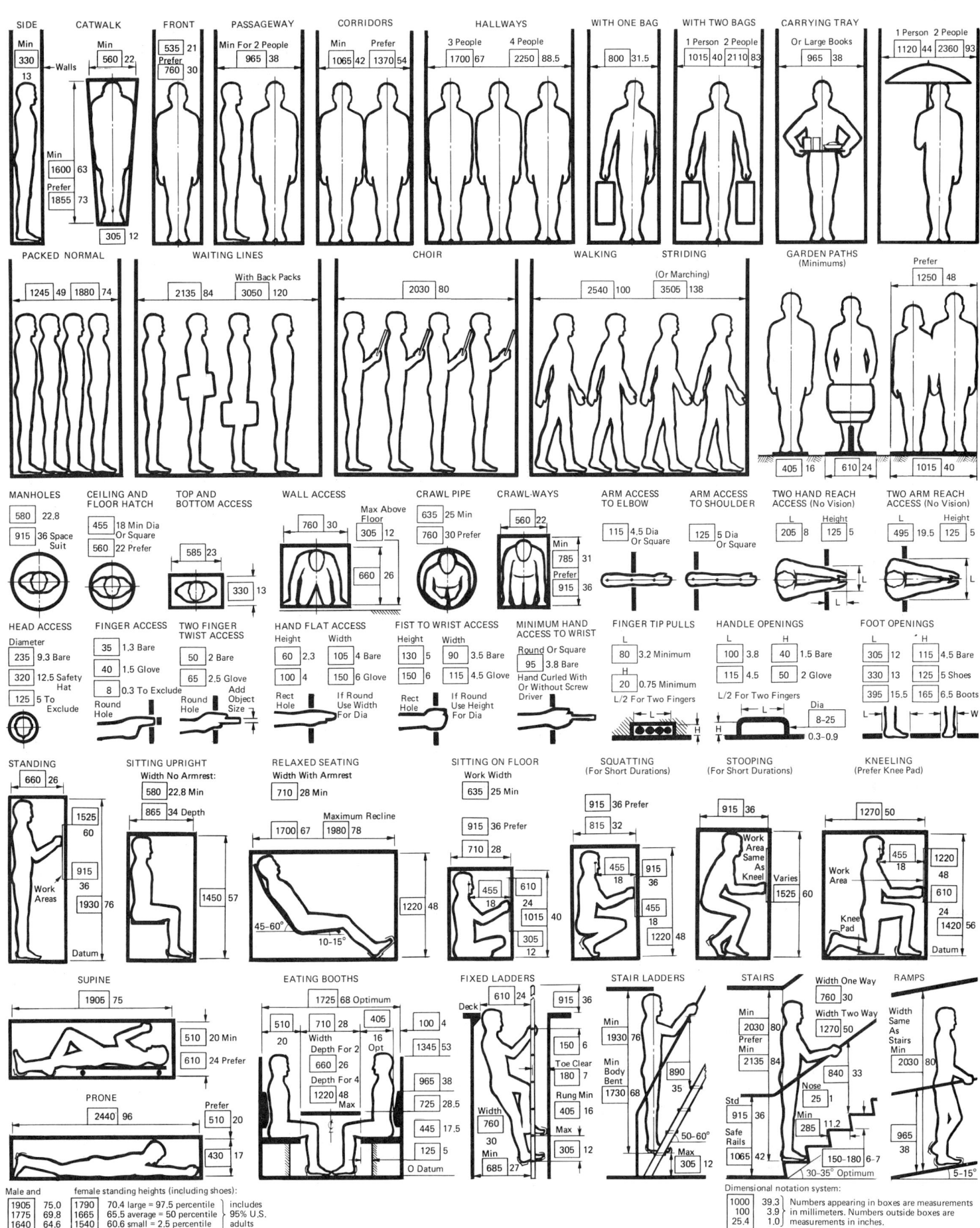

Male and female standing heights (including shoes):

1905	75.0	1790	70.4	large = 97.5 percentile	includes
1775	69.8	1665	65.5	average = 50 percentile	95% U.S.
1640	64.6	1540	60.6	small = 2.5 percentile	adults

Dimensional notation system:

1000	39.3	Numbers appearing in boxes are measurements
100	3.9	in millimeters. Numbers outside boxes are
25.4	1.0	measurements in inches.

Niels Diffrient, Alvin R. Tilley; Henry Dreyfuss Associates; New York, New York

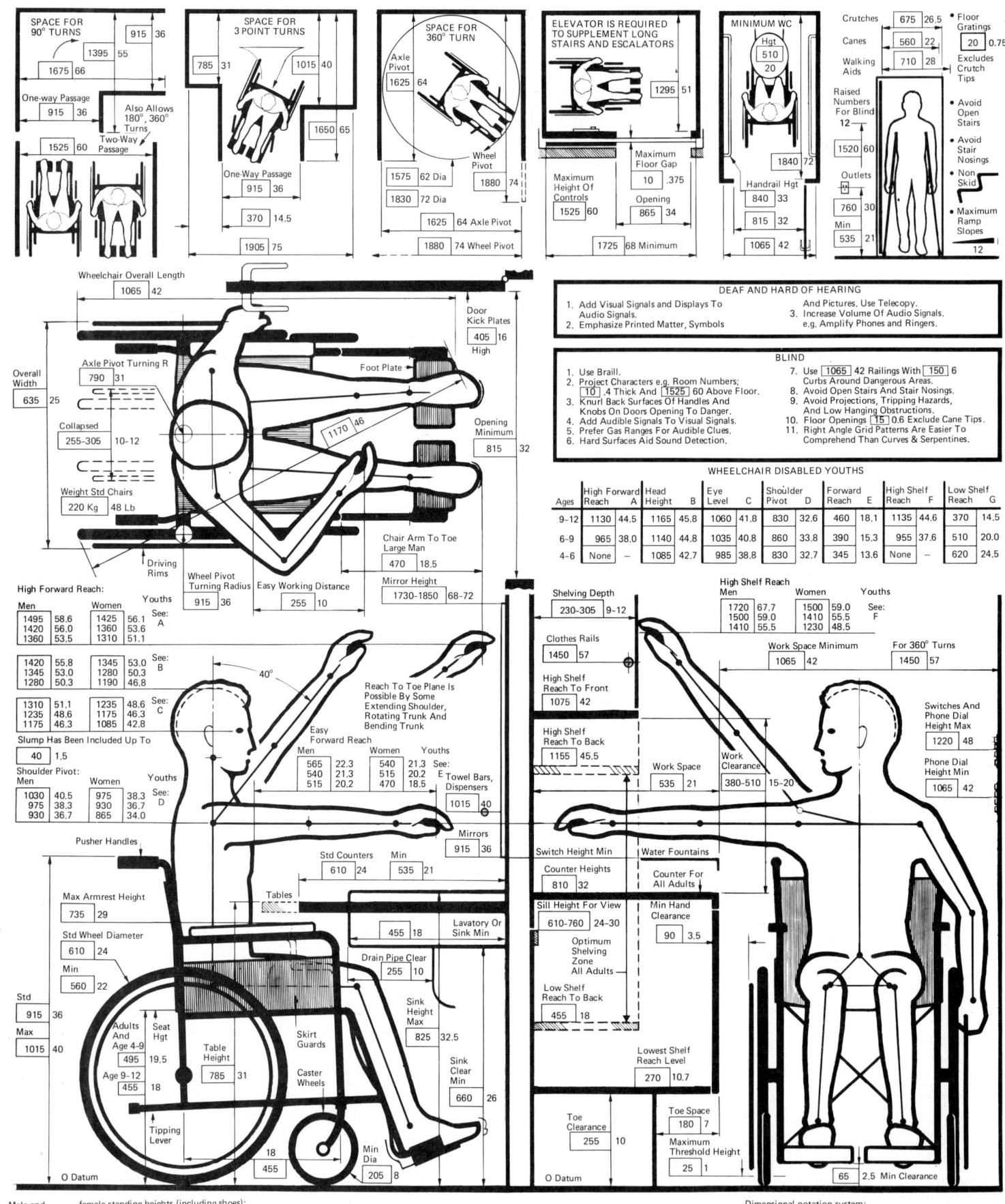

SPACE FOR 90° TURNS
915 | 36
1395 | 55
1675 | 66

One-way Passage
915 | 36

Also Allows 180°, 360° Turns

Two-Way Passage
1525 | 60

SPACE FOR 3 POINT TURNS
785 | 31
1015 | 40
1650 | 65

One-Way Passage
915 | 36
370 | 14.5
1905 | 75

SPACE FOR 360° TURN
Axle Pivot 1625 | 64
Wheel Pivot
1575 | 62 Dia
1830 | 72 Dia
1625 | 64 Axle Pivot
1880 | 74 Wheel Pivot

ELEVATOR IS REQUIRED TO SUPPLEMENT LONG STAIRS AND ESCALATORS
1295 | 51
Maximum Height Of Controls
1525 | 60
Maximum Floor Gap
10 | .375
Opening
865 | 34
1725 | 68 Minimum

MINIMUM WC
Hgt 510 20
1840 | 72
Handrail Hgt
840 | 33
815 | 32
1065 | 42

Crutches 675 | 26.5
Canes 560 | 22
Walking Aids 710 | 28

Floor Gratings 20 | 0.75
Excludes Crutch Tips

Raised Numbers For Blind 12
1520 | 60

Outlets 760 | 30
Min 535 | 21

• Avoid Open Stairs
• Avoid Stair Nosings
• Non Skid
• Maximum Ramp Slopes 12

Wheelchair Overall Length
1065 | 42

Door Kick Plates
405 | 16 High

Overall Width
635 | 25

Axle Pivot Turning R
790 | 31

Foot Plate

Collapsed
255-305 | 10-12

1170 | 46

Opening Minimum
815 | 32

Weight Std Chairs
220 Kg | 48 Lb

Chair Arm To Toe Large Man
470 | 18.5

Driving Rims

Wheel Pivot Turning Radius
915 | 36

Easy Working Distance
255 | 10

Mirror Height
1730-1850 | 68-72

DEAF AND HARD OF HEARING
1. Add Visual Signals and Displays To Audio Signals.
2. Emphasize Printed Matter, Symbols
And Pictures. Use Telecopy.
3. Increase Volume Of Audio Signals. e.g. Amplify Phones and Ringers.

BLIND
1. Use Braill.
2. Project Characters e.g. Room Numbers; 10 | .4 Thick And 1525 | 60 Above Floor.
3. Knurl Back Surfaces Of Handles And Knobs On Doors Opening To Danger.
4. Add Audible Signals To Visual Signals.
5. Prefer Gas Ranges For Audible Clues.
6. Hard Surfaces Aid Sound Detection.
7. Use 1065 | 42 Railings With 150 | 6 Curbs Around Dangerous Areas.
8. Avoid Open Stairs And Stair Nosings.
9. Avoid Projections, Tripping Hazards, And Low Hanging Obstructions.
10. Floor Openings 15 | 0.6 Exclude Cane Tips.
11. Right Angle Grid Patterns Are Easier To Comprehend Than Curves & Serpentines.

WHEELCHAIR DISABLED YOUTHS

Ages	High Forward Reach A		Head Height B		Eye Level C		Shoulder Pivot D		Forward Reach E		High Shelf Reach F		Low Shelf Reach G	
9-12	1130	44.5	1165	45.8	1060	41.8	830	32.6	460	18.1	1135	44.6	370	14.5
6-9	965	38.0	1140	44.8	1035	40.8	860	33.8	390	15.3	955	37.6	510	20.0
4-6	None	—	1085	42.7	985	38.8	830	32.7	345	13.6	None	—	620	24.5

High Forward Reach:

Men		Women		Youths
1495	58.6	1425	56.1	See: A
1420	56.0	1360	53.6	
1360	53.5	1310	51.1	
1420	55.8	1345	53.0	See: B
1345	53.0	1280	50.3	
1280	50.3	1190	46.8	
1310	51.1	1235	48.6	See: C
1235	48.6	1175	46.3	
1175	46.3	1085	42.8	

Slump Has Been Included Up To
40 | 1.5

Shoulder Pivot:

Men		Women		Youths
1030	40.5	975	38.3	See: D
975	38.3	930	36.7	
930	36.7	865	34.0	

Pusher Handles

Max Armrest Height
735 | 29

Std Wheel Diameter
610 | 24
Min
560 | 22

Std 915 | 36
Max 1015 | 40

Adults And Age 4-9
495 | 19.5
Age 9-12
455 | 18

Seat Hgt

Table Height
785 | 31

Tipping Lever

Skirt Guards

Caster Wheels

18
Min Dia
455
205 | 8

40°

Reach To Toe Plane Is Possible By Some Extending Shoulder, Rotating Trunk And Bending Trunk

Easy Forward Reach

Men		Women		Youths
565	22.3	540	21.3	See: E
540	21.3	515	20.2	
515	20.2	470	18.5	

Towel Bars, Dispensers
1015 | 40

Mirrors
915 | 36

Std Counters
610 | 24
Min
535 | 21

Tables

Lavatory Or Sink Min
455 | 18

Drain Pipe Clear
255 | 10

Sink Height Max
825 | 32.5

Sink Clear Min
660 | 26

Shelving Depth
230-305 | 9-12

Clothes Rails
1450 | 57

High Shelf Reach To Front
1075 | 42

High Shelf Reach To Back
1155 | 45.5

Switch Height Min

Counter Heights
810 | 32

Sill Height For View
610-760 | 24-30

Optimum Shelving Zone All Adults

Low Shelf Reach To Back
455 | 18

Lowest Shelf Reach Level
270 | 10.7

Toe Clearance
255 | 10

Water Fountains
Counter For All Adults

Min Hand Clearance
90 | 3.5

Toe Space
180 | 7

Maximum Threshold Height
25 | 1

High Shelf Reach

Men		Women		Youths
1720	67.7	1500	59.0	See: F
1500	59.0	1410	55.5	
1410	55.5	1230	48.5	

Work Space Minimum
1065 | 42

For 360° Turns
1450 | 57

Work Space
535 | 21

Work Clearance
380-510 | 15-20

Switches And Phone Dial Height Max
1220 | 48

Phone Dial Height Min
1065 | 42

O Datum

65 | 2.5 Min Clearance

Male and female standing heights (including shoes):

1905	75.0	1790	70.4	large = 97.5 percentile
1775	69.8	1665	65.5	average = 50 percentile
1640	64.6	1540	60.6	small = 2.5 percentile

includes 95% U.S. adults

Dimensional notation system:

1000	39.3
100	3.9
25.4	1.0

Numbers appearing in boxes are measurements in millimeters. Numbers outside boxes are measurements in inches.

Niels Diffrient, Alvin R. Tilley; Henry Dreyfuss Associates; New York, New York

1   DESIGN ELEMENTS

NOTES

1. Codes and standards used on this page:
   ANSI = American National Standards Institute.
   BOCA = Building Officials and Code Administrators.
   NBC = National Building Code.
   SBCC = Southern Building Code Congress.
   UBC = Uniform Building Code.
2. T = tread; R = riser.
3. Maximum height between landings is 12 ft (most codes).

RULE-OF-THUMB FORMULAS

INTERIOR STAIRS

1. Riser + tread = 17 or $17\frac{1}{2}$ in.; $7\frac{1}{2}$ in. R + 10 in. T = $17\frac{1}{2}$ in.
2. Riser x tread = 70 or 75; thus 7.5 in. R x 10 in. T = 75 in.
3. 2(riser) + tread $\geq$ 24 in. $\leq$ 25 in.
4. Within any flight $3/16$ in. max. variation in riser or tread height or width is permitted.

EXTERIOR STAIRS

Exterior stairs generally are not as steep as interior stairs, since space for wider treads and lower risers is usually available outdoors. Also, more dangerous conditions exist (ice, snow, rain). Wider treads and lower risers make exterior steps safer. The following formula has been devised by Thomas Church in "Gardens Are For People": 2(riser) + tread = 26 in.; thus for a 6 in. riser, 6 x 2 = 12 in., subtracted from 26 = 14 in. tread.

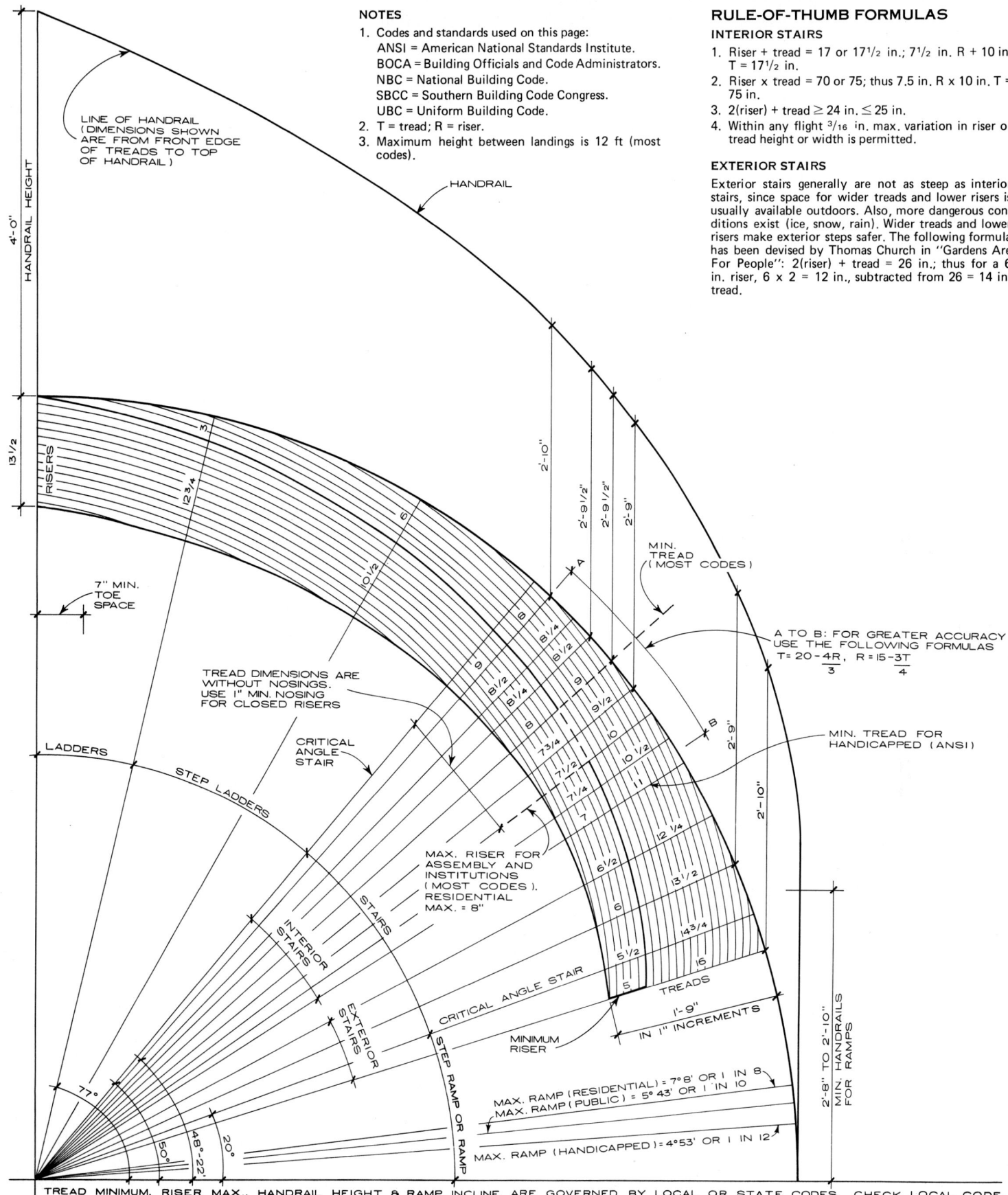

A TO B: FOR GREATER ACCURACY USE THE FOLLOWING FORMULAS $T = 20 - \frac{4R}{3}$, $R = 15 - \frac{3T}{4}$

TREAD MINIMUM, RISER MAX., HANDRAIL HEIGHT & RAMP INCLINE ARE GOVERNED BY LOCAL OR STATE CODES. CHECK LOCAL CODE.

TREADS AND RISERS

Paul Vaughan, AIA; Charleston, West Virginia

BED SIZES

TYPES	W	L
Crib	30''	53''
Daybed	30''	75''
Single bed	39''	82''
Double bed	54''	82''
Queen size	60''	82''
King size	72''	84''

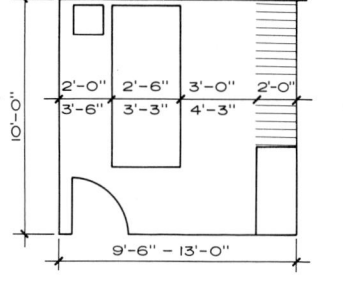

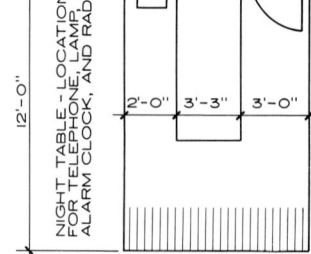

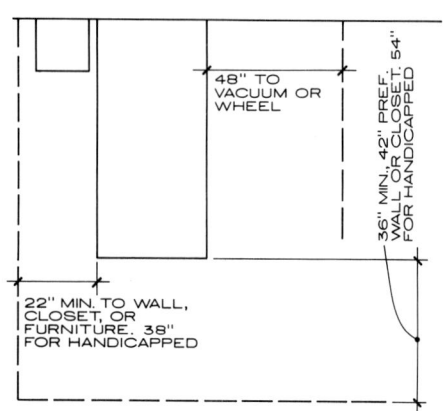

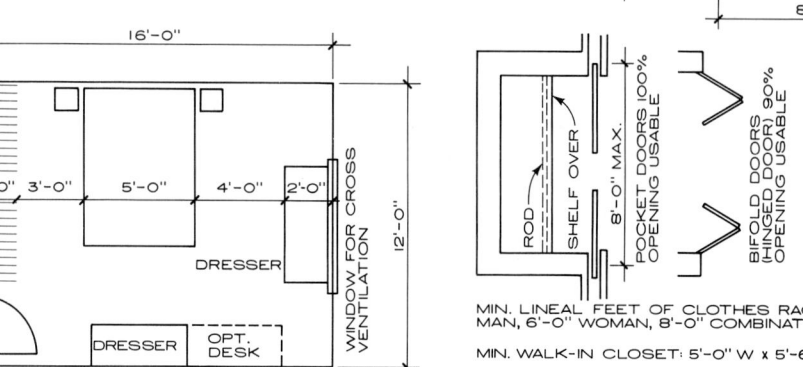

BED CLEARANCES   ARRANGEMENTS   CLOSETS

MIN. LINEAL FEET OF CLOTHES RACK: 4'-0" MAN, 6'-0" WOMAN, 8'-0" COMBINATION

MIN. WALK-IN CLOSET: 5'-0" W x 5'-6" LNG.

BEDROOM FURNITURE

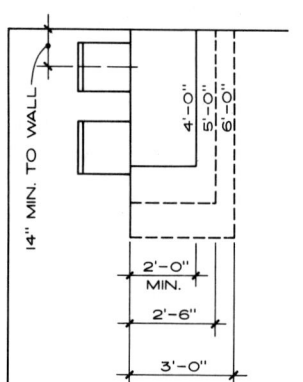

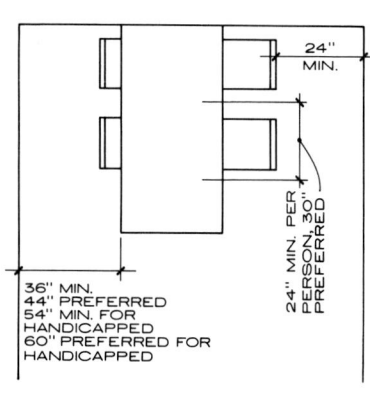

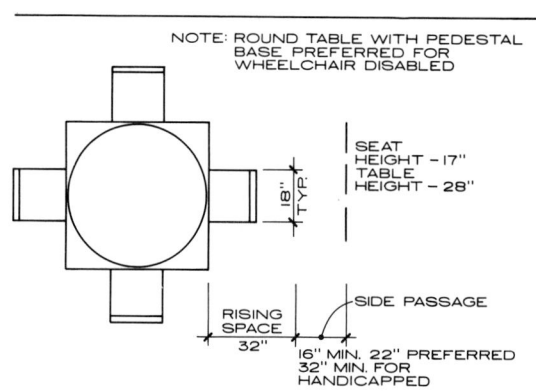

RECTANGULAR TABLES (IN.)

SIZE	SEAT	WHEELCHAIR
24 x 48	4	
30 x 48	4	2
30 x 60	4-6	4
36 x 72	4-6	4-6
36 x 84	6-8	6

SQUARE TABLES (IN.)

SIZE	SEAT	WHEELCHAIR
30 x 30	2	
36 x 36	2-4	
42 x 42	4	2 (tight)
48 x 48	4-8	2
54 x 54	4-8	4

ROUND TABLES (IN.)

SIZE	SEAT	WHEELCHAIR
30	2	
36	2-4	
42	4-5	
48	5-6	2
54	5-6	4

DINING ROOM FURNITURE

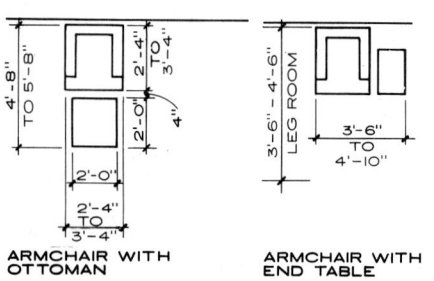

ARMCHAIR WITH OTTOMAN   ARMCHAIR WITH END TABLE

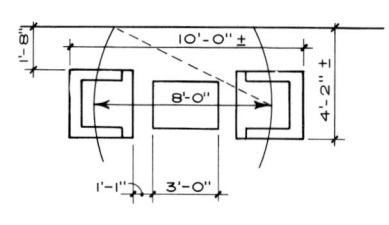

TWO ARMCHAIRS AND COFFEE TABLE, SHOWING ARC OF CONVERSATION

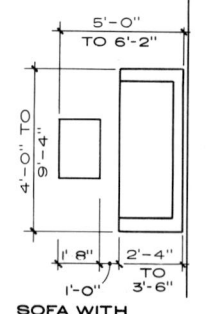

SOFA WITH COFFEE TABLE

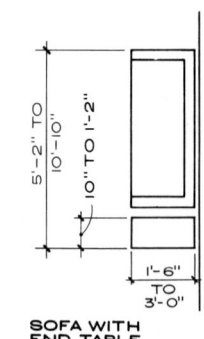

SOFA WITH END TABLE

LIVING ROOM FURNITURE

Arthur J. Pettorino, AIA; Hicksville, New York

1   **DESIGN ELEMENTS**

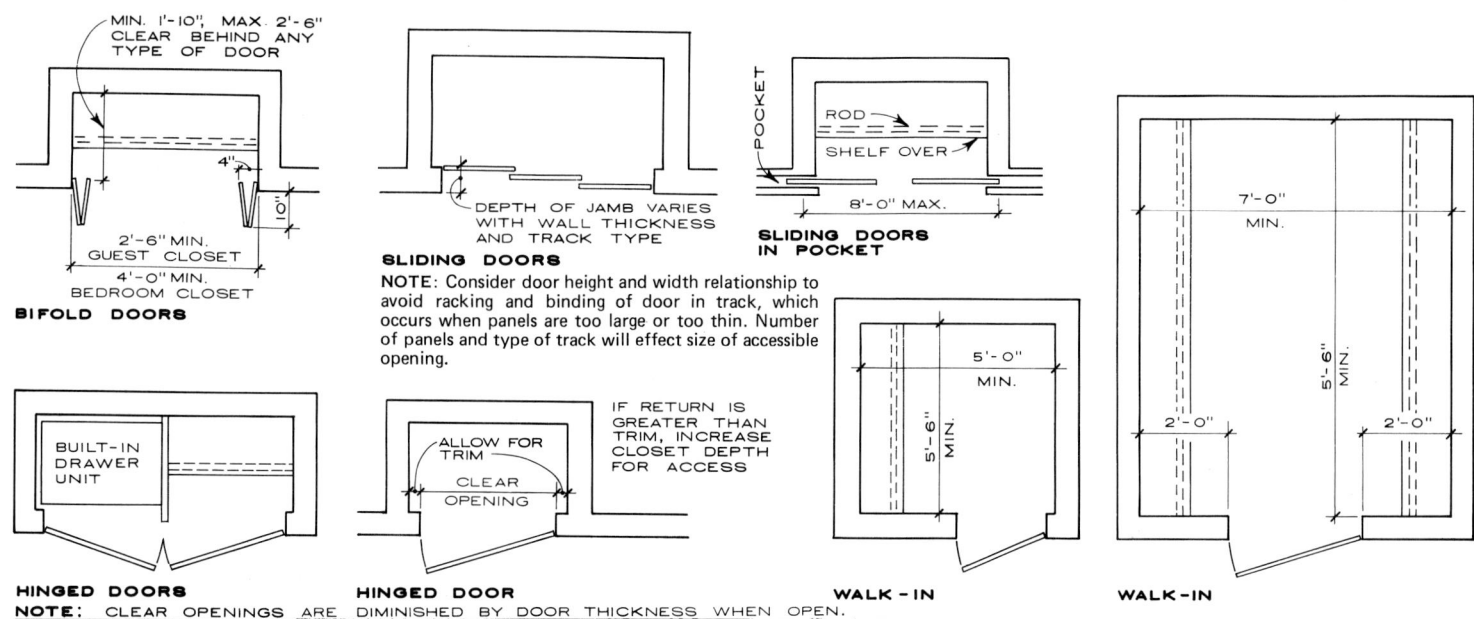

MIN. 1'-10", MAX. 2'-6"
CLEAR BEHIND ANY
TYPE OF DOOR

4"

2'-6" MIN.
GUEST CLOSET

4'-0" MIN.
BEDROOM CLOSET

BIFOLD DOORS

DEPTH OF JAMB VARIES
WITH WALL THICKNESS
AND TRACK TYPE

SLIDING DOORS

NOTE: Consider door height and width relationship to avoid racking and binding of door in track, which occurs when panels are too large or too thin. Number of panels and type of track will effect size of accessible opening.

POCKET

ROD

SHELF OVER

8'-0" MAX.

SLIDING DOORS IN POCKET

5'-0" MIN.

5'-6" MIN.

7'-0" MIN.

5'-6" MIN.

2'-0"   2'-0"

BUILT-IN
DRAWER
UNIT

HINGED DOORS

ALLOW FOR TRIM

CLEAR OPENING

IF RETURN IS GREATER THAN TRIM, INCREASE CLOSET DEPTH FOR ACCESS

HINGED DOOR

WALK-IN

WALK-IN

NOTE: CLEAR OPENINGS ARE DIMINISHED BY DOOR THICKNESS WHEN OPEN.

CLOSETS

NOTES

1. No closet bifold door should exceed 2 ft panel. Largest door stock in pocket and sliding door is 4 ft.
2. All closet doors should allow easy access to top shelves.
3. Doors for children's closets can be used as tackboards, chalkboards, or mirrors.
4. Consider use of hinged doors for storage fittings and mirrors.
5. Walk-in closets should be properly ventilated and lit.
6. Pole and shelf height for wheelchair-handicapped persons is 54 in. maximum.
7. Accessibility of closets varies with door types used. Figure bifold doors allow $66^{2}/_{3}$% minimum of closet to be opened at once, pocket slides 100%, sliding doors 50% or more, and hinged doors 90%, allowing for trim.

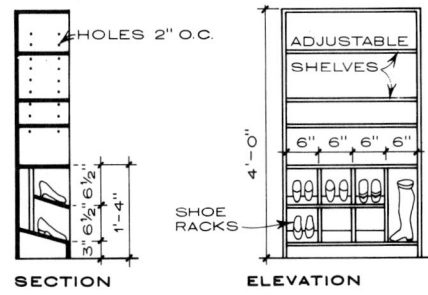

HOLES 2" O.C.

ADJUSTABLE SHELVES

4'-0"

6" 6" 6" 6"

SHOE RACKS

3" 6½" 6½" 6½" 1'-4"

SECTION   **ELEVATION**

SHELVES WITH SHOE RACKS UNDER

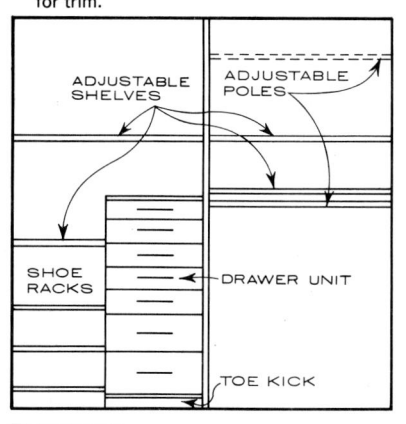

ADJUSTABLE SHELVES

ADJUSTABLE POLES

SHOE RACKS

DRAWER UNIT

TOE KICK

ELEVATION

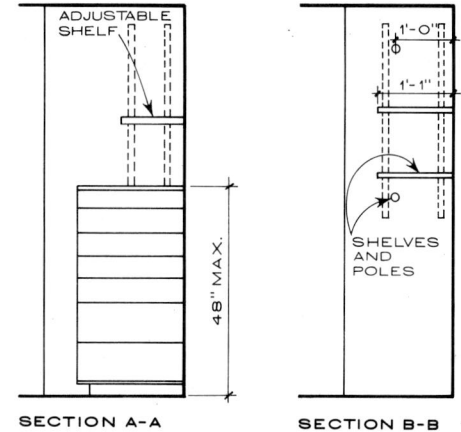

ADJUSTABLE SHELF

48" MAX.

SECTION A-A

1'-0"

1'-1"

SHELVES AND POLES

SECTION B-B

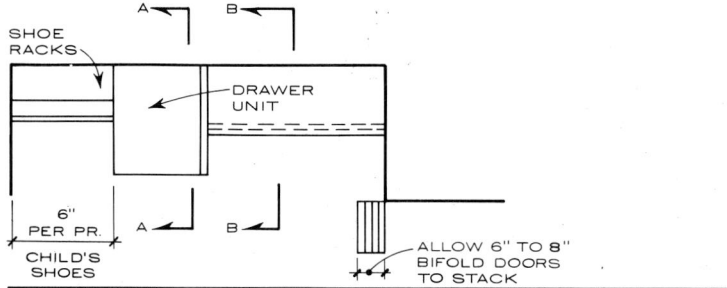

SHOE RACKS

A   B

DRAWER UNIT

A   B

6" PER PR.

CHILD'S SHOES

ALLOW 6" TO 8" BIFOLD DOORS TO STACK

CHILDREN'S CLOSETS

R. L. Speas, Jr.; Hugh N. Jacobsen, FAIA; Washington, D.C.

RESIDENTIAL STORAGE

SHELVING Standard shelving sizes are 6, 8, 10, and 12 in., although shelving up to 18 in. deep is desirable for closet shelving. Shelving may be either fixed or adjustable.

DRAWERS Typical drawers are from 16 to 24 in. deep, 12 to 36 in. wide, and 2 to 8 in. deep or deeper. Often built into casework, drawers may be of wood, metal, or molded plastic.

CABINETS AND CUPBOARDS Cabinets may be built in, as in kitchen and bathroom vanities, or freestanding. Base cabinets are typically 18 to 24 in. deep and from 24 to 42 in. wide or wider, and may be fitted with drawers, shelving, and special storage features. Doors are typically hinged. Wall hung cabinets usually are 12 in. deep.

CLOSETS Standard closet depth is 24 to 30 in. for clothing and 16 to 20 in. for linens.

BOXES Closet storage fittings such as boxes and garment bags can be used for supplemental or seasonal storage.

STORAGE REQUIREMENTS

BEDROOM Allow 4 to 6 ft of hanging space per person. Allow 12 in. of hanging space for 6 suits, 12 shirts, 8 dresses, or 6 pairs of pants.

LINEN STORAGE Place near bedrooms and bathrooms in a closet with 12 to 18 in. deep shelves. Supplemental storage in bins or baskets may be needed.

BATHROOMS A mirrored wall cabinet 4 to 6 in. deep is typical bathroom storage, supplemented by space for supplies of soap, toothpaste, and other toiletries.

GARDEN AND AUTOMOTIVE SUPPLIES Typically, a garage or storage shed is used for garden, automotive supplies, and outdoor furniture. Sheds should be located for convenient use.

COATS A closet near an entry door for coats and rainwear is desirable in most areas of the country.

CLEANING EQUIPMENT A closet at least 24 in. wide for storage of vacuum cleaners and household cleaning supplies is helpful.

KITCHEN/DINING See pages on kitchen planning for recommendations.

OTHER STORAGE Most families have additional storage needs. For custom design work, these needs must be analyzed and storage planned. Storage rooms and attic and basement areas are possible supplemental storage locations.

KITCHEN SPACE PLANNING

The layouts shown here, together with their general area requirements, are based on studies of furniture appliances, storage, and clearances for the average residential kitchen. They have been developed to accommodate storage, work, and required floor areas for various functions, but the location of appliances and their order should be determined by individual preferences, check clearances, traffic flow, and appliance functions rather than total square footage in determining kitchen size during early planning stages.

To simplify comparison of the various room types, basic sizes of furniture, appliances, and clearances have been standardized. However, the appliances shown in the kitchenettes are the more compact units available from some manufacturers (see Equip. pgs.). In all cases, the depth of the counter is assumed as 24", the depth of base storage units as 20", and the depth of wall storage units as 12". Their widths vary in relation to their location.

A useful rule-of-thumb to determine storage area requirements for residential kitchens is: Provide a minimum of 18 square feet of space for basic storage with an additional 6 square feet for each person usually served.

The letters A, B, and C shown below refer to the "work centers" described on another page.

A—Refrigerator center
B—Sink center
C—Range center

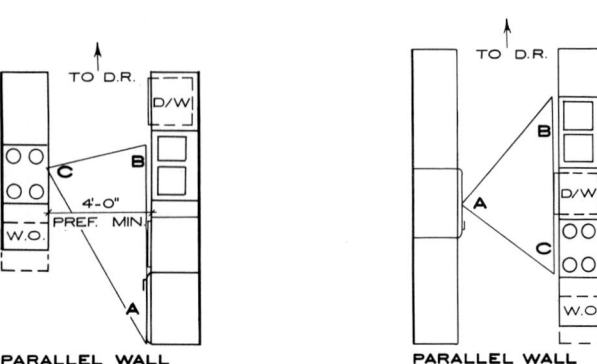

PARALLEL WALL
AREA: APPROX. 68 SQ. FT. FOR 3 PERSONS TO 86 SQ. FT. FOR 6 PERSONS

PARALLEL WALL

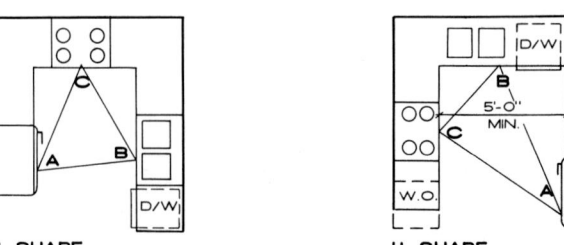

U-SHAPE
AREA: APPROX. 80 SQ. FT. FOR 3 PERSONS TO 92 SQ. FT. FOR 6 PERSONS

AISLE CLEARANCE: 3'-0" MIN. BUT NOT DESIRABLE. 4'-0" IS ADEQUATE. THE DISTANCE BETWEEN A,B,C, SHOULD AVERAGE 15" TO 20" MAX.

U-SHAPE

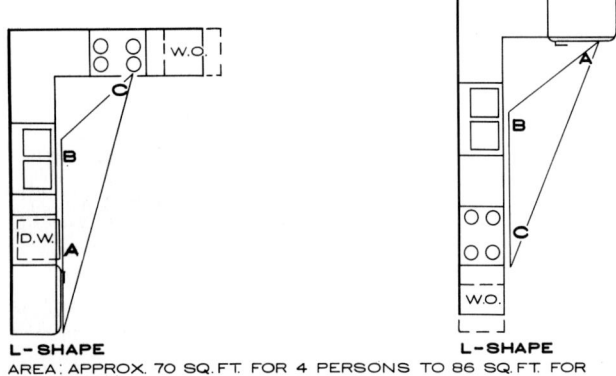

L-SHAPE
AREA: APPROX. 70 SQ. FT. FOR 4 PERSONS TO 86 SQ. FT. FOR 6 PERSONS

L-SHAPE

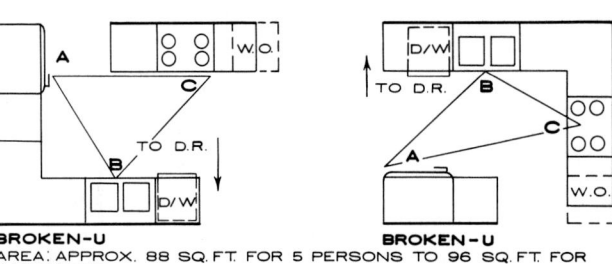

BROKEN-U
AREA: APPROX. 88 SQ. FT. FOR 5 PERSONS TO 96 SQ. FT. FOR 7 PERSONS

OPTION: ISLAND COUNTER CAN BE USED FOR COOKING AND SERVING CENTER

BROKEN-U

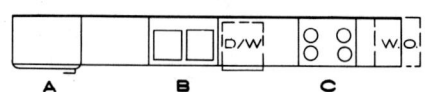

SINGLE WALL
AREA: APPROX. 93 SQ. FT. FOR 3 PERSONS TO 111 SQ. FT. FOR 6 PERSONS

RESIDENTIAL KITCHEN ARRANGEMENTS

NOTE: SMALL KITCHENS USUALLY HAVE UP TO 10 RUNNING FEET OF COUNTER & EQUIPMENT; AVERAGE KITCHEN HAS UP TO 20 FEET OF COUNTER & EQUIPMENT

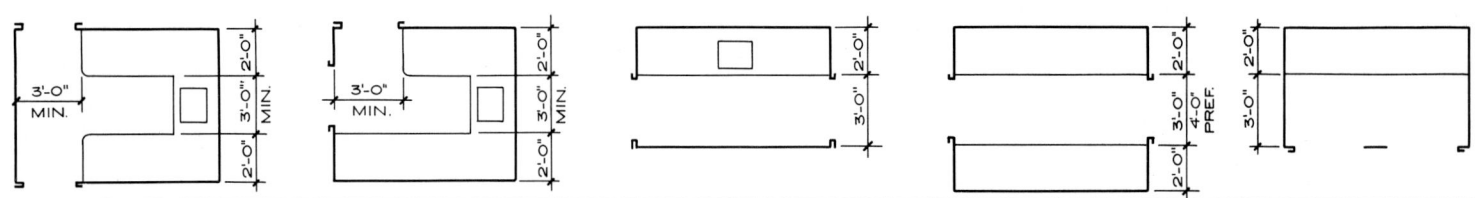

PANTRY TYPES USUAL EQUIPMENT INCLUDES DRAWER & CABINET SPACE FOR GLASSWARE, CHINA, LINENS; SINK & UNDER-COUNTER REFRIG

ABBREVIATIONS:
D/W = DISHWASHER
W.O. = WALL OVEN
D.R. = DINING ROOM

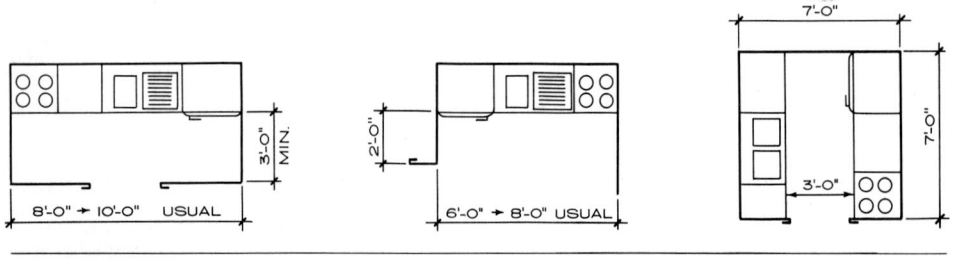

KITCHENETTES

R. E. Powe, Jr., AIA; Hugh N. Jacobsen, FAIA; Washington, D.C.

GENERAL NOTES

1. For equipment not shown, such as covered ranges and under-counter refrigerators see manufacturers' literature.

2. Consult local building codes for kitchenette requirements.

1 DESIGN ELEMENTS

KITCHEN WORK CENTERS

A residential kitchen may be considered in terms of three interconnected work centers, A, B and C, as shown below. Each encompasses a distinct phase of kitchen activity, and storage should be provided for the items that are most used in connection with each center.

The functions of the sink center are most common to the other two centers. It is recommended, therefore, that the sink center's location be convenient to each of the others (usually between them). The refrigerator center is best located near the entry and the range center near the dining area.

CABINETS SHOULD PROJECT FLUSH OVER REFRIGERATOR

FASCIA TO CLOSE OFF TOP OF CABINETS MAY BE PROVIDED

FASCIA (OR BULKHEAD) SPACE MAY BE USED FOR EXTRA CABINETS FOR RARELY USED ITEMS

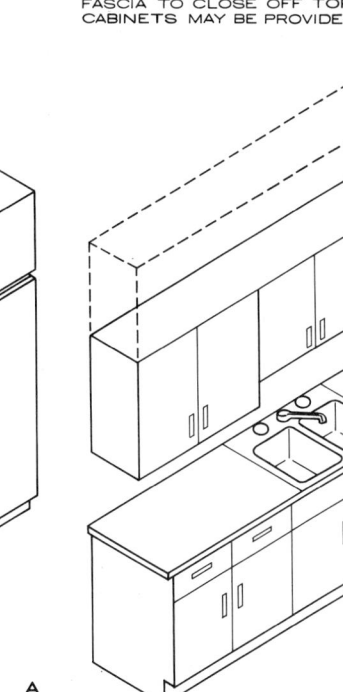

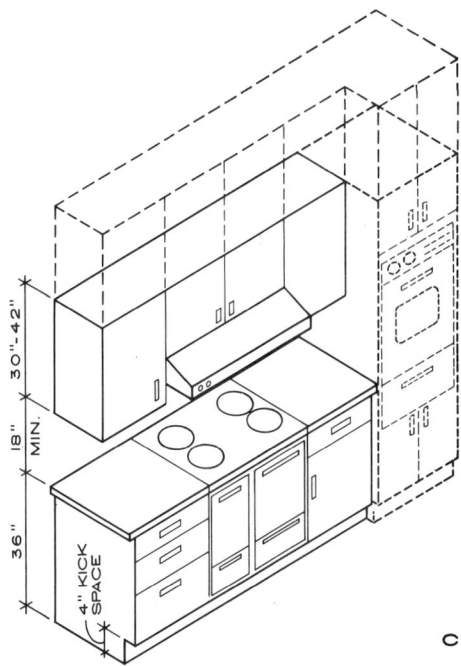

A   B   C

REFRIGERATOR CENTER
(RECEIVING AND FOOD PREPARATION)

Provide storage for mixer and mixing bowls; other utensils: sifter, grater, salad molds, cake and pie tins, occasional dishes, condiments, staples, canned goods, brooms, and miscellaneous items.

SINK CENTER
(FOOD PREPARATION, CLEANING, AND CLEANUP)

Provide storage for everyday dishes, glassware, pots and pans, cutlery, silver, pitchers and shakers, vegetable bins, linen, towel rack, wastebasket, cleaning materials and utensils, garbage can or disposal, and dishdrain. Some codes require louvres or other venting provision in the doors under enclosed sinks.

RANGE CENTER
(COOKING AND SERVING)

Provide storage for pots, potholders, frying pans, roaster, cooking utensils, grease container, seasoning, canned goods, bread bin, bread board, toaster, plate warmer, platters, serving dishes, and trays.

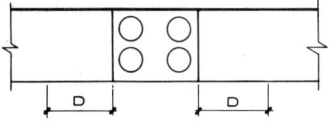

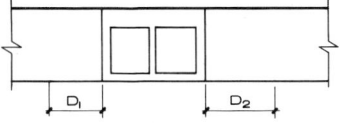

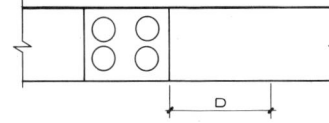

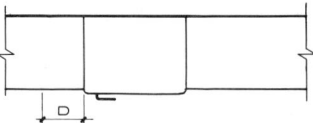

D = 18″ to 24″
D = counter distance on either side of a cooking facility.

D₁ = 18″ to 36″
$D_1 = 18″$ to 36″
$D_2 = 24″$ to 36″
Provide work space on both sides of sink. If dishwasher is used allow at least 24″ to the right or left.

D = 36″ to 42″
D = counter space between range and nearest piece of equipment.

D = 15″ minimum
Provide room at latch side of refrigerator for loading and unloading.

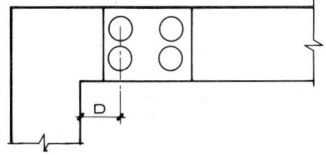

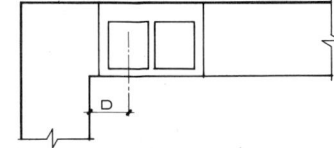

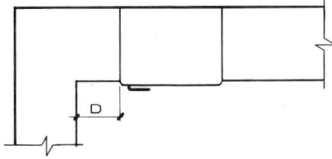

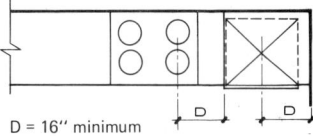

D = 14″ minimum
D = clearance between the center of the front unit (or burner) and the turn of the counter.

D = 14″ minimum
D = clearance between the center of the sink bowl and the turn of the counter.

D = 16″ minimum
D = clearance between latch side of refrigerator door and turn of the counter.

D = 16″ minimum
D = clearance between center of front burner and nearest piece of high equipment or nearest wall; or between the center of a wall oven and an adjoining wall.

CLEARANCES AND COUNTER WIDTHS

KITCHENS FOR THE HANDICAPPED

The preferred cooktop and counter height is 30 to 33 in., but may be standard 36 in. if a pullout workshelf is provided at 30 to 33 in. Open floor space is necessary for wheelchair maneuverability; observe a 5 ft minimum turning radius. Smooth, nonskid flooring is required. Indoor-outdoor carpet is preferred, but difficult to maintain in a kitchen. Linoleum or vinyl asbestos tile is acceptable. Knee space is necessary under sink counter. Insulate pipes to avoid scalding. Provide cooktop controls at front to avoid reaching across hot surfaces. Wall ovens should preferably be set so that top of open oven door is 2 ft 7 in. above floor. Side-by-side refrigerator-freezer is preferred, although units with freezer on bottom are acceptable. Dishwashers should be front loading.

Round tables with pedestal base are preferred. A 4 ft diameter will accommodate two wheelchair users; a 4 ft 6 in. diameter will accommodate four wheelchair users.

Storage considerations for the wheelchair disabled include use of pegboard for pots, pans, and utensils. Vertical drawers in base cabinets allow for storage of food that would otherwise be out of reach of wheelchair users. Narrow shelving mounted to the backs of doors in cabinets or closets provides accessible storage for food and utensils.

Arthur J. Pettorino, AIA; Hicksville, New York

R. E. Powe, Jr., AIA; Hugh N. Jacobsen, FAIA; Washington, D.C.

DESIGN ELEMENTS 1

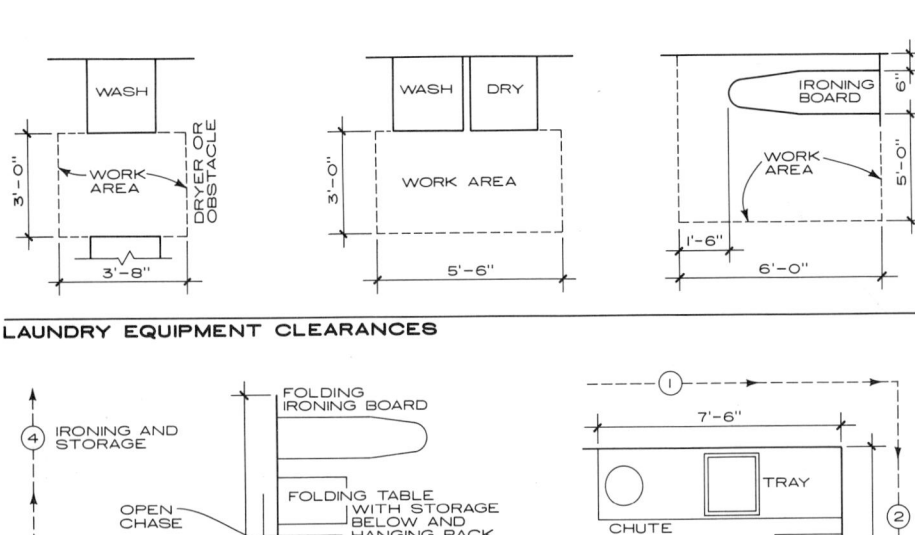

LAUNDRY EQUIPMENT CLEARANCES

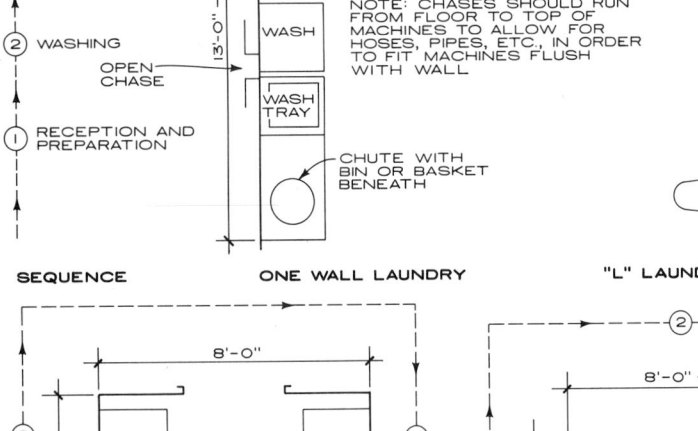

SEQUENCE   ONE WALL LAUNDRY   "L" LAUNDRY

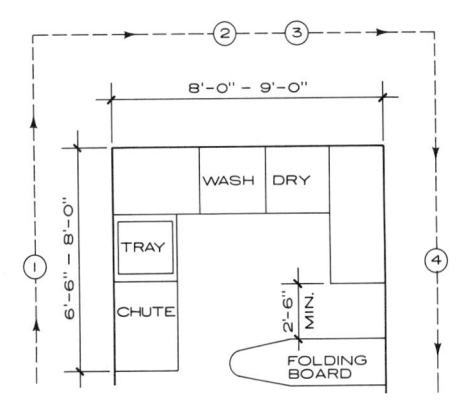

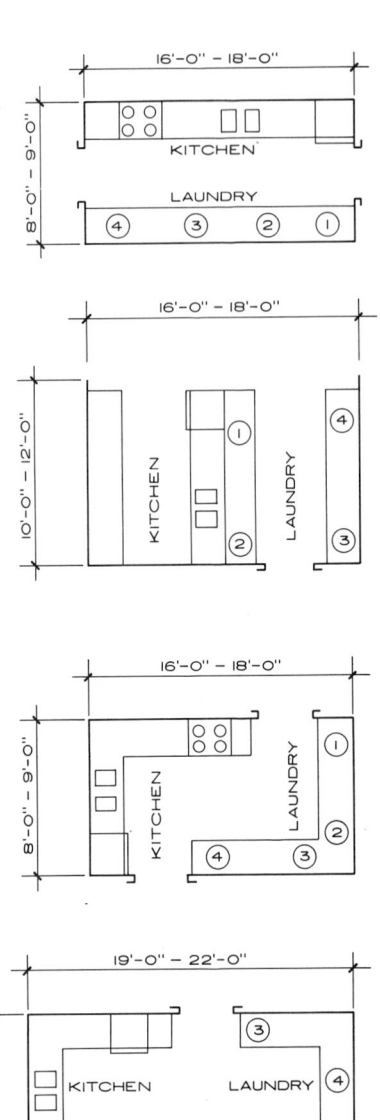

NOTE: CHASES SHOULD RUN FROM FLOOR TO TOP OF MACHINES TO ALLOW FOR HOSES, PIPES, ETC., IN ORDER TO FIT MACHINES FLUSH WITH WALL

PARALLEL LAUNDRY   "U" LAUNDRY

TYPICAL LAUNDRIES

LAUNDRIES WITH KITCHEN

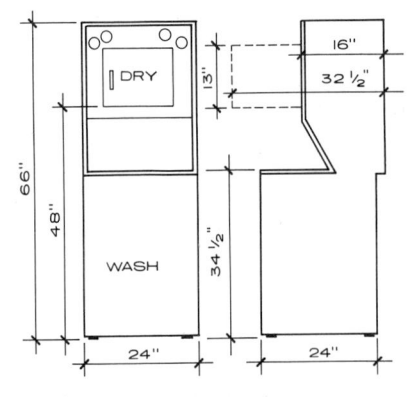

LAUNDRIES FOR THE HANDICAPPED

For the chairborne homemaker, having laundry facilities close to the kitchen is a practical way of coordinating several time consuming activities with a minimum of movement from place to place.

The basic necessities are an efficient automatic washer, a dryer, storage space for supplies, a good lightweight steam iron, and an adjustable ironing board that can be set at a comfortable seated-work height of about 29 in.

Look for a front loading drum type of washer. It is more accessible than the usual top loader, which is too high and has a tub that is too deep for the average wheelchair homemaker.

Most automatic dryers are designed as front loaders. Select a model with controls up front and within reach.

CONSULT MANUFACTURERS FOR VARIOUS MODELS

COMPACT LAUNDRY

APARTMENT HOUSE LAUNDRIES

In apartment house complexes, laundry rooms are usually located in the basement or on the ground floor of the building. This is a logical choice, as it is close to mechanical equipment, piping, and venting, which are necessary to laundry room operations. In addition, these areas, resting on grade, form an excellent surface for washer and dryer placement, for vibrations on this level do not affect apartment dwellers. Easy access is also provided. Folding tables and vending machines for soaps should also be incorporated into the laundry room design. Laundry rooms should be open to visual inspection to ensure the safety of the users. It is important to note that laundry rooms in large apartment buildings tend to become social gathering areas and should be designed to accommodate this function.

Arthur J. Pettorino, AIA; Hicksville, New York

R. E. Powe, Jr., AIA; Hugh N. Jacobsen, FAIA; Washington, D.C.

1   DESIGN ELEMENTS

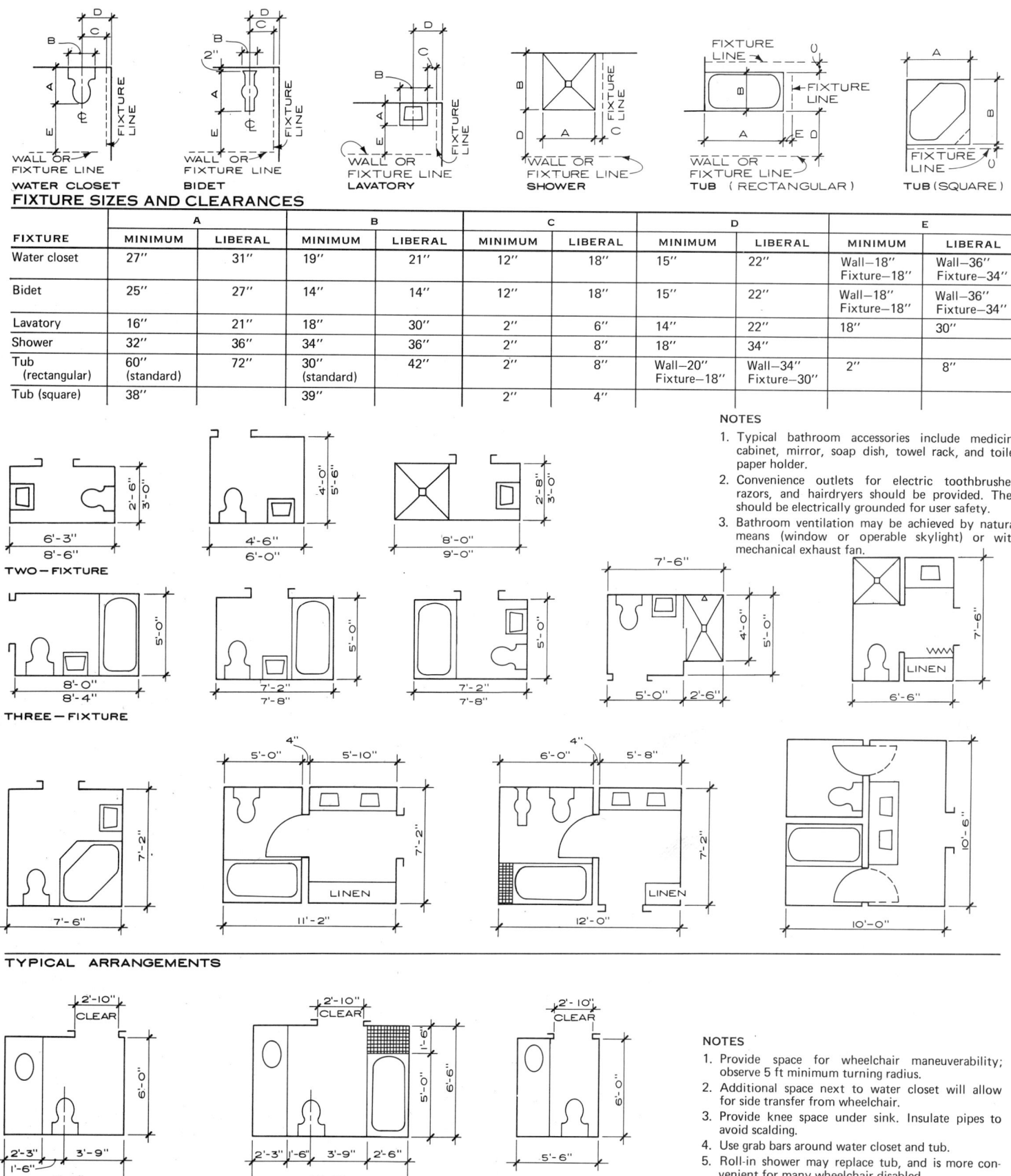

WATER CLOSET   BIDET   LAVATORY   SHOWER   TUB (RECTANGULAR)   TUB (SQUARE)

FIXTURE SIZES AND CLEARANCES

FIXTURE	A MINIMUM	A LIBERAL	B MINIMUM	B LIBERAL	C MINIMUM	C LIBERAL	D MINIMUM	D LIBERAL	E MINIMUM	E LIBERAL
Water closet	27″	31″	19″	21″	12″	18″	15″	22″	Wall—18″ Fixture—18″	Wall—36″ Fixture—34″
Bidet	25″	27″	14″	14″	12″	18″	15″	22″	Wall—18″ Fixture—18″	Wall—36″ Fixture—34″
Lavatory	16″	21″	18″	30″	2″	6″	14″	22″	18″	30″
Shower	32″	36″	34″	36″	2″	8″	18″	34″		
Tub (rectangular)	60″ (standard)	72″	30″ (standard)	42″	2″	8″	Wall—20″ Fixture—18″	Wall—34″ Fixture—30″	2″	8″
Tub (square)	38″		39″		2″	4″				

NOTES

1. Typical bathroom accessories include medicine cabinet, mirror, soap dish, towel rack, and toilet paper holder.
2. Convenience outlets for electric toothbrushes, razors, and hairdryers should be provided. They should be electrically grounded for user safety.
3. Bathroom ventilation may be achieved by natural means (window or operable skylight) or with mechanical exhaust fan.

TWO – FIXTURE

THREE – FIXTURE

TYPICAL ARRANGEMENTS

RECOMMENDED

MINIMUM (DIFFICULT)

NOTES

1. Provide space for wheelchair maneuverability; observe 5 ft minimum turning radius.
2. Additional space next to water closet will allow for side transfer from wheelchair.
3. Provide knee space under sink. Insulate pipes to avoid scalding.
4. Use grab bars around water closet and tub.
5. Roll-in shower may replace tub, and is more convenient for many wheelchair disabled.
6. Bathroom door to be minimum 32 in. clear opening and to swing outward. Use lever hardware on both sides.

ARRANGEMENTS FOR THE WHEELCHAIR DISABLED

Arthur J. Pettorino, AIA; Hicksville, New York

DESIGN ELEMENTS   1

NOTES

Commercial kitchens are normally defined as those providing food to be consumed away from home. Typical of these are kitchens within restaurants, hotels/motels, cafeterias, snack bars/coffee shops, schools/colleges, office buildings, hospitals, and other institutions. The size, type, quantity, and layout of equipment in the kitchen and the related service areas is a direct function of the menu, amount of patronage, and the time in which the items are to be served.

The schematic drawings shown here do not attempt to present kitchen design solutions, but rather to familiarize the reader with the typical characteristics of commercial kitchen design.

FUNCTIONAL FLOW DIAGRAM

NOTES

Workers and materials should travel minimum distances. They should proceed in a logical sequence with minimum of crisscrossing and backtracking. Delay and storage of materials in processing and serving should be reduced to a minimum. Garbage and trash disposal facilities are required for all functions.

GENERAL INFORMATION

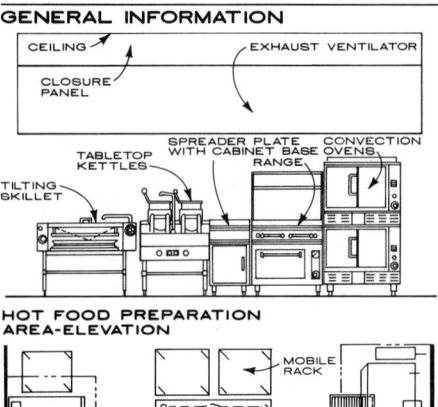

HOT FOOD PREPARATION AREA–ELEVATION

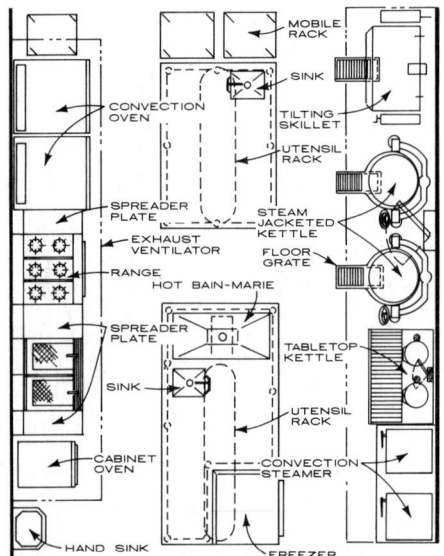

HOT FOOD PREPARATION AREA–CAFETERIA/BANQUET

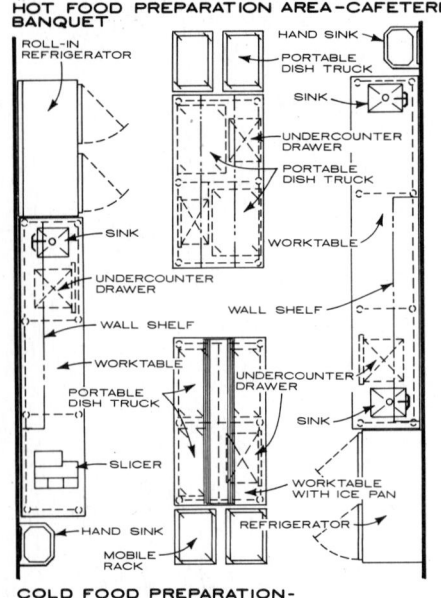

COLD FOOD PREPARATION– CAFETERIA/BANQUET

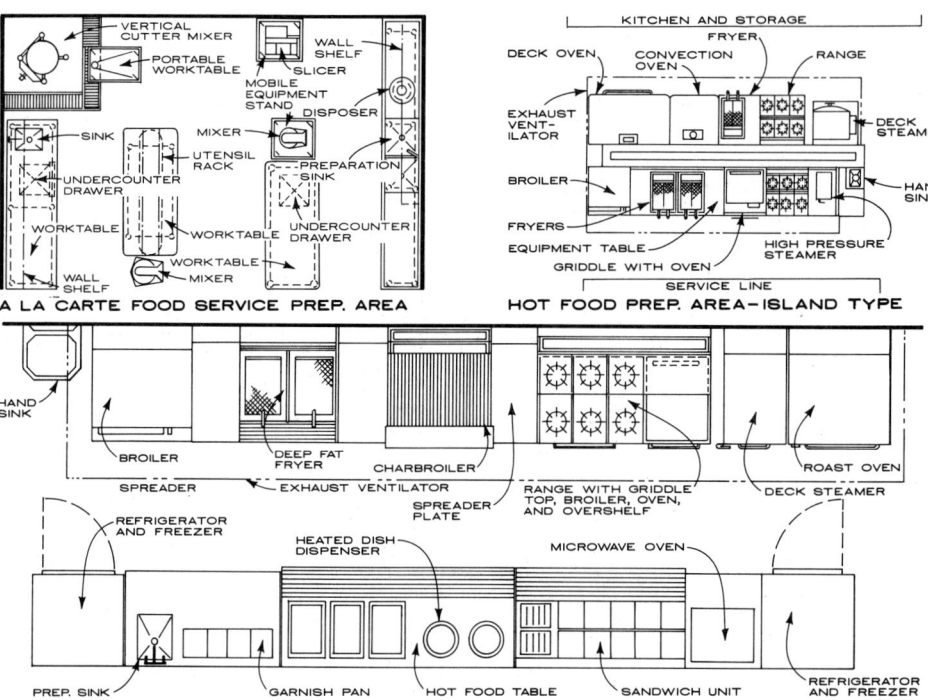

A LA CARTE FOOD SERVICE PREP. AREA

HOT FOOD PREP. AREA–ISLAND TYPE

A LA CARTE FOOD SERVICE AREA

CAFETERIA

NOTES

Numerous layouts are being used for cafeterias today. "Free flow" design permits fast movement through the line and a more diversified menu; it is limited by the capacity of the cashier. The "hollow square" design consists of separate feeding lines using the same central service facility. This increases capacity without increasing staff. The "straight line" is utilized in a low volume operation that is limited by the capacity of the cashier. The service line length is directly related to the variety of the menu.

RECOMMENDED STORAGE TEMPERATURES

1. DRY FOOD STORAGE: 65°F (15°C). Stored 4 in. off floor, 2 in. from wall.
2. COMMON STORAGE: 50°–60°F (10°–15°C).
3. FREEZER STORAGE: –10°F (–23°C).
4. REFRIGERATED STORAGE: 31°–40°F (–0.5°–4°C).

RECOMMENDED WARE WASHING TEMPERATURES

1. PRERINSE: 120°–140°F (49°–60°C).
2. WASH: 140°F (60°C).
3. RINSE: 180°F (82°C) for 10 sec. 170°F (77°C) for 30 sec or longer.

(If sanitizing agent is used –140°F (60°C) is acceptable for all ware washing functions.)

NOTE: Check local codes for requirements.

VENTILATORS

Ventilators are generally required over all types of major cooking equipment. The exhaust system should be either a canopy type or high speed backshelf exhaust. Grease removal should be accomplished through the use of filters or internal centrifugal extraction. Fire extinguishing equipment should be installed in compliance with the National Fire Protection Association and local codes. The NFPA has standard codes for fire extinguishing equipment that must be strictly adhered to. At present, the most commonly used systems are the Carbon Dioxide and Dry Chemical Extinguishing Systems in conjunction with Portable Fire Extinguishers.

Ventilator installations should completely cover the equipment being ventilated with minimum overhangs on all sides regulated by National and local codes. Maximum floor to canopy height should be approximately 7 ft, and the canopy from bottom to top should be 2 ft or more.

Cini-Grissom Associates, Inc.; Food Service Consultants; Washington, D.C.

1   DESIGN ELEMENTS

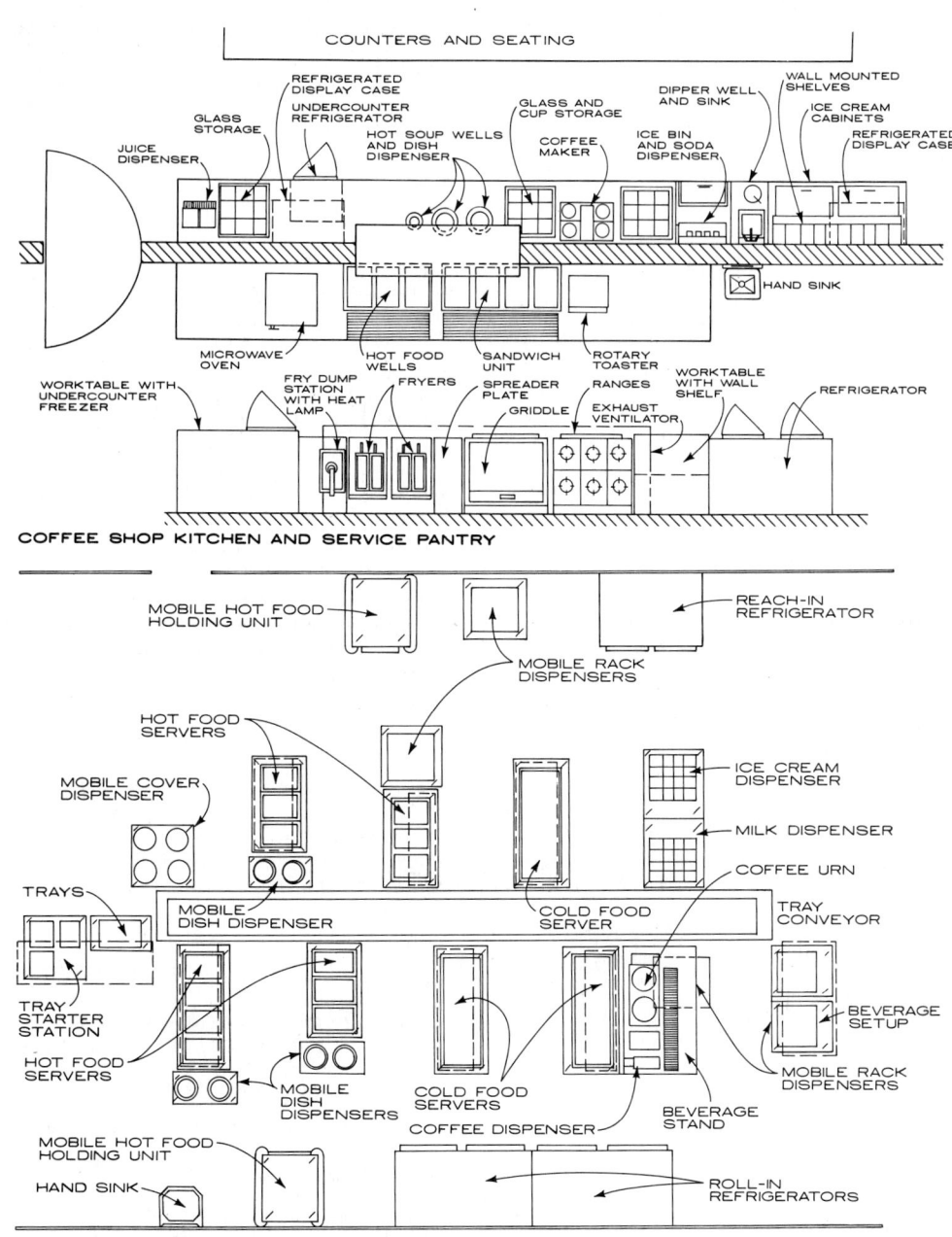

COFFEE SHOP KITCHEN AND SERVICE PANTRY

HOSPITAL PATIENT TRAY ASSEMBLY SYSTEM

INSTITUTIONAL

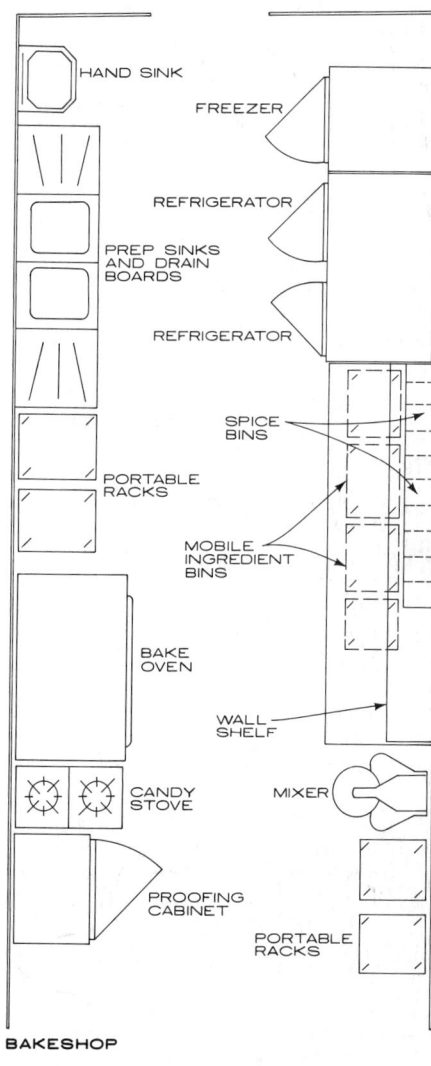

BAKESHOP

NOTE

This system is designed for trays made up in advance of service. It is most commonly used in hospitals, extended care facilities, and hospices. In some cafeteria situations, this design may be modified for reduced customer food handling. Because of the modular design, the system may accommodate a wide variety of menu items.

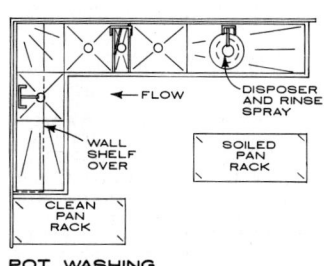

POT WASHING

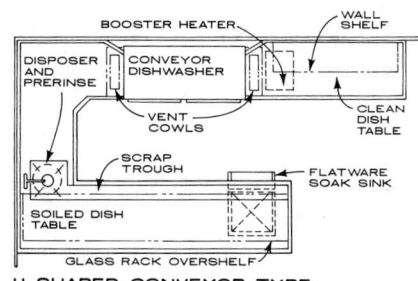

U-SHAPED CONVEYOR TYPE

NOTE

The conveyor type dish machine is less costly than a circular system and has a larger volume capacity than a straight-through machine. Many table configurations are available.

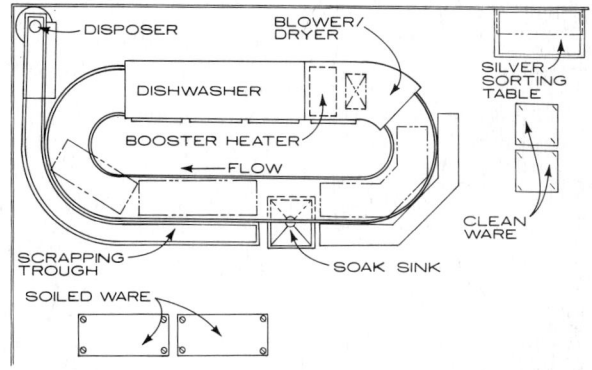

CIRCULAR TYPE

NOTE

The circular system is overall less labor intensive than other designs. It is most useful in a large volume operation.

WARE WASHING SYSTEMS

Cini-Grissom Associates, Inc.; Food Service Consultants; Washington, D.C.

DESIGN ELEMENTS 1

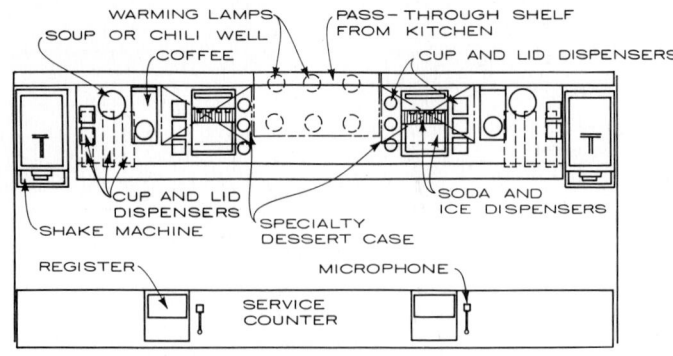

BEVERAGE AND SERVICE COUNTER

NOTE

Design of the service counter will depend on the number of stations required for efficient service and the amount of space available.

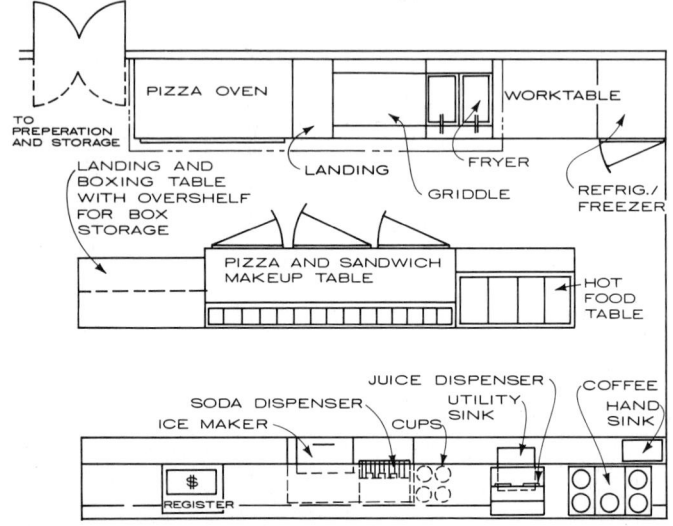

PIZZA AND SANDWICH SHOP

NOTE

This type of operation has many variables. Sandwiches and hot entrees may or may not be offered. The equipment requirements are directly related to the menu, volume, and style of service.

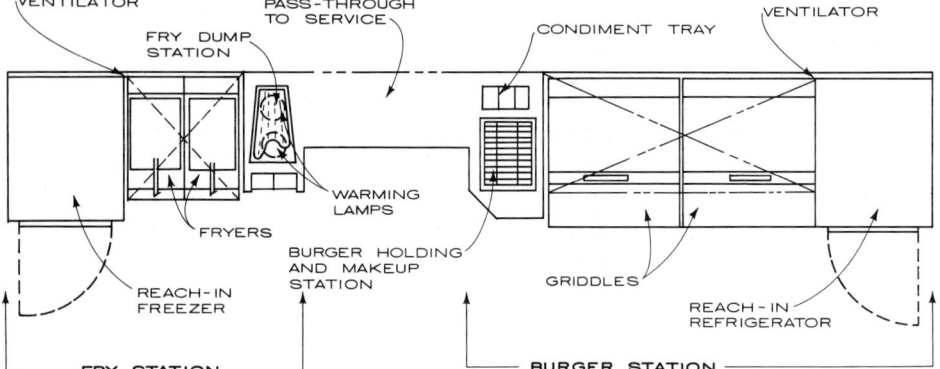

NOTE

The area will vary depending on the menu and method of preparation. Alternate equipment would include a charbroiler, conveyor charbroiler, and more fry space for expanded fry menu items.

HAMBURGER AND FRENCH FRY PREPARATION AREA

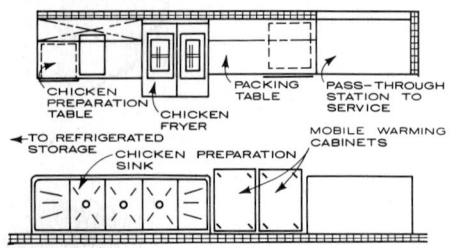

NOTE

This area has been designed for preportioned refrigerated chicken parts. An alternate layout includes ovens for prebreaded, frozen portions.

CHICKEN PREPARATION

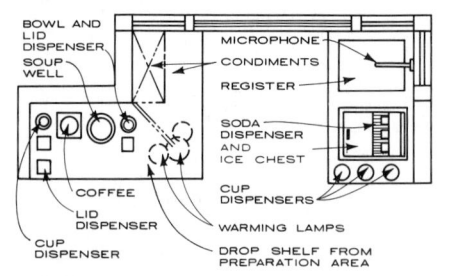

NOTE

The window serves the same menu as the inside operation. Service may be pass-window or bank-drawer type.

DRIVE-UP WINDOW

Cini-Grissom Associates, Inc.; Food Service Consultants; Washington, D.C.

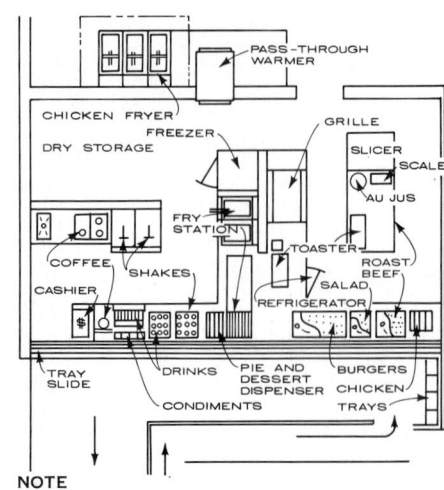

NOTE

The design is an alternative to the service counter operation. The walk-through situation requires less service personnel.

CAFETERIA STYLE BURGER, ROAST BEEF, AND CHICKEN

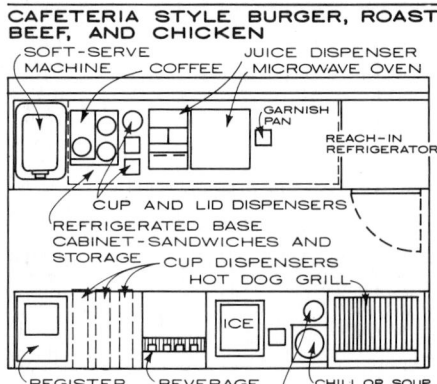

NOTE

Snack bars are most commonly found in stadiums, sports centers, and transportation terminals. They serve a limited menu with prepackaged foods. Most items will be prepared in a commissary situation.

SNACK BAR

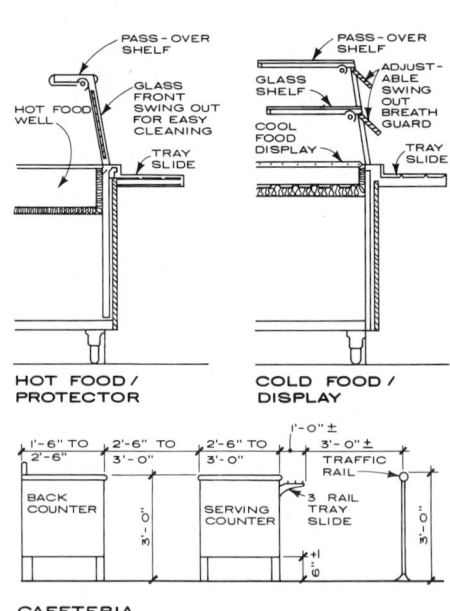

CAFETERIA COUNTERS

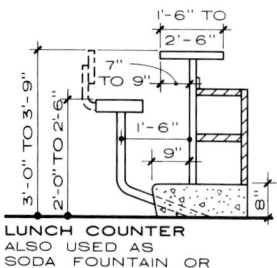

LUNCH COUNTER
ALSO USED AS
SODA FOUNTAIN OR
DINING COUNTER

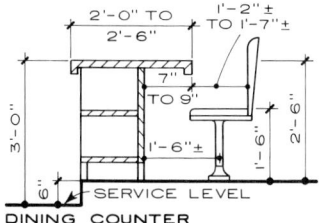

DINING COUNTER
FOR CHAIR HEIGHT STOOL.
IF ABOVE 1'-6" AND COUNTER
HEIGHT ABOVE 2'-6", USE STEP
OR FOOT RAIL

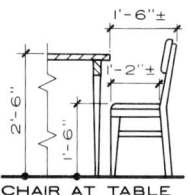

CHAIR AT TABLE

SECTIONS THROUGH COUNTERS, TABLES, AND SEATS

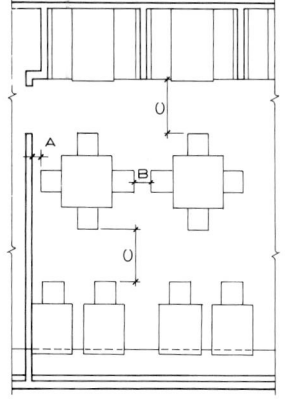

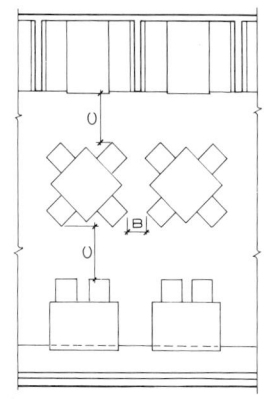

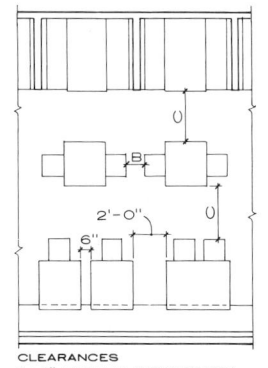

CLEARANCES
A = 6" MINIMUM (NO PASSAGE)
B = 1'-6" LIMITED PASSAGE
C = 2'-6" TO 3'-0" SERVICE AISLE

TYPICAL SEATING ARRANGEMENTS

AVERAGE CAPACITIES PER PERSON

TYPE OF ROOM	SQUARE FEET
Banquet	10–12
Cafeteria	12–15
Tearoom	10–14
Lunchroom/coffee shop	12–16
Dining room/restaurant	13–16
Specialty/formal dining	17–22

NOTE

Figures are general and represent minimum average dimensions. No maximum exists. Seating allowances and requirements may vary to suit individual operations.

GENERAL DESIGN CRITERIA

Service aisles: 30–42 in.

1. Square seating, 66 in. minimum between tables, 30 in. aisle plus two chairs back to back.
2. Diagonal seating, 36 in. minimum between corners of tables.
3. Wall seating, 30 in. minimum between wall and seat back.
4. Minimum of 30 in. for bus carts and flaming service carts.

Customer aisles:

1. Refer to local codes for restrictions on requirements.
2. Wheelchair requirements, 35–44 in. aisle.
3. Wall seating, 30 in. minimum between walls and table.

Tables:

1. Average 29 in. high.
2. Allow space around doors and food service areas.

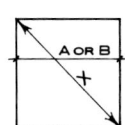

SQUARE

PERSONS	A OR B	X
2	2'-0" to 2'-6"	2'-10" to 3'-6"
4	2'-6" to 3'-0"	3'-6" to 4'-3"

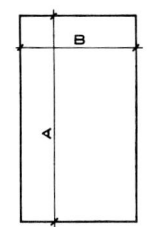

RECTANGLE

PERSONS	A	B
2	2'-6" to 3'-0"	2'-0" to 2'-6"
2 (on one side)	3'-4" to 4'-0"	
6	5'-10" to 6'-0"	2'-6" to 3'-0"
8	6'-10" to 7'-0"	

Tables wider than 2'-6" will seat one at each end.

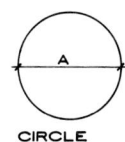

CIRCLE

PERSONS	A
4–5	3'-6" to 4'-0"
6–7	4'-6" to 5'-0"
7–8	5'-6" to 6'-4"
8–10	6'-0" to 7'-2"

Round tables are usually recommended only for seating 5 persons or more.

"A" dim. depends on the perimeter (1'-10"–1'-2" per person) necessary to seat required number. For cocktails, 1'-6" is sufficient.

NOTE

Minimum sizes are satisfactory for drink service; larger sizes for food. Tables with widespread bases are more practical than four legged tables.

Tables and arrangements are affected by the type of operations and the style of service. The use of flaming trays, busing carts, high chairs for children, and handicapped access must be considered.

TABLES

NOTE

All dimensions are minimum clearances. Seating layouts show general configurations and are not intended to depict any specific type of operation. Tables may be converted from square to round to enlarge seating capacity. Booth seating makes effective use of corner space.

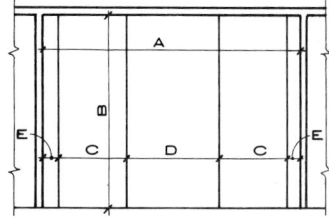

PLAN

A Seat back to seat back: 5'-0" to 6'-2".
B One person per side: 2'-0" to 2'-6".
  Two persons per side: 3'-6" to 4'-6".
  Recommended max. for serving and cleaning 4'-0".
C 1'-6" ±
D 2'-0" to 2'-6".
E 0" to 4"

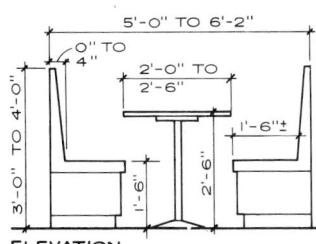

ELEVATION

NOTE

Local regulations determine actual booth sizes. Tables are often 2 in. shorter than seats, and may have rounded ends. Circular booths have overall diameter of 6 ft 4 in. +.

BOOTHS

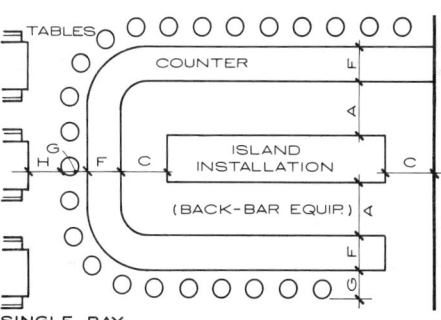

SINGLE BAY

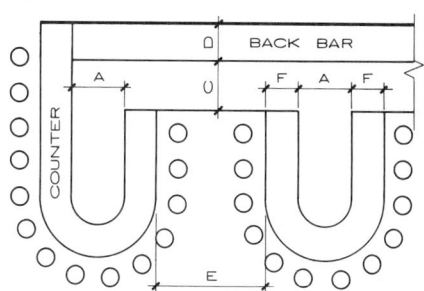

MULTIPLE BAY

STRAIGHT

A = 2'-3" to 3'-0"	E = 5'-0" to 5'-6"
B = 2'-0" to 2'-2"	F = 1'-6" to 2'-6"
C = 2'-3" to 3'-0"	G = 1'-3" to 1'-6"
D = 1'-6" to 2'-9"	H = 3'-0" to 4'-0"

TYPICAL COUNTER ARRANGEMENTS

Cini-Grissom Associates, Inc.; Food Service Consultants; Washington, D.C.

THEATER DESIGN CRITERIA

The planning of seating areas in places of assembly should involve the following considerations:

1. EFFICIENCY: The floor area efficiency in square feet per seat is a function of the row spacing, the average chair width, and the space allocation per seat for aisles. See following pages for further discussion of these factors.

Efficiency (F) = seat factor + aisle factor

$$F \text{ (sq ft/seat)} = \frac{W_s T}{144} + \frac{IT}{144} \times \frac{1}{S_{avg}}$$

where W_s = average seat width (in.)
T = row to row spacing (tread) (in.)
I = average aisle width (in.) (42 in. width is typical)
S_{avg} = average number of seats in a row per single aisle: 8 or fewer—inefficient layout; 14 to 16—maximum efficiency (multiple aisle seating); 18 to 50 and more—continental seating.

2. CAPACITY AND AUDIENCE AREA: Audience area = capacity x efficiency.

35-75	Classroom
75-150	Lecture room, experimental theater
150-300	Large lecture room, small theater
300-750	Average drama theater in educational setting
750-1500	Small commercial theater, repertory theater, recital hall
1500-2000	Medium large theater, large commercial theater
2000-3000	Average civic theater, concert hall, multiple use hall
3000-6000	Very large auditorium
Over 6000	Special assembly facilities

3. PERFORMING AREA (not including adjacent support area) (sq ft):

	MINIMUM	AVERAGE	MAXIMUM
Lectures (single speaker)	150	240	500
Revue, nightclub	350	450	700
Legitimate drama	250	550	1000
Dance	700	950	1200
Musicals, folk opera	800	1200	1800
Symphonic concerts	1500	2000	2500
Opera	1000	2500	4000
Pageant	2000	3500	5000

4. ORIENTATION OR SEATED SPECTATOR: Head strain is minimized by orienting chairs or rows of chairs so that spectators face the center of action of the performing area.

5. ANGLE OF VISION OF SPECTATOR: The human eye has a peripheral spread of vision of about 130°. This angle of view from chairs in the front rows will define the outer limits of the maximum sized performing area.

6. ANGLE OF ENCOUNTER: The angle of encounter is defined by the 130° peripheral spread of vision of a single performer standing at the "point of command." Patrons seated outside the spread of this angle will not have simultaneous eye contact with performer. Natural sound communication will also deteriorate for these patrons.

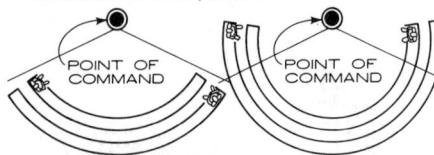

7. DISTANCE BETWEEN PERFORMANCE AND LAST ROW OF SPECTATORS: Achievement of visual and sound communication is enhanced by minimizing this distance while satisfying the preceding parameters.

Peter H. Frink; Frink and Beuchat: Architects; Philadelphia, Pennsylvania

SCREEN PROJECTION

- The minimum distance between the first row and the screen (D_F) is determined by the maximum allowable angle between the sightline from the first row to the top of the screen and the perpendicular to the screen at that point. A maximum angle of 30 to 35° is recommended.
- The maximum distance between the screen and the most distant viewer (MDV) should not exceed eight times the height of the screen image. An MDV two to three times the screen width is preferred.
- Screen width (W) is determined by the use of the appropriate aspect ratio between the screen image width and height.
- Curvature of screens may reduce the amount of apparent distortion for a larger audience area. Curvature of larger screens may help to keep the whole of the image in focus and may provide a more uniform distribution of luminance.

ZERO ENCIRCLEMENT (PROSCENIUM STAGE, PICTURE FRAME STAGE, END STAGE)

- The angle of audience spread in front of a masking frame is determined by the maximum size of the corner cutoff from a rectangularly shaped performing area that can be tolerated by seats at the side.
- Audience may not fill angle of encounter from point of command.
- Audience farthest from performing area.
- Large range in choice of size of performing area.
- Provisions for a large amount of scenic wall surfaces without masking sightlines.
- Horizontal movement of scenery typically made in both perpendicularly and parallel to centerline.
- Possibility of short differences in arrival time between direct and reflected sound at the spectator. This may be beneficial to music performances.

90° TO 130° ENCIRCLEMENT (PICTORIAL OPEN STAGE, WIDE FAN, HYBRID, THRUST STAGE)

- Audience spread defined and limited by angle of encounter from point of command.
- Performing area shape trapezoidal, rhombic, or circular.
- Audience closer to performing area than with zero encirclement.
- Picture frame less dominant.
- Range in choice of size of performing area.
- Provision for an amount of scenic wall surfaces possible without obscuring the performing area.
- Horizontal movement of scenery is possible in directions at 45° to and parallel to centerline.
- Shape of seating area places maximum number of seats within the directional limits of the sound of the unaided voice, beneficial for speech performance.

180° TO 270° ENCIRCLEMENT (GREEK THEATER, PENINSULAR, THREE-SIDED, THRUST STAGE, 3/4 ARENA STAGE, ELIZABETHAN STAGE)

- Audience spread well beyond angle of encounter from point of command in order to bring audience closer to performing area.
- Simultaneous eye contact between performer and all spectators not possible.
- Minimum range of choice in size of performing area.
- Provision of a small amount of scenic wall surfaces possible without masking sightlines.
- Horizontal movement of scenery is possible only parallel to centerline.
- Large encirclement by audience usually demands actor vomitory entrance through or under audience.

360° ENCIRCLEMENT (ARENA STAGE, THEATER IN THE ROUND, ISLAND STAGE, CENTER STAGE)

- Performer always seen from rear by some spectators.
- Simultaneous eye contact between performer and all spectators not possible.
- Audience closest to performance.
- No range of choice in size of performing area.
- No scenic wall surfaces possible without obscuring the view of the performing area.
- Horizontal movement of scenery not readily possible.
- Encirclement by audience demands actor vomitory entrance through audience area.

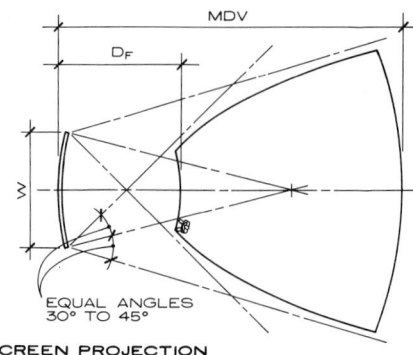

SCREEN PROJECTION

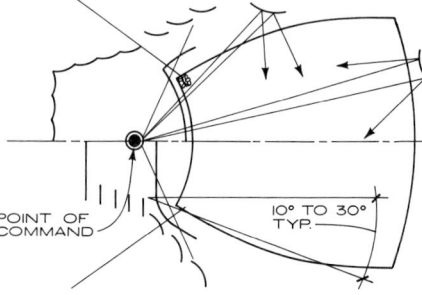

ZERO ENCIRCLEMENT

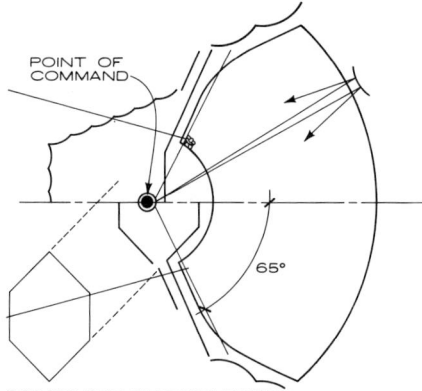

90° TO 130° ENCIRCLEMENT

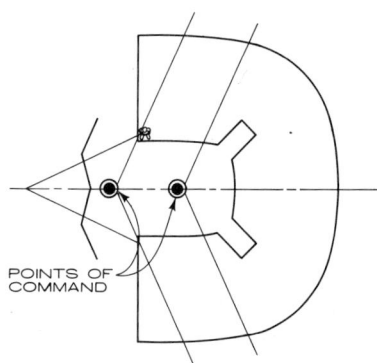

180° TO 270° ENCIRCLEMENT

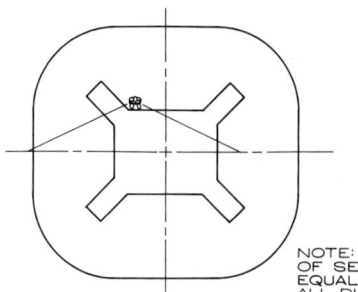

NOTE: AREA OF SEATING EQUAL FOR ALL DIAGRAMS

360° ENCIRCLEMENT

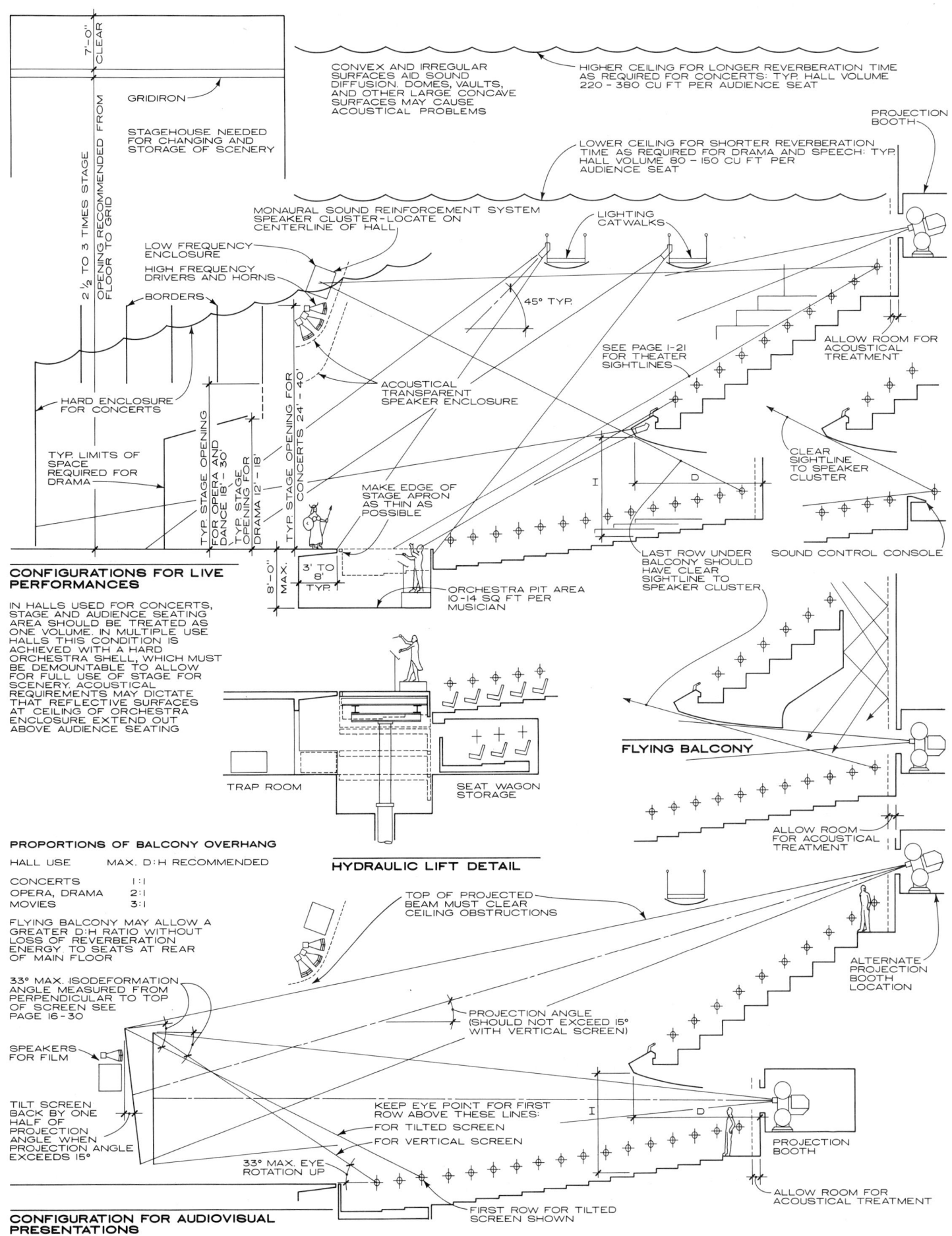

7'-0" CLEAR

GRIDIRON

STAGEHOUSE NEEDED FOR CHANGING AND STORAGE OF SCENERY

2½ TO 3 TIMES STAGE OPENING RECOMMENDED FROM FLOOR TO GRID

CONVEX AND IRREGULAR SURFACES AID SOUND DIFFUSION. DOMES, VAULTS, AND OTHER LARGE CONCAVE SURFACES MAY CAUSE ACOUSTICAL PROBLEMS

HIGHER CEILING FOR LONGER REVERBERATION TIME AS REQUIRED FOR CONCERTS: TYP. HALL VOLUME 220 - 380 CU FT PER AUDIENCE SEAT

PROJECTION BOOTH

LOWER CEILING FOR SHORTER REVERBERATION TIME AS REQUIRED FOR DRAMA AND SPEECH: TYP. HALL VOLUME 80 - 150 CU FT PER AUDIENCE SEAT

MONAURAL SOUND REINFORCEMENT SYSTEM SPEAKER CLUSTER-LOCATE ON CENTERLINE OF HALL

LIGHTING CATWALKS

LOW FREQUENCY ENCLOSURE

HIGH FREQUENCY DRIVERS AND HORNS

BORDERS

45° TYP.

ALLOW ROOM FOR ACOUSTICAL TREATMENT

HARD ENCLOSURE FOR CONCERTS

SEE PAGE 1-21 FOR THEATER SIGHTLINES

ACOUSTICAL TRANSPARENT SPEAKER ENCLOSURE

TYP. LIMITS OF SPACE REQUIRED FOR DRAMA

TYP. STAGE OPENING FOR OPERA AND DANCE 18' - 30'

TYP. STAGE OPENING FOR DRAMA 12'-18'

TYP. STAGE OPENING FOR CONCERTS 24' - 40'

CLEAR SIGHTLINE TO SPEAKER CLUSTER

MAKE EDGE OF STAGE APRON AS THIN AS POSSIBLE

I

D

8'-0" MAX.

3' TO 8' TYP.

ORCHESTRA PIT AREA 10-14 SQ FT PER MUSICIAN

LAST ROW UNDER BALCONY SHOULD HAVE CLEAR SIGHTLINE TO SPEAKER CLUSTER

SOUND CONTROL CONSOLE

CONFIGURATIONS FOR LIVE PERFORMANCES

IN HALLS USED FOR CONCERTS, STAGE AND AUDIENCE SEATING AREA SHOULD BE TREATED AS ONE VOLUME. IN MULTIPLE USE HALLS THIS CONDITION IS ACHIEVED WITH A HARD ORCHESTRA SHELL, WHICH MUST BE DEMOUNTABLE TO ALLOW FOR FULL USE OF STAGE FOR SCENERY. ACOUSTICAL REQUIREMENTS MAY DICTATE THAT REFLECTIVE SURFACES AT CEILING OF ORCHESTRA ENCLOSURE EXTEND OUT ABOVE AUDIENCE SEATING

TRAP ROOM

SEAT WAGON STORAGE

FLYING BALCONY

ALLOW ROOM FOR ACOUSTICAL TREATMENT

PROPORTIONS OF BALCONY OVERHANG

HALL USE	MAX. D:H RECOMMENDED
CONCERTS	1:1
OPERA, DRAMA	2:1
MOVIES	3:1

HYDRAULIC LIFT DETAIL

FLYING BALCONY MAY ALLOW A GREATER D:H RATIO WITHOUT LOSS OF REVERBERATION ENERGY TO SEATS AT REAR OF MAIN FLOOR

33° MAX. ISODEFORMATION ANGLE MEASURED FROM PERPENDICULAR TO TOP OF SCREEN SEE PAGE 16-30

TOP OF PROJECTED BEAM MUST CLEAR CEILING OBSTRUCTIONS

PROJECTION ANGLE (SHOULD NOT EXCEED 15° WITH VERTICAL SCREEN)

ALTERNATE PROJECTION BOOTH LOCATION

SPEAKERS FOR FILM

TILT SCREEN BACK BY ONE HALF OF PROJECTION ANGLE WHEN PROJECTION ANGLE EXCEEDS 15°

KEEP EYE POINT FOR FIRST ROW ABOVE THESE LINES: FOR TILTED SCREEN FOR VERTICAL SCREEN

I

D

PROJECTION BOOTH

33° MAX. EYE ROTATION UP

FIRST ROW FOR TILTED SCREEN SHOWN

ALLOW ROOM FOR ACOUSTICAL TREATMENT

CONFIGURATION FOR AUDIOVISUAL PRESENTATIONS

Peter H. Frink; Frink and Beuchat: Architects; Philadelphia, Pennsylvania

DESIGN ELEMENTS 1

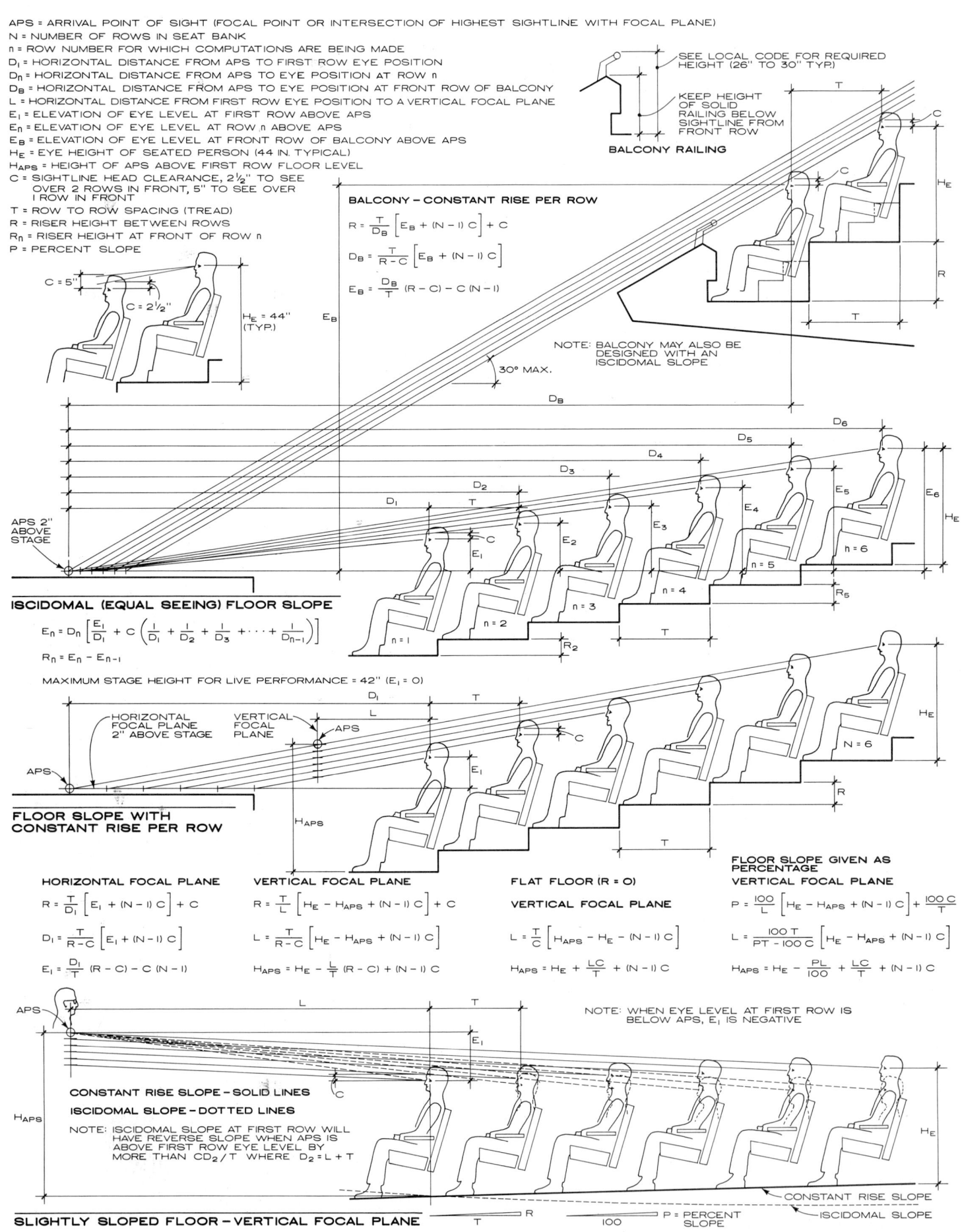

APS = ARRIVAL POINT OF SIGHT (FOCAL POINT OR INTERSECTION OF HIGHEST SIGHTLINE WITH FOCAL PLANE)
N = NUMBER OF ROWS IN SEAT BANK
n = ROW NUMBER FOR WHICH COMPUTATIONS ARE BEING MADE
D_1 = HORIZONTAL DISTANCE FROM APS TO FIRST ROW EYE POSITION
D_n = HORIZONTAL DISTANCE FROM APS TO EYE POSITION AT ROW n
D_B = HORIZONTAL DISTANCE FROM APS TO EYE POSITION AT FRONT ROW OF BALCONY
L = HORIZONTAL DISTANCE FROM FIRST ROW EYE POSITION TO A VERTICAL FOCAL PLANE
E_1 = ELEVATION OF EYE LEVEL AT FIRST ROW ABOVE APS
E_n = ELEVATION OF EYE LEVEL AT ROW n ABOVE APS
E_B = ELEVATION OF EYE LEVEL AT FRONT ROW OF BALCONY ABOVE APS
H_E = EYE HEIGHT OF SEATED PERSON (44 IN. TYPICAL)
H_{APS} = HEIGHT OF APS ABOVE FIRST ROW FLOOR LEVEL
C = SIGHTLINE HEAD CLEARANCE, 2½" TO SEE OVER 2 ROWS IN FRONT, 5" TO SEE OVER 1 ROW IN FRONT
T = ROW TO ROW SPACING (TREAD)
R = RISER HEIGHT BETWEEN ROWS
R_n = RISER HEIGHT AT FRONT OF ROW n
P = PERCENT SLOPE

C = 5"
C = 2½"
H_E = 44" (TYP.)
E_B

SEE LOCAL CODE FOR REQUIRED HEIGHT (26" TO 30" TYP.)
KEEP HEIGHT OF SOLID RAILING BELOW SIGHTLINE FROM FRONT ROW
BALCONY RAILING

BALCONY – CONSTANT RISE PER ROW

$$R = \frac{T}{D_B}\left[E_B + (N-1)C\right] + C$$

$$D_B = \frac{T}{R-C}\left[E_B + (N-1)C\right]$$

$$E_B = \frac{D_B}{T}(R-C) - C(N-1)$$

NOTE: BALCONY MAY ALSO BE DESIGNED WITH AN ISCIDOMAL SLOPE

30° MAX.

D_B

APS 2" ABOVE STAGE

ISCIDOMAL (EQUAL SEEING) FLOOR SLOPE

$$E_n = D_n\left[\frac{E_1}{D_1} + C\left(\frac{1}{D_1} + \frac{1}{D_2} + \frac{1}{D_3} + \cdots + \frac{1}{D_{n-1}}\right)\right]$$

$$R_n = E_n - E_{n-1}$$

MAXIMUM STAGE HEIGHT FOR LIVE PERFORMANCE = 42" (E_1 = 0)

HORIZONTAL FOCAL PLANE 2" ABOVE STAGE
VERTICAL FOCAL PLANE
APS

FLOOR SLOPE WITH CONSTANT RISE PER ROW

H_{APS}

HORIZONTAL FOCAL PLANE	VERTICAL FOCAL PLANE	FLAT FLOOR (R = 0)	FLOOR SLOPE GIVEN AS PERCENTAGE
			VERTICAL FOCAL PLANE
$R = \frac{T}{D_1}\left[E_1 + (N-1)C\right] + C$	$R = \frac{T}{L}\left[H_E - H_{APS} + (N-1)C\right] + C$	**VERTICAL FOCAL PLANE**	$P = \frac{100}{L}\left[H_E - H_{APS} + (N-1)C\right] + \frac{100C}{T}$
$D_1 = \frac{T}{R-C}\left[E_1 + (N-1)C\right]$	$L = \frac{T}{R-C}\left[H_E - H_{APS} + (N-1)C\right]$	$L = \frac{T}{C}\left[H_{APS} - H_E - (N-1)C\right]$	$L = \frac{100T}{PT - 100C}\left[H_E - H_{APS} + (N-1)C\right]$
$E_1 = \frac{D_1}{T}(R-C) - C(N-1)$	$H_{APS} = H_E - \frac{L}{T}(R-C) + (N-1)C$	$H_{APS} = H_E + \frac{LC}{T} + (N-1)C$	$H_{APS} = H_E - \frac{PL}{100} + \frac{LC}{T} + (N-1)C$

APS

NOTE: WHEN EYE LEVEL AT FIRST ROW IS BELOW APS, E_1 IS NEGATIVE

CONSTANT RISE SLOPE – SOLID LINES

ISCIDOMAL SLOPE – DOTTED LINES

NOTE: ISCIDOMAL SLOPE AT FIRST ROW WILL HAVE REVERSE SLOPE WHEN APS IS ABOVE FIRST ROW EYE LEVEL BY MORE THAN CD_2/T WHERE $D_2 = L + T$

H_{APS}

CONSTANT RISE SLOPE
ISCIDOMAL SLOPE

SLIGHTLY SLOPED FLOOR – VERTICAL FOCAL PLANE

$\frac{R}{T}$ $\frac{100}{}$ P = PERCENT SLOPE

Peter H. Frink; Frink and Beuchat: Architects; Philadelphia, Pennsylvania

1 DESIGN ELEMENTS

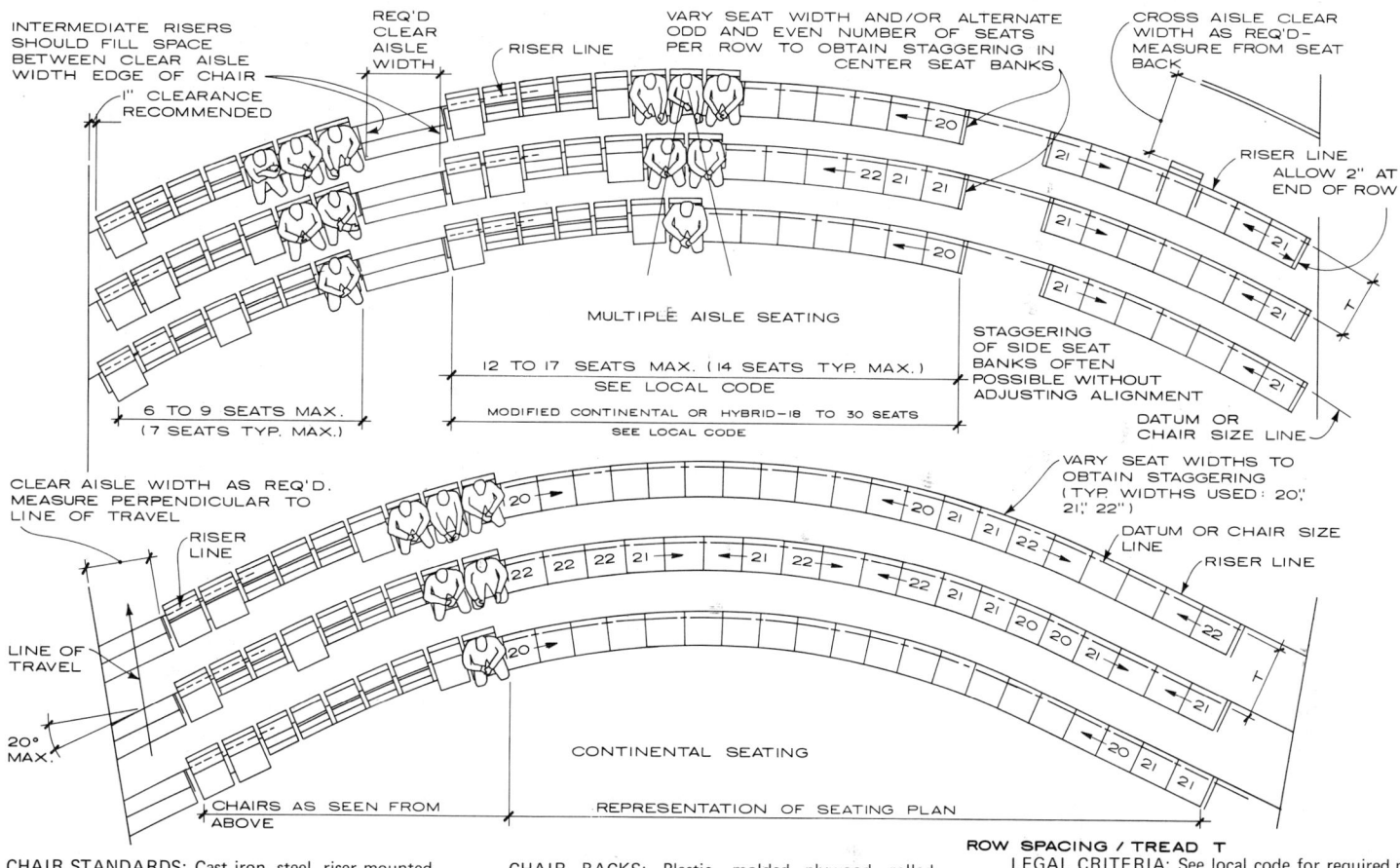

INTERMEDIATE RISERS SHOULD FILL SPACE BETWEEN CLEAR AISLE WIDTH EDGE OF CHAIR

1" CLEARANCE RECOMMENDED

REQ'D CLEAR AISLE WIDTH

RISER LINE

VARY SEAT WIDTH AND/OR ALTERNATE ODD AND EVEN NUMBER OF SEATS PER ROW TO OBTAIN STAGGERING IN CENTER SEAT BANKS

CROSS AISLE CLEAR WIDTH AS REQ'D- MEASURE FROM SEAT BACK

RISER LINE ALLOW 2" AT END OF ROW

6 TO 9 SEATS MAX. (7 SEATS TYP. MAX.)

MULTIPLE AISLE SEATING

12 TO 17 SEATS MAX. (14 SEATS TYP. MAX.) SEE LOCAL CODE

MODIFIED CONTINENTAL OR HYBRID-18 TO 30 SEATS SEE LOCAL CODE

STAGGERING OF SIDE SEAT BANKS OFTEN POSSIBLE WITHOUT ADJUSTING ALIGNMENT

DATUM OR CHAIR SIZE LINE

CLEAR AISLE WIDTH AS REQ'D. MEASURE PERPENDICULAR TO LINE OF TRAVEL

RISER LINE

LINE OF TRAVEL

20° MAX.

CHAIRS AS SEEN FROM ABOVE

CONTINENTAL SEATING

REPRESENTATION OF SEATING PLAN

VARY SEAT WIDTHS TO OBTAIN STAGGERING (TYP. WIDTHS USED: 20", 21", 22")

DATUM OR CHAIR SIZE LINE

RISER LINE

CHAIR STANDARDS: Cast iron, steel, riser mounted and floor mounted. Also pedestal mounting using continuous beam support or cantilevered standards. Folding tablet arms usually available.

CHAIR ARMS: Upholstered fabric, wood, plastic, metal.

CHAIR BACKS: Plastic, molded plywood, rolled stamped metal, upholstered front, rear. Higher backs and bottom extension for scuff protection also available.

CHAIR SEATS: Upholstered, plywood, plastic, metal pan, coil or serpentine springs, polyurethane foam.

ROW SPACING / TREAD T

LEGAL CRITERIA: See local code for required minimum spacing. Codes typically stipulate a minimum clear plumbline distance measured between the unoccupied chair and the rear of the back of the chair in front.

32"-33": typical minimum for multiple aisle seating
34"-37": typical minimum for modified continental seating
38"-42": typical minimum for continental seating

COMFORT FOR THE SEATED PERSON:

32": knees will touch chair back; uncomfortable
34": minimum spacing for comfort
36": ideal spacing for maximum comfort
38" and up: audience cohesiveness may suffer

EASE OF PASSAGE IN FRONT OF SEATED PERSONS:

32"-34": seated person must rise to allow passage
36"-38": some seated persons will rise
40" and up: passage in front of seated persons possible

SAFETY: Excessive plumbline distance may entice exiting persons to squeeze ahead and cause jam.

EFFICIENCY: Choice of minimum spacing satisfying criteria above reduces maximum distance to stage.

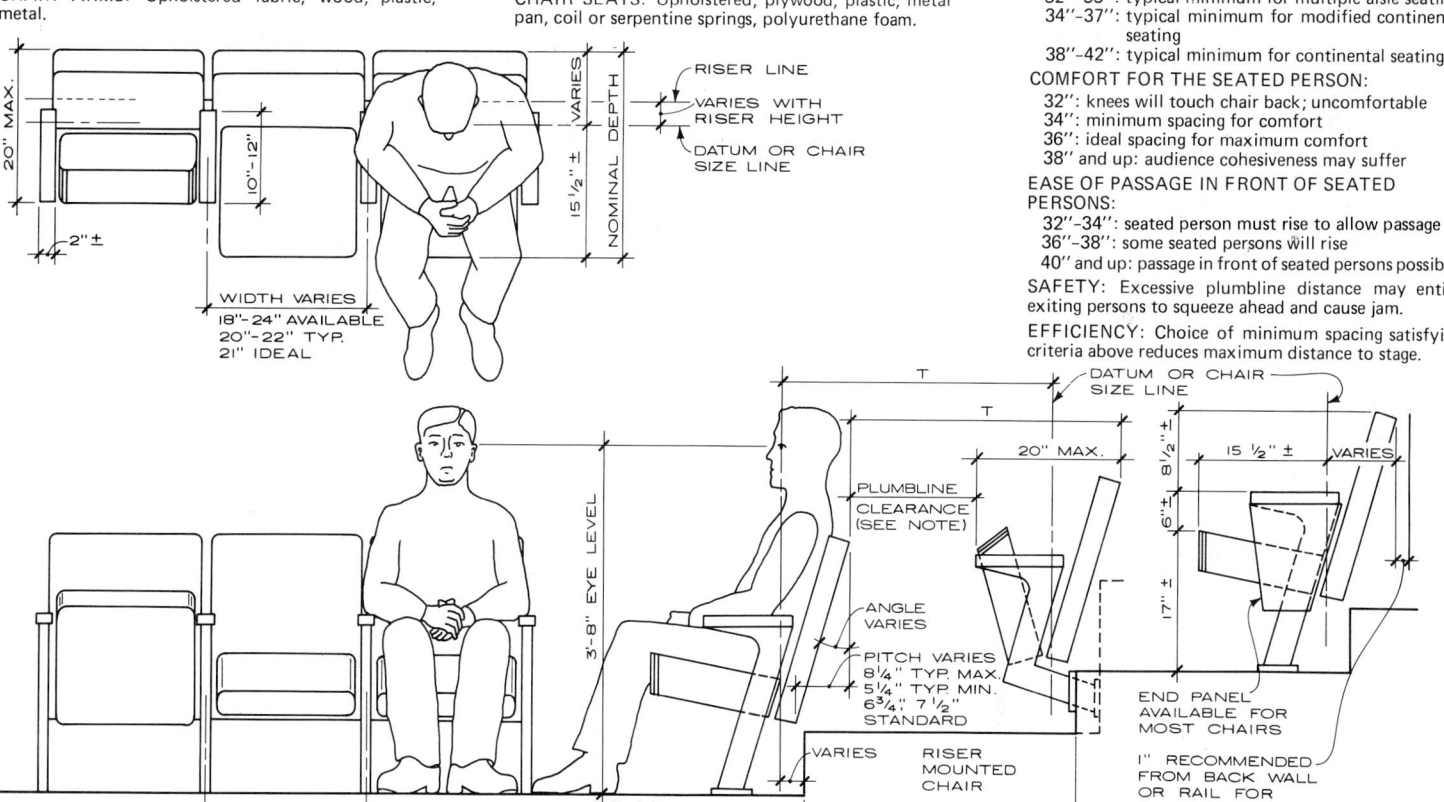

20" MAX.

10"-12"

2" ±

WIDTH VARIES
18"-24" AVAILABLE
20"-22" TYP.
21" IDEAL

RISER LINE

VARIES WITH RISER HEIGHT

DATUM OR CHAIR SIZE LINE

NOMINAL DEPTH

15 ½" ±

3'-8" EYE LEVEL

CHAIR WIDTH

FLOOR MOUNTED CHAIR

PLUMBLINE CLEARANCE (SEE NOTE)

ANGLE VARIES

PITCH VARIES
8¼" TYP. MAX.
5¼" TYP. MIN.
6¾", 7½" STANDARD

VARIES

RISER MOUNTED CHAIR

DATUM OR CHAIR SIZE LINE

20" MAX.

8½" ±

15 ½" ±

VARIES

6" ±

17" ±

END PANEL AVAILABLE FOR MOST CHAIRS

1" RECOMMENDED FROM BACK WALL OR RAIL FOR STANDEE

Peter H. Frink; Frink and Beuchat; Architects; Philadelphia, Pennsylvania

DESIGN ELEMENTS 1

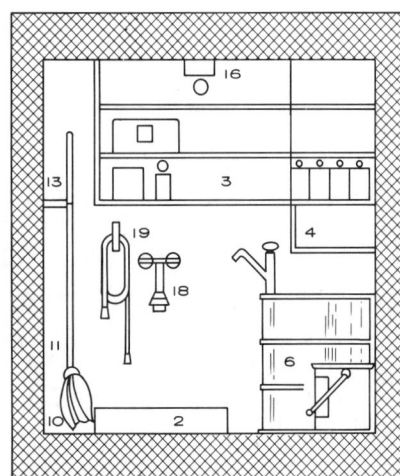

PLAN

NOTE

Housekeeping and maintenance facilities are an important program item in practically every building. Provide adequate space for all standard custodial functions, and add space for special equipment if required.

KEY—OPTIMUM CUSTODIAL CLOSET

1   Storage area for hoses, extension wands, pipes, etc.
2   Built in ceramic tile floor sink with drain (second choice: wall mounted utility sink).
3   Shelves over utility sink 9 in. deep, 12 in. spacing.
4   Storage shelving over floor stock, 18 in. deep, 12 in. spacing.
5   Mopping outfit in stored position.
6   Floor stock (drums, cans, etc.).
7   Floor machine in stored position.
8   Vacuum in stored position.
9   Accessories, fittings, and tools mounted on pegboard.
10 Aluminum or ceramic drip tray.
11 Mop in stored position.
12 Trigrip tool holders.
13 4-in. spacer to keep mops away from wall.
14 Bulletin board containing instructions, schedules, etc.
15 30 in. wide door with louver—location of door interchangeable with accessories pegboard if necessary because of orientation of area.
16 Ceiling light providing minimum 40 ft-c; light should be shielded to prevent damage.
17 Floor of ceramic tile or concrete with floor drain if possible.
18 Bibb (threaded) faucet with brace.
19 Length of hose for washing equipment. A custodial cabinet should be used where there is insufficient space to install a custodial closet.

SECTION

OPTIMUM CUSTODIAL CLOSET (6' × 9' INSIDE)

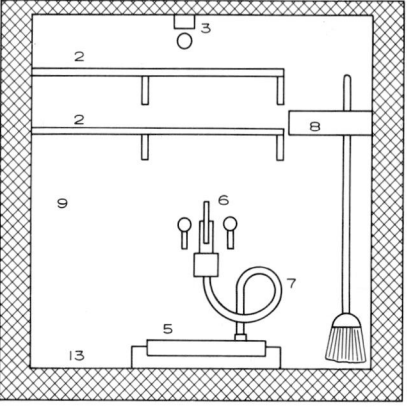

PLAN

SECTION

KEY—MINIMUM CUSTODIAL CLOSET

1   Dimensions: 8 ft long, $4\frac{1}{2}$ ft deep (36 ft^2).
2   Shelving 10 in. deep with bracket supports.
3   75 W lamp with door hinge switch.
4   Two 30 in. doors pierced for ventilation.
5   Utility floor sink with stainless steel lip cover; note off center.
6   Bibb faucet with support hanger.
7   4-ft length of hose.
8   Tool holder.
9   Walls ceramic to 4 ft, painted enamel (including ceiling) above 4 ft.
10 Location for custodial cart or waste hamper.
11 Location for two bucket (or three bucket) mopping outfit.
12 Location for floor machine or vacuum.
13 Floor—concrete, ceramic, or terrazzo (not resilient).

MINIMUM CLOSET (4½' × 8')

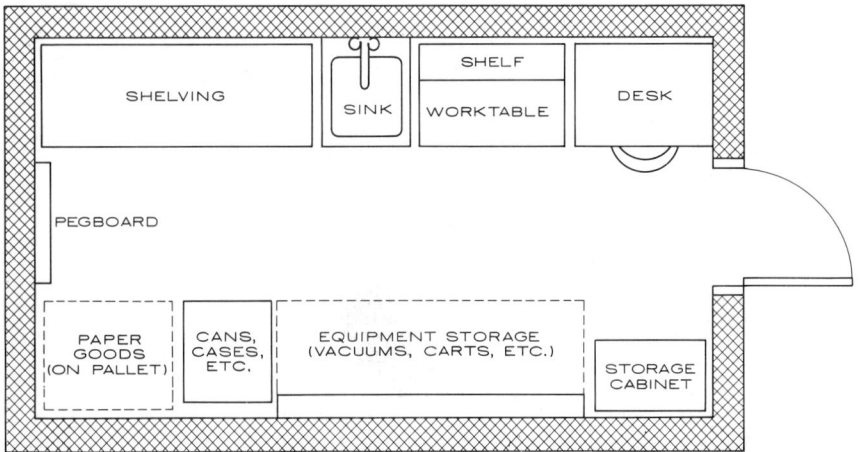

SMALL CENTRAL STORAGE AREA (8' × 15' INSIDE)

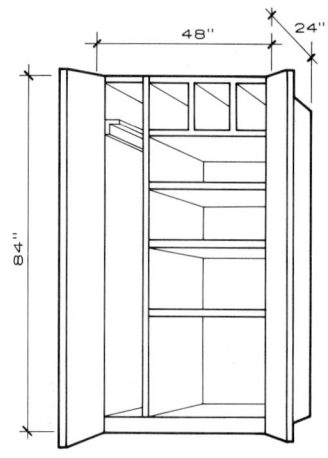

TYPICAL CUSTODIAL CABINET (METAL)

Edwin B. Feldman, P. E.; Service Engineering Associates, Inc.; Atlanta, Georgia

1 DESIGN ELEMENTS

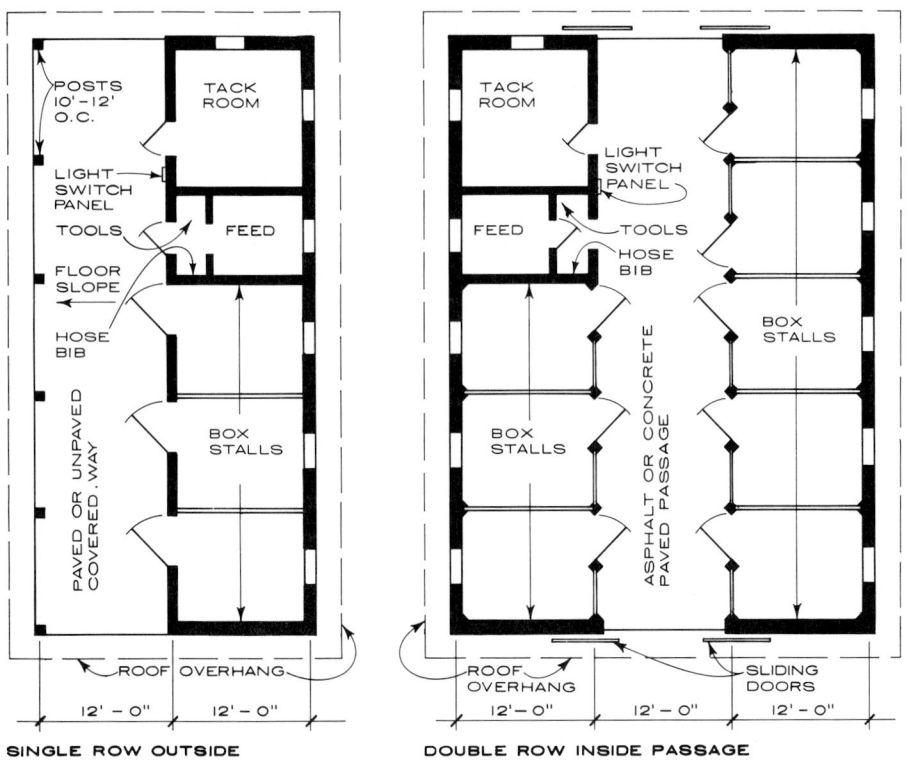

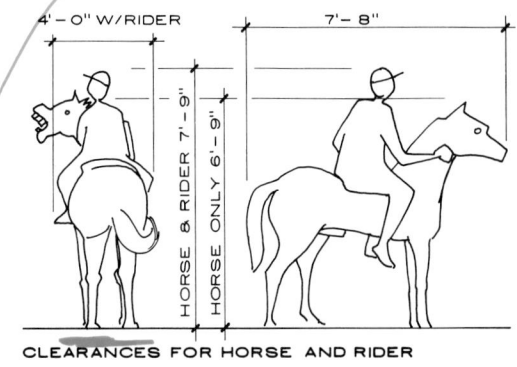

CLEARANCES FOR HORSE AND RIDER

- 4'-0" W/RIDER
- 7'-8"
- HORSE & RIDER 7'-9"
- HORSE ONLY 6'-9"

ARRANGEMENTS OF STALLS, TACK AND FEED ROOMS

SINGLE ROW OUTSIDE

POSTS 10'-12' O.C.

TACK ROOM

LIGHT SWITCH PANEL

TOOLS

FEED

FLOOR SLOPE

HOSE BIB

BOX STALLS

PAVED OR UNPAVED COVERED WAY

ROOF OVERHANG

12'-0" | 12'-0"

DOUBLE ROW INSIDE PASSAGE

TACK ROOM

LIGHT SWITCH PANEL

FEED

TOOLS

HOSE BIB

BOX STALLS

BOX STALLS

ASPHALT OR CONCRETE PAVED PASSAGE

ROOF OVERHANG

SLIDING DOORS

12'-0" | 12'-0" | 12'-0"

NOTES

Double row outside arrangements with stalls back to back are sometimes used at fairgrounds. Woven wire screening between stalls is omitted in racing stables, and wood is carried to full partition height. Combination protected incandescent lighting and heat lamps, frostproof hose bib and water supply are recommended where weather conditions warrant same. Passage lighting should be strip fluorescent type (40 foot-candles). Windows shown are glass jalousie type with fixed inside screen (plus woven wire guard for box stalls). Hardware for stalls should be heavy-duty galvanized, surface-applied type, "T" strap hinges and slide bolts for stall doors. Provide conventional heavy-duty hardware with locks for tack, feed and tool rooms. If exterior walls of stalls are masonry, furr out and finish interior surfaces with hardwood. Passages are sized to accept machinery. A tack room serves up to forty stalls.

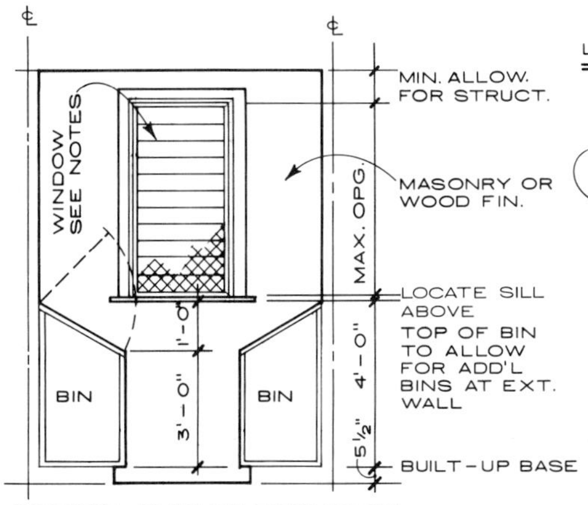

DETAILS OF FEED, TOOL, TACK ROOMS AND BOX STABLE

SECTION - ELEV. OF FEED ROOM

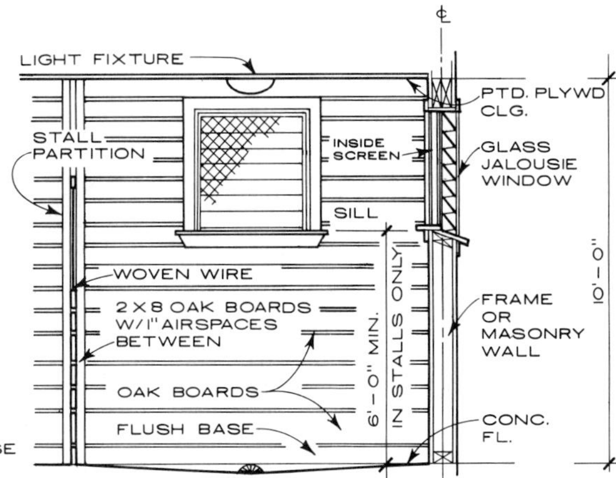

MIN. ALLOW. FOR STRUCT.

WINDOW SEE NOTES

MASONRY OR WOOD FIN.

MAX. OPG.

LOCATE SILL ABOVE TOP OF BIN TO ALLOW FOR ADD'L BINS AT EXT. WALL

BIN | BIN

BUILT-UP BASE

4'-0" 3'-0" 5½"

SECT. - ELEV. STALL EXT. WALL

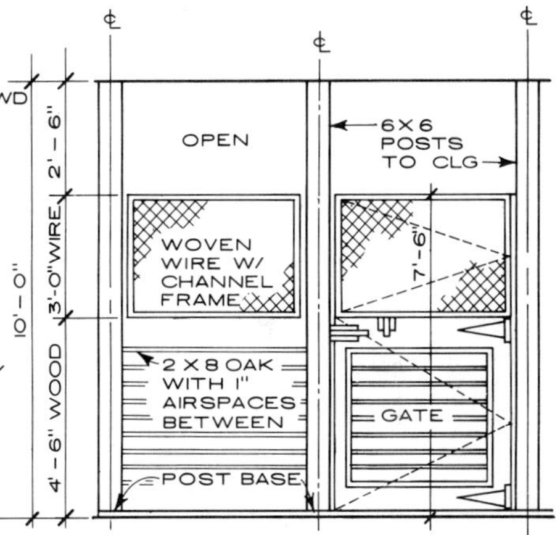

LIGHT FIXTURE

STALL PARTITION

INSIDE SCREEN

PTD. PLYWD CLG.

GLASS JALOUSIE WINDOW

SILL

WOVEN WIRE

2 X 8 OAK BOARDS W/ 1" AIRSPACES BETWEEN

OAK BOARDS

FLUSH BASE

FRAME OR MASONRY WALL

CONC. FL.

6'-0" MIN. IN STALLS ONLY

ELEVATION OF BOX STALL

6 X 6 POSTS TO CLG

OPEN

WOVEN WIRE W/ CHANNEL FRAME

2 X 8 OAK WITH 1" AIRSPACES BETWEEN

GATE

POST BASE

3'-0" WIRE 2'-6" 4'-6" WOOD 10'-0" 7'-6"

PLAN OF FEED & TOOL ROOMS

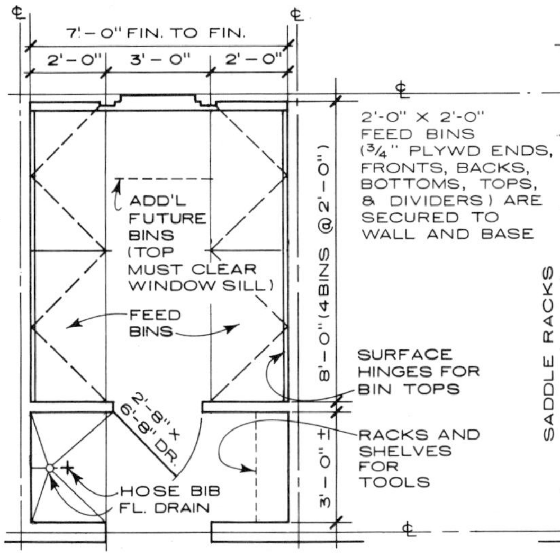

7'-0" FIN. TO FIN.

2'-0" | 3'-0" | 2'-0"

ADD'L FUTURE BINS (TOP MUST CLEAR WINDOW SILL)

FEED BINS

2'-0" X 2'-0" FEED BINS (¾" PLYWD ENDS, FRONTS, BACKS, BOTTOMS, TOPS, & DIVIDERS) ARE SECURED TO WALL AND BASE

SURFACE HINGES FOR BIN TOPS

RACKS AND SHELVES FOR TOOLS

HOSE BIB FL. DRAIN

2'-8" X 6'-8" DR

8'-0" (4 BINS @ 2'-0") 3'-0"

PLAN OF TACK ROOM

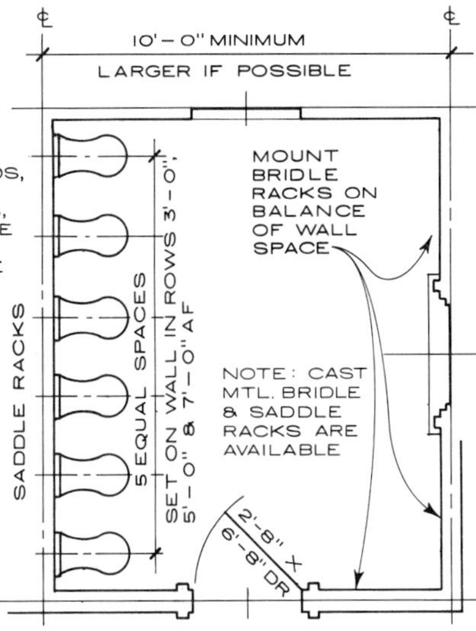

10'-0" MINIMUM

LARGER IF POSSIBLE

SADDLE RACKS

MOUNT BRIDLE RACKS ON BALANCE OF WALL SPACE

NOTE: CAST MTL. BRIDLE & SADDLE RACKS ARE AVAILABLE

SET ON WALL IN ROWS 5'-0" & 7'-0" AF

5 EQUAL SPACES

2'-8" X 6'-8" DR

PLAN OF BOX STALL

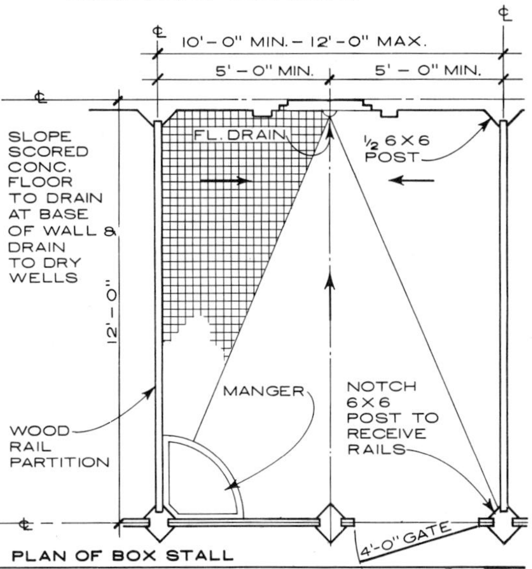

10'-0" MIN. - 12'-0" MAX.

5'-0" MIN. | 5'-0" MIN.

SLOPE SCORED CONC. FLOOR TO DRAIN AT BASE OF WALL & DRAIN TO DRY WELLS

WOOD RAIL PARTITION

FL. DRAIN

½ 6 X 6 POST

MANGER

NOTCH 6 X 6 POST TO RECEIVE RAILS

12'-0"

4'-0" GATE

Douglas S. Stenhouse, AIA, AICP; Los Angeles, California

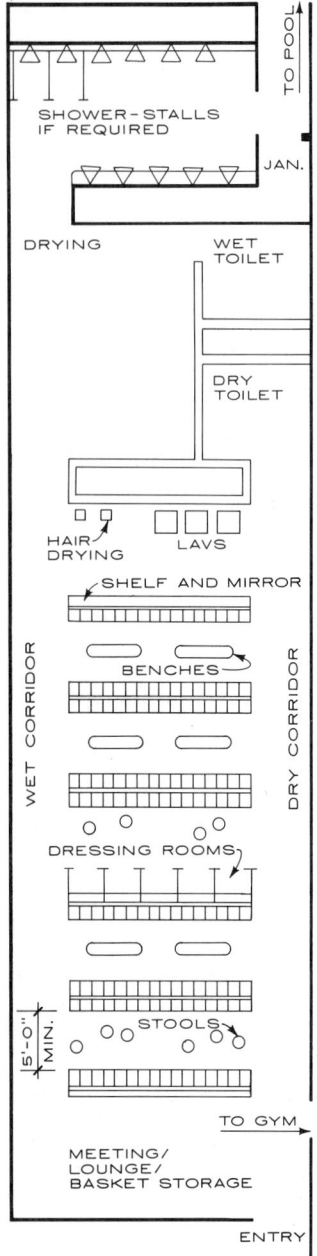

LOCKER/SHOWER UNIT

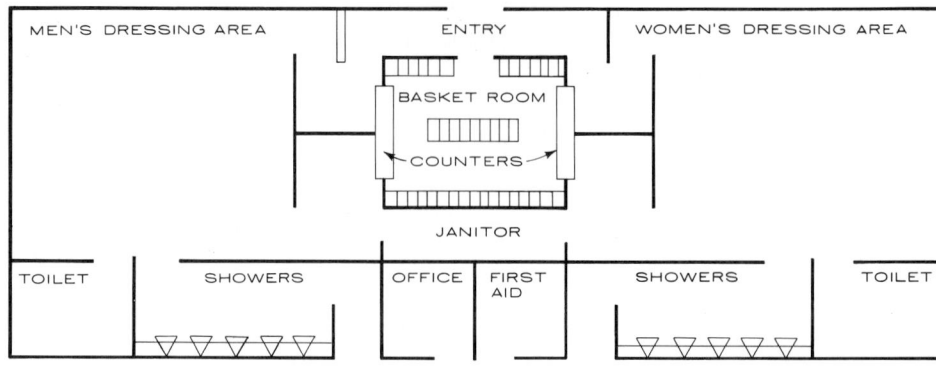

DRESSING UNIT FOR POOL

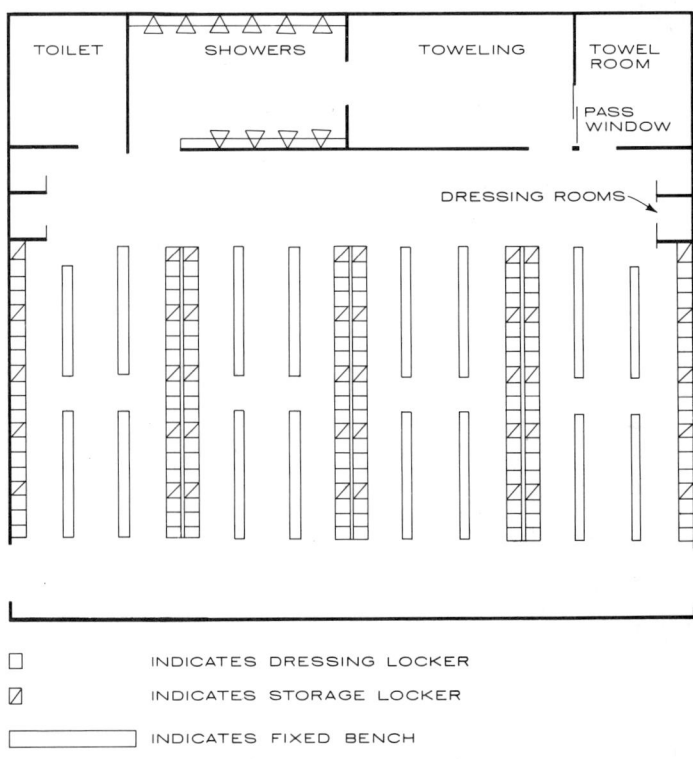

☐ INDICATES DRESSING LOCKER

▨ INDICATES STORAGE LOCKER

▭ INDICATES FIXED BENCH

TO SERVE GYMNASIUM AND POOL

NOTES

The best arrangement of lockers is the bay system, with a minimum 4 ft circulation aisle at each end of the bays. Ordinarily, the maximum number of lockers in a bay is 16. Locate dry (shoe) traffic at one end of the bays and wet (barefoot) traffic at the other end. For long bays with a single bench, make 3 ft breaks at 15 ft intervals.

Supervision of school lockers is the easiest if they are located in single banks along the two long walls, providing one or more bays that run the length of the room.

The number of lockers in a locker room depends on the anticipated number of members and/or size of classes. Separate locker areas should be encouraged. In small buildings interconnecting doors provide flexibility and allow for the handling of peak loads.

Individual dressing and shower compartments may be required for women's and girls' locker and shower rooms and for men's clubs. A shower stall for the handicapped may also be required.

YMCA Building and Furnishings Service; New York, New York

GYMNASIUM LOCKER ROOM

Basket storage, if included, is self-service. Maximum height is 8 tiers. A dehumidifying system should be provided to dry out basket contents overnight. Separate auxiliary locker rooms may be required. These may serve teams, part time instructors, the faculty, or volunteer leaders. A small room for the coach's use may be desirable.

The shower rooms should be directly accessible to the toweling room and the locker room that it serves. When a shower room is designed to serve a swimming pool, the room should be located so that all must pass through the showers prior to reaching the pool deck.

Separate wet and dry toilet areas are recommended. Wet toilets should be easily accessible from the shower room. When designed for use with a swimming pool, wet toilets should be located so that users must pass through the shower room after use of toilets.

Locker room entrance and exit doors should have vision barriers.

All facilities should be barrier free.

Floors should be of impervious material such as ceramic or quarry tile, with a Carborundum impregnated surface, and should slope toward the drains. Concrete floors (nonslip surface), if used, should be treated with a hardener to avoid the penetration of odors and moisture.

Walls should be of materials resistant to moisture and should have surfaces that are easily cleaned. All exterior corners in the locker rooms should be rounded.

Heavy duty, moisture resistant doors at locker room entrances and exits should be of sufficient size to handle the traffic flow and form natural vision barriers. Entrance/exit doors for the lockers should be equipped with corrosion resistant hardware.

Ceilings in shower areas should be of ceramic tile or other material impervious to moisture. Locker room ceilings should be acoustically treated with a material impervious to moisture and breakage. Floor drains should be kept out of the line of traffic where possible.

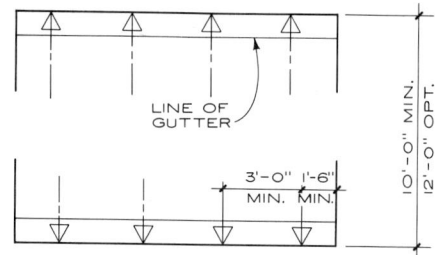

PLAN

GROUP SHOWERS

There must be a sufficient number of shower heads. Educational facilities with time constraints should have 10 shower heads for the first 30 persons and 1 shower head for every 4 additional persons. In recreational facilities 1 shower head for each 10 dressing lockers is a minimum. Temperature controls are necessary to keep water from exceeding 110°F. Both individual and master controls are needed for group showers.

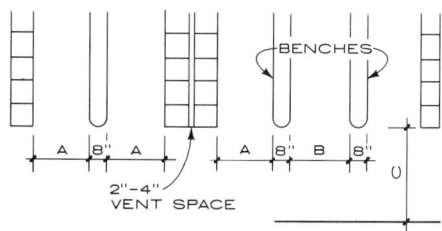

PLAN

AISLE SPACE FOR DRESSING ROOM
AISLE SPACE

	A	B	C
Recreation	2'-2''	1'-8''	3'-6''
School	2'-6''	2'-6''	4'-0''

Bench should be minimum 8 in. in width and 16 in. from the floor. Traffic breaks 3 ft minimum wide should occur at maximum intervals of 12 ft. Main traffic aisle to be wider for large number of locker bays. Avoid lockers that meet at 90° corner.

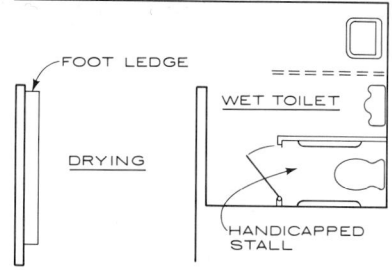

PLAN

DRYING ROOM AND WET TOILET

The drying room should have about the same area as the shower room. Provision for drainage should be made. Heavy duty towel rails, approximately 4 ft from the floor, are recommended. A foot drying ledge, 18 in. high and 8 in. wide as shown in the drawing, is desirable. An adjacent wet toilet is suggested. Avoid curbs between drying room and adjacent space. Towel service is desirable in a school. Size of area varies with material to be stored (can be used for distributing uniforms), with 200 sq ft usually being sufficient.

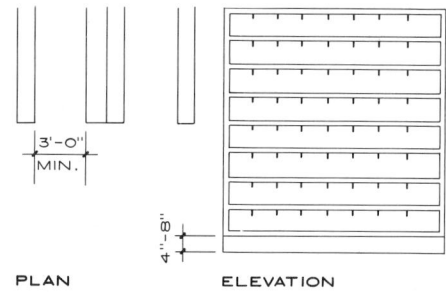

PLAN **ELEVATION**

BASKET ROOM AND BASKET RACK

Basket racks vary from 7 to 10 tiers in height. Wide baskets require 1 ft shelf space, small baskets 10 in. shelf space, both fit 1 to 1½ ft deep shelf. Back-to-back shelving is 2 ft 3 in. wide. Height shelf-to-shelf is 9¼ in.

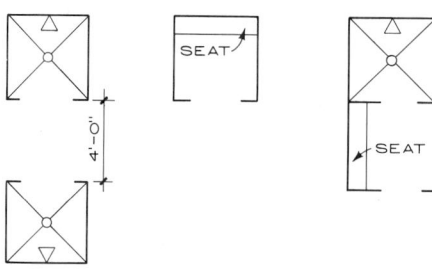

PLAN

INDIVIDUAL SHOWERS AND DRESSING ROOMS

INDIVIDUAL ROOMS	MINIMUM	OPTIMUM
Showers	3'-0'' x 3'-6''	3'-6'' x 3'-6''
Dressing Rooms	3'-0'' x 3'-6''	3'-6'' x 4'-0''

Individual dressing rooms and showers can be combined in a variety of configurations to obtain 1:1, 2:1, 3:1, and 4:1 ratios, respectively.

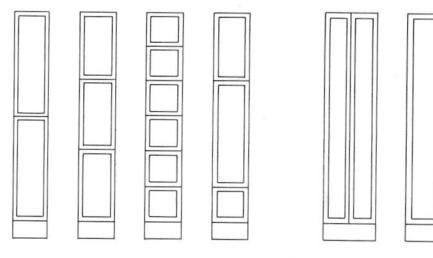

STORAGE **DRESSING**

LOCKERS
STANDARD SIZES

Width	9'', 12'', 15'', 18''
Depth	12'', 15'', 18''
Height	60'', 72'' (overall)

For schools, standard storage locker is 9 in. or 12 in. x 12 in. x 12 in. to 24 in. One storage locker per student enrolled plus 10% for expansion. Standard dressing lockers are 12 in. x 12 in. x 60 in. or 72 in. Number of dressing lockers should be equal to the peak period load plus 10 to 15% for variation.

LOCKER ROOM FACILITIES

ITEMS TO BE PROVIDED

1. Fixed benches 16 in. high.
2. Lockers on raised base.
3. Locker numbering system.
4. Hair dryers—one per 20 lockers.
5. Mirrors at lavatory.
6. Makeup mirror and shelf.
7. Drinking fountain (height as required).
8. Bulletin board.
9. Dressing booths if required.
10. Full length mirror.
11. Clock.
12. Door signs.
13. Sound system speaker if required.
14. Lighting at mirrors for grooming.
15. Lighting located over aisles and passages.
16. Adequate ventilation for storage lockers.
17. Windows located with regard to height and arrangement of lockers.
18. Visual supervision from adjacent office.

YMCA Building and Furnishings Service; New York, New York

RECOMMENDED MOUNTING HEIGHTS

Shower valve	4'-0''
Shower head	
Men	6'-6''
Women	6'-0''
Children	5'-0''
Hand dryer outlet	
Men	3'-8''
Women	3'-6''
Teenagers	3'-1''
Preteens	2'-8''
Hair dryer outlet	
Men	6'-0''
Women	5'-5''
Teenagers	5'-0''
Preteens	5'-0''
Clock	6'-6'' min.
Robe hook	6'-3''
Towel bar	4'-0''

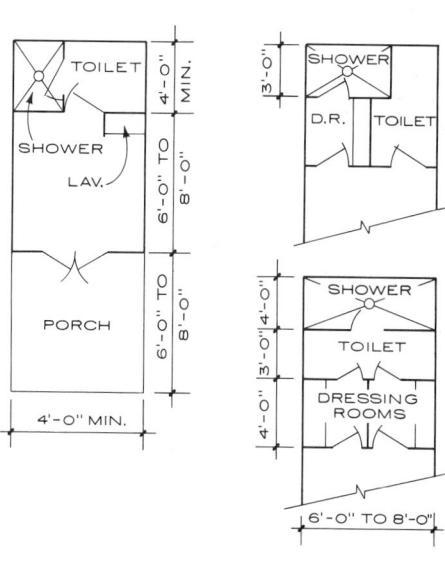

CABANAS

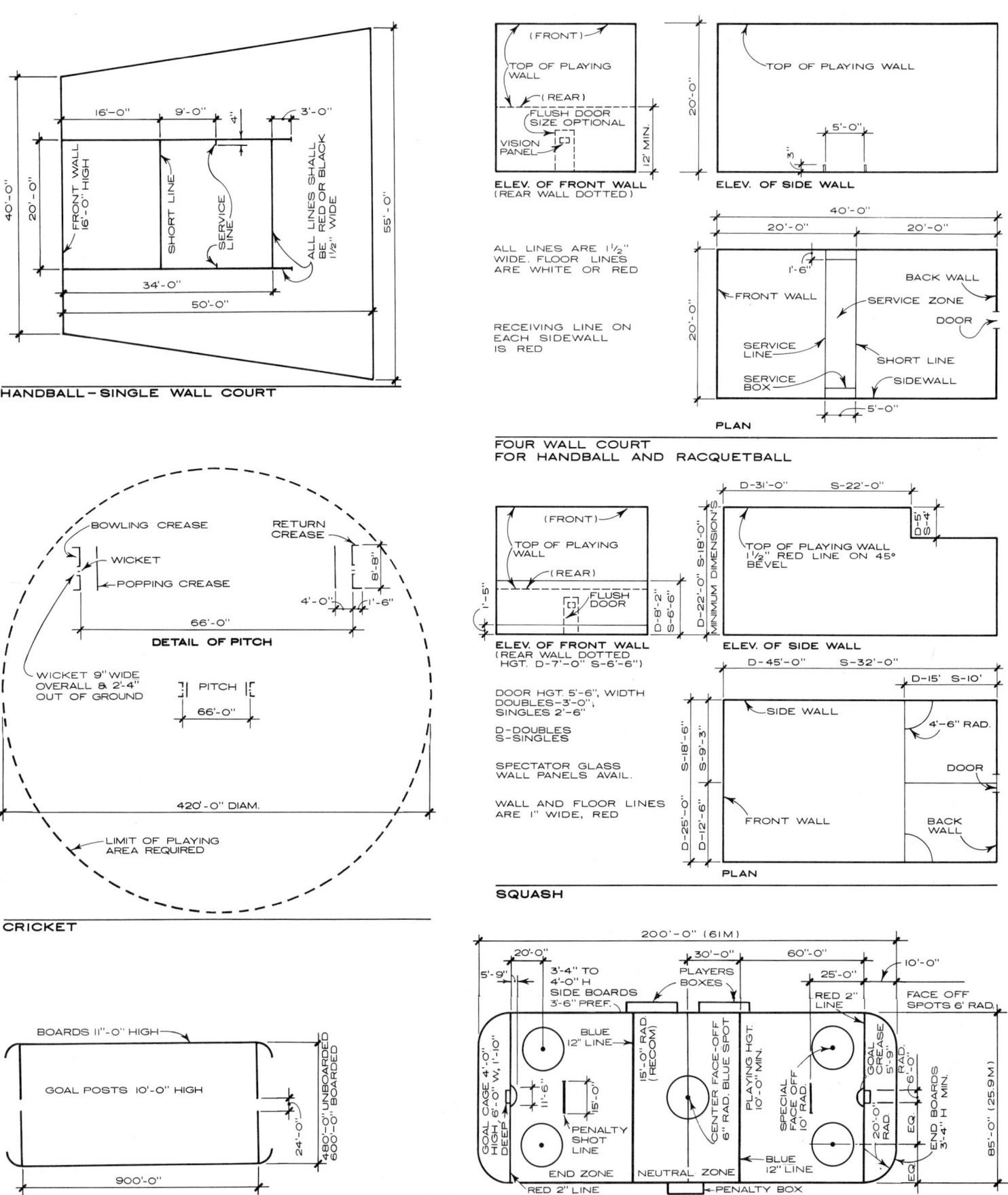

HANDBALL–SINGLE WALL COURT

FOUR WALL COURT
FOR HANDBALL AND RACQUETBALL

CRICKET

SQUASH

POLO

ICE HOCKEY

NOTE: This information is for preliminary planning and design only. For final layouts and design investigate current rules and regulations of the athletic organization or other authority whose standards will govern.

Charles F. D. Egbert, AIA, Architect; Washington, D.C.

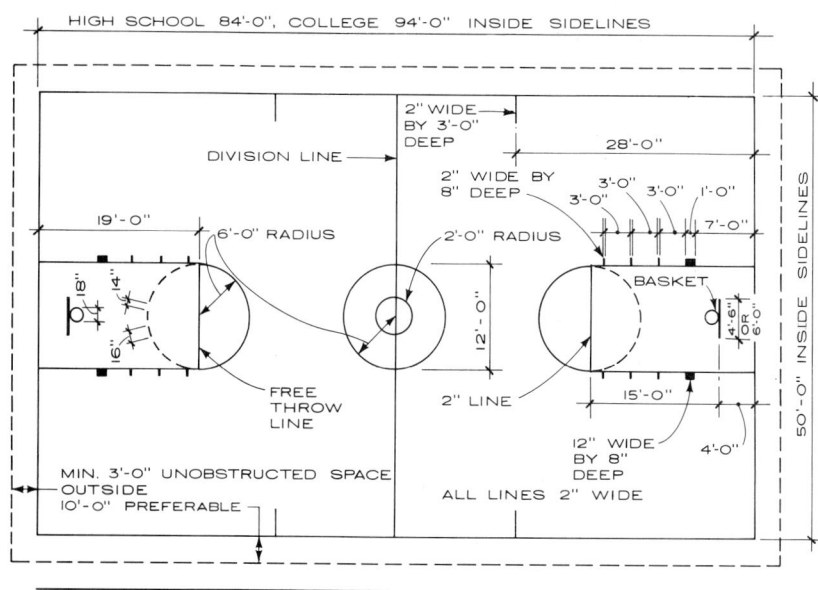

BASKETBALL COURT
NATIONAL COLLEGIATE ATHLETIC ASSOCIATION
AMATEUR ATHLETIC UNION

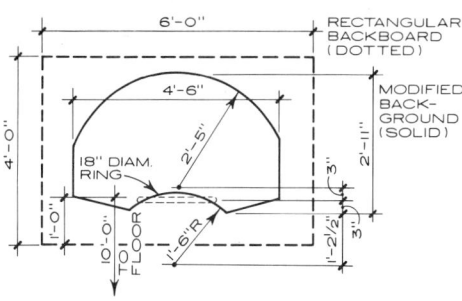

BACKBOARD DETAIL
COLLEGE – TRANSPARENT RECTANGULAR
BACKBOARD
HIGH SCHOOL – EITHER TYPE WITH FAN
SHAPE REQUIRED IN NEW
EQUIPMENT

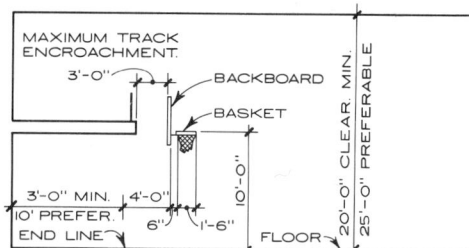

SECTION SHOWING BASKET AND ENCROACHMENTS

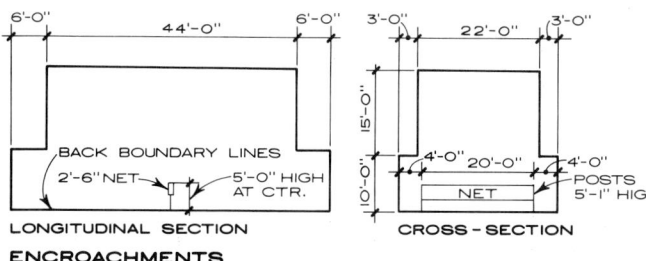

LONGITUDINAL SECTION

ENCROACHMENTS

CROSS-SECTION

5'-0" BETWEEN COURTS

LINED FOR BOTH
DOUBLES AND
SINGLES ALL
LINES 1½" WIDE.

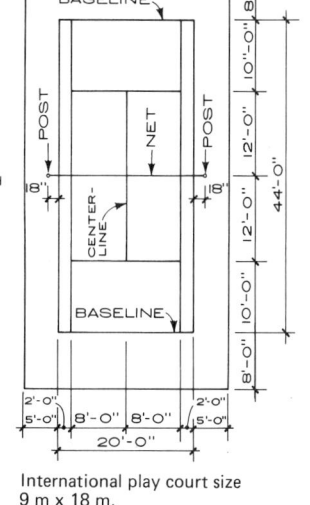

International play court size
9 m x 18 m.

PLATFORM TENNIS
WIRE: 16 GAUGE, 1" MESH,
12' HIGH. NET: 34" AT
CENTER. PLATFORM: 60' X
30'; BASELINES
20' X 44'

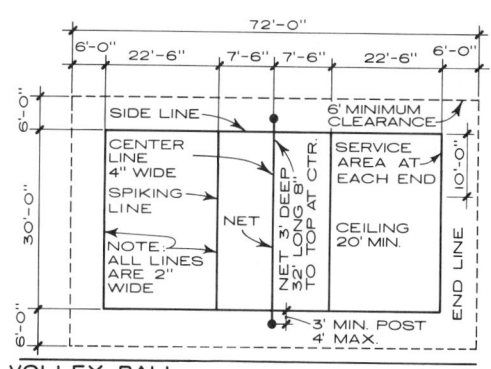

VOLLEY BALL
USVB ASSOCIATION: RULES AND GUIDE

U.S. Volley Ball Association: dimensions for unofficial
games. Court may be varied to suit players. (for
children and the less agile). Min. clearance 3'-0". See
page on womens sports.

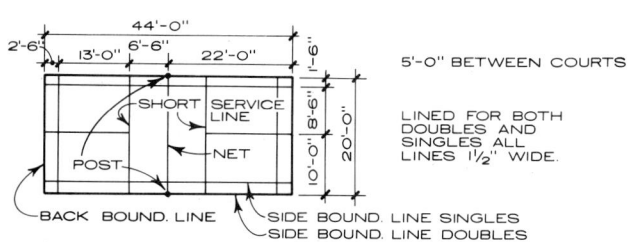

BADMINTON
AMERICAN BADMINTON ASSOCIATION

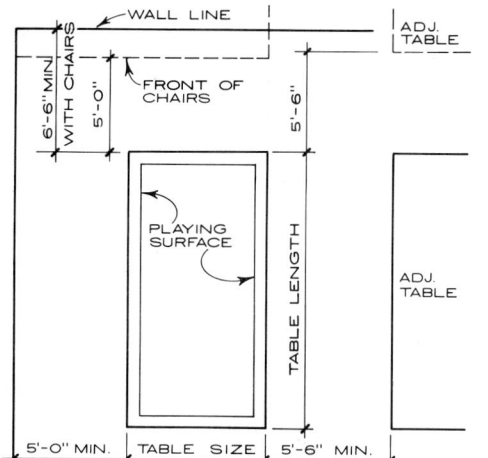

BILLIARDS AND POCKET BILLIARDS (POOL)
BILLIARD CONGRESS OF AMERICA

DIMENSIONS FOR BILLIARDS AND POCKET BILLIARDS

TYPE OF TABLE	PLAYING SURFACE		TABLE SIZE	
	W.	L.	W.	L.
ENGLISH (SNOOKER)	6'-0"	12'-0"	6'-9"	12'-9"
STANDARD POOL OR BILL.	5'-0"	10'-0"	5'-9"	10'-9"
STANDARD POOL OR BILL.	4'-6"	9'-0"	5'-3"	9'-9"
STANDARD POOL OR BILL.	4'-0"	8'-0"	4'-9"	8'-9"
JUNIOR POOL	3'-6"	7'-0"	4'-3"	7'-9"
JUNIOR POOL	3'-0"	6'-0"	3'-9"	6'-9"
TABLE HEIGHT 2'-6" ±				

BASKET– 18" DIAMETER
8' HEIGHT ELEMENT. SCH. USE
9' HEIGHT JUNIOR H.S.
10' HEIGHT H.S. AND COLLEGE

OUTDOOR
20' TO 30'R
INDOOR
15' TO 25'R

½ RADIUS
OF COURT

4' RADIUS

GOAL-HI COURT

NOTE: This information is for preliminary planning and design only. For final layouts and design investigate current rules and regulations of the athletic organization or other authority whose standards will govern.

Charles F. D. Egbert, AIA, Architect; Washington, D.C.

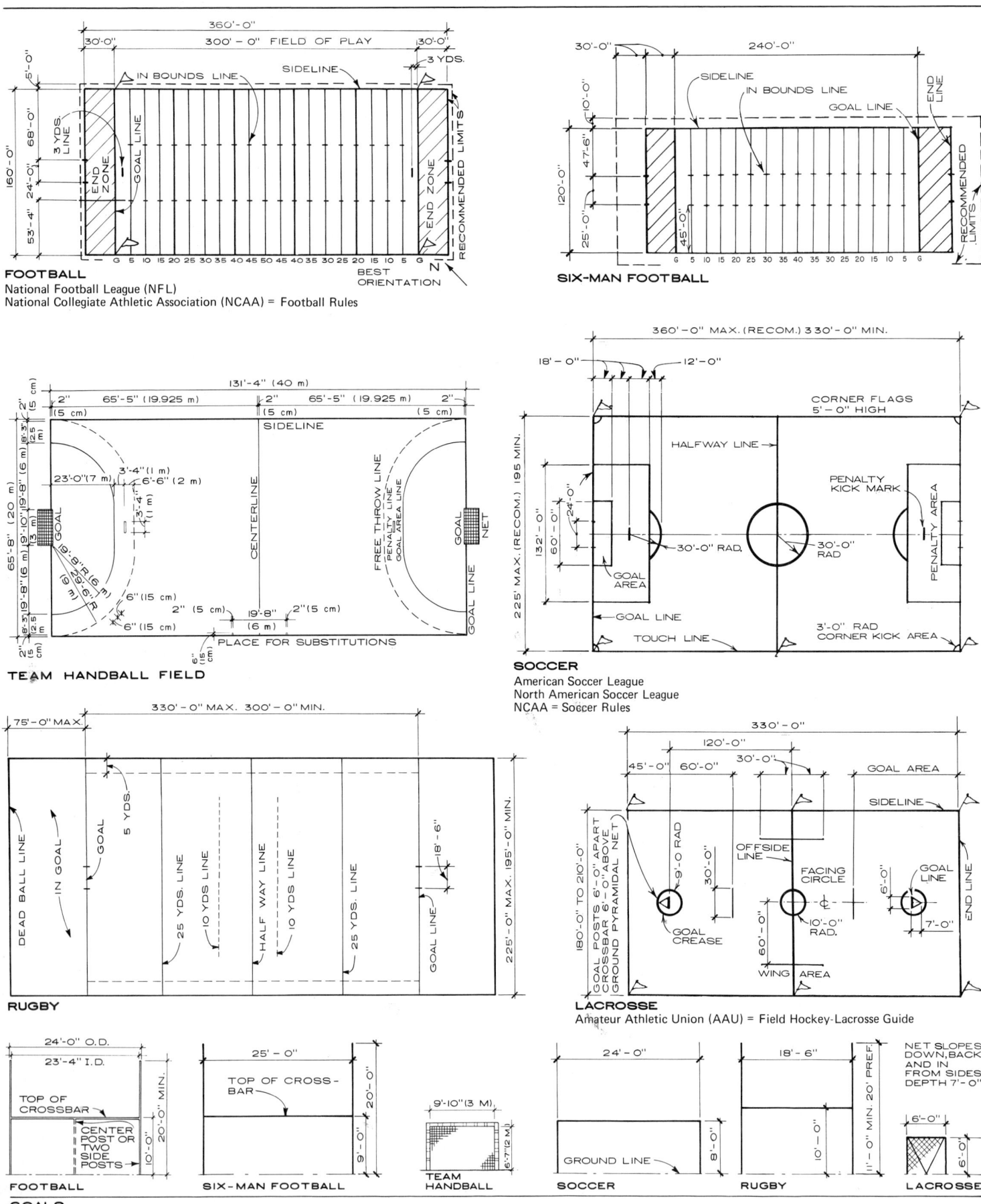

FOOTBALL
National Football League (NFL)
National Collegiate Athletic Association (NCAA) = Football Rules

SIX-MAN FOOTBALL

TEAM HANDBALL FIELD

SOCCER
American Soccer League
North American Soccer League
NCAA = Soccer Rules

RUGBY

LACROSSE
Amateur Athletic Union (AAU) = Field Hockey-Lacrosse Guide

GOALS

NOTE

This information is for preliminary planning and design only. For final layouts and design investigate current rules and regulations of the athletic organization or other authority whose standards will govern.

Charles F. D. Egbert, AIA; Architect; Washington, D. C.

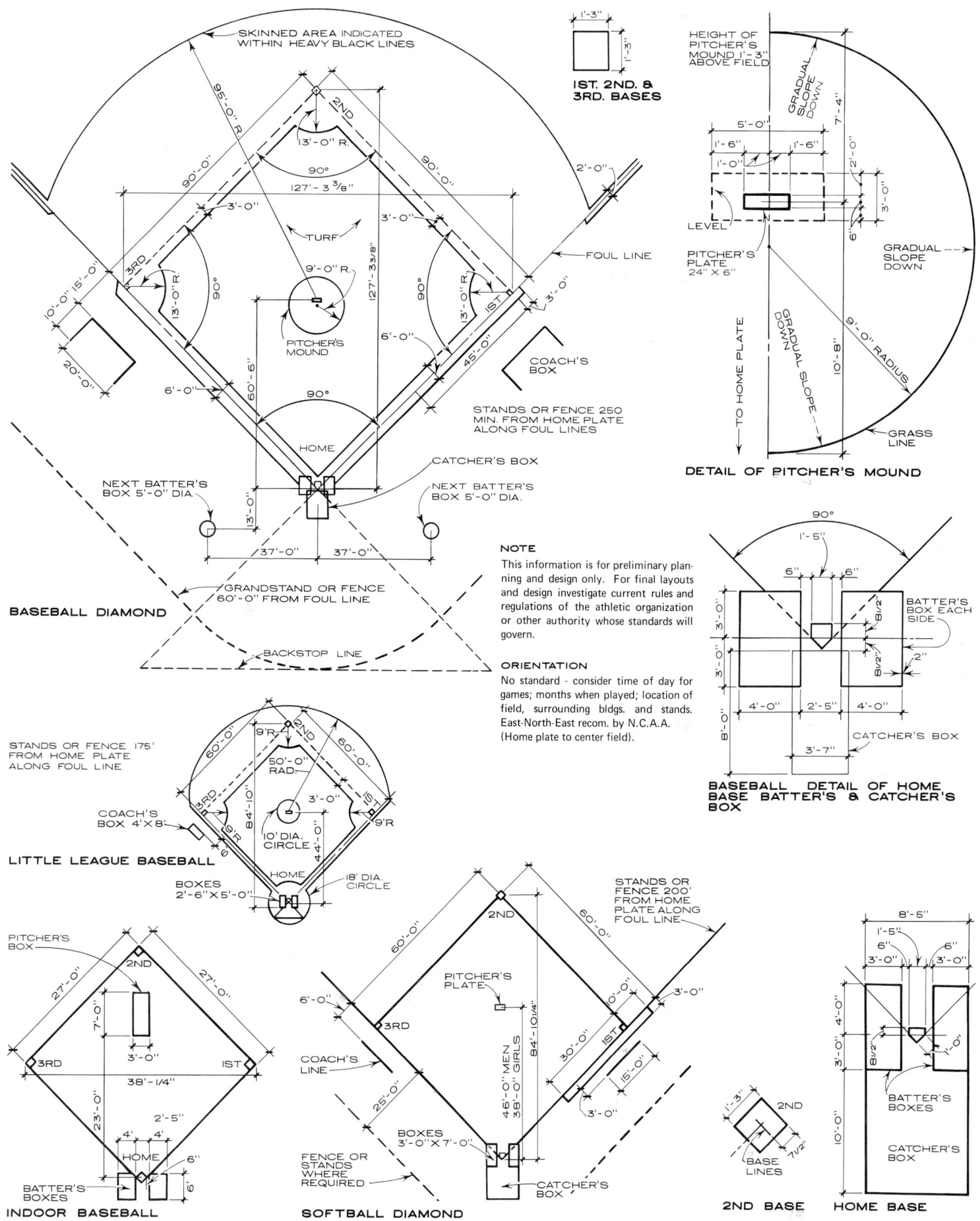

SKINNED AREA INDICATED WITHIN HEAVY BLACK LINES

1ST. 2ND. & 3RD. BASES

HEIGHT OF PITCHER'S MOUND 1'-3" ABOVE FIELD

GRADUAL SLOPE DOWN

LEVEL

PITCHER'S PLATE 24" X 6"

TO HOME PLATE

GRADUAL SLOPE DOWN

9'-0" RADIUS

GRASS LINE

DETAIL OF PITCHER'S MOUND

2ND

13'-0" R.

90°

127'-3 3/8"

TURF

95'-0" R.

90'-0"

90'-0"

127'-3 3/8"

9'-0" R.

PITCHER'S MOUND

3RD

13'-0" R.

90°

10'-0" 15'-0"

20'-0"

3'-0"

90°

13'-0" R.

1ST

3'-0"

6'-0"

45'-0"

FOUL LINE

2'-0"

3'-0"

COACH'S BOX

60'-6"

90°

HOME

STANDS OR FENCE 250 MIN. FROM HOME PLATE ALONG FOUL LINES

NEXT BATTER'S BOX 5'-0" DIA.

CATCHER'S BOX

NEXT BATTER'S BOX 5'-0" DIA.

13'-0"

37'-0"   37'-0"

BASEBALL DIAMOND

GRANDSTAND OR FENCE 60'-0" FROM FOUL LINE

BACKSTOP LINE

NOTE

This information is for preliminary planning and design only. For final layouts and design investigate current rules and regulations of the athletic organization or other authority whose standards will govern.

ORIENTATION

No standard - consider time of day for games; months when played; location of field, surrounding bldgs. and stands. East-North-East recom. by N.C.A.A. (Home plate to center field).

BASEBALL DETAIL OF HOME BASE BATTER'S & CATCHER'S BOX

90°

1'-5"

6"   6"

3'-0"

8 1/2"

BATTER'S BOX EACH SIDE

3'-0"

8 1/2"

2"

8'-0"

4'-0"   2'-5"   4'-0"

8'-0"

CATCHER'S BOX

3'-7"

STANDS OR FENCE 175' FROM HOME PLATE ALONG FOUL LINE

2ND

9'R

60'-0"

60'-0"

50'-0" RAD.

3'-0"

COACH'S BOX 4'X8'

3RD

84'-10"

44'-0"

1ST

9'R

10' DIA. CIRCLE

9'R

HOME

18' DIA. CIRCLE

LITTLE LEAGUE BASEBALL

BOXES 2'-6"X 5'-0"

PITCHER'S BOX

27'-0"

2ND

27'-0"

7'-0"

3'-0"

3RD

38'-1/4"

1ST

23'-0"

2'-5"

4'   4'

HOME

6"

BATTER'S BOXES

INDOOR BASEBALL

2ND

60'-0"

60'-0"

PITCHER'S PLATE

6'-0"

3RD

84'-10 1/4"

46'-0" MEN 38'-0" GIRLS

30'-0"

1ST

3'-0"

STANDS OR FENCE 200' FROM HOME PLATE ALONG FOUL LINE

3'-0"

15'-0"

25'-0"

COACH'S LINE

3'-0"

BOXES 3'-0"X 7'-0"

FENCE OR STANDS WHERE REQUIRED

CATCHER'S BOX

SOFTBALL DIAMOND

8'-5"

1'-5"

6"   6"

3'-0"   3'-0"

4'-0"

3'-0"

8 1/2"

1'-0"

BATTER'S BOXES

10'-0"

CATCHER'S BOX

1'-3"

2ND

7 1/2"

BASE LINES

2ND BASE

HOME BASE

Charles F. D. Egbert, AIA; Architect; Washington, D. C.

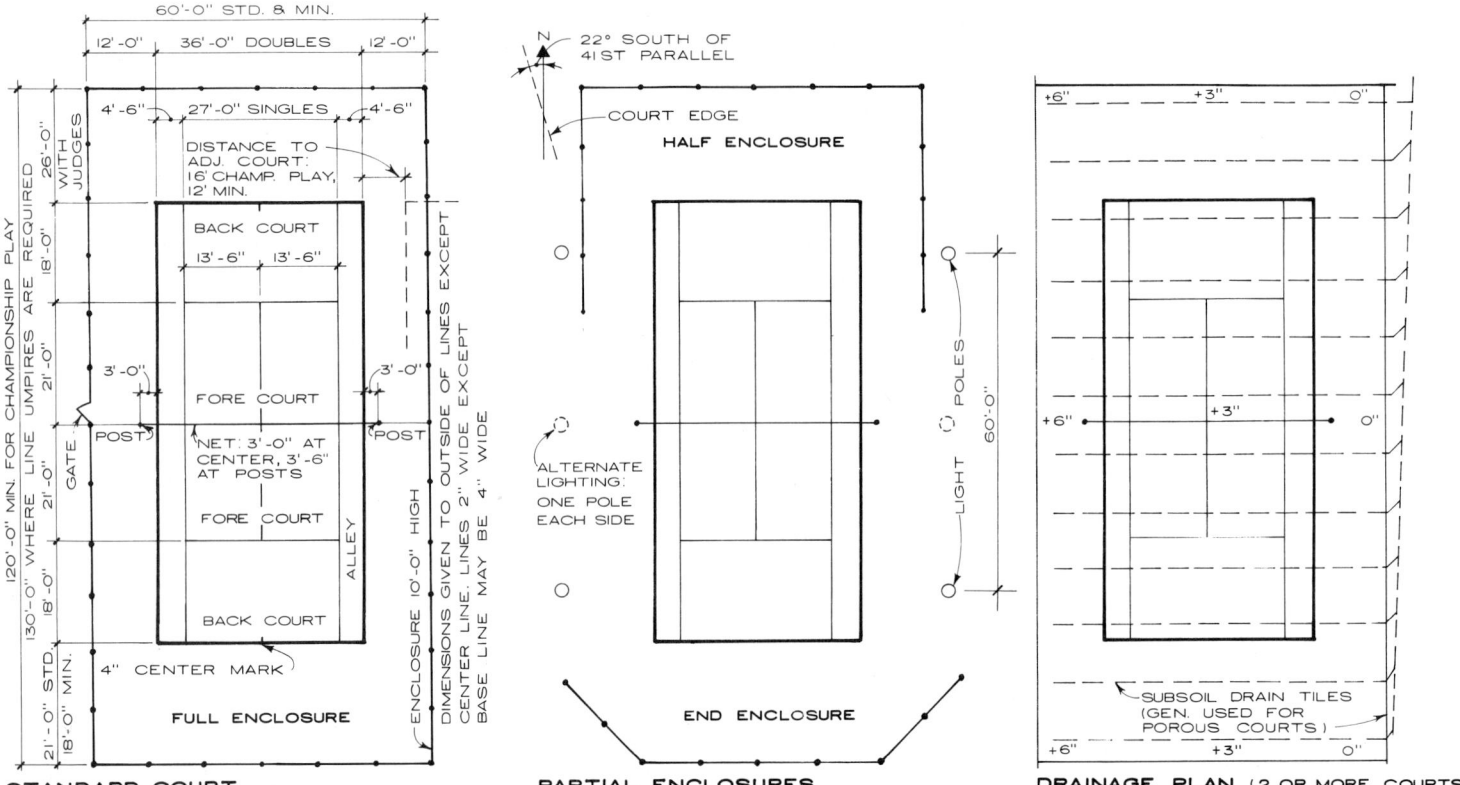

STANDARD COURT   **PARTIAL ENCLOSURES**   **DRAINAGE PLAN** (2 OR MORE COURTS)

ORIENTATION

For the northern states the north-south orientation is recommended. North-northwest by south-southeast at approximately 22° (true north) is recommended for outdoor courts south of the 41st parallel. Particular site characteristics, length of tennis season, and latitude should be taken into consideration when deciding on the most desirable court orientation angle.

NOTES

1. SURFACE DRAINAGE: Pitch 1 in. per 10 ft for porous and nonporous courts. Each court should be in one plane and pitch side to side; *never* up or down to middle court.
2. SUBSOIL DRAINAGE: Need for drainage systems depends on soil conditions.

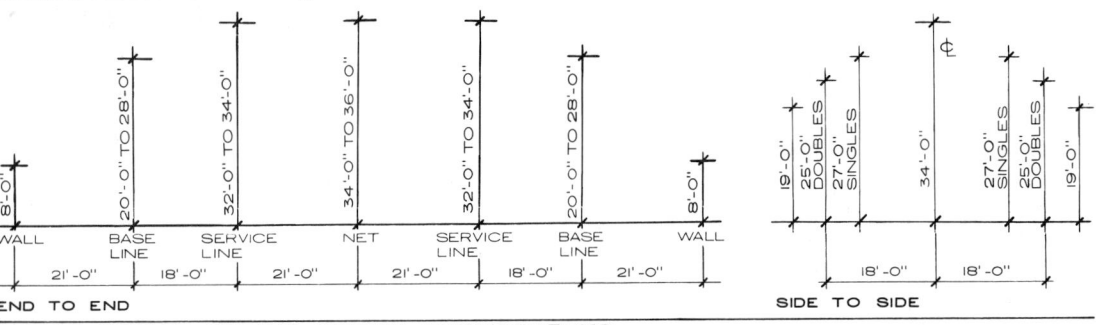

END TO END   **SIDE TO SIDE**

INDOOR TENNIS CEILING HEIGHT REQUIREMENTS

NOTE

This information is for preliminary planning and design only. For final layouts and design investigate current rules and regulations of the athletic organization or other authority whose standards will govern.

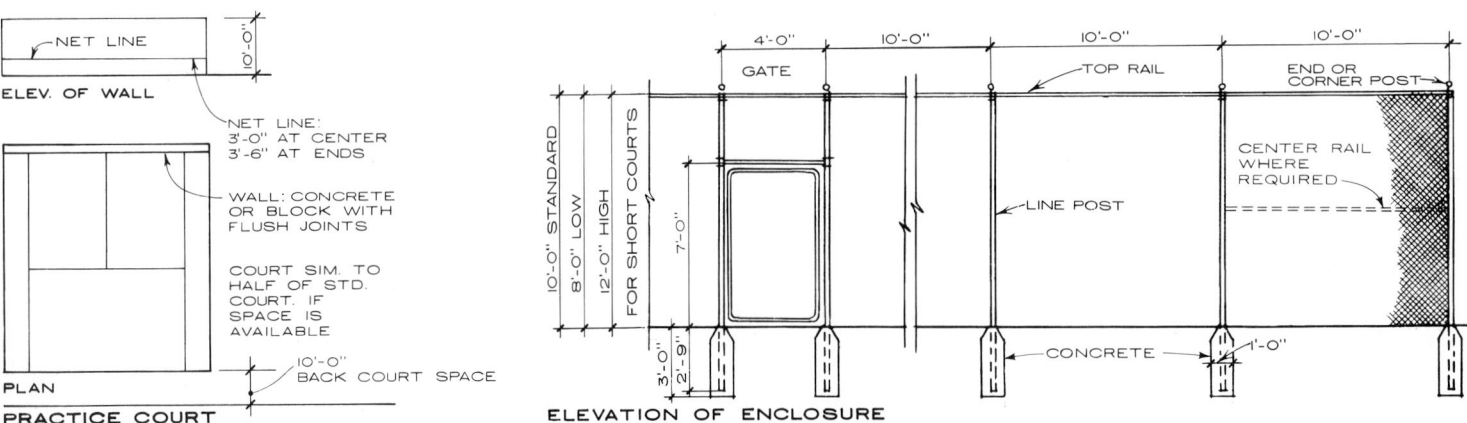

ELEV. OF WALL

PLAN

PRACTICE COURT

ELEVATION OF ENCLOSURE

Pecsok, Jelliffe & Randall, AIA, Architects; Indianapolis, Indiana

1 RECREATION

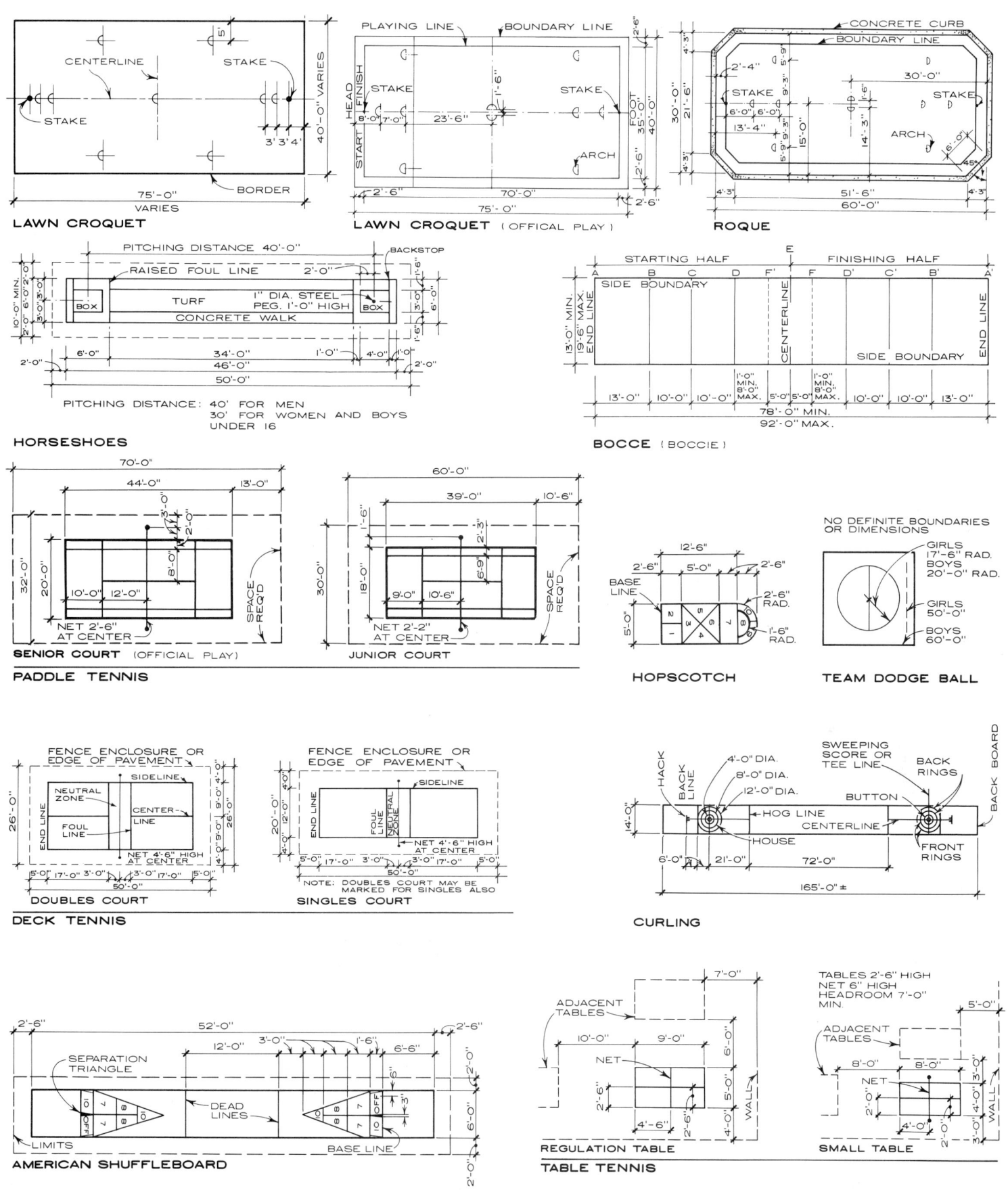

LAWN CROQUET

LAWN CROQUET (OFFICAL PLAY)

ROQUE

HORSESHOES

PITCHING DISTANCE: 40' FOR MEN
30' FOR WOMEN AND BOYS
UNDER 16

BOCCE (BOCCIE)

PADDLE TENNIS

SENIOR COURT (OFFICIAL PLAY)

JUNIOR COURT

HOPSCOTCH

TEAM DODGE BALL

NO DEFINITE BOUNDARIES
OR DIMENSIONS

DECK TENNIS

DOUBLES COURT

SINGLES COURT

NOTE: DOUBLES COURT MAY BE
MARKED FOR SINGLES ALSO

CURLING

AMERICAN SHUFFLEBOARD

TABLE TENNIS

REGULATION TABLE

SMALL TABLE

TABLES 2'-6" HIGH
NET 6" HIGH
HEADROOM 7'-0"
MIN.

NOTE: This information is for preliminary planning and design only. For final layouts and design investigate current rules and regulations of the athletic organization or other authority whose standards will govern.

Charles F. D. Egbert, AIA, Architect; Washington, D.C.

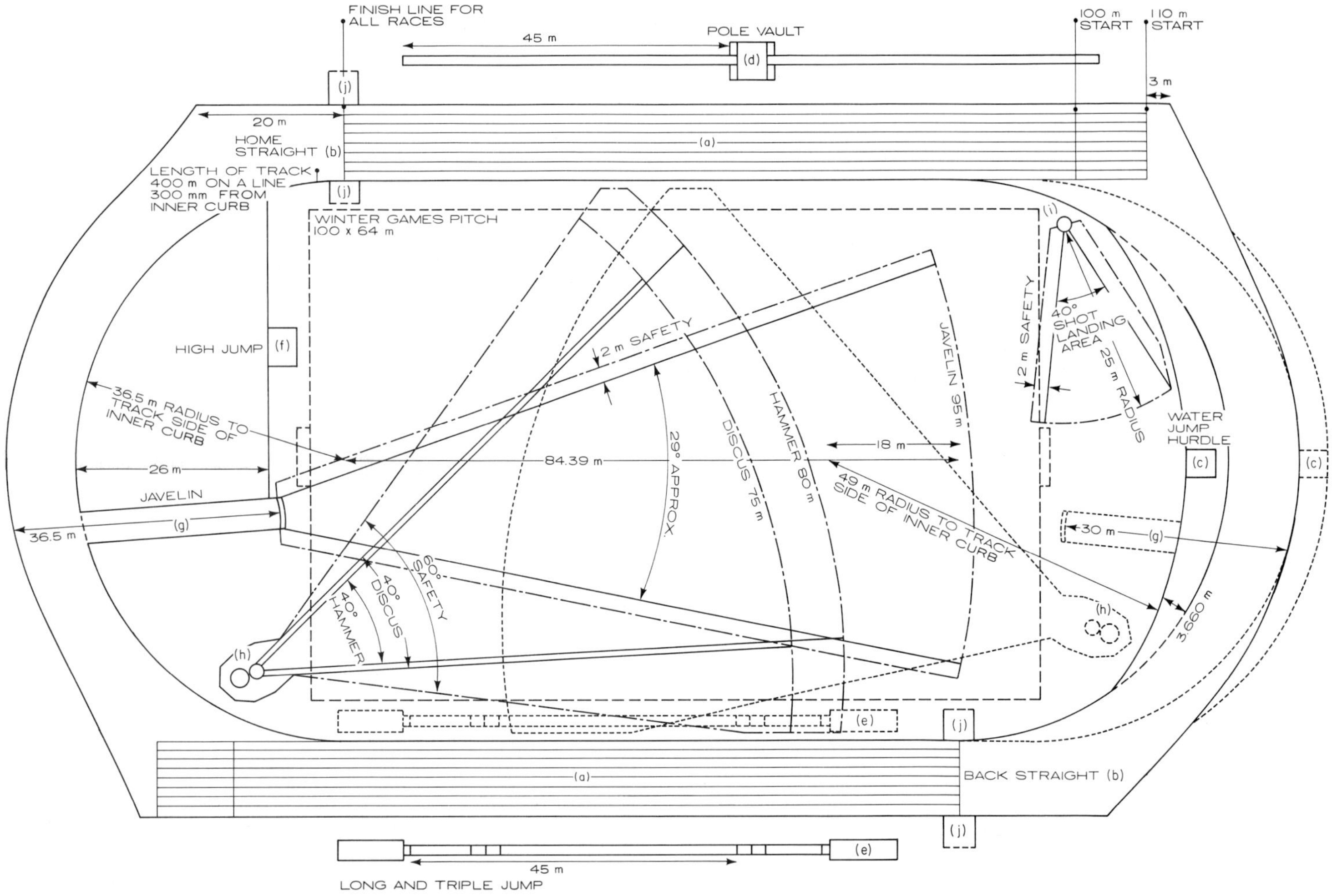

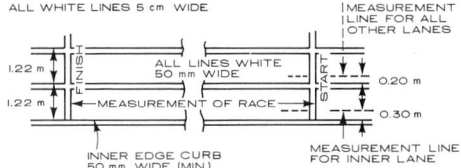

The large diagram labels (as they appear):

FINISH LINE FOR ALL RACES

POLE VAULT — (d)

100 m START — 110 m START

45 m

3 m

(j)

20 m

HOME STRAIGHT (b)

(a)

LENGTH OF TRACK 400 m ON A LINE 300 mm FROM INNER CURB

(j)

WINTER GAMES PITCH 100 x 64 m

(i)

HIGH JUMP (f)

2 m SAFETY

40° SHOT LANDING AREA

2 m SAFETY

25 m RADIUS

36.5 m RADIUS TO TRACK SIDE OF INNER CURB

JAVELIN 95 m

WATER JUMP HURDLE

(c)

(c)

26 m

84.39 m

29° APPROX.

DISCUS 75 m

HAMMER 80 m

18 m

49 m RADIUS TO TRACK SIDE OF INNER CURB

JAVELIN

36.5 m

(g)

30 m — (g)

40° HAMMER

40° DISCUS

60° SAFETY

(h)

3.660 m

(h)

(e)

(j)

BACK STRAIGHT (b)

(a)

(j)

45 m

(e)

LONG AND TRIPLE JUMP

LAYOUT GUIDE FOR 400 m RUNNING TRACK AND FIELD EVENT LOCATIONS

NOTES

(a) Number of lanes
(b) Straights
(c) Steeplechase and water jump
(d) Pole vault
(e) Long and triple jumps

(f) High jump
(g) Javelin
(h) Hammer and discus in cage
(i) Putting and shot
(j) Paved areas

NATIONAL AND INTERNATIONAL COMPETITION

The diagram indicates how a 400 m track with a synthetic surface might be laid out for national and international competition. Different arrangements are possible to suit particular circumstances. For high level competition, however, alternatives for the siting of the throwing circles are of necessity limited if maximum distances are to be safely thrown. For Rules of Competition reference should be made to the Handbook of the International Amateur Athletic Federation.

TRACK AND LANES

The length of the running track should be not less than 400 m. The track should be not less than 7.32 m in width and should, if possible, be bordered on the inside with concrete or other suitable material, approximately 50 mm high, minimum 50 mm wide. The curb may be raised to permit surface water to drain away, in which case a maximum height of 65 mm must not be exceeded.

Where it is not possible for the inner edge of the running track to have a raised border, the inner edge shall be marked with lines 50 mm wide.

The measurement shall be taken 0.30 m outward from the inner border of the track or, where no border exists, 0.20 m from the line marking the inside of the track.

In all races up to and including 400 m, each competitor shall have a separate lane, with a minimum width

Diagram labels (center):
ALL WHITE LINES 5 cm WIDE
MEASUREMENT LINE FOR ALL OTHER LANES
1.22 m
FINISH
ALL LINES WHITE 50 mm WIDE
START
0.20 m
1.22 m
MEASUREMENT OF RACE
0.30 m
INNER EDGE CURB 50 mm WIDE (MIN.)
MEASUREMENT LINE FOR INNER LANE

METHOD OF MARKING LANES

of 1.22 m and a maximum width of 1.25 m to be marked by lines 50 mm in width. The inner lane shall be measured as stated in the preceding text, but the remaining lanes shall be measured 0.20 m from the outer edges of the lines.

In international meetings the track should allow for at least six lanes and, where possible, for eight lanes, particularly for major international events.

The maximum allowance for lateral inclination of tracks shall not exceed 1:100, and the inclination in the running direction shall not exceed 1:1000.

The lateral inclination of the track should wherever possible be toward the inside lane.

SURFACE

Synthetic materials provide a consistently good surface capable of continuous and unlimited use in most weather conditions. Maintenance is minimal, consisting of periodic cleaning by hosing down or brushing, the repainting when necessary of the line markings, and an occasional repair.

Cinder surfaces require considerable maintenance by a skilled groundsman every time a track is used. They are not all-weather and seldom provide a consistently good running surface. They are, however, much cheaper to construct and are suitable for club use and training.

On cinder tracks an extra lane is necessary so that

sprint and hurdle events can be run on the six outer lanes to avoid the inner lane, which is subject to heavy use during long distance events.

ORIENTATION

It is often difficult to reconcile the requirements of wind directions and the need to avoid an approach into the setting sun. For these reasons it is now becoming common practice to provide, where possible, alternative directions for running, jumping, and throwing.

NUMBER OF LANES

Synthetic all-weather:

International competition:	8 lanes (9.76 m)
Area or regional competition:	6 lanes (7.32 m)

Cinder:

International competition:	8 lanes (9.76 m)
	9 lanes (straights)
Area or regional competition:	7 lanes (8.54 m)

THE FINISH

Two white posts shall denote the extremities of the finish line, and shall be placed at least 30 cm from the edge of the track.

The finish posts shall be of rigid construction about 1.4 m high, 80 mm wide, and 20 mm thick.

FORMULA FOR OTHER TRACK PROPORTIONS

Where a track of wider or narrower proportions or of different length is required, the appropriate dimensions can be calculated from the following formula:

$$L = 2P + 2 \quad (R + 300 \text{ mm})$$

where L = length of track (m)
P = length of parallels or distance apart of centers of curves (m)
R = radius to track side of inner curb (m)
π = 3.1416 (not $^{22}/_7$)

It is recommended that the radius of the semicircles should not normally be less than 32 m or more than 42 m for a 400 m circuit.

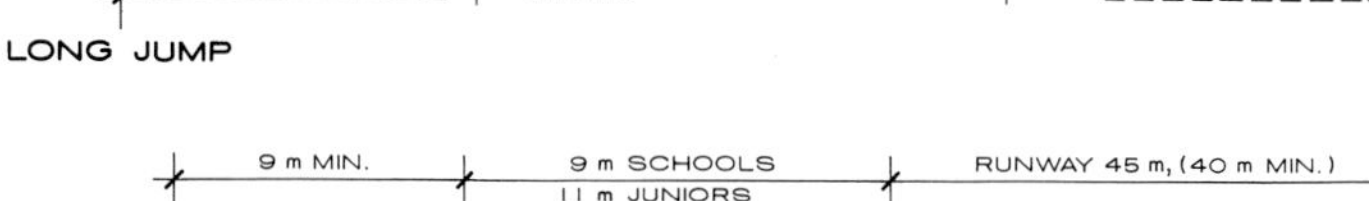

LONG JUMP

10 m MIN.
RUNWAY 45 m, (40 m MIN.)
2.750 m MIN.
LANDING AREA
1 m MIN.
1.220 m MIN.

TRIPLE JUMP

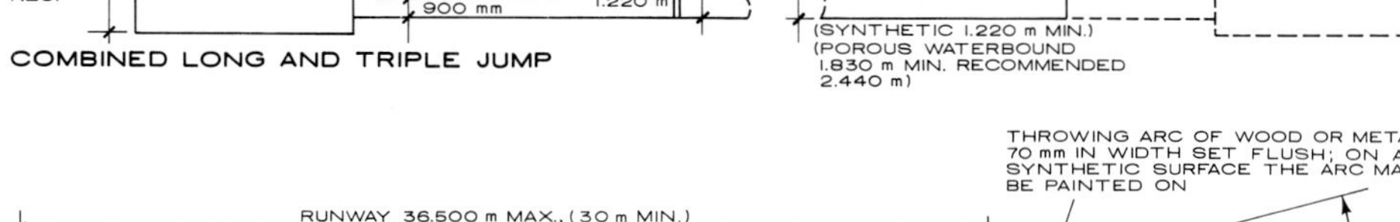

9 m MIN.
9 m SCHOOLS
11 m JUNIORS
13 m SENIORS
RUNWAY 45 m, (40 m MIN.)
2.750 m MIN.
1.220 m MIN.

COMBINED LONG AND TRIPLE JUMP

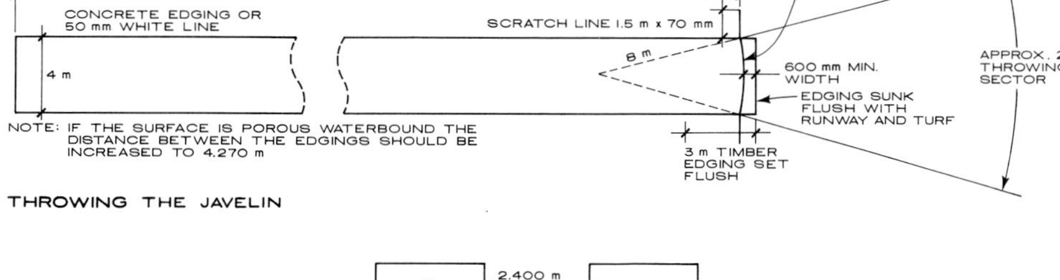

10 m MIN.
RUNWAY 45 m, (40 m MIN.)
3.350 m MIN
3.960 m REC.
760 mm MIN.
PREFERABLY NOT LESS THAN 900 mm
1.220 m
(SYNTHETIC 1.220 m MIN.)
POROUS WATERBOUND
1.830 m MIN. RECOMMENDED
2.440 m)

THROWING THE JAVELIN

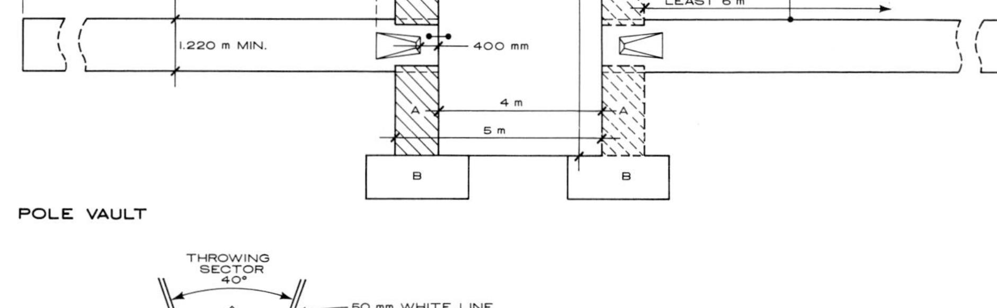

RUNWAY 36.500 m MAX., (30 m MIN.)
CONCRETE EDGING OR 50 mm WHITE LINE
4 m
SCRATCH LINE 1.5 m x 70 mm
8 m
THROWING ARC OF WOOD OR METAL 70 mm IN WIDTH SET FLUSH; ON A SYNTHETIC SURFACE THE ARC MAY BE PAINTED ON
600 mm MIN. WIDTH
EDGING SUNK FLUSH WITH RUNWAY AND TURF
3 m TIMBER EDGING SET FLUSH
APPROX. 29° THROWING SECTOR

NOTE: IF THE SURFACE IS POROUS WATERBOUND THE DISTANCE BETWEEN THE EDGINGS SHOULD BE INCREASED TO 4.270 m

POLE VAULT

RUNWAY 45 m, 40 m MIN.
1.220 m MIN.
2.400 m
B   B
A   5 m   A
400 mm
EDGING SET FLUSH WITH RUNWAY FOR AT LEAST 6 m
A   A
4 m
5 m
B   B

THROWING CIRCLE

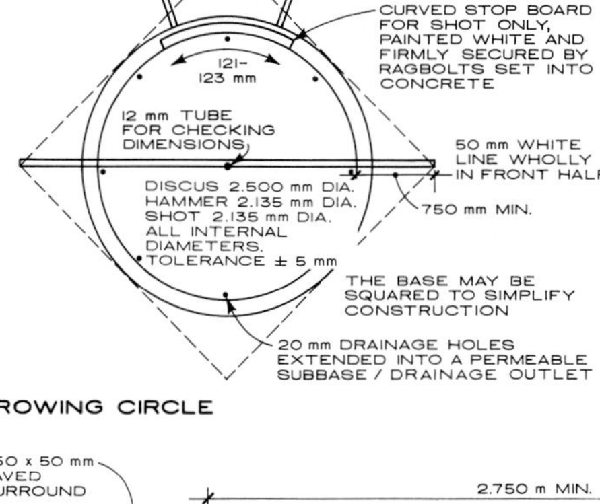

THROWING SECTOR 40°
50 mm WHITE LINE
CURVED STOP BOARD FOR SHOT ONLY, PAINTED WHITE AND FIRMLY SECURED BY RAGBOLTS SET INTO CONCRETE
121– 123 mm
12 mm TUBE FOR CHECKING DIMENSIONS
DISCUS 2.500 mm DIA.
HAMMER 2.135 mm DIA.
SHOT 2.135 mm DIA.
ALL INTERNAL DIAMETERS.
TOLERANCE ± 5 mm
50 mm WHITE LINE WHOLLY IN FRONT HALF
750 mm MIN.
THE BASE MAY BE SQUARED TO SIMPLIFY CONSTRUCTION
20 mm DRAINAGE HOLES EXTENDED INTO A PERMEABLE SUBBASE / DRAINAGE OUTLET

HIGH JUMP

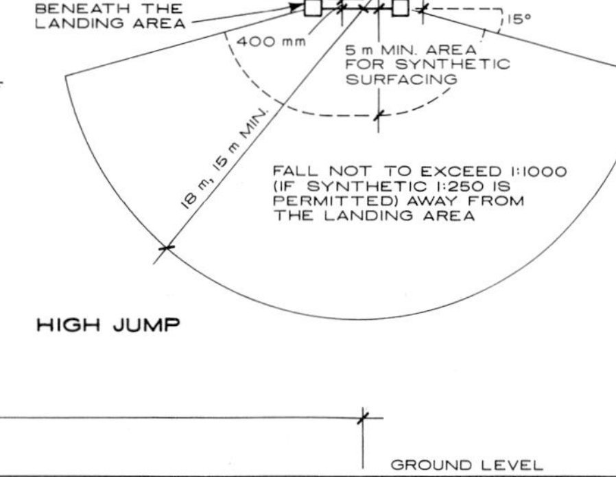

910 x 910 mm CONCRETE SLABS SET FLUSH WITH THE TAKEOFF AREA. THESE ARE NOT NECESSARY IF A SYNTHETIC SURFACE IS USED AND EXTENDED BENEATH THE LANDING AREA
5.320 m
ABOUT 3.500 m
4 m
15°
400 mm
5 m MIN. AREA FOR SYNTHETIC SURFACING
18, 15 m MIN.
FALL NOT TO EXCEED 1:1000 (IF SYNTHETIC 1:250 IS PERMITTED) AWAY FROM THE LANDING AREA

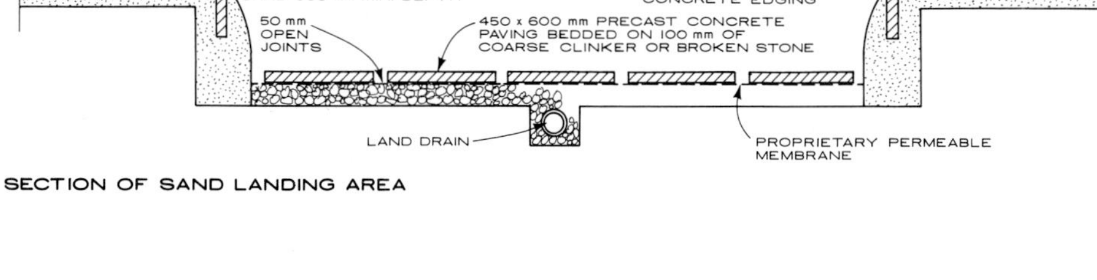

SECTION OF SAND LANDING AREA

450 x 50 mm PAVED SURROUND
2.750 m MIN.
SAND LEVEL SAME AS THE RUNWAY
GROUND LEVEL
250 x 50 mm CONCRETE EDGING
SAND 380 mm MIN. DEPTH
50 mm OPEN JOINTS
450 x 600 mm PRECAST CONCRETE PAVING BEDDED ON 100 mm OF COARSE CLINKER OR BROKEN STONE
LAND DRAIN
PROPRIETARY PERMEABLE MEMBRANE

---

400 m TRACK AND FIELD EVENTS—CONSTRUCTION DETAILS

These details are based on international standards. For additional information consult the IAAF, which is the International Amateur Athletic Federation. These details were provided by the National Playing Fields Association, London, England.

NOTE

To avoid adverse wind conditions during competition, landing areas for the long and triple jumps are desirable at both ends of the runway. A surround of paving slabs (450 x 600 mm) is an advantage. Takeoff board to be of wood or other suitable rigid material, set level with surface and painted white. See detail.

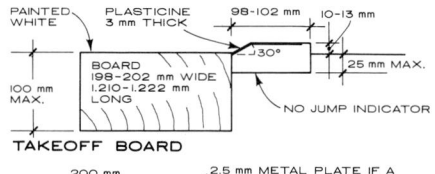

PAINTED WHITE
PLASTICINE 3 mm THICK
98–102 mm
10–13 mm
100 mm MAX.
BOARD 198–202 mm WIDE 1.210–1.222 m LONG
30°
25 mm MAX.
NO JUMP INDICATOR

TAKEOFF BOARD

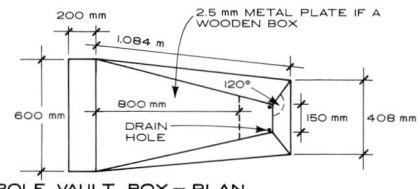

200 mm
1.084 m
2.5 mm METAL PLATE IF A WOODEN BOX
600 mm
800 mm
120°
DRAIN HOLE
150 mm
408 mm

POLE VAULT BOX – PLAN

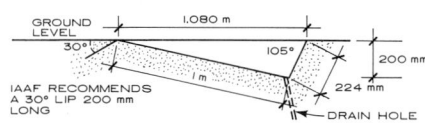

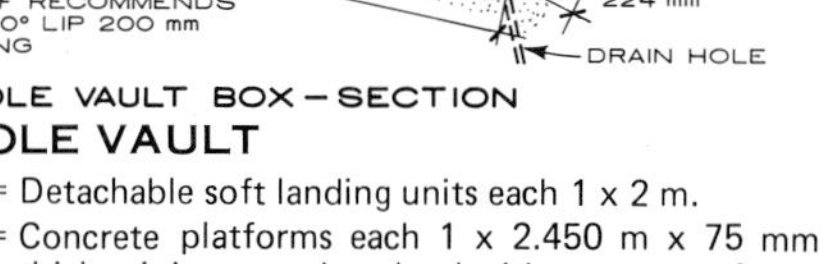

GROUND LEVEL
1.080 m
30°
105°
200 mm
IAAF RECOMMENDS A 30° LIP 200 mm LONG
1 m
224 mm
DRAIN HOLE

POLE VAULT BOX – SECTION

POLE VAULT

A = Detachable soft landing units each 1 x 2 m.

B = Concrete platforms each 1 x 2.450 m x 75 mm thick minimum and set level with runway surface.

The soft landing area to be 5 x 5 m minimum. The distance between uprights or extension arms to be 3.660 m minimum/4.370 m maximum. A larger soft landing unit with a 1.300 m extension for the pole vault box cutout giving a total size of 5 x 6.300 m may be provided. The diagram shows a double runway with detachable A units and thus gives a choice of runways according to the wind direction.

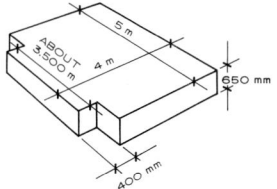

ABOUT 3.500 m
5 m
4 m
650 mm
400 mm

HIGH JUMP SOFT LANDING AREA

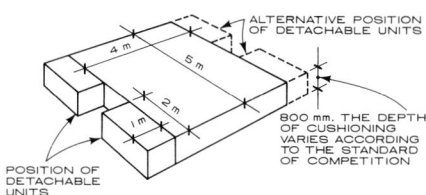

ALTERNATIVE POSITION OF DETACHABLE UNITS
4 m
5 m
2 m
1 m
POSITION OF DETACHABLE UNITS
800 mm. THE DEPTH OF CUSHIONING VARIES ACCORDING TO THE STANDARD OF COMPETITION

POLE VAULT SOFT LANDING AREA

For outdoor use soft landing units should be laid on duckboards on an ash base or other suitable materials (e.g., precast concrete paving on a porous base with 50 mm open joints).

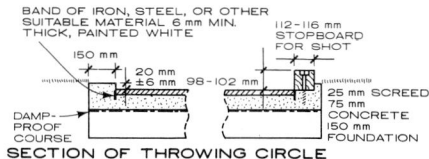

BAND OF IRON, STEEL, OR OTHER SUITABLE MATERIAL 6 mm MIN. THICK, PAINTED WHITE
112–116 mm STOPBOARD FOR SHOT
150 mm
20 mm ± 6 mm
98–102 mm
25 mm SCREED
75 mm CONCRETE
150 mm FOUNDATION
DAMP-PROOF COURSE

SECTION OF THROWING CIRCLE

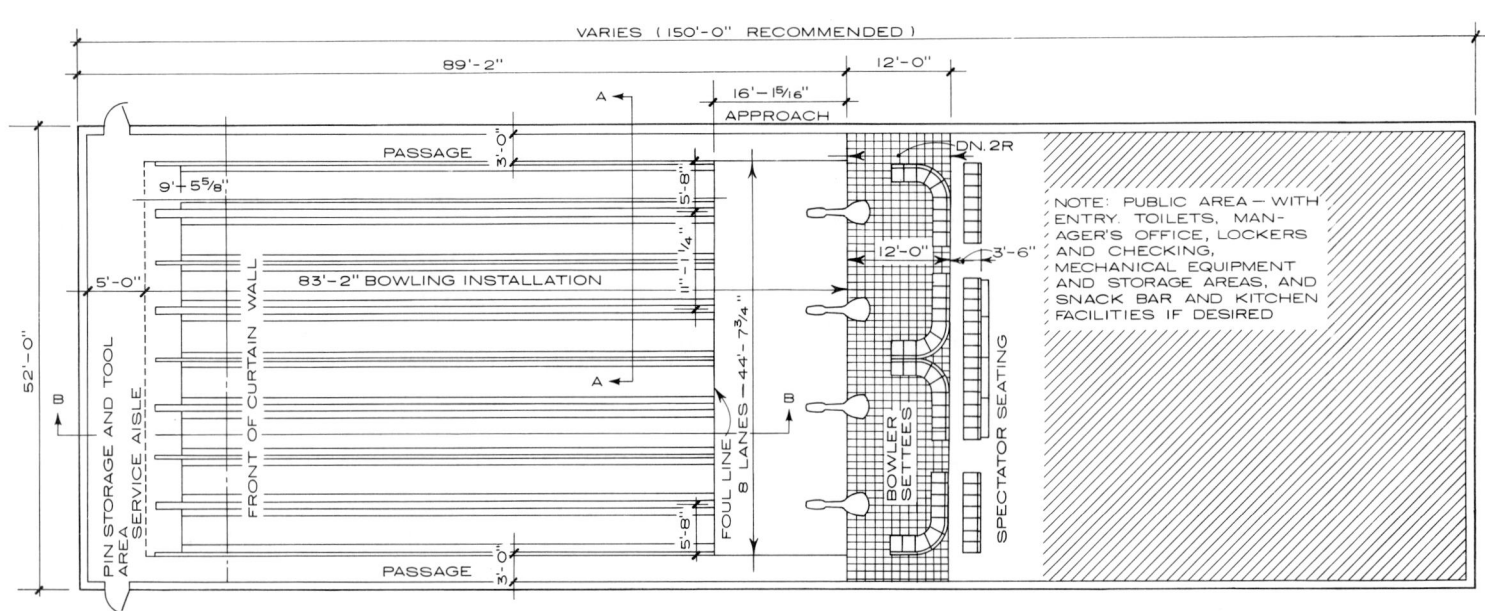

TYPICAL 8 – LANE INSTALLATION LAYOUT – SUBWAY BALL RETURN

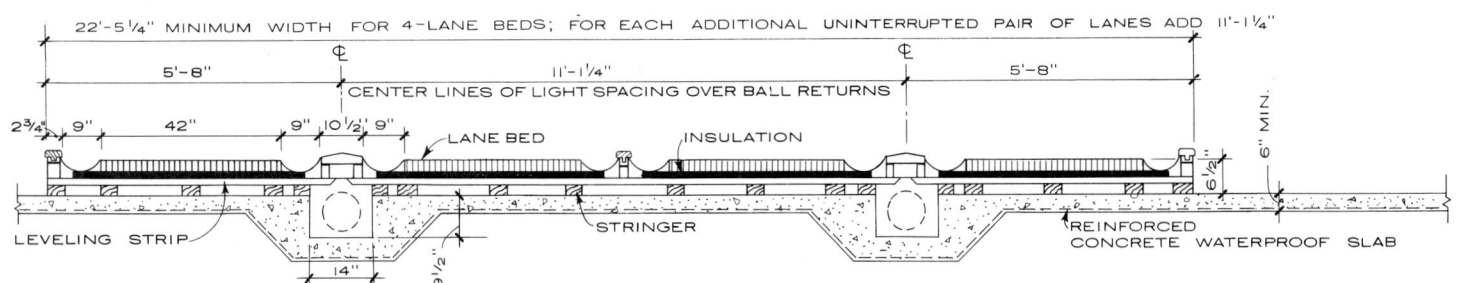

STRINGER FOUNDATION – SUBWAY BALL RETURN, SECTION A-A

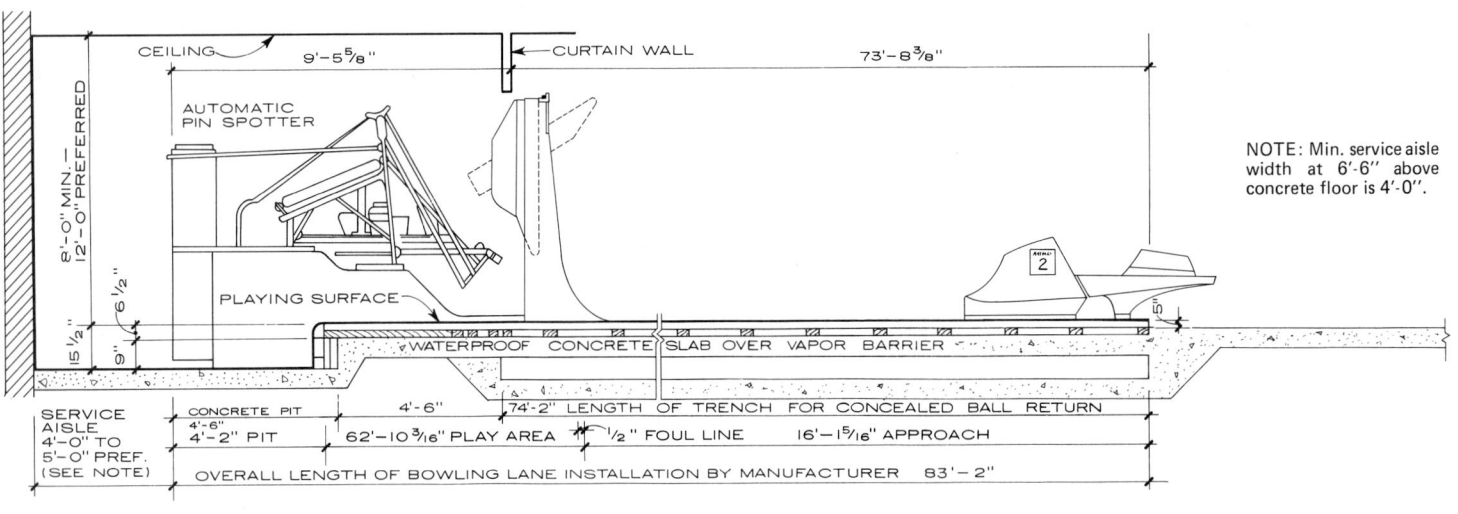

STRINGER FOUNDATION – SUBWAY BALL RETURN, LONGITUDINAL SECTION B-B

BOWLING LANE WIDTHS

LANES	MINIMUM WIDTH (FT AND IN.)	LANES	MINIMUM WIDTH (FT AND IN.)	LANES	MINIMUM WIDTH (FT AND IN.)
2	*11-4	18	100-2	34	189-0
4	*22-5 1/4	20	111-3 1/4	36	200-1 1/4
6	*33-6 1/2	22	122-4 1/2	38	211-2 1/2
8	*44-7 3/4	24	133-5 3/4	40	222-3 3/4
10	55-9	26	144-7	42	233-5
12	66-10 1/4	28	155-8 1/4	44	244-6 1/4
14	77-11 1/2	30	166-9 1/2	46	255-7 1/2
16	89-0 3/4	32	177-10 3/4	48	266-8 3/4

Charles F. D. Egbert, AIA; Architect; Washington, D.C.

NOTES

1. Asterisks (*) in the table indicate ideal sizes for churches, clubs, schools, hospitals, condominiums, and apartment complexes.
2. The dimensions in the table are net measurements of uninterrupted lane widths only; therefore, additions should be made for columns, walls, and passages between lanes or beside them. For each additional pair of lanes add 11 ft 1 1/4 in.
3. CEILING HEIGHT: Generally ranges from 10 ft to 14 ft above lanes. A 12-ft ceiling height is recommended for installations up to 24 lanes.
4. CRIB FOUNDATION: Can be used where a pit depression cannot be provided. Consult with manufacturers.

1 RECREATION

STAGGERED BUTT RIFLE RANGE   BUTT–IN–LINE RIFLE RANGE

OUTDOOR RIFLE AND PISTOL RANGES

NOTES

1. Orientation: North-south (desirable).
2. Earth berm 15 to 20 ft high, ideal for maximum safety.
3. Small bore ranges: 50 and 100 yd and 50 and 100 m.
4. Pistol ranges: 25 and 50 yd and 25 and 50 m.
5. High power rifle range: 200, 300, 600, and 1000 yd or m.
6. Spacing of targets:
   Pistol   4'-0'' O.C. min.
   Small bore rifle 5'-0'' O.C. min.
   High power rifle 8'-0'' O.C. min.
7. General purpose ranges: 50 to 300 yd or m.

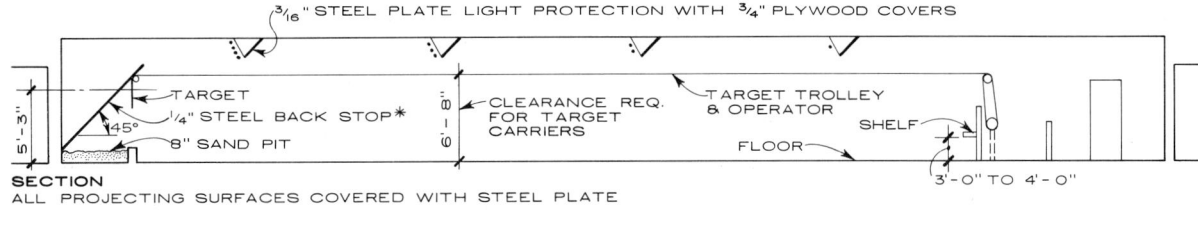

SECTION
ALL PROJECTING SURFACES COVERED WITH STEEL PLATE

DESIGN PROBLEMS

1. Safety.
   a. Trap safety.
   b. Firing line safety— use stalls.
   c. Spectator safety.
   d. Ricochet protection.
   e. Safety from spilled powder explosion.
2. Ventilation.
3. Noise.
4. Lighting.

The use of range design consultants is advisable. Contact National Rifle Association for information.

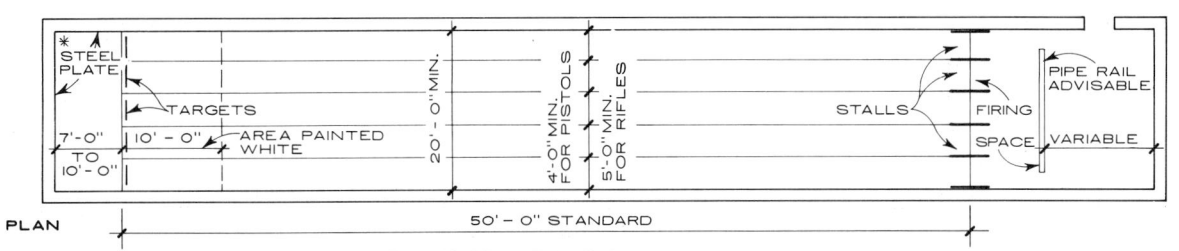

PLAN

INDOOR REGULATION RIFLE AND PISTOL RANGE
* "MULTIBAFFLE AND ESCALATOR" TYPE BULLET TRAPS AVAILABLE; COST GREATER AND HAS LESS MAINTENANCE THAN PLATE AND PIT TYPE SHOWN.
  NATIONAL RIFLE ASSOCIATION

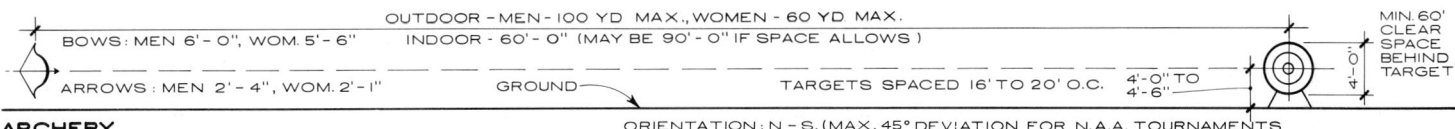

ARCHERY
NATIONAL ARCHERY ASSOCIATION

ORIENTATION: N–S. (MAX. 45° DEVIATION FOR N.A.A. TOURNAMENTS)

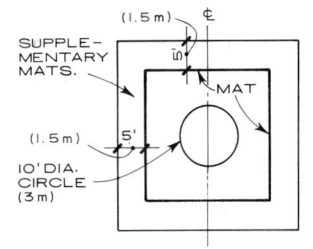

PLAN

MAT SIZES

1. INTERCOLLEGIATE COMPETITION: 32' x 32' (9.8 x 9.8 m) minimum and standard.
2. INTERNATIONAL COMPETITION: 6 x 6 m. (19'-8¼'') min. 1.10 m raised platform.
3. OLYMPIC COMPETITION: 8 x 8 m. (26'-3'') minimum.

   32' diam. mat also available.

WRESTLING
N.C.A.A.

NOTES

1. Rope and raised platform illegal (NCAA Rules).

2. Raised platform legal in other rules but not recommended.

PLAN
IF RING IS ON FLOOR EXTEND PADS 2'-0'' BEYOND ROPES.

PLATFORM MAX. 4'-0'' ABOVE FLOOR.

RING SIZES

MIN. 16' x 16'
MAX. 24' x 24'

BOXING
A.A.U.

REGULATION PISTE (STRIP) FOR ALL THREE WEAPONS

G— ON GUARD LINE   R— EXTENSION OF PISTE
C— CENTER (LINE)
AV— WARNING LINE (ALL WEAPONS)
F— REAR LIMIT. FOIL 12 m (39'-4''), EPEE 24 m (78'-8'') SABRE 14 m (46'-0'')

WIDTH OF PISTE: 1.8 m (5'-11'') TO 2 m (6'-7'')
WEAPON SIZES: FOIL AND EPEE 110 cm (43¼'')
                 SABRE 105 cm (41³⁄₈'')

FENCING
Amateur Fencers League of America

NOTE

This information is for preliminary planning and design only. For final layout and design investigate current rules and regulations of the athletic organization or other authority whose authority will govern.

Charles F. D. Egbert, AIA; Architect; Washington, D. C.

NOTES

1. Trap Field can be super-
    imposed over Skeet Field.

2. Consult manufacturers
    for trap house details.

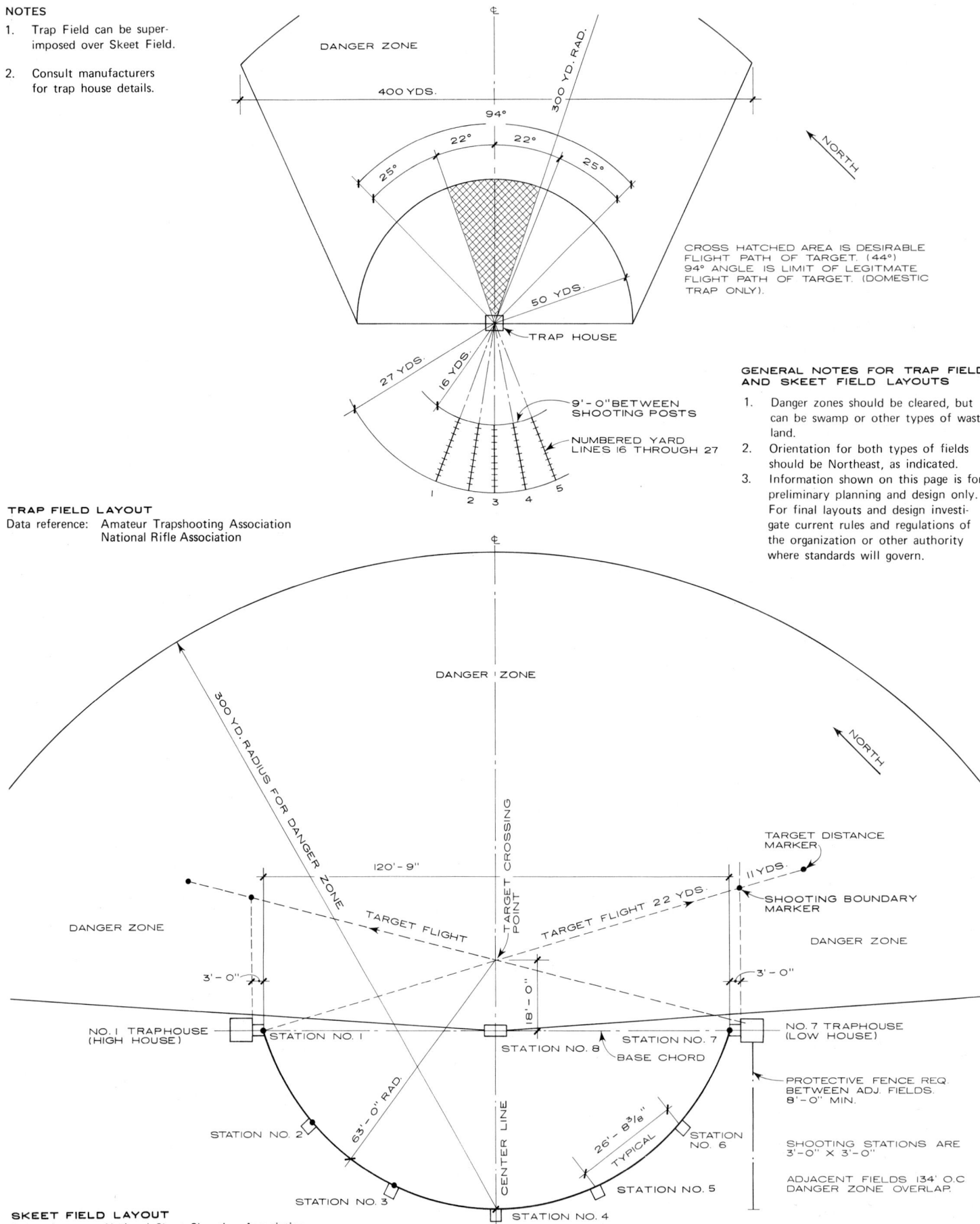

CROSS HATCHED AREA IS DESIRABLE
FLIGHT PATH OF TARGET. (44°)
94° ANGLE IS LIMIT OF LEGITMATE
FLIGHT PATH OF TARGET. (DOMESTIC
TRAP ONLY).

DANGER ZONE

400 YDS.

94°

22° 22°

25° 25°

300 YD. RAD.

NORTH

50 YDS.

TRAP HOUSE

27 YDS. 16 YDS.

9'-0" BETWEEN
SHOOTING POSTS

NUMBERED YARD
LINES 16 THROUGH 27

1 2 3 4 5

TRAP FIELD LAYOUT
Data reference: Amateur Trapshooting Association
National Rifle Association

GENERAL NOTES FOR TRAP FIELD
AND SKEET FIELD LAYOUTS

1. Danger zones should be cleared, but
    can be swamp or other types of waste-
    land.

2. Orientation for both types of fields
    should be Northeast, as indicated.

3. Information shown on this page is for
    preliminary planning and design only.
    For final layouts and design investi-
    gate current rules and regulations of
    the organization or other authority
    where standards will govern.

DANGER ZONE

300 YD. RADIUS FOR DANGER ZONE

TARGET DISTANCE
MARKER

120'-9"

TARGET FLIGHT

TARGET CROSSING POINT

TARGET FLIGHT 22 YDS.

11 YDS.

SHOOTING BOUNDARY
MARKER

DANGER ZONE

DANGER ZONE

3'-0"

18'-0"

3'-0"

NO. 1 TRAPHOUSE
(HIGH HOUSE)

STATION NO. 1

STATION NO. 8

STATION NO. 7

NO. 7 TRAPHOUSE
(LOW HOUSE)

BASE CHORD

PROTECTIVE FENCE REQ.
BETWEEN ADJ. FIELDS.
8'-0" MIN.

STATION NO. 2

63'-0" RAD.

STATION NO. 6

26'-8³⁄₈"

TYPICAL

STATION NO. 5

CENTER LINE

STATION NO. 3

STATION NO. 4

SHOOTING STATIONS ARE
3'-0" X 3'-0"

ADJACENT FIELDS 134' O.C
DANGER ZONE OVERLAP.

SKEET FIELD LAYOUT
Data reference: National Skeet Shooting Association
National Rifle Association

Charles F. D. Egbert, AIA; Architect; Washington, D. C.

1 **RECREATION**

GENERAL

Public pools are generally considered to be those that belong to municipalities, schools, country clubs, hotels, motels, apartments, and resorts. Permits for their construction are required in most areas from local and state boards of health as well as the departments of building, plumbing, and electricity.

Community pools should be integrated with existing and projected recreational facilities, such as picnic areas and parks, for maximum usage. Transportation access should be good, and there should be ample parking space. In a hot climate, enough shade should be provided, particularly in the lounging areas, and be so located that it can be easily converted to spectator space by erecting bleachers.

POOL DESIGN

Formerly most public pools were designed to meet competitive swimming requirements. The trend today is to provide for all-around use. The following should be considered:

1. Ratio of shallow water to deep water. Formerly 60% of pool area 5 ft deep and less was considered to be adequate. Now 80% is considered more realistic.

2. Ratio of loungers to bathers. Generally, no more than one-third of people attending a public pool are in the water at one time. Consequently the 6 to 8 ft walks formerly surrounding pools and used for lounging have been enlarged so that lounging area now approximates pool size.

3. For capacity formula see "Public Swimming Pool Capacity" diagram on another page.

RECOMMENDED DIMENSIONS

RELATED DIVING EQUIPMENT		MINIMUM DIMENSIONS								MINIMUM WIDTH OF POOL AT:		
MAX. BOARD LENGTH	MAX. HEIGHT OVER WATER	D_1	D_2	R	L_1	L_2	L_3	L_4	L_5	PT.A	PT.B	PT.C
10'	2/3 m 26"	2.13 m 7'-0"	2.59 m 8'-6"	1.68 m 5'-6"	0.76 m 2'-6"	2.44 m 8'-0"	3.20 m 10'-6"	2.13 m 7'-0"	8.53 m 28'-0"	4.88 m 16'-0"	5.49 m 18'-0"	5.49 m 18'-0"
12'	3/4 m 30"	2.29 m 7'-6"	2.74 m 9'-0"	1.83 m 6'-0"	0.91 m 3'-0"	2.74 m 9'-0"	3.66 m 12'-0"	1.22 m 4'-0"	8.53 m 28'-0"	5.49 m 18'-0"	6.10 m 20'-0"	6.10 m 20'-0"
16'	1 m	2.59 m 8'-6"	3.05 m 10'-0"	2.13 m 7'-0"	1.22 m 4'-0"	3.05 m 10'-0"	4.57 m 15'-0"	0.61 m 2'-0"	9.45 m 31'-0"	6.10 m 20'-0"	6.71 m 22'-0"	6.71 m 22'-0"
16'	3 m	3.35 m 11'-0"	3.66 m 12'-0"	2.59 m 8'-6"	1.83 m 6'-0"	3.20 m 10'-6"	6.40 m 21'-0"	0	11.43 m 37'-6"	6.70 m 22'-0"	7.32 m 24'-0"	7.32 m 24'-0"

Data source: National Swimming Pool Institute.

L_2, L_3, and L_4 combined represent the minimum distance from the tip of board to pool wall opposite diving equipment.

For board heights exceeding 3 m in height or platform diving shall comply with dimensional requirements of FINA, AAU, NCAA, N.F., etc.

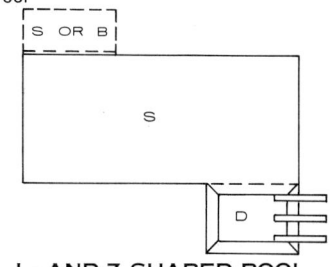

NOTE: Placement of boards shall observe the following minimum dimensions. With multiple board installations minimum pool widths must be increased accordingly.

1 m or deck level board to pool side	9' (2.74 m)
3 m board to pool side	11' (3.35 m)
1 m or deck level board to 3 m board	10' (3.05 m)
1 m or deck level to another 1 m or deck level board	8' (2.44 m)
3 m to another 3 m board	10' (3.05 m)

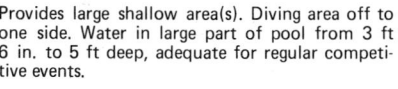

T-SHAPED POOL

Provides large shallow area(s). Diving area off to one side. Water in large part of pool from 3 ft 6 in. to 5 ft deep, adequate for regular competitive events.

L- AND Z-SHAPED POOL

These two shapes generally desired for large 50 m pools.

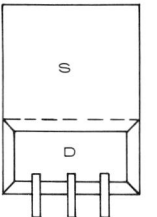

RECTANGULAR POOL

Standard design. Good for competitive swimming and indoor pool design. Shallow area often inadequate.

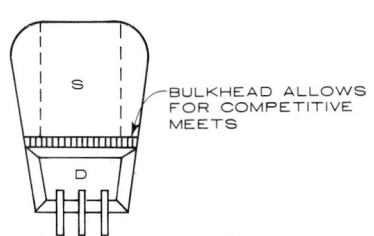

BULKHEAD ALLOWS FOR COMPETITIVE MEETS

FAN SHAPED POOL

Successful where there is a high percentage of children. Largest area for shallow depth. Deep area can be roped off or separated by bulkhead.

FREE FORM POOL

Kidney and oval shapes are the most common free forms. Use only where competitive meets are not a consideration.

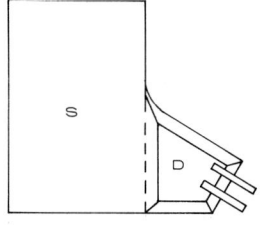

MODIFIED L POOL

Provides for separate diving area. Shallow area with 4 ft min. depth may be roped off for competitive meets.

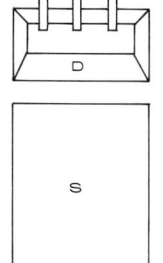

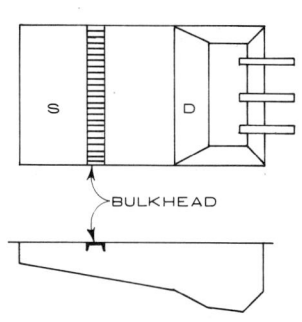

BULKHEAD

MULTIPLE POOLS

Separate pools for beginners, divers and swimmers. Ultimate in desirability especially if pool is intended for large numbers of people. Variation at left shows single pool and bulkhead over it with advantage that swimmers are kept out of area reserved for beginners. Both designs may use common filtration system.

WADING POOLS

Generally provided in connection with community and family club pools. Placed away from swimming area to avoid congestion. If near swimming pool, wading area should be fenced off for children's protection. To add play appeal provide spray fittings and small fountains in pool. Also provide seats and benches for adults who accompany children to pool.

PUBLIC POOL SHAPES

NOTE: S = swimming pool, D = diving pool, B = beginner's pool.

R. Jackson Smith, AIA; Designed Environments, Inc.; Stamford, Connecticut

National Swimming Pool Institute; Washington, D.C.

NOTES

1. The drawings below illustrate the use of a 7-point dimension grid that expresses the minimum desirable dimensions to be used when either specifying or designing a rectangular shaped pool for residential use.
2. Width, length, and depth dimensions may apply to residential pools of any shape.
3. The minimum length with diving board and wading area is 30 ft. The average length of a residential pool is 30 to 40 ft.
4. Standards for residential swimming pools have been published by the National Swimming Pool Institute (1972). The Fédération Internationale de Natation Amateur has published a new handbook, which is available from the AAU in Indianapolis, Indiana.

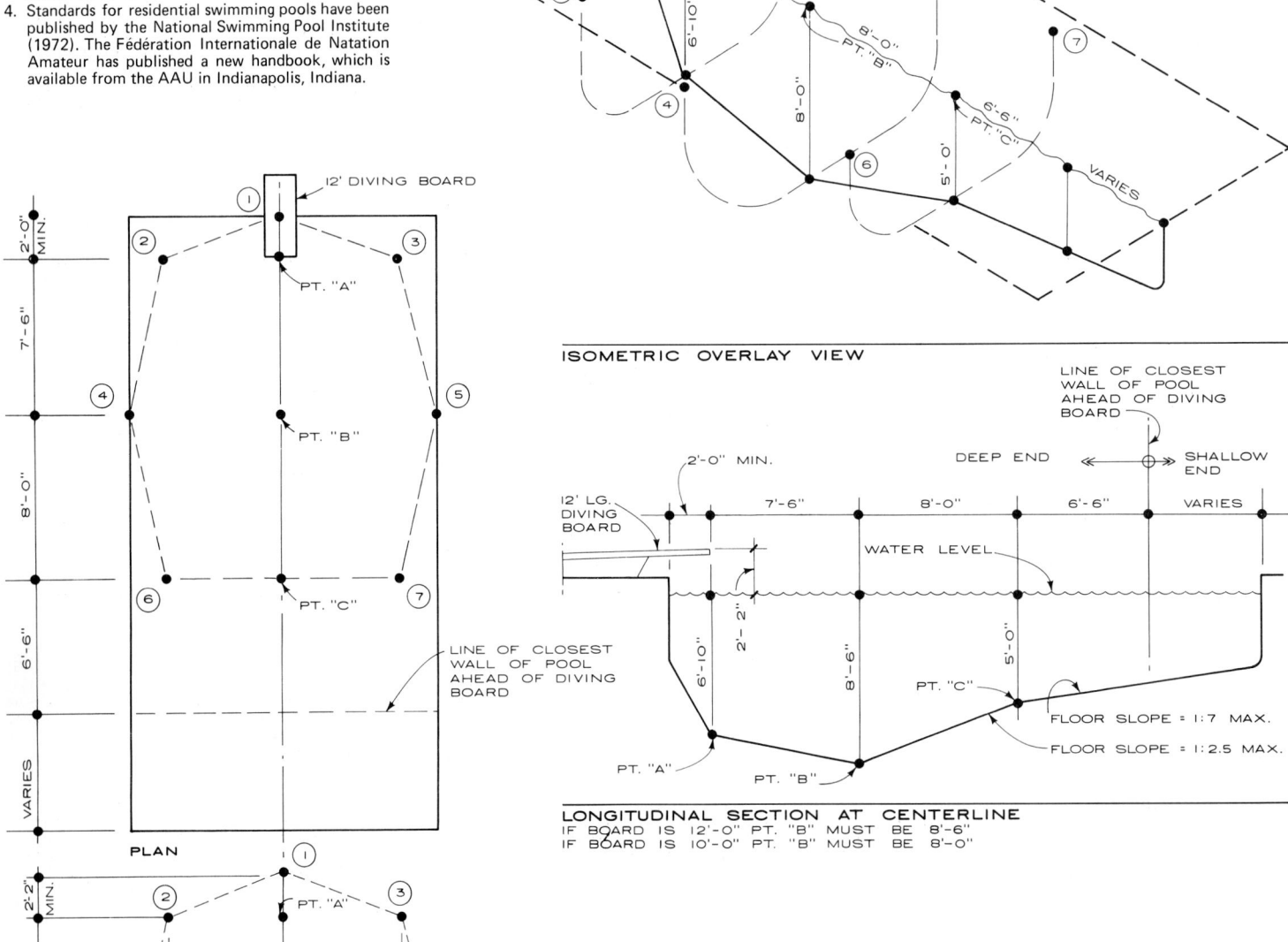

ISOMETRIC OVERLAY VIEW

LONGITUDINAL SECTION AT CENTERLINE
IF BOARD IS 12'-0" PT. "B" MUST BE 8'-6"
IF BOARD IS 10'-0" PT. "B" MUST BE 8'-0"

7-POINT GRID DIMENSION PLAN

Haver, Nunn and Collamer; Phoenix, Arizona

PERMITS AND RESTRICTIONS

Required in most areas from building, health, plumbing, and electrical departments and zoning boards. Check for setback restrictions and easements covering power and telephone lines, sewers, and storm drains.

SITE CONSIDERATIONS

Check the site for the following conditions, each of which will considerably increase the cost.

1. Fill that is more than 3 ft below pool deck.
2. Hard rock that requires drilling and blasting.
3. Underground water or springs that necessitate pumping or drains.
4. Accessibility of the site for mechanical equipment, minimum entry 8 ft wide by 7 ft 8 in. high, with a grade easy enough for a truck to reach the site.
5. Place the pool where it will get the most sun during swimming season. If possible, place deep end so a diver dives away from, not into, the afternoon sun. Avoid overhanging tree branches near the pool.
6. The slope of the site should be as level as possible; a steep slope requires retaining walls for the pool.

CONSTRUCTION AND SHAPES

Pools may be made of reinforced concrete (poured on the job, precast, or gunite sprayed), concrete block, steel, aluminum, or plastic with or without block backup. Concrete, aluminum, fiberglass, and steel pools are available in any shape—rectangular, square, kidney, oval or free form. Complete plastic installations and plastic pool liners with various backups are available only in manufacturers' standard shapes and sizes.

A rectangular pool is the most practical if site permits, since it gives the longest swimming distance.

POOL CAPACITY

Rule of thumb: 36 sq ft for each swimmer, 100 sq ft for each diver. A pool of 20 x 40 ft accommodates 14 persons at a time, but since not everyone is in the pool at once, pool and surroundings are adequate for 30 to 40 people.

FILTER REQUIREMENTS

Filter, motor, and electrical equipment shall be sheltered and waterproofed.

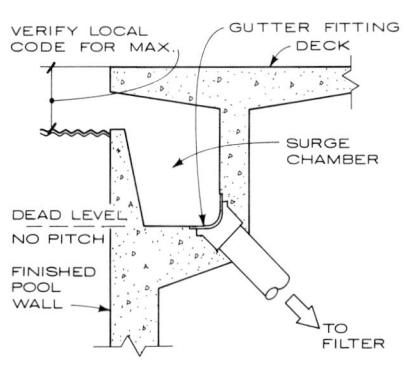

FULLY RECESSED OVERFLOW GUTTER

RIMFLOW SYSTEM

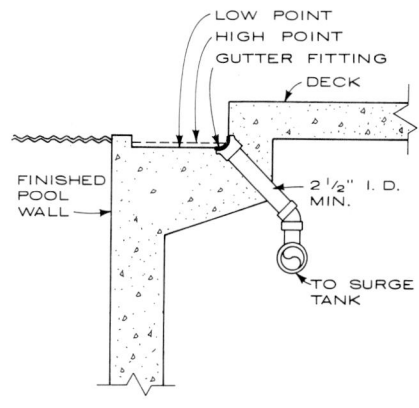

ROLL OUT OVERFLOW

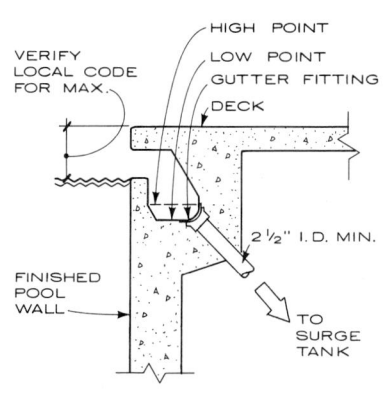

FULLY RECESSED GUTTER

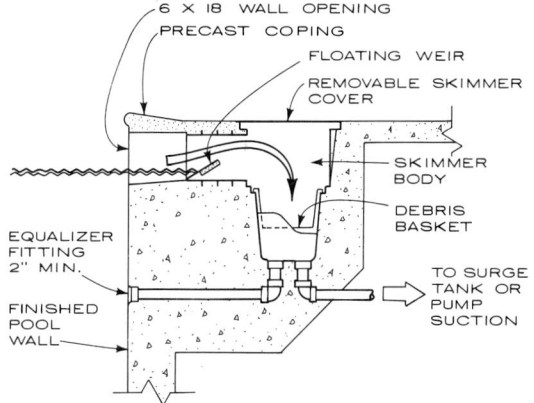

SURFACE SKIMMER

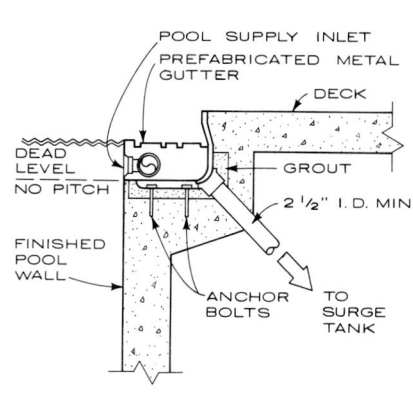

TYPICAL PREFABRICATED OVERFLOW

PERIMETER OVERFLOW SYSTEMS

NOTES

1. A perimeter overflow system must be provided on all public swimming pools. It must be designed and constructed so that the water level of the pool is maintained at the operating level of the overflow rim or weir device. Dimension from the deck to the water level is determined by applicable codes.

2. Perimeter type overflow systems, when used as the only overflow system on the pool, must extend around a minimum 50% of the swimming pool perimeter. Perimeter overflow systems must be connected to the circulation system with a system surge capacity of not less than 1 gal/sq ft of pool surface.

3. The perimeter overflow system in combination with the upper rim of the pool must constitute a handhold. It must be designed to prevent the entrapment of swimmer's arms, legs, or feet and to permit inspection and cleaning.

4. The hydraulic capacity of the overflow system must be sufficient to handle 100% of the circulation flow.

5. When roll-out or flush deck type of perimeter overflows are used on competitive pools, the ends of the pool must be provided with a visual barrier that can be seen by swimmers.

6. Perimeter overflows are commonly used on public swimming pools. Some state health departments do not approve skimmers on public swimming pools that exceed a certain surface area. Current state codes or swimming pool regulations must be checked to determine limits of use, minimum dimensions, and other factors dealing with overflow design.

7. Metal swimming pool systems are available that have a built-in perimeter overflow. In addition to the overflow channel, the metal liner may also contain the return waterline from the filtration system. A metal liner that incorporates a cove between wall and floor is desirable to facilitate cleaning.

8. Deck areas adjoining the overflow system are generally required to slope away from it to separate drains. When deck is sloped to pool overflow, provide for diverting pool overflow to waste during deck cleaning.

YMCA Building and Furnishings Service; New York, New York

National Swimming Pool Institute; Washington, D.C.

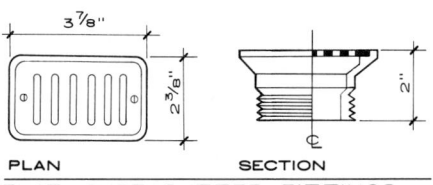

PLAN   **SECTION**

FLAT TYPE GUTTER FITTINGS

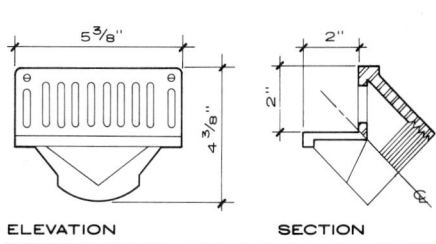

ELEVATION   **SECTION**

ANGLE TYPE GUTTER FITTINGS

9. Perimeter type overflows may be custom built to conform to the design selected. Ceramic tile is the preferred material for the top 6 in. of the pool wall, the pool rim, the gutter, and the deck for indoor swimming pools. Gratings for deep overflow gutters may be of precast concrete, plastic, or metal.

10. Proprietary overflow systems are available that have the characteristics of many of the perimeter overflow types shown. Stainless steel is commonly used because of its corrosion resistance. Aluminum overflow systems have a coating or enamel finish. Slotted precast concrete units are also available.

11. Surfaces subject to traffic must be nonslip.

SURFACE SKIMMERS

When surface skimmers are used, one must be provided for each 500 sq ft, or fraction thereof, of the pool surface. When two or more skimmers are used, they must be located so as to maintain effective skimming action over the entire surface of the swimming pool. Skimmers may not be permitted on larger pools. See local health department codes for limitation on public pools. Skimmers are not recommended for competitive pools.

Surface skimmers are available from many swimming pool suppliers. Metal or plastic units are available in various capacities. An access cover in the deck permits removal and cleaning of the strainer. Surface skimmers should comply with the joint National Swimming Pool Institute—National Sanitation Foundation performance standards.

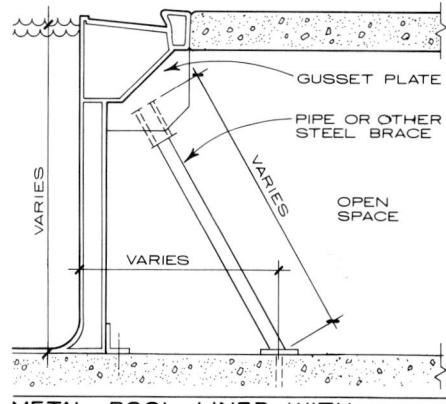

METAL POOL LINER WITH OVERFLOW

Often used in rooftop or other above grade installations where weight is a primary factor in design.

LENGTH OF POOLS

25 yards is the minimum length for American records, and meets interscholastic and intercollegiate requirements. (Pool should be 75'-1½'' long to allow for electronic timing panels at one end.)

Standards for International Competition are shown on 50 meter pool page.

WIDTH OF POOLS

Drawing below shows 7' lanes, with pool width of 45' (6 lanes). Strictly competitive pools should have 8' lanes, with pool width of 83' (10 lanes). Minimum widths include additional 18'' width outside lanes on both sides of pool.

NOTES

Gutters at sides of pool are desirable to reduce wave action in swimming meets or water polo. See lighting standards and diving board standards on other pages of this series for additional requirements for competitive pools.

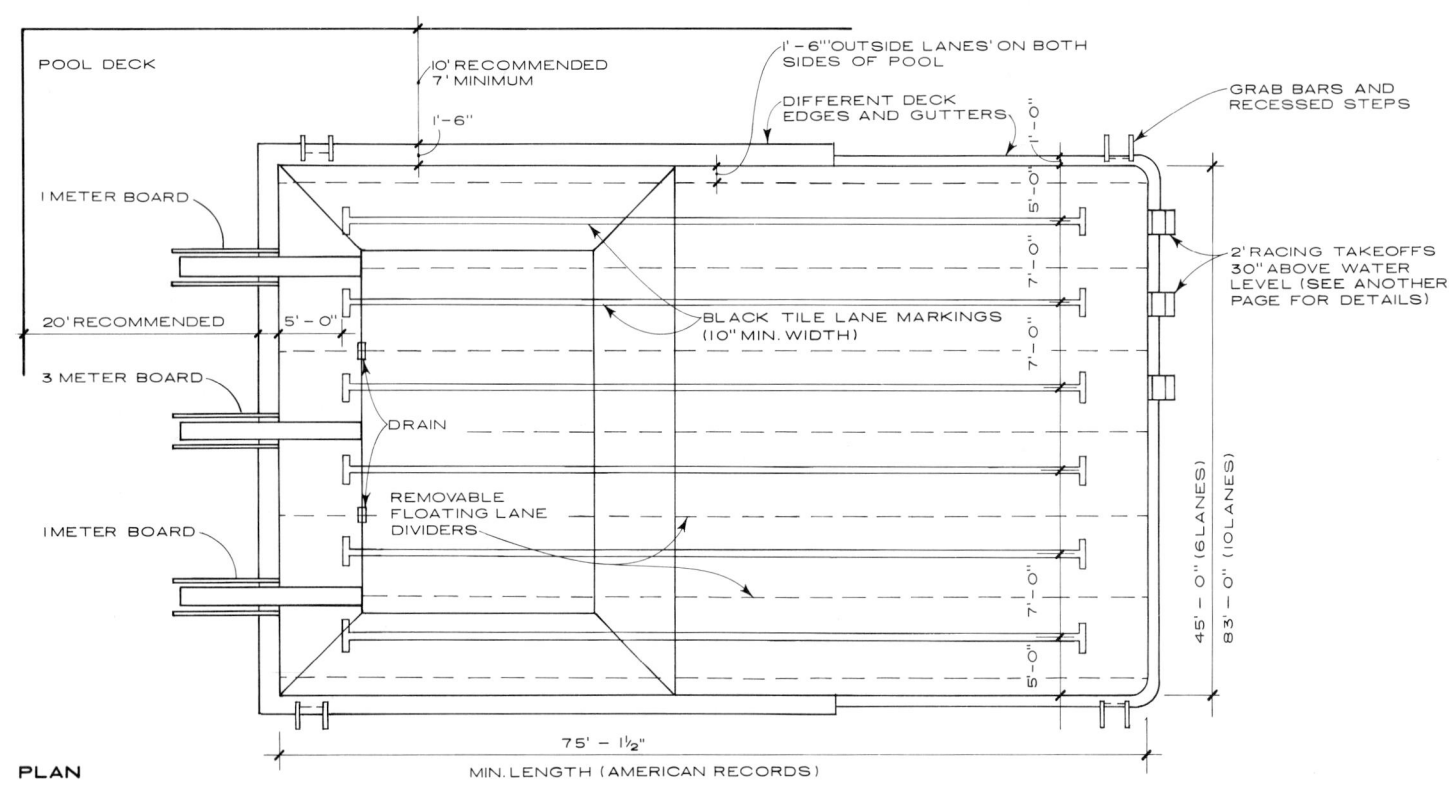

PLAN

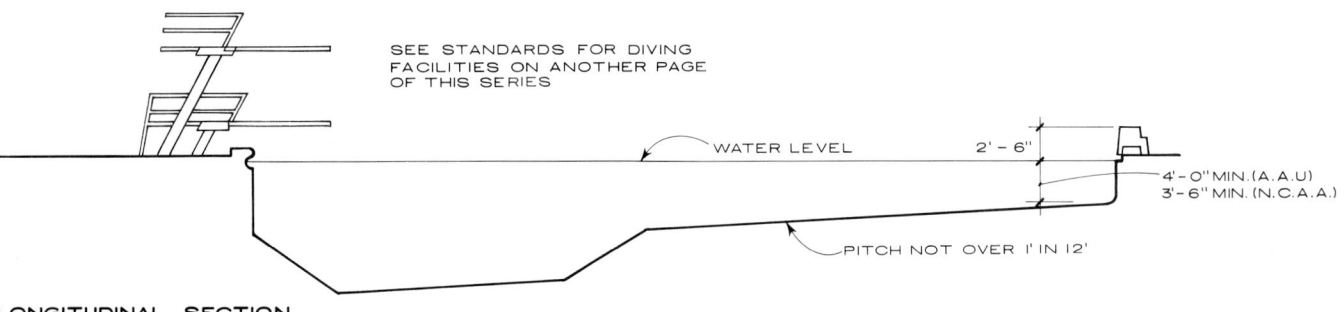

LONGITUDINAL SECTION

25 YARD POOL

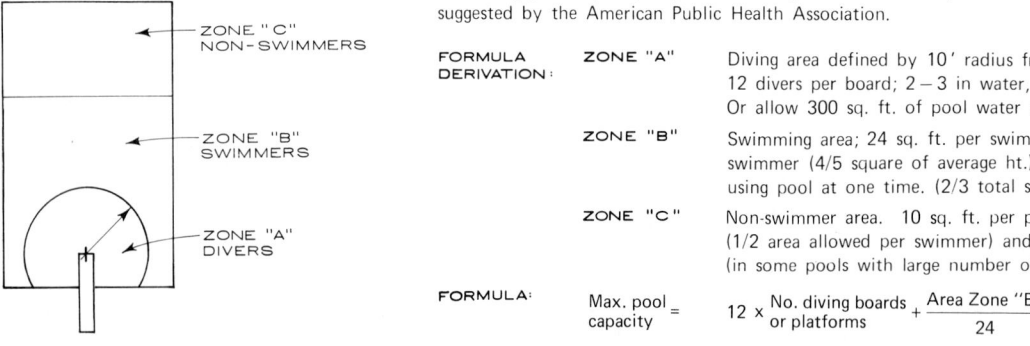

Swimming pool capacity requirements vary from one locality to another: check local regulations. The following is suggested by the American Public Health Association.

FORMULA DERIVATION:

ZONE "A"   Diving area defined by 10' radius from diving board or platform. 12 divers per board; 2 – 3 in water, the rest on shore. Or allow 300 sq. ft. of pool water surface per board.

ZONE "B"   Swimming area; 24 sq. ft. per swimmer. Based on volume displaced by each swimmer (4/5 square of average ht.) and adjusted by the number of swimmers using pool at one time. (2/3 total swimmers).

ZONE "C"   Non-swimmer area. 10 sq. ft. per person. Based on volume displaced by person (1/2 area allowed per swimmer) and adjusted by number not using water—50% (in some pools with large number of non-swimmers, figure may be as high as 75%).

FORMULA: $\text{Max. pool capacity} = 12 \times \dfrac{\text{No. diving boards or platforms}}{} + \dfrac{\text{Area Zone "B"}}{24} + \dfrac{\text{Area Zone "C"}}{10}$

PUBLIC SWIMMING POOL CAPACITY

R. Jackson Smith, AIA; Designed Environment, Inc.; Stamford, Connecticut

RECREATION

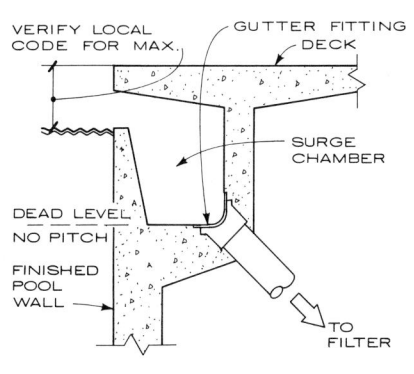

FULLY RECESSED OVERFLOW GUTTER

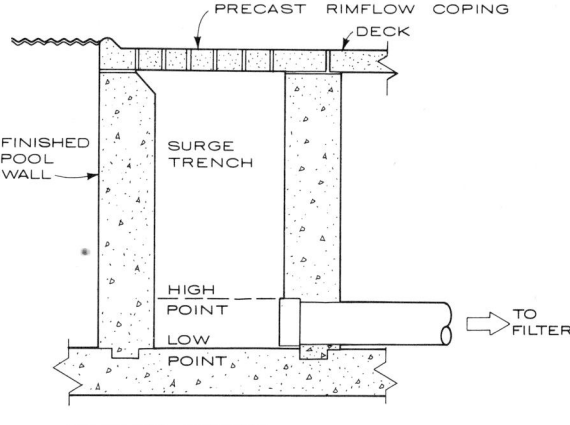

RIMFLOW SYSTEM

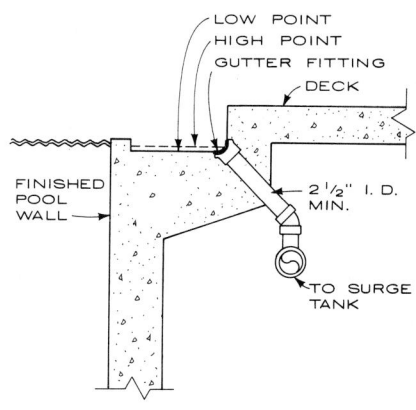

ROLL OUT OVERFLOW

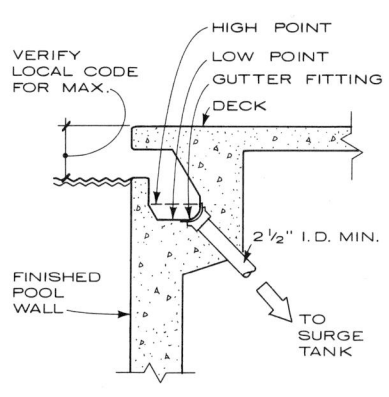

FULLY RECESSED GUTTER

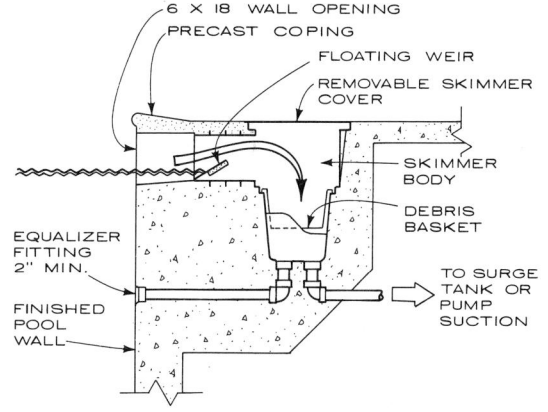

SURFACE SKIMMER

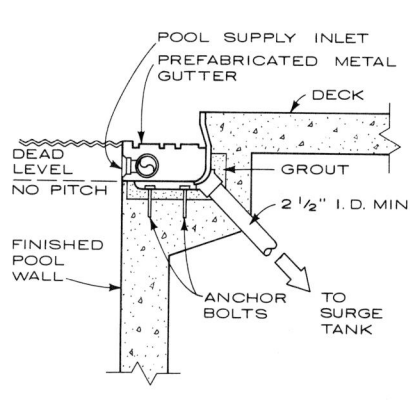

TYPICAL PREFABRICATED OVERFLOW

PERIMETER OVERFLOW SYSTEMS

NOTES

1. A perimeter overflow system must be provided on all public swimming pools. It must be designed and constructed so that the water level of the pool is maintained at the operating level of the overflow rim or weir device. Dimension from the deck to the water level is determined by applicable codes.

2. Perimeter type overflow systems, when used as the only overflow system on the pool, must extend around a minimum 50% of the swimming pool perimeter. Perimeter overflow systems must be connected to the circulation system with a system surge capacity of not less than 1 gal/sq ft of pool surface.

3. The perimeter overflow system in combination with the upper rim of the pool must constitute a handhold. It must be designed to prevent the entrapment of swimmer's arms, legs, or feet and to permit inspection and cleaning.

4. The hydraulic capacity of the overflow system must be sufficient to handle 100% of the circulation flow.

5. When roll-out or flush deck type of perimeter overflows are used on competitive pools, the ends of the pool must be provided with a visual barrier that can be seen by swimmers.

6. Perimeter overflows are commonly used on public swimming pools. Some state health departments do not approve skimmers on public swimming pools that exceed a certain surface area. Current state codes or swimming pool regulations must be checked to determine limits of use, minimum dimensions, and other factors dealing with overflow design.

7. Metal swimming pool systems are available that have a built-in perimeter overflow. In addition to the overflow channel, the metal liner may also contain the return waterline from the filtration system. A metal liner that incorporates a cove between wall and floor is desirable to facilitate cleaning.

8. Deck areas adjoining the overflow system are generally required to slope away from it to separate drains. When deck is sloped to pool overflow, provide for diverting pool overflow to waste during deck cleaning.

YMCA Building and Furnishings Service; New York, New York

National Swimming Pool Institute; Washington, D.C.

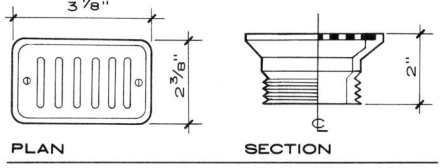

PLAN   SECTION

FLAT TYPE GUTTER FITTINGS

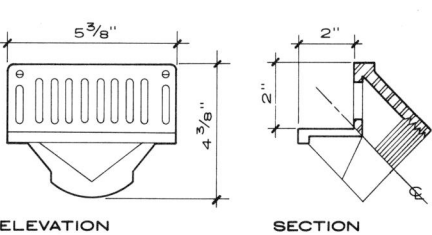

ELEVATION   SECTION

ANGLE TYPE GUTTER FITTINGS

9. Perimeter type overflows may be custom built to conform to the design selected. Ceramic tile is the preferred material for the top 6 in. of the pool wall, the pool rim, the gutter, and the deck for indoor swimming pools. Gratings for deep overflow gutters may be of precast concrete, plastic, or metal.

10. Proprietary overflow systems are available that have the characteristics of many of the perimeter overflow types shown. Stainless steel is commonly used because of its corrosion resistance. Aluminum overflow systems have a coating or enamel finish. Slotted precast concrete units are also available.

11. Surfaces subject to traffic must be nonslip.

SURFACE SKIMMERS

When surface skimmers are used, one must be provided for each 500 sq ft, or fraction thereof, of the pool surface. When two or more skimmers are used, they must be located so as to maintain effective skimming action over the entire surface of the swimming pool. Skimmers may not be permitted on larger pools. See local health department codes for limitation on public pools. Skimmers are not recommended for competitive pools.

Surface skimmers are available from many swimming pool suppliers. Metal or plastic units are available in various capacities. An access cover in the deck permits removal and cleaning of the strainer. Surface skimmers should comply with the joint National Swimming Pool Institute—National Sanitation Foundation performance standards.

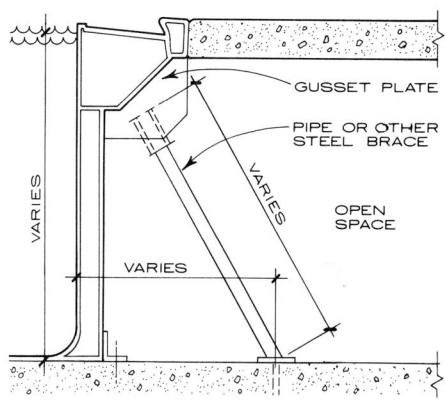

METAL POOL LINER WITH OVERFLOW

Often used in rooftop or other above grade installations where weight is a primary factor in design.

RECREATION 1

LENGTH OF POOLS

25 yards is the minimum length for American records, and meets interscholastic and intercollegiate requirements. (Pool should be 75'-1½'' long to allow for electronic timing panels at one end.)

Standards for International Competition are shown on 50 meter pool page.

WIDTH OF POOLS

Drawing below shows 7' lanes, with pool width of 45' (6 lanes). Strictly competitive pools should have 8' lanes, with pool width of 83' (10 lanes). Minimum widths include additional 18'' width outside lanes on both sides of pool.

NOTES

Gutters at sides of pool are desirable to reduce wave action in swimming meets or water polo. See lighting standards and diving board standards on other pages of this series for additional requirements for competitive pools.

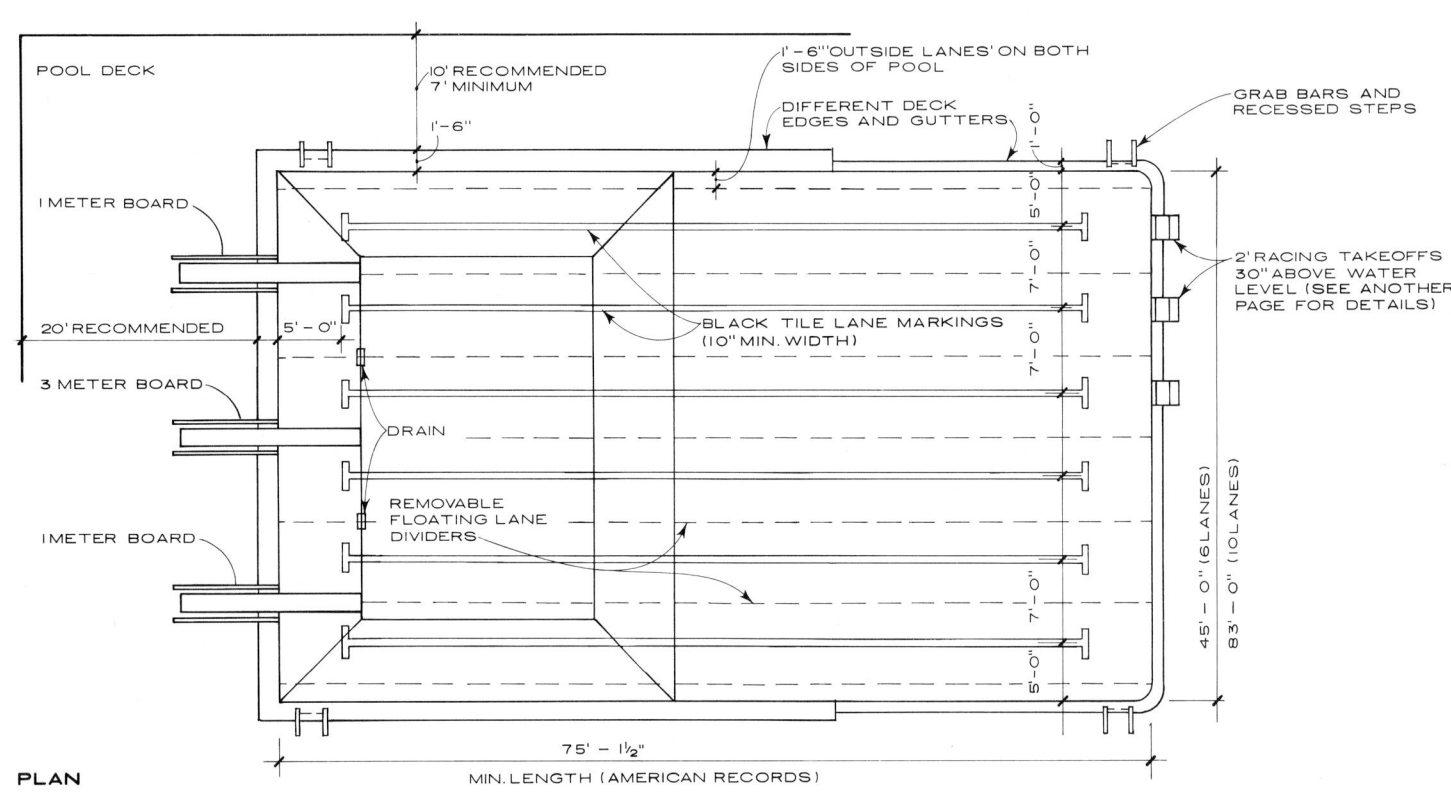

PLAN

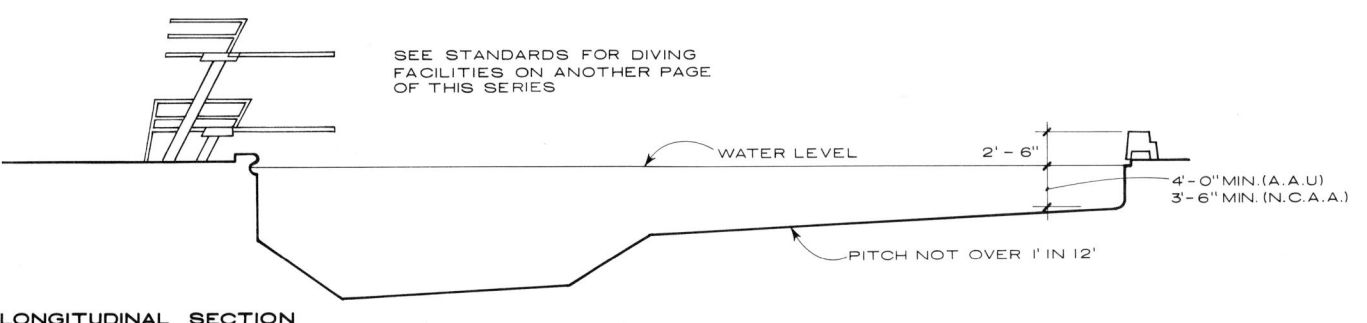

LONGITUDINAL SECTION
25 YARD POOL

Swimming pool capacity requirements vary from one locality to another: check local regulations. The following is suggested by the American Public Health Association.

FORMULA DERIVATION:

ZONE "A" Diving area defined by 10' radius from diving board or platform.
12 divers per board; 2 – 3 in water, the rest on shore.
Or allow 300 sq. ft. of pool water surface per board.

ZONE "B" Swimming area; 24 sq. ft. per swimmer. Based on volume displaced by each swimmer (4/5 square of average ht.) and adjusted by the number of swimmers using pool at one time. (2/3 total swimmers).

ZONE "C" Non-swimmer area. 10 sq. ft. per person. Based on volume displaced by person (1/2 area allowed per swimmer) and adjusted by number not using water—50% (in some pools with large number of non-swimmers, figure may be as high as 75%).

FORMULA:

$$\text{Max. pool capacity} = 12 \times \text{No. diving boards or platforms} + \frac{\text{Area Zone "B"}}{24} + \frac{\text{Area Zone "C"}}{10}$$

PUBLIC SWIMMING POOL CAPACITY

R. Jackson Smith, AIA; Designed Environment, Inc.; Stamford, Connecticut

RECREATION

GENERAL NOTES

For judging competitive meets, F.I.N.A. officials recommend the springboard and diving platform arrangement indicated below in plan. Diving dimensions meet minimum F.I.N.A. standards. Fifty meters is minimum length for world records.

NOTE

*Length should be 50.03 m allowing an extra .03 m to compensate for possible future tile facing, structural defects and electrical timing panels.

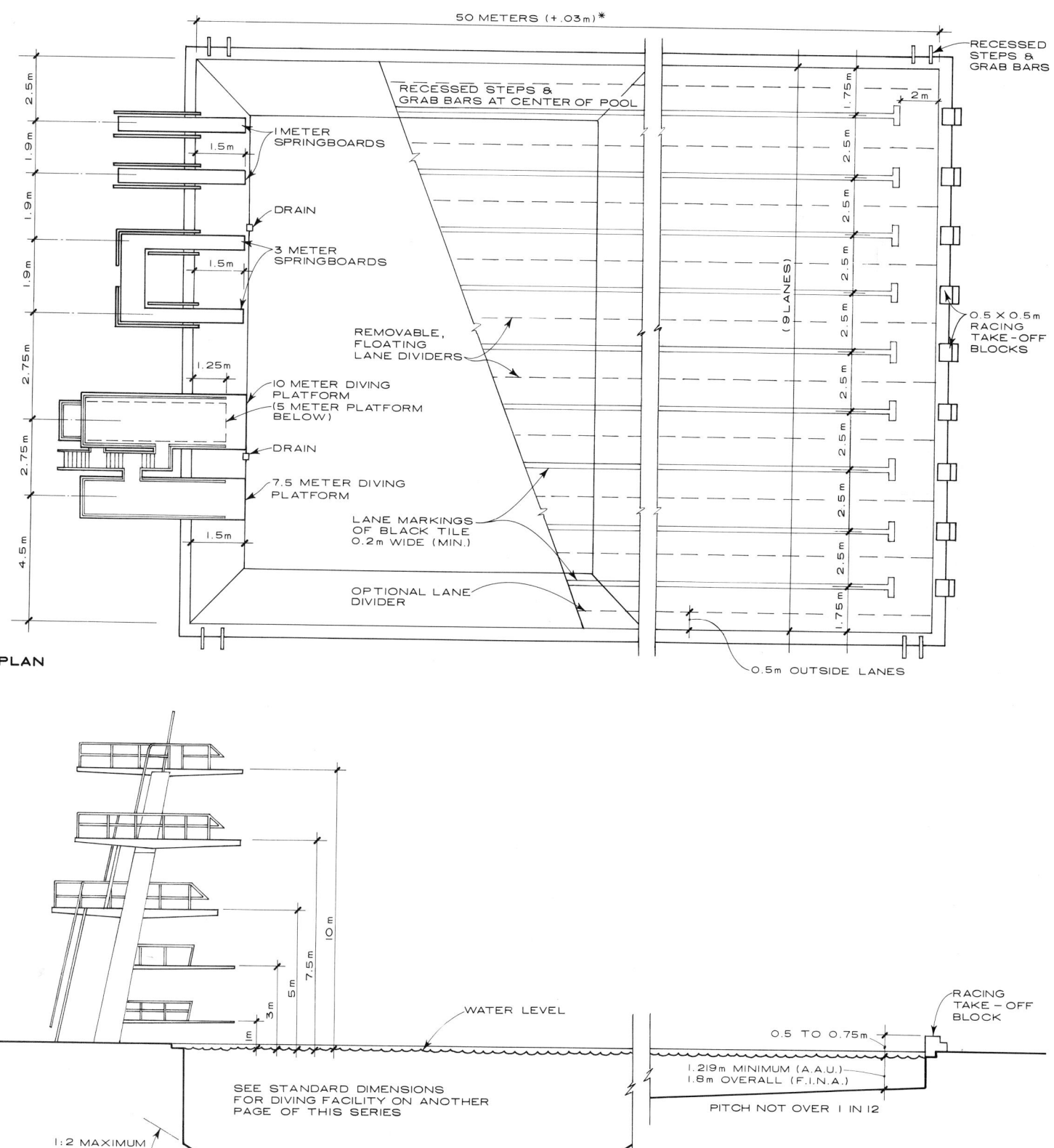

PLAN

LONGITUDINAL SECTION

R. Jackson Smith, AIA; Designed Environment, Inc.; Stamford, Connecticut

RECREATION **1**

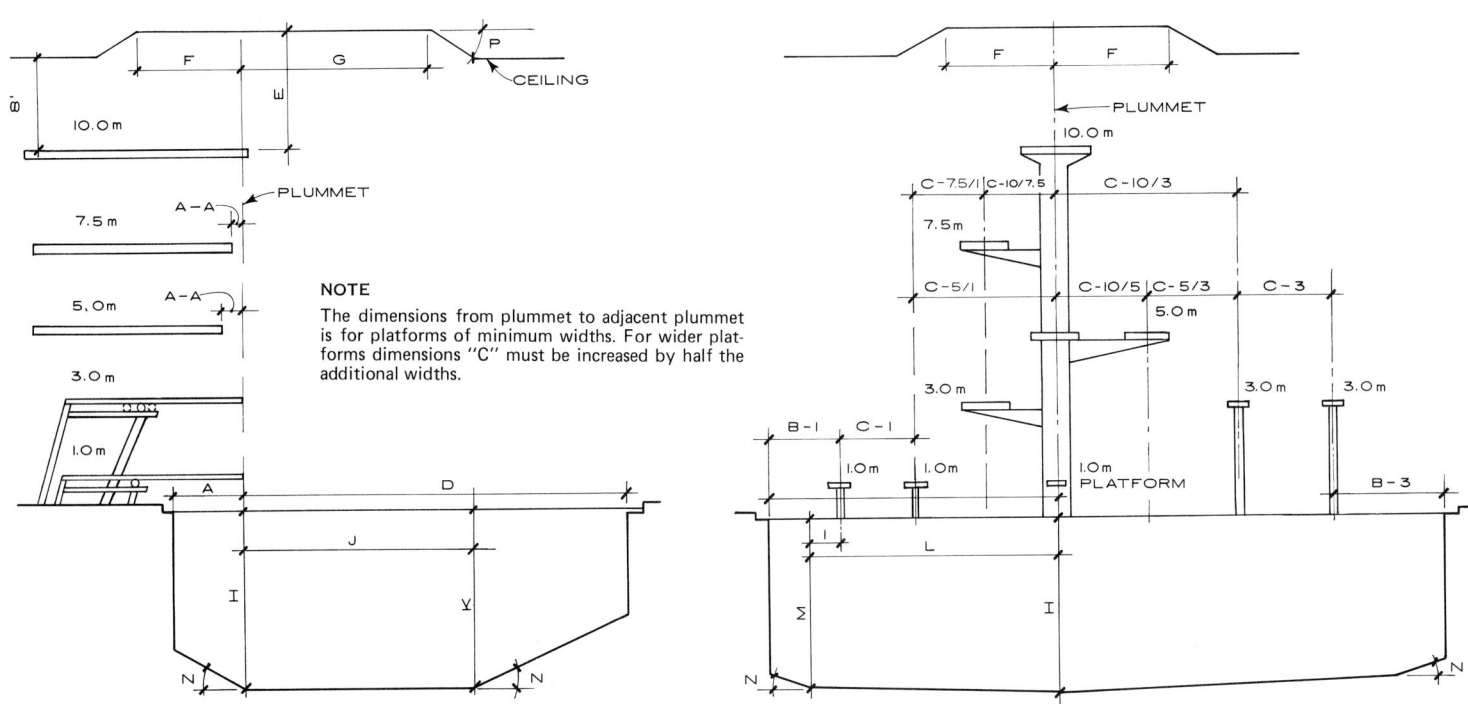

NOTE

The dimensions from plummet to adjacent plummet is for platforms of minimum widths. For wider platforms dimensions "C" must be increased by half the additional widths.

DIAGRAMMATIC LONGITUDINAL SECTION   DIAGRAMMATIC CROSS SECTION

FINA INTERNATIONAL AMATEUR SWIMMING AND DIVING FEDERATION STANDARDS

DIMENSIONS FOR DIVING FACILITIES			SPRINGBOARDS				PLATFORMS							
			1 METER	3 METER		1 METER	3 METER	5 METER		7.5 METER		10 METER		
	LENGTH		5.0	5.0		4.5	5.0	6.0		6.0		6.0		
	WIDTH		0.5	0.5		0.6	0.8	1.5		1.5		2.0		
	HEIGHT		1.0	3.0		1.0	0.8	5.0		7.5		10.0		
A	FROM PLUMMET: BACK TO POOL WALL	DESIG.	A-1	A-3		A-1 (PL)	A-3 (PL)	A-5		A-7.5		A-10		
		MIN.	1.50	1.50		0.75	1.25	1.25		1.50		1.50		
		PREF.	1.80	1.80				1.50						
A-A	FROM PLUMMET: BACK TO PLATFORM DIRECTLY BELOW	DESIG.						AA-5/1		A-7.5/3		AA-10/5		
		MIN.						0.75		0.75		0.75		
		PREF.								1.50		1.50		
B	FROM PLUMMET: TO POOL WALL AT SIDE	DESIG.	B-1	B-3		B-1 (PL)	B-3 (PL)	B-5		B-7.5		B-10		
		MIN.	2.50	3.50		2.30	2.90	4.25		4.50		5.25		
		PREF.	3.00											
C	FROM PLUMMET TO ADJACENT PLUMMET	DESIG.	C-1	C-3	C-3/1	C-1/1 (PL)	C-3/1 (PL)	C-5/3 (PL)	C-5/1	C-7.5/3/1	C-107.5	C-10/7.5/3	C 10/3/1	
		MIN.	2.40	2.60	2.60	1.65	2.10	2.50	2.50	2.50	2.50	2.75	2.75	
		PREF.	2.40	2.40	1.4/3.0									
D	FROM PLUMMET TO POOL WALL AHEAD	DESIG.	D-1	D-3		D-1 (PL)	D-3 (PL)	D-5		D-7.5		D-10		
		MIN.	9.00	10.25		8.00	9.50	10.25		11.00		13.50		
		PREF.												
E	PLUMMET, FROM BOARD TO CEILING OVERHEAD	DESIG.	E-1	E-3		E-1 (PL)	E-3 (PL)		E-5	E-7.5		E-10		
		MIN.	5.00	5.00		3.00	3.00		3.00	3.20		3.40		
		PREF.							3.40	3.40		5 00		
F	CLEAR OVERHEAD, BEHIND AND EACH SIDE OF PLUMMET	DESIG.	F-1	E-1	F-3	E-3	F-1 (PL)	F-3 (PL)	F-5	E-5	F-7.5	E-7.5	F-10	E-10
		MIN.	2.50	5.00	2.50	5.00	2.75	2.75	2.75	3.00	2.75	3.20	2.75	3.40
		PREF.								3.40		3.40		5.00
G	CLEAR OVERHEAD, AHEAD OF PLUMMET	DESIG.	G-1	E-1	G-3	E-3	G-1 (PL)	G-3 (PL)	G-5	E-5	G-7.5	E-7.5	G-10	E-10
		MIN.	5.00	5.00	5.00	5.00	5.00	5.00	5.00	3.00	5.00	3.20	6.00	3.40
		PREF.								3.40		3.40		5.00
H	DEPTH OF WATER AT PLUMMET	DESIG.	H-1		H-3		H-1 (PL)	H-3 (PL)		H-5		H-7.5		H-10
		MIN.	3.40		3.80		3.40	3.60		3.80		4.10		4.50
		PREF.	3.80		4.00			3.80		4.00		4.50		5.00
J-K	DISTANCE, DEPTH OF WATER, AHEAD OF PLUMMET	DESIG.	J-1	K-1	J-3	K-3	J/K-1 (PL)	J/K-3 (PL)	J-5	K-5	J-7.5	K-7.5	J-10	K-10
		MIN.	5.00	3.30	6.00	3.70	5.0/3.3	6.0/3.3	6.00	3.70	8.00	4.00	11.00	4.25
		PREF.		3.70		3.90				3.90		4.40		4.75
L-M	DISTANCE, DEPTH OF WATER, EACH SIDE OF PLUMMET	DESIG.	L-1	M-1	L-3	M-3	L/M-1 (PL)	L/M-3 (PL)	L-5	M-5	L-7.5	M-7.5	L-10	M-10
		MIN.	2.50	3.30	3.25	3.70	2.05/3.3	2.65/3.5	4.25	3.70	4.50	4.00	5.25	4.25
		PREF.		3.70		3.90		3.70		3.90		4.40		4.75
N P	MAXIMUM ANGLE OF SLOPE TO REDUCE DIMENSIONS BEYOND FULL REQUIREMENTS	POOL BOTTOM	= 30 Degrees (Approximately 1 foot vertical to 2 feet horizontal)											
		CEILING HEIGHT	= 30 Degrees											

R. Jackson Smith, AIA; Designed Environment, Inc.; Stamford, Connecticut

GENERAL NOTES

Both 1 m and 3 m boards are required for amateur, collegiate, and international meets. All boards shall have a nonslip surface. Consult FINA Handbook. FINA is the Fédération Internationale de Natation Amateur.

Foundations are shown to approximate scale but dimensions should be determined by engineer.

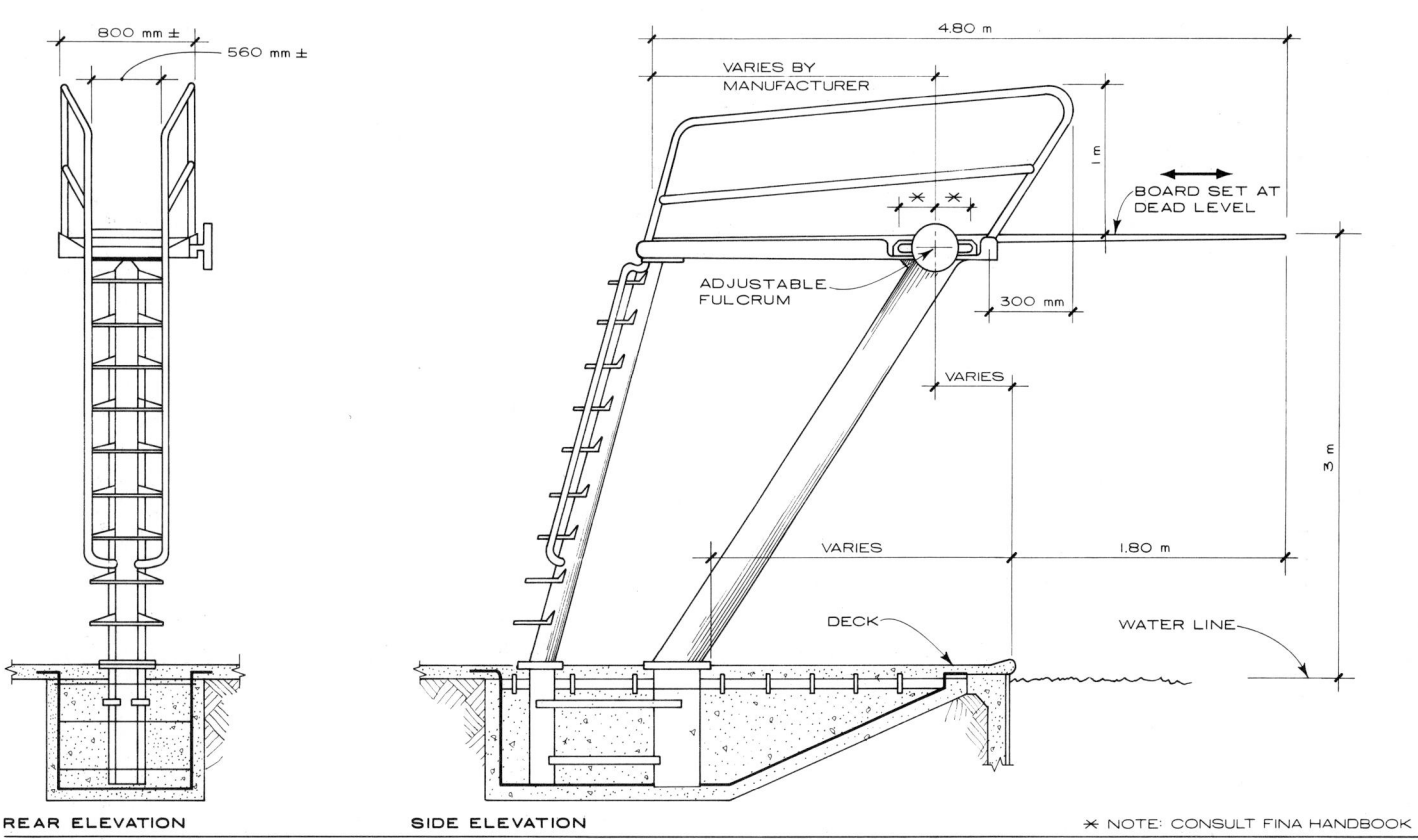

3 METER DIVING BOARD
NOTE: FOR ADDITIONAL INFORMATION ON DIVING SEE PAGE TITLED "STANDARD DIMENSIONS FOR DIVING FACILITIES (FINA)"

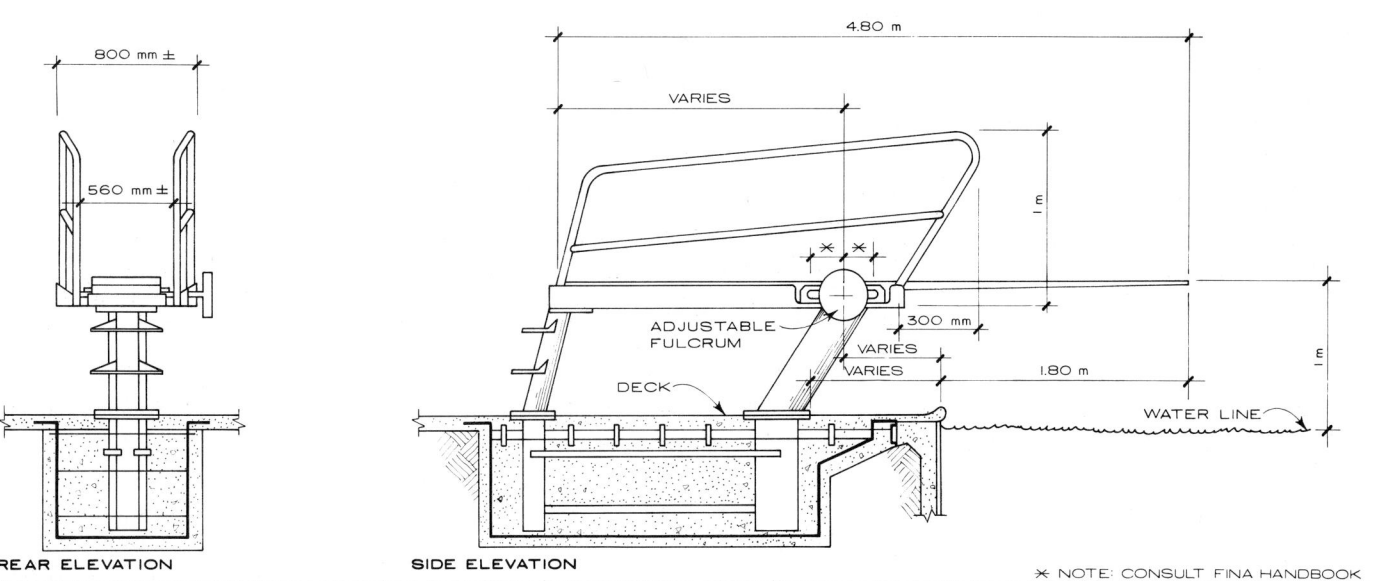

1 METER DIVING BOARD

R. Jackson Smith, AIA; Designed Environment, Inc.; Stamford, Connecticut

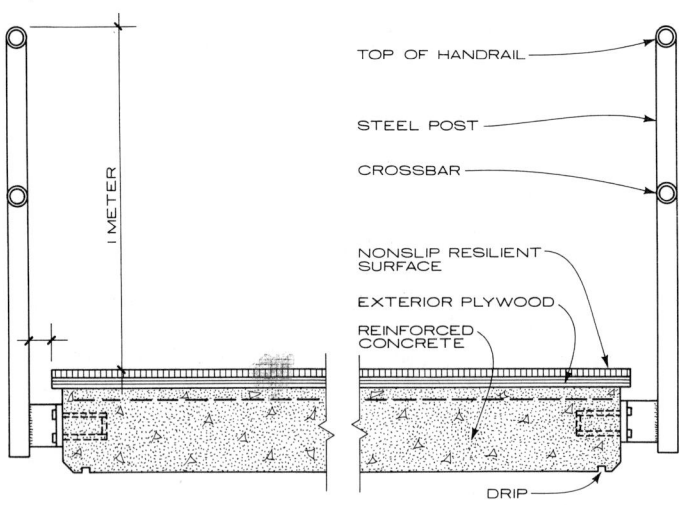

Top of handrail — Steel post — Crossbar — Nonslip resilient surface — Exterior plywood — Reinforced concrete — 1 meter — Drip

PLATFORM DECK – SECTION AA

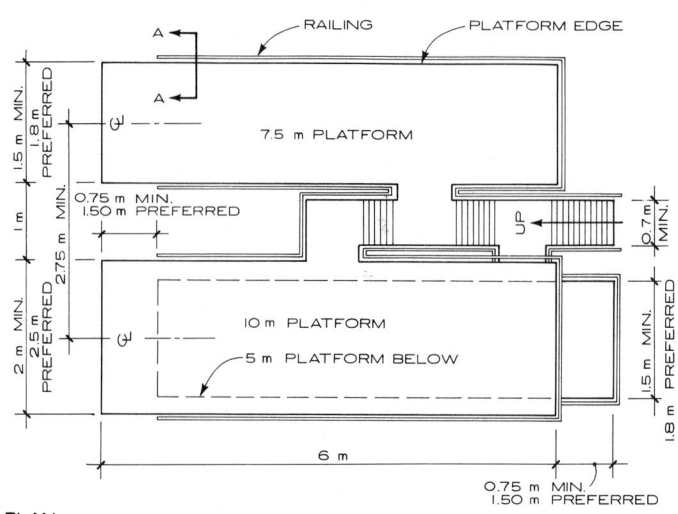

A — Railing — Platform edge
1.5 m MIN. / 1.8 m PREFERRED
7.5 m Platform
0.75 m MIN. / 1.50 m PREFERRED
2.75 m MIN. / PREFERRED
UP — 0.7 m MIN.
2 m MIN. / 2.5 m PREFERRED
10 m Platform
5 m Platform below
1.5 m MIN. / 1.8 m PREFERRED
6 m
0.75 m MIN. / 1.50 m PREFERRED

PLAN

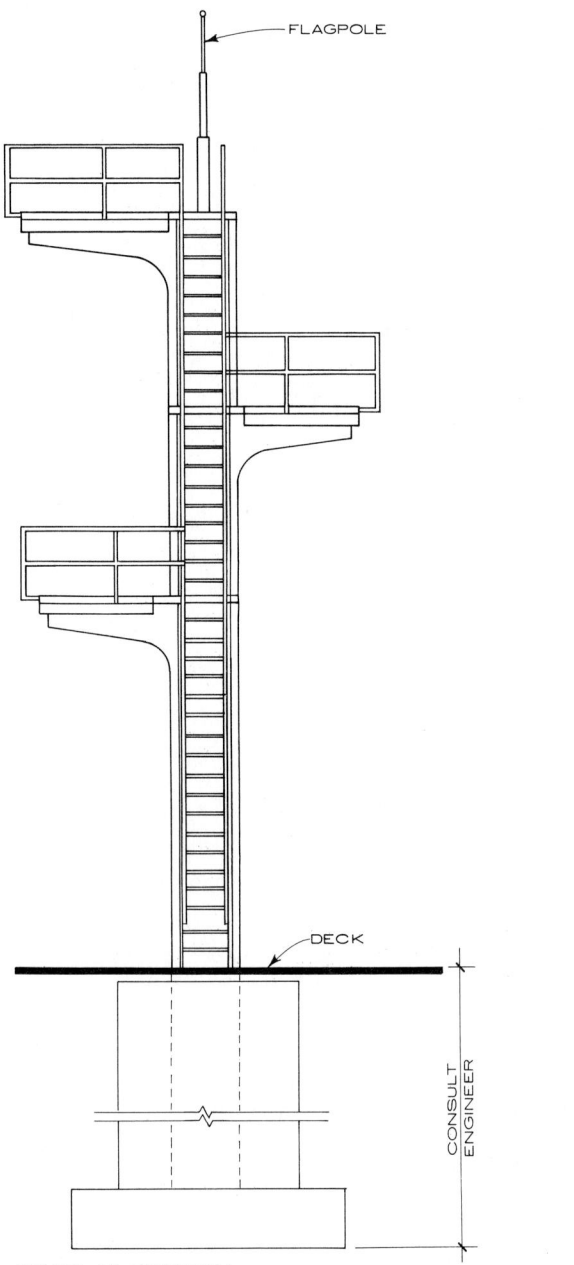

Flagpole — Deck — Consult engineer

REAR ELEVATION

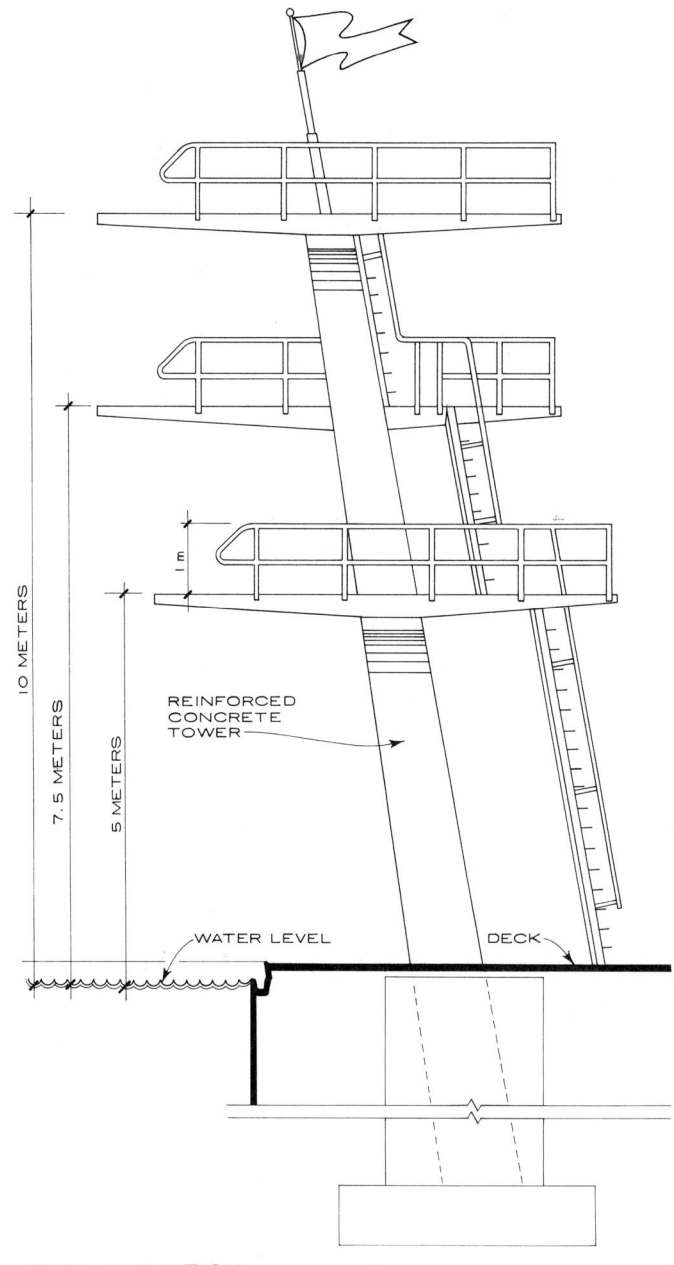

Reinforced concrete tower — Water level — Deck — 10 meters — 7.5 meters — 5 meters — 1 m

SIDE ELEVATION

R. Jackson Smith, AIA; Designed Environments, Inc.; Stamford, Connecticut

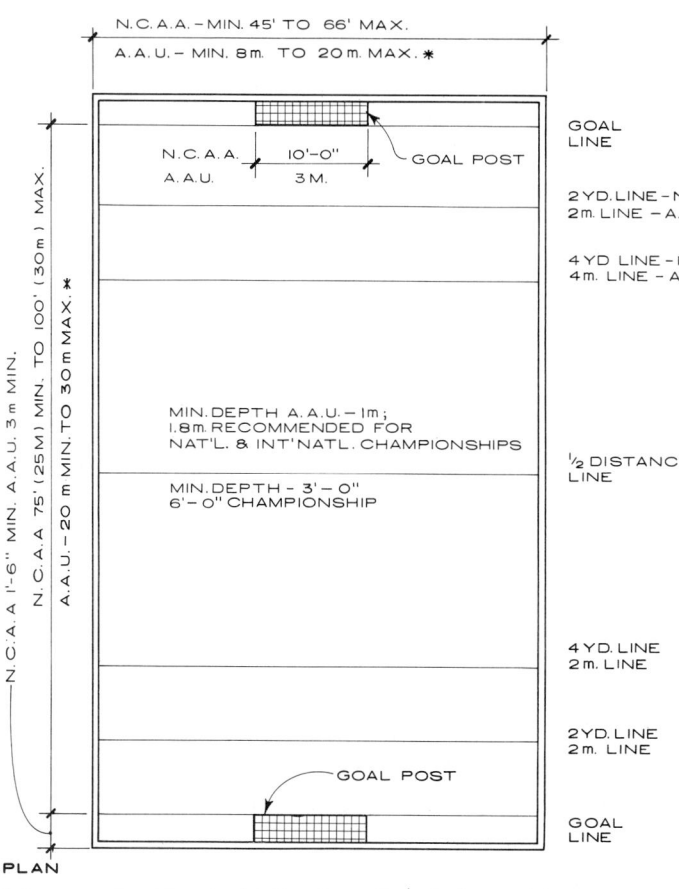

PLAN

* For womens' matches, the A.A.U. recommends measurements of 25 m. x 17 m.

One meter equals 3.28 ft. To obtain equivalent dimensions in feet, multiply by 3.28. A.A.U. figures are expressed in meters.

WATER POLO
N.C.A.A. : WATER POLO RULES
A.A.U. : WATER POLO RULES

SCORER'S FLAG
12" RED SQUARE

BALL
27"–28" CIRCUMFERENCE YELLOW RUBBER FABRIC

REFEREE'S FLAG
WHITE
12"X12"
DARK BLUE

SIDE ELEVATIONS
1'–6" MIN.
8' WHEN WATER IS LESS THAN 5' DEEP
STRAP ANCHOR
3' WHEN WATER IS MORE THAN 5' DEEP
METAL BASE

FRONT ELEVATION
CROSSBAR
4" WIPE FACING
10'–0"

N.C.A.A. GOALS

NOTES

Distinctive marks must be provided on both sides of field of play indicating goal lines, 2 & 4 yd. (or meter) lines, and 1/2 distance between goal lines. These must be clearly visable from any position within the field of play. Allow sufficient space on walkways so referees may move freely from end to end of field of play. Provide space at goal lines for goal judges.

GOAL REQUIREMENTS

Posts and crossbar, rigid and perpendicular. A.A.U., wood or metal, 3" sq., painted white; N.C.A.A., metal, 1 1/2 dia., painted yellow or orange. Nets to hang loosely on frame.

For A.A.U., the underside of the crossbar must be 0.90 meters above water surface when water is 1.50 meters or more in depth, and 2.40 meters from the bottom of the bath when the depth of the water is less than 1.50 meters.

Frames are custom made with bracing placed where necessary. It is recommended that they be collapsible for easy storage. Anchorage methods depend on pool design, with those above commonly used, or brass couplings may be placed in pool walls to which frame is attached. If pool is longer than required length, one of the goals may be floated & anchored with guy wires.

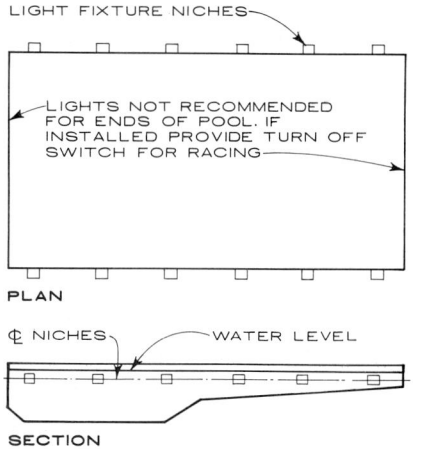

UNDERWATER POOL LIGHTING

NOTES FOR WET AND DRY NICHE UNDERWATER LIGHTS

Underwater lighting type and distance "A" should be in accordance with NEC (Article 680) regulations.

Underwater lights will require 0.5 to 2.0 watts per sq. ft. of water area and should be sized accordingly.

Box connections for dry or wet niches should be a minimum of 4'–0" away from the side wall of the pool and 8" above the deck. Low voltage wiring should be used for all dry or wet niche lighting fixtures. This requires a transformer located, by code, a specific distance away from pool wall and above deck.

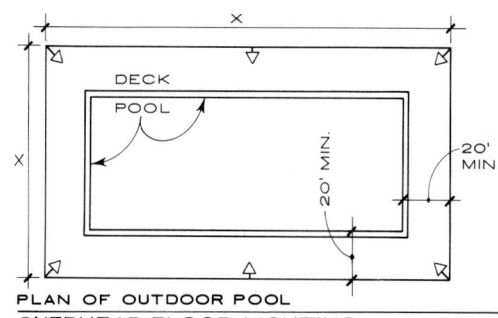

PLAN OF OUTDOOR POOL
OVERHEAD FLOOD LIGHTING

NOTE

Distance "X" for spacing of lights not to exceed four times the actual mounting height of lamp in light fixture.

INTERIOR ABOVE WATER LIGHTING

The A.A.U. states that "sufficient over head lighting be installed with concentration directly over finish line. 40 foot-candles at a height of 3 ft. above the water surface is recommended. Buildings housing indoor pools should not have windows facing pool-ends, to prevent glare at finish and turns."

SWIMMING POOL LIGHTING

R. Jackson Smith, AIA; Designed Environment, Inc.; Stamford, Connecticut

OUTDOOR ABOVE WATER LIGHTING

Flood lights should be mounted at least 20 ft. above the water. Select lamps to allow 1.0 watt per sq. ft. min. for floodlights. Consult A.A.U. or N.C.A.A. for specific requirements for championship meets. A.A.U. rules for championship meets require a minimum of 40 foot-candles 3 feet above the water surface.

GENERAL NOTE

Each **DESIGN VEHICLE** in Groups I, II, and III represents a composite of the critical dimensions of the real vehicles within each group below. Parking lot dimensions on a following page are based on these groups and dimensions. For parking purposes, both compact and standard size vehicles are in Group II. Turning dimensions R, RI, and C are shown on the next page.

DESIGN VEHICLE

GROUP I		SMALL CARS
L	Length	15'-5''
W	Width	5'-10''
H	Height	4'-10''
WB	Wheelbase	9'-2''
OF	Overhang front	2'-6''
OR	Overhang rear	3'-9''
OS	Overhang sides	0'-7''
T	Track	4'-9''

GROUP II		COMPACTS
L	Length	16'-11''
W	Width	6'-3''
H	Height	5'-0''
WB	Wheelbase	10'-0''
OF	Overhang front	2'-8''
OR	Overhang rear	4'-3''
OS	Overhang sides	0'-8''
T	Track	4'-10''

GROUP III		STANDARD
L	Length	17'-9''
W	Width	6'-8''
H	Height	5'-2''
WB	Wheelbase	10'-7''
OF	Overhang front	2'-10''
OR	Overhang rear	4'-4''
OS	Overhang side	0'-9''
T	Track	5'-2''

GROUP IV		LARGE CARS
L	Length	18'-0''
W	Width	6'-8''
H	Height	5'-4''
WB	Wheelbase	10'-8''
OF	Overhang front	2'-11''
OR	Overhang rear	4'-5''
OS	Overhang side	0'-9''
T	Track	5'-2''

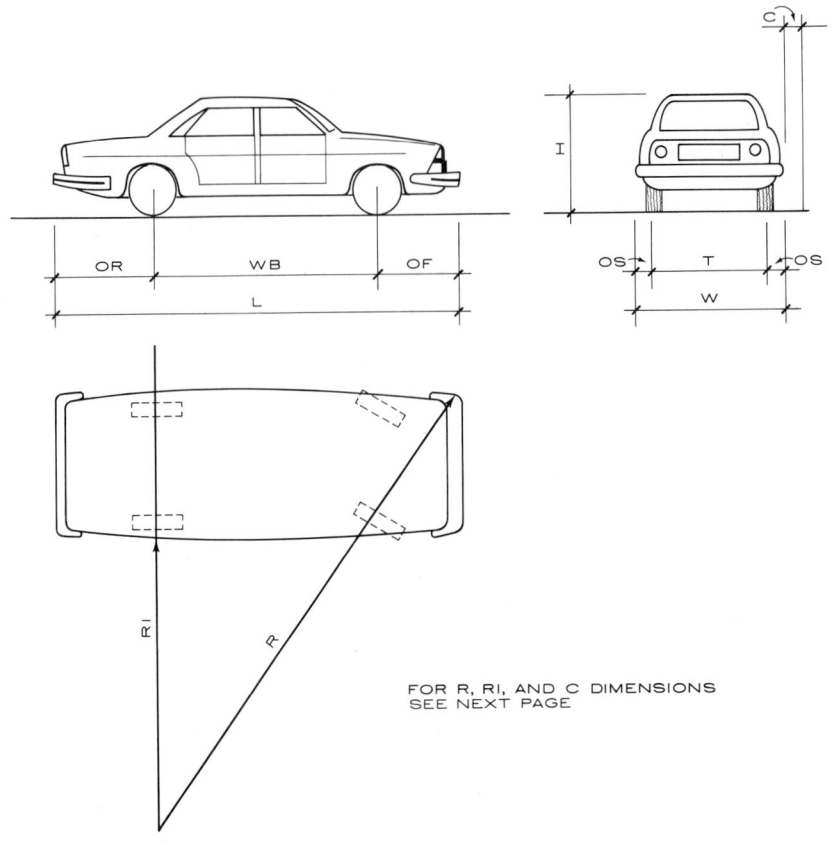

FOR R, RI, AND C DIMENSIONS
SEE NEXT PAGE

LARGE VEHICLE DIMENSIONS*

VEHICLE	(L) LENGTH	(W) WIDTH	(OR) OVERHANG REAR
Intercity bus	45'-0''	9'-0''	10'-1''
City bus	40'-0''	8'-6''	6'-6''
School bus	39'-6''	8'-0''	12'-8''
Ambulance	20'-10¼''	6'-11''	5'-4''
Paramedic van	18'-0''	6'-7''	5'-2''
Hearse	20'-10¼''	6'-11''	5'-4''
Airport limousine	22'-5¾''	6'-4''	3'-11''
Trash truck	28'-2''	8'-0''	6'-0''
U.P.S. truck	23'-2''	7'-7''	8'-2''
Fire truck	31'-4''	8'-1''	10'-0''

*Exact sizes of large vehicles may vary.

NOTE
ANGLES SHOWN BELOW MAY VARY DEPENDING ON SPEED, LOAD, TIRE PRESSURE, AND CONDITION OF SHOCK ABSORBERS

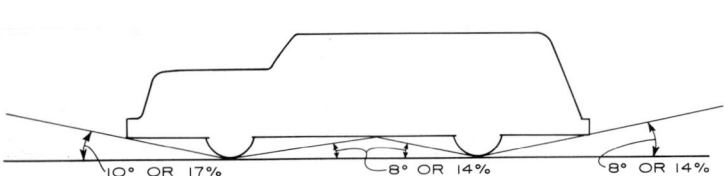

10° OR 17%   8° OR 14%   8° OR 14%

COMPOSITE VEHICLE WITH MAXIMUM WB, OF, AND OR

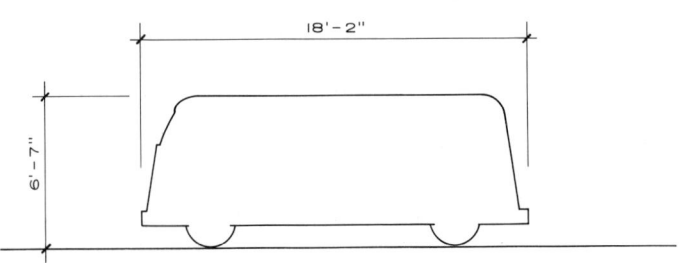

LARGE VAN

William T. Mahan, AIA; Santa Barbara, California

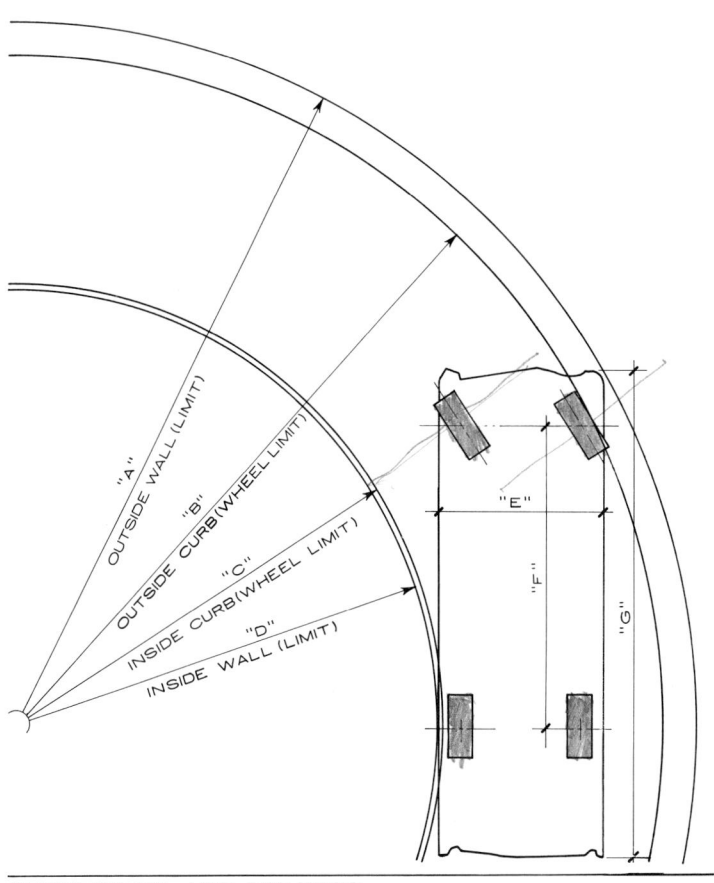

GOLF CARTS GASOLINE OR ELECTRIC POWER

3 WHEELS		4 WHEELS
46 3/4″	Overall Height	47 1/8″
10 3/4″	Floorboard Height	11 1/4″
27 3/4″	Seat Height	28 1/4″
102″	Length	102″
47″	Width	47″
68″	Wheel Base	68 3/4″
—	Front Wheel Tread	34″
34 5/8″	Rear Wheel Tread	34 5/8″
4 5/8″	Ground Clearance	4 5/8″
19′–6″	Clearance Circle	24′–0″

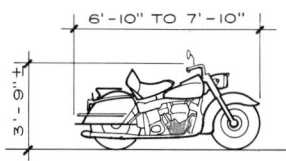

Consult manufacturers' information for width of motorcycle and sidecar.

WIDTH AT HANDLEBAR 2'-7" TO 3'-3"

When parked on stand motorcycle leans about 10°. Large vehicle requires about 3'-8" of space.

HEAVYWEIGHTS WEIGH FROM ABOUT 400 LB TO 661 LB

HEAVYWEIGHT MOTORCYCLES

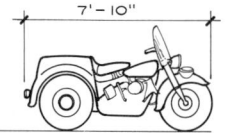

POLICE TRICYCLE WIDTH AT BOX 4"-0"±

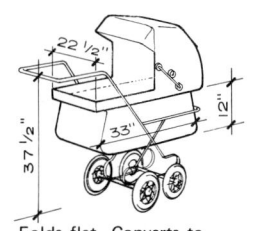

Folds flat. Converts to stroller. Body makes car bed.
BABY CARRIAGE

Handlebar width 23″ and up.
Weight about 230 lb to about 300 lb

LIGHTWEIGHT MOTORCYCLE

AMBULANCES AND HEARSES
DIMENSIONS AND TURNING RADII

MAKE OF CAR	"A"	"B"	"C"	"D"	"E"	"F"	"G"
Cadillac	30'–0″	28'–6″	18'–11 1/2″	18'–9″	6'–11″	13'–0″	20'–10 1/4″
Dodge	23'–4″	21'–9″	13'–4 1/2″	12'–10 3/4″	6'–8″		18'–4″

AIRPORT LIMOUSINE

Checker	28'–3″				6'–4″	15'–9″	22'–5 3/4″

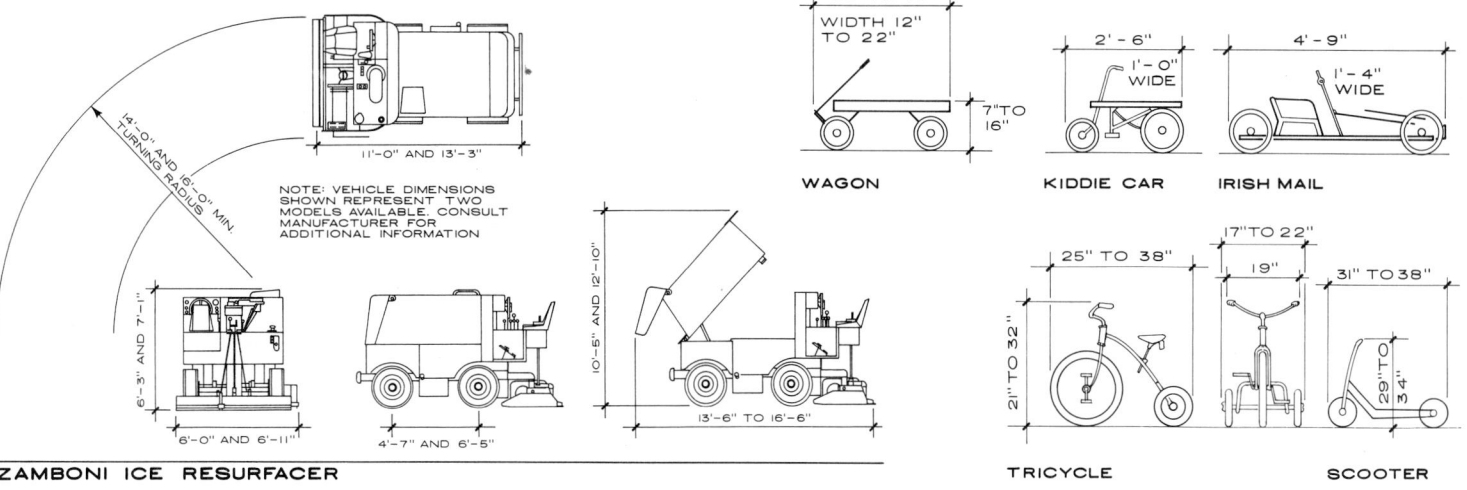

NOTE: VEHICLE DIMENSIONS SHOWN REPRESENT TWO MODELS AVAILABLE. CONSULT MANUFACTURER FOR ADDITIONAL INFORMATION

ZAMBONI ICE RESURFACER

WAGON

KIDDIE CAR

IRISH MAIL

TRICYCLE

SCOOTER

Foster C. Parriott; James M. Hunter & Associates; Boulder, Colorado

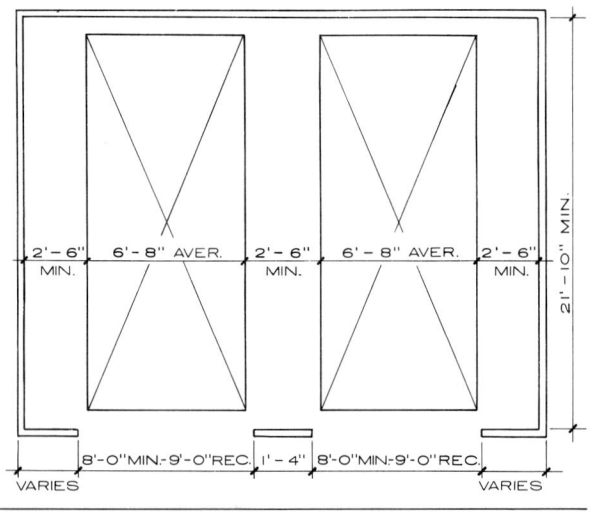

TWO-CAR GARAGE

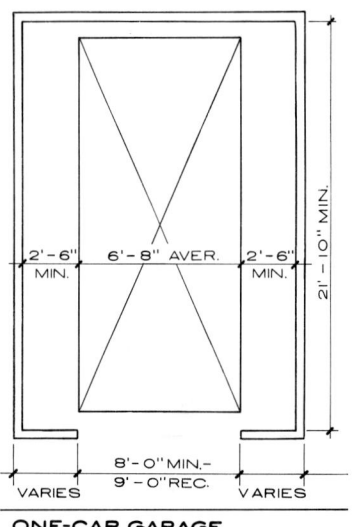

ONE-CAR GARAGE

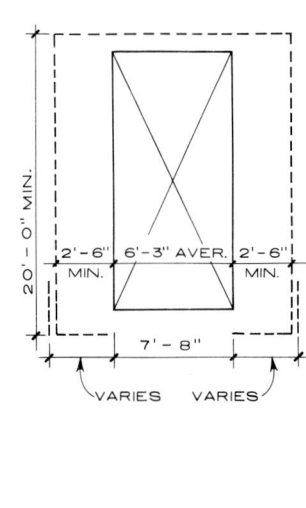

COMPACT CAR GARAGE

NOTES: Garages may be enlarged to provide ease of circulation by allowing spaces of 2'-6'' minimum between all walls and other vehicles; also to provide space for work areas, photography laboratories, laundry room, and storage.

JAMB CLEARANCE – WIDTH OF DR.
SINGLE DOOR

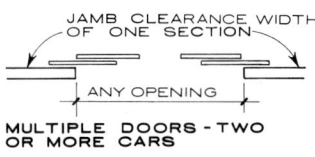

MULTIPLE DOORS – TWO OR MORE CARS

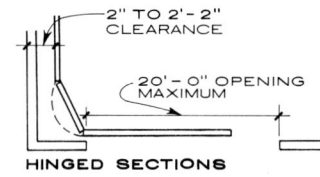

HINGED SECTIONS

NOTE
6 1/2'' to 9'' necessary from top of opening to ceiling (all sliding doors).

SLIDING DOORS

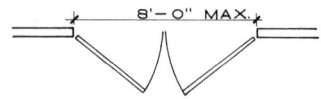

DOUBLE OR TRIPLE HINGED

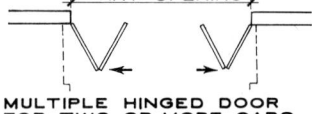

MULTIPLE HINGED DOOR FOR TWO OR MORE CARS

OFFSETHINGE – MULTI-LEAVE

NOTE: For multiple and offset hinged doors, swinging to one or both sides, hinged in or out and used for 2' or more cars: 6 1/2'' to 11'' necessary from top of opening to ceiling.

HINGED DOORS

WIDTHS OF GARAGE HINGED DOORS

OPENING	TWO-DOOR	THREE-DOOR	FOUR-DOOR
8'-0''	4'-0''	2'-8''	2'-0''
8'-6''	4'-3''	2'-10''	2'-1 1/2''
9'-0''	4'-6''	3'-0''	2'-3''

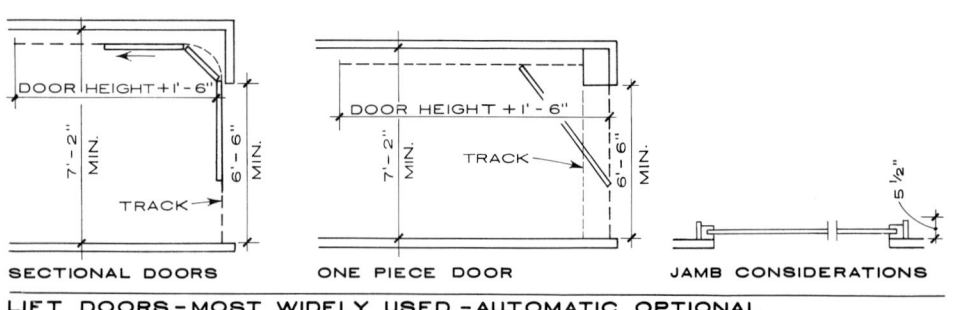

SECTIONAL DOORS   ONE PIECE DOOR   JAMB CONSIDERATIONS

LIFT DOORS – MOST WIDELY USED – AUTOMATIC OPTIONAL

NOTE

Heights: 6'-6'', 6'-10'', 7'-0'', 7'-6'' and 8'-0''.
Lift doors generally 4'-0'' sections high, sometimes 2'-0'' or 3'-0''

R. E. Powe, Jr., AIA; Hugh N. Jacobsen, FAIA; Washington, D.C.

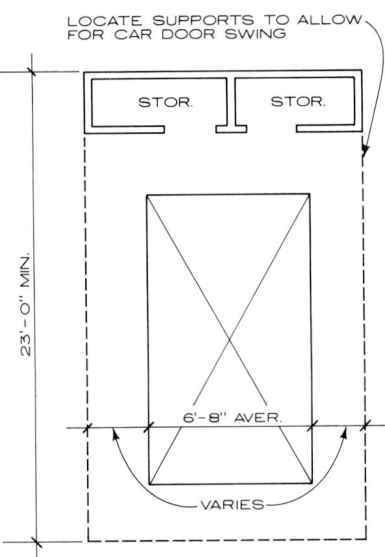

BACKOUT TYPE CARPORT

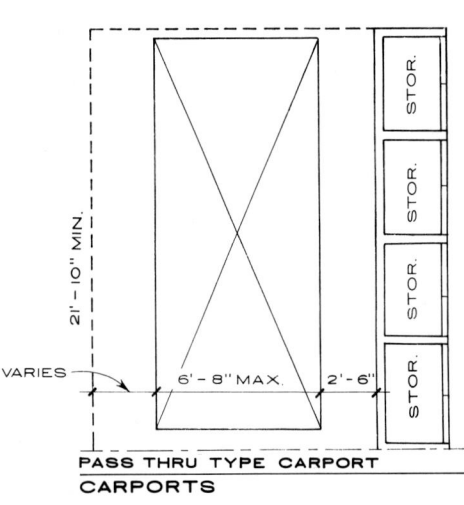

PASS THRU TYPE CARPORT
CARPORTS

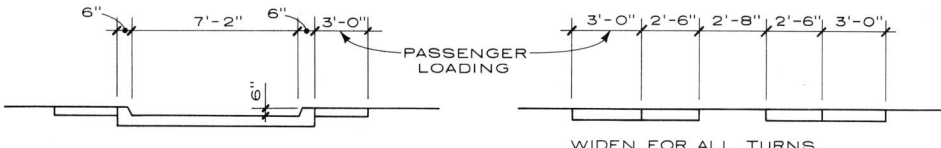

CONCRETE RUNWAYS TO GARAGE

RAMP	APPROACH	APRON
4%	0% to 4%	0% to 2%
5%	0% to 3%	0% to 2%
6%	0% to 2%	0% to 2%
7%	0% to 1%	0% to 1%
8%	0%	0%

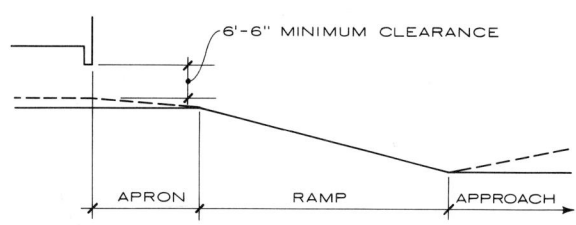

ROAD TO GARAGE RAMPS

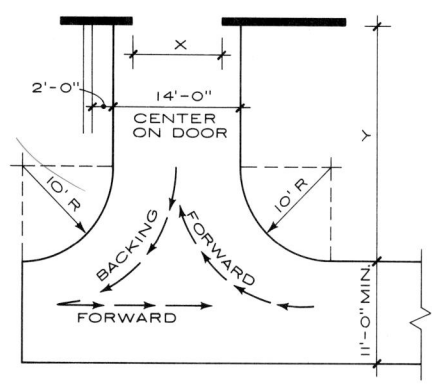

90° IN—BACK OUT (1 CAR)

X	8'-9"	9'-0"	10'-0"	11'-0"	12'-0"
Y	25'-0"	24'-6"	23'-8"	23'-0"	22'-0"

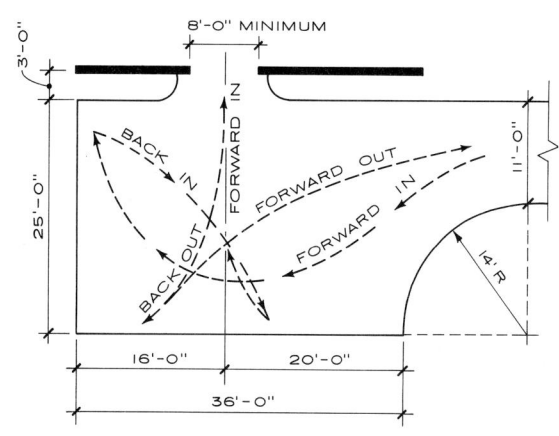

NOTE

Three maneuver entrance for single car garage. Employ only when space limitations demand use. Dimensioned for large car.

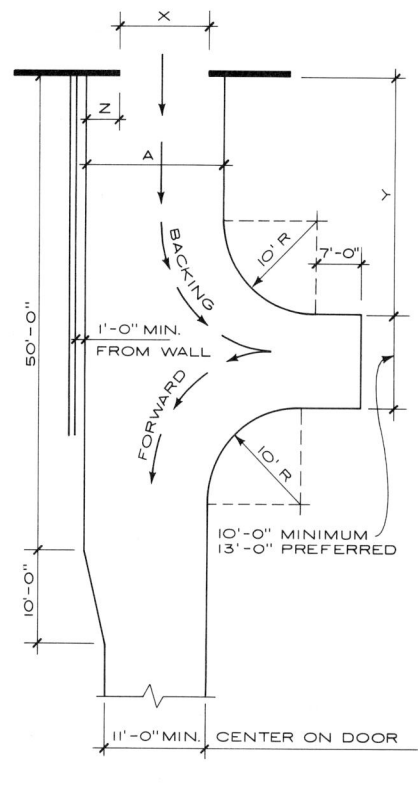

STRAIGHT IN—BACK OUT

X	9'-0"	10'-0"	12'-0"	16'-0"
Y	26'-0"	25'-0"	23'-6"	24'-0"
Z	3'-4"	3'-1"	2'-0"	3'-0"
A	14'-4"	14'-5"	14'-8"	20'-0"

PRIVATE DRIVEWAYS TO GARAGES

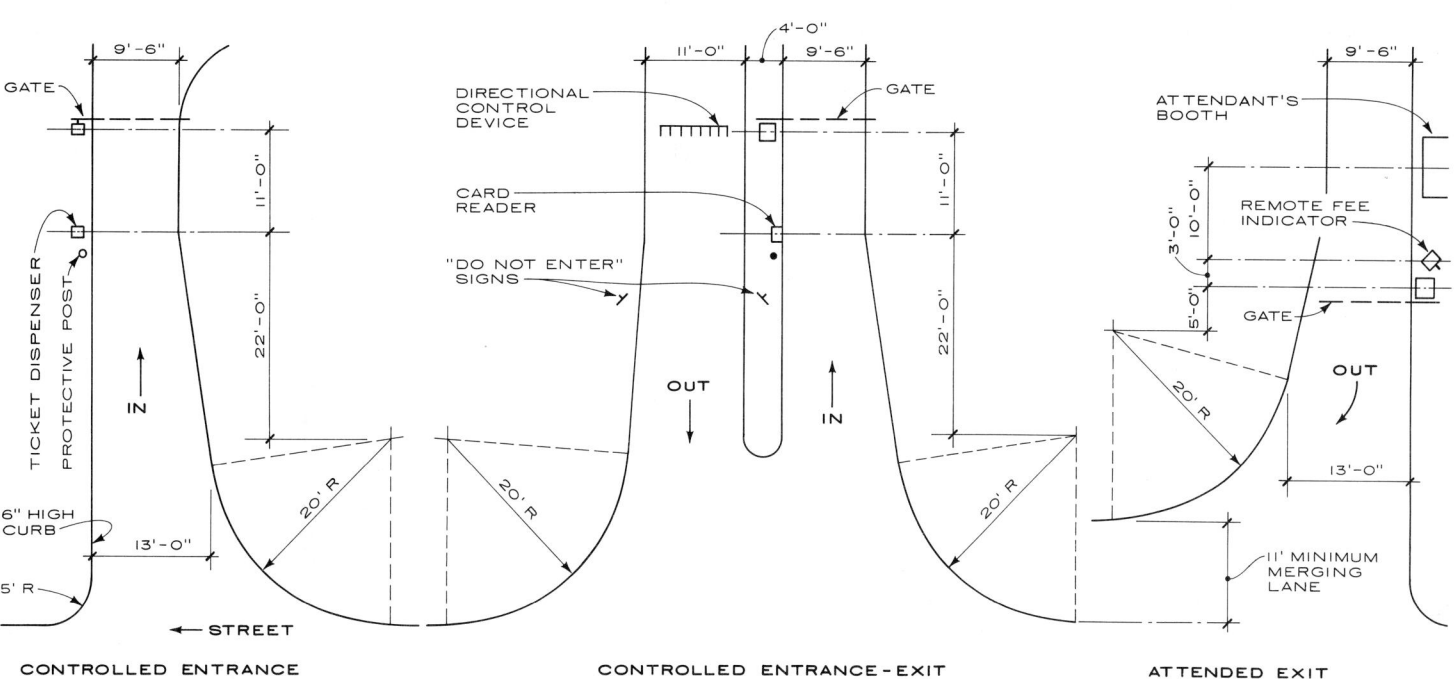

CONTROLLED ENTRANCE   CONTROLLED ENTRANCE-EXIT   ATTENDED EXIT

DRIVEWAYS FOR PARKING FACILITIES

William T. Mahan, AIA; Santa Barbara, California

TRANSPORTATION 1

GENERAL NOTES

Examples shown are for easy driving at moderate speed. See the preceding page for vehicle dimensions (L, W, and OR). The "U" drive shown below illustrates a procedure for designating any drive configuration, given the vehicle's dimensions and turning radii. The T (tangent) dimensions given here are approximate minimums only and may vary with the driver's ability and speed.

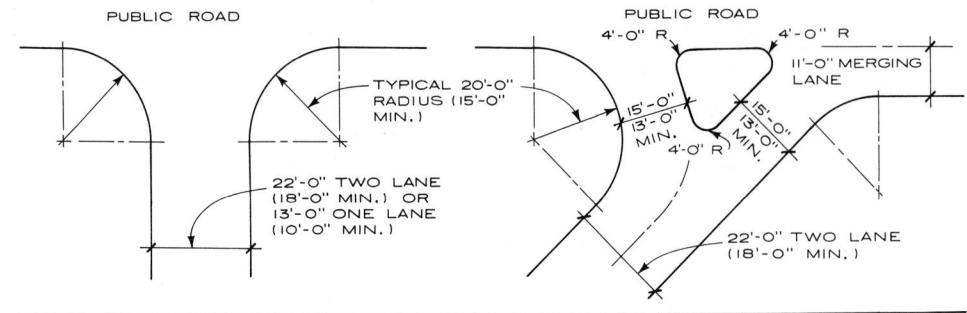

PRIVATE ROADS INTERSECTING PUBLIC ROADS

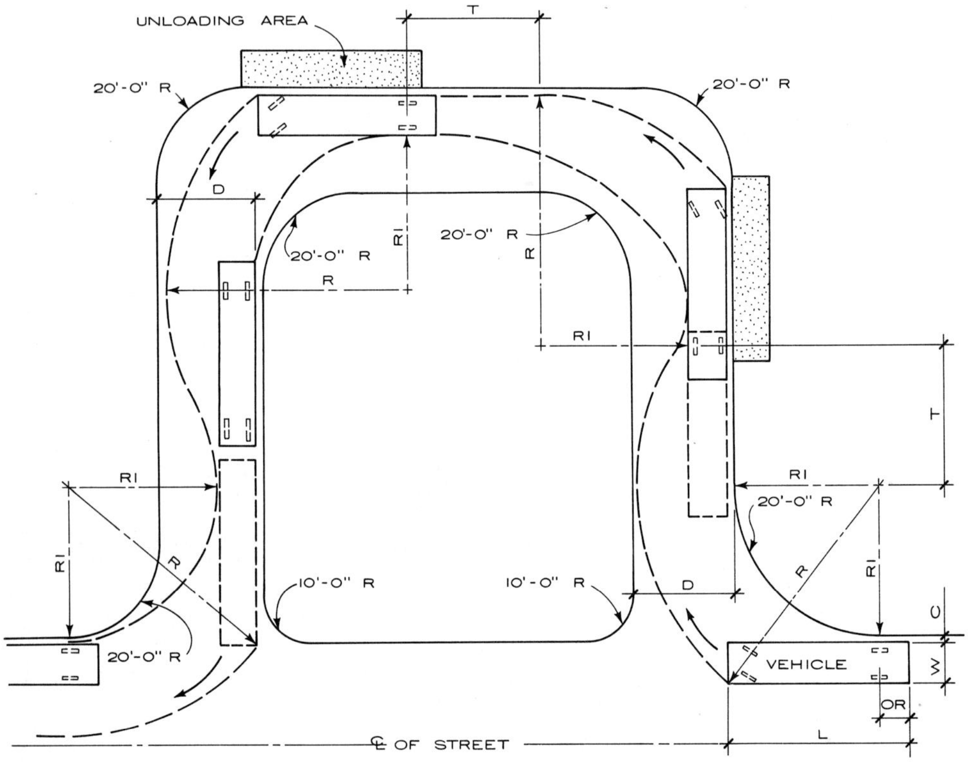

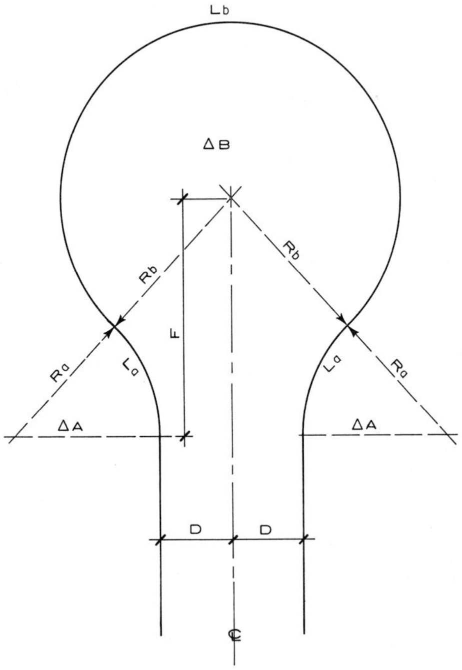

"U" DRIVE AND VEHICLE TURNING DIMENSIONS

VEHICLE	R	RI	T	D	C
Small car	19'-10''	10'-9''	12'-0''	10'-0'	6''
Compact car	21'-6''	11'-10''	15'-0''	10'-10''	7''
Standard car	22'-5''	12'-7''	15'-0''	11'-2''	8''
Large car	23'-0''	12'-7''	15'-0''	12'-0''	9''
Intercity bus*	55'-0''	33'-0''	30'-0''	22'-6''	1'-0''
City bus	53'-6''	33'-0''	30'-0''	22'-6''	1'-0''
School bus	43'-6''	26'-0''	30'-0''	19'-5''	1'-0''
Ambulance	30'-0''	18'-9''	25'-0''	13'-3''	1'-0''
Paramedic van	25'-0''	14'-0''	25'-0''	13'-0''	1'-0''
Hearse	30'-0''	18'-9''	20'-0''	13'-3''	1'-0''
Airport limousine	28'-3''	15'-1½''	20'-0''	15'-1½''	1'-0''
Trash truck†	32'-0''	18'-0''	20'-0''	16'-0''	1'-0''
U.P.S. truck	28'-0''	16'-0''	20'-0''	14'-0''	1'-0''
Fire truck	48'-0''	34'-4'	30'-0''	15'-8''	1'-0''

*Headroom = 14'.
†Headroom = 15'.

William T. Mahan, AIA; Santa Barbara, California

CUL-DE-SAC

	SMALL	LARGE
O	16'-0''	22'-0''
F	50'-11''	87'-3''
A	46.71°	35.58°
B	273.42°	251.15°
Ra	32'-0''	100'-0''
Rb	38'-0''	50'-0''
La	26'-1''	61'-8''
Lb	181'-4''	219'-2''

NOTE: R values for vehicles intended to use these culs-de-sac should not exceed Rb.

NOTE: Small car dimensions should be used only in lots designated for small cars or with entrance controls that admit only small cars. Placing small car stalls into a standard car layout is not recommended. Standard car parking dimensions will accommodate all normal passenger vehicles. Large car parking dimensions make parking easier and faster and are recommended for luxury, a high turnover, and use by the elderly. When the parking angle is 60° or less, it may be necessary to add 3 to 6 ft to the bay width to provide aisle space for pedestrians walking to and from their parked cars. Local zoning laws should be reviewed before proceeding.

RECOMMENDED RANGE OF STALL WIDTHS (SW)

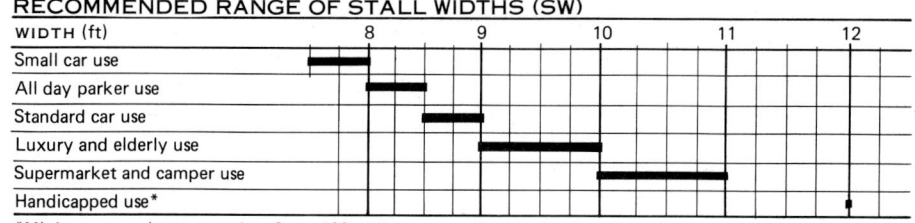

*Minimum requirements = 1 or 2 per 100 stalls or as specified by local, state, or federal law; place convenient to destination.

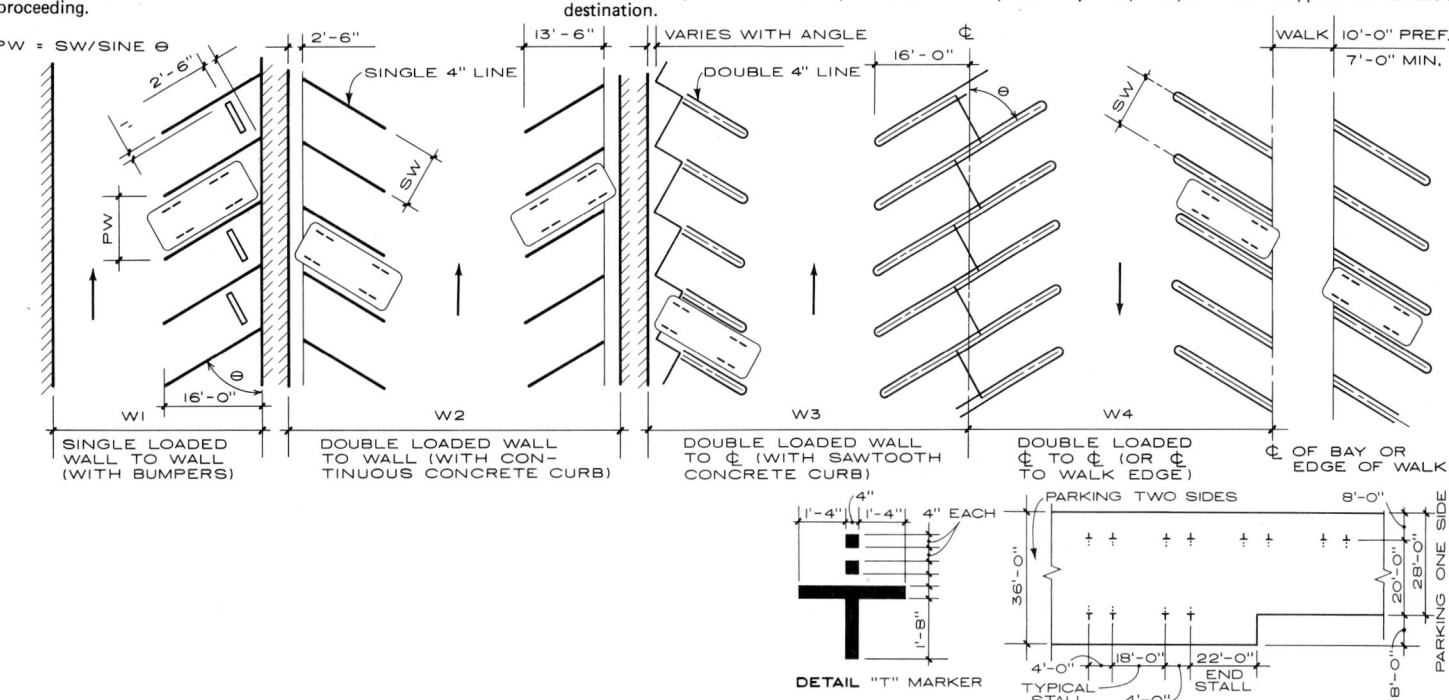

PARALLEL PARKING STALLS AND "T" MARKER DETAIL

PARKING DIMENSIONS IN FEET AND INCHES

	SW	W	45°	50°	55°	60°	65°	70°	75°	80°	85°	90°
						θ ANGLE OF PARK						
Group I: small cars	8'-0"	1	25'-9"	26'-6"	27'-2"	29'-4"	31'-9"	34'-0"	36'-2"	38'-2"	40'-0"	41'-9"
		2	40'-10"	42'-0"	43'-1"	45'-8"	48'-2"	50'-6"	52'-7"	54'-4"	55'-11"	57'-2"
		3	38'-9"	40'-2"	41'-5"	44'-2"	47'-0"	49'-6"	51'-10"	53'-10"	55'-8"	57'-2"
		4	36'-8"	38'-3"	39'-9"	42'-9"	45'-9"	48'-6"	51'-1"	53'-4"	55'-5"	57'-2"
Group II: standard cars	8'-6"	1	32'-0"	32'-11"	34'-2"	36'-2"	38'-5"	41'-0"	43'-6"	45'-6"	46'-11"	48'-0"
		2	49'-10"	51'-9"	53'-10"	56'-0"	58'-4"	60'-2"	62'-0"	63'-6"	64'-9"	66'-0"
		3	47'-8"	49'-4"	51'-6"	54'-0"	56'-6"	59'-0"	61'-2"	63'-0"	64'-6"	66'-0"
		4	45'-2"	46'-10"	49'-0"	51'-8"	54'-6"	57'-10"	60'-0"	62'-6"	64'-3"	66'-0"
	9'-0"	1	32'-0"	32'-9"	34'-0"	35'-4"	37'-6"	39'-8"	42'-0"	44'-4"	46'-2"	48'-0"
		2	49'-4"	51'-0"	53'-2"	55'-6"	57'-10"	60'-0"	61'-10"	63'-4"	64'-9"	66'-0"
		3	46'-4"	48'-10"	51'-4"	53'-10"	56'-0"	58'-8"	61'-0"	63'-0"	64'-6"	66'-0"
		4	44'-8"	46'-6"	49'-0"	51'-6"	54'-0"	57'-0"	59'-8"	62'-0"	64'-2"	66'-0"
	9'-6"	1	32'-0"	32'-8"	34'-0"	35'-0"	36'-10"	38'-10"	41'-6"	43'-8"	46'-0"	48'-0"
		2	49'-2"	50'-6"	51'-10"	53'-6"	55'-4"	58'-0"	60'-6"	62'-8"	64'-6"	65'-11"
		3	47'-0"	48'-2"	49'-10"	51'-6"	53'-11"	57'-0"	59'-8"	62'-0"	64'-3"	65'-11"
		4	44'-8"	45'-10"	47'-6"	49'-10"	52'-6"	55'-9"	58'-9"	61'-6"	63'-10"	65'-11"
Group III: large cars	9'-0"	1	32'-7"	33'-0"	34'-0"	35'-11"	38'-3"	40'-11"	43'-6"	45'-5"	46'-9"	48'-0"
		2	50'-2"	51'-2"	53'-3"	55'-4"	58'-0"	60'-4"	62'-9"	64'-3"	65'-5"	66'-0"
		3	47'-9"	49'-1"	52'-3"	53'-8"	56'-2"	59'-2"	61'-11"	63'-9"	65'-2"	66'-0"
		4	45'-5"	46'-11"	49'-0"	51'-8"	54'-9"	58'-0"	61'-0"	63'-2"	64'-10"	66'-0"
	9'-6"	1	32'-4"	32'-8"	33'-10"	34'-11"	37'-2"	39'-11"	42'-5"	45'-0"	46'-6"	48'-0"
		2	49'-11"	50'-11"	52'-2"	54'-0"	56'-6"	59'-3"	61'-9"	63'-4"	64'-8"	66'-0"
		3	47'-7"	48'-9"	50'-2"	52'-4"	55'-1"	58'-4"	60'-11"	62'-10"	64'-6"	66'-0"
		4	45'-3"	46'-8"	48'-5"	50'-8"	53'-8"	57'-0"	59'-10"	62'-2"	64'-1"	66'-0"
	10'-0"	1	32'-4"	32'-8"	33'-10"	34'-11"	37'-2"	39'-11"	42'-5"	45'-0"	46'-6"	48'-0"
		2	49'-11"	50'-11"	52'-2"	54'-0"	56'-6"	59'-3"	61'-9"	63'-4"	64'-8"	66'-0"
		3	47'-7"	48'-9"	50'-2"	52'-4"	55'-1"	58'-4"	60'-11"	62'-10"	64'-6"	66'-0"
		4	45'-3"	46'-8"	48'-5"	50'-8"	53'-8"	57'-0"	59'-10"	62'-2"	64'-1"	66'-0"

NOTE: θ angles greater than 70° have aisle widths wide enough for two-way travel.

William T. Mahan, AIA; Santa Barbara, California

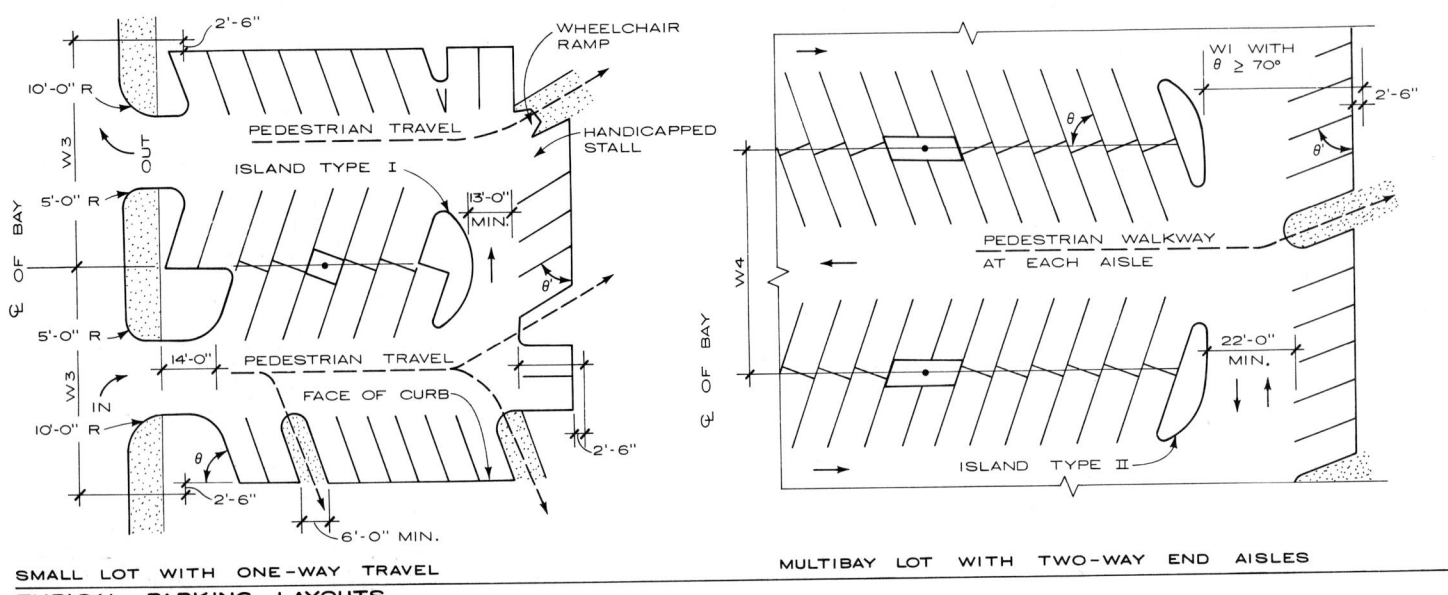

SMALL LOT WITH ONE-WAY TRAVEL   MULTIBAY LOT WITH TWO-WAY END AISLES

TYPICAL PARKING LAYOUTS

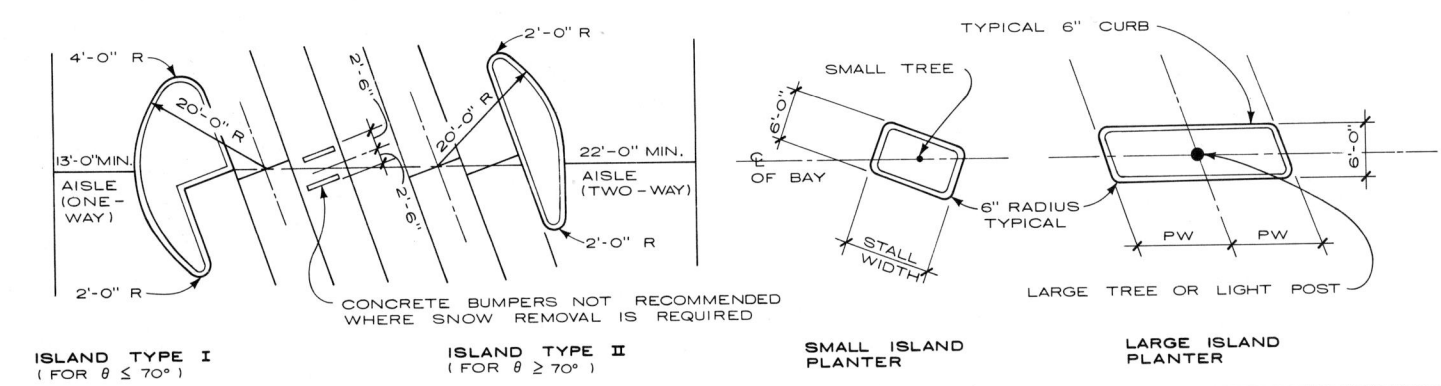

ISLAND TYPE I
(FOR θ ≤ 70°)

ISLAND TYPE II
(FOR θ ≥ 70°)

SMALL ISLAND PLANTER

LARGE ISLAND PLANTER

TYPICAL PLANTER ISLANDS

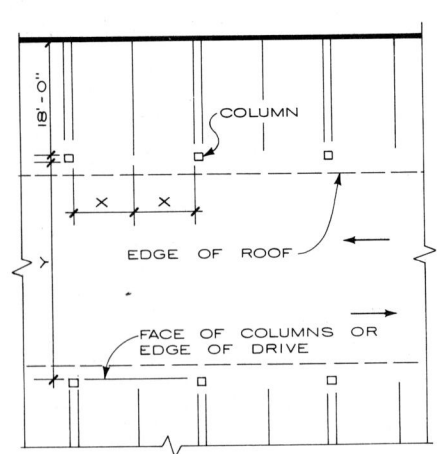

TWO STALL 90° APARTMENT CARPORTS

X	9'-0"	10'-0"	11'-0"	12'-0"
Y	35'-0"	34'-0"	33'-0"	32'-0"

PARKING LAYOUTS WITH COLUMNS

William T. Mahan, AIA; Santa Barbara, California

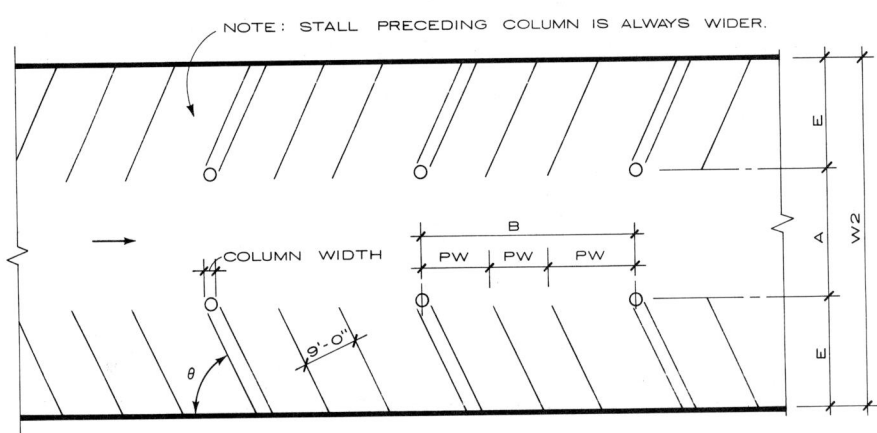

NOTE: STALL PRECEDING COLUMN IS ALWAYS WIDER.

ANGLE PARKING WITH 3 STALLS PER COLUMN

θ	PW	PW'	W2	E	A	B	AREA/STALL
60°	10'-5"	13'-0"	55'-0"	18'-0"	19'-0"	33'-10"	310 sq ft
70°	9'-7"	11'-1"	59'-10"	18'-0"	23'-10"	30'-3"	302 sq ft
80°	9'-1"	10'-2"	63'-4"	18'-0"	27'-4"	28'-4"	300 sq ft

1

TRANSPORTATION

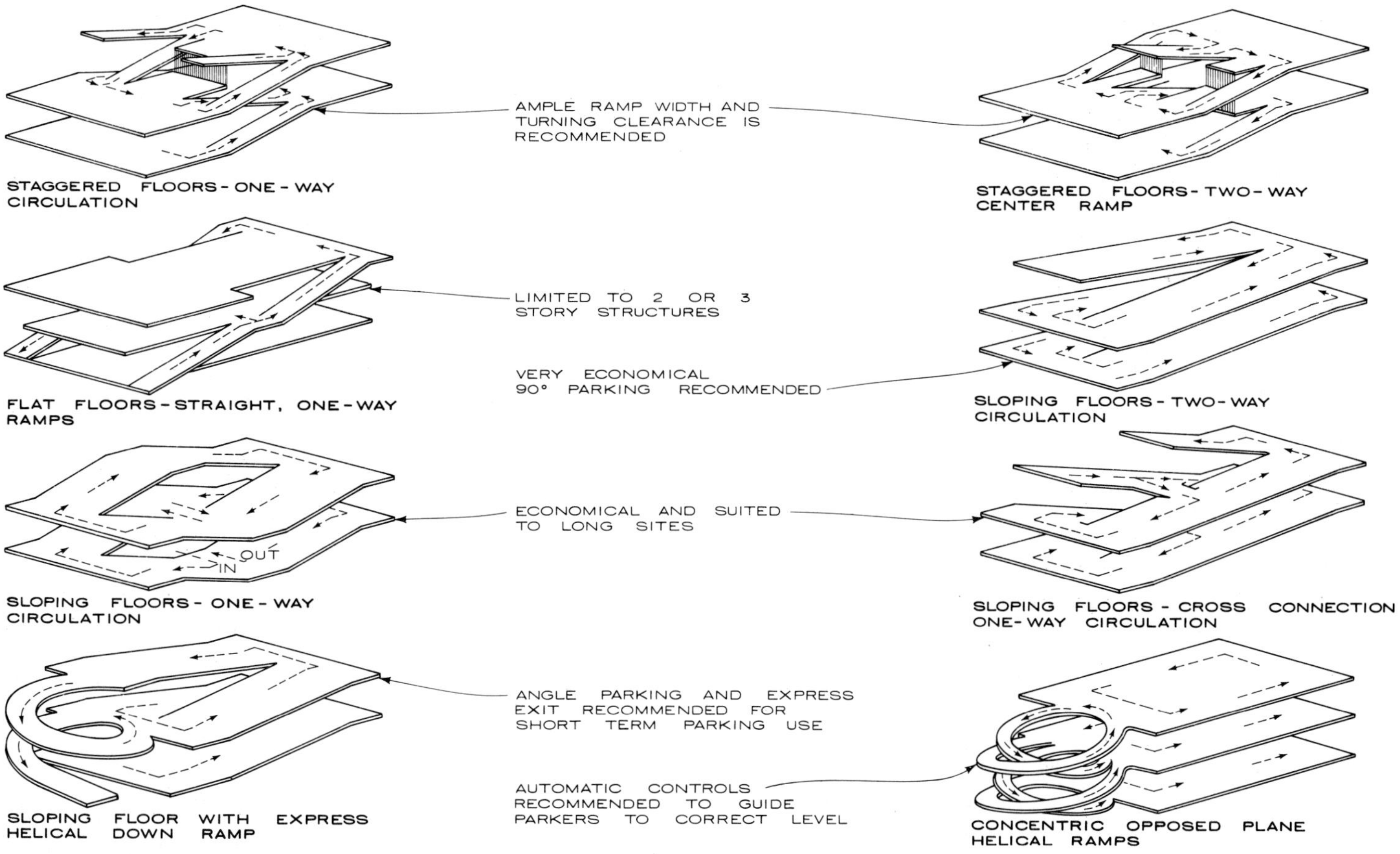

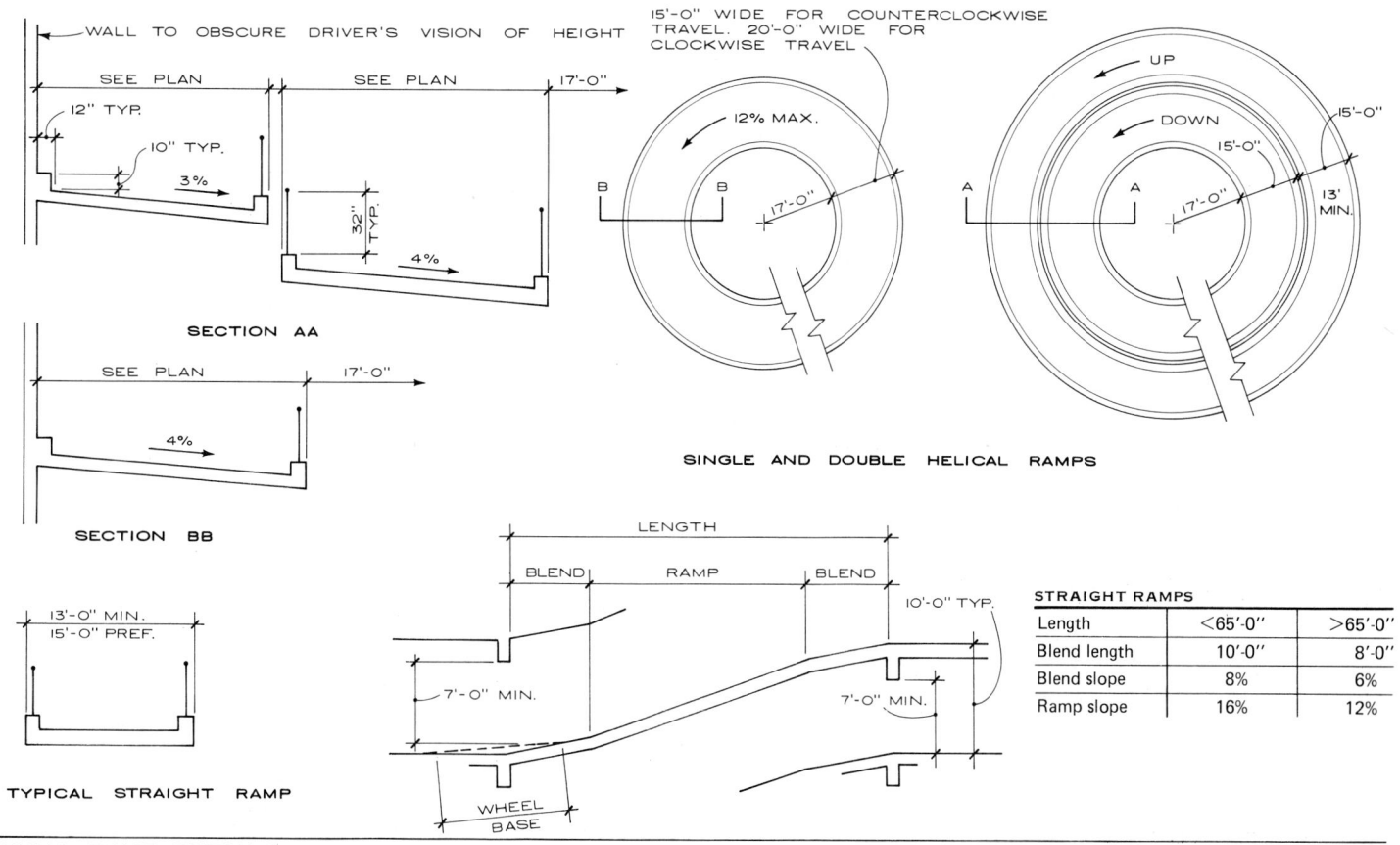

STAGGERED FLOORS - ONE - WAY CIRCULATION

AMPLE RAMP WIDTH AND TURNING CLEARANCE IS RECOMMENDED

STAGGERED FLOORS - TWO - WAY CENTER RAMP

FLAT FLOORS - STRAIGHT, ONE - WAY RAMPS

LIMITED TO 2 OR 3 STORY STRUCTURES

VERY ECONOMICAL 90° PARKING RECOMMENDED

SLOPING FLOORS - TWO - WAY CIRCULATION

SLOPING FLOORS - ONE - WAY CIRCULATION

IN OUT

ECONOMICAL AND SUITED TO LONG SITES

SLOPING FLOORS - CROSS CONNECTION ONE - WAY CIRCULATION

SLOPING FLOOR WITH EXPRESS HELICAL DOWN RAMP

ANGLE PARKING AND EXPRESS EXIT RECOMMENDED FOR SHORT TERM PARKING USE

AUTOMATIC CONTROLS RECOMMENDED TO GUIDE PARKERS TO CORRECT LEVEL

CONCENTRIC OPPOSED PLANE HELICAL RAMPS

TYPICAL RAMP SYSTEMS

WALL TO OBSCURE DRIVER'S VISION OF HEIGHT

SEE PLAN   SEE PLAN   17'-0"

12" TYP.

10" TYP.

3%

32" TYP.

4%

SECTION AA

SEE PLAN   17'-0"

4%

SECTION BB

13'-0" MIN.
15'-0" PREF.

TYPICAL STRAIGHT RAMP

15'-0" WIDE FOR COUNTERCLOCKWISE TRAVEL. 20'-0" WIDE FOR CLOCKWISE TRAVEL

12% MAX.

B   B   17'-0"

UP

DOWN

15'-0"

15'-0"

A   A   17'-0"   13' MIN.

SINGLE AND DOUBLE HELICAL RAMPS

LENGTH

BLEND   RAMP   BLEND

10'-0" TYP.

7'-0" MIN.

7'-0" MIN.

WHEEL BASE

STRAIGHT RAMPS

Length	<65'-0"	>65'-0"
Blend length	10'-0"	8'-0"
Blend slope	8%	6%
Ramp slope	16%	12%

TYPICAL RAMP DETAILS

William T. Mahan, AIA; Santa Barbara, California

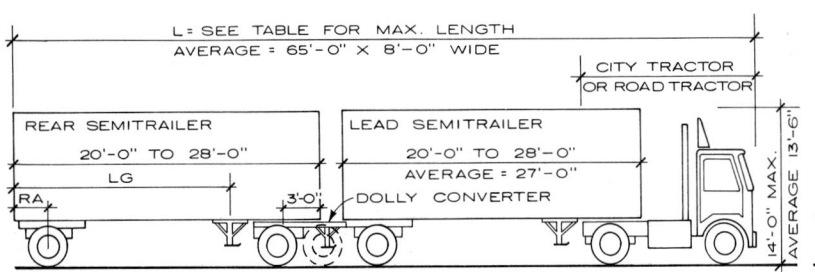

DOUBLE SEMITRAILER AND TRACTOR

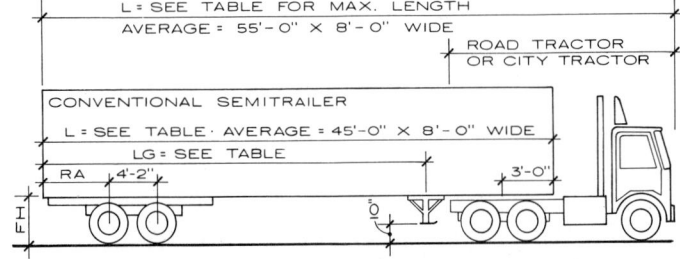

SEMITRAILER AND TRACTOR
TIRE SIZE APPROX. 41″ ± DIA. X 10″ ± WIDE

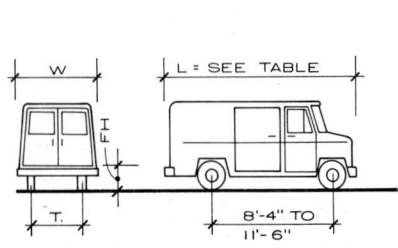

VAN DELIVERY TRUCK

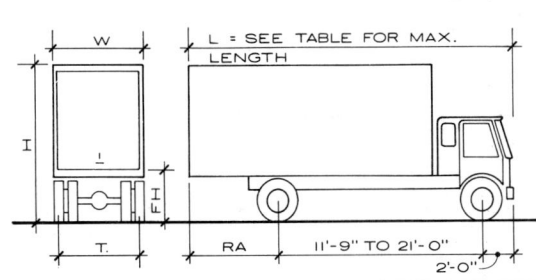

STRAIGHT BODY TRUCK

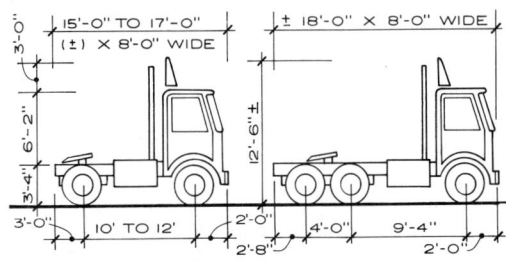

CITY TRACTOR   ROAD TRACTOR

DOUBLE SEMITRAILER AND TRACTOR—MAX. ALLOWABLE LENGTH

65′-0″	In all states except those below
55′-0″	Ga., Miss., N.J., N.Y.
60′-0″	Iowa, Minn., Mont.
70′-0″	Alaska, Nev., S.D.
75′-0″	Idaho, Ore.
85′-0″	Wyo.

NOT PERMITTED in Ala., Conn., Fla., Me., Mass., N.H., N.C., Pa., R.I., S.C., Tenn., Vt., Va., W.Va., Wis., Washington, D.C.

SEMITRAILER AND TRACTOR—MAX. ALLOWABLE LENGTH

55′-0″	In all states except those below
56′-0″	Va., Me.
57′-0″	Ind., Ky.
59′-0″	Wis.
60′-0″	Ark., Calif., Del., Mass., Minn., Mont., Neb., Ohio, Ore., Vt.
65′-0″	Alaska, Ariz., Colo., Idaho, Kans., La., N.M., N.D., Okla., Texas, Utah, Wash.
70′-0″	Nev., S.D.
85′-0″	Wyo.

STRAIGHT BODY TRUCKS—MAX. ALLOWABLE LENGTH

40′-0″	In all states except those below
35′-0″	Colo., Ky., Mass., Miss., N.H., N.J., N.Y., N.D., Wash., Wis.
36′-0″	Ind.
42′-0″	Ill., Kans.
45′-0″	Me., Texas, Utah
55′-0″	Conn., Ga.
60′-0″	Vt., Wyo.

AVERAGE DIMENSIONS OF VEHICLES

	TYPE OF VEHICLES			
	DOUBLE SEMITRAILER	CONVENTIONAL SEMITRAILER	STRAIGHT BODY TRUCK	VAN DELIVERY
Length (L)	65′-0″	55′-0″	17′-0″ to 35′-0″	15′-0″ to 20′-0″
Width (W)	8′-0″	8′-0″	8′-0″	7′-0″
Height (H)	13′-6″	13′-6″	13′-6″	7′-0″
Floor Height (FH)	4′-0″ to 4′-6″	4′-0″ to 4′-4″	3′-0″ to 4′-0″	2′-0″ to 2′-8″
Track (T)	6′-6″	6′-6″	5′-10″	5′-0″ to 5′4″
Rear Axle (RA)	3′-0″ to 4′-0″	4′-0″ to 12′-0″	2′-3″ to 12′-0″	—

VEHICLE HEIGHT—MAX. ALLOWABLE

13′-6″	In all states except those below
12′-6″	Ky., W.Va.
13′-0″	Colo.
14′-0″	Idaho, Nev., Wash., Wyo.
14′-6″	Neb.

LENGTH OF SEMITRAILER (ONLY)—MAX. ALLOWABLE LENGTH

Unrestricted in all states except those below

35′-0″	Ore.
40′-0″	Calif.
45′-0″	Alaska, Ill., Me., Mass., Minn., Ohio, Utah, Wash., Wis.

AVERAGE SEMITRAILER DIMENSIONS

	LENGTH (L)			
	27′-0″	40′-0″	45′-0″	REFRIG. 40′-0″
Floor height (FH)	4′-2″	4′-2″	4′-2″	4′-9″
Rear axle (RA)	3′-0″	5′-2″	5′-10″	4′-5″
Landing gear (LG)	19′-0″	30′-0″	34′-6″	29′-5″
Cubic feet (CU)	1564±	2327±	2620±	2113±

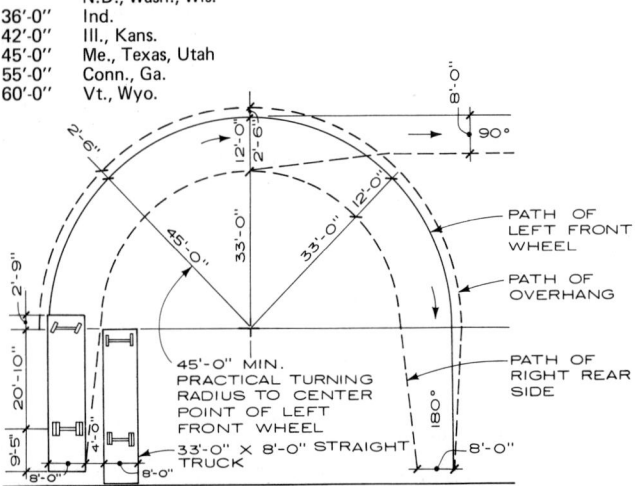

33′-0″ STRAIGHT BODY TRUCK MIN. PRACTICAL TURNING RADIUS OF 45′-0″

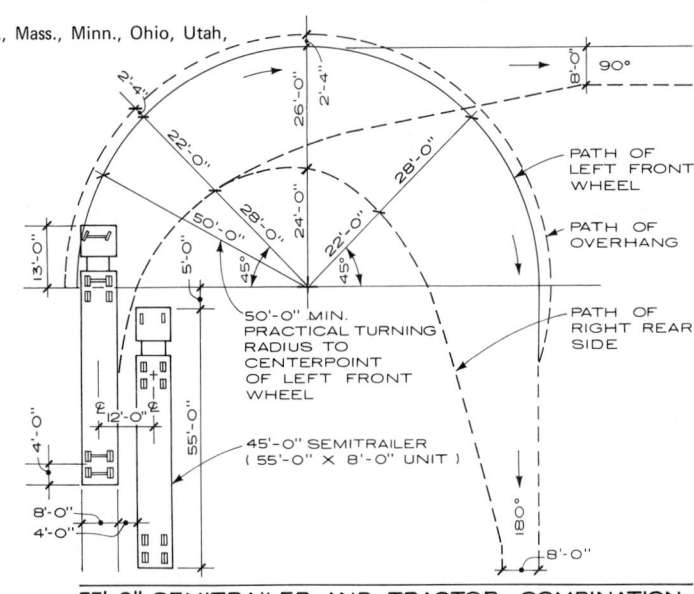

55′-0″ SEMITRAILER AND TRACTOR COMBINATION MIN. PRACTICAL TURNING RADIUS OF 50′-0″

Robert H. Lorenz, AIA; Preston Trucking Company, Inc.; Preston, Maryland

The Operations Council, American Trucking Association; Washington, D.C.

1   TRANSPORTATION

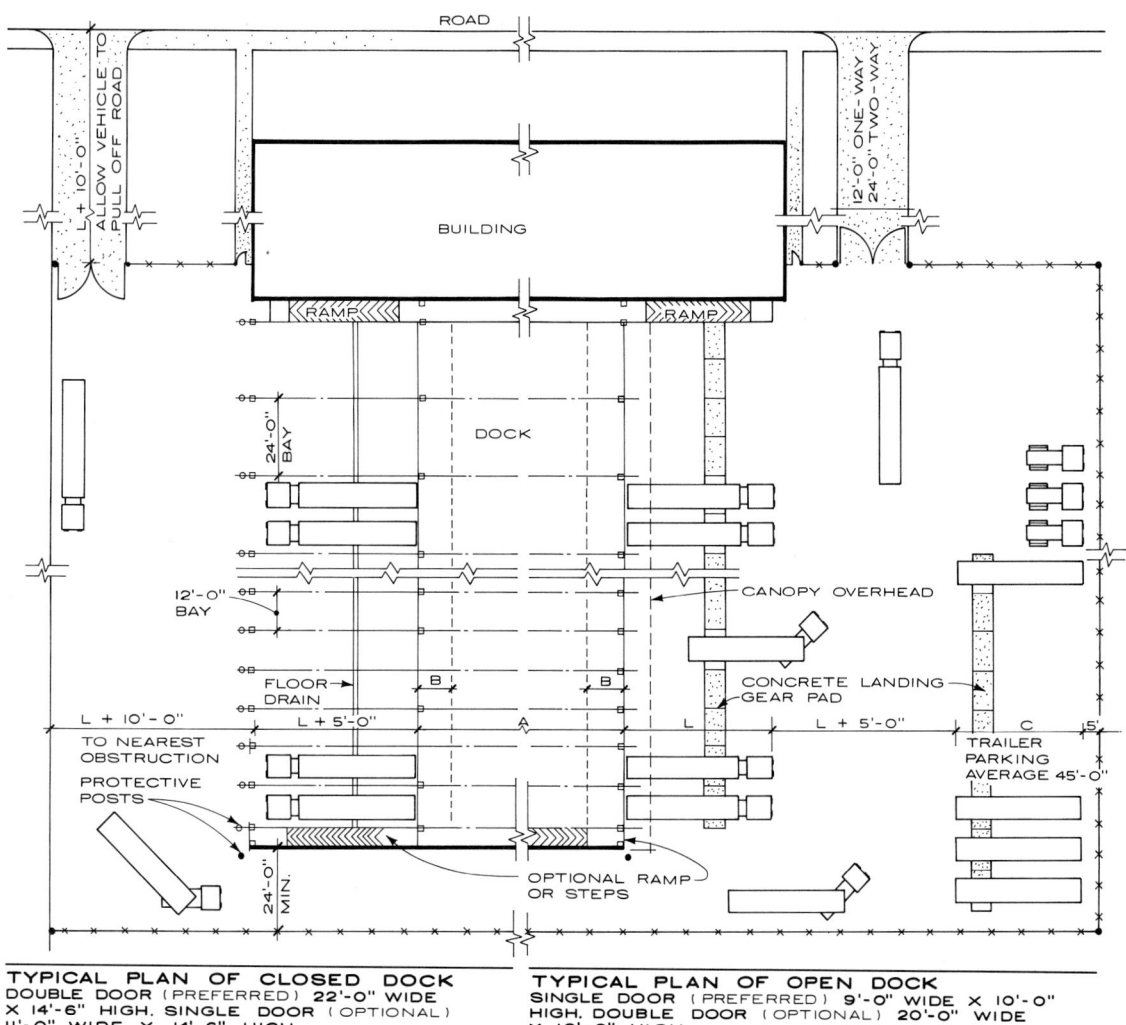

NOTES

1. Allow for off-street employee and/or driver parking.
2. Entrances and exits should be of reinforced concrete when excessive twisting and turning of vehicles are expected.
3. Average gate (swing or slide) 30'-0" wide for two-way traffic. People gate 5'-0" wide with concrete walkway 4'-0" to 6'-0" wide.
4. For yard security use a 6'-0" high chain link fence with barbed wire on top.
5. It is desirable to provide on-site fueling facilities for road units as they leave the yard.
6. Provide general yard lighting from fixtures mounted on building or on 24'-0" high minimum poles at fence line. Mercury vapor or high pressure sodium preferred.
7. Tractor parking requires 12'-0" wide x 20'-0" long slot minimum. Provide motor heater outlets for diesel engines in cold climates.
8. Trailer parking requires 12'-0" wide slot minimum. Provide 10'-0" wide concrete pad for landing gear. Score concrete at 12'-0" o.c. to aid in correct spotting of trailer.
9. 4'-0" wide minimum concrete ramp from dock to grade. 3 to 15% slope (10% average) score surface for traction.
10. Vehicles should circulate in a counterclockwise direction, making left hand turns, permitting driver to see rear of unit when backing into dock.
11. Double trailers are backed into dock separately.

TYPICAL PLAN OF CLOSED DOCK
DOUBLE DOOR (PREFERRED) 22'-0" WIDE X 14'-6" HIGH. SINGLE DOOR (OPTIONAL) 11'-0" WIDE X 14'-6" HIGH

TYPICAL PLAN OF OPEN DOCK
SINGLE DOOR (PREFERRED) 9'-0" WIDE X 10'-0" HIGH. DOUBLE DOOR (OPTIONAL) 20'-0" WIDE X 10'-0" HIGH

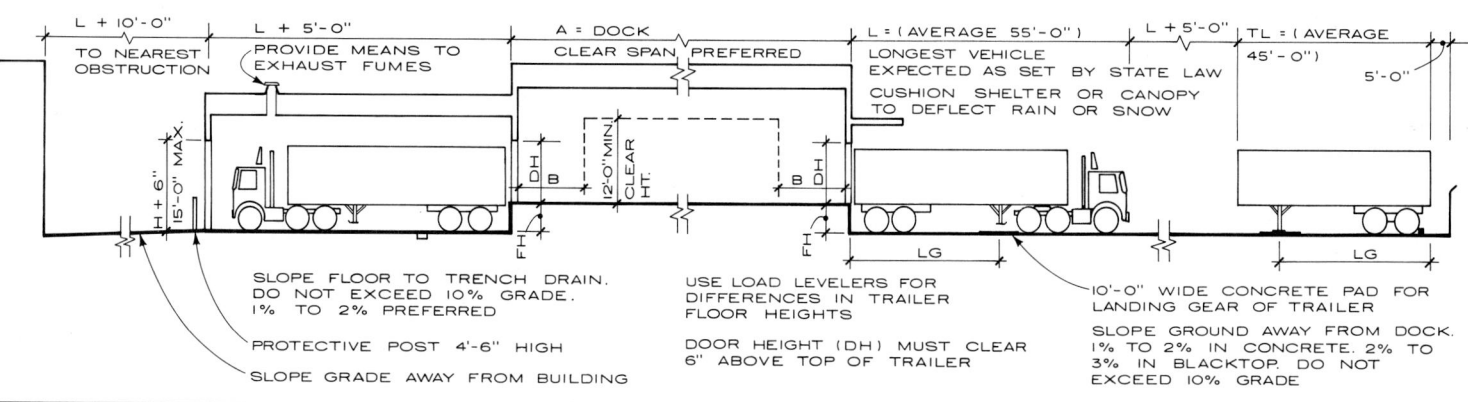

TYPICAL SECTION OF CLOSED DOCK

TYPICAL SECTION OF OPEN DOCK

AVERAGE VEHICLE DIMENSIONS

LENGTH OF VEHICLE (L)	FLOOR HEIGHT (FH)	VEHICLE HEIGHT (H)
55'-0" semitrailer	4'-0" to 4'-6"	14'-0"
37'-0" semitrailer	4'-0" to 4'-2"	13'-6"
25'-0" straight body	3'-8" to 4'-2"	13'-6"
18'-0" van	2'-0" to 2'-8"	7'-0"

NOTE: Refer to other pages for truck and trailer sizes.

Robert H. Lorenz, AIA; Preston Trucking Company, Inc.; Preston, Maryland

The Operations Council, American Trucking Association; Washington, D. C.

AVERAGE WIDTHS OF DOCKS

TYPE OF OPERATION	TWO-WHEEL HAND TRUCK	FOUR-WHEEL HAND TRUCK	FORKLIFT TRUCK	DRAGLINE	AUTO SPUR DRAGLINE
Dock width (A)	50'-0"	60'-0"	60'-0" to 70'-0"	80'-0"	120'-0" to 140'-0"
Work aisle (B)	6'-0"	10'-0"	15'-0"	10'-0" to 15'-0"	10'-0" to 15'-0"

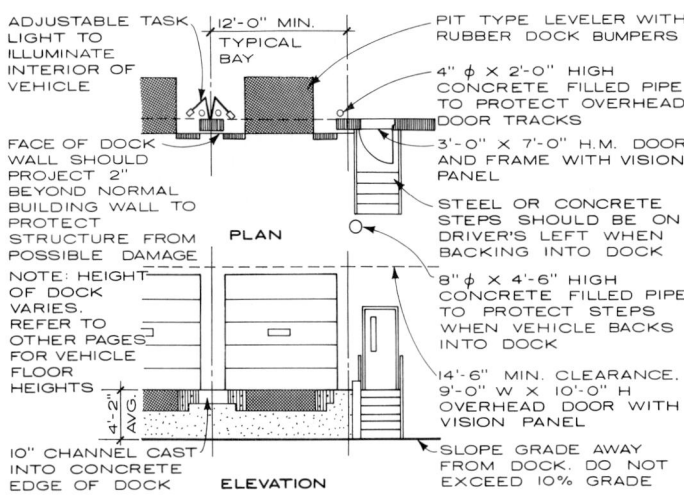

ADJUSTABLE TASK LIGHT TO ILLUMINATE INTERIOR OF VEHICLE

12'-0" MIN. TYPICAL BAY

PIT TYPE LEVELER WITH RUBBER DOCK BUMPERS

4" φ X 2'-0" HIGH CONCRETE FILLED PIPE TO PROTECT OVERHEAD DOOR TRACKS

3'-0" X 7'-0" H.M. DOOR AND FRAME WITH VISION PANEL

FACE OF DOCK WALL SHOULD PROJECT 2" BEYOND NORMAL BUILDING WALL TO PROTECT STRUCTURE FROM POSSIBLE DAMAGE

STEEL OR CONCRETE STEPS SHOULD BE ON DRIVER'S LEFT WHEN BACKING INTO DOCK

PLAN

NOTE: HEIGHT OF DOCK VARIES. REFER TO OTHER PAGES FOR VEHICLE FLOOR HEIGHTS

8" φ X 4'-6" HIGH CONCRETE FILLED PIPE TO PROTECT STEPS WHEN VEHICLE BACKS INTO DOCK

14'-6" MIN. CLEARANCE. 9'-0" W X 10'-0" H OVERHEAD DOOR WITH VISION PANEL

10" CHANNEL CAST INTO CONCRETE EDGE OF DOCK

ELEVATION

SLOPE GRADE AWAY FROM DOCK. DO NOT EXCEED 10% GRADE

TYPICAL LOADING DOCK BAY

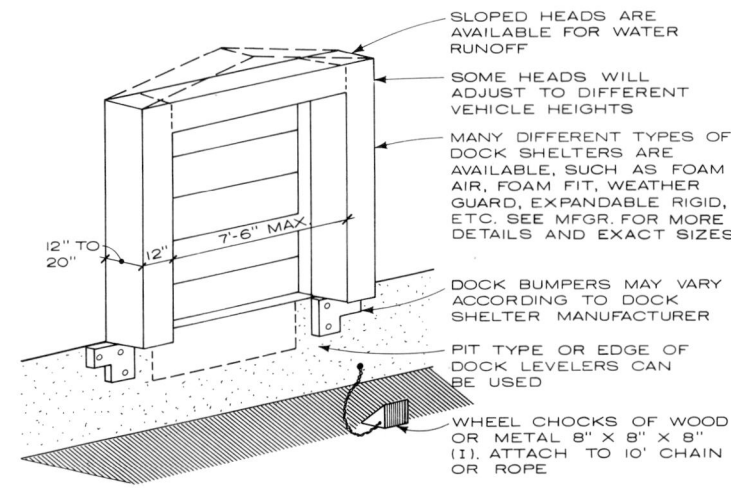

SLOPED HEADS ARE AVAILABLE FOR WATER RUNOFF

SOME HEADS WILL ADJUST TO DIFFERENT VEHICLE HEIGHTS

MANY DIFFERENT TYPES OF DOCK SHELTERS ARE AVAILABLE, SUCH AS FOAM AIR, FOAM FIT, WEATHER GUARD, EXPANDABLE RIGID, ETC. SEE MFGR. FOR MORE DETAILS AND EXACT SIZES

DOCK BUMPERS MAY VARY ACCORDING TO DOCK SHELTER MANUFACTURER

PIT TYPE OR EDGE OF DOCK LEVELERS CAN BE USED

12" TO 20"   12"   7'-6" MAX.

WHEEL CHOCKS OF WOOD OR METAL 8" X 8" X 8" (I). ATTACH TO 10' CHAIN OR ROPE

CUSHIONED DOCK SHELTER

Provides positive weather seal; protects dock from wind, rain, snow, and dirt. Retains constant temperature between dock and vehicle.

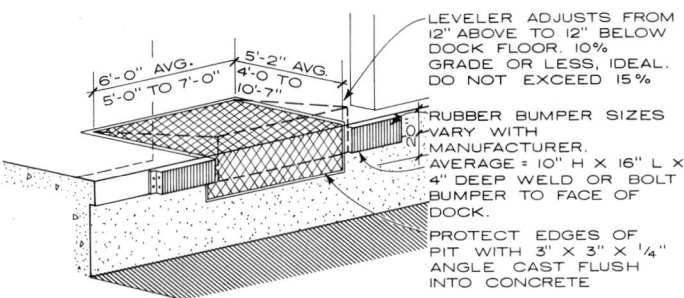

6'-0" AVG. 5'-0" TO 7'-0"   5'-2" AVG. 4'-0" TO 10'-7"

LEVELER ADJUSTS FROM 12" ABOVE TO 12" BELOW DOCK FLOOR. 10% GRADE OR LESS, IDEAL. DO NOT EXCEED 15%

RUBBER BUMPER SIZES VARY WITH MANUFACTURER. AVERAGE = 10" H X 16" L X 4" DEEP WELD OR BOLT BUMPER TO FACE OF DOCK.

PROTECT EDGES OF PIT WITH 3" X 3" X ¼" ANGLE CAST FLUSH INTO CONCRETE

PIT TYPE DOCK LEVELER

Automatic or manual operation for high volume docks where incoming vehicle heights vary widely; must be installed in a preformed concrete pit. Exact dimensions provided by manufacturer.

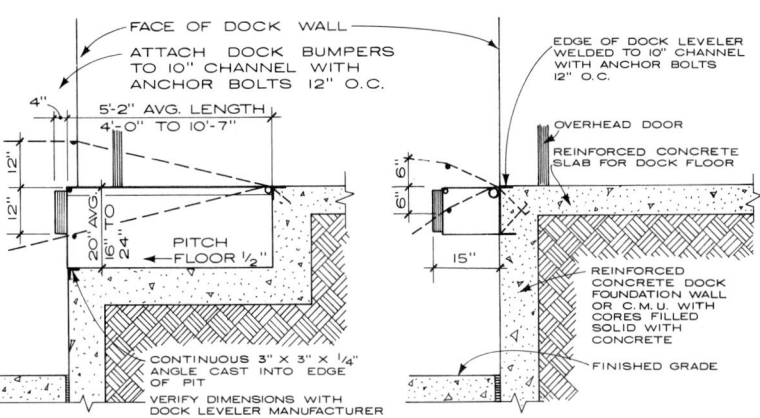

FACE OF DOCK WALL

ATTACH DOCK BUMPERS TO 10" CHANNEL WITH ANCHOR BOLTS 12" O.C.

4"   5'-2" AVG. LENGTH 4'-0" TO 10'-7"

EDGE OF DOCK LEVELER WELDED TO 10" CHANNEL WITH ANCHOR BOLTS 12" O.C.

OVERHEAD DOOR

12"   12"   20" TO 24" 16"   PITCH FLOOR ½"

6"   6"

REINFORCED CONCRETE SLAB FOR DOCK FLOOR

15"

REINFORCED CONCRETE DOCK FOUNDATION WALL OR C.M.U. WITH CORES FILLED SOLID WITH CONCRETE

FINISHED GRADE

CONTINUOUS 3" X 3" X ¼" ANGLE CAST INTO EDGE OF PIT

VERIFY DIMENSIONS WITH DOCK LEVELER MANUFACTURER

SILL FOR PIT LEVELER   **SILL FOR EDGE OF DOCK LEVELER**

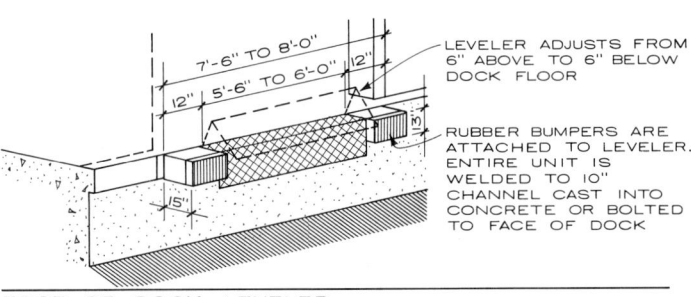

7'-6" TO 8'-0"   12"

12"   5'-6" TO 6'-0"   12"

13"

15"

LEVELER ADJUSTS FROM 6" ABOVE TO 6" BELOW DOCK FLOOR

RUBBER BUMPERS ARE ATTACHED TO LEVELER. ENTIRE UNIT IS WELDED TO 10" CHANNEL CAST INTO CONCRETE OR BOLTED TO FACE OF DOCK

EDGE OF DOCK LEVELER

Manual operation for high or medium volume docks where pit type levelers are impractical or leased facilities are being used.

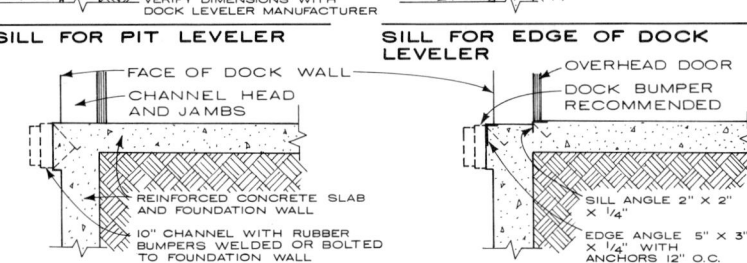

FACE OF DOCK WALL

CHANNEL HEAD AND JAMBS

OVERHEAD DOOR

DOCK BUMPER RECOMMENDED

REINFORCED CONCRETE SLAB AND FOUNDATION WALL

10" CHANNEL WITH RUBBER BUMPERS WELDED OR BOLTED TO FOUNDATION WALL

SILL ANGLE 2" X 2" X ¼"

EDGE ANGLE 5" X 3" X ¼" WITH ANCHORS 12" O.C. SLOPE SILL ½" TO EXTERIOR

DOCK SILL WITHOUT LEVELERS

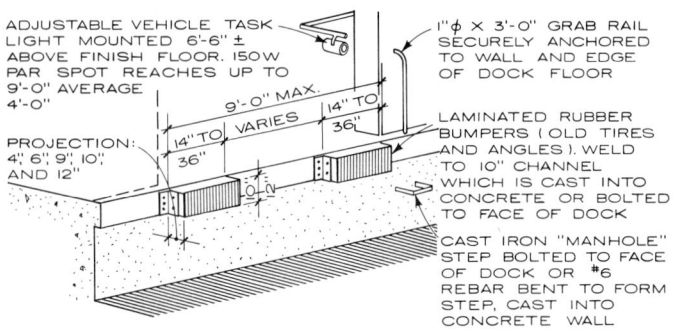

ADJUSTABLE VEHICLE TASK LIGHT MOUNTED 6'-6" ± ABOVE FINISH FLOOR. 150W PAR SPOT REACHES UP TO 9'-0" AVERAGE 4'-0"

1" φ X 3'-0" GRAB RAIL SECURELY ANCHORED TO WALL AND EDGE OF DOCK FLOOR

9'-0" MAX.   14" TO 36"   14" TO 36"

PROJECTION: 4", 6", 9", 10", AND 12"

14" TO 36"   VARIES

LAMINATED RUBBER BUMPERS (OLD TIRES AND ANGLES). WELD TO 10" CHANNEL WHICH IS CAST INTO CONCRETE OR BOLTED TO FACE OF DOCK

CAST IRON "MANHOLE" STEP BOLTED TO FACE OF DOCK OR #6 REBAR BENT TO FORM STEP, CAST INTO CONCRETE WALL

LOADING DOCK WITHOUT LEVELER

Used for low volume docks where incoming vehicle heights do not vary. Use portable type leveler such as a throw plate.

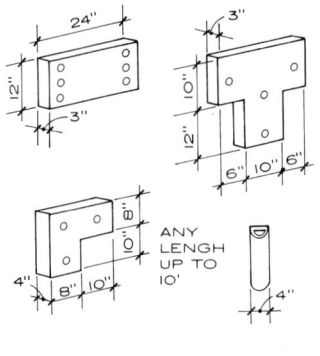

24"   3"

12"   3"   10"   6" 10" 6"

12"   6" 10" 6"

4"   8" 10"

ANY LENGH UP TO 10'

8"

4"

MOLDED HARD RUBBER DOCK BUMPERS

PERCENTAGE OF GRADE FOR EACH 2 IN. RISE FROM TRUCK BED TO DOCK FLOOR

RISE (IN.)	OVERALL LENGTH OF DOCK LEVELER (NOT INCLUDING 16 IN. LONG LIP)					MATERIAL HANDLER
	3'-6"	4'-0"	5'-0"	6'-0"	8'-0"	
2	6.1	5.1	3.9	3.3	2.4	Low lift
4	12.1	10.2	7.8	6.7	4.8	Pallet
6	18.2	15.4	11.8	10.0	7.2	Truck 10% max.
8	24.2	20.4	15.7	13.3	9.6	
10	30.3	25.5	19.6	16.7	11.9	Fork lift
12	36.4	30.5	23.5	20.0	14.3	
14	42.4	35.6	27.4	23.3	16.7	15% max. Marginal to unusable
16	48.5	40.7	31.4	26.7	19.1	
18	54.5	45.7	35.3	30.0	21.5	

Robert H. Lorenz, AIA; Preston Trucking Company, Inc.; Preston, Maryland

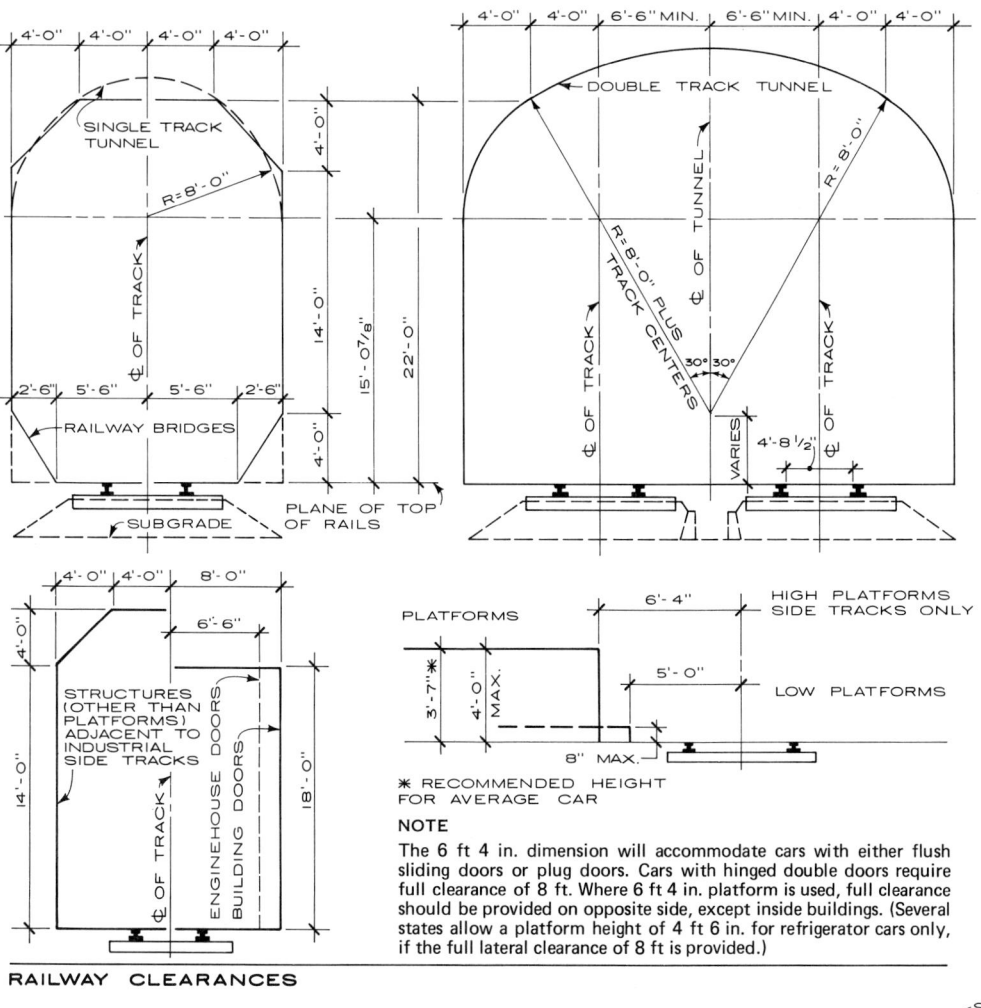

NOTES

1. Given clearances are the recommended minimums of the American Railway Engineering Association. Actual requirements vary from state to state.
2. Clearances shown are for tangent track and new construction. On curved track, lateral clearances should be increased 1 in. per degree of curvature, with a maximum increase of 18 in.
3. Common state requirement for lateral clearance of poles is 8 ft 6 in. (varies from 8 to 12 ft).
4. Standard American railroad gauge of 4 ft 8½ in. is measured between the inner faces of the rails.

NOTE

The 6 ft 4 in. dimension will accommodate cars with either flush sliding doors or plug doors. Cars with hinged double doors require full clearance of 8 ft. Where 6 ft 4 in. platform is used, full clearance should be provided on opposite side, except inside buildings. (Several states allow a platform height of 4 ft 6 in. for refrigerator cars only, if the full lateral clearance of 8 ft is provided.)

RAILWAY CLEARANCES

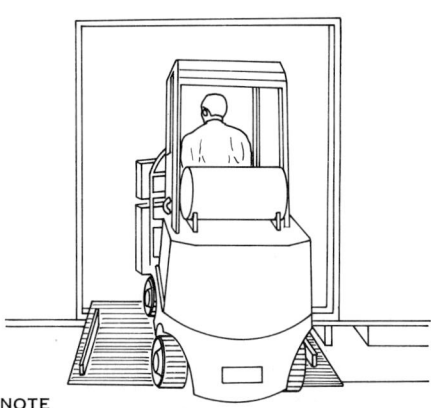

NOTE

Ramp travels laterally on rail mounted to edge of dock for positioning to rail car opening. It adjusts above and below dock level and locks to the rail when in the lowered position. Self-stores in vertical position when not in use. Available in varying lengths and widths.

RAIL DOCK RAMPS

TYPICAL BUMPING POSTS

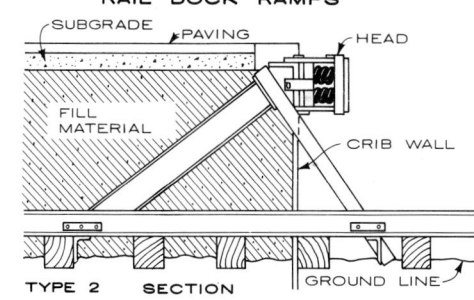

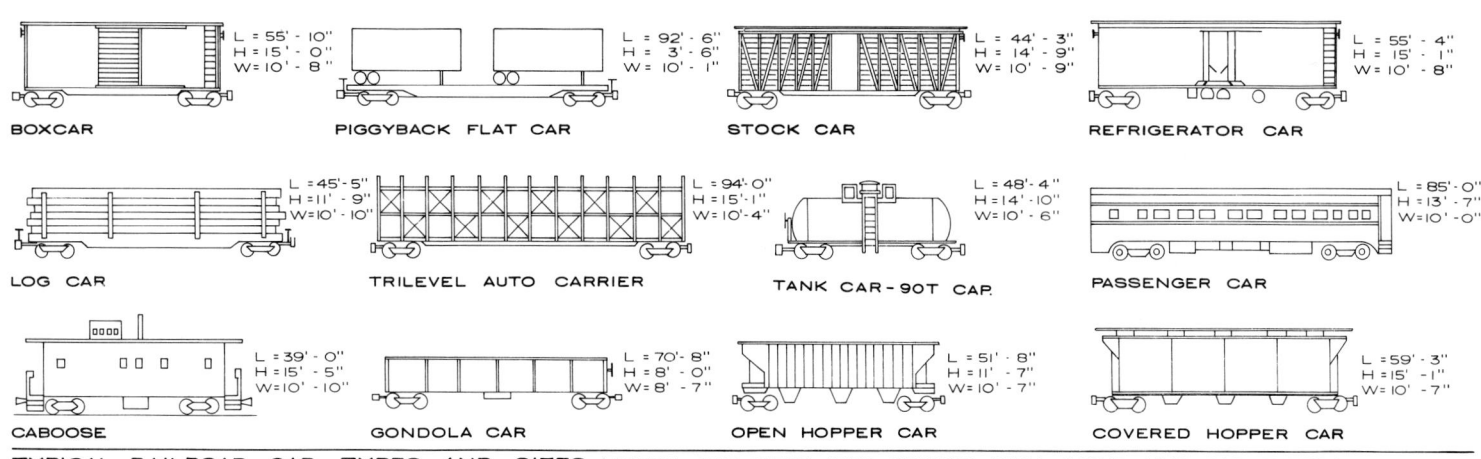

TYPICAL RAILROAD CAR TYPES AND SIZES (ACTUAL CAR SIZES VARY GREATLY EVEN AMONG LIKE CAR TYPES)

Ed Hesner; Rasmussen & Hobbs Architects; Tacoma, Washington

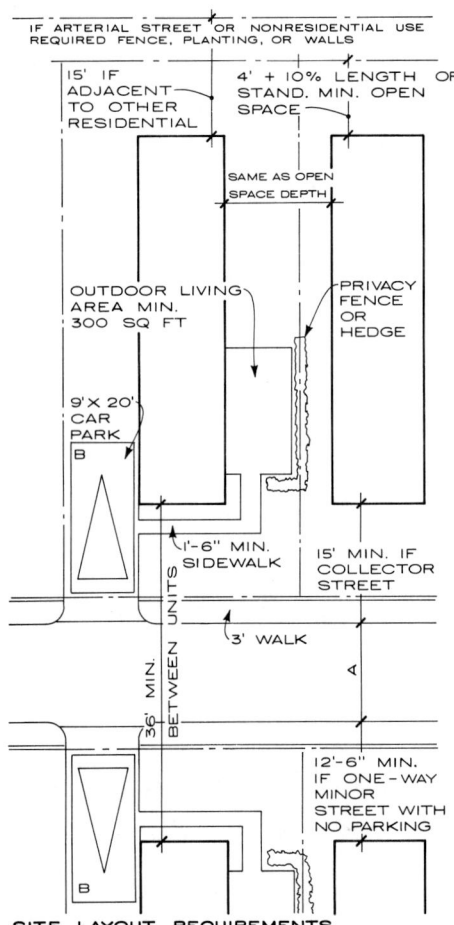

SITE LAYOUT REQUIREMENTS
STREET WIDTHS (A)

36 ft minimum entrance street and collector street with parking on both sides.

30 ft minimum collector street with no parking.

28 ft minimum minor street with parking on one side.

20 ft minimum minor or cul-de-sac with no parking.

11 ft minimum one-way minor street with no parking.

Maximum street length is 500 ft serving 25 stands or less.

NOTE

Width of two-way street may be reduced 2 ft if adjacent sidewalk is provided.

CAR PARKING (B)

One space is required for each mobile home stand plus one additional space for each four stands, for guest parking or service use.

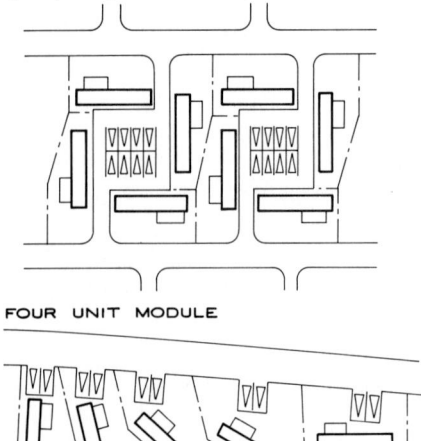

FOUR UNIT MODULE

IRREGULAR
EXAMPLES OF SITE LAYOUTS

Walter Hart, AIA and Frank Gersback, R. A.; North White Plains, New York

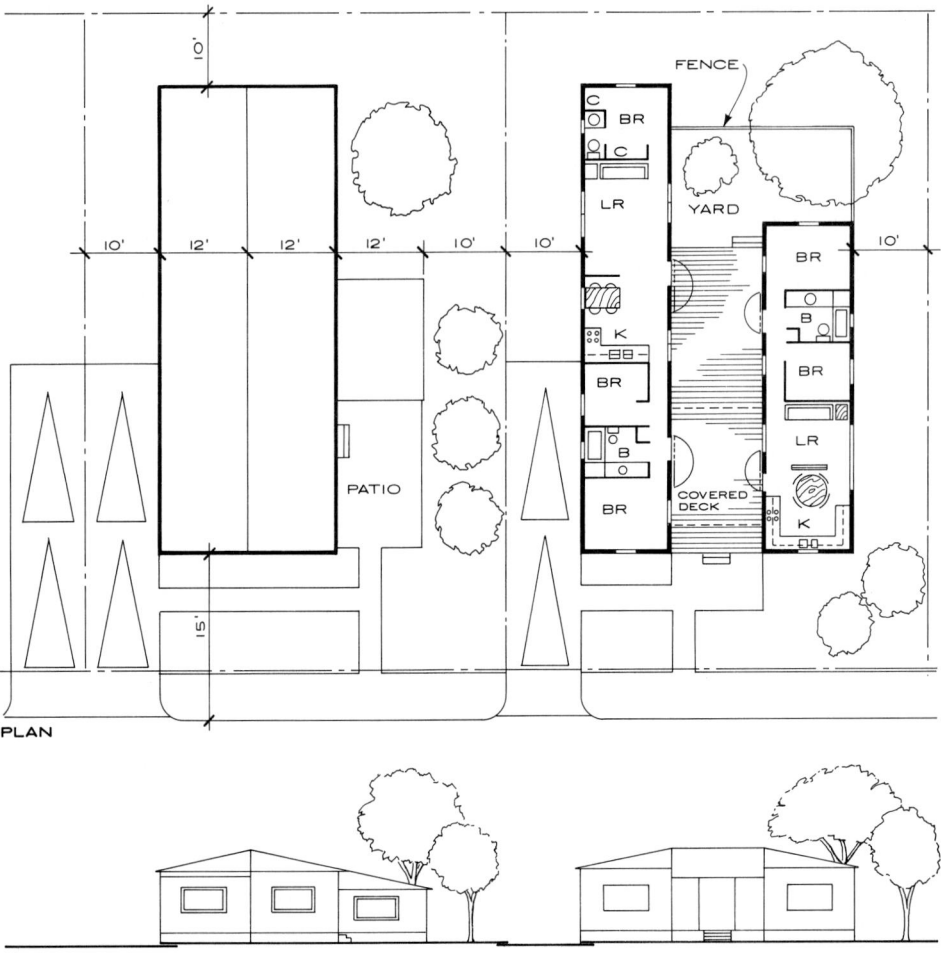

PLAN

ELEVATION
EXAMPLES OF COMBINED UNITS

SERVICE BUILDINGS

For independent mobile homes—provide 1 lavatory and 1 flush toilet each for males and females for emergency use.

For dependent mobile homes—10 units or less:
Male: 1 w.c., 1 urinal, 1 lavatory, 1 shower.
Female: 2 w.c., 1 labatory, 1 shower.
Same for each additional 10 units or less.
Location: 15' to 200' from dependent units.

Construction—permanent, heated, sound retardent wall separating male and female sides, well ventilated.

Many parks provide coin operated laundry facilities for occupants, whether of dependent or independent units.

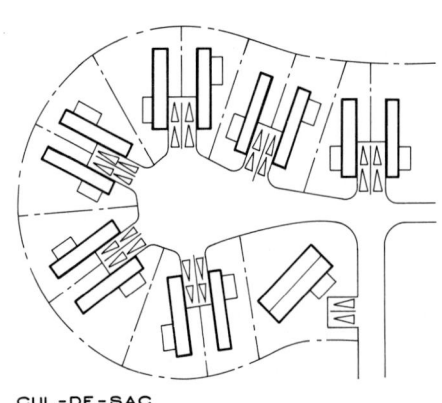

CUL-DE-SAC

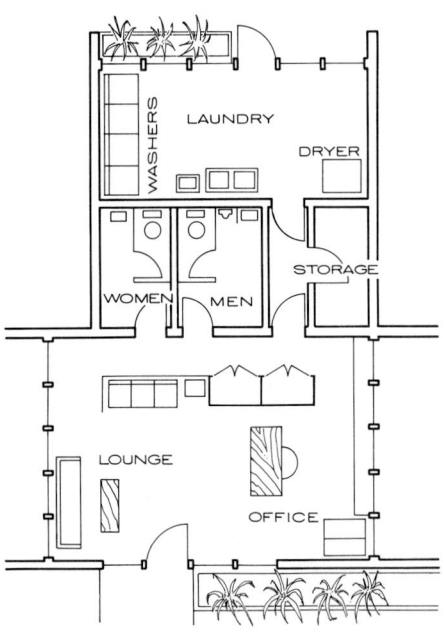

TYPICAL SERVICE BUILDING

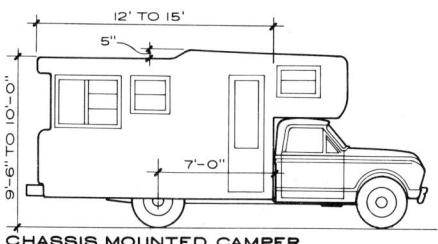

CHASSIS MOUNTED CAMPER
For trucks of 157'' — 159'' wheelbase, dual rear wheels
Side door, rear lounge. Widths: 7'– 6'', 8'– 0''

SLIDE-IN, "CAB OVER" CAMPER
Made to fit 6 ½', 8', 9' pickup beds
Widths vary. 6'– 9'', 7'– 6'', 8'– 0'' typical

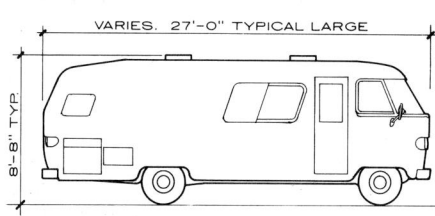

MOTORHOME
Sizes and designs vary. Typical width 8'– 0'' clear

CAMPERS

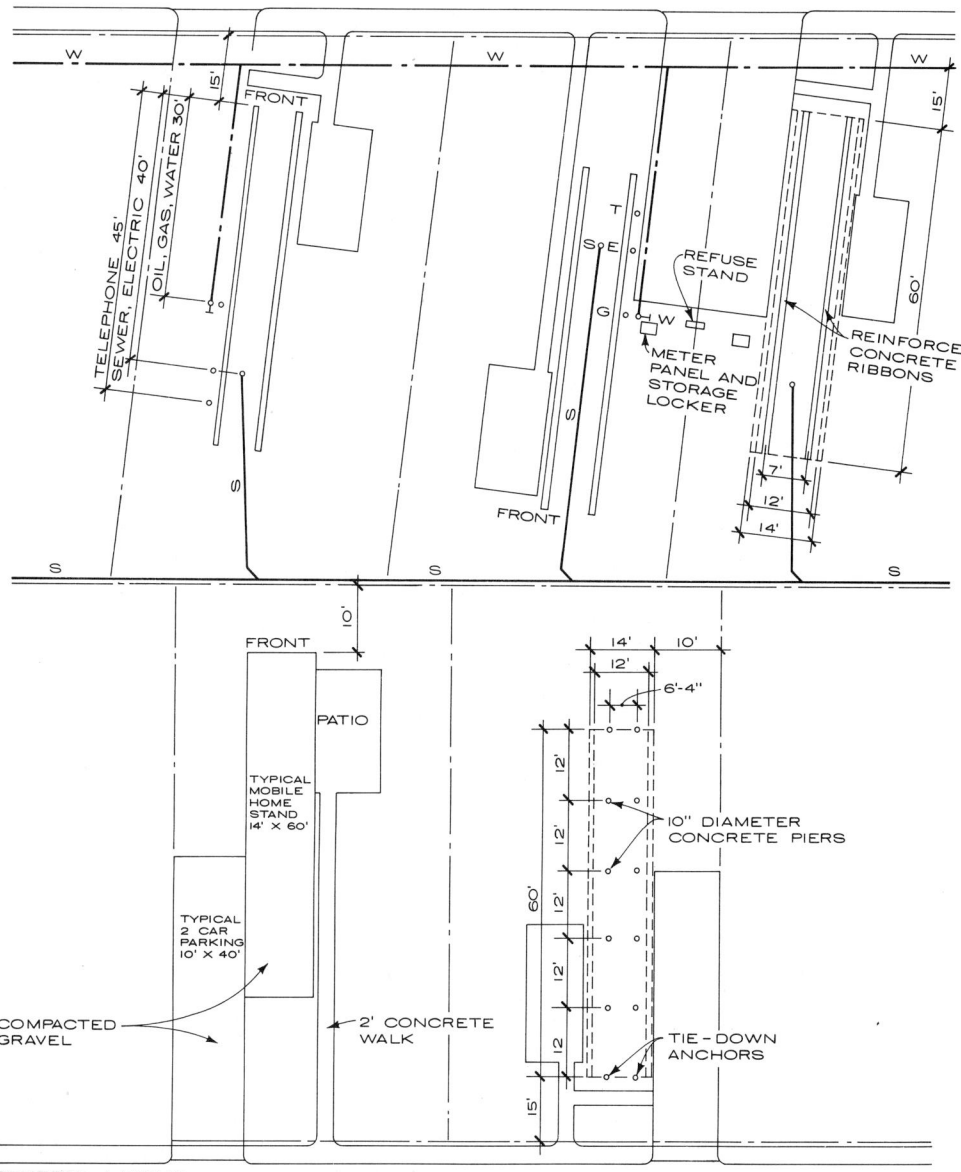

GENERAL LAYOUT
UTILITIES CONNECTIONS, PAVING, AND FOUNDATION REQUIREMENTS

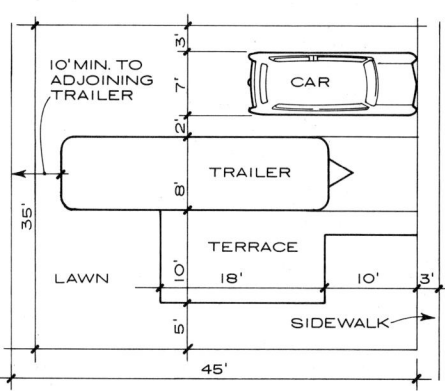

ROADS AND FACILITIES AS REQUIRED FOR MOBILE HOME PARKS

Maximum permissible length of motor vehicle and trailer together varies from 50 to 65 ft, according to the various state statutes.

TOURING TRAILER PARK LOT

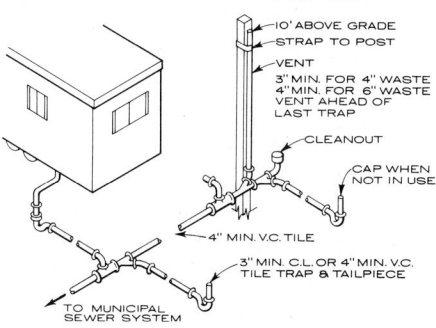

TYPICAL PLUMBING HOOKUP

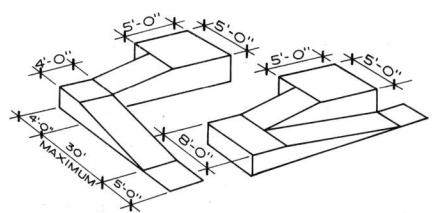

RAMP DESIGN CRITERIA
1. Slope must not exceed 1 in 15.
2. Ramp should be at least 4 ft wide.
3. Handrails on both sides are 2 ft 8 in. high and have rails that are easily grasped.
4. Handrails are extended horizontally 1 ft beyond the top and bottom of the ramp.
5. Large flat platform at the top and large flat paved area at the bottom of ramps should be provided.
6. Long ramps are broken with flat platform area at 30 ft intervals.
7. Ramps and platforms are built of durable weather resistant materials and surfaced with slip resistant material or texture. In cold climates protect ramp surface from snow buildup.

It is recommended that steps be used in conjunction with ramps for the convenience of able-bodied people and those who find ramps difficult to negotiate.

ENTRANCE RAMP FOR HANDICAPPED

NOTES
Consult zoning ordinance for local regulations.

1. WIDTH: 10 to 12 ft standard. Some 14 ft models on the market. Many states restrict width for highway transport.
2. LENGTH: 46 to 60 ft. A 68 ft model is available.
3. WEIGHT OF MOBILE HOMES: 15 to 20 tons.
4. CLASSIFICATIONS OF MOBILE HOMES: Independent is equipped with flush toilet and tub or shower. Dependent is not equipped with plumbing fixtures.

MOBILE HOME PARKS

Walter Hart, AIA and Frank Gersback, R. A.; North White Plains, New York

UTILITY LINES

W = water, S = sewer, G = gas, E = electric, T = telephone.

1. WATER SERVICE: 400 gal/day/unit.
2. GAS SERVICE: Metered. Connect only after inspection and approval. Locate individual storage tanks outside of unit, and rigidly connect them at least 5 ft from any door.
3. ELECTRICAL SERVICE: Metered, 110-120 V. Underground distribution is required by some codes.

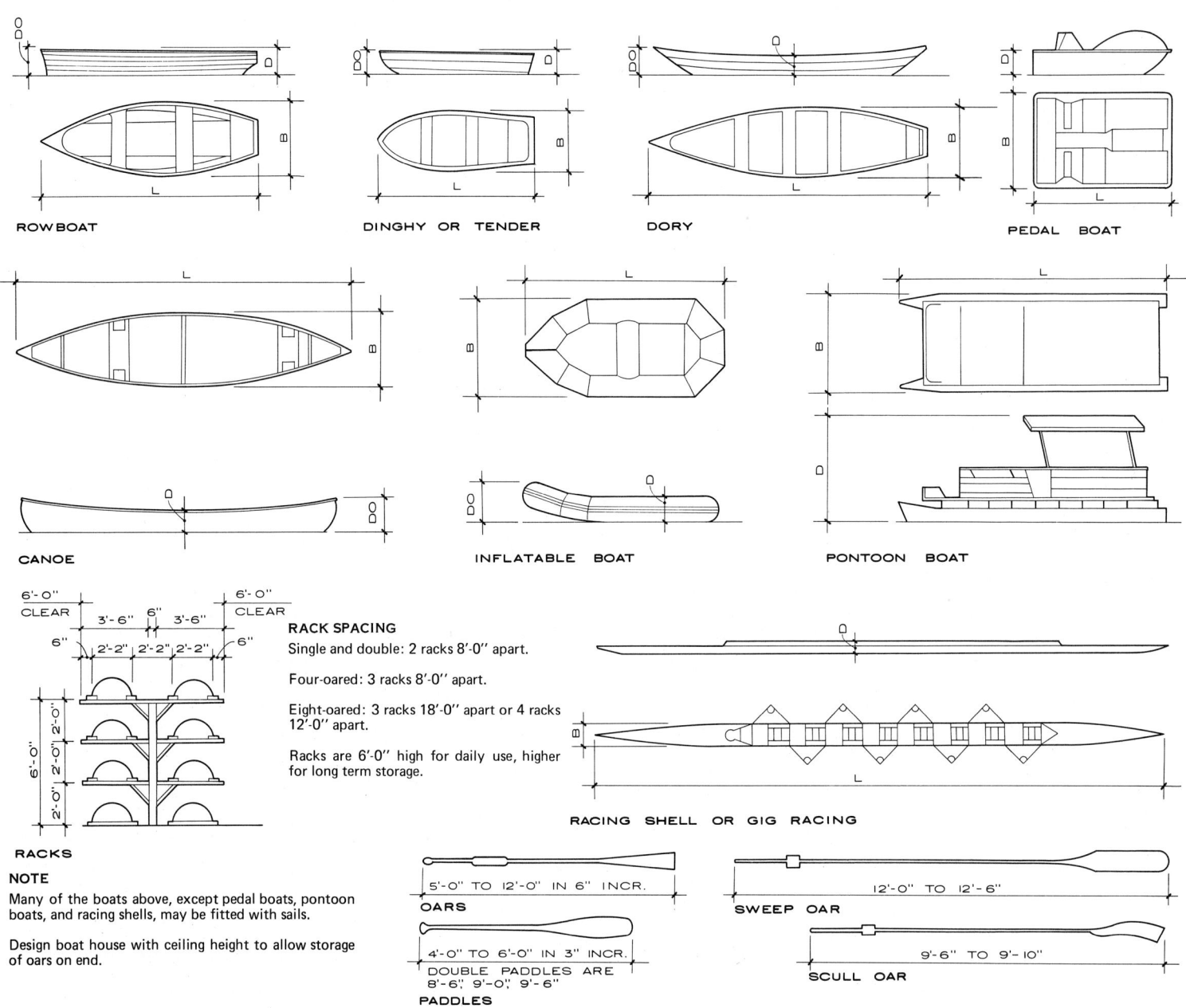

ROW BOAT

DINGHY OR TENDER

DORY

PEDAL BOAT

CANOE

INFLATABLE BOAT

PONTOON BOAT

RACKS

RACK SPACING

Single and double: 2 racks 8'-0'' apart.

Four-oared: 3 racks 8'-0'' apart.

Eight-oared: 3 racks 18'-0'' apart or 4 racks 12'-0'' apart.

Racks are 6'-0'' high for daily use, higher for long term storage.

RACING SHELL OR GIG RACING

NOTE

Many of the boats above, except pedal boats, pontoon boats, and racing shells, may be fitted with sails.

Design boat house with ceiling height to allow storage of oars on end.

5'-0'' TO 12'-0'' IN 6'' INCR.
OARS

4'-0'' TO 6'-0'' IN 3'' INCR.
DOUBLE PADDLES ARE 8'-6'', 9'-0'', 9'-6''
PADDLES

12'-0'' TO 12'-6''
SWEEP OAR

9'-6'' TO 9'-10''
SCULL OAR

TYPES AND SIZES OF TYPICAL SMALL BOATS

LO = LENGTH OVERALL, B = BEAM, D = DEPTH, DO = DEPTH OVERALL

CLASSIFICATION AND TYPE		LENGTH OVERALL	BEAM	DEPTH	DEPTH OVERALL	WEIGHT (LB)
Rowboats (many types and designs)		6'-5'' to 18'-0''	3'-11'' to 5'-5''	1'-2'' to 1'-8''	2'-0'' ±	50 to 270
DINGHY OR TENDER		6'-1'' to 14'-0''	2'-10'' to 5'-5''	1'-6'' to 1'-8''	1'-6'' to 1'-8''	40 to 155
DORY	Lifesaving	18'-0'' ±	4'-6'' ±	1'-8'' ±	1'-11'' ±	275
	Fisherman	12'-0'' to 16'-0''	3'-6'' to 5'-8''	1'-6'' to 1'-8''	1'-6'' to 1'-10''	64 to 320
PEDAL BOAT		7'-2'' to 10'-4''	5'-1'' to 5'-4''	1'-11''		115 to 140
INFLAT-ABLE CANOE	One-man	9'-0'' to 15'-0''	2'-10'' to 3'-0''	1'-0'' ±	2'-0'' to 2'-4''	44 to 85
	Standard	12'-0'' to 17'-0''	3'-0'' to 3'-8''	1'-2''	1'-4''	55 to 79
	Fisherman	16'-0'' to 18'-0''	3'-5'' to 3'-7''	1'-0'' to 1'-1''	2'-0'' to 2'-4''	70 ±
	War	23'-0'' to 35'-0''	3'-8''	1'-3''	2'-3''	225
	Dinghy	8'-2'' to 12'-8''	4'-0'' to 5'-6''	1'-0'' to 1'-4''	1'-6'' to 1'-10''	56 to 119
	Riverboat	13'-9'' to 18'-0''	6'-10'' to 8'-0''	1'-6'' to 1'-9''	2'-0'' to 2'-8''	99 to 154
PONTOON BOAT		20'-0'' to 28'-0''	8'-0''	7'-8''		1015 to 1155
SHELL OR GIG	Single racing	25'-0'' to 28'-0''	1'-2''	6½''	10½''	30
	Double racing	29'-0'' to 33'-0''	1'-4''	7''	11''	60
	Four-oared	40'-0'' to 42'-0''	1'-9''	8½''	1'-0½''	120
	Eight-oared	56'-0'' to 62'-0''	2'-0'' to 2'-4''	1'-4''	1'-2'' to 1'-8''	270

David B. Richards; Rossetti Associates/Architects Planners; Detroit, Michigan

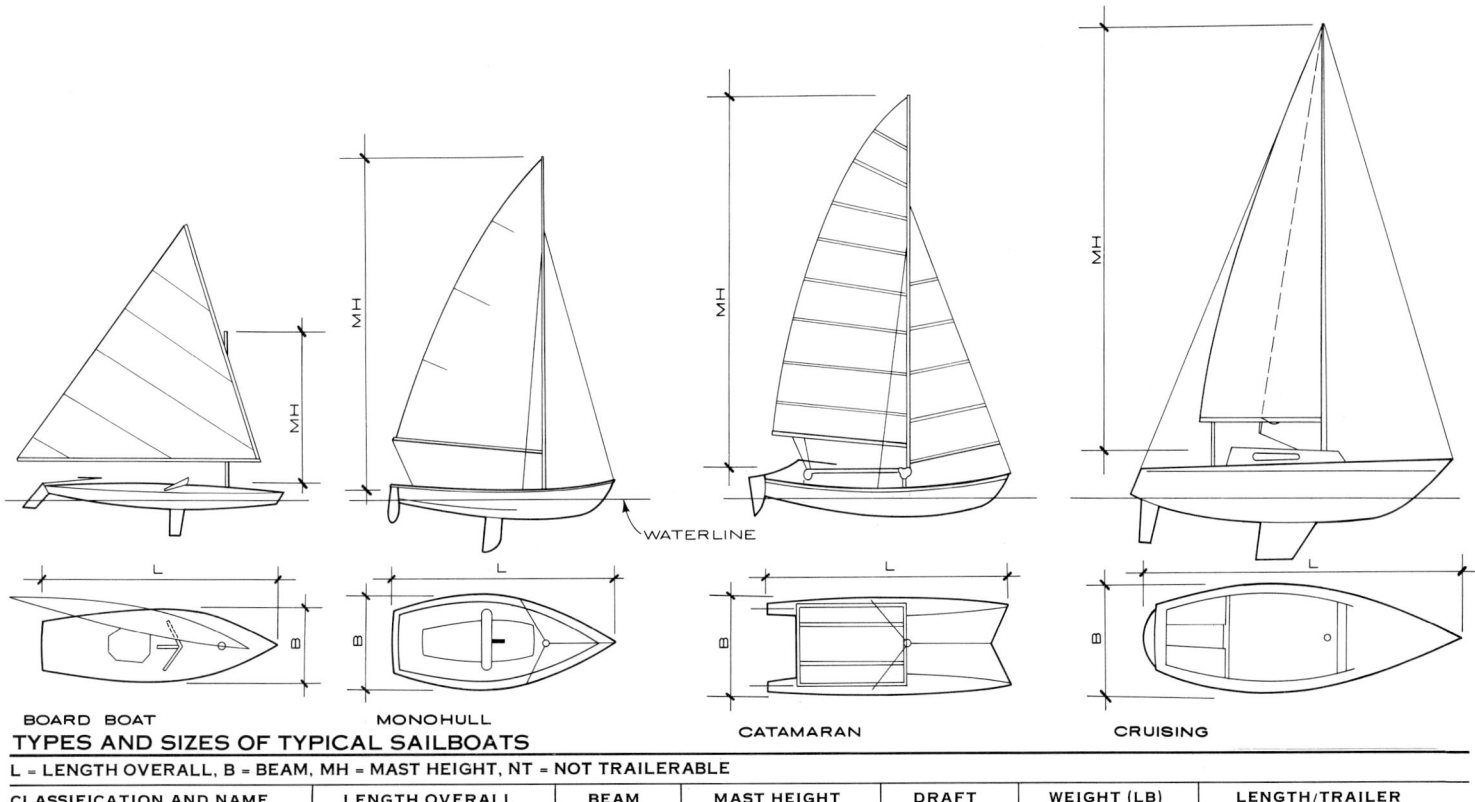

TYPES AND SIZES OF TYPICAL SAILBOATS

L = LENGTH OVERALL, B = BEAM, MH = MAST HEIGHT, NT = NOT TRAILERABLE

CLASSIFICATION AND NAME		LENGTH OVERALL	BEAM	MAST HEIGHT	DRAFT	WEIGHT (LB)	LENGTH/TRAILER
BOARD BOAT	Minifish	11'-9''	3'-10''	9'-0''	2'-4''	83	14'
	Sunfish	13'-9''	4'-0''	10'-0''	2'-8''	139	15'
	Laser	13'-10''	4'-6''	19'-0''	3'-0''	130	16'
MONO-HULL	Puffer	12'-6''	4'-10''	17'-11''	3'-0''	160	15'
	Challenger 15	15'-0''	5'-6''	20'-6''	2'-7''	380	18'
	Flying scot	19'-0''	6'-10''	26'-0''	4'-0''	800	21'
CATA-MARAN	Sol cat 15	15'-0''	7'-10''	25'-4''	8''	290	18'
	Hobie 16	16'-7''	7'-11''	26'-0''	10''	340	19'
	Prindle 18	18'-0''	8'-0''	28'-9''	9$\frac{1}{2}$'	335	21'
CRUISING	O'Day 27	27'-0''	9'-0''	38'-6''	4'-0''	6700	NT
	Pearson 32	31'-8$\frac{1}{2}$''	10'-7''	44'-7''	5'-6''	9400	NT
	CS 36	36'-6''	11'-6''	48'-6''	6'-3''	15,500	NT

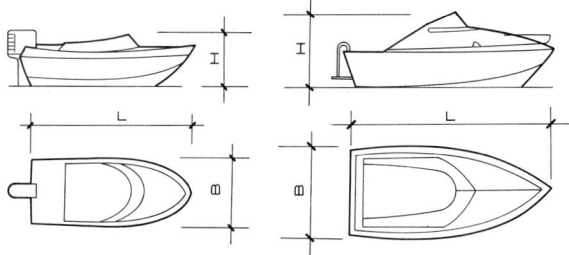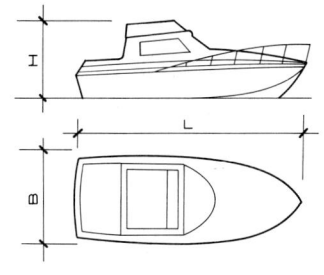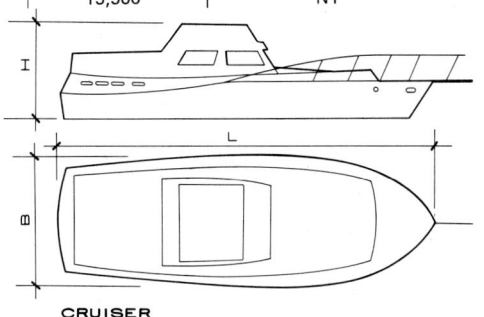

RUNABOUT   SPORT CRUISER   EXPRESS SEDAN CRUISER   CRUISER

TYPES AND SIZES OF TYPICAL POWERBOATS

CLASSIFICATION AND NAME		LENGTH OVERALL	BEAM	HEIGHT	DRAFT	WEIGHT (LB)	LENGTH WITH TRAILER
RUN-ABOUT	Crusader 550	15'-8''	6'-5''	3'-5''	1'-0'	865	19'
	Formula 18	18'-2''	7'-8''	3'-9$\frac{1}{2}$''	2'-4''	2618	21'
	Nordic 22	21'-8''	7'-10''	5'-2''	2'-3''	2800	25'
SPORT CRUISER	V-214	20'-6$\frac{1}{2}$''	8'-0''	6'-0''	2'-8''	6095	25'
	Crusader II	23'-6''	8'-0''	6'-3''	2'-6''	4375	28'
	Formula 255	25'-5''	8'-0''	7'-4''	2'-6''	6095	28'
SEDAN EXPRESS	F-25 Express	25'-0''	9'-4''	8'-4''	2'-2''	4800	NT
	Formula 26 sedan	26'-2''	9'-6''	9'-6''	2'-10''	7200	NT
	F-36 sedan	36'-0''	13'-0''	9'-6''	2'-11''	16,000	NT
CRUISER	F-36	36'-0''	13'-0''	12'-3''	2'-11''	17,000	NT
	F-40	40'-8''	14'-2$\frac{1}{2}$''	13'-1''	3'-7''	26,500	NT
	Viking 43	42'-8''	14'-9''	12'-0''	3'-9''	34,000	NT

David B. Richards; Rossetti Associates/Architects Planners; Detroit, Michigan

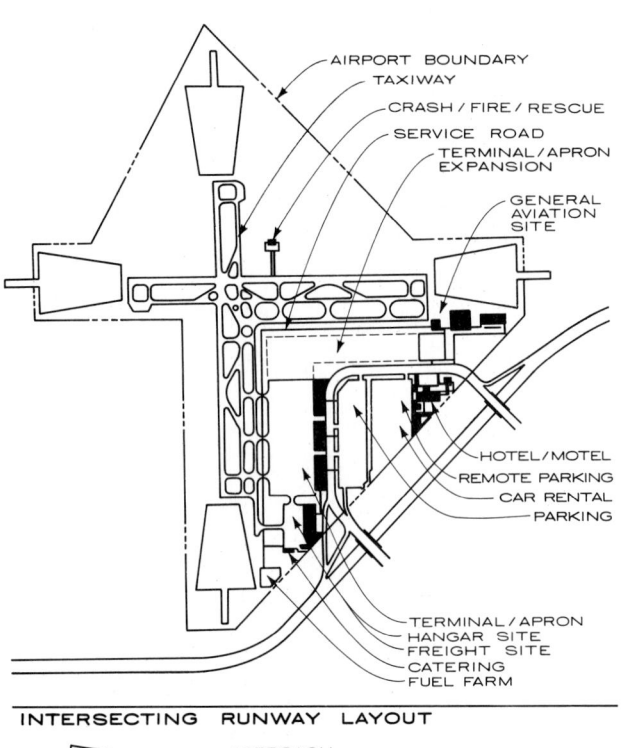

INTERSECTING RUNWAY LAYOUT

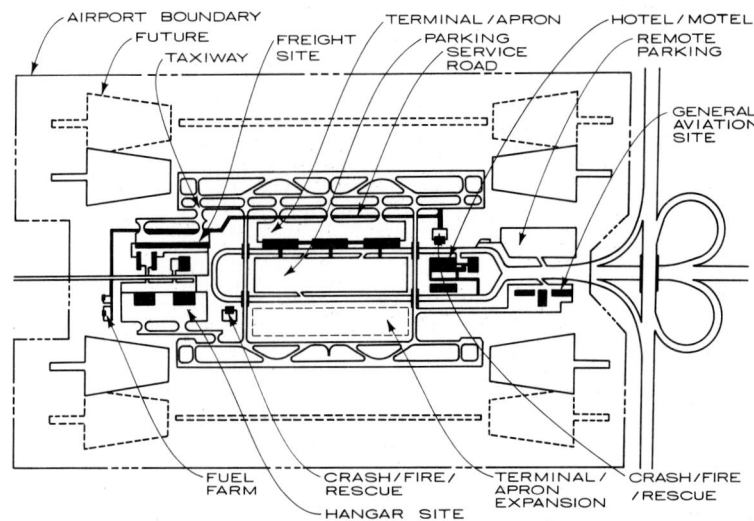

PARALLEL RUNWAY LAYOUT

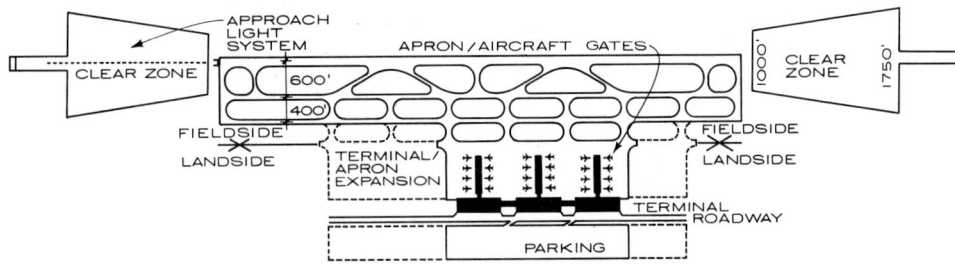

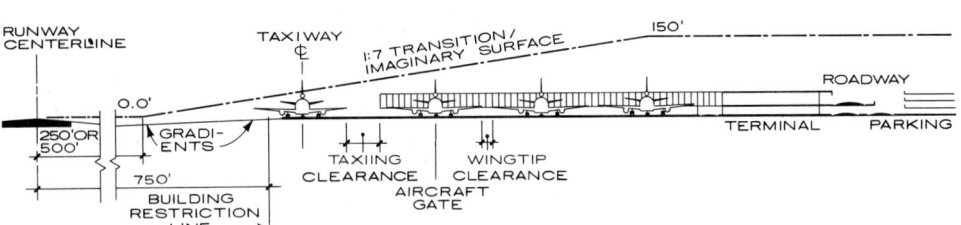

AIRPORT FIELDSIDE - LANDSIDE

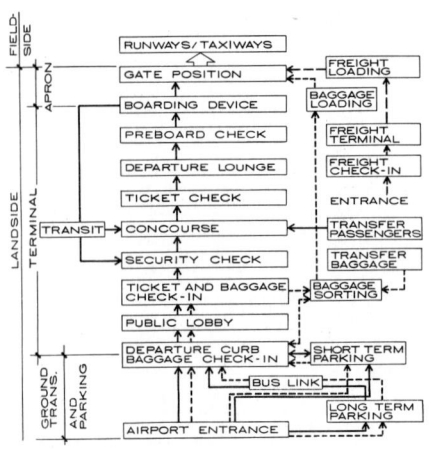

OUTBOUND - U.S. DOMESTIC AND INTERNATIONAL FEDERAL INSPECTION SERVICES (F.I.S.) NOT REQUIRED

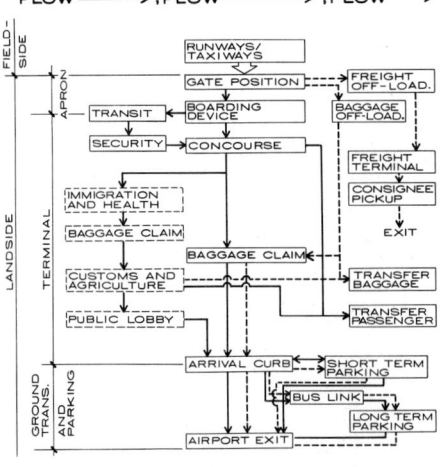

INBOUND - U.S. DOMESTIC AND U.S. INTERNATIONAL FEDERAL INSPECTION SERVICES (F.I.S.) REQUIRED

Runway-taxiway configurations and apron terminal concepts appear in many variations, generally caused by climatic conditions, traffic characteristics, operational requirements, traffic volumes, and historical growth patterns.

Two airport plans are shown: (1) an intersecting runway configuration, total land area small to medium, the landside facilities are arranged within one quadrant, expansion capability is limited; (2) a parallel runway configuration, total land area medium to large, the landside facilities are arranged within the area between the runways, expansion capability is significant.

The airport fieldside consists of the runway-taxiway system, areas for clearances, and areas for navigational aides.

The airport landside consists of the passenger terminal with aircraft apron; airport ground transportation systems, roads, vehicular parking; support facilities, hangars, freight terminals, U.S. mail, catering, car rental, hotels, motels. The fieldside influences the location, plan development, and expansion capabilities of the landside facilities.

Example shows in plan and section the relationship between the runway-taxiway system and the apron terminal system. It is assumed that the runway is equipped with an instrument landing system in both directions.

Requirements, recommendations, minimum criteria for runway-taxiway systems are documented in the United States by the Department of Transportation/ Federal Aviation Administration (DOT/FAA): FAR Part 77 "Objects Affecting the Airspace" and in series of Advisory Circulars. For airports outside the United States the requirements are documented by the International Civil Aviation Organization (ICAO): Aerodromes, Annex 14, 6th ed., September 1971, and Supplement, March 1974.

The following documents will provide more general information on airport master plan development:

1. FAA/AC 150/5070-6 Airport Master Plans.
2. FAA/AC 150/5335-1A Airport Design Standards.
3. Air Transport Association of America (ATA), Runway Capacity Criteria, Air Navigational Control Report No. 118, 5th ed.

Outside the United States:

1. ICAO/Aerodrome Manual, Part 2, Aerodrome Physical Characteristics.
2. ICAO/Airport Planning Manual (Doc. 9184-AN/ 902), Part 1, Master Planning, 1st ed.

OFFICIAL DOCUMENTS FOR PLANNING AIRPORT TERMINALS

1. FAA, Analysis of Concepts for Evaluation of Terminal Buildings, Report No. FAA-RD-73-82.
2. FAA, The Apron & Terminal Planning Report, No. FAA-RD-75-191. Includes aircraft dimensions, turn radii, aircraft jet blast contours for taxing and breakway thrust, and aircraft parking arrangements with staging of ground service equipment.
3. FAA, Advisory Circular No: AC 150/5360-7.
4. ATA, Airline Aircraft Gates and Passenger Terminal Space Approximations, AD/SC Report No. 4.

For airports outside the United States: ICAO, Annex 9, Facilitation; IATA, Airport Terminals Reference Manual, 6th ed.

Walter Hart, AIA; Associates, Frank Gersbach, R.A., Benito Lao, AIA; North White Plains, New York

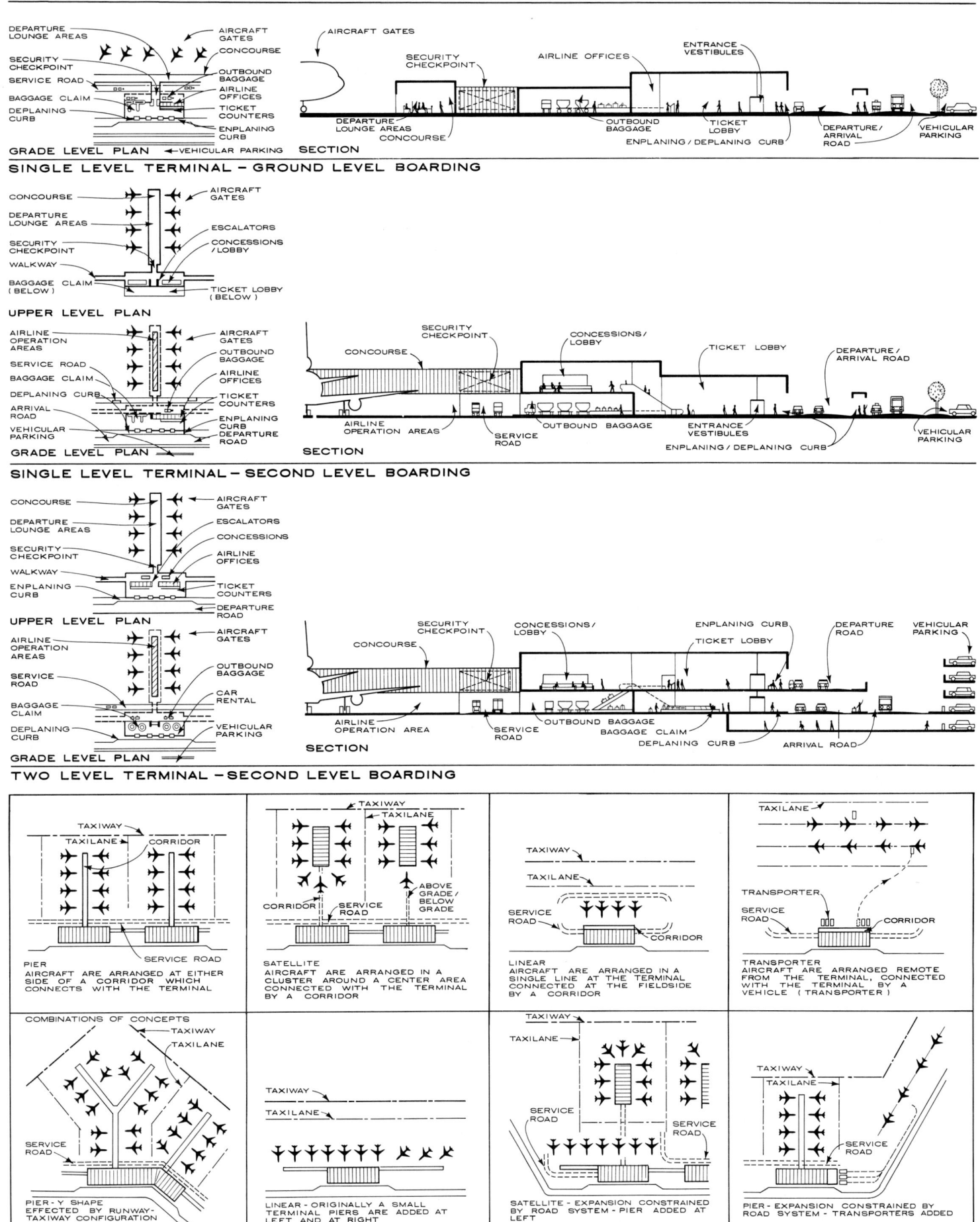

SINGLE LEVEL TERMINAL – GROUND LEVEL BOARDING

SINGLE LEVEL TERMINAL – SECOND LEVEL BOARDING

TWO LEVEL TERMINAL – SECOND LEVEL BOARDING

PIER
AIRCRAFT ARE ARRANGED AT EITHER SIDE OF A CORRIDOR WHICH CONNECTS WITH THE TERMINAL

SATELLITE
AIRCRAFT ARE ARRANGED IN A CLUSTER AROUND A CENTER AREA CONNECTED WITH THE TERMINAL BY A CORRIDOR

LINEAR
AIRCRAFT ARE ARRANGED IN A SINGLE LINE AT THE TERMINAL CONNECTED AT THE FIELDSIDE BY A CORRIDOR

TRANSPORTER
AIRCRAFT ARE ARRANGED REMOTE FROM THE TERMINAL, CONNECTED WITH THE TERMINAL BY A VEHICLE (TRANSPORTER)

COMBINATIONS OF CONCEPTS

PIER-Y SHAPE
EFFECTED BY RUNWAY-TAXIWAY CONFIGURATION

LINEAR – ORIGINALLY A SMALL TERMINAL PIERS ARE ADDED AT LEFT AND AT RIGHT

SATELLITE – EXPANSION CONSTRAINED BY ROAD SYSTEM – PIER ADDED AT LEFT

PIER – EXPANSION CONSTRAINED BY ROAD SYSTEM – TRANSPORTERS ADDED

CONCEPTS

Walter Hart, AIA; Associates, Frank Gersbach, R.A., Benito Lao, AIA; North White Plains, New York

THE NATURE OF SOUND

Sound is a vibration in an elastic medium; its production requires a source and a path; it travels to a receiver (the human ear, usually). Speech, music, mechanical equipment, and footfall noise are types of sound sources. Air, fluids, and building materials are paths; materials possess mass, and therefore inertia; their oscillating motion when excited by acoustical energy is governed by the physical laws of motion.

FREQUENCY OF COMMON SOUNDS

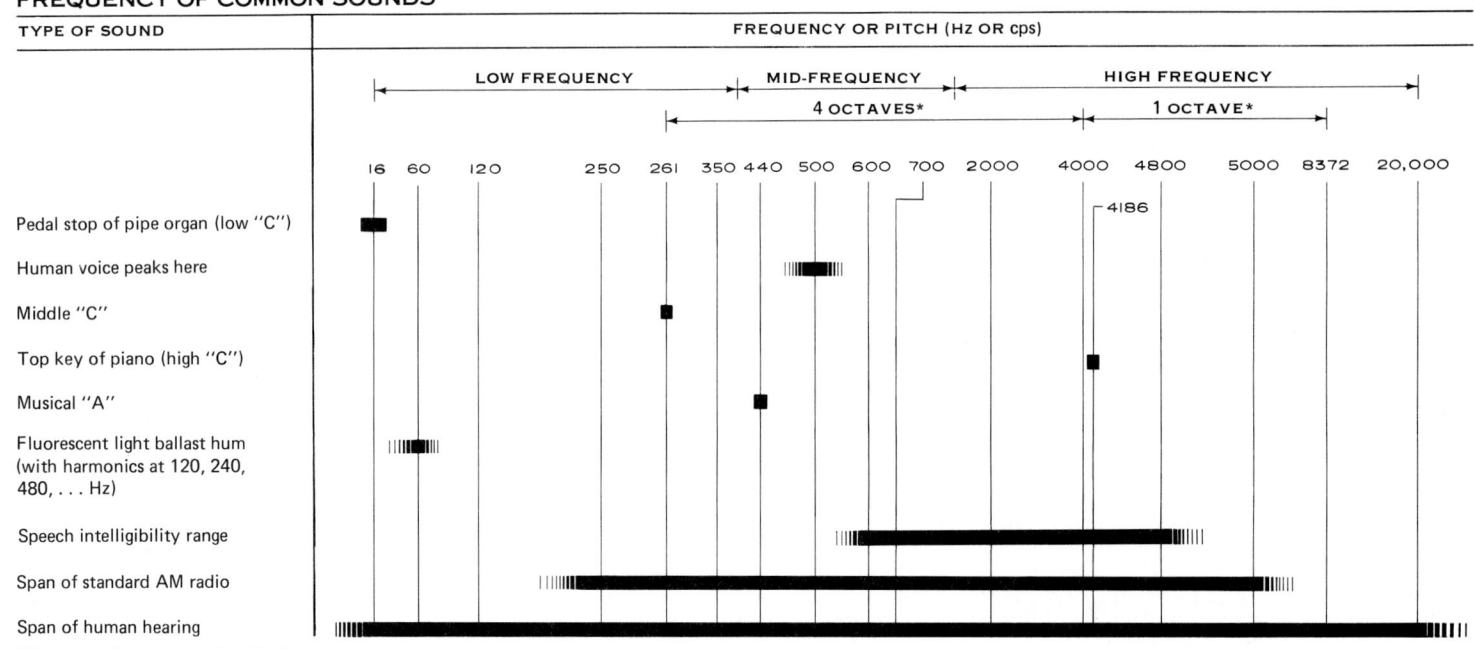

*Octave—a frequency ratio of 2:1.

PHYSICAL FACTORS: RELATIONSHIP OF SOUND INTENSITY, LEVEL, AND LOUDNESS

INTENSITY (RELATIVE ENERGY–UNITS)	A-WEIGHTED SOUND LEVEL (dB)	LOUDNESS
100,000,000,000,000	140	Near jet aircraft and artillery fire
10,000,000,000,000	130	Threshold of pain
1,000,000,000,000	120	Near elevated train
100,000,000,000	110	Inside propeller plane
10,000,000,000	100	
1,000,000,000	90	Full symphony or band
100,000,000	80	Inside auto at high speed
10,000,000	70	Conversation, face to face
1,000,000	60	Inside general office
100,000	50	
10,000	40	Inside private office
1,000	30	Inside bedroom
100	20	Inside quiet theater
10	10	
1	0	Threshold of hearing

NOTE

The decibel number represents a ratio (actually 10 x the logarithm) of the measured intensity to a reference intensity roughly equivalent to the threshold of hearing (10⁻¹⁶ W/sq cm).

A-weighted decibels [dB(A)] is a standard single number rating representing the overall sound energy of a given source. The A-weighting network in a sound level meter filters sound in a manner similar to the human ear, namely, downgrading low frequencies and emphasizing middle and high frequencies to which the ear is most sensitive.

SUBJECTIVE FACTORS: EFFECT OF CHANGE IN SOUND PRESSURE LEVEL

CHANGE IN SOUND PRESSURE LEVEL (+ OR –)	CHANGE IN APPARENT LOUDNESS
3 dB	Just perceptible
5 dB	Clearly noticeable
10 dB	Twice as loud (or ½)
15 dB	Three times as loud (or ⅓)
20 dB	Four times as loud (or ¼)

Don Klabin, AIA; Bolt Beranek and Newman, Inc; Cambridge, Massachusetts

1 ENVIRONMENTAL FACTORS

NOTE

The material below outlines a design procedure, in abbreviated form, for the architect to use in analyzing a noise control problem and developing a solution or solutions. The three major elements of an acoustic circuit—source, path, and receiver—can each be quantified as shown here; hence there is no need for guesswork.

1. SELECT BACKGROUND NOISE DESIGN CRITERIA FOR EACH OCCUPANCY.

TYPE OF SPACE	RECOMMENDED MAXIMUM BACKGROUND NOISE CRITERION CURVE*
Broadcast studios, concert halls	PNC 10-20
Legitimate theaters, churches (no amplification)	PNC 20
Large conference rooms, small auditoriums, orchestra rehearsal rooms, movie theaters, courtrooms	PNC 25-30
Bedrooms (residences, apartments, hotels, hospitals)	PNC 25-40
Small conference rooms, classrooms	PNC 30-35
Small private offices, libraries	PNC 30-40
Restaurants, stores	PNC 35-45
Coliseums for sports only (with amplification)	PNC 40
General offices, computer rooms (typing and business machines)	PNC 40-50
Factories	PNC 50-75

* Each noise criteria curve is a code for specifying permissible sound pressure levels in eight octave bands. It is intended that in none of the frequency bands should the specified level be exceeded.

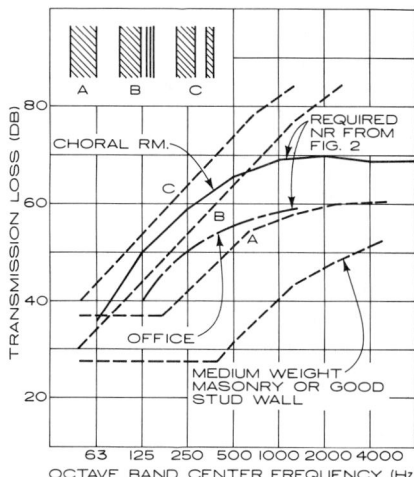

THE PNC CURVES (PREFERRED NOISE CRITERIA) BASED ON HUMAN RESPONSE TO SOUND PRESSURE LEVEL AND FREQUENCY

2. IDENTIFY ALL NOISE SOURCES—INTERIOR AND EXTERIOR: Note proximity of noise sensitive areas to all exterior and interior sources of intrusive background noise—whether speech (in corridors, outdoor play areas, etc.), music (auditorium rehearsal and practice rooms, etc.), impact noise (pedestrian traffic, etc.), activity noise (recreation areas, workrooms, traffic, etc.), or mechanical equipment noise (rooftop, perimeter, basement, etc.). Measured sound pressure level data for all these sources are generally available or can be calculated.

3. CALCULATE REQUIRED NOISE REDUCTION (NR) = SOURCE LEVEL—PNC: To minimize NR requirements, locate noisy spaces next to spaces having a relatively high PNC; when this is not possible, a heavier and more expensive construction assembly is required. See Figs. 1 and 2.

4. SELECT PARTITION TYPES (AND FLOOR/CEILING ASSEMBLIES) WHOSE TRANSMISSION LOSS (TL) CURVES EXCEED REQUIRED NR CURVES.

PLAN A
COMPARATIVE SPACE PLANNING
FIGURE 1

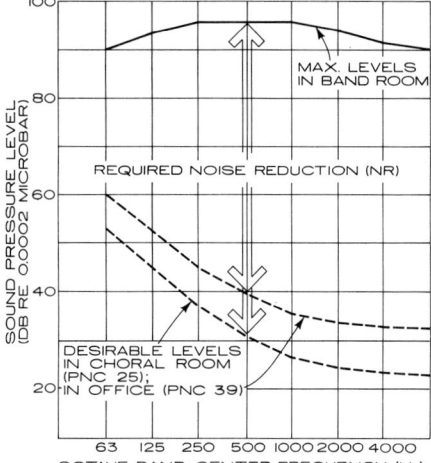

FIGURE 2

FIGURE 3

ACOUSTICAL DESIGN CHECKLIST

1. Build in good acoustical design—sound isolation and reverberation control—from the beginning. It is much cheaper to avoid noise problems in the initial design than to correct them later. Good acoustics is not cosmetics; it must be an integral part of the building design and is not a superficially applied treatment either before or after the fact.

2. Select materials of the proper weight and construction with the proper resiliency. Choose the simplest construction that meets the NR criteria. Detail well and build well; minimize penetrations of walls, floors, and ceilings and make all holes and openings airtight to maintain acoustical integrity. Use materials wisely: do not confuse lightweight, porous, sound absorbing materials (for echo and reverberation control) with heavy, impervious, sound isolating materials (for sound transmission control). Both may be needed, but both cannot be achieved with the same material.

3. Consider the mechanical and electrical equipment as an integral part of the acoustical design. Choose quiet rated fixtures and equipment and beware of the sound "leaks" that the ductwork, piping, and conduit provide. Use as needed vibration isolators and sound absorbing duct lining together with flexible connections and low flow velocities in ducts and pipes.

4. Seek out qualified professional advice for all spaces with critical acoustical requirements. Do not rely solely on rules of thumb.

Don Klabin, AIA; Bolt Beranek and Newman, Inc.; Cambridge, Massachusetts

ENVIRONMENTAL FACTORS 1

INSTRUCTIONS FOR THE PROPER USE OF SOUND TRANSMISSION CLASS (STC) DATA
DESIGN CRITERIA FOR PARTITIONS

STC ratings are a measure of the effectiveness of a given partition construction in reducing airborne sound transmission, not the transmission of impact noise, low frequency noise sources (e.g., HVAC equipment and vehicular traffic), or amplified music. Because of the limited frequency range covered (125-4000 Hz), STC ratings are limited to evaluating the speech privacy potential of the various partitions and therefore are best used in the design of partitions separating adjacent offices, hospital patient rooms, classrooms (with little or no amplified speech or playback of recordings),

dormitories, apartments, courtrooms, small conference rooms, etc. The single number STC ratings should not be relied on, solely, for the selection of partitions separating, say, movie theaters, large conference rooms, auditoriums, music practice rooms, computer and business machine rooms, and mechanical equipment rooms, from, say, private offices and apartments. Typically, a more extensive acoustical analysis is required for such adjacent locations; consult an acoustical engineer for additional information.

Note also that the STC ratings are based on test data measured in a laboratory installation of the given

partitions, that is, under ideal construction conditions. Drywall manufacturers admit to a 5-15 point reduction in the lab ratings for the actual field performance depending on the quality of detailing and workmanship. The importance of communication between the design team and the construction team cannot be overemphasized. The presence of flanking paths—interconnecting ductwork, nonairtight edge joints, inadequate door and window construction, untreated piping and conduit penetrations, and so on—in a completed building can result from improper design, improper construction, or both. The stated criteria assume no flanking paths.

SOUND ISOLATION CRITERIA

TYPE OF OCCUPANCY	WALL OR PARTITION BETWEEN:		SOUND ISOLATION REQUIREMENT (MIN.)
	ROOM CONSIDERED (SOURCE)	ADJACENT AREA (RECEIVER)	
Executive areas, doctors' suites—confidential privacy requirements	Office	Adjacent offices	STC 52
		General office areas	STC 52
		Corridor or lobby	STC 52
		Washrooms and toilet areas	STC 52
		Exterior of building	STC 37-60+*
		Kitchen and dining areas	STC 52
		Manufacturing areas and mechanical equipment rooms	STC 52+†
Normal office areas—normal privacy requirements	Office	Adjacent offices	STC 45
		General office areas	STC 45
		Corridor or lobby	STC 45
		Washrooms and toilet areas	STC 47
		Exterior of building	STC 37-60+*
		Kitchen and dining areas	STC 47
		Manufacturing areas and mechanical equipment rooms	STC 52+†
Any normal occupancy, using conference rooms for group meetings or discussions	Conference rooms	Other conference rooms	STC 45
		Adjacent offices	STC 45
		General office areas	STC 45
		Corridor or lobby	STC 45
		Washrooms and toilet areas	STC 47
		Exterior of building	STC 37-60+*
		Kitchen and dining areas	STC 47
		Manufacturing or other noisy interior areas	STC 52+†
Normal business offices, drafting areas, banking floors, etc.	Large general office areas	Corridors or lobby	STC 37
		Exterior of building	STC 37-60+*
		Data processing areas	STC 42
		Manufacturing areas and mechanical equipment areas	STC 47+
		Kitchen and dining areas	STC 42
Office in manufacturing, laboratory or test areas requiring normal privacy	Shop and laboratory offices	Adjacent offices	STC 42
		Manufacturing, laboratory, or test areas	STC 42+
		Washrooms and toilet areas	STC 42
		Corridor or lobby	STC 37
		Exterior of building	STC 37-60+*
Motels and urban hotels (similar to apartments)	Bedrooms	Adjacent bedrooms, separate occupancy	STC 48+
		Bathrooms, separate occupancy	STC 52+
		Living rooms, separate occupancy	STC 50+
		Dining areas	STC 50+
		Corridor, lobby, or public spaces	STC 48+
		Mechanical equipment rooms	STC 52+†
		Exterior of building	STC 37-60+*
Apartments, multiple dwelling building	Bedrooms	Adjacent bedrooms, separate occupancy	STC 48-55*
		Bathrooms, separate occupancy	STC 52-58*
		Bathrooms, same occupancy	STC 45-52*
		Living rooms, separate occupancy	STC 50-57*
		Living rooms, same occupancy	STC 42-50*
		Kitchen areas, separate occupancy	STC 52-58*
		Kitchen areas, same occupancy	STC 45-52*
		Mechanical equipment rooms	STC 58-65+
		Corridors, lobby, public spaces	STC 48-55*
		Exterior of building	STC 42-60+†

*Depend on the nature of the exterior background noise—its level, spectrum shape, and constancy—as well as on the client's budget and on thermal considerations. Use qualified acoustical consultants for analysis of high noise outdoor environments such as airport areas, highways (with heavy truck traffic especially), and industrial facilities.

†Use acoustical consultants for mechanical equipment rooms housing other than air handling equipment—chillers, pumps, compressors, etc.—and for heavy manufacturing areas employing equipment generating noise levels at or above OSHA allowable levels or generating high vibration levels.

Don Klabin, AIA; Bolt, Beranek and Newman, Inc.; Cambridge, Massachusetts

1 ENVIRONMENTAL FACTORS

Partitions with STC ratings within 1-2 points (1-2 dB) of the listed criteria would still be acceptable given the anticipated tolerances in test results. (Subjectively, the human ear would consider a 1-2 dB change as "just barely audible" at best, which is insignificant.)

The stated performance criteria assume acceptable background noise levels in the source and receiver rooms, that is, some masking of intrusive sounds without loss of speech intelligibility or other interference in listening conditions. The stated criteria are for buildings that fall into an average construction cost range and thus are not weighted toward any one type of con-

struction or geographic region. The primary concern on which these criteria are based is the desire to provide adequate acoustical privacy for the building user. It is clear, however, that these acoustical criteria must be tempered by the designer's consideration of other design parameters—fire ratings, structural loads, energy conservation, and so on—which may downgrade (or even upgrade) the quality of the acoustical design.

For this reason the acoustical criteria listed here tend to be reasonably conservative, rather than lenient, given the many possible compromises.

DESIGN CRITERIA FOR FLOOR/CEILING ASSEMBLIES
1. AIRBORNE SOUND: STC ratings for floor/ceiling assemblies should be equal to or greater than those for the partitions.
2. STRUCTUREBORNE (IMPACT) SOUND: Impact Isolation Class (IIC) ratings should be equal to or greater than the STC ratings.

Both criteria must be met to ensure adequate acoustical privacy.

SOUND ISOLATION DESIGN CRITERIA

TYPE OF OCCUPANCY	WALL OR PARTITION BETWEEN:		SOUND ISOLATION REQUIREMENT (MIN.)
	ROOM CONSIDERED (SOURCE)	ADJACENT AREA (RECEIVER)	
Apartments, multiple dwelling building	(b) Living rooms	Adjacent living rooms, separate occupancy	STC 48-55*
		Bathrooms, separate occupancy	STC 50-57*
		Bathrooms, same occupancy	STC 45-52*
		Kitchen areas, separate occupancy	STC 48-55*
		Mechanical equipment rooms	STC 58-65*
		Exterior of building	STC 37-60+†
Private, singlefamily residences	Bedrooms (living rooms similar)	Adjacent bedrooms	STC 40-48*
		Living rooms	STC 42-50*
		Bathrooms, not directly connected with bedroom	STC 45-52*
		Kitchen areas	STC 45-52*
		Exterior of building	†
School buildings	(a) Classrooms	Adjacent classrooms—speech use only	STC 42
		Adjacent classrooms—speech and audiovisual use	STC 48
		Laboratories	STC 48
		Corridor or public areas	STC 42
		Kitchen and dining areas	STC 47
		Shops	STC 52+
		Recreational areas	STC 52+
		Music rooms	STC 52+
		Mechanical equipment rooms	STC 55+
		Toilet areas	STC 47
		Exterior of building	STC 37-60+†
	(b) Large music or drama areas	Adjacent music or drama rooms	STC 52+
		Corridor or public areas	STC 52
		Practice rooms	STC 52+
		Shops	STC 57
		Recreational areas	STC 57
		Laboratories	STC 52
		Toilet areas	STC 52
		Mechanical equipment rooms	STC 58-65+
		Exterior of building	STC 47+†
	(c) Music practice rooms	Adjacent practice rooms	STC 52+‡
		Corridors and public areas	STC 52+
	(d) Language laboratories	Same as for theaters, concert halls, auditorium, etc.	
	(e) Counseling offices	Same as for executive offices	
Any occupancy where serious performances are given (requirements may be relaxed for elementary schools or other noncritical types of occupancy)	Theaters, concert halls, lecture halls, radio, TV, recording studios	Adjacent similar areas Corridors and public areas Recreational areas Mechanical equipment spaces Classrooms Laboratories Shops Toilet areas Exterior of building	Use qualified acoustical consultants to assist in the design of construction details for these critical occupancies†

*Depend on nighttime, exterior background levels and other factors that affect actual location of building. (Grades I, II, and III are discussed in "A Guide to Airborne, Impact, and Structureborne Noise Control in Multifamily Dwellings," HUD-TS-24, 1974, pp. 10-9 ff.)

†Discretionary—depend on client's budget, climate, interior planning (closed vs. open), site planning, and other factors. Use qualified acoustical consultants for analysis of high noise outdoor environments such as airport areas, industrial facilities, and highways.

‡The STC ratings shown are guidelines only. These situations require, typically, double layer construction with resilient connections between layers or, preferably, structurally independent, "room-within-a-room" construction. The level of continuous background noise, such as that provided by the HVAC system or an electronic masking system, has a significant impact on the quality of construction selected and must be coordinated with the other design parameters.

Don Klabin, AIA; Bolt, Beranek and Newman, Inc.; Cambridge, Massachusetts

ENVIRONMENTAL FACTORS 1

FIGURE I

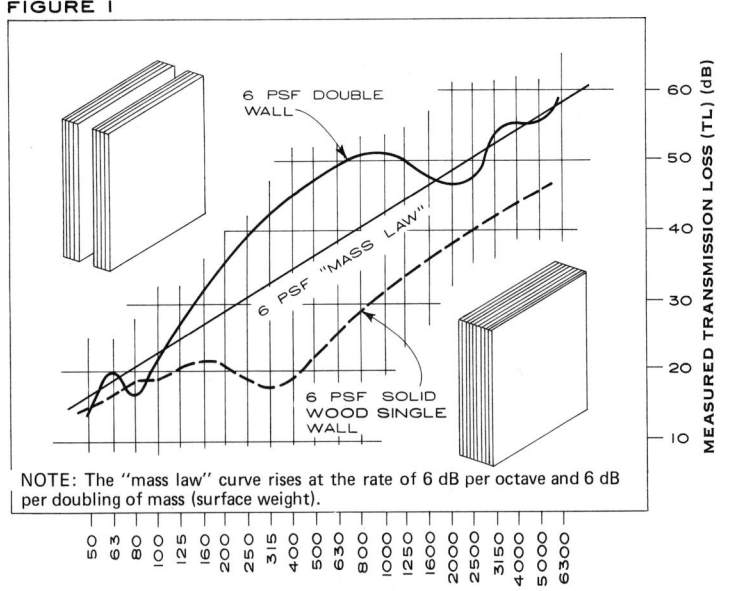

NOTE: The "mass law" curve rises at the rate of 6 dB per octave and 6 dB per doubling of mass (surface weight).

ONE-THIRD OCTAVE BAND CENTER FREQUENCY (Hz) (CPS)

EXPLANATORY NOTES AND DEFINITIONS

1. TRANSMISSION LOSS (TL): The attenuation of airborne sound transmitted through construction when tested in a laboratory according to ASTM E90-75. (Mathematically speaking, TL = SPL source − SPL receiver, where SPL is the measured sound pressure level in either the source room or the receiver room.) The measured test data, as opposed to calculations, provide the most accurate information on which to base the single number STC descriptor.

Sound transmission through walls, floors, and ceilings varies with the frequency of sound, the weight (or mass), the stiffness of the construction, and the cavity absorption. Theoretically, the transmission loss varies at the rate of 6 dB per doubling (or halving) of the surface weight of the construction. For example:

WEIGHT (PSF)	5	10	20	40	80	160
TL at 400 Hz (dB)	33	39	45	51	57	63

A single solid panel behaves less well than the "mass law" would predict, since the "mass law" assumes a homogeneous, infinitely resilient material/wall; hence a true double wall of the same weight with separate, unconnected wythes performs better than the "mass law" predicts. Note in Fig. 1 the significant improvement in TL with increased resiliency—approximately 15 dB± depending on the octave band.

The transmission loss tends to increase about 5 dB for each doubling of the airspace between wythes (minimum effective space approximately 2 in.). For example:

AIRSPACE (IN.)	3	6	12	24	48
TL at 400 Hz (dB)	40	45	50	55	60

Resilient attachment of surface "skins" to studs or structural surfaces provides similar benefit as do separate wythes. Soft, resilient, absorptive materials in the cavity between wythes, particularly for lightweight staggered stud construction, increase transmission loss significantly. "Viscoelastic" (somewhat resilient but not fully elastic) materials, such as certain insulation boards, "dampen" or restrict the vibration of rigid panels such as gypsum board and plywood and thus increase transmission loss appreciably. Installation details recommended by manufacturers should be followed.

FIGURE 2

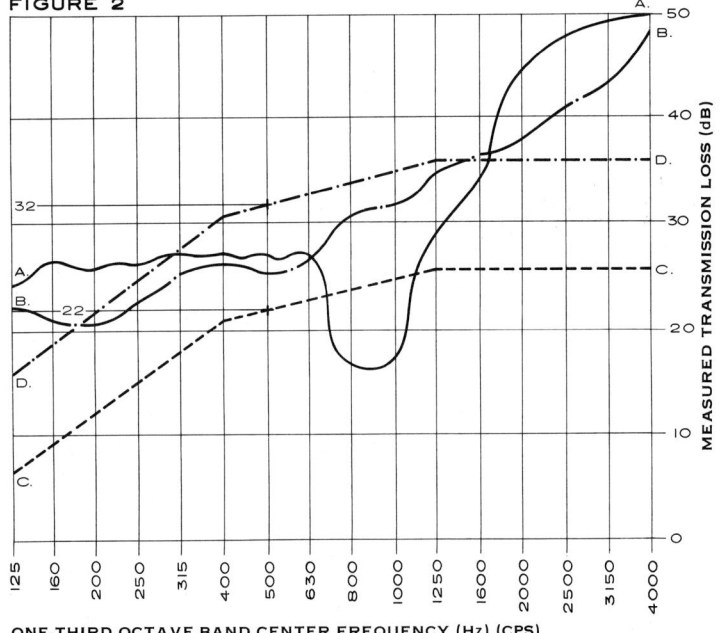

ONE-THIRD OCTAVE BAND CENTER FREQUENCY (Hz) (CPS)

——— A. Partition with 31 dB average, STC 22   ·—·—· B. Partition with 31 dB average, STC 32

- - - - C. STC 22 contour   ·—·—· D. STC 32 contour

2. NOISE REDUCTION (NR): The actual difference in sound pressure level between two spaces being considered. It is what the ear hears and what we are actually interested in, and consists of the transmission loss of the walls, floors, and ceilings as well as the sound absorption present in the receiver room being considered.

3. SOUND TRANSMISSION CLASS (STC): A single number rating system that compares the laboratory TL test curve for a particular material or assembly with a "standard contour" as described in ASTM E413-73. The contour is fitted to the test curve of the constructions allowing for a certain maximum amount of deviation. The STC rating number corresponds to the 500 Hz value for the contour appropriately fitted to the test curve. See Fig. 2 for an example that compares two constructions with identical average TL values but widely differing effectiveness (10 points).

4. SOUND TRANSMISSION CLASS CONTOUR: A three-segment curve shaped to match approximately the ear's evaluation of the importance of the sound pressure in the frequency range spanned by the segments of the curve.

The sound transmission loss at all frequencies, from 125 to 4000 Hz, is important (in varying degrees), so a single TL number or an average is meaningless. The shape of the entire TL test curve as related to the standard contour is important. Deep dips (as in curve A) are harmful, and yet the numerical average misses this dip; the STC contour properly evaluates its effect by downgrading the overall performance accordingly.

Don Klabin, AIA; Bolt, Beranek and Newman, Inc.; Cambridge, Massachusetts

1 ENVIRONMENTAL FACTORS

IMPACT NOISE DESIGN CRITERIA

In addition to "airborne" sound transmission, floors are subject to the impact or structureborne transmission of noises such as footfalls, dropped objects, and scraping furniture. Paralleling the development of laboratory Sound Transmission Class (STC) ratings for partition constructions, Impact Insulation Class (IIC) is a single number rating system developed to evaluate the effectiveness of floor construction in isolating against transmission of impact sounds to spaces below the floor. The current IIC rating method supersedes the previously used Impact Noise Rating (INR) method. To compare the ratings, note that IIC = INR + 51±. (The amount of deviation is relatively small (±2) but should be noted nonetheless.) For example, INR = +4 would be equivalent basically to IIC = 55.

As with STC tests, the IIC tests are performed in a laboratory, not under field conditions. The IIC test method is described fully in ASTM E-492-73T, Annex A-1, which was based on the European test method ISO R140 and employs an impact noise source—a tapping machine—with standardized performance characteristics. The tapping machine sound pressure levels in the source room and in the receiver room below are measured in one-third octave bands in the frequency range of 100-3150 Hz (the STC test method covers 125-4000 Hz), and the algebraic difference between the two sets of data comprise the IIC test curve. Thus the IIC rating can correctly be considered to be a transmission loss (TL) measurement. As shown by the left and right margins of the graph, ISPL (The impact sound pressure level in the receiver room) + IIC = 110, or IIC = 110 – ISPL.

Also as in the STC rating procedure, a standardized three-segment contour is fitted to the curve of the measured laboratory performance for the given construction to determine the single number rating. The three curves shown in the graph indicate the U.S. Department of Housing and Urban Development (HUD) design criteria ("A Guide to Airborne, Impact, and Structureborne Noise Control in Multifamily Dwellings," HUD-TS-24, 1974). Selection among these criteria will depend on the typical nighttime exterior background noise levels in the vicinity of the building site; the higher the background noise level outdoors (and indoors for a given perimeter bedroom), the greater the masking and thus the lower the insulation needed by the building construction. The Grade II (IIC 52) criterion is most often used.

To achieve adequate acoustical privacy in multifamily dwellings and other structures where both airborne and structureborne sound transmission is of concern, the control of impact sound transmission must be at least as good as the control of airborne sound transmission; hence, expressed in its simplest terms, IIC ≥ STC for a given construction. Again as with STC ratings, the higher the IIC number, the greater the sound control.

Note also that often the greatest annoyance caused by footfall noise is generated by low frequency sound energy, which is outside of the standardized test frequency range and is sometimes near or at the resonant frequency of the building structure.

In view of the limitations of the IIC test data, the latest model building codes specify particular construction types rather than IIC performance criteria.

In summary, think resiliency. Wherever possible, use carpet with padding on floors of residential buildings as well as resiliently suspended ceilings with cavity insulation. For especially critical situations—involving pedestrian bridges/tunnels, for example—use an acoustics consultant.

As worthwhile as the current IIC rating method is, there are some limitations that the designer should be aware of. The tapping test method is based on experience gained largely from tests of the heavy masonry floor constructions widely used in European apartment and multifamily buildings, which behave differently from the lightweight, wood joist and other floor constructions common in the United States. As a result, the IIC laboratory test tends to overrate, for example, the effectiveness of such semiresilient floor coverings as linoleum and "resilient" vinyl tile. In addition, the tapping machine test source is not an exact facsimile of a live walker. For this reason, ASTM has developed two alternate impact noise test methods using either a live walker or a modified tapping machine, both of which measure a single number TL in terms of dB(A) rather than a normalized spectrum.

Don Klabin, AIA; Bolt, Beranek and Newman, Inc.; Cambridge, Massachusetts

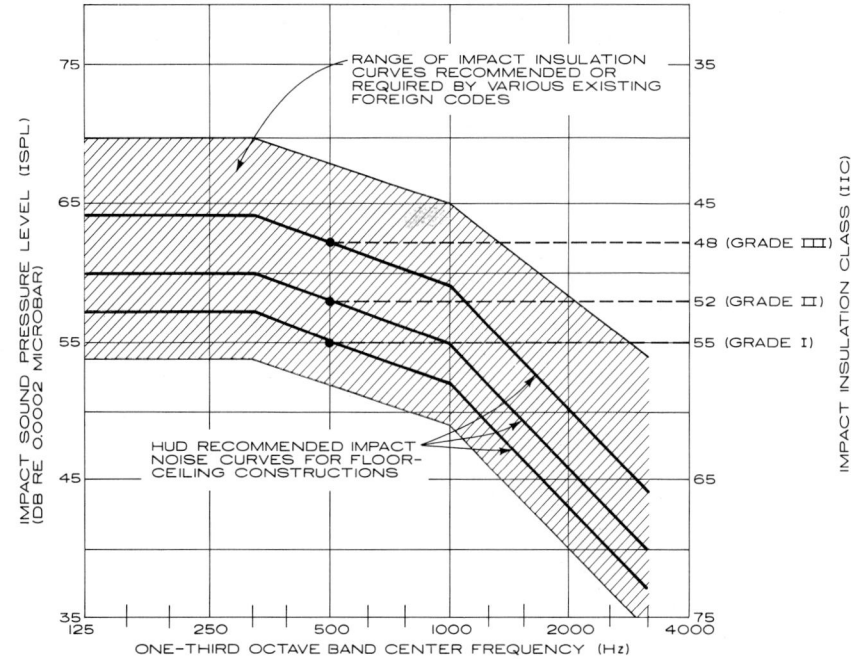

IMPACT NOISE INSULATION CRITERIA

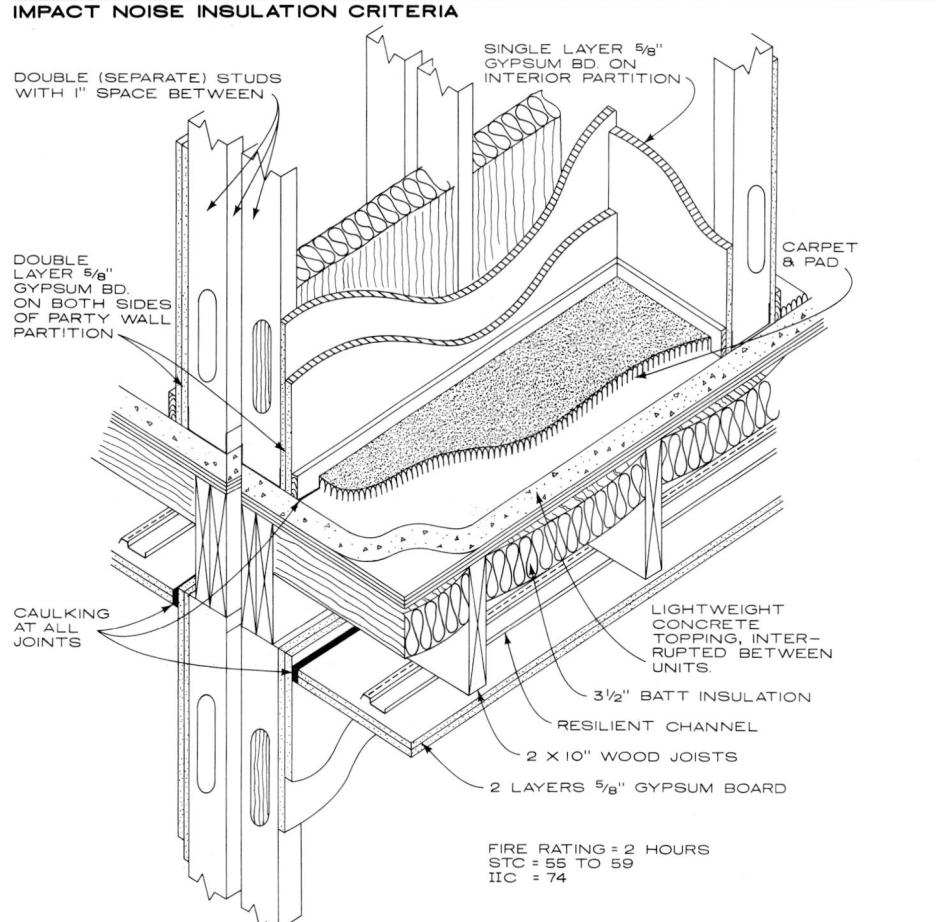

GOOD SOUND ISOLATION CONSTRUCTION

Edge attachment and junctions of walls, partitions, floors, and ceilings can cause large differences in TL performance. The transverse waves set up in continuous, stiff, lightweight walls or floors can carry sound a long distance from the source to other parts of the structure with little attenuation. Curtain walls, thin concrete floors on bar joists, and wood framed structures are particularly subject to this weakness.

Properly designed discontinuities such as interrupted floor slab/toppings are helpful in reducing structural flanking.

A resilient (airtight) joint between exterior wall and partition or partition and floor can appreciably improve TL.

Continuous pipes, conduits, or ducts can act as transmission paths from room to room. Care must be taken to isolate such services from the structure.

USE OF ABSORPTION IN COMMON OCCUPANCIES (1)

| ROOM OCCUPANCY | CEILING | | | | WALL TREATMENT (4) | SPECIAL (5) |
| | FULL | PARTIAL (2) | NRC RANGE (3) | | | |
			0.60–0.75	OVER 0.75		
Auditoriums, churches, theaters, concert halls, lecture halls, radio, recording and T.V. studios, speech and music rooms						●
Classrooms, elementary	●		●			
Classrooms, college		●	●		●	
Commercial kitchens	●			●		
Computer and business machine rooms	●			●	●	
Corridors and lobbies	●		●		●	
Gymnasiums, arenas, and recreational spaces	●			●	●	●
Health care patient rooms	●		●			
Laboratories	●		●			
Libraries	●			●		
Mechanical equipment rooms						●
Meeting and conference rooms	● Small	● Large	●		●	
Open office plan	●			●	●	●
Private offices	●		●			
Restaurants	●		●		●	
Schools and industrial shops, factories	●			●	●	●
Stores and commercial shops	●		●			

NOTES

1. This table lists conservative "rule of thumb" recommendations for the use of absorption in common occupancies.

2. The remainder of the ceiling should be treated with a hard, sound reflecting finish, such as dense (not "acoustical") plaster, solid wood, or gypsum board.

It should be assumed in the use of this table that whenever sound absorbing treatment is not recommended, a hard, sound reflecting finish should be used.

3. NOISE REDUCTION COEFFICIENT: An arithmetic average of sound absorption coefficients of the four middle frequencies (250, 500, 1000, and 2000 Hz) is called the Noise Reduction Coefficient

(NRC). The NRC is a good means of comparing the performance characteristics of similar products.

4. Wall treatment is advisable in addition to ceiling treatment for the reduction of reflections, flutter, or echo. This treatment will further reduce noise and control reverberation.

5. For highly complex applications, consult an acoustical engineer.

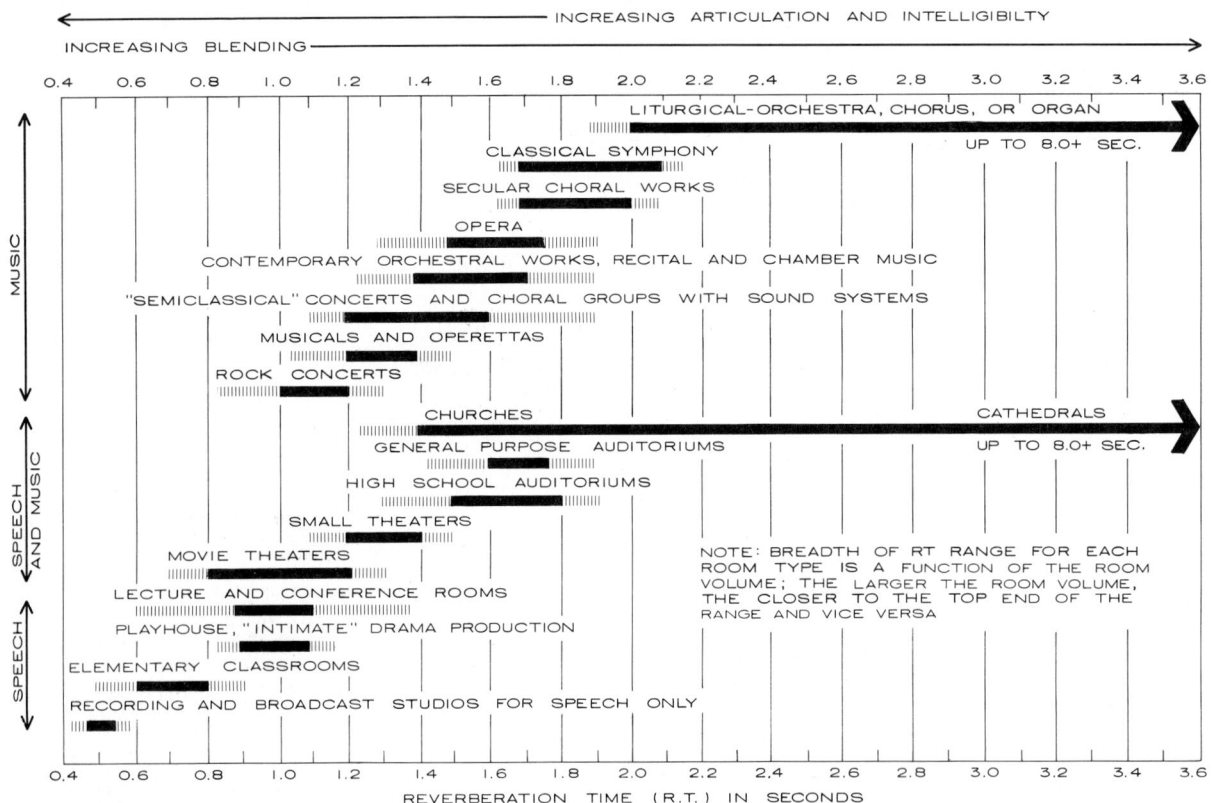

OPTIMUM REVERBERATION TIMES AT MID-FREQUENCIES (500/1000 Hz)
FOR AUDITORIUMS AND SIMILAR FACILITIES

Don Klabin, AIA; Bolt, Beranek and Newman; Cambridge, Massachusetts

1   ENVIRONMENTAL FACTORS

OPEN PLAN OFFICES

Open plan offices utilize partial height screens or space dividers to separate work stations. Since there are no full height partitions or doors to block sound transmission, lack of acoustical privacy is often a serious problem. Speech transmitted between work stations can cause annoyance and distraction to office personnel and can interfere with confidential conversations. Noise from typewriters and business machines, although usually secondary to intruding speech, can also be a source of annoyance to office workers.

Proper acoustical design of open plan offices requires an understanding of the three main factors that are discussed in the three columns below. Specific design elements and guidelines are presented on the bottom half of the page. A thorough study of all of the material is encouraged, since successful acoustical design requires consideration of all elements.

CHARACTERISTICS OF SPEECH

A person talking may use various voice levels ranging from a lowered voice to a shout. In typical open plan office situations we are concerned mainly with normal conversational voice levels. Raised voice levels create serious privacy problems. The intelligibility of speech is contained in the 5 octave frequency bands from 250 to 4000 Hz, with the most important frequency region being around 2000 Hz. Another important characteristic of speech is its directionality. Speech is louder in front of a talker than it is in back of or beside him or her.

SOUND TRANSMISSION PATHS

Sound is transmitted between work stations in open plan offices by a number of different paths: (1) direct or transmitted through screens; (2) diffracted over and around screens; (3) reflected from the ceiling or luminaire; and (4) reflected from walls, windows, and other vertical surfaces. Factors that help reduce the sound transmitted between work stations are distance, the STC rating of the screen, the size and location of the screen, the height and sound absorbing properties of the ceiling, and the location and sound absorbing properties of the vertical surfaces.

SPEECH PRIVACY

Speech privacy and freedom from the distraction of intruding speech depend on how much the intruding speech is masked by the steady background noise in the space. In rare cases, adequate masking is provided by the building ventilation system, but usually an electronic sound masking system is required. The degree of speech privacy can be defined by the articulation index (AI), which is a measure of speech intelligibility. AI can range between 0 and 1. Zero represents no intelligibility and complete privacy; 1 represents complete intelligibility and no privacy.

NORMAL PRIVACY is the degree of privacy required by most office workers. It is achieved if the office occupant is not annoyed or distracted by an intruding conversation, even though hearing and understanding some of the conversation. Normal privacy usually requires an AI of 0.20 or less. This can be achieved without difficulty in well designed open plan offices.

CONFIDENTIAL PRIVACY is required if it is important that a person's conversations not be overheard and understood in adjacent work spaces. This is achieved if the AI is 0.05 or less. Confidential privacy is difficult, though not impossible, to achieve in open plan offices. An acoustic consultant should be retained.

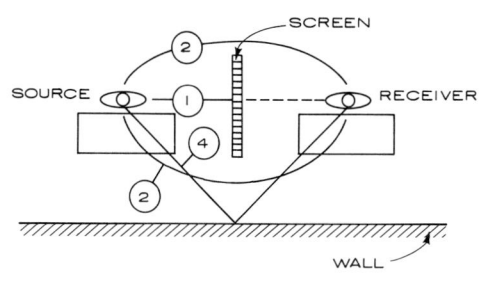

PLAN

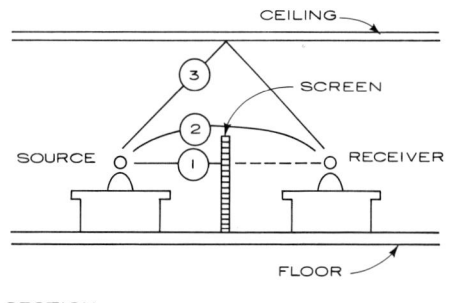

SECTION

SOUND TRANSMISSION PATHS BETWEEN TWO WORK STATIONS

OPEN PLAN GUIDELINES FOR NORMAL PRIVACY

DISTANCE	Noise reduction increases with distance from the source. Locate personnel as far apart as possible commensurate with density requirements. A minimum distance of 8 ft between personnel is desirable.	
ORIENTATION	Privacy can be improved by locating occupants back to back wherever possible in order to take advantage of directionality of the human voice.	
CEILING	Make ceilings as high as possible. Desirable minimum height is 9 ft. Ceiling material should have an NRC of at least 0.70 and a sound absorption coefficient at 2000 Hz of at least 0.90.	
LUMINAIRES	Ceiling mounted luminaires with flat lenses wider than 12 in. should be avoided. 6 in. wide units or units with parabolic louvers reflect less sound energy and are preferable.	NRC = 0.70 MIN.
SCREENS	Screens should break the line of sight between office occupants by 1 ft or more. Minimum screen height should be about 5 ft. All screens should have impervious septums and STC ratings of at least 24. Sound absorbing treatment providing an NRC of at least 0.70 is desirable on all screens.	5'-0" MIN.
FLOORS	Floors should be carpeted to reduce the noise of heel clicks, chair scraping, and other annoying noises originating at the floor. This is the major acoustical benefit of carpeting in open plan offices, and the NRC is not critical.	
SOUND MASKING	Adequate sound masking is an essential part of good open plan design. In most open plan offices an electronic sound masking system is required. The sound level, tonal characteristics, and spatial uniformity of sound masking are critical in order to provide maximum speech masking and minimum annoyance. Loudspeakers usually are located above the acoustical ceiling and produce a sound similar to a well designed ventilating system.	
VERTICAL SURFACES	Provide sound absorbing wall panels on vertical surfaces wherever possible, particularly around copy machines and other noisy equipment. The NRC of these panels should be at least 0.70. Windows can be treated with vertical acoustical blinds, or splayed to reflect sound up to the sound absorbing ceiling. Draperies are acoustically ineffective and should not be used to reduce reflected sound.	SOUND ABSORBING WALL PANELS

Parker W. Hirtle, AIA; Bolt, Beranek and Newman, Inc.; Cambridge, Massachusetts

ENVIRONMENTAL FACTORS 1

TERMS COMMONLY USED IN LIGHTING DESIGN

ENGLISH	SI	MEASURE OF
Candlepower	Candlepower	Intensity
Lumen	Lumen	Light flux
Footcandle (ft-c)	Lux	Density-lumen/ft^2 (lux/m^2)
Reflectance (R)	Reflectance	$R = \dfrac{\text{ft-c (reflected)}}{\text{ft-c (incident)}}$
Transmission (T)		$T = \dfrac{\text{ft-c (transmitted)}}{\text{ft-c (incident)}}$
Footlambert (ft-L)	Candlepower/m^2	Luminance ft-L = ft-c x R

SUBJECTIVE IMPRESSION APPEARS TO BE AFFECTED BY:

Visual clarity	Peripheral wall brightness Luminance in the center of the room Cool color light source and continuous spectrum output
Spaciousness	Peripheral lighting (not affected by color)
Relaxation	Nonuniform, peripheral (wall) lighting
Attention	Intensity of light and contrast Recommended contrast ratios: 2/1: subliminal differences 10/1: minimum for significant focal contrast 100/1: dominating contrast
Privacy, intimacy	Lighting of background and/or inanimate objects (centerpieces)
Gaiety, playfulness	Visual noise and "clutter" such as sparkle, random patterns
Somberness	Dimness and diffusion of light

SEEING

Although many of the characteristics of quality seeing conditions are known, it is a difficult area to define precisely. Research continues in an effort to uncover knowledge of how people see and what kind of lighting conditions are most desirable for every situation.

RECOGNITION OF TASKS

The human ability to recognize detail generally varies with respect to (1) contrast between the details of a task and its immediate surround, (2) luminance (or brightness) of the task, (3) size of the task, and (4) time of viewing.

Maximum visibility is attained when the luminance contrast of details against their background is greatest (e.g., black ink on white paper). Significant savings of electric energy can occur when the task contrast is maximized because the level of illumination needed is reduced. The same opportunity occurs with task size (e.g., large size type on a typewriter saves on the need for illumination). The luminance of the task depends on the amount of incident illumination and the reflectivity of the task. A small amount of light on white paper may be as effective for seeing as a large amount of illumination on dark cloth. With increased time available for viewing, illumination levels can be reduced (e.g., when speed is not critical).

VEILING REFLECTIONS

Substantial losses in contrast, hence in visibility and visual performance, can result when light is reflected from specular visual tasks (the task is "veiled"). This is perhaps the most significant factor in poor seeing conditions. Three factors govern these veiling reflections: (1) the nature of the task, (2) the observer's

Benjamin H. Evans, AIA; Blacksburg, Virginia

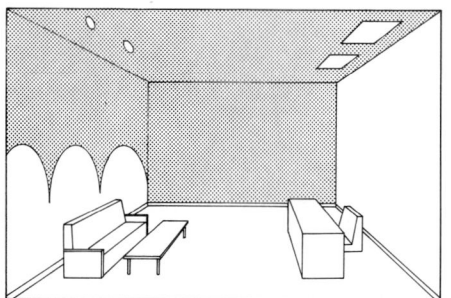

LIGHTING CAN DEFINE A CHANGE OF MOOD BETWEEN DESK AND MORE RELAXED SEATING AREA

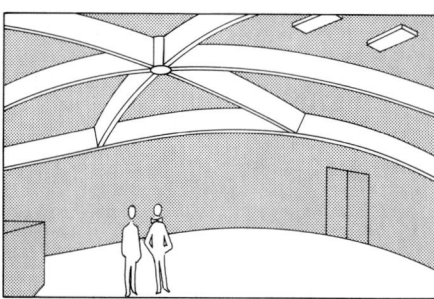

LUMINAIRE PATTERNS THAT CONFLICT WITH STRUCTURE CAN DESTROY HARMONY OF SPACE

ILLUMINATION

Proper illumination depends on the establishment of design goals that define the desired environment, rather than on the equipment needed. Lighting is the most expressive tool available for setting the tone for perception of the environment. It should be thought of as a design tool and not as an "add on" to provide light, and its consideration should be fundamental to any design effort.

Light should be considered to be what we "see by" and not that which we actually see. We do not see footcandles (the measure of quantity). We see luminance as a result of reflected or direct light. (When perceived rather than measured, it is called brightness.) The footlambert is the unit of measurement of brightness.

Of course, there must be enough light. (The unit of measure is the footcandle.) The quantities of illumination necessary for various visual tasks have been

orientation and viewing angle, and (3) the lighting system.

THE TASK

The luminance of the task (e.g., writing or printing on paper) depends on both the amount of light being reflected from it and the bright object or surface (e.g., luminaire) that may be reflected in it. Diffusing or matte papers and inks tend to reduce veiling reflections.

THE OBSERVER

If the eye is in such a position that the rays of light from the "offending zone" are reflected toward it, veiling reflections will occur. This situation can usually be observed in a space by placing a sheet of clear acetate or some other glossy surface over the task

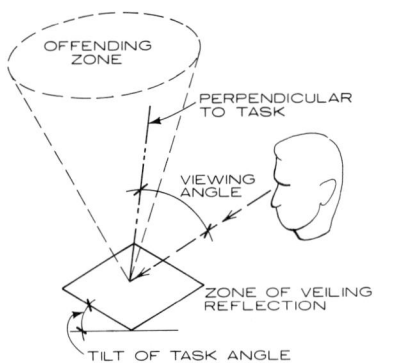

TASK LIGHTING

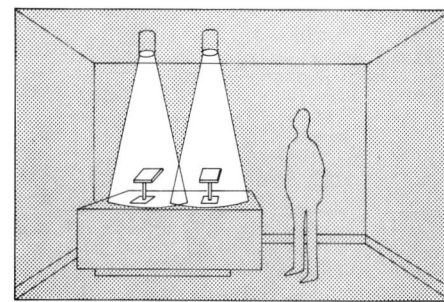

DOWNLIGHTS FOCUS ATTENTION ON OBJECT

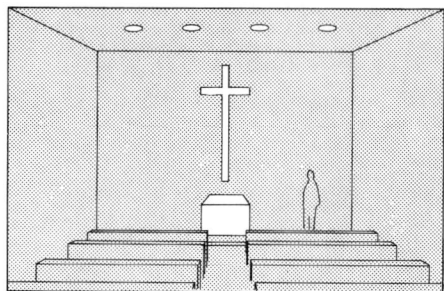

LIGHT CAN DIRECT ATTENTION TO A SPECIFIC FOCAL POINT BY A SHARP CONTRAST OF LIGHT AND DARK SURFACES

recommended by the Illuminating Engineering Society (IES) based on research. But the quantity of illumination needed on walls, floors, ceilings, and so on, for the creation of a beautiful and functional environment is very much left to the designer's logic, experience, and intuition. The proper lighting of all tasks, whether functional or esthetic, is vital to a total design, and recommended footcandle levels should be considered only as targets.

PURPOSE

Lighting can define the intended use of a space by focusing on points of attention and subduing less important areas. It can be used to express structural concepts by silhouetting beams, arches, and columns or to emphasize unusual contours. Mechanical equipment can be made to visually recede with dark paint and the absence of light. Light can help to define space use changes through brightened ceiling areas or changes of light patterns on walls.

(such as a book or paper with writing or printing) and observing the reflections (if any). Sources of light in this offending zone should be minimized for best seeing conditions.

LIGHTING SYSTEMS

The worst condition is a highly concentrated, bright source, above and forward, directed at the task. Paradoxically, it is also the condition under which the worker can most easily escape veiling reflections by tilting or reorienting the task so that the reflected rays do not reach the eye (e.g., as in turning the back so the light comes over the shoulder). Placement of lighting equipment and fenestrations in the general area above and forward of the task (or desk) should be avoided. When the nature of the tasks and their location are known, luminaires can be located to avoid the offending zone. When task locations are not known and flexibility is necessary, as for speculative office space, general low level ambient lighting, which tends to negate the effects of veiling reflections, and task lighting can be provided by plug-in units at the discretion of the tenant.

EQUIVALENT SPHERE ILLUMINATION (ESI)

ESI is a unit adopted by the IES for measuring the visibility potential of a particular task at a particular location and with a specific lighting system. It is a unit of measurement just as is the meterstick. It is not a standard of quality, but a way of taking into consideration those elements by which quality is judged. ESI cannot be measured over the area of a room as simply as raw footcandles, because ESI depends on a task, a location, an orientation, and a lighting system. A task has 50 ESI when it is as visible as it would be when illuminated by 50 ft-c of illuminance produced by a photometric sphere.

TASK AMBIENT LIGHTING

Task ambient (T/A) lighting systems have become popular because they provide higher intensity illumination on the task only and lower levels of ambient light for general circulation, thereby reducing electric energy usage. T/A systems are designed to give localized desk (or task) lighting and, usually, to project some percentage of illumination toward the ceiling for ambient (general purpose) lighting. A T/A lighting system generally requires fewer watts per square foot of floor space (as little as 1.5 W/sq ft) than does the conventional ceiling lighting system (up to 4 or 5 W/sq ft) and thus can be a significant energy saver. However, the principles of good lighting still apply, and not all T/A lighting systems provide sufficient task illumination without producing excessive ceiling reflections. Luminaires should be glarefree; the light source should not be visible from the working position. Direct glare from the normal passing position should be avoided. The downlight should illuminate the back panel of the work station as evenly as possible. A T/A system should not produce excessively bright spots of light on low ceilings and adjacent walls. Poor distribution of illumination on room surfaces can be visually disturbing to occupants.

LUMINAIRE SELECTION PARAMETERS

In selecting a luminaire that will create good seeing conditions several factors should be considered:

1. DIRECT GLARE is produced by excessive luminances in the visual field that affect the visual systems as the individual looks around the environment. It is usually associated with the luminaire zone from 45° to 90°. To minimize direct glare, the luminous intensity should be kept out of the 45° to 90° zone.

2. VISUAL COMFORT PROBABILITY (VCP) is the indicator used to evaluate the direct glare zone area of luminance. Luminaires are given a VCP rating, which indicates the percent of people who, if seated in the most undesirable location, will be expected to find the luminaire acceptable from the standpoint of direct glare (excessive luminances in the visual field).

3. Direct glare may not be a problem if all three of the following conditions are satisfied: (a) The VCP is 70 or more; (b) the ratio of maximum-to-average luminaire luminance does not exceed 5 to 1 at 45°, 55°, 65°, 75°, and 85° from nadir crosswise and lengthwise; (c) maximum luminaire luminances do not exceed:

> 2250 ft-L at 45°
> 1620 ft-L at 55°
> 1125 ft-L at 65°
> 750 ft-L at 75°
> 495 ft-L at 85°

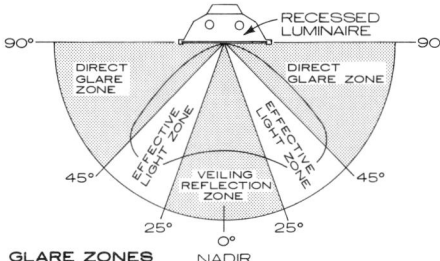

GLARE ZONES

ASHRAE STANDARD 90-75

The American Society for Heating, Refrigeration, and Air Conditioning Engineers has established a procedure for determining a "Lighting Power Budget," which has been adopted in some areas as a mechanism for determining how much electrical energy will be allowed for lighting purposes in new buildings. The lighting power budget is intended only as a mechanism for encouraging energy conservation in lighting and is not a design tool. Once the budget has been established, the designer is free to design the lighting system to achieve the best quality lighting within the budget and for the circumstances. Much can be done to conserve energy while staying within the lighting budget.

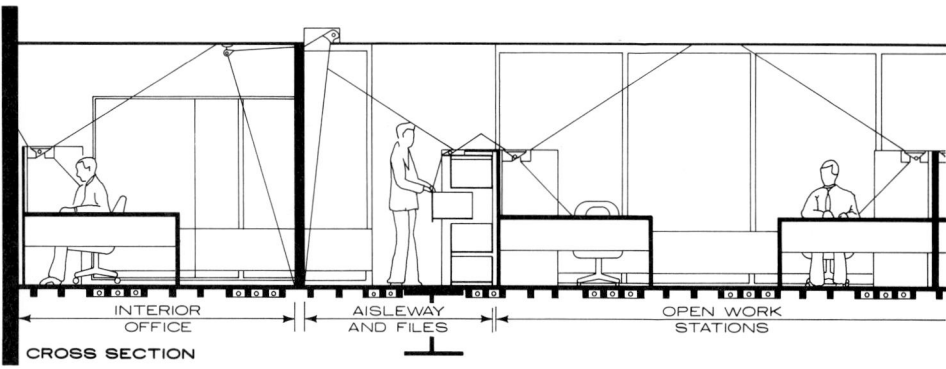

CROSS SECTION — INTERIOR OFFICE / AISLEWAY AND FILES / OPEN WORK STATIONS

SOME USEFUL FORMULAS FOR GENERAL LIGHTING DESIGN

$$\text{NUMBER OF LUMINAIRES} = \frac{\text{footcandles desired x room area}}{\text{CU x LLD x LDD x lamps/luminaire x lumens/lamps}}$$

$$\text{AVERAGE FOOTCANDLES} = \frac{\text{lumens/lamp x lamps/luminaire x CU x LLD x LDD}}{\text{area of room (sq ft)}}$$

$$\text{TOTAL ILLUMINATION (W/sq ft)} = \frac{\text{footcandles desired}}{\text{overall lumens/watt x CU x LLD x LDD}}$$

where   CU = Coefficient of Utilization
LLD = Lamp Lumen Depreciation
LDD = Luminaire Dirt Depreciation

NOTE

See manufacturer's photometric tables or the Lighting Handbook of the Illuminating Engineering Society for tables giving values of CU, LLD, LDD, lumens/lamps, and so on.

TYPICAL EXAMPLES

Room size 25 x 40 ft; ceiling height 9 ft; office area 70 ft-c; 2 x 4 ft recessed troffers with 4–40 W T12 lamps (3100 lm) each. From IES tables, Room Index = E and CU = 0.67 (plastic lens):

$$\text{NUMBER OF FIXTURES} = \frac{70 \times 25 \times 40}{0.67 \times 0.7 \times 4 \times 3100} = 8.4 \text{ (use 8 luminaires)}$$

$$\text{TOTAL ILLUMINATION (W/sq ft)} = \frac{8 \times 200 \text{ W/luminaire}}{25 \times 40} = 1.6 \text{ W/sq ft}$$

MAINTENANCE AND DEPRECIATION

All elements of the building that affect light need to be kept clean. Luminaires, diffusers, lenses, window glass, louvers, blinds, wall surfaces, and so on, tend to collect dust, which reduces their light-controlling efficiency. In the lighting formulas below a Luminaire Dirt Depreciation (LDD) factor is used to account for collected dust and dirt. The LDD figure used will depend on the type of atmosphere in the room and the frequency of cleaning. Also, lamps depreciate with time, with their effective lumen output reduced, which is accounted for in the calculations with the application of the Lamp Lumen Depreciation (LLD) factor.

IES RECOMMENDED ILLUMINATION LEVELS (ESI AT THE TASK)

5 FT-C	10 FT-C	20 FT-C	30 FT-C	50 FT-C	70 FT-C	100 FT-C	150 FT-C	200 FT-C
Exits, at floor	Restaurant	Cleaning	Classrooms	Inspection	Commercial kitchen	Garage repair	Rough drafting	Fine drafting
TV viewing	Parking garages	Hospital room	Waiting rooms	Rough factory assembly	General writing and reading	Office reading	Accounting	Engraving
Theater foyer	Hotel bath	Stairways	Restrooms	Bank lobby	Dormitory desk	Sewing	Office fine work	Color printing inspection
	General residential	Hotel bedroom	Entrance foyers	Church pulpit	Handicraft	Merchandising areas	Proofreading	Critical seeing tasks
			Laundry	Checking and sorting				
			Reading printed material					

Benjamin H. Evans, AIA; Blacksburg, Virginia

DAYLIGHTING

Ample daylight is available throughout North America for lighting interior spaces during a large portion of the working day. This light is thought by many to be psychologically desirable, and there is some evidence that it has biological benefits. Its variability through the day provides some beneficial visual exercise. Its use in place of, or in conjunction with, other light sources can conserve energy. Daylight carries with it significant quantities of heat which, in properly designed buildings, may be used to conserve energy. Daylight produces less interior heat per unit of illumination, however, than do most forms of electric light.

The principles of good lighting apply equally to daylight and electric light. The difference is in the location of the light source, its color spectrum, and its variability.

SOURCE

Daylight comes directly from the sun, from the diffuse sky and clouds, and is reflected from the ground and other surrounding objects. Direct sun penetrating into interior workspaces may cause excessive luminance contrasts. Direct sun should be controlled by proper orientation of the building, or by louvers, overhangs, shades, blinds, or other devices. Diffuse light from the sky may cause excessive luminance contrasts when viewed by eyes concentrating on an interior task. In such cases, the sky should be filtered or shielded from view or the view of the task should be oriented away from the windows. As much as half the light entering a space can be reflected from the ground.

DESIGN GUIDELINES

ROOM DEPTH

The level of illumination will be shallower in the interior than near the window. A rule of thumb is that daylighting can be effective for task illumination up to about 20 to 24 ft away from the windows, but this depends on the size and location of the windows. A window high in the fenestration wall will deliver light deeper into the interior than a low window of the same size. Venetian blinds may be used to reflect daylight against the ceiling and into more remote areas of the space while preventing the penetration of direct sunlight and view of excessively luminous areas on the exterior. The cross-sectional diagrams below show how the depth of the room affects daylight.

FINISHES

Finishes of interior surfaces are important in the control of light and luminous ratios. Light colored surfaces, diffusely reflecting, will aid in the distribution of light and reduce luminance ratios. The diagrams below show how room surfaces affect daylight from a window. The ceiling is the most effective surface for reflecting light and should be very light in color (preferably white). The floor is one of the least significant, and it is here that the designer has the greatest opportunity for use of darker colors, such as those found in carpets, although very dark colors may cause excessive luminance differences.

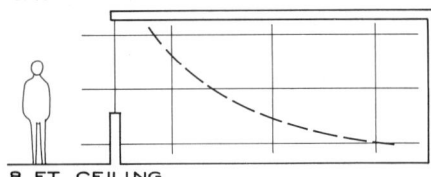

8 FT CEILING

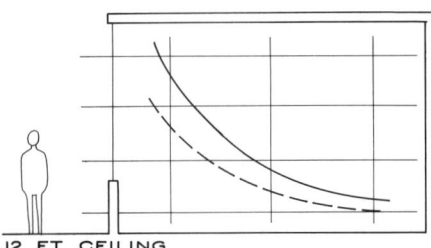

12 FT CEILING

The higher and larger the window, the more light there will be in the interior. The dashed illumination curve for the 8 ft ceiling can be compared with the solid curve for the 12 ft ceiling. Window areas below the level of the work surface are not effective in providing light on the task.

WINDOW HEIGHT

Benjamin H. Evans, AIA; Blacksburg, Virginia

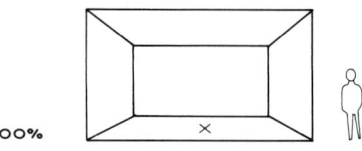

100%

All room surfaces are white, and the illumination level at point x is 100%.

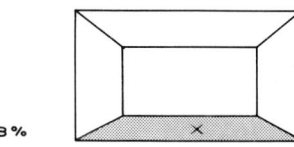

68%

With the floor painted black the illumination level is 68% of the all-white room.

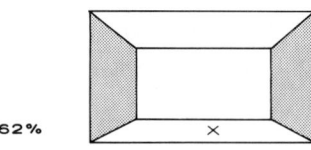

62%

With the sidewalls painted black.

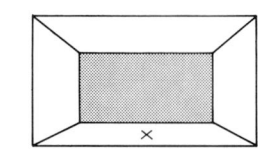

50%

The back wall has been painted black, and the illumination level at point x is only 50% of that in the all-white room.

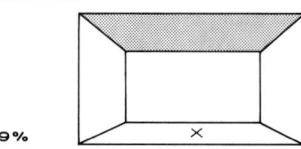

39%

With the ceiling painted black.

SURFACE FINISHES

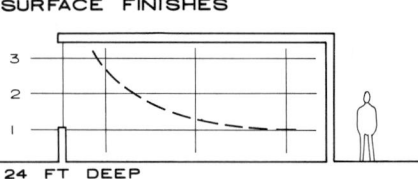

24 FT DEEP

The dashed curve indicates the illumination distribution for a typical 24 ft deep room.

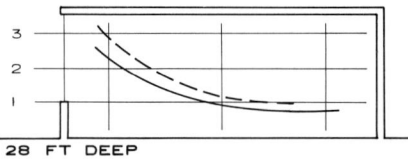

28 FT DEEP

The solid curve indicates the illumination level for a 28 ft deep room and can be compared with the dashed curve from the top diagram.

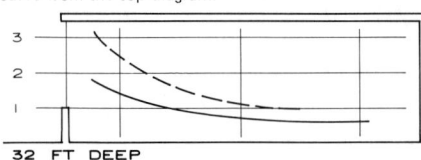

32 FT DEEP

The solid curve indicates the illumination level for a 32 ft deep room and can be compared with the dashed curve from the top diagram.

ROOM DEPTH

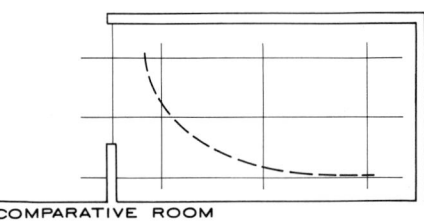

COMPARATIVE ROOM

A particular room produces a distribution of daylight as indicated by the dashed curve (repeated below).

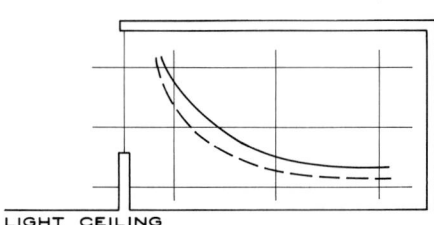

LIGHT CEILING

When the reflectivity of the ceiling is increased (painted white) the illumination level increases as indicated by the solid curve. The distribution curve flattens somewhat, since the increased ceiling reflectance increases illumination most toward the back wall.

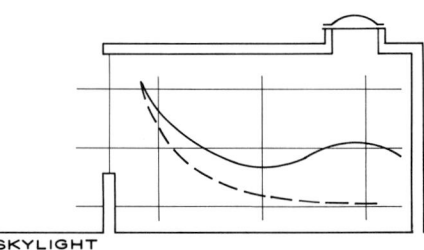

SKYLIGHT

The introduction of a skylight near the back wall increases the illumination in that area. (A clerestory, or a high window in the back wall, would produce similar results.)

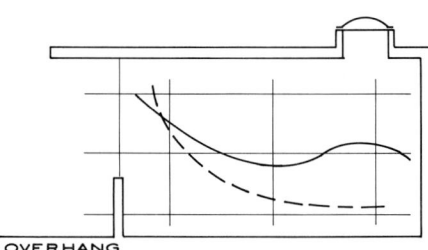

OVERHANG

An overhang can be used to reduce the illumination near the windows to a greater degree than in the back of the room. Another way to do this is with horizontal louvers on the exterior of the window wall or with interior venetian blinds.

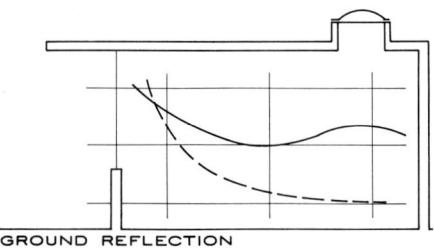

GROUND REFLECTION

Increasing the ground reflectivity (e.g., with a concrete walk) outside the window will increase the general level of interior illumination.

DAYLIGHTING METHODS

1 ENVIRONMENTAL FACTORS

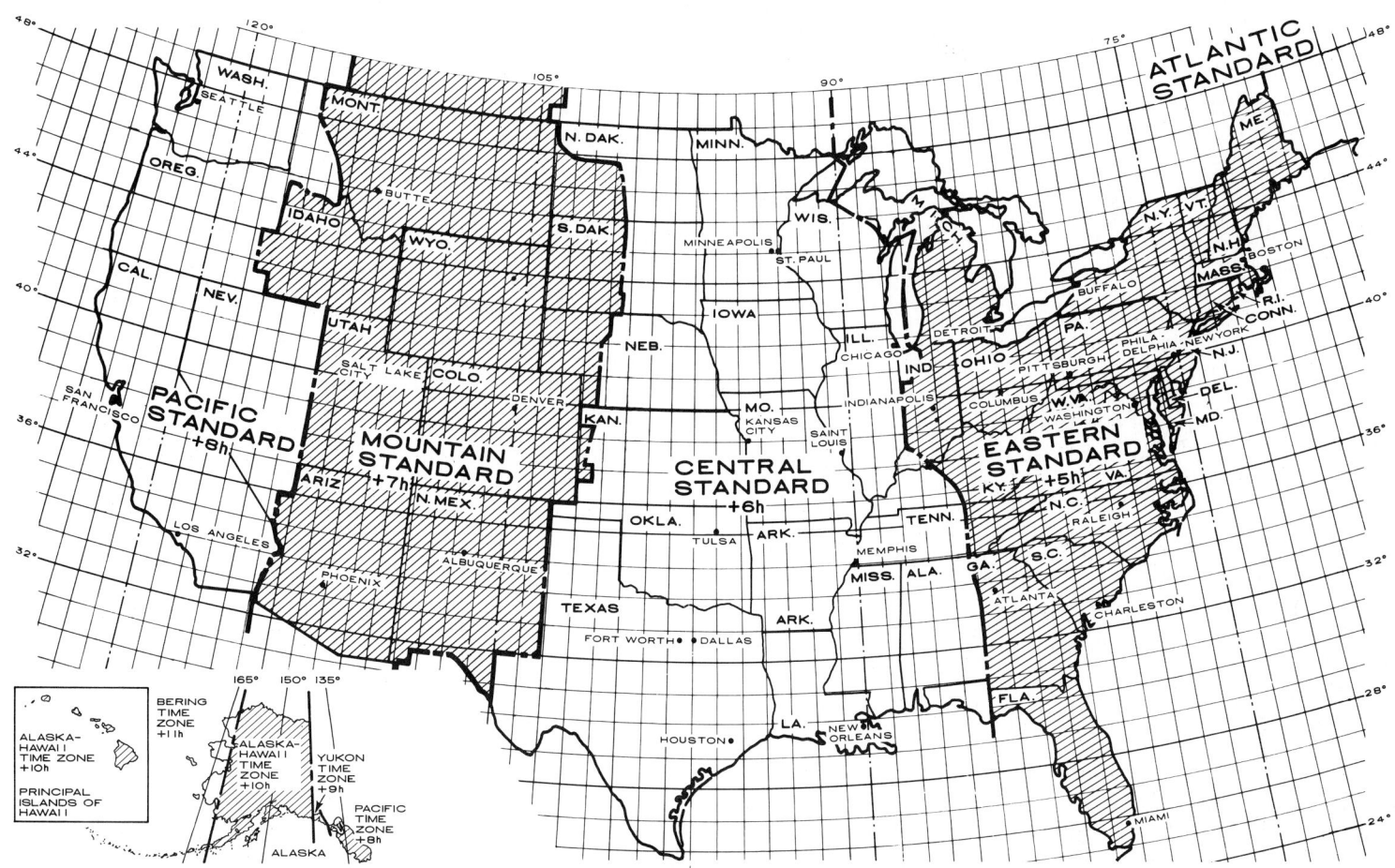

STANDARD TIME ZONES OF THE UNITED STATES
NOTE: Greenwich Standard Time is 0 h.

SOLAR TIME

Solar time generally differs from local standard or daylight saving time, and the difference can be significant, particularly when DST is in effect.

Because the sun appears to move at the rate of 360°/24 hr, its apparent motion is 4 min/1° of longitude. The procedure for finding AST (apparent solar time), explained in detail in the references cited previously, is

$$AST = LST + ET + 4(LSM - LON)$$

where ET = equation of time (min)
LSM = local standard time meridian (degrees of arc)
LON = local longitude, degrees of arc
4 = minutes of time required for 1.0° rotation of earth

The longitudes of the six standard time meridians that affect the United States are: eastern ST, 75°; central ST, 90°; mountain ST, 105°; Pacific ST, 120°; Yukon ST, 135°; Alaska-Hawaii ST, 150°.

The equation of time is the measure, in minutes, of the extent by which solar time, as told by a sundial, runs faster or slower than civil or mean time, as determined by a clock running at a uniform rate. The table below gives values of the declination and the equation of time for the 21st day of each month of a typical year (other than a leap year). This date is chosen because of its significance on four particular days: (a) the winter solstice, December 21, the year's shortest day, $\delta = -23°$ 27 min; (b) the vernal and autumnal equinoxes, March 21 and September 21, when the declination is zero and the day and night are equal in length; and (c) the summer solstice, June 21, the year's longest day, $\delta = +23°$ 27 min.

EXAMPLES

Find AST at noon, local summer time, on July 21 for Washington, D.C., longitude = 77°; and for Chicago, longitude = 87.6°.

SOLUTIONS

In summer, both Washington and Chicago use daylight saving time, and noon, local summer time, is actually 11:00 a.m., local standard time. For Washington, in the eastern time zone, the local standard time meridian is 75° east of Greenwich, and for July 21, the equation of time is -6.2 min. Thus noon, Washington summer time, is actually

$$11:00 - 6.2 \text{ min} + 4 \times (75 - 77) = 10:46 \text{ a.m.}$$

For Chicago, in the central time zone, the local standard time meridian is 90°. Chicago lies 2.4° east of that line, and noon, Chicago summer time, is

$$11:00 - 6.2 \text{ min} + 4 \times 2.4 = 11:03 \text{ a.m.}$$

The hour angle, H, for these two examples would be

for Washington: $H = 0.25 \times (12:00 - 10:46)$
$$= 0.25 \times 74 = 18.8° \text{ east}$$

for Chicago: $H = 0.25 \times (12:00 - 11:03)$
$$= 14.25° \text{ east}$$

YEAR DATE, DECLINATION, AND EQUATION OF TIME FOR THE 21ST DAY OF EACH MONTH; WITH DATA* (A, B, C) USED TO CALCULATE DIRECT NORMAL RADIATION INTENSITY AT THE EARTH'S SURFACE

MONTH	JAN.	FEB.	MAR.	APR.	MAY	JUNE	JULY	AUG.	SEPT.	OCT.	NOV.	DEC.
Day of the year†	21	52	80	111	141	173	202	233	265	294	325	355
Declination, (δ) degrees	-19.9	-10.6	0.0	+11.9	+20.3	+23.45	+20.5	+12.1	0.0	-10.7	-19.9	-23.45
Equation of time (min)	-11.2	-13.9	-7.5	+1.1	+3.3	-1.4	-6.2	-2.4	+7.5	+15.4	+13.8	+1.6
Solar noon	Late			Early		Late			Early			
A: Btuh/sq ft	390	385	376	360	350	345	344	351	365	378	387	391
B: 1/m	0.142	0.144	0.156	0.180	0.196	0.205	0.207	0.201	0.177	0.160	0.149	0.142
C: dimensionless	0.058	0.060	0.071	0.097	0.121	0.134	0.136	0.122	0.092	0.073	0.063	0.057

*A is the apparent solar irradiation at air mass zero for each month; B is the atmospheric extinction coefficient; C is the ratio of the diffuse radiation on a horizontal surface to the direct normal irradiation.
†Declinations are for the year 1964.

John I. Yellott, P.E.; College of Architecture; Arizona State University; Tempe, Arizona

DIAGRAM		A EXCLUDES DIRECT SUN RAYS	B RE-RADIATES HEAT	C CONTROLS SKY GLARE	D CONTROLS GROUND GLARE & HEAT	E EFFECTIVE ORIENTATION	F RESTRICTS VIEW	G HINDERS FREE AIR MOVEMENT	H CONTROLS WINTER RAYS	I MAINTENANCE (NOT CLEANING)
1. OVERHANG	Length of overhang calculated to eliminate summer sun.	Seasonal	No	No	No	South	No	Yes	Yes	Minimum unless otherwise noted
2. VERTICAL SCREEN (WITH OVERHANG)	Length of louver calculated to eliminate summer sun. Length of louver for sky glare dependent on amount of control desired on exterior conditions and occupants normal eye level.	Optional: Completely or seasonal.	Minimal	Yes	Some—amount varies with design.	Any direction. depends on design.	Yes—If opaque blade in louver. No—if tinted glass blade.	Slight	Depends on design	High for louver.
3. VERTICAL SCREEN (WITHOUT OVERHANG)	Length of louver or glass panel calculated to eliminate summer sun. Length of louver for sky glare dependent on amount of control desired on exterior conditions and occupants normal eye level.	Optional: Completely or seasonal.	Minimal	Yes	Some—amount varies with design.	Any direction. depends on design.	Yes—If opaque blade in louver. No—if tinted glass blade.	No—if louvers. Yes—if glass panel unless vent slats are provided.	Depends on design	Low for glazing
4. ADJUSTABLE EXTERIOR HORIZONTAL LOUVERS	Louvers can be adjusted to control direct rays of sun.	Optional	Minimal	No	Yes	Any direction. South is least restrictive to view.	Yes	No	Depends on design	Varies—depending on scale and materials used.
5A. OVERHANG VERTICALLY LOUVERED	Length of overhang calculated to eliminate summer sun.	Seasonal	No	Yes	No	South	No	No	Yes	Varies—depends on material used.
5B. OVERHANG ANGLE LOUVERED	Length of overhang and pitch of louvers calculated to eliminate summer sun and permit winter rays full penetration.	Seasonal	No	No	No	No	No	No	Yes—with louvers as shown, can permit maximum winter sun if desired.	Varies—depends on material used.
6. EXTERIOR VERTICAL LOUVERED	If fixed louvers can be set so as to eliminate low angle sun rays for predetermined orientation. If operable, maximum control any orientation but with various amount of view interference.	Optional: Completely or seasonal depending on orientation or other factors.	Minimal	Some	Some	East or west, south with adequate overhang.	Yes	No	Depends on design	Moderate
		As desired.	Minimal	Can be good see J	Some	Any	Yes	No	Yes	High
7. SPEC. GLAZING (GLASS, PLASTIC, COATED GLASS)	Heat absorbing glazing controls solar heat gain. Heat absorbing and low transmission glazing controls heat gain and sky glare. Sandwich of glass and fixed louvers can control direct sun rays and sky glare and admits greater amounts of useful daylight.	No—reduces—depending on glazing material.	Can be substantial unless double glazing used.	Yes—ideal if darker sheets used in upper portion of window.	Yes	Any	No	See K	Yes—more than others	Low
		Seasonal	Low to minimal.	Yes	Same	Any	Yes	See K	Less than 7A	Low

J. Stanley Sharp, AIA; Handren, Sharp and Associates; New York, New York

1   ENVIRONMENTAL FACTORS

J EFFECT ON INTERIOR LIGHTING	K CAUTIONS	L VARIATIONS
Harsh without ideal exterior conditions, or with no glare control in glass or interior control devices.	Tends to trap warm air. High sash if open may let heat into building.	Overhang with light & heat transmission glass. Overhang with open framing with removable material (fabric, fiber glass). Trellis with plant material—permits entry of winter sun. Fixed awning—similar characteristics, except maintenance is high. Operable awning—also similar, plus lower sun angle control (west), restricts view when down.
Good	Check clearance for operating sash and window cleaning.	Addition of vertical member may be used to cut off low angle oblique rays. Adjustable vertical blinds or awnings afford good control for low sun, or glare from beach or water, without permanent restriction of view. Maintenance is high.
Good	Check clearance for operating sash and window cleaning.	Addition of vertical member may be used to cut off low angle oblique rays. Adjustable vertical blinds or awnings afford good control for low sun, or glare from beach or water, without permanent restriction of view. Maintenance is high.
Good—could be used for darkening device.		Exterior operating shutters have similar characteristics, and can be opened when not required but with loss of sky glare control.
Diffused reflected light from louvers improves quality of daylighting by reducing contrast between interior ceiling and bright sky.		Egg crate overhang instead of louvers to control oblique sun rays. Adjustable louvered awnings (questionable in cold climates) require high maintenance.
Diffused reflected light from louvers improves quality of daylighting by reducing contrast between interior ceiling and bright sky.		Egg crate overhang instead of louvers to control oblique sun rays. Adjustable louvered awnings (questionable in cold climates) require high maintenance.
Varies depending on position in room.	Check clearance for operating sash and window cleaning.	Narrow windows with adequate side reveals or projecting blades have similar sun and glare control.
Good—if a limited view is acceptable.		When used with adequate overhang on south will eliminate all sun in summer months.
Good (see C) w/high levels of artificial light, interior visual comfort is improved as reduces contrast between work surfaces and window area. Good—combine w/7A for ideal sky glare control w/a restricting eye level view.	Open sash may defeat sun & glare control, but is appropriate for a/c buildings. Replacement delay is probable. Open sash may defeat sun & glare control, but is appropriate for a/c buildings.	Allow only storm sash to be tinted to eliminate problem noted under B. Louvered screen placed in front of glazing would control sun but restricts view, maintenance factor if movable, and sky glare control is lost.

J. Stanley Sharp, AIA; Handren, Sharp and Associates; New York, New York

GENERAL NOTES

Uncontrolled glare, generated by the sun's rays, can become uncomfortable in winter; in summer, this glare plus solar heat can be intolerable. Glare can be effectively controlled by either interior or exterior devices, but solar heat gain is best controlled by interception outside the building. Tinted glass and/or interior devices such as shades, horizontal blinds, vertical blinds, as well as various screening methods may be used to control sky glare and glare from the direct rays of the sun. However, they do little to reduce interior air temperature because the sun rays have been allowed to enter the room. Do not use any form of translucent glass where sun will fall directly on it because this will produce glare similar to the dirty windshield of a car. Objectionable glare (i.e., a brightness ratio in excess of 10:1 between peripheral vision and the immediate area of vision) can occur at any orientation, including north, through indirect sources, by reflection from various surfaces. For example, light from a slightly overcast sky or from patches of white clouds can be 30 to 300 times greater than the light reflected from a well-lighted work surface. Provisions for shielding these secondary sources are particularly important to good vision when occupants of a space must remain in relatively fixed positions.

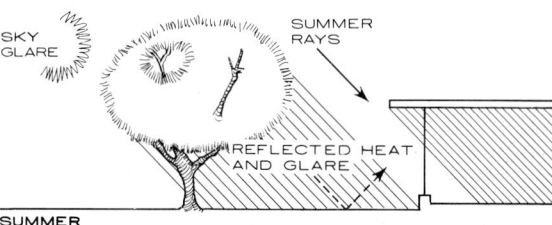

SUMMER
SUN AND GLARE AND HEAT CONTROLLED; I.E. EXCLUDED

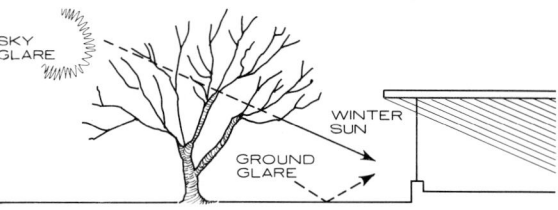

WINTER
SUN ACCEPTED-GLARE CAN BE A PROBLEM (SNOW IN PARTICULAR). CLOSELY SPACED LIMBS CAN CONTROL SKY GLARE.
SOUTH EXPOSURE

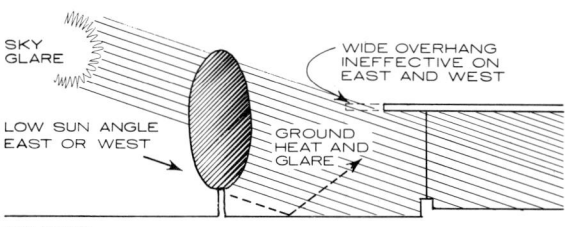

SUMMER
SUN GLARE AND HEAT CONTROLLED

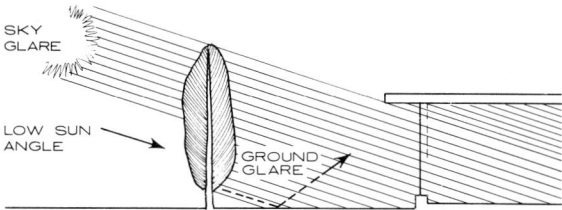

WINTER
LOW SUN ANGLE NOW ACCEPTED; GLARE CONTROLLED BY DENSE BRANCH STRUCTURE; HEAT CAN BE REASONABLY CONTROLLED AS DESIRED BY INSIDE DEVICES (SHADES, BLINDS, OR DRAPES)
EAST AND WEST EXPOSURE

APPLICATIONS IN CONJUNCTION WITH PLANTING
EXAMPLES OF HOW BASIC CONTROL DEVICES CAN BE USED IN CONJUNCTION WITH NATURAL FEATURES TO ACHIEVE GOOD SEASONAL RESULTS

NOTE

For more positive sky glare control in winter and summer, coniferous trees should be used.

SOLAR ANGLES

The position of the sun in relation to specific geographic locations, seasons, and times of day can be determined by several methods. Model measurements, by means of solar machines or shade dials, have the advantage of direct visual observations. Tabulative and calculative methods have the advantage of exactness. However, graphic projection methods are usually preferred by architects, as they are easily understood and can be correlated to both radiant energy and shading calculations.

SOLAR PATH DIAGRAMS

A practical graphic projection is the solar path diagram method. Such diagrams depict the path of the sun within the sky vault as projected onto a horizontal plane. The horizon is represented as a circle with the observation point in the center. The sun's position at any date and hour can be determined from the diagram in terms of its altitude (β) and azimuth (ϕ). (See figure on right.) The graphs are constructed in equidistant projection. The altitude angles are represented at 10° intervals by equally spaced concentric circles; they range from 0° at the outer circle (horizon) to 90° at the center point. These intervals are graduated along the south meridian. Azimuth is represented at 10° intervals by equally spaced radii; they range from 0° at the south meridian to 180° at the north meridian. These intervals are graduated along the periphery. The solar bearing will be to the east during morning hours, and to the west during afternoon hours.

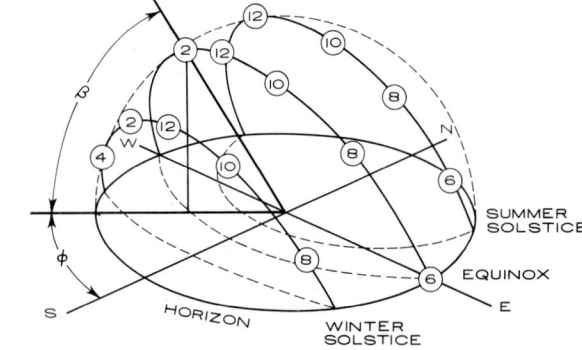

(CONTINUED NEXT PAGE)

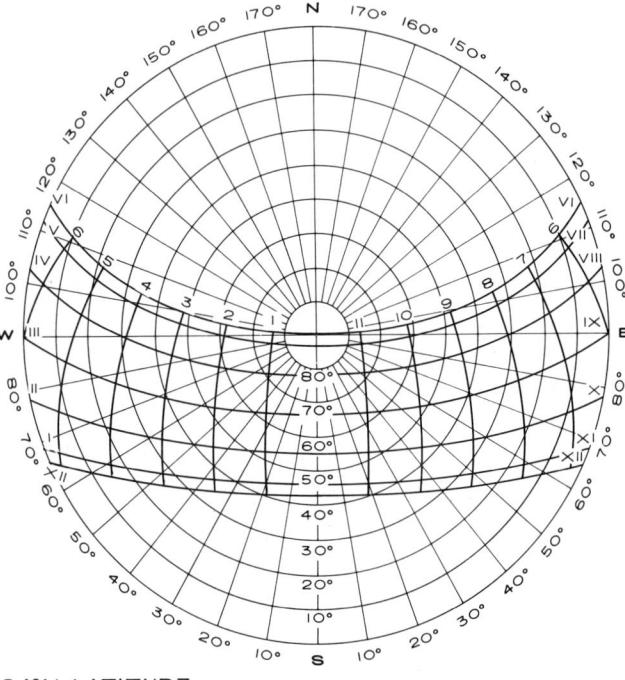

24°N LATITUDE

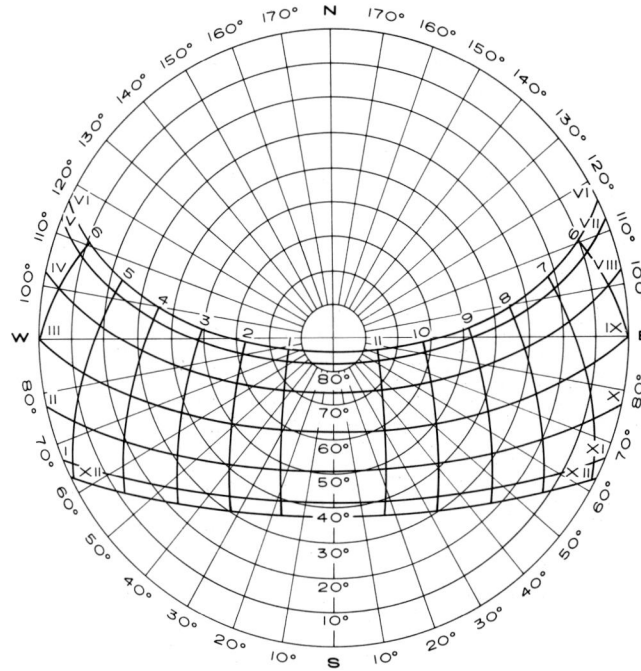

28°N LATITUDE

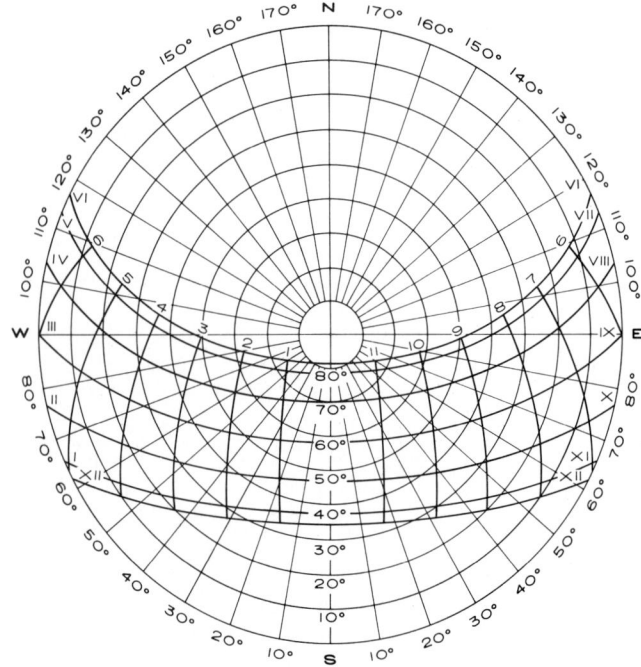

32°N LATITUDE

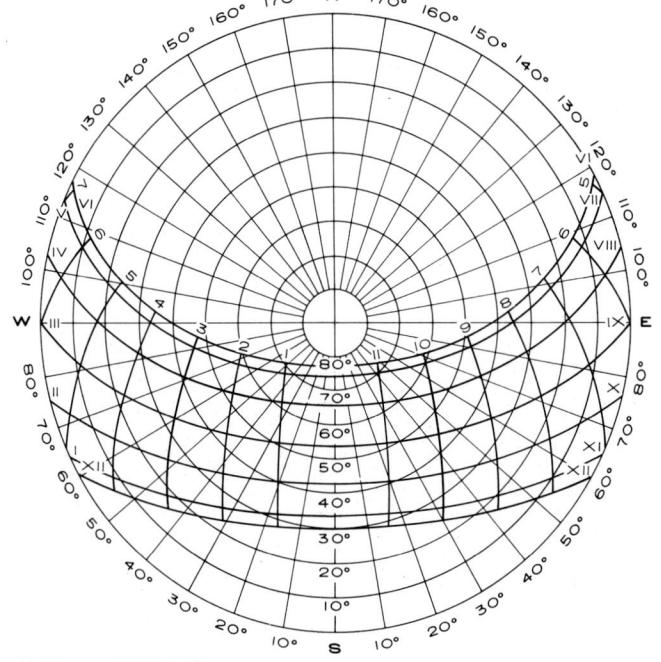

36°N LATITUDE

Victor Olgyay, AIA; Associate Professor; School of Architecture, Princeton University; Princeton, New Jersey

1 ENVIRONMENTAL FACTORS

SOLAR PATH DIAGRAMS (CONTINUED)

The earth's axis is inclined 23°27' to its orbit around the sun and rotates 15° hourly. Thus, from all points on the earth, the sun appears to move across the sky vault on various parallel circular paths with maximum declinations of ±23°27'. The declination of the sun's path changes in a cycle between the extremes of the summer solstice and winter solstice. Thus the sun follows the same path on two corresponding dates each year. Due to irregularities between the calendar year and the astronomical data, here a unified calibration is adapted. The differences, as they do not exceed 41', are negligible for architectural purposes.

DECLINATION OF THE SUN

DATE	DECLINATION	CORRESP. DATE	DECLINATION	UNIFIED CALIBR.
June 21	+23°27'			+23°27'
May 21	+20°09'	July 21	+20°31'	+20°20'
Apr. 21	+11°48'	Aug. 21	+12°12'	+12°00'
Mar. 21	+0°10'	Sep. 21	+0°47'	+0°28'
Feb. 21	−10°37'	Oct. 21	−10°38'	−10°38'
Jan. 21	−19°57'	Nov. 21	−19°53'	−19°55'
Dec. 21	−23°27'			−23°27'

The elliptical curves in the diagrams represent the horizontal projections of the sun's path. They are given on the 21st day of each month. Roman numerals designate the months. A cross grid of curves graduate the hours indicated in arabic numerals. Eight solar path diagrams are shown at 4° intervals from 24°N to 52°N latitude.

EXAMPLE

Find the sun's position in Columbus, Ohio, on February 21, 2 P.M.:

STEP 1. Locate Columbus on the map. The latitude is 40°N.

STEP 2. In the 40° sun path diagram select the February path (marked with II), and locate the 2 hr line. Where the two lines cross is the position of the sun.

STEP 3. Read the altitude on the concentric circles (32°) and the azimuth along the outer circle (35°30'W).

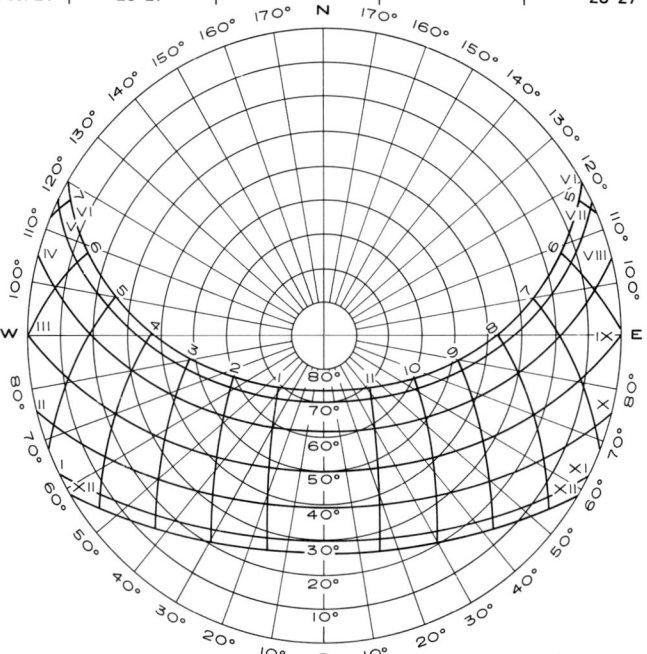

40°N LATITUDE

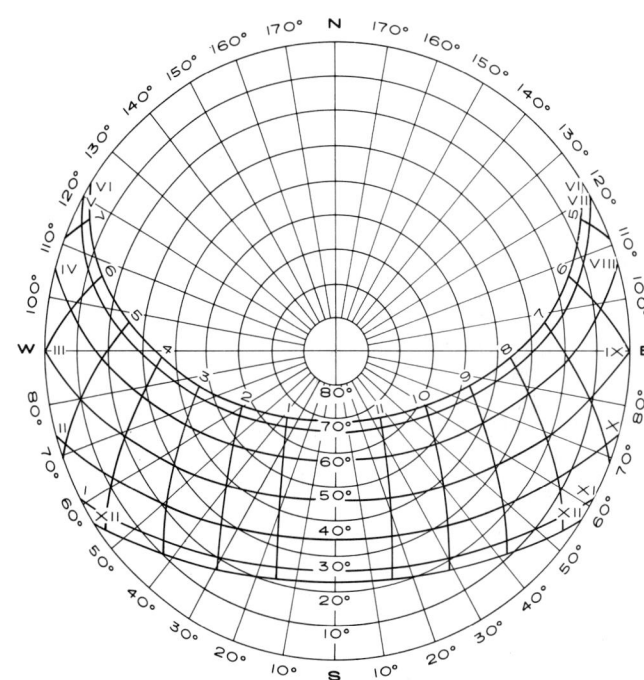

44°N LATITUDE

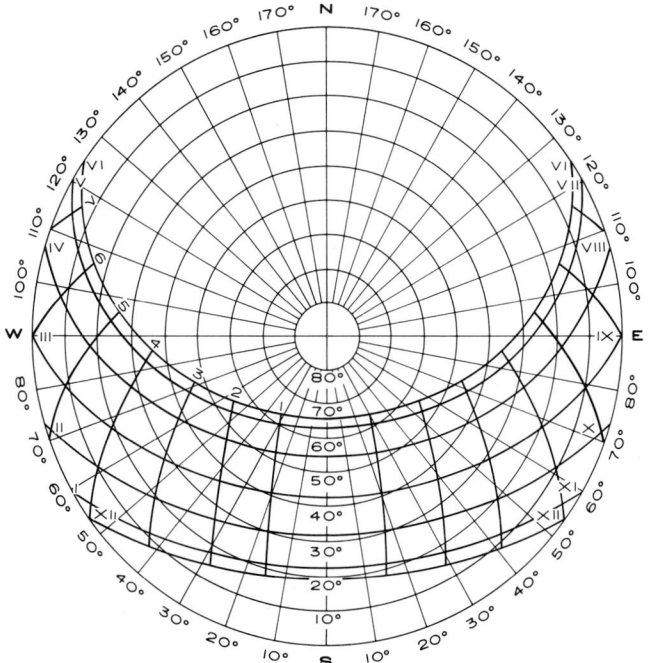

48°N LATITUDE

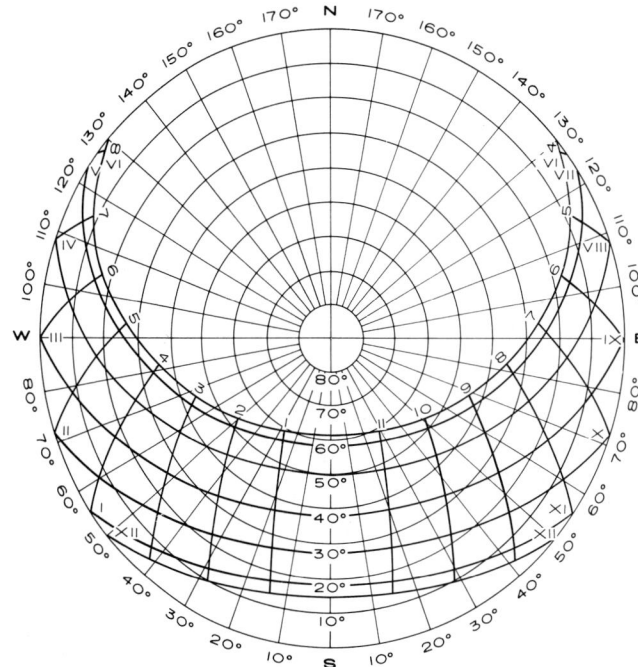

52°N LATITUDE

Victor Olgyay, AIA; Associate Professor; School of Architecture, Princeton University; Princeton, New Jersey

ENVIRONMENTAL FACTORS **1**

SHADING DEVICES

The effect of shading devices can be plotted in the same manner as the solar path was projected. The diagrams show which part of the sky vault will be obstructed by the devices and are projections of the surface covered on the sky vault as seen from an observation point at the center of the diagram. These projections also represent those parts of the sky vault from which no sunlight will reach the observation point; if the sun passes through such an area the observation point will be shaded.

SHADING MASKS

Any building element will define a characteristic form in these projection diagrams, known as "shading masks." Masks of horizontal devices (overhangs) will create a segmental pattern; vertical intercepting elements (fins) produce a radial pattern; shading devices with horizontal and vertical members (eggcrate type) will make a combinative pattern. A shading mask can be drawn for any shading device, even for very complex ones, by geometric plotting. As the shading masks are geometric projections they are independent of latitude and exposed directions, therefore they can be used in any location and at any orientation. By overlaying a shading mask in the proper orientation on the sun-path diagram, one can read off the times when the sun rays will be intercepted. Masks can be drawn for full shade (100% mask) when the observation point is at the lowest point of the surface needing shading; or for 50% shading when the observation point is placed at the halfway mark on the surface. It is customary to design a shading device in such a way that as soon as shading is needed on a surface the masking angle should exceed 50%. Solar calculations should be used to check the specific loads. Basic shading devices are shown below, with their obstruction effect on the sky vault and with their projected shading masks.

SHADING MASK PROTRACTOR

The half of the protractor showing segmental lines is used to plot lines parallel and normal to the observed vertical surface. The half showing bearing and altitude lines is used to plot shading masks of vertical fins or any other obstruction objects. The protractor is in the same projection and scale as the sun-path diagrams (see pages on solar angles); therefore it is useful to transfer the protractor to a transparent overlay to read the obstruction effect.

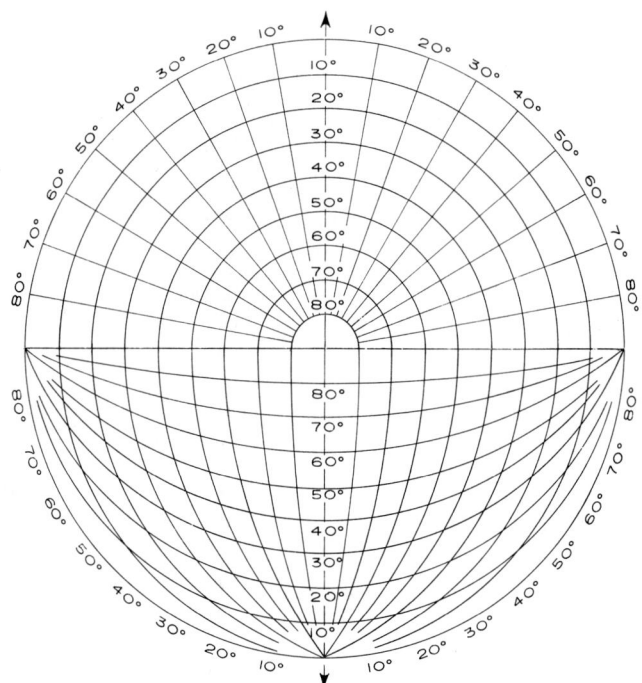

SHADING MASK PROTRACTOR

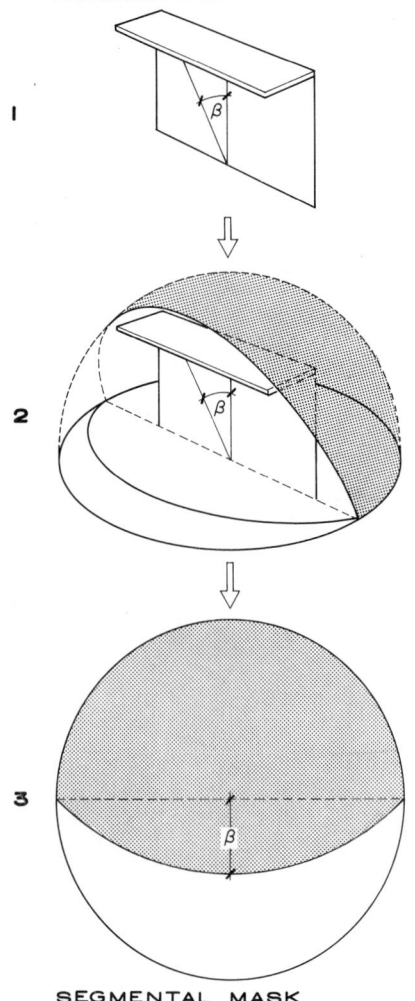

HORIZONTAL

1

2

3

SEGMENTAL MASK

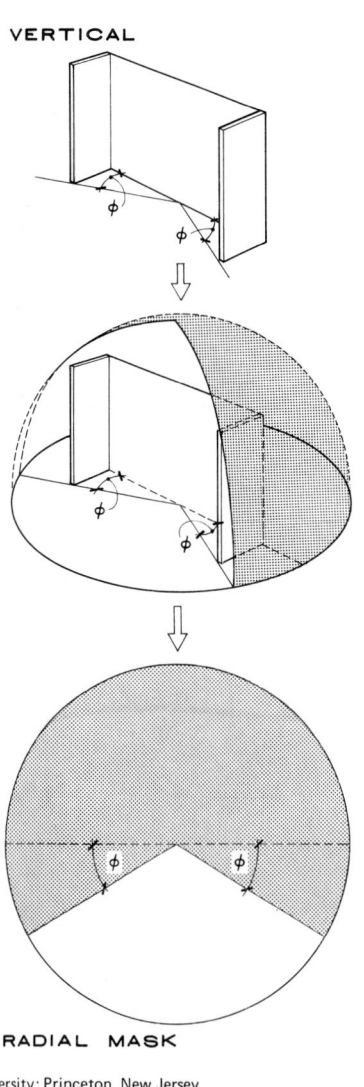

VERTICAL

RADIAL MASK

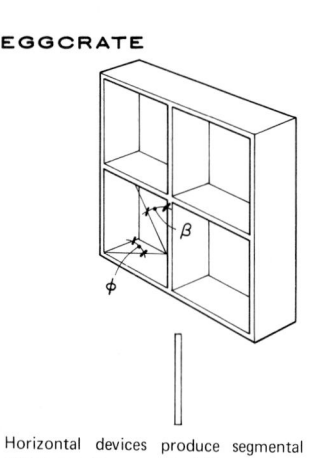

EGGCRATE

Horizontal devices produce segmental obstruction patterns, vertical fins produce radial patterns, and eggcrate devices produce combination patterns.

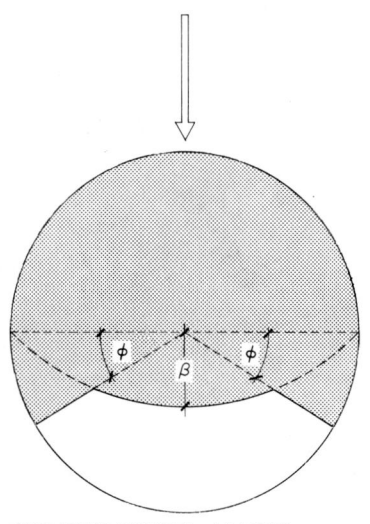

COMBINATION MASK

Victor Olgyay, AIA; Associate Professor; School of Architecture, Princeton University; Princeton, New Jersey

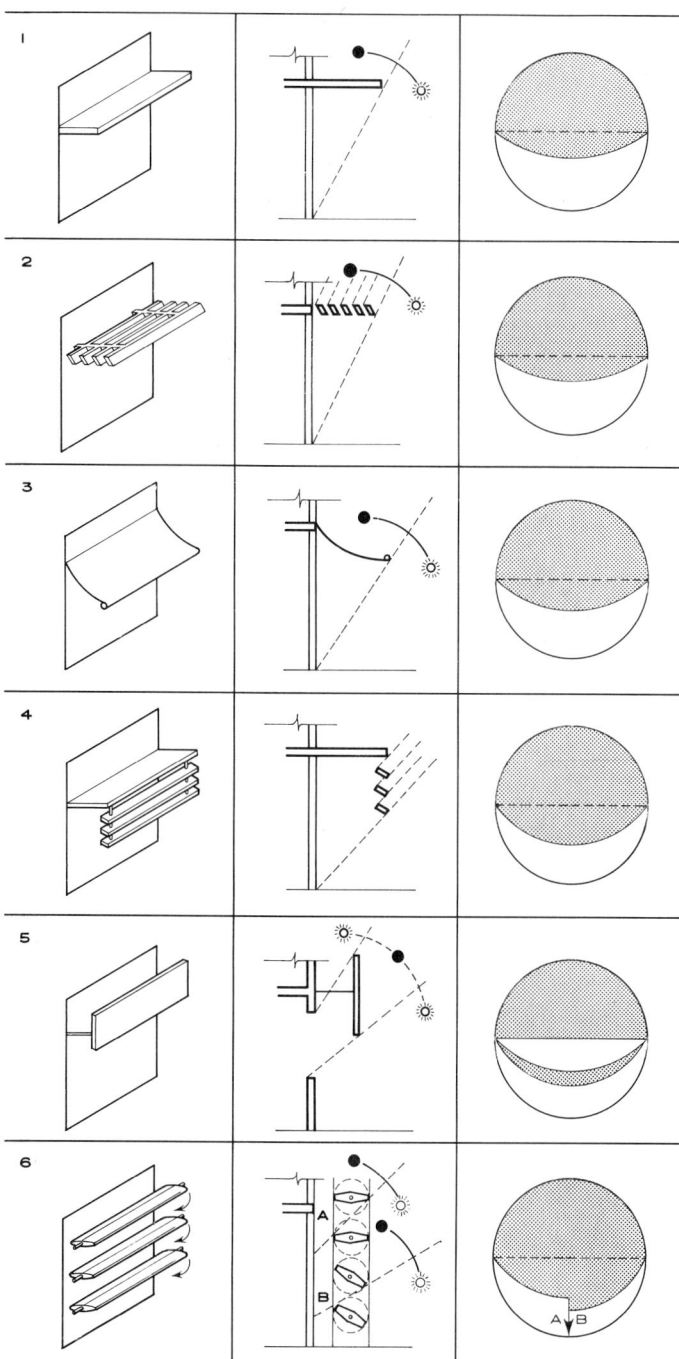

EXAMPLES OF VARIOUS TYPES OF SHADING DEVICES

The illustrations show a number of basic types of devices, classified as horizontal, vertical, and eggcrate types. The dash lines shown in the section diagram in each case indicate the sun angle at the time of 100% shading. The shading mask for each device is also shown, the extent of 100% shading being indicated by the gray area.

General rules can be deduced for the types of shading devices to be used for different orientations. Southerly orientations call for shading devices with segmental mask characteristics, and horizontal devices work in these directions efficiently. For easterly and westerly orientations vertical devices serve well, having radial shading masks. If slanted, they should incline toward the north, to give more protection from the southern positions of the sun. The eggcrate type of shading device works well on walls facing southeast, and is particularly effective for southwest orientations. Because of this type's high shading ratio and low winter head admission; its best use is in hot climate regions. For north walls, fixed vertical devices are recommended; however, their use is needed only for large glass surfaces, or in hot regions. At low latitudes on both south and north exposures eggcrate devices work efficiently.

Whether the shading devices be fixed or movable, the same recommendations apply in respect to the different orientations. The movable types can be most efficiently utilized where the sun's altitude and bearing angles change rapidly: on the east, southeast, and especially, because of the afternoon heat, on the southwest and west.

Victor Olgyay, AIA; Associate Professor; School of Architecture, Princeton University; Princeton, New Jersey

HORIZONTAL TYPES 1. Horizontal overhangs are most efficient toward south, or around southern orientations. Their mask characteristics are segmental. 2. Louvers parallel to wall have the advantage of permitting air circulation near the elevation. Slanted louvers will have the same characteristics as solid overhangs, and can be made retractable. 4. When protection is needed for low sun angles, louvers hung from solid horizontal overhangs are efficient. 5. A solid, or perforated screen strip parallel to wall cuts out the lower rays of the sun. 6. Movable horizontal louvers change their segmental mask characteristics according to their positioning.

VERTICAL TYPES 7. Vertical fins serve well toward the near east and near west orientations. Their mask characteristics are radial. 8. Vertical fins oblique to wall will result in asymmetrical mask. Separation from wall will prevent heat transmission. 9. Movable fins can shade the whole wall, or open up in different directions according to the sun's position.

EGGCRATE TYPES 10. Eggcrate types are combinations of horizontal and vertical types, and their masks are superimposed diagrams of the two masks. 11. Solid eggcrate with slanting vertical fins results in asymmetrical mask. 12. Eggcrate device with movable horizontal elements shows flexible mask characteristics. Because of their high shading ratio, eggcrates are efficient in hot climates.

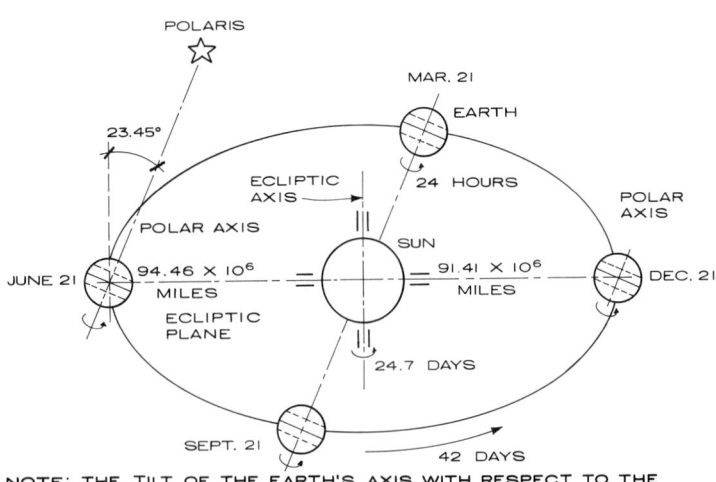

NOTE: THE TILT OF THE EARTH'S AXIS WITH RESPECT TO THE ECLIPTIC AXIS CAUSES THE CHANGING SEASONS AND THE ANNUAL VARIATIONS IN NUMBER OF HOURS OF DAYLIGHT AND DARKNESS.

ANNUAL MOTION OF THE EARTH ABOUT THE SUN

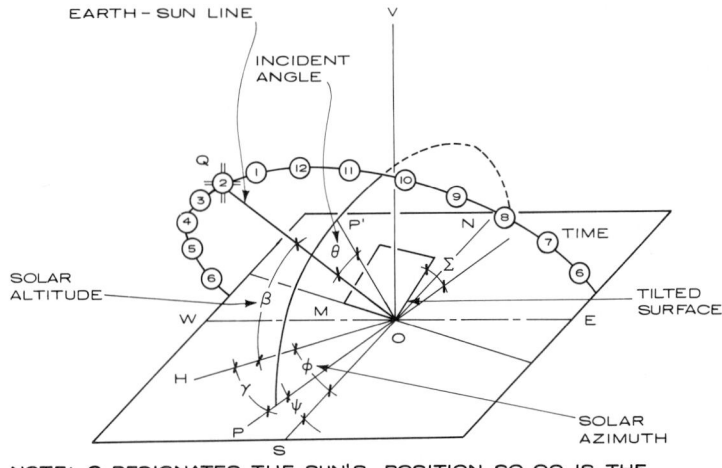

NOTE: Q DESIGNATES THE SUN'S POSITION SO OQ IS THE EARTH – SUN LINE WHILE OP' IS THE NORMAL TO THE TILTED SURFACE AND OP IS PERPENDICULAR TO THE INTERSECTION, OM, BETWEEN THE TILTED SURFACE AND THE HORIZONTAL PLANE.

SOLAR ANGLES WITH RESPECT TO A TILTED SURFACE

SOLAR CONSTANT

The sun is located at one focus of the earth's orbit, and we are only 147.2 million km (91.4 million miles) away from the sun in late December and early January, while the earth-sun distance on July 1 is about 152.0 million km (94.4 million miles).

Solar energy approaches the earth as electromagnetic radiation at wavelengths between 0.25 and 5.0 μm. The intensity of the incoming solar irradiance on a surface normal to the sun's rays beyond the earth's atmosphere, at the average earth-sun distance, is designated as the solar constant, I_{sc}. Although the value of I_{sc} has not yet been precisely determined by verified measurements made in outer space, the most widely used value is 429.2 Btu/sq ft · hr (1353 W/sq m) and the current ASHRAE values are based on this estimate. More recent measurements made at extremely high altitudes indicate that I_{sc} is probably close to 436.6 Btu/sq ft · hr (1377 W/sq m). The unit of radiation that is widely used by meteorologists is the langley, equivalent to one kilogram calorie/square centimeter. To convert from langleys/day to Btu/sq ft · day, multiply Ly/day by 369. To convert from W/sq m to Btu/sq ft · hr, multiply the electrical unit by 0.3172.

SOLAR ANGLES

At the earth's surface the amount of solar radiation received and the resulting atmospheric temperature vary widely, primarily because of the daily rotation of the earth and the fact that the rotational axis is tilted at an angle of 23.45° with respect to the orbital plane. This tilt causes the changing seasons with their varying lengths of daylight and darkness. The angle between the earth-sun line and the orbital plane, called the solar declination, d, varies throughout the year, as shown in the following table for the 21st day of each month.

JAN −19.9° APR +11.9° JUL +20.5° OCT −10.7°
FEB −10.6° MAY +20.3° AUG +12.1° NOV −19.9°
MAR   0.0°   JUN +23.5° SEP   0.0°   DEC −23.5°

Very minor changes in the declination occur from year to year, and when more precise values are needed the almanac for the year in question should be consulted.

The earth's annual orbit about the sun is slightly elliptical, and so the earth-sun distance is slightly greater in summer than in winter. The time required for each annual orbit is actually 365.242 days rather than the 365 days shown by the calendar, and this is corrected by adding a 29th day to February for each year (except century years) that is evenly divisible by 4.

To an observer standing on a particular spot on the earth's surface, with a specified longitude, LON, and latitude, L, it is the sun that appears to move around the earth in a regular daily pattern. Actually it is the earth's rotation that causes the sun's apparent motion. The position of the sun can be defined in terms of its altitude β above the horizon (angle HOQ) and its azimuth ϕ, measured as angle HOS in the horizontal plane.

At solar noon, the sun is, by definition, exactly on the meridian that contains the south-north line, and consequently the solar azimuth ϕ is 0.0°. The noon altitude β is:

$$= 90° - L + \delta$$

Because the earth's daily rotation and its annual orbit around the sun are regular and predictable, the solar altitude and azimuth may be readily calculated for any desired time of day as soon as the latitude, longitude, and date (declination) are specified.

SHADOW CONSTRUCTION WITH TRUE SUN ANGLES

Required information: angle of orientation in relation to north-south axis (C), azimuth ϕ, and altitude angle β of the sun at the desired time (Figure 1).

STEP 1.   Lay out building axis, true south and azimuth ϕ of sun in plan (Figure 2).

STEP 2.   Lay out altitude β upon azimuth ϕ. Construct any perpendicular to ϕ. From the intersection of this perpendicular and ϕ project a line perpendicular to elevation plane (building orientation). Measure distance x along this line from elevation plane. Connect the point at distance x from elevation plane to center to construct sun elevation β (Figure 2).

STEP 3.   Use sun plan $\phi + C$ and sun elevation β to construct shadows in plan and elevation in conventional way (Figure 3).

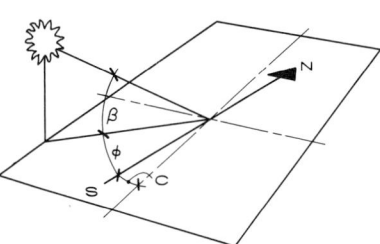

FIGURE 1

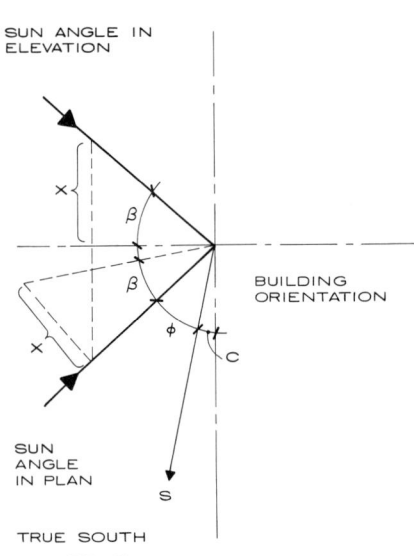

SUN ANGLE IN ELEVATION

BUILDING ORIENTATION

SUN ANGLE IN PLAN

TRUE SOUTH

FIGURE 2

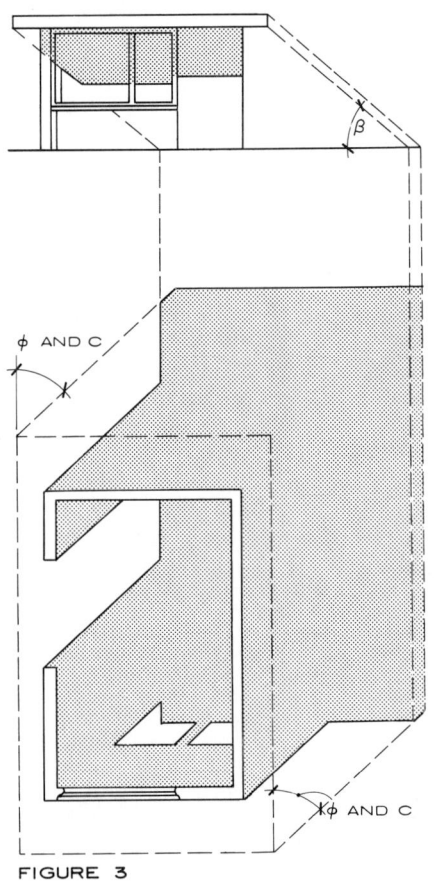

FIGURE 3

John I. Yellot, P.E.; College of Architecture; Arizona State University; Tempe, Arizona

1   ENVIRONMENTAL FACTORS

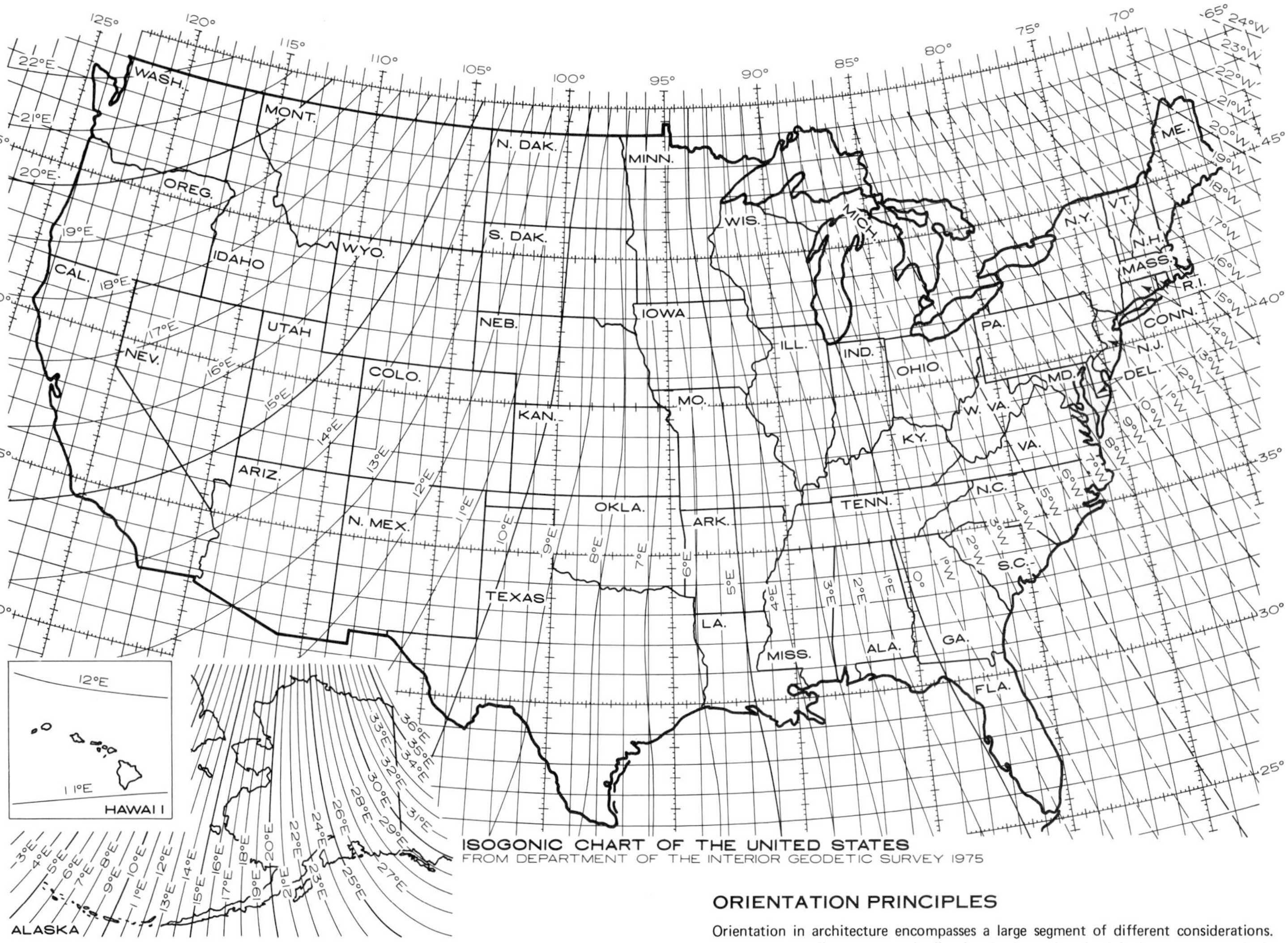

ISOGONIC CHART OF THE UNITED STATES
FROM DEPARTMENT OF THE INTERIOR GEODETIC SURVEY 1975

COMPASS ORIENTATION

The above map is the isogonic chart of the United States. The wavy lines from top to bottom show the compass variations from the true north. At the lines marked E the compass will point east of true north; at those marked W the compass will point west of true north. According to the location, correction should be done from the compass north to find the true north.

EXAMPLE: On a site in Wichita, Kansas, find the true north.

STEP 1.   Find the compass orientation on the site.

STEP 2.   Locate Wichita on the map. The nearest compass variation is the 10°E line.

STEP 3.   Adjust the orientation correction to true north.
The graphical example illustrates a building which lies 25° east with its axis from the compass orientation.

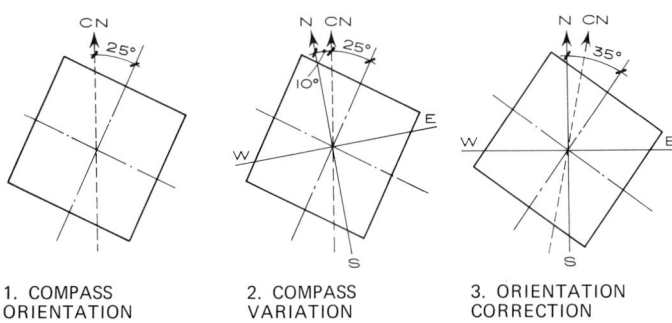

1. COMPASS ORIENTATION   2. COMPASS VARIATION   3. ORIENTATION CORRECTION

ORIENTATION PRINCIPLES

Orientation in architecture encompasses a large segment of different considerations. The expression "total orientation" refers both to the physiological and psychological aspects of the problem.

At the physiological side the factors which affect our senses and have to be taken into consideration are: the thermal impacts—the sun, wind, and temperature effects acting through our skin envelope; the visible impacts—the different illumination and brightness levels affecting our visual senses; the sonic aspects—the noise impacts and noise levels of the surroundings influencing our hearing organs. In addition, our respiratory organs are affected by the smoke, smell, and dust of the environs.

On the psychological side, the view and the privacy are aspects in orientation which quite often override the physical considerations.

Above all, as a building is only a mosaic unit in the pattern of a town organization, the spatial effects, the social intimacy, and its relation to the urban representative directions—aesthetic, political, or social—all play a part in positioning a building.

THERMAL FORCES INFLUENCING ORIENTATION

The climatic factors such as wind, solar radiation, and air temperature play the most eminent role in orientation. The position of a structure in northern latitudes, where the air temperature is generally cool, should be oriented to receive the maximum amount of sunshine without wind exposure. In southerly latitudes, however, the opposite will be desirable; the building should be turned on its axis to avoid the sun's unwanted radiation and to face the cooling breezes instead.

At right the figure shows these regional requirements diagrammatically.

Adaptation for wind orientation is not of great importance in low buildings, where the use of windbreaks and the arrangement of openings in the high and low pressure areas can help to ameliorate the airflow situation. However, for high buildings, where the surrounding terrain has little effect on the upper stories, careful consideration has to be given to wind orientation.

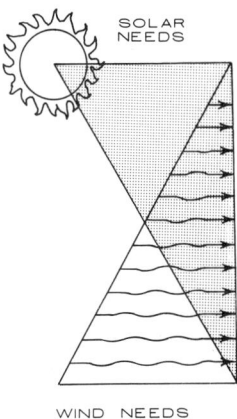

SOLAR NEEDS

WIND NEEDS

Victor Olgyay, AIA; Associate Professor; School of Architecture, Princeton University; Princeton, New Jersey

ENVIRONMENTAL FACTORS 1

NOTES

To visualize the thermal impacts on differently exposed surfaces four locations are shown approximately at the 24°, 32°, 40° and 44° latitudes. The forces are indicated on average clear winter and summer days. The air temperature variation is indicated by the outside concentric circles. Each additional line represents a 2°F difference from the lowest daily temperature. The direction of the impact is indicated according to the sun's direction as temperatures occur. (Note the low temperatures at the east side, and the high ones in westerly directions.)

The total (direct and diffuse) radiation impact on the various sides of the building is indicated with arrows. Each arrow represents 250 Btu/sq ft · day radiation. At the bottom of the page the radiations are expressed in numerical values.

The values show that in the upper latitudes the south side of a building receives nearly twice as much radiation in winter as in summer. This effect is even more pronounced at the lower latitudes, where the ratio is about one to four. Also, in the upper latitudes, the east and west sides receive about 2½ times more radiation in summer than in winter. This ratio is not as large in the lower latitudes; but it is noteworthy that in summer these sides receive two to three times as much radiation as the south elevation. In the summer the west exposure is more disadvantageous than the east exposure, as the afternoon high temperatures combine with the radiation effects. In all latitudes the north side receives only a small amount of radiation, and this comes mainly in the summer. In the low latitudes, in the summer, the north side receives nearly twice the impact of the south side. The amount of radiation received on a horizontal roof surface exceeds all other sides.

Experimental observations were conducted on the thermal behavior of building orientation at Princeton University's Architectural Laboratory. Below are shown the summer results of structures exposed to the cardinal directions. Note the unequal heat distribution and high heat impact of the west exposure compared to the east orientation. The southern direction gives a pleasantly low heat volume, slightly higher, however, than the north exposure.

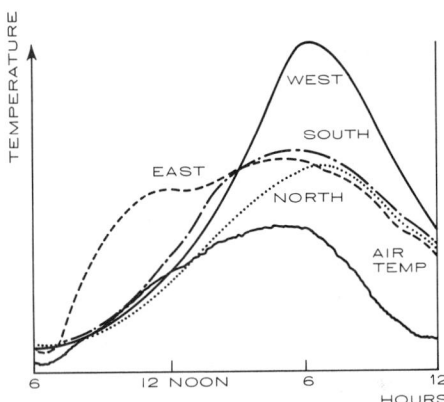

ROOM TEMPERATURE IN DIFFERENTLY ORIENTED HOUSES

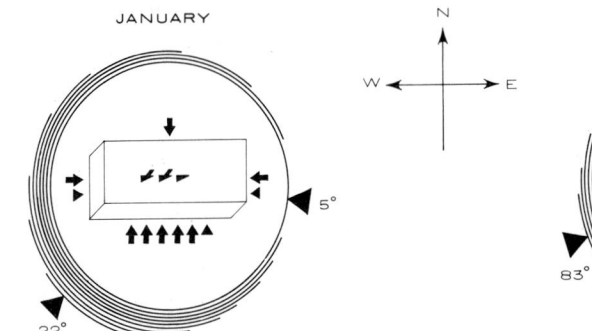

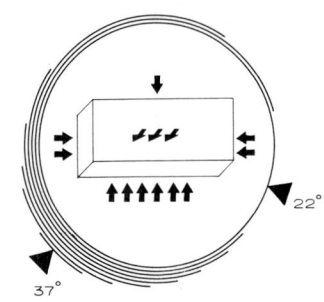

MINNEAPOLIS, MINN.

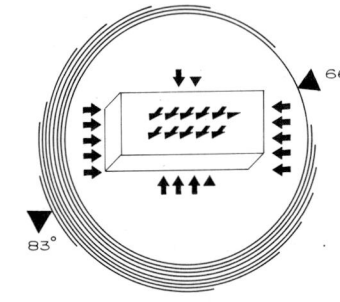

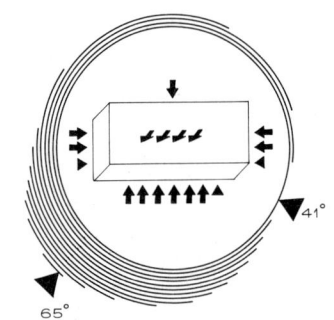

NEW YORK AREA

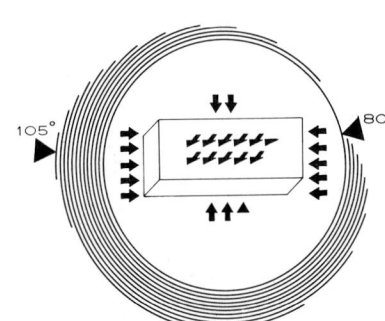

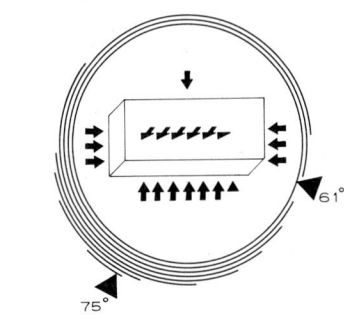

PHOENIX, ARIZ.

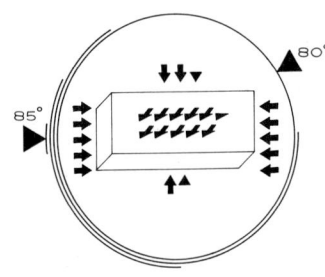

MIAMI, FLA.

ORIENTATION: CONCLUSIONS

1. The optimum orientation will lie near the south; however, will differ in the various regions, and will depend on the daily temperature distribution.
2. In all regions an orientation eastward from south gives a better yearly performance and a more equal daily heat distribution. Westerly directions perform more poorly with unbalanced heat impacts.
3. The thermal orientation exposure has to be correlated with the local wind directions.

Victor Olgyay, AIA; Associate Professor; School of Architecture, Princeton University; Princeton, New Jersey

TOTAL DIRECT AND DIFFUSED RADIATION (BTU/SQ FT · DAY)

LATITUDE	SEASON	EAST	SOUTH	WEST	NORTH	HORIZONTAL
44° LATITUDE	WINTER	416	1374	416	83	654
	SUMMER	1314	979	1314	432	2536
40° LATITUDE	WINTER	517	1489	517	119	787
	SUMMER	1277	839	1277	430	2619
32° LATITUDE	WINTER	620	1606	620	140	954
	SUMMER	1207	563	1207	452	2596
24° LATITUDE	WINTER	734	1620	734	152	1414
	SUMMER	1193	344	1193	616	2568

1 ENVIRONMENTAL FACTORS

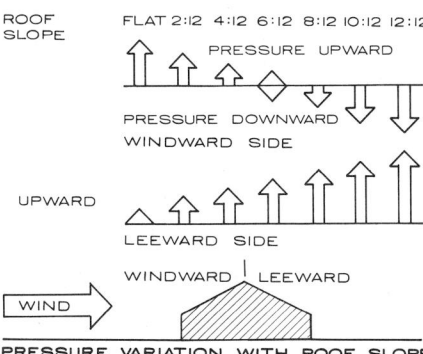

PRESSURE VARIATION WITH ROOF SLOPE

Wind resistant construction requires that roof, wall, floor, and foundation structures be tied together, thus acting in unison to withstand the wind forces acting on the entire structure.

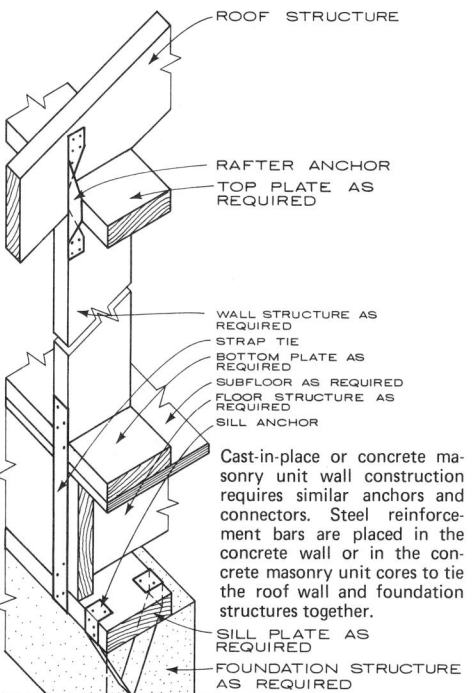

Cast-in-place or concrete masonry unit wall construction requires similar anchors and connectors. Steel reinforcement bars are placed in the concrete wall or in the concrete masonry unit cores to tie the roof wall and foundation structures together.

WIND RESISTANT CONSTRUCTION

MINIMUM DESIGN WIND LOADS

HEIGHT ZONE	HORIZONTAL LOADS		HEIGHT ZONE	HORIZONTAL LOADS
SOUTHERN STD. BLDG. CODE			UNIFORM CODE	
FT	LB/SQ FT		FT	LB/SQ FT
	INLAND REGION	COASTAL REGION		
0–30	10	25	0–60	15
31–50	20	35	60 up	20
51–99	24	45		
100–199	28	50		
200–299	30	50		
300–399	32	50		
Over 400	40	50		

Coastal region is the area lying within 125 miles of the coast.

MINIMUM WIND LOADS ON PITCHED, OR GABLE, ROOFS

1. For roof slopes less than 30°; design to withstand loads acting outward normal to the surface equal to 1¼ times the horizontal loads specified for the corresponding height zone in which the roof is located.

2. For roof slopes greater than 30°; design to withstand loads acting inward normal to the surface equal to those specified for zone, with load applied to windward slope.

Douglas R. Coonley, CHI Housing, Inc.; Hanover, New Hampshire

Protection is provided on the leeward side of hills and in valleys oriented away from prevailing wind directions. Vegetation and trees serve to filter or deflect wind, thus reducing wind loads. Man-made structures provide similar protection to natural forms. However, built structures are usually more angular than trees or hills, causing less predictable and more turbulent airflow.

Proper site planning can substantially increase energy output from wind collector systems. Windward hill crests, open fields, high points of land, valleys oriented in line with prevailing winds, and edges of open bodies of water provide favorable wind collector locations. Increased height above ground level usually gives smoother and faster airflow because of reduced ground interference. Built structures can retard the performance of wind systems if they obstruct the free flow of air. Careful planning, measurement, and expert consultation are necessary to ensure proper design with wind. On-site data collection and analysis are often required to realize a successful and integrated wind design.

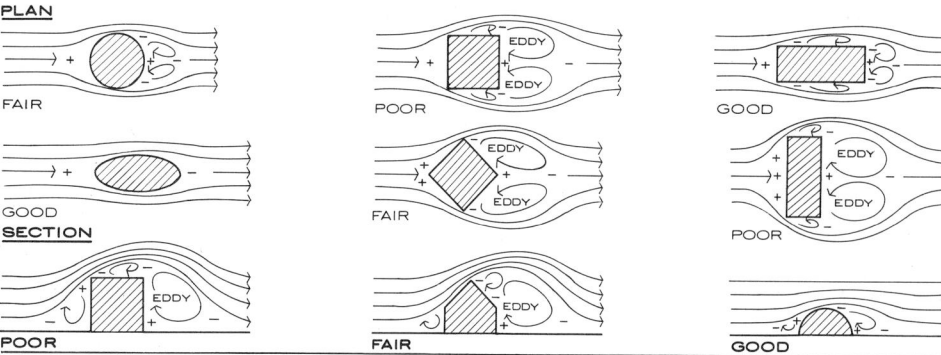

BUILDING SHAPE, ORIENTATION, AND AIRFLOW

Passive wind systems use wind directly without discrete conversion, storage, or distribution systems. Windows, vents, louvers, and roof vents are examples of passive wind systems. Active wind systems use wind indirectly to produce mechanical or electrical energy.

An active wind system includes collector, converter, orientation device, support, storage, distribution, and control. The collector intercepts the wind and drives a converter which changes the collector's motion into a more usable energy form (such as electricity). Generators, gear trains, mechanical linkages, and pumps are examples of converters. An orientation device keeps the wind collector pointed in the proper direction. Tail vanes, gear drives, and collectors are examples of orientation devices. Vertical axis collectors usually do not require an orientation device because of their multi-directional character. The collector system is held aloft by a support structure which may be a tower, post, guy wire, or building (such as a Dutch windmill). A distribution system transmits the energy to places where it is to be used through electric lines, mechanical linkages, or water lines. Energy storage may be provided by batteries, fuel cells, water tanks, or reservoirs. A control system monitors and coordinates these components to provide proper operation and performance of the wind collector system.

Energy output from active collectors depends on wind velocity, collector type, and distribution system. Consult local wind data and wind system distributors for specific information. Active wind systems require shutdown during extreme wind conditions (usually in winds above 40 mph), and usually do not produce energy in winds below 5 mph. The useful working range varies with different wind collector systems and must be coordinated with site conditions to achieve proper performance.

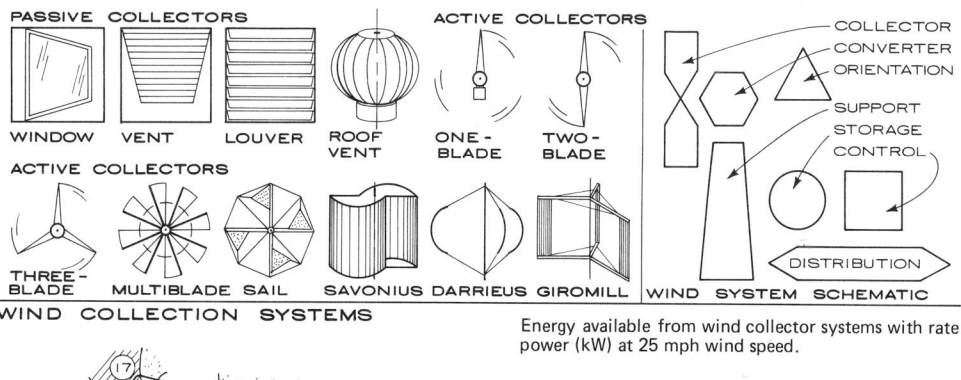

WIND COLLECTION SYSTEMS

Energy available from wind collector systems with rate power (kW) at 25 mph wind speed.

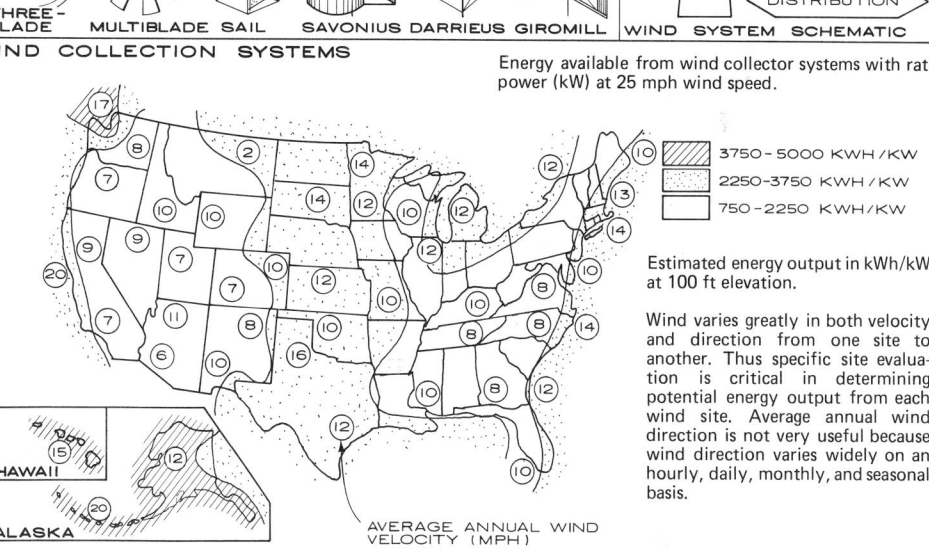

- ▨ 3750 – 5000 KWH/KW
- ░ 2250 – 3750 KWH/KW
- ☐ 750 – 2250 KWH/KW

Estimated energy output in kWh/kW at 100 ft elevation.

Wind varies greatly in both velocity and direction from one site to another. Thus specific site evaluation is critical in determining potential energy output from each wind site. Average annual wind direction is not very useful because wind direction varies widely on an hourly, daily, monthly, and seasonal basis.

AVERAGE ANNUAL WIND VELOCITY (MPH)

ANNUAL AVERAGE WIND VELOCITY AND AVAILABLE ENERGY IN U.S.A.

ENVIRONMENTAL FACTORS **1**

THERMAL COMFORT

Human thermal comfort is determined by the body's ability to dissipate the heat and moisture that are produced continuously by metabolic action. The rate of heat production varies with the size, age, sex, and degree of activity of the individuals whose comfort is under consideration. For men of average size, seated and doing light work, the metabolic rate is about 450 Btu/hr; for women under similar circumstances the comparable rate is about 385 Btu/hr. For a 155 lb man seated and doing moderate to heavy work, the rate ranges from 650 to 800 Btu/hr; standing and walking about while doing moderately heavy work will raise the rate to 1000 Btu/hr while the hardest sustained work will result in a metabolic rate of 2000 to 2400 Btu/hr. For an office with the usual complement of men and women, an average metabolic rate will range from 400 to 450 Btu/hr per person.

Thermal comfort is attained when the environment surrounding the individual can remove the bodily heat and moisture at the rate at which they are being produced. The removal, accomplished by convection, evaporation, and radiation, is regulated by the dry bulb temperature, the vapor pressure, and rate of movement of the air and the mean radiant temperature (MRT) of the surrounding surfaces. MRT is defined by ASHRAE as the temperature of an imaginary black enclosure in which the individual experiences the same rate of radiant heat exchange as in the actual environment. (See 1977 ASHRAE Handbook of Fundamentals, Chapter 8, for more information on MRT and human comfort.)

Heat and moisture removal are also strongly affected by the nature and amount of clothing being worn and by its insulating value. This quality can be evaluated in terms of a thermal resistance unit designated by clo, where 1 clo = 0.88°F/(Btu/hr · sq ft). Typical masculine office attire, complete with warm jacket and light trousers, has an insulating value of 1.12 clo while a woman's office dress is rated at 0.73 clo. Values for other combinations are given in the ASHRAE reference cited above, page 8.7, Tables 1-C and 1-D. Uncomfortably low ambient air temperatures can be made tolerable by putting on more and heavier clothing, thus increasing the clo value; the converse, unfortunately, is not true.

The properties of atmospheric air-water vapor mixtures in the temperature range normally experienced by the human body can be shown effectively on psychrometric charts, which can take many different forms. The most familiar is that put forth by Willis H. Carrier, who is generally regarded as the originator of the air-conditioning industry in the U.S.A. On the Carrier-type chart, shown in modified form in Fig. 1, the humidity ratio of moist air, in pounds or grains (1 lb = 7000 grains) of water vapor per pound of dry air, is plotted against the dry bulb temperature of the air. Significant psychrometric data are given in the table at temperature intervals of 5°F from 50 to 90°F.

The relative humidity of moist air is the ratio, expressed as a percentage, of the amount of water vapor actually present in a given quantity of that air to the amount that the same quantity of air could contain if it were completely saturated at the same temperature and pressure. The uppermost curved line on the chart, called the saturation line, denotes 100% relative humidity. The wet bulb temperature, measured by a thermometer with a water wetted sensor over which the air-vapor

mixture is flowing rapidly (800 to 900 fpm) is used in combination with the dry bulb temperature to find the % RH at conditions other than saturation. For example, at 75°F dry bulb and 60°F wet bulb the relative humidity is seen to be 40%.

The humidity ratio at this condition is 53 grains/lb of dry air while the dew point temperature, found by following the horizontal line of constant humidity ratio to its intersection with the saturation line, is 50°F.

The relatively restricted range of conditions within which most lightly clothed sedentary adults in the U.S.A. will experience thermal comfort is shown by the cross-hatched area on Fig. 1. Known as the ASHRAE comfort zone (also called "comfort envelope"), this area on the psychrometric chart represents the combinations of dry bulb temperature and relative humidity, which, when combined with an air movement of 45 fpm or less, will meet the thermal needs of most adults. For this chart, MRT = dry bulb temperature.

The effective temperature lines shown on Fig. 1 represent combinations of dry bulb temperature and relative humidity that will produce the same rate of heat and moisture dissipation by radiation, convection, and evaporation as an individual would experience in a black enclosure at the specified temperature and 50% relative humidity. As the % RH rises, the dry bulb temperature must be slightly reduced to produce the same feeling of comfort; as the % RH falls toward the 10 to 20% level experienced in desert climates, the dry bulb temperature may rise slightly without inducing discomfort.

The 65°F indoor temperature mandated by federal regulations for winter operation of public buildings is seen to be well below the normal comfort zone. Addition of clothing (higher clo values) may help to offset the discomfort that most occupants will experience at 65°F, regardless of the % RH, but extremities (fingers and toes) will be uncomfortably cold.

The upper range of the comfort zone is close to the 78°F effective temperature line, and so the 78°F dry bulb temperature that is mandated for summer operation of public buildings will be tolerable for most lightly clothed adults until the relative humidity rises above 60 to 65%. At that condition, discomfort will be experienced by many building occupants because of their inability to dissipate metabolic moisture. Increases in air velocity are beneficial under these conditions, but velocities above about 70 fpm will generally result in unpleasant working conditions because of drafts, blowing papers, and so on.

Figure 2 shows another version of the psychrometric chart in which wet bulb temperatures are plotted against dry bulb temperatures, with straight lines of constant % RH running upward from lower left to upper right. The effect of air velocity and clothing thermal resistance (expressed as clo units) is shown by the curved lines near the center of each diagram.

For these conditions, in which the mean radiant temperature equals the dry bulb temperature, relative humidity has only a small effect. As the activity level of the room occupants is lowered, reducing the metabolic rate, the comfortable air temperature range moves upward; as the activity level is increased, cooler air is required.

The effects of radiant energy transfer between individuals and the surfaces surrounding them can have significant influence on sensations of comfort or discomfort. An increase of 1°F in MRT is approximately equivalent to a 1.5°F increase in ambient air temperature. The use of radiant heating from moderately warm surfaces can help to offset the discomfort caused by air temperatures that are significantly below the ASHRAE comfort zone. Conversely, discomfort can be caused by large heated areas, such as sun warmed windows. An excessively high MRT can require a significant reduction in air temperature to create comfort. For an individual exposed to direct sunshine entering through an unshaded window, discomfort is almost certain to result.

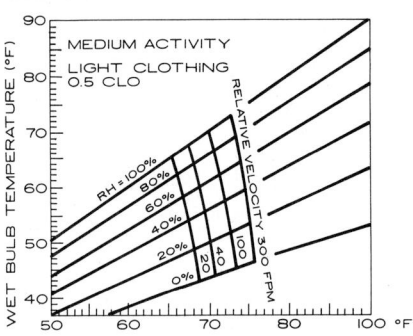

AIR TEMPERATURE = MEAN RADIANT TEMPERATURE

FIGURE 2

NOTE: Modified comfort chart for men, medium activity = 750 Btu/hr, thermal resistance of "light-clothing" = 0.5 clo.

MODIFIED COMFORT CHART

PROPERTIES OF WATER VAPOR AND SATURATED AIR

TEM-PERA-TURE (°F)	VAPOR PRES-SURE (IN. HG)	HUMID-ITY RATIO (GRAINS/LB)	ENTHALPY (BTU/LB)	SPE-CIFIC VOL-UME (CU FT/LB)
50	0.362	53.6	20.30	13.00
55	0.436	64.6	23.32	13.16
60	0.522	80.4	26.46	13.33
65	0.622	92.8	30.06	13.50
70	0.739	110.7	34.09	13.69
75	0.875	131.7	38.61	13.88
80	1.032	156.31	43.69	14.09
85	1.214	184.9	49.43	14.31
90	1.422	218.3	55.93	14.55

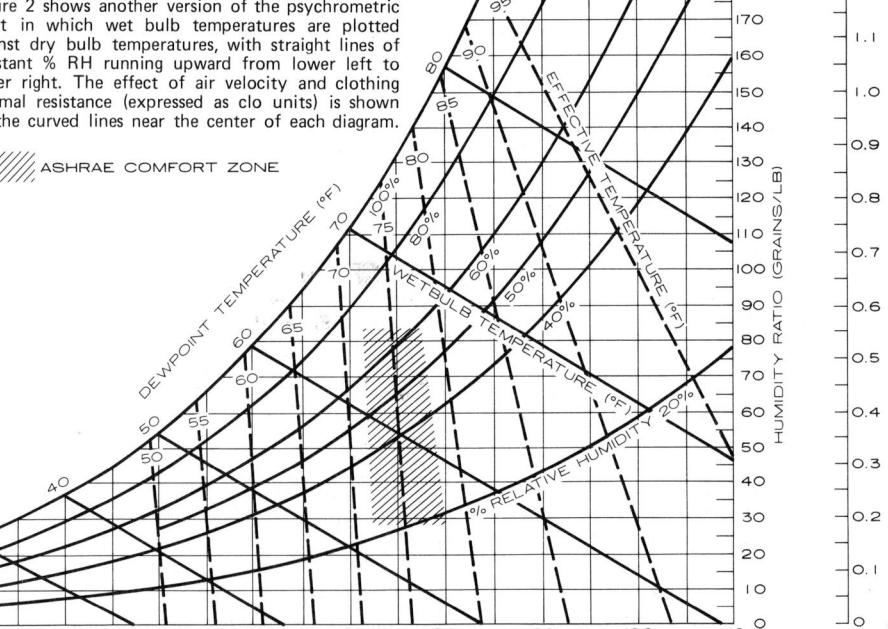

////// ASHRAE COMFORT ZONE

FIGURE 1

PSYCHROMETRIC CHART

John I. Yellott, P. E., Professor Emeritus, College of Architecture, Arizona State University; Tempe, Arizona

1 ENVIRONMENTAL FACTORS

DEFINITIONS AND SYMBOLS

BRITISH THERMAL UNIT (Btu): The quantity of heat required to raise the temperature of one pound of water one degree Fahrenheit (specifically, from 59°F to 60°F).

DEGREE DAYS (DD): A temperature-time unit used in estimating building heating requirements. For any given day, the number of DD equals the difference between the reference temperature, usually 65°F, and the mean temperature of the outdoor air for that day. DD per month or per year are the sum of the daily DD for that period.

DEWPOINT TEMPERATURE: The temperature corresponding to 100% relative humidity for an air-vapor mixture at constant pressure.

EMITTANCE (e): The ratio of the radiant energy emitted by a surface to that emitted by a perfect radiator (a black body) at the same temperature.

HUMIDITY, ABSOLUTE: The weight of water vapor contained in a unit volume of an air-vapor mixture.

HUMIDITY RATIO: The ratio of the mass of water vapor to the mass of dry air in a given air-vapor mixture.

HUMIDITY, RELATIVE (RH): The ratio of the partial pressure of the water vapor in a given air-vapor mixture to the saturation pressure of water at the existing temperature.

ISOTHERM: A line on a graph or map joining points of equal temperature.

OVERALL HEAT TRANSFER COEFFICIENT (U or $1/R_T$): The rate of heat transfer under steady state conditions through a unit area of a building component caused by a difference of one degree between the air temperatures on the two sides of the component. In U.S. practice, the units are Btu/sq ft · hr · °F.

PERM: Unit of water vapor transmission through a material, expressed in grains of vapor per hour per inch of mercury pressure difference (7000 grains = 1 lb).

REFLECTANCE: The ratio of the radiant energy reflected by a surface to the energy incident upon the surface.

SURFACE HEAT TRANSFER COEFFICIENT (h): The rate of heat transfer from a unit area of a surface to the adjacent air and environment caused by a temperature difference of one degree between the surface and the air. In U.S. practice, the units are Btu/sq ft · hr · °F.

THERM: A unit of thermal energy equal to 100,000 Btu.

THERMAL CONDUCTANCE (C or 1/R): Time rate of heat flow through unit area of a material when a temperature difference of one degree is maintained across a specified thickness of the material. In U.S. practice, the units are Btu/hr · sq ft · °F.

THERMAL CONDUCTIVITY (k): Time rate of heat flow through unit area and unit thickness of a homogeneous material when a temperature of gradient of one degree is maintained in the direction of heat flow. In U.S. practice, the units are: Btu/hr · sq ft · (F/in.) or, when thickness is measured in feet, Btu/hr · ft · °F.

THERMAL RESISTANCE (R): Unit of resistance to heat flow, expressed as temperature difference required to cause heat to flow through a unit area of a building component or material at the rate of one heat unit per hour. In U.S. practice, the units are F/Btu/hr · ft^2).

TOTAL THERMAL RESISTANCE (R_t): The total resistance to heat flow through a complete building section or construction assembly, generally expressed as the temperature difference in °F needed to cause heat to flow at the rate of 1 Btu per hour per sq ft of area.

VAPOR BARRIER: A moisture impervious layer applied to surfaces enclosing a humid space to prevent moisture migration to a point where it may condense because of reduced temperature.

VAPOR PERMEABILITY: The property of a material that permits migration of water vapor under the influence of a difference in vapor pressure across the material.

VAPOR PERMEANCE: The ratio of the water vapor flow rate, in grains per hour, through a material of any specified thickness to the vapor pressure difference between the two surfaces of the material, expressed in inches of mercury. The unit is the perm.

VAPOR PRESSURE (P_v): The partial pressure of the water vapor in an air-vapor mixture. It is determined by the dewpoint temperature or by the drybulb temperature and the relative humidity of the mixture. The units are psi or inches of mercury.

VAPOR RESISTANCE: The resistance of a material or an assembly to the passage of water vapor when a vapor pressure difference exists between the two surfaces of the material or assembly. The unit is the rep, which is the reciprocal of the perm.

THERMAL TRANSMISSION

Problems in the performance of building construction materials and assemblies are frequently associated with undesirable flow of heat, moisture, or both. The heat transfer characteristics of most building materials are published in standard references such as the ASHRAE Handbook of Fundamentals. While the published data are subject to manufacturing and testing tolerances and judgment must be used in applying them, they may generally be used with confidence for design purposes.

Heat transmission coefficients are generally expressed as conductivities, k, for which the thickness unit is 1 in., or in conductances, C, for a specified thickness. The resistance to heat flow through a material, R, is the reciprocal of the conductance. For a homogeneous material of thickness L in., the thermal resistance R = L/k.

For a surface or an airspace, where the heat flows by both radiation and convection, combined coefficients are used, symbolized by h with a subscript to designate which particular surface or airspace is being considered. Thermal resistances at surfaces and across airspaces are again designated by R with an appropriate subscript, where R = 1/h. Such R values are strongly influenced by the nature and orientation of the surfaces.

To estimate the rate of heat flow through a building section, the total resistance (R_t) of that section is found by reference to published standard value or by adding the resistances of the individual components of the section. The overall coefficient U is then found as the reciprocal of the total resistance: $U = 1/R_t$. The rate of heat flow Q (Btu/hr) through a wall section of exposed area A sq ft is the product of the overall coefficient U, the area A and the temperature difference $(t_i - t_o)$: $Q = U \times A \times (t_i - t_o)$. This heat flow may be inward or outward, depending on t_i and t_o. The general procedure for finding the total thermal resistance and the U value for a given building section on which the sun is not shining is as follows:

1. Select the design outdoor conditions of air temperature (dry bulb), wind speed, and wind direction from local Weather Service records or ASHRAE recommendations. From this information select an outer surface coefficient h_o which will generally be 4.0 Btu/sq ft · hr · °F for summer and 6.0 for winter. Determine the indoor surface coefficient h_i which will be 1.46 Btu/sq ft · hr · °F under most conditions unless forced airflow exists along the wall of the window. Convert these to resistances with $R_o = 1/h_o$ and $R_i = 1/h_i$.
2. List all of the component elements of the section and determine the thermal resistance of each element by dividing the actual (not the nominal) thickness by its thermal conductivity k, except for airspaces. For airspaces, the thickness is taken into account in the conductance h_{as} and the thermal resistance R_{as} is the reciprocal of the conductance.
3. The total resistance of the building section is simply the sum of the individual resistances (make sure that every component is included properly). The U value of the section is then found from: $U = 1/R_t$. The U x A product is often needed to simplify the calculation of the total heat flow into or out of the building's envelope, as well as for the computations used to determine compliance with building energy performance standards.
4. For such building components as windows, skylights, and doors, U values may be found in standard references, for example, the ASHRAE Handbook of Fundamentals. Thermal resistances for a wide variety of common building materials are given in the table presented later in this section.

GENERAL NOTES

The foregoing does not include consideration of heat losses or gains due to ventilation air in large buildings or to infiltration of outdoor air through openings, cracks around windows and doors, construction imperfections, and so on. The energy required to heat this air in winter or to cool and dehumidify it in summer must be carefully estimated by methods given in the ASHRAE Handbook of Fundamentals. During both summer and winter, effects of the sun on both walls and windows must be taken into account.

The solution to the basic problem of attaining acceptable heat flow rates involves the selection of materials that are appropriate for the intended service and the incorporation of enough insulation within the building section to reduce the inward or outward heat flow to the desired rate. Since the indoor-outdoor temperature difference is one of the essential factors in the heat flow equation, the indoor temperature must be selected to comply with the pertinent code or other restriction. Temperatures from 65 to 72°F are generally used in winter while 75 to 78°F are typical summer values.

Selection of the outdoor design values involves careful consideration of the number of hours per year during which exceptionally low or high temperatures are encountered. National Weather Service temperature data are available for most locations in the United States and similar data exist for principal cities throughout the world. For winter design purposes, dry bulb temperatures are usually listed, which are exceeded by 99 and 97.5% of the total hours (2160) in December, January, and February. The 97.5% value is generally used for designing. Since the 54 hr (approximately) during which the outdoor air temperature will be lower than the stated value are experienced at intervals throughout the winter months. These temperatures are usually encountered in the early morning hours before sunrise, so that winter design heating loads tend to ignore solar effects. In summer, solar loads tend to dominate the air-conditioning picture.

Thermal conductances for walls, roofs, doors, and windows are combined in many of the energy conservation building standards to give a weighted average U value, designated as U_o. Allowable values for U_o depend on the building type and size and the number of heating degree days experienced at the building's location.

$$U_o = \frac{U_{xw} \times A_w + U_f \times A_f + U_d \times A_d}{A_w + A_f + A_d}$$

where the subscripts w, f, and d designate walls, fenestration, and door, respectively.

Allowable U_o values are specified in the ASHRAE Standard 90-75, which has been adopted by many states or other jurisdictions. For commercial buildings higher than three stories, U_o may range from 0.47 to 0.28 as the number of degree days per year increases from 500 to 8000. For commercial and institutional buildings of three stories or less, U_o ranges downward from 0.38 to 0.20 as degree days increase from 500 to 10,000. Estimation of summer cooling loads is also accomplished by using the U x A products as determined above, to which solar loads from fenestration must be added. Thermal resistances may be slightly higher in summer than in winter for the same building section because of variations in surface and airspace coefficients. By far the largest factor in most building heat gains is the load imposed by solar radiation entering through fenestration. Cooling load is also increased by internal heat sources within the structure including lighting, miscellaneous electrical loads, and the people in the building. Latent heat loads from moisture removal must also be considered. Properly qualified consultants should be called in to give advice in this field even before the orientation and fenestration of a proposed new building are fixed.

The energy conservation standards mentioned above also include provisions dealing with summer cooling requirements, which are set primarily by the latitude of the city in which the structure will be erected. The mass of the proposed building in terms of weight per square foot of wall area is also introduced to compensate in part for time lags caused by the thermal capacity of building components. It should be noted that cooling, a year-round requirement in many large buildings with high internal loads, is more costly in terms of energy consumption and cost than is heating. The internal heat gains that are helpful in winter are harmful in summer, since they can add greatly to the building's cooling load.

John I. Yellott, P. E.; College of Architecture; Arizona State University; Tempe, Arizona

MATERIAL & DESCRIPTION		DENSITY (lb per cu ft)	RESISTANCE (R)[a] Per inch thickness (1/k)	For thickness listed (1/C)
BUILDING BOARDS, PANELS, FLOORING, ETC.				
Asbestos-cement board		120	0.25	—
Asbestos-cement board	1/8 in.	120	—	0.033
Gypsum or plaster board	3/8 in.	50	—	0.32
Gypsum or plaster board	1/2 in.	50	—	0.45
Plywood		34	1/25	—
Sheathing, wood fiber (impreg. or coated)	25/32"	20		2.06
		22	2.44	—
		25	2.27	—
Wood fiber board, lam. or homogeneous		26	2.38	—
		33	1.82	—
Wood fiber, hardboard type		65	0.72	—
Wood fiber, hardboard type	1/4 in.	65	—	0.18
Wood subfloor	25/32 in.	—	—	0.98
Wood, hardwood finish	3/4 in.	—	—	0.68
BUILDING PAPER				
Vapor-permeable felt		—	—	0.06
Vapor-seal, 2 layers of mopped 15 lb felt		—	—	0.12
Vapor-seal, plastic film		—	—	Negl.
FINISH FLOORING MATERIALS				
Carpet and fibrous pad		—	—	2.08
Carpet and rubber pad		—	—	1.23
Cork tile	1/8 in.	—	—	0.28
Terrazzo	1 in.	—	—	0.08
Tile-asphalt, linoleum, vinyl, rubber		—	—	0.05
INSULATING MATERIALS				
Blanket and Batt[b]				
Mineral wool, fibrous form processed from rock, slag, or glass		0.5	3.12	—
		1.5–4.0	3.70	—
Wood fiber	AVERAGE TEMP.	3.2–3.6	4.00	—
Boards and Slabs				
Cellular glass	90°F	9	2.44	—
	60°F		2.56	—
	30°F		2.70	—
	0°F		2.86	—
	−30°F		3.00	—
Corkboard	90°F	6.5–8.0	3.57	—
	60°F		3.70	—
	30°F		3.85	—
	0°F		4.00	—
	90°F	12	3.22	—
	60°F		3.33	—
	30°F		3.45	—
	0°F		3.57	—
Glass fiber	90°F	4–9	3.85	—
	60°F		4.17	—
	30°F		4.55	—
	0°F		4.76	—
	−30°F		5.26	—
Expanded rubber (rigid)	75°F	4.5	4.55	—
Expanded polyurethane (R-11 blown)	100°F	1.5–2.5	5.56	—
(Thickness 1 in. & greater)	75°F		5.88	—
	50°F		6.25	—
	25°F		5.88	—
	0°F		5.88	—
Expanded polystyrene, extruded	75°F	1.9	3.85	—
	60°F		4.00	—
	30°F		4.17	—
	0°F		4.55	—
	−60°F		5.26	—
Expanded polystyrene, molded beads	75°F	1.0	3.57	—
	30°F		3.85	—
	0°F		4.17	—
Mineral wool with resin binder	90°F	15	3.45	—
	60°F		3.57	—
	30°F		3.70	—
	0°F		4.00	—
Mineral fiberboard, wet felted				
Core or roof insulation		16–17	2.94	—
Acoustical tile		18	2.86	—
Acoustical tile		21	2.73	—
Mineral fiberboard, wet molded				
Acoustical tile[c]		23	2.38	—
Wood or can fiberboard				
Acoustical tile[c]	1/2 in.	—	—	1.19
Acoustical tile[c]	3/4 in.	—	—	1.78
Interior finish (plank, tile)		15	2.86	—

MATERIAL & DESCRIPTION		DENSITY (lb per cu ft)	RESISTANCE (R)[a] Per inch thickness (1/k)	For thickness listed (1/C)
INSULATING MATERIALS				
Boards and Slabs (continued)				
Insulating roof deck				
Approximately	1-1/2 in.	—	—	4.17
Approximately	2 in.	—	—	5.56
Approximately	3 in.	—	—	8.33
Wood shredded (cemented, preformed slabs)		22	1.67	—
Loose Fill				
Mineral wool	90°F	2.0–5.0	3.33	—
(glass, slag, or rock)	60°F		3.70	—
	30°F		4.00	—
	0°F		4.35	—
Perlite (expanded)	90°F	5.0–8.0	2.63	—
	60°F		2.78	—
	30°F		2.94	—
	0°F		3.12	—
Vermiculite (expanded)	90°F	7.0–8.2	2.08	—
	60°F		2.18	—
	30°F		2.27	—
	0°F		2.38	—
	90°F	4.0–6.0	2.22	—
	60°F		2.33	—
	30°F		2.50	—
	0°F		2.63	—
Roof Insulation[d]				
Preformed, for use above deck				
Approximately	1/2 in.	—	—	1.39
Approximately	1 in.	—	—	2.78
Approximately	1-1/2 in.	—	—	4.17
Approximately	2 in.	—	—	5.26
Approximately	2-1/2 in.	—	—	6.67
Approximately	3 in.	—	—	8.33
Cellular glass		—	2.56	—
MASONRY MATERIALS - CONCRETES				
Cement mortar		116	0.20	—
Gypsum-fiber concrete,				
87-1/2% gypsum, 12-1/2% wood chips		51	0.60	—
Lightweight aggregates including		120	0.19	—
expanded shale, clay or slate;		100	0.28	—
expanded slags; cinders; pumice;		80	0.40	—
perlite; vermiculite; also		60	0.59	—
cellular concretes		40	0.86	—
		30	1.11	—
		20	1.43	—
Sand & gravel or stone aggregate (oven dried)		140	0.11	—
Sand & gravel or stone aggregate (not dried)		140	0.08	—
Stucco		116	0.20	—
MASONRY UNITS				
Brick, common[d]		120	0.20	—
Brick, face[e]		130	0.11	—
Clay tile, hollow: 1 cell deep	3 in.	—	—	0.80
1 cell deep	4 in.	—	—	1.11
2 cells deep	6 in.	—	—	1.52
2 cells deep	8 in.	—	—	1.85

GLASS FIBER INSULATION BOARD

Conductivity $k = 0.25$ Btuh

Resistance $R = \frac{1}{k} = \frac{1}{0.25} = 4.0$

Conductance $C = \frac{k}{x} = \frac{0.25}{4} = 0.063$ Btuh

Resistance $R = \frac{x}{k} = \frac{4}{0.25} = 16.0$

(4 in. in this example)

SAND AND GRAVEL CONCRETE

Conductivity $k = 12$ Btuh

Resistance $R = \frac{1}{k} = \frac{1}{12} = 0.083$

Conductance $C = \frac{k}{x} = \frac{12}{3} = 3$ Btuh

Resistance $R = \frac{x}{k} = \frac{4}{12} = 0.33$

(4 in. in this example)

NOTE: Standard unit of area 1 sq ft. Standard unit temperature differential 1°F.

Owen L. Delevante, AIA; Glen Rock, New Jersey

E. C. Shuman, P. E.; Consulting Engineer; State College, Pennsylvania

1 ENVIRONMENTAL FACTORS

MATERIAL & DESCRIPTION	DENSITY (lb per cu ft)	RESISTANCE (R)[a] Per inch thickness (1/k)	RESISTANCE (R)[a] For thickness listed (1/C)
MASONRY UNITS			
Concrete blocks, three oval core:			
Sand & gravel aggregate 4 in.	—	—	0.71
8 in.	—	—	1.11
12 in.	—	—	1.28
Cinder aggregate 3 in.	—	—	0.86
4 in.	—	—	1.11
8 in.	—	—	1.72
12 in.	—	—	1.89
Lightweight aggregate 3 in.	—	—	1.27
(expanded shale, clay, slate 4 in.	—	—	1.50
or slag; pumice) 8 in.	—	—	2.00
12 in.	—	—	2.27
Concrete blocks, rectangular core:			
Sand & gravel aggregate			
2 core, 8 in. 36 lb. g	—	—	1.04
Lightweight aggregate (expanded			
shale, clay, slate or slag; pumice)			
3 core, 6 in. 19 lb. g 45 F	—	—	1.65
2 core, 8 in. 24 lb. g 45 F	—	—	2.18
3 core, 12 in. 38 lb. g 45 F	—	—	2.48
Granite, marble	150–175	0.05	
Stone, lime or sand	—	0.08	
Gypsum partition tile:			
3 × 12 × 30 in. solid	—	—	1.26
3 × 12 × 30 in. 4-cell	—	—	1.35
4 × 12 × 30 in. 3-cell	—	—	1.67
METALS			
Aluminum	159–175	0.0007	
Brass, red	524–542	0.0014	
Brass, yellow	524–542	0.0014	
Copper, cast rolled	550–555	0.0004	
Iron, gray cast	438–445	0.0030	—
Iron, pure	474–493	0.0023	—
Lead	704	0.0040	—
Steel, cold drawn	490	0.0032	
Steel, stainless, type 304		0.0055	
Zinc, cast		0.0013	
PLASTERING MATERIALS			
Cement plaster, sand aggregate	116	0.20	—
Sand aggregate 1/2 in.	—	—	0.10
Sand aggregate 3/4 in.	—	—	0.15
Gypsum plaster:			
Lightweight aggregate 1/2 in.	45	—	0.32
Lightweight aggregate 5/8 in.	45	—	0.39
Lightweight aggregate, on metal lath 3/4 in.	—	—	0.47
Perlite aggregate	45	0.67	—
Sand aggregate	105	0.18	—
Sand aggregate 1/2 in.	105	—	0.09
Sand aggregate 5/8 in.	105	—	0.11
Sand aggregate, on metal lath 3/4 in.	—	—	0.1
Vermiculite aggregate	45	0.59	—
ROOFING			
Asbestos-cement shingles	120	—	0.21
Asphalt roll roofing	70	—	0.15
Asphalt shingles	70	—	0.44
Built-up roofing 3/8 in.	70	—	0.33
Slate 1/2 in.	—	—	0.05
SIDING MATERIALS (On Flat Surface)			
Shingles:			
Asbestos-cement	120	—	0.21
Wood, 16 in., 7-1/2 in. exposure	—	—	0.87
Wood, double, 16 in., 12 in. exposure	—	—	1.19
Wood, plus insul. backer board, 5/16 in.	—	—	1.40
Siding:			
Asbestos-cement, 1/4 in., lapped	—	—	0.21
Asphalt insulating siding (1/2 in. bd.)	—	—	1.46
Wood, drop, 1 × 8 in.	—	—	0.79
Wood, bevel, 1/2 × 8 in., lapped	—	—	0.81
Wood, bevel, 3/4 × 10 in., lapped	—	—	1.05
Architectural glass	—	—	0.10

MATERIAL & DESCRIPTION	DENSITY (lb per cu ft)	RESISTANCE (R)[a] Per inch thickness (1/k)	RESISTANCE (R)[a] For thickness listed (1/C)
WOODS			
Maple, oak, and similar hardwoods	45	0.91	—
Fir, pine, and similar softwoods	32	1.25	—
Fir, pine, and similar softwoods			
25/32 in.	32	—	0.98
1 1/2 in.	32	—	1.89
2 1/2 in.	32	—	3.12
3 1/2 in.	32	—	4.35
Door, 1-3/4 in. thick solid wood core			1.96

STEEL DOORS (NOMINAL THICKNESS 1 3/4 IN.)

Mineral fiber core	—	—	1.69
Solid urethane foam core*	—	—	5.26
Solid polystyrene core*	—	—	2.13

*With thermal break.

AIR SURFACES

Position of Surface	Direction of Heat Flow	Type of Surface Non-Reflective Materials Resistance (R)	Reflective Aluminum Coated Paper Resistance (R)	Highly Reflective Foil Resistance (R)
STILL AIR				
Horizontal	Upward	0.61	1.10	1.32
45° slope	Upward	0.62	1.14	1.37
Vertical	Horizontal	0.68	1.35	1.70
45° slope	Down	0.76	1.67	2.22
Horizontal	Down	0.92	2.70	4.55
MOVING AIR (any position)				
15 mph wind	Any	0.17 W	—	—
7-1/2 mph wind	Any	0.25 S	—	—

AIR SPACES

Position of Air Space and Thickness (inches)	Heat Flow Dir.	Season	Types of Surfaces on Opposite Sides Both Surfaces Non-Reflective Materials Resistance (R)	Aluminum Coated Paper/ Non-Reflective Materials Resistance (R)	Foil/ Non-Reflective Materials Resistance (R)
Horizontal 3/4	Up	W	0.87	1.71	2.23
3/4		S	0.76	1.63	2.26
4		W	0.94	1.99	2.73
4		S	0.80	1.87	2.75
45° slope 3/4	Up	W	0.94	2.02	2.78
3/4		S	0.81	1.90	2.81
4		W	0.96	2.13	3.00
4		S	0.82	1.98	3.00
Vertical 3/4	Down	W	1.01	2.36	3.48
3/4		S	0.84	2.10	3.28
4		W	1.01	2.34	3.45
4		S	0.91	2.16	3.44
45° slope 3/4	Down	W	1.02	2.40	3.57
3/4		S	0.84	2.09	3.24
4		W	1.08	2.75	4.41
4		S	0.90	2.50	4.36
Horizontal 3/4	Down	W	1.02	2.39	3.55
1-1/2		W	1.14	3.21	5.74
4		W	1.23	4.02	8.94
3/4		S	0.84	2.08	3.25
1-1/2		S	0.93	2.76	5.24
4		S	0.99	3.38	8.08

Owen L. Delevante, AIA; Glen Rock, New Jersey

E. C. Shuman, P. E.; Consulting Engineer; State College, Pennsylvania

ENVIRONMENTAL FACTORS 1

GLASS, GLASS BLOCK AND PLASTIC SHEET

MATERIAL AND DESCRIPTION	OVERALL HEAT TRANSMISSION COEFFICIENT (U)	SEASONS	RESISTANCE (R)
VERTICAL PANELS—EXTERIOR			
Flat Glass			
Single glass	1.10	Winter	0.91
	1.04	Summer	0.96
Insulating glass, two lights of glass			
3/16 in. airspace	0.62	Winter	1.61
	0.65	Summer	1.54
1/4 in. airspace	0.58	Winter	1.72
	0.61	Summer	1.64
1/2 in. airspace	0.49	Winter	2.04
	0.56	Summer	1.79
Insulating glass, three lights of glass			
1/4 in. airspaces	0.39	Winter	2.56
	0.44	Summer	2.22
1/2 in. airspaces	0.31	Winter	3.23
	0.39	Summer	2.56
1/2 in. airspaces, low emittance coating			
e = 0.20	0.32	Winter	3.13
	0.38	Summer	2.63
e = 0.40	0.38	Winter	2.63
	0.45	Summer	2.22
e = 0.60	0.43	Winter	2.33
	0.51	Summer	1.96
Storm windows			
1–4 in. airspace	0.50	Winter	2.00
	0.50	Summer	2.00
Glass Block			
6 x 6 x 4 in. thick (nom.)	0.60	Winter	1.67
	0.57	Summer	1.76
8 x 8 x 4 in. thick (nom.)	0.56	Winter	1.79
	0.54	Summer	1.85
With cavity divider	0.48	Winter	2.08
	0.46	Summer	2.17
12 x 12 x 4 in. thick (nom.)	0.52	Winter	1.92
	0.50	Summer	2.00
With cavity divider	0.44	Winter	2.27
	0.42	Summer	2.38
12 x 12 x 2 in. thick (nom.)	0.60	Winter	1.67
	0.57	Summer	1.76
Single Plastic Sheet			
1/8 in. thick (nom.)	1.06	Winter	0.94
	0.98	Summer	1.02
1/4 in. thick (nom.)	0.96	Winter	1.04
	0.89	Summer	1.12
HORIZONTAL PANELS—EXTERIOR			
Flat Glass			
Single glass	1.23	Winter	0.81
	0.83	Summer	1.20
Insulating glass, two lights of glass			
3/16 in. airspace	0.70	Winter	1.43
	0.57	Summer	1.75
1/4 in. airspace	0.65	Winter	1.54
	0.54	Summer	1.85
1/2 in. airspace	0.59	Winter	1.69
	0.49	Summer	2.04
Glass Block			
11 x 11 x 3 in. thick with cavity divider	0.53	Winter	1.89
	0.35	Summer	2.86
12 x 12 x 4 in. thick with cavity divider	0.51	Winter	1.96
	0.34	Summer	2.94
Plastic Bubbles[k]			
Single walled	1.15	Winter	0.87
	0.80	Summer	1.25
Double walled	0.70	Winter	1.43
	0.46	Summer	2.17

NOTES

The thermal conductivity of glass is relatively high (k = 7.5), and, for single glazing, most of the thermal resistance is imposed at the indoor and outdoor surfaces. Indoors, approximately two-thirds of the heat flows by radiation to the room surfaces and only one-third flows by convection. This can be materially affected by the use of forced airflow from induction units, for example. The inner surface coefficient of heat transfer, h_i, can be substantially reduced by applying a low emittance metallic film to the glass.

For glazing with airspaces, the U value can be reduced to a marked degree by the use of low emittance films. This process imparts a variable degree of reflectance to the glass, thereby reducing its Shading Coefficient. Manufacturers' literature should be consulted for more details on this important subject. Also consult Chapter 26 of the 1977 ASHRAE Handbook of Fundamentals.

FOOTNOTES

a. Resistances are representative values for dry materials and are intended as design (not specification) values for materials in normal use. Unless shown otherwise in descriptions of materials, all values are for 75°C mean temperature.

b. Includes paper backing and facing if any. In cases where insulation forms a boundary (highly reflective or otherwise) of an airspace, refer to appropriate table for the insulating value of the airspace. Some manufacturers of batt and blanket insulation mark their products with R value, but they can ensure only the quality of the material as shipped.

c. Average values only are given, since variations depend on density of the board and on the type, size, and depth of perforations.

d. Thicknesses supplied by different manufacturers may vary depending on the particular material.

e. Values will vary if density varies from that listed.

f. Data on rectangular core concrete blocks differ from the data for oval core blocks because of core configuration, different mean temperature, and different unit weight. Weight data on oval core blocks not available.

g. Weight of units approx. 7⅝ high by 15⅝ long are given to describe blocks tested. Values are for 1 sq ft area.

h. Thermal resistance of metals is so low that in building constructions it is usually ignored. Values shown emphasize relatively easy flow of heat along or through metals so that they are usually heat leaks, inward or outward.

i. Spaces of uniform thickness bounded by moderately smooth surfaces.

j. Values shown not applicable to interior installations of materials listed.

k. Winter is heat flow up; summer is heat flow down.

l. Based on area of opening, not on total surface area.

Based on data from ASHRAE Handbook of Fundamentals, 1977, Chapter 22.

John I. Yellott, P. E.; College of Architecture; Arizona State University; Tempe, Arizona

1 ENVIRONMENTAL FACTORS

SOLAR GAINS THROUGH SUNLIT FENESTRATION

Heat gains through sunlit fenestration constitute major sources of cooling load in summer. In winter, discomfort is often caused by excessive amounts of solar radiation entering through south facing windows. By contrast, passive solar design depends largely on admission and storage of the radiant energy falling on south facing and horizontal surfaces. Admission takes place both by transmission through glazing and by inward flow of absorbed energy. With or without the sun, heat flows through glazing, either inwardly or outwardly, whenever there is a temperature difference between the indoor and outdoor air. These heat flows may be calculated in the following manner.

The solar heat gain is estimated by a two-step process. The first step is to find, either from tabulated data or by calculation, the rate at which solar heat would be admitted under the designated conditions through a single square foot of double strength ($1/8$ in.) clear sheet glass. This quantity, called the solar heat gain factor (SHGF), is set by (a) the local latitude; (b) the date, hence the declination; (c) the time of day (solar time should be used); (d) the orientation of the window.

Tabulated values of SHGF are given in the 1977 ASHRAE Handbook of Fundamentals, Chapter 26, for latitudes from $0°$ (the equator) to $64°$ N by $8°$ increments and for orientations around the compass from N to NNW, by $22.5°$ increments. Selected values from the $40°$ table are given in an adjacent column.

Each individual fenestration system, consisting of glazing and shading devices, has a unique ability to admit solar heat. This property is evaluated in terms of its shading coefficient (SC), which is the ratio of the amount of solar heat admitted by the system under consideration to the solar heat gain factor for the same conditions. In equation form, this becomes:

solar heat gain (Btu/sq ft · hr) = SC × SHGF

Values of the shading coefficient are given in Chapter 26 of the 1977 ASHRAE Handbook of Fundamentals for the most widely used glazing materials alone and in combination with internal and external shading devices. Selected values for single and double glazing are given below:

SHADING COEFFICIENT FOR SELECTED GLAZING SYSTEMS

TYPE OF GLASS	SOLAR TRANS- MISSION	SHADING COEFFICIENT, SC
Clear		
$1/8$ in.	0.86	1.00
$1/4$ in.	0.78	0.94
Heat absorbing		
$1/8$ in.	0.64	0.83
$1/4$ in.	0.46	0.69
Insulating glass, clear both lights		
$1/8 + 1/8$ in.	0.71	0.88
$1/4 + 1/4$ in.	0.61	0.81
Heat absorbing out Clear in, $1/4$ in.	0.36	0.55

For combinations of glazing and shading devices, see the ASHRAE chapter cited above.

The heat flow due to temperature difference is found by multiplying the U-value for the specified fenestration system by the area involved and by the applicable temperature difference:

$$Q = A \times [SC \times SHGF + U \times (t_o - t_i)]$$

The same equation is used for both summer and winter, with appropriate U-values, but in winter the conduction heat flow is usually outward because the outdoor air is colder than the indoor air.

Example: find the total heat gain, in Btu/sq ft · hr, for 1000 sq ft of unshaded $1/4$ in. heat absorbing single glass, facing west, in Denver (40°N latitude) at 4:00 P.M. solar time on October 21. Indoor air temperature is 70°F; outdoor air temperature is 40°F.

Solution: from the accompanying table, for 4:00 P.M. on October 21 find the SHGF for west facing fenestration on October 21 to be 173 Btu/sq ft · hr. For $1/4$ in. heat absorbing glass, SC = 0.69 and U for winter conditions is 1.10 Btu/sq ft · hr · °F.

$$Q = 1000 \times [0.69 \times 173 + 1.10 \times (40 - 70)]$$
$$= 1000 \times (119.4 - 33.0) = 86,400 \text{ Btu/hr}$$

Even though the outdoor air is 30° cooler than the indoor air, the net heat gain through the window in question would be equivalent to 7.2 tons of refrigeration.

For the same window area in summer, on August 21 at 4:00 P.M. solar time, SHGF = 216, and the air temperatures may be taken as 95°F outdoors and 78°F indoors. The total heat gain will be:

$$Q = 1000 \times [0.69 \times 216 + 1.04 \times (95 - 78)]$$
$$= 1000 \times (149.0 + 17.7) = 166,700 \text{ Btu/hr}$$
$$= 13.9 \text{ tons of refrigeration}$$

The cooling load can be reduced by selecting a fenestration system with lower shading coefficient and U-value. Under the same conditions, a double glazed window with two lights of $1/4$ in. clear glass and a highly reflective translucent inner shading device would have U = 0.52 and SC = 0.37. The cooling load would then be reduced to 88,760 Btu/hr or 7.4 tons of refrigeration.

SOLAR INTENSITY AND SOLAR HEAT GAIN FACTORS FOR 40°N LATITUDE

DATE	SOLAR TIME (A.M.)	DIRECT NORMAL (BTUH/SQ FT)	SOLAR HEAT GAIN FACTORS (BTUH/SQ FT)					SOLAR TIME (P.M.)
			N	E	S	W	HOR	
Jan 21	8	142	5	111	75	5	14	4
	10	274	16	124	213	16	96	2
	12	294	20	21	254	21	133	12
Feb 21	8	219	10	183	94	10	43	4
	10	294	21	143	203	21	143	2
	12	307	24	25	241	25	180	12
Mar 21	8	250	16	218	74	16	85	4
	10	297	25	153	171	25	186	2
	12	307	29	31	206	31	223	12
Apr 21	6	89	11	88	5	5	11	6
	8	252	22	224	41	21	123	4
	10	286	31	152	121	31	217	2
	12	293	34	36	154	36	252	12
May 21	6	144	36	141	10	10	31	6
	8	250	27	220	29	25	146	4
	10	277	34	148	83	34	234	2
	12	284	37	40	113	40	265	12
June 21	6	155	48	151	13	13	40	6
	8	246	30	216	29	27	153	4
	10	272	35	145	69	35	238	2
	12	279	38	41	95	41	267	12
Jul 21	6	138	37	137	11	11	32	6
	8	241	28	216	30	26	145	4
	10	269	35	146	81	35	231	2
	12	276	38	41	109	41	262	12
Aug 21	6	81	12	82	6	5	12	6
	8	237	24	216	41	23	122	4
	10	272	32	150	116	32	214	2
	12	280	35	38	149	38	247	12
Sep 21	8	230	17	205	71	17	82	4
	10	280	27	148	165	27	180	2
	12	290	30	32	200	32	215	12
Oct 21	8	204	11	173	89	11	43	4
	10	280	21	139	196	21	140	2
	12	294	25	27	234	27	177	12
Nov 21	8	136	5	108	72	5	14	4
	10	268	16	122	209	16	96	2
	12	288	20	21	250	21	132	12
Dec 21	8	89	3	67	50	3	6	4
	10	261	14	113	146	14	77	2
	12	285	18	19	253	19	113	12
			N	W	S	E	HOR	PM

John I. Yellott, P.E., Professor Emeritus; College of Architecture, Arizona State University; Tempe, Arizona

SOL-AIR TEMPERATURE

When the opaque surfaces of a structure are struck by solar radiation, much of the energy is absorbed by the irradiated surface, raising its temperature and increasing the rate of heat flow into the roof or wall. The time lag between the onset of irradiation and the resulting rise in the indoor surface temperature depends on the thickness and mass per unit area of the building element and on the thermal conductivity, specific heat, and density of the materials. The time lag is negligible for an uninsulated metal roof, but it can be a matter of hours for a massive concrete or masonry wall.

Heat flow through sunlit opaque building elements is estimated by using the sol-air temperature, t_{sa}, defined as an imaginary outdoor temperature that, in the absence of sunshine, would give the same rate of heat flow as actually exists at the specified time under the combined influence of the incident solar radiation and the ambient air temperature.

$$t_{sa} = I \times Abs./h_o$$

where I = solar irradiance (Btu/sq ft · hr)

Abs. = surface absorptance, dimensionless

h_o = outer surface coefficient (Btu/sq ft · hr · °F)

Surface absorptances range from as low as 0.30 for a white surface to 0.95 for a black built-up roof. Values of h_o range from the conventional 4.0 for summer with an assumed wind speed of 7.5 mph to a still air value of 3.0.

Example: find the rate of heat flow through a 1000 sq ft uninsulated black built-up roof, U = 0.3, under strong summer sunshine, I = 300 Btu/sq ft · hr, still air with 100°F outdoors, 78°F indoors.

Solution: the sol-air temperature is found from

$$t_{sa} = 300 \times \frac{0.95}{3.0} + 100 = 195°F$$

The rate of heat flow, neglecting the time lag, is

$$Q = 1000 \times 0.3 \times (195 - 78) = 35,100 \text{ Btu/hr}$$

With no sunshine on the roof, the heat flow is

heat flow = 1000 × 0.3 × (100 − 78) = 6600 Btu/hr

The effect of the solar radiation is thus to increase the heat flow rate by 88%. A more massive roof with a lower U-value would show considerably less effect of the incoming solar radiation.

ENVIRONMENTAL FACTORS   **1**

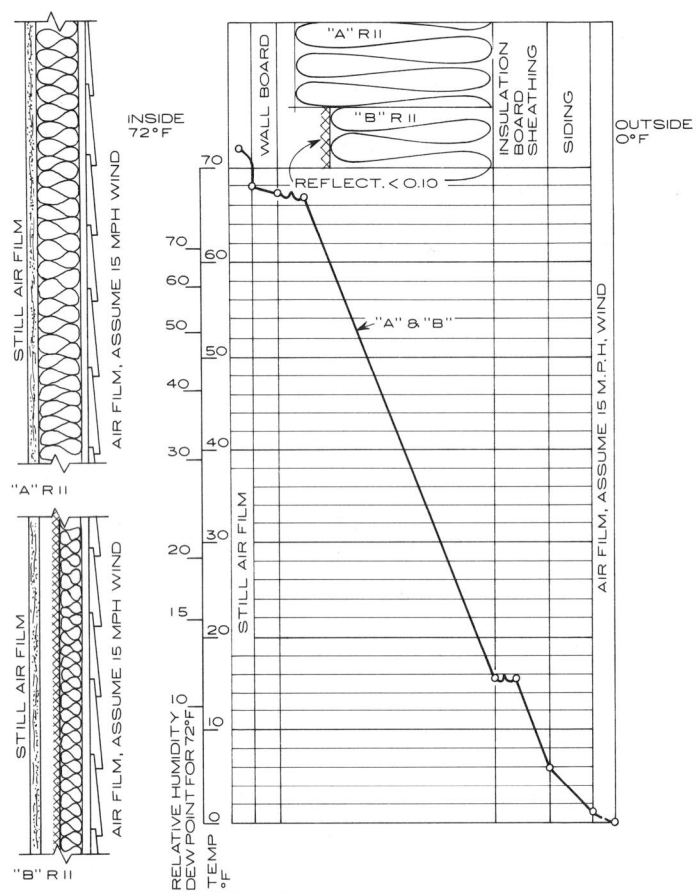

WOOD FRAME CONSTRUCTION

	WALL "A"			WALL "B"		
	R F/Btu*	°F Diff. Due to R*	Temp °F*	R F/Btu*	°F Diff Due to R*	Temp °F*
Indoor room air			72.0			72.0
Still air film (indoor)	0.68	3.2		0.68	3.2	
Indoor face of wall board			68.8			68.8
Gypsum or plaster board (1/2 in.)	0.45	2.1		0.45	2.1	
Back face of wall board			66.7			66.7
Stud air space remaining	negl.	—				
Inner face of insulation			66.7			66.7
Thermal insulation, R11-wo/refl.	11.00	51.37				
-w/refl.				11.00	51.37	
Outer face of insulation			15.3			15.3
Inner face of sheathing			15.3			15.3
Sheathing, 25/32 in., 20 lb.	2.06	9.6		2.06	9.6	
Outer face of sheathing			5.7			5.7
Inner face of siding			5.7			5.7
Siding, wood, 3/4 x 10, lapped	1.05	4.9		1.05	4.95	
Outer face of siding			0.8			0.8
Outdoor air film (15 mph wind)	0.17	0.80		0.17	0.80	
Outdoor air			0			0
TOTALS	15.41	72.0		15.41	72.0	

Heat Loss/sf = $\dfrac{\text{Temp. Diff., Room to Outdoors}}{\text{Total Resistance, R}} = \dfrac{72-0}{15.41} = 4.7$ Btu/hr. applies to insulated areas only; studs and other materials are heat paths which increase heat loss.

Wall "A"—Full thick fibrous insulation R11, non-reflective faces, air spaces insufficient to provide any significant resistance.

Wall "B"—Reflective faced fibrous insulation, R11 with the facing; air space 3/4 in. or more in width required with the facing to provide R11; that space must not be counted a second time.

Insulation thicknesses are not specified but only the R value of the material as manufactured; proper installation is implied.

* Decimals are used to check calculations only — fractional Btu's are usually of no consequence.

MASONRY CAVITY WALL CONSTRUCTION

	WALL "A"			WALL "B"		
	R F/Btu*	°F Diff. Due to R*	Temp °F*	R F/Btu*	°F Diff. Due to R*	Temp °F*
Indoor room air			72.0			72.0
Still air film (indoor)	0.68	10.55		0.68	4.16	
Indoor face of wall board			61.45			67.84
Gypsum or plaster board (1/2 in.)	0.45	6.98		0.45	2.76	
Back face of wall board			54.47			65.08
Furring air space (3/4 in.)	0.90	13.95		0.90	5.52	
Inner face of concrete block			40.52			59.56
Concrete block, 8 in., 3 oval core sand & gravel	1.11	17.10		1.11	6.80	
Outer face of concrete block			23.42			52.76
"A" cavity, 2 in. air space	0.90	13.95		—	—	
"B" cavity, filled w/insulation R8	—	—		8.0	49.04	
Inner face of face brick			9.47			3.72
Face brick, nom. 4 in.	0.44	6.83		0.44	2.70	
Outer face of face brick			2.64			1.02
Outdoor air film (15 mph wind)	0.17	2.63		0.17	1.04	
Outdoor air			0			0
TOTALS	4.65	72.01		11.75	72.02	

Heat Loss/sf = $\dfrac{\text{Temp. Diff., Room to Outdoors}}{\text{Total Resistance, R}} = \dfrac{72-0}{4.65} = 15.5$ Btu/hr. $\dfrac{72-0}{11.75} = 6.13$ Btu/hr.

Wall "A"—2 in. open cavity

Wall "B"—2 in. cavity filled with insulation R8. (Verify if water-repellent type is required.) R value is for material as manufactured; proper installation is implied.

*Decimals are used to check calculations only—fractional Btu's are usually of no consequence.

NOTE: In tabulation the considerable difference between the temperatures of inside surfaces of the two walls. Occupants of conventional rooms with Wall "A" will be less comfortable than with Wall "B" because of colder inside surface temperature; 61°F vs. 68°F.

Owen L. Delevante, AIA; Glen Rock, New Jersey

E. C. Shuman, P. E.; Consulting Engineer; State College, Pennsylvania

1 ENVIRONMENTAL FACTORS

WINTER WEATHER DATA AND DESIGN CONDITIONS FOR THE UNITED STATES AND CANADA

STATE OR PROVINCE	CITY	LATITUDE (° ')	LONGITUDE (° ')	ELEVATION (FT)	WINTER DESIGN TEMP.*	AVE. WINTER TEMP.†	SEPT	OCT	NOV	DEC	JAN	FEB	MAR	APR	MAY	TOTAL
Ala.	Birmingham	33 3	86 5	61	21	54.2	6	93	363	555	592	462	363	108	9	2551
	Mobile	30 4	88 1	119	29	59.9	0	22	213	357	415	300	211	42	0	1560
Alaska	Fairbanks	64 5	147 5	436	−47	6.7	642	1203	1833	2254	2359	1901	1739	1068	555	14,279
	Juneau	58 2	134 4	17	1	32.1	483	725	921	1135	1237	1070	1073	810	601	9075
Ariz.	Flagstaff	35 1	111 4	6973	4	35.6	201	558	867	1073	1169	991	911	651	437	7152
	Tucson	32 1	111 0	2584	32	58.1	0	25	231	406	471	344	242	75	6	1800
Ark.	Little Rock	34 4	92 1	257	20	50.5	9	127	465	716	756	577	434	126	9	3219
Calif.	Bakersfield	35 2	119 0	495	32	55.4	0	37	282	502	546	364	267	105	19	2122
	Sacramento	38 3	121 3	17	32	54.4	0	62	312	533	561	392	310	173	76	2419
	San Diego	32 4	117 1	19	44	59.5	21	43	135	236	298	253	214	135	90	1458
	San Francisco	37 5	122 3	52	40	55.1	102	118	231	388	443	336	319	279	239	3001
Colo.	Alamosa	37 3	105 5	7536	−6	29.7	279	639	1065	1420	1476	1162	1020	696	440	8529
	Denver	39 5	104 5	5283	1	37.6	117	428	819	1035	1132	938	887	558	288	6283
Conn.	Hartford	41 1	73 1	7	9	37.3	117	394	714	1101	1190	1042	908	519	205	6235
Del.	Wilmington	39 4	75 3	78	14	42.5	51	270	588	927	980	874	735	387	112	4930
D.C.	Washington	38 5	77 0	14	17	45.7	33	217	519	834	871	762	626	288	74	4224
Fla.	Miami	25 5	80 2	7	47	71.1	0	0	0	65	74	56	19	0	0	214
	Tallahassee	30 2	84 2	58	30	60.1	0	28	198	360	375	286	202	36	0	1485
Ga.	Atlanta	33 4	84 3	1005	22	51.7	18	124	417	648	636	518	428	147	25	2961
	Savannah	32 1	81 1	52	27	57.8	0	47	246	437	437	353	254	45	0	1819
Hawaii	Honolulu	21 2	158 0	7	63	74.2	0	0	0	0	0	0	0	0	0	0
Idaho	Boise	43 3	116 1	2842	10	39.7	132	415	792	1017	1113	854	722	438	245	5809
Ill.	Chicago	42 0	87 5	658	−4	35.8	117	381	807	1166	1265	1086	939	534	260	6639
	Springfield	39 5	89 4	587	2	40.6	72	291	696	1023	1135	935	769	354	136	5429
Ind.	Indianapolis	39 4	86 2	793	2	39.6	90	316	723	1051	1113	949	809	432	177	5699
Iowa	Des Moines	41 3	93 4	948	−5	35.5	96	363	828	1225	1370	1187	915	438	180	6588
Kan.	Goodland	39 2	101 4	3645	0	37.8	81	381	810	1073	1166	955	884	507	236	6141
	Topeka	39 0	95 4	877	4	41.7	57	270	672	980	1122	893	722	330	124	5182
Ky.	Lexington	38 0	84 4	979	8	43.8	54	239	609	902	946	818	685	325	105	4683
La.	New Orleans	30 0	90 2	3	33	61.8	0	12	165	291	344	241	177	24	0	1254
	Shreveport	32 3	93 5	252	25	56.2	0	47	297	477	552	426	304	81	0	2184
Me.	Portland	43 4	70 2	61	−1	33.0	195	508	807	1215	1339	1182	1042	675	372	7511
Md.	Baltimore	39 1	76 4	146	13	43.7	48	264	585	905	936	820	679	327	90	4654
Mass.	Boston	42 2	71 0	15	9	40.0	60	316	603	983	1088	972	846	513	208	5634
Mich.	Detroit	42 2	83 0	633	6	37.2	87	360	738	1088	1181	1058	936	522	220	6232
	Escanaba	45 4	87 0	594	−7	29.6	243	539	924	1293	1445	1296	1203	777	456	8481
Minn.	Duluth	46 5	92 1	1426	−16	23.4	330	632	1131	1581	1745	1518	1355	840	490	10,000
	Minneapolis	44 5	93 1	822	−12	28.3	189	505	1014	1454	1631	1380	1166	621	288	8322
Miss.	Jackson	32 2	90 1	330	25	55.7	0	65	315	502	546	414	310	87	0	2239
Mo.	Columbia	39 0	92 2	778	4	42.3	54	251	651	967	1076	875	716	324	121	5046
Mont.	Billings	45 5	108 3	3367	−10	34.5	186	487	897	1135	1296	1100	970	570	285	7049
	Missoula	46 5	114 1	3200	−6	31.5	303	651	1035	1287	1420	1120	970	621	391	8125
Neb.	North Platte	41 1	100 4	2779	−4	35.5	123	440	885	1166	1271	1039	930	519	248	6684
	Omaha	41 2	95 5	978	−3	35.6	105	357	828	1175	1355	1126	939	465	208	6612
Nev.	Las Vegas	36 1	115 1	2162	28	53.5	0	78	387	617	688	487	335	111	6	2709
	Reno	39 3	119 5	4404	10	39.3	204	490	801	1026	1073	823	729	510	357	6332
N.H.	Concord	43 1	71 3	339	−3	33.0	177	505	822	1240	1358	1184	1032	636	298	7383
N.J.	Trenton	40 1	74 5	144	14	42.4	57	264	576	924	989	885	753	399	121	4980
N.M.	Albuquerque	35 0	106 4	5310	16	12.0	12	229	642	868	930	703	595	288	81	4348
N.Y.	Buffalo	43 0	78 4	705	6	34.5	141	440	777	1156	1256	1145	1039	645	329	7062
	New York	40 5	74 0	132	15	42.8	30	233	540	902	986	885	760	408	118	4871
N.C.	Charlotte	35 0	81 0	735	22	50.4	6	124	438	691	691	582	481	156	22	3191
	Wilmington	34 2	78 0	30	26	54.6	0	74	291	521	546	462	357	96	0	2347
N.D.	Bismarck	46 5	100 5	1647	−19	26.6	222	577	1088	1463	1708	1442	1203	645	329	8851
Ohio	Cleveland	41 2	81 5	777	5	37.2	105	384	738	1088	1159	1047	918	552	260	6351
	Columbus	40 0	82 5	812	5	39.7	84	347	714	1039	1088	949	809	426	171	5660
Okla.	Oklahoma City	35 2	97 4	1280	13	48.3	15	164	498	766	868	664	527	189	34	3725
	Tulsa	36 1	95 5	650	13	47.7	18	158	522	787	893	683	539	213	47	3860
Ore.	Salem	45 0	123 0	195	23	45.4	111	338	594	729	822	647	611	417	273	4754
Pa.	Pittsburgh	40 3	80 1	1137	5	38.4	105	375	726	1063	1119	1002	874	480	195	5987
	Williamsport	41 1	77 0	527	7	38.5	111	375	717	1073	1122	1002	856	468	177	5934
R.I.	Providence	41 4	71 3	55	9	38.8	96	372	660	1023	1110	988	868	534	236	5954
S.C.	Columbia	34 0	81 1	217	24	54.0	0	84	345	577	570	470	357	81	0	2484
S.D.	Rapid City	44 0	103 0	3165	−7	33.4	165	481	897	1172	1333	1145	1051	615	326	7345
Tenn.	Nashville	36 1	86 4	577	14	48.9	30	158	495	732	778	644	512	189	40	3578
Texas	Brownsville	25 5	97 3	16	39	67.6	0	0	66	149	205	106	74	0	0	600
	Dallas	32 5	96 5	481	22	55.3	0	62	321	524	601	440	319	90	6	2363
	El Paso	31 5	106 2	3918	24	52.9	0	84	414	648	685	445	319	105	0	2700
	Houston	29 4	95 2	50	32	61.0	0	6	183	307	384	288	192	36	0	1396
Utah	Salt Lake City	40 5	112 0	4220	8	38.4	81	419	849	1082	1172	910	763	459	233	6052
Vt.	Burlington	44 3	73 1	331	7	29.4	207	539	891	1349	1513	1333	1187	714	353	8269
Va.	Lynchburg	37 2	79 1	947	16	46.0	51	223	540	822	849	731	605	267	78	4166
Wash.	Seattle	47 4	122 2	14	27	46.9	129	329	543	657	738	599	577	396	242	4424
W. Va.	Charleston	38 2	81 4	939	11	44.8	63	254	591	865	880	770	648	300	96	4476
Wisc.	Green Bay	44 3	88 1	683	−9	30.3	174	484	924	1333	1494	1313	1141	654	305	8029
Wyo.	Casper	42 5	106 3	5319	−5	33.4	192	524	942	1169	1290	1084	1020	651	381	7410
CANADA																
Alta.	Edmonton	53 34	113 31	2219	−25	—	411	738	1215	1603	1810	1520	1330	765	400	10,268
B.C.	Vancouver	49 11	123 10	16	19	—	219	456	657	787	862	723	676	501	310	5515
Man.	Winnipeg	49 54	97 14	786	−27	—	322	683	1251	1757	2008	1719	1465	813	405	10,679
N.S.	Halifax	44 39	63 34	83	5	—	180	457	710	1074	1213	1122	1030	742	487	7361
Ont.	Toronto	43 41	79 38	578	−1	—	151	439	760	1111	1233	1119	1013	616	298	6827
Que.	Montreal	45 28	73 45	98	−10	—	165	521	882	1392	1566	1381	1175	684	316	8203

*Based on 97.5% Design Dry-Bulb values found in ASHRAE Handbook of Fundamentals, 1977.
†October–April, inclusive. ASHRAE Systems Handbook, 1976.
‡Based on the period 1931–1960, inclusive. ASHRAE Systems Handbook, 1976.

ENVIRONMENTAL FACTORS 1

CALCULATION OF SOLAR POSITION

The sun's altitude above the horizontal plane, A, and the solar azimuth, B, as measured toward the north from the south-north line in the horizontal plane, can be calculated accurately for any location, date, and time of day by using the following formulas:

$$\sin A = \cos L \cos d \cos H + \sin L \sin d$$

$$\cos B = \frac{\sin A \sin L - \sin d}{\cos A \cos L}$$

where

d = solar declination (angle between earth-sun line and equatorial plane)

H = hour angle of the sun = 15° × number of hours from local solar noon

Example: find solar altitude and azimuth for L = 40° north; local solar time = 2:00 P.M., H = 30°; date = March 21, d = 0.0°

$$\sin A = 0.766 \times 1.00 \times 0.866 + 0.643 \times 0.00$$

$$= 0.663$$

A = arc sin 0.663 = 41.53°

$$\cos B = \frac{0.663 \times 0.643 - 0.00}{0.749 \times 0.766} = 0.743$$

B = arc cos 0.743 = 41.98°

CALCULATION OF SOLAR IRRADIATION

The amount of solar radiation falling on exposed surfaces must be known before the importance of shading can be properly evaluated. Because shading devices protect surfaces primarily from the sun's direct irradiation, a method is given below for estimating this component of the total irradiation on clear days, for surfaces with varying orientation. For additional details, see 1977 ASHRAE Handbook of Fundamentals, p. 26.26. The intensity of direct solar irradiation depends on the solar altitude, the amount of water vapor in the atmosphere, and the earth-sun distance. When these factors are taken into account in accordance with the ASHRAE procedure, the following values are found for the direct normal irradiance (I_{DN}) in Btu/sq ft · hr:

Solar altitude (degrees)									
5	10	15	20	25	30	35	45	60	90

June 21, declination = +23.45°

| 33 | 106 | 156 | 189 | 212 | 229 | 241 | 258 | 272 | 281 |

March 21, September 21, declination = 0.00°

| 55 | 142 | 195 | 228 | 250 | 266 | 277 | 293 | 306 | 314 |

December 21, declination = −23.45°

| 77 | 173 | 226 | 258 | 279 | 294 | 305 | 320 | 332 | 339 |

At any given solar altitude, I_{DN} is significantly higher in winter than in summer because of the reduced water vapor content of the atmosphere and the shortened earth-sun distance. The direct irradiation $I_{D\theta}$ received by a particular surface is the product of the direct normal irradiance and the cosine of the angle of incidence θ between the solar rays and a line perpendicular to the surface:

$$I_{D\theta} = I_{DN} \cos \theta$$

For horizontal surfaces, the incident angle θ_H is the complement of the solar altitude ($\theta_H = 90 - A$), so:

$$I_{DH} = I_{DN} \times \sin A$$

For vertical surfaces, the incident angle θ_V is found from:

$$\cos \theta_V = \cos A \cos G$$

where the surface-solar azimuth G is the angle between the solar azimuth and the surface azimuth. Then:

$$I_{DV} = I_{DN} \cos A \cos G.$$

SOLAR-SURFACE ANGLES

The direction of the earth-sun line OQ is defined by the solar altitude A (angle HOQ) and the solar azimuth B (angle HOS). These can be calculated when the location (latitude), date (declination), and time of day (hour angle) are known. The surface azimuth S is the angle SOP between the south-north line SON and the normal to the surface OP. The surface-solar azimuth G is the angle HOP.

The angle of incidence θ depends on the orientation and tilt of the irradiated surface. For a horizontal surface, θ_H is the angle QOV between the earth-sun line OQ and the vertical line OV. For the vertical surface shown above as facing SSE, the angle of incidence θ_V is the angle QOP between the earth-sun line OQ and the normal to the surface, OP. For surfaces such as solar collectors, which are generally tilted at some angle T upward from the horizontal, the incident angle θ_T may be found from the equation:

$$\text{cosine } \theta_T = \text{cosine A cosine S sine T} + \text{sine A cosine T}$$

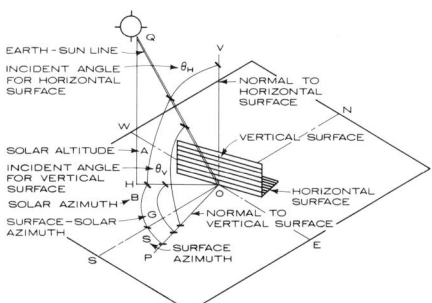

SOLAR ANGLE DIAGRAM

In the tables below, calculated values of the solar position angles in degrees and the direct irradiation values in Btu/sq ft · hr are shown for six vertical orientations and for horizontal surfaces, from 26°N to 46°N latitude by 4° intervals. The values are given for the summer and winter solstices and the spring and fall equinoxes.

26°N LATITUDE

JUNE 21

AM		ALT	AZM	S	SE	E	NE	N	SW	HOR
					BTU/SQ FT · HR					
6	6	10.05	111.30		42	98	96	38		19
7	5	22.82	105.97		91	180	164	52		79
8	4	35.93	101.15		110	193	164	38		143
9	3	49.24	96.45		107	171	134	19		199
10	2	62.69	91.17		87	126	91	3		243
11	1	76.15	82.61	9	53	66	41			271
12		87.45	0.00	13	9				9	281
PM				S	SW	W	NW	N	SE	HOR

MARCH/SEPTEMBER 21

AM		ALT	AZM	S	SE	E	NE	N	SW	HOR
6	6	0.00	90.00							
7	5	13.45	83.30	21	138	175	109			42
8	4	26.71	75.80	56	196	222	117			115
9	3	39.46	66.33	88	205	202	80			181
10	2	51.11	52.79	114	186	150	25			233
11	1	60.25	31.43	130	148	79			36	266
12		64.00	0.00	135	95				95	277
PM				S	SW	W	NW	N	SE	HOR

DECEMBER 21

AM		ALT	AZM	S	SE	E	NE	N	SW	HOR
7	5	2.23	62.48	5	10	9	3			
8	4	13.76	54.88	120	206	171	36			51
9	3	24.12	45.30	177	252	179	1			113
10	2	32.66	33.01	212	248	138			53	162
11	1	38.46	17.65	232	216	74			112	194
12		40.55	0.00	239	169				169	204
PM				S	SW	W	NW	N	SE	HOR

30°N LATITUDE

JUNE 21

AM		ALT	AZM	S	SE	E	NE	N	SW	HOR
					BTU/SQ FT · HR					
6	6	11.48	110.59		50	113	110	42		25
7	5	23.87	104.30		97	184	163	47		84
8	4	36.60	98.26		117	194	157	28		146
9	3	49.53	91.79		117	171	125	5		200
10	2	62.50	83.46	14	99	126	79			243
11	1	75.11	67.48	27	66	66	27			270
12		83.45	0.00	32	23				23	279
PM				S	SW	W	NW	N	SE	HOR

MARCH/SEPTEMBER 21

AM		ALT	AZM	S	SE	E	NE	N	SW	HOR
6	6	0.00	90.00							
7	5	12.95	82.37	23	137	170	104			40
8	4	25.66	73.90	63	199	218	110			109
9	3	37.76	63.43	100	212	200	71			173
10	2	48.59	49.11	128	196	148	14			223
11	1	56.77	28.19	147	159	79			48	254
12		60.00	0.00	153	108				108	265
PM				S	SW	W	NW	N	SE	HOR

DECEMBER 21

AM		ALT	AZM	S	SE	E	NE	N	SE	HOR
7	5	0.38	62.40							
8	4	11.44	54.15	110	185	152	30			38
9	3	21.27	44.12	177	246	171			4	96
10	2	29.28	31.73	217	248	134			59	143
11	1	34.64	16.77	240	221	72			119	173
12		36.55	0.00	247	175				175	183
PM				S	SW	W	NW	N	SE	HOR

Gary L. Powell; College of Architecture; Arizona State University; Tempe, Arizona

1 ENVIRONMENTAL FACTORS

34°N LATITUDE

JUNE 21

AM		ALT	AZM	S	SE	E	NE	N	SW	HOR
						BTU/SQ FT · HR				
5	7	1.47	117.57							
6	6	12.86	109.78		57	126	121	45		
7	5	24.80	102.54		103	188	162	42		34
8	4	37.07	95.28		125	195	151	18		99
9	3	49.49	87.10	9	127	171	115			158
10	2	61.79	76.00	31	111	125	67			205
11	1	73.17	55.10	46	79	66	14			234
12		79.45	0.00	51	36				36	244
	PM			S	SW	W	NW	N	SE	HOR

MARCH/SEPTEMBER 21

AM		ALT	AZM	S	SE	E	NE	N	SW	HOR
6	6	0.00	90.00							
7	5	12.39	81.48	25	134	165	99			37
8	4	24.49	72.11	69	201	215	103			103
9	3	35.89	60.79	110	217	197	61			163
10	2	45.89	45.92	142	204	147	3			211
11	1	53.21	25.60	163	170	78			60	241
12		56.00	0.00	169	120				120	251
	PM			S	SW	W	NW	N	SE	HOR

DECEMBER 21

AM		ALT	AZM	S	SE	E	NE	N	SW	HOR
8	4	9.08	53.57	93	155	126	23			25
9	3	18.38	43.12	173	236	162			8	79
10	2	25.86	30.65	219	246	130			63	123
11	1	30.81	16.05	245	223	70			123	152
12		32.55	0.00	253	179				179	162
	PM			S	SW	W	NW	N	SE	HOR

38°N LATITUDE

JUNE 21

AM		ALT	AZM	S	SE	E	NE	N	SW	HOR
						BTU/SQ FT · HR				
5	7	3.32	117.42		3	9	10	5		1
6	6	14.18	108.87		64	137	130	47		37
7	5	25.60	100.70		109	190	160	36		93
8	4	37.33	92.25		133	195	144	8		149
9	3	49.13	82.47	23	137	171	105			199
10	2	60.58	69.06	48	122	125	55			238
11	1	70.61	45.67	64	92	66	1			262
12		75.45	0.00	70	50				50	270
	PM			S	SW	W	NW	N	SE	HOR

MARCH/SEPTEMBER 21

AM		ALT	AZM	S	SE	E	NE	N	SW	HOR
6	6	0.00	90.00							
7	5	11.77	80.63	26	130	158	93			33
8	4	23.20	70.43	75	202	210	96			96
9	3	33.86	58.38	120	222	194	53			153
10	2	43.03	43.16	155	212	145			7	198
11	1	49.57	23.52	177	180	77			71	227
12		52.00	0.00	185	131				131	236
	PM			S	SW	W	NW	N	SE	HOR

DECEMBER 21

AM		ALT	AZM	S	SE	E	NE	N	SW	HOR
8	4	6.69	53.12	69	114	92	16			13
9	3	15.44	42.30	164	221	149			10	61
10	2	22.40	29.74	216	240	124			66	103
11	1	26.96	15.45	246	222	68			126	130
12		28.55	0.00	255	180				180	139
	PM			S	SW	W	NW	N	SE	HOR

42°N LATITUDE

JUNE 21

AM		ALT	AZM	S	SE	E	NE	N	SW	HOR
						BTU/SQ FT · HR				
5	7	5.15	117.16		11	31	33	16		3
6	6	15.44	107.87		70	147	137	47		43
7	5	26.28	98.78		115	192	157	30		96
8	4	37.38	89.19	3	140	196	136			150
9	3	48.45	77.96	36	146	170	95			196
10	2	58.95	62.79	64	133	125	43			233
11	1	67.64	38.62	82	105	66			12	256
12		71.45	0.00	88	63				63	263
	PM			S	SW	W	NW	N	SE	HOR

MARCH/SEPTEMBER 21

AM		ALT	AZM	S	SE	E	NE	N	SW	HOR
6	6	0.00	90.00							
7	5	11.09	79.84	27	126	151	87			30
8	4	21.81	68.88	79	201	205	89			88
9	3	31.70	56.21	128	225	191	45			142
10	2	40.06	40.79	166	218	143			16	184
11	1	45.88	21.82	190	188	76			81	211
12		48.00	0.00	198	140				140	220
	PM			S	SW	W	NW	N	SE	HOR

DECEMBER 21

AM		ALT	AZM	S	SE	E	NE	N	SW	HOR
8	4	4.28	52.82	35	58	46	8			4
9	3	12.46	41.63	148	197	131			12	44
10	2	18.91	29.00	209	229	116			66	82
11	1	23.09	14.96	242	217	65			125	107
12		24.55	0.00	253	179				179	115
	PM			S	SW	W	NW	N	SE	HOR

46°N LATITUDE

JUNE 21

AM		ALT	AZM	S	SE	E	NE	N	SW	HOR
						BTU/SQ FT · HR				
5	7	6.97	116.78		20	56	60	29		8
6	6	16.63	106.77		76	155	142	47		48
7	5	26.82	96.80		121	194	154	23		99
8	4	37.22	86.15	13	147	195	129			149
9	3	47.47	73.66	50	155	169	85			192
10	2	56.95	57.25	80	144	124	31			226
11	1	64.40	33.33	99	116	65			24	248
12		67.45	0.00	106	75				75	255
	PM			S	SW	W	NW	N	SE	HOR

MARCH/SEPTEMBER 21

AM		ALT	AZM	S	SE	E	NE	N	SW	HOR
6	6	0.00	90.00							
7	5	10.36	79.09	27	120	142	81			26
8	4	20.32	67.45	83	199	199	82			80
9	3	29.42	54.27	134	227	187	37			130
10	2	36.98	38.75	175	223	140			24	169
11	1	42.14	20.43	201	195	75			89	194
12		44.00	0.00	210	148				148	203
	PM			S	SW	W	NW	N	SE	HOR

DECEMBER 21

AM		ALT	AZM	S	SE	E	NE	N	SW	HOR
8	4	1.86	52.65	3	5	4	1			
9	3	9.46	41.12	122	162	107			11	27
10	2	15.41	28.41	194	212	105			63	61
11	1	19.23	14.56	232	207	60			122	84
12		20.55	0.00	244	173				173	92
	PM			S	SW	W	NW	N	SE	HOR

Gary L. Powell; Arizona State University; Tempe, Arizona

PASSIVE SOLAR HEATING

Passive solar heating relies on the natural flow of energy through and around a building to provide comfort. Collection, storage, and distribution of energy are achieved by the three basic heat transfer processes: conduction, convection, and radiation. Efficient operation of passive systems can involve some user control to alter or override energy flows within a building or at its weatherskin.

As part of the development of any passive system, the designer should take into account the elements of energy conserving design. With passive solar heating, prevention and minimization of heat loss from the structure is fundamental in ensuring that the heating system will be effective. This includes proper insulation, orientation, and surface-to-volume ratios, as well as material, texture, and finish choices.

There are three generic categories for passive solar heating: direct gain, indirect gain (thermal storage wall, roof pond), and isolated gain (sunspace, thermosiphon). The primary elements to be considered with each generic category are collection, storage, distribution, and control.

1. SOLAR COLLECTION surfaces are generally of transparent or translucent plastics or fiberglass or are glass oriented in a southerly direction. When considering materials, attention should be paid to material degradation by solar exposure and other weather elements.
2. THERMAL STORAGE materials include concrete, brick, sand, tile, and stone, as well as water or other liquids. Phase change materials such as eutectic salts and paraffins are also feasible. Storage should be well placed to receive maximum solar exposure, either directly or indirectly. Total effective thermal storage capacity should be a minimum of 30 to 45 Btu/°F per sq ft of aperture. Adequate thermal storage capacity will absorb and retain the sun's heat until it is needed, minimizing daily internal temperature fluctuations.
3. HEAT DISTRIBUTION occurs through natural means by conduction, convection, and radiation. Fans or other mechanical equipment to distribute energy are generally avoided, yet sometimes required.
4. CONTROL mechanisms such as vents, dampers, movable insulation, and shading devices are helpful in ensuring a balanced heat distribution.

PASSIVE SOLAR COOLING

Passive solar cooling is simply the tempering of interior spaces by optimizing the use of natural thermal phenomena. A structure designed for natural cooling should incorporate features that minimize heat gain. Adequate insulation, proper overhangs, shading, orientation, and similar factors should be considered. When possible, external heat gain should be controlled before it reaches or penetrates the weatherskin.

When cooling is necessary for internal comfort, dissipation of heat is accomplished by cooling the interior mass, the air, or both. Conduction, convection, radiation, evaporation, and dehumidification are the thermal transfer processes used.

Many passive cooling methods exist: natural cross-ventilation, deep space radiation, day/night closing/opening, induction of precooled air, night cooling of interior air mass, earth mass heat sink, evaporative wicks, dessicant mass, and others. This science integrates traditional architectural solutions, modern developing materials, and a refined knowledge of thermal dynamics, as well as nature's patterns.

The identification and definitions of the three generic cooling categories are as follows:

1. DIRECT LOSS: Heat is lost or dissipated directly from the space.
2. INDIRECT LOSS: The heat loss occurs at the weatherskin.
3. ISOLATED LOSS: Heat loss occurs away from the weatherskin. For example, induced air can be precooled in the earth's mass or cooling ponds.

TYPES	HEATING	COOLING
DIRECT GAIN/LOSS Direct gain is the most common passive solar building approach and most structures utilize it to some degree. Collection and storage are integral with the space. Southerly oriented glazing (collector) admits winter solar radiation to the space beyond. Within the space are adequate amounts of thermal storage incorporated as part of the building structure, which absorbs the solar energy. During the cooling season windows, walls, and roofs can be operable or openable for natural or induced ventilation, cooling both the mass and space.	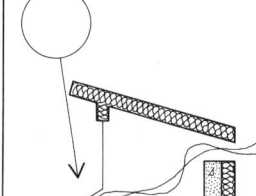	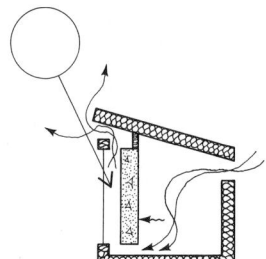
THERMAL STORAGE WALL—MASS WALL Thermal storage walls are a "sun to mass to space" concept. Collection and storage are separated from the space, but linked thermally, transferring energy through the wall by conduction, then to the space by radiation. A mass wall can be vented to the interior if a convective heat flow is warranted during the day. In the mass wall system, storage is generally in masonry or concrete directly behind the south glazing. Mass walls should be vented to the exterior or shaded during summer months.	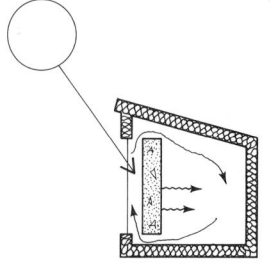	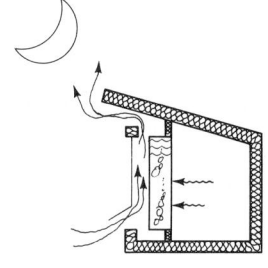
THERMAL STORAGE WALL—WATER WALL In a water wall system a liquid, often held in barrels or tubes directly behind south facing glass, acts as the thermal storage medium. During the winter, solar radiation is absorbed by the contained water. As needed, this energy is gradually released to the interior. Water walls should be shaded or vented to the exterior during cooling periods. Additional cooling can be provided by venting the water wall at night where low nighttime temperatures prevail.	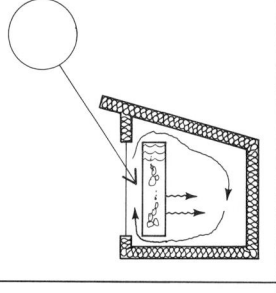	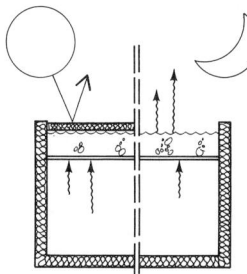
ROOF POND The roof pond system places the liquid storage mass in the ceiling. During the heating season, operable insulation panels are moved during the day to expose the storage mass to the sun. Energy is absorbed by the roof pond, and at night the panels are replaced over the storage, allowing the stored energy to radiate to the building's interior. During summer, this process is reversed. During the day, internal heat is absorbed by the roof pond, which is insulated from the high summer sun. At night, the insulation is opened to allow the storage mass to radiate to deep space.	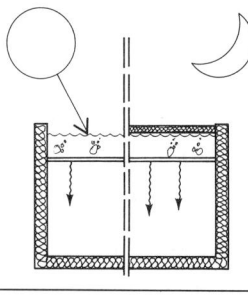	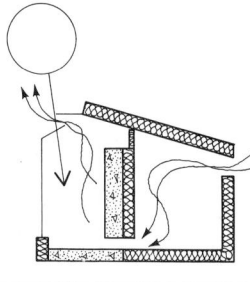
SUNSPACE In sunspace designs, solar collection and primary thermal storage are isolated from all living spaces, although variations are possible. This allows the solar system to function independently of the building interior, although heat can be drawn from the sunspace as the thermal requirements dictate. When cooling is required, the sunspace can be used to induce a convective flow from the exterior, and should be shaded to prevent overheating of the space and storage mass.	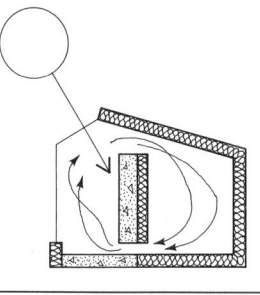	
THERMOSIPHON Thermosiphon, or natural convection, systems rely on the natural rise and fall of a fluid as it is heated and cooled. As the sun warms a collector surface the air rises, simultaneously pulling cooler air from the bottom of the storage and causing a natural convection loop. Heat is convected into the space or stored in the thermal mass until necessary for use. During a cooling season, the collector may be used as a "thermal chimney" to induce precooled air through the storage mass to cool it.	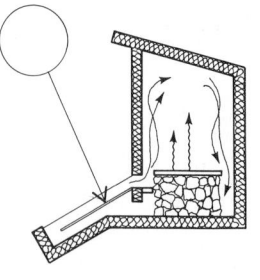	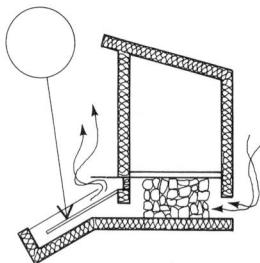

Dennis A. Andrejko, Architect, David Wright, AIA; SEAgroup; Nevada City, California

1 ENVIRONMENTAL FACTORS

PASSIVE SOLAR HEATING—DESIGN PROCEDURE

Passive solar heating systems are integral to building design. The concepts relating to system operation must be applied at the earliest stages of design decision making.

Passive systems demand a skillful and total integration of all the architectural elements within each space—glazing, walls, floor, roof, and in some cases even interior surface colors. The way in which the glazing and thermal mass (heat storage materials, i.e., masonry, water) are designed generally determines the efficiency and level of thermal comfort provided by the system. Two concepts are critical to understanding the thermal performance of passively heated space. They are:

1. That the quantity of south glazing, insulating properties of the space, and the outdoor climatic conditions will determine the number of degrees the average indoor temperature in a space is above the average outdoor temperatures on any given day (Δt).

2. That the size, distribution, material, and in some cases (direct gain systems) surface color of thermal mass in the space will determine the daily fluctuation above and below the average indoor temperature (see Figure 1).

Calculating heat gain and loss is a relatively straightforward procedure. The storage and control of heat in a passively heated space, however, is the major problem confronting most designers. In the process of storing and releasing heat, thermal mass in a space will fluctuate in temperature, yet the object of the heating system is to maintain a relatively constant interior temperature. For each system, the integration of thermal mass in a space will determine the fluctuation of indoor temperature over the day.

EXAMPLE

In a direct gain system, with masonry thermal mass, the major determinant of fluctuations of indoor air temperature is both the amount of exposed surface area of masonry in the space and the distribution of sunlight over the masonry surface; in a thermal storage wall system, it is the thickness of the material used to construct the wall. The following is a procedure for sizing both direct gain and indirect gain thermal storage wall systems (masonry or water) for buildings with skin dominated heating loads.

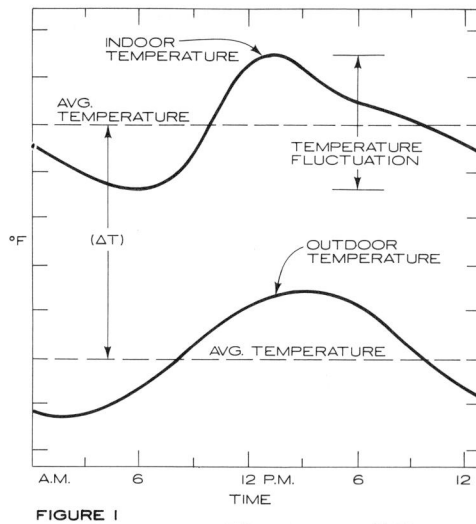

FIGURE I

DAILY TEMPERATURE FLUCTUATION

DIRECT GAIN

The major glass areas (collector) of each space must be oriented to the south ($30°\pm$) for maximum solar heat gain in winter. However, these windows can serve other functions as well, such as openings for light and views.

Each space must also contain enough mass for the storage of solar heat gain. This implies a heavy masonry building, but the masonry can be as thin as 4 in. If an interior water wall is used for heat storage, the lightweight construction (wood frame) can be used.

SOUTH GLAZING: One criterion for a well-designed space using this method is that it gains enough solar energy, on an average sunny day in winter, to maintain an average space temperature of $68°F\pm$ over the 24-hr period. By establishing this criterion, it is possible to develop ratios for the preliminary sizing of south glazing. Table 1 (see next page) lists ratios for various climates and locations that apply to a well-insulated residence.

EXAMPLE

In Denver, Colorado, at 40°N latitude, with an average January temperature of 30°F, a well-insulated space would need approximately 0.20 sq ft of south glazing for each square foot of space floor area (e.g., a 200 sq ft space needs 40 sq ft of south glazing).

In a direct gain system, sunlight can also be admitted into a space through clerestories and skylights, as well as vertical south facing windows. This approach may be taken (1) for privacy; (2) because of shading on the south facades; (3) because spaces are located along facades other than south; and (4) to avoid direct sunlight on people and furniture. Use the following guidelines when designing clerestories and skylights.

1. CLERESTORY: Locate the clerestory at a distance in front of interior thermal storage wall of roughly 1 to 1.5 times the height of the clerestory above the finished floor. Make the ceiling of the clerestory a

light color to reflect and diffuse sunlight down into the space. In regions with heavy snowfall, locate the sill of the clerestory glazing 18 in. or more above the roof surface. (See Figure 2, next page.)

2. SAWTOOTH CLERESTORIES: Make angle α (as measured from horizontal) equal to or smaller than the altitude of the sun at noon on December 21, the winter solstice. Make the underside of the clerestories a light color. (See Figure 3, next page.)

3. SKYLIGHT: Use a south facing or horizontal skylight with a reflector to increase solar gain in winter, and shade both horizontal and south facing skylights in summer to prevent excessive solar gain. (See Figure 4, next page.)

THERMAL STORAGE MASS: The two most common materials used for storing heat are masonry and water. Masonry materials transfer heat from their surface to the interior at a slow rate. If direct sunlight is applied to the surface of a dark masonry material for an extended period of time, it will become uncomfortably hot, thereby giving much of its heat to the air in the space rather than conducting it away from the surface for storage. This results in daytime overheating and large daily temperature fluctuations in the space. To reduce fluctuations, direct sunlight should be spread over a large surface area of masonry. To accomplish this:

1. Construct interior walls and floors of masonry at least 4 in. in thickness.

2. Diffuse direct sunlight over the surface area of the masonry either by using a translucent glazing material—placing a number of small windows so that they admit sunlight in patches—or by reflecting direct sunlight off a light colored interior surface first. (See Figure 5, next page.)

3. Use the following guidelines for selecting interior surface colors and finishes:
   a. Masonry floors of a dark color.

b. Masonry walls of any color.

c. Lightweight construction (little thermal mass) of a light color to reflect sunlight onto masonry surfaces.

d. Avoidance of direct sunlight on dark masonry surfaces for long periods of time.

e. No wall-to-wall carpeting over masonry floors.

By following these recommendations, one can control temperature fluctuations in the space on clear winter days to approximately 10 to 15°F. These temperature fluctuations are for clear winter days and for at least 6 sq ft of exposed masonry surface area (either horizontal or vertical) in direct sunlight for each square foot of south glazing.

For an interior water wall, the volume of water in direct sunlight and the surface color of the container (thin metal or plastic) will determine the temperature fluctuation in a space over the day (see Table 2, next page). When using a water wall for heat storage:

1. Locate the wall so it receives direct sunlight between 10 A.M. and 2 P.M.

2. Make the surface of the container that is exposed to direct sunlight of a dark color (at least 75% solar absorption).

3. Use roughly 1 cu ft (7.48 gal) of water for each square foot of south glazing. (Adjust the volume of water to the temperature fluctuation desired in the space.)

NOTE

With an interior water wall there are few restrictions regarding other wall and floor materials and surface colors in the space. The water can be stored within an interior wall or in freestanding containers, as long as the surface of the water wall is a thin material exposed to direct sunlight.

INDIRECT GAIN—THERMAL STORAGE WALLS

The predominant architectural expression of a thermal storage wall building is south facing glass. The glass functions as a collecting surface only, and admits no natural light into the space. However, windows can be included in the wall to admit natural light and direct heat and to permit a view.

Either water or masonry can be used for a thermal storage wall (a masonry thermal storage wall with thermocirculation vents is often referred to as a Trombe wall). Since the mass is concentrated along the south face of the building, there is no limit to the choice of construction materials and interior finishes in the remainder of the space.

SOUTH GLAZING: The criterion for a double glazed thermal storage wall is the same as for a direct gain system—that it transmit enough heat on an average sunny winter day to supply a space with all its heating needs for that day. Tables 3 and 4 (see next page) list guidelines for sizing the glazing of masonry or water walls, respectively.

EXAMPLE

In Boston, Massachusetts, at 42°N latitude, with an average January temperature of 31.4°F, a well-insulated space will need approximately 0.41 sq ft of double glazed water wall for each square foot of building floor area (e.g., a 200 sq ft space will need about 32 sq ft of glazing).

WALL DETAILS: While the procedure above gives guidelines for the overall size (surface area) of a thermal storage wall, the efficiency of the wall as a heating system depends mainly on its thickness, material, and surface color. (See Table 5, next page.) If the wall is too thin, the space will overheat during the day and be too cool in the evening; if it is too thick, it becomes inefficient as a heating source, since little energy is transmitted through it.

The choice of wall thickness, within the range given for each material in Table 5 (see next page), will determine the air temperature fluctuation in the space over the

day. As a general rule, the greater the wall thickness the smaller the indoor temperature fluctuation. Table 6 (see next page) can be used to select a wall thickness.

The greater the absorption of solar energy at the exterior face of a thermal wall, the greater the quantity of incident energy transferred through the wall into the building. Therefore, make the outside face of the wall dark (preferably black) with a solar absorption of at least 85%.

In cold climates, the addition of thermocirculation vents in a masonry wall will significantly increase the performance of the wall. In mild climates, however, the vents are unnecessary, since winter daytime temperatures are comfortable and heating is usually not needed at that time. To size the vents:

1. Make the total area of each row of vents equal to approximately 1 sq ft for each 100 sq ft of exterior wall surface area.

2. Prevent reverse airflow at night by placing an operable damper over the vents at night.

Edward Mazria, AIA, Architect; Edward Mazria & Associates; Albuquerque, New Mexico

TABLE 1. SIZING SOLAR WINDOWS FOR DIFFERENT CLIMATIC CONDITIONS

AVERAGE WINTER TEMP. (CLEAR DAY)[1]	SQUARE FEET OF GLAZING NEEDED FOR EACH SQUARE FOOT OF FLOOR AREA[2]			
	36°NL	40°NL	44°NL	48°NL
Cold climates				
20°F	0.24	0.25	0.29	0.31 (with night insul.)
25°F	0.22	0.23	0.25	0.28 (with night insul.)
30°F	0.19	0.20	0.22	0.24
Temperate climates				
35°F	0.16	0.17	0.19	0.21
40°F	0.13	0.14	0.16	0.17
45°F	0.10	0.11	0.12	0.13

NOTES

1. Temperatures listed are for December and January (usually the coldest months) and are monthly averages.

2. These ratios apply to a well insulated space with a heat load coefficient (HLC) of 8 Btu/day · sq ft floor · °F. If the rate of space heat loss is higher or lower, adjust the ratios according to the following formula:

$$\text{glazing/floor area} = \frac{HLC(t_i - t_{int}) - t_o}{I_t}$$

where HLC = space heating load coefficient (Btu/day · sq ft floor · °F)

t_i = daily average indoor temperature (normally 68°F for residential applications)

t_{int} = temperature increment due to internal heat generation from people, light, appliances, etc.—normally about 5° for residential applications

t_o = daily average outdoor temperature (clear day)

I_t = daily heat gain (clear day) (Btu/day · sq ft floor)

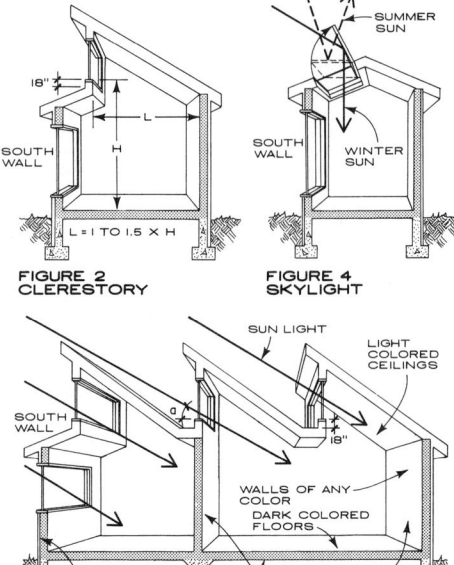

FIGURE 2 CLERESTORY

FIGURE 4 SKYLIGHT

FIGURE 3 SAWTOOTH CLERESTORIES

TABLE 2. DAILY SPACE AIR TEMPERATURE FLUCTUATIONS[1] FOR DIRECT GAIN WATER STORAGE WALL SYSTEMS[2]

SOLAR ABSORPTION (SURFACE COLOR)	VOLUME[3] OF WATER WALL FOR EACH SQUARE FOOT OF SOUTH FACING GLASS			
	1 CU FT	1.5 CU FT	2 CU FT	3 CU FT
75% (dark color)	~17°F	15°F	13°F	12°F
90% (black)	15°F	12°F	10°F	9°F

NOTES

1. Temperature fluctuations are for a clear winter day with approximately 3 sq ft of exposed wall area for each square foot of south glass. If less wall area is exposed in the space, temperature fluctuations will be slightly higher. If additional mass is located in the space (such as masonry walls and/or floor) then fluctuations will be less than those listed and therefore less water can be used.

2. Assumes that 75% of the sunlight entering the space strikes the mass wall.

3. 1 cu ft of water = 62.4 lb or 7.48 gal.

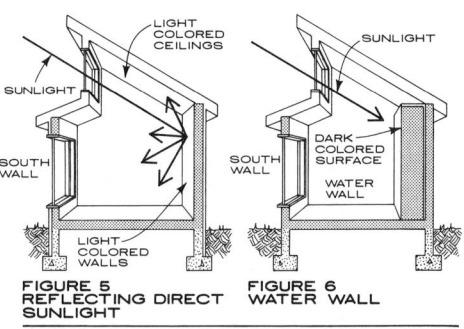

FIGURE 5 REFLECTING DIRECT SUNLIGHT

FIGURE 6 WATER WALL

DIRECT GAIN SYSTEMS

TABLE 3. SIZING AN INDIRECT GAIN MASONRY THERMAL STORAGE WALL (TROMBE WALL) FOR DIFFERENT CLIMATIC CONDITIONS

AVERAGE WINTER TEMP. (CLEAR DAY)	SQUARE FEET OF MASONRY WALL NEEDED FOR EACH SQUARE FOOT OF FLOOR AREA			
	36°NL	40°NL	44°NL	48°NL
Cold climates				
20°F	0.71	0.75	0.85	0.95
25°F	0.59	0.63	0.75	0.84
30°F	0.50	0.53	0.60	0.70
Temperate climates				
35°F	0.40	0.43	0.50	0.55
40°F	0.32	0.35	0.40	0.44
45°F	0.25	0.26	0.30	0.33

NOTE: These tables apply to a well insulated space with a heat load coefficient (HLC) of 8 Btu/day · sq ft floor · °F. If the rate of space heat loss is higher or lower, adjust the ratios accordingly. The surface area of the wall is assumed to be the same size as the glazing. For a thermal wall with a horizontal specular reflector equal to the height of the wall in length or one that utilizes night insulation (R-9), use 60% of the recommended ratios. Since the ratios are very large in cold climates, night insulation is recommended.

TABLE 5. SUGGESTED MATERIAL THICKNESS FOR INDIRECT GAIN THERMAL STORAGE WALLS

MATERIAL	RECOMMENDED THICKNESS
Adobe	8 to 12 in.
Brick (common)	10 to 14 in.
Concrete (dense)	12 to 18 in.
Water	6 in. or more

NOTE: When using water in tubes, cylinders, or other types of circular containers, have a container of at least a 9½ in. diameter or holding ½ cu ft (31 lb, 3.7 gal) of water for each one square foot of glazing.

TABLE 4. SIZING AN INDIRECT GAIN WATER FILLED THERMAL STORAGE WALL FOR DIFFERENT CLIMATIC CONDITIONS

AVERAGE WINTER TEMP. (CLEAR DAY)	SQUARE FEET OF WATER WALL NEEDED FOR EACH SQUARE FOOT OF FLOOR AREA			
	36°NL	40°NL	44°NL	48°NL
Cold climates				
20°F	0.52	0.55	0.65	0.80
25°F	0.45	0.47	0.55	0.64
30°F	0.36	0.39	0.45	0.55
Temperate climates				
35°F	0.28	0.31	0.35	0.40
40°F	0.23	0.25	0.29	0.32
45°F	0.17	0.18	0.20	0.24

NOTE: See note to Table 3.

TABLE 6. APPROXIMATE SPACE TEMPERATURE FLUCTUATIONS AS A FUNCTION OF INDIRECT GAIN THERMAL STORAGE WALL MATERIAL AND THICKNESS

MATERIALS	THICKNESS (IN.)					
	4	8	12	16	20	24
Adobe	—	18°	7°	7°	8°	—
Brick (common)	—	24°	11°	7°	—	—
Concrete (dense)	—	28°	16°	10°	6°	5°
Water (31°F)	—	18°	13°	11°	10°	9°

NOTE: Assumes a double glazed thermal wall. If additional mass is located in the space, such as masonry walls and/or floors, then temperature fluctuations will be less than those listed. Values are given for clear winter days.

Edward Mazria, AIA, Architect; Edward Mazria & Associates; Albuquerque, New Mexico

1 ENVIRONMENTAL FACTORS

PASSIVE SOLAR HEATING— CALCULATION PROCEDURE

The rules of thumb given in the design procedure make it possible to integrate passive solar systems in the schematic design of a building. They give enough detailed information to size a system that will function effectively. After schematic design for the building is complete, it is possible to calculate the thermal performance of each space and make adjustments to the system, if necessary.

The rules of thumb for sizing a system are based on clear day solar radiation and average clear day outdoor temperatures for the winter months. Essentially, this sizing procedure balances the heat lost from a space (kept at $68°F\pm$) over the day with the energy collected from the sun (when shining) that same day. This condition is referred to as the design-day. Because design-day data have been used, it can be expected that the system will not perform as effectively under more severe conditions, although the massive nature of passive buildings tends to moderate the effects of weather extremes. It is reasonable to expect that a sizing procedure for the worst possible winter weather conditions is usually not practical. This would result in spaces that are uncomfortably warm during normal sunny weather and would lead to a design that is oversized and most likely uneconomical to build. For this reason, some form of backup heating system is desirable in most passive solar heated buildings.

Five steps are involved in calculating a system's performance:

1. Calculating the space heat load coefficient.
2. Calculating the monthly space heating requirements.
3. Calculating the monthly solar heating contribution.
4. Determining the average daily indoor temperature.
5. Determining the daily indoor temperature fluctuation.

HEATING LOAD COEFFICIENT

Heat is lost from a space through the skin of a building by two methods: heat loss through the walls, floor, roof, and windows (conduction losses) and heat loss through the exchange of warmed indoor air with cold outdoor air (infiltration losses). The space heat load coefficient is then the sum of the rate of the conduction losses plus the infiltration losses in $Btu/day \cdot °F$.

The building heat load coefficient is computed by using standard ASHRAE space heat loss calculations:

heat load coefficient $(Btu/day \cdot °F)$

$$= \frac{24 \times (\text{space heat loss})}{\text{inside temperature} - \text{outdoor design temperature}}$$

where space heat loss = calculated heat required to maintain the building at a fixed temperature if the outside temperature is equal to the design temperature, in Btu/hr.

MONTHLY SPACE HEATING REQUIREMENT

Compute the monthly space heating requirement $(Q_{r\,month})$ in Btu's by the number of degree-days for the month (DD_{month}).

$$Q_{r\,month} = HLC \times DD_{month}$$

Degree-days for major cities in the United States are given on a page titled WINTER WEATHER DATA AND DESIGN CONDITIONS.

MONTHLY SOLAR HEATING CONTRIBUTION

Three computations are necessary to determine the monthly solar heating contribution $(Q_{c\,month})$ for passive systems.

1. Computing the monthly solar load ratio (SLR) for each space.
2. Determining the fraction of the total space monthly heating requirement supplied by solar energy (SHF).
3. Computing the monthly solar heating contribution in Btu's.

MONTHLY SOLAR LOAD RATIO: The solar load ratio (SLR) is calculated for each month using the formula:

$$SLR = \frac{\text{monthly solar energy absorbed}}{Q_{r\,month}}$$

The monthly solar energy absorbed by a space is calculated by multiplying the total building collector area (A_{gl}) by the solar energy transmitted through the glazing (I_t) for that month and the percentage of energy absorbed within the building (space absorptance):

monthly solar energy absorbed

$$= A_{gl} \times I_t \times \text{space absorptance} \times \text{days per month}$$

where
- A_{gl} = unshaded surface area of collector glazing (sq ft)
- I_t = average daily solar heat gain through on square foot of collector glazing (Btu/day)
- space absorptance = the percentage of solar absorbed within the space. For a masonry or water thermal storage wall, the actual absorptance of the surface can be used. For a direct gain system, use 0.95 for a dark interior or deep space and 0.90 for a light interior or shallow space

FRACTION OF THE TOTAL MONTHLY HEATING REQUIREMENT SUPPLIED BY SOLAR EQUIPMENT

The following graphs present a simple method for determining the fraction of the total monthly space heating requirement supplied by a passive system (SHF). Simply follow a vertical line from the SLR (computed for a particular month in the previous step) on the horizontal scale until it intersects the curve that most closely represents the passive system being used. From this intersection draw a straight line to the scale on the left and read the solar heating fraction for that month. (See Figure 7, next page.)

MONTHLY SOLAR HEATING CONTRIBUTION

To compute the monthly solar heating contribution $(Q_{c\,month})$ in Btu's multiply the monthly space heating requirement $(Q_{r\,month})$ by the solar heating fraction (SHF) for that month, or

$$Q_{c\,month} = Q_{r\,month} \times SHF$$

The percentage of the annual building heating requirement supplied by solar energy is estimated, using the totaled space monthly values (yearly total) for Q_c and Q_r, by the formula:

$$\% \text{ solar year} = 100 \times \frac{\Sigma Q_{c\,month}}{\Sigma Q_{r\,year}}$$

AVERAGE DAILY INDOOR TEMPERATURE

After 1 to 3 days of similar weather conditions (clear or cloudy days in a row) a space will stabilize as a thermal system. This means that temperatures in the space remain roughly the same from day to day. Finding the daily average space temperature for this condition is relatively straightforward.

First, find the total daily solar heat gain for each space. An average sunny January day is a reasonable condition to illustrate a system's performance. For a direct gain system, using clear day January values for solar heat gain transmitted through glazing (I_t) from Mazria, calculate the heat gain through each unshaded skylight, clerestory, and window opening:

$$HG_{sol} = I_t \times A_{gl}$$

where
- L_t = solar heat gain through 1 sq ft of glazing (Btu/day)
- A_{gl} = surface area of the unshaded portion of the glazing (sq ft)

The heat gain into a space from a thermal storage wall (HG_{tm}) can be calculated using the formula:

$$HG_{tm} = A_{gl} \times I_t \times F_r$$

where
- A_{gl} = surface area of the unshaded portion of the glazing (sq ft)
- I_t = solar heat gain through 1 sq ft of glazing (Btu/day)
- F_r = the fraction of incident energy on the face of the wall that is transferred to the space

Values of F_r for double glazed thermal storage walls (black exterior wall surface color) are plotted on graphs in Figures 8a and 8b (see next page). To find the value of F_r, first determine the overall U-value of the space (U_{sp}) by dividing the space HLC by the floor area, or

$$U_{sp} = \frac{HLC}{\text{space floor area}}$$

Next find the ratio of thermal wall area to space floor area. For example a 200 sq ft space with a 100 sq ft concrete thermal wall has a ratio of 100/200 or 0.50. Then from 0.50 on the horizontal scale of the graph, follow a vertical line until it intersects the curve for the overall U-value of space. From this intersection move horizontally to the left and read the fraction of energy transmitted through the wall on the vertical

scale. If, for example, the 200 sq ft space had an overall U-value of 6 $Btu/day \cdot sq\,ft_{floor} \cdot °F$, then F will equal 0.35.

When more than one system provides heat to a space, add the heat gains from each system to arrive at the total space heat gain:

$$HG_{sp} = HG_{sol} + HG_{tm}$$

where HG_{sp} = total space heat gain.

Using the heat load coefficient (HLC) and daily heat gain (HG_{sp}), we find the average daily indoor temperature (t_i) by dividing HG_{sp} by HLC and adding the result to the average daily outdoor temperature (t_o) for the design-day:

$$t_i = \frac{HG_{sp}}{HLC} + t_o$$

In residential buildings to account for additional heat gains from lights, appliances, and people, add 5 to $7°F$ to the average daily indoor temperature. For other than residential applications, compute the temperature increment that is due to internal heat generation.

Because of the complicated nature of building design, there is no ideal average indoor temperature, but as the average temperature approaches $70°F$, enough heat is admitted into a space to supply it with all its heating needs for that day. If the average indoor temperature is too low, it can be raised by reducing the rate of space heat loss (HLC), increasing the area of south glazing, or supplying heat to the space from an auxiliary heat source. If the average indoor temperature is above $70°F$, then overheating can be expected during sunny winter days.

DAILY INDOOR TEMPERATURE FLUCTUATION

The effect of the thermal mass on indoor temperature fluctuations is explained on page titled, PASSIVE SOLAR HEATING—DESIGN PROCEDURE. However, since indoor temperature fluctuations are not always symmetrical about the daily average (an equal number of degrees above and below the average) a series of graphs plotting hourly temperatures for a variety of systems is included. To determine hourly indoor temperatures for a design-day, first select the graph that corresponds to your system. Next, using the average indoor temperature that you calculated in the previous step, plot the number of degrees the indoor air temperature is above or below the average for each hour.

DIRECT GAIN SYSTEMS: Masonry Heat Storage— Since the interior surface area of masonry exposed to direct sunlight greatly influences the indoor air temperature fluctuation over a 24 hr period, two cases are presented. The first case shows a ratio of surface area of exposed masonry to south glazing of 3 to 1 (see Figure 9a, next page). The second, a surface area of exposed masonry to south glazing of 9 to 1 (see Figure 9b, next page).

The following graphs plot hourly indoor temperatures above and below the daily average (t_i) for each case using various masonry materials:

1. DIRECT GAIN SYSTEM: Interior Waterwall. In this case the volume of water in direct sunlight is the major determinant of space temperature fluctuations over the day. The following graph plots indoor temperatures, above and below the daily average, for various quantities of water per square foot of south glazing. The surface of the water wall is assumed to be a dark color. (See Figure 10, next page.)

2. THERMAL STORAGE WALL SYSTEM: The material used to construct a thermal storage wall and the thickness of the wall are the major influences on indoor air temperature fluctuations. The following graphs plot indoor air temperatures for various thicknesses of a concrete masonry wall, brick wall, and a water wall.

REFERENCES

1. For a complete explanation of space heat loss calculations, see the Handbook of Fundamentals, American Society of Heating, Refrigerating, and Air Conditioning Engineers (ASHRAE, New York, 1977).

2. J. D. Balcomb and R. D. McFarland, "A Simple Empirical Method for Estimating the Performance of a Passive Solar Heated Building of the Thermal Storage Wall Type," Proceedings of the 2nd National Passive Solar Conference, Philadelphia, March 1978.

3. Edward Mazria, The Passive Solar Energy Book, Rodale Press, Emmaus, Pa., 1979.

Edward Mazria, AIA, Architect; Edward Mazria & Associates; Albuquerque, New Mexico

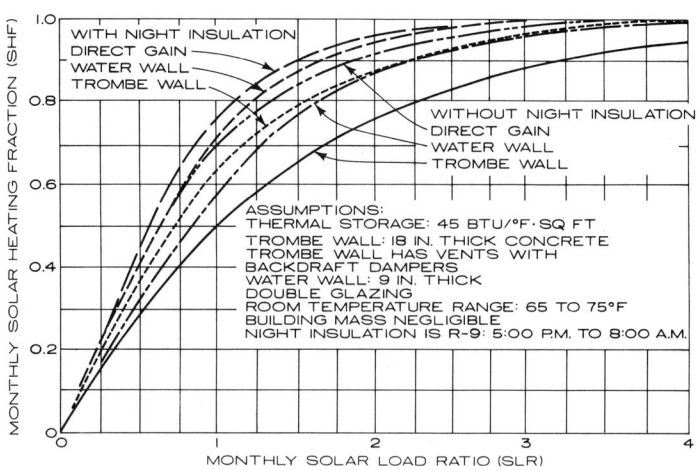

FIGURE 7 FRACTION OF MONTHLY SPACE HEATING REQUIREMENT
SUPPLIED BY SOLAR ENERGY
SOURCE: W.O. WRAY, J.D. BALCOMB AND R.D. McFARLAND
LOS ALAMOS SCIENTIFIC LABORATORY, NEW MEXICO

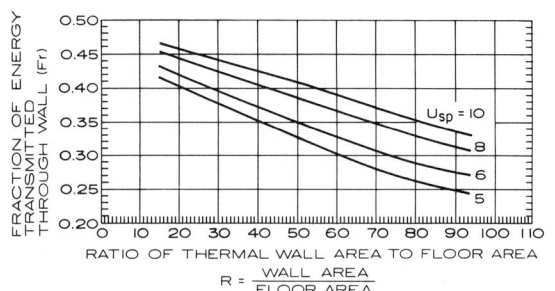

FIGURE 8a CONCRETE THERMAL STORAGE WALL
(I FT THICK)

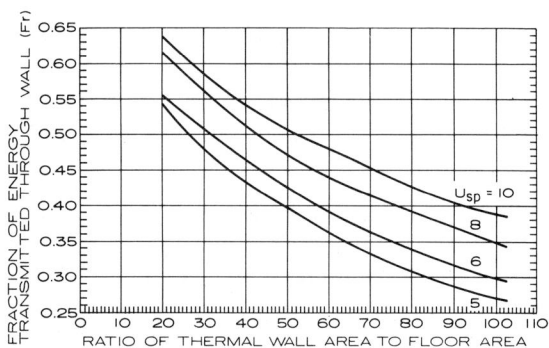

FIGURE 8b WATER THERMAL STORAGE WALL
(ANY THICKNESS)

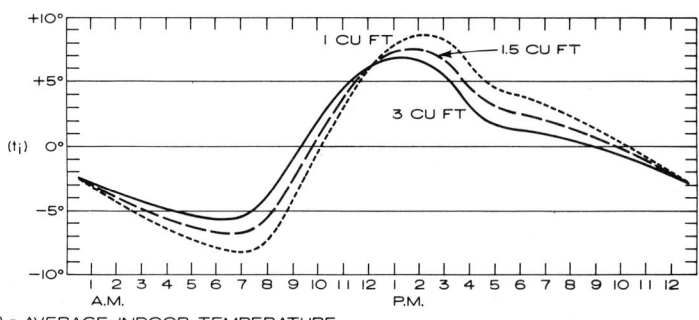

(t_i) = AVERAGE INDOOR TEMPERATURE

FIGURE 10 HOURLY INDOOR TEMPERATURE FOR DIRECT GAIN SYSTEMS
WITH VARIOUS VOLUMES OF WATER STORAGE PER SQUARE FOOT OF
SOUTH FACING GLASS

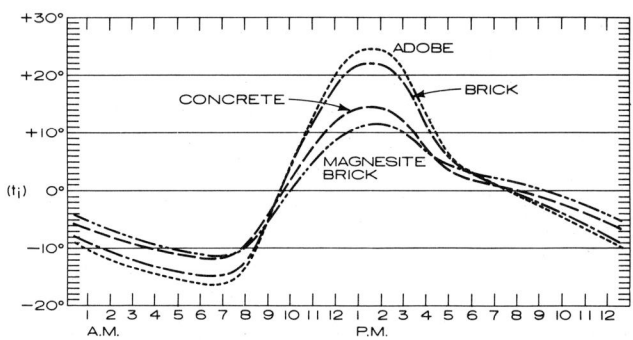

CASE I

FIGURE 9a

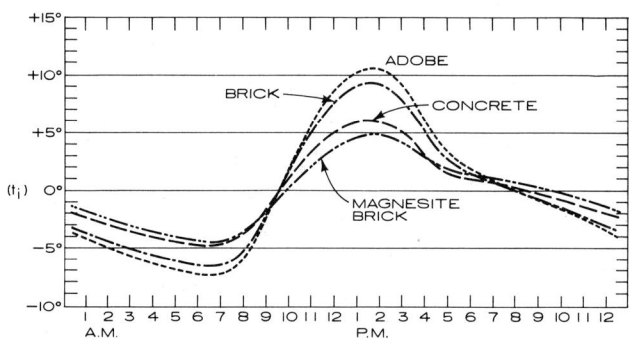

CASE 2 (t_i) = AVERAGE INDOOR TEMPERATURE

FIGURE 9b HOURLY INDOOR TEMPERATURE FOR DIRECT GAIN
SYSTEMS WITH MASONRY HEAT STORAGE

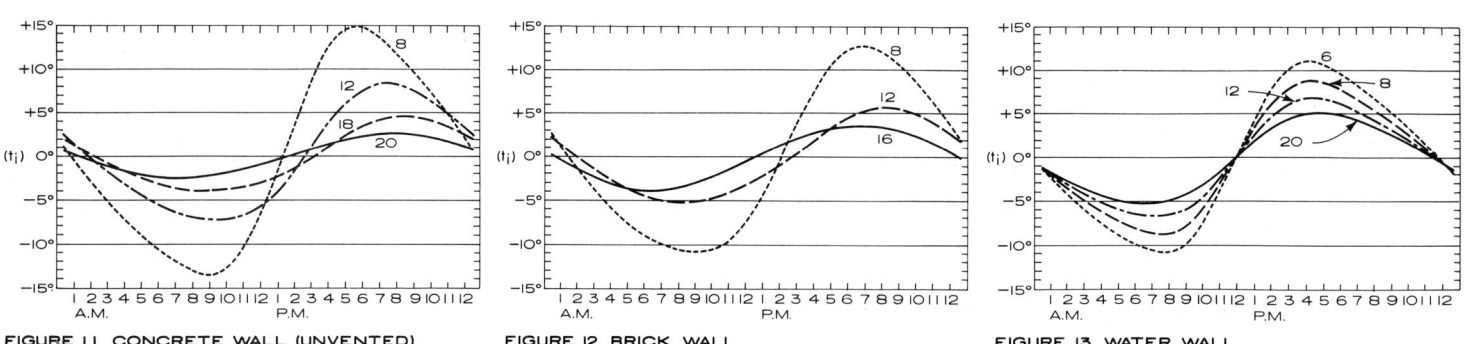

FIGURE II CONCRETE WALL (UNVENTED)   FIGURE I2 BRICK WALL   FIGURE I3 WATER WALL

HOURLY INDOOR TEMPERATURE FOR A THERMAL STORAGE WALL OF VARYING THICKNESS

Edward Mazria, AIA, Architect; Edward Mazria & Associates; Albuquerque, New Mexico

1 ENVIRONMENTAL FACTORS

GENERAL

This three step process evaluates energy conserving alternatives in terms of expected annual savings.

1. Step 1 quantifies peak heating and cooling savings (Btuh).
2. Step 2 converts peak savings to annual savings (Btu).
3. Step 3 establishes a dollar value for annual savings.

Cost benefit analysis involving annual savings and initial cost is a relatively simple matter when the process has been completed.

The following tables provide approximate values for outdoor design temperatures, R values, and ETD. For more detailed and precise information the 1977 ASHRAE Handbook of Fundamentals should be consulted.

TABLE A. OUTDOOR DESIGN TEMPERATURES

CITY	WINTER	SUMMER
Phoenix, AR	34	107
Los Angeles, CA	43	80
San Francisco, CA	40	71
Denver, CO	1	91
Miami, FL	47	90
Chicago, IL	2	91
Bangor, MA	-6	81
Jackson, MS	25	95
Lincoln, NE	-2	95
New York, NY	15	89
Bismarck, ND	-19	91
Muskogee, OK	15	98
Philadelphia, PA	14	90
Dallas, TX	22	100
Seattle, WA	26	81

SOURCE: 1977 ASHRAE Fundamentals, Chapter 23, Table 1.

TABLE B. SELECTED R VALUES (APPROXIMATE)

Glass, single	0.9
Glass, double or storm	1.5
Glass, triple	2.5
Brick (4" thick nominal)	0.1
Concrete brick (4" thick nominal)	0.7
Concrete 1" thick	0.1
Wood 1" thick	1.2
Insulation 1" thick (most materials)	3.5
Insulation polyurethane 1" thick (2 pcf)	5.5
Aluminum foil plus airspace, ceiling	3.0
Aluminum foil plus airspace, wall	2.0

NOTE: For increased thickness, increase R value as appropriate [i.e., 2" wood R = 2.5 (1.25 x 2)].

TABLE C. EQUIVALENT TEMPERATURE DIFFERENCE

DESIGN TEMPERATURE (°F)	90°	95°	100°
Walls—frame or veneer	19	24	29
8" masonry	11	16	21
Ceilings and roof			
Dark color	39	44	49
Light color	31	36	41

For more accurate information consult ASHRAE Fundamentals, 1977, Chapter 25, Table 35.

TABLE D. ENERGY UNITS FOR 1,000,000 BTU

HEATING	UNITS	COOLING	UNITS (kWh)
Coal	100 lb	EER 6	167
Oil	10 gal	EER 7	143
Natural gas	14 therms	EER 8	125
Propane	16 gal	EER 9	111
Electric resistance heat	293 kWh	EER 10	100
Electric heat pump COP 2	147 kWh	EER 11	91

NOTE: Assumes 70% combustion efficiency for heating fuels. If 60%, multiply by 0.86; if 80%, multiply by 1.14. For heat pump C.O.P. above 2, (divide) by COP/2.

F. J. Trost; Texas A & M University; College Station, Texas

EXAMPLE OF INSULATION APPLICATION

A building in Muskogee, OK, is to be reroofed, and the owner is considering adding R-19 insulation. Conditions are as follows: roof area = 1000 sq ft; roof R = 7; roof color = dark; design temperatures = 70°F indoors, 15°F outdoors in winter; 80°F indoors, 98°F outdoors in summer.

STEP 1

Quantify winter peak heat loss in Btuh using the formula:

$$\frac{(area) \times (TD)}{R} = Btuh$$

where area = roof area (sq ft)

TD = temperature difference indoors to outdoors (°F)

R = total resistance value for the roof construction (including all components and air films)

Quantify summer peak heat gain in Btuh using the formula:

$$\frac{(area) \times (ETD)}{R} = Btuh$$

where ETD = equivalent temperature difference (use nearest value; from Table C)

The existing roof has an R value of 7; the new roof will have an R value of 26 (7 plus 19).

Winter heat loss (old)

$$\frac{(1000) \times (55)}{7} = 7857$$

Summer heat gain (old)

$$\frac{1000 \times (49)}{7} = 7000$$

Winter heat loss (new)

$$\frac{(1000) \times (55)}{26} = 2115$$

Summer heat gain (new)

$$\frac{1000 \times (49)}{26} = 1885$$

By subtracting the new values from the old values the peak energy savings are quantified:

Winter savings
5742 Btuh

Summer savings
5115 Btuh

STEP 2

To convert peak savings into annual savings refer to the heating and cooling maps E and F. Multiply the equipment hours by the peak savings in Btuh to obtain the annual Btu savings. For Muskogee, OK, the maps indicate 1200 heating hours and 1500 cooling hours. (Note: local full load hour information will provide more accuracy.)

Annual savings winter:

(1200) x (5742) = 6,890,400, say 6.9 million Btu

Annual savings summer:

(1500) x (5115) = 7,672,500, say 7.7 million Btu

STEP 3

Refer to Table D to determine the units of energy saved and use local utility rates to calculate the annual dollar savings. In this example we use natural gas for heating at X$ per therm and electricity for cooling at Y$ per kWh. Furthermore, we assume an EER of 6 for the air conditioner.

From Table D, 14 therms of gas are required per million Btu heating and 167 kWh per million Btu of cooling.

Annual savings:

(million Btu) (energy units) ($ per unit)

Heating savings:

(6.9) x (14) x (X) = $96.6 (X)

Cooling savings:

(7.7) x (167) x (Y) = $1287 (Y)

sum = total savings/present year

EXAMPLE OF GLAZING APPLICATION

A designer wishes to evaluate double glass for windows in a college dormitory to be constructed in New York City. The dormitory will have 2000 sq ft of window area. Design conditions are 15°F outdoors, 70°F indoors in winter; and 89°F outdoors, 80°F indoors in summer. All windows have external shading so the benefits of double glazing are limited to conducted heat gain and loss only.

STEP 1

Quantify peak heat loss and gain.

Winter heat loss (single)

$$\frac{(2000) \times 55}{0.9} = 122,222$$

Summer heat gain (single)

$$\frac{(2000) \times 9}{0.9} = 20,000$$

Winter heat loss (double)

$$\frac{(2000) \times 55}{1.5} = 73,333$$

Summer heat gain (double)

$$\frac{(2000) \times 9}{1.5} = 12,000$$

By subtracting double values from single values, peak energy savings are quantified.

Winter savings
48,889 Btuh

Summer savings
8000 Btuh

NOTE: Cooling savings are for conducted heat gain only; so the design TD is used as the ETD.

STEP 2

Convert the peak savings to annual savings. Maps indicate 2000 heating hours and 750 cooling hours.

Annual savings, winter

(2000) x (48,889) = 97,778,000, say 98 million Btu

Annual savings, summer

(750) x (8000) = 6,000,000

STEP 3

Calculate the annual utility savings if heating fuel is oil at Z$/gal and cooling is electric, EER = 7, and cost is Y$/kWh.

Heating savings

(98) x (10) x (Y) = $980 (Z)

Cooling savings

(6) x (143) x (Z) = $858 (Y)

sum = total savings/present year

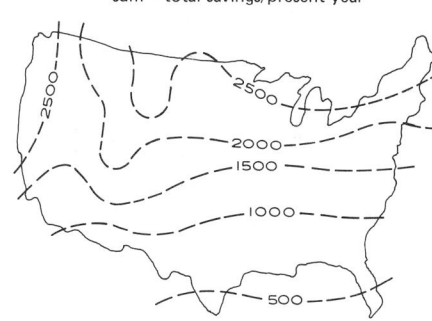

E. HEATING HOURS / YEAR

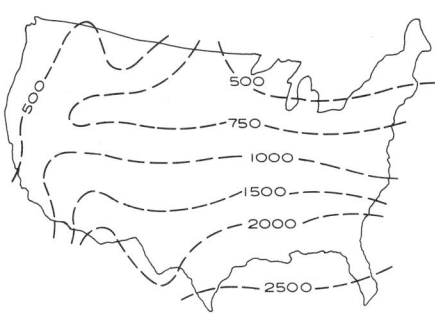

F. COOLING HOURS / YEAR

EQUIVALENT FULL LOAD EQUIPMENT, HOURS / YEAR

ENVIRONMENTAL FACTORS 1

THERMAL STORAGE WALLS

Thermal storage wall designs are passive solar heating approaches that include massive, south facing concrete or masonry walls painted a dark color and covered with glass or some other glazing material. These are known as Trombe walls. Opaque water filled tubes painted a dark color or of clear fiber reinforced plastic (FRP) are often used in lieu of masonry. As solar radiation is transmitted through the glazing material, the thermal storage wall absorbs heat directly, conducts it (and convects it in the case of water containers), and radiates heat to the interior space at night. Vents may be located at the top and bottom of Trombe wall designs to allow for heated air to rise into the living space. Dampers should be included in such vented designs to prevent reverse airflow at night.

Thermal storage walls should either be vented to outside and/or shaded to prevent them from overheating the interior in the summer. However, an unshaded Trombe wall that is vented to the outdoors can effectively induce natural ventilation by the "chimney effect."

Thermal storage walls do not necessarily require insulation but their performance is improved by its application. Exterior hinged insulating panels (which also reflect additional solar radiation onto the wall) or insulating roll shades or curtains may be deployed.

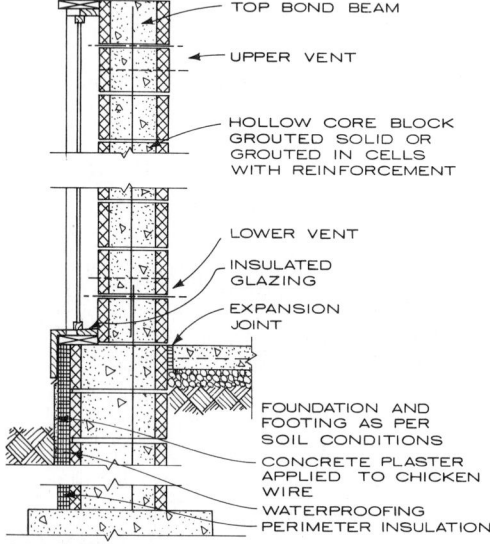

CONCRETE BLOCK STORAGE WALL

The interior finish on the wall must not prevent the wall's heat from radiating to the interior space. A thin plaster coat may be applied, but sheet materials or materials requiring adhesives should not be used.

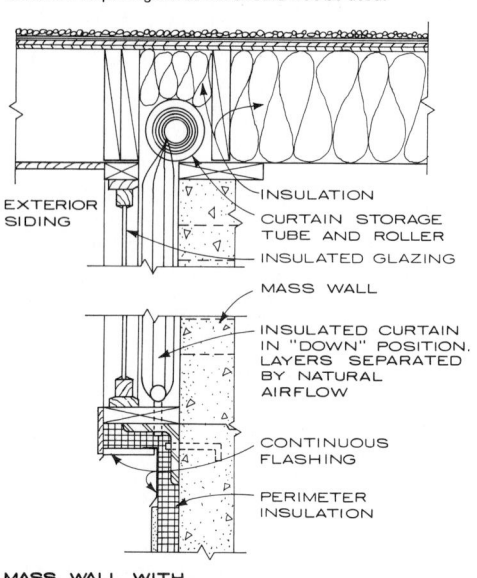

MASS WALL WITH INSULATING CURTAIN

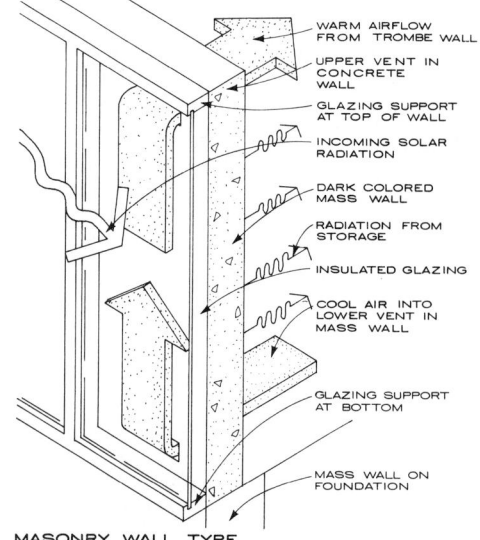

MASONRY WALL TYPE

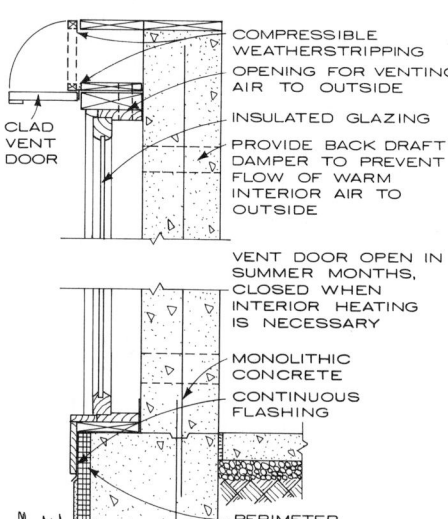

CONCRETE STORAGE WALL WITH OUTSIDE VENT

The exterior glazing component should be mounted 3 to 6 in. out from the wall if natural venting is used or 2 to 4 in. if the system is fan augmented. The use of insulation between the wall and glazing will govern this dimension.

Masonry storage wall designs will vary in thickness (to allow for different time delays of heat movement) depending on the thermal characteristics of the building and the climate in which the building is located.

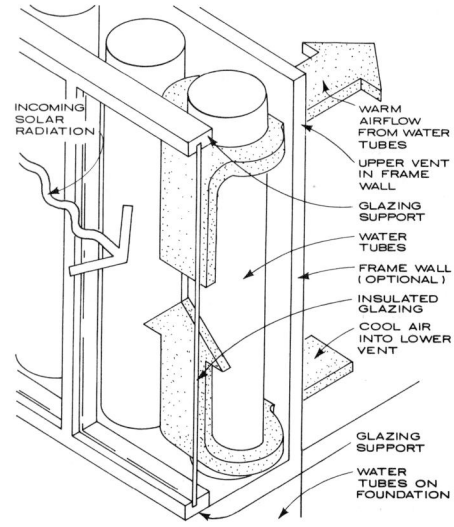

WATER WALL TYPE

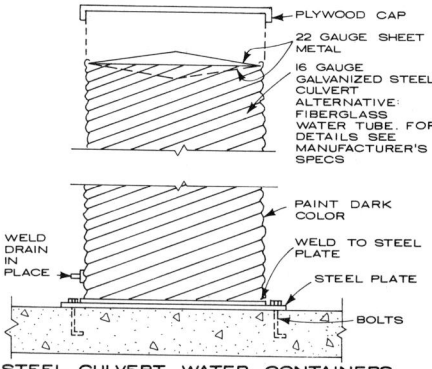

STEEL CULVERT WATER CONTAINERS

WATER WALL

Thermal storage walls of the water container type may be designed as an integral part of the heated space or may be separated from the living space by a vented wall for added comfort control. Corrugated, galvanized steel culverts, FRP, and 55 gal steel drums are the most common containers.

Airspaces in water containers should be provided for the expansion of water. Water in steel containers should also contain a rust inhibitor, while water in FRP tubes should contain algicide to prevent algae growth.

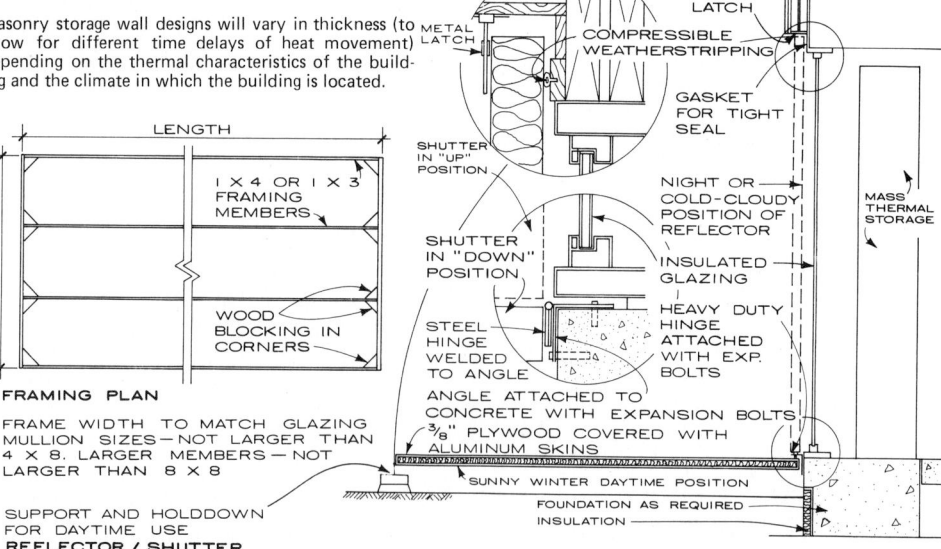

FRAMING PLAN

FRAME WIDTH TO MATCH GLAZING MULLION SIZES—NOT LARGER THAN 4 X 8. LARGER MEMBERS — NOT LARGER THAN 8 X 8

SUPPORT AND HOLDDOWN FOR DAYTIME USE
REFLECTOR / SHUTTER

Professor Kenneth Haggard and Phillip Niles; California Polytechnical State University; San Luis Obispo, California

Lawrence Atkinson and Paul Karius; Atkinson/Karius/Architects; Denver, Colorado

1   ENVIRONMENTAL FACTORS

GENERAL NOTES

Place the collector array where it will receive the maximum amount of available sunlight at your location. A roof mount is most common because it minimizes the possibility of shading due to on- or off-site shading. A roof mount also minimizes the space requirement and safety concerns inherent to ground mounting locations. If an acceptable roof area is not available, collectors may be ground mounted. For further site and installation considerations refer to Installation Guidelines for Solar DHW Systems published by HUD.

COLLECTOR ORIENTATION

It is desirable to mount the collectors to catch as much of the sun's daily rays as possible. Ideally, the collector array should be oriented as nearly as possible to true south, not magnetic south. However, variations of up to 15° east or west of south will have little effect on performance. Typically, it is not worth the added expense to build a special mounting frame to orient collectors true south if the roof is oriented within the ±15° limit. Beyond 15°, the additional calculations must be performed to determine if the expense is justified. Local weather conditions must also be considered when deciding on collector orientation. Although angling the collectors toward the east will start the system earlier in the morning, orientation slightly to the west can increase system performance because ambient temperatures are usually higher in the afternoon. As a result, the collectors will lose less heat and operate more efficiently. If early morning fogs are common in your area, a slight orientation to the west is also desirable.

COLLECTOR TILT

Collector tilt—the angle the surface of the collector makes with the horizon—is also an important factor in collector and overall system performance. Ideally, collector arrays should be positioned where the collector's surface is as nearly perpendicular to the sun's hottest rays as possible. For a solar domestic hot water system, a tilt angle equal to the local north latitude is considered optimum. For a solar space heating or combined space and hot water system, a tilt angle equal to the north latitude + 15° is considered optimum. For a solar swimming pool collector array (summer heating season), a tilt angle equal to the north latitude minus 15° is considered optimum. For example, solar space heating systems located in Denver, Colorado (40°N), would typically be tilted 55° from horizontal for optimum winter collection. Variations of tilt angle ±10° from optimum will not seriously affect the performance of the system.

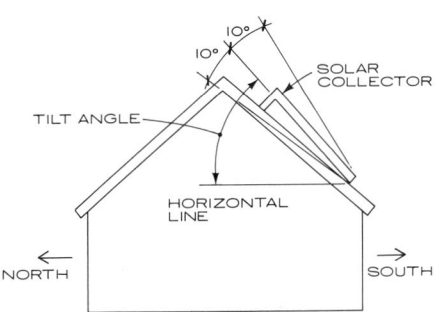

ANGLE/ROOF PITCH CONVERSION TABLE

ANGLE (DEGREES)	ROOF PITCH	ANGLE (DEGREES)	ROOF PITCH
5	1/12	37	9/12
10	2/12	40	10/12
14	3/12	43	11/12
18	4/12	45	12/12
23	5/12	47	13/12
27	6/12	49	14/12
30	7/12	51	15/12
34	8/12	53	16/12

Atkinson/Karius/Architects; Denver, Colorado

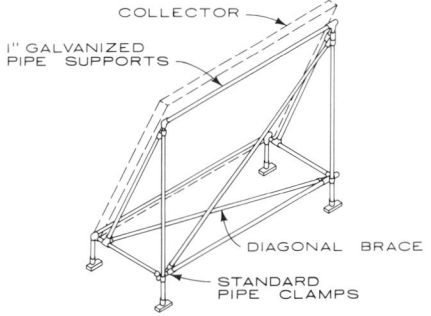

PIPE RACK MOUNTING

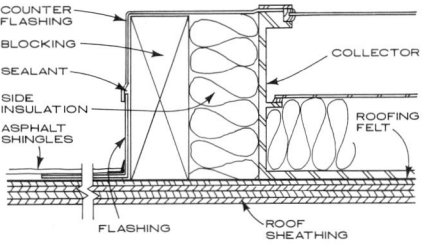

COLLECTOR FLASHING AT SIDES

ATTACHMENTS MADE ACCORDING TO THE SPANNER OR LAG BOLT METHOD BUT WITHOUT MOUNTING BLOCKS. ALTERNATIVE TO PLACING COLLECTORS OVER THE ROOF DECK IS TO INTEGRATE THE COLLECTORS INTO THE ROOF

COLLECTOR FLASHING AT TOP

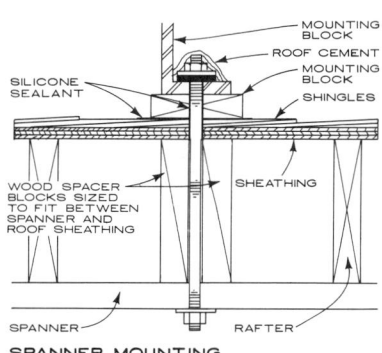

SPANNER MOUNTING

RETROFIT MOUNTING

On retrofit installations, collector arrays should be raised at least 1½ in. above the roof to avoid damage to the shingles. Without that space, moisture buildup could cause growth of fungus, mold, and mildew. Ice dams could also form and draw water under shingles by capillary action. A spanner mount is recommended if the attic is accessible, because the uplift force of wind on the collectors array will be evenly distributed to the roof framing members. Screw or nail 2 x 4 in. spanners directly to the rafters inside the attic, perpendicular to the rafters. If the attic is inaccessible, cut sheetrock and nail wood blocks to the inside of the rafters at least 3 in. short of the ceiling edge. Fasten the spanners on these blocks and bolt. Use threaded through bolts that are at least 3/8 in. in diameter. Replace gypsum board to cover installation. When the attic is completely inaccessible, collectors on the mounting racks can be lag bolted directly to the roof from the outside.

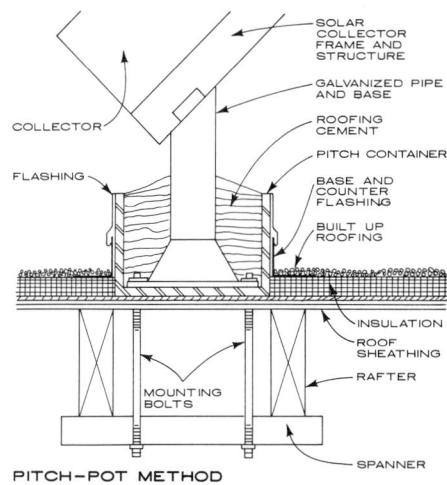

PITCH-POT METHOD

NOTE

An alternative to the pitch pot method is the curb mount. A curb mount requires building up the roof surface with framing members that act as equipment support. The curb is flashed into the roof surface and covered with a sheet metal hood.

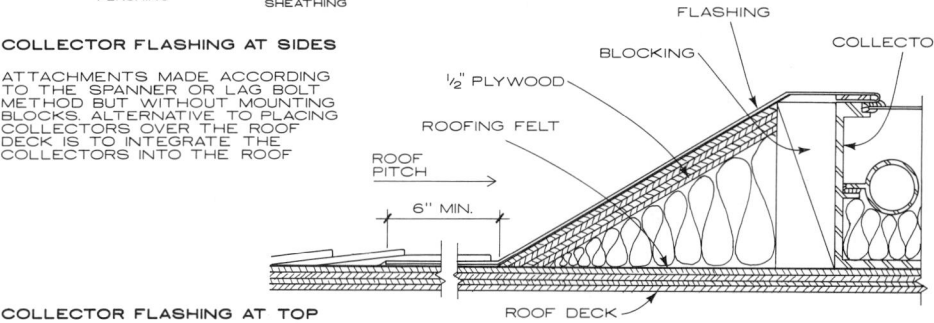

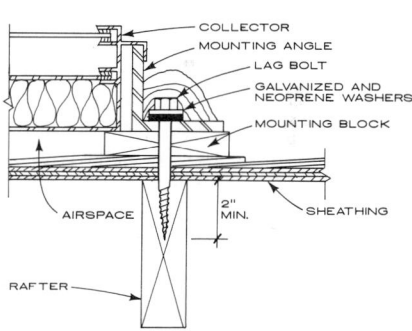

LAG BOLT MOUNTING

RACK MOUNTING (GROUND OR ROOF)

Collectors can be mounted on racks or standoffs to achieve the optimum tilt angle. The collector rack may be made from several materials: galvanized steel pipe, aluminum and steel angle iron, or even wood. If the collector boxes are aluminum, keep the steel and aluminum from contacting each other directly to prevent galvanic corrosion. Slotted steel angle iron of at least 12 gauge and about 1½ x 1½ in. can be cut to any length and bolted together, or 1 in. galvanized pipe and fittings used in awnings or a pipe and fitting system that can be secured with set screws are acceptable. Wood collector racks must be made of redwood, cedar, or treated wood.

In a roof racked array, the bottom of the collectors must be at least 1½ in. off the roof to allow for water and debris passage. All rack should be diagonally braced. If the collectors are ground racked, the bottom edge of the collectors must be a minimum of 18 in. off the ground to prevent mud splashing and snow drifting that may cover the bottom of the panels.

SOLAR RADIANT ENERGY

Solar energy reaches the earth's surface in the form of electromagnetic radiation in the wavelength band between 0.3 and 3.0 micrometers (μm). Beyond the earth's atmosphere, at the average earth-sun distance (about 93 million miles) the radiant flux density on a surface normal to the solar rays is now thought to be 1377 W/sq m or 437 Btu/hr · sq ft. This quantity, known as the solar constant, is apparently subject to minor fluctuations caused by small changes in the sun's output of shortwave (ultraviolet) radiation. An earlier value, 1353 W/sq m or 429.2 Btu/hr · sq ft continues to be widely used pending further measurements from outer space.

At the surface of the earth, solar irradiance falling on horizontal surfaces varies from zero at sunrise to a maximum that, at sea level, may be as high as 325 Btu/hr · sq ft (945 W/sq m) at noon on a clear day. The intensity falls to zero again at sunset. Clear day irradiance values for horizontal and tilted surfaces with varying orientations are given in ASHRAE Publication GRP 170. Values for average day conditions can be found in "Hourly Solar Radiation Data for Vertical and Horizontal Surfaces on Average Days in the United States and Canada" published by the National Bureau of Standards in their Building Science Series 96. A wealth of data on horizontal irradiance is to be found in the "Climatic Atlas of the U.S." and in the publications of the National Weather Service, Asheville, NC. Methods of estimating direct, diffuse, and reflected radiation are given in Chapter 26, 1977 ASHRAE Handbook of Fundamentals.

SOLAR COLLECTION AND UTILIZATION

Solar radiant energy can be put to use at low and moderate temperatures by flat plate collectors, Figure 1, in which a blackened sheet of metal is used to absorb the incoming radiation and covert it to heat. This heat is then conducted to a fluid that passes through tubes or passages integral with or attached to the plate. To minimize loss of heat from the absorber plate, glazing (single or double, with glass or a heat resistant plastic) is used to reduce convection and to suppress longwave radiation exchange with the sky. The rear surface of the collector plate is insulated carefully, preferably with glass fiber that can withstand the relatively high temperatures (300 to 400°F) that can exist under "stagnation" conditions. This occurs when the collector is exposed to full sunshine with no heat transfer fluid flowing through it. The entire unit is contained within a weatherproof box, and connecting pipes or ducts are provided to bring the fluid to the collector and to carry it away after it has been heated. Details of many types of flat plate collectors are given in Chapter 58, 1978 ASHRAE Handbook of Applications. Performance calculations and test data are given in ASHRAE Publication GRP 170.

When high temperatures are required for industrial or power generation applications, concentrating collectors must be used. These reflect or refract a large amount to solar energy onto a relatively small absorber area, thus reducing the surface available for heat loss and enabling the fluid to attain temperatures that can exceed 1000°F. Such collectors must "track the sun" because they can use only the direct beam radiation from the solar disk. Some concentrating collectors remain essentially fixed, but these are limited to concentration ratios of less than 3 : 1.

SOLAR ENERGY UTILIZATION SYSTEMS

A system for using solar energy consists of an array of collectors, a storage subsystem, and another subsystem, which is generally quite conventional, for distributing the heated fluid and returning it to storage. Pumps or fans are used to circulate the heat transfer fluid, and control devices are used to start and stop the circulators. Auxiliary or standby heat sources are generally needed to carry part of the load when demand is exceptionally heavy and the thermal storage is depleted due to long periods of unfavorable weather.

Figure 2 shows a simple system for providing space heating and domestic hot water, using a drain-down procedure in which the collectors are emptied whenever the pump P1 stops. A differential controller senses the temperatures of the collector plate and the water and starts the circulating pump P1 when the sun has heated the plate above the water temperature. The pump is stopped when the plate temperature drops to

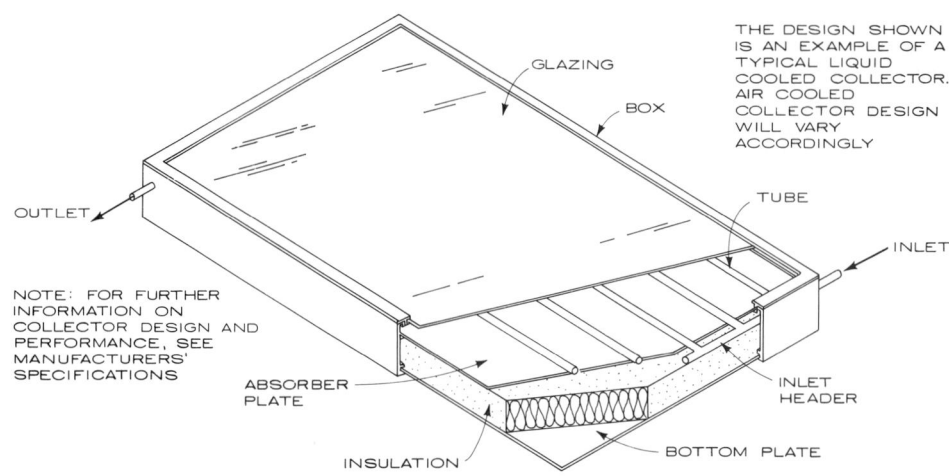

FIGURE I. TYPICAL FLAT PLATE COLLECTOR

THE DESIGN SHOWN IS AN EXAMPLE OF A TYPICAL LIQUID COOLED COLLECTOR. AIR COOLED COLLECTOR DESIGN WILL VARY ACCORDINGLY

NOTE: FOR FURTHER INFORMATION ON COLLECTOR DESIGN AND PERFORMANCE, SEE MANUFACTURERS' SPECIFICATIONS

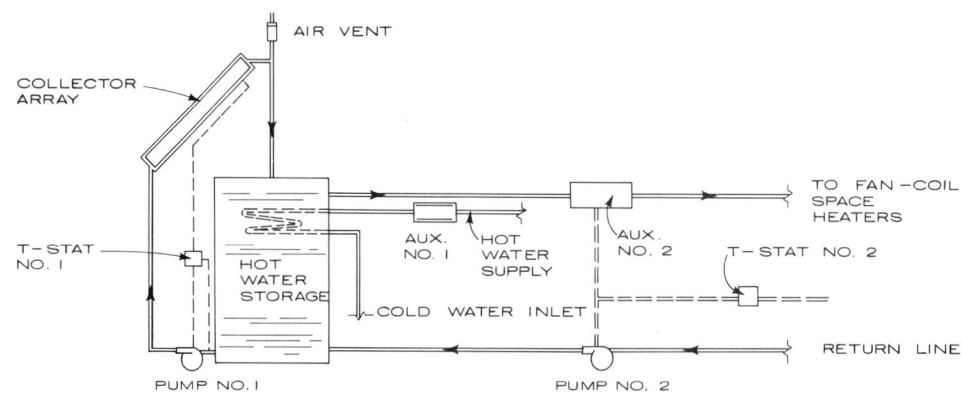

FIGURE 2. DRAIN – DOWN SOLAR WATER SYSTEM

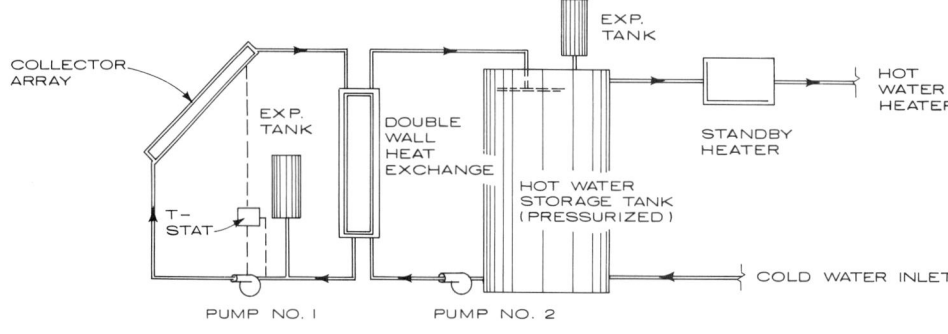

FIGURE 3. SOLAR WATER HEATING SYSTEM

the point where collection of heat is no longer possible.

Domestic hot water is provided by a pipe coil or a small tank located near the top of the main storage tank. The domestic hot water system operates under full line pressure whereas the main tank is at essentially atmospheric pressure, so any leakage would normally be into the main tank. Because of the very remote possibility of a back flow from the main tank into the city water supply, some plumbing codes require a double wall heat exchanger for this service. An auxiliary heater is provided to ensure an adequate supply of hot water at all times.

Since solar heat collection systems work more efficiently when the temperature difference between the collector and the ambient air is relatively low, fancoil units with large areas of finned tube heat transfer surface are generally selected for the space heating assignment. These can be used with water temperatures as low as 100°F. The auxiliary heat source in many solar installations will be electricity, and the heater may use simple direct resistance elements. When cooling is required as well as heating, a heat pump may

prove to be a wise choice, particularly when large amounts of auxiliary energy are likely to be needed.

FREEZE PROTECTION FOR LIQUID SYSTEMS

When water is used as the heat transfer fluid, freeze protection must always be provided, since there is no location within the continental United States where freezing has never been known to occur. The drain-down system shown in Figure 2 is a fail-safe method to provide such protection but it has certain disadvantages that, in many applications, make the use of a freezing point depressant advisable. Figure 3 shows a widely used system in which water plus ethylene glycol or propylene glycol, or some similar antifreeze fluid, is circulated through the collector array by pump P1. A double wall heat exchanger is used to transfer the collected heat to the service hot water which is under full line pressure, and a standby heater is provided to raise the temperature of the sun heated water to the conventional 140°F. Since domestic hot water is rarely actually used at 140°F, it is beneficial to use a lower thermostat setting for the hot water and to use less cold water for dilution.

John I. Yellot, P.E. and Gary Yabumoto; College of Architecture; Arizona State University; Tempe, Arizona

1 ENVIRONMENTAL FACTORS

AIR SYSTEMS

For residences in cold areas, where freezing is a serious problem, air systems are frequently used, since air heaters cannot freeze. Air leakage is generally a minor maintenance problem although it can cause a substantial loss of performance efficiency. Figure 1 shows a typical air system in which domestic hot water is provided by means of a heat exchanger in the duct between the collector array and the rock bed. Operation of this system is similar in principal to that of a water system. By opening dampers 1 and 3 and closing dampers 2 and 4, the air is circulated by blower No.1 through the heater array, through the water heater coil, and into the top of the rock bed. During the daylight hours, when little if any heat is required indoors, the entire output of the collectors can be used to charge the rock bed. Thanks to the stratification that is inherent in a rock bed, the air leaving the bottom of the bed will generally be relatively cool, thus improving the collector efficiency.

When heat is required indoors, the damper setting can be reversed and blower No. 2 goes into action, circulating air from the house upward through the rock bed so that it encounters the hottest rocks as it is leaving the bed on its way back to the house.

SOLAR COOLING SYSTEMS

Cooling can be accomplished by combining an evaporative cooler with a rock bed or by using an indirect plate type heat exchanger so that the humid, evaporatively cooled air will not have to mix with the air being supplied to the space. Such systems are in wide use in Australia and they will become more popular in the United States as the cost of electricity rises.

Heat gathered at moderately high temperatures (175–195°F) by solar collectors can be used successfully to operate lithium bromide-water absorption cooling systems of the type shown schematically in Figure 2. When the unit is in operation, a continuous supply of "rich" lithium bromide-water solution is provided by the generator (A) to the evaporator (B) where water vapor at very low pressure is absorbed by the Li Br-H_2O solution. The chilled water produced by the evaporator is supplied to the fan coil unit to produce the desired cooling effect, and the heat that is picked up within the chiller unit is dissipated by a cooling tower.

The coefficient of performance of an absorption chiller is in the range of 0.5 and 0.7, which is far lower than the C.O.P. of compression systems, but the heat used by the absorption units is generally less expensive than the electricity required by compression machines. The absorption unit in the present stage of its development requires the cooling tower shown in Figure 2, while compression units can use air cooled condensers. Because of both cost and complexity, the absorption unit is better suited to large installations than to residences. The solar apparatus can be used for winter heating by setting the three-way valves V2 and V3 to deliver the sun heated water directly to the fan coil unit and returning it to the storage tank.

Another solar cooling process that is still in the development stage uses Rankine or other thermal power cycle to operate a vapor compression system. If the solar power generator can operate at a sufficiently high temperature, the C.O.P. of the system can be considerably higher than that of an absorption system and air cooled condenser can be used. Equipment to accomplish this at moderate cost is under development by several manufacturers but it is not yet available.

SOLAR ELECTRICITY

Electricity can be generated directly from solar radiation, without the intervention of a thermal cycle, by the use of photovoltaic cells. Developed originally for the U.S. Space Program, silicon solar batteries have been used successfully on the earth's surface for the generation of increasingly large amounts of electric power in the form of low voltage direct current. By employing well-known electronic technology, this can be converted into 120 V alternating current suitable for operating domestic appliances as well as irrigation pumps, communication apparatus, community refrigerators, and so on.

Silicon solar cells can use only a portion of the total

solar spectrum, and they must be kept at temperatures below about 180°F in order to retain acceptable efficiency. Concentrating devices can be employed to increase the amount of solar radiation reaching a single cell and thus to enhance its output, provided that the necessary temperature restrictions are maintained.

This capability is now being put to use by systems similar to Figure 3, in which a fluid stream is used to carry useful heat away from the solar cell array for storage and subsequent use for space heating, domestic hot water, and so on. Conventional lead-acid batteries

are used to store the electricity generated whenever the sun shines for use at night and during cloudy periods.

The system shown in Figure 3 is still in the development stage but it offers promise for providing substantial amounts of electric power and heat at moderate temperatures for residential and commercial use. Extensive research and development work is being carried on to reduce the costs of such systems and thus to make them available for use first in isolated locations without conventional sources of electricity and later for much wider applications.

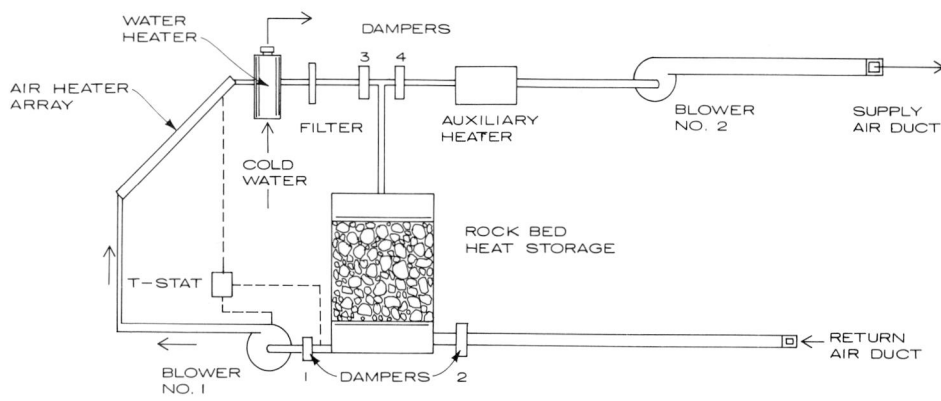

FIGURE 1. SOLAR AIR HEATER SYSTEM WITH ROCK BED STORAGE

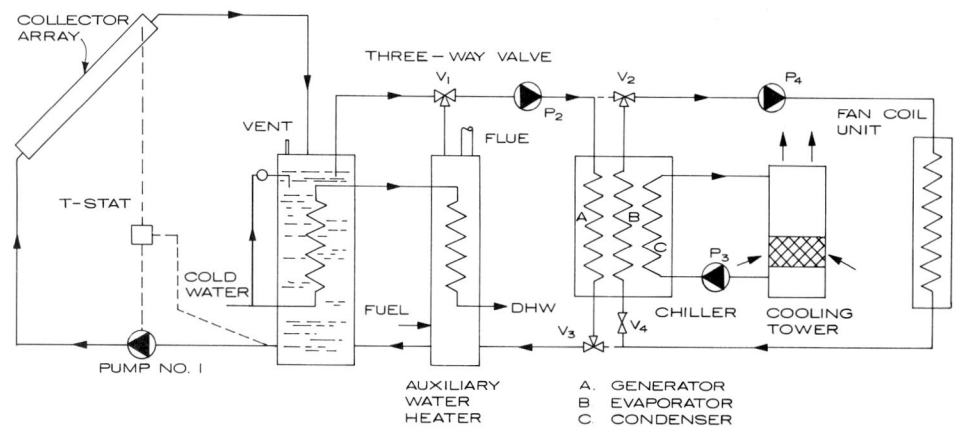

FIGURE 2. SOLAR POWERED ABSORPTION AIR CONDITIONER

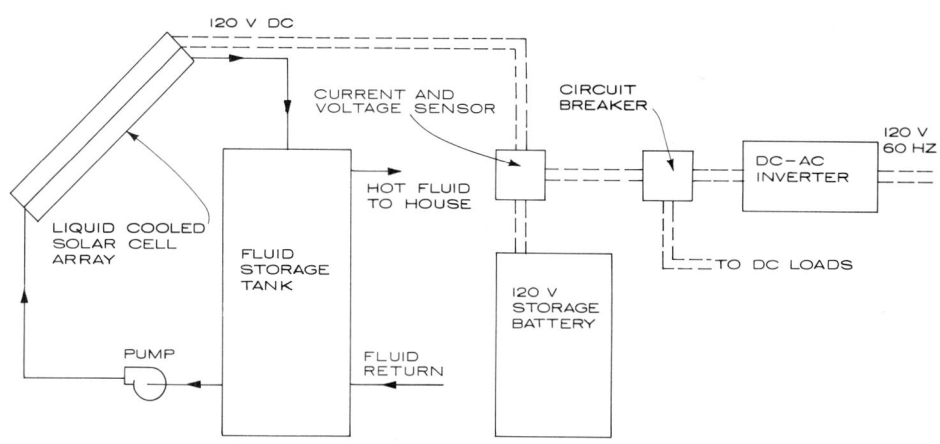

FIGURE 3. LIQUID COOLED PHOTOVOLTAIC SYSTEM FOR PRODUCING 60HZ — 120V POWER AND HEAT

John I. Yellot, P.E. and Gary Yabumoto; College of Architecture; Arizona State University; Tempe, Arizona

ENVIRONMENTAL FACTORS   1

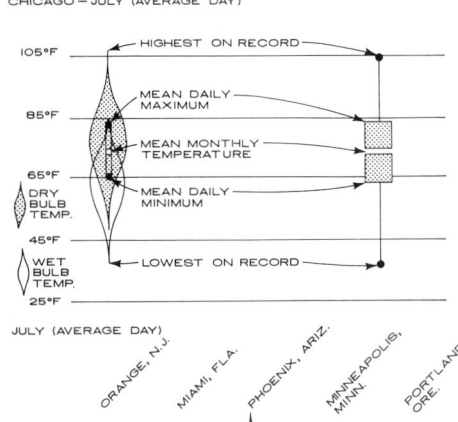

CHICAGO — JULY (AVERAGE DAY)

JULY (AVERAGE DAY)

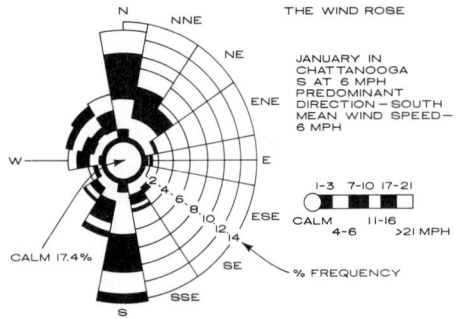

ORANGE, N.J. · MIAMI, FLA. · PHOENIX, ARIZ. · MINNEAPOLIS, MINN. · PORTLAND, ORE.

TEMPERATURE

A record of local daily and monthly temperatures will be a clear indication of the expected monthly heating and cooling loads as well as of the potential for diurnal "time lag" conditioning.

Dry bulb temperature is the sensible air temperature read from a standard thermometer; mean monthly temperatures, mean maximum and minimums, and record highs and lows should be recorded. The diurnal temperature swing is the range between day and night, or minimum and maximum mean temperatures. For load calculations, heating degree days and cooling hours provide a more accurate, cumulative calculation of mean monthly temperatures, measured daily as the number of degrees of difference between outdoor mean temperatures and a design base, usually 65°F.

THE WIND ROSE

JANUARY IN CHATTANOOGA S AT 6 MPH PREDOMINANT DIRECTION — SOUTH MEAN WIND SPEED — 6 MPH

1-3 7-10 17-21
CALM 11-16
4-6 >21 MPH

CALM 17.4%

% FREQUENCY

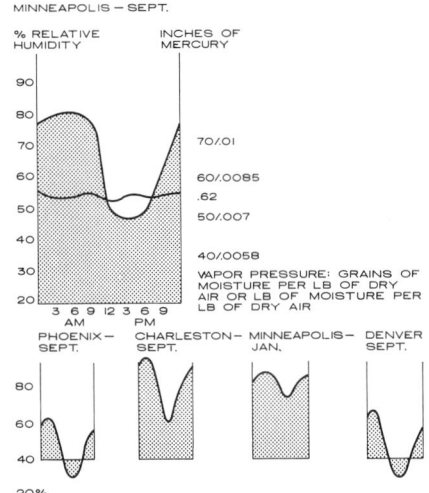

MINNEAPOLIS — SEPT.

% RELATIVE HUMIDITY   INCHES OF MERCURY

70/.01
60/.0085
.62
50/.007
40/.0058

VAPOR PRESSURE: GRAINS OF MOISTURE PER LB OF DRY AIR OR LB OF MOISTURE PER LB OF DRY AIR

PHOENIX — SEPT. · CHARLESTON — SEPT. · MINNEAPOLIS — JAN. · DENVER — SEPT.

20%

RELATIVE HUMIDITY

A record of monthly day and night moisture conditions, coincident with dry bulb temperatures, will indicate the severity of the summer cooling load, as well as the potential for evaporative cooling or the need for dehumidification.

Wet bulb temperature is the measure of the heat held latent in water vapor in the air. The more closely wet bulb temperature matches dry bulb temperatures, the more humid and latently heated is the air. Relative humidity is the amount of moisture in the air expressed as a percentage of the total amount of moisture the air can hold at a given temperature, while vapor pressure represents the amount of moisture actually in the air regardless of temperature. Any two of these factors—wet bulb, dry bulb, relative humidity, and vapor pressure—will give the other two factors on a psychrometric chart.

WIND

A record of monthly wind speeds and direction will indicate the severity of infiltration loads in winter, as well as the potential for natural ventilation in summer.

Wind direction at different times of day and night, in different seasons, will suggest the means to both deflect winter winds and accept summer breezes in building design. Wind speed states the seriousness and the usefulness of these winds, ranging from calm or 0 mph to greater than 20 mph, while wind frequency will reinforce the occurrence of each wind direction and speed.

GROUND TEMPERATURES AND SKY TEMPERATURES

Two additional monthly data points worthy of collection are effective sky temperatures to indicate the potential for radiant cooling and ground temperatures at various depths to indicate the potential for modifying the severity of winter and summer temperatures in harsh climates.

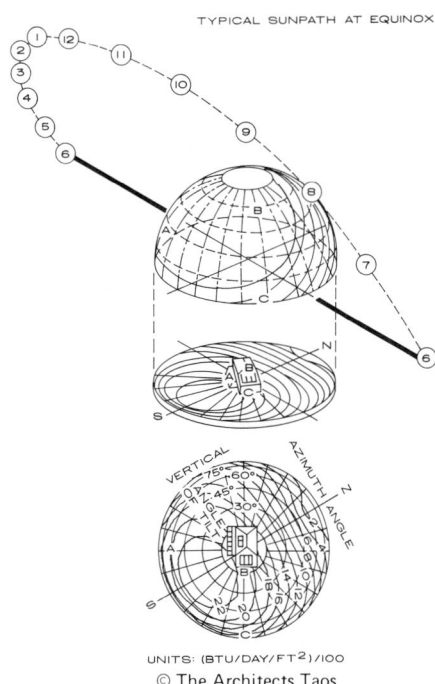

TYPICAL SUNPATH AT EQUINOX

UNITS: (BTU/DAY/FT²)/100

© The Architects Taos

SUN

A record of solar intensity and availability, called irradiation or insolation, will anticipate the cooling loads caused by sun conditions in summer, as well as the potential for solar heating in winter.

Solar intensity is the sun's heat measured in Btu/sq ft · hr, or per day or month, in a given location on horizontal and vertical surfaces.

Solar availability is the time the sun spends in a clear sky, measured in clear sky and cloudiness factors. Degree of altitude represents the sun's height on a vertical axis, higher in summer, and azimuth represents its location on the horizontal, compass directions, a wider range in summer. A north window generally receives bounced diffuse light while a window that sees the sun receives direct and diffuse light.

REFERENCES

National Bureau of Standards, Gaithersburg, Md. Horizontal and Vertical Radiation Data for 48 Cities and SOLMET (Tapes) Solar Radiation Data for 130 Cities.

AIA/House Beautiful's Regional Climate Study 1952, Twelve Regions, Michigan University Press, Ann Arbor, Mich.

ASHRAE's Handbook of Fundamentals, 1977.

National Climatic Center's Asheville N.C., National Climate Summary, 1978, NTIS.

DATA COLLECTION

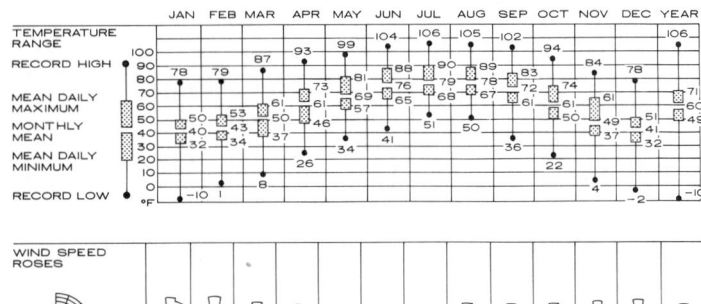

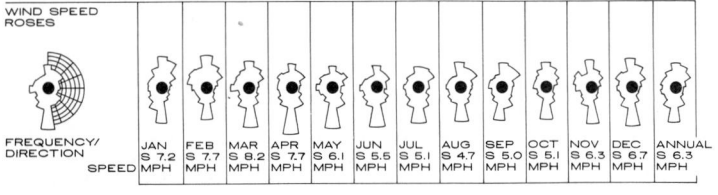

DATA DISPLAY

Vivian Loftness, Kevin Green and Fred Greenberg; AIA Research Corporation; under contract with National Oceanographic and Atmospheric Administration and U.S. Department of Energy

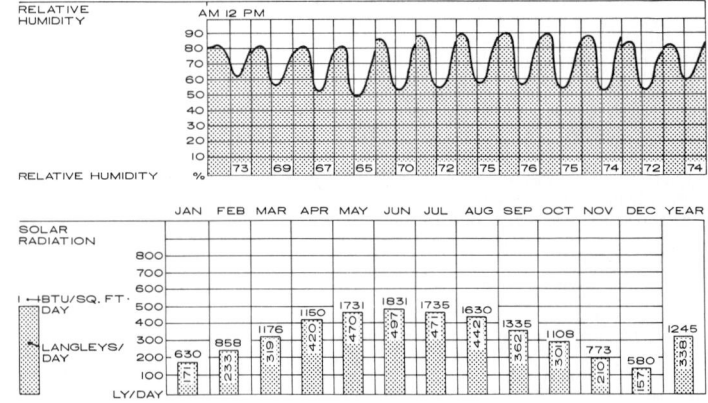

1 ENVIRONMENTAL FACTORS

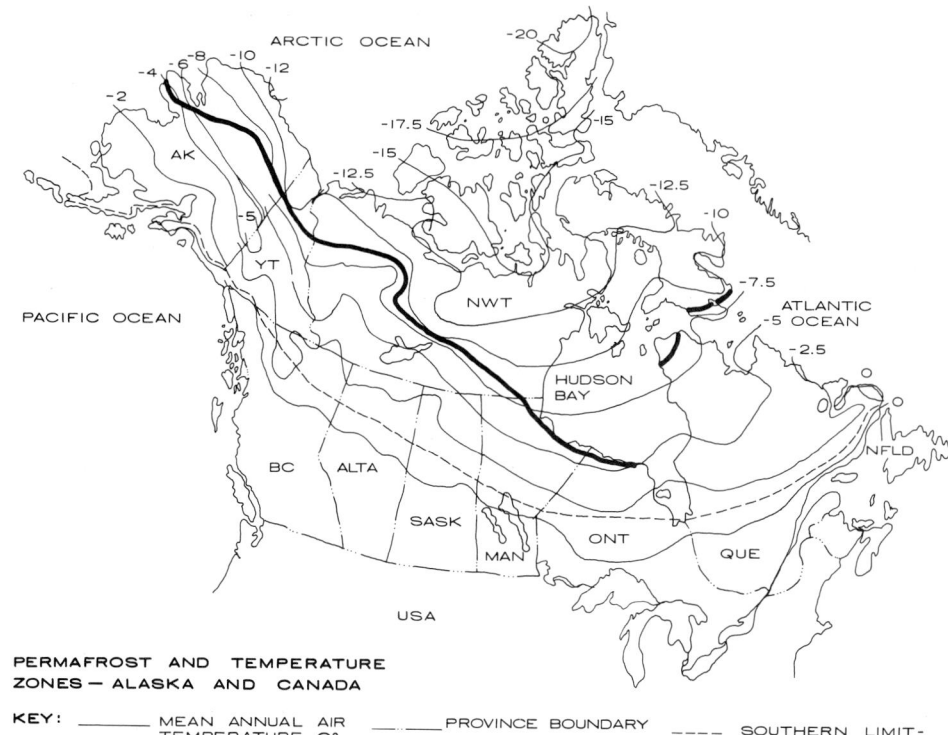

PERMAFROST AND TEMPERATURE ZONES — ALASKA AND CANADA

KEY:
— MEAN ANNUAL AIR TEMPERATURE, C°
— PROVINCE BOUNDARY
---- SOUTHERN LIMIT-DISCONTINUOUS PERMAFROST
▬ SOUTHERN LIMIT CONTINENTAL PERMAFROST
— COUNTRY BOUNDARY

PERMAFROST, ICE WEDGES AND LENSES, AND FROST HEAVE

DEFINITION OF PERMAFROST: Ground of any kind that stays colder than the freezing temperature of water throughout several years.

TERMS

ACTIVE LAYER: Top layer of ground subject to annual freezing and thawing.

FROST HEAVING: Lifting or heaving of soil surface created by the freezing of subsurface frost susceptible material.

FROST SUSCEPTIBLE SOIL: Soil that has enough permeability and capillary action (wickability) to expand upon freezing.

ICE LENSE (TABER ICE): Pocket of ice.

ICE WEDGE: Wedge shaped mass of ice within the soil. Wedges range up to 3 or 4 wide and 10 deep.

PERELETOK: Frozen layer at the base of the active layer that remains unthawed during cold summers.

RESIDUAL THAW ZONE: Layer of unfrozen ground between the permafrost and active layer. This layer does not exist when annual frost extends to the permafrost, but is present during warm winters.

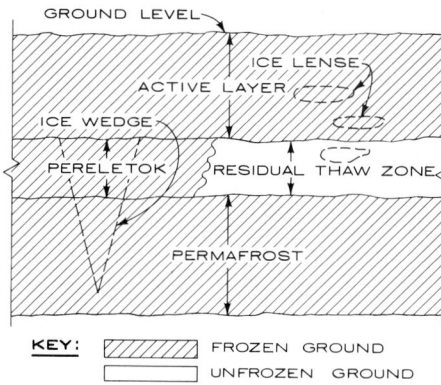

KEY:
▨ FROZEN GROUND
☐ UNFROZEN GROUND

CCC/HOK; Anchorage, Alaska

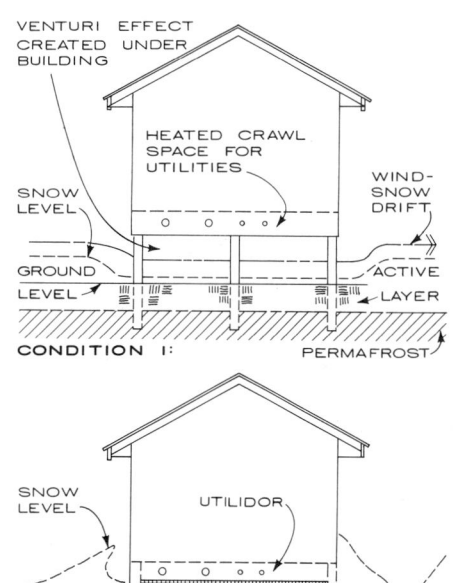

CONDITION 1:

CONDITION 2:

CONDITIONS OF BUILDING ON PERMAFROST

CONDITION 1: Building elevated on piles allows for the dissipation of building heat to help prevent the ground from thawing. Added benefits include winter refreezing of ground by cold winter air and prevention of snowdrift buildup.

CONDITION 2: Building elevated on nonfrost susceptible gravel pad. Benefits include lessening of snowdrift problems and retardation of permafrost thaw. Existing ground cover can remain as insulation. Rigid insulation can also be used.

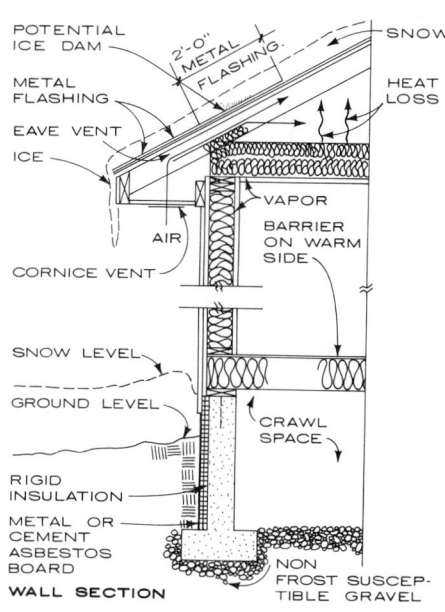

WALL SECTION

EAVE AND FOUNDATION DETAILING IN COLD CLIMATES

Snow buildup on the roof is warmed by heat loss from the building. The melting snow flows down the roof and is refrozen at the eave because of the eave's cold condition. The use of a cornice vent and insulation to create a "cold roof" helps to reduce the problem of ice damming. When an ice dam is created, the water backs up, leaking under roofing materials. The placement of metal flashing on the roof at least 2 ft 0 in. up from the wall line causes the snow and ice to slide off and also prevents moisture penetration.

All vapor barriers in cold and arctic conditions must be on the warm side of the insulation to avoid condensation in the insulation. Use of rigid insulation on the exterior of the foundation wall (with a metal or cement asbestos board cover for protection) creates a heat bank and keeps the utility space from freezing.

PILES

In the arctic, piles are popular because they are a simple way of providing thermal isolation of heated structures, minimize disturbance of existing thermal regime, permit flow of flood waters, and prevent the buildup of drifting snow. However, frost heaving can force the piles upward during the freeze season without allowing the piles to return to the original level when the soil thaws.

Solutions to the problem of pile heaving:

1. Anchor the pile against uplift by placing anchors or notches on the pile within the permafrost zone.
2. Break the bond in the active layer. (Use bond breaking plastic wrap or grease pile in the active layer.)
3. To avoid thaw of the surrounding soil, use one of the three main one-way heat extractors: (a) The gaseous flow system or, (b) the liquid system, containing tubes with "Venturi" funnels to allow warm liquid to rise and cold liquid to sink, and (c) a mechanical refrigeration system. The designer must be careful not to allow heat to be transferred from the building to the pile (thus avoiding thawing the permafrost).

UTILITIES IN COLD CLIMATE AND ARCTIC CONDITIONS

Utilidors or utiliducts are the most common way to provide protection, easy access, and insulation of utility lines to avoid disturbance to the permafrost.

Human waste at isolated facilities may be handled by compost privies (waterless toilets) and chemical toilets, which are commonly referred to as "honey buckets." Disposal systems include incineration and sewage lagoons.

LOCATION

Generally the hot-dry regions of North America are in the SW corner of the United States and the NW corner of Mexico, below the snow line. They consist of valleys and deserts below 3000 ft in elevation with an annual temperature above 65°F.

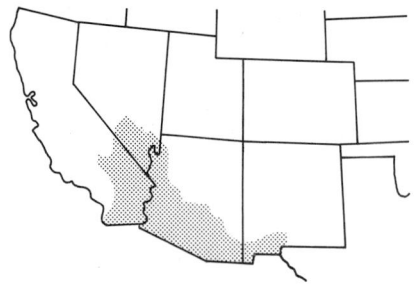

HOT—DRY REGION OF THE U.S.

CLIMATE SUMMARY

Some part of every day or night throughout the year is totally comfortable and pleasant; the balance of the time the climate is usually excessively hot or cold. The 3 to 5 months of summer are the most demanding and establish the critical design parameters; preventing heat gain is the objective. Winter nights are cold but winter days are comfortable. Lack of cloud cover means maximum solar radiation (above 80% annual possible sunshine), little rainfall (average less than 10 in./yr), and high evaporation rate (over 100 in./yr). Summer cooling loads are larger than winter heating loads for all building types.

CLIMATE CHARACTERISTICS

EXCESSIVE RADIATION

Solar radiation and thermal reradiation of heat stored in materials are the prime sources of discomfort. Daily temperature highs average over 100°F from mid-May into September. Clear night skys absorb summer heat but cause heavy frosts every winter.

LOW HUMIDITY

Precipitation averages under 10 in./yr. Infrequent rains are often heavy; resulting runoff produces flash floods. Evaporation rates average over 100 in./yr, resulting in very low relative humidities. Occasional dust storms are encountered.

HIGH DIURNAL TEMPERATURE VARIATION

Range between daily maxima and minima may exceed 50°F. However, in late summer, night temperatures may not drop below 80°F.

HIGH SEASONAL TEMPERATURE VARIATION

Winter lows and summer highs may vary as much as 100°F.

SIGNIFICANT MICROCLIMATES

Both natural and manmade microclimatic variations can occur in a relatively short distance: elevation and landscaping are the major influences.

PLANNING AND SITING

PLANNING

Encourage high density and compact planning; use party or common walls, concentrate development for mutual shading and insulation. Mixed land uses reduce travel time and the need for frequent travel.

PEDESTRIANS

Provide tight, protected circulation; encourage short pedestrian paths. Shading is necessary for pedestrians—use arcades, narrow alleyways, awnings, tree canopies, trellises.

LANDSCAPING

Vegetation is desirable for psychological and evaptranspiration cooling. Prefer native types: riparian near buildings, desert varieties in open areas. Cluster nonnative materials for maximum effect from engineered watering systems; use oasis concepts. Deciduous plants provide a sense of seasons and also winter sun penetration. Vegetative ground cover can reduce ground reflectance, shade the earth, and reduce air temperatures. Include rain holding and percolation areas in site shaping.

BUILDING FORM

ORIENTATION

Minimize exposure to W. Ideal orientation for openings is S. However, orientations from S to 25°E of S can provide appropriate shading control. Northerly orientations for openings are also desirable. Avoid swimming pools on W or N of building.

SHAPE

Compact building forms elongated on an E-W axis are preferable. Design forms to maximize self-shading. Generally keep volume-to-surface ratio high. Avoid courtyard and patio schemes except where building volume/surface ratio is large, or perimeter walls have maximum thermal resistance. Earth contact designs and underground approaches desirable.

MICROCLIMATE

Respond to existing microclimate conditions. Design adjacent microclimates on all sides. Landscape shields on E and W can temper sun and heat impact on buildings. Major elements can direct prevailing cooling breezes. Walled-in gardens and yards can hold cool air pools. Consider water features and heavy vegetation for cooling effect, but watch the costs of water.

FUNCTIONAL ZONING

Use varying construction strategies in a single building. High mass construction is recommended for day use or 24 hr use functions; light, highly insulated low mass construction preferred for occasional use or night use functions; use screened porches, exposed decks, and sheltered terraces for controlled outdoor uses, occupied on time-of-day or season basis.

THERMAL ZONING

Place noninhabited spaces on the W to buffer heat. Isolate heat producing activities. Use vestibules or lobbies in public spaces to provide thermal transitions.

NATURAL LIGHTING

Day lighting (diffuse solar radiation) of work spaces is recommended especially from N. All daylight sources (windows and skylights) should be self-shaded on the exterior. Since smaller window openings are preferred, natural lighting requires special design attention. Use light colored interiors to distribute daylight.

COLOR/TEXTURE

Use light reflective colors on roof and E, S, and W walls to reject summer heat. A greater range of choice is possible on N elevations. Avoid specular reflective surfaces (mirror finishes) because of their focusing nature. Use medium or darker colors adjacent to openings to avoid reflections into interiors. Bright colors are preferable for visual contrast in the bright sunshine of the region; colors in the shadows, such as eaves and soffits, are especially effective.

DESIGN STRATEGIES

Design for cooling by evaporation by considering vegetation, pools, fountains, roof ponds, sprays, landscape watering systems, and so on. Mechanical evaporation cooling systems are effective.

Provide heavy interior thermal mass protected by insulation from exterior temperatures for thermal conservation, combine high mass and low mass in a single structure for different times of use.

Use transitional zones both in construction (i.e., thick wall assemblies) and in planning (i.e., intermediate or transitional areas and seasonal spaces).

Design microclimates using both architectural and landscape materials and forms to modify climate and temper the natural extremes.

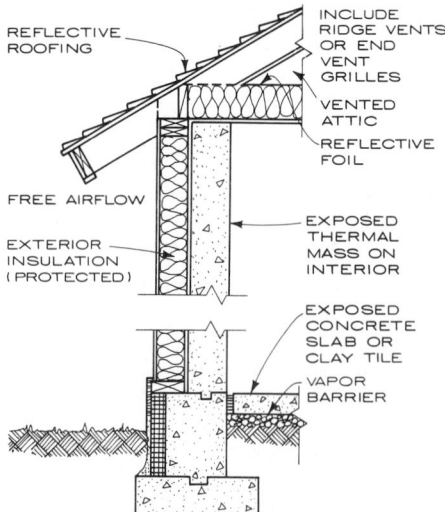

REFLECTIVE ROOFING

INCLUDE RIDGE VENTS OR END VENT GRILLES

VENTED ATTIC

REFLECTIVE FOIL

FREE AIRFLOW

EXTERIOR INSULATION (PROTECTED)

EXPOSED THERMAL MASS ON INTERIOR

EXPOSED CONCRETE SLAB OR CLAY TILE

VAPOR BARRIER

RESIDENTIAL CONSTRUCTION DETAIL

BUILDING ELEMENTS

FOUNDATIONS

Use masonry or concrete in earth contact; slab on grade, basement, or earth-bermed structures. Insulation necessary above grade.

EXTERIOR WALLS

Walls should be seasonally shaded whenever possible. In hot climates shading strategies are critical.

ROOFS

The roof is the most effective location for both shading and insulation. Roof surfaces should be reflective. Overhead insulation values should be approximately 1.5 times thermal resistance of walls. Vented attics are the common method of reducing overhead radiant heat gain. Double roofs, roof ponds, or sprayed roofs are also effective. Roof sprays are more effective than ponds and can bring down surface temperatures approximately 50°F; however, the process is very hard on materials.

THERMAL CAPACITY

Both capacity insulation and resistance insulation materials are important. Heat capacity construction is recommended in excess of 70 lb of heat absorbing building materials per cu ft of space. An ideal strategy is a minimum of a 10 hr heat lag.

THERMAL RESISTANCE

Minimum recommended thermal resistance in roofs is R30 and in walls, R19. Together with caulking, vapor barriers are recommended also to reduce infiltration.

WEATHERING

Masonry, concrete, and ceramic clay products can last indefinitely. Masonry construction requires frequent wetting during setting and curing. Adobe requires maintenance but can have an extended life. Generally, exposed metals show little weathering. Excessive heat and ultraviolet radiation are destructive of many materials such as wood and plastics.

OPENINGS

Doors, windows, and other openings should be selectively shaded according to season. Closures should be tightly fitted and should include weather stripping. Double glazing is cost effective for all elevations. Generally, ratio of opening to floor space should be small (12% or less). Provide for seasonal natural cross-ventilation. Partially movable shading may provide seasonal control. Shading devices should be self-venting by free convection to avoid heat buildup.

EQUIPMENT

EQUIPMENT CHOICES

Select equipment that minimizes heat production.

EVAPORATIVE COOLING

Above 1500 ft elevation conventional evaporative coolers can provide complete comfort more than 90% of the time. Below 1500 ft they can be effective more than 50% of the time. Systems require complete air changes every 2 to 3 min. They provide total comfort if the wet bulb temperature is below 70°F; reasonable comfort when wet bulb temperature is between 70 and 74°F. For wet-bulb temperature above 74°F evaporation coolers only produce relief. Duct sizes must allow air at 1600 ft/min, preferably 1200 ft/min for silence and efficiency.

AIR CONDITIONERS

Heat pumps are a good choice although the cooling load determines sizing. In these climates equipment must operate consistently at higher outdoor air temperatures (115°F and above). Conventional refrigerated air conditioners and heat pumps are normally rated at operating temperatures of 82 and 95°F. Equipment sizing should accommodate load operating conditions.

HEAT SINKS

Generally stable earth temperatures range from 68 to 75°F, thus the earth offers poor cooling sources. Clear night skies can offer 25% conductive/convective, 25% radiative, 50% evaporative cooling potential. Evaporative sprays are the most effective heat sinks; mechanical evaporation systems probably have the most potential.

Professor Jeffrey Cook; College of Architecture; Arizona State University; Tempe, Arizona

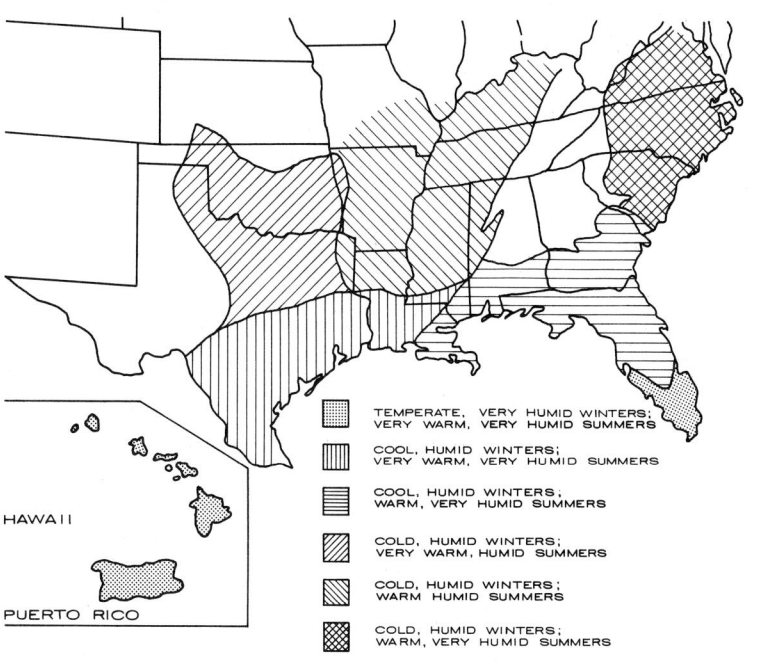

TEMPERATE, VERY HUMID WINTERS;
VERY WARM, VERY HUMID SUMMERS

COOL, HUMID WINTERS;
VERY WARM, VERY HUMID SUMMERS

COOL, HUMID WINTERS;
WARM, VERY HUMID SUMMERS

COLD, HUMID WINTERS;
VERY WARM, HUMID SUMMERS

COLD, HUMID WINTERS;
WARM HUMID SUMMERS

COLD, HUMID WINTERS;
WARM, VERY HUMID SUMMERS

HAWAII

PUERTO RICO

WARM — HUMID REGIONS OF THE UNITED STATES

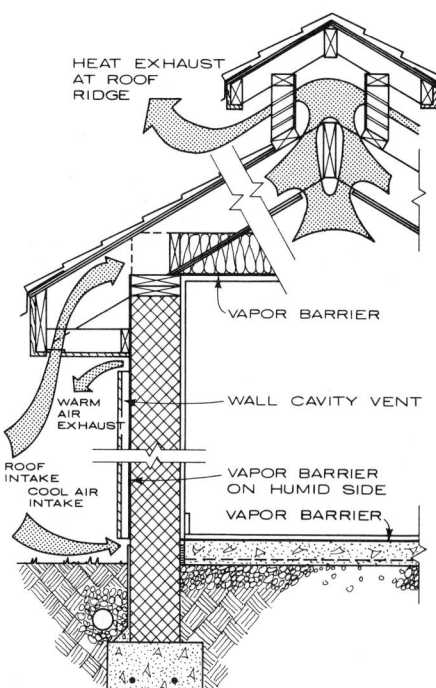

HEAT EXHAUST AT ROOF RIDGE

VAPOR BARRIER

WARM AIR EXHAUST

WALL CAVITY VENT

ROOF INTAKE COOL AIR INTAKE

VAPOR BARRIER ON HUMID SIDE

VAPOR BARRIER

TYPICAL VENTILATION PATTERNS IN WALL SECTION

WARM-HUMID CONSTRUCTION

Characteristics of warm-humid climates are moist air, above average rainfall, variable air movement, damp ground, and air temperatures seldom exceeding skin temperature. Hot humid areas do not exist in the United States.

ORIENTATION

Under all conditions in overheated areas, the building structure must be vented for cooling. Human comfort may be achieved, when natural conditions prevail, by convective cooling of interior space and human skin. Building orientation must accomplish these needs; solar radiation response is of secondary concern as several methods are available to overcome this. When mechanical comfort conditions are employed, solar radiation considerations dominate orientation. Generally, all habitable rooms must have at least two external openings; bathrooms, stores, and kitchens should be placed in the leeward areas of buildings. Stack vents should be used to release heat from kitchens. Corridors, balconies, and terraces assist lateral air movement, while stairwells and elevators encourage vertical motion. Roofs should be pitched because of rainfall, unless needed for activities.

MATERIALS AND CONSTRUCTION METHODS

Diurnal temperatures vary by 10–15°F, so that thermal mass with a long time lag is unnecessary and may be undesirable under certain conditions. Appropriate materials should be poor conductors—wood, plastics, aluminum. Well ventilated structures are essential to prevent mildew or rotting of materials. Regular cleaning of fly screens will allow continuous airflow and control vermin that can be abundant in these regions. Exterior finishes should be of a light color.

SITE AND LANDSCAPE PLANNING

Airflow in and around buildings and urban areas is essential in warm-humid regions. Under natural conditions, single banked buildings should be staggered to achieve this. When mechanically controlled, cooling of the building envelope, only, need be assured. Generous employment of landscaped areas in and around buildings promotes cooling.

BUILDING FORM UNDER MECHANICALLY CONTROLLED CONDITIONS

Envelope must be ventilated with a pitched roof unless it is used for another purpose. Interior volume must be minimal with a low surface/volume ratio. Airflow through the building's interior must be prohibited.

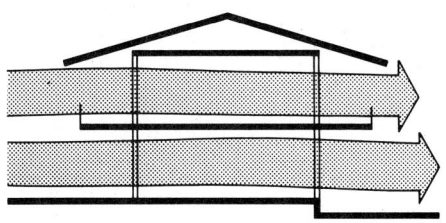

Suburban or rural, single family, where land is plentiful.

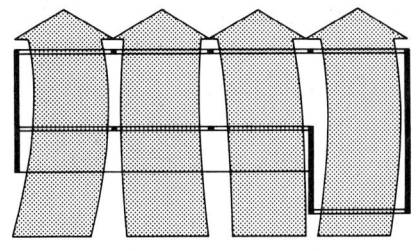

L-shaped plan allows a narrower frontage, screens and doors need perforation and careful attention to detail.

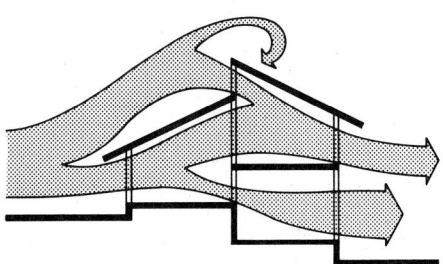

Double banked split level buildings generally stifle air motion, but can allow adequate cross ventilation through careful design.

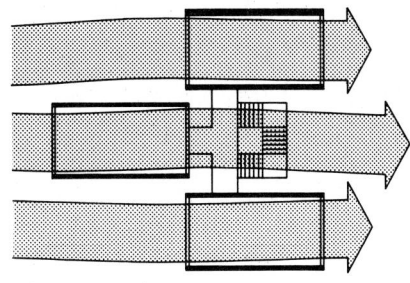

High density, tall apartment buildings must provide maximum external walls for two generous openings per habitable room.

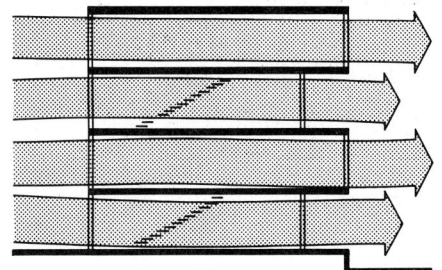

Maisonettes and split-levels can be economical solutions with access balconies, terraces, and corridors assisting in air movement and shading.

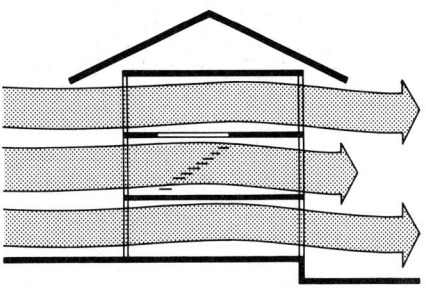

Multistory row development in medium density areas permits cross ventilation when deep room single banked plans are employed.

BUILDING FORM UNDER NATURAL CONDITIONS

Arthur Bowen, RIBA; Professor of Architecture & Planning; University of Miami; Coral Gables, Florida

ENVIRONMENTAL FACTORS 1

NATURAL VENTILATION IN AND AROUND BUILDINGS

Airflow may be gainfully employed in and around buildings for the following tasks:

1. To provide essential air exchange for hygienic purposes—for health and for odor removal.
2. To cool human skin by accelerating conductive and evaporative loss when this is needed.
3. To cool interior space when this is desirable.
4. To cool building fabric in overheated conditions.
5. To remove undesirable moisture from the building's fabric, surfaces, and interior spaces.

GLOBAL AND LOCAL WIND SYSTEMS

Global air movement is governed by three forces: pressure gradient, coriolis, and friction. Local conditions of topography, continentality, and urbanization modify or even supersede prevailing regional systems. Seasonal and diurnal changes are recorded throughout the United States, and this information may be obtained from the National Climate Center, Asheville, North Carolina, and the "Climatic Atlas of the United States" published by the United States Government Printing Office. A wind rose, wedge or matrix, should be compiled for each site, establishing the velocity, frequency, direction, and temperatures that affect it. (Figure 1.)

AIRFLOW PATTERNS

Air will flow from higher (+ve) to a lower (-ve) pressure zone. These pressures exist at a building's boundary and between exterior and interior air. (Figure 2.) Pressures may be manipulated in and around buildings by location and size of openings. Where air velocity is low, it will be accelerated when inlets are smaller than outlets. Where steady, desirable, prevailing winds occur in warm-humid conditions, restricted openings hinder comfort and both inlets and outlets should be large.

Wind flowing against a building causes a high pressure area on the windward side and a low pressure area or wind shadow on the leeward side.

Incoming airstreams may change direction several times, resulting in a decrease in velocities, but promoting turbulence that will improve air movement in areas where stagnation may otherwise occur. Velocities decrease when partitions are located close to the inlet but improve when located nearer the outlet.

CROSS VENTILATION PATTERNS

Partition perpendicular to initial flow alters pattern; back room supplied at cooling speed. (Figure 3.)

Flow is intercepted by partitions; blocking slows flow effect to considerable extent. Cooling effect becomes meager. (Figure 4.)

Partitions parallel to initial flow splits pattern but result remains at adequate high speeds. (Figure 5.)

High inlet and outlet produces poor air movement at body level. (Figure 6.)

Low inlet and outlet produces desirable low level airflow across human body. (Figure 7.)

Poor patterns result when low and high inlets alternate on opposite walls. (Figure 8.)

Louvers can direct airflow upward or downward. (Figure 9.)

Canopies produce an upward airstream that can be corrected by separating the projection from the wall or piercing the canopy. (Figures 10 and 11.)

External barriers reduce air movement through building. (Figure 12.)

Inlet and outlet size and locations radically affect airflow patterns in partitioned rooms. (Figures 13 and 14.)

EFFECTS OF SITE AND LANDSCAPE PLANNING

The building can be exposed or protected from air motion as determined by regional and local conditions. Orientation, shape, and the prudent selection and setting of landscape materials can provide optimum conditions at the building's boundary. Building materials and live plantings may be used individually and in various combinations to create wind barriers or wind scoops in harmony with building needs. Arbors of large canopy trees may reduce ambient temperatures 4–6°F and encourage cool, dense air to flow toward buildings. (Figure 15.)

Arthur Bowen, RIBA; Professor of Architecture & Planning; University of Miami; Coral Gables, Florida

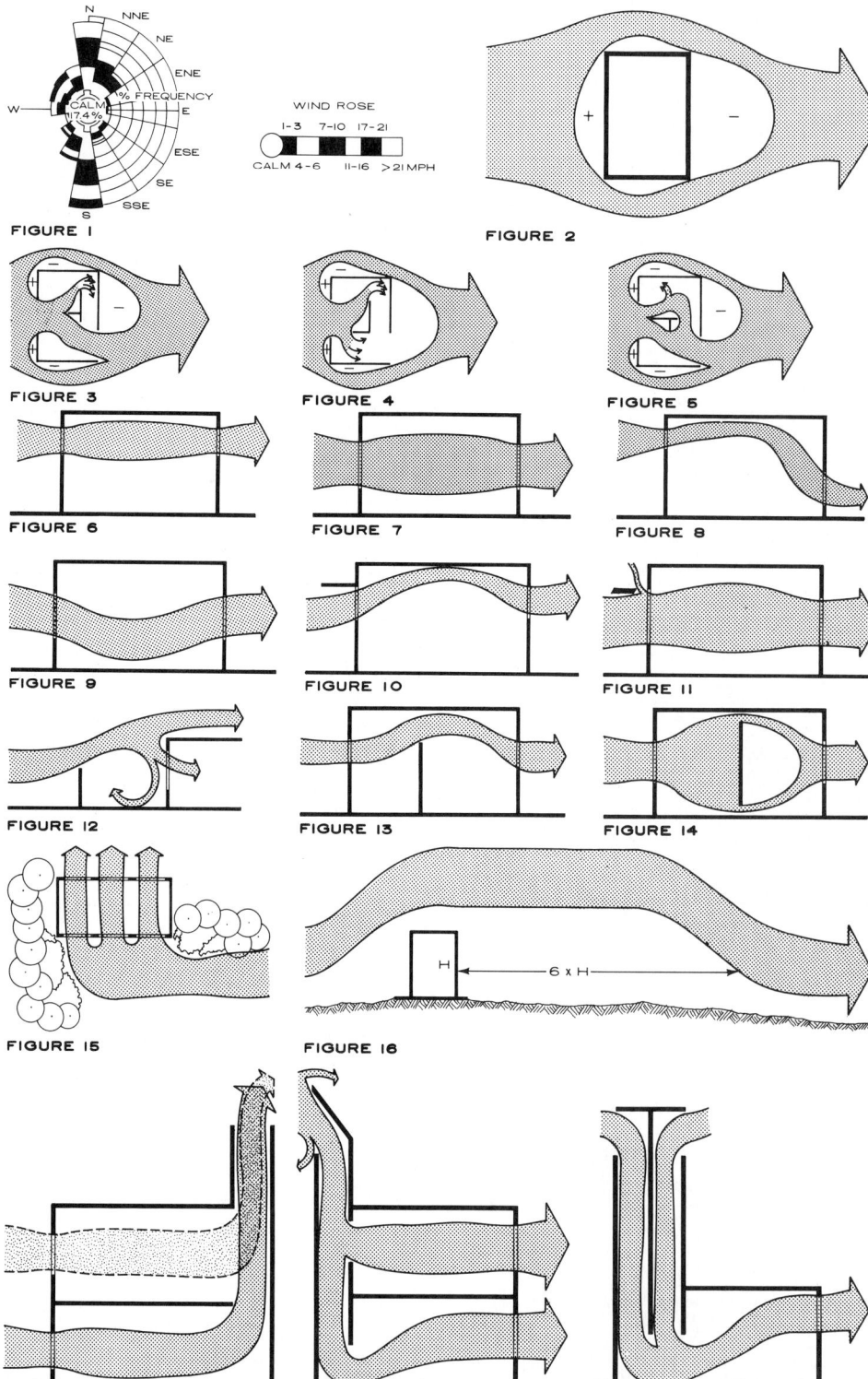

FIGURE I

FIGURE 2

FIGURE 3

FIGURE 4

FIGURE 5

FIGURE 6

FIGURE 7

FIGURE 8

FIGURE 9

FIGURE 10

FIGURE 11

FIGURE 12

FIGURE 13

FIGURE 14

FIGURE 15

FIGURE 16

FIGURE 17

FIGURE 18

FIGURE 19

WIND ROSE

1-3 7-10 17-21

CALM 4-6 11-16 >21MPH

For winds up to 5 mph, a wind shadow is created on the leeward side of buildings, in depth approximately six times the height or width, whichever is the lesser dimension. The depth of the shadow increases with increasing wind velocity. (Figure 16.)

SOLAR INDUCED VENTILATION

Three categories of thermal chimneys can generate airflow: (1) anabatic or "stack effect," which is a conventional method of hot air release from interior space (Figure 17); (2) pressure or "down draft" chimney, which functions efficiently when predictable direction and velocity prevailing winds occur (Figure 18); and (3) "katabatic" or "cold draft" chimneys, which will only function efficiently when large diurnal temperature differences occur (Figure 19).

WALL OPENINGS

Wall openings traditionally are windows and doors. Pivoted and awning windows provide good ventilation. Sliding glass doors and windows provide only 50% of available opening unless rolled back completely. Adjustable louvered doors and windows provide privacy and good ventilation. A louvered "Caribbean" hood provides good rain protection and ventilation at the same time.

1 ENVIRONMENTAL FACTORS

GENERAL NOTES

Building attics, crawl spaces, and basements must be ventilated to remove moisture and water vapor resulting from human activity within the building. Moisture in basements and crawl spaces can occur, in addition, from water in the surrounding soil. The quantity of water vapor depends on building type (e.g., residence, school, hospital), activity (e.g., kitchen, bathroom, laundry), and air temperature and relative humidity. Proper ventilation and insulation must be combined so that the temperature of the ventilated space does not fall below the dew point; this is especially critical with low outdoor temperatures and high inside humidity. Inadequate ventilation will cause condensation and eventual deterioration of framing, insulation, and interior finishes.

The vent types shown allow natural ventilation of roofs and crawl spaces. Mechanical methods (e.g., power attic ventilators, whole house fans) can combine living space and attic ventilation, but openings for natural roof ventilation must still be provided. Protect all vents against insects and vermin with metal or fiberglass screen cloth. Increase net vent areas as noted in table.

VENTILATION REQUIREMENTS TO PREVENT CONDENSATION

SPACE	ROOF TYPE	TOTAL NET AREA OF VENTILATION	REMARKS
Joist (ceiling on underside of joists)	Flat	$1/300$. Uniformly distributed at eaves	Vent each joist space at both ends. Provide at least $1\frac{1}{2}''$ free space above insulation for ventilation
	Sloped	Ditto	Ditto. On gable roofs, drill $1''$ diameter holes through ridge beam in each joist space to provide through-ventilation to both sides of roof
Attic (unheated)	Gable	$1/300$. At least two louvers on opposite sides near ridge	
	Hip	$1/300$. Uniformly distributed at eaves. Provide additional $1/600$ at ridge, with all vents interconnected	Ridge vents create stack effect from eaves; both are recommended over eaves vents alone

Total net vent area = $1/300$ of building area at eaves line. With screens increase net area by: $1/4''$ screen, 1.0; #8 screen, 1.25; #16 screen, 2.00.

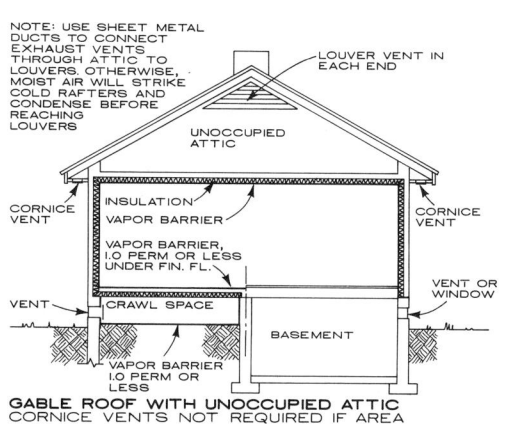

GABLE ROOF WITH UNOCCUPIED ATTIC
CORNICE VENTS NOT REQUIRED IF AREA IS SMALL

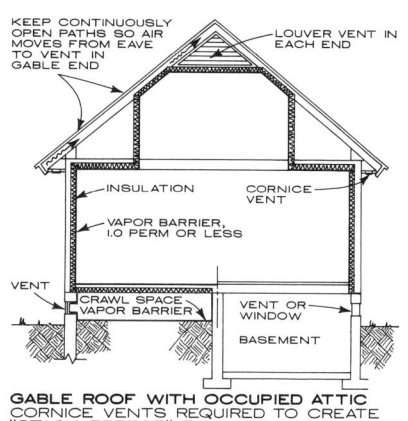

GABLE ROOF WITH OCCUPIED ATTIC
CORNICE VENTS REQUIRED TO CREATE "STACK EFFECT" TO RIDGE

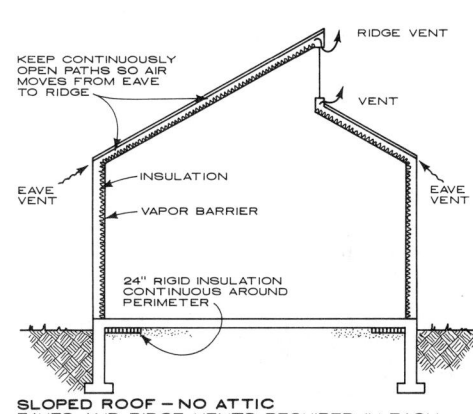

SLOPED ROOF – NO ATTIC
EAVES AND RIDGE VENTS REQUIRED IN EACH JOIST SPACE

TYPICAL ATTIC AND CRAWL SPACE VENTILATION APPLICATIONS

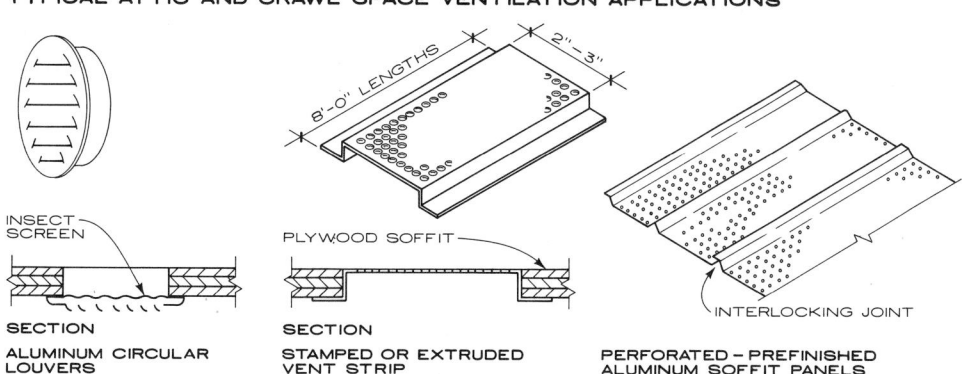

ALUMINUM CIRCULAR LOUVERS
1 INCH – 3 INCH DIAMETER

STAMPED OR EXTRUDED VENT STRIP

PERFORATED – PREFINISHED ALUMINUM SOFFIT PANELS
10'' × 10'-0'' LONG. ALSO IN ROLLS

EAVES VENTILATING MATERIALS

NOTE

Vapor barriers minimize moisture migration to attics and crawl spaces; their use is required for all conditions. Always locate vapor barriers on the warm (room) side of insulation. Provide ventilation on the cold side; this permits cold/hot weather ventilation while minimizing heat gain/loss.

CRAWL SPACES VENTILATION

Crawl spaces under dwellings where earth is damp and uncovered require a high rate of ventilation. Provide at least one opening per side, as high as possible. Calculate total net vent area by the formula:

$$a = \frac{2L}{100} + \frac{A}{300}$$

where

L = crawl space perimeter (linear ft)
A = crawl space area (sq ft)
a = total net vent area (sq ft)

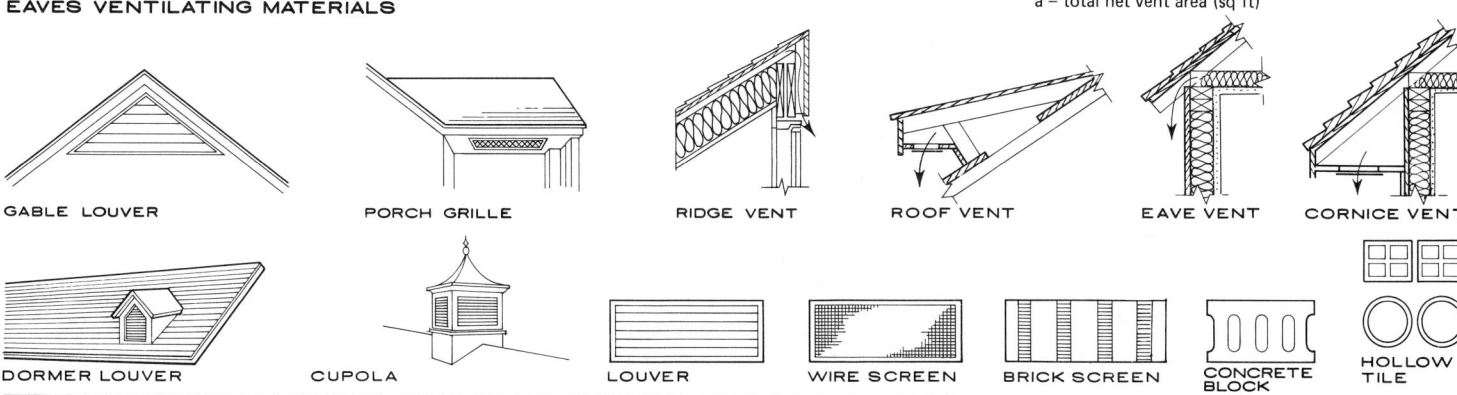

GABLE LOUVER   PORCH GRILLE   RIDGE VENT   ROOF VENT   EAVE VENT   CORNICE VENT

DORMER LOUVER   CUPOLA   LOUVER   WIRE SCREEN   BRICK SCREEN   CONCRETE BLOCK   HOLLOW TILE

TYPICAL ATTIC AND CRAWL SPACE VENT OPENINGS

David Metzger, Architect, CSI; Wilkes and Faulkner Associates; Washington, D.C.

ENVIRONMENTAL FACTORS   **1**

WATER VAPOR MIGRATION

Water is present as vapor in indoor and outdoor air and as absorbed moisture in many building materials. Within the range of temperatures encountered in buildings water may exist in the liquid, vapor, or solid states. Moisture related problems may arise from changes in moisture content, from the presence of excessive moisture, or from the effects of changes of state such as freezing within wall insulation.

In the design and construction of buildings the behavior of moisture must be considered, including particularly the change from vapor to liquid (condensation). Such problems generally arise when moisture in relatively humid indoor air comes in contact with a cold surface such as a window or when the moisture migrates under the influence of vapor pressure differences through walls to enter a region of relatively low temperature where condensation can occur.

Moisture problems in residences generally occur in winter when the outdoor temperature and vapor pressure are low and there are many indoor vapor sources. These may include cooking, laundering, bathing, breathing, and perspiration from the occupants, as well as automatic washers and driers, dishwashers and humidifiers. All of these sources combine to cause vapor pressure indoors to be much higher than outdoors, so that the vapor tends to migrate outward through the building envelope. Vapor cannot permeate glazed windows or metal doors, but most other building materials are permeable to some extent. Walls are particularly susceptible to this phenomenon, and such migration must be prevented or at least minimized by the use of low permeability membranes known as vapor barriers, which should be installed as close as possible to the indoor surface of the building.

Water vapor migration is relatively independent of air motion within the building, since such migration depends primarily on vapor pressure differences. Migration always takes place from regions of higher vapor pressure toward spaces such as wall cavities where the vapor pressure will be lower. When surfaces below the local dewpoint temperature are encountered, condensation will occur and moisture droplets will form. If the local drybulb temperature is at or below 32°F, freezing will occur, which may lead to permanent structural damage.

Moisture in building materials usually increases their thermal conductance to a significant and unpredictable extent. Porous materials that become saturated with moisture lose most of their insulating capability and may not regain it when they dry out. Dust, which usually settles in airspaces, may become permanently affixed to originally reflective surfaces. Moisture migration by evaporation, vapor flow, and condensation can transport significant quantities of latent heat, particularly through fibrous insulating materials.

Positive steps should be taken to prevent migration of moisture in the form of vapor and accumulation in the form of water or ice within building components. Vapor barriers, correctly located near the source of the moisture, are the most effective means of preventing such migration. Venting of moisture laden air from bathrooms, laundry rooms, and kitchens will reduce indoor vapor pressure, as will the introduction of outdoor air with low moisture content.

PERMEANCE AND PERMEABILITY OF MATERIALS TO WATER VAPOR

MATERIAL	PERMEANCE (PERM)	MATERIAL	PERMEANCE (PERM)
MATERIALS USED IN CONSTRUCTION		**BUILDING PAPERS, FELTS, ROOFING PAPERS[3]**	
Concrete (1:2:4 mix)	3.2[5]	Duplex sheet, asphalt laminated, aluminum foil one side (43)[4]	0.176
Brick-masonry (4 in. thick)	0.8-1.1	Saturated and coated roll roofing (326)[4]	0.24
Concrete masonry (8 in. cored, limestone aggregate)	2.4	Kraft paper and asphalt laminated, reinforced 30-120-30 (34)[4]	1.8
Asbestos-cement board (0.2 in. thick)	0.54	Asphalt-saturated, coated vapor-barrier paper (43)[4]	0.6
Plaster on metal lath (³/₄ in.)	15	Asphalt-saturated, not coated sheathing paper (22)[4]	20.2
Plaster on plain gypsum lath (with studs)	20	15-lb asphalt felt (70)[4]	5.6
Gypsum wallboard (³/₈ in. plain)	50	15-lb tar felt (70)[4]	18.2
Structural insulating board (sheathing quality)	20-50[5]	Single kraft, double infused (16)[4]	42
Structural insulating board (interior, uncoated, ¹/₂ in.)	50-90	**LIQUID APPLIED COATING MATERIALS**	
Hardboard (¹/₈ in. standard)	11		
Hardboard (¹/₈ in. tempered)	5		
Built-up roofing (hot mopped)	0.0	Paint—two coats	
Wood, fir sheathing, ³/₄ in.	2.9	Aluminum varnish on wood	0.3-0.5
Plywood (Douglas fir, exterior glue, ¹/₄ in.)	0.7	Enamels on smooth plaster	0.5-1.5
Plywood (Douglas fir, interior, glue, ¹/₄ in.)	1.9	Primers and sealers on interior insulation board	0.9-2.1
Acrylic, glass fiber reinforced sheet, 56 mil	0.12	Miscellaneous primers plus one coat flat oil paint on plastic	1.6-3.0
Polyester, glass fiber reinforced sheet, 48 mil	0.05	Flat paint on interior insulation board	4
THERMAL INSULATIONS		Water emulsion on interior insulation board	30-85
Cellular glass	0.0[5]	Paint—three coats	
Mineral wool, unprotected	29.0	Exterior paint, white lead and oil on wood siding	0.3-1.0
Expanded polyurethane (R-11 blown)	0.4-1.6[5]	Exterior paint, white lead-zinc oxide and oil on wood	0.9
Expanded polystyrene—extruded	1.2[5]	Styrene-butadiene latex coating, 2 oz/sq ft	11
Expanded polystyrene—bead	2.0-5.8[5]	Polyvinyl acetate latex coating, 4 oz/sq ft	5.5
PLASTIC AND METAL FOILS AND FILMS[2]			
Aluminum foil (1 mil)	0.0	Asphalt cutback bastic	
Polyethylene (4 mil)	0.08	¹/₁₆ in. dry	0.14
Polyethylene (6 mil)	0.06	³/₁₆ in. dry	0.0
Polyethylene (8 mil)	0.04	Hot melt asphalt	
Polyester (1 mil)	0.7	2 oz/sq ft	0.5
Polyvinylchloride, unplasticized (2 mil)	0.68	3.5 oz/sq ft	0.1
Polyvinylchloride, plasticized (4 mil)	0.8-1.4		

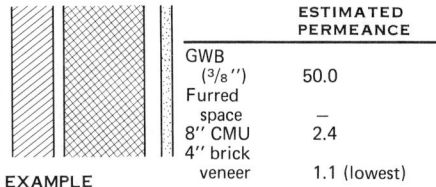

	ESTIMATED PERMEANCE
GWB (³/₈")	50.0
Vapor barrier	0.6 (lowest)
Insulation	29.0
Wood sheathing	2.9
4" brick veneer	1.1 (next)

EXAMPLE

In this example the vapor barrier transmits 1 grain of moisture per square foot per hour for each unit of vapor pressure difference, and nothing else transmits less. However, since the cold brick veneer is nearly as low in permeance it is advisable to make certain that the vapor barrier is expertly installed, with all openings at pipes and with outlet boxes or joints carefully fitted or sealed. Alternatively, the brick veneer may have open mortar joints near the top and bottom to serve both as weep holes and as vapor release openings. They will also ventilate the wall and help to reduce heat gain in summer.

	ESTIMATED PERMEANCE
GWB (³/₈")	50.0
Furred space	—
8" CMU	2.4
4" brick veneer	1.1 (lowest)

EXAMPLE

Vapor (under pressure) would easily pass through the interior finish, be slowed up by the concrete masonry unit, and be nearly stopped by the cold brick veneer. Unless this design is radically improved, the masonry will become saturated and may cause serious water stains or apparent "leaks" in cold weather. In addition, alternating freezing and thawing of condensation within the masonry wall can physically damage the construction.

- List the materials, without surface films or airspaces, in the order of their appearance in the building section, beginning with the inside surface material and working to the outside.
- Against each material list the permeance (or permeability) value from the table or a more accurate value if available from tests or manufacturers' data. Where a range is given, select an average value or use judgment in assigning a value based on the character and potential installation method of the material proposed for use.
- Start at the top of the list and note any material that has less permeance than the materials above it on the list. At that point the possibility exists that vapor leaking through the first material may condense on the second, provided the dew point (condensation point) is reached and the movement is considerable. In that case, provide ventilation through the cold side material or modify the design to eliminate or change the material to one of greater permeance.

NOTES

1. The vapor transmission rates listed will permit comparisons of materials, but selection of vapor barrier materials should be based on rates obtained from the manufacturer or from laboratory tests. The range of values shown indicates variation among mean values for materials that are similar but of different density. Values are intended for design guidance only.
2. Usually installed as vapor barriers. If used as exterior finish and elsewhere near cold side, special considerations are required.
3. Low permeance sheets used as vapor barriers. High permeance use elsewhere in construction.
4. Bases (weight in lb/500 sq ft).
5. Permeability (PERM-in.).

Based on data from "ASHRAE Handbook of Fundamentals," 1977, Chapter 20.

Owen J. Delevante, AIA; Glen Rock, New Jersey

E. C. Shuman, P.E.; Consulting Engineer; State College, Pennsylvania

BUILDING SECTION ANALYSIS FOR POTENTIAL CONDENSATION

Any building section may be analyzed by simple calculations to determine where condensation might occur and what might be done in selecting materials or their method of assembly to eliminate that possibility. The section may or may not contain a vapor barrier or it may contain a relatively imperfect barrier; the building section may include cold side materials of comparatively high resistance to the passage of vapor (which is highly undesirable and is to be avoided). With few exceptions, the vapor resistance at or near the warm surface should be five times that of any components. The table above gives permeances and permeability of building and vapor barrier materials. These values can be used in analyzing building sections by the following simple method:

1

ENVIRONMENTAL FACTORS

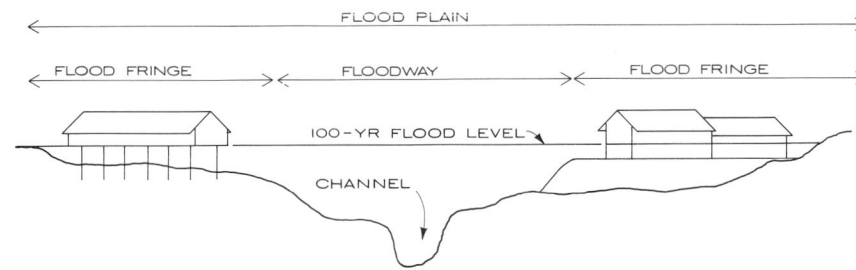

FLOOD PLAIN

FLOOD FRINGE — FLOODWAY — FLOOD FRINGE

100-YR FLOOD LEVEL

CHANNEL

RIVER VALLEY CROSS-SECTION

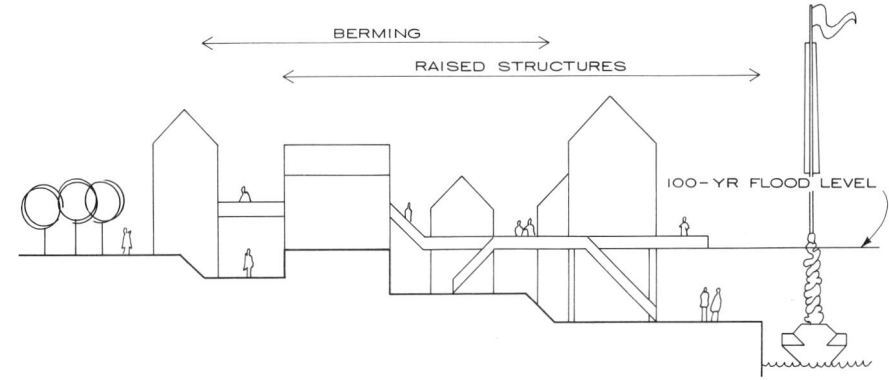

BERMING

RAISED STRUCTURES

100-YR FLOOD LEVEL

PROPOSED WHARF AREA DEVELOPMENT

FLOODWAY DEVELOPMENT

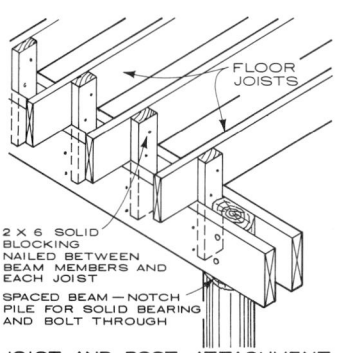

FLOOR JOISTS

2 X 6 SOLID BLOCKING NAILED BETWEEN BEAM MEMBERS AND EACH JOIST

SPACED BEAM—NOTCH PILE FOR SOLID BEARING AND BOLT THROUGH

JOIST AND POST ATTACHMENT

STUD

SOLID SHEATHING NAILED TO ALL MEMBERS

JOIST

HEADER

PIER

PLYWOOD ANCHORAGE

CONSTRUCTION DETAILS

NOTE

Within the United States, the Federal Emergency Management Agency (FEMA) makes the determination of 100-yr flood elevation after review of all technical data. For information, contact office of Federal Insurance and Hazard Mitigation, FEMA. State and regional agencies and the nearest Army Corps of Engineers may be contacted for additional information.

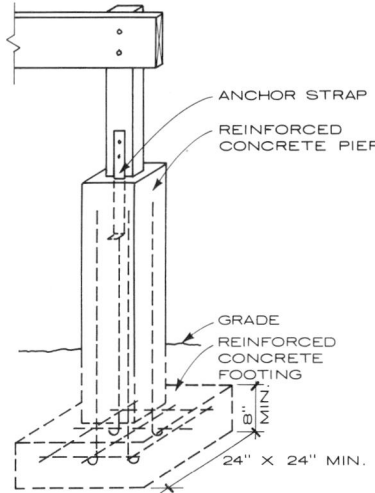

ANCHOR STRAP

REINFORCED CONCRETE PIER

GRADE

REINFORCED CONCRETE FOOTING

8" MIN.

24" X 24" MIN.

REINFORCED CONCRETE PIER AND FOUNDATION

PIER TABLE

PIER MATERIAL	MIN. PIER SIZE	MIN. FOOTING	PIER SPACING		HEIGHT RANGE
			RIGHT ANGLES TO JOIST	PARALLEL TO JOIST	
Brick	12" x 12"	24" x 24" x 8"	8' o.c.	12' o.c.	18" to 6'
Concrete masonry	12" x 12" or 8" x 16"	24" x 24" x 8" 20" x 24" x 8"	8' o.c.	12' o.c.	18" to 8'
Poured-in-place concrete	12" dia. or 10" x 10"	20" x 20" x 8"	Dependant on type of framing and loading conditions		18" to 12' +

Wajeda J. Rab, RLA; Maryland National Capital Park and Planning Commission; Silver Spring, Maryland

Phillip Renfrow, AIA; Komatsu/Brown Architects; Washington, D.C.

DUNE PROTECTION

Dunes provide a natural shoreline defense against storm wave and water level attack that is preferred above all other methods. Often termed a nonstructural coastal protection method, dunes supply short term surges of sediment to high energy wave attack. Material is usually deposited in offshore bars and returns on-shore after storm passage to begin beach rebuilding.

Maintenance of existing dune fields should be performed through vegetation stabilization and sand fencing, which promote further dune growth and limit wind losses. The cutting of roadways or paths should be prohibited and timber crossovers used instead. In areas where no dunes exist and sufficient beach width is present, dune construction using successive tiers of sand fencing will promote further formation.

Dwellings should always be placed behind primary dunes. Construction atop or in front of dunes has historically shown structural damage from storms and should be prohibited.

ENCROACHMENT, FLOODWAY, AND COASTAL HIGH HAZARD ZONES

Development and encroachment, which restrict the flow of flood water has adverse effects. The flood level is raised upstream as well as locally, and the velocity downstream is increased, causing increased scouring and erosion. The floodway concept has been developed for riverine areas to permit local development within flood fringe areas without causing harm to others. The floodplain may be divided into two zones, one intended to carry the full cross section of the 100-yr flood and to be kept clear of obstruction; the other, the flood fringe, only to be developed with adequate precautions.

An analogous concept of the floodway is used for coastal areas. The 100-yr flood plain is divided into the coastal high hazard or velocity area and the general coastal flood plain. Construction may only occur within a coastal high hazard area if the structure is elevated on adequately anchored piles to the 100-yr flood level and if the space below the 100-yr flood level is left free of obstruction to minimize the impact from wave and wind driven water.

Care of the underside of floor deck in a building elevated above grade is one of the major maintenance considerations for building in the 100-yr flood plain. The material used to enclose floor spaces may be inundated by flood waters and thus should be resistant to water damage. Provision must also be made to allow water that may find its way into the floor sandwich to drain out and for the joist spaces to dry out.

Post and pile foundations are braced when it is determined that their size, number, spacing, and embedment condition will not be sufficient to resist lateral forces. 2 x 6 diagonal wood framing, threaded rods, and shear walls are different ways of bracing.

PIER CONSTRUCTION

Pier construction is a common technique for elevating structures in flood hazard areas. The special loading conditions associated with flooding make it essential that an architect or engineer be consulted for the design of pier foundations. Four factors determine pier footing depth: (1) frost depth, (2) flood or wind hazard loadings, (3) scour, (4) high volume change soils. The table below summarizes some of the major requirements for pier construction.

Good anchorage of posts or piles to the ground is essential for preventing wind and flood forces from overturning or uplifting elevated structures. In post construction the hole should be a minimum of 8 in. larger in diameter than the greatest dimension of a post section. This allows for alignment and backfilling. A clean well-consolidated backfill is necessary to ensure a structure of good lateral stability and resistance against wind and water uplifting.

The two critical areas are the connections between floor beams and piers and the connection between floor beams and floor joists in pier foundations designed to resist flood loading conditions. Floor beams can be anchored to piers with steel anchor bolts embedded in the pier and bolted through the beams with nuts and large diameter washers. The bolts should be embedded at least 12 in. in concrete, and 18 in. in masonry piers. Uplift and horizontal movements of joists can be avoided by securely anchoring joists to the beams by (1) metal framing plates and clips, (2) plywood sheating or wood siding, and (3) metal strapping.

ENVIRONMENTAL FACTORS 1

INTRODUCTION

Social impacts are simply the effects on people—the way they live, work, play, and relate to one another—caused by the decision to develop a specific site. Although social impacts can be either beneficial or harmful, it is the latter that are of most concern. Historically, there has been little equity in the distribution of adverse impacts. People who have had to bear the bulk of adverse social impact are members of minority groups, the poor, and the elderly.

Social impacts can occur at any time during the life of a project. There are "anticipatory effects" such as land speculation, which occur when a project is still in the planning stage. Later, during construction, the physical intrusion of heavy machinery accompanied by noise, dust, and fumes may assume great importance. Finally, there are social consequences that accrue after the completion of a project, sometimes many years later. Some negative impacts are short-lived and, at worst, annoying. Others may seriously impair an individual's ability to learn or cope effectively in society; still others may precipitate grief, depression, and occasionally, in the case of the elderly, early death.

Some key questions must be answered in assessing the social impacts of a project:

1. What problems might the project create for the people in the community?
2. How many people will be affected (who gains and who loses)?
3. For how long and how severely will people be affected?
4. What alternatives exist? What happens if development does not take place or if another location is selected?
5. What can be done to lessen the severity of the impact?
6. Is it possible to compensate people adequately for any adverse consequences of the project?

RANKING OF CONSTRUCTION RELATED SOCIAL IMPACTS USING A HIGHWAY CONSTRUCTION PROJECT EXAMPLE

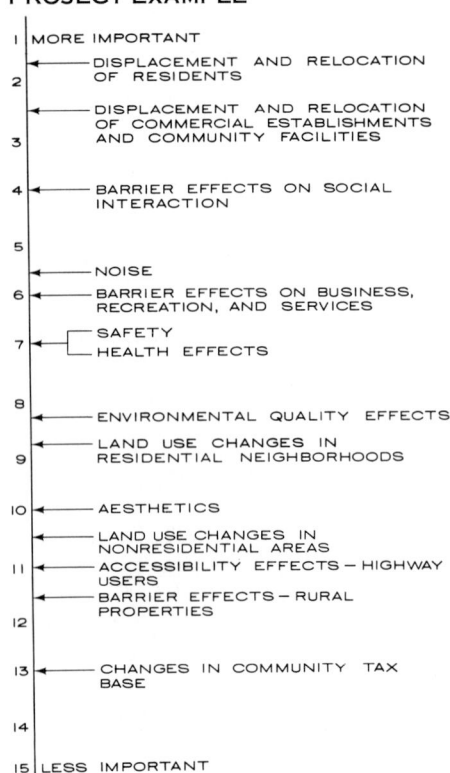

1 MORE IMPORTANT

2 — DISPLACEMENT AND RELOCATION OF RESIDENTS

3 — DISPLACEMENT AND RELOCATION OF COMMERCIAL ESTABLISHMENTS AND COMMUNITY FACILITIES

4 — BARRIER EFFECTS ON SOCIAL INTERACTION

5 — NOISE

6 — BARRIER EFFECTS ON BUSINESS, RECREATION, AND SERVICES

7 — SAFETY / HEALTH EFFECTS

8 — ENVIRONMENTAL QUALITY EFFECTS

9 — LAND USE CHANGES IN RESIDENTIAL NEIGHBORHOODS

10 — AESTHETICS

— LAND USE CHANGES IN NONRESIDENTIAL AREAS

11 — ACCESSIBILITY EFFECTS – HIGHWAY USERS

— BARRIER EFFECTS – RURAL PROPERTIES

12

13 — CHANGES IN COMMUNITY TAX BASE

14

15 LESS IMPORTANT

Lynn G. Llewellyn, Ph.D., Social Psychologist; Rockville, Maryland

The accompanying table shows the relative importance of various social impact categories, using a highway segment as a theoretical construction project. Clearly, other projects ranging in size from a large airport accommodating commercial jets to a single renovated condominium might trigger a somewhat different set of impacts. Although most of the impact categories depicted in the table are valid in other settings, planners must make judgments about the applicability of impacts on a project-by-project basis.

Note that the impacts shown here were ranked by social scientists. Whenever possible, citizens affected by development should be given the opportunity to voice their own set of concerns. The public's priorities may change over time, however, when factors such as the desire for better housing, schools, and access to new employment override other considerations. Moreover, agreements achieved with one group of community representatives may not be honored if changes in leadership occur after elections or for other reasons.

CONSTRUCTION RELATED SOCIAL IMPACTS (HIGHWAY EXAMPLE) RANKED BY ORDER OF SEVERITY

1. DISPLACEMENT AND RELOCATION OF RESIDENTS
   a. Groups most affected:
      (1) Elderly.
      (2) Long term residents of stable communities.
      (3) Low income families.
   b. Range of effects:
      (1) Anxiety, depression.
      (2) Disruption of old friendships.
      (3) Early death for some elderly.
   c. Avoid when elderly involved; provide adequate replacement housing.
2. DISPLACEMENT AND RELOCATION OF COMMERCIAL ESTABLISHMENTS AND COMMUNITY FACILITIES
   a. Groups most affected:
      (1) Small businesses.
      (2) Handicapped, pedestrian-dependent.
      (3) Youth, ethnic minorities.
   b. Range of effects:
      (1) Loss of clientele, new sites inadequate.
      (2) Loss of service to former community.
      (3) Social and cultural disruption.
   c. Avoid if feasible alternative available.
3. BARRIER EFFECTS ON SOCIAL INTERACTION
   a. Groups most affected:
      (1) Schoolchildren, pedestrian-dependent.
      (2) Total neighborhood/community.
      (3) Minorities.
   b. Range of effects:
      (1) Disruption of visiting, neighborhood solidarity.
      (2) Isolation from schools, facilities.
      (3) Travel inconvenience, loss of access.
   c. Avoid bisecting communities; design ample pedestrian walkways.
4. NOISE EFFECTS
   a. Groups most affected:
      (1) Residents adjacent to road system.
      (2) Schoolchildren, older students.
   b. Range of effects:
      (1) Sleep loss, irritability, physical damage.
      (2) Learning impairment, behavior changes.
      (3) Reduced use of outside space.
      (4) Perceived invasion of privacy.
   c. Consider alternative locations; noise shields.
5. BARRIER EFFECTS ON BUSINESS, RECREATION, COMMUNITY SERVICES
   a. Groups most affected:
      (1) Total neighborhood/community.
      (2) Consumers, pedestrian-dependent.
   b. Range of effects:
      (1) Inconvenience, increased travel time.
      (2) Economic loss.
      (3) Impede delivery of emergency service.
   c. Need for careful planning during construction.

6. SAFETY
   a. Groups most affected:
      (1) Children, elderly.
      (2) Bikers, pedestrians.
   b. Range of effects:
      (1) Risk of injury increased.
      (2) Crimes of violence translocated.
   c. Design bikepaths, walkways, ample lighting.
7. HEALTH
   a. Groups most affected:
      (1) Adjacent residents.
      (2) Respiratory patients, elderly.
   b. Range of effects:
      (1) Dust, fumes during construction.
      (2) Airborne lead, asbestos, carbon monoxide.
      (3) Lung disorders, anemia, cramps.
   c. Consider alternative locations carefully.
8. ENVIRONMENTAL QUALITY
   a. Groups most affected: total community.
   b. Range of effects:
      (1) Curtailment of forms of outdoor activity.
      (2) Increased dependence on air conditioning.
      (3) Lower home values, costlier maintenance.
   c. Economic compensation and incentives.
9. LAND USE CHANGES IN NEIGHBORHOODS AND RESIDENTIAL AREAS
   a. Groups most affected: total community.
   b. Range of effects:
      (1) Rapid social change.
      (2) Neighborhood decay.
      (3) Lower property values.
   c. Full public participation in planning.
10. AESTHETICS
    a. Groups most affected: total community.
    b. Range of effects:
       (1) Dominate surrounding landscape.
       (2) Physical intrusion.
       (3) Visual blight.
    c. Design system not to overwhelm backdrop; minimize intrusion of billboards, etc.
11. LAND USE CHANGES IN NONRESIDENTIAL AREAS
    a. Groups most affected:
       (1) Landowners.
       (2) Long term residents.
    b. Range of effects:
       (1) Encourages development, sprawl.
       (2) Population increased.
       (3) Open space, wildlife habitat lost.
    c. Requires thoughtful planning, work with local residents.
12. EFFECTS ON ACCESSIBILITY FOR HIGHWAY USERS
    a. Groups most affected:
       (1) Automobile users, commuters.
       (2) Unemployed.
       (3) Local businesses, property owners.
    b. Range of effects:
       (1) Benefits commuters, truckers.
       (2) Travel convenience.
       (3) Access may encourage burglary.
    c. Alert businesses, property owners of increased crime potential.
13. BARRIER EFFECTS ON PROPERTIES IN RURAL AREAS
    a. Groups most affected: local landowners.
    b. Range of effects:
       (1) Segments property.
       (2) Inconvenience.
       (3) Loss of once productive land.
    c. Carefully examine alternative locations.
14. CHANGES IN COMMUNITY TAX BASE
    a. Groups most affected:
       (1) Property owners.
       (2) Taxpayers.
    b. Range of effects:
       (1) Access raises property values.
       (2) Pollution lowers property values.
       (3) Taxes increase.
    c. Economic compensation plan needed.

1 ENVIRONMENTAL FACTORS

CHAPTER 2   SITEWORK

INTRODUCTION

Site planning for any significant development project should be a sequential process, beginning with broad information-gathering and ending with specific, detailed design drawings. The process involves three basic stages—analysis, design, and implementation. The following chart indicates a planning process; however, specifics of the site—such as physical site characteristics, location, and community criteria—may modify the process. Certain steps in the process may be taken simultaneously, rather than on a precise step-by-step basis.

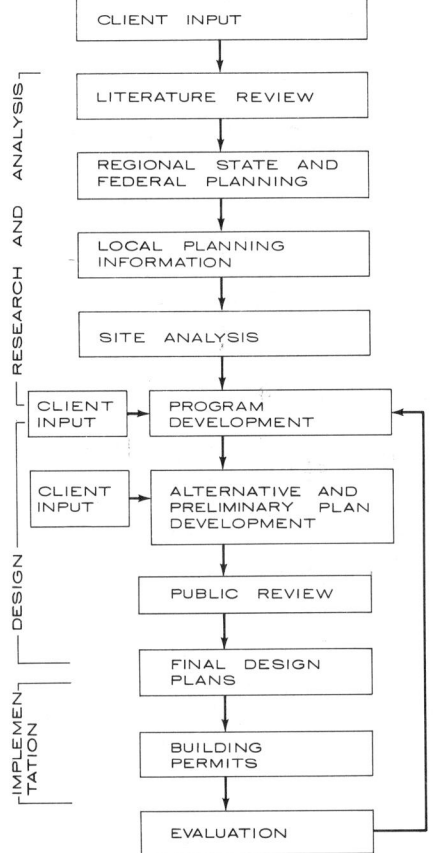

CLIENT CONTACT AND INPUT

The first step is the contact between client and site planner. Although the land planner should be involved as early as possible in the decision making process, the client may already have some broad objectives based on financial capabilities and market feasibility. In many cases, it may be advisable for the client to retain the site planner for assistance in selecting a site that meets the client's basic aims. It is important that the land planner obtain all client data relative to the site planning for the site.

LITERATURE REVIEW

In cases where the site planner has not had extensive exposure to all aspects of site planning, a review of the relevant literature on the subject may be in order. Energy conscious design, for example, is an area where substantial research is now under way and specific literature search may be advisable.

REGIONAL, STATE, AND FEDERAL PLANNING

The site planning process usually begins at the regional level. In some areas of the country, regional planning agencies have been established for the purpose of research and planning of intercommunity regional issues such as water management, transportation, population studies, pollution control, and other regional environmental concerns. Many communities have adopted

Gary Greenan, AIP, ASLA; Miami, Florida

plans that establish regional planning guidelines relative to land use planning. The site planner should discern those regional issues that are pertinent to the design of the site.

Some projects may also come under state and/or national criteria, although this is not a common occurrence. Adopted state plans may address broad issues applicable to large sites or impose constraints on sites involving issues of statewide concern. Additionally, some states require environmental impact statements for large scale projects. At the national level, the National Environmental Policy Act may require impact review particularly if dredge and fill permits are required from the Army Corps of Engineers. Another federal regulation that will affect many coastline projects is the Federal Flood Insurance program, which establishes minimum elevations for potential flood areas.

LOCAL PLANNING INFORMATION

At this stage the site planner becomes involved in collecting local planning information that will influence decisions made in the site planning process. Personal contact with local planning and zoning agencies is important in order to clearly comprehend local criteria. Following is a list of information that should be reviewed.

PLANNING DOCUMENTS

Many communities have adopted comprehensive plans that will indicate in general terms, and in some instances in specific terms, the particular land use and intensity of the site. Also, valuable information on the availability and/or phasing of public services and utilities, environmental criteria, traffic planning information, and population trends can be found in most comprehensive plans. Some communities may require that rezoning meet the criteria provided in their comprehensive plan.

In addition to the comprehensive plan, some communities adopt neighborhood or area studies that refine the comprehensive plan as it relates to subareas. Many of these studies stipulate specific zoning categories for individual parcels of land.

ZONING

The zoning on a tract of land determines specifically the intensity and type of land use that can occur. If the existing zoning does not permit the type of land use and intensity planned for the project, a zoning change will be required.

PUBLIC SERVICES AND UTILITIES

Although some of this information may be provided in the comprehensive plan or neighborhood study, the critical nature of the availability of these public facilities may require additional research, specifically in terms of the following:

1. Availability of public sewer service, access to trunk lines, capacity of the trunk lines, and available increases in the flow. (If sewerage is not immediately available, the projected phasing of these services must be determined, as well as other possible alternatives to sewage collection and treatment.)

2. Availability of potable water, with the same basic research approach as indicated for sewer service determination.

3. Local and state regulations on freshwater wells and septic tanks.

4. Access to public roads, existing and projected carrying capacity, and levels of service of the roads. (State and local road departments can provide this information.)

5. Availability and capacity of schools and other public facilities such as parks and libraries.

SITE ANALYSIS (SITE INVENTORY)

Site analysis is one of the site planner's major responsibilities. All of the on- and off-site environmental design determinants must be evaluated and synthesized during the site analysis process. The site analysis processes follow later in this section.

PROGRAM DEVELOPMENT

At the program development stage, the background research and the site analysis are combined with client input and synthesized into a set of site development concepts and strategies. Elements that form the basis for program development include market and financial criteria, federal, state, regional, and local planning information, development costs, and the client's basic objectives, combined with site opportunities and constraints as developed in the synthesis of environmental site determinants. Trade-offs and a balancing of the various determinants may need to be made in order to develop an appropriate approach to site development. Consideration of dwelling unit type, density, marketing, time phasing, and other similar criteria, as well as graphic studies of the site, constitute the program. Graphic representations depicting design concepts should be clearly developed for presentation to the client and others who may have input to the process. If the program cannot be accomplished under the existing zoning, the decision to request a zone change becomes a part of the program.

If the architect is other than the site planner, he or she should be retained at or before the program development stage. A close working relationship between the architect and site planner is important in the design phase of the site development process to develop architectural solutions that respond to site characteristics. If an impact statement is required, it should be initiated at the beginning of this stage.

ALTERNATIVE AND PRELIMINARY PLAN PREPARATION

Once the program is established and accepted by the client, alternative design solutions that meet the program objectives, including basic zoning criteria, are developed. The accepted alternative is further developed into the preliminary plan. This plan should be a relatively detailed plan showing all spatial relationships, landscaping, and similar information.

PUBLIC REVIEW

If a zone change is required to implement the plan, some form of public review will be required. Some communities will require substantial data, such as impact statements and other narrative and graphic exhibits, while others may only require an application for the zone change. Local requirements for zone changes can be complex, and it is imperative for the site planner or the client's attorney to be familiar with local criteria.

FINAL DESIGN PLANS

At this stage, the preliminary plan is further refined to include any modifications that may have been agreed upon at a public hearing. Final design plans including landscape plans and all required dimensioning must be provided in the final design. In addition, all drawings that are usually prepared by the surveyor or engineer, such as plats, utilities, street, and drainage plans, must be prepared. Upon approval, final design plans are recorded in the public records in the form of plats. Additionally, homeowner association agreements, deed restrictions, and other similar legal documents must be recorded and become binding on all owners and successive owners unless changed by legal processes. Bonding may be required for public facilities.

BUILDING PERMITS

Building permits may be issued when all final documents are recorded and architectural drawings have been reviewed and approved in accordance with local building codes. Depending on the agreement between site planner and client, the planner may continue his or her services into the supervision of the site development.

EVALUATION

This stage may come years later after the community has become a reality. The purpose is to review the process and the resulting program and assess it in the context of the community as it exists. This is an important aspect usually overlooked. It provides the site planner with valuable data for future planning programs.

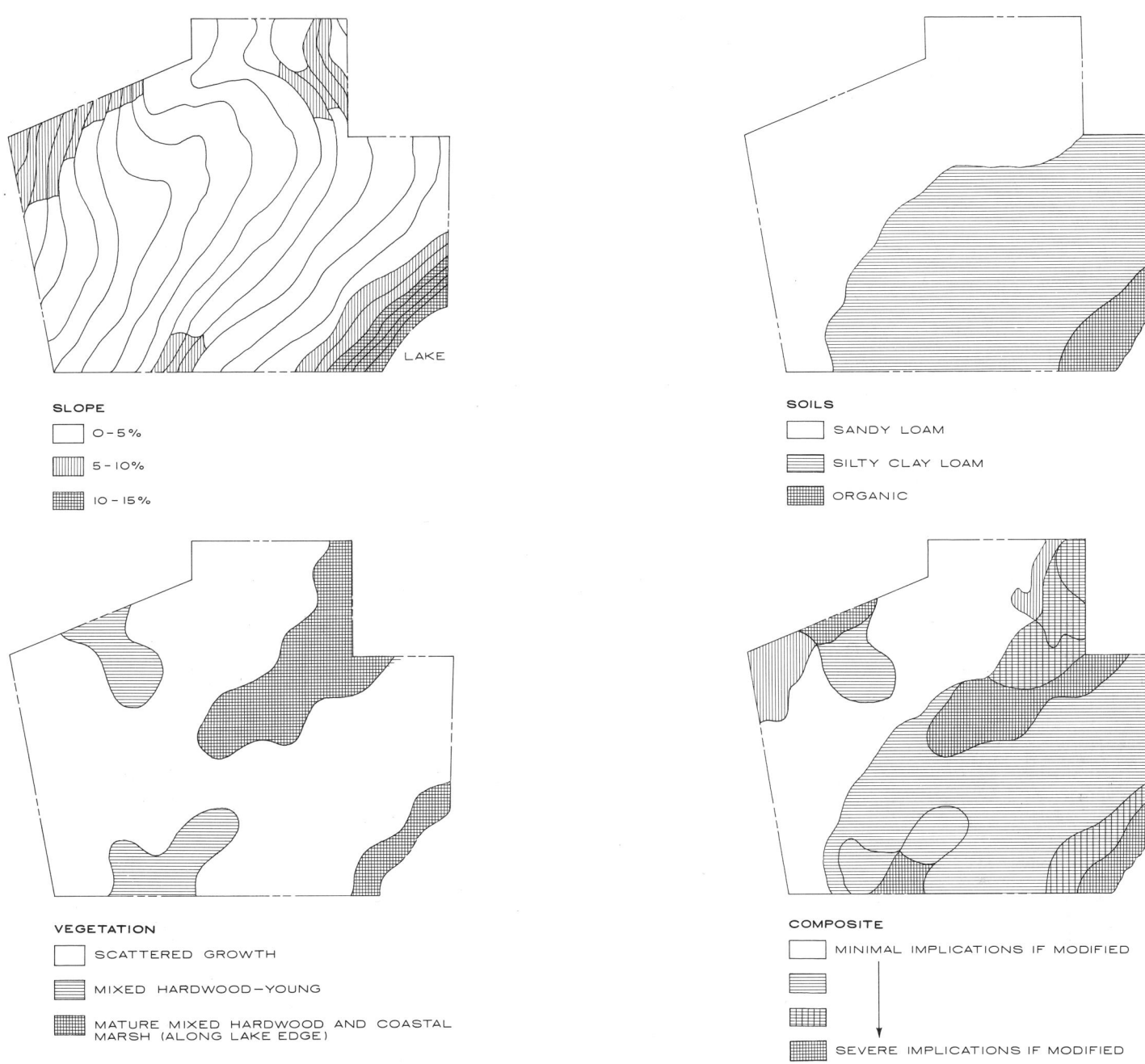

LAKE

SLOPE
- ☐ 0 – 5 %
- ▥ 5 – 10 %
- ▦ 10 – 15 %

SOILS
- ☐ SANDY LOAM
- ▤ SILTY CLAY LOAM
- ▦ ORGANIC

VEGETATION
- ☐ SCATTERED GROWTH
- ▤ MIXED HARDWOOD – YOUNG
- ▦ MATURE MIXED HARDWOOD AND COASTAL MARSH (ALONG LAKE EDGE)

COMPOSITE
- ☐ MINIMAL IMPLICATIONS IF MODIFIED
- ▤
- ▦
- ▦ SEVERE IMPLICATIONS IF MODIFIED

ENVIRONMENTAL SITE ANALYSIS PROCESS

If a site has numerous environmental design determinants, the site planner may need to analyze each environmental system individually in order to comprehend more clearly the environmental character of the site.

By preparing each analysis on transparencies, the site planner can use the overlay approach to site analysis. Each sheet is assigned values based on impact, ranging from areas of the site where change would have minimal effect to areas where change would result in severe disruption of the site. In essence, the separate sheets become abstractions with values assigned by the site planner and associated professionals. As each sheet is superimposed, a composite develops which, when completed, constitutes the synthesis of the environmental design determinants. Lighter tones indicate areas where modification would have minimal influence, darker tones indicate areas more sensitive to change. The sketches shown simulate the overlay process. The site planner may give greater or lesser weight

Gary Greenan, AIP, ASLA; Miami, Florida

Rafael Diaz, Graphics Coordinator; Miami, Florida

to certain parameters depending on the particular situation. In assigning values, the site planner should consider such factors as the value of maintaining the functioning of the individual site systems, the uniqueness of the specific site features, and the cost of modifying the site elements. The composite map is used by the site planner as an input in the site design process.

Following is a list of the environmental design determinants that may, depending on the particular site, need to be considered and included in an overlay format:

1. SLOPE: The slope analysis is developed on the contour map; consideration should include the percentage of slope and orientation of slope relative to the infrastructure and land uses.

2. SOIL PATTERNS: Consideration may include the analysis of soils in terms of erosion potential, compressibility and plasticity, capability of supporting plant growth, drainage capabilities, septic tank location (if relevant), and the proposed land uses and their infrastructure.

3. VEGETATION: Consideration should include indigenous and exotic species (values of each in terms of the environmental system), size and condition, the succession of growth toward climax conditions, uniqueness, the ability of certain species to tolerate construction activities, aesthetic values, and density of undergrowth.

4. WILDLIFE: Consideration of indigenous species, their movement patterns, the degree of changes that each species can tolerate, and feeding and breeding areas.

5. GEOLOGY: Consideration of underlying rock masses, the depth of different rock layers, and the suitability of different geological formations in terms of potential infrastructure and building.

6. SURFACE AND SUBSURFACE WATER: Consideration of natural drainage and patterns, aquifer recharge areas, erosion potential, and flood plains.

7. CLIMATE: Consideration of microclimatic conditions including prevailing breezes (at different times of the year), wind shadows, frost pockets, and air drainage patterns.

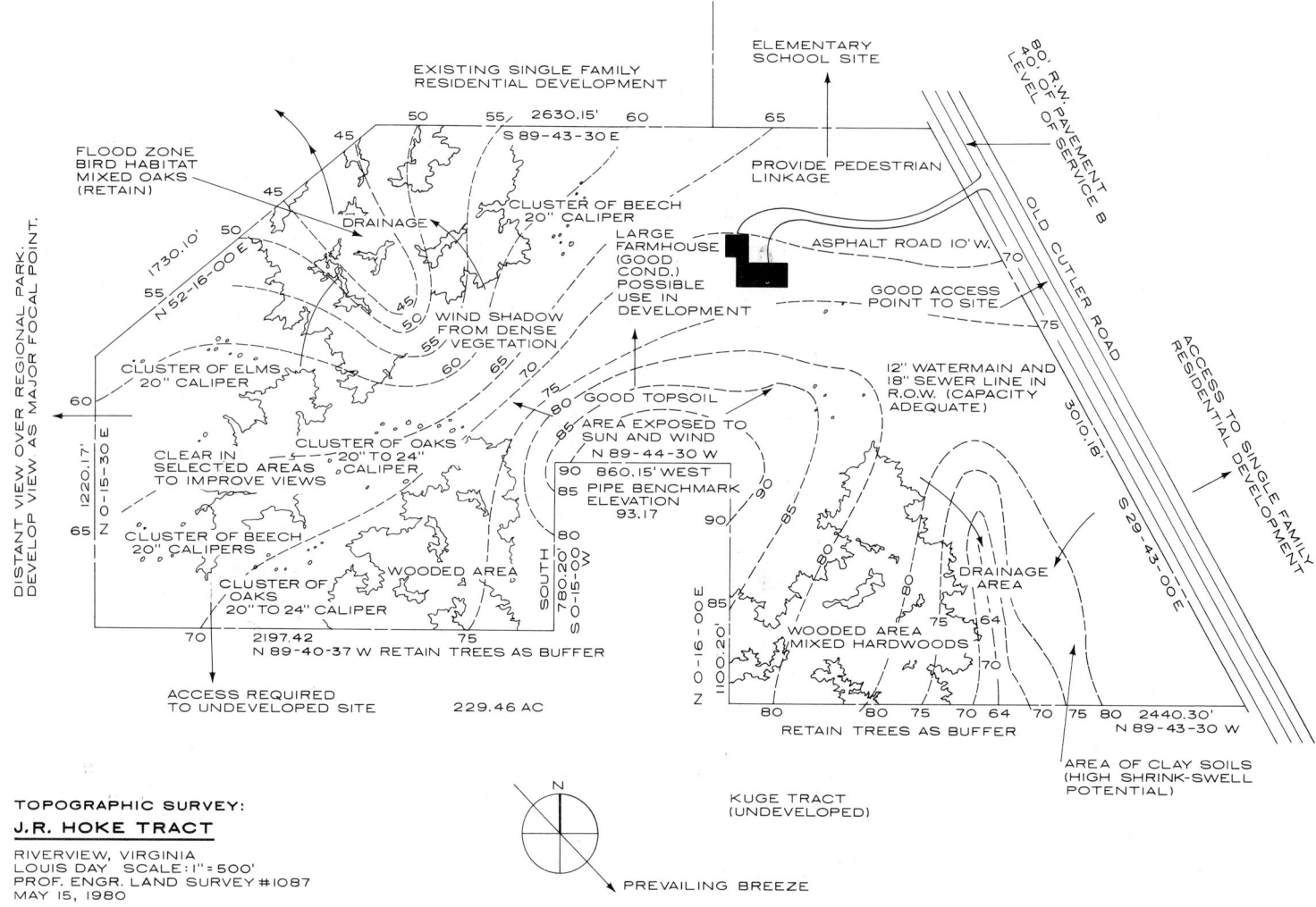

TOPOGRAPHIC SURVEY:

J.R. HOKE TRACT

RIVERVIEW, VIRGINIA
LOUIS DAY   SCALE: 1" = 500'
PROF. ENGR. LAND SURVEY #1087
MAY 15, 1980

KUGE TRACT
(UNDEVELOPED)

PREVAILING BREEZE

SURVEY DATA

The first step in any site analysis is the gathering of physical site data. An aerial photograph and an accurate survey showing the following information are basic to any site analysis process:

1. Scale, north arrow, benchmark and date of survey.

2. Tract boundary lines.

3. Easements: location, width and purpose.

4. Names and locations of existing road rights-of-way on or adjacent to the tract including bridges, curbs, gutters, and culverts.

5. Position of buildings and other structures such as foundations, walls, fences, steps, and paved areas.

6. Utilities on or adjacent to the tract, including:

   a. Location of gas lines, fire hydrants, electric and telephone poles, and street lights.

   b. Direction, distance to and size of nearest water mains and sewers and invert elevation of sewers.

7. Location of swamps, springs, streams, bodies of water, drainage ditches, water shed areas, flood plains, and other physical features.

8. Outline of wooded areas with names and condition of plant material.

9. Contour intervals of 2 to 5 ft, depending on the slope gradients, and spot elevations at breaks in grade, along all drainage channels or swales and selected points as needed.

Gary Greenan, AIP, ASLA; Miami, Florida

Rafael Diaz, Graphics Coordinator; Miami, Florida

ADDITIONAL INFORMATION

Considerable additional information may be needed, depending on design consideration and site complexities such as soil information and studies on the geological structure of the site.

SITE ANALYSIS

As indicated in the previous site planning process, the site analysis is a major responsibility of the site planner. Two interrelated approaches are offered in the text. The first is the physical analysis of the site developed primarily from field inspections.

Using the survey, the aerial photograph, and, where warranted, infrared aerial photographs, the site designer, working in the field and in the office, verifies the survey and notes site design determinants. Site design determinants should include but not be limited to the following:

1. Areas of steep and moderate slopes.
2. Macro- and microclimatic conditions, including:

   a. Sun angles during different seasons.

   b. Prevailing breezes.

   c. Wind shadows.

   d. Frost pockets.

   e. Sectors where high or low points give protection from sun and wind.

   f. Solar energy considerations; if solar energy appears to be feasible, a detailed climatic anal-

ysis must be undertaken considering such factors as:

   Detailed sun charts.

   Daily averages of sunlight and cloud cover.

   Daily rain averages.

   Areas exposed to the sun at different seasons.

   Solar radiation patterns.

   Temperature patterns.

3. Areas of potential flood zones and routes of surface water runoff.

4. Possible road access to the site, including considerations of points of potential conflict with the existing road system and carrying capacities of adjacent roadways. (This information can usually be obtained from local or state road departments.)

5. Natural areas that from an ecological and aesthetic standpoint should be saved; all tree masses with names and condition of tree species and understory.

6. Significant wildlife habitats that would be affected by site modification.

7. Soil conditions relative to supporting plant material, areas suitable for construction, erosion potential, and septic tanks, if relevant.

8. Geological considerations relative to supporting structures.

9. Exceptional views; objectionable views (use on site photographs).

10. Adjacent existing and proposed land uses with notations on compatibility and incompatibility.

INTRODUCTION

These standards should be used only as a basic reference or beginning point in the determination of the spatial site functions. The final determination of intensity and dwelling type of a particular site should evolve as the end of a thorough planning process.

CLUSTER

ATRIUM

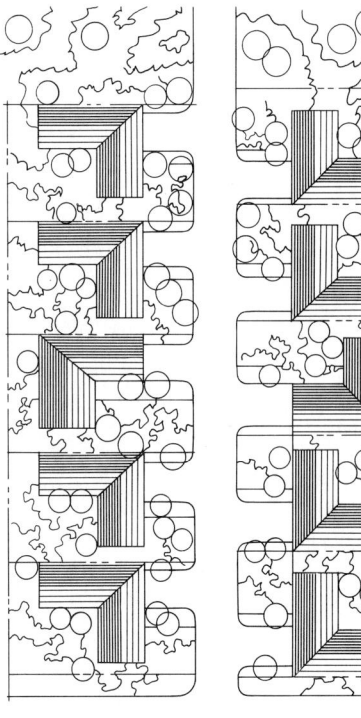

O - LOT LINE

INTENSITY STANDARDS FOR RESIDENTIAL DEVELOPMENT

DWELLING UNIT TYPE	DWELLING UNITS PER ACRE	COMMON OPEN SPACE AS PERCENTAGE OF TOTAL SITE	PARKING PER UNIT (1)	TREES PER ACRE OF TOTAL SITE AREA (2)	PRIVATE OPEN SPACE (3)
Single family estate		Usually not provided	3+	15+	Depends on lot size
Single family	3 to 5 depending on lot size	Usually not provided	2.5+	15+	Depends on lot size
Duplex	5 to 10 depending on lot size	Usually not provided	2+ (4+ for each structure)	15+	Depends on lot size
0-lot line (4)	4 to 7 units per acre	Usually not provided	2.25+	15+	Depends on lot size
Single family cluster (5)	4 to 7	25 to 50%	2.25+	15 to 20± for first 3 acres, 10+ for remaining acreage	Depends on lot size
Atrium (6)	4 to 8 units per acre	Usually not provided	2.25+	15+	25% of total square footage
Suburban townhouse (7)	6 to 9	25% to 40%	2.25+	15 to 20± for first 3 acres, 10± for remaining acreage	500 to 700 sq ft
Urban townhouse (8)	8 to 16	15% to 25% if provided	2.0+	15 to 20± for first 3 acres, 10± for remaining acreage	400 to 600 sq ft
Walk-up apartments	10 to 25	25% to 40%	2.0± depending on number of bedrooms	15 to 20± for first 3 acres, 10± for remaining acreage	Usually not provided except on ground floor apartments
Midrise apartment up to 6 stories	15 to 35	30% to 40%	2.0± depending on number of bedrooms	15 to 20± for first 3 acres, 10± for remaining acreage	Usually not provided except on ground floor apartments
Highrise apartments	30 to 75	35% to 60%	2.0± depending on number of bedrooms	15 to 20± for first 3 acres, 10± for remaining acreage	Usually not provided except on ground floor apartments
Planned unit development (9)	10 to 25 depending on type of planned unit development	25% to 60%	2.0± depending on unit type	15 to 20± for first 3 acres, 10± for remaining acreage	Depends on individual unit type

NOTES

1. PARKING PER UNIT: In determining the parking per unit, the site design should consider the influence of public transportation and location of the development in relation to employment centers and supporting facilities. An excessive amount of parking spaces to accommodate infrequent special activities could result in excess pavement; depending on soil conditions, it is sometimes better to accommodate infrequent overflow parking on grassed areas or, where conditions permit, on commercial parking areas when not in use or at community centers.

2. TREES: Trees provide one of the major unifying design elements and act as climate modifiers; where a substantial number of trees do not already exist, extensive tree planting should be undertaken as part of most planning programs. The determination of the number of trees per acre should be based more on the particular locale than on a uniform standard.

3. PRIVATE OPEN SPACE: Private open space should be private to the unit concerned and may be provided in the form of courtyards, entrance courts, and rear, side, and front yards. Both visual and aural privacy is important in the design of these spaces.

4. 0-LOT LINE: A single family unit located directly on one side property line and possibly on the rear property line; the emphasis is on eliminating small side yards for larger, more usable open spaces.

5. SINGLE FAMILY CLUSTER: Single family units grouped in clusters in order to maximize open space; units may or may not be attached.

6. ATRIUM: A single family unit related to the early Greek and Roman prototypes which incorporate interior living spaces fronting on an interior court.

7. SUBURBAN TOWNHOUSE: A single family unit attached to other single family units with a common party wall; open space is usually a major element in the suburban townhouse development.

8. URBAN TOWNHOUSE: Early prototypes appear in the urban areas of many older cities; similar to suburban townhouse, although densities are usually higher and common open space is usually provided in the form of public open space.

9. PLANNED UNIT DEVELOPMENT: A mixture of housing types with emphasis on total community design; all the housing types included in the chart, plus associated retail support facilities and community amenities, may be found in a PUD development.

Gary Greenan, AIP, ASLA; Miami, Florida

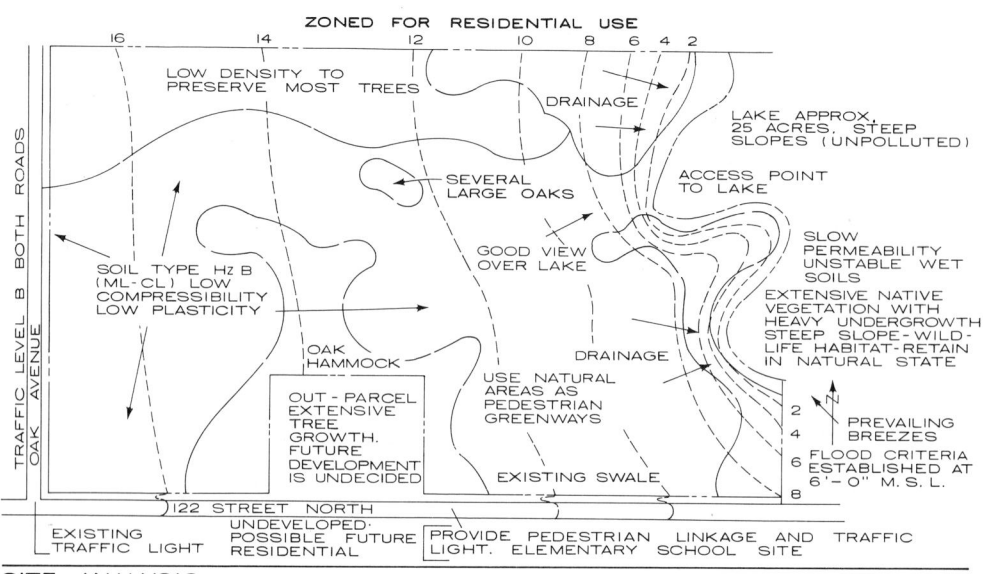

SITE ANALYSIS

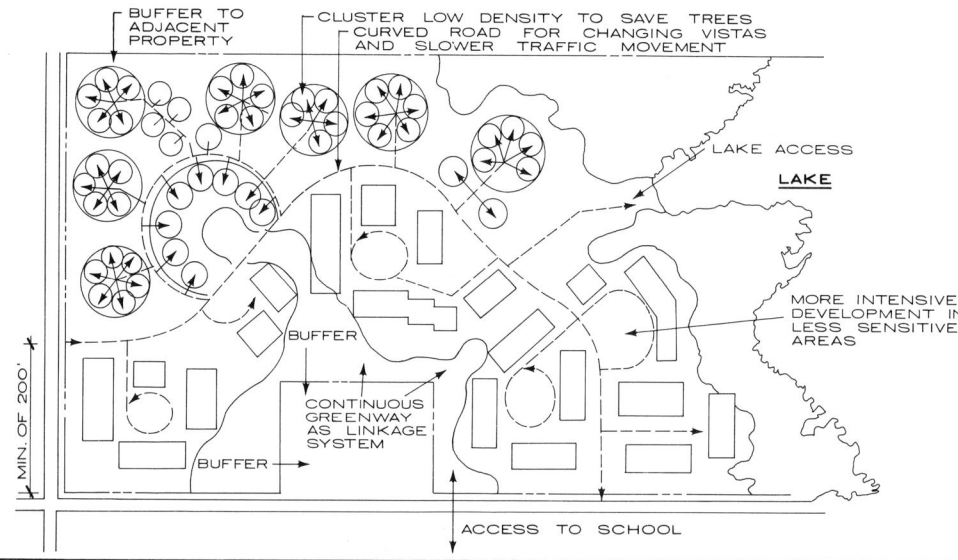

CONCEPT PLANNING

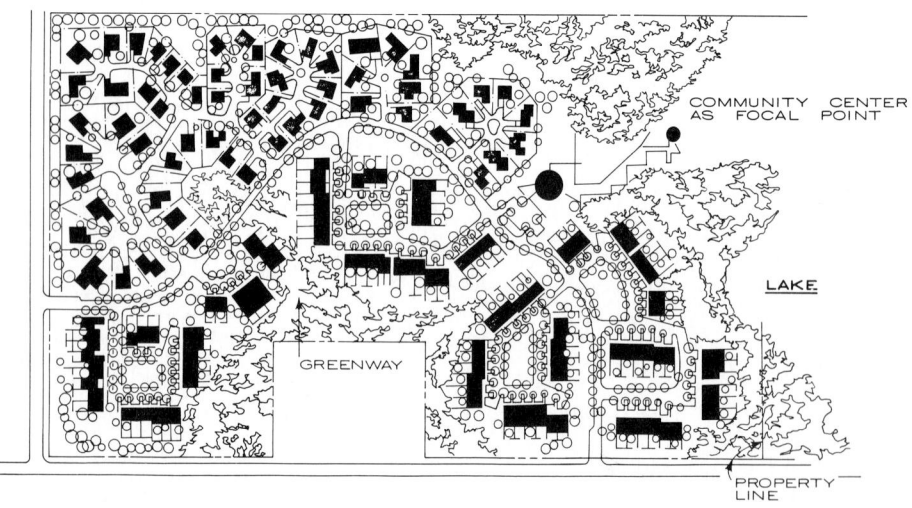

PRELIMINARY PLAN

Gary Greenan, AIP, ASLA; Miami, Florida

Rafael Diaz, Graphics Coordinator; Miami, Florida

INTRODUCTION

The illustrations indicate a design process, including the following:

1. SITE ANALYSIS: A synthesis of the physical environmental design determinants and offsite influences.
2. CONCEPT PLAN: A synthesis of the site analysis, research, and client input into design concepts—several concept plans may be prepared.
3. PRELIMINARY PLAN: A further sophistication and detailing of the concept plan.

DESIGN SCALE

In the design of the site, the site planner should be aware of four interdependent levels of design scale.

COMMUNITY

At the community scale (a neighborhood scale) the site planner should be aware of those elements that create design unity and give identity to the development as a whole. Major natural features, circulation systems, greenway systems, and public use spaces such as schools, shopping, and parks act as focal points and/or linkages in the total design of the project.

SUBCOMMUNITY

The first level down from the community scale is the subcommunity space. These are the spaces created by the grouping or clustering of housing units, associated parking, paths, and landscape into a form that responds to the environmental characteristics of the site and gives identity to the individual clusters.

TRANSITION

Transition spaces, in the form of entrance courts, patios, and yards, are those spaces that provide a transition from the totally private interior spaces to the public spaces. Consideration should be given to privacy for the individual unit and the environmental characteristics of the site such as breezes, sun angles, and landscape.

INTERIOR

This is the smallest scale that the site planner will be involved with. Emphasis should be placed on the interior design of the unit in terms of privacy and its relationship to the exterior microenvironment. A close working relationship between architect and site planner is essential.

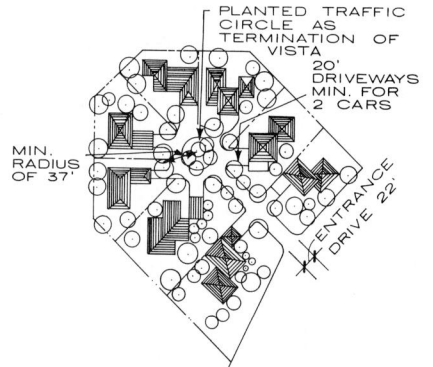

SINGLE FAMILY CLUSTER

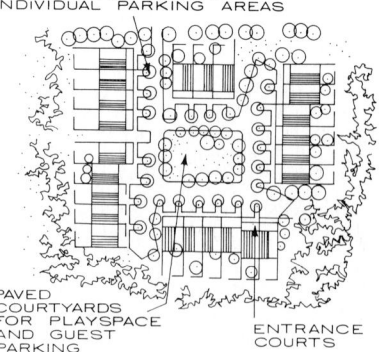

TOWN HOUSE LAYOUT

2 LAND PLANNING AND SITE DEVELOPMENT

FINAL DEVELOPMENT PLANS

After all necessary approvals under the zoning process have been granted, final site development plans are initiated. Unlike the design plans, which are prepared by the architect and landscape architect, the final site development plans are usually prepared by a registered surveyor and/or engineer. The professional preparing these plans should obtain a copy of the local subdivision code and, if available, a copy of the public works manual for specific local requirements. All drawings should show the name and location of the development, the date of preparation and any revisions, the scale, north point, datum, and approvals of local authorities. The following list of exhibits are typical requirements for most communities.

TENTATIVE OR PRELIMINARY PLAT

Platting is the process whereby a piece of land, referred to as the parent tract, is subdivided into two or more parcels. A plat specifically and legally describes the layout of the development. A tentative plat is the first step in the preparation of the final drawings and indicates the layout of the development in terms of lots and sizes of lots, lot frontages, road right-of-ways, setbacks, sidewalks, street offsets, and other graphic information relative to the design of the project. After approval of the tentative plat, the engineer can begin the utility plans and the street paving and drainage plans. Even if the local law does not require a tentative plat, it is advised that the professional prepare a sketch of the plat and meet with local authorities in order to avoid problems later in the final site development plan process.

STREET PAVING AND DRAINAGE PLANS

Street paving and drainage plans are final construction drawings prepared by an engineer indicating the following:

1. Plan for all streets and parking areas with starting points and radii.
2. Typical cross sections (some communities may also require road profiles).
3. Details and specifications of pavement base, surfacing and curbs.
4. Indication of methods to retain storm water runoff within the right-of-way (soil tests for percolation may be required). Also details and specifications for inlets, manholes, catch basins, and surface drainage channels.
5. Indication that roads will meet local, state, and federal flood criteria.

UTILITY PLANS

Utility plans are final drawings prepared by an engineer that indicate the location of water supply lines, sewage disposal lines, fire hydrants, and other utility functions usually located in the road right-of-way. In addition to approval by local public works departments, some communities require review of utility plans by the board of public health, fire department, and departments involved in pollution control.

FINAL PLAT

The final plat is usually the last stage of the final site development process prior to the issuance of building permits. A subdivision plat, when accepted and recorded in the public land records, establishes a legal description of the streets, residential lots and other sites in the development. If roads and other improvements are not constructed at the time of final platting, a bond, usually in excess of the estimated costs of the improvements, will be required. Following is a typical list of information that should be shown on the final plat:

1. Right-of-way lines of streets, easements, and other rights-of-way, and property lines of residential lots and other sites with accurate dimensions, bearings, and curve data.
2. Name and right-of-way width of each street or other right-of-way.
3. Location, dimensions, and purpose of any easements.
4. Identifying number for each lot or site.
5. Purpose for which sites, other than residential lots, are dedicated or reserved.
6. Minimum building setback line on all lots and other sites.
7. Location and description of monuments.
8. Reference to recorded subdivision plats of adjoining platted land by record name, date, and number.
9. Certification by surveyor or engineer.
10. Statement by owner(s) dedicating streets, rights-of-way and any sites for public use.
11. Approval by local authorities.
12. Title, scale, north arrow, and date.

BY RAFAEL DIAZ

SITE PLAN

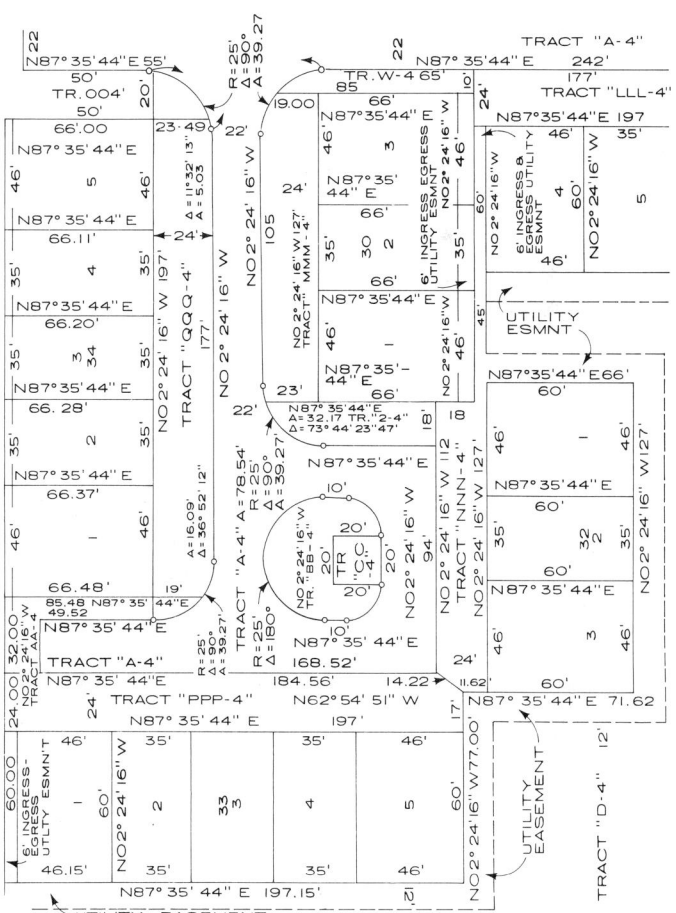

LEGAL PLAT
(SINCE STREETS ARE PRIVATE, THEY ARE INDICATED AS TRACTS)

Gary Greenan, AIP, ASLA; Miami, Florida

Rafael Diaz, Graphics Coordinator; Miami, Florida

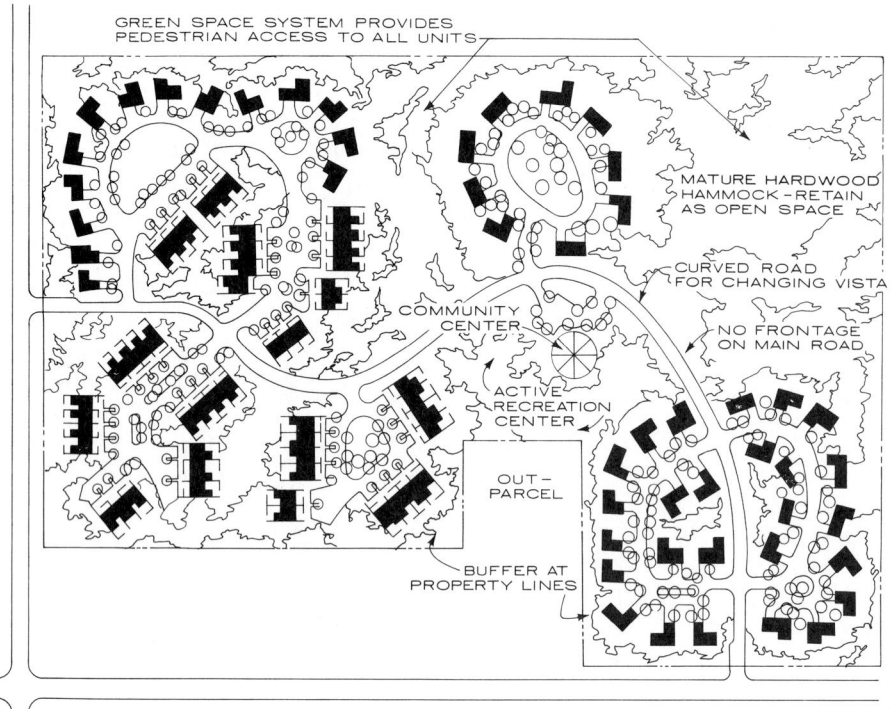

PLANNED UNIT DEVELOPMENT
(SAME NUMBER OF UNITS AS ON CONVENTIONAL PLAN)

The planned unit development ordinance usually incorporates standards for dwelling unit density, open space, and other spatial requirements. PUD ordinances usually place emphasis on total community design, with review of plans by local agencies and public hearing bodies as a primary requirement.

ADVANTAGES OF PLANNED UNIT DEVELOPMENT AND CLUSTER ZONING CONCEPTS

Although the lot-by-lot type of subdivision is still the prevalent development type in many suburban areas, the amenities that can be realized by the planned unit development and cluster zoning concepts are such that these approaches should be seriously considered.

In some communities the terms planned unit development (PUD) and cluster may be synonymous. Usually, however, the PUD is a more comprehensive approach than the cluster, with provisions for both single family and multifamily development and, in some instances, commercial and industrial activities. The term cluster refers to the grouping of single family residences in clusters on lots smaller than permitted by the single family zoning district, and compensating for the smaller lots with common open space areas of substantial and usable configurations.

Both methods offer the designer not only the flexibility of locating structures in a manner that responds to site features, but also the opportunity for developing imaginative architectural forms. A key element of these approaches is the common green space that gives design cohesiveness to the total project.

The responsibility for the maintenance of common space and associated common facilities is a major concern that must be resolved in PUD and cluster developments. The homeowners association is the most commonly accepted approach. The association should be established by recorded agreement before the sale of the first unit by the developer. Each homeowner is automatically a member and is assessed a proportionate share of the cost in maintaining the common facilities. The developer or his attorney should evaluate the best methods of developing a homeowners' association before the initiation of site development. Many jurisdictions require a legal instrument for the association prior to final approval of the project.

The use of common open space usually allows more flexibility in effectively fitting the development to the land than does the more typical lot-by-lot approach. Following are some of the obvious advantages gained by the proper use of the planned unit development concept:

1. With smaller individual lots, excess land can be massed together to provide larger and more useful community recreational space.
2. With the use of connecting community open spaces and fewer through traffic streets, children are better protected from vehicular traffic.
3. With larger amounts of open space, the natural character of the site can be preserved.
4. With the shorter networks of streets and utilities, construction costs can be reduced.

It should be emphasized that the standard subdivision approach still retains a major part of the housing market. Where the program suggests a more typical subdivision layout, the site planner has a responsibility to respond to the same environmental design determinants of the site as for a project being developed under more flexible zoning criteria. Creative planning can be accomplished using either approach.

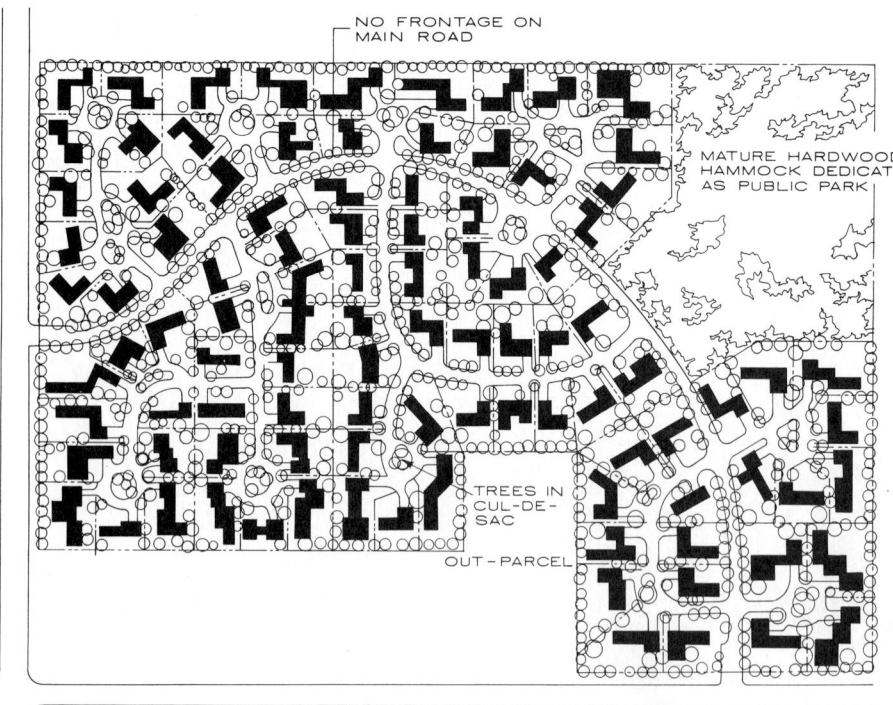

CONVENTIONAL SINGLE FAMILY

Gary Greenan, ASLA, AIP; Miami, Florida

Rafael Diaz, Graphics Coordinator; Miami, Florida

CONVENTIONAL SINGLE FAMILY RESIDENTIAL ZONED DEVELOPMENT

The density determination for conventional single family residential zoning is based on minimum lot size requirements as provided by local ordinances. For planning purposes, the site planner can translate lot size to a net density figure which represents the total number of dwellings per acre within the site, after deducting for roads, parks, school sites, and other public facilities.

INTRODUCTION

The site designer should have a basic understanding of roadway layout in order to design circulation systems that function on the site and are compatible with systems off the site. Specific minimum standards that must be met are in effect for most municipalities.

HIERARCHY OF ROAD SYSTEMS

The site designer should be cognizant of the hierarchy of road systems and the purposes each system serves. At the upper end is the limited access freeway, which carries up to 1000 or 1300 vehicles per lane per hour at high rates of speed and up to 2000 per hour at slower speeds. Freeways are important to the site designer in terms of site selection for accessibility to freeway systems. Major or principal arterials and minor arterials are the intercommunity connectors that can carry, respectively, 600 to 800 cars per lane per hour and 400 to 500 per lane per hour, depending on traffic signals, parking along the street, intersections, and other physical impediments or friction to traffic flow. Arterials are important to the site planner, since these streets usually provide the direct access to a proposed overall development. Collectors that efficiently carry 100 to 250 trips per lane per hour are the street systems laid out by the site planner within the development to collect the traffic from neighborhood or local streets and load this traffic onto the arterials.

ESTIMATING TRAFFIC FLOWS

In larger developments, where traffic may be a major issue, the site designer must make some approximations of trip generations in order to design the appropriate internal collector system(s) and to determine potential impacts on the immediately adjacent roadways.

Many factors influence the number of trips generated by a development during the peak hours (usually 7:00 to 9:00 A.M. and 4:00 to 6:00 P.M.). Type of development (resort, retirement, young married, etc.), the amount of commercial activity, the type of units (single family, apartments, etc.), the availability of mass transit and other forms of public transportation, and the location of the development (rural vs. urban) are some of the factors that influence trip generation.

The figures used for preliminary estimations of peak direction traffic generation, based on middle income subcommunity without major public transportation facilities, are: 0.8± trips per single family residence and 0.6± per multifamily unit during peak hour traffic periods.

For purposes of estimating traffic (see sketch), the site planner counts the number and type of units to determine total estimated trips during peak hours and progressively adds the number of trips along the collector. From this information, the number of lanes for the internal collector can be determined based on vehicles per lane per peak hour, as well as the number of ingress and egress points that may be needed from the site, the type and number of traffic signals, and need for turning bays.

To determine the impact on immediately adjacent roadways, the anticipated direction of travel must be determined. For example, the direction toward the employment center is more significant (usually 70 to 80% of the traffic during morning peak hours) than that toward other areas. The traffic from the development is then added to the existing and/or projected arterial volume to determine existing and/or future carrying volume on the arterial.

ENVIRONMENTAL CONSIDERATIONS

The environmental characteristics of a site affect the location and development of a road system. It is the responsibility of the site designer to develop systems that recognize the ecological constraints of the particular site. Following is a checklist of environmental considerations for road alignment:

1. Minimize the disruption of existing topography by reducing cut and fill requirements and erosion and sedimentation problems.
2. Minimize the disruption of natural overland and subsurface water flows.
3. Minimize disruption of existing vegetation and animal life.
4. Avoid positive drainage along roadways (storm sewer systems) where such systems directly outfall into water bodies and cause pollution. Systems of swales along the roadway help to filter nutrients from the roadway surface before entering natural water bodies, thereby minimizing water pollution.

Gary Greenan, ASLA, AIP; Miami, Florida

Rafael Diaz, Graphic Coordinator; Miami, Florida

ROAD TYPES

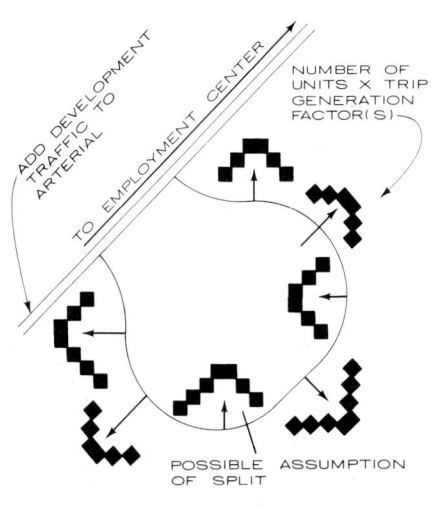

TRAFFIC PROJECTION

NOTES

STEP 1. Calculate number of trips by unit type (peak hour travel).

STEP 2. Progressively add along collector toward ingress/egress points. A certain amount of traffic must be assigned toward each ingress/egress point, depending on minimum travel time toward destination.

STEP 3. Add traffic from development to existing and/or projected arterial traffic to estimate impact.

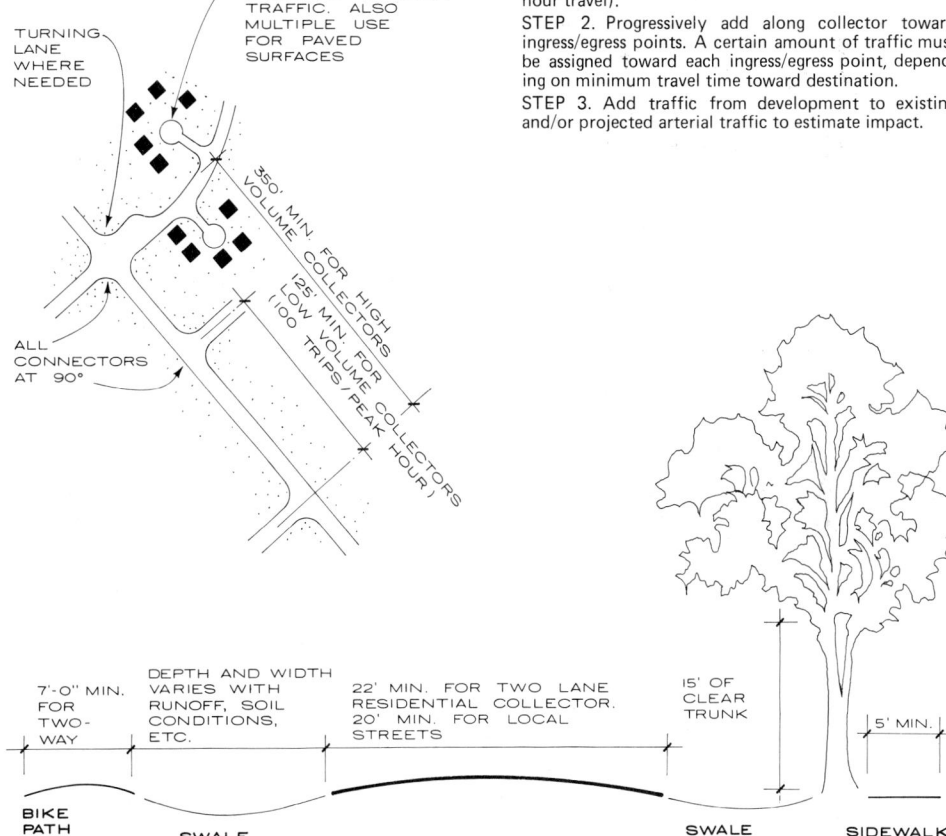

GENERAL DESIGN CONSIDERATION

NOTES

1. BIKE PATH. Grades should not exceed 5 to 6% for short distances (200 to 400 ft) or 2% for long distances. Separate bikepath from roadway with swale, plantings; where possible, bikepaths can be integrated into greenway systems rather than along roadway.

2. TREES. Species should be selected that tolerate smog and dust and whose root systems do not damage underground utilities or pavements. Where snow removal and/or icy conditions occur, trees should be placed far enough from the edge of the roadway to prevent damage from automobiles or chemicals applied to the roadway. Tree spacing should relate to species and desired effect; for example, as a general rule shade trees should be 35 to 50 ft apart.

3. STREET LIGHTING. Spacing should relate to amount of illumination desired, based on type of street, pedestrian use, crime prevention, and similar criteria. An approximate spacing for vehicular street use is 100 to 150 ft between light standards.

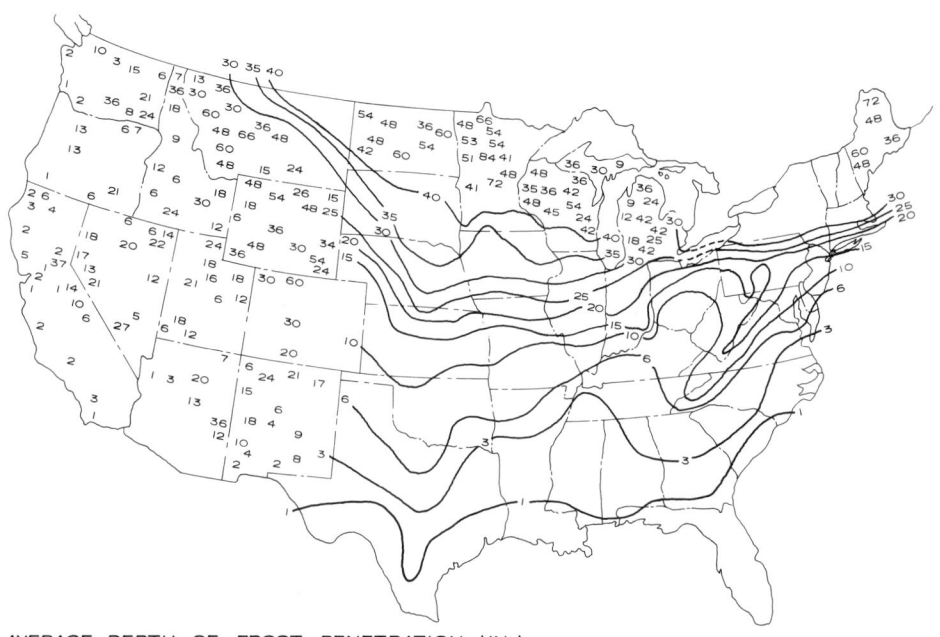

AVERAGE DEPTH OF FROST PENETRATION (IN.)
SOURCE: U.S. DEPT. OF COMMERCE WEATHER BUREAU

PRELIMINARY SUBSURFACE INFORMATION

A. Collect available information for soil, rock and water conditions, including the following:
   1. Topographic and aerial mapping.
   2. Geological survey maps and publications.
   3. Local knowledge (history of site development, experience of nearby structures, flooding, subsidence, etc.).
   4. Existing subsurface data (boreholes, well records, water soundings).
   5. Reconnaissance site survey.
   6. Previous studies.
B. Evaluate available information for site acceptability. If available data are insufficient, consult a geotechnical engineer to perform a limited subsurface investigation to gather basic information.
C. Consult geotechnical engineer for potential foundation performance at each site as part of the selection process.

DETAILED SUBSURFACE INFORMATION

After selection of a potential site a subsurface and laboratory test investigation should be carried out by a qualified geotechnical engineer before design is undertaken.

The investigation should provide an adequate understanding of the subsurface conditions and the information should be assessed to determine potential foundation behavior.

The engineer should evaluate alternative foundation methods and techniques in conjunction with the architect.

The engineer or architect should provide inspection during construction to ensure that material and construction procedures are as specified and to evaluate unexpected soil, rock, or groundwater conditions that may be exposed by excavations.

SOIL TYPES AND THEIR PROPERTIES

| DIVISION | SYMBOLS | | | SOIL DESCRIPTION | VALUE AS A FOUNDATION MATERIAL | FROST ACTION | DRAINAGE |
	LETTER	HATCHING	COLOR				
Gravel and gravelly soils	GW		Red	Well graded gravel, or gravel-sand mixture, little or no fines	Excellent	None	Excellent
	GP		Red	Poorly graded gravel, or gravel-sand mixtures, little or no fines	Good	None	Excellent
	GM		Yellow	Silty gravels, gravel-sand-silt mixtures	Good	Slight	Poor
	GC		Yellow	Clayey-gravels, gravel-clay-sand mixtures	Good	Slight	Poor
Sand and sandy soils	SW		Red	Well-graded sands, or gravelly sands, little or no fines	Good	None	Excellent
	SP		Red	Poorly graded sands, or gravelly sands, little or no fines	Fair	None	Excellent
	SM		Yellow	Silty sands, sand-silt mixtures	Fair	Slight	Fair
	SC		Yellow	Clayey sands, sand-clay mixtures	Fair	Medium	Poor
Silts and clays LL < 50	ML		Green	Inorganic silts, rock flour, silty or clayey fine sands, or clayey silts with slight plasticity	Fair	Very high	Poor
	CL		Green	Inorganic clays of low to medium plasticity, gravelly clays, silty clays, lean clays	Fair	Medium	Impervious
	OL		Green	Organic silt-clays of low plasticity	Poor	High	Impervious
Silts and clays LL > 50	MH		Blue	Inorganic silts, micaceous or diatomaceous fine sandy or silty soils, elastic silts	Poor	Very high	Poor
	CH		Blue	Inorganic clays of high plasticity, fat clays	Very poor	Medium	Impervious
	OH		Blue	Organic clays of medium to high plasticity, organic silts	Very poor	Medium	Impervious
Highly organic soils	Pt		Orange	Peat and other highly organic soils	Not suitable	Slight	Poor

NOTES
1. Consult soil engineers and local building codes for allowable soil bearing capacities.
2. LL indicates liquid limit.

Mueser, Rutledge, Johnston & DeSimone; New York, New York

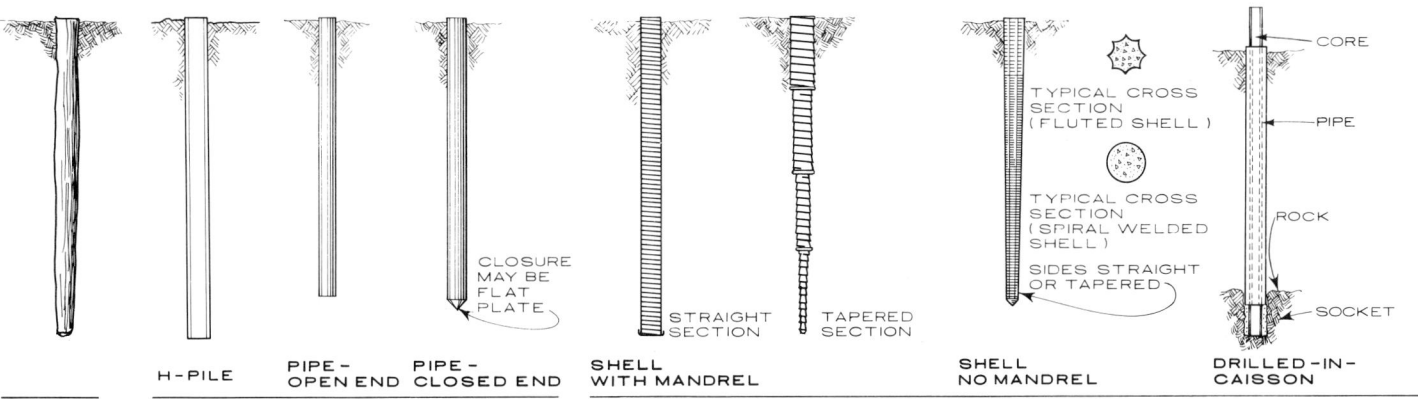

TIMBER STEEL CONCRETE

NOTE: A mandrel is a member inserted into a hollow pile to reinforce the pile shell while it is driven into the ground.

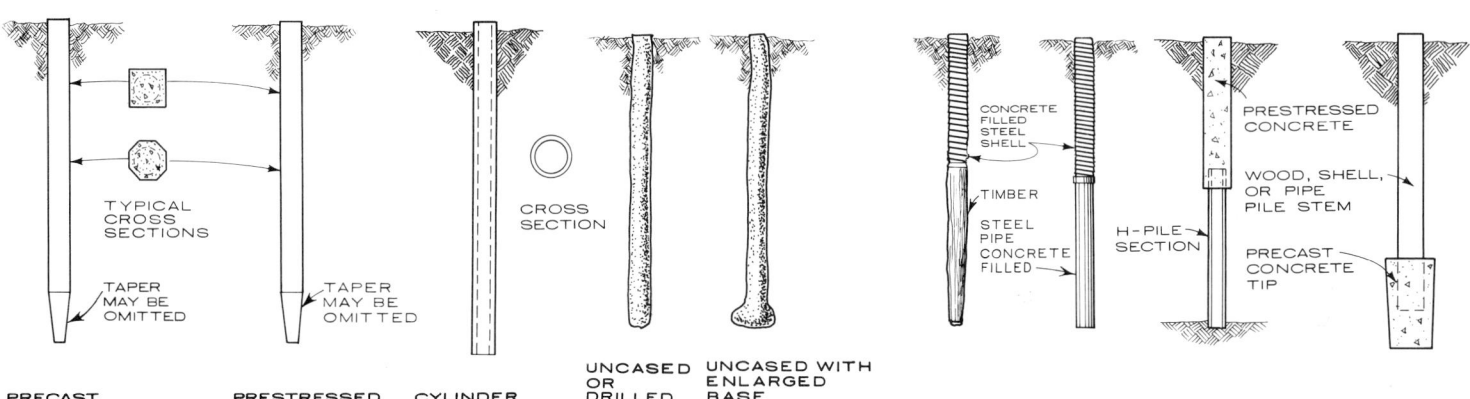

CONCRETE COMPOSITE

GENERAL PILE DATA

PILE TYPE	MAXIMUM LENGTH (FT)	OPTIMUM LENGTH (FT)	SIZE (IN.)	MAXIMUM CAPACITY (TONS)	OPTIMUM LOAD RANGE (TONS)	USUAL SPACING
TIMBER	110	45-65	5-10 tip 12-20 butt	40	15-25	2'6'' to 3'0''
STEEL						
H-pile	250	40-150	8-14	200	50-200	2'6'' to 3'6''
Pipe—open end concrete filled	200	40-120	10-24	250	100-200	3'0'' to 4'0''
Pipe—closed end concrete filled	150	30-80	10-18	100	50-70	3'0'' to 4'0''
Shell—mandrel concrete filled straight or taper	100	40-80	8-18	75	40-60	3'0'' to 3'6''
Shell—no mandrel concrete filled	150	30-80	8-18	80	30-60	3'0'' to 3'6''
Drilled-in caisson concrete filled	250	60-120	24-48	3500	1000-2000	6'0'' to 8'0''
CONCRETE						
Precast	80	40-50	10-24	100	40-60	3'0''
Prestressed	200	60-80	10-24	200	100-150	3'0'' to 3'6''
Cylinder pile	150	60-80	36-54	500	250-400	6'0'' to 9'0''
Uncased or drilled	60	25-40	14-20	75	30-60	3'0'' to 3'6''
Uncased with enlarged base	60	25-40	14-20	150	40-100	6'0''
COMPOSITE						
Concrete—timber	150	60-100	5-10 tip 12-20 butt	40	15-25	3'0'' to 3'6''
Concrete—pipe	180	60-120	10-23	150	40-80	3'0'' to 4'0''
Prestressed concrete H-pile	200	100-150	20-24	200	120-150	3'6'' to 4'0''
Precast concrete tip	80	40	13-35	180	150	4'6''

NOTES

Timber piles must be treated with wood preservative when any portion is above permanent groundwater table.

Applicable material Specifications Concrete—ACL 318; Timber—ASTM D25: Structural Sections ASTM A36, A572 and A696.

For selection of type of pile consult foundation engineer.

Mueser, Rutledge, Johnston & DeSimone; New York, New York

GENERAL INFORMATION

Before an architectural design can proceed a plot or site plan must be drawn to scale, showing the relevant available information about the construction area. This plan should show the relationship of the new building to property lines (and monuments), street lines above and below ground, and other features. It usually will also show the new contour lines and needed elevation information, such as special bench marks.

In simple building layout, key corner marks are placed on pegs or hubs, using the transit and steel tapes to ensure right angles and correct distances. The initial layout on the ground should be established in correct relationship to baselines, property lines, buildings, and so on. Once the building is laid out, diagonals shoud be measured and compared to make certain that all the building angles are square.

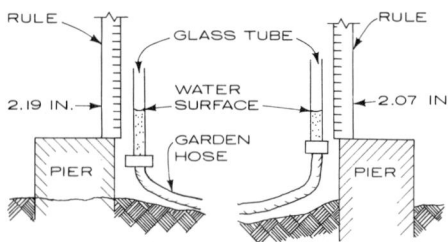

WATER TUBE LEVELING METHOD

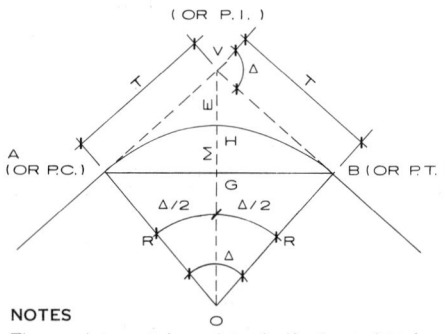

NOTES

The word tangent is used to signify the straight (not curved) portion of the building. From the plan some other relations that may be useful are also seen:

The long chord is c:
$$c = AB = AG + GB$$
$$= 2R \sin \tfrac{1}{2} \Delta$$

The mid-ordinate is M:
$$M = HG = OH - OG$$
$$= R - R \cos \tfrac{1}{2} \Delta$$

The external is E:
$$E = HV = OV - OH$$
$$= R/\cos \tfrac{1}{2} \Delta - R$$

A frequently used relationship, however, is the tangent (or semitangent) of the curve, which is T:
$$T = AV = BV$$
$$= R \tan \tfrac{1}{2} \Delta$$

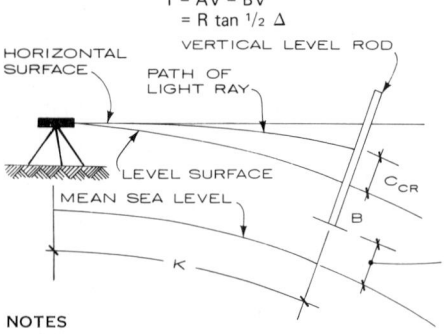

NOTES

Because of the curvature of the earth and the refraction or bending of light rays, the path of the ray of light departs both from the horizontal plane and from the level surface. In any situation employing fairly long sighting, a correction to the rod reading may be needed. The formula for the correction for curvature and refraction is

$$C_{CR} \text{ (ft)} = 0.572k^2$$

$$k = \text{sighted distance (miles)}$$

CURVATURE AND REFRACTION

Walter H. Sobel, FAIA and Associates; Chicago, Illinois

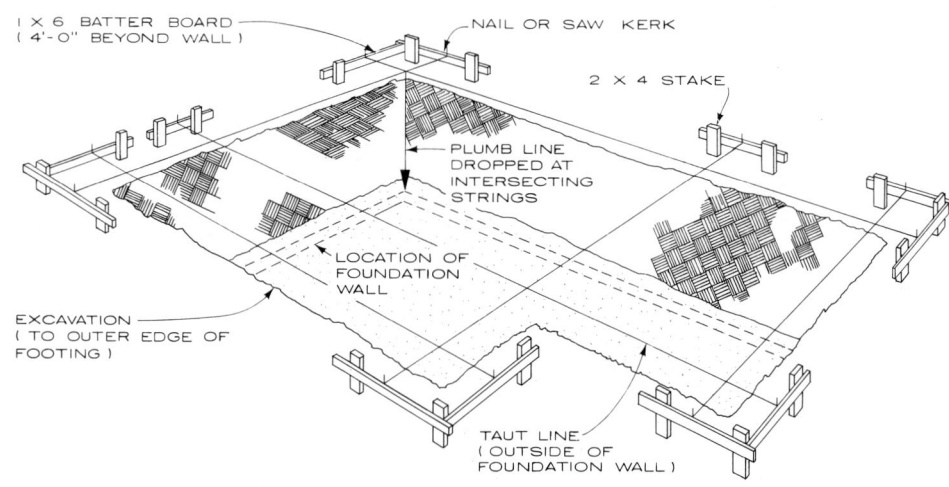

STAKING AND EXCAVATION (RESIDENTIAL)

NOTES

A transit or theodolite is basically an angle measuring instrument (it can also measure distances and elevations). It measures horizontal angles in the horizontal plane about an azimuth (vertical) axis, as well as vertical angles in a vertical plane about an elevation (horizontal) axis. To provide very great accuracy in setting a baseline at any angle to some existing reference line a technique is employed that involves repeated measuring of an angle. Essentially it consists of first laying out the angle, then measuring it carefully, and finally moving the newly set point as needed to achieve the proper angle. An engineer's level is used for surveying work of ordinary accuracy.

NOTES

On a construction site for a structure, it is important to place the project and its several components at the proper elevation. Control leveling will first be made to establish bench marks (BM) nearby to ensure this. Temporary bench marks for construction should be within 100 ft, at most 200 ft, of the location where they will be needed. Their location should be foreseen carefully enough to forstall any need to use a turning point between them and the constructed item (framework, pile, cap, etc.) that needs an elevation check.

A = ANGLE OF INTERSECTION
R = RADIUS OF CURVE
P.I. = POINT OF INTERSECTION (V)
P.C. = POINT OF CURVATURE (A)
P.T. = POINT OF TANGENCY (B)

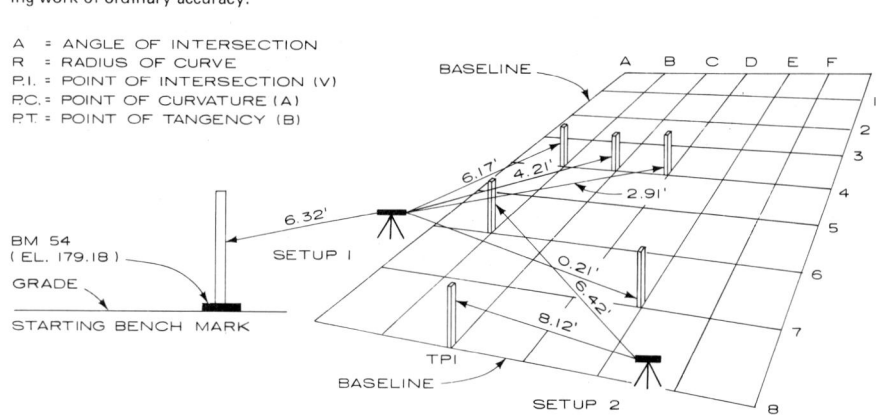

GRID SYSTEM

NOTES

A grid system is used for conveniently identifying the points whose elevation is required periodically. The level is set where both the bench mark and the desired points on the grid iron can be observed. Sighting on a known point (BM 54) gives the elevation of the instrument (H.1 = 185.50), from which elevations of grid points can be found by sighting each point in turn. This method may very well be used to take readings on a concrete floor slab or grade to detect local settlements or to determine that it has been finished to specification.

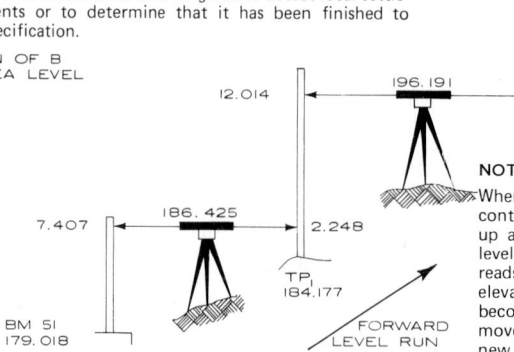

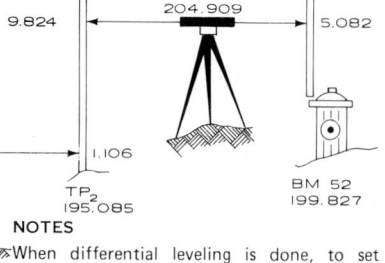

NOTES

When differential leveling is done, to set vertical control points one starts at a known elevation, sets up a transit or leveling device, reads a backsight on a level rod held on the known bench mark, and then reads a foresight on the rod held on a point whose elevation is needed. Temporarily, this new point becomes the known elevation. The instrument is then moved forward, and the process is begun anew to set a new point.

2   **SITE DEVELOPMENT**

Embankment stabilization is required where extremely steep slopes exist that are subject to heavy storm water runoff. The need for mechanical stabilization can be reduced by intercepting the runoff, or slowing the velocity of the runoff down the slope. Diversions are desirable at the tops of slopes to intercept the runoff. Slopes can be shelved or terraced to reduce the velocity of runoff to the point where a major erosion hazard is avoided. Use an armored channel or slope drain if concentrated runoff down a slope must be controlled.

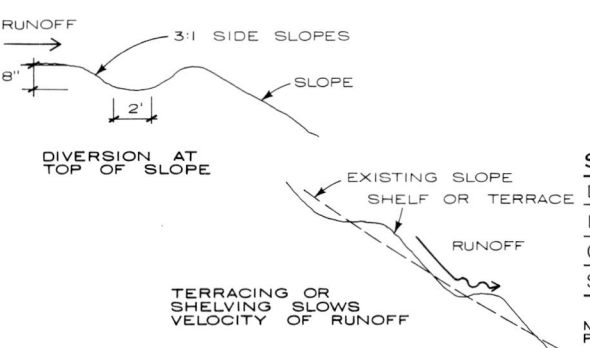

DIVERSION AT
TOP OF SLOPE

TERRACING OR
SHELVING SLOWS
VELOCITY OF RUNOFF

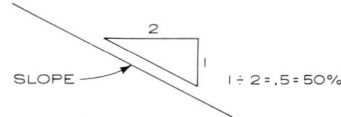

SOIL	GRADIENT	RATIO
Dry sand	33%	3:1
Loam	40%	2.5:1
Compacted clay	80%	1.25:1
Saturated clay	20%	5:1

MAXIMUM GRADIENTS
FOR BARE SOILS

BASIC PRINCIPLES OF SLOPE EROSION CONTROL

For slopes up to 2:1 slope stabilization may be achieved using stone, broken concrete, or wood grid as shown. For slopes up to 1:1, set stone or broken concrete in mortar setting bed and joints. Use retaining walls for extremely steep slopes.

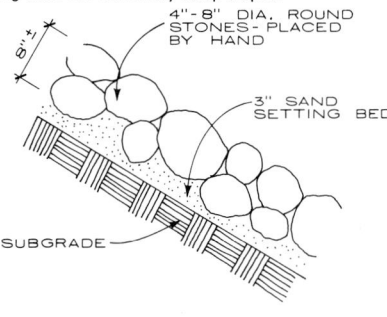

STONE

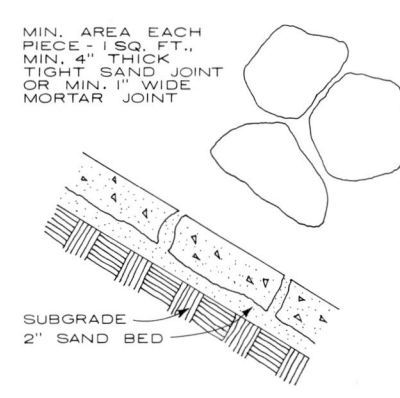

BROKEN CONCRETE

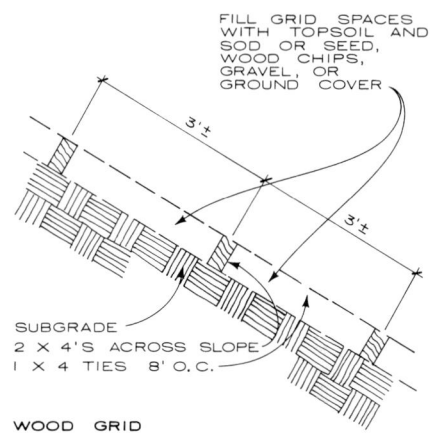

WOOD GRID

SLOPE STABILIZATION WITH RIPRAP

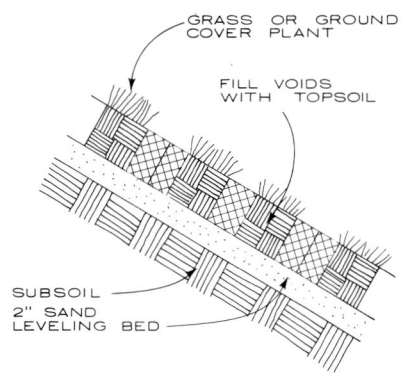

TYPICAL INSTALLATION SECTION

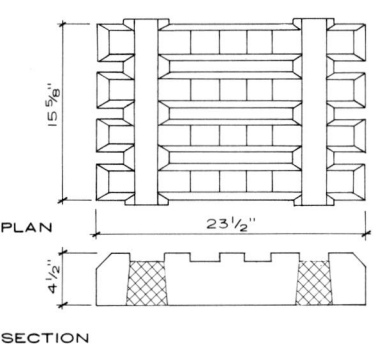

PLAN

SECTION

TYPICAL PRECAST UNITS

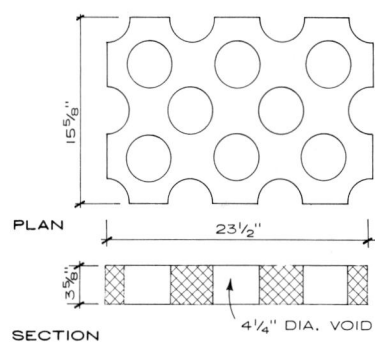

PLAN

SECTION

Precast concrete paving units may be used for slope stabilization up to 1:1 slope. Use retaining walls for steeper slopes.

PRECAST PERFORATED CONCRETE PAVING UNITS

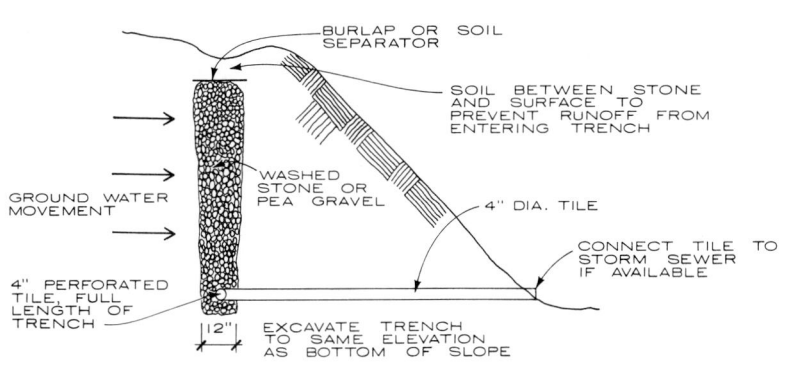

INTERCEPTOR DRAIN FOR WEEPING BANK

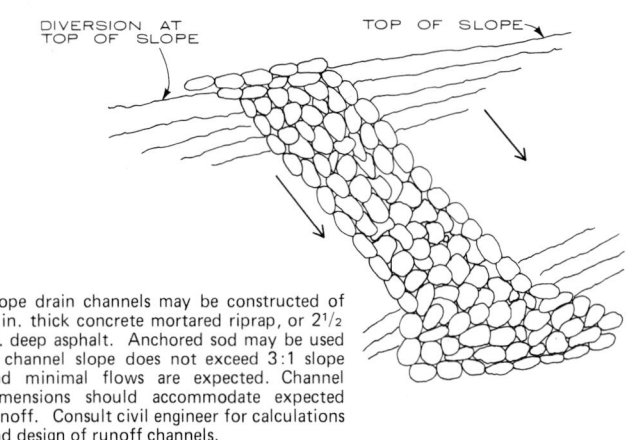

Slope drain channels may be constructed of 4 in. thick concrete mortared riprap, or 2½ in. deep asphalt. Anchored sod may be used if channel slope does not exceed 3:1 slope and minimal flows are expected. Channel dimensions should accommodate expected runoff. Consult civil engineer for calculations and design of runoff channels.

SLOPE DRAIN

John M. Beckett; Beckett, Raeder, Rankin, Inc.; Ann Arbor, Michigan

GENERAL NOTES

Drainage systems are provided to intercept and dispose of the water flow to the degree necessary to prevent inordinate damage to an area or facility from seepage and direct runoff. Each of these two sources requires its own method of control and competent engineering design to ensure a degree of protection commensurate with the hazard potential.

Subsurface drainage systems are designed to lower the natural water table, intercept underground flow, and dispose of infiltration percolating downward through soils from surface sources. These systems are typically used under floors, around foundations, in planters, and under athletic fields and courts. Each system must be provided with a positive outfall either by pumped discharge or gravity drain above expected high water levels.

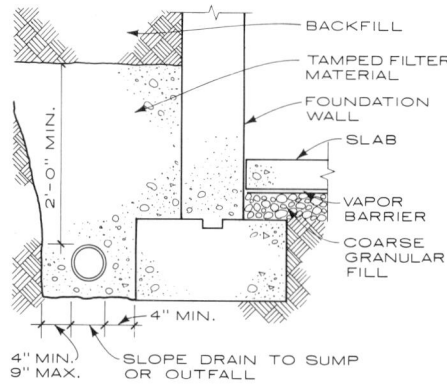

FOOTING DRAIN

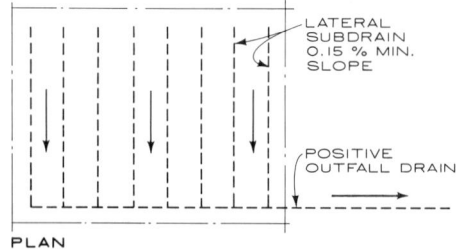

PLAN

Drain layout varies to meet need. May be grid, parallel, herringbone, or random pattern to fit topography.

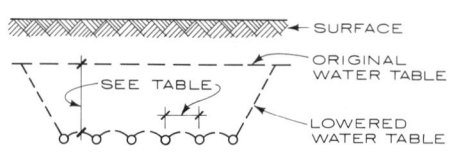

SECTION

Depths indicated in table below are minimum range. Greater depths may be required in order to prevent frost heave in colder climates or where soils have a high capillarity.

SUBSURFACE DRAINAGE SYSTEM

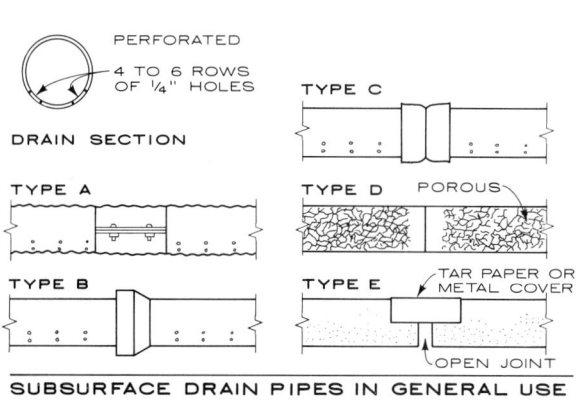

SUBSURFACE DRAIN PIPES IN GENERAL USE

DRAIN TYPE	MATERIAL	JOINT
A	CORRUGATED METAL FLEXIBLE PLASTIC	COLLARS
B	CONCRETE CLAY TILE	BELL AND SPIGOT
C	ASBESTOS CEMENT RIGID PLASTIC	SLEEVE SOCKET
D	POROUS CONCRETE	TONGUE AND GROOVE
E	UNPERFORATED CLAY TILE CONCRETE PLASTIC	BUTT

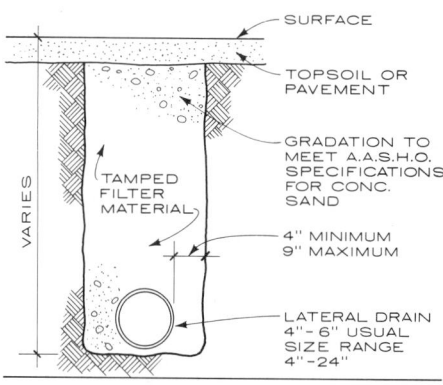

TYPICAL SECTION

If perforated drain is used, it should be installed with the holes facing downward.

When used to intercept sidehill seepage, bottom of trench should be cut into underlying impervious material a minimum of 6 in.

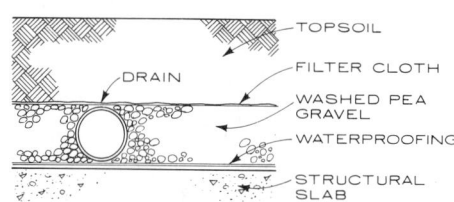

PLANTER DRAIN

DEPTH AND SPACING OF SUBDRAINS RECOMMENDED FOR VARIOUS SOIL CLASSES

SOIL CLASSES	PERCENTAGE OF SOIL SEPARATES			DEPTH OF BOTTOM OF DRAIN (FT)	DISTANCE BETWEEN SUBDRAINS (FT)
	SAND	SILT	CLAY		
Sand	80–100	0–20	0–20	3–4 / 2–3	150–300 / 100–150
Sandy loam	50–80	0–50	0–20	3–4 / 2–3	100–150 / 85–100
Loam	30–50	30–50	0–20	3–4 / 2–3	85–100 / 75–85
Silt loam	0–50	50–100	0–20	3–4 / 2–3	75–85 / 65–75
Sandy clay loam	50–80	0–30	20–30	3–4 / 2–3	65–75 / 55–65
Clay loam	20–50	20–50	20–30	3–4 / 2–3	55–65 / 45–55
Silty clay loam	0–30	50–80	20–30	3–4 / 2–3	45–55 / 40–45
Sandy clay	50–70	0–20	30–50	3–4 / 2–3	40–45 / 35–40
Silty clay	0–20	50–70	30–50	3–4 / 2–3	35–40 / 30–35
Clay	0–50	0–50	30–100	3–4 / 2–3	30–35 / 25–30

DRYWALLS

Drywells are used to provide an underground means of disposal for surface runoff. Their effectiveness is in direct proportion to the porosity of surrounding soils, and they are efficient for draining only small areas. High rates of rainfall runoff cannot be absorbed at the considerably lower percolation rates of most soils, and the difference is temporarily stored in the drywell. Efficiency is reduced during extended periods of wet weather when receiving soils are saturated and the well is refilled prior to draining completely.

Kurt N. Pronske, P. E.; Reston, Virginia

SURFACE DRAINAGE SYSTEMS: Designed to collect and dispose of rainfall runoff. There are two basic types. One, a ditch/swale and culvert, or open system, is generally used in less densely populated and more open areas where natural surfaces predominate. In urbanized areas where much of the land is overbuilt, the second type is used—the pipe, inlet/catchbasin and manhole, or closed system. Combinations of the two are quite common where terrain and density dictate.

SYSTEM NOTES: The location of the storm sewer in the street must be coordinated with other utilities, existing as well as proposed, which may have a priority position in the right-of-way. Detailed design is required in order to determine the most efficient combination of pipe size, slope, and material for a given system.

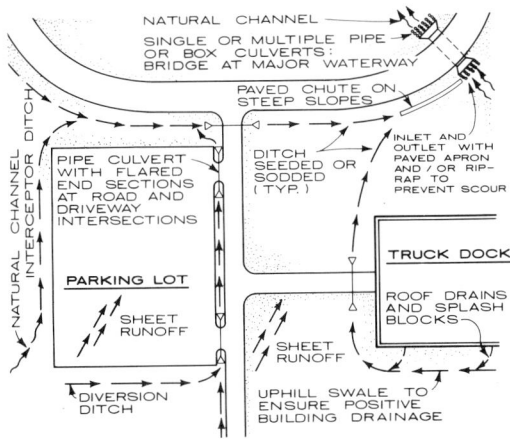

OPEN SYSTEM

CULVERT SECTIONS

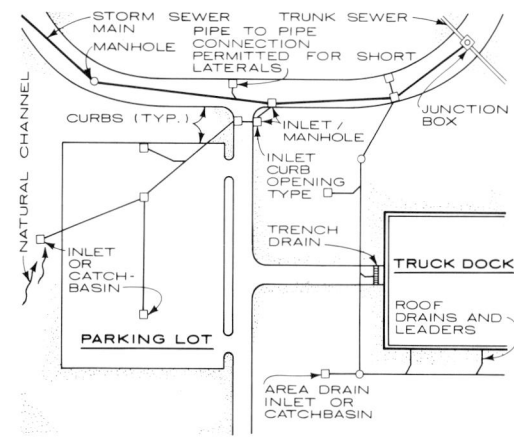

CLOSED SYSTEM

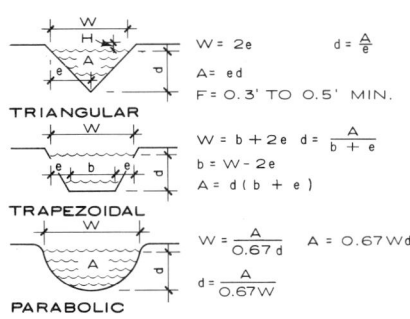
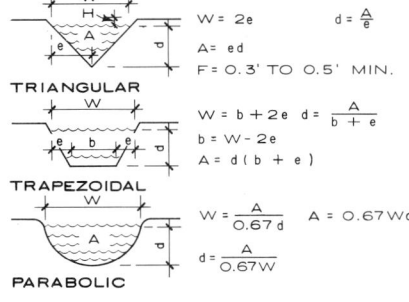

CHANNEL / DITCH SECTIONS

NOTE
Choice of section depends on topography, soil type, and runoff quantities. The ability to withstand erosion is a function of soil type and flow velocity. Most ditches are at least seeded or sodded. Where ditch slopes exceed 4 to 5%, some type of lining pavement is usually required to prevent erosion.

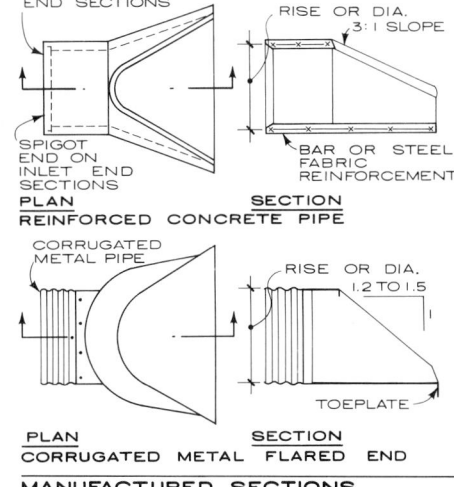

MANUFACTURED SECTIONS

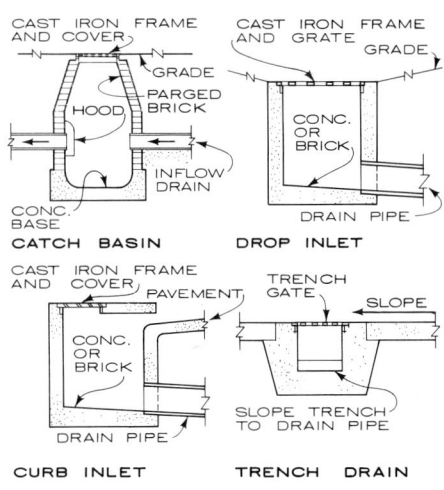

INLETS

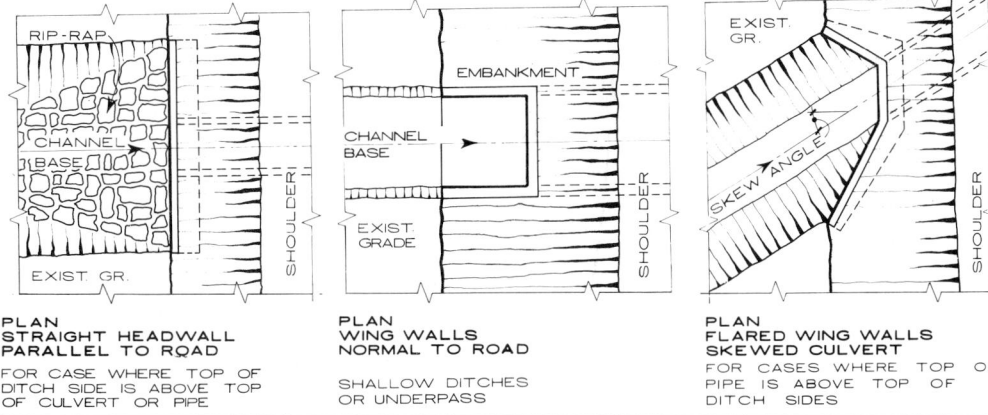

HEADWALL DESIGN AS CONTROLLED BY TOPOGRAPHY

Kurt N. Pronske, P. E.; Reston, Virginia

MANHOLES: Provided at the upper end of sewers and at changes in sewer sizes, slope, or alignment. Maximum distance between manholes varies from 300 to 600 ft for inspection and maintenance depending on size of sewer and local standards and practice.
INLETS AND CATCHBASINS: Provided at low points and periodically along swales and gutters to intercept runoff. Spacing is a function of size and type of unit and slope of gutter or swale in relation to the amount of runoff anticipated. The choice of unit (i.e., drop inlet, curb inlet, grate inlet) is subject to local codes and practice. Catchbasins have a sump below the outlet pipe to trap debris and silt, and are used where storm sewers are expected to flow at less than self-cleaning velocity (2 fps minimum). Catchbasins should not be interconnected and must be cleaned periodically to maintain a proper trap.
INLET/MANHOLE: Combination units used to reduce number of structures in the system.
JUNCTION BOX: Used in lieu of manhole for joining larger sewers, 48 in. and up. Customized design is required for each juncture.
TRENCH DRAINS: Used at the base of truck docks, ramps, and stairs, i.e., wherever it is desirable to intercept runoff along a level plane.

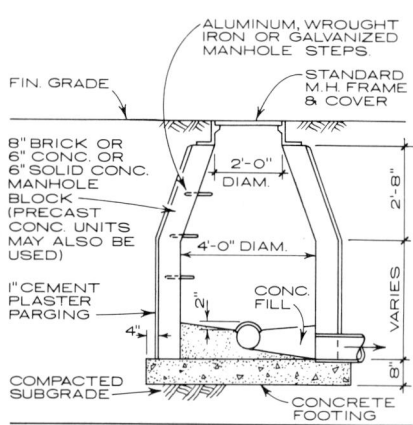

COMBINED OR SANITARY SEWER MANHOLE

NOTES

1. Parging may be omitted in construction of storm sewer manholes.

2. Brick and block walls to be as shown for manholes up to 12 ft deep. For that part of manhole deeper than 12 ft, brick and block walls shall be 12 in. thick. Manholes over 12 ft deep shall have a 12 in. thick base.

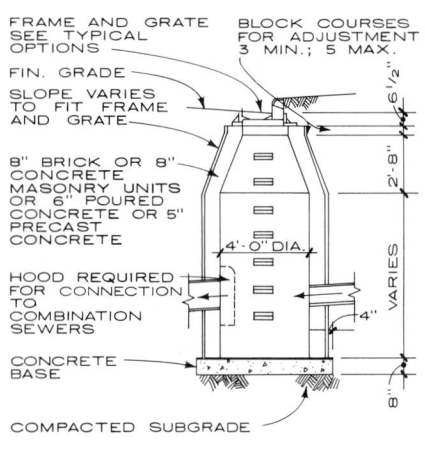

CATCH BASIN

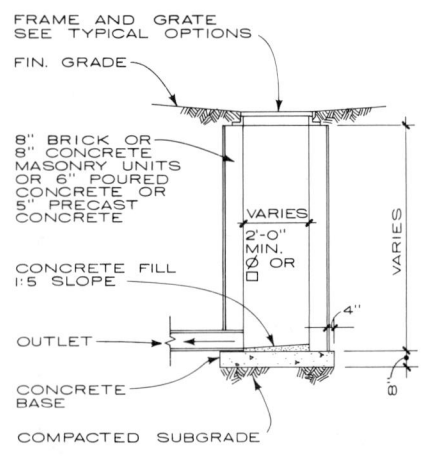

INLET

Kurt N. Pronske, P.E.; Reston, Virginia

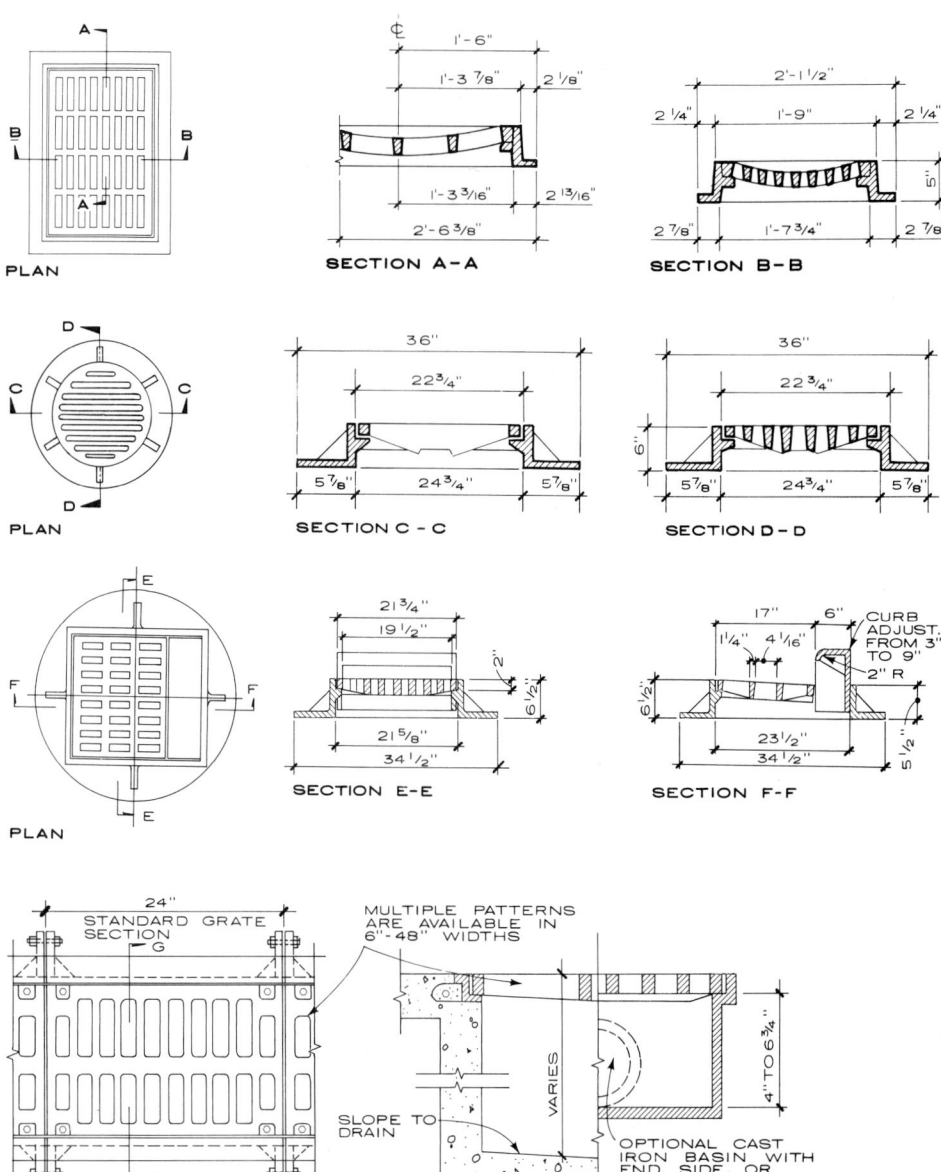

PLAN—TRENCH DRAIN

GRATES, WITHOUT BOLTS ARE AVAILABLE

TYPICAL FRAMES AND GRATES

NOTES

1. A great number of standard shapes and sizes of frames and grates are available. They are constructed of cast or ductile iron for light or heavy duty loading conditions. The available shapes are shown above: round, rectangular or square, and linear. In addition, grates may be flat, concave, or convex. Manufacturers' catalogs and local foundries should be consulted for the full range of castings.

2. Drainage structures with grated openings should be located on the periphery of traveled ways or beyond to minimize their contact with pedestrian or vehicular traffic. Grates that will be susceptible to foot or narrow wheel contact must be so constructed as to prevent penetration by heels, crutch and cane tips, and slim tires, but still serve to provide sufficient drainage. This can be done by reducing the size of each unit opening and increasing the overall size or number of grates. Where only narrow wheel use is expected, slotted gratings can be used if the slots are oriented transversely to the direction of traffic.

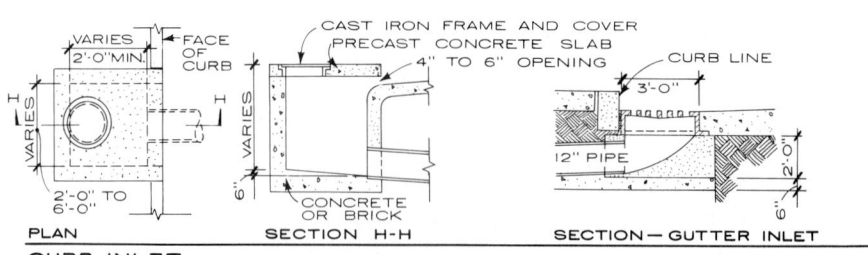

CURB INLET

CHEMICALS AND CONCENTRATIONS

CHEMICALS	CONCENTRATIONS
Aldrin	0.5% applied in water emulsion
Chlordane	1.0% applied in water emulsion
Dieldren	0.5% applied in water emulsion
Heptachlor	0.5% in water emulsion
Chlordane and heptachlor	0.5% chlordane plus 0.25% heptachlor 0.7% solution applied in water emulsion

STANDARD SOIL CLASSIFICATION

SOIL TYPE	PRESSURE (PSI)
Granular — SW, SP, GW, GP	30 — 50
Intermediate — GM, GC, ML, SM, SC, OL, CL	50 — 150
Dense Impermeable clays— MH, CH, OH	150 — 300

NOTES

1. Other materials may be used provided they contain at least one of the abovementioned chemicals in the concentrations recommended.

2. All these chemicals are chlorinated hydrocarbons and are highly toxic. Their use has proved effective for more than 25 years when applied properly by qualified personnel.

3. Oil solutions shall not be used under concrete slabs or where the solution may come in contact with vapor barriers.

4. Where individual water supply systems are used well must be not less than 100 ft from treated area. Horizontal distance from treated area may be reduced to 50 ft where ground surface is effectively separated from water bearing formation by an extensive, continuous, impervious strata of clay, hardpan, rock, etc.

APPLICATION—GENERAL

Treatment shall not be made when the soil or fill is excessively wet or immediately after heavy rains, to avoid surface flow of the toxicant from application site. Surface flow of toxicants toward sources of individual water supply shall be avoided. Unless the treated areas are to be immediately covered, precautions shall be taken to prevent disturbance of the treatment by human or animal contact with the treated soil.

UNDER SLABS

Under entire area of floor slab including porches and entrance platforms. Rate—1 gal/10 sq ft. In gravel fill of coarse material—1 1/2 gal/10 sq ft.

FOUNDATIONS

1. Rate—4 gal/10 lineal ft both sides of foundation, piers, interior foundation walls, around plumbing, etc.

   a. With concrete foundations or slab-on-grade apply to depth of 1 ft.

   b. With masonry foundations increase rate by multiplying by depth of foundation in feet.

2. Voids of unit masonry foundation walls and piers—2 gal/lineal ft to voids at bottom of foundation.

3. Application Methods:

   a. Chemical mixed with soil as it is replaced in trench—1 ft lifts.

   b. Chemical applied by rodding with soil injector rod inserted at 12 in. intervals—6 in. from foundation wall. Penetration of rod to within 6 in. of top of footing. Disperse chemicals through rod under pressure according to soil type.

HAZARD ZONES

REGION 1 VERY HEAVY

REGION 2 MODERATE TO HEAVY

REGION 3 SLIGHT TO MODERATE

NOTE

Lines defining areas approximate only. Local conditions may be more or less severe than indicated by the region classification.

John R. Hoke, Jr., AIA, Architect; Washington, D.C.

Joseph A. Wilkes, FAIA, Wilkes and Faulkner; Washington, D.C.

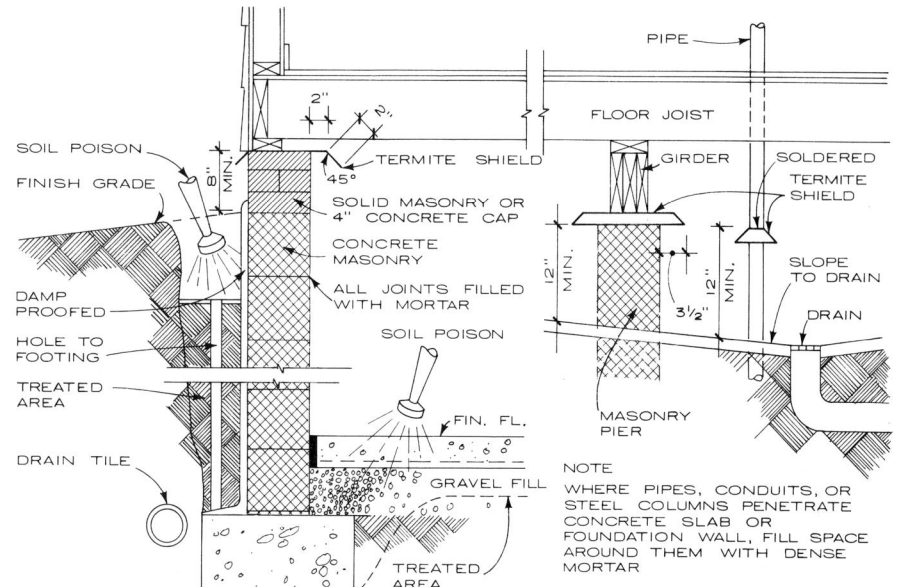

FOUNDATION WALL

Termite infestation occurs in poorly vented, warm, and moist spaces. Avoid leaving wood debris in soil or under crawl spaces. Clearance should be 18 in. minimum in crawl space. Periodic inspection should be made. Termite shields must be continuous to be effective. USDA does not recommend their use.

INTERIOR PIER AND CRAWL SPACE

Materials for metal shields:

1. GALVANIZED IRON: Limited corrosion resistance, 26 gauge minimum.
2. COPPER: 16 oz, tempered.
3. ALUMINUM: 0.019 in. minimum (cannot be soldered).
4. STAINLESS STEEL: 26 gauge.

NOTE

Hawaii and Puerto Rico included in Region 1. Alaska is free of termites.

GEOGRAPHIC DISTRIBUTION OF TERMITE INFESTATION

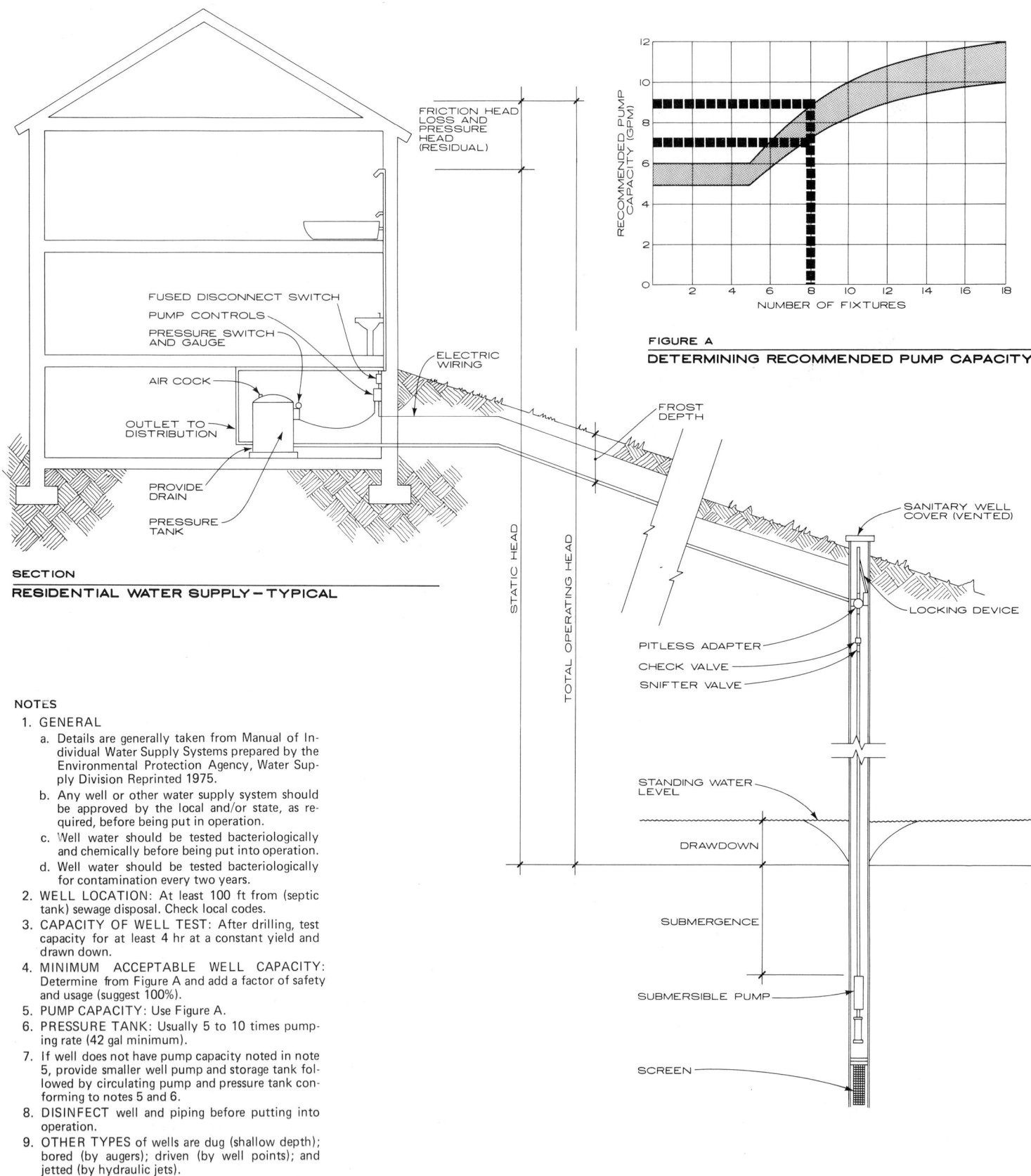

FRICTION HEAD
LOSS AND
PRESSURE
HEAD
(RESIDUAL)

FUSED DISCONNECT SWITCH
PUMP CONTROLS
PRESSURE SWITCH
AND GAUGE
ELECTRIC
WIRING
AIR COCK
OUTLET TO
DISTRIBUTION
PROVIDE
DRAIN
PRESSURE
TANK

SECTION
RESIDENTIAL WATER SUPPLY—TYPICAL

STATIC HEAD
TOTAL OPERATING HEAD

FIGURE A
DETERMINING RECOMMENDED PUMP CAPACITY

FROST
DEPTH

SANITARY WELL
COVER (VENTED)

LOCKING DEVICE

PITLESS ADAPTER
CHECK VALVE
SNIFTER VALVE

STANDING WATER
LEVEL

DRAWDOWN

SUBMERGENCE

SUBMERSIBLE PUMP

SCREEN

FIGURE B
DRILLED WELL—SECTION

NOTES

1. GENERAL
   a. Details are generally taken from Manual of Individual Water Supply Systems prepared by the Environmental Protection Agency, Water Supply Division Reprinted 1975.
   b. Any well or other water supply system should be approved by the local and/or state, as required, before being put in operation.
   c. Well water should be tested bacteriologically and chemically before being put into operation.
   d. Well water should be tested bacteriologically for contamination every two years.
2. WELL LOCATION: At least 100 ft from (septic tank) sewage disposal. Check local codes.
3. CAPACITY OF WELL TEST: After drilling, test capacity for at least 4 hr at a constant yield and drawn down.
4. MINIMUM ACCEPTABLE WELL CAPACITY: Determine from Figure A and add a factor of safety and usage (suggest 100%).
5. PUMP CAPACITY: Use Figure A.
6. PRESSURE TANK: Usually 5 to 10 times pumping rate (42 gal minimum).
7. If well does not have pump capacity noted in note 5, provide smaller well pump and storage tank followed by circulating pump and pressure tank conforming to notes 5 and 6.
8. DISINFECT well and piping before putting into operation.
9. OTHER TYPES of wells are dug (shallow depth); bored (by augers); driven (by well points); and jetted (by hydraulic jets).
10. OTHER TYPES OF WELL PUMPING SYSTEMS:
    a. Centrifugal pump with motor above ground and below water level in well.
    b. Jet pump with pump and motor above ground.
    c. Direct or reciprocating pumps in the well with motor above ground.

Jack L. Staunton, P.E.; Staunton and Freeman, Consulting Engineers; New York, New York

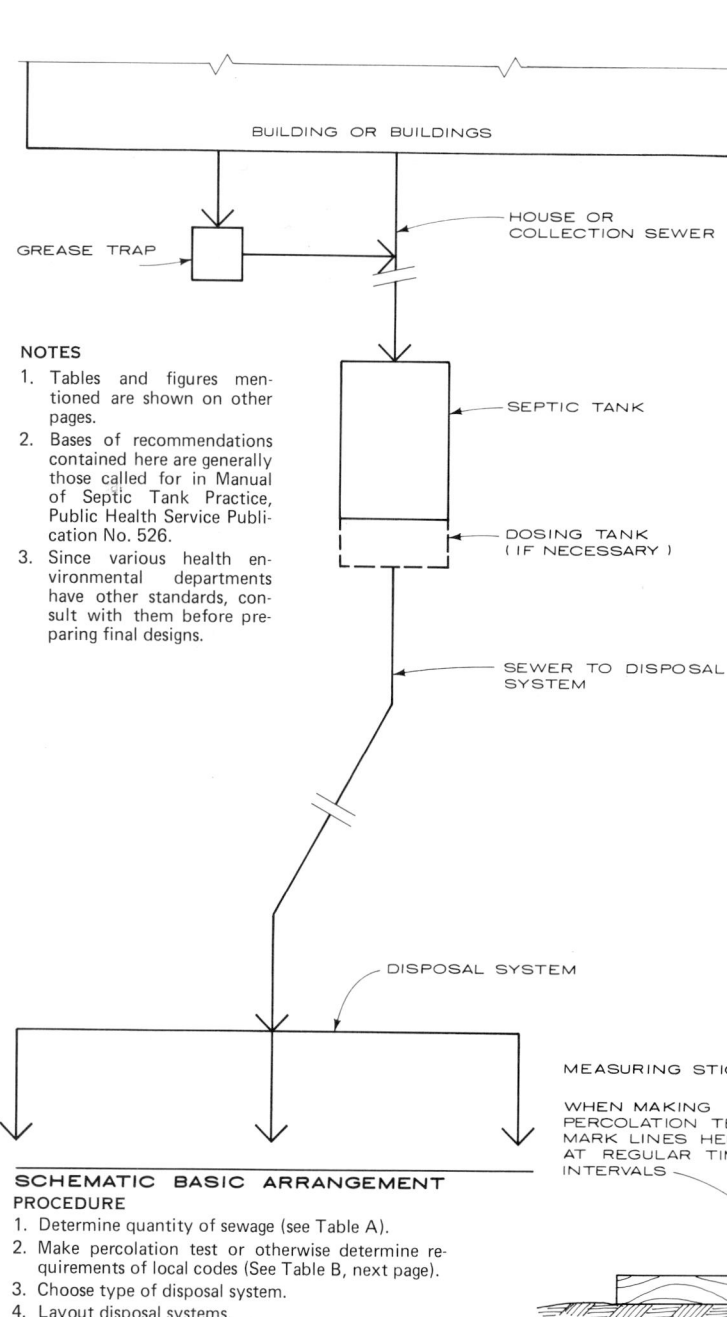

TABLE A   QUANTITIES OF SEWAGE FLOWS

TYPE OF ESTABLISHMENT	GALLONS PER PERSON PER DAY
Airports (per passenger)	5
Bathhouses and swimming pools	10
Camps	
Campground with central comfort stations	35
Day camps (no meals served)	15
Resort camp (night and day) with limited plumbing	50
Cottages and small dwelling with seasonal occupancy[1]	50
Country clubs (per resident member)	100
Country clubs (per nonresident member present)	25
Dwellings	
Boarding houses[1]	50
Multiple family dwellings (apartments)	60
Single family dwellings[1]	75
Factories (gallons per person, per shift, exclusive of industry wastes)	35
Hospitals (per bed space)	250+
Hotels with private baths (2 persons per room)[2]	60
Institutions other than hospitals (per bed space)	125
Laundries, self-service (gallons per wash, i.e., per customer)	50
Mobile home parks (per space)	250
Picnic parks (toilet wastes only, per picnicker)	5
Picnic parks with bathhouses, showers, and flush toilets	10
Restaurants (toilets and kitchen wastes per patron)	10
Restaurants (kitchen wastes per meal served)	3
Restaurants (additional for bars and cocktail lounges)	2
Schools	
Boarding	100
Day, with gyms, cafeteria, and showers	25
Service stations (per vehicle served)	10
Theaters	
Movie (per auditorium seat)	5
Drive-in (per car space)	5
Travel trailer parks with individual water and sewer hookups	100
Workers	
Day, at schools and offices (per shift)	15

NOTES
1. Two people per bedroom.
2. Use also for motels.

SCHEMATIC BASIC ARRANGEMENT

NOTES
1. Tables and figures mentioned are shown on other pages.
2. Bases of recommendations contained here are generally those called for in Manual of Septic Tank Practice, Public Health Service Publication No. 526.
3. Since various health environmental departments have other standards, consult with them before preparing final designs.

PROCEDURE
1. Determine quantity of sewage (see Table A).
2. Make percolation test or otherwise determine requirements of local codes (See Table B, next page).
3. Choose type of disposal system.
4. Layout disposal systems.
5. Design septic tank.
6. Use dosing tank, diversion box and/or trap where necessary.

MATERIALS
Piping may be salt glazed clay bell and spigot, tile pipe, asbestos cement or concrete bell and spigot. If near well or any other water supply, use cast iron.

Where trees or shrubs may cause root stoppage in clay pipe, use cast iron.

Use bituminous joints or rubber ring type joints for clay, concrete, or asbestos cement pipe; use lead for cast iron pipe.

SIZE
4 in. diameter for small installations; 6 in. is better in all cases.

GRADE
In northern latitudes, start sewer approximately 3 ft below grade. In southern latitudes, sewer may start just below grade.

PITCH
Pitch 4 in. sewer $1/4$ in./ft minimum. Pitch 6 in. sewer $1/8$ in./ft minimum.

PROCEDURE
First soak hole by filling at least 12 in. over gravel with water and continue to refill with water so that hole is soaked for 24 hr. After 24 hr adjust the depth of water over the gravel to approximately 6 in. Now measure the drop in water level over a 30 min period.

NOTE: THIS TEST IS RECOMMENDED BY THE ENVIRONMENTAL PROTECTION AGENCY. CHECK LOCAL REQUIREMENTS FOR OTHER TEST CONDITIONS.

METHOD OF MAKING PERCOLATION TEST

Jack L. Staunton, P.E.; Staunton and Freeman Consulting Engineers; New York, New York

SITE UTILITIES   2

TABLE B.   ALLOWABLE RATE OF SEWAGE APPLICATION TO A SOIL ABSORPTION SYSTEM

PERCOLATION RATE [TIME (MIN) FOR WATER TO FALL 1 IN.]	MAXIMUM RATE OF SEWAGE APPLICATION (GAL/SQ FT/DAY)[1] FOR ABSORPTION TRENCHES,[2] SEEPAGE BEDS, AND SEEPAGE PITS[3]	PERCOLATION RATE [TIME (MIN) FOR WATER TO FALL 1 IN.]	MAXIMUM RATE OF SEWAGE APPLICATION (GAL/SQ FT/DAY)[1] FOR ABSORPTION TRENCHES,[2] SEEPAGE BEDS, AND SEEPAGE PITS[3]
1 or less	5.0	10	1.6
2	3.5	15	1.3
3	2.9	30[4]	0.9
4	2.5	45[4]	0.8
5	2.2	60[4,5]	0.6

NOTES

1. Not including effluents from septic tanks that receive wastes from garbage grinders and automatic washing machines.
2. Absorption area is figured as trench bottom area and includes a statistical allowance for vertical sidewall area.
3. Absorption area for seepage pits is effective sidewall area.
4. Over 30 is unsuitable for seepage pits.
5. Over 60 is unsuitable for absorption systems.

If permissible, use sand filtration system. For subsurface sand filters use 1.15 gal/sq ft/day.

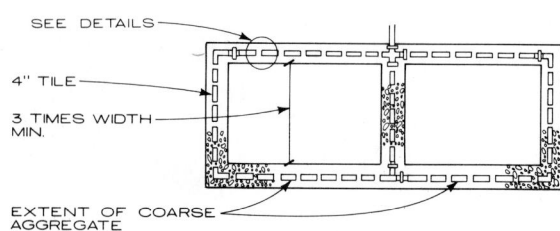

ABSORPTION TRENCH ARRANGEMENT FOR LEVEL GROUND FOR HOUSEHOLD DISPOSAL

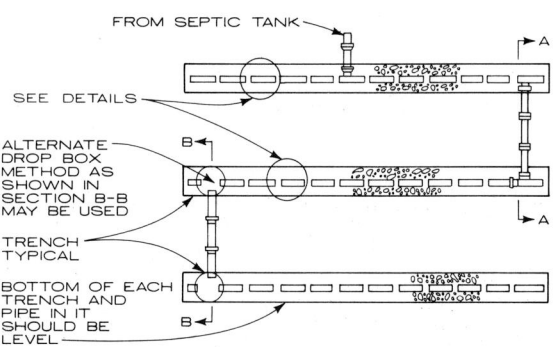

NOTE
INVERT OF THE OVERFLOW PIPE MUST BE AT LEAST 4" LOWER THAN INVERT OF THE SEPTIC TANK OUTLET

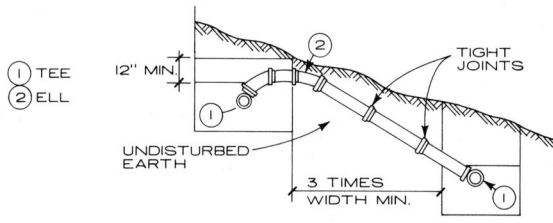

SECTION A-A

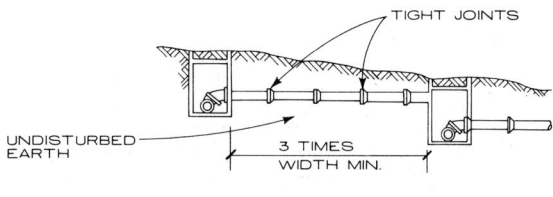

SECTION B-B

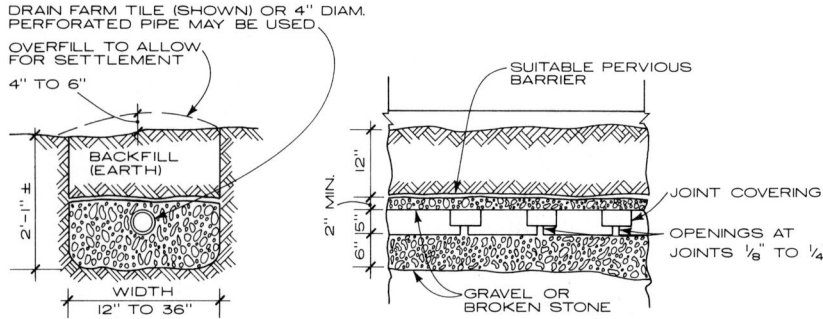

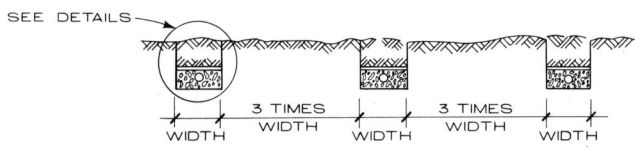

ABSORPTION TRENCH SYSTEM DETAILS

ABSORPTION TRENCH ARRANGEMENT FOR HILLY SITE FOR HOUSEHOLD DISPOSAL

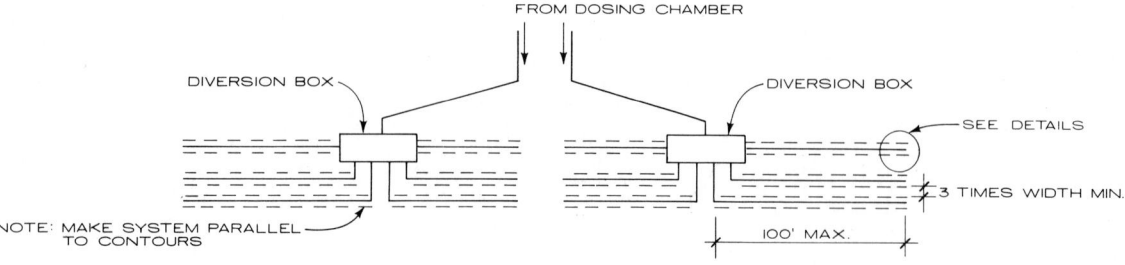

ABSORPTION TRENCH ARRANGEMENT FOR INSTITUTIONAL AND LIGHT COMMERCIAL DISPOSAL

Jack L. Staunton, P. E.; Staunton and Freeman, Consulting Engineers; New York, New York

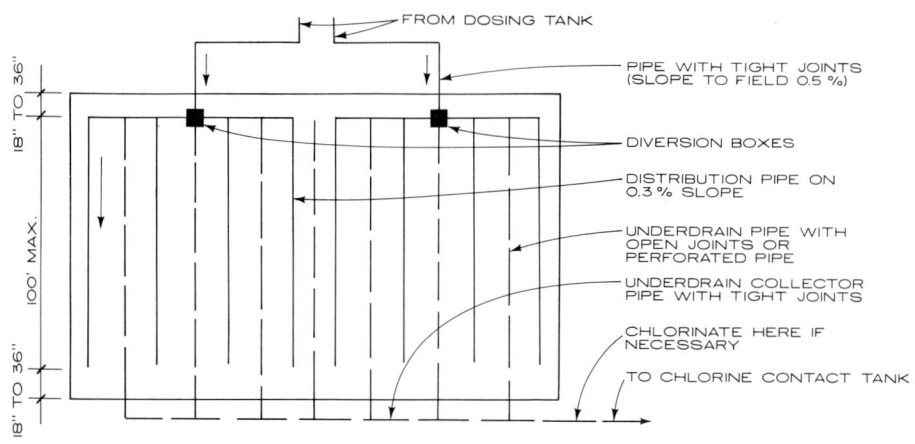

PLAN

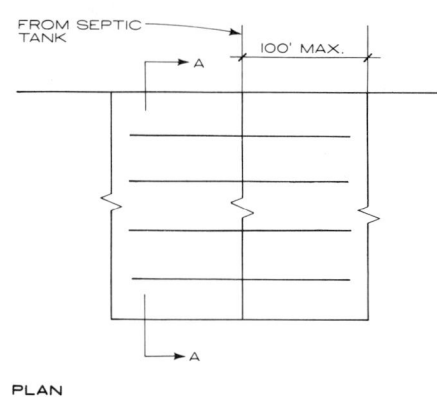

PLAN

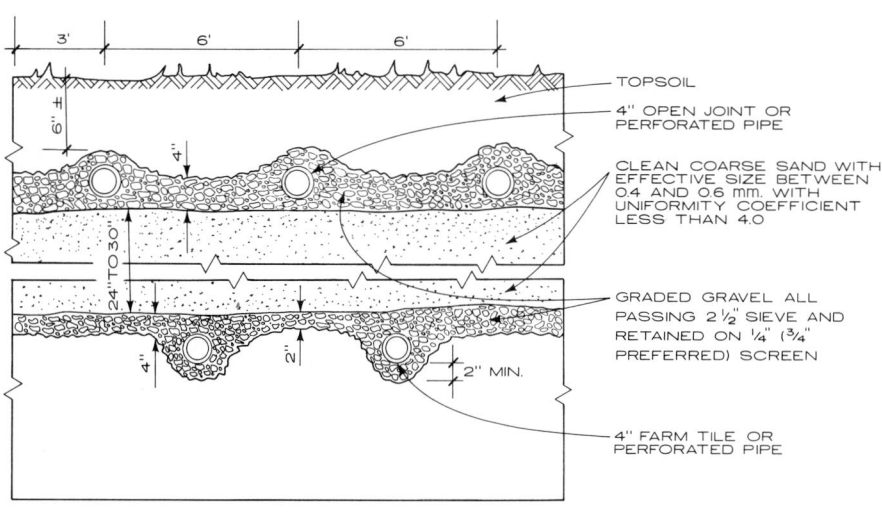

SECTIONAL ELEVATION

SUBSURFACE SAND FILTER

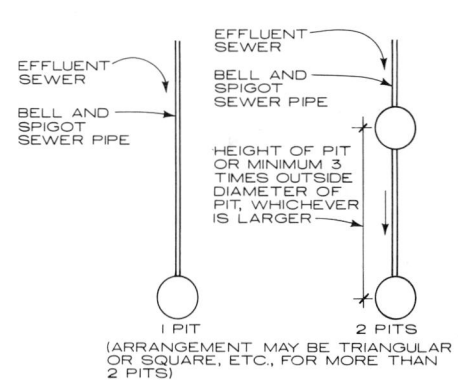

SECTION A-A

SEEPAGE BED

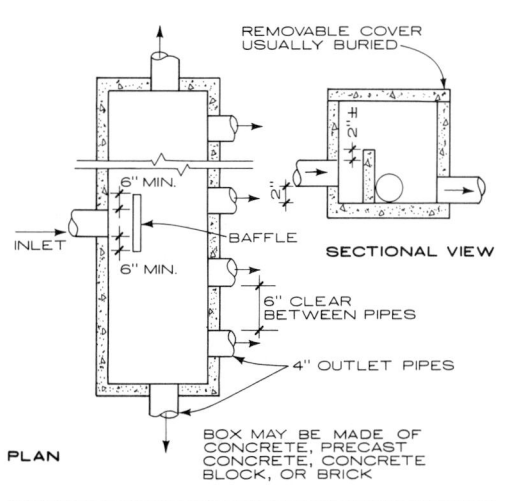

PLAN

DIVERSION BOX

SEEPAGE PITS

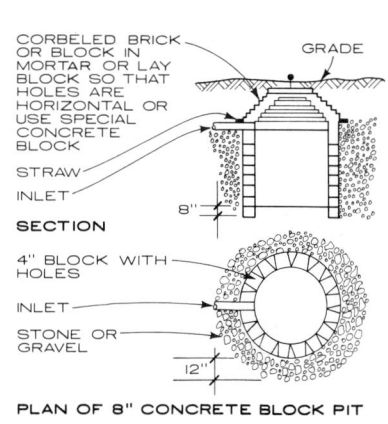

ARRANGEMENT

Jack L. Staunton, P. E.; Staunton and Freeman, Consulting Engineers; New York, New York

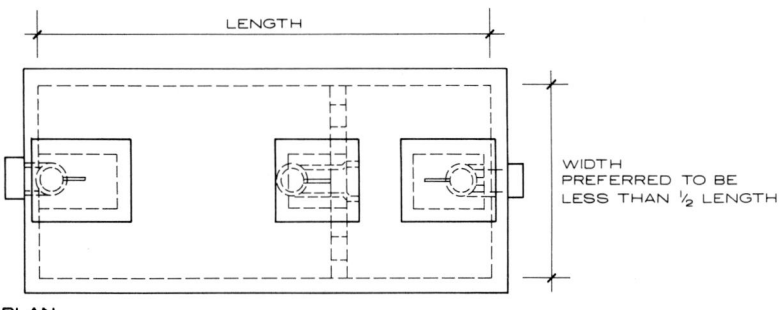

PLAN

WIDTH PREFERRED TO BE LESS THAN ½ LENGTH

LENGTH

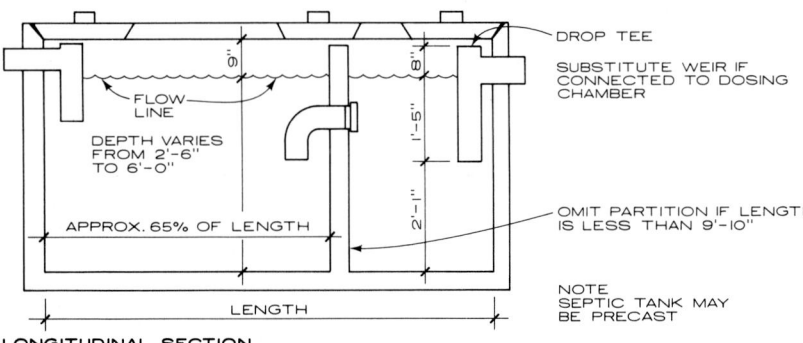

LONGITUDINAL SECTION

DROP TEE

SUBSTITUTE WEIR IF CONNECTED TO DOSING CHAMBER

OMIT PARTITION IF LENGTH IS LESS THAN 9'-10"

NOTE
SEPTIC TANK MAY BE PRECAST

FLOW LINE

DEPTH VARIES FROM 2'-6" TO 6'-0"

APPROX. 65% OF LENGTH

LENGTH

SEPTIC TANK

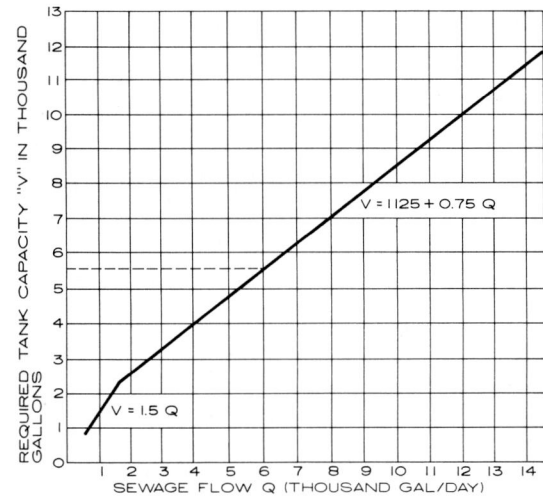

$$V = 1125 + 0.75 Q$$

$$V = 1.5 Q$$

DETERMINATION OF SEPTIC TANK VOLUME

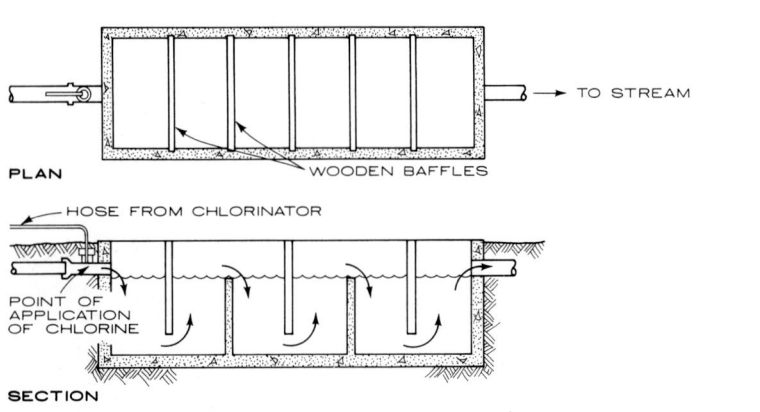

PLAN

WOODEN BAFFLES

TO STREAM

HOSE FROM CHLORINATOR

POINT OF APPLICATION OF CHLORINE

SECTION

CHLORINE CONTACT CHAMBER

Jack L. Staunton, P. E.; Staunton and Freeman, Consulting Engineers; New York, New York

NOTES
• DOSE FROM CHAMBER TO EQUAL ¾ OF FARM TILE OR PERFORATED PIPE IN ONE FIELD
• PIPES MAY BE SUBSTITUTED FOR SIPHONS IF CONDITION DICTATES

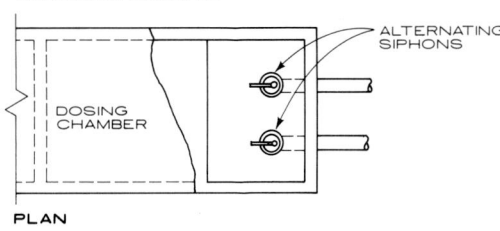

PLAN

ALTERNATING SIPHONS

DOSING CHAMBER

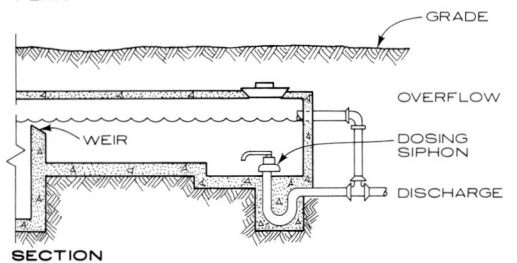

SECTION

GRADE

OVERFLOW

DOSING SIPHON

DISCHARGE

WEIR

DOSING CHAMBER WITH ALTERNATING SIPHONS

NOTE
GREASE TRAPS TO BE USED ONLY IF THEY ARE CLEANED DAILY

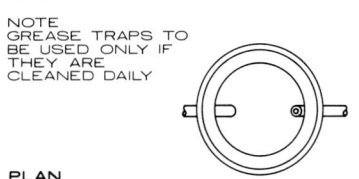

PLAN
(TOP REMOVED)

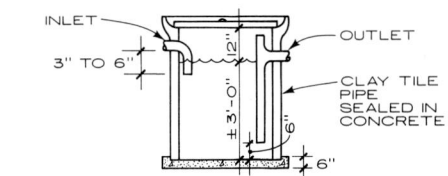

SECTION

INLET

OUTLET

3" TO 6"

CLAY TILE PIPE SEALED IN CONCRETE

PLAN
(TOP REMOVED)

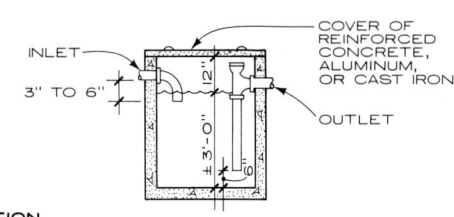

SECTION
CONCRETE BOX

INLET

3" TO 6"

COVER OF REINFORCED CONCRETE, ALUMINUM, OR CAST IRON

OUTLET

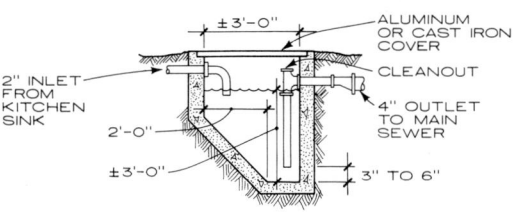

2" INLET FROM KITCHEN SINK

2'-0"

±3'-0"

ALUMINUM OR CAST IRON COVER

CLEANOUT

4" OUTLET TO MAIN SEWER

3" TO 6"

TYPICAL GREASE TRAPS

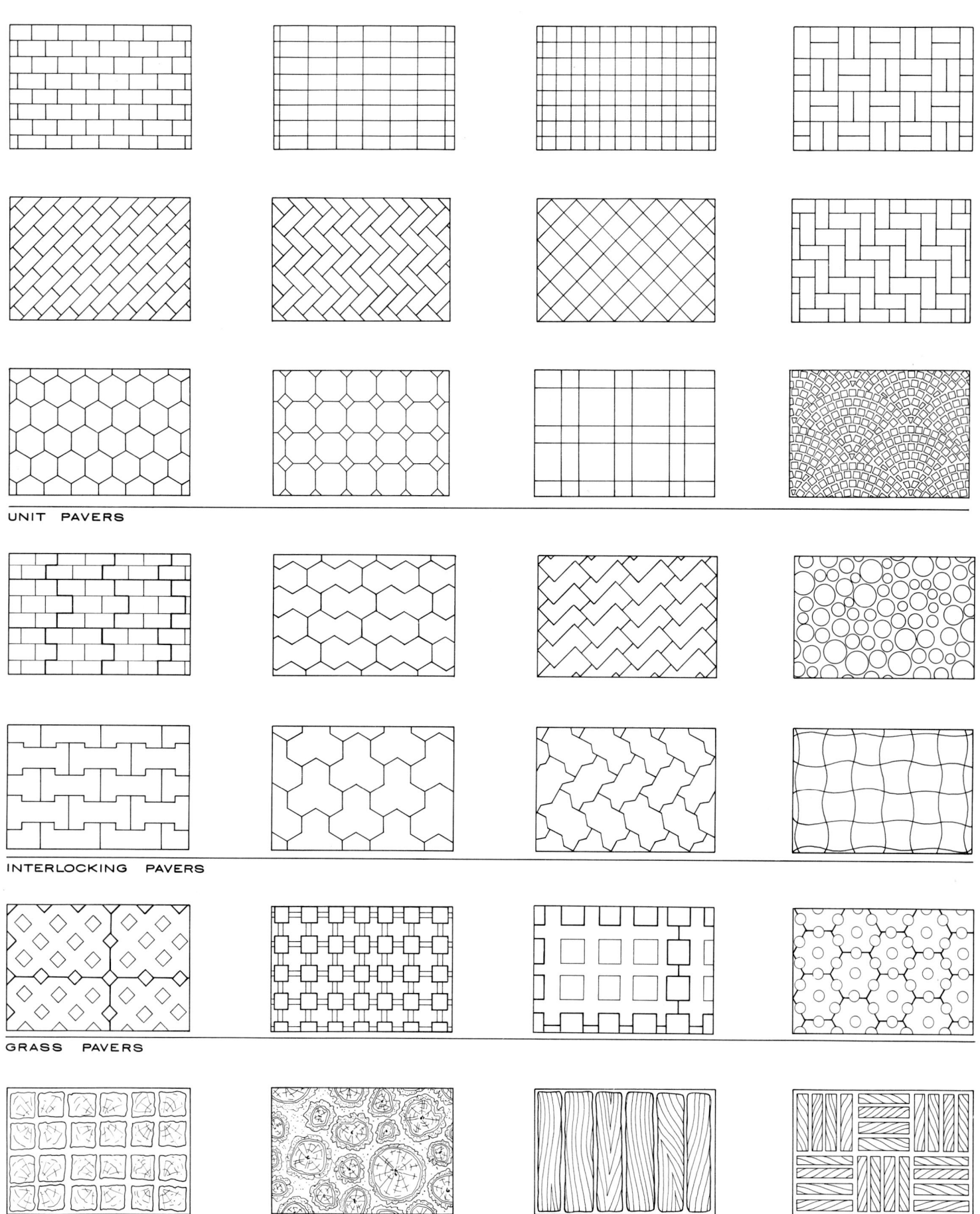

UNIT PAVERS

INTERLOCKING PAVERS

GRASS PAVERS

WOOD PAVERS

John R. Hoke, Jr., AIA, Architect; Washington, D.C.

PAVING AND SURFACING   2

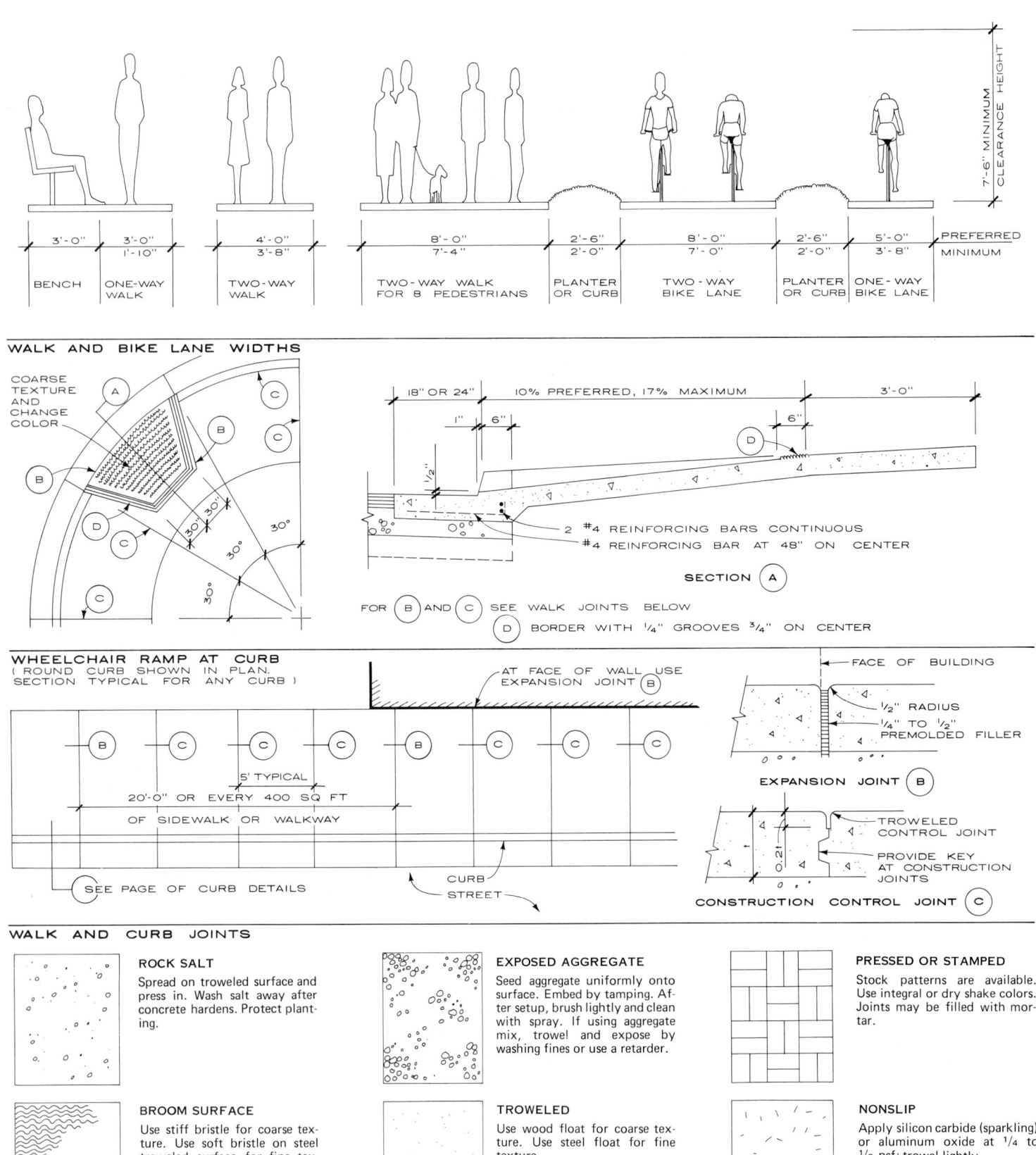

7'-6" MINIMUM CLEARANCE HEIGHT

| BENCH | ONE-WAY WALK | TWO-WAY WALK | TWO-WAY WALK FOR 8 PEDESTRIANS | PLANTER OR CURB | TWO-WAY BIKE LANE | PLANTER OR CURB | ONE-WAY BIKE LANE | PREFERRED MINIMUM |

3'-0" / 3'-0" / 1'-10" / 4'-0" / 3'-8" / 8'-0" / 7'-4" / 2'-6" / 2'-0" / 8'-0" / 7'-0" / 2'-6" / 2'-0" / 5'-0" / 3'-8"

WALK AND BIKE LANE WIDTHS

COARSE TEXTURE AND CHANGE COLOR

18" OR 24" — 10% PREFERRED, 17% MAXIMUM — 3'-0"

2 #4 REINFORCING BARS CONTINUOUS
#4 REINFORCING BAR AT 48" ON CENTER

SECTION (A)

FOR (B) AND (C) SEE WALK JOINTS BELOW
(D) BORDER WITH 1/4" GROOVES 3/4" ON CENTER

WHEELCHAIR RAMP AT CURB
(ROUND CURB SHOWN IN PLAN.
SECTION TYPICAL FOR ANY CURB)

AT FACE OF WALL USE EXPANSION JOINT (B)

FACE OF BUILDING
1/2" RADIUS
1/4" TO 1/2" PREMOLDED FILLER

5' TYPICAL
20'-0" OR EVERY 400 SQ FT
OF SIDEWALK OR WALKWAY

SEE PAGE OF CURB DETAILS

CURB
STREET

EXPANSION JOINT (B)

TROWELED CONTROL JOINT
PROVIDE KEY AT CONSTRUCTION JOINTS

CONSTRUCTION CONTROL JOINT (C)

WALK AND CURB JOINTS

ROCK SALT
Spread on troweled surface and press in. Wash salt away after concrete hardens. Protect planting.

EXPOSED AGGREGATE
Seed aggregate uniformly onto surface. Embed by tamping. After setup, brush lightly and clean with spray. If using aggregate mix, trowel and expose by washing fines or use a retarder.

PRESSED OR STAMPED
Stock patterns are available. Use integral or dry shake colors. Joints may be filled with mortar.

BROOM SURFACE
Use stiff bristle for coarse texture. Use soft bristle on steel troweled surface for fine texture.

TROWELED
Use wood float for coarse texture. Use steel float for fine texture.

NONSLIP
Apply silicon carbide (sparkling) or aluminum oxide at 1/4 to 1/2 psf; trowel lightly.

WALK SURFACES AND TEXTURES

William T. Mahan, AIA; Santa Barbara, California

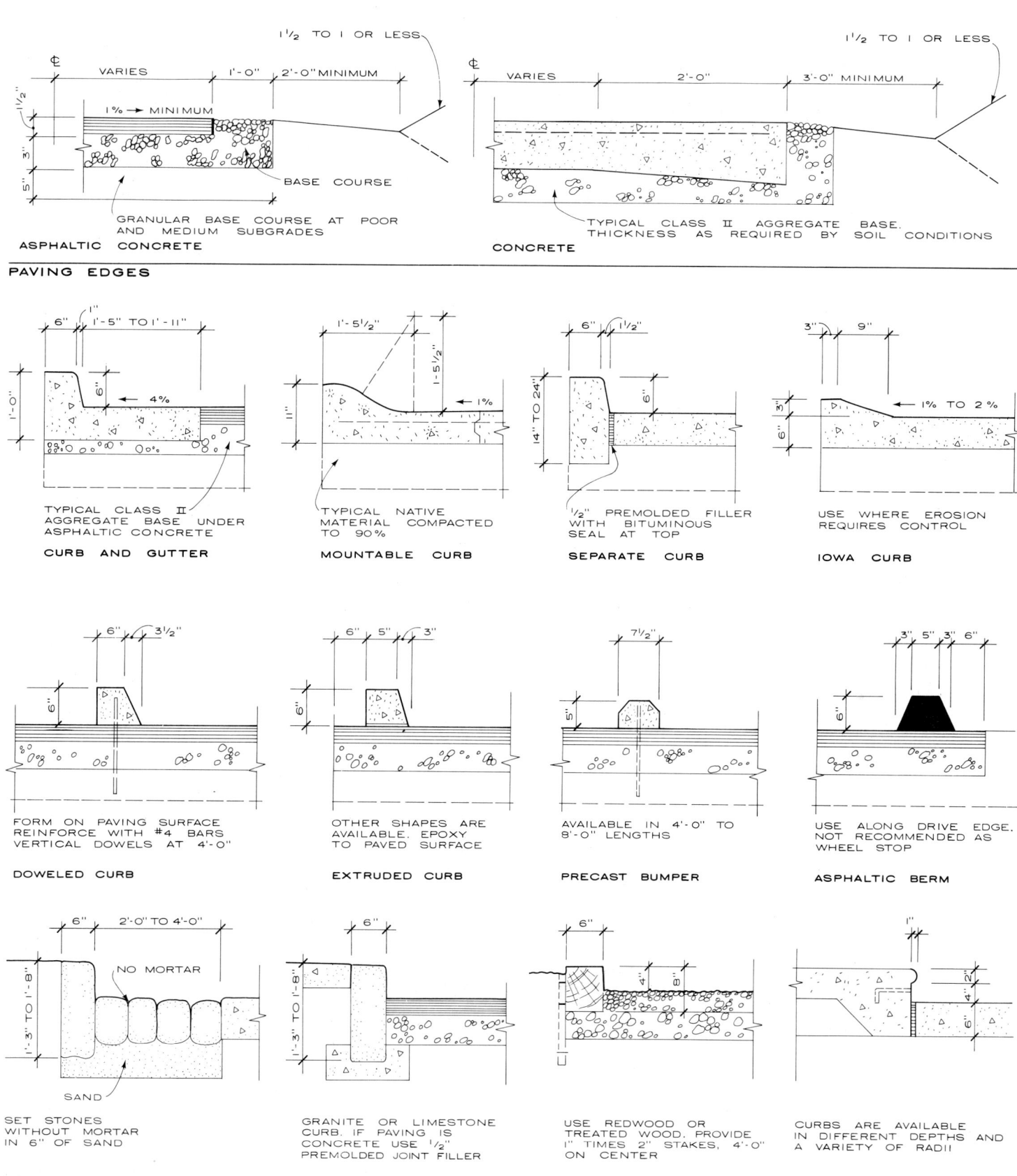

PAVING EDGES

1½ TO 1 OR LESS
VARIES | 1'-0" | 2'-0" MINIMUM
1% → MINIMUM
1½
3"
5"
BASE COURSE
GRANULAR BASE COURSE AT POOR
AND MEDIUM SUBGRADES

ASPHALTIC CONCRETE

1½ TO 1 OR LESS
VARIES | 2'-0" | 3'-0" MINIMUM
TYPICAL CLASS II AGGREGATE BASE.
THICKNESS AS REQUIRED BY SOIL CONDITIONS

CONCRETE

6" | 1'-5" TO 1'-11"
1"
1'-0"
6"
4%
TYPICAL CLASS II
AGGREGATE BASE UNDER
ASPHALTIC CONCRETE

CURB AND GUTTER

1'-5½"
1-5½"
11"
1%
TYPICAL NATIVE
MATERIAL COMPACTED
TO 90%

MOUNTABLE CURB

6" | 1½"
14" TO 24"
6"
½" PREMOLDED FILLER
WITH BITUMINOUS
SEAL AT TOP

SEPARATE CURB

3" | 9"
3"
6"
1% TO 2%
USE WHERE EROSION
REQUIRES CONTROL

IOWA CURB

6" | 3½"
6"
FORM ON PAVING SURFACE
REINFORCE WITH #4 BARS
VERTICAL DOWELS AT 4'-0"

DOWELED CURB

6" | 5" | 3"
6"
OTHER SHAPES ARE
AVAILABLE. EPOXY
TO PAVED SURFACE

EXTRUDED CURB

7½"
5"
AVAILABLE IN 4'-0" TO
8'-0" LENGTHS

PRECAST BUMPER

3" | 5" | 3" | 6"
6"
USE ALONG DRIVE EDGE.
NOT RECOMMENDED AS
WHEEL STOP

ASPHALTIC BERM

6" | 2'-0" TO 4'-0"
NO MORTAR
1'-3" TO 1'-8"
SAND
SET STONES
WITHOUT MORTAR
IN 6" OF SAND

STONE CURB AND GUTTER

6"
1'-3" TO 1'-8"
GRANITE OR LIMESTONE
CURB. IF PAVING IS
CONCRETE USE ½"
PREMOLDED JOINT FILLER

STONE CURB

6"
4" | 8"
USE REDWOOD OR
TREATED WOOD. PROVIDE
1" TIMES 2" STAKES, 4'-0"
ON CENTER

TIMBER CURB

1"
2"
6"
CURBS ARE AVAILABLE
IN DIFFERENT DEPTHS AND
A VARIETY OF RADII

STEEL CURB

CURBS AND GUTTERS

William T. Mahan, AIA; Santa Barbara, California

PAVING AND SURFACING 2

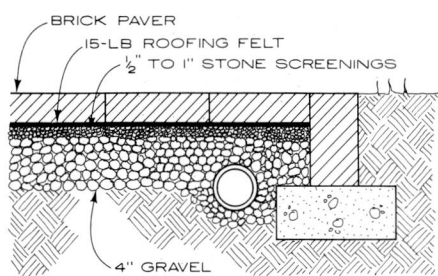

ON FLEXIBLE BASE

BRICK SIZES: 4 x 4, 4 x 8, 4 x 12 in.
6 x 6, 8 x 8, 12 x 12 in.; 5³/₄, 8 and 12 in. hexagon.
Depth varies 1¹/₈ to 2¹/₄ in.

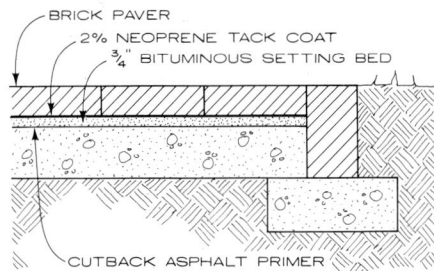

ON RIGID BASE

Surface textures vary from moderately abrasive to smooth. Colors are from light to dark earth tones. Special flashed surfaces are also available. Brick pavers are recommended for residential and light commercial uses.

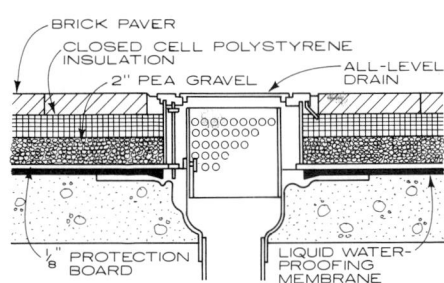

ON SUSPENDED BASE

Installed over waterproofing, roofing, slab, asphalt binder course or crushed stone base on bituminous setting.

BRICK PAVERS

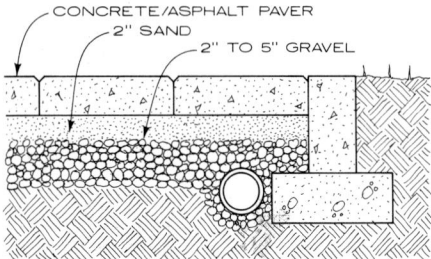

ON FLEXIBLE BASE
CONCRETE SIZES: 4 x 8, 8 x 8, 6 x 12,
12 x 18, 12 x 24, 18 x 18, 24 x 24,
24 x 30, 24 x 36, and 24 in. hexagon.
Depth varies 2 to 4 in.
Surface textures are smooth to coarse.

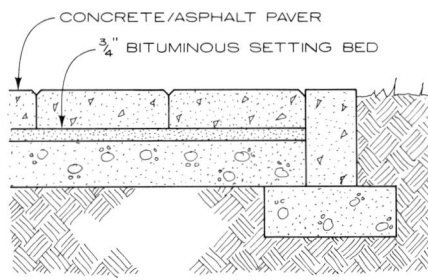

ON RIGID BASE
Colors are usually gray or white but are available with colored aggregates or colored cement matrix.
ASPHALT SIZES
5 x 12, 6 x 12, 8 x 8, and 8 in. hexagon.
Depth varies 1¹/₄ to 3 in.

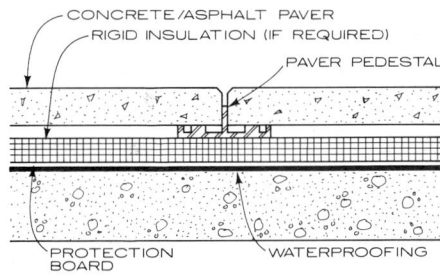

ON SUSPENDED BASE

Surface textures are abrasive but not coarse. Colors are natural black or exposed aggregate finish. Installed over waterproofing, roofing, slab, asphalt binder course, or crushed stone base on bituminous setting bed.

CONCRETE AND ASPHALT PAVERS

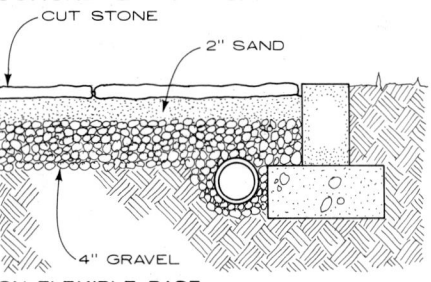

ON FLEXIBLE BASE
TERRA COTTA SIZES
4 x 4, 8 x 8 in.
Depths 1 to 2¹/₂ in.
Surface texture is usually smooth.
Colors are earth tones.
Installed on rigid base and mortar. Avoid frost.

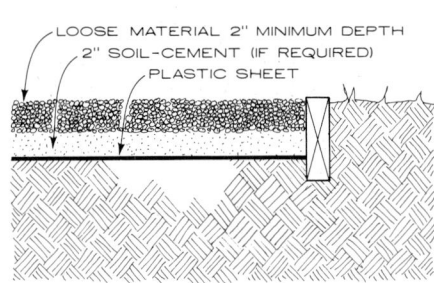

ON RIGID BASE
SLATE SIZES
4 in. min. x random.
Depths ³/₄ to 2¹/₂ in.
Surface texture is smooth.
Colors are grays and reds.
Installed on flexible base, no mortar. Keep well drained.

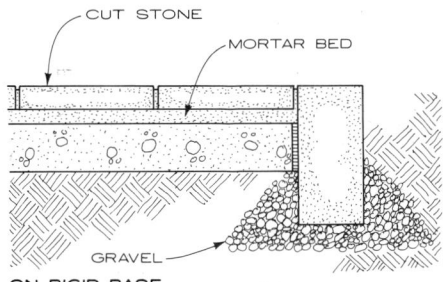

ON RIGID BASE
GRANITE SIZES: 4 x 4, 4 x 8, 5 x 8 in.
8 x 8, 12 x 12, Depth 2, 3, 4, and 10 in.

Surface texture is smooth. Colors are light and dark shades of red, gray and brown. Installed on rigid base and mortar for stability and heavy duty use; on flexible base for light duty use.

CUT STONE PAVERS

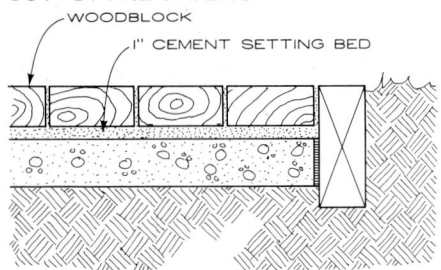

DEPTH: Crosscut = 2 in. min. Rip cut = 3 in. min.
Surface texture is smooth to slippery.
Colors are natural wood or color of preservatives.
Installed on flexible base that is well drained.
Wood should be pressure treated.

WOODBLOCK PAVERS

GENERAL NOTES

Paved areas should slope at a minimum of 0.5%, preferably 1.0%, in any direction. Main traffic areas should be kept dry.

Dan Mock and John M. Weed, ASLA; Houston, Texas

MATERIAL SIZES

Wood chips 1 in. nominal	¹/₂ in. decomposed granite
Shredded bark mulch	³/₄ in. crushed stone
¹/₄ in. stone chips	1–2 in. washed stone
³/₄ in. pea gravel	

Installed on subgrade, plastic or soil-cement base.
Natural materials will decompose.

LOOSE MATERIALS

Pavers in mortar on rigid and suspended bases must have full expansion joint 20 ft on center. Rigid base on expansion soils is to be reinforced and doweled at joints. Porous base or subbase required in cold

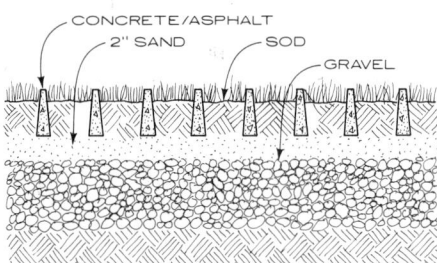

Size: 24 x 24 x 4 in. deep.
Surface texture is moderately abrasive.
Color is standard gray or white.
Installed without slab, mortar, or grout.
A preformed lattice unit used for embankment and storm run-off control, recreation areas, pathways, parking areas, and soil conservation.

GRID PAVING BLOCKS

regions with adequate subsurface drainage.

All pavers require edging members to contain horizontal movement at perimeter.

BIKE PATH CLASSIFICATIONS

Three bike path classifications have been generally accepted in the United States:

1. CLASS I: Completely separated right-of-way designated exclusively for bicycles. Through traffic, whether by motor vehicles or pedestrians, is not allowed. Cross flows by vehicles and pedestrians are allowed but minimized.
2. CLASS II: Restricted right-of-way designated exclusively or semiexclusively for bicycles. Through traffic by motor vehicles or pedestrians is not allowed. Cross flows by vehicles and pedestrians are allowed but minimized.
3. CLASS III: Shared right-of-way designated by signs or stencils. Any pathway that shares its through traffic right-of-way with either moving (but not parked) motor vehicles or pedestrians.

CLASS I: TOTAL SEPARATION / DIVIDING STRIP BETWEEN RIGHTS-OF-WAY ON SEPARATE SURFACES

CLASS II: TOTAL OR PARTIAL SEPARATION / ADJACENT, BUT SEPARATED RIGHTS-OF-WAY ON SAME SURFACE

CLASS III: NO SEPARATION / SHARED RIGHT-OF-WAY ON SAME SURFACE

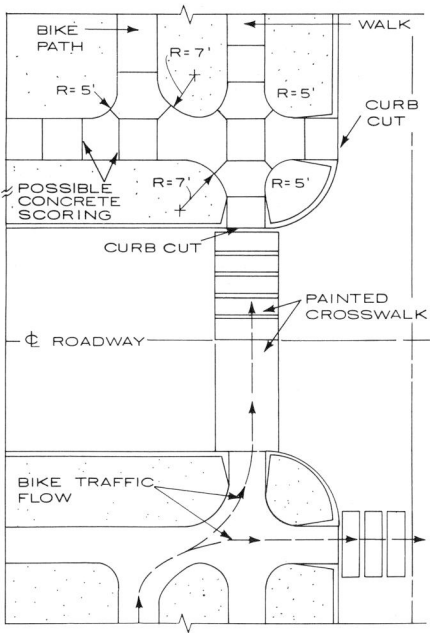

CLASS I: BIKE PATH, ON-GRADE INTERSECTION CONSIDERATIONS

Johnson, Johnson & Roy; Ann Arbor, Michigan

VERTICAL AND HORIZONTAL LAYOUT

The gradients of a bike path are directly related to the amount of use it will get. Extremes of steepness and flatness should be avoided if possible. The following gradients are recommended:

| | LENGTH | |
GRADIENT	NORM	MAXIMUM
1.5%	1000 ft	—
3%	400 ft	800 ft
4.5%	150 ft	300 ft
10%	30 ft	60 ft

The following formula can be used to determine horizontal radii used on bike paths:

$$R = 1.528V + 2.2*$$

where R = the unbraked radius of curvature (ft) negotiated by a bicycle on a flat, dry, bituminous concrete surface and V = the velocity of bicycle (mph).

*Formula applicable to a maximum design speed of 18 mph. Using this formula, the minimum radius acceptable for a 10 mph design speed would be 17.5 ft. The radii used at the base of gradients in excess of 4.5% and running longer than 100 ft should be longer to accept higher design speeds (20-30 mph). Shorter radii can be used along approaches to on-grade intersections to slow cyclists down as they merge with pedestrians.

BIKE PATH INTERSECTIONS

One of the most dangerous elements of a bike path system is the on-grade intersection that brings bicycles, pedestrians, and automobiles together. If possible, Class I bike paths should include complete grade separations. Often this is not economically feasible; therefore, the following recommendations should be considered:

1. If possible, merge bicycles and pedestrians a minimum of 100 ft from the intersection using warning signs for both cyclists and pedestrians.
2. Provide warning signs for motorists indicating special caution at intersections.
3. Maintain adequate lighting (see Chapter 1 on illumination).
4. Install walk-don't walk, electronic crosswalk signals at busy intersections.
5. Control placement and maintenance of plant materials so as to maintain adequate site distance and visibility.

Confusion at intersections tends to increase at Class II and III bike paths. Warning signs are therefore recommended along approaches to intersections for all three types of users (distance from intersections for signs varies with speed of vehicular traffic).

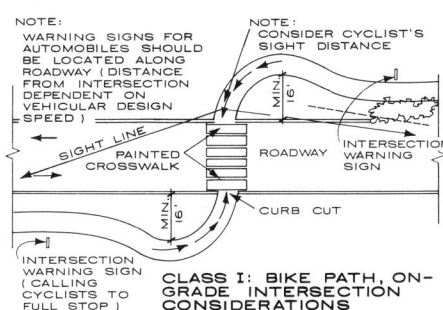

CLASS I: BIKE PATH, ON-GRADE INTERSECTION CONSIDERATIONS

BICYCLE SIZES

FRAME SIZE "W"	FRAME SIZE "F"
16"	12"
20"	13"
24"	16" boys 15" girls
26"	18", 19", 21", 23"
27"	19", 21", 23"

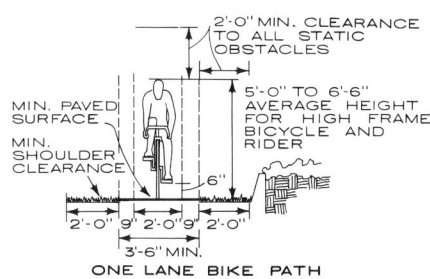

ONE LANE BIKE PATH

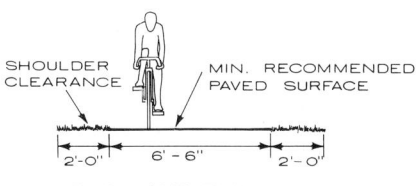

TWO LANE BIKE PATH

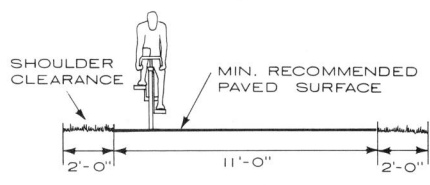

THREE LANE BIKE PATH

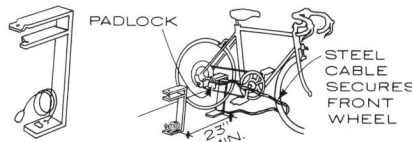

UPRIGHT, METAL BICYCLE RACK

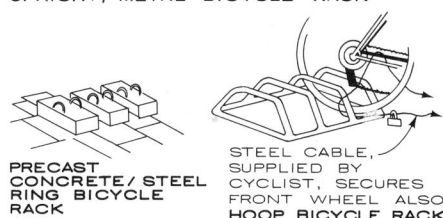

PRECAST CONCRETE/STEEL RING BICYCLE RACK

HOOP BICYCLE RACK

BICYCLE PARKING

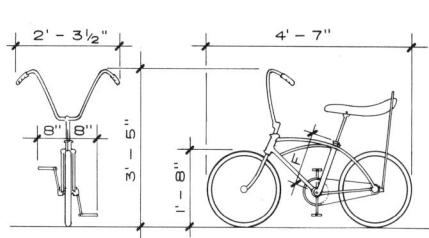

YOUTH'S SPORT W/"HIGHRISE" HANDLEBARS
FRAME SIZE (F) 13½", 14½"

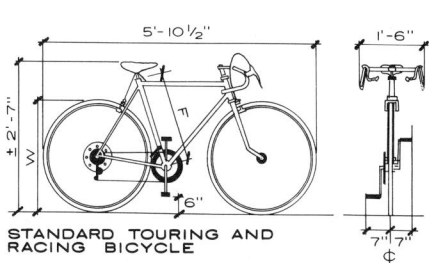

STANDARD TOURING AND RACING BICYCLE

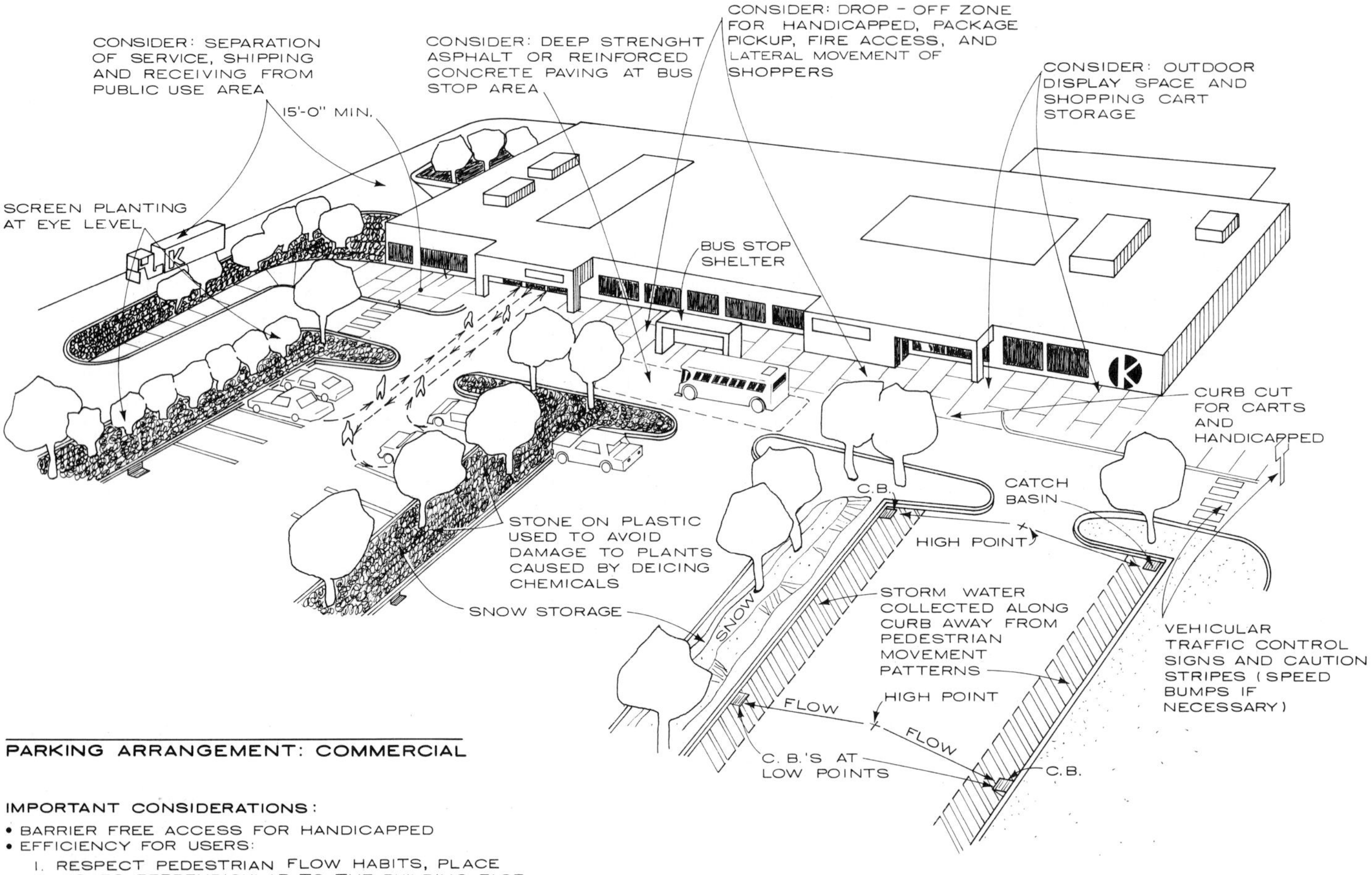

CONSIDER: SEPARATION OF SERVICE, SHIPPING AND RECEIVING FROM PUBLIC USE AREA

15'-0" MIN.

CONSIDER: DEEP STRENGHT ASPHALT OR REINFORCED CONCRETE PAVING AT BUS STOP AREA

CONSIDER: DROP - OFF ZONE FOR HANDICAPPED, PACKAGE PICKUP, FIRE ACCESS, AND LATERAL MOVEMENT OF SHOPPERS

CONSIDER: OUTDOOR DISPLAY SPACE AND SHOPPING CART STORAGE

SCREEN PLANTING AT EYE LEVEL

BUS STOP SHELTER

CURB CUT FOR CARTS AND HANDICAPPED

STONE ON PLASTIC USED TO AVOID DAMAGE TO PLANTS CAUSED BY DEICING CHEMICALS

SNOW STORAGE

C.B.

CATCH BASIN

HIGH POINT

STORM WATER COLLECTED ALONG CURB AWAY FROM PEDESTRIAN MOVEMENT PATTERNS

HIGH POINT

FLOW

FLOW

C.B.'S AT LOW POINTS

C.B.

VEHICULAR TRAFFIC CONTROL SIGNS AND CAUTION STRIPES (SPEED BUMPS IF NECESSARY)

PARKING ARRANGEMENT: COMMERCIAL

IMPORTANT CONSIDERATIONS:
- BARRIER FREE ACCESS FOR HANDICAPPED
- EFFICIENCY FOR USERS:
  1. RESPECT PEDESTRIAN FLOW HABITS, PLACE AISLES PERPENDICULAR TO THE BUILDING FACE
  2. KEEP PEDESTRIAN WALKING AREAS IN PARKING LOT DRY AND FREE OF STANDING WATER

- PROVIDE SPACE FOR SNOW STORAGE
- PROVIDE FOR MASS TRANSIT ACCESS AT LARGER COMMERCIAL CENTERS

DESIGN CONSIDERATIONS

While efficiency (number of spaces per gross acres) is the major practical consideration in the development of parking areas, several other important design questions exist. Barrier free design is mandatory in most communities. Parking spaces for the handicapped should be designated near building entrances. Curb cuts for wheelchairs should be provided at entrances. The lots should not only be efficient in terms of parking spaces provided, but should also allow maximum efficiency for pedestrians once they leave their vehicles.

Pedestrians habitually walk in the aisles behind parked vehicles. This should be recognized in the orientation of the aisles to building entrances. When aisles are perpendicular to the building face, pedestrians can walk to and from the building without squeezing between parked cars with carts and packages. Pedestrian movement areas should be graded to avoid creating standing water in the paths of pedestrians. Space should be provided for snow storage within parking areas, if required.

Johnson, Johnson & Roy, Inc.; Ann Arbor, Michigan

PLANTING CONSIDERATIONS

The distribution and placement of plants in parking areas can help to relieve the visually overwhelming scale of large parking lots. To maximize the impact of landscape materials, the screening capabilities of the plants must be considered. High branching canopy trees do not create a visual screen at eye level. When the landscaped area is concentrated in islands large enough to accommodate a diversified mixture of canopy and flowering trees, evergreen trees, and shrubs, visual screening via plants is much more effective. Planting low branching, densely foliated trees and shrubs can soften the visual impact of large parking areas. Consider the use of evergreens and avoid plants that drop fruit or sap.

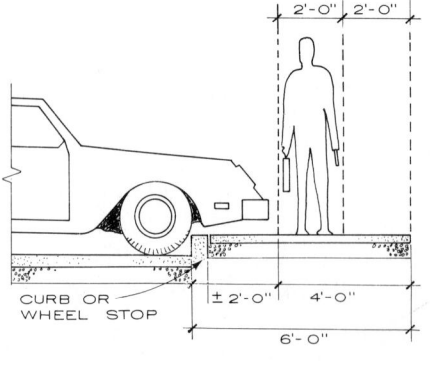

2'-0"   2'-0"

CURB OR WHEEL STOP

± 2'-0"   4'-0"

6'-0"

AUTOMOBILE OVERHANG REQUIREMENT

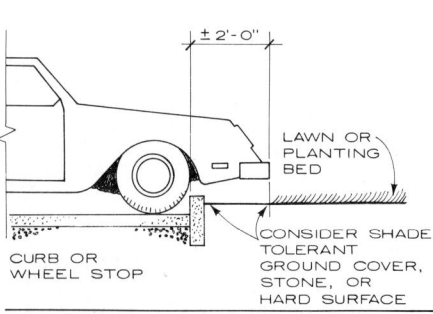

± 2'-0"

LAWN OR PLANTING BED

CURB OR WHEEL STOP

CONSIDER SHADE TOLERANT GROUND COVER, STONE, OR HARD SURFACE

OVERHANGS IN PLANTING AREA

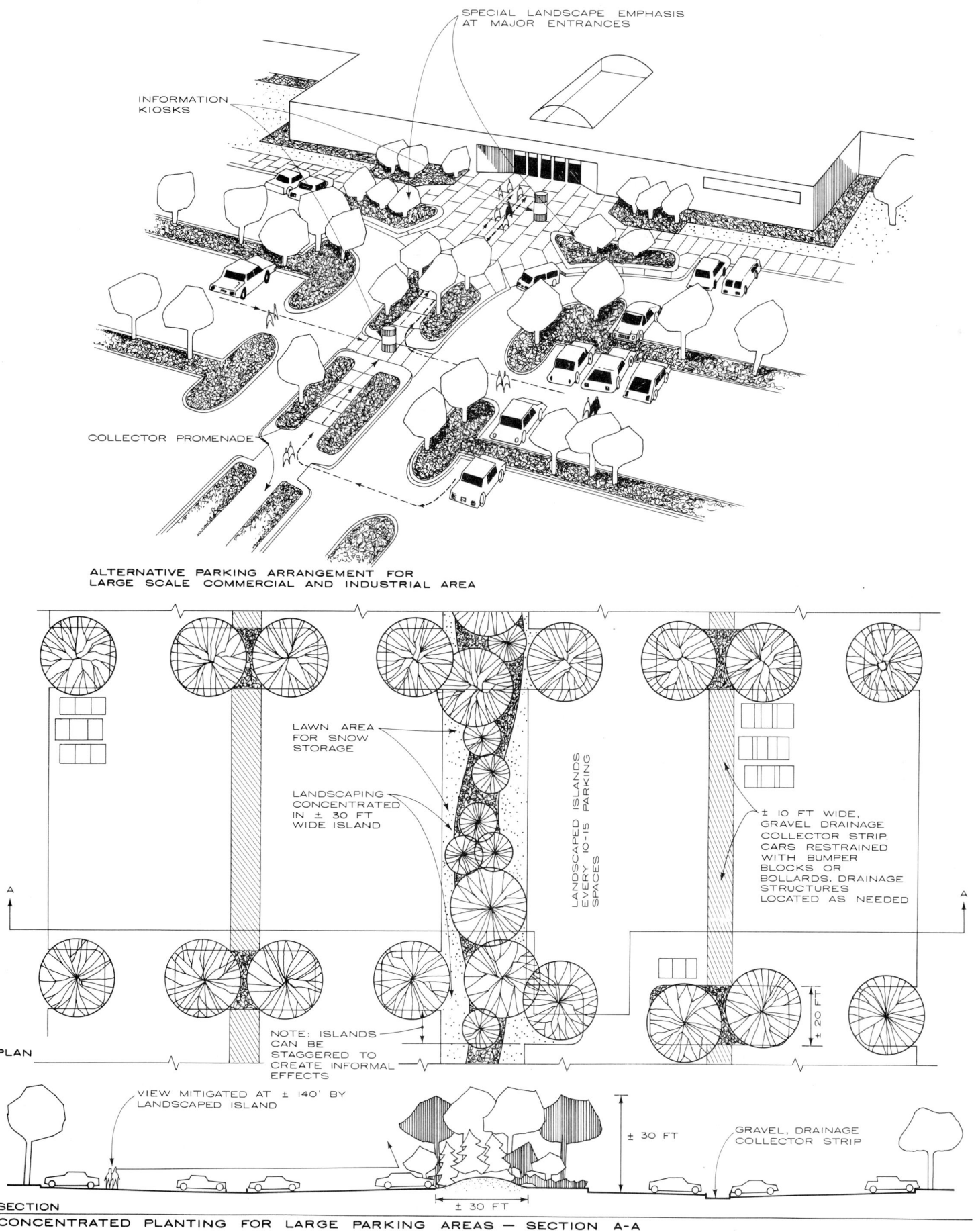

SPECIAL LANDSCAPE EMPHASIS
AT MAJOR ENTRANCES

INFORMATION
KIOSKS

COLLECTOR PROMENADE

ALTERNATIVE PARKING ARRANGEMENT FOR
LARGE SCALE COMMERCIAL AND INDUSTRIAL AREA

LAWN AREA
FOR SNOW
STORAGE

LANDSCAPING
CONCENTRATED
IN ± 30 FT
WIDE ISLAND

LANDSCAPED ISLANDS
EVERY 10-15 PARKING
SPACES

± 10 FT WIDE,
GRAVEL DRAINAGE
COLLECTOR STRIP.
CARS RESTRAINED
WITH BUMPER
BLOCKS OR
BOLLARDS. DRAINAGE
STRUCTURES
LOCATED AS NEEDED

A   A

± 20 FT

PLAN

NOTE: ISLANDS
CAN BE
STAGGERED TO
CREATE INFORMAL
EFFECTS

VIEW MITIGATED AT ± 140' BY
LANDSCAPED ISLAND

± 30 FT

GRAVEL, DRAINAGE
COLLECTOR STRIP

SECTION
± 30 FT

CONCENTRATED PLANTING FOR LARGE PARKING AREAS — SECTION A-A

Johnson, Johnson & Roy, Inc.; Ann Arbor, Michigan

SITE IMPROVEMENTS 2

CONSIDERATIONS

The following factors must be considered when installing or renovating outdoor lighting systems:

1. In general, overhead lighting is more efficient and economical than low level lighting.
2. Fixtures should provide an overlapping pattern of light at a height of about 7 ft.
3. Lighting levels should respond to site hazards such as steps, ramps, and steep embankments.
4. Posts and standards should be placed so that they do not create hazards for pedestrians or vehicles.

NOTE

All exterior installations must be provided with ground fault interruption circuit.

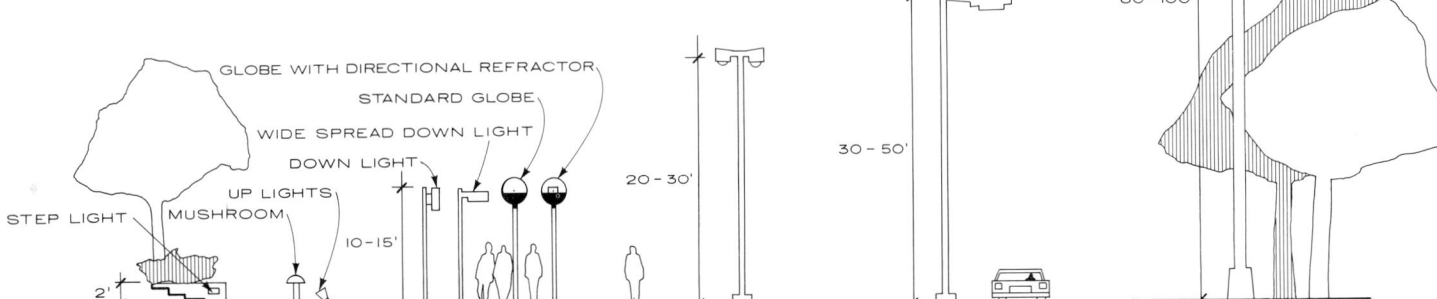

LOW LEVEL
- Heights below eye level
- Very finite patterns with low wattage capabilities
- Incandescent and fluorescent
- Lowest maintenance requirements but highly susceptible to vandals

MALL AND WALKWAY
- 10–15' heights average multi-use because of extreme variety of fixtures and light patterns
- Incandescent, mercury vapor
- Susceptible to vandals

SPECIAL PURPOSE
- 20–30' heights average
- Recreational, commercial, residential, industrial
- Metal halide, mercury vapor
- Fixtures maintained by gantry

PARKING AND ROADWAY
- 30–50' heights average
- Large recreational, commercial, industrial areas; highways
- Mercury vapor, high pressure sodium
- Fixtures maintained by gantry

HIGH MAST
- 60–100' heights average
- Large area lighting—parking, recreational, highway interchanges
- Mercury vapor, high pressure sodium
- Fixtures must lower for maintenance

DEFINITIONS

A lumen is a unit used for measuring the amount of light energy given off by a light source. A footcandle is a unit used for measuring the amount of illumination on a surface. The amount of usable light from any given source is partially determined by the source's angle of incidence and the distance to the illuminated surface. See Chapter 1 on illumination.

RECOMMENDED LIGHTING LEVELS IN FOOTCANDLES

	COMMER-CIAL	INTERME-DIATE	RESIDEN-TIAL
PEDESTRIAN AREAS			
Sidewalks	0.9	0.6	0.2
Pedestrian ways	2.0	1.0	0.5
VEHICULAR ROADS			
Freeway*	0.6	0.6	0.6
Major road and expressway*	2.0	1.4	1.0
Collector road	1.2	0.9	0.6
Local road	0.9	0.6	0.4
Alleys	0.6	0.4	0.2
PARKING AREAS			
Self-parking	1.0	—	—
Attendant parking	2.0	—	—
Security problem area	—	—	5.0
Minimum for television viewing of important interdiction areas	10.0	10.0	10.0
BUILDING AREAS			
Entrances	5.0	—	—
General grounds	1.0	—	—

*Both mainline and ramps.

Johnson, Johnson & Roy; Ann Arbor, Michigan

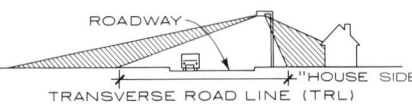

MEASURING LIGHT INTENSITY IN FOOTCANDLES

NOTE

The total intensity of two or more overlapping light patterns equals the sum of their individual intensities.

1. CUTOFF means that maximum of 10% of light source lumens fall outside of TRL area
2. SEMICUTOFF means that maximum of 30% of light source lumens fall outside of the TRL area
3. NONCUTOFF means that no control limitations exist

CUTOFF TERMINOLOGY
(NOTE: "CUTOFF" IS MEASURED ALONG TRL.)

NOTE

Degree of cutoff is determined by one of the following:

(a) design of fixture housing
(b) incorporation of prismatic lens over light source
(c) addition of shield to fixture on "house side"

SHORT = 3.75 × MH
MEDIUM = 6.0 × MH
LONG = 8.0 × MH

TYPES OF DISTRIBUTION
(NOTE: "DISTRIBUTION IS MEASURED ALONG LRL)

VEHICULAR CONSIDERATIONS

There are strong differences between the perceptual performance of the driver and that of the pedestrian. Increasing speed imposes five limitations on man:

1. MAN'S CONCENTRATION INCREASES: While stationary or walking, a person's attention may be widely dispersed. When moving in an automobile, however, he or she concentrates on those factors that are relevant to the driving experience.

2. THE POINT OF CONCENTRATION RECEDES: As speed or motion increases, a person's concentration is directed at a focal point increasingly farther away.

3. PERIPHERAL VISION DIMINISHES: As the eye concentrates on detail at a point of focus a great distance ahead, the angular field of vision shrinks. This shrinking process is a function of focusing distance, angle of vision, and distance of foreground detail.

4. FOREGROUND DETAIL FADES INCREAS-INGLY: While concentrating on more significant distant objects, a person perceives foreground objects to be moving and increasingly blurred.

5. SPACE PERCEPTION BECOMES IMPAIRED: As the time available for perceiving objects decreases, specific details become less noticeable, making spatial perception more difficult.

With an increasing rate of motion, it becomes more and more important that copy, including illustrations and symbols, be created specifically for out-of-doors use and not merely rescaled from other media of communication. The safety of the motorist and passengers can depend on the clarity of messages conveyed by signs.

VEHICLE SPEEDS VERSUS LETTER HEIGHT ON TRAFFIC SIGNS

INITIAL SPEED	DISTANCE TRAVELED WHILE READING	DISTANCE TRAVELED WHILE SLOWING	TOTAL DISTANCE	SIZE OF COPY AT 65 FT/IN.
30 mph	110 ft	200 ft	310 ft	4.8 in.
40 mph	147 ft	307 ft	454 ft	7.0 in.
50 mph	183 ft	360 ft	543 ft	8.4 in.
60 mph	220 ft	390 ft	610 ft	9.4 in.

NOTE: It is recommended that street name signs have 4 in. letters in area where vehicle speeds are 30–35 mph. For speeds of 40 mph and over, a 5 in. letter size is recommended.

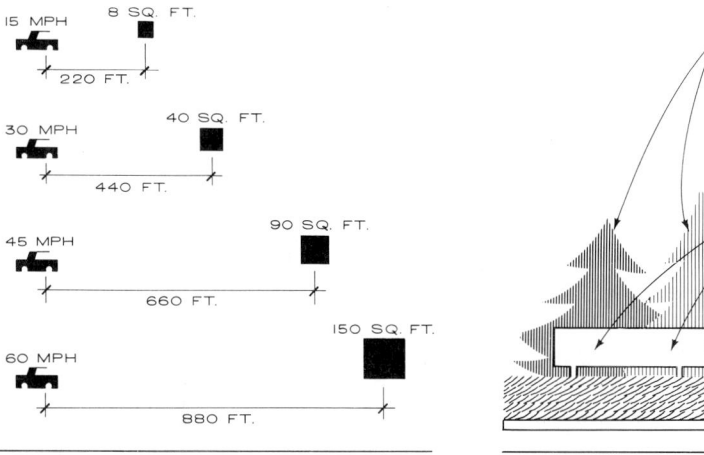

SPEED, SIGHT DISTANCE AND GRAPHIC SIZE RELATION SHIPS

NOTE: LETTERS SHOULD CONSTITUTE APPROXIMATELY 40% OF GRAPHIC'S AREA.

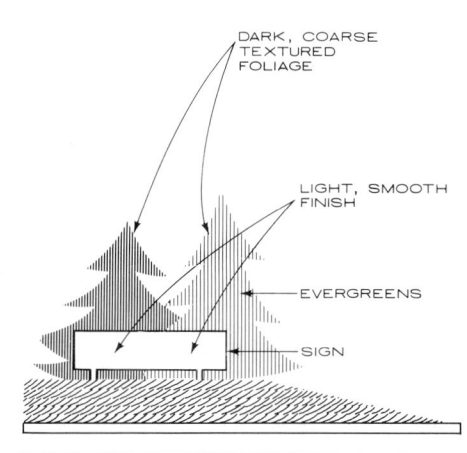

CONSIDER BACKGROUND WHEN CHOOSING COLOR AND MATERIALS

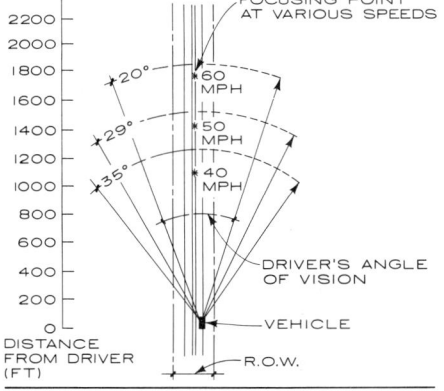

RELATIONSHIP BETWEEN DRIVER'S FOCUSING POINT AND ANGLE OF VISION DOES NOT CONSIDER EFFECT OF PRECEDING TRAFFIC

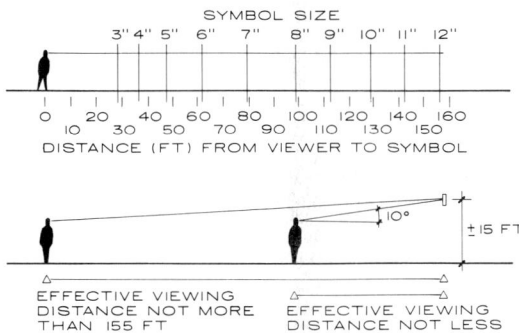

PEDESTRIAN CONSIDERATIONS

Johnson, Johnson & Roy; Ann Arbor, Michigan

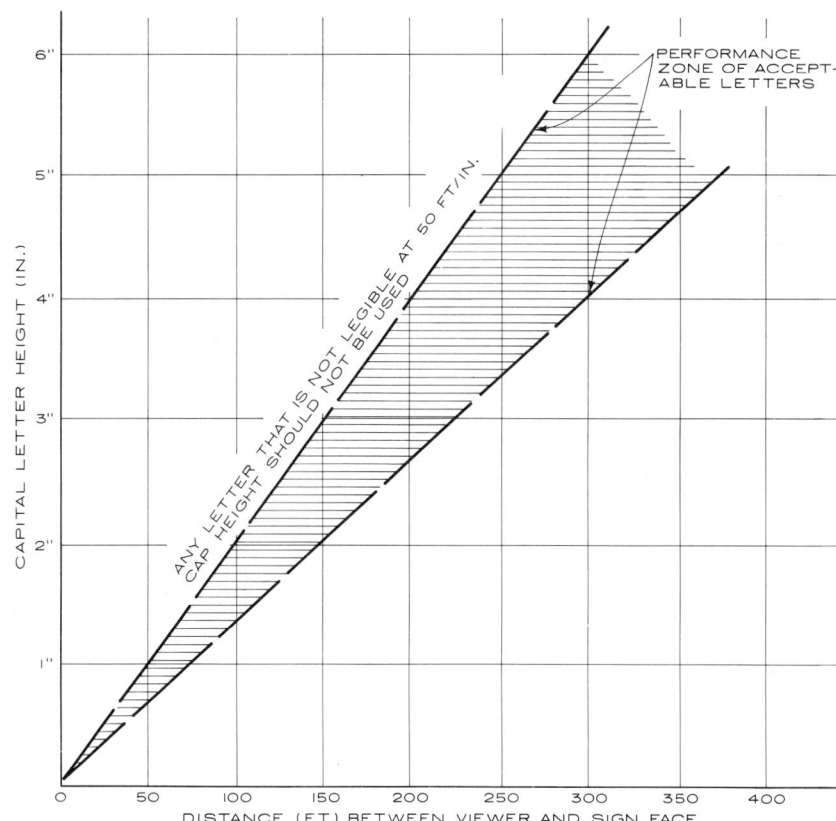

NOTE

Under normal daylight conditions, with normal vision, and an angular distortion of 0° approximately 50 ft/in. of capital height can be taken as a guideline for minimal legibility, as seen from the chart.

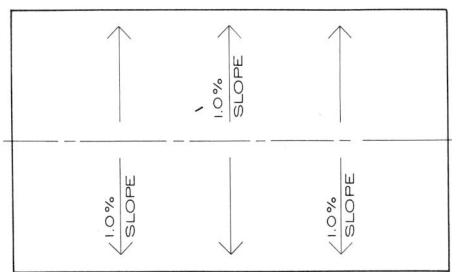

PREFERRED GRADING

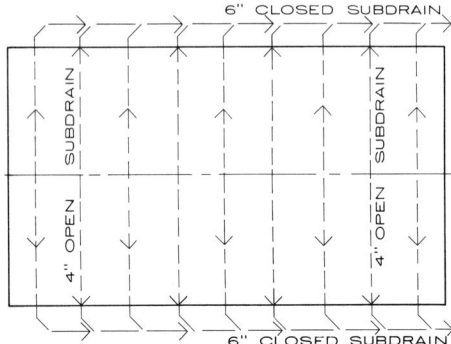

SUBSOIL DRAINAGE

RECTANGULAR SPORTS FIELDS

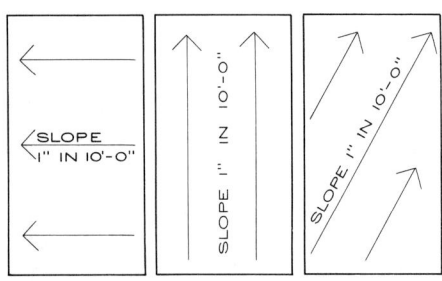

DRAINAGE DIAGRAMS

SPORTS COURTS

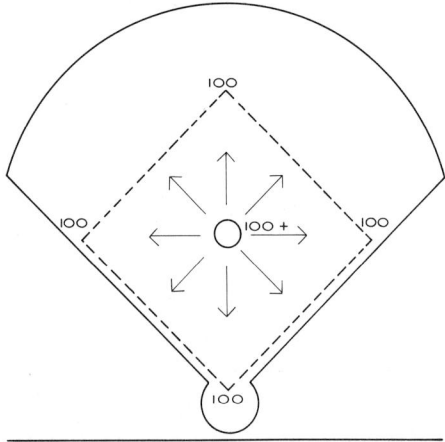

BASEBALL, SOFTBALL DIAMONDS

NOTE

It is preferable that the base lines be level. If the diamond must pitch, the average slope shall be 2.0% from first base to third base or vice versa.

The minimum slope for drainage on turf areas outside the skinned area is 1.0% when adequate subsoil drainage is provided. The maximum is 2.5%.

J. Paul Raeder; Beckett Raeder Rankin, Inc.; Ann Arbor, Michigan

Lawrence Cook & Associates; Falls Church, Virginia

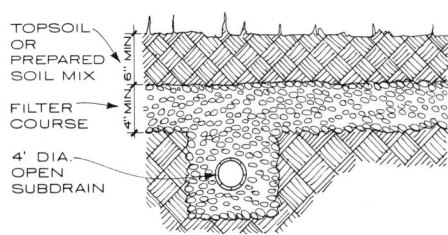

NATURAL TURF

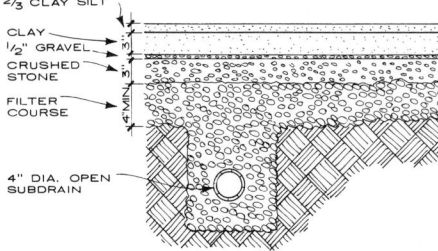

SAND CLAY

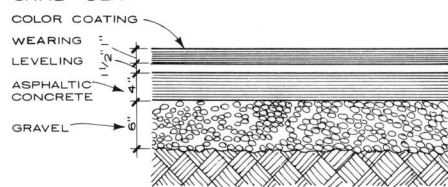

BITUMINOUS CONCRETE

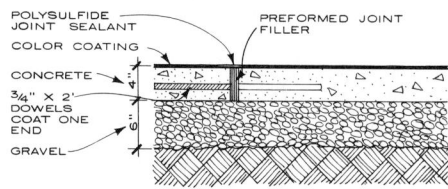

CONSTRUCTION JOINT IN CONCRETE

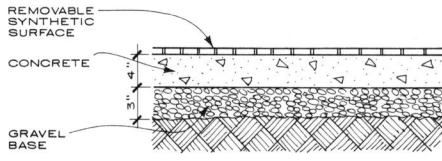

SYNTHETIC SURFACE

PLAYING SURFACES

TYPICAL GRADING AND DRAINAGE DETAILS

COURT SURFACES

Paved playing surfaces should be in one plane and pitched from side to side, end to end, or corner to corner diagonally, instead of in two planes pitched to or from the net. Minimum slope should be 1 in. in 10 ft. Subgrade should slope in the same direction as the surface. Perimeter drains may be provided for paved areas. Underdrains are not recommended beneath paved areas.

PLAYING FIELDS

Preferred grading for rectangular field is a longitudinal crown with 1% slope from center to each side.

Grading may be from side to side or corner to corner diagonally if conditions do not permit the preferred grading.

Subsoil drainage is to slope in the same direction as the surface. Subdrains and filter course are to be used only when subsoil conditions require. Where subsoil drainage is necessary, the spacing of subdrains is dependent on local soil conditions and rainfall.

Subdrains are to have a minimum gradient of 0.15%.

Baseball and softball fields should be graded so that the bases are level.

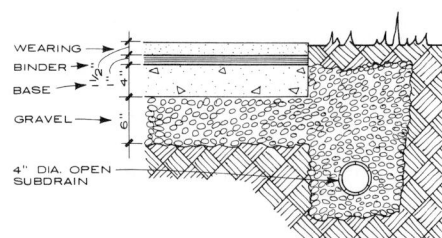

SYNTHETIC TURF

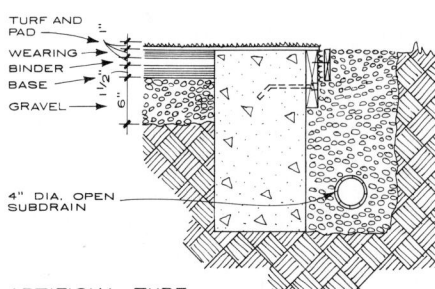

ARTIFICIAL TURF

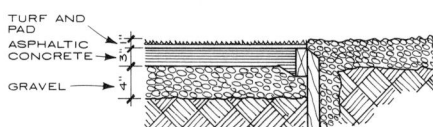

ARTIFICIAL TURF

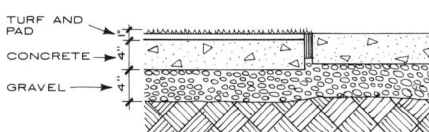

ARTIFICIAL TURF

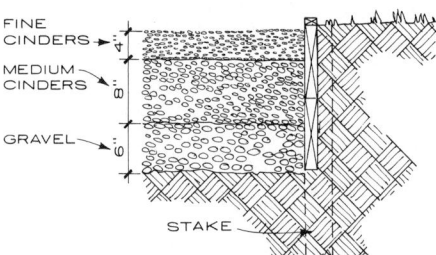

CINDER TRACK

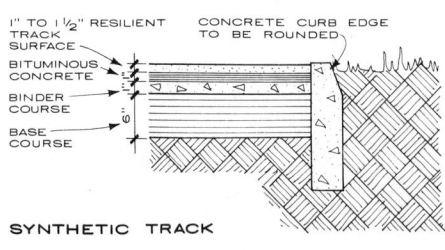

SYNTHETIC TRACK

EDGE CONDITIONS

2 SITE IMPROVEMENTS

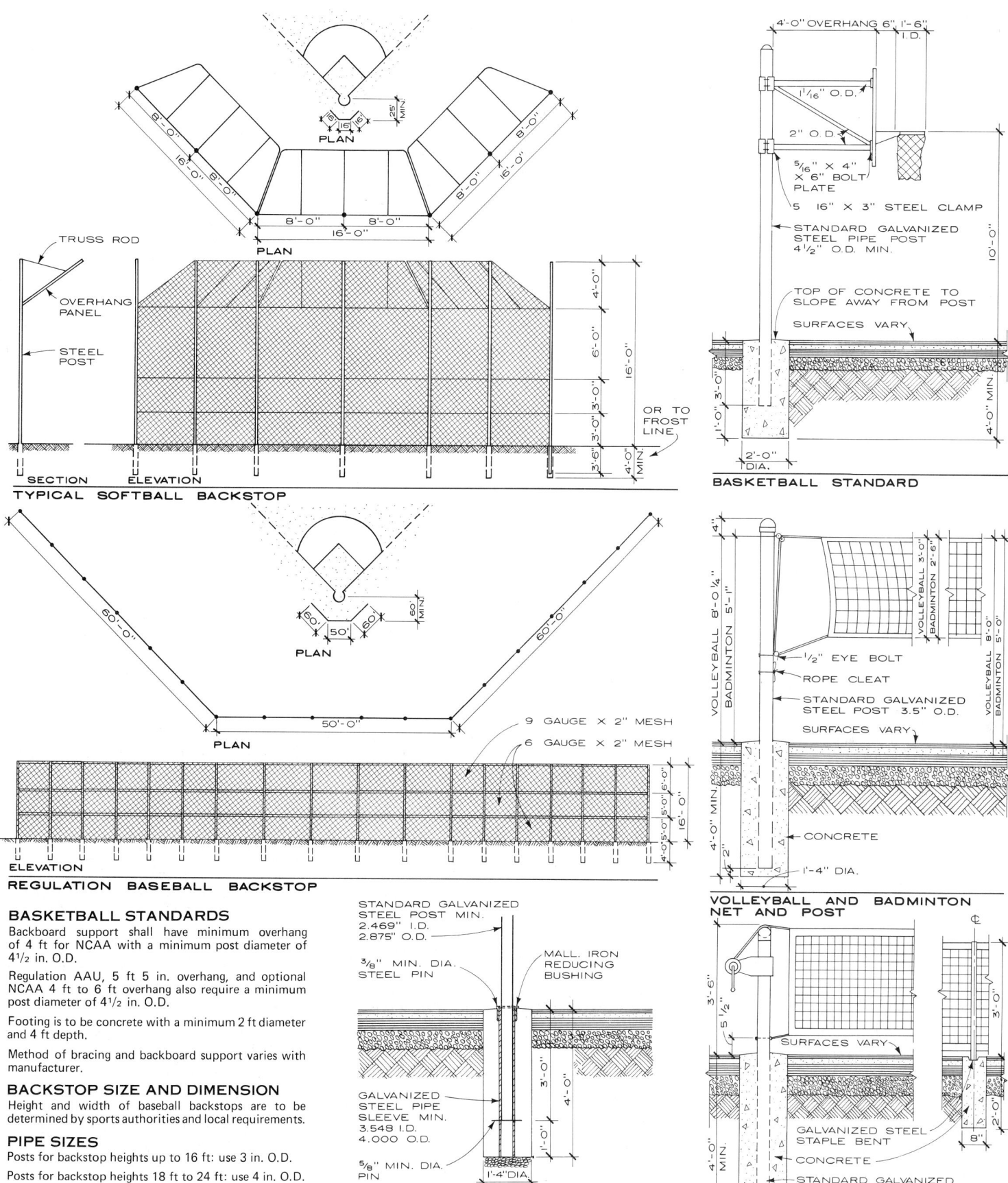

PLAN

PLAN

TRUSS ROD

OVERHANG PANEL

STEEL POST

SECTION   ELEVATION

TYPICAL SOFTBALL BACKSTOP

PLAN

PLAN

9 GAUGE X 2" MESH

6 GAUGE X 2" MESH

ELEVATION

REGULATION BASEBALL BACKSTOP

4'-0" OVERHANG 6" 1'-6" I.D.

1 1/16" O.D.

2" O.D.

5/16" X 4" X 6" BOLT PLATE

5 16" X 3" STEEL CLAMP

STANDARD GALVANIZED STEEL PIPE POST 4 1/2" O.D. MIN.

TOP OF CONCRETE TO SLOPE AWAY FROM POST

SURFACES VARY

2'-0" DIA.

BASKETBALL STANDARD

VOLLEYBALL 8'-0 1/4"
BADMINTON 5'-1"

1/2" EYE BOLT

ROPE CLEAT

STANDARD GALVANIZED STEEL POST 3.5" O.D.

SURFACES VARY

CONCRETE

1'-4" DIA.

VOLLEYBALL 3'-0"
BADMINTON 2'-6"

VOLLEYBALL 8'-0"
BADMINTON 5'-0"

VOLLEYBALL AND BADMINTON NET AND POST

BASKETBALL STANDARDS

Backboard support shall have minimum overhang of 4 ft for NCAA with a minimum post diameter of 4 1/2 in. O.D.

Regulation AAU, 5 ft 5 in. overhang, and optional NCAA 4 ft to 6 ft overhang also require a minimum post diameter of 4 1/2 in. O.D.

Footing is to be concrete with a minimum 2 ft diameter and 4 ft depth.

Method of bracing and backboard support varies with manufacturer.

BACKSTOP SIZE AND DIMENSION

Height and width of baseball backstops are to be determined by sports authorities and local requirements.

PIPE SIZES

Posts for backstop heights up to 16 ft: use 3 in. O.D.

Posts for backstop heights 18 ft to 24 ft: use 4 in. O.D.

Top, intermediate, and bottom rails: 1 5/8 in. O.D.

WIRE MESH FABRIC

Fabric shall be chain link with galvanized coating or aluminized. (Optional polyvinyl chloride coated steel.)

STANDARD GALVANIZED STEEL POST MIN. 2.469" I.D. 2.875" O.D.

3/8" MIN. DIA. STEEL PIN

MALL. IRON REDUCING BUSHING

GALVANIZED STEEL PIPE SLEEVE MIN. 3.548 I.D. 4.000 O.D.

5/8" MIN. DIA. PIN

1'-4" DIA.

REMOVABLE POST

All ferrous metal parts are to be hot dip galvanized after fabrication.

SURFACES VARY

GALVANIZED STEEL STAPLE BENT

CONCRETE

STANDARD GALVANIZED STEEL POST MIN. 2.469" I.D. 2.875" O.D.

1'-4" DIA.

TENNIS NET, POST, AND ANCHOR

J. Paul Raeder; Beckett Raeder Rankin, Inc.; Ann Arbor, Michigan

Lawrence Cook & Associates; Falls Church, Virginia

SITE IMPROVEMENTS   **2**

DECORATIVE POOLS AND FOUNTAINS

Decorative use of water usually falls within one of four basic classifications.

CALM WATER, as in ponds and pools, is appreciated in terms of its overall form and reflective qualities. Water reflections are effective as a compliment to buildings and sculptural pieces. The reflective quality of a pool is attained by keeping the body of water smooth at the surface and the sides and the bottom of the pool dark so these planes do not read through the reflections on the water surface.

FREE-FALLING WATER includes waterfalls or the vertical fall of water in a smooth sheet. Considerable volume of water is required to produce a solid sheet for a vertical distance greater than 3 ft, thereby requiring higher initial cost and ongoing energy cost. However, the masking sound produced by a higher volume of water can be effectively used to isolate an area from urban noise.

FLOWING WATER, used in streams and channels, can produce a variety of visual effects. The shape, size and slope of the channel is an important design consideration. Surface tension retards the rate of fall, keeping more water in motion for any given unit volume. For a 12 ft change in elevation, a free-falling sheet of water requires a flow of about 150 gpm per lineal foot while water directed over a surface requires only 25–35 gpm.

JETS occur when water is being forced upward. Height of jets depends on orifice size and water pressure. A man-made jet can be either a solid stream of water employed in a formal setting or an air entraining jet such as a bubbler employed for greater visual interest. The third type of jet produces a water shape such as a dome or a flower form. Contact manufacturers for a variety of available formed jets.

WATER JET SIZES

JET HEIGHT	ORIFICE SIZE
8'–10'	1/2''
10'–15'	3/4''
15'–25'	1''
Over 25'	1 1/2''
500'	8''

Orifice sizes over 3 in. require special fabrication.

WATERPROOFING

Waterproofing membrane is essential in pool area. Membrane material: tar, felt or spray-on synthetics. Selection is determined by specific installation and manufacturers' data.

DRAINS

Drains are essential for cleaning all fountains except small simple fountains that can be bailed or siphoned out with a garden hose. Drain lines can lead to sewer, dry well, or sump. If water is unchlorinated, drain lines may lead to lawn or garden areas. Check valves should be employed to avoid basin from draining out each time the pump is shut off when the pump is at a lower elevation than the source pipe in a basin or when a filter system in a fountain has basins at higher elevation than the main pool.

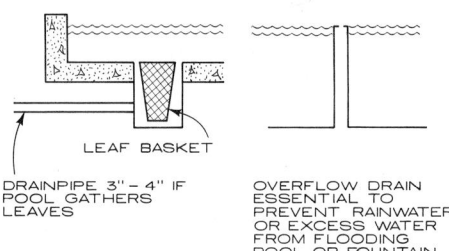
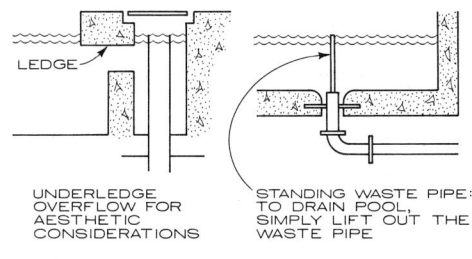

DRAINPIPE 3''–4'' IF POOL GATHERS LEAVES

OVERFLOW DRAIN ESSENTIAL TO PREVENT RAINWATER OR EXCESS WATER FROM FLOODING POOL OR FOUNTAIN

UNDERLEDGE OVERFLOW FOR AESTHETIC CONSIDERATIONS

STANDING WASTE PIPE: TO DRAIN POOL, SIMPLY LIFT OUT THE WASTE PIPE

DRAINS

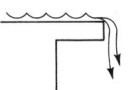
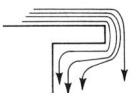
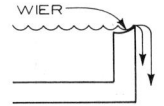
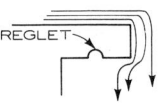

PIPE PENETRATION AND WATERSTOP

JET NOZZLE, PUMP, AND LIGHT FIXTURE

CAST–IN–PLACE POOL BOTTOM UNIT

NOTES
1. Under water lights effect glowing body.
2. White water jets or falls are effective when lighted from outside.
3. Combination of underwater and floodlights may be used for design effects.

CAST–IN–PLACE WALL UNIT

LIGHTING

NOTE
Wier design is critical and should be determined with 1/4 scale model for design effect.

Provide reglet to overcome surface tension if velocity and volume of water are low.

FREE-FALLING WATER

MECHANICAL AND ELECTRICAL EQUIPMENT SPACE

Essential for all fountains that employ pumps except simple fountains using submersible pump. When equipment is large, a room with normal head height and ventilation is needed. Equipment rooms may be located in an underground vault or an adjacent building, and should be inconspicuous.

PUMPS AND CONTROLS

1. SUBMERSIBLE PUMP: For a small fountain or pool; available from 1/50 to 1/3 hp.
2. ISOLATED MANUAL PUMP: Used for small or medium pool or fountains; activated by on-off switches.
3. FULLY AUTOMATIC PUMPS: For large pool or fountain; operated by time clock or electrical switches; reduce maintenance costs for large pools or fountain.

Medium to large fountains have a recirculating system and a filtration system. Recirculating system components include (1) pump, (2) piping, (3) electrical and mechanical controls, and (4) display fittings.

Recirculating system is the heart of decorative fountains. Calculate total flow rate and pressure requirement to select pump.

Filtration system removes sediment, leaves, papers. Heating and chemical systems, if used, are incorporated into the filtration system.

UNDERWATER LIGHTS

1. Use corrosion resistant materials (brass, bronze, stainless steel, or monel) and ground fault circuit interruptors to prevent shocks.
2. Economical lamp types are 2000-hr PAR incandescent, 4000-hr tungsten-halogen, and, 8000-hr locomotive or traffic signal incandescent.

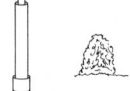

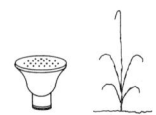

HALF SHEET / FULL SHEET

	AERATED	MORNING GLORY		BUBBLER	GEYSER	WATER CASTLE	JET CLUSTER	SPRAY RING	
A.	4'–5'	2'–2.5' FULL	3'–4' HALF	18''	9'–12'	5'–10'	14'	10'	A.
B.	1'–4'	5'–6'	8'–9'	15''	16''–2'	4'–6'	3'	2'–12'	B.
C.	8''–30'	9'–12'	14'–16'	15'	18'–24'	10'–20'	28'	20'–32'	C.
D.	16''	16''	16''	16''	16''–18''	16''	16''	16''	D.

NOTE: **A.** HEIGHT OF JETS; **B.** TOTAL WATER PATTERN DIAMETER; **C.** RECOMMENDED POOL SIZE; **D.** WATER DEPTH

TYPES OF JETS

Wajeda J. Rab, RLA; Maryland National Capital Park and Planning Commission; Silver Spring, Maryland

SITE IMPROVEMENTS

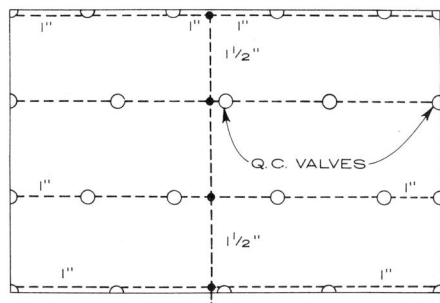

QUICK-COUPLING SYSTEM

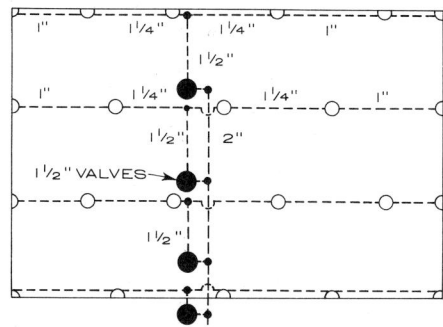

ROTARY POP-UP SYSTEM

TYPICAL LAYOUTS—AREA 1.15 ACRES

DESIGN FACTORS

a. Size of the supply line; b. length of supply line; c. available water pressure. These factors will govern the type of system, type of heads and pipe size to be used.

TYPES OF SYSTEMS

Uses	SPRAY SYSTEM	ROTARY POP-UP	IMPACT SYSTEM
Uses	Residential, light commercial	Commercial, recreational	Commercial, agricultural
Affects of wind/evaporation	Low	Moderate	High
Pressure (psi)	15–30	30–100	25–100
Maximum operating radius (ft) 360°	30	97	117
180°	15	97	77
90°	12	97	77
Head spacing (ft)	10–24	30–100	70–100

TYPES OF PIPE

Polyvinyl chloride or polyethylene piping is commonly used, since it is easily cut and joined together. Steel and copper pipe is also used. Standard pipe is produced in $1/2$ to 12 in. diameters and 20 or 40 ft lengths. Pipe sleeves should be preset under walks and through walls for future extension of the system.

TYPES OF CONTROL

QUICK COUPLER: This system is normally under pressure, and key is inserted where water is needed.
MANUAL: This system is turned on by use of a valve; all heads are in place.

AUTOMATIC: This system is operated from a central control unit. The valves are placed at remote locations with lines from the valves to the control unit. The control lines are buried with the pipe.

PRECIPITATION RATES

The amount of precipitation applied to lawn areas must be adjusted according to the species of grass, the traffic it receives, the subsoil conditions, and the gradient across its surface. Typical precipitation rates range from $1/10$ in./hr for heavy, dense soils to $3/4$ in./hr for light, sandy soils. Final calculations for lawn sprinkler system designs should be entrusted to expert consultants.

John Barclay; Seibert, Hunter, Shute & Plumley; Medford, Oregon

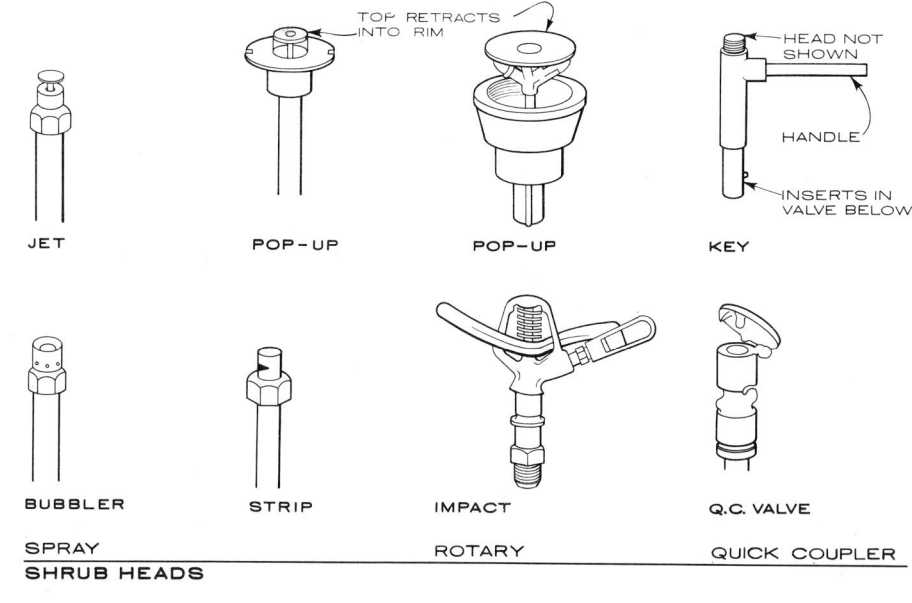

SHRUB HEADS

STANDARD SPRAY HEADS
(OVERTHROW NOT PERMITTED IN SOME AREAS)   OPTIONAL HEADS AVAILABLE

TYPICAL LAYOUT—RESIDENTIAL

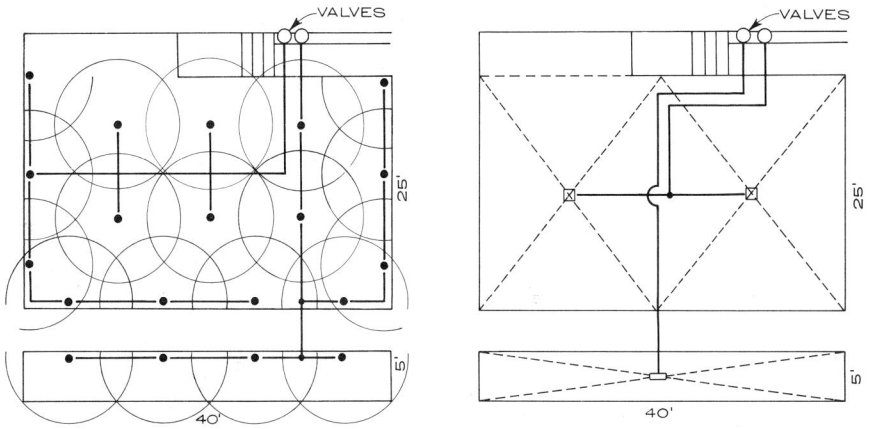

PRECIPITATION PATTERNS

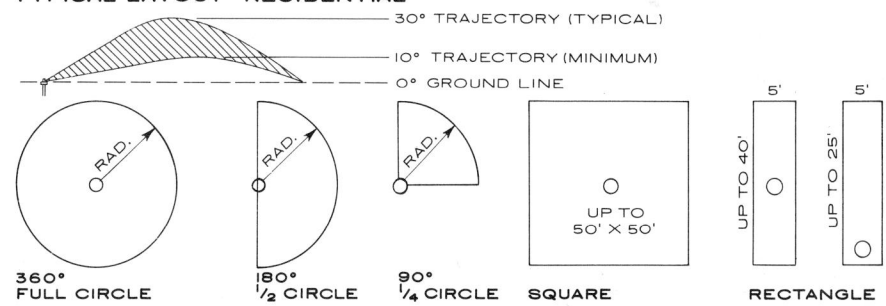

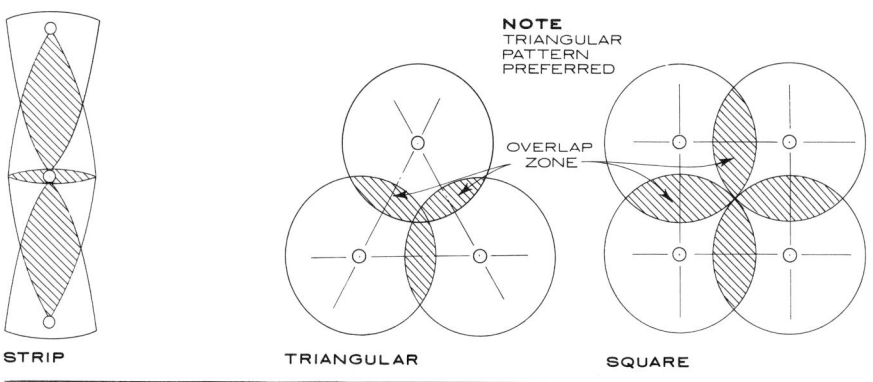

PRECIPITATION COVERAGE

PLAY ELEMENTS

Several basic activities constitute the activity play and concurrently several basic elements can be combined to create a play environment. The physical activities of jumping, climbing, swinging, sliding, crawling, hanging, running, building are essential to play and must be provided by a play area. The social and intellectual aspect of play must also be accommodated; imitation, role playing, interaction with others, and problem solving are essential to a child's growth. A playground must challenge children to maintain their interest and participation. The play equipment should allow the child to challenge himself or herself physically and to expand self-understanding.

GROWTH AND DEVELOPMENT

As children grow their physical abilities change, as does the scale of equipment that will challenge them. Physical growth is accommodated by social development resulting in different levels and types of interaction and activity. A child's play experience must be successful as well as challenging. Therefore play equipment should be designed and selected to meet the physical and intellectual requirements of groups that will use it. The height, distance between levels, and the ability and strength required to use the equipment should be scaled to the size and level of social and intellectual development of the child.

EQUIPMENT COMPONENTS

Several basic elements may be used to create play equipment. These elements are seen in the wide range of manufactured products available. The most commonly used and easily manipulated components are round, square, and rectangular timber, steel pipe and sheets, tires, drums, ladders, and landform, as illustrated below. The greater the variety of combinations to which these components are applied, the more options for play are available to the user.

SINGLE UNIT VS. INTEGRATED PLAY EQUIPMENT

Many types of play equipment are designed to stand alone as units. While they may often be linked to other equipment, they are generally single activity items. Where space or other conditions limit the scope of development such equipment is useful. However, since activity proceeds in a continuous flow, integrated play areas have proved to be more successful than arrangements of individual items. Linking of equipment and equipment that combines several activities on one structure increase the options available to the user and tend to increase the interest and challenge.

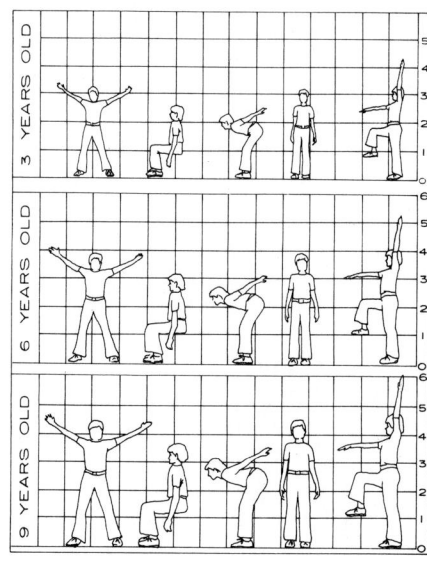

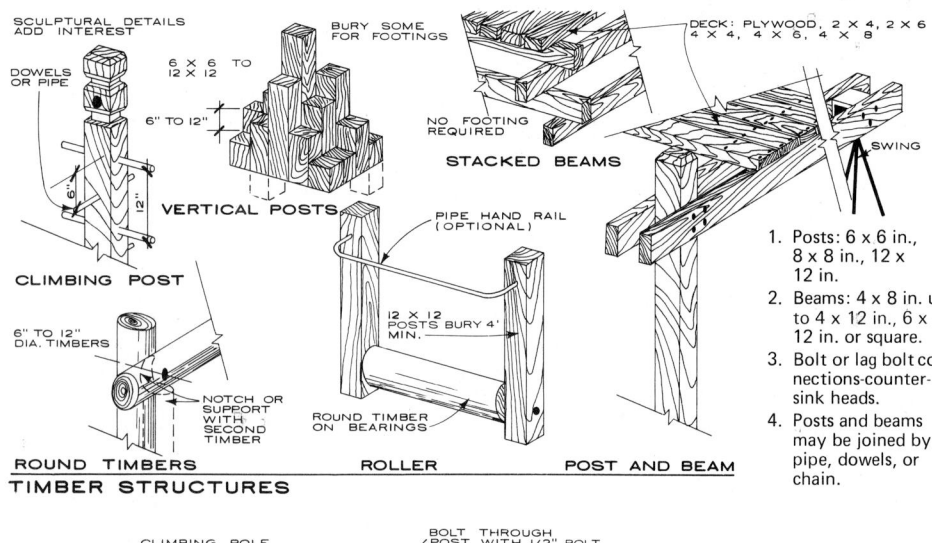

TIMBER STRUCTURES

1. Posts: 6 x 6 in., 8 x 8 in., 12 x 12 in.
2. Beams: 4 x 8 in. up to 4 x 12 in., 6 x 12 in. or square.
3. Bolt or lag bolt connections-countersink heads.
4. Posts and beams may be joined by pipe, dowels, or chain.

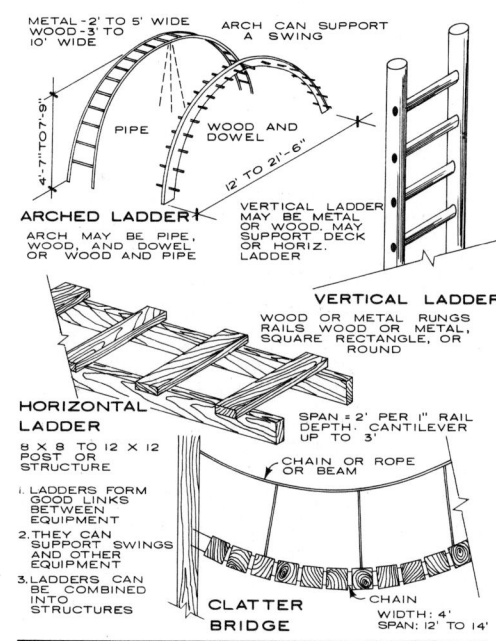

LADDERS

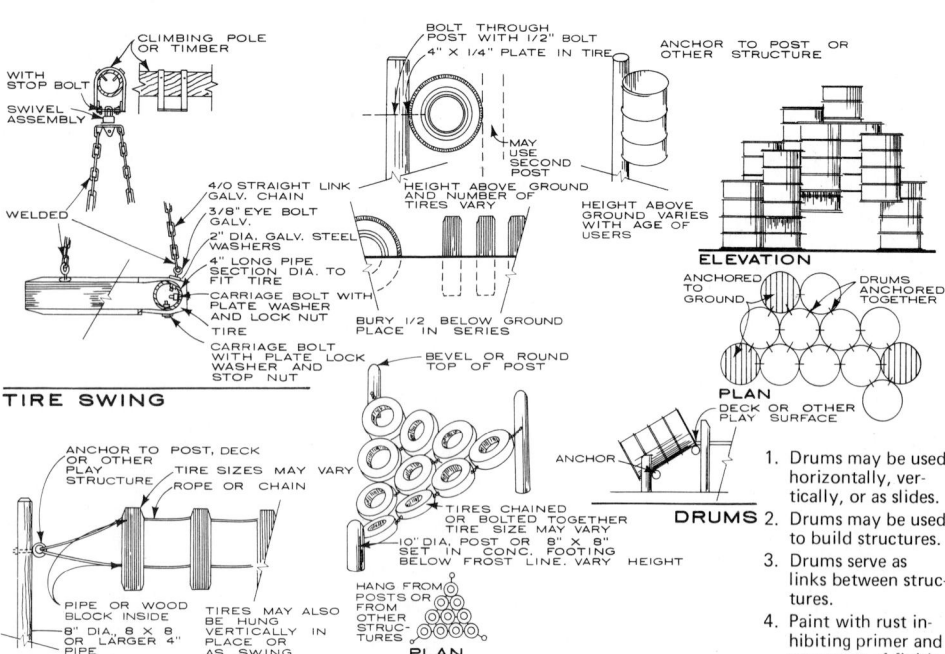

TIRE SWING

TIRE SYSTEMS

TIRE CLIMBER

DRUMS

1. Drums may be used horizontally, vertically, or as slides.
2. Drums may be used to build structures.
3. Drums serve as links between structures.
4. Paint with rust inhibiting primer and two coats of finish color.

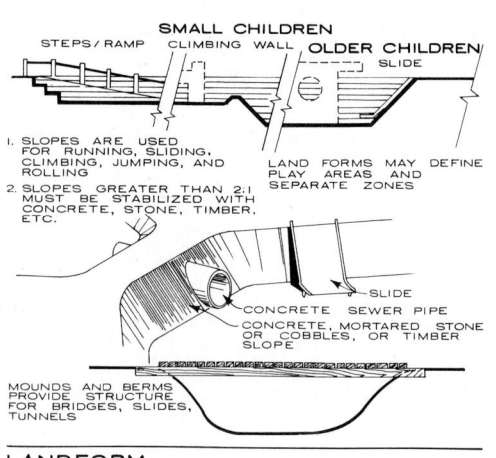

LANDFORM

Bruce A. Rankin; Beckett, Raeder, Rankin, Inc.; Ann Arbor, Michigan

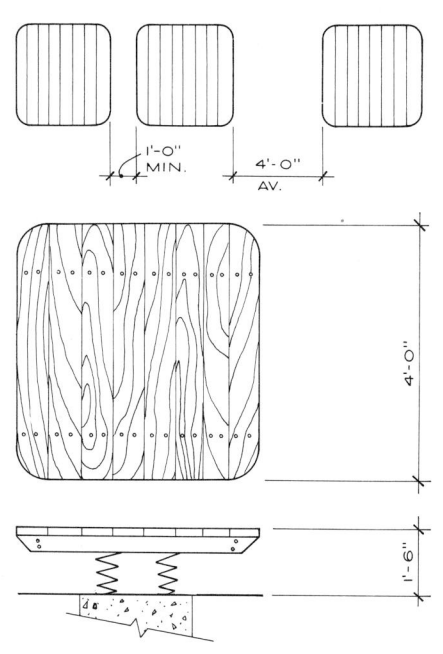

1'-0" MIN.   4'-0" AV.

4'-0"

1'-6"

SPRING PAD

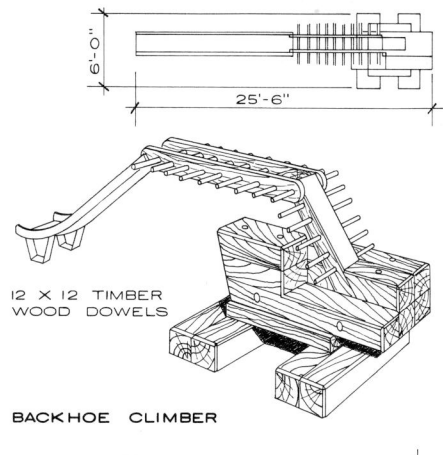

6'-0"   25'-6"

12 X 12 TIMBER
WOOD DOWELS

BACKHOE CLIMBER

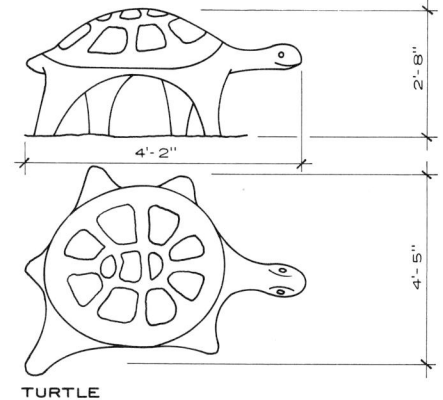

4'-2"

2'-8"

4'-5"

TURTLE

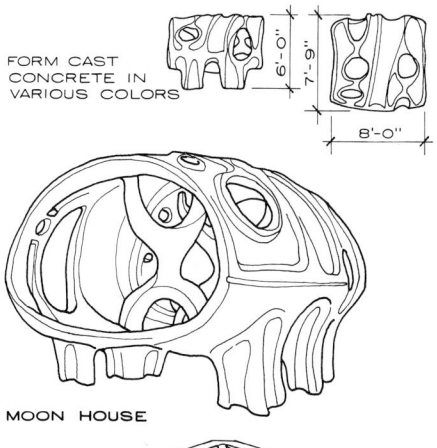

FORM CAST
CONCRETE IN
VARIOUS COLORS

6'-0"   7'-9"

8'-0"

MOON HOUSE

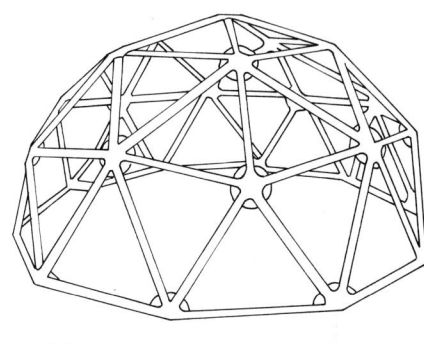

DIA.: 8'-17'; HEIGHT: 4'-7';
GALVANIZED 1⁵⁄₁₆" O.D. PIPE

DOME CLIMBER

NOTE

SINGLE UNIT PLAY EQUIPMENT: Generally designed to provide one or two activities in a specific, controlled location. Where integrated systems are not possible, single units can be used, especially if they are located so that a sequence or sequences of activities can be followed by the users.

SINGLE UNIT PLAY EQUIPMENT

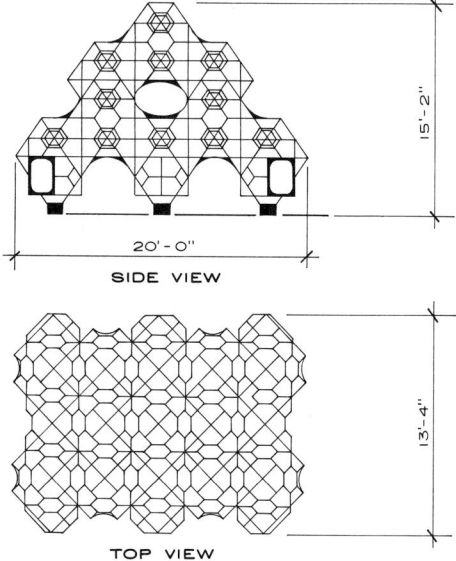

15'-2"

20'-0"

SIDE VIEW

13'-4"

TOP VIEW

³⁄₁₆" CLEAR LEXAN
CURVED SPACE SYSTEM

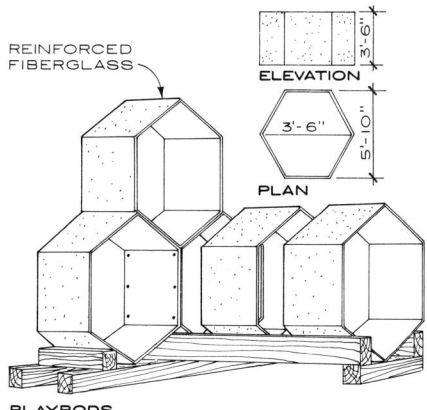

REINFORCED
FIBERGLASS

3'-6"

ELEVATION

3'-6"

5'-10"

PLAN

PLAYPODS

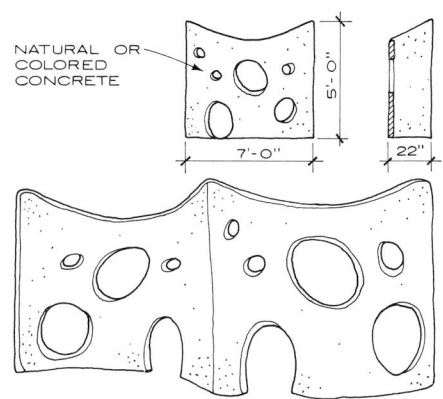

NATURAL OR
COLORED
CONCRETE

5'-0"

7'-0"   22"

PLAYWALL

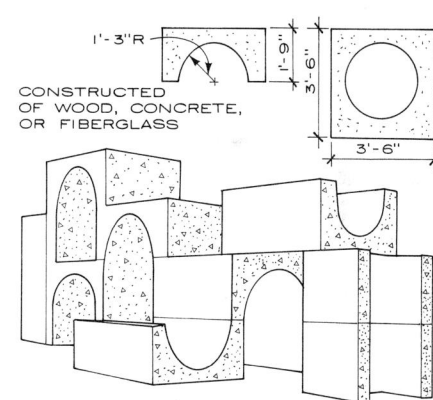

1'-3"R   1'-9"

3'-6"

CONSTRUCTED
OF WOOD, CONCRETE,
OR FIBERGLASS

3'-6"

PRECAST BLOCKS

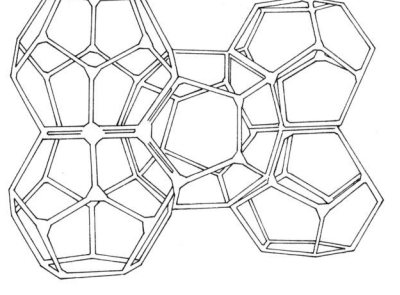

5'-6" DODECAHEDRON UNITS;
ENAMELED 1⁵⁄₈" O.D. STEEL PIPE

PLAY CLIMBERS

NOTE

MODULAR PLAY UNITS: Basic building blocks for a variety of structures through either combinations or juxtapositions. Such units can stand alone or be integrated into a system. They offer the designer considerable latitude in structuring a play area.

MODULAR UNIT PLAY EQUIPMENT

Bruce A. Rankin, Beckett Raeder & Rankin, Inc. Ann Arbor, Michigan
Robin Roberts; Washington, D.C.

INTEGRATED PLAY AREAS

Integrated play areas may be comprised of several types and sizes of elements. The goal of integrating equipment is to establish connections between activities and activity zones so that a continuous flow is maintained. The child may create his or her own sequence of events within a wide variety of options.

Structures that combine several activities stimulate and challenge the user by allowing imagination and interplay with others to determine how the piece of equipment is used. Combining materials on a structure creates further variety and interest.

Play areas should be treated as three-dimensional systems allowing movement of various kinds (swinging, climbing, sliding, etc.) vertically, horizontally, and diagonally at varying levels. They should be flexible and adaptable to the changes in individual growth.

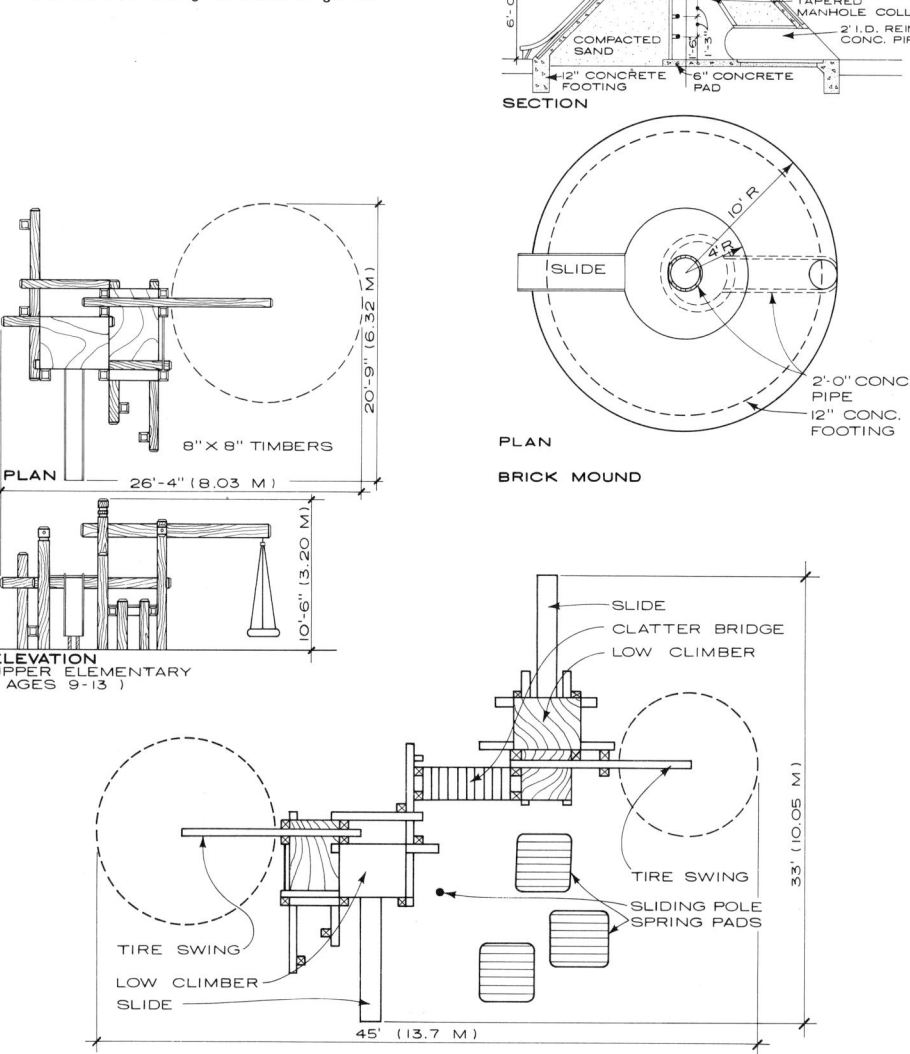

SECTION

PLAN

BRICK MOUND

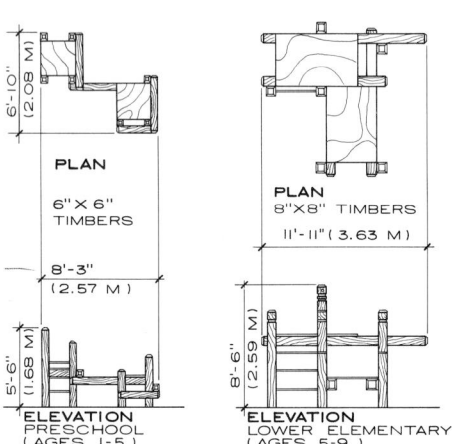

PLAN
6" X 6" TIMBERS

ELEVATION
PRESCHOOL
(AGES 1-5)

PLAN
8"X8" TIMBERS
11'-11" (3.63 M)

ELEVATION
LOWER ELEMENTARY
(AGES 5-9)

8" X 8" TIMBERS
26'-4" (8.03 M)

PLAN

ELEVATION
UPPER ELEMENTARY
(AGES 9-13)

NOTES

Two methods of expanding the capabilities of an integrated playground are linking and juxtapositioning.

1. LINKING OF EQUIPMENT: Connecting activity centers with links that are in themselves play structures, thus multiplying the possible uses of all of the structures involved.
2. JUXTAPOSITIONING EQUIPMENT: Placing units close enough together to generate interaction from one to the other; also increases the play potential and interest of the area.

SLIDE
CLATTER BRIDGE
LOW CLIMBER

TIRE SWING

SLIDING POLE
SPRING PADS

TIRE SWING
LOW CLIMBER
SLIDE

45' (13.7 M)

INTEGRATED PLAY AREA

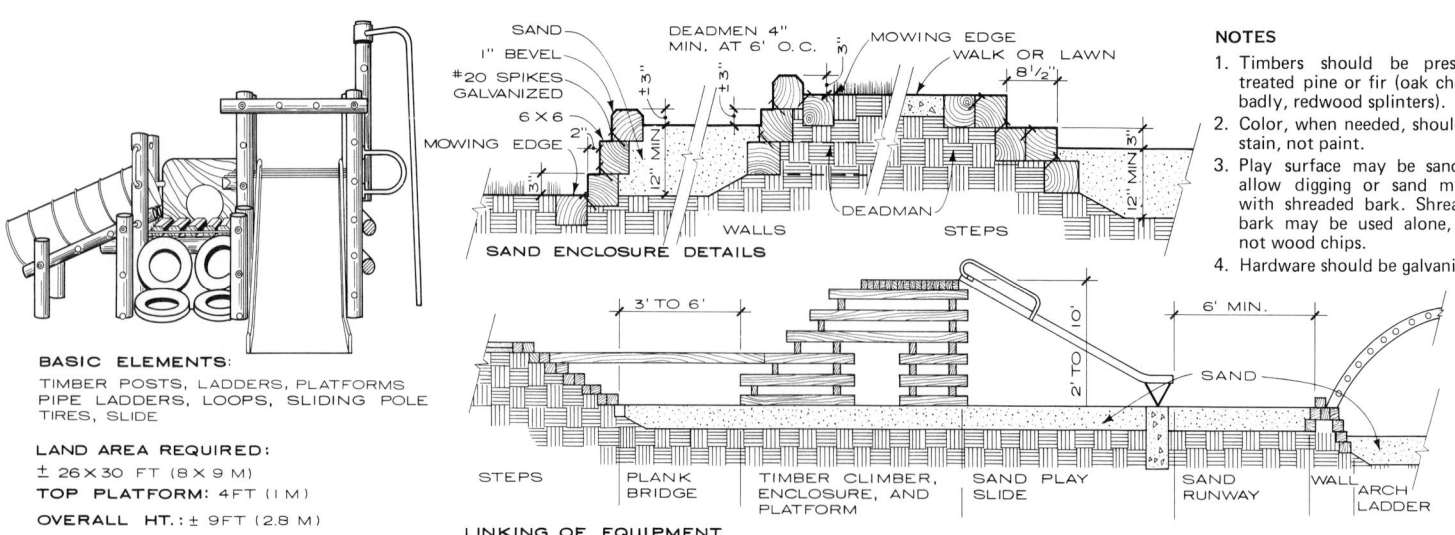

BASIC ELEMENTS:
TIMBER POSTS, LADDERS, PLATFORMS
PIPE LADDERS, LOOPS, SLIDING POLE
TIRES, SLIDE

LAND AREA REQUIRED:
± 26 X 30 FT (8 X 9 M)
TOP PLATFORM: 4FT (1 M)
OVERALL HT.: ± 9FT (2.8 M)

SAND ENCLOSURE DETAILS

LINKING OF EQUIPMENT

STEPS | PLANK BRIDGE | TIMBER CLIMBER, ENCLOSURE, AND PLATFORM | SAND PLAY SLIDE | SAND RUNWAY | WALL ARCH LADDER

NOTES

1. Timbers should be pressure treated pine or fir (oak checks badly, redwood splinters).
2. Color, when needed, should be stain, not paint.
3. Play surface may be sand to allow digging or sand mixed with shreaded bark. Shreaded bark may be used alone, but not wood chips.
4. Hardware should be galvanized.

Bruce A. Rankin; Beckett, Raeder, Rankin, Inc.; Ann Arbor, Michigan

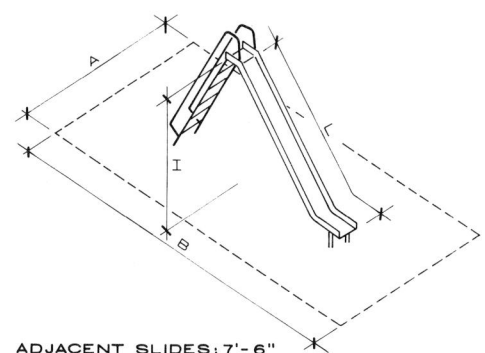

ADJACENT SLIDES: 7'-6"
(CHUTES C.TO C.) OTHERS 10' O.C.

SLIDES

H	L	NURSERY A	NURSERY B	STRAIGHT A	STRAIGHT B	RACER A	RACER B
5	10	8	20				
6	12	8	22				
7	14	8	24				
8	16			12	30	20	30
10	20			12	35	20	35
12	24			15	40	25	40
13½	30			15	45	25	45

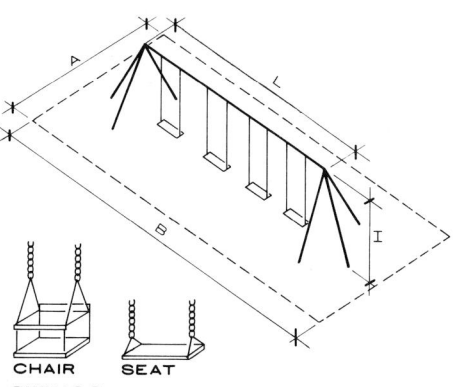

CHAIR   SEAT

SWINGS

NO SWINGS	CHAIR TYPE L	CHAIR TYPE A	CHAIR TYPE B	SEAT TYPE L	SEAT TYPE A	SEAT TYPE B	SEAT TYPE A	SEAT TYPE B	SEAT TYPE A	SEAT TYPE B
2	8	17	24	9	17	25	21	25	25	25
3	10	17	26	15	17	31	21	31	25	31
4	16	17	32	18	17	34	21	34	25	34
6	20,24	17	38	27,30	17	46	21	46	25	46
8				36	17	52	21	52	25	52
9				45	17	61	21	61	25	61
Height	8'			8',10',12'	8'		10'		12'	

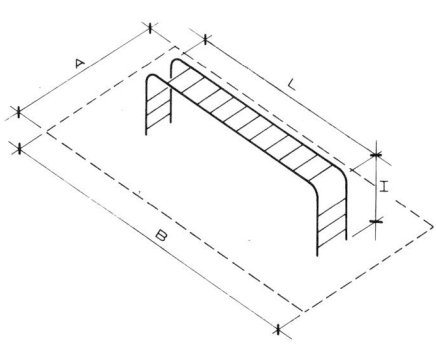

HORIZONTAL LADDER

HEIGHT	LENGTH	A	B
6	12	8	25
7½	16	8	30

GENERAL PLANNING INFORMATION

EQUIPMENT	AREA (SQ FT)	CAPACITY (NUMBER OF CHILDREN)
Slide	450	4-6
Low swing	150	1
High swing	250	1
Horizontal ladder	375	6-8
Seesaw	100	2
Junior climbing gym	180	8-10
General climbing gym	500	15-20

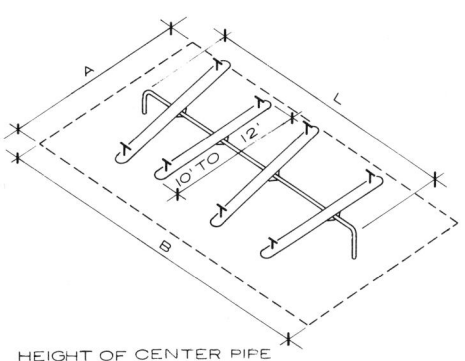

HEIGHT OF CENTER PIPE
1'-0" TO 3'-0" ABOVE GROUND

SEESAWS

BOARDS	1	2	3	4	6
L	3	6	9	12	18
A	20	20	20	20	20
B	5	10	15	20	25

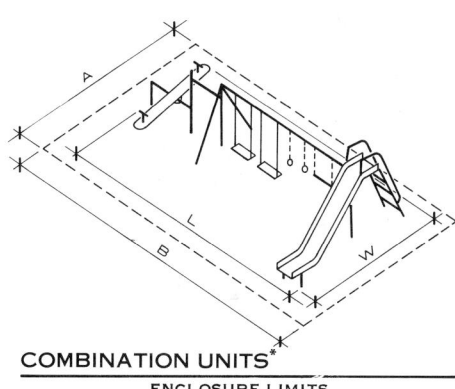

COMBINATION UNITS*

ENCLOSURE LIMITS
A = W + 12'-0"
B = L + 6'-0"

*Types and no. of units are variable.

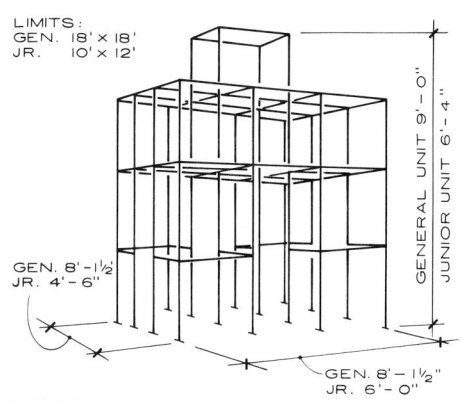

LIMITS:
GEN. 18' × 18'
JR. 10' × 12'

GENERAL UNIT 9'-0"
JUNIOR UNIT 6'-4"

GEN. 8'-1½"
JR. 4'-6"

GEN. 8'-1½"
JR. 6'-0"

N.Y.C. HOUSING AUTH. STANDARD
CLIMBING GYM

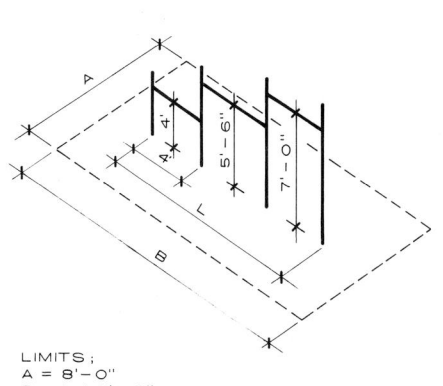

LIMITS;
A = 8'-0"
B = L + 6'-0"
HORIZONTAL BARS

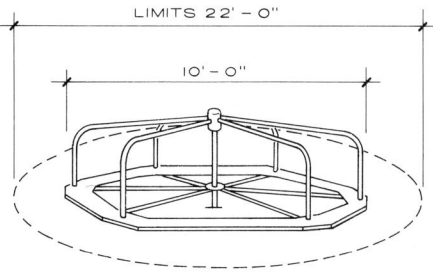

LIMITS 22'-0"
10'-0"

10 FT. DIAMETER IS CONSIDERED STAND-
ARD. OTHER DIAMETERS = 12',14' & 16'
LIMITS 24', 26' & 28' DIA.
MERRY - GO - ROUND

Vincent F. Nauseda; Sasaki, Dawson Associates, Inc.; Watertown, Massachusetts

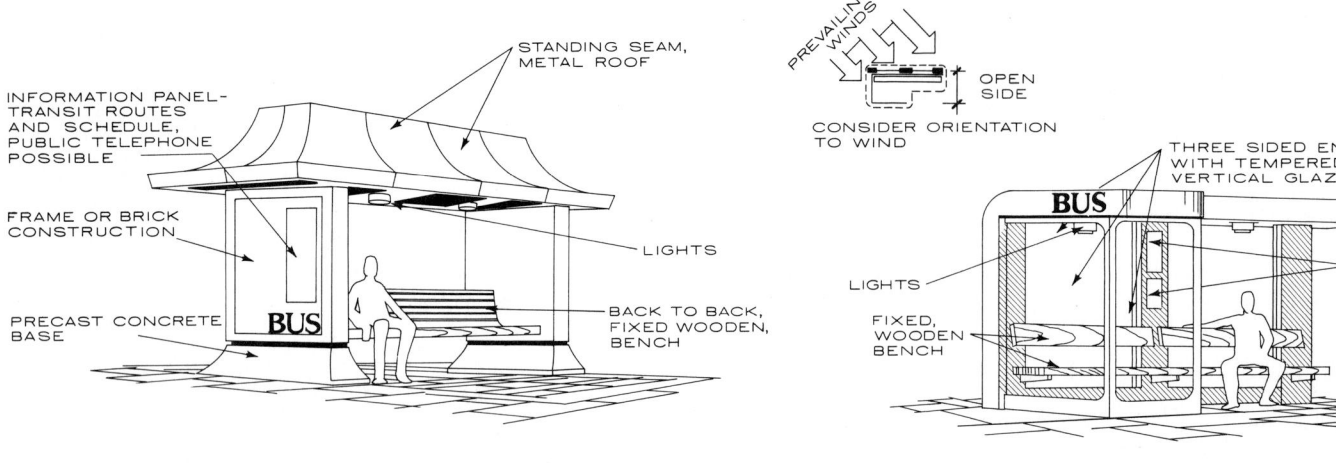

COMMUNITY TRANSIT SHELTER
MILD CLIMATE, OPEN ON TWO SIDES

URBAN TRANSIT SHELTER
COLD CLIMATE, OPEN VISUALLY ON
ALL SIDES FOR EASY SURVEILLANCE

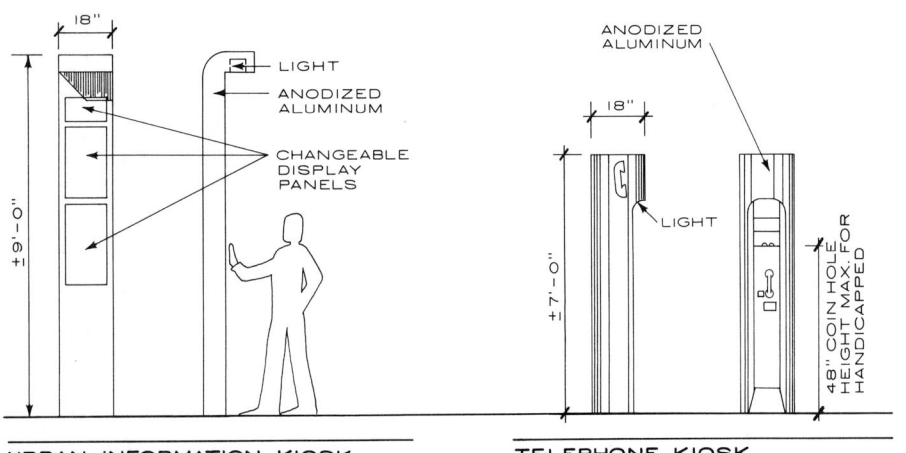

URBAN INFORMATION KIOSK

TELEPHONE KIOSK

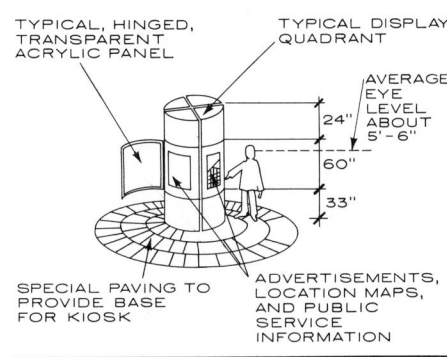

URBAN AREA KIOSK

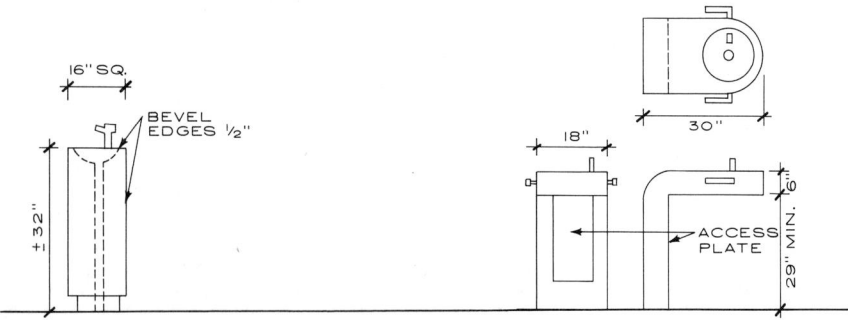

**CONCRETE
DRINKING FOUNTAIN**

**METAL DRINKING FOUNTAIN,
ACCOMMODATES USERS IN
WHEELCHAIRS**

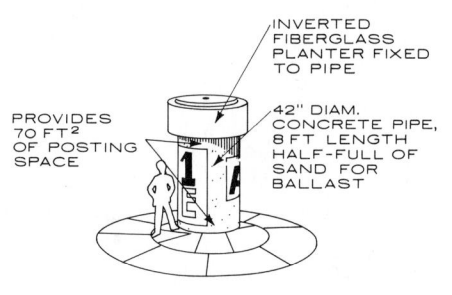

CAMPUS KIOSK

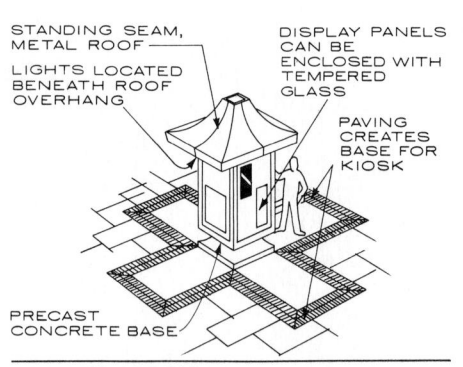

VILLAGE KIOSK

SITE DETAILS

The process of designing and detailing has changed significantly over the last decade with the increased availability of well-designed, cataloged site furnishings. The need for custom designed site furnishings, however, is still felt on many urban design projects. Because of this dual option, the designer is forced to choose the alternative that best serves the project's design objectives. In some cases, both cataloged and custom designed site furnishings are used, defining still a third option.

Among the many considerations in making site detailing decisions are the existing site furnishings in the development area, local codes, the availability of cataloged site furnishings, local maintenance concerns, and cost. Each area of site furnishing detailing emphasizes certain unique considerations. Such considerations involve user habits and needs, maintenance, safety, aesthetics, and construction feasibility. The emphasis of relevant considerations is noted on the above details.

Johnson, Johnson & Roy; Ann Arbor, Michigan

 SITE FURNISHINGS

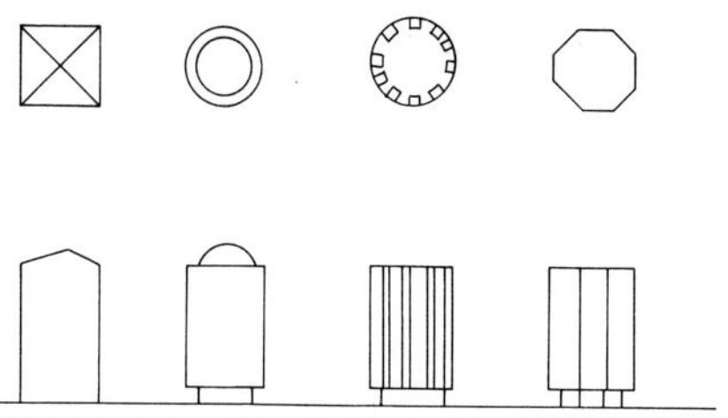

VARIETY OF BOLLARD DESIGN MOTIFS

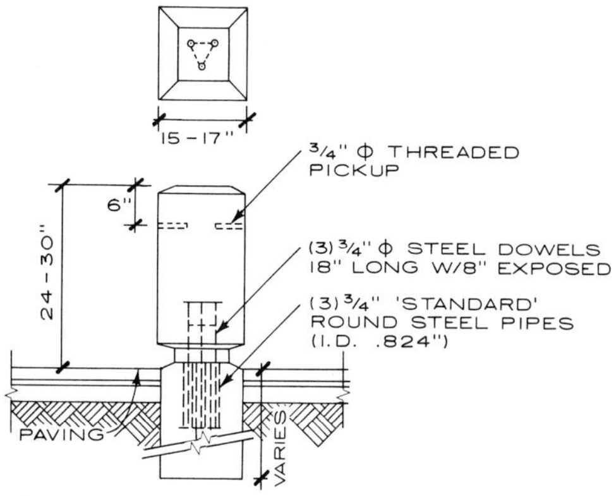

15 - 17"

6"

24 - 30"

3/4" Φ THREADED PICKUP

(3) 3/4" Φ STEEL DOWELS 18" LONG W/8" EXPOSED

(3) 3/4" 'STANDARD' ROUND STEEL PIPES (I.D. .824")

PAVING

VARIES

REMOVABLE BOLLARD

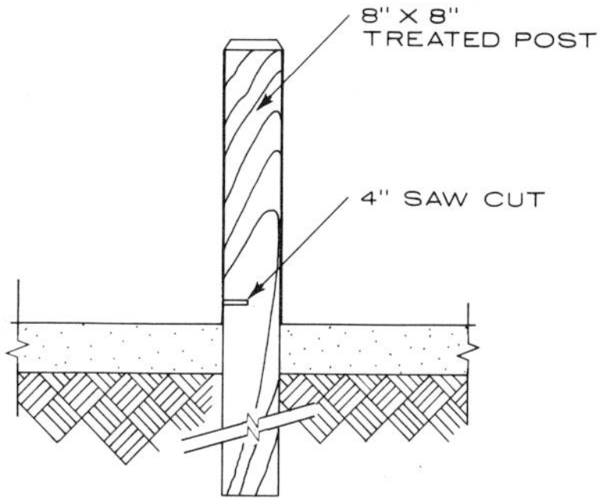

8" X 8" TREATED POST

4" SAW CUT

BREAKAWAY BOLLARD

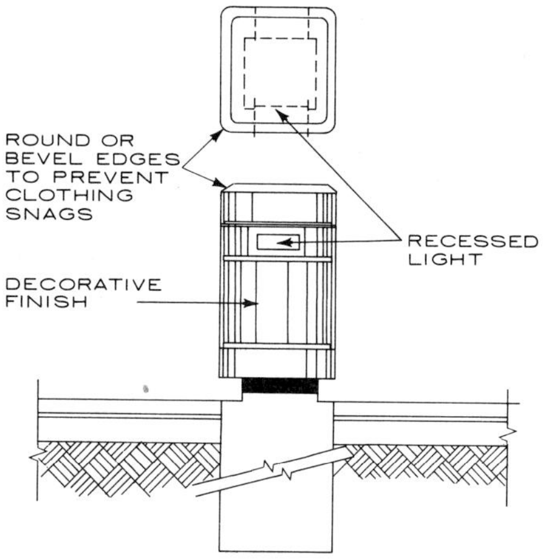

ROUND OR BEVEL EDGES TO PREVENT CLOTHING SNAGS

RECESSED LIGHT

DECORATIVE FINISH

RECESSED LIGHT IN BOLLARD

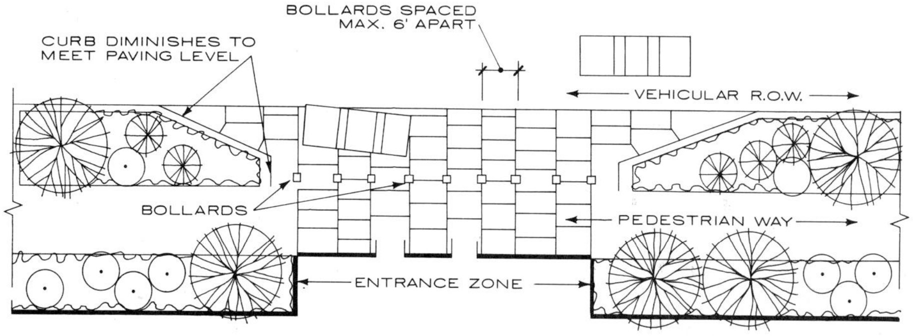

CURB DIMINISHES TO MEET PAVING LEVEL

BOLLARDS SPACED MAX. 6' APART

VEHICULAR R.O.W.

BOLLARDS

PEDESTRIAN WAY

ENTRANCE ZONE

BOLLARD LOCATIONS

MOLDED FIBERGLASS   DOUBLE BACK   CONTOURED WOOD

STONE OR MASONRY   WALL MOUNTED   WOOD WITH CONCRETE BASE

VARIETY OF BENCH DESIGN MOTIFS

NOTE
BENCHES SHOULD BE LOCATED SO AS NOT TO CONFLICT WITH MAJOR PEDESTRIAN FLOW

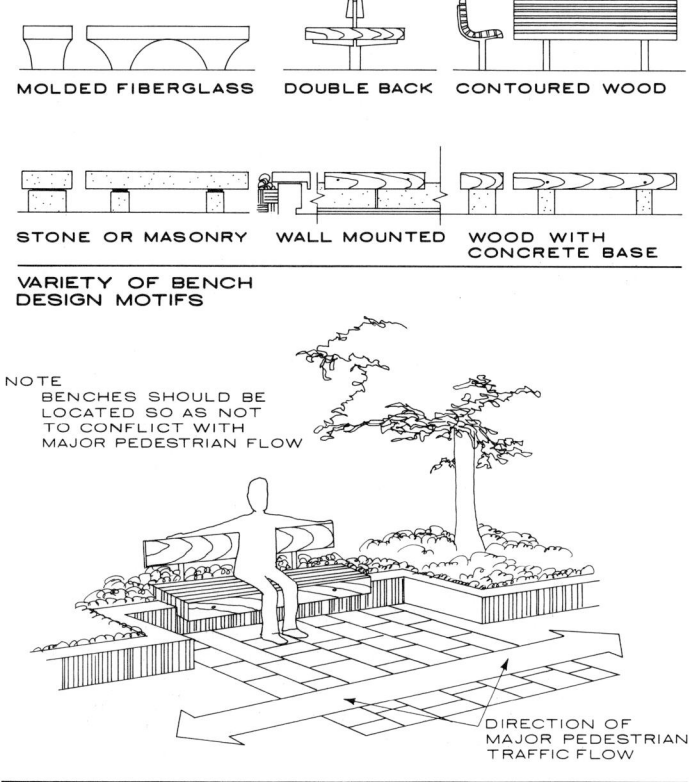

DIRECTION OF MAJOR PEDESTRIAN TRAFFIC FLOW

BENCH LOCATION

Johnson, Johnson & Roy; Ann Arbor, Michigan

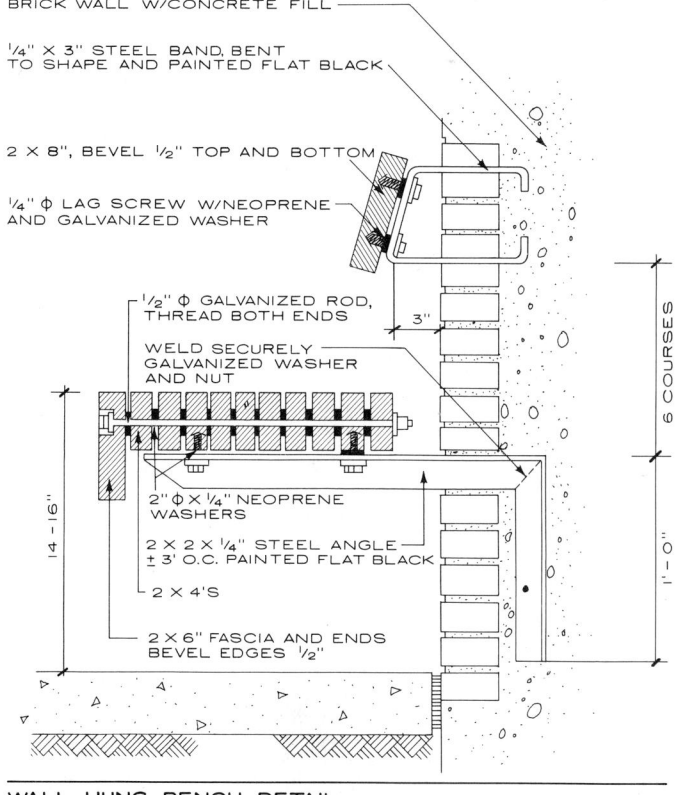

BRICK WALL W/CONCRETE FILL

1/4" X 3" STEEL BAND, BENT TO SHAPE AND PAINTED FLAT BLACK

2 X 8", BEVEL 1/2" TOP AND BOTTOM

1/4" Φ LAG SCREW W/NEOPRENE AND GALVANIZED WASHER

1/2" Φ GALVANIZED ROD, THREAD BOTH ENDS

WELD SECURELY GALVANIZED WASHER AND NUT

3"

6 COURSES

1' - 0"

14 - 16"

2" Φ X 1/4" NEOPRENE WASHERS

2 X 2 X 1/4" STEEL ANGLE ± 3' O.C. PAINTED FLAT BLACK

2 X 4'S

2 X 6" FASCIA AND ENDS BEVEL EDGES 1/2"

WALL HUNG BENCH DETAIL

SITE FURNISHINGS 2

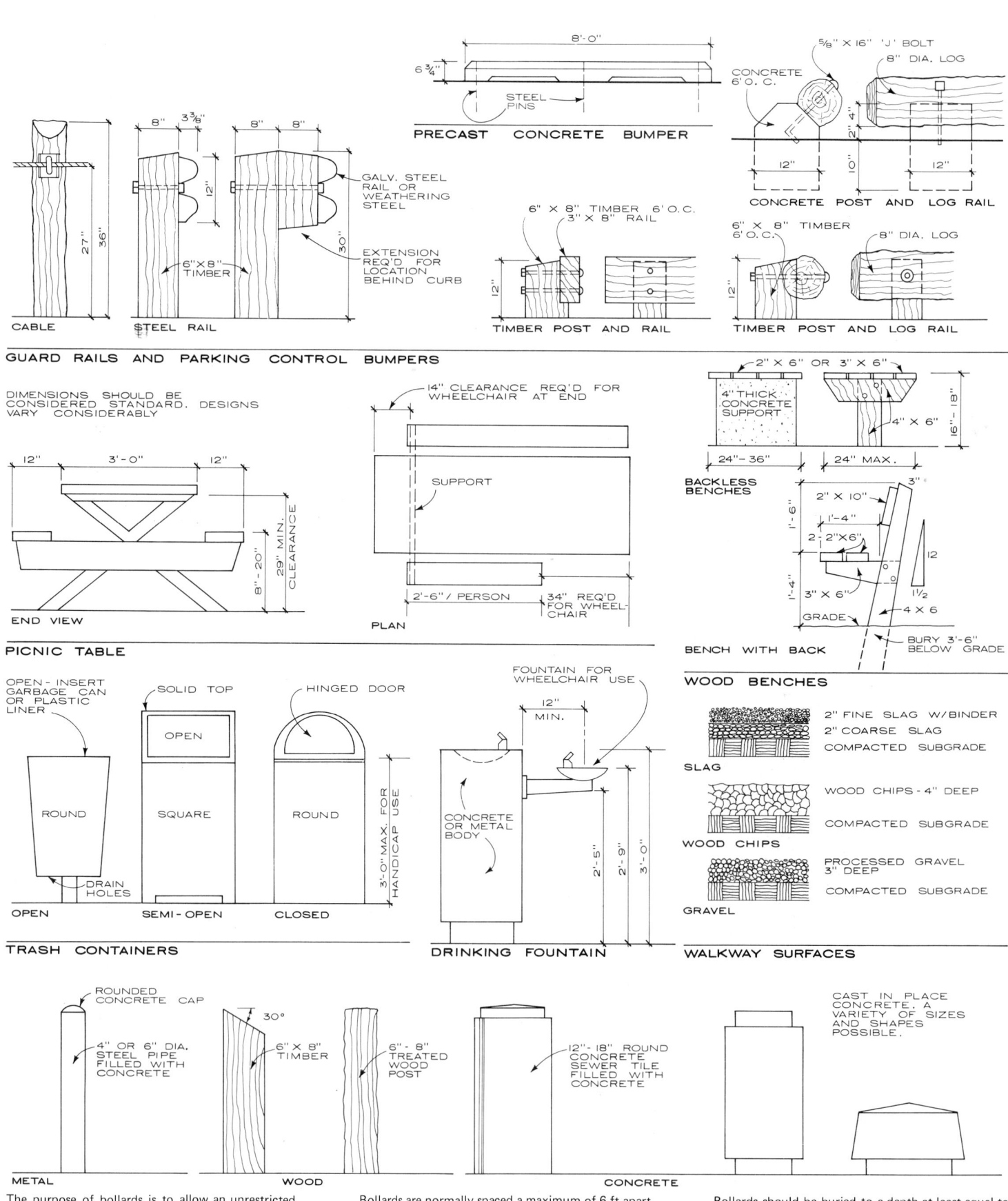

GUARD RAILS AND PARKING CONTROL BUMPERS

PRECAST CONCRETE BUMPER

CONCRETE POST AND LOG RAIL

CABLE

STEEL RAIL

TIMBER POST AND RAIL

TIMBER POST AND LOG RAIL

PICNIC TABLE

DIMENSIONS SHOULD BE CONSIDERED STANDARD. DESIGNS VARY CONSIDERABLY

END VIEW

PLAN

WOOD BENCHES

BACKLESS BENCHES

BENCH WITH BACK

TRASH CONTAINERS

OPEN

SEMI-OPEN

CLOSED

DRINKING FOUNTAIN

WALKWAY SURFACES

SLAG
2" FINE SLAG W/BINDER
2" COARSE SLAG
COMPACTED SUBGRADE

WOOD CHIPS
WOOD CHIPS - 4" DEEP
COMPACTED SUBGRADE

GRAVEL
PROCESSED GRAVEL 3" DEEP
COMPACTED SUBGRADE

METAL

WOOD

CONCRETE

The purpose of bollards is to allow an unrestricted, barrier free flow of pedestrian, bicycle, and wheelchair traffic, while restricting the passage of such vehicles as cars and trucks.

Bollards are normally spaced a maximum of 6 ft apart to restrict vehicles. Spacings of less than 6 ft should be determined in accordance with the height and mass of the unit for desired design effect.

Bollards should be buried to a depth at least equal to the height above ground. Where vehicles may contact the bollard, a concrete footing or encasement should be provided.

BOLLARDS

John M. Beckett; Beckett, Raeder, Rankin, Inc.; Ann Arbor, Michigan

2   SITE FURNISHINGS

NOTES

Several factors should be considered when designing with plants:

1. The physical environment of the site:
   - Soil conditions (acidity, porosity).
   - Available sunlight.
   - Available precipitation.
   - Seasonal temperature range.
   - Exposure of the site (wind).
2. The design needs of the project:
   - Directing movement.
   - Framing vistas.
   - Moderating the environment of the site.
   - Creating space by using plants to develop the base, vertical, and overhead planes.
3. The design character of the plants chosen:
   - Height.
   - Mass.
   - Silhouette (rounded, pyramidal, spreading).
   - Texture (fine, medium, coarse).
   - Color.
   - Seasonal interest (flowers, fruit, fall color).
   - Growth habits (fast or slow growing).

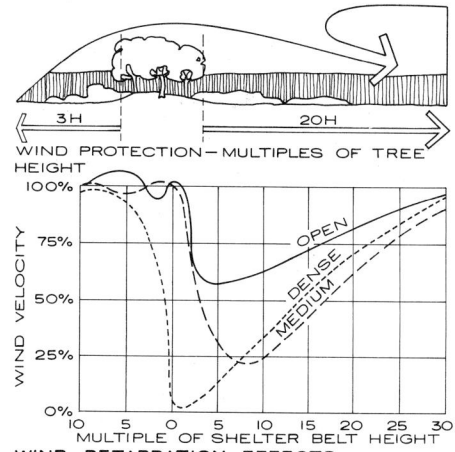

WIND PROTECTION—MULTIPLES OF TREE HEIGHT

WIND RETARDATION EFFECTS:
1. REDUCE EVAPORATION
2. LOWER TEMPERATURE IN SUMMER
3. REDUCE HEAT LOSSES IN WINTER
4. INCREASE RELATIVE HUMIDITY
5. REDUCE DUST AND SNOW BLOWING

DENSITY

The density of a planted wind buffer determines the area that is protected. Height and composition are also factors in wind protection.

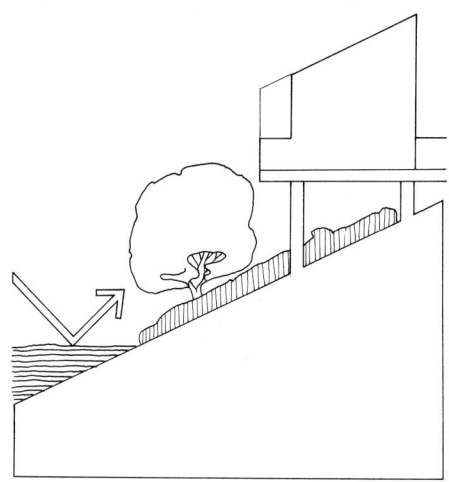

GLARE PROTECTION

The sun's vertical angle changes seasonally; therefore, the area subject to the glare of reflected sunlight varies. Plants of various heights screen glare from adjacent reflective surfaces (water, paving, glass, and building surfaces).

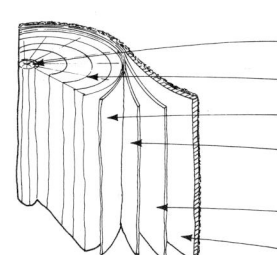

CROWN: THE HEAD OF FOLIAGE OF THE TREE LEAVES — THE FOLIAGE UNIT OF THE TREE THAT FUNCTIONS PRIMARILY IN FOOD MANUFACTURE BY PHOTOSYNTHESIS

HEARTWOOD: THE NONLIVING CENTRAL PART OF THE TREE GIVING STRENGTH AND STABILITY

ANNUAL RINGS: REVEAL AGE OF THE TREE BY SHOWING THE YEARLY GROWTH

SAPWOOD (XYLEM): CARRIES NUTRIENTS AND WATER TO THE LEAVES FROM THE ROOTS

CAMBIUM: LAYER BETWEEN THE XYLEM AND PHLOEM WHERE CELL GROWTH OCCURS, ADDING NEW SAPWOOD TO THE INSIDE AND NEW INNER BARK TO THE OUTSIDE

INNER BARK (PHLOEM): CARRIES FOOD FROM THE LEAVES TO THE BRANCHES, TRUNK, AND ROOTS

OUTER BARK: THE AGED INNER BARK THAT PROTECTS THE TREE FROM DESSICATION AND INJURY

ROOTS: THE ROOTS ANCHOR THE TREE AND HELP HOLD THE SOIL AGAINST EROSION

ROOT HAIRS: THE TINY ROOT HAIRS ABSORB THE MINERALS FROM THE SOIL MOISTURE AND SEND THEM AS NUTRIENT SALTS IN THE SAPWOOD TO THE LEAVES

PHYSICAL CHARACTERISTICS

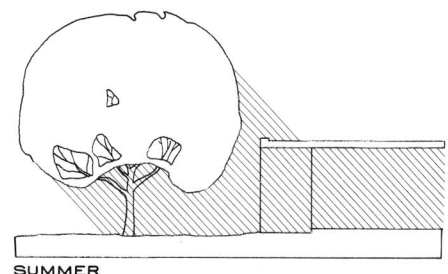

SUMMER

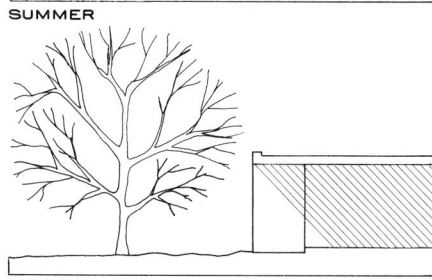

WINTER

RADIATION PROTECTION

In summer deciduous plants obstruct or filter the sun's strong radiation, thus cooling the area beneath them. In winter the sun penetrates through.

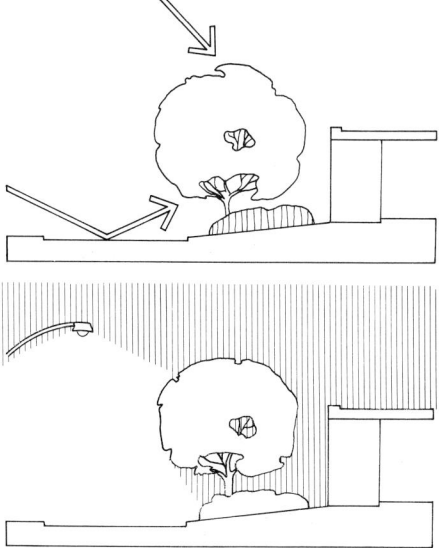

GLARE PROTECTION

Glare and reflection from sunlight and/or artificial sources can be screened or blocked by plants of various height and placement.

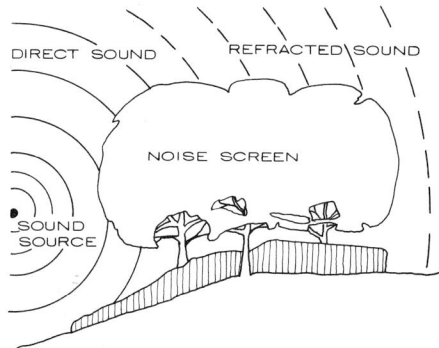

SOUND ATTENUATION

Plantings of deciduous and evergreen materials reduce sound more effectively than deciduous plants alone. Planting on earth mounds increases the attenuating effects of the buffer.

PARTICULATE MATTER TRAPPED ON THE LEAVES IS WASHED TO THE GROUND DURING A RAINFALL. GASEOUS AND OTHER POLLUTANTS ARE ASSIMILATED IN THE LEAVES

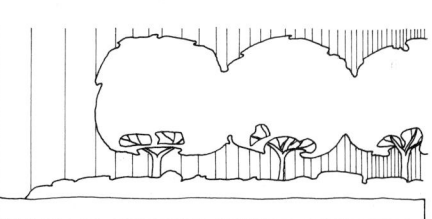

FUMES AND ODORS CAN BE MECHANICALLY MASKED BY FRAGRANT PLANTS AND CHEMICALLY METABOLIZED IN THE PHOTOSYNTHETIC PROCESS

AIR FILTRATION

Large masses of plants physically and chemically filter and deodorize the air to reduce air pollution.

A. E. Bye and Associates, Landscape Architects; Old Greenwich, Connecticut

Robin Roberts; Washington, D.C.

LANDSCAPING 2

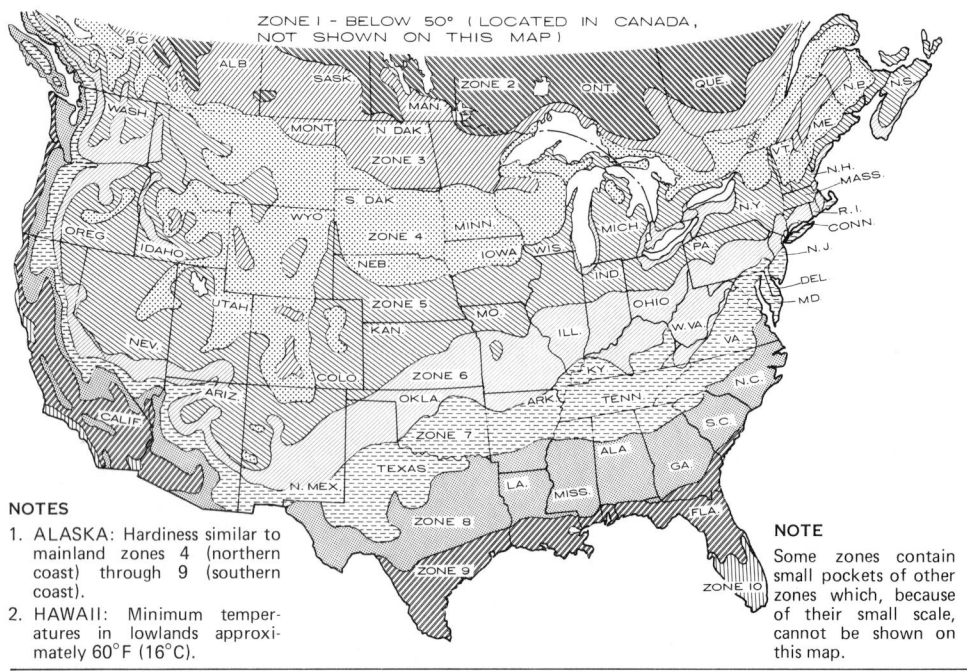

ZONE I – BELOW 50° (LOCATED IN CANADA, NOT SHOWN ON THIS MAP)

NOTE

The zone map shows in moderate detail the expected minimum temperature of most of the horticulturally important areas of the United States. Plants are listed in the coldest zone where they will grow normally, but they can be expected to grow in warmer areas.

APPROXIMATE RANGE OF AVERAGE ANNUAL MINIMUM TEMPERATURES FOR EACH ZONE

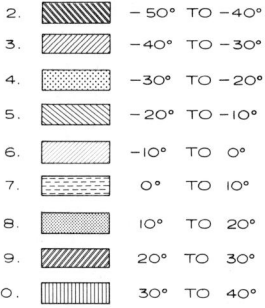

2.	−50° TO −40°
3.	−40° TO −30°
4.	−30° TO −20°
5.	−20° TO −10°
6.	−10° TO 0°
7.	0° TO 10°
8.	10° TO 20°
9.	20° TO 30°
10.	30° TO 40°

NOTES

1. ALASKA: Hardiness similar to mainland zones 4 (northern coast) through 9 (southern coast).
2. HAWAII: Minimum temperatures in lowlands approximately 60°F (16°C).

NOTE

Some zones contain small pockets of other zones which, because of their small scale, cannot be shown on this map.

ZONES OF PLANT HARDINESS
(ADAPTED FROM MAP IN U.S.D.A. PUBLICATION 814)

NEEDLE EVERGREENS—30 FT AND OVER

BOTANICAL NAME	COMMON NAME	Columnar	Conical	Spreading	Slow	Medium	Fast	Urban	Seashore	Ornamental	Windbreak	Green	Light Green	Dark Green	Silver Green	Blue Green	Full Sun	Dry Soil	Moist Soil	Acid	Alkaline	Well Drained	Average	1	2	3	4	5	6	7	8	9	10
Abies concolor	White fir		●			●	●	●		●	●				●	●	●			●								●						
Araucaria excelsa	Norfolk Island pine		●	●				●	●	●				●			●			●														●
Cedrus atlantica glauca	Blue atlas cedar		●	●		●				●	●				●	●		●						●							●			
Cedrus deodara	Deodar cedar		●			●				●	●		●					●						●								●		
Cedrus libani stenocoma	Cedar of Lebanon		●	●		●				●				●				●						●							●			
Chamaecyparis lawsoniana	Lawson false cypress	●	●		●					●	●			●			●		●												●			
Chamaecyparis obtusa	Hinoki false cypress	●	●	●	●					●				●			●		●											●				
Chamaecyparis pisifera	Sawara false cypress	●	●		●				●	●	●						●		●										●					
Cryptomeria japonica	Cryptomeria	●	●		●			●		●				●			●		●	●										●	●			
Cunninghamia lanceolata	Common China fir		●	●						●	●	●					●		●				●								●			
Cupressus sempervirens 'stricta'	Italian pyramidal cypress	●			●					●	●			●			●	●					●								●			
Juniperus chinensis	Chinese juniper		●		●	●	●			●	●	●	●				●		●	●			●						●					
Juniperus scopulorum	Western red cedar	●			●					●	●	●				●	●	●		●	●			●					●					
Juniperus virginiana	Eastern red cedar	●	●		●				●	●	●						●		●	●			●		●									
Larix leptolepis	Japanese larch		●	●		●	●	●		●			●				●		●		●							●						
Libocedrus decurrens	California incense cedar	●	●			●				●	●			●			●		●										●					
Metasequoia glyptostroboides	Dawn redwood		●			●	●			●	●	●					●		●										●					
Picea*	Spruce											●																						
Pinus*	Pine											●																						
Podocarpus macrophyllus	Yew podocarpus	●				●				●	●			●			●															●		
Pseudolarix amabilis	Golden larch		●	●		●				●	●		●				●		●	●									●					
Pseudotsuga menziesii	Douglas fir		●	●		●	●			●	●			●			●		●									●						
Sciadopitys verticulata	Umbrella pine	●	●		●					●	●			●			●		●	●									●					
Sequoiadendron giganteum	Giant sequoia	●			●					●					●	●	●													●				
Taxodium distichum	Bald cypress	●			●				●	●		●					●					●						●						
Taxus Baccata	English yew		●	●	●					●	●			●			●		●	●	●									●				
Taxus Baccata stricta	Irish yew	●			●					●	●			●			●		●	●	●									●				
Thuja occidentalis	American arborvitae	●	●		●				●	●		●					●									●								
Thuja plicata	Giant arborvitae	●	●		●				●	●		●					●											●						
Tsuga canadensis	Canada hemlock		●	●		●	●			●				●			●	●	●	●	●					●								
Tsuga caroliniana	Carolina hemlock		●	●		●			●	●				●			●	●	●	●	●						●						

*See other references for local species and varieties.

A. E. Bye & Associates, Landscape Architects; Old Greenwich, Connecticut

2   LANDSCAPING

BROAD LEAVED EVERGREENS

Botanical Name	Common Name	Under 1 ft	1 to 3 ft	3 to 6 ft	6 to 10 ft	10 ft and over	White	Yellow-orange	Pink-red	Purple-blue	Spring	Summer	Fall	Winter	Partial sun	Full sun	Full shade	Moist soil	Dry soil	Acid soil	Alkaline soil	City	Seashore	Ornamental	Hedge	1	2	3	4	5	6	7	8	9	10
		HEIGHT					**FLOWER COLOR**				**SEASON**				**CULTURAL CONDITIONS**							**USES**				**HARDINESS ZONES**									
Abelia x grandiflora	Glossy abelia			•					•			•			•	•		•				•		•	•						•				
Azalea varieties*	Azalea varieties			•	•		•	•	•		•				•	•		•		•		•		•						•					
Buxus sempervirens	Common box			•											•	•		•		•					•					•					
Calliandra inaequilatera	Pink powder puff			•					•		•					•					•		•											•
Callistemon citrinus	Lemon bottle brush			•	•				•		•	•		•		•			•				•											•	
Calluna vulgaris	Heather		•				•		•	•		•	•			•		•		•				•								•			
Citrus sinensis	Sweet orange				•	•					•	•	•	•	•	•		•		•				•										•	•
Codiaeum variegatum	Croton			•										•	•	•								•	•										
Cotoneaster species*	Cotoneaster species		•	•	•		•				•	•				•							•	•					•	•	•	•			
Daphne cneorum	Rose daphne	•							•		•	•			•	•		•		•	•			•						•					
Elaeagnus pungens	Thorny elaeagnus				•	•	•					•						•	•	•	•	•		•								•			
Enkianthus campanulatus	Redvein enkianthus				•	•			•		•				•	•		•		•				•						•					
Erica carnea	Spring heather		•				•		•		•					•		•		•				•							•				
Eriobotrya japonica	Loquat				•	•							•	•		•			•		•				•								•		
Euonymus japonica	Evergreen euonymus				•							•	•		•		•	•						•									•		
Euphorbia pulcherrima	Poinsetta			•	•					•					•	•		•		•				•											•
Fatsia japonica	Japanese fatsia				•	•							•				•					•	•		•								•		
Ficus benjamina	Weeping fig				•							•				•								•											•
Gardenia jasminoides	Gardenia			•			•				•	•	•		•	•		•		•				•								•		
Gaultheria shallon	Salal			•			•		•		•				•	•	•	•	•	•				•							•			
Hebe traversii	Traverse hebe			•			•				•					•	•						•	•								•			
Hibiscus rosa-sinensis	Chinese hibiscus				•			•	•		•					•		•					•	•										•	
Hypericum species*	Saint-John's-wort species	•						•			•	•				•	•						•								•			
Ilex (evergreen species)**	Holly (evergreen species)		•	•	•	•									•	•		•		•		•		•				•	•	•	•	•	•		
Ixora coccinea	Ixora				•	•	•		•	•	•	•	•	•	•			•						•										•
Jasminum mesnyi	Primrose jasmine				•			•			•	•			•		•	•	•	•				•									•		
Kalmia latifolia	Mountain laurel			•	•		•		•		•				•	•	•	•		•		•		•						•				
Laurus nobilis	Laurel				•	•					•					•		•	•	•				•								•			
Ligustrum japonicum	Japanese privet			•	•	•	•					•				•		•	•	•				•								•			
Mahonia aquifolia	Oregon holly-grape	•							•		•				•		•	•						•						•	•				
Myrtus communis 'compacta'	Compact Myrtle		•	•			•					•				•		•				•	•									•			
Nandina domestica	Nandina			•			•				•					•		•						•							•				
Nerium Oleander	Oleander				•	•	•	•	•	•	•	•			•		•	•	•				•							•				
Olea europarea	Common olive				•	•					•					•			•					•									•		
Osmanthus heterophyllus	Holly osmanthus				•	•						•				•		•						•							•				
Photinia serrulata	Chinese photinia				•	•					•				•									•								•			
Pieris floribunda	Mountain andromeda			•			•				•				•	•	•	•		•				•						•					
Pieris japonica	Japanese andromeda			•			•				•					•		•		•		•		•						•					
Pittosporum tobira	Japanese pittosporum			•			•				•					•		•						•								•			
Plumbago capensis	Cape plumbago		•							•	•	•	•	•		•							•										•		
Prunus laurocerasus 'schipkaenis'	Schipka cherry-laurel			•	•		•				•					•		•						•	•						•	•	•		
Pyracantha coccinea	Firethorn			•			•				•					•		•	•	•				•						•					
Rhododendron species*	Rhododendron species		•	•	•	•	•	•	•		•	•			•	•	•	•		•		•		•				•	•	•	•				
Schinus molle	California pepper tree				•		•				•				•		•	•	•	•				•									•		
Skimmia japonica	Japanese skimmia			•			•				•					•	•							•							•				
Ulmus parvifolia pendens	Evergreen elm					•									•	•	•	•						•											•
Viburnum rhytidophyllum	Leatherleaf viburnum			•	•	•					•			•		•	•							•							•				
Xylosma senticosa	Xylosma		•			•										•		•	•					•								•			

* See other references for local species and varieties.
** Also deciduous ilex available.

A. E. Bye & Associates, Landscape Architects; Old Greenwich, Connecticut

LANDSCAPING **2**

DECIDUOUS TREES—20 TO 50 FT

Botanical Name	Common Name	Rounded	Weeping	Spreading	Conical	Columnar	Oval	Slow	Medium	Fast	Shade Tree	Ornamental	Street Tree	Urban Tree	Seashore Tree	Flowers	Fruit	Leaf Color	Bark	Light Shade	Full Sun	Dry Soil	Moist Soil	Well Drained Soil	Acid Soil	Alkali Soil	1	2	3	4	5	6	7	8	9	10
Acer campestre	Hedge maple	•						•				•	•	•						•	•										•					
Acer ginnala	Amur maple	•							•			•	•	•		•	•	•			•	•							•								
Acer palmatum	Japanese maple	•						•				•		•					•		•	•		•	•							•					
Ailanthus altissima	Tree of heaven	•								•				•	•		•		•		•	•	•		•						•						
Albizia julibrissin	Hardy silk tree			•						•		•	•	•		•	•		•		•	•														•	
Amelanchier laevis	Allegany serviceberry	•								•			•		•	•	•	•	•	•	•	•	•	•								•					
Arbutus unedo	Strawberry tree			•				•					•				•	•		•		•				•									•		
Bauhinia variegata	Buddhist bauhinia	•								•			•				•		•			•	•														•
Betula populifolia	Gray birch			•		•				•			•						•	•		•	•	•						•	•						
Broussonetia papyrifera	Common paper mulberry	•		•						•		•	•	•			•	•		•		•	•	•										•			
Camellia japonica	Common camellia	•						•					•				•		•		•		•											•			
Carpinus caroliniana	American hornbeam	•						•				•	•	•					•	•	•	•							•								
Cassia fistula	Golden shower senna	•								•		•	•				•	•			•	•			•												•
Castanea mollissima	Chinese chestnut			•						•	•			•			•	•				•	•		•							•	•				
Cercis canadensis	Eastern redbud	•		•			•						•				•		•		•	•										•					
Chionanthus virginicus	Fringetree	•		•				•					•				•	•	•		•	•										•					
Cladastris lutea	American yellowwood	•						•			•	•	•	•			•	•	•		•	•				•					•						
Clethera barbinervis	Japanese clethera			•					•				•				•			•	•	•		•								•					
Cornus florida	Flowering dogwood	•	•	•					•				•		•		•	•	•		•	•		•							•					
Cornus kousa	Japanese dogwood			•					•				•		•		•	•	•		•	•									•					
Cornus mas	Cornelian cherry	•		•					•				•				•	•	•		•	•									•					
Crataegus species*	Hawthorne species	•								•	•		•		•	•	•	•			•	•	•				•				•					
Delonix regia	Royal poinciana			•						•	•	•	•	•			•	•			•	•															•
Elaeagnus angustifolia	Russian olive	•		•						•	•	•	•	•		•	•	•	•		•								•								
Firmiana simplex	Chinese parasol tree				•				•	•						•	•			•	•													•			
Fraxinus holotricha	Moraine ash	•		•						•	•										•										•						
Fraxinus velutina glabra	Modesto ash	•								•	•	•							•		•	•			•						•					
Halesia carolina	Carolina silverbell	•		•			•					•		•			•		•		•		•									•					
Koelreuteria paniculata	Goldenrain tree			•						•	•	•	•	•			•	•			•										•					
Laburnum watereri	Waterer laburnum					•				•			•				•				•		•								•					
Magnolia species*	Magnolia	•								•			•				•	•	•		•	•		•							•	•	•	•	•	
Malus species*	Crab apple species	•		•			•						•		•		•	•	•			•		•					•	•	•	•					
Melia azedarach	Chinaberry	•		•					•	•				•			•	•			•	•	•				•							•		
Phellodendron amurense	Amur cork tree			•						•		•		•	•				•	•	•	•	•		•					•						
Prunus species*	Cherries, apricots, plums, peaches	•								•		•		•	•	•	•	•			•	•							•	•	•	•	•				
Pterocarya fraxinifolia	Caucasian wing nut			•						•		•		•				•			•										•					
Pyrus calleryana "Bradford"	Bradford pear				•		•			•		•	•	•			•	•			•										•					
Salix babylonica	Babylon weeping willow		•							•		•						•			•		•									•				
Salix elegantissima	Thurlow weeping willow		•							•		•						•			•										•					
Sapium sebiferum	Chinese tallow tree			•					•	•				•				•			•	•	•												•		
Sorbus alnifolia	Korean mountain ash	•			•					•		•	•	•		•	•	•	•		•									•						
Sorbus aucuparia	Rowan tree	•		•					•	•		•				•	•	•			•									•						
Stewartia koreana	Korean stewartia			•			•			•			•				•	•	•	•	•	•		•								•				
Styrax japonica	Japanese snowbell	•		•				•				•	•				•			•	•									•						
Syringa amurensis japonica	Japanese tree lilac			•	•				•	•		•	•	•			•			•	•									•						
Ulmus parvifolia	Chinese elm		•							•			•	•	•	•	•	•	•	•	•										•					
Viburnum sieboldii	Siebold viburnum	•		•			•						•				•	•	•	•	•	•			•						•					

*See other references for local species and varieties.

A. E. Bye & Associates, Landscape Architects; Old Greenwich, Connecticut

LARGE DECIDUOUS TREES—50 FT AND OVER

Botanical Name	Common Name	Rounded	Weeping	Spreading	Conical	Columnar	Oval	Slow	Medium	Fast	Shade Tree	Ornamental	Street Tree	Urban Tree	Seashore Tree	Flowers	Fruit	Leaf Color	Bark	Light Shade	Full Sun	Dry Soil	Moist Soil	Acid Soil	Alkaline Soil	Well Drained Soil	1	2	3	4	5	6	7	8	9	10
Acacia decurrens dealbata	Silver wattle			•						•		•				•					•					•									•	
Acer platinoides and varieties	Norway maple and varieties	•		•	•				•	•	•	•	•	•	•						•					•			•							
Acer rubrum	Red or swamp maple	•					•		•	•	•		•	•	•	•	•	•			•		•						•							
Acer saccharum	Sugar maple						•	•	•		•		•						•	•	•				•				•							
Aesculus hippocastanum	Horse chestnut	•					•			•		•		•	•	•	•			•	•		•						•							
Betula nigra	River birch			•						•	•	•		•				•	•	•	•		•	•						•						
Betula papyrifera	Canoe or paper birch			•		•				•	•	•						•	•	•	•	•	•					•							
Betula pendula	European birch		•		•	•				•	•	•						•	•	•	•	•	•					•							
Carpinus betulus	European hornbeam	•			•		•			•			•	•						•	•										•					
Cercidiphyllum japonicum	Katsura tree	•					•	•	•	•			•	•					•		•	•	•	•							•					
Cornus controversa	Giant dogwood			•					•			•				•	•			•				•							•					
Eucalyptus species*	Eucalyptus species	•							•	•	•	•	•					•	•	•	•													•	•
Fagus grandifolia	American beech	•					•	•			•	•			•			•		•	•		•						•							
Fagus sylvatica and varieties*	European beech and varieties	•	•	•			•	•			•	•			•			•	•	•	•		•							•						
Fraxinus americana	White ash	•								•	•	•		•				•		•										•						
Fraxinus oregona	Oregon ash				•					•	•	•	•					•		•												•				
Fraxinus pennsylvanica lanceolata	Green ash	•		•						•	•	•						•		•								•								
Ginkgo biloba	Ginkgo			•	•	•	•					•	•					•		•	•	•	•						•							
Gleditsia triacanthos and varieties*	Honey locust and varieties			•					•	•	•	•	•	•				•	•		•										•					
Gordonia lasianthus	Loblolly bay gordonia				•			•			•	•			•				•	•	•		•										•			
Liquidambar styraciflua	Sweet gum				•				•	•	•	•	•	•				•	•	•	•		•								•					
Liriodendron tulipifera	Tulip tree				•				•	•	•	•				•	•	•		•	•		•							•					
Magnolia grandiflora	Southern magnolia			•					•			•	•			•	•						•									•			
Nyssa sylvatica	Black tupelo			•					•			•		•		•		•		•	•		•	•						•					
Pittosporum rhombifolium	Diamond leaf pittosporum	•							•			•	•	•		•					•															•
Platanus acerifolium	London plane tree	•		•					•	•	•	•	•	•	•		•	•	•	•	•				•						•				
Populus alba	White poplar			•		•			•		•	•			•			•	•		•	•							•						
Populus tremuloides	Quaking aspen			•					•	•	•							•	•	•	•	•				•	•	•							
Prunus serotina	Black cherry			•					•		•	•			•	•	•			•									•						
Quercus alba	White oak	•		•			•		•		•	•			•			•	•		•	•		•					•						
Quercus borealis	Red oak	•		•					•		•		•	•				•	•		•			•				•							
Quercus coccinea	Scarlet oak	•		•					•		•		•					•	•		•			•				•							
Quercus falcata	Southern red oak	•		•					•		•							•	•		•			•							•				
Quercus imbricaria	Shingle oak	•		•			•		•		•	•						•	•		•			•							•				
Quercus kelloggii	California black oak	•		•					•		•							•	•		•	•		•									•		
Quercus laurifolia	Laurel oak	•								•		•						•	•		•	•												•		
Quercus palustris	Pin oak			•					•		•		•	•				•	•		•		•	•					•							
Quercus phellos	Willow oak	•		•					•	•	•	•	•	•				•	•		•		•	•							•	•			
Quercus robur and varieties*	English oak and varieties	•			•		•					•						•		•			•							•						
Quercus shumardii	Shumard oak			•					•		•		•					•	•		•		•							•						
Quercus virginiana	Live oak	•		•					•		•	•	•		•			•	•		•	•											•		
Salix alba tristis	Golden weeping willow		•						•		•	•			•			•		•		•					•									
Sassafras albidum	Sassafras			•					•			•				•	•	•		•	•	•	•	•							•					
Sophora japonica	Japanese pagoda tree	•		•					•	•	•	•		•	•		•	•		•	•	•		•							•				
Tilia cordata	Little leaf linden				•		•		•		•	•	•	•	•		•	•		•	•	•	•	•						•						
Tilia euchlora	Crimean linden			•					•		•	•	•	•	•		•	•		•	•	•	•							•						
Tilia tomentosa	Silver linden			•			•		•		•	•	•	•	•		•	•	•		•	•	•	•						•						
Zelkova serrata and varieties*	Japanese zelkova and varieties	•							•	•		•		•	•		•		•		•	•	•				•					•				

*See other references for local species and varieties.

A. E. Bye & Associates, Landscape Architects; Old Greenwich, Connecticut

DECIDUOUS SHRUBS

BOTANICAL NAME	COMMON NAME	HEIGHT				SPECIAL FEATURES						FLOWERS COLOR				SEASON				USES			CULTURAL REQUIREMENTS								HARDINESS ZONES									
		0 to 3 ft	3 to 6 ft	6 to 10 ft	10 ft and over	Flowers	Fruit	Foliage Color	Good Winter Appearance	Rapid Growth	Easy Maintenance	White	Yellow-orange	Pink-red	Blue-purple	Spring	Summer	Fall	Winter	Urban	Seashore	Hedges	Sun	Shade	Light Shade	Acid Soil	Alkaline Soil	Moist Soil	Dry Soil	Well drained Soil	1	2	3	4	5	6	7	8	9	10
Amelanchier stolonifera	Running serviceberry		●			●	●	●			●	●				●					●		●		●	●		●	●	●				●						
Aronia species*	Chokeberry species	●	●	●	●	●	●	●	●		●	●				●				●	●	●	●		●	●	●	●	●					●						
Berberis species*	Barberry species	●	●	●		●	●	●	●		●		●			●				●	●	●	●		●	●	●	●	●					●						
Calycanthus floridus	Sweet shrub		●	●		●		●			●			●		●						●	●		●	●	●	●						●						
Caragana arborescens	Siberian pea tree			●	●	●	●				●		●			●				●		●	●				●	●	●	●		●								
Cercis chinensis	Chinese redbud		●	●		●		●			●			●	●	●							●	●				●											●	
Chaenomeles species*	Quince species	●	●			●	●				●	●	●	●		●				●	●	●	●		●	●	●	●	●					●						
Clethra alnifolia	Summer sweet		●			●		●			●	●		●			●			●		●	●	●	●	●		●							●					
Cornus species*	Dogwood species	●	●	●	●	●	●	●	●	●	●	●		●		●				●		●	●	●	●			●	●				●							
Corylopsis species*	Winter hazel species	●	●	●	●	●		●			●		●			●						●	●	●	●			●										●		
Cotinus species*	Smoke tree species			●	●	●		●			●			●	●	●				●			●				●	●	●									●		
Cotoneaster species*	Cotoneaster species	●	●	●	●	●	●	●	●		●	●		●		●				●	●	●	●				●	●	●					●						
Cytisus species*	Scotch broom species	●	●	●		●			●	●	●	●	●	●	●	●					●		●		●			●	●						●					
Deutzia species*	Deutzia species		●	●		●		●			●	●		●		●	●			●		●	●		●			●	●					●						
Euonymus species*	Euonymus species	●	●	●		●	●	●			●									●	●	●	●	●	●			●	●				●						
Exochorda species*	Pearlbush species		●	●	●	●					●	●				●						●	●					●	●						●					
Forsythia species*	Forsythia species	●	●	●		●			●	●	●		●			●				●		●	●		●			●	●					●						
Fothergilla species*	Fothergilla species	●	●	●		●		●			●	●	●			●							●	●	●	●			●						●					
Hamamelis species*	Witch hazel species		●	●	●	●		●	●		●		●			●	●	●		●		●	●		●			●	●					●						
Hibiscus species*	Rose of Sharon species		●	●	●	●			●		●	●		●	●		●	●		●	●	●	●		●			●		●				●						
Ilex verticillata	Winterberry		●				●	●	●		●									●		●	●	●	●	●			●				●							
Jasminum nudiflorum	Winter jasmine	●	●	●	●	●		●			●		●						●	●		●	●		●			●	●						●					
Kerria japonica	Kerria	●	●			●		●	●		●		●	●		●				●		●	●		●			●						●						
Kolkwitzia amabilis	Beauty bush		●			●	●	●	●		●			●		●				●		●	●		●			●	●					●						
Lagerstroemia indica	Crape myrtle		●	●	●	●		●	●		●		●	●		●				●		●	●		●		●	●												●
Lespedeza species*	Bush clover species		●	●		●					●			●			●	●		●			●				●	●	●					●						
Ligustrum species*	Privet species		●	●	●	●	●			●	●		●			●	●	●		●	●	●	●	●	●	●			●	●				●						
Lindera benzoin	Spicebush		●	●	●	●	●			●		●		●		●				●			●	●	●	●		●						●						
Myrica pensylvanica	Bayberry		●	●			●		●		●									●	●		●		●			●	●			●								
Photinia villosa	Oriental photinia			●	●	●	●			●	●	●				●						●	●					●						●						
Plumeria rubra	Frangipani			●	●	●			●		●	●	●	●		●	●	●			●		●		●			●												●
Potentilla species*	Bush cinquefoil species		●			●				●	●	●	●			●	●	●		●			●					●	●			●								
Rhamnus species*	Buckthorn species			●	●		●	●												●		●	●		●			●	●			●								
Rhododendron	Azalea	●	●	●	●	●		●			●	●	●	●	●	●				●		●	●	●	●	●		●						●						
Rosa species*	'Shrub' rose species		●	●	●	●	●	●	●		●	●	●	●		●	●	●		●	●	●	●					●	●					●						
Spiraea species*	Spiraea species	●	●	●		●		●			●	●		●		●	●			●	●	●	●		●			●	●					●						
Stephanandra species*	Stephanandra species	●	●	●		●		●			●	●				●				●			●		●			●										●		
Stewartia species*	Stewartia species			●	●	●		●	●		●	●					●						●		●	●		●										●		
Symphoricarpos species*	Snowberry species	●	●				●		●		●									●	●	●	●	●	●			●	●			●								
Symplocos paniculata	Sapphireberry			●	●	●	●				●					●							●		●	●		●									●			
Syringa species*	Lilac species	●	●	●	●	●			●		●	●	●	●	●	●				●	●	●	●		●		●	●						●						
Vaccinium corymbosum	Highbush blueberry		●	●		●	●	●			●	●				●				●	●	●	●		●	●			●								●			
Viburnum species*	Viburnum species	●	●	●	●	●	●	●	●		●	●		●		●				●	●	●	●	●	●			●	●					●						

NOTES

*See other references for local species and varieties. Listings in this chart represent large genera of many species and varieties. Other sources need to be consulted to obtain detailed information. The hardiness zone notations indicate that most of the species within the family are hardy to that zone but there are a few that are not.

A. E. Bye & Associates, Landscape Architects; Old Greenwich, Connecticut

2   LANDSCAPING

GROUND COVERS

Column groups: **HEIGHT** (Less than 6 in. / 6 to 12 in. / 12 to 18 in. / 18 in. and over) · **LIGHT REQUIREMENTS** (Sun / Shade / Light Shade) · **SOIL TYPES** (Acid / Alkaline) · **SPECIAL AREAS** (Seashore / City) · **MOISTURE NEEDS** (Moist Soil / Dry Soil / Well-drained Soil) · **FOLIAGE COLOR** (Green / Dark Green / Blue Green / Gray Green / Purple Green) · **FEATURES** (Flowers / Fruit / Mowable / Slopes / Rapid Growth / Easy Maintenance) · **HARDINESS ZONES** (1–10)

Botanical Name	Common Name	<6in	6–12	12–18	18+	Sun	Shade	Lt Shade	Acid	Alk	Seashore	City	Moist	Dry	Well-dr	Green	Dk Grn	Bl Grn	Gy Grn	Pur Grn	Flowers	Fruit	Mowable	Slopes	Rapid	Easy Maint	1	2	3	4	5	6	7	8	9	10
DECIDUOUS																																				
Asperula odorata	Sweet woodruff		•				•		•				•			•					•				•	•				•						
Coronilla varia	Crown vetch			•	•	•		•	•	•			•	•		•					•				•	•	•		•							
Cotoneaster (spreading varieties)	Cotoneaster		•			•			•	•	•				•		•				•	•			•						•					
Gazania uniflora	Trailing gazania	•				•			•	•					•					•		•			•	•									•	
Phlox subulata	Ground pink	•				•									•	•					•				•	•			•							
Rosa wichuraiana	Memorial rose		•			•					•				•		•				•				•	•	•				•					
Trifolium repens	White clover	•				•							•			•					•		•			•			•							
Vaccinium angustifolium laevifolium	Low bush blueberry		•			•	•	•	•				•			•					•	•			•	•			•							
Veronica repens	Creeping speedwell	•					•	•					•			•					•				•	•					•					
Xanthorhiza simplicissima	Yellowroot			•	•			•					•			•					•				•	•				•						
BROAD LEAVED EVERGREENS																																				
Ajuga reptans	Bugleweed	•				•	•	•					•				•	•		•	•				•	•				•						
Anthemis nobilis	Chamomile	•	•			•									•	•					•		•			•				•						
Arabis albida	Wall rockcress	•				•								•					•		•					•				•						
Arctostaphylos uva-ursi	Bearberry		•			•		•			•					•					•	•		•		•			•							
Baccharis pilularis	Coyote bush			•	•	•					•		•	•						•		•			•	•	•							•		
Carissa macrocarpa 'green carpet'	Green carpet natal plum		•			•		•			•					•					•	•													•	
Carpobrotus edulis	Hottentot fig	•				•					•				•				•		•			•	•										•
Ceanothus griseus horizontalis	Carmel creeper			•	•	•					•				•	•					•			•									•		
Ceratostigma plumbaginoides	Leadwort		•			•		•						•	•	•					•				•	•						•			
Cornus canadensis	Bunchberry		•				•	•	•				•			•					•	•			•		•		•							
Cotoneaster dammeri	Bearberry cotoneaster		•			•		•	•	•	•	•	•				•				•	•		•	•					•					
Dichondra repens	Dichondra	•				•	•	•					•	•		•							•	•											•
Drosanthemum hispidum	Rosea ice plant		•			•					•				•				•		•			•	•									•	
Euonymus fortunei coloratus	Purple-leaf wintercreeper	•				•		•	•				•				•			•		•			•					•					
Fragaria chiloensis	Wild strawberry		•			•		•			•	•	•				•				•	•		•	•				•						
Galax aphylla	Galax	•	•				•	•	•				•				•				•				•			•							
Hedera helix	English ivy		•			•	•	•				•	•				•							•	•				•						
Hypericum calycinum	Aaronsbeard Saint-John's-wort		•			•		•						•		•					•			•	•					•					
Iberis sempervirens	Evergreen candytuft		•			•					•		•	•		•					•			•				•							
Leucothoe catesbaei	Drooping leucothoe		•	•	•	•	•	•	•				•			•					•			•				•							
Lotus bertholettii	Parrot's beak, coral gem	•	•			•						•	•			•			•		•			•										•
Micromeria chamissonis	Yerba buena	•				•		•	•				•			•					•			•	•					•					
Pachistma canbyi	Canby pachistima		•	•		•	•	•	•				•			•					•				•				•						
Pachysandra terminalis	Japanese spurge		•				•	•	•				•			•					•	•		•				•							
Rosmarinus officinalis prostratus	Creeping rosemary			•	•	•					•			•	•	•					•			•		•				•					
Saxifraga stolonifera	Strawberry geranium	•						•					•				•		•	•	•			•						•					
Trachelospermum jasminoides	Star jasmine		•	•		•	•	•					•			•					•				•	•				•					
Vinca minor	Myrtle, periwinkle	•					•	•					•			•					•			•	•	•				•					
NEEDLE EVERGREENS																																				
Calluna vulgaris	Scotch heather	•	•	•	•	•		•	•		•		•				•				•				•				•						
Erica carnea	Spring heath		•			•		•		•					•			•			•			•	•					•					
Juniperus chinensis varieties	Varieties of Chinese juniper		•	•	•	•					•	•	•	•	•	•	•		•	•					•				•						
Juniperus conferta	Shore juniper		•			•					•	•		•				•						•					•						
Juniperus horizontalis douglasii	Waukegan juniper	•	•			•					•			•			•		•					•	•			•							
Juniperus horizontalis 'Bar Harbor'	Bar Harbor juniper		•			•					•	•	•	•			•	•	•					•	•			•							
Juniperus horizontalis 'wiltonii'	Wilton carpet juniper	•				•					•		•	•			•							•				•							
Juniperus horizontalis 'plumosa'	Andorra juniper			•		•					•		•	•					•	•				•					•						
Juniperus procumbens 'nana'	Japanese garden juniper	•	•			•					•			•					•					•					•						
Juniperus sabina tamariscifolia	Tamarix juniper			•		•					•	•	•		•	•						•		•				•							
Taxus baccata repandens	Spreading English yew			•	•	•	•	•					•		•		•							•					•						

A. E. Bye & Associates, Landscape Architects; Old Greenwich, Connecticut

LANDSCAPING 2

PLANT CHARTS

The intent of the plant chart is to indicate the wide variety of plants available to the designer. There are many unusual trees, shrubs, and ground covers for every environmental and design situation. In using the charts, the designer will obtain a general perception of the plants listed. It is strongly recommended that more specific information be sought in botanic journals. The charts note the northernmost reaches of the plant listed, but some plants will not grow where winters are too warm. The southern reach of those particular plants has not been included in the charts because of conflicting and inadequate information. There are many regional variations in climate that should be considered when selecting plants. The designer is urged to consult a landscape architect to ensure the best selection for the design.

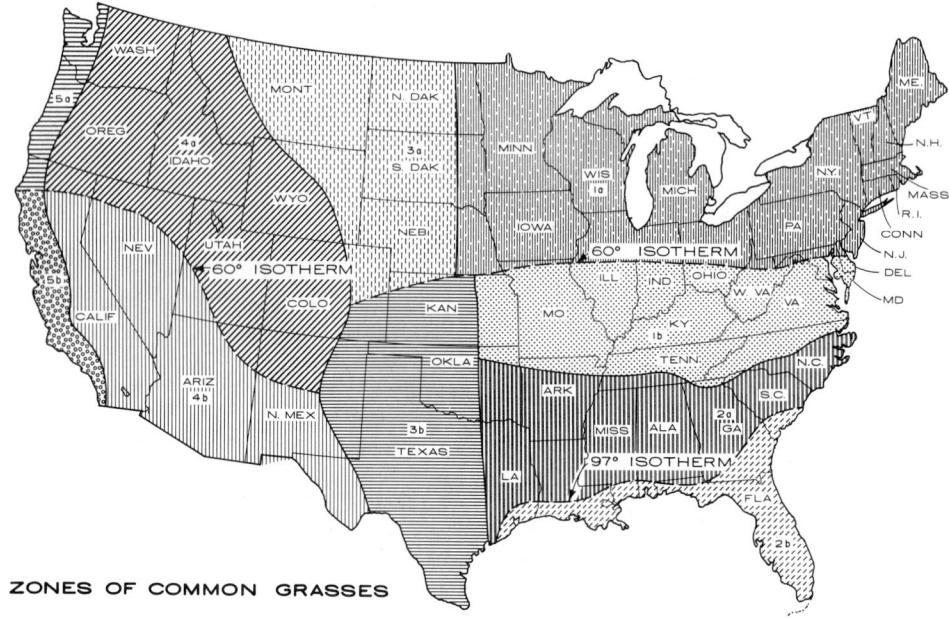

ZONES OF COMMON GRASSES

GRASSES

In selecting a type of grass for lawn development the designer must consider both environmental and use factors. The amount of available sunlight, the temperature range, rainfall, soil type, and drainage will determine the type of grass that will survive in a given location while additional consideration of tolerance to traffic and recuperative rates will ensure the best possible lawn. For example, different grasses are used for athletic fields depending on environmental factors: bluegrasses and fescues in the northern zones; Bermuda grasses and zoysias in the southern zones, and St. Augustine grass in the extreme south. All are rugged, but require different environments to grow well. Another example is bent grass. Although it requires high maintenance, it is desirable for golf courses because of its fine texture and thick growth.

Lawns can be installed by seed, sprigging, or sod at varying costs. Careful installation at the proper time of the year will ensure the health and beauty of the lawn. Proper soil preparation including aerating the soil, adding topsoil, fertilizer, lime, if necessary, good drainage, and the use of high quality certified weedfree seed is important for success. Frequently, mixtures of seeds are used, since growing conditions are rarely uniform throughout the lawn area. This practice can also mitigate the effects of lawn disease. More specific information is available from local agricultural agents.

GRASSES

BOTANICAL NAME	COMMON NAME	Sun	Shade	Light Shade	Well-drained Soil	Moist	Dry	Acid	Alkaline	Cool	Warm	Coarse	Fine	Thick	Hairy	High	Moderate	Minimal	Green	Dark Green	Light Green	Blue Green	Gray Green	Brown (hot weather)	Brown (cold weather)	1a	1b	2a	2b	3a	3b	4a	4b	5a	5b
Agropyron	Wheat	•					•	•	•		•			•			•			•	•									•	•	•			
Agrostis	Bent	•	•		•		•		•	•			•	•		•		•		•				•		•	•		*		*			•	*
Ammophila	Beach	•		•			•		•	•					•			•			•					•	•	•						•	*
Axonopus	Carpet	•	•				•	•		•	•				•			•			•			•				•	•						
Bouteloua	Blue gamma	•				•			•				•				•					•	•							*	•	*	•		
Buchloë	Buffalo	•				•			•		•						•					•	•						•	•	*	*		
Cynodon	Bermuda	•		*	•		•			•		•	•	•		•			•					•				•	•		*		*		•
Eremochloa	Centipede	•	•			*		•		•	•		•				•			•				•				•	•		*		*		*
Festuca	Fescue	•	•	•	•	•	•	•		•			•				•		•							•	•	*		*		•	*	•	
Lolium	Rye	•		•		•		•		•				•			•		•	•						•	•	*	*		*		*	•	
Paspalum notatum	Bahia	•		•		•	*		•		•	•		•			•			•		•						•	•		•				
Poa	Bluegrass	•		*	•		•	•		•				•			•		•			•				•	•		*				•		
Stenotaphrum	St. Augustine	•	•	•		•		•			•	•			•			•			•				•				•		*	•		*	*
Zoysia	Zoysia	•	•	•			•			•		•					•			•				•				•	•	•	*		*	*	•

*Will grow under special conditions: high altitude, proximity to water, or irrigation.

NOTES

1. Consult local agricultural agent, horticulturist, or nurseryman in your area for best grasses for slopes, maintenance concerns, and general planting instructions.
2. Planting slopes: (a) 3 to 1 is maximum for mowed banks. (b) 2 to 1 is maximum for unmowed banks.

A. E. Bye & Associates, Landscape Architects; Old Greenwich, Connecticut

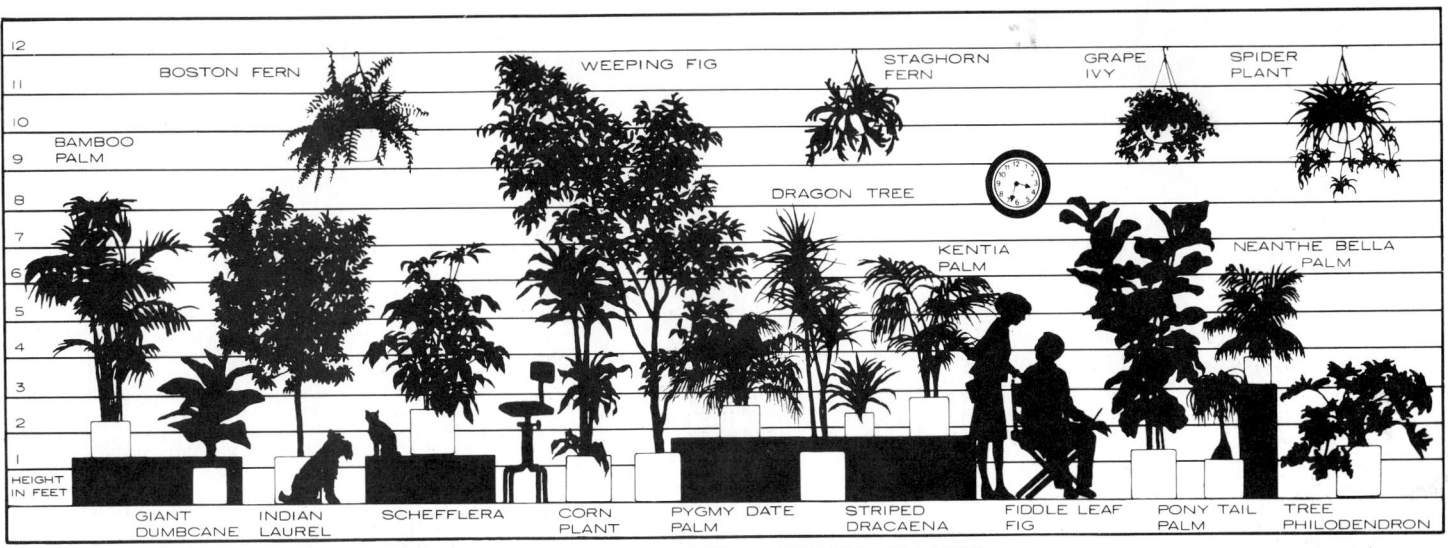

FORM, TEXTURE, AND SIZES OF SOME TYPICALLY USED INTERIOR PLANTS

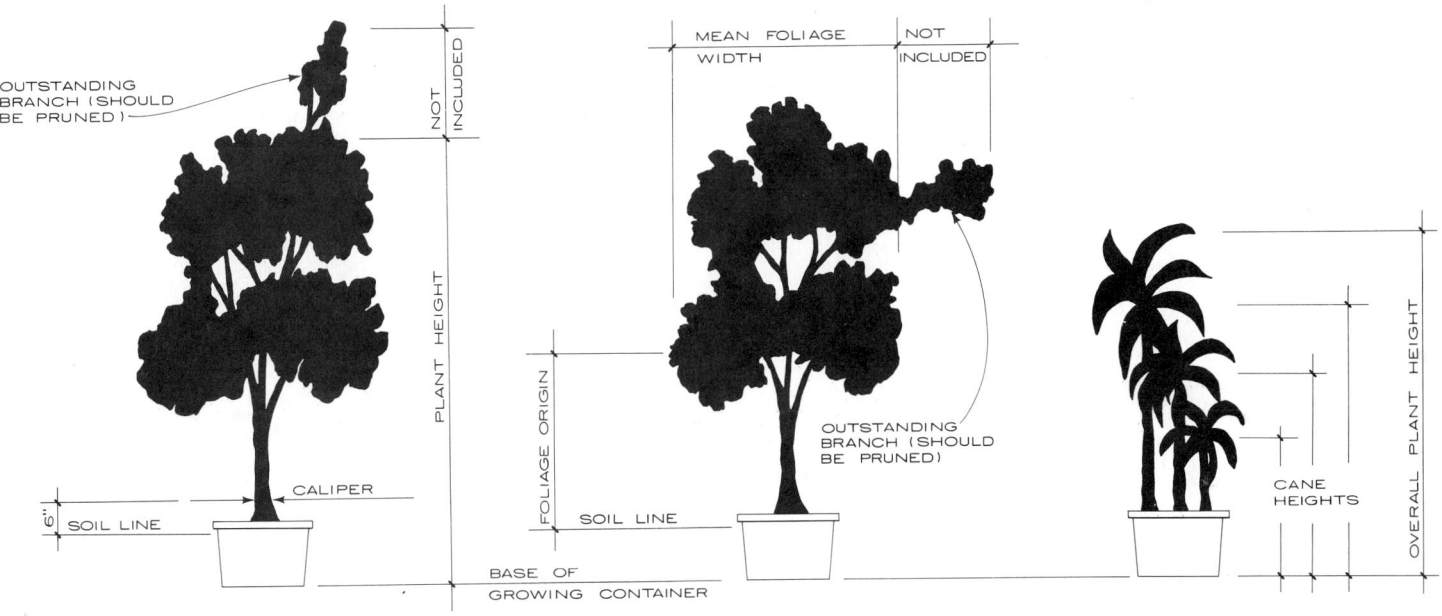

PLANT HEIGHT AND CALIPER   FOLIAGE WIDTH AND ORIGIN   CANE HEIGHTS

INTERIOR PLANT SPECIFICATIONS

NOTE

Plant height should be measured as overall height from the base of the growing container to mean foliage top. Isolated outstanding branches should not be included in height. (Since most plants are installed in movable planters, this overall height measurement should be utilized.)

NOTE

Foliage width should be measured across the nominal mean width dimension. Isolated outstanding branches should not be included in foliage width. Origin or start of foliage should be measured from the soil line.

NOTE

Many plant varieties are grown from rooted canes, with the plant being made up of one or more canes. The number of canes must be specified, if plant form is to be identified. Cane heights should always be measured from the base of the growing container.

OTHER PLANT SPECIFICATION FACTORS

1. Accurately describe plant form (e.g., multistem vs. standard tree form, clump form) and foliage spread desired. Indicate "clear trunk" measurements on trees, if desired. These measurements are from soil line to foliage origin point. Specify caliper, if significant.

2. Indicate lighting intensities designed or calculated for interior space where plants will be installed.

3. Indicate how plants will be used (i.e., in at-grade planter or in movable decorative planter). If movable decorative planters are used, indicate interior diameter and height of planter for each plant specified, since growing container sizes vary considerably.

4. Specify both botanical and common plant names.

5. Indicate any special shipping instructions or limitations.

6. Specify in-plant height column, whether plant height is measured as overall height or above-the-soil line height. Recommended height measurements:

   Interior plants: overall plant height (i.e., from bottom of growing container to mean foliage top).
   Exterior plants: above-the-soil line height.

7. Indicate whether plants are to be container grown or balled and burlapped (B & B) material.

8. Indicate location of all convenient water supply sources on all interior landscaping layouts.

Richard L. Gaines, AIA; Plantscape House; Apopka, Florida

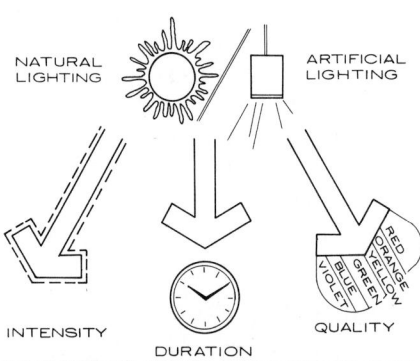

INTERIOR PLANT LIGHTING FACTORS

LIGHTING DURATION NEEDS

1. Adequate lighting is the product of intensity times duration to yield "footcandle-hours"; therefore, compensation between the two exists (e.g., 300 ft-c x 12 hr = 360 ft-c x 10 hr).
2. Recommended rule of thumb: 10–12 hr of continuous lighting on a regular basis, 7 days a week.
3. Generally, it is believed that continuous 24 hr lighting period might be detrimental to plants, but no research bears this out and many projects are under this regime with no apparent bad effects.

LIGHTING INTENSITY NEEDS

1. All plants desire good lighting, but many are tolerant and adaptable to lower light conditions.
2. Because most interior plants are native to areas with intensities of 10–14,000 ft-c, these plants must be "trained" through an acclimatization process of lowered light (2000–4000 ft-c), water and fertilizer levels for survival, and maintained appearance in the interior environment.
3. All plants have varying degrees of interior lighting intensity requirements, best understood as footcandle (lumens/square foot) requirements.
4. Lighting intensity for plants must be planned and is not simply a footcandle measurement after the building is complete (i.e., footcandle meters are "after the fact" instruments).
5. Intensity must always be above the individual light compensation point for each plant variety, for survival. (LCP is the intensity point at which the plant utilizes as much food as it produces; hence no food storage. Eventually, the plant could die with no food backup.)
6. Recommended rule of thumb: design for a MINIMUM of 50 ft-c on the ground plane for fixed floor type of planters and 75 ft-c at desk height for movable decorative floor planters.
7. Flowering plants and flowers require extremely high intensities (above 2000 ft-c) or direct sunlight to bud, flower, or fruit, as well as lighting high in red and far-red energy.

RECOMMENDED LIGHTING SOURCES FOR PLANTS

Lighting sources are listed in order of priority, based on plant growth efficiency, color rendition preference, and energy efficiency.

CEILING HEIGHT	RECOMMENDED LIGHT SOURCE
10 ft and less	Daylight—sidewall glazing Cool white fluorescent Natural light fluorescent Incandescent Plant growth fluorescent

10–15 ft	Daylight
	  Sidewall glazing
	  Major glazing
	  Skylights
	Metal halide lamp, phosphor coated
	Mercury lamp, deluxe white
	Mercury lamp, warm deluxe white
	High pressure sodium (if color rendition not a design factor)
	Quartz halogen lamp
	Incandescent

15 ft and greater	Daylight
	  Sidewall glazing
	  Major glazing
	  Skylights
	Metal halide lamp, clear
	Metal halide lamp, phosphor coated
	Mercury lamp, deluxe white
	Mercury lamp, warm deluxe white
	High pressure sodium (if color rendition not a design factor)
	Quartz halogen lamp
	Incandescent

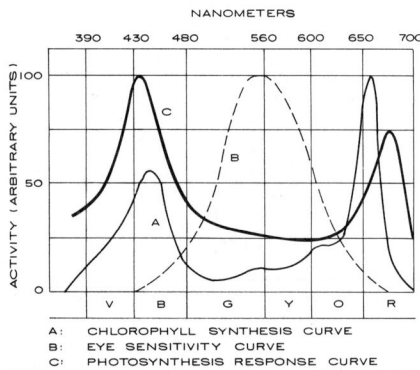

A: CHLOROPHYLL SYNTHESIS CURVE
B: EYE SENSITIVITY CURVE
C: PHOTOSYNTHESIS RESPONSE CURVE

SPECTRAL ENERGY DISTRIBUTION CURVE SHOWING OPPOSING PLANT AND HUMAN EYE RESPONSES

LIGHT QUALITY NEEDS

1. Natural lighting is about twice as efficient as cool white fluorescent lighting for plant growth, because of sunlight's broad range spectrum (i.e., 200 ft-c of CWF = 95 ft-c of natural light).
2. Chlorophyll is most responsive to blue and red wavelength energy in the production of food. The human eye is least responsive to blue and red energy and most responsive to the green-yellow region of the spectrum.
3. High blue energy emitting sources are best for overall plant maintenance (stockier growth, dark green color, little elongation).
4. High red energy emitting sources produce lighter colored foliage, elongated growth, stragglier growth.
5. Designer must be cognizant of color rendition of source, as well as light quality, if lighting is to be used for both plant lighting and illumination. (See Lamp Responses table.)
6. Ultraviolet energy is believed to be somewhat helpful to the photosynthesis process, but is not considered necessary as an integral segment of plant lighting.

Richard L. Gaines, AIA; Plantscape House; Apopka, Florida

LAMP RESPONSES ON INTERIOR PLANTS

BULB	ROOM APPEARANCE	COLORS STRENGTHENED	COLORS GREYED	PLANT RESPONSES
CW	Neutral to cool	Blue, yellow, orange	Red	Green foliage, stem elongates slowly, multiple side shoots, flower life long
WW	Yellow to warm	Yellow, orange	Blue, green, red	
GRO-PL	Purple to pink	Blue, red	Green, yellow	Deep green foliage, stem elongates very slowly, thick stems, multiple side shoots, late flowers on short stems
GRO-WS	Warm	Blue, yellow, red	Green	Light green foliage, stem elongates rapidly, suppressed side shoots, early flowering on long stems, plant matures and dies rapidly
AGRO	Neutral to warm	Blue, yellow, red	Green	
VITA	Neutral to warm	Blue, yellow, red	Green	
HG	Cool	Blue, green, yellow	Red	Green foliage expands, stem elongates slowly, multiple side shoots, flower life long
MH	Cool green	Blue, green, yellow	Red	
HPS	Warm	Green, yellow, orange	Blue, red	Deep green, large foliage, stem elongates very slowly, late flowers, short stems
LPS	Warm	Yellow	All except yellow	Extra deep green foliage, slow, thick stem elongation, multiple side shoots, some flowering, short stems. Some plants require supplemental sun
INC	Warm	Yellow, orange, red	Blue	Pale, thin, long foliage, stems spindly, suppressed side shoots early, short-lived flowers
INC-HG	Warm	Yellow, orange, red	Blue	

KEY

CW: cool white fluorescent.
WW: warm white fluorescent.
GRO-PL: Gro-Lux plant light.
GRO-WS: Gro-Lux wide spectrum.
AGRO: Agro-Lite.
VITA: Vita-Lite.

HG: mercury (all types).
MH: metal halide.
HPS: high pressure sodium.
LPS: low pressure sodium.
INC-HG: incandescent mercury.
INC-PL: incandescent plant light.

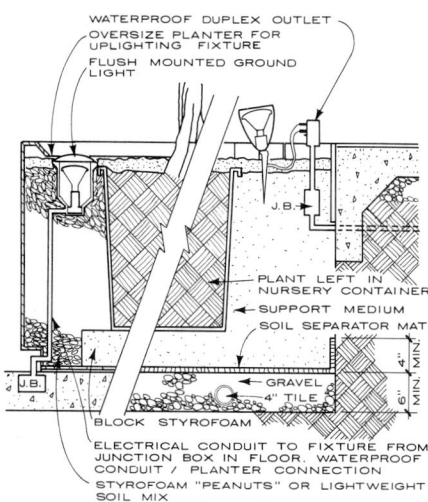

WATERPROOF DUPLEX OUTLET
OVERSIZE PLANTER FOR UPLIGHTING FIXTURE
FLUSH MOUNTED GROUND LIGHT

J.B.

PLANT LEFT IN NURSERY CONTAINER
SUPPORT MEDIUM
SOIL SEPARATOR MAT

GRAVEL
4" TILE

BLOCK STYROFOAM

ELECTRICAL CONDUIT TO FIXTURE FROM JUNCTION BOX IN FLOOR. WATERPROOF CONDUIT / PLANTER CONNECTION
STYROFOAM "PEANUTS" OR LIGHTWEIGHT SOIL MIX

**MOVABLE PLANTER AT-GRADE PLANTER
UPLIGHTING / PLANTING DETAILS**

UPLIGHTING AND ELECTRICAL NEEDS

1. May be of some benefit to plants, but inefficient for plant photosynthesis because of plant physiological structure. Chlorophyll is usually in upper part of leaf.
2. Uplighting should never be utilized as sole lighting source for plants.
3. Waterproof duplex outlets above soil line with a waterproof junction box below soil line are usually adequate for "atmosphere" uplighting and water fountain pumps.

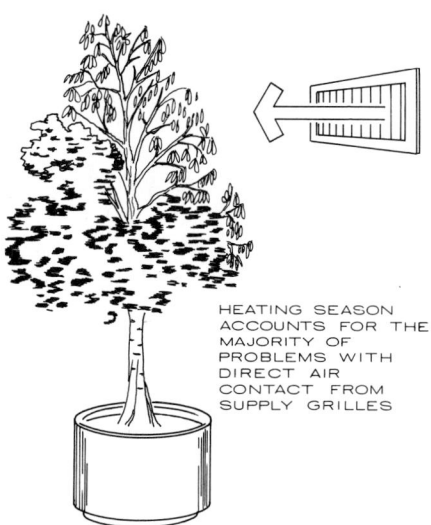

HEATING SEASON ACCOUNTS FOR THE MAJORITY OF PROBLEMS WITH DIRECT AIR CONTACT FROM SUPPLY GRILLES

FOLIAGE BURN FROM DIRECT HEAT CONTACT

HVAC EFFECT ON PLANTS

1. Air-conditioning (cooled air) is rarely detrimental to plants, even if it is "directed" at plants. The ventilation here is what counts! Good ventilation is a must with plants; otherwise oxygen and temperatures build up. Heat supply, on the other hand, when "directed" at plants, can truly be disastrous. Plan for supplies directed away from plants, but maintain adequate ventilation.
2. Extended heat or power failures of sufficient duration can damage plant health. The lower limit of temperature as a steady state is 65°F for plant survival. Brief drops to 55°F (less than 1 hr) are the lower limit before damage. Temperatures up to 85°F for only 2 days a week can usually be tolerated.
3. The relative humidity should not be allowed to fall below 30%, as plants prefer a relative humidity of 50–60%.

Richard L. Gaines, AIA; Plantscape House; Apopka, Florida

DIRECT PLANTING OF PLANT IN NURSERY CONTAINER RESTRICTS GROWTH AND AIDS IN PLANT REMOVAL (PLANTING WITHOUT CONTAINER AIDS IN GROWTH)
LIGHTWEIGHT SOIL OR SOILLESS SUPPORT MEDIUM
MAINTENANCE SURFACE TO PREVENT WATER AND SOIL STAINING

PEAT / BUILDERS SAND / BARK CHIPS OR HORTICULTURAL PERLITE SUPPORT SOIL MEDIUM
MULCH COVER
PROVIDE POTABLE WATER AND WATERPROOF POWER WITH BELOW GRADE JUNCTION BOX PROVIDE BELOW GRADE TEE ON WATER

CEILING CAVITY
WATERPROOFING
STYROFOAM "PEANUTS"
SUMP DRAIN TO BUILDING DRAINAGE SYSTEM

SOIL SEPARATOR MAT
GRAVEL DRAINAGE BED (IF NECESSARY)
PERFORATED DRAINAGE TILE IF EXISTING SOIL IMPERVIOUS

ABOVE—GRADE PLANTER   **AT—GRADE PLANTER
FLOOR PLANTER DETAILS**

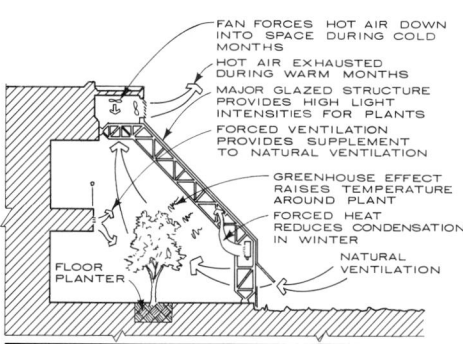

FAN FORCES HOT AIR DOWN INTO SPACE DURING COLD MONTHS
HOT AIR EXHAUSTED DURING WARM MONTHS
MAJOR GLAZED STRUCTURE PROVIDES HIGH LIGHT INTENSITIES FOR PLANTS
FORCED VENTILATION PROVIDES SUPPLEMENT TO NATURAL VENTILATION
GREENHOUSE EFFECT RAISES TEMPERATURE AROUND PLANT
FORCED HEAT REDUCES CONDENSATION IN WINTER
NATURAL VENTILATION
FLOOR PLANTER

GREENHOUSE EFFECT RAISES NEED FOR ADEQUATE VENTILATION

TEMPERATURE REQUIREMENTS

1. Most plants prefer human comfort range: 70-75°F daytime temperatures and 60-65°F nighttime temperatures.
2. An absolute minimum temperature of 50°F must be observed. Plant damage will result below this figure. Rapid temperature fluctuations of 30-40°F can also be detrimental to plants.
3. "Q-10" phenomenon of respiration: for every 10°C rise in temperature, plants' respiration rate and food consumption doubles.
4. Both photosynthesis and respiration decline and stop with time, as temperatures go beyond 80°F. Beware of the greenhouse effect!

WATER SUPPLY REQUIREMENTS

1. Movable and railing planters are often watered by watering can. Provide convenient access to hot and cold potable water by hose bibbs and/or service sinks (preferably in janitor's closet) during normal working hours, with long (min. 24 in.) faucet-to-sink or floor distances. Provide for maximum of 200 ft travel on all floors.
2. At-grade floor planters are usually watered by hose and extension wand. Provide hose bibbs above soil line (for maximum travel of 50 ft) with capped "tee" stub-outs beneath soil line. If soil temperature is apt to get abnormally low in winter, provide hot and cold water by mixer-faucet type hose bibbs.
3. High concentrations of fluoride and chlorine in water supply can cause damage to plants. Provide water with low concentrations of these elements and with a pH value of 5.0-6.0. Higher or lower pH levels can result in higher plant maintenance costs.

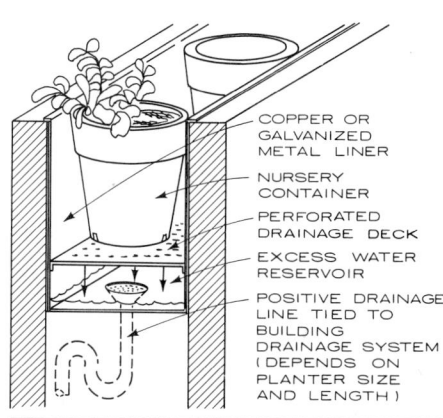

COPPER OR GALVANIZED METAL LINER
NURSERY CONTAINER
PERFORATED DRAINAGE DECK
EXCESS WATER RESERVOIR
POSITIVE DRAINAGE LINE TIED TO BUILDING DRAINAGE SYSTEM (DEPENDS ON PLANTER SIZE AND LENGTH)

RAILING PLANTER DETAIL

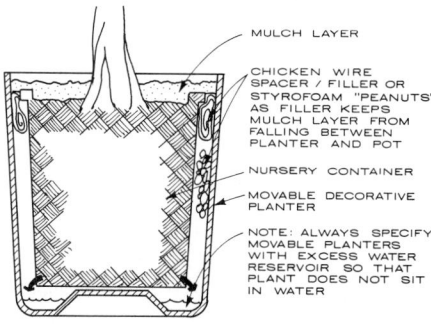

MULCH LAYER
CHICKEN WIRE SPACER / FILLER OR STYROFOAM "PEANUTS" AS FILLER KEEPS MULCH LAYER FROM FALLING BETWEEN PLANTER AND POT
NURSERY CONTAINER
MOVABLE DECORATIVE PLANTER
NOTE: ALWAYS SPECIFY MOVABLE PLANTERS WITH EXCESS WATER RESERVOIR SO THAT PLANT DOES NOT SIT IN WATER

MOVABLE DECORATIVE PLANTER DETAIL

STORAGE REQUIREMENTS

Provide a secured storage space of approximately 30 sq ft for watering equipment and other maintenance materials. It may be desirable to combine water supply and janitor needs in the same storage area.

AIR POLLUTION EFFECTS ON PLANTS

Problems result from inadequate ventilation. Excessive chlorine gas from swimming pool areas can be a damaging problem, as well as excessive fumes from toxic cleaning substances for floor finishes, etc. Ventilation a must here!

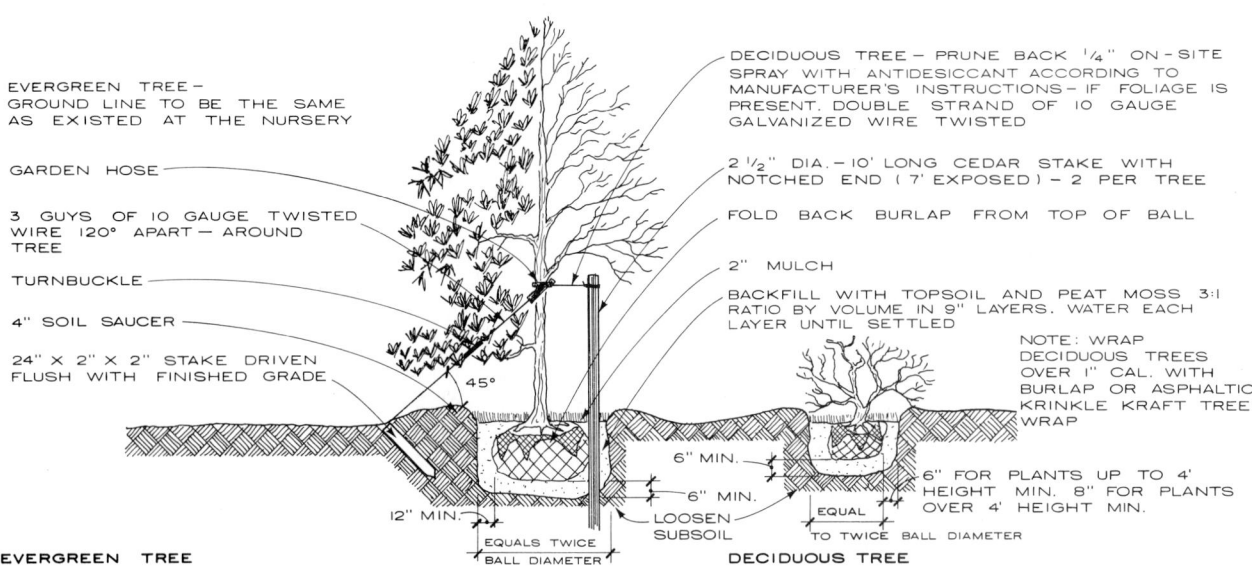

EVERGREEN TREE—
GROUND LINE TO BE THE SAME
AS EXISTED AT THE NURSERY

GARDEN HOSE

3 GUYS OF 10 GAUGE TWISTED
WIRE 120° APART — AROUND
TREE

TURNBUCKLE

4" SOIL SAUCER

24" X 2" X 2" STAKE DRIVEN
FLUSH WITH FINISHED GRADE

DECIDUOUS TREE — PRUNE BACK ¼" ON-SITE
SPRAY WITH ANTIDESICCANT ACCORDING TO
MANUFACTURER'S INSTRUCTIONS — IF FOLIAGE IS
PRESENT. DOUBLE STRAND OF 10 GAUGE
GALVANIZED WIRE TWISTED

2½" DIA.-10' LONG CEDAR STAKE WITH
NOTCHED END (7' EXPOSED) — 2 PER TREE

FOLD BACK BURLAP FROM TOP OF BALL

2" MULCH

BACKFILL WITH TOPSOIL AND PEAT MOSS 3:1
RATIO BY VOLUME IN 9" LAYERS. WATER EACH
LAYER UNTIL SETTLED

NOTE: WRAP
DECIDUOUS TREES
OVER 1" CAL. WITH
BURLAP OR ASPHALTIC
KRINKLE KRAFT TREE
WRAP

45°

6" MIN.

6" MIN.

12" MIN.

EQUALS TWICE
BALL DIAMETER

LOOSEN
SUBSOIL

EQUAL

TO TWICE BALL DIAMETER

6" FOR PLANTS UP TO 4'
HEIGHT MIN. 8" FOR PLANTS
OVER 4' HEIGHT MIN.

EVERGREEN TREE

DECIDUOUS TREE

PLANTING DETAILS — TREES AND SHRUBS

SHRUBS AND MINOR TREES BALLED AND BURLAPPED

HEIGHT RANGE (FT)	MINIMUM BALL DIAMETER (IN.)	MINIMUM BALL DEPTH (IN.)
1½–2	10	8
2–3	12	9
3–4	13	10
4–5	15	11
5–6	16	12
6–7	18	13
7–8	20	14
8–9	22	15
9–10	24	16
10–12	26	17

NOTE: Ball sizes should always be of a diameter to encompass the fibrous and feeding root system necessary for the full recovery of the plant.

STANDARD SHADE TREES—BALLED AND BURLAPPED

CALIPER* (IN.)	HEIGHT RANGE (FT)	MAXIMUM HEIGHTS (FT)	MINIMUM BALL DIAMETER (IN.)	MINIMUM BALL DEPTH (IN.)
½–¾	5–6	8	12	9
¾–1	6–8	10	14	10
1–1¼	7–9	11	16	12
1¼–1½	8–10	12	18	13
1½–1¾	10–12	14	20	14
1¾–2	10–12	14	22	15
2–2½	12–14	16	24	16
2½–3	12–14	16	28	19
3–3½	14–16	18	32	20
3½–4	14–16	18	36	22
4–5	16–18	22	44	26
5–6	18 and up	26	48	29

*Caliper indicates the diameter of the trunk taken 6 in. above the ground level up to and including 4 in. caliper size and 12 in. above the ground level for larger sizes.

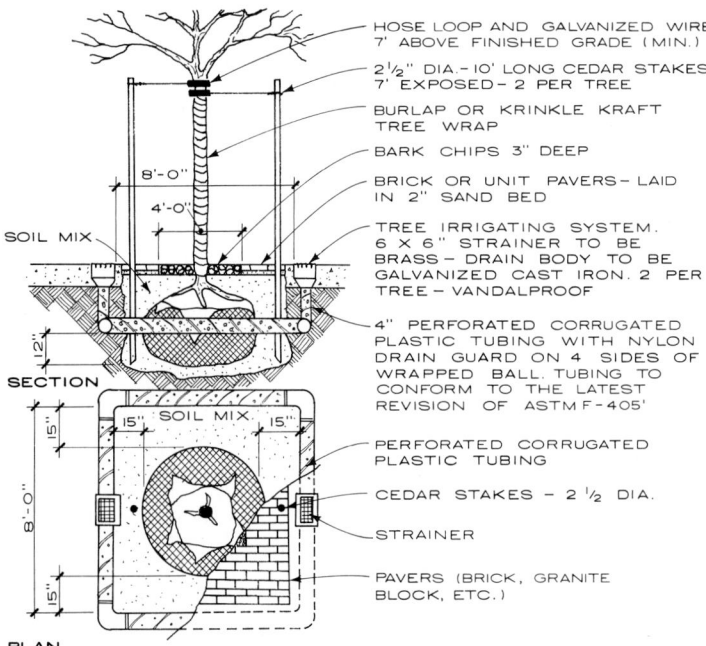

HOSE LOOP AND GALVANIZED WIRE
7' ABOVE FINISHED GRADE (MIN.)

2½" DIA.-10' LONG CEDAR STAKES
7' EXPOSED- 2 PER TREE

BURLAP OR KRINKLE KRAFT
TREE WRAP

BARK CHIPS 3" DEEP

BRICK OR UNIT PAVERS — LAID
IN 2" SAND BED

TREE IRRIGATING SYSTEM.
6 X 6" STRAINER TO BE
BRASS — DRAIN BODY TO BE
GALVANIZED CAST IRON. 2 PER
TREE — VANDALPROOF

4" PERFORATED CORRUGATED
PLASTIC TUBING WITH NYLON
DRAIN GUARD ON 4 SIDES OF
WRAPPED BALL. TUBING TO
CONFORM TO THE LATEST
REVISION OF ASTM F-405'

PERFORATED CORRUGATED
PLASTIC TUBING

CEDAR STAKES – 2½ DIA.

STRAINER

PAVERS (BRICK, GRANITE
BLOCK, ETC.)

SOIL MIX

8'-0"

4'-0"

12"

SECTION

15" 15"

SOIL MIX

8'-0"

15"

PLAN

PLANTING DETAIL — TREE IN PAVING

A. E. Bye & Associates, Landscape Architects; Old Greenwich, Connecticut

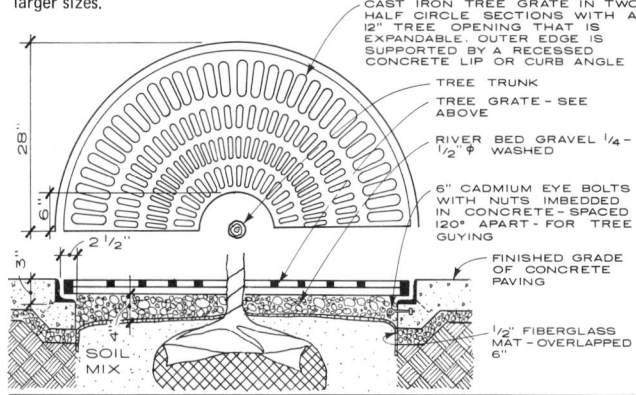

CAST IRON TREE GRATE IN TWO
HALF CIRCLE SECTIONS WITH A
12" TREE OPENING THAT IS
EXPANDABLE. OUTER EDGE IS
SUPPORTED BY A RECESSED
CONCRETE LIP OR CURB ANGLE

TREE TRUNK

TREE GRATE — SEE
ABOVE

RIVER BED GRAVEL ¼–
½" φ WASHED

6" CADMIUM EYE BOLTS
WITH NUTS IMBEDDED
IN CONCRETE – SPACED
120° APART – FOR TREE
GUYING

FINISHED GRADE
OF CONCRETE
PAVING

½" FIBERGLASS
MAT – OVERLAPPED
6"

28"

6"

2½"

3"

SOIL
MIX

TREE GRATE DETAIL

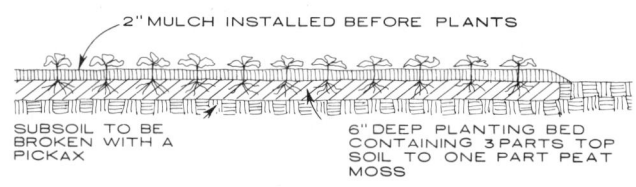

2" MULCH INSTALLED BEFORE PLANTS

SUBSOIL TO BE
BROKEN WITH A
PICKAX

6" DEEP PLANTING BED
CONTAINING 3 PARTS TOP
SOIL TO ONE PART PEAT
MOSS

GROUND COVER PLANTING DETAIL
NOTE: GROUND COVERS SHOULD BE POT OR CONTAINER GROWN

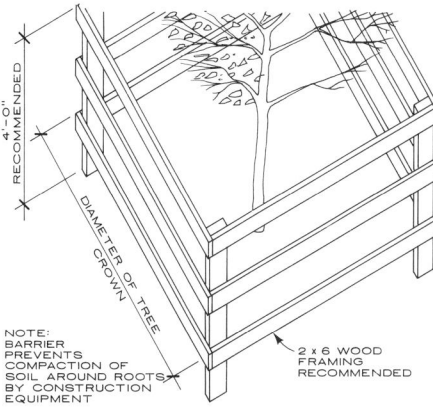

NOTE: BARRIER PREVENTS COMPACTION OF SOIL AROUND ROOTS BY CONSTRUCTION EQUIPMENT

TREE PROTECTION BARRIER

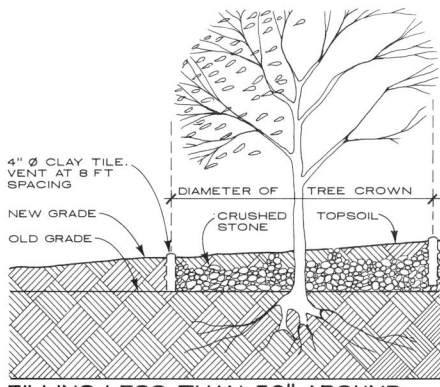

FILLING LESS THAN 30" AROUND EXISTING TREE

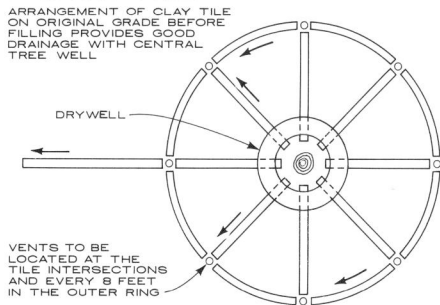

PLAN

FILLING OVER 30" AROUND EXISTING TREE

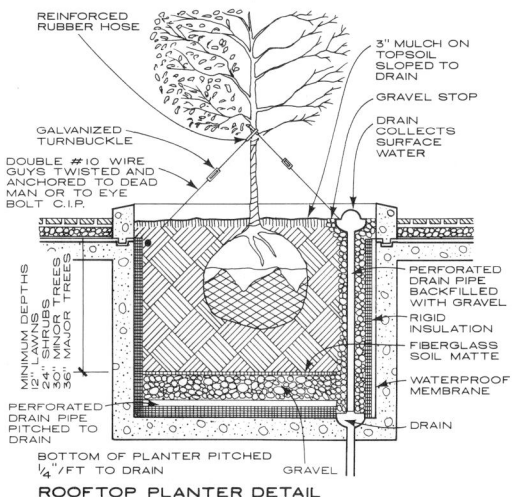

ROOFTOP PLANTER DETAIL

PLANTING ON STRUCTURES

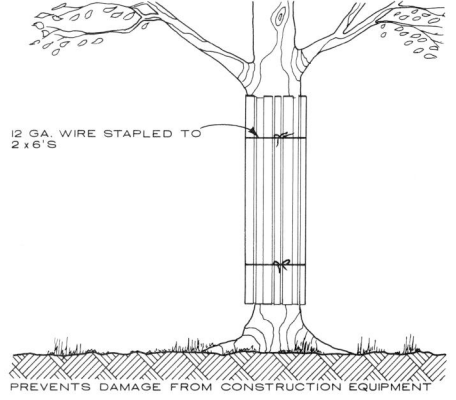

12 GA. WIRE STAPLED TO 2 x 6'S

PREVENTS DAMAGE FROM CONSTRUCTION EQUIPMENT

TREE TRUNK PROTECTION

CUTTING AROUND EXISTING TREES

Extreme care should be taken not to compact the earth within the crown of the tree. Compaction can cause severe root damage and reduce the air and water holding capacity of the soil.

If no surrounding barrier is provided, care should be taken not to operate equipment or store materials within the crown spread of the tree. If this area should be compacted, it would be necessary to aerate the soil thoroughly in the root zone immediately following construction. Certain tree species are severely affected by manipulation of the water table, and great care should be exercised to minimize this condition.

SPECIAL USE OF TREES

Trees for special uses should be branched or pruned naturally according to type. Where a form of growth is desired that is not in accordance with a natural growth habit, this form should be specified. For example:

1. BUSH FORM: Trees that start to branch close to the ground in the manner of a shrub.
2. CLUMPS: Trees with three or more main stems starting from the ground.
3. CUT BACK OR SHEARED: Trees that have been pruned back so as to multiply the branching structure and to develop a more formal effect.
4. ESPALIER: Trees pruned and trained to grow flat against a building or trellis, usually in a predetermined pattern or design.
5. PLEACHING: A technique of severe pruning, usually applied to a row or bosque of trees to produce a geometrically formal or clipped hedgelike effect.
6. POLLARDING: The technique in which annual severe pruning of certain species of trees serves to produce abundant vigorous growth the following year.
7. TOPIARY: Trees sheared or trimmed closely in a formal geometric pattern, or sculptural shapes frequently resembling animals or flowers.

SELECTING PLANTS FOR ROOFTOPS

WIND TOLERANCE

Higher elevations and exposure to wind can cause defoliation and increased transpiration rate. High parapet walls with louvers screen wind velocity and provide shelter for plants.

HIGH EVAPORATION RATE

Drying effects of wind and sun on soil around planter reduce available soil moisture rapidly. Irrigation, mulches, moisture holding soil additives (perlite, vermiculite and peat moss), and insulation assist in reducing this moisture loss.

RAPID SOIL TEMPERATURE FLUCTUATION

The conduction capacity of planter materials tends to produce a broad range of soil temperatures. Certain plant species suffer severe root damage because of cold or heat. Use of rigid insulation lining planter alleviates this condition.

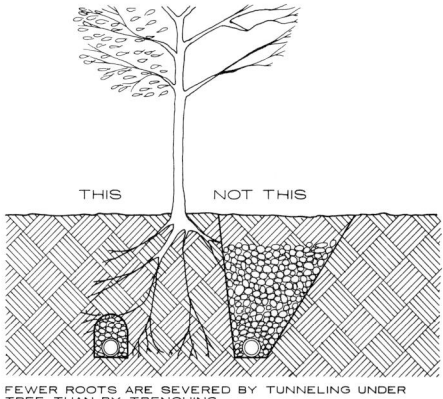

THIS   NOT THIS

FEWER ROOTS ARE SEVERED BY TUNNELING UNDER TREE THAN BY TRENCHING

UNDERGROUND UTILITIES NEAR EXISTING TREES

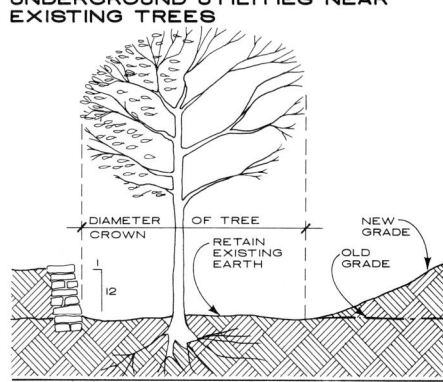

FILLING GRADE AROUND EXISTING TREE

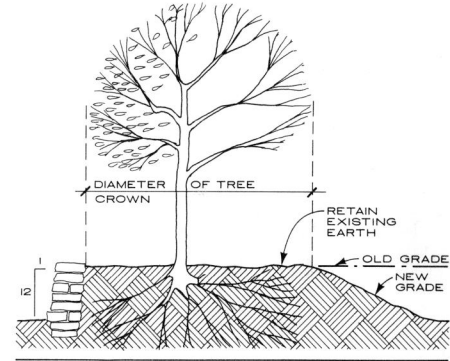

CUTTING GRADE AROUND EXISTING TREE

TOPSOIL

Topsoil in planters should be improved to provide the optimum growing condition. A general formula would add fertilizer (as per soil testing) plus 1 part peat moss or vermiculite (high water holding capacity) to 3 parts topsoil. More specific requirements for certain varieties of plants or grasses should be considered.

ROOT CAPACITY

Plant species should be carefully selected to adapt to the size of the plant bed. If species with shallow fibrous roots are used instead of species with a tap root system consult with nurseryman. Consider the ultimate maturity of the plant species in sizing planter.

Jim E. Miller and David W. Wheeler; Saratoga Associates; Saratoga Springs, New York

Erik Johnson; Lawrence Cook and Associates; Falls Church, Virginia

LANDSCAPING 2

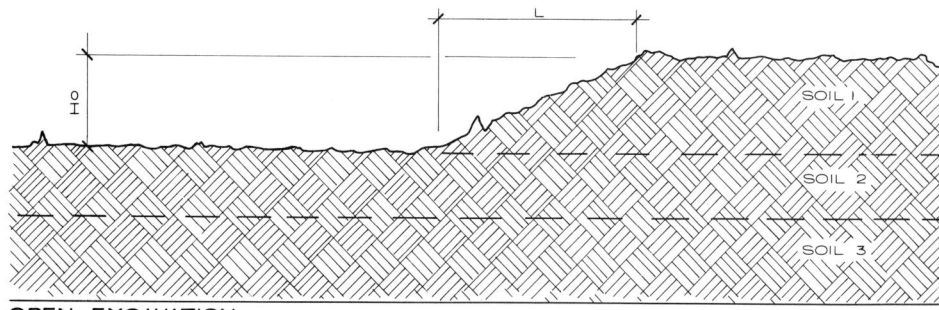

OPEN EXCAVATION

EMBANKMENT STABILITY
CONSULT FOUNDATION ENGINEER

SOIL TYPES			L/HO	REMARKS
S1	S2	S3		
Fill	Rock		>1.5	Check sliding of S1
Soft clay	Hard clay	Rock	>1.0	Check sliding of S1
Sand	Soft clay	Hard clay	>1.5	Check lateral displacement of S2
Sand	Sand	Hard clay	>1.5	
Hard clay	Soft clay	Sand	<1.0	Check lateral displacement of S2

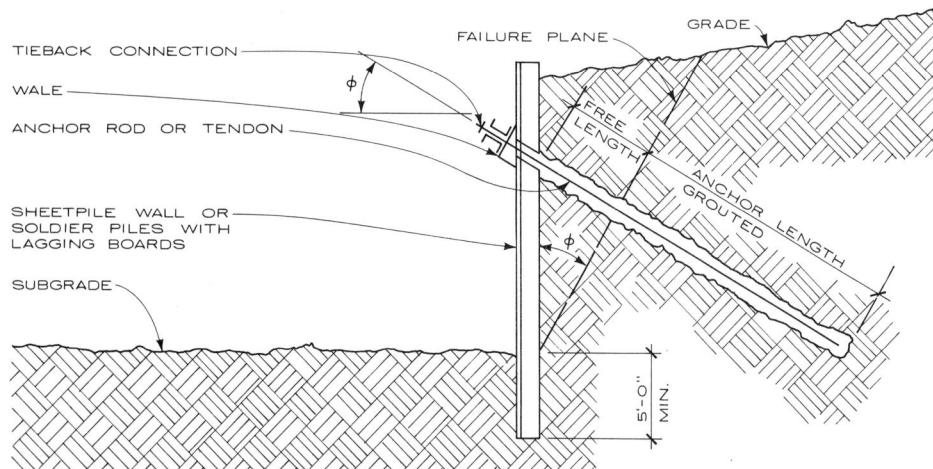

BRACED EXCAVATION USING RAKERS

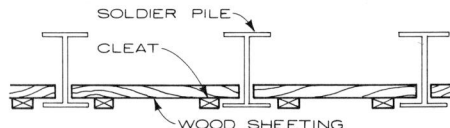

TIMBER LAGGING

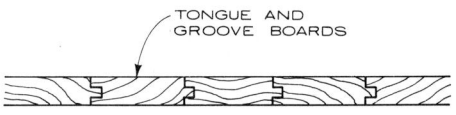

TIMBER SHEETING

STEEL SHEETING

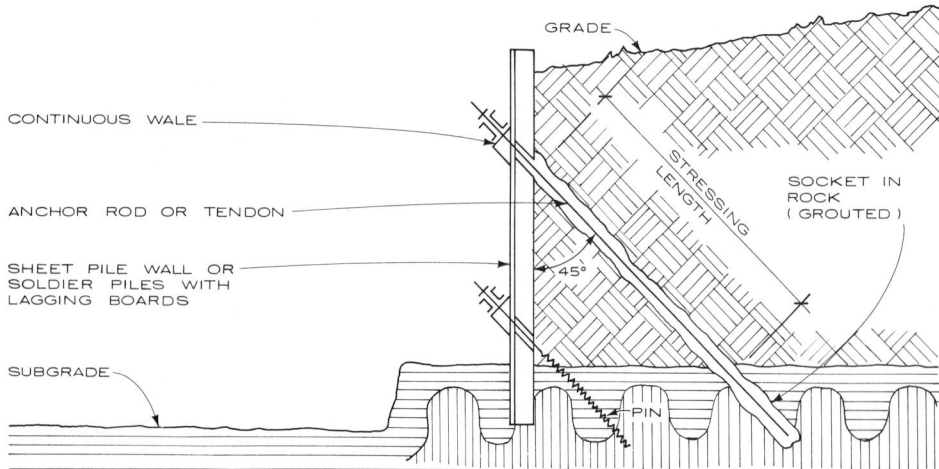

BRACED EXCAVATION USING EARTH ANCHORS

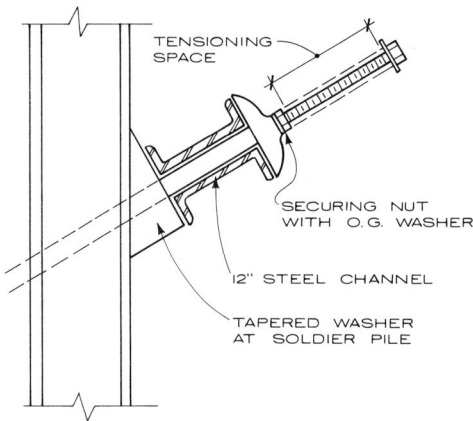

CHANNEL WALER DETAIL

NOTES
1. For shallow depths of excavation cantilever sheeting may be used, if driven to sufficient depth.
2. For deep excavations, several tiers of bracing may be necessary.
3. If subgrade of excavation is used for installation of spreadfootings or mats, proper dewatering procedures may be required to avoid disturbance of bearing level.
4. At times it may be possible to improve the bearing stratum by excavation of compressible materials and their replacement with compacted granular backfill.
5. For evaluation of problems encountered with sheeting and shoring, a foundation engineer should be consulted.
6. Local codes and OSHA regulations must be considered.
7. Proximity of utilities and other structures must be considered in design.

BRACED EXCAVATION USING ROCK ANCHORS

Mueser, Rutledge, Johnston & DeSimone; New York, New York

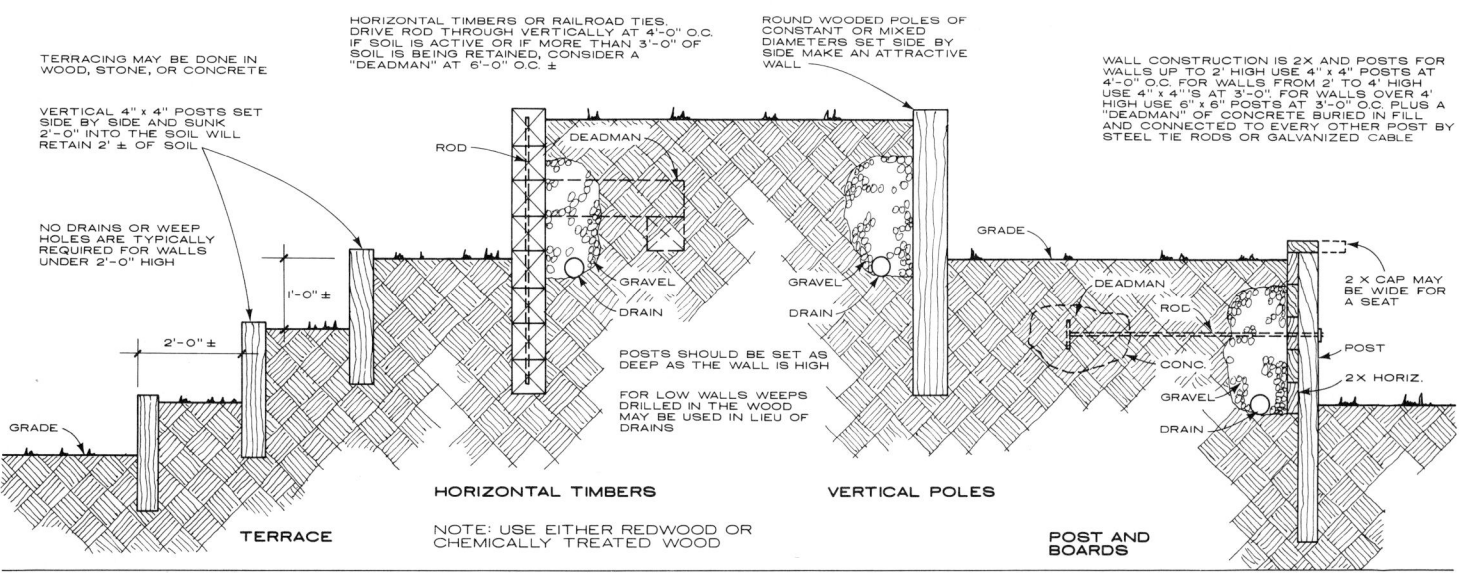

TERRACING MAY BE DONE IN WOOD, STONE, OR CONCRETE

VERTICAL 4" x 4" POSTS SET SIDE BY SIDE AND SUNK 2'-0" INTO THE SOIL WILL RETAIN 2' ± OF SOIL

NO DRAINS OR WEEP HOLES ARE TYPICALLY REQUIRED FOR WALLS UNDER 2'-0" HIGH

HORIZONTAL TIMBERS OR RAILROAD TIES. DRIVE ROD THROUGH VERTICALLY AT 4'-0" O.C. IF SOIL IS ACTIVE OR IF MORE THAN 3'-0" OF SOIL IS BEING RETAINED, CONSIDER A "DEADMAN" AT 6'-0" O.C. ±

ROUND WOODED POLES OF CONSTANT OR MIXED DIAMETERS SET SIDE BY SIDE MAKE AN ATTRACTIVE WALL

WALL CONSTRUCTION IS 2X AND POSTS FOR WALLS UP TO 2' HIGH USE 4" x 4" POSTS AT 4'-0" O.C. FOR WALLS FROM 2' TO 4' HIGH USE 4" x 4"'S AT 3'-0". FOR WALLS OVER 4' HIGH USE 6" x 6" POSTS AT 3'-0" O.C. PLUS A "DEADMAN" OF CONCRETE BURIED IN FILL AND CONNECTED TO EVERY OTHER POST BY STEEL TIE RODS OR GALVANIZED CABLE

ROD

DEADMAN

GRAVEL DRAIN

GRAVEL DRAIN

GRADE

DEADMAN

ROD

CONC

GRAVEL

DRAIN

2 X CAP MAY BE WIDE FOR A SEAT

POST

2 X HORIZ.

POSTS SHOULD BE SET AS DEEP AS THE WALL IS HIGH

FOR LOW WALLS WEEPS DRILLED IN THE WOOD MAY BE USED IN LIEU OF DRAINS

GRADE

TERRACE

HORIZONTAL TIMBERS

VERTICAL POLES

POST AND BOARDS

NOTE: USE EITHER REDWOOD OR CHEMICALLY TREATED WOOD

WOOD APPLICATIONS

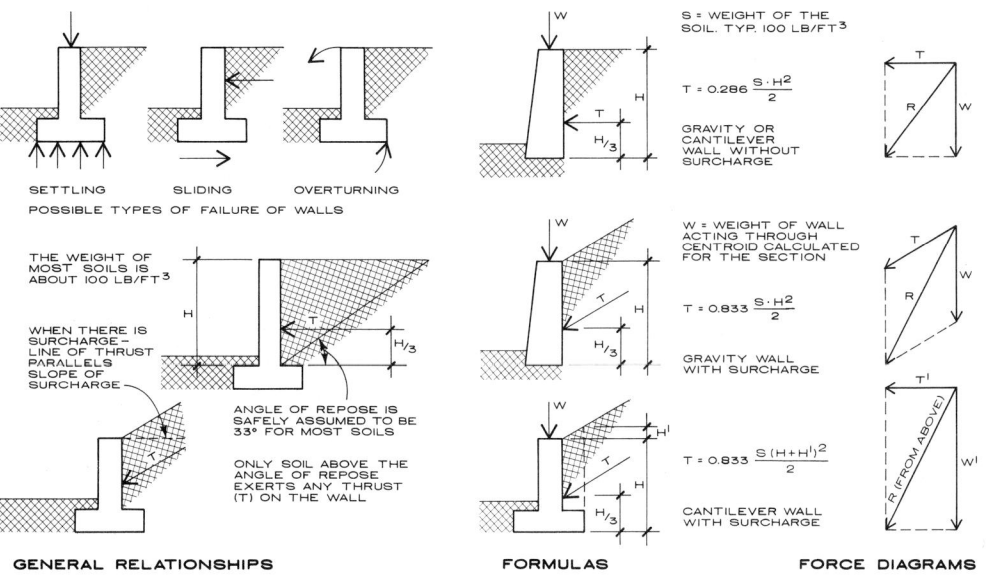

SETTLING   SLIDING   OVERTURNING

POSSIBLE TYPES OF FAILURE OF WALLS

THE WEIGHT OF MOST SOILS IS ABOUT 100 LB/FT³

WHEN THERE IS SURCHARGE - LINE OF THRUST PARALLELS SLOPE OF SURCHARGE

ANGLE OF REPOSE IS SAFELY ASSUMED TO BE 33° FOR MOST SOILS

ONLY SOIL ABOVE THE ANGLE OF REPOSE EXERTS ANY THRUST (T) ON THE WALL

GENERAL RELATIONSHIPS

S = WEIGHT OF THE SOIL. TYP. 100 LB/FT³

$$T = 0.286 \frac{S \cdot H^2}{2}$$

GRAVITY OR CANTILEVER WALL WITHOUT SURCHARGE

W = WEIGHT OF WALL ACTING THROUGH CENTROID CALCULATED FOR THE SECTION

$$T = 0.833 \frac{S \cdot H^2}{2}$$

GRAVITY WALL WITH SURCHARGE

$$T = 0.833 \frac{S(H + H')^2}{2}$$

CANTILEVER WALL WITH SURCHARGE

FORMULAS

FORCE DIAGRAMS

SLIDING

The thrust on the wall must be resisted. The resisting force is the weight of the wall times the coefficient of soil friction. Use a safety factor of 1.5. Therefore:

$$W(C.F.) \geq 1.5T$$

Average coefficients:

Gravel	0.6
Silt/dry clay	0.5
Sand	0.4
Wet clay	0.3

OVERTURNING

The overturning moment equals T(H/3). This is resisted by the resisting moment. For symmetrical sections, resisting moment equals W times (width of base/2). Use a safety factor of 2.0. Therefore:

$$M_R \geq 2(M_0)$$

SETTLING

Soil bearing value must resist vertical force. For symmetrical sections that force is W (or W')/bearing area. Use a safety factor of 1.5. Therefore:

$$S.B. \geq 1.5(W/A)$$

STRUCTURAL DESIGN CONSIDERATIONS

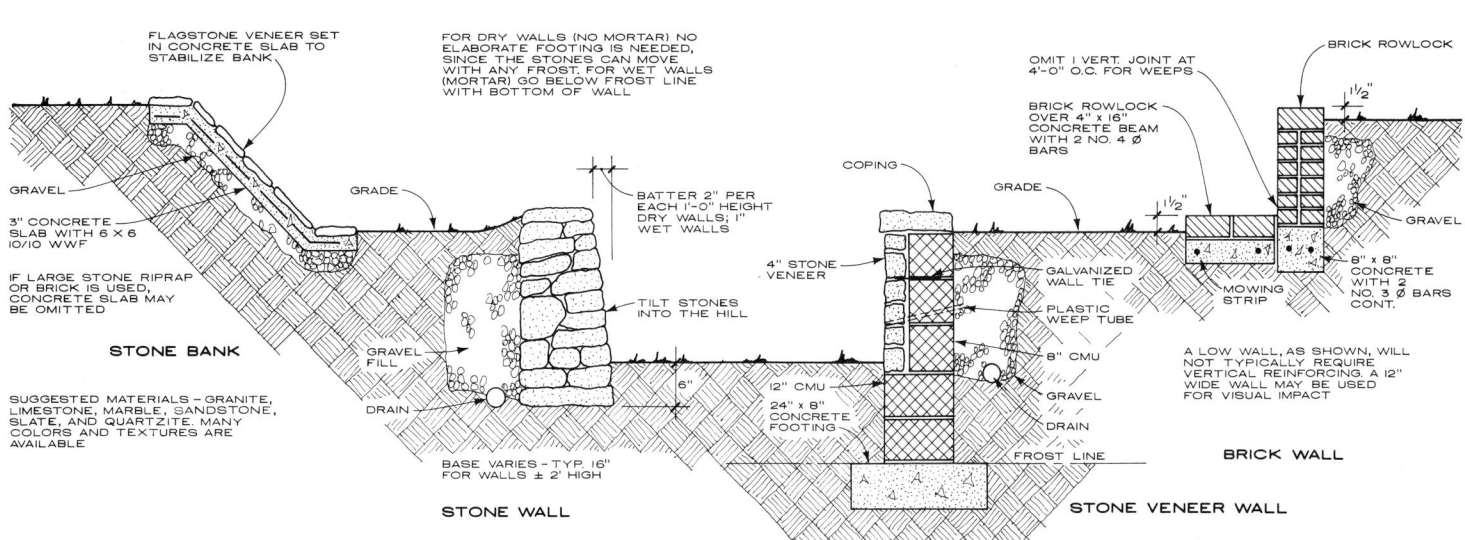

FLAGSTONE VENEER SET IN CONCRETE SLAB TO STABILIZE BANK

GRAVEL

3" CONCRETE SLAB WITH 6 X 6 10/10 WWF

IF LARGE STONE, RIPRAP OR BRICK IS USED, CONCRETE SLAB MAY BE OMITTED

STONE BANK

SUGGESTED MATERIALS — GRANITE, LIMESTONE, MARBLE, SANDSTONE, SLATE, AND QUARTZITE. MANY COLORS AND TEXTURES ARE AVAILABLE

FOR DRY WALLS (NO MORTAR) NO ELABORATE FOOTING IS NEEDED, SINCE THE STONES CAN MOVE WITH ANY FROST. FOR WET WALLS (MORTAR) GO BELOW FROST LINE WITH BOTTOM OF WALL

GRADE

BATTER 2" PER EACH 1'-0" HEIGHT DRY WALLS; 1" WET WALLS

TILT STONES INTO THE HILL

GRAVEL FILL

DRAIN

BASE VARIES - TYP. 16" FOR WALLS ± 2' HIGH

STONE WALL

COPING

4" STONE VENEER

GALVANIZED WALL TIE

PLASTIC WEEP TUBE

8" CMU

12" CMU

24" x 8" CONCRETE FOOTING

FROST LINE

STONE VENEER WALL

OMIT 1 VERT. JOINT AT 4'-0" O.C. FOR WEEPS

BRICK ROWLOCK OVER 4" x 16" CONCRETE BEAM WITH 2 NO. 4 Ø BARS

GRADE

BRICK ROWLOCK

GRAVEL

8" x 8" CONCRETE WITH 2 NO. 3 Ø BARS CONT.

MOWING STRIP

GRAVEL

DRAIN

A LOW WALL, AS SHOWN, WILL NOT TYPICALLY REQUIRE VERTICAL REINFORCING. A 12" WIDE WALL MAY BE USED FOR VISUAL IMPACT

BRICK WALL

STONE AND MASONRY APPLICATIONS

Charles R. Heuer, AIA; Washington, D.C.

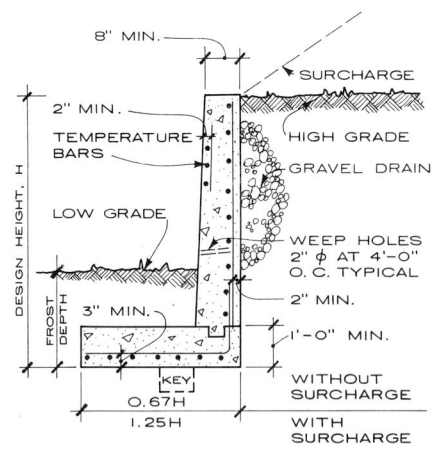

Place base below frost line. Dimensions are approximate.

CONCRETE OUTLINES FOR L TYPE RETAINING WALL

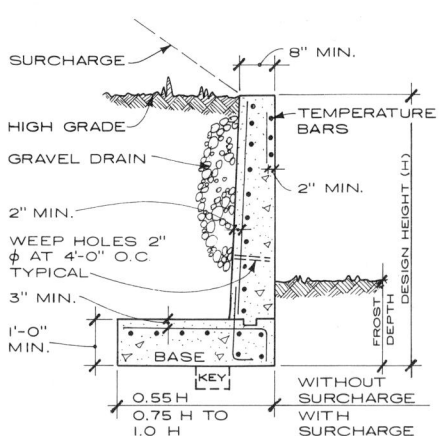

Soil pressure at toe equals 0.2 times the height in kips per square foot. Dimensions are preliminary.

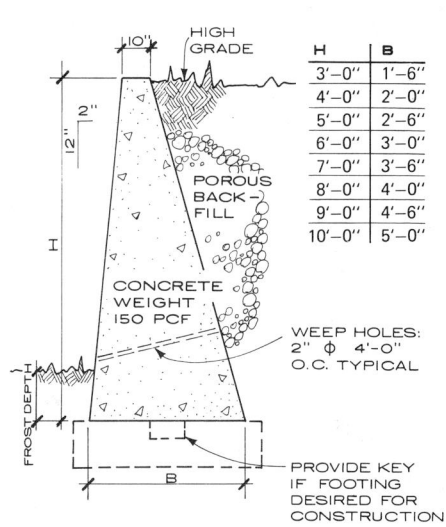

H	B
3'-0"	1'-6"
4'-0"	2'-0"
5'-0"	2'-6"
6'-0"	3'-0"
7'-0"	3'-6"
8'-0"	4'-0"
9'-0"	4'-6"
10'-0"	5'-0"

MASS CONCRETE RETAINING WALL WITHOUT SURCHARGE

RETAINING WALL – VERTICAL CONTROL JOINT

RETAINING WALL – VERTICAL EXPANSION JOINT

NOTES

Provide control and/or construction joints in concrete retaining walls about every 25 ft and expansion joints about every fourth control and/or construction joint. Coated dowels should be used if average wall height on either side of a joint is different.

Consult with a structural engineer for final design of concrete retaining walls.

Use temperature bars if wall is more than 12 in. thick.

Keys shown dashed may be required to prevent sliding in high walls and those on moist clay.

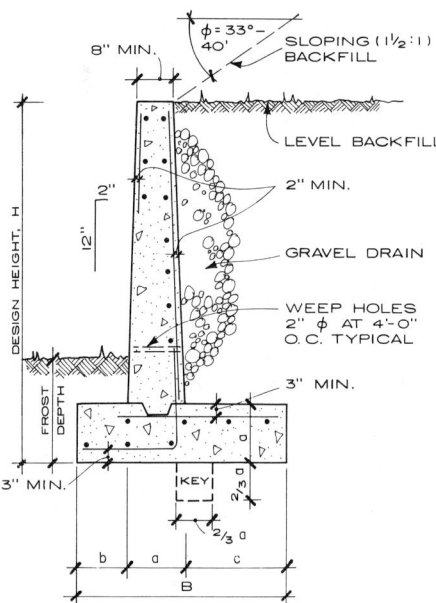

PRELIMINARY DIMENSIONS

HEIGHT OF WALL = H (FT)	BACKFILL SLOPING φ = 33° - 40' (1½:1) CONCRETE OUTLINES				HEIGHT OF WALL = H (FT)	BACKFILL LEVEL—NO SURCHARGE CONCRETE OUTLINES			
	B (FT)	a (FT)	b (FT)	c (FT)		B (FT)	a (FT)	b (FT)	c (FT)
3	2'-6"	0'-11"	0'-7"	1'-0"	3	1'-9"	0'-10½"	0'-4"	0'-6½"
4	3'-2"	1'-0"	0'-9"	1'-5"	4	2'-2"	0'-11"	0'-5"	0'-10"
5	3'-10"	1'-1"	1'-0"	1'-9"	5	2'-8"	0'-11"	0'-5"	1'-4"
6	4'-6"	1'-2"	1'-3"	2'-1"	6	3'-3"	1'-0"	0'-8"	1'-7"
7	5'-3"	1'-3"	1'-6"	2'-6"	7	3'-10"	1'-0"	1'-0"	1'-10"
8	5'-11"	1'-4"	1'-9"	2'-10"	8	4'-3"	1'-1"	1'-1"	2'-1"
9	6'-8"	1'-5"	2'-0"	3'-3"	9	4'-9"	1'-1"	1'-1"	2'-7"
10	7'-5"	1'-6"	2'-3"	3'-8"	10	5'-4"	1'-2"	1'-4"	2'-10"
11	8'-1"	1'-7"	2'-6"	4'-0"	11	5'-10"	1'-2"	1'-6"	3'-2"
12	8'-10"	1'-8"	2'-9"	4'-5"	12	6'-6"	1'-3"	1'-8"	3'-7"
13	9'-6"	1'-9"	3'-0"	4'-9"	13	7'-0"	1'-4"	1'-8"	4'-0"
14	10'-3"	1'-10"	3'-3"	5'-2"	14	7'-8"	1'-4"	2'-1"	4'-3"
15	11'-0"	1'-11"	3'-6"	5'-7"	15	8'-1"	1'-5"	2'-1"	4'-7"
16	11'-10"	2'-0"	3'-10"	6'-0"	16	8'-6"	1'-5"	2'-2"	4'-11"
17	12'-7"	2'-1"	4'-1"	6'-5"	17	9'-0"	1'-6"	2'-3"	5'-3"
18	13'-4"	2'-2"	4'-4"	6'-10"	18	9'-6"	1'-7"	2'-4"	5'-7"
19	14'-2"	2'-3"	4'-8"	7'-3"	19	10'-2"	1'-7"	2'-6"	6'-1"
20	15'-0"	2'-4"	5'-0"	7'-8"	20	10'-5"	1'-8"	2'-6"	6'-3"

Key shown dashed may be required to prevent sliding in high walls and those on moist clay.

CONCRETE OUTLINES FOR "T" TYPE RETAINING WALL WITH LEVEL AND SLOPING BACKFILL

Neubaur · Sohn, Engineers; Washington, D.C.

DIMENSIONS AND REINFORCEMENT

WALL	H	B	T	A	VERTICAL RODS IN THE WALL	HORIZONTAL RODS IN FOOTING
8 in. thickness	3'-4"	2'-4"	9"	8"	3/8" @ 32"	3/8" @ 27"
	4'-0"	2'-9"	9"	10"	1/2" @ 32"	3/8" @ 27"
	4'-8"	3'-3"	10"	12"	5/8" @ 32"	3/8" @ 27"
	5'-4"	3'-8"	10"	14"	1/2" @ 16"	1/2" @ 30"
	6'-0"	4'-2"	12"	15"	1/2" @ 24"	1/2" @ 25"

NOTE

These dimensions and reinforcement are for level backfill. Consult structural engineer for walls over 6 ft high, sloping fill, or vehicular loads.

LINE ONE SIDE OF CORE WITH BUILDING PAPER

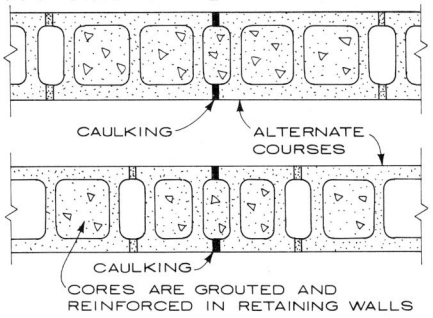

CAULKING — ALTERNATE COURSES

CAULKING

CORES ARE GROUTED AND REINFORCED IN RETAINING WALLS

SHEAR-RESISTING CONTROL JOINT

NOTE

Long retaining walls should be broken into panels 20 to 30 ft in length by means of vertical control joints. Joints should be designed to resist shear and other lateral forces while permitting longitudinal movement.

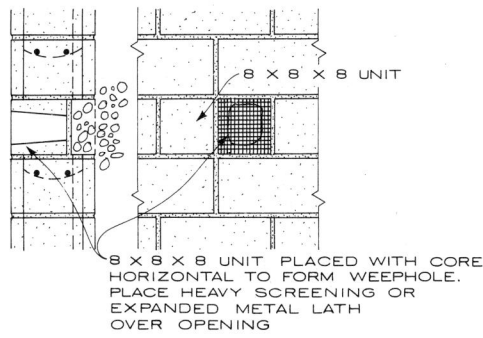

8 X 8 X 8 UNIT

8 X 8 X 8 UNIT PLACED WITH CORE HORIZONTAL TO FORM WEEPHOLE. PLACE HEAVY SCREENING OR EXPANDED METAL LATH OVER OPENING

ALTERNATE WEEPHOLE DETAIL

NOTE

Four inch diameter weepholes located at 5 to 10 ft spacing along the base of the wall should be sufficient. Place about 1 cu ft of gravel or crushed stone around the intake of each weephole.

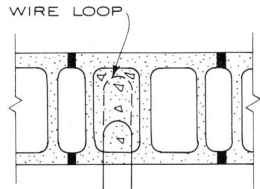

WIRE LOOP

PLAN VERTICAL ROD

NOTE

Place wire loop extending into core in mortar joints as wall is laid up. Loosen before mortar sets. After inserting bar, pull wire loop and bar to proper position and secure wire by tying free ends.

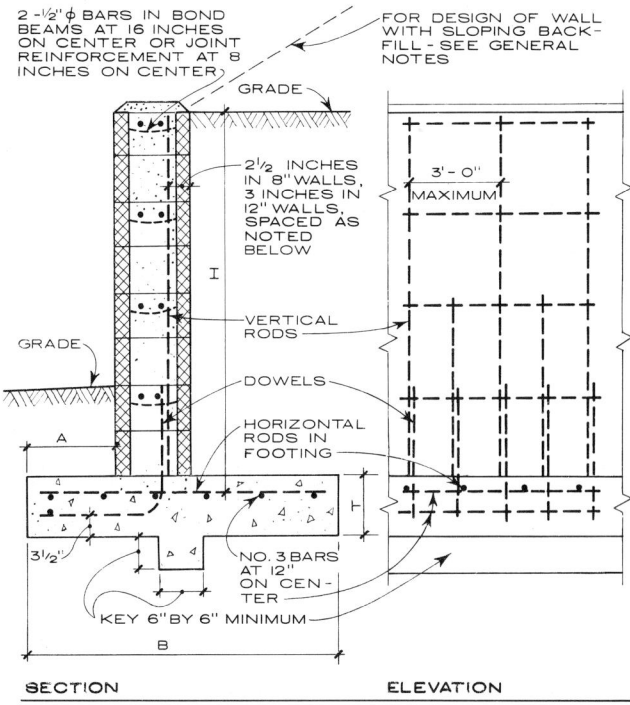

2 - 1/2"∅ BARS IN BOND BEAMS AT 16 INCHES ON CENTER OR JOINT REINFORCEMENT AT 8 INCHES ON CENTER

FOR DESIGN OF WALL WITH SLOPING BACK-FILL - SEE GENERAL NOTES

GRADE

2 1/2 INCHES IN 8" WALLS, 3 INCHES IN 12" WALLS, SPACED AS NOTED BELOW

3'-0" MAXIMUM

VERTICAL RODS

GRADE

DOWELS

HORIZONTAL RODS IN FOOTING

3 1/2"

NO. 3 BARS AT 12" ON CENTER

KEY 6" BY 6" MINIMUM

B

SECTION — ELEVATION

TYPICAL CANTILEVER RETAINING WALL

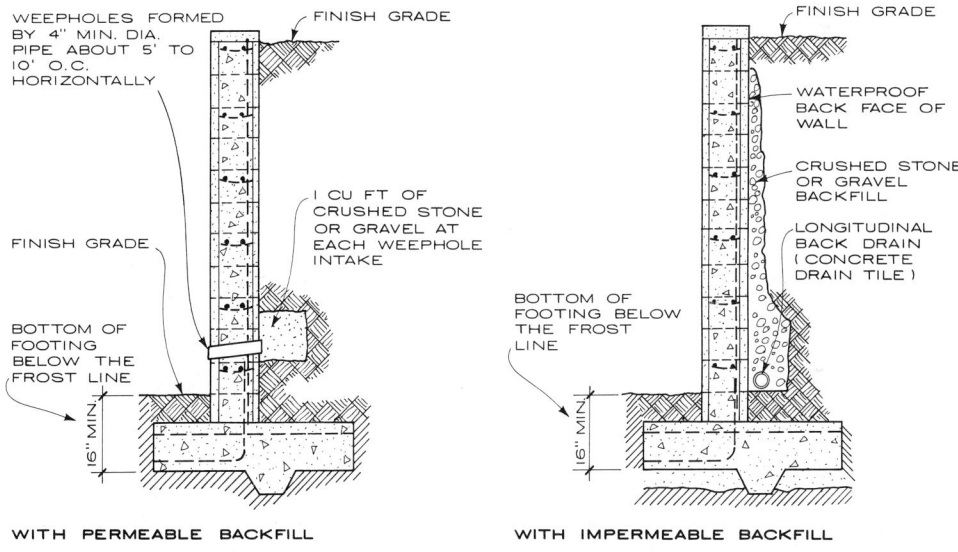

WEEPHOLES FORMED BY 4" MIN. DIA. PIPE ABOUT 5' TO 10' O.C. HORIZONTALLY

FINISH GRADE

1 CU FT OF CRUSHED STONE OR GRAVEL AT EACH WEEPHOLE INTAKE

FINISH GRADE

BOTTOM OF FOOTING BELOW THE FROST LINE

16" MIN.

WITH PERMEABLE BACKFILL

FINISH GRADE

WATERPROOF BACK FACE OF WALL

CRUSHED STONE OR GRAVEL BACKFILL

LONGITUDINAL BACK DRAIN (CONCRETE DRAIN TILE)

BOTTOM OF FOOTING BELOW THE FROST LINE

16" MIN.

WITH IMPERMEABLE BACKFILL

BACKFILLING PROCEDURES AND DRAINAGE

GENERAL NOTES

1. Concrete for footings should be mixed in the following approximate proportions: 1 part portland cement, 2 3/4 parts sand, and 4 parts gravel. Gravel should be well graded and not exceed 1 1/2 in. in size. Amount of water used for each bag of cement should not exceed 5 1/2 gal unless the sand is very dry.

2. Use fine grout where grout space is less than 3 in. in least dimension. Use coarse grout where the least dimension of the grout space is 3 in. or more.

3. Steel reinforcement should be clean, free from harmful rust, and in compliance with applicable ASTM standards for deformed bars and steel wire.

4. Alternate vertical bars may be stopped at the midheight of the wall. Vertical reinforcement is usually secured in place after the masonry work has been completed and before grouting.

5. Designs herein are based on an assumed soil weight (vertical pressure) of 100 pcf. Horizontal pressure is based on an equivalent fluid weight for the soil of 45 pcf.

6. Walls shown are designed with a safety factor against overturning of not less than 2 and a safety factor against horizontal sliding of not less than 1.5. Computations in the table for wall heights are based on level backfill. One method of providing for additional loads due to sloping backfill or surface loads is to consider them as an additional depth of soil, that is, an extra load of 300 psf can be treated as 3 ft of extra soil weighing 100 psf.

7. Top of masonry retaining walls should be capped or otherwise protected to prevent the entry of water into unfilled hollow cells and spaces. If bond beams are used, steel is placed in the beams as the wall is constructed. If desired, horizontal joint reinforcement may be placed in each joint (8 in. o.c.) and the bond beams omitted.

8. Allow 24 hr for masonry to set before grouting. Pour grout in 4 ft layers, 1 hr between each pour. Break long walls into panels of 20 to 30 ft in length with vertical control joints. Allow 7 days for finished wall to set before backfilling. Prevent water from accumulating behind wall by means of 4 in. diameter weepholes at a 5 to 10 ft spacing (with screen and graded stone) or by a continuous drain with felt covered open joints in combination with waterproofing.

9. Where backfill exceeds 6 ft in height, provide a key under the base of the footing to resist the tendency of the wall to slide horizontally.

10. Heavy equipment used in backfilling should not approach closer to the top of the wall than a distance equal to the height of the wall.

Stephen J. Zipp, AIA; Wilkes and Faulkner Associates; Washington, D.C.

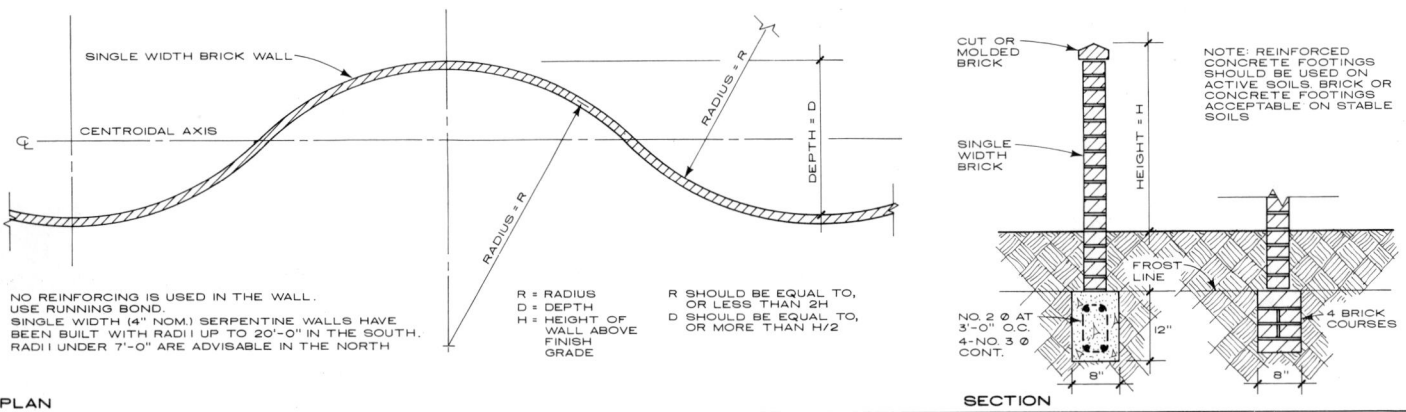

NO REINFORCING IS USED IN THE WALL.
USE RUNNING BOND.
SINGLE WIDTH (4" NOM.) SERPENTINE WALLS HAVE
BEEN BUILT WITH RADII UP TO 20'-0" IN THE SOUTH.
RADII UNDER 7'-0" ARE ADVISABLE IN THE NORTH

R = RADIUS
D = DEPTH
H = HEIGHT OF
WALL ABOVE
FINISH
GRADE

R SHOULD BE EQUAL TO,
OR LESS THAN 2H
D SHOULD BE EQUAL TO,
OR MORE THAN H/2

PLAN

SECTION

SERPENTINE GARDEN WALLS

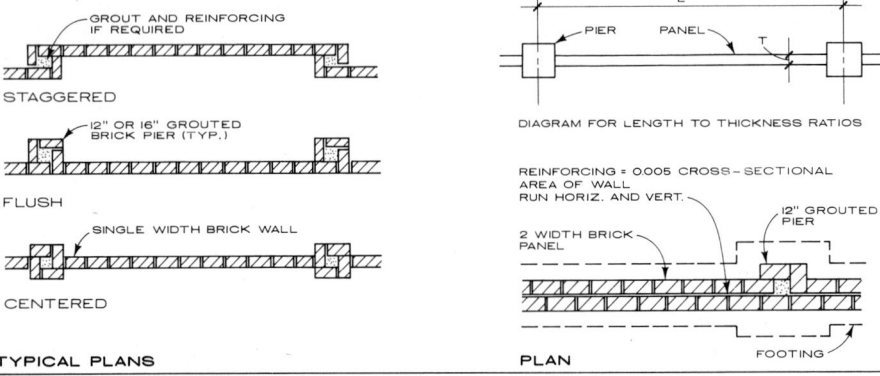

STAGGERED

FLUSH

CENTERED

TYPICAL PLANS

DIAGRAM FOR LENGTH TO THICKNESS RATIOS

REINFORCING = 0.005 CROSS-SECTIONAL
AREA OF WALL
RUN HORIZ. AND VERT.

PLAN

LENGTH TO THICKNESS RATIOS

WIND PRESSURE (LB/FT^2)	MAXIMUM L/T RATIO
5	35
10	25
15	20
20	18
25	16
30	14
35	13
40	12

PIER AND PANEL WALLS

WIND PRESSURE CHART

HEIGHT ZONE (FT)	WIND PRESSURE MAP AREAS (PSF)						
	20	25	30	35	40	45	50
Less than 30	15	20	25	25	30	35	40

POUNDS PER
SQUARE FOOT
20 25 30 35 40 45 50

ANALYSIS OF SECTIONS

M_0 = OVERTURNING MOMENT
M_r = RESISTING MOMENT
W = WEIGHT OF WALL AND
FOOTING (LB)
P = WIND LOAD (FROM
TABLE) (LB/FT^2)
$M_0 = PL_1$ $M_r = WL_2$
FOR STABILITY $M_r \geq M_0$;
IF NOT, REDESIGN

CANTILEVER FOOTINGS
ARE OFTEN USED AT
PROPERTY LINES OR TO
INCREASE RESISTANCE
TO OVERTURNING. BE
SURE TO CHECK FOR
WIND FROM EITHER
DIRECTION

W = WEIGHT OF
WALL AND
FOOTING

P = WIND LOAD

LOCATION OF
CENTROID MUST
BE CALCULATED
FOR EACH
ECCENTRIC
WALL
SITUATION

CALCULATE FOR
BOTH P_1 AND P_2

FINISH GRADE

CONCRETE
FOOTING.
SIZE AND
REINFORCING
AS REQUIRED

SYMMETRICAL   CANTILEVER/ECCENTRIC

HORIZONTAL LOADING – FREESTANDING WALLS

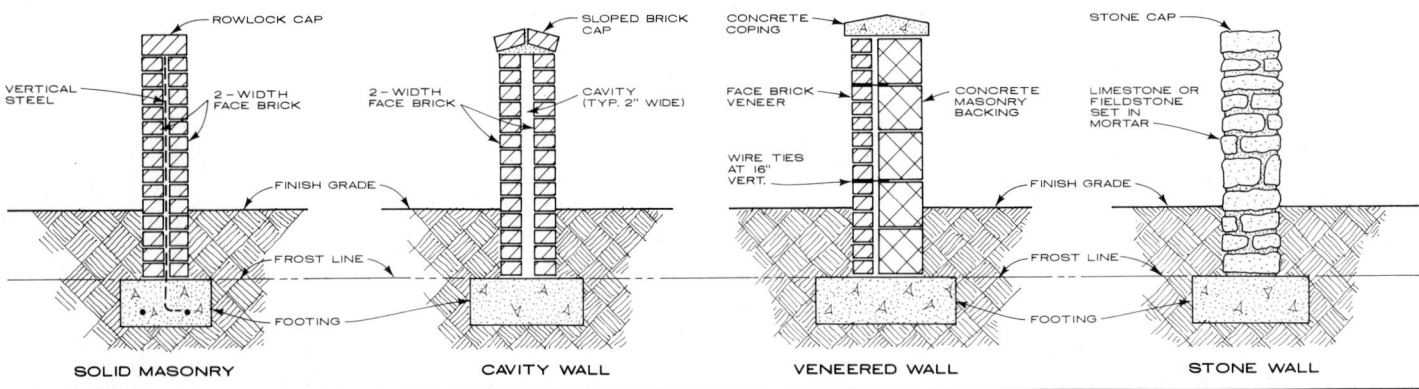

SOLID MASONRY   CAVITY WALL   VENEERED WALL   STONE WALL

FREESTANDING WALL TYPES

Charles R. Heuer, AIA; Washington, D. C.

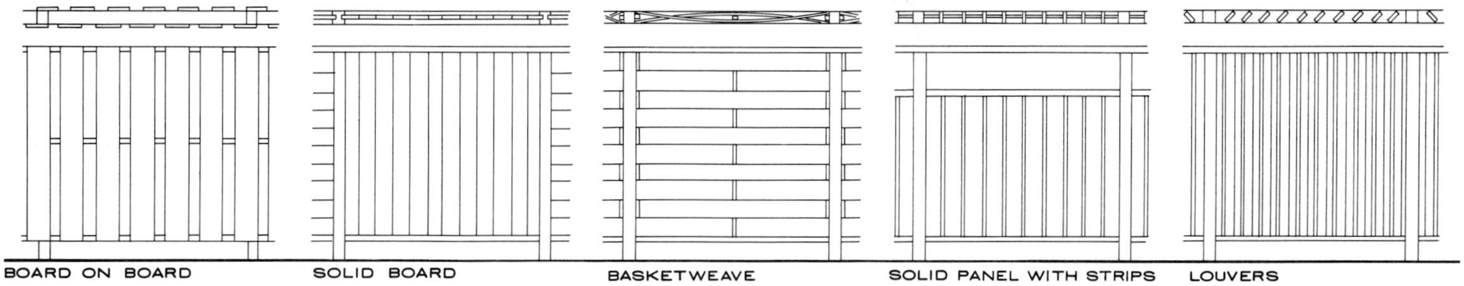

BOARD ON BOARD   **SOLID BOARD**   **BASKETWEAVE**   **SOLID PANEL WITH STRIPS**   **LOUVERS**

SOLID FENCE TYPES

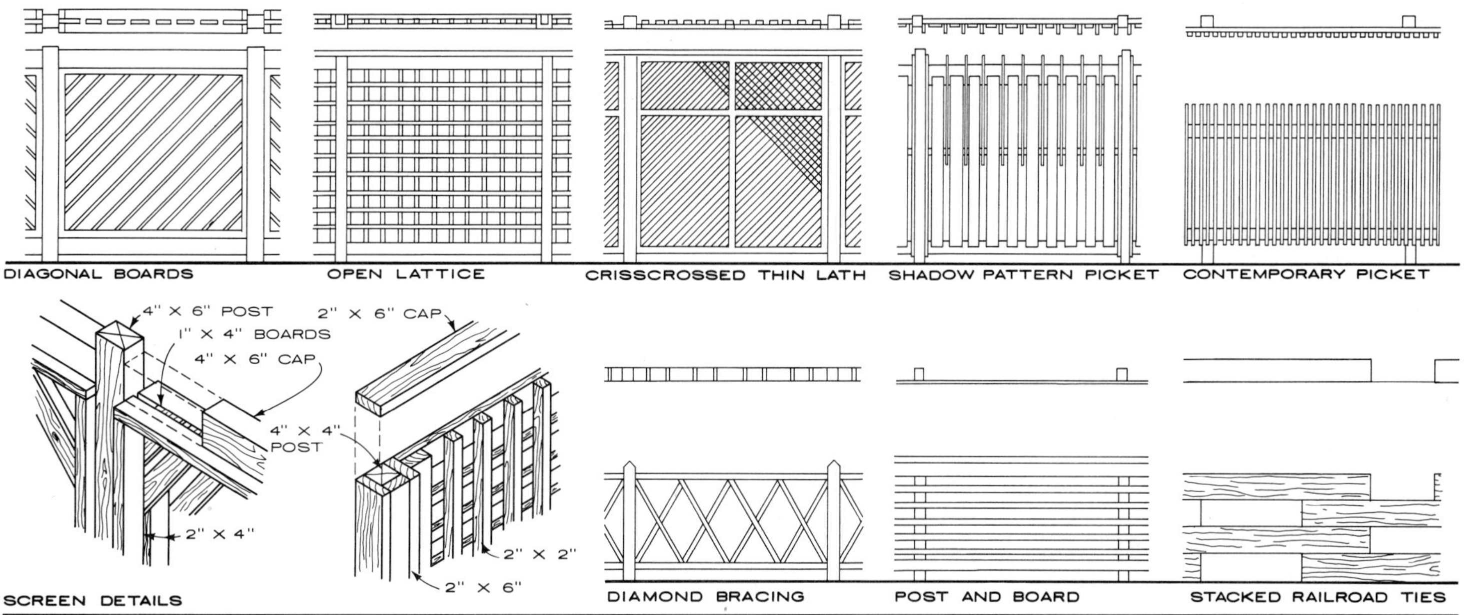

DIAGONAL BOARDS   **OPEN LATTICE**   **CRISSCROSSED THIN LATH**   **SHADOW PATTERN PICKET**   **CONTEMPORARY PICKET**

4" X 6" POST
1" X 4" BOARDS
4" X 6" CAP
2" X 6" CAP
4" X 4" POST
2" X 4"
2" X 2"
2" X 6"

SCREEN DETAILS

DIAMOND BRACING   **POST AND BOARD**   **STACKED RAILROAD TIES**

TRANSPARENT FENCES AND SCREENS

GENERAL NOTES

The following issues should be considered when selecting a wood fence pattern:

1. The topography of the site and the prevailing wind conditions.
2. The architectural style of surrounding buildings as well as the adjacent use of land.
3. The required height of the fence and the size of the property to be enclosed.

Wood fences can be constructed as solid walls and used near buildings for protection and privacy of outdoor spaces. A semitransparent wood screen is often used to enclose an outdoor room without totally obstructing views or restricting natural ventilation. Long open fence patterns are best used at the property line to define boundaries or limit access to a site.

MATERIALS

Wood posts and rails are usually made of red or white oak, western larch, many species of pine, eastern red cedar, or redwood. Wood or aluminum caps should be used wherever end grains are exposed to the weather.

Most heartwoods, especially cedar and redwood, have superior natural resistance to decay. Other exposed wood members should be treated with water soluble preservatives such as chromated copper arsenate (CCA) or pentachlorophenol dissolved in a volatile solvent. Creosote or pentachlorophenal in an oil solvent should be avoided, since they do not mix with stains or paints.

Uncoated wood rapidly weathers to a shade of gray. A broad range of colors are obtainable with standard paints, bleaches, and stains. Clear water repellents may be used with redwood and cedar. Natural finishes or penetrating stains allow more of the wood grain to show than paint and are preferable for severe weather exposures. Varnishes deteriorate rapidly in sunlight and water.

Fasteners should be of noncorrosive aluminum alloy or stainless steel. Top quality, hot dip galvanized steel is acceptable. Metal flanges, cleats, bolts, and screws are better than common nails.

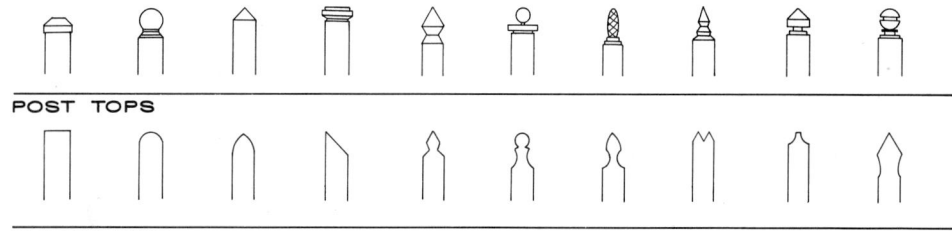

POST TOPS

PICKET TOPS

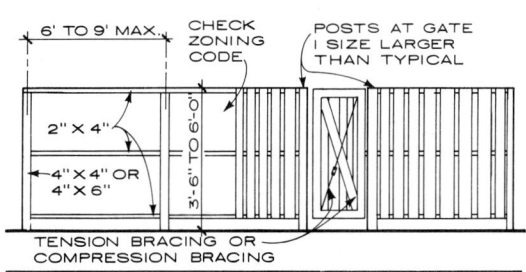

6' TO 9' MAX.
CHECK ZONING CODE
POSTS AT GATE 1 SIZE LARGER THAN TYPICAL
2" X 4"
4" X 4" OR 4" X 6"
3'-6" TO 6'-0"
TENSION BRACING OR COMPRESSION BRACING

TYPICAL FENCE DIMENSIONS

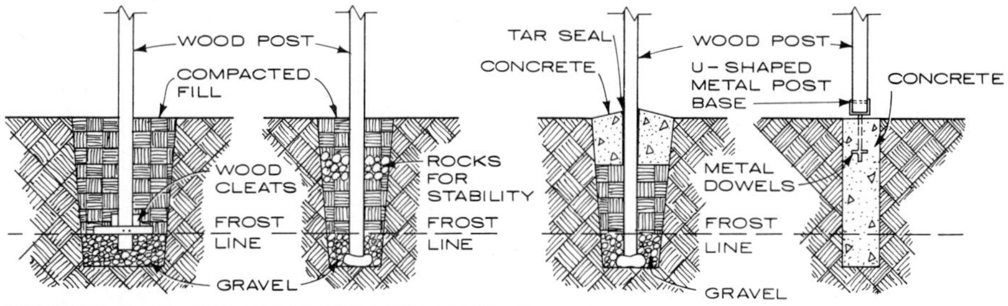

WOOD POST
COMPACTED FILL
WOOD CLEATS
FROST LINE
GRAVEL

ROCKS FOR STABILITY
FROST LINE

TAR SEAL
CONCRETE
U-SHAPED METAL POST BASE
METAL DOWELS
FROST LINE
GRAVEL

WOOD POST
CONCRETE
METAL DOWELS
FROST LINE

FOOTING DETAILS

Charles R. Heuer, AIA; Washington, D.C.

WALLS AND FENCES 2

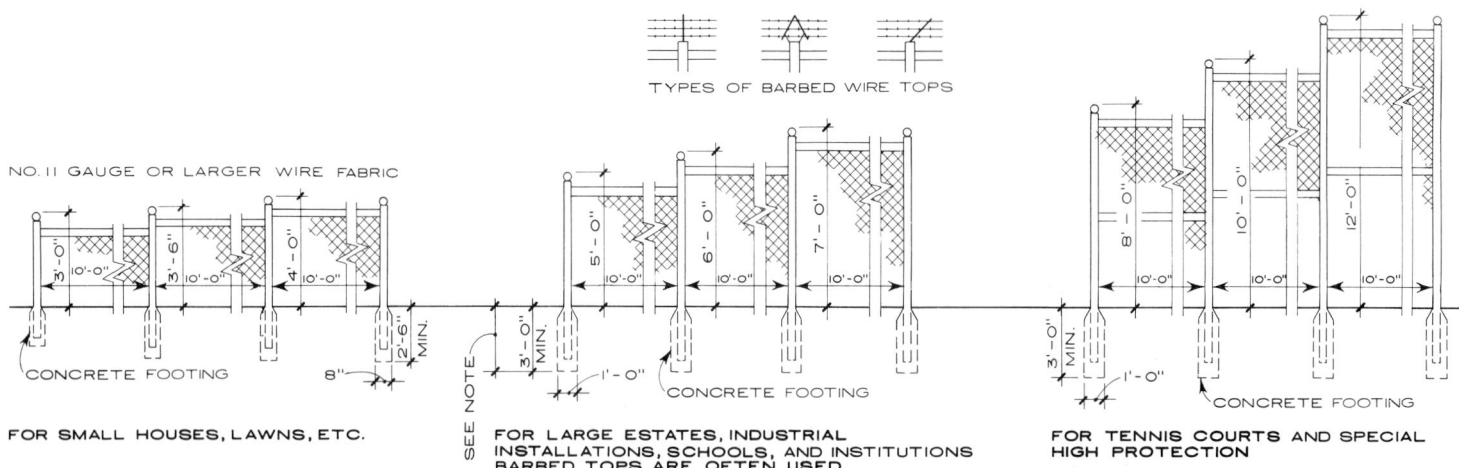

TYPES OF BARBED WIRE TOPS

NO. 11 GAUGE OR LARGER WIRE FABRIC

CONCRETE FOOTING   8"

SEE NOTE

CONCRETE FOOTING

CONCRETE FOOTING

FOR SMALL HOUSES, LAWNS, ETC.

FOR LARGE ESTATES, INDUSTRIAL INSTALLATIONS, SCHOOLS, AND INSTITUTIONS BARBED TOPS ARE OFTEN USED

FOR TENNIS COURTS AND SPECIAL HIGH PROTECTION

HEIGHTS OF FENCES FOR VARIOUS USES

See note at middle right for depth of concrete footings.

MATERIALS

SIZES GIVEN ARE NOT STANDARD BUT REPRESENT THE AVERAGE SIZES USED

Wire gauge	Usually No. 11 or No. 9 W & M. For specially rugged use use No. 6. For tennis courts usually No. 11
Wire mesh	Usually 2″. For tennis courts usually 1⅝″ or 1¾″ of chain link steel hot dip galvanized after weaving. Top and bottom salvage may be barbed or knuckled
Corner and end posts	For lawn fences usually 2″ O.D. For estate fences 2″ for low and 2½″ for medium and 3″ O.D. for heavy or high For tennis courts 3″ O.D.
Line or intermediate posts	For lawn 1⅜″ or 2″ O.D. round For estate etc. 2″, 2¼″, 2½″ H or I sections For tennis courts 2½″ round O.D. or 2¼″ H or I sections
Gate posts	The same or next size larger than the corner posts. Footings for gate posts 3′-6″ deep
Top rails	1⅝″ O.D. except some lawn fence may be 1⅜″ O.D.
Middle rails	On 12′-0″ fence same as top rail
Gates	Single or double any width desired
Post spacing	Line posts 10′-0″ O.C., 8′-0″ O.C. may be used on heavy construction

O.D. = outside diameter.

POST SIZES FOR HEAVY DUTY GATES

A.S.A. SCHEDULE 40 PIPE SIZES	SWING GATE OPENINGS	
	SINGLE GATE	DOUBLE GATE
2½″	To 6′-0″	Up to 12′-0″
3½″	Over 6′ to 18′	Over 12′ to 26′
6″	Over 13′ to 18′	Over 26′ to 36′
8″	Over 18′ to 32′	Over 36′ to 64′

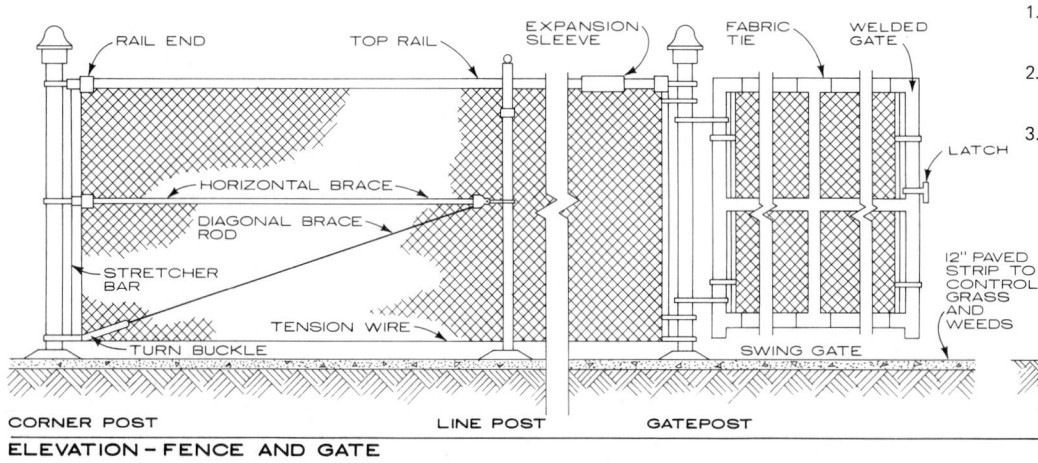

RAIL END   TOP RAIL   EXPANSION SLEEVE   FABRIC TIE   WELDED GATE

HORIZONTAL BRACE

DIAGONAL BRACE ROD

STRETCHER BAR

TENSION WIRE

TURN BUCKLE

LATCH

12″ PAVED STRIP TO CONTROL GRASS AND WEEDS

SWING GATE

CORNER POST   LINE POST   GATEPOST

ELEVATION – FENCE AND GATE

NOTE

For fences 5′-0″ and taller a horizontal or diagonal brace, or both, is used for greater stability. Post spacing should be equidistant and should not exceed 10′-0″ O.C.

Charles Driesen; Ewing Cole Erdman & Eubank; Philadelphia, Pennsylvania

CONCRETE FOOTING

Bottom of concrete footing to be set below frost line (see local code). Concrete footing sizes shown are the recommended minimum; they should be redesigned for conditions where soil is poor.

TYPES OF WIRE FABRIC MESH

VINYL-COATED: Suitable for residential, commercial or industrial applications.
Mesh sizes: 1, 1¼, 1½, 1¾, and 2 in.
Gauge sizes: 11, 9, 6, and 3.

REDWOOD SLATS

Used for visual privacy and appearance. Suitable for homes, swimming pools, and gardens.
Mesh size: 3½ x 5 in.
Gauge size: 9.

1. PREGALVANIZED: Should be restricted to such residential applications as residential perimeter fencing, swimming pool enclosures, private tennis courts, dog kennels, and interior industrial storage.
   Mesh sizes: 1½, 1¾, and 2 in. Gauge sizes: 13, 11, and 9.

2. HOT DIPPED GALVANIZED: Suitable for highway enclosures, institutional security fencing, highway bridge enclosures, exterior industrial security fences, parking lot enclosures, recreational applications, and any other environment where resistance to abuse and severe climatic conditions exist.
   Mesh sizes: 1½, 2¾, and 2 in. Gauge sizes: 9 and 6.

COATINGS

Protective coatings used on fencing, such as zinc and aluminum. Various decorative coatings can be applied including vinyl bonded and organic coatings available from most manufacturers.

SPECIAL FENCING

1. ORNAMENTAL: Vertical struts only—no chain link fabric required. Ideal for landscape or as barrier fence.

2. ELEPHANT FENCE: This fence can actually stop an elephant, hold back a rock slide, or bring a small truck to a halt. Size: 3 gauges x 2-in. mesh.

3. SECURITY FENCE: This fabric is nonclimbable and cannot be penetrated by gun muzzles, knives, or other weapons. Suitable as security barrier for police stations, prisons, reformatories, hospitals, and mental institutions. Mesh size: ⅜ in. for maximum security, ½ in. for high security, ⅝ in. for supersecurity, and 1 in. for standard security.

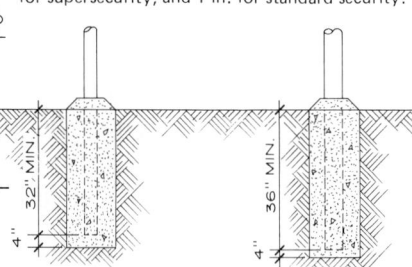

LINE POST   CORNER AND GATEPOST

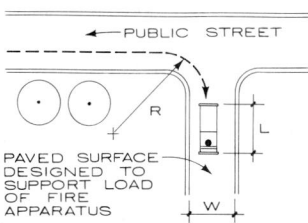

FIRE APPARATUS ACCESS

Fire apparatus (i.e., pumpers, ladder trucks, tankers) should have unobstructed access to buildings. Check with local fire department for apparatus turning radius (R), length (L), and other operating characteristics.

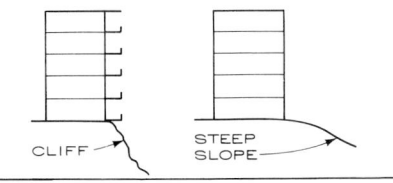

RESTRICTED ACCESS

Be sure that buildings constructed near cliffs or steep slopes do not restrict access by fire apparatus to only one side of building. Grades greater than 10% make operation of fire apparatus difficult and dangerous.

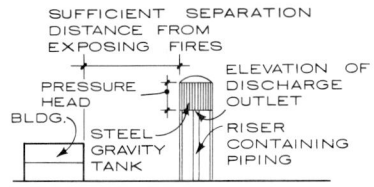

GRAVITY TANK

Gravity tanks can provide reliable source of pressure to building standpipe or sprinkler systems. Available pressure head increases by 0.434 psi/ft increase of water above tank discharge outlet. Tank capacity in gallons depends on fire hazard, water supply, and other factors. Tanks require periodic maintenance and protection against freezing during cold weather. Locations subject to seismic forces or high winds require special consideration. Gravity tanks also can be integrated within building design.

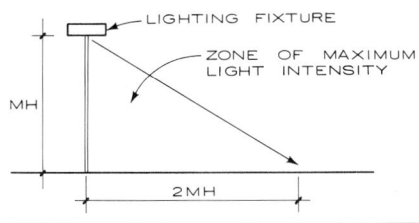

OUTDOOR LIGHTING

Streets that are properly lighted enable fire fighters to locate hydrants quickly and to position apparatus at night. Avoid layouts that place hydrants and standpipe connections in shadows. In some situations, lighting fixtures can be integrated into exterior of buildings. All buildings should have a street address number on or near the main entrance.

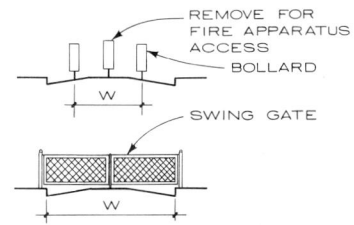

ACCESS OBSTRUCTIONS

Bollards used for traffic control and fences for security should allow sufficient open road width (W) for access by fire apparatus. Bollards and gates can be secured by standard fire department keyed locks (check with department having jurisdiction).

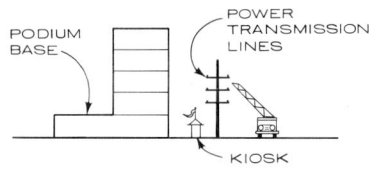

STREET FURNITURE AND ARCHITECTURAL OBSTRUCTIONS

Utility poles can obstruct use of aerial ladders for rescue and fire supression operations. Kiosks, outdoor sculpture, fountains, newspaper boxes, and the like can also seriously impede fire fighting operations. Wide podium bases can prevent ladder access to the upper stories of buildings. Canopies and other non-structural building components can also prevent fire apparatus operations close to buildings.

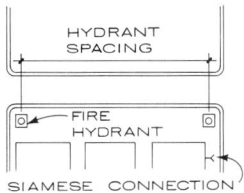

FIRE HYDRANT AND STANDPIPE CONNECTION LAYOUT

Locate fire hydrants at street intersections and at intermediate points along roads so that spacing between hydrants does not exceed about 300 ft. (Check with local authority having fire jurisdiction for specific requirements.) Hydrants should be placed 2 to 10 ft from curb lines. Siamese connections to standpipes should be visible, marked conspicuously, and be within 200 ft of hydrant to allow rapid connection by fire fighters.

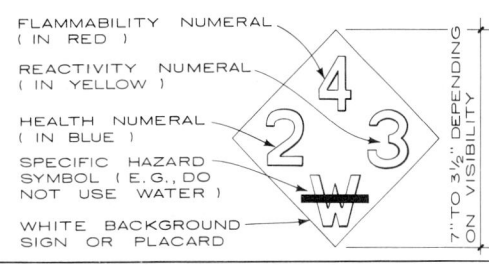

NFPA 704 DIAMOND SYMBOLS

Standard diamond symbols provide information fire fighters need to avoid injury from hazardous building contents. 0 numeral is the lowest degree of hazard, 4 is highest. Locate symbols near building entrances. Correct spatial arrangement for two kinds of diamond symbols are shown. Consider integrating symbols with overall graphics design of building. (Refer to "Identification of the Fire Hazards of Materials," NFPA No. 704, available from the National Fire Protection Association.)

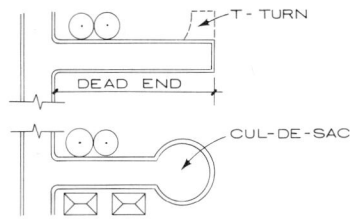

DRIVEWAY LAYOUTS

Long dead ends (greater than 150 ft) can cause time consuming, hazardous backup maneuvers. Use t-turns, culs-de-sacs, and curved driveway layouts to allow unimpeded access to buildings.

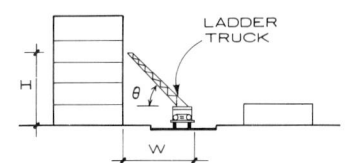

DRIVEWAY WIDTHS

For full extension of aerial ladders at a safe climbing angle (θ), sufficient driveway width (W) is required. Estimate the required width in feet by: $W = (H - 6) \cot \theta + 4$, where preferred climbing angles are 60 to 80°. Check with local fire department for aerial apparatus operating requirements.

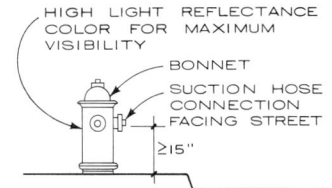

FIRE HYDRANT PLACEMENT

Fire hose connections should be at least 15" above grade. Do not bury hydrants or locate them behind shrubs or other visual barriers. Avoid locations where runoff water and snow can accumulate. Bollards and fences used to protect hydrants from vehicular traffic must not obstruct fire fighters' access to hose connections. Suction hose connection should usually face the side of arriving fire apparatus.

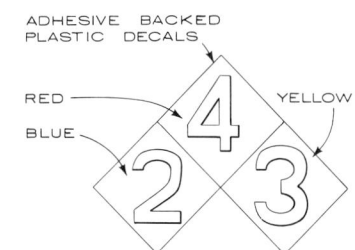

M. David Egan, P.E.; College of Architecture, Clemson University; Clemson, South Carolina

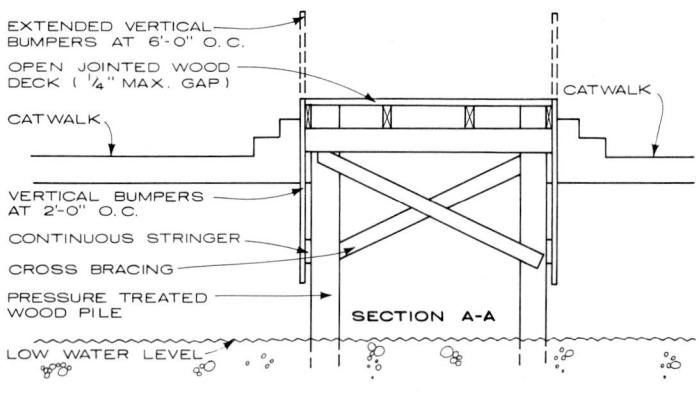

SECTION A-A

EXTENDED VERTICAL BUMPERS AT 6'-0" O.C.
OPEN JOINTED WOOD DECK (¼" MAX. GAP)
CATWALK
CATWALK
VERTICAL BUMPERS AT 2'-0" O.C.
CONTINUOUS STRINGER
CROSS BRACING
PRESSURE TREATED WOOD PILE
LOW WATER LEVEL

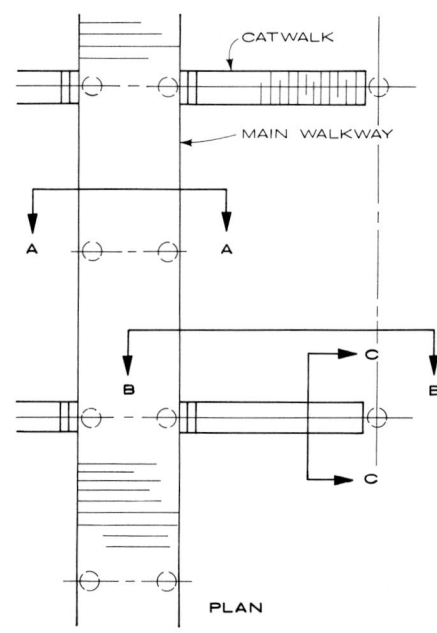

CATWALK
MAIN WALKWAY
PLAN

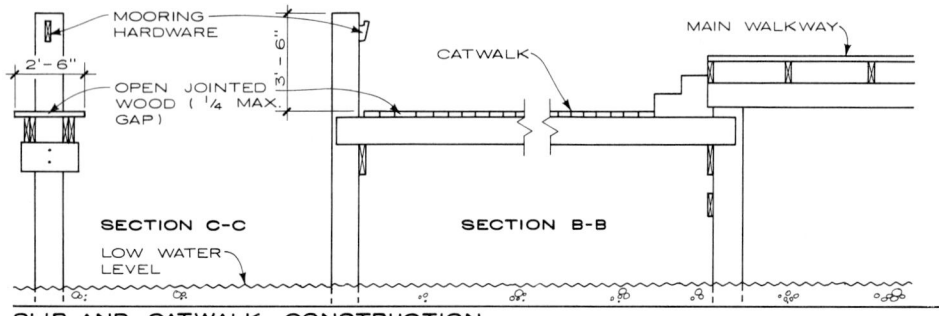

MOORING HARDWARE
2'-6"
OPEN JOINTED WOOD (¼ MAX. GAP)
3'-6"
CATWALK
MAIN WALKWAY
SECTION C-C
LOW WATER LEVEL
SECTION B-B

SLIP AND CATWALK CONSTRUCTION

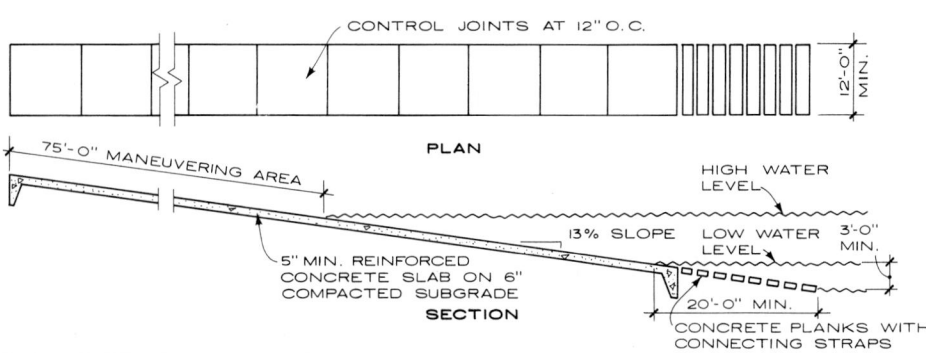

CONTROL JOINTS AT 12" O.C.
12'-0" MIN.
PLAN

75'-0" MANEUVERING AREA
5" MIN. REINFORCED CONCRETE SLAB ON 6" COMPACTED SUBGRADE
13% SLOPE
HIGH WATER LEVEL
LOW WATER LEVEL
3'-0" MIN.
20'-0" MIN.
CONCRETE PLANKS WITH CONNECTING STRAPS
SECTION

BOAT LAUNCHING RAMP

GENERAL NOTES

1. Wood marine construction must be pressure treated with a preservative. Wood preservatives for use in marine applications fall into two general categories, creosote and waterborne. To select a specific preservative from within these categories, the decaying agents must be identified. A preservative may then be chosen based on the recommendations of the American Wood Preservers Institute.
2. Waterborne preservatives are recommended for decks because creosote stains shoes and bare feet.
3. The preservatives selected should be approved by the Environmental Protection Agency.
4. Dock height above water is determined by average deck levels and probable water level. Maintain a 12 in. minimum dimension between water and deck. Floating docks may be required in tidal waters. Consult manufacturer for construction information.
5. Cross bracing should be minimized to avoid entanglement of swimmers.

LAUNCHING RAMPS

1. Launching ramps are for sheltered waters only.
2. A catwalk may be provided alongside the ramp.
3. Floating ramps may be required in tidal waters.

TABLE OF DIMENSIONS FOR SLIPS AND CATWALKS TO BE USED WITH DIAGRAM

LENGTH GROUP FOR BOAT	BEAM TO BE PROVIDED FOR	MIN. CLEAR WIDTH OF SLIP	GROSS SLIP WIDTH TYPE A	GROSS SLIP WIDTH TYPE B	GROSS SLIP WIDTH TYPE C	1ST CATWALK SPAN LENGTH D	2ND CATWALK SPAN LENGTH E	3RD CATWALK SPAN LENGTH F	DISTANCE G TO ANCHOR PILE
Up to 14'	6'–7"	8'–10"	10'–9"	10'–6"	11'–2"	12'–0"			17'–0"
Over 14' to 16'	7'–4"	9'–8"	11'–7"	11'–4"	12'–0"	12'–0"			19'–0"
Over 16' to 18'	8'–0"	10'–5"	12'–4"	12'–1"	12'–9"	14'–0"			21'–0"
Over 18' to 20'	8'–7"	11'–1"	13'–0"	12'–9"	13'–5"	8'–0"	8'–0"		23'–0"
Over 20' to 22'	9'–3"	11'–9"	13'–8"	13'–5"	14'–1"	10'–0"	8'–0"		25'–0"
Over 22' to 25'	10'–3"	13'–1"	15'–0"	14'–9"	15'–5"	10'–0"	8'–0"		28'–0"
Over 25' to 30'	11'–3"	14'–3"	16'–2"	15'–11"	16'–7"	10'–0"	10'–0"		33'–0"
Over 30' to 35'	12'–3"	15'–8"	17'–7"	17'–4"	18'–0"	12'–0"	10'–0"		38'–0"
Over 35' to 40'	13'–3"	16'–11"	18'–10"	18'–7"	19'–3"	12'–0"	12'–0"		43'–0"
Over 40' to 45'	14'–1"	17'–11"	19'–10"	19'–7"	20'–3"	14'–0"	12'–0"		48'–0"
Over 45' to 50'	14'–11"	19'–0"	20'–11"	20'–8"	21'–4"	9'–0"	9'–0"	10'–0"	53'–0"
Over 50' to 60'	16'–6"	21'–0"	22'–11"	22'–8"	23'–4"	11'–0"	11'–0"	12'–0"	63'–0"
Over 60' to 70'	18'–1"	23'–0"	26'–8"	24'–8"	25'–4"	11'–0"	11'–0"	12'–0"	73'–0"
Over 70' to 80'	19'–9"	24'–11"	28'–7"	26'–7"	26'–3"	11'–0"	11'–0"	12'–0"	83'–0"

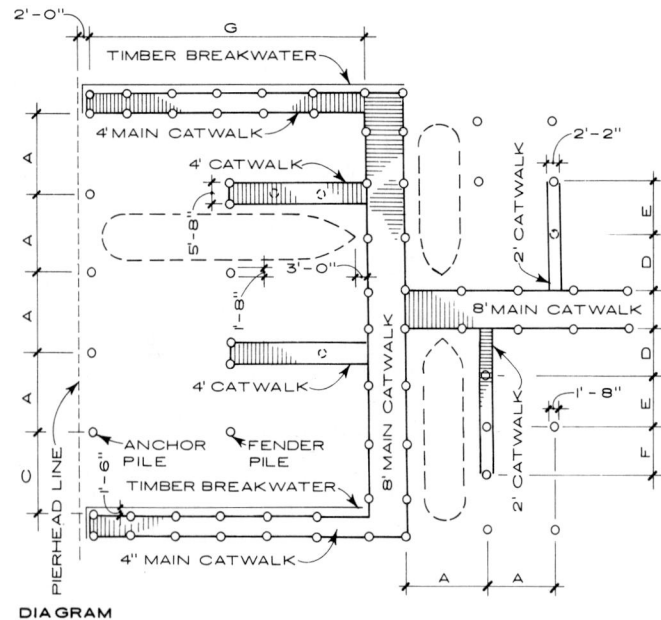

2'-0"
TIMBER BREAKWATER
G
4' MAIN CATWALK
4' CATWALK
2'-2"
2' CATWALK
5'-8"
3'-0"
1'-8"
8' MAIN CATWALK
4' CATWALK
2' CATWALK
1'-8"
1'-6"
ANCHOR PILE
FENDER PILE
TIMBER BREAKWATER
PIERHEAD LINE
4" MAIN CATWALK
8' MAIN CATWALK
A   A   D   E   F

DIAGRAM

David E. Rose; Rossen/Neumann Associates; Southfield, Michigan

CHAPTER 3 CONCRETE

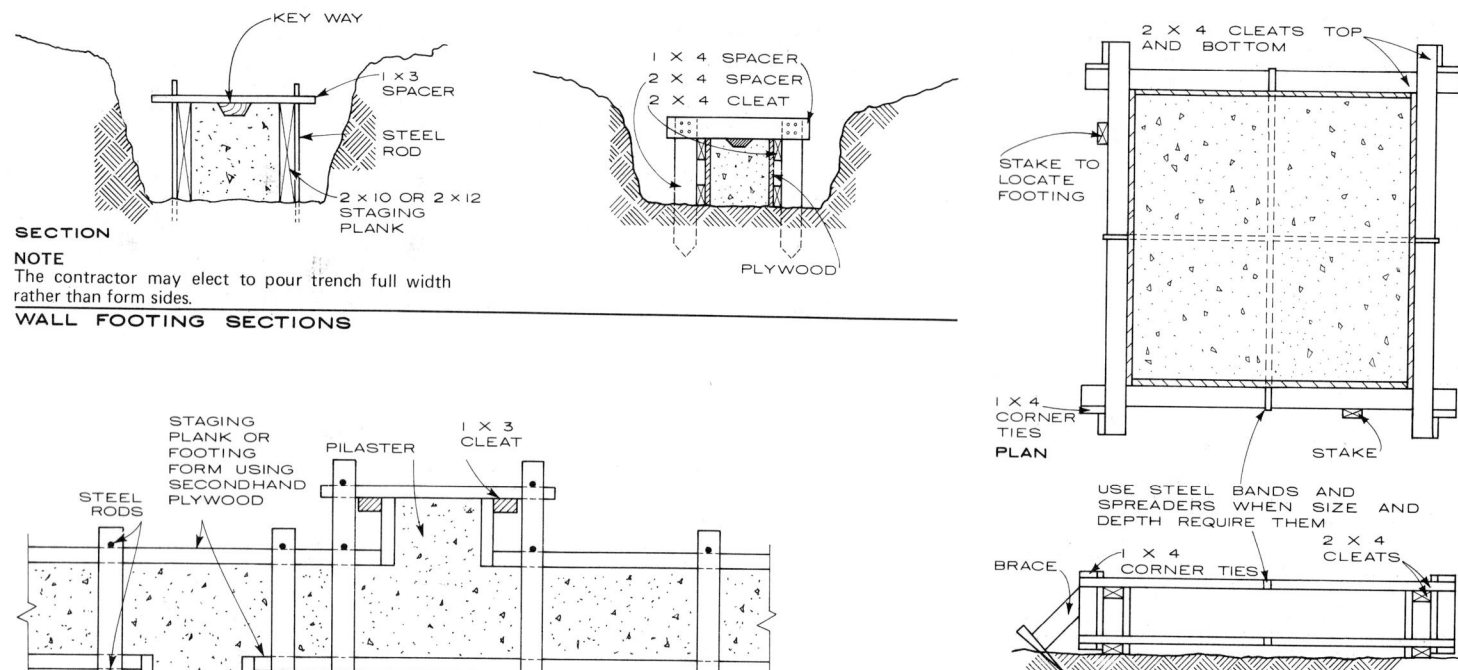

SECTION

NOTE
The contractor may elect to pour trench full width rather than form sides.

WALL FOOTING SECTIONS

PLAN

ELEVATION
COLUMN FOOTINGS

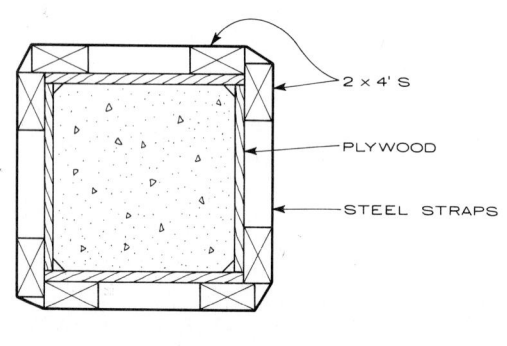

PLAN OF WALL FOOTINGS

PLAN
SQUARE COLUMNS

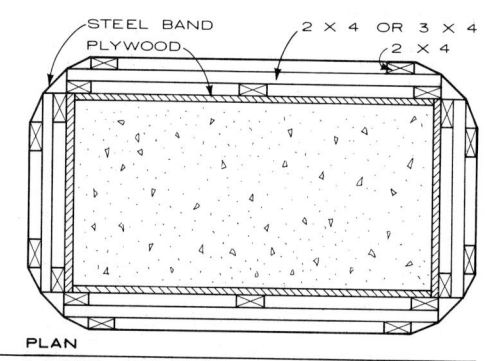

PLAN
LARGE COLUMN

NOTE

Height of column will change thickness and spaces of steel bands. Consult manufacturers' catalogs. Selection of sheathing (or plywood), type of column clamps (job built or patented metal types), and their spacing will depend on column height, rate of concrete pour (ft/hr), and concrete temperature (°F), as well as on whether the concrete is to be vibrated during pour. Consult design guides for correct selection of materials to ensure safe column forms.

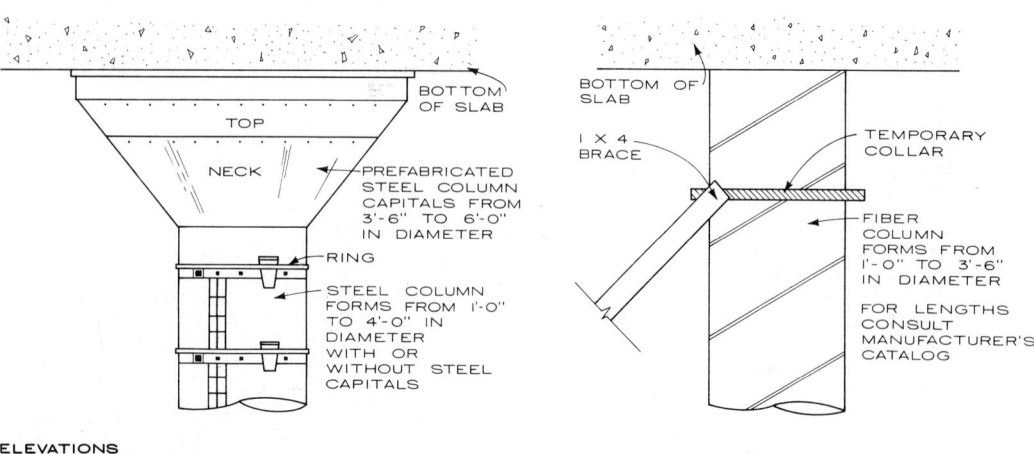

ELEVATIONS
ROUND COLUMNS

Tucker Concrete Form Co.; Malden, Massachusetts

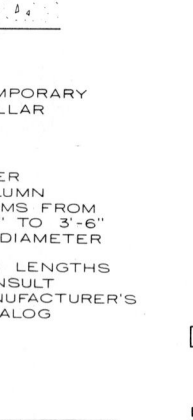

PLAN
TYPICAL PATENTED COLUMN CLAMP

3 CONCRETE FORMWORK

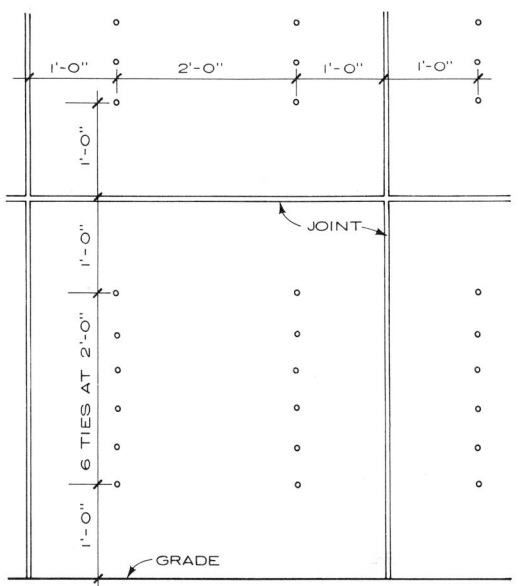

ELEVATION

EXPOSED CONCRETE WITH RUSTICATION STRIP (IF DESIRED)

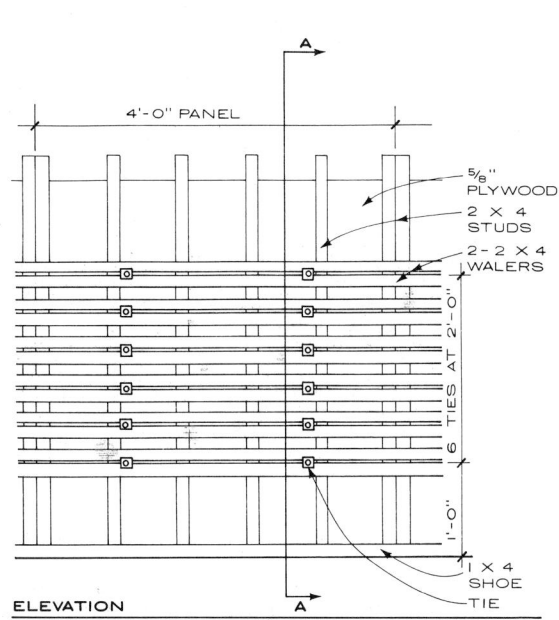

ELEVATION

SAMPLE WALL FORM

Mortar-tight forms are required for architectural exposed concrete. Consult manufacturers' literature on the proper use of metal forms or plywood forms with metal frames.

SECTION A-A

The section above will change if there are any variations in the thickness of plywood used, the type and strength of ties, or the size of studs and walers.

HORIZONTAL STRIP

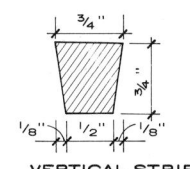

VERTICAL STRIP

RUSTICATION STRIPS

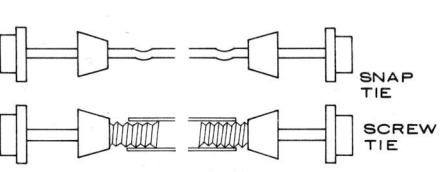

1" TO 2" CONES —WOOD, PLASTIC, STEEL ARE AVAILABLE

TYPICAL TIES

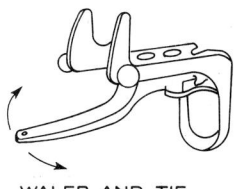

WALER AND TIE BRACKET

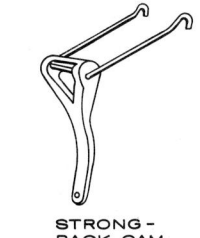

STRONG-BACK CAM

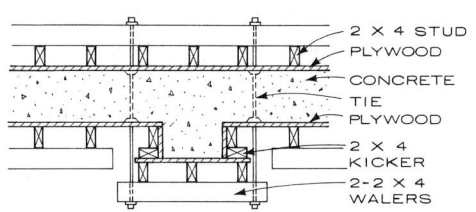

PLAN

SMALL PILASTER

PLAN

TYPICAL CORNER

PLAN

TYPICAL WALL WITH OFFSET

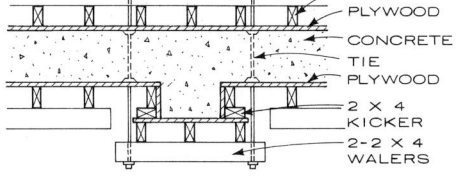

PLAN

LARGE PILASTER

PLAN

TYPICAL "T" WALL JUNCTION

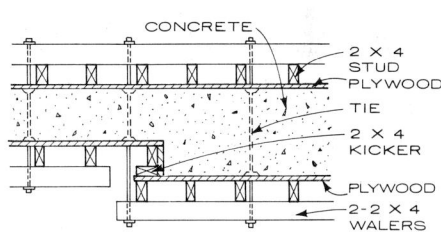

FORM DESIGN NOTES

1. Pressure depends on rate of pour (ft/hr) and concrete temperature (°F). Vibration of concrete is also a factor in form pressure.
2. Provide cleanout doors at bottom of wall forms.
3. Various types of form ties are on the market. Some are not suitable for architectural concrete work, i.e., they cannot be withdrawn from the concrete.
4. Various plastic cones 1½ in. in diameter and ½ in. deep can be used and the holes are left ungrouted to form a type of architectural feature.
5. Consult manufacturers' catalogs for form design and tie strength information.

Tucker Concrete Form Company; Malden, Massachusetts

CONCRETE FORMWORK 3

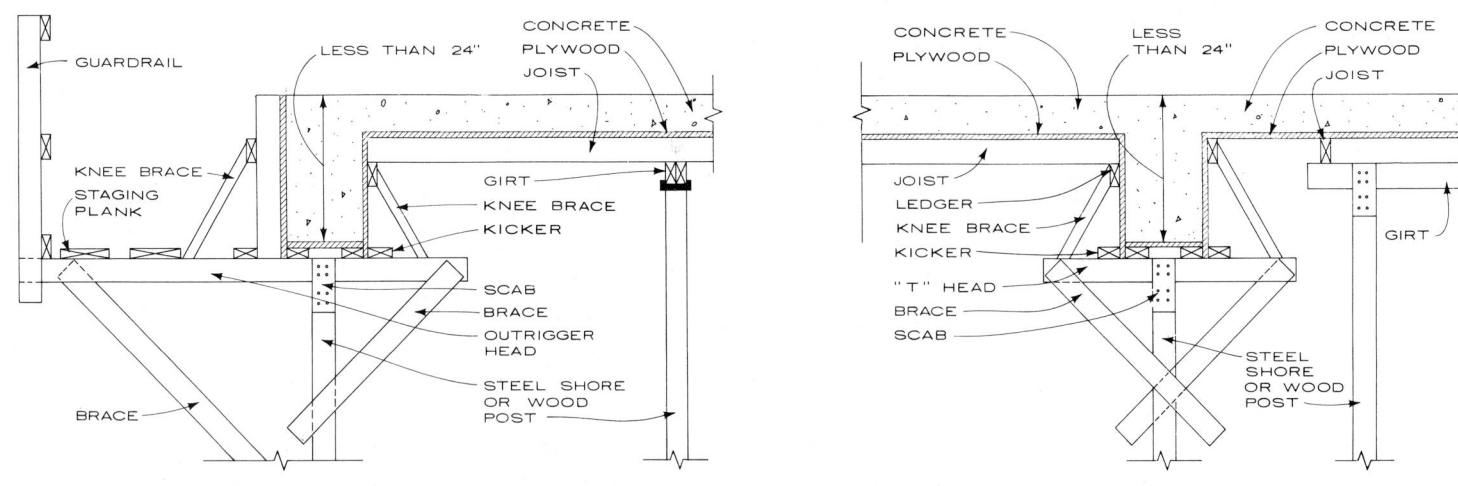

TYPICAL SLAB AND SHALLOW BEAM FORMING

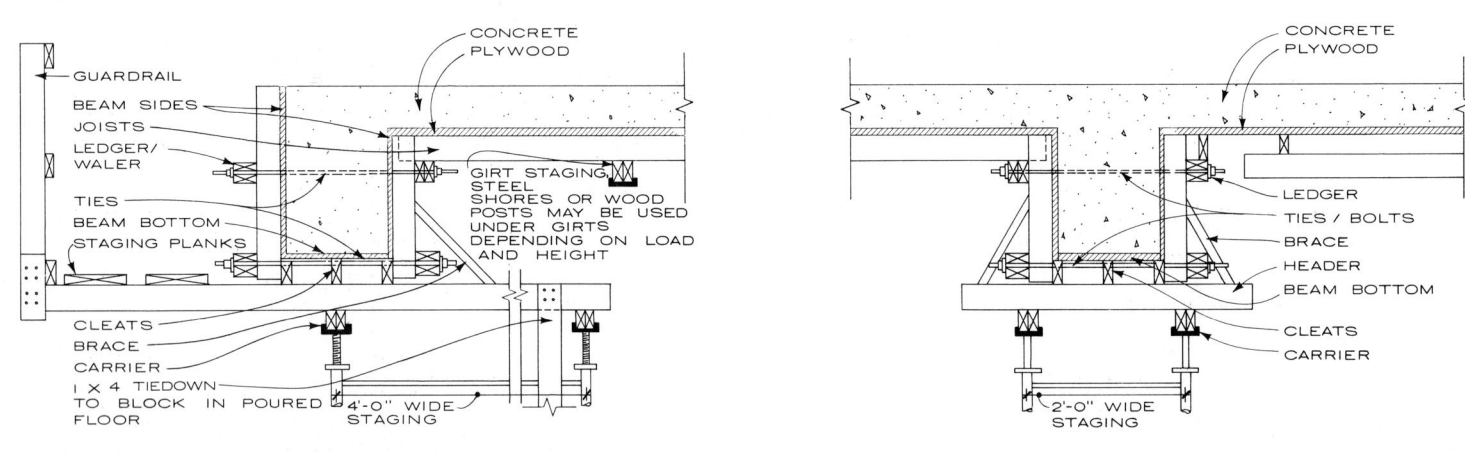

TYPICAL SLAB AND HEAVY BEAM FORMING

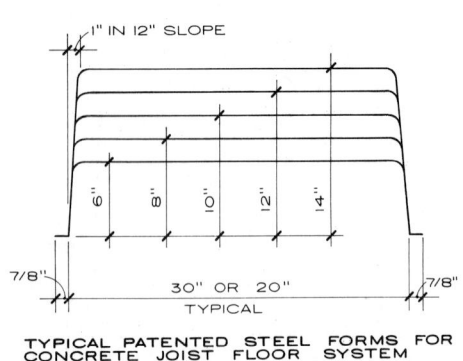

TYPICAL PATENTED STEEL FORMS FOR CONCRETE JOIST FLOOR SYSTEM

NOTE

Smaller filler sizes are available for nontypical conditions.

See manufacturer's catalogs.
Fiber forms also on market in similar size.
Plywood deck is required for forming.

TYPICAL CENTERING

ALTERNATE SYSTEM

NOTES

1. Staging, steel shores, or wood posts may be used under girts depending on loads and height requirements.

2. For flat slabs of flat plate forming, metal "flying forms" are commonly used.

3. Patented steel forms or fillers are also available for nontypical conditions on special order. See manufacturer's catalogs. Fiber forms, too, are on the market in similar sizes. Plywood deck is required for forming.

4. $5/8$ in. exterior plywood is the thickness of stock used on all details.

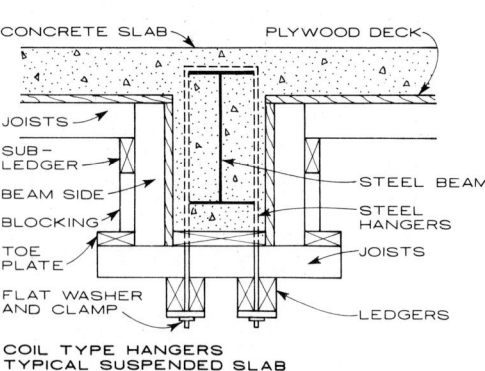

COIL TYPE HANGERS
TYPICAL SUSPENDED SLAB

Tucker Concrete Form Co.; Malden, Massachusetts

CONCRETE FORMWORK

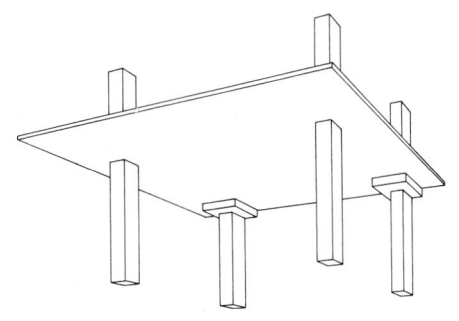

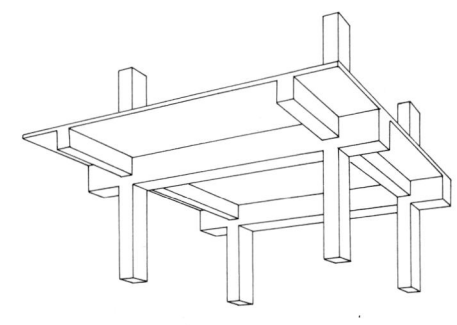

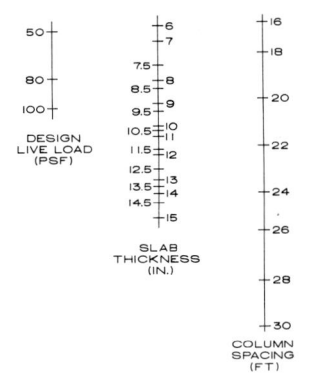

FLAT SLABS TO HAVE DROP
PANELS OR COLUMN CAPITALS.
FOR SUPERIMPOSED LOADS
OVER 100 PSF, USE BOTH DROP
PANELS AND COLUMN CAPITALS

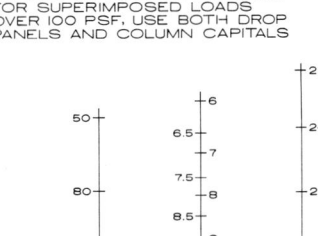

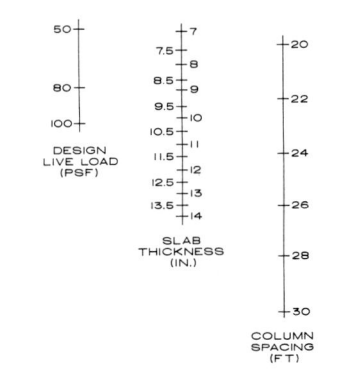

FLAT PLATE

FLAT SLAB

TWO-WAY SOLID SLAB

TAPERED PANS AT GIRDER TO
RESIST SHEAR FORCES

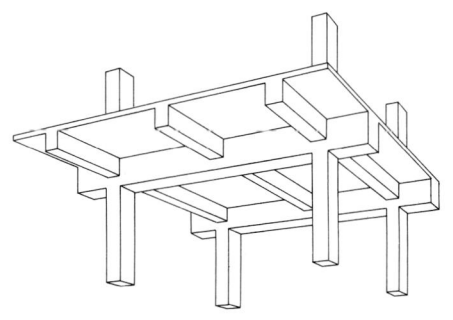

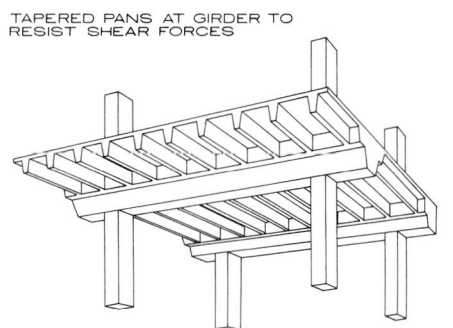

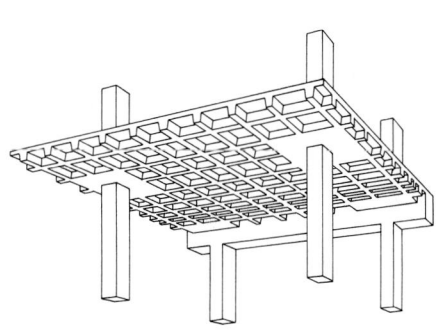

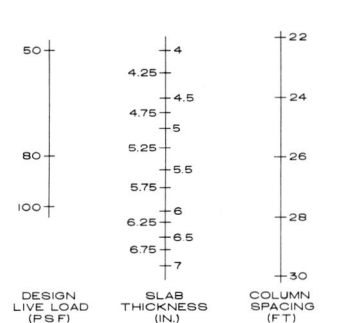

20" FORMS WITH
6" RIBS = 26" C. TO C.

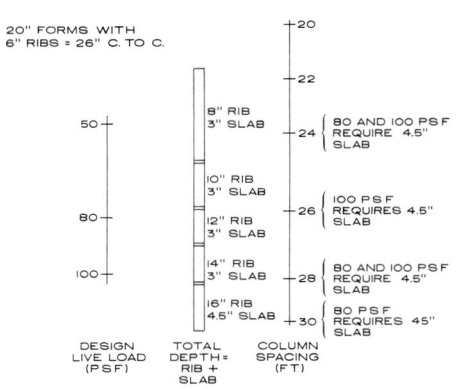

19" x 19" FORMS WITH
5" RIBS = 24" C. TO C.

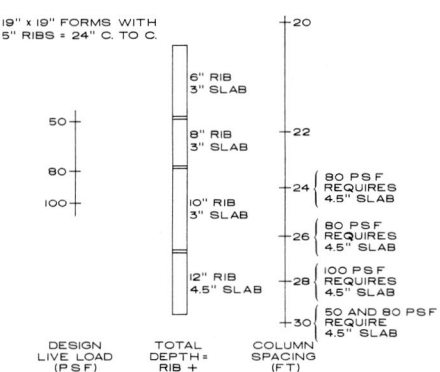

ONE-WAY SOLID SLAB
(SPAN = ½ THE COLUMN SPACING)

ONE-WAY JOISTS WITH BEAMS
(METAL PAN CONSTRUCTION)

TWO-WAY JOISTS WITHOUT BEAMS
(WAFFLE FLAT PLATE
CONSTRUCTION)

To use bar graphs, lay straight edge across chart and
line up with design live load required on left bar and
with selected column spacing on right bar. Slab
thickness required is indicated where straight edge
intersects center bar.

The examples above are all calculated by the ultimate
design strength method around the following parameters:

1. Concrete strength of 4000 psi at 28 days.
2. Steel reinforcing strength of 60,000 psi.
3. Steel to concrete ratio of minimum steel.

The information represented on this page is intended
to be used as a preliminary design guide only and not
to replace complete analysis and calculation of each
project condition by a licensed professional engineer.

Killebrew/Rucker/Associates, Inc.; Architects/Planners/Engineers; Wichita Falls, Texas

CAST-IN-PLACE CONCRETE 3

CAST-IN-PLACE CONCRETE CONSTRUCTION: PRELIMINARY DATA

REINFORCED CONCRETE

Reinforced concrete consists of concrete and reinforcing steel; the concrete resists the compressive stresses and the reinforcing steel resists the tensile stresses.

Concrete is a mixture of hydraulic cement (usually portland cement), aggregate, admixtures, and water. The concrete strength develops by the hydration of the portland cement, which binds the aggregates together.

TYPES OF CEMENT

Five types of portland cement are manufactured to meet ASTM standards.

Type I is a general purpose cement for all uses when special properties, such as resistance to sulfate attack by water in the soil or the heat of hydration would be undesirable, are not required.

Type II cement provides moderate protection from sulfate attack for concrete in drainage structures and a lower heat of hydration for concrete use in heavy retaining walls, piers, and abutments.

Type III cement provides high strengths at an early age, a week or less. Type III is used when rapid removal of forms is desired and in cold weather to reduce time of controlled curing conditions.

Type IV cement has a low heat of hydration and is used for massive concrete structures such as gravity dams.

Type V cement is sulfate resisting cement for use where the soil and groundwater have a high sulfate content.

ADMIXTURES

Admixtures are various compounds, other than cement, water, and aggregates, added to a mixture to modify the fresh or hardened properties of concrete.

Air entraining admixtures disperse small air bubbles in the concrete, which improves the concrete's resistance to freezing and thawing and to scaling by deicing chemicals. Recommended total air contents are shown in Table 1 for different exposure conditions and for maximum size of aggregate.

Water reducing admixtures reduce the quantity of mixing water needed for a given consistency and may delay the set time and entrain air.

Other mixtures are used to retard or accelerate the set of concrete.

Some water reducing and accelerating admixtures may increase dry shrinkage.

Pozzolans can be used to reduce the amount of cement in a concrete mix.

Superplasticizers allow for much lower water-cement ratios to be used than with the usual water reducing admixtures.

AGGREGATES

The aggregate portion of a concrete mix is divided into fine and coarse aggregates. The fine aggregate generally is sand of particles less than $3/8$ in. large. The coarse aggregate is crushed stone or gravel greater than $3/8$ in. Sand, crushed rock, or gravel concrete weighs 135 to 165 pcf. Lightweight aggregate is manufactured from expanded shale, slate, clay, or slag, and the concrete weighs from 85 to 115 pcf.

Normal weight aggregates must meet ASTM Specification C33.

The aggregate represents 60 to 80% of the volume of the concrete, and the gradation (range of particle sizes) affects the amount of cement and water required in the mix, the physical properties during placing and finishing, and the compressive strength. Aggregates should be clean, hard, strong, and free of surface materials.

REINFORCING STEEL

Reinforcing steel, manufactured as round rods with raised deformations for adhesion and resistance to slip in the concrete, is available in several grades (yield strengths) and diameters manufactured to ASTM standards. Commonly used reinforcing rods have yield strengths of 40,000 and 60,000 psi available in sizes from #3 to #18, the size being the diameter in eighths of an inch. Welded wire mesh has yield strengths of 60,000 to 70,000 psi, and the wire is either plain or deformed.

Table 3 summarizes the various grades of reinforcing steel, and Figure 1 shows the system of reinforcing rod identification.

SLUMP TEST

The standard slump cone test is only to determine the consistency among batches of concrete of the same mix design; it should not be used to compare mixes of greatly different mix proportions. A slump test mold is a funnel shaped sheet metal form that is 12 in. high, 8 in. in diameter at the base, and 4 in. in diameter at the top. The slump mold is filled from the top in three levels, each level being tamped 25 times with a $5/8$ in. diameter rod. After the top is smoothed evenly, the mold is slowly removed, allowing the concrete to slump down from its original height. The metal mold is placed next to the slumped concrete, and the difference from the tops of each is measured in inches. A "right" slump consistency does not exist for all concrete work. It can vary from 1 to 6 in., depending on the specific requirements of the job. Table 2 lists typical slumps for various types of construction. Workability is the ease or difficulty of placing, consolidating, and finishing the concrete. Concrete should be workable and should not segregate or bleed excessively before finishing.

CYLINDER TEST

A major problem with concrete tests is that the most important data, the compressive strength, cannot be determined until after curing has begun. This occasionally has caused the removal of deficient concrete several weeks after it was placed. A compression test is made by placing three layers of concrete in a cardboard cylinder 6 in. in diameter and 12 in. high. Each layer is rodded 25 times with a $5/8$ in. diameter steel rod. The cyclinder should be protected from damage but placed in the same temperature and humidity environment as the concrete from which the sample was obtained. At the end of the test curing time, usually determined to be 7 or 28 days, the outer cylinder is removed and placed in a press. The point at which the cylinder fails in compression is registered on a gauge in pounds, and the strength of the concrete is calculated in pounds per square inch.

PLACING CONCRETE

Concrete should be placed as near its final position as possible and should not be moved horizontally in forms because segregation of the mortar from the coarser material may occur. Concrete should be placed in horizontal layers of uniform thickness, each layer being thoroughly consolidated before the next layer is positioned.

Consolidation of concrete can be achieved either by hand tamping or rodding and by mechanical internal or external vibration. The frequency and amplitude of an internal mechanical vibration should be appropriate for the plastic properties (stiffness or slump) and space in the forms to prevent segregation of the concrete during placing.

External vibration can be accomplished by surface vibration for thin sections (slabs) that cannot be practically consolidated by internal vibration. Surface vibrators may be used directly on the surface of slabs or with plates attached to the concrete form stiffeners. External vibration must be done for a longer time (1 to 2 min) than for internal vibration (5 to 15 sec) to achieve the same consolidation.

TABLE 1. RECOMMENDED AIR CONTENT PERCENTAGE

NOMINAL MAXIMUM SIZE OF COARSE AGGREGATE (IN.)	EXPOSURE	
	MILD	EXTREME
$3/8$ (10 mm)	4.5	7.5
$1/2$ (13 mm)	4.0	6.0
$3/4$ (19 mm)	3.5	6.0
1 (25 mm)	3.0	6.0
$1^1/_2$ (40 mm)	2.5	5.5
2 (50 mm)	2.0	5.0
3 (75 mm)	1.5	4.5

TABLE 2. RECOMMENDED SLUMPS FOR VARIOUS TYPES OF CONSTRUCTION

CONCRETE CONSTRUCTION	SLUMP (IN.)	
	MAXIMUM*	MINIMUM
Reinforced foundation walls and footings	3	1
Plain footings, caissons, and substructure walls	3	1
Beams and reinforced walls	4	1
Building columns	4	1
Pavements and slabs	3	1
Mass concrete	2	1

*May be increased 1 in. for consolidation by hand methods such as rodding and spading.

Quentin L. Reutershan, AIA, Architect; Potsdam, New York

Gordon B. Batson, P.E.; Potsdam, New York

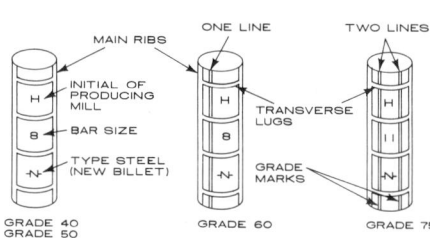

FIGURE 1. REINFORCING BAR IDENTIFICATION

TABLE 3. REINFORCING STEEL GRADES AND STRENGTHS

DEFORMED BILLET	MINIMUM YIELD POINT OR YIELD STRENGTH (PSI)	ULTIMATE STRENGTH (PSI)
ASTM A-615		
Grade 40	40,000	70,000
Grade 50	50,000	90,000
Rail steel ASTM A-616		
Grade 50	50,000	80,000
Grade 60	60,000	90,000
Axly steel ASTM A-617		
Grade 40	40,000	70,000
Grade 60	50,000	90,000
Deformed wire ASTM A-496 Welded fabric	70,000	80,000
Cold drawn ASTM A-82 Welded fabric		
< W 1.2 Size	56,000	70,000
≥ W 1.2	65,000	75,000

CAST-IN-PLACE CONCRETE

CAST-IN-PLACE CONCRETE CONSTRUCTION: PRELIMINARY DATA

PROPERTIES OF CONCRETE

Minimum concrete compressive strength at 28 days of age is generally stated in contract specifications for the concrete in various structural elements, such as columns, beams, slabs, and foundations. The normal 28-day compressive strength for commercial-ready mix concrete is 3000 to 4000 psi; however, higher strengths of 5000 to 7000 psi are generally required for pre- or posttensioned concrete and higher strengths of 10,000 to 12,000 psi may be required for highrise concrete structures.

A design mix for 3000 psi concrete with a 20% safety factor would be 517 lb of cement ($5\frac{1}{2}$ sacks), 1300 lb of sand, 1800 lb of gravel, and 34 gal of water (6.2 gal per sack), which would yield a cu yd of concrete, the standard unit of measure.

The compressive strength depends primarily on the type of cement, water-cement ratio, and the quality of the aggregate; the most important strength determining parameter is the water-cement ratio. The lower the water-cement ratio, the greater the compressive strength for workable mixes.

Figure 2 shows the general relationship between compressive strength of Type I cements and the water-cement ratio expressed in terms of weight of water per 100 lb of cement cured for 1 and 28 days. Table 4 lists recommended water-cement ratios for different types of structures and exposures, and Table 5 lists maximum water-cement ratios.

When cement, aggregate, and water are mixed, a chemical reaction is started that is independent of drying. Concrete does not need air to cure. It can set under water. Water starts the reaction. Concrete sets or becomes firm within hours after it has been mixed, but curing, the process of attaining strength, takes considerably longer. Standard (Type 1) cement is assumed to achieve 100% of its designed compressive strength 28 days after mixing. The majority of the strength is achieved in the first days of curing. Approximately 50% of the total compressive strength is reached in 3 days; 70% is reached in 7 days. The remaining 30% occurs in the last 21 days at a much slower rate. The compressive strength of the concrete may continue to increase beyond the designed strength, as shown in Figure 3.

Normal unit weight concrete is 145 to 155 pcf, and lightweight concrete varies from 100 to 115 pcf. Lightweight concrete can be used to reduce the dead load of a structure.

CURING AND PROTECTION

Two physical properties have a very pronounced effect on the final compressive strength and curing attained by concrete—temperature and the rate at which the water used in mixing is allowed to leave the concrete. The optimum temperature for curing concrete is 73°F

(22.8°C). Any great variance from this mark reduces its compressive strength. Freezing concrete during curing not only affects the compressive strength but also greatly reduces the ability of the material to resist weathering.

Proper curing of concrete is essential if the design strength of concrete mix is to be obtained. This requires that moisture be available for the hydration of the cement at temperatures above 50°F and that the concrete be protected against temperatures below 40°F during the early stages of curing.

Hydration is a chemical reaction between the water and the lime in the cement when concrete is curing. The longer the water is presented in the concrete, the longer the reaction takes place, hence the stronger it becomes.

Moisture conditions can be maintained by sprinkling wet coverings of burlap or mats, waterproof paper, or plastic sheets over concrete, plastic sheets placed on ground before slab is poured, liquid curing compound sprayed on the surface of fresh concrete, and concrete left in forms for a longer period.

HOT AND COLD WEATHER CONSTRUCTION

Hot and cold weather construction requires that additional precautions be taken to ensure proper curing of the concrete. High temperatures accelerate the hardening of concrete and more water is needed to maintain the consistency of the mix and more cement is required to prevent a strength reduction due to the added water. Chilled water or ice may be used to reduce the temperature of the aggregates, and admixtures can be used to retard the initial set. Hot weather construction begins at temperatures ranging from 75°F to 100°F.

Generally in cold weather heat must be provided to keep the concrete above 40°F during placing and the early stages of curing for a period of 7 days. Protection against freezing may be necessary for up to 2 weeks. This is accomplished by covering the concrete with plastic sheets and heating the interior space with a portable heater called a salamander. Type III and IIIA cement, low water-cement ratio, accelerator type admixtures, and steam curing can be employed to reduce the time the concrete must be protected. Concrete should never be placed directly on frozen ground. Fresh concrete that has frozen during curing should be removed and replaced because frozen concrete containing ice crystals has very little strength.

PROPORTION OF STRUCTURAL ELEMENTS

Rules of thumb for approximating proportions of solid rectangular beams and slabs are one inch of depth for each foot of span, and the beam width is about two-thirds the depth. The area of steel will vary from 1 to 2% of cross-sectional area of the beam or slab. Columns will generally have higher steel percentages than beams. The maximum for columns is 8% of the cross-sectional area; however, the common range is 3 to 6%.

TABLE 4. MAXIMUM WATER-CEMENT RATIOS FOR VARIOUS EXPOSURE CONDITIONS

EXPOSURE CONDITION	NORMAL WEIGHT CONCRETE, ABSOLUTE WATER-CEMENT RATIO BY WEIGHT
Concrete protected from exposure to freezing and thawing or application of deicer chemicals	Select water-cement ratio on basis of strength, workability, and finishing needs
Watertight concrete* In fresh water In seawater	 0.50 0.45
Frost resistant concrete* Thin sections; any section with less than 2-in. cover over reinforcement and any concrete exposed to deicing salts All other structures	 0.45 0.50
Exposure to sulfates* Moderate Severe	 0.50 0.45
Placing concrete under water	Not less than 650 lb of cement per cubic yard (386 kg/m³)
Floors on grade	Select water-cement ratio for strength, plus minimum cement requirements

*Contain entrained air within the limits of Table 1.

TABLE 5. MAXIMUM PERMISSIBLE WATER-CEMENT RATIOS FOR CONCRETE WHEN STRENGTH DATA FROM TRIAL BATCHES OR FIELD EXPERIENCE ARE NOT AVAILABLE

SPECIFIED COMPRESSIVE STRENGTH F_c' (PSI*)	MAXIMUM ABSOLUTE PERMISSIBLE WATER-CEMENT RATIO, BY WEIGHT	
	NON AIR ENTRAINED CONCRETE	AIR ENTRAINED CONCRETE
2500	0.67	0.54
3000	0.58	0.46
3500	0.51	0.40
4000	0.44	0.35
4500	0.38	†
5000	†	†

NOTE: 1000 psi ≃ 7 MPa.
*28-day strength. With most materials, the water-cement ratios shown will provide average strengths greater than required.
†For strengths above 4500 psi (non air entrained concrete) and 4000 psi (air entrained concrete), proportions should be established by the trial batch method.

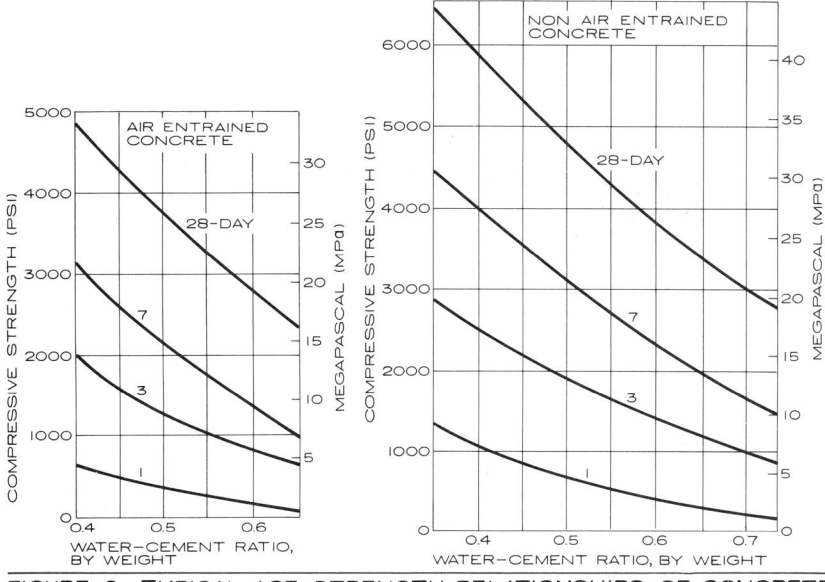

FIGURE 2. TYPICAL AGE-STRENGTH RELATIONSHIPS OF CONCRETE BASED ON COMPRESSION TESTS OF CYLINDERS, USING TYPE I CEMENT AND MOIST-CURING AT 70°F

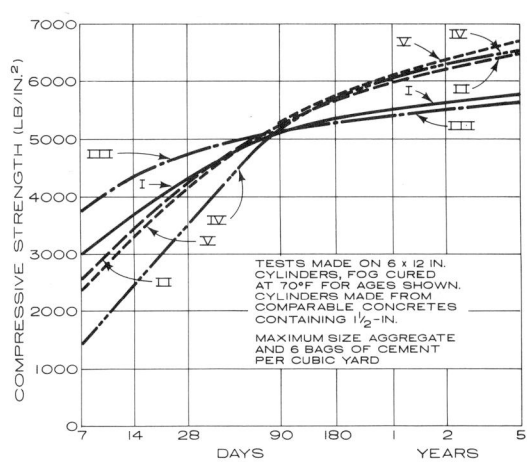

FIGURE 3. RATES OF STRENGTH DEVELOPMENT FOR CONCRETE MADE WITH VARIOUS TYPES OF CEMENT

Quentin L. Reutershan, AIA, Architect; Potsdam, New York

Gordon B. Batson, P.E.; Potsdam, New York

ASTM STANDARD REINFORCING BAR SIZES— NOMINAL DIAMETER

BAR SIZE DESIGNATION	WEIGHT PER FOOT		DIAMETER		CROSS-SECTIONAL AREA SQUARED	
	LB	KG	IN.	CM	IN.	CM
#3	0.376	0.171	0.375	0.953	0.11	0.71
#4	0.668	0.303	0.500	1.270	0.20	1.29
#5	1.043	0.473	0.625	1.588	0.31	2.00
#6	1.502	0.681	0.750	1.905	0.44	2.84
#7	2.044	0.927	0.875	2.223	0.60	3.87
#8	2.670	1.211	1.000	2.540	0.79	5.10
#9	3.400	1.542	1.128	2.865	1.00	6.45
#10	4.303	1.952	1.270	3.226	1.27	8.19
#11	5.313	2.410	1.410	3.581	1.56	10.07
#14	7.650	3.470	1.693	4.300	2.25	14.52
#18	13.600	6.169	2.257	5.733	4.00	25.81

COMMON STOCK STYLES OF WELDED WIRE FABRIC

NEW DESIGNATION SPACING—CROSS SECTIONAL AREA (IN.)—(SQ IN./100)	OLD DESIGNATION SPACING—WIRE GAUGE (IN.)—(AS & W)	STEEL AREA PER FOOT				APPROX-IMATE WEIGHT PER 100 SQ FT	
		LONGITU-DINAL		TRANS-VERSE			
		IN.	CM	IN.	CM	LB	KG
6 x 6—W1.4 x W1.4	6 x 6—10 x 10	0.028	0.071	0.028	0.071	21	9.53
6 x 6—W2.0 x W2.0	6 x 6—8 x 8 (1)	0.040	0.102	0.040	0.102	29	13.15
6 x 6—W2.9 x W2.9	6 x 6—6 x 6	0.058	0.147	0.058	0.147	42	19.05
6 x 6—W4.0 x W4.0	6 x 6—4 x 4	0.080	0.203	0.080	0.203	58	26.31
4 x 4—W1.4 x W1.4	4 x 4—10 x 10	0.042	0.107	0.042	0.107	31	14.06
4 x 4—W2.0 x W2.0	4 x 4—8 x 8 (1)	0.060	0.152	0.060	0.152	43	19.50
4 x 4—W2.9 x W2.9	4 x 4—6 x 6	0.087	0.221	0.087	0.221	62	28.12
4 x 4—W4.0 x W4.0	4 x 4—4 x 4	0.120	0.305	0.120	0.305	85	38.56
6 x 6—W2.9 x W2.9	6 x 6—6 x 6	0.058	0.147	0.058	0.147	42	19.05
6 x 6—W4.0 x W4.0	6 x 6—4 x 4	0.080	0.203	0.080	0.203	58	26.31
6 x 6—W5.5 x W5.5	6 x 6—2 x 2 (2)	0.110	0.279	0.110	0.279	80	36.29
4 x 4—W4.0 x W4.0	4 x 4—4 x 4	0.120	0.305	0.120	0.305	85	38.56

(Rolls: first group; Sheets: second group)

NOTES
1. Exact W-number size for 8 gauge is W2.1.
2. Exact W-number size for 2 gauge is W5.4.

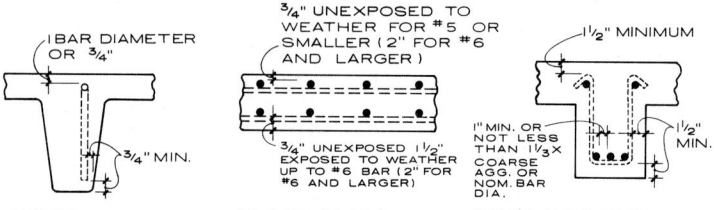

JOISTS   FLOOR SLABS   BEAM OR GIRDER

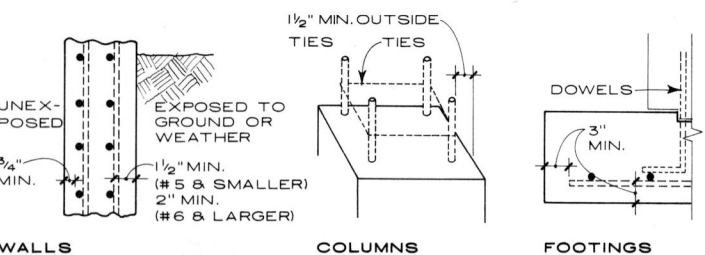

WALLS   COLUMNS   FOOTINGS

PROTECTION FOR REINFORCEMENT

LAP SPLICE REQUIREMENTS
1977 CODE IN BAR DIAMETERS

F_y (KSI)	SPIRAL COLUMN	TIED COLUMN	LOOSE
40	15.0	16.6	20
50	18.75	20.75	25
60	22.5	24.9	30
75	32.6	36.2	43.5
80	36.0	39.9	48.0

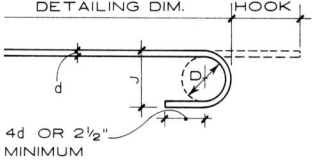

NOTES
1. These requirements are for compression lap splices only.
2. Lap splice lengths are minimum for $Fc' \geq 3000$ psi.
3. Minimum lap is 12 in.
4. Maximum reinforcing bar size permitted in lap splice is No. 11.

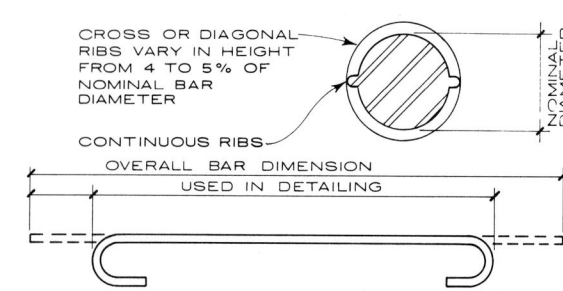

REINFORCING BAR DIMENSIONING

STANDARD STEEL WIRE SIZES AND GAUGES

A.S.&W GAUGE	DIAMETER		AREA SQUARED		WEIGHT PER FOOT	
	IN.	CM	IN.	CM	LB	KG
00	0.3310	0.8407	0.0860	0.5549	0.2922	0.1325
0	0.3065	0.7785	0.0738	0.4762	0.2506	0.1137
1	0.2830	0.7188	0.0629	0.4058	0.2136	0.0969
2	0.2625	0.6668	0.0541	0.3491	0.1829	0.0830
— (1/4")	0.2500	0.6350	0.0491	0.3168	0.1667	0.0756
3	0.2437	0.6190	0.0466	0.3007	0.1584	0.0718
4	0.2253	0.5723	0.0397	0.2561	0.1354	0.0614
5	0.2070	0.5258	0.0337	0.2174	0.1143	0.0518
6	0.1920	0.4877	0.0290	0.1871	0.0983	0.0446
7	0.1770	0.4496	0.0246	0.1587	0.0836	0.0379
8	0.1620	0.4115	0.0206	0.1329	0.0700	0.0318
9	0.1483	0.3767	0.0173	0.1116	0.0587	0.0266
10	0.1350	0.3429	0.0143	0.0922	0.0486	0.0220
11 (1/8")	0.1250	0.3175	0.0114	0.0736	0.0387	0.0176
12	0.1055	0.2680	0.0087	0.0561	0.0297	0.0135
13	0.0915	0.2324	0.0066	0.0426	0.0223	0.0101
14	0.0800	0.2032	0.0050	0.0323	0.0171	0.0078
15	0.0720	0.1838	0.0041	0.0265	0.0138	0.0063
16 (1/16")	0.0625	0.1588	0.0031	0.0200	0.0104	0.0047

180° HOOK

d = (1) Bar Diameter
D = 6d for No. 3 to No. 8 Bars
D = 8d for No. 9 to No. 11 Bars
J = D + 2d
H = 5d + D/2 (or) 2 1/2" + d + D/2 minimum

90° HOOK

d = (1) Bar Diameter
D = 6d for No. 3 to No. 8 bars
D = 8d for No. 9 to No. 11 bars
J = 13d + D/2

135° HOOK STIRRUP — TIES SIMILAR

d = (1) Bar Diameter
D = 1 1/2" for No. 3
D = 2" for No. 4
D = 2 1/2" for No. 5
D = 6d for No. 6 to No. 8

STANDARD REINFORCING BAR HOOK DETAILS

TEMPERATURE REINFORCEMENT FOR STRUCTURAL FLOOR AND ROOF SLAB (ONE WAY) (IN PERCENTAGE OF CROSS-SECTIONAL AREA OF CONCRETE)

REINFORCEMENT		CONCRETE SLABS	
GRADE	TYPE		
40/50	Deformed bars	0.20%	Max. spacing five times slab thickness
—	Welded wire fabric	0.18%	
60	Deformed bars	0.18%	

Dave Keppler; Haver, Nunn and Collamer; Phoenix, Arizona

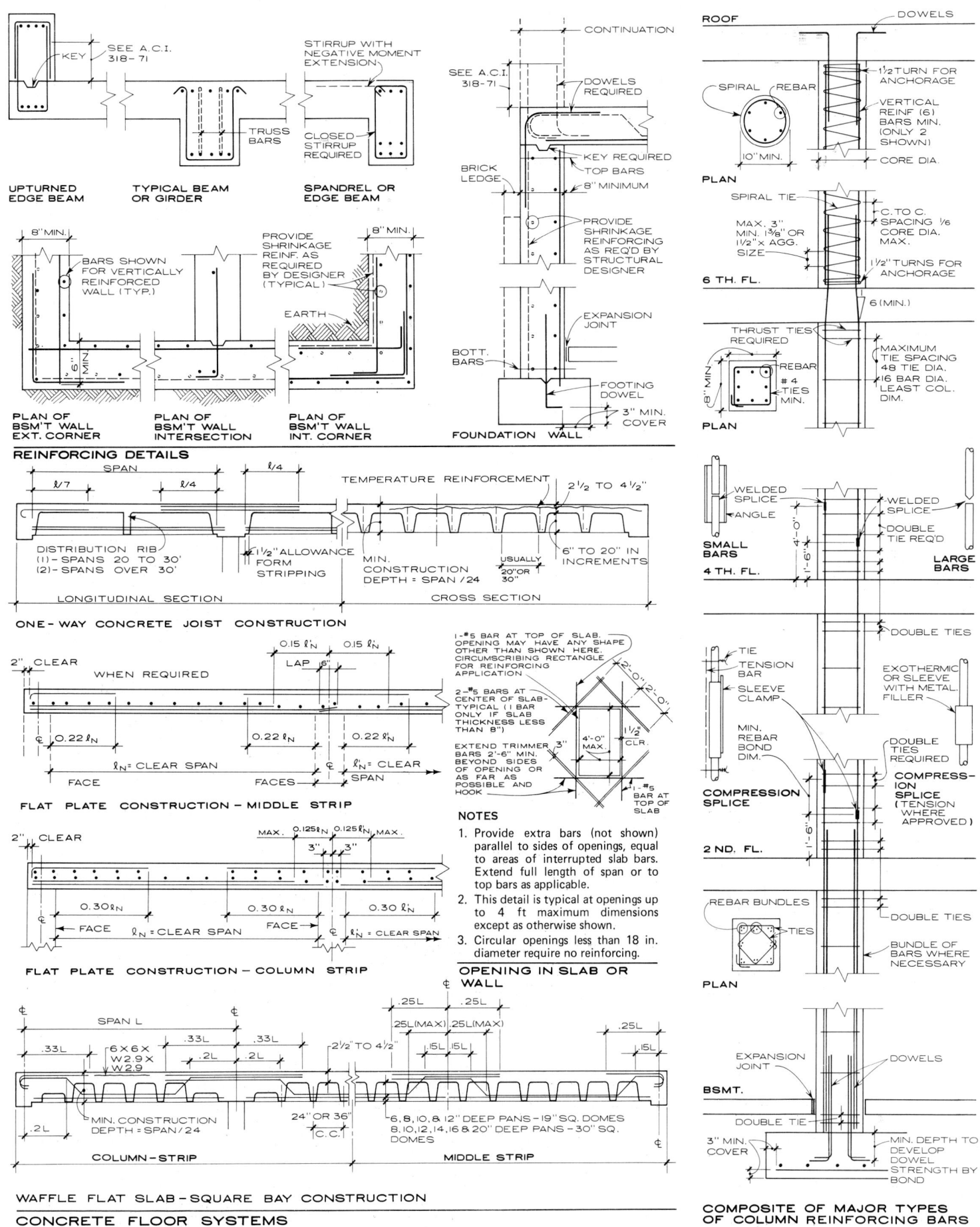

REINFORCING DETAILS

ONE-WAY CONCRETE JOIST CONSTRUCTION

FLAT PLATE CONSTRUCTION – MIDDLE STRIP

FLAT PLATE CONSTRUCTION – COLUMN STRIP

NOTES

1. Provide extra bars (not shown) parallel to sides of openings, equal to areas of interrupted slab bars. Extend full length of span or to top bars as applicable.

2. This detail is typical at openings up to 4 ft maximum dimensions except as otherwise shown.

3. Circular openings less than 18 in. diameter require no reinforcing.

OPENING IN SLAB OR WALL

WAFFLE FLAT SLAB – SQUARE BAY CONSTRUCTION

CONCRETE FLOOR SYSTEMS

Thomas A. Lines; Haver, Nunn and Collamer; Phoenix, Arizona

COMPOSITE OF MAJOR TYPES OF COLUMN REINFORCING BARS

CONCRETE REINFORCEMENT 3

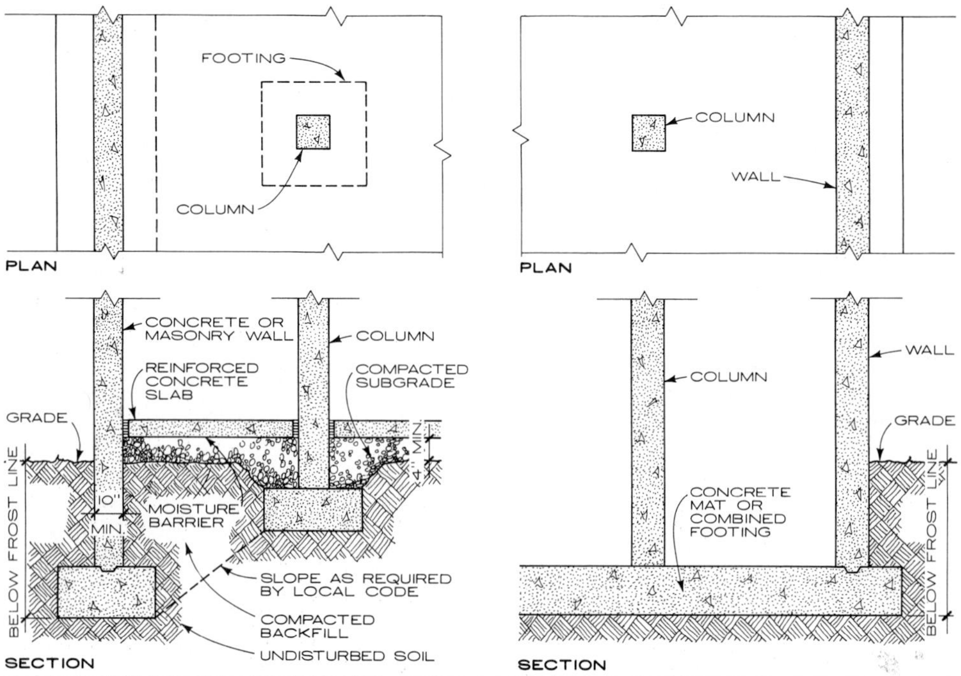

SPREAD FOOTINGS

PLAN

- FOOTING
- COLUMN

SECTION

- CONCRETE OR MASONRY WALL
- COLUMN
- REINFORCED CONCRETE SLAB
- COMPACTED SUBGRADE
- GRADE
- BELOW FROST LINE
- 10" MIN
- MOISTURE BARRIER
- SLOPE AS REQUIRED BY LOCAL CODE
- COMPACTED BACKFILL
- UNDISTURBED SOIL

PLAN

- COLUMN
- WALL

SECTION

- COLUMN
- WALL
- GRADE
- BELOW FROST LINE
- CONCRETE MAT OR COMBINED FOOTING

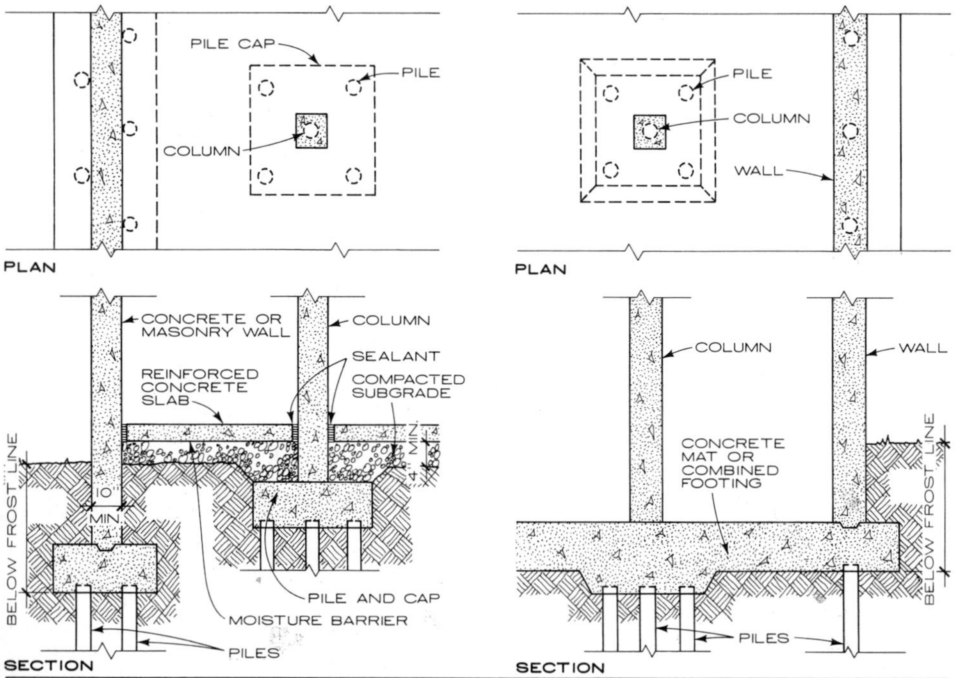

PILE SUPPORTED FOUNDATIONS

PLAN

- PILE CAP
- PILE
- COLUMN

SECTION

- CONCRETE OR MASONRY WALL
- COLUMN
- REINFORCED CONCRETE SLAB
- SEALANT
- COMPACTED SUBGRADE
- BELOW FROST LINE
- 10" MIN
- PILE AND CAP
- MOISTURE BARRIER
- PILES

PLAN

- PILE
- COLUMN
- WALL

SECTION

- COLUMN
- WALL
- CONCRETE MAT OR COMBINED FOOTING
- BELOW FROST LINE
- PILES

AREAWAY WALL

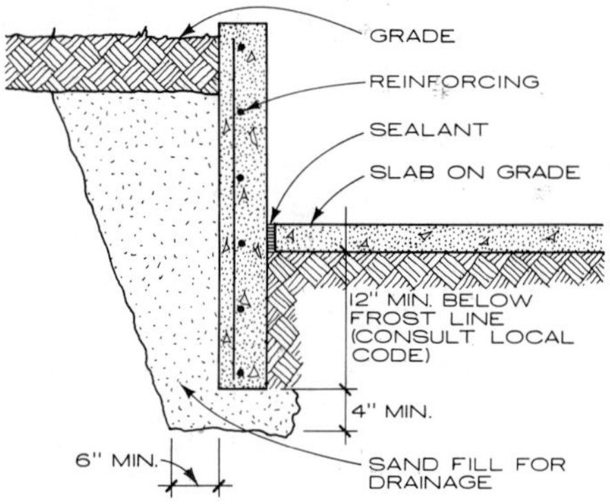

- GRADE
- REINFORCING
- SEALANT
- SLAB ON GRADE
- 12" MIN BELOW FROST LINE (CONSULT LOCAL CODE)
- 4" MIN.
- 6" MIN.
- SAND FILL FOR DRAINAGE

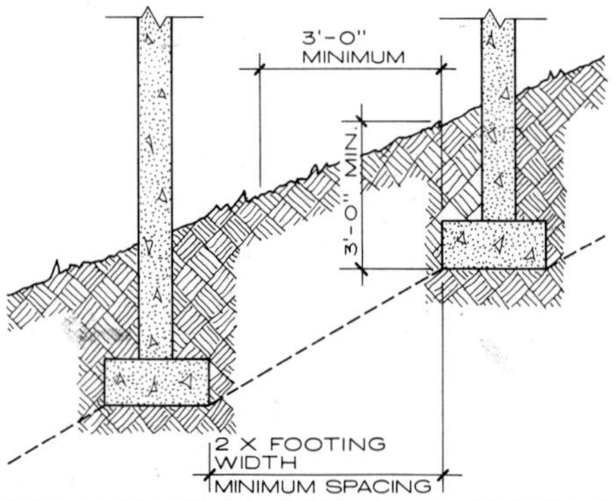

STEP FOOTINGS
MAX. STEEPNESS: 1/2 HORIZONTAL TO 1 VERTICAL

- 3'-0" MINIMUM
- 3'-0" MIN.
- 2 X FOOTING WIDTH MINIMUM SPACING

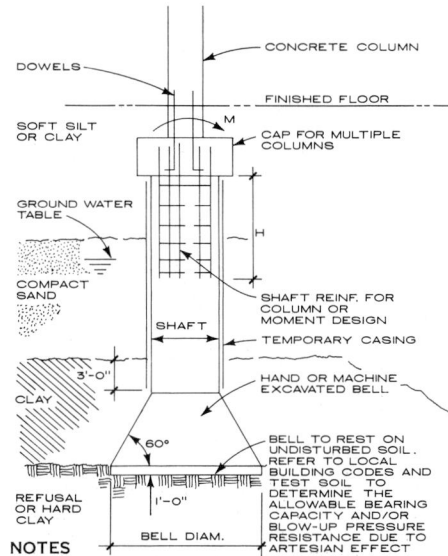

BELL PIER FOUNDATION

- CONCRETE COLUMN
- DOWELS
- FINISHED FLOOR
- SOFT SILT OR CLAY
- M
- CAP FOR MULTIPLE COLUMNS
- GROUND WATER TABLE
- H
- COMPACT SAND
- SHAFT REINF. FOR COLUMN OR MOMENT DESIGN
- SHAFT
- TEMPORARY CASING
- 3'-0"
- HAND OR MACHINE EXCAVATED BELL
- CLAY
- 60°
- BELL TO REST ON UNDISTURBED SOIL. REFER TO LOCAL BUILDING CODES AND TEST SOIL TO DETERMINE THE ALLOWABLE BEARING CAPACITY AND/OR BLOW-UP PRESSURE RESISTANCE DUE TO ARTESIAN EFFECT
- REFUSAL OR HARD CLAY
- 1'-0"
- BELL DIAM.

NOTES

1. H is a function of the passive resistance of the soil, generated by the moment applied to the caisson cap.
2. Caissons may be used under grade beams or concrete walls. For very heavy loads, pier foundations may be more economical than piles.

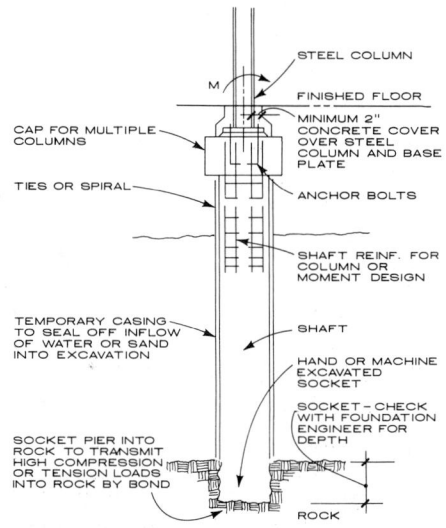

SOCKET PIER FOUNDATION

- STEEL COLUMN
- M
- FINISHED FLOOR
- CAP FOR MULTIPLE COLUMNS
- MINIMUM 2" CONCRETE COVER OVER STEEL COLUMN AND BASE PLATE
- TIES OR SPIRAL
- ANCHOR BOLTS
- SHAFT REINF. FOR COLUMN OR MOMENT DESIGN
- TEMPORARY CASING TO SEAL OFF INFLOW OF WATER OR SAND INTO EXCAVATION
- SHAFT
- HAND OR MACHINE EXCAVATED SOCKET
- SOCKET – CHECK WITH FOUNDATION ENGINEER FOR DEPTH
- SOCKET PIER INTO ROCK TO TRANSMIT HIGH COMPRESSION OR TENSION LOADS INTO ROCK BY BOND
- ROCK

NOTES

1. Pier shaft should be poured in the dry if possible, but tremie pours can be used with appropriate control.
2. Grout bottom of shaft against artesian water or sulphur gas intrusion into the excavation.

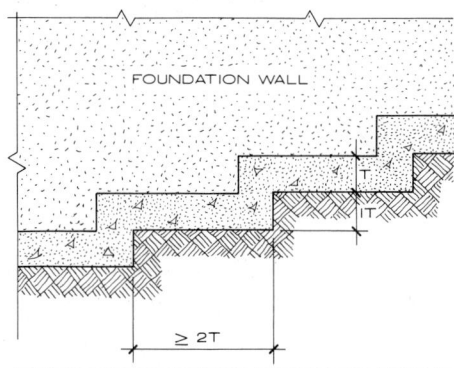

STEP FOOTING (FOR CONTINUOUS WALL)
MAX. STEEPNESS: 2 HORIZONTAL TO 1 VERTICAL

- FOUNDATION WALL
- ≥ 2T
- T

Mueser, Rutledge, Johnston & DeSimone; New York, New York

CONCRETE FOUNDATIONS

GENERAL NOTES

Factors to consider in construction of all concrete slabs on grade include assurance of uniform subgrade, quality of concrete, adequacy of structural capacity, type and spacing of joints, finishing, curing, and the application of special surfaces. It is vital to design and construct the subgrade as carefully as the floor slab itself. The subgrade support must be reasonably uniform, and the upper portion of the subgrade should be of uniform material and density. A subbase, a thin layer of granular material placed on the subgrade, should be used in most cases to cushion the slab.

Wear resistance is directly related to concrete strength. A low water-cement ratio improves the surface hardness and finishability as well as internal strength of concrete. Low water-cement ratio, low slump, and well graded aggregates with coarse aggregate size as large as placing and finishing requirements will permit and enhance the quality of concrete.

Exterior concrete subjected to freeze-thaw cycles should have 6 to 8% entrained air. Reinforcement is unnecessary where frequent joint spacing is used. Where less frequent joint spacing is necessary, reinforcement is put in the top one third depth to hold together any shrinkage cracks that form. Control joint spacing of 15 to 25 ft square is recommended. Checkerboard pouring patterns allow for some shrinkage between pours, but the process is more costly and is not recommended for large areas. The total shrinkage process takes up to one year. Strip pouring, allowing for a continuous pour with control joints cut after concrete has set, is a fast economical method, recommended for large areas.

Three types of joints are recommended:

1. ISOLATION JOINTS (also called expansion joints): Allow movement between slab and fixed parts of the building such as columns, walls, and machinery bases.
2. CONTROL JOINTS: Induce cracking at preselected locations.
3. CONSTRUCTION JOINTS: Provide stopping places during floor construction. Construction joints also function as control and isolation joints.
Sawcut control joints should be made as early as is practical after finishing the slab and should be filled in areas with wet conditions, hygienic and dust control requirements, or considerable traffic

by hard wheeled vehicles, such as forklift trucks. A semirigid filler with Shore Hardness "A" of at least 80 should be used.

Concrete floor slabs are monolithically finished by floating and troweling the concrete to a smooth dense finish. Depressions of more than $1/8$ in. in 10 ft or variations of more than $1/4$ in. from a level plane are undesirable. Special finishes are available to improve appearance. These include sprinkled (shake) finishes and high strength concrete toppings, either monolithic or separate (two-stage floor).

A vaporproof barrier should be placed under all slabs on grade where the passage of water vapor through the floor is undesirable. Permeance of vapor barrier should not exceed 0.20 perms.

Generally the controlling factor in determining the thickness of a floor on ground is the heaviest concentrated load it will carry, usually the wheel load plus impact of an industrial truck. Because of practical considerations, the minimum recommended thickness for an industrial floor is about 5 in. For Class 1, 2, and 3 floors, the minimum thickness should be 4 in.

The floor thickness required for wheel loads on relatively small areas may be obtained from the table for concrete; an allowable flexural tensile stress (psi) can be estimated from the approximate formula $f_t = 4.6 \sqrt{f_c'}$ in which f_c' is the 28-day concrete compressive strength. If f_t is not 300 psi, the table can be used by multiplying the actual total load by the ratio of 300 to the stress used and entering the chart with that value.

Assume that a 5000 psi concrete slab is to be designed for an industrial plant floor over which there will be considerable traffic—trucks with loads of 10,000 lb/wheel, each of which has a contact area of about 30 sq in. Assume that operating conditions are such that impact will be equivalent to about 25% of the load. The equivalent static load will then be 12,500 lb. The allowable flexural tensile stress for 5000 psi concrete is

$$4.6 \sqrt{5000} = 325 \text{ psi}$$

The allowable loads in the table are based on a stress of 300 psi, so that the design load must be corrected by the factor 300/325. Thus 11,500 lb on an area of 30 sq in. requires a slab about $7\frac{1}{2}$ in. thick.

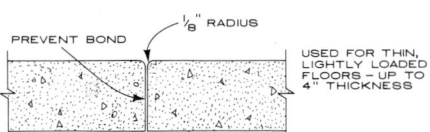

BUTT TYPE CONSTRUCTION JOINT

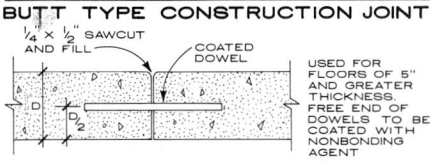

BUTT TYPE CONSTRUCTION JOINT WITH DOWELS

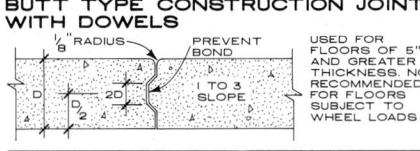

TONGUE AND GROOVE CONSTRUCTION JOINT

SAWED OR PREMOLDED CONTROL JOINT FOR SLABS < 4"

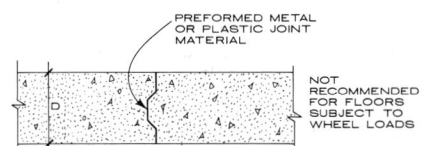

TONGUE AND GROOVE CONTROL JOINT

CONTROL JOINT WITH DOWELS

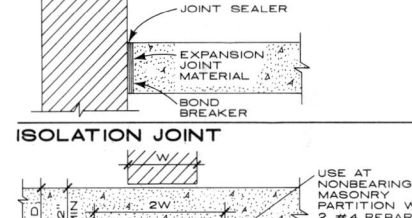

ISOLATION JOINT

THICKENED SLAB

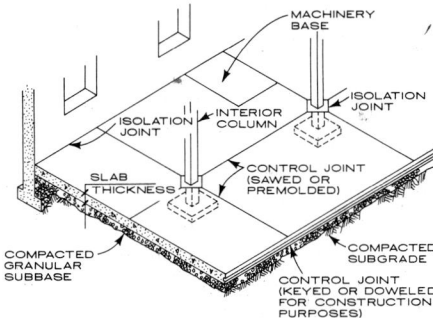

CONTROL JOINTS FOR A SLAB ON GRADE

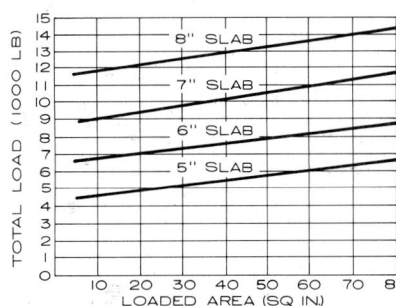

MAXIMUM WHEEL LOADS FOR INDUSTRIAL FLOORS (FLEXURAL TENSILE STRESS = 300 PSI)

CLASSIFICATION OF CONCRETE SLABS ON GRADE

CLASS	SLUMP RANGE (IN.)	MINIMUM COMPRESSIVE STRENGTH (PSI)	USUAL TRAFFIC	USE	SPECIAL CONSIDERATION	CONCRETE FINISHING TECHNIQUE
1	2-4	3500	Light foot	Residential or tile covered	Grade for drainage; plane smooth for tile	Medium steel trowel
2	2-4	3500	Foot	Offices, schools, hospitals, residential	Nonslip aggregate, mix in surface Color shake, special	Steel trowel; special finish for nonslip Steel trowel, color exposed aggregate
3	2-4	3500	Light foot and pneumatic wheels	Drives, garage floors, sidewalks for residences	Crown; pitch joints	Float, trowel, and broom
4	1-3	4000	Foot and pneumatic wheels	Light industrial, commercial	Careful curing	Hard steel trowel and brush for nonslip
5	1-3	4500	Foot and wheels— abrasive wear	Single course industrial, integral topping	Careful curing	Special hard aggregate, float and trowel
6	2-4	3500	Foot and steel tire vehicles—severe abrasion	Bonded two-course, heavy industrial	Base: textured surface and bond Top: special aggregate	Base: surface leveled by screeding Top: special power floats
7	1-3	4000	Same as Classes 3, 4, 5, 6	Unbonded topping	Mesh reinforcing; bond breaker on old concrete surface	—

Setter, Leach & Lindstrom, Inc.; Minneapolis, Minnesota

GENERAL CONSIDERATIONS

1. Concrete strength usually 5000 psi at 28 days and at least 3000 psi at time of prestressing. Hardrock aggregate or lightweight concrete used. Low slump controlled mix is required to reduce shrinkage. Shrinkage after prestressing increases prestress losses.

2. Post-tensioning systems can be divided into three categories depending on whether the tendon is wire, strand, or bar. Wire systems use 0.25 in. diameter wires that have a minimum strength of 240,000 psi and are usually cut to length in the shop. Strand systems use tendons composed of seven wires wrapped together that have a minimum strength of 270,000 psi and are cut in the field. Bar systems use bars ranging in diameter from $5/8$ to $1 3/8$ in. in diameter, with a minimum strength of 145,000 psi; they may be smooth or deformed. The system used will determine the type of anchorage used, which in turn will affect the size of blockout required in the edge of slab or beam for the anchorage to be recessed.

3. Tendons are greased and wrapped, or placed in conduits to reduce frictional losses during stressing operations. Length of continuous tendons limited to about 100 ft if stressed from one end. Long tendons require simultaneous stressing from both ends to reduce friction losses. Tendons may be grouted after stressing or left unbonded. Bonded tendons have structural advantages that are more important for beams and primary structural members.

4. Minimum average prestress (net prestress force/area of concrete) = 150 to 250 psi for flat plates, 200 to 500 psi for beams. Exceeding these values very much will cause excessive prestress losses because of creep.

5. Field inspection of post-tensioned concrete is critical to ensure proper size and location of tendons and to monitor the tendon stress. Tendon stress should be checked by measuring elongation of the tendon, and by gauge pressures on the stressing jack.

6. Provisions must be made for the shortening of post-tensioned beams and slabs caused by elastic compression, shrinkage, and creep. Shearwalls, curtain walls, or other stiff elements that adjoin post-tensioned members should be built after the post-tensioning has been done or should be isolated from these members with an expansion joint. Otherwise, additional post-tensioning force will be required to overcome the stiffness of the walls; cracking of the walls may also occur.

7. Fire tests have been conducted on prestressed beam and slab assemblies according to ASTM E119 test procedures; they compare favorably with conventionally reinforced concrete. There is little difference between beams using grouted tendons and those using ungrouted tendons.

8. References for further study:
   a. Post-Tensioning Institute, "Post-Tensioning Manual."
   b. Prestressed Concrete Institute, "Design Handbook for Precast and Prestressed Concrete."
   c. Lin, T.Y., "Design of Prestressed Concrete Structures."
   d. American Concrete Institute, "Building Code Requirements for Reinforced Concrete" (ACI-318-77).

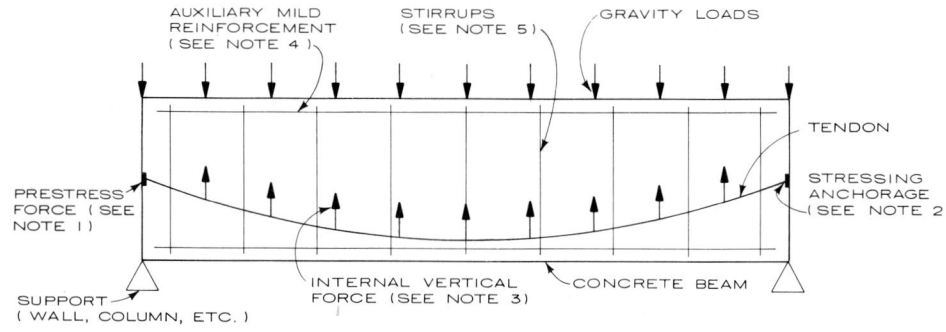

PRESTRESSED OR POST—TENSIONED BEAM

NOTES

1. Prestressing force puts entire beam cross-section into compression, thereby reducing unwanted tension cracks.

2. Permanent tension is introduced into tendon and "locked in" with the stressing anchorage in one of two ways. In prestressed concrete, the tendon is elongated in a stressing bed before the concrete is poured. In post-tensioned concrete, the tendon is elongated after concrete has been poured and allowed to cure by means of hydraulic jacks pushing against the beam itself. The principle in both cases is the same. Post-tensioned beams permit casting at the site for members too large or heavy for transporting from factory to site.

3. Vertical internal force on beam is caused by tendency of tendon to "straighten out" under tension.

It reduces downward beam deflection and allows shallower beams and longer spans than in conventionally reinforced beams.

4. Auxiliary mild reinforcement provides additional strength, controls cracking, and produces more ductile behavior.

5. Stirrups are used to provide additional shear strength in the beam and to support the tendons and longitudinal mild reinforcement. Stirrups should be open at the top to allow the reinforcing to be fabricated and placed before the tendon is placed.

6. Shoring must be left in place until the post-tensioning operation is performed. After stressing, reshoring may be required to prevent overloading during additional construction.

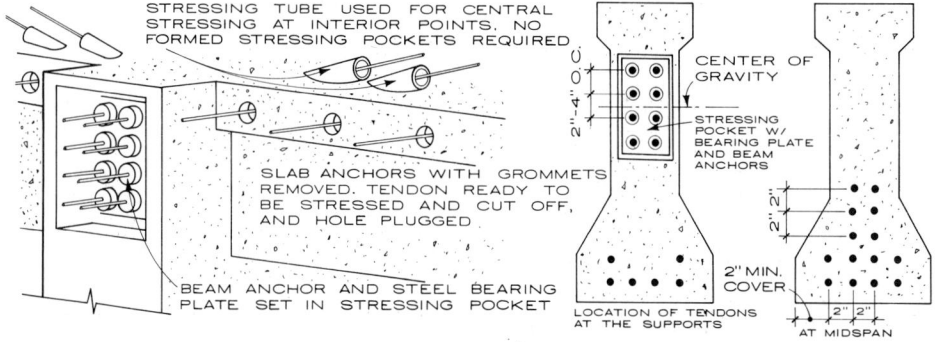

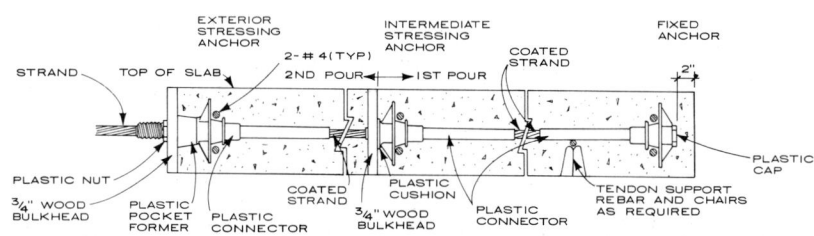

TYPICAL UNBONDED SINGLE STRAND TENDON INSTALLATION

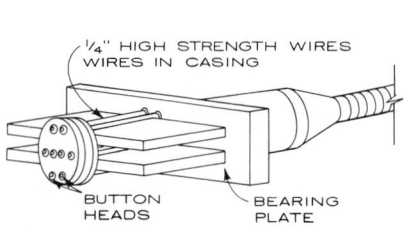

8 WIRE BBRV POST-TENSIONING ANCHOR (GROUTED)

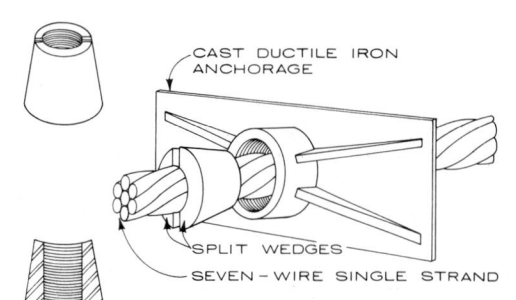

SINGLE STRAND TENDON ANCHORAGE (UNBONDED)

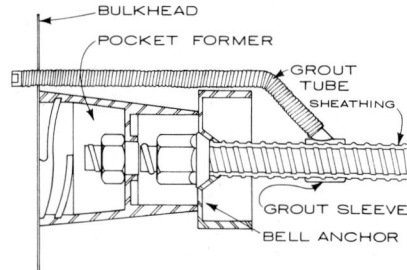

THREAD BAR ANCHORAGE (GROUTED)

Leo A. Daly, Architecture-Engineering-Planning; Omaha, Nebraska

PRECAST CONCRETE

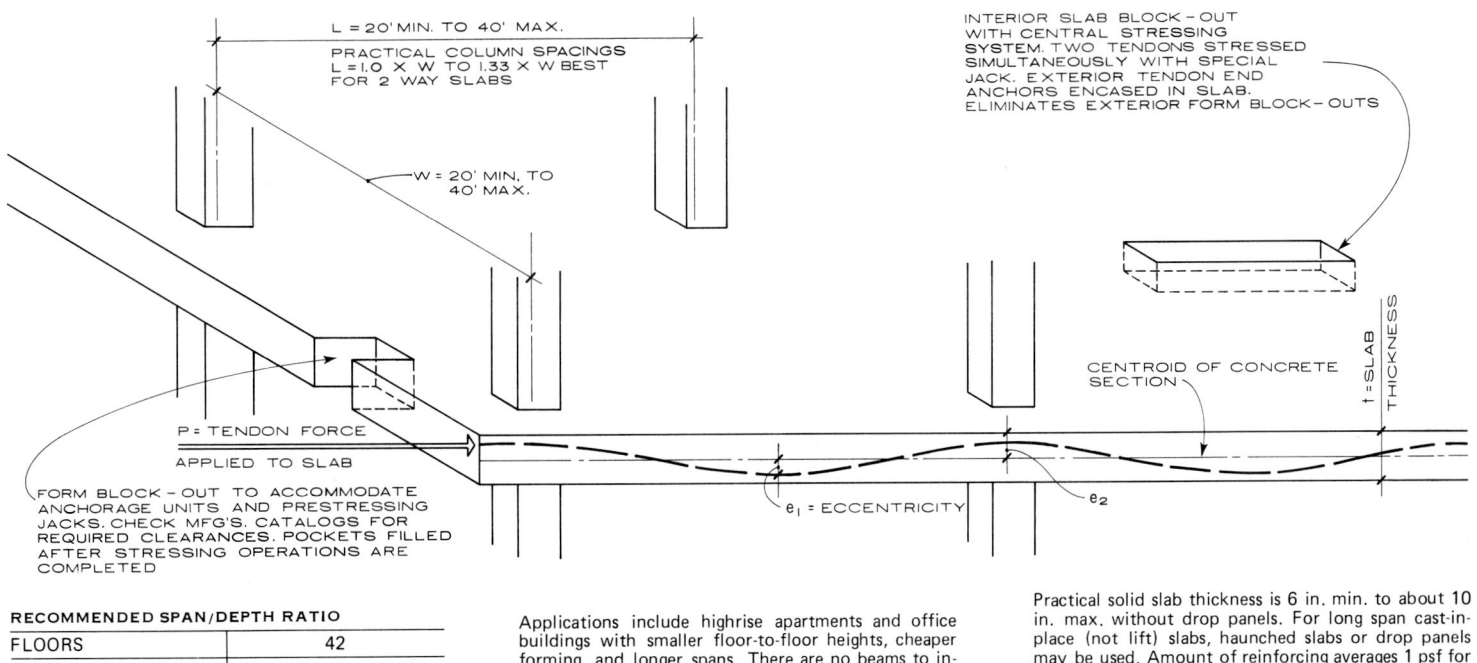

RECOMMENDED SPAN/DEPTH RATIO	
FLOORS	42
ROOF	48

Check deflections and vibration

Applications include highrise apartments and office buildings with smaller floor-to-floor heights, cheaper forming, and longer spans. There are no beams to interfere with ducts and piping, and a sprayed-on ceiling may be applied directly to slab soffit.

Practical solid slab thickness is 6 in. min. to about 10 in. max. without drop panels. For long span cast-in-place (not lift) slabs, haunched slabs or drop panels may be used. Amount of reinforcing averages 1 psf for 24 to 28 ft bays, as compared to 2 to 3 psf for conventional concrete.

FLAT PLATE CONSTRUCTION

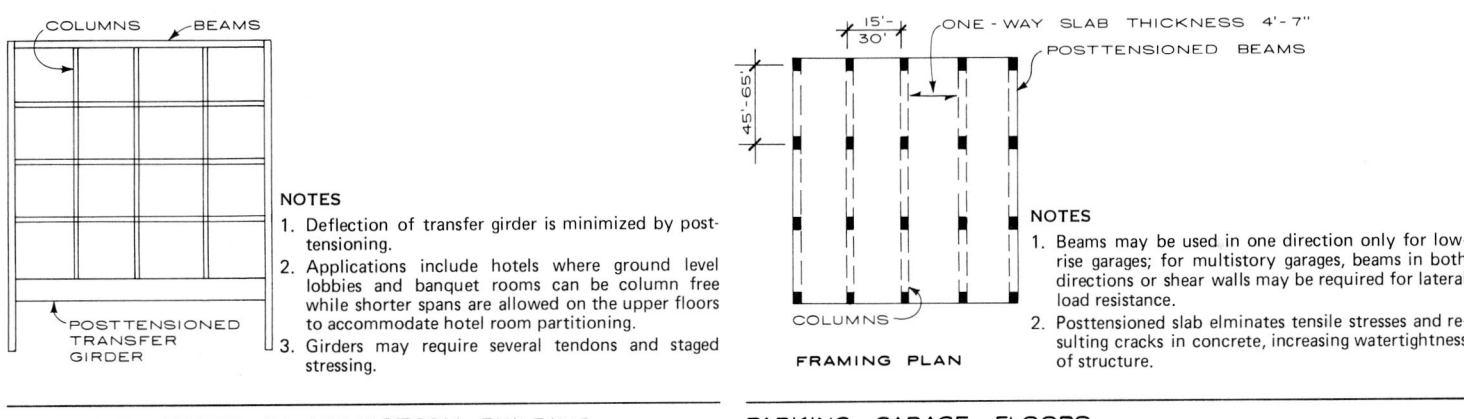

NOTES

1. Deflection of transfer girder is minimized by post-tensioning.
2. Applications include hotels where ground level lobbies and banquet rooms can be column free while shorter spans are allowed on the upper floors to accommodate hotel room partitioning.
3. Girders may require several tendons and staged stressing.

TRANSFER GIRDER IN MULTISTORY BUILDING

NOTES

1. Beams may be used in one direction only for low-rise garages; for multistory garages, beams in both directions or shear walls may be required for lateral load resistance.
2. Posttensioned slab eliminates tensile stresses and resulting cracks in concrete, increasing watertightness of structure.

PARKING GARAGE FLOORS

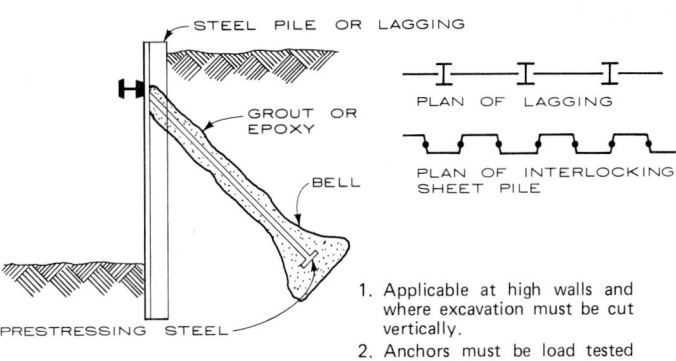

1. Applicable at high walls and where excavation must be cut vertically.
2. Anchors must be load tested after installation.

TIE BACK RETAINING WALL

MISCELLANEOUS APPLICATIONS

1. GRANDSTANDS: Cantilevered posttensioned roofs can eliminate columns that interrupt sight lines.
2. DOMED STRUCTURES: Posttensioned rings may be used to resist the thrust at the base of the dome.
3. MAT FOUNDATIONS: Posttensioned mat foundations distribute column loads over the entire area of the mat and may be more economical than pile foundations.
4. SLABS-ON-GROUND: Posttensioning is often used to eliminate cracking resulting from swelling soils which are a problem in many parts of the United States. Other types of construction where posttensioning may be used include waffle slabs, folded plates, and shell structures.

APPLICATIONS OF POSTTENSIONED CONCRETE

Leo A. Daly, Architecture-Engineering-Planning; Omaha, Nebraska

PRECAST CONCRETE 3

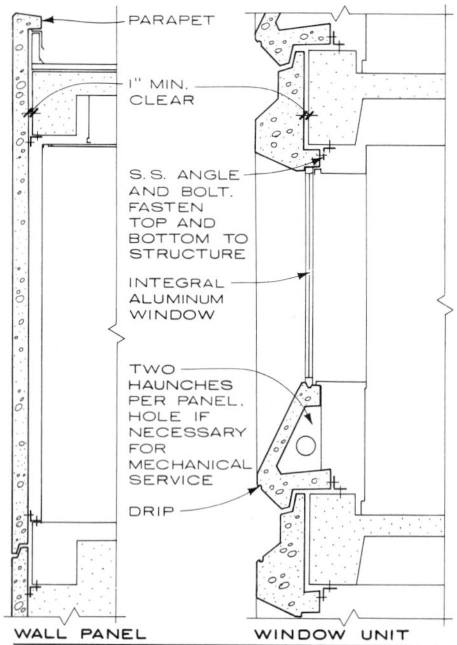

NONSTRUCTURAL FACING UNITS

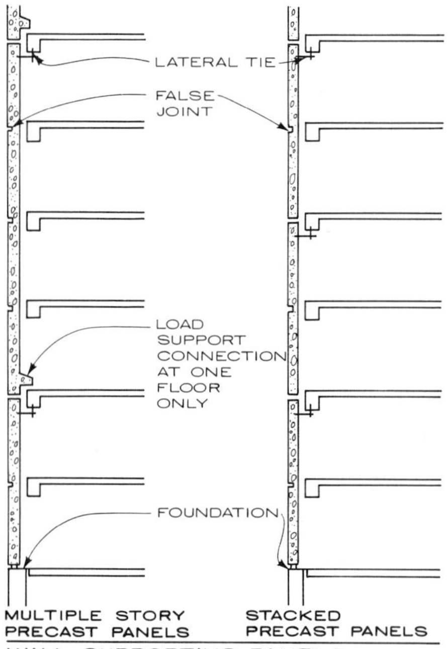

PARAPET

1" MIN. CLEAR

S.S. ANGLE AND BOLT. FASTEN TOP AND BOTTOM TO STRUCTURE

INTEGRAL ALUMINUM WINDOW

TWO HAUNCHES PER PANEL. HOLE IF NECESSARY FOR MECHANICAL SERVICE

DRIP

WALL PANEL   WINDOW UNIT

WALL SUPPORTING PANELS

LATERAL TIE

FALSE JOINT

LOAD SUPPORT CONNECTION AT ONE FLOOR ONLY

FOUNDATION

MULTIPLE STORY PRECAST PANELS   STACKED PRECAST PANELS

PRECAST PANEL JOINT TOLERANCES

JOINT TOLERANCES

FACE WIDTH OF JOINTS
JOINT TAPER

± 3/16 IN.

1/40 IN./FT LENGTH (MAX. LENGTH OF TAPERING IN ONE DIRECTION OF 10 FT)

STEP IN FACE 1/4 IN. JOG IN ALIGNMENT OF EDGE 1/4 IN.

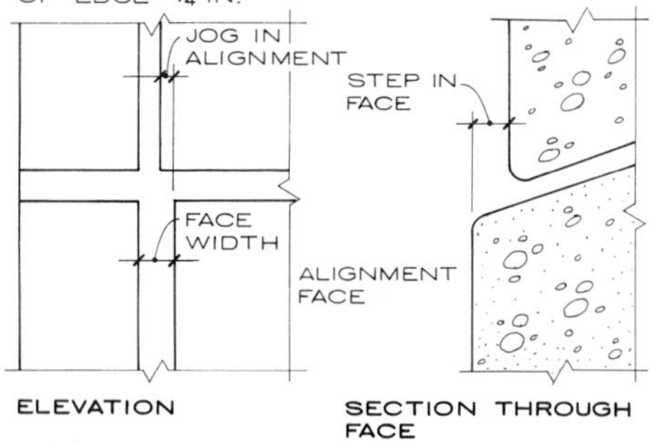

JOG IN ALIGNMENT

STEP IN FACE

FACE WIDTH

ALIGNMENT FACE

ELEVATION   SECTION THROUGH FACE

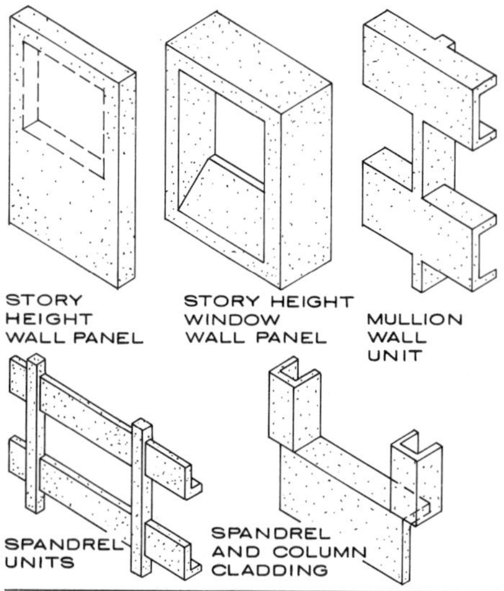

BASIC ELEVATIONAL APPROACHES TO PRECAST CLADDING

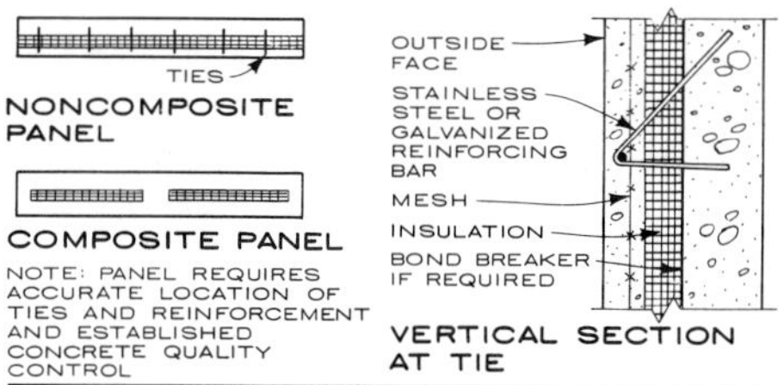

STORY HEIGHT WALL PANEL

STORY HEIGHT WINDOW WALL PANEL

MULLION WALL UNIT

SPANDREL UNITS

SPANDREL AND COLUMN CLADDING

SANDWICH WALL CONSTRUCTION

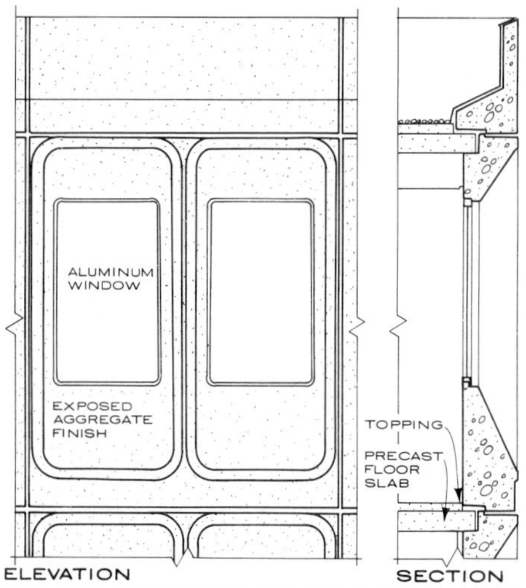

TIES

NONCOMPOSITE PANEL

COMPOSITE PANEL

NOTE: PANEL REQUIRES ACCURATE LOCATION OF TIES AND REINFORCEMENT AND ESTABLISHED CONCRETE QUALITY CONTROL

OUTSIDE FACE

STAINLESS STEEL OR GALVANIZED REINFORCING BAR

MESH

INSULATION

BOND BREAKER IF REQUIRED

VERTICAL SECTION AT TIE

LOAD BEARING WALL PANEL

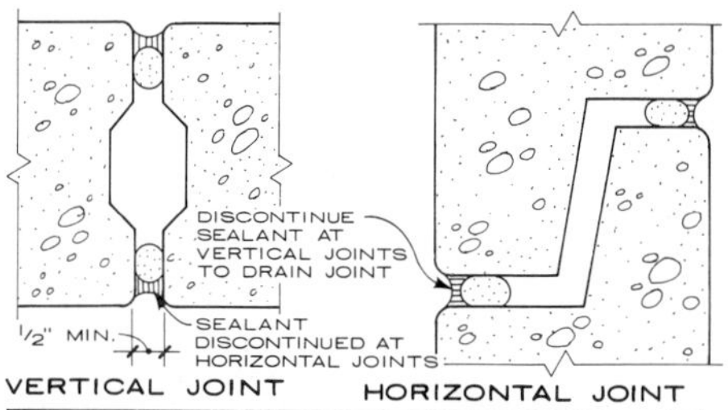

ALUMINUM WINDOW

EXPOSED AGGREGATE FINISH

TOPPING

PRECAST FLOOR SLAB

ELEVATION   SECTION

TWO-STAGE SEALANT JOINTS

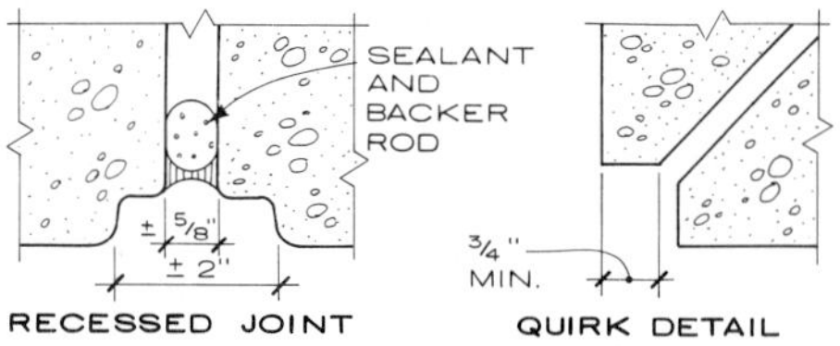

DISCONTINUE SEALANT AT VERTICAL JOINTS TO DRAIN JOINT

1/2" MIN.

SEALANT DISCONTINUED AT HORIZONTAL JOINTS

VERTICAL JOINT   HORIZONTAL JOINT

JOINT DETAILS

SEALANT AND BACKER ROD

± 5/8 ± 2"

3/4" MIN.

RECESSED JOINT   QUIRK DETAIL

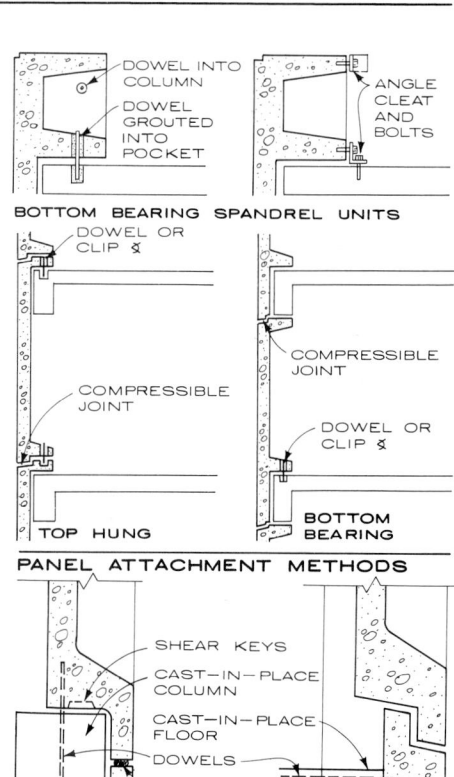

PANEL ATTACHMENT METHODS

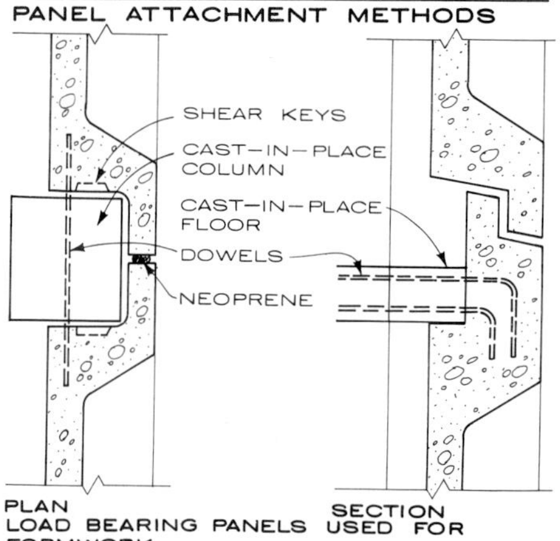

DOWEL INTO COLUMN

DOWEL GROUTED INTO POCKET

ANGLE CLEAT AND BOLTS

BOTTOM BEARING SPANDREL UNITS

DOWEL OR CLIP Ⅎ

COMPRESSIBLE JOINT

COMPRESSIBLE JOINT

DOWEL OR CLIP Ⅎ

TOP HUNG   BOTTOM BEARING

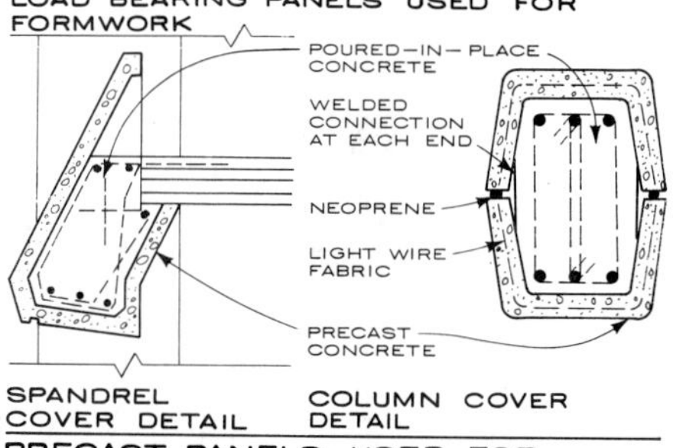

PRECAST PANELS USED FOR FORMWORK

SHEAR KEYS

CAST-IN-PLACE COLUMN

CAST-IN-PLACE FLOOR

DOWELS

NEOPRENE

PLAN
LOAD BEARING PANELS USED FOR FORMWORK

SECTION

POURED-IN-PLACE CONCRETE

WELDED CONNECTION AT EACH END

NEOPRENE

LIGHT WIRE FABRIC

PRECAST CONCRETE

SPANDREL COVER DETAIL   COLUMN COVER DETAIL

PANEL VARIATIONS

Panels are available in many forms, such as decorative, single or multistory, shear walls, insulated, or factory assembled with integral glazing units, interior finish, or HVAC subsystems. Consult with manufacturers to determine factors affecting design; verify transportation and erection limitations.

FINISHES

A wide variety of concrete finishes are available. Before casting, concrete molds provide smooth or textured finishes depending on the design of the form liner. Finish treatment after casting, but prior to hardening, includes exposed aggregate (light, medium, or deep exposure), broom, travel, screen, float, or strippled finishes. After hardening, finishes include acid etching, sandblasting, honed, polished, bush-hammered, or hammered rib finishes.

COLORS

In smooth finish concrete, the color of the cement (plus pigment) is dominant. If color uniformity is essential, use white cement from one source only. Gray cement is generally subject to color variations even when supplied from one source. Use of pigments requires a high quality of manufacture and controlled curing standards. Where the color depends mainly on the fine aggregates, control of the graduation of the mixture is required. Coarse aggregates selected for color should be chosen for durability and appearance.

Bruce Lambert, Architect; Washington, D.C.

PRECAST CONCRETE

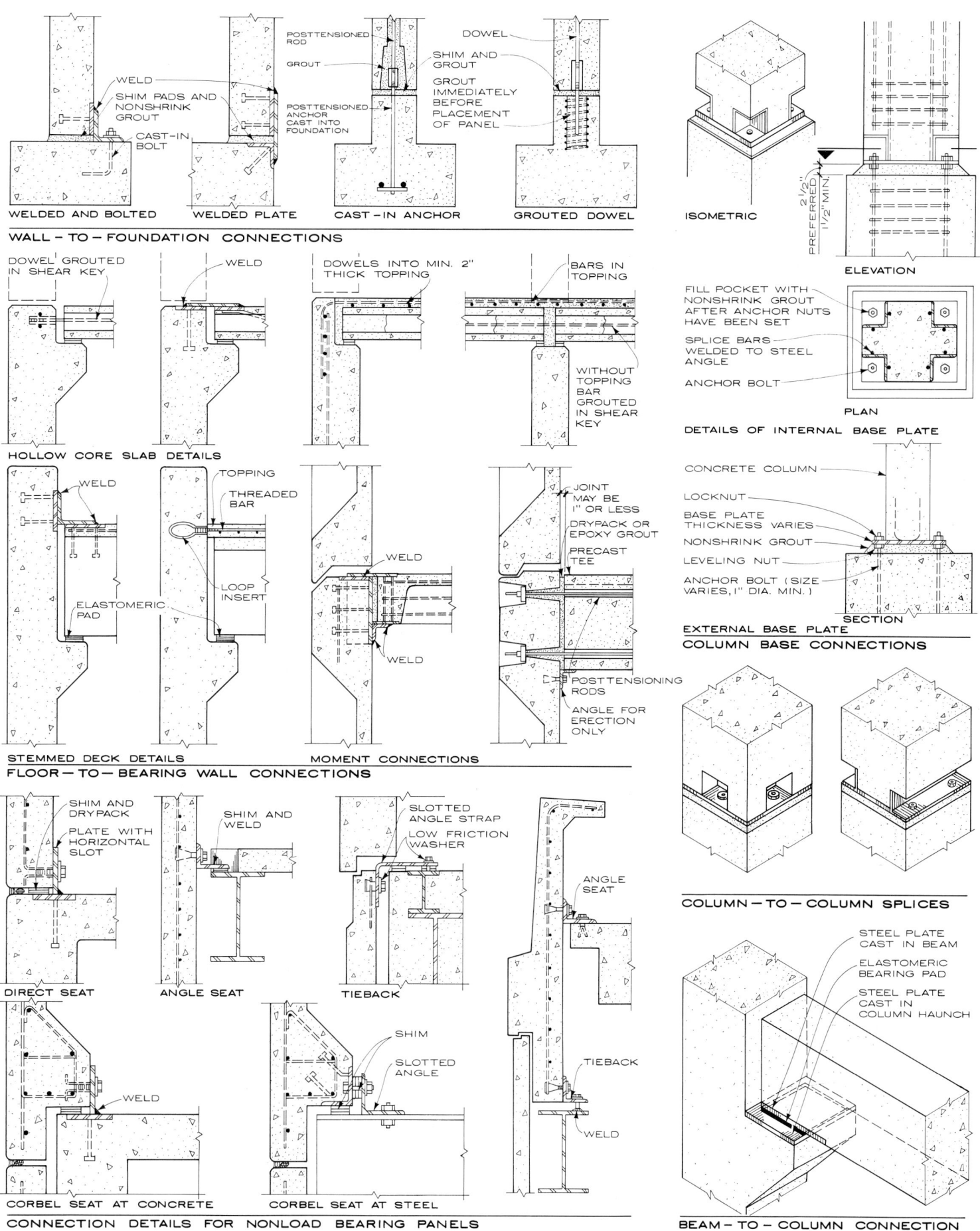

WELD
SHIM PADS AND NONSHRINK GROUT
CAST-IN BOLT

WELDED AND BOLTED

POSTTENSIONED ROD
GROUT
POSTTENSIONED ANCHOR CAST INTO FOUNDATION

WELDED PLATE

DOWEL
SHIM AND GROUT
GROUT IMMEDIATELY BEFORE PLACEMENT OF PANEL

CAST-IN ANCHOR

DOWEL

GROUTED DOWEL

WALL - TO - FOUNDATION CONNECTIONS

DOWEL GROUTED IN SHEAR KEY

WELD

DOWELS INTO MIN. 2" THICK TOPPING

BARS IN TOPPING

WITHOUT TOPPING BAR GROUTED IN SHEAR KEY

HOLLOW CORE SLAB DETAILS

WELD

TOPPING
THREADED BAR

WELD

JOINT MAY BE 1" OR LESS
DRYPACK OR EPOXY GROUT
PRECAST TEE

ELASTOMERIC PAD

LOOP INSERT

WELD

POSTTENSIONING RODS
ANGLE FOR ERECTION ONLY

STEMMED DECK DETAILS   **MOMENT CONNECTIONS**

FLOOR - TO - BEARING WALL CONNECTIONS

SHIM AND DRYPACK
PLATE WITH HORIZONTAL SLOT

DIRECT SEAT

SHIM AND WELD

ANGLE SEAT

SLOTTED ANGLE STRAP
LOW FRICTION WASHER

TIEBACK

ANGLE SEAT

WELD

CORBEL SEAT AT CONCRETE

SHIM
SLOTTED ANGLE

WELD

CORBEL SEAT AT STEEL

TIEBACK

WELD

CONNECTION DETAILS FOR NONLOAD BEARING PANELS

Bruce Lambert, Architect; Washington, D.C.

ISOMETRIC

2½" PREFERRED 1½" MIN.

ELEVATION

FILL POCKET WITH NONSHRINK GROUT AFTER ANCHOR NUTS HAVE BEEN SET
SPLICE BARS WELDED TO STEEL ANGLE
ANCHOR BOLT

PLAN

DETAILS OF INTERNAL BASE PLATE

CONCRETE COLUMN
LOCKNUT
BASE PLATE THICKNESS VARIES
NONSHRINK GROUT
LEVELING NUT
ANCHOR BOLT (SIZE VARIES, 1" DIA. MIN.)

SECTION

EXTERNAL BASE PLATE

COLUMN BASE CONNECTIONS

COLUMN - TO - COLUMN SPLICES

STEEL PLATE CAST IN BEAM
ELASTOMERIC BEARING PAD
STEEL PLATE CAST IN COLUMN HAUNCH

BEAM - TO - COLUMN CONNECTION

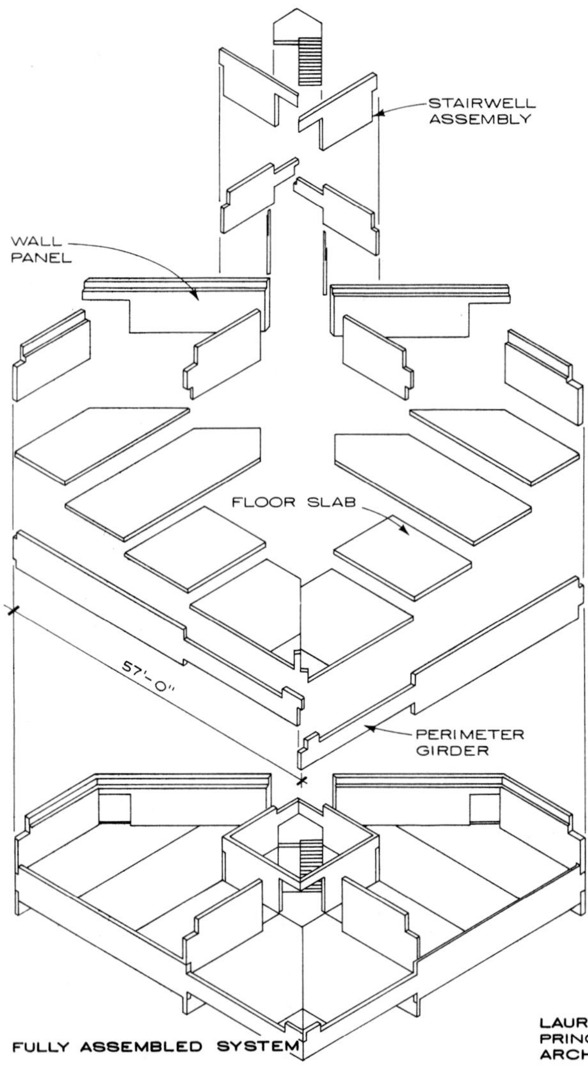

STAIRWELL ASSEMBLY

WALL PANEL

FLOOR SLAB

57'-0"

PERIMETER GIRDER

FULLY ASSEMBLED SYSTEM

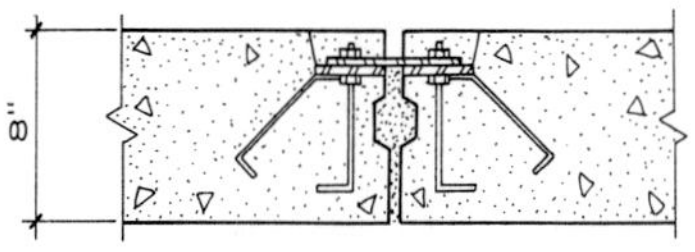

SLAB AND PANEL SYSTEM

NOTE

This precast wall system utilizes load bearing precast window panel units measuring 12 ft high, 10 ft wide, and 3 ft deep to support the precast concrete double tee floor. Units are attached to the floor and top and bottom with welded plates.

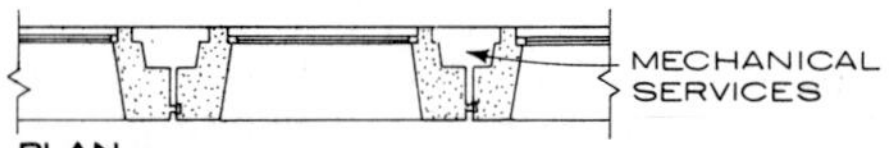

MECHANICAL SERVICES

PLAN

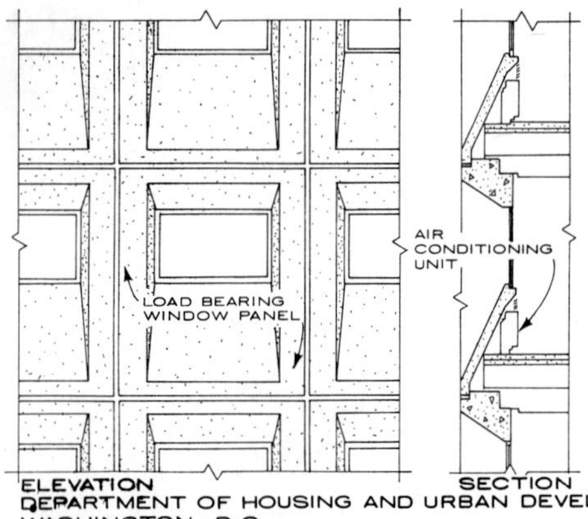

LOAD BEARING WINDOW PANEL

AIR CONDITIONING UNIT

ELEVATION   **SECTION**

DEPARTMENT OF HOUSING AND URBAN DEVELOPMENT
WASHINGTON, D.C.
ARCHITECT: MARCEL BREUER AND HERBERT BECKHARD,
NOLEN·SWINBURNE AND ASSOCIATES

WALL PANEL SYSTEM

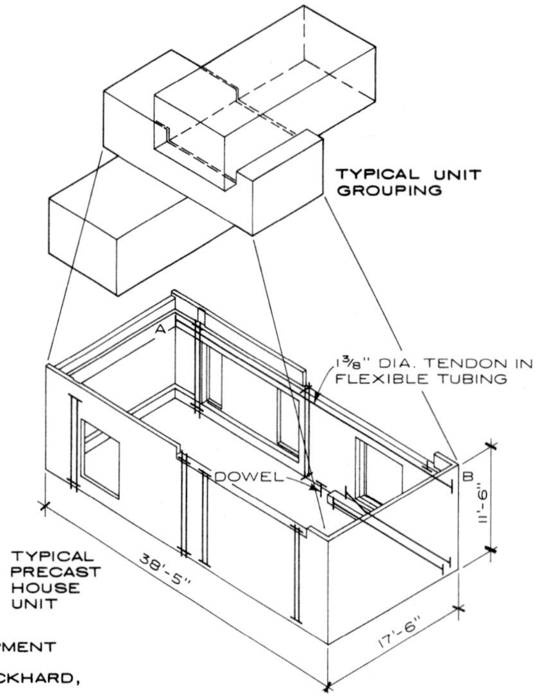

Bruce Lambert, Architect; Washington, D.C.

8"

SLAB TO SLAB DETAIL

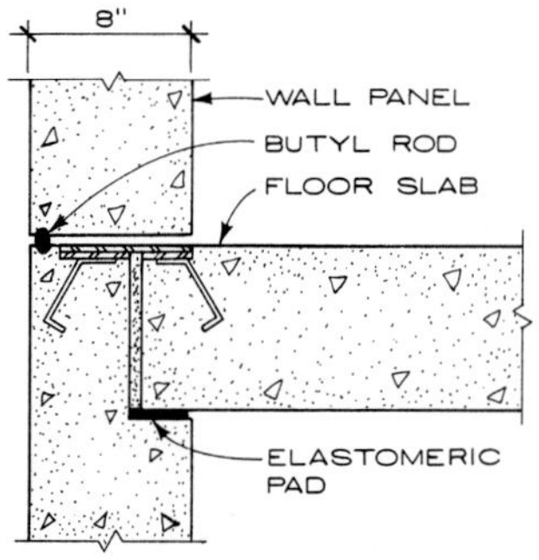

8"

WALL PANEL
BUTYL ROD
FLOOR SLAB

ELASTOMERIC PAD

SLAB TO WALL DETAIL

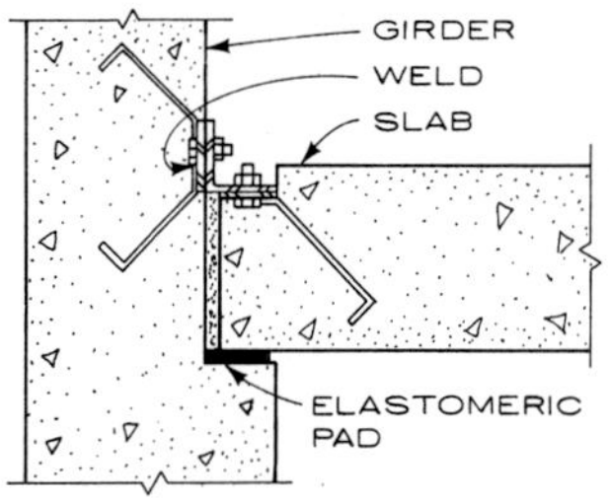

GIRDER
WELD
SLAB

ELASTOMERIC PAD

SLAB TO GIRDER DETAIL

NOTE

This precast prestressed floor, wall, and girder system is shop fabricated and field assembled to form a completed structure. Slab and wall panels are welded to posttensioned girders. All members are left exposed throughout and utilize 5000 psi concrete using buff gray cement.

LAURA SPELMAN ROCKEFELLER HALL
PRINCETON UNIVERSITY, PRINCETON, N.J.
ARCHITECT: I.M. PEI AND PARTNERS

TYPICAL UNIT GROUPING

1³⁄₈" DIA. TENDON IN FLEXIBLE TUBING

DOWEL

TYPICAL PRECAST HOUSE UNIT

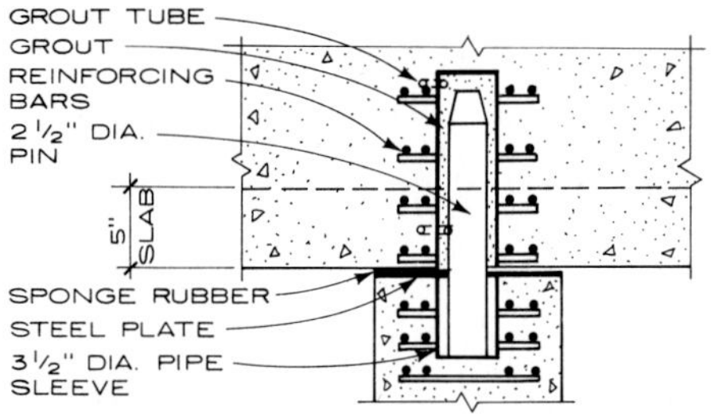

38'-5"

11'-6"

17'-6"

BOX SYSTEM

PRECAST CONCRETE PLANTER

PRECAST CONCRETE DOUBLE "TEE"

ELASTOMERIC PAD

METAL RAILING

PRECAST CONCRETE "L" BEAM

PRECAST CONCRETE "TREE" COLUMN

CAST-IN-PLACE CONCRETE FOOTINGS

CONSTRUCTION JOINT

SLAB ON GRADE

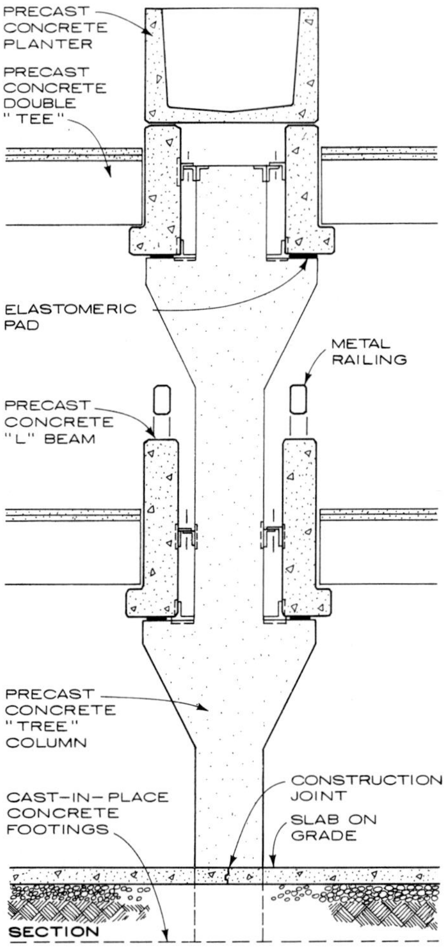

SECTION

NOTE

This precast prestressed column and beam system consists of precast double tees spanning 57.5 ft to precast leader beams. Ledger beams are bolted and welded to 18 x 24 in. full height haunched column to stiffen the structural frame.

PARKING STRUCTURE, FNMA HEADQUARTERS
WASHINGTON, D.C.
ARCHITECT: JOHN CARL WARNECKE, FAIA

COLUMN AND BEAM SYSTEM

GROUT TUBE
GROUT
REINFORCING BARS
2¹⁄₂" DIA. PIN

5" SLAB

SPONGE RUBBER
STEEL PLATE
3¹⁄₂" DIA. PIPE SLEEVE

DOWEL DETAIL

NOTE

This three dimensional precast posttensioned concrete system utilizes a five sided building envelope that is cast monolithically and then stacked and connected together in a variety of groupings. Walls are typically 5 in. thick. Services run vertically outside the units.

HABITAT '67, MONTREAL, CANADA
ASSOCIATED ARCHITECTS: MOSHE
SAFDIE AND DAVID, BAROTT, BOULVA

PRECAST CONCRETE

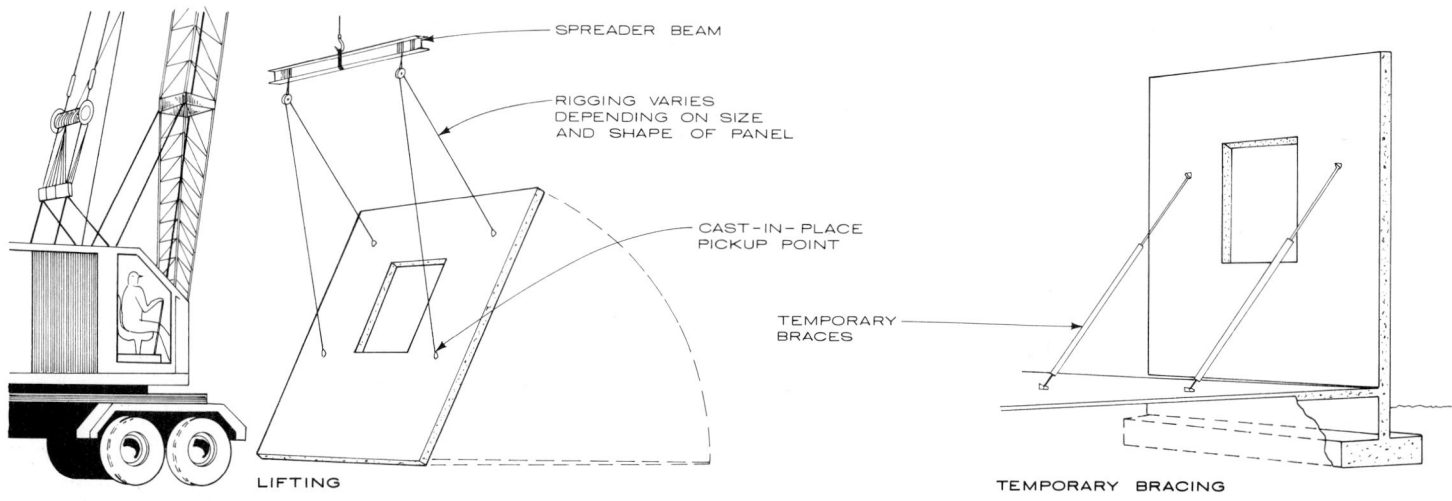

SPREADER BEAM

RIGGING VARIES DEPENDING ON SIZE AND SHAPE OF PANEL

CAST-IN-PLACE PICKUP POINT

TEMPORARY BRACES

LIFTING

TEMPORARY BRACING

CONSTRUCTION PROCEDURES

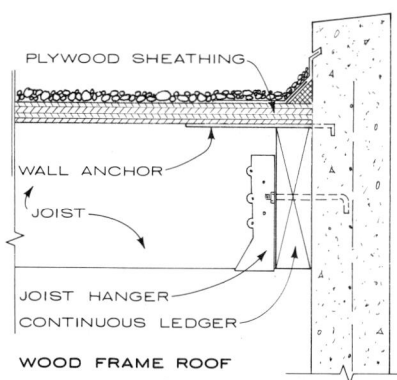

PLYWOOD SHEATHING

WALL ANCHOR

JOIST

JOIST HANGER

CONTINUOUS LEDGER

WOOD FRAME ROOF

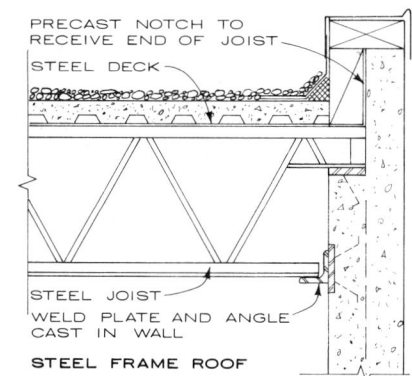

PRECAST NOTCH TO RECEIVE END OF JOIST

STEEL DECK

STEEL JOIST

WELD PLATE AND ANGLE CAST IN WALL

STEEL FRAME ROOF

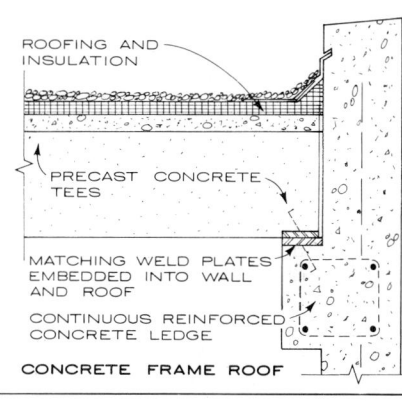

ROOFING AND INSULATION

PRECAST CONCRETE TEES

MATCHING WELD PLATES EMBEDDED INTO WALL AND ROOF

CONTINUOUS REINFORCED CONCRETE LEDGE

CONCRETE FRAME ROOF

PANEL CONNECTIONS AT ROOF

GENERAL NOTES

Tilt-up construction is a form of precast concrete construction. Walls are cast on the site in a horizontal position, tilted to the vertical position, set in place, and made an integral part of the completed structure. The designer should consult with possible contractors before the design and construction details are definitely established. Even small changes in design or construction procedure may result in an appreciable saving in time and money as well as providing a better structure.

APPLICATIONS

Tilt-up walls are very economical and are adaptable to a wide range of architectural uses. They have been used in many types of structures from private homes and garages to multistory office buildings, although by far the greatest use has been in one-story industrial and commercial buildings.

DESIGN

Wall panels must be designed for the conditions to which they will be subjected during erection and in the completed structure. The general design of the building determines whether the walls are load bearing or nonload bearing either with a continuous footing or supported on the column footings only. The panels are designed like walls of reinforced concrete built in the conventional manner, the only difference being in the details.

LIFTING STRESSES

Lifting a wall panel creates stresses not encountered in conventional cast-in-place construction, and with some pickup arrangements the exact determination of these stresses can be complicated. The method of attaching the lifting equipment must be known in order to determine the stresses. Rigging details will vary depending on the size and shape of the individual panel.

Harnish, Morgan, and Causey, Architects; Ontario, California

Taylor & Gaines, Structural Engineers; Pasadena, California

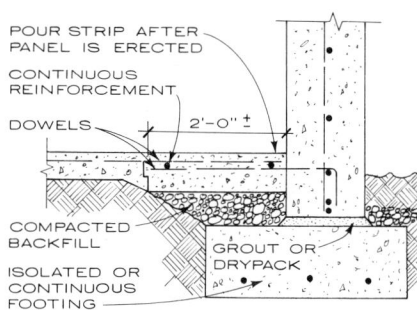

POUR STRIP AFTER PANEL IS ERECTED

CONTINUOUS REINFORCEMENT

DOWELS

2'-0" ±

COMPACTED BACKFILL

ISOLATED OR CONTINUOUS FOOTING

GROUT OR DRYPACK

SLAB AND FOOTING DETAIL

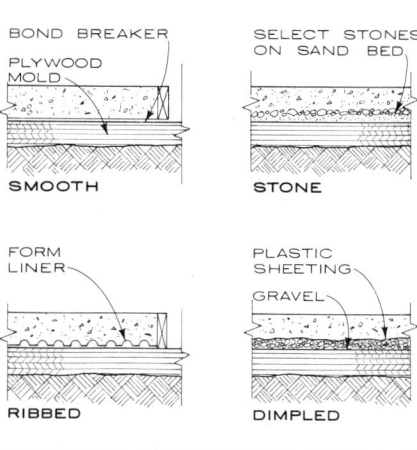

BOND BREAKER

PLYWOOD MOLD

SMOOTH

SELECT STONES ON SAND BED

STONE

FORM LINER

RIBBED

PLASTIC SHEETING

GRAVEL

DIMPLED

SURFACE TREATMENTS

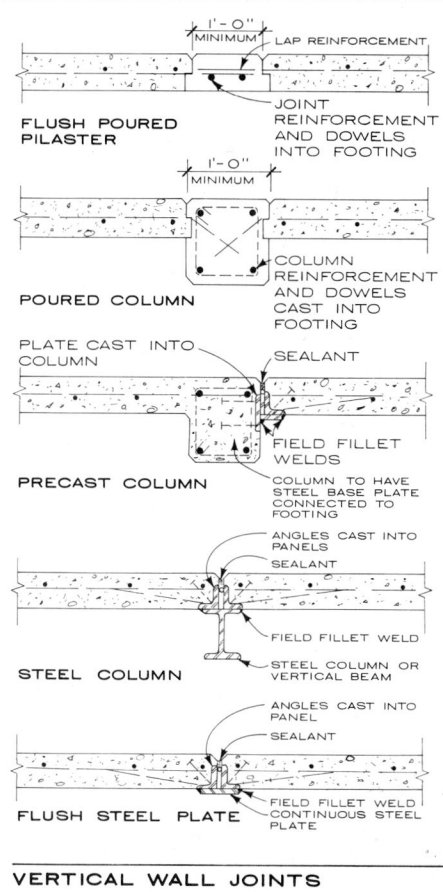

1'-0" MINIMUM   LAP REINFORCEMENT

FLUSH POURED PILASTER

JOINT REINFORCEMENT AND DOWELS INTO FOOTING

1'-0" MINIMUM

POURED COLUMN

COLUMN REINFORCEMENT AND DOWELS CAST INTO FOOTING

PLATE CAST INTO COLUMN

SEALANT

PRECAST COLUMN

FIELD FILLET WELDS

COLUMN TO HAVE STEEL BASE PLATE CONNECTED TO FOOTING

ANGLES CAST INTO PANELS

SEALANT

STEEL COLUMN

FIELD FILLET WELD

STEEL COLUMN OR VERTICAL BEAM

ANGLES CAST INTO PANEL

SEALANT

FLUSH STEEL PLATE

FIELD FILLET WELD

CONTINUOUS STEEL PLATE

VERTICAL WALL JOINTS

PRECAST CONCRETE 3

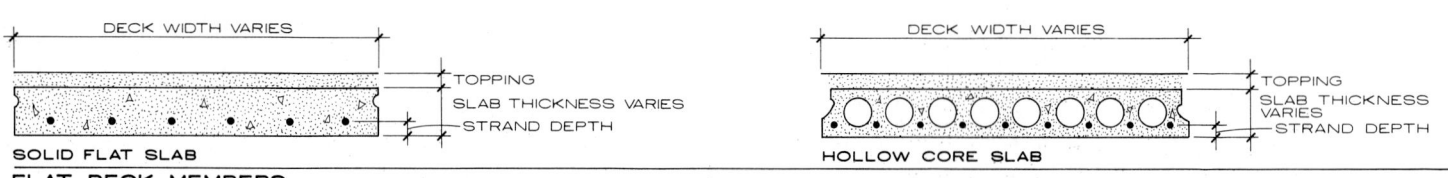

SOLID FLAT SLAB   **HOLLOW CORE SLAB**

FLAT DECK MEMBERS

TABLE 1 *
SAFE SUPERIMPOSED SERVICE LOADS (PSF) FOR SOLID FLAT SLABS

SLAB THICKNESS (IN.)	SLAB DESIGNATION	TOPPING THICKNESS (IN.)	SPAN (FT)															
			12	14	16	18	20	22	24	26	28	30	32	34	36	38	40
4"	FS4	NONE	160	105	68												
	FS4+2	2	284	167	91												
6"	FS6	NONE		261	182	128	90	61									
	FS6+2	2			262	172	108	60									
8"	FS8	NONE				227	165	119	84								
	FS8+2	2				298	206	139	87								

TABLE 2 *
SAFE SUPERIMPOSED SERVICE LOADS (PSF) FOR HOLLOW CORE SLABS (4 FT WIDTH)

SLAB THICKNESS (IN.)	SLAB DESIGNATION	TOPPING THICKNESS (IN.)	SPAN (FT)															
			12	14	16	18	20	22	24	26	28	30	32	34	36	38	40
6"	4HC6	NONE		291	225	168	126	96	73								
	4HC6+2	2				222	158	111	75	47							
8"	4HC8	NONE				269	213	169	135	107	85	66	52				
	4HC8+2	2					264	205	154	115	83	58					
10"	4HC10	NONE					274	232	186	150	122	100	81	66	52		
	4HC10+2	2						270	215	172	137	103	76	54			
12"	4HC12	NONE									166	138	115	95	79	66	54
	4HC12+2	2							234	209	182	149	122	97	74	55	

LOAD TABLES FOR FLAT DECK MEMBERS

* NOTE: 1. NORMAL WEIGHT (150 PCF) CONCRETE SLAB AND TOPPING
2. SLABS f_c = 5000 PSI
3. STRAND DESIGNATION CODE = 50-S

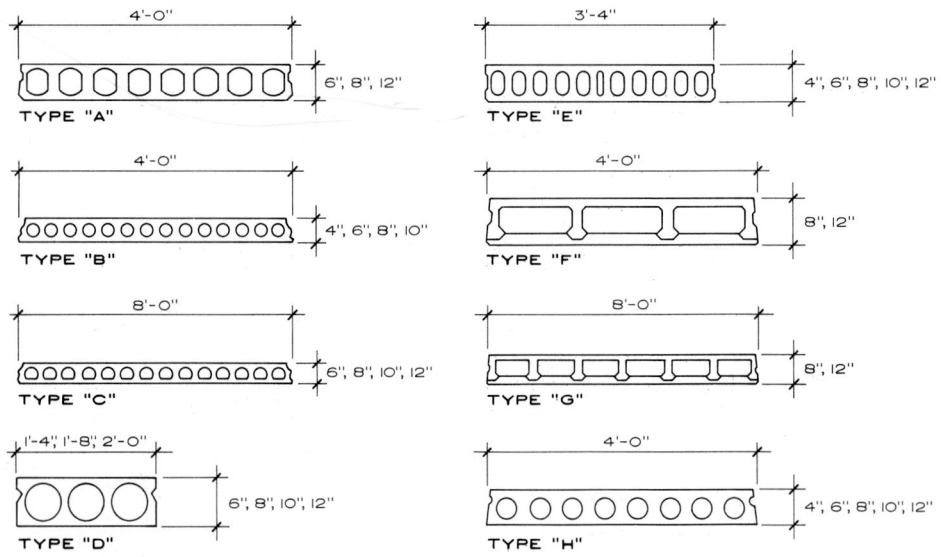

TYPE "A" — 4'-0" — 6", 8", 12"
TYPE "E" — 3'-4" — 4", 6", 8", 10", 12"
TYPE "B" — 4'-0" — 4", 6", 8", 10"
TYPE "F" — 4'-0" — 8", 12"
TYPE "C" — 8'-0" — 6", 8", 10", 12"
TYPE "G" — 8'-0" — 8", 12"
TYPE "D" — 1'-4", 1'-8", 2'-0" — 6", 8", 10", 12"
TYPE "H" — 4'-0" — 4", 6", 8", 10", 12"

NOTES

1. Normal weight (150 pcf) or lightweight concrete (115 pcf) is used in standard slab construction. Topping concrete is usually normal weight concrete with a cylinder strength of 3000 psi. All units are prestressed with strand release when concrete strength is 3500 psi.
2. Strands are available in various sizes and strengths according to individual manufacturers. Strand placement may vary, which will change load capacity, camber values, and fire resistance. Contact the local supplier for strand placement and allowable loading.
3. Camber will vary substantially depending on slab design, span, and loading. Nonstructural components attached to members may be affected by camber variations. Calculations of topping quantities should recognize camber variations.
4. Safe superimposed service loads include a dead load of 10 psf for untopped concrete and 15 psf for topped concrete. The remainder is live load.
5. Smooth or textured soffits may be available in some types; check with the supplier.

HOLLOW CORE SLAB TYPES
ALL SECTIONS ARE NOT AVAILABLE FROM ALL PRODUCERS
CHECK AVAILABILITY WITH LOCAL MANUFACTURERS

Bruce Lambert, Architect; Washington D.C.

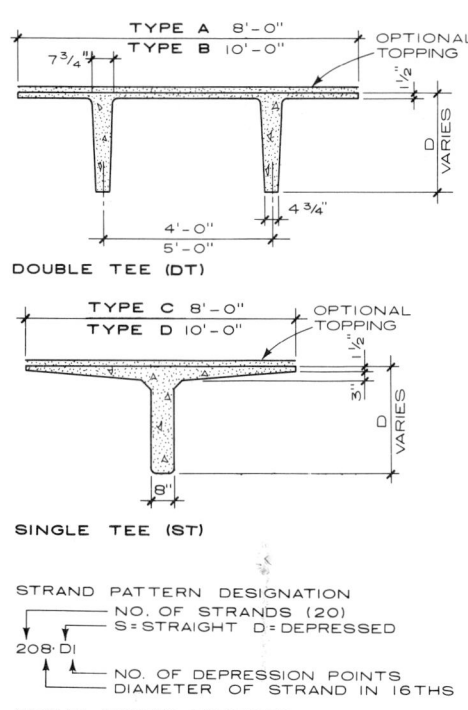

STRAND PATTERN DESIGNATION

NO. OF STRANDS (20)
S = STRAIGHT D = DEPRESSED

208 · D1

NO. OF DEPRESSION POINTS
DIAMETER OF STRAND IN 16THS

NORMAL WEIGHT CONCRETE
f'_c = 5000 PSI

NOTES

1. Safe loads shown indicate dead load of 10 psf for untopped members and 15 psf for topped members. Remainder is live load.
2. Designers should contact the manufacturers in the geographic area of the proposed structure to determine availability, exact dimensions, and load tables for various sections.
3. Camber should be checked for its effect on non-structural members (i.e., partitions, folding doors, etc.), which should be placed with adequate allowance for error. Calculations of topping quantities should also recognize camber variations.
4. Normal weight concrete is assumed to be 150 lb/cu ft; lightweight concrete is assumed to be 115 lb/cu ft.

STEMMED DECK MEMBERS
SEE CHART FOR APPROXIMATE MAX. SPANS

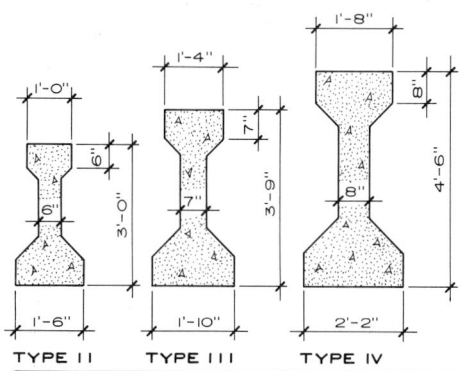

TYPE II   TYPE III   TYPE IV

AASHTO GIRDERS

TABLE OF SAFE SUPERIMPOSED SERVICE LOAD* (PLF) FOR AASHTO GIRDER

DESIG-NATION	NO. OF STRANDS	SPAN (FT)						
		36	40	44	48	52	56	60
Type II	14	3520	2785	2241	1826			
Type III	22	7231	5757	4667	3837	3192	2679	2266
Type IV	32		9848	7996	6588	5492	4622	3920

Bruce Lambert, Architect; Washington, D.C.

APPROXIMATE MAXIMUM SPAN FOR STEMMED DECK SECTIONS

DECK TYPE	DEPTH D (IN.)	CONCRETE WEIGHT	DESIGNATION	TOPPING DEPTH (IN.)	STRAND DESIGNATION	MAX. SPAN (FT)	SAFE LOAD (PSF)
A	12	Normal weight	8DT12	0	88 · D1	40	40
			8DT12 + 2	2	68 · D1	34	39
		Lightweight	8LDT12	0	68 · D1	40	35
			8LDT12 + 2	2	68 · D1	36	36
A	18	Normal weight	8DT18	0	108 · D1	58	34
			8DT18 + 2	2	88 · D1	46	48
		Lightweight	8LDT18	0	108 · D1	60	37
			8LDT18 + 2	2	88 · D1	50	39
A	24	Normal weight	8DT24	0	148 · D1	74	38
			8DT24 + 2	2	128 · D1	60	56
		Lightweight	8LDT24	0	148 · D1	80	35
			8LDT24 + 2	2	108 · D1	62	44
A	32	Normal weight	8DT32	0	228 · D1	88	56
			8DT32 + 2	2	208 · D1	76	76
		Lightweight	8LDT32	0	228 · D1	100	41
			8LDT32 + 2	2	208 · D1	82	67
B	32	Normal weight	10DT32	0	228 · D1	86	49
			10DT32 + 2	2	208 · D1	74	62
		Lightweight	10LDT32	0	228 · D1	98	35
			10LDT32 + 2	2	208 · D1	78	59
C	36	Normal weight	8ST36	0	228 · D1	100	44
			8ST36 + 2	2	188 · D1	82	61
		Lightweight	8LST36	0	228 · D1	110	38
			8LST36 + 2	2	168 · D1	86	50
D	48	Normal weight	10ST48	0	248 · D1	112	42
		Lightweight	10LST48	0	248 · D1	120	41

TABLE OF SAFE SUPERIMPOSED SERVICE LOAD* (PLF) FOR PRECAST BEAM SECTIONS

TYPE	DESIGNATION	NO. STRAND	H (IN.)	H1/H2 (IN.)	SPAN (FT)								
					18	22	26	30	34	38	42	46	50
RECTANGULAR BEAM	12RB24	10	24		6726	4413	3083	2248	1684	1288	1000		
	12RB32	13	32			7858	5524	4059	3080	2394	1894	1519	1230
	16RB24	13	24		8847	5803	4052	2954	2220	1705	1330		
	16RB32	18	32				7434	5464	4147	3224	2549	2036	1642
	16RB40	22	40					8647	6599	5163	4117	3332	2728
L-SHAPED BEAM	18LB20	9	20	12/8	5068	3303	2288	1650	1218				
	18LB28	12	28	16/12		6578	4600	3360	2531	1949	1524	1200	
	18LB36	16	36	24/12			7903	5807	4405	3422	2706	2168	1755
	18LB44	19	44	28/16				8729	6666	5219	4166	3370	2754
	18LB52	23	52	36/16					9538	7486	5992	4871	4007
	18LB60	27	60	44/16							8116	6630	5481
INVERTED TEE BEAM	24IT20	9	20	12/8	5376	3494	2412	1726	1266				
	24IT28	13	28	16/12		6951	4848	3529	2648	2030			
	24IT36	16	36	24/12			8337	6127	4644	3598	2836	2265	1825
	24IT44	20	44	28/16				9300	7075	5514	4378	3525	2868
	24IT52	24	52	36/16					7916	6326	5132	4213	
	24IT60	28	60	44/16							8616	7025	5800

*Safe loads shown indicate 50% dead load and 50% live load; 800 psi top tension has been allowed, therefore additional top reinforcement is required.

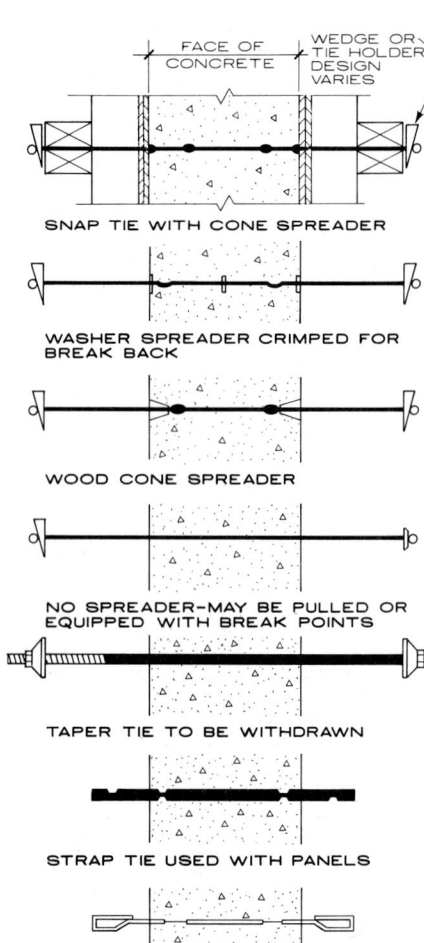

SNAP TIE WITH CONE SPREADER

WASHER SPREADER CRIMPED FOR BREAK BACK

WOOD CONE SPREADER

NO SPREADER–MAY BE PULLED OR EQUIPPED WITH BREAK POINTS

TAPER TIE TO BE WITHDRAWN

STRAP TIE USED WITH PANELS

LOOP END TIE USED WITH PANELS

TYPICAL SINGLE MEMBER TIES

CONCRETE SURFACES—GENERAL

The variety of architectural finishes is as extensive as the cost and effort expended to achieve them. There are three basic ways to improve or change the appearance of concrete:

1. Changing materials, that is, using a colored matrix and exposed aggregates.
2. Changing the mold or form by such means as a form liner.
3. By treating or tooling the concrete surface in the final stages of hardening.

The aim is to obtain maximum benefit from one of three features—color, texture, and pattern—all of which are interrelated. Color is the easiest method of changing the appearance of concrete. It should not be used on a plain concrete surface with a series of panels, since color matches are difficult to achieve. The exception is possible when white cement is used, usually as a base for the pigment to help reduce changes of color variation. Since white cement is expensive, many effects are tried with gray cement to avoid an entire plain surface. Colored concrete is most effective when it is used with an exposed aggregate finish.

FORM LINERS

1. Sandblasted Douglas fir or long leaf yellow pine dressed one side away from the concrete surface.
2. Flexible steel strip formwork adapted to curbed surfaces (Schwellmer System).
3. Resin coated, striated, or sandblasted plywood.
4. Rubber mats.
5. Thermoplastic sheets with high glass or texture laid over stone, for example.
6. Formed plastics.
7. Plaster of Paris molds for sculptured work.
8. Clay (sculpturing and staining concrete).
9. Hardboard (screen side).

D. Neil Rankins; SHWC, Inc.; Dallas, Texas

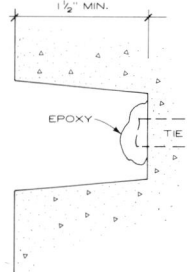

EPOXY OVER TIE

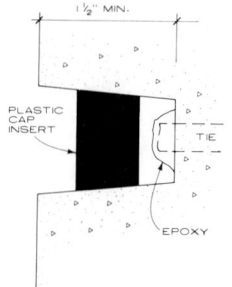

EPOXY AND PLASTIC CAP

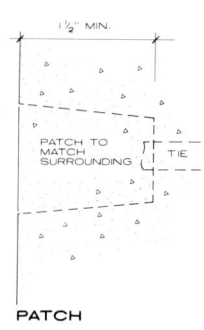

PATCH

TIE HOLE TREATMENT OPTIONS

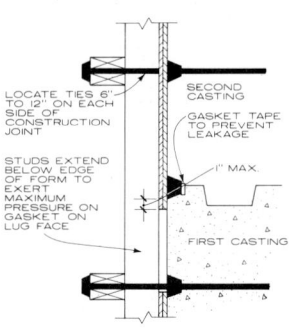

TYPICAL CONSTRUCTION JOINT

10. Standard steel forms.
11. Wood boarding and reversed battens.
12. Square edged lumber dressed one side.
13. Resawn wood boards.

RELEASE AGENTS

1. Oils, petroleum based, used on wood, concrete, and steel forms.
2. Soft soaps.
3. Talcum.
4. Whitewash used on wood with tannin in conjunction with oils.
5. Calcium stearate powder.
6. Silicones used on steel forms.
7. Plastics used on wood forms.
8. Lacquers used on plywood and plaster forms.
9. Resins used on plywood forms.
10. Sodium silicate.
11. Membrane used over any form.
12. Grease used on plaster forms.
13. Epoxy resin plastic used on plywood.

CATEGORIES OF COMMON AGGREGATE

1. QUARTZ: Clear, white, rose.
2. MARBLE: Green, yellow, red, pink, blue, gray, white, black.
3. GRANITE: Pink, gray, black, white.
4. CERAMIC: Full range.
5. VITREOUS/GLASS: Full range.

CRITICAL FACTORS AFFECTING SURFACES

DESIGN DRAWINGS should show form details, including openings, control joints, construction joints, expansion joints, and other important specifics.

1. CEMENT: Types and brands.
2. AGGREGATES: Sources of coarse and fine aggregates.
3. TECHNIQUES: Uniformity in mixing and placing.
4. FORMS: Closure techniques or concealing joints in formwork materials.
5. SLUMP CONTROL: Ensure compliance with design.
6. CURING METHODS: Ensure compliance with design.

RUSTICATION AT CONSTRUCTION JOINT

TIES

A concrete tie is a tensile unit adapted to hold concrete forms secure against the lateral pressure of unhardened concrete. Two general types of concrete ties exist:

1. Continuous single member where the tensile unit is a single piece and the holding device engages the tensile unit against the exterior of the form. Standard types: working load = 2500 to 5000 lb.
2. Internal disconnecting where the tensile unit has an inner part with threaded connections to removable external members, which have suitable devices of securing them against the outside of the form. Working load = 6000 to 36,000 lb.

GUIDELINES FOR PATCHING

1. Design the patch mix to match the original, with small amount of white cement; may eliminate coarse aggregate or hand place it. Trial and error is the only reliable match method.
2. Saturate area with water and apply bonding agent to base of hole and to water of patch mix.
3. Pack patch mix to density of original.
4. Place exposed aggregate by hand.
5. Bristle brush after setup to match existing material.
6. Moist cure to prevent shrinking.
7. Use form or finish to match original.

CHECKLIST IN PLANNING FOR ARCHITECTURAL CONCRETE PLACING TECHNIQUES:

Pumping vs. bottom drop or other type of bucket.

1. FORMING SYSTEM: Evaluate whether architectural concrete forms can also be used for structural concrete.
2. SHOP DRAWINGS: Determine form quality and steel placement.
3. VIBRATORS: Verify that proper size, frequency, and power are used.
4. RELEASE AGENTS: Consider form material, color impact of agents, and possible use throughout job.
5. CURING COMPOUND: Determine how fast it wears off.
6. WORK CREW: Make certain that a good foreman is supervising the project.
7. SAMPLES: Require approval of forms and finishes.

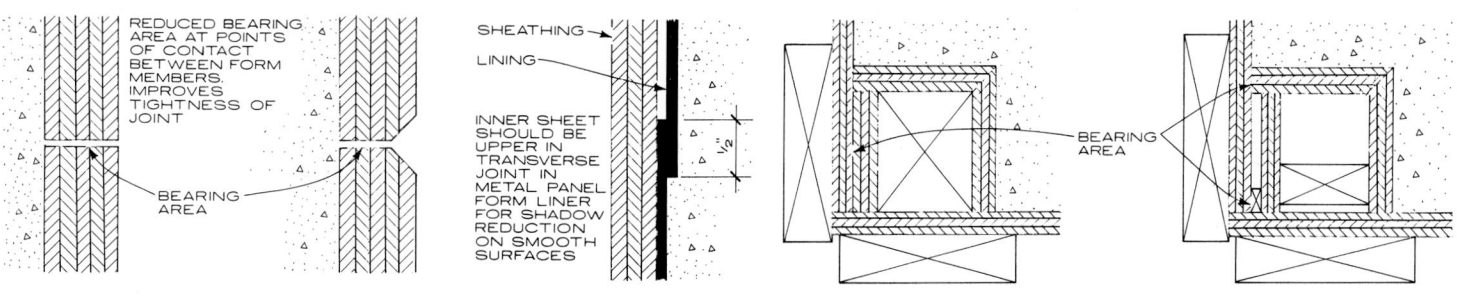

USUAL   RECOMMENDED   LINER JOINT   USUAL   RECOMMENDED

FORM JOINTS

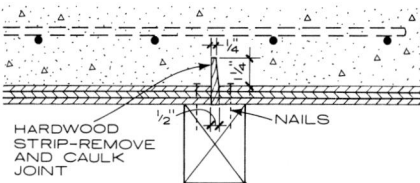

RUBBER FORM INSERT

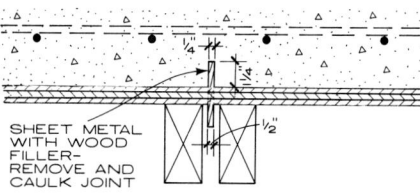

WOOD FORM INSERT

SHEET METAL
WITH WOOD
FILLER-
REMOVE AND
CAULK JOINT

SHEET METAL FORM INSERT

CONTROL JOINTS

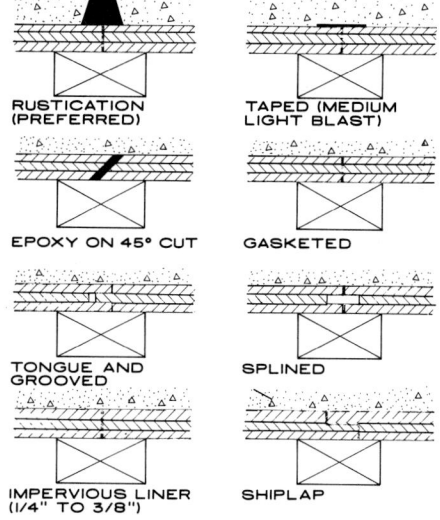

RUSTICATION (PREFERRED)   TAPED (MEDIUM LIGHT BLAST)

EPOXY ON 45° CUT   GASKETED

TONGUE AND GROOVED   SPLINED

IMPERVIOUS LINER (1/4" TO 3/8")   SHIPLAP

PLYWOOD BUTT JOINTS FOR EXPOSED AGGREGATE FINISHES

D. Neil Rankins; SHWC, Inc.; Dallas, Texas

CATEGORIES OF ARCHITECTURAL CONCRETE SURFACES

CATEGORY	FINISH	COLOR	FORMS	CRITICAL DETAILS
1. As cast	Remains as is after form removal—usually board marks or wood grain	Cement first influence, fine aggregate second influence	Plastic best All others • Wire brushed plywood • Sandblasted plywood • Exposed grain plywood • Unfinished sheathing lumber • Ammonia sprayed wood • Tongue + groove bands spaced	Slump = $2^1/_2$–$3^1/_2$'' Joinery of forms Proper release agent Point form joints to avoid marks
2. Abrasive blasted surfaces A. Brush blast	Uniform scour cleaning	Cement + fine aggregate have = influence	All smooth	Scouring after 7 days Slump = $2^1/_2$–$3^1/_2$''
B. Light blast	Sandblast to expose fine and some coarse aggregate	Fine aggregate primary coarse aggregate + cement secondary	All smooth	10% more coarse aggregate Slump = $2^1/_2$–$3^1/_2$'' Blasting between 7 and 45 days
C. Medium exposed aggregate	Sandblasted to expose coarse aggregate	Coarse aggregate	All smooth	Higher than normal coarse aggregate Slump = 2–3'' Blast before 7 days
D. Heavy exposed aggregate	Sandblasted to expose coarse aggregate 80% viable	Coarse aggregate	All smooth	Special mix coarse aggregate Slump = 0–2'' Blast within 24 hr Use high frequency vibrator
3. Chemical retardation of surface set	Chemicals expose aggregate Aggregate can be adhered to surface	Coarse aggregate and cement	Glass fiber best and all smooth	Grade of chemical determines depth of etch Stripping scheduled to prevent long drying between stripping and washoff
4. Mechanically fractured surfaces, scaling, bush hammering, jackhammering tooling	Varied	Cement Fine and coarse Aggregate	Textured	Aggregate particles $^3/_8$'' for scaling and tooling Aggregate particles
5. Combination/ fluted	Striated/abrasive blasted/irregular pattern Corrugated/abrasive Vertical rusticated/abrasive blasted Reeded and bush hammered Reeded and hammered Reeded and chiseled	The shallower the surface, the more influence aggregate fines and cement have	Wood or rubber strips, corrugated sheet metal, glass fiber, or asbestos cement	Depends on type of finish desired Wood flute kerfed and nailed loosely

NOTES
1. See page on stair dimensions for code requirements for stairs.
2. Structural designer to determine reinforcement and verify structural assumptions.
 *Denotes BOCA Code.
**Denotes ANSI A117.1.

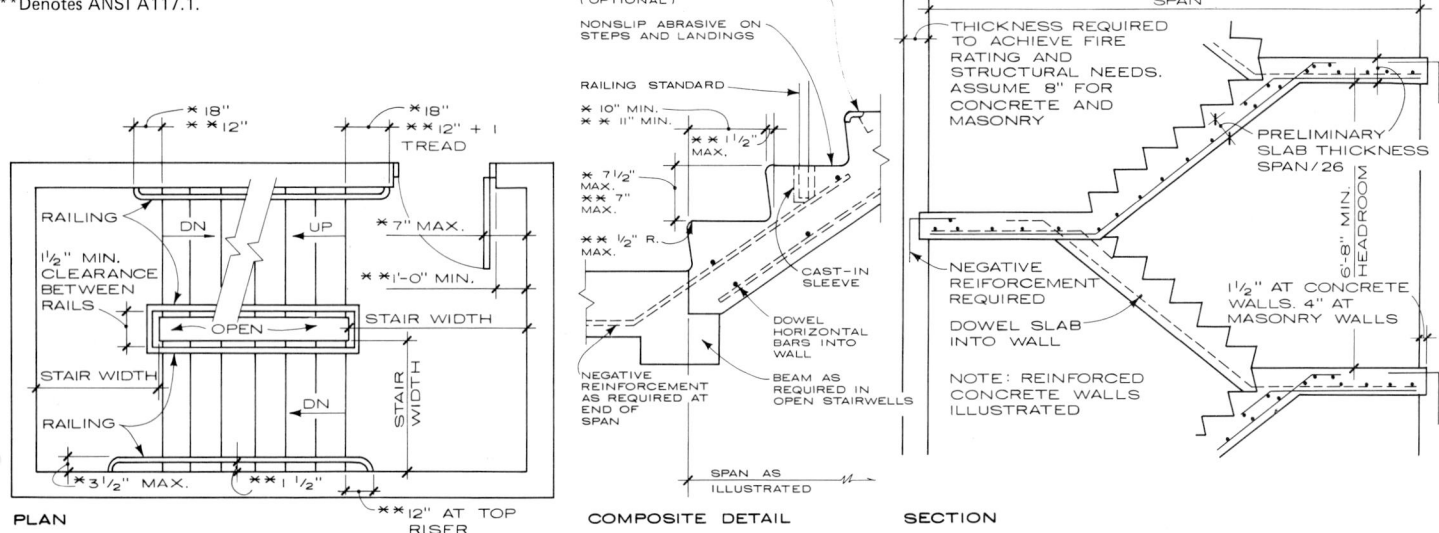

PLAN

U — TYPE CONCRETE STAIRS

COMPOSITE DETAIL   SECTION

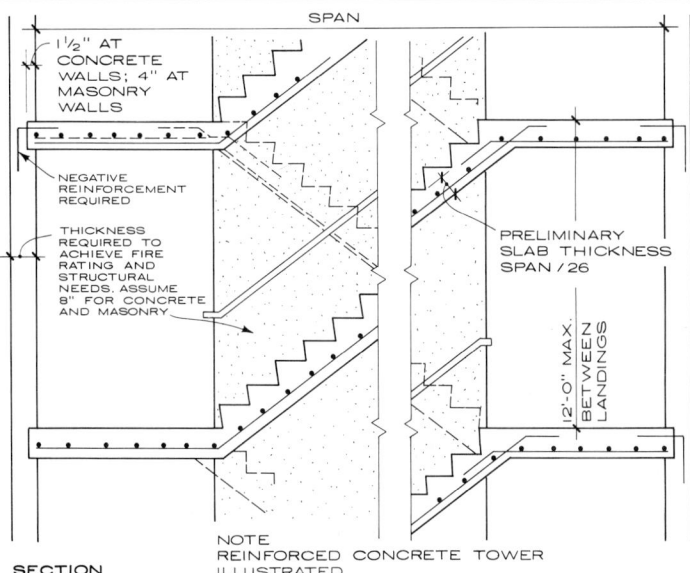

PLAN

SCISSOR TYPE CONCRETE STAIRS

SECTION

NOTE
REINFORCED CONCRETE TOWER
ILLUSTRATED

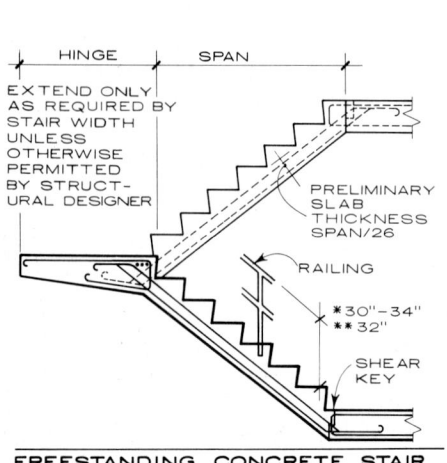

FREESTANDING CONCRETE STAIR

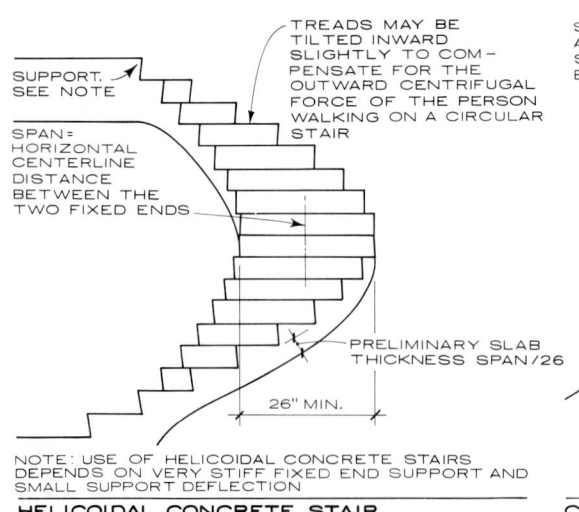

NOTE: USE OF HELICOIDAL CONCRETE STAIRS
DEPENDS ON VERY STIFF FIXED END SUPPORT AND
SMALL SUPPORT DEFLECTION

HELICOIDAL CONCRETE STAIR

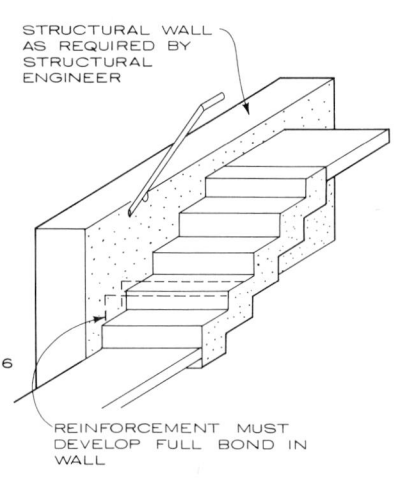

CANTILEVER CONCRETE STAIR

Karlsberger and Associates, Inc.; Columbus, Ohio

3 **ARCHITECTURAL CONCRETE**

CHAPTER 4 MASONRY

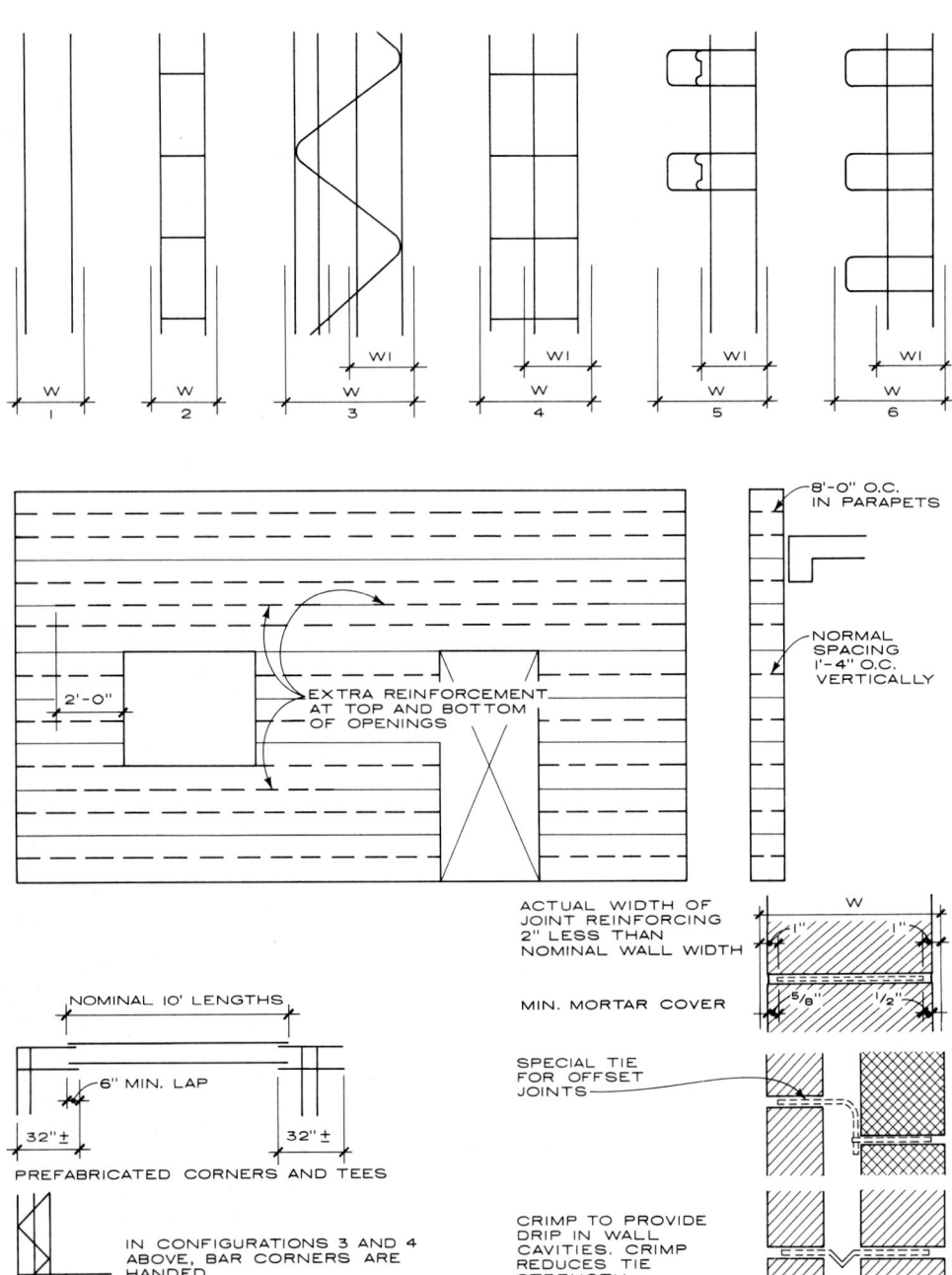

HORIZONTAL JOINT REINFORCEMENT

Horizontal joint reinforcement is used in masonry walls to control shrinkage cracks, to bond multi-wythe (composite) walls, to anchor veneer and cavity wall facing to backup masonry, and to increase the structural strength of the wall.

Reinforcing is available in a great variety of sizes and configurations. Not all manufacturers make all combinations of constructions. Consult local suppliers.

Typical configurations shown are available in both truss and ladder designs. Truss designs provide greater flexural strength.

Refer to the reinforcing configurations shown at the left of this column.

1. Truss configuration with two longitudinal rods suitable for single wythe and lightly reinforced composite walls. Meets most code requirements for bonding multiwythe walls when spaced 16 in. on center vertically and collar joint is filled with mortar.
2. Ladder version of 1.
3. Combination reinforcement and tie for composite and cavity walls. Suitable for anchoring brick veneer or to tie brick cavity wall facing to masonry backup.
4. Similar to 3 but providing four longitudinal wires.
5. Ladder reinforcing with separate adjustable veneer anchor.
6. Ladder reinforcing with tab type tie for anchoring brick facing to backup.

NORMAL CONSTRUCTIONS

1. Metal:
   Plain steel wire.
   Plain steel wire with galvanized cross wire.
   Galvanized wire.
   Hot dip galvanized after fabrication.
   Stainless steel.
2. Width:
   Nominal wall thickness (W) minus 2 in.
   Available backup widths (W) in.: 3, 4, 6, 8, 10, 12, 13, 14, 16.
   Available backup widths (WI) in.: 3, 4, 6, 8, 10.
3. Size of wire (cross wires may be different from longitudinal wires):
   10 gauge: light interior.
   9 gauge: standard.
   8 gauge: heavy duty.
   $3/16$ gauge: extra heavy duty.

SELECTION

Corrosion resistance is required by most codes for reinforcing in exterior walls. Severity of exposure determines selection of metal finish and thickness.

Nine gauge wire develops strength adequate to control shrinkage in concrete masonry walls at normal spacing. Heavier weights increase corrosion resistance and provide greater flexural strength.

PRECAUTIONS

Sections of reinforcing must be lapped 6 in. to prevent a point of weakness.

Do not continue reinforcing through control joints.

Avoid placing flashings in the same joint as reinforcing.

Use prefabricated corners and tees to prevent excessive metal thickness where lapped sections cross.

STEEL BAR REINFORCEMENT

Concrete reinforcing bars may be used to reinforce masonry wall in lieu of horizontal joint reinforcement. Place steel and grout as described on page concerned with reinforced masonry.

Reinforced bond beams spaced 4 ft o.c. vertically may be substituted for horizontal joint reinforcing used to control shrinkage. Vertical reinforcing may be required for earthquake design and for walls without support at the top. Consult local codes.

HORIZONTAL JOINT REINFORCEMENT

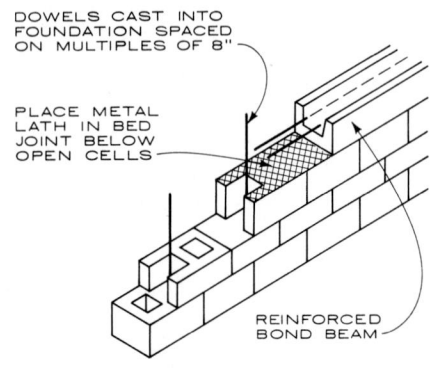

HORIZONTAL AND VERTICAL REINFORCEMENT

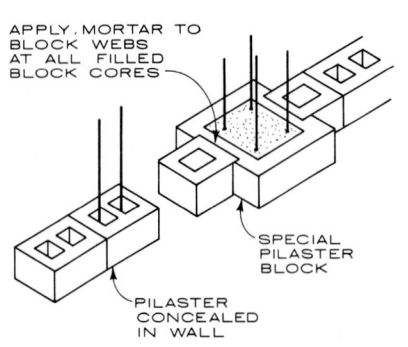

REINFORCED PILASTERS

STEEL BAR REINFORCEMENT

Metz Train Olson & Youngren; Chicago, Illinois

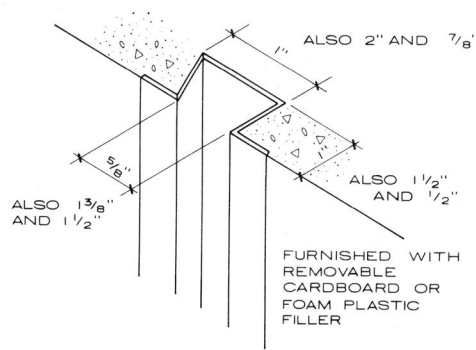

ALSO 2" AND 7/8"

1"

5/8"

ALSO 1 3/8" AND 1 1/2"

ALSO 1 1/2" AND 1/2"

FURNISHED WITH REMOVABLE CARDBOARD OR FOAM PLASTIC FILLER

22 OR 24 GA. GALVANIZED STEEL USUAL. ALSO AVAILABLE IN 16, 18, 20 AND 26 GA. GALVANIZED STEEL AND STAINLESS STEEL, COPPER AND ZINC ALLOY

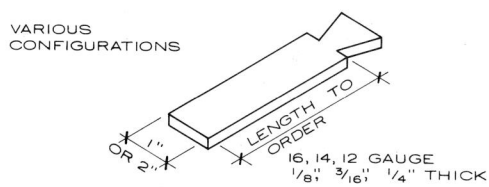

VARIOUS CONFIGURATIONS

LENGTH TO ORDER

OR 1" OR 2"

16, 14, 12 GAUGE 1/8", 3/16", 1/4" THICK

AVAILABLE IN GALVANIZED STEEL, COPPER, BRASS, ZINC ALLOY

DOVETAIL SLOTS — FOR INSTALLATION IN POURED CONCRETE WALLS AND COLUMNS

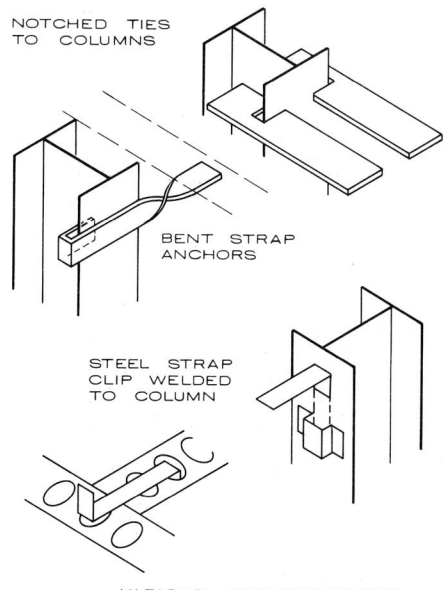

NOTCHED TIES TO COLUMNS

BENT STRAP ANCHORS

STEEL STRAP CLIP WELDED TO COLUMN

VARIOUS CONFIGURATIONS 1/8", 3/16", 1/4" X 1" OR 1 1/2" X 24" STEEL, GALVANIZED STEEL, STAINLESS STEEL

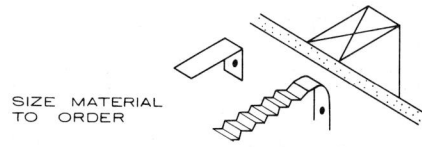

SIZE MATERIAL TO ORDER

MISCELLANEOUS ANCHORS

Metz Train Olson & Youngren; Chicago, Illinois

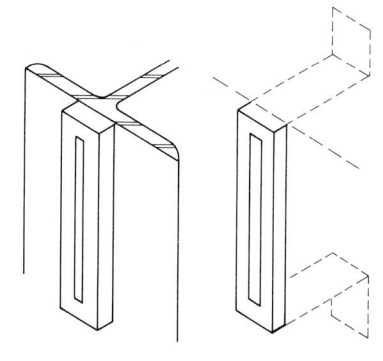

WELDED TO STEEL

WITH MASONRY ANCHORS

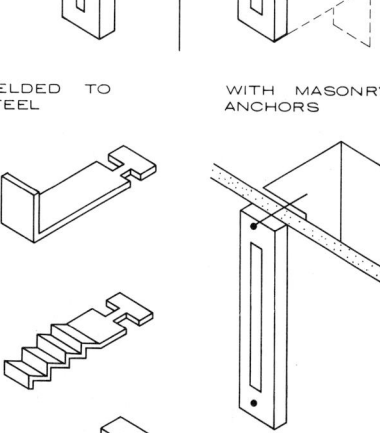

WELDED TO STEEL

SCREWED TO STUDS

CHANNEL SLOTS

CHANNELS AVAILABLE IN PAINTED STEEL, GALVANIZED STEEL, STAINLESS STEEL. MATCHING TIES AVAILABLE IN SAME METALS AND 16 GA., 1/8", 3/16" AND 1/4" THICKNESSES

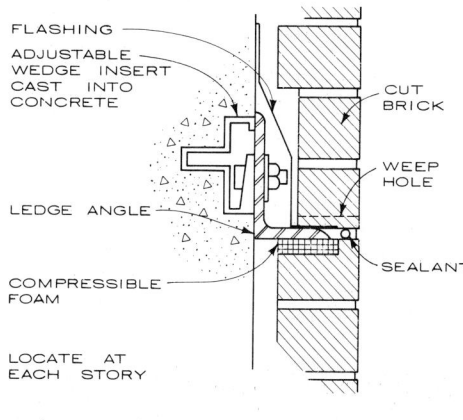

FLASHING

ADJUSTABLE WEDGE INSERT CAST INTO CONCRETE

CUT BRICK

WEEP HOLE

LEDGE ANGLE

COMPRESSIBLE FOAM

SEALANT

LOCATE AT EACH STORY

STRESS RELIEVING ANGLE

NOTE

Masonry veneer and facing must be anchored to backup construction. Codes usually require one anchor for 3 sq ft of surface area. Inserts are usually spaced 2 ft on center horizontally and ties spaced 16 to 18 in. on center vertically. Spandrel beams over 18 in. deep require inserts and anchors for tieing masonry facing to the beam. Most anchor systems permit differential movement in one or two directions. Select an anchoring system that permits movement only in the directions desired.

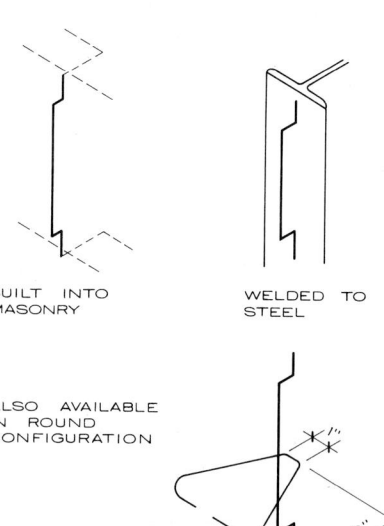

BUILT INTO MASONRY

WELDED TO STEEL

ALSO AVAILABLE IN ROUND CONFIGURATION

1"

3, 5, 7, 9"

WIRE TIES AND ANCHORS FABRICATED OF GALVANIZED WIRE, STAINLESS STEEL, COPPERWELD AND ZINC ALLOY. WIRE SIZE: 9, 8, 6 GAUGE 1/8", 3/16", 1/4" DIAMETER WIRE

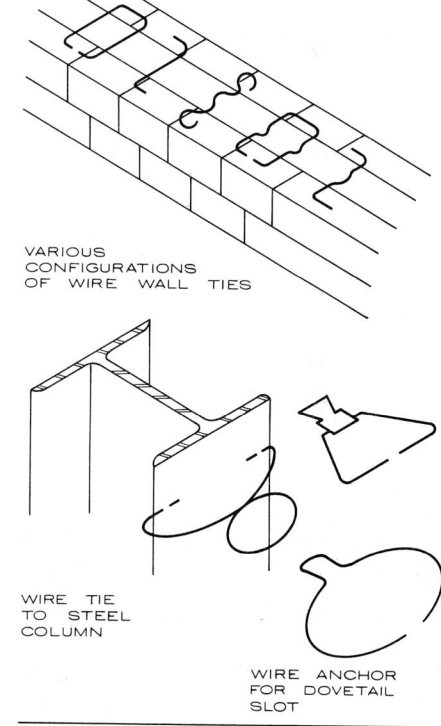

VARIOUS CONFIGURATIONS OF WIRE WALL TIES

WIRE TIE TO STEEL COLUMN

WIRE ANCHOR FOR DOVETAIL SLOT

WIRE TIES

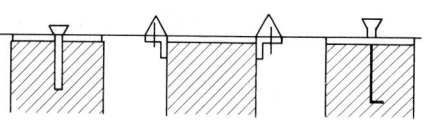

DOVETAIL SLOT WITH NUT AND BOLT

ANGLE CLIPS BOLTED TO STRUCTURE

INSERT CAST IN CONCRETE WITH BOLT

PARTITION ANCHORAGE TO STRUCTURE ABOVE

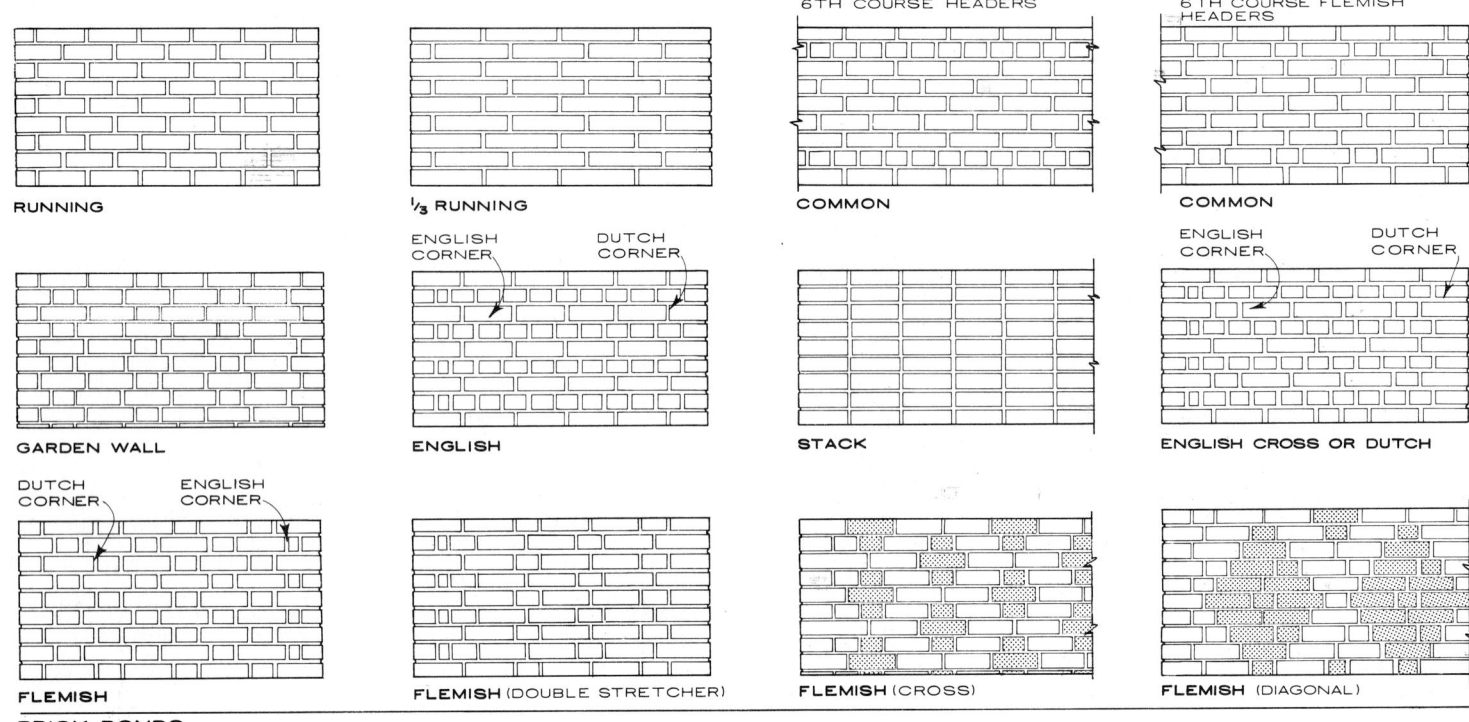

RUNNING

¹/₃ RUNNING

COMMON — 6TH COURSE HEADERS

COMMON — 6TH COURSE FLEMISH HEADERS

GARDEN WALL

ENGLISH — ENGLISH CORNER / DUTCH CORNER

STACK

ENGLISH CROSS OR DUTCH — ENGLISH CORNER / DUTCH CORNER

FLEMISH — DUTCH CORNER / ENGLISH CORNER

FLEMISH (DOUBLE STRETCHER)

FLEMISH (CROSS)

FLEMISH (DIAGONAL)

BRICK BONDS

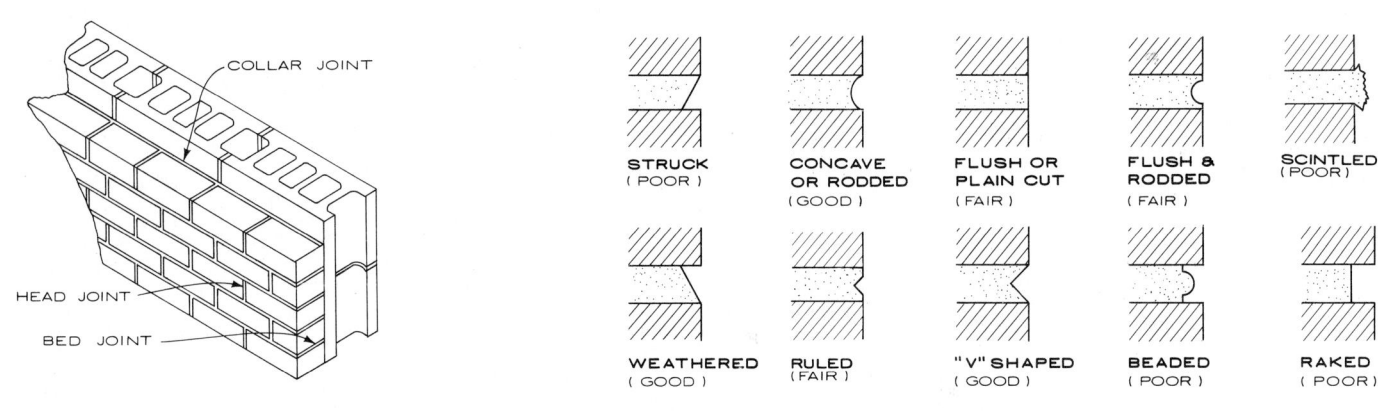

COLLAR JOINT

HEAD JOINT

BED JOINT

TERMS APPLIED TO JOINTS

STRUCK (POOR)

CONCAVE OR RODDED (GOOD)

FLUSH OR PLAIN CUT (FAIR)

FLUSH & RODDED (FAIR)

SCINTLED (POOR)

WEATHERED (GOOD)

RULED (FAIR)

"V" SHAPED (GOOD)

BEADED (POOR)

RAKED (POOR)

TYPES OF JOINTS (WEATHERABILITY)

BRICK JOINTS

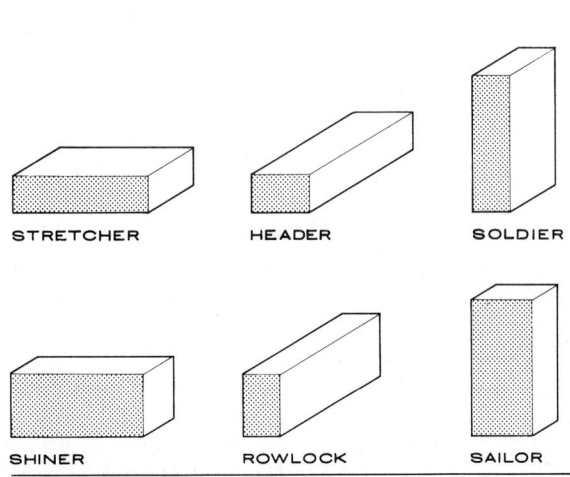

STRETCHER

HEADER

SOLDIER

SHINER

ROWLOCK

SAILOR

TERMS APPLIED TO VARIED BRICK POSITIONS

Brick Institute of America; McLean, Virginia

SIZES OF MODULAR BRICK

UNIT DESIGNATION	NOMINAL DIMENSIONS			MODULAR COURSING
	THICKNESS	HEIGHT	LENGTH	
MODULAR	4″	2²/₃″	8″	3C = 8″
ENGINEER	4″	3¹/₅″	8″	5C = 16″
ECONOMY	4″	4″	8″	1C = 4″
DOUBLE	4″	5¹/₃″	8″	3C = 16″
ROMAN	4″	2″	12″	2C = 4″
NORMAN	4″	2²/₃″	12″	3C = 8″
NORWEGIAN	4″	3¹/₅″	12″	5C = 16″
UTILITY[1]	4″	4″	12″	1C = 4″
TRIPLE	4″	5¹/₃″	12″	3C = 16″
SCR BRICK	6″	2²/₃″	12″	3C = 8″
6″ NORWEGIAN	6″	3¹/₅″	12″	5C = 16″
6″ JUMBO	6″	4″	12″	1C = 4″
8″ JUMBO	8″	4″	12″	1C = 4″
8″ SQUARE	4″	8″	8″	1C = 8″
12″ SQUARE	4″	12″	12″	1C = 12″

[1] Also called Norman Economy, General and King Norman.
*For special shapes contact local brick manufacturers.

4   UNIT MASONRY

STANDARD MODULAR
4" x 2 2/3" x 8" NOMINAL

BRICK SIZES:
* For 3/8" Joint   3 5/8" x 2 1/4" x 7 5/8"
** For 1/2" Joint   3 1/2" x 2 3/16" x 7 1/2"

NORMAN
4" x 2 2/3" x 12" NOMINAL

BRICK SIZES:
* For 3/8" Joint   3 5/8" x 2 1/4" x 11 5/8"
** For 1/2" Joint   3 1/2" x 2 3/16" x 11 1/2"

SCR BRICK
6" x 2 2/3" x 12" NOMINAL
For 1/2" Joint   5 1/2" x 2 1/8" x 11 1/2"

Joint selected determines brick size
3 courses = 2 modules (8")

NOMINAL HEIGHT OF 2 2/3" COURSES

31	6' – 10 2/3"	61	13' – 6 2/3"
30	6' – 8"	60	13' – 4"
29	6' – 5 1/3"	59	13' – 1 1/3"
28	6' – 2 2/3"	58	12' – 10 2/3"
27	6' – 0"	57	12' – 8"
26	5' – 9 1/3"	56	12' – 5 1/3"
25	5' – 6 2/3"	55	12' – 2 2/3"
24	5' – 4"	54	12' – 0"
23	5' – 1 1/3"	53	11' – 9 1/3"
22	4' – 10 2/3"	52	11' – 6 2/3"
21	4' – 8"	51	11' – 4"
20	4' – 5 1/3"	50	11' – 1 1/3"
19	4' – 2 2/3"	49	10' – 10 2/3"
18	4' – 0"	48	10' – 8"
17	3' – 9 1/3"	47	10' – 5 1/3"
16	3' – 6 2/3"	46	10' – 2 2/3"
15	3' – 4"	45	10' – 0"
14	3' – 1 1/3"	44	9' – 9 1/3"
13	2' – 10 2/3"	43	9' – 6 2/3"
12	2' – 8"	42	9' – 4"
11	2' – 5 1/3"	41	9' – 1 1/3"
10	2' – 2 1/3"	40	8' – 10 2/3"
9	2' – 0"	39	8' – 8"
8	1' – 9 1/3"	38	8' – 5 1/3"
7	1' – 6 2/3"	37	8' – 2 2/3"
6	1' – 4"	36	8' – 0"
5	1' – 1 1/3"	35	7' – 9 1/3"
4	10 2/3"	34	7' – 6 2/3"
3	8"	33	7' – 4"
2	5 1/3"	32	7' – 1 1/3"
1	2 2/3"		

NOTES
Not all sizes made in all sections of U.S.; check with local manufacturers for sizes available.

Brick Institute of America; McLean, Virginia

ENGINEER
4" x 3 1/5" x 8" NOMINAL

BRICK SIZES:
* For 3/8" Joint   3 5/8" x 2 13/16" x 7 5/8"
For 1/2" Joint   3 1/2" x 2 11/16" x 7 1/2"

Joint selected determines brick size.
5 courses = 4 modules (16").

NOMINAL HEIGHTS OF 3 1/5" COURSES

29	7' – 8 4/5"	59	15' – 8 4/5"
28	7' – 5 3/5"	58	15' – 5 3/5"
27	7' – 2 2/5"	57	15' – 2 2/5"
26	6' – 11 1/5"	56	14' – 11 1/5"
25	6' – 8"	55	14' – 8"
24	6' – 4 4/5"	54	14' – 4 4/5"
23	6' – 1 3/5"	53	14' – 1 3/5"
22	5' – 10 2/5"	52	13' – 10 2/5"
21	5' – 7 1/3"	51	13' – 7 1/5"
20	5' – 4"	50	13' – 4"
19	5' – 0 4/5"	49	13' – 0 4/5"
18	4' – 9 3/5"	48	12' – 9 3/5"
17	4' – 6 2/5"	47	12' – 6 2/5"
16	4' – 3 1/5"	46	12' – 3 1/5"
15	4' – 0"	45	12' – 0"
14	3' – 8 4/5"	44	11' – 8 4/5"
13	3' – 5 3/5"	43	11' – 5 3/5"
12	3' – 2 2/5"	42	11' – 2 2/5"
11	2' – 11 1/5"	41	10' – 11 1/5"
10	2' – 8"	40	10' – 8"
9	2' – 4 4/5"	39	10' – 4 4/5"
8	2' – 1 3/5"	38	10' – 1 3/5"
7	1' – 10 2/5"	37	9' – 10 2/5"
6	1' – 7 1/5"	36	9' – 7 1/5"
5	1' – 4"	35	9' – 4"
4	1' – 0 4/5"	34	9' – 0 4/5"
3	9 3/5"	33	8' – 9 3/5"
2	6 2/5"	32	8' – 6 2/5"
1	3 1/5"	31	8' – 3 1/5"
		30	8' – 0"

*3/8" Joint used for facing brick.
**1/2" Joint used for glazed and structural units and building brick.

ECONOMY
4" x 4" x 8" NOMINAL

BRICK SIZES:
* For 3/8" Joint   3 5/8" x 3 5/8" x 7 5/8"
** For 1/2" Joint   3 1/2" x 3 1/2" x 7 1/2"

UTILITY
4" x 4" x 12" NOMINAL

BRICK SIZES:
For 3/8" Joint   3 5/8" x 3 5/8" x 11 5/8"
For 1/2" Joint   3 1/2" x 3 1/2" x 11 1/2"

Joint selected determines brick size.
1 course = 1 module (4")

NOMINAL HEIGHTS OF 4" COURSES

21	7' – 0"	43	14' – 4"
20	6' – 8"	42	14' – 0"
19	6' – 4"	41	13' – 8"
18	6' – 0"	40	13' – 4"
17	5' – 8"	39	13' – 0"
16	5' – 4"	38	12' – 8"
15	5' – 0"	37	12' – 4"
14	4' – 8"	36	12' – 0"
13	4' – 4"	35	11' – 8"
12	4' – 0"	34	11' – 4"
11	3' – 8"	33	11' – 0"
10	3' – 4"	32	10' – 8"
9	3' – 0"	31	10' – 4"
8	2' – 8"	30	10' – 0"
7	2' – 4"	29	9' – 8"
6	2' – 0"	28	9' – 4"
5	1' – 8"	27	9' – 0"
4	1' – 4"	26	8' – 8"
3	1' – 0"	25	8' – 4"
2	8"	24	8' – 0"
1	4"	23	7' – 8"
		22	7' – 4"

Grid lines (—·—·—) are 4" modules. Vertical dimensions are from bottom of mortar joint to bottom of mortar joint.

VERTICAL BRICK COURSES

NUMBER OF BRICKS AND JOINTS	HEIGHT 3/8" JOINTS	HEIGHT 1/2" JOINTS
1 brk. & 1 jt.	2 5/8"	2 3/4"
2 brks. & 2 jts.	5 1/4"	5 1/2"
3 brks. & 3 jts.	7 7/8"	8 1/4"
4 brks. & 4 jts.	10 1/2"	11"
5 brks. & 5 jts.	1'-1 1/8"	1'-1 3/4"
6 brks. & 6 jts.	1'-3 3/4"	1'-4 1/2"
7 brks. & 7 jts.	1'-6 3/8"	1'-7 1/4"
8 brks. & 8 jts.	1'-9"	1'-10"
9 brks. & 9 jts.	1'-11 5/8"	2'-0 3/4"
10 brks. & 10 jts.	2'-2 1/4"	2'-3 1/2"
11 brks. & 11 jts.	2'-4 7/8"	2'-6 1/4"
12 brks. & 12 jts.	2'-7 1/2"	2'-9"
13 brks. & 13 jts.	2'-10 1/8"	2'-11 3/4"
14 brks. & 14 jts.	3'-0 3/4"	3'-2 1/2"
15 brks. & 15 jts.	3'-3 5/8"	3'-5 1/4"
16 brks. & 16 jts.	3'-6"	3'-8"
17 brks. & 17 jts.	3'-8 5/8"	3'-10 3/4"
18 brks. & 18 jts.	3'-11 1/4"	4'-1 1/2"
19 brks. & 19 jts.	4'-1 7/8"	4'-4 1/4"
20 brks. & 20 jts.	4'-4 1/2"	4'-7"
21 brks. & 21 jts.	4'-7 1/8"	4'-9 3/4"
22 brks. & 22 jts.	4'-9 3/4"	5'-0 1/2"
23 brks. & 23 jts.	5'-0 3/8"	5'-3 1/4"
24 brks. & 24 jts.	5'-3"	5'-6"
25 brks. & 25 jts.	5'-5 5/8"	5'-8 3/4"
26 brks. & 26 jts.	5'-8 1/4"	5'-11 1/2"
27 brks. & 27 jts.	5'-10 7/8"	6'-2 1/4"
28 brks. & 28 jts.	6'-1 1/2"	6'-5"
29 brks. & 29 jts.	6'-4 1/8"	6'-7 3/4"
30 brks. & 30 jts.	6'-6 3/4"	6'-10 1/2"
31 brks. & 31 jts.	6'-9 3/8"	7'-1 1/4"
32 brks. & 32 jts.	7'-0"	7'-4"
33 brks. & 33 jts.	7'-2 5/8"	7'-6 3/4"
34 brks. & 34 jts.	7'-5 1/4"	7'-9 1/2"
35 brks. & 35 jts.	7'-7 7/8"	8'-0 1/4"
36 brks. & 36 jts.	7'-10 1/2"	8'-3"
37 brks. & 37 jts.	8'-1 1/8"	8'-5 3/4"
38 brks. & 38 jts.	8'-3 3/4"	8'-8 1/2"
39 brks. & 39 jts.	8'-6 3/8"	8'-11 1/4"
40 brks. & 40 jts.	8'-9"	9'-2"
41 brks. & 41 jts.	8'-11 5/8"	9'-4 3/4"
42 brks. & 42 jts.	9'-2 1/4"	9'-7 1/2"
43 brks. & 43 jts.	9'-4 7/8"	9'-10 1/4"
44 brks. & 44 jts.	9'-7 1/2"	10'-1"
45 brks. & 45 jts.	9'-10 1/8"	10'-3 3/4"
46 brks. & 46 jts.	10'-0 3/4"	10'-6 1/2"
47 brks. & 47 jts.	10'-3 3/8"	10'-9 1/4"
48 brks. & 48 jts.	10'-6"	11'-0"
49 brks. & 49 jts.	10'-8 5/8"	11'-2 3/4"
50 brks. & 50 jts.	10'-11 1/4"	11'-5 1/2"
51 brks. & 51 jts.	11'-1 7/8"	11'-8 1/4"
52 brks. & 52 jts.	11'-4 1/2"	11'-11"
53 brks. & 53 jts.	11'-7 1/8"	12'-1 3/4"
54 brks. & 54 jts.	11'-9 3/4"	12'-4 1/2"
55 brks. & 55 jts.	12'-0 3/8"	12'-7 1/4"
56 brks. & 56 jts.	12'-3"	12'-10"
57 brks. & 57 jts.	12'-5 5/8"	13'-0 3/4"
58 brks. & 58 jts.	12'-8 1/4"	13'-3 1/2"
59 brks. & 59 jts.	12'-10 7/8"	13'-6 1/4"
60 brks. & 60 jts.	13'-1 1/2"	13'-9"
61 brks. & 61 jts.	13'-4 1/8"	13'-11 3/4"
62 brks. & 62 jts.	13'-6 3/4"	14'-2 1/2"
63 brks. & 63 jts.	13'-9 3/8"	14'-5 1/4"
64 brks. & 64 jts.	14'-0"	14'-8"
65 brks. & 65 jts.	14'-2 5/8"	14'-10 3/4"
66 brks. & 66 jts.	14'-5 1/4"	15'-1 1/2"
67 brks. & 67 jts.	14'-7 7/8"	15'-4 1/4"
68 brks. & 68 jts.	14'-10 1/2"	15'-7"
69 brks. & 69 jts.	15'-1 1/8"	15'-9 3/4"
70 brks. & 70 jts.	15'-3 3/4"	16'-0 1/2"
71 brks. & 71 jts.	15'-6 3/8"	16'-3 1/4"
72 brks. & 72 jts.	15'-9"	16'-6"
73 brks. & 73 jts.	15'-11 5/8"	16'-8 3/4"
74 brks. & 74 jts.	16'-2 1/4"	16'-11 1/2"
75 brks. & 75 jts.	16'-4 7/8"	17'-2 1/4"
76 brks. & 76 jts.	16'-7 1/2"	17'-5"

HORIZONTAL BRICK COURSES

NUMBER OF BRICKS AND JOINTS	LENGTH OF COURSE 3/8" JOINTS	LENGTH OF COURSE 1/2" JOINTS
1 brk. & 0 jt.	0'-8"	0'-8"
1 1/2 brks. & 1 jt.	1'-0 3/8"	1'-0 1/2"
2 brks. & 1 jt.	1'-4 3/8"	1'-4 1/2"
2 1/2 brks. & 2 jts.	1'-8 3/4"	1'-9"
3 brks. & 2 jts.	2'-0 3/4"	2'-1"
3 1/2 brks. & 3 jts.	2'-5 1/8"	2'-5 1/2"
4 brks. & 3 jts.	2'-9 1/8"	2'-9 1/2"
4 1/2 brks. & 4 jts.	3'-1 1/2"	3'-2"
5 brks. & 4 jts.	3'-5 1/2"	3'-6"
5 1/2 brks. & 5 jts.	3'-9 7/8"	3'-10 1/2"
6 brks. & 5 jts.	4'-1 7/8"	4'-2 1/2"
6 1/2 brks. & 6 jts.	4'-6 1/4"	4'-7"
7 brks. & 6 jts.	4'-10 1/4"	4'-11"
7 1/2 brks. & 7 jts.	5'-2 5/8"	5'-3 1/2"
8 brks. & 7 jts.	5'-6 5/8"	5'-7 1/2"
8 1/2 brks. & 8 jts.	5'-11"	6'-0"
9 brks. & 8 jts.	6'-3"	6'-4"
9 1/2 brks. & 9 jts.	6'-7 3/8"	6'-8 1/2"
10 brks. & 9 jts.	6'-11 3/8"	7'-0 1/2"
10 1/2 brks. & 10 jts.	7'-3 3/4"	7'-5"
11 brks. & 10 jts.	7'-7 3/4"	7'-9"
11 1/2 brks. & 11 jts.	8'-0 1/8"	8'-1 1/2"
12 brks. & 11 jts.	8'-4 1/8"	8'-5 1/2"
12 1/2 brks. & 12 jts.	8'-8 1/2"	8'-10"
13 brks. & 12 jts.	9'-0 1/2"	9'-2"
13 1/2 brks. & 13 jts.	9'-4 7/8"	9'-6 1/2"
14 brks. & 13 jts.	9'-8 7/8"	9'-10 1/2"
14 1/2 brks. & 14 jts.	10'-1 1/4"	10'-3"
15 brks. & 14 jts.	10'-5 1/4"	10'-7"
15 1/2 brks. & 15 jts.	10'-9 5/8"	10'-11 1/2"
16 brks. & 15 jts.	11'-1 5/8"	11'-3"
16 1/2 brks. & 16 jts.	11'-6"	11'-8"
17 brks. & 16 jts.	11'-10"	12'-0"
17 1/2 brks. & 17 jts.	12'-2 3/8"	12'-4 1/2"
18 brks. & 17 jts.	12'-6 3/8"	12'-8 1/2"
18 1/2 brks. & 18 jts.	12'-10 3/4"	13'-1"
19 brks. & 18 jts.	13'-2 3/4"	13'-5"
19 1/2 brks. & 19 jts.	13'-7 1/8"	13'-9 1/2"
20 brks. & 19 jts.	13'-11 1/8"	14'-1 1/2"
20 1/2 brks. & 20 jts.	14'-3 1/2"	14'-6"
21 brks. & 20 jts.	14'-7 1/2"	14'-10"
21 1/2 brks. & 21 jts.	14'-11 7/8"	15'-2 1/2"
22 brks. & 21 jts.	15'-3 7/8"	15'-6 1/2"
22 1/2 brks. & 22 jts.	15'-8 1/4"	15'-11"
23 brks. & 22 jts.	16'-0 1/4"	16'-3"
23 1/2 brks. & 23 jts.	16'-4 5/8"	16'-7 1/2"
24 brks. & 23 jts.	16'-8 5/8"	16'-11 1/2"
24 1/2 brks. & 24 jts.	17'-1"	17'-4"
25 brks. & 24 jts.	17'-5"	17'-8"
25 1/2 brks. & 25 jts.	17'-9 3/8"	18'-0 1/2"
26 brks. & 25 jts.	18'-1 3/8"	18'-4 1/2"
26 1/2 brks. & 26 jts.	18'-5 3/4"	18'-9"
27 brks. & 26 jts.	18'-9 3/4"	19'-1"
27 1/2 brks. & 27 jts.	19'-2 1/8"	19'-5 1/2"
28 brks. & 27 jts.	19'-6 1/8"	19'-9 1/2"
28 1/2 brks. & 28 jts.	19'-10 1/2"	20'-2"
29 brks. & 28 jts.	20'-2 1/8"	20'-6"
29 1/2 brks. & 29 jts.	20'-6 7/8"	20'-10 1/2"
30 brks. & 29 jts.	20'-10 7/8"	21'-2 1/2"
30 1/2 brks. & 30 jts.	21'-3 1/4"	21'-7"
31 brks. & 30 jts.	21'-7 1/4"	21'-11"
31 1/2 brks. & 31 jts.	21'-11 5/8"	22'-3 1/2"
32 brks. & 31 jts.	22'-3 5/8"	22'-7 1/2"
32 1/2 brks. & 32 jts.	22'-8"	23'-0"
33 brks. & 32 jts.	23'-0"	23'-4"
33 1/2 brks. & 33 jts.	23'-4 3/8"	23'-8 1/2"
34 brks. & 33 jts.	23'-8 3/8"	24'-0 1/2"
34 1/2 brks. & 34 jts.	24'-0 3/4"	24'-5"
35 brks. & 34 jts.	24'-4 3/4"	24'-9"
35 1/2 brks. & 35 jts.	24'-9 1/8"	25'-1 1/2"
36 brks. & 35 jts.	25'-1 1/8"	25'-5 1/2"
36 1/2 brks. & 36 jts.	25'-5 1/2"	25'-10"
37 brks. & 36 jts.	25'-9 1/2"	26'-2"
37 1/2 brks. & 37 jts.	26'-1 7/8"	26'-6 1/2"
38 brks. & 37 jts.	26'-5 7/8"	26'-10 1/2"
38 1/2 brks. & 38 jts.	26'-10 1/4"	27'-3"
39 brks. & 38 jts.	27'-2 1/4"	27'-7"
39 1/2 brks. & 39 jts.	27'-6 5/8"	27'-11 1/2"
40 brks. & 39 jts.	27'-10 5/8"	28'-3 1/2"
40 1/2 brks. & 40 jts.	28'-3"	28'-8"
41 brks. & 40 jts.	28'-7"	29'-0"
41 1/2 brks. & 41 jts.	28'-11 3/8"	29'-4 1/2"
42 brks. & 41 jts.	29'-3 3/8"	29'-8 1/2"
42 1/2 brks. & 42 jts.	29'-7 3/4"	30'-1"
43 brks. & 42 jts.	29'-11 3/4"	30'-5"
43 1/2 brks. & 43 jts.	30'-4 1/8"	30'-9 1/2"
44 brks. & 43 jts.	30'-8 1/8"	31'-1 1/2"
44 1/2 brks. & 44 jts.	31'-0 1/2"	31'-6"
45 brks. & 44 jts.	31'-4 1/2"	31'-10"
45 1/2 brks. & 45 jts.	31'-8 7/8"	32'-2 1/2"
46 brks. & 45 jts.	32'-0 7/8"	32'-6 1/2"
46 1/2 brks. & 46 jts.	32'-5 1/4"	32'-11"
47 brks. & 46 jts.	32'-9 1/4"	33'-3"
47 1/2 brks. & 47 jts.	33'-1 5/8"	33'-7 1/2"
48 brks. & 47 jts.	33'-5 5/8"	33'-11 1/2"
48 1/2 brks. & 48 jts.	33'-10"	34'-4"
49 brks. & 48 jts.	34'-2"	34'-8"
49 1/2 brks. & 49 jts.	34'-6 3/8"	35'-0 1/2"
50 brks. & 49 jts.	34'-10 3/8"	35'-4 1/2"
50 1/2 brks. & 50 jts.	35'-2 3/4"	35'-9"
51 brks. & 50 jts.	35'-6 3/4"	36'-1"
51 1/2 brks. & 51 jts.	35'-11 1/8"	36'-5 1/2"
52 brks. & 51 jts.	36'-3 1/8"	36'-9 1/2"
52 1/2 brks. & 52 jts.	36'-7 1/2"	37'-2"
53 brks. & 52 jts.	36'-11 1/2"	37'-6"
53 1/2 brks. & 53 jts.	37'-3 7/8"	37'-10 1/2"
54 brks. & 53 jts.	37'-7 7/8"	38'-2 1/2"
54 1/2 brks. & 54 jts.	38'-0 1/4"	38'-7"
55 brks. & 54 jts.	38'-4 1/4"	38'-11"
55 1/2 brks. & 55 jts.	38'-8 5/8"	39'-3 1/2"
56 brks. & 55 jts.	39'-0 5/8"	39'-7 1/2"
56 1/2 brks. & 56 jts.	39'-5"	40'-0"
57 brks. & 56 jts.	39'-9"	40'-4"
57 1/2 brks. & 57 jts.	40'-1 3/8"	40'-8 1/2"
58 brks. & 57 jts.	40'-5 3/8"	41'-0 1/2"
58 1/2 brks. & 58 jts.	40'-9 3/4"	41'-5"
59 brks. & 58 jts.	41'-1 3/4"	41'-9"
59 1/2 brks. & 59 jts.	41'-6 1/8"	42'-1 1/2"
60 brks. & 59 jts.	41'-10 1/8"	42'-5 1/2"

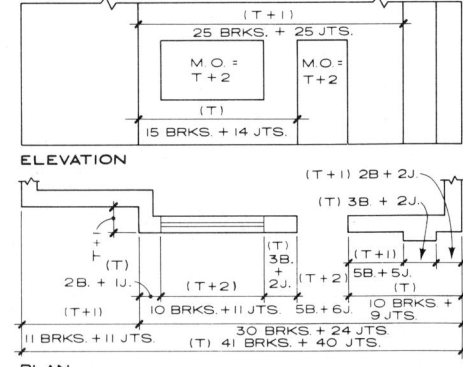

ELEVATION

PLAN

EXAMPLE SHOWING USE OF TABLE

T: Dimensions and number of joints as given in the table, that is, one joint less than the number of bricks.

T + 1: One brick joint added to figure given in the table, that is, the number of bricks is equal to the number of joints.

T + 2: Two brick joints added to figure given in the table, that is, one joint more than the number of bricks.

Brick Institute of America; McLean, Virginia

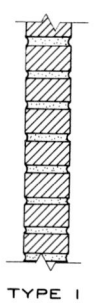 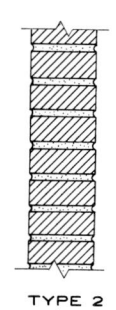 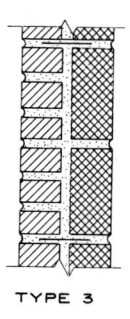 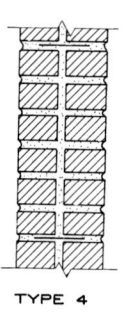 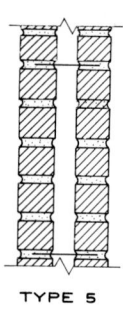 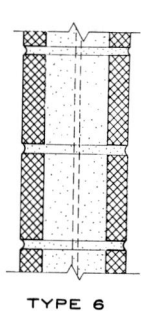

TYPE 1	TYPE 2	TYPE 3	TYPE 4	TYPE 5	TYPE 6
4" BRICK WALL MODULAR BRICK 4" × 2²⁄₃" × 8"	6" BRICK WALL SCR BRICK 6" × 2²⁄₃" × 12"	4" MODULAR BRICK 4" C.M.U. WALL METAL TIED	8" BRICK WALL METAL TIED 4" × 2²⁄₃" × 8"	8" BRICK CAVITY WALL KING SIZE BRICK 3" × 2⁵⁄₈" × 9⁵⁄₈"	10" REINFORCED C.M.U. WALL

PROPERTIES OF MASONRY WALLS

WALL TYPE NUMBER		1	2	3	4	5[1]	6
Allowable compressive load (lb/linear ft)	Type M mortar	9	27,000[2]	7778[2,3]	36,600[2,3]	9	9
	Type S mortar		23,625[2]	6863[2,3]	32,025[2,3]		
	Type N mortar		20,250[2]	6405[2,3]	27,450[2,3]		
Lateral support spacing (ft-in.)	Load bearing		9'-0"	12'-0"	13'-4"		
Material quantity (per 100 sq ft)[7]	Mortar (cu ft)	5.5	7.9	11	14.1	7.8	
	Brick/C.M.U.	675	450	675/113	1350	960	
U value (Btu/sq ft · hr · F°)	Uninsulated	0.78	0.66	0.30-0.49[8]	0.58	0.40	
U value with 1 in. rigid insulation	(Polystyrene)	0.15	0.15	0.11-0.13[8]	0.14	0.13	
Wall weight (lb/sq ft)	Unplastered	40	60	52-69[8]	80	60	
Average sound resistance (S.T.C.)	Unplastered	45	51	45-50[8]	52	49(est.)	
Fire resistance (hr)	Unplastered	1	2	4	2-4[8]	3	

 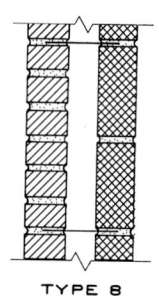 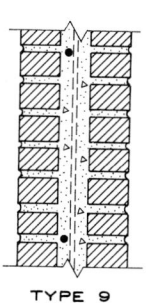 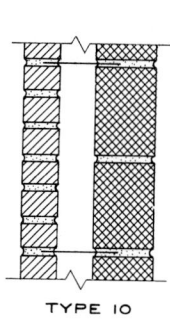 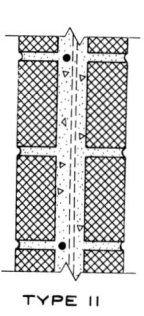 

TYPE 7	TYPE 8	TYPE 9	TYPE 10	TYPE 11	TYPE 12
10" CAVITY WALL SPLIT FACE C.M.U. 4" C.M.U.	10" CAVITY WALL-4" BRICK AND 4" C.M.U.	10" REINFORCED BRICK MASONRY WALL (R.B.M.)	12" CAVITY WALL-4" BRICK AND 6" C.M.U.	10" REINFORCED C.M.U. WALL	6" C.M.U. WALL

PROPERTIES OF MASONRY WALLS

WALL TYPE NUMBER		7[1]	8[1]	9	10[1]	11	12
Allowable compressive load (lb/linear ft)	Type M mortar	6090	6090	9	7770	9	5738
	Type S mortar	5220	5220		6660		5063
	Type N mortar	4785	4785		6105		4725
Lateral support spacing (ft-in.)	Load bearing	12'-0"	12'-0"		15'-0"		9'-0"
Material quantity (per 100 sq ft)	Mortar (cu ft)	12	15	11/18.8	15		6
	Brick/C.M.U.	113/113	675/113	1350	675/113		113
U value (Btu/sq ft · hr · F°)	Uninsulated	0.23-0.33[8]	0.23-0.33[8]	0.44	0.22-0.32[8]		0.32-0.59[8]
U value with 1 in. rigid insulation	(Polystyrene)	0.11-0.12[8]	0.11-0.12[8]	0.13	0.11-0.12[8]		0.12-0.14[8]
Wall weight (lb/sq ft)	Unplastered	52-69[8]	52-69[8]	94.2	58-84[8]		20-46[8]
Average sound resistance (S.T.C.)	Unplastered	55	55	59	55		30-45[8]
Fire resistance (hr)	Unplastered	4	4	4	4		1-2[8]

NOTES

1. Use straight metal wire ties—no drips.
2. Brick compressive strength: 8000 psi plus.
3. Collar joints filled with mortar (½").
4. If loads bear on only one wythe, allowable loads are reduced by 20%.
5. Masonry compressive strength (F'M) = 3000 psi h/t = 25.
6. Load bearing strengths are based on allowable compressive strengths, taken from the empirical ANSI A41.1, American Standard Building Code Requirements for masonry.

7. Waste is not included, as this will vary with the job. A waste factor of 2 to 5% is frequently applied for masonry units and 10 to 20% for mortar.
8. A range of values is shown for several categories because of aggregate type and density of units.
9. Rational design and engineered masonry should be used in order to handle all variables under load bearing conditions.

Robert Joseph Sangiamo, AIA; New York, New York

Davis, Brody & Associates; New York, New York

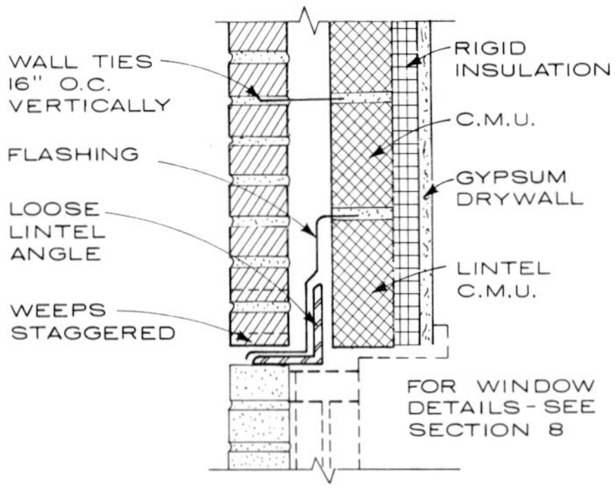

SECTION AT HEAD

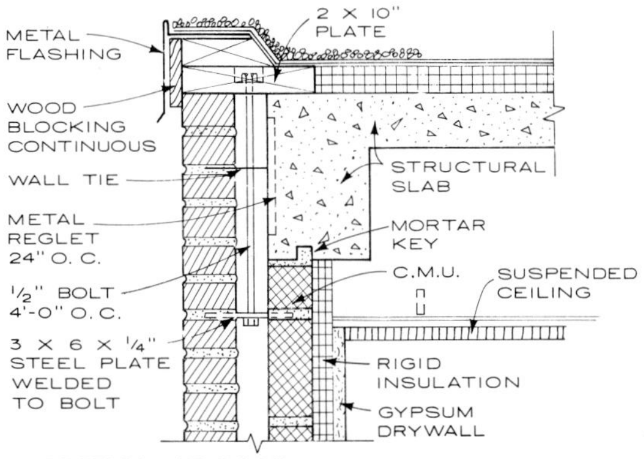

WALL TIES 16" O.C. VERTICALLY
RIGID INSULATION
C.M.U.
FLASHING
GYPSUM DRYWALL
LOOSE LINTEL ANGLE
LINTEL C.M.U.
WEEPS STAGGERED
FOR WINDOW DETAILS - SEE SECTION 8

SECTION AT SILL

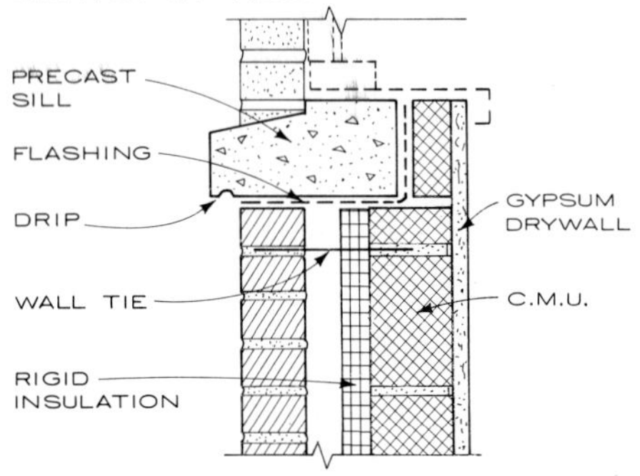

PRECAST SILL
FLASHING
DRIP
GYPSUM DRYWALL
WALL TIE
C.M.U.
RIGID INSULATION

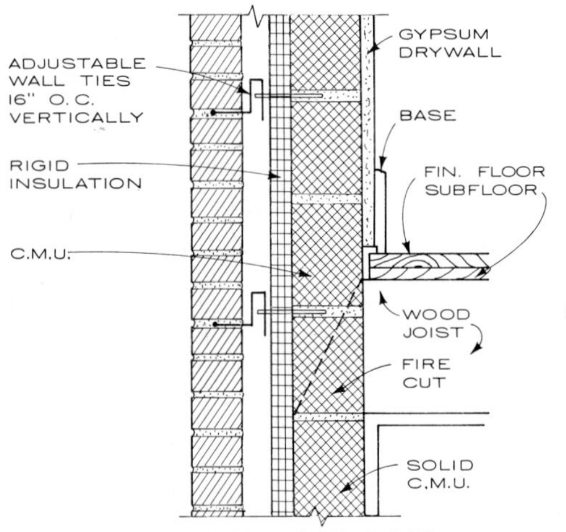

SECTION AT WOOD JOIST FLOOR

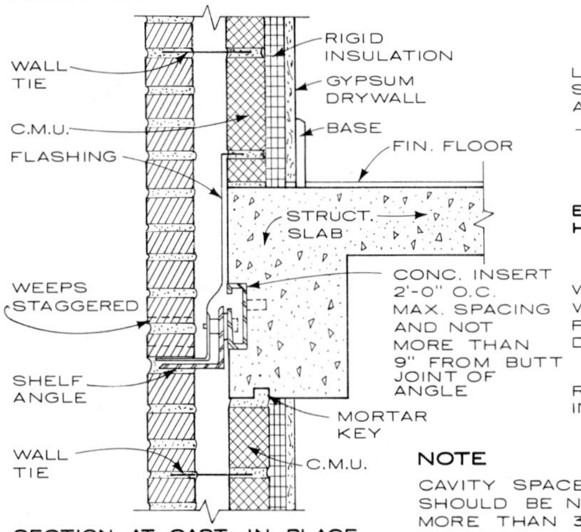

ADJUSTABLE WALL TIES 16" O.C. VERTICALLY
GYPSUM DRYWALL
BASE
RIGID INSULATION
FIN. FLOOR SUBFLOOR
C.M.U.
WOOD JOIST
FIRE CUT
SOLID C.M.U.

SECTION AT GRADE

WALL TIE
RIGID INSULATION
FLASHING
GYPSUM DRYWALL
WEEPS STAGGERED
C.M.U.
FILL WITH MORTAR
BASE
GRADE
STRUCTURAL SLAB
MEMBRANE W. P.
RIGID INSULATION
POROUS BACKFILL
HABITABLE SPACE BELOW

SECTION AT ROOF

METAL FLASHING
2 X 10" PLATE
WOOD BLOCKING CONTINUOUS
WALL TIE
STRUCTURAL SLAB
METAL REGLET 24" O.C.
MORTAR KEY
1/2" BOLT 4'-0" O.C.
C.M.U.
SUSPENDED CEILING
3 X 6 X 1/4" STEEL PLATE WELDED TO BOLT
RIGID INSULATION
GYPSUM DRYWALL

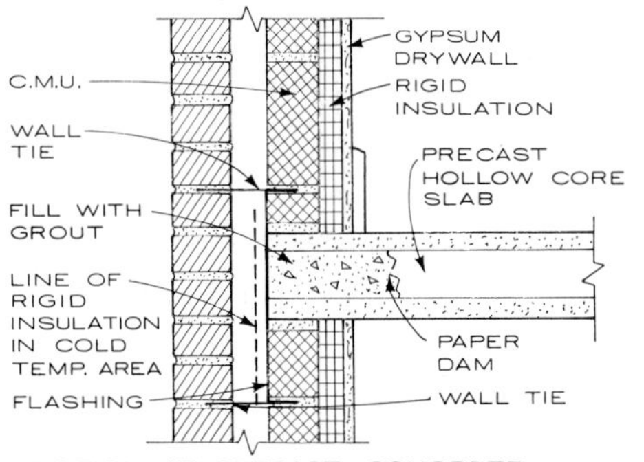

SECTION AT PRECAST CONCRETE FLOOR SLAB

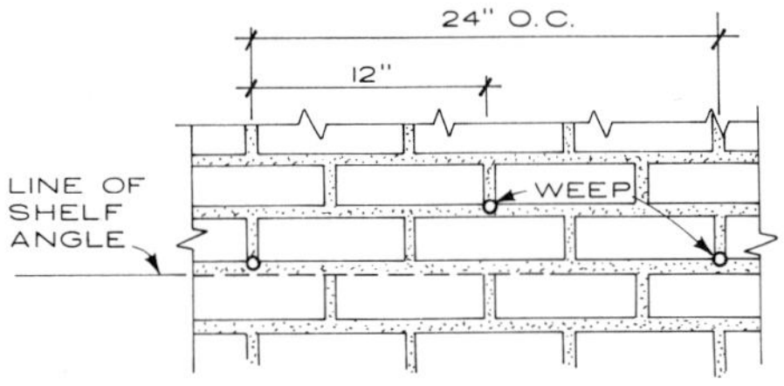

GYPSUM DRYWALL
RIGID INSULATION
C.M.U.
WALL TIE
PRECAST HOLLOW CORE SLAB
FILL WITH GROUT
LINE OF RIGID INSULATION IN COLD TEMP. AREA
PAPER DAM
FLASHING
WALL TIE

SECTION AT CAST-IN-PLACE FLOOR SLAB

WALL TIE
RIGID INSULATION
GYPSUM DRYWALL
C.M.U.
BASE
FLASHING
FIN. FLOOR
STRUCT. SLAB
WEEPS STAGGERED
CONC. INSERT 2'-0" O.C. MAX. SPACING AND NOT MORE THAN 9" FROM BUTT JOINT OF ANGLE
SHELF ANGLE
WALL TIE
MORTAR KEY
C.M.U.

NOTE
CAVITY SPACE SHOULD BE NO MORE THAN 3", NO LESS THAN 2"

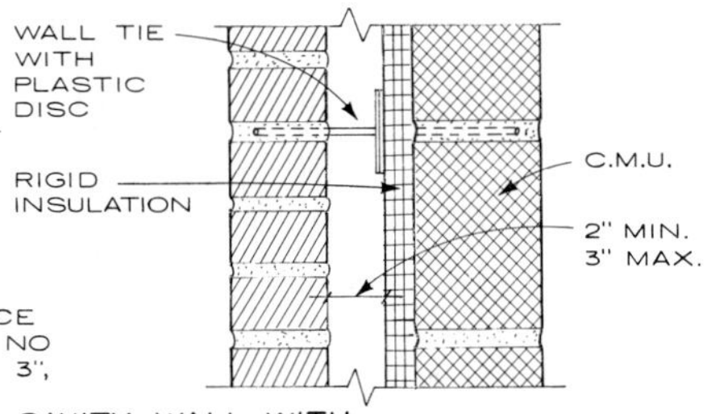

SECTION AT GRADE

WALL TIES
RIGID INSULATION
FLASHING
GYPSUM DRYWALL
WEEPS STAGGERED
C.M.U.
FLOOR SLAB
FILL WITH MORTAR
MOISTURE PROTECTION
GRADE
C.M.U. FOUNDATION WALL
POROUS FILL
PRIMETER INSULATION

Z TIE   RECTANGULAR TIE

ADJUSTABLE TIES

TRUSS TYPE REINFORCEMENT   LADDER TYPE REINFORCEMENT

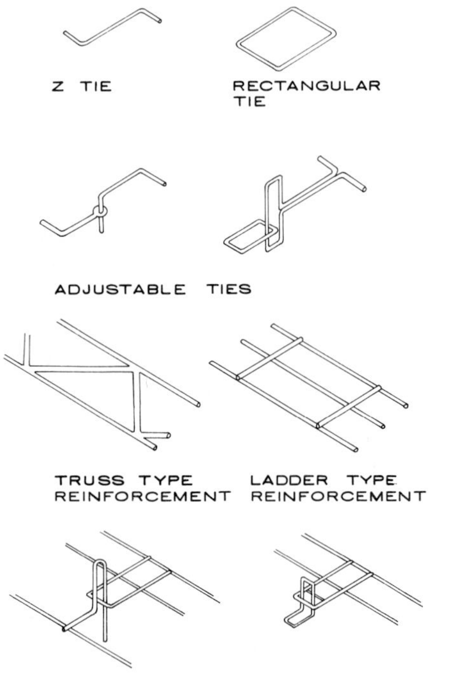

ADJUSTABLE REINFORCEMENT CAVITY WALL TIES

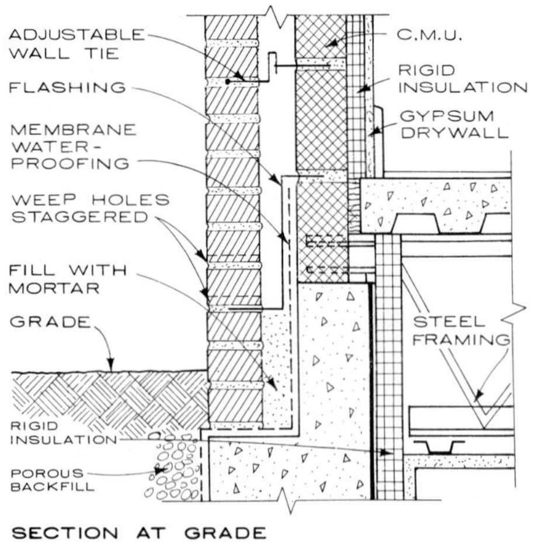

ELEVATION OF WEEP HOLE LOCATIONS

24" O.C.
12"
LINE OF SHELF ANGLE
WEEP

CAVITY WALL WITH RIGID INSULATION

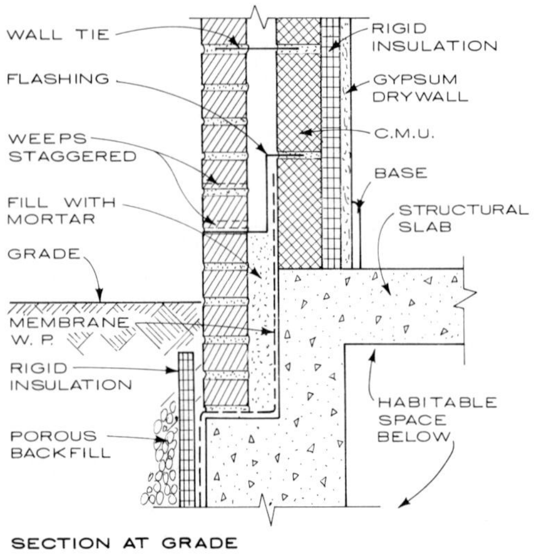

WALL TIE WITH PLASTIC DISC
C.M.U.
RIGID INSULATION
2" MIN. 3" MAX.

SECTION AT GRADE

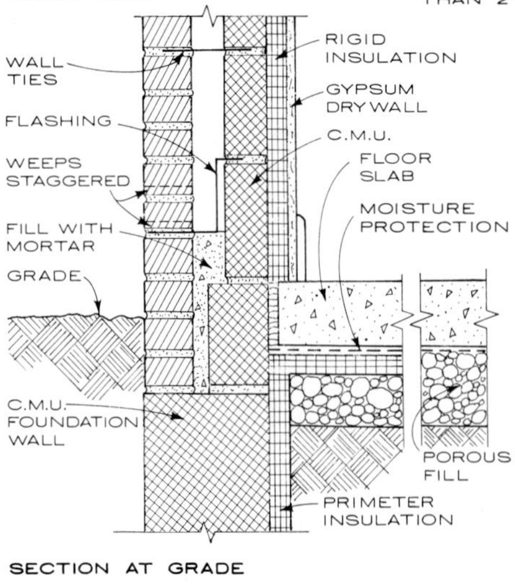

ADJUSTABLE WALL TIE
C.M.U.
RIGID INSULATION
FLASHING
GYPSUM DRYWALL
MEMBRANE WATER-PROOFING
WEEP HOLES STAGGERED
FILL WITH MORTAR
GRADE
STEEL FRAMING
RIGID INSULATION
POROUS BACKFILL

Robert J. Sangiamo, AIA; New York, New York
Davis, Brody & Associates; New York, New York

 UNIT MASONRY

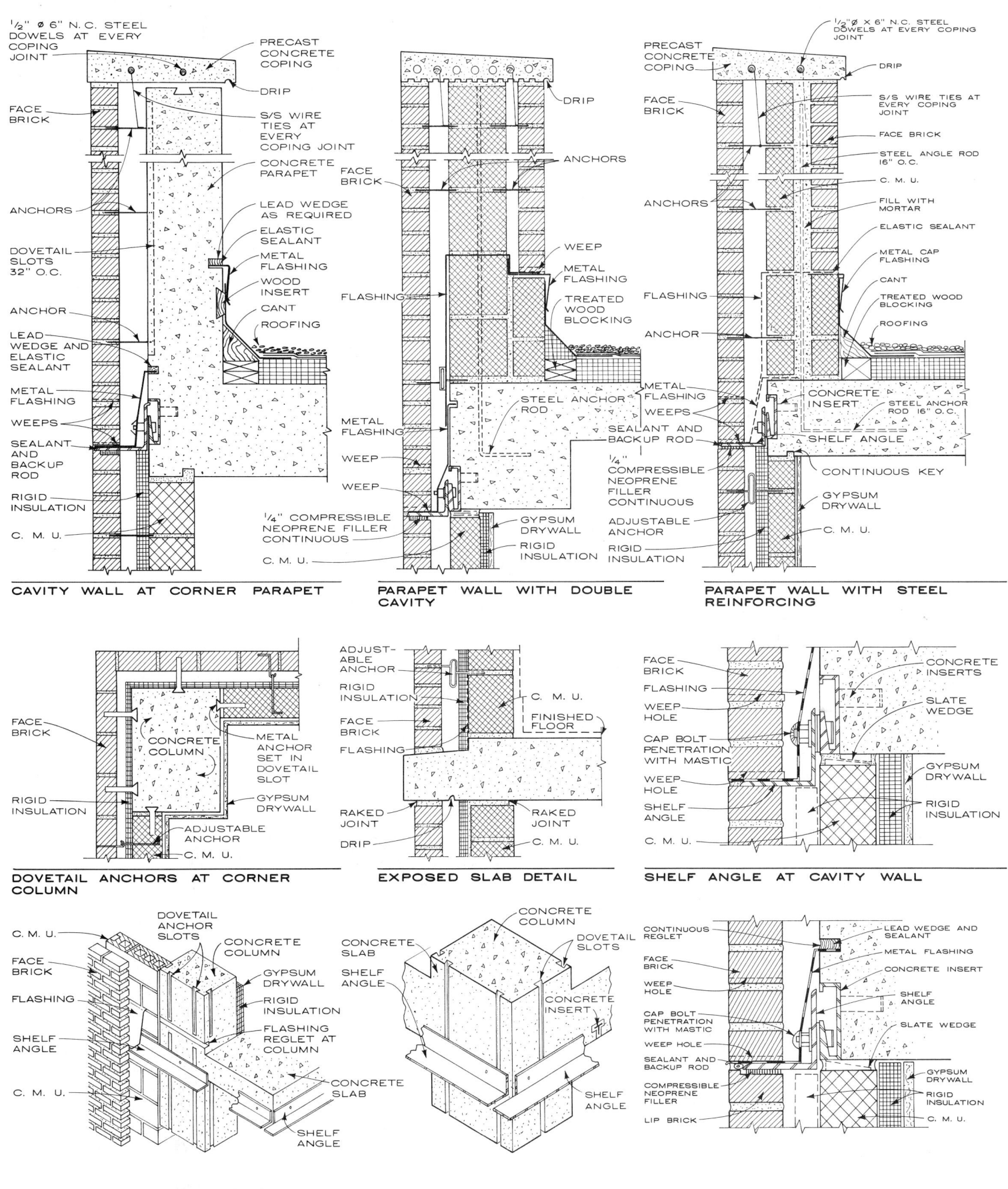

1/2" ⌀ 6" N.C. STEEL DOWELS AT EVERY COPING JOINT
PRECAST CONCRETE COPING
DRIP
FACE BRICK
S/S WIRE TIES AT EVERY COPING JOINT
CONCRETE PARAPET
ANCHORS
LEAD WEDGE AS REQUIRED
ELASTIC SEALANT
METAL FLASHING
WOOD INSERT
CANT
ROOFING
DOVETAIL SLOTS 32" O.C.
ANCHOR
LEAD WEDGE AND ELASTIC SEALANT
METAL FLASHING
WEEPS
SEALANT AND BACKUP ROD
RIGID INSULATION
C. M. U.

CAVITY WALL AT CORNER PARAPET

FACE BRICK
ANCHORS
FLASHING
METAL FLASHING
WEEP
WEEP
DRIP
WEEP
METAL FLASHING
TREATED WOOD BLOCKING
STEEL ANCHOR ROD
1/4" COMPRESSIBLE NEOPRENE FILLER CONTINUOUS
GYPSUM DRYWALL
RIGID INSULATION
C. M. U.

PARAPET WALL WITH DOUBLE CAVITY

1/2" ⌀ X 6" N.C. STEEL DOWELS AT EVERY COPING JOINT
PRECAST CONCRETE COPING
DRIP
FACE BRICK
S/S WIRE TIES AT EVERY COPING JOINT
FACE BRICK
STEEL ANGLE ROD 16" O.C.
C. M. U.
FILL WITH MORTAR
ELASTIC SEALANT
METAL CAP FLASHING
CANT
TREATED WOOD BLOCKING
ROOFING
ANCHORS
FLASHING
ANCHOR
METAL FLASHING
WEEPS
SEALANT AND BACKUP ROD
CONCRETE INSERT
STEEL ANCHOR ROD 16" O.C.
SHELF ANGLE
CONTINUOUS KEY
ADJUSTABLE ANCHOR
GYPSUM DRYWALL
C. M. U.
RIGID INSULATION

PARAPET WALL WITH STEEL REINFORCING

FACE BRICK
CONCRETE COLUMN
METAL ANCHOR SET IN DOVETAIL SLOT
GYPSUM DRYWALL
RIGID INSULATION
ADJUSTABLE ANCHOR
C. M. U.

DOVETAIL ANCHORS AT CORNER COLUMN

ADJUSTABLE ANCHOR
RIGID INSULATION
FACE BRICK
FLASHING
RAKED JOINT
DRIP
C. M. U.
FINISHED FLOOR
RAKED JOINT
C. M. U.

EXPOSED SLAB DETAIL

FACE BRICK
FLASHING
WEEP HOLE
CAP BOLT PENETRATION WITH MASTIC
WEEP HOLE
SHELF ANGLE
C. M. U.
CONCRETE INSERTS
SLATE WEDGE
GYPSUM DRYWALL
RIGID INSULATION

SHELF ANGLE AT CAVITY WALL

C. M. U.
FACE BRICK
FLASHING
SHELF ANGLE
C. M. U.
DOVETAIL ANCHOR SLOTS
CONCRETE COLUMN
GYPSUM DRYWALL
RIGID INSULATION
FLASHING REGLET AT COLUMN
CONCRETE SLAB
SHELF ANGLE

SHELF ANGLE AT CORNER COLUMN

CONCRETE COLUMN
CONCRETE SLAB
SHELF ANGLE
DOVETAIL SLOTS
CONCRETE INSERT
SHELF ANGLE

CONTINUOUS REGLET
FACE BRICK
WEEP HOLE
CAP BOLT PENETRATION WITH MASTIC
WEEP HOLE
SEALANT AND BACKUP ROD
COMPRESSIBLE NEOPRENE FILLER
LIP BRICK
LEAD WEDGE AND SEALANT
METAL FLASHING
CONCRETE INSERT
SHELF ANGLE
SLATE WEDGE
GYPSUM DRYWALL
RIGID INSULATION
C. M. U.

HORIZONTAL EXPANSION JOINT

Robert J. Sangiamo, AIA; New York, New York

Davis, Brody & Associates; New York, New York

UNIT MASONRY **4**

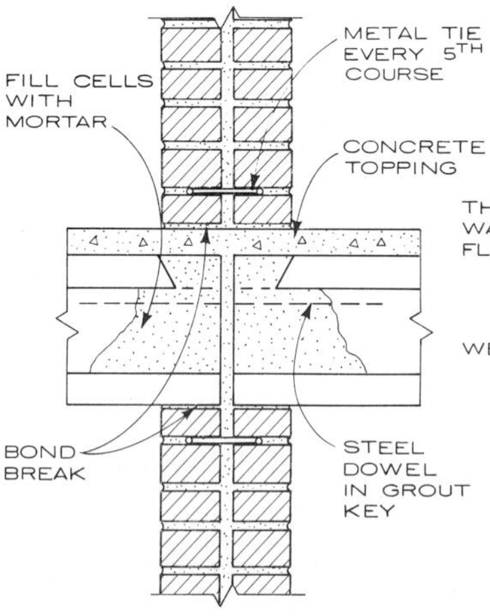

FILL CELLS WITH MORTAR

METAL TIE EVERY 5TH COURSE

CONCRETE TOPPING

BOND BREAK

STEEL DOWEL IN GROUT KEY

8" BRICK BEARING WALL — PRECAST CONCRETE FLOOR

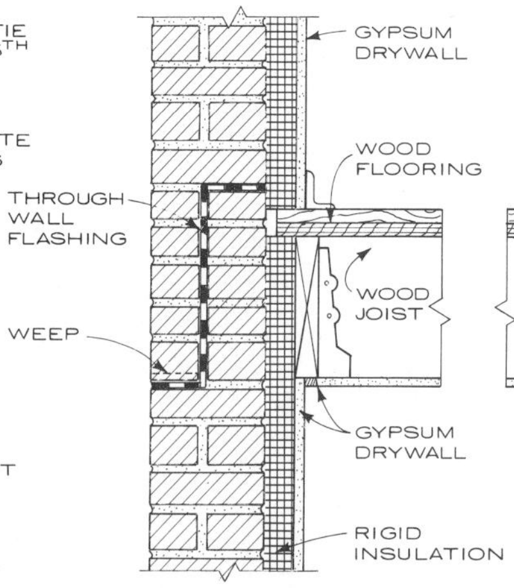

GYPSUM DRYWALL

THROUGH WALL FLASHING

WOOD FLOORING

WEEP

WOOD JOIST

GYPSUM DRYWALL

RIGID INSULATION

8" BRICK BEARING WALL — WOOD JOIST FLOOR

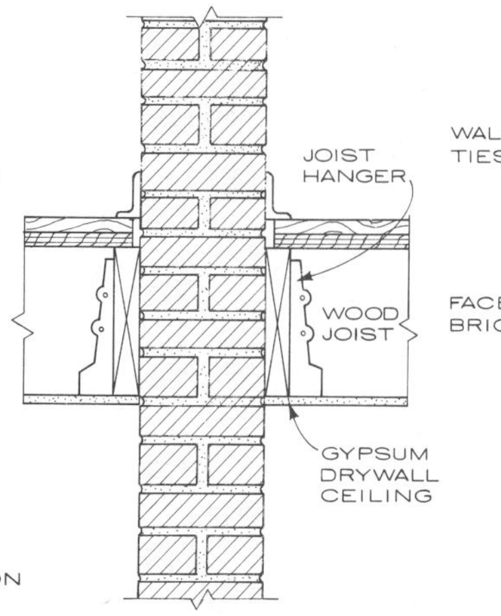

JOIST HANGER

WOOD JOIST

GYPSUM DRYWALL CEILING

8" BRICK BEARING WALL — WOOD JOIST FLOOR

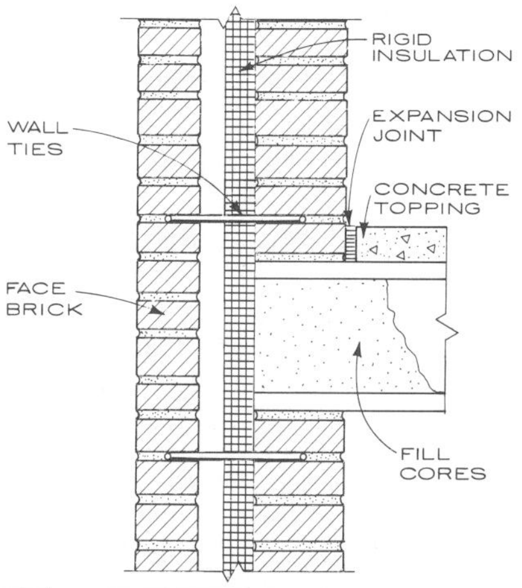

RIGID INSULATION

WALL TIES

EXPANSION JOINT

CONCRETE TOPPING

FACE BRICK

FILL CORES

BRICK BEARING CAVITY WALL — PRECAST CONCRETE FLOOR

JOINT REINF.

HORIZONTAL ANCHOR

CONCRETE TOPPING

VERTICAL REINF.

JOINT REINF.

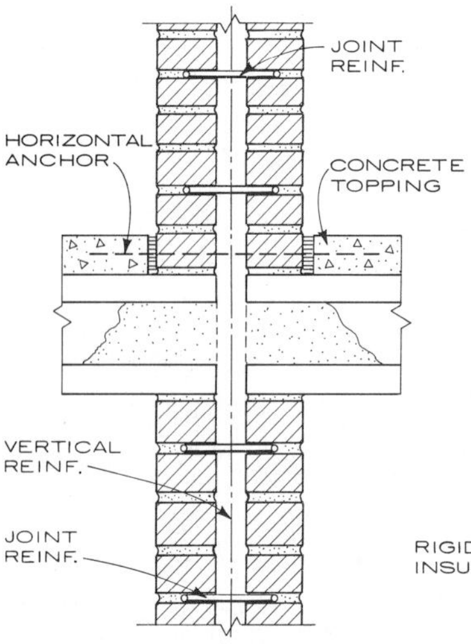

10" R.B.M. BEARING WALL — PRECAST CONCRETE FLOOR

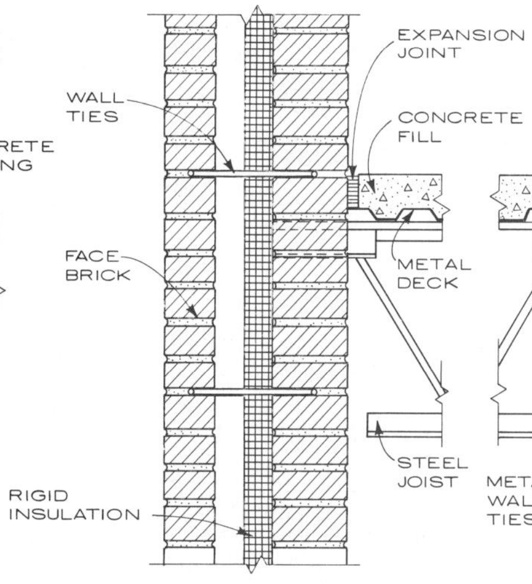

WALL TIES

EXPANSION JOINT

CONCRETE FILL

FACE BRICK

METAL DECK

STEEL JOIST

RIGID INSULATION

BRICK BEARING CAVITY WALL — STEEL JOIST FLOOR

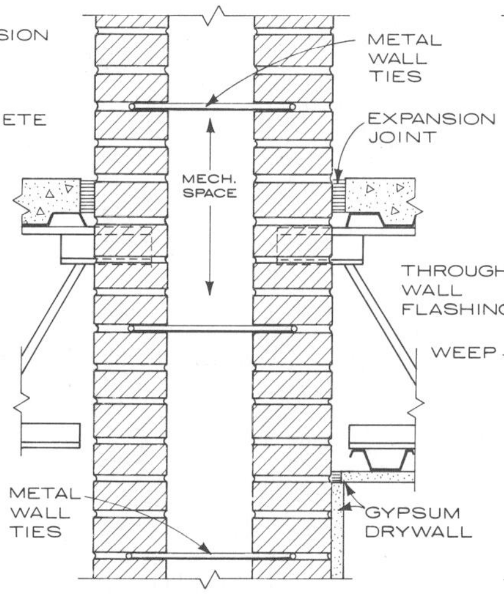

METAL WALL TIES

EXPANSION JOINT

MECH. SPACE

METAL WALL TIES

GYPSUM DRYWALL

BRICK BEARING PARTITION FOR MECHANICAL SPACE

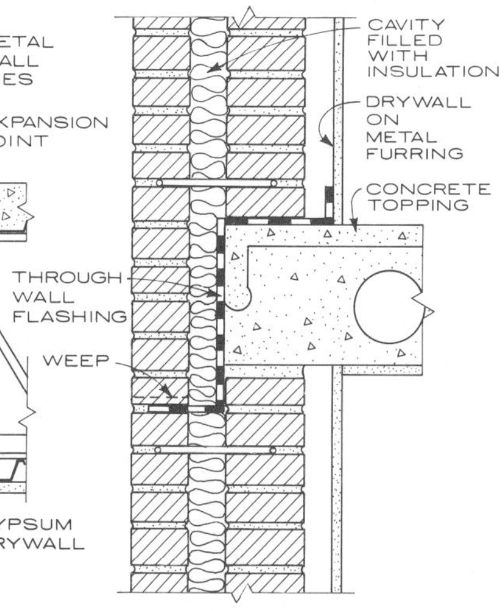

CAVITY FILLED WITH INSULATION

DRYWALL ON METAL FURRING

CONCRETE TOPPING

THROUGH WALL FLASHING

WEEP

BRICK BEARING CAVITY WALL — PRECAST CONCRETE FLOOR

CEMENT PLASTER FINISH

HORIZONTAL REINF.

INSULATION AND FINISH IF REQUIRED

WOOD FLOOR

BLOCKING

VERTICAL REINF.

JOIST ANCHOR 4'-0" O.C.

WOOD LEDGER

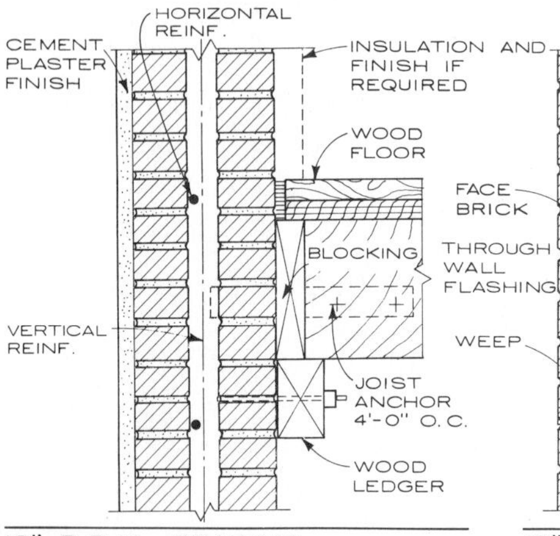

10" R.B.M. BEARING WALL — WOOD JOIST FLOOR

RIGID INSULATION

GYPSUM DRYWALL

FACE BRICK

THROUGH WALL FLASHING

WEEP

CONCRETE FILL

STEEL BEAM

GYPSUM DRYWALL

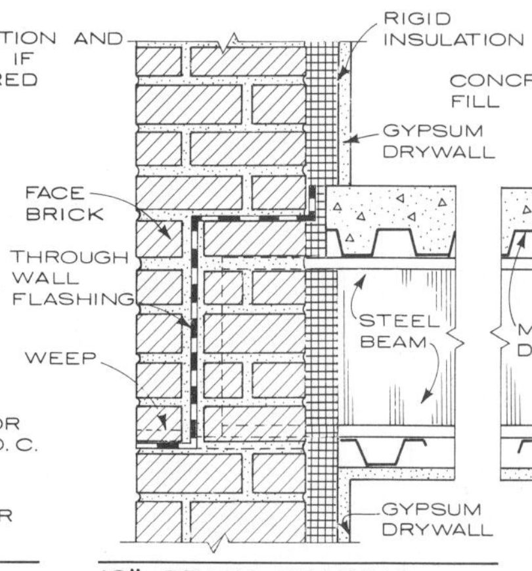

12" BRICK BEARING WALL — STEEL BEAM AND METAL DECK FLOOR

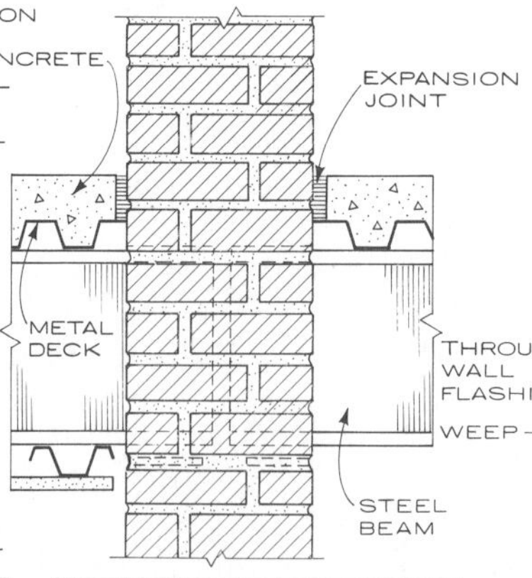

CONCRETE FILL

EXPANSION JOINT

METAL DECK

STEEL BEAM

12" INTERIOR BRICK BEARING PARTITION

GYPSUM DRYWALL

RIGID INSULATION

CONCRETE TOPPING

THROUGH WALL FLASHING

WEEP

FILL CORES

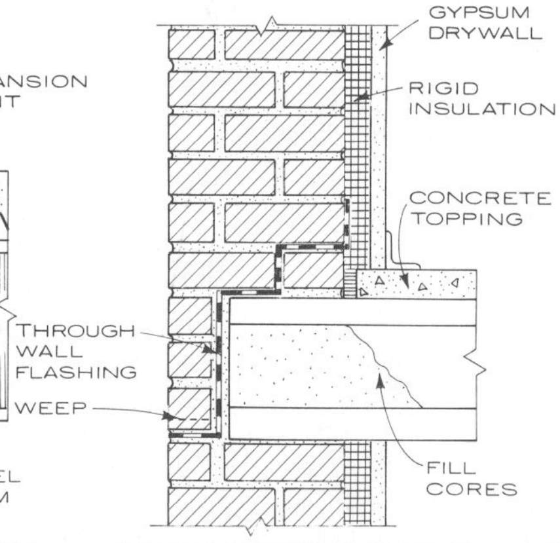

12" BRICK BEARING WALL — PRECAST CONCRETE FLOOR

Robert Joseph Sangiamo, AIA; New York, New York

Davis, Brody & Associates; New York, New York

UNIT MASONRY

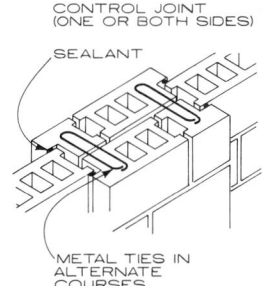

CONTROL JOINT AT PIER

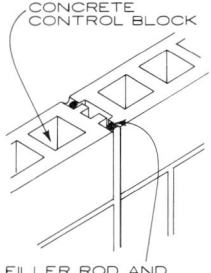

FLUSH WALL AND PLASTER CONTROL JOINTS

CONTROL JOINT BLOCK

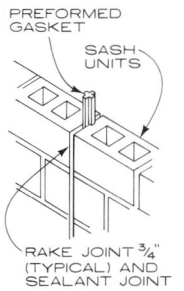

FLUSH WALL CONTROL JOINTS

PRINCIPLES

Masonry materials expand and contract in response to temperature changes. Dimensional changes also occur in masonry because of moisture variations. To compensate for these dimensional changes and thus control cracking in masonry, keep the following in mind:

1. Proper product specifications and construction procedures limit moisture related movements. For example, Type I moisture controlled concrete masonry units are manufactured to minimize moisture related movement.
2. Proper steel reinforcing, including horizontal joint reinforcing, increases the tensile resistance of masonry walls.
3. Properly placed expansion joints and control joints accommodate movement and provide for controlled crack locations.

EXPANSION JOINTS

The purpose of expansion joints is to relieve tension and compression between separate portions of a masonry wall resulting from temperature and/or moisture induced dimensional movements.

Exterior and interior masonry wythes of cavity walls should be connected with flexible metal ties. Horizontal expansion joints should be located below shelf angles or structural frames supporting masonry walls or panels. Shelf angles should contain sufficient interruptions to accommodate thermal movements. Horizontal expansion joints (soft joints, slip channel, etc.) should also be provided above exterior masonry walls or panels abutting structural frames and at interior non-load-bearing masonry walls abutting the underside of floor or roof structures above.

CONTROL JOINTS

The purpose of control joints is to provide tension relief between individual portions of a masonry wall that may change from their original dimensions. They must provide for lateral stability across the joint and contain a through wall seal.

Control joints should be located in long straight walls, at major changes in wall heights, at changes in wall thickness, above joints in foundations, at columns and pilasters, at one or both sides of wall openings, near wall intersections, and near junctions of walls in L, T, or U shaped buildings. Joints should continue through roof parapets.

SEALANTS

The type of sealant recommended varies depending on the surface to which it is applied. Some sealants require a primer but one part primerless sealants are available that are capable of withstanding compression and extension up to 50% in a single direction. A variety of colors are available to blend with masonry. Polyethylene foam rod backup material should be used so that, when compressed, it will fit tightly. Sealant depth should equal the joint width up to 1/2 in. wide; for joints over 1/2 in. wide, the caulking depth should be 1/2 in. As a general rule, use one part silicones, urethanes, or thiokols for exterior caulking and acrylics for interior caulking. Joint width should be three times the expected movement for low modulus silicones and four times the expected movement for other elastomers (polysulfides and urethanes).

Setter, Leach & Lindstrom, Inc.; Minneapolis, Minnesota

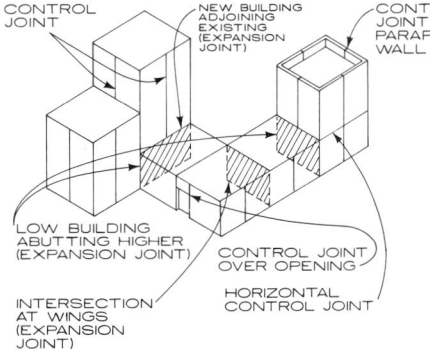

LOCATION OF CONTROL AND EXPANSION JOINTS

CONTROL JOINT SPACING FOR MOISTURE CONTROLLED ASTM C90 TYPE I BLOCK UNITS

RECOMMENDED SPACING OF CONTROL JOINTS	VERTICAL SPACING OF JOINT REINFORCEMENT			
	NONE	24''	16''	8''
Expressed as ratio of panel length to height (L/H)	2	2 1/2	3	4
Panel length (L) not to exceed (regardless of height (H))	40'	45'	50'	60'

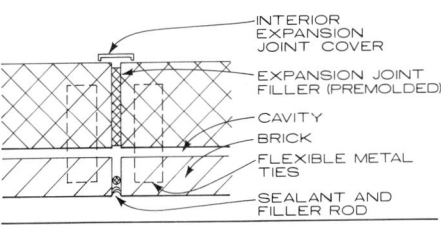

EXPANSION JOINT AT WALL

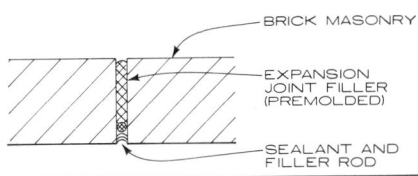

EXPANSION JOINT AT MASONRY CAVITY WALL

EXPANSION JOINT AT WALL

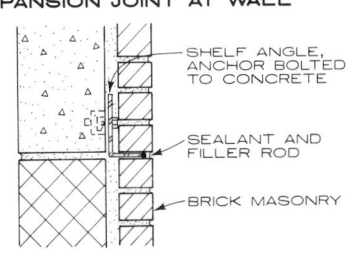

HORIZONTAL EXPANSION JOINT

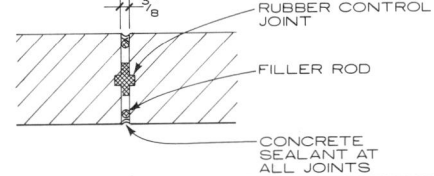

CONTROL JOINT AT STRAIGHT WALL

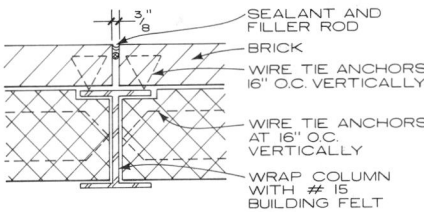

CONTROL JOINT AT STEEL COLUMN

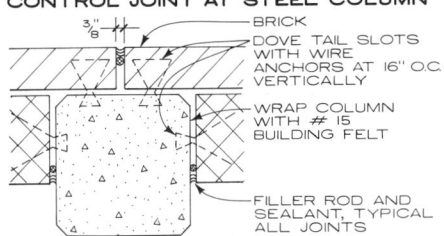

CONTROL JOINT AT CONCRETE COLUMN

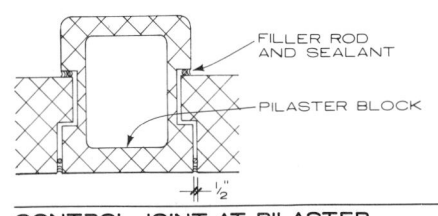

CONTROL JOINT AT PILASTER

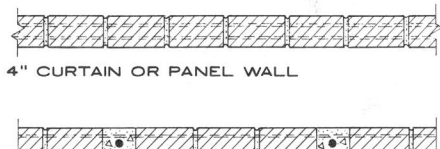

4" CURTAIN OR PANEL WALL

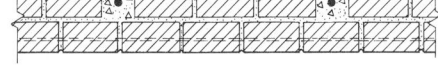

8" GROUTED POCKET WALL

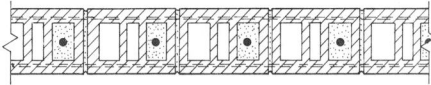

8" GROUTED HOLLOW BRICK WALL.
OTHER THICKNESSES OF RBM HOLLOW
BRICK ARE ALSO AVAILABLE IN 4, 6 AND 10 IN.

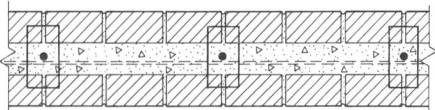

12" GROUTED CAVITY WALL

NOTE: ALL JOINTS ARE CONCAVED OR
V-TOOLED

TYPICAL REINFORCED BRICK MASONRY WALLS

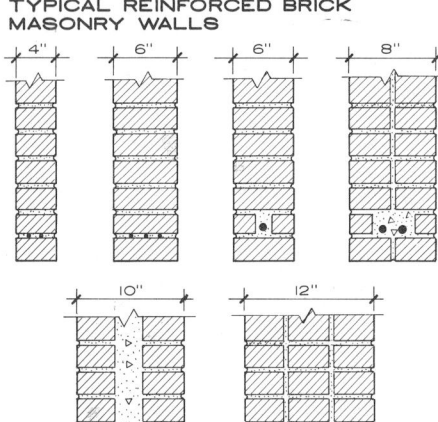

TYPICAL LINTEL DETAILS

TYPICAL RETAINING WALL DESIGN VALUES

H	B	L	D BARS	V BARS	F BARS
2'-0''	1'-9''	1'-10''	#3 @ 40''		#3 @ 40''
2'-6''	1'-9''	2'-4''	#3 @ 40''		#3 @ 40''
3'-0''	2'-0''	2'-10''	#3 @ 40''		#3 @ 40''
3'-6''	2'-0''	3'-4''	#3 @ 40''		#3 @ 40''
4'-0''	2'-4''	1'-4''	#3 @ 27'' #4 @ 40''	#3 @ 27'' #3 @ 40''	#3 @ 27'' #3 @ 40''
4'-6''	2'-8''	1'-6''	#3 @ 19'' #4 @ 35''	#3 @ 38'' #3 @ 35''	#3 @ 19'' #3 @ 35''
5'-0''	3'-0''	1'-8''	#3 @ 14'' #4 @ 25'' #5 @ 40''	#3 @ 28'' #3 @ 25'' #4 @ 40''	#3 @ 14'' #3 @ 25'' #4 @ 40''
5'-6''	3'-3''	1'-10''	#3 @ 11'' #4 @ 20'' #5 @ 31''	#3 @ 22'' #4 @ 40'' #4 @ 31''	#3 @ 11'' #3 @ 20'' #4 @ 31''
6'-0''	3'-6''	2'-0''	#3 @ 8'' #4 @ 14'' #5 @ 20''	#3 @ 16'' #4 @ 28'' #4 @ 20''	#3 @ 8'' #3 @ 14'' #4 @ 20''

NOTE: For convenience, this table was developed to aid the nondesigner in a typical application. However, materials must meet these additional minimum requirements:

1. Brick strength in excess of 6000 psi in compression.
2. Steel design tensile strength, F_s, of 20,000 psi.
3. No surcharge.

For additional information, consult a qualified engineer and the Brick Institute of America.

John R. Hoke, Jr., AIA, Architect; Washington, D.C.

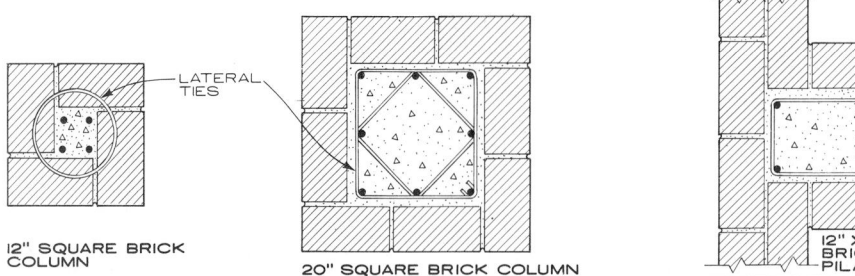

12" SQUARE BRICK COLUMN

20" SQUARE BRICK COLUMN

12" X 16" BRICK PILASTER

REINFORCED COLUMNS AND PILASTER

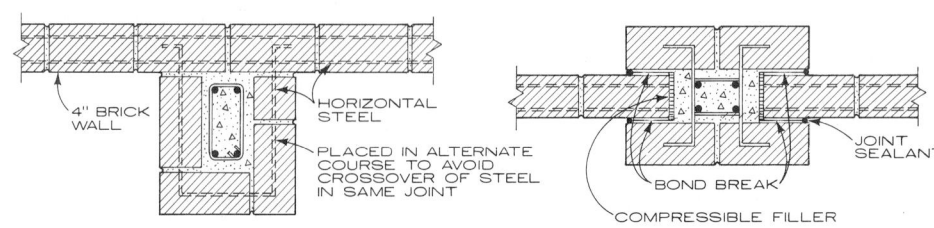

REINFORCED BRICK MASONRY COLUMN

REINFORCED BRICK MASONRY PILASTER

STEEL COLUMN

REINFORCED CONCRETE COLUMN

TYPICAL 4 IN. PANEL WALL DETAILS

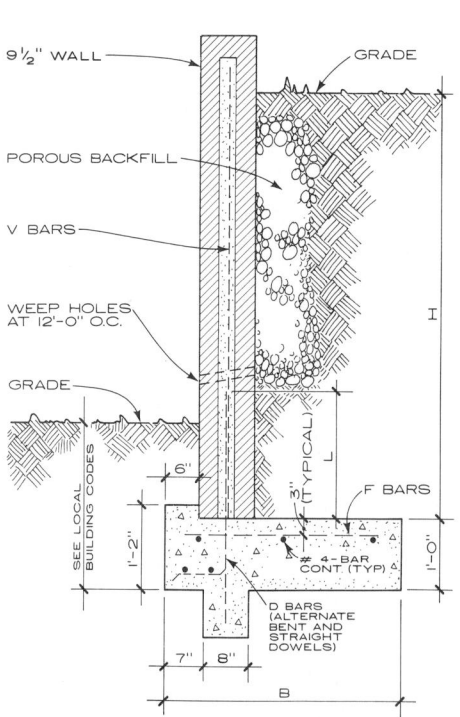

LOW BRICK MASONRY RETAINING WALL (LESS THAN 6'-0")

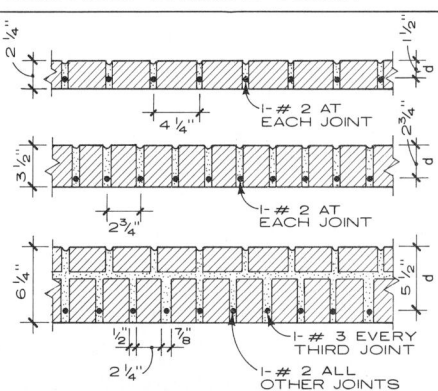

REINFORCED BRICK MASONRY SLABS

LIVE LOADS (PSF)	MAXIMUM CLEAR SPAN		
	T = 2¼'' 1 #2 EACH JOINT	T = 3½'' 1 #2 EACH JOINT	T = 6¼'' 1 #3 EVERY JOINT 1 #2 REMAINING JOINT
30	6'-10''	10'-5''	14'-5''
40	6'-3''	9'-9''	13'-8''
50	5'-10''	9'-2''	13'-1''
100	4'-6''	7'-3''	10'-11''
250	1'-10''	5'-0''	7'-10''

NOTE: Design parameters for the table are as follows: The brick compressive strength average is 8000 psi. The mortar is type M (1:¼:3)—portland cement, lime, and sand. Reinforcement steel is ASTM A 82-66, f_s = 20,000 psi. A simple span loading condition was assumed:

$$\left(M = \frac{wl^2}{8} \right)$$

All mortar joints are ½ in. thick for the slabs shown, except as noted.

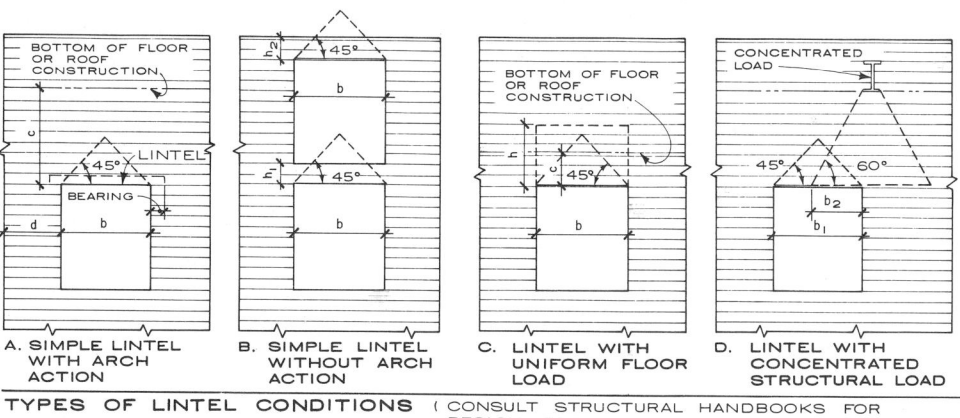

A. SIMPLE LINTEL WITH ARCH ACTION
B. SIMPLE LINTEL WITHOUT ARCH ACTION
C. LINTEL WITH UNIFORM FLOOR LOAD
D. LINTEL WITH CONCENTRATED STRUCTURAL LOAD

TYPES OF LINTEL CONDITIONS (CONSULT STRUCTURAL HANDBOOKS FOR DESIGN FORMULAS)

NOTES FOR LINTEL CONDITIONS

A. Simple lintel with arch action carries wall load only in triangle above opening:

$$c \geq b \quad \text{and} \quad d \geq b$$

B. Simple lintel without arch action carries less wall load than triangle above opening:

$$h_1 \text{ or } h_2 < 0.6b$$

C. Lintel with uniform floor load carries both wall and floor loads in rectangle above opening:

$$c < b$$

D. Lintel with concentrated load carries wall and portion of concentrated load distributed along length b_2.

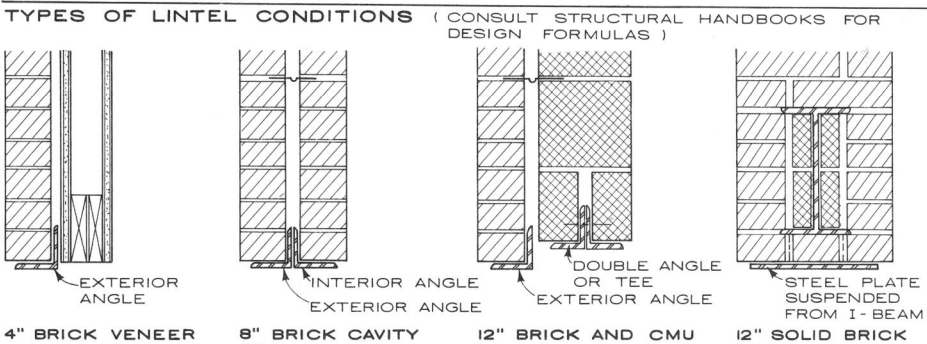

4" BRICK VENEER — EXTERIOR ANGLE
8" BRICK CAVITY WALL — INTERIOR ANGLE, EXTERIOR ANGLE
12" BRICK AND CMU — DOUBLE ANGLE OR TEE, EXTERIOR ANGLE
12" SOLID BRICK WALL — STEEL PLATE SUSPENDED FROM I-BEAM

NOTES ON STEEL LINTELS

1. Consult a structural engineer in the case of long span lintels, lintels in bearing walls, and any loading conditions not covered here.
2. Deflections greater than 1/700 result in local cracking at corners of opening.
3. Long lintels should be set with control joint at ends to provide space for thermal expansion.
4. Heavily loaded lintels bearing directly on masonry units may cause localized spalling of the masonry unit.

 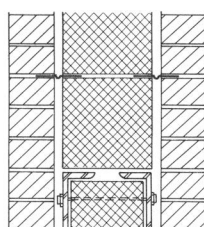 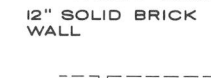 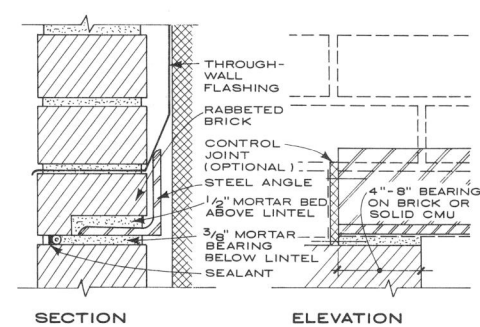

12" BRICK AND CMU — STEEL PLATE WELDED TO CHANNEL, EXTERIOR ANGLE
16" BRICK AND CMU — STEEL CHANNEL AND ANGLE ASSEMBLY
BEARING END DETAILS — SECTION, ELEVATION

THROUGH-WALL FLASHING / RABBETED BRICK / CONTROL JOINT (OPTIONAL) / STEEL ANGLE / ½" MORTAR BED ABOVE LINTEL / 4"–8" BEARING ON BRICK OR SOLID CMU / ⅜" MORTAR BEARING BELOW LINTEL / SEALANT

LOOSE STEEL LINTELS FOR MASONRY WALLS

STEEL LINTELS FOR MASONRY
NUMBER AND SIZE OF ANGLES REQUIRED
No superimposed loads

CLEAR SPAN (MAX.)	EXTERIOR ANGLES	INTERIOR ANGLES
4'-0"	$\angle 3\frac{1}{2}" \times 3\frac{1}{2}" \times \frac{5}{16}"$	$2 \angle s\ 3\frac{1}{2}" \times 3\frac{1}{2}" \times \frac{5}{16}"$
6'-0"	$\angle 4" \times 3\frac{1}{2}" \times \frac{5}{16}"$	$2 \angle s\ 4" \times 3\frac{1}{2}" \times \frac{5}{16}"$
8'-0"	$\angle 5" \times 3\frac{1}{2}" \times \frac{5}{16}"$	$2 \angle s\ 5" \times 3\frac{1}{2}" \times \frac{5}{16}"$

NOTES

1. Design based on 4 in. face brick with 8 in. CMU backup.
2. $F_y = 36,000$ psi.
3. Allow 6 in. bearing at each end.

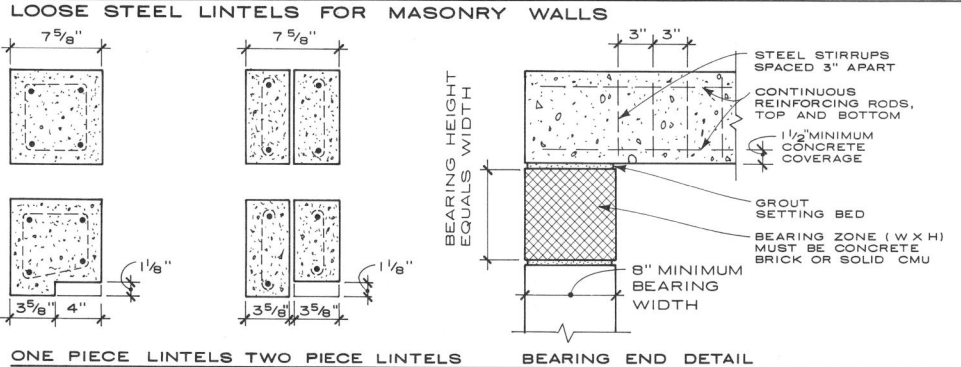

STEEL STIRRUPS SPACED 3" APART / CONTINUOUS REINFORCING RODS, TOP AND BOTTOM / 1½" MINIMUM CONCRETE COVERAGE / GROUT SETTING BED / BEARING ZONE (W X H) MUST BE CONCRETE BRICK OR SOLID CMU / 8" MINIMUM BEARING WIDTH / BEARING HEIGHT EQUALS WIDTH

ONE PIECE LINTELS **TWO PIECE LINTELS** **BEARING END DETAIL**

REINFORCED CONCRETE LINTELS

PRECAST CONCRETE AND REINFORCED CMU LINTELS—
NUMBER AND SIZE OF REBARS REQUIRED
No superimposed loads

LINTEL TYPE	CLEAR SPAN (MAX.)	8" BRICK WALL (80 LB/SQ FT)	8" CMU WALL (50 LB/SQ FT)
Reinforced concrete (7⅝" square)	4'-0"	4-#3	4-#3
	6'-0"	4-#4	4-#3
	8'-0"	4-#5	4-#4
Precast CMU (7⅝" square)	4'-0"	2-#4	2-#4
	6'-0"	2-#5	2-#4
	8'-0"	2-#6	2-#5

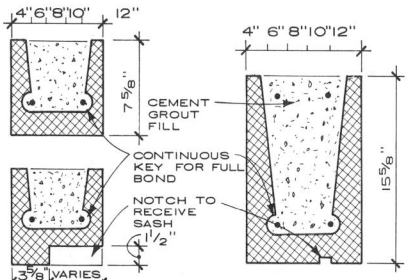 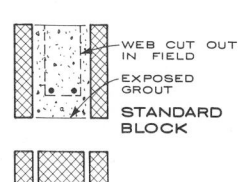

CEMENT GROUT FILL / CONTINUOUS KEY FOR FULL BOND / NOTCH TO RECEIVE SASH
COMMON U-BLOCK / STANDARD BLOCK / DOUBLE CORE / SAWED UNIT

CEMENT GROUT FILL / REINFORCING STEEL BARS / WEB CUT OUT IN FIELD / EXPOSED GROUT

STANDARD SECTIONS **BOND BEAMS** **KNOCKOUT BOND BEAMS**

PRECAST CONCRETE MASONRY LINTELS

NOTES

1. Weight of lintel included in all reinforcing calculations.
2. Reinforced CMU lintels designed without shear reinforcing stirrups.
3. Allow 7⅝ in. bearing: both types of lintel.
4. $f'_c = 3000$ lb/sq in. for both precast concrete and CMU grout.
5. $f_y = 60,000$ lb/sq in.

Metz, Train, Olson and Youngren, Inc.; Chicago, Illinois

UNIT MASONRY **4**

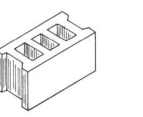

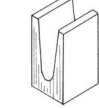
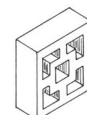

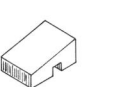

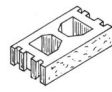
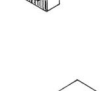
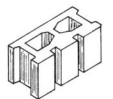
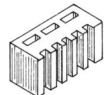
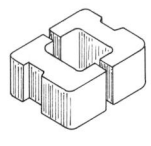
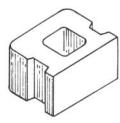
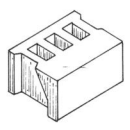
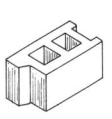
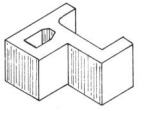

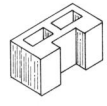
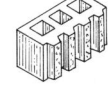

STRETCHER   CONTROL JOINT   LINTEL   SCREEN

CORNER   BOND BEAM   SILL   SPLIT FACE

CORNER RETURN   HEADER   SASH   JOIST UNIT   SOFFIT   RIBBED OR SCORED   FLUTED

COLUMN   GRADE   JAMB   PILASTER INSERT   SCREEN   OFFSET FACE   SPLIT RIBBED

TYPICAL CONCRETE MASONRY UNIT SHAPES

CONCRETE MASONRY UNIT SPECIFICATIONS AND FIRE RESISTANCE DATA

1. A solid (load bearing) concrete block is a unit whose cross-sectional area in every plane parallel to the bearing surface is not less than 75% of the gross cross-sectional area measured in the same plane. (ASTM C145—75.)

2. A hollow concrete block is a unit whose cross-sectional area in every plane parallel to the bearing surface is less than 75% of the gross cross-sectional area measured in the same plane. (ASTM C90—75.)

3. Actual dimension is 3/8 to 1/2 in. less than nominal shown.

4. All shapes shown are available in all dimensions given in chart except for width (W) which may be otherwise noted.

5. Because the number of shapes and sizes for concrete masonry screen units is virtually unlimited, it is advisable for the designer to check on availability of any specific shape during early planning.

6. Screen units should be of high quality, even though they seldom are employed in load bearing construction. When tested with their hollow cells parallel to the direction of the load, screen units should have a compressive strength exceeding 1000 psi of gross area; a quality of concrete unit comparable to "Specifications for Hollow Load-Bearing Concrete Masonry Units" ASTM C90—75.

7. Building codes are quite specific in the degree of fire protection required in various areas of buildings. Local building regulations will govern the concrete masonry wall section best suited for specific applications. Fire resistance ratings of concrete masonry walls are based on fire tests made at Underwriters' Laboratories, Inc., National Bureau of Standards, Portland Cement Association, and other recognized laboratories. Methods of test are described in ASTM E119 "Standard Method of Fire Tests of Building Construction and Materials."

8. The fire resistance ratings of most concrete masonry walls are determined by heat transmission measured by temperature rise on the cold side. Fire endurance can be calculated as a function of the aggregate type used in the block unit,

and the solid thickness of the wall, or the equivalent solid thickness of the wall when working with hollow units.

9. Equivalent thickness of hollow units is calculated from actual thickness and the percentage of solid materials. Both needed items of information are normally reported by the testing laboratory using standard ASTM procedures, such as ASTM C140 "Methods of Sampling and Testing Concrete Masonry Units." When walls are plastered or otherwise faced with fire resistant materials, the thickness of these materials is included in calculating the equivalent thickness effective for fire resistance. Estimated fire resistance ratings shown in the table are for fully protected construction in which all structural members are of incombustible materials. Where combustible members are framed into walls, equivalent solid thickness protecting each such member should not be less than 93% of the thicknesses shown. Plaster is effective in increasing fire resistance when combustible members are framed into masonry walls, as is filling core spaces with various fire resistant materials.

10. The following are minimum equivalent thicknesses for rating of:

	1 HR	2 HR	3 HR	4 HR
Expanded slag	2.2	3.3	4.2	5.0
Expanded shale or clay	2.5	3.7	4.7	5.5
Limestone, scoria, cinders unexpanded slag	2.7	4.0	5.0	5.9
Calcareous gravel	2.8	4.2	5.3	6.2
Siliceous gravel	3.0	4.5	5.7	6.7

Equivalent thickness is the solid thickness that would be obtained if the same amount of concrete contained in a hollow unit were recast without core holes. Calculate fire resistance as follows: equivalent thickness equals the percentage of block solidity (based on aggregate type) times actual block thickness (in.). Refer to table for hour rating of wall.

NOMINAL DIMENSIONS OF TYPICAL CONCRETE MASONRY UNIT SHAPES

Height (H) = 4", 8"
Length (L) = 8", 12", 16", 18", 24"
Width (W) = 2", 3", 4", 6", 8", 10", 12"

R VALUE OF SINGLE WYTHE CONCRETE MASONRY UNITS

NOMINAL UNIT THICKNESS (IN.)	DENSITY OF CONCRETE IN CMU (PCF)				
	60	80	100	120	140
4	2.07	1.68	1.40	1.17	0.77
6	2.25	1.83	1.53	1.29	0.86
8	2.30	2.12	1.75	1.46	0.98
10	3.00	2.40	1.97	1.63	1.08
12	3.29	2.62	2.14	1.81	1.16

U VALUE OF SINGLE WYTHE CONCRETE MASONRY UNITS

NOMINAL UNIT THICKNESS (IN.)	DENSITY OF CONCRETE IN CMU (PCF)				
	60	80	100	120	140
4	0.34	0.40	0.44	0.50	0.62
6	0.32	0.37	0.42	0.47	0.59
8	0.32	0.34	0.38	0.43	0.55
10	0.26	0.31	0.35	0.40	0.52
12	0.24	0.29	0.34	0.38	0.50

Robert J. Sangiamo, AIA, and Davis, Brody & Associates; New York, New York

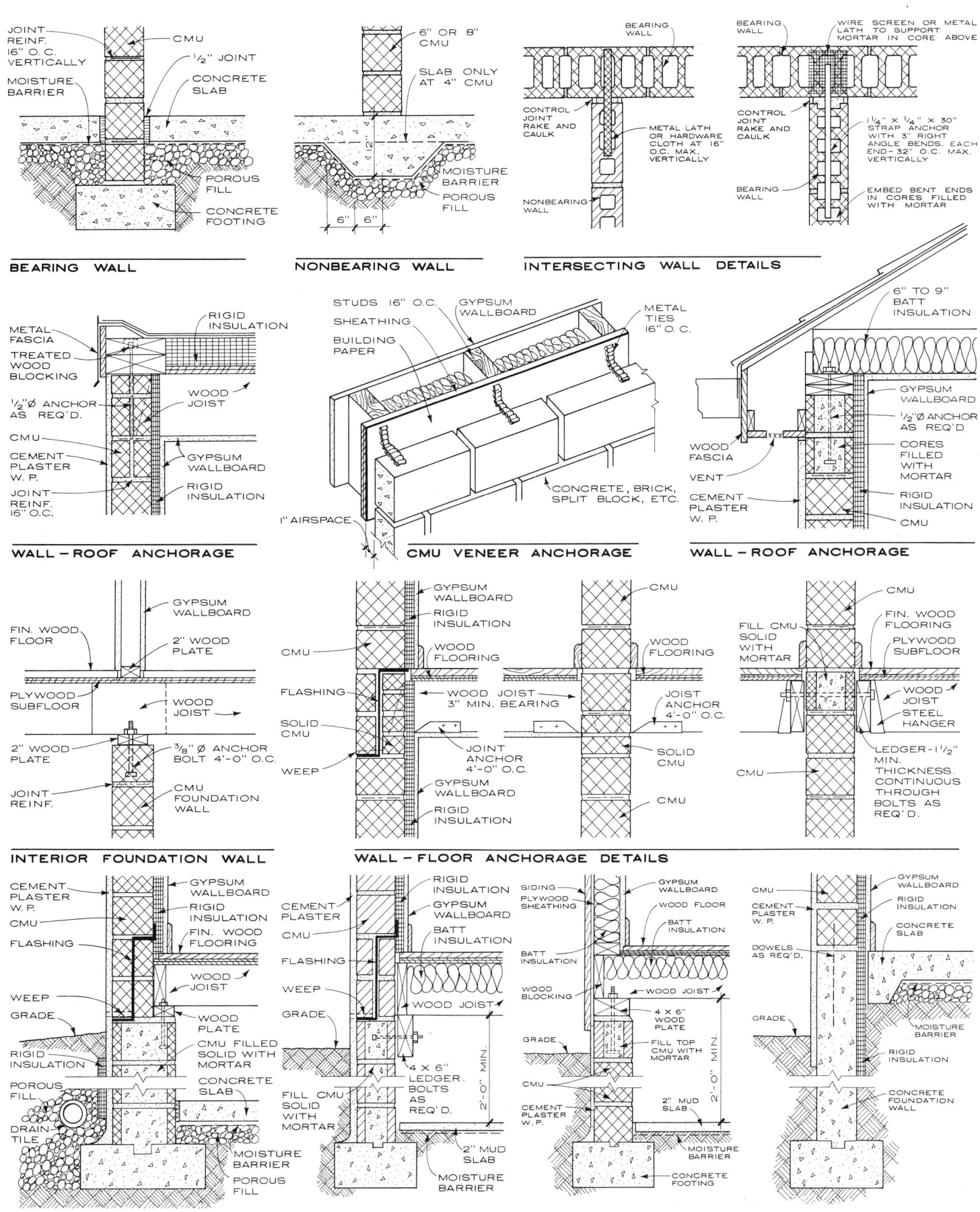

BEARING WALL

JOINT REINF. 16" O.C. VERTICALLY
CMU
1/2" JOINT
CONCRETE SLAB
MOISTURE BARRIER
POROUS FILL
CONCRETE FOOTING

NONBEARING WALL

6" OR 8" CMU
SLAB ONLY AT 4" CMU
MOISTURE BARRIER
POROUS FILL
6" 6"

INTERSECTING WALL DETAILS

BEARING WALL
CONTROL JOINT RAKE AND CAULK
METAL LATH OR HARDWARE CLOTH AT 16" O.C. MAX. VERTICALLY
NONBEARING WALL

BEARING WALL
WIRE SCREEN OR METAL LATH TO SUPPORT MORTAR IN CORE ABOVE
CONTROL JOINT RAKE AND CAULK
1 1/4" x 1/4" x 30" STRAP ANCHOR WITH 3" RIGHT ANGLE BENDS. EACH END- 32" O.C. MAX. VERTICALLY
BEARING WALL
EMBED BENT ENDS IN CORES FILLED WITH MORTAR

WALL - ROOF ANCHORAGE

METAL FASCIA
TREATED WOOD BLOCKING
1/2"Ø ANCHOR AS REQ'D.
CMU
CEMENT PLASTER W. P.
JOINT REINF. 16" O.C.
RIGID INSULATION
WOOD JOIST
GYPSUM WALLBOARD
RIGID INSULATION

CMU VENEER ANCHORAGE

STUDS 16" O.C.
SHEATHING
BUILDING PAPER
GYPSUM WALLBOARD
METAL TIES 16" O. C.
CONCRETE, BRICK, SPLIT BLOCK, ETC.
1" AIRSPACE

WALL - ROOF ANCHORAGE

6" TO 9" BATT INSULATION
WOOD FASCIA
VENT
CEMENT PLASTER W. P.
GYPSUM WALLBOARD
1/2"Ø ANCHOR AS REQ'D
CORES FILLED WITH MORTAR
RIGID INSULATION
CMU

INTERIOR FOUNDATION WALL

FIN. WOOD FLOOR
GYPSUM WALLBOARD
2" WOOD PLATE
PLYWOOD SUBFLOOR
WOOD JOIST
2" WOOD PLATE
3/8"Ø ANCHOR BOLT 4'-0" O.C.
JOINT REINF.
CMU FOUNDATION WALL

WALL - FLOOR ANCHORAGE DETAILS

GYPSUM WALLBOARD
RIGID INSULATION
CMU
WOOD FLOORING
FLASHING
SOLID CMU
WEEP
WOOD JOIST 3" MIN. BEARING
JOINT ANCHOR 4'-0" O.C.
GYPSUM WALLBOARD
RIGID INSULATION

CMU
WOOD FLOORING
JOINT ANCHOR 4'-0" O.C.
SOLID CMU
CMU

FILL CMU SOLID WITH MORTAR
CMU
FIN. WOOD FLOORING
PLYWOOD SUBFLOOR
WOOD JOIST
STEEL HANGER
LEDGER- 1 1/2" MIN. THICKNESS. CONTINUOUS THROUGH BOLTS AS REQ'D.

FOUNDATION DETAILS—WOOD FRAME BUILDINGS

CEMENT PLASTER W. P.
CMU
FLASHING
WEEP
GRADE
RIGID INSULATION
POROUS FILL
DRAIN TILE
GYPSUM WALLBOARD
RIGID INSULATION
FIN. WOOD FLOORING
WOOD JOIST
WOOD PLATE
CMU FILLED SOLID WITH MORTAR
CONCRETE SLAB
MOISTURE BARRIER
POROUS FILL

CEMENT PLASTER
CMU
FLASHING
WEEP
GRADE
RIGID INSULATION
GYPSUM WALLBOARD
BATT INSULATION
WOOD JOIST
FILL CMU SOLID WITH MORTAR
4 x 6" LEDGER. BOLTS AS REQ'D.
2" MUD SLAB
MOISTURE BARRIER
2'-0" MIN.

SIDING
PLYWOOD SHEATHING
BATT INSULATION
WOOD BLOCKING
GRADE
CMU
CEMENT PLASTER W. P.
GYPSUM WALLBOARD
WOOD FLOOR
BATT INSULATION
WOOD JOIST
4 x 6" WOOD PLATE
FILL TOP CMU WITH MORTAR
2" MUD SLAB
MOISTURE BARRIER
CONCRETE FOOTING
2'-0" MIN.

CMU
CEMENT PLASTER W. P.
DOWELS AS REQ'D.
GRADE
GYPSUM WALLBOARD
RIGID INSULATION
CONCRETE SLAB
MOISTURE BARRIER
RIGID INSULATION
CONCRETE FOUNDATION WALL

Robert J. Sangiamo, AIA; New York, New York

Davis, Brody & Associates; New York, New York

UNIT MASONRY 4

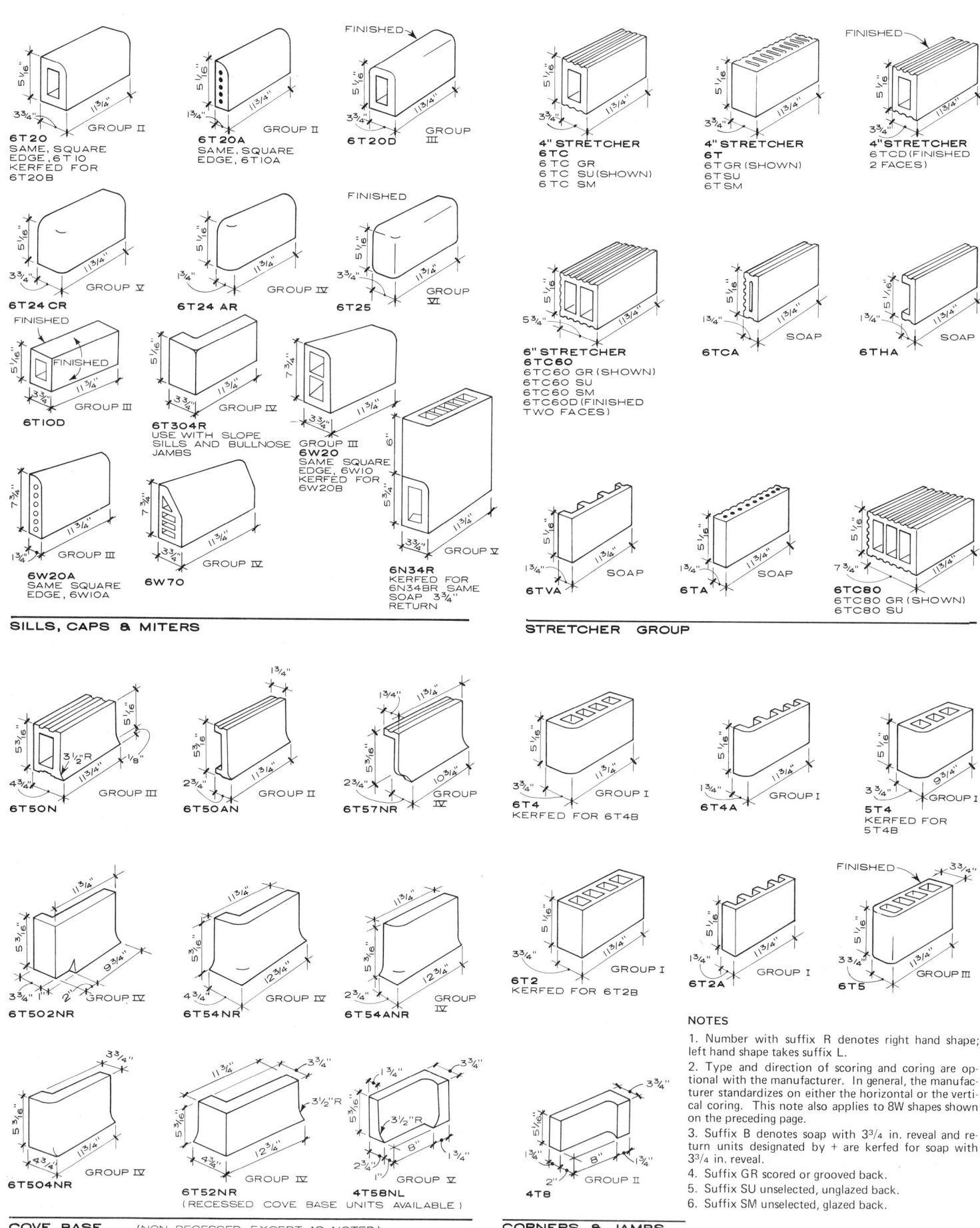

6T20
SAME, SQUARE EDGE, 6T10 KERFED FOR 6T20B
GROUP II

6T20A
SAME, SQUARE EDGE, 6T10A
GROUP II

6T20D
GROUP III

4" STRETCHER 6TC
6TC GR
6TC SU (SHOWN)
6TC SM

4" STRETCHER 6T
6TGR (SHOWN)
6TSU
6TSM

4" STRETCHER 6TCD (FINISHED 2 FACES)

6T24CR
GROUP V

6T24AR
GROUP IV

6T25
GROUP VI

6" STRETCHER 6TC60
6TC60 GR (SHOWN)
6TC60 SU
6TC60 SM
6TC60D (FINISHED TWO FACES)

6TCA
SOAP

6THA
SOAP

6T10D
GROUP III

6T304R
USE WITH SLOPE SILLS AND BULLNOSE JAMBS
GROUP IV

6W20
GROUP III
SAME SQUARE EDGE, 6W10 KERFED FOR 6W20B

6W20A
SAME SQUARE EDGE, 6W10A
GROUP III

6W70
GROUP IV

6N34R
KERFED FOR 6N34BR SAME SOAP 3¾ RETURN
GROUP V

6TVA
SOAP

6TA
SOAP

6TC80
6TC80 GR (SHOWN)
6TC80 SU

SILLS, CAPS & MITERS

STRETCHER GROUP

6T50N
GROUP III

6T50AN
GROUP II

6T57NR
GROUP IV

6T4
KERFED FOR 6T4B
GROUP I

6T4A
GROUP I

5T4
KERFED FOR 5T4B
GROUP I

6T502NR
GROUP IV

6T54NR
GROUP IV

6T54ANR
GROUP IV

6T2
KERFED FOR 6T2B
GROUP I

6T2A
GROUP I

6T5
GROUP III

6T504NR
GROUP IV

6T52NR
GROUP IV
(RECESSED COVE BASE UNITS AVAILABLE)

4T58NL
GROUP V

4T8
GROUP II

COVE BASE (NON RECESSED EXCEPT AS NOTED)

CORNERS & JAMBS

NOTES

1. Number with suffix R denotes right hand shape; left hand shape takes suffix L.

2. Type and direction of scoring and coring are optional with the manufacturer. In general, the manufacturer standardizes on either the horizontal or the vertical coring. This note also applies to 8W shapes shown on the preceding page.

3. Suffix B denotes soap with 3¾ in. reveal and return units designated by + are kerfed for soap with 3¾ in. reveal.

4. Suffix GR scored or grooved back.

5. Suffix SU unselected, unglazed back.

6. Suffix SM unselected, glazed back.

Facing Tile Institute; Washington, D.C.

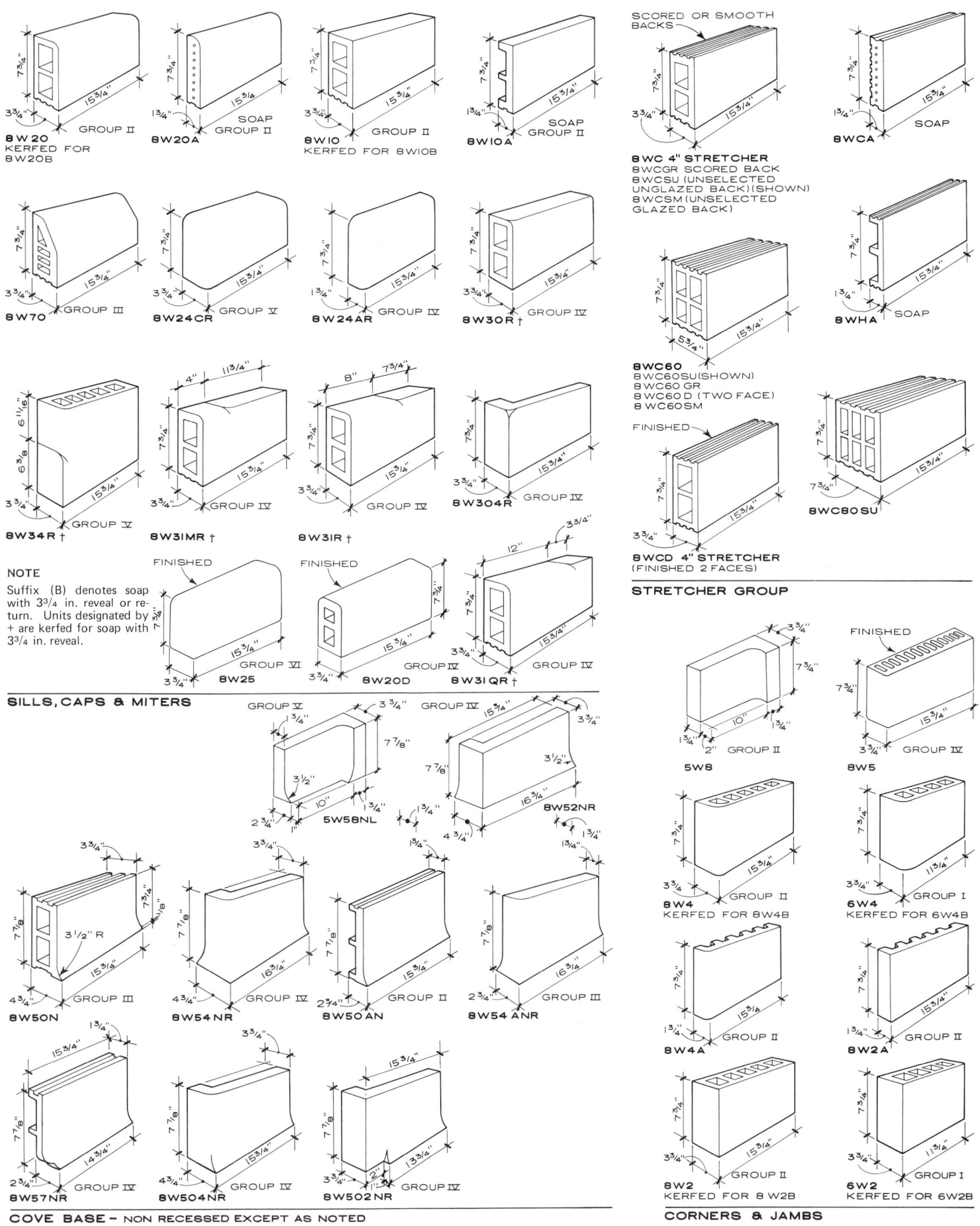

8W20
KERFED FOR
8W20B
7 3/4" 15 3/4" 3 3/4"
GROUP II

8W20A
SOAP
GROUP II
7 3/4" 15 3/4" 1 3/4"

8W10
KERFED FOR 8W10B
GROUP II
7 3/4" 15 3/4" 3 3/4"

8W10A
SOAP
GROUP II
7 3/4" 15 3/4" 1 3/4"

SCORED OR SMOOTH BACKS
8WC 4" STRETCHER
8WCGR SCORED BACK
8WCSU (UNSELECTED
UNGLAZED BACK)(SHOWN)
8WCSM (UNSELECTED
GLAZED BACK)
7 3/4" 15 3/4" 3 3/4"

8WCA
SOAP
7 3/4" 15 3/4" 1 3/4"

8W70
GROUP III
7 3/4" 15 3/4" 3 3/4"

8W24CR
GROUP V
7 3/4" 15 3/4" 3 3/4"

8W24AR
GROUP IV
7 3/4" 15 3/4" 1 3/4"

8W30R †
GROUP IV
7 3/4" 15 3/4" 3 3/4"

8WC60
8WC60SU(SHOWN)
8WC60 GR
8WC60 D (TWO FACE)
8WC60SM
7 3/4" 15 3/4" 5 3/4"

8WHA
SOAP
7 3/4" 15 3/4" 1 3/4"

8W34R †
GROUP V
6 1/16" 6 3/8" 15 3/4" 3 3/4"

8W31MR †
GROUP IV
4" 11 3/4" 7 3/4" 15 3/4" 3 3/4"

8W31R †
GROUP IV
8" 7 3/4" 15 3/4" 3 3/4"

8W304R
GROUP IV
7 3/4" 15 3/4" 3 3/4"

FINISHED
8WCD 4" STRETCHER
(FINISHED 2 FACES)
7 3/4" 15 3/4" 3 3/4"

NOTE
Suffix (B) denotes soap with 3 3/4 in. reveal or return. Units designated by † are kerfed for soap with 3 3/4 in. reveal.

FINISHED
8W25
GROUP VI
15 3/4" 3 3/4"

FINISHED
8W20D
GROUP IV
15 3/4" 3 3/4"

8W31QR †
GROUP IV
3 3/4" 12" 7 3/4" 15 3/4" 3 3/4"

STRETCHER GROUP

5W8
GROUP II
10" 7 3/4" 15 3/4" 1 3/4" 2" 3 3/4"

FINISHED
8W5
GROUP IV
7 3/4" 15 3/4" 3 3/4"

SILLS, CAPS & MITERS

GROUP V
5W58NL
7 7/8" 3 1/2" 10" 2 3/4" 1" 1 3/4" 3 3/4"

GROUP IV
8W52NR
7 7/8" 3 1/2" 16 3/4" 4 3/4" 1 3/4" 1 3/4" 3 3/4" 15 3/4"

8W50N
GROUP III
3 3/4" 7 7/8" 3 1/2" R 15 3/4" 4 3/4"

8W54NR
GROUP IV
3 3/4" 7 7/8" 16 3/4" 4 3/4"

8W50AN
GROUP II
7 7/8" 15 3/4" 2 3/4"

8W54ANR
GROUP III
7 7/8" 16 3/4" 2 3/4"

8W4
GROUP II
KERFED FOR 8W4B
7 3/4" 15 3/4" 3 3/4"

6W4
GROUP I
KERFED FOR 6W4B
7 3/4" 11 3/4" 3 3/4"

8W4A
GROUP II
7 3/4" 15 3/4" 1 3/4"

8W2A
GROUP II
7 3/4" 11 3/4" 1 3/4"

8W57NR
GROUP IV
15 3/4" 7 7/8" 14 3/4" 2 3/4"

8W504NR
GROUP IV
3 3/4" 7 7/8" 15 3/4" 4 3/4"

8W502NR
GROUP IV
15 3/4" 7 7/8" 13 3/4" 3 3/4" 2"

8W2
GROUP II
KERFED FOR 8W2B
7 3/4" 15 3/4" 3 3/4"

6W2
GROUP I
KERFED FOR 6W2B
7 3/4" 11 3/4" 3 3/4"

COVE BASE - NON RECESSED EXCEPT AS NOTED

CORNERS & JAMBS

Facing Tile Institute; Washington, D.C.

VERTICAL COURSING

NUMBER OF COURSES	5 1/3" NOMINAL HEIGHT	8" NOMINAL HEIGHT
1	5 5/16"	8"
2	10 5/8"	1' 4"
3	1' 4"	2' 0"
4	1' 9 5/16"	2' 8"
5	2' 2 5/8"	3' 4"
6	2' 8"	4' 0"
7	3' 1 5/16"	4' 8"
8	3' 6 5/8"	5' 4"
9	4' 0"	6' 0"
10	4' 5 5/16"	6' 8"
11	4' 10 5/8"	7' 4"
12	5' 4"	8' 0"
13	5' 9 5/16"	8' 8"
14	6' 2 5/8"	9' 4"
15	6' 8"	10' 0"
16	7' 1 5/16"	10' 8"
17	7' 6 5/8"	11' 4"
18	8' 0"	12' 0"
19	8' 5 5/16"	12' 8"
20	8' 10 5/8"	13' 4"
21	9' 4"	14' 0"
22	9' 9 5/16"	14' 8"
23	10' 2 5/8"	15' 4"
24	10' 8"	16' 0"
25	11' 1 5/16"	16' 8"
26	11' 6 5/8"	17' 4"
27	12' 0"	18' 0"
28	12' 5 5/16"	18' 8"
29	12' 10 5/8"	19' 4"
30	13' 4"	20' 0"
31	13' 9 5/16"	20' 8"
32	14' 2 5/8"	21' 4"
33	14' 8"	22' 0"
34	15' 1 5/16"	22' 8"
35	15' 6 5/8"	23' 4"
36	16' 0"	24' 0"
37	16' 5 5/16"	24' 8"
38	16' 10 5/8"	25' 4"
39	17' 4"	26' 0"
40	17' 9 5/16"	26' 8"
41	18' 2 5/8"	27' 4"
42	18' 8"	28' 0"
43	19' 1 5/16"	28' 8"
44	19' 6 5/8"	29' 4"
45	20' 0"	30' 0"
46	20' 5 5/16"	30' 8"
47	20' 10 5/8"	31' 4"
48	21' 4"	32' 0"
49	21' 9 5/16"	32' 8"
50	22' 2 5/8"	33' 4"

Note: For convenience in using scale, 1/3" dimensions are changed to 5/16"

Bucks should be filled with mortar to provide sound attenuation

Panic-safe internal corners are possible using standard stretcher units in block bond with as few as 5 units, 3/8" joints producing a quarter circle with radius of 1' 1 1/8" or 9 units, 1/4" joints with a radius of 1'-11". See mfgrs data.

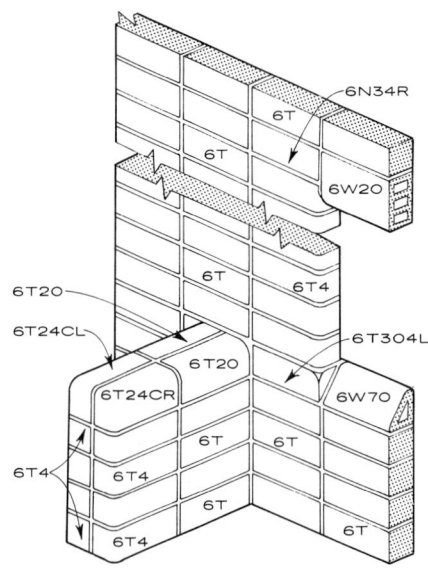

EIGHT INCH DOUBLE-FACED WING WALL BONDED TO MAIN WALL WITH TYPICAL BUTT JOINTS, STACK BOND

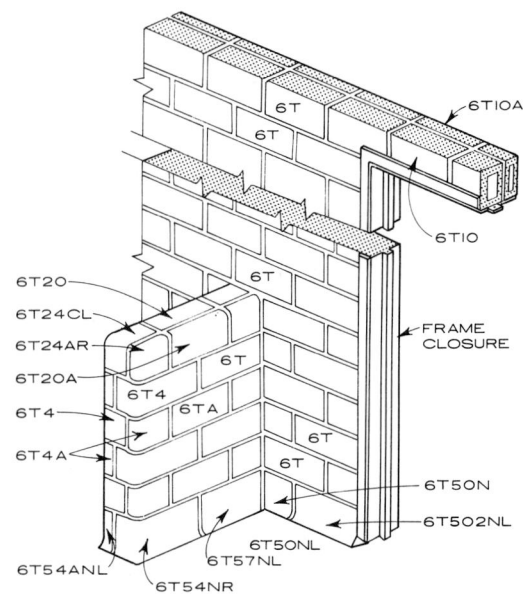

SIX INCH DOUBLE-FACED WING WALL BONDED TO MAIN WALL WITH TYPICAL BUTT JOINTS

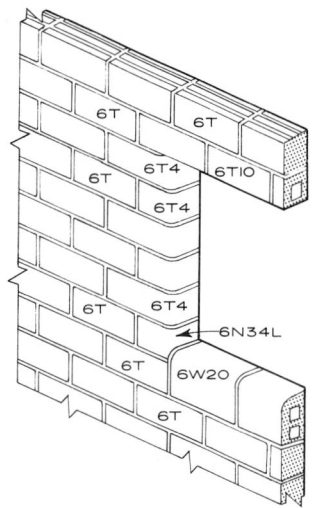

FOUR INCH SINGLE-FACED WALL WITH BULLNOSE SILL AND JAMB. SQUARE LINTEL RUNNING BOND

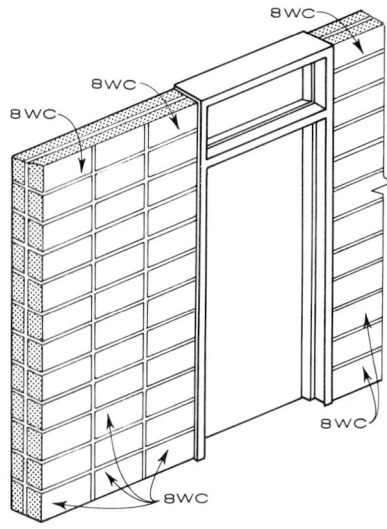

ECONOMY WALL CONSTRUCTION NO SHAPES REQUIRED FULL HEIGHT TRANSOM. 8W SERIES STACK BOND

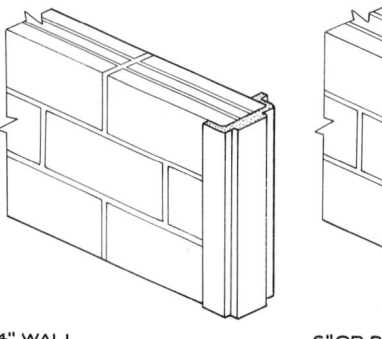

4" WALL

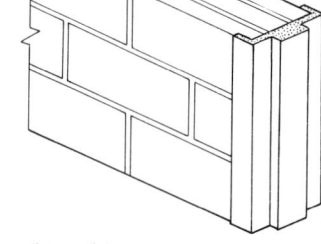

6" OR 8" WALL

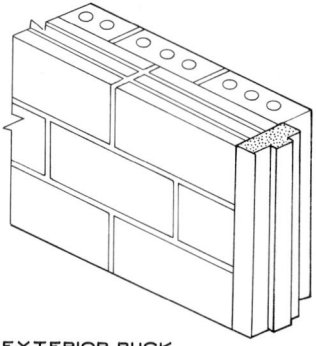

EXTERIOR BUCK

FRAME FITTINGS

Facing Tile Institute; Washington, D.C.

 UNIT MASONRY

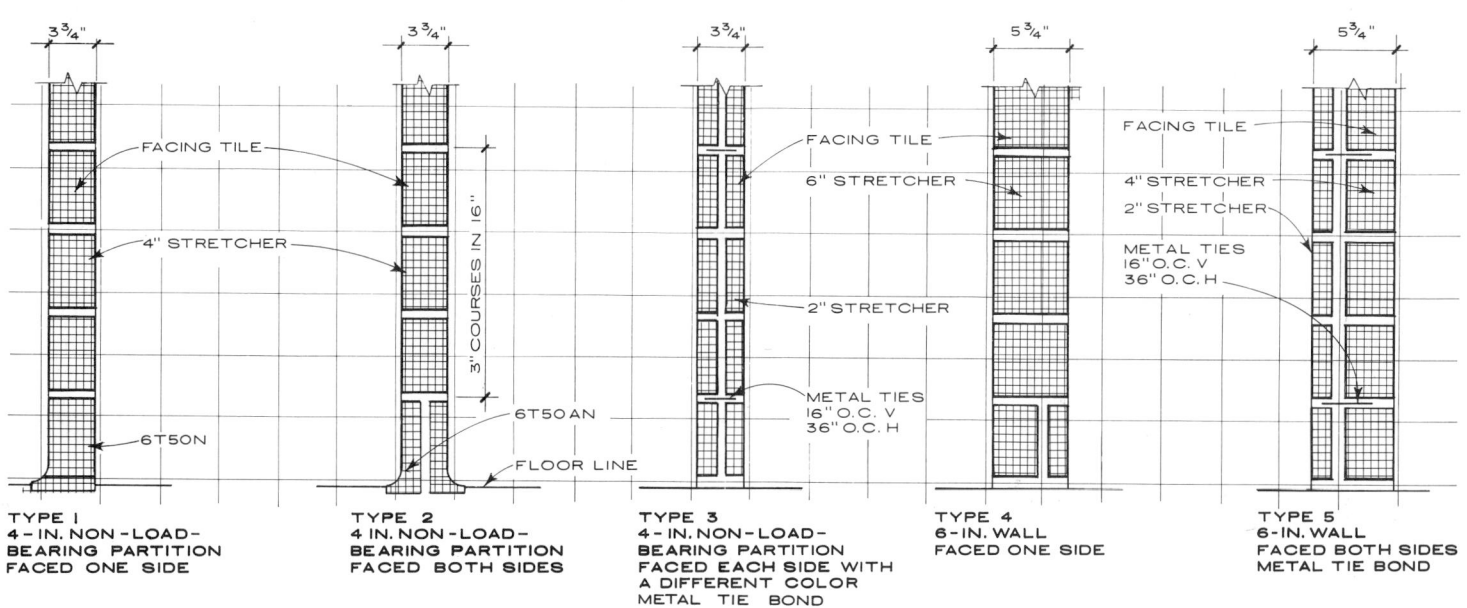

TYPE 1
4-IN. NON-LOAD-
BEARING PARTITION
FACED ONE SIDE

TYPE 2
4 IN. NON-LOAD-
BEARING PARTITION
FACED BOTH SIDES

TYPE 3
4-IN. NON-LOAD-
BEARING PARTITION
FACED EACH SIDE WITH
A DIFFERENT COLOR
METAL TIE BOND

TYPE 4
6-IN. WALL
FACED ONE SIDE

TYPE 5
6-IN. WALL
FACED BOTH SIDES
METAL TIE BOND

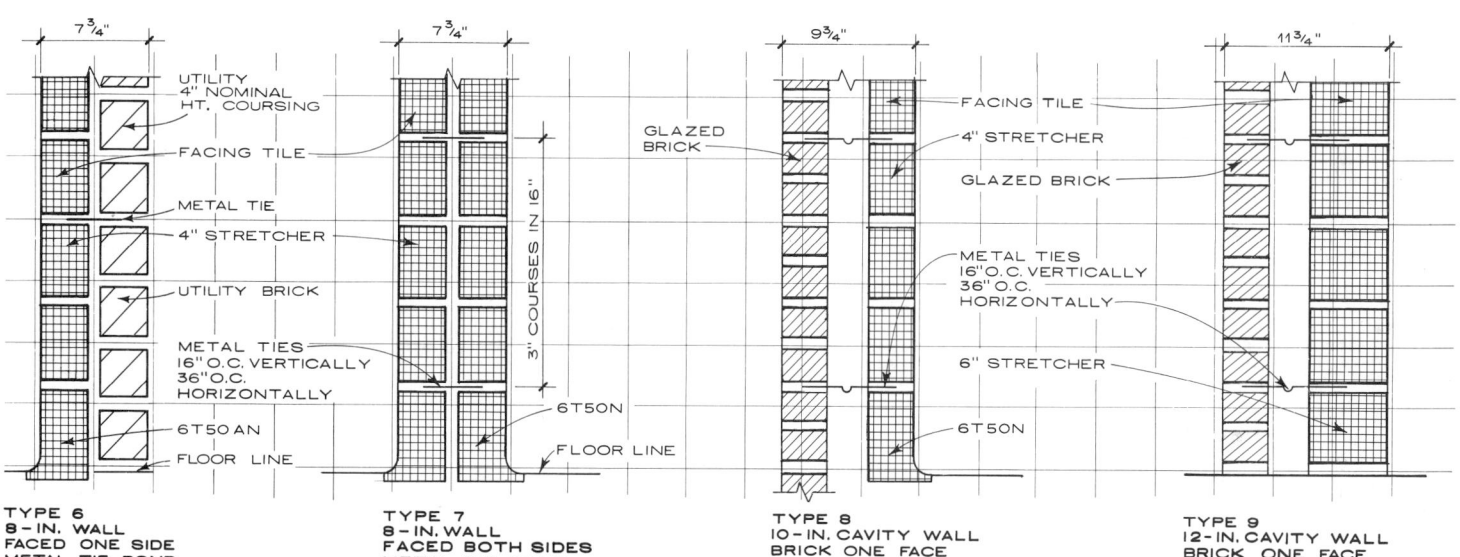

TYPE 6
8-IN. WALL
FACED ONE SIDE
METAL TIE BOND

TYPE 7
8-IN. WALL
FACED BOTH SIDES
METAL TIE BOND

TYPE 8
10-IN. CAVITY WALL
BRICK ONE FACE
TILE ONE FACE

TYPE 9
12-IN. CAVITY WALL
BRICK ONE FACE
TILE ONE FACE

WALL SECTIONS AND PROPERTIES

WALL TYPE NUMBER		1	2	3	4	5	6	7	8	9
Allowable load (lb/linear ft)	Type M mortar (85 psi)				5870	5870	5870	7900	6300[2]	7970[2]
	Type S mortar (75 psi)				5180	5180	5180	6980	5400[2]	6840[2]
	Type N mortar (70 psi)				4830	4830	4830	6510	4950[2]	6270[2]
Material quantity (per 100 sq ft)	Mortar (cu ft) 25% waste added	2.19	2.19	2.19	3.36	3.36[1]	3.36	4.531[1]	6.97	8.14
	Facing tile 2% waste added	230	230	460	230	230	230	460	230	230
	Brick 5% waste added						230		709	709
	Metal ties 2% waste added			25.5		25.5	25.5	25.5	25.5	25.5
U Values (BTU/sq ft · hr · °F)	Unplastered partition	0.40	0.40	0.39	0.35	0.34	0.34	0.30		
	Exterior wall								0.30	0.23
	With 2 in. insulation								0.08	0.08
Lateral support spacing required (ft)	Non-load bearing	12	12	12	18	18	18	24	24	30
	Load-bearing				9	9	9	12	12	15
Wall weight	Unplastered	30	30	33	41	47	47	60	67	79
Sound resistance (dB)	Unplastered	45	45	46	47	48	48	50	54	58
Fire resistance (hr)	Regular coring	*	*	1	1	2		2	3	4
	Fire rated coring	1	1	1	2	3		4	4	4

NOTE

*3/4 in. plaster on back of these units will produce 1 hour fire rating.

[1] If collar joint is filled, add 2.6 cu ft per 100 sq ft of wall.

[2] Eccentrically loaded. For concentric loading increase allowable load 25 per cent.

Facing Tile Institute; Washington, D.C.

UNIT MASONRY **4**

GENERAL NOTES

Natural stone has a wide variety of applications in building, as a facing, a veneer, or decoration. The major factors and dangers in the suitability and use of stone fall under two broad but overlapping headings: strength properties and aesthetic qualities. The three features of building stone that most affect their selection by architects for aesthetic reasons are color, pattern, and texture.

To obtain an accurate picture of stone colors, it is recommended that you use a color chart, such as the Rock Color Chart, published by the Geological Society of America (Boulder, Colorado 80302).

Patterns are highly varied and impart the special features that make building stones a unique material.

Texture also is varied and ranges from coarse fragments to fine grains and crystalline structures. It varies with the hardness of minerals composing the stone and the manner in which the stone is fabricated, such as cleavage and polishing.

The three classes of rock are igneous, sedimentary, and metamorphic. The common construction stones are marketed under the names given in the following table, although specialty stones such as soapstone or serpentine are sold under their names. Each type of stone listed has various commercial grades. Limestone, for example, is sold under three categories quarried in different locations, of two types (oolitic and dolomitic). Travertine is also classed as a limestone.

Factors in selecting stone include strength and aesthetic qualities. Color, pattern, and texture are important features of stone, affected by fabrication methods and finish. Granites and slates tend to hold their colors, while limestone may change under exposure.

Physical characteristics of stone must be suitable for its intended use. Moisture penetration, weatherability, and resistance to pollution may be decisive factors for exterior facing, as well as anchorage and joint design.

Consideration may be given to the following minimum list of selection factors:

1. Price.
2. Availability.
3. Finishes available.
4. Absorption, weatherability.
5. Color.
6. Thickness limitations.

Developments in the detailing of stone have helped to control cost, using new systems of installation. Factors involved in detailing include design of joints, selection of mortars, and the use of sealants. Proper attention to anchorage of each piece of stone is important, and the use of relieving angles may be required to prevent excessive compressive loads.

Since detailing varies with each installation, the designer should be aware of the technical aspects of designing with stone and should work closely with the stone suppliers and the stone setting specialty contractors.

STONE CLASSIFIED ACCORDING TO QUALITIES AFFECTING USE

CLASS	COLOR	TEXTURE	SPECIAL FEATURES	PARTINGS	HARDNESS	CHIEF USES
Sandstone	Very light buff to light chocolate brown or brick red; may tarnish to brown	Granular, showing sand grains, cemented together	Ripple marks; oblique color bands ("cross bedding")	Bedding planes; also fractures transverse to beds	Fairly hard if well cemented	General; walls; building; flagstone
Limestone	White, light gray to light buff	Fine to crystalline; may have fossils	May show fossils	Parallel to beds; also fractures across beds	Fairly soft; steel easily scratches	All building uses
Marble	Highly varied: snow white to black; also blue-gray and light to dark olive green; also pinkish	Finely granular to very coarsely crystalline showing flat-sided crystals	May show veins of different colors or angular rock pieces or fossils	Usually not along beds but may have irregular fractures	Slightly harder than limestone	May be used for building stone but usually in decorative panels
Granite (light igneous rock)	Almost white to pink-and-white or gray-and-white	Usually coarsely crystalline; crystals may be varicolored; may be fine grained	May be banded with pink, white or gray streaks and veins	Not necessarily any regular parting but fractures irregularly	Harder than limestone and marble; keeps cut shape well	Building stone, but also in paneling if attractively colored
Dark igneous rock	Gray, dark olive green to black; Laurvikite is beautifully crystalline	Usually coarsely crystalline if quarried but may be fine grained	May be banded with lighter and darker gray bands and veins	Not necessarily any regular parting but may facture irregularly	About like granite; retains cut shape well	Building stone but also used in panels if nicely banded or crystalline
Lavas	Varies: pink, purple, black; if usable, rarely almost white	Fine grained; may have pores locally	Note rare porosity	Not necessarily any regular parting, as a rule, but some have parallel fractures	About as strong as granite; if light colored, usually softer	Good foundation and building stone; not decorative
Quartzite	Variable: white, buff, red, brown	Dense, almost glassy	Very resistant to weather and impact	Usually no special parting	Very hard if well cemented, as usually the case	Excellent for building but hard to "shape"
Slate	Grayish-green, brick red or dark brown, usually gray; may be banded	Finely crystalline; flat crystals give slaty fracture	Some slates have color-fading with age	Splits along slate surface, often crossing color bands	Softer than granite or quartzite; scratches easily	Roofing; blackboards; paving
Gneiss	Usually gray with some pink, white or light gray bands	Crystalline, like granite, often with glassy bands (veins)	Banding is decorative; some bands very weak, however	No special parting; tends to break along banding	About like granite	Used for buildings; also may be decorative if banded

STRUCTURAL PROPERTIES OF REPRESENTATIVE STONES

STRUCTURAL PROPERTY		IGNEOUS ROCK		SEDIMENTARY ROCK		METAMORPHIC ROCK	
		GRANITE	TRAPROCK	LIMESTONE	SANDSTONE	MARBLE	SLATE
Composition—ultimate strength	(psi)	15,000–30,000	20,000	4,000–20,000	3,000–20,000	10,000–23,000	10,000–15,000
Composition—allowable working stress	(psi)	800–1,500		500–1,000	400–700	500–900	1,000
Shear—ultimate strength	(psi)	1,800–2,700		1,000–2,000	1,200–2,500	900–1,700	
Shear—allowable working stress	(psi)	200		200	150	150	
Tension—allowable working stress	(psi)	150		125	75	125	
Weight	(psf)	156–170	180–185	147–170	135–155	165–178	170–180
Specific gravity		2.4–2.7	2.96	2.1–2.8	2.0–2.6	2.4–2.8	2.7–2.8
Absorption of water (parts by weight)		1/750		1/38	1/24	1/300	1/430
Modulus of elasticity	(psi)	6–10,000,000	12,000,000	4–14,000,000	1–7,500,000	4–13,500,000	12,000,000
Coefficient of expansion	(psf)	0.0000040		0.0000045	0.0000055	0.0000045	0.0000058

NOTE: Individual samples vary greatly.

The McGuire & Shook Corporation; Indianapolis, Indiana

STONE

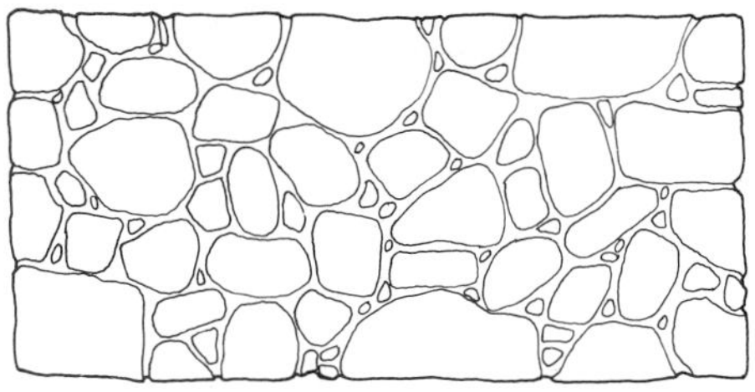

UNCOURSED FIELDSTONE PATTERN

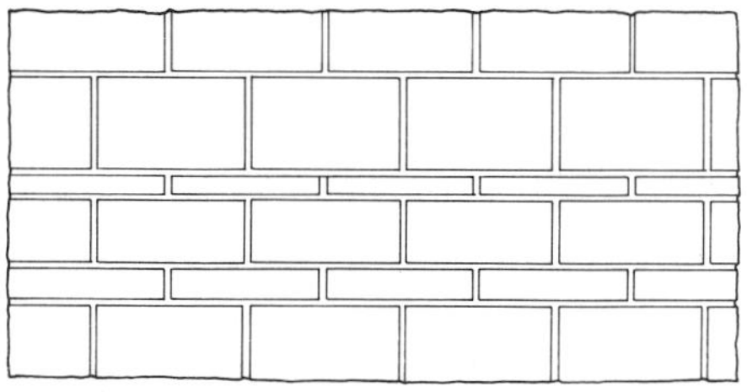

COURSED ASHLAR-RUNNING BOND

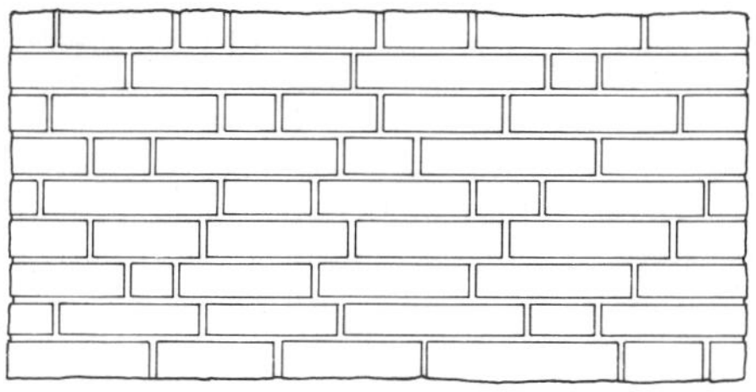

ONE-HEIGHT PATTERN (SINGLE RISE)

UNCOURSED LEDGEROCK PATTERN

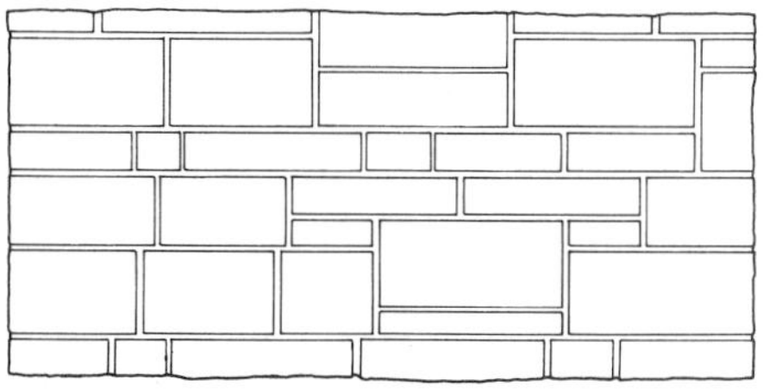

RANDOM COURSED ASHLAR

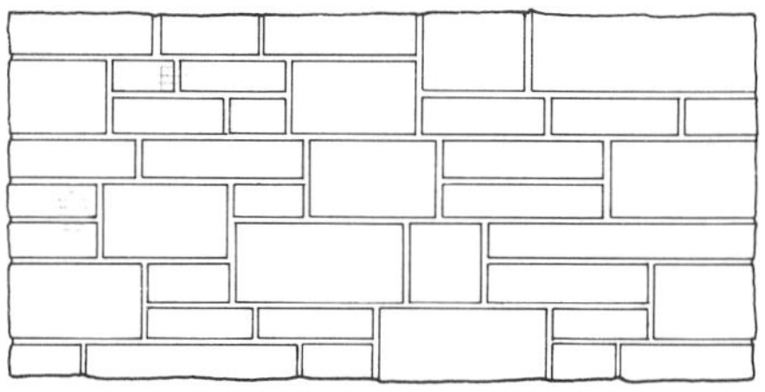

TWO-HEIGHT PATTERN (40% - 2¼"; 60% - 5")

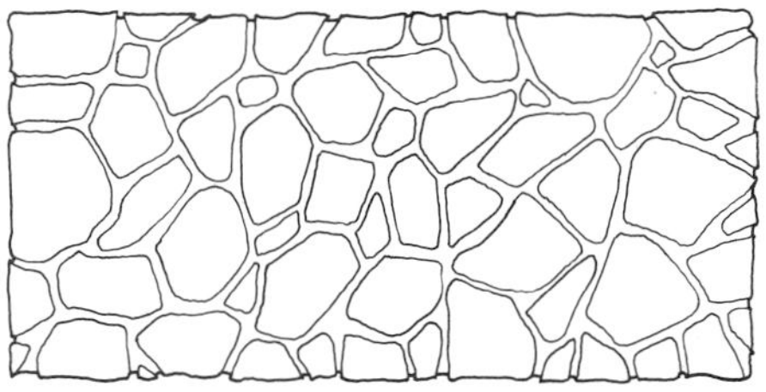

UNCOURSED WEB WALL OR MOSAIC PATTERN

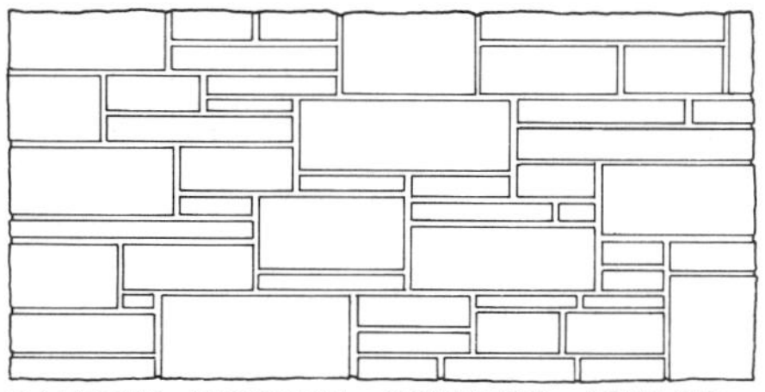

RANDOM BROKEN COURSED ASHLAR

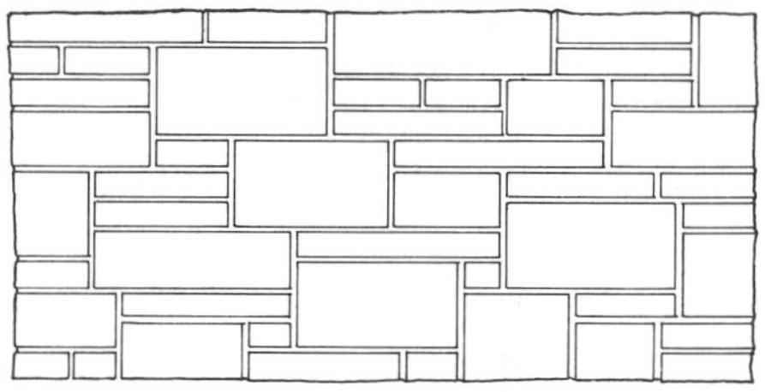

THREE-HEIGHT PATTERN (15% - 2¼"; 40% - 5"; 45% - 7¾")

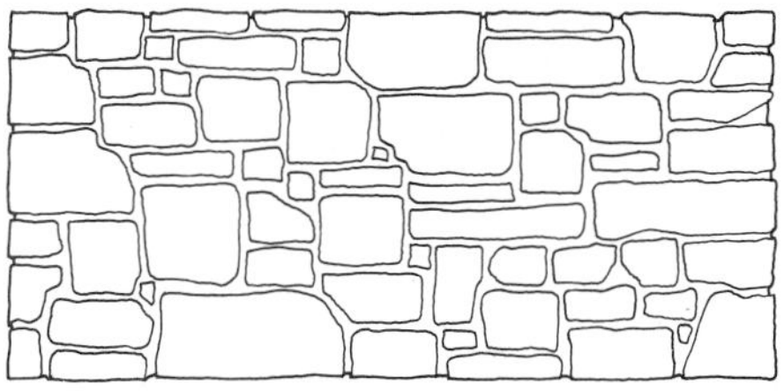

UNCOURSED ROUGHLY SQUARED PATTERN

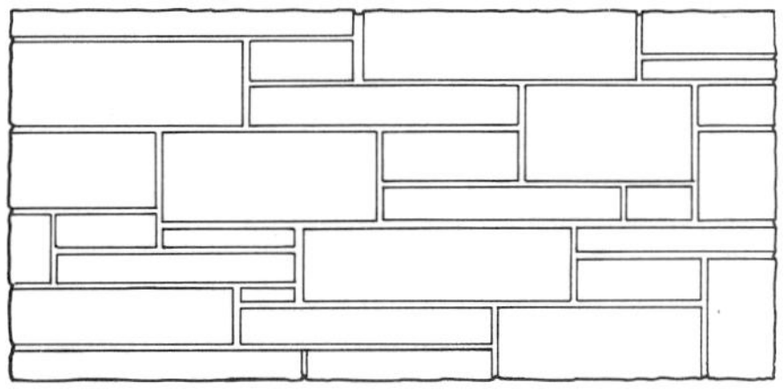

RANDOM ROUGH BEDDED ASHLAR

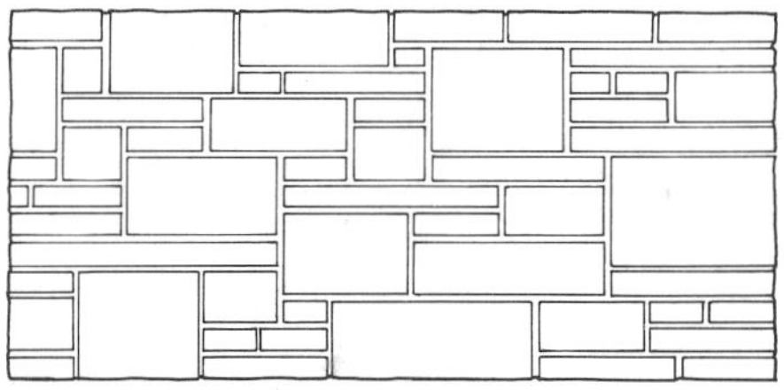

FOUR-HEIGHT PATTERN

RUBBLE STONE MASONRY PATTERNS—ELEVATIONS

SPLIT STONE MASONRY PATTERNS—ELEVATIONS

SPLIT STONE MASONRY HEIGHT PATTERNS—ELEVATIONS

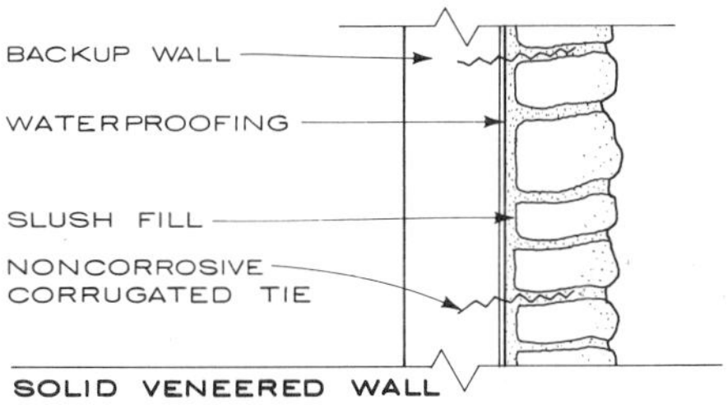

BACKUP WALL
WATERPROOFING
SLUSH FILL
NONCORROSIVE CORRUGATED TIE

SOLID VENEERED WALL

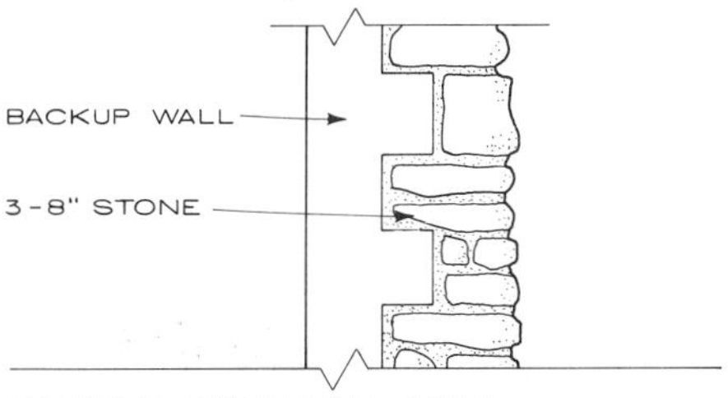

BACKUP WALL
3 - 8" STONE

BONDED VENEERED WALL
(TIES RECOMMENDED IN SOME CASES, E.G., LIMESTONE)

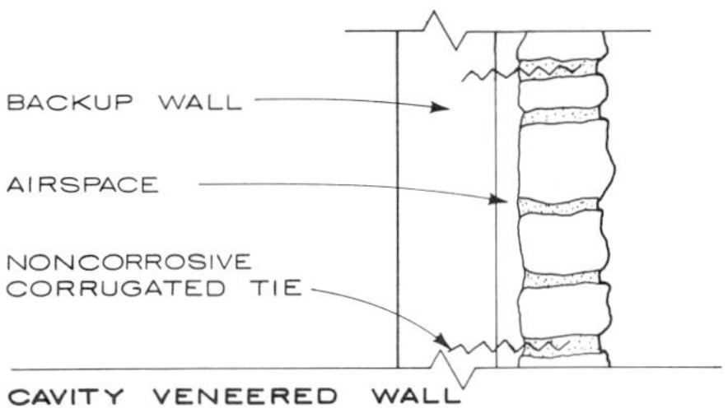

BACKUP WALL
AIRSPACE
NONCORROSIVE CORRUGATED TIE

CAVITY VENEERED WALL

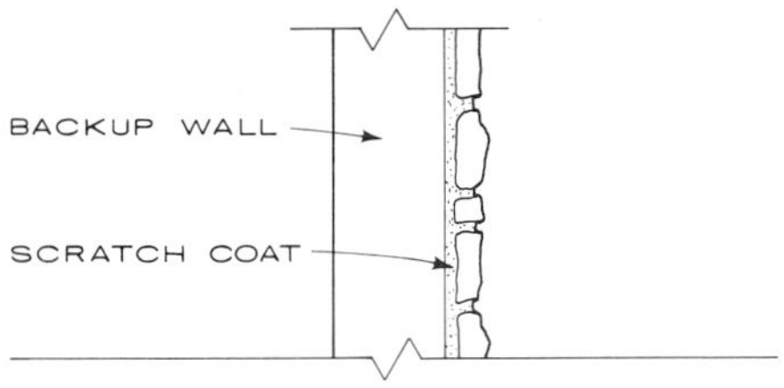

BACKUP WALL
SCRATCH COAT

THIN VENEERED WALL

TYPICAL WALL SECTIONS

GENERAL NOTES

1. A course is a horizontal row of stone. Bond pattern is described by the horizontal arrangement of vertical joints. (See also Brickwork.) Structural bond refers to the physical tying together of load bearing and veneer portions of a composite wall. Structural bond can be accomplished with metal ties or with stone units set as headers through veneer and into the backup.

2. Ashlar masonry is composed of squared-off building stone units of various sizes. Cut Ashlar is dressed to specific design dimensions at the mill. Ashlar is often used in random lengths and heights, with jointing worked out on the job.

3. All ties and anchors must be made of noncorrosive material. Chromium-nickel stainless steel types 302 and 304 and eraydo alloy zinc are the most resistant to corrosion and staining. Hot dipped galvanized is widely used, but is not as resistant, hence is prohibited by some building codes. Copper, brass, and bronze will stain under some conditions. Local building codes often govern the types of metal that may be used for stone anchors.

4. Nonstaining cement mortar should be used on porous and light colored stones. At all corners use extra ties and, when possible, larger stones. Joints are usually ½ to 1½ in. for rough work and ⅜ to ¾ in. for Ashlar.

Building Stone Institute; New York, New York

George M. Whiteside, III, AIA and James D. Lloyd; Kennett Square, Pennsylvania

Alexander Keyes; Darrel Rippeteau, Architect; Washington, D.C.

STONE 4

NOTES
1. Throughout this section, flashing, sealants, and other ancillary materials necessary for sound weatherproof construction have sometimes been omitted for the sake of clarity. See other pages for flashing and sealant details.
2. Refer to earlier editions of Architectural Graphic Standards for examples of classical moulding detailing.

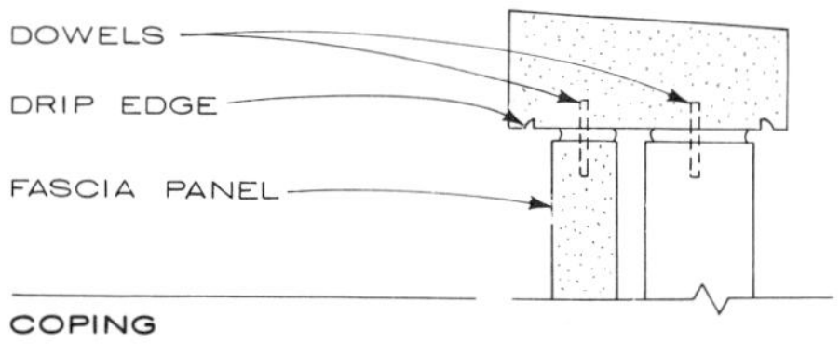

DOWELS
DRIP EDGE
FASCIA PANEL

COPING

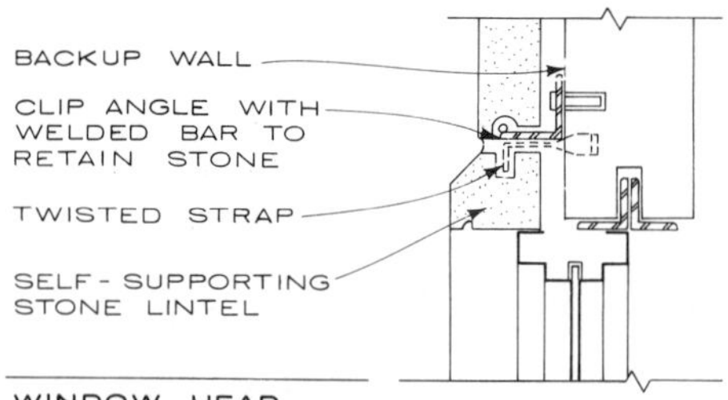

BACKUP WALL
CLIP ANGLE WITH WELDED BAR TO RETAIN STONE
TWISTED STRAP
SELF-SUPPORTING STONE LINTEL

WINDOW HEAD

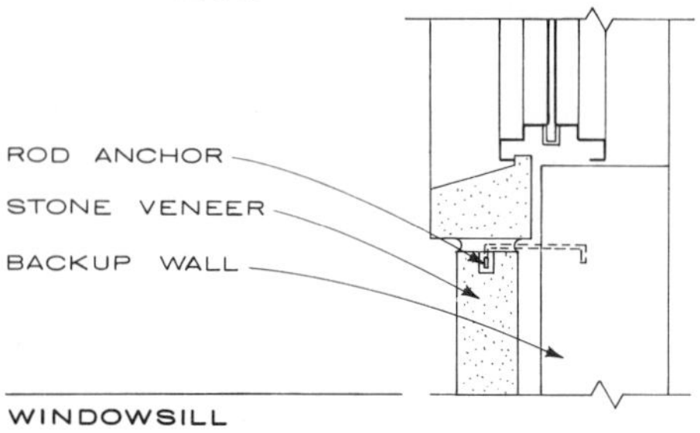

ROD ANCHOR
STONE VENEER
BACKUP WALL

WINDOWSILL

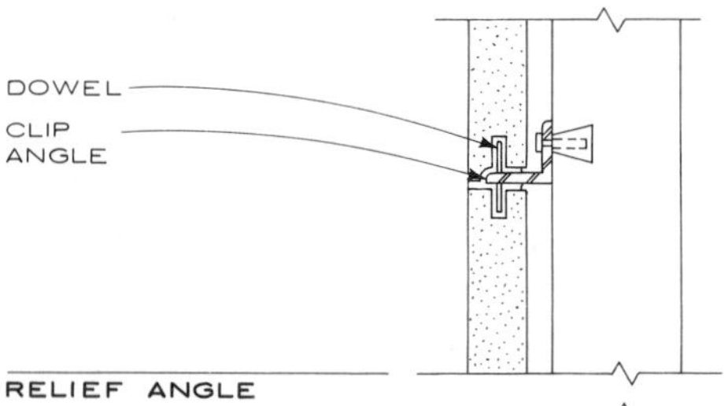

DOWEL
CLIP ANGLE

RELIEF ANGLE

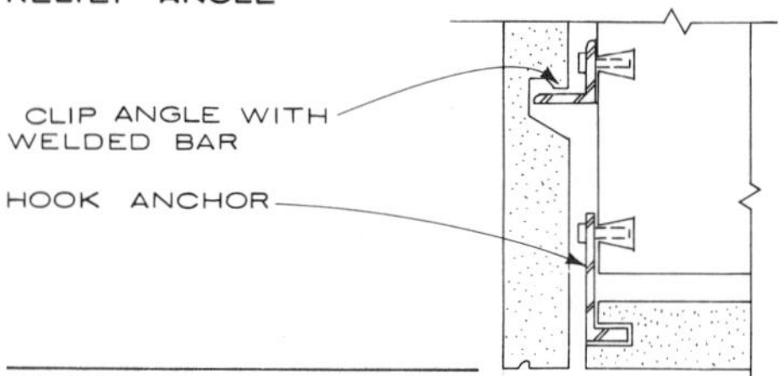

CLIP ANGLE WITH WELDED BAR
HOOK ANCHOR

SOFFIT

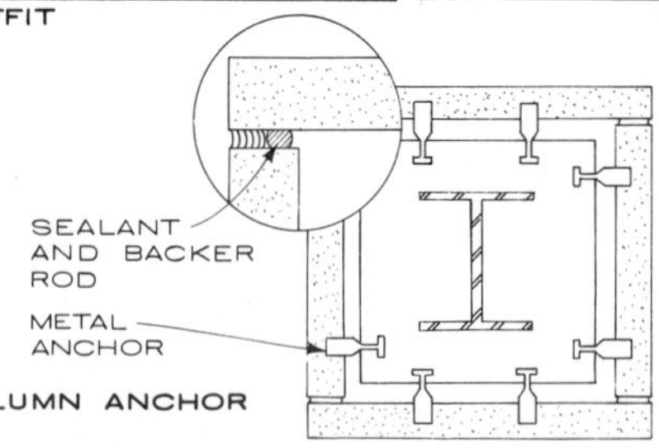

SEALANT AND BACKER ROD
METAL ANCHOR

COLUMN ANCHOR

STONE VENEER ON CONCRETE WITH MASONRY BACKUP

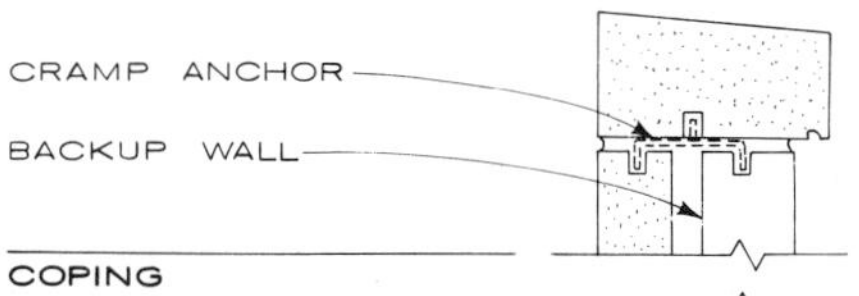

CRAMP ANCHOR
BACKUP WALL

COPING

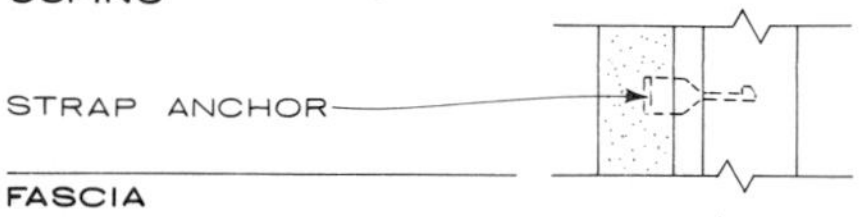

STRAP ANCHOR

FASCIA

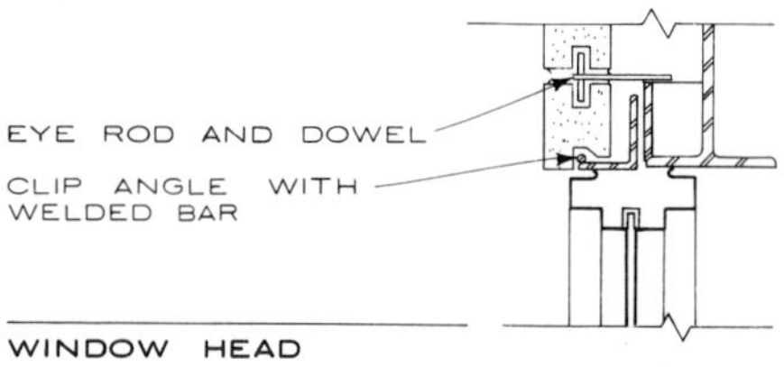

EYE ROD AND DOWEL
CLIP ANGLE WITH WELDED BAR

WINDOW HEAD

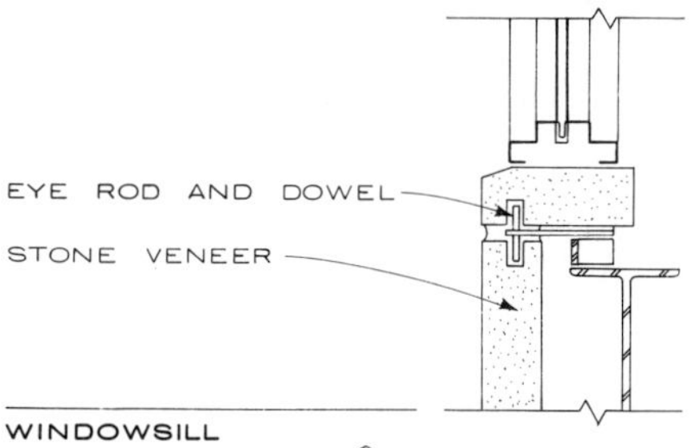

EYE ROD AND DOWEL
STONE VENEER

WINDOWSILL

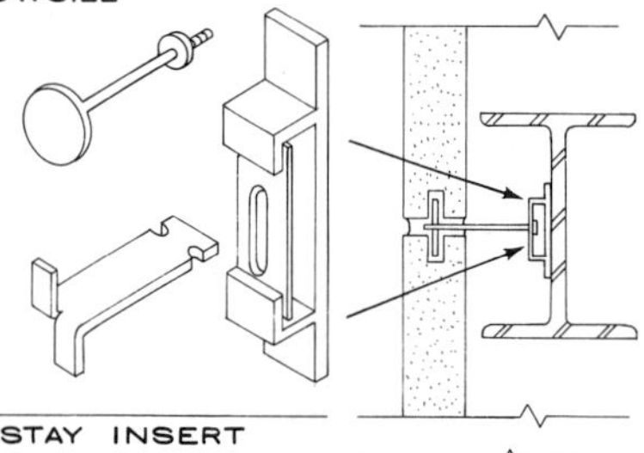

GRIP STAY INSERT

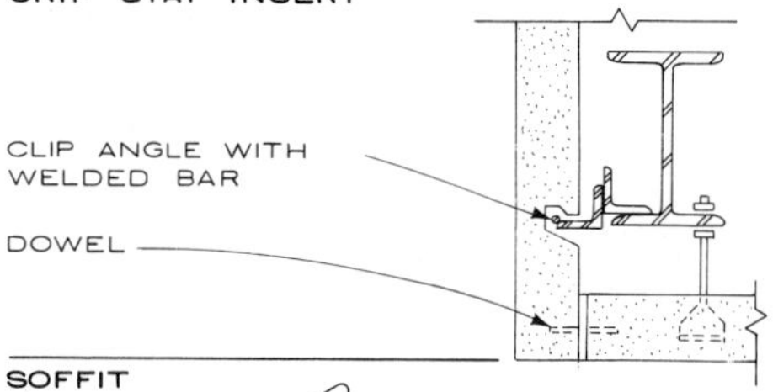

CLIP ANGLE WITH WELDED BAR
DOWEL

SOFFIT

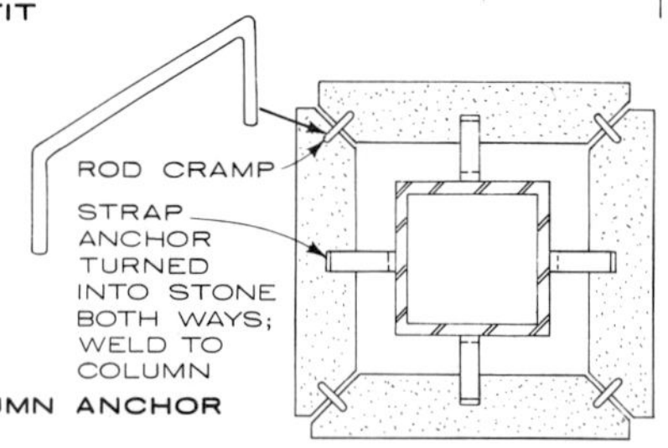

ROD CRAMP
STRAP ANCHOR TURNED INTO STONE BOTH WAYS; WELD TO COLUMN

COLUMN ANCHOR

STONE VENEER ON STEEL FRAME

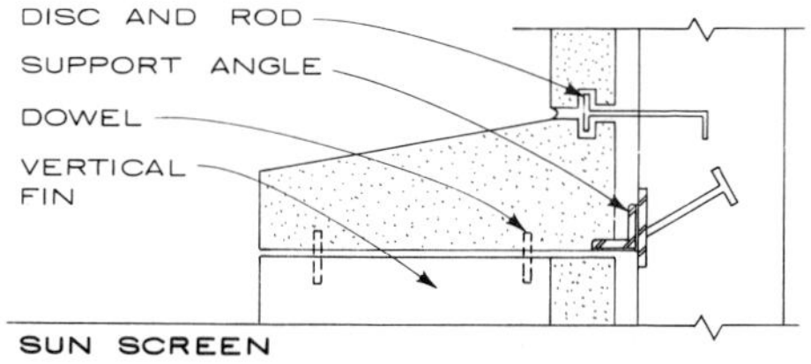

DISC AND ROD
SUPPORT ANGLE
DOWEL
VERTICAL FIN

SUN SCREEN

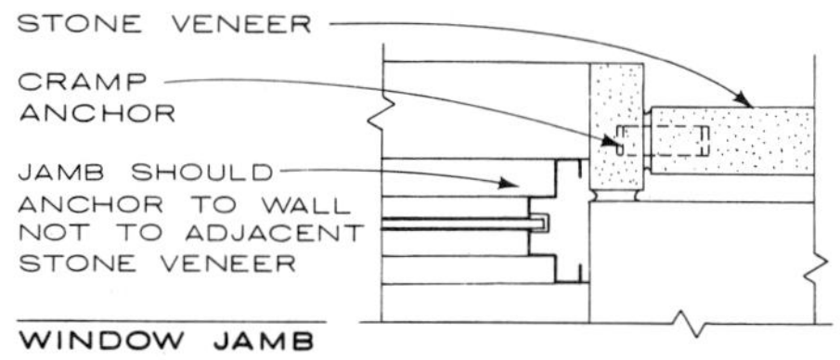

STONE VENEER
CRAMP ANCHOR
JAMB SHOULD ANCHOR TO WALL NOT TO ADJACENT STONE VENEER

WINDOW JAMB

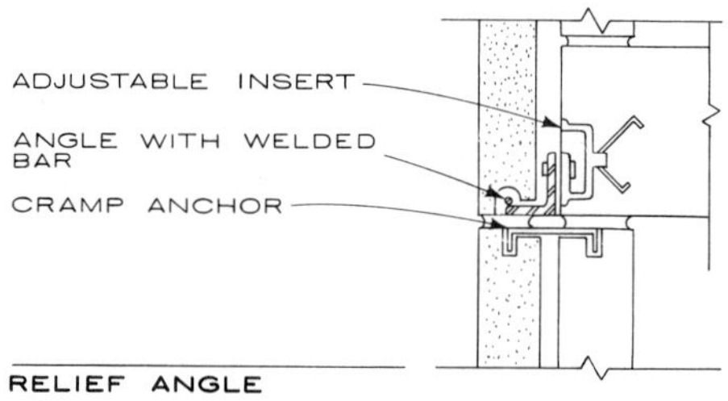

ADJUSTABLE INSERT
ANGLE WITH WELDED BAR
CRAMP ANCHOR

RELIEF ANGLE

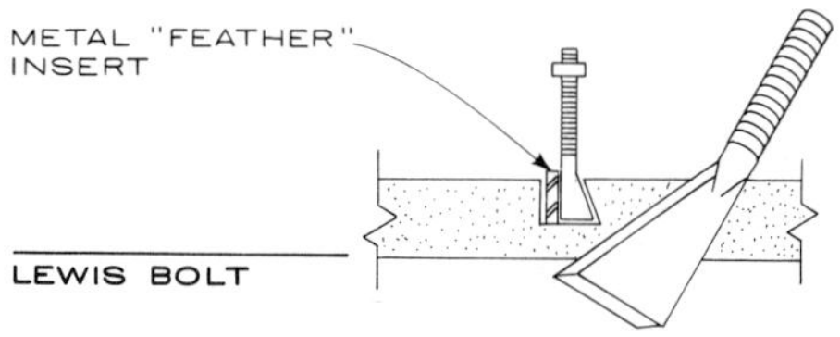

METAL "FEATHER" INSERT

LEWIS BOLT

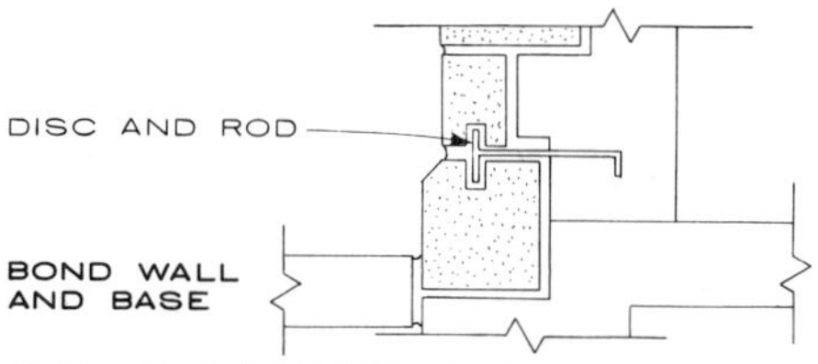

DISC AND ROD

BOND WALL AND BASE

STONE VENEER DETAILS; OPTIONS

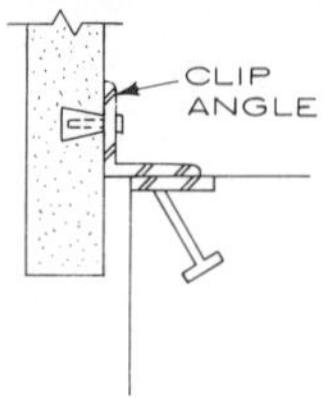

CLIP ANGLE

EXPANSION BOLT

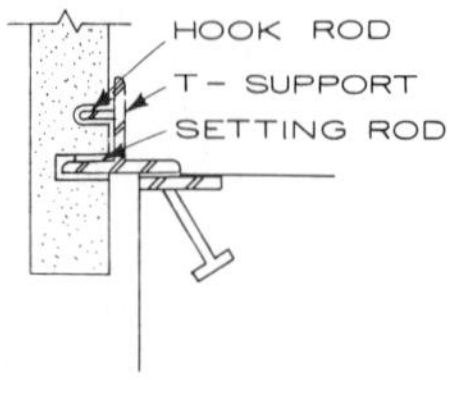

HOOK ROD
T-SUPPORT
SETTING ROD

HOOK ROD ANCHOR

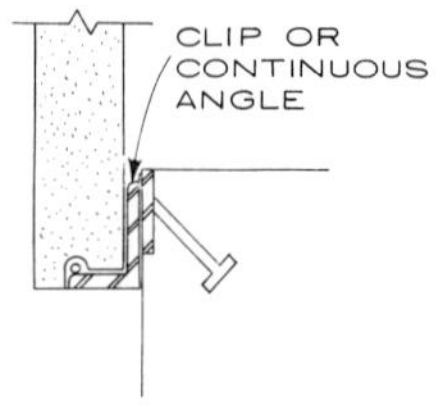

CLIP OR CONTINUOUS ANGLE

ANGLE WITH WELDED BAR

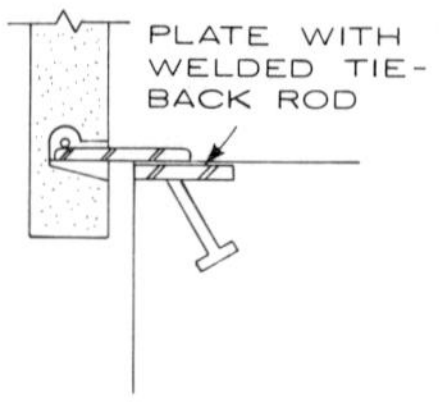

PLATE WITH WELDED TIE-BACK ROD

PLATE WITH WELDED BAR

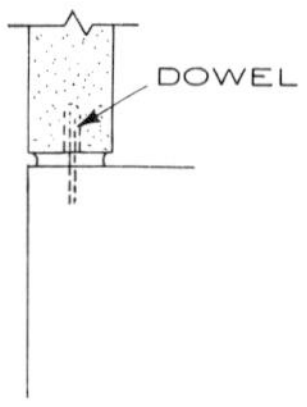

DOWEL

DOWEL PIN CONNECTION

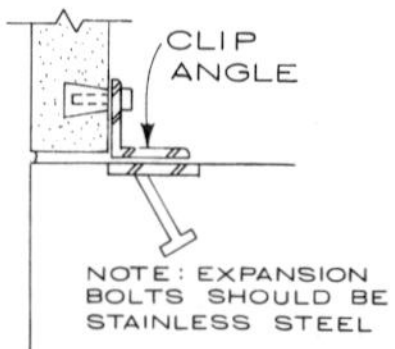

CLIP ANGLE

NOTE: EXPANSION BOLTS SHOULD BE STAINLESS STEEL

EXPANSION BOLT

BASE DETAILS

Building Stone Institute; New York, New York
George M. Whiteside, III, AIA and James D. Lloyd; Kennett Square, Pennsylvania
Alexander Keyes; Darrel Rippeteau, Architect; Washington, D.C.

STONE

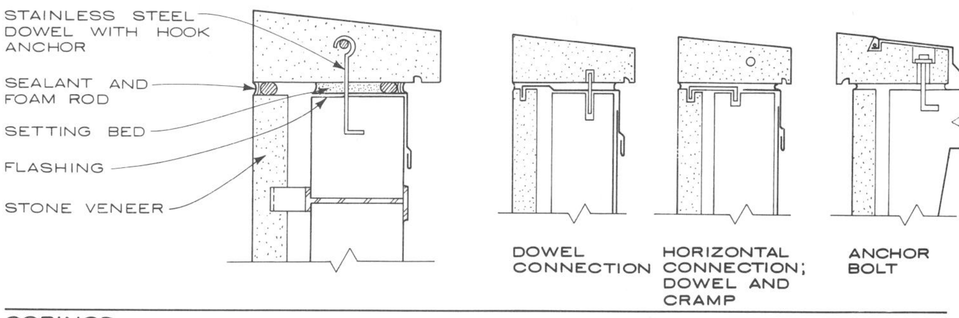

COPINGS

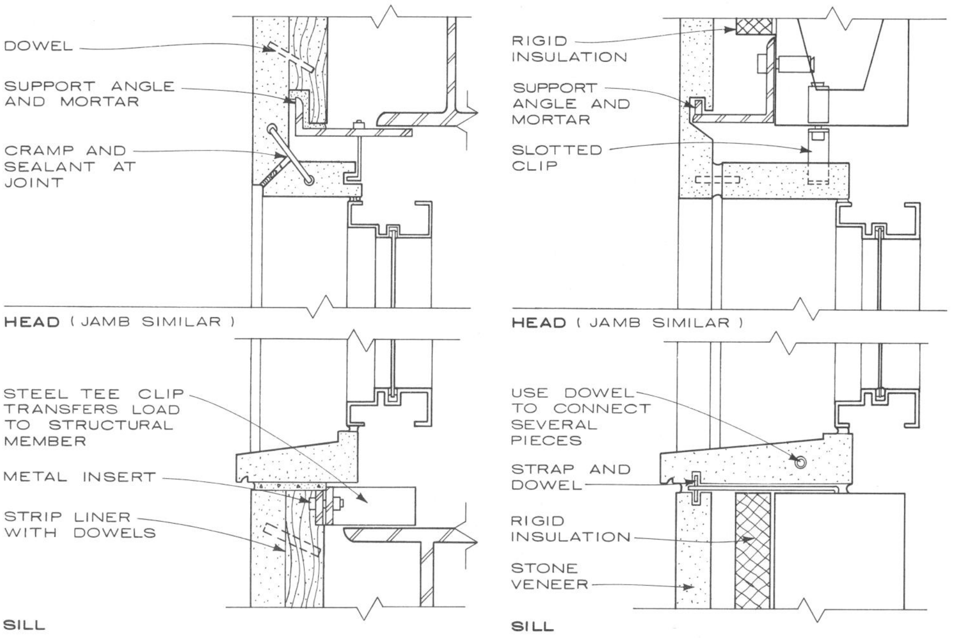

STAINLESS STEEL DOWEL WITH HOOK ANCHOR

SEALANT AND FOAM ROD

SETTING BED

FLASHING

STONE VENEER

DOWEL CONNECTION

HORIZONTAL CONNECTION; DOWEL AND CRAMP

ANCHOR BOLT

ANCHOR DIMENSIONS

Standard flat stock anchors are made from strap 1 and 1¼ in. wide by ⅛, 3/16, and ¼ in. thick. Lengths vary up to 6, 8, 10, and 12 in. standards. Dovetail anchors are usually 4¼ in. overall with 3½ in. projection from face of concrete. Bends are ¾, 1, and 1¼ in.

Round stock anchors are made from stock of any diameter: ¼ and ⅜ in. are most common for rods; ⅛ (#11 gauge) through 3/16 in. (#6 gauge) for wire anchors; and ¼ and ⅜ in. are most common for dowels. Dowel lengths are usually 2 to 6 in.

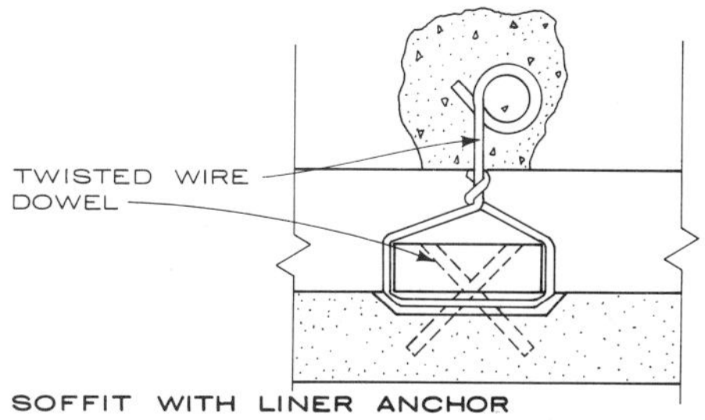

TWISTED WIRE DOWEL

SOFFIT WITH LINER ANCHOR

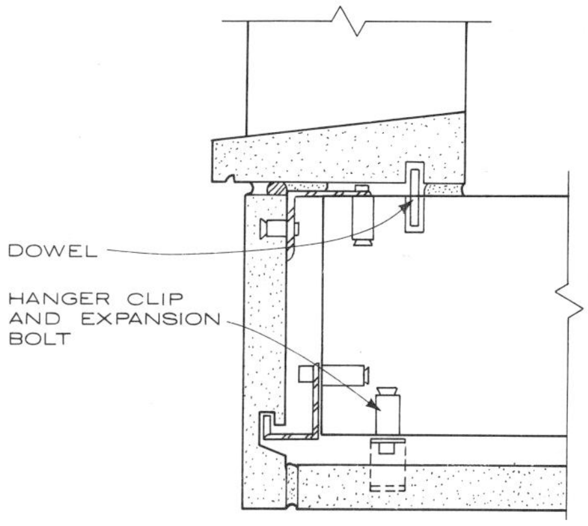

WINDOW DETAILS

DOWEL

SUPPORT ANGLE AND MORTAR

CRAMP AND SEALANT AT JOINT

HEAD (JAMB SIMILAR)

RIGID INSULATION

SUPPORT ANGLE AND MORTAR

SLOTTED CLIP

HEAD (JAMB SIMILAR)

STEEL TEE CLIP TRANSFERS LOAD TO STRUCTURAL MEMBER

METAL INSERT

STRIP LINER WITH DOWELS

SILL

USE DOWEL TO CONNECT SEVERAL PIECES

STRAP AND DOWEL

RIGID INSULATION

STONE VENEER

SILL

DOWEL

HANGER CLIP AND EXPANSION BOLT

SOFFIT AND SILL DETAIL

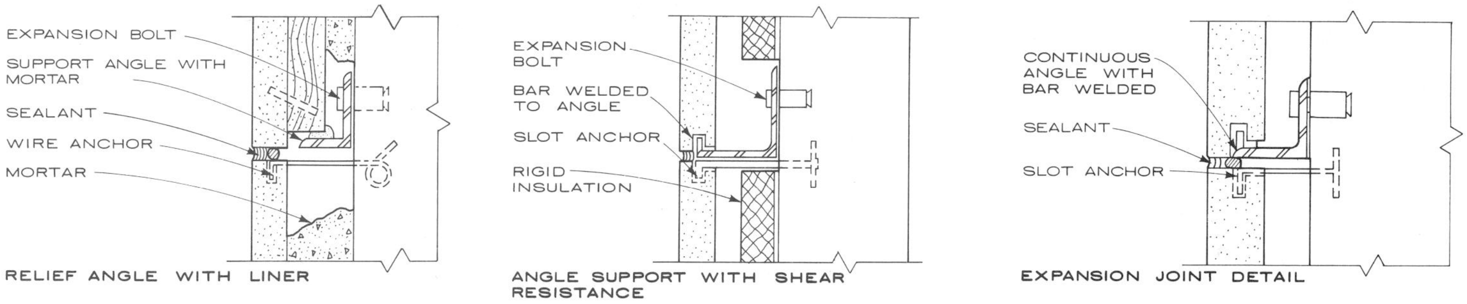

RELIEF ANGLE SUPPORTS

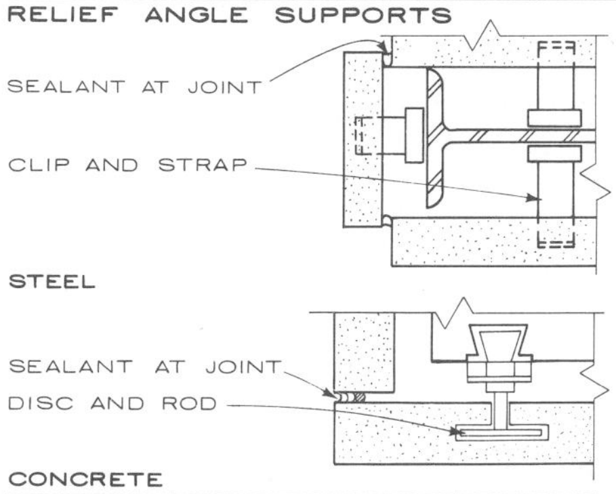

EXPANSION BOLT

SUPPORT ANGLE WITH MORTAR

SEALANT

WIRE ANCHOR

MORTAR

RELIEF ANGLE WITH LINER

EXPANSION BOLT

BAR WELDED TO ANGLE

SLOT ANCHOR

RIGID INSULATION

ANGLE SUPPORT WITH SHEAR RESISTANCE

CONTINUOUS ANGLE WITH BAR WELDED

SEALANT

SLOT ANCHOR

EXPANSION JOINT DETAIL

CORNER DETAILS

SEALANT AT JOINT

CLIP AND STRAP

STEEL

SEALANT AT JOINT

DISC AND ROD

CONCRETE

BASE DETAILS

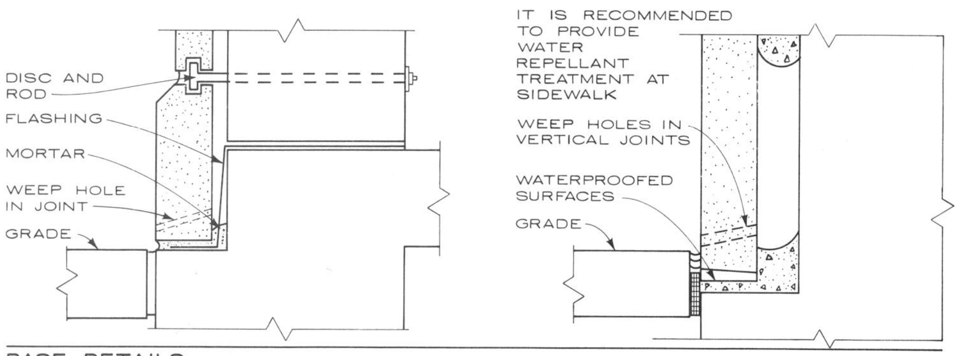

DISC AND ROD

FLASHING

MORTAR

WEEP HOLE IN JOINT

GRADE

IT IS RECOMMENDED TO PROVIDE WATER REPELLANT TREATMENT AT SIDEWALK

WEEP HOLES IN VERTICAL JOINTS

WATERPROOFED SURFACES

GRADE

Building Stone Institute; New York, New York

George M. Whiteside, III, AIA and James D. Lloyd; Kennett Square, Pennsylvania

Alexander Keyes; Darrel Rippeteau, Architect; Washington, D.C.

STONE

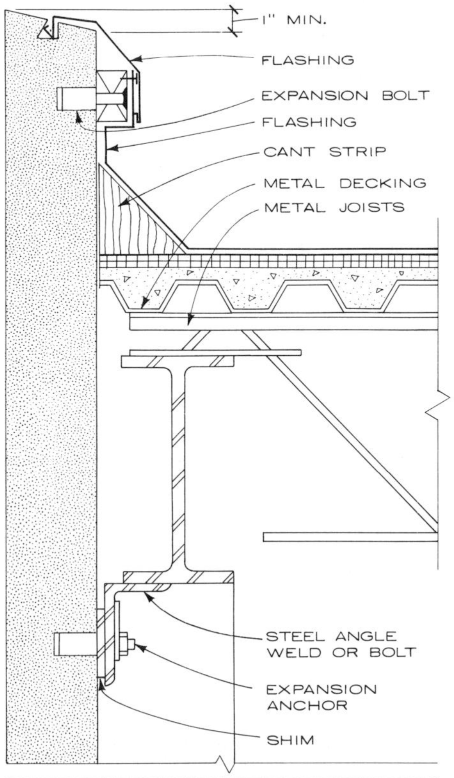

1" MIN.
FLASHING
EXPANSION BOLT
FLASHING
CANT STRIP
METAL DECKING
METAL JOISTS

STEEL ANGLE
WELD OR BOLT

EXPANSION
ANCHOR

SHIM

PARAPET

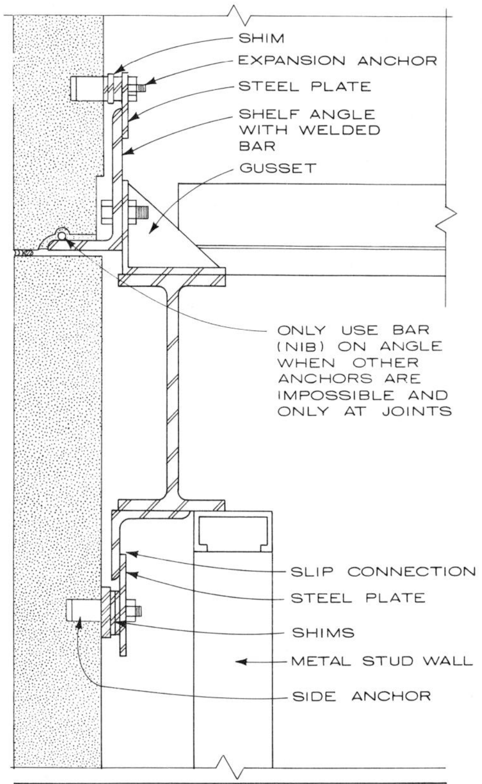

SHIM
EXPANSION ANCHOR
STEEL PLATE
SHELF ANGLE
WITH WELDED
BAR
GUSSET

ONLY USE BAR
(NIB) ON ANGLE
WHEN OTHER
ANCHORS ARE
IMPOSSIBLE AND
ONLY AT JOINTS

SLIP CONNECTION
STEEL PLATE
SHIMS
METAL STUD WALL
SIDE ANCHOR

**STONE PANELS ANCHORED
ON STEEL FRAME**

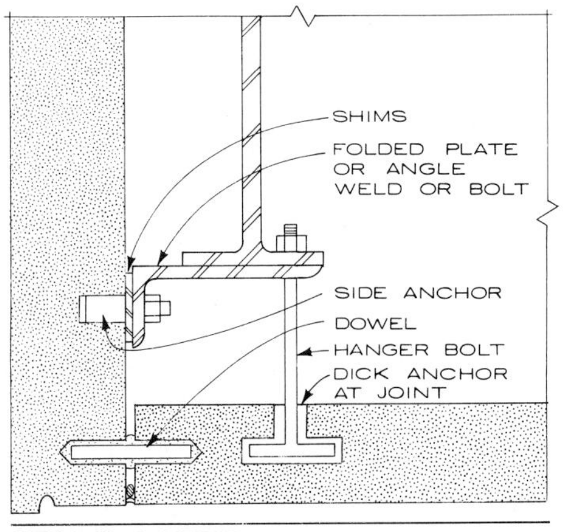

SHIMS
FOLDED PLATE
OR ANGLE
WELD OR BOLT

SIDE ANCHOR
DOWEL
HANGER BOLT
DICK ANCHOR
AT JOINT

STONE SOFFIT

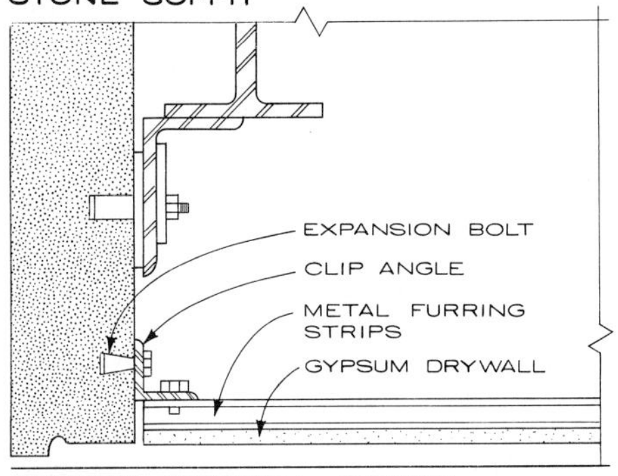

EXPANSION BOLT
CLIP ANGLE
METAL FURRING
STRIPS
GYPSUM DRYWALL

GYPSUM DRYWALL SOFFIT

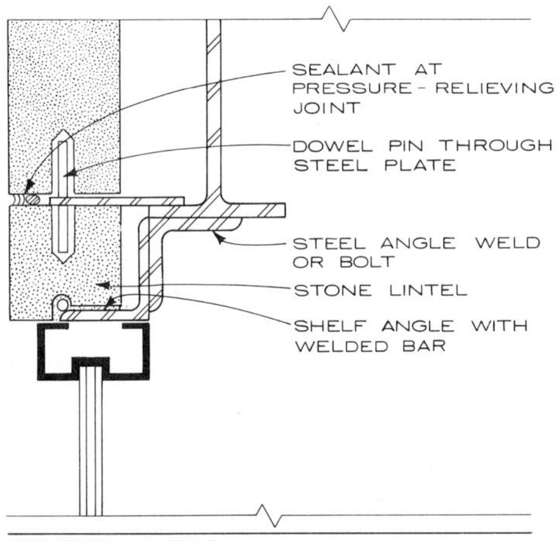

SEALANT AT
PRESSURE-RELIEVING
JOINT
DOWEL PIN THROUGH
STEEL PLATE

STEEL ANGLE WELD
OR BOLT
STONE LINTEL
SHELF ANGLE WITH
WELDED BAR

WINDOW HEAD

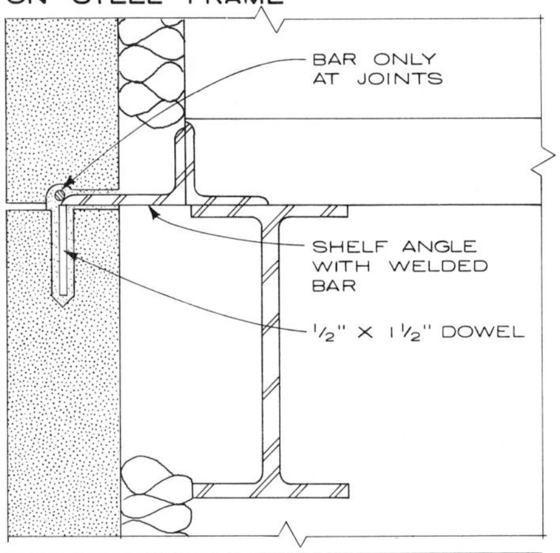

BAR ONLY
AT JOINTS

SHELF ANGLE
WITH WELDED
BAR

1/2" X 1 1/2" DOWEL

**STONE PANELS ANCHORED AT
FLOOR SLAB**

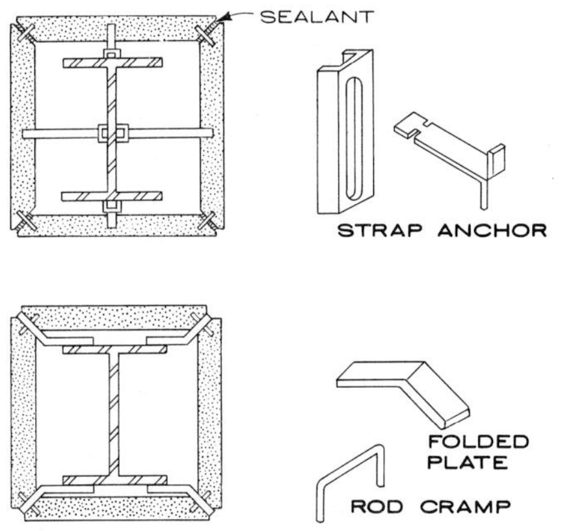

SEALANT

STRAP ANCHOR

**FOLDED
PLATE**

ROD CRAMP

COLUMN FACINGS

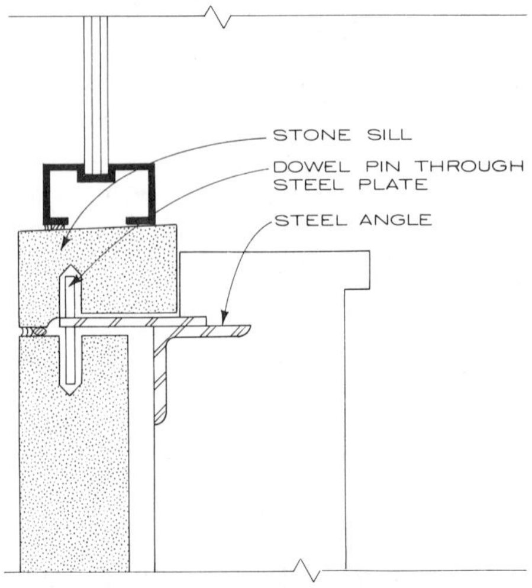

STONE SILL
DOWEL PIN THROUGH
STEEL PLATE
STEEL ANGLE

WINDOW SILL

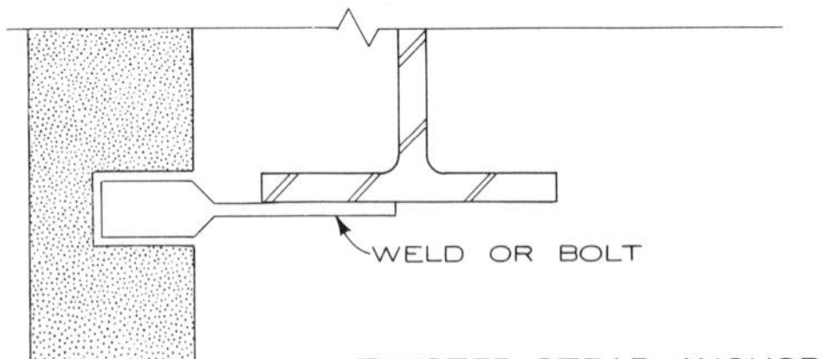

WELD OR BOLT

TWISTED STRAP ANCHOR

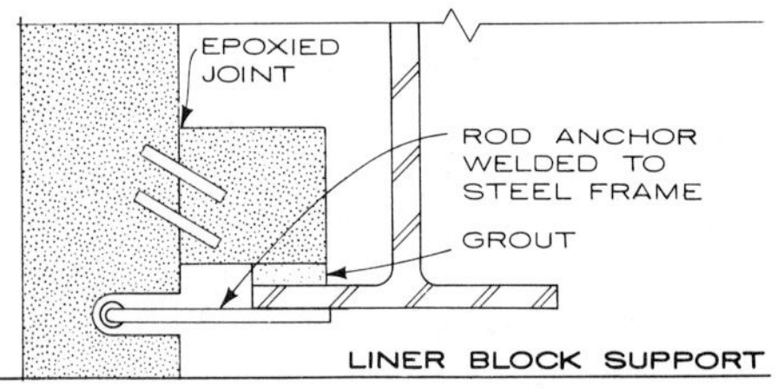

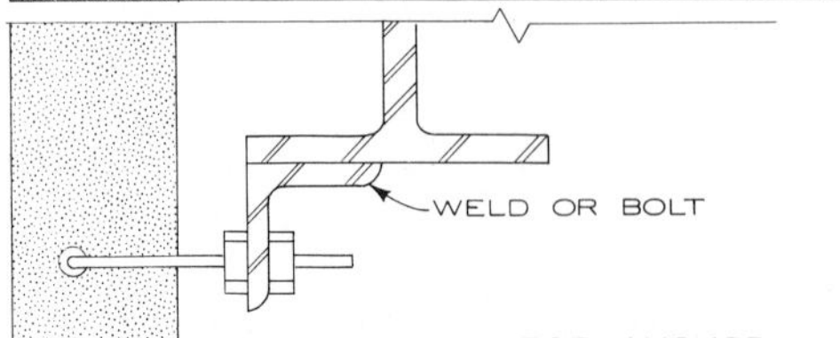

WELD OR BOLT

HOOK ROD ANCHOR

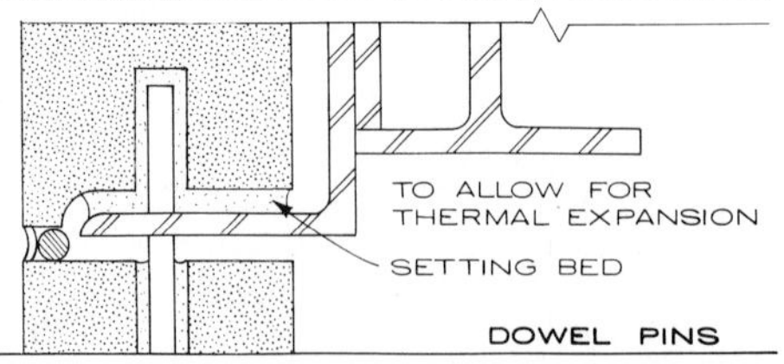

TYPICAL STONE PANEL CONNECTIONS

EPOXIED
JOINT

ROD ANCHOR
WELDED TO
STEEL FRAME
GROUT

LINER BLOCK SUPPORT

TO ALLOW FOR
THERMAL EXPANSION
SETTING BED

DOWEL PINS

Building Stone Institute; New York, New York
George M. Whiteside, III, AIA, and James D. Lloyd; Kennett Square, Pennsylvania
Alexander Keyes; Darrel Rippeteau, Architect; Washington, D.C.

4   STONE

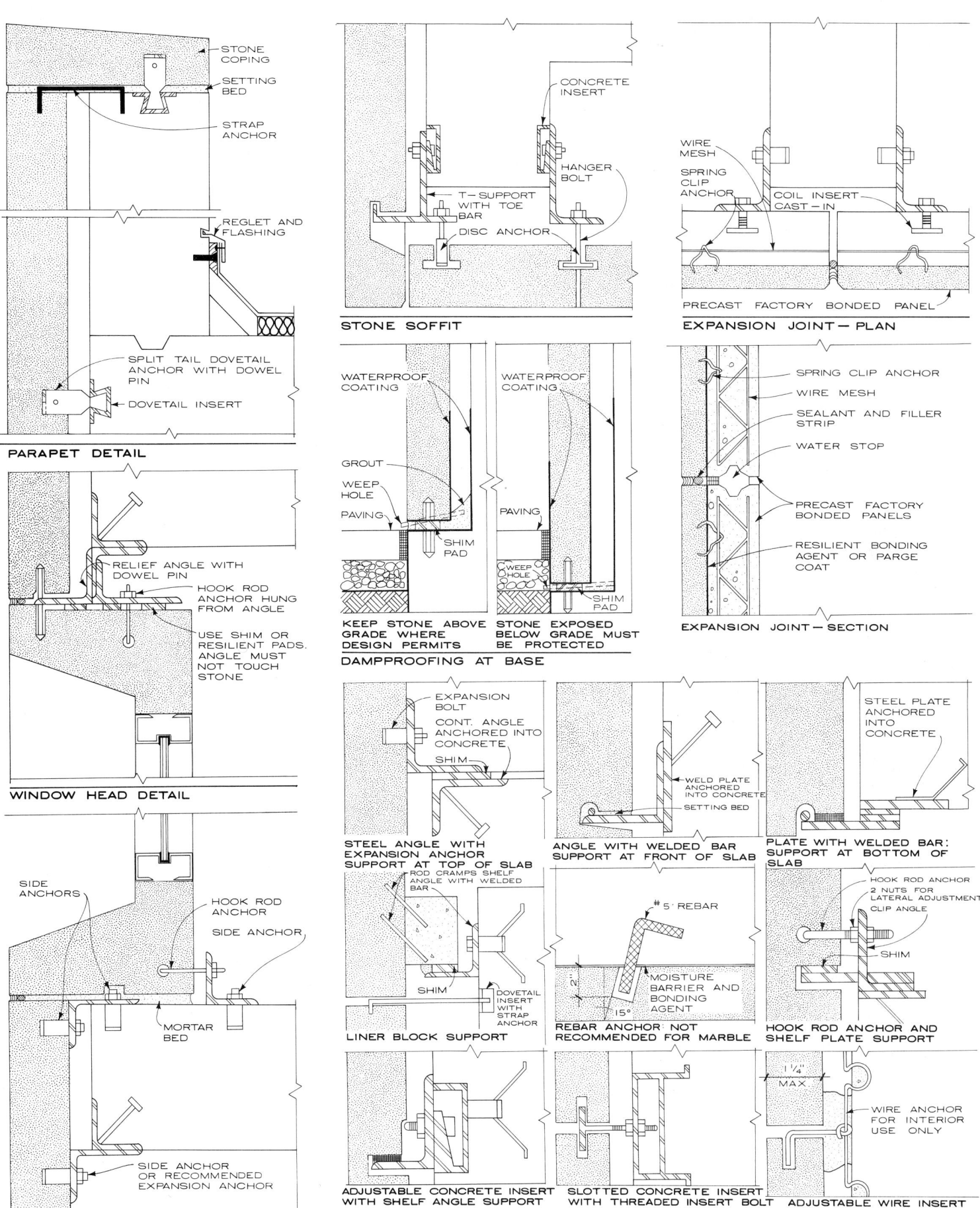

PARAPET DETAIL

- STONE COPING
- SETTING BED
- STRAP ANCHOR
- REGLET AND FLASHING
- SPLIT TAIL DOVETAIL ANCHOR WITH DOWEL PIN
- DOVETAIL INSERT

WINDOW HEAD DETAIL

- RELIEF ANGLE WITH DOWEL PIN
- HOOK ROD ANCHOR HUNG FROM ANGLE
- USE SHIM OR RESILIENT PADS. ANGLE MUST NOT TOUCH STONE

WINDOW SILL DETAIL

- SIDE ANCHORS
- HOOK ROD ANCHOR
- SIDE ANCHOR
- MORTAR BED
- SIDE ANCHOR OR RECOMMENDED EXPANSION ANCHOR

STONE SOFFIT

- CONCRETE INSERT
- HANGER BOLT
- T-SUPPORT WITH TOE BAR
- DISC ANCHOR

DAMPPROOFING AT BASE

- WATERPROOF COATING
- GROUT
- WEEP HOLE
- PAVING
- SHIM PAD
- KEEP STONE ABOVE GRADE WHERE DESIGN PERMITS
- WATERPROOF COATING
- PAVING
- WEEP HOLE
- SHIM PAD
- STONE EXPOSED BELOW GRADE MUST BE PROTECTED

EXPANSION JOINT — PLAN

- WIRE MESH
- SPRING CLIP ANCHOR
- COIL INSERT CAST-IN
- PRECAST FACTORY BONDED PANEL

EXPANSION JOINT — SECTION

- SPRING CLIP ANCHOR
- WIRE MESH
- SEALANT AND FILLER STRIP
- WATER STOP
- PRECAST FACTORY BONDED PANELS
- RESILIENT BONDING AGENT OR PARGE COAT

TYPICAL CONNECTIONS OF STONE PANELS TO CONCRETE FRAME

STEEL ANGLE WITH EXPANSION ANCHOR SUPPORT AT TOP OF SLAB
- EXPANSION BOLT
- CONT. ANGLE ANCHORED INTO CONCRETE
- SHIM

ANGLE WITH WELDED BAR SUPPORT AT FRONT OF SLAB
- WELD PLATE ANCHORED INTO CONCRETE
- SETTING BED

PLATE WITH WELDED BAR: SUPPORT AT BOTTOM OF SLAB
- STEEL PLATE ANCHORED INTO CONCRETE

LINER BLOCK SUPPORT
- ROD CRAMPS SHELF ANGLE WITH WELDED BAR
- SHIM
- DOVETAIL INSERT WITH STRAP ANCHOR

REBAR ANCHOR NOT RECOMMENDED FOR MARBLE
- #5 REBAR
- MOISTURE BARRIER AND BONDING AGENT
- 2"
- 15°

HOOK ROD ANCHOR AND SHELF PLATE SUPPORT
- HOOK ROD ANCHOR 2 NUTS FOR LATERAL ADJUSTMENT CLIP ANGLE
- SHIM

ADJUSTABLE CONCRETE INSERT WITH SHELF ANGLE SUPPORT

SLOTTED CONCRETE INSERT WITH THREADED INSERT BOLT

ADJUSTABLE WIRE INSERT
- 1¼" MAX
- WIRE ANCHOR FOR INTERIOR USE ONLY

Building Stone Institute; New York, New York

George M. Whiteside, III, AIA and James D. Lloyd; Kennett Square, Pennsylvania

Alexander Keyes; Darrel Rippeteau, Architect; Washington, D.C.

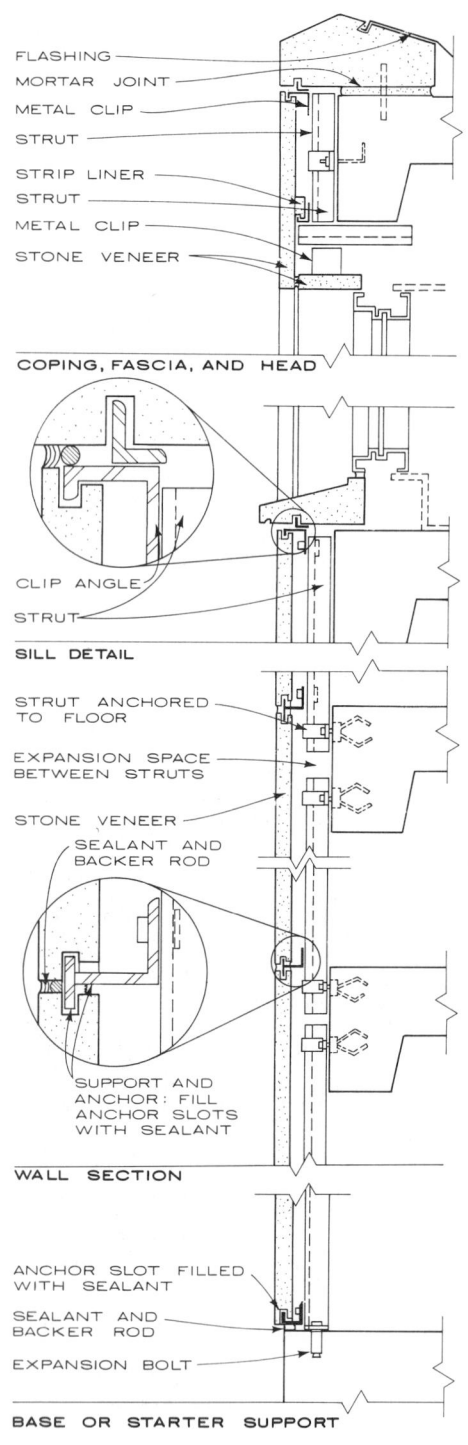

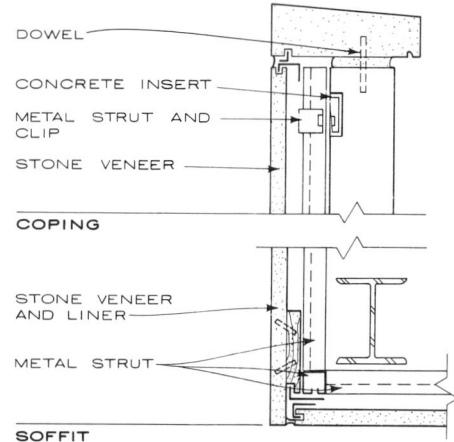

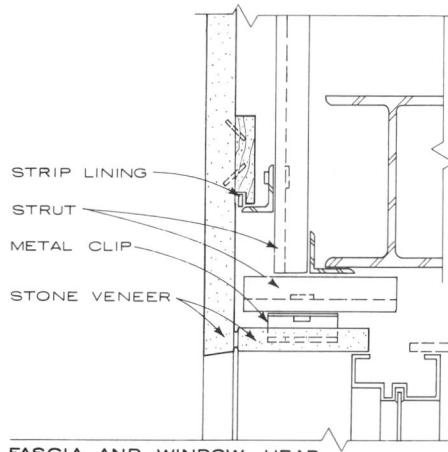

COPING, FASCIA, AND HEAD

FLASHING
MORTAR JOINT
METAL CLIP
STRUT
STRIP LINER
STRUT
METAL CLIP
STONE VENEER

DOWEL
CONCRETE INSERT
METAL STRUT AND CLIP
STONE VENEER

COPING

STRIP LINING
STRUT
METAL CLIP
STONE VENEER

FASCIA AND WINDOW HEAD

CLIP ANGLE
STRUT

SILL DETAIL

STONE VENEER AND LINER
METAL STRUT

SOFFIT

STRUT ANCHORED TO FLOOR
EXPANSION SPACE BETWEEN STRUTS
STONE VENEER
SEALANT AND BACKER ROD
SUPPORT AND ANCHOR: FILL ANCHOR SLOTS WITH SEALANT

WALL SECTION

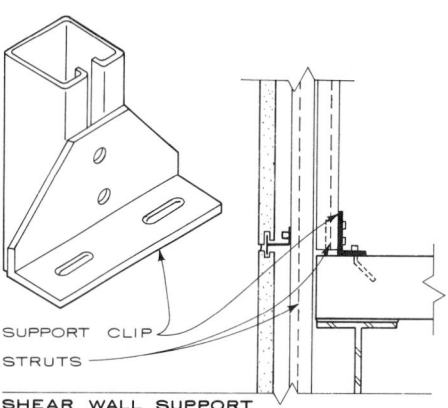

SUPPORT CLIP
STRUTS

SHEAR WALL SUPPORT

STRUTS ANCHORED TO EXISTING BUILDING FACING
EXISTING WALL

CONNECTION TO EXISTING FACING

ANCHOR SLOT FILLED WITH SEALANT
SEALANT AND BACKER ROD
EXPANSION BOLT

BASE OR STARTER SUPPORT

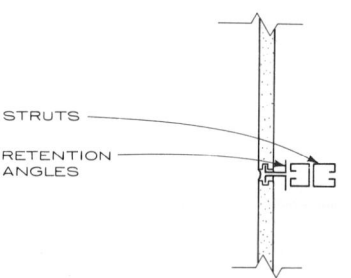

STRUTS
RETENTION ANGLES

SHEAR WALL SIDE RETENTION (PLAN)

GRID STRUT SYSTEM — METAL FRAME

GRID STRUT SPACING RELATIVE TO SLAB HEIGHT—MARBLE

HEIGHT OF SLAB UP TO	GRID STRUT SPACING	
	⁷⁄₈'' THICK	1¼'' THICK
2'-6''	4'-9''	4'-0''
3'-0''	4'-6''	3'-9''
3'-6''	4'-3''	3'-6''
4'-0''	4'-0''	3'-3''
4'-6''	3'-9''	3'-0''
5'-0''*	3'-6''	2'-9''
5'-6''*	3'-3''	2'-6''
6'-0''*	3'-3''	2'-3''

*For slabs over 4'-6'' height use intermediate vertical joint anchoring.

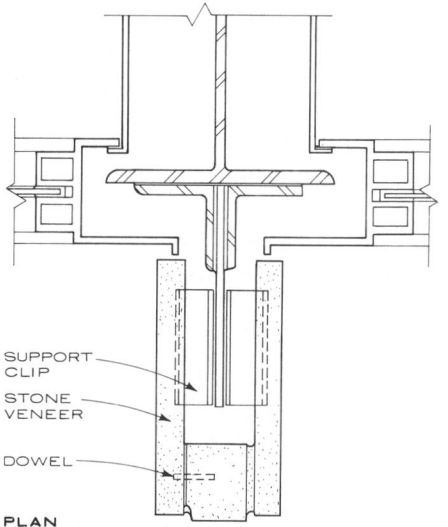

SUPPORT CLIP
STONE VENEER
DOWEL

PLAN
COLUMN RETURN

GRID ANCHOR SPACING AND STRUT SIZE—MARBLE

MAXIMUM SPACING	ANCHOR	STRUT SIZE
⁷⁄₈'' THICK	1¼'' THICK	WIDTH, DEPTH, AND SHAPE
4'-0''	4'-0''	1⁵⁄₈'' x 1⁵⁄₈''
7'-0''	6'-0''	1⁵⁄₈'' x 2⁷⁄₁₆''
10'-0''	9'-0''	1⁵⁄₈'' x 3¼''
15'-0''	13'-0''	1⁵⁄₈'' x 4⁷⁄₈''

NOTES
1. ''X'' = dimension between strut and outside face of stone.
2. ''X'' = 1⁵⁄₈'' for ⁷⁄₈'' marble.
3. ''X'' = 1¾'' for 1¼'' marble.

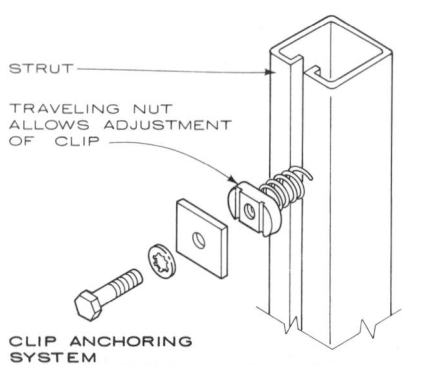

STRUT
TRAVELING NUT ALLOWS ADJUSTMENT OF CLIP

CLIP ANCHORING SYSTEM

GRID STRUT SYSTEM — CONCRETE FRAME

NOTE: Engineering design of all supports for this type of construction is essential.

Building Stone Institute; New York, New York
George M. Whiteside, III, AIA and James D. Lloyd; Kennett Square, Pennsylvania
Alexander Keyes; Darrel Rippeteau, Architect; Washington, D.C.

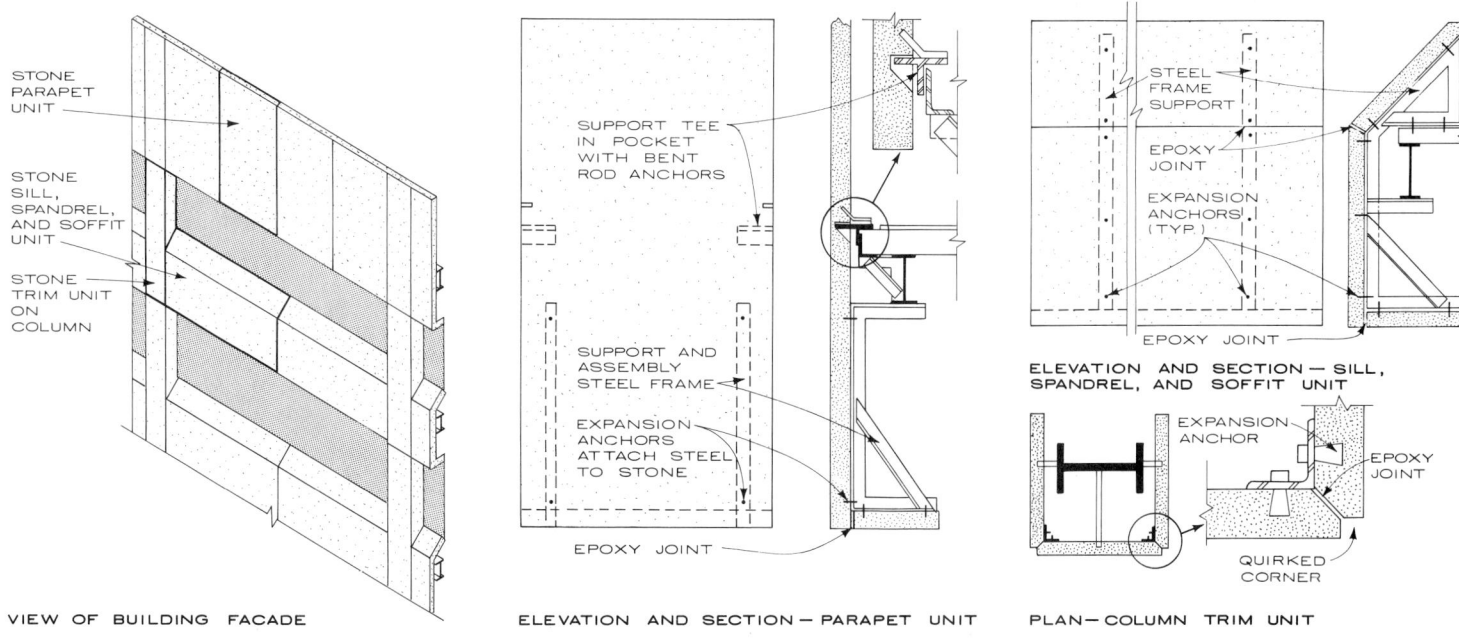

VIEW OF BUILDING FACADE

STONE PARAPET UNIT

STONE SILL, SPANDREL, AND SOFFIT UNIT

STONE TRIM UNIT ON COLUMN

ELEVATION AND SECTION — PARAPET UNIT

SUPPORT TEE IN POCKET WITH BENT ROD ANCHORS

SUPPORT AND ASSEMBLY STEEL FRAME

EXPANSION ANCHORS ATTACH STEEL TO STONE

EPOXY JOINT

PLAN — COLUMN TRIM UNIT

STEEL FRAME SUPPORT

EPOXY JOINT

EXPANSION ANCHORS (TYP.)

EPOXY JOINT

ELEVATION AND SECTION — SILL, SPANDREL, AND SOFFIT UNIT

EXPANSION ANCHOR

EPOXY JOINT

QUIRKED CORNER

PREASSEMBLED STONE UNIT WITH EPOXY ON STEEL FRAME

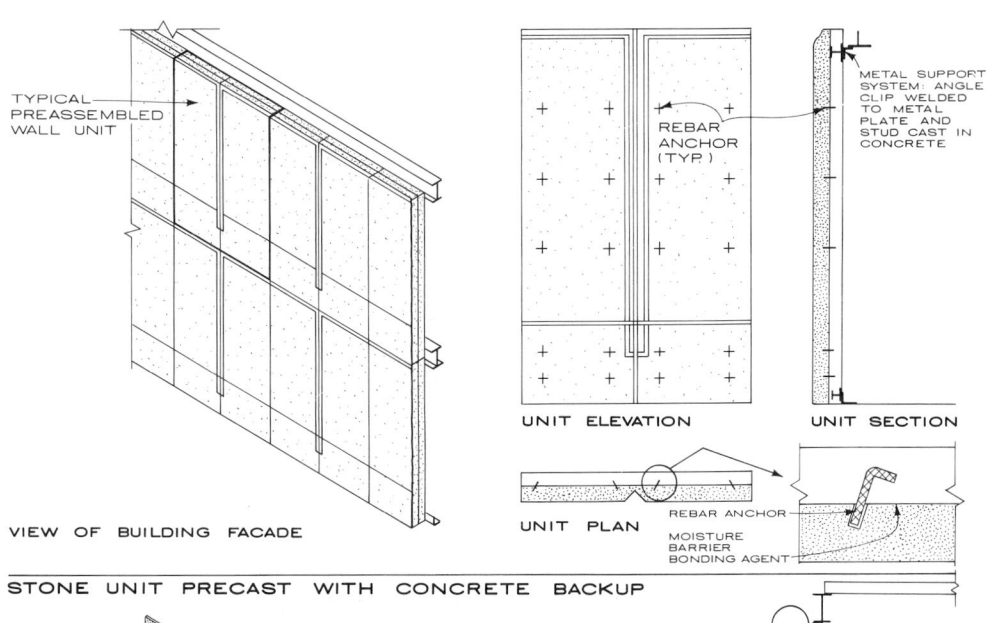

TYPICAL PREASSEMBLED WALL UNIT

VIEW OF BUILDING FACADE

METAL SUPPORT SYSTEM: ANGLE CLIP WELDED TO METAL PLATE AND STUD CAST IN CONCRETE

REBAR ANCHOR (TYP.)

UNIT ELEVATION

UNIT SECTION

UNIT PLAN

REBAR ANCHOR

MOISTURE BARRIER BONDING AGENT

STONE UNIT PRECAST WITH CONCRETE BACKUP

PREASSEMBLED PANELS

Preassembled stone panel technology provides savings in on-site labor and allows precision joining of component stone units.

STONE ON STEEL FRAME WITH EPOXY JOINTS

Stone units are mounted on a steel frame with expansion bolts and dowel pins (as recommended by manufacturer). Joints in stone are epoxied and are held to approximately $1/8$ in. when finished for delivery. All stones in the assembly are anchored as a unit to the structure. Installation of preassembled units reduces the leveling, plumbing, and aligning of individual pieces, and on-site joint sealing is not as extensive as with individual stone panel technology. On-site installation joints of $1/4$ and $3/8$ in. are recommended.

COMPOSITE ASSEMBLIES OF STONE AND CONCRETE

Stone units are bonded to reinforced precast concrete panels with bent stainless steel rebars. A moisture barrier and bonding agent is installed between the stone and concrete in conditions where concrete alkali salts may stain stone units.

STONE AND STEEL ASSEMBLIES WITH SEALANT JOINTS

Stone units are shimmed and anchored to a steel frame using standard stone connecting hardware. Joints may be sealed at site, along with joints between assemblies.

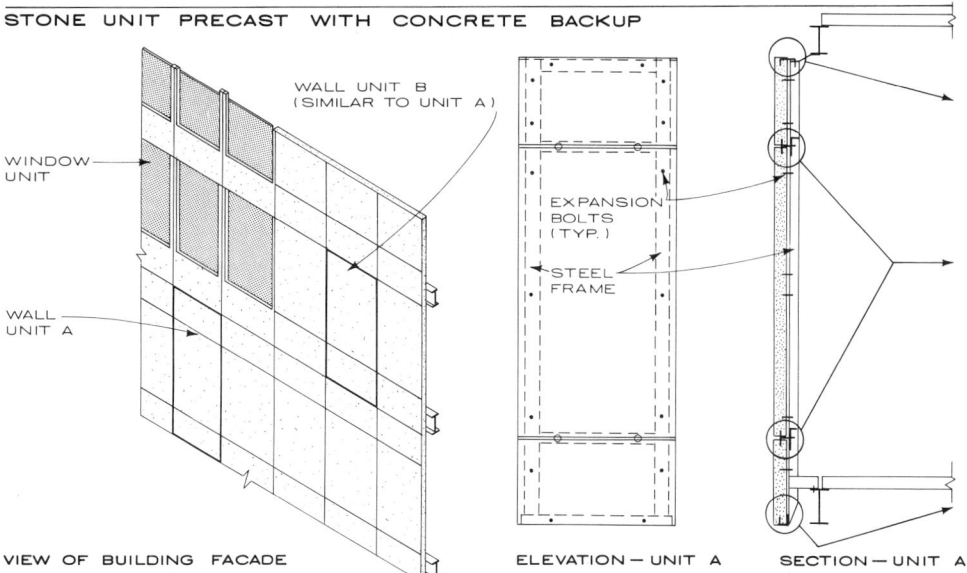

WALL UNIT B (SIMILAR TO UNIT A)

WINDOW UNIT

WALL UNIT A

VIEW OF BUILDING FACADE

EXPANSION BOLTS (TYP.)

STEEL FRAME

ELEVATION — UNIT A

SECTION — UNIT A

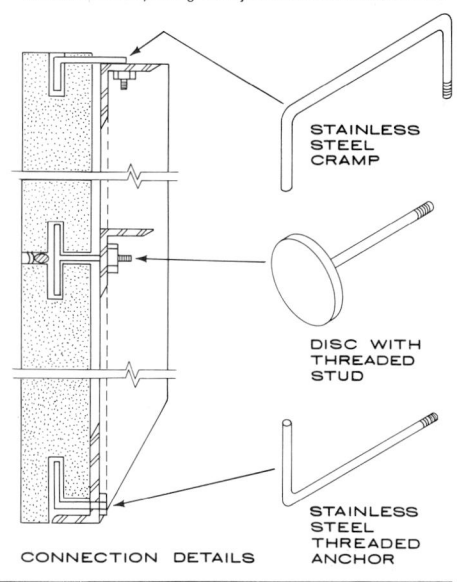

STAINLESS STEEL CRAMP

DISC WITH THREADED STUD

STAINLESS STEEL THREADED ANCHOR

CONNECTION DETAILS

PREASSEMBLED STONE UNIT ON STEEL FRAME

Building Stone Institute; New York, New York

George M. Whiteside, III, AIA, and James D. Lloyd; Kennett Square, Pennsylvania

Alexander Keyes; Darrel Rippeteau, Architect; Washington, D.C.

STONE 4

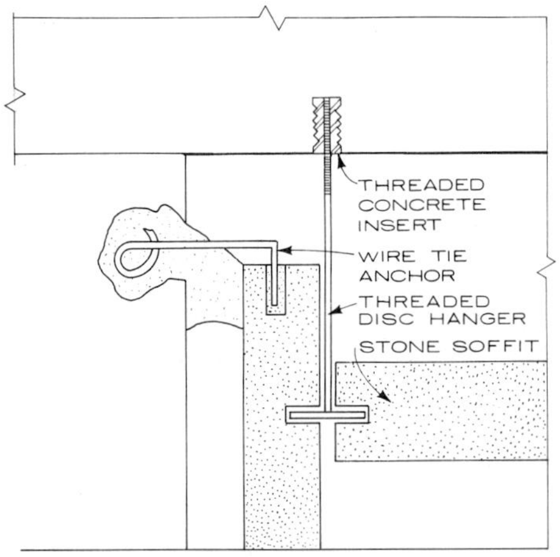

SOFFIT DETAIL AT WALL

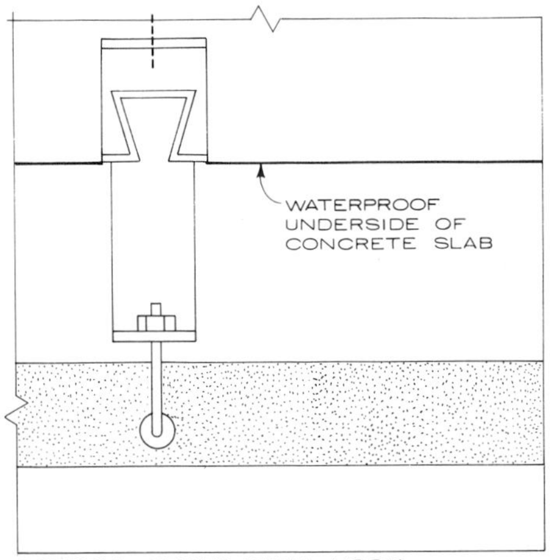

THREADED
CONCRETE
INSERT

WIRE TIE
ANCHOR

THREADED
DISC HANGER

STONE SOFFIT

VERTICAL JOINT DETAIL

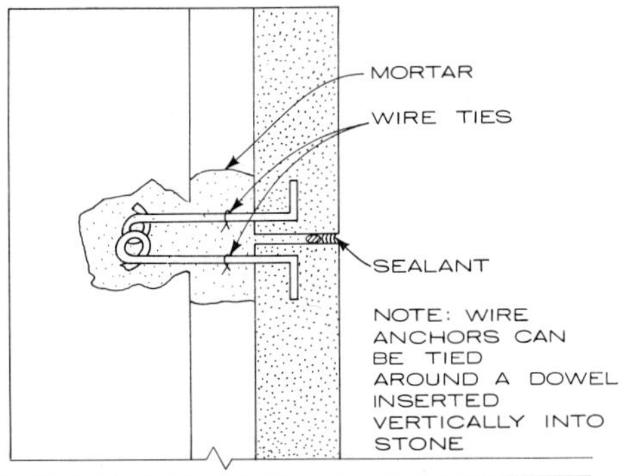

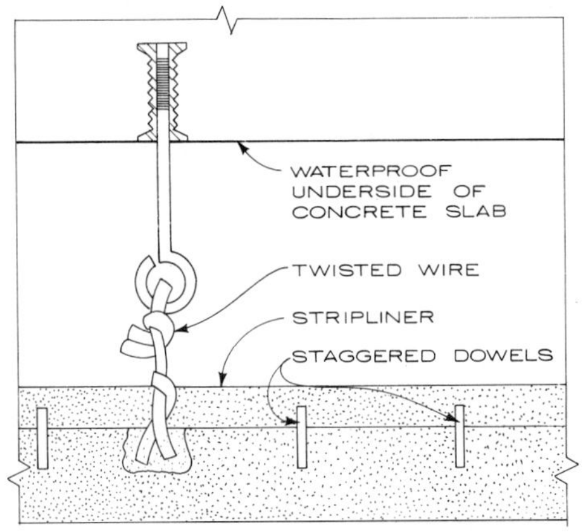

MORTAR

WIRE TIES

SEALANT

NOTE: WIRE
ANCHORS CAN
BE TIED
AROUND A DOWEL
INSERTED
VERTICALLY INTO
STONE

BASE DETAIL

WIRE ANCHOR

FLOOR

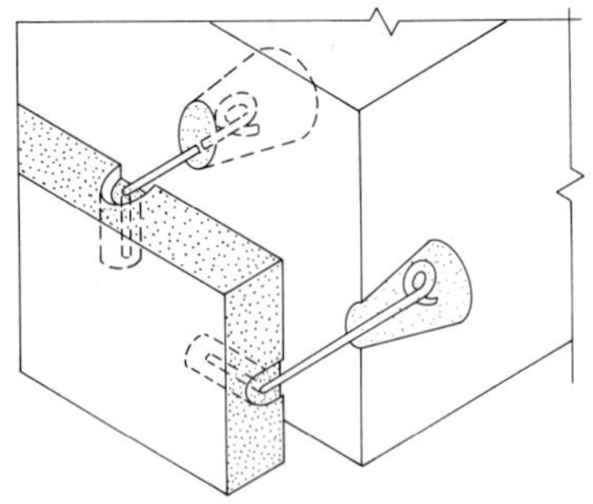

SIMPLE WIRE ANCHOR CONNECTION

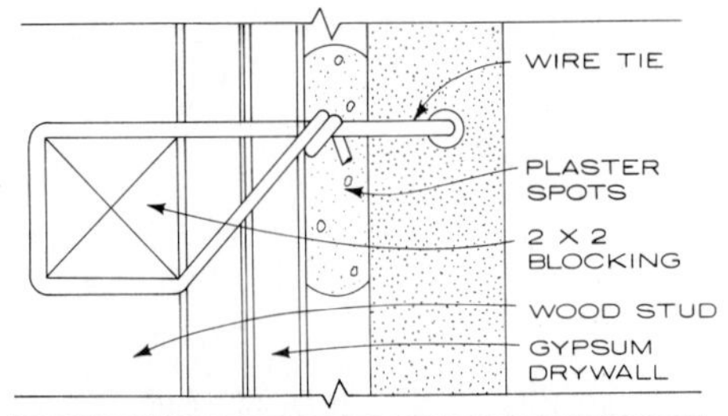

STONE PANEL ON WOOD STUDS

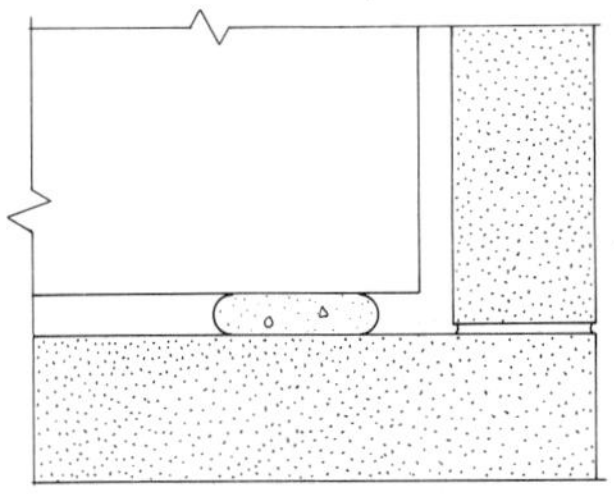

WIRE TIE

PLASTER
SPOTS

2 X 2
BLOCKING

WOOD STUD

GYPSUM
DRYWALL

DOVETAIL STRAP WITH HOOK ROD ANCHOR

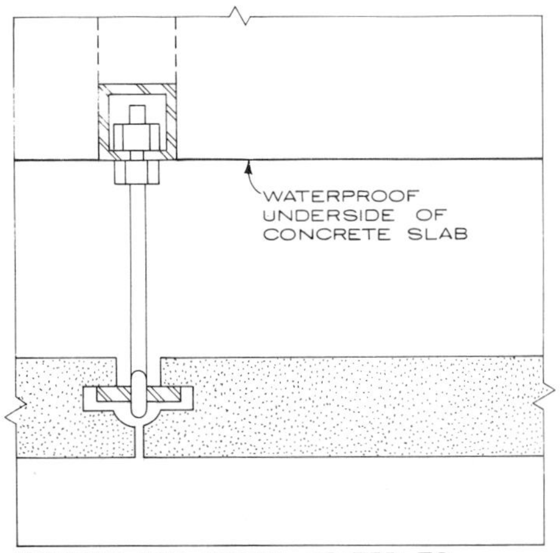

WATERPROOF
UNDERSIDE OF
CONCRETE SLAB

EYEBOLT AND DOWEL BOLTED TO THREADED CONCRETE INSERT

WATERPROOF
UNDERSIDE OF
CONCRETE SLAB

THREADED INSERT AND EYEBOLT

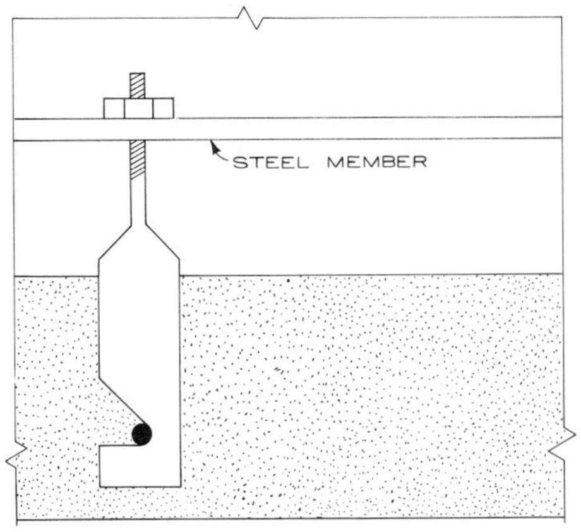

WATERPROOF
UNDERSIDE OF
CONCRETE SLAB

TWISTED WIRE

STRIPLINER

STAGGERED DOWELS

FLAT HOOK ANCHOR AND DOWEL

STEEL MEMBER

TYPICAL SYSTEMS FOR HANGING INTERIOR VENEER STONE

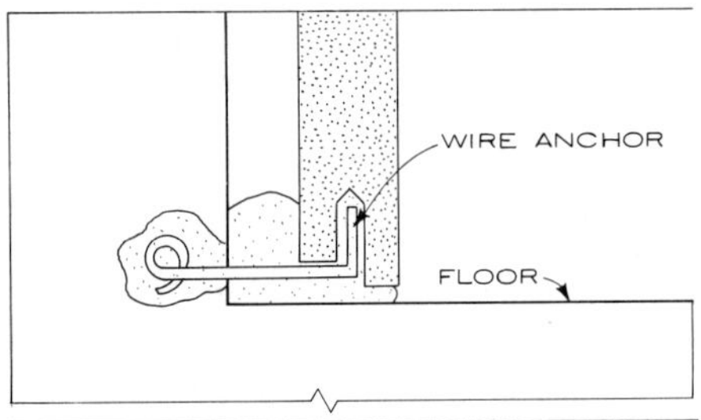

CORNER BUTT

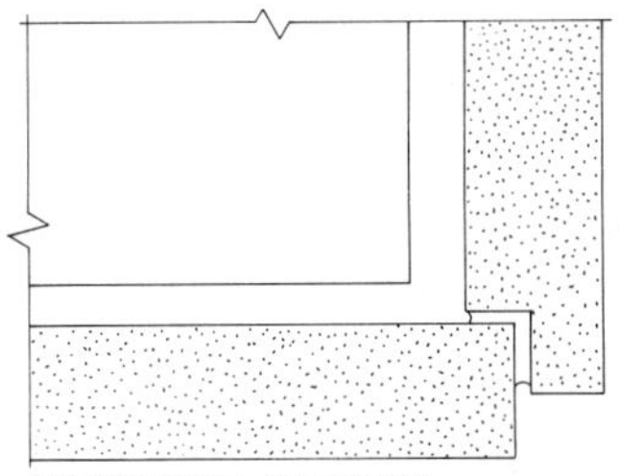

RABBETED CORNER

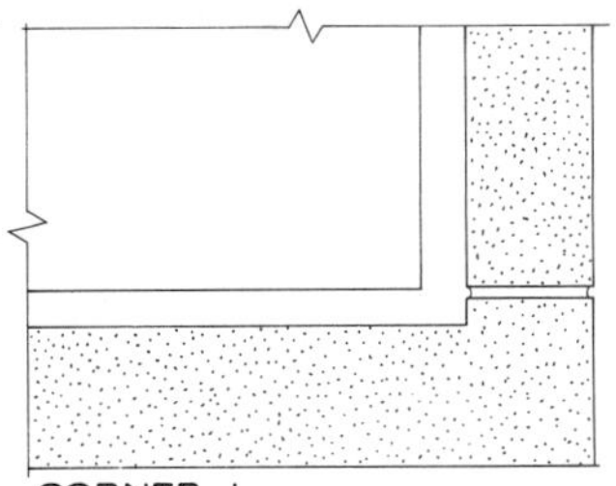

CORNER L

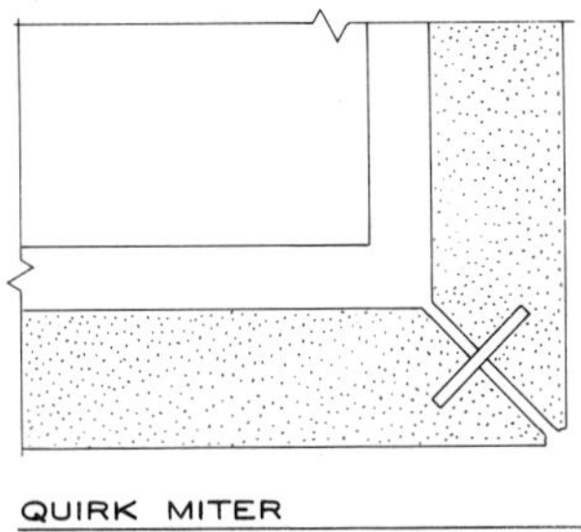

QUIRK MITER

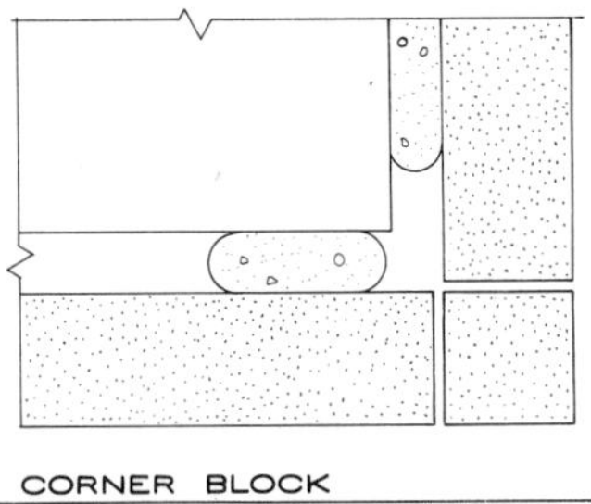

CORNER BLOCK

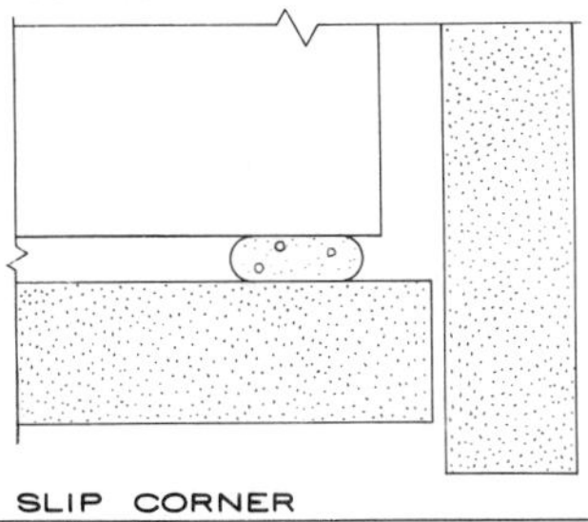

SLIP CORNER

TYPICAL CORNER DETAILS

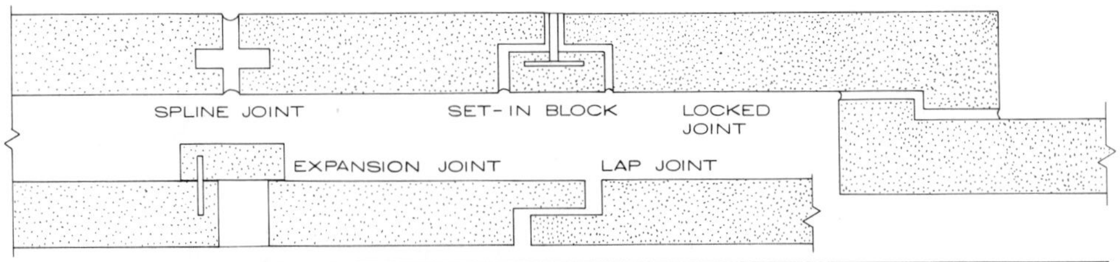

SPLINE JOINT

SET-IN BLOCK

LOCKED
JOINT

EXPANSION JOINT

LAP JOINT

TYPICAL HORIZONTAL JOINTS

Building Stone Institute; New York, New York
George M. Whiteside, III, AIA and James D. Lloyd; Kennett Square, Pennsylvania
Alexander Keyes; Darrel Rippeteau, Architect; Washington, D.C.

STONE

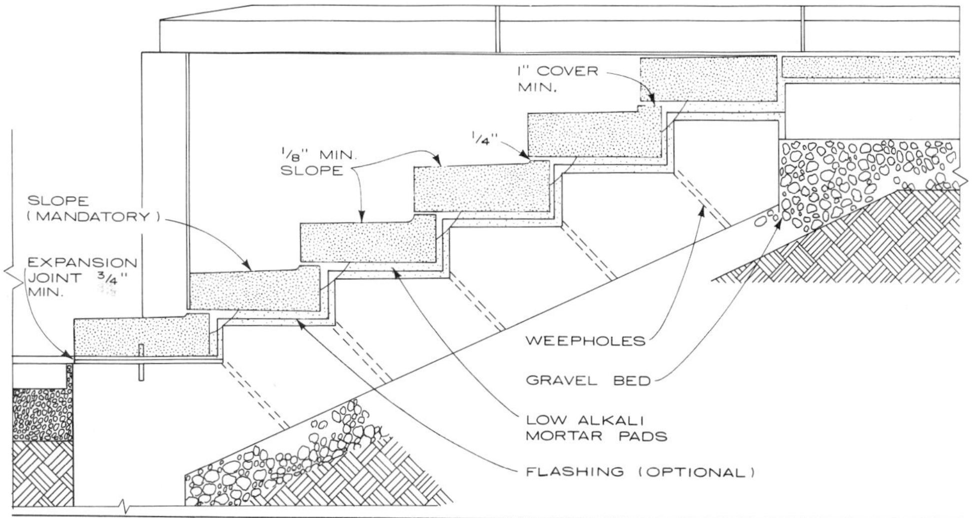

EXTERIOR STAIR SECTION

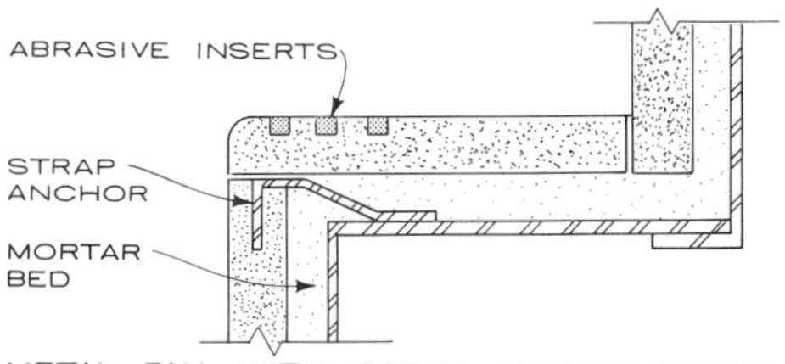

SLOPE (MANDATORY)

EXPANSION JOINT ³/₄" MIN.

1" COVER MIN.

¹/₈" MIN SLOPE

¹/₄"

WEEPHOLES

GRAVEL BED

LOW ALKALI MORTAR PADS

FLASHING (OPTIONAL)

STONE STAIRS WITH STEEL FRAME

ABRASIVE INSERTS

STRAP ANCHOR

MORTAR BED

METAL PAN WITH STONE SAFETY TREAD

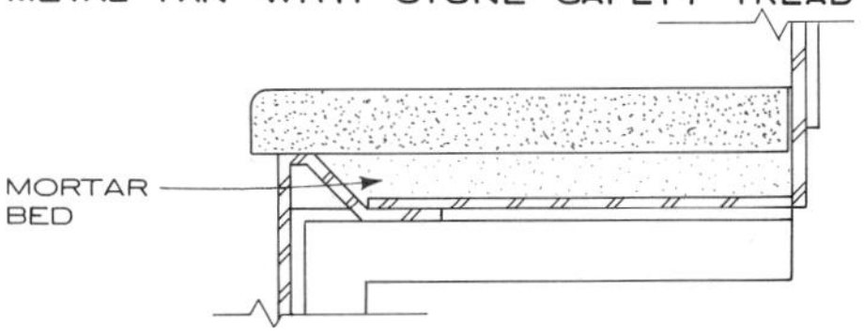

MORTAR BED

STEEL SUBTREAD AND RISER WITH STONE TREAD

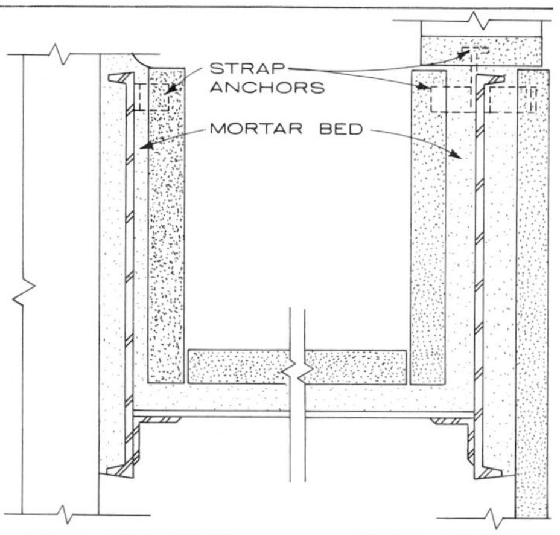

STRAP ANCHORS

MORTAR BED

WALL STRINGER   OPEN STRINGER

STONE FLOORING

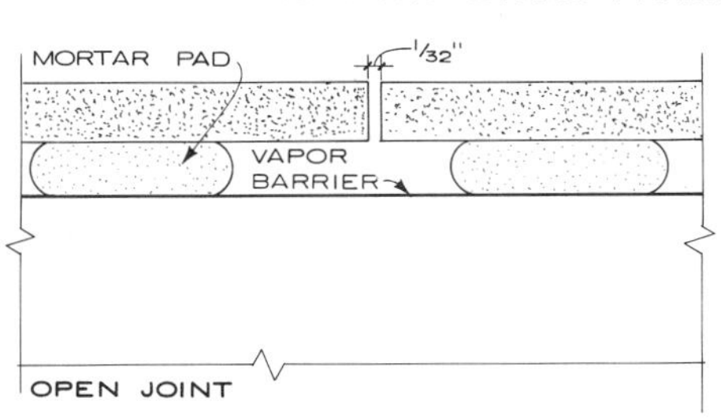

MORTAR PAD   ¹/₃₂"

VAPOR BARRIER

OPEN JOINT

LATEX MORTAR

THIN SET

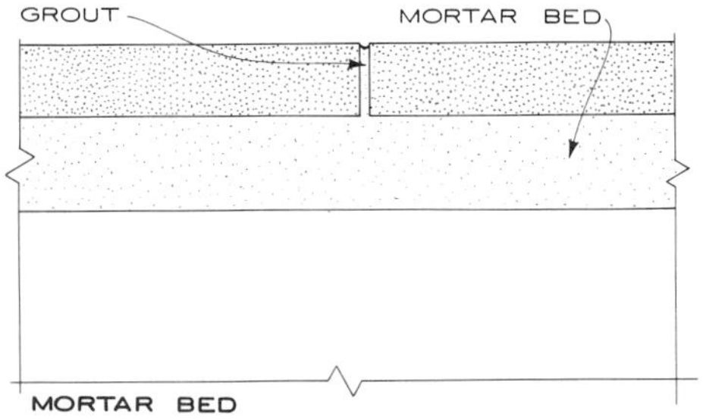

GROUT   MORTAR BED

MORTAR BED

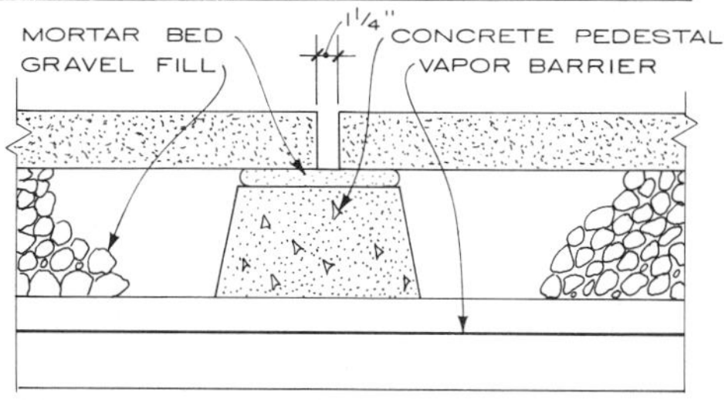

MORTAR BED GRAVEL FILL

1¹/₄"

CONCRETE PEDESTAL VAPOR BARRIER

OPEN JOINT — PEDESTAL

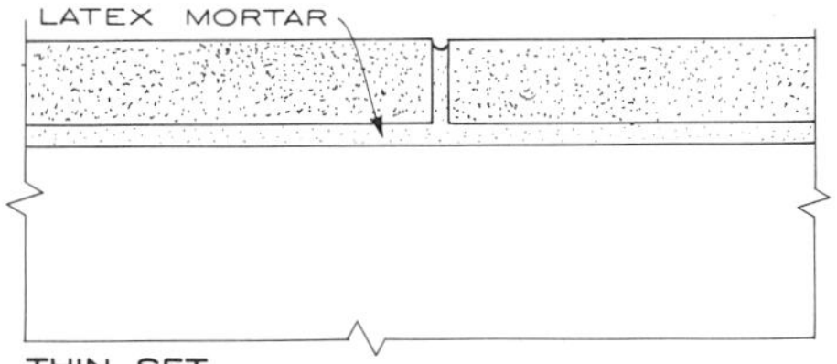

SEALANT

MORTAR BED

FILLER STRIP

CONCRETE

VAPOR BARRIER

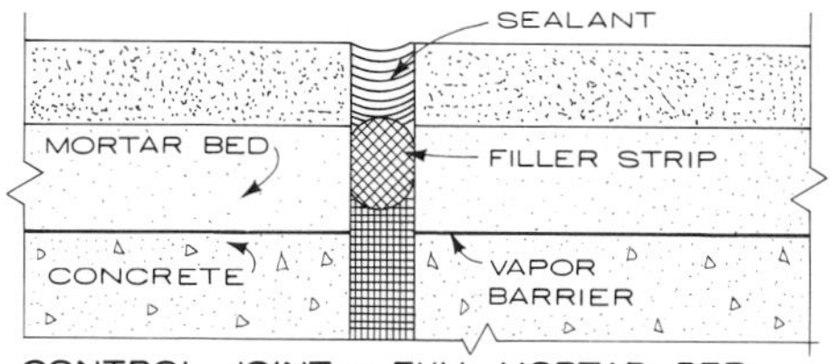

CONTROL JOINT — FULL MORTAR BED

MORTAR BED WITH REINFORCING

GROUT

ROOFING FELT OR POLYETHYLENE FILM

WOOD SUBFLOOR

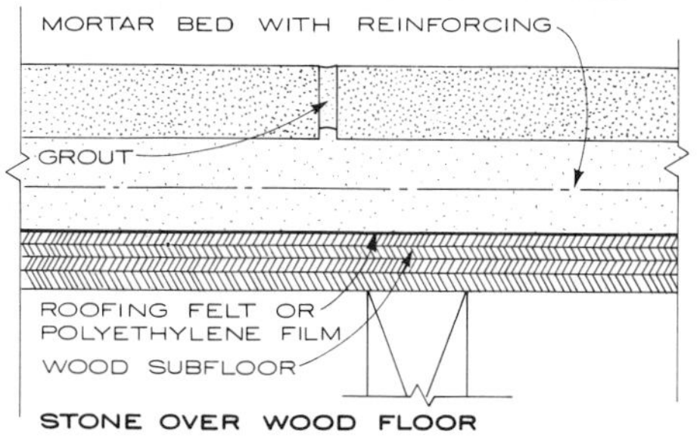

STONE OVER WOOD FLOOR

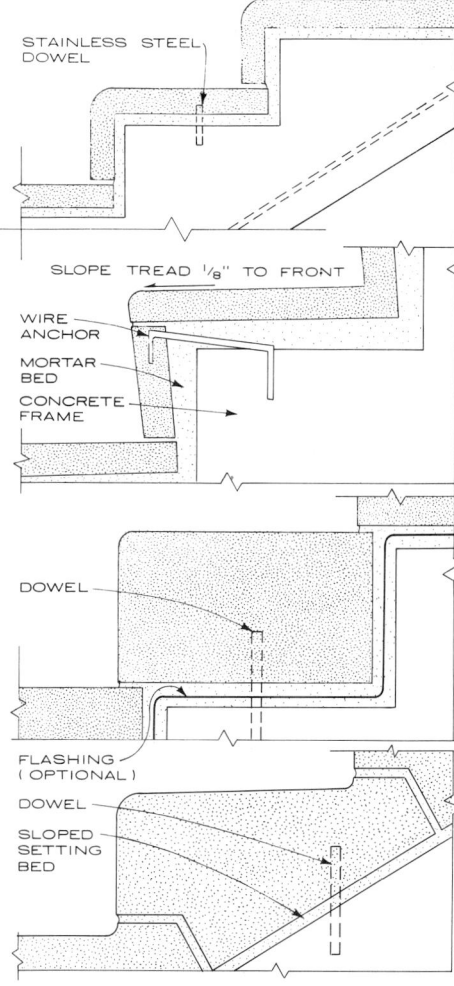

STAINLESS STEEL DOWEL

SLOPE TREAD ¹/₈" TO FRONT

WIRE ANCHOR

MORTAR BED

CONCRETE FRAME

DOWEL

FLASHING (OPTIONAL)

DOWEL

SLOPED SETTING BED

STONE STAIRS WITH CONCRETE FRAME

DESIGN FACTORS FOR STONE STAIRS

Stone used for steps should have an abrasive resistance of 10 (measured on a scale from a minimum of 6 to a maximum of 17). When different varieties of stone are used, their abrasive hardness should be similar to prevent uneven wear.

Dowels and anchoring devices should be noncorrosive.

If a safety tread is not used on stairs, a light bush hammered soft finish or nonslip finish is recommended.

To prevent future staining, dampproof the face of all concrete or concrete block, specify low alkali mortar, and provide adequate drainage (slopes and weepholes).

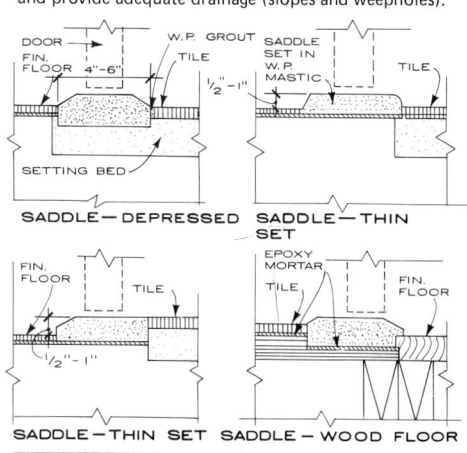

DOOR FIN. FLOOR 4"–6"

W.P. GROUT   TILE

SADDLE SET IN W.P. MASTIC

TILE

¹/₂"–1"

SETTING BED

SADDLE—DEPRESSED   SADDLE—THIN SET

FIN. FLOOR   TILE

¹/₂"–1"

EPOXY MORTAR   TILE   FIN. FLOOR

SADDLE—THIN SET   SADDLE—WOOD FLOOR

STONE THRESHOLDS

Building Stone Institute; New York, New York

George M. Whiteside, III, AIA and James D. Lloyd; Kennett Square, Pennsylvania

Alexander Keyes; Darrel Rippeteau, Architect; Washington, D.C.

STONE 4

SEGMENTAL

3 COURSE
2 COURSE
SPRING LINE
ROWLOCK COURSE

JACK

SKEWBACK - 1/2" PER FT. OF SPAN FOR EACH 4" OF ARCH DEPTH
ALL JOINTS ARE UNIFORM
CAMBER - 1/8" PER FT. OF SPAN
EQ   EQ
STONE SKEWBACK
STONE JOINTS 1/4"

TUDOR

BRICK   STONE
SPRING LINE

ELLIPTICAL

FULL BRICK WIDTH HERE
MINOR AXIS
MAJOR AXIS
SPRING LINE

ROMAN

LAY OUT FULL BRICK PLUS JOINT ON PERIMETER
RADIUS
STONES EQUAL

GOTHIC

CENTERS ALWAYS ON SPRING LINE

NOTE: Walls, piers, or abutments adjacent to masonry arches must be of sufficient strength to resist horizontal thrusts.

PARABOLIC

SPRING LINE MAJOR ARCH
ALTERNATING ROWLOCK AND SOLDIER COURSES
SPRING LINE MINOR ARCH

ARCH TERMINOLOGY

RISE (F)
ARCH AXIS
CROWN
EXTRADOS
DEPTH (D)
SKEW-BACK
SOFFIT
RISE (R)
INTRADOS
ABUT-MENT
SPRING LINE (MINOR ARCH)
SPRING LINE (MAJOR ARCH)
SPAN (S)
SPAN (L)

Brick Institute of America; McLean, Virginia

ARCHES

INTRODUCTION

A traditional masonry fireplace with its foundation, hearth, and chimney is a special element in a building and requires special design consideration. The masonry chimney is usually the heaviest single part of a wood frame structure and therefore requires a special foundation. The same holds true for masonry buildings where walls are not thick enough to incorporate the chimney or where the chimney is not designed into a masonry wall. Beyond the structural requirements, a fireplace and chimney must be designed with the proper spaces and relationships between spaces to sustain combustion and to carry smoke away safely. In the latter area, fireplace design is bound by the physical laws of nature and by various building codes. The internal diagram of a working fireplace (right) shows the several required parts and their vertical organization. Each part is further illustrated on succeeding pages in details of practical designs.

An ordinary masonry fireplace is only about one-third as efficient for heating as is a good stove or circulating heater. Other pages describe more efficient prefabricated fireplace units which incorporate air heating and circulating devices. A fireplace should not be located near doors to the exterior.

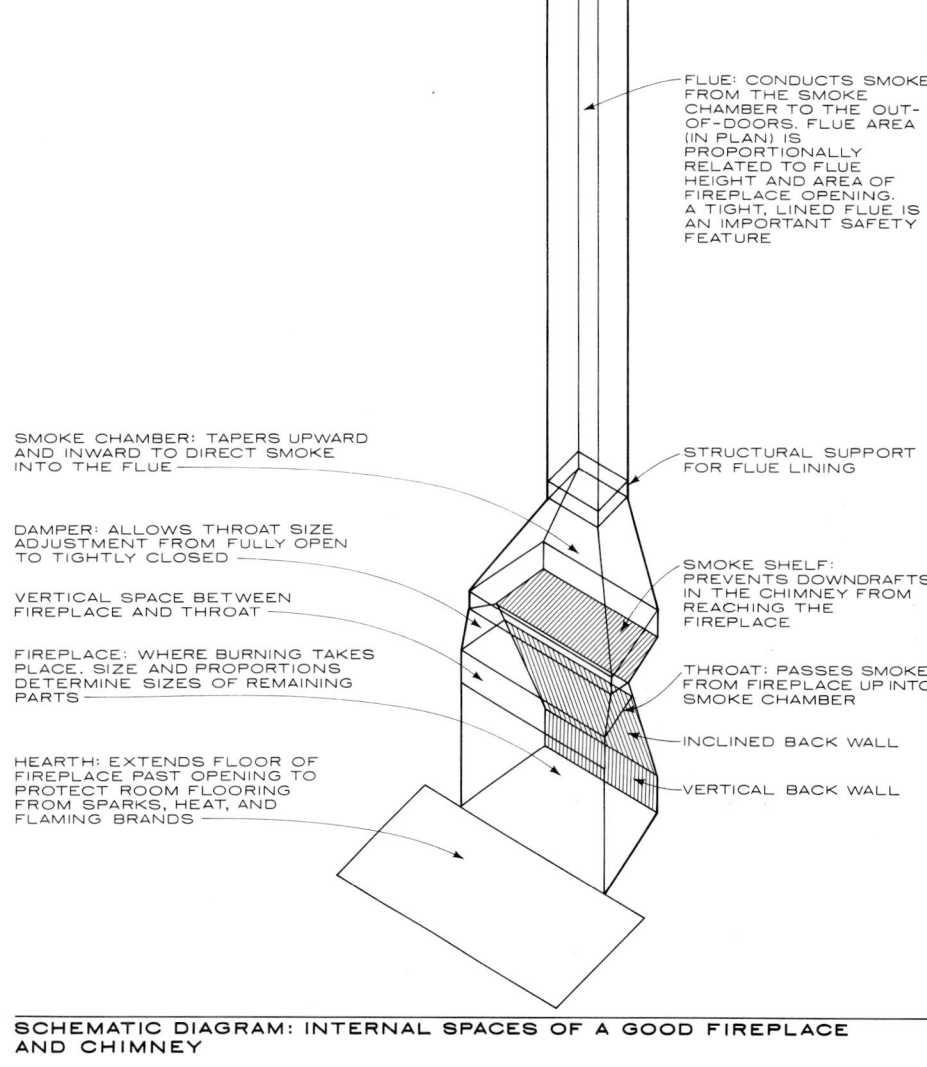

NOTE: FLUE TERMINATION MUST BE PROPERLY RELATED TO ADJACENT ROOFS, WALLS. AS AN EXTERIOR BUILDING PART, IT REQUIRES EXTRA CONSIDERATION FOR WEATHERPROOFING

FLUE: CONDUCTS SMOKE FROM THE SMOKE CHAMBER TO THE OUT-OF-DOORS. FLUE AREA (IN PLAN) IS PROPORTIONALLY RELATED TO FLUE HEIGHT AND AREA OF FIREPLACE OPENING. A TIGHT, LINED FLUE IS AN IMPORTANT SAFETY FEATURE

SMOKE CHAMBER: TAPERS UPWARD AND INWARD TO DIRECT SMOKE INTO THE FLUE

DAMPER: ALLOWS THROAT SIZE ADJUSTMENT FROM FULLY OPEN TO TIGHTLY CLOSED

VERTICAL SPACE BETWEEN FIREPLACE AND THROAT

FIREPLACE: WHERE BURNING TAKES PLACE. SIZE AND PROPORTIONS DETERMINE SIZES OF REMAINING PARTS

HEARTH: EXTENDS FLOOR OF FIREPLACE PAST OPENING TO PROTECT ROOM FLOORING FROM SPARKS, HEAT, AND FLAMING BRANDS

STRUCTURAL SUPPORT FOR FLUE LINING

SMOKE SHELF: PREVENTS DOWNDRAFTS IN THE CHIMNEY FROM REACHING THE FIREPLACE

THROAT: PASSES SMOKE FROM FIREPLACE UP INTO SMOKE CHAMBER

INCLINED BACK WALL

VERTICAL BACK WALL

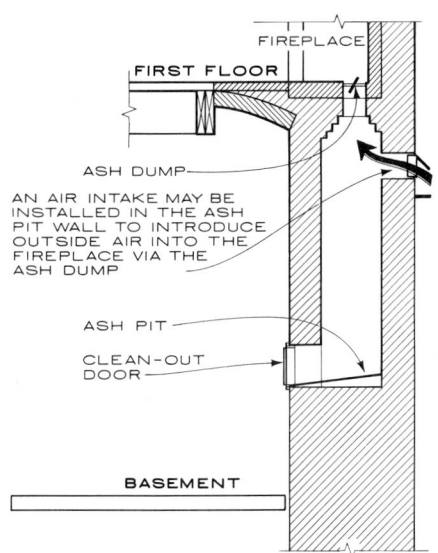

FIREPLACE

FIRST FLOOR

ASH DUMP

AN AIR INTAKE MAY BE INSTALLED IN THE ASH PIT WALL TO INTRODUCE OUTSIDE AIR INTO THE FIREPLACE VIA THE ASH DUMP

ASH PIT

CLEAN-OUT DOOR

BASEMENT

OPTIONAL ACCESSORY SPACES FOR IMPROVED FIREPLACE OPERATION

SCHEMATIC DIAGRAM: INTERNAL SPACES OF A GOOD FIREPLACE AND CHIMNEY

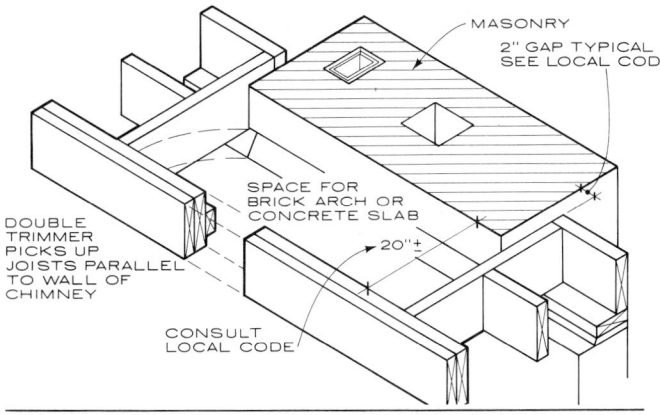

MASONRY

2" GAP TYPICAL SEE LOCAL CODE

SPACE FOR BRICK ARCH OR CONCRETE SLAB

DOUBLE TRIMMER PICKS UP JOISTS PARALLEL TO WALL OF CHIMNEY

20"±

CONSULT LOCAL CODE

WOOD FLOOR FRAMING AROUND CHIMNEY AND HEARTH

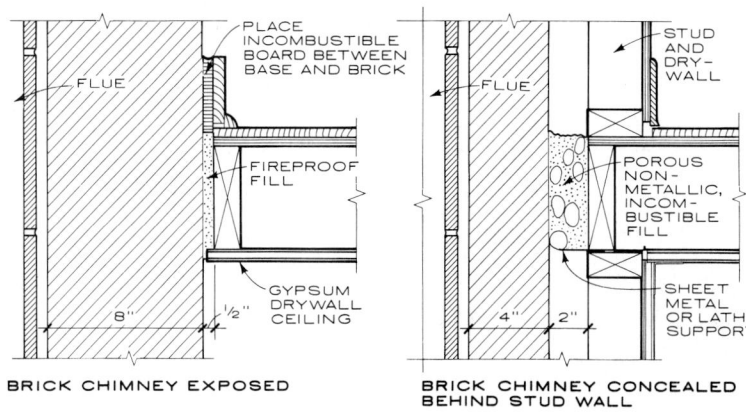

FLUE

PLACE INCOMBUSTIBLE BOARD BETWEEN BASE AND BRICK

FIREPROOF FILL

GYPSUM DRYWALL CEILING

8"

1/2"

BRICK CHIMNEY EXPOSED

STUD AND DRY-WALL

FLUE

POROUS NON-METALLIC, INCOM-BUSTIBLE FILL

SHEET METAL OR LATH SUPPORT

4"

2"

BRICK CHIMNEY CONCEALED BEHIND STUD WALL

INSULATION OF WOOD FRAMING MEMBERS AT A CHIMNEY

Darrel Rippeteau, Architect; Washington, D.C.

FIREPLACES **4**

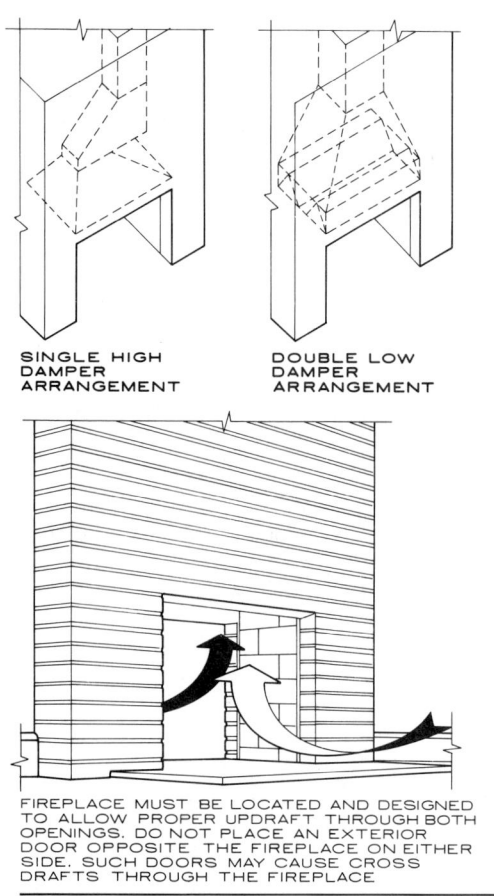

SINGLE HIGH
DAMPER
ARRANGEMENT

DOUBLE LOW
DAMPER
ARRANGEMENT

FIREPLACE MUST BE LOCATED AND DESIGNED
TO ALLOW PROPER UPDRAFT THROUGH BOTH
OPENINGS. DO NOT PLACE AN EXTERIOR
DOOR OPPOSITE THE FIREPLACE ON EITHER
SIDE. SUCH DOORS MAY CAUSE CROSS
DRAFTS THROUGH THE FIREPLACE

FIREPLACE OPEN FRONT AND BACK

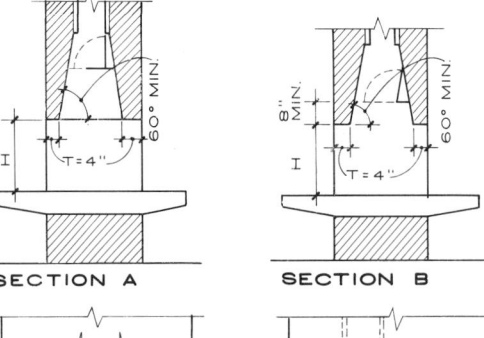
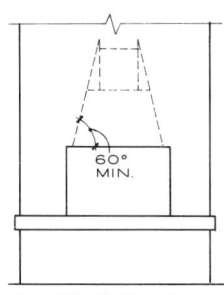
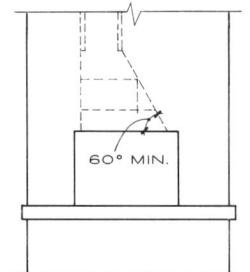

SECTION A   SECTION B

ELEVATION A   ELEVATION B

PLAN A   PLAN B

FIREPLACE OPEN FRONT AND BACK

H Height from top of hearth to bottom of facing.

B (Depth of burning area) $5/8$ H minus 8 in. but never less than 16 in.

W (Width of fireplace) B + 2T.

D (Damper at bottom of flue, see Section A) equal to free area of flue.

D (Damper closer to fire, see Section B) equal to twice the free area of flue. Set damper a minimum of 8 in. from bottom of smoke chamber. Open damper should extend entire length of smoke chamber.

TYPICAL FIREPLACE DIMENSIONS

L	H	B	FLUE
28	24	16	13 x 13
30	28	16	13 x 18
36	30	17	18 x 18
48	32	19	20 x 24
54	36	22	24 x 24

NOTE: W should not be less than 24".

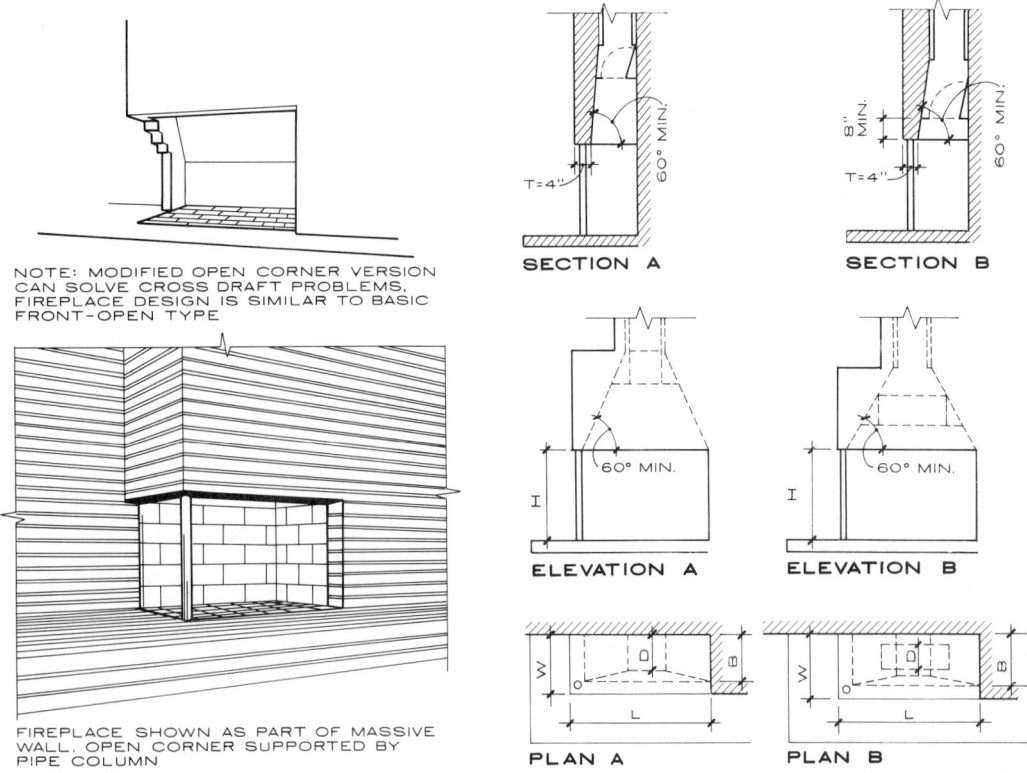

NOTE: MODIFIED OPEN CORNER VERSION
CAN SOLVE CROSS DRAFT PROBLEMS.
FIREPLACE DESIGN IS SIMILAR TO BASIC
FRONT-OPEN TYPE

FIREPLACE SHOWN AS PART OF MASSIVE
WALL. OPEN CORNER SUPPORTED BY
PIPE COLUMN

SECTION A   SECTION B

ELEVATION A   ELEVATION B

PLAN A   PLAN B

FIREPLACE OPEN FRONT AND SIDE

H Height from top of hearth to bottom of facing.

B (Depth of burning area) $2/3$ H minus 4 in.

W (Width of fireplace) B + T.

D (Damper at bottom of flue, see Section A) equal to twice the free area of the flue. Set damper a minimum of 8 in. from bottom of smoke chamber.

TYPICAL FIREPLACE DIMENSIONS

L	H	B	FLUE
28	24	16	12 x 12
30	28	18	13 x 18
36	30	20	13 x 18
48	32	22	18 x 18

FIREPLACE OPEN FRONT AND SIDE

Darrel Rippeteau, Architect; Washington, D.C.

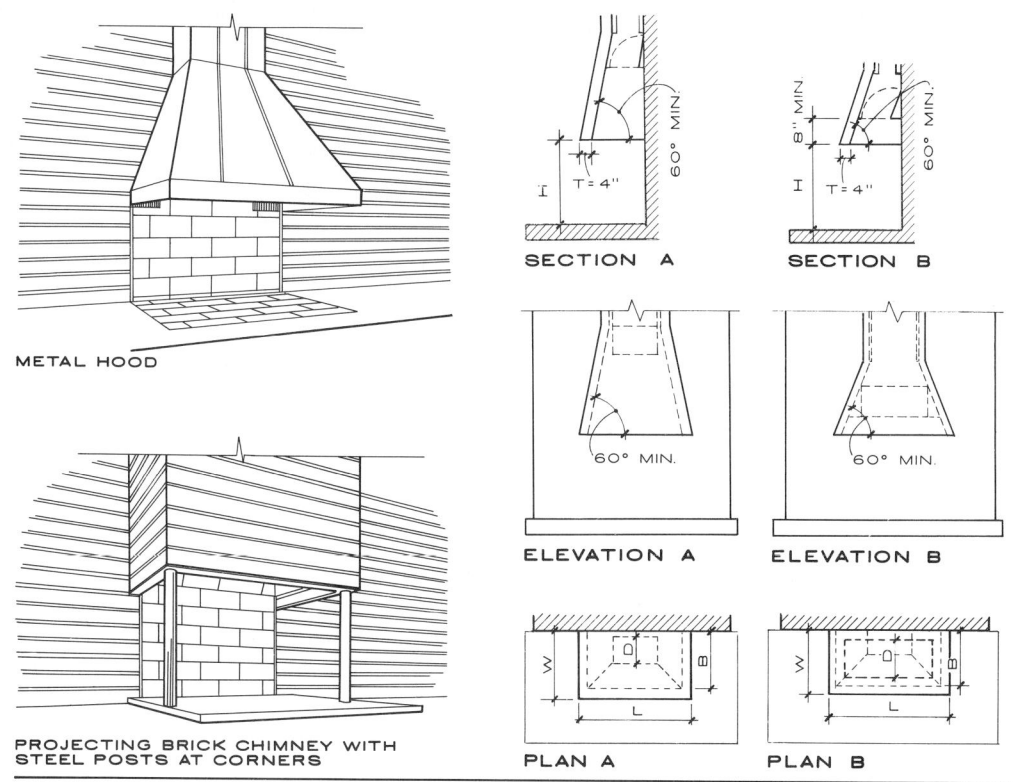

METAL HOOD

PROJECTING BRICK CHIMNEY WITH STEEL POSTS AT CORNERS

SECTION A

SECTION B

ELEVATION A

ELEVATION B

PLAN A

PLAN B

FIREPLACE PROJECTING FROM WALL (ONE LONG SIDE AND TWO SHORT SIDES)

H Height from top of hearth to bottom of facing.

B (Depth of burning area) $\frac{2}{3}$H minus 4 in.

W (Width of fireplace) B + T.

D (Damper at bottom of flue, Section A) equal to free area of flue.

D (Damper closer to fire, Section B) equal to twice free area of flue. Set damper minimum 8 in. from bottom of smoke chamber. Open damper should extend entire length of smoke chamber.

FREE AREA OF FLUE (MINIMUM): $\frac{1}{12}$ of H x (L + 2W).

GENERAL NOTE FOR ALL FIREPLACES

In tightly sealed buildings, a positive supply of outdoor air must be provided to support combustion at the fireplace. Size air intakes to admit air in the volumes computed from the following formulas:

1. Fireplace open front and side: CFM fresh air = (L + W) x H x 60.
2. Fireplace open front and back: CFM fresh air = 2L x H x 60.
3. Fireplace open three sides (one long and two short): CFM fresh air = (L + 2W) x H x 60.
4. Fireplace open three sides (two long and one short): CFM fresh air = (2L + W) x H x 60.
5. Fireplace open four sides (or around circumference of circle): CFM fresh air = perimeter x H x 60.

FIREPLACE PROJECTING FROM WALL: ONE LONG SIDE, TWO SHORT SIDES OPEN

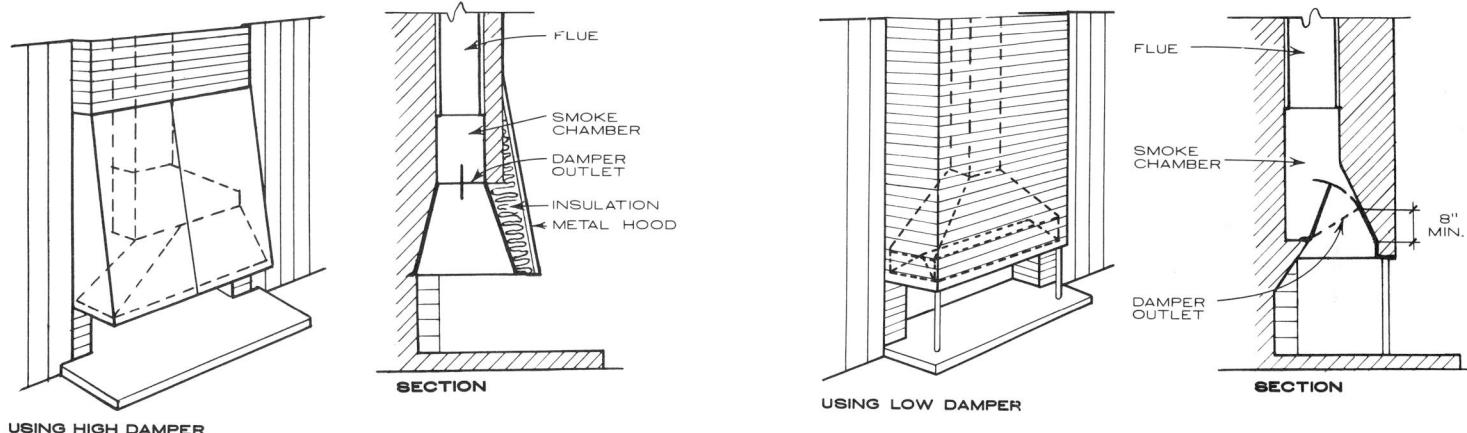

USING HIGH DAMPER

SECTION

FLUE
SMOKE CHAMBER
DAMPER OUTLET
INSULATION
METAL HOOD

USING LOW DAMPER

SECTION

FLUE
SMOKE CHAMBER
8" MIN.
DAMPER OUTLET

FIREPLACE PARTIALLY RECESSED IN WALL: ONE LONG SIDE, TWO SHORT SIDES OPEN

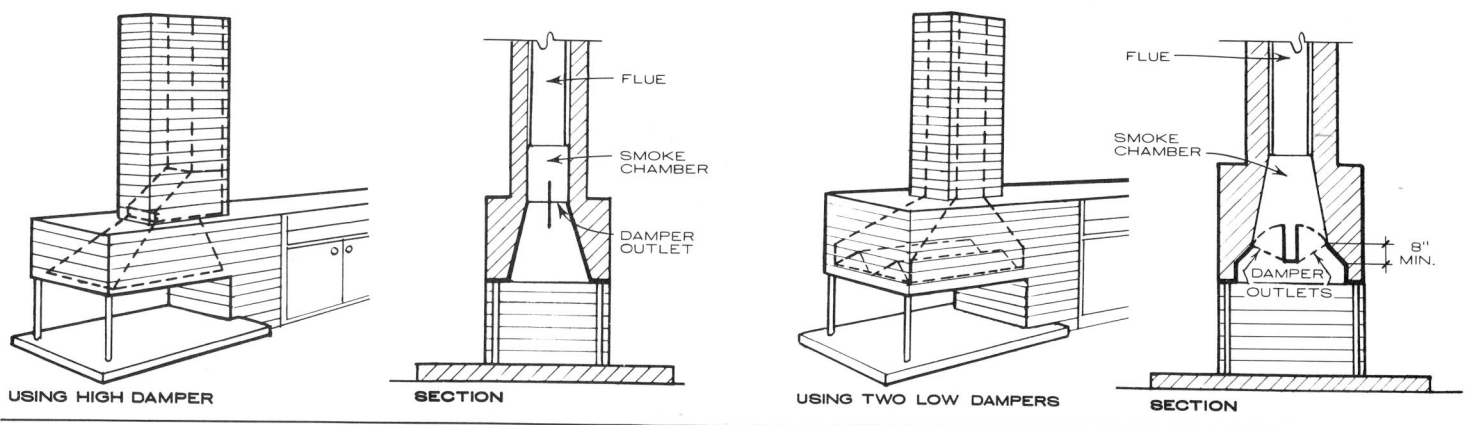

USING HIGH DAMPER

SECTION

FLUE
SMOKE CHAMBER
DAMPER OUTLET

USING TWO LOW DAMPERS

SECTION

FLUE
SMOKE CHAMBER
8" MIN.
DAMPER OUTLETS

FIREPLACE AS PENINSULA IN ROOM: TWO LONG SIDES, ONE SHORT SIDE OPEN

Darrel Rippeteau, Architect; Washington, D.C.

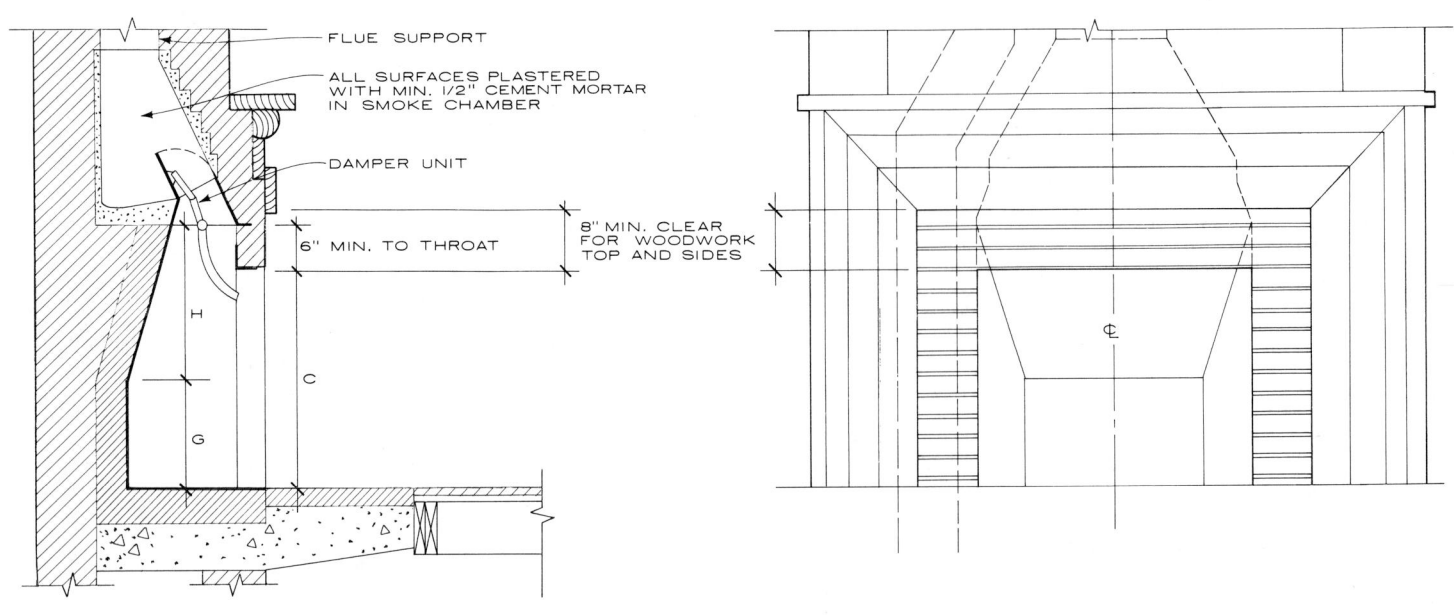

SECTION

ELEVATION

RECOMMENDED DIMENSIONS FOR WOOD BURNING FIREPLACES, HEARTH, AND FLUE (IN.)

FIREPLACE OPENING			BACK-WALL WIDTH (MIN.)	VERTICAL BACKWALL HEIGHT	INCLINED BACKWALL HEIGHT	FLUE LINING	
WIDTH B	HEIGHT C	DEPTH A	F	G	H	RECTANGULAR (OUTSIDE)	ROUND (INSIDE)
24	24	16–18	14	14	16	8½ x 13	10
28	24	16–18	14	14	16	8½ x 13	10
30	28–30	16–18	16	14	18	8½ x 13	10
36	28–30	16–18	22	14	18	8½ x 13	12
42	28–30	16–18	28	14	18	13 x 13	12
48	32	18–20	32	14	24	13 x 13	15
54	36	18–20	36	14	28	13 x 18	15
60	36	18–20	44	14	28	13 x 18	15
54	40	20–22	36	17	29	13 x 18	15
60	40	20–22	44	17	30	18 x 18	18
66	40	20–22	44	17	30	18 x 18	18
72	40	22–28	51	17	30	18 x 18	18

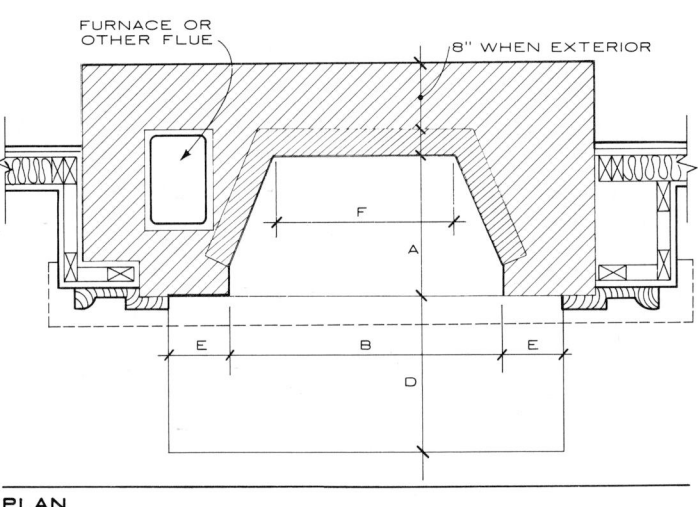

PLAN

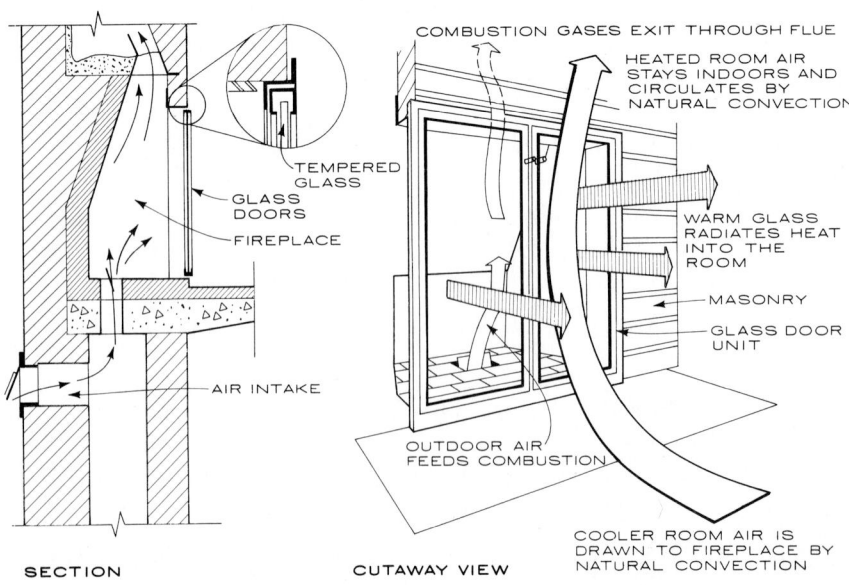

SECTION

CUTAWAY VIEW

TRADITIONAL MASONRY FIREPLACE WITH ENERGY CONSERVATION MODIFICATIONS

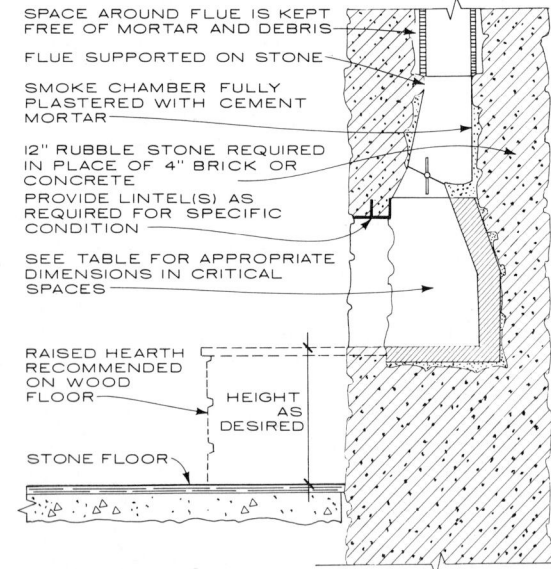

RAISED FIREPLACE IN MASSIVE STONE WALL – SECTION

Darrel Rippeteau, Architect; Washington, D.C.

HEAT CIRCULATING FIREPLACE FOR INSTALLATION IN MASONRY

These special fireplaces are constructed of steel and must be properly enclosed in masonry to obtain a complete wood burning unit. When placed on a firebrick hearth, the steel fireplace includes all of the essential combustion and smoke handling spaces described earlier in the chapter. In addition, the circulator provides a heat transfer chamber with inlets and outlets that draw in cool air, heat it, and expel warm air by natural convection. The air heating cycle can be augmented with electric fans in the intakes (not in the outlets). The steel shell provides a form for the masonry enclosure, but it is not a structural element. Enclosing masonry must be held at least 1/2 in. away from the shell to allow for expansion and contraction in the metal. The 1/2 in. space is taken up with fireproof insulation that covers the entire circulator.

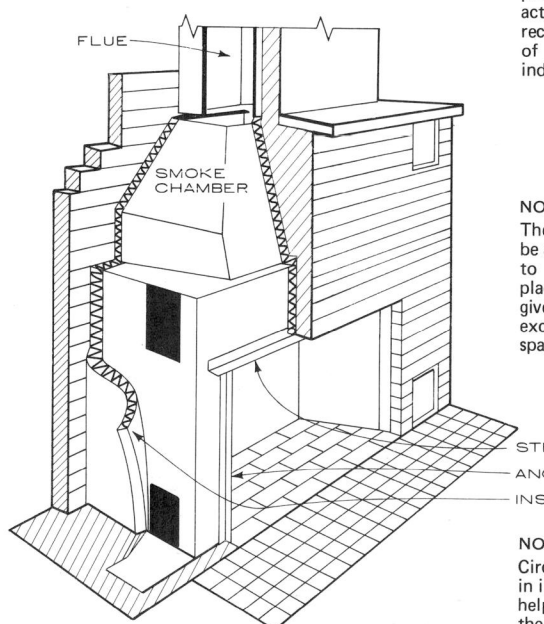

CUTAWAY VIEW

NOTE
Steel circulatory fireplaces are manufactured in various sizes with proportions set for proper burning action and air heating. An incorrect flue size may negate the design of the fireplace. The flue must be independently supported.

NOTE
The rear wall of the fireplace should be at least 8 in. thick if it is exposed to the exterior. Placing the fireplace within the exterior stud wall gives better thermal insulation in exchange for some lost indoor floor space.

NOTE
Circulator must be entirely wrapped in insulation for heat control and to help space the masonry away from the steel shell.

ELEVATION: CIRCULATOR IN BRICK

PLAN: CIRCULATOR IN BRICK

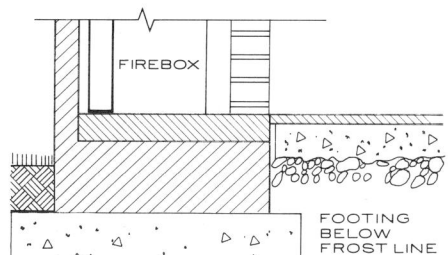

HEARTH FOR SLAB-ON-GRADE BUILDING

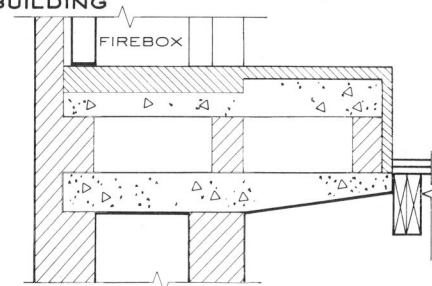

RAISED HEARTH

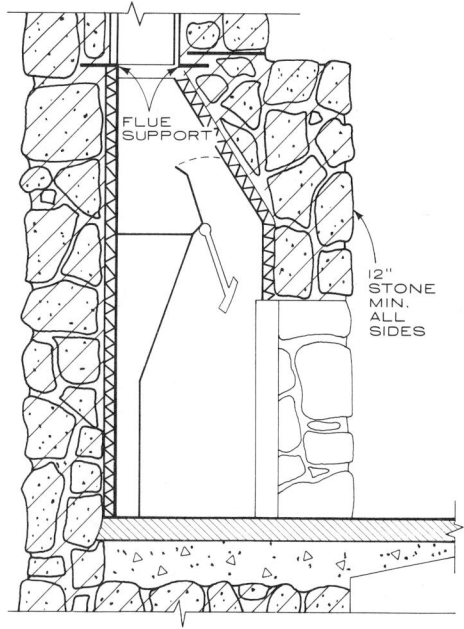

SECTION: CIRCULATOR IN STONE

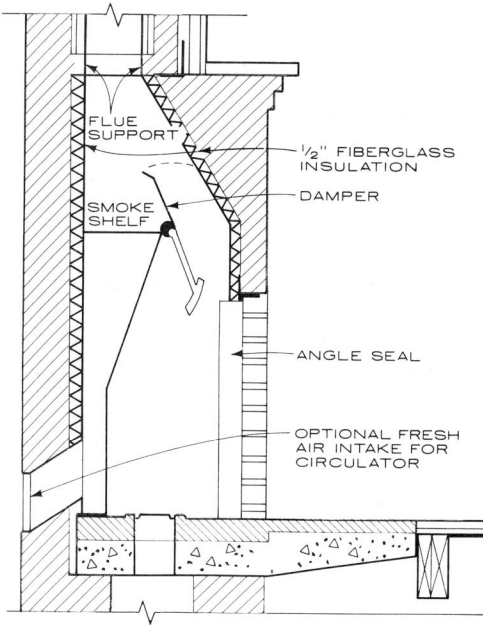

SECTION: CIRCULATOR IN BRICK

Darrel Rippeteau, Architect; Washington, D.C.

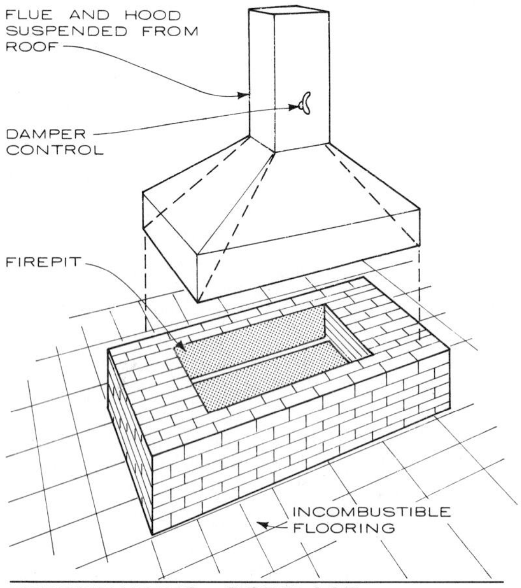

FLUE AND HOOD SUSPENDED FROM ROOF

DAMPER CONTROL

FIREPIT

INCOMBUSTIBLE FLOORING

FREESTANDING FIREPLACE

OPERABLE FLUE CAP CAN BE USED INSTEAD OF DAMPER.

NOTE: ALL SEAMS MUST BE SMOKEPROOF BUT NOT SOLDERED

CAP CONTROL LEVER

ALLOW GENEROUS HOOD OVERHANG

45° MIN.

FIREPIT

PERIMETER HEARTH SHOULD BE PROVIDED

MASONRY PIT REQUIRES ITS OWN FOUNDATION

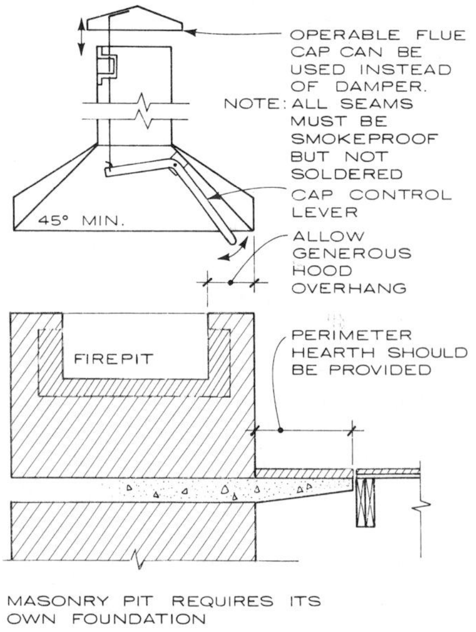

DESIGN CONSIDERATIONS

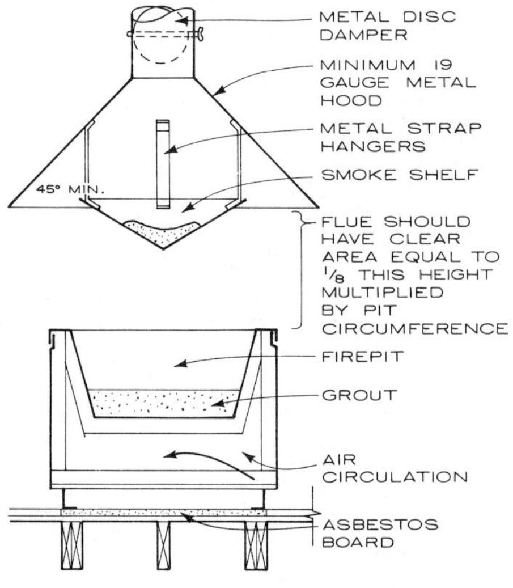

FREESTANDING FIREPLACES

Fireplaces that are open on all sides are more subject to disturbance by air currents and human movements in a room than are other more conventional fireplaces. Placement of the freestanding fireplace should be made with consideration for nearby doors, windows, and circulation paths.

Since the freestanding fireplace is open on all sides, a tremendous quantity of air is readily available for combustion. A large flue is required to vent off the substantial products generated by combustion. Typically the flue clear area should equal or exceed one-eighth of the total clear area between the fireplace pit and the hood above it. This large flue is a serious heat leak when the fireplace is not in use, hence a flue damper or operable flue cap is required. The operable flue cap keeps the flue warm (at indoor temperature) when it is closed, which promotes instant updraft when the cap is opened.

With large quantities of air rushing up the flue, uncomfortable drafts may occur in the room. If infiltration air is not sufficient to feed the fire, billows of smoke can occur and spread into the room. Both problems can be reduced by providing a direct supply of outdoor air to the firepit through ductwork and grilles.

METAL DISC DAMPER

MINIMUM 19 GAUGE METAL HOOD

METAL STRAP HANGERS

SMOKE SHELF

45° MIN.

FLUE SHOULD HAVE CLEAR AREA EQUAL TO $\frac{1}{8}$ THIS HEIGHT MULTIPLIED BY PIT CIRCUMFERENCE

FIREPIT

GROUT

AIR CIRCULATION

ASBESTOS BOARD

METAL FIREPIT AND HOOD

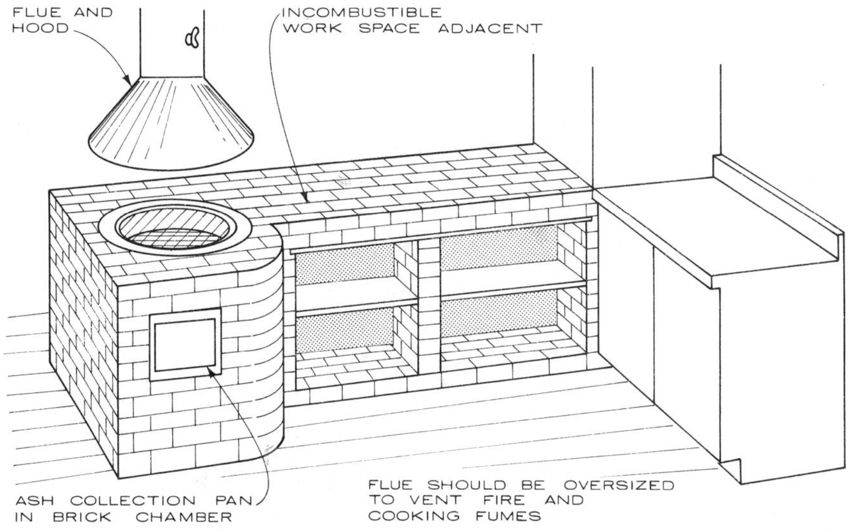

FLUE AND HOOD

INCOMBUSTIBLE WORK SPACE ADJACENT

ASH COLLECTION PAN IN BRICK CHAMBER

FLUE SHOULD BE OVERSIZED TO VENT FIRE AND COOKING FUMES

KITCHEN BARBECUE PIT

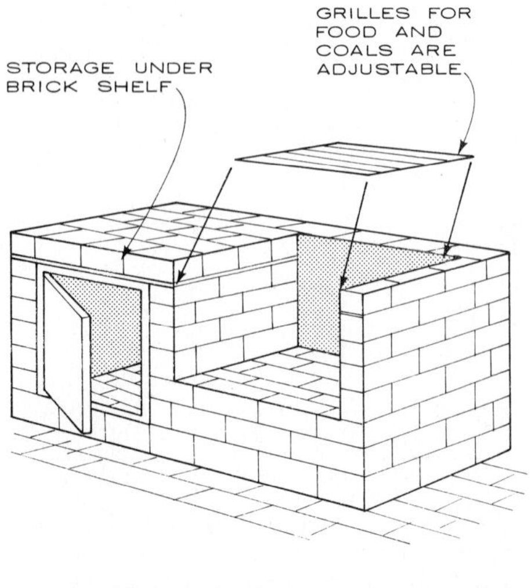

STORAGE UNDER BRICK SHELF

GRILLES FOR FOOD AND COALS ARE ADJUSTABLE

OUTDOOR BARBECUE

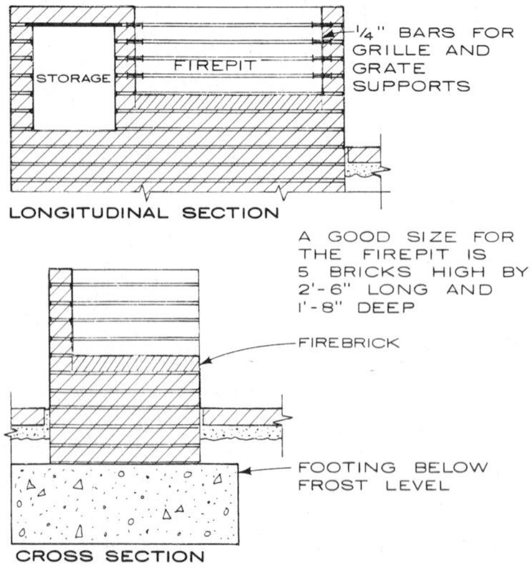

STORAGE

FIREPIT

$\frac{1}{4}$" BARS FOR GRILLE AND GRATE SUPPORTS

LONGITUDINAL SECTION

A GOOD SIZE FOR THE FIREPIT IS 5 BRICKS HIGH BY 2'-6" LONG AND 1'-8" DEEP

FIREBRICK

FOOTING BELOW FROST LEVEL

CROSS SECTION

DETAIL SECTIONS

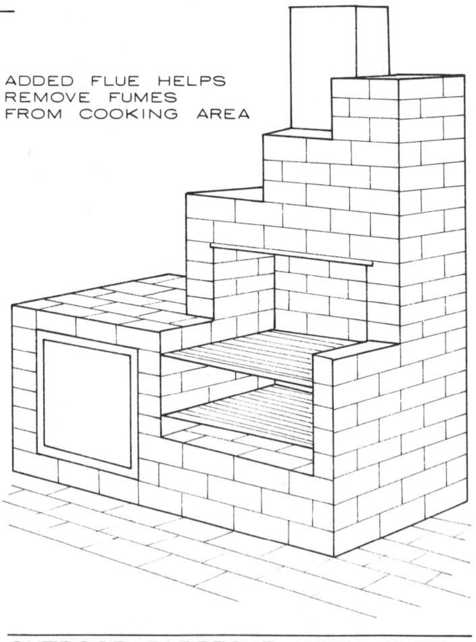

ADDED FLUE HELPS REMOVE FUMES FROM COOKING AREA

OUTDOOR BARBECUE WITH FLUE

Darrel Rippeteau, Architect; Washington, D.C.

FIREPLACES

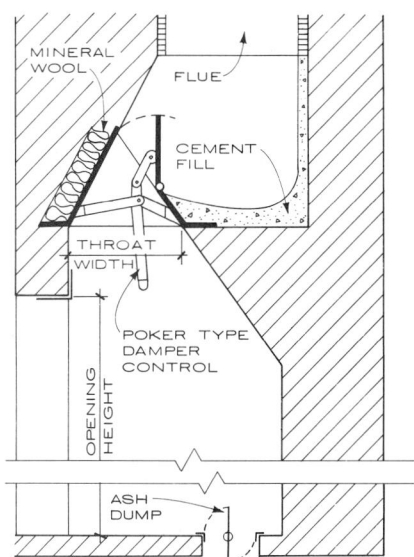

ONE-SIDED FIREPLACE WITH FORM DAMPER

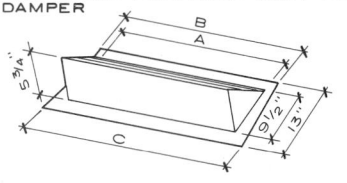

FORM DAMPER (IN.)

WIDTH OF FIREPLACE OPENING	DAMPER DIMENSIONS		
	A	B	C
24–26	24	26 3/4	28 1/4
27–30	28	30 3/4	32 1/4
31–34	32	34 3/4	36 1/4
35–38	36	38 3/4	40 1/4
39–42	40	42 3/4	44 1/4
43–46	44	46 3/4	48 1/4
47–50	48	50 3/4	52 1/4
51–54	52	54 3/4	56 1/4
57–60	58	60 3/4	62 1/2

FORM STEEL DAMPERS are designed to provide the correct ratio of throat-to-fireplace opening, producing maximum draft. These dampers are equipped with poker type control and are easily installed.

FORM DAMPERS

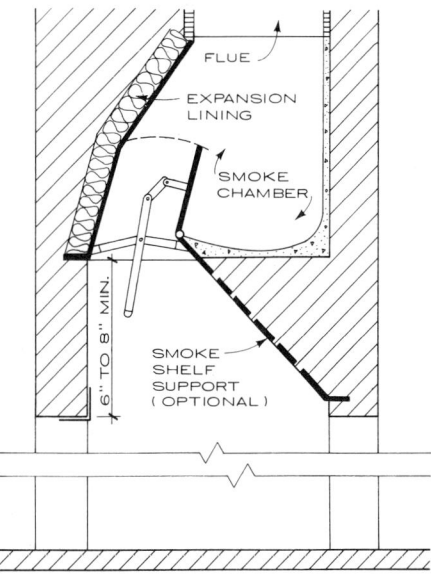

TWO-SIDED FIREPLACE WITH HIGH FORM DAMPER

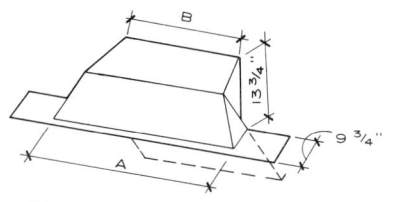

HIGH FORM DAMPER (IN.)

A	24	28	32	36	40	44	48
B	7 1/4	11 1/4	15 1/4	19 1/4	23 1/4	27 1/4	31 1/4

HIGH FORM DAMPERS provide correct ratio of throat-to-fireplace opening with an optional preformed smoke shelf, which can reduce material and labor requirements. They are useful for both single and multiple opening fireplaces.

NOTES

1. Locate bottom of damper minimum 6 to 8 in. from top of fireplace opening.
2. Mineral wool blanket allows for expansion of metal damper walls.
3. Dampers are available in heavy gauge steel or cast iron. Check with local suppliers for specific forms and sizes.

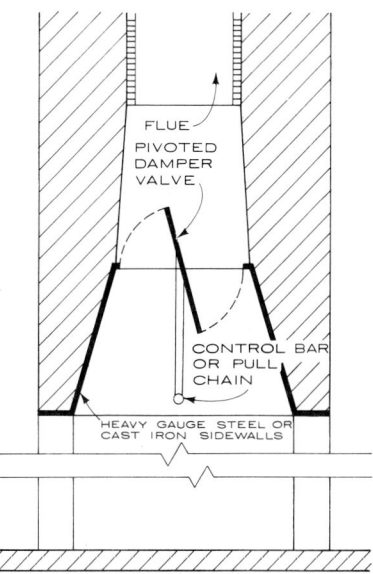

THREE-SIDED FIREPLACE WITH SQUARE FORM DAMPER

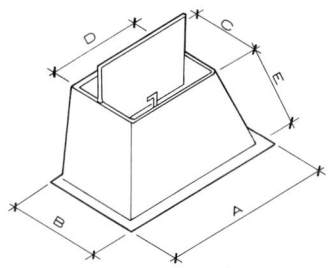

SQUARE FORM DAMPER (IN.)

A	B	C	D	E
30	16	12	17	17
34	20	17	17	17
38	20	17	17	25
42	20	17	23	25
50	24	21	23	28

SQUARE FORM DAMPERS have high sloping sides that promote even draw on all sides of multiple opening fireplaces. They are properly proportioned for a strong draft and smokefree operation.

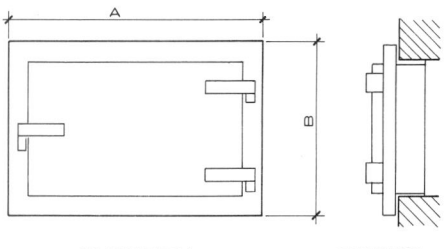

ELEVATION   SECTION

DOOR DIMENSIONS (IN.)

A	B
6	8
8	8, 10
10	10, 12
12	8, 10, 12, 16, 18
16	16, 18, 20, 24
18	18, 24, 30
20	16, 20, 30

CLEANOUT OR ASHPIT DOORS

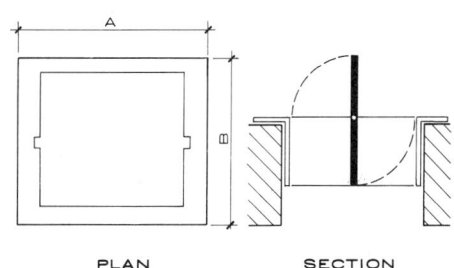

PLAN   SECTION

DUMP DIMENSIONS (IN.)

A	3 1/2	4 1/2	7
B	7	9	10

NOTE

Ash dumps and cleanout doors are available in heavy gauge steel or cast iron. See local manufacturers for available types and sizes.

ASH DUMPS

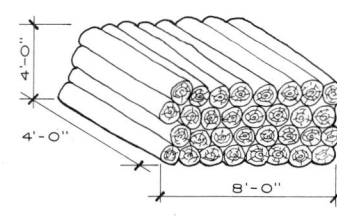

CORD (ONE CORD = 128 CU FT)

NOTES

1. A face cord of wood consists of 64 cu ft, or a stack 4 ft high and 8 ft wide, with logs 2 ft long.
2. Logs are cut to lengths of 1 ft 4 in., 2 ft 0 in., 2 ft 6 in., and 4 ft. Allow 3 in. minimum clearance between logs and each side of fireplace.

LOGS

Olga Barmine; Darrel Rippeteau, Architect; Washington, D.C.

FIREPLACES **4**

HEIGHT OF ADJACENT FLUES
SHOULD VARY APPROX. 4"

WASH

4" MIN.

FLAT ROOF + 3'
PITCHED ROOF PEAK + 2'

ROOF LINE

CORBEL BRICKWORK
TO PROVIDE FULL 8"
WHERE EXPOSED TO
WEATHER

60°

60°

A   A   A   A

ATTIC FLOOR

FLUE LININGS
EACH FIREPLACE OR
STOVE REQUIRES ITS
OWN SEPARATE FLUE

4"
MIN.

SECOND FLOOR

ASH
CHUTE

FLUE ANGLE NOT LESS
THAN 60° CUT FLUE
TO ENSURE TIGHT
JOINTS. MAINTAIN
FULL FREE AREA

60°

DAMPER

FIREPLACE

FIRST FLOOR

ASH
CHUTE

FURNACE THIMBLE

ASH PIT

CLEANOUT DOORS

2' TYP.

BASEMENT

TYPICAL RESIDENTIAL CHIMNEY ELEVATION   SECTION

Darrel Rippeteau, Architect; Washington, D.C.

NOTE: FLUE LININGS SHOULD STAND FREE OF
SURROUNDING MASONRY, WITH JUST
ENOUGH MORTAR CONTACT TO MAINTAIN
SPACING

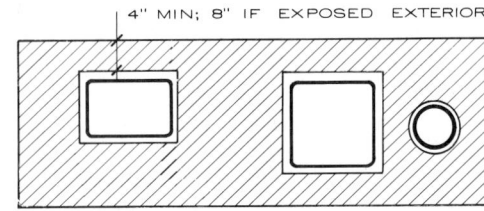

4" MIN; 8" IF EXPOSED EXTERIOR

TYPICAL CONSTRUCTION FOR RESIDENTIAL
CHIMNEY

PLAN SECTION A-A

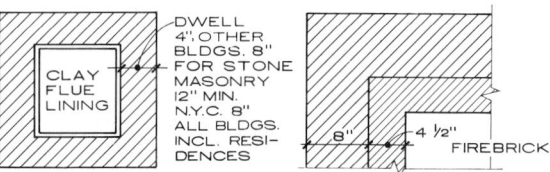

CLAY
FLUE
LINING

DWELL
4", OTHER
BLDGS. 8"
FOR STONE
MASONRY
12" MIN.
N.Y.C. 8"
ALL BLDGS.
INCL. RESI-
DENCES

8"   4 1/2"
FIREBRICK

Chimneys for stoves, cooking
ranges, warm air, hot water
and low pressure steam heating furnaces, low heat industrial appliances, portable type
incinerators, fireplaces.

**LOW HEAT
APPLIANCES**

Chimneys for high pressure
steam boilers, smokehouses,
and other medium heat appliances other than incinerators.
Continue firebrick up 25' min.
N.Y.C. firebrick up 50' min.

**MEDIUM HEAT
APPLIANCES**

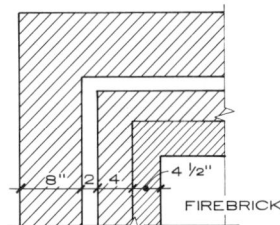

8"   2 4   4 1/2"
FIREBRICK

Chimneys for cupolas, brass
furnaces, porcelain baking
kilns, and other high heat appliances.

**HIGH HEAT
APPLIANCES**

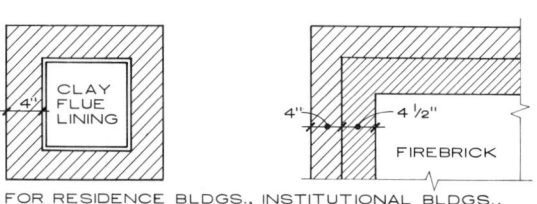

CLAY
FLUE
LINING

4"

4"   4 1/2"
FIREBRICK

FOR RESIDENCE BLDGS., INSTITUTIONAL BLDGS.,
CHURCHES, SCHOOLS AND RESTAURANTS.

For domestic type incinerators
where firebox or charging compartment is not larger than 5
cu ft

For apartment house type incinerators. Continue firebrick
up 10' above roof of combustion chamber for grate area 7 □'
or less; 40' above for grate
area exceeding 7 □'

CHIMNEYS FOR INCINERATORS

**CHIMNEY REQUIREMENTS - VARIOUS USE
TYPES**

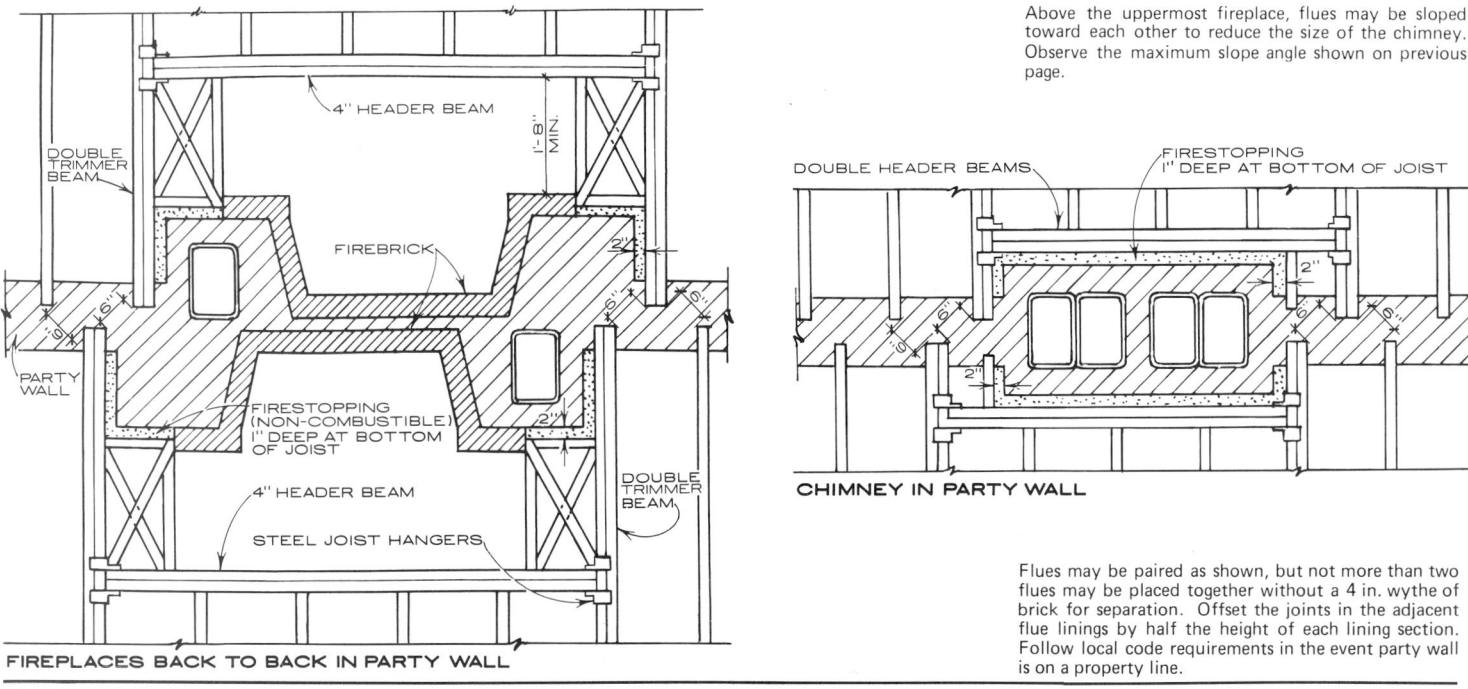

Above the uppermost fireplace, flues may be sloped toward each other to reduce the size of the chimney. Observe the maximum slope angle shown on previous page.

FIREPLACES BACK TO BACK IN PARTY WALL

CHIMNEY IN PARTY WALL

Flues may be paired as shown, but not more than two flues may be placed together without a 4 in. wythe of brick for separation. Offset the joints in the adjacent flue linings by half the height of each lining section. Follow local code requirements in the event party wall is on a property line.

FIREPLACES CONSTRUCTED INTEGRALLY WITH BRICK PARTY WALL

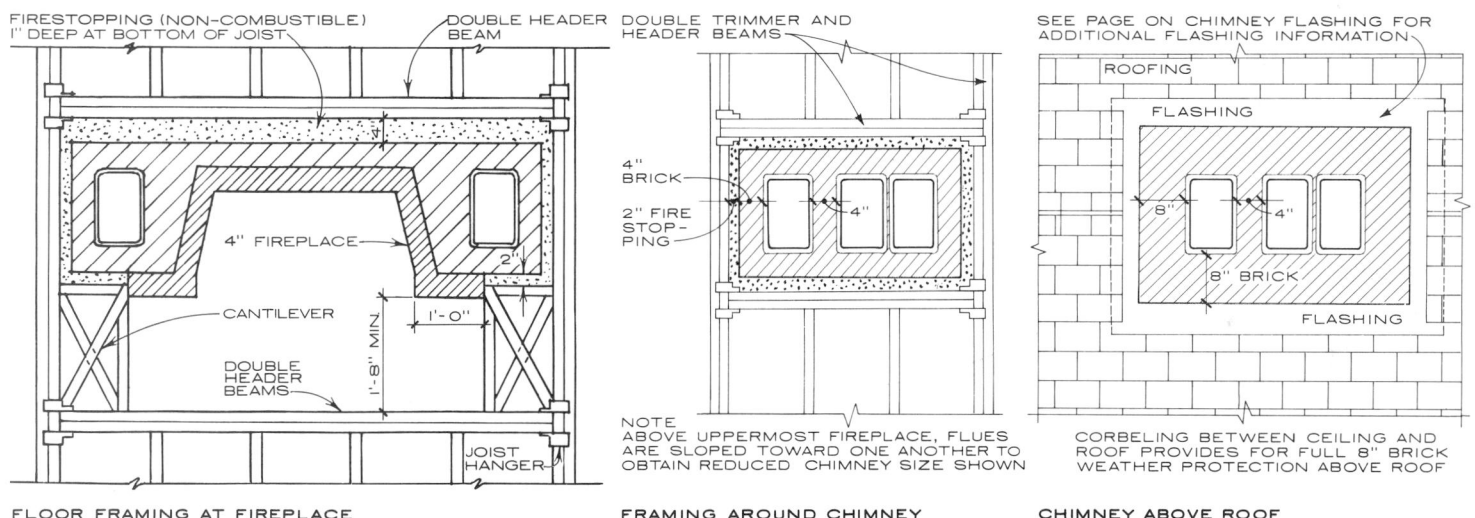

NOTE
ABOVE UPPERMOST FIREPLACE, FLUES ARE SLOPED TOWARD ONE ANOTHER TO OBTAIN REDUCED CHIMNEY SIZE SHOWN

CORBELING BETWEEN CEILING AND ROOF PROVIDES FOR FULL 8" BRICK WEATHER PROTECTION ABOVE ROOF

FLOOR FRAMING AT FIREPLACE   **FRAMING AROUND CHIMNEY**   **CHIMNEY ABOVE ROOF**

FIREPLACES AND CHIMNEY CONSTRUCTED AS FREESTANDING TOWER INSIDE WOOD FRAME HOUSE

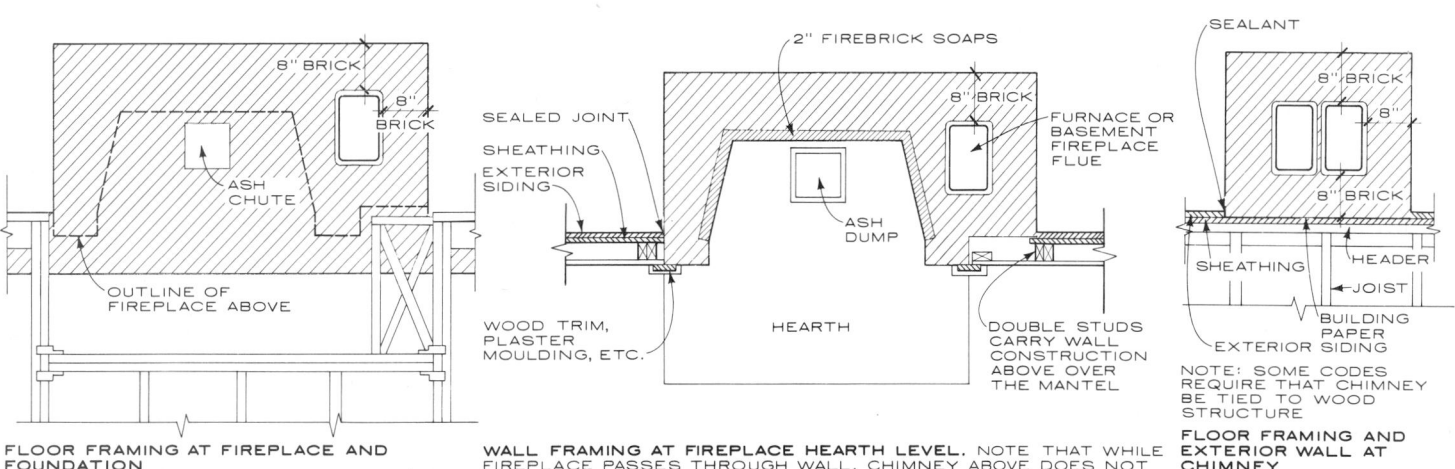

FLOOR FRAMING AT FIREPLACE AND FOUNDATION

WALL FRAMING AT FIREPLACE HEARTH LEVEL. NOTE THAT WHILE FIREPLACE PASSES THROUGH WALL, CHIMNEY ABOVE DOES NOT

FLOOR FRAMING AND EXTERIOR WALL AT CHIMNEY

NOTE: SOME CODES REQUIRE THAT CHIMNEY BE TIED TO WOOD STRUCTURE

FIREPLACES AND CHIMNEY CONSTRUCTED AS FREESTANDING TOWER OUTSIDE WOOD FRAME HOUSE

Darrel Rippeteau, Architect; Washington, D.C.

FIREPLACES   **4**

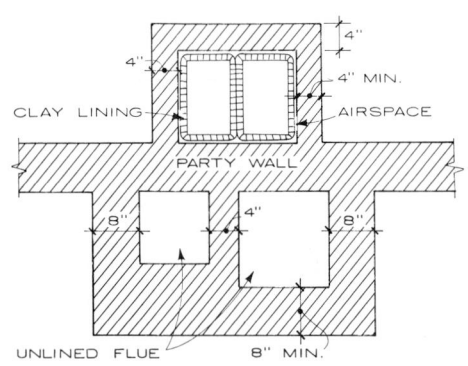

FLUE ARRANGEMENT — PARTY WALL

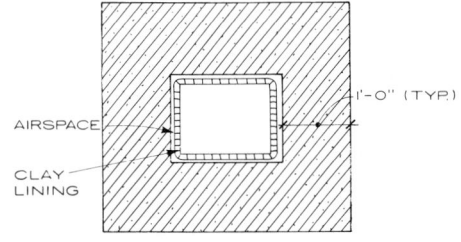

FLUE ARRANGEMENT —
RUBBLE STONE CHIMNEY

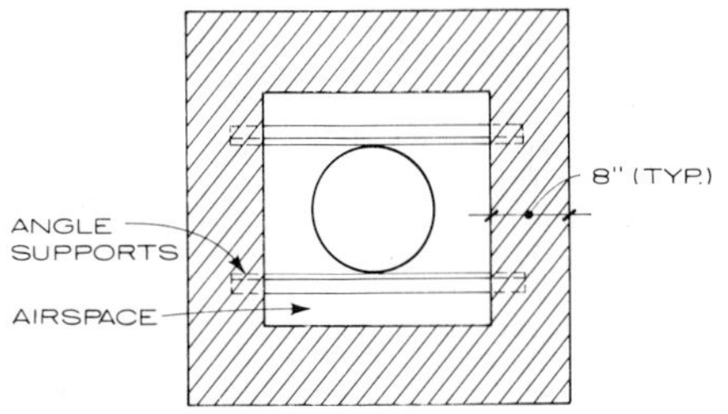

STEEL STACK SURROUNDED BY
BRICK — FOR LARGE BOILERS

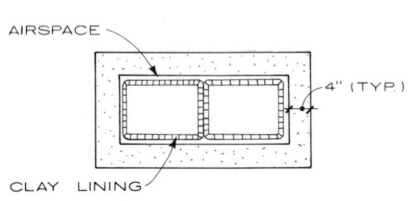

FLUE ARRANGEMENT —
DRESSED STONE CHIMNEY

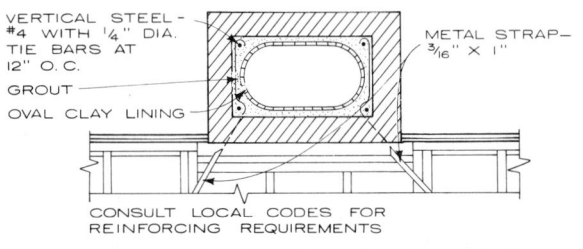

REINFORCED CHIMNEY WITH OVAL FLUE
LININGS IN AREAS SUBJECT TO
EARTHQUAKES AND HIGH WINDS

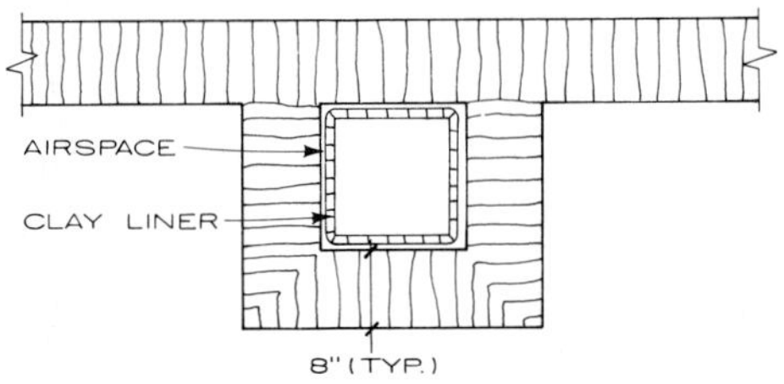

FLUE LINING IN EXTERIOR
TILE WALL

FLUE ARRANGEMENTS AND CHIMNEY TYPES

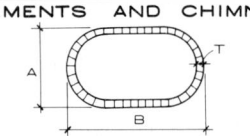

OVAL FLUE LINING

NOMINAL SIZE	AREA (SQ IN.)	A	B
8½″ x 13″	69	8½″	12¾″
8½″ x 17″	87	8½″	16¾″
10″ x 18″	112	10″	17¾″
10″ x 21″	138	10″	21″
13″ x 17″	134	12¾″	16¾″
13″ x 21″	173	12¾″	21″
17″ x 17″	171	16¾″	16¾″
17″ x 21″	223	16¾″	21″
21″ x 21″	269	21″	21″

RECTANGULAR FLUE LINING (STANDARD)

AREA (SQ IN.)	A	B	T
51	8½″	8½″	⅝″
79	8½″	13″	¾″
108	8½″	18″	⅞″
125	13″	13″	⅞″
168	13″	18″	⅞″
232	18″	18″	1⅛″
279	20″	20″	1⅜″
338	20″	24″	1½″
420	24″	24″	1½″

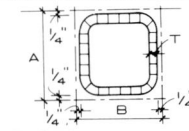

RECTANGULAR FLUE LINING (MODULAR)

AREA (SQ IN.)	A	B	T
57	8″	12″	¾″
74	8″	16″	⅞″
87	12″	12″	⅞″
120	12″	16″	1″
162	16″	16″	1⅛″
208	16″	20″	1¼″
262	20″	20″	1⅜″
320	20″	24″	1½″
385	24″	24″	1⅝″

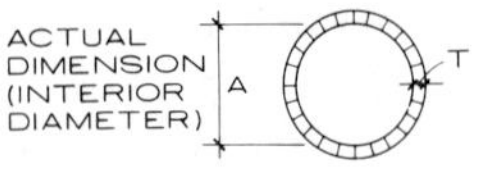

ACTUAL DIMENSION (INTERIOR DIAMETER)

ROUND FLUE LINING

AREA (SQ IN.)	A	T	LENGTH
47	8″	¾″	2′-0″
74.5	10″	⅞″	2′-0″
108	12″	1″	2′-0″
171	15″	1⅛″	2′-0″
240	18″	1¼″	2′-0″
298	20″	1⅜″	2′-0″
433	24″	1⅝″	2′-0″

CLAY FLUE LININGS

NOTES

1. Availability of specific clay flue lining shapes varies according to location. Generally, oval and round flue linings, used in construction with steel reinforcing bars, are available in the western states, while rectangular flue linings are found commonly throughout the eastern states. Check with local manufacturers for available types and sizes.

2. U.L. approved lightweight concrete flues are available in the western states in modular sizes 8 x 8 in. and 16 x 16 in.

3. Nominal flue size for round flues is interior diameter; nominal flue sizes for standard rectangular flues are the exterior dimensions and, for modular flue linings, the outside dimensions plus ½ in.

4. Areas shown are net minimum inside areas.

5. Wall thicknesses shown are minimum required. Flue dimensions vary ±½ in. about the nominal sizes shown.

6. All flue linings listed are generally available in 2 ft lengths. Verify other lengths with local supplier.

7. Fireplace flue sizes: One-tenth the area of fireplace opening recommended; one-eighth the area of opening recommended if chimney is higher than 20 ft and rectangular flues are used; one-twelfth the area is minimum required; verify with local codes.

8. Flue area should never be less than 70 sq in. for fireplace of 840 sq in. opening or smaller.

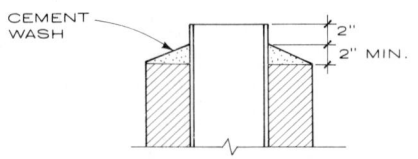

SETTING OF FLUE LINING

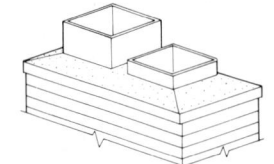

9. Unequal projection of flues is a safeguard against smoke pouring out of one flue and down the other.

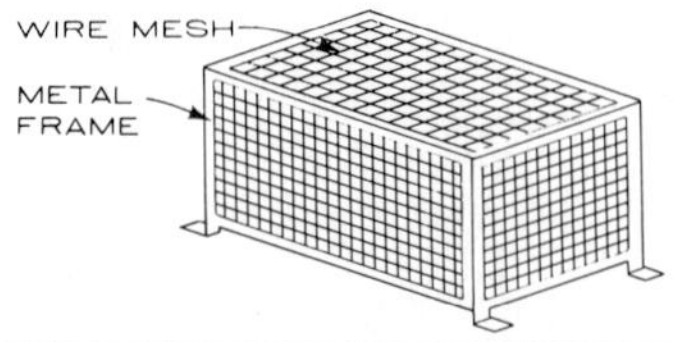

SPARK ARRESTOR

10. Consult local codes for required size and mesh openings.

Alexander Keyes; Darrel Rippeteau, Architect; Washington, D.C.

FIREPLACES

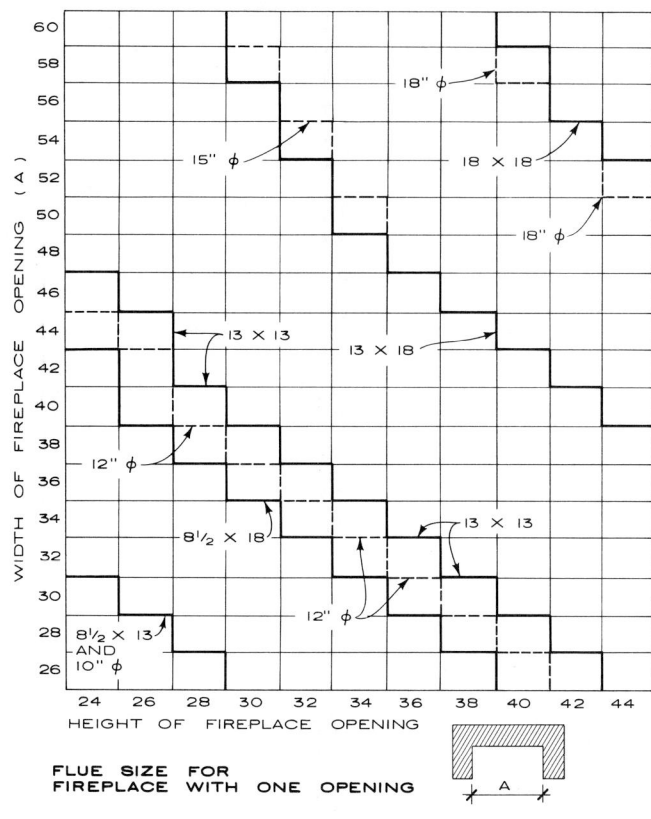

FLUE SIZE FOR
FIREPLACE WITH ONE OPENING

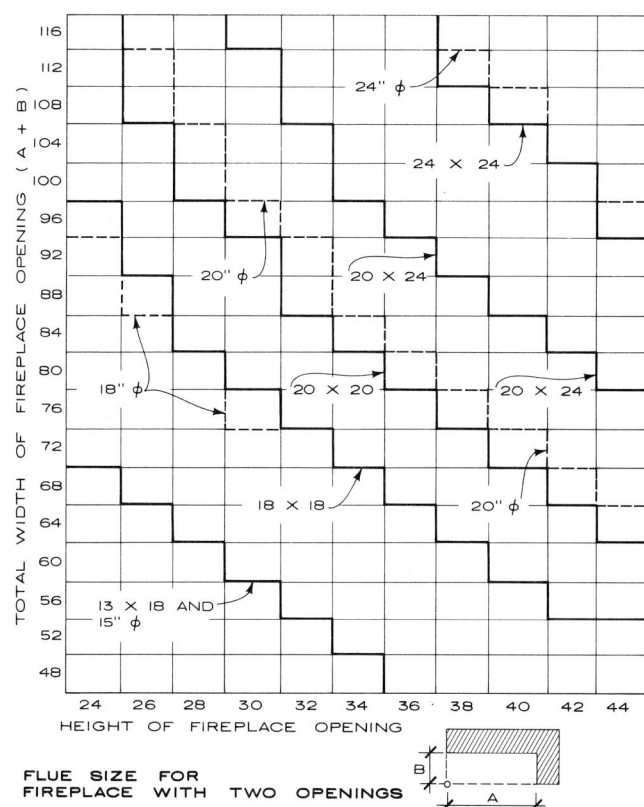

FLUE SIZE FOR
FIREPLACE WITH TWO OPENINGS

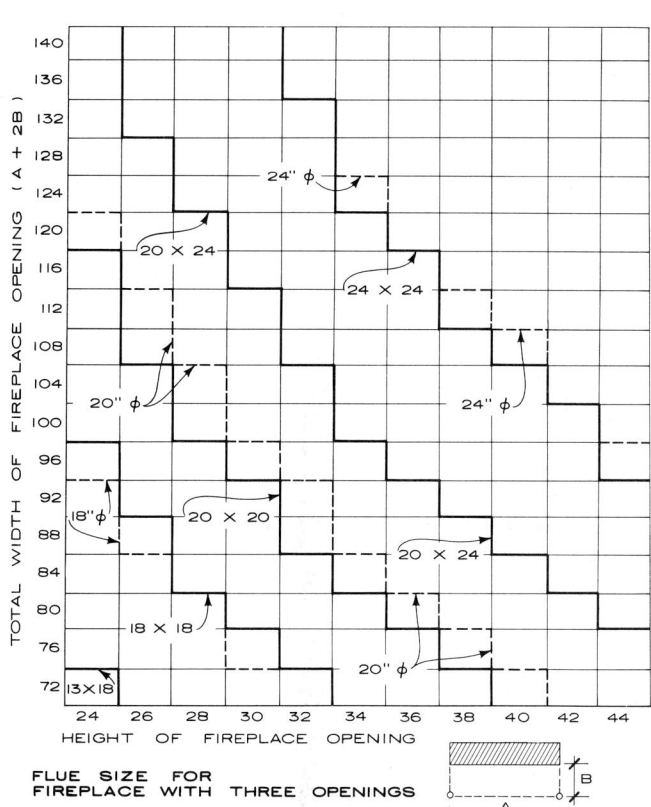

FLUE SIZE FOR
FIREPLACE WITH THREE OPENINGS

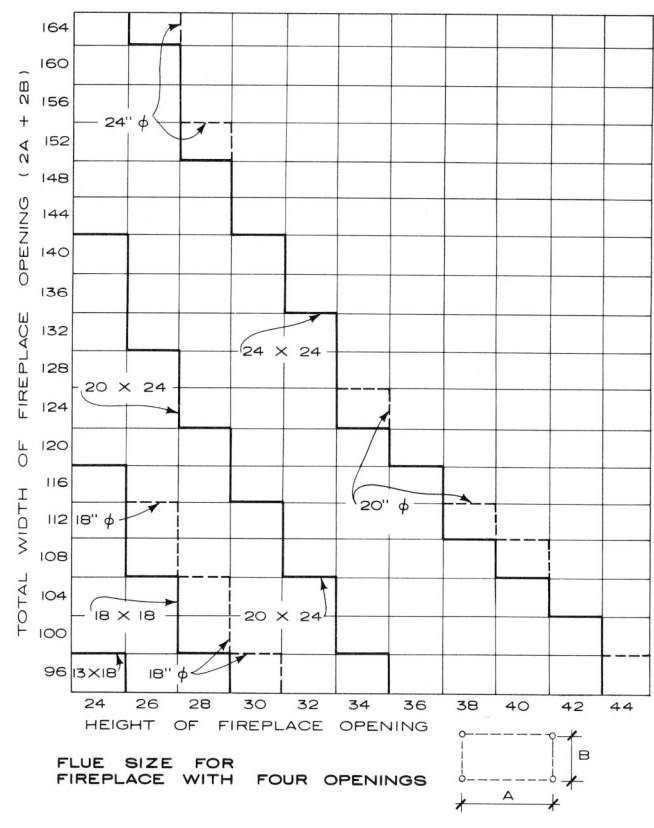

FLUE SIZE FOR
FIREPLACE WITH FOUR OPENINGS

KEY

—————— Rectangular flue.
-- -- -- -- Round flue.

Based on recommended sizes, 1/10 of fireplace area.

Alexander Keyes; Darrel Rippeteau, Architect; Washington, D.C.

EXPLANATION

Flue size is indicated by the area of graph that lies within (or below) the designated solid or dashed line.

NOTES

Charts are based on minimum net inside area of standard rectangular and round terra cotta flue linings. Where rectangular (and round) flue designations coincide, the designation for rectangular flue is shown.

FIREPLACES 4

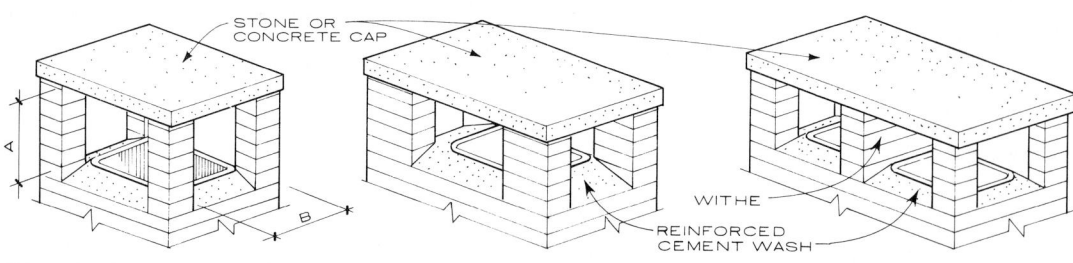

Chimney hoods to prevent downdraft due to adjoining hills, buildings, trees, etc.

A should be ¼ greater than B in all hooded chimneys

Chimney hoods also serve as water protection for seldom used flues

Withe between flues is the best method of preventing downdraft

CHIMNEY HOODS

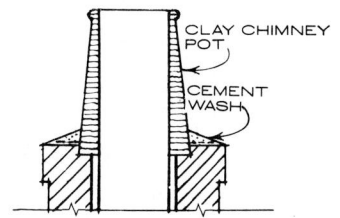

CHIMNEY POT

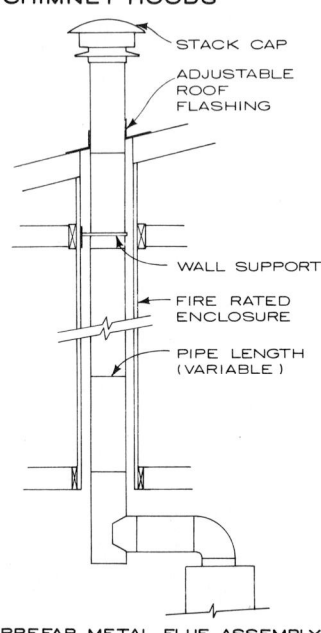

PREFAB METAL FLUE ASSEMBLY

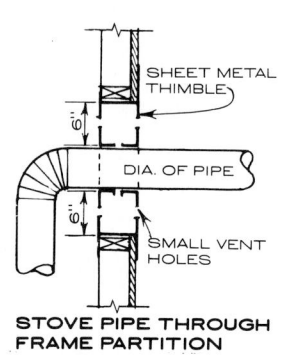

STOVE PIPE THROUGH FRAME PARTITION

Metal chimneys, connections, and flues are designed to be assembled with other pipes and accessory parts of the same model without requiring field construction. Pipes are single, double, or triple metal walls separated by ½ to 1 in. airspace. Sizes range from 3 to 14 in. I.D. round pipe and 4⁵⁄₆ in. oval pipe for use in 2 x 6 stud walls. Provide 1 to 2 in. clearance from enclosure walls and roof structure. Verify with manufacturer's listings for approved uses and specifications.

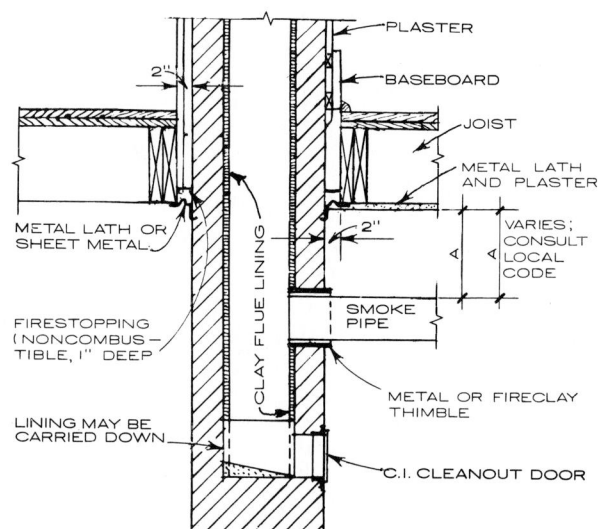

SMOKE PIPE FOR STOVES, H.W. HEATERS AND SMALL RANGES—CONNECTIONS AND CLEARANCES

FLUES, VENTS, AND SMOKE CONNECTIONS—RESIDENTIAL

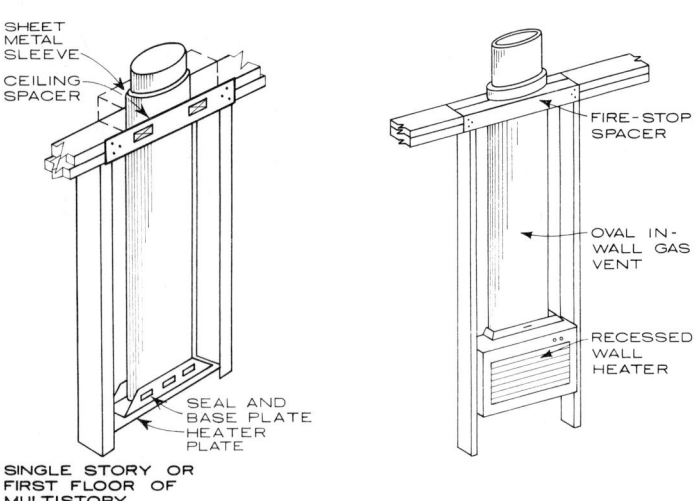

SINGLE STORY OR FIRST FLOOR OF MULTISTORY

Use only type BW vent system (approved for use with recessed heater), acceptable for use in 2 x 6 walls. This system consists of pipe-base plated, seal, ceiling spacer, and fire-stop spacer. Type BW gas vents shall have listed capacity not less than that of the listed vented wall furnaces to which they are connected.

RECESSED WALL HEATER FLUE SYSTEM

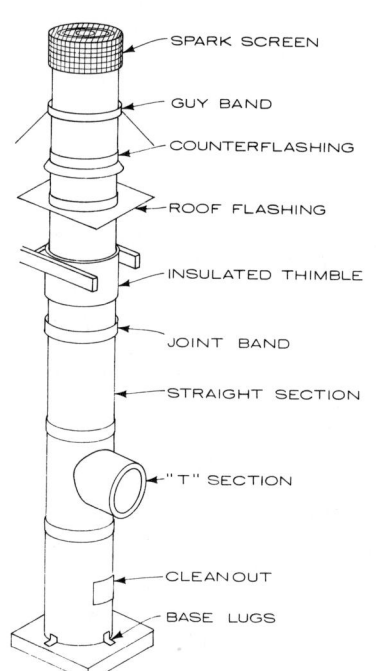

U.L. approved metal chimney systems with refractory linings are available in 10 to 60 in. I.D. in 4 ft lengths.

INDUSTRIAL CHIMNEY SYSTEM

Alexander Keyes; Darrel Rippeteau, Architect; Washington, D.C.

FIREPLACES

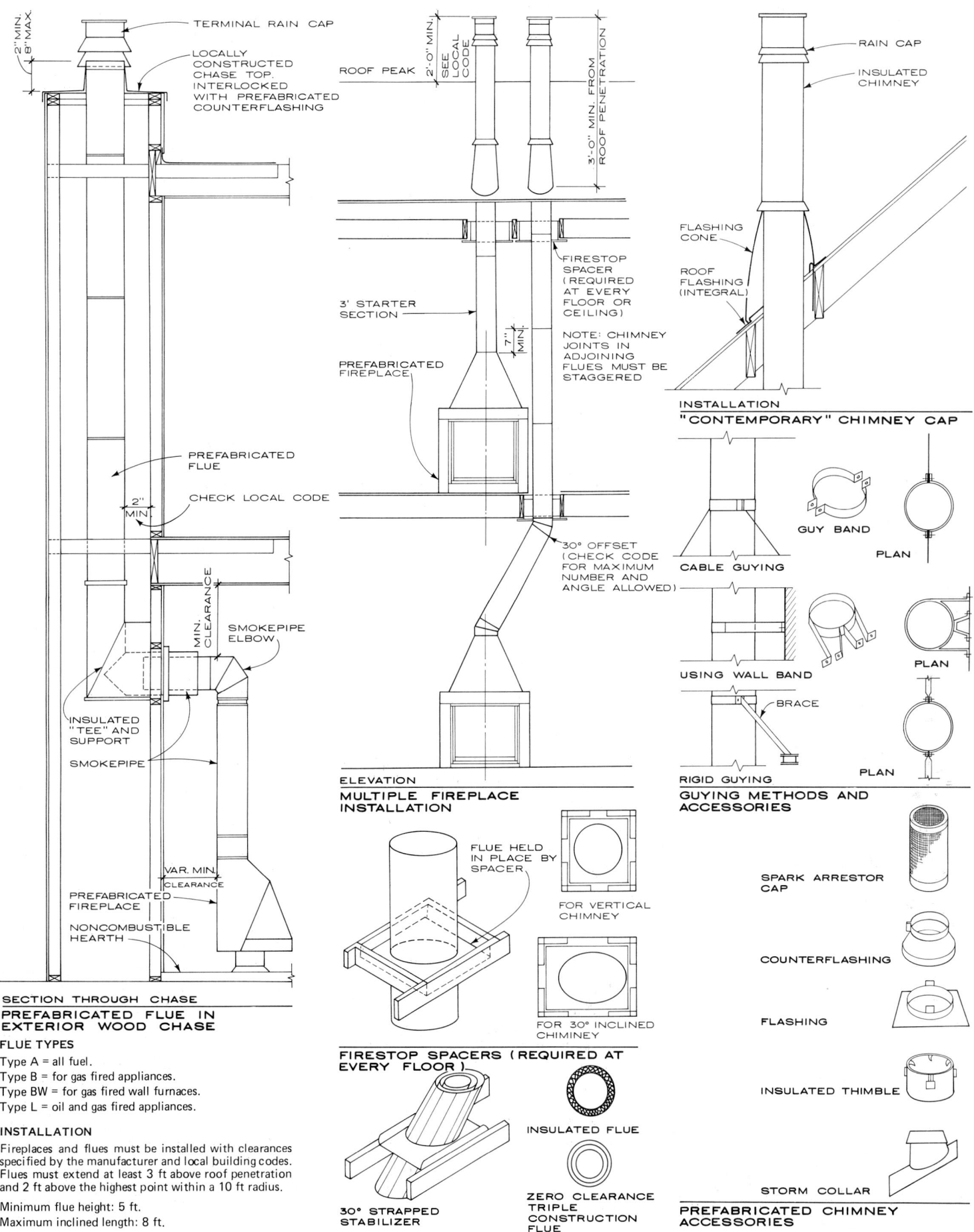

TERMINAL RAIN CAP

LOCALLY CONSTRUCTED CHASE TOP. INTERLOCKED WITH PREFABRICATED COUNTERFLASHING

2" MIN. 8" MAX.

ROOF PEAK

2'-0" MIN. SEE LOCAL CODE

3'-0" MIN. FROM ROOF PENETRATION

RAIN CAP

INSULATED CHIMNEY

PREFABRICATED FLUE

3' STARTER SECTION

CHECK LOCAL CODE

2" MIN.

PREFABRICATED FIREPLACE

FIRESTOP SPACER (REQUIRED AT EVERY FLOOR OR CEILING)

7" MIN.

NOTE: CHIMNEY JOINTS IN ADJOINING FLUES MUST BE STAGGERED

FLASHING CONE

ROOF FLASHING (INTEGRAL)

INSTALLATION "CONTEMPORARY" CHIMNEY CAP

MIN. CLEARANCE

SMOKEPIPE ELBOW

INSULATED "TEE" AND SUPPORT

SMOKEPIPE

30° OFFSET (CHECK CODE FOR MAXIMUM NUMBER AND ANGLE ALLOWED)

GUY BAND

PLAN

CABLE GUYING

USING WALL BAND

PLAN

BRACE

RIGID GUYING

PLAN

GUYING METHODS AND ACCESSORIES

VAR. MIN. CLEARANCE

PREFABRICATED FIREPLACE

NONCOMBUSTIBLE HEARTH

SECTION THROUGH CHASE

PREFABRICATED FLUE IN EXTERIOR WOOD CHASE

ELEVATION
MULTIPLE FIREPLACE INSTALLATION

FLUE HELD IN PLACE BY SPACER

FOR VERTICAL CHIMNEY

FOR 30° INCLINED CHIMNEY

FIRESTOP SPACERS (REQUIRED AT EVERY FLOOR)

30° STRAPPED STABILIZER

INSULATED FLUE

ZERO CLEARANCE TRIPLE CONSTRUCTION FLUE

SPARK ARRESTOR CAP

COUNTERFLASHING

FLASHING

INSULATED THIMBLE

STORM COLLAR

PREFABRICATED CHIMNEY ACCESSORIES

FLUE TYPES

Type A = all fuel.
Type B = for gas fired appliances.
Type BW = for gas fired wall furnaces.
Type L = oil and gas fired appliances.

INSTALLATION

Fireplaces and flues must be installed with clearances specified by the manufacturer and local building codes. Flues must extend at least 3 ft above roof penetration and 2 ft above the highest point within a 10 ft radius.

Minimum flue height: 5 ft.
Maximum inclined length: 8 ft.

Olga Barmine; Darrel Rippeteau, Architect; Washington, D.C.

FIREPLACES 4

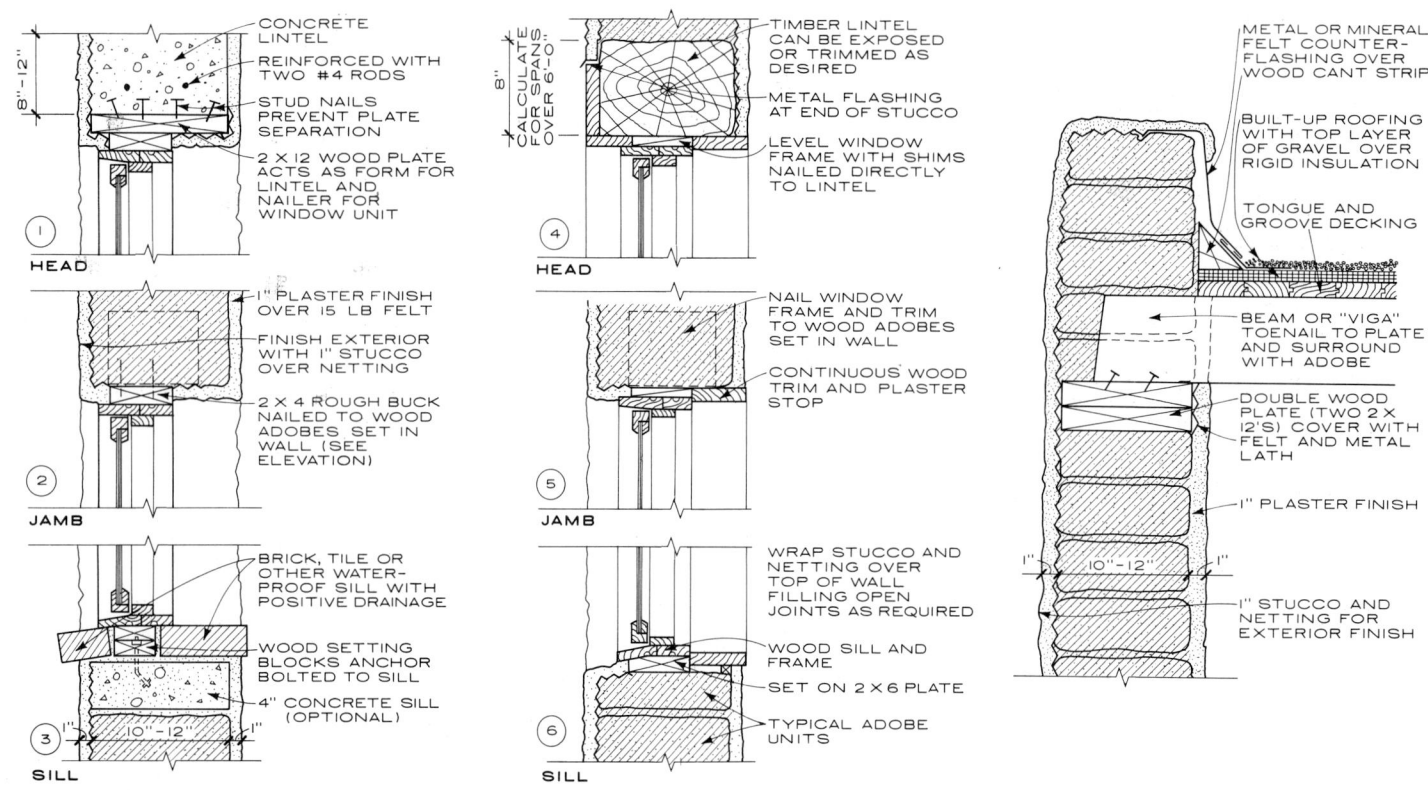

CONCRETE LINTEL

REINFORCED WITH TWO #4 RODS

STUD NAILS PREVENT PLATE SEPARATION

2 X 12 WOOD PLATE ACTS AS FORM FOR LINTEL AND NAILER FOR WINDOW UNIT

8″-12″

① HEAD

I″ PLASTER FINISH OVER 15 LB FELT

FINISH EXTERIOR WITH I″ STUCCO OVER NETTING

2 X 4 ROUGH BUCK NAILED TO WOOD ADOBES SET IN WALL (SEE ELEVATION)

② JAMB

BRICK, TILE OR OTHER WATER-PROOF SILL WITH POSITIVE DRAINAGE

WOOD SETTING BLOCKS ANCHOR BOLTED TO SILL

4″ CONCRETE SILL (OPTIONAL)

③ SILL   10″-12″   1″

TIMBER LINTEL CAN BE EXPOSED OR TRIMMED AS DESIRED

METAL FLASHING AT END OF STUCCO

LEVEL WINDOW FRAME WITH SHIMS NAILED DIRECTLY TO LINTEL

8″ CALCULATE FOR SPANS OVER 6′-0″.

④ HEAD

NAIL WINDOW FRAME AND TRIM TO WOOD ADOBES SET IN WALL

CONTINUOUS WOOD TRIM AND PLASTER STOP

⑤ JAMB

WRAP STUCCO AND NETTING OVER TOP OF WALL FILLING OPEN JOINTS AS REQUIRED

WOOD SILL AND FRAME

SET ON 2 X 6 PLATE

TYPICAL ADOBE UNITS

⑥ SILL

WINDOW DETAILS (SEE ELEVATION FOR ANCHORAGE OF FRAME)

METAL OR MINERAL FELT COUNTER-FLASHING OVER WOOD CANT STRIP

BUILT-UP ROOFING WITH TOP LAYER OF GRAVEL OVER RIGID INSULATION

TONGUE AND GROOVE DECKING

BEAM OR "VIGA" TOENAIL TO PLATE AND SURROUND WITH ADOBE

DOUBLE WOOD PLATE (TWO 2 X 12'S) COVER WITH FELT AND METAL LATH

I″ PLASTER FINISH

I″ STUCCO AND NETTING FOR EXTERIOR FINISH

1″   10″-12″   1″

BATTER PARAPET (PUEBLO STYLE)

NOTES

The details here deal with the use of sundried mud bricks. They may be stabilized with additives or simply made of mud. Proportions for the mud mixture of sand, silt, and clay normally are not critical. Gravel and small stones can also be present if they do not exceed 50% of the volume. Adobe is approved by local building officials in areas where adobe use is traditional or familiar to builders or construction officials. Information concerning local codes should be sought.

Nailing anchors are best provided by the use of wood adobes ("Gringo blocks"), either solid or made of scrap lumber, laid up with the wall in locations where door and window jambs may require attachment. Nails will not hold permanently when nailed into adobe bricks unless additionally secured by plaster or other material. Later attachments can be made by the use of wooden triple wedges driven into a pilot hole. Channels for wiring, pipes, and decorative features may be easily cut in the wall after it is in place.

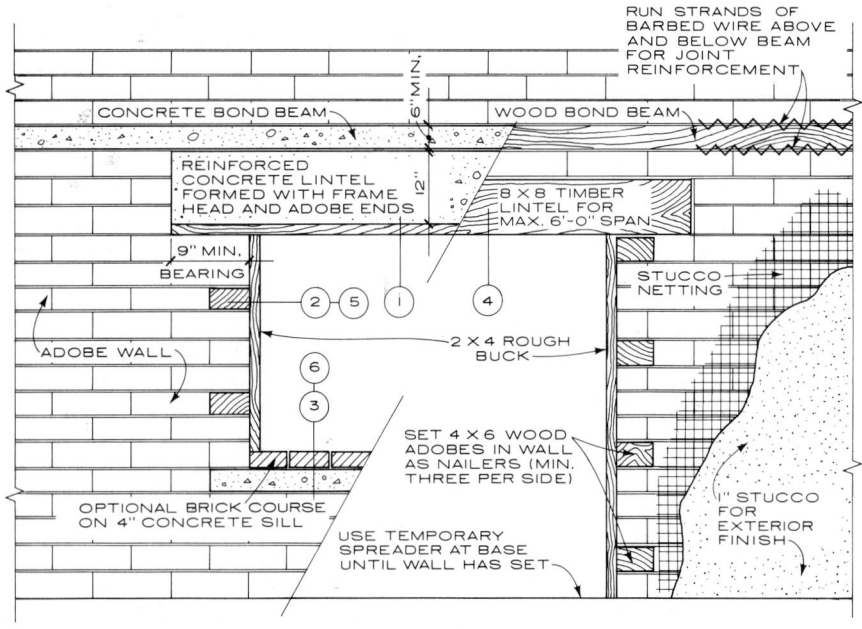

RUN STRANDS OF BARBED WIRE ABOVE AND BELOW BEAM FOR JOINT REINFORCEMENT

CONCRETE BOND BEAM   WOOD BOND BEAM

REINFORCED CONCRETE LINTEL FORMED WITH FRAME HEAD AND ADOBE ENDS

9″ MIN. BEARING

8 X 8 TIMBER LINTEL FOR MAX. 6′-0″ SPAN

6″ MIN.   12″

② ⑤ ① ④

STUCCO NETTING

ADOBE WALL

2 X 4 ROUGH BUCK

⑥ ③

OPTIONAL BRICK COURSE ON 4″ CONCRETE SILL

SET 4 X 6 WOOD ADOBES IN WALL AS NAILERS (MIN. THREE PER SIDE)

USE TEMPORARY SPREADER AT BASE UNTIL WALL HAS SET

I″ STUCCO FOR EXTERIOR FINISH

ELEVATION OF TYPICAL FRAMED OPENINGS

P. G. McHenry, Jr.; Corrales, New Mexico

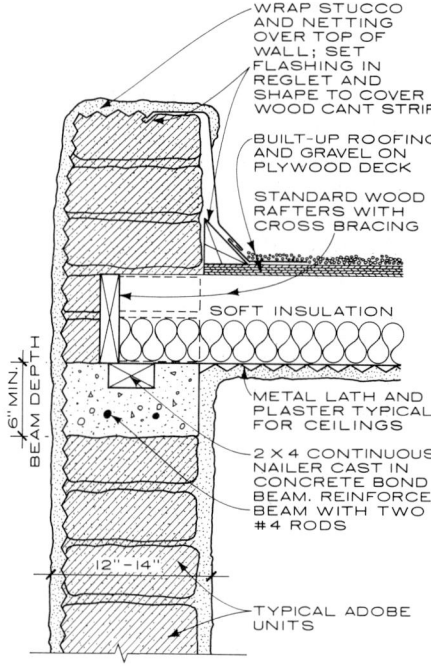

WRAP STUCCO AND NETTING OVER TOP OF WALL; SET FLASHING IN REGLET AND SHAPE TO COVER WOOD CANT STRIP

BUILT-UP ROOFING AND GRAVEL ON PLYWOOD DECK

STANDARD WOOD RAFTERS WITH CROSS BRACING

SOFT INSULATION

METAL LATH AND PLASTER TYPICAL FOR CEILINGS

2 X 4 CONTINUOUS NAILER CAST IN CONCRETE BOND BEAM. REINFORCE BEAM WITH TWO #4 RODS

6″ MIN. BEAM DEPTH

12″-14″

TYPICAL ADOBE UNITS

PARAPET WITH CONCRETE COLLAR

GENERAL NOTE

Some building codes may require additional thicknesses and reinforcement of concrete bond beams. The anchorage of pitched roof structures may be done by normal attachment to the bond beams shown.

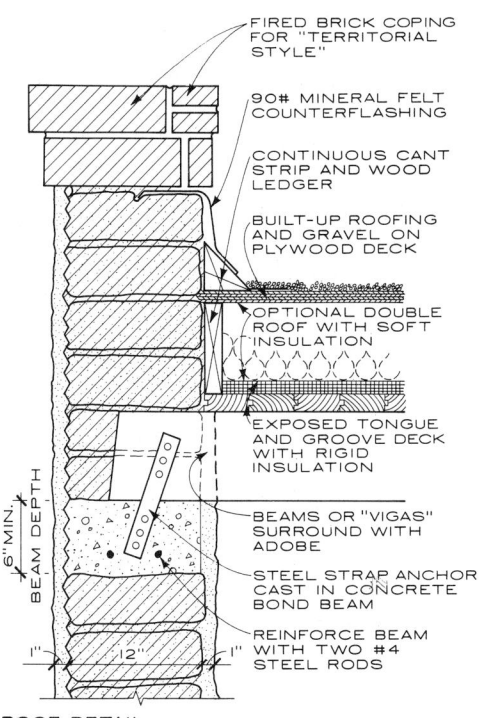

FIRED BRICK COPING FOR "TERRITORIAL STYLE"

90# MINERAL FELT COUNTERFLASHING

CONTINUOUS CANT STRIP AND WOOD LEDGER

BUILT-UP ROOFING AND GRAVEL ON PLYWOOD DECK

OPTIONAL DOUBLE ROOF WITH SOFT INSULATION

EXPOSED TONGUE AND GROOVE DECK WITH RIGID INSULATION

BEAMS OR "VIGAS" SURROUND WITH ADOBE

STEEL STRAP ANCHOR CAST IN CONCRETE BOND BEAM

REINFORCE BEAM WITH TWO #4 STEEL RODS

6" MIN. BEAM DEPTH

1" 12" 1"

ROOF DETAIL

CLAY TILE FLOORING SET IN 2" MORTAR BED OVER PLYWOOD AND FELT SUBFLOORING

EXPOSED TONGUE AND GROOVE DECKING

FLOOR JOISTS WITH CROSS BRACING

STEEL STRAP ANCHOR

CONCRETE BOND BEAM WITH THREE #4 STEEL RODS

1" PLASTER

1" STUCCO AND NET FOR EXTERIOR FINISH

6" MIN. BEAM DEPTH

1" 18" 1"

SECOND FLOOR DETAIL

OPTIONAL WOOD BASE

TILE FLOORING ON REINFORCED CONCRETE SLAB

KEY TOP OF PIER AND WATERPROOF

REINFORCED CONCRETE STEM WALL

1" SAND BED WITH VAPOR BARRIER

PERIMETER INSULATION

6" MIN.

18"

FOUNDATION DETAIL

WALL SECTIONS (TERRITORIAL STYLE)

P. G. McHenry, Jr.; Corrales, New Mexico

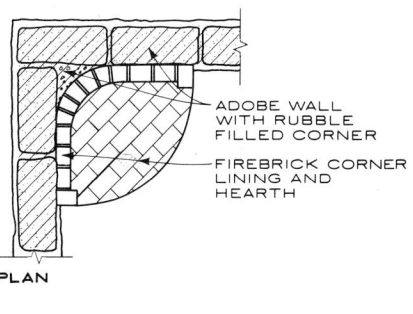

ADOBE WALL WITH RUBBLE FILLED CORNER

FIREBRICK CORNER LINING AND HEARTH

PLAN

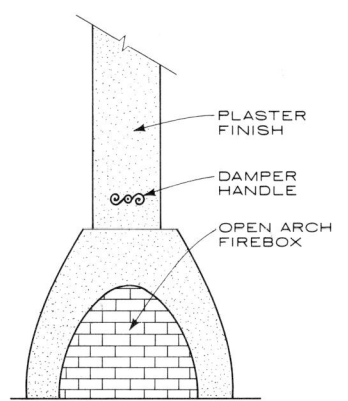

PLASTER FINISH

DAMPER HANDLE

OPEN ARCH FIREBOX

ELEVATION

"HORNO" FIREPLACES

TYPICAL SIZES OF ADOBE BRICK

HEIGHT	LENGTH	WIDTH
4"	8"	16"
4"	10"	16"
4"	9"	18"
4"	12"	18"
5"	12"	16"
5"	10"	20"
5"	12"	18"
6"	12"	24"

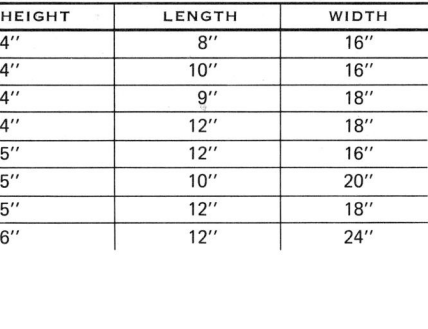

WATER BRUSH EXPOSED MASONRY FOR OPTIONAL INTERIOR FINISH

WOOD PLANK FLOORING OVER PLYWOOD AND FELT BASE

FLOOR JOISTS WITH CROSS BRACING

ANCHOR PLATE TO CONCRETE FILLED CORE OF CMU PIER

VENTED CRAWL SPACE

WATERPROOF TOP OF PIER

CMU FOUNDATION WALL FILLED WITH EARTH OR REINFORCED CONCRETE

PERIMETER INSULATION

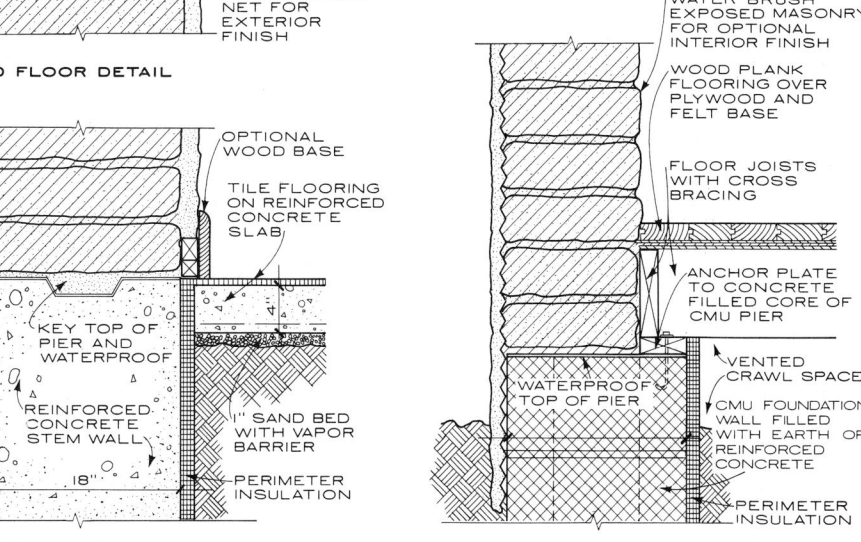

FIREPLACES

A traditional feature of most adobe homes is one or more corner "Kiva" or "Horno" fireplaces. The main masonry structure is provided by the adobe wall at a corner. If a corner is not available, sometimes a "Padercita" (little wall) is projected from another wall to provide a corner. The corner is lined with firebrick, and a masonry shell encloses the firebox and fireplace flue. A vitreous flue liner or masonry flue is projected through the roof. The curved back wall and open firebox reflect heat efficiently into the room, and the curve provides a smoke shelf. A butterfly damper in the flue or throat is controlled by a decorative wrought iron handle.

New seismic requirements in some areas require vertical steel reinforcement in the masonry of fireplaces.

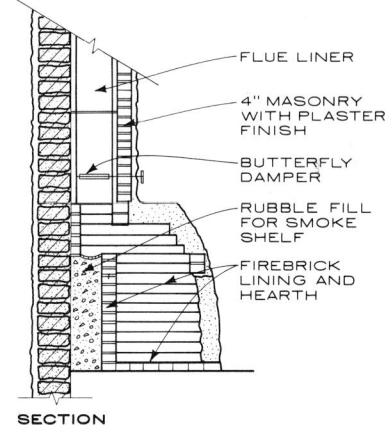

FLUE LINER

4" MASONRY WITH PLASTER FINISH

BUTTERFLY DAMPER

RUBBLE FILL FOR SMOKE SHELF

FIREBRICK LINING AND HEARTH

SECTION

ADOBE WALL CONSTRUCTION

The strength of an adobe wall lies in its mass and homogeneous nature, using the same material, mud, for mortar. The addition of reinforcing bars or anchor bolts may weaken joints. An international use standard for adobe wall thickness-height ratio is approximately 1:10. Uniform sizes for sundried bricks vary widely with different locales. The bricks should be made near the point of use and will vary with tradition and the standards of the manufacturer. Larger sizes of great weight will increase the labor cost. Minimum bonding distance is approximately 4 in.

One story walls should be 12 in. thick in Arizona and 10 in. in New Mexico and should not exceed 12 ft in height. Two story walls should be 18 in. thick at first floor and 12 in. at second and not over 22 ft in height.

Avoidance of flowing water on mud surfaces is the most important detail consideration. Rising damp is of no consequence if the site immediately adjacent is well drained and moisture is not trapped by waterproofing materials. Unstabilized mud brick or plaster (without the addition of waterproofing compounds) bonds well to itself and to wood without the use of normal lathing reinforcement. Rain erosion of unstabilized mud surfaces will only approximate 1 in. in 20 years in rainfall areas of 10 to 25 in. per year. Monolithic slab/foundations are not desirable with mud adobe because possible concentrations of rainwater on the slab during construction may damage lower courses.

"Effective" U values for insulation are more significant than the ASHRAE "steady-state" values in common use. The "effective" values take into account the thermal mass, storage, insulation gains in various climate zones, wall compass orientation, and color.

"Burned adobe," which is merely a low fired brick, should be dealt with in the manner normal for brick masonry. Its use is not recommended in climate zones where high daily temperature fluctuations can cause severe freeze-thaw cycle damage. Mud bricks can be stabilized (waterproofed) by the addition of cement, asphalt emulsion, or other compounds. These materials often do not bond well with themselves in repeated layers and may accelerate the deterioration at the point of contact with the mud material.

ADOBE   **4**

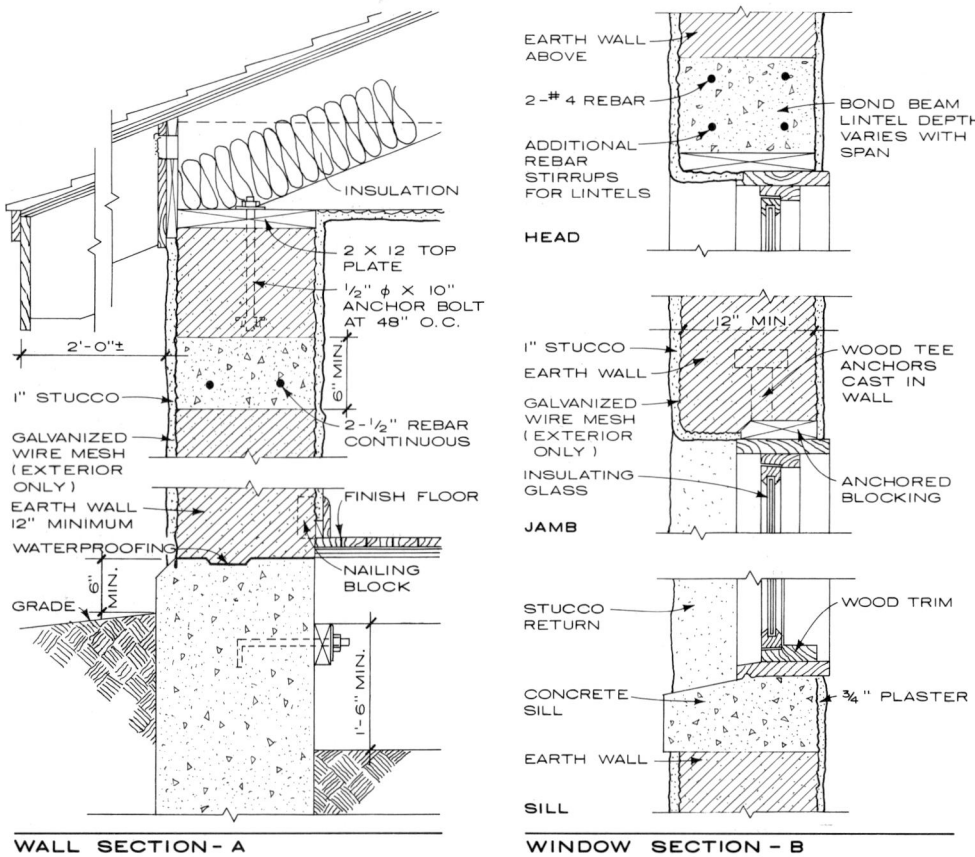

WALL SECTION - A

HEAD

JAMB

SILL

WINDOW SECTION - B

NOTES

1. Rammed earth wall construction is an old technique used effectively in many parts of the world. The basic material is earth, with allowable proportions of clay, silt, and aggregate, commonly found almost everywhere. The soil in most locations has naturally usable proportions that do not require further tempering. The ideal soil mixture will have less than 50% clay and silt, and a maximum aggregate size of 1/4 in. The solid is dampened to a moisture content of approximately 10% by weight, of dry soil. Saltwater should not be used under any circumstances.

2. The walls are constructed by the use of slip forms, (24 to 36 in. high x 8 to 12 ft long) placed level and secure. The forms are filled with damp (not wet) earth in 4 in. lifts. Each lift is rammed with a tamper until full compaction is reached. The tamp should be flat, approximately 6 x 6 in., weighing 18 to 25 lb, tamped by hand or mechanically. Full compaction can be determined by a ringing sound when the tamp compacts the fill. When the form is full and compacted, it is moved to a new location and secured and the process is repeated. The corners should be placed first, with special corner forms. When the full circumference is completed, the next course is started. The form heights (courses) are best coordinated with heights of window and door lintels. Form replacement can begin as soon as compaction is reached, without further drying.

3. Exterior wall thickness should be a minimum of 12 in. for one story, 18 in. to support a second story, and interior walls of not less than 9 in. Wall thickness can be increased as appropriate to the design. Basic rammed earth walls have many of the same characteristics of sundried adobe. The insulation value of the walls is not as great as more efficient insulating materials, but will provide thermal mass for heat storage, sound control, and other benefits.

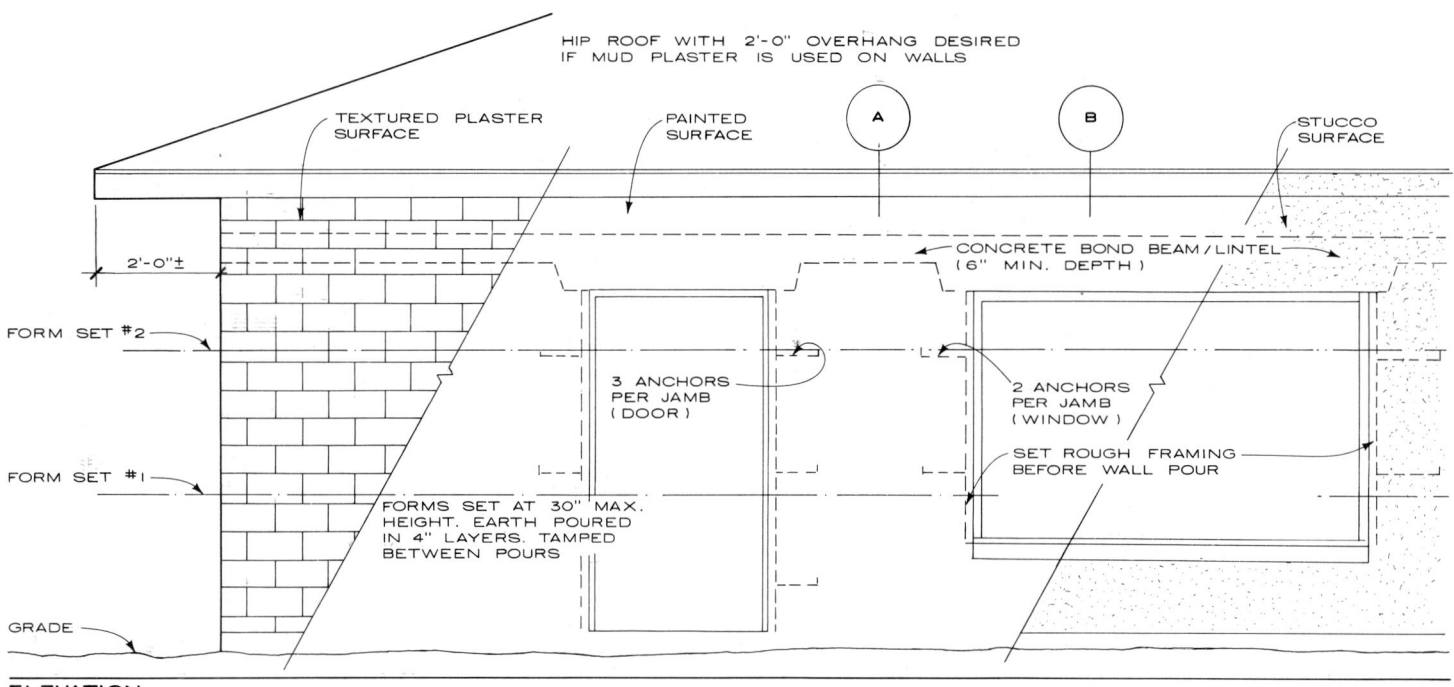

ELEVATION

NOTES

1. Foundations are normally conventional spread footings of sufficient width to support the heavy (3000 # per lin ft) walls. The foundation wall should be of a waterproof material, topped with a vapor barrier to prevent capillary moisture rise. Attachment anchors in the form of wood tees or plugs are placed in the wall as it is erected, in the positions required to secure window and door frames. A continuous steel reinforced concrete beam (6 in. thick) is placed as a continuous lintel beam to support walls above the openings.

2. A top plate of wood is secured by means of anchor bolts cast in the top of the walls. The plate provides load distribution and an attachment point for the roof structure. Interior and exterior walls can be finished by the application of conventional stucco or plaster. Simpler treatment can be achieved by smoothing or texturing the earth wall with a sponge rubber float, wet burlap, or sheepskin, and painting it. Sealing and preparation of the surface before painting is the same as for plaster. If waterproof stucco is not used, roof overhangs should be of sufficient width to protect the walls from rain erosion.

P.G. McHenry, Jr.; Corrales, New Mexico

RAMMED EARTH

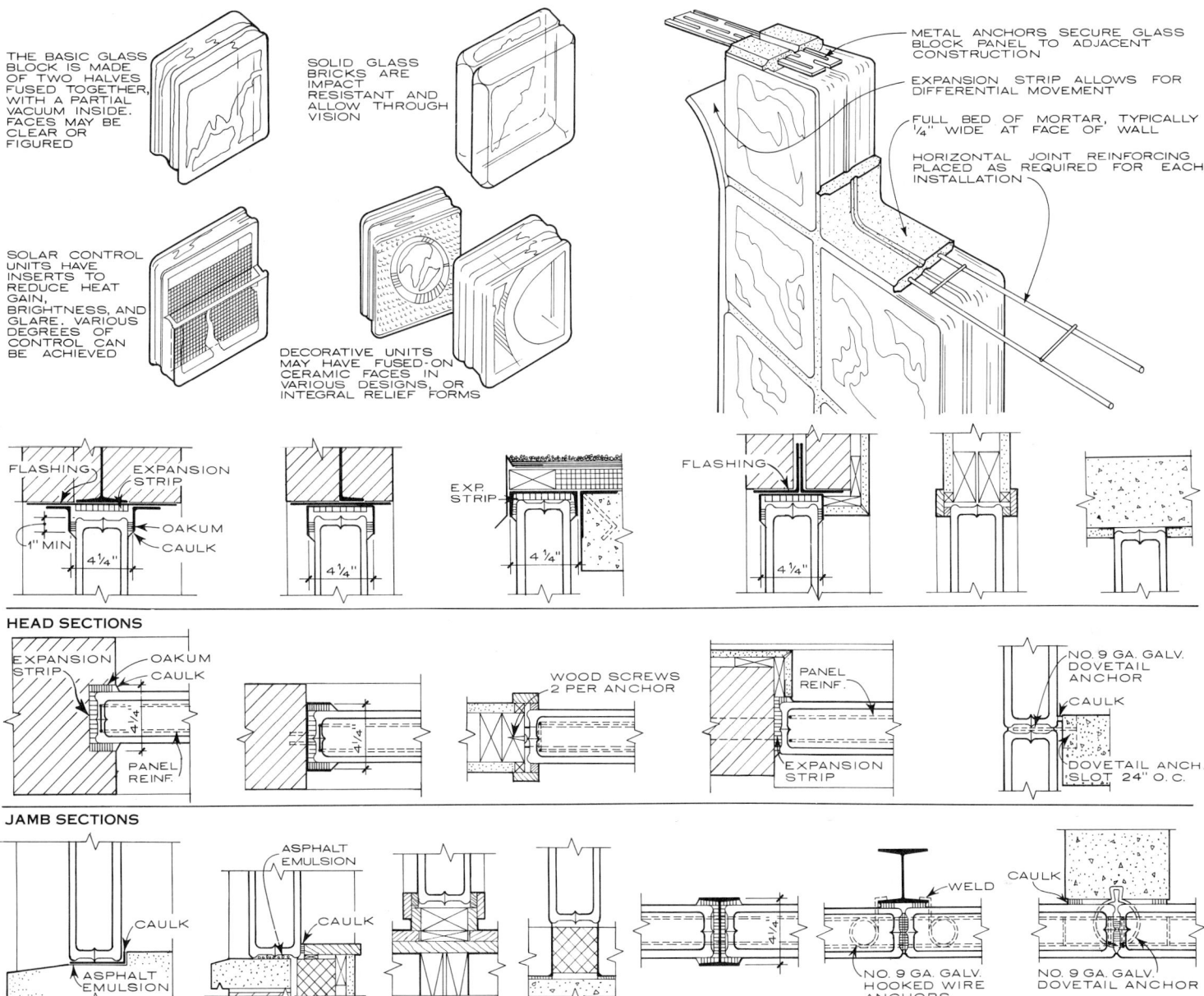

THE BASIC GLASS BLOCK IS MADE OF TWO HALVES FUSED TOGETHER, WITH A PARTIAL VACUUM INSIDE. FACES MAY BE CLEAR OR FIGURED

SOLID GLASS BRICKS ARE IMPACT RESISTANT AND ALLOW THROUGH VISION

SOLAR CONTROL UNITS HAVE INSERTS TO REDUCE HEAT GAIN, BRIGHTNESS, AND GLARE. VARIOUS DEGREES OF CONTROL CAN BE ACHIEVED

DECORATIVE UNITS MAY HAVE FUSED-ON CERAMIC FACES IN VARIOUS DESIGNS, OR INTEGRAL RELIEF FORMS

METAL ANCHORS SECURE GLASS BLOCK PANEL TO ADJACENT CONSTRUCTION

EXPANSION STRIP ALLOWS FOR DIFFERENTIAL MOVEMENT

FULL BED OF MORTAR, TYPICALLY 1/4" WIDE AT FACE OF WALL

HORIZONTAL JOINT REINFORCING PLACED AS REQUIRED FOR EACH INSTALLATION

HEAD SECTIONS

JAMB SECTIONS

SILL SECTIONS

STIFFENER SECTIONS

LIGHT TRANSMISSION

BLOCK TYPE	% LIGHT TRANSMISSION
Glass brick	80
Clear block	75
Clear block with irregular glass	43
Block with light diffusing face	39
Diffusing block with solar control	20

NOTES

1. Heat gain resulting from direct radiation passing through a glass block may be controlled by using block with appropriate transmission properties.

2. For general planning purposes, a glass block wall can provide daylight illumination to a depth of about 20 ft, unless panels are exceptionally high.

HEAT TRANSMISSION

BLOCK SIZE AND TYPE	U-VALUE (BTU/HR · SQ FT · °F)
6" sq single cavity	0.60
8" sq single cavity	0.56
8" sq double cavity	0.48
12" sq single cavity	0.52
12" sq double cavity	0.44
4 x 12" single cavity	0.60
4 x 12" double cavity	0.52
For comparison: single sheet of glass	1.10

NOTES

1. Glass block panels prove to be an excellent control of ambient heat transmission. Block inserts give a double cavity system which further enhances transmission control.

2. If glass block panels face within 10° of either side of true north where sunlight never strikes the panel, then nonsun exposure units should be installed.

3. Panel facing further south will receive direct sunlight at some time. Solar controlling units should be used unless panel is adequately shaded by external factors.

ACTUAL BLOCK DIMENSIONS AND WEIGHT

DIMENSIONS (IN.)		AVERAGE WEIGHT PER BLOCK (LB)
NOMINAL	ACTUAL	
AVERAGE THICKNESS 3⅞"		
6 x 6"	5¾ x 5¾"	4
8 x 8"	7¾ x 5¾"	6
12 x 12"	11¾ x 11¾"	16
4 x 8"	3¾ x 7¾"	4
4 x 12"	3¾ x 11¾"	5
5" sq brick	5 x 5 x 2⅝"	6
8" sq brick	7⅝ x 7⅝ x 3"	15

NOTES

1. While single panels of glass block are limited to a maximum of 144 sq ft, panel and curtain wall sections up to a maximum area of 250 sq ft may be erected if properly braced to limit movement and settlement.

2. Any glass block installation that is made in a frame construction shall have the wood adjacent to the mortar properly primed with asphalt emulsion.

3. Underwriters' listing: glass block panels may be used for window opening subject to the light fire exposure (class F openings).

Darrel Rippeteau, Architect; Washington, D.C.

GLASS BLOCK   **4**

CHAPTER 5 METALS

STRUCTURAL ECONOMY—STEEL FRAMING

The most commonly used strength grade of structural steel is 36,000 psi yield strength (ASTM A36). For heavily loaded members such as columns, girders, or trusses where buckling, lateral stability, deflection, or vibration does not control member selection, higher yield strength steels may be economically utilized. A 50,000 psi yield strength is most frequently used among high strength, low alloy steels.

The Manual of Steel Construction of the AISC contains column and beam load tables for both 36,000 and 50,000 psi yield strengths.

High strength, low alloy steels are available in several grades, and some possess superior corrosion resistance to such a degree that they are classified as "weathering steel." Table 1 contains data for several ASTM alloys used for structural members.

TABLE 1 STRUCTURAL STEEL DATA

ATSM DESIGNATION	STRENGTH GRADES (KSI)	ATMOSPHERIC CORROSION RESISTANCE	REMARKS
A572	42, 45, 50, 55, 60, 65	Same as carbon steel	Most commonly used of low alloy steels
A441	40, 42, 46, 50	Twice the resistance of carbon steel	Primarily for welded structures—not frequently used
A242	42, 46, 50*	5 to 8 times the resistance of carbon steel	Used exposed as "weathering steel" or painted
A588	42, 46, 50*	4 times the resistance of carbon steel	Used exposed as "weathering steel" or painted

*50 KSI normally provided, but reduced for thicker material.

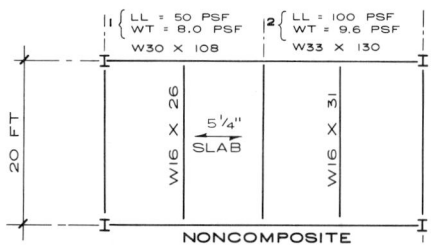

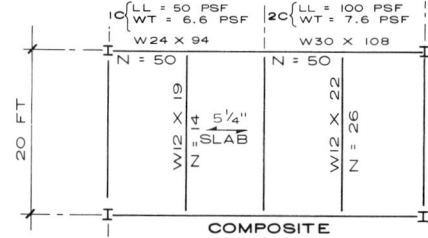

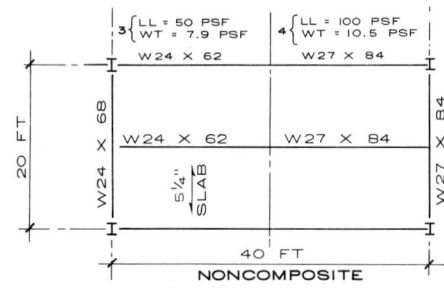

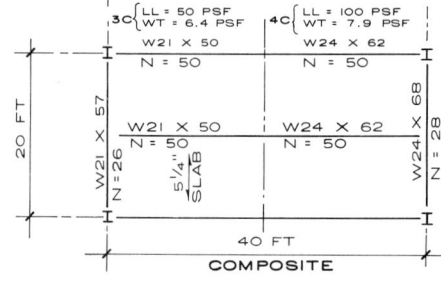

TABLE 2 ALTERNATE FRAMING

	SHORT BEAMS, LONG GIRDERS				LONG BEAMS, SHORT GIRDERS			
	LL = 50 PSF		LL = 100 PSF		LL = 50 PSF		LL = 100 PSF	
	1	1C	2	2C	3	3C	4	4C
Girder depth	30"	24"	33"	30"	24"	21"	27"	24"
Steel weight per bay (lb)	6400	5280	7680	6080	6320	5140	8400	6320
Weight ratio— Noncomposite : composite	1.21 : 1		1.26 : 1		1.23 : 1		1.33 : 1	
No. shear studs	0	106	0	154	0	126	0	128
Cost ratio (see Note 5)	1.16 : 1		1.19 : 1		1.16 : 1		1.27 : 1	

NOTES

1. Floor slab: 5¼ in. total thickness—3¼ in. lightweight concrete over 2 in. composite metal deck, all schemes. This provides a 2 hr fire rating without spraying the deck.
2. Additional dead load allowance for finishes, etc.: 30 psf, all schemes.
3. All steel ASTM A36.
4. Shear studs: ¾ in. dia. x 3½ in. long. N = 50 indicates total number of studs per beam.
5. The cost ratio between noncomposite and composite floor steel is approximately 95% of the weight ratio. The cost of studs accounts for the difference.
6. Vibration of floor beams should be analyzed.

Walter D. Shapiro, P.E.; Tor, Shapiro & Associates; New York, New York

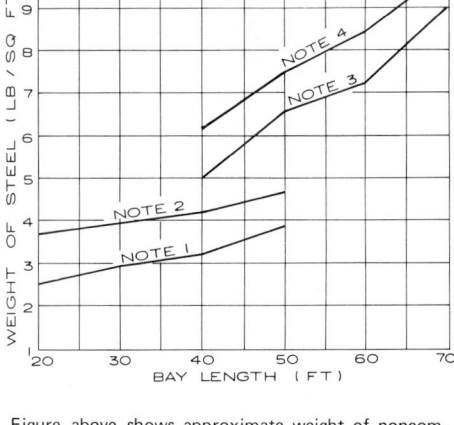

Figure above shows approximate weight of noncomposite structural steel floor or roof framing versus bay size.

NOTES

1. Roof of 15 ft high one-story structure, H-series open web joists on continuous A36 girders (weight of A36 columns included). Joist span = 30 ft.
2. Same as (1) except that joist span = 45 ft.
3. Typical level of five-story garage, V-50 steel throughout (weight of columns included) bay width = 20 ft.
4. Same as (3) except that bay width = 30 ft.

NOTES

The weight of structural steel per square foot of floor area increases with bay size, as does the depth of the structure. Cost of structural steel may not rise as rapidly as weight if savings can be realized by reducing the number of pieces to be fabricated and erected. Improved space utilization afforded by larger bay sizes is offset by increases in wall area and building volume resulting from increased structure depth.

Steel frame economy can be improved by incorporating as many of these cost reducing factors into the structure layout and design as architectural requirements permit:

1. Keep columns in line in both directions and avoid offsets or omission of columns.
2. Design for maximum repetition of member sizes within each level and from floor to floor.
3. Reduce the number of beams and girders per level to reduce fabrication and erection time and cost.
4. Maximize the use of simple beam connections by bracing the structure at a limited number of moment resisting bents or by the most efficient method, cross-bracing.
5. Utilize high strength steels for columns and floor members where studies indicate that cost can be reduced while meeting other design parameters.
6. Use composite design, but consider effect of in-slab electric raceways or other discontinuities.
7. Consider open web steel joists, especially for large roofs of one-story structures, and for floor framing in many applications.

An analysis of alternate framing schemes for a 20 x 40 ft interior floor bay appears in Table 2.

One constant relationship that may be noted in the analysis is the decrease in girder depth when using long beams and short girders. The weight of steel for roofs or lightly loaded floors is generally least when long beams and short girders are used. For heavier loadings long girders and short filler beams should result in less steel weight. The most economical framing type (composite, noncomposite, continuous, simple spans, etc.) and arrangement must be determined for each structure, considering such factors as structure depth, building volume, wall area, mechanical system requirements, deflection or vibration limitations, wind or seismic load interaction between floor system, and columns or shear walls.

Composite construction combines two different materials or two different grades of a material to form a structural member that utilizes the most desirable properties of each material. Examples of composite construction are all around us but may go unrecognized as such. Perhaps the earliest composite structural unit was the mud brick reinforced with straw. Other common examples are: nineteenth century trusses of wood and iron; modern trusses and open web joists of wood and steel; reinforced concrete, which combines the tensile strength of steel with the compressive strength of concrete; cable supported concrete roofs and bridges; fiberglass reinforced plastics; wire reinforced safety glass; plywood; glued laminated wood beams.

Composite systems currently used in building construction include:

1. Concrete topped composite steel decks.
2. Steel beams acting compositely with concrete slabs.
3. Steel columns encased by or filled with concrete.
4. Open web joists of wood and steel or joists with plywood webs and wood chords.
5. Trusses combining wood and steel.
6. Hybrid girders utilizing steels of different strengths.
7. Cast-in-place concrete slab on precast concrete joists or beams.

To make two different materials act compositely as one unit they must be joined at their interface by one or a combination of these means:

1. Chemical bonding (concrete).
2. Gluing (plywood, glulam).
3. Welding (steel, aluminum).
4. Screws (sheet metal, wood).
5. Bolts (steel, wood).
6. Shear studs (steel to concrete).
7. Keys or embossments (steel deck to concrete, concrete to concrete).
8. Dowels (concrete to concrete).
9. Friction (positive clamping force must be present).

Individual elements of the composite unit must be securely fastened to prevent slippage with respect to one another. This principle can be demonstrated by bending a telephone book at its free edges and then trying to bend the book at its binding—the binding makes all the pages resist bending in a combined effort, unlike the free edges where pages slip and slide, offering little resistance.

The illustrations of composite systems show points of potential slippage, which occur where load is transferred from one element of the composite member to another.

Comparative designs are shown below for a floor beam and a roof joist to demonstrate possible reductions in structure weight and cost savings through use of composite design. Additional information on structural economy is presented in this chapter.

FLOOR: DEAD LOAD = 80 PSF   ROOF: D.L. = 20 PSF
         LIVE LOAD = <u>100</u> PSF   L.L. = <u>30</u> PSF
            TOTAL = 180 PSF   TOTAL = 50 PSF

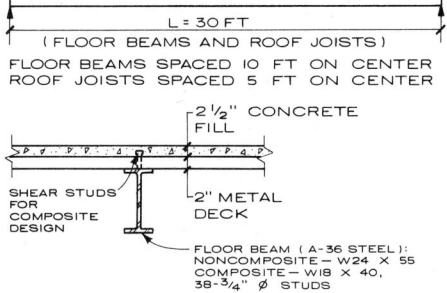

L = 30 FT
(FLOOR BEAMS AND ROOF JOISTS)
FLOOR BEAMS SPACED 10 FT ON CENTER
ROOF JOISTS SPACED 5 FT ON CENTER

SHEAR STUDS FOR COMPOSITE DESIGN

2½" CONCRETE FILL

2" METAL DECK

FLOOR BEAM (A-36 STEEL): NONCOMPOSITE—W24 × 55 COMPOSITE—W18 × 40, 38-¾" ⌀ STUDS

ROOF JOIST:
STEEL BEAM (A-36)—W14 × 22 #/FT
STEEL JOIST—24J6 (9.9 #/FT) OR 20H5 (8.4#/FT)
WOOD-STEEL JOIST—26" DEEP(5#/FT) DOUBLE 1.5" × 2.3" MICRO-LAM CHORDS, STEEL TUBE DIAGONALS—1½" TO 1" DIA.
(SEE DET. 4B ABOVE)

COMPARATIVE DESIGN EXAMPLE

Walter D. Shapiro, P. E.; Tor, Shapiro & Associates; New York, New York

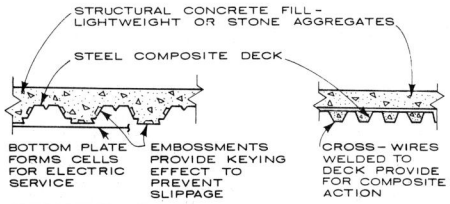

1. CONCRETE TOPPED STEEL DECKING

STRUCTURAL CONCRETE FILL-LIGHTWEIGHT OR STONE AGGREGATES

STEEL COMPOSITE DECK

BOTTOM PLATE FORMS CELLS FOR ELECTRIC SERVICE

EMBOSSMENTS PROVIDE KEYING EFFECT TO PREVENT SLIPPAGE

CROSS-WIRES WELDED TO DECK PROVIDE FOR COMPOSITE ACTION

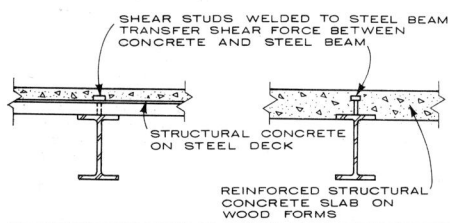

SHEAR STUDS WELDED TO STEEL BEAM TRANSFER SHEAR FORCE BETWEEN CONCRETE AND STEEL BEAM

STRUCTURAL CONCRETE ON STEEL DECK

REINFORCED STRUCTURAL CONCRETE SLAB ON WOOD FORMS

2. STEEL BEAM WITH STUD IN CONCRETE SLAB

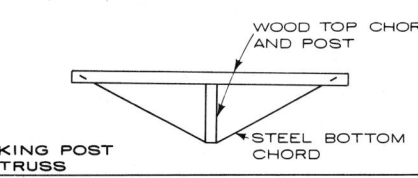

WOOD TOP AND BOTTOM CHORDS AND COMPRESSION DIAGONALS

STEEL TENSION MEMBERS

HOWE TRUSS

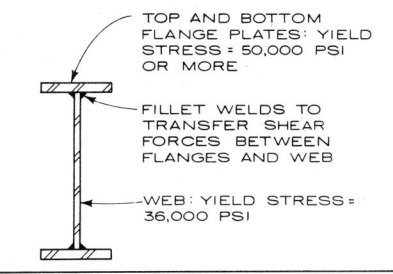

WOOD TOP CHORD AND POST

STEEL BOTTOM CHORD

KING POST TRUSS

5. WOOD AND STEEL TRUSSES

 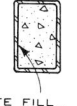 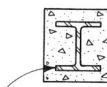

CONCRETE FILL BONDS TO STEEL PIPE OR TUBE

CONCRETE ENCASEMENT BONDS TO STRUCTURAL STEEL COLUMN AND REBARS FOR COMPOSITE ACTION

3. STEEL AND CONCRETE COLUMNS

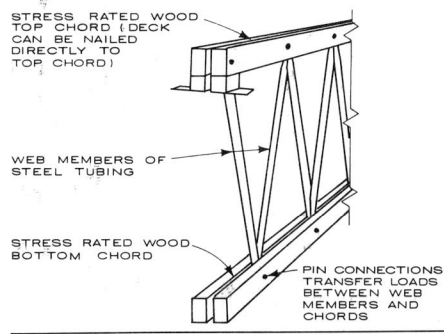

STRESS RATED WOOD TOP CHORD (DECK CAN BE NAILED DIRECTLY TO TOP CHORD)

WEB MEMBERS OF STEEL TUBING

STRESS RATED WOOD BOTTOM CHORD

PIN CONNECTIONS TRANSFER LOADS BETWEEN WEB MEMBERS AND CHORDS

4A. WOOD AND STEEL JOIST

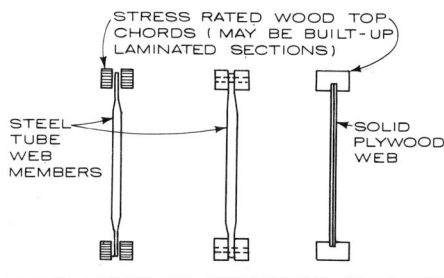

STRESS RATED WOOD TOP CHORDS (MAY BE BUILT-UP LAMINATED SECTIONS)

STEEL TUBE WEB MEMBERS

SOLID PLYWOOD WEB

4. TYPICAL COMPOSITE JOISTS

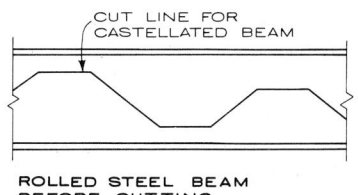

TOP AND BOTTOM FLANGE PLATES: YIELD STRESS = 50,000 PSI OR MORE

FILLET WELDS TO TRANSFER SHEAR FORCES BETWEEN FLANGES AND WEB

WEB: YIELD STRESS = 36,000 PSI

6A. HYBRID GIRDERS (USING DIFFERENT STRENGTH STEELS)

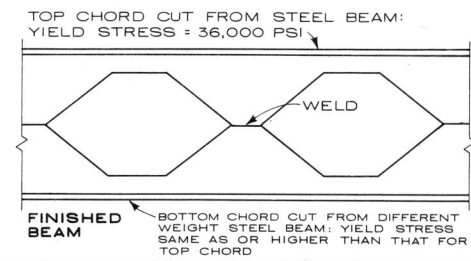

STRUCTURAL CONCRETE SLAB ACTS AS COMPRESSION FLANGE OF COMPOSITE MEMBER

SHEAR STUDS

LIGHT TEE: YIELD STRESS = 36,000 PSI

HEAVY TEE: YIELD STRESS SAME AS TOP TEE OR HIGHER

WELD TO TRANSFER SHEAR FORCES BETWEEN TEES

CUT LINE FOR CASTELLATED BEAM

ROLLED STEEL BEAM BEFORE CUTTING

TOP CHORD CUT FROM STEEL BEAM: YIELD STRESS = 36,000 PSI

WELD

FINISHED BEAM

BOTTOM CHORD CUT FROM DIFFERENT WEIGHT STEEL BEAM: YIELD STRESS SAME AS OR HIGHER THAN THAT FOR TOP CHORD

6 CASTELLATED BEAMS

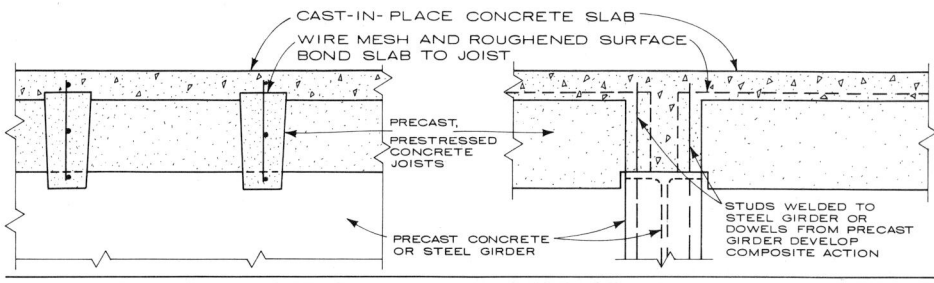

CAST-IN-PLACE CONCRETE SLAB

WIRE MESH AND ROUGHENED SURFACE BOND SLAB TO JOIST

PRECAST, PRESTRESSED CONCRETE JOISTS

PRECAST CONCRETE OR STEEL GIRDER

STUDS WELDED TO STEEL GIRDER OR DOWELS FROM PRECAST GIRDER DEVELOP COMPOSITE ACTION

7. REINFORCED CONCRETE SLAB AND PRECAST JOIST

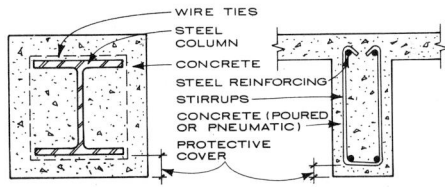

CONCRETE ENCASEMENT

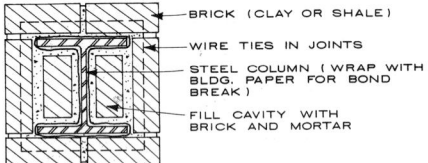

MASONRY ENCLOSURE

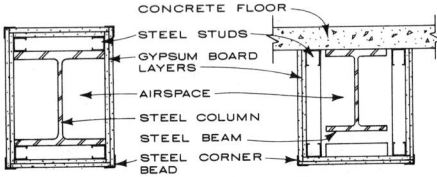

GYPSUM MEMBRANE ENCLOSURE

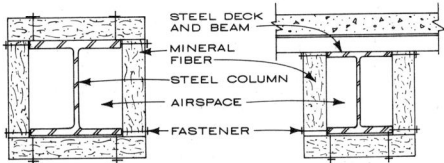

MINERAL FIBER MEMBRANE ENCLOSURE

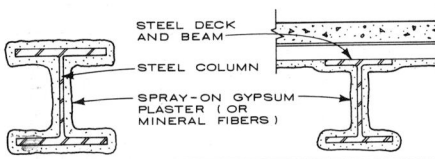

SPRAY-ON CONTOUR

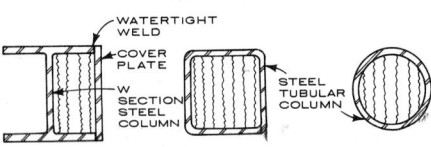

LIQUID FILLED COLUMN

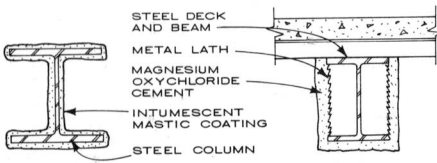

COATINGS

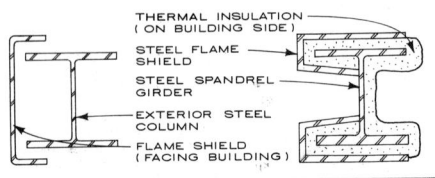

FLAME SHIELDS

M. David Egan, P.E.; College of Architecture, Clemson University, Clemson, South Carolina

UNPROTECTED STEEL

At temperatures greater than 1000°F, mild steel loses about one half of its ultimate room temperature strength. Consequently, fire tests on steel beams and columns are terminated when the steel's surface temperatures reach a predetermined limit or when the applied design loading can no longer be sustained (specific alternate test procedures are given by ASTM Standard Methods E 119). Fire resistance ratings are expressed in terms of duration in hours of fire exposure to standard temperature conditions in a test furnace (e.g., 3/4 hr, 1 hr, 2 hr, 3 hr). For further information on fire resistance tests and fire protection of steel, see American Iron and Steel Institute's handbook, "Fire-Resistant Steel-Frame Construction."

CONCRETE ENCASEMENT

Achieved fire resistance for steel members encased in concrete depends on thickness of protective concrete cover, concrete mixture, and structural restraint (i.e., method of support and method of confining thermal expansion). Lightweight aggregate concrete has better fire resistance than normal weight concrete because of its higher moisture content and higher thermal resistance to heat flow. Heavier members require less cover for equivalent fire resistance, since they have greater mass. For data on columns encased in concrete, see National Fire Protection Association's "Fire Protection Handbook." Gunite, a mixture of cement, sand, and water, can be spray-applied by air pressure, but requires steel reinforcing. For exterior applications, reinforcing steel with less than 2 in. of concrete cover usually requires corrosion resistant primers.

MASONRY ENCLOSURE

Masonry materials (brick, concrete block, gypsum block, hollow clay tile) can be used to encase steel columns. The cores (or cells), which provide openings for reinforcing, also can be filled with mortar or insulating materials such as vermiculite to increase thermal resistance to heat flow. For data on fire resistance of masonry constructions, see National Concrete Masonry Association's "Fire Safety with Concrete Masonry."

GYPSUM MEMBRANE ENCLOSURE

Gypsum board or troweled plaster (e.g., vermiculite-gypsum, perlite-gypsum) or lath can be used to protect steel at building locations not exposed to moisture. Gypsum retards heat flow to steel by releasing chemically combined water (called "calcination") at temperatures above 180°F. To protect steel columns, gypsum board layers can be attached to steel studs by means of self-tapping screws or installed behind a galvanized or stainless sheet steel cover. For data on fire resistance of gypsum constructions, see Gypsum Association's "Fire Resistance Design Data Manual."

MINERAL FIBER MEMBRANE ENCLOSURE

When exposed to fire, mineral fiber (made from molten rock or slag) retards heat flow to steel because of its low thermal conductivity (it can withstand temperatures above 2000°F without melting). Mineral fiber requires a protective covering when exposed to outdoor conditions or the possibility of damage from accidental impact or abrasion.

SPRAY-ON CONTOUR

Spray-on applied cementitious mixtures (lightweight aggregate plasters with insulating fibers or vermiculite) or mineral fibers mixed with inorganic binders provide thermal barrier to heat from fire. The steel surface must be clean and free of loose paint, rust, oil, and grease before spraying, and a protective primer may be required. In addition, spraying should not be scheduled during cold conditions. Lightweight spray-on contours can be easily damaged during installation of nearby gas and water pipes, air ducts, and the like, and they are subject to flaking during normal use. Pins, studs, and other mechanical fasteners can be used to secure moisture or abrasion resistant protective finish coatings. Applications more than 2 in. thick generally require wire mesh or lath reinforcement.

LIQUID FILLED COLUMNS

During a fire the liquid, circulating by convection from fire floor columns, removes heat. Storage tanks or city water mains can be used to replace water converted to steam (vented by pressure relief valves or rupture discs). Pumps also may be used to avoid stagnant areas within an interconnected water circulation system of columns and piping. To prevent corrosion, use a rust inhibitor such as potassium nitrate. To prevent freezing in cold climates, use an antifreeze such as potassium carbonate. During construction, strict quality control is essential to achieve a watertight system.

COATINGS

Intumescent mastic coatings can be spray-applied like paint. When exposed to fire, the coating absorbs heat above about 300°F by expanding into a thick, lightweight thermal barrier more than about 150 times its initial thickness. This gas filled multicellular layer retards heat flow by releasing cooling gases and blocks off oxygen supply. Coatings should only be applied to steel surfaces that are free of dirt, scale, and oil. A multilayer system, consisting of intumescent mastic layers with glass fiber reinforcing between, is needed to achieve fire resistance ratings greater than 1 hr.

When exposed to heat, magnesium oxychloride cement retards heat flow to steel by releasing water of hydration at temperatures above about 570°F. Corrosion resistant priming may be required to assure proper adhesion of magnesium oxychloride to steel surfaces. In high intensity fires (e.g., flammable liquid or gas fires), magnesium oxychloride does not spall and the magnesium oxide residue acts as an efficient heat reflector.

FLAME SHIELDS

Steel flame shields can deflect heat and flames from burning building away from exterior structural steel members. For example, girder top and bottom flanges avoid direct flame impingement during fire by having flame shield protection with thermal insulation behind girder.

NOTES

1. Check prevailing building code for required fire resistance ratings of building constructions. Begin planning steel fire protection during the early stages of a project so that it can be integrated into building design. Consult early with authority having jurisdiction and insurance underwriting groups such as Industrial Risk Insurers, American Insurance Association, or Factory Mutual System.
2. Refer to fire resistance data based on ASTM E 119 test procedures from Underwriters' Laboratories, Factory Mutual, and other nationally recognized testing laboratories.
3. In general, fire resistance of constructions with cavity airspace (e.g., walls, floor-ceilings) will be greater than similar identical weight constructions without airspace.
4. If possible, locate cavity airspace on side of construction opposite potential fire exposure.
5. For most situations, fire resistance of constructions with thermal insulating materials such as mineral fiber and glass fiber in cavity airspace (e.g., doors, walls) will be greater than identical constructions without cavity insulation. Be careful, however, since adding thermal insulation to suspended floor-ceiling assemblies may lower fire resistance by causing metal suspension grid system to buckle or warp from elevated surface temperatures.
6. When plenum spaces above suspended ceilings are used for mechanical system return airflow, fire resistance of floor-ceiling assemblies will be diminished. Conversely, plenums under positive pressure from supply airflow can achieve greater fire resistances than under neutral pressure conditions (e.g., no air circulation in plenum).
7. For beams and columns, the higher the ratio of weight (e.g., pounds per unit length) to heated perimeter (i.e., surface area exposed to fire) the greater the fire resistance.
8. Beams and columns with membrane enclosure protection will have less surface area exposed to fire than identical members with spray-on applied contour protection. In addition, membrane enclosures (e.g., gypsum board, mineral fiber, magnesium oxychloride, or metal lath) form airspaces on both sides of W and S section webs.

MAXIMUM ALLOWABLE UNIFORM LOAD (KIPS) FOR BEAMS LATERALLY SUPPORTED—ASTM A-36 STEEL*

LENGTH (FT)	DEPTH† WEIGHT	w6 8.5	12	16	w8 10	13	15	17	20	24	28	31	w10 11.5	15	17	19	21	25	29	33	w12 14	16.5	19	22	27	31	36	40	m14 17.2	w14 22	26
6		13	19	27	20	26	31	38	45	55	65	67	27	37	43	50	57	71	82	83	39	47	57	67	82	93	108		56	77	94
8		10	14	20	15	20	24	28	34	42	49	54	20	28	32	38	43	53	62	69	29	35	43	51	68	79	92	102	42	58	70
10		8	12	16	12	16	19	23	27	33	39	43	16	22	26	30	34	42	49	55	23	28	34	40	55	63	73	83	34	46	56
12		6	10	13	10	13	16	19	23	28	32	36	14	18	22	25	29	35	41	46	19	23	28	34	45	53	61	69	28	39	47
14					9	11	13	16	19	24	28	31	12	16	18	21	25	30	35	39	17	20	24	29	39	45	52	59	24	33	40
16					8	10	12	14	17	21	24	27	10	14	16	19	22	26	31	34	15	17	21	25	34	39	46	52	21	29	35
18													9	12	14	17	19	23	27	31	13	16	19	22	30	35	41	46	19	26	31
20													8	11	13	15	17	21	25	28	12	14	17	20	27	32	37	42	17	23	28
22																					11	13	15	18	25	29	33	38	15	21	25
24																					10	12	14	17	23	26	31	35	14	19	23

NOTE: Verify lateral support with structural engineering consultant.

*For capacity of beams that are not shown see "AISC Manual of Steel Construction."
†Depth = steel designation (in.); weight = lb/ft; Kip = 1000 lb.

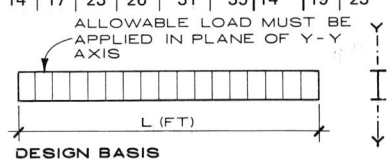

ALLOWABLE LOAD MUST BE APPLIED IN PLANE OF Y-Y AXIS

L (FT)

DESIGN BASIS

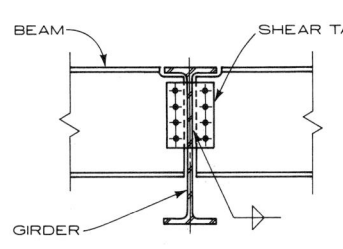

SHOP WELDED TAB FIELD HIGH STRENGTH BOLTED
SHEAR CONNECTION BEAM TO GIRDER

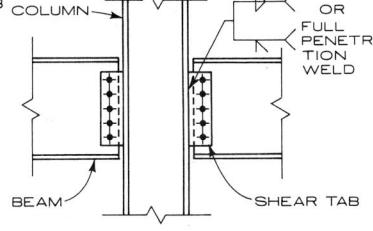

SHOP WELDED TAB FIELD H.S. BOLTED
NONMOMENT CONNECTION BEAM TO COLUMN FLANGE

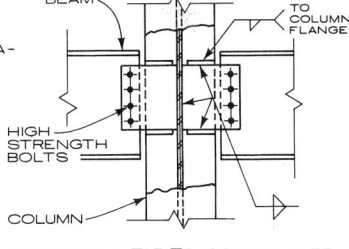

SHOP WELD TAB TO COLUMN WEB AND PLATES FIELD H.S. BOLTED
NONMOMENT CONNECTION BEAM TO COLUMN WEB

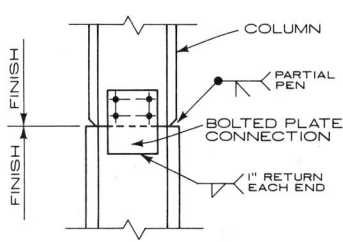

WEB-FIELD H.S. BOLTED FLANGE–PARTIAL PENETRATION
COLUMN SPLICE FLANGE AND WEB

MAXIMUM ALLOWABLE CONCENTRIC LOAD (KIPS) FOR COLUMNS OF ASTM A-36 STEEL (W SHAPES AND TUBING)

DESIGNATION	*	EFFECTIVE LENGTH IN FEET "KH" WITH RESPECT TO LEAST RADIUS OF GYRATION 6	7	8	9	10	11	12	13	14	15	16	17	18	19	20	21	22	23
W 4	13	62	57	51	45	39	32	27	23	20	17	15							
W 6	15.5	84	81	77	73	69	65	60	55	50	45	39	35	31	28	25	23	21	19
	20	109	105	100	96	91	85	80	74	68	61	54	48	43	39	35	32	29	26
	25	137	132	126	120	114	108	101	94	86	78	70	62	55	49	45	41	37	34
W 8	24	133	128	123	118	113	107	101	94	88	81	73	66	59	53	47	43	39	36
	28	155	150	144	138	132	125	118	111	103	95	86	78	69	62	56	51	46	42
	31	178	174	169	164	159	154	148	142	136	130	123	117	110	102	95	87	79	72
TS 3½" OD	0.216	38	36	34	31	28	25	22	19	16	14	12	11	10	9				
	0.300	52	48	45	41	37	33	28	24	21	18	16	14	12	11				
	0.600	91	84	77	69	60	51	43	37	32	28	24	22						
TS 4" OD	0.226	48	46	44	41	38	35	32	29	25	22	19	17	15	14	12	11	10	
	0.318	66	63	59	55	51	47	43	38	33	29	25	23	20	18	16			
TS 4½" OD	0.237	59	57	54	52	49	46	43	40	36	33	29	26	23	21	19	17	15	14
	0.337	81	78	75	71	67	63	59	54	49	44	39	34	31	28	25	23	21	19
	0.674	147	140	133	126	118	109	100	91	81	70	62	55	49	44	40	36	33	
TS 5½" OD	0.258	83	81	78	76	73	71	68	65	61	58	55	51	47	43	39	36	32	29
	0.375	118	114	111	107	103	99	95	91	86	81	76	71	65	59	54	49	44	40
	0.750	216	209	202	195	187	178	170	160	151	141	130	119	108	97	87	79	72	67
TS 6⅝" OD	0.280	110	108	106	103	101	98	95	92	89	86	82	79	75	71	67	63	59	55
	0.432	166	162	159	155	151	146	142	137	132	127	122	116	111	105	99	92	86	79
	0.864	306	299	292	284	275	266	257	247	237	227	216	205	193	181	168	155	142	130
TS 4 x 4	0.250	66	63	60	57	54	51	48	44	40	36	32	29	25	23	21	19	17	16
TS 5 x 5	0.250	88	86	83	81	78	75	72	69	66	62	59	55	51	47	43	39	35	32
TS 6 x 6	0.250	110	108	106	103	101	98	95	93	90	87	83	80	77	73	69	66	62	58
TS 5 x 3	0.250	61	58	54	50	45													
TS 6 x 3	0.250	71	67	62	58	53													
TS 6 x 4	0.250	85	82	79	76	72													
TS 8 x 4	0.250	105	101	98	94	89													

NOTE: For additional columns and actual dimensions of tubing see "AISC Manual of Steel Construction."

*Weight per foot for w columns. Wall thickness for tubing. KIP = 1000 lb; K = effective length factor (verify with structural engineering consultant).

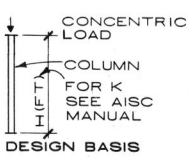

CONCENTRIC LOAD

COLUMN

FOR K SEE AISC MANUAL

DESIGN BASIS

H. Thompson, P.E.; Thompson & Czark; Hempstead, Long Island, New York

W SHAPES-DIMENSIONS FOR DETAILING

DESIGNATION	DEPTH d (IN.)	FLANGE WIDTH b_f (IN.)	FLANGE THICKNESS t_f (IN.)	WEB THICKNESS t_w (IN.)
W36 x 300	36-3/4	16-5/8	1-11/16	15/16
x 280	36-1/2	16-5/8	1-9/16	7/8
x 260	36-1/4	16-1/2	1-7/16	13/16
x 245	36-1/8	16-1/2	1-3/8	13/16
x 230	35-7/8	16-1/2	1-1/4	3/4
W36 x 210	36-3/4	12-1/8	1-3/8	13/16
x 194	36-1/2	12-1/8	1-1/4	3/4
x 182	36-3/8	12-1/8	1-3/8	3/4
x 170	36-1/8	12	1-1/8	11/16
x 160	36	12	1	5/8
x 150	35-7/8	12	15/16	5/8
x 135	35-1/2	12	13/16	5/8
W33 x 241	34-1/8	15-7/8	1-3/8	13/16
x 221	33-7/8	15-3/4	1-1/4	3/4
x 201	33-5/8	15-3/4	1-1/8	11/16
W33 x 152	33-1/8	11-5/8	1-1/16	5/8
x 141	33-1/4	11-1/2	15/16	5/8
x 130	33-1/8	11-1/2	7/8	9/16
x 118	32-7/8	11-1/2	3/4	9/16
W30 x 211	31	15-1/8	1-5/16	3/4
x 191	30-5/8	15	1-3/16	11/16
x 173	30-1/2	15	1-1/16	5/8
W30 x 132	30-1/4	10-1/2	1	5/8
x 124	30-1/8	10-1/2	15/16	9/16
x 116	30	10-1/2	7/8	9/16
x 108	29-7/8	10-1/2	3/4	9/16
x 99	29-5/8	10-1/2	11/16	1/2
W27 x 178	27-3/4	14-1/8	1-3/16	3/4
x 161	27-5/8	14	1-1/16	11/16
x 146	27-3/8	14	1	5/8
W27 x 114	27-1/4	10-1/4	15/16	9/16
x 102	27-1/8	10	13/16	1/2
x 94	26-7/8	10	3/4	1/2
x 84	26-3/4	10	5/8	7/16
W24 x 162	25	13	1-1/4	11/16
x 146	24-3/4	12-7/8	1-1/16	5/8
x 131	24-1/2	12-7/8	15/16	5/8
x 117	24-1/4	12-3/4	7/8	1/2
x 104	24	12-3/4	3/4	1/2
W24 x 94	24-1/4	9-1/4	7/8	1/2
x 84	24-1/8	9	3/4	1/2
x 76	23-7/8	9	11/16	7/16
x 68	23-3/4	9	9/16	7/16
W24 x 62	23-3/4	7	9/16	7/16
x 55	23-5/8	7	1/2	3/8
W21 x 147	22	12-1/2	1-1/8	3/4
x 132	21-7/8	12-1/2	1-1/16	5/8
x 122	21-5/8	12-3/8	15/16	5/8
x 111	21-1/2	12-3/8	7/8	9/16
x 101	21-3/8	12-1/4	13/16	1/2
W21 x 93	21-5/8	8-3/8	15/16	9/16
x 83	21-3/8	8-3/8	13/16	1/2
x 73	21-1/4	8-1/4	3/4	7/16
x 68	21-1/8	8-1/4	11/16	7/16
x 62	21	8-1/4	5/8	3/8
W21 x 57	21	6-1/2	5/8	3/8
x 50	20-7/8	6-1/2	9/16	3/8
x 44	20-5/8	6-1/2	7/16	3/8
W18 x 119	19	11-1/4	1-1/16	5/8
x 106	18-3/4	11-1/4	15/16	9/16
x 97	18-5/8	11-1/8	7/8	9/16
x 86	18-3/8	11-1/8	3/4	1/2
x 76	18-1/4	11	11/16	7/16

DESIGNATION	DEPTH d (IN.)	FLANGE WIDTH b_f (IN.)	FLANGE THICKNESS t_f (IN.)	WEB THICKNESS t_w (IN.)
W18 x 71	18-1/2	7-5/8	13/16	1/2
x 65	18-3/8	7-5/8	3/4	7/16
x 60	18-1/4	7-1/2	11/16	7/16
x 55	18-1/8	7-1/2	5/8	3/8
x 50	18	7-1/2	9/16	3/8
W18 x 46	18	6	5/8	3/8
x 40	17-7/8	6	1/2	5/16
x 35	17-3/4	6	7/16	5/16
W16 x 100	17	10-3/8	1	9/16
x 89	16-3/4	10-3/8	7/8	1/2
x 77	16-1/2	10-1/4	3/4	7/16
x 67	16-3/4	10-1/4	11/16	3/8
W16 x 57	16-3/8	7-1/8	11/16	7/16
x 50	16-1/4	7-1/8	5/8	3/8
x 45	16-1/8	7	9/16	3/8
x 40	16	7	1/2	5/16
x 36	15-7/8	7	7/16	5/16
W16 x 31	15-7/8	5-1/2	7/16	1/4
x 26	15-3/4	5-1/2	3/8	1/4
W14 x 730	22-3/8	17-7/8	4-15/16	3-1/16
x 665	21-5/8	17-5/8	4-1/2	2-13/16
x 605	20-7/8	17-3/8	4-3/16	2-5/8
x 550	20-1/4	17-1/4	3-13/16	2-3/8
x 500	19-5/8	17	3-1/2	2-3/16
x 455	19	16-7/8	3-3/16	2
W14 x 426	18-5/8	16-3/8	3-1/16	1-7/8
x 398	18-1/4	16-5/8	2-7/8	1-3/4
x 370	17-7/8	16-1/2	2-11/16	1-5/8
x 342	17-1/2	16-3/8	2-1/2	1-9/16
x 311	17-1/8	16-1/4	2-1/4	1-7/16
x 283	16-3/4	16-1/8	2-1/16	1-5/16
x 257	16-3/8	16	1-7/8	1-3/16
x 233	16	15-7/8	1-3/4	1-1/16
x 211	15-3/4	15-3/4	1-9/16	1
x 193	15-1/2	15-3/4	1-7/16	7/8
x 176	15-1/4	15-5/8	1-5/16	13/16
x 159	15	15-5/8	1-3/16	3/4
x 145	14-3/4	15-1/2	1-1/16	11/16
W14 x 132	14-5/8	14-3/4	1	5/8
x 120	14-1/2	14-5/8	15/16	9/16
x 109	14-3/8	14-5/8	7/8	1/2
x 99	14-1/8	14-5/8	3/4	1/2
x 90	14	14-1/2	11/16	7/16
W14 x 82	14-1/4	10-1/8	7/8	1/2
x 74	14-1/8	10-1/8	13/16	1/2
x 68	14	10	3/4	7/16
x 61	13-7/8	10	5/8	3/8
W14 x 53	13-7/8	8	11/16	3/8
x 48	13-3/4	8	5/8	3/8
x 43	13-5/8	8	1/2	5/16
W14 x 38	14-1/8	6-3/4	1/2	5/16
x 34	14	6-3/4	7/16	5/16
x 30	13-7/8	6-3/4	3/8	1/4
W14 x 26	13-7/8	5	7/16	1/4
x 22	13-3/4	5	5/16	1/4
W12 x 336	16-7/8	13-3/8	2-15/16	1-3/4
x 305	16-3/8	13-1/4	2-11/16	1-5/8
x 279	15-7/8	13-1/8	2-1/2	1-1/2
x 252	15-3/8	13	2-1/4	1-3/8
x 230	15	12-7/8	2-1/16	1-5/16
x 210	14-3/4	12-3/4	1-7/8	1-3/16

DESIGNATION	DEPTH d (IN.)	FLANGE WIDTH b_f (IN.)	FLANGE THICKNESS t_f (IN.)	WEB THICKNESS t_w (IN.)
W12 x 190	14-3/8	12-5/8	1-3/4	1-1/16
x 170	14	12-5/8	1-9/16	15/16
x 152	13-3/4	12-1/2	1-3/8	7/8
x 136	13-3/8	12-3/8	1-1/4	13/16
x 120	13-1/8	12-3/8	1-1/8	11/16
x 106	12-7/8	12-1/4	1	5/8
x 96	12-3/4	12-1/8	7/8	9/16
x 87	12-1/2	12-1/8	13/16	1/2
x 79	12-3/8	12-1/8	3/4	1/2
x 72	12-1/4	12	11/16	7/16
x 65	12-1/8	12	5/8	3/8
W12 x 58	12-1/4	10	5/8	3/8
x 53	12	10	9/16	3/8
W12 x 50	12-1/4	8-1/8	5/8	3/8
x 45	12	8	9/16	5/16
x 40	12	8	1/2	5/16
W12 x 35	12-1/2	6-1/2	1/2	5/16
x 30	12-3/8	6-1/2	7/16	1/4
x 26	12-1/4	6-1/2	3/8	1/4
W12 x 22	12-1/4	4	7/16	1/4
x 19	12-1/8	4	3/8	1/4
x 16	12	4	1/4	1/4
x 14	11-7/8	4	1/4	3/16
W10 x 112	11-3/8	10-3/8	1-1/4	3/4
x 100	11-1/8	10-3/8	1-1/8	11/16
x 88	10-7/8	10-1/8	1	5/8
x 77	10-5/8	10-1/4	7/8	1/2
x 68	10-3/8	10-1/8	3/4	1/2
x 60	10-1/4	10-1/8	11/16	7/16
x 54	10-1/8	10	5/8	3/8
x 49	10	10	9/16	5/16
W10 x 45	10-1/8	8	5/8	3/8
x 39	9-7/8	8	1/2	5/16
x 33	9-3/4	8	7/16	5/16
W10 x 30	10-1/2	5-3/4	1/2	5/16
x 26	10-3/8	5-3/4	7/16	1/4
x 22	10-1/8	5-3/4	3/8	1/4
W10 x 19	10-1/4	4	3/8	1/4
x 17	10-1/8	4	5/16	1/4
x 15	10	4	1/4	1/4
x 12	9-7/8	4	3/16	3/16
W8 x 67	9	8-1/4	15/16	9/16
x 58	8-3/4	8-1/4	13/16	1/2
x 48	8-1/2	8-1/8	11/16	3/8
x 40	8-1/4	8-1/8	9/16	3/8
x 35	8-1/8	8	1/2	5/16
x 31	8	8	7/16	5/16
W8 x 28	8	6-1/2	7/16	5/16
x 24	7-7/8	6-1/2	3/8	1/4
W8 x 21	8-1/4	5-1/4	3/8	1/4
x 18	8-1/8	5-1/4	5/16	1/4
W8 x 15	8-1/4	4	5/16	1/4
x 13	8	4	1/4	1/4
x 10	7-7/8	4	3/16	3/16
W6 x 25	6-3/8	6-1/8	7/16	5/16
x 20	6-1/4	6	3/8	1/4
x 15	6	6	1/4	1/4
W6 x 16	6-1/4	4	3/8	1/4
x 12	6	4	1/4	1/4
x 9	5-7/8	4	3/16	3/16
W5 x 19	5-1/8	5	7/16	1/4
x 16	5	5	3/8	1/4
W4 x 13	4-1/8	4	3/8	1/4

M SHAPES-DIMENSIONS FOR DETAILING

DESIGNATION	DEPTH d (IN.)	FLANGE WIDTH b_f (IN.)	FLANGE THICKNESS t_f (IN.)	WEB THICKNESS t_w (IN.)
M 14 x 17.2	14	4	1/4	3/16
M 12 x 11.8	12	3-1/8	1/4	3/16
M 10 x 29.1	9-7/8	5-7/8	3/8	7/16
x 22.9	9-7/8	5-3/4	3/8	1/4
M 10 x 9	10	2-3/4	3/16	3/16
M 8 x 37.7	8-1/8	8	1/2	3/8
x 34.3	8	8	7/16	3/8
x 32.6	8	8	7/16	5/16
M 8 x 22.5	8	5-3/8	3/8	3/8
x 18.5	8	5-1/4	3/8	1/4
M 8 x 6.5	8	2-1/4	3/16	1/8
M 7 x 5.5	7	2-1/8	3/16	1/8
M 6 x 33.75	6-1/4	6-1/8	5/8	1/2
x 22.5	6	6	3/8	3/8
x 20	6	6	3/8	1/4
M 6 x 4.4	6	1-7/8	3/16	1/8
M 5 x 18.9	5	5	7/16	5/16
M 4 x 16.3	4-1/4	4	1/2	5/16
x 13.8	4	4	3/8	5/16
x 13	4	4	3/8	1/4

S SHAPES—DIMENSIONS FOR DETAILING

DESIGNATION	DEPTH d (IN.)	FLANGE WIDTH b_f (IN.)	FLANGE AVERAGE THICKNESS t_f (IN.)	WEB THICKNESS t_w (IN.)
S 24 x 120	24	8	$1\frac{1}{8}$	$\frac{13}{16}$
x 105.9	24	$7\frac{7}{8}$	$1\frac{1}{8}$	$\frac{5}{8}$
S 24 x 100	24	$7\frac{1}{4}$	$\frac{7}{8}$	$\frac{3}{4}$
x 90	24	$7\frac{1}{8}$	$\frac{7}{8}$	$\frac{5}{8}$
x 79.9	24	7	$\frac{7}{8}$	$\frac{1}{2}$
S 20 x 95	20	$7\frac{1}{4}$	$\frac{15}{16}$	$\frac{13}{16}$
x 85	20	7	$\frac{15}{16}$	$\frac{5}{8}$
S 20 x 75	20	$6\frac{3}{8}$	$\frac{13}{16}$	$\frac{5}{8}$
x 65.4	20	$6\frac{1}{4}$	$\frac{13}{16}$	$\frac{1}{2}$
S 18 x 70	18	$6\frac{1}{4}$	$\frac{11}{16}$	$\frac{11}{16}$
x 54.7	18	6	$\frac{11}{16}$	$\frac{7}{16}$
S 15 x 50	15	$5\frac{5}{8}$	$\frac{5}{8}$	$\frac{9}{16}$
x 42.9	15	$5\frac{1}{2}$	$\frac{5}{8}$	$\frac{7}{16}$
S 12 x 50	12	$5\frac{1}{2}$	$\frac{11}{16}$	$\frac{11}{16}$
x 40.8	12	$5\frac{1}{4}$	$\frac{11}{16}$	$\frac{7}{16}$
S 12 x 35	12	$5\frac{1}{8}$	$\frac{9}{16}$	$\frac{7}{16}$
x 31.8	12	5	$\frac{9}{16}$	$\frac{3}{8}$
S 10 x 35	10	5	$\frac{1}{2}$	$\frac{5}{8}$
x 25.4	10	$4\frac{5}{8}$	$\frac{1}{2}$	$\frac{5}{16}$
S 8 x 23	8	$4\frac{1}{8}$	$\frac{7}{16}$	$\frac{7}{16}$
x 18.4	8	4	$\frac{7}{16}$	$\frac{1}{4}$
S 7 x 20	7	$3\frac{7}{8}$	$\frac{3}{8}$	$\frac{7}{16}$
x 15.3	7	$3\frac{5}{8}$	$\frac{3}{8}$	$\frac{1}{4}$
S 6 x 17.25	6	$3\frac{5}{8}$	$\frac{3}{8}$	$\frac{7}{16}$
x 12.5	6	$3\frac{5}{8}$	$\frac{3}{8}$	$\frac{1}{4}$
S 5 x 14.75	5	$3\frac{1}{4}$	$\frac{5}{16}$	$\frac{1}{2}$
x 10	5	3	$\frac{5}{16}$	$\frac{3}{16}$
S 4 x 9.5	4	$2\frac{3}{4}$	$\frac{5}{16}$	$\frac{5}{16}$
x 7.7	4	$2\frac{5}{8}$	$\frac{5}{16}$	$\frac{3}{16}$
S 3 x 7.5	3	$2\frac{1}{2}$	$\frac{1}{4}$	$\frac{3}{8}$
x 5.7	3	$2\frac{3}{8}$	$\frac{1}{4}$	$\frac{3}{16}$

HP SHAPES—DIMENSIONS FOR DETAILING

DESIGNATION	DEPTH d (IN.)	FLANGE WIDTH b_f (IN.)	FLANGE AVERAGE THICKNESS t_f (IN.)	WEB THICKNESS t_w (IN.)
HP14 x 117	$14\frac{1}{4}$	$14\frac{7}{8}$	$\frac{13}{16}$	$\frac{13}{16}$
x 102	14	$14\frac{3}{4}$	$\frac{11}{16}$	$\frac{11}{16}$
x 89	$13\frac{7}{8}$	$14\frac{3}{4}$	$\frac{5}{8}$	$\frac{5}{8}$
x 73	$13\frac{5}{8}$	$14\frac{5}{8}$	$\frac{1}{2}$	$\frac{1}{2}$
HP12 x 74	$12\frac{1}{8}$	$12\frac{1}{4}$	$\frac{5}{8}$	$\frac{5}{8}$
x 53	$11\frac{3}{4}$	12	$\frac{7}{16}$	$\frac{7}{16}$
HP10 x 57	10	$10\frac{1}{4}$	$\frac{9}{16}$	$\frac{9}{16}$
x 42	$9\frac{3}{4}$	$10\frac{1}{8}$	$\frac{7}{16}$	$\frac{7}{16}$
HP8 x 36	8	$8\frac{1}{8}$	$\frac{7}{16}$	$\frac{7}{16}$

AMERICAN STANDARD CHANNELS

DESIGNATION	DEPTH d (IN.)	FLANGE WIDTH b_f (IN.)	FLANGE AVERAGE THICKNESS t_f (IN.)	WEB THICKNESS t_w (IN.)
C 15 x 50	15	$3\frac{3}{4}$	$\frac{5}{8}$	$\frac{11}{16}$
x 40	15	$3\frac{1}{2}$	$\frac{5}{8}$	$\frac{1}{2}$
x 33.9	15	$3\frac{3}{8}$	$\frac{5}{8}$	$\frac{3}{8}$
C 12 x 30	12	$3\frac{1}{8}$	$\frac{1}{2}$	$\frac{1}{2}$
x 25	12	3	$\frac{1}{2}$	$\frac{3}{8}$
x 20.7	12	3	$\frac{1}{2}$	$\frac{5}{16}$
C 10 x 30	10	3	$\frac{7}{16}$	$\frac{11}{16}$
x 25	10	$2\frac{7}{8}$	$\frac{7}{16}$	$\frac{1}{2}$
x 20	10	$2\frac{3}{4}$	$\frac{7}{16}$	$\frac{3}{8}$
x 15.3	10	$2\frac{5}{8}$	$\frac{7}{16}$	$\frac{1}{4}$
C 9 x 20	9	$2\frac{5}{8}$	$\frac{7}{16}$	$\frac{7}{16}$
x 15	9	$2\frac{1}{2}$	$\frac{7}{16}$	$\frac{5}{16}$
x 13.4	9	$2\frac{3}{8}$	$\frac{7}{16}$	$\frac{1}{4}$
C 8 x 18.75	8	$2\frac{1}{2}$	$\frac{3}{8}$	$\frac{1}{2}$
x 13.75	8	$2\frac{3}{8}$	$\frac{3}{8}$	$\frac{5}{16}$
x 11.5	8	$2\frac{1}{4}$	$\frac{3}{8}$	$\frac{1}{4}$
C 7 x 14.75	7	$2\frac{1}{4}$	$\frac{3}{8}$	$\frac{7}{16}$
x 12.25	7	$2\frac{1}{4}$	$\frac{3}{8}$	$\frac{5}{16}$
x 9.8	7	$2\frac{1}{8}$	$\frac{3}{8}$	$\frac{3}{16}$
C 6 x 13	6	$2\frac{1}{8}$	$\frac{5}{16}$	$\frac{7}{16}$
x 10.5	6	2	$\frac{5}{16}$	$\frac{5}{16}$
x 8.2	6	$1\frac{7}{8}$	$\frac{5}{16}$	$\frac{3}{16}$
C 5 x 9	5	$1\frac{7}{8}$	$\frac{5}{16}$	$\frac{5}{16}$
x 6.7	5	$1\frac{3}{4}$	$\frac{5}{16}$	$\frac{3}{16}$
C 4 x 7.25	4	$1\frac{3}{4}$	$\frac{5}{16}$	$\frac{5}{16}$
x 5.4	4	$1\frac{5}{8}$	$\frac{5}{16}$	$\frac{3}{16}$
C 3 x 6	3	$1\frac{5}{8}$	$\frac{1}{4}$	$\frac{3}{8}$
x 5	3	$1\frac{1}{2}$	$\frac{1}{4}$	$\frac{1}{4}$
x 4.1	3	$1\frac{3}{8}$	$\frac{1}{4}$	$\frac{3}{16}$

MISCELLANEOUS CHANNELS—DIMENSIONS FOR DETAILING

DESIGNATION	DEPTH d (IN.)	FLANGE WIDTH b_f (IN.)	FLANGE AVERAGE THICKNESS t_f (IN.)	WEB THICKNESS t_w (IN.)
MC 18 x 58	18	$4\frac{1}{4}$	$\frac{11}{16}$	$\frac{5}{8}$
x 51.9	18	$4\frac{1}{8}$	$\frac{5}{8}$	$\frac{5}{8}$
x 45.8	18	4	$\frac{1}{2}$	$\frac{5}{8}$
x 42.7	18	4	$\frac{7}{16}$	$\frac{5}{8}$
MC 13 x 50	13	$4\frac{3}{8}$	$\frac{13}{16}$	$\frac{5}{8}$
x 40	13	$4\frac{1}{8}$	$\frac{9}{16}$	$\frac{5}{8}$
x 35	13	$4\frac{1}{8}$	$\frac{9}{16}$	$\frac{5}{8}$
x 31.8	13	4	$\frac{3}{8}$	$\frac{5}{8}$
MC 12 x 50	12	$4\frac{1}{8}$	$\frac{13}{16}$	$\frac{11}{16}$
x 45	12	4	$\frac{11}{16}$	$\frac{11}{16}$
x 40	12	$3\frac{7}{8}$	$\frac{9}{16}$	$\frac{11}{16}$
x 35	12	$3\frac{3}{4}$	$\frac{7}{16}$	$\frac{11}{16}$
MC 12 x 37	12	$3\frac{5}{8}$	$\frac{5}{8}$	$\frac{5}{8}$
x 32.9	12	$3\frac{1}{2}$	$\frac{1}{2}$	$\frac{5}{8}$
x 30.9	12	$3\frac{1}{2}$	$\frac{7}{16}$	$\frac{5}{8}$
MC 12 x 10.6	12	$1\frac{1}{2}$	$\frac{5}{16}$	$\frac{3}{16}$
MC 10 x 41.1	10	$4\frac{3}{8}$	$\frac{13}{16}$	$\frac{9}{16}$
x 33.6	10	$4\frac{1}{8}$	$\frac{9}{16}$	$\frac{9}{16}$
x 28.5	10	4	$\frac{7}{16}$	$\frac{9}{16}$
MC 10 x 28.3	10	$3\frac{1}{2}$	$\frac{1}{2}$	$\frac{9}{16}$
x 25.3	10	$3\frac{1}{2}$	$\frac{7}{16}$	$\frac{1}{2}$
x 24.9	10	$3\frac{3}{8}$	$\frac{3}{8}$	$\frac{9}{16}$
x 21.9	10	$3\frac{1}{2}$	$\frac{5}{16}$	$\frac{1}{2}$
MC 10 x 8.4	10	$1\frac{1}{2}$	$\frac{3}{16}$	$\frac{1}{4}$
MC 10 x 6.5	10	$1\frac{1}{8}$	$\frac{1}{8}$	$\frac{3}{16}$
MC 9 x 25.4	9	$3\frac{1}{2}$	$\frac{9}{16}$	$\frac{7}{16}$
9 x 23.9	9	$3\frac{1}{2}$	$\frac{9}{16}$	$\frac{3}{8}$
MC 8 x 22.8	8	$3\frac{1}{2}$	$\frac{1}{2}$	$\frac{7}{16}$
x 21.4	8	$3\frac{1}{2}$	$\frac{1}{2}$	$\frac{3}{8}$
MC 8 x 20	8	3	$\frac{1}{2}$	$\frac{3}{8}$
x 18.7	8	3	$\frac{1}{2}$	$\frac{3}{8}$
MC 8 x 8.5	8	$1\frac{7}{8}$	$\frac{5}{16}$	$\frac{3}{16}$
MC 7 x 22.7	7	$3\frac{5}{8}$	$\frac{1}{2}$	$\frac{1}{2}$
x 19.1	7	$3\frac{1}{2}$	$\frac{1}{2}$	$\frac{3}{8}$
MC 7 x 17.6	7	3	$\frac{1}{2}$	$\frac{3}{8}$
MC 6 x 18	6	$3\frac{1}{2}$	$\frac{1}{2}$	$\frac{3}{8}$
x 15.3	6	$3\frac{1}{2}$	$\frac{3}{8}$	$\frac{5}{16}$
MC 6 x 16.3	6	3	$\frac{1}{2}$	$\frac{3}{8}$
x 15.1	6	3	$\frac{1}{2}$	$\frac{5}{16}$
MC 6 x 12	6	$2\frac{1}{2}$	$\frac{3}{8}$	$\frac{5}{16}$

ANGLES (EQUAL LEGS)—DIMENSIONS FOR DETAILING

SIZE AND THICKNESS (IN.)	SIZE AND THICKNESS (IN.)
L 8 x 8 x $1\frac{1}{8}$	L $3\frac{1}{2}$ x $3\frac{1}{2}$ x $\frac{1}{2}$
1	$\frac{7}{16}$
$\frac{7}{8}$	$\frac{3}{8}$
$\frac{3}{4}$	$\frac{5}{16}$
$\frac{5}{8}$	$\frac{1}{4}$
$\frac{9}{16}$	L 3 x 3 x $\frac{1}{2}$
$\frac{1}{2}$	$\frac{7}{16}$
L 6 x 6 x 1	$\frac{3}{8}$
$\frac{7}{8}$	$\frac{5}{16}$
$\frac{3}{4}$	$\frac{1}{4}$
$\frac{5}{8}$	$\frac{3}{16}$
$\frac{9}{16}$	L $2\frac{1}{2}$ x $2\frac{1}{2}$ x $\frac{1}{2}$
$\frac{1}{2}$	$\frac{3}{8}$
$\frac{7}{16}$	$\frac{5}{16}$
$\frac{3}{8}$	$\frac{1}{4}$
$\frac{5}{16}$	$\frac{3}{16}$
L 5 x 5 x $\frac{7}{8}$	L 2 x 2 x $\frac{3}{8}$
$\frac{3}{4}$	$\frac{5}{16}$
$\frac{5}{8}$	$\frac{1}{4}$
$\frac{1}{2}$	$\frac{3}{16}$
$\frac{7}{16}$	$\frac{1}{8}$
$\frac{3}{8}$	L $1\frac{3}{4}$ x $1\frac{3}{4}$ x $\frac{1}{4}$
$\frac{5}{16}$	$\frac{3}{16}$
L 4 x 4 x $\frac{3}{4}$	$\frac{1}{8}$
$\frac{5}{8}$	L $1\frac{1}{2}$ x $1\frac{1}{2}$ x $\frac{1}{4}$
$\frac{1}{2}$	$\frac{3}{16}$
$\frac{7}{16}$	$\frac{5}{32}$
$\frac{3}{8}$	$\frac{1}{8}$
$\frac{5}{16}$	L $1\frac{1}{4}$ x $1\frac{1}{4}$ x $\frac{1}{4}$
$\frac{1}{4}$	$\frac{3}{16}$
	$\frac{1}{8}$
	L 1 x 1 x $\frac{1}{4}$
	$\frac{3}{16}$
	$\frac{1}{8}$

ANGLES (UNEQUAL LEGS)—DIMENSIONS FOR DETAILING

SIZE AND THICKNESS (IN.)	SIZE AND THICKNESS (IN.)	SIZE AND THICKNESS (IN.)	SIZE AND THICKNESS (IN.)
L 9 x 4 x 1	L 6 x 4 x $\frac{7}{8}$	L 4 x $3\frac{1}{2}$ x $\frac{5}{8}$	L 3 x 2 x $\frac{1}{2}$
$\frac{7}{8}$	$\frac{3}{4}$	$\frac{1}{2}$	$\frac{7}{16}$
$\frac{3}{4}$	$\frac{5}{8}$	$\frac{7}{16}$	$\frac{3}{8}$
$\frac{5}{8}$	$\frac{9}{16}$	$\frac{3}{8}$	$\frac{5}{16}$
$\frac{9}{16}$	$\frac{1}{2}$	$\frac{5}{16}$	$\frac{1}{4}$
$\frac{1}{2}$	$\frac{7}{16}$	$\frac{1}{4}$	$\frac{3}{16}$
L 8 x 6 x 1	$\frac{3}{8}$	L 4 x 3 x $\frac{5}{8}$	L $2\frac{1}{2}$ x 2 x $\frac{3}{8}$
$\frac{7}{8}$	$\frac{5}{16}$	$\frac{1}{2}$	$\frac{5}{16}$
$\frac{3}{4}$	$\frac{1}{4}$	$\frac{7}{16}$	$\frac{1}{4}$
$\frac{5}{8}$	L 6 x $3\frac{1}{2}$ x $\frac{1}{2}$	$\frac{3}{8}$	$\frac{3}{16}$
$\frac{9}{16}$	$\frac{3}{8}$	$\frac{5}{16}$	L $2\frac{1}{2}$ x $1\frac{1}{2}$ x $\frac{5}{16}$
$\frac{1}{2}$	$\frac{5}{16}$	$\frac{1}{4}$	$\frac{1}{4}$
$\frac{7}{16}$	$\frac{1}{4}$	L $3\frac{1}{2}$ x 3 x $\frac{1}{2}$	$\frac{3}{16}$
L 8 x 4 x 1	L 5 x $3\frac{1}{2}$ x $\frac{3}{4}$	$\frac{7}{16}$	L 2 x $1\frac{1}{2}$ x $\frac{1}{4}$
$\frac{7}{8}$	$\frac{5}{8}$	$\frac{3}{8}$	$\frac{3}{16}$
$\frac{3}{4}$	$\frac{1}{2}$	$\frac{5}{16}$	$\frac{1}{8}$
$\frac{5}{8}$	$\frac{7}{16}$	$\frac{1}{4}$	L 2 x $1\frac{1}{4}$ x $\frac{1}{4}$
$\frac{9}{16}$	$\frac{3}{8}$	L $3\frac{1}{2}$ x $2\frac{1}{2}$ x $\frac{1}{2}$	$\frac{3}{16}$
$\frac{1}{2}$	$\frac{5}{16}$	$\frac{7}{16}$	$\frac{1}{8}$
$\frac{7}{16}$	$\frac{1}{4}$	$\frac{3}{8}$	L $1\frac{3}{4}$ x $1\frac{1}{4}$ x $\frac{1}{4}$
L 7 x 4 x $\frac{7}{8}$	L 5 x 3 x $\frac{1}{2}$	$\frac{5}{16}$	$\frac{3}{16}$
$\frac{3}{4}$	$\frac{7}{16}$	$\frac{1}{4}$	$\frac{1}{8}$
$\frac{5}{8}$	$\frac{3}{8}$	L 3 x $2\frac{1}{2}$ x $\frac{1}{2}$	
$\frac{9}{16}$	$\frac{5}{16}$	$\frac{7}{16}$	
$\frac{1}{2}$	$\frac{1}{4}$	$\frac{3}{8}$	
$\frac{7}{16}$		$\frac{5}{16}$	
$\frac{3}{8}$		$\frac{1}{4}$	
		$\frac{3}{16}$	

STRUCTURAL TEES CUT FROM W SHAPES—DIMENSIONS FOR DETAILING

DESIGNATION	DEPTH OF SECTION d (IN.)	FLANGE WIDTH b_f (IN.)	FLANGE AVERAGE THICKNESS t_f (IN.)	STEM THICKNESS t_w (IN.)
WT18 x 150	18.370	16.655	1.680	0.945
x 140	18.260	16.595	1.570	0.885
x 130	18.130	16.550	1.440	0.840
x 122.5	18.040	16.510	1.350	0.800
x 115	17.950	16.470	1.260	0.760
WT18 x 105	18.345	12.180	1.360	0.830
x 97	18.245	12.115	1.260	0.765
x 91	18.165	12.075	1.180	0.725
x 85	18.085	12.030	1.100	0.680
x 80	18.005	12.000	1.020	0.650
x 75	17.925	11.975	0.940	0.625
x 67.5	17.775	11.950	0.790	0.600
WT16.5 x 120.5	17.090	15.860	1.400	0.830
x 110.5	16.965	15.805	1.275	0.775
x 100.5	16.840	15.745	1.150	0.715
WT16.5 x 76	16.745	11.565	1.055	0.635
x 70.5	16.650	11.535	0.960	0.605
x 65	16.545	11.510	0.855	0.580
x 59	16.430	11.480	0.740	0.550
WT15 x 105.5	15.470	15.105	1.315	0.775
x 95.5	15.340	15.040	1.185	0.710
x 86.5	15.220	14.985	1.065	0.655
WT15 x 66	15.155	10.545	1.000	0.615
x 62	15.085	10.515	0.930	0.585
x 58	15.005	10.495	0.850	0.565
x 54	14.915	10.475	0.760	0.545
x 49.5	14.825	10.450	0.670	0.520
WT13.5 x 89	13.905	14.085	1.190	0.725
x 80.5	13.795	14.020	1.080	0.660
x 73	13.690	13.965	0.975	0.605
WT13.5 x 57	13.645	10.070	0.930	0.570
x 51	13.545	10.015	0.830	0.515
x 47	13.460	9.990	0.745	0.490
x 42	13.355	9.960	0.640	0.460
WT12 x 81	12.500	12.955	1.220	0.705
x 73	12.370	12.900	1.090	0.650
x 65.5	12.240	12.855	0.960	0.605
x 58.5	12.130	12.800	0.850	0.550
x 52	12.030	12.750	0.750	0.500
WT12 x 47	12.155	9.065	0.875	0.515
x 42	12.050	9.020	0.770	0.470
x 38	11.960	8.990	0.680	0.440
x 34	11.865	8.965	0.585	0.415
WT12 x 31	11.870	7.040	0.590	0.430
x 27.5	11.785	7.005	0.505	0.395
WT10.5 x 73.5	11.030	12.510	1.150	0.720
x 66	10.915	12.440	1.035	0.650
x 61	10.840	12.390	0.960	0.600
x 55.5	10.755	12.340	0.875	0.550
x 50.5	10.680	12.290	0.800	0.500
WT10.5 x 46.5	10.810	8.420	0.930	0.580
x 41.5	10.715	8.355	0.835	0.515
x 36.5	10.620	8.295	0.740	0.455
x 34	10.565	8.270	0.685	0.430
x 31	10.495	8.240	0.615	0.400
WT10.5 x 28.5	10.530	6.555	0.650	0.405
x 25	10.415	6.530	0.535	0.380
x 22	10.330	6.500	0.450	0.350

DESIGNATION	DEPTH OF SECTION d (IN.)	FLANGE WIDTH b_f (IN.)	FLANGE AVERAGE THICKNESS t_f (IN.)	STEM THICKNESS t_w (IN.)
WT9 x 59.5	9.485	11.265	1.060	0.655
x 53	9.365	11.200	0.940	0.590
x 48.5	9.295	11.145	0.870	0.535
x 43	9.195	11.090	0.770	0.480
x 38	9.105	11.035	0.680	0.425
WT9 x 35.5	9.235	7.635	0.810	0.495
x 32.5	9.175	7.590	0.750	0.450
x 30	9.120	7.555	0.695	0.415
x 27.5	9.055	7.530	0.630	0.390
x 25	8.995	7.495	0.570	0.355
WT9 x 23	9.030	6.060	0.605	0.360
x 20	8.950	6.015	0.525	0.315
x 17.5	8.850	6.000	0.425	0.300
WT8 x 50	8.485	10.425	0.985	0.585
x 44.5	8.375	10.365	0.875	0.525
x 38.5	8.260	10.295	0.760	0.455
x 33.5	8.165	10.235	0.665	0.395
WT8 x 28.5	8.215	7.120	0.715	0.430
x 25	8.130	7.070	0.630	0.380
x 22.5	8.065	7.035	0.565	0.345
x 20	8.005	6.995	0.505	0.305
x 18	7.930	6.985	0.430	0.295
WT8 x 15.5	7.940	5.525	0.440	0.275
x 13	7.845	5.500	0.345	0.250
WT7 x 365	11.210	17.890	4.910	3.070
x 332.5	10.820	17.650	4.520	2.830
x 302.5	10.460	17.415	4.160	2.595
x 275	10.120	17.200	3.820	2.380
x 250	9.800	17.010	3.500	2.190
x 227.5	9.510	16.835	3.210	2.015
WT7 x 213	9.335	16.695	3.035	1.875
x 199	9.145	16.590	2.845	1.770
x 185	8.960	16.475	2.660	1.655
x 171	8.770	16.360	2.470	1.540
x 155.5	8.560	16.230	2.260	1.410
x 141.5	8.370	16.110	2.070	1.290
x 128.5	8.190	15.995	1.890	1.175
x 116.5	8.020	15.890	1.720	1.070
x 105.5	7.860	15.800	1.560	0.980
x 96.5	7.740	15.710	1.440	0.890
x 88	7.610	15.650	1.310	0.830
x 79.5	7.490	15.565	1.190	0.745
x 72.5	7.390	15.500	1.090	0.680
WT7 x 66	7.330	14.725	1.030	0.645
x 60	7.240	14.670	0.940	0.590
x 54.5	7.160	14.605	0.860	0.525
x 49.5	7.080	14.565	0.780	0.485
x 45	7.010	14.520	0.710	0.440
WT7 x 41	7.155	10.130	0.855	0.510
x 37	7.085	10.070	0.785	0.450
x 34	7.020	10.035	0.720	0.415
x 30.5	6.945	9.995	0.645	0.375
WT7 x 26.5	6.960	8.060	0.660	0.370
x 24	6.895	8.030	0.595	0.340
x 21.5	6.830	7.995	0.530	0.305
WT7 x 19	7.050	6.770	0.515	0.310
x 17	6.990	6.745	0.455	0.285
x 15	6.920	6.730	0.385	0.270
WT7 x 13	6.955	5.025	0.420	0.255
x 11	6.870	5.000	0.335	0.230

DESIGNATION	DEPTH OF SECTION d (IN.)	FLANGE WIDTH b_f (IN.)	FLANGE AVERAGE THICKNESS t_f (IN.)	STEM THICKNESS t_w (IN.)
WT6 x 95	7.190	12.670	1.735	1.060
x 85	7.015	12.570	1.560	0.960
x 76	6.855	12.480	1.400	0.870
x 68	6.705	12.400	1.250	0.790
x 60	6.560	12.320	1.105	0.710
x 53	6.445	12.220	0.990	0.610
x 48	6.355	12.160	0.900	0.550
x 43.5	6.265	12.125	0.810	0.515
x 39.5	6.190	12.080	0.735	0.470
x 36	6.125	12.040	0.670	0.430
x 32.5	6.060	12.000	0.605	0.390
WT6 x 29	6.095	10.010	0.640	0.360
x 26.5	6.030	9.995	0.575	0.345
WT6 x 25	6.095	8.080	0.640	0.370
x 22.5	6.030	8.045	0.575	0.335
x 20	5.970	8.005	0.515	0.295
WT6 x 17.5	6.250	6.560	0.520	0.300
x 15	6.170	6.520	0.440	0.260
x 13	6.110	6.490	0.380	0.230
WT6 x 11	6.155	4.030	0.425	0.260
x 9.5	6.080	4.005	0.350	0.235
x 8	5.995	3.990	0.265	0.220
x 7	5.955	3.970	0.225	0.200
WT5 x 56	5.680	10.415	1.250	0.755
x 50	5.550	10.340	1.120	0.680
x 44	5.420	10.265	0.990	0.605
x 38.5	5.300	10.190	0.870	0.530
x 34	5.200	10.130	0.770	0.470
x 30	5.110	10.080	0.680	0.420
x 27	5.045	10.030	0.615	0.370
x 24.5	4.990	10.000	0.560	0.340
WT5 x 22.5	5.050	8.020	0.620	0.350
x 19.5	4.960	7.985	0.530	0.315
x 16.5	4.865	7.960	0.435	0.290
WT5 x 15	5.235	5.810	0.510	0.300
x 13	5.165	5.770	0.440	0.260
x 11	5.085	5.750	0.360	0.240
WT5 x 9.5	5.120	4.020	0.395	0.250
x 8.5	5.055	4.010	0.330	0.240
x 7.5	4.995	4.000	0.270	0.230
x 6	4.935	3.960	0.210	0.190
WT4 x 33.5	4.500	8.280	0.935	0.570
x 29	4.375	8.220	0.810	0.510
x 24	4.250	8.110	0.685	0.400
x 20	4.125	8.070	0.560	0.360
x 17.5	4.060	8.020	0.495	0.310
x 15.5	4.000	7.995	0.435	0.285
WT4 x 14	4.030	6.535	0.465	0.285
x 12	3.965	6.495	0.400	0.245
WT4 x 10.5	4.140	5.270	0.400	0.250
x 9	4.070	5.250	0.330	0.230
WT4 x 7.5	4.055	4.015	0.315	0.245
x 6.5	3.995	4.000	0.255	0.230
x 5	3.945	3.940	0.205	0.170
WT3 x 12.5	3.190	6.080	0.455	0.320
x 10	3.100	6.020	0.365	0.260
x 7.5	2.995	5.990	0.260	0.230
WT3 x 8	3.140	4.030	0.405	0.260
x 6	3.015	4.000	0.280	0.230
x 4.5	2.950	3.940	0.215	0.170

STRUCTURAL TEES CUT FROM S SHAPES—DIMENSIONS FOR DETAILING

DESIGNATION	d	b_f	t_f	t_w
ST12 x 60	12.00	8.048	1.102	0.798
x 52.95	12.00	7.875	1.102	0.625
ST12 x 50	12.00	7.247	0.871	0.747
x 45	12.00	7.124	0.871	0.624
x 39.95	12.00	7.001	0.871	0.501
ST10 x 47.5	10.00	7.200	0.916	0.800
x 42.5	10.00	7.053	0.916	0.653
ST10 x 37.5	10.00	6.391	0.789	0.641
x 32.7	10.00	6.250	0.789	0.500
ST9 x 35	9.00	6.251	0.691	0.711
x 27.35	9.00	6.001	0.691	0.461

DESIGNATION	d	b_f	t_f	t_w
ST7.5 x 25	7.50	5.640	0.622	0.550
x 21.45	7.50	5.501	0.622	0.411
ST6 x 25	6.00	5.477	0.659	0.687
x 20.4	6.00	5.252	0.659	0.462
ST6 x 17.5	6.00	5.078	0.544	0.428
x 15.9	6.00	5.000	0.544	0.350
ST5 x 17.5	5.00	4.944	0.491	0.594
x 12.7	5.00	4.661	0.491	0.311
ST4 x 11.5	4.00	4.171	0.425	0.441
x 9.2	4.00	4.001	0.425	0.271

DESIGNATION	d	b_f	t_f	t_w
ST3.5 x 10	3.50	3.860	0.392	0.450
x 7.65	3.50	3.662	0.392	0.252
ST3 x 8.625	3.00	3.565	0.359	0.465
x 6.25	3.00	3.332	0.359	0.232
ST2.5 x 7.375	2.50	3.284	0.326	0.494
x 5	2.50	3.004	0.326	0.214
ST2 x 4.75	2.00	2.796	0.293	0.326
x 3.85	2.00	2.663	0.293	0.193
ST1.5 x 3.75	1.50	2.509	0.260	0.349
x 2.85	1.50	2.330	0.260	0.170

NOTE

The following tables show sizes and shapes usually stocked or readily available. Manufacturers' data should be checked for availability of sizes other than those in these tables. Where necessary, and where extra cost is warranted, other sections may be produced by welding, cutting, or other methods.

STEEL CHANNEL

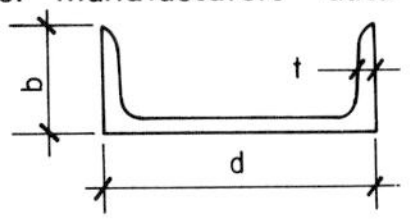

STEEL CHANNELS—BAR SIZE (IN.)

d x b x t	d x b x t	d x b x t
3/4 x 5/16 x 1/8	1 1/4 x 1/2 x 1/8	2 x 9/16 x 3/16
3/4 x 3/8 x 1/8	1 1/2 x 1/2 x 1/8	2 x 5/8 x 1/4
7/8 x 3/8 x 1/8	1 1/2 x 9/16 x 3/16	2 x 1 x 1/8
7/8 x 7/16 x 1/8	1 1/2 x 3/4 x 1/8	2 x 1 x 3/16
1 x 3/8 x 1/8	1 1/2 x 1 1/2 x 3/16	2 1/2 x 5/8 x 3/16
1 x 1/2 x 1/8	1 3/4 x 1/2 x 3/16	
1 1/8 x 9/16 x 3/16	2 x 1/2 x 1/8	

NOTE: For structural channel sizes (d = 3 in. and larger) see Dimensions of Channel Shapes in this chapter.

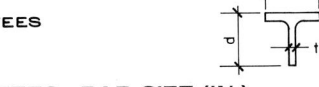

STEEL TEES

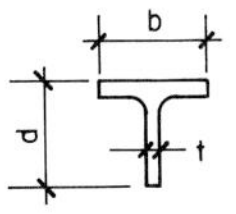

STEEL TEES—BAR SIZE (IN.)

b x d x t	b x d x t	b x d x t
3/4 x 3/4 x 1/8	1 1/2 x 1 1/2 x 3/16	2 x 2 x 5/16
1 x 1 x 1/8	1 1/2 x 1 1/2 x 1/4	2 1/4 x 2 1/4 x 1/4
1 x 1 x 3/16	1 3/4 x 1 3/4 x 3/16	2 1/2 x 2 1/4 x 1/4
1 1/4 x 1 1/4 x 1/8	1 3/4 x 1 3/4 x 1/4	2 1/2 x 2 1/2 x 5/16
1 1/4 x 1 1/4 x 3/16	2 x 1 1/2 x 1/4	2 1/2 x 2 1/2 x 3/8
1 1/4 x 1 1/4 x 1/4	2 x 2 x 1/4	
STRUCTURAL		
3 x 2 1/2 x 5/16	3 x 3 x 3/8	4 x 4 x 1/2
3 x 3 x 5/16	4 x 3 x 3/8	5 x 3 1/8 x 1/2

ALUMINUM ANGLE STRUCTURAL

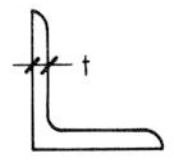

ALUMINUM ANGLES—STRUCTURAL—EQUAL LEGS (IN.)

SIZE x t	SIZE x t	SIZE x t
3/4 x 3/4 x 1/8	2 x 2 x 3/16	3 1/2 x 3 1/2 x 1/4
1 x 1 x 1/8	2 x 2 x 1/4	3 1/2 x 3 1/2 x 3/8
1 x 1 x 3/16	2 x 2 x 5/16	3 1/2 x 3 1/2 x 1/2
1 x 1 x 1/4	2 x 2 x 3/8	4 x 4 x 1/4
1 1/4 x 1 1/4 x 1/8	2 1/2 x 2 1/2 x 1/8	4 x 4 x 5/16
1 1/4 x 1 1/4 x 3/16	2 1/2 x 2 1/2 x 3/16	4 x 4 x 3/8
1 1/4 x 1 1/4 x 1/4	2 1/2 x 2 1/2 x 1/4	4 x 4 x 1/2
1 1/2 x 1 1/2 x 1/8	2 1/2 x 2 1/2 x 5/16	4 x 4 x 3/4
1 1/2 x 1 1/2 x 3/16	2 1/2 x 2 1/2 x 3/8	5 x 5 x 3/8
1 1/2 x 1 1/2 x 1/4	3 x 3 x 3/16	5 x 5 x 1/2
1 3/4 x 1 3/4 x 1/8	3 x 3 x 1/4	6 x 6 x 3/8
1 3/4 x 1 3/4 x 3/16	3 x 3 x 5/16	6 x 6 x 1/2
1 3/4 x 1 3/4 x 1/4	3 x 3 x 3/8	8 x 8 x 1/2
2 x 2 x 1/8	3 x 3 x 1/2	
UNEQUAL LEGS (IN.)		
1 1/2 x 1 1/4 x 1/8	2 1/2 x 2 x 5/16	4 x 3 x 1/2
1 1/2 x 1 1/4 x 3/16	2 1/2 x 2 x 3/8	5 x 3 x 3/8
1 1/2 x 1 1/4 x 1/4	3 x 2 x 3/16	5 x 3 x 1/2
1 3/4 x 1 1/4 x 1/8	3 x 2 x 1/4	5 x 3 1/2 x 5/16
1 3/4 x 1 1/4 x 3/16	3 x 2 x 3/8	5 x 3 1/2 x 3/8
1 3/4 x 1 1/4 x 1/4	3 x 2 1/2 x 1/4	5 x 3 1/2 x 1/2
2 x 1 1/2 x 1/8	3 x 2 1/2 x 3/8	6 x 3 1/2 x 5/16
2 x 1 1/2 x 3/16	3 1/2 x 2 1/2 x 1/4	6 x 3 1/2 x 1/2
2 x 1 1/2 x 1/4	3 1/2 x 2 1/2 x 3/8	6 x 4 x 3/8
2 1/2 x 1 1/2 x 1/4	3 1/2 x 3 x 1/4	6 x 4 x 1/2
2 1/2 x 2 x 3/16	4 x 3 x 1/4	6 x 4 x 5/8
2 1/2 x 2 x 1/4	4 x 3 x 3/8	8 x 6 x 3/4

Harnish, Morgan, and Causey, Architects; Ontario, California

STEEL ANGLES UNEQUAL LEGS

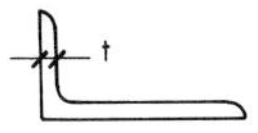

STEEL ANGLES—UNEQUAL LEGS—BAR SIZE (IN.)

SIZE x t	SIZE x t	SIZE x t
1 x 5/8 x 1/8	2 x 1 1/4 x 1/4	2 1/2 x 1 1/2 x 5/16
1 x 3/4 x 1/8	2 x 1 1/2 x 1/8	2 1/2 x 2 x 3/16
1 3/8 x 7/8 x 1/8	2 x 1 1/2 x 3/16	2 1/2 x 2 x 1/4
1 3/8 x 7/8 x 3/16	2 x 1 1/2 x 1/4	2 1/2 x 2 x 5/16
1 1/2 x 1 1/4 x 3/16	2 1/4 x 1 1/2 x 3/16	2 1/2 x 2 x 1/8
1 3/4 x 1 1/4 x 1/8	2 1/2 x 1 1/2 x 3/16	
2 x 1 1/4 x 3/16	2 1/2 x 1 1/2 x 1/4	

NOTE: For structural angle sizes (3 x 2 x 3/16 in. and larger) see Dimensions of Angle Shapes in this chapter.

STEEL ZEES

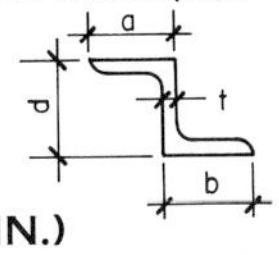

STEEL ZEES—BAR SIZE (IN.)

d x a x b x t	d x a x b x t
1 x 1/2 x 5/8 x 1/8	1 3/8 x 3/4 x 1 3/16 x 1/8
1 3/16 x 5/8 x 3/4 x 1/8	1 3/4 x 1 1/4 x 3/4 x 3/16
STRUCTURAL	
3 x 2 11/16 x 2 11/16 x 1/4	4 1/8 x 3 3/16 x 3 3/16 x 3/8
3 x 2 11/16 x 2 11/16 x 3/8	5 x 3 1/4 x 3 1/4 x 5/16
3 x 2 11/16 x 2 11/16 x 1/2	5 x 3 1/4 x 3 1/4 x 1/2
4 x 3 1/16 x 3 1/16 x 1/4	5 1/16 x 3 5/16 x 3 5/16 x 3/8
4 1/16 x 3 1/8 x 3 1/8 x 5/16	6 x 3 1/2 x 3 1/2 x 3/8

ALUMINUM ANGLE SQUARE CORNERS

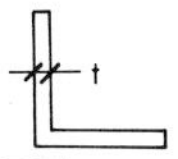

ALUMINUM ANGLES—SQUARE CORNERS—EQUAL LEGS (IN.)

SIZE x t	SIZE x t	SIZE x t
1/2 x 1/2 x 1/16	1 1/8 x 1 1/8 x 3/16	2 x 2 x 3/16
1/2 x 1/2 x 1/8	1 1/4 x 1 1/4 x 1/8	2 x 2 x 1/4
5/8 x 5/8 x 1/8	1 1/4 x 1 1/4 x 3/16	2 1/2 x 2 1/2 x 1/8
3/4 x 3/4 x 1/16	1 1/2 x 1 1/2 x 1/8	3 x 3 x 1/8
3/4 x 3/4 x 1/8	1 1/2 x 1 1/2 x 3/16	3 x 3 x 3/16
1 x 1 x 1/16	1 1/2 x 1 1/2 x 1/4	3 1/2 x 3 1/2 x 1/8
1 x 1 x 1/8	1 3/4 x 1 3/4 x 1/8	4 x 4 x 1/8
1 x 1 x 3/16	2 x 2 x 1/8	
UNEQUAL LEGS (IN.)		
3/4 x 3/8 x 3/32	2 x 3/4 x 1/8	3 1/2 x 2 x 1/8
1 x 1/2 x 1/8	2 x 1 x 1/8	3 1/2 x 2 1/2 x 1/8
1 x 3/4 x 1/8	2 x 1 x 3/16	3 1/2 x 3 x 1/8
1 1/4 x 1/2 x 1/8	2 x 1 1/2 x 1/8	4 x 2 x 1/8
1 1/2 x 1/2 x 1/8	2 1/2 x 1 x 1/8	4 x 3 x 1/8
1 1/2 x 3/4 x 1/8	2 1/2 x 1 1/2 x 1/8	5 x 3 x 1/8
1 1/2 x 1 x 1/8	2 1/2 x 2 x 1/8	5 x 4 x 1/8
1 3/4 x 1 x 1/8	3 x 1 x 1/8	5 1/4 x 2 1/4 x 1/8
1 3/4 x 1 1/2 x 1/8	3 x 2 x 1/8	
2 x 1/2 x 1/8	3 1/2 x 1 1/4 x 1/8	

ALUMINUM ZEES SQUARE CORNERS

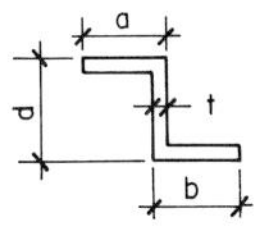

ALUMINUM ZEES—SQUARE CORNERS (IN.)

d x a x b x t	d x a x b x t
1/2 x 1/2 x 1/2 x 3/32	1 x 1 1/8 x 1 1/8 x 1/8
3/4 x 3/4 x 3/4 x 1/8	1 x 5/8 x 7/8 x 1/8
7/8 x 3/4 x 3/4 x 1/8	

STEEL ANGLES EQUAL LEGS

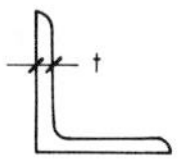

STEEL ANGLES—EQUAL LEGS—BAR SIZE (IN.)

SIZE x t	SIZE x t	SIZE x t
1/2 x 1/2 x 1/8	1 1/4 x 1 1/4 x 3/16	2 x 2 x 3/16
5/8 x 5/8 x 1/8	1 1/4 x 1 1/4 x 1/4	2 x 2 x 1/4
3/4 x 3/4 x 1/8	1 1/2 x 1 1/2 x 1/8	2 x 2 x 5/16
7/8 x 7/8 x 1/8	1 1/2 x 1 1/2 x 3/16	2 x 2 x 3/8
1 x 1 x 1/8	1 1/2 x 1 1/2 x 1/4	2 1/2 x 2 1/2 x 3/16
1 x 1 x 3/16	1 3/4 x 1 3/4 x 1/8	2 1/2 x 2 1/2 x 1/4
1 x 1 x 1/4	1 3/4 x 1 3/4 x 3/16	2 1/2 x 2 1/2 x 5/16
1 1/8 x 1 1/8 x 1/8	1 3/4 x 1 3/4 x 1/4	2 1/2 x 2 1/2 x 3/8
1 1/4 x 1 1/4 x 1/8	2 x 2 x 1/8	2 1/2 x 2 1/2 x 1/2

NOTE: For structural angle sizes (3 x 3 x 3/16 in. and larger) see Dimensions of Angle Shapes in this chapter.

ALUMINUM CHANNEL SQUARE CORNERS

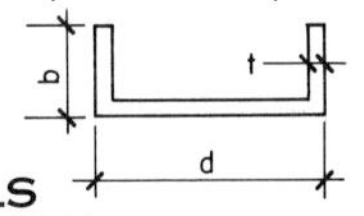

ALUMINUM CHANNELS—SQUARE CORNERS (IN.)

d x b x t	d x b x t	d x b x t
3/8 x 3/8 x 7/64	1 1/4 x 3/4 x 1/8	2 1/2 x 3/4 x 1/8
1/2 x 3/8 x 1/8	1 1/4 x 1 1/4 x 1/8	2 1/2 x 1 1/2 x 1/8
1/2 x 1/2 x 3/32	1 1/2 x 1/2 x 1/8	2 1/2 x 2 1/2 x 1/8
1/2 x 3/4 x 1/8	1 1/2 x 5/8 x 1/8	3 x 1/2 x 1/8
5/8 x 5/8 x 1/8	1 1/2 x 3/4 x 1/8	3 x 1 x 1/8
5/8 x 1 x 1/8	1 1/2 x 1 x 1/8	3 x 2 x 1/8
3/4 x 3/8 x 1/8	1 1/2 x 1 1/2 x 1/8	3 x 3 x 1/8
3/4 x 1/2 x 1/8	1 3/4 x 1/2 x 1/8	4 x 1 1/2 x 1/8
3/4 x 3/4 x 1/8	1 3/4 x 3/4 x 1/8	4 1/2 x 2 x 1/8
1 x 1/2 x 1/8	1 3/4 x 1 x 1/8	5 x 2 x 3/16
1 x 3/4 x 1/8	2 x 1/2 x 1/8	
1 x 1 x 1/8	2 x 1 x 1/8	
1 1/4 x 1/2 x 1/8	2 x 2 x 1/8	
1 1/4 x 5/8 x 1/8	2 1/4 x 7/8 x 1/8	

NOTE: For aluminum channels in American Standard sizes and Aluminum Association Standard sizes, see Dimensions of Channel Shapes in this chapter.

ALUMINUM TEES SQUARE CORNERS

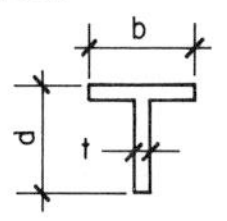

ALUMINUM TEES—SQUARE CORNERS (IN.)

b x d x t	b x d x t	b x d x t
3/4 x 3/4 x 1/8	1 1/8 x 1/2 x 3/8	2 x 3/4 x 1/8
3/4 x 1 1/4 x 1/8	1 1/8 x 1 1/8 x 1/8	2 x 2 x 3/16
1 x 3/4 x 1/8	1 1/4 x 7/8 x 1/8	
1 x 1 x 1/8	1 1/2 x 1 1/2 x 1/8	

ALUMINUM TEES SQUARE CORNERS

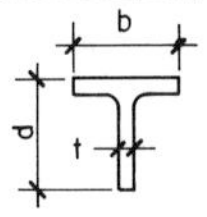

STRUCTURAL (IN.)

1 1/2 x 1 1/2 x 1/4	2 1/4 x 2 1/4 x 1/4	4 x 4 x 3/8
2 x 2 x 1/4	3 x 3 x 3/8	

STAINLESS STEEL ANGLES

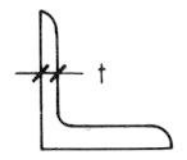

STAINLESS STEEL ANGLES (IN.)

SIZE x t	SIZE x t	SIZE x t
3/4 x 3/4 x 1/8	1 1/2 x 1 1/2 x 3/16	2 1/2 x 2 1/2 x 1/4
1 x 1 x 1/8	1 1/2 x 1 1/2 x 1/4	3 x 3 x 1/4
1 x 1 x 3/16	2 x 2 x 1/8	3 x 3 x 5/16
1 1/4 x 1 1/4 x 1/8	2 x 2 x 3/16	3 x 3 x 3/8
1 1/4 x 1 1/4 x 3/16	2 x 2 x 1/4	
1 1/2 x 1 1/2 x 1/8	2 1/2 x 2 1/2 x 3/16	

RECTANGULAR TUBING

RECTANGULAR ALUMINUM TUBING

ROUND PIPE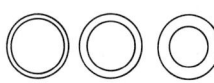

RECTANGULAR TUBING—STEEL

SIZE (IN.)	T = WALL THICKNESS (BW GAUGE OR IN.)				
$1^1/_2$ x $3/_4$	0.073				
$1^1/_2$ x 1	16	14	11		
2 x 1	16	14	11		
2 x $1^1/_4$	14				
2 x $1^1/_2$	11				
$2^1/_2$ x 1	14				
$2^1/_2$ x $1^1/_4$	14				
$2^1/_2$ x $1^1/_2$	14	0.145	7	5	$1/_4$''
3 x 1	14				
3 x $1^1/_2$	16	14	11	7	
3 x 2	14	11	$9/_{64}$''	$3/_{16}$''	$1/_4$''
4 x 2	14	11	$5/_{32}$''	$3/_{16}$''	$1/_4$''
4 x $2^1/_2$	11				
4 x 3	11	$5/_{32}$''	$3/_{16}$''	$1/_4$''	$5/_{16}$''
5 x 2	$3/_{16}$''	$1/_4$''			
5 x $2^1/_2$	11	7			
5 x 3	$3/_{16}$''	$1/_4$''	$5/_{16}$''	$3/_8$''	$1/_2$''
6 x 2	$3/_{16}$''	$1/_4$''			
6 x 3	$3/_{16}$''	$1/_4$''	$5/_{16}$''	$3/_8$''	$1/_2$''
6 x 4	$3/_{16}$''	$1/_4$''	$5/_{16}$''	$3/_8$''	$1/_2$''
7 x 4	$1/_4$''	$3/_8$''			
7 x 5	$3/_{16}$''	$1/_4$''	$5/_{16}$''	$3/_8$''	$1/_2$''
8 x 2	$3/_{16}$''				
8 x 3	$3/_{16}$''	$1/_4$''			
8 x 4	$3/_{16}$''	$1/_4$''	$5/_{16}$''	$3/_8$''	$1/_2$''
8 x 6	$3/_{16}$''	$1/_4$''	$5/_{16}$''	$3/_8$''	$1/_2$''
10 x 2	$3/_{16}$''				
10 x 4	$3/_{16}$''	$1/_4$''			
10 x 5	$1/_4$''				
10 x 6	$1/_4$''	$5/_{16}$''	$3/_8$''	$1/_2$''	
10 x 8	$1/_4$''	$3/_8$''	$1/_2$''		
12 x 2	$3/_{16}$''				
12 x 4	$1/_4$''	$3/_8$''			
12 x 6	$1/_4$''	$3/_8$''	$1/_2$''		

ALUMINUM

SIZE (IN.)		
2 x 3	$3/_{16}$''	
2 x 4	$3/_{16}$''	
2 x 6	$3/_{16}$''	

STAINLESS STEEL

SIZE (IN.)	
$1/_2$ x $1^1/_2$	0.065
$3/_4$ x $1^1/_4$	0.065
$3/_4$ x $1^1/_2$	0.065
1 x $1^1/_2$	0.065
1 x 2	0.065
$1^1/_4$ x $2^1/_2$	0.065
$1^3/_4$ x 3	0.065
$1^3/_4$ x 4	0.065

ROUND TUBING—COPPER

SIZE (IN.) NOMINAL INSIDE DIA.	OUTSIDE DIA. (BW GAUGE)	INSIDE DIAMETER (BW GAUGE)			
		TYPE K	TYPE L	TYPE M	TYPE DWV
$1/_4$	0.375	0.305	0.315		
$1/_2$	0.625	0.527	0.545	0.569	
$3/_4$	0.875	0.745	0.785	0.811	
1	1.125	0.995	1.025	1.055	
$1^1/_2$	1.625	1.481	1.505	1.527	1.541
2	2.125	1.959	1.985	2.009	2.041
4	4.125	3.857	3.905	3.935	4.009

RECTANGULAR ALUMINUM TUBING (IN.)

SIZE x T	SIZE x T	SIZE x T
$1/_2$ x 1 x $1/_8$	$1^1/_2$ x $2^1/_2$ x $1/_8$	2 x 3 x $1/_8$
$3/_4$ x $1^1/_2$ x $1/_8$	$1^1/_2$ x 6 x $1/_8$	2 x 4 x $1/_8$
1 x $1^1/_2$ x $1/_8$	$1^3/_4$ x $2^1/_4$ x $1/_8$	2 x 5 x $1/_8$
1 x 2 x $1/_8$	$1^3/_4$ x 3 x $1/_8$	2 x 6 x $1/_8$
1 x 3 x $1/_8$	$1^3/_4$ x $3^1/_2$ x $1/_8$	3 x 5 x $1/_8$
$1^1/_4$ x $2^1/_2$ x $1/_8$	$1^3/_4$ x 4 x $1/_8$	3 x 5 x $1/_8$
$1^1/_4$ x 3 x $1/_8$	$1^3/_4$ x $4^1/_2$ x $1/_8$	
$1^1/_2$ x 2 x $1/_8$	$1^3/_4$ x 5 x $1/_8$	

SQUARE ALUMINUM TUBING

SQUARE ALUMINUM TUBING (IN.)

SIZE x T	SIZE x T	SIZE x T
$1/_2$ x $1/_2$ x $1/_{16}$	$1^1/_4$ x $1^1/_4$ x $5/_{64}$	2 x 2 x $1/_8$
$5/_8$ x $5/_8$ x $1/_{16}$	$1^1/_4$ x $1^1/_4$ x $1/_8$	$2^1/_2$ x $2^1/_2$ x $1/_8$
$3/_4$ x $3/_4$ x $1/_{16}$	$1^1/_2$ x $1^1/_2$ x $5/_{64}$	3 x 3 x $1/_8$
$3/_4$ x $3/_4$ x $1/_8$	$1^1/_2$ x $1^1/_2$ x $1/_8$	4 x 4 x $1/_8$
1 x 1 x $1/_{16}$	$1^3/_4$ x $1^3/_4$ x $1/_8$	
1 x 1 x $1/_8$	2 x 2 x $5/_{64}$	

NOTE: Rectangular and square aluminum tubing with sharp corners is usually used for miscellaneous architectural metalwork.

NOTE

Round tubing, usually manufactured for mechanical purposes, is used for architectural metalwork to supplement round pipe. Round tubing is measured by the outside diameter and the wall thickness by gauge, fractions, or decimals of an inch. Round tubing is used where a high grade finish is required and exact diameters are necessary.

Round tubing is available in steel, aluminum, copper, stainless steel, and other metals. Individual manufacturers' catalogs should be consulted for availability of materials and sizes.

 DMV

 M

 L

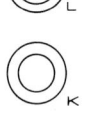 K

ROUND TUBING COPPER

ROUND PIPE—STEEL

SIZE (IN.) NOMINAL INSIDE DIA.	OUTSIDE DIA. (BW GAUGE)	INSIDE DIAMETER (BW GAUGE)		
		STANDARD	EXTRA STRONG	DOUBLE EXTRA STRONG
$1/_8$	0.405	0.269	0.215	
$1/_4$	0.540	0.364	0.302	
$3/_8$	0.675	0.493	0.423	
$1/_2$	0.840	0.622	0.546	0.252
$3/_4$	1.050	0.824	0.742	0.434
1	1.315	1.049	0.957	0.599
$1^1/_4$	1.660	1.380	1.278	0.896
$1^1/_2$	1.900	1.610	1.500	1.100
2	2.375	2.067	1.939	1.503
$2^1/_2$	2.875	2.469	2.323	1.771
3	3.500	3.068	2.900	2.300
$3^1/_2$	4.000	3.548	3.364	2.728
4	4.500	4.026	3.826	3.152
5	5.563	5.047	4.813	4.063
6	6.625	6.065	5.761	4.897
8	8.625	7.981	7.625	6.875
10	10.750	10.020	9.750	8.750
12	12.750	12.000	11.750	10.750

NOTE

Round pipe is made in primarily three weights: Standard, Extra Strong (or Extra Heavy), and Double Extra Strong (or Double Extra Heavy). Outside diameters of the three weights of pipe in each size are always the same, extra thickness always being on the inside and therefore reducing the inside diameter of the heavier pipe. All sizes are specified by what is known as the "nominal inside diameter."

Round pipe is also available in aluminum and stainless steel. Individual manufacturers' catalogs should be consulted for sizes.

SQUARE TUBING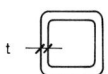

SQUARE TUBING—STEEL

SIZE (IN.)	T = WALL THICKNESS (BW GAUGE OR IN.)								SIZE (IN.)	T
$1/_2$ x $1/_2$	18	16							**ALUMINUM**	
$5/_8$ x $5/_8$	18	0.060	16						2 x 2	0.120
$3/_4$ x $3/_4$	20	18	0.060	16	11				3 x 3	$3/_{16}$''
$7/_8$ x $7/_8$	18	16							4 x 4	$3/_{16}$''
1 x 1	20	18	0.060	16	14	13	0.102	12	**STAINLESS STEEL**	11
$1^1/_8$ x $1^1/_8$	18	16							$3/_4$ x $3/_4$	0.049
$1^1/_4$ x $1^1/_4$	18	0.060	16	0.075	0.090	11	$3/_{16}$''		1 x 1	0.049 / 0.065
$1^1/_2$ x $1^1/_2$	18	0.060	16	14	11	0.140	7	$3/_{16}$'' / $1/_4$''	$1^1/_4$ x $1^1/_4$	0.065
$1^3/_4$ x $1^3/_4$	16	14	13	11					$1^1/_2$ x $1^1/_2$	0.065
2 x 2	0.060	18	16	14	11	$1/_8$''	0.145	$3/_{16}$'' / $1/_4$''	$1^3/_4$ x $1^3/_4$	0.065
$2^1/_2$ x $2^1/_2$	16	14	11	0.141	$1/_4$''				2 x 2	0.065
3 x 3	16	14	13	11	$3/_{16}$''	$1/_4$''				
$3^1/_2$ x $3^1/_2$	11	$5/_{32}$''	5	$1/_4$''						
4 x 4	14	11	$3/_{16}$''	$1/_4$''	$3/_8$''	$1/_2$''				
$4^1/_2$ x $4^1/_2$	$3/_{16}$''	$1/_4$''								
5 x 5	$3/_{16}$''	$1/_4$''	$5/_{16}$''	$3/_8$''						
6 x 6	$3/_{16}$''	$1/_4$''	$5/_{16}$''	$3/_8$''						
7 x 7	$3/_{16}$''	$1/_4$''	$5/_{16}$''	$3/_8$''						
8 x 8	$1/_4$''	$5/_{16}$''	$3/_8$''	$1/_2$''						
10 x 10	$1/_4$''	$5/_{16}$''	$3/_8$''	$1/_2$''						

Harnish, Morgan, and Causey, Architects; Ontario, California

GENERAL INFORMATION

GAUGE NO.	GRAPHIC SIZES	US STD. REVISED		UNITED STATES STANDARD (USS)		AMERICAN STEEL WIRE OR WASHBURN & MOEN (W & M)		BROWN AND SHARP (B & S) OR AMERICAN WIRE (AW)		BIRMINGHAM WIRE (BWG) OR STUBS IRON WIRE		MACHINE AND WOOD SCREWS		GRAPHIC SIZES	GAUGE NO.
		For hot and cold rolled steel sheets.		For stainless steel and monel metal sheets.		For iron and steel wire.		For aluminum, copper, brass, bronze, and nickel silver sheets, strips, and wire. Small sizes in copper and brass tubing.		For hot and cold rolled steel strips. Rivets, spring steel, and flat steel wire. Steel, aluminum, bronze, monel stainless, and large size copper and brass tubing.		For machine screws and ferrous and non-ferrous wood screws.			
		DECIMAL	FRACTION	DECIMAL	FRACTION	DECIMAL	FRACTION	DECIMAL	FRACTION	DECIMAL		DECIMAL	FRACTION		
000		.3750"	3/8"	.3750"	3/8"	.3625"	23/64"	.4096"	13/32"+	.425"	27/64"+	GRAPHIC SIZES DO NOT APPLY TO THIS COLUMN			000
00		.3437"	11/32"	.3437"	11/32"	.3310"	21/64"+	.3648"	23/64"+	.380"	3/8"+				00
0		.3125"	5/16"	.3125"	5/16"	.3065"	5/16"-	.3249"	21/64"-	.340"	11/32"-	.060"	1/16"		0
1		.2812"	9/32"	.2812"	9/32"	.2830"	9/32"	.2893"	19/64"-	.300"	19/64"+	.073"	5/64"-		1
2		.2656"	17/64"	.2656"	17/64"	.2625"	17/64"-	.2576"	1/4"+	.284"	9/32"+	.086"	3/32"-		2
3		.2391"	15/64"+	.2500"	1/4"	.2437"	1/4"-	.2294"	15/64"-	.259"	17/64"-	.099"	3/32"+		3
4		.2242"	7/32"+	.2344"	15/64"	.2253"	7/32"+	.2043"	13/64"+	.238"	15/64"+	.112"	7/64"+		4
5		.2092"	13/64"+	.2187"	7/32"	.2070"	13/64"+	.1819"	3/16"-	.220"	7/32"+	.125"	1/8"		5
6		.1943"	3/16"+	.2031"	13/64"	.1920"	3/16"+	.1620"	5/32"+	.203"	13/64"	.138"	9/64"-		6
7		.1793"	11/64"+	.1875"	3/16"	.1770"	11/64"+	.1443"	9/64"+	.180"	3/16"-	.151"	5/32"-		7
8		.1644"	11/64"-	.1719"	11/64"	.1620"	5/32"+	.1285"	1/8"+	.165"	11/64"-	.164"	11/64"-		8
9		.1495"	5/32"-	.1562"	5/32"	.1483"	9/64"+	.1144"	7/64"+	.148"	9/64"+	.177"	11/64"+		9
10		.1345"	9/64"-	.1406"	9/64"	.1350"	9/64"-	.1019"	7/64"-	.134"	9/64"-	.190"	3/16"+		10
11		.1196"	1/8"-	.1250"	1/8"	.1205"	1/8"-	.0907"	3/32"-	.120"	1/8"-	.203"	13/64"		11
12		.1046"	7/64"-	.1094"	7/64"	.1055"	7/64"-	.0808"	5/64"+	.109"	7/64"	.216"	7/32"-		12
13		.0897"	3/32"-	.0938"	3/32"	.0915"	3/32"-	.0719"	5/64"-	.095"	3/32"+	–	–		13
14		.0747"	5/64"-	.0781"	5/64"	.0800"	5/64"+	.064"	1/16"+	.083"	5/64"+	.242"	1/4"-		14
15		.0673"	1/16"+	.0703"	5/64"-	.0720"	5/64"-	.0571"	1/16"-	.072"	5/64"-	–	–		15
16		.0598"	1/16"-	.0625"	1/16"	.0625"	1/16"	.0508"	3/64"+	.065"	1/16"+	.268"	17/64"+		16
17		.0538"	3/64"+	.0562"	1/16"-	.0540"	3/64"+	.0453"	3/64"-	.058"	1/16"-	–	–		17
18		.0478"	3/64"+	.0500"	3/64"+	.0475"	3/64"+	.0403"	3/64"-	.049"	3/64"+	.294"	19/64"		18
19		.0418"	3/64"-	.0437"	3/64"-	.0410"	3/64"-	.0359"	1/32"+	.042"	3/64"-	–	–		19
20		.0359"	1/32"+	.0375"	1/32"+	.0348"	1/32"+	.0320"	1/32"+	.035"	1/32"+	.320"	5/16"+		20
21		.0329"	1/32"+	.0344"	1/32"+	.0318"	1/32"+	.0285"	1/32"	.032"	1/32"+	–	–		21
22		.0299"	1/32"-	.0312"	1/32"	.0286"	1/32"	.0253"	1/32"-	.028"	1/32"-	–	–		22
23		.0269"	1/32"-	.0281"	1/32"-	.0258"	1/32"-	.0226"	1/64"+	.025"	1/32"-	–	–		23
24		.0239"	1/32"-	.0250"	1/32"-	.0230"	1/64"+	.0201"	1/64"+	.022"	1/64"+	.372"	3/8"-		24
25		.0209"	1/64"+	.0219"	1/64"+	.0204"	1/64"+	.0179"	1/64"+	.020"	1/64"+	–	–		25
26		.0179"	1/64"+	.0187"	1/64"+	.0181"	1/64"+	.0159"	1/64"+	.018"	1/64"+	–	–		26
27		.0164"	1/64"+	.0172"	1/64"+	.0173"	1/64"+	.0142"	1/64"-	.016"	1/64"+	–	–		27
28		.0149"	1/64"-	.0156"	1/64"	.0162"	1/64"+	.0126"	1/64"-	.014"	1/64"	–	–		28
29		.0135"	1/64"-	.0141"	1/64"-	.0150"	1/64"-	.0113"	1/64"-	.013"	1/64"-	–	–		29
30		.0120"	1/64"-	.0125"	1/64"-	.0140"	1/64"-	.0100"	1/64"-	.012"	1/64"-	.450"	29/64"		30

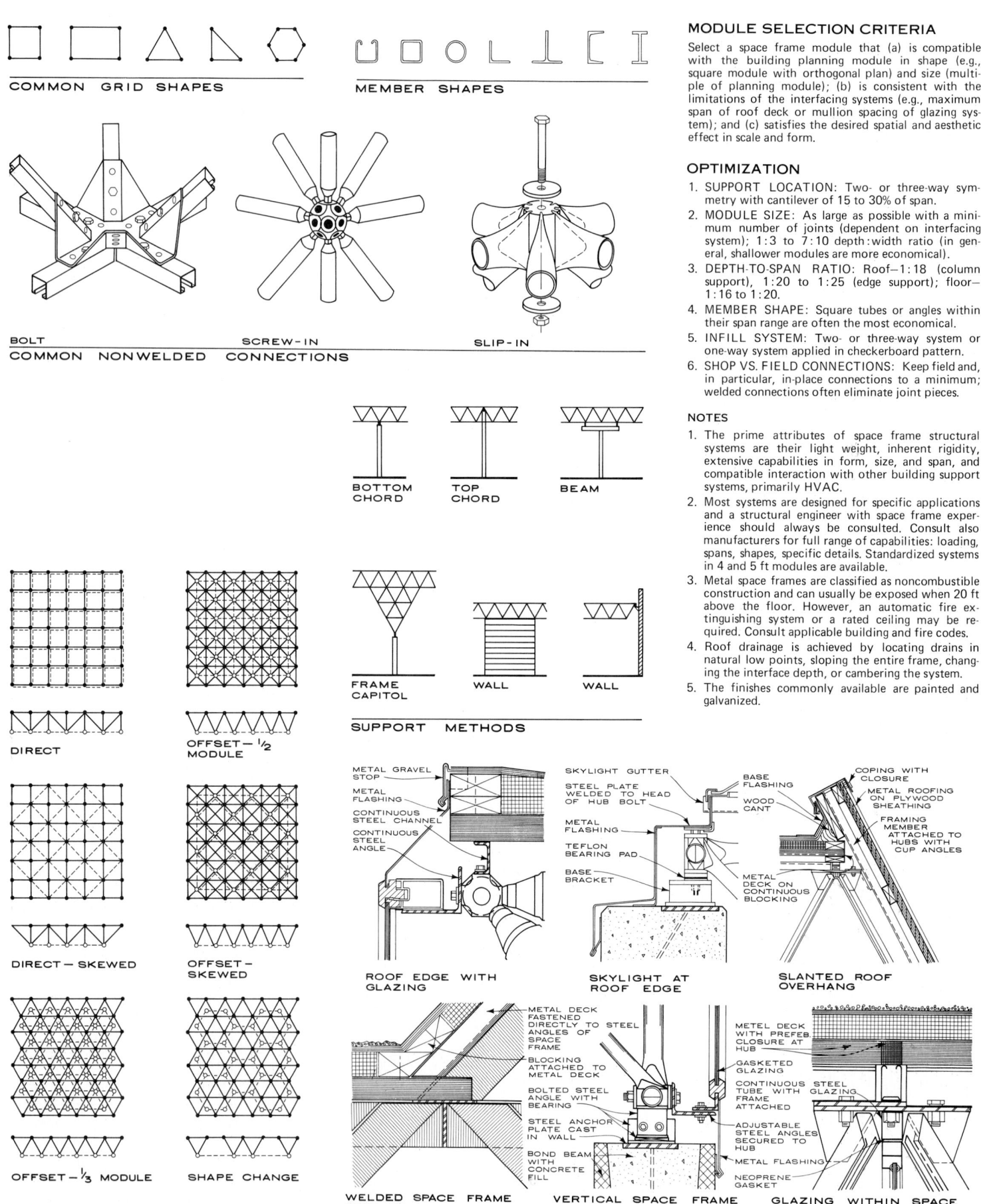

COMMON GRID SHAPES

MEMBER SHAPES

BOLT   **SCREW-IN**   **SLIP-IN**

COMMON NONWELDED CONNECTIONS

BOTTOM CHORD   **TOP CHORD**   **BEAM**

DIRECT   **OFFSET—½ MODULE**

DIRECT—SKEWED   **OFFSET—SKEWED**

OFFSET—⅓ MODULE   **SHAPE CHANGE**

COMMON PATTERNS

FRAME CAPITOL   **WALL**   **WALL**

SUPPORT METHODS

MODULE SELECTION CRITERIA

Select a space frame module that (a) is compatible with the building planning module in shape (e.g., square module with orthogonal plan) and size (multiple of planning module); (b) is consistent with the limitations of the interfacing systems (e.g., maximum span of roof deck or mullion spacing of glazing system); and (c) satisfies the desired spatial and aesthetic effect in scale and form.

OPTIMIZATION

1. SUPPORT LOCATION: Two- or three-way symmetry with cantilever of 15 to 30% of span.
2. MODULE SIZE: As large as possible with a minimum number of joints (dependent on interfacing system); 1:3 to 7:10 depth:width ratio (in general, shallower modules are more economical).
3. DEPTH-TO-SPAN RATIO: Roof—1:18 (column support), 1:20 to 1:25 (edge support); floor—1:16 to 1:20.
4. MEMBER SHAPE: Square tubes or angles within their span range are often the most economical.
5. INFILL SYSTEM: Two- or three-way system or one-way system applied in checkerboard pattern.
6. SHOP VS. FIELD CONNECTIONS: Keep field and, in particular, in-place connections to a minimum; welded connections often eliminate joint pieces.

NOTES

1. The prime attributes of space frame structural systems are their light weight, inherent rigidity, extensive capabilities in form, size, and span, and compatible interaction with other building support systems, primarily HVAC.
2. Most systems are designed for specific applications and a structural engineer with space frame experience should always be consulted. Consult also manufacturers for full range of capabilities: loading, spans, shapes, specific details. Standardized systems in 4 and 5 ft modules are available.
3. Metal space frames are classified as noncombustible construction and can usually be exposed when 20 ft above the floor. However, an automatic fire extinguishing system or a rated ceiling may be required. Consult applicable building and fire codes.
4. Roof drainage is achieved by locating drains in natural low points, sloping the entire frame, changing the interface depth, or cambering the system.
5. The finishes commonly available are painted and galvanized.

ROOF EDGE WITH GLAZING

- METAL GRAVEL STOP
- METAL FLASHING
- CONTINUOUS STEEL CHANNEL
- CONTINUOUS STEEL ANGLE

SKYLIGHT AT ROOF EDGE

- SKYLIGHT GUTTER
- STEEL PLATE WELDED TO HEAD OF HUB BOLT
- METAL FLASHING
- TEFLON BEARING PAD
- BASE BRACKET
- BASE FLASHING
- WOOD CANT
- METAL DECK ON CONTINUOUS BLOCKING

SLANTED ROOF OVERHANG

- COPING WITH CLOSURE
- METAL ROOFING ON PLYWOOD SHEATHING
- FRAMING MEMBER ATTACHED TO HUBS WITH CUP ANGLES

WELDED SPACE FRAME STEP-UP

- METAL DECK FASTENED DIRECTLY TO STEEL ANGLES OF SPACE FRAME
- BLOCKING ATTACHED TO METAL DECK
- BOLTED STEEL ANGLE WITH BEARING
- STEEL ANCHOR PLATE CAST IN WALL
- BOND BEAM WITH CONCRETE FILL

VERTICAL SPACE FRAME WITH GLAZING

GLAZING WITHIN SPACE FRAME

- METEL DECK WITH PREFEB. CLOSURE AT HUB
- GASKETED GLAZING
- CONTINUOUS STEEL TUBE WITH FRAME ATTACHED
- ADJUSTABLE STEEL ANGLES SECURED TO HUB
- METAL FLASHING
- NEOPRENE GASKET

DETAILS

Steven W. Henkelman, R.A.; Cope, Linder, Walmsley; Philadelphia, Pennsylvania

5 **STRUCTURAL METAL FRAMING**

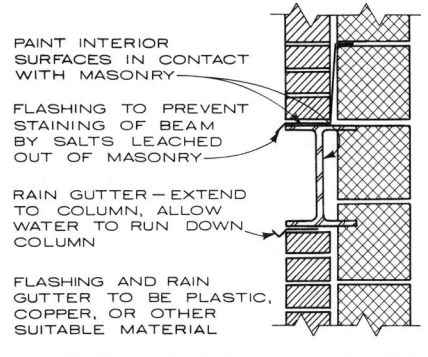

PAINT INTERIOR SURFACES IN CONTACT WITH MASONRY

FLASHING TO PREVENT STAINING OF BEAM BY SALTS LEACHED OUT OF MASONRY

RAIN GUTTER — EXTEND TO COLUMN, ALLOW WATER TO RUN DOWN COLUMN

FLASHING AND RAIN GUTTER TO BE PLASTIC, COPPER, OR OTHER SUITABLE MATERIAL

EXPOSED SPANDREL IN MASONRY WALL

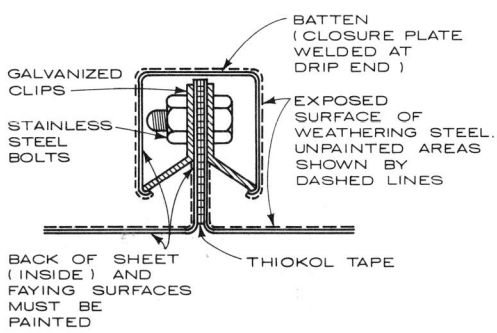

BATTEN (CLOSURE PLATE WELDED AT DRIP END)

GALVANIZED CLIPS

STAINLESS STEEL BOLTS

EXPOSED SURFACE OF WEATHERING STEEL. UNPAINTED AREAS SHOWN BY DASHED LINES

BACK OF SHEET (INSIDE) AND FAYING SURFACES MUST BE PAINTED

THIOKOL TAPE

TYPICAL ROOF BATTEN

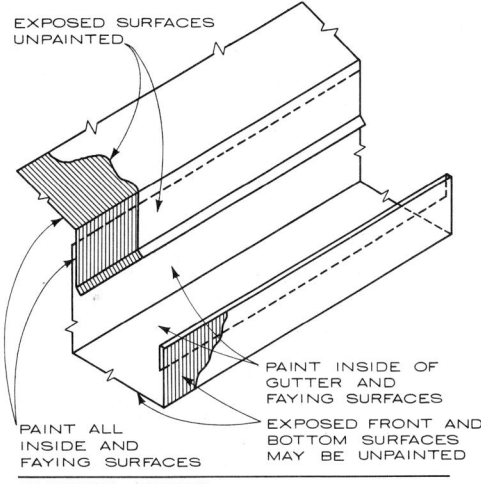

EXPOSED SURFACES UNPAINTED

PAINT ALL INSIDE AND FAYING SURFACES

PAINT INSIDE OF GUTTER AND FAYING SURFACES

EXPOSED FRONT AND BOTTOM SURFACES MAY BE UNPAINTED

GUTTER DETAIL

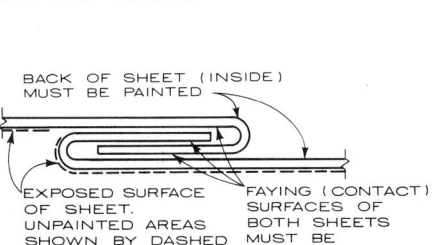
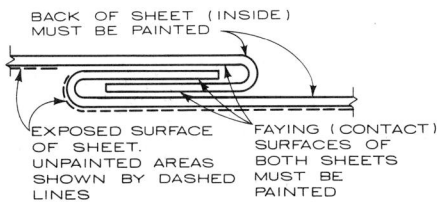

BACK OF SHEET (INSIDE) MUST BE PAINTED

EXPOSED SURFACE OF SHEET. UNPAINTED AREAS SHOWN BY DASHED LINES

FAYING (CONTACT) SURFACES OF BOTH SHEETS MUST BE PAINTED

SHEET STEEL DETAIL

TROUGH IN PIER

CONCRETE PIER

COLUMN

NOTCH IN PIER

GRAVEL BED

PLAN

GRAVEL BED OR TROUGH TO PREVENT STAINING OF PAVEMENT BY RUNOFF FROM ELEMENTS ABOVE

TROUGH

EXPOSED COLUMN

CONCRETE PIER

GRAVEL BED

NOTCH IN PIER DIRECTS RUNOFF INTO GRAVEL BED

ELEVATION

COLUMN AND PIER WITH RUNOFF BED

GENERAL

The term "weathering steel" is used to identify steels that are corrosion resistant when boldly exposed to normal atmospheric conditions, by virtue of a self-forming, self-sealing oxide film. This dense, tightly adherent oxide coating starts to form upon exposure to the elements and grows progressively darker in tone for a period of 18 months to 3 years or more, depending on the atmospheric environment.

Color starts as a "rusty" red-orange and deepens to a purple-brown, brown-black, or bluish black, depending on exposure, lighting, and the eye of the viewer. The color is darker in industrial atmospheres and lighter in rural environments, and the weathering process is quite slow in arid climates. The oxide film does not form satisfactorily in an indoor, controlled environment. The action of natural wetting and drying on the surface is required to fully develop the normal oxide film.

DESIGN

Detailed design guidelines have been published by the major manufacturers of weathering steel, and their literature should be consulted for complete information concerning the limitations and expected performance of the respective weathering steels.

Design of structures utilizing bare weathering steel requires careful detailing to avoid or minimize ledges, crevices, and other areas that can hold water or collect debris. Water draining or dripping from the steel can deposit oxide particles on adjacent construction materials and cause "rusty" stains or streaks. Porous materials are particularly susceptible to such discoloration.

Permanent design details should be developed to divert runoff water away from adjacent vulnerable materials. Gutter and downspout systems, ample overhangs, drip plates, flashings, and brown gravel beds at column bases are examples. Weathering steel is not recommended for gutter systems; if so used, all inside surfaces in contact with water should be painted and maintained.

MATERIALS

Selection of suitable materials resistant to staining for use in areas adjacent to weathering steel is another approach available to the designer. Materials considered suitable include glossy porcelain enamel coatings, anodized or unanodized aluminum, stainless steel, extruded neoprene, ceramic tile, glazed brick, and glass. Glass requires frequent cleaning during the period when oxide is forming on steel, but acid cleaning solutions should not be used, since they will attack the protective oxide film where they splash on or run down the surface of adjacent weathering steel.

Unsuitable materials include porous materials such as concrete, stucco, and unglazed brick, unpainted galvanized steel, matte porcelain enamels, stone, and wood. Other materials should be investigated for past performance in similar applications before being incorporated in a new design.

Weathering sheet steel is not recommended as a general roofing and siding material. If used, special provisions should be made and manufacturer's details should be consulted. Attention to detail in using weathering sheet steel is of the utmost importance. Sensitive areas include the backside of the sheet, which must be painted, and all faying (contact) surfaces of both sheets at lap seams. Before fabricating foam filled panels with weathering sheet steel, the foam must be checked for compatibility with the weathering steel.

FASTENERS

High strength structural bolts are available that are made from the same steel as noted in the table or to ASTM A325 Type 3 specifications. These will weather to a color and texture that is close to the members on which the bolts are used. Galvanized carbon steel bolts should not be used. Welding electrodes are available that will deposit weld material compatible with the base steel, and welded joints will weather to a point where they are almost indistinguishable.

PAINTING

Paint protection is required on any weathering steel surfaces that are not boldly exposed to the atmosphere, such as those that are in contact with other architectural materials, including gaskets or sealants, and on all other interior surfaces. All such unexposed surfaces, including all faying (contact) surfaces, are to be treated as if they were carbon steel and must be painted.

When weathering steel is painted, it is as readily coated as carbon steel, and paint should last significantly longer than when applied to carbon steel. The paint manufacturer's recommendations on surface preparation and paint selection should be consulted.

APPLICATIONS

Weathering steels are not recommended for use in the bare condition in certain environments:

1. Atmospheres containing concentrated, corrosive industrial fumes.
2. Marine locations exposed to recurrent wetting by saltwater spray or salt laden fog.
3. Where steel may be continuously submerged in saltwater or freshwater or buried in soil.

For architectural applications, all exposed surfaces of hot rolled products must be blast cleaned to remove mill scale. Cold rolled steel does not require any surface preparation other than removal of foreign matter, grease, oil, chalk, crayon marks, etc. During construction, care should be exercised to keep surfaces that will be exposed free of foreign matter. Otherwise, cleaning after installation may be necessary to promote uniform weathering of steel.

The higher cost of weathering steel and the special details required in its use can be partially offset by the elimination of other materials normally required for protection of steel and by a reduction in steel weight due to greater strength of weathering steels. The decision to use weathering steel is based principally on architectural considerations.

WEATHERING STEEL DATA

ASTM DESIGNATION	STRENGTH (KSI)	ATMOSPHERIC CORROSION RESISTANCE
A242, Type 1	50, (42, 46)	Approximately five to eight times the resistance of carbon steel
A588	50, (42, 46)	Approximately four times the resistance of carbon steel

NOTE: 50 ksi is the yield strength provided for most sections, but yield strengths are reduced for thick sections. See manufacturer's data or ASTM requirements for limitations.

Walter D. Shapiro, P.E.; Tor, Shapiro & Associates; New York, New York

STRUCTURAL METAL FRAMING 5

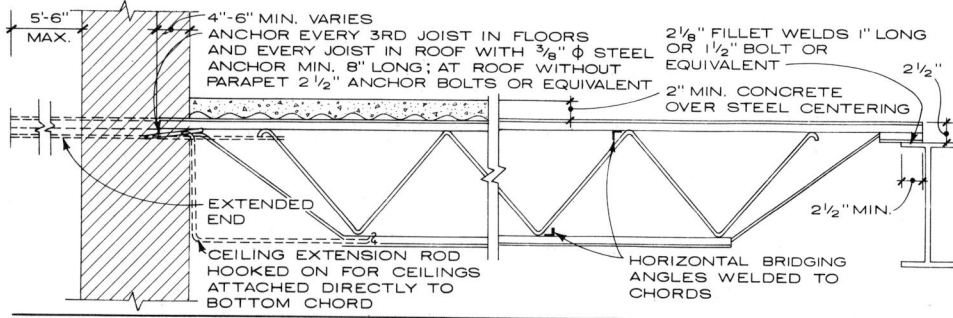

SECTION THROUGH JOIST BEARING

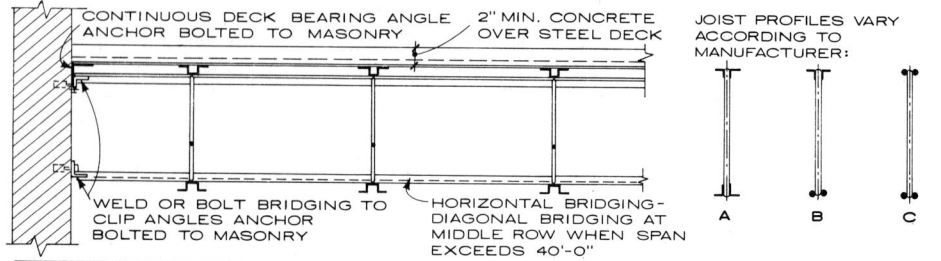

SECTION THROUGH JOISTS

NOTES
The following information applies to both open web and long span steel joists.

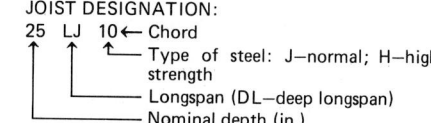

JOIST DESIGNATION:
25 LJ 10 ← Chord
— Type of steel: J—normal; H—high strength
— Longspan (DL—deep longspan)
— Nominal depth (in.)

Because of increased popularity of H-series joists, J-series joists have been eliminated from the load tables by the Steel Joist Institute.

1. ROOF CONSTRUCTION: Joists are usually covered by steel deck topped with either rigid insulation board or lightweight concrete fill and built-up felt and gravel roof. Plywood, poured gypsum, or structural wood fiber deck systems can also be used with built-up roof.

2. CEILINGS: Ceiling supports can be suspended from or mounted directly to bottom chords of joists, although suspended systems are recommended because of dimensional variations in actual joist depths.

3. FLOOR CONSTRUCTION: Joists usually covered by 2 to $2\frac{1}{2}$ in. concrete on steel centering. Concrete thickness may be increased for electrical conduit or electrical/communications raceways. Precast concrete, gypsum planks, or plywood can also be used for the floor system.

4. VIBRATION: Objectionable vibrations can occur in open web joist and $2\frac{1}{2}$ in. concrete slab designs for open floor areas at spans between 24 and 40 ft, especially at 28 ft. When a floor area cannot have partitions, objectionable vibrations can be prevented or reduced by increasing slab thickness, joist spacing, or floor spans. Attention should also be given to support framing beams which can magnify a vibration problem.

5. OPENINGS IN FLOOR OR ROOF SYSTEMS: Small openings between joists are framed with angles of channel supported on the adjoining two joists. Larger openings necessitating interruption of joists are framed with steel angle or channel headers spanning the adjoining two joists. The interrupted joists bear on the headers.

6. ROOF DRAINAGE: Roof drainage should be carefully considered on level or near level roofs especially with parapet walls. Roof insulation can be sloped, joists can be sloped or obtained with sloping top chords in one or both directions, and overflow scuppers should be provided in parapet walls.

PRELIMINARY JOIST SELECTION: The tables below are not to be used for final joist design but are intended as an aid in speeding selection of steel joists for preliminary design and planning. The final design must be a separate and thorough process, involving a complete investigation of the pertinent conditions. This page is not for that purpose. Consult structural engineer.

EXAMPLE: Assume a particular clear span. By assuming a joist spacing and estimating the total load a joist can immediately be selected from the table. Then proceed with preliminary design studies.

NOTES
1. Total safe load = live load + dead load. Dead load includes weight of joist. For dead loads and recommended live loads, see pages on weights of materials. Local codes will govern.
2. Span not to exceed a depth 24 times that of a nominal joist.
3. For more detailed information refer to standard specifications and load tables adopted jointly by the Steel Joist Institute and the American Institute of Steel Construction.

NUMBER OF ROWS OF BRIDGING (FT)
DISTANCES ARE CLEAR SPAN DIMENSIONS

CHORD SIZE*	1 ROW	2 ROWS	3 ROWS	4 ROWS	5 ROWS†
#3	Up to 13	13–17	17–28	—	—
#4	Up to 16	16–21	21–32	—	—
#5	Up to 16	16–21	21–33	33–38	38–40
#6	Up to 18	18–22	22–36	36–40	40–48
#7	Up to 20	20–25	25–41	41–46	46–48
#8	Up to 21	21–27	27–43	43–48	48–60
#9	Up to 23	23–30	30–46	46–52	52–60
#10	Up to 24	24–30	30–47	47–53	53–60
#11	Up to 24	24–31	31–48	48–55	55–60

*Last digit(s) of joist designation shown on load table below.
†Where five rows of bridging are required and spans are over 40 ft, the middle row shall be diagonal with bolted connections at chords and intersections.

SELECTED LOAD TABLES: H SERIES— TOTAL SAFE UNIFORMLY DISTRIBUTED LOAD (LB/FT)

JOIST DESIGNATION		CLEAR SPAN (FT)											
		8	12	16	20	24	28	32	36	42	48	54	60
H Series f_s = 30,000 psi	8H3	600	400	232									
	10H3		417	302	193								
	12H4		533	400	300	208							
	14H5			475	380	300	220						
	16H6			575	460	383	293	224					
	18H7				520	433	371	303	240				
	20H7				540	450	386	325	257				
	22H8					483	414	363	322	247			
	24H8					500	429	375	333	271	207		
	26H9						514	450	400	343	268		
	28H9						514	450	400	343	289	229	
	30H10							506	450	386	338	276	224
	30H11							544	483	414	363	319	259

NOTE: Number preceding letter is joist depth; 14H5 is 14 in. deep.

Setter, Leach & Lindstrom, Inc.; Minneapolis, Minnesota

METAL JOISTS

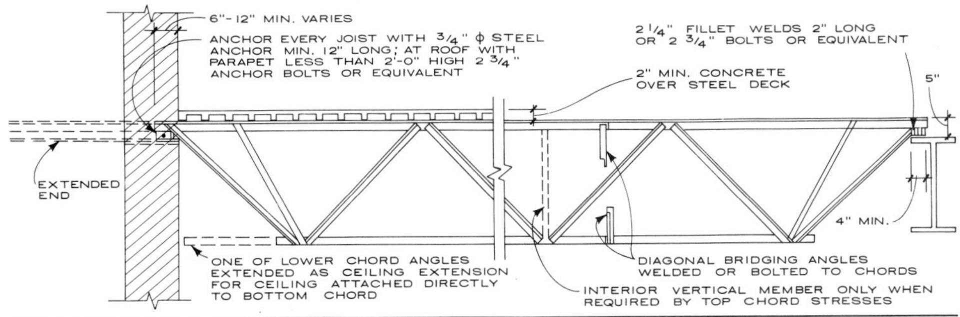

SECTION THROUGH JOIST BEARING

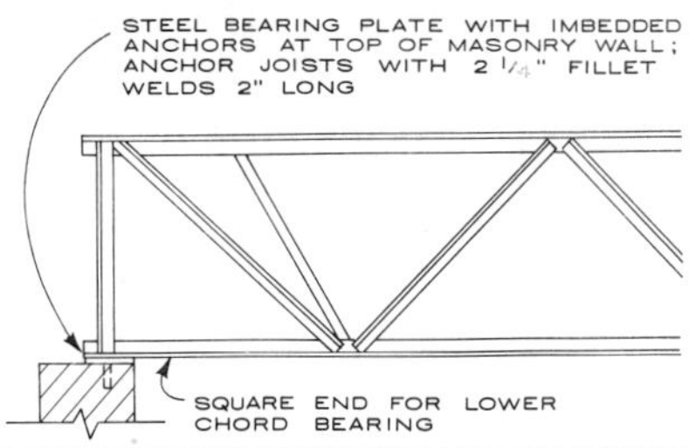

SQUARE END

BRIDGING SPACING (FT)*

LH CHORD SIZE†	MAXIMUM SPACING (FT)
02-09	11
10-14	16
15-17	21
DHL CHORD SIZE†	**MAXIMUM SPACING (FT)**
10	14
11-14	16
15-17	21
18-19	26

*Joist span not to exceed 24 x depth for roofs, 20 x depth for floors.
†Last two digits of joist designation shown in load tables.

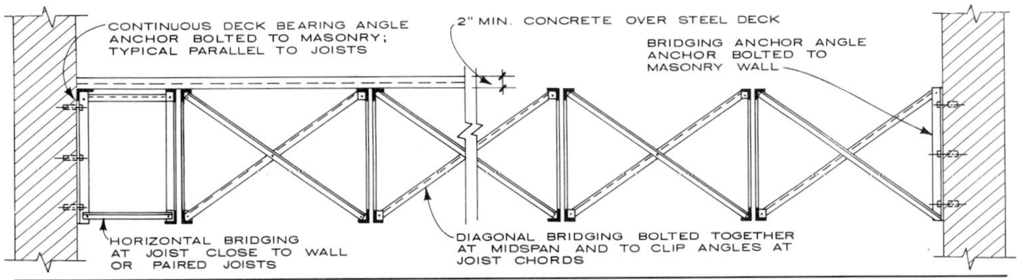

SECTION THROUGH JOISTS

PRELIMINARY JOIST SELECTION

The tables below are not to be used for final joist design but are intended as an aid in speeding selection of steel joists for preliminary design and planning.

The final design must be a separate thorough process, involving a complete investigation of the pertinent conditions. This page is not for that purpose. Consult a structural engineer.

EXAMPLE

Assume a particular clear span. By assuming a joist spacing and estimating the total load a joist can immediately be selected from the table. Then proceed with preliminary design studies.

NOTES

1. Total safe load = live load + dead load. Dead load includes weight of joist. For dead loads and recommended live loads, see pages on weights of materials. Local codes will govern.
2. Span not to exceed a depth 24 times that of a nominal joist.
3. For more detailed information refer to standard specifications and load tables adopted jointly by the Steel Joist Institute and the American Institute of Steel Construction.

FIRE RESISTANCE RATINGS

TIME (HR)	FLOOR ASSEMBLIES	TIME (HR)	ROOF ASSEMBLIES
1 or 1 1/2	2" reinforced concrete, listed 1/2" (5/8" for 1 1/2 hr) acoustical tile ceiling, concealed ceiling grid suspended from joists	1	Built-up roofing on 2" structural wood fiber units, listed 3/4" acoustical ceiling tiles, concealed ceiling grid suspended from joists
	2" reinforced concrete, listed 1/2" acoustical board ceiling listed exposed ceiling grid suspended from joists		Built-up roofing and insulation on 26 gauge min. steel deck, listed 5/8" acoustical ceiling boards, listed exposed ceiling grid suspended from joists
	2" reinforced concrete, listed 1/2 " gypsum board ceiling fastened to joists		Built-up roofing over 2" vermiculite on centering, listed 1/2" acoustical ceiling boards, listed exposed ceiling grid suspended from joists
2	2 1/2" reinforced concrete, listed 5/8" acoustical tile ceiling, listed concealed ceiling grid suspended from joists		
	2 1/2" reinforced concrete, listed 1/2" acoustical board ceiling, listed exposed ceiling grid suspended from joists	2	Built-up roofing on 2" listed gypsum building units, listed 5/8" acoustical ceiling boards, listed exposed ceiling grid suspended from joists
	2" reinforced concrete, listed 5/8" gypsum board ceiling fastened to joists		Built-up roofing on 22 gauge min. steel deck, suspended 7/8" metal lath and plaster ceiling
	2 1/2" reinforced concrete, listed 1/2" gypsum board ceiling fastened to joists		

NOTE: Listed by Underwriters Laboratories or Factory Mutual approved, as appropriate. Ratings are the result of tests made in accordance with ASTM Standard E 119. A more complete list can be obtained from the SJI Technical Digest concerning the design of fire resistive assemblies with steel joists.

SELECTED LOAD TABLES: LH AND DLH SERIES—TOTAL SAFE UNIFORMLY DISTRIBUTED LOAD (LB/FT)

JOIST DESIGNATION		CLEAR SPAN (FT)												
		28	32	36	42	48	54	60	66	72	78	84	90	96
LH Series f_s = 30,000 psi	18LH05	581	448	355										
	20LH06	723	560	444										
	24LH07			588	446	343								
	28LH09				639	499	401							
	32LH10						478	389						
	36LH11							451	378	322				
	40LH12								472	402	346			
	44LH13										423	369		
	48LH14											444	390	346
		90	96	102	108	114	120	126	132	138	144			
DLH Series f_s = 30,000 psi	52DLH13	433	381	338										
	56DLH14			411	368									
	60DLH15				442	398	361							
	64DLH16					466	421	382						
	68DLH17							460	420					
	72DLH18								505	463	426			

NOTE: Number preceding letter is joist depth; 32LH10 is 32 in. deep.

Setter, Leach & Lindstrom, Inc.; Minneapolis, Minnesota

EXAMPLES OF THE MANY TYPES OF DECK AVAILABLE (SEE TABLES):

1. Roof deck.
2. Floor deck (noncomposite).
3. Composite floor deck interacting with concrete.
4. Permanent forms for self-supporting concrete slabs.
5. Cellular deck (composite or noncomposite).
6. Acoustical roof deck.
7. Acoustic cellular deck (composite or non-composite).
8. Electric raceway cellular deck.
9. Prevented roof deck (used with lightweight insulating concrete fill).

All metal floor and roof decks must be secured to all supports, generally by means of "puddle welds" made through the deck to supporting steel. Steel sheet lighter than 22 gauge (0.0295 in. thick) should be secured by use of welding washers (see illustration).

Shear studs welded through floor deck also serve to secure the deck to supporting steel. Power actuated and pneumatically driven fasteners may also be used in certain applications.

Side laps between adjacent sheets of deck must be secured by button-punching standing seams, welding, or screws, in accordance with manufacturer's recommendations.

Decks used as lateral diaphragms must be welded to steel supports around their entire perimeter to ensure development of diaphragm action. More stringent requirements may govern the size and/or spacing of attachments to supports and side lap fasteners or welds.

Roof deck selection must take into consideration construction and maintenance loads as well as the capacity to support uniformly distributed live loads. Consult current Steel Deck Institute recommendations and Factory Mutual requirements.

Floor deck loadings are virtually unlimited in scope, ranging from light residential and institutional loads to heavy duty industrial floors utilizing composite deck with slabs up to 24 in. thick. The designer can select the deck type, depth, and gauge most suitable for the application.

Fire resistance ratings for roof deck assemblies are published by Underwriters Laboratories and Factory Mutual. Ratings of 1 to 2 hr are achieved with spray-on insulation: a 1 hr rating with suspended acoustical ceiling and a 2 hr rating with a metal lath and plaster ceiling.

Floor deck assembly fire resistive ratings are available both with and without spray-applied fireproofing, and with regular weight or lightweight concrete fill. From 1 to 3 hr ratings are possible using only concrete fill—consult Underwriters Laboratory Fire Resistance Index for assembly ratings.

Consult manufacturer's literature and technical representatives for additional information. Consult "Steel Deck Institute Design Manual for Floor Decks and Roof Decks" and "Tentative Recommendations for the Design of Steel Deck Diaphragms" by the Steel Deck Institute.

ADVANTAGES OF METAL ROOF DECKS:

1. High strength-to-weight ratio reduces roof dead load.
2. Can be erected in most weather conditions.
3. Variety of depths and rib patterns available.
4. Acoustical treatment is possible.
5. Serve as base for insulation and roofing.
6. Fire ratings can be obtained with standard assemblies.
7. Provide lateral diaphragm.
8. Can be erected quickly.
9. Can be erected economically.

The use of vapor barriers on metal deck roofs is not customary for normal building occupancies. For high relative humidity exposure a vapor barrier may be provided as part of the roofing system, but the user should be aware of the great difficulties encountered in installing a vapor barrier on metal deck. Punctures of the vapor barrier over valleys might reduce or negate entirely the effectiveness of the vapor barrier.

EAVE PLATE   CANT STRIP   RIDGE AND VALLEY PLATE

ROOF DECK ACCESSORIES

MAXIMUM OPENING = 10" X 10" OR 10" DIAMETER

REINFORCING PLATE

Small openings (up to 6 x 6 in. or 6 in. dia.) may usually be cut in roof or floor deck without reinforcing the deck. Openings up to 10 x 10 in. or 10 in. dia. require reinforcing of the deck by either welding a reinforcing plate to the deck all around the opening, or by providing channel shaped headers and/or supplementary reinforcing parallel to the deck span. Reinforcing plates should be 14 gauge sheets with a minimum projection of 6 in. beyond all sides of the opening, and they should be welded to each cell of the deck.

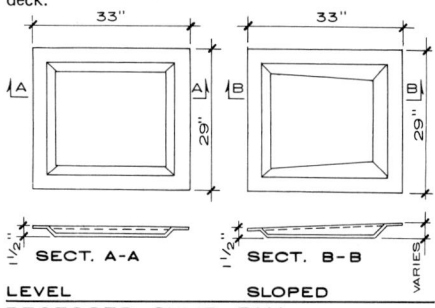

SECT. A-A   SECT. B-B
LEVEL   SLOPED

RECESSED SUMP PAN

Preformed recessed sump pans are available from deck manufacturers for use at roof drains.

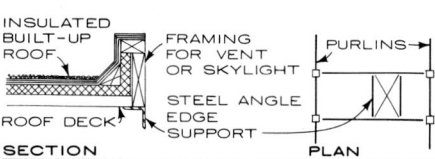

SECTION   PLAN

FRAMED OPENING

Larger openings should be framed with supplementary steel members so that all free edges of deck are supported.

Roof-mounted mechanical equipment should not be placed directly on metal roof deck. Equipment on built-up or prefabricated curbs should be supported directly on main and supplementary structural members and the deck must also be supported along all free edges (see illustration). Heavy items such as cooling towers which must be elevated should be supported by posts extending through pitch pockets directly onto structural members below the deck. Openings through the deck may be handled as previously discussed.

ROOF DECK (ACOUSTICAL ROOF DECKS ARE AVAILABLE IN MANY OF THESE PROFILES – CONSULT MANUFACTURERS)

TYPICAL EXAMPLES	ECONOMICAL SPANS	USUAL WIDTH	MAX. LENGTH AVAILABLE
1½" NARROW RIB	4'- 6'	24" – 36"	36'- 42'
1½" INTERMEDIATE RIB	5'- 7'	24"- 36"	40'- 42'
1½" WIDE RIB	6'- 9'	24"- 30"	32'- 42'
(3" profile)	8'- 16'	24"	40'
(4½" profile)	15'- 18'	12"	32'
(1½" profile)	7'- 11'	24"	32'
(3½" profile)	10'- 20'	24"	40'
(7½" profile)	12'- 30'	12"	40'- 42'
(7½" profile)	13'- 33'	24"	40'

Walter D. Shapiro, P.E.; Tor, Shapiro & Associates; New York, New York

FLOOR DECK – COMPOSITE WITH CONCRETE FILL

TYPICAL EXAMPLES	ECONOMICAL SPANS	USUAL WIDTH	MAX. LENGTH AVAILABLE
1½"	4'- 9'	30"	36'
2"	8'- 12'	30"	40'- 45'
3"	8'- 15'	24"	40'
7½", 6", 4½", 3", 2"	8'- 24'	12"	40'

FLOOR DECK – COMPOSITE CELLULAR (ACOUSTIC DECK AVAILABLE IN SOME PROFILES; CONSULT MANUFACTURERS)

	ECONOMICAL SPANS	USUAL WIDTH	MAX. LENGTH AVAILABLE
1½" 6"	6'- 12'	24"	40'
⅝"	6'- 12'	24"	40'
2"	6'- 12'	30"	36'- 45'
3"	10'- 16'	24"	40'
7½", 6", 4½", 3"	8'- 24'	24"	40'

CORRUGATED FORMS FOR CONCRETE SLABS – NONCOMPOSITE

	ECONOMICAL SPANS	USUAL WIDTH	MAX. LENGTH AVAILABLE
½"	1'- 2'	96"	2'- 6'
9/16"	1'- 6"- 3'	30"	40'
15/16"	3'- 5'	29"	40'
1" 4"	3'- 5'	28"	30'- 40'
15/16" 4½"	4'- 9'	27"	30'- 40'
2" 6"	7'- 12'	24"	30'- 40'

Walter D. Shapiro, P.E.; Tor, Shapiro & Associates; New York, New York

ADVANTAGES OF METAL FLOOR DECKS:

1. Provide a working platform, eliminating temporary wood planking in highrise use.
2. Composite decks provide positive reinforcement for concrete slabs.
3. Noncomposite and composite decks serve as forms for concrete, eliminate forming and stripping.
4. Fire ratings can be achieved without spray-on fireproofing or rated ceilings.
5. Acoustical treatment is possible.
6. Electric raceways may be built into floor slab.
7. Economical floor assemblies.

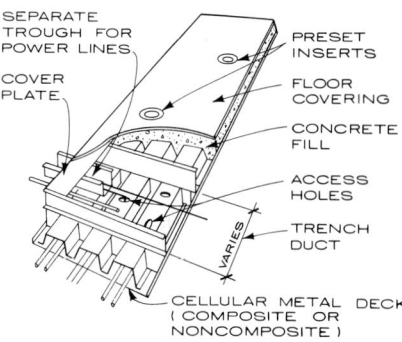

ELECTRICAL TRENCH DUCT

Electric raceways may be built into floor slabs by use of cellular deck or special units that are blended with plain deck. Two-way distribution is achieved by use of trench ducts that sit astride the cellular units at right angles. Use of trench ducts with composite floor deck may reduce or eliminate entirely the effectiveness of composite action at the trench duct. This is also true for composite action between steel floor beams and concrete fill. Trench duct locations must be taken into account in deciding whether composite action is possible.

Openings in composite deck may be blocked out on top of the deck and the deck can be burned out after the concrete has set and become self-supporting. Reinforcing bars can be added alongside openings to replace positive moment deck steel area lost at openings.

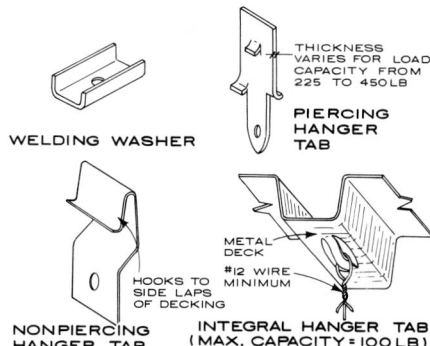

DECKING ATTACHMENTS

A convenient and economical means for supporting lightweight acoustical ceilings is by attaching suspension system to hanger tabs at side laps, piercing tabs driven through deck, or prepunched tabs in roof deck (see illustrations above). These tabs and metal decks must not be used to support plaster ceilings, piping, ductwork, electric equipment, or other heavy loads. Such elements must be supported directly from structural joists, beams, girders, and so on, or from supplementary subframing, and not from metal deck.

ALLOWABLE LOADS FOR SIMPLE SPAN STEEL "C" JOISTS (LB/LINEAR FOOT) MADE OF 40 KSI MATERIAL

SPAN	SECTION (DEPTH/GAUGE)	SINGLE MEMBER		DOUBLE MEMBER	
		TOTAL ALLOWABLE LOAD	ALLOWABLE LIVE LOAD	TOTAL ALLOWABLE LOAD	ALLOWABLE LIVE LOAD
8'	6"/18	201	189	402*	378
	6"/16	245	230	490	460
	6"/14	301	283	602	566
	8"/18	295	295	590*	590
	8"/16	359	359	718*	718
	8"/14	442	442	884*	884
	10"/16	506	506	1012*	1012
	10"/14	627	627	1254*	1254
10'	6"/18	129	97	258	194
	6"/16	157	118	314	236
	6"/14	193	144	386	288
	8"/18	188	186	376*	372
	8"/16	230	228	460*	456
	8"/14	283	280	566	560
	10"/16	326	326	652*	652
	10"/14	401	401	802*	802
12'	6"/18	89	56	178	112
	6"/16	109	68	218	136
	6"/14	134	83	268	166
	8"/18	131	108	262*	216
	8"/16	159	131	318	262
	8"/14	196	162	392	324
	10"/16	226	226	452*	452
	10"/14	278	278	556*	556
14'	6"/18	65	35	130	70
	6"/16	80	43	160	86
	6"/14	98	52	196	204
	8"/18	96	68	192	136
	8"/16	117	83	234	166
	8"/14	144	102	288	204
	10"/16	166	150	332*	300
	10"/14	204	184	408	368
16'	6"/18	50	23	100	46
	6"/16	61	28	122	56
	6"/14	75	35	150	70
	8"/18	73	45	146	90
	8"/16	89	55	178	110
	8"/14	110	68	220	136
	10"/16	127	100	254	200
	10"/14	156	123	312	246
18'	8"/18	58	32	116	64
	8"/16	71	39	142	78
	8"/14	87	48	174	96
	10"/16	100	70	200	140
	10"/14	123	86	246	172
20'	8"/18	47	23	94	46
	8"/16	57	28	114	56
	8"/14	70	35	140	70
	10"/16	81	51	162	102
	10"/14	100	63	200	126
22'	8"/18	39	17	78	34
	8"/16	47	21	94	42
	8"/14	58	26	116	52
	10"/16	67	38	134	76
	10"/14	82	47	164	94
24'	10"/16	56	29	112	58
	10"/14	69	36	138	72

NOTES
The tables on this page are not to be used for final design.
They are intended to serve only as aides in the preliminary selection of members.
Consult appropriate manufacturers' literature for final and/or additional information.
*Ends of members require additional reinforcing, such as by end clips.

Ed Hesner; Rasmussen & Hobbs Architects; Takoma, Washington

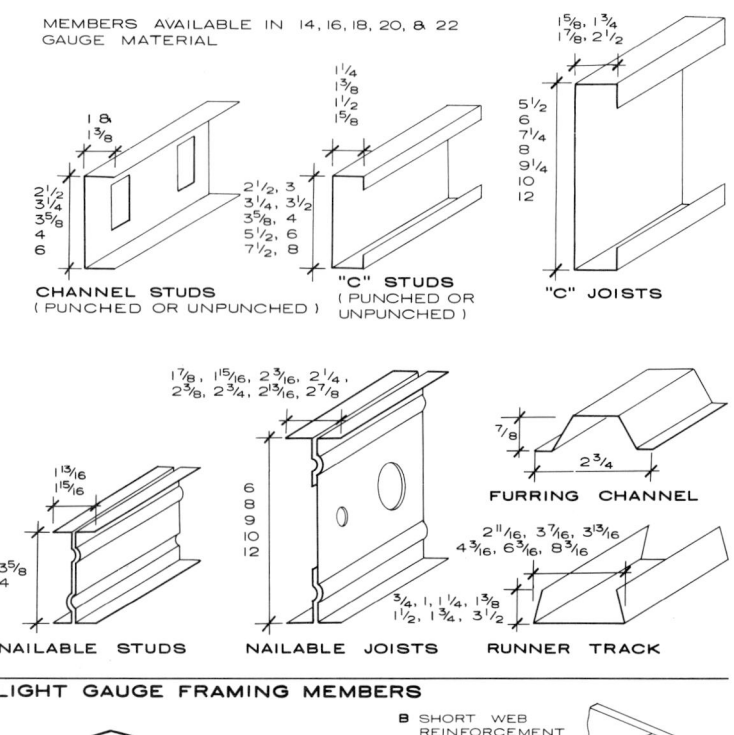

MEMBERS AVAILABLE IN 14, 16, 18, 20, & 22 GAUGE MATERIAL

CHANNEL STUDS (PUNCHED OR UNPUNCHED) · "C" STUDS (PUNCHED OR UNPUNCHED) · "C" JOISTS · FURRING CHANNEL · NAILABLE STUDS · NAILABLE JOISTS · RUNNER TRACK

LIGHT GAUGE FRAMING MEMBERS

L = OVERALL TRUSS WIDTH · BUILDING OVERHANG · BALCONY OR ROOF CANTILEVER

A NO REINFORCEMENT AT SUPPORT

B SHORT WEB REINFORCEMENT AT SUPPORT — LENGTH = WIDTH AT SUPPORT + 2"

C LONG SIDE PIECE REINFORCEMENT AT SUPPORT — LENGTH = 2 X OVERHANG OR CANTILEVER

REQUIRED WEB REINFORCEMENT

SECTION (DEPTH/GAUGE)	OVER-HANG DEPTH (FT)	BUILDING OVERHANGS											
		L = 28'-0"				L = 32'-0"				L = 40'-0"			
		TOTAL ROOF LOAD				TOTAL ROOF LOAD				TOTAL ROOF LOAD			
		30 PSF		40 PSF		30 PSF		40 PSF		30 PSF		40 PSF	
		JOIST SPACING		JOIST SPACING		JOIST SPACING		JOIST SPACING		JOIST SPACING		JOIST SPACING	
		16"	24"	16"	24"	16"	24"	16"	24"	16"	24"	16"	24"
6"/16	1	B	B	B	B	B	B	B	C	B	C	B	C
	1½	B	C	B	C	B	C	B	—	B	—	C	—
	2	B	—	C	—	B	—	C	—	C	—	—	—
6"/14	1	A	B	A	B	A	B	A	B	A	B	B	C
	1½	A	B	A	B	A	B	B	B	A	B	B	—
	2	A	C	B	—	A	C	B	—	C	—	C	—
8"/16	1	B	B	B	B	B	B	B	C	B	C	B	C
	1½	B	B	B	B	B	B	B	C	B	C	B	C
	2	B	B	B	C	B	C	B	C	B	C	B	—
8"/14	1	A	B	A	B	A	B	A	B	A	B	B	B
	1½	A	B	A	B	A	B	A	B	A	B	B	B
	2	A	B	A	B	A	B	B	B	B	B	B	C
10"/16	1	B	B	B	B	B	B	B	C	B	C	B	C
	1½	B	B	B	B	B	B	B	C	B	C	B	C
	2	B	B	B	B	B	B	B	C	B	C	B	C
10"/14	1	A	B	A	B	A	B	A	B	A	B	B	B
	1½	A	B	A	B	A	B	A	B	A	B	B	B
	2	A	B	A	B	A	B	B	B	B	B	B	B

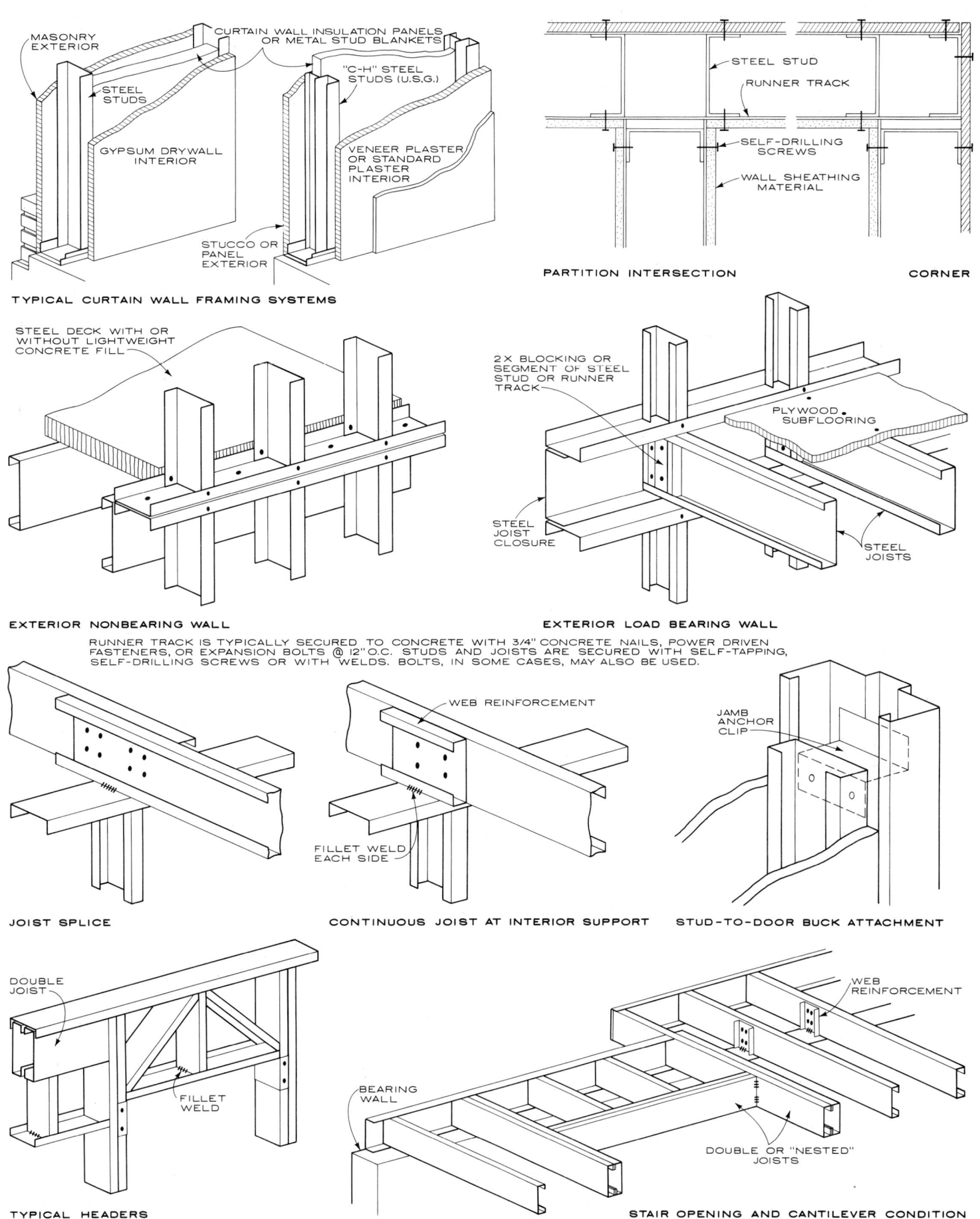

TYPICAL CURTAIN WALL FRAMING SYSTEMS

MASONRY EXTERIOR

STEEL STUDS

GYPSUM DRYWALL INTERIOR

CURTAIN WALL INSULATION PANELS OR METAL STUD BLANKETS

"C-H" STEEL STUDS (U.S.G.)

VENEER PLASTER OR STANDARD PLASTER INTERIOR

STUCCO OR PANEL EXTERIOR

PARTITION INTERSECTION **CORNER**

STEEL STUD

RUNNER TRACK

SELF-DRILLING SCREWS

WALL SHEATHING MATERIAL

EXTERIOR NONBEARING WALL

STEEL DECK WITH OR WITHOUT LIGHTWEIGHT CONCRETE FILL

EXTERIOR LOAD BEARING WALL

2 X BLOCKING OR SEGMENT OF STEEL STUD OR RUNNER TRACK

PLYWOOD SUBFLOORING

STEEL JOIST CLOSURE

STEEL JOISTS

RUNNER TRACK IS TYPICALLY SECURED TO CONCRETE WITH 3/4" CONCRETE NAILS, POWER DRIVEN FASTENERS, OR EXPANSION BOLTS @ 12"O.C. STUDS AND JOISTS ARE SECURED WITH SELF-TAPPING, SELF-DRILLING SCREWS OR WITH WELDS. BOLTS, IN SOME CASES, MAY ALSO BE USED.

JOIST SPLICE

WEB REINFORCEMENT

FILLET WELD EACH SIDE

CONTINUOUS JOIST AT INTERIOR SUPPORT

JAMB ANCHOR CLIP

STUD-TO-DOOR BUCK ATTACHMENT

DOUBLE JOIST

FILLET WELD

TYPICAL HEADERS

WEB REINFORCEMENT

BEARING WALL

DOUBLE OR "NESTED" JOISTS

STAIR OPENING AND CANTILEVER CONDITION

Ed Hesner; Rasmussen & Hobbs Architects; Takoma, Washington

LIGHTGAUGE METAL FRAMING 5

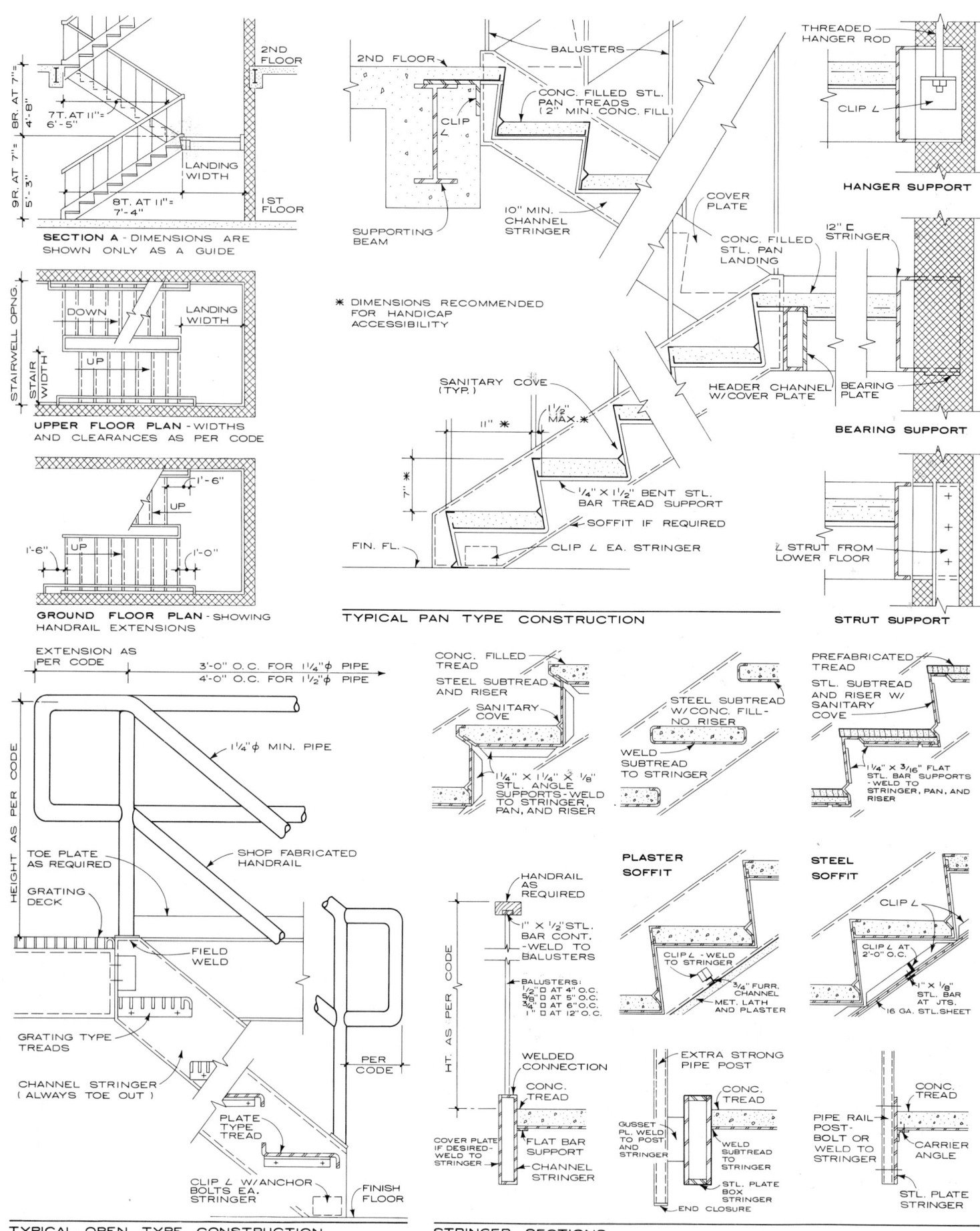

SECTION A - DIMENSIONS ARE SHOWN ONLY AS A GUIDE

UPPER FLOOR PLAN - WIDTHS AND CLEARANCES AS PER CODE

GROUND FLOOR PLAN - SHOWING HANDRAIL EXTENSIONS

TYPICAL PAN TYPE CONSTRUCTION

HANGER SUPPORT

BEARING SUPPORT

STRUT SUPPORT

* DIMENSIONS RECOMMENDED FOR HANDICAP ACCESSIBILITY

TYPICAL OPEN TYPE CONSTRUCTION

STRINGER SECTIONS

John D. Harvey, AIA; Wheatley Associates; Charlotte, North Carolina

5 **METAL FABRICATION**

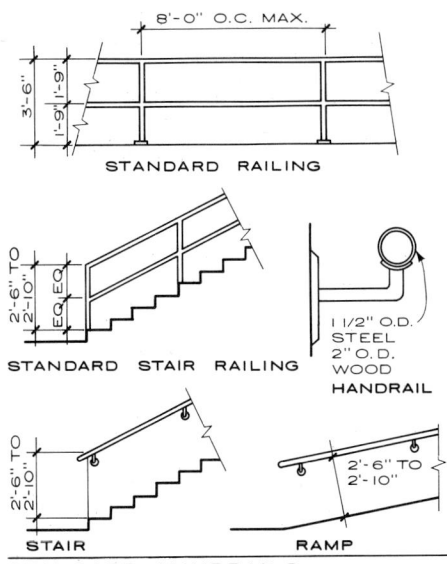

STANDARD RAILING

STANDARD STAIR RAILING

1 1/2" O.D. STEEL
2" O.D. WOOD
HANDRAIL

STAIR

RAMP

STANDARD HANDRAILS

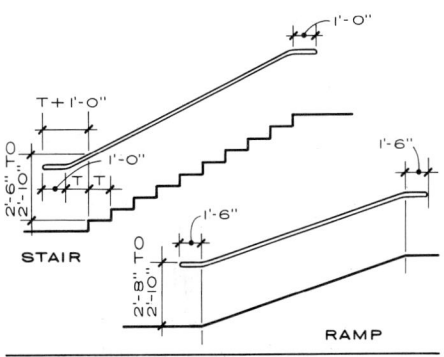

STAIR

RAMP

OSHA RAILING STANDARDS

NOTE: MANY BUILDING CODES CONTAIN MORE RESTRICTIVE REQUIREMENTS ESPECIALLY FOR POST AND RAIL SPACING AND STRUCTURAL LOAD CAPACITY

RAILING STANDARDS (OSHA)

1. All floor openings, including open sides of stair landings, must be protected by a standard railing or be covered.
2. Open sides of all stairs must be protected by a standard stair railing.
3. Handrails are required on all stairs as follows:
   a. Open sided stairs less than 44 in. wide, the stair railing will suffice.
   b. Closed sided stairs less than 44 in. wide, one standard handrail (preferably on right side descending).
   c. Stairs between 44 and 88 in. wide, one standard handrail each side or standard stair railing if open.
   d. Stairs more than 88 in. wide, one handrail or stair rail each side and one intermediate handrail in center.
4. All railings and handrails must be designed to support a load of 200 lb applied at any point in any direction.

HANDRAIL STANDARDS (ANSI)

Handrails are required on both sides of stairs or ramps at a height of 30 to 34 in. If children are the principal users, an additional rail is required at a height of 24 in. Extensions of 1 ft beyond the top riser at the top and bottom of ramps and an extension of 1 ft plus one tread width at the bottom of stairs are required. Continuity of rails is required along the entire length of the stair or ramp and on at least one side of landings. The inside rail on switchback stairs must be continuous.

Clearance between rail and wall shall be a maximum of 1 1/2 in. Projecting ends of handrails must be returned smoothly to wall, floor, or post.

John C. Lunsford, AIA; Varney, Sexton, Sydnor Associates-Architects; Phoenix, Arizona

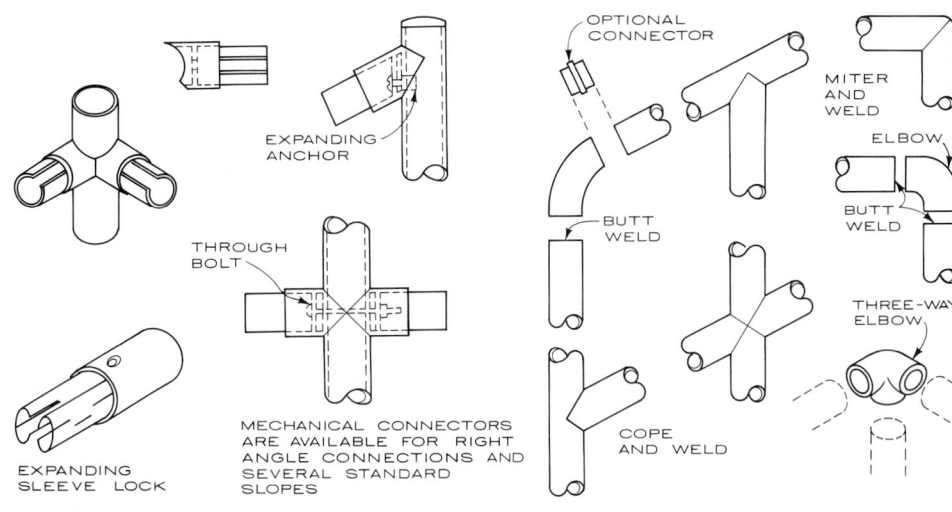

TYPICAL PIPE RAILING CONNECTIONS

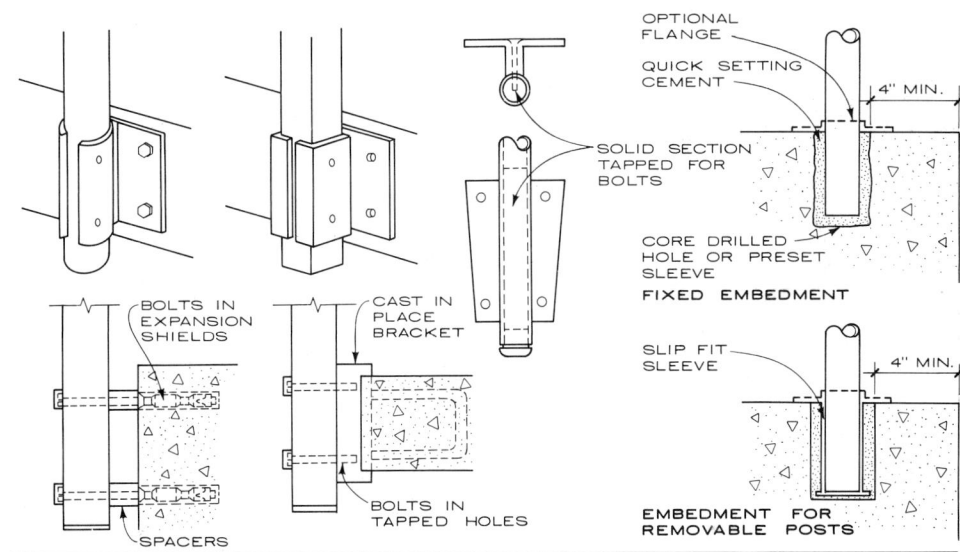

POST ANCHORS AND BRACKETS

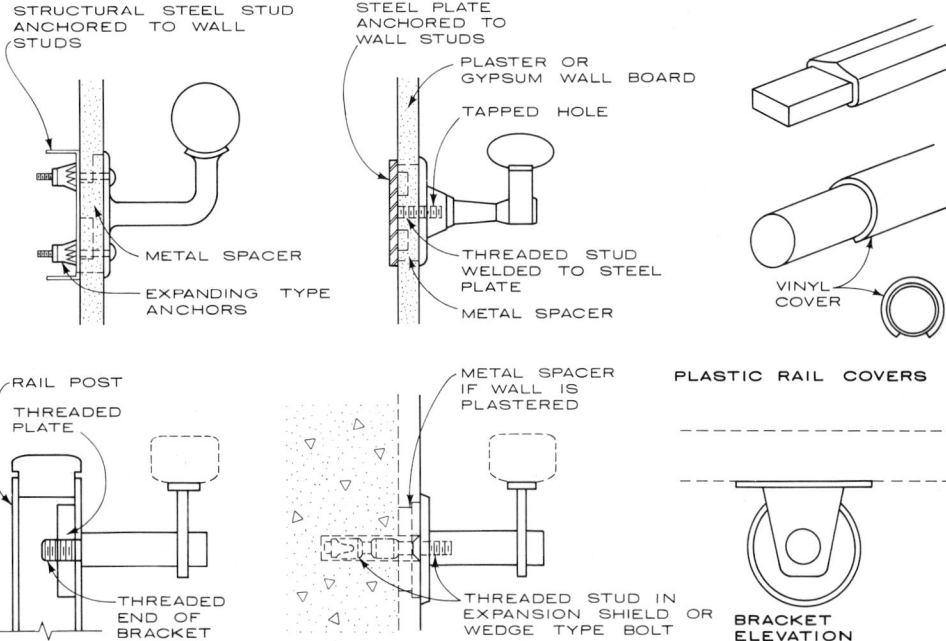

HANDRAIL BRACKETS AND ANCHORAGE

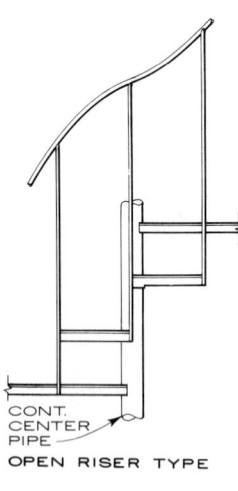

CONT.
CENTER
PIPE

OPEN RISER TYPE

CONT.
CENTER
PIPE

CLOSED RISER TYPE

GENERAL NOTES

1. C.I., stl, or alum. stairs are identified by treads. When al. treads are specified all parts are alum.

2. Center pipe may terminate at platform, or be capped above well rail, or be extended and secured to clg.

3. Balusters: 1 Per tread. 3/4" bar or 3/4" O.D. for stl/al, 15/16" for C.I. At quarter points 1 1/4" O.D. for C.I.

4. Formed steel floor plate tread is welded to steel collar and web for cantilever type, or to steel collar and riser assembly for open riser type.

5. Cantilever treads are secured and held in position by set screws in the hub, or welded.

6. Plated screw and bolt fasteners for stl and C.I. stairs. SST fasteners for al. stairs.

7. Platform sizes are 1" larger than stair radius and anchored to suit well opening construction.

8. Design reference must be made to applicable codes and regulations.

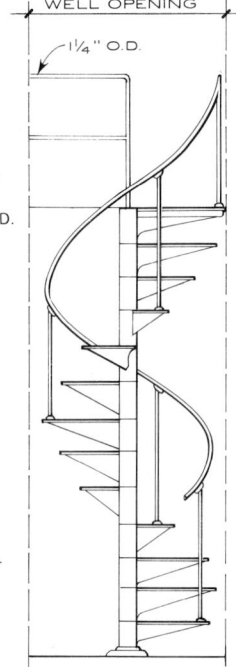

WELL OPENING

1 1/4" O.D.

ELEVATION
CANTILEVER TYPE

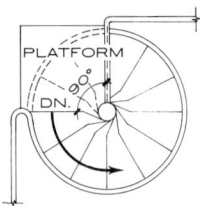

PLATFORM

DN.

PLAN
SQUARE WELL
LEFT HAND STAIR
RAILING ON LEFT
GOING UP

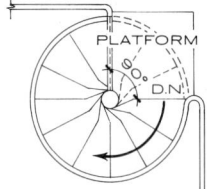

PLATFORM

D.N.

PLAN
SQUARE WELL
RIGHT HAND STAIR
RAILING ON RIGHT
GOING UP

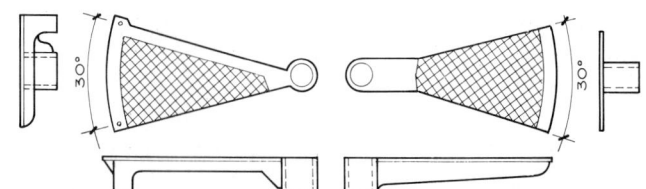

OPEN RISER TREADS   **CANTILEVER TREADS**

TREAD DEGREE	NO. OF TREADS IN A CIRCLE	RISER SIZE	HEAD◊ ROOM	REMARKS
22°–30'	16	7"	7'–0"	Narrowest treads, Lowest riser
28°–0'	12–13	7 5/8"–7 3/4"	6'–9"	
30°–0'	12–13	8 3/8"–9"	6'–9"	Widest treads, Highest riser

◊ Head room calculated on a basis of 3/4 of a circle.

Surfaces of treads and platforms

Cast Iron:
Raised diamond abrasive

Steel:
Checkered plate abrasive,
expanded metal grating,
bar grating

Aluminum:
Checkered plate, abrasive
bar grating

Special:
Wood or rubber cemented to steel tread,
or plywood treads for carpeting

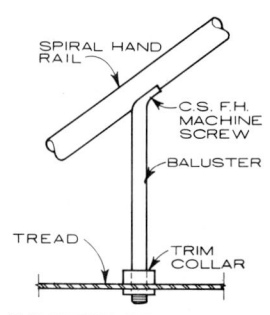

SPIRAL HAND
RAIL

C.S. F.H.
MACHINE
SCREW

BALUSTER

TREAD

TRIM
COLLAR

BALUSTER DETAIL

STANDARD SIZES OF STAIRS, PLATFORMS AND WELLS

*DIA. OF STAIR (IN)	CENTER PIPE, O.D. (IN)		PLATFORM SIZE (IN) SQ/ 1/4 CIRCLE	WELL OPEN'G (IN) SQ/CIRCULAR
	C.I.	STL/AL		
42	3 1/2	3 1/2	22	44
48 †	3 1/2	3 1/2	25	50
54 †	4 1/2	3 1/2	28	56
60 †	4 1/2	3 1/2	31	62
66	4 1/2	5	34	68
72	4 1/2	5	37	74

*Also available in 78" 84" 90" & 98" - special sizes.
†Most residential stairs - with 28° treads, larger dia.
  Residential stairs usually 22°–30'

SPIRAL STAIRS OF CAST IRON, STEEL OR ALUMINUM

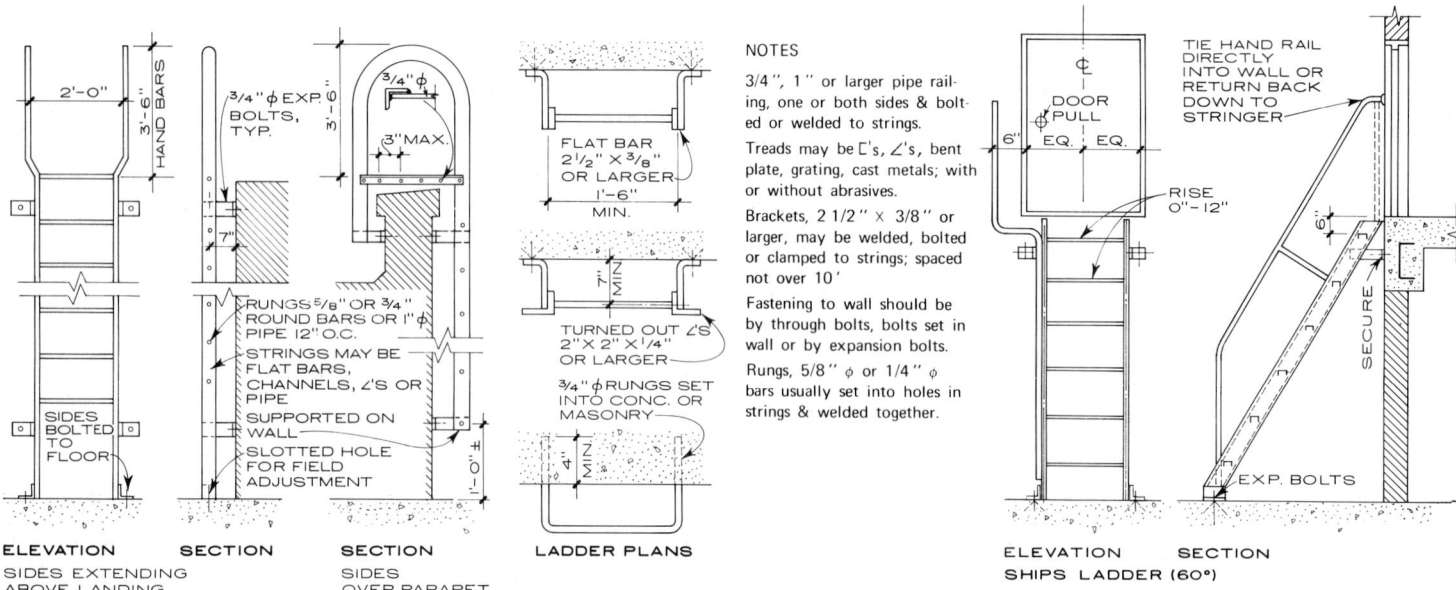

2'-0"

3'-6" HAND BARS

3/4" φ EXP. BOLTS, TYP.

3'-6"

3/4" φ

3" MAX.

7"

RUNGS 5/8" OR 3/4" ROUND BARS OR 1" φ PIPE 12" O.C.

STRINGS MAY BE FLAT BARS, CHANNELS, ∠'S OR PIPE

SUPPORTED ON WALL

SLOTTED HOLE FOR FIELD ADJUSTMENT

SIDES BOLTED TO FLOOR

FLAT BAR 2 1/2" X 3/8" OR LARGER 1'-6" MIN.

7" MIN.

TURNED OUT ∠'S 2" X 2" X 1/4" OR LARGER

3/4" φ RUNGS SET INTO CONC. OR MASONRY

4" MIN.

NOTES

3/4", 1" or larger pipe railing, one or both sides & bolted or welded to strings.

Treads may be ⊏'s, ∠'s, bent plate, grating, cast metals; with or without abrasives.

Brackets, 2 1/2" X 3/8" or larger, may be welded, bolted or clamped to strings; spaced not over 10'.

Fastening to wall should be by through bolts, bolts set in wall or by expansion bolts.

Rungs, 5/8" φ or 1/4" φ bars usually set into holes in strings & welded together.

TIE HAND RAIL DIRECTLY INTO WALL OR RETURN BACK DOWN TO STRINGER

DOOR PULL

6" EQ. EQ.

RISE 0"–12"

SECURE

EXP. BOLTS

ELEVATION   SECTION

ELEVATION   SECTION   SECTION   LADDER PLANS
SIDES EXTENDING   SIDES   SIDES
ABOVE LANDING   OVER PARAPET

SHIPS LADDER (60°)

VERTICAL AND SHIPS LADDERS

Paul R. Schieve, Sr. and Joseph Hornyak; Tippetts, Abbett, McCarthy, Stratton; New York, New York

METAL FABRICATION

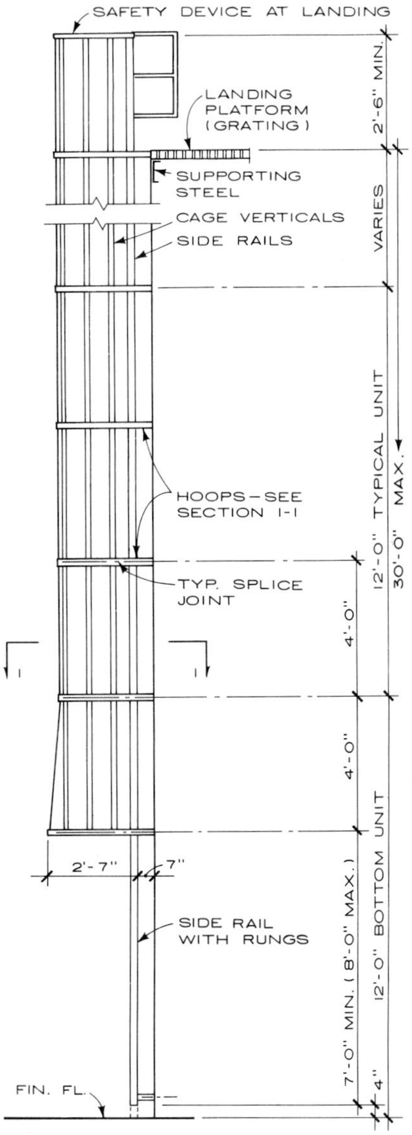
SAFETY DEVICE AT LANDING
LANDING PLATFORM (GRATING)
SUPPORTING STEEL
CAGE VERTICALS
SIDE RAILS
HOOPS—SEE SECTION 1-1
TYP. SPLICE JOINT
SIDE RAIL WITH RUNGS
FIN. FL.
2'-6" MIN.
VARIES
12'-0" TYPICAL UNIT
30'-0" MAX.
4'-0"
4'-0"
2'-7"
7"
7'-0" MIN. (8'-0" MAX.)
12'-0" BOTTOM UNIT
4"

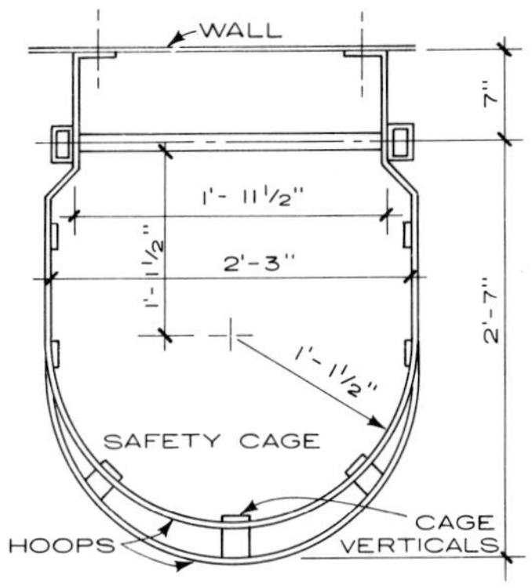
WALL
1'-11½"
2'-3"
1'-1½"
1'-1½"
7"
2'-7"
SAFETY CAGE
HOOPS
CAGE VERTICALS

SECTION 1-1

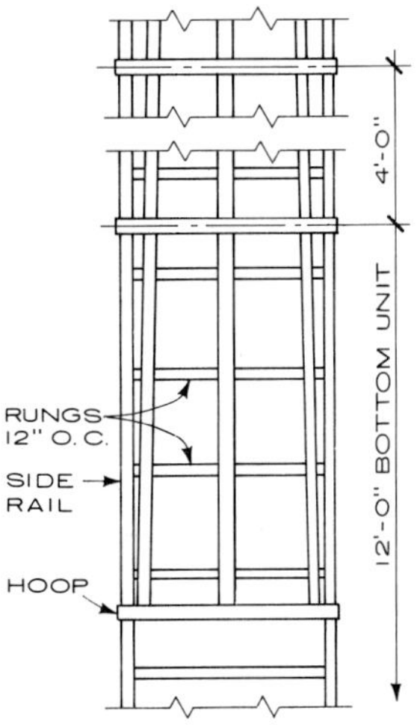
4'-0"
12'-0" BOTTOM UNIT
RUNGS 12" O.C.
SIDE RAIL
HOOP

PART. ELEVATION

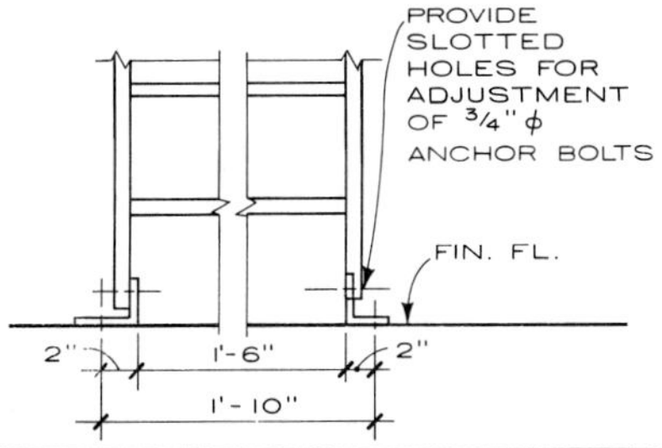
PROVIDE SLOTTED HOLES FOR ADJUSTMENT OF ¾" ϕ ANCHOR BOLTS
FIN. FL.
2"
1'-6"
2"
1'-10"

TYPICAL SIDE ELEVATION
(EXTRUDED ALUMINUM LADDER)
MEETS OSHA REQUIREMENTS AND ANSI SPECIFICATIONS A 14.3

TYPICAL LADDER FOOTING CONNECTIONS

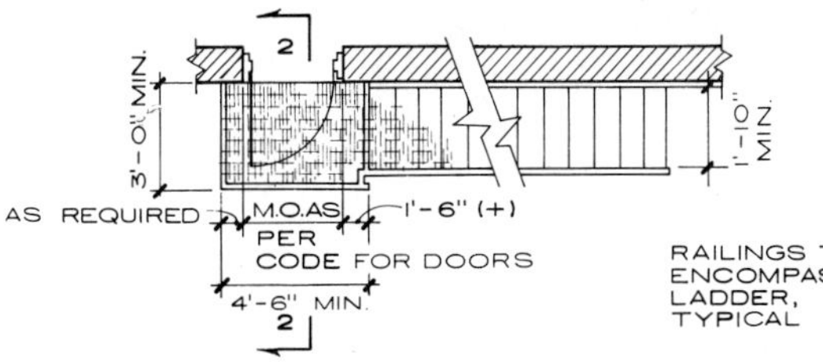
2
3'-0" MIN.
1'-10" MIN.
AS REQUIRED
M.O.AS PER CODE FOR DOORS
1'-6" (+)
4'-6" MIN.
2

PLAN

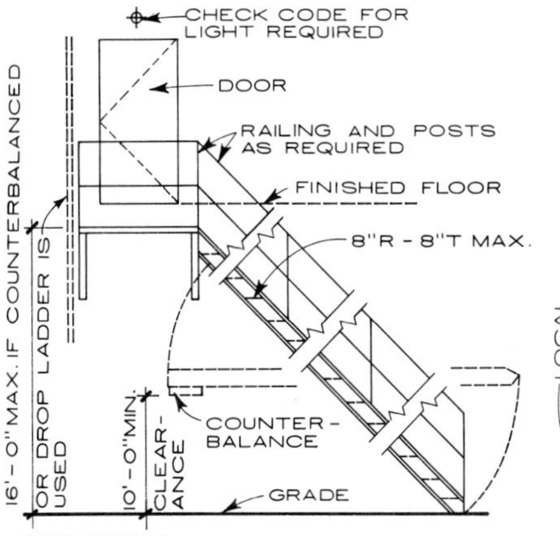
CHECK CODE FOR LIGHT REQUIRED
DOOR
RAILING AND POSTS AS REQUIRED
FINISHED FLOOR
8"R - 8"T MAX.
COUNTER-BALANCE
GRADE
16'-0" MAX. IF COUNTERBALANCED OR DROP LADDER IS USED
10'-0" MIN. CLEARANCE

ELEVATION

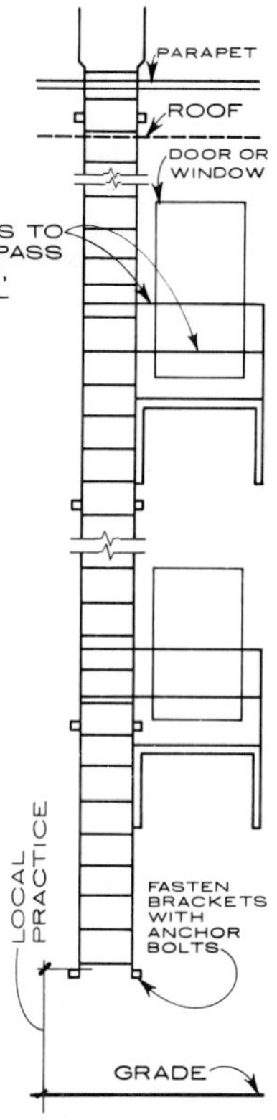
PARAPET
ROOF
DOOR OR WINDOW
RAILINGS TO ENCOMPASS LADDER, TYPICAL
LOCAL PRACTICE
FASTEN BRACKETS WITH ANCHOR BOLTS
GRADE

ELEVATION

NOTE: WEATHER PROTECTION FROM ICE AND SNOW IS REQUIRED IN SOME AREAS

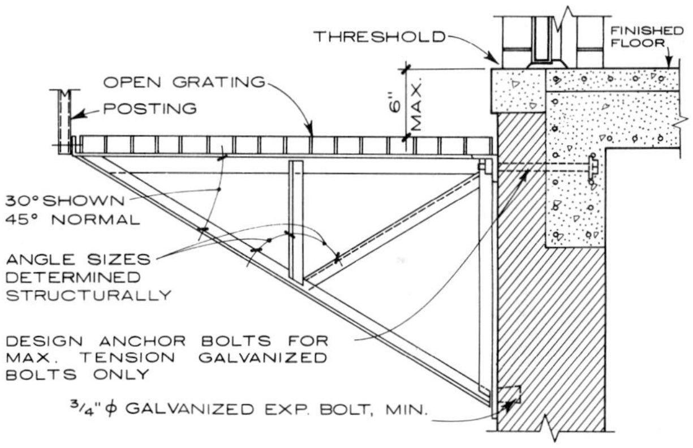
THRESHOLD
FINISHED FLOOR
OPEN GRATING
POSTING
6" MAX.
30° SHOWN
45° NORMAL
ANGLE SIZES DETERMINED STRUCTURALLY
DESIGN ANCHOR BOLTS FOR MAX. TENSION GALVANIZED BOLTS ONLY
¾" ϕ GALVANIZED EXP. BOLT, MIN.

SECTION 2-2

TYPICAL FIRE ESCAPE DETAILS

SUGGESTED STEEL LADDER FRAMING

MEMBER	SIZE	SUPPORT SPACING
Ladder side rails	2½" x ⅜"	8'-0" maximum
	3" x ⅜"	12'-0" maximum
	3½" x ⅜"	16'-0" maximum
Cage hoop	5" x ⅜"	20'-0" maximum top and bottom
	2" x ⅜"	All intermediates
Cage verticals	2" x ⅜"	See Section 1-1 above
Ladder rungs	¾" ϕ plug welded into side rails	

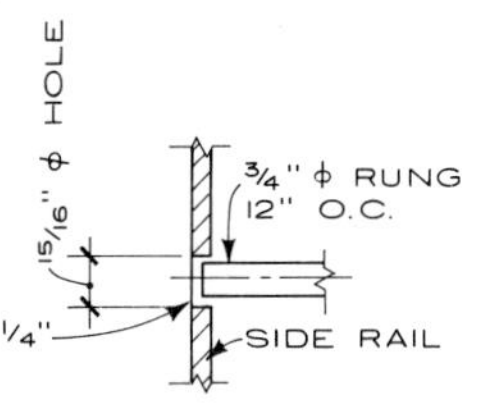
¹⁵⁄₁₆" ϕ HOLE
¾" ϕ RUNG 12" O.C.
¼"
SIDE RAIL

LADDER RUNG DETAIL

GENERAL NOTES: FOUR BASIC TYPES

1. Vertical ladders with platforms at exit door and windows. This type is used only for industrial buildings of low height.
2. Stairways supported on brackets attached to building walls with platforms at exits. This type is used for any building height permitted by code. Lowest section may be counterbalanced or drop ladder. Fire escape stairs may be used as required means of exit only in existing buildings, subject to occupancy provisions: ". . . not more than 50 percent of required exit capacity in any case" (NFPA 101 Life Safety Code 1976) (5-2.9.1.1.2).
3. Freestanding stairways independently supported on steel columns, with platforms and walkways at exits. This type is used on buildings to which construction scaffolding cannot be attached.
4. Chutes-fire escapes. This type is used chiefly in institutional buildings.
   a. Fire escapes must be designed in accordance with state or local laws and ordinances.
   b. Frames for platforms can be angles, as shown, or channels bolted to brackets; grating can be bolted or welded to frame or set loose in it. Alternate bracket may be round or square steel, usually 1 or 1¼ in.

NOTE

All ladder safety devices such as those that incorporate lifebelts, friction brakes, and sliding attachments shall meet the design requirements of fire escape ladders; by U.S. Department of Labor-Occupational Safety and Health Administration.

Max O. Urbahn Associates, Inc.; New York, New York

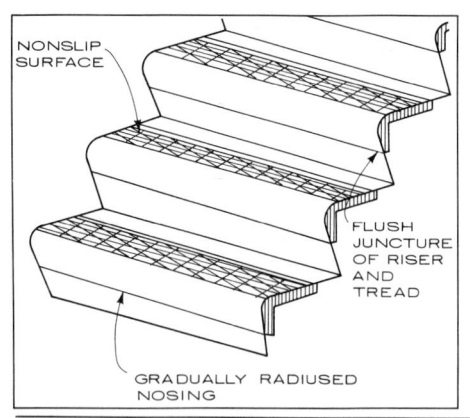

NONSLIP SURFACE

FLUSH JUNCTURE OF RISER AND TREAD

GRADUALLY RADIUSED NOSING

TREAD SIZE

Riser and tread dimensions must be uniform for the length of the stair. ANSI specifications recommend a minimum tread dimension of 11 in., nosing to nosing, and a riser height of 5 to 7 in. for maximum secure footing. Stairs with tread dimensions of less than 9 in. must be open riser stairs. These are a hazard for persons with leg braces, however, and should be used only where another stair, elevator, or ramp that complies with the standards is available.

TREAD COVERING

OSHA standards require finishes to be "reasonably slip resistant" with nosings of nonslip finish. Treads without nosings are acceptable provided that the tread is serrated or is of definite nonslip design. Uniform color and texture are recommended for clear delineation of edges.

NOSING DESIGN

ANSI specifications recommend nosings without abrupt edges which project no more than 1½ in. beyond the edge of the riser. A "safe stair" will use a slightly rounded, abrasive nosing, firmly anchored to the tread, with no overhangs and a clearly visible edge.

RAILINGS

Handrails should be mounted at height 32 to 34 in. above the nosings and should be graspable for their entire length. A 1¾ to 2 in. diameter rounded handrail is recommended. It should extend 1 ft to 1 ft 6 in. beyond the top and bottom of the stair.

LIGHTING

Illumination of the stair with directional lighting from the lower landing will increase the visibility of the tread edge.

DESIGN OF A "SAFE" STAIR, USABLE BY THE PHYSICALLY HANDICAPPED

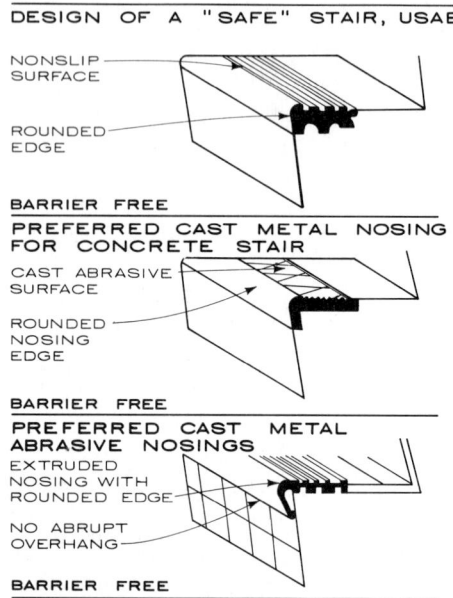

NONSLIP SURFACE
ROUNDED EDGE
BARRIER FREE
PREFERRED CAST METAL NOSING FOR CONCRETE STAIR

CAST ABRASIVE SURFACE
ROUNDED NOSING EDGE
BARRIER FREE
PREFERRED CAST METAL ABRASIVE NOSINGS

EXTRUDED NOSING WITH ROUNDED EDGE
NO ABRUPT OVERHANG
BARRIER FREE
PREFERRED ALUMINUM NOSINGS

FLUSH ABRASIVE NOSING WITH ROUNDED EDGE CAST INTO CONCRETE STAIR
CONCRETE ANCHORS
BARRIER FREE
PREFERRED ABRASIVE EXPOXY FILLED NOSINGS

NONSLIP RUBBER BUTT TYPE NOSING WITH ROUNDED EDGE
NO TREAD OVERHANG
BARRIER FREE
PREFERRED VINYL AND RUBBER NOSING DETAIL

FLUSH SERRATED NOSING WITH ROUNDED EDGE
GRADUAL RETURN
BARRIER FREE
PREFERRED STEEL SUBTREAD DETAIL

ABRASIVE STRIPS
ROUNDED EDGE
MARBLE RISER
MARBLE TREAD
BARRIER FREE
PREFERRED STONE TREAD DETAIL

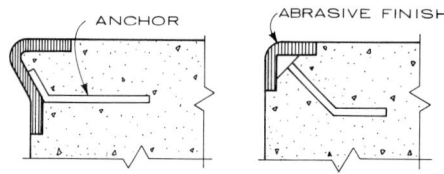
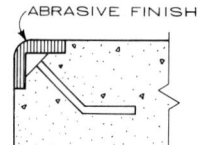
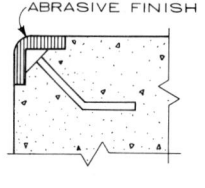
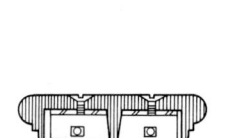
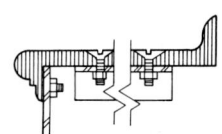

ANCHOR
ABRASIVE FINISH
WOOD OR CONCRETE
SERRATED METAL NOSING
METAL PAN INSTALLATION
CAST METAL ABRASIVE STRUCTURAL TREAD TYPES
OTHER CAST METAL NOSINGS

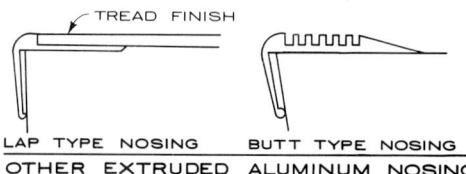

TREAD FINISH
LAP TYPE NOSING
BUTT TYPE NOSING
OTHER EXTRUDED ALUMINUM NOSINGS

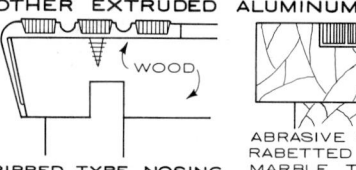
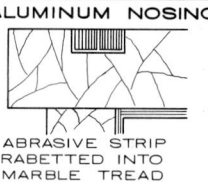

WOOD
RIBBED TYPE NOSING
ABRASIVE STRIP RABETTED INTO MARBLE TREAD
OTHER ALUMINUM NOSINGS WITH ABRASIVE FILLER

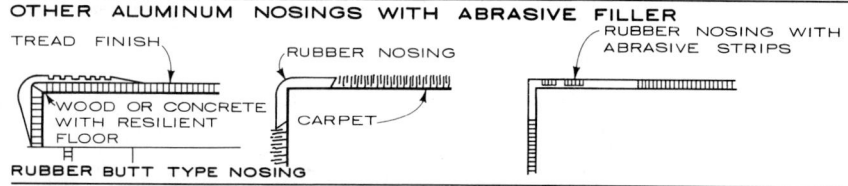

TREAD FINISH
RUBBER NOSING
RUBBER NOSING WITH ABRASIVE STRIPS
WOOD OR CONCRETE WITH RESILIENT FLOOR
CARPET
RUBBER BUTT TYPE NOSING
OTHER NONSLIP VINYL AND RUBBER NOSINGS

SANITARY COVE
LINOLEUM OR TILE
STEEL SUBTREAD WITH FORMED NOSING
STEEL SUBTREAD AND RISER, WITH STEEL ANGLE NOSING
OTHER CEMENT FILLED STEEL SUBTREADS

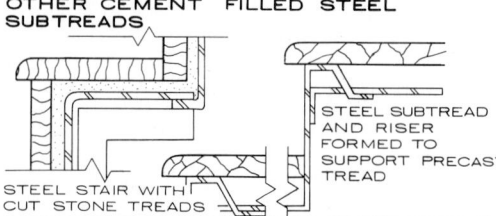
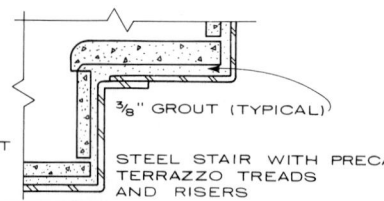

STEEL SUBTREAD AND RISER FORMED TO SUPPORT PRECAST TREAD
STEEL STAIR WITH CUT STONE TREADS
⅜" GROUT (TYPICAL)
STEEL STAIR WITH PRECAST TERRAZZO TREADS AND RISERS
OTHER STONE AND TERRAZZO TREAD DETAILS

NOTE

Cast nosings for concrete stairs are iron, aluminum, or bronze, custom made to exact size. Nosings and treads come with factory drilled countersunk holes or riveted strap anchors, or with wing type anchors.

NOTE

Abrasive materials are used as treads, nosings, or inlay strips for new work, and also as surface mounted replacement treads for old work. A homogeneous epoxy abrasive is cured on an extruded aluminum base for a smoother surface or is used as filler between aluminum ribs.

Olga Barmine; Darrel Rippeteau, Architect; Washington, D.C.

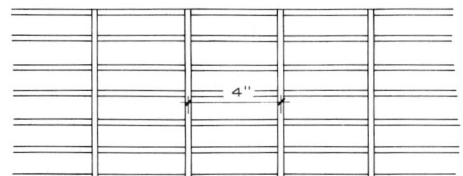

WITH SPACER BARS WELDED 4" O.C.   WITH SPACER BARS WELDED 2" O.C.

RECTANGULAR (WELDED OR PRESSURE LOCKED)

NOTES

Constructed of flat bearing bars of steel or aluminum I-bars, with spacer bars at right angles. Spacer bars may be square, rectangular, or of another shape. Spacer bars are connected to bearing bars by pressing them into prepared slots or by welding. They have open ends or perhaps ends banded with flat bars that are of about the same size as welded bearing bars. Standard bar spacings are $^{15}/_{16}$ and $1^{3}/_{16}$ in.

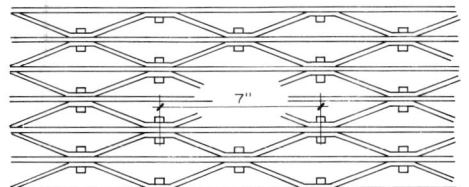

WITH SPACER BARS RIVETED APPROX. 7" O.C.
USED FOR AVERAGE INSTALLATION

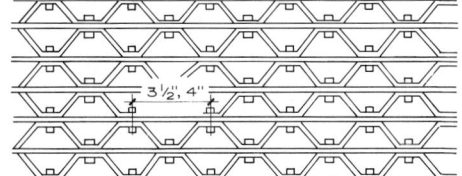

WITH SPACER BARS RIVETED $3^{1}/_{2}$" OR 4"
USED FOR HEAVY TRAFFIC AND WHERE
WHEELED EQUIPMENT IS USED

RETICULATED (RIVETED)

NOTES

Flat bearing bars are made of steel or aluminum, and continuous bent spacer or reticulate bars are riveted to the bearing bars. Usually they have open ends or ends that are banded with flat bars of the same size as bearing bars, welded across the ends. Normal spacing of bars: $^{3}/_{4}$, $1^{1}/_{8}$, or $2^{5}/_{16}$ in. Many bar gratings cannot be used in areas of public pedestrian traffic (crutches, canes, pogo sticks, women's shoes, etc.). Close mesh grating ($^{1}/_{4}$ in.) is available in steel and aluminum, for use in pedestrian traffic areas.

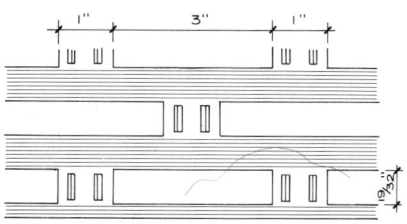

PLAN

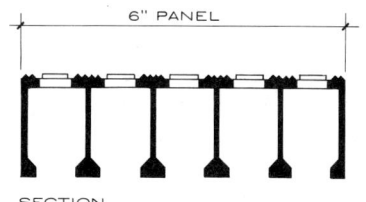

6" PANEL

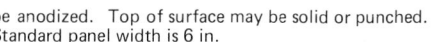

SECTION

ALUMINUM PLANK

NOTES

Grating is extruded from aluminum alloy in one piece with integral I-beam ribs and can have a natural finish or be anodized. Top of surface may be solid or punched. Standard panel width is 6 in.

NOSING OF ANGLE AND ABRASIVE
STRIP AND BAR ENDS

HEAVY FRONT AND BACK BEARING
BARS AND BAR END PLATES

FLOOR PLATE NOSING, BAR END
PLATES

NOSING OF CLOSELY SPACED BARS,
ANGLE ENDS

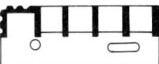

CHECKER PLATE NOSING, BAR END
PLATES

EXTRUDED ALUMINUM CORRUGATED
NOSING, BAR END PLATES

TREADS

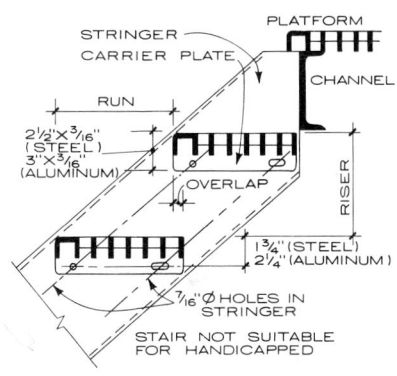

STAIR STRINGER AND TREAD CARRIER

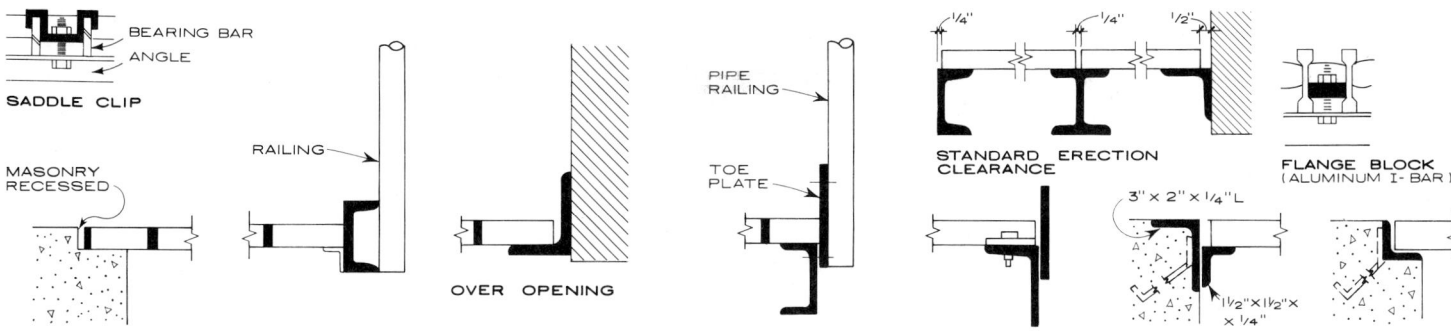

SADDLE CLIP

OVER OPENING

STANDARD ERECTION CLEARANCE

FLANGE BLOCK
(ALUMINUM I-BAR)

USUALLY ATTACHED BY WELDING, WHERE SUPPORT AND GRATE ARE CONSTRUCTED AS A UNIT

FIXED OR LOOSE GRATINGS

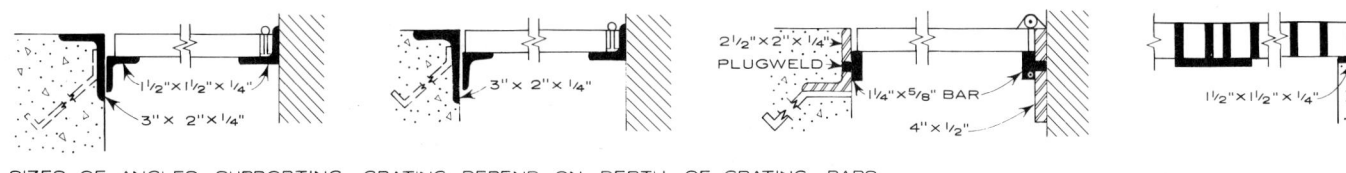

SIZES OF ANGLES SUPPORTING GRATING DEPEND ON DEPTH OF GRATING BARS

HINGED AREA GRATINGS

Vicente Cordero, AIA; Arlington, Virginia

METAL FABRICATION 5

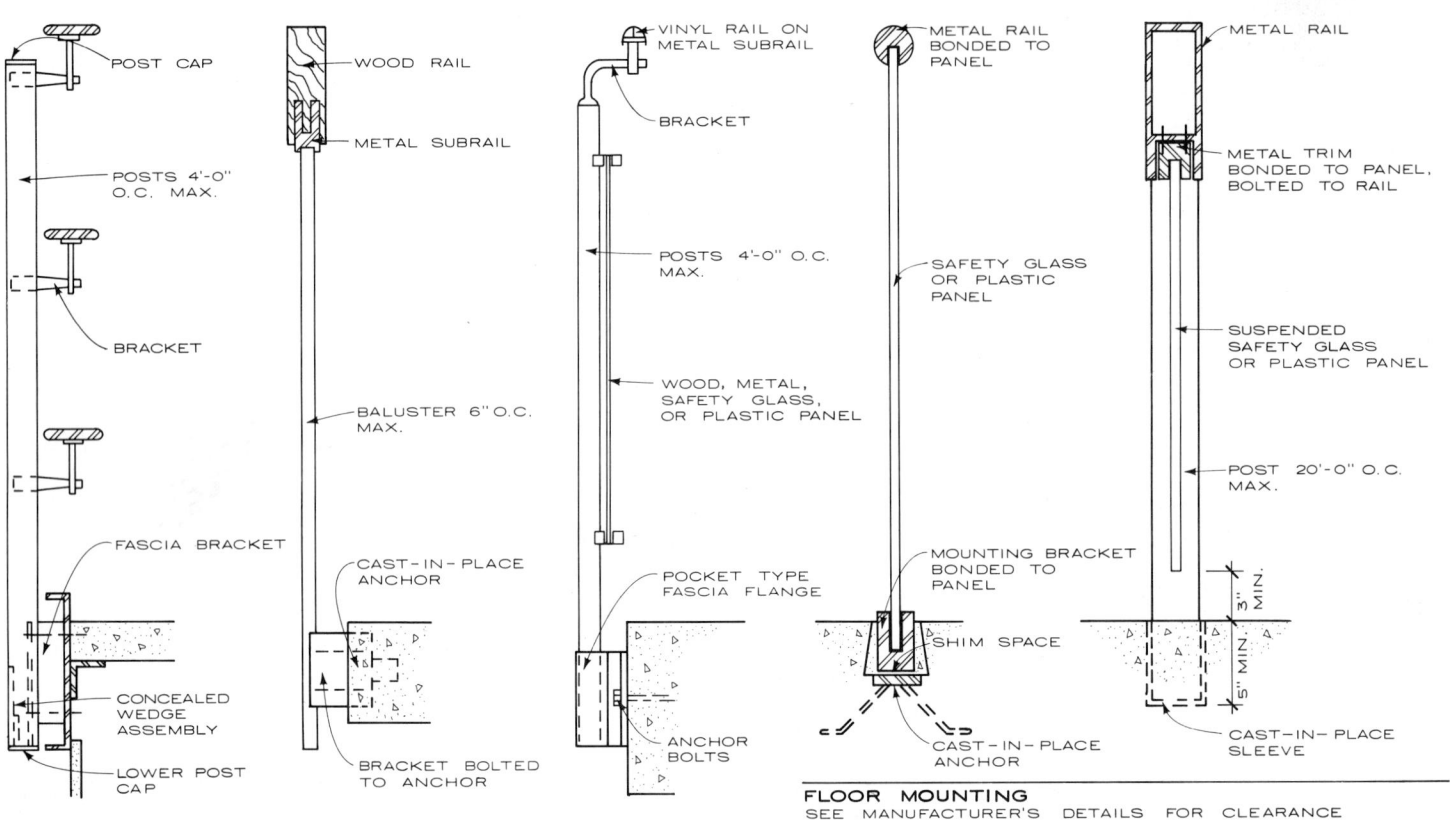

SIDE MOUNTING

FLOOR MOUNTING
SEE MANUFACTURER'S DETAILS FOR CLEARANCE
BETWEEN FLOOR EDGE AND RAIL

CONSULT CODE FOR RAILING HEIGHT, POST RAIL, AND BALUSTER SPACING, AND LOADING REQUIREMENTS

TYPICAL POST AND RAIL DETAILS

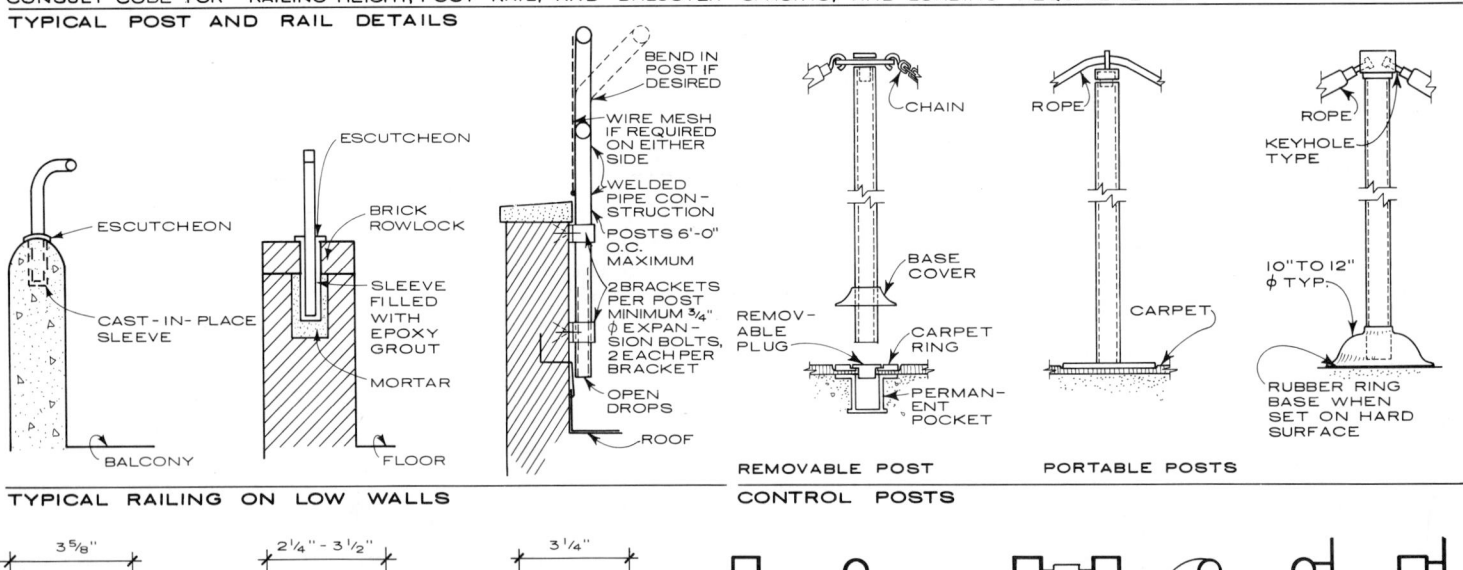

TYPICAL RAILING ON LOW WALLS

REMOVABLE POST   PORTABLE POSTS

CONTROL POSTS

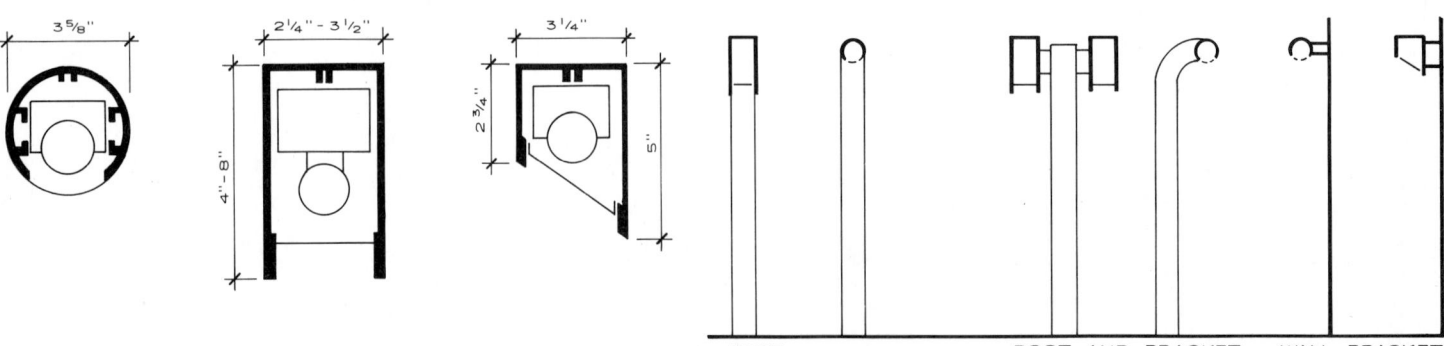

FLUORESCENT FIXTURES AND PLASTIC DIFFUSERS, SMALLER
HANDRAILS AVAILABLE WITH INCANDESCENT FIXTURES

LIGHTED HANDRAILS

POST   POST AND BRACKET   WALL BRACKET

John McCartney, AIA; Washington, D.C.

5 ORNAMENTAL METAL

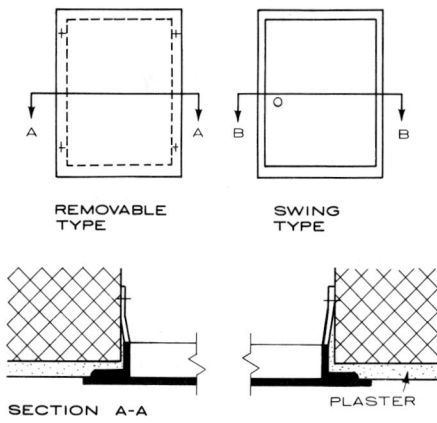

REMOVABLE TYPE   SWING TYPE

SECTION A-A   PLASTER

NOTES

1. Frames are usually set into the building construction and the door constructed later to fit. Doors may be hinged, set in with clips, or fastened with screws. Hinges may be butt, pivot, or surface. Assorted stock sizes range from 8 x 8 to 24 x 36 in.
2. Access panels should have a fire rating similar to the wall in which it occurs. Access panels of more than 144 sq in. require automatic closers.

ACCESS DOORS

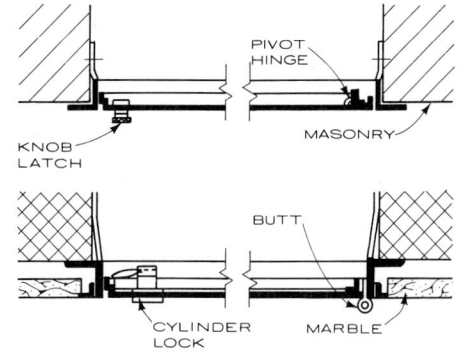

PIVOT HINGE   MASONRY
KNOB LATCH
CYLINDER LOCK   BUTT   MARBLE

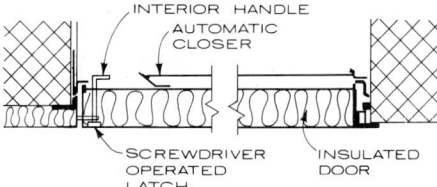

INTERIOR HANDLE AUTOMATIC CLOSER
SCREWDRIVER OPERATED LATCH   INSULATED DOOR

SECTION B-B

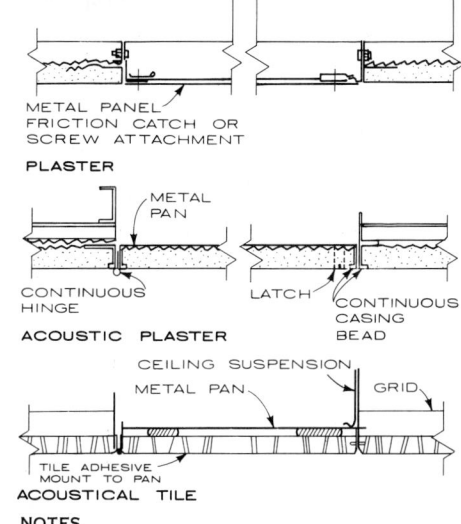

METAL PANEL FRICTION CATCH OR SCREW ATTACHMENT
PLASTER

METAL PAN
CONTINUOUS HINGE   LATCH   CONTINUOUS CASING BEAD
ACOUSTIC PLASTER

CEILING SUSPENSION
METAL PAN   GRID
TILE ADHESIVE MOUNT TO PAN
ACOUSTICAL TILE

NOTES

1. Spring operated swing down panels as well as swing up panels for ceiling access are frequently used.
2. Standard sizes: 12 x 12 to 24 x 36 in.
3. Other finish ceiling types—detail similar to that for acoustic tiles.

CEILING ACCESS PANELS

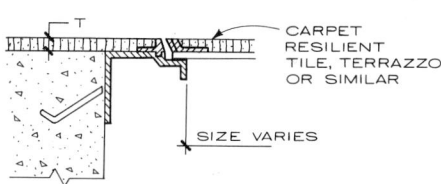

CARPET RESILIENT TILE, TERRAZZO OR SIMILAR
SIZE VARIES
FLOOR HATCH – SECTION C-C

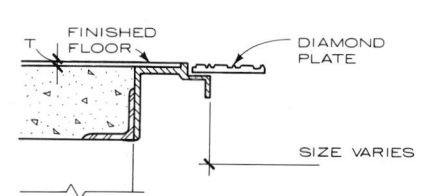

FINISHED FLOOR   DIAMOND PLATE
SIZE VARIES
FLOOR HATCH – SECTION C-C

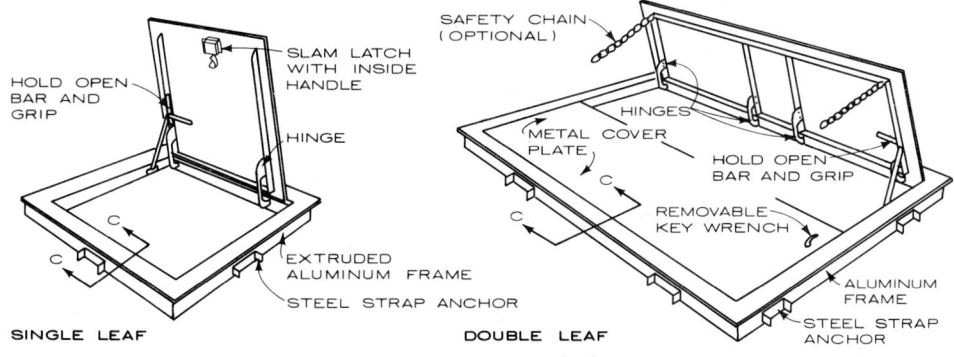

SLAM LATCH WITH INSIDE HANDLE
HOLD OPEN BAR AND GRIP
HINGE
EXTRUDED ALUMINUM FRAME
STEEL STRAP ANCHOR
SINGLE LEAF

SAFETY CHAIN (OPTIONAL)
HINGES
METAL COVER PLATE
HOLD OPEN BAR AND GRIP
REMOVABLE KEY WRENCH
ALUMINUM FRAME
STEEL STRAP ANCHOR
DOUBLE LEAF

1. MATERIAL: Steel or aluminum.
2. SIZES:
   Single leaf—2'-0'' x 2'-0'', 2'-6'' x 2'-6'', 3'-0'' x 3'-0''.
   Double leaf—3'-6'' x 3'-6'', 4'-0'' x 4'-0'', 4'-0'' x 6'-0'', 5'-0'' x 5'-0''.

Thickness "T"—varies from 1/8 in. for resilient flooring to 3/16 in. for carpet; some manufacturers offer 3/4 in. for terrazzo and tile floor.

Double leaf floor hatch is recommended for areas where there is danger of persons' falling into the opening. Safety codes require that floor openings be protected.

FLOOR HATCHES

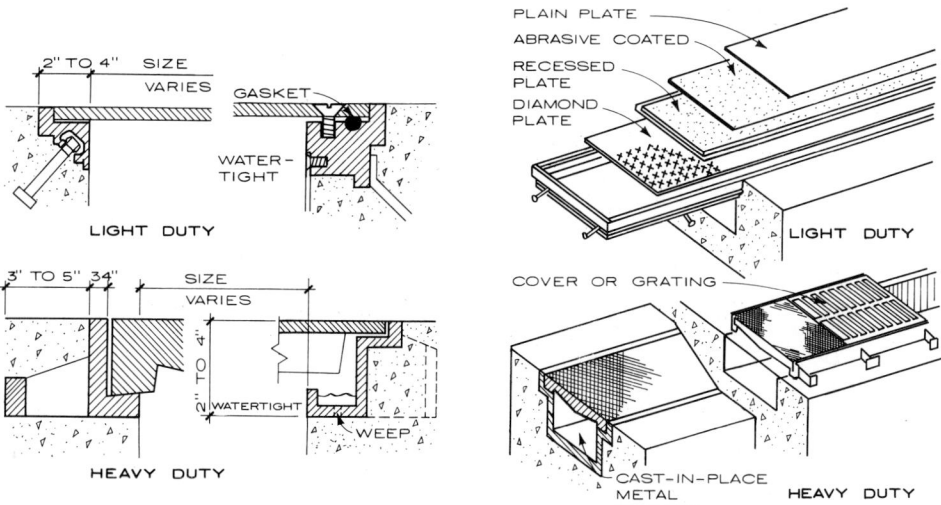

2" TO 4"   SIZE VARIES   GASKET
WATER-TIGHT
LIGHT DUTY

3" TO 5"   3/4"   SIZE VARIES
WATERTIGHT   WEEP
HEAVY DUTY

PLAIN PLATE
ABRASIVE COATED
RECESSED PLATE
DIAMOND PLATE
LIGHT DUTY

COVER OR GRATING
HEAVY DUTY
CAST-IN-PLACE METAL TROUGH

LIGHT DUTY TRENCH COVERS

1. MATERIAL: Extruded aluminum.
2. SIZE: 2 to 36 in. wide. Side frames are available in cut length of 20 ft stocks and may be spliced to meet any length. Recessed cover plates are available in 20 ft stock; other covers in 10 and 12 ft.
3. Side frames are normally cast in concrete around trough form.

HEAVY DUTY TRENCH COVER

1. MATERIAL: Cast iron or ductile iron.
2. SIZES: Heavy duty cast iron trench cover should be planned carefully to use standard stock length to avoid cutting, or special length casting should be ordered.
3. STOCK COVER SIZE: 2 to 48 in. wide and 24 in. long. Frames are manufactured in standard lengths of 24 or 36 in. depending on size and manufacturer. Cast iron troughs are 8 in. deep, 6 to 24 in. wide, and 48 in. in stock length.

TRENCH COVERS

Cohen, Karydas & Associates, Chartered; Washington, D.C.

ORNAMENTAL METAL   **5**

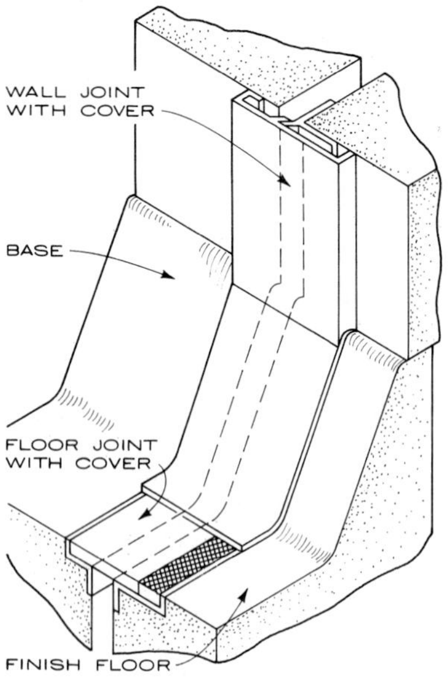

WALL JOINT
WITH COVER

BASE

FLOOR JOINT
WITH COVER

FINISH FLOOR

AT PROJECTING BASE

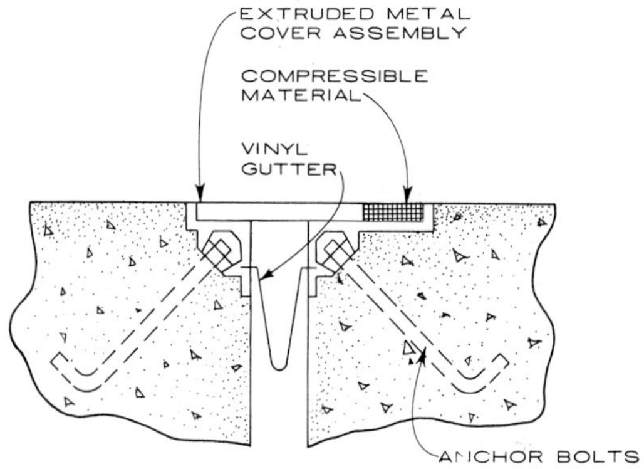

EXTRUDED METAL
COVER ASSEMBLY

COMPRESSIBLE
MATERIAL

VINYL
GUTTER

ANCHOR BOLTS

AT FLOOR

PREMOLDED
EXPANSION JOINT
FILLER (OPTIONAL)

RETAINER CLIPS

EXTRUDED METAL
COVER

AT WALL

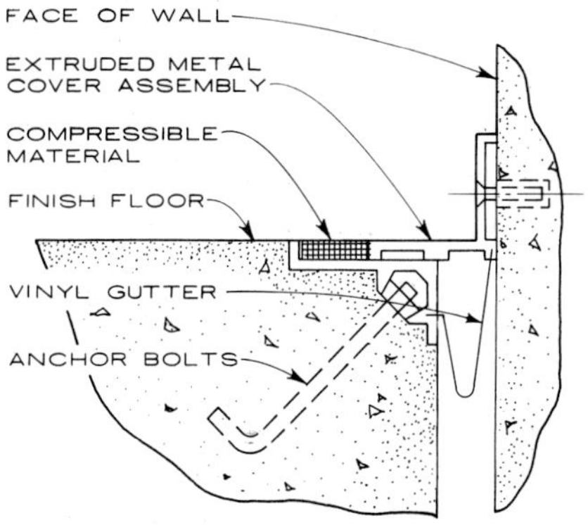

FACE OF WALL

EXTRUDED METAL
COVER ASSEMBLY

COMPRESSIBLE
MATERIAL

FINISH FLOOR

VINYL GUTTER

ANCHOR BOLTS

AT FLOOR AND WALL

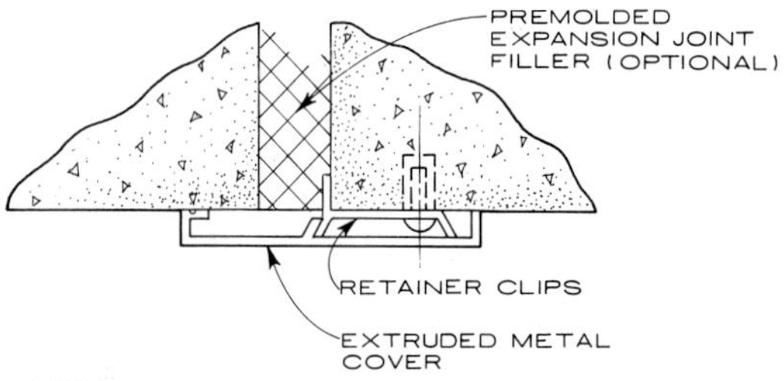

PREMOLDED
EXPANSION JOINT
FILLER (OPTIONAL)

EXTRUDED METAL
COVER

RETAINER CLIPS

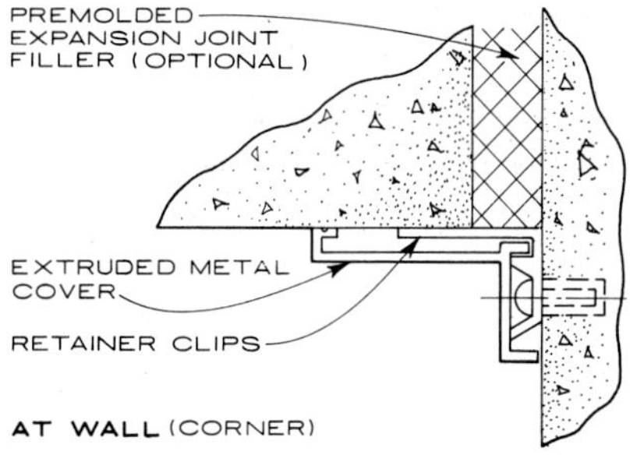

AT WALL (CORNER)

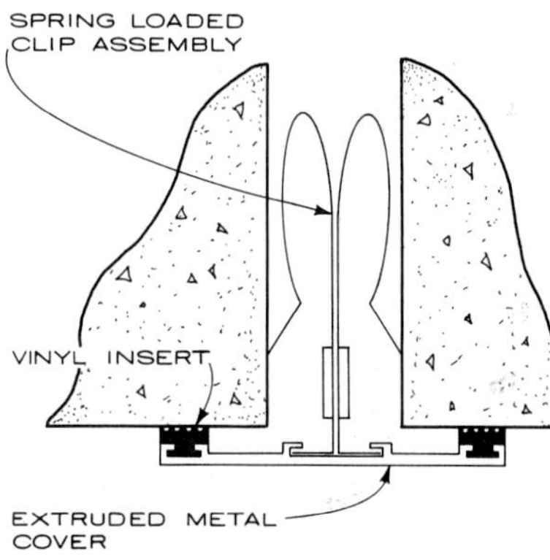

SPRING LOADED
CLIP ASSEMBLY

VINYL INSERT

EXTRUDED METAL
COVER

AT WALL OR CEILING

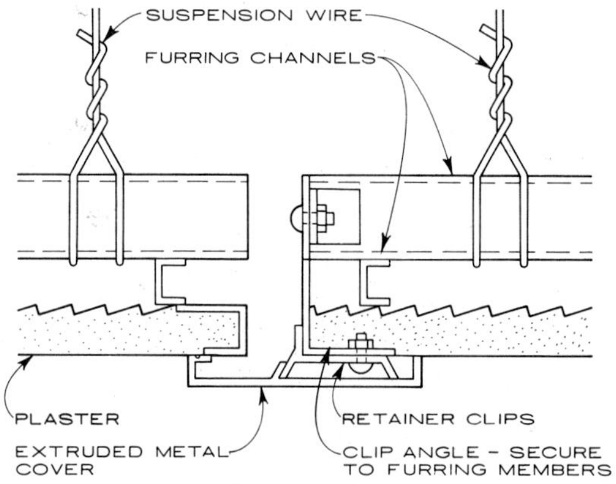

SUSPENSION WIRE

FURRING CHANNELS

PLASTER

EXTRUDED METAL
COVER

RETAINER CLIPS

CLIP ANGLE – SECURE
TO FURRING MEMBERS

AT SUSPENDED CEILING

COMPRESSIBLE
MATERIAL

EXTRUDED METAL
COVER ASSEMBLY

PREMOLDED
EXPANSION JOINT
FILLER (OPTIONAL)

ANCHOR BOLTS

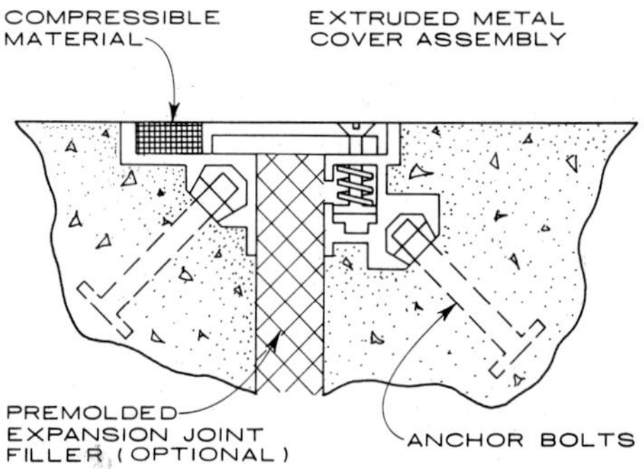

SEISMIC FLOOR JOINT COVER

NOTE

Expansion joint covers that will respond to differential movement, both laterally and horizontally should be provided at joints in structures located where seismic action (earth tremors and quakes) may be expected or where differential settlement is anticipated.

PREFABRICATED INTERIOR EXPANSION JOINT COVERS

NOTE

A large selection of prefabricated assemblies to cover interior expansion joints are available from various manufacturers to satisfy most joint and finish conditions.

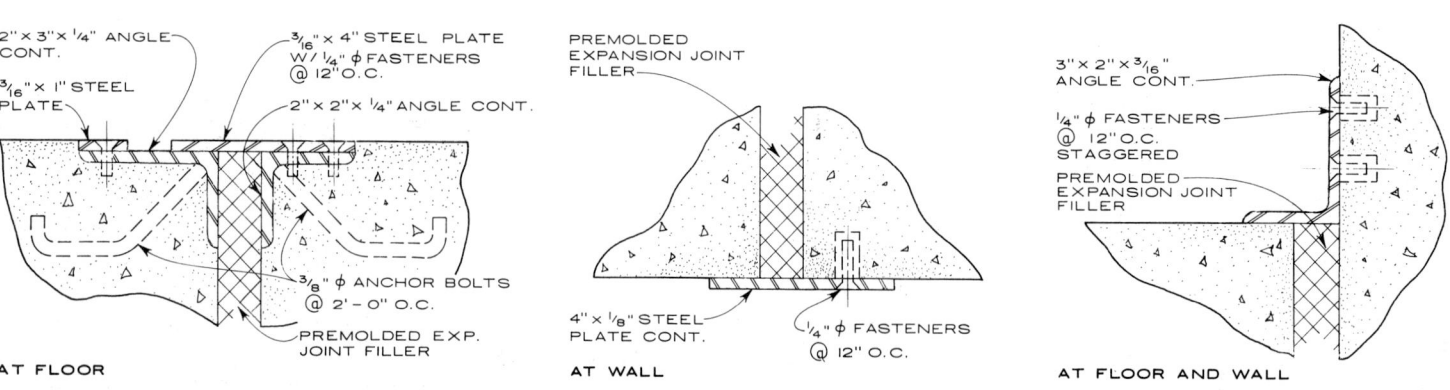

2" x 3" x ¼" ANGLE
CONT.

³⁄₁₆" x 1" STEEL
PLATE

³⁄₁₆" x 4" STEEL PLATE
W/ ¼" φ FASTENERS
@ 12" O.C.

2" x 2" x ¼" ANGLE CONT.

³⁄₈" φ ANCHOR BOLTS
@ 2'-0" O.C.

PREMOLDED EXP.
JOINT FILLER

AT FLOOR

PREMOLDED
EXPANSION JOINT
FILLER

4" x ⅛" STEEL
PLATE CONT.

¼" φ FASTENERS
@ 12" O.C.

AT WALL

3" x 2" x ³⁄₁₆"
ANGLE CONT.

¼" φ FASTENERS
@ 12" O.C.
STAGGERED

PREMOLDED
EXPANSION JOINT
FILLER

AT FLOOR AND WALL

PLATE AND ANGLE TYPE INTERIOR EXPANSION JOINT COVERS

Robert D. Abernathy; J. N. Pease Associates; Charlotte, North Carolina

 ORNAMENTAL METAL

GENERAL NOTES

Many variations of the typical types shown are available such as slanted, rounded, or tapered tops and ends; grooved, ribbed, fluted and shaped faces; as well as other decorative treatment.

Refer to   a) Standard   b) Metal
the following   Metal   Stair
sections for: Shapes   Nosings

MATERIALS AND FINISHES :

Aluminum
Regular polish: bright or satin texture.
Clear or color anodized: smooth, spun, or hammered texture.
Stainless Steel: satin finish.
Screws: nickel plated where exposed.
Insert strips: bronze or plastic—standard colors.

LEGEND

D.O.F. = DEPTH OF FACE

INDICATES BACK-UP MATERIAL (PLYWOOD, PLASTER OR OTHER DENSE SURFACE)

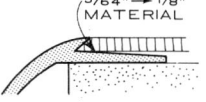

BUTT TYPE
5/16" → 1/8" MATERIAL
5/8" → 1 1/2" D.O.F.

OVERLAP TYPE
5/64" → 1/8" MATERIAL
13/16" → 1 3/32" D.O.F.

ROLL DOWN TYPE
1/16" → 1/8" MATERIAL
3/4" → 1 1/16" D.O.F.

CONCEALED FLANGES: TAPERED OR STRAIGHT

13/32" & 11/16" OVERLAP
7/8" → 1 3/8" D.O.F.

1/4" OVERLAP
3/4" → 1 1/4" D.O.F.

1/2" & 5/8" OVERLAP
13/16" → 1 1/2" D.O.F.

3/16" & 1/4" OVERLAP
5/16" → 2" D.O.F.

APPLIED AFTER TYPES

1/8" & 3/16" OVERLAP
5/16" → 1/2" INSERT
3/4" → 1 1/4" D.O.F.

TEE TYPE
5/16" → 1 25/32" FACE

NOSINGS

5/64" → 1/8" MATERIAL

1/8" & 1/4" UNDER FLANGE

1/16" → 3/16" MATERIAL

1/16" → 1/8" MATERIAL

SINK (FLAT RIM) OR DOORWAY: BUTT & ROLL DOWN TYPES
CONCEALED FLANGES: TAPERED OR STRAIGHT

1/8" & 3/16" MATERIAL

1/8" & 3/16" MATERIAL

BUTT TYPES

EDGINGS

3/32" → 5/32" MATERIAL
3/8" → 1 3/16" WIDTHS

EDGE BINDER OVERLAP TYPES

3/4" → 1 9/32" WIDTHS

SEAM BINDER

1" → 2 1/2" WIDTHS

OVERLAP TYPE CARPET EDGE BINDERS

13/64" → 2 1/8" WIDTHS

TAP DOWN TYPE

EDGINGS

1/16" → 9/32" MATERIAL

1/32" → 1/4" MATERIAL

OUTSIDE TYPES
CONCEALED FLANGES: TAPERED

1/16" → 1/8" MATERIAL

INSIDE TYPE

1/16" → 3/8" MATERIAL

2 1/64" OVERLAP

OUTSIDE APPLIED AFTER TYPE

SLOTTED HOLES
1/32" → 1/2" MATERIAL

CONCEALED FLANGE

CORNERS

CAP MOULDING

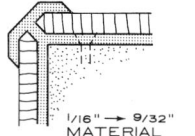

1/32" → 3/8" MATERIAL

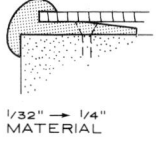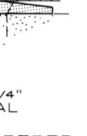

1/16" → 5/32" MATERIAL

CONCEALED FLANGE – TAPERED

COVE AND BATHTUB EDGING

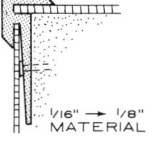

7/16" → 2" FACE

APPLIED AFTER
COVE

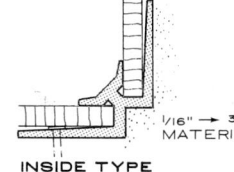

HANDLE MOULDINGS FOR 1/4" MATERIAL

SHOW CASE MOULDINGS

BOWL LEDGES UP TO 1/2", 1/2" TO 3/4", 3/4" TO 1 1/8"

SINK AND LAVATORY FRAME

1/16" → 1/2" MATERIAL

CONCEALED FLANGE

DIVISION BAR

TAG PLACED HERE

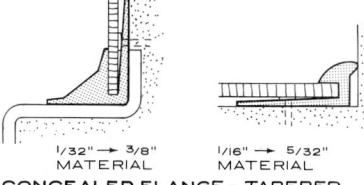

7/8" → 3 11/16" WIDTHS
3/4" → 3 1/2" TAGS

STRAIGHT

1/2" → 1" BACK FASTENING
1-1/16" → 2 3/16" FACE
7/8" → 2" TAGS

CURVED

TAG MOULDINGS

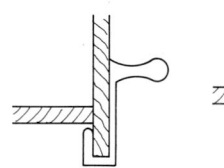

INSIDE   OUTSIDE   RIGHT/LEFT
CORNERS   **END STOPS**
UP TO 5/32" MATERIAL

COVE BASE

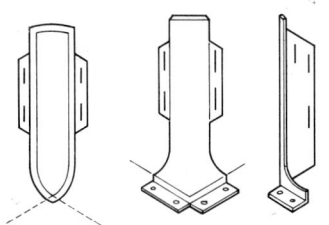

NOTE: ALL WOOD SIZES ARE NOMINAL

ROUGH CARPENTRY

	PENNY	INCHES	TYPE OF NAIL
1'' thick stock	8	2 $\frac{1}{2}$	Common nails.
2'' thick stock	16 to 20	3 $\frac{1}{2}$ or 4	Common nails.
3'' thick stock	40 to 60	5 or 6	Common nails or spikes.
Concrete Forms	variable		Common or double headed nails.
Framing for general use and for large members	10, 16, 20, 60	3, 3 $\frac{1}{2}$, 4, 6	Common nails or spikes depending on size of members.
Toe nailing studs, joists, etc.	10	3	Common nails.
Spiking usual plates and sills	16	3 $\frac{1}{2}$	Common nails.
Toe nailing rafters and plates	10	3	Common nails.
Sheathing — roof and wall	8	2 $\frac{1}{2}$	Common nails, may be zinc coated.
Finished rough flooring	8	2 $\frac{1}{2}$	Common nails, may be zinc coated.

FINISH CARPENTRY

	PENNY	INCHES	TYPE OF NAIL
Moldings —— Sizes as required		$\frac{7}{8}$ to 1 $\frac{1}{4}$	Molding nails (brads).
Carpet strips, shoes	8	2 $\frac{1}{2}$	Finishing or casing nails.
Door and window stops and members $\frac{1}{4}$'' to $\frac{1}{2}$'' thick	4	1 $\frac{1}{2}$	Finishing or casing nails.
Ceiling, trim, casing, picture mold, base balusters and members $\frac{1}{2}$'' to $\frac{3}{4}$'' thick	6	2	Finishing or casing nails.
Ceiling, trim, casing, base, jambs, trim and members $\frac{3}{4}$'' to 1'' thick	8	2 $\frac{1}{2}$	Finishing or casing nails.
Doors and window trim, boards and other members 1'' to 1 $\frac{1}{4}$'' thick	10	3	Finishing or casing nails.
Drop siding, 1'' thick	7 or 9	2 $\frac{1}{4}$ or 2 $\frac{3}{4}$	Siding nails (7d), Casing nails (9d).
Bevel siding, $\frac{1}{2}$'' thick	6 or 8	2 or 2 $\frac{1}{2}$	Finishing nails (6d), Siding nails (8d).

WOOD FLOORING

See wood flooring page for nail sizes and types recommended.			Cut steel, wire, finishing, wire casing, flooring brads, parquet and flooring nails.

LATHING

	PENNY	INCHES	TYPE OF NAIL
Wood lath	3	1 $\frac{1}{4}$	Blued lath nail.
Gypsum lath	3	1 $\frac{1}{4}$	Blued common.
Fiber lath			
Metal lath, interior		1	Blued lath nails, staples or offset head nails.
Metal lath, exterior	3	1 $\frac{1}{4}$	Self furring nails (double heads). Staples or cement coated.

SHEATHING OR SIDING

	PENNY	INCHES	TYPE OF NAIL
Asbestos $\frac{3}{8}$'' thick		1 $\frac{1}{4}$	Galvanized roofing nail with $\frac{7}{16}$'' diameter head.
Fiber board $\frac{1}{2}$'' and 2 $\frac{5}{32}$''		1 $\frac{1}{2}$ to 2	Galvanized roofing nail with $\frac{7}{16}$'' diameter head.
Gypsum board $\frac{1}{2}$''		1 $\frac{3}{4}$	Galvanized roofing nail with $\frac{7}{16}$'' diameter head.
Plywood $\frac{5}{16}$'' and $\frac{3}{8}$'' thick	6	2	Common nails.
Plywood $\frac{1}{2}$'' and $\frac{5}{8}$'' thick	8	2 $\frac{1}{2}$	Common nails.

ROOFING & SHEET METAL

		PENNY	INCHES	TYPE OF NAIL
Aluminum roofing		1	1 $\frac{3}{4}$ to 2 $\frac{1}{2}$	Aluminum nail, neoprene washer optional.
Asbestos, corrugated or sheets		Depends on thickness		Leakproof roofing nails.
Asbestos shingles			1 to 2	See "Asbestos Cement Roofing and Siding."
Asphalt shingles				Galvanized large head roofing.
Copper cleats and flashing to wood				Copper wire or cut slating nails.
Copper cleats and flashing to prevent joints				Barbed copper nails.
Clay tile		4 to 6	1 $\frac{1}{2}$ to 2	Copper nails.
Prepared felt roofing			1 to 1 $\frac{1}{4}$	Zinc roofing nails or large head roofing nails (barbed preferred). Heads may be reinforced.
Shingles, wood	usual size	3 to 4	1 $\frac{1}{4}$ to 1 $\frac{1}{2}$	Zinc coated, copper wire shingle, copper clad shingle, cut iron
	for heavy butts	4 to 8	1 $\frac{1}{2}$ to 2 $\frac{1}{2}$	or cut steel.
Slate		Use nails 1'' larger than thickness of slate		Copper wire slating nail (large head). In dry climates zinc coated or copper clad nails may be used.
Tin, zinc roofing				Zinc coated nails (roofing or slating).
Monel roofing				Monel nail.
Nailing to sheet metal				Self tapping screws, helical drive screws.

TO CONCRETE OR CEMENT MORTAR

See following pages of fastening devices.			Concrete or cement nails (hardened), helical drive nails or drive bolts.

GENERAL NOTES

1. Nail diameter, length, shape and surface affect holding power (withdrawal resistance and lateral resistance). See NFPA publications.

2. Materials: Zinc, brass, monel, copper, aluminum, iron or steel, stainless steel, copper bearing steel, muntz metal.

3. Coatings: Tin, copper, cement, brass plated, zinc, nickel, chrome, cadmium, etched acid, parkerized.

4. Forms: Smooth, barbed, helical, annular-ring.

5. Colors: Blue, bright, coppered, black (annealed).

6. Gauges shown are for steel wire (Washburn and Moen).

7. Abbreviations (for the following pages of nails only):

B = blunt	F = flat	O = oval
CS = countersunk	L = long	PC = pointing cone
D = diamond	N = narrow	R = round

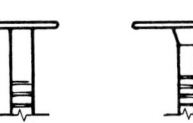   

FLAT COMMON | LARGE FLAT | LARGE FLAT REINFORCED | WIRE SPIKE | CHECKERED ROOFING

   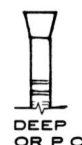 

SINKERS CORKER | TWINHEAD FLAT-CS | L N ALSO BRAD | DEEP OR P C | CUPPED CS

OVAL | ROUND | OVAL CS | ROUND CS | OFFSET

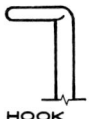    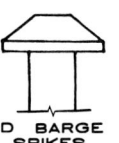

HOOK | NON-LEAK | CONE | HEADLESS DOWELS | D BARGE SPIKES

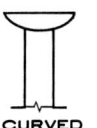  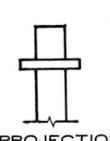   

CURVED | CURLICUE | PROJECTION | NUMERAL & LETTERED | CUT NAIL | BRAD HEAD

TYPES OF NAIL HEADS

 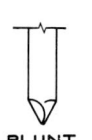   

ROUND | BLUNT | DIAMOND | LONG DIAMOND | NEEDLE

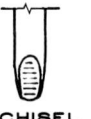   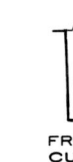 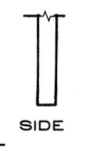

CHISEL POINT | FRONT SHEARED | SIDE BEVEL | FRONT CUT NAIL | SIDE

TYPES OF NAIL POINTS

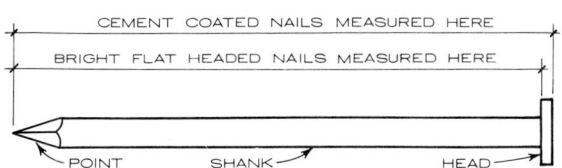

CEMENT COATED NAILS MEASURED HERE
BRIGHT FLAT HEADED NAILS MEASURED HERE
POINT — SHANK — HEAD

COMMON NAIL (STEEL WIRE)

LENGTH (IN INS.)	PENNY	GAUAGE	DIAM. OF HEAD (IN INS.)	NO. OF NAILS PER LB.	SAFE WORKING RESISTANCE TO LATERAL SHEAR-LB.
1	2	15	$^{11}/_{64}$	847	
$1\,^1/_4$	3	14	$^{13}/_{64}$	543	
$1\,^1/_2$	4	$12\,^1/_2$	$^1/_4$	296	
$1\,^3/_4$	5	$12\,^1/_2$	$^1/_4$	254	
2	6	$11\,^1/_2$	$^{17}/_{64}$	167	48
$2\,^1/_4$	7	$11\,^1/_2$	$^{17}/_{64}$	150	
$2\,^1/_2$	8	$10\,^1/_4$	$^9/_{32}$	101	64
$2\,^3/_4$	9	$10\,^1/_4$	$^9/_{32}$	92.1	
3	10	9	$^5/_{16}$	66	80
$3\,^1/_4$	12	9	$^5/_{16}$	66.1	96
$3\,^1/_2$	16	8	$^{11}/_{32}$	47.4	128
4	20	6	$^{13}/_{32}$	29.7	160
$4\,^1/_2$	30	5	$^7/_{16}$	22.7	
5	40	4	$^{15}/_{32}$	17.3	
$5\,^1/_2$	50	3	$^1/_2$	13.5	
6	60	2	$^{17}/_{32}$	10.7	

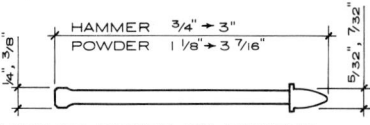

HAMMER 3/4" → 3"
POWDER 1 1/8" → 3 7/16"

HAMMER DRIVEN OR POWDER DRIVEN PIN

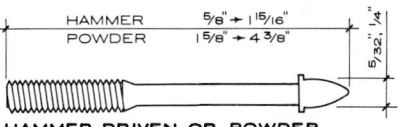

HAMMER 5/8" → 1 15/16"
POWDER 1 5/8" → 4 3/8"

HAMMER DRIVEN OR POWDER DRIVEN HEADLESS THREADED STUD

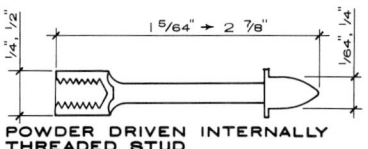

1 5/64" → 2 7/8"

POWDER DRIVEN INTERNALLY THREADED STUD

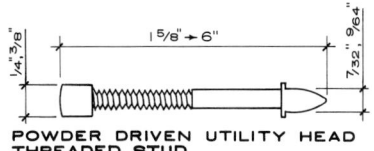

1 5/8" → 6"

POWDER DRIVEN UTILITY HEAD THREADED STUD

NOTE

1. Thread sizes and lengths vary.

2. Hammer and powder driven studs are intended for insertion into materials such as concrete, steel, etc.

3. Different stud heads and various attaching devices are available.

NAIL TYPE		SIZE		MATERIAL
F D #14 GAUGE	BARBED NAILS	1/4" TO 1 1/2"		CEMENT COATED, BRASS, STEEL
LCSN D #14 GAUGE	CASING NAILS	2d TO 40d 6d TO 10d		BRIGHT, CEMENT COATED CUPPED HEADS AVAILABLE IN ALUMINUM
O ALSO FLAT HEAD CS D #5 TO #10 GAUGE	CEMENT NAILS ALSO CALLED CONCRETE NAILS & HARDENED NAILS	1/2" TO 3"		SMOOTH, BRIGHT OIL QUENCHED
L N F CUP HEAD AVAILABLE #15 TO #2 GAUGE	COMMON BRAD	2d TO 60d		BRIGHT—MAY BE SECURED WITH CUPPED HEAD, CEMENT COATED—USUALLY MADE IN HEAVY GAUGES
F	CUT COMMON NAILS OR CUT COMMON SPIKE	2d TO 60d 20d TO 100d		STEEL OR IRON PLAIN OR ZINC COATED
L N F D GAUGE	COMMON NAILS (SHINGLE NAILS)	2d TO 60d		COPPER—CLAD
F D LIGHT GAUGE 095" HEAVY GAUGE 120"	COMMON BRASS WIRE NAILS	LIGHT GAUGE	1/2", 1" TO 3 1/2"	BRASS, ALUMINUM
		HEAVY GAUGE	3/4"—6"	
F D 109 (ABOUT 12 GAUGE)	COMMON NAILS; (SHINGLE NAILS)	5/8" TO 6"		COPPER WIRE, ALUMINUM
F	STANDARD CUT NAILS (NON-FERROUS)	5/8" TO 6"		COPPER, MUNTZ METAL OR ZINC
F 2" LONG D #11 1/2 GAUGE DOUBLE HEADED		1 3/4", 2", 2 1/4", 2 1/2", 2 3/4", 3", 3 1/2", 4", 4 1/2"		BRIGHT, CEMENT COATED, MADE IN SEVERAL DESIGNS
CUPPED HEAD AVAILABLE D MADE IN 5 DIAMETERS	DOWEL PINS	5/8" TO 2"		BARBED — CUPPED HEAD AVAILABLE
O D MADE IN 3 GAUGES	ESCUTCHEON PINS	1/4" TO 2"		BRIGHT STEEL, BRASS PLATED, BRASS, ALSO NICKEL, SILVER, COPPER, ALUMINUM
F 6d—2" D #10 GAUGE FENCE NAILS		5d TO 20d		SMOOTH; BRIGHT, CEMENT COATED (GAUGE HEAVIER THAN COMMON)
L N F D #15 GAUGE	FINISHING NAIL, WIRE	2d TO 20d		SMOOTH; CUPPED HEADS AVAILABLE (SMALLER GAUGE THAN USUAL COMMON BRAD)
	FINISHING NAILS	STANDARD FINE	3d TO 20d 6d TO 10d	CUT IRON AND STEEL
3d—1 1/8" #15 & #16 GAUGE	FINE NAILS	2d & 2d EX.FINE 3d & 3d EX.FINE		BRIGHT—SMALLER GAUGE & HEADS THAN COMMON NAILS
PC B (ALSO WITH D. POINT) FLOORING NAILS #14 GAUGE		3d TO 20d 6d TO 20d		BRIGHT & CEMENT COATED (DIFFERENT GAUGE) CUPPED HEADS AVAILABLE
L N CS 6d—2" D OR BLUNT D #11 GAUGE FLOORING BRAD		6d TO 20d		SMOOTH; BRIGHT & CEMENT COATED CUPPED HEADS AVAILABLE

NAIL TYPE	SIZE		MATERIAL
NCSF 1⅛" NEEDLE #15 GAUGE PARQUET FLOORING NAIL OR BRAD	1", 1⅛," 1¼"		SMOOTH OR BARBED
FLOORING NAILS	4d TO 10d		IRON OR STEEL (CUT)
OVAL, - ALSO CS HEAD ¼" HEAVY CHISEL HINGE NAILS	HEAVY: ¼" TO ⅜" DIA.	1½"TO 4"LONG	SMOOTH, BRIGHT OR ANNEALED
	LIGHT-3/16" TO ¼" DIA		
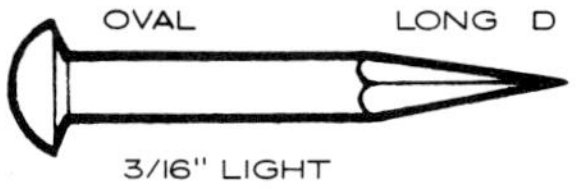 OVAL LONG D 3/16" LIGHT HINGE NAILS	HEAVY-¼" DIA.	1½"TO 3"ALSO TO 4"	SMOOTH, BRIGHT OR ANNEALED
	LIGHT - 3/16" DIA.		
F 3d-1⅛" D #15 GAUGE LATH NAILS (WOOD)	2d, 2d LIGHT 3d 3d, LIGHT,3d HEAVY 4d.		BRIGHT (NOT RECOMMENDED) BLUED OR CEMENT COATED
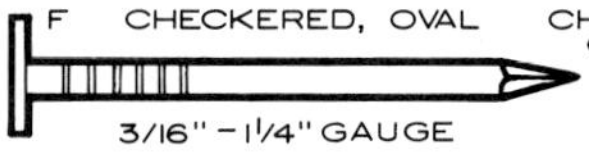 F CHECKERED, OVAL CHISEL OR D 3/16" – 1¼" GAUGE GUTTER SPIKES	6" TO 10"		STEEL, ZINC COATED
O R #6½" GAUGE HINGE NAILS	1½" TO 3"		STEEL, ZINC COATED
HOOK 1⅛" #12 GAUGE LATH NAILS (METAL)	1⅛"		BRIGHT, BLUED, ZINC COATED, ANNEALED
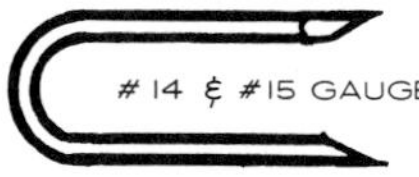 #14 ¢ #15 GAUGE LATH STAPLES	1" TO 1½"		BRIGHT, BLUED, ZINC COATED, ANNEALED
 OFFSET F D #10 GAUGE LATH OFFSET HEAD NAILS FOR SELF FURRING METAL LATH	1¼" TO 1¾"		BRIGHT, ZINC COATED
 F #7 - #9 GAUGE MASONRY NAILS USED FOR FURRING STRIPS CLEATS, PLATES	½" TO 4"		HIGH CARBON STEEL, HEATED ¢ TEMPERED
 NCSF NEEDLE #14 GAUGE MOLDING NAILS (BRADS)	⅞" TO 1¼"		SMOOTH, BRIGHT OR CEMENT COATED
½" D #9 OR #10 GAUGE PLASTER-BOARD NAILS USED ALSO FOR WALL-BOARD ROCK LATH (5/16" HEAD)	1" TO 1¾" 1⅛" TO 1½"		SMOOTH, BRIGHT OR CEMENT COATED, BLUED ALUMINUM
 F D #10 GAUGE ROOFING NAILS (STANDARD)	¾" TO 2"		BRIGHT, CEMENT COATED, ZINC COATED BARBED
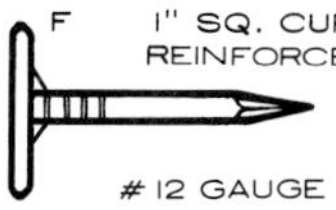 F 1" SQ. CUP REINFORCED D #12 GAUGE ROOFING NAILS FOR BUILT-UP ROOFING	⅜" TO 2"		STEEL, ZINC COATED
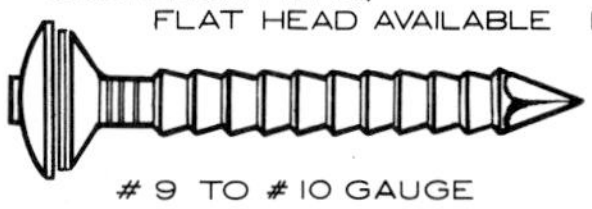 UMBRELLA HEAD, FLAT HEAD AVAILABLE D #9 TO #10 GAUGE NEOPRENE WASHER ROOFING NAILS	1½" TO 2½"		STEEL, ZINC COATED
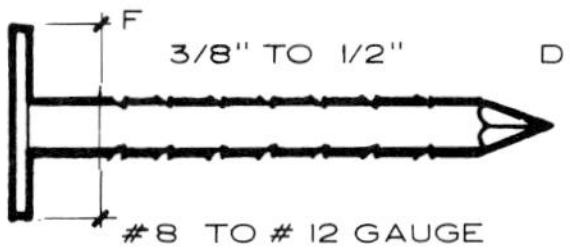 F 3/8" TO ½" D #8 TO #12 GAUGE ROOFING NAILS LARGE HEAD	¾" TO 1¾" ALSO 2" ¾" TO 2½"		BARBED, BRIGHT OR ZINC COATED CHECKERED HEAD AVAILABLE ALUMINUM (ETCHED) NEOPRENE WASHER OPTIONAL

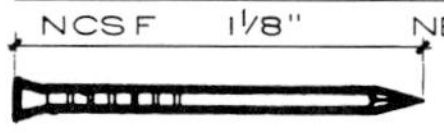

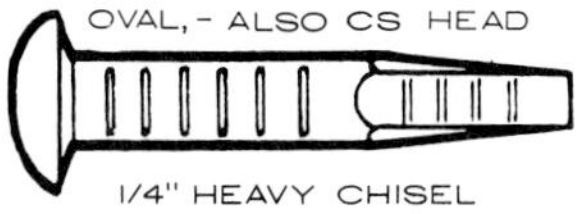

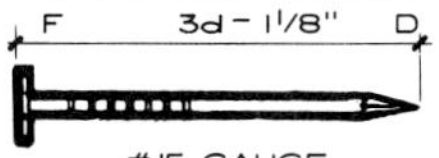

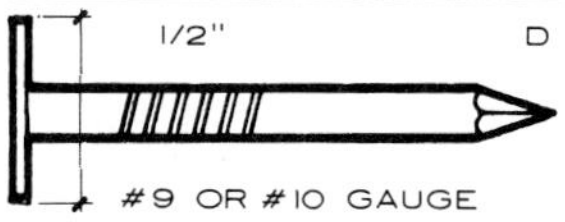

NAIL TYPE	SIZE	MATERIAL
ROOFING NAILS LARGE HEAD — F REINFORCED 5/8" DIA. 1¼" — NEEDLE OR D — #11 TO #12 GAUGE ALSO #10 GAUGE	3/4" TO 1¼"	BRIGHT OR ZINC COATED
NON-LEAKING ROOFING NAIL — #10 GAUGE	1¾" TO 2"	ZINC COATED, ALSO WITH LEAD HEADS
CUT SHEATHING NAILS	3/4" TO 3"	COPPER OR MUNTZ METAL
SHINGLE NAILS — F LARGE HEAD AVAILABLE 1/4" TO 9/32" 5/16" DIA. — #12 GAUGE D	3d TO 6d 2d TO 6d	SMOOTH, BRIGHT, ZINC, CEMENT COATED, LIGHT AND HEAVY ALUMINUM
CUT SHINGLE NAILS	2d TO 6d	IRON OR STEEL (CUT) PLAIN OR ZINC COATED
SIDING NAILS — F D — #14 GAUGE	2d TO 40d 6d TO 10d	SMOOTH, BRIGHT OR CEMENT COATED SMALLER DIAMETER THAN COMMON NAILS ALUMINUM
SIDING NAILS USED FOR FENCES, TANKS, GATES, ETC. — F D — #11 GAUGE	2½" TO 3"	STEEL ZINC COATED
SLATING NAILS — F 5/16" TO 3/8" — SEVERAL GAUGES	3/8" HEAD 1"TO 2" SMALL HEADS 1"TO 2" COPPER WIRE 7/8"-1½"	ZINC COATED, BRIGHT, CEMENT COATED, COPPER CLAD, COPPER
CUT SLATING NAILS, NON-FERROUS	1¼" TO 2"	COPPER, ZINC OR MUNTZ METAL
BARGE SPIKE, SQUARE — OVAL, SQUARE OR ROUND HEAD CHISEL POINT — 1/4" TO 5/8" SQ.	3" TO 12" ALSO 16"	PLAIN AND ZINC COATED USED FOR HARDWOOD
BOAT SPIKE, SQUARE — SQUARE OR DIAMOND HEAD 7/32" TO 1⅛" DIA. CHISEL POINT — 1/4" TO 5/8" SQ.	3" TO 12"	PLAIN AND ZINC COATED USED FOR HARD WOOD
ROOF DECK NAILS — 1" HEAD	1" AND 1¾"	GALVANIZED - NAILS STEEL TUBE
ROUND WIRE SPIKES — F OR OCS D OR CHISEL POINT — #6 TO 3/8" GAUGE	10d TO 60d & 7" TO 12" ALSO 16"	SMOOTH, BRIGHT OR ZINC COATED

SCREW & BOLT LENGTHS (IN INCHES)

DIAMETER (IN INCHES)	CAP SCREWS		BOLTS			
	BUTTON HEAD	FLAT HEAD	HEXAGON HEAD	FILLISTER HEAD	MACHINE BOLT	CARRIAGE BOLT
$1/4$	$1/2 - 2\,1/4$	$1/2 - 3\,1/2$	$3/4 - 3$	$1/2 - 8$	$3/4 - 8$	
$5/16$	$1/2 - 2\,3/4$	$1/2 - 3\,1/2$	$3/4 - 3\,3/4$	$1/2 - 8$	$3/4 - 8$	
$3/8$	$5/8 - 3$	$1/2 - 4$	$3/4 - 3\,1/2$	$3/4 - 12$	$3/4 - 12$	
$7/16$	$3/4 - 3$	$3/4 - 4$	$3/4 - 3\,3/4$	$3/4 - 12$	$1 - 12$	
$1/2$	$3/4 - 4$	$3/4 - 4\,1/2$	$3/4 - 4$	$3/4 - 24$	$1 - 20$	
$9/16$	$1 - 4$	$1 - 4\,1/2$	$1 - 4$	$1 - 30$	$1 - 20$	
$5/8$	$1 - 4$	$1 - 5$	$1\,1/4 - 4\,1/2$	$1 - 30$	$1 - 20$	
$3/4$	$1 - 4$	$1\,1/4 - 5$	$1\,1/2 - 4\,1/2$	$1 - 30$	$1 - 20$	
$7/8$		$2 - 6$	$1\,3/4 - 5$	$1\,1/2 - 30$		
1		$2 - 6$	$2 - 5$	$1\,1/2 - 30$		

Length intervals = $1/8''$ increments up to $1''$, $1/4''$ increments from $1\,1/4''$ to $4''$, $1/2''$ increments from $4\,1/2''$ to $6''$.

Length intervals = $1/4''$ increments up to $6''$, $1/2''$ increments from $6\,1/2''$ to $12''$, $1''$ increments over $12''$.

MACHINE SCREW & STOVE BOLT (IN INCHES)

STOVE BOLT DIAMETER (IN INS)	MACHINE SCREW DIAMETER	ROUND HEAD	FLAT HEAD	FILLISTER HEAD	OVAL HEAD	OVEN HEAD
	2	$1/8 - 7/8$			$1/8 - 7/8$	
	3	$1/8 - 7/8$			$1/8 - 7/8$	
	4	$1/8 - 1\,1/2$	40 N.C.		$1/8 - 1\,1/2$	
	4	$1/8 - 1\,1/2$	36 N.C.		$1/8 - 1\,1/2$	$1/8 - 3/4$
$1/8$	5	$1/8 - 2$			$1/8 - 2$	$3/8 - 2$
	6	$1/8 - 2$			$1/8 - 2$	$1/8 - 1$
$5/32$	8	$3/16 - 3$			$3/16 - 3$	$3/16 - 2$
$3/16$	10	$3/16 - 6$			$3/16 - 3$	$1/4 - 6$
	12	$1/4 - 3$			$1/4 - 3$	
$1/4$	$1/4$	$5/16 - 6$			$5/16 - 3$	$3/8 - 6$
$5/16$	$5/16$	$3/8 - 6$			$3/8 - 3$	$3/4 - 6$
$3/8$	$3/8$	$1/2 - 5$			$1/2 - 3$	$3/4 - 5$
$1/2$	$1/2$	$1 - 4$				

Length intervals = $1/16''$ increments up to $1/2''$, $1/8''$ increments from $5/8''$ to $1\,1/4''$, $1/4''$ increments from $1\,1/2''$ to $3''$, $1/2''$ increments from $3\,1/2''$ to $6''$.

NUTS

SQUARE   HEXAGON   CAP   WING

HEADS

PHILLIPS

SLOTTED

NUT SIZES

Square and hexagon head nuts are available for all screws and bolts listed; Cap nuts for all except nos. 2, 3, 4 (40 N.C. only), 5, and $9/16''$. Wing nuts for all except nos. 2, 3, 4 (40 N.C.), 5, $9/16''$, $5/8''$, $3/4''$, $7/8''$ and $1''$.

American Standard sizes by the American Institute of Bolt, Nut and Rivet Manufacturers. Many of listed items also stocked in aluminum, brass, copper, stainless steel, monel and bronze. Stove bolts have wider tolerances than machine screws.

SHEET METAL & THREADING SCREWS

SHEET METAL GIMLET POINT.

Hardened, self-tapping. Used in 28 to 6 gauge sheet metal; aluminum, plastic, slate, etc. Usual head types.

SHEET METAL BLUNT POINT.

Hardened, self-tapping. Used in 28 to 18 gauge sheet metal. Made in 4 to 14 sizes and usual heads.

THREAD CUTTING-CUTTING SLOT.

Hardened. Used in metals up to $1/4''$ thick. Sizes: 4 to $5/16''$, in usual head types. (Flat, oval, round, etc.).

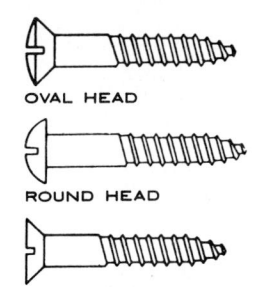

OVAL HEAD

ROUND HEAD

FLAT HEAD

WOOD SCREWS (IN INCHES)

DIAM.	DECI. EQUIV.	LENGTH
0	.060	$1/4 - 3/8$
1	.073	$1/4 - 1/2$
2	.086	$1/4 - 3/4$
3	.099	$1/4 - 1$
4	.112	$1/4 - 1\,1/2$
5	.125	$3/8 - 1\,1/2$
6	.138	$3/8 - 2\,1/2$
7	.151	$3/8 - 2\,1/2$
8	.164	$3/8 - 3$
9	.177	$1/2 - 3$
10	.190	$1/2 - 3\,1/2$
11	.203	$5/8 - 3\,1/2$
12	.216	$5/8 - 4$
14	.242	$3/4 - 5$
16	.268	$1 - 5$
18	.294	$1\,1/4 - 5$
20	.320	$1\,1/2 - 5$
24	.372	$3 - 5$

Length intervals = $1/8''$ increments up to $1''$, $1/4''$ increments from $1\,1/4''$ to $3''$, $1/2''$ increments from $3\,1/2''$ to $5''$.

LAG BOLT (IN INCHES)

DIAM. (IN INS)	DECI. EQUIV.	LENGTH
$1/4$	.250	$1 - 6$
$5/16$	.313	$1 - 10$
$3/8$	.375	$1 - 12$
$7/16$	.438	$1 - 12$
$1/2$	.500	$1 - 12$
$5/8$	.625	$1\,1/2 - 16$
$3/4$	.750	$1\,1/2 - 16$
$7/8$	.875	$2 - 16$
1	1.00	$2 - 16$

Length intervals = $1/2''$ increments up to $8''$, $1''$ increments over $8''$.

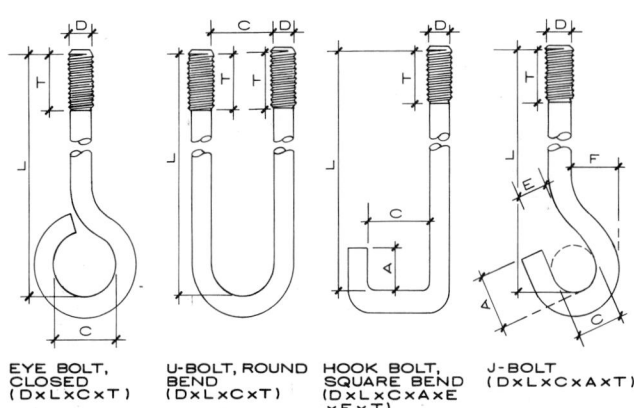

EYE BOLT, CLOSED (D×L×C×T)

U-BOLT, ROUND BEND (D×L×C×T)

HOOK BOLT, SQUARE BEND (D×L×C×A×E ×F×T)

J-BOLT (D×L×C×A×T)

BENT BOLT DETAILS

NOTES

1. Bent bolts are specialty items made to order.
2. D = diameter of bolt. C = inside opening width. T = length of thread. L = inside length of bolt. A = inside depth.

SQUARE HEAD **HEADLESS**

SET SCREWS

Headless type with socket or slotted top made in sizes 4 to $1/2$"; in $1/2$" to 5" lengths.

Square head sizes $1/4$" to 1"; $1/2$" to 5" lengths.

SOCKET TOP

SLOTTED TOP

CUT
Of steel and non-ferrous metals.

O.G. CAST
Made of cast metal.

SPRING LOCK
Of steel, monel metal, bronze and stainless steel.

FAIRING
Of aluminum

INTERNAL TOOTH LOCK **EXTERNAL / INTERNAL TOOTH LOCK** **COUNTERSUNK TOOTH LOCK** **EXTERNAL TOOTH LOCK**

WASHERS
All types for bolts and screws of all sizes.

Tooth lock washers of steel, monel metal, bronze, beryllium, copper, and stainless steel

LOCKING SLEEVE

DRAW BOLT

THREAD SIZE 1/4" 20-2A

TIGHTENING BOLT

$4 \, 1/16$"

1"

$7/8$"

FLUSH JOINT WOOD FASTENER

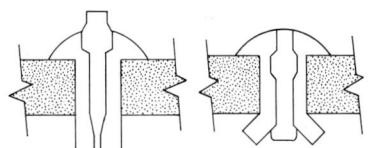

ROUND **TRUSS** **FLAT** **COUNTER SUNK** **PAN**

RIVETS

Standard Rivets available with solid, tubular and split shanks of steel, brass, copper, aluminum, monel metal and stainless steel; in diameters of $1/8$" up to $7/16$" and lengths of $3/16$" up to 4 inches.

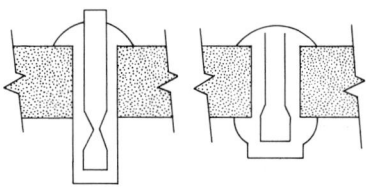

DRIVE PIN

PULL MANDREL

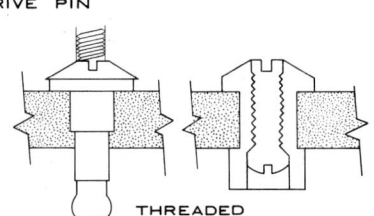

THREADED

CHEMICALLY EXPANDED

BLIND RIVETS FOR USE IN A JOINT THAT IS ACCESSIBLE FROM ONLY ONE SIDE

SPLIT RING (IN INCHES)

INSIDE DIAMETER	$2\,1/2$	4
DEPTH	$3/4$	1
BOLT DIAMETER	$1/2$	$3/4$
LUMBER MIN. DIMS. — RING-1 FACE	$1 \times 3\,5/8$	$1 \times 5\,1/2$
RING-2 FACE	$1\,5/8 \times 3\,5/8$	$1\,5/8 \times 5\,1/2$

Made from SAE 1010 carbon steel.

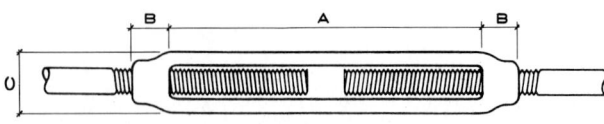

B A B

TURNBUCKLE WITH STUB ENDS

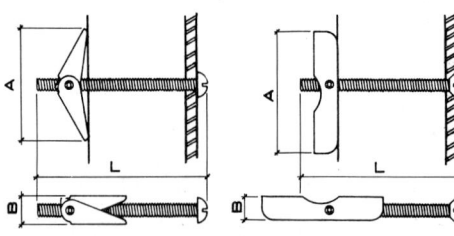

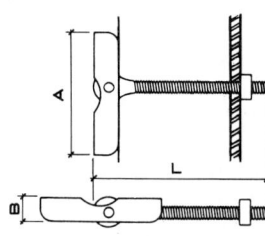

SPRING WING **TUMBLE** **RIVETED TUMBLE**

A L B

EYE **HOOK**

TURNBUCKLES (IN INCHES)

DIAMETER	$1/4$	$5/16$	$3/8$	$1/2$	$5/8$	$3/4$	$7/8$	1
DECI. EQUIV.	.250	.313	.375	.500	.625	.750	.875	1.00
A	4	$4\,1/2$	6"	6" 9" 12"	6" 9" 12"	6" 9" 12"	6" 12"	6" 12"
B		$7/16$	$1/2$	$9/16$	$3/4$	$2\,9/32$	$1\,1/16$	$1\,7/32$	$1\,3/8$
C		$3/4$	$7/8$	$3\,1/32$	$1\,7/32$	$1\,1/2$	$1\,23/32$	$1\,7/8$	$2\,1/32$

DIAMETERS OVER 1" AVAILABLE, NOT ALWAYS STOCKED.

TOGGLE BOLTS (IN INCHES)

DIAMETER		$1/8$	$5/32$	$3/16$	$1/4$	$5/16$	$3/8$	$1/2$
DECIMAL EQUIV.		.138	.164	.190	.250	.313	.375	.500
SPRING WING	A	1.438	1.875	1.875	2.063	2.750	2.875	4.625
	B	.375	.500	.500	.688	.875	1.000	1.250
	L	2 – 4	$2\,1/2$ – 4	2 – 6	$2\,1/2$ – 6	3 – 6	3 – 6	4 – 6
TUMBLE	A	1.250	2.000	2.000	2.250	2.750	2.750	
	B	.375	.500	.500	.688	.875	.875	
	L	2 – 4	$2\,1/2$ – 4	3 – 6	3 – 6	3 – 6	3 – 6	
RIVETED TUMBLE	A		2.000	2.000	2.250	2.750	2.750	3.375
	B		.375	.375	.500	.625	.688	.875
	L		$2\,1/2$ – 4	3 – 6	3 – 6	3 – 6	3 – 6	3 – 6

MACHINE BOLT ANCHORS AND SHIELDS (IN.)

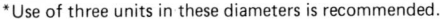

BOLT DIAM.	THPS PER INCH	DECIMAL EQUIV. (IN.)	SINGLE EXPANDING ANCHOR (CALKING)		SINGLE EXPANDING ANCHOR (NONCALKING)		MULTIPLE EXPANDING ANCHOR (PLAIN STYLE)			MULTIPLE EXPANDING ANCHOR (THREADED STYLE)			DOUBLE ACTING SHIELD	
								L UNITS			L UNITS			
			A	L	A	L	A	2	3	A	2	3	A	L
6	32	.138	5/16	1/2										
8	32	.164	5/16	1/2										
10	24	.190	3/8	5/8										
12	24	.216	1/2	7/8										
1/4	20	.250	1/2	7/8	1/2	1 3/8	1/2"	1 1/8		1/2	1		1/2	1 1/4
5/16	18	.312	5/8	1	5/8	1 5/8							5/8	1 1/2
3/8	16	.375	3/4	1 1/4	5/8	1 5/8	3/4	1 1/2		3/4	1 1/2		3/4	1 3/4
1/2	13	.500	7/8	1 1/2	7/8	2 1/2	1	1 3/4	2 3/8	1	1 3/4	2 1/4	7/8	2 1/4
5/8	11	.625	1 1/8	2	1	2 3/4	1 1/8	*	2 5/8	1 1/8	*	2 1/2	1	2 1/2
3/4	10	.750	1 1/4	2 1/4	1 1/4	2 7/8	1 3/8	*	3	1 3/8	*	3 1/8	1 1/4	3 1/2
7/8	9	.875					1 1/2	*	3 1/2	1 1/2	*	3 5/8	1 5/8	4"
1	8	1.00					1 5/8	*	3 7/8	1 5/8	*	3 3/4	1 3/4	4 1/4

*Use of three units in these diameters is recommended.

NOTE
1. Extension sleeve for deep setting.
2. Expansion shields and anchors shown are representative of many types, some of which may be used in single or multiple units.

Many are threaded for use with the head of the screw outside, some with the head inside and some types require setting tools to install.
In light construction plastic expansion shields are used frequently.

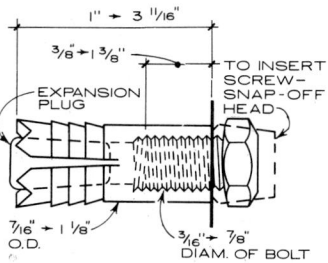

SELF DRILLING EXPANSION ANCHOR (SNAP-OFF TYPE)

NOTE
1. Refer to manufacturers for size variations within the limits shown, and for different types of bolts.
2. The anchor is made of case hardened steel and drawn carburizing steel.

HOLLOW WALL ANCHORS

ANCHOR DIAM. (IN.)	A	L	A	L
1/8	5/16	1-2 9/16		XS-L
3/16	7/16	2 1/4-3 1/2		
1/4	1/2	2 1/4-3 1/2		

SHIELDS FOR LAG BOLTS AND WOOD SCREWS (IN.)

LAG SCREW DIAM. (IN.)	WOOD SCREW SIZES	DECIMAL EQUIV. (IN.)	LAG BOLT EXPANSION SHIELD A	L SHORT	LONG	LEAD SHIELD FOR LAG BOLT OR WOOD SCREW A	L
	6	.138				1/4	3/4-1 1/2
	8	.164				1/4	3/4-1 1/2
	10	.190				5/16	1-1 1/2
	12	.216				5/16	1-1 1/2
1/4	14	.250	1/2	1	1 1/2	5/16	1-1 1/2
	16	.268				3/8	1 1/2
	18	.294				3/8	1 1/2
5/16	20	.320	1/2	1 1/4	1 3/4	7/16	1 3/4
3/8	24	.372	5/8	1 3/4	2 1/2	7/16	1 3/4
1/2		.500	3/4	2	3		
5/8		.625	7/8	2	3 1/2		
3/4		.750	1	2	3 1/2		

ONE PIECE ANCHORS (IN.)

ANCHOR SIZE AND DRILL SIZE	DECIMAL EQUIV. (IN.)	WEDGE ANCHOR L	MIN. HOLE DEPTH D	STUD ANCHOR L	MIN. HOLE DEPTH D	SLEEVE ANCHOR L	MIN. HOLE DEPTH D	HEAD STYLE
1/4	.250	1 3/4-3 1/4	1 3/8	1 3/4-3 1/4	1 3/8	5/8-2 1/4	1/2-1 1/8	Acorn nut
5/16	.320					1 1/2-2 1/2	1 1/8	Hex nut
3/8	.375	2 1/4-5	1 3/4	2 1/4-6	1 5/8	1 7/8-3	1 1/2	"
1/2	.500	2 3/4-7	2 1/8	2 3/4-5 1/4	1 7/8	2 1/4-4	1 7/8	"
5/8	.625	3 1/2-8 1/2	2 5/8	3 3/8-7	2 3/8	2 1/4-6	2	"
3/4	.750	4 1/4-10	3 1/4	4 1/4-8 1/2	2 7/8	2 1/2-8	2 1/4-5 1/2	"
7/8	.875	6-10	3 3/4					
1	1.00	6-12	4 1/2					
1 1/4	1.25	9-12	5 1/2					

Sleeve anchors available in acorn nut, hex nut, flat head, round head, Phillips round head, and tie wire head styles.

EMBOSSED STEEL SHEETS are cold rolled carbon steel sheets with a decorative design rolled into the surface of the metal. The base metal is normally a low carbon steel and is available in three grades: commercial quality (CQ), drawing quality (DQ), and drawing quality special killed (DQSK).

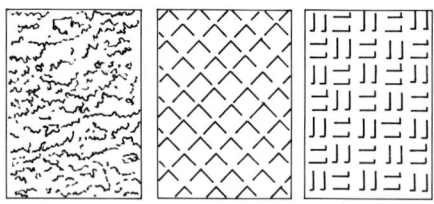

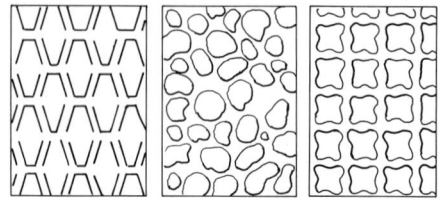

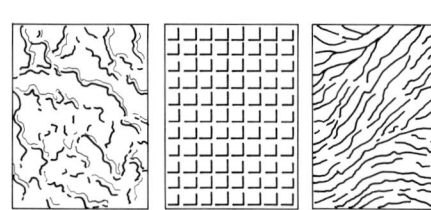

FINISH PERFORMANCE

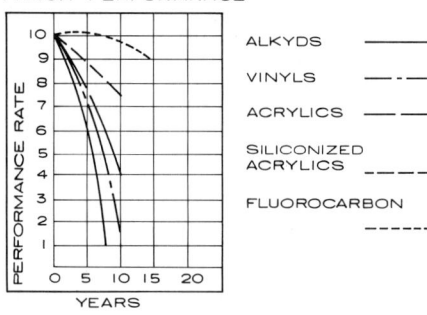

ALKYDS ——————

VINYLS ———·———

ACRYLICS ——— ——

SILICONIZED ACRYLICS ——— ———

FLUOROCARBON ------

NOTE

Performance rating is a weighted average of the factors that affect total performance of the coated metal: chalk resistance, gloss retention, color retention, erosion resistance, and abrasion resistance.

METAL CHARACTERISTICS

METAL	WEATHERED FINISH	PROBLEMS	REMARKS
Aluminum	Uniform gray patina	Avoid contact with dissimilar metals or concrete	High resistant atmospheric corrosion
Copper	Brown shades and finally to blue-green and gray-green patina		Weathered coating that resists corrosion
Lead	Soft gray patina	Reacts with uncured concrete or mortar if not protected by a bituminous or similar coating	Allowance must be made for its high thermal expansion
Steel (stainless)	Weather resistant		Various finishes from non-reflective matte to mirror
Steel (weathering)	Dark purple brown patina	Conditions where moisture collects and will not permit weathering oxide to form	Requires no painting or other maintenance
Terne	Should be painted	Avoid contact with aluminum copper or acidic metals	Low coefficient of expansion, requires relatively few expansion seams
Zinc	Gray matte patina	Avoid contact with acidic wood or with metals	Excellent forming properties and requires no paint

Mark E. Lord; R. D. Design Associates; Newport Beach, California

PAINTED FINISHES

FINISH	ADVANTAGES	TYPICAL USES
Fluorocarbons	Unexcelled in formability, color retention, resistance to solvents, and chalking	Curtain walls, residential siding, and industrial building components
Fluorocarbon film laminates	Provide long life and durability	Exterior siding and other exterior building products
Vinyl film laminates	Largest selection of colors, patterns, and third dimension	Televisions, humidifiers, store fixtures and shelving, lock seam tubing, and water coolers
Strippable coatings	Protection of polished or coated metals during forming and shipment	Exterior building panels and siding to be cut or formed at the construction site and appliance housings

CHEMICAL FINISHES

Alkaline etches	Wide variety of matte finishes. Diffuse reflector finishes. Deep etching and chemical milling. Cleaning prior to subsequent finishing procedures
Acid etches	Removal of stains and films. Variety of matte finishes. Chemical milling and deep etching
Bright dip	Finishes of superior luster and reflectance
Chemical milling	Selective deep removal of metal in a controlled manner by alkaline or acid etching
Immersion plating	Deposition of thin, metallic films of tin, zinc, lead silver, and copper by displacement reaction
Electroless plating	Deposition of nickel, cobalt, copper, gold, and palladium by autocatalytic reduction
Conversion coating	Inexpensive protective and decorative films of oxide, chromate, and phosphate coatings

MECHANICAL FINISHES

Grinding	Removes coarse surface irregularities
Polishing	Smooths the surface and imparts a texture
Buffing	Smooths the surface to a bright finish
Satin finishing	Brushes the surface to a semi-lustrous texture
Coining and embossing	Stamps and embosses the surface with various patterns
Abrasive blasting	Blasts the surface to a textured matte finish
Shot peening	Peens the surface to a deep textured patterned finish
Barrel burnishing	Burnishes the surface bright and smooth

ANODIC FINISHES

Chromic acid coatings	Corrosion resistant coating primarily used as base for paint
Hard anodic coatings	Especially thick, dense coatings for wear resistance
Conventional anodic coatings	Durable, decorative, and protective
Integral colors	Colored anodic coatings largely dependent on alloy and electrolyte. Exhibit superior light fastness
Impregnated colors	1. Organic colorants provide a wide variety of colors and shades suitable for most interior applications and limited outdoor use 2. Inorganic colorants provide limited colors. Light fastness generally superior to organic colorants
Electrolytically deposited colors	Anodic coatings colored by electrolytic deposition of inorganic pigments. Also exhibit superior light-fastness

ELECTROPLATED FINISHES

Silver	For electrical equipment. Decrease contact resistance or improve surface conductivity
Tin or cadmium	For cable connectors, electrical contacts, and soldering applications, as well as for reducing friction on bearing surfaces
Brass	For decorative use
Copper or tin	For facilitating soft soldering
Chromium	For reducing friction or increasing wear resistance
Zinc	For a nontarnishing surface with high electrical conductivity, as in electronic applications
Lead or lead-tin	For soldering and to minimize galling
Rhodium over silver	For electronic use
Nickel	For decorative use and corrosion resistance

CHAPTER ⑥ WOOD

DESIGN VALUES FOR VISUALLY GRADED STRUCTURAL LUMBER—DESIGN VALUES LISTED ARE FOR NORMAL LOADING CONDITIONS

Species and Commercial Grade (Surfaced Dry or Surfaced Green. Used at 19% max. M.C.)	Size Classification	Extreme Fiber in Bending, F_b — Single Member Uses	Extreme Fiber in Bending, F_b — Repetitive Member Uses	Tension Parallel to Grain F_t	Horizontal Shear F_v	Compression Perpendicular to Grain $F_{c\perp}$	Compression Parallel to Grain F_c	Modulus of Elasticity	Grading Rules Agency
BALSAM FIR, EASTERN SPRUCE									
Select Structural	2-4" thick	1350	1550	800	60	170	1050	1,200,000	NELMA NHPMA (see footnotes 1–6)
No. 1	2-4" wide	1150	1300	675	60	170	825	1,200,000	
No. 2		950	1100	550	60	170	650	1,100,000	
No. 3		525	600	300	60	170	400	900,000	
Stud		525	600	300	60	170	400	900,000	
Construction	2-4" thick	675	800	400	60	170	750	900,000	
Standard	4" wide	375	450	225	60	170	625	900,000	
Utility		175	200	100	60	170	400	900,000	
Select Structural	2-4" thick	1150	1350	775	60	170	925	1,200,000	NELMA (see footnotes 1–6)
No. 1	5" and wider	1000	1150	650	60	170	825	1,200,000	
No. 2		825	950	425	60	170	700	1,100,000	
No. 3		475	550	550	60	170	450	900,000	
Stud		475	550	250	60	170	450	900,000	
CALIFORNIA REDWOOD									
Select Decking*	Decking	1850	2150	—	—	—	—	1,400,000	RIS (see footnotes 1, 2, 6)
Select Decking	2" thick	1450	1700	—	—	—	—	1,100,000	
Commercial Decking	6" and wider	1200	1350	—	—	—	—	1,000,000	
DOUGLAS FIR-LARCH									
Select Structural	2-4" thick	2100	2400	1200	95	385	1600	1,800,000	
No. 1	2-4" wide	1750	2050	1050	95	385	1250	1,800,000	
No. 2		1450	1650	850	95	385	1000	1,700,000	
No. 3		800	925	475	95	385	600	1,500,000	
Appearance		1750	2050	1050	95	385	1500	1,800,000	
Stud		800	925	475	95	385	600	1,500,000	
Construction	2-4" thick	1050	1200	625	95	385	1150	1,500,000	WCLIB WWPA (see footnotes 1–6)
Standard	4" wide	600	675	350	95	385	925	1,500,000	
Utility		275	325	175	95	385	600	1,500,000	
Dense Select Structural	2-4" thick	2100	2400	1400	95	455	1650	1,900,000	
Select Structural	5" and wider	1800	2050	1200	95	385	1400	1,800,000	
Dense No. 1		1800	2050	1200	95	455	1450	1,900,000	
No. 1		1500	1750	1000	95	385	1250	1,800,000	
Dense No. 2		1450	1700	775	95	455	1250	1,700,000	
No. 2		1250	1450	650	95	385	1050	1,700,000	
No. 3		725	850	375	95	385	675	1,500,000	
Appearance		1500	1750	1000	95	385	1500	1,800,000	
Stud		725	850	375	95	385	675	1,500,000	
Dense Select Structural	Beams and stringers	1900	—	1100	85	455	1300	1,700,000	WCLIB (see footnotes 1–6)
Selected Structural		1600	—	950	85	385	1100	1,600,000	
Dense No. 1		1550	—	775	85	455	1100	1,700,000	
No. 1		1300	—	675	85	385	925	1,600,000	
Dense Select Structural	Posts and timbers	1750	—	1150	85	455	1350	1,700,000	
Select Structural		1500	—	1000	85	385	1150	1,600,000	
Dense No. 1		1400	—	950	85	455	1200	1,700,000	
No. 1		1200	—	825	85	385	1000	1,600,000	
Selected Decking	Decking	—	2000	—	—	—	—	1,600,000	WWPA (see footnotes 1–7)
Commercial Decking		—	1650	—	—	—	—	1,700,000	
Selected Decking	Decking	—	2150	(Surfaced at 15% max. m.c. and used at 15% max. m.c.)			—	1,900,000	
Commercial Decking		—	1800				—	1,700,000	
ENGELMANN SPRUCE-ALPINE FIR (ENGELMANN SPRUCE-LODGEPOLE PINE)									
Select Structural	2-4" thick	1350	1550	800	70	195	950	1,300,000	
No. 1	2-4" wide	1150	1250	675	70	195	750	1,300,000	
No. 2		950	1100	550	70	195	600	1,100,000	
No. 3		525	600	300	70	195	375	1,000,000	
Appearance		1150	1350	674	70	195	900	1,300,000	
Stud		525	600	300	70	195	375	1,000,000	
Construction	2-4" thick	700	800	400	70	195	675	1,000,000	
Standard	4" wide	375	450	225	70	195	550	1,000,000	
Utility		175	200	100	70	195	375	1,000,000	
Select Structural	2-4" thick	1200	1350	775	70	195	850	1,300,000	WWPA (see footnotes 1–7)
No. 1	5" and wider	1000	1150	675	70	195	750	1,300,000	
No. 2		825	950	425	70	195	625	1,100,000	
No. 3		475	550	250	70	195	400	1,000,000	
Appearance		1000	1150	675	70	195	900	1,300,000	
Stud		475	550	250	70	195	400	1,000,000	
Select Structural	Beams and stringers	1050	—	700	65	195	675	1,100,000	
No. 1		875	—	600	65	195	550	1,100,000	
Select Structural	Posts and timbers	975	—	650	65	195	700	1,100,000	
No. 1		800	—	525	65	195	625	1,100,000	
Selected Decking	Decking	—	1300	—	—	—	—	1,300,000	
Commercial Decking		—	1100	—	—	—	—	1,100,000	
Selected Decking	Decking	—	1400	(Surfaced at 15% max. m.c. and used at 15% max. m.c.)			—	1,300,000	
Commercial Decking		—	1200				—	1,200,000	

*Close grain.

National Forest Products Association; Washington, D.C.

GENERAL INFORMATION

DESIGN VALUES FOR VISUALLY GRADED STRUCTURAL LUMBER—DESIGN VALUES LISTED ARE FOR NORMAL LOADING CONDITIONS

SPECIES AND COMMERCIAL GRADE (SURFACED DRY OR SURFACED GREEN. USED AT 19% MAX. M.C.)	SIZE CLASSIFICATION	EXTREME FIBER IN BENDING, F_b SINGLE MEMBER USES	REPETITIVE MEMBER USES	TENSION PARALLEL TO GRAIN F_t	HORIZONTAL SHEAR F_v	COMPRESSION PERPENDICULAR TO GRAIN $F_{c\perp}$	COMPRESSION PARALLEL TO GRAIN F_c	MODULUS OF ELASTICITY	GRADING RULES AGENCY
HEM-FIR									
Select Structural	2-4" thick	1650	1900	975	75	245	1300	1,500,000	
No. 1	2-4" wide	1400	1600	825	75	245	1050	1,500,000	
No. 2		1150	1350	675	75	245	825	1,400,000	
No. 3		650	725	375	75	245	500	1,200,000	
Appearance		1400	1600	825	75	245	1250	1,500,000	
Stud		650	725	375	75	245	500	1,200,000	
Construction	2-4" thick	825	975	500	75	245	925	1,200,000	WCLIB
Standard	4" wide	475	550	275	75	245	775	1,200,000	WWPA
Utility		225	250	125	75	245	500	1,200,000	(see footnotes 1-6)
Select Structural	2-4" thick	1400	1650	950	75	245	1150	1,500,000	
No. 1	5" and wider	1200	1400	800	75	245	1050	1,500,000	
No. 2		1000	1150	525	75	245	875	1,400,000	
No. 3		575	675	300	75	245	550	1,200,000	
Appearance		1200	1400	800	75	245	1250	1,500,000	
Stud		575	675	300	75	245	550	1,200,000	
Select Structural	Beams and	1300	—	750	70	245	925	1,300,000	
No. 1	stringers	1050	—	525	70	245	750	1,300,000	WCLIB
Select Structural	Posts and	1200	—	800	70	245	975	1,300,000	(see footnotes 1-6)
No. 1	timbers	975	—	650	70	245	850	1,300,000	
Selected Decking	Decking	—	1600	—	—	—	—	1,500,000	
Commercial Decking		—	1350	—	—	—	—	1,400,000	
Selected Decking	Decking	—	1700	(Surfaced at 15% max. m.c. and used at 15% max. m.c.)			—	1,600,000	WWPA
Commercial Decking		—	1450				—	1,400,000	(see footnotes 1-7)
IDAHO WHITE PINE									
Selected Decking	Decking	—	1300	—	—	—	—	1,400,000	
Commercial Decking		—	1050	—	—	—	—	1,300,000	WWPA
Selected Decking	Decking	—	1400	(Surfaced at 15% max. m.c. and used at 15% max. m.c.)			—	1,500,000	(see footnotes 1-7)
Commercial Decking		—	1150				—	1,400,000	
NORTHERN PINE									
Select structural	2-4" thick	1650	1850	950	70	280	1200	1,400,000	
No. 1	2-4" wide	1400	1600	825	70	280	875	1,400,000	
No. 2		1150	1200	675	70	280	775	1,300,000	
No. 3		625	725	375	70	280	475	1,100,000	
Appearance		1200	1400	800	70	280	1150	1,400,000	
Stud		625	725	375	70	280	475	1,100,000	
Construction	2-4" thick	825	950	475	70	280	875	1,100,000	NELMA
Standard	4" wide	450	525	275	70	280	725	1,100,000	NHPMA
Utility		225	250	125	70	280	475	1,100,000	(see footnotes 1-6)
Select Structural	2-4" thick	1400	1600	950	70	280	1100	1,400,000	
No. 1	5" and wider	1200	1400	800	70	280	975	1,400,000	
No. 2		950	1100	525	70	280	825	1,300,000	
No. 3		575	650	300	70	280	525	1,100,000	
Appearance		1200	1400	800	70	280	1150	1,400,000	
Stud		575	650	300	70	280	525	1,100,000	
PONDEROSA PINE-SUGAR PINE (PONDEROSA PINE-LODGEPOLE PINE)									
Select Structural	2-4" thick	1400	1650	825	70	235	1050	1,200,000	
No. 1	2-4" wide	1200	1400	700	70	235	850	1,200,000	
No. 2		1000	1150	575	70	235	675	1,100,000	
No. 3		550	625	325	70	235	400	1,000,000	
Appearance		1200	1400	700	70	235	1000	1,200,000	
Stud		550	625	325	70	235	400	1,000,000	
Construction	2-4" thick	725	825	425	70	235	775	1,000,000	
Standard	4" wide	400	450	225	70	235	625	1,000,000	
Utility		200	225	100	70	235	400	1,000,000	
Select Structural	2-4" thick	1200	1400	825	70	235	950	1,200,000	WWPA
No. 1	5" and wider	1050	1200	700	70	235	850	1,200,000	(see footnotes 1-7)
No. 2		850	975	450	70	235	700	1,100,000	
No. 3		500	575	250	70	235	450	1,000,000	
Appearance		1050	1200	700	70	235	1000	1,200,000	
Stud		500	575	250	70	235	450	1,000,000	
Selected Decking	Decking	—	1350	—	—	—	—	1,200,000	
Commercial Decking		—	1150	—	—	—	—	1,200,000	
Selected Decking	Decking	—	1450	(Surfaced at 15% max. m.c. and used at 15% max. m.c.)			—	1,300,000	
Commercial Decking		—	1250				—	1,100,000	

National Forest Products Association; Washington, D.C.

DESIGN VALUES FOR VISUALLY GRADED STRUCTURAL LUMBER—DESIGN VALUES LISTED ARE FOR NORMAL LOADING CONDITIONS

SPECIES AND COMMERCIAL GRADE (SURFACED DRY OR SURFACED GREEN. USED AT 19% MAX. M.C.)	SIZE CLASSIFICATION	EXTREME FIBER IN BENDING, F_b SINGLE MEMBER USES	REPETITIVE MEMBER USES	TENSION PARALLEL TO GRAIN F_t	HORIZONTAL SHEAR F_v	COMPRESSION PERPENDICULAR TO GRAIN $F_{c\perp}$	COMPRESSION PARALLEL TO GRAIN F_c	MODULUS OF ELASTICITY	GRADING RULES AGENCY
SOUTHERN PINE*									
Select Structural	2–4″ thick 2–4″ wide	2150	2500	1250	105	405	1800	1,800,000	
No. 1		1850	2100	1050	105	405	1450	1,200,000	
No. 2		1550	1750	900	95	405	1150	1,600,000	
No. 3		850	975	500	95	405	675	1,500,000	
Stud		850	975	500	95	405	675	1,500,000	
Construction	2–4″ thick 4″ wide	1100	1250	650	105	405	1300	1,500,000	
Standard		625	725	375	95	405	1050	1,500,000	
Utility		275	300	175	95	405	675	1,500,000	
Select Structural	2–4″ thick 5″ and wider	1850	2150	1200	95	405	1600	1,800,000	SPIB (see footnotes 1, 3, 4, 5, 8)
Dense Select Structural		2200	2500	1450	95	475	1850	1,900,000	
No. 1		1600	1850	1050	95	405	1450	1,800,000	
No. 1 Dense		1850	2150	1250	95	475	1700	1,900,000	
No. 2		1300	1500	675	95	405	1200	1,600,000	
No. 2 Dense		1550	1750	800	95	475	1400	1,700,000	
No. 3		750	875	400	95	405	725	1,500,000	
No. 3 Dense		875	1000	450	95	475	850	1,500,000	
Stud		800	900	400	95	405	725	1,500,000	
Dense Standard Decking	2–4″ thick 2″ and wider Decking	2150	2450	—	—	475	—	1,900,000	
Select Decking		1150	1750	—	—	405	—	1,600,000	
Dense Select Decking		1800	2050	—	—	475	—	1,700,000	
Commercial Decking		1550	1750	—	—	405	—	1,600,000	
Dense Commercial Decking		1800	2050	—	—	475	—	1,700,000	
SOUTHERN PINE†									
Select Structural	2–4″ thick 2–4″ wide	2000	2300	1150	100	405	1550	1,700,000	
No. 1		1700	1950	1000	100	405	1250	1,700,000	
No. 2		1400	1650	825	90	405	975	1,600,000	
No. 3		775	900	450	90	405	575	1,400,000	
Stud		775	900	450	90	405	575	1,400,000	
Construction	2–4″ thick 4″ wide	1000	1150	600	100	405	1100	1,400,000	
Standard		575	675	350	90	405	900	1,400,000	
Utility		275	300	150	90	405	575	1,400,000	
Select Structural	2–4″ thick 5″ and wider	1750	2000	1150	90	405	1350	1,700,000	SPIB (see footnotes 1, 3, 4, 5, 8)
Dense Select Structural		2050	2350	1300	90	475	1600	1,800,000	
No. 1		1450	1700	975	90	405	1250	1,700,000	
No. 1 Dense		1700	200	1150	90	475	1450	1,800,000	
No. 2		1200	1400	625	90	405	1000	1,600,000	
No. 2 Dense		1400	1650	725	90	475	1200	1,600,000	
No. 3		700	800	350	90	405	625	1,400,000	
No. 3 Dense		825	925	425	90	475	725	1,500,000	
Stud		725	850	350	90	405	625	1,400,000	
Dense Standard Decking	2–4″ thick 2″ and wider Decking	2000	2300	—	—	475	—	1,800,000	
Select Decking		1400	1650	—	—	405	—	1,600,000	
Dense Select Decking		1650	1900	—	—	475	—	1,600,000	
Commercial Decking		1400	1650	—	—	405	—	1,600,000	
Dense Commercial Decking		1650	1900	—	—	475	—	1,600,000	
SOUTHERN PINE‡									
Select Structural	2½–4″ thick 2½–4″ wide	1600	1850	925	95	270	1050	1,500,000	
No. 1		1350	1550	800	95	270	825	1,500,000	
No. 2		1150	1300	675	85	270	650	1,400,000	
No. 3		625	725	375	85	270	400	1,200,000	
Stud		625	725	375	85	270	400	1,200,000	
Construction	2½–4″ thick 4″ wide	825	925	475	95	270	725	1,200,000	
Standard		475	525	275	85	270	600	1,200,000	
Utility		200	250	125	85	270	400	1,200,000	
Select Structural	2½–4″ thick 5″ and wider	1400	1600	900	85	270	900	1,500,000	
Dense Select Structural		1600	1850	1050	85	315	1050	1,600,000	
No. 1		1200	1350	775	85	270	825	1,500,000	
No. 1 Dense		1400	1600	925	85	315	950	1,600,000	
No. 2		975	1100	500	85	270	675	1,400,000	SPIB (see footnotes 1, 3, 4, 5, 8)
No. 2 Dense		1150	1300	600	85	315	800	1,400,000	
No. 3		550	650	300	85	270	425	1,200,000	
No. 3 Dense		650	750	350	85	315	475	1,300,000	
Stud		575	675	300	85	270	425	1,200,000	
Dense Standard Decking	2½–4″ thick 2″ and wider Decking	1600	1800	—	—	315	—	1,600,000	
Select Decking		1150	1300	—	—	270	—	1,400,000	
Dense Select Decking		1350	1500	—	—	315	—	1,400,000	
Commercial Decking		1150	1300	—	—	270	—	1,400,000	
Dense Commercial Decking		1350	1500	—	—	315	—	1,400,000	
No. 1 SR	5″ and thicker	1350	—	875	110	270	775	1,500,000	
No. 1 Dense SR		1550	—	1050	110	315	925	1,600,000	
No. 2 SR		1100	—	725	95	270	625	1,400,000	
No. 2 Dense SR		1250	—	850	95	315	725	1,400,000	

*Surfaced at 15% maximum moisture content, K. D. Used at 15% max. m.c.
†Surfaced dry. Used at 19% max. m.c.
‡Surfaced green. Used at any condition.

National Forest Products Association; Washington, D.C.

GENERAL INFORMATION

DESIGN VALUES FOR VISUALLY GRADED STRUCTURAL LUMBER— DESIGN VALUES LISTED ARE FOR NORMAL LOADING CONDITIONS

SPECIES AND COMMERCIAL GRADE (SURFACED DRY OR SURFACED GREEN. USED AT 19% MAX. M.C.)	SIZE CLASSIFICATION	EXTREME FIBER IN BENDING, F_b — SINGLE MEMBER USES	REPETITIVE MEMBER USES	TENSION PARALLEL TO GRAIN F_t	HORIZONTAL SHEAR F_v	COMPRESSION PERPENDICULAR TO GRAIN $F_{c\perp}$	COMPRESSION PARALLEL TO GRAIN F_c	MODULUS OF ELASTICITY	GRADING RULES AGENCY
SPRUCE-PINE-FIR									
Select Structural	2-4" thick 2-4" wide	1450	1650	850	70	265	1100	1,500,000	NLGA (a Canadian agency; see footnotes 1–6)
No. 1		1200	1400	725	70	265	875	1,500,000	
No. 2		1000	1150	600	70	265	675	1,300,000	
No. 3		550	650	325	70	265	425	1,200,000	
Appearance		1200	1400	700	70	265	1050	1,500,000	
Stud		550	650	325	70	265	425	1,200,000	
Construction	2-4" thick 4" wide	725	850	425	70	265	775	1,200,000	
Standard		400	475	225	70	265	650	1,200,000	
Utility		175	225	100	70	265	425	1,200,000	
Select Structural	2-4" thick 5" and wider	1250	1450	825	70	265	975	1,500,000	
No. 1		1050	1200	700	70	265	875	1,500,000	
No. 2		875	100	450	70	265	725	1,300,000	
No. 3		500	575	275	70	265	450	1,200,000	
Appearance		1050	1200	700	70	265	1050	1,500,000	
Stud		500	575	275	70	265	450	1,200,000	
Select	Decking	1200	1400	—	—	265	—	1,500,000	
Commercial		1000	1150	—	—	265	—	1,300,000	
WESTERN CEDAR									
Selected Decking	Decking	—	1450	—	—	—	—	1,100,000	WWPA (see footnotes 1–6)
Commercial Decking		—	1200	—	—	—	—	1,000,000	
Selected Decking	Decking	—	1550	(Surfaced at 15% max. m.c. and used at 15% max. m.c.)			—	1,100,000	
Commercial Decking		—	1300				—	1,000,000	
WESTERN HEMLOCK									
Select Structural	2-4" thick 2-4" wide	1800	2100	1050	90	280	1450	1,600,000	WCLIB WWPA (see footnotes 1–6)
No. 1		1550	1800	900	90	280	1150	1,600,000	
No. 2		1300	1450	750	90	280	900	1,400,000	
No. 3		700	800	425	90	280	550	1,300,000	
Appearance		1550	1800	900	90	280	1350	1,600,000	
Stud		700	800	425	90	280	550	1,300,000	
Construction	2-4" thick 4" wide	925	1050	550	90	280	1050	1,300,000	
Standard		525	600	300	90	280	850	1,300,000	
Utility		250	275	150	90	280	550	1,300,000	
Select Structural	2-4" thick 5" and wider	1550	1800	1050	90	280	1300	1,600,000	
No. 1		1350	1550	900	90	280	1150	1,600,000	
No. 2		1100	1250	575	90	280	975	1,400,000	
No. 3		650	750	325	90	280	625	1,300,000	
Appearance		1350	1550	900	90	280	1350	1,600,000	
Stud		650	750	325	90	280	625	1,300,000	
Select Structural	Beams and stringers	1400	—	825	85	280	1000	1,400,000	WCLIB (see footnotes 1–6)
No. 1		1150	—	575	85	280	850	1,400,000	
Select Structural	Posts and timbers	1300	—	875	85	280	1100	1,400,000	
No. 1		1050	—	700	85	280	950	1,400,000	
Select Dex	Decking	1500	1750	—	—	280	—	1,600,000	
Commercial Dex		1300	1450	—	—	280	—	1,400,000	
Selected Decking	Decking	—	1750	—	—	—	—	1,600,000	WWPA (see footnotes 1–7)
Commercial Decking		—	1450	—	—	—	—	1,400,000	
Selected Decking	Decking	—	1900	(Surfaced at 15% max. m.c. and used at 15% max. m.c.)			—	1,700,000	
Commercial Decking		—	1600				—	1,500,000	
WHITE WOODS (WESTERN WOODS)									
Select Structural	2-4" thick 2-4" wide	1350	1150	775	70	190	950	1,100,000	WWPA (see footnotes 1–7)
No. 1		1150	1300	650	70	190	750	1,100,000	
No. 2		925	1050	550	70	190	600	1,000,000	
No. 3		525	600	300	70	190	375	900,000	
Appearance		1150	1300	650	70	190	900	1,100,000	
Stud		525	600	300	70	190	375	900,000	
Construction	2-4" thick 4" wide	675	775	400	70	190	675	900,000	
Standard		375	425	225	70	190	550	900,000	
Utility		175	200	100	70	190	375	900,000	
Select Structural	2-4" thick 5" and wider	1150	1300	775	70	190	850	1,100,000	
No. 1		975	1100	650	70	190	750	1,100,000	
No. 2		800	925	425	70	190	625	1,000,000	
No. 3		475	550	250	70	190	400	900,000	
Appearance		975	1100	650	70	190	900	1,100,000	
Stud		475	550	250	70	190	400	900,000	
Select Structural	Beams and stringers	1000	—	700	65	190	675	1,000,000	
No. 1		850	—	575	65	190	550	1,000,000	
Select Structural	Posts and timbers	950	—	650	65	190	700	1,000,000	
No. 1		775	—	525	65	190	625	1,000,000	
Selected Decking	Decking	—	1300	—	—	—	—	1,100,000	
Commercial Decking		—	1050	—	—	—	—	1,000,000	
Selected Decking	Decking	—	1400	(Surfaced at 15% max. m.c. and used at 15% max. m.c.)			—	1,100,000	
Commercial Decking		—	1150				—	1,000,000	

NOTES ON VISUALLY GRADED LUMBER

1. Grading rules agencies listed include the following:

   NELMA—Northeastern Lumber Manufacturers Association, Incorporated

   NHPMA—Northern Hardwood and Pine Manufacturers Association, Incorporated

   NLGA—National Lumber Grades Authority (Canada)

   RIS—Redwood Inspection Service

   SPIB—Southern Pine Inspection Bureau

   WCLIB—West Coast Lumber Inspection Bureau

   WWPA—Western Wood Products Association

2. The design values are applicable to lumber that will be used under dry conditions. For 2 to 4 in. thick lumber the DRY surfaced size shall be used in member design.

3. Tabulated tension parallel to grain values for all species for 5 in. and wider, 2 to 4 in. thick (and 2½ to 4 in. thick) size classifications apply to 5 and 6 in. widths only, for grades of Select Structural, No. 1, No. 2, No. 3. Appearance and Stud, including dense grades. For lumber wider than 6 in. in these grades, the tabulated F_t values shall be multiplied by the following factors:

4. Design values for all species of Stud grade in 5 in. and wider size classifications apply to 5 and 6 in. widths only.

5. Values for F_b, F_t, and F_c for all species of grades of Construction, Standard, and Utility apply only to 4 in. widths. Design values for 2 and 3 in. widths of these grades are available from NELMA, NLGA, RIS, SPIB, WCLIB, and WWPA (see Note 1).

7. When decking graded to WWPA rules is surfaced at 15% maximum moisture content and used where the moisture content will exceed 15% for an extended period of time, the tabulated design values for decking surfaced at 15% maximum moisture content shall be multiplied by the following factors: extreme fiber in bending F_b, -0.79; modulus of elasticity E, -0.92.

8. When 2 to 4 in. thick southern pine lumber is surfaced dry or at 15% maximum moisture content (KD) and is designed for use where the moisture content will exceed 19% for an extended period of time, the design values for the corresponding grades of 2½ to 4 in. thick surfaced green southern pine lumber shall be used. The net green size may be used in such designs.

GRADE

(2 TO 4 IN. THICK, 5 IN. AND WIDER) (2½ TO 4 IN. THICK, 5 IN. AND WIDER) (INCLUDES "DENSE" GRADES)	MULTIPLY TABULATED F_t VALUES BY		
	5 AND 6 IN. WIDE	8 IN. WIDE	10 IN. AND WIDER
Select Structural	1.00	0.90	0.80
No. 1, No. 2, No. 3 and Appearance	1.00	0.80	0.60
Stud	1.00	—	—

6. When 2 to 4 in. thick lumber is manufactured at a maximum moisture content of 15% and used in a condition where the moisture content does not exceed 15%, the design values for surfaced dry or surfaced green lumber may be multiplied by the following factors (for southern pine use tabulated design values without adjustment):

2 TO 4 IN. THICK LUMBER MANUFACTURED AND USED AT 15% MAXIMUM MOISTURE CONTENT (MC 15)

EXTREME FIBER IN BENDING IN F_b	TENSION PARALLEL TO GRAIN F_t	HORIZONTAL SHEAR F_v	COMPRESSION PERPENDICULAR TO GRAIN $F_{c\perp}$	COMPRESSION* PARALLEL TO GRAIN F_c	MODULUS* OF ELASTICITY E
1.08	1.08	1.05	1.00	1.17	1.05
				1.15	1.04

*For redwood use only.

When 2 to 4 in. thick lumber is designed for use where the moisture content will exceed 19% for an extended period of time, the design values shown here shall be multiplied by the following factors (except for southern pine, to which note 8 applies):

2 TO 4 IN. THICK LUMBER USED WHERE MOISTURE CONTENT WILL EXCEED 19%

EXTREME FIBER IN BENDING IN F_b	TENSION PARALLEL TO GRAIN F_t	HORIZONTAL SHEAR F_v	COMPRESSION PERPENDICULAR TO GRAIN $F_{c\perp}$	COMPRESSION PARALLEL TO GRAIN F_c	MODULUS OF ELASTICITY E
0.86	0.84	0.97	0.67	0.70	0.97

When lumber 5 in. and thicker is designed for use where the moisture content will exceed 19% for an extended period of time, the design values shown (except those for southern pine) shall be multiplied by the following factors:

5 IN. AND THICKER LUMBER USED WHERE MOISTURE CONTENT WILL EXCEED 19%

EXTREME FIBER IN BENDING IN F_b	TENSION PARALLEL TO GRAIN F_t	HORIZONTAL SHEAR F_v	COMPRESSION PERPENDICULAR TO GRAIN $F_{c\perp}$	COMPRESSION PARALLEL TO GRAIN F_c	MODULUS OF ELASTICITY E
1.00	1.00	1.00	0.67	0.91	1.00

National Forest Products Association; Washington, D.C.

LUMBER

The DESIGN VALUES FOR VISUALLY GRADED STRUCTURAL LUMBER presented on the four previous pages are obtained from grading rules published by seven agencies: National Lumber Grades Authority (a Canadian agency), Northeastern Lumber Manufacturers Association, Northern Hardwood and Pine Manufacturers Association, Redwood Inspection Service, Southern Pine Inspection Bureau, West Coast Lumber Inspection Bureau, and Western Wood Products Association. The grading rules promulgated by these agencies, including design values, have been approved by the Board of Review of the American Lumber Standards Committee and certified for conformance with U.S. Department of Commerce Voluntary Product Standard PS 20-70, "American Softwood Lumber Standard."

Design values for visually graded lumber are based on the provisions of ASTM Designation D245, "Methods for Establishing Structural Grades and Related Allowable Properties for Visually Graded Lumber." These methods involve adjusting the strength properties of small clear specimens of wood, as given in ASTM Designation D2555, "Methods for Establishing Clear Wood Strength Values," for the effects of knots, slope of grain, splits, checks, size, duration of load, moisture content, and other influencing factors, to obtain design values applicable to normal conditions of service. Lumber structures designed on the basis of working stresses derived from ASTM D245 procedures and standard design criteria have a long history of satisfactory performance.

The appropriateness of lumber design values is regularly evaluated on the basis of experience and experimental data developed on the properties and performance of clear wood specimens or full size lumber pieces. Reduced tension parallel to grain values for some sizes of visually graded lumber reflect new test information on actual lumber grades and sizes. Such modifications in stresses for individual pieces of lumber may not always be reflected in changed usage of trusses or other structural assemblies involving appropriately joined pieces of lumber or other materials. Performance of these assemblies depends not only on design values for the individual elements, but also on assumptions made in estimating the stresses induced in each member, assumptions regarding fastener rigidity, the relationship between assumed and actual loads on the structure, estimated versus actual environmental exposure conditions, and the quality of fabrication. These factors are all subject to adjustment or revision based on experimental evidence, experience, and the application of improved stress analysis procedures.

Design values for machine stress rated (MSR) lumber presented on the following page are based on nondestructive stiffness testing of individual pieces. Certain visual grade requirements also apply to such lumber. The stress rating system for MSR lumber is regularly checked by the responsible grading agency for conformance to established certification and quality control procedures.

For additional information on the development and applicability of lumber design values, the grading rules published by the individual agencies and the referenced ASTM Standards should be consulted.

CONDITIONS OF USE

Design values presented for lumber are for normal loading under dry conditions of service. Because the strength of wood varies with conditions under which it is used, these design values should only be applied in conjunction with appropriate design and service recommendations from the "National Design Specification for Wood Construction," available from the National Forest Products Association.

GENERAL INFORMATION

DECAY AND INSECT RESISTANT WOOD

WOLMANIZED PRESSURE TREATED WOOD AND OUTDOOR BRAND WOOD

Wolmanized wood has been pressure treated with a water solution of preservative chemicals. Has outstanding durability under any condition of exposure. Use is limited to the treatment of fully air seasoned or kiln dried material. Wolman salts, the preservative used, impart a light green, blue-green, or brownish color to the wood, depending on the species. Wolmanized wood weathers to a silver gray.

1. GENERAL USE: In the ground; in water; in contact with masonry, or when the wood will be exposed to wetting.
2. SPECIFIC USE: Decks, patios, walkways, fences, boat docks, sills plates, soffits, facia, all weather wood foundations, pole houses, and pole buildings.
3. ADVANTAGES: Provides lasting protection against decay producing fungi, and insects. Clean, oil free. Odorless. Can be painted or stained. Preservative chemicals are fiberfixed in the wood to prevent leaching. Harmless to people, plants, and animals.
4. LIMITATIONS: Air seasoning or kiln drying is required after treatment to make Wolmanized lumber paintable and to guard further against shrinkage in service. Moisture content should be 19% or less. Because undercoated steel rusts quickly, nails or bolts should be galvanized.

CELLON PRESSURE TREATED WOOD

The Cellon pressure treatment process utilizes liquefied butane gas as a solvent to carry pentachlorophenol, the preservative, deep into the wood. After treatment, the solvent is evaporated. Particularly suitable for treating hardwoods and all plywoods.

1. GENERAL USE: Ground contact, in contact with masonry, or when the wood will be exposed to wetting.
2. SPECIFIC USE: Glue-lam beams, lighting standards, pole houses and pole buildings, decking.
3. ADVANTAGES: Provides lasting protection against decay producing fungi and insects. Clean and dry to the touch. Can be painted, stained, and glued. Since neither water nor oil is used in the Cellon process, air seasoning and kiln drying are not required after treatment. Retains the wood's original texture and color. Weathers naturally.
4. LIMITATIONS: Will not protect against attack from marine organisms. Certain species such as Douglas fir, southern pine, and ponderosa pine may exude resin from knots and heartwood after treatment. Wood rich in tannin, such as redwood and oak, may develop a blue-black surface stain if the lumber has not been well seasoned prior to treatment; however, the sun's rays will bleach out the stain in several months.

PENTACHLOROPHENOL PRESSURE TREATED WOOD

Pentachlorophenol is the principal preservative in the "oil borne" category. Toxic to insects and fungi.

1. GENERAL USE: In the ground.
2. SPECIFIC USE: Industrial and farm buildings; fence posts.
3. ADVANTAGES: Protects against fungi and insect attack. Seasoned hardwoods and softwoods can be treated without fear of grain raising, checking, or splitting.
4. LIMITATIONS: Penta treated forest products may become blotchy when exposed to the weather; this condition disappears after extended service. Penta-in-oil treated wood would NOT be used as a subflooring, or in contact with materials subject to staining (plaster, wallboard). Not readily paintable; would not be used in direct contact with roofing felt, since it can cause the tar to drip. Not recommended for use in saltwater.

Domenic F. Valente, AIA; D. F. Valente, Architect & Planner; Medford, Massachusetts

CREOSOTE

Creosote is the oldest commercial wood preservative currently being used. It has demonstrated, through years of actual service, outstanding durability, dependability, and general utility. Creosote contains a multitude of chemical compounds which are toxic to fungi, insects, and most marine organisms. Average life expectancy of a creosoted wood pole in the ground is 35 to 40 years, but some creosoted poles are still standing fast after more than 75 years of rugged service.

1. GENERAL USE: In the ground and in water.
2. SPECIFIC USE: Foundation piles, landscape ties, fence posts, highway guard rails, marine piling, and bulkheads.
3. ADVANTAGES: Creosote is a coal tar product that derives its effectiveness from its persistent high toxicity to wood destroying insects and fungi. Creosote effectively protects wood from the ravages of most marine organisms.
4. LIMITATIONS: Pressure creosoted lumber should NOT be used as a subflooring or in contact with materials subject to staining (plaster, wallboard). It is not readily paintable, and should not be used in direct contact with roofing felt, since it can cause the tar to drip.

CORROSION RESISTANT WOOD

KP RESIN IMPREGNATED WOOD

KP resin impregnated wood has been impregnated with a phenolic resin solution to obtain a high degree of acid resistance and excellent dimensional stability. The treatment is limited to southern pine, hard maple, cativo, and kempas. Natural wood color.

1. GENERAL USE: Where corrosion resistance or dimensional stability is required.
2. SPECIFIC USE: Filter press plates and frames, flumes, stacks, tank covers, tanks, troughs and trays, die models.
3. ADVANTAGES: High degree of acid resistance. Dimensional stability far greater than untreated wood. Can be machined. Gouging the surface does not reduce the protection.
4. LIMITATIONS: Should not be exposed to alkaline solutions, aniline, chlorine gas, strong bleaching solutions, strong oxidizing acids.

ASIDBAR IMPREGNATED WOOD

Asidbar impregnated wood has been impregnated with topped coal tar material that provides the natural structural properties of wood as well as the chemical resistant properties of coal tar composites. Color is coal-tar black. Treatment is for southern pine lumber, and southern pine and Douglas fir plywood.

1. GENERAL USE: Where corrosion resistance is required.
2. SPECIFIC USE: Beams, interior wall cladding, decking, effluent systems, platforms, roof systems, walkways.
3. ADVANTAGES: High degree of acid resistance. Gouging of surface does not reduce the protection.
4. LIMITATIONS: Tends to soften and expand in severe temperatures above 130°F. Not suitable for use with acetate solvents, benzene or benzol, ethers, trichloroethylene, xylene, or xylol.

FIRE RETARDANT TREATED WOOD

NON-COM FIRE RETARDANT TREATED WOOD

Non-Com fire retardant treated wood is used indoors where the relative humidity is normally below 80%. The wood is pressure impregnated with inorganic salts that react chemically at temperatures below the ignition point of untreated wood. This chemical reaction reduces the flammable vapors emitted by wood subjected to fire. A protective char is formed and wood underneath remains structurally sound longer than untreated and surface treated wood.

1. CLASSIFIED: Non-Com fire retardant treated lumber and plywood have an Underwriters' Laboratories designated rating of FRS, which means that the material has a fire hazard classification of 25 or less for flame spread, fuel contributed, and smoke developed, and shows no sign of progressive combustion when the 10 minute fire hazard classification test is continued for an additional 20 minutes.
2. APPROVED: The Factory Mutual Engineering Division, the Factory Insurance Association, all state insurance rating bureaus, and all branches of the Insurance Services Office frequently permit the use of Non-Com fire retardant treated wood as an alternative to materials classified as noncombustible.
3. GENERAL USE: In buildings (interior).
4. SPECIFIC USE: Studs, wall plates, and fire stops with metal lath and plaster or drywall construction of interior nonbearing walls and partitions in fire resistive buildings. Roof systems including deck, purlins, and joists.
5. ADVANTAGES: Reduces flame spread and fuel contributed. Requires no maintenance to retain its fire retardant properties. Can be installed by regular carpenter crews. Low sound transmission makes it an excellent product for remodeling as well as for new construction.
6. LIMITATIONS: If Non-Com is to be painted, sealed, or varnished, it must be kiln dried to a maximum moisture content of 12%. Not recommended for use in the ground or for exposed locations that are subject to weathering or humidity normally above 80%. At jobsite, dry lumber should be stored indoors if possible. Otherwise, it should be stored on raised platforms and covered with suitable weatherproof protective covering such as tarpaulins or polyethylene film. NOTE: NCX fire retardant treated wood is recommed for architectural appearance applications.

NCX FIRE RETARDANT TREATED WOOD

NCX fire retardant treated wood is used outside or where the relative humidity is frequently above 80%. The wood is pressure impregnated with a fire retardant monomeric resin solution. After impregnation, the wood is kiln dried to cure the chemicals in the wood. The cured chemicals in the wood are not affected by direct outdoor weather exposure and high humidity.

1. CLASSIFIED: NCX fire retardant treated lumber and plywood have an Underwriters' Laboratories designated rating of FRS, which means that the material has a fire hazard classification of 25 or less for flame spread, fuel contributed, and smoke developed, and shows no sign of progressive combustion when the 10 minute fire hazard classification test is continued for an additional 20 minutes.
2. APPROVED: The Factory Mutual Engineering Division, the Factory Insurance Association, all state insurance rating bureaus, and all branches of the Insurance Services Office frequently permit the use of NCX as an alternative to materials classified as noncombustible.
3. RECOGNIZED: For certain applications by numerous state and city building codes. Also by BOCA, ICBO, SBCC, Southern Standard, AIA, and American Insurance Association.
4. GENERAL USE: Exterior use and where humidity is frequently above 80%. Also, interior appearance applications.
5. SPECIFIC USE: Balconies and steps. Roof systems. Soffit and fascia. Architectural hardwood moulding and paneling. Western red cedar shingles and shakes.
6. ADVANTAGES: Suitable for exposure to the weather or high humidity conditions. Clear architectural finishes can be applied without causing below-film blushes.
7. LIMITATIONS: Although NCX wood has excellent weathering characteristics, it is not recommended for use in the ground or in ground contact. Treatment may darken wood slightly, but basic tone or hue remains almost unchanged. Treated wood may show sticker marks after drying. Underwriters' Laboratories permits milling of some species after drying. Where marks are objectionable, milling is recommended.

DESIGN VALUES FOR MACHINE STRESS RATED STRUCTURAL LUMBER (1)

DESIGN VALUES LISTED ARE FOR NORMAL LOADING CONDITIONS. SEE NOTES BELOW, AND OTHER PROVISIONS IN THE NATIONAL DESIGN SPECIFICATION, FOR ADJUSTMENTS OF TABULATED VALUES (2)

GRADE DESIGNATION	GRADING RULES AGENCY (SEE NOTES 3–6)	SIZE CLASSIFICATION	DESIGN VALUES (PSI)				
			EXTREME FIBER IN BENDING, F_b		TENSION PARALLEL TO GRAIN, F_t	COMPRESSION PARALLEL TO GRAIN, F_c	MODULUS OF ELASTICITY, E
			SINGLE MEMBER USES	REPETITIVE MEMBER USES			
900f-1.0E	7		900	1050	350	725	1,000,000
1200f-1.2E	5, 6, 7, 8		1200	1400	650	950	1,200,000
1350f-1.3E	6, 8		1350	1550	750	1100	1,300,000
1450f-1.3E	5, 7, 8		1450	1650	800	1150	1,300,000
1500f-1.4E	5, 6, 7, 8		1500	1750	900	1200	1,400,000
1650f-1.5E	5, 6, 7, 8		1650	1900	1020	1320	1,500,000
1800f-1.6E	5, 6, 7, 8	Machine rated lumber, 2 in. thick or less, all widths	1800	2050	1175	1450	1,600,000
1950f-1.7E	5, 6, 8		1950	2250	1375	1550	1,700,000
2100f-1.8E	5, 6, 7, 8		2100	2400	1575	1700	1,800,000
2250f-1.9E	5, 6, 8		2250	2600	1750	1800	1,900,000
2400f-2.0E	5, 6, 7, 8		2400	2750	1925	1925	2,000,000
2550f-2.1E	5, 6, 8		2550	2950	2050	2050	2,100,000
2700f-2.2E	5, 6, 7, 8		2700	3100	2150	2150	2,200,000
2850f-2.3E	6, 8		2850	3300	2300	2300	2,300,000
3000f-2.4E	5, 6, 8		3000	3450	2400	2400	2,400,000
3150f-2.5E	6, 8		3150	3600	2500	2500	2,500,000
3300f-2.6E	6, 8		3300	3800	2650	2650	2,600,000
900f-1.0E	5, 6, 7, 8		900	1050	350	725	1,000,000
900f-1.2E	5, 6, 7, 8		900	1050	350	725	1,200,000
1200f-1.5E	5, 6, 7, 8	See note 7	1200	1400	600	950	1,500,000
1350f-1.8E	5, 6, 8		1350	1550	750	1075	1,800,000
1500f-1.8E	7		1500	1750	900	1200	1,800,000
1800f-2.1E	5, 6, 7, 8		1800	2050	1175	1450	2,100,000

NOTES

1. Stresses apply at 19% maximum moisture content.
2. Notes 1, 2, and 6 on the preceding page also apply to machine stress rated lumber.
3. National Lumber Grades Authority grading rules.
4. Southern Pine Inspection Bureau grading rules.
5. West Coast Lumber Inspection Bureau grading rules.
6. Western Wood Products Association grading rules.
7. Size classifications for these grades are:
   NLGA—machine rated lumber; 2 in. thick or less; all widths.
   SPIB—machine rated lumber; 2 in. thick or less; all widths.
   WCLIB—machine rated joists; 2 in. thick or less; 6 in. and wider.
   WWPA—machine rated lumber; 2 in. thick or less; all widths.

Tabulated extreme fiber values in bending values F_b is applicable to lumber loaded on edge. When loaded flat, these values may be increased by multiplying by the following factors:

Nominal width (in.)	3	4	5	6	8	10	12	14
Factor	1.06	1.10	1.12	1.15	1.19	1.22	1.25	1.28

Design values for horizontal shear F_v (DRY) and compression perpendicular to grain $F_{c\perp}$ (DRY) are:

CEDAR (WWPA/WCLIB)	DOUGLAS FIR-LARCH (WWPA/WCLIB/NLGA)	DOUGLAS FIR SOUTH (WWPA)	ENGLEMANN SPRUCE (WWPA)	HEM-FIR (WWPA/WCLIB/NLGA)	MIXED SPECIES (WCLIB)	PINE (WWPA)	SOUTHERN PINE (SPIB)	SPRUCE PINE-FIR (NLGA)	WESTERN HEMLOCK (WWPA/WCLIB)
HORIZONTAL SHEAR F_v (DRY)									
75	95	90	70	75	70	70	90 / 95 For Southern pine KD	70	90
COMPRESSION PERPENDICULAR TO GRAIN $F_{c\perp}$ (DRY)									
265	385	335	195	245	190	190	405	265	280

NOTE: Cedar includes incense or Western red cedar. Pine includes Idaho white pine, lodgepole pine, ponderosa pine, or sugar pine.

National Forest Products Association; Washington, D.C.

GENERAL INFORMATION

NOMINAL AND MINIMUM DRESSED SIZES OF LUMBER PRODUCTS (IN.)
The thicknesses apply to all widths and all widths to all thicknesses.

LUMBER PRODUCT	THICKNESSES NOMINAL	MINIMUM DRESSED DRY	MINIMUM DRESSED GREEN	FACE WIDTHS NOMINAL	MINIMUM DRESSED DRY	MINIMUM DRESSED GREEN
Boards	1	3/4	25/32	2	1 1/2	1 9/16
				3	2 1/2	2 9/16
				4	3 1/2	3 9/16
				5	4 1/2	4 5/8
	1 1/4	1	1 1/32	6	5 1/2	5 5/8
				7	6 1/2	6 5/8
				8	7 1/4	7 1/2
	1 1/2	1 1/4	1 9/32	9	8 1/4	8 1/2
				10	9 1/4	9 1/2
				11	10 1/4	10 1/2
				12	11 1/4	11 1/2
				14	13 1/4	13 1/2
				16	15 1/4	15 1/2
Dimension lumber	2	1 1/2	1 9/16	2	1 1/2	1 9/16
	2 1/2	2	2 1/16	3	2 1/2	2 9/16
	3	2 1/2	2 9/16	4	3 1/2	3 9/16
	3 1/2	3	3 1/16	5	4 1/2	4 5/8
				6	5 1/2	5 5/8
				8	7 1/4	7 1/2
				10	9 1/4	9 1/2
				12	11 1/4	11 1/2
				14	13 1/4	13 1/2
				16	15 1/4	15 1/2
	4	3 1/2	3 9/16	2	1 1/2	1 9/16
	4 1/2	4	4 1/16	3	2 1/2	2 9/16
				4	3 1/2	3 9/16
				5	4 1/2	4 5/8
				6	5 1/2	5 5/8
				8	7 1/4	7 1/2
				10	9 1/4	9 1/2
				12	11 1/4	11 1/2
				14		13 1/2
				16		15 1/2
Timbers	5 and thicker		1/2 off	5 and wider		1/2 off
Shiplap 3/8″ lap	1	3/4	25/32	4	3 1/8	3 3/16
				6	5 1/8	5 1/4
				8	6 7/8	7 1/8
				10	8 7/8	9 1/8
				12	10 7/8	11 1/8
				14	12 7/8	13 1/8
				16	14 7/8	15 1/8
Shiplap 1/2″ lap	1	3/4	25/32	4	3	3 1/16
				6	5	5 1/8
				8	6 3/4	7
				10	8 3/4	9
				12	10 3/4	11
				14	12 3/4	13
				16	14 3/4	15
Centermatch 1/4″ tongue	1	3/4	25/32	4	3 1/8	3 3/16
	1 1/4	1	1 1/32	5	4 1/8	4 1/4
	1 1/2	1 1/4	1 9/32	6	5 1/8	5 1/4
				8	6 7/8	7 1/8
				10	8 7/8	9 1/8
				12	10 7/8	11 1/8
2″ dressed and matched 3/8″ tongue	2	1 1/2	1 9/16	4	3	3 1/16
				6	5	5 1/8
				8	6 3/4	7
				10	8 3/4	9
				12	10 3/4	11
2″ shiplap 1/2″ lap	2	1 1/2	1 9/16	4	3	3 1/16
				6	5	5 1/8
				8	6 3/4	7
				10	8 3/4	9
				12	10 3/4	11

NOTE: For dry lumber moisture content is 19% or less and for green lumber moisture content is in excess of 19%.

NOMINAL AND MINIMUM DRESSED DRY SIZES OF LUMBER PRODUCTS (IN.)
The thicknesses apply to all widths and all widths to all thicknesses.

LUMBER PRODUCT	THICKNESSES NOMINAL	THICKNESSES MINIMUM DRESSED	FACE WIDTHS NOMINAL	FACE WIDTHS MINIMUM DRESSED
Finish	3/8	5/16	2	1 1/2
	1/2	7/16	3	2 1/2
	5/8	9/16	4	3 1/2
	3/4	5/8	5	4 1/2
	1	3/4	6	5 1/2
	1 1/4	1	7	6 1/2
	1 1/2	1 1/4	8	7 1/4
	1 3/4	1 3/8	9	8 1/4
	2	1 1/2	10	9 1/4
	2 1/2	2	11	10 1/4
	3	2 1/2	12	11 1/4
	3 1/2	3	14	13 1/4
	4	3 1/2	16	15 1/4
Flooring; dimension given is face dimension excluding tongue	3/8	5/16	2	1 1/8
	1/2	7/16	3	2 1/8
	5/8	9/16	4	3 1/8
	1	3/4	5	4 1/8
	1 1/4	1	6	5 1/8
	1 1/2	1 1/4		
Ceiling	3/8	5/16	3	2 1/8
	1/2	7/16	4	3 1/8
	5/8	9/16	5	4 1/8
	3/4	11/16	6	5 1/8
Partition	1	23/32	3	2 1/8
			4	3 1/8
			5	4 1/8
			6	5 1/8
Stepping	1	3/4	8	7 1/4
	1 1/4	1	10	9 1/4
	1 1/2	1 1/4	12	11 1/4
	2	1 1/2		
Bevel siding	1/2	7/16 butt, 3/16 tip	4	3 1/2
	9/16	15/32 butt, 3/16 tip	5	4 1/2
	5/8	9/16 butt, 3/16 tip	6	5 1/2
	3/4	11/16 butt, 3/16 tip	8	7 1/4
	1	3/4 butt, 3/16 tip	10	9 1/4
			12	11 1/4
Bungalow siding	3/4	11/16 butt, 3/16 tip	8	7 1/4
			10	9 1/4
			12	11 1/4
Rustic and drop siding shiplapped 3/8″	5/8	9/16	4	3
	1	23/32	5	4
			6	5
Rustic and drop siding shiplapped 1/2″	5/8	9/16	4	2 7/8
	1	23/32	5	3 7/8
			6	4 7/8
			8	6 5/8
			10	8 5/8
			12	10 5/8
Rustic and drop siding dressed and matched	5/8	9/16	4	3 1/8
	1	23/32	5	4 1/8
			6	5 1/8
			8	6 7/8
			10	8 7/8

NOTE: Maximum moisture content is 19%.

NOTE

For additional information reference should be made to the National Bureau of Standards, Product Standard PS20-70 American Softwood Lumber Standard. Available through U.S. Government Printing Office.

CEILING JOISTS—10 LB/SQ FT LIVE LOAD (GYPSUM WALLBOARD CEILING)
No attic storage and roof slope not steeper than 3 IN 12.

MAXIMUM ALLOWABLE LENGTHS L BETWEEN SUPPORTS

JOIST SIZE (NOMINAL) (IN.)	JOIST SPACING (NOMINAL) (IN.)	SPAN L LIMITED BY DEFLECTION AND F_b IS EXTREME FIBER STRESS			
		E =	1,000,000	1,200,000	1,400,000	1,600,000
2 x 4	12	L = F_b =	10-7 830	11-3 930	11-10 1030	12-5 1130
	16	L = F_b =	9-8 910	10-3 1030	10-9 1140	11-3 1240
	24	L = F_b =	8-5 1040	8-11 1170	9-5 1300	9-10 1420
2 x 6	12	L = F_b =	16-8 830	17-8 930	18-8 1030	19-6 1130
	16	L = F_b =	15-2 910	16-1 1030	16-11 1140	17-8 1240
	24	L = F_b =	13-3 1040	14-1 1170	14-9 1300	15-6 1420
2 x 8	12	L = F_b =	21-11 830	23-4 930	24-7 1030	25-8 1130
	16	L = F_b =	19-11 910	21-2 1030	22-4 1140	23-4 1240
	24	L = F_b =	17-5 1040	18-6 1170	19-6 1300	20-5 1420
2 x 10	12	L = F_b =	28-0 830	29-9 930	31-4 1030	32-9 1130
	16	L = F_b =	25-5 910	27-1 1030	28-6 1140	29-9 1240
	24	L = F_b =	22-3 1040	23-8 1170	24-10 1300	26-0 1420

NOTE: L in feet and inches; E and F_b in pounds per square inch as shown above.

DESIGN CRITERIA

1. Maximum allowable deflection = 1/240 of span length.
2. Live load of 10 lb/sq ft plus dead load of 5 lb/sq ft determine required fiber stress value.

CEILING JOISTS—20 LB/SQ FT LIVE LOAD (GYPSUM WALLBOARD CEILING)
Limited attic storage where development of future rooms is not possible.

MAXIMUM ALLOWABLE LENGTHS L BETWEEN SUPPORTS

JOIST SIZE (NOMINAL) (IN.)	JOIST SPACING (NOMINAL) (IN.)	SPAN L LIMITED BY DEFLECTION AND F_b IS EXTREME FIBER STRESS			
		E =	1,000,000	1,200,000	1,400,000	1,600,000
2 x 4	12	L = F_b =	8-5 1040	8-11 1170	9-5 1300	9-10 1420
	16	L = F_b =	7-8 1140	8-1 1290	8-7 1430	8-11 1570
	24	L = F_b =	6-8 1310	7-1 1480	7-6 1640	7-10 1790
2 x 6	12	L = F_b =	13-3 1040	14-1 1170	14-9 1300	15-6 1420
	16	L = F_b =	12-0 1140	12-9 1290	13-5 1430	14-1 1570
	24	L = F_b =	10-6 1310	11-2 1480	11-9 1640	12-3 1790
2 x 8	12	L = F_b =	17-5 1040	18-6 1170	19-6 1300	20-5 1420
	16	L = F_b =	15-10 1140	16-10 1290	17-9 1430	18-6 1570
	24	L = F_b =	13-10 1310	14-8 1480	15-6 1640	16-2 1790
2 x 10	12	L = F_b =	22-3 1040	23-8 1170	24-10 1300	26-0 1420
	16	L = F_b =	20-2 1140	21-6 1290	22-7 1430	23-8 1570
	24	L = F_b =	17-8 1310	18-9 1480	19-9 1640	20-8 1790

NOTE: L in feet and inches; E and F_b in pounds per square inch as shown above.

DESIGN CRITERIA

1. Maximum allowable deflection = 1/240 of span length.
2. Live load of 20 lb/sq ft plus dead load of 10 lb/sq ft determine required fiber stress value.

NOTE

For rafters, design values in F_b may be greater than the design values for normal duration of load, by the following amounts:

15% for 2 months' duration as for snow.
25% for 7 days' duration, as for construction loading.

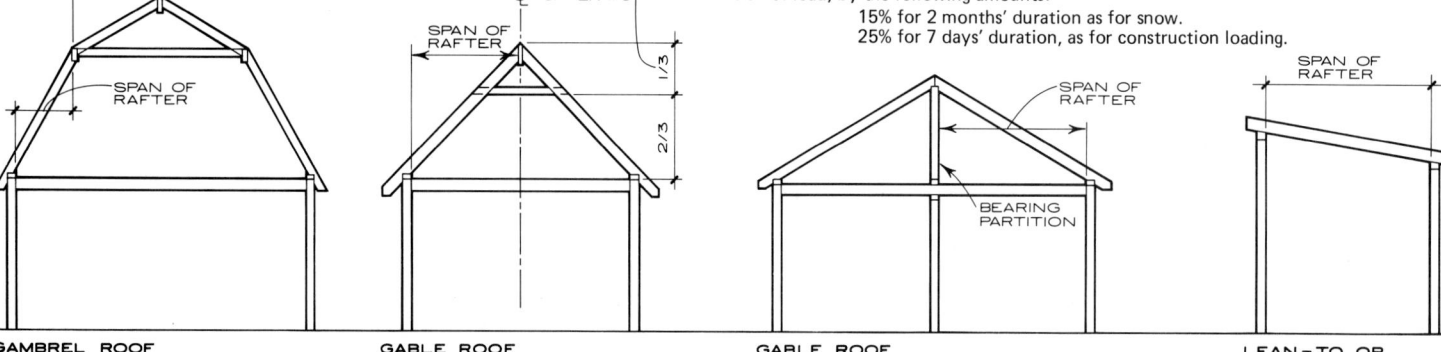

GAMBREL ROOF   GABLE ROOF (SLOPE OVER 3 IN 12)   GABLE ROOF (SLOPE UNDER 3 IN 12)   LEAN-TO OR SHED ROOF

SECTION MODULUS

LUMBER SIZES (NOMINAL)	S (INCHES³)
2 x 3	1.56
2 x 4	3.06
2 x 6	7.56
2 x 8	13.41
2 x 10	21.39
2 x 12	31.64
3 x 6	12.60
3 x 8	21.90
3 x 10	35.65
3 x 12	52.73
3 x 14	73.15
4 x 4	7.15
4 x 6	17.65
4 x 8	30.66
4 x 10	49.91
4 x 12	73.82

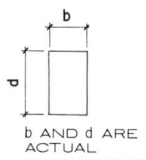

SECTION MODULUS

$$S = \frac{bd^2}{6}$$

(INCHES³)

b AND d ARE ACTUAL DIMENSIONS.

NOTE

(Applicable to this and the following pages on joist and rafter sizes.)

SPANS LIMITED BY DEFLECTION: Computed for the assumed loads to cause a deflection not exceeding $\frac{1}{360}$ of the span. The weight of plaster itself was ignored in the assumed loads for the deflection computations, because the initial deflection from the dead load occurs before plaster sets. The influence of live loads, rather than dead loads, when the ratio of live to dead loads is relatively high, is the principal factor to be considered. Also with joisted floors, flooring and bridging serve to distribute moving or concentrated loads to adjoining members. The omission of the plaster weight in load assumption applies to deflection computations only; the full dead and live load is considered when computing for strength.

SPANS LIMITED BY BENDING STRENGTH OF PIECE: May be used where ceilings are not plastered and deflection is not objectionable.

National Forest Products Association; Washington, D. C.

E = modulus of elasticity
F_b = extreme fiber stress in bending
L = span length between supports

LIVE LOAD ASSUMPTIONS: Uniformly distributed.

PARTITIONS: Spans shown are computed for the given live load plus the dead load and do not provide for additional loads such as partitions. Where concentrated load are imposed the spans should be recomputed to provide for them.

DESIGN CRITERIA

STRENGTH: 15 psf dead load plus 20 psf live load determines required fiber stress.

DEFLECTION: For 20 psf live load. Limited to span in inches divided by 240.

RAFTERS: Spans are measured along the horizontal projection, and loads are considered as applied on the horizontal projection.

FLAT OR SLOPED RAFTERS—20 LB LIVE LOAD
FLAT ROOF OR CATHEDRAL CEILING WITH NO ATTIC SPACE—SUPPORTING GYPSUM WALLBOARD CEILING

RAFTER SIZE, SPACING (IN.)		EXTREME FIBER STRESS IN BENDING, F_b (PSI)														
		500	600	700	800	900	1000	1100	1200	1300	1400	1500	1600	1700	1800	1900
2 x 6	12	8-6 / 0.26	9-4 / 0.35	10-0 / 0.44	10-9 / 0.54	11-5 / 0.64	12-0 / 0.75	12-7 / 0.86	13-2 / 0.98	13-8 / 1.11	14-2 / 1.24	14-8 / 1.37	15-2 / 1.51	15-8 / 1.66	16-1 / 1.81	16-7 / 1.96
	16	7-4 / 0.23	8-1 / 0.30	8-8 / 0.38	9-4 / 0.46	9-10 / 0.55	10-5 / 0.65	10-11 / 0.75	11-5 / 0.85	11-10 / 0.96	12-4 / 1.07	12-9 / 1.19	13-2 / 1.31	13-7 / 1.44	13-11 / 1.56	14-4 / 1.70
	24	6-0 / 0.19	6-7 / 0.25	7-1 / 0.31	7-7 / 0.38	8-1 / 0.45	8-6 / 0.53	8-11 / 0.61	9-4 / 0.70	9-8 / 0.78	10-0 / 0.88	10-5 / 0.97	10-9 / 1.07	11-1 / 1.17	11-5 / 1.28	11.8 / 1.39
2 x 8	12	11-2 / 0.26	12-3 / 0.35	13-3 / 0.44	14-2 / 0.54	15-0 / 0.64	15-10 / 0.75	16-7 / 0.86	17-4 / 0.98	18-0 / 1.11	18-9 / 1.24	19-5 / 1.37	20-0 / 1.51	20-8 / 1.66	21-3 / 1.81	21-10 / 1.96
	16	9-8 / 0.23	10-7 / 0.30	11-6 / 0.38	12-3 / 0.46	13-0 / 0.55	13-8 / 0.65	14-4 / 0.75	15-0 / 0.85	15-7 / 0.96	16-3 / 1.07	16-9 / 1.19	17-4 / 1.31	17-10 / 1.44	18-5 / 1.56	18-11 / 1.70
	24	7-11 / 0.19	8-8 / 0.25	9-4 / 0.31	10-0 / 0.38	10-7 / 0.45	11-2 / 0.53	11-9 / 0.61	12-3 / 0.70	12-9 / 0.78	13-3 / 0.88	13-8 / 0.97	14-2 / 1.07	14-7 / 1.17	15-0 / 1.28	15-5 / 1.39
2 x 10	12	14-3 / 0.26	15-8 / 0.35	16-11 / 0.44	18-1 / 0.54	19-2 / 0.64	20-2 / 0.75	21-2 / 0.86	22-1 / 0.98	23-0 / 1.11	23-11 / 1.24	24-9 / 1.37	25-6 / 1.51	26-4 / 1.66	27-1 / 1.81	27.10 / 1.96
	16	12-4 / 0.23	13-6 / 0.30	14-8 / 0.38	15-8 / 0.46	16-7 / 0.55	17-6 / 0.65	18-4 / 0.75	19-2 / 0.85	19-11 / 0.96	20-8 / 1.07	21-5 / 1.19	22-1 / 1.31	22-10 / 1.44	23-5 / 1.56	24.1 / 1.70
	24	10-1 / 0.19	11-1 / 0.25	11-11 / 0.31	12-9 / 0.38	13-6 / 0.45	14-3 / 0.53	15-0 / 0.61	15-8 / 0.70	16-3 / 0.78	16-11 / 0.88	17-6 / 0.97	18-1 / 1.07	18-7 / 1.17	19-2 / 1.28	19-8 / 1.39
2 x 12	12	17-4 / 0.26	19-0 / 0.35	20-6 / 0.44	21-11 / 0.54	23-3 / 0.64	24-7 / 0.75	25-9 / 0.86	26-11 / 0.98	28-0 / 1.11	29-1 / 1.24	30-1 / 1.37	31-1 / 1.51	32-0 / 1.66	32-11 / 1.81	33-10 / 1.96
	16	15-0 / 0.23	16-6 / 0.30	17-9 / 0.38	19-0 / 0.46	20-2 / 0.55	21-3 / 0.65	22-4 / 0.75	23-3 / 0.85	24-3 / 0.96	25-2 / 1.07	26-0 / 1.19	26-11 / 1.31	27-9 / 1.44	28.6 / 1.56	29-4 / 1.70
	24	12-3 / 0.19	13-5 / 0.25	14-6 / 0.31	15-6 / 0.38	16-6 / 0.45	17-4 / 0.53	18-2 / 0.61	19-0 / 0.70	19-10 / 0.78	20-6 / 0.88	21-3 / 0.97	21-11 / 1.07	22-8 / 1.17	23-3 / 1.28	23-11 / 1.39

NOTE: The required modulus of elasticity, E, in 1,000,000 psi is shown below each span.

DESIGN CRITERIA

STRENGTH: 15 psf dead load plus 30 psf live load determines required fiber stress.

DEFLECTION: For 30 psf live load. Limited to span in inches divided by 240.

RAFTERS: Spans are measured along the horizontal projection, and loads are considered as applied on the horizontal projection.

FLAT OR SLOPED RAFTERS—30 LB LIVE LOAD
FLAT ROOF OR CATHEDRAL CEILING WITH NO ATTIC SPACE—SUPPORTING GYPSUM WALLBOARD CEILING

RAFTER SIZE, SPACING (IN.)		EXTREME FIBER STRESS IN BENDING, F_b (PSI)														
		500	600	700	800	900	1000	1100	1200	1300	1400	1500	1600	1700	1800	1900
2 x 6	12	7-6 / 0.27	8-2 / 0.36	8-10 / 0.45	9-6 / 0.55	10-0 / 0.66	10-7 / 0.77	11-1 / 0.89	11-7 / 1.01	12-1 / 1.14	12-6 / 1.28	13-0 / 1.41	13-5 / 1.56	13-10 / 1.71	14-2 / 1.86	14-7 / 2.02
	16	6-6 / 0.24	7-1 / 0.31	7-8 / 0.39	8-2 / 0.48	8-8 / 0.57	9-2 / 0.67	9-7 / 0.77	10-0 / 0.88	10-5 / 0.99	10-10 / 1.10	11-3 / 1.22	11-7 / 1.35	11-11 / 1.48	12-4 / 1.61	12-8 / 1.75
	24	5-4 / 0.19	5-10 / 0.25	6-3 / 0.32	6-8 / 0.39	7-1 / 0.46	7-6 / 0.54	7-10 / 0.63	8-2 / 0.72	8-6 / 0.81	8-10 / 0.90	9-2 / 1.00	9-6 / 1.10	9-9 / 1.21	10-0 / 1.31	10-4 / 1.43
2 x 8	12	9-10 / 0.27	10-10 / 0.36	11-8 / 0.45	12-6 / 0.55	13-3 / 0.66	13-11 / 0.77	14-8 / 0.89	15-3 / 1.01	15-11 / 1.14	16-6 / 1.28	17-1 / 1.41	17-8 / 1.56	18-2 / 1.71	18-9 / 1.86	19-3 / 2.02
	16	8-7 / 0.24	9-4 / 0.31	10-1 / 0.39	10-10 / 0.48	11-6 / 0.57	12-1 / 0.67	12-8 / 0.77	13-3 / 0.88	13-9 / 0.99	14-4 / 1.10	14-10 / 1.22	15-3 / 1.35	15-9 / 1.48	16-3 / 1.61	16-8 / 1.75
	24	7-0 / 0.19	7-8 / 0.25	8-3 / 0.32	8-10 / 0.39	9-4 / 0.46	9-10 / 0.54	10-4 / 0.63	10-10 / 0.72	11-3 / 0.81	11-8 / 0.90	12-1 / 1.00	12-6 / 1.10	12-10 / 1.21	13-3 / 1.31	13-7 / 1.43
2 x 10	12	12-7 / 0.27	13-9 / 0.36	14-11 / 0.45	15-11 / 0.55	16-11 / 0.66	17-10 / 0.77	18-8 / 0.89	19-6 / 1.01	20-4 / 1.14	21-1 / 1.28	21-10 / 1.41	22-6 / 1.56	23-3 / 1.71	23-11 / 1.86	24-6 / 2.02
	16	10-11 / 0.24	11-11 / 0.31	12-11 / 0.39	13-9 / 0.48	14-8 / 0.57	15-5 / 0.67	16-2 / 0.77	16-11 / 0.88	17-7 / 0.99	18-3 / 1.10	18-11 / 1.22	19-6 / 1.35	20-1 / 1.48	20-8 / 1.61	21-3 / 1.75
	24	8-11 / 0.19	9-9 / 0.25	10-6 / 0.32	11-3 / 0.39	11-11 / 0.46	12-7 / 0.54	13-2 / 0.63	13-9 / 0.72	14-4 / 0.81	14-11 / 0.90	15-5 / 1.00	15-11 / 1.10	16-5 / 1.21	16-11 / 1.31	17-4 / 1.43
2 x 12	12	15-4 / 0.27	16-9 / 0.36	18-1 / 0.45	19-4 / 0.55	20-6 / 0.66	21-8 / 0.77	22-8 / 0.89	23-9 / 1.01	24-8 / 1.14	25-7 / 1.28	26-6 / 1.41	27-5 / 1.56	28-3 / 1.71	29-1 / 1.86	29-10 / 2.02
	16	13-3 / 0.24	14-6 / 0.31	15-8 / 0.39	16-9 / 0.48	17-9 / 0.57	18-9 / 0.67	19-8 / 0.77	20-6 / 0.88	21-5 / 0.99	22-2 / 1.10	23-0 / 1.22	23-9 / 1.35	24-5 / 1.48	25-2 / 1.61	25-10 / 1.75
	24	10-10 / 0.19	11-10 / 0.25	12-10 / 0.32	13-8 / 0.39	14-6 / 0.46	15-4 / 0.54	16-1 / 0.63	16-9 / 0.72	17-5 / 0.81	18-1 / 0.90	18-9 / 1.00	19-4 / 1.10	20-0 / 1.21	20-6 / 1.31	12-1 / 1.43

NOTE: The required modulus of elasticity, E, in 1,000,000 psi is shown below each span.

National Forest Products Association; Washington, D.C.

DESIGN CRITERIA

STRENGTH: 10 psf dead load plus 20 psf live load determines required fiber stress.

DEFLECTION: For 20 psf live load. Limited to span in inches divided by 240.

RAFTERS: Spans are measured along the horizontal projection, and loads are considered as applied on the horizontal projection.

FLAT OR LOW SLOPE RAFTERS—20 LB LIVE LOAD
NO CEILING LOAD—SLOPE 3 IN 12 OR LESS

RAFTER SIZE, SPACING (IN.)		EXTREME FIBER STRESS IN BENDING, F_b (PSI)													
		500	600	700	800	900	1000	1100	1200	1300	1400	1500	1600	1700	1800	1900
2 x 6	12	9-2 / 0.33	10-0 / 0.44	10-10 / 0.55	11-7 / 0.67	12-4 / 0.80	13-0 / 0.94	13-7 / 1.09	14-2 / 1.24	14-9 / 1.40	15-4 / 1.56	15-11 / 1.73	16-5 / 1.91	16-11 / 2.09	17-5 / 2.28	17-10 / 2.47
	16	7-11 / 0.29	8-8 / 0.38	9-5 / 0.48	10-0 / 0.58	10-8 / 0.70	11-3 / 0.82	11-9 / 0.94	12-4 / 1.07	12-10 / 1.21	13-3 / 1.35	13-9 / 1.50	14-2 / 1.65	14-8 / 1.81	15-1 / 1.97	15-6 / 2.14
	24	6-6 / 0.24	7-1 / 0.31	7-8 / 0.39	8-2 / 0.48	8-8 / 0.57	9-2 / 0.67	9-7 / 0.77	10-0 / 0.88	10-5 / 0.99	10-10 / 1.10	11-3 / 1.22	11-7 / 1.35	11-11 / 1.48	12-4 / 1.61	12-8 / 1.75
2 x 8	12	12-1 / 0.33	13-3 / 0.44	14-4 / 0.55	15-3 / 0.67	16-3 / 0.80	17-1 / 0.94	17-11 / 1.09	18-9 / 1.24	19-6 / 1.40	20-3 / 1.56	20-11 / 1.73	21-7 / 1.91	22-3 / 2.09	22-11 / 2.28	23-7 / 2.47
	16	10-6 / 0.29	11-6 / 0.38	12-5 / 0.48	13-3 / 0.58	14-0 / 0.70	14-10 / 0.82	15-6 / 0.94	16-3 / 1.07	16-10 / 1.21	17-6 / 1.35	18-2 / 1.50	18-9 / 1.65	19-4 / 1.81	19-10 / 1.97	20-5 / 2.14
	24	8-7 / 0.24	9-4 / 0.31	10-1 / 0.39	10-10 / 0.48	11-6 / 0.57	12-1 / 0.67	12-8 / 0.77	13-3 / 0.88	13-9 / 0.99	14-4 / 1.10	14-10 / 1.22	15-3 / 1.35	15-9 / 1.48	16-3 / 1.61	16-8 / 1.75
2 x 10	12	15-5 / 0.33	16-11 / 0.44	18-3 / 0.55	19-6 / 0.67	20-8 / 0.80	21-10 / 0.94	22-10 / 1.09	23-11 / 1.24	24-10 / 1.40	25-10 / 1.56	26-8 / 1.73	27-7 / 1.91	28-5 / 2.09	29-3 / 2.28	30-1 / 2.47
	16	13-4 / 0.29	14-8 / 0.38	15-10 / 0.48	16-11 / 0.58	17-11 / 0.70	18-11 / 0.82	19-10 / 0.94	20-8 / 1.07	21-6 / 1.21	22-4 / 1.35	23-2 / 1.50	23-11 / 1.65	24-7 / 1.81	25-4 / 1.97	26-0 / 2.14
	24	10-11 / 0.24	11-11 / 0.31	12-11 / 0.39	13-9 / 0.48	14-8 / 0.57	15-5 / 0.67	16-2 / 0.77	16-11 / 0.88	17-7 / 0.99	18-3 / 1.10	18-11 / 1.22	19-6 / 1.35	20-1 / 1.48	20-8 / 1.61	21-3 / 1.75
2 x 12	12	18-9 / 0.33	20-6 / 0.44	22-2 / 0.55	23-9 / 0.67	25-2 / 0.80	26-6 / 0.94	27-10 / 1.09	29-1 / 1.24	30-3 / 1.40	31-4 / 1.56	32-6 / 1.73	33-6 / 1.91	34-7 / 2.09	35-7 / 2.28	36-7 / 2.47
	16	16-3 / 0.29	17-9 / 0.38	19-3 / 0.48	20-6 / 0.58	21-9 / 0.70	23-0 / 0.82	24-1 / 0.94	25-2 / 1.07	26-2 / 1.21	27-2 / 1.35	28-2 / 1.50	29-1 / 1.65	29-11 / 1.81	30-10 / 1.97	31-8 / 2.14
	24	13-3 / 0.24	14-6 / 0.31	15-8 / 0.39	16-9 / 0.48	17-9 / 0.57	18-9 / 0.67	19-8 / 0.77	20-6 / 0.88	21-5 / 0.99	22-2 / 1.10	23-0 / 1.22	23-9 / 1.35	24-5 / 1.48	25-2 / 1.61	25-10 / 1.75

NOTE: The required modulus of elasticity, E, in 1,000,000 psi is shown below each span.

DESIGN CRITERIA

STRENGTH: 10 psf dead load plus 30 psf live load determines required fiber stress.

DEFLECTION: For 30 psf live load. Limited to span in inches divided by 240.

RAFTERS: Spans are measured along the horizontal projection, and loads are considered as applied on the horizontal projection.

FLAT OR LOW SLOPE RAFTERS—30 LB LIVE LOAD
NO CEILING LOAD—SLOPE 3 IN 12 OR LESS

RAFTER SIZE, SPACING (IN.)		EXTREME FIBER STRESS IN BENDING, F_b (PSI)													
		500	600	700	800	900	1000	1100	1200	1300	1400	1500	1600	1700	1800	1900
2 x 6	12	7-11 / 0.32	8-8 / 0.43	9-5 / 0.54	10-0 / 0.66	10-8 / 0.78	11-3 / 0.92	11-9 / 1.06	12-4 / 1.21	12-10 / 1.36	13-3 / 1.52	13-9 / 1.69	14-2 / 1.86	14-8 / 2.04	15-1 / 2.22	15-6 / 2.41
	16	6-11 / 0.28	7-6 / 0.37	8-2 / 0.47	8-8 / 0.57	9-3 / 0.68	9-9 / 0.80	10-2 / 0.92	10-8 / 1.05	11-1 / 1.18	11-6 / 1.32	11-11 / 1.46	12-4 / 1.61	12-8 / 1.76	13-1 / 1.92	13-5 / 2.08
	24	5-7 / 0.23	6-2 / 0.30	6-8 / 0.38	7-1 / 0.46	7-6 / 0.55	7-11 / 0.65	8-4 / 0.75	8-8 / 0.85	9-1 / 0.96	9-5 / 1.08	9-9 / 1.19	10-0 / 1.31	10-4 / 1.44	10-8 / 1.57	10-11 / 1.70
2 x 8	12	10-6 / 0.32	11-6 / 0.43	12-5 / 0.54	13-3 / 0.66	14-0 / 0.78	14-10 / 0.92	15-6 / 1.06	16-3 / 1.21	16-10 / 1.36	17-6 / 1.52	18-2 / 1.69	18-9 / 1.86	19-4 / 2.04	19-10 / 2.22	20-5 / 2.41
	16	9-1 / 0.28	9-11 / 0.37	10-9 / 0.47	11-6 / 0.57	12-2 / 0.68	12-10 / 0.80	13-5 / 0.92	14-0 / 1.05	14-7 / 1.18	15-2 / 1.32	15-8 / 1.46	16-3 / 1.61	16-9 / 1.76	17-2 / 1.92	17-8 / 2.08
	24	7-5 / 0.23	8-1 / 0.30	8-9 / 0.38	9-4 / 0.46	9-11 / 0.55	10-6 / 0.65	11-0 / 0.75	11-6 / 0.85	11-11 / 0.96	12-5 / 1.08	12-10 / 1.19	13-3 / 1.31	13-8 / 1.44	14-0 / 1.57	14-5 / 1.70
2 x 10	12	13-4 / 0.32	14-8 / 0.43	15-10 / 0.54	16-11 / 0.66	17-11 / 0.78	18-11 / 0.92	19-10 / 1.06	20-8 / 1.21	21-6 / 1.36	22-4 / 1.52	23-2 / 1.69	23-11 / 1.86	24-7 / 2.04	25-4 / 2.22	26-0 / 2.41
	16	11-7 / 0.28	12-8 / 0.37	13-8 / 0.47	14-8 / 0.57	15-6 / 0.68	16-4 / 0.80	17-2 / 0.92	17-11 / 1.05	18-8 / 1.18	19-4 / 1.32	20-0 / 1.46	20-8 / 1.61	21-4 / 1.76	21-11 / 1.92	22-6 / 2.08
	24	9-5 / 0.23	10-4 / 0.30	11-2 / 0.38	11-11 / 0.46	12-8 / 0.55	13-4 / 0.65	14-0 / 0.75	14-8 / 0.85	15-3 / 0.96	15-10 / 1.08	16-4 / 1.19	16-11 / 1.31	17-5 / 1.44	17-11 / 1.57	18-5 / 1.70
2 x 12	12	16-3 / 0.32	17-9 / 0.43	19-3 / 0.54	20-6 / 0.66	21-9 / 0.78	23-0 / 0.92	24-1 / 1.06	25-2 / 1.21	26-2 / 1.36	27-2 / 1.52	28-2 / 1.69	29-1 / 1.86	29-11 / 2.04	30-10 / 2.22	31-8 / 2.41
	16	14-1 / 0.28	15-5 / 0.37	16-8 / 0.47	17-9 / 0.57	18-10 / 0.68	19-11 / 0.80	20-10 / 0.92	21-9 / 1.05	22-8 / 1.18	23-6 / 1.32	24-4 / 1.46	25-2 / 1.61	25-11 / 1.76	26-8 / 1.92	27-5 / 2.08
	24	11-6 / 0.23	12-7 / 0.30	13-7 / 0.38	14-6 / 0.46	15-5 / 0.55	16-3 / 0.65	17-0 / 0.75	17-9 / 0.85	18-6 / 0.96	19-2 / 1.08	19-11 / 1.19	20-6 / 1.31	21-2 / 1.44	21-9 / 1.57	22-5 / 1.70

NOTE: The required modulus of elasticity, E, in 1,000,000 psi is shown below each span.

National Forest Products Association; Washington, D.C.

DESIGN LOAD TABLES

DESIGN CRITERIA

STRENGTH: 15 psf dead load plus 20 psf live load determines required fiber stress.

DEFLECTION: For 20 psf live load. Limited to span in inches divided by 180.

RAFTERS: Spans are measured along the horizontal projection, and loads are considered as applied on the horizontal projection.

MEDIUM OR HIGH SLOPE RAFTERS—20 LB LIVE LOAD
HEAVY ROOF COVERING—NO CEILING LOAD—SLOPE OVER 3 IN 12

RAFTER SIZE, SPACING (IN.)		EXTREME FIBER STRESS IN BENDING, F_b (PSI)														
		500	600	700	800	900	1000	1100	1200	1300	1400	1500	1600	1700	1800	1900
2 x 4	12	5-5 / 0.20	5-11 / 0.26	6-5 / 0.33	6-10 / 0.40	7-3 / 0.48	7-8 / 0.56	8-0 / 0.65	8-4 / 0.74	8-8 / 0.83	9-0 / 0.93	9-4 / 1.03	9-8 / 1.14	9-11 / 1.24	10-3 / 1.36	10-6 / 1.47
	16	4-8 / 0.17	5-1 / 0.23	5-6 / 0.28	5-11 / 0.35	6-3 / 0.41	6-7 / 0.49	6-11 / 0.56	7-3 / 0.64	7-6 / 0.72	7-10 / 0.80	8-1 / 0.89	8-4 / 0.98	8-7 / 1.08	8-10 / 1.17	9-1 / 1.27
	24	3-10 / 0.14	4-2 / 0.18	4-6 / 0.23	4-10 / 0.28	5-1 / 0.34	5-5 / 0.40	5-8 / 0.46	5-11 / 0.52	6-2 / 0.59	6-5 / 0.66	6-7 / 0.73	6-10 / 0.80	7-0 / 0.88	7-3 / 0.96	7-5 / 1.04
2 x 6	12	8-6 / 0.20	9-4 / 0.26	10-0 / 0.33	10-9 / 0.40	11-5 / 0.48	12-0 / 0.56	12-7 / 0.65	13-2 / 0.74	13-8 / 0.83	14-2 / 0.93	14-8 / 1.03	15-2 / 1.14	15-8 / 1.24	16-1 / 1.36	16-7 / 1.47
	16	7-4 / 0.17	8-1 / 0.23	8-8 / 0.28	9-4 / 0.35	9-10 / 0.41	10-5 / 0.49	10-11 / 0.56	11-5 / 0.64	11-10 / 0.72	12-4 / 0.80	12-9 / 0.89	13-2 / 0.98	13-7 / 1.08	13-11 / 1.17	14-4 / 1.27
	24	6-0 / 0.14	6-7 / 0.18	7-1 / 0.23	7-7 / 0.28	8-1 / 0.34	8-6 / 0.40	8-11 / 0.46	9-4 / 0.52	9-8 / 0.59	10-0 / 0.66	10-5 / 0.73	10-9 / 0.80	11-1 / 0.88	11-5 / 0.96	11-8 / 1.04
2 x 8	12	11-12 / 0.20	12-3 / 0.26	13-3 / 0.33	14-2 / 0.40	15-0 / 0.48	15-10 / 0.56	16-7 / 0.65	17-4 / 0.74	18-0 / 0.83	18-9 / 0.93	19-5 / 1.03	20-0 / 1.14	20-8 / 1.24	21-3 / 1.36	21-10 / 1.47
	16	9-8 / 0.17	10-7 / 0.23	11-6 / 0.28	12-3 / 0.35	13-0 / 0.41	13-8 / 0.49	14-4 / 0.56	15-0 / 0.64	15-7 / 0.72	16-3 / 0.80	16-9 / 0.89	17-4 / 0.98	17-10 / 1.08	18-5 / 1.17	18-11 / 1.27
	24	7-11 / 0.14	8-8 / 0.18	9-4 / 0.23	10-0 / 0.28	10-7 / 0.34	11-2 / 0.40	11-9 / 0.46	12-3 / 0.52	12-9 / 0.59	13-3 / 0.66	13-8 / 0.73	14-2 / 0.80	14-7 / 0.88	15-0 / 0.96	15-5 / 1.04
2 x 10	12	14-3 / 0.20	15-8 / 0.26	16-11 / 0.33	18-1 / 0.40	19-2 / 0.48	20-2 / 0.56	21-2 / 0.65	22-1 / 0.74	23-0 / 0.83	23-11 / 0.93	24-9 / 1.03	25-6 / 1.14	26-4 / 1.24	27-1 / 1.36	27-10 / 1.47
	16	12-4 / 0.17	13-6 / 0.23	14-8 / 0.28	15-8 / 0.35	16-7 / 0.41	17-6 / 0.49	18-4 / 0.56	19-2 / 0.64	19-11 / 0.72	20-8 / 0.80	21-5 / 0.89	22-1 / 0.98	22-10 / 1.08	23-5 / 1.17	24-1 / 1.27
	24	10-1 / 0.14	11-1 / 0.18	11-11 / 0.23	12-9 / 0.28	13-6 / 0.34	14-3 / 0.40	15-0 / 0.46	15-8 / 0.52	16-3 / 0.59	16-11 / 0.66	17-6 / 0.73	18-1 / 0.80	18-7 / 0.88	19-2 / 0.96	19-8 / 1.04

NOTE: The required modulus of elasticity, E, in 1,000,000 psi is shown below each span.

DESIGN CRITERIA

STRENGTH: 15 psf dead load plus 30 psf live load determines required fiber stress.

DEFLECTION: For 30 psf live load. Limited to span in inches divided by 180.

RAFTERS: Spans are measured along the horizontal projection, and loads are considered as applied on the horizontal projection.

MEDIUM OR HIGH SLOPE RAFTERS—30 LB LIVE LOAD
HEAVY ROOF COVERING—NO CEILING LOAD—SLOPE OVER 3 IN 12

RAFTER SIZE, SPACING (IN.)		EXTREME FIBER STRESS IN BENDING, F_b (PSI)														
		500	600	700	800	900	1000	1100	1200	1300	1400	1500	1600	1700	1800	1900
2 x 4	12	4-9 / 0.20	5-3 / 0.27	5-8 / 0.34	6-0 / 0.41	6-5 / 0.49	6-9 / 0.58	7-1 / 0.67	7-5 / 0.76	7-8 / 0.86	8-0 / 0.96	8-3 / 1.06	8-6 / 1.17	8-9 / 1.28	9-0 / 1.39	9-3 / 1.51
	16	4-1 / 0.18	4-6 / 0.23	4-11 / 0.29	5-3 / 0.36	5-6 / 0.43	5-10 / 0.50	6-1 / 0.58	6-5 / 0.66	6-8 / 0.74	6-11 / 0.83	7-2 / 0.92	7-5 / 1.01	7-7 / 1.11	7-10 / 1.21	8-0 / 1.31
	24	3-4 / 0.14	3-8 / 0.19	4-0 / 0.24	4-3 / 0.29	4-6 / 0.35	4-9 / 0.41	5-0 / 0.47	5-3 / 0.54	5-5 / 0.61	5-8 / 0.68	5-10 / 0.75	6-0 / 0.83	6-3 / 0.90	6-5 / 0.99	6-7 / 1.07
2 x 6	12	7-6 / 0.20	8-2 / 0.27	8-10 / 0.34	9-6 / 0.41	10-0 / 0.49	10-7 / 0.58	11-1 / 0.67	11-7 / 0.76	12-1 / 0.86	12-6 / 0.96	13-0 / 1.06	13-5 / 1.17	13-10 / 1.28	14-2 / 1.39	14-7 / 1.51
	16	6-6 / 0.18	7-1 / 0.23	7-8 / 0.29	8-2 / 0.36	8-8 / 0.43	9-2 / 0.50	9-7 / 0.58	10-0 / 0.66	10-5 / 0.74	10-10 / 0.83	11-3 / 0.92	11-7 / 1.01	11-11 / 1.11	12-4 / 1.21	12-8 / 1.31
	24	5-4 / 0.14	5-10 / 0.19	6-3 / 0.24	6-8 / 0.29	7-1 / 0.35	7-6 / 0.41	7-10 / 0.47	8-2 / 0.54	8-6 / 0.61	8-10 / 0.68	9-2 / 0.75	9-6 / 0.83	9-9 / 0.90	10-0 / 0.99	10-4 / 1.07
2 x 8	12	9-10 / 0.20	10-10 / 0.27	11-8 / 0.34	12-6 / 0.41	13-3 / 0.49	13-11 / 0.58	14-8 / 0.67	15-3 / 0.76	15-11 / 0.86	16-6 / 0.96	17-1 / 1.06	17-8 / 1.17	18-2 / 1.28	18-9 / 1.39	19-3 / 1.51
	16	8-7 / 0.18	9-4 / 0.23	10-1 / 0.29	10-10 / 0.36	11-6 / 0.43	12-1 / 0.50	12-8 / 0.58	13-3 / 0.66	13-9 / 0.74	14-4 / 0.83	14-10 / 0.92	15-3 / 1.01	15-9 / 1.11	16-3 / 1.21	16-8 / 1.31
	24	7-0 / 0.14	7-8 / 0.19	8-3 / 0.24	8-10 / 0.29	9-4 / 0.35	9-10 / 0.41	10-4 / 0.47	10-10 / 0.54	11-3 / 0.61	11-8 / 0.68	21-1 / 0.75	12-6 / 0.83	12-10 / 0.90	13-3 / 0.99	13-7 / 1.07
2 x 10	12	12-7 / 0.20	13-9 / 0.27	14-11 / 0.34	15-11 / 0.41	15-11 / 0.49	17-10 / 0.58	18-8 / 0.67	19-6 / 0.76	20-4 / 0.86	21-1 / 0.96	21-10 / 1.06	22-6 / 1.17	23-3 / 1.28	23-11 / 1.39	24-6 / 1.51
	16	10-11 / 0.18	11-11 / 0.23	12-11 / 0.29	13-9 / 0.36	14-8 / 0.43	15-5 / 0.50	16-2 / 0.58	16-11 / 0.66	17-7 / 0.74	18-3 / 0.83	18-11 / 0.92	19-6 / 1.01	20-1 / 1.11	20-8 / 1.21	21-3 / 1.31
	24	8-11 / 0.14	9-9 / 0.19	10-6 / 0.24	11-3 / 0.29	11-11 / 0.35	12-7 / 0.41	13-2 / 0.47	13-9 / 0.54	14-4 / 0.61	14-11 / 0.68	15-5 / 0.75	15-11 / 0.83	16-5 / 0.90	16-11 / 0.99	17-4 / 1.07

NOTE: The required modulus of elasticity, E, in 1,000,000 psi is shown below each span.

National Forest Products Association; Washington, D.C.

DESIGN CRITERIA

STRENGTH: 7 psf dead load plus 20 psf live load determines required fiber stress.

DEFLECTION: For 20 psf live load. Limited to span in inches divided by 180.

RAFTERS: Spans are measured along the horizontal projection, and loads are considered as applied on the horizontal projection.

MEDIUM OR HIGH SLOPE RAFTERS—20 LB LIVE LOAD
LIGHT ROOF COVERING—NO CEILING LOAD—SLOPE OVER 3 IN 12

RAFTER SIZE, SPACING (IN.)		EXTREME FIBER STRESS IN BENDING, F_b (PSI)														
		500	600	700	800	900	1000	1100	1200	1300	1400	1500	1600	1700	1800	1900
2 x 4	12	6-2 0.29	6-9 0.38	7-3 0.49	7-9 0.59	8-3 0.71	8-8 0.83	9-1 0.96	9-6 1.06	9-11 1.23	10-3 1.37	10-8 1.52	11-0 1.68	11-4 1.84	11-8 2.00	12-0 1.17
	16	5-4 0.25	5-10 0.33	6-4 0.42	6-9 0.51	7-2 0.61	7-6 0.72	7-11 0.83	8-3 0.94	8-7 1.06	8-11 1.19	9-3 1.32	9-6 1.45	9-10 1.59	10-1 1.73	10-5 1.88
	24	4-4 0.21	4-9 0.27	5-2 0.34	5-6 0.42	5-10 0.50	6-2 0.59	6-5 0.68	6-9 0.77	7-0 0.87	7-3 0.97	7-6 1.08	7-9 1.19	8-0 1.30	8-3 1.41	8-6 1.53
2 x 6	12	9-8 0.29	10-7 0.38	11-5 0.49	12-3 0.59	13-0 0.71	13-8 0.83	14-4 0.96	15-0 1.09	15-7 1.23	16-2 1.37	16-9 1.52	17-3 1.68	17-10 1.84	18-4 2.00	18-10 2.17
	16	8-4 0.25	9-2 0.33	9-11 0.42	10-7 0.51	11-3 0.61	11-10 0.72	12-5 0.83	13-0 0.94	13-6 1.06	14-0 1.19	14-6 1.32	15-0 1.45	15-5 1.59	15-11 1.73	16-4 1.88
	24	6-10 0.21	7-6 0.27	8-1 0.34	8-8 0.42	9-2 0.50	9-8 0.59	10-2 0.68	10-7 0.77	11-0 0.87	11-5 0.97	11-10 1.08	12-3 1.19	12-7 1.30	13-0 1.41	13-4 1.53
2 x 8	12	12-9 0.29	13-11 0.38	15-1 0.49	16-1 0.59	17-1 0.71	18-0 0.83	18-11 0.96	19-9 1.09	20-6 1.23	21-4 1.37	22-1 1.52	22-9 1.68	23-6 1.84	24-2 2.00	24-10 2.17
	16	11-0 0.25	12-1 0.33	13-1 0.42	13-11 0.51	14-10 0.61	15-7 0.72	16-4 0.83	17-1 0.94	17-9 1.06	18-5 1.19	19-1 1.32	19-9 1.45	20-4 1.59	20-11 1.73	21-6 1.88
	24	9-0 0.21	9-10 0.27	10-8 0.34	11-5 0.42	12-1 0.50	12-9 0.59	13-4 0.68	13-11 0.77	14-6 0.87	15-1 0.97	15-7 1.08	16-1 1.19	16-7 1.30	17-1 1.41	17-7 1.53
2 x 10	12	16-3 0.29	17-10 0.38	19-3 0.49	20-7 0.59	21-10 0.71	23-0 0.83	24-1 0.96	25-2 1.09	26-2 1.23	27-2 1.37	28-2 1.52	29-1 1.68	30-0 1.84	30-10 2.00	31-8 2.17
	16	14-1 0.25	15-5 0.33	16-8 0.42	17-10 0.51	18-11 0.61	19-11 0.72	20-10 0.83	21-10 0.94	22-8 1.06	23-7 1.19	24-5 1.32	25-2 1.45	25-11 1.59	26-8 1.73	27-5 1.88
	24	11-6 0.21	12-7 0.27	13-7 0.34	14-6 0.42	15-5 0.50	16-3 0.59	17-1 0.68	17-10 0.77	18-6 0.87	19-3 0.97	19-11 1.08	20-7 1.19	21-2 1.30	21-10 1.41	22-5 1.53

NOTE: The required modulus of elasticity, E, in 1,000,000 psi is shown below each span.

DESIGN CRITERIA

STRENGTH: 7 psf dead load plus 30 psf live load determines required fiber stress.

DEFLECTION: For 30 psf live load. Limited to span in inches divided by 180.

RAFTERS: Spans are measured along the horizontal projection, and loads are considered as applied on the horizontal projection.

MEDIUM OR HIGH SLOPE RAFTERS—30 LB LIVE LOAD
LIGHT ROOF COVERING—NO CEILING LOAD—SLOPE OVER 3 IN 12

RAFTER SIZE, SPACING (IN.)		EXTREME FIBER STRESS IN BENDING, F_b (PSI)														
		500	600	700	800	900	1000	1100	1200	1300	1400	1500	1600	1700	1800	1900
2 x 4	12	5-3 0.27	5-9 0.36	6-3 0.45	6-8 0.55	7-1 0.66	7-5 0.77	7-9 0.89	8-2 1.02	8-6 1.15	8-9 1.28	9-1 1.42	9-5 1.57	9-8 1.72	10-0 1.87	10-3 2.03
	16	4-7 0.24	5-0 0.31	5-5 0.39	5-9 0.48	6-1 0.57	6-5 0.67	6-9 0.77	7-1 0.88	7-4 0.99	7-7 1.11	7-11 1.23	8-2 1.36	8-5 1.49	8-8 1.62	8-10 1.76
	24	3-9 0.19	4-1 0.25	4-5 0.32	4-8 0.39	5-0 0.47	5-3 0.55	5-6 0.63	5-9 0.72	6-0 0.81	6-3 0.91	6-5 1.01	6-8 1.11	6-10 1.21	7-1 1.32	7-3 1.43
2 x 6	12	8-3 0.27	9-1 0.36	9-9 0.45	10-5 0.55	11-1 0.66	11-8 0.77	12-3 0.89	12-9 1.02	13-4 1.15	13-10 1.28	14-4 1.42	14-9 1.57	15-3 1.72	15-8 1.87	16-1 2.03
	16	7-2 0.24	7-10 0.31	8-5 0.39	9-1 0.48	9-7 0.57	10-1 0.67	10-7 0.77	11-1 0.88	11-6 0.99	12-0 1.11	12-5 1.23	12-9 1.36	13-2 1.49	13-7 1.62	13-11 1.76
	24	5-10 0.19	6-5 0.25	6-11 0.32	7-5 0.39	7-10 0.47	8-3 0.55	8-8 0.63	9-1 0.72	9-5 0.81	9-9 0.91	10-1 1.01	10-5 1.11	10-9 1.21	11-1 1.32	11-5 1.43
2 x 8	12	10-11 0.27	11-11 0.36	12-10 0.45	13-9 0.55	14-7 0.66	15-5 0.77	16-2 0.89	16-10 1.02	17-7 1.15	18-2 1.28	18-10 1.42	19-6 1.57	20-1 1.72	20-8 1.87	21-3 2.03
	16	9-5 0.24	10-4 0.31	11-2 0.39	11-11 0.48	12-8 0.57	13-4 0.67	14-0 0.77	14-7 0.88	15-2 0.99	15-9 1.11	16-4 1.23	16-10 1.36	17-4 1.49	17-11 1.62	18-4 1.76
	24	7-8 0.19	8-5 0.25	9-1 0.32	9-9 0.39	10-4 0.47	10-11 0.55	11-5 0.63	11-11 0.72	12-5 0.81	12-10 0.91	13-4 1.01	13-9 1.11	14-2 1.21	14-7 1.32	15-0 1.43
2 x 10	12	13-11 0.27	15-2 0.36	16-5 0.45	17-7 0.55	18-7 0.66	19-8 0.77	20-7 0.89	21-6 1.02	22-5 1.15	23-3 1.28	24-1 1.42	24-10 1.57	25-7 1.72	26-4 1.87	27-1 2.03
	16	12-0 0.26	13-2 0.34	14-3 0.43	15-2 0.53	16-2 0.63	17-0 0.74	17-10 0.85	18-7 0.97	19-5 1.09	20-1 1.22	20-10 1.35	21-6 1.49	22-2 1.63	22-10 1.78	23-5 1.93
	24	9-10 0.19	10-9 0.25	11-7 0.32	12-5 0.39	13-2 0.47	13-11 0.55	14-7 0.63	15-2 0.72	15-10 0.81	16-5 0.91	17-0 1.01	17-7 1.11	18-1 1.21	18-7 1.32	19-2 1.43

NOTE: The required modulus of elasticity, E, in 1,000,000 psi is shown below each span.

National Forest Products Association; Washington, D.C.

DESIGN LOAD TABLES

DESIGN CRITERIA

STRENGTH: Live load of 30 psf plus dead load of 10 psf determines the required fiber stress value.
DEFLECTION: For 30 psf live load. Limited to span in inches divided by 360.

FLOOR JOISTS—30 LB LIVE LOAD

ALL ROOMS USED FOR SLEEPING AREAS AND ATTIC FLOORS

JOIST (IN.) SIZE	SPACING	| MODULUS OF ELASTICITY, E, IN 1,000,000 PSI														
		0.5	0.6	0.7	0.8	0.9	1.0	1.1	1.2	1.3	1.4	1.5	1.6	1.7	1.8	1.9
2 x 6	12	8-0 / 510	8-6 / 570	8-11 / 640	9-4 / 700	9-9 / 750	10-1 / 810	10-5 / 860	10-9 / 910	11-0 / 960	11-3 / 1010	11-7 / 1060	11-10 / 1100	12-0 / 1150	12-3 / 1200	12-6 / 1240
	16	7-3 / 560	7-9 / 630	8-2 / 700	8-6 / 770	8-10 / 830	9-2 / 890	9-6 / 950	9-9 / 1000	10-0 / 1060	10-3 / 1110	10-6 / 1160	10-9 / 1220	10-11 / 1270	11-2 / 1320	11-4 / 1360
	24	6-4 / 640	6-9 / 720	7-1 / 800	7-5 / 880	7-9 / 950	8-0 / 1020	8-3 / 1080	8-6 / 1150	8-9 / 1210	8-11 / 1270	9-2 / 1330	9-4 / 1390	9-7 / 1450	9-9 / 1510	9-11 / 1560
2 x 8	12	10-7 / 510	11-3 / 570	11-10 / 640	12-4 / 700	12-10 / 750	13-4 / 810	13-9 / 860	14-2 / 910	14-6 / 960	14-11 / 1010	15-3 / 1060	15-7 / 1100	15-10 / 1150	16-2 / 1200	16-6 / 1240
	16	9-7 / 560	10-2 / 630	10-9 / 700	11-13 / 770	11-8 / 830	12-1 / 890	12-6 / 950	12-10 / 1000	13-2 / 1060	13-6 / 1110	13-10 / 1160	14-2 / 1220	14-5 / 1270	14-8 / 1320	15-0 / 1360
	24	8-5 / 640	8-11 / 720	9-4 / 800	9-10 / 880	10-2 / 950	10-7 / 1020	10-11 / 1080	11-3 / 1150	11-6 / 1210	11-10 / 1270	12-1 / 1330	12-4 / 1390	12-7 / 1450	12-10 / 1510	13-1 / 1560
2 x 10	12	13-6 / 510	14-4 / 570	15-1 / 640	15-9 / 700	16-5 / 750	17-0 / 810	17-6 / 860	18-0 / 910	18-6 / 960	19-0 / 1010	19-5 / 1060	19-10 / 1100	20-3 / 1150	20-8 / 1200	21-0 / 1240
	16	12-3 / 560	13-0 / 630	13-8 / 700	14-4 / 770	14-11 / 830	15-5 / 890	15-11 / 950	16-5 / 1000	16-10 / 1060	17-3 / 1110	17-8 / 1160	18-0 / 1220	18-5 / 1270	18-9 / 1320	19-1 / 1360
	24	10-8 / 640	11-4 / 720	11-11 / 800	12-6 / 880	13-0 / 950	13-6 / 1020	13-11 / 1080	14-4 / 1150	14-8 / 1210	15-1 / 1270	15-5 / 1330	15-9 / 1390	16-1 / 1450	16-5 / 1510	16-8 / 1560
2 x 12	12	16-5 / 510	17-5 / 570	18-4 / 640	19-2 / 700	19-11 / 750	20-8 / 810	21-4 / 860	21-11 / 910	22-6 / 960	23-1 / 1010	23-7 / 1060	24-2 / 1100	24-8 / 1150	25-1 / 1200	25-7 / 1240
	16	14-11 / 560	15-10 / 630	16-8 / 700	17-5 / 770	18-1 / 830	18-9 / 890	19-4 / 950	19-11 / 1000	20-6 / 1060	21-0 / 1110	21-6 / 1160	21-11 / 1220	22-5 / 1270	22-10 / 1320	23-3 / 1360
	24	13-0 / 640	13-10 / 720	14-7 / 800	15-2 / 880	15-10 / 950	16-5 / 1020	16-11 / 1080	17-5 / 1150	17-11 / 1210	18-4 / 1270	18-9 / 1330	19-2 / 1390	19-7 / 1450	19-11 / 1510	20-3 / 1560

NOTE: The required extreme fiber stress in bending, F_b, in psi is shown below each span.

DESIGN CRITERIA

STRENGTH: Live load of 40 psf plus dead load of 10 psf determines the required fiber stress value.
DEFLECTION: For 40 psf live load. Limited to span in inches divided by 360.

FLOOR JOISTS—40 LB LIVE LOAD

ALL ROOMS EXCEPT THOSE USED FOR SLEEPING AREAS AND ATTIC FLOORS

JOIST (IN.) SIZE	SPACING	| MODULUS OF ELASTICITY, E, IN 1,000,000 PSI														
		0.5	0.6	0.7	0.8	0.9	1.0	1.1	1.2	1.3	1.4	1.5	1.6	1.7	1.8	1.9
2 x 6	12	7-3 / 520	7-9 / 590	8-2 / 660	8-6 / 720	8-10 / 780	9-2 / 830	9-6 / 890	9-9 / 940	10-0 / 990	10-3 / 1040	10-6 / 1090	10-9 / 1140	10-11 / 1190	11-2 / 1230	11-4 / 1280
	16	6-7 / 580	7-0 / 650	7-5 / 720	7-9 / 790	8-0 / 860	8-4 / 920	8-7 / 980	8-10 / 1040	9-1 / 1090	9-4 / 1150	9-6 / 1200	9-9 / 1250	9-11 / 1310	10-2 / 1360	10-4 / 1410
	24	5-9 / 660	6-2 / 750	6-6 / 830	6-9 / 900	7-0 / 980	7-3 / 1050	7-6 / 1120	7-9 / 1190	7-11 / 1250	8-2 / 1310	8-4 / 1380	8-6 / 1440	8-8 / 1500	8-10 / 1550	9-0 / 1610
2 x 8	12	9-7 / 520	10-2 / 590	10-9 / 660	11-3 / 720	11-8 / 780	12-1 / 830	12-6 / 890	12-10 / 940	13-2 / 990	13-6 / 1040	13-10 / 1090	14-2 / 1140	14-5 / 1190	14-8 / 1230	15-0 / 1280
	16	8-9 / 580	9-3 / 650	9-9 / 720	10-2 / 790	10-7 / 850	11-0 / 920	11-4 / 980	11-8 / 1040	12-0 / 1090	12-3 / 1150	12-7 / 1200	12-10 / 1250	13-1 / 1310	13-4 / 1360	13-7 / 1410
	24	7-7 / 660	8-1 / 750	8-6 / 830	8-11 / 900	9-3 / 980	9-7 / 1050	9-11 / 1120	10-2 / 1190	10-6 / 1250	10-9 / 1310	11-0 / 1380	11-3 / 1440	11-5 / 1500	11-8 / 1550	11-11 / 1610
2 x 10	12	12-3 / 520	13-0 / 590	13-8 / 660	14-4 / 720	14-11 / 780	15-5 / 830	15-11 / 890	16-5 / 940	16-10 / 990	17-3 / 1040	17-8 / 1090	18-0 / 1140	18-5 / 1190	18-9 / 1230	19-1 / 1280
	16	11-1 / 580	11-10 / 650	12-5 / 720	13-0 / 790	13-6 / 850	14-0 / 920	14-6 / 980	14-11 / 1040	15-3 / 1090	15-8 / 1150	16-0 / 1200	16-5 / 1250	16-9 / 1310	17-0 / 1360	17-4 / 1410
	24	9-9 / 660	10-4 / 750	10-10 / 830	11-4 / 900	11-10 / 980	12-3 / 1050	12-8 / 1120	13-0 / 1190	13-4 / 1250	13-8 / 1310	14-0 / 1380	14-4 / 1440	14-7 / 1500	14-11 / 1550	15-2 / 1610
2 x 12	12	14-11 / 520	15-10 / 590	16-8 / 660	17-5 / 720	18-1 / 780	18-9 / 830	19-4 / 890	19-11 / 940	20-6 / 990	21-0 / 1040	21-6 / 1090	21-11 / 1140	22-5 / 1190	22-10 / 1230	23-3 / 1280
	16	13-6 / 580	14-4 / 650	15-2 / 720	15-10 / 790	16-5 / 860	17-0 / 920	17-7 / 980	18-1 / 1040	18-7 / 1090	19-1 / 1150	19-6 / 1200	19-11 / 1250	20-4 / 1310	20-9 / 1360	21-1 / 1410
	24	11-10 / 660	12-7 / 750	13-3 / 830	13-10 / 900	14-4 / 980	14-11 / 1050	15-4 / 1120	15-10 / 1190	16-3 / 1250	16-8 / 1310	17-0 / 1380	17-5 / 1440	17-9 / 1500	18-1 / 1550	18-5 / 1610

NOTE: The required extreme fiber stress in bending, F_b, in psi is shown below each span.

National Forest Products Association; Washington, D.C.

DESIGN LOAD TABLES

GENERAL DESIGN INFORMATION

For floor construction where live loading is heavier than customarily found in residential occupancies, tabular data are provided.

The tabulated spans are based on bending strength using the live load indicated in each table heading plus a dead load of 10 psf. In calculating the required modulus of elasticity for the tabulated span, the live load only was used, since this is in accordance with established practice for design of floor joists.

SPAN

While the effective span length for an isolated beam

is customarily taken as the distance from face to face of supports plus one-half the required length of bearing at each end, it is the practice in designing joists spaced not over 24 in. apart to consider the span as the clear distance between supports.

NET SIZES OF LUMBER

Joists are customarily specified in terms of nominal sizes, but calculations to determine the allowable span and required modulus of elasticity are based on actual sizes.

DESIGN STRESSES

Unit design values for design of wood joists are given in the National Design Specification for Wood Construc-

tion, available from the National Forest Products Association.

ADJUSTMENT OF MODULUS OF ELASTICITY

The modulus of elasticity values listed in the span tables for joists are those required for the tabulated spans if deflection under the live load is limited to $\ell/360$. Where other deflection limits are acceptable, the tabular E values may be adjusted by multiplying them by the following factors:

For limit of $\ell/360$: 0.833
For limit of $\ell/240$: 0.667
For limit of $\ell/180$: 0.500

FLOOR JOISTS—50 LB LIVE LOAD

JOIST (IN.)			EXTREME FIBER STRESS IN BENDING, F_b (PSI)									
SIZE	SPACING		900	1000	1100	1200	1300	1400	1500	1600	1800	2000
2 x 6	12		8-8 / 1.063	9-2 / 1.246	9-7 / 1.437	10-0 / 1.637	10-5 / 1.846	10-10 / 2.063	11-3 / 2.289	11-7 / 2.521	12-3 / 3.007	12-11 / 3.522
	16		7-6 / 0.924	7-11 / 1.083	8-4 / 1.249	8-8 / 1.423	9-1 / 1.605	9-5 / 1.794	9-9 / 1.989	10-0 / 2.191	10-7 / 2.614	11-2 / 3.062
	24		6-1 / 0.744	6-5 / 0.871	6-9 / 1.005	7-1 / 1.144	7-4 / 1.291	7-7 / 1.443	7-11 / 1.600	8-2 / 1.762	8-7 / 2.103	9-1 / 2.463
2 x 8	12		11-5 / 1.063	12-1 / 1.246	12-7 / 1.437	13-3 / 1.631	13-9 / 1.846	14-3 / 2.063	14-9 / 2.289	15-3 / 2.521	16-2 / 3.007	17-1 / 3.522
	16		9-11 / 0.924	10-5 / 1.083	11-0 / 1.249	11-6 / 1.423	11-11 / 1.605	12-5 / 1.794	12-10 / 1.989	13-3 / 2.191	14-0 / 2.614	14-10 / 3.062
	24		8-1 / 0.744	8-6 / 0.871	8-11 / 1.005	9-4 / 1.144	9-8 / 1.291	10-1 / 1.443	10-5 / 1.600	10-9 / 1.762	11-5 / 2.103	12-0 / 2.463
2 x 10	12		14-7 / 1.063	15-5 / 1.246	16-2 / 1.437	16-10 / 1.637	17-6 / 1.846	18-2 / 2.063	18-10 / 2.289	19-5 / 2.521	20-7 / 3.007	21-9 / 3.522
	16		12-7 / 0.924	13-4 / 1.083	14-0 / 1.249	14-7 / 1.423	15-3 / 1.605	15-10 / 1.794	16-4 / 1.989	16-10 / 2.191	17-11 / 2.614	18-11 / 3.062
	24		10-3 / 0.744	10-10 / 0.871	11-4 / 1.005	11-10 / 1.144	12-4 / 1.291	12-10 / 1.443	13-3 / 1.600	13-9 / 1.762	14-7 / 2.103	15-4 / 2.463
2 x 12	12		17-9 / 1.063	18-9 / 1.246	19-7 / 1.437	20-6 / 1.637	21-4 / 1.846	22-2 / 2.063	22-11 / 2.289	23-8 / 2.521	25-1 / 3.007	26-6 / 3.522
	16		15-5 / 0.924	16-3 / 1.083	17-1 / 1.249	17-10 / 1.423	18-6 / 1.605	19-2 / 1.794	19-10 / 1.989	20-6 / 2.191	21-9 / 2.614	23-0 / 3.062
	24		12-6 / 0.744	13-2 / 0.871	13-10 / 1.005	14-5 / 1.144	15-0 / 1.291	15-7 / 1.443	16-2 / 1.600	16-7 / 1.762	17-8 / 2.103	18-10 / 2.463
2 x 14	12		20-11 / 1.063	22-1 / 1.246	23-2 / 1.437	24-2 / 1.637	25-2 / 1.846	26-1 / 2.063	27-0 / 2.289	27-11 / 2.521	29-7 / 3.007	31-2 / 3.522
	16		18-2 / 0.924	19-2 / 1.083	20-1 / 1.249	20-11 / 1.423	21-9 / 1.605	22-7 / 1.794	23-5 / 1.989	24-2 / 2.191	25-7 / 2.614	27-0 / 3.062
	24		14-9 / 0.744	15-6 / 0.871	16-3 / 1.005	17-0 / 1.144	17-8 / 1.291	18-4 / 1.443	19-0 / 1.600	19-7 / 1.762	20-10 / 2.103	22-0 / 2.463
3 x 6	12		11-2 / 1.373	11-10 / 1.608	12-5 / 1.855	12-11 / 2.113	13-6 / 2.383	14-0 / 2.663	14-6 / 2.953	14-11 / 3.254	15-10 / 3.882	16-9 / 4.547
	16		9-9 / 1.193	10-3 / 1.397	10-9 / 1.612	11-3 / 1.836	11-8 / 2.071	12-2 / 2.314	12-7 / 2.567	12-11 / 2.827	13-9 / 3.374	14-6 / 3.952
	24		7-11 / 0.960	8-4 / 1.124	8-9 / 1.297	9-2 / 1.478	9-6 / 1.666	9-10 / 1.862	10-2 / 2.065	10-6 / 2.275	11-2 / 2.714	11-9 / 3.179
3 x 8	12		14-9 / 1.373	15-7 / 1.608	16-4 / 1.855	17-1 / 2.113	17-9 / 2.383	18-5 / 2.663	19-1 / 2.953	19-9 / 3.254	20-11 / 3.882	22-1 / 4.537
	16		12-10 / 1.193	13-6 / 1.397	14-2 / 1.612	14-10 / 1.836	15-5 / 2.071	16-0 / 2.314	16-7 / 2.567	17-1 / 2.827	18-1 / 3.374	19-1 / 3.952
	24		10-5 / 0.960	11-0 / 1.124	11-6 / 1.297	12-0 / 1.478	12-6 / 1.666	13-0 / 1.862	13-5 / 2.065	13-10 / 2.275	14-8 / 2.714	15-6 / 3.179
3 x 10	12		18-10 / 1.373	19-10 / 1.608	20-10 / 1.855	21-9 / 2.113	22-7 / 2.383	23-6 / 2.663	24-4 / 2.953	25-1 / 3.254	26-7 / 3.882	28-1 / 4.547
	16		16-4 / 1.193	17-3 / 1.397	18-1 / 1.612	18-10 / 1.836	19-7 / 2.071	20-5 / 2.314	21-1 / 2.567	21-10 / 2.827	23-2 / 3.374	24-5 / 3.952
	24		13-3 / 0.960	14-0 / 1.124	14-8 / 1.297	15-4 / 1.478	16-0 / 1.666	16-7 / 1.862	17-2 / 2.065	17-8 / 2.275	18-9 / 2.714	19-10 / 3.179
3 x 12	12		22-11 / 1.373	24-2 / 1.608	25-4 / 1.855	26-5 / 2.113	27-6 / 2.383	28-7 / 2.663	29-7 / 2.953	30-7 / 3.254	32-5 / 3.882	34-2 / 4.547
	16		19-11 / 1.193	20-11 / 1.397	21-11 / 1.612	22-11 / 1.836	23-11 / 2.071	24-10 / 2.314	25-8 / 2.567	26-6 / 2.827	28-1 / 3.374	29-7 / 3.952
	24		16-2 / 0.960	17-0 / 1.124	17-10 / 1.297	18-8 / 1.478	19-5 / 1.666	20-2 / 1.862	20-10 / 2.065	21-6 / 2.275	22-10 / 2.714	24-1 / 3.179
3 x 14	12		27-0 / 1.373	28-5 / 1.608	29-10 / 1.855	31-2 / 2.113	32-5 / 2.383	33-8 / 2.663	34-10 / 2.953	36-0 / 3.254	38-2 / 3.882	40-3 / 4.547
	16		23-5 / 1.193	24-8 / 1.397	25-11 / 1.612	27-1 / 1.836	28-2 / 2.071	29-3 / 2.314	30-3 / 2.567	31-3 / 2.827	33-1 / 3.374	34-11 / 3.952
	24		19-0 / 0.960	20-0 / 1.124	21-0 / 1.297	22-0 / 1.478	22-11 / 1.666	23-9 / 1.862	24-7 / 2.065	25-5 / 2.275	26-11 / 2.714	28-4 / 3.179

NOTE: The required modulus of elasticity, E, in 1,000,000 psi is shown below each span, if deflection under the live load is limited to $\ell/360$.

National Forest Products Association; Washington, D.C.

DESIGN LOAD TABLES

GENERAL DESIGN INFORMATION

For floor construction where live loading is heavier than customarily found in residential occupancies, tabular data are provided.

The tabulated spans are based on bending strength using the live load indicated in each table heading plus a dead load of 10 psf. In calculating the required modulus of elasticity for the tabulated span, the live load only was used, since this is in accordance with established practice for design of floor joists.

SPAN

While the effective span length for an isolated beam is customarily taken as the distance from face to face of supports plus one-half the required length of bearing at each end, it is the practice in designing joists spaced not over 24 in. apart to consider the span as the clear distance between supports.

NET SIZES OF LUMBER

Joists are customarily specified in terms of nominal sizes, but calculations to determine the allowable span and required modulus of elasticity are based on actual sizes.

DESIGN STRESSES

Unit design values for design of wood joists are given in the National Design Specification for Wood Construc-

tion, available from the National Forest Products Association.

ADJUSTMENT OF MODULUS OF ELASTICITY

The modulus of elasticity values listed in the span tables for joists are those required for the tabulated spans if deflection under the live load is limited to $\ell/360$. Where other deflection limits are acceptable, the tabular E values may be adjusted by multiplying them by the following factors:

For limit of $\ell/360$: 0.833
For limit of $\ell/240$: 0.667
For limit of $\ell/180$: 0.500

FLOOR JOISTS—60 LB LIVE LOAD

JOIST (IN.)		EXTREME FIBER STRESS IN BENDING, F_b (PSI)									
SIZE	SPACING	900	1000	1100	1200	1300	1400	1500	1600	1800	2000
2 x 6	12	8-1 1.012	8-6 1.186	8-11 1.368	9-3 1.558	9-8 1.757	10-0 1.964	10-5 2.179	10-9 2.400	11-5 2.863	12-0 3.353
	16	7-0 0.880	7-4 1.031	7-9 1.189	8-1 1.355	8-5 1.528	8-8 1.708	9-0 1.894	9-4 2.191	9-10 2.489	10-5 2.915
	24	5-8 0.708	6-0 0.829	6-4 0.957	6-7 1.089	6-10 1.229	7-1 1.374	7-4 1.523	7-7 1.677	8-0 2.002	8-5 2.345
2 x 8	12	10-7 1.012	11-2 1.186	11-9 1.368	12-3 1.558	12-9 1.757	13-3 1.964	13-8 2.179	14-1 2.400	15-0 2.863	15-10 3.353
	16	9-2 0.880	9-8 1.031	10-2 1.189	10-7 1.355	11-0 1.528	11-5 1.708	11-10 1.894	12-3 2.191	13-0 2.489	13-8 2.915
	24	7-6 0.708	7-11 0.829	8-3 0.957	8-7 1.089	9-0 1.229	9-4 1.374	9-7 1.523	9-11 1.677	10-7 2.002	11-2 2.345
2 x 10	12	13-6 1.012	14-3 1.186	14-11 1.368	15-7 1.558	16-3 1.757	16-10 1.964	17-5 2.179	18-0 2.400	19-1 2.863	20-2 3.353
	16	11-9 0.880	12-3 1.031	13-0 1.189	13-6 1.355	14-0 1.528	14-6 1.708	15-1 1.894	15-7 2.191	16-7 2.489	17-6 2.915
	24	9-6 0.708	10-0 0.829	10-6 0.957	11-0 1.089	11-6 1.229	11-11 1.374	12-4 1.523	12-9 1.677	13-6 2.002	14-3 2.345
2 x 12	12	16-6 1.012	17-4 1.186	18-2 1.368	19-0 1.558	19-9 1.757	20-6 1.964	21-3 2.179	21-11 2.400	23-3 2.863	24-6 3.353
	16	14-3 0.880	15-0 1.031	15-9 1.189	16-6 1.355	17-2 1.528	17-10 1.708	18-5 1.894	19-0 2.191	20-2 2.489	21-3 2.915
	24	11-7 0.708	12-3 0.829	12-10 0.957	13-5 1.089	13-11 1.229	14-5 1.374	14-11 1.523	15-5 1.677	16-5 2.002	17-5 2.345
2 x 14	12	19-5 1.012	20-5 1.186	21-5 1.368	22-4 1.558	23-3 1.757	24-2 1.964	25-0 2.179	25-10 2.400	27-5 2.863	28-11 3.353
	16	16-10 0.880	17-8 1.031	18-6 1.189	19-4 1.355	20-2 1.528	20-11 1.708	21-8 1.894	22-5 2.191	23-9 2.489	25-1 2.915
	24	13-8 0.708	14-5 0.829	15-1 0.957	15-9 1.089	16-5 1.229	17-0 1.374	17-7 1.523	18-2 1.677	19-3 2.002	20-4 2.345
3 x 6	12	10-4 1.037	10-11 1.531	11-6 1.766	12-0 2.012	12-6 2.269	13-0 2.535	13-5 2.811	13-10 3.098	14-8 3.696	15-6 4.329
	16	9-0 1.136	9-6 1.330	10-0 1.535	10-5 1.748	10-10 1.972	11-3 2.203	11-8 2.444	12-0 2.691	12-9 3.212	13-5 3.762
	24	7-4 0.914	7-9 1.070	8-1 1.235	8-5 1.406	8-9 1.586	9-1 1.773	9-5 1.966	9-9 2.166	10-4 2.584	10-11 3.026
3 x 8	12	13-8 1.307	14-5 1.531	15-2 1.766	15-10 2.012	16-6 2.269	17-1 2.535	17-8 2.811	18-3 3.098	19-4 3.696	20-5 4.329
	16	11-10 1.136	12-6 1.330	13-1 1.535	13-8 1.748	14-3 1.972	14-10 2.203	15-4 2.444	15-10 2.691	16-9 3.212	17-8 3.762
	24	9-7 0.914	10-1 1.070	10-7 1.235	11-1 1.406	11-7 1.586	12-0 1.773	12-5 1.966	12-10 2.166	13-7 2.584	14-4 3.026
3 x 10	12	17-5 1.307	18-5 1.531	19-4 1.766	20-2 2.012	21-0 2.269	21-9 2.535	22-7 2.811	23-4 3.098	24-9 3.696	26-1 4.329
	16	15-2 1.136	16-0 1.330	16-9 1.535	17-6 1.748	18-2 1.972	18-10 2.203	19-6 2.444	20-2 2.691	21-5 3.212	22-7 3.762
	24	12-4 0.914	13-0 1.070	13-7 1.235	14-2 1.406	14-9 1.586	15-4 1.773	15-10 1.966	16-4 2.166	17-5 2.584	18-4 3.026
3 x 12	12	21-3 1.307	22-4 1.531	23-5 1.766	24-6 2.012	25-6 1.269	26-6 2.535	27-5 2.811	28-4 3.098	30-0 3.696	31-7 4.329
	16	18-5 1.136	19-5 1.330	20-4 1.535	21-3 1.748	22-2 1.972	23-0 2.203	23-9 2.444	24-6 2.691	26-0 3.212	27-5 3.762
	24	15-0 0.914	15-9 1.070	16-6 1.235	17-3 1.406	18-0 1.586	18-8 1.773	19-4 1.966	20-0 2.166	21-2 2.584	22-4 3.036
3 x 14	12	25-0 1.307	26-4 1.531	27-7 1.766	28-10 2.012	30-1 2.269	31-3 2.535	32-4 2.811	33-4 3.098	35-4 3.696	37-4 4.329
	16	21-8 1.136	22-10 1.330	24-0 1.535	25-1 1.748	26-1 1.972	27-1 2.203	28-0 2.444	28-11 2.691	30-8 3.212	32-4 3.762
	24	17-7 0.914	18-7 1.070	19-6 1.235	20-4 1.406	21-2 1.586	22-0 1.773	22-9 1.966	23-6 2.166	24-11 2.584	26-3 3.026

NOTE: The required modulus of elasticity, E, in 1,000,000 psi is shown below each span, if deflection under the live load is limited to $\ell/360$.

National Forest Products Association; Washington, D.C.

DESIGN LOAD TABLES

GENERAL DESIGN INFORMATION

For floor construction where live loading is heavier than customarily found in residential occupancies, tabular data are provided.

The tabulated spans are based on bending strength using the live load indicated in each table heading plus a dead load of 10 psf. In calculating the required modulus of elasticity for the tabulated span, the live load only was used, since this is in accordance with established practice for design of floor joists.

SPAN

While the effective span length for an isolated beam is customarily taken as the distance from face to face of supports plus one-half the required length of bearing at each end, it is the practice in designing joists spaced not over 24 in. apart to consider the span as the clear distance between supports.

NET SIZES OF LUMBER

Joists are customarily specified in terms of nominal sizes, but calculations to determine the allowable span and required modulus of elasticity are based on actual sizes.

DESIGN STRESSES

Unit design values for design of wood joists are given in the National Design Specification for Wood Construc-

tion, available from the National Forest Products Association.

ADJUSTMENT OF MODULUS OF ELASTICITY

The modulus of elasticity values listed in the span tables for joists are those required for the tabulated spans if deflection under the live load is limited to $\ell/360$. Where other deflection limits are acceptable, the tabular E values may be adjusted by multiplying them by the following factors:

For limit of $\ell/360$: 0.833
For limit of $\ell/240$: 0.667
For limit of $\ell/180$: 0.500

FLOOR JOISTS—70 LB LIVE LOAD

JOIST (IN.)			EXTREME FIBER STRESS IN BENDING, F_b (PSI)									
SIZE	SPACING		900	1000	1100	1200	1300	1400	1500	1600	1800	2000
2 x 10	12		12-8 0.963	13-4 1.133	14-0 1.306	14-7 1.488	15-2 1.678	15-9 1.875	16-4 2.081	16-10 2.292	17-11 2.733	18-10 3.201
	16		11-1 0.840	11-7 0.984	12-1 1.135	12-7 1.294	13-2 1.459	13-8 1.631	14-2 1.808	14-7 1.992	15-6 2.376	16-4 2.783
	24		8-11 0.676	9-5 0.792	9-10 0.914	10-3 1.040	10-8 1.174	11-1 1.312	11-6 1.454	11-11 1.602	12-7 1.912	13-3 2.239
2 x 12	12		15-5 0.963	16-3 1.133	17-0 1.306	17-9 1.488	18-6 1.678	19-2 1.875	19-10 2.081	20-6 2.292	21-9 2.733	22-11 3.201
	16		13-4 0.840	14-1 0.984	14-9 1.135	15-5 1.294	16-0 1.459	16-7 1.631	17-3 1.808	17-10 1.992	18-10 2.376	19-11 2.783
	24		10-10 0.676	11-5 0.792	12-0 0.914	·12-6 1.040	13-0 1.174	13-6 1.312	14-0 1.454	14-5 1.602	15-4 1.912	16-4 2.239
2 x 14	12		18-2 0.963	19-1 1.133	20-0 1.306	20-11 1.488	21-9 1.678	22-7 1.875	23-5 2.081	24-2 2.292	25-7 2.733	27-0 3.201
	16		15-9 0.840	16-7 0.984	17-5 1.135	18-2 1.294	18-11 1.459	19-7 1.631	20-3 1.808	20-11 1.992	22-3 2.376	23-5 2.783
	24		12-9 0.676	13-6 0.792	14-2 0.914	14-9 1.040	15-4 1.174	15-11 1.312	16-6 1.454	17-0 1.602	18-1 1.912	19-1 2.239
3 x 8	12		12-10 1.248	13-6 1.462	14-2 1.686	14-9 1.921	15-4 2.166	15-11 2.421	16-6 2.684	17-1 2.958	18-1 3.529	19-1 4.133
	16		11-1 1.084	11-8 1.270	12-3 1.465	12-10 1.669	13-4 1.883	13-10 2.103	14-4 2.333	14-10 2.570	15-8 3.067	16-7 3.592
	24		9-0 0.873	9-6 1.022	10-0 1.179	10-5 1.344	10-10 1.514	11-3 1.693	11-8 1.877	12-0 2.068	12-9 2.467	13-5 2.900
3 x 10	12		16-4 1.248	17-3 1.462	18-1 1.686	18-10 1.921	19-7 2.166	20-4 2.421	21-1 2.684	21-9 2.958	23-1 3.529	24-4 4.133
	16		14-2 1.084	14-11 1.270	15-8 1.465	16-4 1.669	17-0 1.883	17-8 2.103	18-3 2.333	18-11 2.570	20-1 3.067	21-1 3.592
	24		11-6 0.873	12-2 1.022	12-9 1.179	13-3 1.344	13-10 1.514	14-4 1.693	14-10 1.877	15-4 2.068	16-3 2.467	17-2 2.900
3 x 12	12		19-11 1.248	20-11 1.462	21-11 1.686	22-22 1.921	23-10 2.166	24-9 2.421	25-8 2.684	26-6 2.958	28-1 3.529	29-7 4.133
	16		17-3 1.084	18-2 1.270	19-1 1.465	19-11 1.669	20-9 1.883	21-6 2.103	22-3 2.333	23-0 2.570	24-4 3.067	25-8 3.592
	24		14-0 0.873	14-9 1.022	15-6 1.179	16-2 1.344	16-10 1.514	17-6 1.693	18-1 1.877	18-7 2.068	19-9 2.467	20-10 2.900
3 x 14	12		23-4 1.248	24-7 1.462	25-10 1.686	27-0 1.921	28-1 2.166	29-2 2.421	30-2 2.684	21-2 2.958	33-1 3.529	34-11 4.133
	16		20-3 1.084	21-4 1.270	22-5 1.465	23-5 1.669	24-5 1.883	25-4 2.103	26-2 2.333	27-0 2.570	28-8 3.067	30-3 3.592
	24		16-6 0.873	17-4 1.022	18-7 1.179	19-0 1.344	19-9 1.514	20-6 1.693	21-3 1.877	22-0 2.068	23-4 2.467	24-7 2.900
4 x 8	12		15-2 1.490	16-0 1.745	16-10 2.015	17-7 2.295	18-3 2.588	18-11 2.891	19-7 3.207	20-3 3.533	21-6 4.217	22-7 4.939
	16		13-2 1.300	13-11 1.533	14-7 1.757	15-3 2.002	15-11 2.257	16-6 2.522	17-1 2.799	17-7 3.082	18-7 3.676	19-7 4.306
	24		10-9 1.054	11-4 1.234	11-11 1.425	12-5 1.625	12-11 1.831	13-5 2.046	13-11 2.268	14-4 2.500	15-2 2.922	16-0 3.492
4 x 10	12		19-5 1.490	20-5 1.745	21-5 2.015	22-5 2.295	22-4 2.588	24-2 2.891	25-0 3.207	25-10 3.533	27-5 4.217	28-9 4.939
	16		16-10 1.300	17-9 1.533	18-7 1.757	19-5 2.002	20-3 2.257	21-0 2.522	21-9 2.799	22-5 3.082	23-10 3.676	25-1 4.306
	24		13-8 1.054	14-5 1.234	15-2 1.425	15-10 1.625	16-6 1.831	17-1 2.046	17-8 2.268	18-3 2.500	19-3 2.922	20-5 3.492
4 x 12	12		23-7 1.490	24-10 1.745	26-1 2.015	27-3 2.295	28-4 2.588	29-5 2.891	20-5 3.207	31-5 2.533	33-4 4.217	35-2 4.939
	16		20-6 1.300	21-7 1.533	22-7 1.757	23-7 2.002	24-7 2.257	25-6 2.522	26-5 2.799	27-4 3.082	28-5 3.676	30-6 4.306
	24		16-8 1.054	17-7 1.234	18-5 1.425	19-3 1.625	20-1 1.831	20-10 2.046	21-6 2.268	22-2 2.500	23-6 2.922	24-10 3.492

NOTE: The required modulus of elasticity, E, in 1,000,000 psi is shown below each span, if deflection under the live load is limited to $\ell/360$.

National Forest Products Association; Washington, D.C.

DESIGN LOAD TABLES

GENERAL DESIGN INFORMATION

For floor construction where live loading is heavier than customarily found in residential occupancies, tabular data are provided.

The tabulated spans are based on bending strength using the live load indicated in each table heading plus a dead load of 10 psf. In calculating the required modulus of elasticity for the tabulated span, the live load only was used, since this is in accordance with established practice for design of floor joists.

SPAN

While the effective span length for an isolated beam is customarily taken as the distance from face to face of supports plus one-half the required length of bearing at each end, it is the practice in designing joists spaced not over 24 in. apart to consider the span as the clear distance between supports.

NET SIZES OF LUMBER

Joists are customarily specified in terms of nominal sizes, but calculations to determine the allowable span and required modulus of elasticity are based on actual sizes.

DESIGN STRESSES

Unit design values for design of wood joists are given in the National Design Specification for Wood Construc-tion, available from the National Forest Products Association.

ADJUSTMENT OF MODULUS OF ELASTICITY

The modulus of elasticity values listed in the span tables for joists are those required for the tabulated spans if deflection under the live load is limited to $\ell/360$. Where other deflection limits are acceptable, the tabular E values may be adjusted by multiplying them by the following factors:

For limit of $\ell/360$: 0.833
For limit of $\ell/240$: 0.667
For limit of $\ell/180$: 0.500

FLOOR JOISTS— 80 LB LIVE LOAD

JOIST (IN.)		EXTREME FIBER STRESS IN BENDING, F_b (PSI)									
SIZE	SPACING	900	1000	1100	1200	1300	1400	1500	1600	1800	2000
2 x 10	12	11-11 / 0.926	12-7 / 1.084	13-2 / 1.250	13-9 / 1.423	14-4 / 1.604	14-11 / 1.795	15-5 / 1.988	15-11 / 2.191	16-10 / 2.617	17-9 / 3.062
	16	10-4 / 0.803	10-11 / 0.941	11-5 / 1.086	11-11 / 1.236	12-5 / 1.395	12-11 / 1.561	13-4 / 1.730	13-9 / 1.903	14-7 / 2.273	15-5 / 2.662
	24	8-5 / 0.646	8-10 / 0.758	9-3 / 0.873	9-8 / 0.995	10-1 / 1.124	10-6 / 1.254	10-10 / 1.390	11-2 / 1.533	11-10 / 1.829	12-6 / 2.143
2 x 12	12	14-6 / 0.926	15-4 / 1.084	16-1 / 1.250	16-9 / 1.423	17-5 / 1.604	18-1 / 1.795	18-9 / 1.988	19-4 / 2.191	20-6 / 2.617	21-7 / 3.062
	16	11-3 / 0.803	12-7 / 0.947	13-11 / 1.089	14-6 / 1.236	15-1 / 1.395	15-8 / 1.561	16-3 / 1.730	16-9 / 1.903	17-9 / 2.273	18-9 / 2.662
	24	10-3 / 0.646	10-9 / 0.758	11-3 / 0.873	11-9 / 0.995	12-3 / 1.124	12-9 / 1.254	13-2 / 1.390	13-7 / 1.533	14-5 / 1.829	15-5 / 2.143
2 x 14	12	17-1 / 0.926	18-0 / 1.084	18-10 / 1.250	19-8 / 1.423	20-6 / 1.604	21-4 / 1.795	22-1 / 1.988	22-9 / 2.191	24-2 / 2.617	25-5 / 3.062
	16	14-10 / 0.803	15-7 / 0.941	16-4 / 1.086	17-1 / 1.236	17-10 / 1.395	18-6 / 1.561	19-2 / 1.730	19-9 / 1.903	20-11 / 2.273	22-1 / 2.662
	24	12-0 / 0.646	12-8 / 0.758	13-4 / 0.873	13-11 / 0.995	14-5 / 1.124	15-0 / 1.254	15-6 / 1.390	16-0 / 1.533	17-0 / 1.829	18-0 / 2.143
3 x 8	12	12-0 / 1.195	12-8 / 1.399	13-4 / 1.614	13-11 / 1.838	14-6 / 2.073	15-1 / 2.317	15-7 / 2.569	16-1 / 2.831	17-1 / 3.377	18-0 / 3.956
	16	10-6 / 1.038	11-0 / 1.215	11-7 / 1.402	12-1 / 1.597	12-7 / 1.082	13-1 / 2.013	13-6 / 2.233	13-11 / 2.459	14-9 / 2.935	15-7 / 3.438
	24	8-6 / 0.835	9-0 / 0.978	9-5 / 1.128	9-10 / 1.286	10-3 / 1.449	10-7 / 1.620	11-0 / 1.797	11-4 / 1.979	12-0 / 2.361	12-8 / 2.766
3 x 10	12	15-5 / 1.195	16-3 / 1.399	17-0 / 1.614	17-9 / 1.838	18-6 / 2.073	19-2 / 2.317	19-10 / 2.569	20-6 / 2.831	21-8 / 3.377	22-11 / 3.956
	16	13-4 / 1.038	14-1 / 1.215	14-9 / 1.402	15-5 / 1.597	16-0 / 1.802	16-7 / 2.013	17-3 / 2.233	17-9 / 2.459	18-10 / 2.935	19-11 / 3.438
	24	10-10 / 0.835	11-5 / 0.978	12-0 / 1.128	12-6 / 1.286	13-0 / 1.446	13-6 / 1.620	14-0 / 1.797	14-5 / 1.979	15-4 / 2.361	16-2 / 2.766
3 x 12	12	18-9 / 1.195	19-9 / 1.399	20-8 / 1.614	21-7 / 1.838	22-6 / 2.073	23-4 / 2.317	24-2 / 2.569	25-0 / 2.831	26-5 / 3.377	27-11 / 3.956
	16	16-3 / 1.038	17-1 / 1.215	17-11 / 1.402	18-9 / 1.597	19-6 / 1.802	20-3 / 2.013	20-11 / 2.233	21-7 / 2.459	22-11 / 2.935	24-2 / 3.438
	24	13-2 / 0.835	13-11 / 0.978	14-7 / 1.128	15-3 / 1.286	15-10 / 1.449	16-5 / 1.620	17-0 / 1.797	17-7 / 1.979	18-7 / 2.361	19-7 / 2.766
3 x 14	12	22-1 / 1.195	23-3 / 1.399	24-4 / 1.614	25-5 / 1.838	26-6 / 2.073	27-6 / 2.317	28-6 / 2.569	29-5 / 2.831	31-2 / 3.377	32-10 / 3.956
	16	19-2 / 1.038	20-2 / 1.215	21-2 / 1.402	22-1 / 1.597	23-0 / 1.802	23-10 / 2.013	24-8 / 2.233	25-6 / 2.459	27-1 / 2.935	28-6 / 3.438
	24	15-6 / 0.835	16-4 / 0.978	17-2 / 1.128	17-11 / 1.286	18-8 / 1.449	19-5 / 1.620	20-1 / 1.797	20-9 / 1.979	22-0 / 2.361	23-2 / 2.776
4 x 8	12	14-4 / 1.426	15-1 / 1.670	15-10 / 1.928	16-6 / 2.196	17-2 / 2.475	17-10 / 2.766	18-5 / 3.068	19-0 / 3.379	20-3 / 4.034	21-4 / 4.725
	16	12-5 / 1.243	13-1 / 1.457	13-9 / 1.681	14-4 / 1.915	14-11 / 2.159	15-6 / 2.413	16-1 / 2.677	16-7 / 2.948	17-7 / 3.516	18-6 / 4.119
	24	10-2 / 1.009	10-8 / 1.180	11-2 / 1.363	11-8 / 1.554	12-2 / 1.752	12-6 / 1.957	13-1 / 2.170	13-6 / 2.391	14-4 / 2.795	15-1 / 3.340
4 x 10	12	18-3 / 1.426	19-3 / 1.670	20-2 / 1.928	21-1 / 2.196	21-11 / 2.475	22-9 / 2.766	23-7 / 3.068	24-4 / 3.379	25-10 / 4.034	27-3 / 4.725
	16	15-10 / 1.243	16-8 / 1.457	17-6 / 1.681	18-4 / 1.915	19-1 / 2.159	19-10 / 2.413	20-6 / 2.677	21-2 / 2.948	22-5 / 3.516	23-7 / 4.119
	24	12-11 / 1.009	13-7 / 1.180	14-3 / 1.363	14-11 / 1.554	15-6 / 1.752	16-1 / 1.957	16-8 / 2.170	17-2 / 2.391	18-2 / 2.795	19-3 / 3.340
4 x 12	12	22-3 / 1.426	23-5 / 1.670	25-6 / 1.928	25-7 / 2.196	26-8 / 2.475	27-8 / 2.766	28-8 / 3.068	29-7 / 3.379	31-5 / 4.034	33-2 / 4.725
	16	19-3 / 1.243	20-4 / 1.457	21-4 / 1.681	22-3 / 1.915	23-2 / 2.159	24-1 / 2.413	24-11 / 2.677	25-9 / 2.948	27-3 / 3.516	28-9 / 4.119
	24	15-9 / 1.009	16-7 / 1.180	17-4 / 1.363	18-1 / 1.554	18-10 / 1.752	19-7 / 1.957	20-3 / 2.170	20-11 / 2.391	22-2 / 2.795	23-5 / 3.340

NOTE: The required modulus of elasticity, E, in 1,000,000 psi is shown below each span, if deflection under the live load is limited to $\ell/360$.

National Forest Products Association; Washington, D.C.

DESIGN LOAD TABLES

UNIT AXIAL STRESSES: SIMPLE SOLID COLUMNS— ℓ/d FROM 11 TO 30

E	Fc	11+	12	13	14	15	16	17	18	19	20	21	22	23	24	25	26	27	28	29	30
1,800,000	1500	1475	1464	1451	1434	1413	1388	1357	1320	1277	1226	1167	1098	1020	938	864	799	741	689	642	600
	1400	1380	1371	1360	1346	1329	1309	1284	1254	1218	1177	1129	1073	1010	937	864	799	741	689	642	600
	1300	1284	1277	1268	1257	1243	1227	1207	1188	1155	1121	1083	1039	988	930	864	799	741	689	642	600
	1200	1187	1182	1175	1166	1156	1142	1127	1108	1086	1060	1029	994	954	909	857	799	741	689	642	600
1,700,000	1500	1472	1460	1445	1426	1403	1374	1339	1298	1249	1192	1126	1050	964	885	816	754	700	651	606	567
	1400	1377	1368	1355	1340	1321	1298	1269	1236	1196	1150	1096	1034	963	885	816	754	700	651	606	567
	1300	1282	1274	1264	1252	1237	1218	1195	1169	1137	1100	1057	1007	950	885	816	754	700	651	606	567
	1200	1186	1180	1172	1162	1150	1135	1118	1097	1072	1043	1009	969	925	873	816	754	700	651	606	567
1,600,000	1500	1468	1455	1438	1417	1390	1358	1319	1272	1217	1153	1078	992	907	833	768	710	658	612	571	533
	1400	1374	1363	1350	1332	1311	1284	1253	1215	1170	1118	1057	987	907	833	768	710	658	612	571	533
	1300	1279	1271	1260	1246	1228	1207	1182	1152	1116	1074	1025	969	905	833	768	710	658	612	571	533
	1200	1184	1177	1168	1157	1144	1127	1107	1083	1055	1022	984	940	889	831	768	710	658	612	571	533
	1100	1087	1082	1076	1067	1057	1044	1029	1010	988	963	934	900	861	816	766	710	658	612	571	533
	1000	991	987	982	975	967	958	946	933	916	897	875	849	820	787	749	706	658	612	571	533
	900	893	890	887	882	876	869	861	851	839	825	809	790	769	744	717	686	651	612	571	533
1,500,000	1400	1371	1358	1343	1323	1298	1268	1232	1189	1138	1079	1010	930	851	781	720	666	617	574	535	500
	1300	1276	1267	1254	1238	1219	1195	1166	1131	1091	1043	987	923	851	781	720	666	617	574	535	500
	1200	1181	1174	1164	1151	1136	1117	1094	1067	1035	998	954	904	846	781	720	666	617	574	535	500
	1100	1086	1080	1072	1063	1051	1036	1019	998	973	944	911	872	828	777	720	666	617	574	535	500
	1000	989	985	979	972	963	952	939	923	905	883	858	829	795	757	714	666	617	574	535	500
	900	892	889	885	880	873	865	855	844	830	815	796	775	751	723	692	656	617	574	535	500
	800	795	792	789	786	781	775	769	761	751	740	727	712	695	676	654	629	601	570	535	500
	700	696	695	693	690	687	684	679	674	667	660	651	641	630	617	602	585	567	546	523	497
	600	598	597	595	594	592	590	587	583	579	575	569	563	556	548	538	528	516	503	488	472
1,400,000	1200	1179	1170	1159	1144	1127	1105	1079	1048	1011	968	918	860	794	729	672	621	576	536	499	467
	1100	1084	1077	1068	1057	1043	1027	1007	983	954	921	883	838	787	729	672	621	576	536	499	467
	1000	988	983	976	968	957	945	930	912	891	866	837	803	765	721	672	621	576	536	499	467
	900	891	887	883	876	869	860	849	836	820	802	781	757	729	697	661	620	576	536	499	467
	800	794	791	788	783	778	772	764	755	744	731	716	699	680	657	632	604	571	536	499	467
	700	696	694	692	689	685	681	676	670	662	654	644	633	619	604	587	568	547	523	496	467
1,300,000	1100	1081	1073	1063	1050	1034	1015	992	964	931	893	848	796	737	677	624	577	535	497	464	433
	1000	986	980	972	963	951	936	919	898	873	844	811	772	727	677	624	577	535	497	464	433
	900	890	885	880	873	864	853	841	825	807	786	762	734	701	664	623	577	535	497	464	433
	800	793	790	786	781	775	767	758	748	735	720	703	683	660	635	605	572	535	497	464	433
	700	695	693	690	687	683	678	672	665	656	647	635	622	607	589	569	547	522	495	464	433
1,200,000	1100	1078	1068	1057	1042	1023	1000	973	940	902	857	804	744	681	625	576	533	444	459	428	400
	1000	983	976	967	956	942	925	905	880	851	817	778	732	680	625	576	533	444	459	428	400
	900	888	883	876	868	858	845	830	813	791	767	738	705	667	624	576	533	444	459	428	400
	800	791	788	783	778	770	762	751	739	724	706	686	663	636	606	571	533	444	459	428	400
	700	694	692	689	685	680	674	667	659	649	637	624	608	590	570	547	521	492	459	428	400
	600	596	595	593	591	588	584	579	574	568	560	552	542	531	518	504	487	469	448	425	400
	500	498	497	496	495	493	491	488	485	481	477	472	467	460	453	444	435	424	412	399	384
	400	399	398	398	397	396	395	394	392	390	388	386	383	380	376	371	367	361	355	348	341
1,100,000	900	885	879	872	862	850	835	817	796	771	741	707	668	622	573	528	488	453	421	392	397
	800	790	786	780	773	765	754	742	727	709	689	665	637	605	569	528	488	453	421	392	397
	700	693	690	687	682	676	669	661	651	639	625	609	591	569	545	518	487	453	421	392	397
	600	596	594	592	589	585	581	575	569	562	553	543	531	518	503	485	466	444	419	392	397
	500	498	496	495	493	491	489	486	482	478	473	467	460	452	444	434	422	410	395	380	362
	400	399	398	398	397	396	394	393	391	389	386	383	380	376	371	366	360	354	346	338	329
1,000,000	700	692	688	684	678	671	663	653	641	626	610	590	568	542	513	479	444	412	383	357	333
	600	595	593	590	586	582	577	570	563	554	543	531	517	501	482	461	438	411	383	357	333
	500	497	496	494	492	490	487	483	478	473	467	460	452	442	432	420	406	391	374	354	333
	400	398	398	397	396	395	393	391	389	386	383	380	375	371	365	359	352	344	335	325	315
	300	299	299	299	298	298	297	296	295	294	293	291	290	288	285	283	280	276	273	269	264

UNIT AXIAL STRESSES: SIMPLE SOLID COLUMNS— ℓ/d FROM 30 TO 50

E	Fc	30	31	32	33	34	35	36	37	38	39	40	41	42	43	44	45	46	47	48	49	50
1,800,000	900 or more	600	562	527	496	467	441	417	394	374	355	338	321	306	292	279	267	255	244	234	225	216
1,700,000	900 or more	567	531	498	468	441	416	394	373	353	335	319	303	289	276	263	252	241	231	221	212	204
1,600,000	800 or more	533	499	469	441	415	392	370	351	332	316	300	286	272	260	248	237	227	217	208	200	192
1,500,000	800 or more	500	468	439	413	389	367	347	329	312	296	281	268	255	243	232	222	213	204	195	187	180
1,400,000	700 or more	467	437	410	386	363	343	324	307	291	276	263	250	238	227	217	207	198	190	182	175	168
1,300,000	700 or more	433	406	381	358	337	318	301	285	270	256	244	232	221	211	201	193	184	177	169	162	156
1,200,000	600 or more	400	375	352	331	311	294	278	263	249	237	225	214	204	195	186	178	170	163	156	150	144
1,100,000	600 or more	367	343	322	303	285	269	255	241	229	217	206	196	187	178	170	163	156	149	143	137	132
1,000,000	500 or more	333	312	293	275	260	245	231	219	208	197	188	178	170	162	155	148	142	136	130	125	120

NOTES

1. Obtain design values for E and F_C from the National Design Specification for Wood Construction.
2. Modify F_C for different load duration, if applicable.
3. Calculate ℓ/d where ℓ = unsupported length of column (in.) and d = applicable least actual dimension of column cross section.
4. Determine value of F_C' from table.
5. Total design load on column = cross-sectional area (sq in.) x F_C' value.

National Forest Products Association; Washington, D.C.

DESIGN LOAD TABLES

FLOOR AND ROOF BEAMS – DESIGN TABLES 20 POUNDS PSF

Required values for fiber stress in bending (f) and modulus of elasticity (E) for the sizes shown to support safely a live load of 20 pounds per square foot with a deflection limitation of $^1/_{300}$
l = span in inches.

MINIMUM f & E IN PSI FOR BEAMS SPACED:

SPAN OF BEAM	NOMINAL SIZE OF BEAM	6'-0" f	6'-0" E	7'-0" f	7'-0" E	8'-0" f	8'-0" E
10'	2-3x6	1020	925000	1190	1080000	1360	1240000
	1-3x8	1100	730000	1280	855000	1460	970000
	2-2x8	890	590000	1030	690000	1180	790000
	1-4x8	790	530000	920	620000	1050	705000
	3-2x8	590	395000	690	460000	790	525000
	2-3x8	550	365000	640	425000	730	485000
	2-2x10	550	290000	640	340000	730	390000
11'	2-3x6	1230	1130000	1440	1440000	1640	1650000
	1-3x8	1320	970000	1540	1140000	1760	1300000
	2-2x8	1070	785000	1250	920000	1430	1050000
	1-4x8	960	705000	1120	825000	1270	940000
	3-2x8	710	525000	830	615000	950	700000
	2-3x8	660	485000	780	565000	880	650000
	2-2x10	660	390000	780	455000	880	520000
12'	2-3x6	1470	1600000				
	1-3x8	1580	1260000	1840	1470000	1700	1360000
	2-2x8	1270	1020000	1490	1190000	1510	1220000
	1-4x8	1140	915000	1330	1070000	1510	1220000
	3-2x8	850	680000	990	795000	1130	910000
	2-3x8	790	630000	920	735000	1050	840000
	1-6x8	750	605000	880	705000	1000	805000
	2-2x10	790	505000	920	590000	1050	670000
13'	1-3x8	1850	1600000				
	2-2x8	1500	1300000	1740	1440000	1990	1730000
	1-4x8	1340	1160000	1550	1280000	1780	1550000
	3-2x8	990	865000	1160	960000	1330	1160000
	2-3x8	920	800000	1080	885000	1230	1070000
	1-6x8	880	770000	1030	850000	1180	1020000
	2-2x10	920	640000	1080	705000	1230	850000
	1-3x10	1150	790000	1350	875000	1540	1050000
	1-4x10	830	570000	970	630000	1110	760000
14'	3-2x8	1150	1080000	1350	1260000	1540	1440000
	2-3x8	1070	1000000	1250	1170000	1430	1340000
	1-6x8	1030	960000	1200	1120000	1370	1280000
	1-3x10	1340	990000	1570	1150000	1780	1320000
	2-2x10	1070	810000	1260	935000	1430	1070000
	1-4x10	970	715000	1130	835000	1290	955000
	3-2x10	720	525000	840	625000	960	710000
	2-3x10	670	495000	780	575000	890	660000
	1-6x10	640	470000	750	550000	850	630000
	4-2x10	540	405000	630	417000	720	535000
	2-2x12	740	450000	870	525000	990	600000
15'	3-2x8	1320	1330000	1550	1540000	1770	1770000
	2-3x8	1230	1230000	1440	1430000	1640	1640000
	1-6x8	1180	1170000	1370	1370000	1570	1570000
	1-3x10	1540	1210000	1800	1410000	2050	1610000
	2-2x10	1230	1020000	1440	1140000	1640	1310000
	1-4x10	1110	875000	1300	1020000	1480	1170000
	3-2x10	820	655000	960	761000	1100	872000
	2-3x10	770	605000	900	705000	1030	805000
	1-6x10	740	580000	860	675000	980	770000
	4-2x10	620	510000	725	570000	830	655000
	2-2x12	850	553000	990	645000	1140	737000
	1-4x12	760	495000	890	576000	1020	660000
16'	2-3x8	1410	1490000	1650	1740000		
	2-2x10	1410	1190000	1650	1390000	1880	1590000
	1-4x10	1260	1070000	1470	1240000	1680	1420000
	3-2x10	940	795000	1100	930000	1250	1060000
	2-3x10	880	740000	1020	860000	1170	985000
	1-6x10	840	705000	970	820000	1110	935000
	4-2x10	700	595000	820	695000	940	795000
	1-8x10	610	515000	710	600000	810	690000
	1-3x12	1200	830000	1400	970000	1600	1110000
	2-2x12	970	670000	1130	785000	1290	895000
	1-4x12	870	600000	1010	705000	1150	805000
	3-2x12	650	448000	750	522000	860	597000

SPAN OF BEAM	NOMINAL SIZE OF BEAM	6'-0" f	6'-0" E	7'-0" f	7'-0" E	8'-0" f	8'-0" E
17'	2-2x10	1590	1430000	1860	1670000		
	1-4x10	1430	1280000	1670	1490000	1900	1710000
	3-2x10	1060	955000	1240	1110000	1410	1270000
	2-3x10	990	885000	1150	1030000	1310	1180000
	1-6x10	940	845000	1100	980000	1250	1120000
	4-2x10	790	715000	930	835000	1060	955000
	1-8x10	690	620000	810	720000	920	825000
	1-3x12	1350	1000000	1580	1160000	1800	1330000
	2-2x12	1090	805000	1280	940000	1450	1080000
	1-4x12	980	720000	1140	840000	1300	960000
	3-2x12	730	535000	850	625000	970	715000
	2-3x12	680	500000	790	580000	900	665000
18'	1-4x10	1600	1520000	1870	1780000		
	3-2x10	1190	1130000	1370	1320000	1570	1510000
	2-3x10	1110	1050000	1300	1230000	1480	1400000
	1-6x10	1060	1000000	1230	1170000	1410	1340000
	4-2x10	890	850000	1040	995000	1190	1130000
	1-8x10	780	735000	910	860000	1030	980000
	1-3x12	1520	1190000	1780	1380000	2020	1580000
	2-2x12	1230	960000	1430	1120000	1630	1280000
	1-4x12	1100	855000	1280	1000000	1460	1140000
	3-2x12	820	640000	960	745000	1090	850000
	2-3x12	760	595000	890	690000	1010	790000
	1-6x12	720	570000	840	660000	960	750000
19'	3-2x10	1320	1340000	1550	1560000	1760	1780000
	2-3x10	1230	1240000	1440	1440000	1650	1650000
	1-6x10	1170	1180000	1370	1370000	1570	1570000
	4-2x10	990	1000000	1160	1170000	1320	1340000
	2-4x10	890	900000	1040	1040000	1190	1190000
	1-8x10	860	870000	1010	1010000	1150	1160000
	1-3x12	1680	1400000	1970	1630000		
	2-2x12	1360	1130000	1590	1320000	1820	1510000
	1-4x12	1220	1010000	1430	1180000	1630	1350000
	3-2x12	910	755000	1060	825000	1210	1000000
	2-3x12	840	700000	980	815000	1130	930000
	1-6x12	800	670000	940	780000	1070	890000
20'	3-2x10	1470	1550000				
	2-3x10	1370	1440000	1600	1680000		
	1-6x10	1300	1370000	1520	1600000		
	4-2x10	1100	1160000	1280	1360000	1470	1550000
	2-4x10	990	1040000	1150	1220000	1320	1390000
	1-8x10	960	1010000	1120	1180000	1280	1340000
	2-2x12	1510	1310000	1770	1530000	2020	1750000
	1-4x12	1350	1170000	1580	1370000	1800	1570000
	3-2x12	1010	873000	1180	1020000	1350	1160000
	2-3x12	940	810000	1090	950000	1250	1080000
	1-6x12	890	775000	1040	905000	1190	1030000
	4-2x12		655000		765000		875000
21'	2-3x10	1500	1670000				
	1-6x10	1430	1590000	1680	1850000		
	4-2x10	1210	1350000	1420	1570000		
	2-4x10	1090	1210000	1270	1410000	1450	1610000
	1-8x10	1050	1170000	1230	1360000	1400	1550000
	2-2x12	1660	1520000	1950	1770000		
	1-4x12	1490	1360000	1740	1580000	1990	1810000
	3-2x12	1110	1010000	1300	1180000	1480	1350000
	2-3x12	1030	940000	1200	1100000	1380	1250000
	1-6x12	970	895000	1130	1050000	1310	1200000
	4-2x12	830	740000	970	885000	1110	1010000
	2-4x12	750	680000	870	795000	990	907000
22'	4-2x10	1330	1550000				
	2-4x10	1200	1380000	1400	1620000		
	1-8x10	1160	1350000	1350	1570000	1550	1790000
	1-4x12	1640	1560000				
	3-2x12	1220	1160000	1420	1360000	1630	1550000
	2-3x12	1130	1080000	1320	1260000	1520	1440000
	1-6x12	1080	1030000	1260	1210000	1450	1370000
	4-2x12	920	870000	1070	1020000	1230	1160000
	2-4x12	820	785000	960	915000	1100	1040000
	5-2x12	730	700000	860	815000	980	930000
	3-3x12	750	720000	880	840000	1010	960000

National Forest Products Association; Washington, D. C.

FLOOR AND ROOF BEAMS – DESIGN TABLES 30 POUNDS PSF

Required values for fiber stress in bending (f) and modulus of elasticity (E) for the sizes shown to support safely a live load of 30 pounds per square foot with a deflection limitation of $1/300$
1 = span in inches.

SPAN OF BEAM	NOMINAL SIZE OF BEAM	6'-0" f	6'-0" E	7'-0" f	7'-0" E	8'-0" f	8'-0" E
10'	2-3x6	1360	1390000	1590	1620000		
	1-3x8	1460	1090000	1700	1280000	1950	1460000
	1-4x8	1050	795000	1220	925000	1400	1060000
	3-2x8	790	590000	920	690000	1050	790000
	2-3x8	730	545000	850	640000	970	730000
	2-4x8	530	400000	610	465000	700	530000
	2-2x10	740	435000	860	515000	980	585000
11'	1-3x8	1770	1460000	2060	1690000		
	1-4x8	1270	1060000	1490	1240000	1700	1410000
	3-2x8	950	790000	1110	920000	1270	1050000
	2-3x8	880	730000	1030	850000	1180	970000
	2-4x8	640	530000	750	620000	850	710000
	2-2x10	890	585000	1040	680000	1180	780000
	1-3x10	1100	720000	1290	840000	1480	960000
12'	1-4x8	1510	1370000	1770	1600000		
	2-2x8	1130	1020000	1320	1190000	1510	1360000
	2-3x8	1050	945000	1230	1100000	1400	1260000
	2-4x8	760	685000	880	800000	1010	915000
	1-6x8	1000	905000	1170	1050000	1340	1210000
	2-2x10	1060	755000	1230	880000	1410	1010000
	3-2x10	750	505000	820	590000	940	675000
	2-3x10	660	465000	760	545000	880	620000
13'	1-4x8	1780	1750000				
	3-2x8	1330	1300000	1550	1520000	1770	1740000
	2-3x8	1230	1210000	1440	1400000	1650	1600000
	2-4x8	890	875000	1040	1020000	1190	1170000
	1-6x8	1180	1050000	1370	1350000	1570	1540000
	2-2x10	1240	965000	1450	1120000	1650	1280000
	3-2x10	830	640000	970	750000	1100	855000
	2-3x10	770	595000	900	695000	1030	790000
	1-4x10	1110	860000	1300	1000000	1480	1150000
14'	3-2x8	1540	1620000				
	2-3x8	1430	1500000	1670	1750000		
	2-4x8	1030	1090000	1210	1280000	1380	1450000
	1-6x8	1370	1440000	1600	1680000		
	2-2x10	1490	1200000	1680	1400000	1930	1600000
	3-2x10	960	800000	1120	935000	1280	1070000
	2-3x10	890	740000	1050	865000	1200	980000
	1-4x10	1290	1070000	1510	1250000	1720	1430000
	1-6x10	850	710000	1000	825000	1140	940000
	2-4x10	650	535000	750	625000	860	715000
15'	2-4x8	1190	1340000	1380	1560000	1580	1780000
	1-6x8	1570	1770000				
	2-2x10	1650	1480000	1930	1720000		
	3-2x10	1100	985000	1280	1150000	1470	1310000
	2-3x10	1030	910000	1200	1060000	1370	1220000
	1-4x10	1480	1320000	1730	1540000	1970	1760000
	1-6x10	980	870000	1140	1020000	1300	1060000
	2-4x10	740	660000	865	770000	990	880000
	4-2x10	830	740000	960	860000	1100	980000
	1-8x10	720	640000	840	745000	960	850000
	2-2x12	1040	830000	1330	970000	1510	1110000
	1-4x12	1020	745000	1190	870000	1350	990000
16'	2-2x10	1880	1780000				
	3-2x10	1250	1190000	1460	1390000	1670	1590000
	2-3x10	1170	1100000	1360	1290000	1550	1470000
	1-4x10	1690	1600000				
	1-6x10	1110	1050000	1300	1230000	1480	1410000
	2-4x10	840	810000	980	950000	1120	1070000
	4-2x10	940	895000	1100	1040000	1250	1190000
	1-8x10	830	720000	950	905000	1090	1030000
	2-2x12	1290	1010000	1510	1180000	1720	1340000
	1-4x12	1160	900000	1350	1050000	1540	1200000
	3-2x12	860	670000	1000	785000	1150	895000
	2-3x12	800	620000	930	730000	1070	830000

SPAN OF BEAM	NOMINAL SIZE OF BEAM	6'-0" f	6'-0" E	7'-0" f	7'-0" E	8'-0" f	8'-0" E
17'	3-2x10	1420	1430000	1650	1670000		
	2-3x10	1320	1330000	1540	1550000	1760	1770000
	1-6x10	1260	1260000	1470	1480000	1680	1690000
	2-4x10	950	960000	1110	1120000	1270	1280000
	4-2x10	1060	1070000	1240	1250000	1420	1430000
	1-8x10	920	930000	1080	1080000	1230	1240000
	2-2x12	1460	1210000	1700	1410000	1950	1610000
	1-4x12	1310	1080000	1520	1260000	1750	1440000
	3-2x12	970	805000	1140	1080000	1300	1070000
	2-3x12	900	750000	1060	870000	1210	1000000
	4-2x12	730	605000	850	705000	970	805000
	2-4x12	650	545000	760	635000	870	725000
18'	2-3x10	1480	1580000				
	1-6x10	1410	1510000	1650	1760000		
	2-4x10	1070	1140000	1250	1330000	1430	1520000
	4-2x10	1190	1280000	1390	1490000	1590	1700000
	1-8x10	1040	1100000	1210	1290000	1380	1470000
	2-2x12	1640	1440000	1910	1680000		
	1-4x12	1470	1290000	1710	1500000	1950	1710000
	3-2x12	1090	960000	1270	1120000	1460	1280000
	2-3x12	1010	890000	1180	1040000	1350	1190000
	4-2x12	820	720000	960	840000	1090	960000
	2-4x12	730	650000	860	755000	980	860000
	5-2x12	660	575000	770	670000	870	765000
19'	1-6x10	1570	1770000				
	2-4x10	1190	1340000	1390	1560000	1590	1780000
	4-2x10	1330	1500000	1550	1750000		
	1-8x10	1150	1300000	1340	1510000	1540	1720000
	1-4x12	1630	1510000	1900	1760000		
	3-2x12	1220	1120000	1420	1310000	1620	1500000
	2-3x12	1140	1040000	1320	1220000	1500	1390000
	4-2x12	910	845000	1060	980000	1210	1120000
	2-4x12	820	760000	950	885000	1090	1010000
	5-2x12	730	675000	850	785000	970	900000
	1-6x12	1070	995000	1250	1160000	1430	1330000
	3-3x12	750	695000	880	810000	1000	925000
20'	1-8x10	1150	1510000	1340	1760000		
	3-2x12	1210	1310000	1410	1530000	1620	1750000
	2-3x12	1120	1220000	1310	1420000	1500	1630000
	4-2x12	910	1090000	1060	1150000	1210	1310000
	2-4x12	810	885000	950	1030000	1090	1180000
	5-2x12	730	790000	850	920000	970	1050000
	1-6x12	1070	1160000	1250	1360000	1430	1550000
	3-3x12	750	810000	880	945000	1000	1080000
	1-8x12	790	850000	920	995000	1050	1140000
	1-10x12	620	670000	720	780000	830	895000
	4-3x12	560	610000	660	710000	750	815000
	2-3x14	810	755000	950	880000	1090	1010000
21'	3-2x12	1490	1640000				
	2-3x12	1380	1470000	1600	1700000		
	4-2x12	1110	1180000	1300	1370000	1480	1570000
	2-4x12	1000	1060000	1160	1240000	1330	1410000
	5-2x12	890	945000	1040	1100000	1190	1260000
	1-6x12	1310	1400000	1530	1620000		
	3-3x12	920	975000	1070	1130000	1220	1290000
	1-8x12	970	1030000	1020	1190000	990	1360000
	1-10x12	760	805000	880	940000	1010	1450000
	4-3x12	690	730000	800	850000	920	970000
	2-3x14	1000	905000	1160	1050000	1330	1200000
	1-6x14	950	865000	1110	1010000	1270	1150000
22'	4-2x12	1220	1310000	1420	1530000	1630	1740000
	2-4x12	1090	1180000	1280	1370000	1460	1570000
	5-2x12	980	1050000	1140	1225000	1300	1400000
	1-6x12	1430	1550000	1680	1800000		
	3-3x12	1010	1080000	1180	1260000	1340	1440000
	1-8x12	1050	1040000	1230	1330000	1410	1510000
	1-10x12	830	890000	970	1040000	1110	1190000
	4-3x12	750	810000	880	945000	1010	1080000
	2-3x14	1090	1000000	1280	1170000	1460	1340000
	1-6x14	1040	960000	1220	1120000	1390	1280000
	3-3x14	730	670000	850	780000	970	890000
	2-4x14	790	725000	920	845000	1060	965000

National Forest Products Association; Washington, D. C.

DESIGN LOAD TABLES

FLOOR AND ROOF BEAMS – DESIGN TABLES 40 POUNDS PSF

Required values for fiber stress in bending (f) and modulus of elasticity (E) for the sizes shown to support safely a live load of 40 pounds per square foot within a deflection limitation of $1/360$

1 = span in inches.

SPAN OF BEAM	NOMINAL SIZE OF BEAM	6'-0" f	6'-0" E	7'-0" f	7'-0" E	8'-0" f	8'-0" E
10'	1-3x8	1820	1460000	2130	1690000		
	2-2x8	1480	1180000	1720	1380000	1970	1580000
	1-4x8	1320	1060000	1540	1230000	1750	1410000
	1-6x8	870	700000	1020	815000	1160	930000
	2-2x10	920	585000	1070	680000	1220	775000
	1-3x10	1140	885000	1330	840000	1520	960000
	1-4x10	820	520000	960	610000	1090	695000
11'	2-2x8	1780	1570000				
	1-4x8	1600	1410000	1860	1650000		
	1-6x8	1060	930000	1230	1090000	1410	1240000
	2-2x10	1110	775000	1300	905000	1490	1035000
	1-3x10	1380	960000	1610	1120000	1840	1280000
	1-4x10	1000	695000	1160	810000	1330	925000
	3-2x10	740	515000	860	605000	990	690000
12'	1-6x8	1250	1210000	1460	1410000	1670	1610000
	3-2x8	1410	1360000	1650	1590000	1890	1820000
	2-2x10	1360	1010000	1560	1180000	1760	1340000
	1-3x10	1630	1250000	1910	1450000	2190	1660000
	1-4x10	1180	900000	1380	1050000	1580	1200000
	3-2x10	880	670000	1030	785000	1170	895000
	2-3x10	810	620000	950	730000	1090	830000
	1-6x10	780	595000	910	695000	1040	790000
	2-4x10	590	450000	690	535000	790	600000
13'	1-6x8	1470	1530000				
	2-3x8	1540	1600000				
	2-4x8	1110	1170000	1300	1360000	1490	1550000
	3-2x10	1010	855000	1180	1000000	1380	1140000
	2-2x10	1550	1280000	1810	1500000	2070	1710000
	1-3x10	1920	1580000				
	2-3x10	960	790000	1120	925000	1280	1150000
	1-4x10	1390	1150000	1620	1340000	1850	1530000
	2-4x10	690	575000	810	670000	920	765000
14'	2-4x8	1290	1450000	1510	1690000		
	3-2x10	1200	1070000	1400	1240000	1600	1420000
	2-3x10	1110	990000	1300	1150000	1490	1320000
	1-4x10	1610	1430000	1890	1660000		
	2-4x10	800	715000	940	830000	1070	950000
	3-3x10	740	660000	870	765000	990	880000
	1-6x10	1060	940000	1240	1100000	1420	1260000
	1-8x10	780	690000	910	805000	1040	920000
	4-2x10	900	800000	1050	930000	1200	1060000
	2-2x12	1250	900000	1440	1050000	1650	1200000
15'	3-2x10	1380	1310000	1610	1530000	1840	1750000
	2-3x10	1290	1220000	1500	1420000	1710	1620000
	2-4x10	930	880000	1080	1020000	1240	1170000
	3-3x10	860	810000	1000	945000	1140	1080000
	1-6x10	1220	1160000	1430	1350000	1630	1540000
	1-8x10	900	850000	1050	990000	1200	1130000
	4-2x10	1030	985000	1210	1150000	1380	1310000
	2-2x12	1420	1110000	1660	1290000	1900	1480000
	3-2x12	950	735000	1110	860000	1260	985000
	1-3x12	1760	1370000	2050	1600000		
	4-2x12	710	555000	830	645000	950	740000
	2-3x12	880	685000	1030	800000	1170	915000
16'	3-2x10	1570	1590000				
	2-3x10	1460	1480000	1700	1720000		
	2-4x10	1050	1070000	1230	1250000	1410	1430000
	3-3x10	970	985000	1130	1150000	1290	1310000
	1-6x10	1390	1410000	1630	1640000		
	1-8x10	1020	1030000	1190	1200000	1360	1380000
	4-2x10	1170	1190000	1370	1390000	1570	1590000
	2-2x12	1610	1340000	1880	1570000		
	3-2x12	1080	895000	1260	1050000	1440	1200000
	4-2x12	810	670000	940	785000	1080	895000
	5-2x12	640	550000	750	630000	860	720000
	2-3x12	1000	830000	1170	970000	1330	1110000

SPAN OF BEAM	NOMINAL SIZE OF BEAM	6'-0" f	6'-0" E	7'-0" f	7'-0" E	8'-0" f	8'-0" E
17'	2-3x10	1640	1760000				
	2-4x10	1190	1280000	1390	1490000	1580	1700000
	3-3x10	1100	1180000	1280	1370000	1460	1570000
	1-8x10	1150	1240000	1340	1440000	1530	1650000
	3-2x12	1220	1070000	1420	1250000	1620	1430000
	4-2x12	910	805000	1060	940000	1210	1070000
	5-2x12	730	645000	850	750000	970	860000
	2-3x12	1130	995000	1310	1160000	1500	1330000
	3-3x12	750	665000	880	770000	1000	885000
	2-4x12	820	725000	950	840000	1090	965000
	1-6x12	1070	950000	1250	1110000	1430	1270000
	1-8x12	790	700000	920	810000	1050	930000
18'	2-4x10	1330	1510000	1550	1770000		
	3-3x10	1230	1390000	1430	1630000		
	1-8x10	1290	1460000	1510	1720000		
	3-2x12	1360	1270000	1590	1490000	1810	1700000
	4-2x12	1020	950000	1190	1120000	1360	1270000
	5-2x12	820	760000	950	890000	1090	1020000
	2-3x12	1270	1180000	1480	1380000	1680	1580000
	3-3x12	840	785000	980	920000	1120	1050000
	2-4x12	920	855000	1070	1000000	1220	1145000
	1-6x12	1200	1120000	1400	1320000	1600	1520000
	1-8x12	880	825000	1030	970000	1180	1100000
	3-4x12	610	570000	710	665000	810	760000
19'	3-3x10	1370	1640000				
	3-2x12	1520	1500000	1770	1750000		
	4-2x12	1140	1130000	1330	1310000	1520	1500000
	5-2x12	910	900000	1060	1050000	1210	1200000
	2-3x12	1410	1390000	1650	1620000		
	3-3x12	940	925000	1100	1080000	1250	1230000
	2-4x12	1020	1010000	1190	1180000	1360	1350000
	1-6x12	1340	1330000	1560	1550000	1790	885000
	1-8x12	990	975000	1150	1140000	1310	1300000
	3-4x12	680	675000	790	785000	910	895000
	4-3x12	700	695000	820	810000	940	925000
	2-6x12	670	665000	780	770000	890	885000
20'	3-2x12	1680	1750000				
	4-2x12	1260	1310000	1470	1530000	1680	1750000
	5-2x12	1010	1050000	1180	1230000	1350	1400000
	3-3x12	1040	1080000	1210	1260000	1390	1440000
	2-4x12	1130	1180000	1320	1370000	1510	1570000
	1-6x12	1460	1550000				
	1-8x12	1090	1140000	1270	1330000	1450	1520000
	3-4x12	750	785000	880	920000	1000	1050000
	4-3x12	780	810000	910	950000	1040	1080000
	2-6x12	740	775000	870	905000	990	1030000
	1-10x12	850	890000	1000	1040000	1140	1190000
	2-3x14	1130	1000000	1320	1170000	1510	1340000
21'	4-2x12	1390	1520000	1620	1770000		
	5-2x12	1110	1210000	1300	1420000	1490	1620000
	3-3x12	1150	1250000	1340	1460000	1530	1670000
	2-4x12	1240	1360000	1450	1590000		
	1-8x12	1200	1320000	1400	1540000	1600	1750000
	3-4x12	830	910000	970	1060000	1110	1210000
	4-3x12	860	940000	1000	1100000	1150	1260000
	2-6x12	820	895000	960	1040000	1090	1190000
	1-10x12	940	1030000	1100	1210000	1260	1380000
	2-3x14	1240	1160000	1450	1360000	1660	1550000
	1-6x14	1190	1110000	1390	1300000	1590	1480000
	2-4x14	900	840000	1050	980000	1200	1120000
22'	4-2x12	1530	1750000				
	5-2x12	1220	1400000	1430	1620000		
	3-3x12	1260	1440000	1470	1680000		
	3-4x12	910	1050000	1060	1220000	1210	1390000
	4-3x12	940	1080000	1100	1260000	1260	1440000
	2-6x12	900	1030000	1050	1190000	1200	1370000
	1-10x12	1040	1190000	1210	1390000	1380	1590000
	2-3x14	1360	1340000	1590	1560000	1820	1780000
	1-6x14	1310	1280000	1530	1490000	1740	1700000
	2-4x14	990	970000	1160	1130000	1320	1280000
	3-3x14	910	895000	1060	1040000	1210	1190000
	3-4x14	660	645000	770	750000	880	865000

National Forest Products Association; Washington, D.C.

DESIGN LOAD TABLES   6

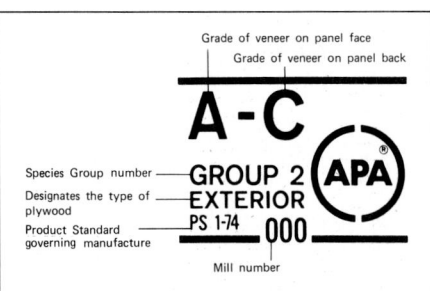

APPEARANCE GRADE STAMP

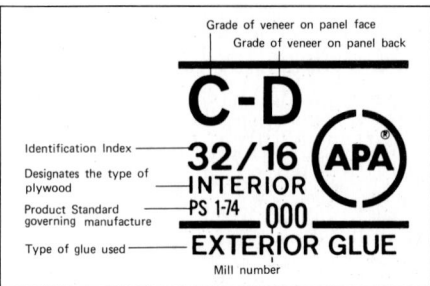

ENGINEERED GRADE STAMP

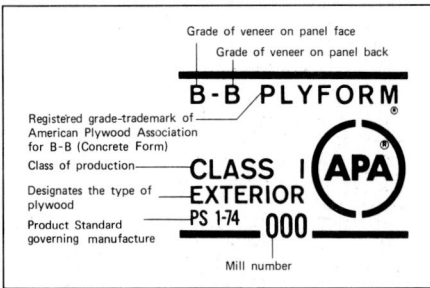

CONCRETE FORM STAMP

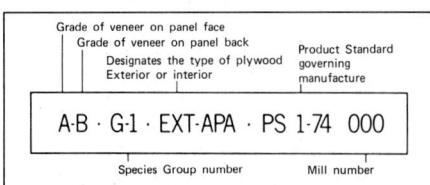

EDGE STAMP

KEY DEFINITIONS

TYPE

1. EXTERIOR: 100% waterproof glueline, for permanent applications outdoors or under continuing moist or extremely humid conditions.
2. INTERIOR: Highly moisture resistant glueline (100% waterproof glueline may be used).

GROUP

Wood species are grouped, by stiffness and strength, in five classification groups, with group 1 being the best. Listed group number is the weakest species used in face and back, except in decorative and sanded panels 3/8 in. or less in thickness where group refers to face species. Refer to National Bureau of Standards Product Standard PS I for a listing of 70 species in all groups.

APPEARANCE GRADES

APPEARANCE GRADING DESIGNATIONS: N, A, B, C, and D, with best veneers being N and A. Panel grades are based on veneer grade of panel face and back and by glueline (interior or exterior). Refer to National Bureau of Standards Product Standard PS I for allowable characteristics and repairs.

ENGINEERED GRADES

In engineering grades strength is more important than appearance. Design properties include nail bearing, shear, compression, and tension.

C-D INTERIOR AND C-D INTERIOR WITH EXTERIOR GLUE (CDX)

Interior panels are suitable for sheathing and will withstand limited moisture during construction because they are bonded with exterior glue. They are not exterior grade plywood. Structural I C-D is limited to Group 1 species, Structural II C-D permits Group 1, 2, or 3 species.

IDENTIFICATION INDEX

APA two-number identification index applies to basic unsanded grades of plywood, such as C-D sheathing, C-C Exterior, and Structural I and II C-C and C-D. The left-hand number refers to maximum recommended spacing of roof framing in inches (sheathing), and the right-hand number refers to maximum spacing of floor framing (subflooring); for example, 24/0, 32/16. Numbers are based on two or more spans with face grain across supports.

IMPORTANT NOTE

Published span tables must be checked with applicable code limitations.

CLASS I, CLASS II

This identification applies to wood species for plywood grades used for concrete forms. Class I: Group 1 faces, Groups 1 and 2 crossbands, and Group 1, 2, 3, or 4 center ply. Class II: Group 1 or 2 (Group 3 in certain conditions) and Groups 1, 2, 3, or 4 inner plies.

VENEER GRADES

1. N AND A: Smooth surface "natural finish" veneer. Select all heartwood or all sapwood. Free of open defects. Allows not more than six repairs, wood only, per 4 x 8 panel, made parallel to grain and well matched for grain and color. Smooth, paintable. Not more than 18 neatly made repairs, boat, sled or router type and parallel to grain, permitted. May be used for natural finish in less demanding applications.

2. B: Solid surface. Shims, circular repair plugs, and tight knots to 1 in. across grain permitted. Some minor splits permitted.

3. C PLUGGED: Improved C veneer with splits limited to 1/8 in. width and knotholes limited to 1/4 by 1/2 in. Admits some broken grain. Synthetic repairs permitted.

4. C: Tight knots to 1 1/2 in. Knotholes to 1 in. across grain and some to 1/2 in. if total width of knots and knotholes is within specified limits. Synthetic or wood repairs. Discoloration and sanding defects that do not impair strength are permitted. Limited splits allowed. Stitching permitted.

5. D: Knots and knotholes to 2 1/2 in. width across grain and 1/2 in. larger within specified limits. Limited splits are permitted. Stitching permitted. Limited to interior grades of plywood.

C-D INT-APA C-C EXT-APA

THICK-NESS (IN.)	GROUP 1 AND STRUC-TURAL I	GROUP 2 OR 3 (1) AND STRUCTURAL II (1,3)	GROUP 4 (2)
5/16	20/0	16/0	12/0
3/8	24/0	20/0	16/0
1/2	32/16	24/0	24/0
5/8	42/20	32/16	30/12 (3)
3/4	48/24	42/20	36/16 (3)
7/8	—	48/24	42/20

NOTES
1. Panels with Group 2 outer plies and special thickness and construction requirements, or Structural II panels with Group 1 faces, may carry the Identification Index numbers shown for Group 1 panels.
2. Panels made with Group 4 outer plies may carry the Identification Index numbers shown for Group 3 panels when they conform to special thickness and construction requirements.
3. Check local availability.

CLASSIFICATION OF SPECIES

GROUP 1	GROUP 2	GROUP 3		GROUP 4	GROUP 5
Apitong (1,2)	Cedar, Port Orford	Maple, black	Alder, red	Aspen	Basswood
Beech, American	Cypress	Mengkulang (1)	Birch, paper	Bigtooth	Poplar, balsam
Birch	Douglas fir No. 2 (3)	Meranti, red (1,4)	Cedar, Alaska	Quaking	
Sweet	Fir	Mersawa	Fir, subalpine	Cativo	
Yellow	Balsam	Pine	Hemlock, Eastern	Cedar	
Douglas fir No. 1 (3)	California red	Pond	Maple, bigleaf	Incense	
Kapur	Grand	Red	Pine	Western red	
Keruing (1,2)	Noble	Virginia	Jack	Cottonwood	
Larch, Western	Pacific silver	Western white	Lodgepole	Eastern	
Maple, sugar	White	Spruce	Ponderosa	Black (Western poplar)	
Pine	Hemlock, Western	Black	Spruce	Pine	
Caribbean	Lauan	Red	Redwood	Eastern white	
Ocote	Almon	Sitka	Spruce	Sugar	
Pine, Southern	Bagtikan	Sweetgum	Engelmann		
Loblolly	Mayapis	Tamarack	White		
Longleaf	Red Lauan	Yellow poplar			
Shortleaf	Tangile				
Slash	White Lauan				
Tanoak					

NOTES
1. Each name represents a trade group of woods consisting of a number of closely related species.
2. Species from the genus Dipterocarpus are marketed collectively. Apitong if originating in the Philippines; Keruing if originating in Malaysia or Indonesia.
3. Douglas fir from trees grown in Washington, Oregon, California, Idaho, Montana, Wyoming, and the Canadian Provinces of Alberta and British Columbia shall be classed as Douglas fir No. 1. Douglas fir from trees grown in Nevada, Utah, Colorado, Arizona, and New Mexico shall be classed as Douglas fir No. 2.
4. Red Meranti shall be limited to species having a specific gravity of 0.41 or more based on green volume and oven dry weight.

John D. Bloodgood, Architects, P.C.; Des Moines, Iowa

INTERIOR TYPE PLYWOOD

APPEARANCE (1, 3)

GRADE (2)	COMMON USES	FACE	MIDDLE	BACK	1/4	5/16	3/8	1/2	5/8	3/4
N-N, N-A, N-B INT-APA	Cabinet quality. For natural finish furniture. Special order items	N	C	NA / B						●
N-D INT-APA	For natural finish paneling. Special orders	N	D	D	●					
A-A INT-APA	For applications where both sides are visible. Smooth face; suitable for painting	A	D	A	●		●	●	●	●
A-B INT-APA	Use where view of one side is less important but two solid surfaces are needed	A	D	B	●		●	●	●	●
A-D INT-APA	Use where only one side is visible	A	D	D	●		●	●	●	●
B-B INT-APA	Utility panel with two solid sides	B	D	B	●		●	●	●	●
B-D INT-APA	Utility panel with one solid side	B	D	D	●		●	●	●	●
DECORATIVE PANELS-APA	Rough sawn, brushed, grooved, or striated faces for walls and built-ins	A B C	D	D		●	●	●	●	
PLYRON INT-APA	Hardboard face on both sides, tempered smooth or screened for counters and doors	HB	C D	HB				●	●	●

ENGINEERED (3)

GRADE	COMMON USES	FACE	MIDDLE	BACK	1/4	5/16	3/8	1/2	5/8	3/4
C-D INT-APA (8,12)	Commonly available with intermediate glue for sheathing and subflooring. Specify exterior glue for better durability and treated wood foundations	C	D	D		●	●	●	●	●
STRUCTURAL I C-D INT-APA / STRUCTURAL II C-D INT-APA	Unsanded structural grades where plywood strength properties are of maximum importance. Made only with exterior glue for beams, plates, and panels	C (10)	D (10)	D (10)		●	●	●	●	●
UNDERLAYMENT INT-APA (2,5,8)	For combination subfloor and underlayment under resilient flooring or carpet. Specify exterior glue where moisture is present. Available in tongue and groove	C PLUGGED	C / D (11)	D	●		●	●	●	●
C-D PLUGGED INT-APA (2,5,8)	For built-ins or tile backing. Not a substitute for underlayment, as it lacks underlayment's impact resistance. Touch sanded	C PLUG.	D	D		●	●	●	●	●
2.4.1 INT-APA (8,9,13)	Combination subfloor underlayment. Use 2.4.1 with exterior glue in areas subject to moisture; or if construction may be delayed as in site built floors. Unsanded or touch sanded as specified	C PLUGGED	C D	D						1 1/8

EXTERIOR TYPE PLYWOOD

APPEARANCE (1, 3)

GRADE (2)	COMMON USES	FACE	MIDDLE	BACK	1/4	5/16	3/8	1/2	5/8	3/4
A-A EXT-APA(5)	Use where both sides are visible	A	C	A	●		●	●	●	●
A-B EXT-APA(5)	Use where view of one side is less important	A	C	B	●		●	●	●	●
A-C EXT-APA(5)	Use where only one side is visible	A	C	C	●		●	●	●	●
B-B EXT-APA(5)	Utility panel with two solid faces	B	C	B	●		●	●	●	●
B-C EXT-APA(5)	Utility panel. Also used as base for exterior coatings on walls and roofs	B	C	C	●		●	●	●	●
HDO EXT-APA(5)	High density overlay plywood has a hard, semiopaque resin fiber overlay on both faces. Abrasion resistant. Use for concrete forms, cabinets, and counter tops	A B PLUG.	C C	A B			●	●	●	●
MDO EXT-APA(5)	Medium density overlay with smooth resin fiber overlay on one or two faces. Recommended for siding and other outdoor applications. Ideal base for paint	B	C	B C			●	●	●	●
303 SIDING EXT-APA (7)	Special surface treatment such as V-groove channel groove, striated, brushed, rough sawn	(6)	C	C				●	●	●
T1-11 EXT-APA (7)	Special 303 panel having grooves 1/4" deep, 3/8" wide, spaced 4 or 8" o.c. Other spacing optional. Edges shiplapped. Available unsanded, textured, and medium density overlay	A B C	C	C						●
PLYRON EXT-APA	Hardboard faces both sides, tempered, smooth or screened	HB	C	HB				●	●	●
MARINE EXT-APA	Made only with Douglas fir or Western larch. Special solid jointed core construction. Subject to special limitations on core gaps and number of face repairs. Also available with HDO or MDO faces	A B	B	A B	●		●	●	●	●

ENGINEERED (3)

GRADE	COMMON USES	FACE	MIDDLE	BACK	1/4	5/16	3/8	1/2	5/8	3/4
C-C EXT-APA (12)	Unsanded grade with waterproof bond	C	C	C		●	●	●	●	●
STRUCTURAL I C-C EXT-APA / STRUCTURAL II C-C EXT-APA	For engineered applications in construction and industry where full exterior type panels are required. Unsanded. See Note 5 for species group requirements	C	C	C		●	●	●	●	●
UNDERLAYMENT C-C PLUGGED EXT-APA / C-C PLUGGED EXT-APA (2,5)	For underlayment or combination subfloor underlayment under resilient floor coverings where severe moisture conditions exist, as in balcony decks. Use for tile backing in atmosphere controlled rooms. Touch sanded and tongue and groove	C PLUGGED	C (11)	C	●		●	●	●	●
B-B PLYFORM CLASS I AND CLASS II EXT-APA (4)	Concrete form grades with high reuse factor. Sanded on both sides. Mill oiled unless otherwise specified. Special restrictions on species. Also available in HDO	B	C	B					●	●

GENERAL NOTES

1. Sanded on both sides except where decorative or other surfaces specified.
2. Available in Group 1, 2, 3, 4, or 5 unless otherwise noted.
3. Standard 4 x 8 panel sizes; other sizes available.
4. Also available in Structural I.
5. Also available in Structural I (all plies limited to Group 1 species) and Structural II (all plies limited to Group 1, 2, or 3 species).
6. C or better for five plies; C Plugged or better for three-ply panels.
7. Stud spacing is shown on grade stamp.
8. Also made with exterior glue.
9. Made only in woods of certain species to conform to APA specifications.
10. Special improved grade for structural panels.
11. Special construction to resist indentation from concentrated loads.
12. Made in many different species combinations. Specify by identification index.
13. Can be special ordered in exterior type for porches and patio decks, roof overhangs, and exterior balconies.

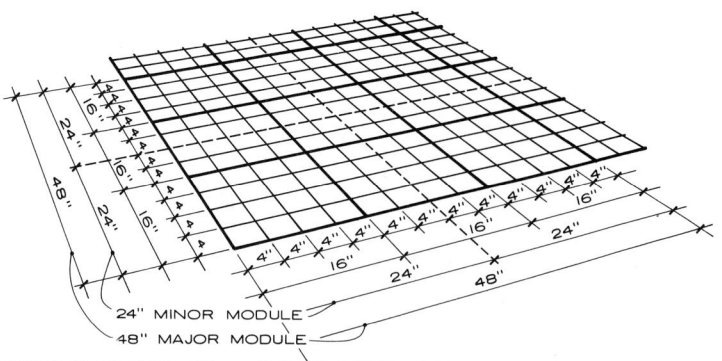

MODULAR PLANNING GRID

THE MODULAR PLAN

The key to cost savings in frame construction is preplanning, using standard lumber and panel sizes. The major consideration is the 4 x 8 building unit panel dimension. Since most building components are based on this unit of measurement, a preplanned modular system can eliminate unnecessary waste of material and labor. The modular planning grid is divided into 4, 16, 24, 48 in. units, with 48 in. being the major module and 24 in. the minor module. These can be used as the planning guides for exterior overall dimensioning. Floor, ceiling, and roof construction can easily be coordinated with these dimensions.

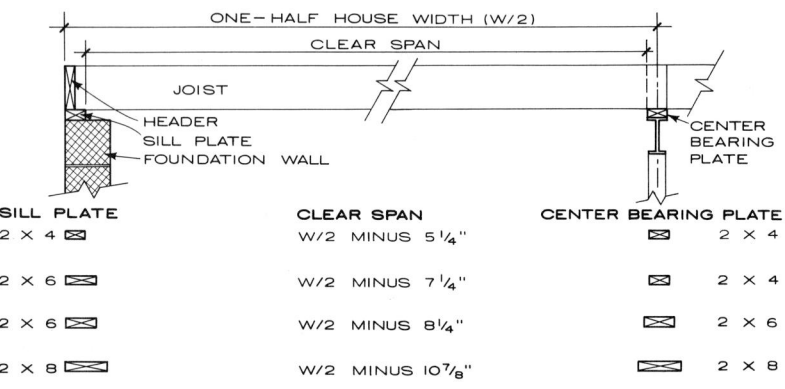

SILL PLATE	CLEAR SPAN	CENTER BEARING PLATE
2 × 4 ⊠	W/2 MINUS 5¼"	⊠ 2 × 4
2 × 6 ⊠	W/2 MINUS 7¼"	⊠ 2 × 4
2 × 6 ⊠	W/2 MINUS 8¼"	⊠ 2 × 6
2 × 8 ⊠	W/2 MINUS 10⅞"	⊠ 2 × 8

NOTE: USE OF WIDER BEARING PLATES TO REDUCE CLEAR SPANS

CLEAR SPAN OF JOIST

FLOOR PLANNING

Most common joist spacing is at 12, 16, 24 in. on center, depending on the design floor loads. Joists can also be spaced at 13.7, 19.2 in. on center, thus dividing the 8 ft length of plywood subfloor panels into seven and five equal parts, respectively. Use of the 48 in. module on house width permits greater use of full 4 x 8 plywood subflooring and minimizes cutting and waste. A maximum savings can be achieved with the 48 in. house width module if the largest of the subfloor panels are preplanned. Full 48 in. wide panels can be used without ripping for the 24, 28, and 32 ft house width when joists are either lapped or trimmed to meet correct dimension.

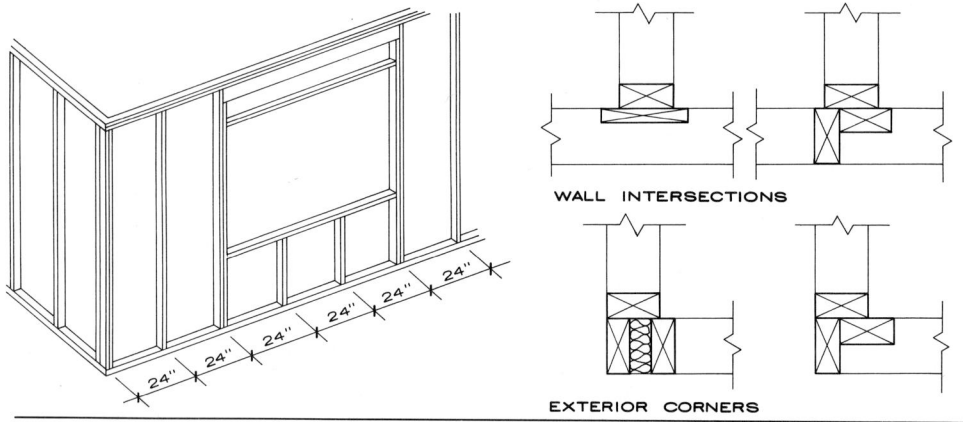

WALL FRAMING

WALL INTERSECTIONS

EXTERIOR CORNERS

WALLS, DOORS, AND WINDOWS

Cost savings will be greatest when the overall size of the house plus the size and location of wall openings coincide with standard modular stud spacing. A simple practical approach to this kind of modular preplanning is to separate the exterior wall elements to the minor and major division points with stud spacing at the minor module dimension of 24 in. o.c.

Maximum flexibility in placing window and door openings is achieved by having the 16 in. module coincide with the 24 in. module. The precise location of wall openings on the 16 in. module eliminates extra wall framing frequently required in nonmodular residential construction. Test and structural analysis show that, for many installations, 24 in. on center 2 x 4 construction can be used for walls supporting the upper roof of two-story units.

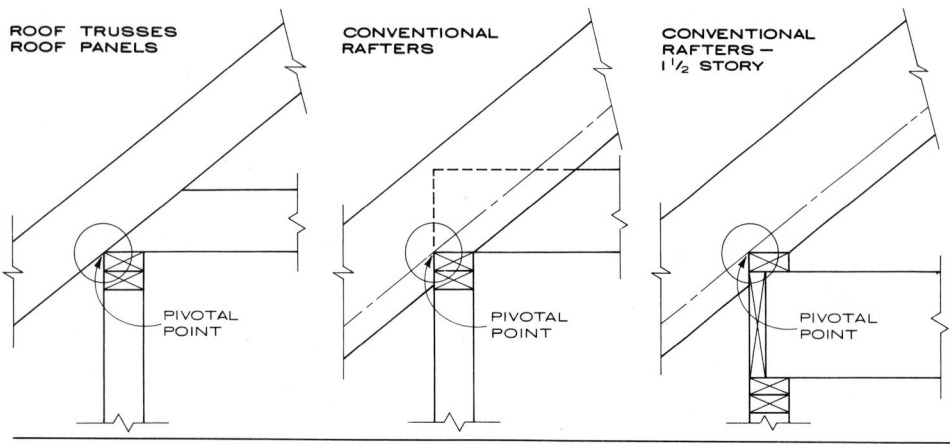

ROOF TRUSSES ROOF PANELS

CONVENTIONAL RAFTERS

CONVENTIONAL RAFTERS – 1½ STORY

PIVOTAL POINT OF ROOF

ROOF FRAMING

Increments for house width are in 24 in. multiples. Six 48 in. module depths and five 24 in. module widths fulfill most roof span requirements. Standard roof slopes combined with modular house width provide all dimensions required for design of rafter, truss, and panel roofs. The pivotal point shown is the fixed point of reference in the module line of the exterior wall. Modular roof design and construction dimensions are determined from this point.

Haver, Nunn, Collamer; Phoenix, Arizona

Robin A. Roberts; Washington, D.C.

 MODULAR PLANNING

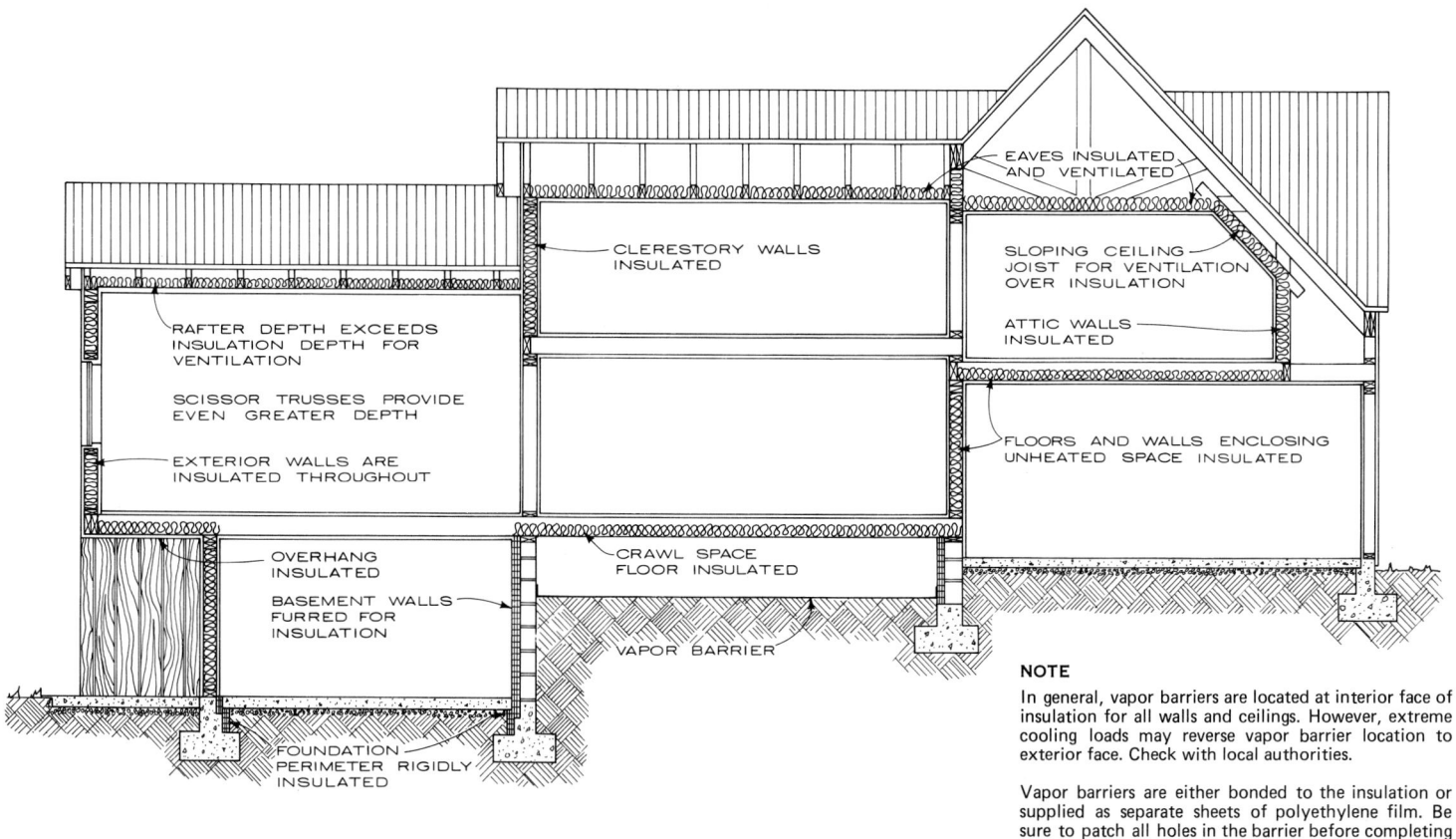

CLERESTORY WALLS INSULATED

EAVES INSULATED AND VENTILATED

SLOPING CEILING JOIST FOR VENTILATION OVER INSULATION

ATTIC WALLS INSULATED

RAFTER DEPTH EXCEEDS INSULATION DEPTH FOR VENTILATION

SCISSOR TRUSSES PROVIDE EVEN GREATER DEPTH

EXTERIOR WALLS ARE INSULATED THROUGHOUT

FLOORS AND WALLS ENCLOSING UNHEATED SPACE INSULATED

OVERHANG INSULATED

CRAWL SPACE FLOOR INSULATED

BASEMENT WALLS FURRED FOR INSULATION

VAPOR BARRIER

FOUNDATION PERIMETER RIGIDLY INSULATED

NOTE

In general, vapor barriers are located at interior face of insulation for all walls and ceilings. However, extreme cooling loads may reverse vapor barrier location to exterior face. Check with local authorities.

Vapor barriers are either bonded to the insulation or supplied as separate sheets of polyethylene film. Be sure to patch all holes in the barrier before completing construction.

INSULATED FRAME RESIDENCE

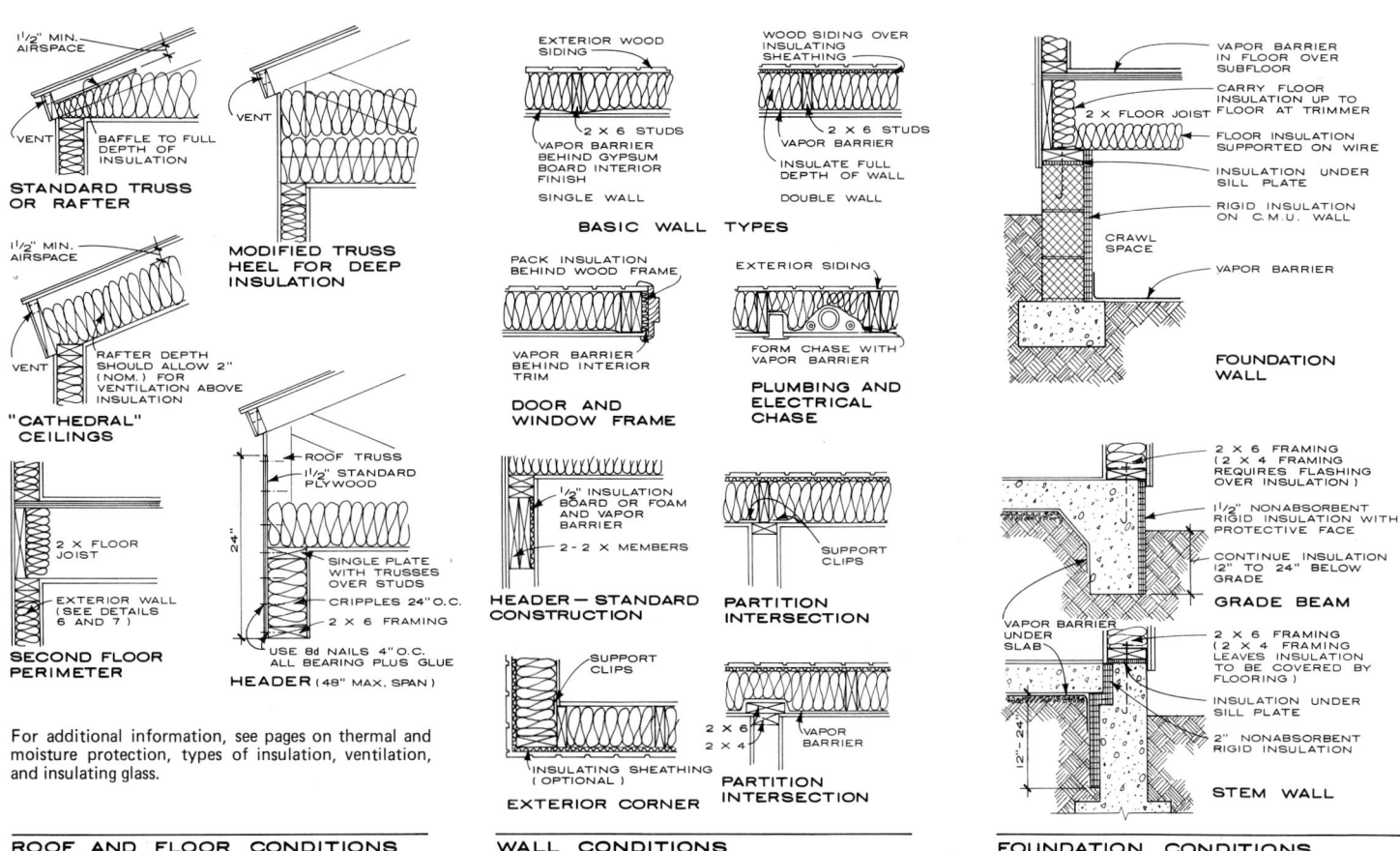

1½" MIN. AIRSPACE

VENT

BAFFLE TO FULL DEPTH OF INSULATION

STANDARD TRUSS OR RAFTER

VENT

MODIFIED TRUSS HEEL FOR DEEP INSULATION

1½" MIN. AIRSPACE

VENT

RAFTER DEPTH SHOULD ALLOW 2" (NOM.) FOR VENTILATION ABOVE INSULATION

"CATHEDRAL" CEILINGS

2 X FLOOR JOIST

EXTERIOR WALL (SEE DETAILS 6 AND 7)

SECOND FLOOR PERIMETER

ROOF TRUSS

1½" STANDARD PLYWOOD

24"

SINGLE PLATE WITH TRUSSES OVER STUDS

CRIPPLES 24" O.C.

2 X 6 FRAMING

USE 8d NAILS 4" O.C. ALL BEARING PLUS GLUE

HEADER (48" MAX. SPAN)

EXTERIOR WOOD SIDING

2 X 6 STUDS

VAPOR BARRIER BEHIND GYPSUM BOARD INTERIOR FINISH

SINGLE WALL

WOOD SIDING OVER INSULATING SHEATHING

2 X 6 STUDS VAPOR BARRIER

INSULATE FULL DEPTH OF WALL

DOUBLE WALL

BASIC WALL TYPES

PACK INSULATION BEHIND WOOD FRAME

VAPOR BARRIER BEHIND INTERIOR TRIM

DOOR AND WINDOW FRAME

EXTERIOR SIDING

FORM CHASE WITH VAPOR BARRIER

PLUMBING AND ELECTRICAL CHASE

½" INSULATION BOARD OR FOAM AND VAPOR BARRIER

2 - 2 X MEMBERS

HEADER — STANDARD CONSTRUCTION

SUPPORT CLIPS

PARTITION INTERSECTION

SUPPORT CLIPS

INSULATING SHEATHING (OPTIONAL)

EXTERIOR CORNER

2 X 6
2 X 4
VAPOR BARRIER

PARTITION INTERSECTION

VAPOR BARRIER IN FLOOR OVER SUBFLOOR

CARRY FLOOR INSULATION UP TO FLOOR AT TRIMMER

2 X FLOOR JOIST

FLOOR INSULATION SUPPORTED ON WIRE

INSULATION UNDER SILL PLATE

RIGID INSULATION ON C.M.U. WALL

CRAWL SPACE

VAPOR BARRIER

FOUNDATION WALL

2 X 6 FRAMING (2 X 4 FRAMING REQUIRES FLASHING OVER INSULATION)

1½" NONABSORBENT RIGID INSULATION WITH PROTECTIVE FACE

CONTINUE INSULATION 12" TO 24" BELOW GRADE

GRADE BEAM

2 X 6 FRAMING (2 X 4 FRAMING LEAVES INSULATION TO BE COVERED BY FLOORING)

VAPOR BARRIER UNDER SLAB

INSULATION UNDER SILL PLATE

12"-24"

2" NONABSORBENT RIGID INSULATION

STEM WALL

For additional information, see pages on thermal and moisture protection, types of insulation, ventilation, and insulating glass.

ROOF AND FLOOR CONDITIONS

WALL CONDITIONS

FOUNDATION CONDITIONS

Ralph D. Provencal, AIA; Olympia, Washington

MONOPLANER WOOD TRUSSES, LIGHT METAL PLATE CONNECTED OR PLYWOOD

Monoplaner trusses usually of 2'' nominal lumber, spaced 2'– 0'' o.c. Camber as required. Dry wall ceiling may be attached directly to trusses. Plywood sheathing staggered joints.

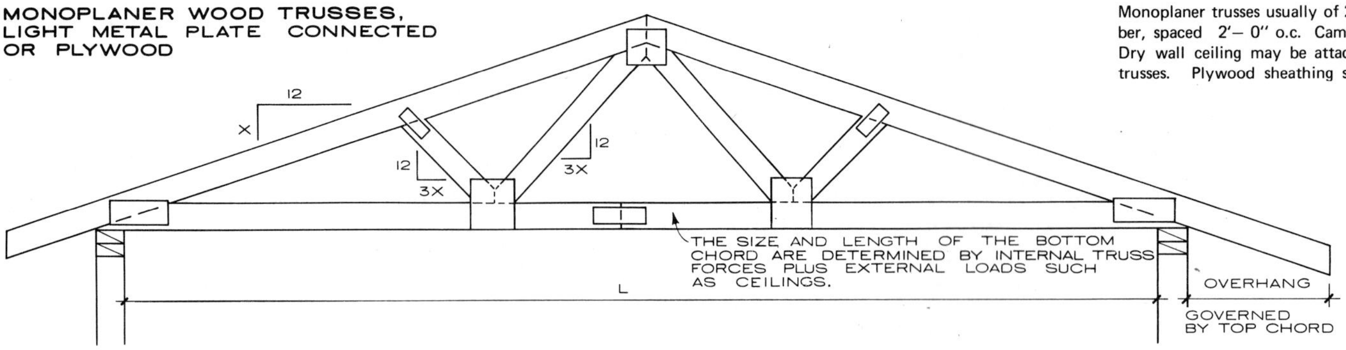

THE SIZE AND LENGTH OF THE BOTTOM CHORD ARE DETERMINED BY INTERNAL TRUSS FORCES PLUS EXTERNAL LOADS SUCH AS CEILINGS.

OVERHANG GOVERNED BY TOP CHORD

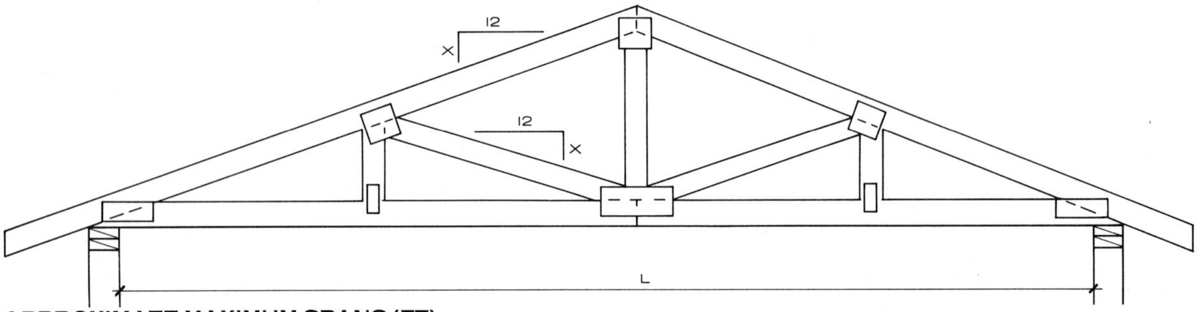

APPROXIMATE MAXIMUM SPANS (FT)

	L FOR 2 x 4		L FOR 2 x 4	
X	40 psf	50 psf	40 psf	50 psf
2	22	19	33	28
3	25	21	38	32
4	26	22	41	35
5	27	23	42	36
6	27	24	42	37

FOUR PANEL TRUSSES

Approximate maximum spans for 2 x 4 and 2 x 6 top chords for trusses above (4 panel) using machine stress rated (MSR) lumber with f = 1200 psi and E = 1,200,000 psi. Trusses spaced 2 ft o.c. (Assume 15% of live load increase for snow load condition.) All web members 2 x 4. All bottom chords 2 x 4 except where ceiling or external loads required.

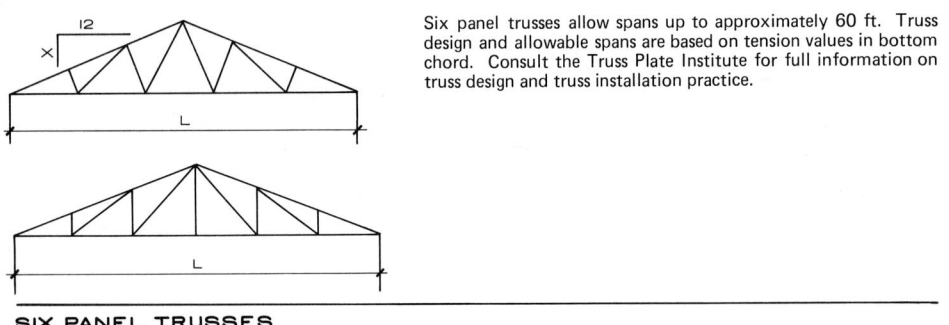

SIX PANEL TRUSSES

Six panel trusses allow spans up to approximately 60 ft. Truss design and allowable spans are based on tension values in bottom chord. Consult the Truss Plate Institute for full information on truss design and truss installation practice.

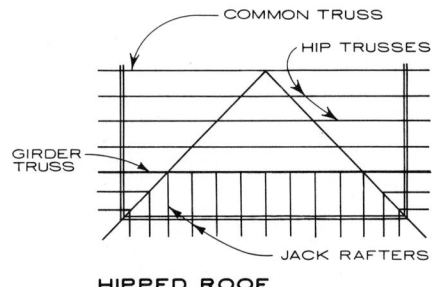

HIPPED ROOF

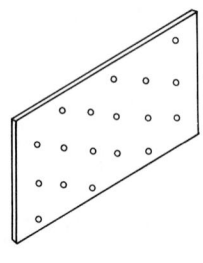

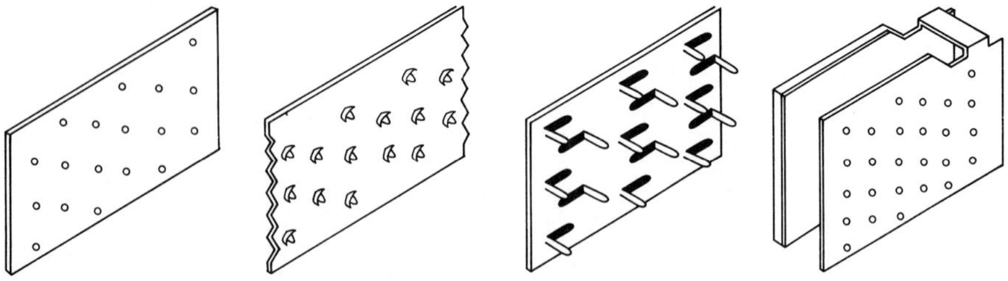

NAIL–ON 18-20 GAUGE

PRONGS 18-20 GAUGE

TEETH 14-20 GAUGE

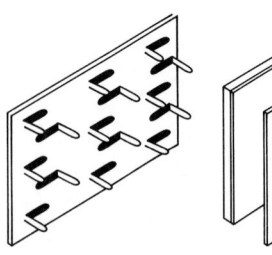

SELF–CLINCHING NAILS 20 GAUGE

Plates manufactured from zinc coated (hot dip process) sheet steel conforming to current ASTM A446 Grade A. Plates applied to both sides of joint. Where nails are required through connector plates they shall be 1½ in. long with $9/32$ in. head and a 0.12 in. (8d) deformed or annular ringed shank.

PLATE TYPES

GENERAL NOTES

1. Trusses designed in accordance with Truss Plate Institute Design Specifications and National Design Specifications for wood construction.
2. Plates sized for axial loads, eccentricity, net section of metal and fastener design value.

3. Truss members should be clamped in a mechanical or hydraulic jig with sufficient pressure to bring members into reasonable contact at all joints during application of connector plates.

4. Provide adequate anchorage and erection bracing as specified by plate manufacturer or as designed in accordance with NDS. Refer also to Bracing Wood Trusses, BWT-76.

Joseph A. Wilkes, FAIA; Wilkes and Faulkner; Washington, D.C.

WOOD TRUSSES

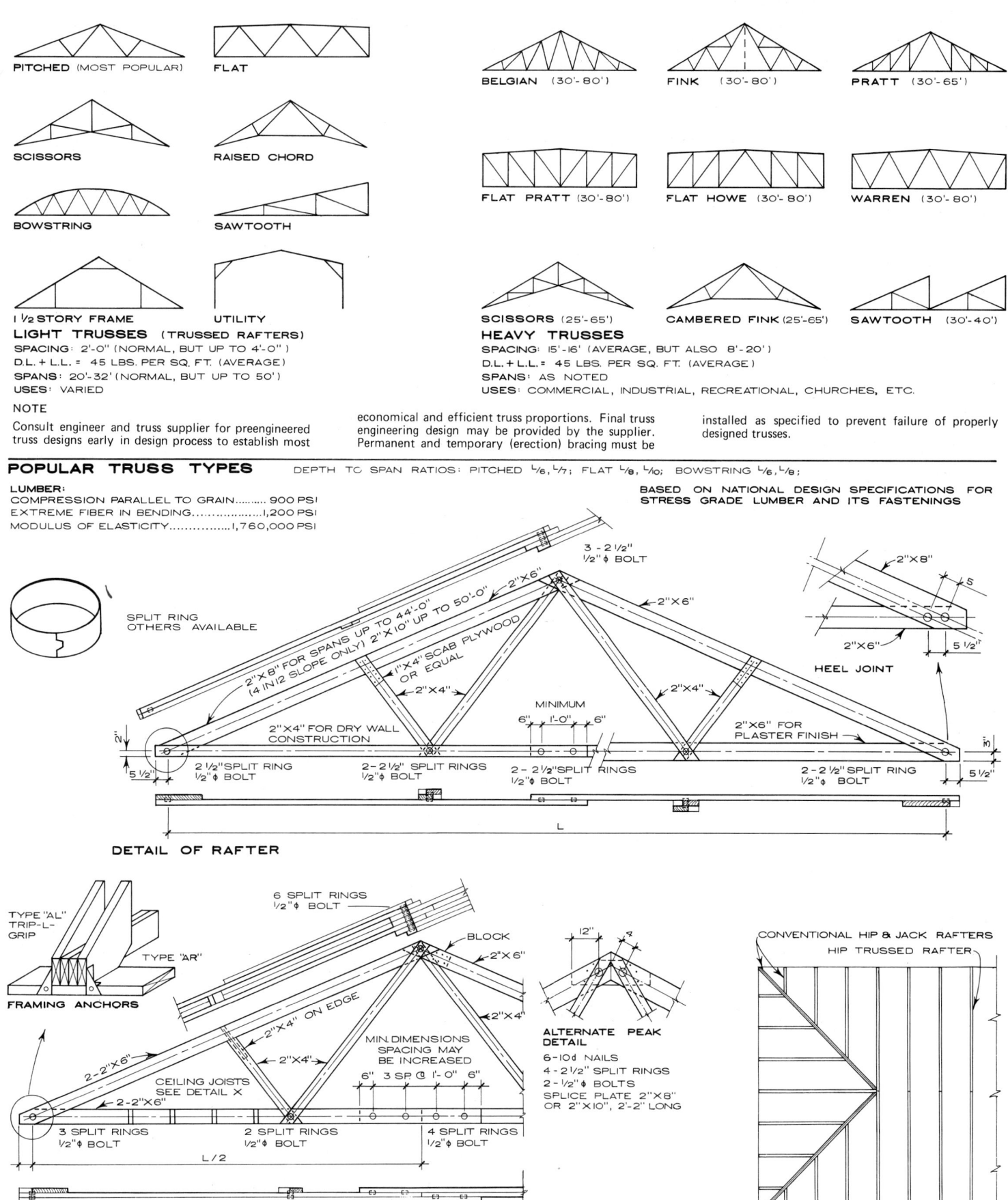

PITCHED (MOST POPULAR)   FLAT

SCISSORS   RAISED CHORD

BOWSTRING   SAWTOOTH

1 1/2 STORY FRAME   UTILITY

LIGHT TRUSSES (TRUSSED RAFTERS)
SPACING: 2'-0" (NORMAL, BUT UP TO 4'-0")
D.L.+ L.L.= 45 LBS. PER SQ. FT. (AVERAGE)
SPANS: 20'-32' (NORMAL, BUT UP TO 50')
USES: VARIED

BELGIAN (30'-80')   FINK (30'-80')   PRATT (30'-65')

FLAT PRATT (30'-80')   FLAT HOWE (30'-80')   WARREN (30'-80')

SCISSORS (25'-65')   CAMBERED FINK (25'-65')   SAWTOOTH (30'-40')

HEAVY TRUSSES
SPACING: 15'-16' (AVERAGE, BUT ALSO 8'-20')
D.L.+ L.L.= 45 LBS. PER SQ. FT. (AVERAGE)
SPANS: AS NOTED
USES: COMMERCIAL, INDUSTRIAL, RECREATIONAL, CHURCHES, ETC.

NOTE

Consult engineer and truss supplier for preengineered truss designs early in design process to establish most economical and efficient truss proportions. Final truss engineering design may be provided by the supplier. Permanent and temporary (erection) bracing must be installed as specified to prevent failure of properly designed trusses.

POPULAR TRUSS TYPES
DEPTH TO SPAN RATIOS: PITCHED L/6, L/7; FLAT L/8, L/10; BOWSTRING L/6, L/8;

LUMBER:
COMPRESSION PARALLEL TO GRAIN.......... 900 PSI
EXTREME FIBER IN BENDING..................1,200 PSI
MODULUS OF ELASTICITY..............1,760,000 PSI

BASED ON NATIONAL DESIGN SPECIFICATIONS FOR STRESS GRADE LUMBER AND ITS FASTENINGS

SPLIT RING
OTHERS AVAILABLE

3 - 2 1/2"
1/2"φ BOLT

2"X8"

2"X6"

2"X6"

2"X6"

2"X8" FOR SPANS UP TO 44'-0"
(4 IN 12 SLOPE ONLY) 2"X10" UP TO 50'-0"

1"X4" SCAB PLYWOOD
OR EQUAL

2"X4"

2"X4"

HEEL JOINT

2"X6"

5 1/2"

MINIMUM

6"   1'-0"   6"

2"X4" FOR DRY WALL
CONSTRUCTION

2"X6" FOR
PLASTER FINISH

2"

2 1/2" SPLIT RING
1/2"φ BOLT

2 - 2 1/2" SPLIT RINGS
1/2"φ BOLT

2 - 2 1/2" SPLIT RINGS
1/2"φ BOLT

2 - 2 1/2" SPLIT RING
1/2"φ BOLT

5 1/2"

5 1/2"

L

DETAIL OF RAFTER

TYPE "AL"
TRIP-L-GRIP

TYPE 'AR'

FRAMING ANCHORS

6 SPLIT RINGS
1/2"φ BOLT

BLOCK

2"X6"

2"X4"

2"X4" ON EDGE

2"X6"

2"X4"

2-2"X6"

CEILING JOISTS
SEE DETAIL X

2"X4"

MIN. DIMENSIONS
SPACING MAY
BE INCREASED

6"   3 SP @ 1'-0"   6"

2-2"X6"

3 SPLIT RINGS
1/2"φ BOLT

2 SPLIT RINGS
1/2"φ BOLT

4 SPLIT RINGS
1/2"φ BOLT

L/2

12"   4

ALTERNATE PEAK DETAIL
6-10d NAILS
4 - 2 1/2" SPLIT RINGS
2 - 1/2"φ BOLTS
SPLICE PLATE 2"X8"
OR 2"X10", 2'-2" LONG

CONVENTIONAL HIP & JACK RAFTERS
HIP TRUSSED RAFTER

HIP TRUSSED RAFTER
FOR SPANS UP TO 32'-0" &
SLOPES OF 4,5,6 & 7 ON 12

FRAMING PLAN

RING CONNECTOR TRUSSES

Joseph A. Wilkes; FAIA; Wilkes and Faulkner; Washington, D.C.

WOOD TRUSSES   6

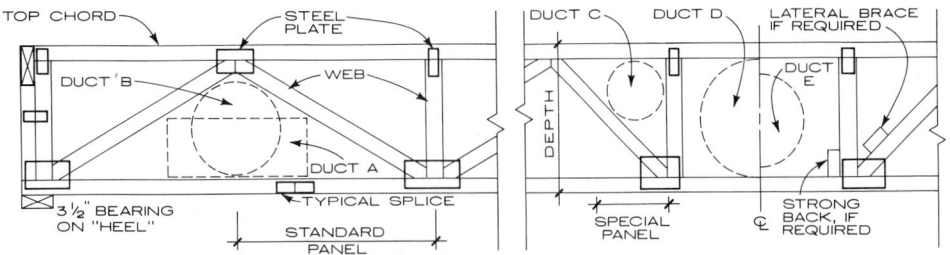

RESIDENTIAL TYPE TRUSSED FLOOR JOIST STEEL PLATE CONNECTED

WOOD TRUSSED RAFTERS SPANS

	RESIDENTIAL LIVE LOADS								
	FLOORS 55 PSF (A)			ROOFS 40 PSF (B)		55 PSF (C)		(DOUBLE CHORDS) 55 PSF (C)	
	TRUSSED RAFTERS SPACING (C TO C)								
DEPTH	12″	16″	24″	16″	24″	16″	24″	16″	24″
12″	23-6	21-0	17-1	24-0	21-4	21-11	18-2		
13″	24-11	22-0	17-11						
14″	26-4	22-11	18-8	27-5	23-3	24-5	19-10		
15″	27-7	23-10	19-5						
16″	28-7	24-9	20-1	30-3	25-0	26-4	21-4	31-10	27-10
18″	30-6	26-4	21-5	32-11	26-9	28-1	22-9	35-1	30-7
20″	32-4	27-11	22-8	34-8	28-0	29-7	23-11	38-1	33-1
22″	34-0	26-9	23-11						
24″	35-8	30-10	25-0	38-3	30-11	32-7	26-4	43-10	36-7
28″				41-6	33-6	35-5	28-7	49-2	39-11
32″				44-3	35-7	37-8	30-4	52-9	42-9
36″				47-0	37-10	40-1	32-3	56-3	45-7
48″								60-0	53-3

	COMMERCIAL LIVE LOADS								
	FLOORS 80 PSF (D)			100 PSF (E)			120 PSF (F)		
	TRUSSED RAFTERS SPACING (C TO C)								
DEPTH	12″	16″	24″	12″	16″	24″	12″	16″	24″
12″	19-0	17-3	15-1	17-3	15-8	13-7	16-0	14-7	12-4
14″	21-4	19-4	16-6	19-4	17-7	14-9	18-0	16-4	13-6
16″	23-6	21-5	17-10	21-5	19-5	15-11	19-10	17-11	14-6
18″	25-8	23-4	19-0	23-4	21-0	17-0	21-8	19-2	15-6
20″	27-8	24-10	20-2	25-2	22-3	18-0	23-4	20-3	16-5
24″	31-6	27-5	22-2	28-5	24-6	19-10	25-11	22-4	18-1
16″*	27-7	25-1	21-11	25-1	22-9	19-11	23-2	21-2	18-5
24″*	38-0	34-6	30-1	34-6	31-4	27-4	32-0	29-1	25-1
32″*	47-1	42-9	36-1	42-9	38-10	32-3	39-8	36-1	29-5

Top chord live load	40 psf	20 psf		35 psf	60 psf		80 psf	100 psf
Top chord dead load	10 psf	10 psf		10 psf	10 psf		10 psf	10 psf
Bottom chord dead load	5 psf	10 psf		10 psf	10 psf		10 psf	10 psf
Total load	(A) 55 psf	(B) 40 psf	(C) 55 psf	(D) 80 psf	(E) 100 psf	(F) 120 psf		

NOTES

1. Spans are clear, inside to inside, for bottom chord bearing. Values shown would vary very slightly for a truss with top chord loading.
2. Spans should not exceed 24 x depth of truss.
3. Designed deflection limit under total load is ℓ/240 for roofs, ℓ/360 for residential floors, and ℓ/480 for commercial floors.
4. Roof spans include a +15% short term stress.

5. Asterisk (*) indicates that truss has double chords, top and bottom.
6. Spans shown are for only one type of lumber; in this case—#2 Southern pine, with an f_b value of 1550. Charts are available for other grades and species. Lumber and grades may be mixed in the same truss, but chord size must be identical. Repetitive member bending stress is used in this chart.

GENERAL

Monoplaner trusses are usually made up from 2 x 4 or 2 x 6 lumber. Spacing, normally 24 in. o.c., varies for special uses, especially in agriculture. Camber is designed for dead load only. Bottom chord furring generally is not required for drywall ceiling. Joints in plywood floor or roof should be staggered. Many trusses are approved by model codes, such as BOCA, ICBO, FHA, and SBC.

$$\text{CAMBER (USUAL)} = \frac{L(FT)}{60}$$

BRACING

Adequate bracing of trusses is vital. Sufficient support at right angles to plane of truss must be provided to hold each truss member in its designated position. Consider bracing during design, fabrication, and erection. In addition, provide permanent bracing/anchorage as an integral part of the building. Strongbacks are often used.

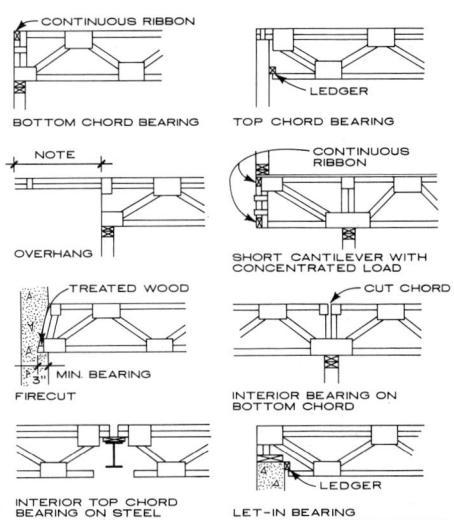

FRAMING DETAILS

Several types of manufactured trusses are shown below. Span limits are for a 55 psf total load, truss 24 in. o.c. Spans: small—20 to 40 ft, medium—40 to 60 ft, long—60 to 80 ft, very long—80 to 100 ft. This information is for initial design only.

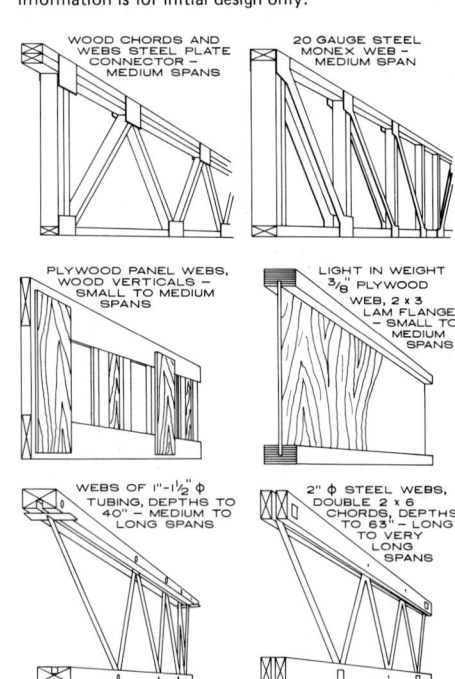

TYPES OF WOOD TRUSSED RAFTERS

DUCT SIZES

Ease of running electrical and mechanical services through framing is a major advantage of trussed joists. Most manufacturers provide a large rectangular open panel at midspan; this void will generally accommodate a trunk line.

Sizes given here are approximations. Because web size and angles vary with different brands, the designer is cautioned to verify individual sizes carefully. Note that shape E is the duct that will fit in a flat truss with double chords top and bottom.

Michael Bengis, AIA; Hopatcong, N.J.

DEPTH OF TRUSS AND SIZE OF DUCTWORK

DEPTH	12″	16″	20″	24″
SHAPE				
A	4 x 9	6 x 12	7 x 13	8 x 14
B	7″	10″	12″	14″
C	5″	7″	8″	9″
D	9″	13″	17″	21″
E	6″	10″	14″	18″

WOOD TRUSSES

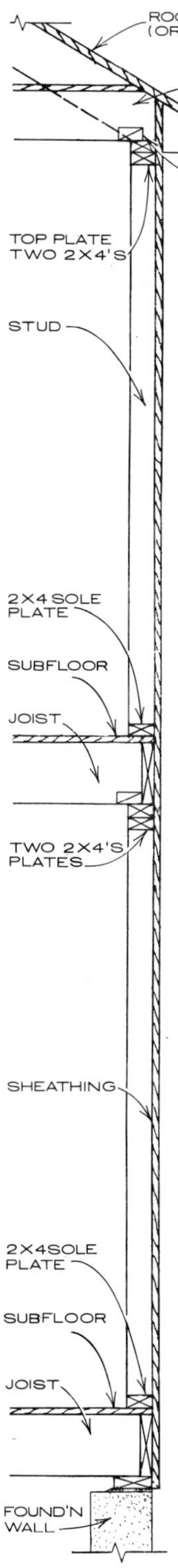

ROOF SHEATHING
(OR SHINGLE LATH)

RAFTER

NAILER
FOR
CEILING

TOP PLATE
TWO 2×4'S

STUD

2×4 SOLE
PLATE

SUBFLOOR

JOIST

TWO 2×4'S
PLATES

SHEATHING

2×4 SOLE
PLATE

SUBFLOOR

JOIST

FOUND'N
WALL

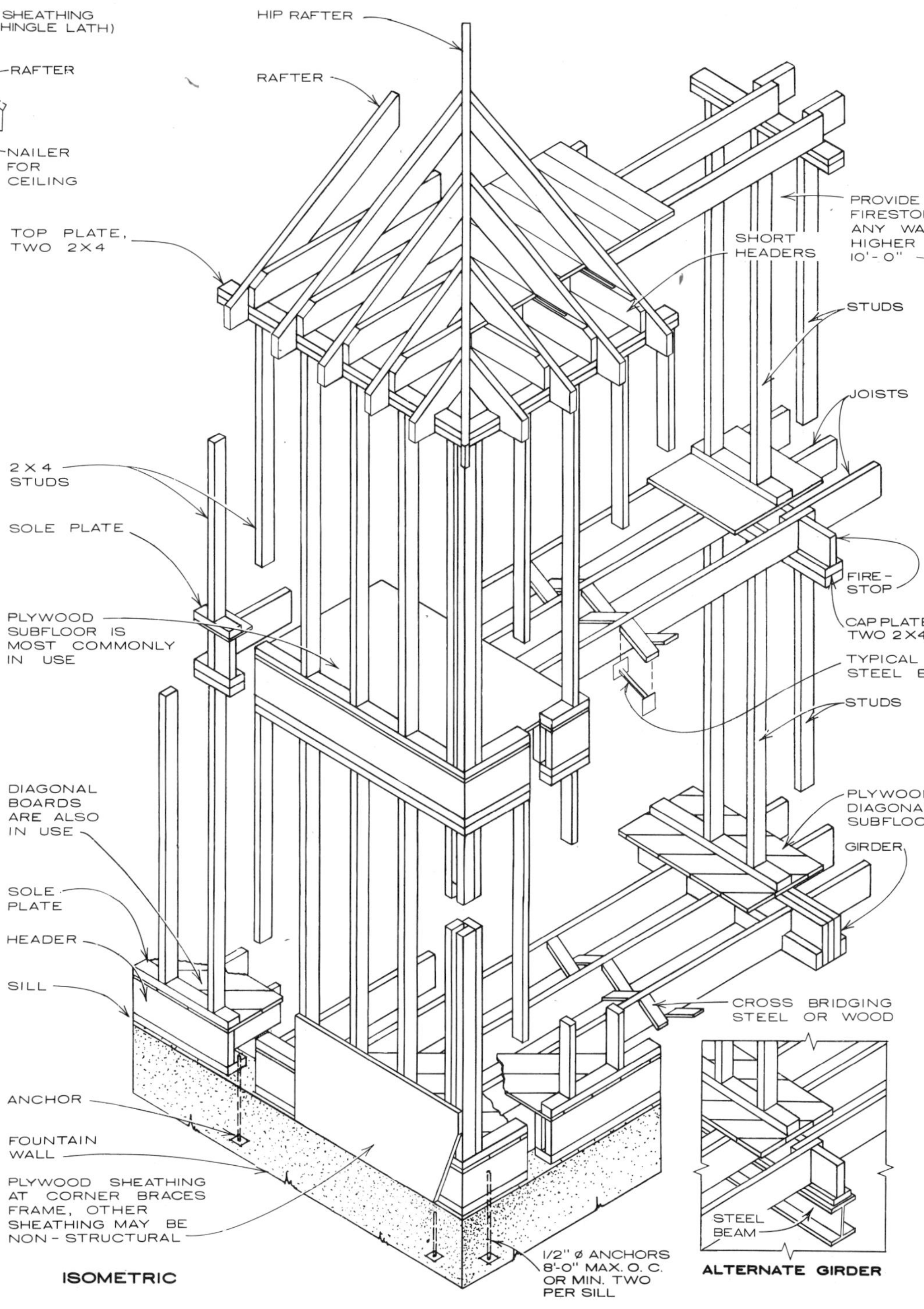

HIP RAFTER

RAFTER

TOP PLATE,
TWO 2×4

2 × 4
STUDS

SOLE PLATE

PLYWOOD
SUBFLOOR IS
MOST COMMONLY
IN USE

DIAGONAL
BOARDS
ARE ALSO
IN USE

SOLE
PLATE

HEADER

SILL

ANCHOR

FOUNTAIN
WALL

PLYWOOD SHEATHING
AT CORNER BRACES
FRAME, OTHER
SHEATHING MAY BE
NON-STRUCTURAL

ISOMETRIC

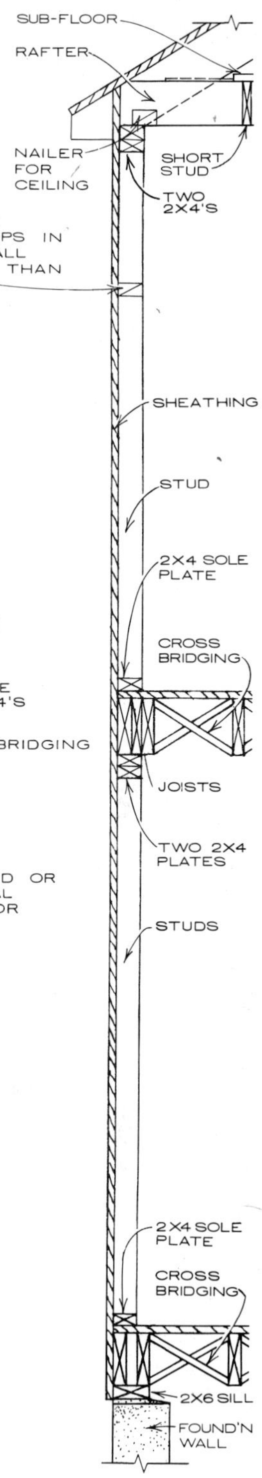

SUB-FLOOR

RAFTER

NAILER
FOR
CEILING

SHORT
STUD

TWO
2×4'S

PROVIDE
FIRESTOPS IN
ANY WALL
HIGHER THAN
10'-0"

SHORT
HEADERS

STUDS

JOISTS

SHEATHING

STUD

2×4 SOLE
PLATE

CROSS
BRIDGING

FIRE-
STOP

CAP PLATE
TWO 2×4'S

TYPICAL
STEEL BRIDGING

STUDS

JOISTS

TWO 2×4
PLATES

PLYWOOD OR
DIAGONAL
SUBFLOOR

GIRDER

STUDS

CROSS BRIDGING
STEEL OR WOOD

2×4 SOLE
PLATE

CROSS
BRIDGING

STEEL
BEAM

ALTERNATE GIRDER

2×6 SILL

FOUND'N
WALL

1/2" Ø ANCHORS
8'-0" MAX. O.C.
OR MIN. TWO
PER SILL

**SECTION-CEILING JOISTS PARALLEL TO
RAFTERS: FLOOR JOISTS PERPENDICULAR
TO EXTERIOR WALLS   SCALE 3/8"=1'-0"**

**SECTION- CEILING JOISTS PERPENDICULAR
TO RAFTERS: FLOOR JOISTS PARALLEL TO
EXTERIOR WALLS. SCALE:3/8"=1'-0"**

NOTES

WESTERN OR PLATFORM FRAMING

Subfloor extends to outer edge of the frame and provides a
flat, work surface at each floor. Common practice is to
assemble walls on subfloor and tilt them into place.
Arrangement of members in platform framing equilizes vertical shrinkage within the structure.

FIRESTOPPING

All concealed spaces in framing with 2" blocking, fitted to
openings and arranged to prevent drafts between spaces.

Joseph A. Wilkes; FAIA; Wilkes and Faulkner; Washington, D.C.

EXTERIOR WALL FRAMING

One Story Buildings: 2x4's, 16'' or 24'' o.c.
Two & Three Stories: 2x4's, 16'' o.c.

BRACING EXTERIOR WALLS

Suitable sheathing acts as bracing. Where required for additional stiffness or bracing, 1x4's may be let into outer face
of studs at 45° angle secured top, bottom and to studs.

BRIDGING FOR FLOOR JOISTS

May be omitted when flooring is properly nailed to joists.
However, where nominal depth-to-thickness ratio of joists
exceeds 6 bridging should be installed at 8' − 0'' intervals.
(F.H.A. also allows omission of bridging under certain
conditions--see F.H.A. publication No. 300, 1963, revised 1965.)

Steel bridging is available. Some types do not require
nails.

LIGHT WOOD FRAMING

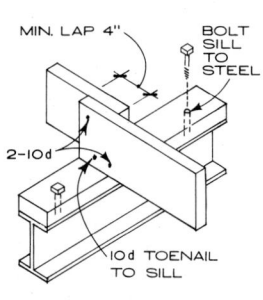

MIN. LAP 4"
BOLT SILL TO STEEL
2-10d
10d TOENAIL TO SILL

LAPPED OVER WOOD SILL

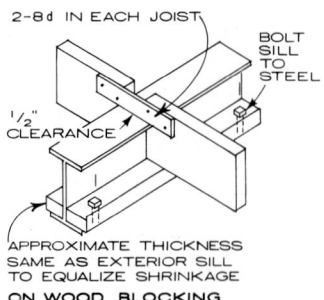

2-8d IN EACH JOIST
STEEL STRAP OR WOOD SCAB

ON LOWER FLANGE

2-8d IN EACH JOIST
BOLT SILL TO STEEL
1/2" CLEARANCE
APPROXIMATE THICKNESS SAME AS EXTERIOR SILL TO EQUALIZE SHRINKAGE

ON WOOD BLOCKING

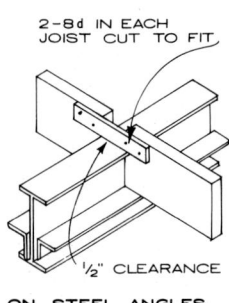

2-8d IN EACH JOIST CUT TO FIT
1/2" CLEARANCE

ON STEEL ANGLES

WOOD JOISTS SUPPORTED ON STEEL GIRDERS

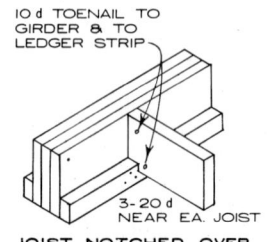

10d TOENAIL TO GIRDER & TO LEDGER STRIP
3-20d NEAR EA. JOIST

JOIST NOTCHED OVER LEDGER STRIP
NOTCHING OVER BEARING NOT RECOMMENDED

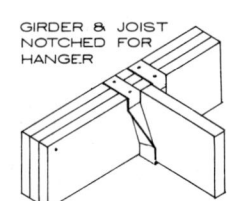

GIRDER & JOIST NOTCHED FOR HANGER

JOIST IN JOIST HANGER IRON
ALSO CALLED STIRRUP OR BRIDLE IRON

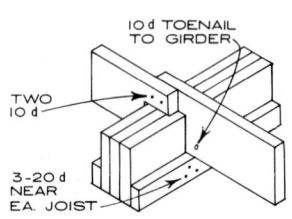

10d TOENAIL TO GIRDER
TWO 10d
3-20d NEAR EA. JOIST

OVERLAPPING JOISTS NOTCHED OVER GIRDER
BEARING ONLY ON LEDGER, NOT ON TOP OF GIRDER

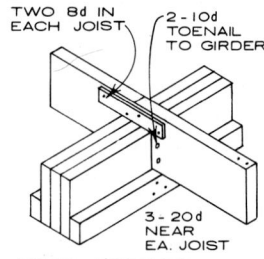

TWO 8d IN EACH JOIST
2-10d TOENAIL TO GIRDER
3-20d NEAR EA. JOIST

JOISTS NOTCHED OVER GIRDER
BEARING ONLY ON LEDGER, NOT ON TOP OF GIRDER

WOOD JOISTS SUPPORTED ON WOOD GIRDERS

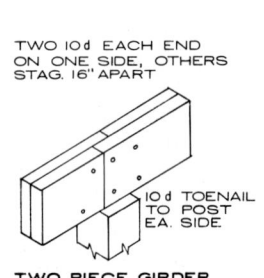

TWO 10d EACH END ON ONE SIDE, OTHERS STAG. 16" APART
10d TOENAIL TO POST EA. SIDE

TWO PIECE GIRDER
GIRDER JOINTS ONLY AT SUPPORTS STAGGER JOINTS

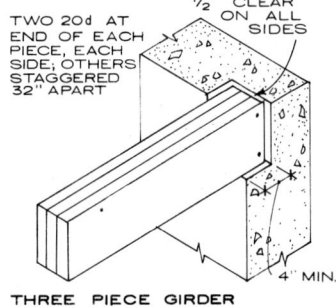

1/2" CLEAR ON ALL SIDES
TWO 20d AT END OF EACH PIECE, EACH SIDE; OTHERS STAGGERED 32" APART
4" MIN.

THREE PIECE GIRDER
FOR FOUR PIECE GIRDER ADD NAILED WITH 20d TO THREE PC.

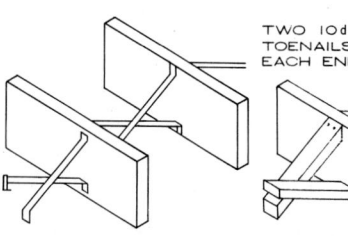

TWO 10d TOENAILS EACH END

STEEL BRIDGING
SOME HAVE BUILT-IN TEETH, NEEDS NO NAILS

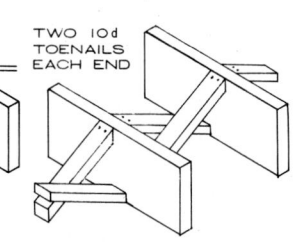

1" X 3" CROSS BRIDGING
LOWER ENDS NOT NAILED UNTIL FLOORING IS LAYED

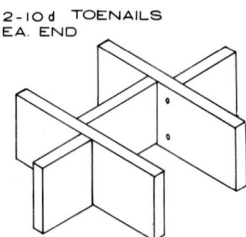

2-10d TOENAILS EA. END

SOLID BRIDGING
USED UNDER PARTITIONS FOR HEAVY LOADING STAGGER BOARDS FOR EASE OF NAILING

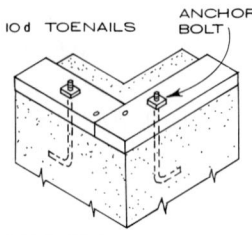

10d TOENAILS
ANCHOR BOLT

2 X 6 SILL

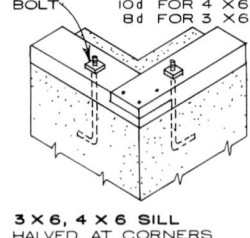

ANCHOR BOLT
10d FOR 4 X 6
8d FOR 3 X 6

3 X 6, 4 X 6 SILL
HALVED AT CORNERS

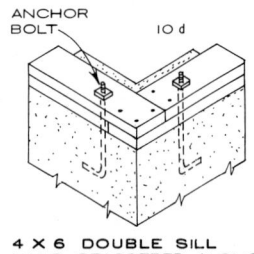

ANCHOR BOLT
10d

4 X 6 DOUBLE SILL
NAILS STAGGERED ALONG SILL 24" ON CENTER

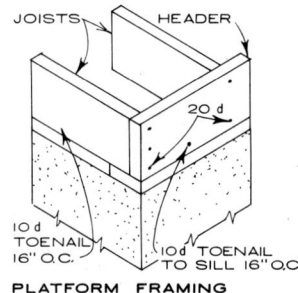

JOISTS
HEADER
20d
10d TOENAIL 16" O.C.
10d TOENAIL TO SILL 16" O.C.

PLATFORM FRAMING
TOENAIL TO SILL NOT REQUIRED IF DIAGONAL SHEATHING USED

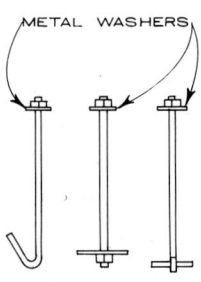

METAL WASHERS

TYPES OF SILL ANCHOR BOLTS

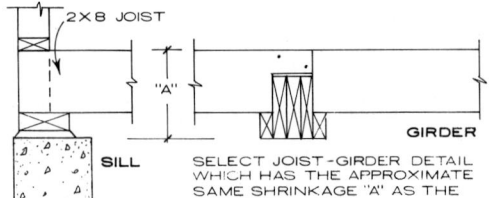

2X8 JOIST
"A"
SILL
GIRDER

SHRINKAGE
SELECT JOIST-GIRDER DETAIL WHICH HAS THE APPROXIMATE SAME SHRINKAGE "A" AS THE SILL DETAIL USED

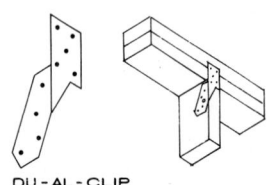

DU-AL-CLIP

METAL FRAMING DEVICES

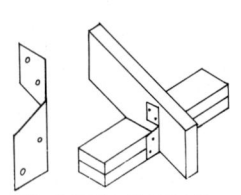

TY-DOWN ANCHOR

16 - 18 GAUGE ZINC COATED STEEL

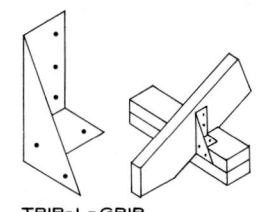

TRIP-L-GRIP

Joseph A. Wilkes, FAIA; Wilkes and Faulkner; Washington, D.C.

LIGHT WOOD FRAMING

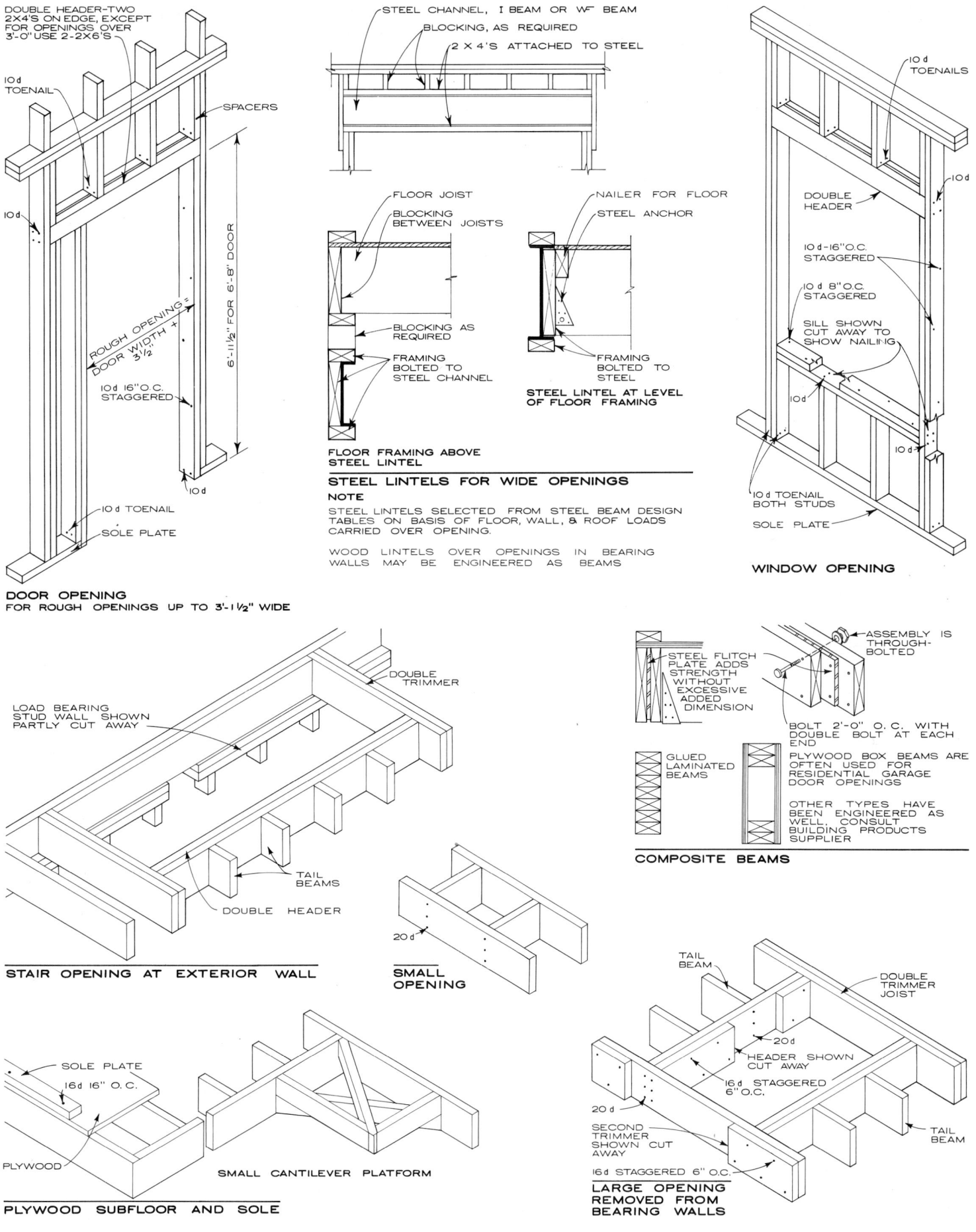

DOUBLE HEADER–TWO
2X4'S ON EDGE, EXCEPT
FOR OPENINGS OVER
3'-0" USE 2-2X6'S

10 d TOENAIL

SPACERS

10 d

ROUGH OPENING =
DOOR WIDTH + 3½"

6'-11½" FOR 6'-8' DOOR

10d 16"O.C.
STAGGERED

10 d

10 d TOENAIL

SOLE PLATE

DOOR OPENING
FOR ROUGH OPENINGS UP TO 3'-1½" WIDE

STEEL CHANNEL, I BEAM OR W⁻ BEAM

BLOCKING, AS REQUIRED

2 X 4'S ATTACHED TO STEEL

FLOOR JOIST

BLOCKING
BETWEEN JOISTS

BLOCKING AS
REQUIRED

FRAMING
BOLTED TO
STEEL CHANNEL

**FLOOR FRAMING ABOVE
STEEL LINTEL**

NAILER FOR FLOOR

STEEL ANCHOR

FRAMING
BOLTED TO
STEEL

**STEEL LINTEL AT LEVEL
OF FLOOR FRAMING**

STEEL LINTELS FOR WIDE OPENINGS
NOTE
STEEL LINTELS SELECTED FROM STEEL BEAM DESIGN
TABLES ON BASIS OF FLOOR, WALL, & ROOF LOADS
CARRIED OVER OPENING.

WOOD LINTELS OVER OPENINGS IN BEARING
WALLS MAY BE ENGINEERED AS BEAMS

10 d TOENAILS

DOUBLE
HEADER

10 d

10 d –16"O.C.
STAGGERED

10 d 8"O.C.
STAGGERED

SILL SHOWN
CUT AWAY TO
SHOW NAILING

10 d

10 d

10 d TOENAIL
BOTH STUDS

SOLE PLATE

WINDOW OPENING

LOAD BEARING
STUD WALL SHOWN
PARTLY CUT AWAY

DOUBLE
TRIMMER

TAIL
BEAMS

DOUBLE HEADER

STAIR OPENING AT EXTERIOR WALL

20 d

**SMALL
OPENING**

STEEL FLITCH
PLATE ADDS
STRENGTH
WITHOUT
EXCESSIVE
ADDED
DIMENSION

ASSEMBLY IS
THROUGH-
BOLTED

BOLT 2'-0" O. C. WITH
DOUBLE BOLT AT EACH
END

GLUED
LAMINATED
BEAMS

PLYWOOD BOX BEAMS ARE
OFTEN USED FOR
RESIDENTIAL GARAGE
DOOR OPENINGS

OTHER TYPES HAVE
BEEN ENGINEERED AS
WELL. CONSULT
BUILDING PRODUCTS
SUPPLIER

COMPOSITE BEAMS

SOLE PLATE

16d 16" O.C.

PLYWOOD

SMALL CANTILEVER PLATFORM

PLYWOOD SUBFLOOR AND SOLE

TAIL
BEAM

DOUBLE
TRIMMER
JOIST

20 d

HEADER SHOWN
CUT AWAY

16 d STAGGERED
6" O.C.

TAIL
BEAM

20 d

SECOND
TRIMMER
SHOWN CUT
AWAY

16 d STAGGERED 6" O.C.

**LARGE OPENING
REMOVED FROM
BEARING WALLS**

Joseph A. Wilkes, FAIA; Wilkes and Faulkner; Washington, D.C.

LIGHT WOOD FRAMING 6

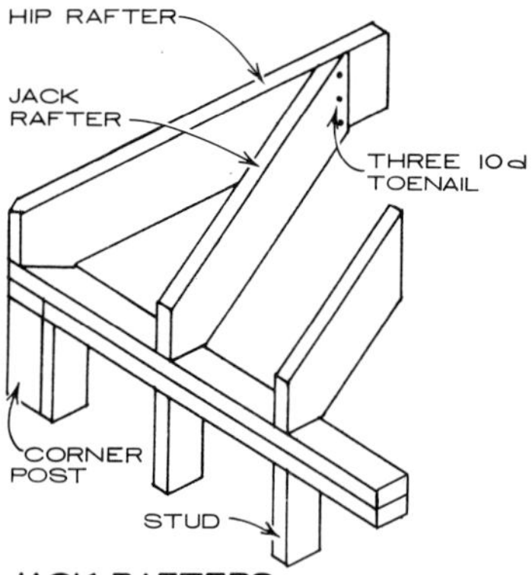

JACK RAFTERS

HIP RAFTER

JACK RAFTER

THREE 10d TOENAIL

CORNER POST

STUD

NOTE: 10d = 10 PENNY

ROOF PEAK

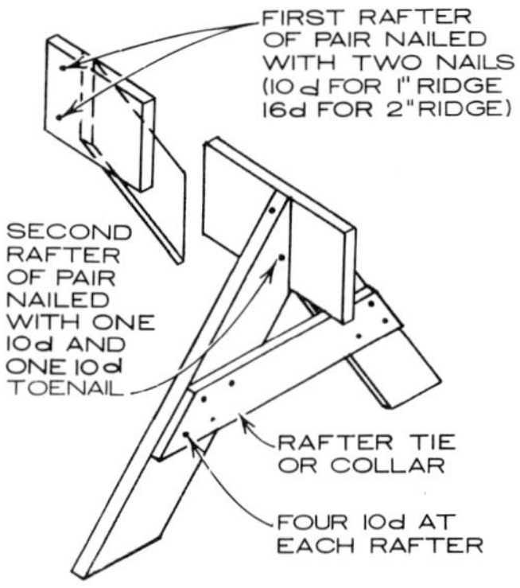

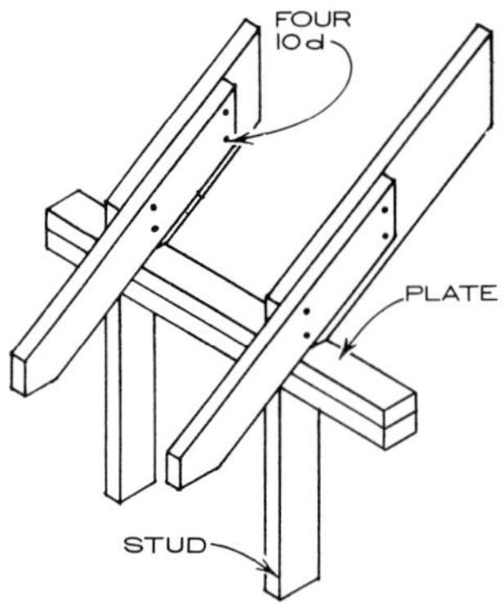

FIRST RAFTER OF PAIR NAILED WITH TWO NAILS (10d FOR 1" RIDGE 16d FOR 2" RIDGE)

SECOND RAFTER OF PAIR NAILED WITH ONE 10d AND ONE 10d TOENAIL

RAFTER TIE OR COLLAR

FOUR 10d AT EACH RAFTER

RAFTER ENDS

FOUR 10d

PLATE

STUD

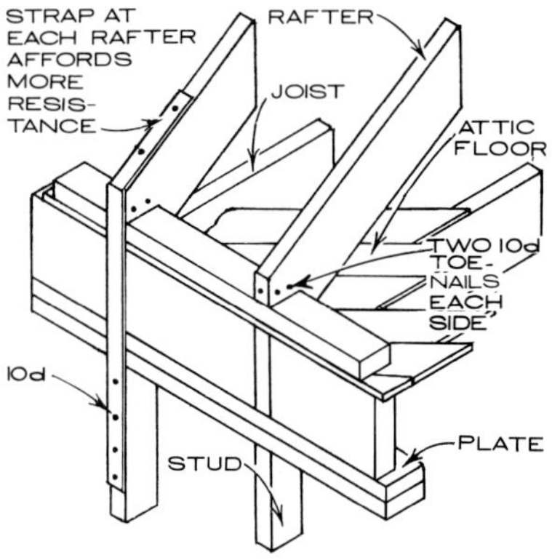

BEVELED RAFTERS BACK NOTCHED OVER PLATE

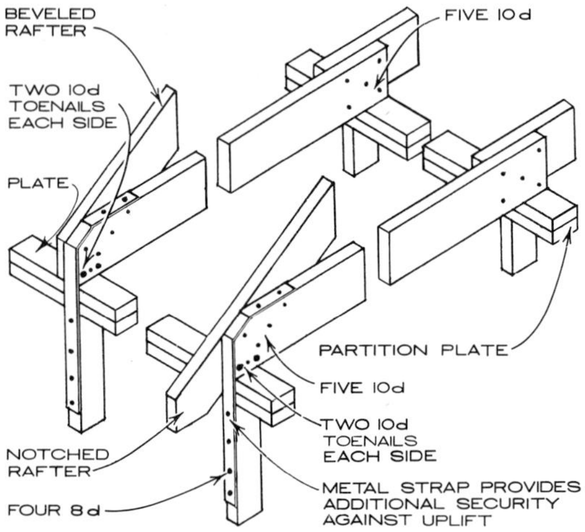

STRAP AT EACH RAFTER AFFORDS MORE RESISTANCE

RAFTER

JOIST

ATTIC FLOOR

TWO 10d TOENAILS EACH SIDE

10d

STUD

PLATE

RAFTERS AND CEILING JOISTS RESTING ON WALL PLATES

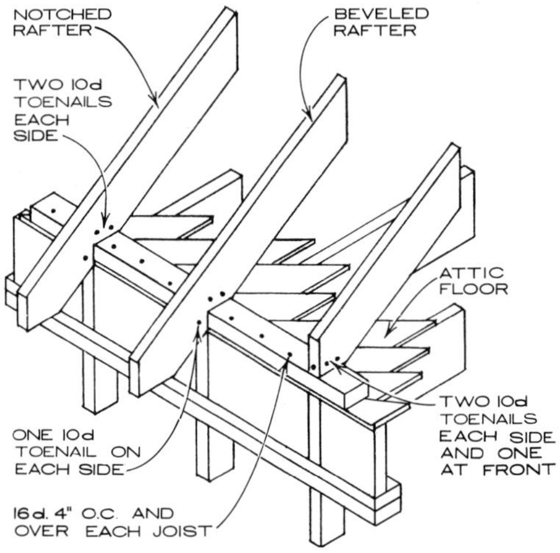

BEVELED RAFTER

TWO 10d TOENAILS EACH SIDE

PLATE

NOTCHED RAFTER

FOUR 8d

FIVE 10d

PARTITION PLATE

FIVE 10d

TWO 10d TOENAIL EACH SIDE

METAL STRAP PROVIDES ADDITIONAL SECURITY AGAINST UPLIFT

NOTCHED OR BEVELED RAFTERS RESTING ON PLATE

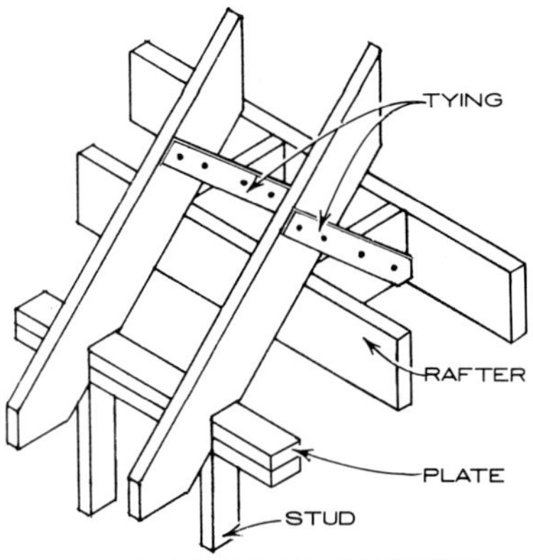

NOTCHED RAFTER

BEVELED RAFTER

TWO 10d TOENAILS EACH SIDE

ATTIC FLOOR

ONE 10d TOENAIL ON EACH SIDE

TWO 10d TOENAILS EACH SIDE AND ONE AT FRONT

16d 4" O.C. AND OVER EACH JOIST

BRACING OF ROOF RAFTERS ARE AT RT. ANGLES TO JOISTS

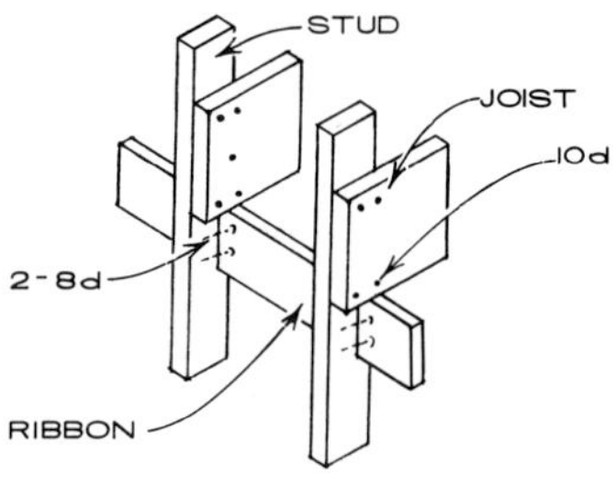

TYING

RAFTER

PLATE

STUD

JOISTS BEARING ON RIBBON

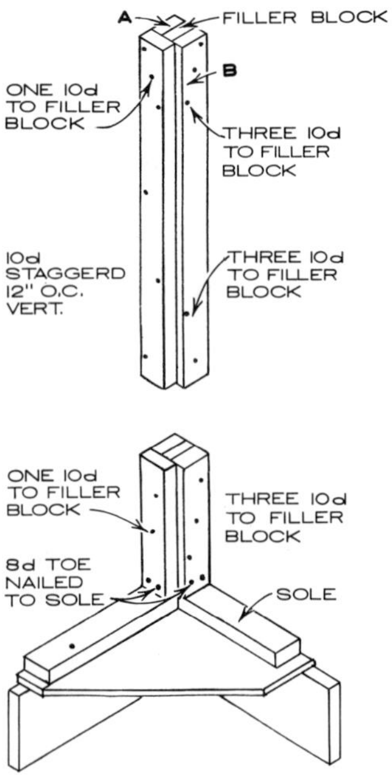

STUD

JOIST

10d

2-8d

RIBBON

TWO NAILS IN EACH JOIST ARE SUFFICIENT IF FULL STORY ABOVE RIBBON

CORNER POST

A FILLER BLOCK

ONE 10d TO FILLER BLOCK

B

THREE 10d TO FILLER BLOCK

10d STAGGERD 12" O.C. VERT.

THREE 10d TO FILLER BLOCK

ONE 10d TO FILLER BLOCK

8d TOE NAILED TO SOLE

THREE 10d TO FILLER BLOCK

SOLE

STUD "A" TO HAVE SAME NAILING TO FILLER BLOCK AS STUD "B"

TOP PLATE AND BRACING

10d STAGGERED 16 O.C.

16d

FILLER BLOCK

10d

10d

16d

1 X 4 MIN. OR 1¼" WIDE 16 GA. STEEL STRAP BRACE AT 45°

PLYWOOD PANEL WILL ALSO SUFFICE

8d

PLYWOOD SUBFLOOR

8d TOE NAILS

SOLE PLATE

10d

FILLER BLOCK

8d TOENAILS

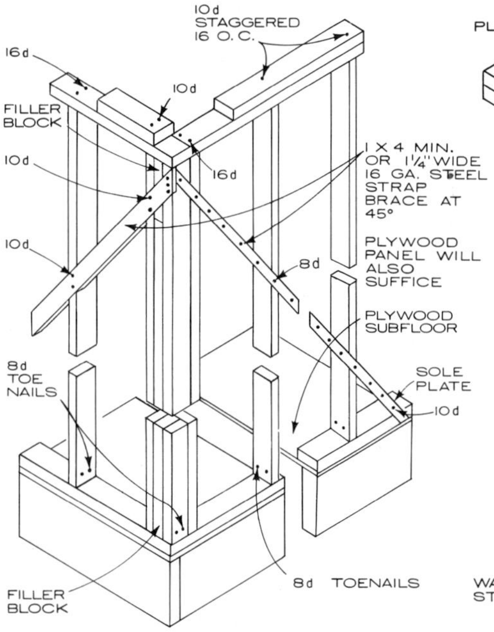

ONE TOENAIL THRU STUDS TO SOLE PLATE SUFFICIENT IF DIAGONAL SHEATHING USED

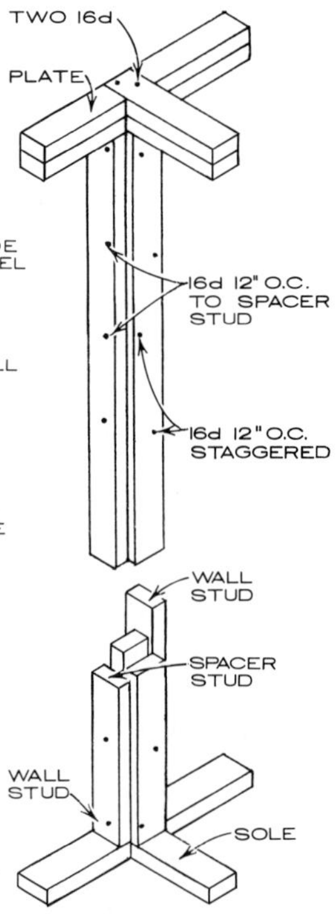

PARTITION TO WALL CONNECTION

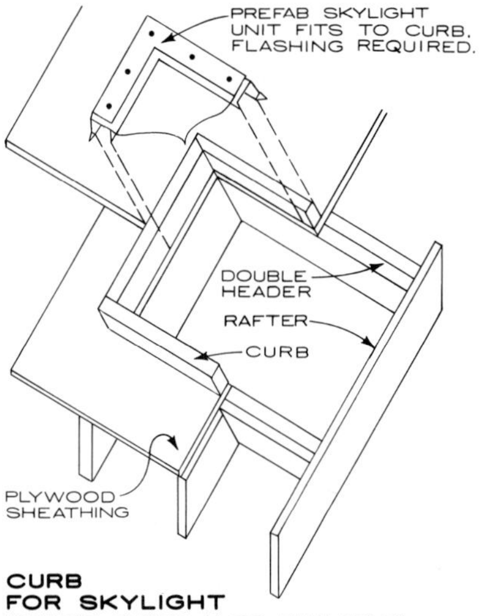

TWO 16d

PLATE

16d 12" O.C. TO SPACER STUD

16d 12" O.C. STAGGERED

WALL STUD

SPACER STUD

WALL STUD

SOLE

CURB FOR SKYLIGHT
(PREFAB CURBS ALSO AVAILABLE)

PREFAB SKYLIGHT UNIT FITS TO CURB. FLASHING REQUIRED.

DOUBLE HEADER

RAFTER

CURB

PLYWOOD SHEATHING

Joseph A. Wilkes; FAIA; Wilkes and Faulkner; Washington, D.C.

LIGHT WOOD FRAMING

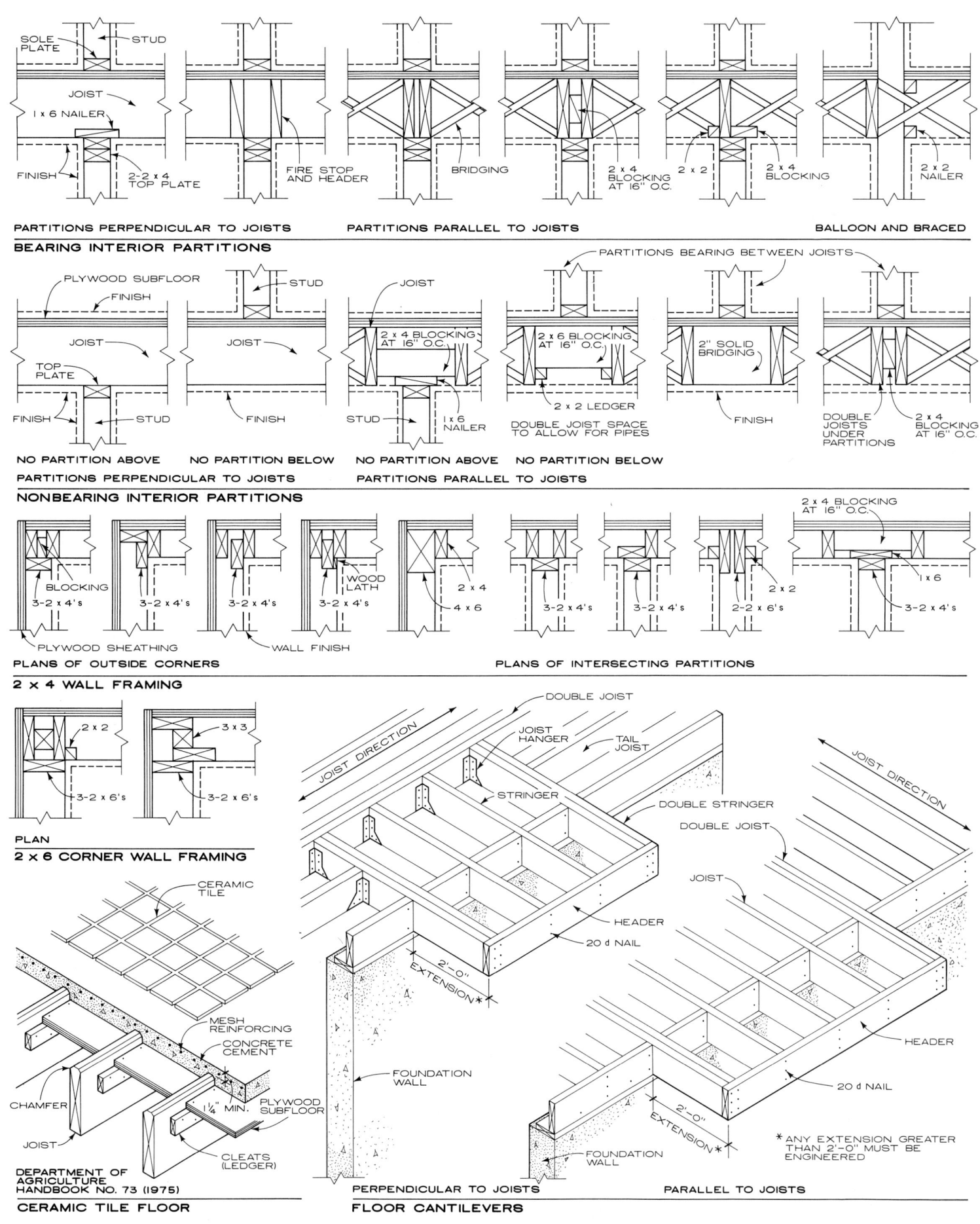

BEARING INTERIOR PARTITIONS

PARTITIONS PERPENDICULAR TO JOISTS   PARTITIONS PARALLEL TO JOISTS   BALLOON AND BRACED

NONBEARING INTERIOR PARTITIONS

NO PARTITION ABOVE   NO PARTITION BELOW   NO PARTITION ABOVE   NO PARTITION BELOW

PARTITIONS PERPENDICULAR TO JOISTS   PARTITIONS PARALLEL TO JOISTS

2 x 4 WALL FRAMING

PLANS OF OUTSIDE CORNERS   PLANS OF INTERSECTING PARTITIONS

2 x 6 CORNER WALL FRAMING

PLAN

CERAMIC TILE FLOOR

DEPARTMENT OF AGRICULTURE HANDBOOK NO. 73 (1975)

FLOOR CANTILEVERS

PERPENDICULAR TO JOISTS   PARALLEL TO JOISTS

* ANY EXTENSION GREATER THAN 2'-0" MUST BE ENGINEERED

John R. Hoke, Jr., AIA, Architect; Washington, D.C.

LIGHT WOOD FRAMING 6

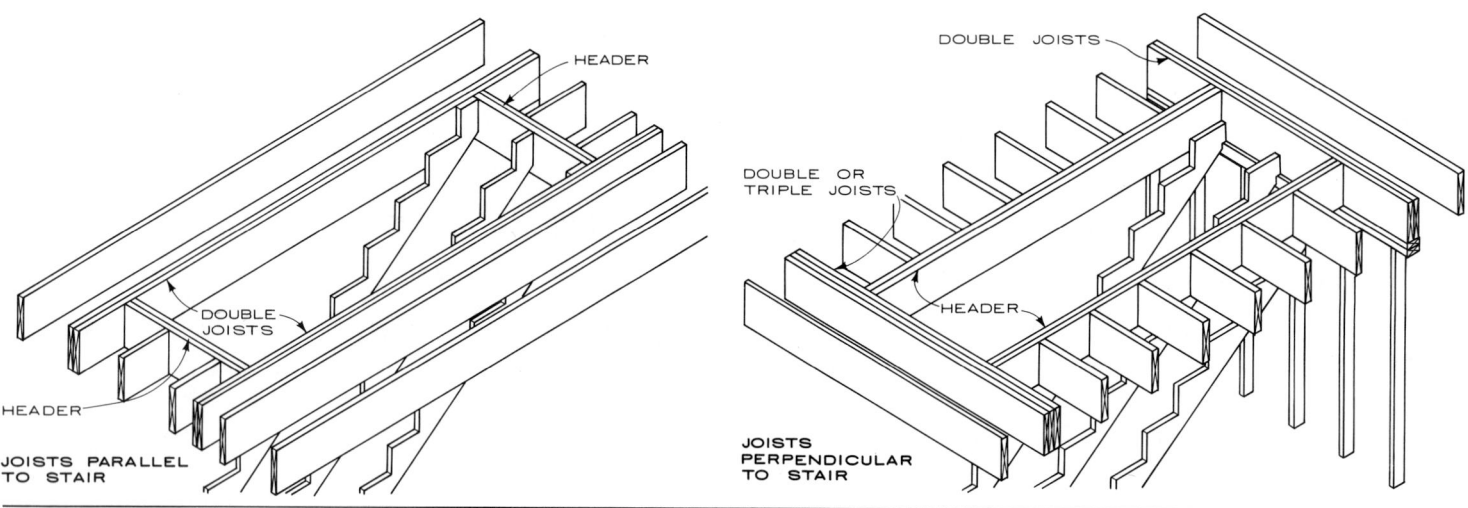

FLOOR OPENINGS

JOISTS PARALLEL TO STAIR

JOISTS PERPENDICULAR TO STAIR

HEADER

DOUBLE JOISTS

DOUBLE JOISTS

DOUBLE OR TRIPLE JOISTS

HEADER

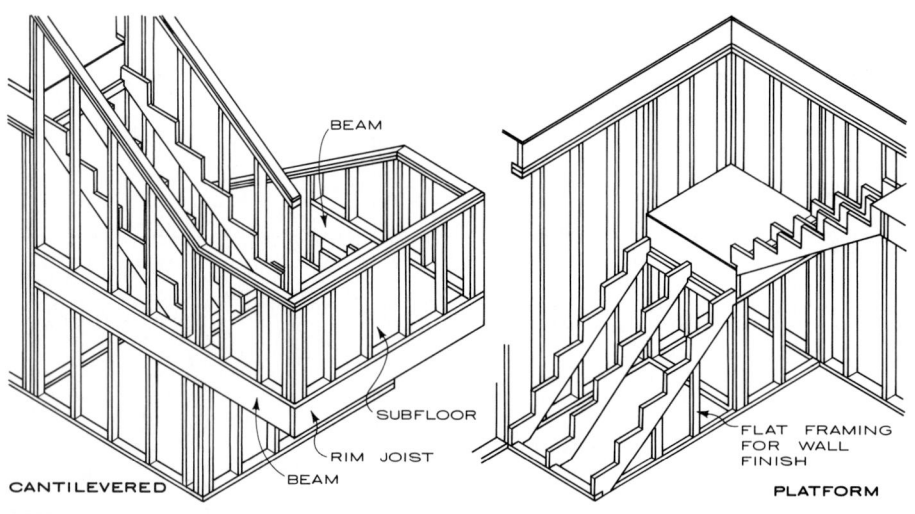

LANDINGS

CANTILEVERED

PLATFORM

BEAM

SUBFLOOR

RIM JOIST

BEAM

FLAT FRAMING FOR WALL FINISH

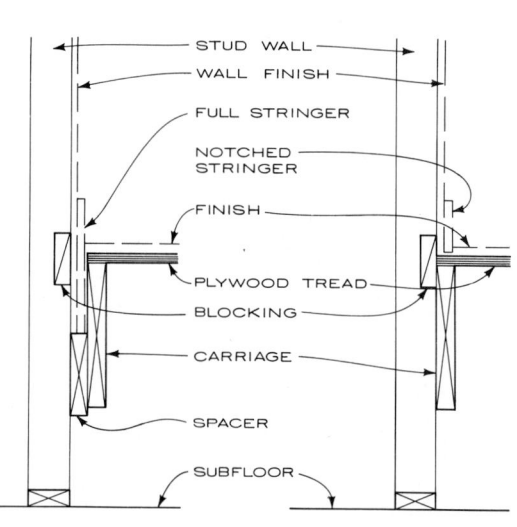

ANCHORS AT END OF SOLID RAIL

ALTERNATE: STEEL FLAT BAR WITH LAG BOLTS TO RAIL END AND JOIST BLOCKING

STEEL PIPE WITH ANCHOR PLATE

BLOCKING JOISTS SUBFLOOR

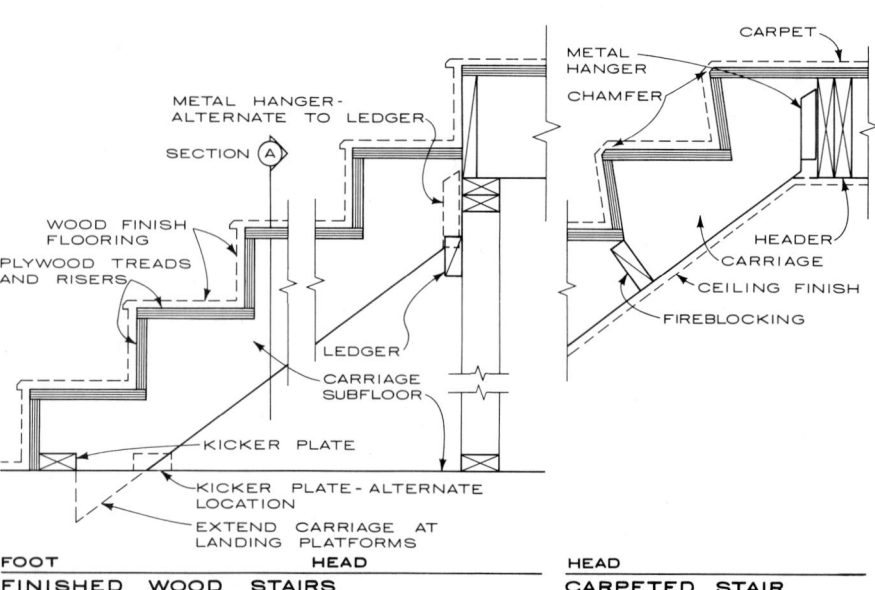

FINISHED WOOD STAIRS

FOOT

HEAD

CARPETED STAIR

HEAD

METAL HANGER-ALTERNATE TO LEDGER

SECTION A

WOOD FINISH FLOORING

PLYWOOD TREADS AND RISERS

LEDGER

CARRIAGE SUBFLOOR

KICKER PLATE

KICKER PLATE-ALTERNATE LOCATION

EXTEND CARRIAGE AT LANDING PLATFORMS

CARPET

METAL HANGER

CHAMFER

HEADER

CARRIAGE

CEILING FINISH

FIREBLOCKING

STUD WALL

WALL FINISH

FULL STRINGER

NOTCHED STRINGER

FINISH

PLYWOOD TREAD

BLOCKING

CARRIAGE

SPACER

SUBFLOOR

SECTION 'A' : FRAMING FULL STRINGER

SECTION 'A' : FRAMING NOTCHED STRINGER

CARRIAGE DETAILS FOR CARPENTER BUILT STAIRS

The Bumgardner Partnership/Architects; Seattle, Washington

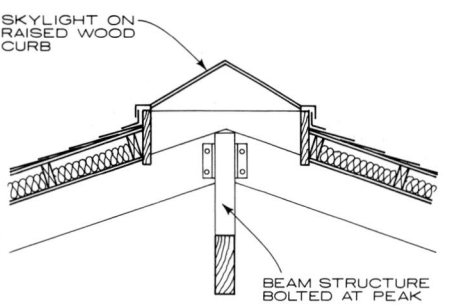

PYRAMID SKYLIGHT AT ROOF PEAK

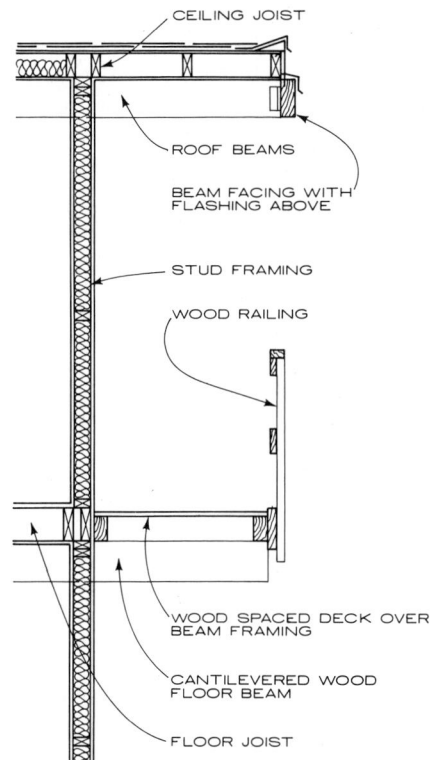

BALCONY FRAMING

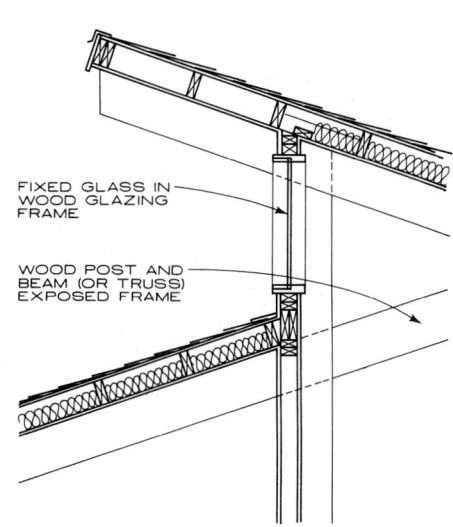

A fixed glass light is shown in wood glazing frame, with wood mullions coincident with structural beam or truss framing members. Intermediate mullions may be used, if desired, to divide clerestory glazing into smaller panels. Continuous strip glazing is possible between roof curb and soffit finish using minimum mullions (i.e., small structural gaskets or the like) with supporting structure located behind. Care should be taken to avoid solar glare; because of height above floor, interior shading from drapes or similar devices is difficult to accomplish.

CLERESTORY WINDOW (FIXED)

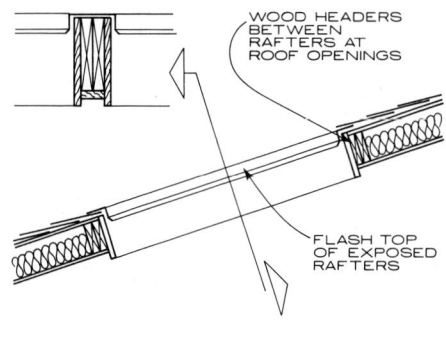

OPENINGS IN ROOFS

EXPOSED WOOD BEAM DETAILS

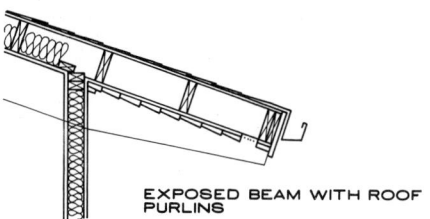

EXPOSED BEAM WITH ROOF PURLINS

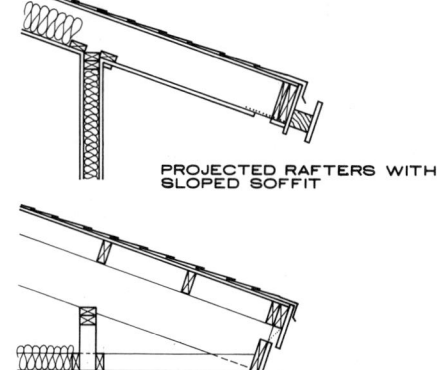

PROJECTED RAFTERS WITH SLOPED SOFFIT

CONCEALED BEAMS WITH STEPPED FASCIA AND FLAT SOFFIT

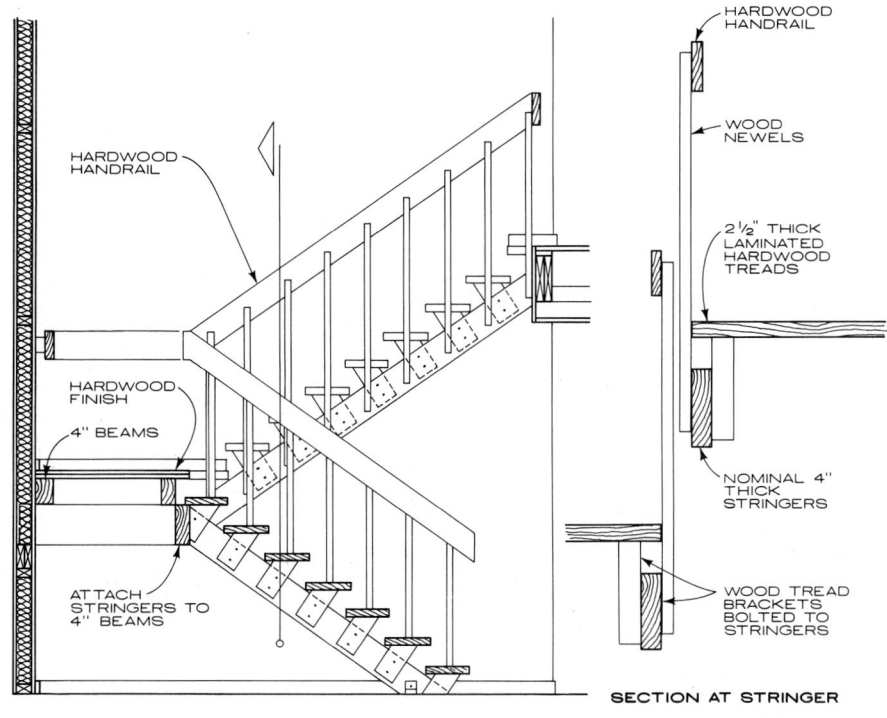

SECTION AT STRINGER

OPEN STAIRWELL AND BEAM FRAMED STAIR

Knight and Koonce and Associates; Bogalusa, Louisiana

NOTE: Design of eave overhang should take into account such factors as the following:

1. Whether overhang protection is required.
2. The need for gutters or downspouts.
3. Economy of soffit materials.
4. Maximum cantilever distance for projected rafters or beams (structural).
5. Eave ventilation of attic spaces.
6. Decay resistance of exposed beam ends, fascia boards, and other materials exposed to the weather.

EAVE OVERHANG DETAILS

LIGHT WOOD FRAMING 6

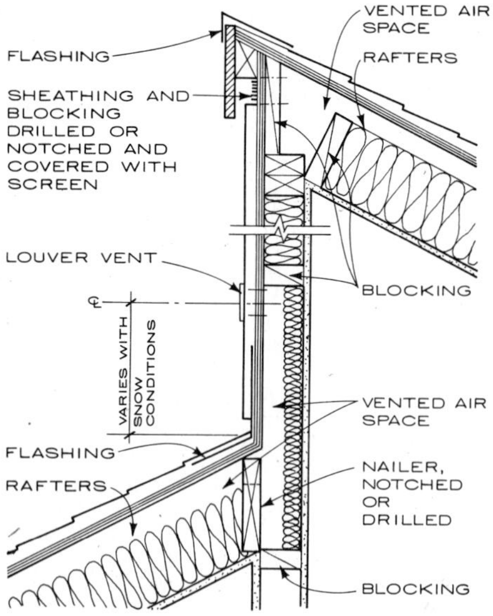

FLASHING

SHEATHING AND BLOCKING DRILLED OR NOTCHED AND COVERED WITH SCREEN

VENTED AIR SPACE

RAFTERS

LOUVER VENT

VARIES WITH SNOW CONDITIONS

BLOCKING

FLASHING

RAFTERS

VENTED AIR SPACE

NAILER, NOTCHED OR DRILLED

BLOCKING

SHED ROOF / PEAK AND WALL INTERSECTION

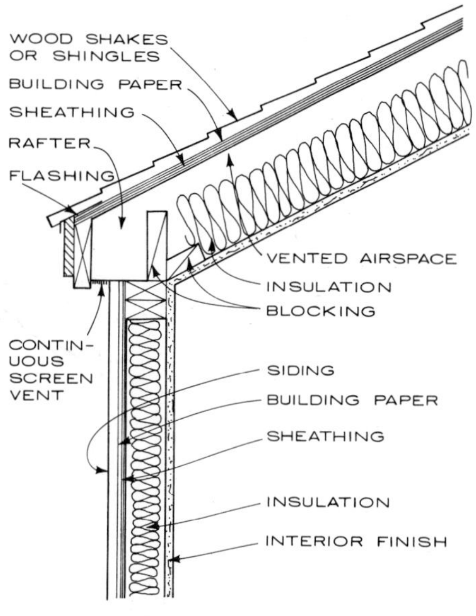

WOOD SHAKES OR SHINGLES

BUILDING PAPER

SHEATHING

RAFTER

FLASHING

VENTED AIRSPACE

INSULATION

BLOCKING

CONTINUOUS SCREEN VENT

SIDING

BUILDING PAPER

SHEATHING

INSULATION

INTERIOR FINISH

VENTED EAVE

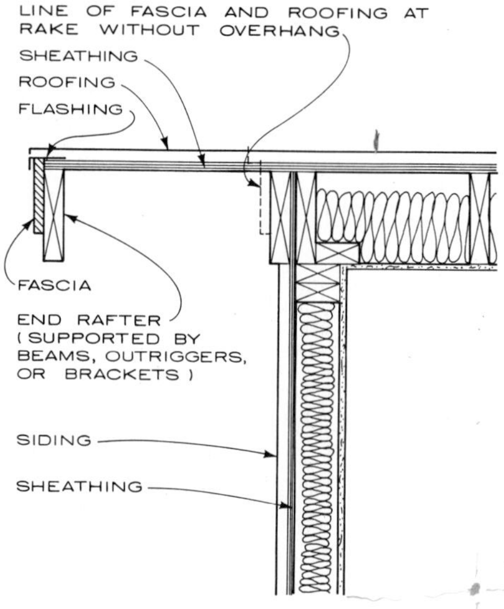

LINE OF FASCIA AND ROOFING AT RAKE WITHOUT OVERHANG

SHEATHING

ROOFING

FLASHING

FASCIA

END RAFTER (SUPPORTED BY BEAMS, OUTRIGGERS, OR BRACKETS)

SIDING

SHEATHING

RAKE OVERHANG

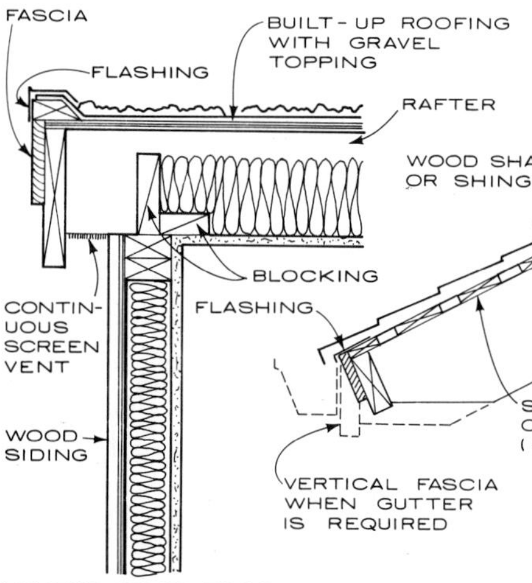

FASCIA

FLASHING

BUILT-UP ROOFING WITH GRAVEL TOPPING

RAFTER

BLOCKING

FLASHING

CONTINUOUS SCREEN VENT

WOOD SIDING

VERTICAL FASCIA WHEN GUTTER IS REQUIRED

VENTED ROOF EDGE

FRONT VIEW OF EAVE BLOCKING SHOWING DRILLED VENT HOLES WITH SCREEN ON BACK

WOOD SHAKES OR SHINGLES

NOTCHED RAFTER

BLOCKING

FLASHING

STRIPPING AT OVERHANG (OPTIONAL)

WOOD SHINGLE SIDING

EXPOSED RAFTERS

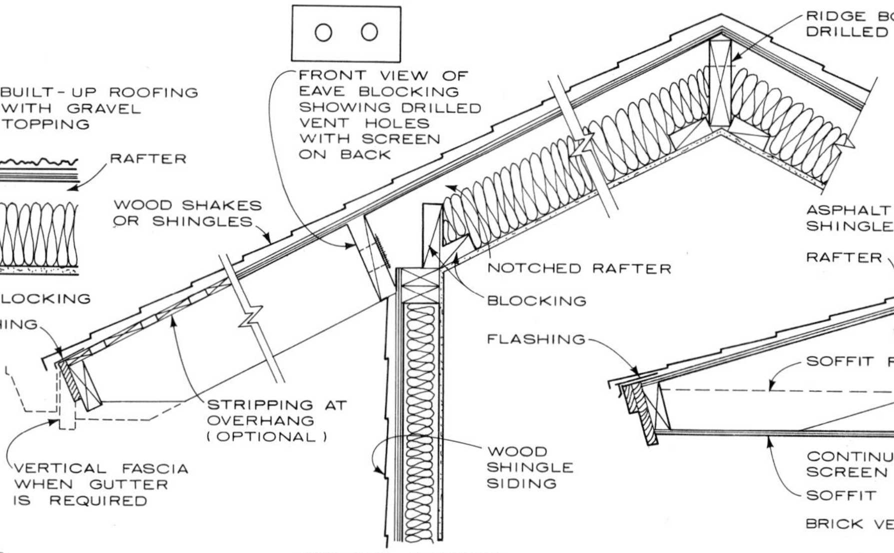

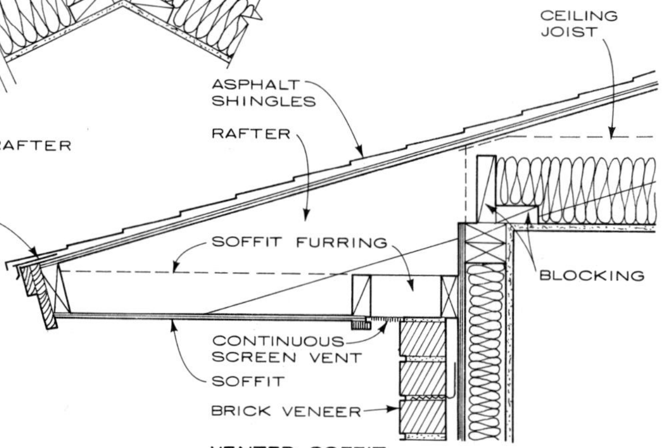

RIDGE BOARD — NOTCHED OR DRILLED FOR CROSS VENTILATION

CEILING JOIST

ASPHALT SHINGLES

RAFTER

SOFFIT FURRING

BLOCKING

FLASHING

CONTINUOUS SCREEN VENT

SOFFIT

BRICK VENEER

VENTED SOFFIT

EAVE AND OVERHANG SECTIONS

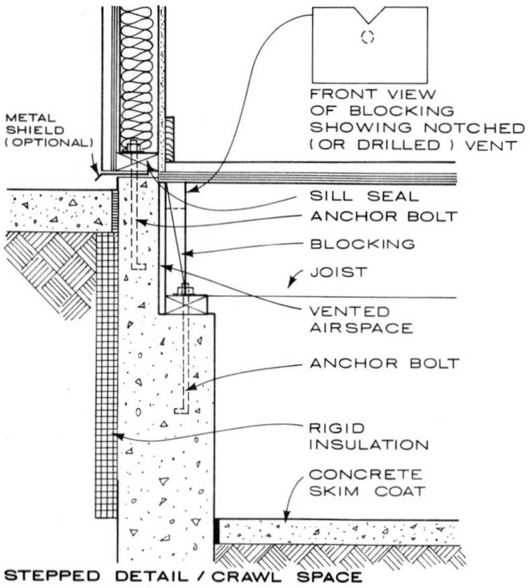

METAL SHIELD (OPTIONAL)

FRONT VIEW OF BLOCKING SHOWING NOTCHED (OR DRILLED) VENT

SILL SEAL

ANCHOR BOLT

BLOCKING

JOIST

VENTED AIRSPACE

ANCHOR BOLT

RIGID INSULATION

CONCRETE SKIM COAT

STEPPED DETAIL / CRAWL SPACE

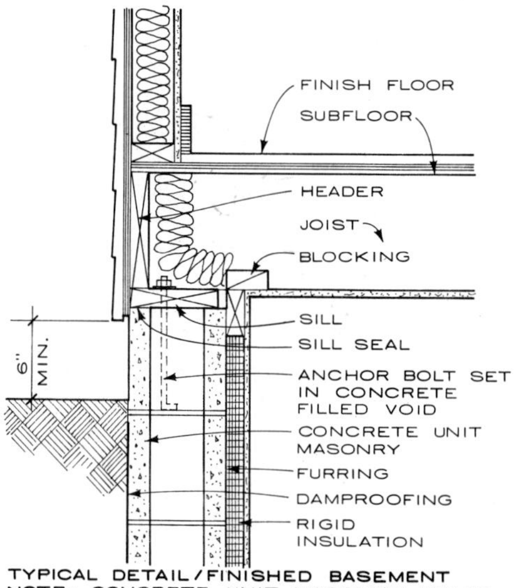

FINISH FLOOR

SUBFLOOR

HEADER

JOIST

BLOCKING

SILL

SILL SEAL

6" MIN.

ANCHOR BOLT SET IN CONCRETE FILLED VOID

CONCRETE UNIT MASONRY

FURRING

DAMPROOFING

RIGID INSULATION

TYPICAL DETAIL / FINISHED BASEMENT
NOTE: CONCRETE UNIT MASONRY WALLS VARY WIDELY. CHECK LOCAL CODES

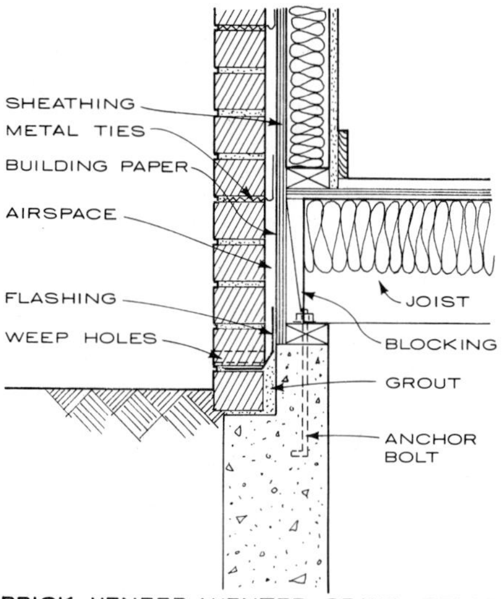

SHEATHING

METAL TIES

BUILDING PAPER

AIRSPACE

FLASHING

WEEP HOLES

JOIST

BLOCKING

GROUT

ANCHOR BOLT

BRICK VENEER / VENTED CRAWL SPACE OR UNFINISHED BASEMENT (UNHEATED)

FOUNDATION WALL SECTIONS

The Bumgardner Partnership/Architects; Seattle, Washington

 LIGHT WOOD FRAMING

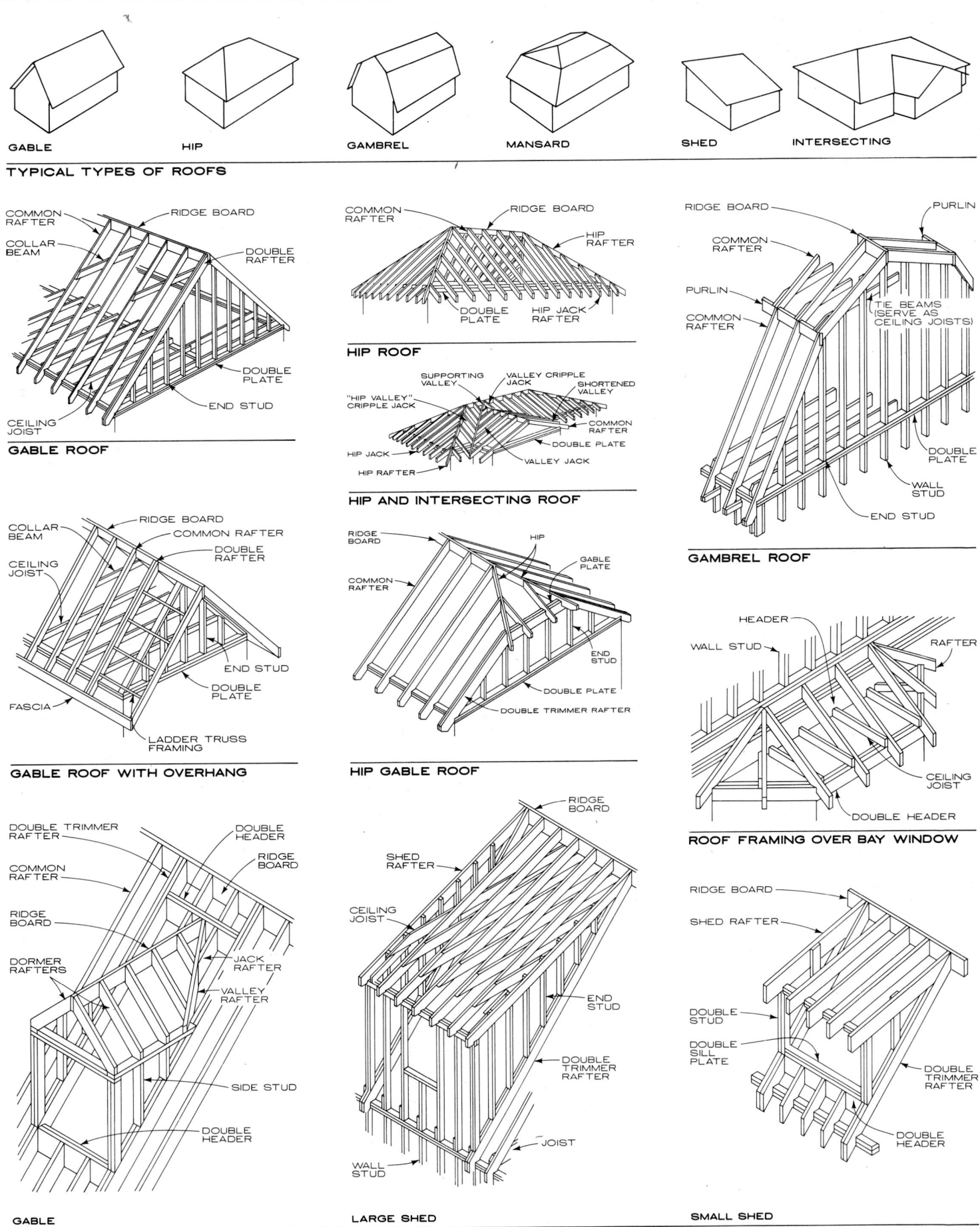

TYPICAL TYPES OF ROOFS

GABLE   HIP   GAMBREL   MANSARD   SHED   INTERSECTING

GABLE ROOF

COMMON RAFTER, RIDGE BOARD, COLLAR BEAM, DOUBLE RAFTER, DOUBLE PLATE, END STUD, CEILING JOIST

GABLE ROOF WITH OVERHANG

COLLAR BEAM, RIDGE BOARD, COMMON RAFTER, DOUBLE RAFTER, CEILING JOIST, END STUD, DOUBLE PLATE, FASCIA, LADDER TRUSS FRAMING

GABLE

DORMERS

DOUBLE TRIMMER RAFTER, DOUBLE HEADER, COMMON RAFTER, RIDGE BOARD, RIDGE BOARD, DORMER RAFTERS, JACK RAFTER, VALLEY RAFTER, SIDE STUD, DOUBLE HEADER

HIP ROOF

COMMON RAFTER, RIDGE BOARD, HIP RAFTER, DOUBLE PLATE, HIP JACK RAFTER

HIP AND INTERSECTING ROOF

SUPPORTING VALLEY, VALLEY CRIPPLE JACK, SHORTENED VALLEY, "HIP VALLEY" CRIPPLE JACK, COMMON RAFTER, HIP JACK, DOUBLE PLATE, VALLEY JACK, HIP RAFTER

HIP GABLE ROOF

RIDGE BOARD, HIP, GABLE PLATE, COMMON RAFTER, END STUD, DOUBLE PLATE, DOUBLE TRIMMER RAFTER

LARGE SHED

RIDGE BOARD, SHED RAFTER, CEILING JOIST, END STUD, DOUBLE TRIMMER RAFTER, JOIST, WALL STUD

GAMBREL ROOF

RIDGE BOARD, PURLIN, COMMON RAFTER, PURLIN, COMMON RAFTER, TIE BEAMS (SERVE AS CEILING JOISTS), DOUBLE PLATE, WALL STUD, END STUD

ROOF FRAMING OVER BAY WINDOW

HEADER, WALL STUD, RAFTER, CEILING JOIST, DOUBLE HEADER

SMALL SHED

RIDGE BOARD, SHED RAFTER, DOUBLE STUD, DOUBLE SILL PLATE, DOUBLE TRIMMER RAFTER, DOUBLE HEADER

John R. Hoke, Jr., AIA, Architect; Washington, D.C.

LIGHT WOOD FRAMING   6

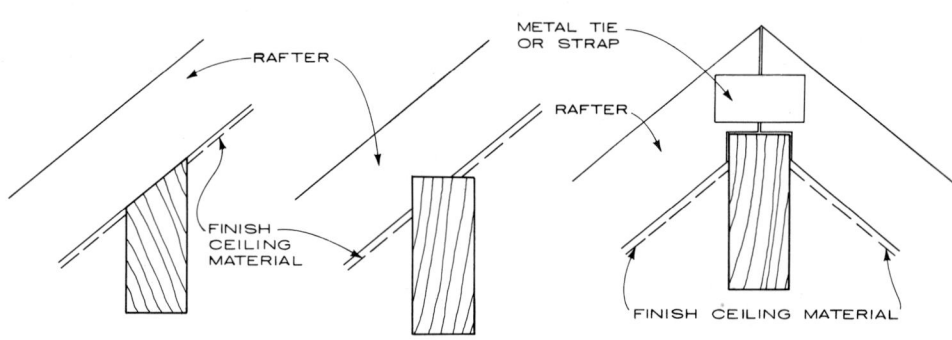

SLOPED BEAM   BIRD'S MOUTH   RIDGE BEAM

EXPOSED BEAMS AT SLOPING RAFTERS

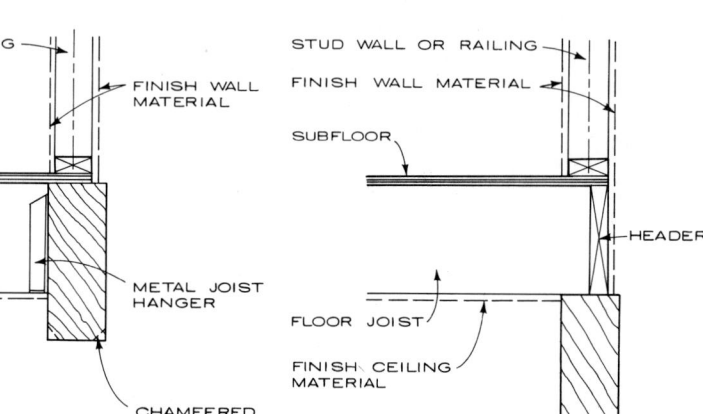

EXPOSED BEAMS AT FLOORS

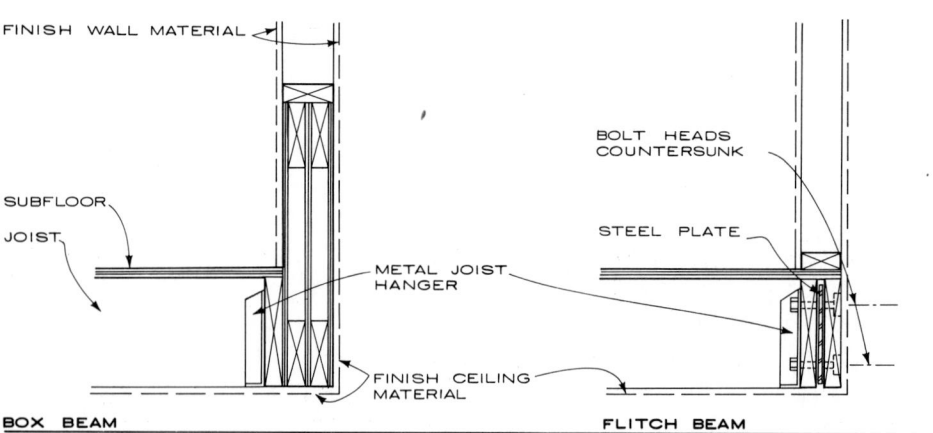

BOX BEAM   FLITCH BEAM

CONCEALED BUILT-UP BEAMS AT FLOORS

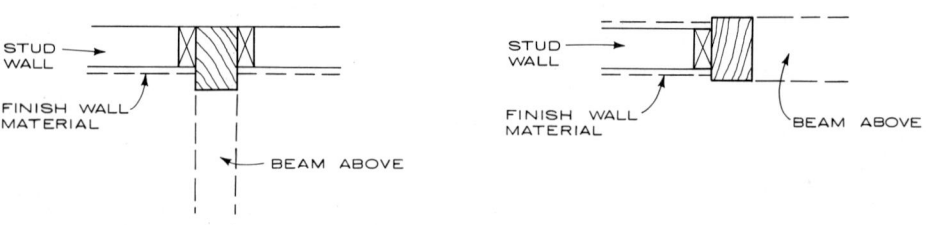

EXPOSED POSTS AT STUD WALLS

The Bumgardner Partnership/Architects; Seattle, Washington

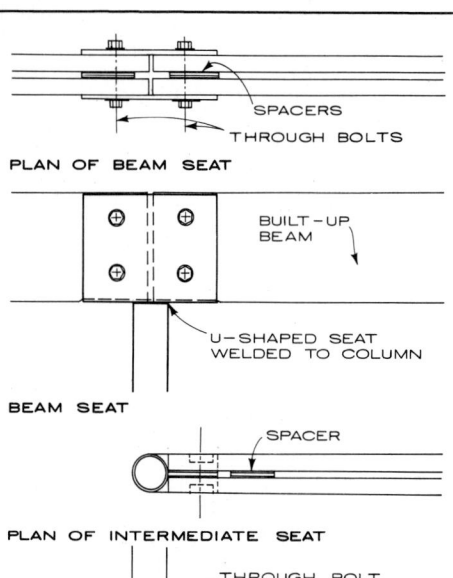

PLAN OF BEAM SEAT

BEAM SEAT

PLAN OF INTERMEDIATE SEAT

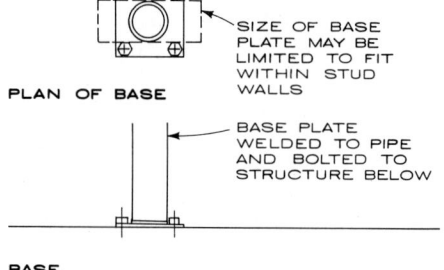

INTERMEDIATE BEAM SEAT

PLAN OF BASE

BASE

STEEL PIPE COLUMNS

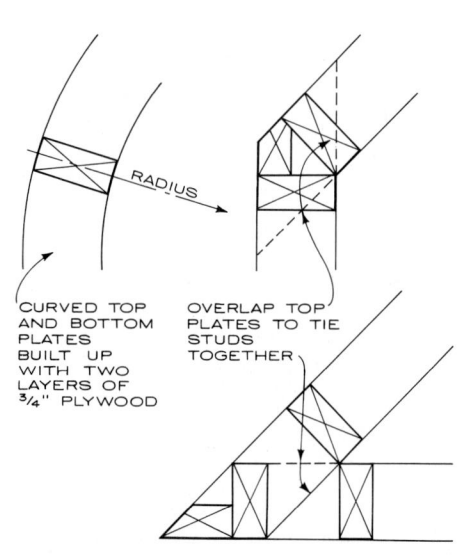

NON-RIGHT ANGLE WALL CORNERS

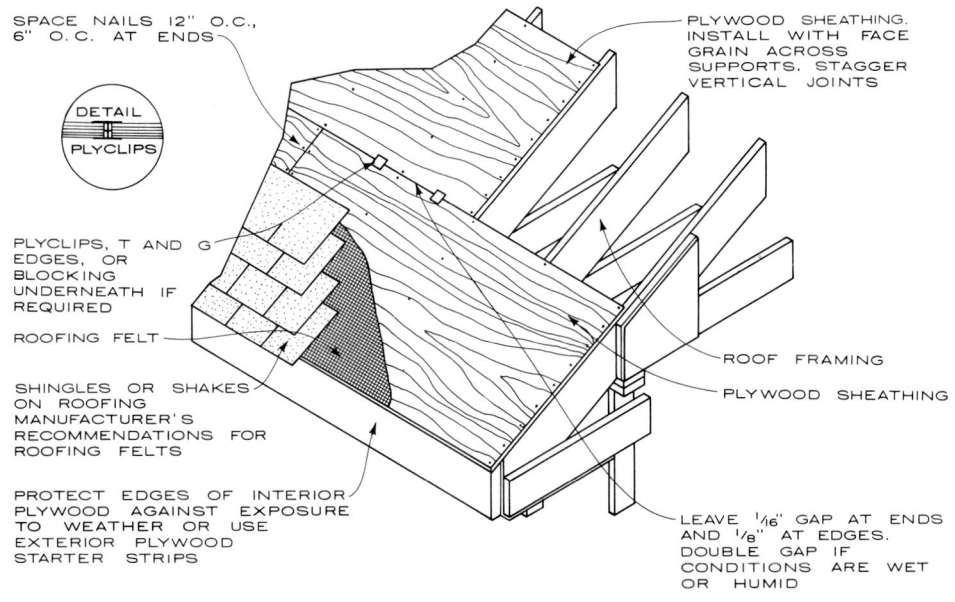

SPACE NAILS 12" O.C., 6" O.C. AT ENDS

DETAIL PLYCLIPS

PLYCLIPS, T AND G EDGES, OR BLOCKING UNDERNEATH IF REQUIRED

ROOFING FELT

SHINGLES OR SHAKES ON ROOFING MANUFACTURER'S RECOMMENDATIONS FOR ROOFING FELTS

PROTECT EDGES OF INTERIOR PLYWOOD AGAINST EXPOSURE TO WEATHER OR USE EXTERIOR PLYWOOD STARTER STRIPS

PLYWOOD SHEATHING. INSTALL WITH FACE GRAIN ACROSS SUPPORTS. STAGGER VERTICAL JOINTS

ROOF FRAMING

PLYWOOD SHEATHING

LEAVE 1/16" GAP AT ENDS AND 1/8" AT EDGES. DOUBLE GAP IF CONDITIONS ARE WET OR HUMID

PLYWOOD ROOF SHEATHING

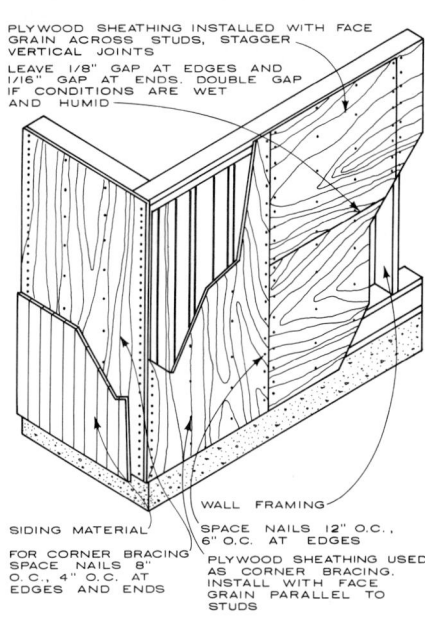

PLYWOOD SHEATHING INSTALLED WITH FACE GRAIN ACROSS STUDS, STAGGER VERTICAL JOINTS

LEAVE 1/8" GAP AT EDGES AND 1/16" GAP AT ENDS. DOUBLE GAP IF CONDITIONS ARE WET AND HUMID

WALL FRAMING

SIDING MATERIAL

FOR CORNER BRACING SPACE NAILS 8" O.C., 4" O.C. AT EDGES AND ENDS

SPACE NAILS 12" O.C., 6" O.C. AT EDGES

PLYWOOD SHEATHING USED AS CORNER BRACING. INSTALL WITH FACE GRAIN PARALLEL TO STUDS

PLYWOOD WALL SHEATHING

PLYWOOD ROOF SHEATHING

Plywood grades commonly used for roof (and wall) sheathing are C-D interior, C-D exterior, and Structural I and II, C-C or C-D, interior or exterior. Refer to American Plywood Association recommendations for unsupported edges.

PLYWOOD WALL SHEATHING

Common grade is same as used in roof sheathing. Use Plyclips, tongue and groove panels, or blocking between studs to support edges. Refer to American Plywood Association recommendations for unsupported edges.

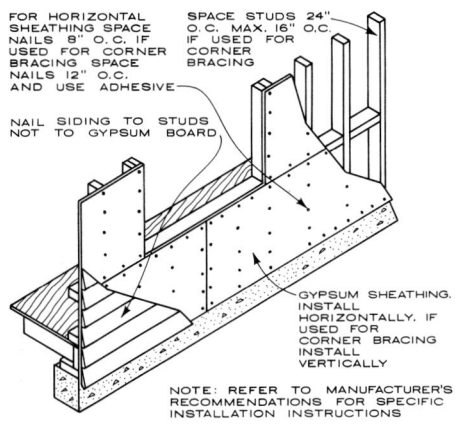

FOR HORIZONTAL SHEATHING SPACE NAILS 8" O.C. IF USED FOR CORNER BRACING SPACE NAILS 12" O.C. AND USE ADHESIVE

NAIL SIDING TO STUDS NOT TO GYPSUM BOARD

SPACE STUDS 24" O.C. MAX. 16" O.C. IF USED FOR CORNER BRACING

GYPSUM SHEATHING. INSTALL HORIZONTALLY. IF USED FOR CORNER BRACING INSTALL VERTICALLY

NOTE: REFER TO MANUFACTURER'S RECOMMENDATIONS FOR SPECIFIC INSTALLATION INSTRUCTIONS

GYPSUM WALL SHEATHING

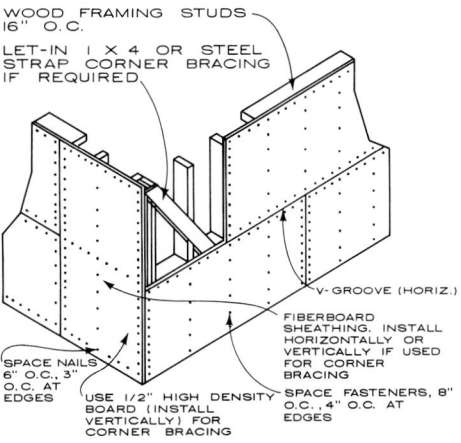

WOOD FRAMING STUDS 16" O.C.

LET-IN 1 X 4 OR STEEL STRAP CORNER BRACING IF REQUIRED

V-GROOVE (HORIZ.)

FIBERBOARD SHEATHING. INSTALL HORIZONTALLY OR VERTICALLY IF USED FOR CORNER BRACING

SPACE NAILS 6" O.C., 3" O.C. AT EDGES

USE 1/2" HIGH DENSITY BOARD (INSTALL VERTICALLY) FOR CORNER BRACING

SPACE FASTENERS, 8" O.C., 4" O.C. AT EDGES

FIBERBOARD SHEATHING

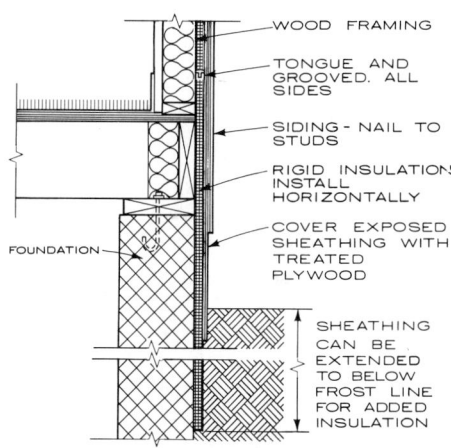

WOOD FRAMING

TONGUE AND GROOVED. ALL SIDES

SIDING - NAIL TO STUDS

RIGID INSULATION. INSTALL HORIZONTALLY

COVER EXPOSED SHEATHING WITH TREATED PLYWOOD

FOUNDATION

SHEATHING CAN BE EXTENDED TO BELOW FROST LINE FOR ADDED INSULATION

PLASTIC SHEATHING

GYPSUM WALL SHEATHING

Fire rated panels are available in 1/2 and 5/8 in. thicknesses. Gypsum board is not an effective vapor barrier.

FIBERBOARD SHEATHING

Also called insulation board. Can be treated or impregnated with asphalt. Available in regular or 1/2 in. high density panels.

PLASTIC SHEATHING

Usually made of polyurethane or polystyrene. Can be considered an effective vapor barrier, hence wall must be effectively vented. All edges are usually tongue and groove.

SHEATHING MATERIALS

CHARACTERISTICS	PLYWOOD	GYPSUM	FIBERBOARD	PLASTIC
Available base	Yes	No	Only high density	No
Vapor barrier	No	No	If asphalt treated	Yes
Insulation value "R" (1/2 in. thickness)	1.2	0.7	2.6	6.25
Corner bracing	Yes	Yes (see manufacturer's recommendation)	Only high density	No
Panel sizes (ft)	4 x 8, 4 x 9, 4 x 10	4 x 8, 4 x 10, 4 x 12, 4 x 14	4 x 8, 4 x 9, 4 x 10, 4 x 12	16 x 96, 24 x 48, 24 x 96
Panel thickness (in.)	5/16, 3/8, 1/2, 5/8, 3/4	1/4, 3/8, 1/2, 5/8	1/2, 25/32	3/4-6 (for roof)

John D. Bloodgood, Architects, P.C.; Des Moines, Iowa

ROUGH CARPENTRY

6

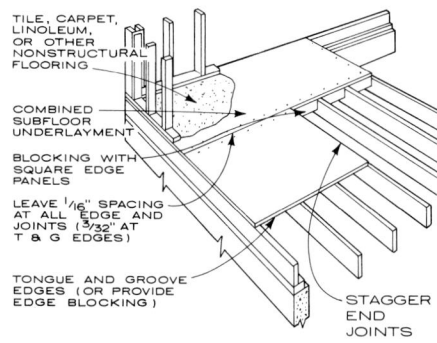

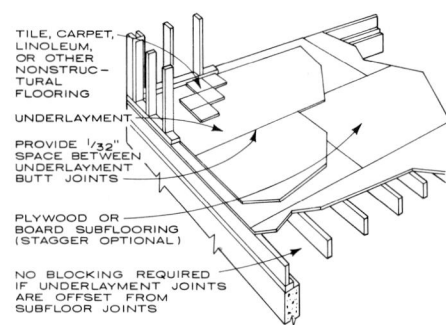

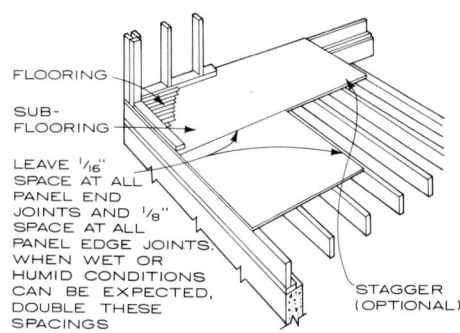

PLYWOOD SUBFLOOR/ UNDERLAYMENT COMBINED SUBFLOOR/ UNDERLAYMENT

PLYWOOD UNDERLAYMENT

PLYWOOD SUBFLOOR

PLYWOOD UNDERLAYMENT (1)

PLYWOOD GRADES AND SPECIES GROUP	APPLICATION (2)	MINIMUM PLYWOOD THICK-NESS (IN.)
Groups 1, 2, 3, 4, 5 UNDERLAYMENT INT-APA (with interior or exterior glue), or UNDERLAYMENT EXT-APA (C-C plugged)	Over plywood sub-floor	1/4
	Over lumber sub-floor or other uneven surfaces	3/8
Same grades as above, but Group 1 only.	Over lumber floor up to 4 in. wide. Face grain must be perpendicular to boards	1/4

1. For floors to receive tile, carpeting, linoleum, or other nonstructural flooring.
2. Where floors may be subject to unusual moisture conditions, use panels with exterior glue or UNDERLAYMENT C-C Plugged, EXT-APA. C-D. Plugged is not an adequate substitute for underlayment grade, since it does not ensure equivalent dent resistance.
3. Recommended grades have a solid surface backed with a special inner ply construction that resists punch-through, dents, and concentrated loads.

NAILING SCHEDULE

Use 3d ring shank nails for underlayment up to 1/2 in. thickness, 4d for 5/8 in. and thicker. Use 16 gauge staples, except that 18 gauge may be used with 1/4 in. thick underlayment. Crown width should be 3/8 in. for 16 gauge staples, 3/16 in. for 18 gauge. Length should be sufficient to penetrate subflooring at least 5/8 in. or extend completely through. Space fasteners at 3 in. along panel edges and at 6 in. each way in the panel interior, except for 3/8 in. or thicker underlayment applied with ring shank nails. In this case, use 6 in. spacing along edges and 8 in. spacing each way in the panel interior. Unless subfloor and joists are of thoroughly seasoned material and have remained dry during construction, countersink nail heads 1 ft 16 in. below surface of the underlayment just prior to laying finish floors to avoid nail popping. Staples should be countersunk 1/32 in.

NOTES

1. For complete information on glued floors, including joist span tables (based on building code criteria and lumber sizes), application sequence, and list of recommended adhesives and adhesive dispensing equipment, contact the American Plywood Association.
2. Place UNDERLAYMENT APA T&G plywood across the joists with end joints staggered. Leave 1/16 in. space at all end and edge joints (3/32 in. at T&G edges).
3. UNDERLAYMENT grade may be 19/32 in.
4. UNDERLAYMENT grade may be 23/32 in.
5. Although T&G is used most often, square edge may be used if 2 x 4 blocking is placed under panel edge joints between joists.

NAILING SCHEDULE

The plywood panels should be secured with power driven fasteners or nailed with 6d deformed shank nails, spaced 12 in. at all supports. (8d common smooth nails may be substituted.)

PLYWOOD SUBFLOORING (1)

PANEL IDENTIFI-CATION INDEX	PLYWOOD THICK-NESS (IN.)	MAXIMUM SPACING (2, 3, 6) (IN.)
30/12	5/8	12 (4)
32/16	1/2, 5/8	16 (5)
36/16	3/4	16 (5)
42/20	5/8, 3/4, 7/8	20 (5)
48/24	3/4, 7/8	24
1 1/8" groups (1, 2)	1 1/8	48
1 1/4" groups (3, 4)	1 1/4	48
2.4.1 groups (1, 2, 3)	1 1/8	32 (2X joists) 48 (4X joists)

1. Applies to STRUCTURAL I & II C-C, C-D, CD interior sheathing and C-C exterior grades only.
2. The spans assume plywood continuous over two or more spans with face grain across supports.
3. In some nonresidential buildings special conditions may require construction in excess of minimums given.
4. May be 16 in. if 25/32 in. wood strip flooring is installed at right angles to joists.
5. May be 24 in. if 25/32 in. wood strip flooring is installed at right angles to joists.
6. Spans are limited to the values shown because of the possible effect of concentrated loads.

NAILING SCHEDULE

Use 6d common nails for 1/2 in. plywood, 8d for thicknesses from 5/8 to 7/8 in., and 10d for 1 1/8 and 1 1/4 in. thicknesses. Space nails at 6 in. along panel edges for all thicknesses. Along intermediate supports, space nails at 10 in.; when plywood spans 48 in., however, space nails at 6 in. For 2.4.1 panels, use 8d ring shank or, if supports are well-seasoned, 10d common smooth. Nail at 6 in. on center along panel edges. Along intermediate supports, space nails 6 in. apart for 48 in. span and 10 in. apart for 32 in. spans.

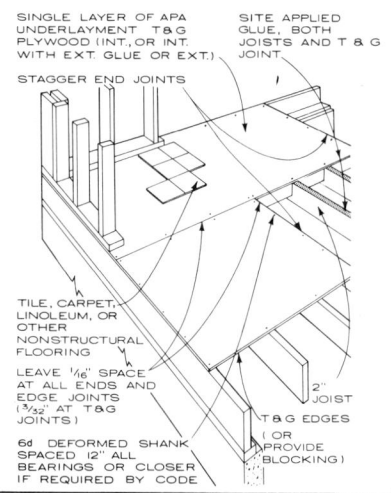

APA GLUED FLOOR SYSTEM

NAILING SCHEDULE

To minimize the effects of framing shrinkage, ring shank or spiral thread nails should be used. Use 6d deformed shank nails for thicknesses through 3/4 in. Use 8d for panels 7/8 in. and thicker. Space nails at 6 in. along panel edges and at 10 in. along intermediate supports. Nails should be driven flush or preferably slightly set below surface of the underlayment. Do not fill nail holes. If resilient flooring is to be applied, fill and thoroughly sand joints.

ALLOWABLE CLEAR SPANS FOR APA (1): GLUED FLOOR SYSTEM (PARTIAL LIST)

		APA GLUED FLOOR SPANS			
SPECIES-GRADE	JOIST SIZE	1/2" PLYWOOD JOISTS AT 16"	5/8" PLYWOOD (3) JOISTS AT 16"	3/4" PLYWOOD (4) JOISTS AT 16"	3/4" PLYWOOD (4) JOISTS AT 24"
Douglas fir Larch-No. 2	2 x 6	10'-6''	10'-6''	10'-6''	8'-7''
	2 x 8	13'-10''	13'-10''	13'-10''	11'-3''
	2 x 10	17'-7''	17'-7''	17'-7''	14'-5''
	2 x 12	21'-2''	21'-5''	21'-5''	17'-6''
Douglas fir South-No. 1	2 x 6	10'-2''	10'-5''	10'-8''	9'-1''
	2 x 8	13'-2''	13'-6''	13'-9''	12'-0''
	2 x 10	16'-7''	16'-11''	17'-2''	15'-4''
	2 x 12	20'-0''	20'-4''	20'-7''	18'-5''
Hem-fir No. 1	2 x 6	10'-3''	10'-3''	10'-3''	8'-5''
	2 x 8	13'-5''	13'-7''	13'-7''	11'-1''
	2 x 10	16'-11''	17'-3''	17'-4''	14'-2''
	2 x 12	20'-5''	20'-9''	21'-0''	17'-2''
Mountain hemlock No. 2	2 x 6	9'-6''	9'-6''	9'-6''	7'-9''
	2 x 8	12'-4''	12'-7''	12'-7''	10'-3''
	2 x 10	15'-6''	15'-10''	16'-0''	13'-1''
	2 x 12	18'-8''	19'-0''	19'-3''	15'-11''
Southern pine KD No. 2	2 x 6	10'-7''	10'-8''	10'-8''	8'-8''
	2 x 8	13'-8''	14'-0''	14'-0''	11'-6''
	2 x 10	17'-3''	17'-6''	17'-10''	14'-8''
	2 x 12	20'-10''	21'-1''	21'-4''	17'-9''

COMBINED SUBFLOOR/ UNDERLAYMENT

PLYWOOD GRADE	PLYWOOD SPECIES GRADE	MAXIMUM SUPPORT		
		16 IN. O.C.	20 IN. O.C.	SPACING (2) (3) 24 IN. O.C.
		MIN. PANEL THICKNESS (IN.)	MIN. PANEL THICKNESS (IN.)	MIN. PANEL THICKNESS (IN.)
UNDERLAYMENT INT-APA (with interior or exterior glue), or UNDERLAYMENT EXT-APA (C-C plugged)	1	1/2	5/8	3/4
	2 & 3	5/8	3/4	7/8
	4	3/4	7/8	1

1. For direct application of tile, carpeting, linoleum, or other nonstructural flooring.
2. Plywood is assumed continuous over two or more spans, with face grain across supports.
3. In some nonresidential buildings special conditions require construction in excess of minimums given.

John D. Bloodgood, Architects, P.C.; Des Moines, Iowa

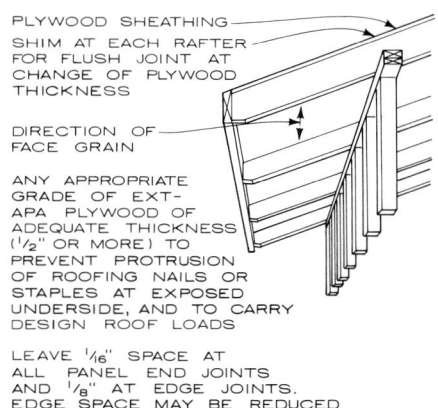

PLYWOOD SHEATHING

SHIM AT EACH RAFTER FOR FLUSH JOINT AT CHANGE OF PLYWOOD THICKNESS

DIRECTION OF FACE GRAIN

ANY APPROPRIATE GRADE OF EXT-APA PLYWOOD OF ADEQUATE THICKNESS (1/2" OR MORE) TO PREVENT PROTRUSION OF ROOFING NAILS OR STAPLES AT EXPOSED UNDERSIDE, AND TO CARRY DESIGN ROOF LOADS

LEAVE 1/16" SPACE AT ALL PANEL END JOINTS AND 1/8" AT EDGE JOINTS. EDGE SPACE MAY BE REDUCED TO 1/16" IF JOINT WILL BE VISIBLE

OPEN SOFFIT

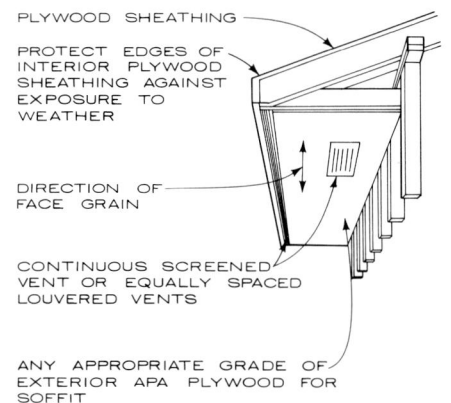

PLYWOOD SHEATHING

PROTECT EDGES OF INTERIOR PLYWOOD SHEATHING AGAINST EXPOSURE TO WEATHER

DIRECTION OF FACE GRAIN

CONTINUOUS SCREENED VENT OR EQUALLY SPACED LOUVERED VENTS

ANY APPROPRIATE GRADE OF EXTERIOR APA PLYWOOD FOR SOFFIT

CLOSED SOFFIT

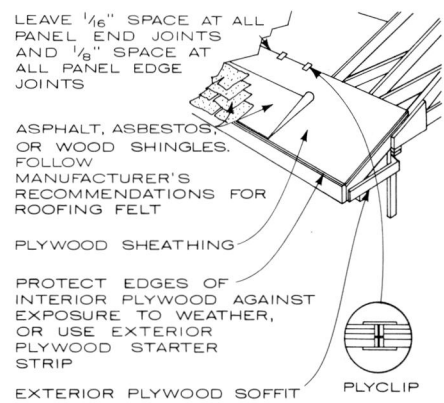

LEAVE 1/16" SPACE AT ALL PANEL END JOINTS AND 1/8" SPACE AT ALL PANEL EDGE JOINTS

ASPHALT, ASBESTOS, OR WOOD SHINGLES. FOLLOW MANUFACTURER'S RECOMMENDATIONS FOR ROOFING FELT

PLYWOOD SHEATHING

PROTECT EDGES OF INTERIOR PLYWOOD AGAINST EXPOSURE TO WEATHER, OR USE EXTERIOR PLYWOOD STARTER STRIP

EXTERIOR PLYWOOD SOFFIT

PLYCLIP

GABLE ROOF

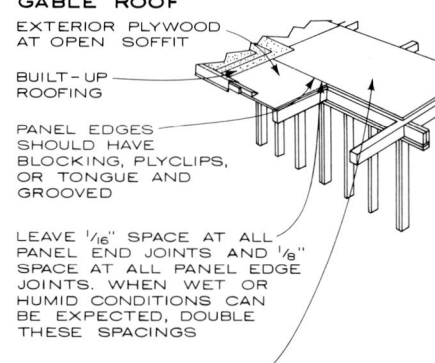

EXTERIOR PLYWOOD AT OPEN SOFFIT

BUILT-UP ROOFING

PANEL EDGES SHOULD HAVE BLOCKING, PLYCLIPS, OR TONGUE AND GROOVED

LEAVE 1/16" SPACE AT ALL PANEL END JOINTS AND 1/8" SPACE AT ALL PANEL EDGE JOINTS. WHEN WET OR HUMID CONDITIONS CAN BE EXPECTED, DOUBLE THESE SPACINGS

PLYWOOD SHEATHING

FLAT – LOW PITCHED ROOF

EXTERIOR OPEN PLYWOOD SOFFITS/ COMBINED CEILING/DECKING (1)

PANEL DESCRIPTIONS, MINIMUM RECOMMENDATIONS	GROUP	MAXIMUM SPAN (IN.)
7/16" APA 303 siding	1, 2, 3, 4	16
1/2" APA sanded	1, 2, 3, 4	
1/2" APA sanded	1, 2, 3	24
5/8" APA 303 siding	1, 2, 3, 4	
5/8" APA sanded	1, 2, 3, 4	
3/4" APA 303 siding	1, 2, 3, 4	
5/8" APA sanded	1	32 (2)
3/4" APA 303 siding	1, 2, 3	
3/4" APA sanded	1, 2, 3, 4	
1 1/8" APA textured	1, 2, 3, 4	48 (2)

NOTES

1. Plywood is assumed to be continuous across two or more spans with face grain across supports.
2. For spans of 32 or 48 in. in open soffit construction, provide adequate blocking, tongue-and-groove edges, or other support such as Plyclips. Minimum loads are at least 40 psf live load, plus 5 psf dead load, except for 1 1/8 in. panels of Group 2, 3, or 4 species, which support 35 psf live load.

NAILING SCHEDULE: For open soffits, use 6d common smooth, ring shank, or spiral thread nails for 1/2 in. or smaller thicknesses; use 8d nails for plywood 5/8 to 1 in. thick. Use 8d ring shank or spiral thread or 10d common smooth shank nails for 1 to 1/8 in. textured panels. Space nails 6 in. at panel edges, 12 in. at intermediate supports, except for 48 in. spans where nails should be spaced 6 in. at all supports.

EXTERIOR CLOSED PLYWOOD SOFFITS

NOMINAL PLYWOOD THICKNESS	GROUP	MAXIMUM SPAN (IN.) ALL EDGES SUPPORTED
5/16" APA 303 siding 3/8" APA sanded		24
7/16" APA 303 siding 1/2" sanded	1, 2, 3, 4	32
5/8" APA 303 siding or APA sanded		48

NOTE: Plywood is assumed to be continuous across two or more spans with face grain across supports.

NAILING SCHEDULE: For closed soffits, use non-staining box or casing nails, 6d for 5/16 and 7/16 in. panels and 8d for 5/8 in. panels. Space nails 6 in. at panel edges and 12 in. along intermediate supports.

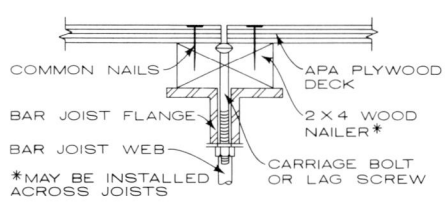

COMMON NAILS

APA PLYWOOD DECK

BAR JOIST FLANGE

2 X 4 WOOD NAILER*

BAR JOIST WEB

*MAY BE INSTALLED ACROSS JOISTS

CARRIAGE BOLT OR LAG SCREW

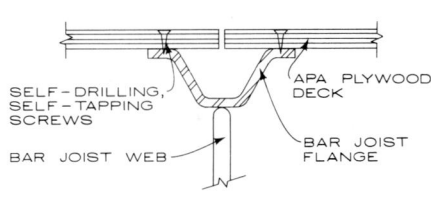

SELF-DRILLING, SELF-TAPPING SCREWS

APA PLYWOOD DECK

BAR JOIST WEB

BAR JOIST FLANGE

CONNECTIONS TO OPEN WEB STEEL JOISTS

PLYWOOD ROOF DECKING (1)

IDENTIFICATION INDEX	PLYWOOD THICKNESS (IN.)	MAXIMUM SPAN (IN.)	UNSUPPORTED EDGE— MAXIMUM LENGTH (IN.)	ALLOWABLE LIVE LOADS (PSF) (2-4) SPACING OF SUPPORTS CENTER TO CENTER (IN.)									
				12	16	20	24	30	32	36	42	48	60
12/0	5/16	12	12	150									
16/0	5/16, 3/8	16	16	160	75								
20/0	5/16, 3/8	20	20	190	105	65							
24/0	3/8	24	20	250	140	95	50						
	1/2		24										
32/16	1/2, 5/8	32	28	385	215	150	95	50	40				
42/20	5/8, 3/4, 7/8	42	32		330	230	145	90	75	50	35		
48/24	3/4, 7/8	48	36			300	190	120	105	65	45	35	
48/24 (5)	3/4, 7/8	48	36				225	125	105	75	55	40	
2-4-1	1 1/8	72	48				390	245	215	135	100	75	45
1 1/8" groups 1, 2	1 1/8	72	48				305	195	170	105	75	55	35
1 1/4" groups 3, 4	1 1/4	72	48				355	225	195	125	90	65	40

NOTES

1. Apply to C-D Interior APA, C-C Exterior APA; Structural I and II C-D Interior APA and Structural I and II C-C Interior APA.
2. Values assume 5 psf dead load. Uniform load deflection limit is 1/180 span under live load plus dead load, or 1/240 under live load only.
3. Special conditions may require construction in excess of the given minimums.
4. Plywood is assumed to be continuous across two or more spans with face grain across supports.
5. Loads apply only to C-C Exterior-APA, Structural I C-D Interior APA, and Structural I C-C Exterior APA. Check availability before specifying.

NAILING SCHEDULE: Use 6d common smooth, ring shank, or spiral thread nails for plywood 1/2 in. thick or thinner and 8d for plywood to 1 in. thick. Use 8d ring shank or spiral thread or 10d common smooth for 2-4-1, 1 1/8 and 1 1/4 in. panels. Space nails 6 in. at panel edges and 12 in. at intermediate supports, except for 48 in. or longer spans where nails should be spaced 6 in. at all supports.

John D. Bloodgood, Architects, P.C.; Des Moines, Iowa

ROUGH CARPENTRY

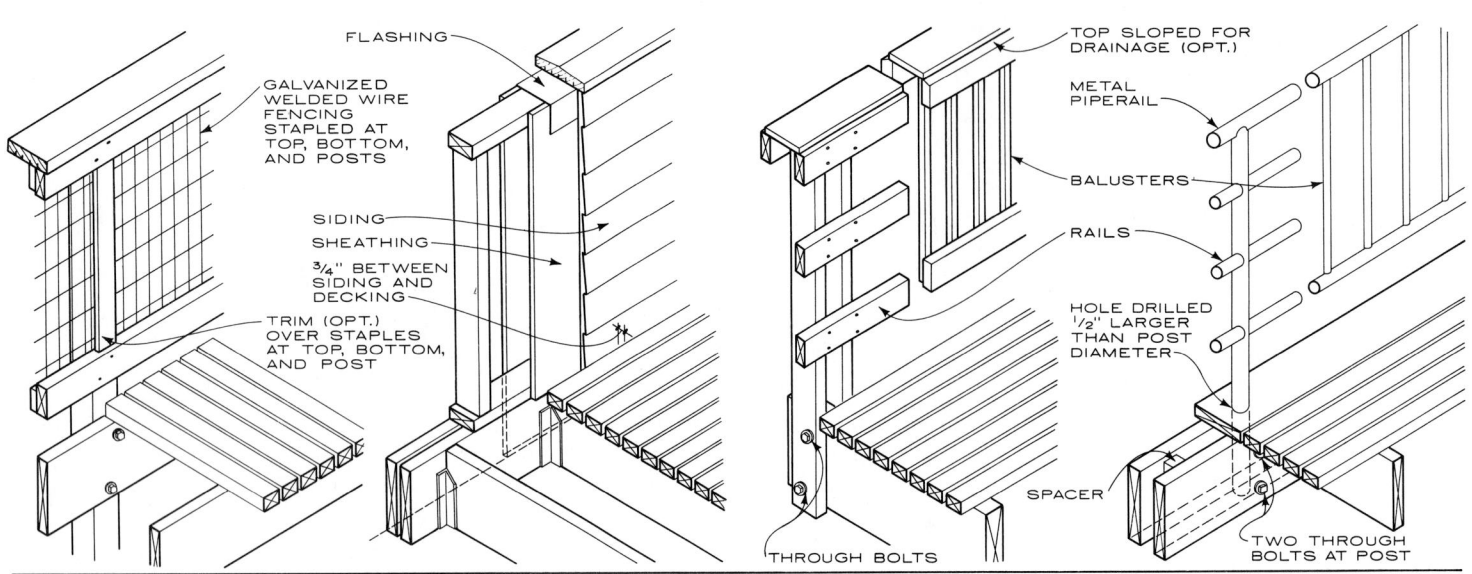

RAILINGS

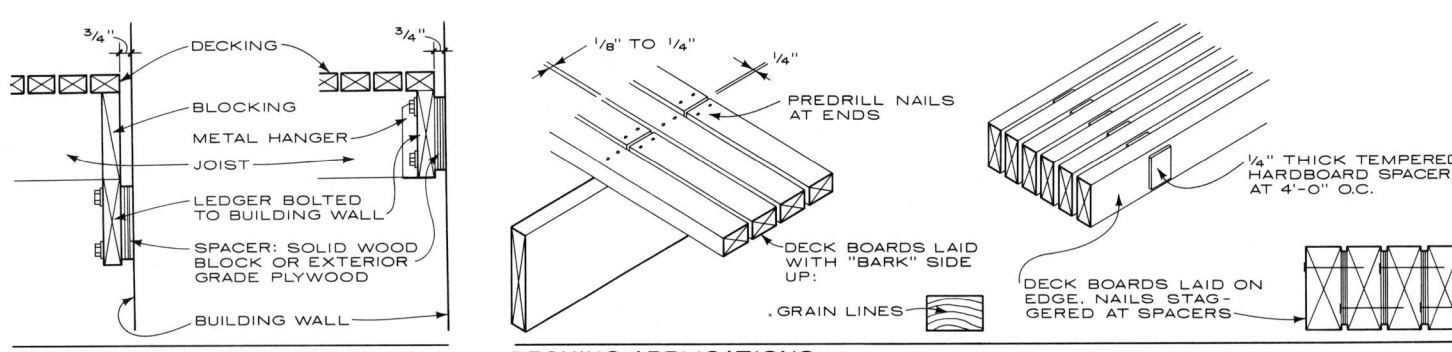

CONNECTIONS AT BUILDING WALL

DECKING APPLICATIONS

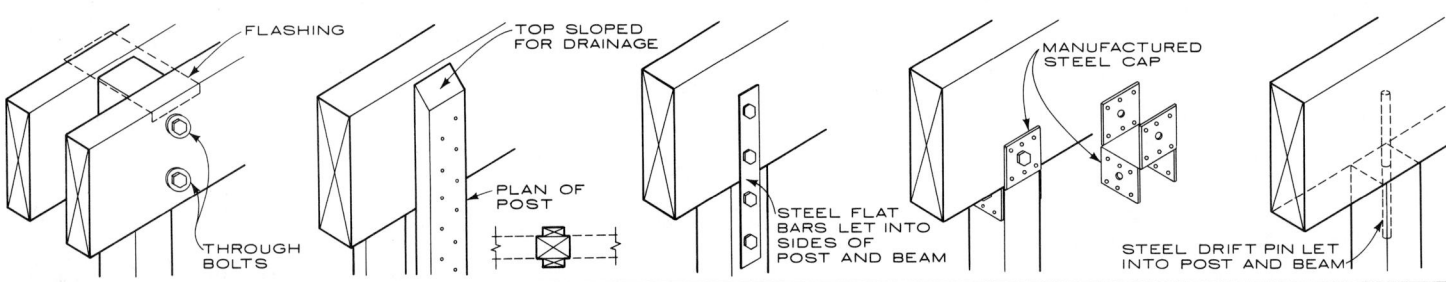

POST AND BEAM CONNECTIONS

RELATIVE COMPARISON OF VARIOUS QUALITIES OF WOOD USED IN DECK CONSTRUCTION

	DOUGLAS FIR—LARCH	SOUTHERN PINE	HEMLOCK FIR*	SOFT PINES†	WESTERN RED CEDAR	REDWOOD	SPRUCE	CYPRESS
Hardness	Fair	Fair	Poor	Poor	Poor	Fair	Poor	Fair
Warp resistance	Fair	Fair	Fair	Good	Good	Good	Fair	Fair
Ease of working	Poor	Fair	Fair	Good	Good	Fair	Fair	Fair
Paint holding	Poor	Poor	Poor	Good	Good	Good	Fair	Good
Stain acceptance‡	Fair	Fair	Fair	Fair	Good	Good	Fair	Fair
Nail holding	Good	Good	Poor	Poor	Poor	Fair	Fair	Fair
Heartwood decay resistance	Fair	Fair	Poor	Poor	Good	Good	Poor	Good
Proportion of heartwood	Good	Poor	Poor	Fair	Good	Good	Poor	Good
Bending strength	Good	Good	Fair	Poor	Poor	Fair	Fair	Fair
Stiffness	Good	Good	Good	Poor	Poor	Fair	Fair	Fair
Strength as a post	Good	Good	Fair	Poor	Fair	Good	Fair	Fair
Freedom from pitch	Fair	Poor	Good	Fair	Good	Good	Good	Good

*Includes West Coast and eastern hemlocks.
†Includes western and northeastern pines.
‡Categories refer to semitransparent oil base stain.

The Bumgardner Partnership/Architects; Seattle, Washington

MAXIMUM SPAN OF DECK BOARDS

	FLAT		ON EDGE	
	1 x 4	2 x 2 (x3)(x4)	2 x 3	2 x 4
Douglas fir, larch, and southern pine	1'-4''	5'-0''	7'-6''	12'-0''
Hemlock-fir, Douglas-fir, southern	1'-2''	4'-0''	6'-6''	10'-0''
Western pines and cedars, redwoods, spruce	1'-0''	3'-6''	5'-6''	9'-0''

NOTE

Size and spacing of joists, posts, and beams may be selected according to other pages in chapter.

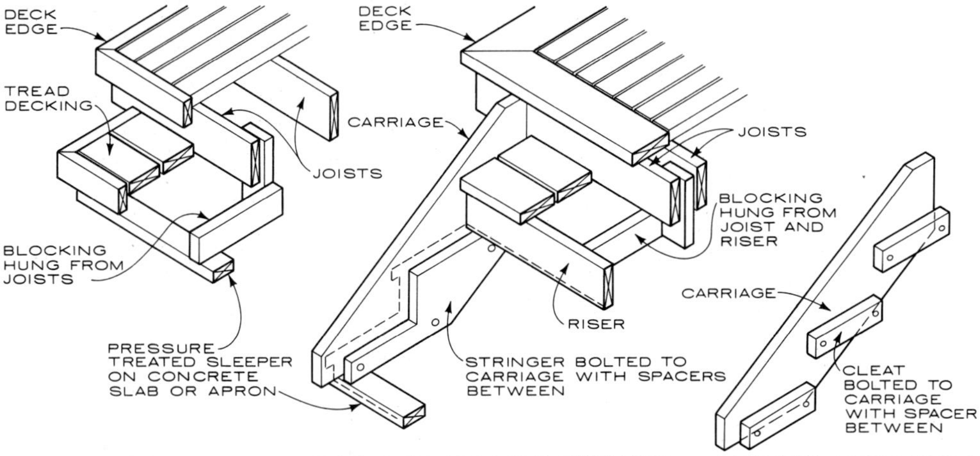

DECK EDGE

TREAD DECKING

BLOCKING HUNG FROM JOISTS

PRESSURE TREATED SLEEPER ON CONCRETE SLAB OR APRON

DECK EDGE

CARRIAGE

JOISTS

JOISTS

BLOCKING HUNG FROM JOIST AND RISER

RISER

STRINGER BOLTED TO CARRIAGE WITH SPACERS BETWEEN

CARRIAGE

CLEAT BOLTED TO CARRIAGE WITH SPACER BETWEEN

STEP PLATFORM   **STAIR CARRIAGE WITH STRINGER**   **CARRIAGE WITH CLEATS**

STEPS AND STAIRS

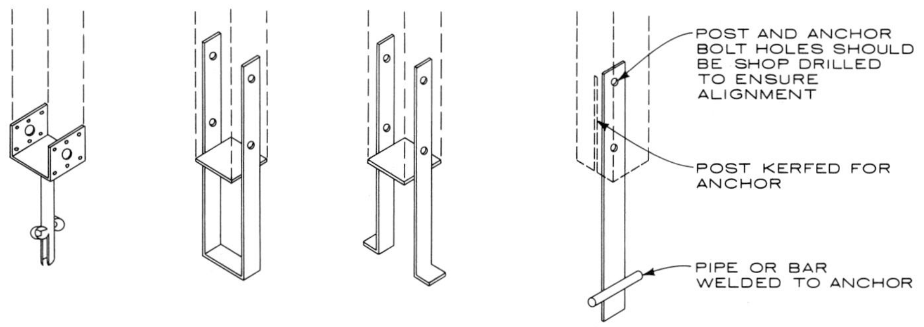

POST AND ANCHOR BOLT HOLES SHOULD BE SHOP DRILLED TO ENSURE ALIGNMENT

POST KERFED FOR ANCHOR

PIPE OR BAR WELDED TO ANCHOR

STANDARD MANUFACTURED   **SHOP FABRICATED**

STEEL POST ANCHORS

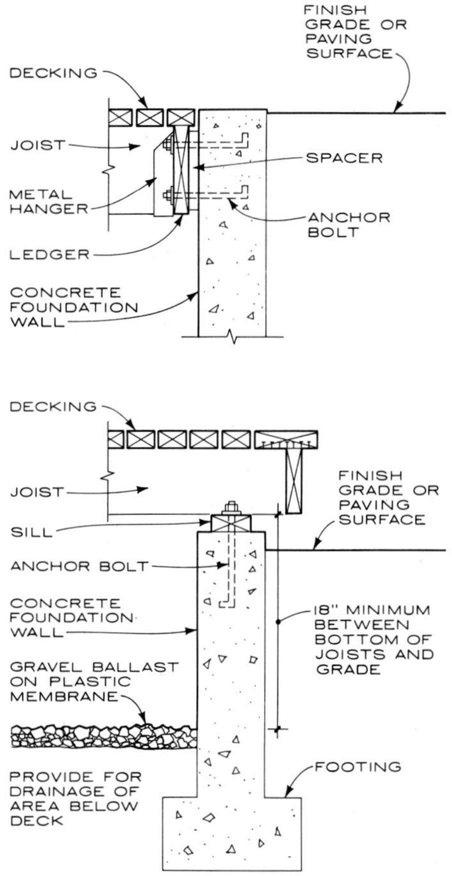

DECKING

JOIST

METAL HANGER

LEDGER

CONCRETE FOUNDATION WALL

FINISH GRADE OR PAVING SURFACE

SPACER

ANCHOR BOLT

DECKING

JOIST

SILL

ANCHOR BOLT

CONCRETE FOUNDATION WALL

GRAVEL BALLAST ON PLASTIC MEMBRANE

PROVIDE FOR DRAINAGE OF AREA BELOW DECK

FINISH GRADE OR PAVING SURFACE

18" MINIMUM BETWEEN BOTTOM OF JOISTS AND GRADE

FOOTING

LOW DECK EDGES

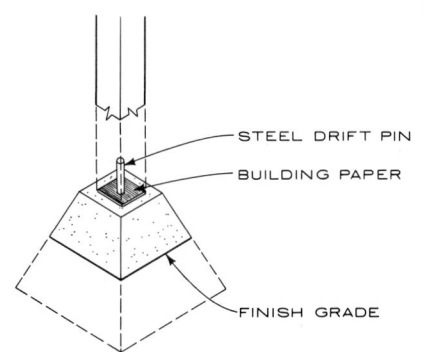

STEEL DRIFT PIN

BUILDING PAPER

FINISH GRADE

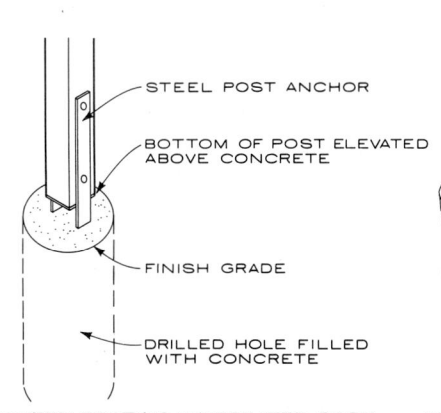

STEEL POST ANCHOR

BOTTOM OF POST ELEVATED ABOVE CONCRETE

FINISH GRADE

DRILLED HOLE FILLED WITH CONCRETE

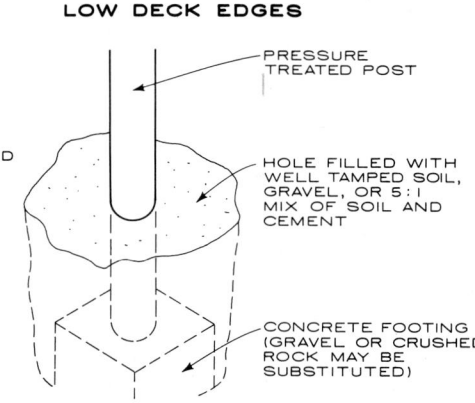

PRESSURE TREATED POST

HOLE FILLED WITH WELL TAMPED SOIL, GRAVEL, OR 5:1 MIX OF SOIL AND CEMENT

CONCRETE FOOTING (GRAVEL OR CRUSHED ROCK MAY BE SUBSTITUTED)

PRECAST CONCRETE PLINTH/UNTREATED POST   **POURED FOOTING/UNTREATED POST**   **POURED OR PRECAST FOOTING/TREATED POST**

POSTS AND FOOTINGS

FASTENERS

1. Smooth shank nails lose holding strength after repeated wet/dry cycles. Ring or spiral grooved shank nails are preferable.
2. Use galvanized or plated fasteners to avoid corrosion and staining.
3. To reduce board splitting by nailing: blunt nail points; predrill ($3/4$ of nail diameter); stagger nailing; place nails no closer to edge than one half of board thickness.
4. Avoid end grain nailing and toe nailing if possible.
5. Use flat washers under heads of lag screws and bolts, and under nuts.

MOISTURE PROTECTION

1. All wood members should be protected from weather by pressure treatment or field application of preservatives, stains, or paints.
2. All wood in direct contact with soil must be pressure treated.
3. Bottoms of posts on piers should be 6 in. above grade.
4. Sterilize or cover soil with membrane to keep plant growth away from wood members so as to minimize moisture exchange.
5. Treat all ends, cuts, holes, and so on with preservative prior to placement.
6. Decking and flat trim boards, 2 x 6 and wider, should be kerfed on the underside with $3/4$ in. deep saw cuts at 1 in. on center to prevent cupping.
7. Avoid horizontal exposure of endgrain or provide adequate protection by flashing or sealing. Avoid or minimize joint situations where moisture may be trapped by using spacers and/or flashing, caulking, sealant, plastic roofing cement.

CONSTRUCTION

1. WOOD SELECTION: Usual requirements are good decay resistance, nonsplintering, fair stiffness, strength, hardness, and warp resistance. Selection varies according to local climate and exposure.
2. BRACING: On large decks, or decks where post heights exceed 5 ft, lateral stability should be achieved with horizontal bracing (metal or wood diagonal ties on top or bottom of joists, or diagonal application of decking) in combination with vertical bracing (rigid bolted or gusseted connections at top of posts, knee bracing, or "X" bracing between posts), and/or connection to a braced building wall. Lateral stability should be checked by a structural engineer.

The Bumgardner Partnership/Architects; Seattle, Washington

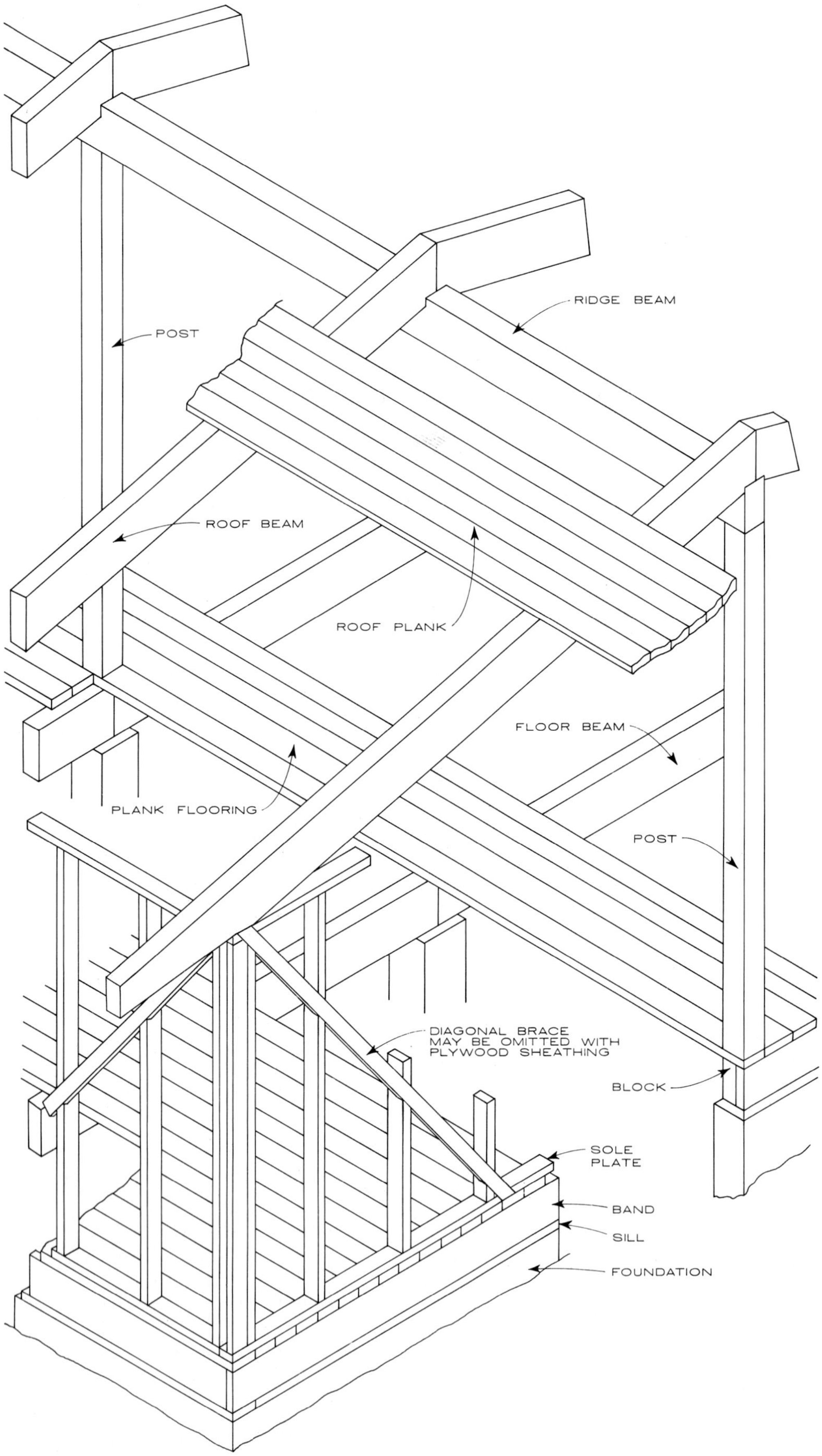

DESCRIPTION

Use of two inch nominal thickness plank for subfloors or roofs supported on beams spaced 6 to 8 feet apart.

PRINCIPLES OF DESIGN

Two inch plank used more efficiently when continuous over more than one span.

Uses standard lumber lengths such as 12, 14 and 16 feet with beams 6, 7 or 8 feet apart.

Design permitting, end joints between supports allows use of random lengths.

ADVANTAGES OF SYSTEM

Architectural effect provided by exposed plank and beam ceiling. Added effective height of ceiling at no increase in wall height.

Fewer members permits savings in labor.

Cross-bridging not required.

LIMITATIONS OF SYSTEM

Bearing partitions and heavy loads such as bathtubs, refrigerators etc., may require additional framing. Concealment must be provided for wiring, piping and duct work.

Insulation value of two inch deck may be adequate, but where additional insulation is required it may be attached below deck or as rigid insulation above deck under roofing.

CONSTRUCTION DETAILS AND FASTENING

Members of built-up beams should be securely spiked together from both outside faces. Spaced beams should be blocked at frequent intervals, and each member should be securely nailed to blocking. Where planks butt over a single member, a nominal beam width of three or more inches is necessary to provide a suitable bearing and nailing surface for the planks. Planks should be both blind and face-nailed to the beam. In this construction posts (rather than studs) carry the loads, which are concentrated and must be designed for conditions, but not smaller than 4 x 4 inches. Built-up posts should be spiked together.

When solid beams butt at a column, a nominal column dimension of 6 or more inches parallel to direction of beam is recommended to provide suitable bearing. Spike bearing blocks to column where necessary to increase bearing surface.

RIDGE BEAM

POST

ROOF BEAM

ROOF PLANK

FLOOR BEAM

PLANK FLOORING

POST

DIAGONAL BRACE
MAY BE OMITTED WITH
PLYWOOD SHEATHING

BLOCK

SOLE
PLATE

BAND

SILL

FOUNDATION

TYPICAL PLANK AND BEAM FRAMING FOR ONE STORY HOUSE

Joseph A. Wilkes, FAIA; Wilkes and Faulkner; Washington, D.C.

⑥ **HEAVY TIMBER**

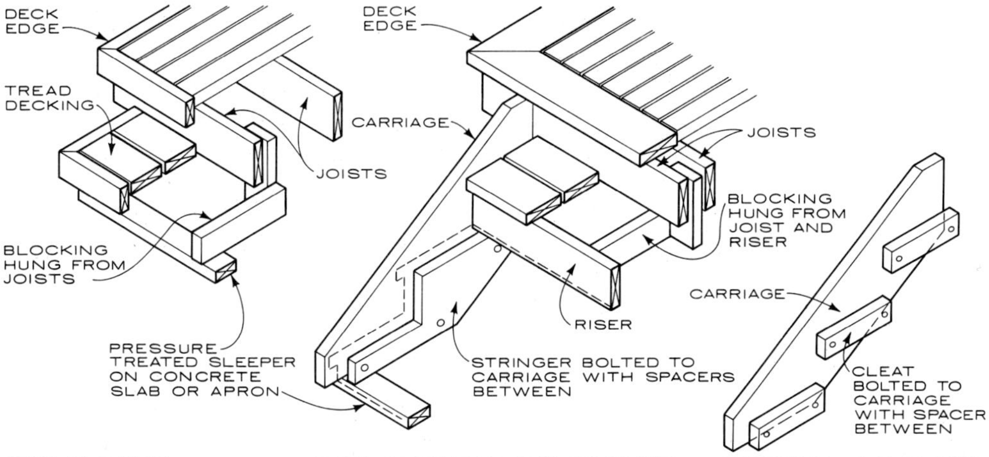

STEPS AND STAIRS

DECK EDGE

TREAD DECKING

JOISTS

BLOCKING HUNG FROM JOISTS

PRESSURE TREATED SLEEPER ON CONCRETE SLAB OR APRON

STEP PLATFORM

DECK EDGE

CARRIAGE

JOISTS

RISER

STRINGER BOLTED TO CARRIAGE WITH SPACERS BETWEEN

STAIR CARRIAGE WITH STRINGER

JOISTS

BLOCKING HUNG FROM JOIST AND RISER

CARRIAGE

CLEAT BOLTED TO CARRIAGE WITH SPACER BETWEEN

CARRIAGE WITH CLEATS

FINISH GRADE OR PAVING SURFACE

DECKING

JOIST

METAL HANGER

LEDGER

CONCRETE FOUNDATION WALL

SPACER

ANCHOR BOLT

STEEL POST ANCHORS

POST AND ANCHOR BOLT HOLES SHOULD BE SHOP DRILLED TO ENSURE ALIGNMENT

POST KERFED FOR ANCHOR

PIPE OR BAR WELDED TO ANCHOR

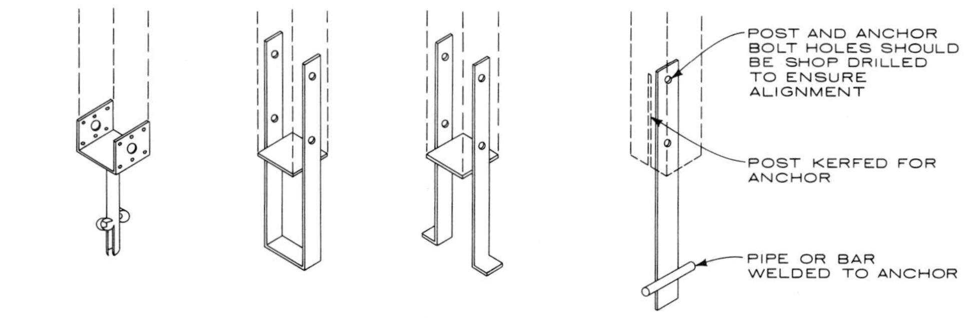

STANDARD MANUFACTURED   **SHOP FABRICATED**

DECKING

JOIST

SILL

ANCHOR BOLT

CONCRETE FOUNDATION WALL

GRAVEL BALLAST ON PLASTIC MEMBRANE

PROVIDE FOR DRAINAGE OF AREA BELOW DECK

FINISH GRADE OR PAVING SURFACE

18" MINIMUM BETWEEN BOTTOM OF JOISTS AND GRADE

FOOTING

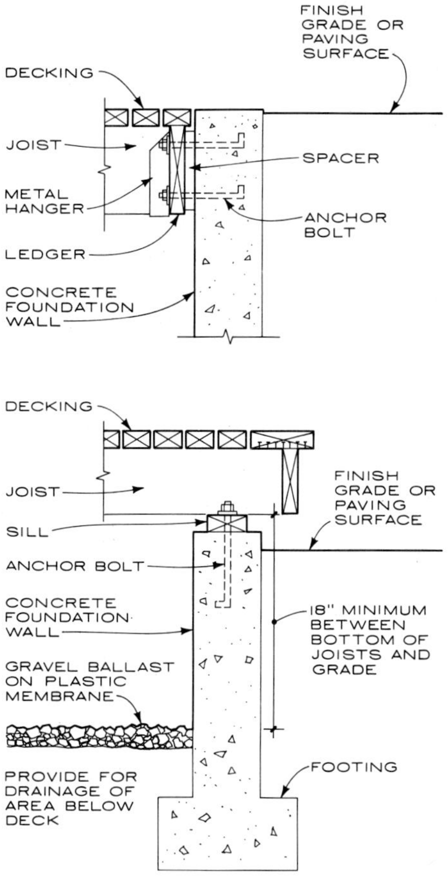

LOW DECK EDGES

POSTS AND FOOTINGS

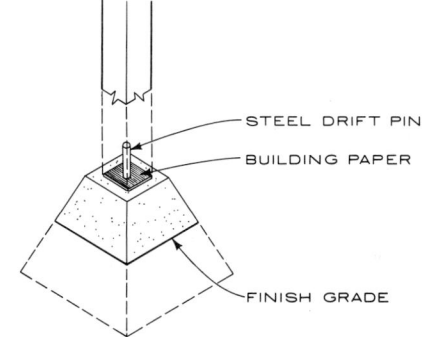

STEEL DRIFT PIN

BUILDING PAPER

FINISH GRADE

PRECAST CONCRETE PLINTH/UNTREATED POST

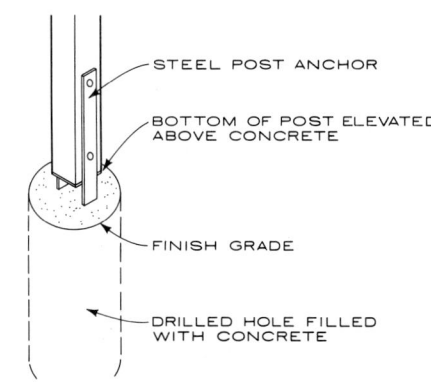

STEEL POST ANCHOR

BOTTOM OF POST ELEVATED ABOVE CONCRETE

FINISH GRADE

DRILLED HOLE FILLED WITH CONCRETE

POURED FOOTING/UNTREATED POST

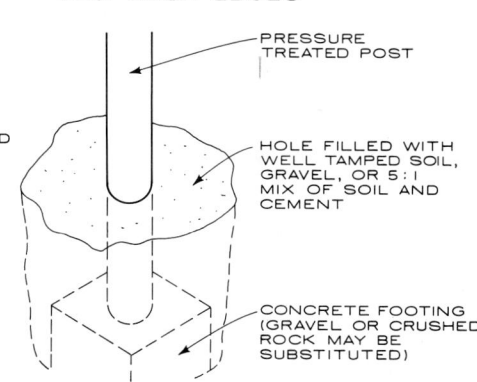

PRESSURE TREATED POST

HOLE FILLED WITH WELL TAMPED SOIL, GRAVEL, OR 5:1 MIX OF SOIL AND CEMENT

CONCRETE FOOTING (GRAVEL OR CRUSHED ROCK MAY BE SUBSTITUTED)

POURED OR PRECAST FOOTING/TREATED POST

FASTENERS

1. Smooth shank nails lose holding strength after repeated wet/dry cycles. Ring or spiral grooved shank nails are preferable.
2. Use galvanized or plated fasteners to avoid corrosion and staining.
3. To reduce board splitting by nailing: blunt nail points; predrill ($3/4$ of nail diameter); stagger nailing; place nails no closer to edge than one half of board thickness.
4. Avoid end grain nailing and toe nailing if possible.
5. Use flat washers under heads of lag screws and bolts, and under nuts.

MOISTURE PROTECTION

1. All wood members should be protected from weather by pressure treatment or field application of preservatives, stains, or paints.
2. All wood in direct contact with soil must be pressure treated.
3. Bottoms of posts on piers should be 6 in. above grade.
4. Sterilize or cover soil with membrane to keep plant growth away from wood members so as to minimize moisture exchange.
5. Treat all ends, cuts, holes, and so on with preservative prior to placement.
6. Decking and flat trim boards, 2 x 6 and wider, should be kerfed on the underside with $3/4$ in. deep saw cuts at 1 in. on center to prevent cupping.
7. Avoid horizontal exposure of endgrain or provide adequate protection by flashing or sealing. Avoid or minimize joint situations where moisture may be trapped by using spacers and/or flashing, caulking, sealant, plastic roofing cement.

CONSTRUCTION

1. WOOD SELECTION: Usual requirements are good decay resistance, nonsplintering, fair stiffness, strength, hardness, and warp resistance. Selection varies according to local climate and exposure.
2. BRACING: On large decks, or decks where post heights exceed 5 ft, lateral stability should be achieved with horizontal bracing (metal or wood diagonal ties on top or bottom of joists, or diagonal application of decking) in combination with vertical bracing (rigid bolted or gusseted connections at top of posts, knee bracing, or "X" bracing between posts), and/or connection to a braced building wall. Lateral stability should be checked by a structural engineer.

The Bumgardner Partnership/Architects; Seattle, Washington

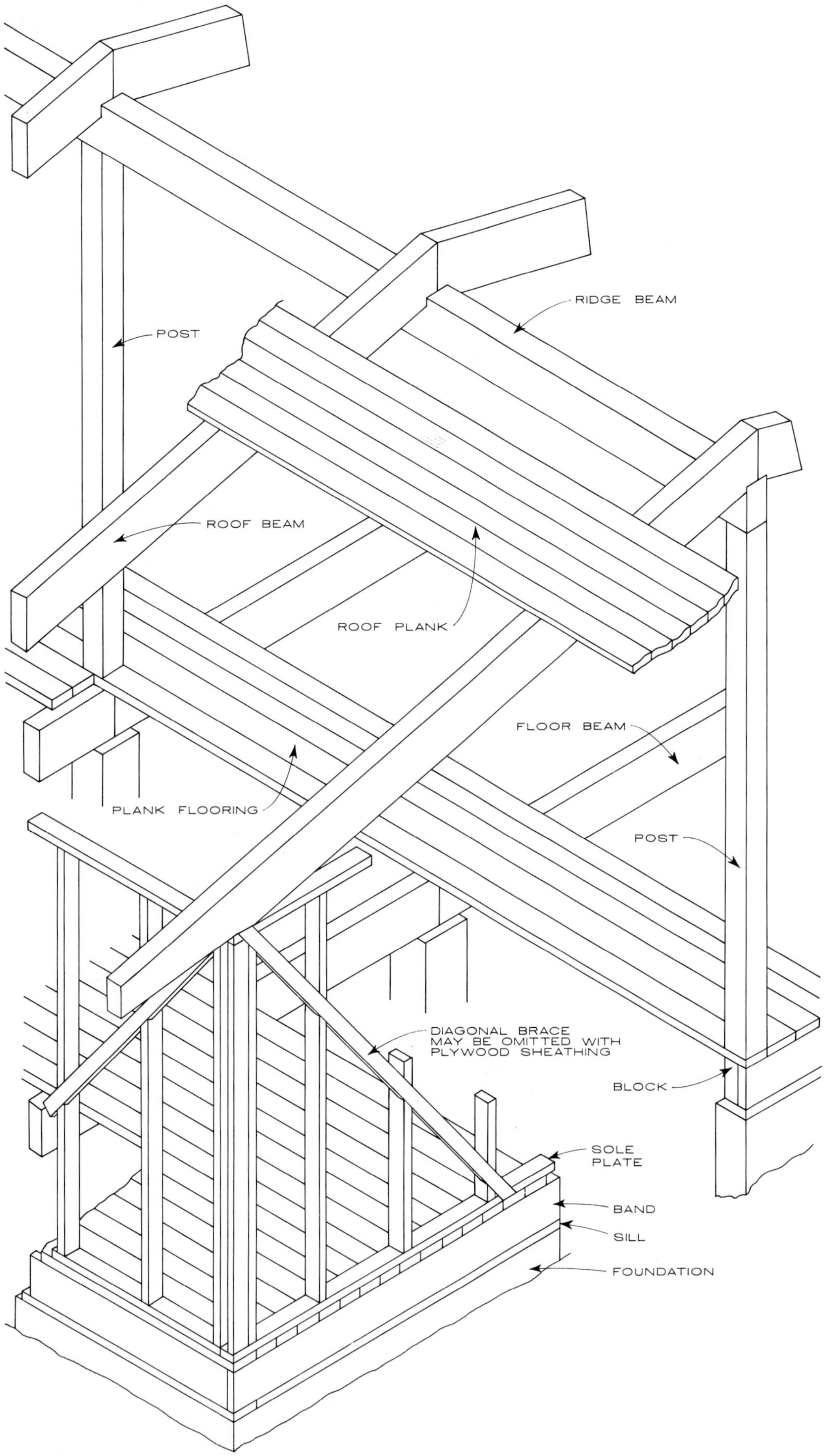

DESCRIPTION

Use of two inch nominal thickness plank for subfloors or roofs supported on beams spaced 6 to 8 feet apart.

PRINCIPLES OF DESIGN

Two inch plank used more efficiently when continuous over more than one span.

Uses standard lumber lengths such as 12, 14 and 16 feet with beams 6, 7 or 8 feet apart.

Design permitting, end joints between supports allows use of random lengths.

ADVANTAGES OF SYSTEM

Architectural effect provided by exposed plank and beam ceiling. Added effective height of ceiling at no increase in wall height.

Fewer members permits savings in labor.

Cross-bridging not required.

LIMITATIONS OF SYSTEM

Bearing partitions and heavy loads such as bathtubs, refrigerators etc., may require additional framing. Concealment must be provided for wiring, piping and duct work.

Insulation value of two inch deck may be adequate, but where additional insulation is required it may be attached below deck or as rigid insulation above deck under roofing.

CONSTRUCTION DETAILS AND FASTENING

Members of built-up beams should be securely spiked together from both outside faces. Spaced beams should be blocked at frequent intervals, and each member should be securely nailed to blocking. Where planks butt over a single member, a nominal beam width of three or more inches is necessary to provide a suitable bearing and nailing surface for the planks. Planks should be both blind and face-nailed to the beam. In this construction posts (rather than studs) carry the loads, which are concentrated and must be designed for conditions, but not smaller than 4 x 4 inches. Built-up posts should be spiked together.

When solid beams butt at a column, a nominal column dimension of 6 or more inches parallel to direction of beam is recommended to provide suitable bearing. Spike bearing blocks to column where necessary to increase bearing surface.

POST

RIDGE BEAM

ROOF BEAM

ROOF PLANK

FLOOR BEAM

PLANK FLOORING

POST

DIAGONAL BRACE
MAY BE OMITTED WITH
PLYWOOD SHEATHING

BLOCK

SOLE
PLATE

BAND

SILL

FOUNDATION

TYPICAL PLANK AND BEAM FRAMING FOR ONE STORY HOUSE

Joseph A. Wilkes, FAIA; Wilkes and Faulkner; Washington, D.C.

HEAVY TIMBER

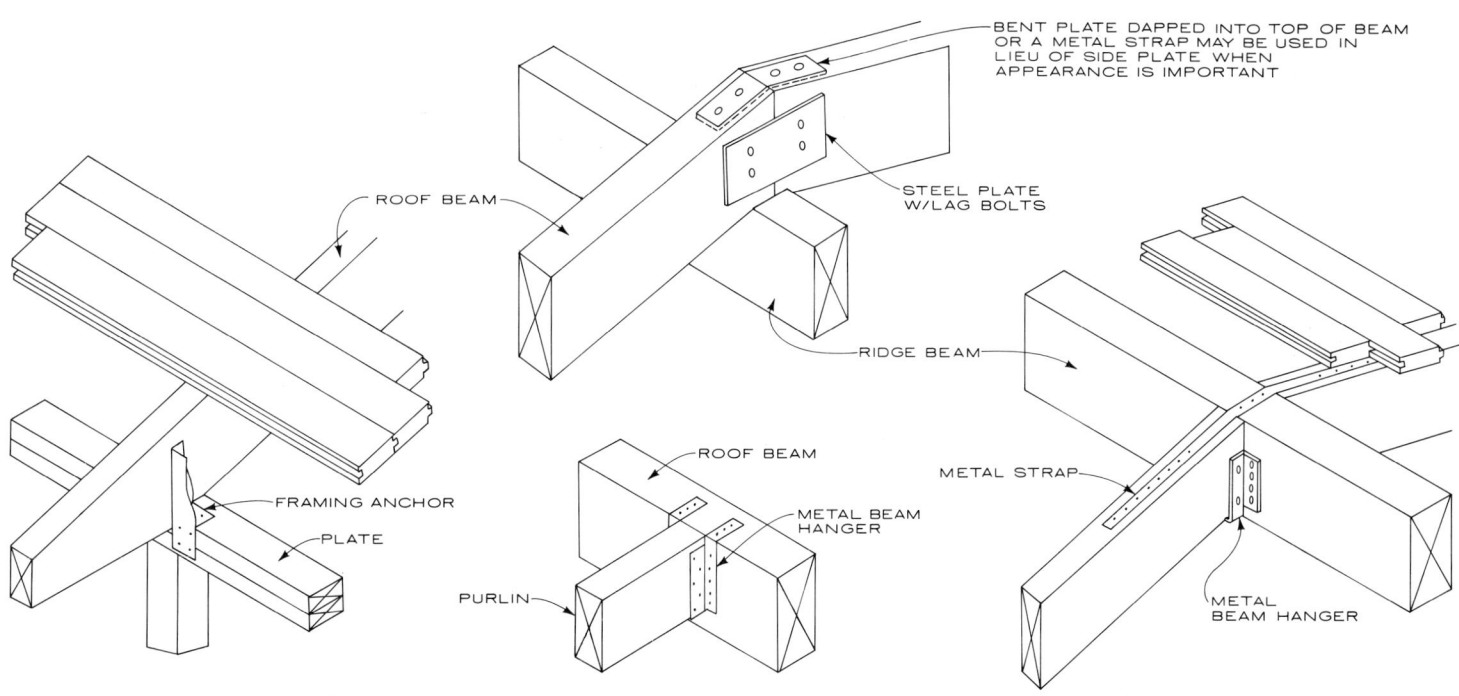

BENT PLATE DAPPED INTO TOP OF BEAM OR A METAL STRAP MAY BE USED IN LIEU OF SIDE PLATE WHEN APPEARANCE IS IMPORTANT

ROOF BEAM ANCHORAGE DETAILS

DESIGN TABLE FOR NOMINAL 2 IN. PLANK

REQUIRED VALUES FOR FIBER STRESS IN BENDING (f) AND MODULUS OF ELASTICITY (E) TO SUPPORT SAFELY A LIVE LOAD OF 20, 30, OR 40 LB/SQ FT WITHIN A DEFLECTION LIMITATION OF $\ell/240$, $\ell/300$, OR $\ell/360$.

SPAN (FT)	LIVE LOAD (PSF)	DEFLECTION LIMIT	TYPE A SINGLE SPAN f (PSI)	TYPE A SINGLE SPAN E (PSI)	TYPE B DOUBLE SPAN f (PSI)	TYPE B DOUBLE SPAN E (PSI)	TYPE C THREE SPAN f (PSI)	TYPE C THREE SPAN E (PSI)	TYPE D COMBINATION SINGLE AND DOUBLE SPAN f (PSI)	TYPE D COMBINATION SINGLE AND DOUBLE SPAN E (PSI)	TYPE E RANDOM LAYUP f (PSI)	TYPE E RANDOM LAYUP E (PSI)
6	20	$\ell/240$	360	576,000	360	239,000	288	305,000	360	408,000	360	442,000
		$\ell/300$	360	720,000	360	299,000	288	381,000	360	509,000	360	553,000
		$\ell/360$	360	864,000	360	359,000	288	457,000	360	611,000	360	664,000
	30	$\ell/240$	480	864,000	480	359,000	384	457,000	480	611,000	480	664,000
		$\ell/300$	480	1,080,000	480	448,000	384	571,000	480	764,000	480	829,000
		$\ell/360$	480	1,296,000	480	538,000	384	685,000	480	917,000	480	995,000
	40	$\ell/240$	600	1,152,000	600	478,000	480	609,000	600	815,000	600	885,000
		$\ell/300$	600	1,440,000	600	598,000	480	762,000	600	1,019,000	600	1,106,000
		$\ell/360$	600	1,728,000	600	717,000	480	914,000	600	1,223,000	600	1,327,000
7	20	$\ell/240$	490	915,000	490	380,000	392	484,000	490	647,000	490	702,000
		$\ell/300$	490	1,143,000	490	475,000	392	605,000	490	809,000	490	878,000
		$\ell/360$	490	1,372,000	490	570,000	392	726,000	490	971,000	490	1,054,000
	30	$\ell/240$	653	1,372,000	653	570,000	522	726,000	653	971,000	653	1,054,000
		$\ell/300$	653	1,715,000	653	712,000	522	907,000	653	1,213,000	653	1,317,000
		$\ell/360$	653	2,058,000	653	854,000	522	1,088,000	653	1,456,000	653	1,581,000
	40	$\ell/240$	817	1,829,000	817	759,000	653	968,000	817	1,294,000	817	1,405,000
		$\ell/300$	817	1,187,000	817	949,000	653	1,209,000	817	1,618,000	817	1,756,000
		$\ell/360$	817	2,744,000	817	1,139,000	653	1,451,000	817	1,941,000	817	2,107,000
8	20	$\ell/240$	640	1,365,000	640	567,000	512	722,000	640	966,000	640	1,049,000
		$\ell/300$	640	1,707,000	640	708,000	512	903,000	640	1,208,000	640	1,311,000
		$\ell/360$	640	2,048,000	640	850,000	512	1,083,000	640	1,449,000	640	1,573,000
	30	$\ell/240$	853	2,048,000	853	850,000	682	1,083,000	853	1,449,000	853	1,573,000
		$\ell/300$	853	2,560,000	853	1,063,000	682	1,345,000	853	1,811,000	853	1,966,000
		$\ell/360$	853	3,072,000	853	1,275,000	682	1,625,000	853	2,174,000	853	2,359,000
	40	$\ell/240$	1,067	2,731,000	1,067	1,134,000	853	1,144,000	1,067	1,932,000	1,067	2,097,000
		$\ell/300$	1,067	3,413,000	1,067	1,417,000	853	1,805,000	1,067	2,145,000	1,067	2,621,000
		$\ell/360$	1,067	4,096,000	1,067	1,700,000	853	2,166,000	1,067	2,898,000	1,067	3,146,000

Ed Hesner; Rasmussen & Hobbs Architects, AIA; Takoma, Washington

HEAVY TIMBER

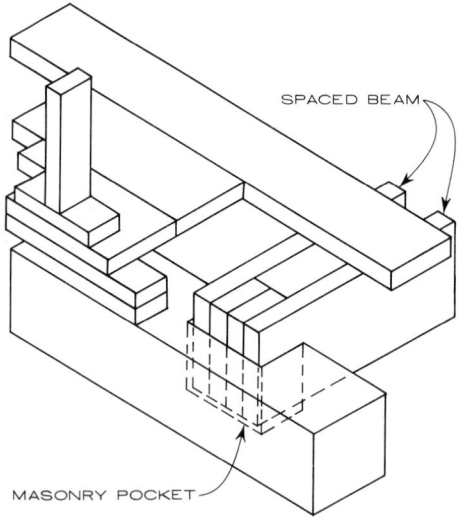

FIRST FLOOR FRAMING AT EXTERIOR WALL BEAM SET IN FOUNDATION

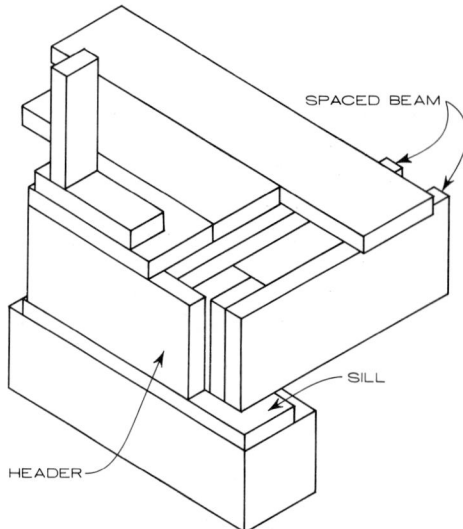

FIRST FLOOR FRAMING AT EXTERIOR WALL BEAM BEARING ON SILL

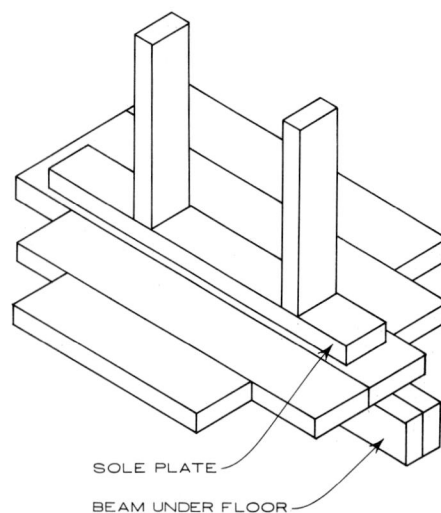

NON-BEARING PARTITION PARALLEL TO PLANK SUPPORTED BY BEAM UNDER FLOOR

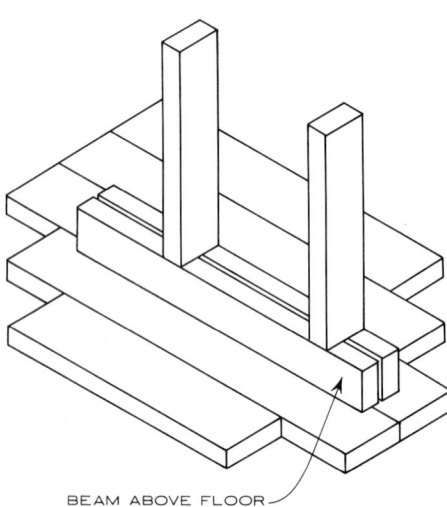

NON-BEARING PARTITION PARALLEL TO PLANK SUPPORTED BY BEAM ABOVE FLOOR

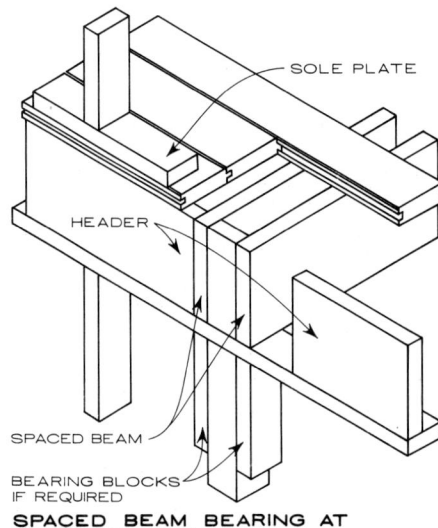
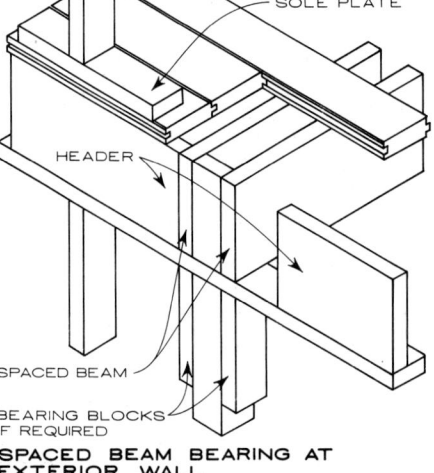

SPACED BEAM BEARING AT EXTERIOR WALL

The details in this column are preferable from the standpoint of equalizing shrinkage of horizontal lumber partition supports.

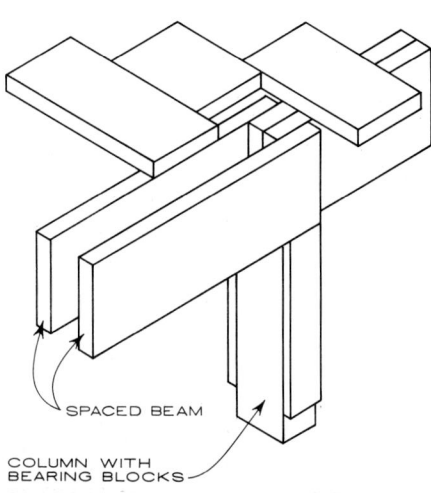

SPACED BEAM BEARING OVER BASEMENT SUPPORT

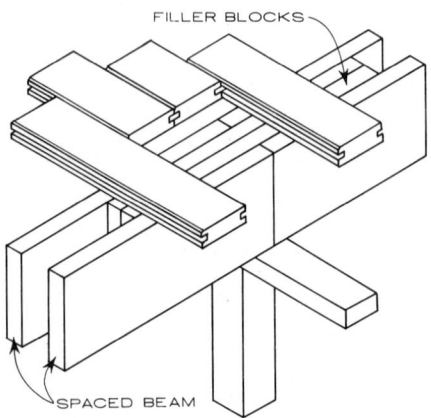
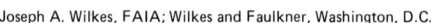

SPACED BEAM BEARING OVER INTERIOR POST

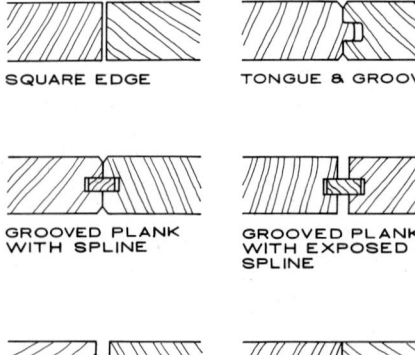

SQUARE EDGE | TONGUE & GROOVE

GROOVED PLANK WITH SPLINE | GROOVED PLANK WITH EXPOSED SPLINE

GROOVED PLANK MOULDED SPLINE | RABBETED PLANK BATTEN INSERT

JOINT TYPES IN EXPOSED PLANK CEILINGS

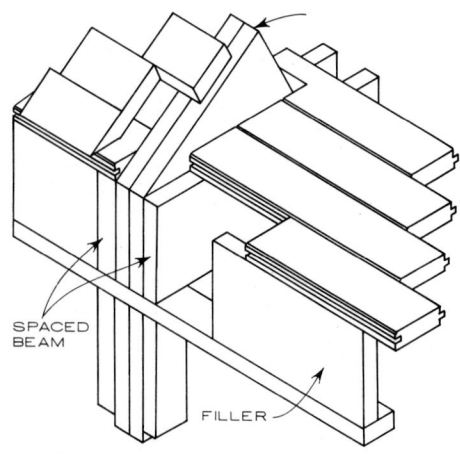

SOLID ROOF BEAM AND SPACED FLOOR BEAM BEARING ON EXTERIOR WALL

Joseph A. Wilkes, FAIA; Wilkes and Faulkner, Washington, D.C.

 HEAVY TIMBER

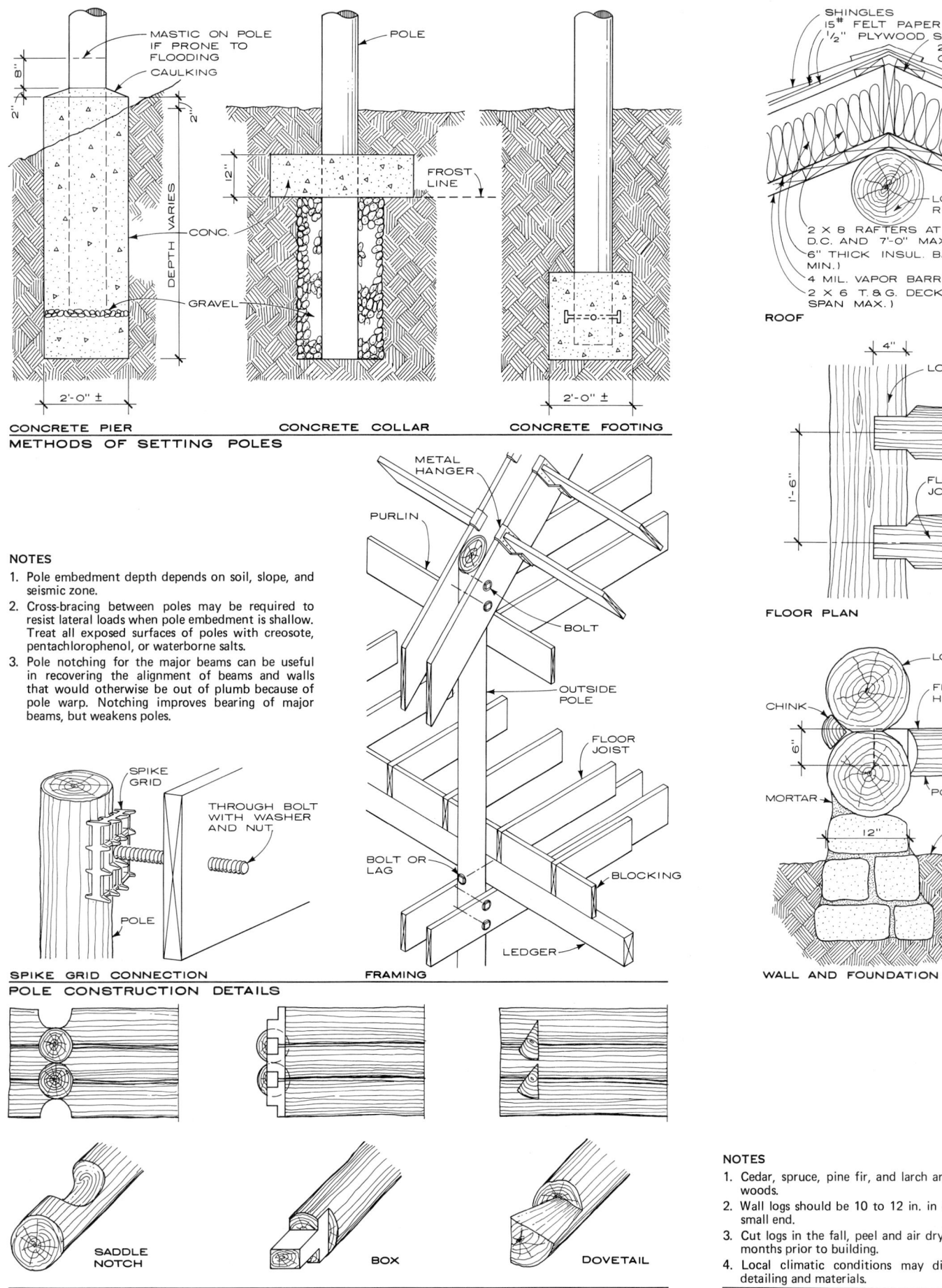

MASTIC ON POLE IF PRONE TO FLOODING

POLE

CAULKING

8"

2"

2"

CONC.

DEPTH VARIES

GRAVEL

2'-0" ±

CONCRETE PIER

POLE

12"

FROST LINE

CONCRETE COLLAR

METHODS OF SETTING POLES

POLE

2'-0" ±

CONCRETE FOOTING

ROOF

SHINGLES
15# FELT PAPER
½" PLYWOOD SHEATHING
2 X 4 AT 16" O.C. NAILERS

LOG RIDGE

2 X 8 RAFTERS AT 48" O.C. D.C. AND 7'-0" MAX. SPAN
6" THICK INSUL. BATT (R.19 MIN.)
4 MIL. VAPOR BARRIER
2 X 6 T. & G. DECK (6'-0" SPAN MAX.)

FLOOR PLAN

4"

LOG WALL

1'-6"

FLOOR JOIST

NOTES

1. Pole embedment depth depends on soil, slope, and seismic zone.
2. Cross-bracing between poles may be required to resist lateral loads when pole embedment is shallow. Treat all exposed surfaces of poles with creosote, pentachlorophenol, or waterborne salts.
3. Pole notching for the major beams can be useful in recovering the alignment of beams and walls that would otherwise be out of plumb because of pole warp. Notching improves bearing of major beams, but weakens poles.

SPIKE GRID

THROUGH BOLT WITH WASHER AND NUT

POLE

SPIKE GRID CONNECTION

POLE CONSTRUCTION DETAILS

METAL HANGER

PURLIN

BOLT

OUTSIDE POLE

FLOOR JOIST

BOLT OR LAG

BLOCKING

LEDGER

FRAMING

LOG WALL

FLOOR JOIST HEW LEVEL

CHINK

6"

MORTAR

POLE LEVEL

12"

GRADE

WALL AND FOUNDATION

SADDLE NOTCH

BOX

DOVETAIL

LOG CONSTRUCTION CORNER DETAILS

NOTES

1. Cedar, spruce, pine fir, and larch are the preferred woods.
2. Wall logs should be 10 to 12 in. in diameter at the small end.
3. Cut logs in the fall, peel and air dry on skids for 6 months prior to building.
4. Local climatic conditions may dictate different detailing and materials.

LOG CONSTRUCTION DETAILS

Robert T. Gordon, Architect, and Dan Williams, Architect; Bruce Hawtin, AIA; Jackson, Wyoming

HEAVY TIMBER   6

BEAM HANGER

When supported members are seasoned material, the top of the supported member may be set flush with the top of the hanger strap.

When supported members are of unseasoned material, the hangers should be so dimensioned that the top edge of the supported member is raised above the top of the supporting member, or top of hanger strap to allow for shrinkage as the members season in place. For supported members with moisture content at or above fiber saturation when installed, the distance raised should be about 5% of the members depth above its bearing point.

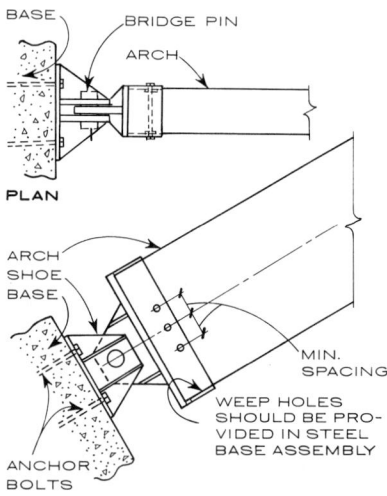

PLAN

SIDE ELEVATION
TRUE HINGE ANCHORAGE FOR ARCHES

Recommended for arches where true hinge action is desired

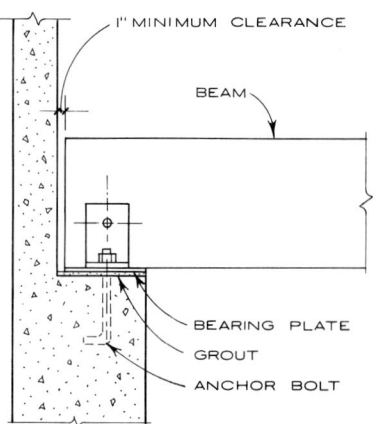

BEAM ANCHORAGE

This detail is intended for anchorages which are required to resist both uplift and horizontal forces. It may have one or more anchor bolts in masonry and one or more bolts with or without shear plates through the beam.

Provide minimum of one inch clearance or impervious moisture barrier on all wall contact surfaces, ends, sides and tops (if masonry exists above beam end).

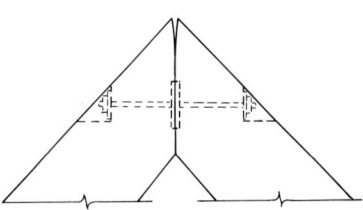

ARCH PEAK CONNECTIONS

This connection is intended for arches with a slope of 4:12 and greater, and will transfer both vertical forces (shear) and horizontal forces (tension and compression). It consists of two shear plates back to back and a through bolt or threaded rod with washers counterbored into the arch. To avoid local crushing of the peak tips of the arch due to dead load deflection, the tips are often beveled off as shown.

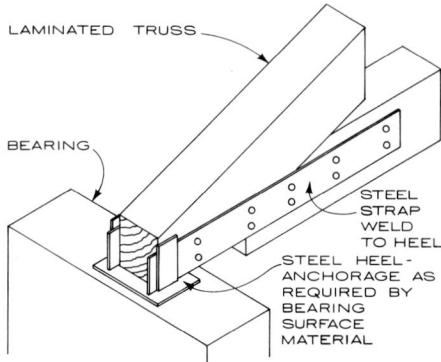

TRUSS HEEL CONNECTION

If substantial cross grain shrinkage is anticipated, double steel straps may be used in place of a single strap.

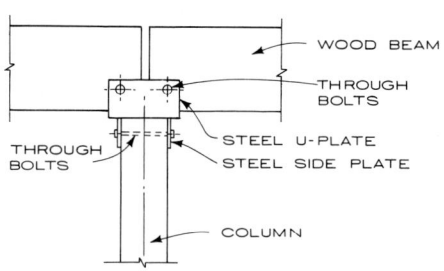

BEAM TO COLUMN CONNECTION

Steel U-plate passes under abutting beams and is welded to steel plates bolted to column. U-plate may also be welded directly to steel pipe column support where applicable.

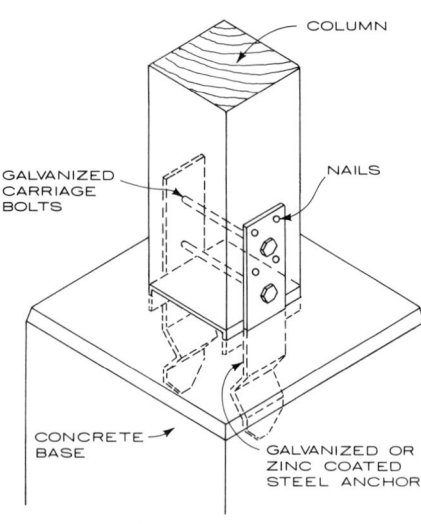

WET POST ANCHORAGE TO CONCRETE BASE

This detail is recommended for heavy duty use where moisture protection is desired. Anchor is set and leveled in wet concrete after screeding.

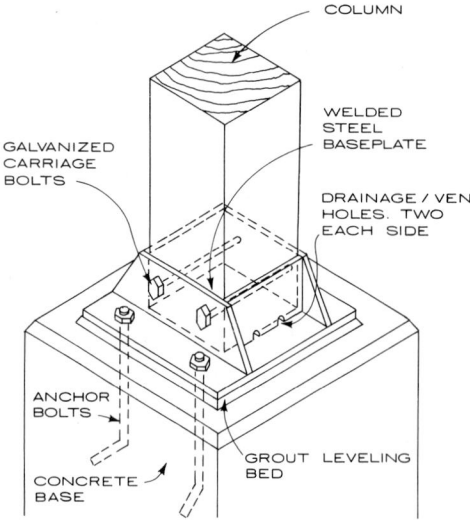

WOOD COLUMN ANCHORED WITH STEEL BASEPLATE

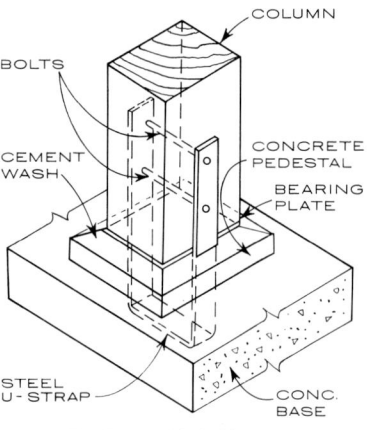

U-STRAP COLUMN ANCHORAGE TO CONCRETE BASE

This detail is recommended for industrial buildings and warehouses to resist both horizontal forces and uplift. Moisture barrier is recommended. It may be used with shear plates.

Douglas W. Brewer, AIA; Brown and Page Architects; Alexandria, Virginia

HEAVY TIMBER

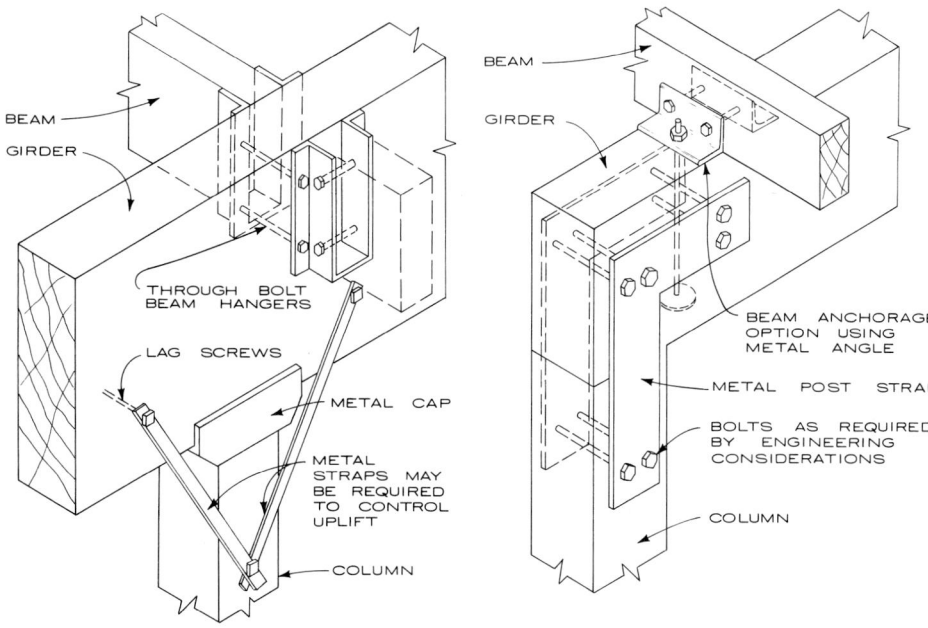

WOOD COLUMN, GIRDER, AND BEAM

- BEAM
- GIRDER
- THROUGH BOLT BEAM HANGERS
- LAG SCREWS
- METAL CAP
- METAL STRAPS MAY BE REQUIRED TO CONTROL UPLIFT
- COLUMN

GIRDER TO COLUMN CONNECTION

- BEAM
- GIRDER
- BEAM ANCHORAGE OPTION USING METAL ANGLE
- METAL POST STRAP
- BOLTS AS REQUIRED BY ENGINEERING CONSIDERATIONS
- COLUMN

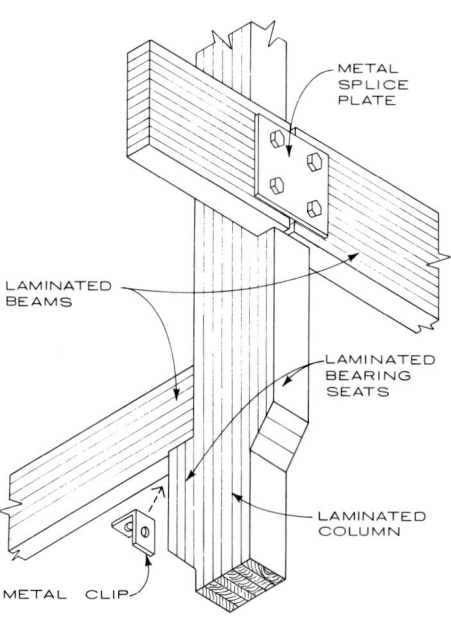

LAMINATED COLUMN WITH INTEGRALLY LAMINATED BEARING SEATS

- METAL SPLICE PLATE
- LAMINATED BEAMS
- LAMINATED BEARING SEATS
- LAMINATED COLUMN
- METAL CLIP

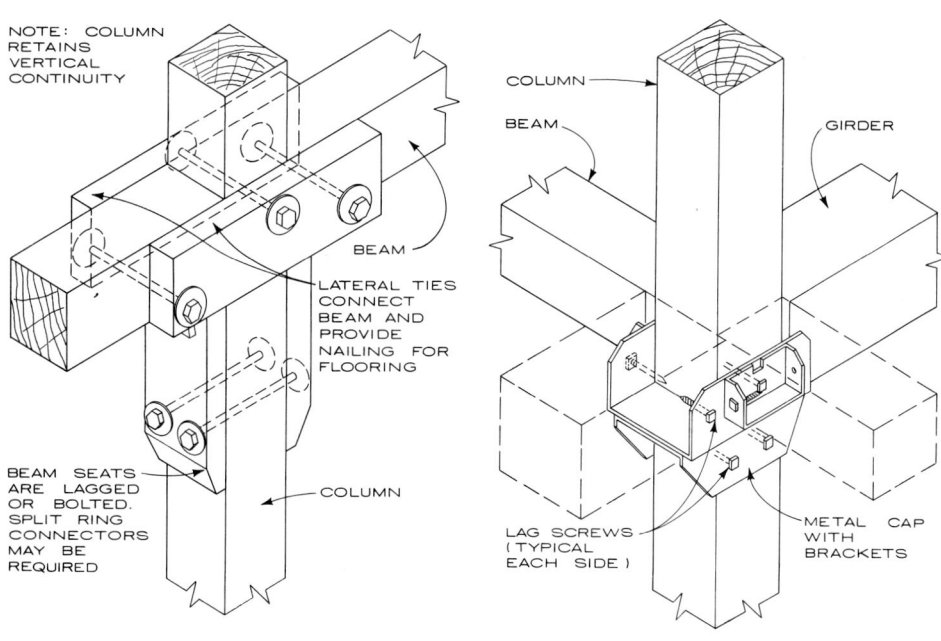

FLOOR BEAM FRAMING AT COLUMN

- NOTE: COLUMN RETAINS VERTICAL CONTINUITY
- BEAM
- LATERAL TIES CONNECT BEAM AND PROVIDE NAILING FOR FLOORING
- BEAM SEATS ARE LAGGED OR BOLTED. SPLIT RING CONNECTORS MAY BE REQUIRED
- COLUMN

METAL COLUMN CAP WITH BEAM SEATS

- COLUMN
- BEAM
- GIRDER
- LAG SCREWS (TYPICAL EACH SIDE)
- METAL CAP WITH BRACKETS

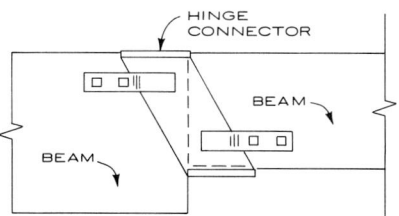

HINGE CONNECTOR

- HINGE CONNECTOR
- BEAM
- BEAM

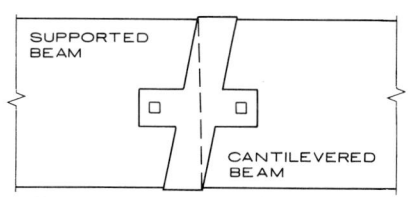

WELDED STEEL PLATE SPLICE

- SUPPORTED BEAM
- CANTILEVERED BEAM

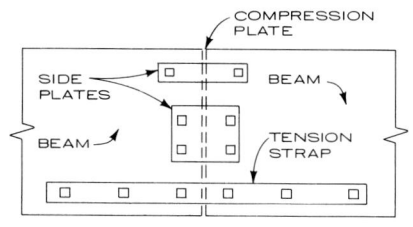

MOMENT SPLICING

- COMPRESSION PLATE
- SIDE PLATES
- BEAM
- BEAM
- TENSION STRAP

BEAM SPLICING

MOMENT SPLICE: Compression stress is taken in bearing on the wood through a steel compression plate. Tension is taken across the splice by means of steel straps and sheer plates. Side plates and straps are used to hold sides and tops of members in position. Shear is taken by shear plates in end grain. Bolts and shear plates are used as design and construction considerations require.

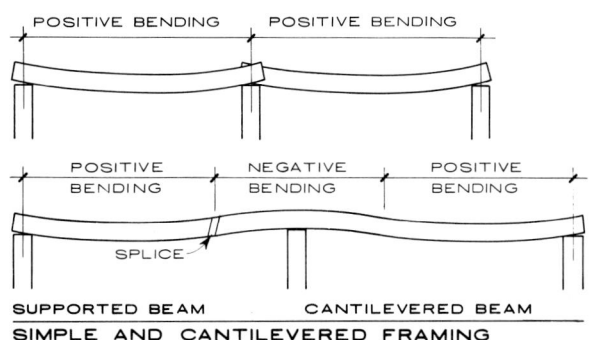

- POSITIVE BENDING
- POSITIVE BENDING
- POSITIVE BENDING
- NEGATIVE BENDING
- POSITIVE BENDING
- SPLICE
- SUPPORTED BEAM
- CANTILEVERED BEAM

SIMPLE AND CANTILEVERED FRAMING

SIMPLE FRAMING: This illustration shows the "positive" or downward bending that occurs in conventional framing with simple spans.

CANTILEVERED FRAMING: This illustration shows the combination of "positive" (downward) and "negative" (upward) bending that occurs with beams spliced at quarterpoint producing supported beam and cantilevered beam. The two types of bending counterbalance each other, which produces more uniform stresses and uses material more efficiently. In-line joists simplify plywood subflooring.

Joseph A. Wilkes, FAIA; Wilkes and Faulkner; Washington, D.C.

HEAVY TIMBER

STRUCTURAL GLUED LAMINATED TIMBER

The term "structural glued laminated timber" refers to an engineered, stress rated product of a timber laminating plant, comprising assemblies of suitably selected and prepared wood laminations securely bonded together with adhesives. The grain of all laminations is approximately parallel longitudinally. Laminations may be comprised of pieces end joined to form any length, of pieces placed or glued edge to edge to make wider ones, or of pieces bent to curved form during gluing.

STANDARD DEPTHS

Dimension lumber, surfaced to 1 1/2 in. (38 mm), is normally used to laminate straight members and those curved members that have radii of curvature within the bending radius limitations for the species. Boards, surfaced to 3/4 in. (19 mm), are recommended for laminating curved members when the bending radius is too short to permit the use of dimension lumber, provided that the bending radius limitations for the species are observed. Other lamination thicknesses may be used to meet special requirements.

STANDARD WIDTHS

Nominal width	in.	3	4	6	8	10	12	14	16
Net finished width	in.	2 1/4	3 1/8	5 1/8	6 3/4	8 3/4	10 3/4	12 1/4	14 1/4
	mm	57	79	130	171	222	273	311	362

CAMBER

Camber is curvature (circular or parabolic) fabricated into structural glued laminated beams opposite to the anticipated deflection movement. The recommended minimum camber is on the order of one and one half times dead load deflection which, after plastic deformation has taken place, will usually produce a near level floor or roof beam under dead load conditions. Additional camber or slope should be provided to ensure proper drainage at roof beams. On level roof beams of long span and floor beams of multistory buildings it may be desirable to provide additional camber to counter the optical illusion that the beam sags.

FIRE SAFETY

The self-insulating qualities of heavy timber sizes create a slow burning characteristic. Good structural details, elimination of concealed spaces, and use of fire stops to interfere with passage of flames up or across a structure contribute to the fire performance of heavy timber construction in fire. While timber will burn, it retains its strength under fire longer than unprotected metals, which lose their strength quickly under extreme heat.

Building codes generally exempt heavy timber framing from interior finish requirements for preventing flame spread.

Fire retardant treatments may be applied to glued laminated timber but they do not substantially increase the fire resistance of heavy timber construction. When fire retardant treatments are used, the reduction of strength as related to type and penetration of treatment, the compatibility of treatment and adhesive, the use of special gluing procedures, difficulty of application, and the effect on wood color as well as on fabricating procedures should be investigated.

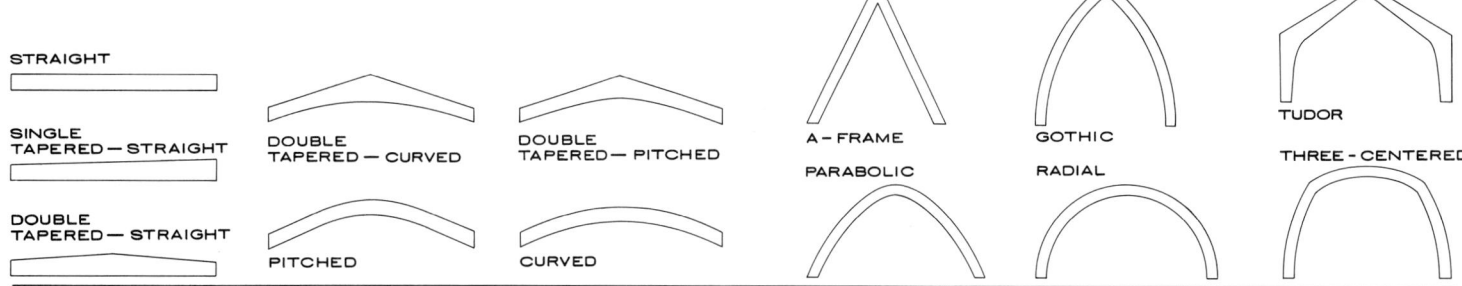

STRUCTURAL GLUED LAMINATED TIMBER SHAPES

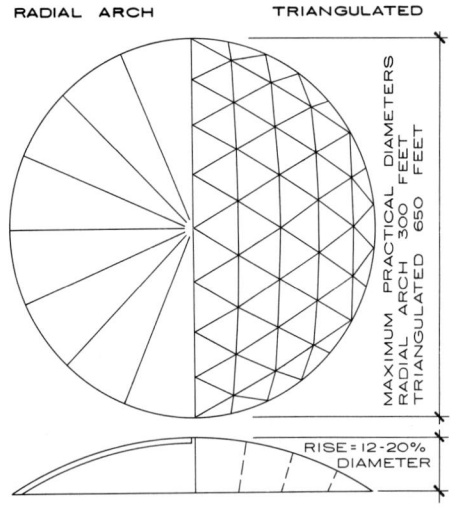

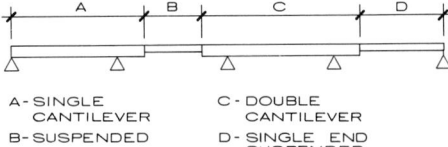

A - SINGLE CANTILEVER
B - SUSPENDED
C - DOUBLE CANTILEVER
D - SINGLE END SUSPENDED

NOTES ON SHAPES

1. Beam names describe top and bottom surfaces of the beam. "S" designates a sawn or "tapered" surface. Sloped or "pitched" surfaces should be used on the tension side of the beam.
2. More complex shapes may be fabricated. Contact the American Institute of Timber Construction (AITC).

LAMINATED DOME SYSTEMS

The triangulated and the radial arch are the two basic types of structural glued laminated wood dome systems available. Both systems require a tension ring at the dome spring line to convert axial thrusts to vertical loads. Consideration must be given to the perimeter bond beam design since wind forces will produce loads in this member. The length of main members of the radial arch system, which must span a distance greater than half the dome diameter, limit the maximum practical dome diameter. The far smaller members of the triangulated dome result in the greater diameters. The triangulated system can be designed for five or more segments with an equal number of peripheral supports at each segment.

CANTILEVERED AND CONTINUOUS SPAN SYSTEMS

Cantilever beam systems may be comprised of any of the various types and combinations of beams shown above. Cantilever systems generally permit longer spans or larger loads per a given size member than do simple span systems. Substantial design economies can be effected by decreasing the depths of the members in the suspended portions of a cantilever system. For economy the negative bending moment at the support of a cantilevered beam should be equal in magnitude to the positive moment.

Continuous span beams are commonly used in both building and bridge construction to reduce maximum moments, thus reducing section size required.

ALLOWABLE UNIT STRESS RANGES FOR STRUCTURAL GLUED LAMINATED TIMBER—NORMAL DURATION OF LOADING

SPECIES	EXTREME FIBER IN BENDING, F_b (PSI)	TENSION PARALLEL TO GRAIN, F_t (PSI)	COMPRESSION PARALLEL TO GRAIN, F_c (PSI)	HORIZONTAL SHEAR F_v (PSI)	COMPRESSION PERPENDICULAR TO GRAIN, $F_{c\perp}$ (PSI)	MODULUS OF ELASTICITY, E (MILLION PSI)
DRY CONDITIONS OF USE = MOISTURE CONTENT IN SERVICE LESS THAN 16%						
Douglas fir and larch	1600 to 2600	900 to 1100	1500	165	385 to 450	1.6 to 1.8
Hem-fir	1800 to 2400	900	1250	155	245	1.6 to 1.7
Southern pine	1600 to 2600	800 to 1100	700 to 1500	140 to 200	385 to 450	1.5 to 1.8
California redwood	1600 to 2200	1100 to 1200	1600 to 2000	125	325	1.4
WET CONDITIONS OF USE = MOISTURE CONTENT IN SERVICE 16% OR MORE (REQUIRES WET USE ADHESIVES)						
Douglas fir and larch	1280 to 2080	720 to 880	1100	145	260 to 300	1.3 to 1.5
Hem-fir	1440 to 1920	720	910	135	165	1.3 to 1.4
Southern pine	1280 to 2080	640 to 880	510 to 1100	125 to 175	260 to 300	1.25 to 1.5
California redwood	1280 to 1760	880 to 960	1170 to 1460	110	220	1.2

The Hodne/Stageberg Partners, Inc.; Minneapolis, Minnesota

APPEARANCE GRADES

Structural glued laminated timber is produced in three appearance grades:

1. INDUSTRIAL: For use where appearance is not a primary concern.
2. ARCHITECTURAL: For use where appearance is a factor.
3. PREMIUM: For uses that demand the finest appearance.

These appearance grades do not modify design stresses, fabrication controls, grades of lumber used, or other provisions of the applicable standards. Descriptions of the three grades follow. A textured ("rough sawn") surface may be called for instead of the surfacing described. In all grades laminations will possess the natural growth characteristics of the lumber grade.

INDUSTRIAL APPEARANCE GRADE

Void filling is not required. The wide face of laminations exposed to view will be free of loose knots and open knot holes. Edge joints will not be filled. Members will be surfaced two sides only, an occasional miss being permitted along individual laminations.

ARCHITECTURAL APPEARANCE GRADE

In exposed surfaces, knot holes and other voids measuring over 3/4 in. (19 mm) will be replaced with clear wood inserts or a neutral colored filler. Inserts will be selected with reasonable care for similarity of the grain and color to the adjacent wood in the lamination. The wide face of laminations exposed to view will be free of loose knots and open knot holes. The material will be selected with reasonable care for similarity of the grain and color of laminations at end and edge joints. Voids greater than 1/16 in. (2 mm) wide in edge joints appearing on the wide face of laminations exposed to view will be filled. When an opaque finish is specified, requirements for similarity of grain and color will be disregarded, exposed faces will be surfaced smooth. Misses are not permitted. The corners on the wide face of laminations exposed to view will be eased. Current practice for eased edges is for a radius between 1/8 in. (3 mm) and 1/2 in. (13 mm).

PREMIUM APPEARANCE GRADE

Similar to Architectural Grade except that in exposed surfaces, all knot holes and other voids will be replaced with wood inserts or a neutral colored filler as de-scribed for Architectural Grade. In addition, knots will be limited in size to 20% of the net face width of the lamination, with not over two maximum size knots occurring in a 6 ft (1.8 m) length of the exposed wide face of the laminations.

FINISHES

Available finishes for glued laminated timber include sealers, stains and paints.

End sealers retard moisture transmission and minimize checking and are normally applied to the ends of all members.

Surface sealers increase resistance to soiling, control grain raising, minimize checking, and serve as a moisture retardant. They fall within two classifications. Penetrating sealers provide limited protection and are suitable for use when final finish requires staining or a natural finish. Primer and sealer coats provide maximum protection by sealing the surface of the wood, but should not be specified when the final finish requires a natural or stained finish. Wood color is modified by any sealer application. Wood sealers followed by staining will look different from stained untreated wood.

GLUED LAMINATED COLUMNS

Structural glued laminated timber columns offer higher allowable stresses, controlled appearance, and the ability to fabricate variable sections.

For simple rectangular columns, the "slenderness ratio," or the ratio of the unsupported length between points of lateral support to the least column dimension, may not exceed 50.

The least dimension for tapered columns is taken as the sum of the smaller dimension and one-third the difference between the smaller and greater dimensions.

Spaced columns consist of two or more members with their longitudinal axes parallel, separated at the ends and at the midpoint by blocking, and joined at the ends by shear fastenings. The members are considered to act together to carry the total column load, and because of the end fixity developed, a greater slenderness ratio than that allowed for solid columns is permitted.

NOTES ON BEAM DESIGN CHART

1. Total load carrying capacity includes beam weight. Floor beams are designed for uniform loads of 40 psf live load and 10 psf dead load.
2. Allowable stresses: F_b = 2400 psi (reduced by size factor), F_v = 165 psi, E = 1,800,000 psi.
3. Deflection limits = roof = 1/180, floor = 1/360.
4. Values are for preliminary design purposes only. For more complete information see the AITC "Timber Construction Manual."

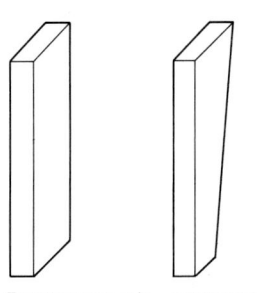 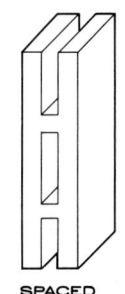

RECTANGULAR   TAPERED   SPACED

LAMINATED FLOOR, ROOF BEAM, AND PURLIN DESIGN CHART—
TYPICAL SINGLE SPAN SIMPLY SUPPORTED GLUED LAMINATED BEAMS (MEMBER SIZES IN INCHES)

| SPAN (FT) | SPACING (FT) | TOTAL LOAD CARRYING CAPACITY (PSF) | | | | | | FLOOR BEAMS |
		30 PSF	35 PSF	40 PSF	45 PSF	50 PSF	55 PSF	50 PSF
12	6	3¹/₈ x 6	3¹/₈ x 6	3¹/₈ x 7¹/₂	3¹/₈ x 7¹/₂	3¹/₈ x 7¹/₂	3¹/₈ x 7¹/₂	3¹/₈ x 9
	8	3¹/₈ x 6	3¹/₈ x 7¹/₂	3¹/₈ x 9	3¹/₈ x 9	3¹/₈ x 9	3¹/₈ x 9	3¹/₈ x 10¹/₂
	10	3¹/₈ x 7¹/₂	3¹/₈ x 7¹/₂	3¹/₈ x 9	3¹/₈ x 9	3¹/₈ x 9	3¹/₈ x 10¹/₂	3¹/₈ x 10¹/₂
	12	3¹/₈ x 7¹/₂	3¹/₈ x 9	3¹/₈ x 9	3¹/₈ x 9	3¹/₈ x 10¹/₂	3¹/₈ x 10¹/₂	3¹/₈ x 12
16	8	3¹/₈ x 9	3¹/₈ x 9	3¹/₈ x 10¹/₂	3¹/₈ x 10¹/₂	3¹/₈ x 12	3¹/₈ x 12	3¹/₈ x 13¹/₂
	12	3¹/₈ x 10¹/₂	3¹/₈ x 12	3¹/₈ x 12	3¹/₈ x 12	3¹/₈ x 13¹/₂	3¹/₈ x 13¹/₂	3¹/₈ x 15
	14	3¹/₈ x 12	3¹/₈ x 12	3¹/₈ x 13¹/₂	3¹/₈ x 13¹/₂	3¹/₈ x 15	3¹/₈ x 15	3¹/₈ x 15
	16	3¹/₈ x 12	3¹/₈ x 13¹/₂	3¹/₈ x 13¹/₂	3¹/₈ x 15	3¹/₈ x 15	3¹/₈ x 16¹/₂	3¹/₈ x 15
20	8	3¹/₈ x 12	3¹/₈ x 12	3¹/₈ x 13¹/₂	3¹/₈ x 13¹/₂	3¹/₈ x 13¹/₂	3¹/₈ x 15	3¹/₈ x 16¹/₂
	12	3¹/₈ x 13¹/₂	3¹/₈ x 13¹/₂	3¹/₈ x 15	3¹/₈ x 16¹/₂	3¹/₈ x 16¹/₂	5¹/₈ x 13¹/₂	5¹/₈ x 15
	16	3¹/₈ x 15	3¹/₈ x 16¹/₂	3¹/₈ x 18	3¹/₈ x 18	5¹/₈ x 15	5¹/₈ x 16¹/₂	5¹/₈ x 18
	20	3¹/₈ x 16	3¹/₈ x 18	5¹/₈ x 15	5¹/₈ x 16¹/₂	5¹/₈ x 16¹/₂	5¹/₈ x 18	5¹/₈ x 18
24	8	3¹/₈ x 13¹/₂	3¹/₈ x 15	3¹/₈ x 15	3¹/₈ x 16¹/₂	3¹/₈ x 16¹/₂	3¹/₈ x 18	5¹/₈ x 19¹/₂
	12	3¹/₈ x 16¹/₂	3¹/₈ x 16¹/₂	3¹/₈ x 18	5¹/₈ x 15	5¹/₈ x 16¹/₂	5¹/₈ x 16¹/₂	5¹/₈ x 21
	16	3¹/₈ x 18	5¹/₈ x 16¹/₂	5¹/₈ x 16¹/₂	5¹/₈ x 18	5¹/₈ x 18	5¹/₈ x 19¹/₂	5¹/₈ x 24
	20	5¹/₈ x 16¹/₂	5¹/₈ x 16¹/₂	5¹/₈ x 18	5¹/₈ x 19¹/₂	5¹/₈ x 19¹/₂	5¹/₈ x 21	5¹/₈ x 25¹/₂
28	8	3¹/₈ x 16¹/₂	3¹/₈ x 16¹/₂	3¹/₈ x 18	3¹/₈ x 18	5¹/₈ x 16¹/₂	5¹/₈ x 16¹/₂	5¹/₈ x 19¹/₂
	12	3¹/₈ x 18	5¹/₈ x 16¹/₂	5¹/₈ x 18	5¹/₈ x 18	5¹/₈ x 18	5¹/₈ x 19¹/₂	5¹/₈ x 21
	16	5¹/₈ x 18	5¹/₈ x 18	5¹/₈ x 19¹/₂	5¹/₈ x 19¹/₂	5¹/₈ x 21	5¹/₈ x 22¹/₂	5¹/₈ x 24
	20	5¹/₈ x 18	5¹/₈ x 19¹/₂	5¹/₈ x 21	5¹/₈ x 22¹/₂	5¹/₈ x 24	5¹/₈ x 25¹/₂	5¹/₈ x 25¹/₂
32	8	3¹/₈ x 18	5¹/₈ x 16¹/₂	5¹/₈ x 18	5¹/₈ x 18	5¹/₈ x 18	5¹/₈ x 19¹/₂	5¹/₈ x 21
	12	5¹/₈ x 18	5¹/₈ x 19¹/₂	5¹/₈ x 19¹/₂	5¹/₈ x 21	5¹/₈ x 21	5¹/₈ x 22¹/₂	5¹/₈ x 24
	16	5¹/₈ x 19¹/₂	5¹/₈ x 21	5¹/₈ x 22¹/₂	5¹/₈ x 22¹/₂	5¹/₈ x 24	5¹/₈ x 25¹/₂	5¹/₈ x 27
	20	5¹/₈ x 21	5¹/₈ x 22¹/₂	5¹/₈ x 24	5¹/₈ x 25¹/₂	5¹/₈ x 27	5¹/₈ x 28¹/₂	6³/₄ x 27
40	12	5¹/₈ x 22¹/₂	5¹/₈ x 24	5¹/₈ x 24	5¹/₈ x 25¹/₂	5¹/₈ x 27	6³/₄ x 25¹/₂	6³/₄ x 28¹/₂
	16	5¹/₈ x 24	5¹/₈ x 25¹/₂	5¹/₈ x 27	5¹/₈ x 28¹/₂	6³/₄ x 27	6³/₄ x 28¹/₂	6³/₄ x 31¹/₂
	20	5¹/₈ x 27	5¹/₈ x 28¹/₂	5¹/₈ x 27	6³/₄ x 28¹/₂	6³/₄ x 30	6³/₄ x 31¹/₂	6³/₄ x 33
	24	5¹/₈ x 28¹/₂	6³/₄ x 27	6³/₄ x 28¹/₂	6³/₄ x 31¹/₂	6³/₄ x 33	6³/₄ x 34¹/₂	6³/₄ x 36
48	12	5¹/₈ x 27	5¹/₈ x 28¹/₂	5¹/₈ x 30	5¹/₈ x 30	6³/₄ x 28¹/₂	6³/₄ x 30	6³/₄ x 33
	16	5¹/₈ x 30	6³/₄ x 28¹/₂	6³/₄ x 30	6³/₄ x 30	6³/₄ x 31¹/₂	6³/₄ x 34¹/₂	6³/₄ x 37¹/₂
	20	6³/₄ x 28¹/₂	6³/₄ x 30	6³/₄ x 31¹/₂	6³/₄ x 34¹/₂	6³/₄ x 36	6³/₄ x 36	8³/₄ x 36
	24	6³/₄ x 30	6³/₄ x 33	6³/₄ x 34¹/₂	6³/₄ x 37¹/₂	6³/₄ x 39	8³/₄ x 36	8³/₄ x 39
60	12	6³/₄ x 30	6³/₄ x 31¹/₂	6³/₄ x 33	6³/₄ x 34¹/₂	6³/₄ x 36	6³/₄ x 37¹/₂	8³/₄ x 39
	16	6³/₄ x 33	6³/₄ x 34¹/₂	6³/₄ x 36	6³/₄ x 39	8³/₄ x 36	8³/₄ x 37¹/₂	8³/₄ x 42
	20	6³/₄ x 36	6³/₄ x 37¹/₂	8³/₄ x 36	8³/₄ x 37¹/₂	8³/₄ x 40¹/₂	8³/₄ x 42	8³/₄ x 45
	24	6³/₄ x 39	8³/₄ x 36	8³/₄ x 39	8³/₄ x 42	8³/₄ x 43¹/₂	8³/₄ x 45	8³/₄ x 48

The Hodne/Stageberg Partners, Inc.; Minneapolis, Minnesota

PATTERNED

EXTRA THICK

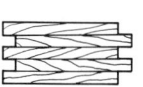
DOUBLE T & G

GLUE LAMINATED

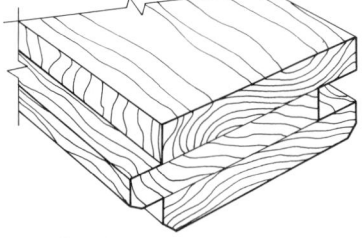

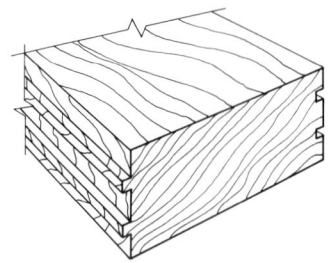

SINGLE T & G

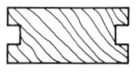
SPLINE

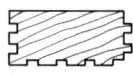
PATTERNED

MACHINE SHAPED

GLUE LAMINATED SIZES

THICKNESS		WIDTH	
NOMINAL	ACTUAL	NOMINAL	ACTUAL
3″	2³/₁₆″, 2¼″	6″ and 8″ are standard	5³/₈″, 7⅛″
3″ super	2⅞″		
5″	2²¹/₃₂″		
	1⅞″	6″, 8″	5³/₈″, 7⅛″
	2¼″	8″	7⅛″
	3″		
	3¾″	6″, 8″	5³/₈″, 7⅛″
	4¼″	6″	5³/₈″

NOTE: Verify sizes with manufacturers.

MACHINE SHAPED SIZES

THICKNESS		WIDTH	
NOMINAL	ACTUAL	NOMINAL	ACTUAL
2″	1½″	6″ std (others available)	5¼″
3″	2½″		
4″	3½″		

NOTES

General availability is decreasing. Check source for the sizes and quantities available in desired species.

WEIGHT AND INSULATION FACTORS
(U FACTOR IN BTU/HR · SQ FT · °F)

SPECIES	NOMINAL THICKNESS	WEIGHT (PSF)	U VALUE
Inland red cedar	3″	4.5	0.24
	3″ thick	5.8	0.20
	5″	7.5	0.15
White fir Idaho white pine	3″	5.0	0.27
	3″ thick	7.3	0.22
	5″	9.5	0.17
Southern yellow pine Douglas fir Larch	3″	6.5	0.30
	3″ thick	8.1	0.25
	5″	10.5	0.20

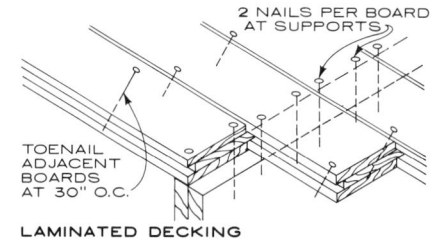

2 NAILS PER BOARD AT SUPPORTS

TOENAIL ADJACENT BOARDS AT 30″ O.C.

LAMINATED DECKING

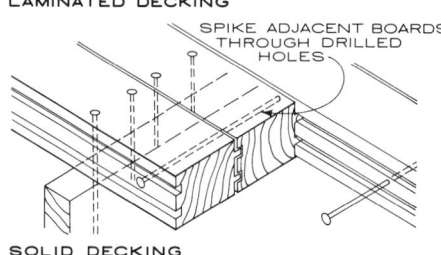

SPIKE ADJACENT BOARDS THROUGH DRILLED HOLES

SOLID DECKING

FASTENING

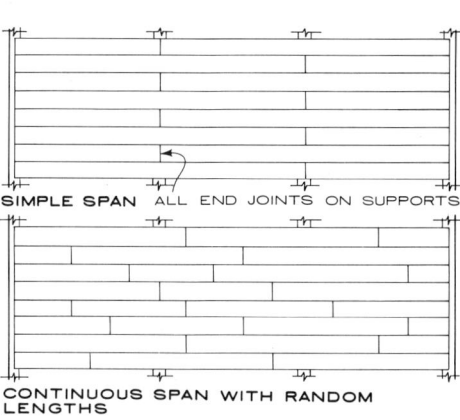

SIMPLE SPAN ALL END JOINTS ON SUPPORTS

CONTINUOUS SPAN WITH RANDOM LENGTHS

NOTES

Use of random lengths reduces waste. The deck must be continuous over at least three spans (four supports). End joint requirements are critical; consult deck manufacturers.

LAMINATED DECK—ALLOWABLE UNIFORMLY DISTRIBUTED TOTAL LOADS GOVERNED BY DEFLECTION

			INLAND RED CEDAR E = 1.2 (INLAND RED CEDAR FACE AND BACK) F = 1590						INLAND RED CEDAR E = 1.3 (IDAHO WHITE PINE OR WHITE FIR BACK) F = 1590						IDAHO WHITE PINE E = 1.2 INLAND WHITE FIR E = 1.2 F = 1850						DOUGLAS FIR/LARCH E = 1.8 SOUTHERN PINE E = 2640					
			SIMPLE SPAN			CONTINUOUS SPAN WITH RANDOM LENGTHS			SIMPLE SPAN			CONTINUOUS SPAN WITH RANDOM LENGTHS			SIMPLE SPAN			CONTINUOUS SPAN WITH RANDOM LENGTHS			SIMPLE SPAN			CONTINUOUS SPAN WITH RANDOM LENGTHS		
DEFLECTION			¹/₁₈₀	¹/₂₄₀	¹/₃₆₀	¹/₁₈₀	¹/₂₄₀	¹/₃₆₀	¹/₁₈₀	¹/₂₄₀	¹/₃₆₀	¹/₁₈₀	¹/₂₄₀	¹/₃₆₀	¹/₁₈₀	¹/₂₄₀	¹/₃₆₀	¹/₁₈₀	¹/₂₄₀	¹/₃₆₀	¹/₁₈₀	¹/₂₄₀	¹/₃₆₀	¹/₁₈₀	¹/₂₄₀	¹/₃₆₀
DECK THICKNESS		SPAN (FT)	PSF	PSF	PSF	PSF	PSF	PSF	PSF	PSF	PSF	PSF	PSF	PSF	PSF	PSF	PSF	PSF	PSF	PSF	PSF	PSF	PSF	PSF	PSF	PSF
NOMINAL	ACTUAL																									
3″	2¼″ 2³/₁₆″	8	71	53	35	121	91	60	76	57	38	129	98	64	89	67	44	150	113	75	115	86	57	195	146	97
		9	50	38	25	85	64	42	54	41	27	92	69	46	63	47	31	106	79	53	81	61	40	137	103	68
		10	37	27	18	62	46	31	40	29	20	67	49	33	46	34	23	77	58	38	59	44	29	100	75	50
		11	27	21	13	46	35	23	29	22	14	49	37	24	34	26	17	58	44	29	44	33	22	75	56	37
		12	21	16	10	36	27	18	22	17	11	39	29	19	26	20	13	45	34	22	34	26	17	58	43	29
		13	17	12	8	28	21	14	18	13	9	30	22	15	21	16	10	35	26	17	27	20	13	45	34	22
3″	2⅞″ 2⅞″	13	39	29	19	65	49	32	43	33	21	73	54	36	48	36	24	82	61	41	58	43	29	98	73	49
		14	31	23	15	52	39	26	34	26	17	58	44	29	39	29	19	65	49	32	47	34	23	78	59	39
		15	25	18	12	42	32	21	28	20	14	48	35	24	32	24	16	53	40	26	38	28	19	63	48	31
		16	20	16	10	35	26	17	23	18	11	39	29	19	26	19	13	44	33	22	31	23	15	53	40	26
		17	17	13	8	29	22	14	20	14	10	33	24	16	21	16	10	37	28	18	26	19	13	44	33	22
5″	3²¹/₃₂″ 3²¹/₃₂″	16	42	32	21	71	53	35	46	34	23	77	58	38	53	39	26	89	67	44	63	47	31	107	80	53
		17	35	26	17	59	45	29	38	29	19	64	48	32	44	33	22	74	56	37	53	40	26	89	67	44
		18	30	22	15	50	38	25	32	24	16	54	41	27	37	28	18	63	47	31	44	33	22	75	56	37
		19	25	19	12	43	32	21	27	20	13	46	35	23	31	24	15	53	40	26	38	28	19	64	48	32
		20	22	16	11	37	27	18	23	18	11	40	30	20	27	20	13	46	34	23	32	24	16	55	41	27
		21	19	14	9	32	24	16	20	15	10	34	26	17	23	17	11	39	40	19	28	21	14	47	35	23

NOTES

1. Tabulated loads derived from data provided by the Potlatch Corporation.

2. Numerous other deck thicknesses and wood species are available.

3. Actual deck design should be based on manufacturers' specifications for each deck board type.

Darrel Rippeteau, Architect; Washington, D.C.

FINISH CARPENTRY

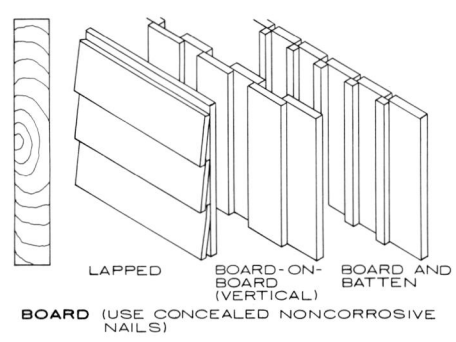

LAPPED   BOARD-ON-BOARD (VERTICAL)   BOARD AND BATTEN

BOARD (USE CONCEALED NONCORROSIVE NAILS)

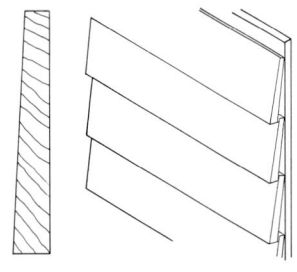

BEVELED BOARD

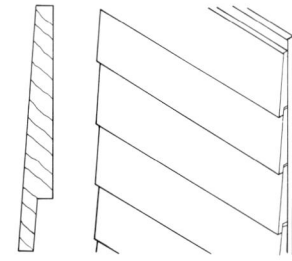

RABBETED BEVELED BOARD

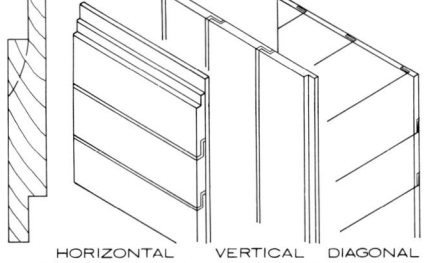

HORIZONTAL   VERTICAL   DIAGONAL

SHIPLAP (USE CONCEALED NONCORROSIVE NAILS)

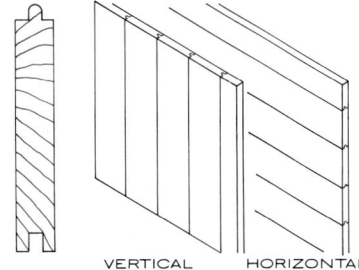

VERTICAL   HORIZONTAL

TONGUE AND GROOVE

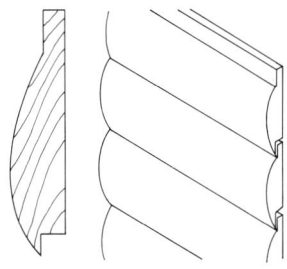

LOG CABIN

SIDING PATTERNS

Numerous additional standard patterns are available, cedar, redwood, spruce, white pine, and various species of West Coast woods. Board thickness typically ranges from ½ to 1½ in. (actual), while width ranges from 2¼ to 11½ in. (actual).

Fastening should be as directed by siding manufacturer. Nail length must be sufficient to accommodate sheathing as well as siding. Nails should be rust resistant, high tensile strength aluminum or galvanized steel. Siding boards may be obtained with smooth face or saw textured face surfaces. Consult individual manufacturers.

Final surface finish may be painted with alkyd, oil base, or latex paints or it may be stained. Stains include those that hide the grain or those that reveal and enhance grain patterns. Water repellents may be used to protect the wood without hiding its natural fresh sawn appearance. Weathering agents can bleach wood to a uniformly aged appearance.

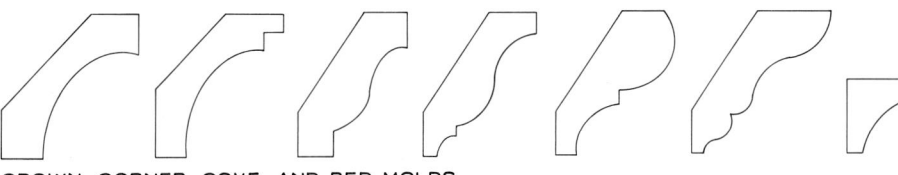

CROWN, CORNER, COVE, AND BED MOLDS

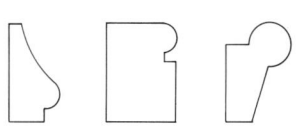

BRICK MOLDS, CAPS, PICTURE MOLDS

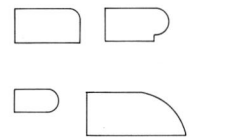

STOPS, NOSINGS   CASING BASES

ROUNDS, HALF ROUNDS, ETC.

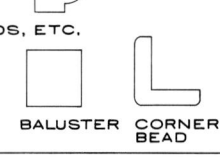

WINDOW STOOL   BASE SHOE   BALUSTER   CORNER BEAD

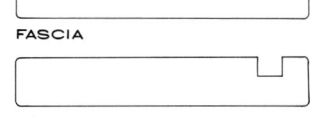

FASCIA

DRIP CAP   PLOWED FASCIA

MOLDING AND TRIM

Numerous patterns and dimensions of trim are produced in a variety of hard and soft woods for interior and exterior use. For a complete line of patterns, sizes, and wood species available, contact lumber associations active in area of use.

Material thickness and panel patterns are major cost factors. Patterns shown here represent only a few of the many shapes available. One pattern is often available in a choice of dimensions.

Custom designs can be economically manufactured if designed with thought to minimum handling, simple cutting, and use of standard finish sizes.

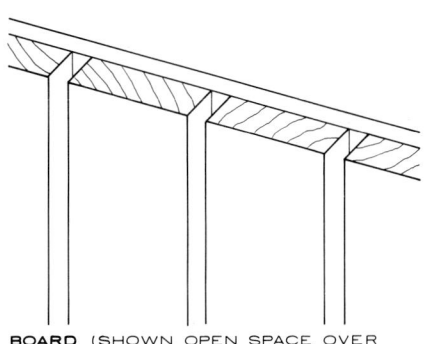

BOARD (SHOWN OPEN SPACE OVER WALLBOARD)

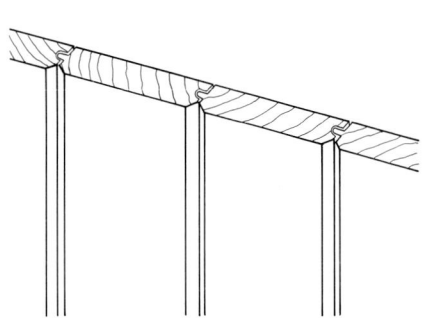

V-JOINTED TONGUE AND GROOVE

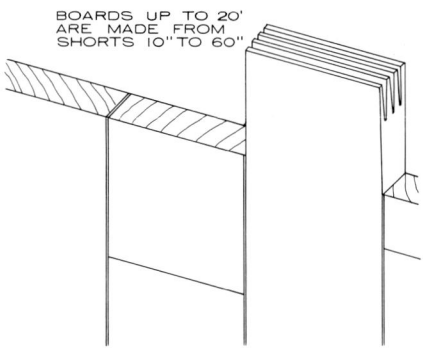

BOARDS UP TO 20' ARE MADE FROM SHORTS 10" TO 60"

FINGER-JOINTED SHORT BOARDS

PANEL PATTERNS

Darrel Rippeteau, Architect; Washington, D.C.

FINISH CARPENTRY 6

GENERAL NOTES

1. Height of handrail 2 ft 6 in. to 2 ft 10 in. Height of railing at landings 3 ft to 3 ft 6 in.

2. Extensions of handrails at top and bottom of stairs may effect total length of required run. Verify with local code.

3. Stringer (10 to 12 in. wide, $^5/_4$ to $^6/_4$ in. thick) to be accurately cut to receive risers, treads, and wedges. Wedges to be glued and driven up tight.

4. Block riser and tread between stringers as shown. Blocks to be glued and screwed in place. Omit blocks when center carriage is used.

5. Stair width: 36 in. minimum. (See local code requirements.)

6. No more than 9 ft vertical between landings.

7. Rise not to exceed 7$^1/_2$ in. and run not to be less than 10 in.

8. See other pages for handicapped requirements.

9. Construction details on this page are for a shop built stair reflecting Architectural Woodwork Institute Premium Grade standards.

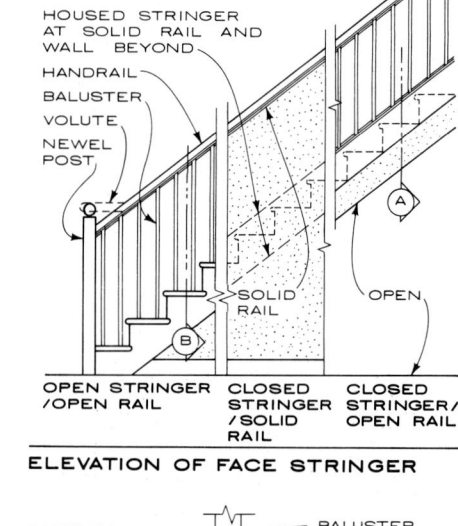

ELEVATION OF FACE STRINGER

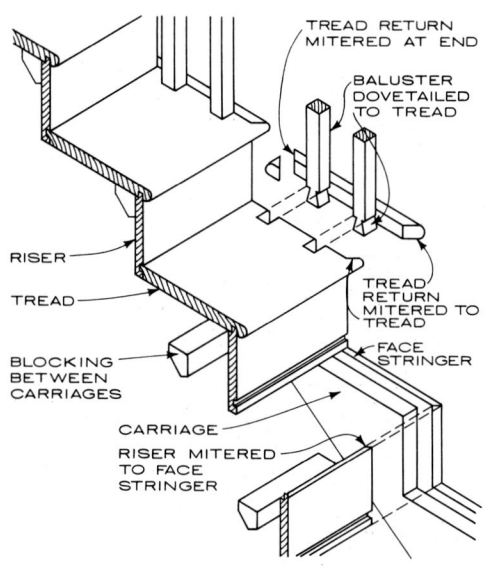

BALUSTERS AND TRIM AT FACE STRINGER

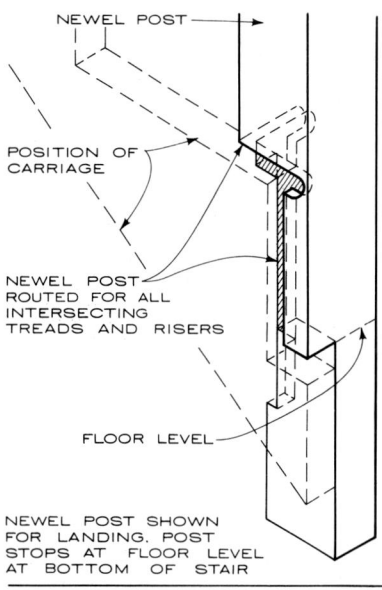

NEWEL POST

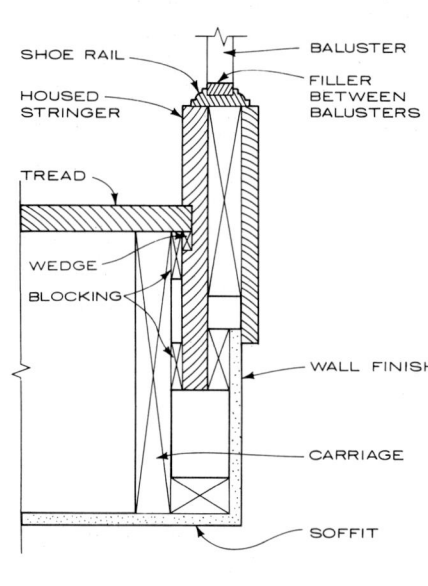

SECTION A

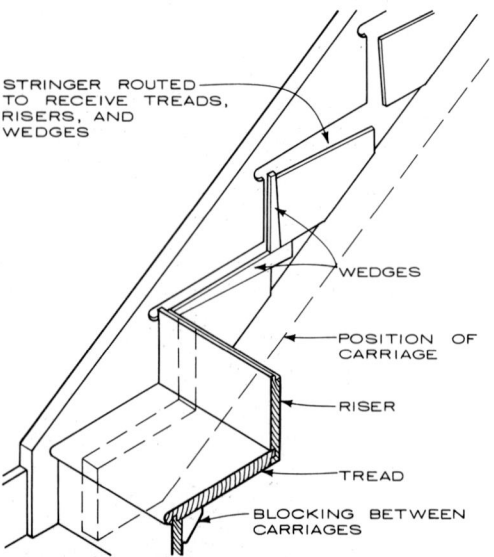

TREADS AND RISERS AT HOUSED STRINGER

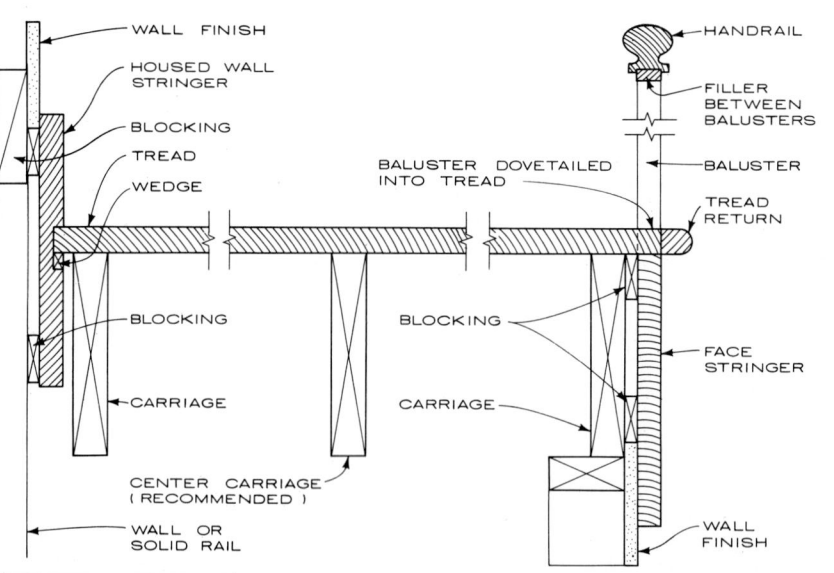

SECTION B

The Bumgardner Partnership/Architects; Seattle, Washington

FINISH CARPENTRY

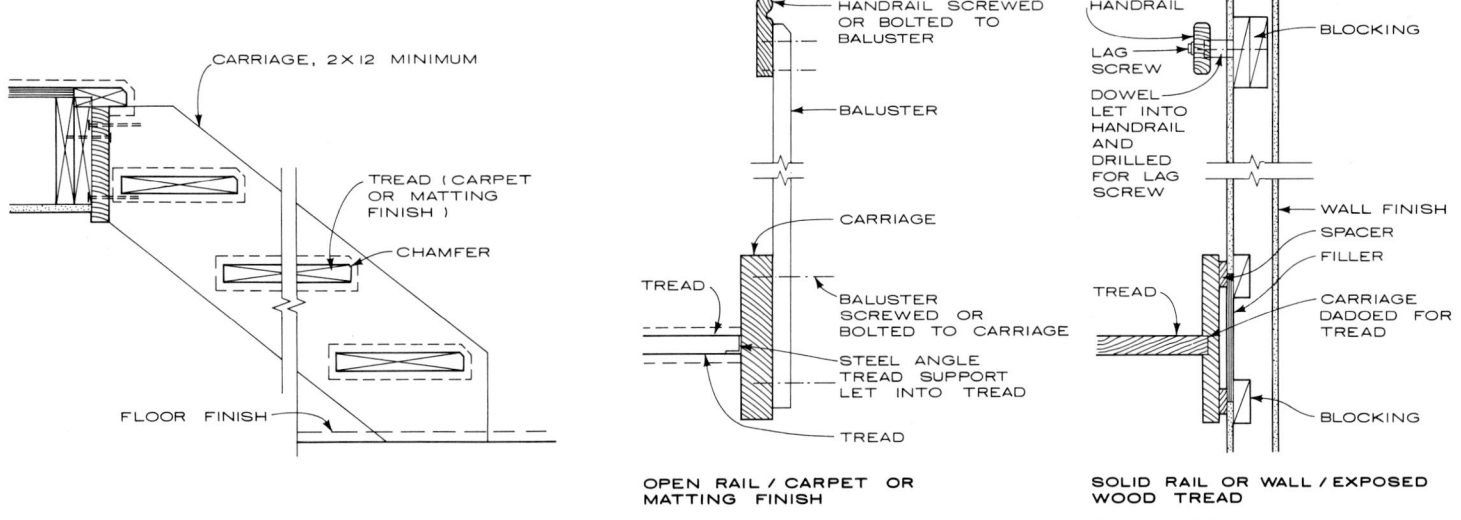

OPEN RAIL / CARPET OR MATTING FINISH

SOLID RAIL OR WALL / EXPOSED WOOD TREAD

OPEN RISER STAIR

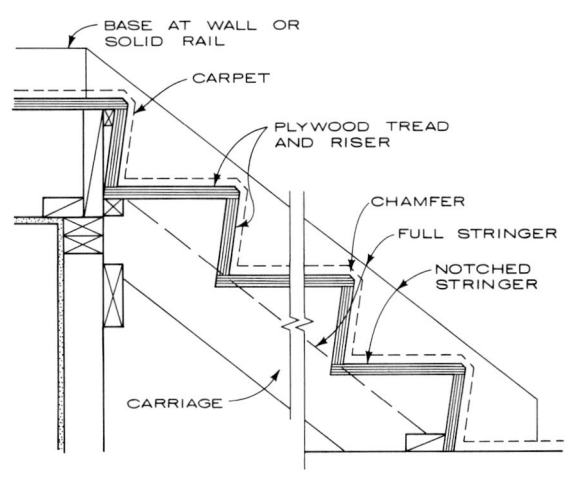

CLOSED RISER STAIR / CARPET FINISH

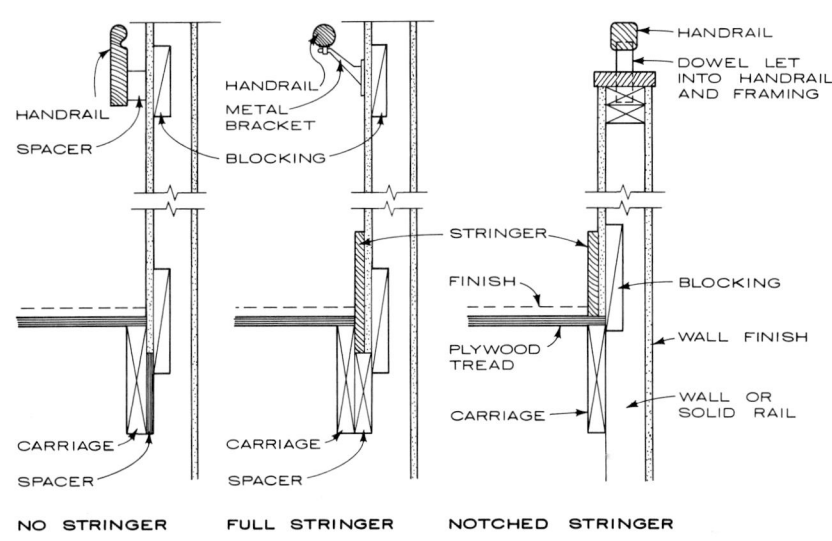

NO STRINGER   FULL STRINGER   NOTCHED STRINGER

CLOSED RISER STAIRS AT WALLS AND SOLID RAILING WALLS

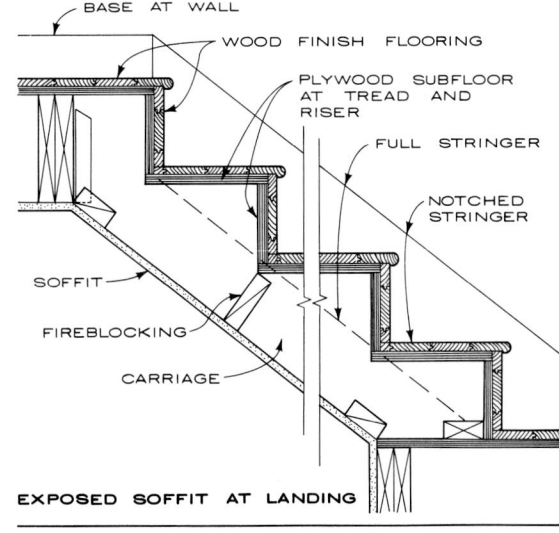

EXPOSED SOFFIT AT LANDING

CLOSED RISER STAIR / WOOD FINISH

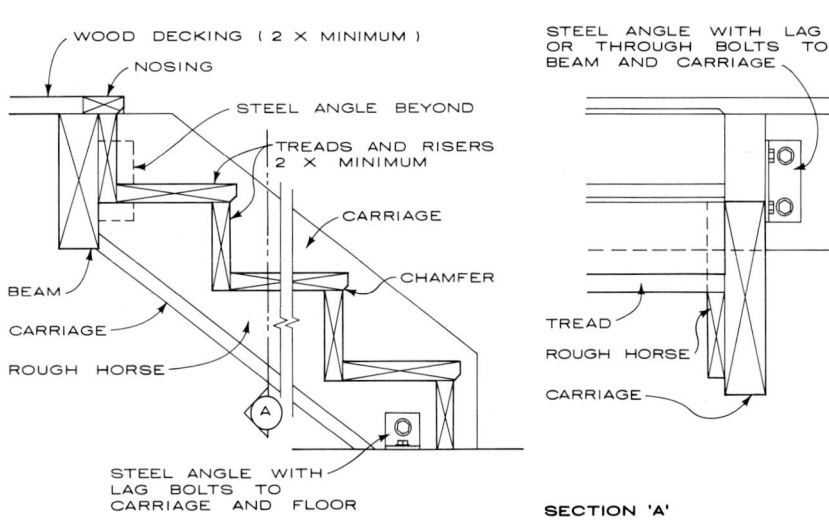

SECTION 'A'

HEAVY TIMBER STAIR

The Bumgardner Partnership/Architects; Seattle, Washington

COMPARATIVE TABLE FOR SELECTION OF WOOD SPECIES—CONSULT WITH THE ARCHITECTURAL WOODWORK INSTITUTE

SPECIES	HARDNESS	PRINCIPAL USES	APPEARANCE			REMARKS
			COLOR	FIGURE	GRAIN	
Ash, white	Hard	Trim, cabinetry	Creamy white to light brown	High	Open	Excellent strength; bold grain
Basswood	Soft	Decorative moldings and carvings	Creamy white	No figure	Closed	Good for moldings; uniform grain
Beech	Hard	Semiexposed cabinet parts	White to reddish brown	Medium	Closed	Good utility hardwood
Birch, yellow-"natural"	Hard	Trim, paneling and cabinetry	White to dark red	Medium	Closed	Excellent architectural wood, plentiful supply
Birch, yellow-"select red" (heartwood)	Hard	Trim, paneling and cabinetry	Dark red	Medium	Closed	Rich color
Birch, yellow-"select white" (sapwood)	Hard	Trim, paneling and cabinetry	Creamy white	Medium	Closed	Uniform appearance
Butternut	Medium	Trim, paneling and cabinetry	Pale brown	High	Open	Beautiful wood
Cedar, western red	Soft	Trim, paneling exterior and interior	Reddish brown to nearly white sapwood	Medium	Closed	Decay resistant; rough texture
Cherry, American black	Hard	Trim, paneling and cabinetry	Reddish brown	High	Closed	Beautiful wood
Chestnut-wormy	Medium	Paneling and trim	Greyish brown	High	Open with wormholes	Very limited supply
Cypress, yellow	Medium	Trim, frames and special siding	Yellowish brown	High	Closed	Subject to regional availability
Fir, Douglas-flat grain	Medium	Trim, frames and paneling	Reddish tan	High	Closed	Good supply
Fir, Douglas-vertical grain	Medium	Trim, frames and paneling	Reddish tan	Low	Closed	Very limited supply
Mahogany, African-plain sawn	Medium	Trim, frames, paneling, and cabinetry	Reddish brown	Medium	Open	Fine hardwood
Mahogany, African-quarter sawn	Medium	Trim, frames, paneling, and cabinetry	Reddish brown	Low	Open	Limited supply
Mahogany, tropical American-"Honduras"	Medium	Trim, frames, paneling, and cabinetry	Rich golden brown	Medium	Open	One of the world's finest cabinet woods
Maple, hard-natural	Very hard	Trim, paneling and cabinetry	White to reddish brown	Medium	Closed	Plentiful supply; excellent properties
Maple, hard-select white (sapwood)	Very hard	Trim, paneling and cabinetry	White	Medium	Closed	Uniform appearance
Maple, soft-natural	Medium	Trim, semiexposed cabinet parts	White to reddish brown	Low	Closed	Good utility hardwood
Oak, English brown	Hard	Veneered paneling and cabinetry	Leathery brown	High	Open	Distinctive appearance; high cost
Oak, red-plain sawn	Hard	Trim, paneling and cabinetry	Reddish tan to brown	High	Open	Excellent architectural wood; plentiful supply
Oak, red-rift sawn	Hard	Trim, paneling and cabinetry	Reddish tan to brown	Low	Open	Closer grain pattern; limited supply
Oak, red-quarter sawn	Hard	Trim, paneling and cabinetry	Reddish tan to brown	Low	Open	Shows flakes; limited supply
Oak, white-plain sawn	Hard	Trim, paneling and cabinetry	Greyish tan	High	Open	Excellent architectural wood; moderate supply
Oak, white-rift sawn	Hard	Trim, paneling and cabinetry	Greyish tan	Low	Open	Close grain pattern; limited supply
Oak, white-quarter sawn	Hard	Trim, paneling and cabinetry	Greyish tan	Low figure accented with flakes	Open	Shows flakes; limited supply
Pecan	Hard	Trim, paneling and cabinetry	Reddish brown with brown stripes	Medium	Open	Subject to regional availability; attractive
Pine, eastern or northern white	Soft	Trim, frames, paneling, and cabinetry	Creamy white to pink	Medium	Closed	True white pine, wide range of applications for general use
Pine, Idaho, sugar	Soft	Trim, frames, paneling, and cabinetry	Creamy white	Low	Closed	True white pine, wide range of applications for general use
Pine, ponderosa	Soft	Trim, frames, paneling, and cabinetry	White to pale yellow	Medium	Closed	Most widely used pine, wide range of application for general use
Pine, southern yellow-shortleaf	Soft	Trim, frames, paneling, and cabinetry	White to pale yellow	High	Closed	Wide range of applications for general use
Poplar, yellow	Medium	Trim, paneling and cabinetry	White to brown with green cast	Medium	Closed	Good utility hardwood; excellent paintability
Redwood, flat grain (heartwood)	Soft	Trim, frames and paneling	Deep red	High	Closed	Superior exterior wood, high natural decay resistance
Redwood, vertical grain (heartwood)	Soft	Trim, frames and paneling	Deep red	Low	Closed	Superior exterior wood, high natural decay resistance
Rosewood, Brazilian	Very hard	Veneered paneling and cabinetry	Mixed reds, browns, and blacks	High	Open	Exotic figure; high cost
Spruce, Sitka	Soft	Trim, frames	Light yellowish tan	High	Closed	Limited general availability

Architectural Woodwork Institute; Arlington, Virginia

 TABLE OF WOOD SPECIES

COMPARATIVE TABLE FOR SELECTION OF WOOD SPECIES—CONSULT WITH THE ARCHITECTURAL WOODWORK INSTITUTE

SPECIES	HARDNESS	PRINCIPAL USES	APPEARANCE			REMARKS
			COLOR	FIGURE	GRAIN	
Teak	Hard	Trim, paneling and cabinetry	Tawny yellow to dark brown	High	Open	Outstanding wood for decorative applications; high cost
Walnut, American black	Hard	Trim, paneling and cabinetry	Chocolate brown	High	Open	Fine domestic hardwood; extremely limited width/length; readily available veneer
Zebrawood, African-quarter sawn	Hard	Trim, paneling and cabinetry	Light gold color/streaked and dark brown to black	High	Closed	Highly decorative

COMPARATIVE TABLE OF WOOD SPECIES FOR DESIGN CRITERIA—CONSULT WITH THE ARCHITECTURAL WOODWORK INSTITUTE

SPECIES	BOTANICAL NAME	FINISHING		PRACTICAL SIZE LIMITATIONS			AVAILABILITY OF MATCHING PLYWOOD (A)	DIMENSIONAL STABILITY (B)
		PAINT	TRANSPARENT	MAX. PRACTICAL THICKNESS WITHOUT LAMINATION	MAX. PRACTICAL WIDTH	MAX. PRACTICAL LENGTH		
Ash, white	Fraxinus americana	Not normally used	Excellent	1 1/2"	7 1/2"	12'	3	10/64"
Basswood	Tilia, americana	Excellent	Excellent	1 1/2"	7 1/2"	10'	4	10/64"
Beech	Fagus grandifolia	Excellent	Good	1 1/2"	7 1/2"	12'	4	14/64"
Birch, yellow–"natural"	Betula alleghaniensis	Excellent	Good	1 1/2"	7 1/2"	12'	1	12/64"
Birch, yellow–"select red" (heartwood)	Betula alleghaniensis	Not normally used	Excellent	1 1/2"	5 1/2"	11'	2	12/64"
Birch, yellow–"select white" (sapwood)	Betula alleghaniensis	Not normally used	Excellent	1 1/2"	5"	11'	2	12/64"
Butternut	Juglans cinerea	Not normally used	Excellent	1 1/2"	5 1/2"	8'	3	8/64"
Cedar, western red	Thuja plicata	Not normally used	Good	3 1/4"	11"	16'	1 & 3	10/64"
Cherry, American black	Prunus serotina	Not normally used	Excellent	1 1/2"	5 1/2"	7'	2	9/64"
Chestnut–wormy	Castanea dentata	Not normally used	Excellent	3/4"	7 1/2"	10'	4	9/64"
Cypress, yellow	Taxodium distichum	Good	Good	2 1/2"	9 1/2"	16'	4	8/64"
Fir, Douglas–flat grain	Pseudotsuga taxifolia	Fair	Fair	3 1/4"	11"	16'	1	10/64"
Fir, Douglas–vertical grain	Pseudotsuga taxifolia	Good	Good	1 1/2"	11"	16'	4	6/64"
Mahogany, African–plain sawn	Khaya ivorensis	Good	Excellent	2 1/2"	11"	15'	3	7/64"
Mahogany, African–quarter sawn	Khaya ivorensis	Not normally used	Excellent	2 1/2"	7 1/2"	15'	3	5/64"
Mahogany, tropical American– "Honduras"	Sweitenia macrophylla	Not normally used	Excellent	2 1/2"	11"	15'	3	6/64"
Maple, hard–natural	Acer saccharum	Excellent	Good	3 1/2"	9 1/2"	12'	3	12/64"
Maple, hard–select white (sapwood)	Acer saccharum	Not normally used	Excellent	2 1/2"	9 1/2"	12'	3	12/64"
Maple, soft–natural	Acer saccharum	Excellent	Not normally used	3 1/4"	9 1/2"	12'	4	9/64"
Oak, English brown	Quercus robur	Not normally used	Excellent	1 1/2"	5 1/2"	8'	3	
Oak, red–plain sawn	Quercus rubra	Not normally used	Excellent	1 1/2"	7 1/4"	12'	1	11/64"
Oak, red–rift sawn	Quercus rubra	Not normally used	Excellent	1 1/16"	5 1/2"	10'	3	7/64"
Oak, red–quarter sawn	Quercus rubra	Not normally used	Excellent	1 1/6"	5 1/2"	8'	3	7/64"
Oak, white–plain sawn	Quercus alba	Not normally used	Excellent	1 1/2"	5 1/2"	10'	2	11/64"
Oak, white–rift sawn	Quercus alba	Not normally used	Excellent	3/4"	4 1/2"	10'	3	7/64"
Oak, white–quarter sawn	Quercus alba	Not normally used	Excellent	3/4"	4 1/2"	10'	3	7/64"
Pecan	Carya species	Not normally used	Good	1 1/2"	5 1/2"	12'	3	11/64"
Pine, eastern or northern white	Pinus strobus	Good	Good	1 1/2"	9 1/2"	14'	3	8/64"
Pine, Idaho, sugar	Pinus monticola	Good	Good	1 1/2"	9 1/2"	14'	4	8/64"
Pine, ponderosa	Pinus ponderosa	Good	Good	1 1/2"	9 1/2"	16'	3	8/64"
Pine, southern yellow–shortleaf	Pinus echinata	Fair	Good	1 1/2"	7 1/2"	16'	3	10/64"
Poplar, yellow	Liriodendron tulipfera	Excellent	Good	2 1/2"	7 1/2"	12'	3	9/64"
Redwood, flat grain (heartwood)	Sequoia sempervirens	Good	Good	2 1/2"	11"	16'	1 & 3	6/64"
Redwood, vertical grain (heartwood)	Sequoia sempervirens	Excellent	Excellent	2 1/2"	11"	16'	3	3/64"
Rosewood, Brazilian	Dalbergia nigra	Not normally used	Excellent				3	
Spruce, Sitka	Picea sitchensis	Fair	Fair	3 1/4"	9 1/2"	16'	4	10/64"
Teak	Tectona grandis	Not normally used	Excellent	1 1/2"	7 1/2"	10'	2	6/64"
Walnut, American black	Juglans	Not normally used	Excellent	1 1/2"	4 1/2"	6'	1	10/64"
Zebrawood, African-quarter sawn	Brachystegia fleuryana	Not normally used	Excellent	1 1/2"	9"	16'	3	7/64"

(A) Rated from 1 to 4 as follows:

1. Warehouse stock in good quantities and fair assortment of thicknesses and lengths.
2. Warehouse stock in fair quantity but not in thicknesses other than 1/4 and 3/4 in.; or sizes other than 4 x 8 feet.
3. Produced on a special order only.
4. Not generally available.

(B) These figures represent possible width change in a 12 in. board when moisture content is reduced from 10 to 5%. Figures are for plain sawn unless indicated otherwise in species column.

Architectural Woodwork Institute; Arlington, Virginia

TABLE OF WOOD SPECIES ⑥

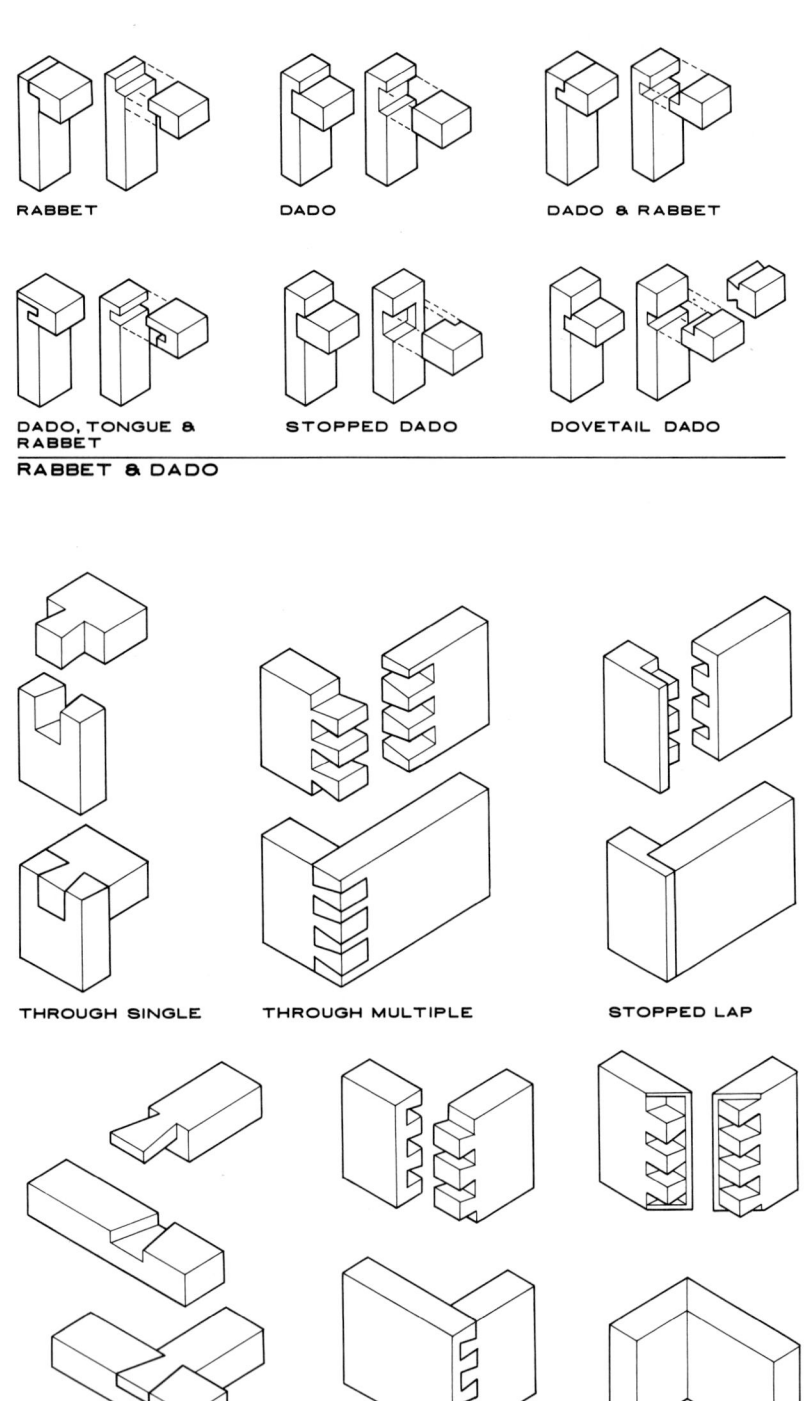

RABBET

DADO

DADO & RABBET

DADO, TONGUE & RABBET

STOPPED DADO

DOVETAIL DADO

RABBET & DADO

THROUGH SINGLE

THROUGH MULTIPLE

STOPPED LAP

HALF LAP

LAP (OR HALF BLIND)

BLIND MITER

DOVETAIL

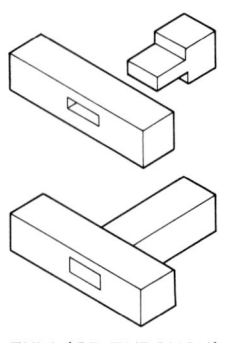

FULL (OR THROUGH)

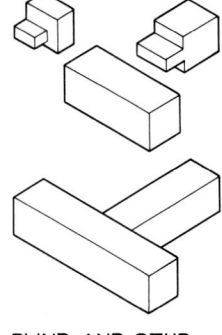

BLIND AND STUB

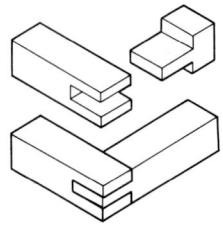

SHIP (OR OPEN)

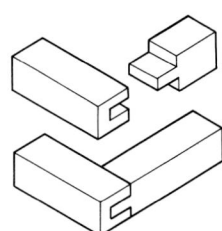

HALF BLIND

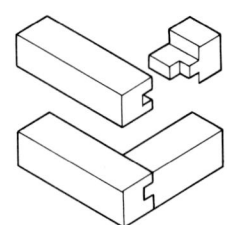

HAUNCH

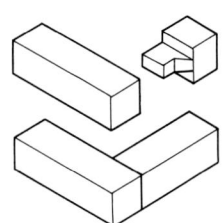

HAUNCH — BLIND

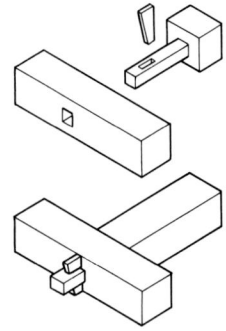

KEYED

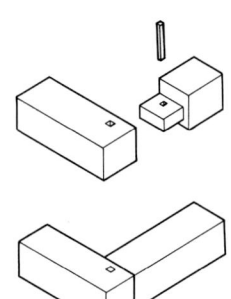

PINNED BLIND

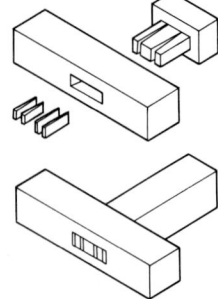

WEDGED

MORTISE & TENON

NOTES

1. Wood joints may be grouped into three classes: (1) right angle joints, (2) end joints, and (3) edge joints.

2. End joints are used to increase the length of a wood member. By proper utilization of end joints short lengths can be used which might otherwise have been wasted.

3. Edge joints are used to increase the width of a wood member. By giving narrow widths greater use of narrow stock may result.

4. A rabbet (rebate) is a right angle cut made along a corner edge of a wood member. A dado is a rectangular groove cut across the grain of a wood member. If this groove extends along the edge or face of a wood member (being cut parallel to the grain) it is known as a plough (plow).

ARCHITECTURAL WOODWORK

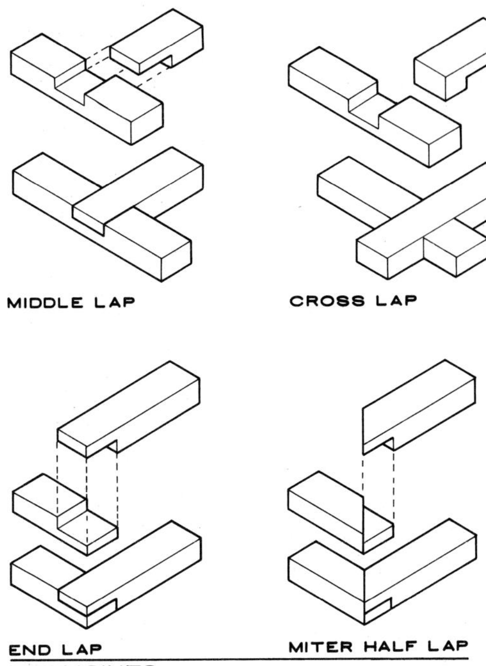

MIDDLE LAP

CROSS LAP

END LAP

MITER HALF LAP

LAP JOINTS

RIGHT ANGLE JOINTS

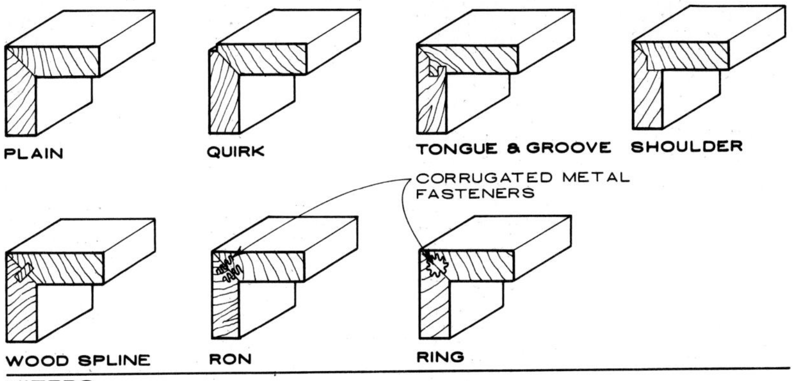

PLAIN

QUIRK

TONGUE & GROOVE

SHOULDER

CORRUGATED METAL FASTENERS

WOOD SPLINE

RON

RING

MITERS

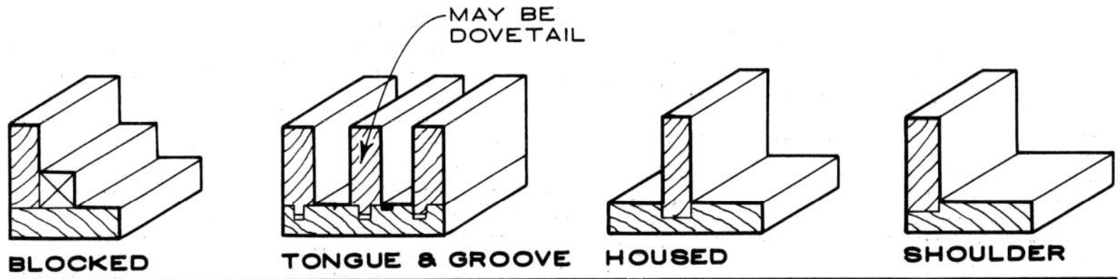

MAY BE DOVETAIL

BLOCKED

TONGUE & GROOVE

HOUSED

SHOULDER

TYPICAL PANELING JOINTS

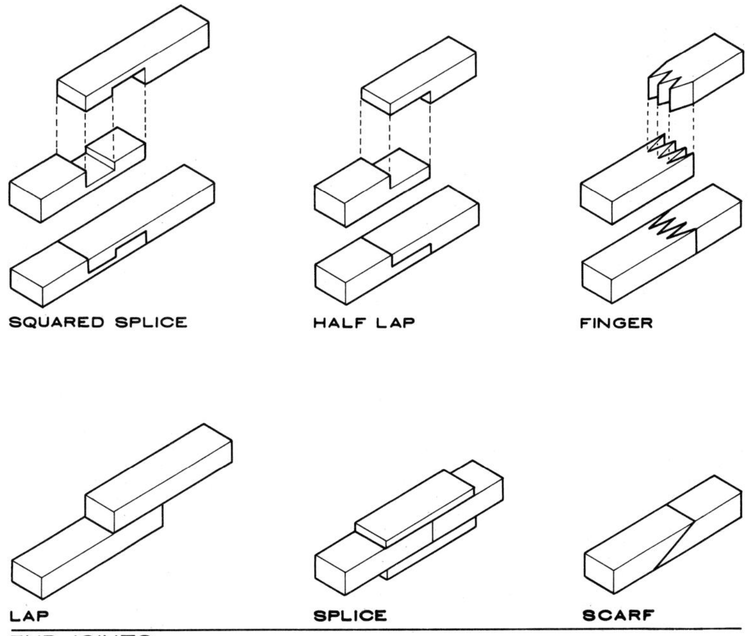

SQUARED SPLICE

HALF LAP

FINGER

LAP

SPLICE

SCARF

END JOINTS

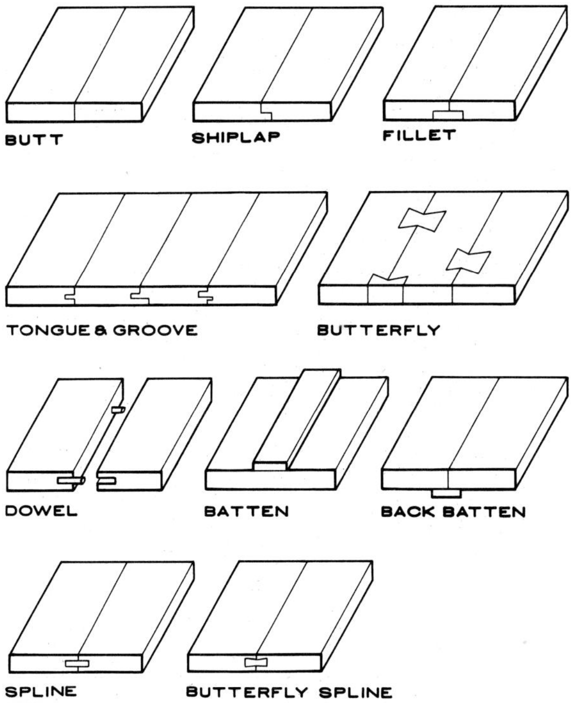

BUTT

SHIPLAP

FILLET

TONGUE & GROOVE

BUTTERFLY

DOWEL

BATTEN

BACK BATTEN

SPLINE

BUTTERFLY SPLINE

EDGE JOINTS

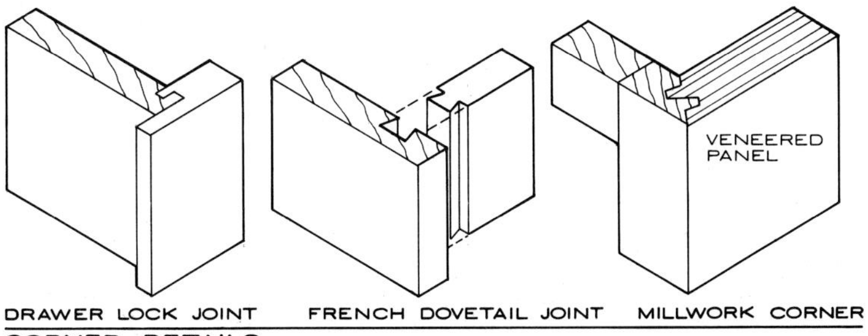

DRAWER LOCK JOINT

FRENCH DOVETAIL JOINT

MILLWORK CORNER

VENEERED PANEL

CORNER DETAILS

THROUGH DADO

STOP DADO

BLIND DADO

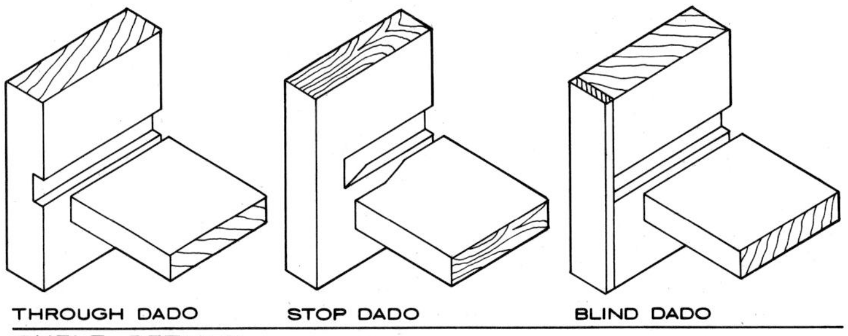

SHELF DETAILS

ARCHITECTURAL WOODWORK 6

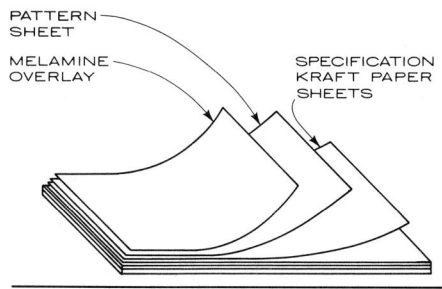

LAMINATED PLASTIC VENEER

PATTERN SHEET
MELAMINE OVERLAY
SPECIFICATION KRAFT PAPER SHEETS

NOTES

1. HIGH PRESSURE LAMINATE: A "sandwich" of 8 to 10 layers of resin impregnated papers converted by heat and pressure into a plastic-like material. The face is a translucent sheet of melamine treated paper; the second layer is the pattern or color sheet also melamine impregnated; the balance of the plies are phenolic resin impregnated kraft filler papers.

2. FINISHES: The method of creating the various available surface finishes vary. Gloss, satin, furniture finishes, velvet, low glare, oil rub, and textured surfaces are available. Since most are unique to specific manufacturers, check their brochures.

3. GRADES

   a. $1/16$ IN. GENERAL PURPOSE GRADE is the most universally used. It is suitable for either horizontal or vertical surfaces, and affords the maximum selection of colors, patterns, and finishes.

   b. $1/32$ IN. VERTICAL SURFACE GRADE, as the name implies, is suitable for vertical surfaces only, such as wall panels and cabinet surfaces, if maximum durability is not a prerequisite. Its use is not recommended on surfaces wider than 24 in.

   c. 0.050 IN. POST FORMING GRADE is manufactured so that it can be heated and bent to small radii. Its other properties and uses are similar to $1/16$ in. General Purpose Grade.

   d. 0.025 CABINET LINER GRADE is intended for the interior of cabinet surfaces. It costs considerably less than the facing grades, yet still affords surface durability and structural balance and prevents moisture absorption. Color selection is usually limited to white, black, and a few neutral solid colors.

4. GLUES AND ADHESIVES

   a. RIGID GLUES, such as urea formaldehyde and resorcinol, require press pressure to effect adhesion.

   b. CONTACT TYPE ADHESIVES, made of neoprene, are either water emulsion or solvent based and are characterized by their ability to adhere when two coated surfaces are subjected to momentary pressure.

   c. HOT MELT GLUES are increasingly used for the application of laminate edges.

5. BALANCING OR BACKING LAMINATE SHEETS: $1/16$, 0.05, 0.03, and 0.02 in. unfinished plastic laminates should be used to inhibit moisture absorption through the back and to attain structural balance.

6. CORE TYPE: Plywood with heavy grained or rotary cut top ply should not be used.

   a. PARTICLE BOARD has inherent stability and defect free surface, comes in multiple sizes, and is moderately priced. It is being increasingly used. Either use rigid glue or contact adhesives.

   b. HARDWOOD FACED FIR CORE PLYWOOD costs more than particle board. This type of core is recommended if high structural strength is required. Use either rigid glue or contact adhesive.

   c. FIR PLYWOOD is largely being supplanted by particle board, for it can produce grain patterns through laminate face. Use contact adhesive only. If the laminate assembly is to be subjected to prolonged high humidity or free water, use waterproof type plywood.

7. HARDWARE: Increased weight of doors warrants the use of heavier duty hinges. All screw attachments must be done from unexposed areas.

8. FIRE RESISTANT LAMINATES: Test variations between the products are provided by each manufacturer when applied with approved glues to a fire retardant core.

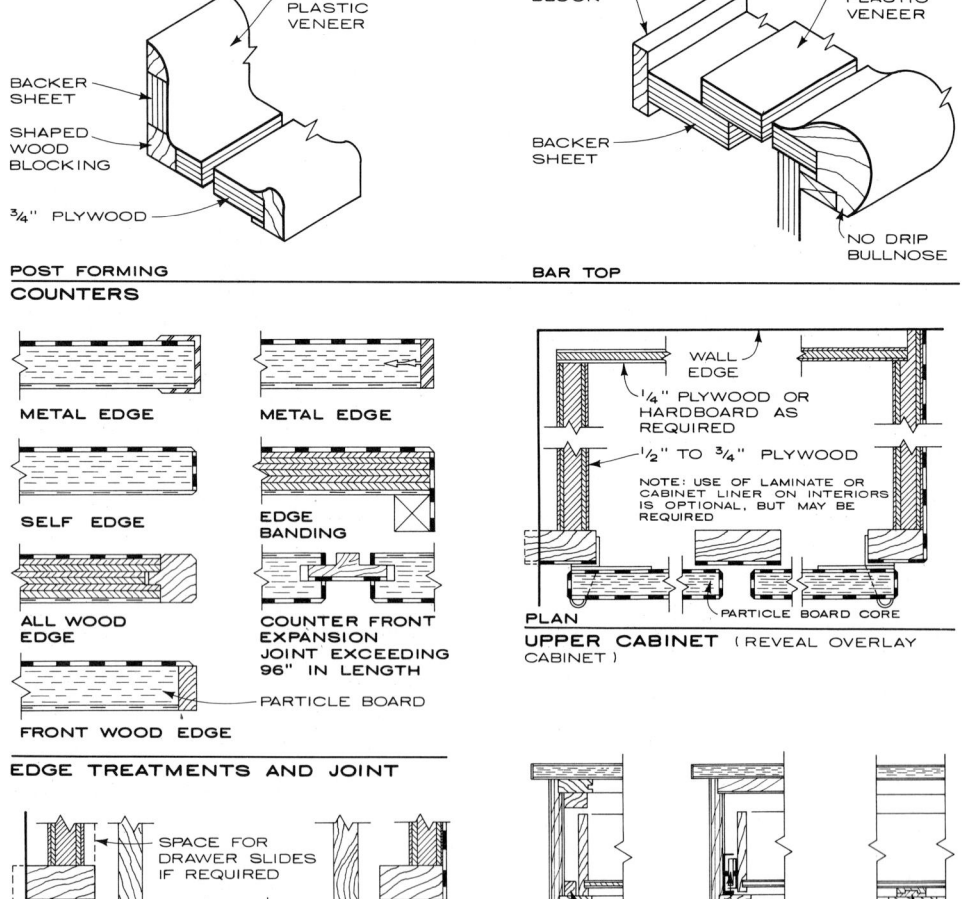

POST FORMING

COUNTERS

LAMINATED PLASTIC VENEER
BACKER SHEET
SHAPED WOOD BLOCKING
$3/4$" PLYWOOD

BAR TOP

FINISHED BLOCK
LAMINATED PLASTIC VENEER
BACKER SHEET
NO DRIP BULLNOSE

UPPER CABINET (REVEAL OVERLAY CABINET)

SECTION

SCRIBE
CEILING EDGE
PARTICLE BOARD CORE
$1/2$" TO $3/4$" PLYWOOD
$1/4$" PLYWOOD OR HARDBOARD
ADJUSTABLE SHELF SUPPORTS, 4 PER CABINET
12"

EDGE TREATMENTS AND JOINT

METAL EDGE
METAL EDGE
SELF EDGE
EDGE BANDING
ALL WOOD EDGE
COUNTER FRONT EXPANSION JOINT EXCEEDING 96" IN LENGTH
PARTICLE BOARD
FRONT WOOD EDGE

PLAN

UPPER CABINET (REVEAL OVERLAY CABINET)

WALL EDGE
$1/4$" PLYWOOD OR HARDBOARD AS REQUIRED
$1/2$" TO $3/4$" PLYWOOD
NOTE: USE OF LAMINATE OR CABINET LINER ON INTERIORS IS OPTIONAL, BUT MAY BE REQUIRED
PARTICLE BOARD CORE

SECTION

BASE CABINET (REVEAL OVERLAY CABINET)

WALL EDGE
PARTICLE BOARD CORE
PLASTIC LAMINATE
HARDWOOD
$1/4$" PLYWOOD
DUST PANEL
FLOOR
BASE
$3 1/2$"

PLAN

DRAWER DETAIL (REVEAL OVERLAY CABINET)

SPACE FOR DRAWER SLIDES IF REQUIRED
WALL EDGE

CABINET DRAWER CONSTRUCTION

WOOD, DRAW-SLIDE
METAL, DRAW-SLIDE
CONTINUOUS HARDWOOD GUIDE, METAL ALSO AVAILABLE

John R. Hoke, Jr., AIA, Architect; Washington, D.C.

ARCHITECTURAL WOODWORK

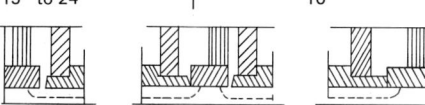

CABINET DIMENSIONS

SUGGESTED MINIMUM SIZES FOR CABINET PARTS

CABINET PARTS	THICKNESS
Face frame	3/4''
Web members or stretcher	3/4'' x 2''
Ends and divisions	
Economy	1/2''
Custom and premium	5/8''
Flush overlay	3/4''
Shelves, tops and bottoms	
Economy plywood	5/8''
Solid stock or particleboard	3/4''
Over 3'-6'' in length or adjustable	1''
Backs	
Economy untempered hardboard	1/8''
Custom and premium—plywood or tempered hardboard	1/4''
Exposed backs	3/4''
Door faces—all grades	3/4''
Drawers	
Fronts, sides and backs	
Economy	7/16''
Custom and premium	1/2''
Bottoms	
Economy (up to 18'' width)	1/8''
Economy (over 18'' width)	1/4''
Custom and premium	1/4''
Breadboards	3/4''

CLASSIFICATION OF CABINETS

Cabinets can be identified into three classifications: economy, the lowest grade; custom, the average grade; and premium, the top of the line. The economy grade cabinet has no back and usually has a lipped door. The underside of the counter is not specially treated and thus may produce some warpage. The custom grade cabinet does have a back in all of its construction. The edges of all the exposed plywood are covered; the ends and divisions between one area and another are solid as opposed to just a frame, and the drawers have hardwood guides for better wear. The premium grade cabinets are made with the best construction procedures and materials possible. The corners are mitered, solid panels between drawers to prevent dust travel. Drawers are made completely of hardwood and use high quality hardware. The countertops are attached with hidden clips or screwed, not nailed down, and all joints are screwed or glued with blocks.

TYPES OF CABINET DOORS

There are basically three types of doors. Variations of them do exist but fundamentally they are exposed face frame (flush and lipped); flush overlay; and reveal overlay. The exposed face frame is recommended for hard service applications because of its superior strength. However, it is an expensive design, because of the necessity of careful fitting and alignment of doors and drawers. The lipped design is more economical, since fitting tolerances are less critical. The flush overlay has gained popularity because it offers very clean and simple lines, and only the door and drawer fronts are visible. A requirement of the flush overlay design is heavy duty hardware. The reveal overlay incorporates most of the advantages of the flush overlay and exposed face frame designs. The reveal between the door and drawer fronts reduces the problem of alignment. The architect has the option of utilizing the reveals vertically and/or horizontally, and the width of the reveal is variable.

SHELVING DIMENSIONS

DEPTH OF SHELF	VERTICAL SPACING (MIN.)
4'' to 6''	5''
6'' to 10''	6''
10'' to 15''	7''
15'' to 24''	10''

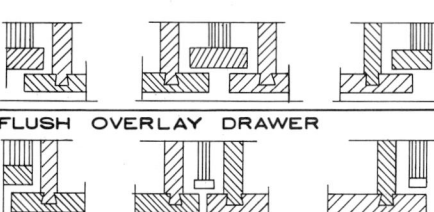

EXPOSED FACE FRAME DRAWER

FLUSH OVERLAY DRAWER

REVEAL OVERLAY DRAWER

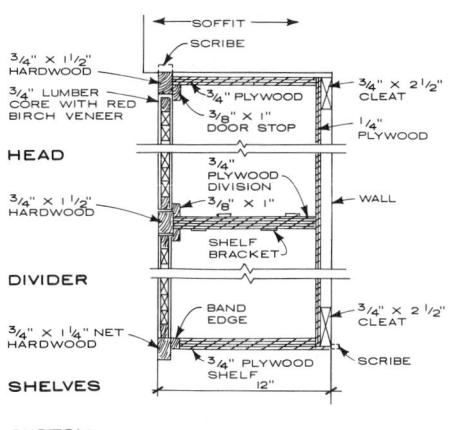

ECONOMY

TYPICAL BASE CABINET DETAILS

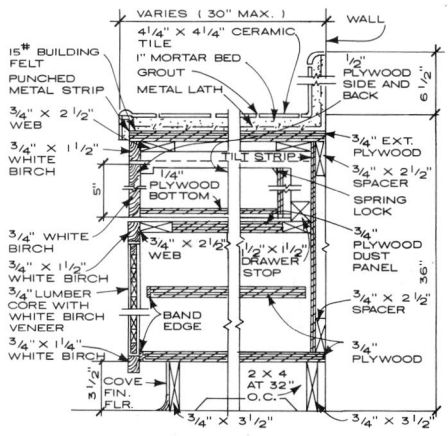

CUSTOM AND PREMIUM

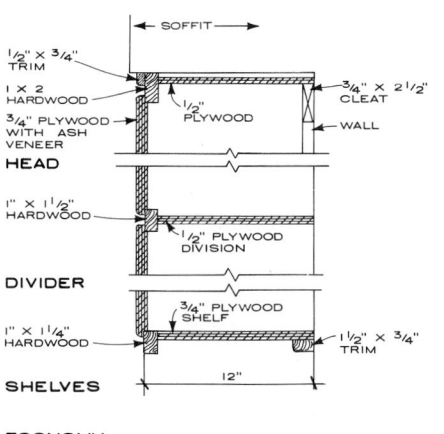

ECONOMY

TYPICAL WALL CABINET DETAILS

CUSTOM

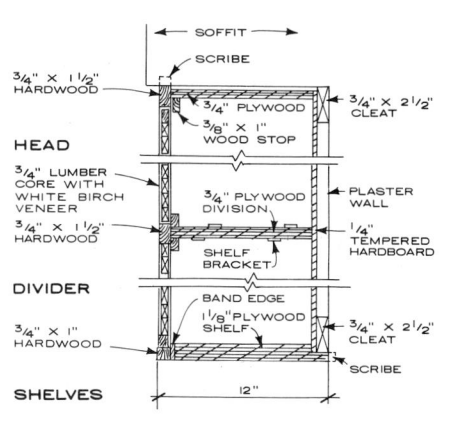

PREMIUM

Robert T. Gordon, Architect; Jackson, Wyoming

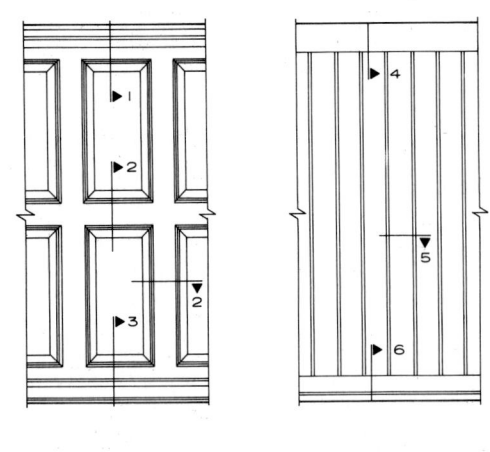

NOTES

1. For flush plywood paneling refer to interior plywood pages.
2. For fire protection refer to local and state building codes. Fire retardant classifications determined by tunnel test (ASTM #84) and flame spread are considered the most important:

   Class I   (A)   0-25.
   Class II   (B)   26-75.
   Class III (C)   76-200.

   Since treated lumber can discolor considerably, treated core veneered construction with untreated face veneers is preferred. Conventional nitrocellulose lacquers increase flame spread. Conversion varnish or a similar catalyzed finish is neutral in flame spread.

3. For acoustics refer to acoustical pages. Generally, slats have higher sound absorption coefficients than flat panels.
4. For specification of architectural woodwork refer to Architectural Woodworking Institute (AWI) Quality Standard: lumber grades, section 100; standing and running trim, section 300; stile and rail paneling, section 500c; finishing, section 1500.
5. Shape and size of various elements vary with individual design as well as with the availability of lumber size.

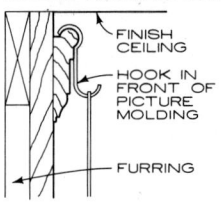
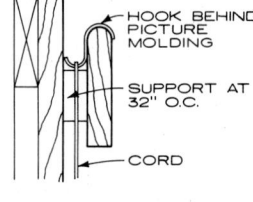
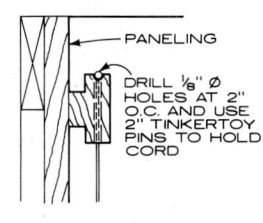

WOOD PANELING ELEVATIONS

WOOD RAILING ELEVATIONS

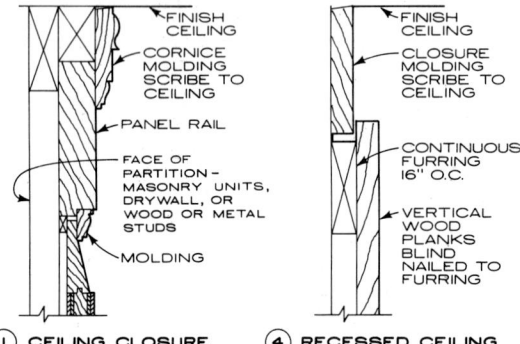

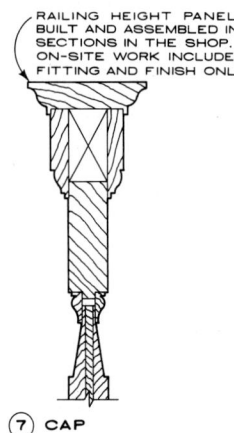
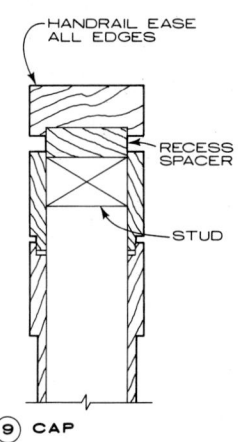
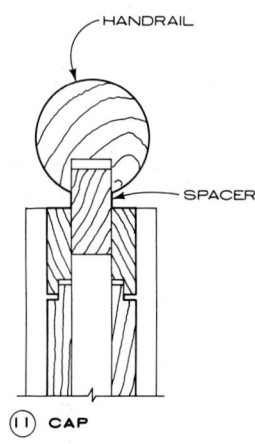

(1) CEILING CLOSURE

(4) RECESSED CEILING CLOSURE

EXPOSED HOOK   CONCEALED HOOK   CONCEALED PIN

PICTURE MOLDING DETAILS

(2) RAIL OR STILE

(5) BATTEN

(7) CAP

(9) CAP

(11) CAP

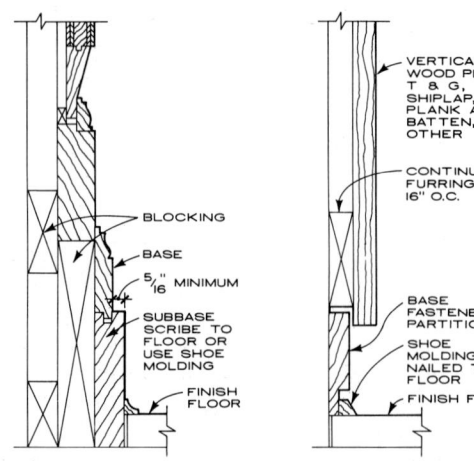
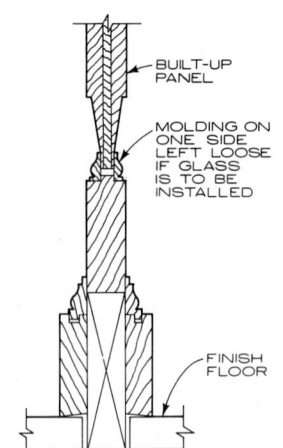
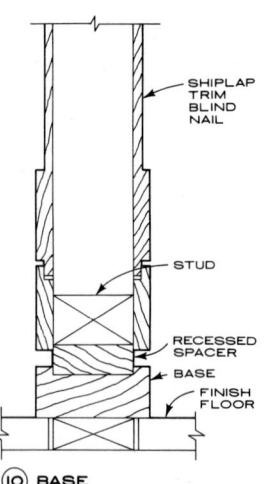
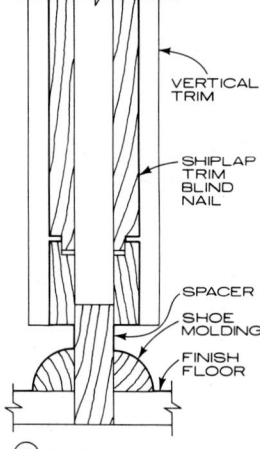

(3) BASE

(6) RECESSED BASE

(8) BASE

(10) BASE

(12) BASE

SECTIONS

SECTIONS

WOOD PANELING DETAILS

WOOD RAILING DETAILS

Charles Szoradi, AIA; Washington, D.C.

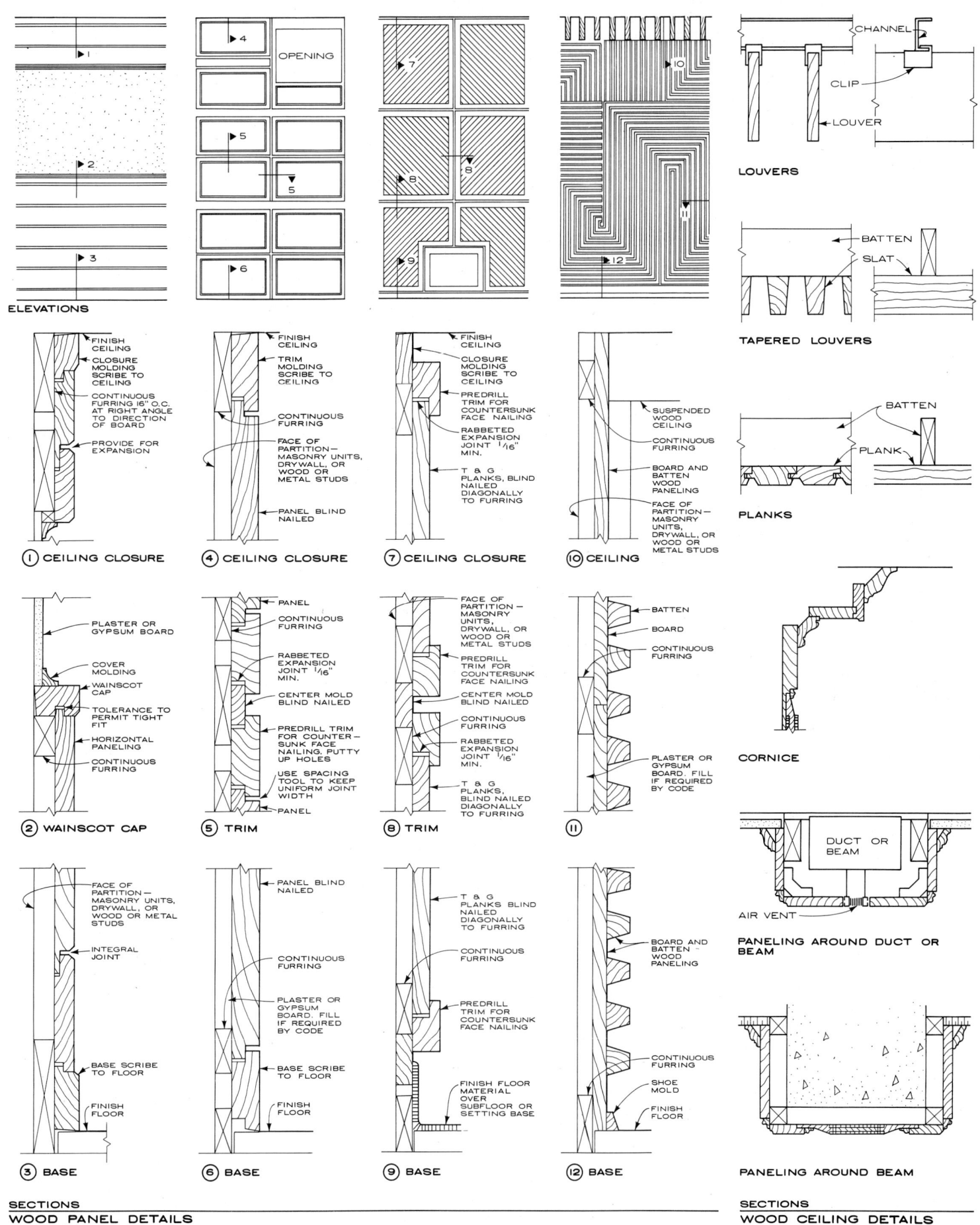

ELEVATIONS

① CEILING CLOSURE

FINISH CEILING
CLOSURE MOLDING SCRIBE TO CEILING
CONTINUOUS FURRING 16" O.C. AT RIGHT ANGLE TO DIRECTION OF BOARD
PROVIDE FOR EXPANSION

② WAINSCOT CAP

PLASTER OR GYPSUM BOARD
COVER MOLDING
WAINSCOT CAP
TOLERANCE TO PERMIT TIGHT FIT
HORIZONTAL PANELING
CONTINUOUS FURRING

③ BASE

FACE OF PARTITION — MASONRY UNITS, DRYWALL, OR WOOD OR METAL STUDS
INTEGRAL JOINT
BASE SCRIBE TO FLOOR
FINISH FLOOR

④ CEILING CLOSURE

FINISH CEILING
TRIM MOLDING SCRIBE TO CEILING
CONTINUOUS FURRING
FACE OF PARTITION — MASONRY UNITS, DRYWALL, OR WOOD OR METAL STUDS
PANEL BLIND NAILED

⑤ TRIM

PANEL
CONTINUOUS FURRING
RABBETED EXPANSION JOINT 1/16" MIN.
CENTER MOLD BLIND NAILED
PREDRILL TRIM FOR COUNTER-SUNK FACE NAILING. PUTTY UP HOLES
USE SPACING TOOL TO KEEP UNIFORM JOINT WIDTH
PANEL

⑥ BASE

PANEL BLIND NAILED
CONTINUOUS FURRING
PLASTER OR GYPSUM BOARD. FILL IF REQUIRED BY CODE
BASE SCRIBE TO FLOOR
FINISH FLOOR

⑦ CEILING CLOSURE

FINISH CEILING
CLOSURE MOLDING SCRIBE TO CEILING
PREDRILL TRIM FOR COUNTERSUNK FACE NAILING
RABBETED EXPANSION JOINT 1/16" MIN.
T & G PLANKS, BLIND NAILED DIAGONALLY TO FURRING

⑧ TRIM

FACE OF PARTITION — MASONRY UNITS, DRYWALL, OR WOOD OR METAL STUDS
PREDRILL TRIM FOR COUNTERSUNK FACE NAILING
CENTER MOLD BLIND NAILED
CONTINUOUS FURRING
RABBETED EXPANSION JOINT 1/16" MIN.
T & G PLANKS, BLIND NAILED DIAGONALLY TO FURRING

⑨ BASE

T & G PLANKS BLIND NAILED DIAGONALLY TO FURRING
CONTINUOUS FURRING
PREDRILL TRIM FOR COUNTERSUNK FACE NAILING
FINISH FLOOR MATERIAL OVER SUBFLOOR OR SETTING BASE

⑩ CEILING

SUSPENDED WOOD CEILING
CONTINUOUS FURRING
BOARD AND BATTEN WOOD PANELING
FACE OF PARTITION — MASONRY UNITS, DRYWALL, OR WOOD OR METAL STUDS

⑪

BATTEN
BOARD
CONTINUOUS FURRING
PLASTER OR GYPSUM BOARD. FILL IF REQUIRED BY CODE

⑫ BASE

BOARD AND BATTEN WOOD PANELING
CONTINUOUS FURRING
SHOE MOLD
FINISH FLOOR

SECTIONS
WOOD PANEL DETAILS

LOUVERS
CHANNEL
CLIP
LOUVER

TAPERED LOUVERS
BATTEN
SLAT

PLANKS
BATTEN
PLANK

CORNICE

PANELING AROUND DUCT OR BEAM
DUCT OR BEAM
AIR VENT

PANELING AROUND BEAM

SECTIONS
WOOD CEILING DETAILS

Charles Szoradi, AIA; Washington, D.C.

ARCHITECTURAL WOODWORK   6

TYPES OF HARDWOOD PLYWOOD

Technical	Fully waterproof bond—approx. equal strength in two directions
Type 1 (ext.)	Fully waterproof bond—full weather exposure, resist organisms
Type 11 (int.)	Water resistant bond
Type 111 (int.)	Moisture—resistant bond

GRADES OF HARDWOOD PLYWOOD

Premium Grade (A)	Slight imperfections
Good Grade (1)	For natural finishes, no sharp contrasts
Sound Grade (2)	For smooth painted surfaces
Utility Grade (3)	Open defects permitted but limited in size, species not selected, no matching
Backing Grade (4)	Many flaws permitted, species not selected. No matching
Specialty Grade (SP)	Nonconforming for special uses, matching, etc. Grade and type by agreement

NUMBER OF PLIES

Odd number in pairs on opposite sides of core. For Technical Type, plies parallel to finish plies provide 40–60% of total thickness.

SOME POPULAR SPECIES OF HARDWOOD VENEERS

DENSE: white ash, yellow birch, black maple, red oak, rosewood, teak.
MEDIUM DENSE: black ash, gum, African mahogany, red maple, prima vera, American walnut.
LOW DENSITY: aspen, American basswood, American chestnut, yellow poplar.

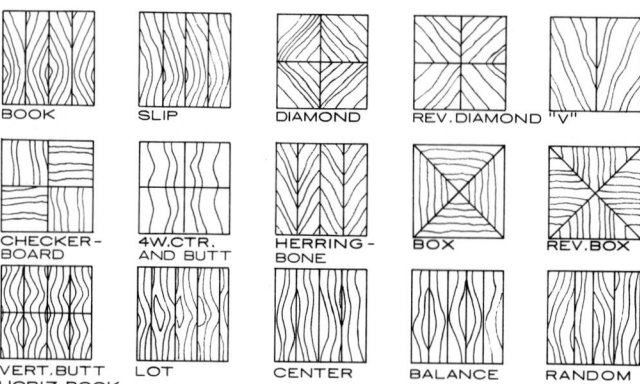

VENEER MATCHING

BOOK · SLIP · DIAMOND · REV.DIAMOND "V"
CHECKER-BOARD · 4W.CTR. AND BUTT · HERRING-BONE · BOX · REV.BOX
VERT.BUTT HORIZ.BOOK · LOT · CENTER · BALANCE · RANDOM

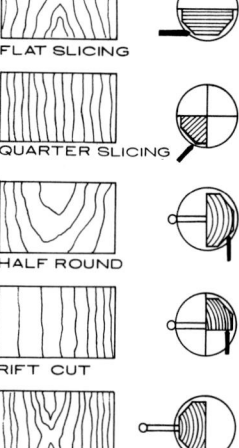

VENEER CUTTING

ROTARY
FLAT SLICING
QUARTER SLICING
HALF ROUND
RIFT CUT
BACK CUT

STANDARD SIZES AND THICKNESSES OF HARDWOOD PLYWOOD

WIDTHS: 48″	Tolerance ± $1/32$″
LENGTHS: 84″, 96″, 120″	Tolerance ± $1/32$″
THICKNESSES: $1/8$″ to $3/4$″	

Tolerances: Unsanded panels: ± $1/32$″
Sanded panels: + 0″ – $1/32$″ except that $1/4$″ or more wall panels + 0″ – $3/64$″

Data supplied by Hardwood Plywood Manufacturers' Association and by Champion Building Products, Division of Champion International

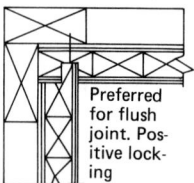

INSIDE CORNER — Preferred for flush joint. Positive locking

OUTSIDE CORNER — Usually used. Joint is glued

Spline usually $1/4$″ x $5/8$″. Dowels 6″ to 12″ o.c.

DOWEL AND SPLINE

Tongue usually $1/4$″ wide, $5/16$″ deep. Dowels sometimes added

TONGUE AND GROOVE

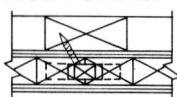

2 $1/2$″ TO 3″

Glue spirals No. 8–10 dowels approx. $3/8$″

DOWEL

VENEER **EXPOSED PLYWOOD SPLINE**

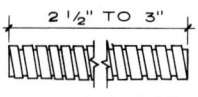

2 nails, 1 face hole, colored putty. Screws hidden by joint preferred for possible removal of panels. #10 or #12 size usual

NAILS AND SCREWS RECOMMENDED

3″ x 2″ clips 16″ o.c. Allow 1″ at ceiling to drop panel into place

METAL CLIPS

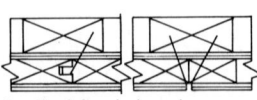

MATCHING HARDWOOD END · CONCEALED CROSSBAND · VENEER EDGEBAND

PANEL EDGES

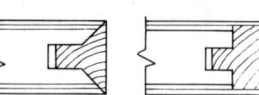

DETAILS FOR QUALITY INTERIOR HARDWOOD PLYWOOD PANELING
LUMBER CORE PLYWOOD SHOWN

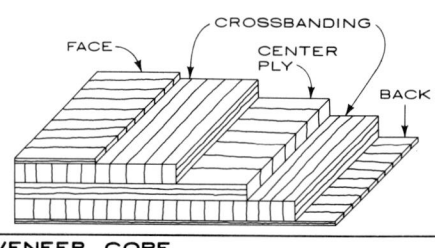

FACE · CROSSBANDING · CENTER PLY · BACK

VENEER CORE

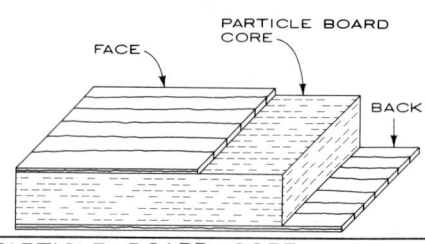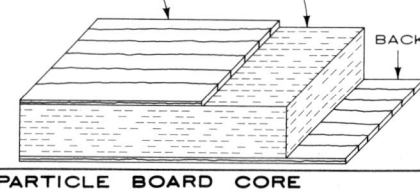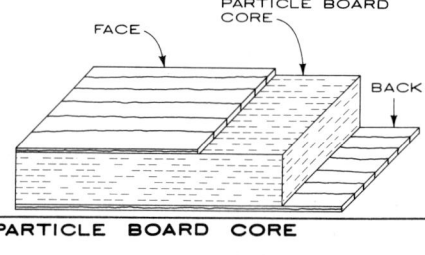

FACE · PARTICLE BOARD CORE · BACK

PARTICLE BOARD CORE

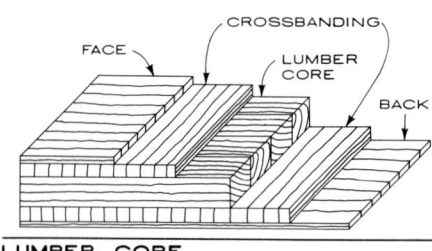

FACE · CROSSBANDING · LUMBER CORE · BACK

LUMBER CORE

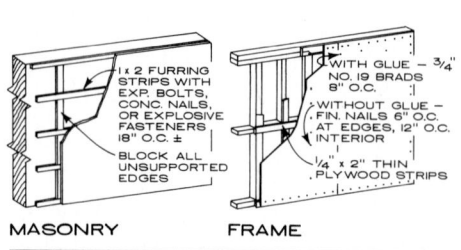

1 x 2 FURRING STRIPS WITH EXP. BOLTS, CONC. NAILS, OR EXPLOSIVE FASTENERS 18″ O.C. ±
BLOCK ALL UNSUPPORTED EDGES
WITH GLUE – $3/4$″ NO. 19 BRADS 8″ O.C.
WITHOUT GLUE – FIN. NAILS 6″ O.C. AT EDGES, 12″ O.C. INTERIOR
$1/4$″ x 2″ THIN PLYWOOD STRIPS

MASONRY · FRAME

INTERIOR WALL AND FURRING APPLICATION

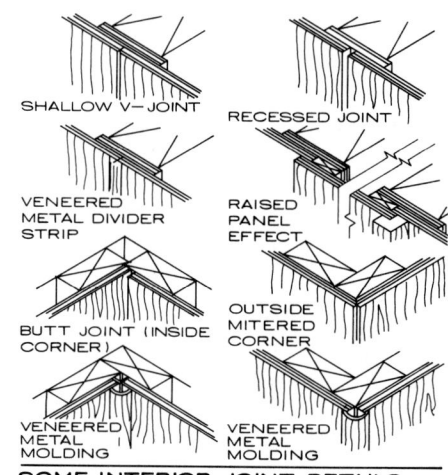

SHALLOW V–JOINT · RECESSED JOINT
VENEERED METAL DIVIDER STRIP · RAISED PANEL EFFECT
BUTT JOINT (INSIDE CORNER) · OUTSIDE MITERED CORNER
VENEERED METAL MOLDING · VENEERED METAL MOLDING

SOME INTERIOR JOINT DETAILS

LAMINATED HARDWOOD BLOCK FLOORING

Standard size	9″ x 9″ x $1/2$″	
Grades	Prime	finished or unfinished
	Standard	
Species listed in accordance with hardness and wearing capacity	(1) Pecan (2) Hard maple (3) Oak (red and white) (4) Birch (5) Ash (6) Beech (7) Walnut (8) Cherry	
Plies	Three at right angles; tongue on corresponding groove on each of four edges	
Application	Laid in mastic over concrete or other suitable subflooring	

NOTE: Samples tested under ANSI–010.2-1975.

Foster C. Parriott; James M. Hunter & Associates; Boulder, Colorado

ARCHITECTURAL WOODWORK

CHAPTER 7 THERMAL AND MOISTURE PROTECTION

BUILT-UP ROOFING

DECK OR SUBSTRATE	SURFACING	SLOPE (IN./FT)	BASE SHEET	PLYSHEETS	PLY BITUMEN (LB/SQ/PLY)	SURFACING BITUMEN (LB/SQ)	NOTES TO DESIGNER/SPECIFIER
Nonnailable decks or roof insulations (Consult manufacturer for approved types of roof insulation)	Gravel: 400 lb/sq OR Slag: 300 lb/sq OR White marble chips: 500 lb/sq	Inclines up to 1/2	43 lb coated base spot mopped in asphalt to deck or solid mopped in asphalt to insulation	3 coal tar saturated felts (perforated)	Coal tar @ 25	Coal tar @ 75	• U.L. Class A on most deck and insulation types (1) • Requires complete surfacing daily • For ponded roofs, add 4th ply of felt and double flood and double gravel surface • Base flashings must be installed in flashing cement • Same configuration possible on slopes of 1/2–3 in./ft (2) using Type III asphalt
			Organic base felts 43 lb mopped. 43 lb coated base spot mopped in asphalt to deck or solid mopped in asphalt to insulation	3 organic or asbestos felts (perforated)	Type II asphalt @ 25	Type I asphalt @ 60	
		Inclines up to 1/2	Fiberglas ® base or OCF approved base for specific deck/substrate spot mopped to deck or solid mopped to insulation (3)	2 Perma-Ply R ® plysheets, ASTM D2178 Type IV (3)	Coal tar @ 30	Coal tar @ 75	• U.L. Class A on most deck and insulation types (1) • Roofing may be left up to 6 months before surfacing • For ponded roofs, add 3rd ply of Perma-Ply R and double flood and double gravel surface • Base flashings must be installed in flashing cement
				2 Perma-Ply R ® plysheets (3)	Type II asphalt @ 30	Type I asphalt @ 60	• Same configuration possible on slopes of 1/2–3 in./ft (2) using Type III asphalt
	Mineral surface cap sheet (72–80 lb)	1/4–12 (2)	Fiberglass base spot mopped to deck or solid mopped to insulation	2 fiberglass plysheets	Asphalt @ 25–30	Asphalt @ 25–30 for cap sheet	• U.L. Class A, B, or C depending on deck substrate, slope, and manufacturer (1) • Consult manufacturer for specific regional requirements • Fiberglass systems may be left up to 6 months before surfacing • Proper application of mineral cap sheet requires warm weather • Cold process fiberglass systems also possible; consult manufacturer • Asbestos systems should be glaze coated if surfacing is delayed
			Asbestos base spot mopped to deck or solid mopped to insulation	2 asbestos felts (perforated)	Asphalt @ 25	Asphalt @ 25–30 for cap sheet	
	Smooth surface	1/4–12 (2)	Fiberglass base spot mopped to deck or solid mopped to insulation	3 fiberglass plysheets	Asphalt @ 25–30	Asphalt/ clay emulsion @ 6 gal/sq	• U.L. Clsss A, B, or C depending on deck/ substrate, slope, and manufacturer (1) • Consult manufacturer for specific regional requirements • Fiberglass systems may be left up to 6 months before surfacing • Reflective coatings are recommended over smooth surface systems • Asbestos systems should be lightly glaze coated if surfacing is delayed
			Asbestos base spot mopped to deck or solid mopped to insulation	3 asbestos felts (perforated)	Asphalt @ 25	Asphalt/ clay emulsion @ 6 gal/sq	

NOTES

1. Underwriters Laboratories test for Fire-Hazard Classification by assembling particular constructions using specific products of stated manufacturers; consult U.L. or the manufacturer to verify classifications for specific roofing systems for given project conditions.

2. On slopes of 1 in./ft or greater, plies should be strapped (laid parallel to slope) and back nailed to prevent slippage, and Type III or Type IV asphalt should be called for; if roofing is on roof insulation, wood insulation stops/nailers should be provided.

3. Fiberglas and Perma-Ply R: registered trademarks of Owens/Corning Fiberglas Corporation.

ROLL ROOFING

TYPE	DESCRIPTION	SLOPE (IN./FT) MIN.	SLOPE (IN./FT) MAX.	WEIGHT (LB/SQ)	SIZE	UNDERLAY	FASTENERS	EXPOSURE	COLOR AND TEXTURE	U.L. RATING
Asphalt Roll Roofing	Smooth surface	0	6	50	36″ x 36′		Nails and cement	33″	Black	C-wind resistant
				65						
	Mineral surface			90	36″ x 36′					
	Double coverage fiberglass	1/2	4	60	36″ x 36′			17″	Various color blends	A-wind resistant
	Fiberglass reinforced mineral fiber	1/8	4	75	36″ x 72′				Black	B-wind resistant

Walter H. Sobel, FAIA & Associates; Chicago, Illinois

Kent Wong; Hewlett, Jamison, Atkinson & Luey Portland, Oregon; from data furnished by A. Larry Brown; Owens/Corning Fiberglas Corporation

GENERAL INFORMATION

BUILT-UP ROOFING (CONT.)

DECK OR SUBSTRATE	SURFACING	SLOPE (IN./FT)	BASE SHEET	PLYSHEETS	PLY BITUMEN (LB/SQ/PLY)	SURFACING BITUMEN (LB/SQ)	NOTES TO DESIGNER/SPECIFIER
Wood or other nailable decking (Over wood board decks, one ply of sheathing paper should be applied under base felt next to deck) (Consult manufacturers for approved decks and fasteners)	Gravel: 400 lb/sq OR Slag: 300 lb/sq OR White marble chips: 500 lb/sq	Inclines up to 1/2	43 lb coated base mechanically attached	3 coal tar saturated felts (perforated)	Coal tar @ 25	Coal tar @ 75	• U.L. Class A on most deck types (1) • Requires complete surfacing daily • For ponded roofs, add a 4th ply of felt and double flood and double gravel surface • Base flashings must be installed in flashing cement
			43 lb organic bar felt mechanically attached	3 organic or asbestos felts	Type II asphalt @ 25	Type I asphalt @ 60	• Same configuration possible on slopes of 1/2–3 in./ft (2) using Type III asphalt
		Inclines up to 1/2	Fiberglas ® base mechanically attached (3)	2 Perma-Ply R ® plysheets ASTM D2178 Type IV (3)	Coal tar @ 30	Coal tar @ 75	• U.L. Class A on most deck types (1) • Roofing may be left up to 6 months before surfacing • For ponded roofs, add a 3rd ply of Perma-Ply R and double flood and double gravel surface • Base flashings must be installed in flashing cement
			Fiberglas ® base mechanically attached (3)	2 Perma-Ply R ® plysheets ASTM D2178 Type IV (3)	Type II asphalt @ 30	Type I asphalt @ 60	• Same configuration possible on slopes of 1/2–3 in./ft (2) using Type III asphalt
	Mineral surface cap sheet (72–80 lb)	1/4–12 (2)	Fiberglass base mechanically attached	2 fiberglass plysheets, ASTM D2178 Type III or IV	Asphalt @ 30	Asphalt @ 30 for cap sheet	• U.L. Class A, B, or C depending on deck type, slope, and manufacturer (1) • Consult manufacturer for specific regional requirements for various types of plysheets • Fiberglass roofing may be left up to 6 months before surfacing • Proper application of mineral cap sheet requires warm weather
			43 lb organic base mechanically attached	2 fiberglass plysheets, ASTM D2178 Type III or IV	Asphalt @ 30	Asphalt @ 30 for cap sheet	
		1/4–12 (2)	Asbestos base (25–55 lb) mechanically attached	2 asbestos felts (perforated)	Asphalt @ 25	Asphalt @ 25 for cap sheet	• U.L. Class A, B, or C depending on deck type, slope, and manufacturer (1) • Consult manufacturer for specific requirements for various weights of base sheets • Fiberglass mineral cap sheet is recommended over asbestos mineral cap sheet • Roofing should be glaze coated if surfacing is delayed • Proper application of cap sheet requires warm weather
	Smooth surface	1/4–12 (2)	Fiberglass or asbestos base mechanically attached	3 fiberglass or asbestos plysheets, ASTM D2178 Type III or IV; ASTM D250 Type II	Asphalt @ 25–30	Asphalt/ clay emulsion @ 6 gal/sq	• U.L. Class A, B, or C depending on deck type, slope, and manufacturer (1) • Consult manufacturer for specific regional requirements • Asbestos system should be lightly glaze coated if surfacing is delayed • Reflective coatings are recommended over smooth surface systems

SHINGLES

TYPE	DESCRIPTION	SLOPE (IN./FT) MIN.	SLOPE (IN./FT) MAX.	WEIGHT (LB/SQ)[3]	SIZE	UNDERLAY	FASTENERS	EXPOSURE	COLOR AND TEXTURE	U.L. RATING
Asphalt Organic Felt[1,2]	3 tab	4	12	235	12″ x 36″	15 lb asphalt felt	Galvanized steel or aluminum roofing nails	5″	Various colors; granular texture	
	2 tab	4	12	300	12″ x 36″					
	Random edged	4	12	345	12″ x 36″				Varied; smooth	C-wind resistant
	No cutout	2	12	290	12″ x 36″					
	Interlocking			180	19 3/4″ x 20 1/2″			—	Varied; smooth	C-wind resistant
	Basketweave			245	18 1/2″ x 20″					
Fiberglass	Random edged Laminated Overlay	4	12	300	14″ x 35 9/16″	15 lb asphalt felt	Galvanized steel or aluminum roofing nails	6″	Varied; smooth	A-wind resistant
	3 tab	4	12	225	12″ x 36″			5″		
	2 tab	4	12	260	12″ x 36″			5″	Varied; granular texture	
	No cutout Random edged	4	12	225	12″ x 36 1/4″			5″	Varied; smooth	

NOTES

1. These shingles may be used on slopes down to 2 in./ft when over a two ply felt underlayment.

2. All shingles are self-sealing.

3. A SQUARE is a term used to describe 100 sq ft of roof area.

Walter H. Sobel, FAIA & Associates; Chicago, Illinois

Kent Wong; Hewlett, Jamison, Atkinson & Luey Portland, Oregon; from data furnished by A. Larry Brown; Owens/Corning Fiberglas Corporation

SHINGLES AND ROOFING TILES

TYPE	DESCRIPTION	APPLICATION	SLOPE MINIMUM (IN./FT)	WEIGHT (LB/SQ)	UNDERLAY	FASTENERS	COLOR AND TEXTURE	SIZE (IN.) L X W	BUTT THICKNESS	EXPOSURE DATA
Wood: red cedar; most types and sizes available in cypress, redwood, white cedar; shakes	Handsplit and resawn	Roofs and sidewall panels for institutional, commercial, residential use	4	200–450	Spaced sheathing 30 lb felt interlayment with shakes	Corrosion resistant nails	Natural or various stains Various textures	Length 15–24 Width random	1/2–3/4 in.	5–7 1/2 in.
	Taper split			260				Length 24 Width random	1/2 in.	10 in.
	Straight split			200–260				Length 18–24 Width random	3/8 in.	3 in. overlap
Wood: red cedar; most types and sizes available in cypress, redwood, white cedar; shingles	No. 1 Blue Label No. 2 Red Label No. 3 Black Label	Roofs and sidewall panels for institutional, commercial, residential use	4	None given	Open or solid sheathing Open sheathing shall be 1 x 4 or 1 x 6 in. boards	Corrosion resistant nails	Natural or various stains Various textures	Length 16 / 18 / 24	3/8 in.	5 in. / 5 1/2 in. / 7 1/2 in.
	No. 4							16 / 18		
	Undercoursing									
	No. 1 or No. 2 Rebutted-rejointed							16 / 18 / 24 Width random		
Clay tile	Shingle—flat	Institutional, commercial, residential	3	800–1600	One layer 30 lb or 45 lb felt over plywood	Noncorrosive copper nails	Various finishes	l w 15 x 7	3/8 in. minimum	Exposed length 6 1/2 in. Exposed width 7 in.
	Interlocking flat			800				14 x 9	7/8 in. minimum	Exposed length 11 in. Exposed width 8 1/4 in.
	French			940–1000				16 1/4 x 9	2 in.	Exposed length 13 1/8 in. Exposed width 8 1/8 in.
	Spanish		4	850				13 1/4 x 9 3/4	1/2 in.	Exposed length 10 1/2 in. Exposed width 8 1/4 in.
Concrete[1]	Shingle—flat	Institutional, commercial, residential	4	950	One layer 30 lb felt over plywood	10 penny corrosion resistant galvanized copper, or colors stainless steel box nail	Various colors	13 x 16	1 in.	3 in. overlap
	Barreled mission curved									
Slate	Commercial grade—smooth	Institutional, commercial, residential	4	700–800	One layer 30 lb asphalt saturated rag felt over plywood	Slaters hard copper wire nails cut copper, cut brass, or cut yellow metal slat nails	Blue-black	Various sizes	3/16, 1/4 in.	3 in. overlap
	Quarry—run rough			825–3600					3/8, 1/2, 3/4 in.	

NOTES

1. Specifier should ask for concrete tile freeze-thaw test.
2. Underwriters Laboratories Standard UL 580 classifies roof deck assemblies as Class 30, Class 60, and Class 90. The nominal uplift pressures and wind velocities commonly related in technical studies and literature are the following:

RATING	NOMINAL UPLIFT PRESSURE	NOMINAL WIND VELOCITY
Class 30	30 psf	100 mph
Class 60	60 psf	142 mph
Class 90	90 psf	174 mph

Consult local manufacturer or agent for roofing system rating.

3. Underwriters Laboratories classifies prepared roof covering materials as Class A, B, or C. CLASS A includes roof coverings that are effective against severe fire exposure. Roof coverings of this class are then not readily flammable and do not carry or communicate fire; afford a fairly high degree of fire protection to the roof deck; do not slip from position; possess no flying brand hazard; and do not require frequent repairs in order to maintain their fire resisting properties.

Walter H. Sobel, FAIA & Associates; Chicago, Illinois

SEAMED METAL ROOFING

TYPE	DESCRIPTION	MIN. SLOPE (IN./FT)	SIZE	THICKNESS	WEIGHT (LB/SQ)	UNDERLAY	FASTENER
Aluminum coated steel	Polyurethane insulation sandwiched between two layers of steel[1] standing seam	1/4	40" x 32'	2½"	250	None	Panels are clipped to structurals, and interlocking seams sealed
Copper coated galvanized steel	Standing seam, pan, or roll method	3	20" x 30' max.	24 gauge	130	30 lb felt	Anchor clips and galvanized nails or screws
			22" x 30' max.				
Prepainted galvanized steel	Batten seam pan method	3	24" x 30' max.				
Zinc-copper titanium alloy	Batten or standing seam pan method	3	20", 24", or 28" x 8', 10', 12', or 14'	0.027"	100	Roofing felt	Galvanized U channel or L seam support spacer with screw or nails
Terne coated stainless[2,3,5]	Standing or batten seam	3	20", 24", 28", or 36" x 96", or 120"	0.015"	89	Roofing felt and rosin paper	TCS cleats and stainless steel nails
	Flat locked seam	3	20" x 28"				
Terne plate[4,6]	Batten seam	3	20" x 120" max.	26 gauge	62	Rosin paper	Terne cleats and roofing nails
	Standing seam	3	14", 20"	28 gauge			
			24" x 120" max.	30 gauge			
	Flat locked seam (wood deck only)	3	14" x 20"	28 gauge			
			20" x 28"	30 gauge			
	Horizontal seam (wood deck only)	3½	24" x 96" max.	26 gauge			
				28 gauge			
Painted aluminum	Standing seam	1/2	12" x 60"–80"	0.032"	72.5	None	Anchor clips
			16" x 60"–80"	0.040"	90.4		

NOTES

1. This is a composite section providing structural deck, insulation, and weathertight roof. U value is 0.50; class I fire rating.
2. Terne coated steel is 304 nickel-chrome stainless steel covered on both sides with terne alloy (80% lead, 20% tin).
3. Terne coated steel can be painted without special preparation of the surface.
4. Terne plate is prime copper bearing steel coated with lead-tin alloy.
5. Expansion seams must be provided on runs exceeding 30 ft where both ends are free to move or exceeding 15 ft where ends are securely fastened.
6. Terne must be shop coated or painted one coat underside and primed and painted two coats on exposed side.

METAL SHINGLES AND TILES

TYPE	DESCRIPTION	APPLICATION	SLOPE MINIMUM (IN./FT)	WEIGHT (LB/SQ)	UNDERLAY	FASTENERS	COLOR AND TEXTURE	SIZE (IN.) L X W	BUTT THICKNESS	EXPOSURE DATA
Aluminum	California mission tile	Institutional, commercial, residential	3	48	One layer 30 lb asphalt saturated rag felt over plywood	Aluminum nails, screws	Tile red / Burnt red	10½ x 17 / 5 x 14	30 gauge aluminum	2 in. overlap
	Shake—shingle	Institutional, commercial, residential	4	36–88	One layer 30 lb felt over plywood	Anchor clip nailed	Various baked enamel finishes	12 x 48	Variable up to 1³⁄₁₆ in.	12 in.
Porcelain enamel on aluminum	Individual American method	Institutional, commercial, residential	3	225	One layer 30 lb felt plus 18 in. felt strips between tile	Special sealing nails supplied with tile	Various finishes	10 x 10	Prefinish for tiles custom fabricated to fit roof	

Walter H. Sobel, FAIA & Associates; Chicago, Illinois

CORRUGATED AND CRIMPED ROOFING

TYPE		SLOPE, MIN. (IN./FT)	MAX. SPAN (IN.)	WEIGHT (LB/SQUARE)	SIZE	WEIGHT OR THICKNESS	EXPOSURE OR LAP	COLOR AND TEXTURE	FASTENER
Iron and steel or galvanized iron	2.67" corrugations with 7/8, 3/4, or 1/2" depth	3	81-51[1]	Uncoated from 548 to 69. Coated from 568 to 90. Add approx. 10% for 3" corrugations	Width 34-5/8", 39-1/8", length 2-45'	Gauges 18-26	31 1/2", 36". End lap 6" min.	Uncoated galvanized or several colors of coatings	Corrosion resistant self-tapping screws, bolts, welded studs, power driven fasteners or nails in wood. All use neoprene washers
Protected metal (steel)[3]	Corrugated sheet 2.67" corrugations with 3/4 or 1/2" depth	4	88-44[1]	From 244 to 147	Width 33", length to 12'	Gauges 18-24	29-3/4" wide. End lap 6" min.	Smooth black or several colors	Same as corrugated steel
	Mansard sheet, 6 beads per sheet				Width 30", length to 12'				
	V-beam sheet, 5.4" pitch and 1 5/8" deep, 5 vees per sheet			From 278 to 167					
Aluminum	Corrugated sheet, 2.67" corrugations, 7/8" depth	3	77-55[1] 91-64 102-72	42 56 70	Widths 35 or 48", length 3-40'	0.024 0.032 0.040	1 1/2" corrugation side lap. 6" min. end lap. 1 vee side lap[6]	Plain mill or stucco in natural and various colors of acrylic enamel	Same as for corrugated steel, except use aluminum nails and sheet metal screws
	Curved corrugated sheet, same corrugations[5]			55.2	Width 33 3/4", length 3-40'	0.032			
	V-beam sheet, 4 7/8" pitch and 1 5/8" deep, top and bottom flats 3/4"		130-92[1] 152-107 173-122	58.4 72.2 90.3	Width 41 5/8", length 3-40'	0.032 0.040 0.050			
	Concealed clip panels (Reynolds Metals Co.)[7]			68.9 86.1 107.7	Width 13.35", length 3-40'	0.032 0.040 0.050	Width 12". End lap 6" min.	Stucco only; same colors as above	Clips with sheets locked at side laps
Corrugated asbestos cement	4.2" corrugations, 1 1/2" deep	3	54	410	Width 42", length 6-12'	3/8"	1 corrugation side lap. 6" min. end lap	Smooth natural or various colors of acrylic enamel	Bolts and clips, self-tapping screws, or drive screws over wood
	Curved sheet, min. radius (length) 5', min. radius (width) 4'								
Corrugated fiberglass, reinforced plastic	1 1/4" corrugations, 1/4" deep	3	40-22[2]	Approx. 40	Width 26" (max. 50") length 4-39'	5, 6, 8 oz/sq ft	1, 1 1/2 or 2 corrugation side lap. 6" min. end lap	Many colors, translucent opaque; or smooth or pebble finish.	Self-tapping screws, drive screws and nails. All with neoprene washers
	2 1/2" corrugations, 1/2" deep		65-32[2]		Widths 26" (max. 50") length 4-39'	4, 5, 6, 8, 10, 12 oz/sq ft			
	4.2" corrugations, 1 1/16" deep		72-50[2]		Widths 42, 50 3/8", length 4-39'	5-12 oz/sq ft			
	2.67" corrugations, 7/8" deep		70-42[2]		Width 50", length 4-39'	5-12 oz/sq ft			
	5-V crimp, 1/2" deep		65-32[2]		Width 26", length 4-39'	5-8 oz/sq ft			
	5.3-V crimp, 1" deep		84-60[2]		Width 41 5/8", 45", length 4-39'	5-12 oz/sq ft			
Corrugated plastic, nonreinforced plastic	2.67" corrugations, 9/16" deep	1	70-42[2]	Approx. 40	Width 50 1/2", length 8, 10, 12, 15, 20'	5-8 oz/sq ft	1 corrugation side lap. 8" min. end lap	Same as for reinforced plastic	Same as for reinforced plastic

NOTES

1. For 20 to 40 psf.
2. For 15 to 40 psf.
3. For use in chemical atmospheres. Panels are made of steel core, with both sides covered by a dry film at least 4 mils thick. The film has a special liquid resin coating, which is fused under high heat to a special corrosion resistant bond coat over chemically treated galvanized steel.
4. Corrugated and mansard sheets may be used on 4 in. min. slope with laps unsealed and on 3 in. min. slope with laps sealed. V-beam sheets may be used on 3 in. min. slope with laps unsealed and on 1 1/2 in. min. slope with laps sealed.
5. Minimum curvature radius 18 in.
6. Use 9 in. min. side laps on slopes from 2 to 3 in. Use 6 in. min. side laps on slopes above 3 in.
7. May be used on min. 1/2 in. slope only when one course used on slope. When more than one slope, the min. slope is 4 in.
8. Available in General Purpose, Type I, and Fire Retardant, Type II, except Type I has 5 oz weight only.

INSULATION

Many roof panel systems are available with foamed-in-place insulation. Their applications are subject to temperature limitations and various building codes, however. Check codes and manufacturers' fire ratings. Certain applications of roofing systems can also be applied directly over fiberglass batts.

VAPOR BARRIERS

To control a moderate level of relative humidity in living spaces, vapor resistant membranes must be utilized:

1. To control the moisture level within the structure.
2. To prevent moisture from passing through the insulation to a cold point where it can condense into water, possibly causing structural damage or rot.

Walter H. Sobel, FAIA & Associates; Chicago, Illinois

 GENERAL INFORMATION

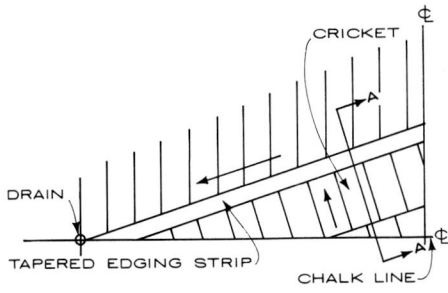

SECTION A-A

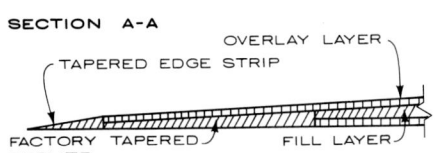

TAPERED INSULATION

NOTES

TAPERED INSULATION SYSTEMS: Consist of a series of factory prefabricated panels that are tapered to provide a positive slope on flat roof decks when used in conjunction with fill insulation of appropriate thickness. The tapered panels are produced from perlite, foam glass, urethane, and/or polystyrene. Standard available slopes vary from 1/8 to 1/2 in./ft. After installation of the fill layer and the tapered layers of insulation, an overlay layer is applied. As in the installation of any insulation system, joints of successive layers must be staggered in both dimensions. In the system, each block is identified for positions by a code number on the block. It is important that shop drawings, showing complete roof layout including drains, valleys, and cricket details, be provided.

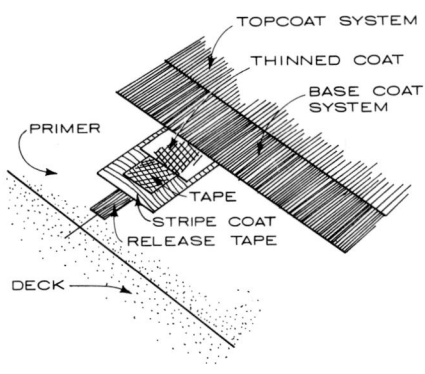

FLUID ROOFING

NOTES

NEOPRENE HYPALON: A single component, air curing, liquid coating designed to yield elastomeric films for high strength waterproof membranes for roof, deck, wall, floor, and subgrade applications over a wide variety of substrates such as concrete, plywood, insulation, metal, and built-up roofing. They are not recommended for continuous water emersion or for long term exposure to severe weathering. Coatings exposed to weather and some chemical environments require a hypalon topcoat.

Hypalon coatings are leadfree, air curing, liquid elastomeric coating. Used as weathering, ultraviolet protective, fire retardant coating.

Neoprene coating is applied in sufficient coats to secure a total minimum coverage of 3 gal/square (wet film thickness of 48 mils). Dry film 12 mils. Hypalon is applied in two coats with a wet film thickness of 16 mils/coat. Using not less than 1 gal/square per coat.

Robert E. Fehlberg, FAIA; CTA Architects Engineers; Billings, Montana

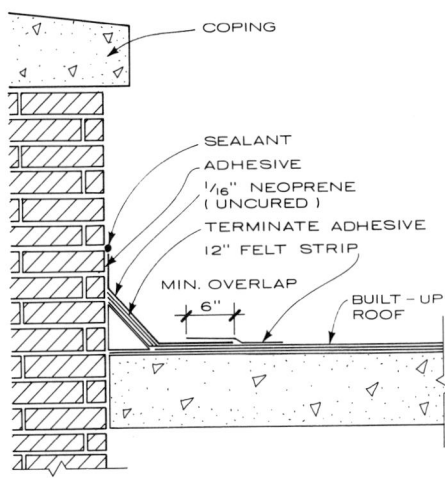

ELASTOMERIC FLASHING

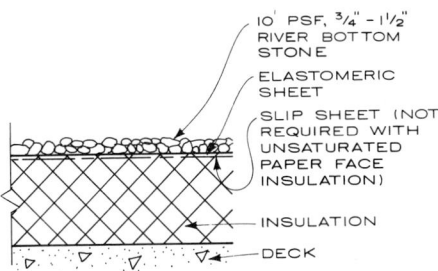

TYPICAL ROOF MEMBRANE APPLICATION

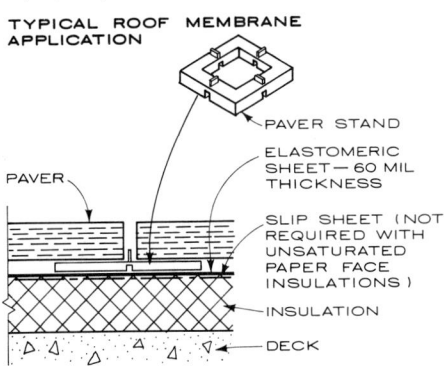

WITH WALKING SURFACE

SHEET ELASTOMERIC ROOF

NOTES

ELASTOMERIC SHEET ROOFING: This loosely laid roof consists of an elastomeric sheet that covers the entire roof continuously from edge to edge. The vapor barrier, insulation, and roof membrane are laid loosely. The polyvinyl sheet is seamed into a homogeneous skin, which is fastened to the deck only at roof edges and roof interruptions. This creates a one-piece loose membrane over the whole surface of the roof, which moves with the structure. Every seam and point where water could enter the roof are sealed with the same material as the roof itself and desolved in a solvent that cures to become an integral part of the roof.

The whole assembly is then ballasted with washed river bottom gravel—3/4 to 1 1/2 in. in its smallest dimension. This ballast protects the roof from casual traffic and aging and reduces peak temperatures of the roof during the summer by as much as 40°F.

Loosely laid membrane materials may be PVC (polyvinyl chloride), CPE (chlorinated polyethylene), or EPDM (ethylene propylene diene monomer). CPE and EPDM are recommended occasionally for certain applications; the most common material specified is PVC—unsupported or reinforced.

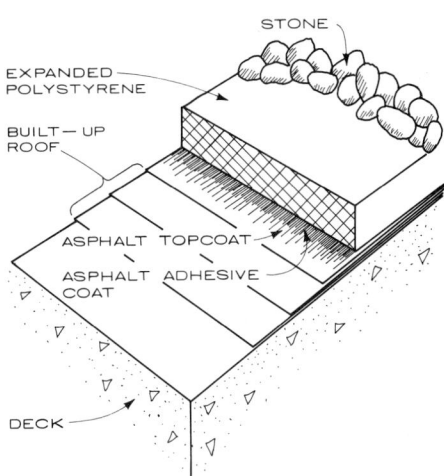

INSULATED ROOF MEMBRANE APPLICATION

NOTES

INSULATED ROOF MEMBRANE: Apply directly to the roof deck and with insulation on top of it. The membrane is on the warm side of the insulation and is practically invulnerable. It is not subject to roof traffic, ultraviolet degradation, thermocycling, and exposure that cause alligatoring, splitting, ridging, and other deterioration. These causes of roof failure are substantially reduced or totally eliminated. The heat gain or loss is just the same as if the insulation were installed under the membrane, because the expanded polystyrene does not absorb water. And, even in high humidity buildings, there is no need to install a vapor barrier because the membrane is the vapor barrier.

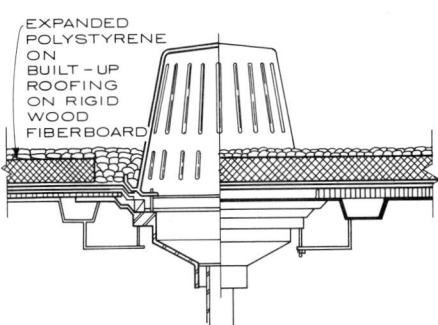

ROOF DRAIN DETAIL

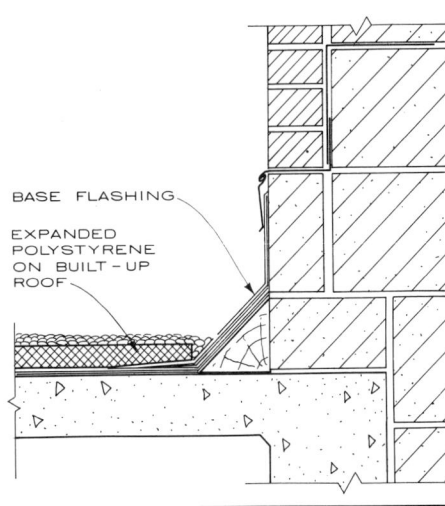

INSULATED ROOF MEMBRANE

ROOFING SYSTEMS **7**

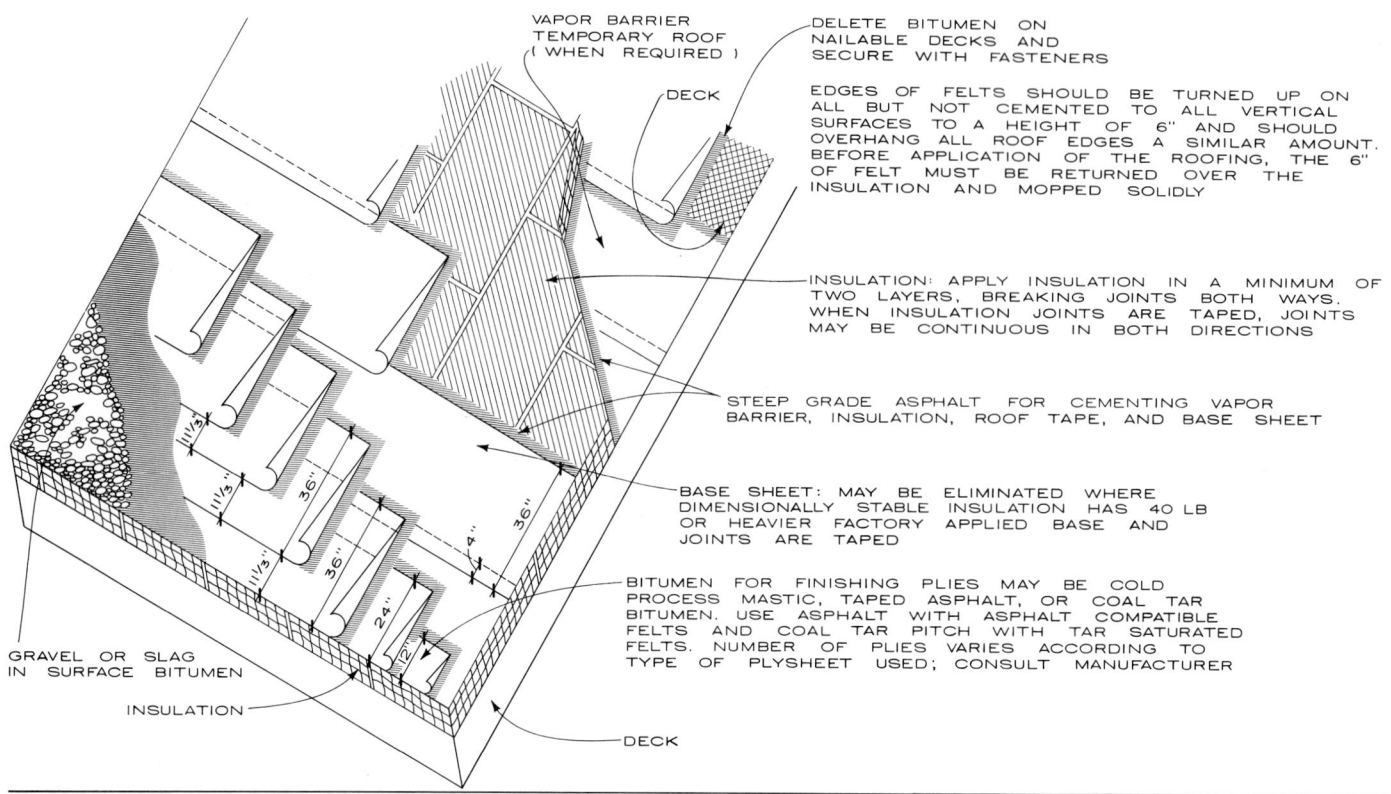

VAPOR BARRIER TEMPORARY ROOF (WHEN REQUIRED)

DECK

DELETE BITUMEN ON NAILABLE DECKS AND SECURE WITH FASTENERS

EDGES OF FELTS SHOULD BE TURNED UP ON ALL BUT NOT CEMENTED TO ALL VERTICAL SURFACES TO A HEIGHT OF 6" AND SHOULD OVERHANG ALL ROOF EDGES A SIMILAR AMOUNT. BEFORE APPLICATION OF THE ROOFING, THE 6" OF FELT MUST BE RETURNED OVER THE INSULATION AND MOPPED SOLIDLY

INSULATION: APPLY INSULATION IN A MINIMUM OF TWO LAYERS, BREAKING JOINTS BOTH WAYS. WHEN INSULATION JOINTS ARE TAPED, JOINTS MAY BE CONTINUOUS IN BOTH DIRECTIONS

STEEP GRADE ASPHALT FOR CEMENTING VAPOR BARRIER, INSULATION, ROOF TAPE, AND BASE SHEET

BASE SHEET: MAY BE ELIMINATED WHERE DIMENSIONALLY STABLE INSULATION HAS 40 LB OR HEAVIER FACTORY APPLIED BASE AND JOINTS ARE TAPED

BITUMEN FOR FINISHING PLIES MAY BE COLD PROCESS MASTIC, TAPED ASPHALT, OR COAL TAR BITUMEN. USE ASPHALT WITH ASPHALT COMPATIBLE FELTS AND COAL TAR PITCH WITH TAR SATURATED FELTS. NUMBER OF PLIES VARIES ACCORDING TO TYPE OF PLYSHEET USED; CONSULT MANUFACTURER

GRAVEL OR SLAG IN SURFACE BITUMEN

INSULATION

DECK

20 YEAR TYPE BUILT-UP ROOF OVER INSULATION

NOTES

1. For smooth surface roofs omit gravel or slag and add additional ply, using inorganic plysheets only.
2. On slopes over 1 in./ft all felts along top edge must usually be strapped and back-nailed.

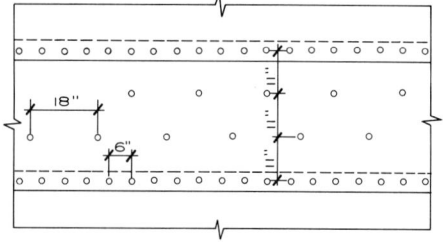

PATTERN FOR NAILING BASE SHEET OR VAPOR BARRIER OVER NAILABLE DECK

NOTES

1. Over nonnailable deck or insulation omit rosin paper and cement with asphalt. Nailing strips must be provided.
2. Minimum slope for organic felt = $1/2$ in./ft. EXCEPTION: In coal-tar systems the minimum slope is 0 in./ft.
3. Minimum slope for asbestos felt = $1/4$ in./ft.
4. Minimum slope for fiberglass felt = 0 in./ft.

STAGGER NAILS AT 12" O.C.

NAILABLE DECK

MINERAL SURFACE ROOFING. 2" SIDE LAPS IF SELVAGE IS UNGRANULATED; 3" SIDE LAPS IF SELVAGE IS GRANULATED

STEEP GRADE ASPHALT

ROSIN PAPER (OVER WOOD, EXCEPT PLYWOOD)

ASPHALT BETWEEN PLIES OF 15 LB FELT. ASPHALT TYPE (I, II, III, OR IV) DETERMINED BY ROOF SLOPE

MINERAL SURFACE BUILT-UP ROOF

SCHEDULE OF FELT OVERLAP (INCHES)

Organic base sheet	4
Fiberglass or asbestos base sheet	2
2-ply felts/plysheets	19
3-ply felts/plysheets	$24^2/_3$
4-ply felts/plysheets	$27^1/_2$
Fiberglass or asbestos mineral	3 if selvage granulated
Surface cap sheet	2 if selvage granulated

Kent Wong; Hewlett, Jamison, Atkinson & Luey; Portland, Oregon

Developed by Angelo J. Forlidas, AIA; Charlotte, North Carolina; from data furnished by Robert M. Stafford, P.E., Consulting Engineer; Charlotte, North Carolina

7 ROOFING SYSTEMS

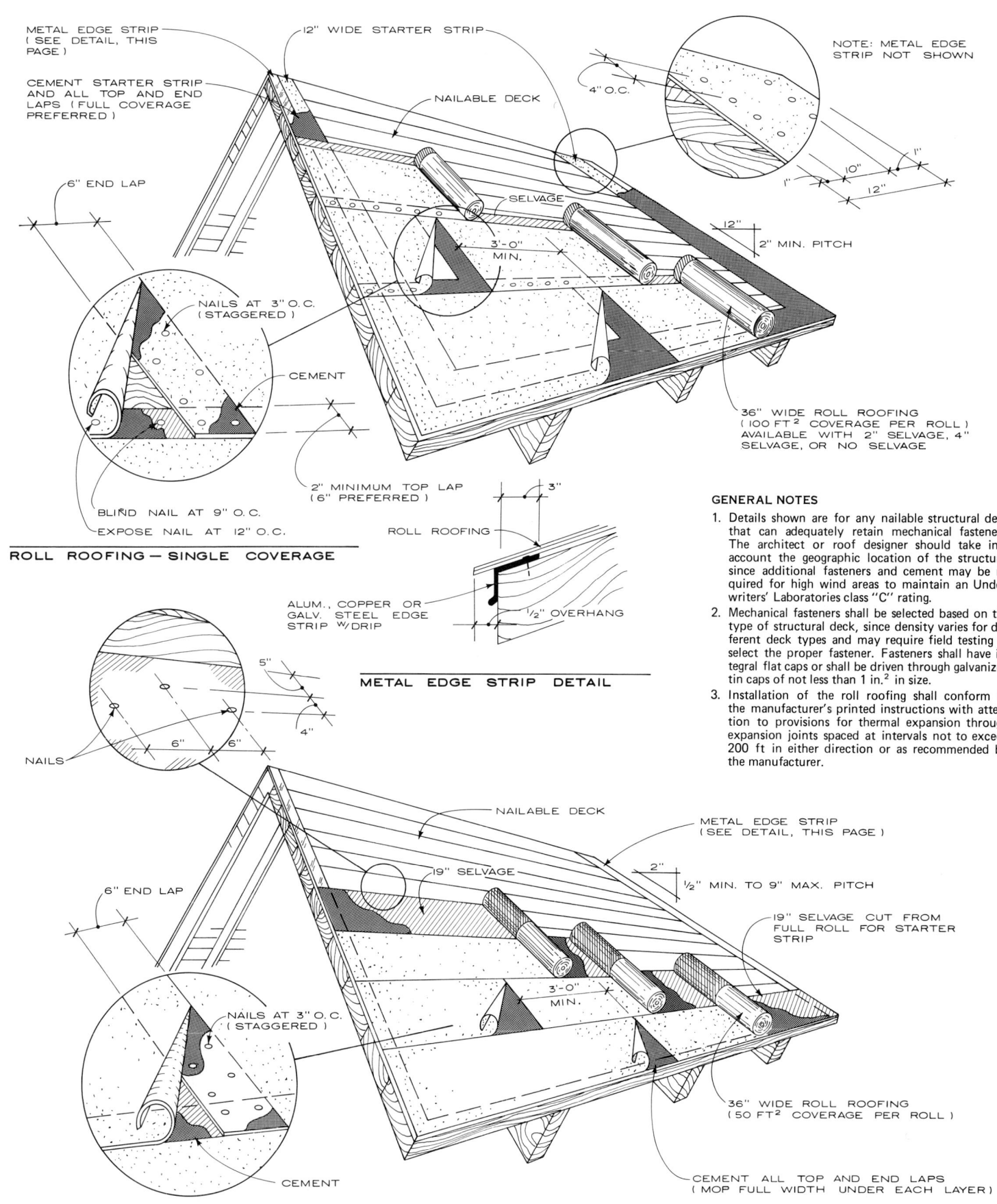

METAL EDGE STRIP
(SEE DETAIL, THIS
PAGE)

CEMENT STARTER STRIP
AND ALL TOP AND END
LAPS (FULL COVERAGE
PREFERRED)

6" END LAP

12" WIDE STARTER STRIP

NAILABLE DECK

NOTE: METAL EDGE
STRIP NOT SHOWN

4" O.C.

SELVAGE

3'-0"
MIN.

12"

2" MIN. PITCH

1"   10"   1"

12"

NAILS AT 3" O.C.
(STAGGERED)

CEMENT

BLIND NAIL AT 9" O.C.
EXPOSE NAIL AT 12" O.C.

36" WIDE ROLL ROOFING
(100 FT² COVERAGE PER ROLL)
AVAILABLE WITH 2" SELVAGE, 4"
SELVAGE, OR NO SELVAGE

ROLL ROOFING — SINGLE COVERAGE

2" MINIMUM TOP LAP
(6" PREFERRED)

3"

ROLL ROOFING

ALUM., COPPER OR
GALV. STEEL EDGE
STRIP W/DRIP

½" OVERHANG

METAL EDGE STRIP DETAIL

5"

4"

6"   6"

NAILS

NAILABLE DECK

METAL EDGE STRIP
(SEE DETAIL, THIS PAGE)

19" SELVAGE

2"

½" MIN. TO 9" MAX. PITCH

19" SELVAGE CUT FROM
FULL ROLL FOR STARTER
STRIP

6" END LAP

NAILS AT 3" O.C.
(STAGGERED)

3'-0"
MIN.

36" WIDE ROLL ROOFING
(50 FT² COVERAGE PER ROLL)

CEMENT

CEMENT ALL TOP AND END LAPS
(MOP FULL WIDTH UNDER EACH LAYER)

**ROLL ROOFING — DOUBLE COVERAGE
CONCEALED NAILING**

GENERAL NOTES

1. Details shown are for any nailable structural deck that can adequately retain mechanical fasteners. The architect or roof designer should take into account the geographic location of the structure, since additional fasteners and cement may be required for high wind areas to maintain an Underwriters' Laboratories class "C" rating.

2. Mechanical fasteners shall be selected based on the type of structural deck, since density varies for different deck types and may require field testing to select the proper fastener. Fasteners shall have integral flat caps or shall be driven through galvanized tin caps of not less than 1 in.² in size.

3. Installation of the roll roofing shall conform to the manufacturer's printed instructions with attention to provisions for thermal expansion through expansion joints spaced at intervals not to exceed 200 ft in either direction or as recommended by the manufacturer.

James E. Phillips, AIA, Liles/Associates/Architects; Greenville, South Carolina

ROOFING SYSTEMS   7

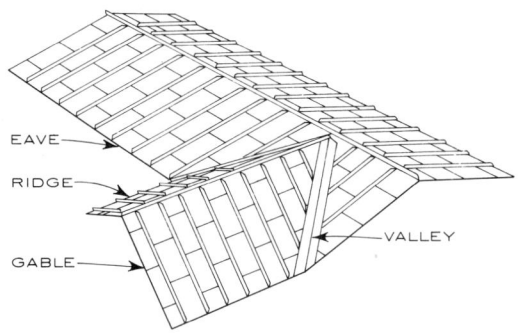

STANDING SEAM METAL ROOF

GAUGE AND PAN WIDTHS FOR STANDING SEAM ROOFS

WIDTH OF SHEET (IN.)	WIDTH OF PAN (INCHES)			RECOMMENDED GAGES		
	SEAM HEIGHT 7/8 IN.	SEAM HEIGHT 1 IN.	SEAM HEIGHT 1 1/4 IN.	GALV. STEEL (GAUGE)	COPPER (OZ.)	PAINTED TERNE 40 LB COATING
20	17 1/4	16 3/4	16 1/4	26	16	0.015 in.
22	19 1/4	18 3/4	18 1/4	26	16	0.015 in.
24	21 1/4	20 3/4	20 1/4	26	16	0.015 in.
26	23 1/4	22 3/4	22 1/4	24	20	0.0178 in.
28	25 1/4	24 3/4	24 1/4	24	20	0.0178 in.

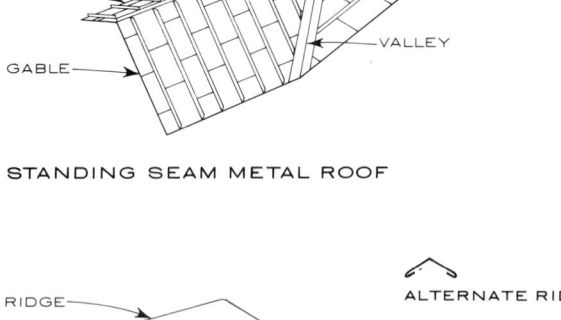

DETAIL I - RIDGE CONSTRUCTION

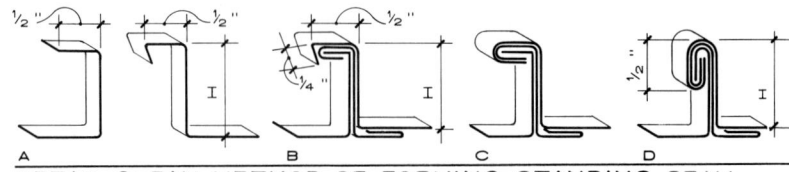

DETAIL 2 - PAN METHOD OF FORMING STANDING SEAM

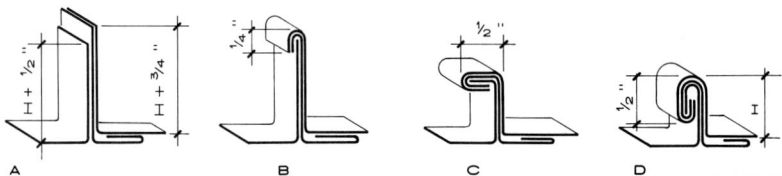

DETAIL 3 - FIELD METHOD OF FORMING STANDING SEAM

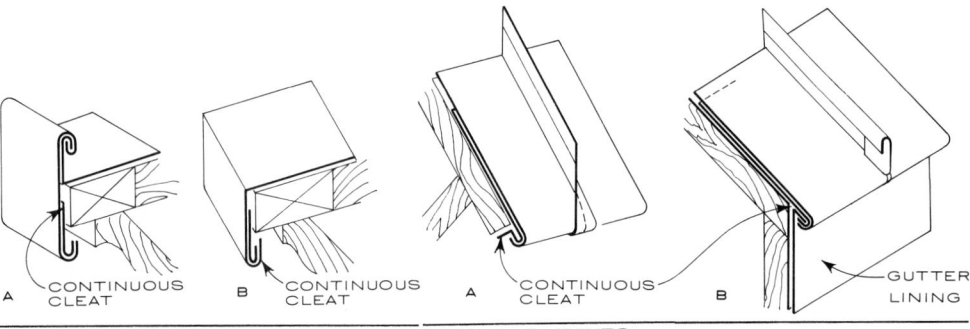

DETAIL 4 - GABLES   DETAIL 5 - EAVES

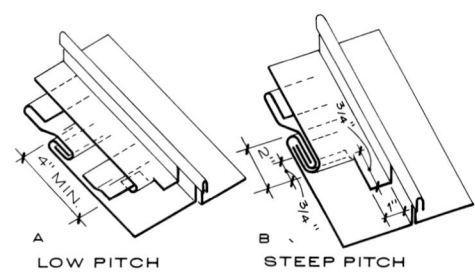

DETAIL 6 - TRANSVERSE SEAM

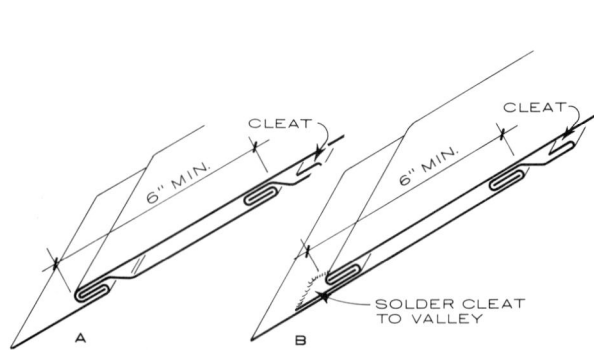

DETAIL 7 - VALLEY

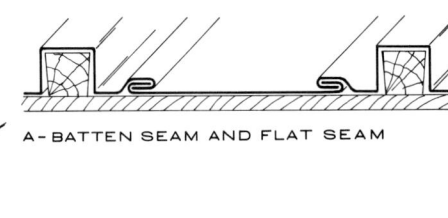

A - BATTEN SEAM AND FLAT SEAM

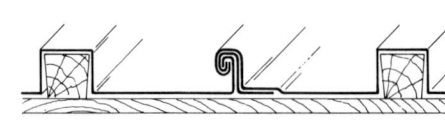

B - BATTEN SEAM AND STANDING SEAM

DETAIL 8 - COMBINATION ROOFS

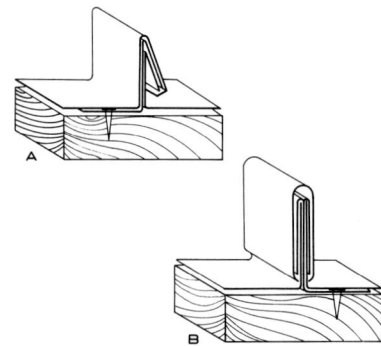

DETAIL 9 - PREFABRICATED SEAMS

NOTES

1. Standing seam roofing may be applied on slopes of 3 in./ft or greater. If the surface to receive the roofing is other than wood, nailing strips must be provided to receive the cleats. See general notes on metal roofs for recommended surface preparation.

2. The spacing of seams may vary between reasonable limits to suit the architectural style of a given building. The two methods of installing standing seam roofing are the pan and the roll method. In the pan method, the sides of the sheets are formed as shown in A of detail 2. Top and bottom edges of pans are formed as shown in A and B of detail 6. Pans are installed with cleats spaced not more than 12 inches on center. Each pan is locked to the one below as shown in A and B of detail 7. The adjacent row of pans is next installed and the standing seams completed as in C and D of detail 2.

3. The roll method consists of a series of long sheets joined together at their ends with double flat lock seams and sent to the job in rolls. The standing seam is field formed as shown in A of detail 3. The roofing is installed in lengths reaching from the eave to the ridge and attached with cleats spaced not more than 12 in. on center. After a second length is installed and cleated in place, the standing seam is formed as shown in detail 3.

4. A of detail 5 shows method of terminating metal roofing at the eave where roofing is locked over a continuous cleat. B of detail 5 shows method of terminating metal roofing at a built-in gutter. Roofing is loose locked to a continuous cleat and the flange on back edge of gutter. Seam terminations must be soldered.

5. A and B of detail 9 show two common prefabricated standing seams now in use. The use of newly developed electronic seaming machines is recommended for long runs of standing seams.

See also Metal Roofs for general notes.

Straub, VanDine, Dziurman/Architects; Troy, Michigan

Emory E. Hinkel, Jr.; A. G. Odell, Jr. and Associates; Charlotte, North Carolina

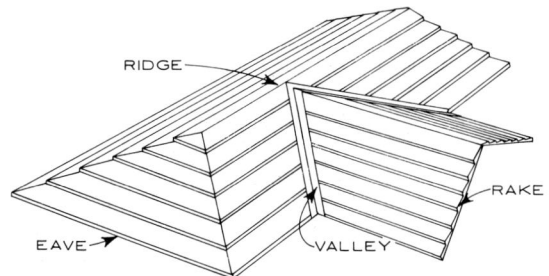

BERMUDA TYPE METAL ROOF

RECOMMENDED GAUGES OR WEIGHTS FOR PAN WIDTHS

WIDTH OF SHEET (IN.)	WIDTH OF PAN "D" (IN.)	COPPER (OZ)	GALVANIZED STEEL (GAUGE)	STAINLESS STEEL (GAUGE)	PAINTED TERNE 40 LB COATING
20	16½	16	26	28	0.015 IN.
22	18½	16	26	28	0.015 IN.
24	20½	16	26	26	0.015 IN.
26	22½	20	24	26	0.0178 IN.
28	24½	20	24	26	0.0178 IN.

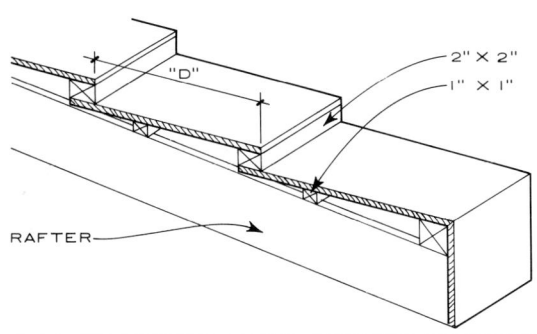

DETAIL I-WOOD FRAMING

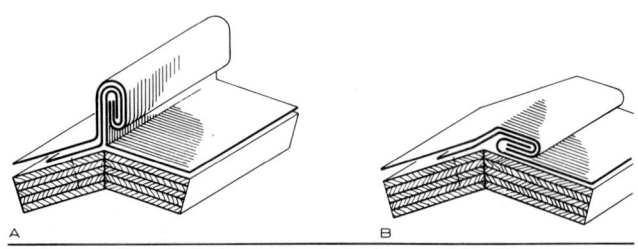

DETAIL 2-SEAM TYPES AT HIP OR RIDGE

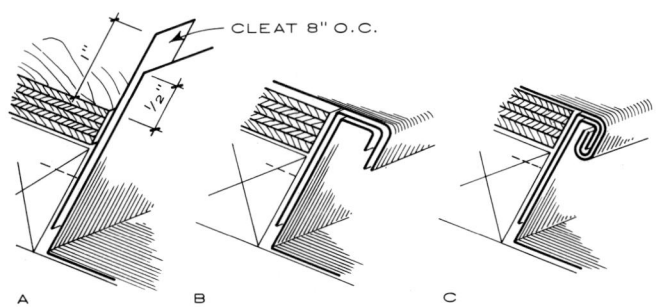

DETAIL 3-CONSTRUCTION AT BATTEN

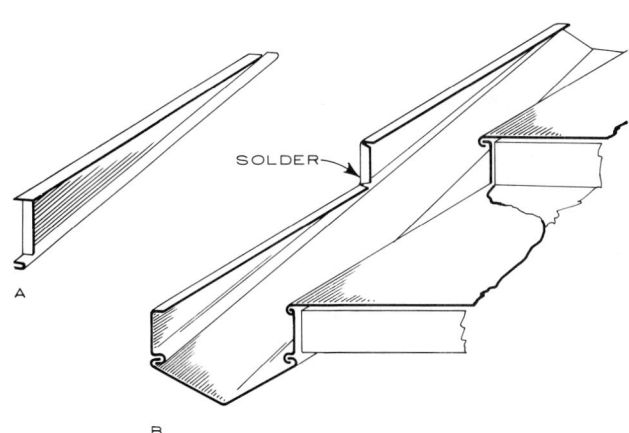

DETAIL 4-CONSTRUCTION AT CLOSURE AND VALLEY

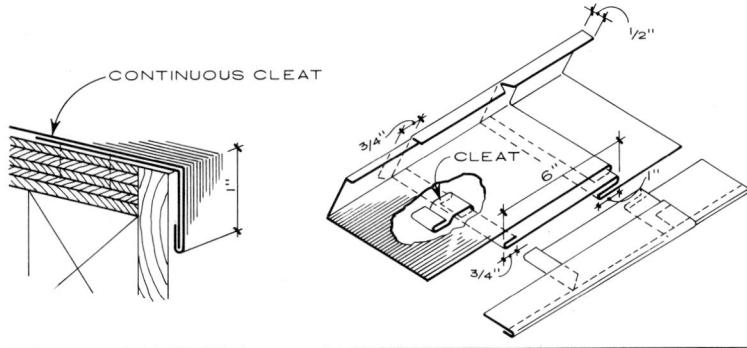

DETAIL 5-EAVE **DETAIL 6-EXPANSION JOINT**

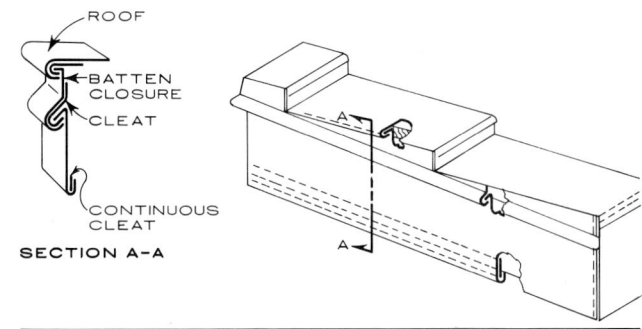

DETAIL 7-CONSTRUCTION AT RAKE

NOTES

1. The Bermuda roof may be used for roofs having a slope greater than 2½ in./ft. Wood framing must be provided as shown in detail 1. Dimension "D" and gauge of metal will depend on the size of sheet used. See chart. Consult general notes on metal roofs for recommended surface preparation.

2. Bermuda roof is applied beginning at the eave. The first pan is hooked over a continuous cleat as shown in detail 5. The upper portion of the first and each succeeding pan is attached as shown in detail 3. Cleats spaced on 8 in. centers are nailed to batten

as in A of detail 3. Joint is developed as shown in B of detail 3 and malleted against batten as shown in C of detail 3. All cross seams are single locked and soldered except at expansion joints. Cross seams should be staggered. Expansion joints should be used at least every 25 ft and formed as shown in detail 6. Roofing is joined at hip or ridge by use of a standing seam as shown in A of detail 2. Seam may be malleted down as shown in B of detail 2.

3. Detail 4 shows the method of forming valleys. Valley sections are lapped 8 in. in direction of flow.

Individual closures for sides of valley are formed as shown in A of detail 4 and must be soldered as indicated in B of detail 4. A method of terminating the roof at rake is shown in detail 7. The face plate (optional) is held in place by continuous cleats at both top and bottom. The batten closure is formed as a cleat to hold edge of roof pan as shown in section A-A of detail 7.

See also Metal Roofs for general notes.

Straub, VanDine, Dziurman/Architects; Troy, Michigan

Emory E. Hinkel, Jr.; A. G. Odell, Jr. and Associates; Charlotte, North Carolina

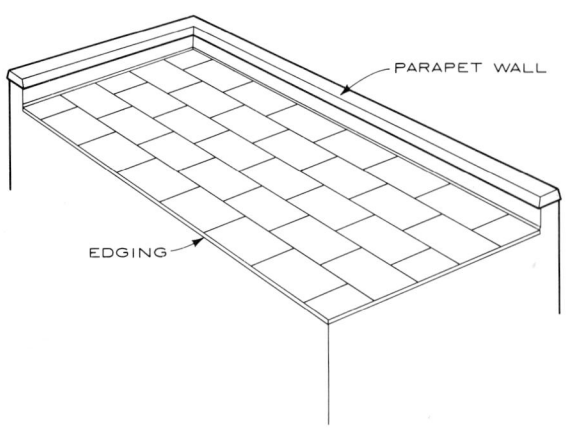

FLAT SEAM ROOF

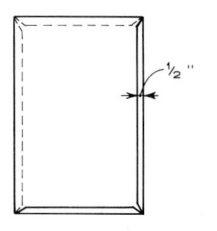

DETAIL 1- ROOFING SHEET

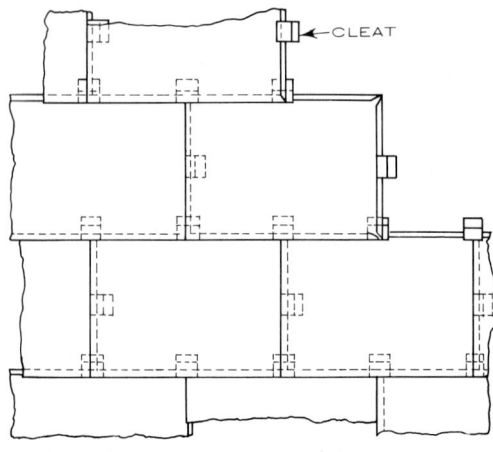

DETAIL 2- FLAT SEAM ROOF

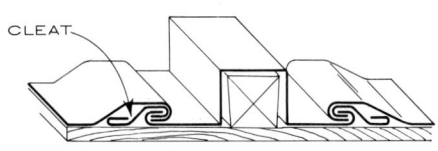

DETAIL 3- EXPANSION BATTEN

DETAIL 4- JUNCTION AT PARAPET WALL

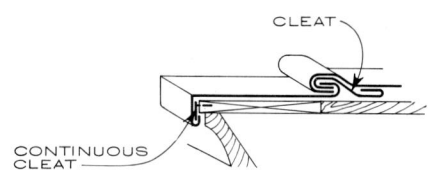

DETAIL 5- ROOF EDGE

NOTES

1. The flat seam method of roofing as illustrated is most commonly used on roofs of slight pitch or for the covering of curved surfaces such as towers or domes.
2. The joints connecting the sheets of roofs having a pitch greater than 1/2 in./ft may be sealed with caulking compound or white lead. The joints of roofs having a pitch of less than 1/2 in./ft must be malleted and thoroughly sweated full with solder.
3. Roofs of slight pitch should be divided by expansion batten as shown in detail 3, into sections not exceeding maximum total areas of 30 ft².

4. Consult general notes on metal roofs for recommended surface preparation.
5. The metal sheets may be pretinned if required, 1 1/2 in. back from all edges and on both sides of the sheet. Pans are formed by notching and folding the sheets as shown in detail 1.
6. The pans are held in place by cleating as shown. After pans are in place, all seams are malleted and soldered or sealed.

7. Detail 4 shows the junction of a roof and a parapet wall. Metal base flashing is cleated to deck on 2 ft centers and extended up wall; 8 in. pans are locked and soldered to base flashing. Metal counter flashing covers 4 in. of the base flashing. Detail 5 illustrates the installation of flashing at edge of roof. Flashing is formed as shown and attached to the face by a continuous cleat nailed on 1 ft centers and cleated to the roof deck. Pans are locked and soldered or sealed to the flashing. See also general notes below.

GENERAL NOTES

1. Detail drawings for metal roof types are diagrammatic only. The indication of adjoining construction is included merely to establish its relation to the sheet metal work and is not intended as a recommendation of architectural design. Any details that may suggest an architectural period do not limit the application of sheet metal to that or any other architectural style.
2. Weights of metals and roof slopes indicated on detail drawings are minimum as recommended by the Sheet Metal and Air Conditioning Contractors'

National Association and may vary from recommendations of some manufacturers.
3. Metals used must be of a thickness or gauge heavy enough and in correct proportion to the breadth and scale of the work. Provide expansion joints for freedom of movement.
4. Prevent direct contact of metal roofing with dissimilar metals that cause electrolysis.
5. A wide range of metals, alloys, and finishes are available for metal roofing. The durability as well as the maintenance requirements of each should be

taken into consideration when selecting roofing.
6. The surface to receive the metal roofing should be thoroughly dry and covered by a saturated roofing felt in case of leakage due to construction error or wind driven moisture. A rosin paper should be applied over the felt to avoid bonding between felt and metal.
7. Many of the prefabricated batten and standing seam devices are not as watertight as with conventional methods and are therefore more suitable for steeply pitched roofs such as mansards.

Straub, VanDine, Dziurman/Architects; Troy, Michigan

Emory E. Hinkel, Jr.; A. G. Odell, Jr. and Associates; Charlotte, North Carolina

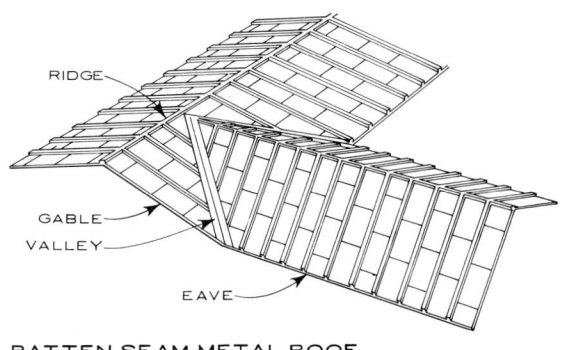

BATTEN SEAM METAL ROOF

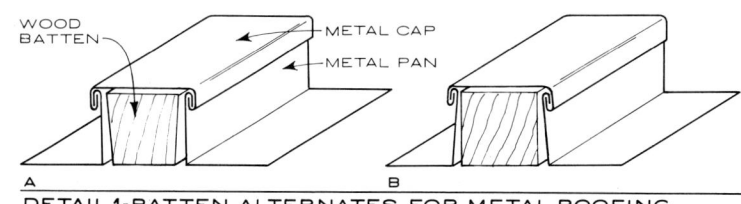

DETAIL 1-BATTEN ALTERNATES FOR METAL ROOFING

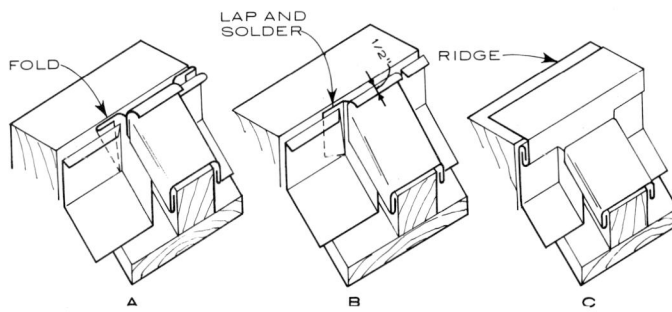

DETAIL 2 - RIDGE CONSTRUCTION

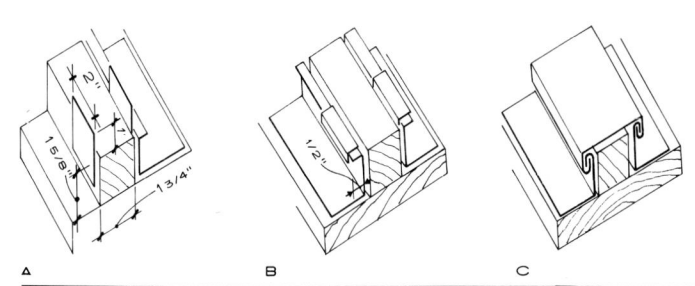

DETAIL 3 - BATTEN JOINT CONSTRUCTION

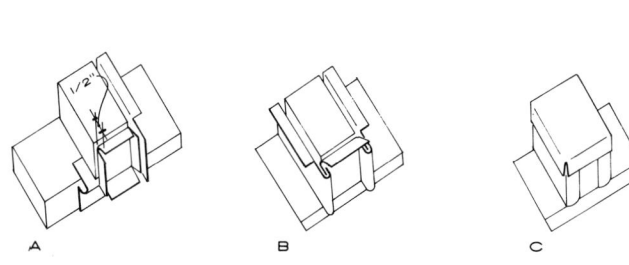

DETAIL 4 - BATTEN CAP CONSTRUCTION

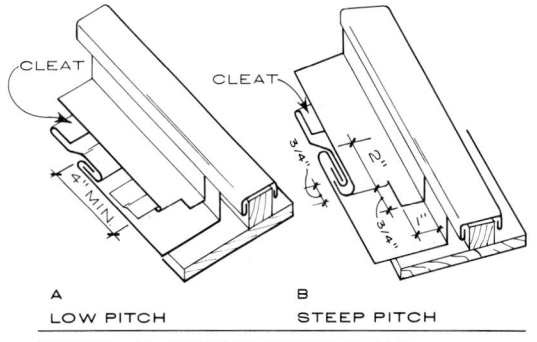

DETAIL 5 - TRANSVERSE SEAM

LOW PITCH   STEEP PITCH

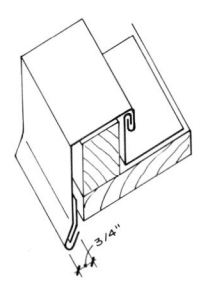

DETAIL 6 - GABLE

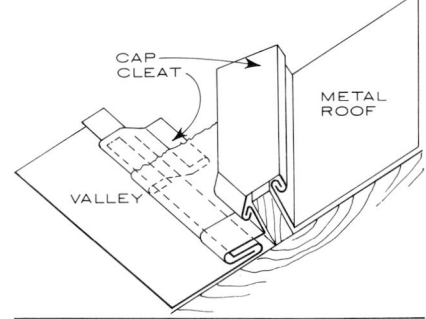

DETAIL 7 - VALLEY

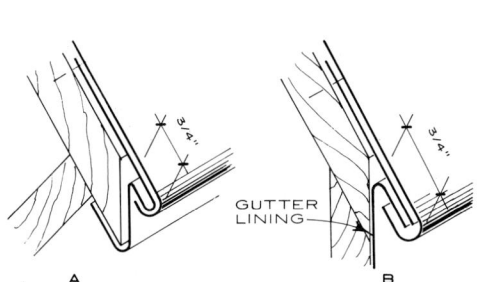

DETAIL 8 - EAVES

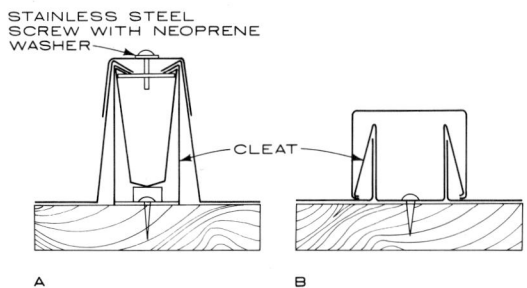

DETAIL 9 - PREFABRICATED BATTENS

NOTES

1. Batten seam roofing may be applied on slopes of 3 in./ft or greater. If the surface to receive the roofing is other than wood, the battens should be bolted into place. All batten fasteners must be countersunk into battens. See general notes on Metal Roofs for recommended surface preparation.

2. The spacing of the wood battens may vary within reasonable limits to suit the architectural style and scale of the building, but the recommended maximum distance is 20 in. between battens. Care should be taken to space the battens in such a manner that waste of metal is held to a minimum. Battens may be shaped as shown in A or B of detail 1.

A is preferred, since it automatically makes allowance for expansion. When battens shown in B are used, care must be taken to provide for expansion by bending the metal where it meets the batten at greater than 90°.

3. Sheets are formed into pans with each side turned up 2 1/8 in. A 1/2 in. flange is turned toward the center of the pan as shown in B of detail 3. At lower end of the pan, the sheet is notched and a hook edge is formed as in A or B of detail 5. For low pitched roofs the upper end of the sheet is formed as in A of detail 5. On steeper roofs the upper end is formed as shown in B of detail 5. Pans

are installed, starting at the eave, and held in place with cleats spaced not over 12 in. on center as shown in A of detail 3. Each pan is hooked to the one below it and cleated into place. After pans are in place, a cap is installed over the batten as shown in B and C of detail 3.

4. A number of manufacturers have developed metal roofing systems using several prefabricated devices. A and B of detail 9 show two common prefabricated battens in use.

5. See also Standing Seam Metal Roofing for details on combination batten and standing or flat seam roofing. See also Metal Roofs for general notes.

Straub, VanDine, Dziurman/Architects; Troy, Michigan

Emory E. Hinkel, Jr.; A. G. Odell, Jr. and Associates; Charlotte, North Carolina

METAL ROOFING   **7**

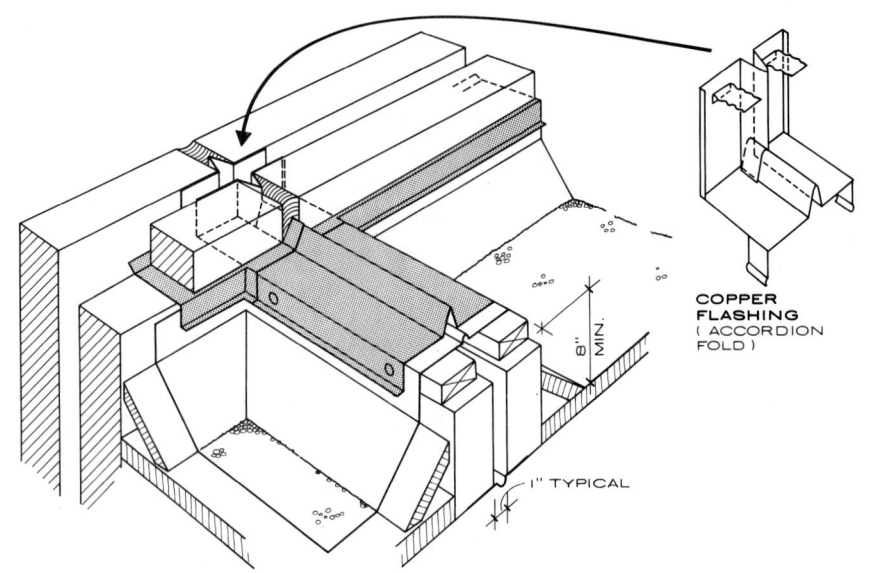

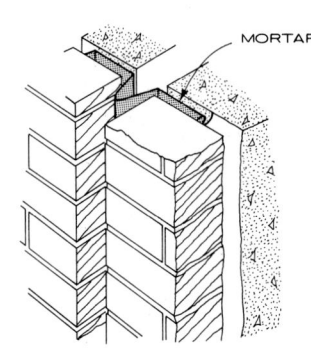

MORTAR

WATERSTOPS SHOULD RUN CONTINUOUS FROM FOOTING TO TOP OF BUILDING. LAP JOINT 4" IN DIRECTION OF FLOW

COPPER FLASHING (ACCORDION FOLD)

8" MIN.

1" TYPICAL

EXPANSION JOINT AT INTERSECTION OF WALL AND PARAPET

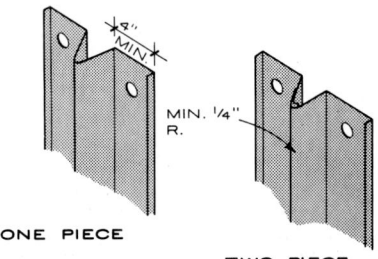

MIN. ¼" R.

ONE PIECE

TWO PIECE

VERTICAL EXPANSION JOINT AT WALL

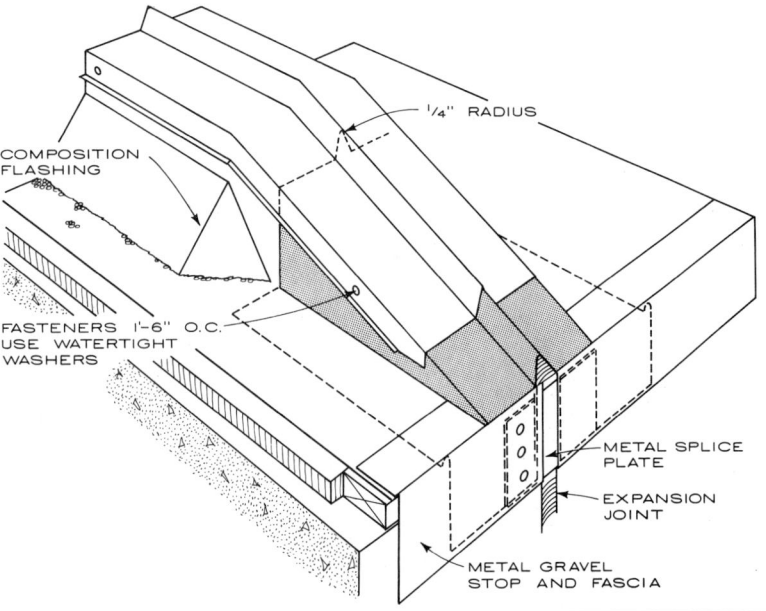

¼" RADIUS

COMPOSITION FLASHING

FASTENERS 1'-6" O.C. USE WATERTIGHT WASHERS

METAL SPLICE PLATE

EXPANSION JOINT

METAL GRAVEL STOP AND FASCIA

EXPANSION JOINT TRANSITION AT EAVE

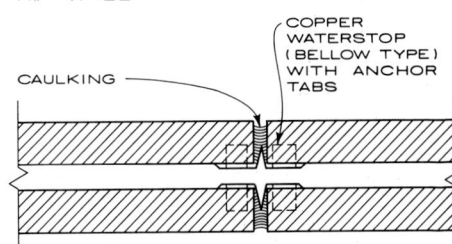

CAULKING

COPPER WATERSTOP (BELLOW TYPE) WITH ANCHOR TABS

PLAN SECTION AT PARAPET WALL

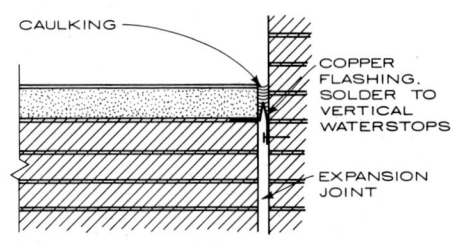

CAULKING

COPPER FLASHING. SOLDER TO VERTICAL WATERSTOPS

EXPANSION JOINT

VERTICAL SECTION AT PARAPET COPING

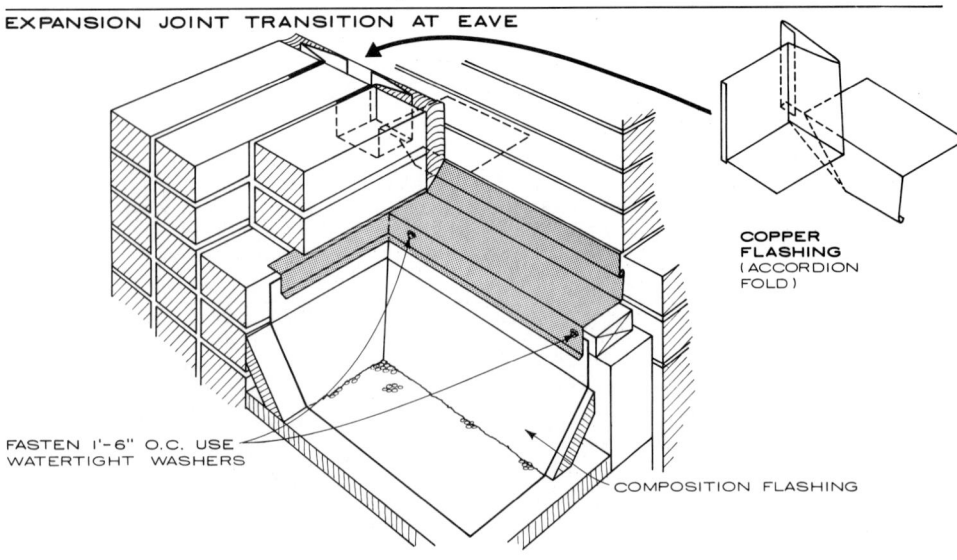

COPPER FLASHING (ACCORDION FOLD)

FASTEN 1'-6" O.C. USE WATERTIGHT WASHERS

COMPOSITION FLASHING

EXPANSION JOINT AT INTERSECTION OF WALL AND PARAPET

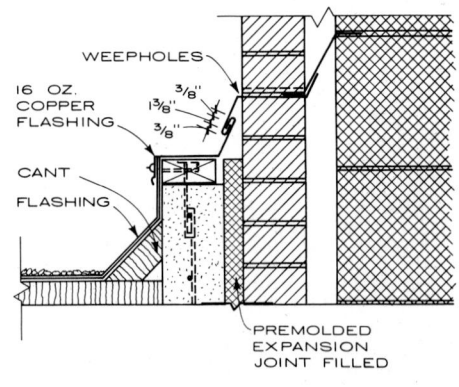

WEEPHOLES

16 OZ. COPPER FLASHING

3/8"

1 3/8"

3/8"

CANT

FLASHING

PREMOLDED EXPANSION JOINT FILLED

EXPANSION JOINT AT ROOF AND WALL

CTA Architects Engineers; Billings, Montana

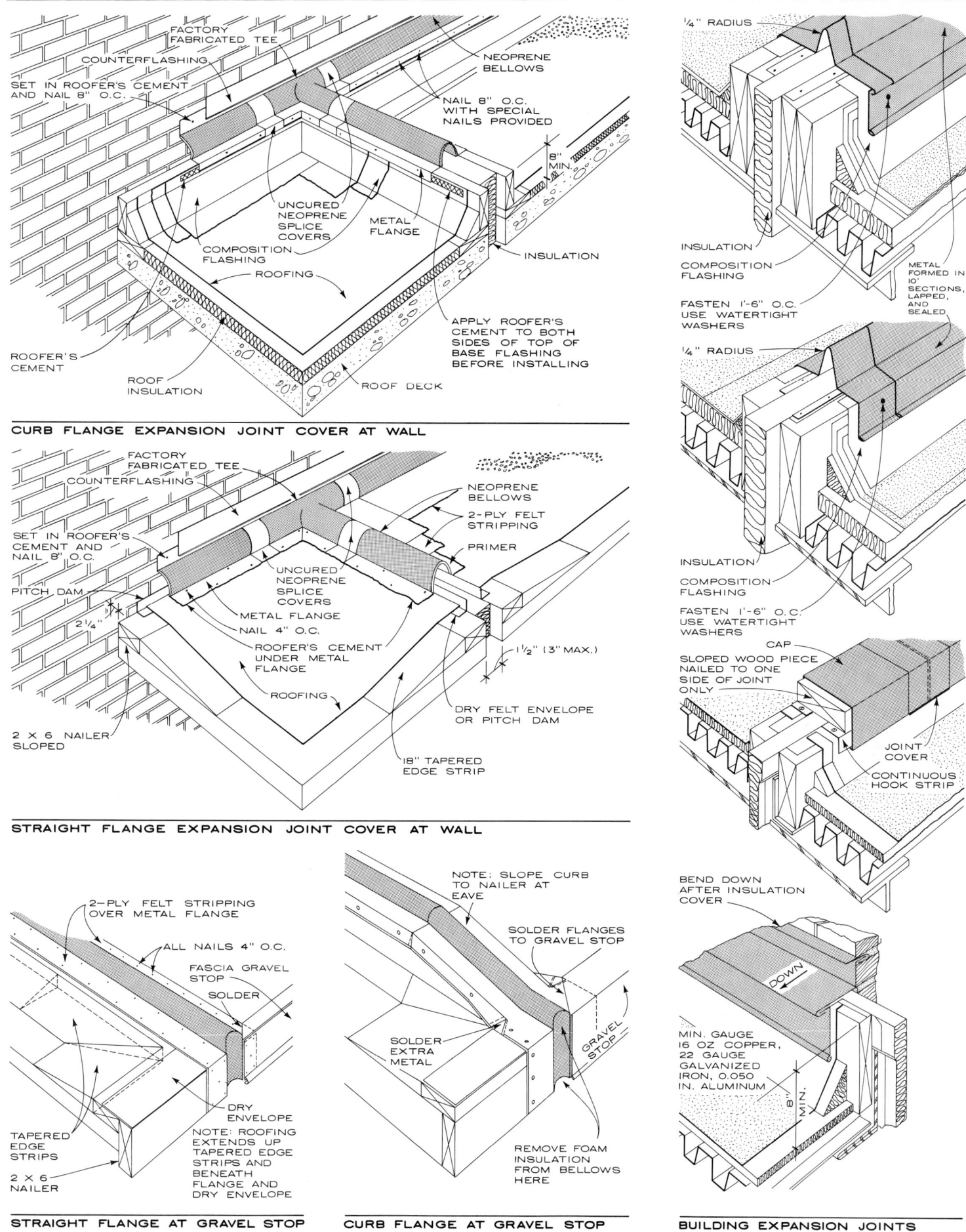

FACTORY FABRICATED TEE
COUNTERFLASHING
SET IN ROOFER'S CEMENT AND NAIL 8" O.C.
NEOPRENE BELLOWS
NAIL 8" O.C. WITH SPECIAL NAILS PROVIDED
8" MIN.
UNCURED NEOPRENE SPLICE COVERS
METAL FLANGE
COMPOSITION FLASHING
ROOFING
INSULATION
ROOFER'S CEMENT
ROOF INSULATION
APPLY ROOFER'S CEMENT TO BOTH SIDES OF TOP OF BASE FLASHING BEFORE INSTALLING
ROOF DECK

CURB FLANGE EXPANSION JOINT COVER AT WALL

FACTORY FABRICATED TEE
COUNTERFLASHING
SET IN ROOFER'S CEMENT AND NAIL 8" O.C.
NEOPRENE BELLOWS
2-PLY FELT STRIPPING
PRIMER
PITCH DAM
2 1/4"
UNCURED NEOPRENE SPLICE COVERS
METAL FLANGE
NAIL 4" O.C.
ROOFER'S CEMENT UNDER METAL FLANGE
ROOFING
2 X 6 NAILER SLOPED
1 1/2" (3" MAX.)
DRY FELT ENVELOPE OR PITCH DAM
18" TAPERED EDGE STRIP

STRAIGHT FLANGE EXPANSION JOINT COVER AT WALL

2-PLY FELT STRIPPING OVER METAL FLANGE
ALL NAILS 4" O.C.
FASCIA GRAVEL STOP
SOLDER
TAPERED EDGE STRIPS
2 X 6 NAILER
DRY ENVELOPE
NOTE: ROOFING EXTENDS UP TAPERED EDGE STRIPS AND BENEATH FLANGE AND DRY ENVELOPE

STRAIGHT FLANGE AT GRAVEL STOP

NOTE: SLOPE CURB TO NAILER AT EAVE
SOLDER FLANGES TO GRAVEL STOP
SOLDER EXTRA METAL
GRAVEL STOP
REMOVE FOAM INSULATION FROM BELLOWS HERE

CURB FLANGE AT GRAVEL STOP

1/4" RADIUS
INSULATION
COMPOSITION FLASHING
FASTEN 1'-6" O.C. USE WATERTIGHT WASHERS
METAL FORMED IN 10' SECTIONS, LAPPED, AND SEALED

1/4" RADIUS
NEOPRENE BELLOWS
INSULATION
COMPOSITION FLASHING
FASTEN 1'-6" O.C. USE WATERTIGHT WASHERS

CAP
SLOPED WOOD PIECE NAILED TO ONE SIDE OF JOINT ONLY
JOINT COVER
CONTINUOUS HOOK STRIP

BEND DOWN AFTER INSULATION COVER
DOWN
MIN. GAUGE 16 OZ COPPER, 22 GAUGE GALVANIZED IRON, 0.050 IN. ALUMINUM
8" MIN.

BUILDING EXPANSION JOINTS

CTA Architects Engineers; Billings, Montana

ROOF SPECIALTIES 7

WIDTH OF RECTANGULAR GUTTERS FOR GIVEN ROOF AREAS AND RAINFALL INTENSITIES

NOTE

The terms "leader," "conductor," and "down-spout" all mean the same thing.

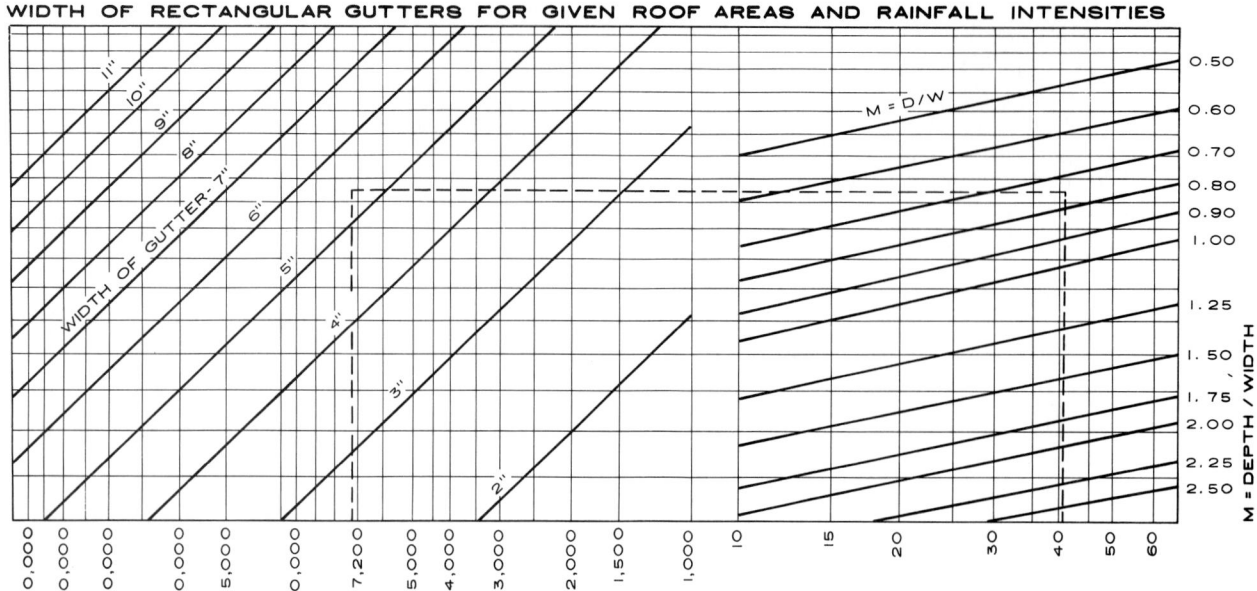

IA = RAINFALL INTENSITY X AREA

L = LENGTH OF GUTTER IN FEET

SAMPLE PROBLEM

To size rectangular gutter for a building 120 x 30 ft. located in New York City. This building has a flat roof with a raised roof edge on three sides. A gutter is to be located on one of the 120 ft. sides. So that each section of gutter will not exceed 50 ft., three downspouts will be used with 2 gutter expansion joints. The area to be drained by each section of gutter will be 1200 sq. ft., the rainfall intensity from map below is 6 in., the length of each gutter section is 40 ft., and the ratio of gutter depth to width is 0.75. On chart above find the vertical line representing L = 40. Proceed vertically along this line to its intersection with the oblique line representing M = 0.75. Pass horizontally to the left to intersect the vertical line representing IA = 7200. The point of intersection occurs between the oblique line representing gutter widths of 5 and 6 in. The required width of gutter is, therefore, 6 in. and its depth need be only 4 $\frac{1}{2}$ in.

DESIGN AREAS FOR PITCHED ROOFS

PITCH	FACTOR
LEVEL TO 3 IN./FT.	1.00
4 TO 5 IN./FT.	1.05
6 TO 8 IN./FT.	1.10
9 TO 11 IN./FT.	1.20
12 IN./FT.	1.30

NOTE: When a roof is sloped neither the plan nor actual area should be used in sizing drainage. Multiply the plan area by the factor shown above to obtain design area.

INFLUENCE OF GUTTER SHAPE ON DESIGN

1. RECTANGULAR GUTTERS:

Use graph at top of page.

2. IRREGULAR SHAPES:

Determine equivalent rectangular size and use same method.

3. SEMICIRCULAR GUTTERS:

First size downspout from tables below. Then use gutter 1 inch larger in diameter.

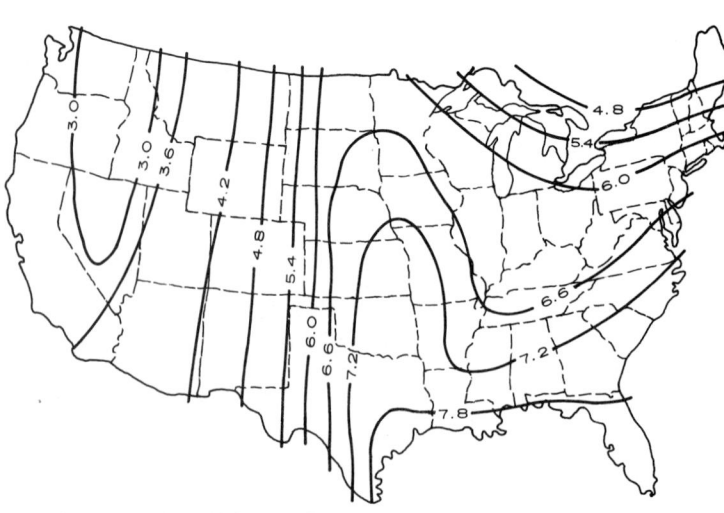

RAINFALL INTENSITY MAP
NOTE

Map shows hourly rainfall intensity in inches per hour for 5 minute periods to be expected once in 10 years. Normally this is adequate for design, but some storms have been twice as intense in some areas. See local records.

Lawrence W. Cobb; Columbia, South Carolina

DOWNSPOUT CAPACITY

INTENSITY IN IN./HR. LASTING 5 MIN.	SQ. FT. ROOF/ SQ. IN. DOWN-SPOUT
2	600
3	400
4	300
5	240
6	200
7	175
8	150
9	130
10	120
11	110

GENERAL NOTES

Most gutters are run level for appearance. However, a slope of $\frac{1}{16}$ in. per foot is desirable for drainage.

For residential work allow 100 sq. ft. of roof area per 1 sq. in. of downspout.

DOWNSPOUT SIZES

TYPE	AREA SQ. IN.	NOM. SIZE IN.	ACT. SIZE IN.
PLAIN ROUND	7.07	3	3
	12.57	4	4
	19.63	5	5
	28.27	6	6
CORR. ROUND	5.94	3	3
	11.04	4	4
	17.72	5	5
	25.97	6	6
CORR. RECT.	3.80	2	$1\frac{3}{4}$ x $2\frac{1}{4}$
	7.73	3	$2\frac{3}{8}$ x $3\frac{1}{4}$
	11.70	4	$2\frac{3}{4}$ x $4\frac{1}{4}$
	18.75	5	$3\frac{3}{4}$ x 5
PLAIN RECT.	3.94	2	$1\frac{1}{4}$ x $2\frac{1}{4}$
	6.00	3	2 x 3
	12.00	4	3 x 4
	20.00	5	$3\frac{3}{4}$ x $4\frac{1}{4}$
	24.00	6	4 x 6

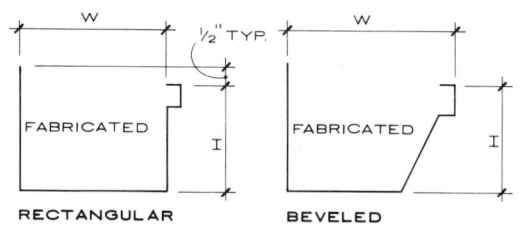

RECTANGULAR   BEVELED

OGEE OR STYLE "K"

2 1/2 " H x 3 " W		
2 3/4 " H x 4 " W	G	A
3 3/4 " H x 5 " W	G	A
4 3/4 " H x 6 " W	G	
5 1/4 " H x 7 " W		
6 " H x 8 " W		

STOCK

SEMICIRCULAR OR HALF – ROUND

4 " W	G
5 " W	G A
6 " W	G A
7 " W	G
8 " W	G

NOTE: Stock sizes—G = galvanized,   A = aluminum.

METAL GUTTER NOTES

Various sizes and other shapes available.

Always keep front 1/2 inch lower than back of gutter.

Do not use width less than 4 inches except for canopies and small porches. Min. ratio of depth to width should be 3 to 4.

METAL GUTTER SHAPES AND SIZES

NOTES

1. Continuous gutters may be formed at the installation site with cold forming equipment, thus eliminating joints in long runs of gutter.

2. Girth is width of sheet metal from which gutter is fabricated.

3. Sizes listed in table to the left but not marked as stock are available on special order.

4. Aluminum and stainless steel are more commonly used, whereas copper and especially galvanized steel are least used.

5. All jointing methods are applicable to most gutter shapes. Seal all joints with mastic or by soldering. Lock, slip, or lap joints do not provide expansion.

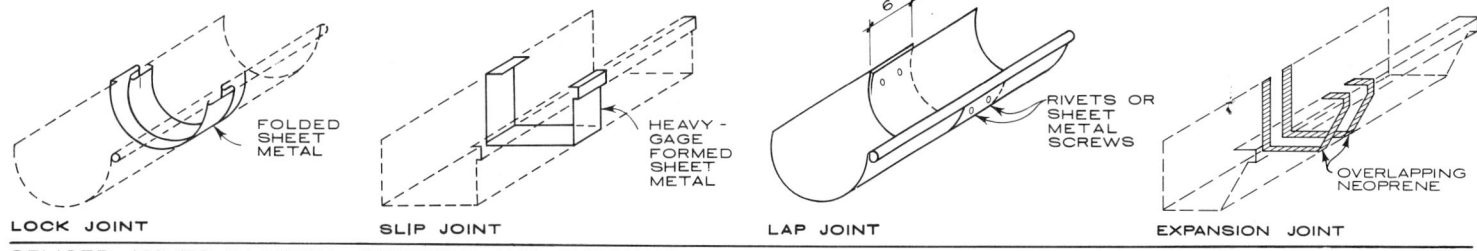

LOCK JOINT — FOLDED SHEET METAL

SLIP JOINT — HEAVY-GAGE FORMED SHEET METAL

LAP JOINT — RIVETS OR SHEET METAL SCREWS

EXPANSION JOINT — OVERLAPPING NEOPRENE

SPLICED JOINTS IN METAL GUTTERS AND EXPANSION JOINT

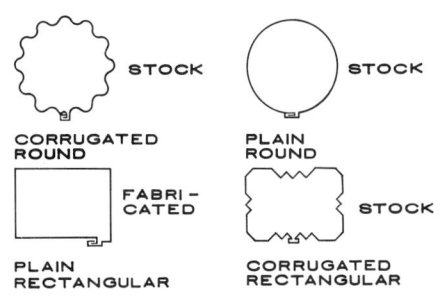

CORRUGATED ROUND — STOCK

PLAIN ROUND — STOCK

PLAIN RECTANGULAR — FABRICATED

CORRUGATED RECTANGULAR — STOCK

NOTES

Space downspouts 20 ft. min., 50 ft. max., generally. Extreme max. 60 ft.

Do not use size smaller than 7.00 in area except for canopies.

Corrugated shapes resist freezing better than plain shapes.

Elbows available: 45°, 60°, 75°, 90°.

STANDARD DOWNSPOUT SHAPES

EXPANSION JOINTS

Expansion joints should be used on all hip roof installations and on straight runs over 40 ft. In a 10 ft section of gutter and a 100° temperature change linear expansion will be:

EXPANSION OF METAL GUTTERS IN 40 FT

METAL	COEFFICIENT OF EXPANSION	MOVEMENT
Aluminum	$^{11}/_{64}$ x 4.0 =	0.68"
Copper	$^{7}/_{64}$ x 4.0 =	0.45"
Galvanized steel	$^{5}/_{64}$ x 4.0 =	0.31"

RECOMMENDED MINIMUM GAUGES FOR METAL GUTTER

GIRTH–INCHES	GALV. STEEL GAUGE	COPPER OZ.	ALUMINUM INCHES	STAINLESS STEEL GAUGE
UP TO 15	26	16	0.025	26
16 TO 20	24	16	0.032	26
21 TO 25	22	20	0.051	24
26 TO 30	20	24	0.064	22
31 TO 35	18	24	—	20
OVER 35	16	—	—	18

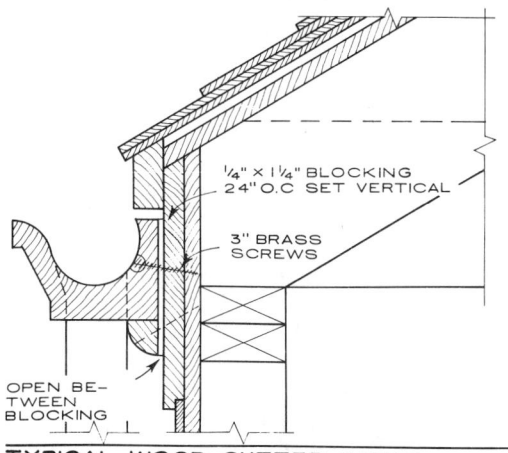

1/4" x 1 1/4" BLOCKING 24" O.C SET VERTICAL

3" BRASS SCREWS

OPEN BETWEEN BLOCKING

TYPICAL WOOD GUTTER DETAIL

PROFILES VARY

REDWOOD	FIR
3 " H x 4 " W	3 " H x 4 " W
4 " H x 4 " W	4 " H x 5 " W
4 " H x 6 " W	4 " H x 6 " W
	5 " H x 7 " W

NOTE

Wood gutters are still in use in New York State and the New England States.

WOOD GUTTERS

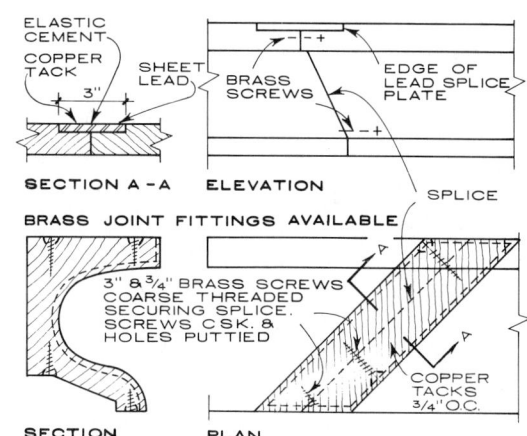

ELASTIC CEMENT — COPPER TACK — SHEET LEAD — BRASS SCREWS — EDGE OF LEAD SPLICE PLATE

SECTION A-A   ELEVATION

SPLICE

BRASS JOINT FITTINGS AVAILABLE

3" & 3/4" BRASS SCREWS COARSE THREADED SECURING SPLICE. SCREWS CSK. & HOLES PUTTIED

COPPER TACKS 3/4" O.C.

SECTION   PLAN

SPLICED JOINT IN WOOD GUTTER

Lawrence W. Cobb; Columbia, South Carolina

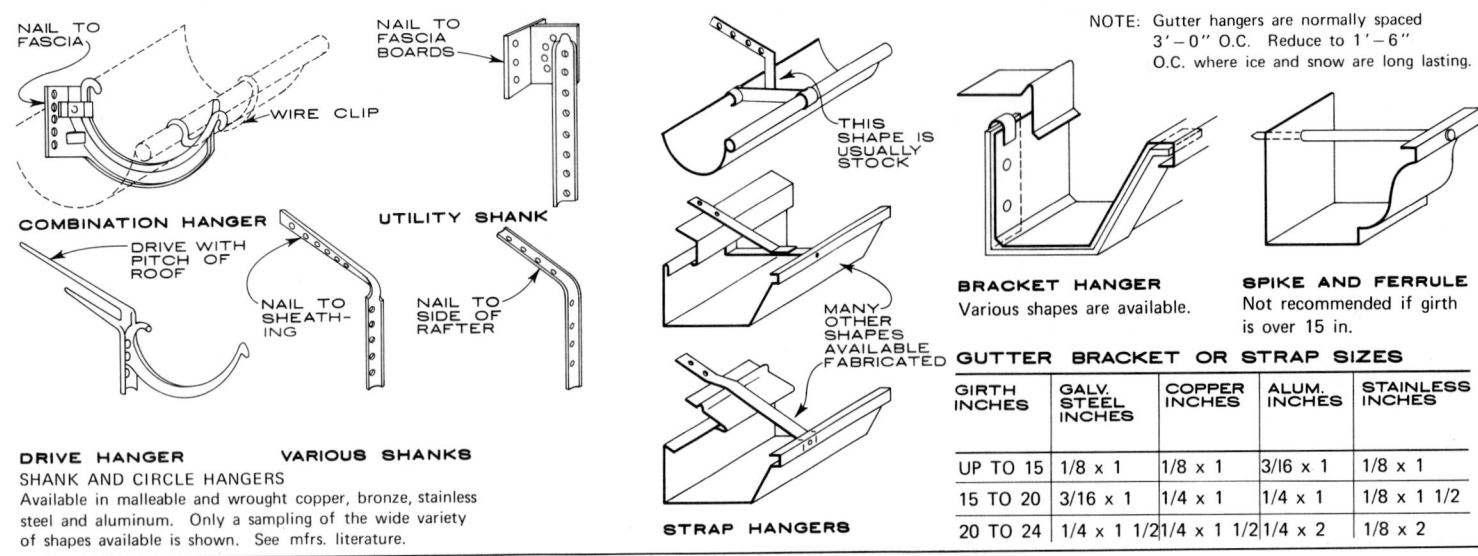

COMBINATION HANGER   **UTILITY SHANK**

DRIVE HANGER   VARIOUS SHANKS

SHANK AND CIRCLE HANGERS
Available in malleable and wrought copper, bronze, stainless steel and aluminum. Only a sampling of the wide variety of shapes available is shown. See mfrs. literature.

STRAP HANGERS

BRACKET HANGER
Various shapes are available.

SPIKE AND FERRULE
Not recommended if girth is over 15 in.

NOTE: Gutter hangers are normally spaced 3'-0" O.C. Reduce to 1'-6" O.C. where ice and snow are long lasting.

GUTTER BRACKET OR STRAP SIZES

GIRTH INCHES	GALV. STEEL INCHES	COPPER INCHES	ALUM. INCHES	STAINLESS INCHES
UP TO 15	1/8 x 1	1/8 x 1	3/16 x 1	1/8 x 1
15 TO 20	3/16 x 1	1/4 x 1	1/4 x 1	1/8 x 1 1/2
20 TO 24	1/4 x 1 1/2	1/4 x 1 1/2	1/4 x 2	1/8 x 2

GUTTER HANGERS

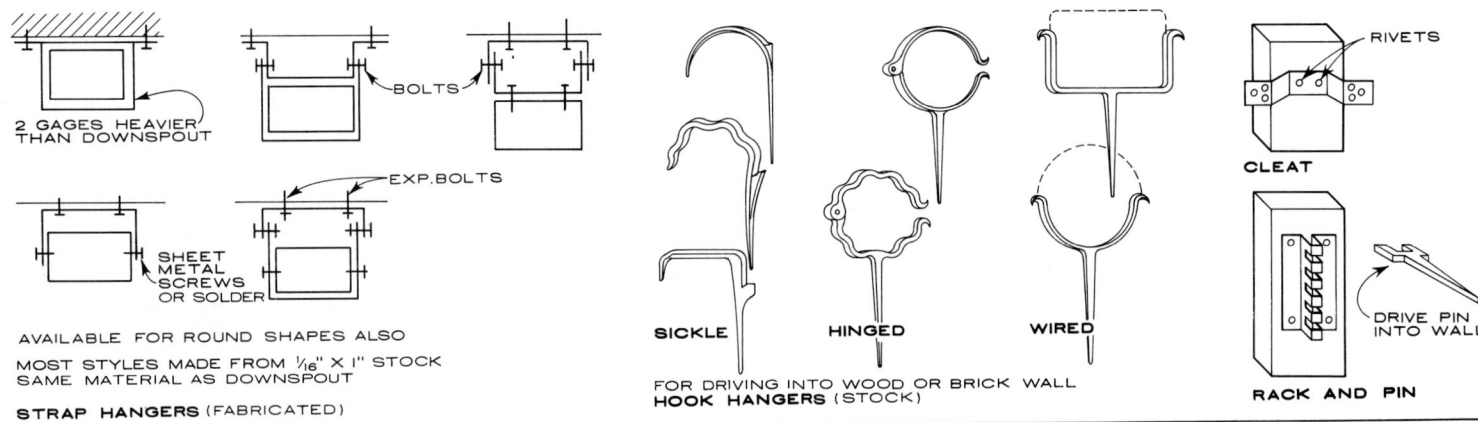

2 GAGES HEAVIER THAN DOWNSPOUT

AVAILABLE FOR ROUND SHAPES ALSO

MOST STYLES MADE FROM 1/16" X 1" STOCK SAME MATERIAL AS DOWNSPOUT

STRAP HANGERS (FABRICATED)

SICKLE   **HINGED**   **WIRED**

FOR DRIVING INTO WOOD OR BRICK WALL
HOOK HANGERS (STOCK)

CLEAT

RACK AND PIN

DOWNSPOUT HANGERS

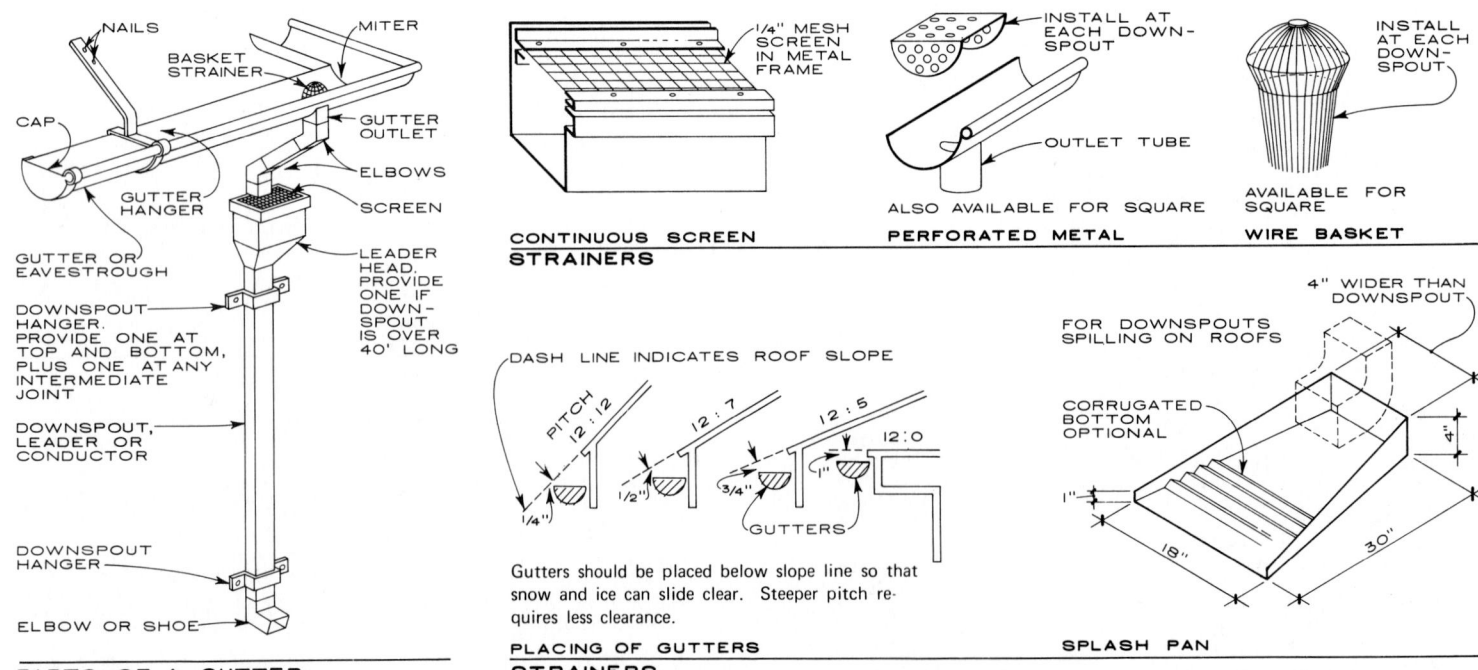

PARTS OF A GUTTER

CONTINUOUS SCREEN   **PERFORATED METAL**   **WIRE BASKET**
STRAINERS

1/4" MESH SCREEN IN METAL FRAME

INSTALL AT EACH DOWN-SPOUT

OUTLET TUBE

ALSO AVAILABLE FOR SQUARE

INSTALL AT EACH DOWN-SPOUT

AVAILABLE FOR SQUARE

DASH LINE INDICATES ROOF SLOPE

Gutters should be placed below slope line so that snow and ice can slide clear. Steeper pitch requires less clearance.

PLACING OF GUTTERS
STRAINERS

FOR DOWNSPOUTS SPILLING ON ROOFS

CORRUGATED BOTTOM OPTIONAL

4" WIDER THAN DOWNSPOUT

SPLASH PAN

Lawrence W. Cobb; Columbia, South Carolina

7 ROOF SPECIALTIES

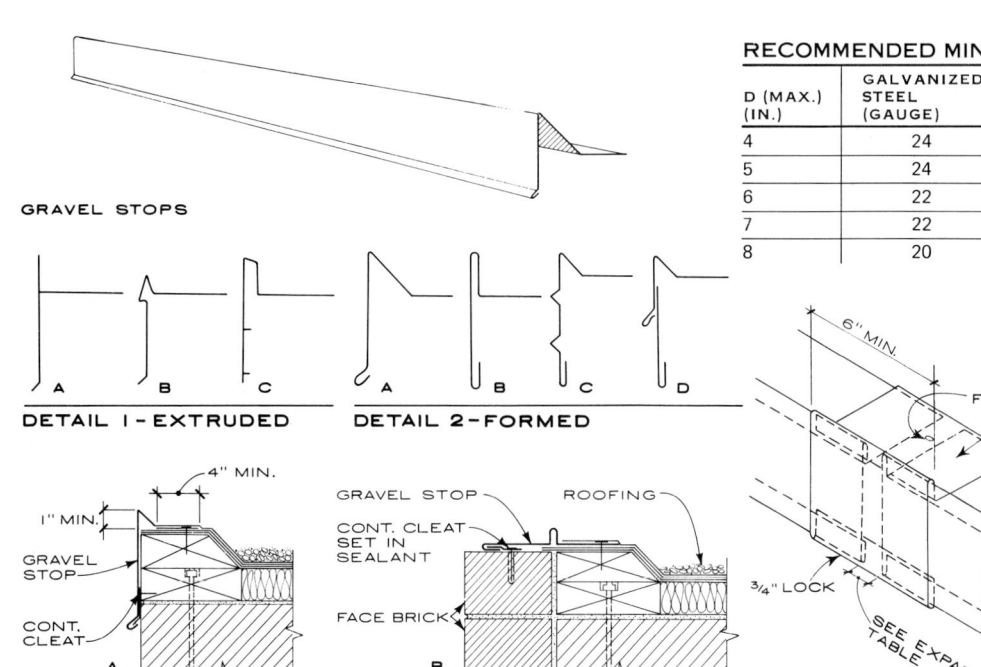

GRAVEL STOPS

A   B   C
DETAIL I-EXTRUDED

A   B   C   D
DETAIL 2-FORMED

4" MIN.
1" MIN.
GRAVEL STOP
CONT. CLEAT

A

GRAVEL STOP   ROOFING
CONT. CLEAT SET IN SEALANT
FACE BRICK

B

NOTE: LEAKAGE MAY OCCUR IF IMPROPERLY INSTALLED AND MAINTAINED

DETAIL 3- GRAVEL STOP INSTALLATION

RECOMMENDED MINIMUM GAUGES GRAVEL STOP—FASCIA

D (MAX.) (IN.)	GALVANIZED STEEL (GAUGE)	COPPER (OZ)	ALUMINUM (IN.)	ZINC ALLOY (IN.)	STAINLESS STEEL (GAUGE)
4	24	16	0.025	0.020	26
5	24	16	0.032	0.027	26
6	22	20	0.040	0.027	24
7	22	20	0.040	–	22
8	20	20	0.050	–	20

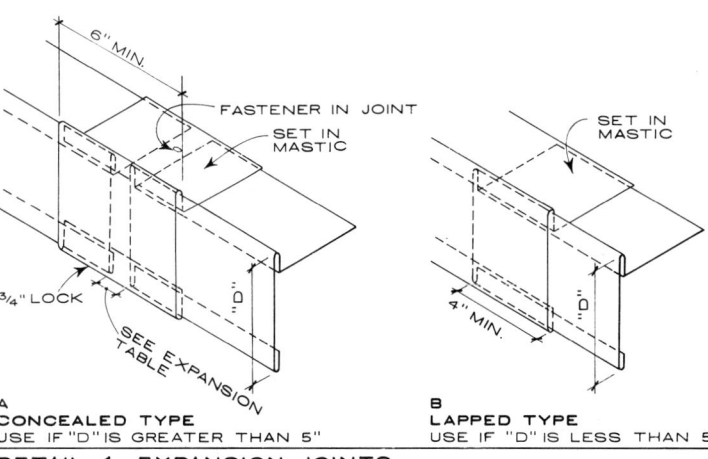

6" MIN.
FASTENER IN JOINT
SET IN MASTIC
SET IN MASTIC
3/4" LOCK
SEE EXPANSION TABLE
"D"

A
CONCEALED TYPE
USE IF "D" IS GREATER THAN 5"

4" MIN.
"D"

B
LAPPED TYPE
USE IF "D" IS LESS THAN 5"

DETAIL 4-EXPANSION JOINTS

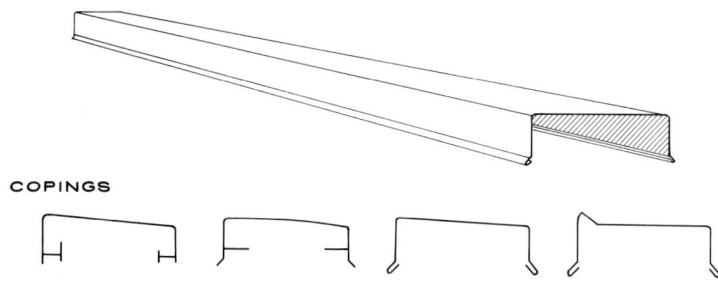

COPINGS

DETAIL 5-EXTRUDED   **DETAIL 6-FORMED**

RECOMMENDED MINIMUM GAUGES FOR COPING

WIDTH OF COPING TOP (IN.)	GALVANIZED STEEL (GAUGE)	STAINLESS STEEL (GAUGE)	ALUMINUM (IN.)	COPPER (OZ)
Through 12	24	26	0.232	16
13 to 18	22	24	0.040	20

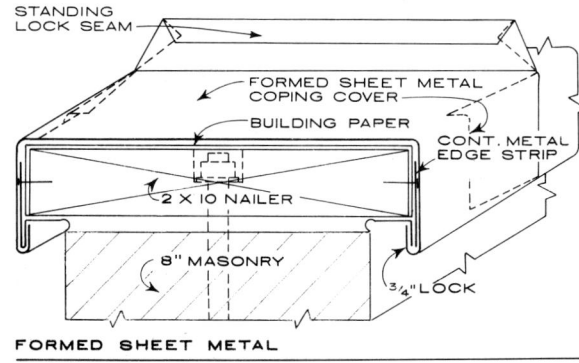

STANDING LOCK SEAM
FORMED SHEET METAL COPING COVER
BUILDING PAPER
CONT. METAL EDGE STRIP
2 X 10 NAILER
8" MASONRY
3/4" LOCK

FORMED SHEET METAL
DETAIL 7 - COPING SEAM

3/4" LOCK
1 1/4"
C
STANDING LOCK SEAM

AS REQUIRED
3/4" LOCK
SOLDER ONE SIDE
B
STANDING CAPPED TYPE

1/2"   1 1/2"
FILL WITH SOFT CAULKING
A
FLAT LOOSE LOCK TYPE

DETAIL 8-EXPANSION SEAMS

BEND
TAPER
FASCIA   SLIT   FASCIA
WIDTH OF NAILER
3/4" LOCK   TAB   3/4" LOCK
BEND
STANDING LOCK SEAM

DETAIL 9 - SEAM PATTERN

NOTES

1. A large variety of metal copings and gravel stops are available in both extruded aluminum and formed metals. Illustrated here are only a few of those offered. A multitude of colors, textures and finishes are also available.

2. For additional strength, longitudinal breaks may be formed in wide fascia as shown in C of detail 2. Two piece construction as shown in D of detail 2 is also recommended for wide fascia.

3. Where the fascia exceeds 5 in., a continuous cleat should be used at the drip edge.

4. Nailing the gravel stop or coping directly to the wall is not recommended because of temperature differentials between the metal and the wall. The use of a watertight washer such as neoprene at all fasteners is recommended.

5. All gravel stops should be installed on a raised curb with a 1 in. lip formed as shown in detail 3. This places the junction between the gravel stop and roofing membrane above standing water.

6. B of detail 3 shows a concealed gravel stop. Extreme care must be exercised when installing this type of gravel stop because it is somewhat more vulnerable to weather and moisture. A of detail 3 shows a more typical gravel stop installation procedure.

7. Allowance for expansion and contraction at joints should be made as shown in A and B of detail 4. Soldered or welded joints are not recommended except at corners. All joints should be set in mastic. Expansion joints for metal copings similar to detail 4.

8. In areas of extreme temperature changes, galvanized steel may require more maintenance than other metals mentioned.

Straub, Van Dine, Dziurman/Architects; Troy, Michigan

Ferebee, Walters and Associates; Charlotte, North Carolina

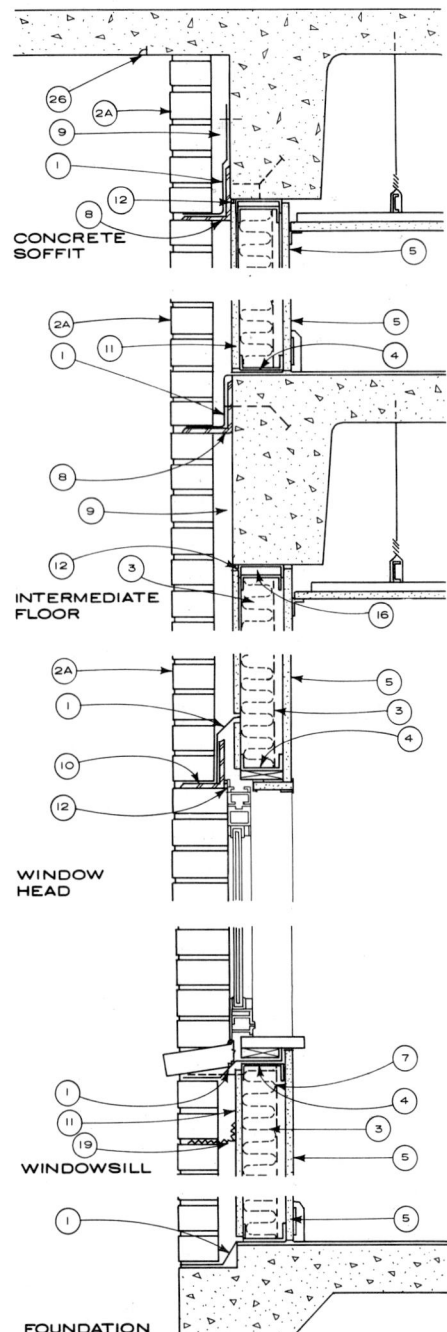

CONCRETE SOFFIT

INTERMEDIATE FLOOR

WINDOW HEAD

WINDOWSILL

FOUNDATION

GYPSUM CURTAIN WALL WITH BRICK VENEER

KEY

1 CONTINUOUS FLASHING: With weep holes at exterior face; up inside face of stud.

2 EXTERIOR FINISH:
   A Brick, or
   B Stucco: cement lime. Mixture applied to galvanized metal lath.

3 FIBERGLASS INSULATION:
   3½ in.   R-11
   3⅝ in.   R-13
   6 in.   R-19
   Fill cavity with insulation.

4 STUDS AND RUNNERS: 3⅝ to 7½ in. 20 gauge galvanized steel minimum. Check local codes for loading requirements. Optional double partition eliminates conduction through studs.

5 INTERIOR FINISH: Any system compatible with metal stud construction.

6 CONTROL JOINTS: Check manufacturer's recommendation for maximum spacing.

7 VAPOR BARRIER: Polyethylene film. Integral with insulation or foil back gypsum board.

8 RELIEVING ANGLES FOR BRICK VENEER: Check local building codes for maximum spacing.

9 AIRSPACE: 1 in. minimum.

10 LINTEL ANGLE REQUIRED AT OPENINGS: With brick exterior finish. Note that flashing and weepholes are required.

11 GYPSUM SHEATHING.

12 SEALANT BACKER AND SEALANT.

13 CORNER BEAD WITH DRIP.

14 CASING BEAD.

15 DRIP CAP.

16 FLEXIBLE JOINT: At top of studs and runners under structural frame members.

17 METAL FASCIA SYSTEM.

18 ROOFING.

19 NONCORROSIVE MASONRY TIE: Fasten to metal studs. Check local codes for spacing requirements.

20 PREFABRICATED SCREED AND DRIP.

21 CONTROL JOINT: Check manufacturer's recommendations for type and maximum spacing.

22 9 IN. MINIMUM WIDE FELT STRIPS: Stapled to sheathing.

23 THERMAL INSULATION.

24 SEALANT.

25 STRUCTURAL FRAME MEMBER.

26 DRIP.

27 STEEL CLIP ANGLE: Fastened to structural members.

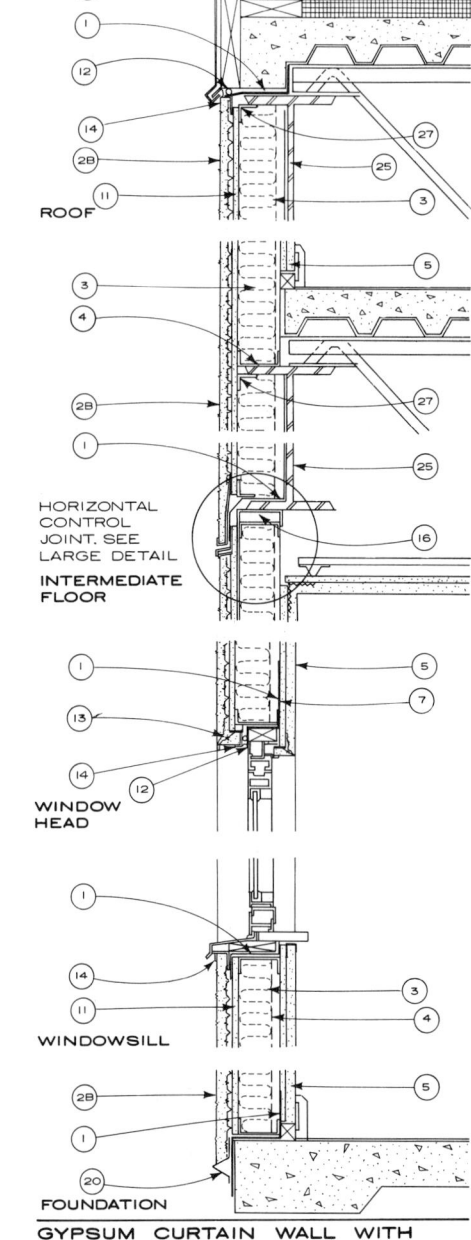

ROOF

INTERMEDIATE FLOOR

HORIZONTAL CONTROL JOINT. SEE LARGE DETAIL

WINDOW HEAD

WINDOWSILL

FOUNDATION

GYPSUM CURTAIN WALL WITH STUCCO

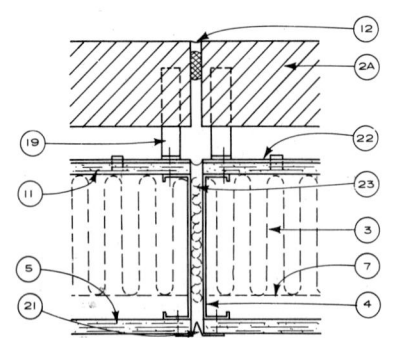

VERTICAL CONTROL JOINT AT BRICK VENEER

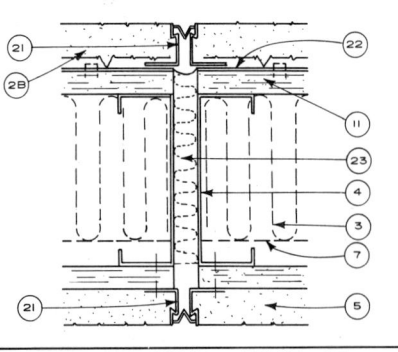

VERTICAL CONTROL JOINT AT STUCCO

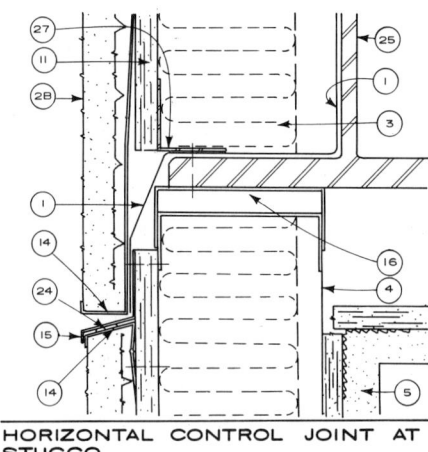

HORIZONTAL CONTROL JOINT AT STUCCO

Isaak and Isaak, Architects; Professional Association; Manchester, New Hampshire

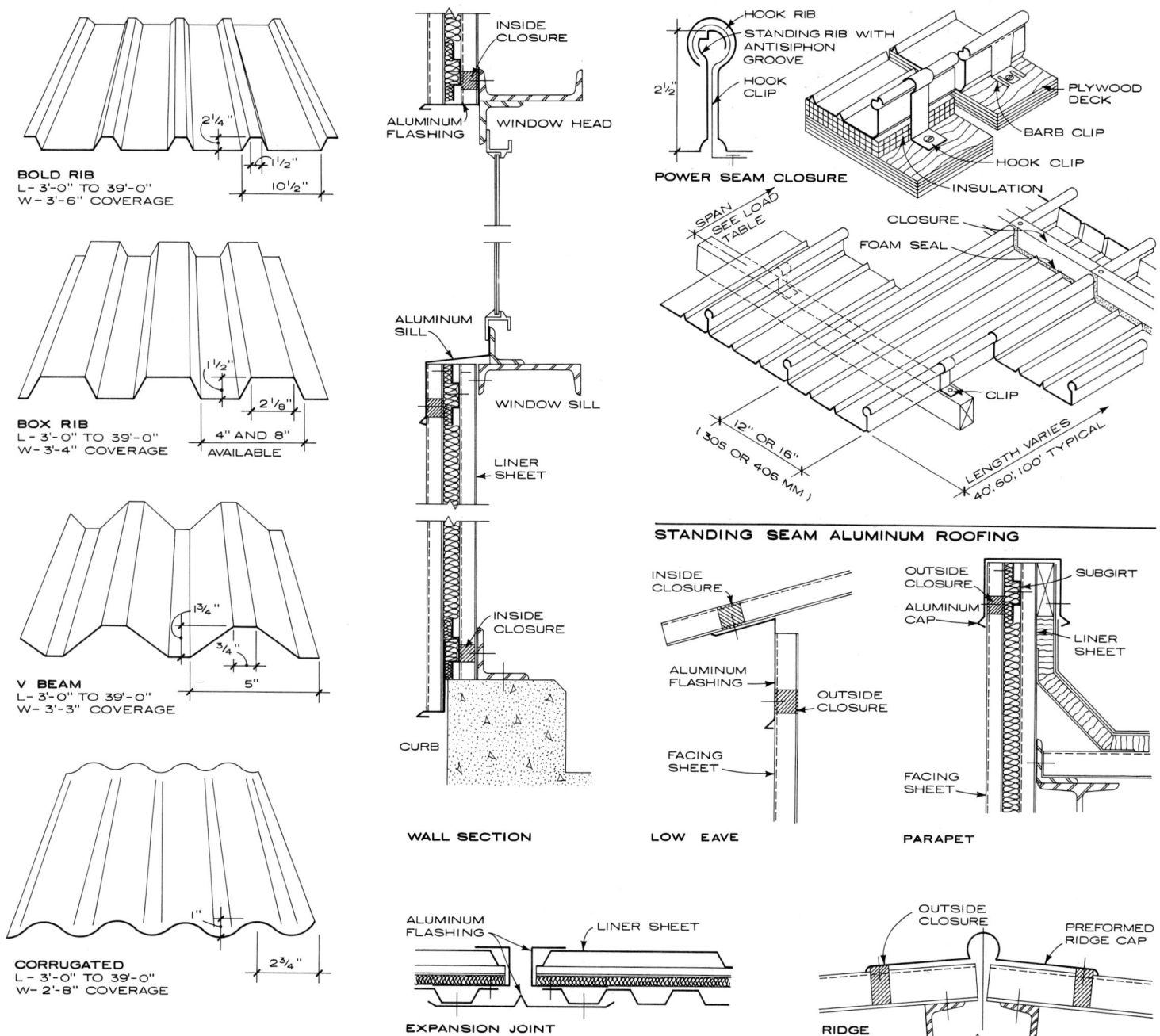

BOLD RIB
L – 3'-0" TO 39'-0"
W – 3'-6" COVERAGE

BOX RIB
L – 3'-0" TO 39'-0"
W – 3'-4" COVERAGE
4" AND 8" AVAILABLE

V BEAM
L – 3'-0" TO 39'-0"
W – 3'-3" COVERAGE

CORRUGATED
L – 3'-0" TO 39'-0"
W – 2'-8" COVERAGE

INSIDE CLOSURE
ALUMINUM FLASHING
WINDOW HEAD
ALUMINUM SILL
WINDOW SILL
LINER SHEET
INSIDE CLOSURE
CURB
WALL SECTION

HOOK RIB
STANDING RIB WITH ANTISIPHON GROOVE
HOOK CLIP
POWER SEAM CLOSURE
PLYWOOD DECK
BARB CLIP
HOOK CLIP
INSULATION
SPAN SEE LOAD TABLE
CLOSURE
FOAM SEAL
CLIP
12" OR 16" (305 OR 406 MM)
LENGTH VARIES 40', 60', 100' TYPICAL

STANDING SEAM ALUMINUM ROOFING

INSIDE CLOSURE
ALUMINUM FLASHING
OUTSIDE CLOSURE
FACING SHEET
LOW EAVE

OUTSIDE CLOSURE
SUBGIRT
ALUMINUM CAP
LINER SHEET
FACING SHEET
PARAPET

ALUMINUM FLASHING
LINER SHEET
EXPANSION JOINT

OUTSIDE CLOSURE
PREFORMED RIDGE CAP
RIDGE

FORMED ALUMINUM ROOFING AND SIDING

NOTES

1. Endlaps for roofing and siding shall be at least 6 in. and fastened at every rib. Two fasteners may be required when designing for a negative (uplift) loading condition.
2. Minimum sidelaps shall be equal to one rib or corrugation and laid away from prevailing wind. Fasteners shall be spaced a maximum of 12 in. on center for all types of roofing and siding.
3. For roofing, fasteners shall pierce only the high corrugation. For siding, fasteners shall pierce either the high or low corrugation. Consult manufacturer for proper sheet metal fasteners and accessories.
4. Minimum slopes for sheet roofing are as follows:
   a. 1 in. depth corrugated—3 in 12.
   b. 1½ in. depth ribbed—2 in 12.
   c. 1¾ in. v-corrugated—2 in 12.
5. See page on Metal Walls for insulation details and fire rated wall assemblies.

John A. Schulte; Hellmuth, Obata & Kassabaum, Inc.; St. Louis, Missouri

MAXIMUM SPAN TABLE FOR FORMED ALUMINUM ROOFING AND SIDING (IN.)

DESIGN LOAD (PSF)	BOLD RIB		4" BOX RIB		V BEAM		CORRUGATED		STANDING SEAM	
	0.032 IN. THICK	0.040 IN. THICK	0.032 IN. THICK	0.040 IN. THICK	0.032 IN. THICK	0.040 IN. THICK	0.032 IN. THICK	0.040 IN. THICK	0.032 IN. THICK	0.040 IN. THICK
20	95	123	100	120	131	151	90	98	103	124
30	77	100	82	98	107	124	73	80	86	104
40	67	87	71	85	92	107	64	69	77	92
50	60	76	63	76	83	96	57	62	70	83

NOTE: Values are based on uniform positive (downward) and walking loads on single span only.

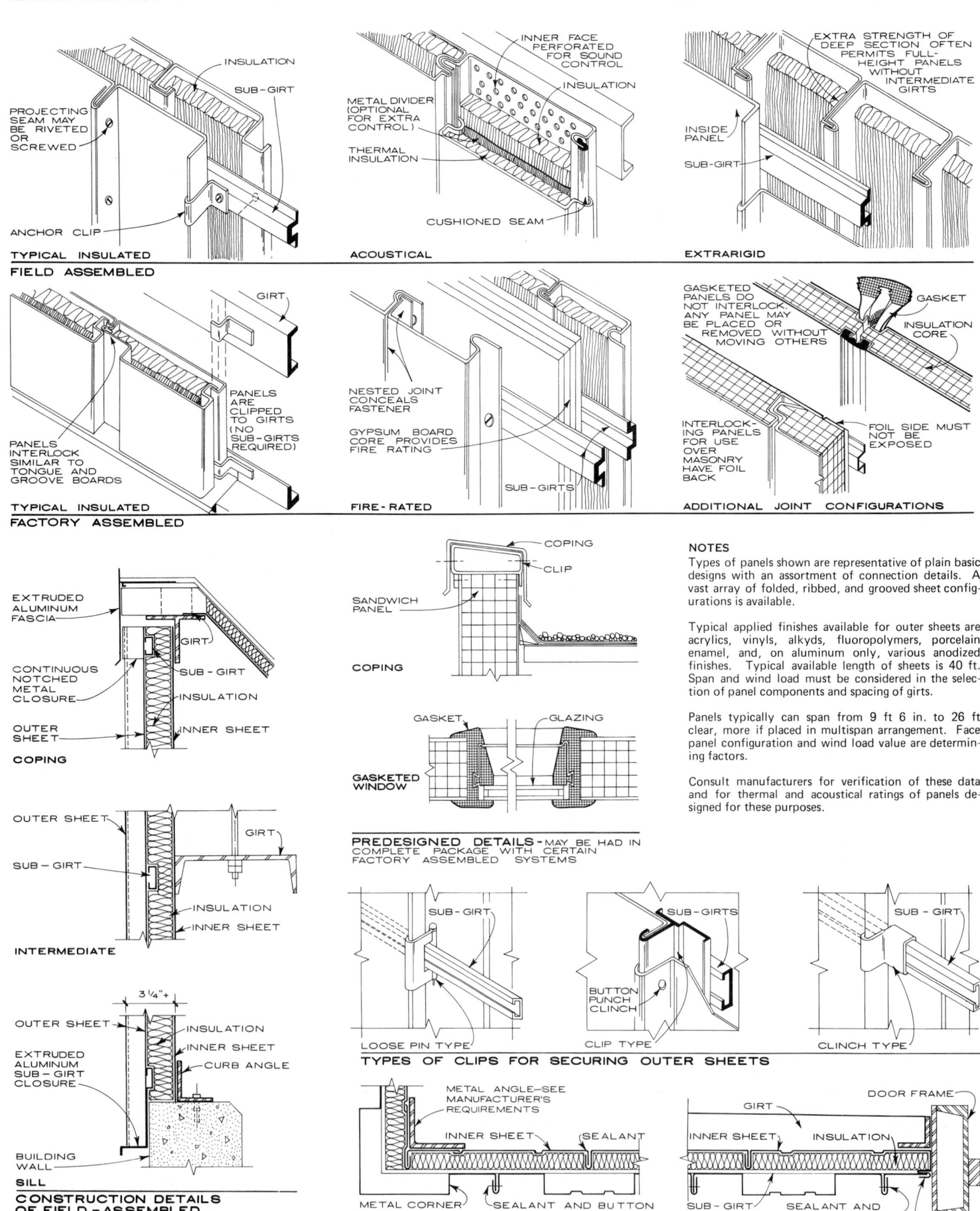

TYPICAL INSULATED FIELD ASSEMBLED

INSULATION

SUB-GIRT

PROJECTING SEAM MAY BE RIVETED OR SCREWED

ANCHOR CLIP

ACOUSTICAL

INNER FACE PERFORATED FOR SOUND CONTROL

INSULATION

METAL DIVIDER (OPTIONAL FOR EXTRA CONTROL)

THERMAL INSULATION

CUSHIONED SEAM

EXTRARIGID

EXTRA STRENGTH OF DEEP SECTION OFTEN PERMITS FULL-HEIGHT PANELS WITHOUT INTERMEDIATE GIRTS

INSIDE PANEL

SUB-GIRT

TYPICAL INSULATED FACTORY ASSEMBLED

GIRT

PANELS ARE CLIPPED TO GIRTS (NO SUB-GIRTS REQUIRED)

PANELS INTERLOCK SIMILAR TO TONGUE AND GROOVE BOARDS

FIRE-RATED

NESTED JOINT CONCEALS FASTENER

GYPSUM BOARD CORE PROVIDES FIRE RATING

SUB-GIRTS

ADDITIONAL JOINT CONFIGURATIONS

GASKETED PANELS DO NOT INTERLOCK. ANY PANEL MAY BE PLACED OR REMOVED WITHOUT MOVING OTHERS

GASKET

INSULATION CORE

INTERLOCKING PANELS FOR USE OVER MASONRY HAVE FOIL BACK

FOIL SIDE MUST NOT BE EXPOSED

COPING

EXTRUDED ALUMINUM FASCIA

CONTINUOUS NOTCHED METAL CLOSURE

OUTER SHEET

GIRT

SUB-GIRT

INSULATION

INNER SHEET

INTERMEDIATE

OUTER SHEET

SUB-GIRT

GIRT

INSULATION

INNER SHEET

SILL

3 1/4"+

OUTER SHEET

EXTRUDED ALUMINUM SUB-GIRT CLOSURE

INSULATION

INNER SHEET

CURB ANGLE

BUILDING WALL

CONSTRUCTION DETAILS OF FIELD-ASSEMBLED INSULATED METAL WALLS

COPING

COPING

CLIP

SANDWICH PANEL

GASKETED WINDOW

GASKET

GLAZING

PREDESIGNED DETAILS - MAY BE HAD IN COMPLETE PACKAGE WITH CERTAIN FACTORY ASSEMBLED SYSTEMS

TYPES OF CLIPS FOR SECURING OUTER SHEETS

SUB-GIRT

LOOSE PIN TYPE

SUB-GIRTS

BUTTON PUNCH CLINCH

CLIP TYPE

SUB-GIRT

CLINCH TYPE

OUTSIDE CORNER

METAL ANGLE—SEE MANUFACTURER'S REQUIREMENTS

INNER SHEET

SEALANT

METAL CORNER

SEALANT AND BUTTON PUNCH

JAMB AT DOOR

DOOR FRAME

GIRT

INNER SHEET

INSULATION

SUB-GIRT

SEALANT AND BUTTON PUNCH

SEALANT

NOTES

Types of panels shown are representative of plain basic designs with an assortment of connection details. A vast array of folded, ribbed, and grooved sheet configurations is available.

Typical applied finishes available for outer sheets are acrylics, vinyls, alkyds, fluoropolymers, porcelain enamel, and, on aluminum only, various anodized finishes. Typical available length of sheets is 40 ft. Span and wind load must be considered in the selection of panel components and spacing of girts.

Panels typically can span from 9 ft 6 in. to 26 ft clear, more if placed in multispan arrangement. Face panel configuration and wind load value are determining factors.

Consult manufacturers for verification of these data and for thermal and acoustical ratings of panels designed for these purposes.

FACING MATERIALS AVAILABLE

1. Aluminum.
2. Aluminized steel.
3. Galvanized steel.

FINISHES AVAILABLE

1. Anodized aluminum.
2. 50% silicone—modified polyester baked enamel paint.
3. Fluorocarbon baked enamel paint.
4. Porcelain enamel on aluminized steel.

INSULATING VALUES	MAX. U FACTOR
2 in. urethane core	0.065
3 in. honeycomb core	0.41
2 in. honeycomb with fill	0.107

NOTE

Some codes restrict the use of the urethane core panel. The honeycomb panels are more acceptable.

Urethane panel = 25 flame spread rating
Honeycomb panel = 15 flame spread rating
See manufacturer for span tables.

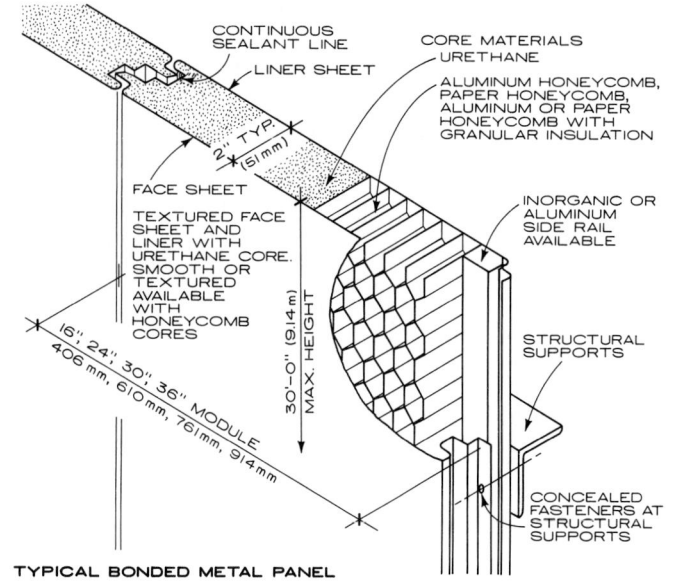

TYPICAL BONDED METAL PANEL

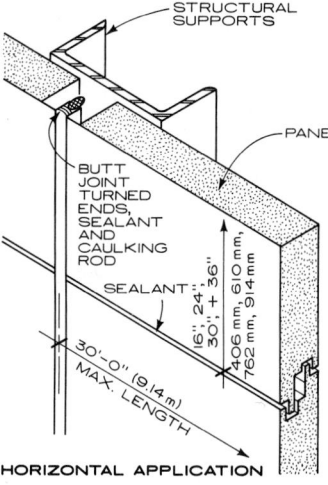

HORIZONTAL APPLICATION

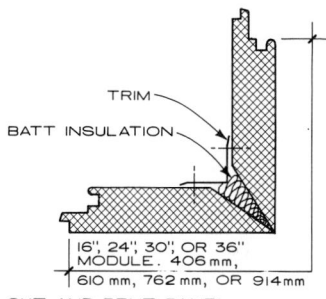

CUT AND BENT PANEL

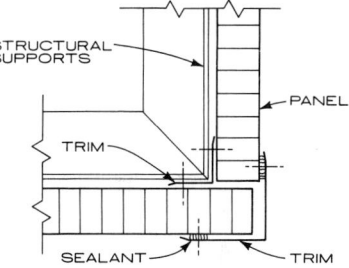

EXPOSED TRIM

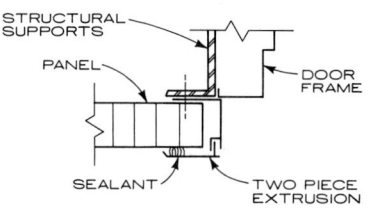

DOOR JAMB

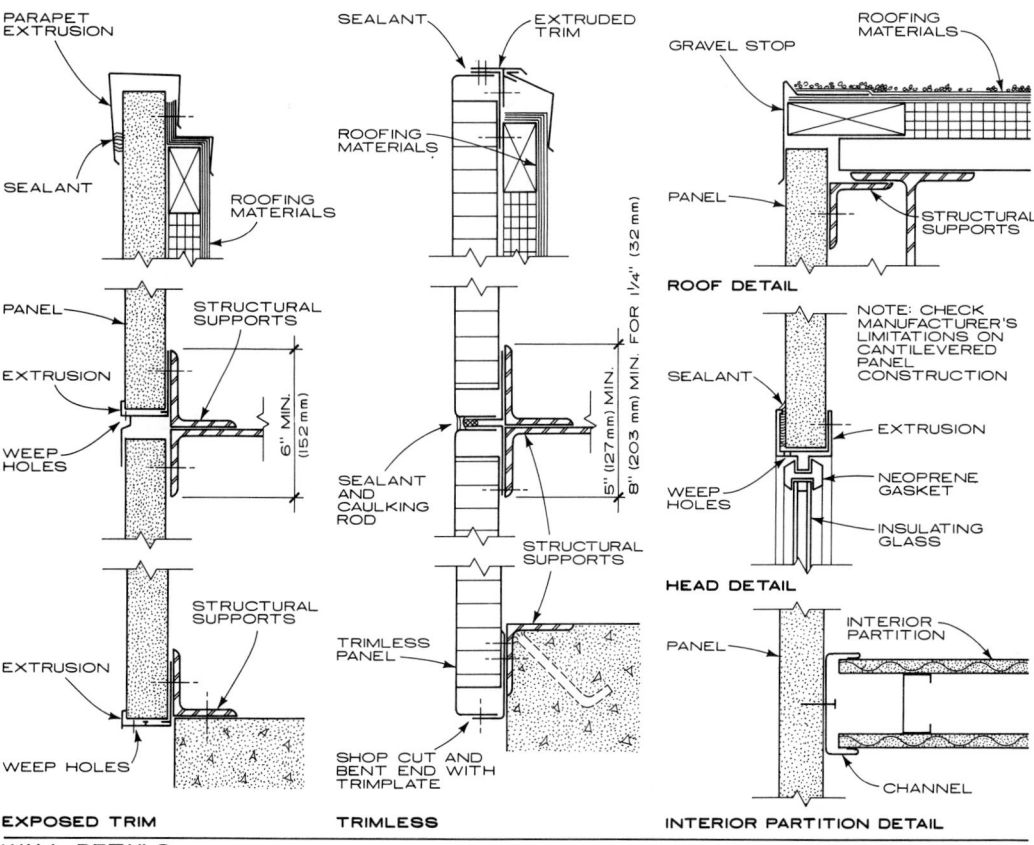

WALL DETAILS

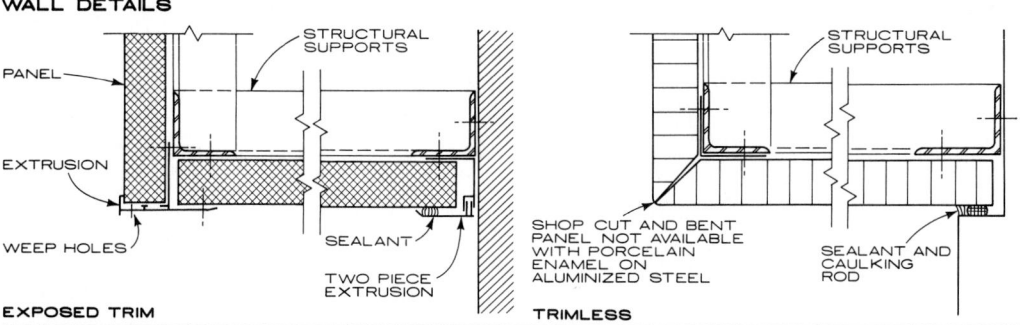

SOFFIT DETAILS

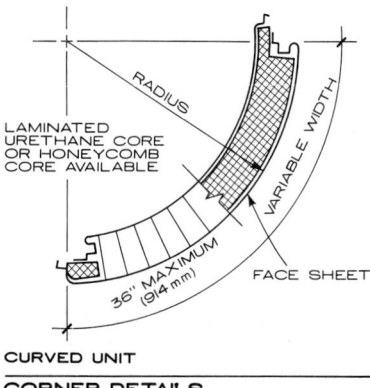

CURVED UNIT

CORNER DETAILS

John A. Schutle; Hellmuth, Obata, & Kassabaum, Inc.; St. Louis, Missouri

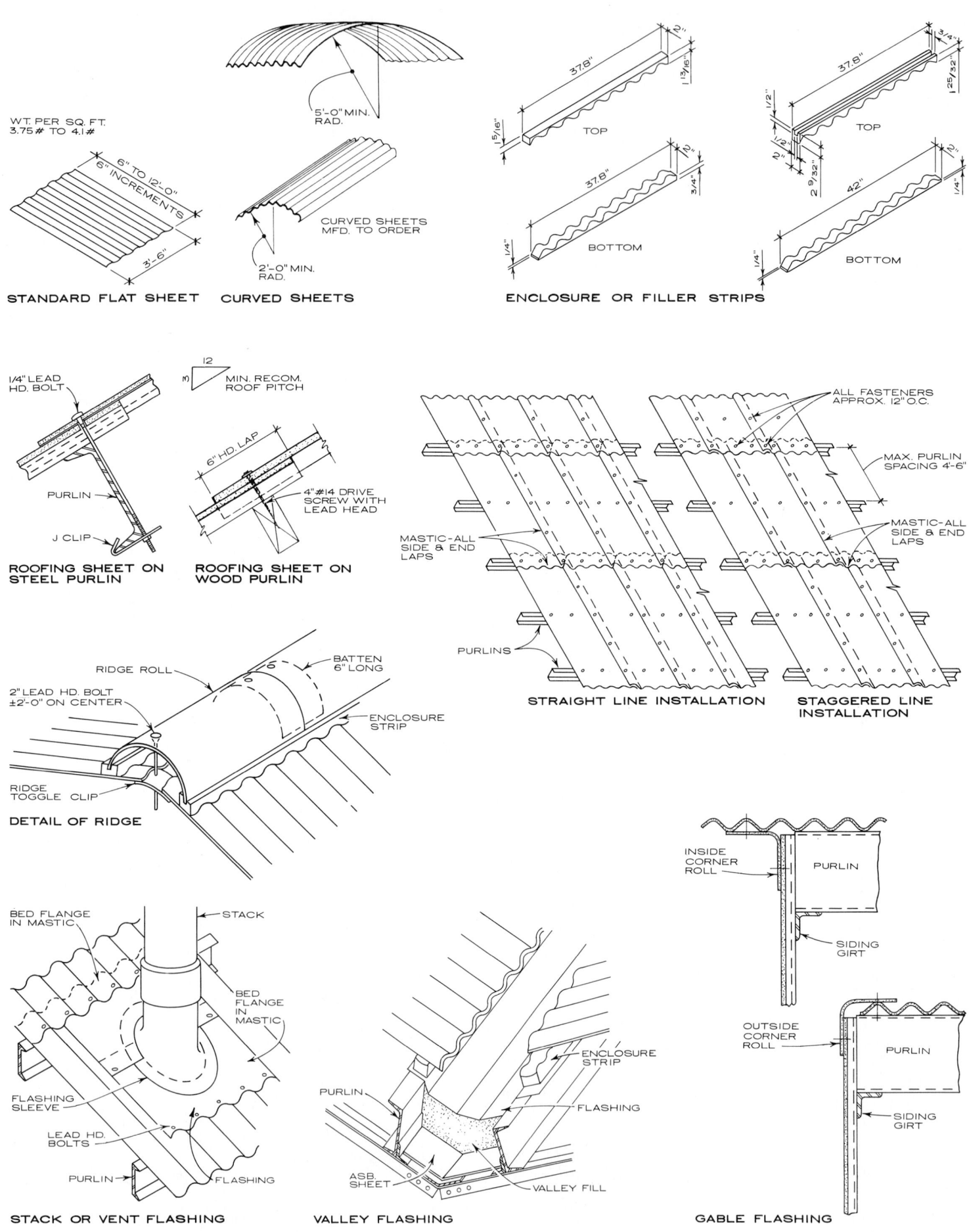

WT. PER SQ. FT.
3.75# TO 4.1#

6" TO 12'-0"
6" INCREMENTS

3'-6"

STANDARD FLAT SHEET

5'-0" MIN. RAD.

CURVED SHEETS MF'D. TO ORDER

2'-0" MIN. RAD.

CURVED SHEETS

37.8"

TOP

BOTTOM

37.8"

ENCLOSURE OR FILLER STRIPS

TOP

BOTTOM

42"

1/4" LEAD HD. BOLT

PURLIN

J CLIP

ROOFING SHEET ON STEEL PURLIN

12

3

MIN. RECOM. ROOF PITCH

6" HD. LAP

4" #14 DRIVE SCREW WITH LEAD HEAD

ROOFING SHEET ON WOOD PURLIN

ALL FASTENERS APPROX. 12" O.C.

MAX. PURLIN SPACING 4'-6"

MASTIC-ALL SIDE & END LAPS

MASTIC-ALL SIDE & END LAPS

PURLINS

STRAIGHT LINE INSTALLATION   **STAGGERED LINE INSTALLATION**

RIDGE ROLL

BATTEN 6" LONG

2" LEAD HD. BOLT ±2'-0" ON CENTER

ENCLOSURE STRIP

RIDGE TOGGLE CLIP

DETAIL OF RIDGE

BED FLANGE IN MASTIC

STACK

BED FLANGE IN MASTIC

FLASHING SLEEVE

LEAD HD. BOLTS

PURLIN

FLASHING

STACK OR VENT FLASHING

ENCLOSURE STRIP

PURLIN

FLASHING

ASB. SHEET

VALLEY FILL

VALLEY FLASHING

INSIDE CORNER ROLL

PURLIN

SIDING GIRT

OUTSIDE CORNER ROLL

PURLIN

SIDING GIRT

GABLE FLASHING

7 **COMPOSITE BUILDING PANELS**

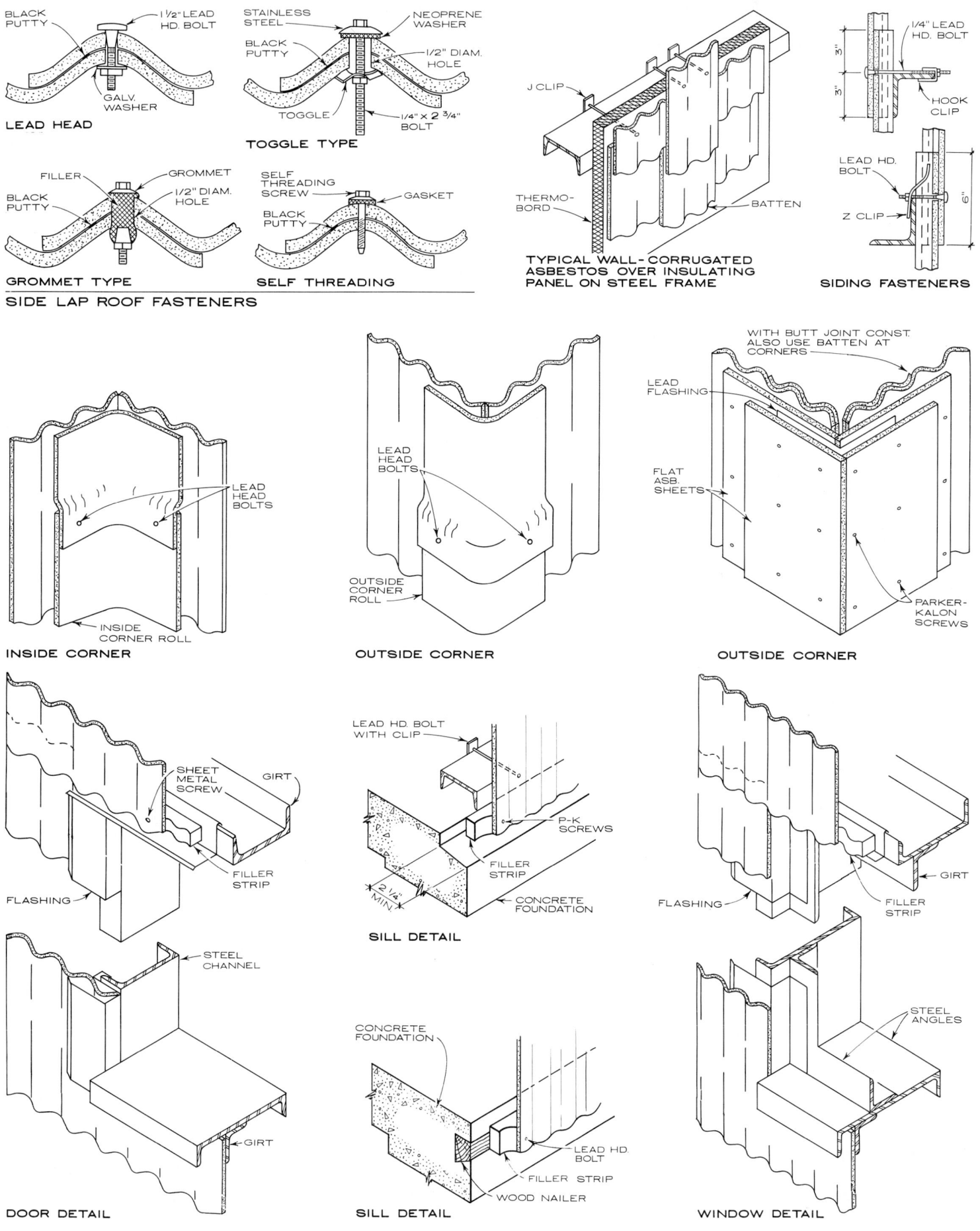

LEAD HEAD

TOGGLE TYPE

GROMMET TYPE

SELF THREADING

SIDE LAP ROOF FASTENERS

TYPICAL WALL-CORRUGATED
ASBESTOS OVER INSULATING
PANEL ON STEEL FRAME

SIDING FASTENERS

INSIDE CORNER

OUTSIDE CORNER

OUTSIDE CORNER

SILL DETAIL

DOOR DETAIL

SILL DETAIL

WINDOW DETAIL

COMPOSITE BUILDING PANELS **7**

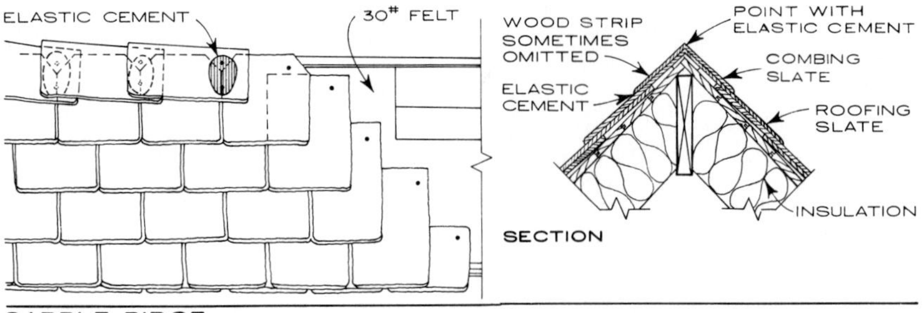

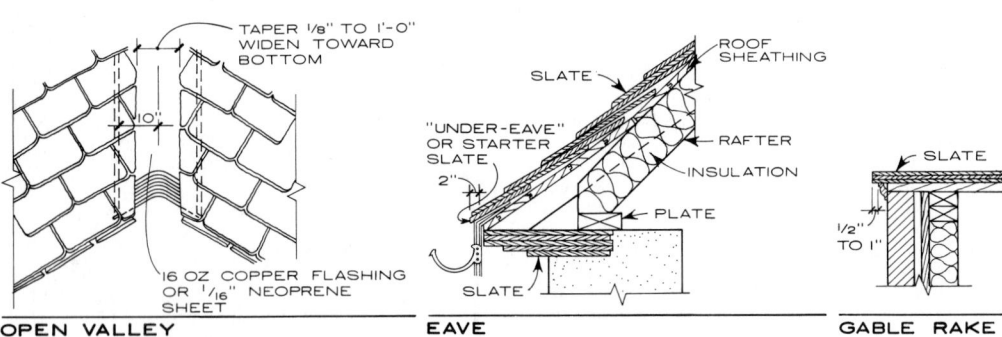

SADDLE RIDGE

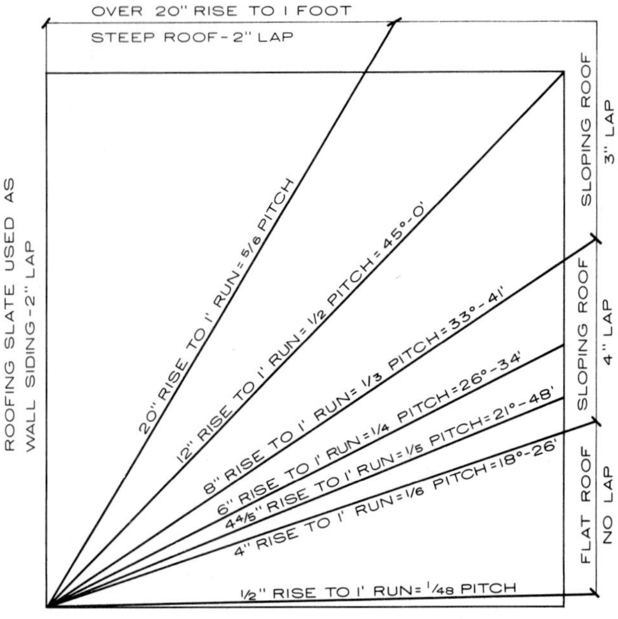

ELASTIC CEMENT · WOOD STRIP SOMETIMES OMITTED · 30# FELT · ELASTIC CEMENT · POINT WITH ELASTIC CEMENT · COMBING SLATE · ROOFING SLATE · INSULATION · SECTION

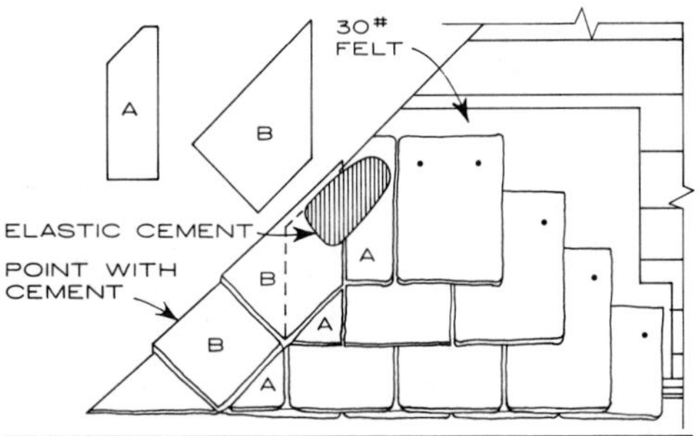

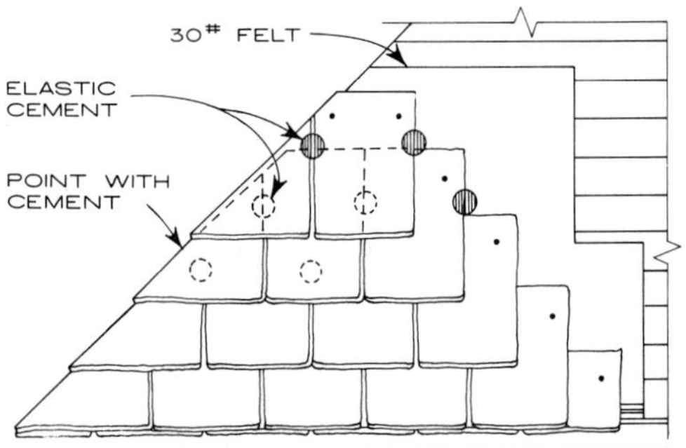

SADDLE HIP

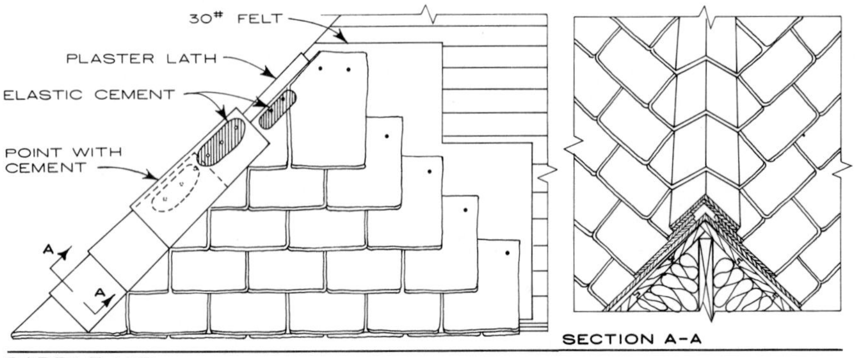

30# FELT · PLASTER LATH · ELASTIC CEMENT · POINT WITH CEMENT

SECTION A-A

BOSTON HIP

30# FELT · ELASTIC CEMENT · POINT WITH CEMENT

MITERED HIP

30# FELT · ELASTIC CEMENT · POINT WITH CEMENT

OPEN VALLEY

TAPER 1/8" TO 1'-0" WIDEN TOWARD BOTTOM · 10" · 16 OZ COPPER FLASHING OR 1/16" NEOPRENE SHEET

EAVE

ROOF SHEATHING · SLATE · "UNDER-EAVE" OR STARTER SLATE · 2" · RAFTER · INSULATION · PLATE · SLATE

GABLE RAKE

SLATE · 1/2" TO 1"

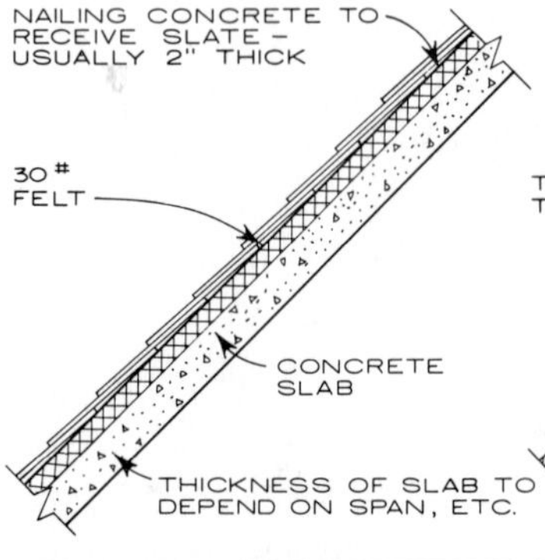

NAILING CONCRETE ON CONCRETE SLAB

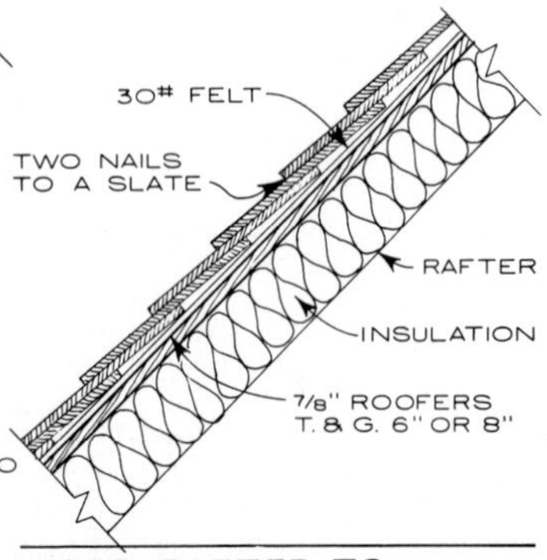

NAILING CONCRETE TO RECEIVE SLATE – USUALLY 2" THICK · 30# FELT · CONCRETE SLAB · THICKNESS OF SLAB TO DEPEND ON SPAN, ETC.

WOOD RAFTER TO RECEIVE SLATE

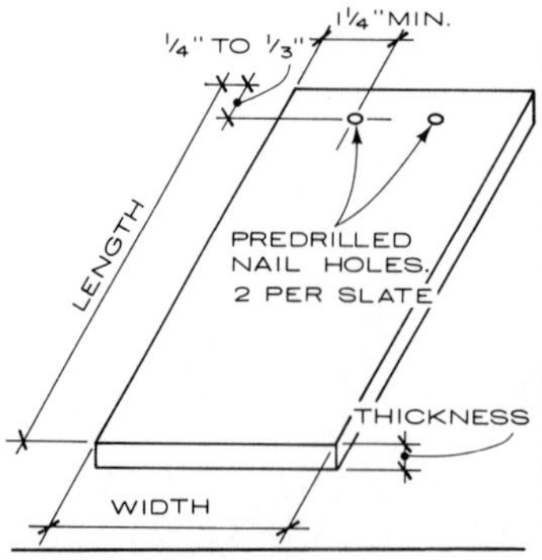

30# FELT · TWO NAILS TO A SLATE · RAFTER · INSULATION · 7/8" ROOFERS T. & G. 6" OR 8"

ROOFING SLATE

1/4" TO 1/3" · 1 1/4" MIN. · PREDRILLED NAIL HOLES, 2 PER SLATE · LENGTH · WIDTH · THICKNESS

ROOFING SLATE USED AS WALL SIDING-2" LAP

OVER 20" RISE TO 1 FOOT · STEEP ROOF-2" LAP

20" RISE TO 1' RUN = 5/3 PITCH

12" RISE TO 1' RUN = 1/2 PITCH = 45°-0'

8" RISE TO 1' RUN = 1/3 PITCH = 33°-41'

6" RISE TO 1' RUN = 1/4 PITCH = 26°-34'

4 4/5" RISE TO 1' RUN = 1/5 PITCH = 21°-48'

4" RISE TO 1' RUN = 1/6 PITCH = 18°-26'

1/2" RISE TO 1' RUN = 1/48 PITCH

SLOPING ROOF 3" LAP · SLOPING ROOF 4" LAP · FLAT ROOF NO LAP

DIAGRAM OF PROPER LAP FOR RISE/RUN

GENERAL NOTES

1. COMMERCIAL STANDARD: The quarry run of $3/16$ in. thickness; includes tolerable variations above and below $3/16$ in.
2. TEXTURAL: A rough textured slate roof with uneven butts; the slates vary in thickness and size, which is generally not true of slate more than $3/8$ in. thick.
3. GRADUATED: A textural roof of large slates; more variation in thickness, size, and color.
4. A SQUARE OF ROOFING SLATE: A number of slates of any size sufficient to cover 100 ft² with a 3 in. lap. Weight per square: $3/16$ in.—800 lb; $1/4$ in. —900 lb; $3/8$ in.—1100 lb; $1/2$ in.—1700 lb; $3/4$ in.— 2600 lb.
5. STANDARD NOMENCLATURE FOR SLATE COLOR: Black, blue black, mottled gray, purple, green, mottled purple and green, purple variegated, red; to be preceded by the word "Unfading" or "Weathering." Other colors and combinations are termed specials.
6. PROPER JOINTING FOR PITCHED ROOFS: Requires a 3 in. minimum vertical overlap. Overlap varies with pitch; see graph above.
7. FELT: With Commercial Standard Slate use 30# saturated felt. With graduated roofs use 30# for $1/4$ in. slate and 45#, 55#, or 65# prepared roll roofing for heavier slate.
8. NAIL FASTENING: Use large head, slaters' hard copper wire nails, cut copper, cut brass, or cut yellow metal slating nails. Each slate punched with two nail holes. Use nails that are 1 in. longer than thickness of slate. Cover all exposed heads with elastic cement. In dry climates hot dip galvanized nails may be used.

STANDARD SLATE DIMENSIONS*

LENGTH (IN.)	WIDTH (IN.)
10†	6, 7, 8
12†	6, 7, 8, 9, 10
14†	7, 8, 9, 10, 11, 12
16	8, 9, 10, 11, 12, 14
18	9, 10, 11, 12, 13, 14
20	9, 10, 11, 12, 13, 14
22	10, 11, 12, 13, 14
24	11, 12, 13, 14, 16

*The slates are split in these thicknesses: $3/16$, $1/4$, $1/8$, $1/2$, and $3/4$ in.
†$1/2$ in. and larger slates are not often used in these sizes. Random widths are usually used.

Domenic F. Valente, AIA, Architect & Planner; Medford, Massachusetts

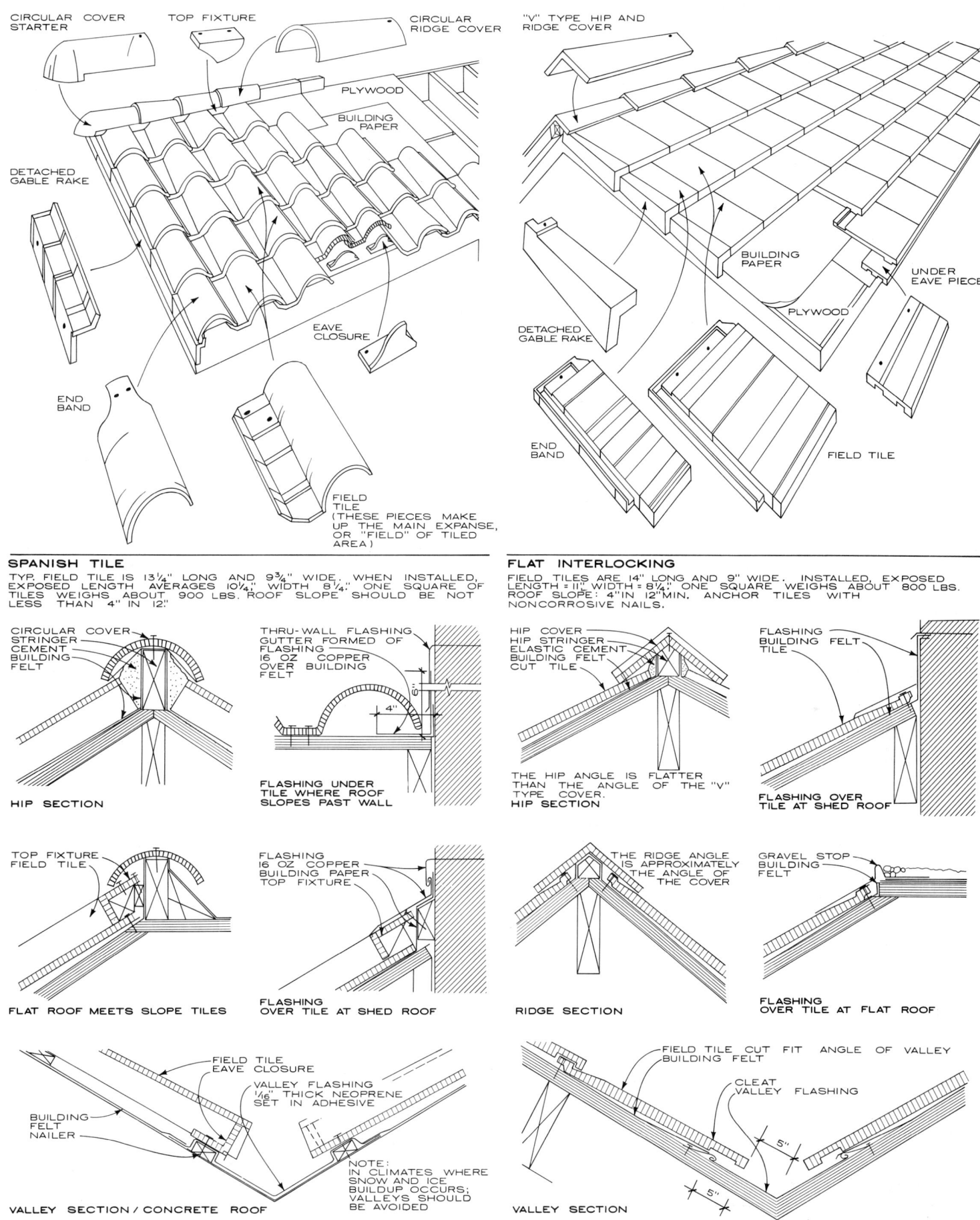

CIRCULAR COVER STARTER

TOP FIXTURE

CIRCULAR RIDGE COVER

"V" TYPE HIP AND RIDGE COVER

PLYWOOD

BUILDING PAPER

DETACHED GABLE RAKE

EAVE CLOSURE

END BAND

FIELD TILE (THESE PIECES MAKE UP THE MAIN EXPANSE, OR "FIELD" OF TILED AREA)

BUILDING PAPER

DETACHED GABLE RAKE

UNDER EAVE PIECE

PLYWOOD

END BAND

FIELD TILE

SPANISH TILE

TYP. FIELD TILE IS 13¼" LONG AND 9¾" WIDE. WHEN INSTALLED, EXPOSED LENGTH AVERAGES 10¼" WIDTH 8¼." ONE SQUARE OF TILES WEIGHS ABOUT 900 LBS. ROOF SLOPE SHOULD BE NOT LESS THAN 4" IN 12."

FLAT INTERLOCKING

FIELD TILES ARE 14" LONG AND 9" WIDE. INSTALLED, EXPOSED LENGTH = 11" WIDTH = 8¼." ONE SQUARE WEIGHS ABOUT 800 LBS. ROOF SLOPE: 4" IN 12" MIN. ANCHOR TILES WITH NONCORROSIVE NAILS.

CIRCULAR COVER STRINGER CEMENT BUILDING FELT

THRU-WALL FLASHING GUTTER FORMED OF FLASHING 16 OZ COPPER OVER BUILDING FELT

6"

4"

HIP COVER HIP STRINGER ELASTIC CEMENT BUILDING FELT CUT TILE

FLASHING BUILDING FELT TILE

HIP SECTION

FLASHING UNDER TILE WHERE ROOF SLOPES PAST WALL

THE HIP ANGLE IS FLATTER THAN THE ANGLE OF THE "V" TYPE COVER.
HIP SECTION

FLASHING OVER TILE AT SHED ROOF

TOP FIXTURE FIELD TILE

FLASHING 16 OZ COPPER BUILDING PAPER TOP FIXTURE

THE RIDGE ANGLE IS APPROXIMATELY THE ANGLE OF THE COVER

GRAVEL STOP BUILDING FELT

FLAT ROOF MEETS SLOPE TILES

FLASHING OVER TILE AT SHED ROOF

RIDGE SECTION

FLASHING OVER TILE AT FLAT ROOF

FIELD TILE EAVE CLOSURE

VALLEY FLASHING ¹⁄₁₆" THICK NEOPRENE SET IN ADHESIVE

BUILDING FELT NAILER

NOTE: IN CLIMATES WHERE SNOW AND ICE BUILDUP OCCURS; VALLEYS SHOULD BE AVOIDED

FIELD TILE CUT FIT ANGLE OF VALLEY BUILDING FELT

CLEAT VALLEY FLASHING

5"

5"

VALLEY SECTION / CONCRETE ROOF

VALLEY SECTION

Darrel Rippeteau, Architect; Washington, D.C.

RED CEDAR HANDSPLIT SHAKES

GRADE	LENGTH AND THICKNESS	DESCRIPTION
No. 1 handsplit and resawn	15″ starter-finish 18 x 1/2″ medium 18 x 3/4″ heavy 24 x 3/8″ 24 x 1/2″ medium 24 x 3/4″ heavy	These shakes have split faces and sawn backs. Cedar logs are first cut into desired lengths. Blanks or boards of proper thickness are split and then run diagonally through a bandsaw to produce two tapered shakes from each blank
No. 1 tapersplit	24 x 1/2″	Produced largely by hand, using a sharp bladed steel froe and a wooden mallet. The natural shinglelike taper is achieved by reversing the block, end-for-end, with each split
No. 1 straight	18 x 3/8″ side wall 18 x 3/8″ 24 x 3/8″	Produced in the same manner as tapersplit shakes except that by splitting from the same end of the block, the shakes acquire the same thickness throughout

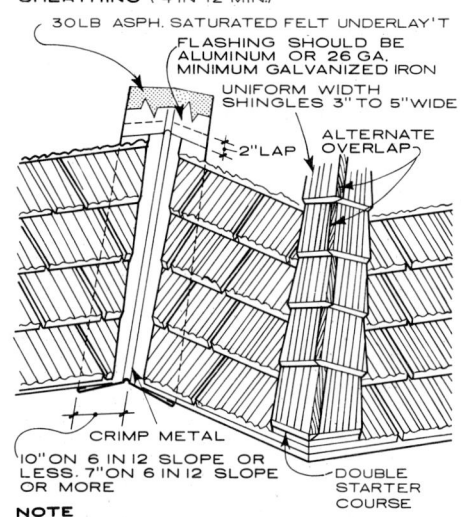

INSTALLATION OF SHAKES OVER SPACED SHEATHING (4 IN 12 MIN.)

RED CEDAR SHINGLES

	NO. 1 BLUE LABEL*			NO. 2 RED LABEL†			NO. 3 BLACK LABEL‡		
	MAXIMUM EXPOSURE RECOMMENDED FOR ROOFS								
ROOF PITCH	16″	18″	24″	16″	18″	24″	16″	18″	24″
3 in 12 to 4 in 12	3 3/4″	4 1/4″	5 3/4″	3 1/2″	4″	5 1/2″	3″	3 1/2″	5″
4 in 12 and steeper	5″	5 1/2″	7 1/2″	4″	4 1/2″	6 1/2″	3 1/2″	4″	5 1/2″

*Premium Grade: 100% heartwood, 100% clear, 100% edge grain, for highest quality.
†Intermediate Grade: not less then 10″ clear on 16″ shingles, 11″ clear on 18″ shingles, 16″ clear on 24″ shingles. Flat grain and limited sapwood permitted.
‡Utility Grade: 6″ clear on 16″ and 18″ shingles, 10″ clear on 24″ shingles. For economy applications.

UNDERLAYMENT AND SHEATHING

ROOFING TYPE	SHEATHING	UNDERLAYMENT	NORMAL SLOPE		LOW SLOPE	
Wood shakes and shingles	Solid or spaced	No. 30 asphalt saturated felt (interlayment)	4 in 12 and up	Underlayment starter course; interlayment over entire roof	3 in 12 to 4 in 12	Single layer underlayment over entire roof; interlayment over entire roof

NOTES
1. Shakes not recommended on slopes less than 4 in 12.
2. Breathing type building paper—such as deadening felt—may be applied over either type of sheating, although paper is not used in most applications.

NOTE
Copper flashing should not be used with red cedar.

VALLEY HIP AND RIDGE APPLICATION OF SHAKES & SHINGLES

SHINGLES AND SHAKES USED FOR ROOFING

EXPOSURE FOR SHINGLES & SHAKES USED FOR SIDING

SHINGLE LENGTH	EXPOSURE OF SHINGLES	
	SGL. COURSE	DBL. COURSE
16″	6″ TO 7 1/2″	8″ TO 12″
18″	6″ TO 8 1/2″	9″ TO 14″
24″	8″ TO 11 1/2″	12″ TO 20″

SINGLE COURSING APPLICATION

DOUBLE COURSING APPLICATION

WOOD SHINGLES AND SHAKES FOR SIDING

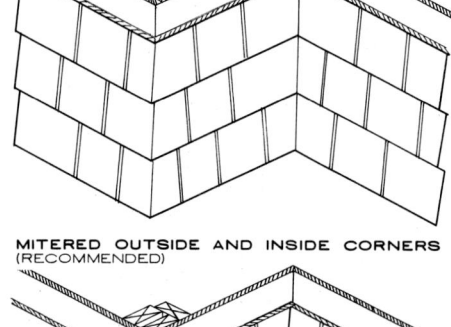

MITERED OUTSIDE AND INSIDE CORNERS
(RECOMMENDED)

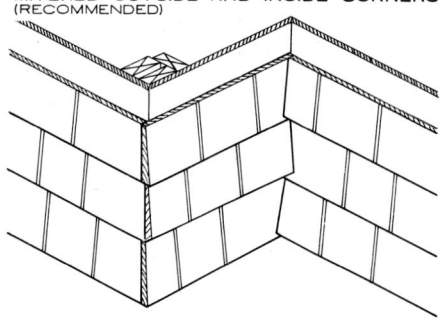

WOVEN OUTSIDE AND INSIDE CORNERS
(MORE ECONOMICAL)

CORNER BOARDS OUTSIDE AND INSIDE CORNERS

NAILING (DEFORMED SHANK NON-FERROUS)

THICKNESS AND NAILS

16″ long	5 butts = 2″	3d
18″ long	5 butts = 2 1/4″	3d
24″ long	4 butts = 2″	4d
25″ to 27″	1 butt = 1/2″	5 or 6d
25″ to 27″	1 butt = 5/8″ to 1 1/4″	7 or 8d

SHEATHING NOTES

Sheathing may be strip-type, solid 1″ x 6″ diagonal type, plywood, fiberboard or gypsum. Horizontal wood nailing strips, 1″ x 2″, should be used over fiberboard and gypsum sheathing. Space strips equal to shingle exposure.

Developed by: Holroyd and Gray, Architects; Charlotte, North Carolina; from data furnished by: Robert M. Stafford, P. E.; Consulting Engineer; Charlotte, North Carolina

7 SHINGLES AND ROOFING TILES

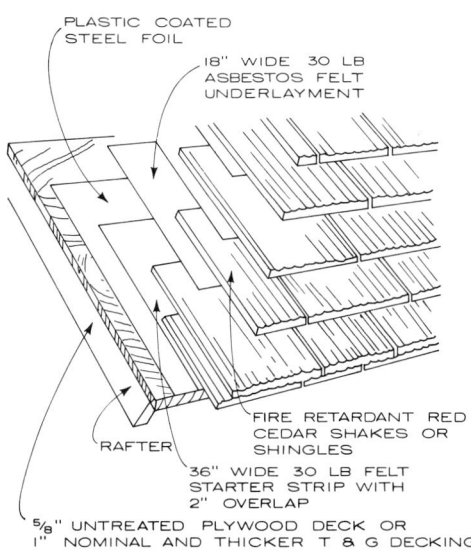

FIRE RATED ROOF CONSTRUCTION

PLASTIC COATED STEEL FOIL

18" WIDE 30 LB ASBESTOS FELT UNDERLAYMENT

FIRE RETARDANT RED CEDAR SHAKES OR SHINGLES

RAFTER

36" WIDE 30 LB FELT STARTER STRIP WITH 2" OVERLAP

⅝" UNTREATED PLYWOOD DECK OR 1" NOMINAL AND THICKER T & G DECKING

NOTES

In treating shakes, fire retardant chemicals are pressure impregnated into the wood cells, and chemicals are then fixed in the wood to prevent leaching. Treatment does not alter appearance. Fire retardant red cedar shakes are classified as Class C by U.L. With the addition of the deck constructed of ⅝ in. plywood with exterior glue or 1 in. nominal T&G boards, overlaid with a layer of approved asbestos felt lapped 2 in. on all joints and between each shake is an 18 in. wide strip of approved asbestos felt not exposed to the weather, Class B classification by U.L. is used. Decorative stains may be applied.

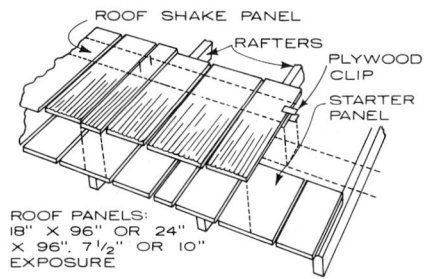

ROOF SHAKE PANEL

RAFTERS

PLYWOOD CLIP

STARTER PANEL

ROOF PANELS: 18" X 96" OR 24" X 96". 7½" OR 10" EXPOSURE

ROOF PANEL

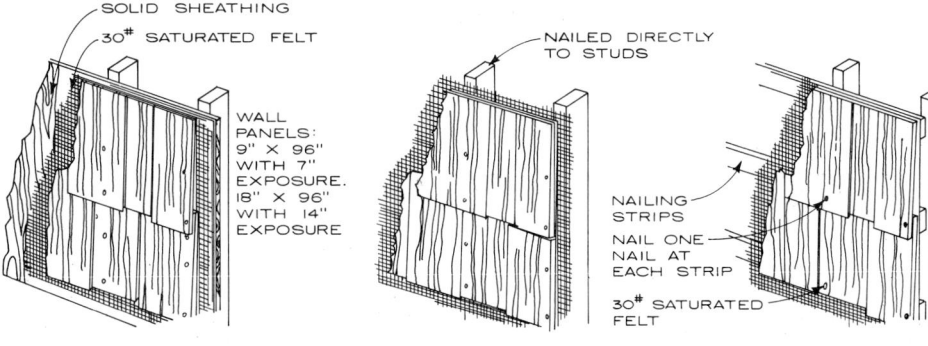

SOLID SHEATHING

30# SATURATED FELT

WALL PANELS: 9" X 96" WITH 7" EXPOSURE. 18" X 96" WITH 14" EXPOSURE

NAILED DIRECTLY TO STUDS

NAILING STRIPS

NAIL ONE NAIL AT EACH STRIP

30# SATURATED FELT

APPLIED TO SHEATHING   **APPLIED DIRECTLY TO STUD**   **APPLIED TO NAILING STRIPS**

NOTES

8 ft sidewall panels are of three-ply construction.

1. Surface layer of individual #1 grade shingles or shakes.
2. Cross binder core of plywood veneer.

SIDEWALL PANELS

Robert E. Fehlberg, FAIA; CTA Architects—Engineers; Billings, Montana

---

REMOVE OLD RIDGE COVERING. REPLACE WITH CEDAR BEVEL SIDING

1 X 4

OLD ROOFING

30 LB FELT   ROOF RAFTERS

REMOVE 6" WIDE STRIP OF OLD ROOFING. APPLY 1 X 6

METAL VALLEY SHEET 20" MIN. WIDTH

NEW CEDAR SHAKES USE LONGER NAILS TO PENETRATE SHEATHING

WOOD SHAKES APPLIED TO EXISTING ROOF

NOTES

Shakes can also be applied over any existing wall or roof. Brick or other masonry requires vertical frameboards and horizontal nailing strips.

Over stucco, horizontal nailing strips are attached directly to wall. Nails should penetrate shading or studs. Over wood, apply shakes directly just as if on new sheathing.

NOTES

Shakes and shingles plus sheathing go up in one operation. 8 ft roof panels have 16 individual handsplit shakes bonded to 6 in. wide ½ in. plywood strip, which form a solid deck when the panels are nailed. A 4 to 12 in. or steeper roof pitch is recommended.

After application of starter panels, attach panels directly to rafters. Although designed to center on 16 or 24 in. spacing, they may meet between rafters. Use two 6d nails at each rafter.

3. Undercourse layer of shingle backing panels.

Panels can be applied to nailing strips or directly to studs where Code permits. Use 30 lb saturated fill lapped 3 in. vertically and horizontally. Stagger joints between panels. Matching sidewall or mansard style corners are available.

NOMENCLATURE

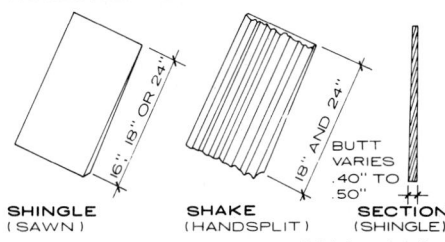

SHINGLE (SAWN)   SHAKE (HANDSPLIT)   SECTION (SHINGLE)

16", 18" OR 24"   18" AND 24"   BUTT VARIES .40" TO .50"

Species: Shingles and shakes are available in red cedar, redwood, and tidewater red cypress.

GENERAL NOTES

1. Wood shingles and shakes are manufactured from wood species that are naturally resistant to water, sunlight, rot, and hail. They are typically installed in the natural state, although stains, primers, and paint may be applied.
2. Nails must be hot dipped in zinc or aluminum. Nail heads should be driven flush with the surface of the shingle or shake, but never into the wood.
3. Underlayment and sheathing should be designed to augment the protection provided by the shingles or shakes, depending on roof pitch and climate. For instance, a low pitched roof in an area subject to wind driven snow should have solid sheathing and an additional underlayment.

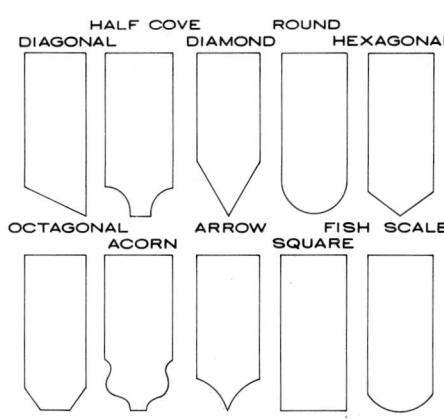

HALF COVE   ROUND
DIAGONAL   DIAMOND   HEXAGONAL

OCTAGONAL   ARROW   FISH SCALE
ACORN   SQUARE

NOTE

Fancy butt shingles are 5 in. wide and 7½ in. long. Custom produced to individual orders.

FANCY BUTT RED CEDAR SHINGLES

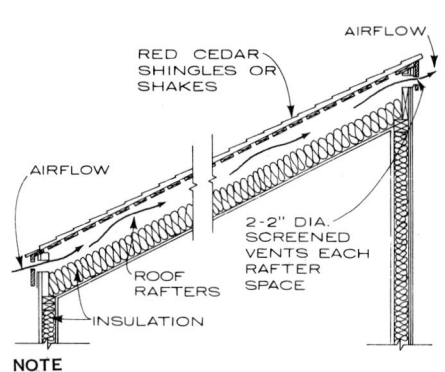

AIRFLOW

RED CEDAR SHINGLES OR SHAKES

AIRFLOW

2-2" DIA. SCREENED VENTS EACH RAFTER SPACE

ROOF RAFTERS

INSULATION

NOTE

A recommended ratio of total free area to adding area should not be less than 1:150 for adequate ventilation.

SECTION

VENTILATION OF ROOF

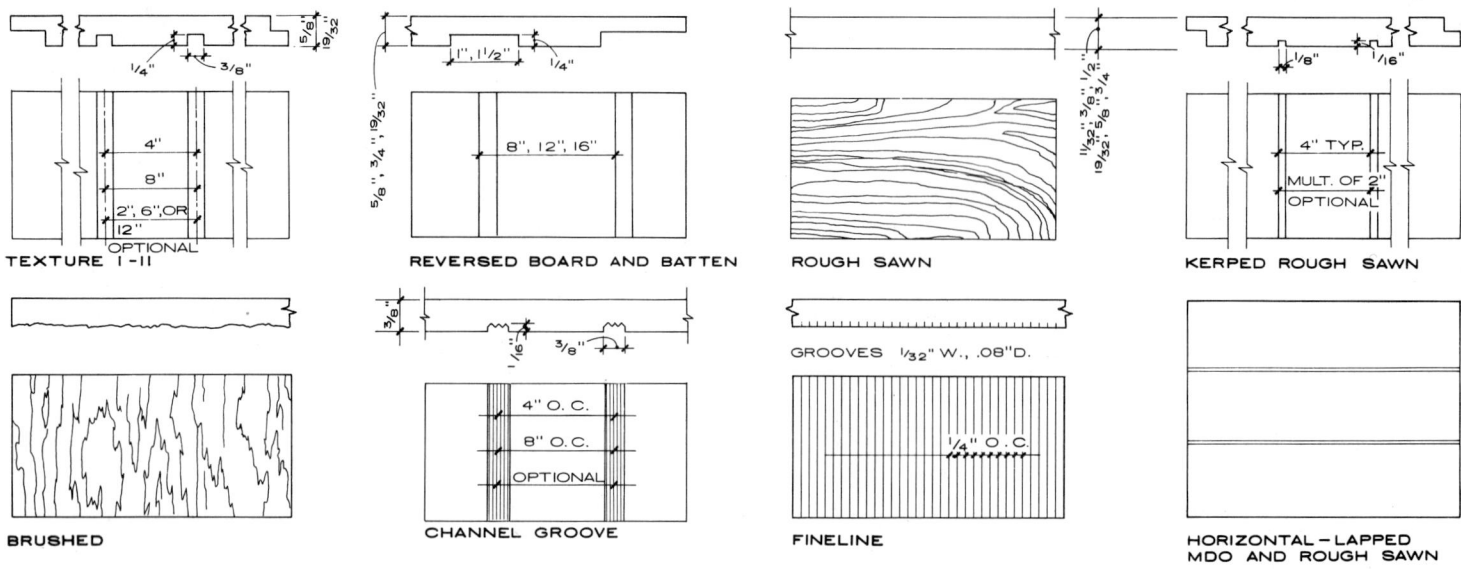

PLYWOOD SIDING T 1-11 AND 303 SPECIAL

Medium density overlay (MDO) plywood lap siding: standard thickness is ³/₈ in. in lengths to 16 ft on order; standard widths are 12 or 16 in.

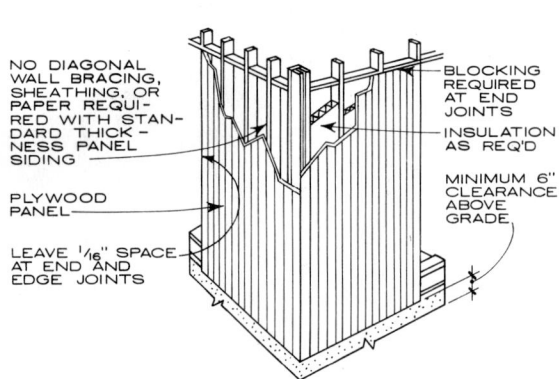

PANEL SIDING VERTICAL APPLICATION

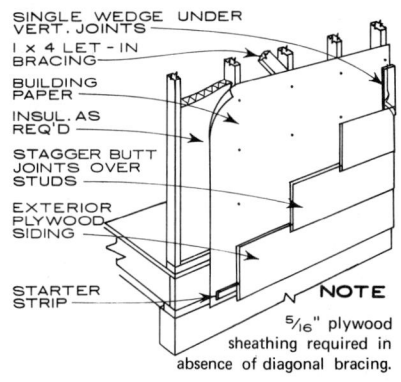

NOTE

⁵/₁₆" plywood sheathing required in absence of diagonal bracing.

PLYWOOD LAP SIDING APPLICATION

PANEL SIDING HORIZONTAL APPLICATION

NAILING CHART FOR PLYWOOD SIDING

APPLICATION	PLYWOOD THICKNESS (IN.)	MAX. SPACING OF SUPPORTS (C.—C.)	NAIL SIZE AND TYPE (a)	NAIL SPACING (IN.)	
				PANEL EDGES	INTERMEDIATE
Panel siding (b)	³/₈" (c)	16"	6d casing or siding	6"	12"
	¹/₂"	24"	6d casing or siding	6"	12"
	⁵/₈" or thicker	24"	8d casing or siding	6"	12"
Lap siding or bevel siding	³/₈" (d)	16"	6d casing or siding	One nail per stud along bottom edge	4" at vert. joint 8" at studs (siding wider than 12")
	⁷/₁₆"	24"	8d casing or siding		

NOTES

(a) Use galvanized, aluminum, or other noncorrosive nails. Use same schedule for panel siding and siding over sheathing.

(b) Battens applied with 8d noncorrosive casing nails spaced 12" o.c. staggered.

(c) Over separate sheathing ³/₈" panel siding may be used over supports 24" o.c.

(d) Over separate sheathing ⁵/₁₆" MDO plywood lap siding may be used over supports spaced 16" o.c.

MINIMUM BENDING RADII FOR PLYWOOD PANELS

The following are found to be appropriate minimum radii for mill run panels, thickness as shown, bent dry. Shorter radii can be developed by selection for bending of areas free of knots and short grain, and/or by wetting or steaming. Exterior type of plywood should be used for such wetting or steaming. Panels to be glued should be redried before gluing. The radii given are minimum; an occasional panel may develop localized fractures at these radii. Bending radii (ft) for panel bent in direction:

1. Panel thickness (in.): ¹/₄, ⁵/₁₆, ³/₈, ¹/₂, ⁵/₈, and ³/₄.

2. Across grain: 2, 2, 3, 6, 8, and 12.

3. Parallel to grain: 5, 6, 8, 12, 16, and 20.

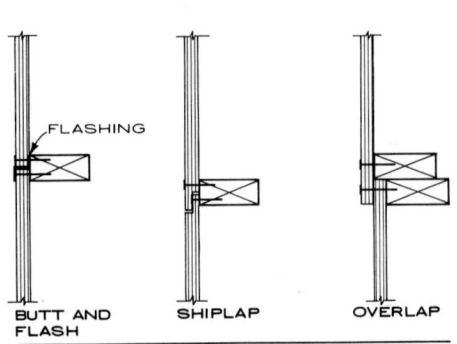

HORIZONTAL JOINTS

John D. Bloodgood, Architect, P.C.; Des Moines, Iowa

NOTES

The types of plywood recommended for exterior siding are: A.P.A. grade trademarked medium density overlay (MDO), Type 303 siding or Texture 1-11 (T1-11 special 303 siding). T1-11 plywood siding is manufactured with ³/₈ in. wide parallel grooves and shiplapped edges. MDO is recommended for paint finishes and is available in variety of surfaces. 303 plywood panels are also available in a wide variety of surfaces. The most common A.P.A. plywood siding panel dimensions are 4 x 8 ft but the panels are also available in 9 and 10 ft lengths, lap siding to 16 ft.

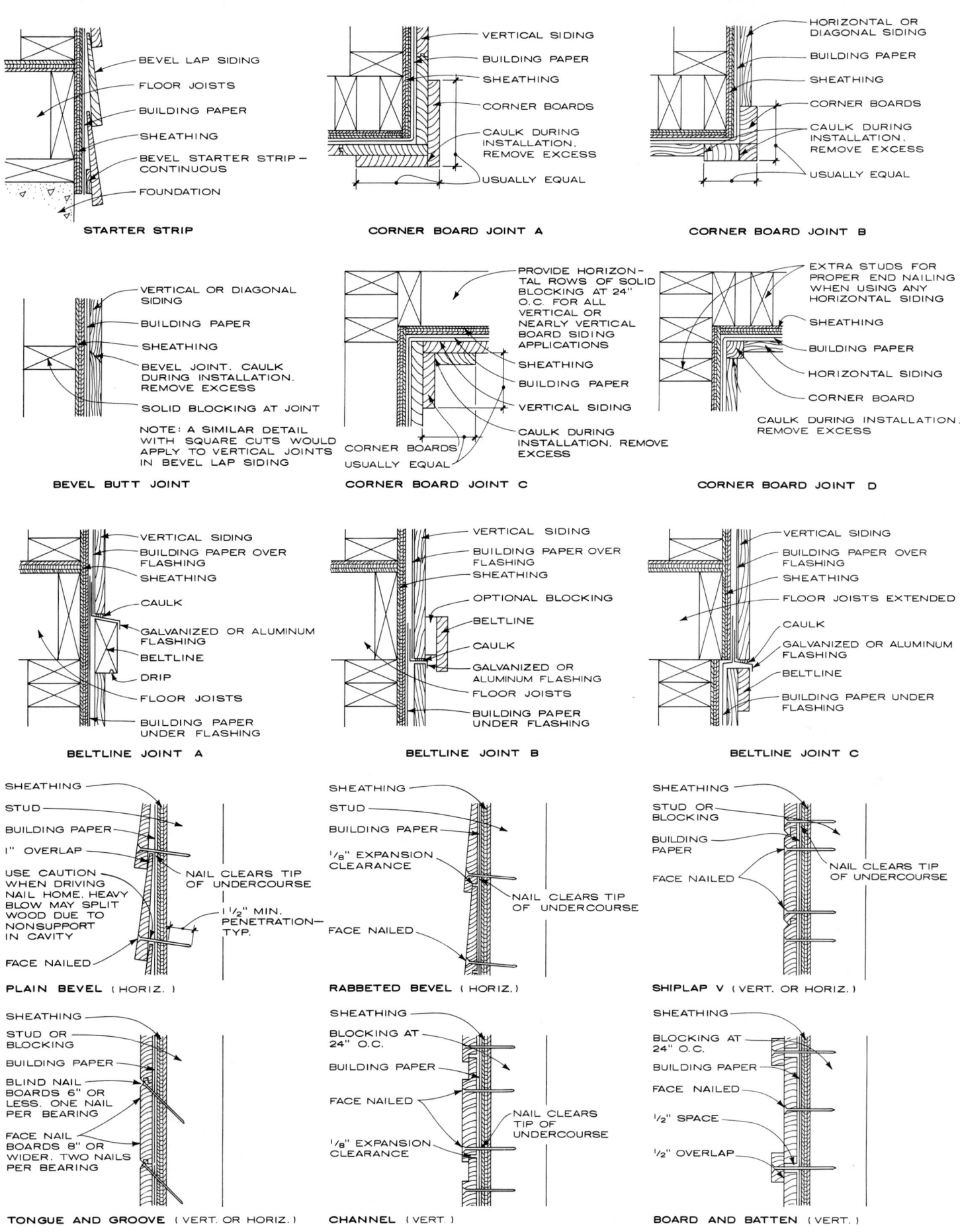

STARTER STRIP
- BEVEL LAP SIDING
- FLOOR JOISTS
- BUILDING PAPER
- SHEATHING
- BEVEL STARTER STRIP — CONTINUOUS
- FOUNDATION

CORNER BOARD JOINT A
- VERTICAL SIDING
- BUILDING PAPER
- SHEATHING
- CORNER BOARDS
- CAULK DURING INSTALLATION. REMOVE EXCESS
- USUALLY EQUAL

CORNER BOARD JOINT B
- HORIZONTAL OR DIAGONAL SIDING
- BUILDING PAPER
- SHEATHING
- CORNER BOARDS
- CAULK DURING INSTALLATION. REMOVE EXCESS
- USUALLY EQUAL

BEVEL BUTT JOINT
- VERTICAL OR DIAGONAL SIDING
- BUILDING PAPER
- SHEATHING
- BEVEL JOINT. CAULK DURING INSTALLATION. REMOVE EXCESS
- SOLID BLOCKING AT JOINT

NOTE: A SIMILAR DETAIL WITH SQUARE CUTS WOULD APPLY TO VERTICAL JOINTS IN BEVEL LAP SIDING

CORNER BOARD JOINT C
- PROVIDE HORIZONTAL ROWS OF SOLID BLOCKING AT 24" O.C. FOR ALL VERTICAL OR NEARLY VERTICAL BOARD SIDING APPLICATIONS
- SHEATHING
- BUILDING PAPER
- VERTICAL SIDING
- CAULK DURING INSTALLATION. REMOVE EXCESS
- CORNER BOARDS USUALLY EQUAL

CORNER BOARD JOINT D
- EXTRA STUDS FOR PROPER END NAILING WHEN USING ANY HORIZONTAL SIDING
- SHEATHING
- BUILDING PAPER
- HORIZONTAL SIDING
- CORNER BOARD
- CAULK DURING INSTALLATION. REMOVE EXCESS

BELTLINE JOINT A
- VERTICAL SIDING
- BUILDING PAPER OVER FLASHING
- SHEATHING
- CAULK
- GALVANIZED OR ALUMINUM FLASHING
- BELTLINE
- DRIP
- FLOOR JOISTS
- BUILDING PAPER UNDER FLASHING

BELTLINE JOINT B
- VERTICAL SIDING
- BUILDING PAPER OVER FLASHING
- SHEATHING
- OPTIONAL BLOCKING
- BELTLINE
- CAULK
- GALVANIZED OR ALUMINUM FLASHING
- FLOOR JOISTS
- BUILDING PAPER UNDER FLASHING

BELTLINE JOINT C
- VERTICAL SIDING
- BUILDING PAPER OVER FLASHING
- SHEATHING
- FLOOR JOISTS EXTENDED
- CAULK
- GALVANIZED OR ALUMINUM FLASHING
- BELTLINE
- BUILDING PAPER UNDER FLASHING

PLAIN BEVEL (HORIZ.)
- SHEATHING
- STUD
- BUILDING PAPER
- 1" OVERLAP
- USE CAUTION WHEN DRIVING NAIL HOME. HEAVY BLOW MAY SPLIT WOOD DUE TO NONSUPPORT IN CAVITY
- FACE NAILED
- NAIL CLEARS TIP OF UNDERCOURSE
- 1 1/2" MIN. PENETRATION — TYP.

RABBETED BEVEL (HORIZ.)
- SHEATHING
- STUD
- BUILDING PAPER
- 1/8" EXPANSION CLEARANCE
- NAIL CLEARS TIP OF UNDERCOURSE
- FACE NAILED

SHIPLAP V (VERT. OR HORIZ.)
- SHEATHING
- STUD OR BLOCKING
- BUILDING PAPER
- FACE NAILED
- NAIL CLEARS TIP OF UNDERCOURSE

TONGUE AND GROOVE (VERT. OR HORIZ.)
- SHEATHING
- STUD OR BLOCKING
- BUILDING PAPER
- BLIND NAIL BOARDS 6" OR LESS. ONE NAIL PER BEARING
- FACE NAIL BOARDS 8" OR WIDER. TWO NAILS PER BEARING

CHANNEL (VERT.)
- SHEATHING
- BLOCKING AT 24" O.C.
- BUILDING PAPER
- FACE NAILED
- 1/8" EXPANSION CLEARANCE
- NAIL CLEARS TIP OF UNDERCOURSE

BOARD AND BATTEN (VERT.)
- SHEATHING
- BLOCKING AT 24" O.C.
- BUILDING PAPER
- FACE NAILED
- 1/2" SPACE
- 1/2" OVERLAP

Jerry Graham; CTA Architects Engineers; Billings, Montana

CLADDING AND SIDING   7

SCHEDULE OF UNDERLAYMENT

SLOPE	TYPE OF UNDERLAYMENT
Normal slope: 4 in 12 and up	Single layer of 15 lb asphalt saturated felt over entire roof
Low slope: 2 in 12 to 4 in 12	Two layers of 15 lb asphalt saturated felt over entire roof

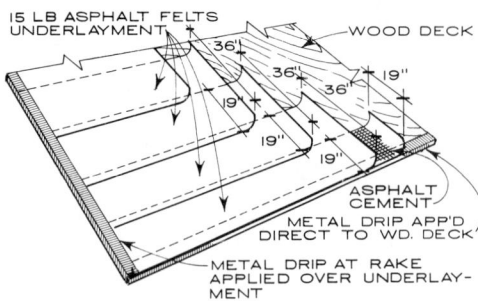

15 LB ASPHALT FELTS UNDERLAYMENT
WOOD DECK
36'
36'
19'
36'
19'
19'
19'
ASPHALT CEMENT
METAL DRIP APP'D DIRECT TO WD. DECK
METAL DRIP AT RAKE APPLIED OVER UNDERLAYMENT

Use only enough nails to hold underlayment in place until shingles are laid.

APPLICATION OF UNDERLAYMENT ON LOW SLOPE ROOFS

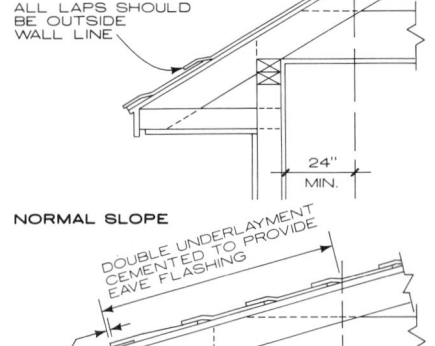

EAVES FLASHING STRIP PREVENTS BACKUP DAMAGE
ALL LAPS SHOULD BE OUTSIDE WALL LINE
24" MIN.

NORMAL SLOPE

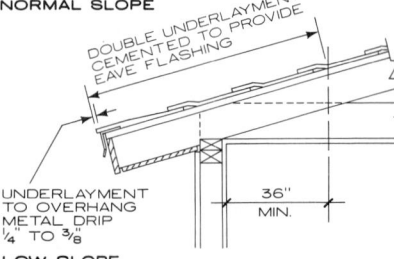

DOUBLE UNDERLAYMENT CEMENTED TO PROVIDE EAVE FLASHING
UNDERLAYMENT TO OVERHANG METAL DRIP 1/4 TO 3/8
36" MIN.

LOW SLOPE

EAVE FLASHING

EAVE FLASHING

Eave flashing is required wherever the January daily average temperature is 25°F or less or where there is a possibility of ice forming along the eaves.

NORMAL SLOPE—4 IN./FT OR OVER

A course of 90 lb mineral surfaced roll roofing or a course of 50 lb smooth roll roofing is installed to overhang the underlay and metal edge from 1/4 to 3/8 in. Extend up the roof far enough to cover a point at least 24 in. inside the interior wall line of the building. When the overhang requires flashing wider than 36 in., the horizontal lap joint is cemented and located on the roof deck extending beyond the exterior line of the building.

LOW SLOPE—2 TO 4 IN./FT

Cover the deck with two layers of 15# asphalt saturated felt. Begin with a 19 in. starter course laid along the eaves, followed by a 36 in. wide sheet laid even with the eaves and completely overlapping the starter course. The starter course is covered with asphalt cement. Thereafter, 36 in. sheets are laid in asphalt cement, each to overlap the preceding course 19 in., exposing 17 in. of the underlying sheet.

The plies are placed in asphalt cement to a point at least 36 in. inside the interior wall line of the building.

SCHEDULE OF SHINGLE TYPES

DESCRIPTION	DESIGN	MATERIAL	U.L. RATING	WEIGHT	SIZE
Three-tab square butt		Fiberglass Organic felts	A C	215–225 lb/sq 235–300 lb/sq	36" x 12"
Two-tab square butt		Fiberglass Organic felts	A C	260–325 lb/sq 300 lb/sq	36" x 12"
Laminated overlay		Fiberglass Organic felts	A C	300 lb/sq 330–380 lb/sq	36" x 14"
Random edge cut		Fiberglass Organic felts	A C	225–260 lb/sq 250 lb/sq	36" x 12"

NOTE: Exposure 5", edge lap 2".

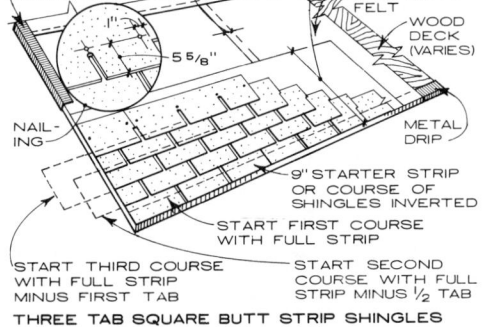

MET. DRIP EDGE APP'D OVER FELT ALONG RAKE
2" TOP LAP
4" TOP LAP
EAVES FLASH'G STRIP 36" MIN.
UNDERLAYM'T 15 LB ASPH. FELT
WOOD DECK (VARIES)
1"
5 5/8"
NAILING
METAL DRIP
9" STARTER STRIP OR COURSE OF SHINGLES INVERTED
START FIRST COURSE WITH FULL STRIP
START THIRD COURSE WITH FULL STRIP MINUS FIRST TAB
START SECOND COURSE WITH FULL STRIP MINUS 1/2 TAB

THREE TAB SQUARE BUTT STRIP SHINGLES

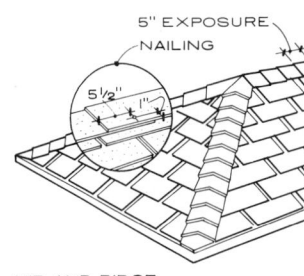

5" EXPOSURE
NAILING
5 1/2"
1"

HIP AND RIDGE

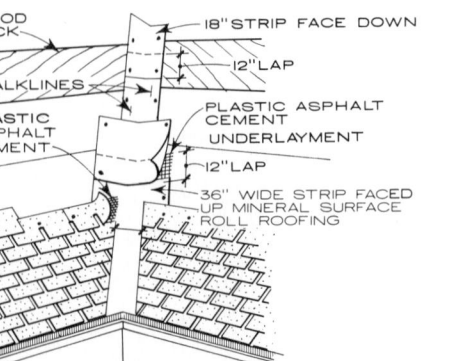

WOOD DECK
18" STRIP FACE DOWN
12" LAP
CHALKLINES
PLASTIC ASPHALT CEMENT
PLASTIC ASPHALT CEMENT
UNDERLAYMENT
12" LAP
36" WIDE STRIP FACED UP MINERAL SURFACE ROLL ROOFING

OPEN VALLEY

*Valley width should be 6" wide at ridge and spread wider at the rate of 1/8"/foot downward to eave. Establish valley width using chalkline from ridge to cove.

WOOD DECK
36" ROLL ROOFING AT LEAST 55 LB OR 1/16" SHEET NEOPRENE
EACH STRIP TO EXTEND AT LEAST 12" BEYOND CENTER OF VALLEY
6" MINIMUM
UNDERLAYMENT
EXTRA NAIL IN END OF STRIP

CLOSED VALLEY

APPLICATION DIAGRAMS

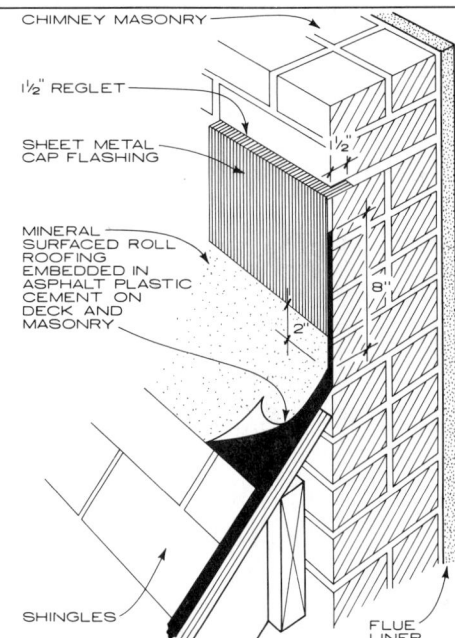

CHIMNEY MASONRY
1 1/2" REGLET
1/2"
SHEET METAL CAP FLASHING
MINERAL SURFACED ROLL ROOFING EMBEDDED IN ASPHALT PLASTIC CEMENT ON DECK AND MASONRY
8"
2"
SHINGLES
FLUE LINER

METHOD OF SECURING CAP FLASHING TO CHIMNEY MASONRY

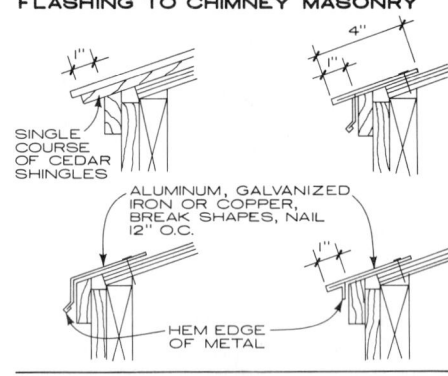

1"
1"
4"
1"
SINGLE COURSE OF CEDAR SHINGLES
ALUMINUM, GALVANIZED IRON OR COPPER, BREAK SHAPES, NAIL 12" O.C.
HEM EDGE OF METAL

DRIP EDGE DETAILS

SMOOTH
ANNULAR THREADED
SCREW THREADED

NAIL TYPES

NAILING OF SHINGLES RECOMMENDATION	
DECK TYPE	NAIL LENGTH
1" Wood sheathing	1 1/4"
3/8" Plywood	7/8"
1/2" Plywood	1"
Reroofing over asphalt shingles	1 3/4"

Robert E. Fehlberg, FAIA; CTA Architects Engineers; Billings, Montana

MINIMUM THICKNESS (GAUGES OR WEIGHT) FOR COMMON FLASHING CONDITIONS

CONDITIONS MATERIALS	BASE COURSE	WALL OPENINGS HEAD AND SILL	THROUGH WALL AND SPANDREL	CAP AND BASE FLASHING	VERTICAL AND HORIZONTAL SURFACES	ROOF EDGE RIDGES AND HIPS	CRICKETS VALLEY OR GUTTER	CHIMNEY PAN	LEDGE FLASHING	ROOF PENETRATIONS	COPING WIDTH UP TO 12"	COPING WIDTH ABOVE 12"	EDGE STRIPS	CLEATS	NOTE
Copper	10 oz	10 oz	10 oz	16 oz	16 oz	16 oz	16 oz	16 oz	16 oz	16 oz	16 oz	20 oz	20 oz	16 oz	
Aluminum	0.019"	0.019"	0.019"	0.019"	0.019"	0.019"	0.019"	0.019"	0.019"	0.040"	0.032"	0.040"	0.024"	✕	Note 6
Stainless steel	30 GA	30 GA	30 GA	26 GA	30 GA	26 GA	26 GA	30 GA	26 GA	26 GA	26 GA	24 GA	24 GA	✕	Note 5
Galvanized steel	26 GA	26 GA	26 GA	26 GA	26 GA	24 GA	24 GA	26 GA	24 GA	24 GA	24 GA	22 GA	26 GA	22 GA	Note 2
Zinc alloy	0.027"	0.027"	0.027"	0.027"	0.027"	0.027"	0.027"	0.027"	0.027"	0.027"	0.027"	0.032"	0.040"	0.027"	Note 4
Lead	3#	2½#	2½#	2½#	3#	3#	3#	3#	3#	3#	3#	3#	3#	3#	Note 3
Painted terne	40#	40#	40#	20#	40#	20#	40#	20#	40#	40#	✕	✕	20#	40#	Note 8
1/16" elastomeric sheet	See Note 7	✕	✕	✕	✕	✕	✕	✕	See Note 7	✕	✕	✕	✕	✕	Note 7

GENERAL NOTES

1. All sizes and weights of material given in chart are minimum. Actual conditions may require greater strength.
2. All galvanized steel must be painted.
3. With lead flashing use 16 oz copper cleats. If any part is exposed, use 3# lead cleats.
4. Coat zinc with asphaltum paint when in contact with redwood or cedar. High acid content (in these woods only) develops stains.
5. Type 302 stainless steel is an all purpose flashing type. Cleats not needed.
6. Use only aluminum manufactured for the purpose of flashing. Cleats not needed.
7. See manufacturer's literature for use and types of elastic flashing.
8. In general cleats will be of the same material as flashing, but heavier weight or thicker gauge.
9. In selecting metal flashing precaution must be taken not to place flashing in direct contact with dissimilar metals that cause electrolysis.
10. Spaces marked ✕ in the table are uses not recommended for that material.

GALVANIC CORROSION (ELECTROLYSIS) POTENTIAL BETWEEN COMMON FLASHING MATERIALS AND SELECTED CONSTRUCTION MATERIALS

FLASHING MATERIALS \ CONSTRUCTION MATERIALS	COPPER	ALUMINUM	STAINLESS STEEL	GALVANIZED STEEL	ZINC	LEAD	BRASS	BRONZE	MONEL	UNCURRED MORTAR OR CEMENT	WOODS WITH ACID (REDWOOD AND RED CEDAR)	IRON/STEEL
Copper		●	●	◐	●	◐	◐	◐	◐	○	○	●
Aluminum	○		○	○	◐	●	●	●	○	●	●	◐
Stainless steel	◐	●		◐	◐	●	●	●	○	○	○	◐
Galvanized steel	○	○	◐		◐	◐	◐	◐	○	○	◐	●
Zinc alloy	○	●	●	◐		●	●	●	○	●	●	●
Lead							◐	◐	◐	●	○	○

● Galvanic action will occur, hence direct contact should be avoided.
◐ Galvanic action may occur under certain circumstances and/or over a period of time.
○ Galvanic action is insignificant, metals may come into direct contact under normal circumstances.

GENERAL NOTE: Galvanic corrosion is apt to occur when water runoff from one material comes in contact with a potentially reactive material.

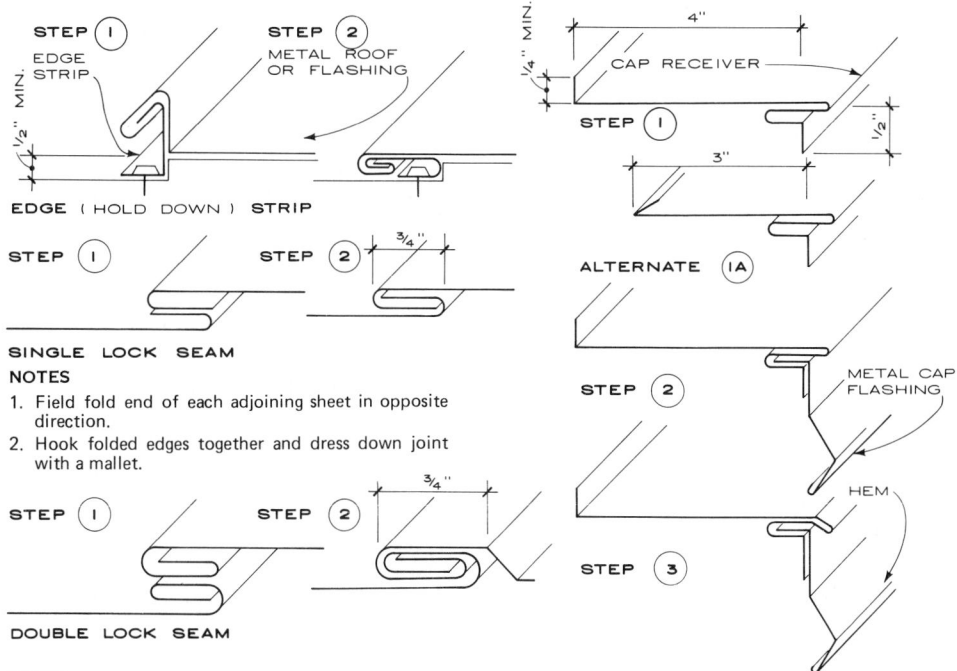

STEP ①   EDGE STRIP   STEP ②   METAL ROOF OR FLASHING

1/2" MIN.

EDGE (HOLD DOWN) STRIP

STEP ①   STEP ②   3/4"

SINGLE LOCK SEAM

NOTES

1. Field fold end of each adjoining sheet in opposite direction.
2. Hook folded edges together and dress down joint with a mallet.

STEP ①   STEP ②   3/4"

DOUBLE LOCK SEAM

NOTES

1. Double fold end of each adjoining sheet in opposite direction with bar folder.
2. Slide edges together and dress down joint with a mallet.

2" MIN.   4"   1/4"   CAP RECEIVER

STEP ①

3"   1/2"

ALTERNATE ⒶⒶ

STEP ②   METAL CAP FLASHING

HEM

STEP ③

DEVELOPMENT OF CAP FLASHING
NOTE
Hem in cap flashing recommended for stiffness; but may be omitted if heavier gauge material used.

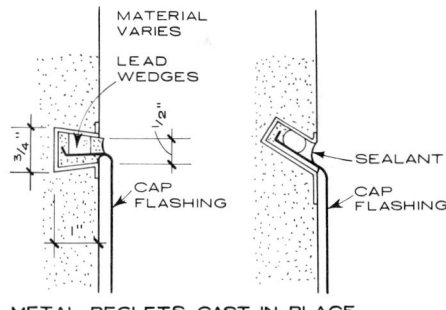

MATERIAL VARIES   LEAD WEDGES

3/4"   1/2"   1"   CAP FLASHING   SEALANT   CAP FLASHING

METAL REGLETS CAST IN PLACE

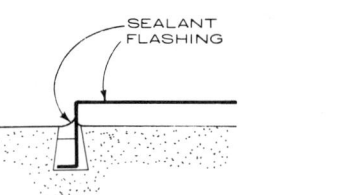

SEALANT FLASHING

REGLET SAWED IN MATERIAL

TYPICAL REGLETS

NOTE
Various types of metal reglets are available for cast in place and masonry work; see manufacturer's literature. Where material permits, reglets may be sawn. Flashing is secured in reglets with lead wedges at max. 12" cc, fill reglet with nonhardening water proof compound.

Michael Scott Rudden, The Stephens Associates P.C.—Architects; Albany, New York

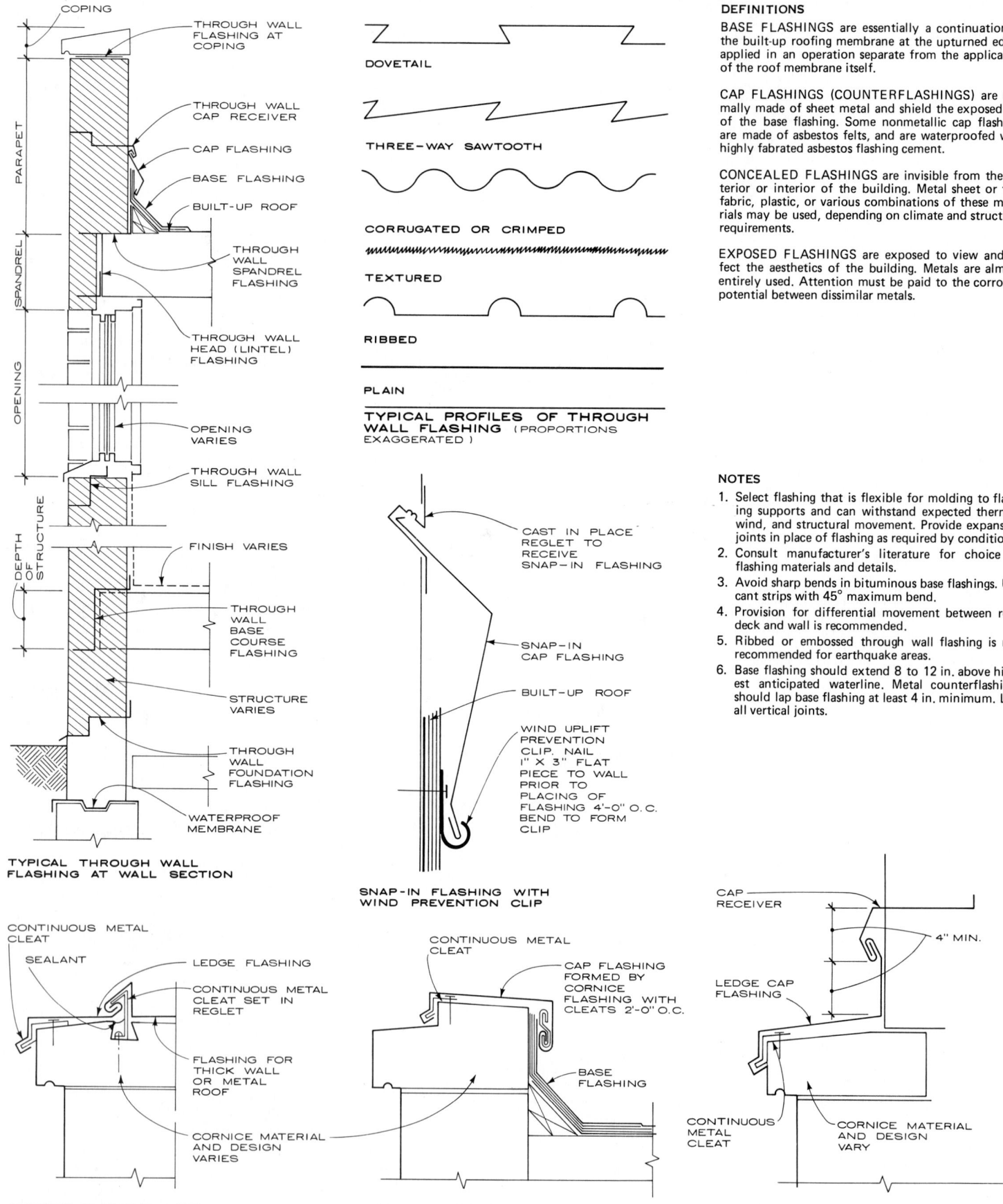

DOVETAIL

THREE-WAY SAWTOOTH

CORRUGATED OR CRIMPED

TEXTURED

RIBBED

PLAIN

TYPICAL PROFILES OF THROUGH WALL FLASHING (PROPORTIONS EXAGGERATED)

DEFINITIONS

BASE FLASHINGS are essentially a continuation of the built-up roofing membrane at the upturned edges, applied in an operation separate from the application of the roof membrane itself.

CAP FLASHINGS (COUNTERFLASHINGS) are normally made of sheet metal and shield the exposed top of the base flashing. Some nonmetallic cap flashings are made of asbestos felts, and are waterproofed with highly fabrated asbestos flashing cement.

CONCEALED FLASHINGS are invisible from the exterior or interior of the building. Metal sheet or foil, fabric, plastic, or various combinations of these materials may be used, depending on climate and structural requirements.

EXPOSED FLASHINGS are exposed to view and affect the aesthetics of the building. Metals are almost entirely used. Attention must be paid to the corrosive potential between dissimilar metals.

NOTES

1. Select flashing that is flexible for molding to flashing supports and can withstand expected thermal, wind, and structural movement. Provide expansion joints in place of flashing as required by conditions.
2. Consult manufacturer's literature for choice of flashing materials and details.
3. Avoid sharp bends in bituminous base flashings. Use cant strips with 45° maximum bend.
4. Provision for differential movement between roof deck and wall is recommended.
5. Ribbed or embossed through wall flashing is not recommended for earthquake areas.
6. Base flashing should extend 8 to 12 in. above highest anticipated waterline. Metal counterflashings should lap base flashing at least 4 in. minimum. Lap all vertical joints.

TYPICAL THROUGH WALL FLASHING AT WALL SECTION

SNAP-IN FLASHING WITH WIND PREVENTION CLIP

CORNICE FLASHING WITH METAL ROOF

CORNICE FLASHING WITH CAP FLASHING

CORNICE LEDGE CAP FLASHING AND RECEIVER

CORNICE FLASHING

Michael Scott Rudden, The Stephens Associates P.C.—Architects; Albany, New York

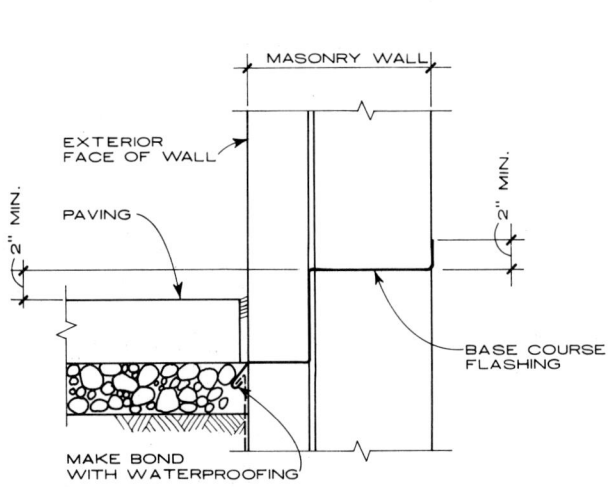

DAMP COURSE AT PAVING AND WALL

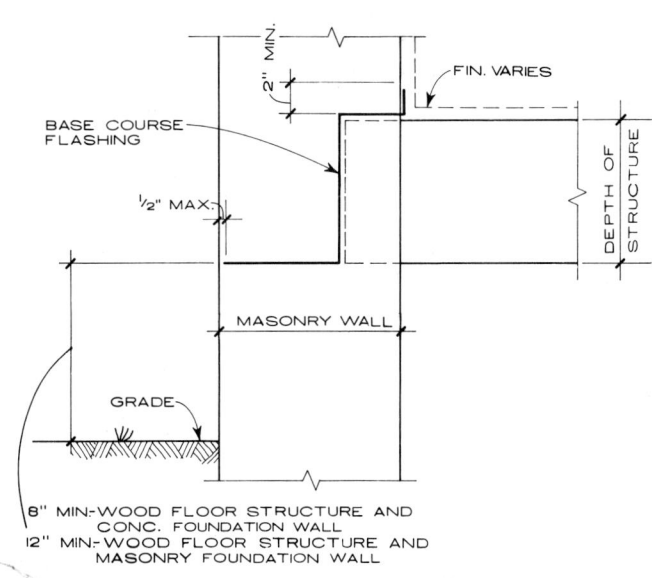

DAMP COURSE AT FLOOR CONSTRUCTION

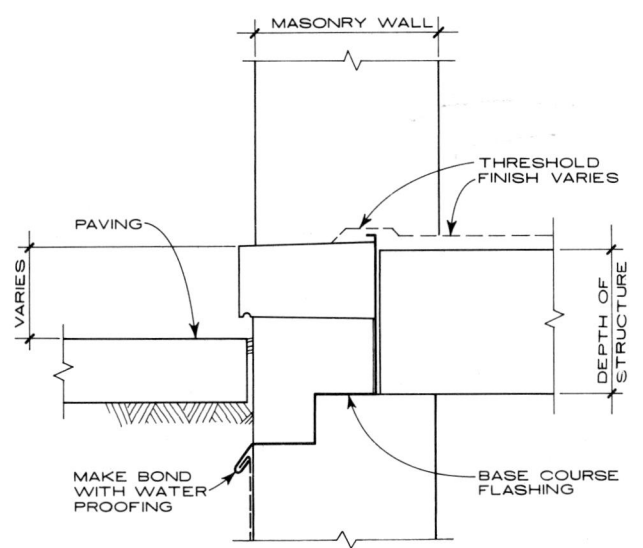

DAMP COURSE AT SILL OF MASONRY CONSTRUCTION

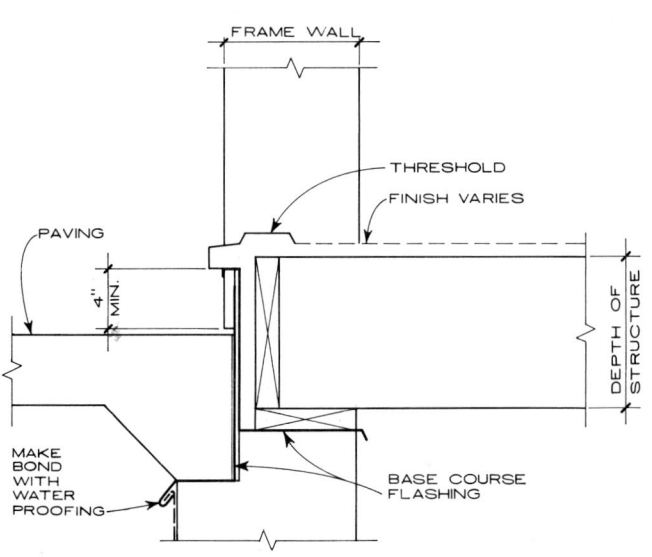

DAMP COURSE AT SILL OF FRAME CONSTRUCTION

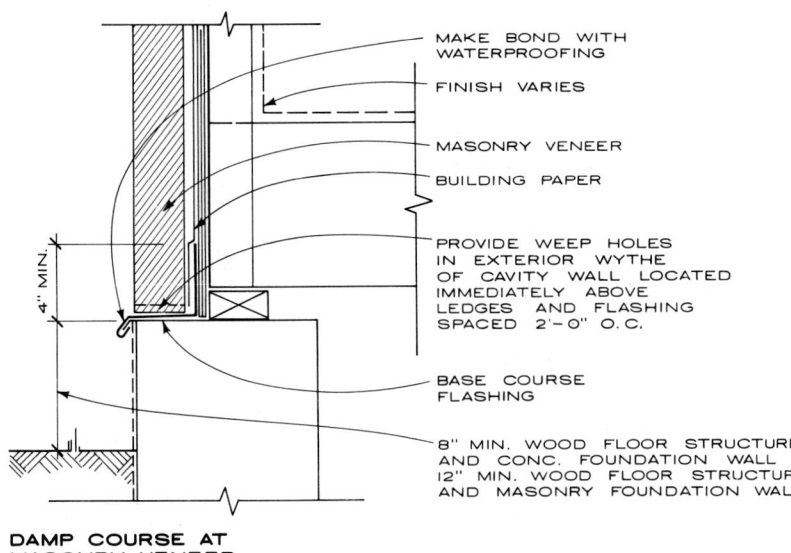

DAMP COURSE AT MASONRY VENEER

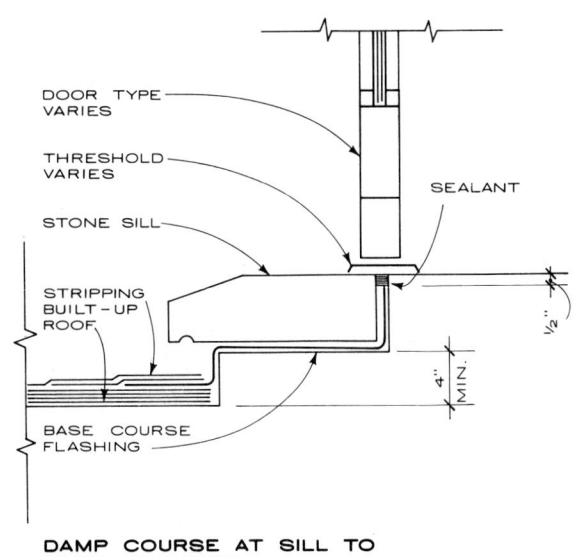

DAMP COURSE AT SILL TO BUILT-UP ROOF

Michael Scott Rudden, The Stephens Associates P.C.—Architects; Albany, New York

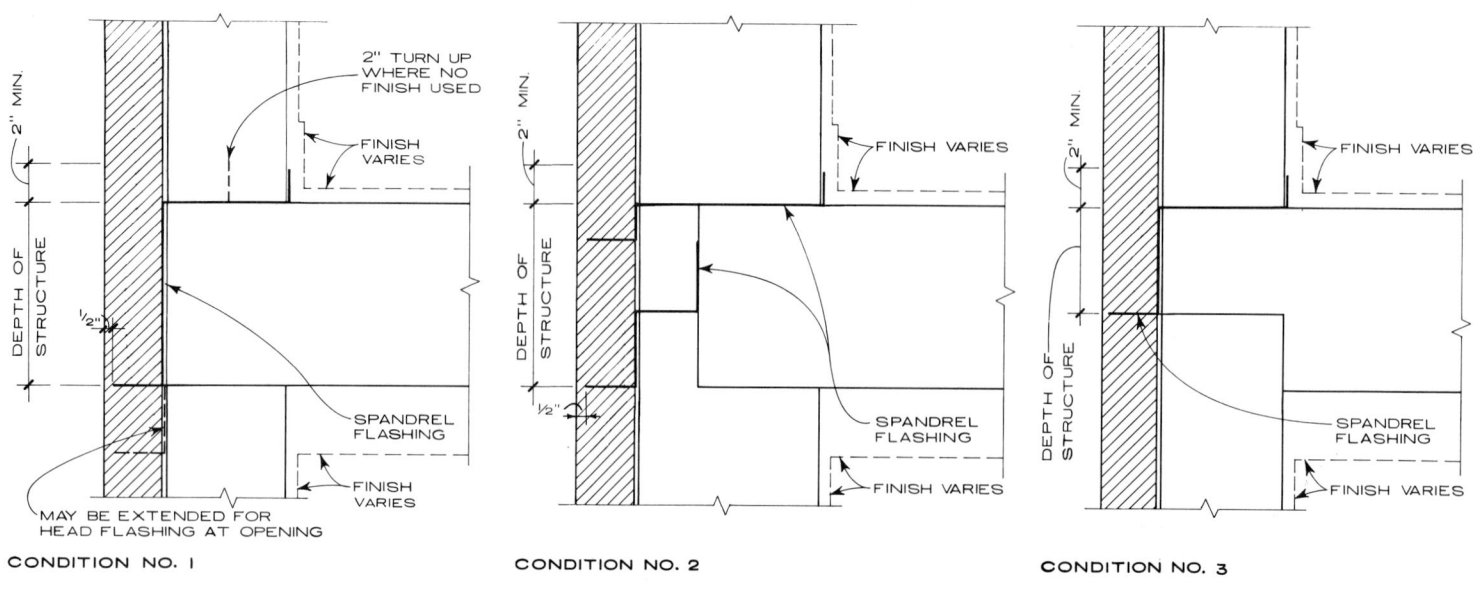

2" TURN UP WHERE NO FINISH USED

FINISH VARIES

2" MIN.

DEPTH OF STRUCTURE

1/2"

SPANDREL FLASHING

FINISH VARIES

MAY BE EXTENDED FOR HEAD FLASHING AT OPENING

CONDITION NO. 1

FINISH VARIES

2" MIN.

DEPTH OF STRUCTURE

1/2"

SPANDREL FLASHING

FINISH VARIES

CONDITION NO. 2

FINISH VARIES

2" MIN.

DEPTH OF STRUCTURE

SPANDREL FLASHING

FINISH VARIES

CONDITION NO. 3

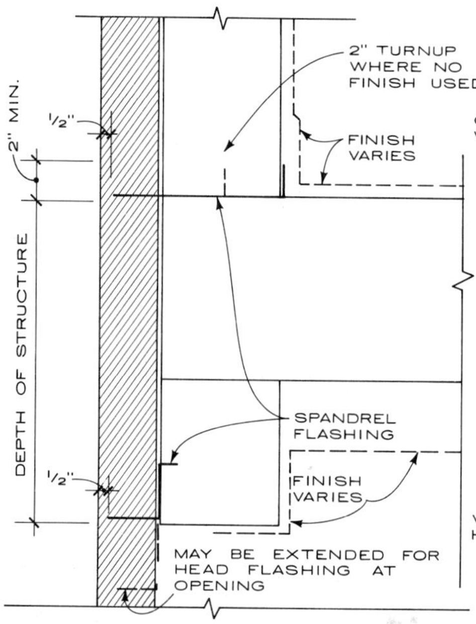

2" TURNUP WHERE NO FINISH USED

2" MIN.

1/2"

FINISH VARIES

DEPTH OF STRUCTURE

1/2"

SPANDREL FLASHING

FINISH VARIES

MAY BE EXTENDED FOR HEAD FLASHING AT OPENING

CONDITION NO. 4

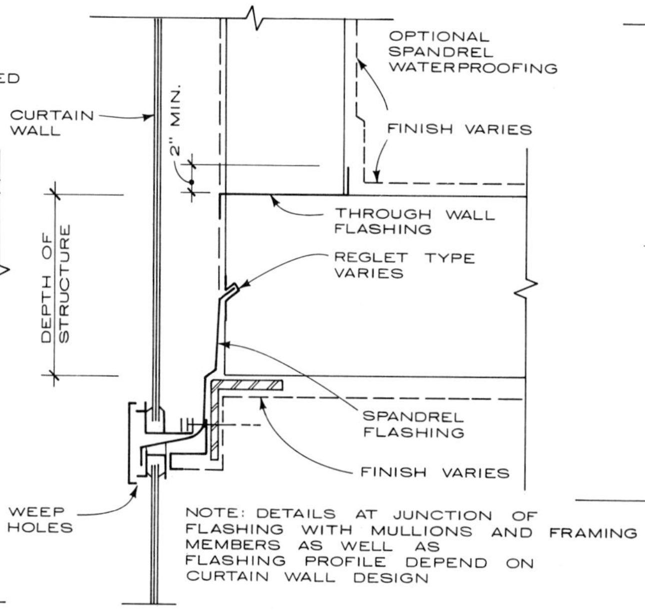

CURTAIN WALL

2" MIN.

DEPTH OF STRUCTURE

THROUGH WALL FLASHING

REGLET TYPE VARIES

OPTIONAL SPANDREL WATERPROOFING

FINISH VARIES

SPANDREL FLASHING

FINISH VARIES

WEEP HOLES

NOTE: DETAILS AT JUNCTION OF FLASHING WITH MULLIONS AND FRAMING MEMBERS AS WELL AS FLASHING PROFILE DEPEND ON CURTAIN WALL DESIGN

CONDITION NO. 5

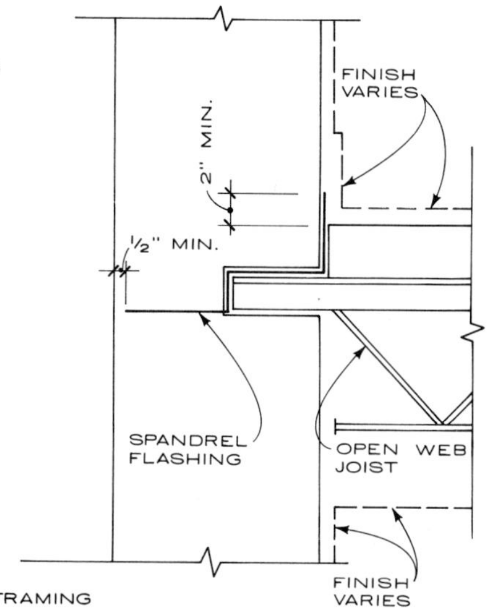

FINISH VARIES

2" MIN.

1/2" MIN.

SPANDREL FLASHING

OPEN WEB JOIST

FINISH VARIES

CONDITION NO. 6

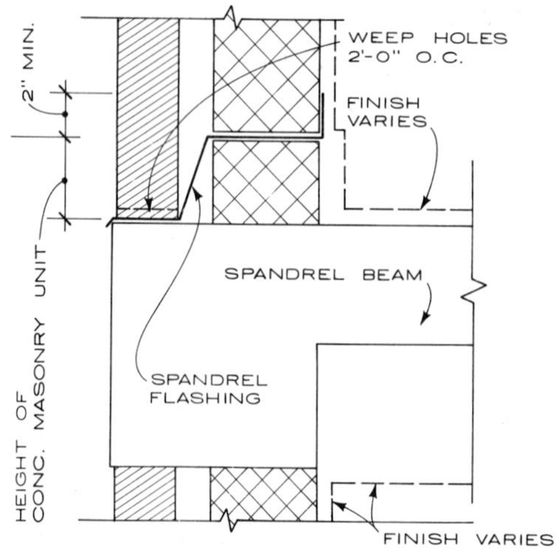

WEEP HOLES 2'-0" O.C.

FINISH VARIES

2" MIN.

SPANDREL BEAM

SPANDREL FLASHING

HEIGHT OF CONC. MASONRY UNIT

FINISH VARIES

CONDITION NO. 7

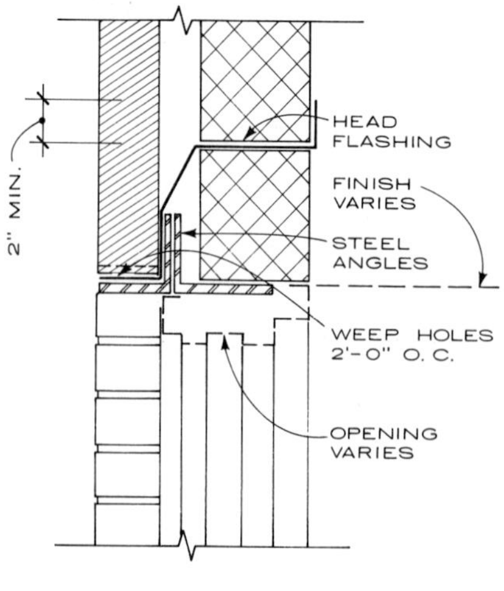

HEAD FLASHING

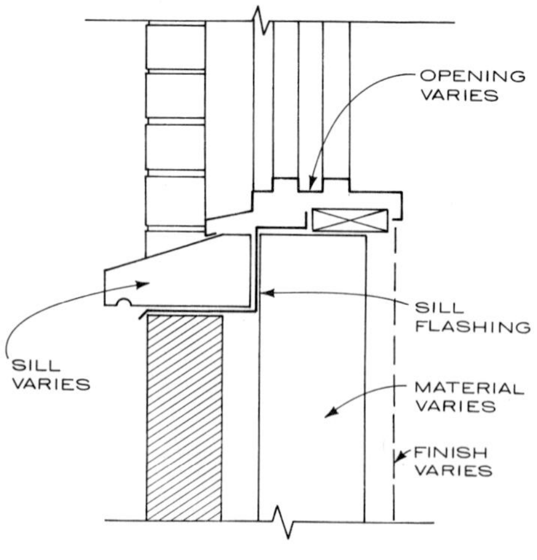

FINISH VARIES

STEEL ANGLES

WEEP HOLES 2'-0" O.C.

OPENING VARIES

2" MIN.

HEAD FLASHING

OPENING VARIES

SILL FLASHING

SILL VARIES

MATERIAL VARIES

FINISH VARIES

SILL FLASHING

Michael Scott Rudden, The Stephens Associates P.C.—Architects; Albany, New York

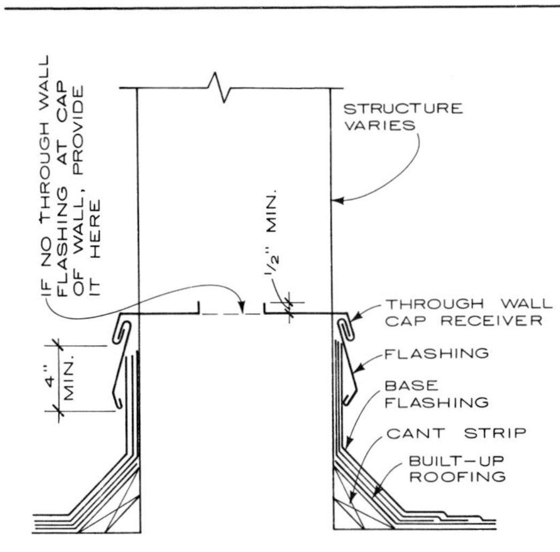

FIRE WALL

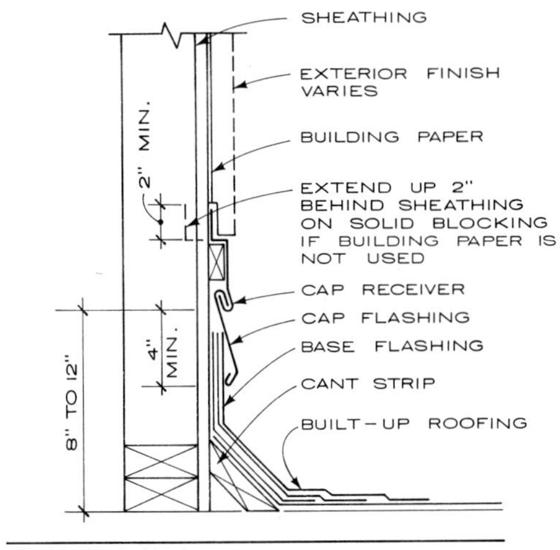

IF NO THROUGH WALL FLASHING AT CAP OF WALL, PROVIDE IT HERE

STRUCTURE VARIES

1/2" MIN.

THROUGH WALL CAP RECEIVER

FLASHING

BASE FLASHING

CANT STRIP

BUILT-UP ROOFING

4" MIN.

FRAME WALL

SHEATHING

EXTERIOR FINISH VARIES

BUILDING PAPER

EXTEND UP 2" BEHIND SHEATHING ON SOLID BLOCKING IF BUILDING PAPER IS NOT USED

CAP RECEIVER

CAP FLASHING

BASE FLASHING

CANT STRIP

BUILT-UP ROOFING

2" MIN.

8" TO 12"

4" MIN.

MASONRY WALL

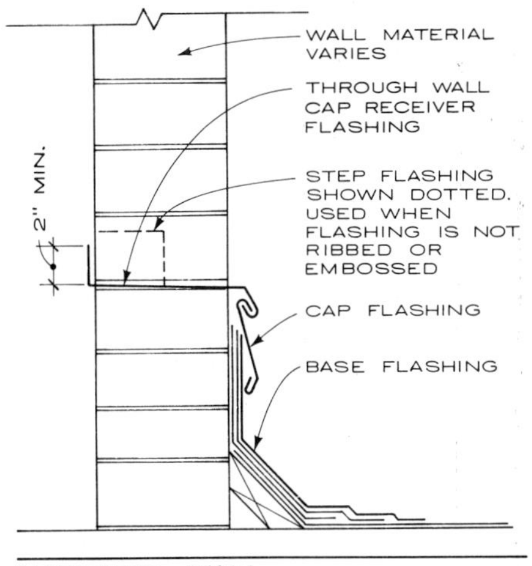

WALL MATERIAL VARIES

THROUGH WALL CAP RECEIVER FLASHING

STEP FLASHING SHOWN DOTTED. USED WHEN FLASHING IS NOT RIBBED OR EMBOSSED

CAP FLASHING

BASE FLASHING

2" MIN.

CAST IN PLACE CONC. WALL

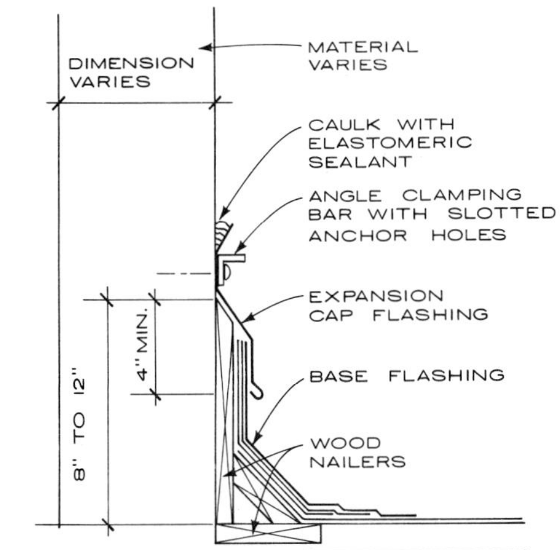

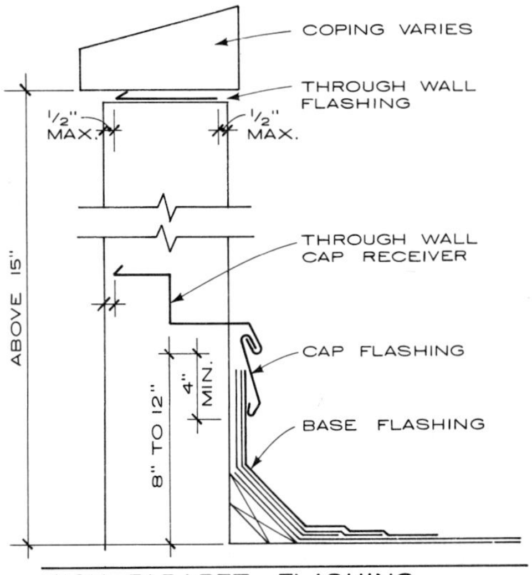

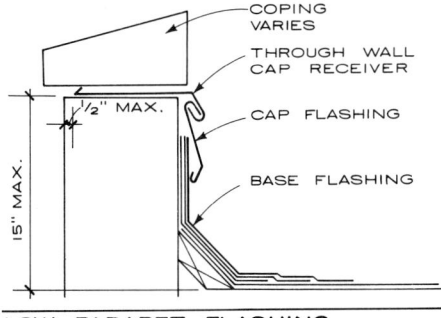

DIMENSION VARIES

MATERIAL VARIES

CAULK WITH ELASTOMERIC SEALANT

ANGLE CLAMPING BAR WITH SLOTTED ANCHOR HOLES

EXPANSION CAP FLASHING

BASE FLASHING

WOOD NAILERS

4" MIN.

8" TO 12"

HIGH PARAPET FLASHING

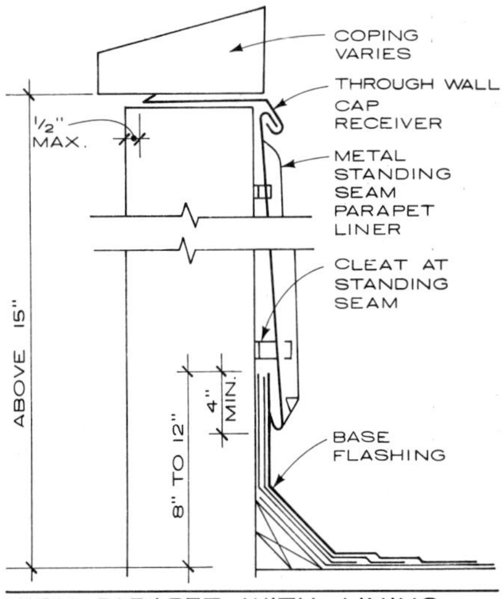

COPING VARIES

THROUGH WALL FLASHING

1/2" MAX. 1/2" MAX.

THROUGH WALL CAP RECEIVER

CAP FLASHING

BASE FLASHING

ABOVE 15"

8" TO 12" 4" MIN.

HIGH PARAPET WITH LINING

COPING VARIES

THROUGH WALL CAP RECEIVER

METAL STANDING SEAM PARAPET LINER

CLEAT AT STANDING SEAM

BASE FLASHING

1/2" MAX.

ABOVE 15"

8" TO 12" 4" MIN.

LOW PARAPET FLASHING

COPING VARIES

THROUGH WALL CAP RECEIVER

CAP FLASHING

BASE FLASHING

1/2" MAX.

15" MAX.

GENERAL NOTES

1. Select flashing that is flexible for molding to flashing supports and can withstand expected thermal, wind, and structural movement. Provide expansion joints in place of flashing as required by conditions.
2. Consult manufacturer's literature for choice of flashing materials and details.
3. Avoid sharp bends in bituminous base flashings. Use cant strips with 45° maximum bend.
4. Provision for differential movement between roof deck and wall is recommended.
5. A ribbed or embossed pattern should be used for all through wall flashing. Through wall flashing is not recommended for earthquake areas.
6. Base flashing should extend 8 to 12 in. above highest anticipated waterline. Metal counterflashing should lap base flashing by at least 4 in. Lap all vertical joints.

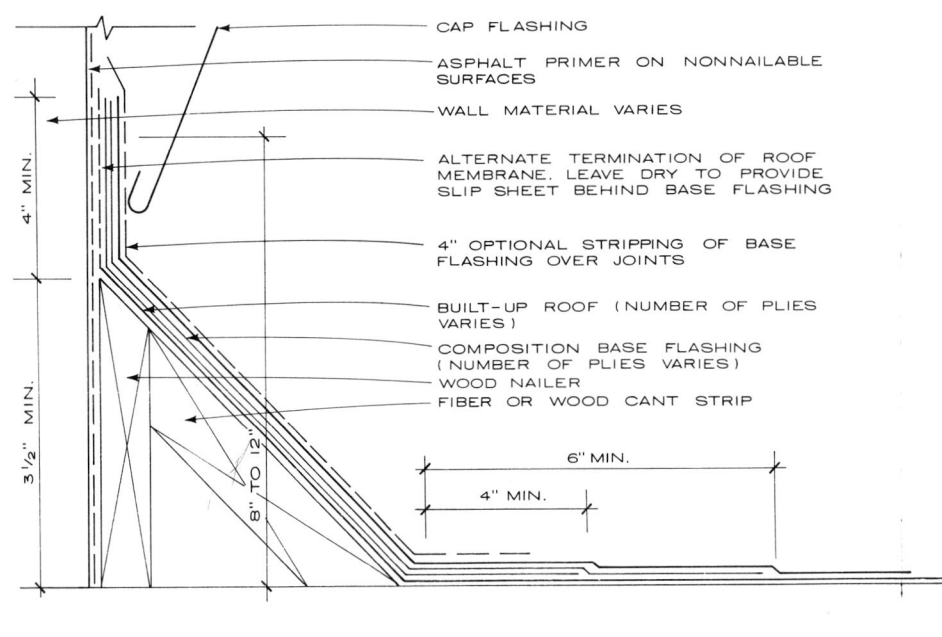

CAP FLASHING

ASPHALT PRIMER ON NONNAILABLE SURFACES

WALL MATERIAL VARIES

ALTERNATE TERMINATION OF ROOF MEMBRANE. LEAVE DRY TO PROVIDE SLIP SHEET BEHIND BASE FLASHING

4" OPTIONAL STRIPPING OF BASE FLASHING OVER JOINTS

BUILT-UP ROOF (NUMBER OF PLIES VARIES)

COMPOSITION BASE FLASHING (NUMBER OF PLIES VARIES)

WOOD NAILER

FIBER OR WOOD CANT STRIP

4" MIN.

3 1/2" MIN.

8" TO 12"

6" MIN.

4" MIN.

TYPICAL BASE FLASHING

Michael Scott Rudden, The Stephens Associates P.C.—Architects; Albany, New York

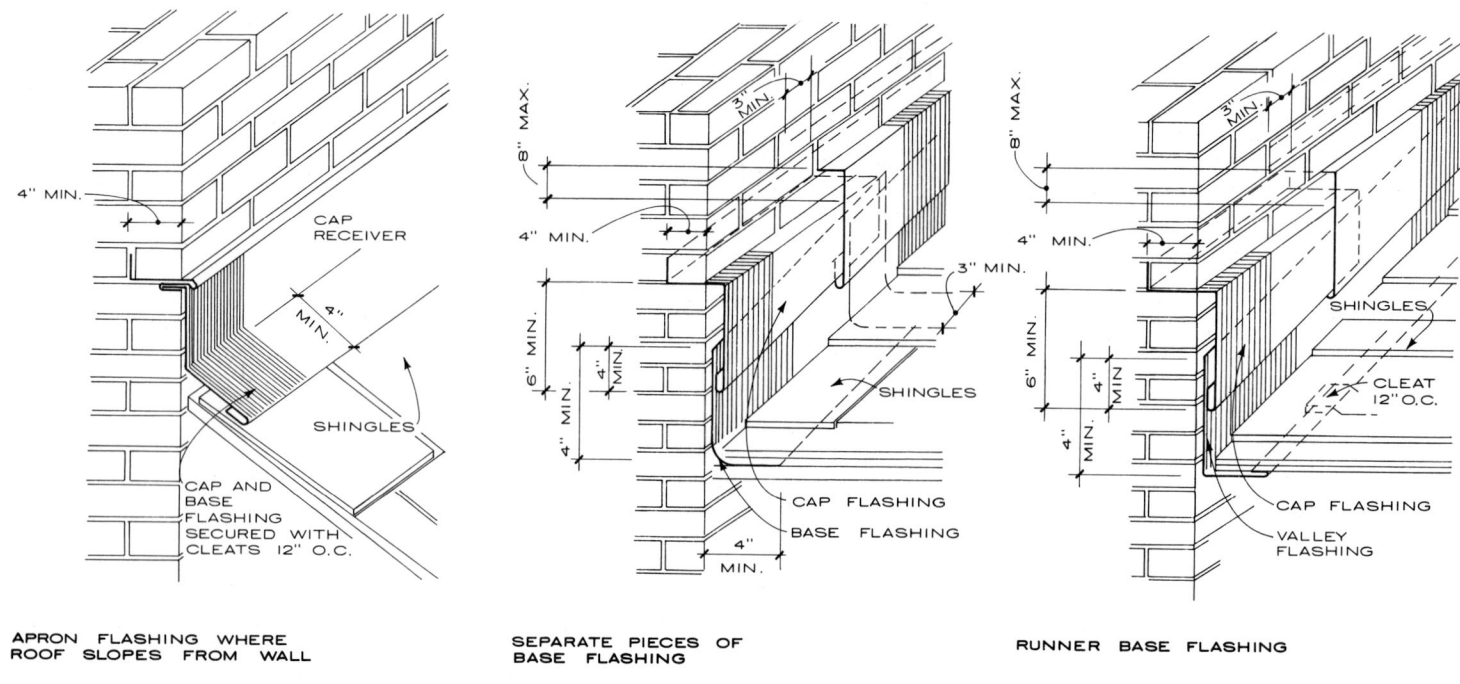

APRON FLASHING WHERE
ROOF SLOPES FROM WALL

SEPARATE PIECES OF
BASE FLASHING

RUNNER BASE FLASHING

PITCHED ROOF WITH WALL FLASHING

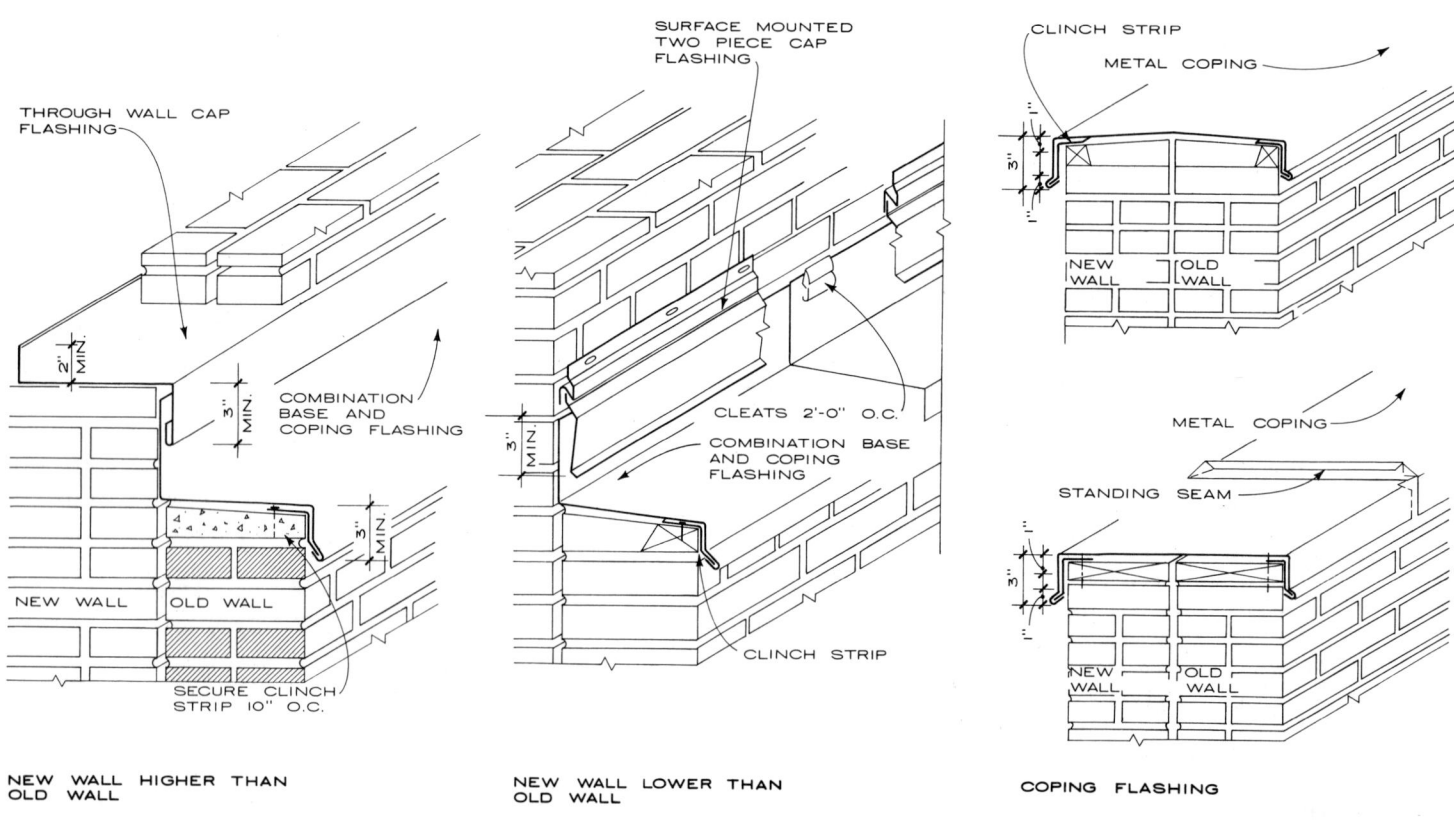

NEW WALL HIGHER THAN
OLD WALL

NEW WALL LOWER THAN
OLD WALL

COPING FLASHING

NEW WALL TO OLD WALL FLASHING

NOTE

Through wall flashing not recommended in earthquake
areas.

Michael Scott Rudden; The Stephens Associates P.C.—Architects; Albany, New York

 FLASHING

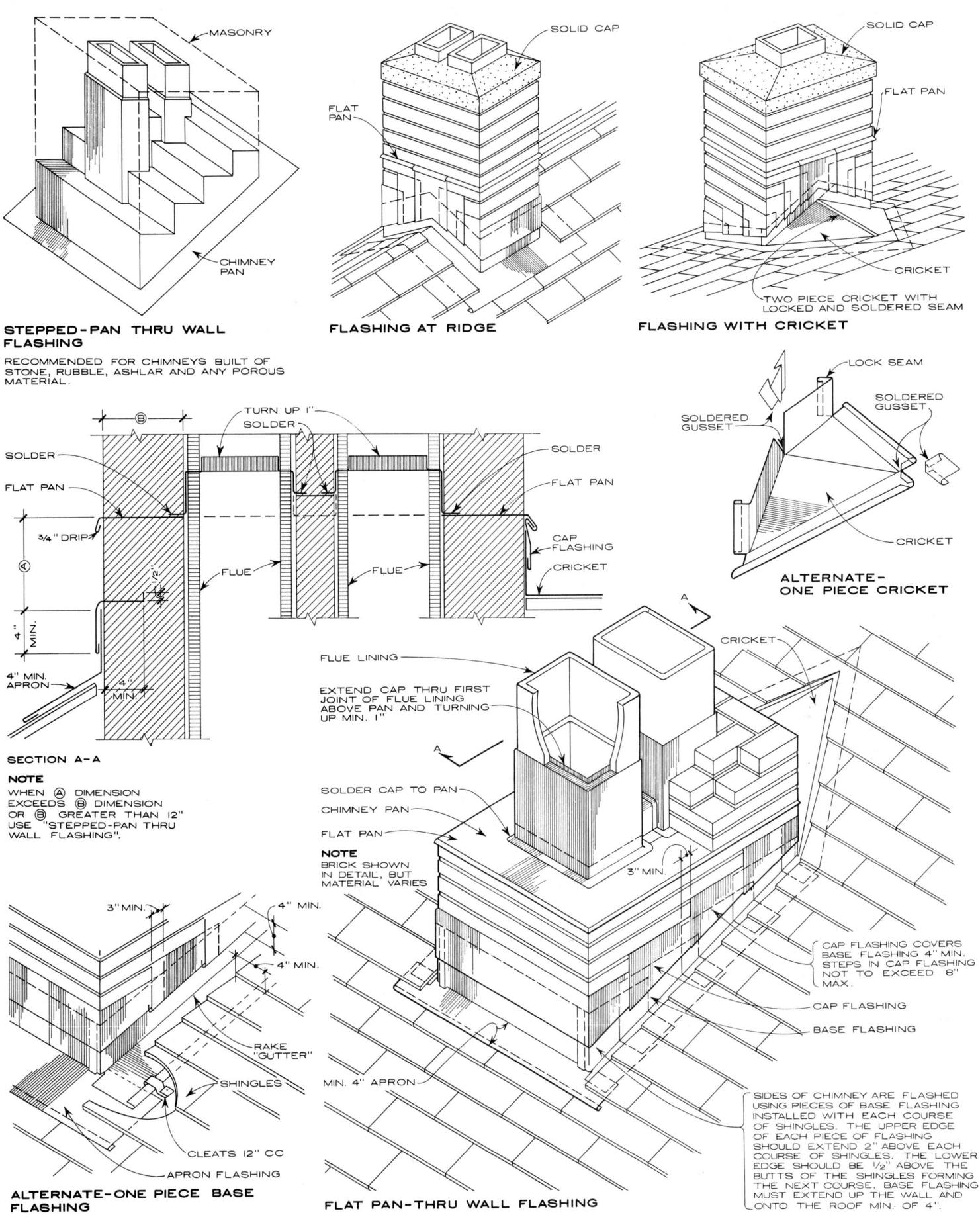

STEPPED-PAN THRU WALL FLASHING

RECOMMENDED FOR CHIMNEYS BUILT OF STONE, RUBBLE, ASHLAR AND ANY POROUS MATERIAL.

MASONRY

CHIMNEY PAN

FLASHING AT RIDGE

SOLID CAP

FLAT PAN

FLASHING WITH CRICKET

SOLID CAP

FLAT PAN

CRICKET

TWO PIECE CRICKET WITH LOCKED AND SOLDERED SEAM

ALTERNATE-ONE PIECE CRICKET

LOCK SEAM

SOLDERED GUSSET

SOLDERED GUSSET

CRICKET

TURN UP 1"
SOLDER

SOLDER

FLAT PAN

3/4" DRIP

1/2"

4" MIN.

4" MIN.
APRON

4" MIN.

SOLDER

FLAT PAN

CAP FLASHING

CRICKET

FLUE

FLUE

SECTION A-A

NOTE

WHEN Ⓐ DIMENSION EXCEEDS Ⓑ DIMENSION OR Ⓑ GREATER THAN 12" USE "STEPPED-PAN THRU WALL FLASHING".

3" MIN.

4" MIN.

4" MIN.

RAKE "GUTTER"

SHINGLES

CLEATS 12" CC

APRON FLASHING

ALTERNATE-ONE PIECE BASE FLASHING

FLUE LINING

EXTEND CAP THRU FIRST JOINT OF FLUE LINING ABOVE PAN AND TURNING UP MIN. 1"

SOLDER CAP TO PAN

CHIMNEY PAN

FLAT PAN

NOTE
BRICK SHOWN IN DETAIL, BUT MATERIAL VARIES

MIN. 4" APRON

CRICKET

3" MIN.

CAP FLASHING COVERS BASE FLASHING 4" MIN. STEPS IN CAP FLASHING NOT TO EXCEED 8" MAX.

CAP FLASHING

BASE FLASHING

SIDES OF CHIMNEY ARE FLASHED USING PIECES OF BASE FLASHING INSTALLED WITH EACH COURSE OF SHINGLES. THE UPPER EDGE OF EACH PIECE OF FLASHING SHOULD EXTEND 2" ABOVE EACH COURSE OF SHINGLES. THE LOWER EDGE SHOULD BE 1/2" ABOVE THE BUTTS OF THE SHINGLES FORMING THE NEXT COURSE. BASE FLASHING MUST EXTEND UP THE WALL AND ONTO THE ROOF MIN. OF 4".

FLAT PAN-THRU WALL FLASHING

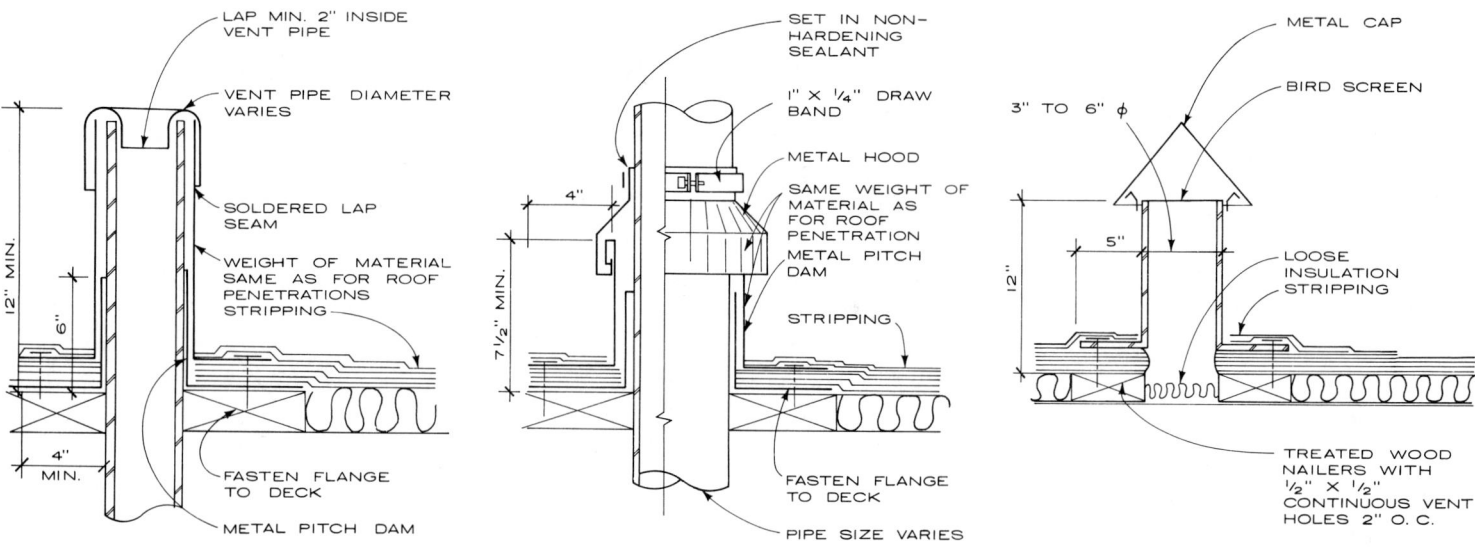

VENT PIPE

FLAGPOLES AND TALL POLES

ROOF RELIEF VENT

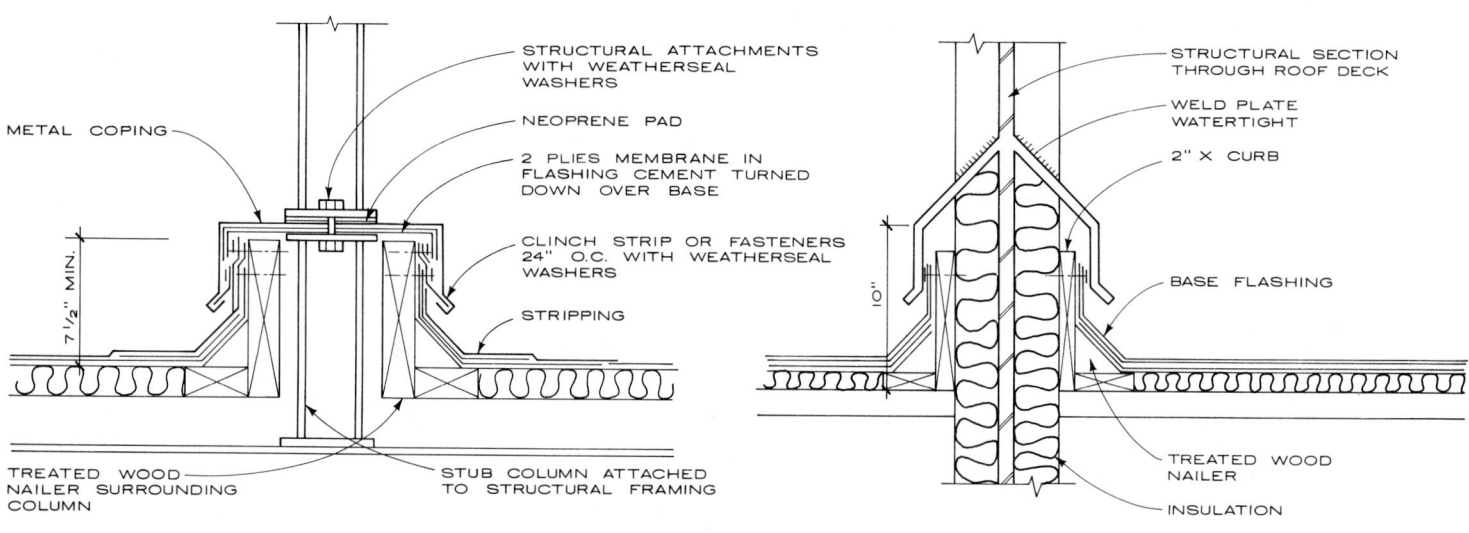

FUTURE COLUMNS, SIGN SUPPORTS, AND STEEL ANGLES

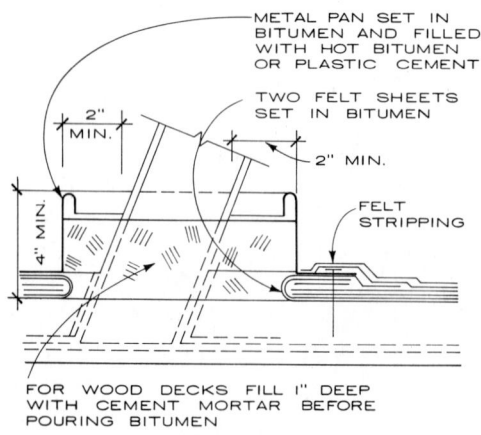

NOTE
Whenever possible avoid the use of pitch pockets in favor of curbs with base and cap flashing around the penetrating member.

PITCH POCKET

NOTE
To obtain proper drainage, roof drains should be located at points of the lowest expected deflection in roof deck.

ROOF DRAIN

Michael Scott Rudden, The Stephens Associates, P.C.—Architects; Albany, New York

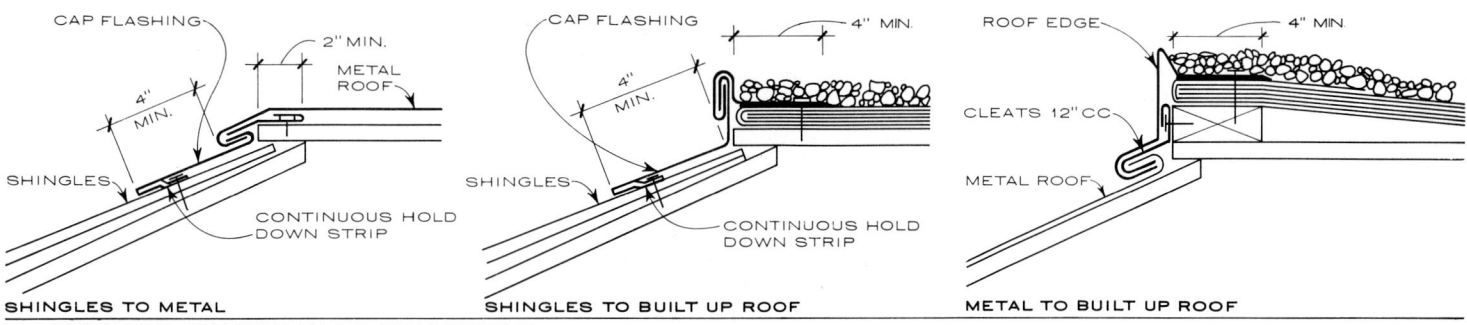

CAP FLASHING · 2" MIN. · METAL ROOF · 4" MIN. · SHINGLES · CONTINUOUS HOLD DOWN STRIP

SHINGLES TO METAL

CAP FLASHING · 4" MIN. · 4" MIN. · SHINGLES · CONTINUOUS HOLD DOWN STRIP

SHINGLES TO BUILT UP ROOF

ROOF EDGE · 4" MIN. · CLEATS 12" CC · METAL ROOF

METAL TO BUILT UP ROOF

FLASHING AT CHANGE IN ROOF MATERIAL

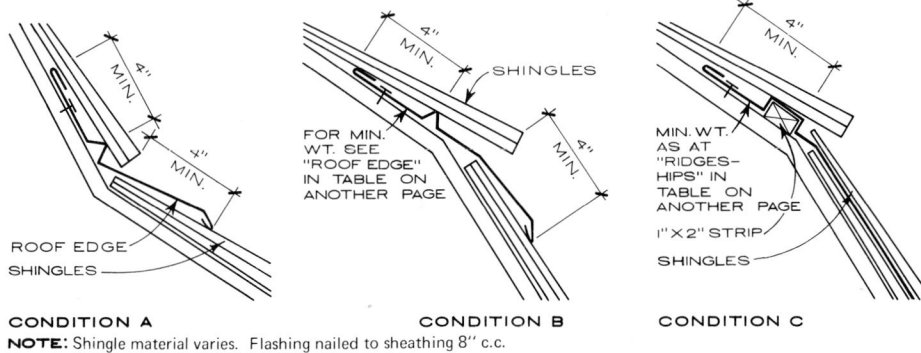

4" MIN. · 4" MIN. · ROOF EDGE · SHINGLES

CONDITION A

4" MIN. · SHINGLES · FOR MIN. WT. SEE "ROOF EDGE" IN TABLE ON ANOTHER PAGE · 4" MIN.

CONDITION B

4" MIN. · MIN. WT. AS AT "RIDGES-HIPS" IN TABLE ON ANOTHER PAGE · 1" X 2" STRIP · SHINGLES

CONDITION C

NOTE: Shingle material varies. Flashing nailed to sheathing 8" c.c.

FLASHING OF BREAK IN SLOPE OF SHINGLE ROOFS

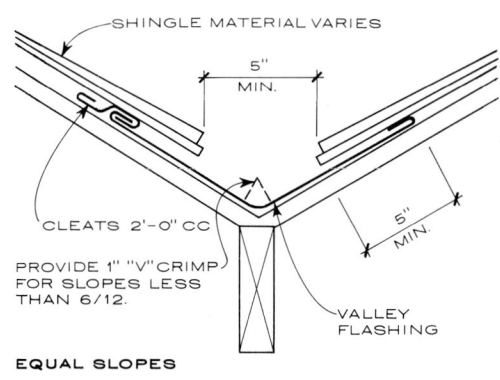

SHINGLE MATERIAL VARIES · 5" MIN. · 5" MIN. · CLEATS 2'-0" CC · PROVIDE 1" "V" CRIMP FOR SLOPES LESS THAN 6/12. · VALLEY FLASHING

EQUAL SLOPES
OPEN VALLEY FLASHING

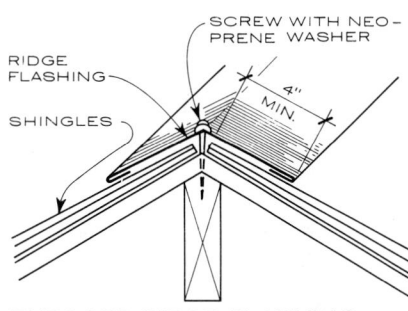

RIDGE FLASHING · SHINGLES · 4" MIN.

CONCEALED RIDGE FLASHING
NOTE.

Ridge flashing formed in 10' lengths and lapped 4". Flashing is nailed to sheathing after shingles are installed, then flashing is covered with ridge shingles.

SCREW WITH NEO-PRENE WASHER · RIDGE FLASHING · SHINGLES · 4" MIN.

EXPOSED RIDGE FLASHING
NOTE.

Ridge flashing formed in 10' lengths and lapped 4".

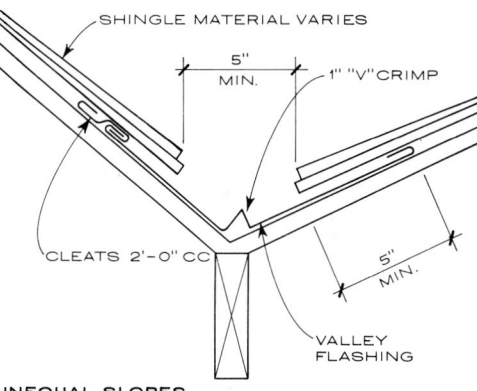

SHINGLE MATERIAL VARIES · 5" MIN. · 1" "V" CRIMP · CLEATS 2'-0" CC · 5" MIN. · VALLEY FLASHING

UNEQUAL SLOPES
OPEN VALLEY FLASHING

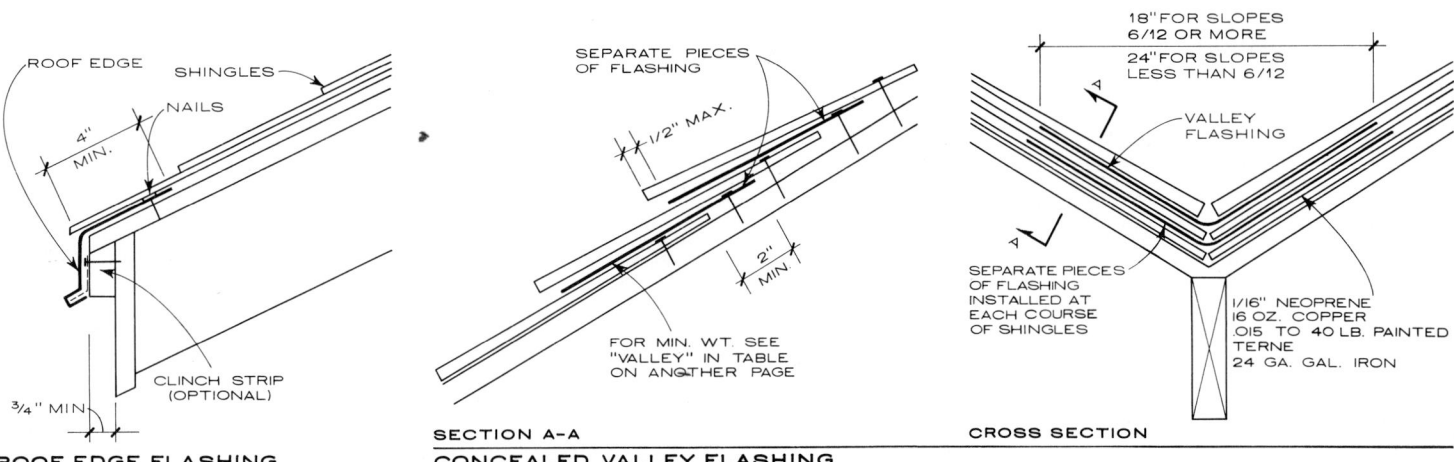

ROOF EDGE · SHINGLES · NAILS · 4" MIN. · CLINCH STRIP (OPTIONAL) · 3/4" MIN.

ROOF EDGE FLASHING

SEPARATE PIECES OF FLASHING · 1/2" MAX. · 2" MIN. · FOR MIN. WT. SEE "VALLEY" IN TABLE ON ANOTHER PAGE

SECTION A-A
CONCEALED VALLEY FLASHING

18" FOR SLOPES 6/12 OR MORE · 24" FOR SLOPES LESS THAN 6/12 · VALLEY FLASHING · SEPARATE PIECES OF FLASHING INSTALLED AT EACH COURSE OF SHINGLES · 1/16" NEOPRENE · 16 OZ. COPPER · .015 TO 40 LB. PAINTED TERNE · 24 GA. GAL. IRON

CROSS SECTION

Michael Scott Rudden; The Stephens Associates, P.C.–Architects; Albany, New York

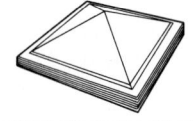

PYRAMID SKYLIGHT

SINGLE OR DOUBLE GLAZED
OUTSIDE CURB DIMENSIONS

33½" x 33½"	8" RISE
40¼" x 40¼"	10" RISE
49½" x 49½"	12" RISE
58¼" x 58¼"	14" RISE
78¼" x 78¼"	18" RISE

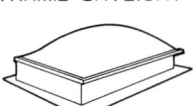

INSULATED CURB

SINGLE OR DOUBLE GLAZED
STANDARD CURB HEIGHT
4" OR 9"–12" IS AVAILABLE
SIZES AS FOR SQUARE AND
RECTANGULAR

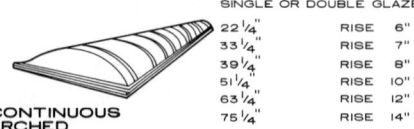

CONTINUOUS ARCHED

SINGLE OR DOUBLE GLAZED

22¼"	RISE 6"
33¼"	RISE 7"
39¼"	RISE 8"
51¼"	RISE 10"
63¼"	RISE 12"
75¼"	RISE 14"

BUILT-UP CURB SQUARE

SINGLE OR DOUBLE GLAZED

22¼" x 22¼"	RISE 5"
25½" x 25½"	RISE 7"
33½" x 33½"	RISE 8"
40¼" x 40¼"	RISE 10"
49½" x 49½"	RISE 12"
58¼" x 58¼"	RISE 14"
78¼" x 78¼"	RISE 18"

BUILT-UP CURB RECTANGULAR

SINGLE OR DOUBLE GLAZED

25½" x 49½"	RISE 7"
33½" x 49½"	RISE 10"
33½" x 72¾"	RISE 10"
40¼" x 78¼"	RISE 12"
49½" x 92¾"	RISE 13"
60¾" x 72¾"	RISE 16"
60¾" x 92¾"	RISE 16"

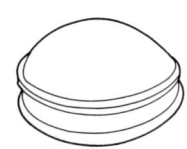

CIRCULAR

SINGLE OR DOUBLE GLAZED
INSIDE DIAMETER

31"	DOME RISE	11"
43"	DOME RISE	13"
54"	DOME RISE	19"
67"	DOME RISE	22"
79"	DOME RISE	25"

STANDARD CURB HEIGHT
4" OR 9"–12" AVAILABLE

RIDGE LIGHT

SINGLE GLAZED
RAKE DIMENSION

24"–30"–36"–42"–48"

STANDARD SKYLIGHT TYPES

FRAMING SYSTEMS

In selecting the structural members, the designer should consider the thermal movement differential between the aluminum and the glazing materials.

Framing systems should provide complete control of both condensation and water infiltration.

Gutter systems should be as simple and functional as possible. Design must take into account compatibility of materials and provision of adequate slope for drainage.

The supporting structure, as well as the enclosure itself, must be engineered to carry the total resultant forces of the particular live load, wind load, and dead load in accordance with state and local codes.

The minimum rise to span on curved (vaulted or domed) structures should be 22%, the point at which maximum economy is achieved.

SKYLIGHTS WITH MOVABLE SECTIONS

Most skylights can be designed with movable sections. Consideration must be given to design and aesthetic acceptance of motors, tracks, and other operating parts.

FINISHES

Finishes for aluminum components are available in the following:

1. Mill finish.
2. Clear anodized.
3. Duranodic bronze or black.
4. Acrylic enamel.
5. Fluorocarbons.

GLAZING

The thickness and geometric profile of all glass and acrylic glazing materials should be carefully selected for compliance with building codes and manufacturer's recommendations.

The following glazing materials are listed in an approximate order of cost, from lowest to highest:

1. Textured, obscure wire glass.
2. Flat acrylic.
3. Clear polished wire glass.
4. Formed acrylic.
5. Tempered glass.
6. Polycarbonates.
7. Laminated glass.
8. Insulated units of tempered, reflective, and/or laminated glass.

ACRYLIC AND POLYCARBONATE GLAZING

Glazing with flat sheet plastics should usually be restricted to the arched enclosures. Its thickness should be selected based on cold formed radii, rabbet dimensions, and design loading. For other applications of plastic glazing, consult manufacturer's design data.

Domes or other thermoformed acrylic shapes should not exceed a maximum base dimension of 10 x 10 ft. The structural properties of formed acrylic units are determined by both geometry and thickness. Tinted acrylics, for economy, should be limited to the ¼ in. thickness.

Because of the thermal movement and moisture infiltration, hermetically sealed insulating units, incorporating acrylics or polycarbonates, should not be used.

Mar resistant coatings for plastics should be specified if frequent cleaning or heavy pedestrian contact is anticipated.

GLASS

The use of plate glass in skylights should be avoided. Most building codes permit or approve the use of wire or laminated safety glass. Note that wire glass is not available in tinted shades. The maximum available widths for the wire and laminated glasses are 60 and 48 in., respectively.

Careful consideration should be given to glazing overhead enclosures with tempered glass. The maximum width dimension for tempered should be no more than 72 in.

Glazing with high performance insulated glass units provides important energy savings and offers the architect numerous functional and aesthetic design choices.

The actual size of a glass unit is governed by total design loading and manufacturer's recommendations.

AVAILABLE LIGHT ZONES

PERCENTAGE OF ROOF AREA REQUIRED FOR SKYLIGHTING

LIGHT ZONE	LIGHT DESIGN LEVELS		
	30 FT-C	60 FT-C	120 FT-C
1	3.3	5.2	13.3
2	2.8	4.3	10.8
3	1.8	3.2	6.9
4	1.5	2.8	4.0

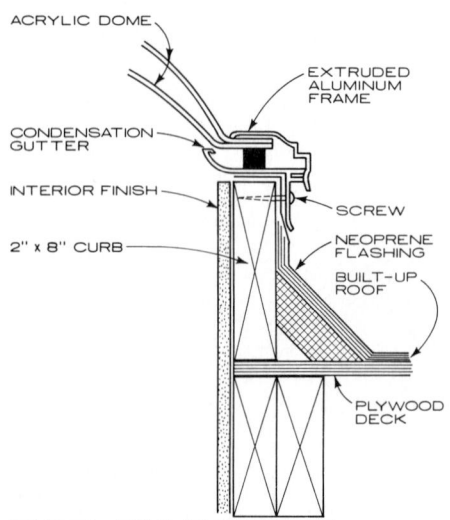

PYRAMID – BUILT-UP SQUARE OR RECTANGULAR

ACRYLIC DOME
EXTRUDED ALUMINUM FRAME
CONDENSATION GUTTER
INTERIOR FINISH
2" x 8" CURB
SCREW
NEOPRENE FLASHING
BUILT-UP ROOF
PLYWOOD DECK

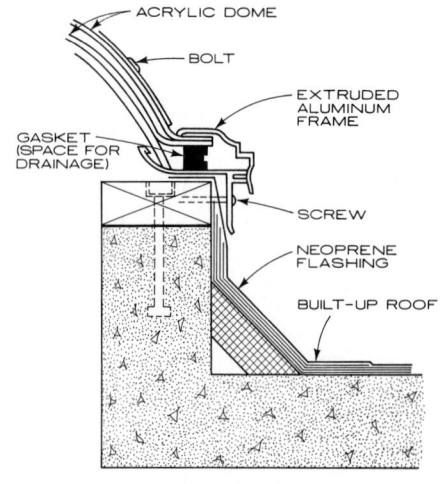

CONTINUOUS ARCH

ACRYLIC DOME
BOLT
EXTRUDED ALUMINUM FRAME
GASKET (SPACE FOR DRAINAGE)
SCREW
NEOPRENE FLASHING
BUILT-UP ROOF

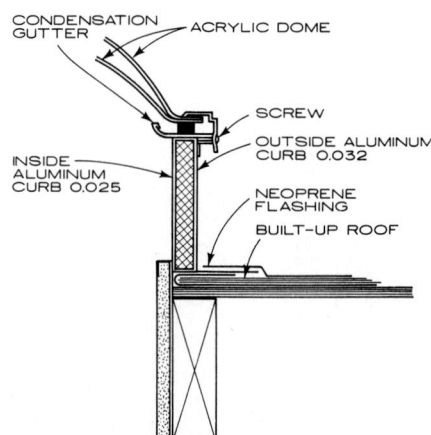

INSULATED CURB – CIRCULAR OR RECTANGULAR

CONDENSATION GUTTER
ACRYLIC DOME
INSIDE ALUMINUM CURB 0.025
SCREW
OUTSIDE ALUMINUM CURB 0.032
NEOPRENE FLASHING
BUILT-UP ROOF

CURB DETAILS

Jerry Graham; CTA Architects Engineers; Billings, Montana

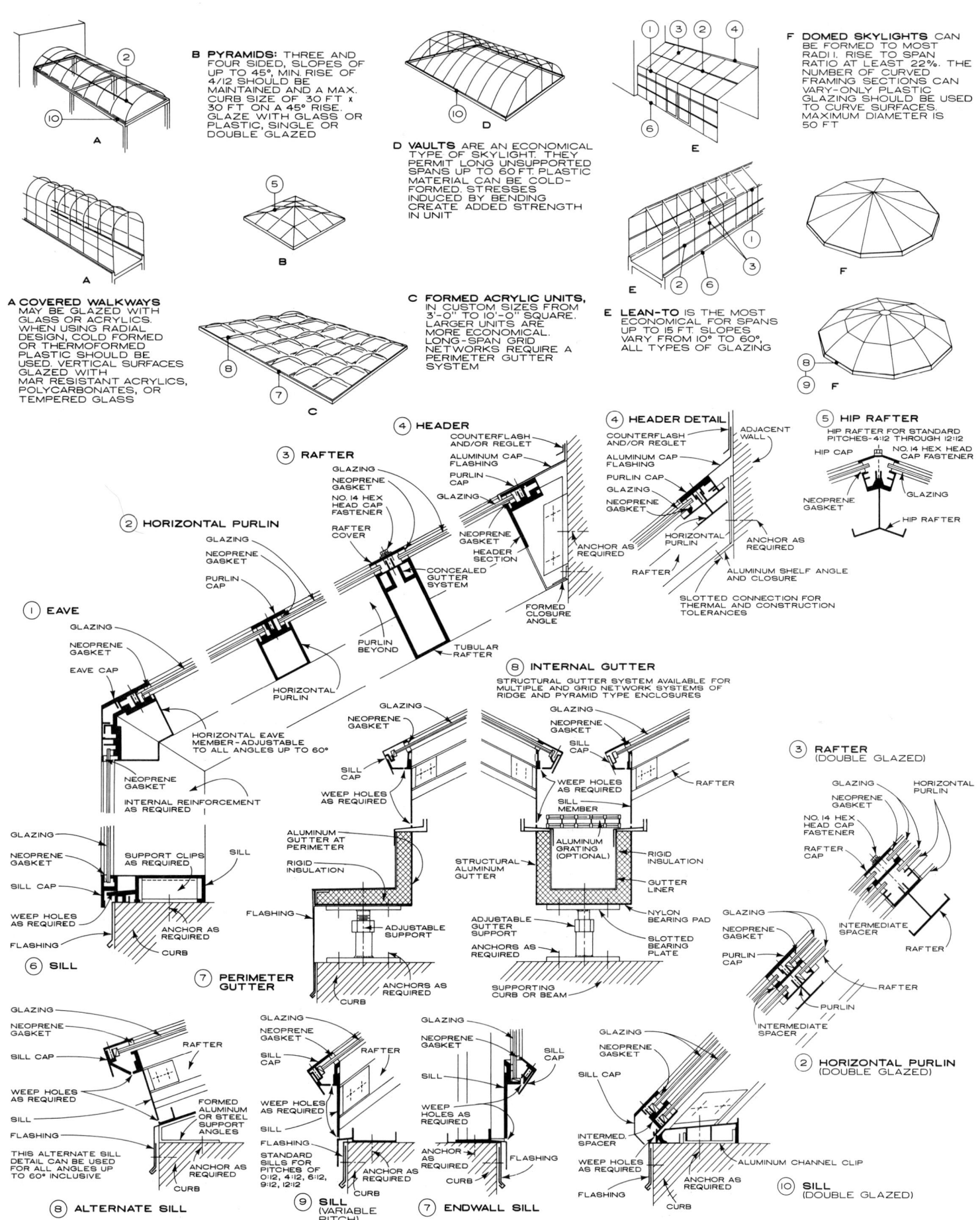

B PYRAMIDS: THREE AND FOUR SIDED, SLOPES OF UP TO 45°, MIN. RISE OF 4/12 SHOULD BE MAINTAINED AND A MAX. CURB SIZE OF 30 FT x 30 FT ON A 45° RISE. GLAZE WITH GLASS OR PLASTIC, SINGLE OR DOUBLE GLAZED

D VAULTS ARE AN ECONOMICAL TYPE OF SKYLIGHT. THEY PERMIT LONG UNSUPPORTED SPANS UP TO 60 FT. PLASTIC MATERIAL CAN BE COLD-FORMED. STRESSES INDUCED BY BENDING CREATE ADDED STRENGTH IN UNIT

F DOMED SKYLIGHTS CAN BE FORMED TO MOST RADII. RISE TO SPAN RATIO AT LEAST 22%. THE NUMBER OF CURVED FRAMING SECTIONS CAN VARY-ONLY PLASTIC GLAZING SHOULD BE USED TO CURVE SURFACES. MAXIMUM DIAMETER IS 50 FT

A COVERED WALKWAYS MAY BE GLAZED WITH GLASS OR ACRYLICS. WHEN USING RADIAL DESIGN, COLD FORMED OR THERMOFORMED PLASTIC SHOULD BE USED. VERTICAL SURFACES GLAZED WITH MAR RESISTANT ACRYLICS, POLYCARBONATES, OR TEMPERED GLASS

C FORMED ACRYLIC UNITS, IN CUSTOM SIZES FROM 3'-0" TO 10'-0" SQUARE. LARGER UNITS ARE MORE ECONOMICAL. LONG-SPAN GRID NETWORKS REQUIRE A PERIMETER GUTTER SYSTEM

E LEAN-TO IS THE MOST ECONOMICAL FOR SPANS UP TO 15 FT. SLOPES VARY FROM 10° TO 60°, ALL TYPES OF GLAZING

CTA Architects Engineers; Billings, Montana

ROOF ACCESSORIES 7

THERMAL INSULATION

Thermal insulation controls heat flow under temperatures ranging from absolute zero to 3000°F. This broad range can be subdivided into four general temperature regimes that classify applications for various types of insulation:

1. LOW TEMPERATURES: Insulation for vessels containing cryogenic materials, such as liquified natural gas.
2. AMBIENT TEMPERATURES: Insulation for building structures.
3. MEDIUM TEMPERATURES: Insulation for tanks, pipes, and equipment in industrial process heat applications.
4. HIGH TEMPERATURES: Refractory or other specialized insulation materials used in foundry work, nuclear power facilities, the aerospace industry, and so on.

Architects and builders are generally concerned with the design and material performance of building insulations that operate within ambient temperature limits. As temperatures range much above or below ambient conditions, design and performance requirements change and must be matched with insulation materials that withstand the stress introduced by extreme temperatures, large temperature differentials, and thermal cycling.

BUILDING INSULATION—THERMAL FUNCTIONS

The two major functions of building insulations are to (1) control temperatures of inside surfaces that affect the comfort of occupants and aid or deter condensation and (2) conserve energy by reducing heat transmission through building sections that determine the energy requirements for both heating and cooling. Economics in fuel consumption can be calculated with reasonable accuracy and balanced against initial costs of insulation and the costs for heating and cooling with equipment (see figure).

ADDITIONAL FUNCTIONS

Thermal insulations may also perform several other functions:

1. Add structural strength to a wall, ceiling, or floor section.
2. Provide support for a surface finish.
3. Impede water vapor transmission.
4. Prevent or reduce damage to equipment and structure from exposure to fire and freezing conditions.
5. Reduce noise and vibration.

BASIC MATERIALS

Thermal insulation is made from the following basic materials:

1. MINERAL FIBROUS: Material such as glass, rock, slag, or asbestos that is melted and spun into thin fibers.
2. MINERAL CELLULAR: Material such as foamed glass, calcium silicate, perlite, vermiculite, foamed concrete, or ceramic.
3. ORGANIC FIBROUS: Material such as wood, cane, cotton, hair, cellulose, or synthetic fibers.
4. ORGANIC CELLULAR: Material such as cork, foamed rubber, polystyrene, or polyurethane.
5. METALLIC: Aluminum or other foils, or metallized organic reflective membranes that must face air, gas filled, or evacuated spaces.

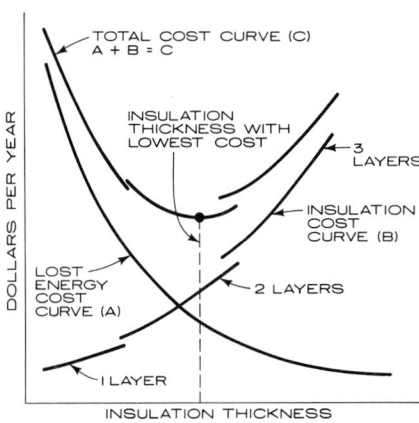

DETERMINATION OF ECONOMIC THICKNESS OF INSULATION

PHYSICAL STRUCTURE AND FORM

Thermal insulation is available in the following physical forms:

1. LOOSE FILL: Dry granules, nodules, or fibers poured or blown into place.
2. FLEXIBLE OR SEMIRIGID: Blankets and batts of woollike material.
3. RIGID: Boards and blocks.
4. MEMBRANE: Reflective insulation.
5. SPRAY APPLIED: Mineral fiber or insulating concrete.
6. POURED-IN-PLACE: Insulating concrete.
7. FOAMED-IN-PLACE: Polyurethane, urea formaldehyde.

MECHANISMS OF HEAT TRANSFER

Heat flows through materials and space by conduction, convection, and radiation. Convection and conduction are functions of the roughness of surfaces, air movement, and the temperature difference between the air and surface. Mass insulations, by their low densities, are designed to suppress conduction and convection across their sections by the entrapment of air molecules within their structure. Convective air currents are stilled by the surrounding matrix of fibers or cells, and the chances of heat transfer by the collision of air molecules is reduced. Radiant heat transfer between objects operates independently of air currents and is controlled by the character of the surfaces (emissivity) and the temperature difference between warm objects emitting radiation and cooler object absorbing radiation.

The resistance of these modes of heat transfer may be retarded by the elements of a building wall section.

1. OUTSIDE SURFACE FILMS: The outside surface traps a thin film of air, which resists heat flow. This film varies with wind velocity and surface roughness.
2. MATERIAL LAYERS: Each layer of material contributes to the resistance of heat flow, usually according to its density. A layer of suitable insulation is normally many times more effective in resisting heat transfer than the combination of all other materials in the section.
3. AIRSPACE: Each measureable airspace also adds to the overall resistance. Foil faced surfaces of low emissivities that form the boundaries of the airspace can further reduce the rate of radiant transfer across the space.
4. INSIDE SURFACE FILM: The inside surface of the building section also traps a thin film of air. The air film thus formed is usually thicker because of much lower air velocities.

NOTE: RECOMMENDED INSULATION ZONES FOR HEATING AND COOLING

MAP OF INSULATION ZONES

RECOMMENDED MINIMUM THERMAL RESISTANCES (R) OF INSULATION

ZONE	CEILING	WALL	FLOOR
1	19	11	11
2	26	13	11
3	26	19	13
4	30	19	19
5	33	19	22
6	38	19	22

NOTE: The minimum insulation R values recommended for various parts of the United States as delineated on the zone map above.

David F. Hill; Burt Hill Kosar Rittelmann Associates; Butler, Pennsylvania

Donald Bosserman, AIA; Saunders, Cheng & Appleton; Alexandria, Virginia

COEFFICIENT OF HEAT TRANSMISSION

Calculations of heating and cooling loads are based on the rate of heat flow through building sections along with ventilation and moisture requirements. The symbol U designates the overall coefficient of heat transmission for any section of building shell. The units for U are Btu's per square foot of building section per hour per °F temperature difference between inside and outside air (Btu/sq ft · hr · °F).

U-values of composite building sections are calculated by first determining the individual conductivities (k) or conductances (C) of each material comprising the section. The conductivity of a homogeneous material is measured as Btu's per square foot per hour per °F temperature difference per inch thickness of the material. The reciprocal, R, is the thermal resistivity. The resistance of any thickness of a material is its resistivity per inch times its total thickness. Nonhomogeneous materials such as concrete masonry units are given conductance and resistance values for their standard thicknesses. In calculating the overall U-coefficients only the resistances are used. The sum is taken of the resistance values of all the materials in the section plus the resistance values of the inside and outside surface films to yield an overall R-value. The reciprocal, 1/R equals the U-coefficient.

FACTORS AFFECTING INSULATION PERFORMANCE

The most serious factor affecting the performance of building insulation is the presence of water. While the effect of moisture is not too serious when moisture exists in the vapor phase, the conductivity is greatly increased by the presence of condensed moisture. Water or ice in insulation will impair or destroy the insulating value; it may cause deterioration of the insulation or eventual structural damage by rot, corrosion, or the expansion action of freezing water. Whether or not moisture accumulates within the insulation depends on the operating temperatures, ambient conditions, and the effectiveness of water vapor barriers in relation to other vapor resistances within the composite structure.

The moisture resistance depends on the basic material of the insulation and the type of physical structure. Most insulations are hygroscopic and will gain or lose moisture in proportion to the relative humidity of the air in contact with the insulation. Fibrous and granular insulations permit transmission of water vapor to the colder side of the structure. A vapor barrier should, therefore, be used with the materials and installed on the warm side where moisture transmission is a factor. Certain insulations with a closed cellular structure are relatively impervious to water and water vapor. Often, these materials are marketed as rigid boards and installed on the outside of stud work as sheathing. To avoid moisture accumulation, in this application their vapor permeance should be at least five times that of the interior vapor barrier, or they should be modified by perforations or venting along their joints to allow water vapor to escape.

Conductivity also varies with density. A change in density due to the degree of compaction of fibrous or granular types of insulation increases conductivity. For fibrous types, minimum conductivity is ideally obtained when fibers are uniformly spaced and are perpendicular to the direction of heat flow. Other factors such as the diameter of the fiber or the amount of binder that influence the bond or contact of the fiber may also affect conductivity.

For cellular insulation a specific combination of cell size and density will produce an optimum thermal conductivity. The type of gas trapped in the cells also affects conductivity. Flourocarbon gas, having a lower conductivity than air, is used to expand rigid urethane to maximize its thermal resistance. Unless encased in a gas impermeable membrane, urethane conductivities usually increase over time as oxygen and nitrogen seep into the cell structure and the flourocarbon gas diffuses out.

THE IMPORTANCE OF PROPER DESIGN AND INSTALLATION

To perform at maximum efficiency, insulation systems must be properly designed and their installation closely supervised. Vapor barriers must be properly located in the wall section and carefully placed to fully cover all areas. Edges should be sealed and joints overlapped. Attachment by glueing instead of stapling should be practiced if possible because the effectiveness of vapor barriers may be greatly reduced if openings, even very small ones, exist in the barrier.

Low density fibrous and loose fill insulations, though widely used, are most susceptible to increased heat transfer by improper installation. If batts or granular materials are compacted, conductivities increase because of higher densities. These types of insulations should also completely fill the space between studs or rafters to prevent convective air currents and infiltration. The performance of fibrous batts installed vertically with airspaces on either side is seriously impaired because of the air interchange between the two voids. Special attention should also be given to the sources of greatest heat loss. Insulating and sealing window frames, wall plates at foundations, and electrical outlets along perimeter walls is crucial for reducing air infiltration. The perimeter of the floor joist system in frame construction, ordinarily overlooked, should be detailed to allow space for application of insulation along its length.

ECONOMIC THICKNESS

The cost of lost energy is directly related to the rate of heat transfer through the insulation and the dollar value of that energy. As shown in the figure, the cost of lost energy decreases as insulation thickness increases. Since the optimal economic thickness is the lowest total cost of lost energy plus the installed insulation over the life of the insulation, these two costs must be compared on similar terms. Either the cost of insulation must be annualized and compared to the average annual cost of the lost energy, or the cost of the energy lost each year must be expressed in present dollars and compared to the annual cost of the insulation investment.

The economic thickness will be affected by the length of time over which the insulation cost is annualized. With the life cycle–cost method the economic thickness is usually greatest because the fuel savings that would accrue over the many years the insulation is in service can be used to pay for the most insulation (i.e., the payback period = the life cycle). If a shorter payback is required for the insulation, this maximum life cycle economic thickness becomes thinner because there are fewer years of energy savings allotted to pay for the insulation.

The annualized cost of installed insulation must be adjusted for the cost of money that can be a discount rate including the desired rate of return on the insulation investment. Cost of maintenance should also be included in the annual costs.

The cost of fuel including efficiency conversion plus the expected yearly price escalation above the inflation rate or the average cost of fuel over the life cycle or payback period should be forecast as accurately as possible before calculating economic thickness.

MATERIAL PROPERTIES OF COMMON BUILDING INSULATION

BUILDING INSULATIONS	DENSITY (LB/CU FT)	RESISTANCE (R) (HR/SQ FT·°F· BTU PER 1 IN. THICKNESS)	WATER VAPOR PERMEABILITY (PERM-IN.)	WATER ABSORPTION (% BY WEIGHT)	FIRE RESISTANCE FLAME SPREAD	FIRE RESISTANCE FUEL CONTRIBUTED	FIRE RESISTANCE SMOKE DEVELOPED	TOXICITY	EFFECTS OF AGING DIMENSIONAL STABILITY	DEGRADATION DUE TO TEMPERATURE	DEGRADATION DUE TO MOISTURE	DEGRADATION DUE TO FUNGAL OR BACTERIAL GROWTH	DEGRADATION DUE TO WEATHERING	CORROSIVENESS
Fiberglass	0.6–1.0	3.16	100	1%	15–20	5–15	0–20	Some fumes if burned	None	OK below 180°F	None	None	None	None
Rock or slag wool	1.5–2.5	3.2–3.7	100	2%	15	0	0	None	None	None	Transient	None	None	None
Cellulose	2.2–3.0	3.2–3.7	High	5–20%	15–40	0–40	0–45	CO if burned	Settles 0–20%	None	Not severe	Maybe	?	Steel Aluminum Copper
Molded polystyrene	0.8–2.0	3.8–4.4	1.2–3.0	4%[1]	5–25	5–80	10–400	CO if burned	None	If above 165°F	None	None	UV degrades	None
Extruded polystyrene	0.8–2.0	3.8–4.4	1.2–3.0	0.7%	5–25	5–80	10–400	CO if burned	None	If above 165°F	None	None	UV degrades	None
Polyurethane	2.0	5.8–6.2[2]	2–3	Negligible	30–50	10–25	155–200	CO if burned	0–12% change	If above 250°F	?	None	None	None
Polyisocyanurate	2.0	5.8–6.2[2]	2–3	Negligible	25	5	55–200	CO if burned	0–12% change	If above 250°F	?	None	None	None
Urea formaldehyde	0.6–0.9	4.2	4.5–100	18%[3]	0–25	0–30	0–10	Negligible	Shrinks 1–4% in 28 days	If above 415°F	?	None	?	?
Perlite (loose fill)	2–11	2.5–3.7	High	Low	0	0	0	None	None	If above 1200°F	None	None	None	None
Vermiculite (loose fill)	4–10	2.4–3.0	High	None	0	0	0	None	None	If above 1000°F	None	None	None	None
Insulating concrete	12–88	0.85[4]/1.2[5]	Varies with density	?	0	0	0	None	None	If above 1000°C	None	None	Below 30#/ft³	None

NOTES
1. By volume.
2. Aged unfaced or spray applied.
3. At 60% rh, 65°F.
4. At 40 lb/cu ft.
5. At 25 lb/cu ft.

David F. Hill; Burt Hill Kosar Rittelmann Associates; Butler, Pennsylvania

INSULATION 7

DEFINITIONS

Waterproofing is a system intended to prevent the passage of water through walls and floors.

Dampproofing is to prevent the passage of moisture or collection of water vapors. This system is not capable of withstanding hydrostatic pressures.

GENERAL NOTES

1. Membrane, hydrolithic and chemical admixtures in concrete are typical types of waterproofing and dampproofing systems. Choice of the appropriate system depends upon the prevailing hydrostatic conditions. Consult manufacturers for system properties and uses.
2. Specify installation to conform strictly to the recommendations of the manufacturer of the system selected.
3. The details on the following pages are typical conditions only.

TYPICAL SYSTEMS

TYPE	DESCRIPTION	GENERAL USES
MEMBRANES	Tar or asphalt bitumens on and between layer(s) of felt made of rag, asbestos and wood fiber or of fabric made of cotton and glass. Butyl rubber and polyvinyl chloride sheets with laps sealed with adhesives and cements.	Exterior, below grade on walls and under floors. Under walking surfaces of roofs.
HYDROLITHIC COATINGS	Sprayed, troweled or brushed on coatings of asphaltic bitumens and plastics. Coatings of plaster or cement mixed with ferrous particles.	Exterior, below grade on walls. Interior, below grade on walls and floors.
CONCRETE ADMIXTURES	Liquid, paste or powder admixtures used integrally to render concrete impermeable.	Walls and floors above and below grade, concrete canopies and covered walks.
METAL WATERPROOFING	Plain metal sheets, and metal sheets coated with fabric and/or plastic sheets sealed by soldering, adhesives and cements. Generally the metal is lead or copper.	Shower stalls and pans, pools, around floor and roof drains. Under walking surfaces on roofs.

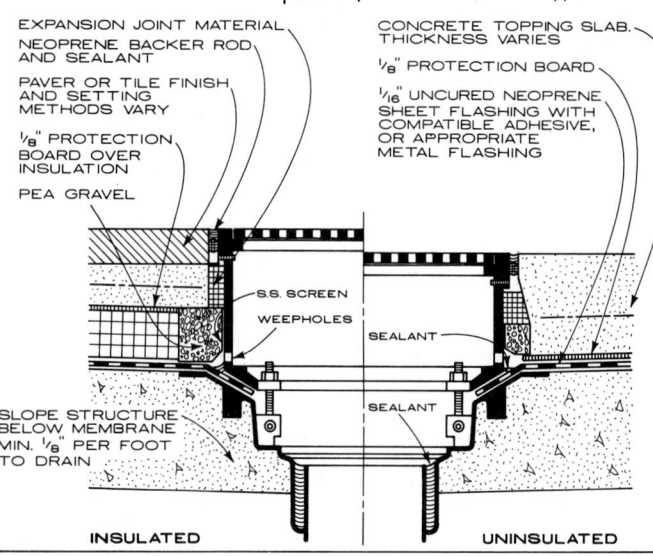

DECK DRAIN

EXPANSION JOINT MATERIAL NEOPRENE BACKER ROD AND SEALANT

PAVER OR TILE FINISH AND SETTING METHODS VARY

1/8" PROTECTION BOARD OVER INSULATION

PEA GRAVEL

CONCRETE TOPPING SLAB. THICKNESS VARIES

1/8" PROTECTION BOARD

1/16" UNCURED NEOPRENE SHEET FLASHING WITH COMPATIBLE ADHESIVE, OR APPROPRIATE METAL FLASHING

S.S. SCREEN

WEEPHOLES

SEALANT

SEALANT

SLOPE STRUCTURE BELOW MEMBRANE MIN. 1/8" PER FOOT TO DRAIN

INSULATED   UNINSULATED

CONCEALED DECK DRAIN

OPEN JOINT BRICK OR STONE PAVERS

SQUARE 12 GAUGE S.S. FRAME WITH SPACERS

PEA GRAVEL DRAINAGE COURSE-DEPTH VARIES-2" MIN.

1/8" PROTECTION BOARD OVER INSULATION

PAVER DRAIN COVER

1/8" PROTECTION BOARD

1/16" UNCURED NEOPRENE SHEET FLASHING WITH COMPATIBLE ADHESIVE, OR APPROPRIATE METAL FLASHING

S.S. SCREEN

WEEPHOLES

SEALANT

SEALANT

SLOPE STRUCTURE BELOW MEMBRANE MIN. 1/8" PER FOOT TO DRAIN

INSULATED   UNINSULATED

SIDEWALK VAULT – MEMBRANE AND METAL WATERPROOFING

EXPANSION JOINT

4" MIN. REINFORCED CONCRETE SLAB. SLOPE WITH STRUCTURAL SLAB MIN. 1/8" PER FOOT

1/8" PROTECTION BOARD OVER INSULATION

EXPANSION JOINT AT CURB

VINYL OR METAL WATERSTOP

1/2" PROTECTION BOARD OVER INSULATION

1/16" UNCURED NEOPRENE SHEET FLASHING WITH COMPATIBLE ADHESIVE, OR APPROPRIATE METAL FLASHING

STRUCTURES VARY

DOUBLE CONCRETE SLAB. DESIGN FOR UPLIFT WHERE HYDRAULIC PRESSURE EXISTS

VINYL OR METAL WATERSTOP

DRAIN TILE

DECK PENETRATION

SEALANT AND NEOPRENE BACKING ROD

PAVER OR TILE FINISH AND SETTING METHODS VARY

1/8" PROTECTION BOARD OVER INSULATION

SHEET METAL FLANGE SOLDERED TO PIPE AND SET IN MASTIC ON MEMBRANE

2-PLY FABRIC REINFORCEMENT

1/16" UNCURED NEOPRENE SHEET FLASHING WITH COMPATIBLE ADHESIVE, OR APPROPRIATE METAL FLASHING

PIPE SLEEVE

CAULKING

PIPE OR CONDUIT

CONCRETE TOPPING SLAB. THICKNESS VARIES

SLOPE STRUCTURE BELOW MEMBRANE MIN. 1/8" PER FOOT TO DRAINS

INSULATED   UNINSULATED

Jerry Graham; CTA Architects-Engineers; Billings, Montana

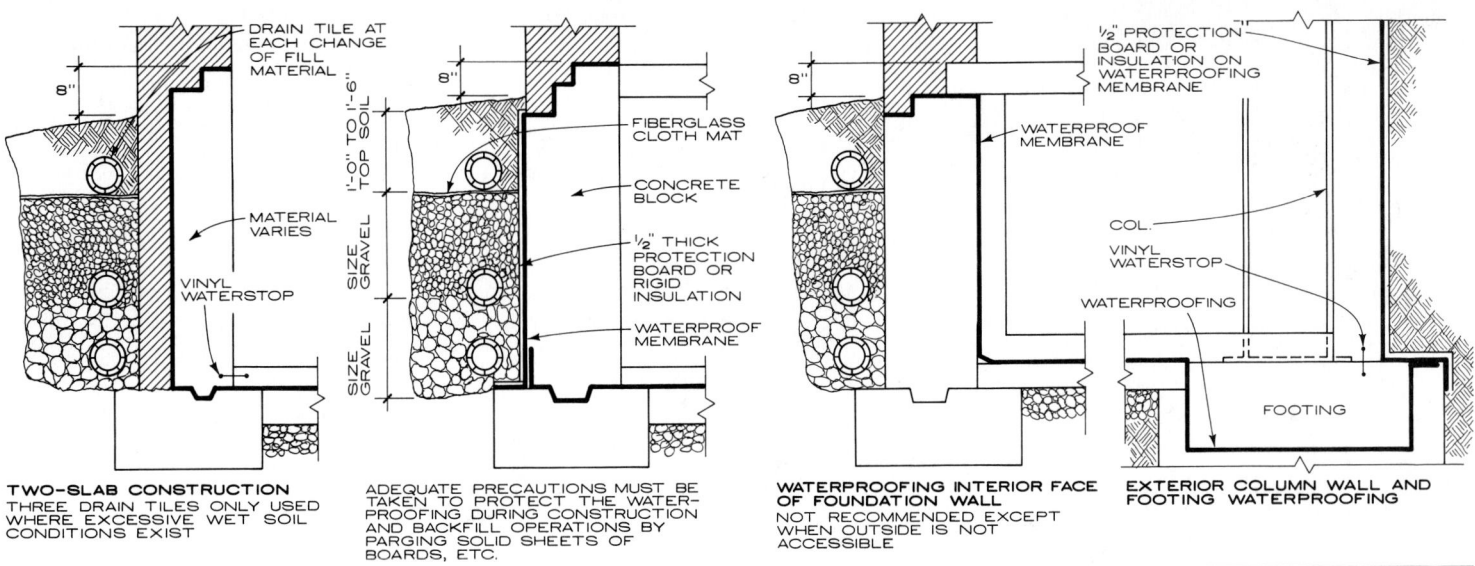

TWO-SLAB CONSTRUCTION
THREE DRAIN TILES ONLY USED WHERE EXCESSIVE WET SOIL CONDITIONS EXIST

ADEQUATE PRECAUTIONS MUST BE TAKEN TO PROTECT THE WATER-PROOFING DURING CONSTRUCTION AND BACKFILL OPERATIONS BY PARGING SOLID SHEETS OF BOARDS, ETC.

WATERPROOFING INTERIOR FACE OF FOUNDATION WALL
NOT RECOMMENDED EXCEPT WHEN OUTSIDE IS NOT ACCESSIBLE

EXTERIOR COLUMN WALL AND FOOTING WATERPROOFING

EXTERIOR WALLS – TWO-SLAB CONSTRUCTION, MEMBRANE AND METAL TYPES

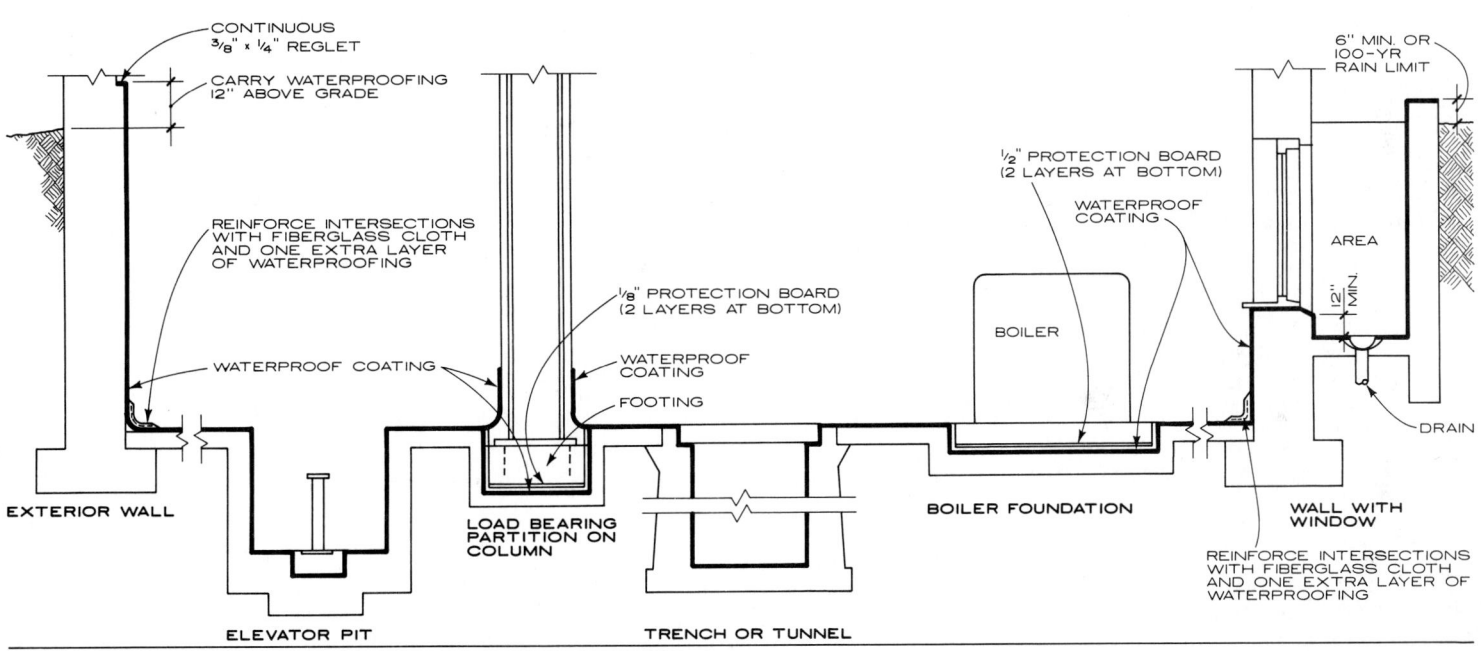

EXTERIOR WALL

LOAD BEARING PARTITION ON COLUMN

ELEVATOR PIT

TRENCH OR TUNNEL

BOILER FOUNDATION

WALL WITH WINDOW

WATERPROOF COATING METHOD – HYDROLITHIC TYPE
RECOMMENDED ONLY WHEN OUTSIDE IS NOT ACCESSIBLE

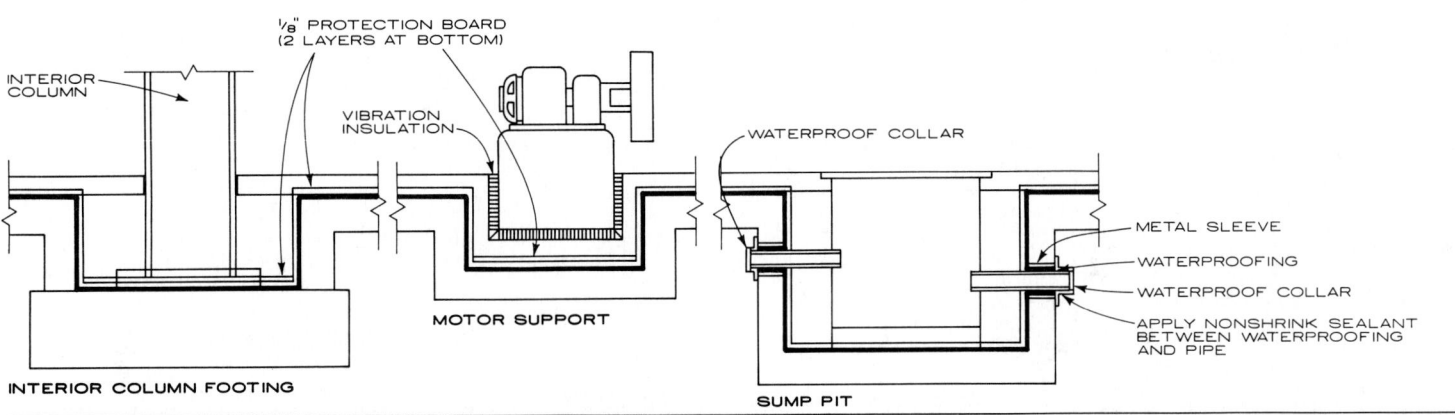

INTERIOR COLUMN FOOTING

MOTOR SUPPORT

SUMP PIT

WATERPROOFING WITH PROTECTIVE SLAB – MEMBRANE TYPE

Larry O. Opseth, AIA; Meyers and Bennett Architects/BRW; Minneapolis, Minnesota

William C. Nichols, AIA; Atlanta, Georgia

WATERPROOFING SYSTEMS **7**

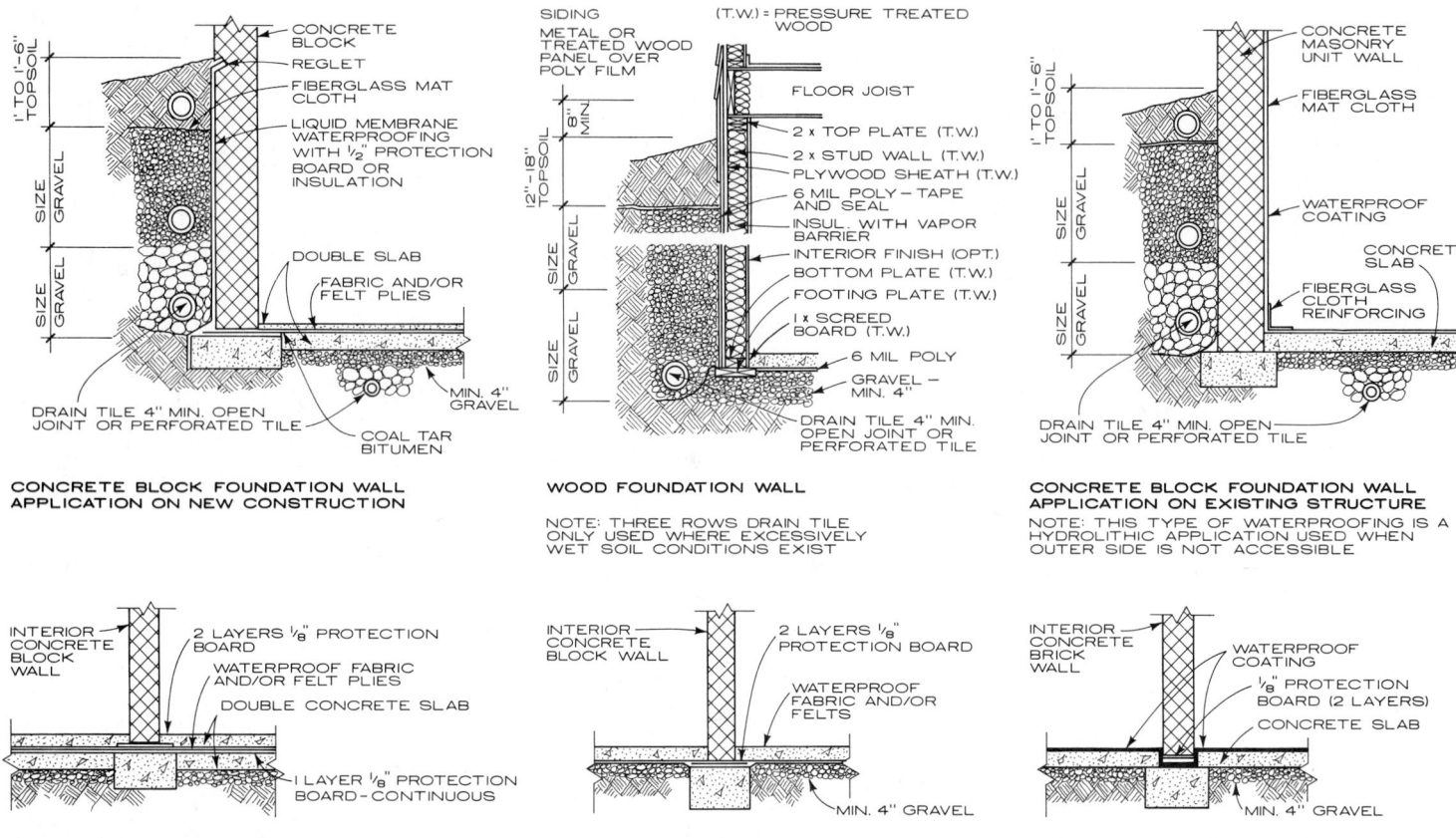

CONCRETE BLOCK FOUNDATION WALL APPLICATION ON NEW CONSTRUCTION

WOOD FOUNDATION WALL

NOTE: THREE ROWS DRAIN TILE ONLY USED WHERE EXCESSIVELY WET SOIL CONDITIONS EXIST

CONCRETE BLOCK FOUNDATION WALL APPLICATION ON EXISTING STRUCTURE

NOTE: THIS TYPE OF WATERPROOFING IS A HYDROLITHIC APPLICATION USED WHEN OUTER SIDE IS NOT ACCESSIBLE

DOUBLE CONCRETE SLAB

SINGLE CONCRETE SLAB

HYDROLITHIC APPLICATION

RESIDENTIAL WATERPROOFING — BASEMENTS BELOW GRADE

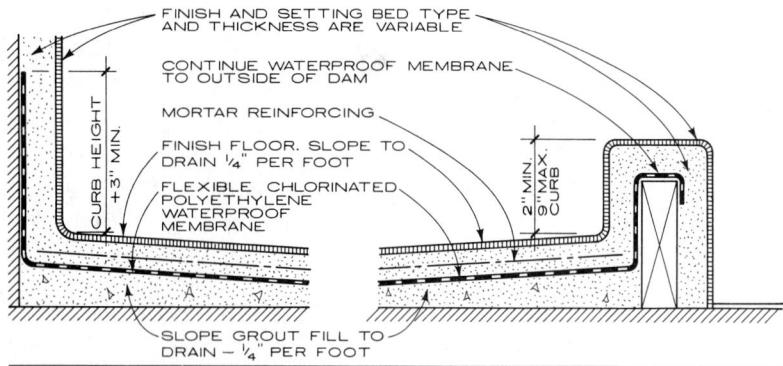

SHOWER RECEPTOR MEMBRANE APPLICATION
NOTE: MOP RECEPTOR SIMILAR

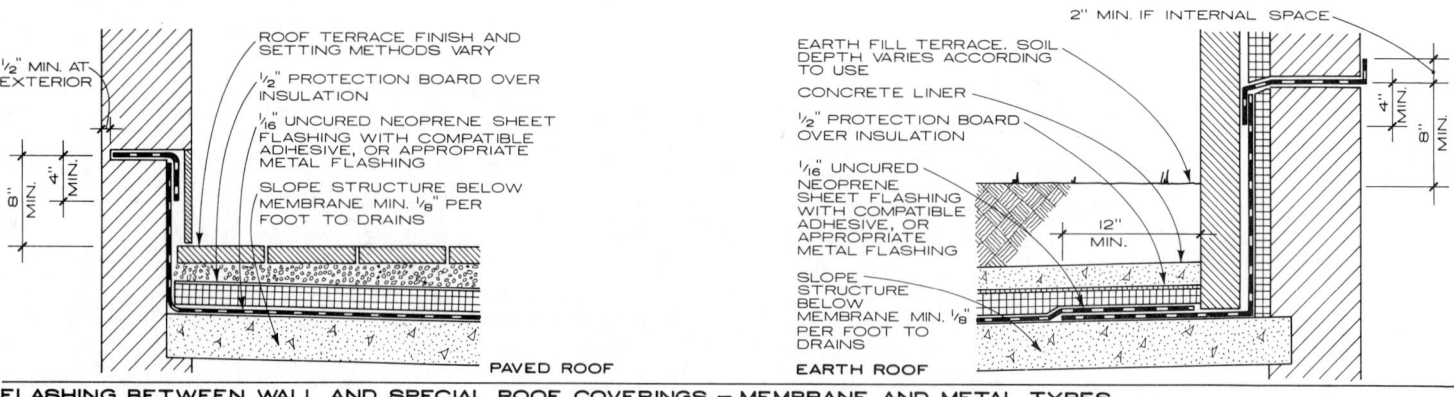

PAVED ROOF

EARTH ROOF

FLASHING BETWEEN WALL AND SPECIAL ROOF COVERINGS — MEMBRANE AND METAL TYPES

Larry O. Opseth, AIA; Meyers and Bennett Architects/BRW; Minneapolis, Minnesota

Jerry Graham; CTA Architects Engineers; Billings, Montana

7 WATERPROOFING SYSTEMS

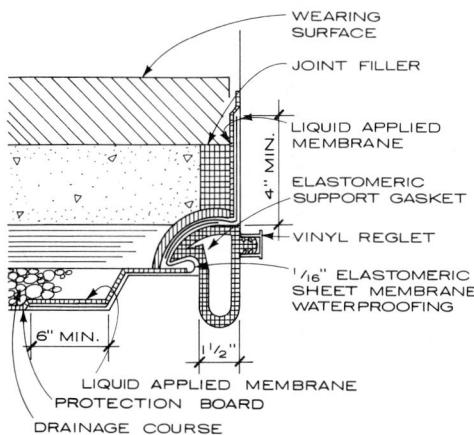

WATERSHED EXPANSION JOINT

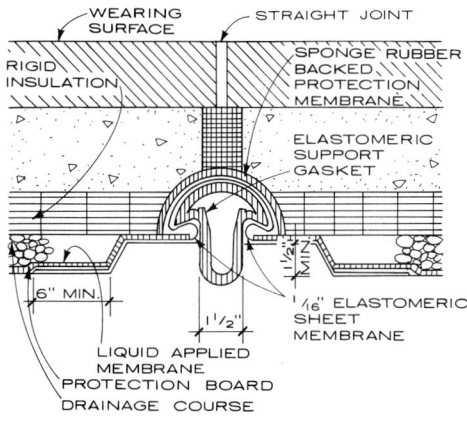

WATERSHED EXPANSION JOINT

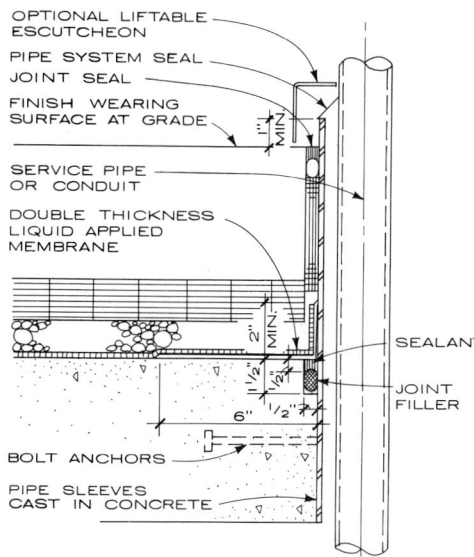

CONDITION AT PIPE PENETRATION

NOTES

1. Slope the monolithic concrete substrate under the membrane a minimum of 1/8 in./ft away from expansion joints and walls to the drains.

2. Use a drainage course to increase the rate of flow to drains.

3. Drainage at wearing surface: (a) by an open system that allows rainwater to penetrate down to membrane level; (b) closed joint system.

   These systems remove most water by slope-to-surface drains.

Robert E. Fehlberg, FAIA; CTA Architects-Engineers; Billings Montana

Charles J. Parise, FAIA, FASTM; Smith, Hinchman & Grylls; Detroit, Michigan

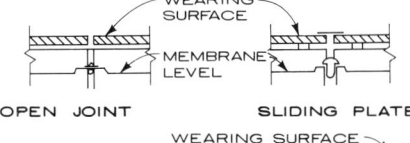

BASIC COMPONENTS OF ELASTOMERIC MEMBRANE

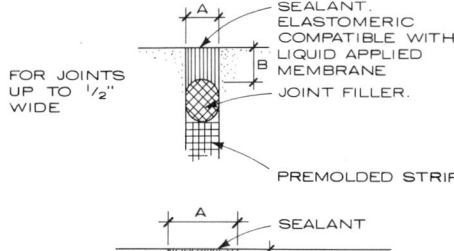

SCHEMATIC EXPANSION JOINTS

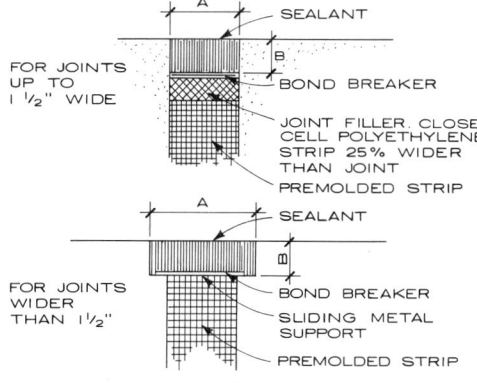

SEE OTHER PAGES FOR JOINT DESIGN AND DIMENSIONS

WET SEALANT DETAILS AT WEARING SURFACE

NOTES

1. A liquid applied waterproofing membrane has the capability of adhering to the structural slab and should be so applied as to take optimum advantage of this inherent characteristic.

2. Dry film thickness of membrane shall be 60 mil (1.5 mm). Double coating at drain, wall, penetration terminations and at joints. A preparation coat(s) totaling 100 mils (2.5 mm) of liquid applied membrane shall be applied that extends 6 in. (150 mm) onto the horizontal surface and up the wall to termination height before application of final 60 mil membrane.

3. The information on this page is based on ASTM C898-78, Standard Guide for Use of High Solids Content, Cold Liquid-Applied Elastomeric Waterproofing Membrane with Separate Wearing Course. This standard was prepared by ASTM Committee C-24 on Building Seals and Sealants.

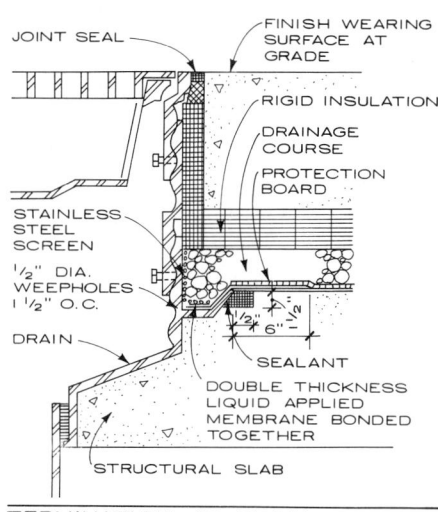

TERMINATION AT DRAIN

CONCRETE WALL BELOW WEARING SURFACE

MASONRY ABOVE WEARING SURFACE

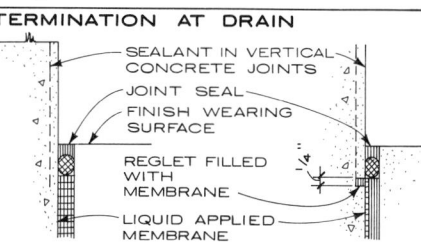

TERMINAL CONDITION AT CONCRETE WALL

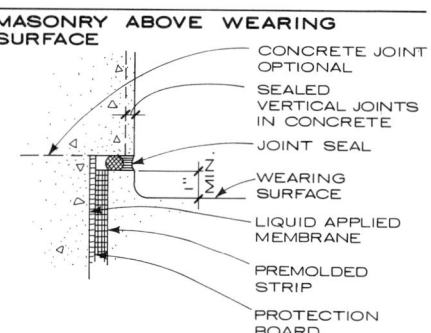

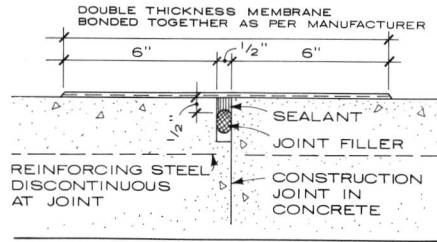

BUTT JOINT IN CONCRETE SLAB

MAJOR COMPONENTS

The major components of a good joint seal are the substrate, primer, joint-filler, bond breaker, and sealant.

SUBSTRATE

The more common substrates are masonry concrete, metal, and glass. These are generally classified as porous or nonporous.

Some substrates may not be suitable for achieving a joint unless treated mechanically, chemically, or both.

When the substrate has a coating, the coating must be compatible with the sealant and its bond to the substrate and sealant must be adequate.

Proprietary treatments or protective coatings on metal and waterproofing or water repellent treatments on concrete may inhibit bonding. Consult both substrate and sealant manufacturers for suitable joint preparation methods and the primers to be used before applying joint materials. Adhesion testing of trial applications in the field is recommended.

Surface laitance and incompatible or bond inhibiting, form release agents on concrete surfaces must be removed.

Substrates must be clean, dry, sound, and free of loose particles, contaminants, foreign matter, water soluble material, and frost.

Joints in masonry and concrete should be sealed before cleaning exposed surfaces and applying required protective barriers.

PRIMER

The purpose of a primer is to improve the adhesion of a sealant to a substrate. Many sealants require primers on all substrates, some on only certain substrates or on none at all. Most require a primer for maximum adhesion to concrete and masonry surfaces.

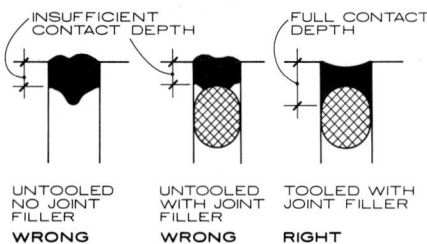

INSUFFICIENT CONTACT DEPTH — UNTOOLED NO JOINT FILLER — **WRONG**

FULL CONTACT DEPTH — UNTOOLED WITH JOINT FILLER — **WRONG**

TOOLED WITH JOINT FILLER — **RIGHT**

PURPOSE FOR JOINT-FILLER AND TOOLING

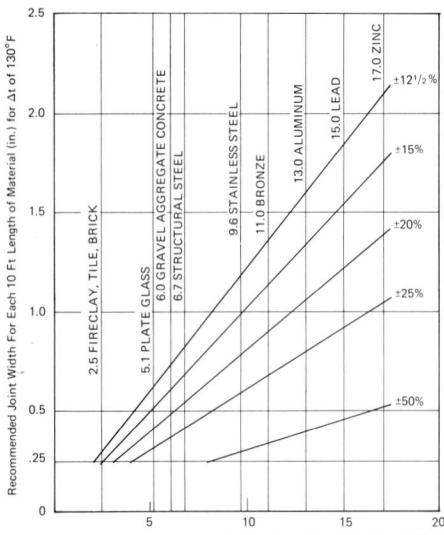

RECOMMENDED JOINT WIDTH FOR SEALANTS WITH VARIOUS MOVEMENT CAPABILITIES

JOINT DESIGN

The geometry of a joint seal is related to numerous factors including desired appearance, spacing of joints,

Charles J. Parise, FAIA; FASTM; Smith, Hinchman & Grylls; Detroit, Michigan

---

Normally the sealant manufacturer's standard published recommendations should be adhered to regarding the use of primers or surface conditioners for optimum adhesion. However, field tests may be required to determine the proper treatment and sealant/primer selection.

JOINT-FILLERS

A joint-filler is used to control the depth of sealant in the joint and permit full wetting of the intended interface when tooled. It can also serve as a temporary joint seal for weather protection when conditions are unsuitable for immediate sealant application, but normally should be replaced before sealant is applied with a new permanent joint-filler.

Some joint-fillers may be incompatible with the substrate and sealant, causing stains on either one of them or both. Some may be factory coated with a suitable material that provides a barrier to staining. To confirm its suitability, the barrier coating should be acceptable to both the sealant and joint-filler manufacturers.

Joint-fillers for vertical application may be flexible, compatible, closed cell plastic foam or sponge rubber rod stock and elastomeric tubing of such materials as neoprene, butyl, and EPDM. They should resist permanent deformation before and during sealant application, and be nonabsorbent to water or gas, and resist flowing upon mild heating, since this can cause bubbling of the sealant. Open cell sponge type materials such as urethane foam may be satisfactory, provided that their water absorption characteristics are recognized. The sealant should be applied immediately after joint-filler placement to prevent water absorption from rain. Elastomeric tubing of neoprene, butyl, or EPDM may be applied immediately as a temporary seal until the primary sealant is put in place, after which they serve to a limited degree as a secondary water barrier. When used as temporary seals, joint-fillers should be

movement in joint, movement capability of sealant to be used, required sealant width to accommodate anticipated movement, and tooling method.

SEALANT WIDTH

The required width of the sealant is determined by the application temperature range of the sealant, the temperature extremes anticipated at the site location, and the movement capability of the sealant to be used.

An application temperature from 40 to 100°F should be assumed in determining the anticipated amount of joint movement in the design of joints.

The minimum joint widths for various building materials in 10 ft sections and for sealants with the movement capability range indicated are shown in the accompanying table.

SEALANT DEPTH

The sealant depth, when applied, depends on the sealant width. The following guidelines are normally accepted practice.

1. For a recommended minimum width of $^1/_4$ in., the depth should be $^1/_4$ in.
2. For joints in concrete masonry or stone, the depth of the sealant may be equal to the sealant width in joints up to $^1/_2$ in. For joints $^1/_2$ to 1 in. wide, the sealant depth should be $^1/_2$ in. For joints 1 to 2 in. wide, the sealant depth should not be greater than one half the sealant width. For widths exceeding 2 in., the depth should be determined by the sealant manufacturer.
3. For sealant widths over $^1/_4$ in. in metal, glass, and other nonporous surface joints, the sealant depth should be a minimum of one half the sealant width and should in no case exceed the width.

When determining location of the joint-filler in the joint, consideration should be given to the reduction in sealant depth with concave and recessed tooled joints and the joint should be designed accordingly.

APPLICATION

Thoroughly clean all joints, removing all foreign matter such as dust, paint (unless it is a permanent protective coating), oil, grease, waterproofing or water repellent treatments, water, surface dirt, and frost.

Clean porous materials such as concrete, masonry, and unglazed surfaces of ceramic tile by brushing, grinding, blast cleaning, mechanical abrading, acid washing, or a combination of these methods to provide

---

able to remain resilient at temperatures down to −15°F and have low compression set.

Joint-fillers for horizontal application for floors, pavements, sidewalks, patios, and other light traffic areas may be compatible, extruded, closed cell, high density, flexible foams, cork board, resin impregnated fiberboard, or elastomeric tubing or rods. These joint-fillers should remain resilient down to −15°F, exhibit good recovery, not cause the sealant to bubble in the joint because of heat, and be capable of supporting the sealant in traffic areas. They should not exude liquids under compression, which could hydraulically cause sealant failure by forcing the sealant from the joint. Combinations of joint-filler materials can be used to satisfy the several requirements of a joint seal. A premolded joint-filler may be used to form a joint in concrete, and an additional joint-filler material may be installed under compression across the width and to the proper depth just before the sealant is applied to provide a clean, dry, compatible backup.

BOND BREAKER

A bond breaker may be necessary to prevent adhesion of the sealant to any surface or material where such adhesion would be detrimental to the performance of the sealant.

The use of a joint-filler to which the sealant will not adhere may preclude the need for a bond breaker.

The bond breaker may be a polyethylene tape with pressure sensitive adhesive on one side or various liquid applied compounds as recommended by the sealant manufacturer.

SEALANT

Sealants are classified as single component or multicomponent, nonsag or self-leveling, and traffic or nontraffic use, as well as according to movement capability. Characteristics of some generic types are listed in the accompanying table.

a clean, sound substrate for optimum sealant adhesion. The surface of concrete may be cut back to remove contaminants and expose a clean surface when acceptable to the purchaser.

Remove laitance from concrete by acid washing, grinding, or mechanical abrading.

Remove form oils from concrete by blast cleaning.

Remove loose particles originally present or resulting from grinding, abrading, or blast cleaning by blowing out joints with oilfree compressed air (or vacuuming) prior to application of primer or sealant.

Clean nonporous surfaces, such as metal, glass, porcelain enamel, and glazed surfaces of ceramic tile chemically or by other means that are not harmful to the substrate and are acceptable to the substrate manufacturer.

Remove temporary protective coatings on metallic surfaces by a solvent that leaves no residue. Apply the solvent with clean oilfree cloths or lintless paper towels. Do not allow the solvent to air-dry without wiping. Wipe dry with a clean dry cloth or lintless paper towels. Permanent coatings that are to remain must not be removed or damaged.

Install masking tape at joint edges when necessary to avoid undesirable sealant smears on exposed visible surfaces. Use a nonstaining, nonabsorbent, compatible type.

Install primer when and as recommended by the sealant manufacturer for optimum adhesion.

Install compatible joint-filler uniformly to proper depth without twisting and braiding.

Install sealant in strict accordance with the manufacturer's recommendations and precautions. Completely fill the recess provided in the joint. Sealants are more safely applied at temperatures above 40°F. Joints must be dry.

Tool sealant so as to force it into the joint, eliminating air pockets and ensuring contact of the sealant with the sides of the joint. Use appropriate tool to provide a concave, flush, or recessed joint as required.

Immediately after tooling the joint remove masking tape carefully, if used, without disturbing the sealant.

Reference: ASTM Committee C-24 ''Standard Guide For Use of Chemically Curing Elastomeric Sealants.'' Highlights of text, graph, and figures are reprinted with permission from the American Society for Testing and Materials.

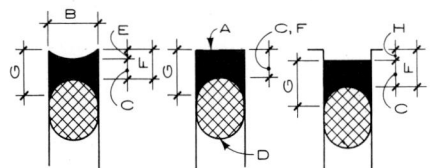

A — sealant
B — sealant width
C — sealant depth
D — joint-filler

E — tooling depth
F — joint-filler depth
G — sealant contact depth
H — sealant recess depth

TYPICAL VERTICAL APPLICATIONS, PROFILES AND TERMINOLOGY

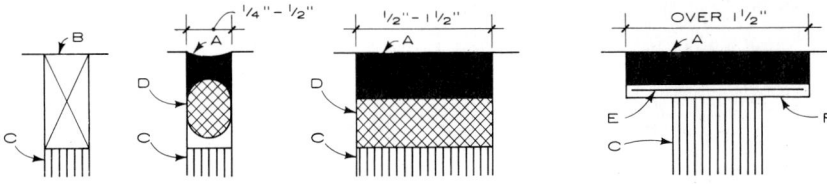

A — sealant
B — removable joint-filler
C — premolded joint-filler cast in concrete
D — joint-filler installed under compression

E — bond breaker (use over sliding metal support in relatively wide joints)
F — concrete shoulder provides vertical support

USE OF MULTIPLE JOINT-FILLERS IN HORIZONTAL APPLICATIONS IN CAST-IN-PLACE CONCRETE

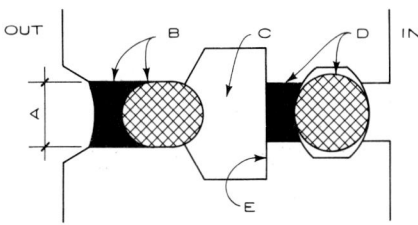

A — 1″ minimum for access to interior air seal
B — sealant and joint-filler preferred for rain screen; preformed compression seal also used
C — pressure equalization chamber; vent to outside, and chamber baffles at every second floor vertically and same distance horizontally
D — sealant and joint-filler installed from outside to facilitate continuity of air seal; building framework hinders application of continuous air seal from interior
E — concrete shoulders required for tooling screed

TWO-STAGE PRESSURE EQUALIZED JOINT SEAL

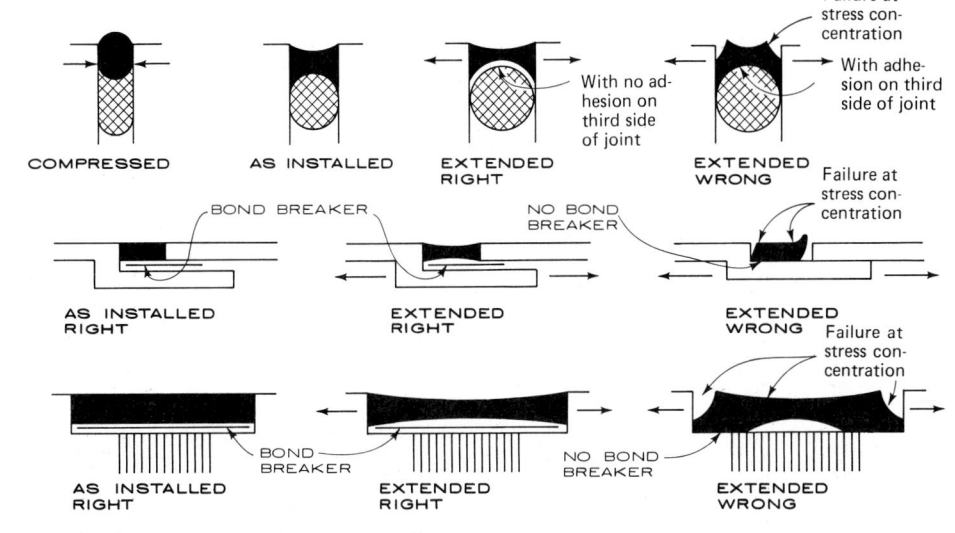

SEALANT CONFIGURATIONS WITH MOVEMENT AND EFFECT OF THREE-SIDED ADHESION

CHARACTERISTICS OF COMMON ELASTOMERIC SEALANTS

	ACRYLIC (SOLVENT RELEASES) (ONE-PART)	POLYSULFIDE		POLYURETHANE		SILICONE (ONE-PART)
		TWO-PART	ONE-PART	TWO-PART	ONE-PART	
Chief ingredients	Acrylic terpolymer, inert pigments, stabilizer, and selected fillers	Polysulfide polymers, activators, pigments, plasticizers, inert fillers, gelling, and curing agents		Polyurethane prepolymer, inert fillers, pigment, plasticizers, accelerators, activators, and extenders	Polyurethane prepolymer, inert fillers, pigment, and plasticizers	Siloxane polymer, pigment, and selected fillers
Percent solids	85–95	95–100	95–100	95–100	95–100	95–100
Curing process	Solvent release and very slow chemical cure	Chemical reaction with curing agent	Chemical reaction with moisture in the air	Chemical reaction with curing agent	Chemical reaction with moisture in air	Chemical reaction with moisture in the air
Curing characteristics	Skins on exposed surface; interior remains soft and tacky	Cures uniformly throughout; rate affected by temperature and humidity	Skins over, cures progressively inward; final cure uniform throughout	Cures uniformly throughout; rate affected by temperature and humidity	Skins over, cures progressively inward, final cure uniform throughout	Cures progressively inward; final cure uniform throughout
Primer	Generally not required	Manufacturer's approved primer required for porous surfaces, sometimes for other surfaces		Manufacturer's approved primer required for most surfaces		Manufacturer's approved primer required for most surfaces
Application temperature (°F)	40–120, must be heated	40–100	60–100	40–120	40–120	0–120
Tackfree time	1–7 days	6–24 hr	6–72 hr	1–24 hr	Slightly tacky until weathered	1 hr or less
Hardness, Shore A Cured 1 to 6 months, aged 5 years	0–25 / 45–55	15–45 / 30–60	25–35 / 40–50	20–40 / 35–55	25–45 / 30–50	20–40 / 35–55
Toxicity	Nontoxic	Curing agent is toxic	Contains toxic ingredients	Toxic; gloves recommended for handling		Nontoxic
Use characteristics	Excellent adhesion; poor low temperature flexibility; not usable in traffic areas; unpleasant odor 5–12 days	Wide range of appropriate applications; curing time depends on temperature and humidity	Unpleasant odor; broad range of cured hardnesses available	Sets very fast; broad range of cured hardnesses; excellent for concrete joints and traffic areas	Excellent for concrete joints and traffic areas, but substrate must be absolutely dry; short package stability	Requires contact with air for curing; low abrasion resistance; not tough enough for use in traffic areas

Charles J. Parise, FAIA; FASTM; Smith, Hinchman & Grylls; Detroit, Michigan

CHAPTER 8 DOORS AND WINDOWS

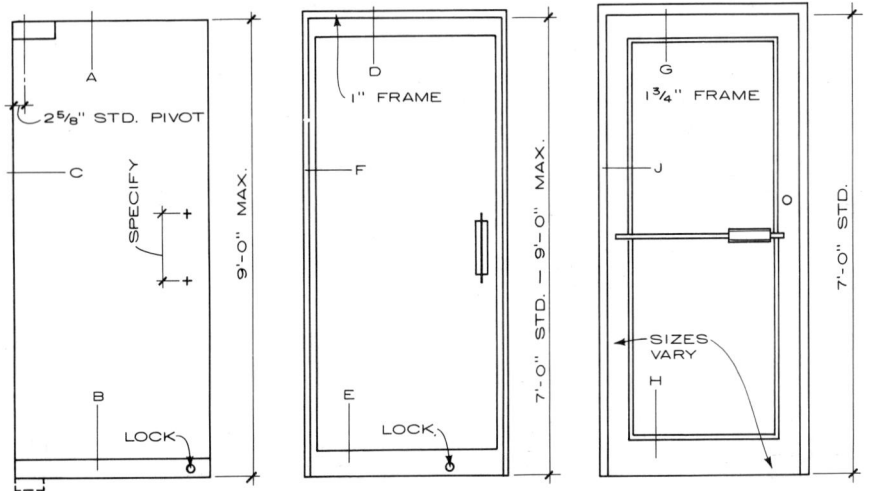

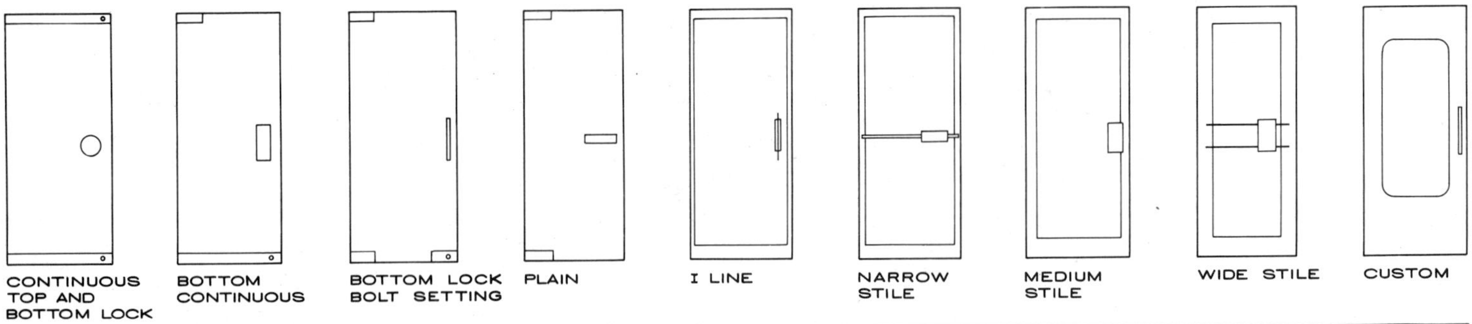

CONTINUOUS TOP AND BOTTOM LOCK | BOTTOM CONTINUOUS | BOTTOM LOCK BOLT SETTING | PLAIN | I LINE | NARROW STILE | MEDIUM STILE | WIDE STILE | CUSTOM

DOOR TYPES

FRAMELESS DOOR — 2⅝" STD. PIVOT, SPECIFY, 9'-0" MAX., LOCK

NARROW FRAMED DOOR — 1" FRAME, 7'-0" STD. - 9'-0" MAX., SIZES VARY, LOCK

STANDARD FRAMED DOOR — 1¾" FRAME, 7'-0" STD., SIZES VARY

ELEVATION — TYPICAL GLASS DOORS

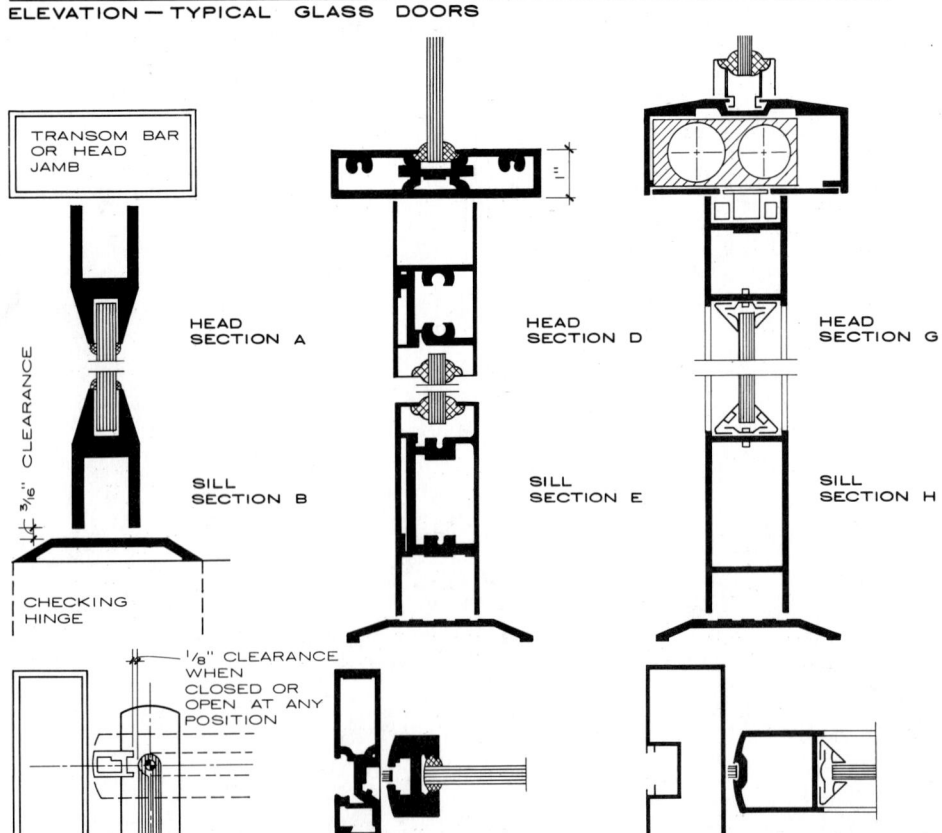

TRANSOM BAR OR HEAD JAMB

HEAD SECTION A

SILL SECTION B

CHECKING HINGE

3/16 CLEARANCE

HEAD SECTION D

SILL SECTION E

1"

HEAD SECTION G

SILL SECTION H

⅛" CLEARANCE WHEN CLOSED OR OPEN AT ANY POSITION

JAMB SECTION C

JAMB SECTION F

JAMB SECTION J

DETAILS — TYPICAL GLASS DOORS

G. Lawson Drinkard, III, AIA; The Vickery Partnership, Architects; Charlottesville, Virginia

CLOSED POSITION | PARTLY OPEN | COMPLETELY OPEN

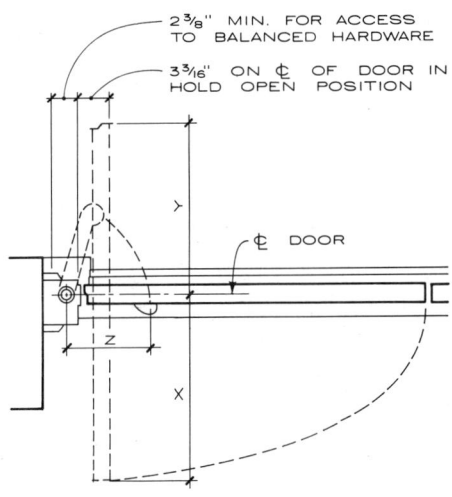

2⅜" MIN. FOR ACCESS TO BALANCED HARDWARE

3³/₁₆" ON ℄ OF DOOR IN HOLD OPEN POSITION

℄ DOOR

PLAN
BALANCED DOOR

SPACE REQUIREMENTS—VARIOUS DOOR WIDTHS (IN.)

	34	36	38	40	42	44
X	21¼	23¼	25¼	23¼	25¼	27¼
Y	12¾			16¼		
Z	7⅛			8⅞		

NOTES

1. Consult applicable building codes for glass size, thickness, tempering, and safety rail requirements.
2. ½ in. frameless glass doors are available in clear, grey, or bronze tints in sizes up to 60 x 108 in. Glass doors in ¾ in. thickness are available in clear only, in sizes up to 48 x 108 in.
3. Consult manufacturer's data for structural adequacy against prevailing wind loads and provision for increased reinforcement for frames and transom bars.
4. Aluminum doors and frames are available in all standard aluminum finishes in sizes up to 6 x 7 ft.

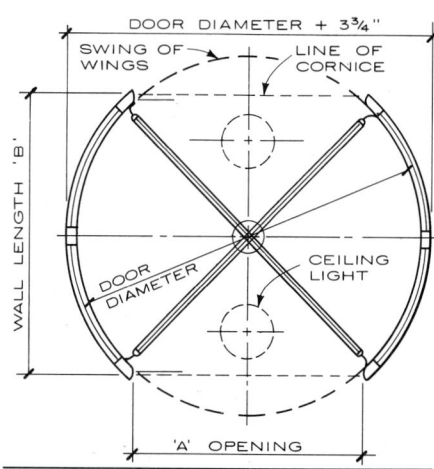

KEY TO TABLE DIMENSIONS

STANDARD DOOR DIMENSIONS

DIAMETER	A (OPENING)	B (WALL LENGTH)
6'-6''	4'-5¼''	4'-11⅝''
6'-8''	4'-6¹¹⁄₁₆''	5'-1¹⁄₁₆''
6'-10''	4'-8⅛''	5'-2½''
7'-0''	4'-9½''	5'-3⅞''
7'-2''	4'-10¹⁵⁄₁₆''	5'-5⁵⁄₁₆''
7'-4''	5'-0⅜''	5'-6¾''
7'-6''	5'-1¾''	5'-8⅛''

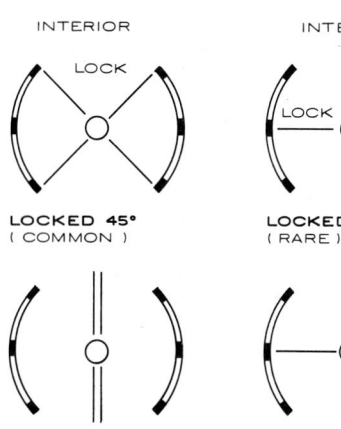
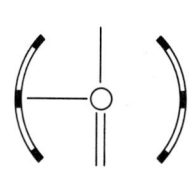
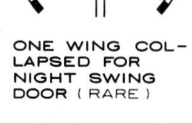

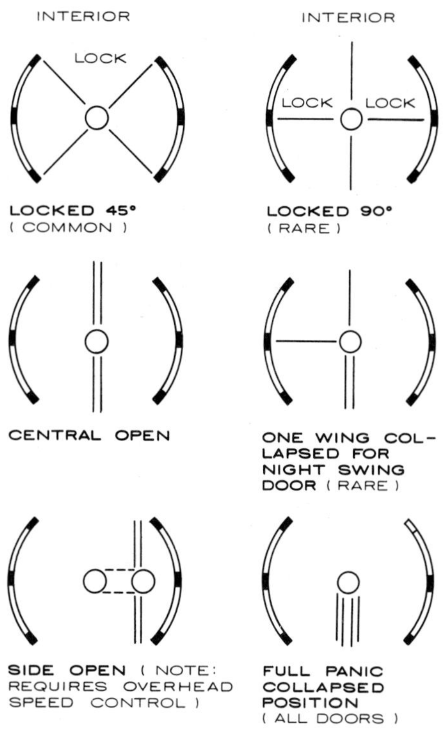

Curved sliding night door available for security if code permits. Enclosure walls and wings may be designed to roll aside.

PLANS SHOWING LOCKED AND FOLDED WING POSITIONS

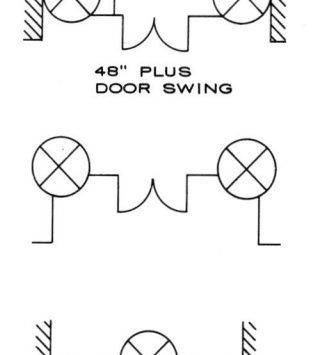

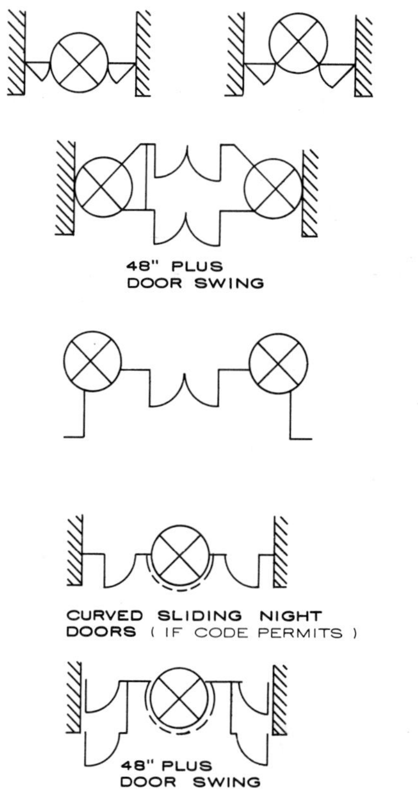

LAYOUT TYPES

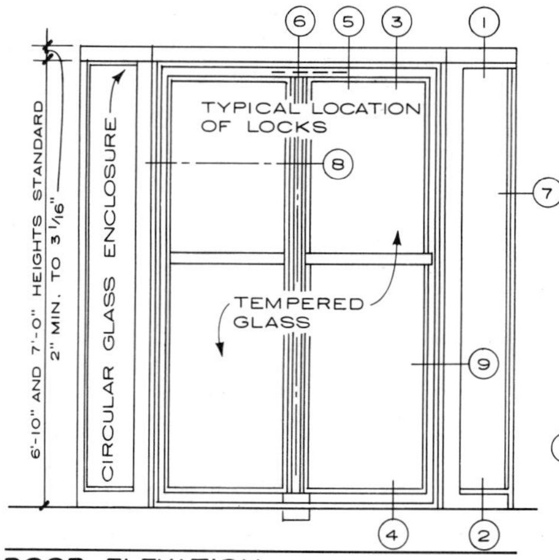

DOOR ELEVATION

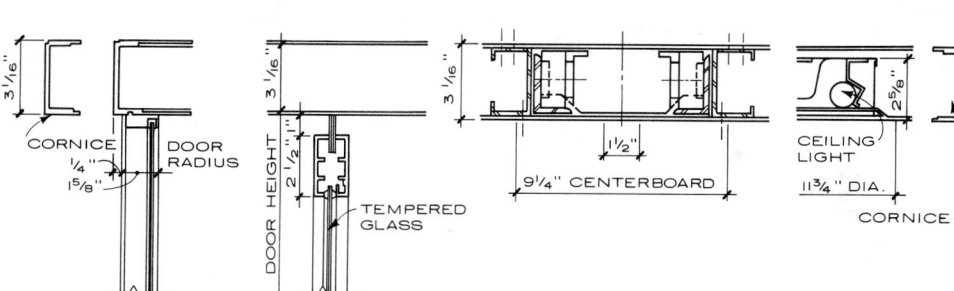

① SECTION—ENCLOSURE HEAD AT CEILING   ③ SECTION—WING HEAD AT CEILING   ⑤ DETAIL AT PIVOT HEAD   ⑥ CEILING LIGHT DETAIL

NOTES

1. Circular glass enclosure walls may be simply annealed ¼ in. glass. However, this varies with different government bodies. Some jurisdictions require laminated or wire glass. Tempered glass is not available for this use. Refer to Consumer Products Safety Commission Standards for Glazing.
2. Theoretical capacity each way = 2880 per hour. Practical capacity = 2000 per hour.
3. Doors fabricated from stainless steel, aluminum, or bronze sections are available. Wall enclosure may be all metal, all glass, partial glass, or housed-in construction.
4. Provide heating and cooling source integral with or immediately adjacent to enclosure.
5. Motor drive recommended with constant low speed.
6. For general use, use 6 ft 6 in. diameter. For hotels, department stores, or other large traffic areas, use 7 ft or greater diameter.
7. Codes may allow 50% of legal exiting requirements by means of revolving doors. Some do not credit any and require hinged doors adjacent. Verify with local authorities.

② SECTION—ENCLOSURE SILL AT FLOOR   ④ SECTION—WING SILL AT FLOOR

⑦ PLAN—ENCLOSURE AT MULLION

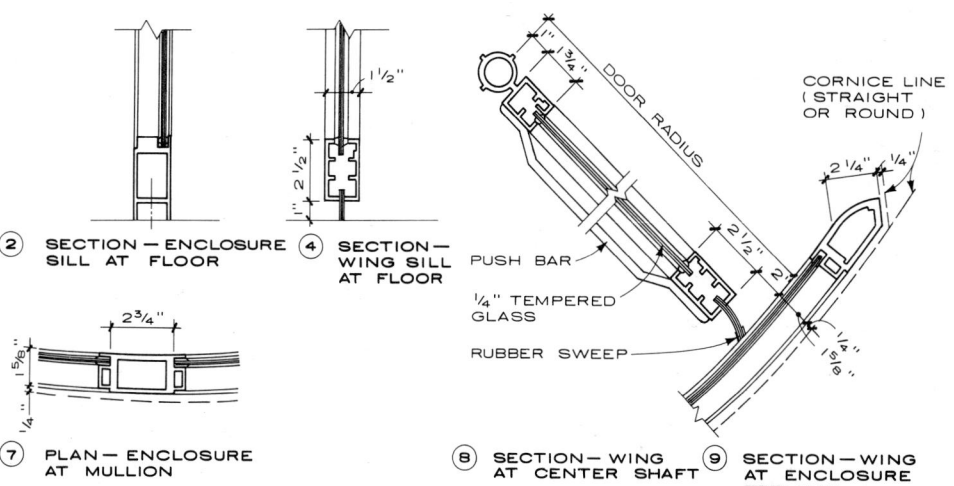

⑧ SECTION—WING AT CENTER SHAFT   ⑨ SECTION—WING AT ENCLOSURE TERMINAL

TYPICAL DOOR DETAILS

Skidmore, Owings & Merrill

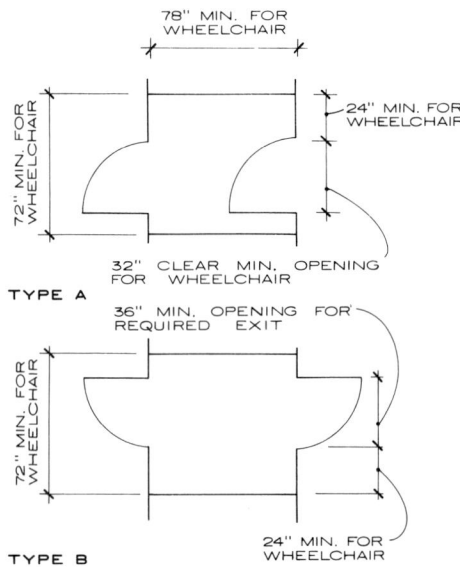

TYPE A

TYPE B

1. Provide doors for handicapped to operate at less than 8 lb pressure.
2. Minimum turning radius of wheelchair is 36 in.; desirable space is 60 x 60 in.

VESTIBULES

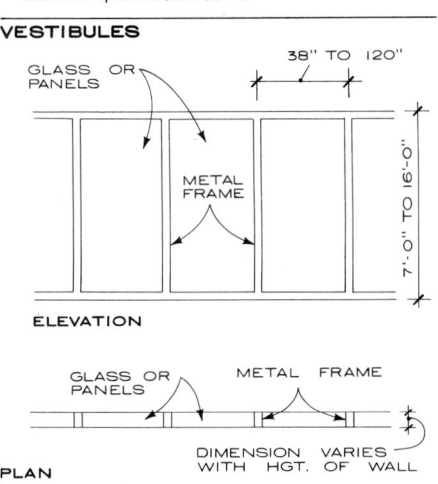

ELEVATION

PLAN
METAL FRAME SYSTEM

Design each component part (other than glass) so that deflections normal to wall plane at full locally required loading will not exceed $1/200$ of the clear span of the component part, but limit deflection of glass supporting members to $1/300$ of the distance over which such glass is supported. Do not permit deflections parallel to wall plane to exceed 75% of the glass edge clearances or other clearances provided between component parts. Base calculations for such deflections on the combination of maximum direct loading, building deflections, thermal stresses, and erection tolerances. Do not permit permanent deflections in this type of work.

Glass or panel thickness varies with width and height. Consult span charts in glass manufacturer's structural data sheets, then confirm data with the manufacturer.

Comply with the requirements of local and state laws or ordinances with respect to the use and application of safety glazing materials at all locations of both indoor and outdoor glass walls.

LARGE GLASS WALLS

Skidmore, Owings and Merrill

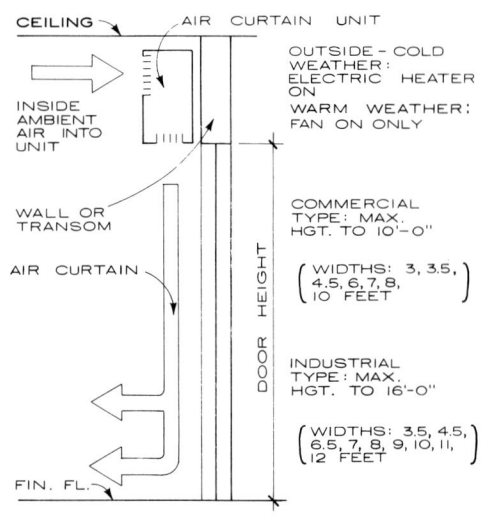

AIR CURTAIN ENTRANCE

Consult manufacturers' data regarding energy conservation, sound, installation details, and limitations of use.

SPECIAL ENTRANCES

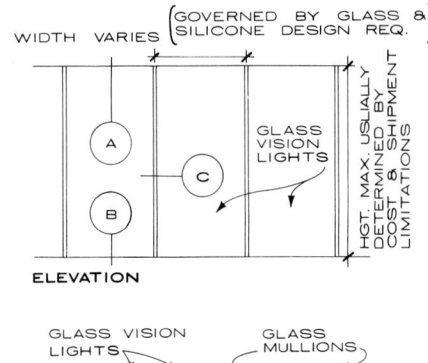

ELEVATION

PLAN
ALL GLASS SYSTEM

All glass wall systems are engineered, custom fabricated combinations of clear glass vertical mullion lights and silicone structural sealant at the mullion and vision interfaces.

Glass mullion systems replace the conventional masonry, wood, or metal supports for large glass walls and may be used inside or out. No opaque materials are used except for simple metal sections at the head and sill. Engineers usually rely on $3/4$ in. thick mullions as the principal supporting element. The thickness and width of the large vision lights for clear glass (or, under special conditions, tinted glass) are governed by glass and silicone design requirements at the design wind load. Reputable glass manufacturers with expertise in this type of construction should be consulted at the very beginning of a project where an all glass system is proposed.

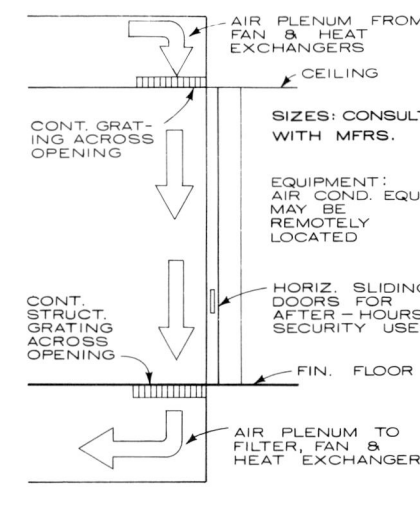

AIR ENTRANCE SYSTEM

Consult manufacturers' data regarding energy conservation, soil, installation details, limitations, and first costs and maintenance costs early in the design phase.

Hand or floor mat activated and pneumatic, hydraulic, or electric powered automatic doors are available from various sources. This type of door is either horizontally sliding (both single and biparting) or pivotal (single or double). Both types usually have "break out" features from inside that allow them to be used as exit doors. "Power-off" safety features can be provided to ensure safe passage by the general public, including the handicapped. Minimum clear opening width for the handicapped is 32 in.

All glass used in doors, sidelights, and vestibule return lights, within 48 in. of a doorjamb, must be safety glazed. See Glass Doors: Entrances.

AUTOMATIC DOORS (POWER OPER.)

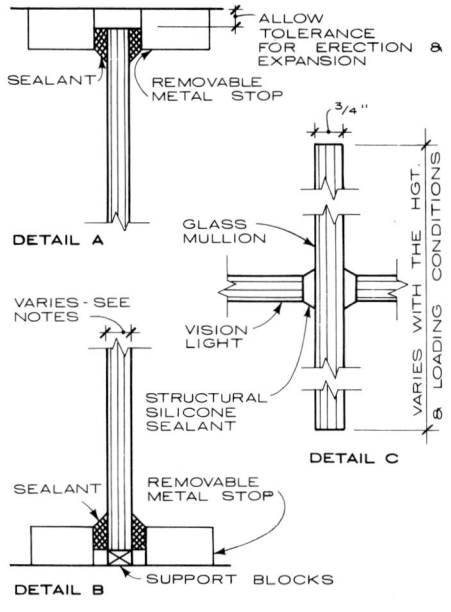

DETAIL A

DETAIL B

DETAIL C

ALL GLASS DETAILS

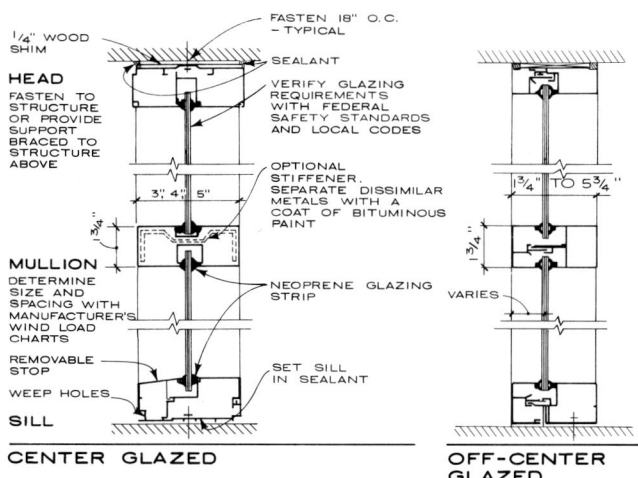

CENTER GLAZED

OFF-CENTER GLAZED

Various anodized color finishes are available. Class I (0.7 mil) or Class II (0.4 mil) in black, bronze, or clear is standard with most manufacturers.

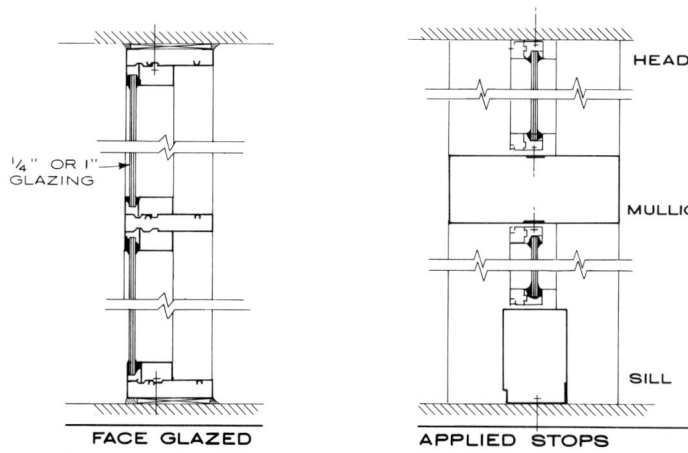

FACE GLAZED

APPLIED STOPS

NOTES

1. Review tinted and coated glass applications and details to eliminate possibility of thermal breakage.
2. Weep holes are required at sill for double glazing.
3. For specific applications, refer to manufacturers' current recommendations.
4. Other materials such as hollow metal or wood can be used for custom work.

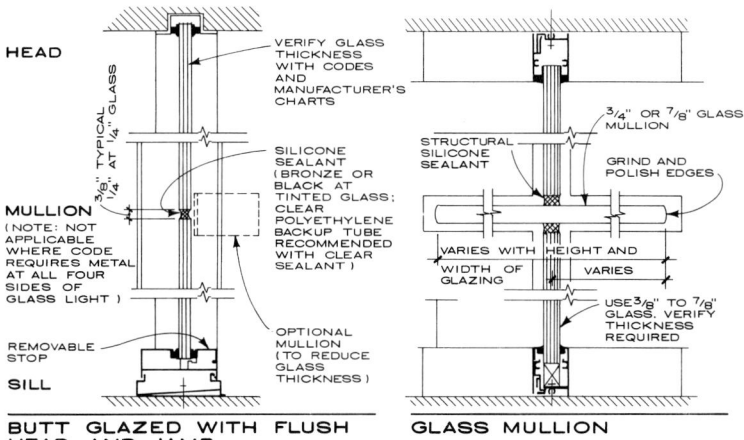

BUTT GLAZED WITH FLUSH HEAD AND JAMB

GLASS MULLION

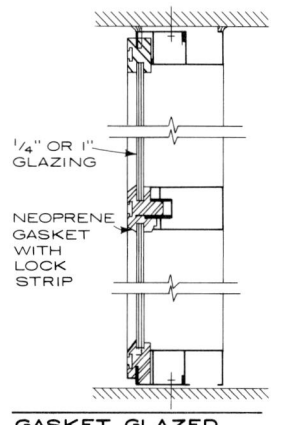

GASKET GLAZED

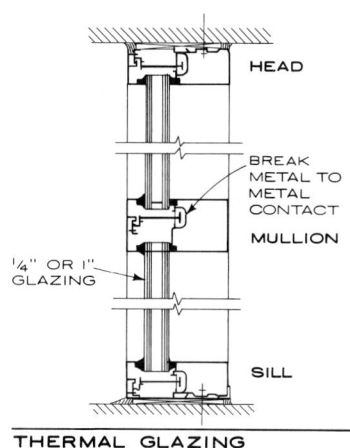

THERMAL GLAZING

Mitered glass edges at corners are not recommended. Maximum vertical span for butt glazing is 10 x 8 ft wide.

Mullions are clear glass. Tinted or coated glass lights may be considered for small areas. Maximum vertical span is 30 x 9 ft wide.

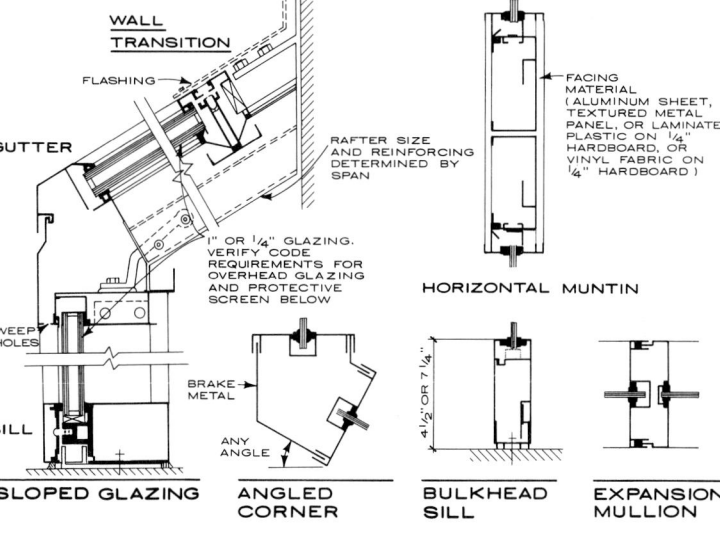

SLOPED GLAZING

ANGLED CORNER

BULKHEAD SILL

EXPANSION MULLION

HORIZONTAL MUNTIN

DOOR TRANSOM WITH CLOSER AND ILLUMINATED EXIT SIGN

HEAD WITH RECEPTOR

VARIABLE POCKET GLAZING

Care should be taken to protect the public from the possibility of overhead glass breakage.

Higher bulkheads can be built up with aluminum tubing and applied stops. Locate expansion mullions 20 ft o.c.

Use variable pocket glazing where deflection or dimensional tolerance problems exist.

O'Leary Terasawa & Takahashi, AIA Architects; Los Angeles, California

ENTRANCES AND STOREFRONTS   8

GLASS: DEFINITION

A hard and brittle amorphous substance, made by fusing silica (sometimes in combination with the oxides of boron or phosphorus) with certain basic oxides (notably those of sodium, potassium, calcium, magnesium, and lead) and cooling the product rapidly to prevent crystallization or devitrification. Most glasses melt between 800 and 950°C. Heat resisting glass generally contains a high proportion of boric oxide. The brittleness of glass is such that minute surface scratches during manufacture greatly reduce its strength.

INDUSTRY QUALITY STANDARDS

FEDERAL SPECIFICATION DD-G-451: Establishes the thickness and dimensional tolerances and the quality characteristics of flat glass products.

FEDERAL SPECIFICATION DD-G-1403: Establishes standards for tempered glass, heat strengthened glass, and spandrel glass.

AMERICAN NATIONAL STANDARD 2971: Establishes standards for testing safety glazing material.

NOTE: Because of the continuing revisions in available processes, qualities, finishes, colors, sizes, thicknesses, and limitations consult glass manufacturers for current information. The information that follows represents the guidelines of one or more manufacturers.

BASIC TYPES OF GLASS
(CLEAR GLASS)

WINDOW AND SHEET GLASS

Manufactured by a horizontally flat or vertical draw process and then annealed slowly to produce natural flat fired, high gloss surfaces. Generally has residential and industrial applications. Inherent surface waves are noticeable in sizes larger than 4 sq ft. For minimum distortion, install the larger sizes with the wave running horizontally. When specifying, list the width first.

FLOAT GLASS

Generally accepted as the successor to polished plate glass, it has become the quality standard of the glass industry in architectural, mirror, and specialty applications. Manufactured by floating on a surface of molten tin and then annealed slowly to produce a transparent flat glass, thus eliminating grinding and polishing.

PLATE GLASS

Transparent flat glass ground and polished after rolling. Cylindrical and conic shapes may, within limits, be bent to desired curvature.

VARIATIONS OF BASIC TYPES
OF GLASS

PATTERNED GLASS

Known also as rolled or figured glass, it is made by passing molten glass through rollers that are etched to produce the appropriate design. Most often only one side of the glass is imprinted with a pattern; it is possible to imprint both sides, however.

WIRE GLASS

Available as clear polished glass or in various patterns, most commonly with embedded welded square or diamond wire. Some distortion, wire discoloration, and misalignment are inherent. Some 1/4 in. (6 mm) wired glass products are recognized as certified safety glazing materials for use in hazardous locations. For applicable fire and safety codes that govern their use, refer to ANSI Z97.1.

CATHEDRAL GLASS

Known also as art glass, stained glass, or opalescent glass. It is produced in many colors, textures, and patterns, is usually 1/8 in. thick, and is used primarily in decorating leaded glass windows. Specialty firms usually contract this highly exacting art.

OBSCURE GLASS

For the purpose of obscurity or for the creation of a design, the entire surface on one or both sides of glass can be sandblasted, acid etched, or both. When a glass surface is altered by any of these methods, the glass is weakened and may become difficult to clean.

Skidmore, Owings and Merrill

HEAT ABSORBING OR TINTED GLASS

The glass absorbs much of the sun's energy because of admixture contents and then dissipates the heat to both the exterior and interior. The exterior glass surfaces reflect a portion of the energy depending on the sun's position. Heat absorbing glass has a higher temperature when exposed to the sun than does clear glass; thus the central area will expand more than the cooler shaded edges, causing edge tensile stress buildup.

DESIGN CONSIDERATIONS

1. It is advantageous to provide conditions that cause the glass edges to warm as rapidly as do the other lights, such as framing systems with low heat capacity and minimal glass grip or stops to avoid shading problems. Structural rubber gaskets have been used.
2. The thicker the glass the greater the solar energy absorbtion.
3. Indoor shading devices such as blinds and draperies reflect energy back through the glass, thus increasing temperature. The spaces between indoor shading and the glass, including ceiling pockets, should be properly vented. Heating elements should always be located on the interior side of shading devices, directing warm air away from the glass.

REFLECTIVE GLASS

Reflective glass coatings may be applied to float, plate, heat strengthened, tempered, laminated, or insulated spandrel glass. The vast number of combinations precludes listing them all.

Glass utilizing reflective coatings may be divided into three basic classifications:

1. Single glazing with a coating on one surface.
2. Laminated glass with the coating either between the glass plys or on the exterior surface.
3. Insulating glass units with the coating on the exterior surface or on either of the interior surfaces.

The application of the reflective coating on the exterior surface allows for the creation of a visually uniform surface composed of components of any or all of these glass classifications. Extreme care must be observed in handling, glazing, and cleaning this type of glass to avoid scratching the coating.

HEAT STRENGTHENED AND TEMPERED GLASS

Produced by reheating and rapidly cooling annealed glass, it has greatly increased mechanical strength and resistance to thermal stresses. Neither type can be altered after fabrication; hence the manufacturer, taking into account all limitations, must furnish the exact desired size and shape. Glazing problems may be encountered because of inherent warpage. Refer to Federal Specifications DD-G-1404 for allowable tolerances.

HEAT STRENGTHENED GLASS

Twice as strong as annealed glass. Does not pulverize into crystal-like form when broken, as does tempered glass.

TEMPERED GLASS

Four to five times the strength of annealed glass; breaks into innumerable small, cubelike fragments, but much safer than annealed glass. Shallow patterned glass may be tempered also. Visible tong marks are usually prevalent along the short side near the edge, since the glass is held in a vertical position during tempering. Some manufacturers can eliminate these marks. Strain patterns are inherent and may be observed under certain lighting conditions or by viewing with polarized eyeglasses.

SPANDREL GLASS

Heat strengthened through the process of firefusing an opaque ceramic color to the interior surface of sheet, plate, or float glass. May be fully tempered if GSA guide specification No. PBS-4-0885 is conformed with.

A variety of standard colors and special finishes are available. Supplied with a color frit only or with integral insulation and one of the following: (1) foil vapor barrier, (2) sheet metal backing, or (3) cement asbestos board backing. Pinholes and nonuniformity of color are apparent if used without solid opaque backup. If supplied without integral insulation, at least 1/2 in. air space is required between glass back and backup material.

LAMINATED GLASS
SAFETY GLASS

(See also Wire Glass, Mirrors)

A tough, clear sheet of plastic film (sometimes known as the interlayer) 0.015 in. (0.636 mm) minimum thickness sandwiched under heat and pressure between piles of sheet, plate, float, wired, heat absorbing tinted, reflective, heat strengthened, full tempered glass, or a number of combinations of each.

When fractured, particles tend to adhere to the plastic film. Always weep the glazing cavity to the exterior.

ACOUSTICAL GLASS

Safety glass with a plastic film of 0.045 in. (1.143 mm) minimum thickness.

SECURITY GLASS

Safety glass with a plastic film of 0.060 in. (1.5 mm) minimum thickness for bullet resistant and burglar resistant glass. Bullet resisting glass consists of three to five plies from 3/4 to 3 in. in overall thickness. Avoid sealants with organic solvents or oil which can react with the plastic film. (See Plastics in Glazing.)

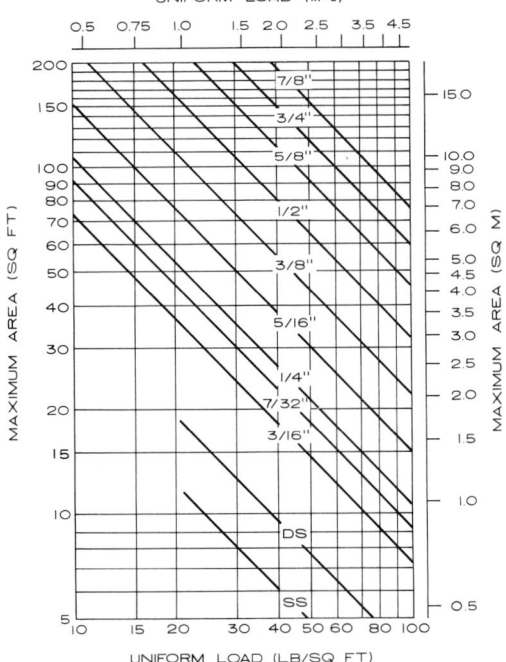

GRAPH A
Float and sheet glass supported four edges

Example: If it is determined from Graph A that a light of 1/4" (6 mm) float should withstand 20 psf (0.96 kPa), 1/4" (6 mm) Tuf-flex of the same size would be expected to withstand 80 psf (3.8 kPa) and 1/4" (6 mm), wired glass 10 psf (0.48 kPa).

$$\text{Design load for use with graphs} = \frac{\text{chosen design factor}}{2.5} \times \text{actual design load}$$

GLAZING

INSULATING GLASS

The primary function is to reduce the air-to-air heat transfer. Insulating glass units are manufactured from two or more pieces of glass, separated by a hermetically sealed air space. Two types of units are available:

1. GLASS EDGE OR GLASS SEAL UNIT: Primarily for residential use, constructed by fusing edges of two lights of glass together with 3/16 in. (5 mm) space filled with a dry gas at atmospheric pressure. Use at high altitudes is not recommended. Do not glaze with lockstrip structural gaskets.

2. ORGANIC SEALED EDGE UNIT: Primarily for commercial and industrial use, as well as for some residential applications. Constructed with two sheets of glass separated by a metal or organic spacer (filled with a moisture absorbing material) around the edges and hermetically sealed. It is available either with or without metal edge banding. Units without banding allow for inspection of glass edges before installation.

Available with 1/4 and 1/2 in. air space in plate, float, patterned, heat absorbing, tinted, reflective, heat strengthened, tempered, and laminated glass. The thickness of the two glass panes, however, should not differ by more than 1/16 in. Performance characteristics, glass thickness, maximum fabricated sizes, and a multitude of various combinations may be found in the manufacturer's literature.

Heat absorbing units must have the heat absorbing glass to the exterior. In sloped insulated glazing, located over populated areas, heat strengthened laminated glass should be considered for use in the interior light; the glass manufacturer and governing codes and authorities on fire and safety should be consulted, however. Triple glazing units are available for special applications. Provide for the drainage of any moisture that might collect and destroy the organic seal. On metal edge units the sealant must extend above the metal edge.

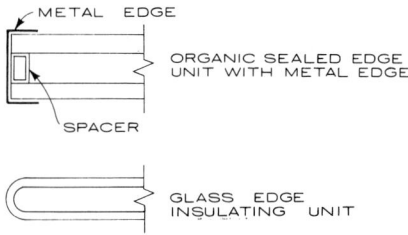

INSULATING GLASS UNITS

INSULATING GLASS

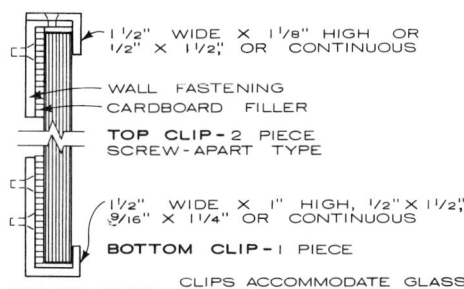

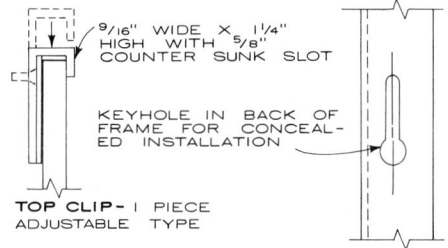

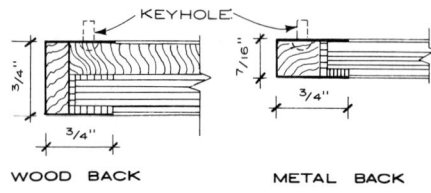

MIRROR WITH METAL FRAME
AVAILABLE IN BRASS, BRONZE & NICKEL SILVER WITH ANY POLISHED OR PLATED FINISH

MIRROR CLIPS — CLIPS ACCOMMODATE GLASS FROM 1/4" TO 3/8." AVAILABLE IN BRASS-BRIGHT CHROME FINISH; NICKEL PLATED STEEL; BRASS, NICKEL SILVER, BRONZE-ANY FINISH, BRASS-NICKEL PLATED

MIRROR GLAZING DETAILS

MIRRORS

Most commonly manufactured from surfacing sheet, float, or plate glass, hermetically sealing a silver coating with a uniform film of electrolytic copper plating. A protective coating of paint is then applied to seal out moisture from the silver. When sheet glass is used, the quality should be A-silvering or B-silvering. Float or plate glass should be selected for mirror glazing quality. Incidental applications include safety, observation (two-way), and institutional uses.

For applications of mirrored acrylic plastics, see Glazing with Plastics.

CONVEX AND CONCAVE MIRRORS

Mirrors can be used to provide both security and safety for "blind spots" from visual vantage points. Twisted or bent mirrors are used to create distorted images.

SAFETY MIRRORS

Used for cladding full height, hinged, pivoted, or sliding doors. Commonly manufactured by one of the following methods:

1. Silvering fully tempered glass—visually inferior to regular glass mirrors because of inherent warpage of tempered glass.
2. Silvering the back of laminated glass—visually inferior.
3. Silvering a light of glass and laminating it to another glass light with the silvering inside the unit—visually the best of the three.

OBSERVATION (ONE-WAY OR TWO-WAY) MIRRORS

Commonly used for research and security in observation areas. Designed to provide vision through one side while reflecting images when viewed from the opposite side. To facilitate this function, the observers' area should have dull, subdued colors and low lighting levels with controlled dimming. The area to be observed should have light colors and a high illumination level, as suggested in the light ratio table.

Light ratio = observed area : viewing area.

Skidmore, Owings and Merrill

LIGHT RATIO TABLE

BASE GLASS	DESCRIPTION	LIGHT RATIO PREFERRED	ACCEPTABLE
Float	Clear	10:1	5:1
	Laminated	10:1	5:1
	Gray	4:1	2:1

Observation mirrors can be manufactured in the following forms (for comments, see Safety Mirrors):

1. Single glazed, for interior applications. Extreme care must be taken to avoid damaging the reflective coating through abrasion.
2. Safety tempered.
3. Safety laminated. The mirror coating is usually located between the two bonded plys of glass, thus protecting it against abrasion.
4. Security laminated. A single light of observation mirror glass that is laminated between two lights of clear glass with a plastic film interlayer.

INSTITUTIONAL MIRRORS

Used in detention or security areas and in areas involving high risk to personal safety. Often made of highly polished noncorrosive metal with reinforced rounded corners and edges. Commonly made for attachment to masonry walls with flat head spanner screws.

MOUNTING APPLICATIONS

Mirrors can be mounted by way of frames or they can be surface mounted frameless by any of the following methods:

1. MASTIC: Mastic specifically made for mirrors is not generally recommended for use without clips, channels, or other auxiliary supportive devices. Certain design considerations, mirror sizes, and weights may, however, make this type of installation desirable. Mounting surfaces should be clean, dry, smooth, and plumb. Avoid applying to papered surfaces. Paint the back of the mirror with an extra coat of water resistant paint. Spot apply mastic to dry mirror back; it should not cover more than approximately 25% of the mirror area or exceed 1/2 to 5/8 in. in thickness, so as to allow for trueing the mirror and adequate ventilation. Always provide support along the bottom edge and brace the mirror until the mastic sets.
2. DOUBLE FACED TAPE: The tape must be compatible with the mirror backing and supportive surface. Thicknesses and quantities depend on adhesive qualities of the tape. A tape with a capability of 1 lb for every 1/2 sq in. is recommended. To prevent moisture collection, install tape vertically, cutting the top edge to a point. Provide a bottom edge support that allows for drainage.
3. BOTTOM CHANNEL AND CLIPS.
4. WOOD FRAME BACK: Used to level a single mirror or multiple mirrors in a uniform plane. Paint the surface facing the mirror back to prevent wood resins from spoiling the silver. All mechanical fastening devices should be countersunk into the frame. Use clips at the bottom edge; provide paper padding to prevent metal contact.
5. ROSETTES OR SCREWS: Only experienced glaziers should undertake this type of work, since extreme care is needed. To prevent the glass from coming in contact with the metal screw anchor, make the hole in the mirror of adequate size to accommodate a rubber sleeve fitting around the screw. A felt cushion should be placed behind the rosette on the face of the glass. It is recommended that mirrors up to 10 sq ft in area be supported at each corner, 4 in. in from the edges; mirrors over 10 sq ft in area should have holes about 36 in. on centers.

Surface mounted, frameless mirrors should have all exposed edges ground and polished. If a continuous bottom channel is used, the bottom edge should be ground and painted to protect it from possible moisture intrusion. The paint must be water resistant and compatible with the coating on the mirror's back, as it must overlap the back to seal the edge. To avoid moisture penetration, mirrors should not be mounted directly against felt or felt paper and unpainted plaster, wood, or plywood.

When walls are entirely covered with mirrors, either in vertical panels or rectilinear stacked panels, the mirror edges must be flat polished with an appropriate thin 1/16 in. divider strip placed between all butt joints. In working with large areas, use a wood frame system, with members behind each vertical and horizontal joint, to allow for proper leveling.

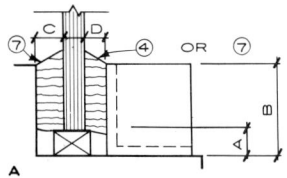

A
TAPE GLAZING

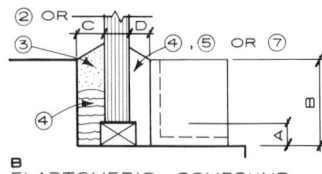

B
ELASTOMERIC COMPOUND WITH TAPE

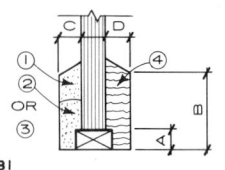

B1
OIL-BASE GLAZING COMPOUND & TAPE OR PREFORMED SEALANT

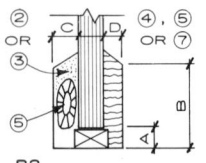

B2
TAPE AND PREFORMED SEALANT

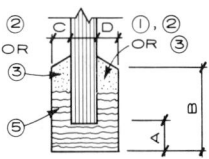

B3
OIL-BASE GLAZING COMPOUND WITH PREFORMED SEALANT

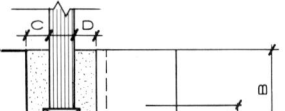

C
IMPREGNATED POLYURETHANE FOAM

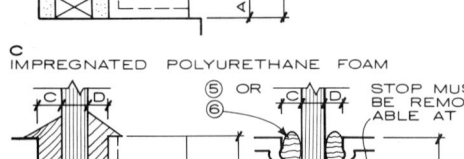

D
GASKET GLAZING

E
STOREFRONT SETTING AT HEAD & JAMBS (ROLL-IN BEADS)

STOP MUST BE REMOVABLE AT SILL

WEEP

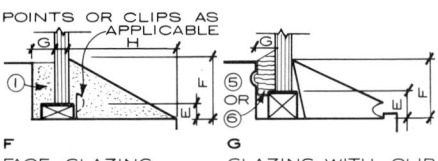

POINTS OR CLIPS AS APPLICABLE

F
FACE GLAZING (WOOD OR METAL)

G
GLAZING WITH CLIP (SLIDING WINDOWS & DOORS)

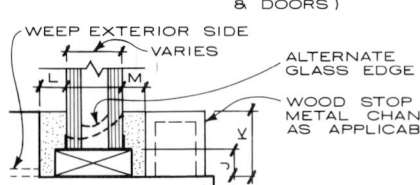

WEEP EXTERIOR SIDE
VARIES
ALTERNATE GLASS EDGE
WOOD STOP OR METAL CHANNEL AS APPLICABLE

H
GLAZING WITH STOP (WOOD OR METAL)

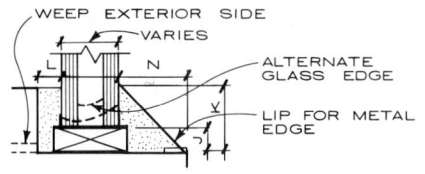

WEEP EXTERIOR SIDE
VARIES
ALTERNATE GLASS EDGE
LIP FOR METAL EDGE

I
FACE GLAZING (WOOD OR METAL)

GLAZING DETAILS: E, F, G, AND H EDGE CLEARANCES

GLASS TYPE	THICK-NESS (IN.)	GLASS AREA (SQ FT)	SIZE WIDTH HEIGHT (IN.)	E DIMENSION (IN.) ALLOW CLEARANCE FOR HEAD, SILL, JAMB	F DIMENSION (IN.) RABBET DEPTH (MIN.)	G DIMENSION (IN.) (MIN.)	H DIMENSION (IN.)
Sheet	ss $3/32$	5	40	$1/16$	$3/8$	$1/16$	$3/8$
	ss $3/32$	14	50	$1/6$	$7/16$	$1/8$	$3/8$
	ds $1/8$	5	40	$1/16$	$3/6$	$1/8$	$3/8$
	ds $1/8$	25	80	$1/8$	$7/16$	$1/8$	$3/8$
	hs $3/16$	25	120	$11/62$	$1/2$	$1/8$	$3/8$
	hs $3/16$	70	120	$15/62$	$5/8$	$1/8$	$3/8$
	hs $7/32$	25	120	$11/64$	$1/2$	$1/8$	$3/8$
	hs $7/32$	70	120	$15/64$	$5/8$	$1/8$	$3/8$
Spandrel and heat strengthened	$1/4$	25	80	$5/32$	$1/2$	$1/8$	$3/8$
	$1/4$	84	168	$1/4$	$5/8$	$1/8$	$3/8$
	$3/8$	25	80	$5/32$	$1/2$	$1/8$	$3/8$
	$3/8$	84	168	$1/4$	$5/8$	$1/8$	$3/8$
Flat glass	$1/8$	25	128	$11/64$	$1/2$	$1/8$	$3/8$
	$1/8$	67	128	$15/64$	$5/8$	$1/8$	$3/8$
	$1/4$	100	120	$11/64$	$1/2$	$1/8$	$3/8$
	$1/4$	140	156	$1/4$	$5/8$	$1/8$	$3/8$
	$1/4$	207	229	$11/32$	$3/4$	$1/8$	$3/8$
	$5/16$	207	229	$11/32$	$3/4$	$1/8$	$3/8$
	$3/8$	258	286	$3/8$	$3/4$	$1/8$	$3/8$
	$3/8$	258	286	$7/16$	$7/8$	$1/8$	$3/8$
	$1/2$	258	286	$7/16$	$7/8$	$1/8$	$3/8$

GLAZING DETAILS: A, B, C, AND D EDGE CLEARANCES

CLEAR-ANCE	SIZE (SQ FT)	THICKNESS (IN.)					C AND D DIMENSION
		$3/16$	$7/32$	$1/4$	$5/16$	$3/8 - 1/2$	
A edge	Up to 70	$1/4$	$1/4$	$1/4$	$1/4$	$1/4$	$1/8$
	Over 70 to 84			$1/4$	$1/4$	$1/4$	$1/8$
	Over 84			$1/4$	$1/4$	$9/32$	$1/8$
Rabbet depth B	Up to 25	$5/8$	$5/8$	$5/8$	$5/8$	$5/8$	$1/8$
	Over 25 to 70	$3/4$	$3/4$	$3/4$	$3/4$	$3/4$	$1/8$
	Over 70			$3/4$	$3/4$	$7/8$	$1/8$

GLAZING DETAILS: J, K, L, M, AND N EDGE CLEARANCES

GLASS TYPE	THICKNESS (IN.)		MAXIMUM (SQ FT)	MINIMUM DIMENSION (IN.)				
				J	K	L	M	N
Glass edge ss	$3/8$		To 10	$1/8$	$5/8$	$1/8$	$1/8$	$1/2$
Glass edge ds Metal edge	$7/16$		To 24	$1/8$	$5/8$	$1/8$	$1/8$	$1/2$
	$9/16$	$13/16$	12	$1/8$	$5/8$	$1/8$	$1/8$	$1/2$
Metal edge	$11/16$	$15/16$	27	$1/4$	$3/4$	$1/8$	$1/8$	$5/8$
Metal edge	$13/16$	$1-1/16$	70	$1/4$	$3/4$	$1/8$	$1/8$	$5/8$

SEALANT MATERIALS

1.	Oil base glazing compound	Wet
2.	Two-part rubber base compound—polysulfide	Wet
3.	One-part elastic compound—polysulfide, silicone	Wet
4.	Polybutene ribbon or tape	Wet
5.	Neoprene or butyl—cured*	Dry
6.	Polyvinyl chloride*	Dry
7.	Butyl ribbon or tape—partially cured	Wet

*Good practice requires that either inside or outside gaskets have welded corners.

NOTES

1. In all cases refer to current manufacturers' information.
2. Details shown apply also to thick glass, including insulating glass and panels.
3. Except in details B3 and D, use setting blocks at bottom edge and resilient spacer shims at all other edges.
4. For all glass over 6 sq ft in area, set setting blocks at quarter points.

ABBREVIATIONS

ss—single strength; ds—double strength; hs—heavy sheet.

SINGLE & DOUBLE GLAZING

NOM. GL. SIZE
NOM. FRAME SIZE

$1/8"$

MOUNTING ON METAL FRAME

NOM. GL. SIZE
NOM. FRAME SIZE

$1/4"$

MOUNTING ON PRECAST FRAME

NOM. GL. SIZE
NOM. FRAME SIZE

MOUNTING IN PVC REGLET

WEEP TO THE EXTERIOR

MOUNTING ON METAL FRAME

VERTICALLY STACKED

MULLION

STRUCTURAL GASKETS

Skidmore, Owings and Merrill

GLAZING

ACRYLIC PLASTIC AND POLYCARBONATE SHEETS

Both materials are relatively tough, break, shatter, or crack resistant thermoplastics. They are commonly used in the clear transparent form for glazing in schools, factories, skylights, domes, display cases, and protective shields for stained glass assemblies. Certain conditions of varying temperatures and/or humidity on opposing surfaces of a single light may cause it to bow in the direction of the higher temperature and/or humidity. Though this does not affect visibility, it may cause distorted reflections. The surfaces of these materials are susceptible to scratching and abrasions. Progress is being made in developing abrasion resistant coatings. As compared with clear glass of equal size and thickness, they maintain greater resistance to impact and breakage and are lighter in weight. Polycarbonates have softer surfaces and are more impact resistant than acrylics. Acrylics generally weather better than polycarbonates. Because of a somewhat higher coefficient of thermal expansion than in clear glass and other materials with which they are used in construction, acrylics and polycarbonates are subject to a greater degree of dimensional change. In applications that must allow for wide ranges of thermal expansion, avoid inflexible installation methods. Both may be produced with or without light absorbing properties. The allowable continuous service temperature for polycarbonates is slightly higher than that for acrylics. Both may be cold formed to a smooth arc if the resulting radius of curvature is at least 100 times the thickness of the sheet for polycarbonates (180 times for acrylics) and both are supported by curved channel supports following this radius.

Mirrored coatings applied to acrylic sheets are available for interior applications and may be installed with recommended contact cements, double faced tape, clip and channel mounting, and through fastening. Distortion problems indicate that they should not be used for precise image reflectance requirements.

Certain polycarbonate sheets may be used in some bullet resisting and burglar resisting applications.

Consult the manufacturers for current information. Refer to and adhere to all applicable codes and governing authorities on fire and safety.

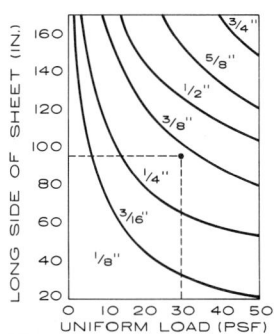

FLAT DOUBLE PANEL ON A JOB BUILT CURB

PLASTIC SKYLIGHT DETAIL

Skidmore, Owings & Merrill

POLYCARBONATE GLAZING

	POLY-CARBONATE SHEET THICKNESS	SHORT DIMEN-SION	RABBET DEPTH
Small lights	1/8″	24″	1/2″
Intermediate lights	3/16″ / 1/4″	36″ / 48″	3/4″ / 3/4″
Large lights	3/8″ / 1/2″	60″ / 72″	1″ / 1″

NOTES
1. Rabbet width is determined by sheet thickness plus sealant and tape as recommended by sealant tape manufacturers.
2. To select polycarbonate sheet thickness based on wind loads refer to manufacturers' information.

SMALL ACRYLIC LIGHTS

Major dimension to 24″
Minimum thickness—0.100″
Minimum rabbet depth 7/16″

INTERMEDIATE ACRYLIC LIGHTS

ACRYLIC THICK-NESS	MAXIMUM SASH OPENING SQUARE	RECTAN-GULAR	RABBET DIMENSIONS DEPTH	WIDTH
0.125″	40″ x 40″	30″ x 42″	1/2″	3/8″
0.125″	55″ x 55″	36″ x 68″	3/4″	3/8″
0.187″	42″ x 42″	30″ x 45″	1/2″	7/16″
0.187″	63″ x 63″	36″ x 72″	3/4″	7/16″
0.250″	44″ x 44″	30″ x 46″	1/2″	1/2″
0.250″	69″ x 69″	36″ x 72″	3/4″	1/2″

LARGE ACRYLIC LIGHTS

ACRYLIC THICKNESS	LONG DIMENSIONS	RABBET DIMENSIONS* DEPTH	WIDTH
3/16″	72″ to 108″	1″	9/16″
1/4″	72″ to 108″	1″	5/8″
1/4″	108″ to 144″	1 1/8″	3/4″
3/8″	72″ to 108″	1″	3/4″
3/8″	108″ to 144″	1 1/8″	7/8″
1/2″	108″ to 144″	1 1/8″	1″
5/8″	108″ to 144″	1 1/8″	1 1/8″

* When darker (less than 60% light transmittance) transparent tints of acrylic plastic are used, rabbet depth shown above should be increased by 1/4″ to allow for greater thermal expansion resulting from solar energy absorption.

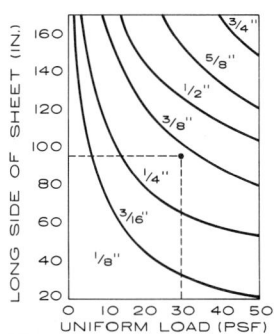

ACRYLIC GLAZING GRAPH
Design load data—large area acrylic glazing

Problem:
Size = 48 x 96 in.
Design load = 30 psf

Solution:
Select 1/4 in.
Sheet thickness

Data apply to square and rectangular lights of acrylic sheets when the length is no more than three times the width. All edges continuously held.

Sheet thickness section is based on total deflection under uniform load limited to 5% of the short side, or 3 in., whichever is smaller.

PLASTIC SHEET EXPANSION ALLOWANCE

SASH LENGTH OR HEIGHT	REDUCE PLASTIC GLAZING LENGTH OR HEIGHT CLEAR ACRYLIC	POLYCARBONATE
0″ to 12″	1/16″	1/16″
12″ to 24″	1/16″	1/8″
24″ to 36″	1/16″	3/16″
36″ to 48″	1/8″	1/4″
48″ to 60″	1/8″	5/16″
60″ to 72″	3/16″	3/8″
72″ to 84″	3/16″	7/16″
84″ to 96″	3/16″	1/2″
96″ to 132″	1/4″	—
132″ to 144″	5/16″	—

NOTE: Both length and height must be reduced according to this table.

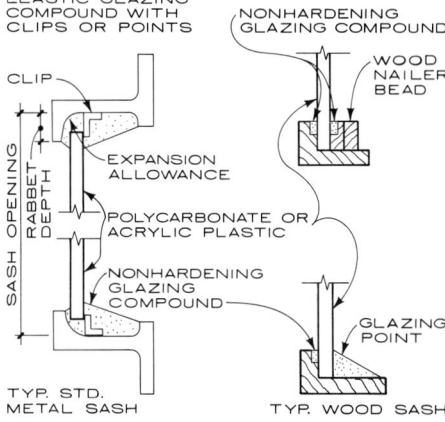

SMALL LIGHTS

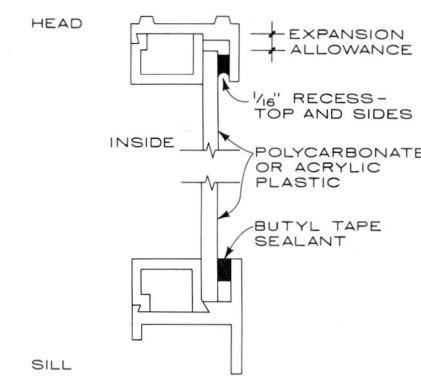

INTERMEDIATE LIGHTS

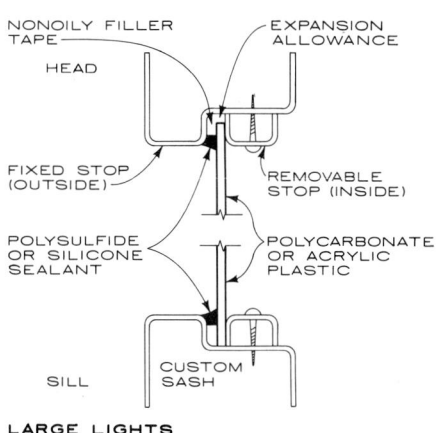

LARGE LIGHTS

PLASTIC GLAZING DETAILS

GLAZING 8

EXAMPLES	EXTERIOR DESIGN ELEMENTS				FRAME DESIGN ELEMENTS			
	WINDBREAKS Arborvitae, basket weave fence, open masonry wall	**SHADES** Sunscreen, louvers, awnings, architectural projections	**COVERINGS** Roll blinds, shutters, storm sash	**SUN ORIENTATION** South facing windows	**INSULATED FRAMES** Wood or metal with a thermal break	**OPENING TYPE** Casement, awning, double hung, sliding, pivoting, and hopper	**WEATHER-STRIP** Pile, vinyl, foam, brass, or copper	**HARDWARE** Latches, operating devices, locks, and hinges
A. Airtightness B. Watertightness	Reduced potential for water or air leakage to the extent that the windbreak shields the window, reducing wind and water velocity	Reduced potential for water or air leakage to the extent the device shields the window. Provide positive drainage for trapped water. Lack of drainage and freezing can cause air and water leakage		May or may not coincide with optimum orientation for prevailing summer breezes versus winter wind. Correct conflicting orientation requirements by using other design elements	As important as insulating value. Performance varies greatly with quality of window and type of operation. Hinged windows tend to be more airtight than vertical or horizontal sliding units. Excellent to minimum performance: 0.1 to 0.5 cfm per crack foot at 26 mph wind, ASTM E283-73 test. Note: specify manufacturer's production average. Provide positive drainage and keep weeps clear. Hopper, awning, and jalousie provide some rain protection when open		Ease of replacement essential. Keep paint off pile or foam weatherstrip	By cam action hardware can force tight closure of sash. Improper design can twist frame, causing increased air and water infiltration
C. Natural ventilation	May alter summer wind direction and increase or decrease local velocity	May impede natural ventilation. Even insect screen reduces airflow by 50%				Direction and axis of opening directs airflow. Openable free area critical	Pile type W, fin desirable for sliding units; use compression or spring type for hinged units	May limit how window opens, thus affecting quantity and quality of ventilation
D. Insulation	Reduce rate of erosion of insulating layer of air at surface of glass to the extent window is shielded from wind	Dead airspace between covering and window insulates. More airtight coverings better		Sol-air temperature useful concept. See ASHRAE Handbook of Fundamentals	Should be specified with multiple glazing in moderate and severe climates			
E. Solar admittance	Overgrown planted windbreaks can block beneficial solar energy	Ventilate space between window and shade at top and bottom. Remove or adjust to admit winter sun	Reduced solar gain according to shading coefficient. Adjust to admit winter sun	Locate spaces to receive winter sun during time of occupancy	Broadface area of frame reduces glass area and solar gain per window			
F. Day lighting	Overgrown planted windbreaks can block daylight	Too much shading can necessitate expensive electric lighting. Ideally, device should reflect light to ceiling for maximum depth of daylight penetration into room		Intensive solar exposure for winter heating may cause glare. Provide control, using design elements	Frame interior faces should be light in color to reduce contrast glare. Position window head near ceiling for maximum room depth of daylight penetration			
G. Visual separation	Opportunity to provide privacy as desired	Some types as seen from outside are opaque during day but transparent at night						
H. Acoustical isolation	Principal benefit is psychological; provide minimal actual sound isolation	Decreases as distance of noise increases. Overhangs can reflect noise to the window	Can be effective if airtight and layers not same thickness or density		Airtightness critical to "sound tightness"			
I. Safety	Depending on distance from window, could keep children away from window	Projections within 7 ft of grade may be hazardous to pedestrians	Can reduce frequency or severity of breakage related accidents			Windows projecting in or out can be hazardous, depending on location	Should not require excessive force to open or close window	Can limit opening dimensions to prevent children from falling out
J. Access/egress	Must be located so as not to block emergency access or egress	Must be easily removable from inside for emergency exiting through code required egress windows. Must not reduce area or dimension below minimum required			Must not interfere with easy exiting	Typical exit window: 3 sq ft min. area, 16 in. min. dimension, 44 in. max. sill height	Should not inhibit the easy opening of windows used for emergency egress	Should facilitate rapid opening for emergency egress
K. Ease of operation	Accumulated organic debris may reduce ease of operation	Interior operation of exterior devices desirable to meet changing exterior conditions or interior requirements			Frame rigidity must prevent distortion of sash or frame during operation	Location affects ease of operation of different window types	Should not require excessive force to open or close window	Gear reduction or leverage can increase ease of operation
L. Forced entry resistance	May provide cover for intruders or act as partial barrier	May deter intruders, depending on ease of removal or noise from breakage. Locked shutters or roll blinds very effective			Rigidity of frame and sash important to resist prying	No exposed removable hinges. Sash or glass should be removable from inside only	Soft weatherstripping can permit insertion of wire to unlock window	Function, quality, placement, and anchorage critical to security
M. Durability/ maintenance	Require pruning, feeding, watering (plants), painting (fences)	Must withstand wind, rain, ice, and intense solar radiation. May require seasonal removal. Some are self-storing—e.g., roller awnings. Detail installation to avoid staining adjacent materials			Thermal break material must be UV stable or protected from sunlight	The more movable parts, the greater the possible need for maintenance	Must be detailed to permit periodic replacement	

S. Robert Hastings and Porter Driscoll, AIA, Architect; Center for Building Technology, National Bureau of Standards; Washington, D.C.

ENVIRONMENTAL FACTORS

GLAZING DESIGN ELEMENTS				INTERIOR DESIGN ELEMENTS				
MULTI-GLAZING Fused edge or organically sealed insulating glass	**REFLECTIVE GLAZING** Reflective coated glass or films	**PLASTIC GLAZING** Polycarbonate (pc), or acrylic (ac) sheet	**GLASS BLOCK** Hollow masonry units of glass	**INTERIOR SHADING** Venetian or vertical blinds, open weave drapery	**INTERIOR COVERINGS** Roll shades, inside storm sash, heavy drapery, shutters	**INTEGRATED LIGHTING** Task lighting, light sensing automatic controls	**INTERIOR MASS** Masonry, concrete, stone, water	**EXAMPLES**
		Large thermal movement requires large edge clearance, deep containment, gaskets, or flexible sealants	Seal at joint between adjacent construction and glass block important, expansion can be great	Negligible	Solid weather-stripped shutters improve airtightness			A. Airtightness
Drain sill channels well to prevent failure of organic edge seal of glass							Water container seams critical. Also see (M) below	B. Water-tightness
		See ease of operation	Operable vents available that fit block module	Concurrent shading and ventilation desirable	Closed mode may preclude natural ventilation		Mass cooled by night air can provide daytime cooling	C. Natural ventilation
Storm = 0.5 Double = 0.6 (1/2″ space)	Single glass U-value (winter) = 1.10		12″ sq face 1 cavity = 0.52 2 cavity = 0.44	Minimal if free movement of room air between device and window	Depends on airtightness of covering and tightness of edge fit		Daytime heat loss reduced because mass absorbs heat, reducing overheating of space	D. Insulation
	I. R. refl. ≅ 0.7 Sol. refl. ≅ 0.9	Polycarbonate or acrylic = 1.06						
1/8″ glass: shading coeff. (sc) = 1.0, % sol transmission (sol) = 87				Shading coeff. 1/8″ gl = 1.0 ven. blind = 0.6* open weave curtains = 0.8* roll shutters = 0.3* tight weave curtains = 0.3* *closed			Solar heat absorbed by mass permits greater glass area, without overheating	E. Solar admittance
(1/8 + 1/8) clear: sc = 0.89 % sol = 69	Low example sc = 0.38 % sol = 17	sc = 0.98 ac = 0.98 pc % sol = 85 ac = 82 pc	High example sc = 0.65 % sol = 60					
1/8″ glass: % visible transmission (vis) = 90				Experimental reflective ven. blind. Contact: 1 Oak Ridge Lab 2 Lawrence Berkeley Lab	Can be effective for complete blackout	Daylight sensing control operation: on/off or continuous dimming	Dark color for solar absorption reduces room daylighting	F. Day lighting
% vis = 81	Low example % vis = 15	% vis = 92 ac = 88 pc	High example % vis = 75					
	Tend to distort color rendition of view and correct sense of time	Scratches can detract from quality of view out	View out/in distorted or entirely obscured depending on type	See exterior shading and coverings			"Trombe" walls provide complete visual separation and passive solar heat	G. Visual separation
1/8″ single glass sound transmission (vis) = 90				Negligible	Depends on airtightness as in (D) above	No ballast hum with daylight	Mass provides the best acoustical isolation if no penetrations	H. Acoustical isolation
1/2″ cavity = 32 6″ cavity = 40		1/4″ thick = 29 ac = 31 pc	Stand blk. = 38 Solid blk. = 45					
Insulating glass eliminates hazard of installing/removing storm sash	May cause disorienting glare to pedestrians/drivers	Reduced probability of breakage related accidents		May help prevent direct contact with glass in impact situations			Additives for water may be toxic. Caution in disposal	I. Safety
See (L) below	Avoid creating reflections that could confuse emergency exiting	Popout gasketing desirable for egress through fixed units	Essentially impenetrable for emergency egress	Should not hide windows, thus reducing the likelihood of their use for emergency egress, nor impede any quick opening qualities				J. Access/egress
Increased weight makes operation more difficult due to inertia, friction	Requires no management by the occupant	Decreased weight makes operation easier		Good ease of operation due to greater accessibility, increased likelihood of effective use		No occupant operation required with automatic controls	No operation required	K. Ease of operation
Greater hazard to enter/exit through broken-out window	Impedes outside daytime surveillance	1/8″ glass (1/4 lb steel ball dropped on 12″ sq sample) = 24″ drop		Can prevent burglar's surveillance of interior	Can discourage penetration if locked closed	Controls can be integrated with security system		L. Forced entry resistance
		ac = 72″ to 1000″ pc = 1000″	Stand blk. = 200″ Solid = marred at 320″					
Durability of edge seal of insulating glazing critical	Ideally reflective surface is on a cavity surface of insulating glass	Easily scratched. May increase frequency of replacement	Very durable	Periodic removal/cleaning make ease of removal desirable		Increased daylight use increases lamp life	Water may require antifreeze, rust inhibitor, or algicide	M. Durability maintenance

S. Robert Hastings and Porter Driscoll, AIA, Architect; Center for Building Technology, National Bureau of Standards; Washington, D.C.

SWINGING DOOR ASSEMBLIES

A door, in addition to providing a portal for entry, should resist unwanted intruders. This resistance can be accommodated by requiring that all exterior doors comply with ANSI/ASTM standard F476-76 Standard Test Methods for Security of Swinging Door Assemblies. The security of a door assembly depends not only on the lock but also on the strike, buck, hinge, door, and even the surrounding wall. Test requirements included in the ANSI/ASTM standard are based on the most common burglary attacks and include requirements for the entire door assembly and components. Criteria for four grades are included—from Grade 10 for the minimum level to a Grade 40 for a high level of resistance.

GRADE SELECTION FACTORS

GRADE 10
Minimum security level; adequate for single family residential buildings located in stable, comparatively low crime areas.

GRADE 20
Low to medium security level; provides security for residential buildings located in average crime rate areas or for apartments in both low and average crime rate areas.

GRADE 30
Medium to high security level; provides security for residential buildings located in higher than average crime rate areas or for small commercial buildings in average or low crime rate areas.

GRADE 40
High security level; provides security for commercial buildings located in medium to high crime rate areas.

The following items should be considered when designing and selecting components for an entrance door:

1. LOCATION: If the doorway is hidden from public view, or if security lighting is not provided, a higher grade is required than that normally used in the area.
2. ACCESS: If entry is controlled by a guard or protected by a detection device, a lower grade should be adequate.
3. USE: If the doorway provides access to particularly valuable or desirable property, a higher grade is required.
4. TYPE: In a double door, each door should be tested. If the door has solid or glazed panels make sure they meet the test requirements; mail slots are not recommended in the door.

SUGGESTED MATERIALS AND METHODS FOR DOORS

1. GRADE 40: Hollow metal steel doors, 16 gauge.
2. GRADE 30: Hollow metal, 18 gauge; flush wood, lumber core, 1³/₄ in. thick.
3. GRADE 20: Flush wood, particle core, 1³/₄ in. thick, lock block of dense solid wood at least 6 in. wide x 24 in. high. Hinge blocks, 6 in. wide, x 12 in. high.
4. GRADE 10: Flush wood, particle core, 1³/₄ in. thick; wood panel door with minimum thickness of panel at ¹/₂ in. including rebate, stiles minimum dimension 1³/₄ x 6 in.

NOTE: A lock installation in wood doors can weaken that area unless the lock, in effect, reinforces its required void.

VISION PANELS

Not recommended unless polycarbonate or laminated glass is used; sidelights should also be of polycarbonate or laminated glass; vision panels and sidelights should be unremovable from the outside; make sure that all glazing within 36 in. of door lock meets test requirements; use a peephole if vision panel is not practical.

FRAME

The stiffness of the bucks is critical; wood bucks should be a minimum of 2 in. thick and have solid, secure shims for 24 in. at the locking point and 12 in. at each hinge point; stops should be milled integral with the buck; wood bucks for Grade 20 should be of hard wood premium grade; Grade 20 bucks should be 16 gauge steel; Grade 40 bucks should be 15 gauge steel; all steel bucks should be grouted full.

STRIKE

The strike plate is a critical element in any doorway; it must be strong and secured against failure when

DOOR PERFORMANCE REQUIREMENTS—SUMMARY OF ANSI/ASTM F476-76

COMPONENT/TEST		GRADE 10	GRADE 20	GRADE 30	GRADE 40
DOOR					
1. Impact resistance		(Equivalent to an average man) 2 blows at 59 ft-lb force	(Strong man) Grade 10 requirements + 2 blows at 89 ft-lb force	(Man with sledge) Grade 20 requirements + 2 blows at 118 ft-lb force	(2 men with ram) Grade 30 requirements + 2 blows at 148 ft-lb force
VISION PANEL					
2. Impact resistance		(Equivalent to an average man + hammer) 1 blow at 74 ft-lb force	(Average man + hammer) 2 blows at 74 ft-lb force	(Average man + hammer) 5 blows at 74 ft-lb force	(Average man + hammer) 10 blows at 74-ft lb force
BUCKS					
3. Jimmying resistance		(Equivalent to a screw driver) 1350 lb force	(Short pry bar) 1800 lb force	(Long pry bar) 3600 lb force	(Auto jack) 4950 lb force
4. Impact resistance of strike plate		Same as #1	Same as #1	Same as #1	Same as #1
LOCK					
5. BOLT	Impact	Same as #1	Same as #1	Same as #1	Same as #1
	End pressure	150 lb force	150 lb force	150 lb force	150 lb force
6. CYLINDER	Tension	290 lb force	1080 lb force	2470 lb force	3600 lb force
	Torque	n.a.	n.a.	81 lb force—ft	118 lb force—ft
	Impact	n.a.	n.a.	5 blows at 74 ft-lb force	10 blows at 74 ft-lb force
7. KNOB (key-in)	Impact	Same as #2	Same as #2	Same as #2	Same as #2
	Torque	18.5 lb force—ft	37 lb force—ft	81 lb force—ft	118 lb force—ft
HINGES		For outswinging doors, pins must be nonremovable			
8. Impact resistance		Same as #1	Same as #1	Same as #1	Same as #1

NOTE: These forces are applied with equipment and methods specified in the Standard. In addition, the assembly cannot be "manipulated" or disassembled from outside.

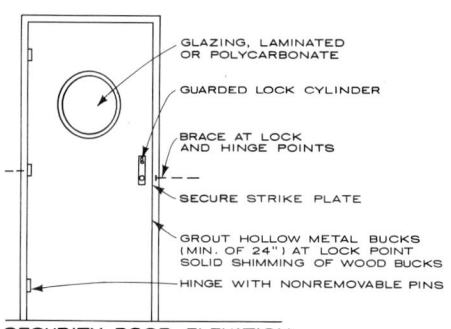

SECURITY DOOR ELEVATION

- GLAZING, LAMINATED OR POLYCARBONATE
- GUARDED LOCK CYLINDER
- BRACE AT LOCK AND HINGE POINTS
- SECURE STRIKE PLATE
- GROUT HOLLOW METAL BUCKS (MIN. OF 24") AT LOCK POINT SOLID SHIMMING OF WOOD BUCKS
- HINGE WITH NONREMOVABLE PINS

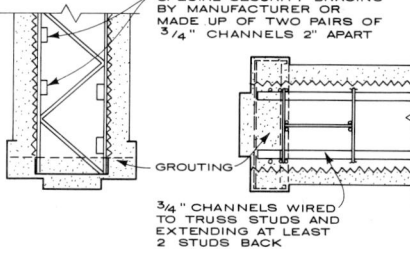

DOOR BUCK DETAIL — HEAD — JAMB

- SPECIAL SECURITY BRACING BY MANUFACTURER OR MADE UP OF TWO PAIRS OF ³/₄" CHANNELS 2" APART
- GROUTING
- ³/₄" CHANNELS WIRED TO TRUSS STUDS AND EXTENDING AT LEAST 2 STUDS BACK

NOTE: Brace at lock point is essential; brace at hinge points for additional security. If two hinges, braces required at both; if three hinges, brace only at middle hinge. Braces should extend two studs back.

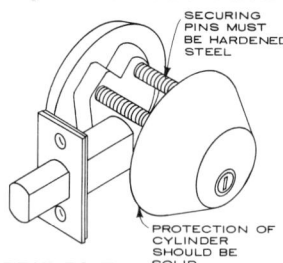

DEAD BOLT

- SECURING PINS MUST BE HARDENED STEEL
- PROTECTION OF CYLINDER SHOULD BE SOLID

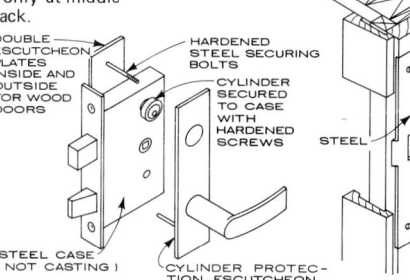

MORTISE LOCK

- DOUBLE ESCUTCHEON PLATES INSIDE AND OUTSIDE FOR WOOD DOORS
- HARDENED STEEL SECURING BOLTS
- CYLINDER SECURED TO CASE WITH HARDENED SCREWS
- STEEL CASE (NOT CASTING)
- CYLINDER PROTECTION, ESCUTCHEON

STRIKE PLATE

- SHIM SOLID FOR 24" (12" ABOVE AND BELOW) AT LOCK POINT
- PRIME SCREWS SET BACK FROM FACE
- SCREWS ARE LONG ENOUGH TO SECURE TO SUBFRAMING
- STEEL
- 10" OR MORE

attacked; the standard strike plate is usually not adequate for a wood buck; this can be accommodated by securing the strike plate to the subframing or reinforcing the buck.

WALL

Fire stops or braces should be located at the lock point and each hinge point—for one stud space at Grade 10, two stud spaces for Grade 20 and above; if wood studs appear, plywood sheathing should be used on both sides of the studs for two stud spaces to each side of the doorway; if it is a masonry wall, grout all space between frame and wall.

HARDWARE

All entry doors should have a dead locking bolt with a minimum projection of ⁵/₈ in. for Grades 10 and 20 and ³/₄ in. for Grades 30 and 40; key-in-knob locks are not recommended except for Grade 10, and they must have a deadlocking device or latch guard. A manufacturer could, however, provide a key-in-knob lock that will pass tests for Grade 20 under certain restrictions specified (i.e., that they be used with particular doors and frames); Grade 40 locks should be pick resistant, with special pin tumblers; Grade 20 and above locks should have tempered securing bolts, a minimum of ¹/₄ in. diameter, and be secured directly to the cylinder; stop works are not recommended for mortise locks requiring a security rating; lock cases of cast material are not recommended; Grade 40 locks should have at least hardened steel bolts.

John Stroik, Architect and Porter Driscoll, AIA, Architect; Center for Building Technology, National Bureau of Standards; Washington, D.C.

SECURITY

WINDOW UNITS

Window units should at least comply with ANSI/ASTM F 588-79 Standard Test Methods for Resistance of Window Assemblies to Forced Entry, for a minimum grade performance, and with NILECJ-STD-0316 Physical Security of Window Units, for higher grade performance. As with a door assembly, the security of a window does not rely on the lock alone.

Windows are tested only as complete units installed in a particular test wall or in a wall duplicating their intended location.

Since glass is subject to breakage, the type of glazing and method of securing the glazing are important. Regular glass can be used with Grade 10 doors, since the danger and noise of breaking glass is a limited deterrent. Locks should be dead locking (fixed in locked position, resistant to pressure on bolt) and located at opposite corners; cam locks are not recommended. If sash is removable or reversible for window washing, lock for this operation should be inside; hinges should not be accessible.

The following items should be considered when designing and selecting windows:

1. LOCATION: If accessible (residential: 12 ft vertical, 6 ft horizontal; commercial: 18 ft vertical, 10 ft horizontal) and hidden from public view, a higher grade is required.
2. PROTECTED: If windows are protected by a detection device, shutters, security screens, or bars, the window grade could be irrelevant. If security screens, bars, or shutters are used, requirements for fire exiting must be met.

MATERIALS AND METHODS FOR WINDOWS

1. CLASS IV (Grade 40): Very heavy fixed frames with laminated glass over 1/4 in. thick or security screen, bars, or shutters with special locking device.
2. CLASS III (Grade 30): Heavy duty sash with laminated glass over 1/4 in. thick or polycarbonate glazing 1/4 in. thick. Lock should include at least two heavy duty dead locking bolts.
3. CLASS II (Grade 20): Heavy duty sash with laminated glass or polycarbonate glazing; if wood, sash must be reinforced or heavy; double locks required.
4. CLASS I (Grade 10): Regular glazing in commercial sash with double locks; can be wood frame.

ATTACK PREVENTION METHODS FOR WINDOWS

WINDOW ATTACKS	PREVENTION
Break glazing—reach in to open and enter	Laminated or polycarbonate glazing, security grill/screen, key operated locks and small openings
Pry or break—sash frame and open	Heavy or reinforced sash frame and dead bolts
Disassemble component(s) and open	All fasteners concealed from outside
Loiding (slip-knife) or break lock and open	Interlocking meeting member Deadlocking with "strong" bolt

NOTE: Particular criteria can be specified by using the referenced standards.

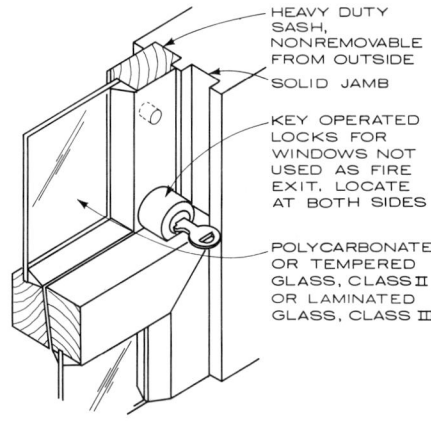

HEAVY DUTY SASH, NONREMOVABLE FROM OUTSIDE
SOLID JAMB
KEY OPERATED LOCKS FOR WINDOWS NOT USED AS FIRE EXIT. LOCATE AT BOTH SIDES
POLYCARBONATE OR TEMPERED GLASS, CLASS II OR LAMINATED GLASS, CLASS III

DOUBLE HUNG WINDOW

WINDOW PERFORMANCE REQUIREMENTS—SUMMARY OF NILECJ-STD. 0316

COMPONENT/TEST	CLASS I (GRADE 10)	CLASS II (GRADE 20)	CLASS III (GRADE 30)	CLASS IV (GRADE 40)
LOCK				
1. Stability	50 cycles of unlocking motion			
2. Strength	49 lb force load	151 lb force load	300 lb force load	753 lb force load
SASH				
3. Strength	49 lb force primary load	100 lb force primary load	100 lb force primary load	100 lb force primary load
	49 lb force secondary load	151 lb force secondary load	300 lb force secondary load	753 lb force secondary load
4. Impact	n.a.	1 at 37 ft-lb force	1 at 74 ft-lb force	10 at 74 ft-lb force
GLASS				
5. Impact	n.a.	1 at 37 ft-lb force	1 at 74 ft-lb force	10 at 74 ft-lb force

NOTE: Based on information supplied by National Institute for Law Enforcement and Criminal Justice; LEAA; Department of Justice.

SLIDING DOOR UNITS

Sliding glass doors are a particular concern in securing a building. Performance requirements specified in the NILECJ-STD-0318, Physical Security of Sliding Glass Door Units should be complied with.

Sliding glass doors are tested only as complete units installed in a particular test wall or in a wall duplicating their intended location. As in windows, the glazing is critical, and polycarbonate or glazing is recommended. At this writing, tests for higher grades of security have not been developed, but a modification of the tests for swinging doors could be used; security shutters and detection devices should be considered for higher security locations.

The locking devices should include vertical rod, or lever bolts, at top and bottom; the frame should be solid or reinforced at the locking points; the stile must also be reinforced at the lock points. The operating panels should be designed so that they cannot be lifted out of their tracks when in the locked position.

Glazing and other components should be installed from the inside so that entry cannot be gained by disassembly. As with windows and other doors, a hidden location requires a higher grade.

ATTACK PREVENTION METHODS FOR DOORS

DOOR ATTACKS	PREVENTION
Bodily force—kicking, shoving, pushing, lifting (sliding doors), ramming	"Strong" door, lock, bolt, strike, and frame Sliding door, nonremovable when locked
Bolt attacks (a) Loiding (slip-knife) (b) Cutting (c) Prying and spreading	(a) Dead bolt (b) "Strong" dead bolt (c) Stiff bucks
Lock attacks (a) Smashing cylinder (b) Pulling out the cylinder core (c) Wrenching the cylinder (d) Picking	(a) "Strong" cylinder and case (b) Fail-safe core attachment (c) Cylinder guard (d) Special cylinder core
Disassemble component(s) and open	All fasteners concealed from the outside; nonremovable hinge pins
Break panel (glass or solid), unlock door by reaching in	Laminated or polycarbonate glazing, peephole viewer, double cylinder lock

SLIDING GLASS DOOR PERFORMANCE REQUIREMENTS— SUMMARY OF NILECJ-STD. 0318

COMPONENT/TEST	CLASS I (GRADE 10)	CLASS II (GRADE 20)	CLASS III & IV (GRADE 30 + 40)
LOCK			
1. Stability	50 lb force horiz. + (50 lb force + weight of panel) – ten times at each bottom corner	50 lb force horiz. + (50 lb force + weight of panel) – ten times at each bottom corner	Not applicable at this time— if custom design is desired, the manufacturer should increase the criteria proportionally or shutters and grilles should be used
2. Strength	301 lb force	600 lb force	
PANEL			
3. Removal	101 lb force horiz. 301 lb force + panel weight – vert.	101 lb force horiz. 600 lb force + panel weight – vert.	
4. Meeting stile strength	151 lb force	301 lb force	
GLASS			
5. Impact	4 impacts—1 each 74; 143; 222; 295 ft-lb force	10 impacts—1 each 74; 148; 222; 295; 369; 443; 517; 590; 664; 738 ft-lb force	

NOTE: These forces are applied with equipment and methods specified in the Standards. In addition, windows and sliding door units cannot be manipulated or disassembled from outside. Based on information supplied by National Institute for Law Enforcement and Criminal Justice; LEAA, Department of Justice.

John Stroik, Architect and Porter Driscoll, AIA, Architect; Center for Building Technology, National Bureau of Standards; United States of America

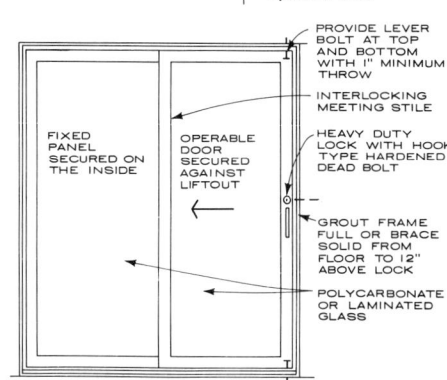

PROVIDE LEVER BOLT AT TOP AND BOTTOM WITH 1" MINIMUM THROW
INTERLOCKING MEETING STILE
HEAVY DUTY LOCK WITH HOOK TYPE HARDENED DEAD BOLT
GROUT FRAME FULL OR BRACE SOLID FROM FLOOR TO 12" ABOVE LOCK
POLYCARBONATE OR LAMINATED GLASS
FIXED PANEL SECURED ON THE INSIDE
OPERABLE DOOR SECURED AGAINST LIFTOUT

SLIDING GLASS DOOR

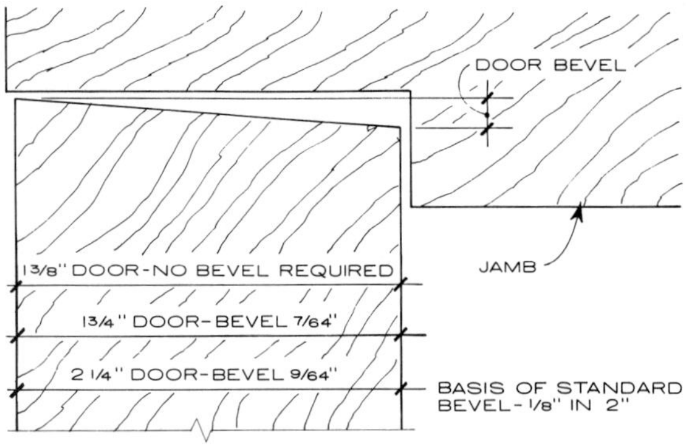

13/8" DOOR-NO BEVEL REQUIRED

13/4" DOOR-BEVEL 7/64'

2 1/4" DOOR-BEVEL 9/64'

DOOR BEVEL

JAMB

BASIS OF STANDARD
BEVEL- 1/8" IN 2"

DOOR BEVELS

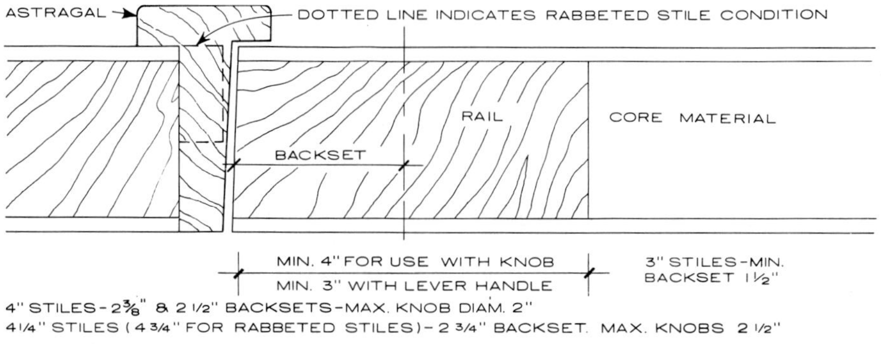

ASTRAGAL   DOTTED LINE INDICATES RABBETED STILE CONDITION

RAIL   CORE MATERIAL

BACKSET

MIN. 4" FOR USE WITH KNOB
MIN. 3" WITH LEVER HANDLE

3" STILES-MIN.
BACKSET 1 1/2"

4" STILES- 2 3/8" & 2 1/2" BACKSETS-MAX. KNOB DIAM. 2"
4 1/4" STILES (4 3/4" FOR RABBETED STILES)-2 3/4" BACKSET. MAX. KNOBS 2 1/2"

DOUBLE DOORS WITH FLAT ASTRAGAL (ALSO APPLIES TO DOORS WITH RABBETED MEETING STILES)

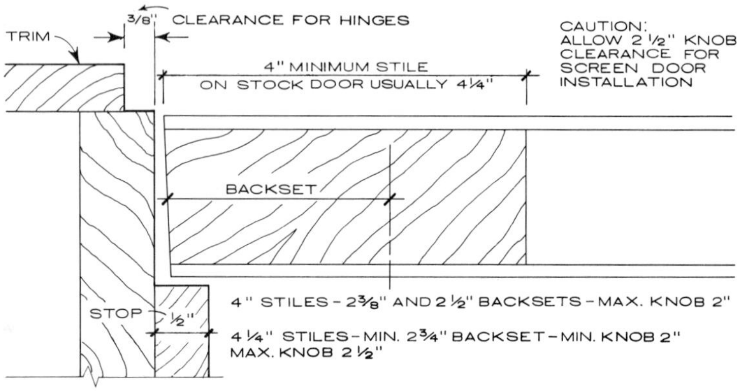

TRIM   3/8" CLEARANCE FOR HINGES

4" MINIMUM STILE
ON STOCK DOOR USUALLY 4 1/4"

CAUTION:
ALLOW 2 1/2" KNOB
CLEARANCE FOR
SCREEN DOOR
INSTALLATION

BACKSET

STOP 1/2"

4" STILES - 2 3/8" AND 2 1/2" BACKSETS - MAX. KNOB 2"
4 1/4" STILES-MIN. 2 3/4" BACKSET-MIN. KNOB 2"
MAX. KNOB 2 1/2"

DOOR WITH KNOB USING CYLINDER LOCK

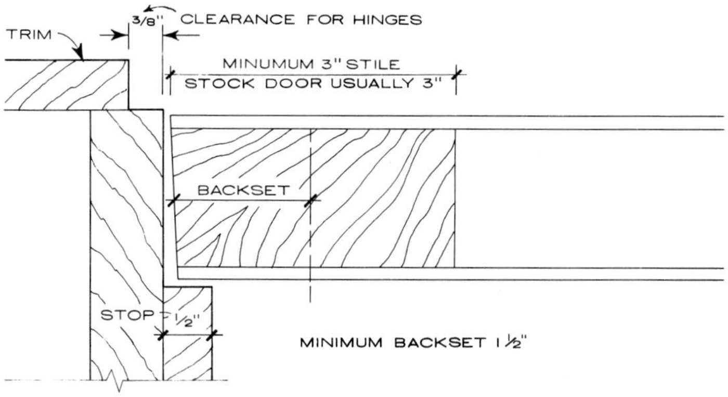

TRIM   3/8" CLEARANCE FOR HINGES

MINIMUM 3" STILE
STOCK DOOR USUALLY 3"

BACKSET

STOP 1/2"

MINIMUM BACKSET 1 1/2"

DOOR WITH LEVER HANDLE USING CYLINDER LOCK

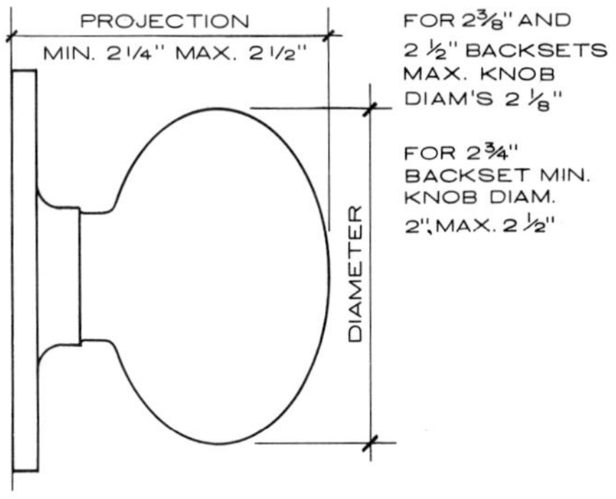

PROJECTION
MIN. 2 1/4" MAX. 2 1/2"

FOR 2 3/8" AND
2 1/2" BACKSETS
MAX. KNOB
DIAM'S 2 1/8"
FOR 2 3/4"
BACKSET MIN.
KNOB DIAM.
2", MAX. 2 1/2"

DIAMETER

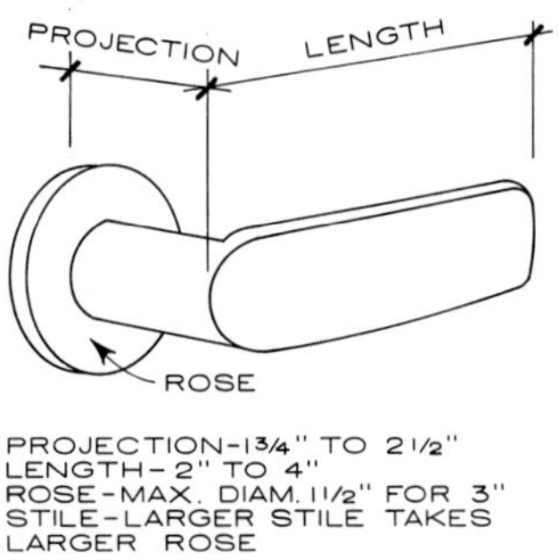

DOOR KNOBS

PROJECTION   LENGTH

ROSE

PROJECTION-1 3/4" TO 2 1/2"
LENGTH-2" TO 4"
ROSE-MAX. DIAM. 1 1/2" FOR 3"
STILE-LARGER STILE TAKES
LARGER ROSE

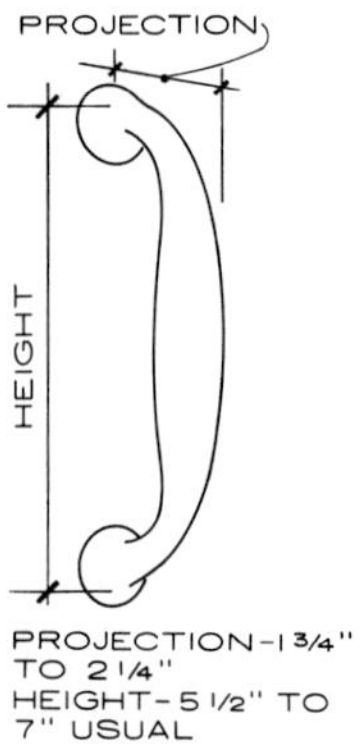

LEVER HANDLES

PROJECTION

HEIGHT

PROJECTION-1 3/4"
TO 2 1/4"
HEIGHT-5 1/2" TO
7" USUAL

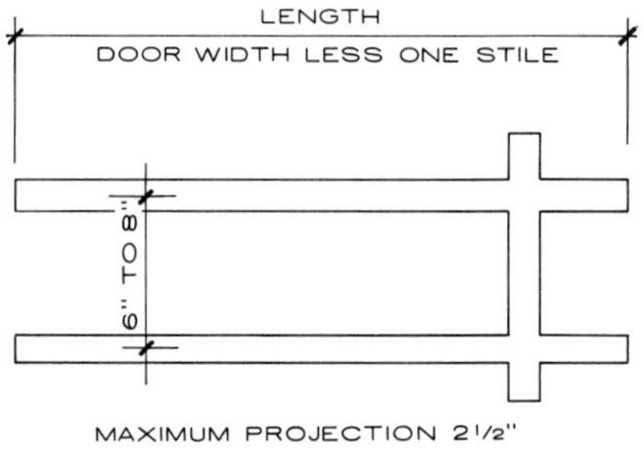

DOOR PULL

LENGTH
DOOR WIDTH LESS ONE STILE

6" TO 8"

MAXIMUM PROJECTION 2 1/2"

PUSH BARS

NOTE: FOR MOUNTING HEIGHTS SEE NEXT PAGE - REFER TO MANUFACTURER'S CATALOGS FOR EXACT HARDWARE SIZES AND DIMENSIONS

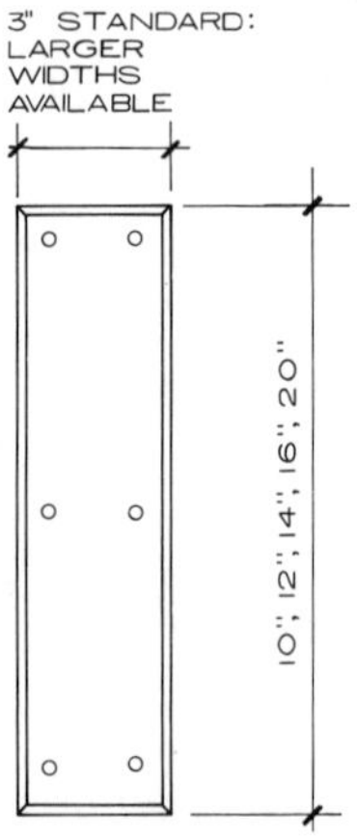

3" STANDARD:
LARGER
WIDTHS
AVAILABLE

10",12",14",16", 20"

PUSH PLATE

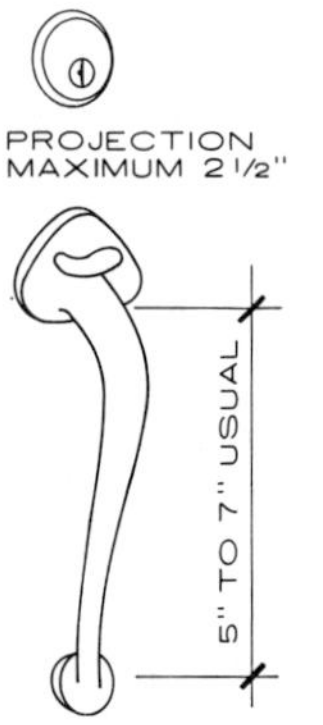

PROJECTION
MAXIMUM 2 1/2"

5" TO 7" USUAL

**ENTRANCE
HANDLE**

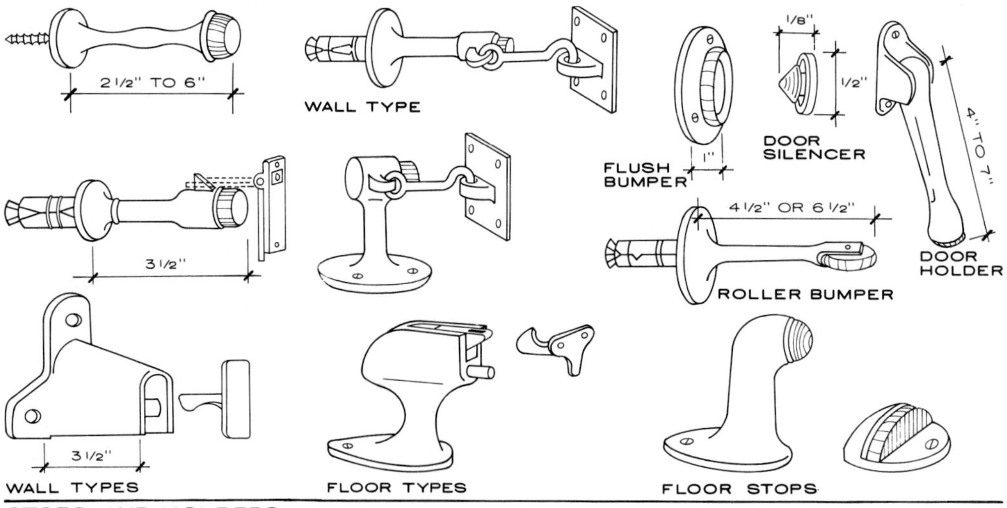

2 1/2" TO 6"

WALL TYPE

3 1/2"

3 1/2"

WALL TYPES

FLOOR TYPES

1/8"

1/2"

DOOR
SILENCER

FLUSH
BUMPER   1"

4 1/2" OR 6 1/2"

ROLLER BUMPER

4" TO 7"

DOOR
HOLDER

FLOOR STOPS

STOPS AND HOLDERS

F. J. Trost, SMS Architects; New Caanan, Connecticut
Door and Hardware Institute; Arlington, Virginia

HARDWARE

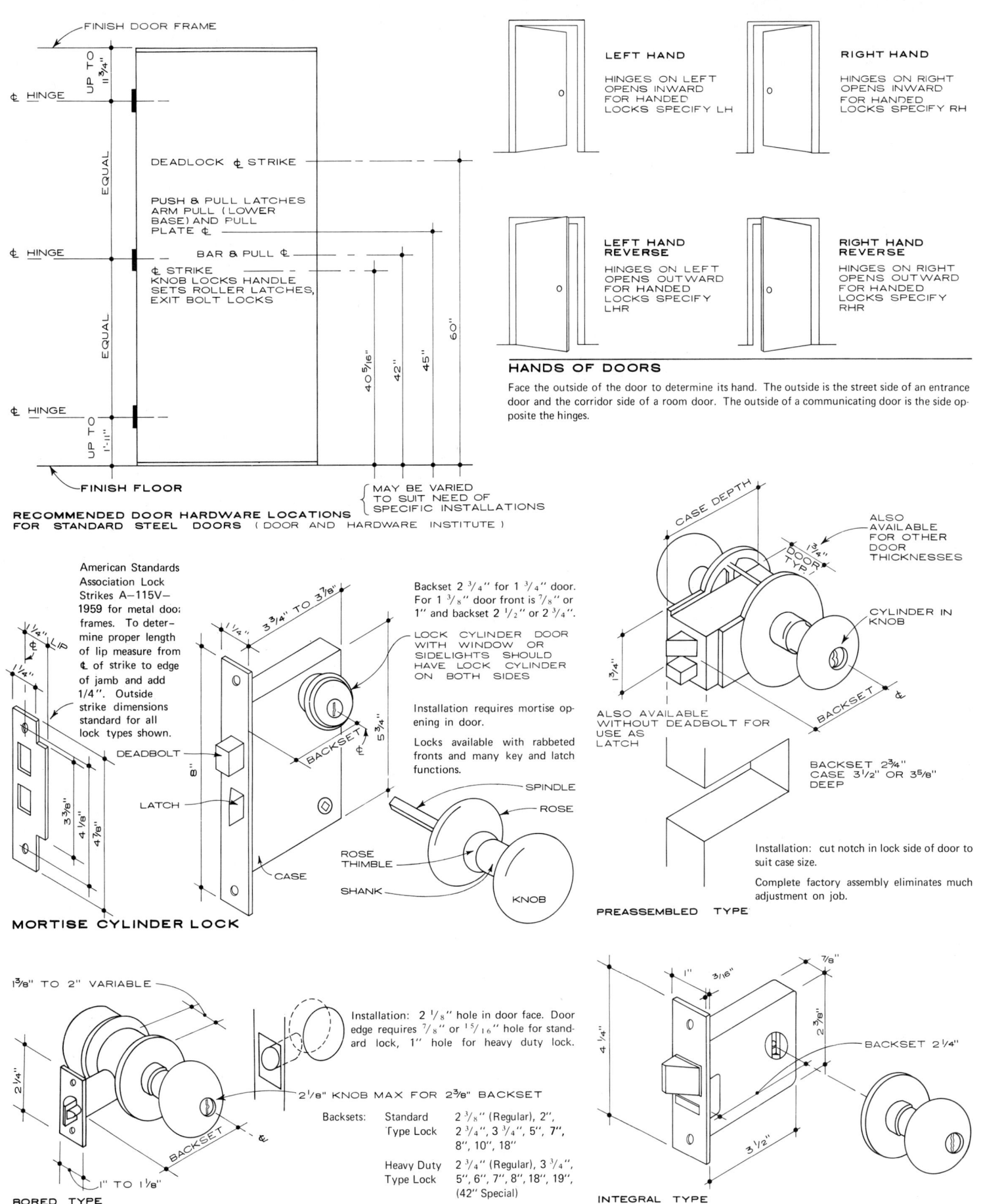

HANDS OF DOORS

Face the outside of the door to determine its hand. The outside is the street side of an entrance door and the corridor side of a room door. The outside of a communicating door is the side opposite the hinges.

RECOMMENDED DOOR HARDWARE LOCATIONS FOR STANDARD STEEL DOORS (DOOR AND HARDWARE INSTITUTE)

American Standards Association Lock Strikes A–115V–1959 for metal door frames. To determine proper length of lip measure from ℄ of strike to edge of jamb and add 1/4″. Outside strike dimensions standard for all lock types shown.

MORTISE CYLINDER LOCK

Backset 2 3/4″ for 1 3/4″ door. For 1 3/8″ door front is 7/8″ or 1″ and backset 2 1/2″ or 2 3/4″.

LOCK CYLINDER DOOR WITH WINDOW OR SIDELIGHTS SHOULD HAVE LOCK CYLINDER ON BOTH SIDES

Installation requires mortise opening in door.

Locks available with rabbeted fronts and many key and latch functions.

ALSO AVAILABLE FOR OTHER DOOR THICKNESSES

CYLINDER IN KNOB

ALSO AVAILABLE WITHOUT DEADBOLT FOR USE AS LATCH

BACKSET 2 3/4″ CASE 3 1/2″ OR 3 5/8″ DEEP

Installation: cut notch in lock side of door to suit case size.

Complete factory assembly eliminates much adjustment on job.

PREASSEMBLED TYPE

Installation: 2 1/8″ hole in door face. Door edge requires 7/8″ or 15/16″ hole for standard lock, 1″ hole for heavy duty lock.

2 1/8″ KNOB MAX FOR 2 3/8″ BACKSET

Backsets:	Standard Type Lock	2 3/8″ (Regular), 2″, 2 3/4″, 3 3/4″, 5″, 7″, 8″, 10″, 18″
	Heavy Duty Type Lock	2 3/4″ (Regular), 3 3/4″ 5″, 6″, 7″, 8″, 18″, 19″ (42″ Special)

BORED TYPE

Available in standard type (residential & light commercial) & heavy duty-type (institutional commercial)

BACKSET 2 1/4″

INTEGRAL TYPE

Mortise type installation. Combines features of mortise and cylinder locks.

F. J. Trost, SMS Architects; New Canaan, Connecticut

Door and Hardware Institute; Arlington, Virginia

HARDWARE 8

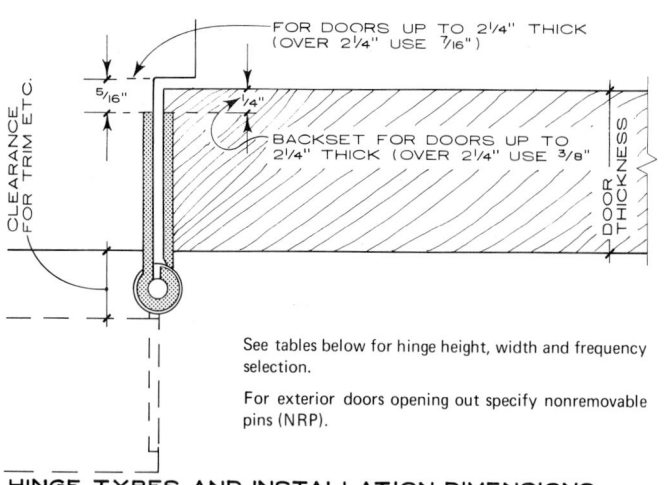

HINGE TYPES AND INSTALLATION DIMENSIONS

TEMPLATE

NON-TEMPLATE (FOR WOOD DOORS)

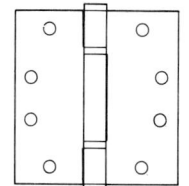

STANDARD FOR
ALL HINGES

ROUNDED TO AVOID
ATTACHING WEARING
APPAREL ETC.

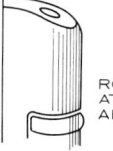

BUTTON TIP **HOSPITAL TIP**
CONSULT MANUFACTURERS FOR OTHER
AVAILABLE TIPS

NOTE

1. Use 2 hinges on doors less than 5'—0'' high. Add 1 hinge for each additional 2'—6'' of door height. Always specify 3 hinges per door.

2. Use ball bearing hinges on doors equipped with closers.

3. Use high frequency hinges on high frequency openings, average frequency hinges on average frequency openings, low frequency hinges on low frequency openings.

4. 2 or 4 ball or oilite bearings available on most hinge types (4 for extra heavy).

See tables below for hinge height, width and frequency selection.

For exterior doors opening out specify nonremovable pins (NRP).

HINGE SELECTION TABLES

HINGE HEIGHT—DETERMINED BY DOOR WIDTH AND THICKNESS

DOOR THICKNESS	DOOR WTH.	HINGE HGT.
3/4'' to 1 1/8'' CABINET	to 24	2 1/2
7/8'' & 1 1/8'' SCREEN OR COMB.	to 36	3
1 3/8''	to 36	3 1/2
1 3/4''	to 36	4
	over 36-41	4 1/2
	42 to 48	4 1/2*
2'', 2 1/4'', 2 1/2''	to 42	5
	over 42	6
TRANSOMS		
1 1/4'' & 1 3/8''		3
1 3/4''		3 1/2
2'', 2 1/4'', 2 1/2''		4

NOTE: Height of a hinge is always first dimension not including tips.
* Extra heavy hinges should be specified for heavy doors and doors where high frequency service is expected. Extra heavy hinges should be 4 1/2'', 5'', & 6'' sizes.

HINGE WIDTH—DETERMINED BY DOOR THICKNESS AND CLEARANCE REQUIRED

DOOR THICKNESS	CLEARANCE REQUIRED *	HINGE WIDTH
1 3/8	1 1/4	3 1/2
	1 3/4	4
1 3/4	1	4
	1 1/2	4 1/2
	2	5
	3	6
2	1	4 1/2
	1 1/2	5
	2 1/2	6
2 1/4	1	5
	2	6
2 1/2	3/4	5
	1 3/4	6
3	3/4	6
	2 3/4	8
	4 3/4	10

* NOTE: Clearance is computed for door flush with casing.

FREQUENCY OF DOOR OPERATION

TYPE OF BUILDING AND DOOR	ESTIMATED FREQUENCY		
	DAILY	YEARLY	
LARGE DEPT. STORE ENTRANCE	5,000	1,500,000	HIGH FREQUENCY
LARGE OFFICE BUILDING ENTRANCE	4,000	1,200,000	
THEATER ENTRANCE PERFORMANCE	1,000	450,000	
SCHOOL ENTRANCE	1,250	225,000	
SCHOOL TOILET DOOR	1,250	225,000	
STORE OR BANK ENTRANCE	500	150,000	
OFFICE BUILDING TOILET DOOR	400	118,000	
SCHOOL CORRIDOR DOOR	80	15,000	AVERAGE FREQUENCY
OFFICE BUILDING CORRIDOR DOOR	75	22,000	
STORE TOILET DOOR	60	18,000	
DWELLING ENTRANCE	40	15,000	
DWELLING TOILET DOOR	25	9,000	LOW FREQ.
DWELLING CORRIDOR DOOR	10	3,600	
DWELLING CLOSET DOOR	6	2,200	

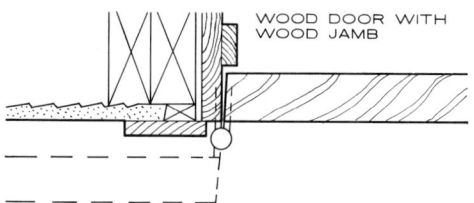

WOOD DOOR WITH WOOD JAMB

FULL MORTISE NON TEMPLATE

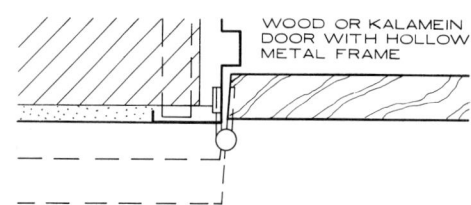

WOOD OR KALAMEIN DOOR WITH HOLLOW METAL FRAME

FULL MORTISE TEMPLATE

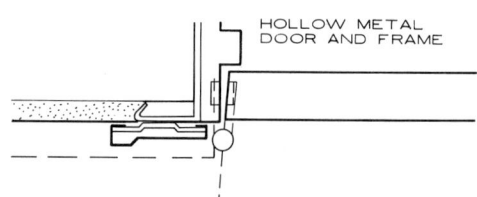

HOLLOW METAL DOOR AND FRAME

FULL MORTISE TEMPLATE

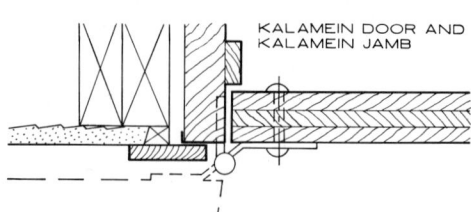

KALAMEIN DOOR AND KALAMEIN JAMB

HALF SURFACE TEMPLATE

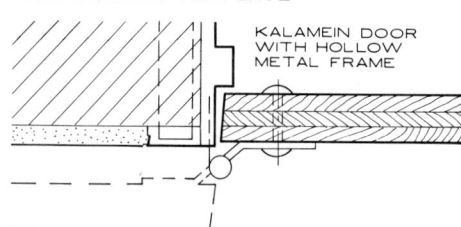

KALAMEIN DOOR WITH HOLLOW METAL FRAME

HALF SURFACE TEMPLATE

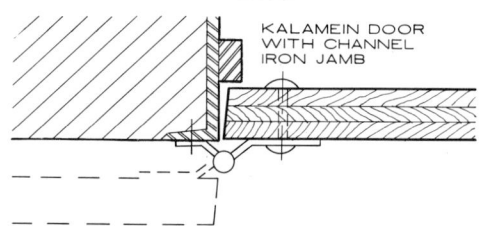

KALAMEIN DOOR WITH CHANNEL IRON JAMB

FULL SURFACE TEMPLATE

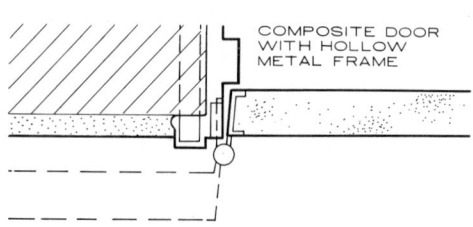

COMPOSITE DOOR WITH HOLLOW METAL FRAME

FULL MORTISE TEMPLATE

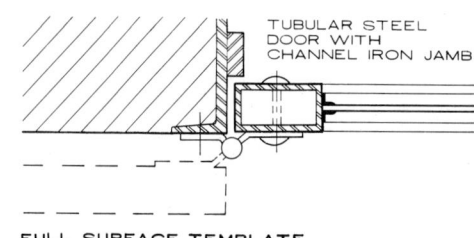

TUBULAR STEEL DOOR WITH CHANNEL IRON JAMB

FULL SURFACE TEMPLATE

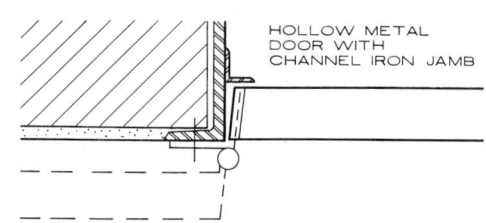

HOLLOW METAL DOOR WITH CHANNEL IRON JAMB

HALF MORTISE TEMPLATE

F. J. Trost, SMS Architects; New Caanan, Connecticut

Door and Hardware Institute; Arlington, Virginia

HARDWARE

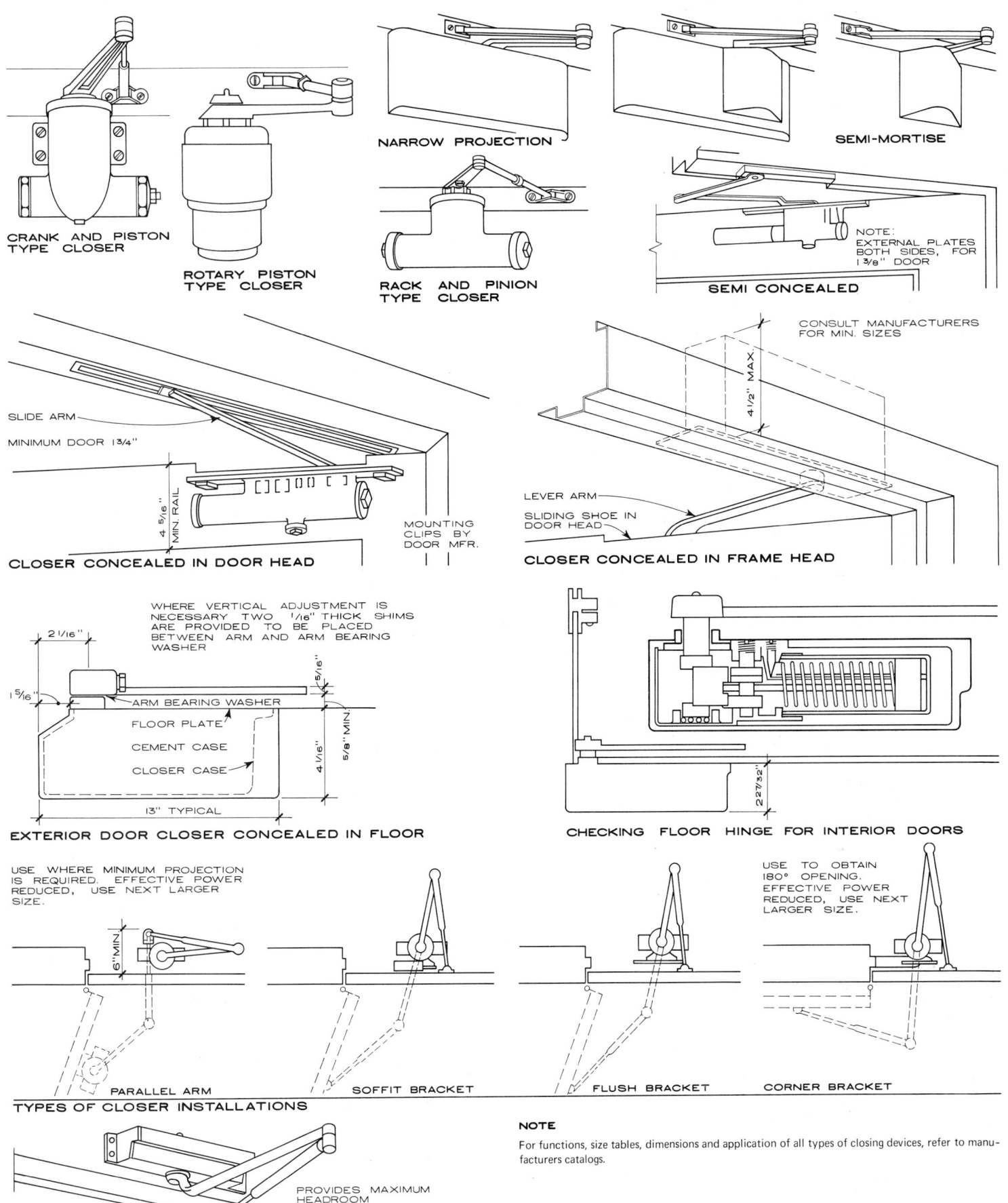

CRANK AND PISTON TYPE CLOSER

ROTARY PISTON TYPE CLOSER

NARROW PROJECTION

RACK AND PINION TYPE CLOSER

SEMI-MORTISE

SEMI CONCEALED

NOTE: EXTERNAL PLATES BOTH SIDES, FOR 1 3/8" DOOR

SLIDE ARM

MINIMUM DOOR 1 3/4"

4 5/16" MIN. RAIL

MOUNTING CLIPS BY DOOR MFR.

CLOSER CONCEALED IN DOOR HEAD

CONSULT MANUFACTURERS FOR MIN. SIZES

4 1/2" MAX.

LEVER ARM

SLIDING SHOE IN DOOR HEAD

CLOSER CONCEALED IN FRAME HEAD

WHERE VERTICAL ADJUSTMENT IS NECESSARY TWO 1/16" THICK SHIMS ARE PROVIDED TO BE PLACED BETWEEN ARM AND ARM BEARING WASHER

2 1/16"

1 5/16"

5/16"

ARM BEARING WASHER

FLOOR PLATE

CEMENT CASE

CLOSER CASE

4 1/16"

5/8" MIN.

13" TYPICAL

EXTERIOR DOOR CLOSER CONCEALED IN FLOOR

2 27/32"

CHECKING FLOOR HINGE FOR INTERIOR DOORS

USE WHERE MINIMUM PROJECTION IS REQUIRED. EFFECTIVE POWER REDUCED, USE NEXT LARGER SIZE.

6" MIN

PARALLEL ARM

SOFFIT BRACKET

FLUSH BRACKET

USE TO OBTAIN 180° OPENING. EFFECTIVE POWER REDUCED, USE NEXT LARGER SIZE.

CORNER BRACKET

TYPES OF CLOSER INSTALLATIONS

PROVIDES MAXIMUM HEADROOM

TOP JAMB INSTALLATION

NOTE

For functions, size tables, dimensions and application of all types of closing devices, refer to manufacturers catalogs.

CAUTION

Check headroom on brackets for low projection.

F. J. Trost, SMS Architects; New Caanan, Connecticut
Door and Hardware Institute; Arlington, Virginia

HARDWARE 8

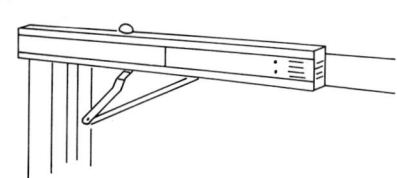

CLOSER, HOLDER, AND DETECTOR
PUSH-SIDE MOUNTED

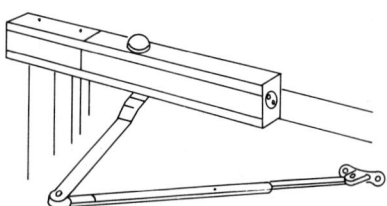

CLOSER AND HOLDER ONLY
PUSH-SIDE MOUNTED

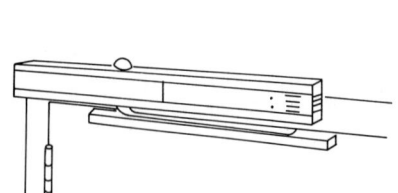

CLOSER, HOLDER, AND DETECTOR
PULL-SIDE MOUNTED

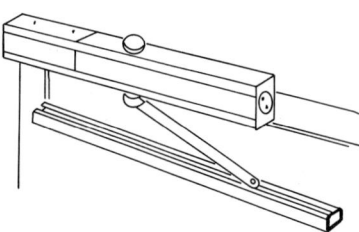

CLOSER AND HOLDER ONLY
PULL-SIDE MOUNTED

A COMBINATION CLOSER, HOLDER, AND DE-TECTOR is available with either ionization, photoelectric, or heat sensing detectors for discovering the presence of smoke or any of the products of combustion and for closing the door for life safety.

A COMBINATION CLOSER AND HOLDER (only) will hold door in open position when incorporated with an independent detector or wired into any type of fire detecting system.

All these units have unlimited hold-open from 0° to approximately 170°, or limited hold-open from 85° to 170° for cross corridor doors.

SURFACE MOUNTED COMBINATION CLOSERS, HOLDERS, AND DETECTORS

FIRE AND SMOKE DETECTION SYSTEMS

1. Heat sensing detectors operate on the basis of fixed temperature or a rate of temperature rise. Door closers are activated upon release of a heat activated device such as a fusable link. Closing mechanisms may consist of gravity operated weights or wound steel springs.

2. Smoke sensing detectors detect both visible and invisible airborne particles. Various operating principles include ionization, photoelectric, resistance, sampling, and cloud chamber detection.

   a. Ionization detection closers contain a small quantity of radioactive material within the sensing chamber. The resulting ionized air permits an electric current flow between electrodes. When entrance of smoke particles reduces the flow to a preset level, the detection circuit responds. Closing mechanisms usually consist of a detector, electromechanical holding device, and a door closer.

      Ionization detectors will sense ordinary products of combustion from such sources as kitchens, motors, power tools, and automobile exhausts.

   b. Photoelectric detection closers consists of a light source and a photoelectric cell. Actuation occurs when smoke becomes dense enough to change the reflectance of light reaching the photoelectric device. Photoelectric detectors may be of spot or beam type. Closing mechanisms consist of a detector, electromechanical holding device, and a door closer.

   c. Other types of smoke detectors include electrical bridging, sampling, and cloud chambers. Each has operating characteristics similar to ionization and photoelectric detectors.

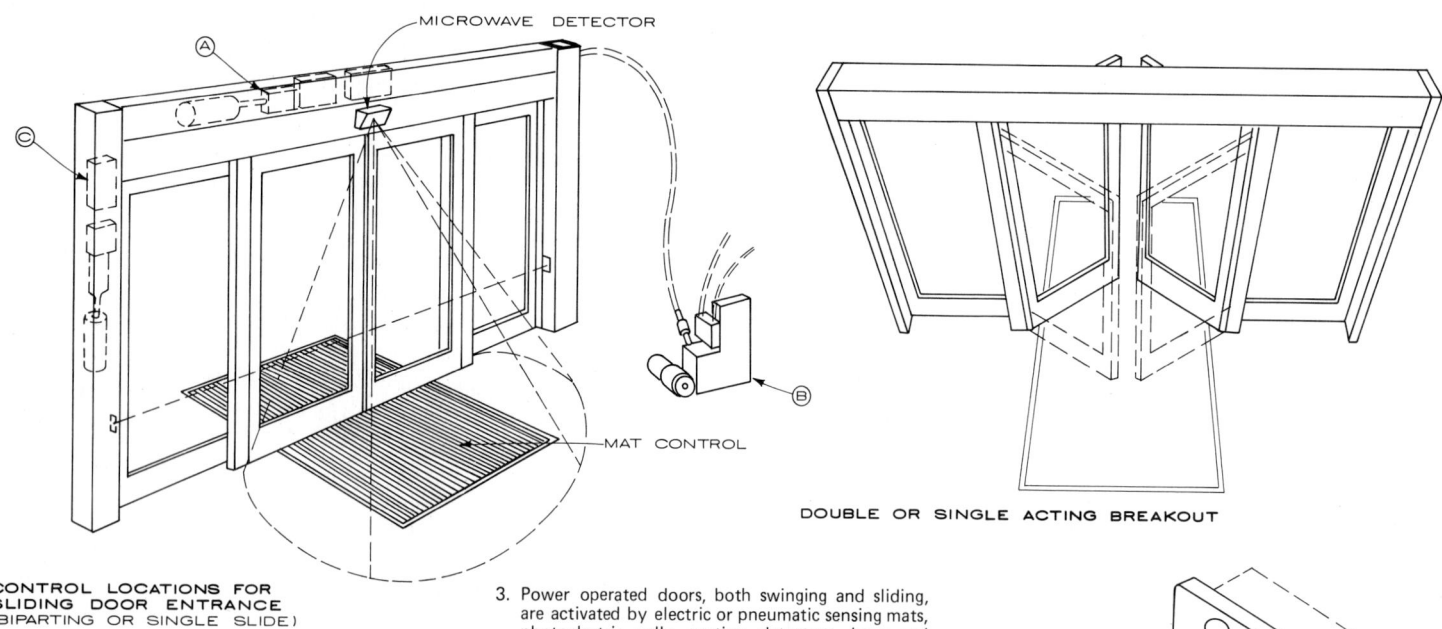

CONTROL LOCATIONS FOR
SLIDING DOOR ENTRANCE
(BIPARTING OR SINGLE SLIDE)

DOUBLE OR SINGLE ACTING BREAKOUT

PUSH-PLATE SWITCH
AVAILABLE FOR HANDICAPPED

Power unit mounting locations:
A. Header—concealed above header.
B. Remote—concealed away from door.
C. Vertical—concealed in side jamb.

3. Power operated doors, both swinging and sliding, are activated by electric or pneumatic sensing mats, photoelectric cells, motion detectors, keys and switches, and so on. Fire rated openings require an approved detection device that will deactivate and exhaust the operator and positively close the door by spring action. Manual operation of the door as an emergency exit must not be restricted. Door design should comply with handicapped accessibility regulations.

   Sliding power operated doors are ideal for all disabled persons. Motion detectors and swinging power operated doors can be potentially hazardous to the blind or visually impaired individual.

AUTOMATIC SLIDING DOOR OPENING DEVICES

Lee A. Anderson; SRGF, Inc., Architects; Champaign, Illinois

HARDWARE

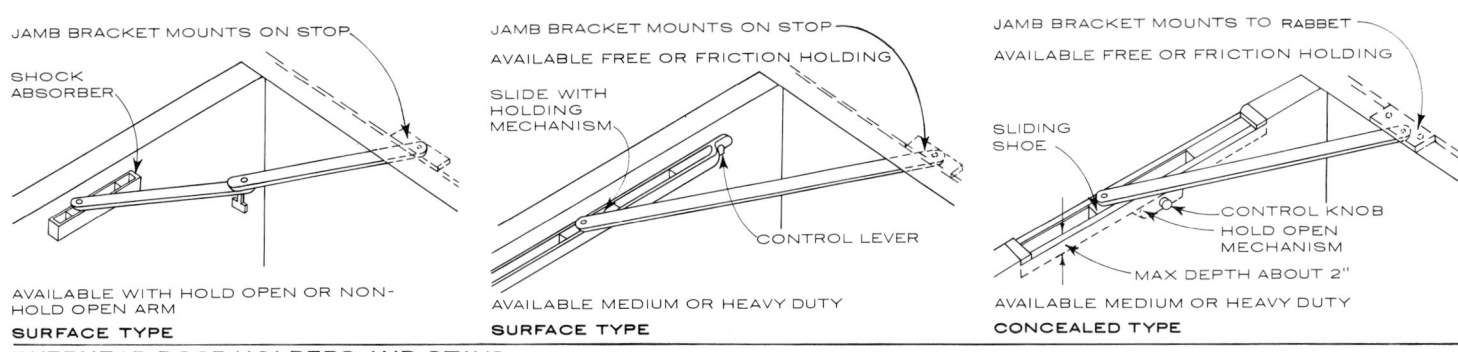

JAMB BRACKET MOUNTS ON STOP

SHOCK ABSORBER

AVAILABLE WITH HOLD OPEN OR NON-HOLD OPEN ARM

SURFACE TYPE

JAMB BRACKET MOUNTS ON STOP

AVAILABLE FREE OR FRICTION HOLDING

SLIDE WITH HOLDING MECHANISM

CONTROL LEVER

AVAILABLE MEDIUM OR HEAVY DUTY

SURFACE TYPE

JAMB BRACKET MOUNTS TO RABBET

AVAILABLE FREE OR FRICTION HOLDING

SLIDING SHOE

CONTROL KNOB

HOLD OPEN MECHANISM

MAX DEPTH ABOUT 2"

AVAILABLE MEDIUM OR HEAVY DUTY

CONCEALED TYPE

OVERHEAD DOOR HOLDERS AND STAYS

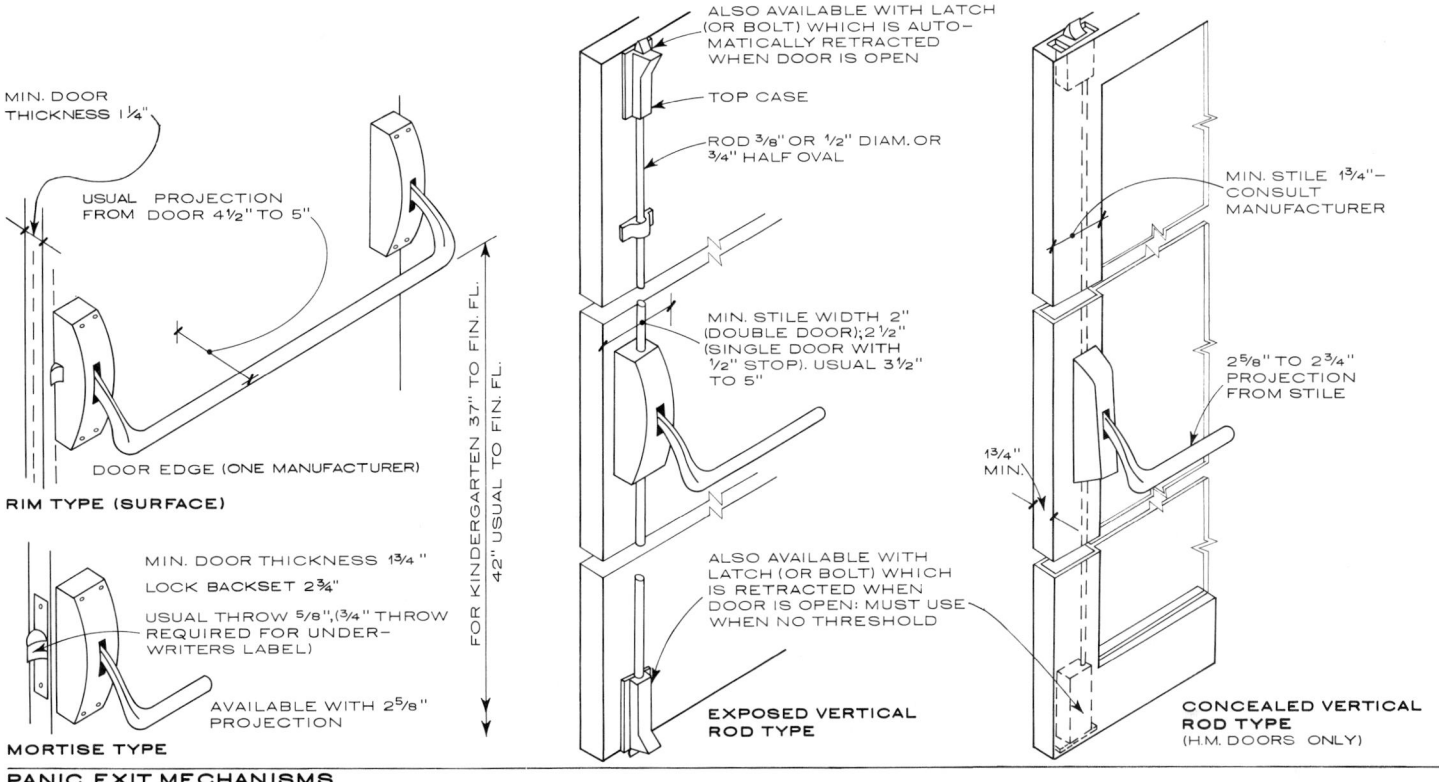

MIN. DOOR THICKNESS 1¼"

USUAL PROJECTION FROM DOOR 4½" TO 5"

DOOR EDGE (ONE MANUFACTURER)

RIM TYPE (SURFACE)

MIN. DOOR THICKNESS 1¾"

LOCK BACKSET 2¾"

USUAL THROW ⅝", (¾" THROW REQUIRED FOR UNDERWRITERS LABEL)

AVAILABLE WITH 2⅝" PROJECTION

MORTISE TYPE

FOR KINDERGARTEN 37" TO FIN. FL. 42" USUAL TO FIN. FL.

ALSO AVAILABLE WITH LATCH (OR BOLT) WHICH IS AUTOMATICALLY RETRACTED WHEN DOOR IS OPEN

TOP CASE

ROD ⅜" OR ½" DIAM. OR ¾" HALF OVAL

MIN. STILE WIDTH 2" (DOUBLE DOOR); 2½" (SINGLE DOOR WITH ½" STOP). USUAL 3½" TO 5"

ALSO AVAILABLE WITH LATCH (OR BOLT) WHICH IS RETRACTED WHEN DOOR IS OPEN: MUST USE WHEN NO THRESHOLD

EXPOSED VERTICAL ROD TYPE

MIN. STILE 1¾" – CONSULT MANUFACTURER

2⅝" TO 2¾" PROJECTION FROM STILE

1¾" MIN.

CONCEALED VERTICAL ROD TYPE (H.M. DOORS ONLY)

PANIC EXIT MECHANISMS

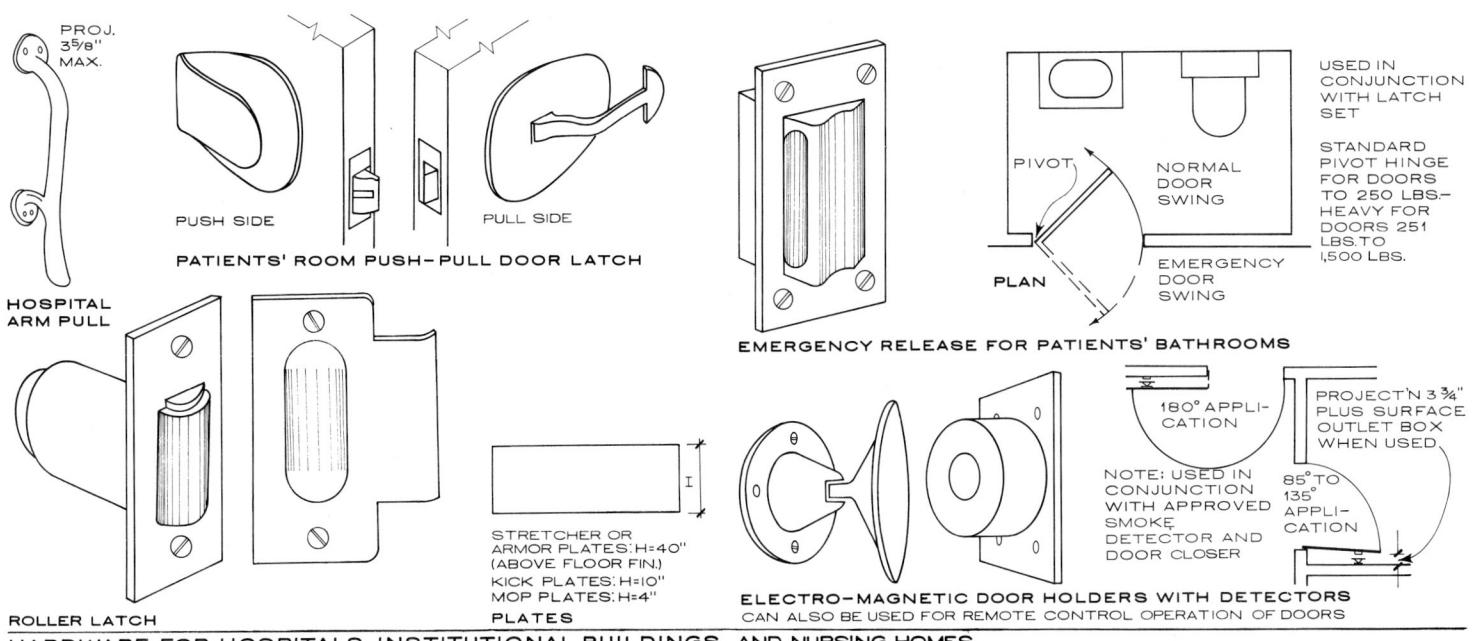

PROJ. 3⅝" MAX.

PUSH SIDE

PULL SIDE

PATIENTS' ROOM PUSH-PULL DOOR LATCH

HOSPITAL ARM PULL

ROLLER LATCH

STRETCHER OR ARMOR PLATES: H=40" (ABOVE FLOOR FIN.) KICK PLATES: H=10" MOP PLATES: H=4"

PLATES

PIVOT

NORMAL DOOR SWING

PLAN

EMERGENCY DOOR SWING

EMERGENCY RELEASE FOR PATIENTS' BATHROOMS

USED IN CONJUNCTION WITH LATCH SET

STANDARD PIVOT HINGE FOR DOORS TO 250 LBS. – HEAVY FOR DOORS 251 LBS. TO 1,500 LBS.

NOTE: USED IN CONJUNCTION WITH APPROVED SMOKE DETECTOR AND DOOR CLOSER

180° APPLICATION

PROJECT'N 3¾" PLUS SURFACE OUTLET BOX WHEN USED

85° TO 135° APPLICATION

ELECTRO-MAGNETIC DOOR HOLDERS WITH DETECTORS CAN ALSO BE USED FOR REMOTE CONTROL OPERATION OF DOORS

HARDWARE FOR HOSPITALS, INSTITUTIONAL BUILDINGS, AND NURSING HOMES

F. J. Trost, SMS Architects; New Canaan, Connecticut

Door and Hardware Institute; Arlington, Virginia

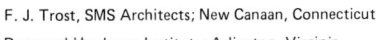

HARDWARE 8

HARDWARE SYMBOLS & FINISHES

SYMBOL	FINISH
USP	Primed For Painting
US 3	Bright Brass
US 4	Dull Brass
US 10	Dull Bronze
US 10B	Dull Bronze, Oxidized And Oil Rubbed
US 14	Nickel Plated, Bright
US 26	Chromium Plated, Bright
US 26D	Chromium Plated, Dull
US 27	Satin Aluminum, Lacquered
US 28	Satin Aluminum, Anodized
US 32	Stainless Steel, Polished
US 32D	Stainless Steel, Dull

NOTE

Finishes noted are federal approved with samples on file (except US 10 B – no sample). For other finishes consult manufacturers.

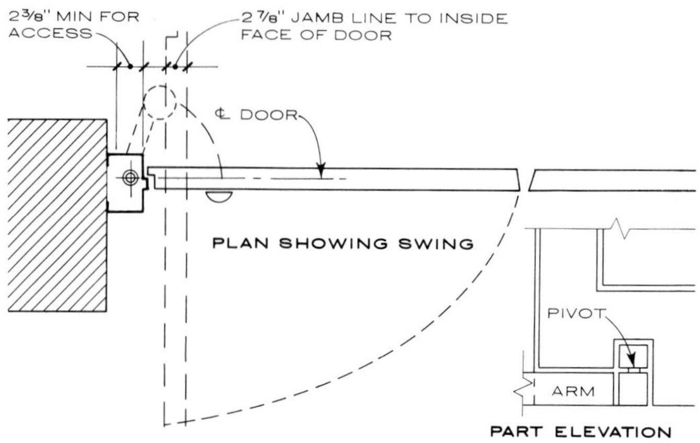
2⅜" MIN FOR ACCESS
2 ⅞" JAMB LINE TO INSIDE FACE OF DOOR
℄ DOOR
PLAN SHOWING SWING
PIVOT
ARM
PART ELEVATION

BALANCED DOOR

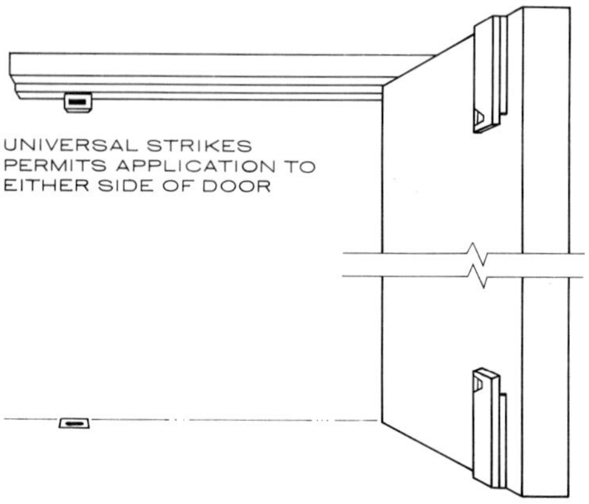
UNIVERSAL STRIKES PERMITS APPLICATION TO EITHER SIDE OF DOOR

SURFACE BOLTS

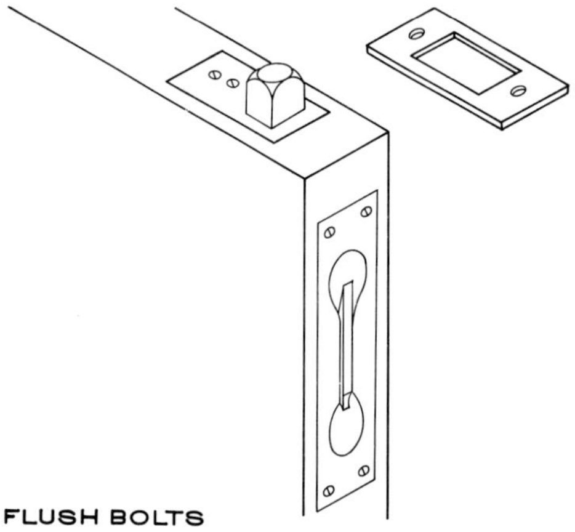

FLUSH BOLTS

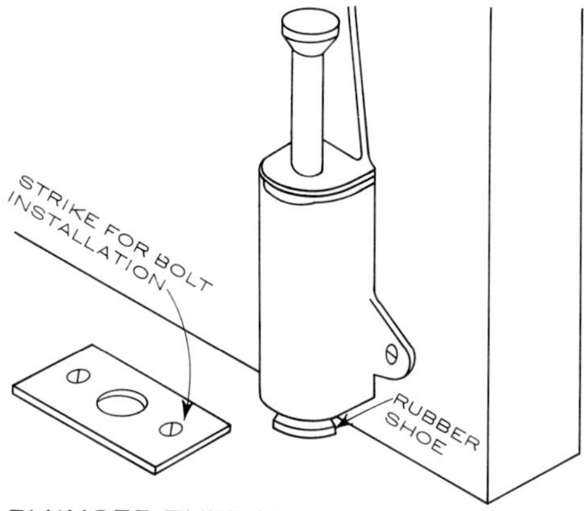
STRIKE FOR BOLT INSTALLATION
RUBBER SHOE

PLUNGER TYPE HOLDER OR BOLT

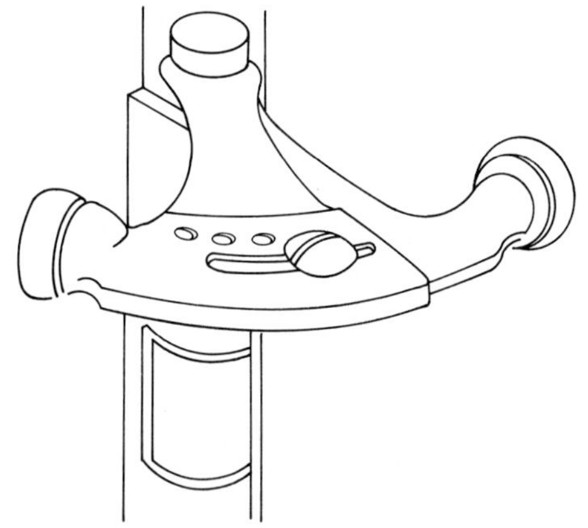

HINGE PIN DOOR STOP

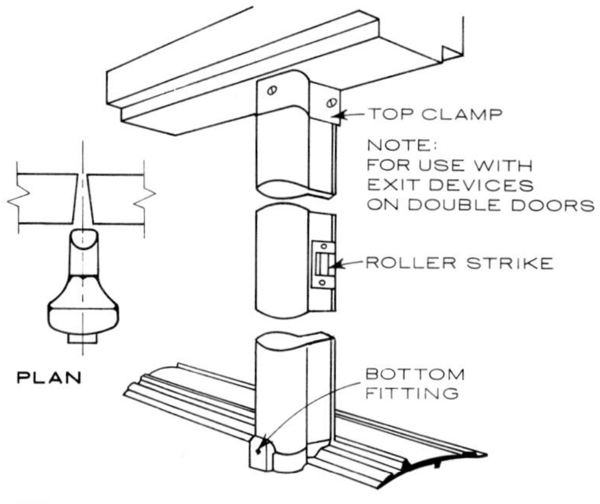
TOP CLAMP
NOTE: FOR USE WITH EXIT DEVICES ON DOUBLE DOORS
ROLLER STRIKE
PLAN
BOTTOM FITTING

REMOVABLE MULLION

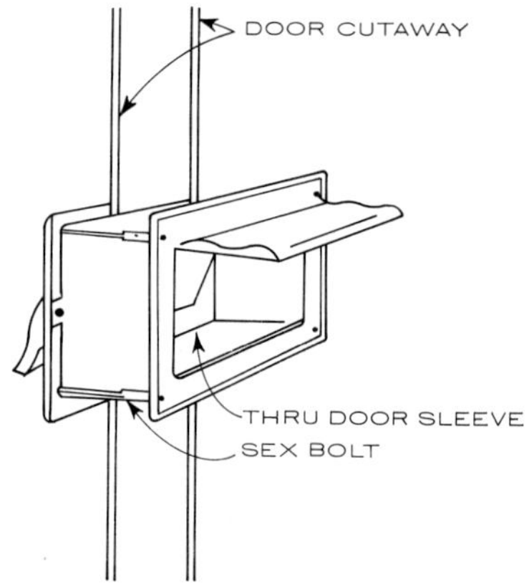
DOOR CUTAWAY
THRU DOOR SLEEVE
SEX BOLT

DOOR LETTER BOX

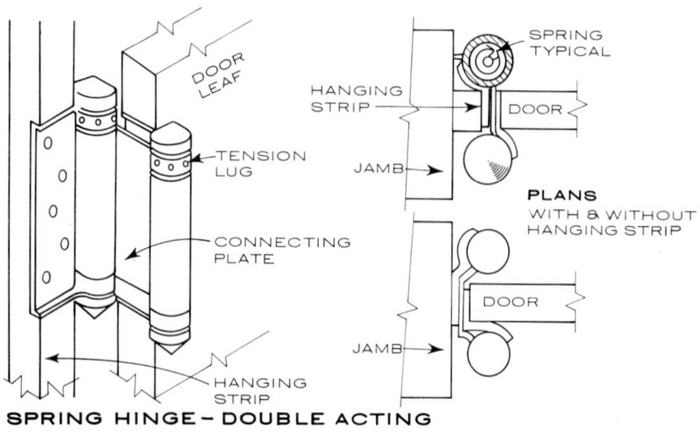
DOOR LEAF
TENSION LUG
CONNECTING PLATE
HANGING STRIP
SPRING TYPICAL
HANGING STRIP
DOOR
JAMB
PLANS
WITH & WITHOUT HANGING STRIP
DOOR
JAMB

SPRING HINGE – DOUBLE ACTING

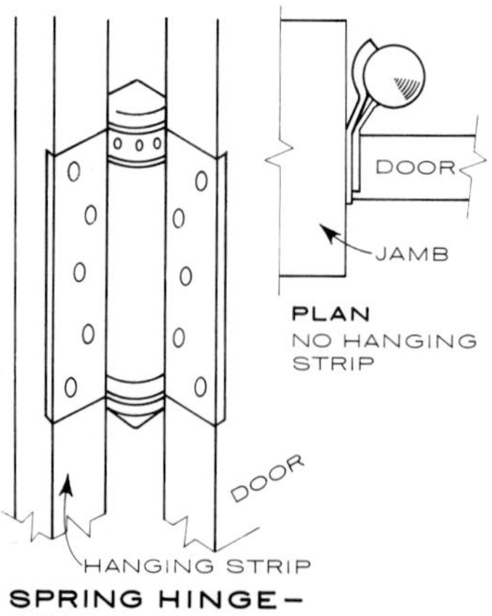
DOOR
JAMB
PLAN
NO HANGING STRIP
DOOR
HANGING STRIP

SPRING HINGE – SINGLE ACTING

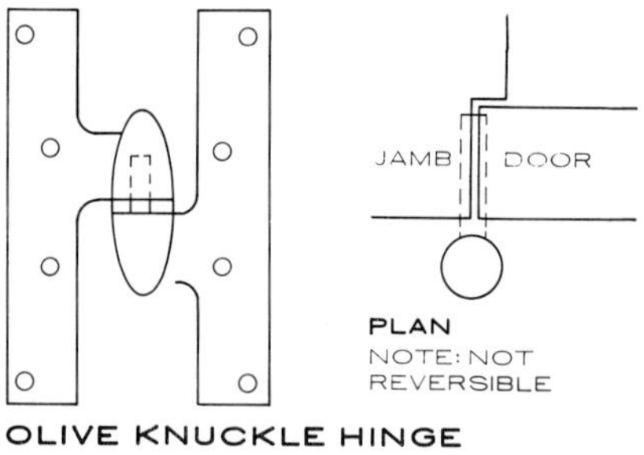
JAMB
DOOR
PLAN
NOTE: NOT REVERSIBLE

OLIVE KNUCKLE HINGE

F. J. Trost, SMS Architects; New Canaan, Connecticut
Door and Hardware Institute; Arlington, Virginia

NOTE

Threshold profiles vary from mfr. to mfr. Consult mfr. catalog for additional sizes. Std. length is 18' to 20' or saddles may be cut to size. Anchors to wood floors are screws; to terrazzo or cement floors, screws in fiber plugs or expansive metal anchors; to concrete, screws tapped to clips set in concrete.

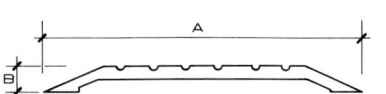

FLUTED TYPES

BRASS		ALUM.		BRONZE		STEEL	
A	B	A	B	A	B	A	B
3, 3 1/2		3, 4		3	5/16"	3 & 4	1/2"
4,5	1/2"	5,6			3/8"	5 1/2"	9/16"
& 6		6 1/4"	1/2"	4, 4 1/2		5 1/2	5/8"
		7		5, 6	1/2"	& 7	
		7 1/2		& 7			
		3, 4		6 & 7			
		5 & 6	5/8"	6 & 7	5/8"		

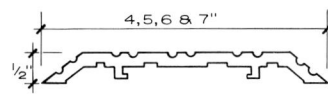
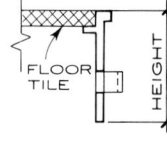
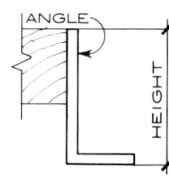

JOINT STRIP

Used for division of floors of different materials

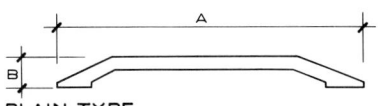

PLAIN TYPE

BRASS		ALUMINUM				BRONZE	
A	B	A	B	A	B	A	B
3"	1/4"	4 5/64"	3/32"	4"		2 1/2 & 3	1/4"
2 1/4"	3/16"	2 1/4"	3/16"	4 5/64"	1/2"	4,5	
4,5	1/2"	2 1/2, 3"	1/4"	5 & 6		& 6	1/2"
& 6		2 1/4"	3/16"	4"	7/16"		

PLAIN AND FLUTED SADDLES AND JOINT STRIPS FOR INTERIORS

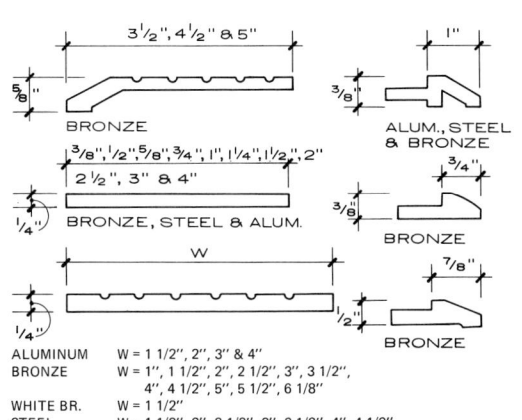

ASSEMBLED SADDLE COMPONENTS

ALUMINUM	W = 1 1/2", 2", 3" & 4"
BRONZE	W = 1", 1 1/2", 2", 2 1/2", 3", 3 1/2", 4", 4 1/2", 5", 5 1/2", 6 1/8"
WHITE BR.	W = 1 1/2"
STEEL	W = 1 1/2", 2", 2 1/2", 3", 3 1/2", 4", 4 1/2"

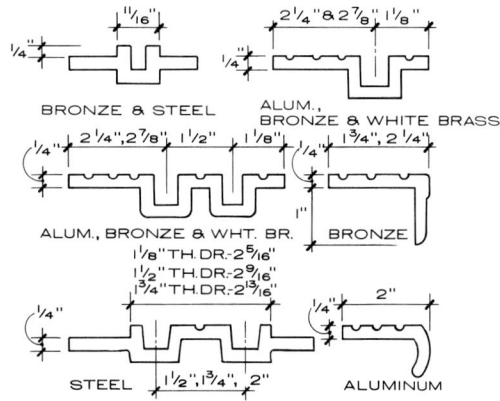

SLIDING DOOR SADDLE COMPONENTS

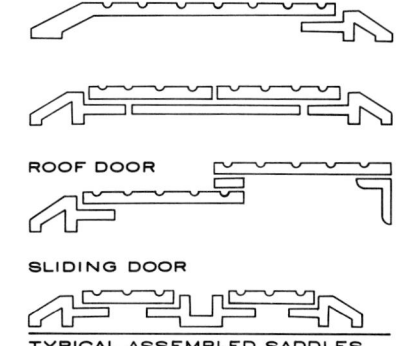

TYPICAL ASSEMBLED SADDLES

By combining components saddles may be made to any width, joints will not show as fluting pattern is identical.

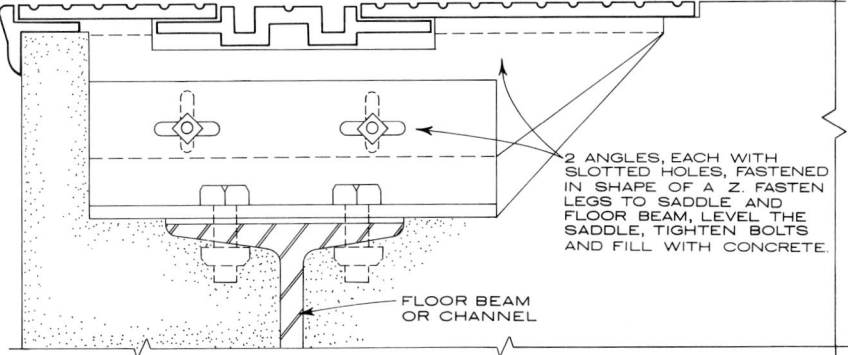

ELEVATOR SADDLE CONSTRUCTION

2 ANGLES, EACH WITH SLOTTED HOLES, FASTENED IN SHAPE OF A Z. FASTEN LEGS TO SADDLE AND FLOOR BEAM, LEVEL THE SADDLE, TIGHTEN BOLTS AND FILL WITH CONCRETE.

CUTOUT FOR FLOOR HINGES

Threshold assemblies may also be cut or notched to fit mullions or columns.

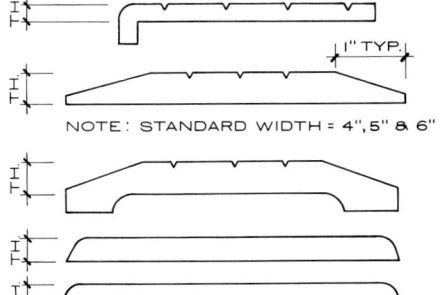

NOTE: STANDARD WIDTH = 4", 5" & 6"

RECOMMENDED PRACTICE

TH.	IRON	BRONZE	ALUMINUM	NICKEL
1/4		to 6" wide	to 10" wide	to 6" wide
5/16	to 6" wide	to 10" wide	to 18" wide	to 10" wide
3/8	to 12" wide	to 18" wide	to 24" wide	to 14" wide
7/16	to 24" wide	to 24" wide	to 36" wide	to 18" wide
1/2	to 30" wide	to 30" wide	to 42" wide	to 24" wide
5/8	to 42" wide	to 42" wide	to 42" wide	to 30" wide
3/4	to 42" wide	to 42" wide	to 42" wide	to 30" wide

Length, to 9'-6". When width exceeds 32", length should not exceed 7'-6".

Minimum thickness — 1/2" for iron. 3/8" for bronze, aluminum and nickel

ELEVATOR DOOR SADDLE

Saddles with floor hinge cut-outs, as shown above also available.

CAST METAL ABRASIVE SURFACE SADDLES

Dan Cowling and Associates, Inc.; Little Rock, Arkansas

HARDWARE **8**

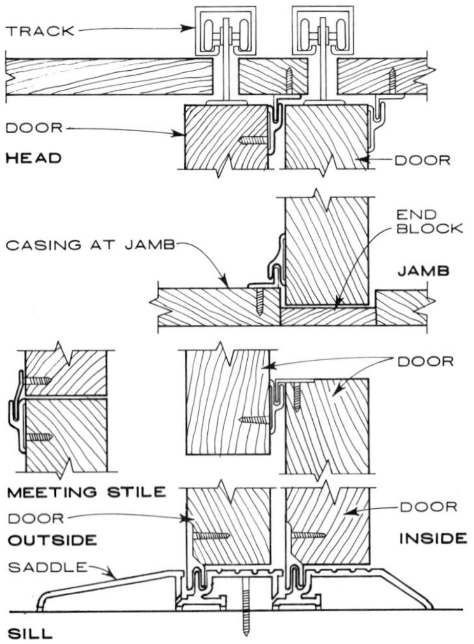

TRACK

DOOR

HEAD

CASING AT JAMB

END BLOCK

JAMB

DOOR

MEETING STILE

DOOR

OUTSIDE

DOOR

INSIDE

SADDLE

SILL

SLIDING DOORS

DOOR   DOOR

SPRING BRONZE, STAIN. STL. OR ALUM.

SPRING BRONZE, STAIN. STL. OR ALUM.

DOOR   DOOR

MEETING STILES

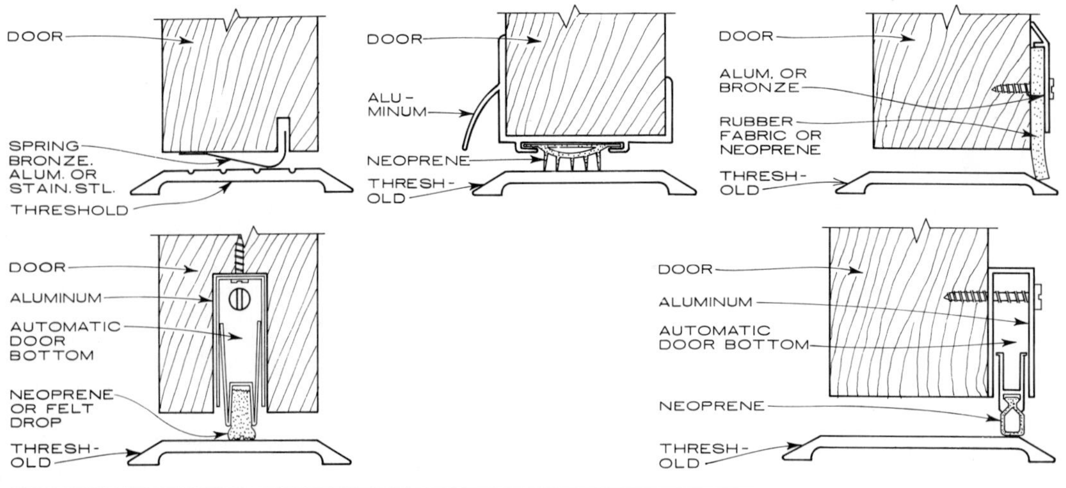

NEOPRENE IN ALUM. HOLDER.

DOOR   DOOR

MAGNETIC INSERTS AVAILABLE

NEOPRENE IN ALUM. OR BR.

DOOR   DOOR

DOOR — SPRING BRONZE STAIN. STL. OR ALUM. — FRAME

FOR LOCK & HINGE SIDE

DOOR — SPRING BRONZE STAIN. STL. OR ALUM. — FRAME

FOR LOCK & HINGE SIDE

DOOR — SPRING BRONZE OR ZINC — FRAME

FOR LOCK SIDE ONLY

DOOR — VINYL INSERT — WOOD STOP — FRAME

FOR LOCK & HINGE SIDE

DOOR — SPONGE PLASTIC OR RUBBER — FRAME

FOR LOCK & HINGE SIDE

DOOR — VINYL GASKET — BRONZE OR ALUM. — FRAME

FOR LOCK & HINGE SIDE

DOOR — VINYL GASKET — BRONZE OR ALUM. — FRAME

FOR LOCK & HINGE SIDE

DOOR — SPONGE PLASTIC — BRONZE OR ALUM. — FRAME

FOR LOCK & HINGE SIDE

DOOR — ALUM. OR BRONZE — FRAME

FOR JAMB ONLY - AT HINGE SIDE

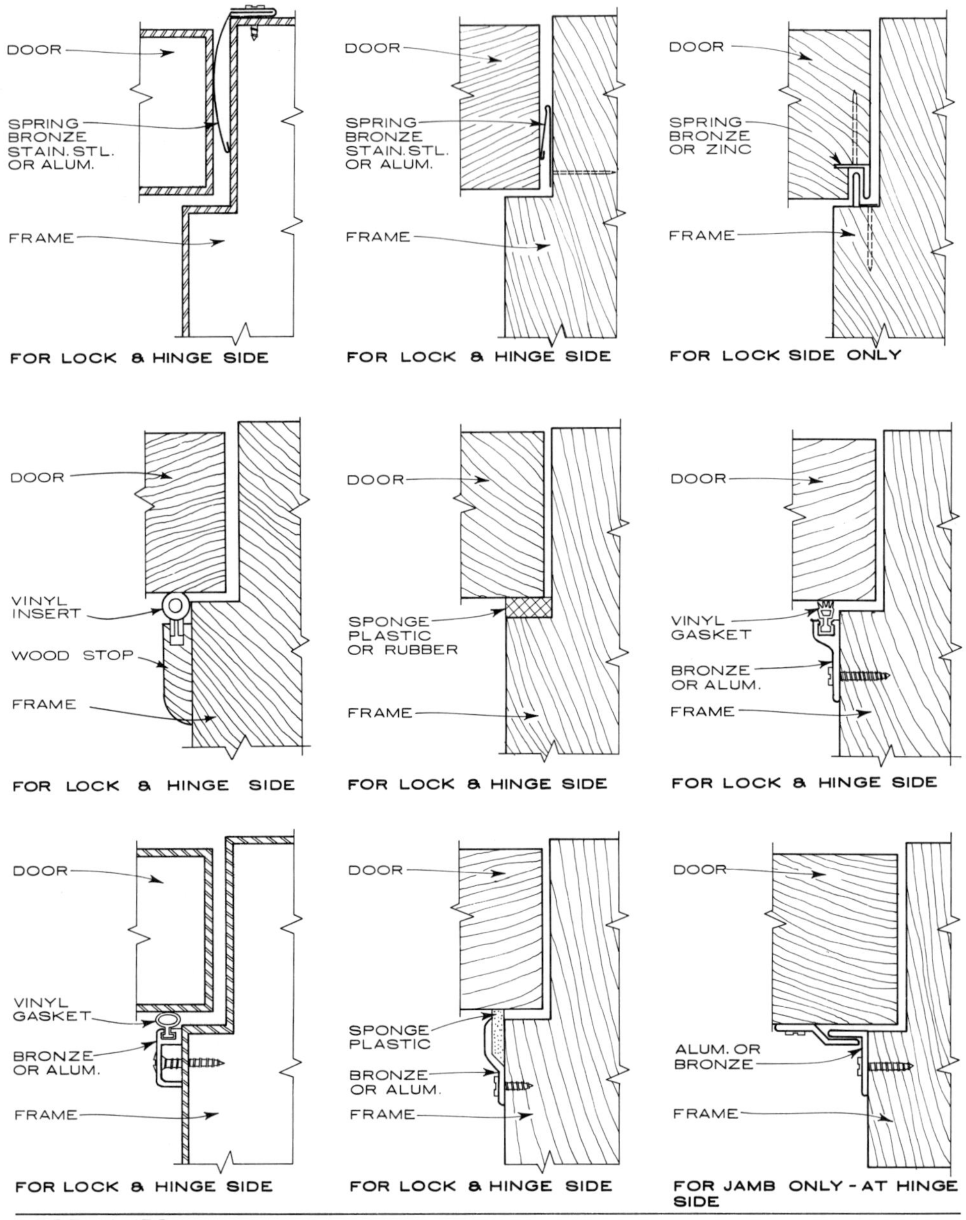

DOOR JAMBS

NOTE: Door heads are similar except where noted otherwise.

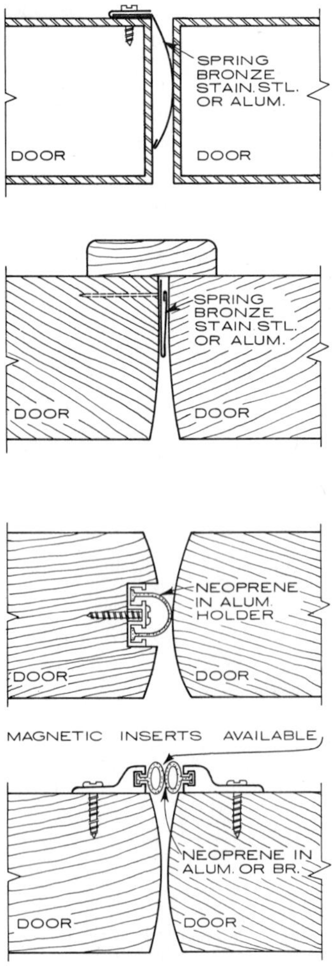

DOOR — SPRING BRONZE, ALUM. OR STAIN. STL. — THRESHOLD

DOOR — ALUMINUM — NEOPRENE — THRESHOLD

DOOR — ALUM. OR BRONZE — RUBBER FABRIC OR NEOPRENE — THRESHOLD

DOOR — ALUMINUM — AUTOMATIC DOOR BOTTOM — NEOPRENE OR FELT DROP — THRESHOLD

DOOR — ALUMINUM — AUTOMATIC DOOR BOTTOM — NEOPRENE — THRESHOLD

DOOR SILLS

Dan Cowling and Associates, Inc.; Little Rock, Arkansas

HARDWARE

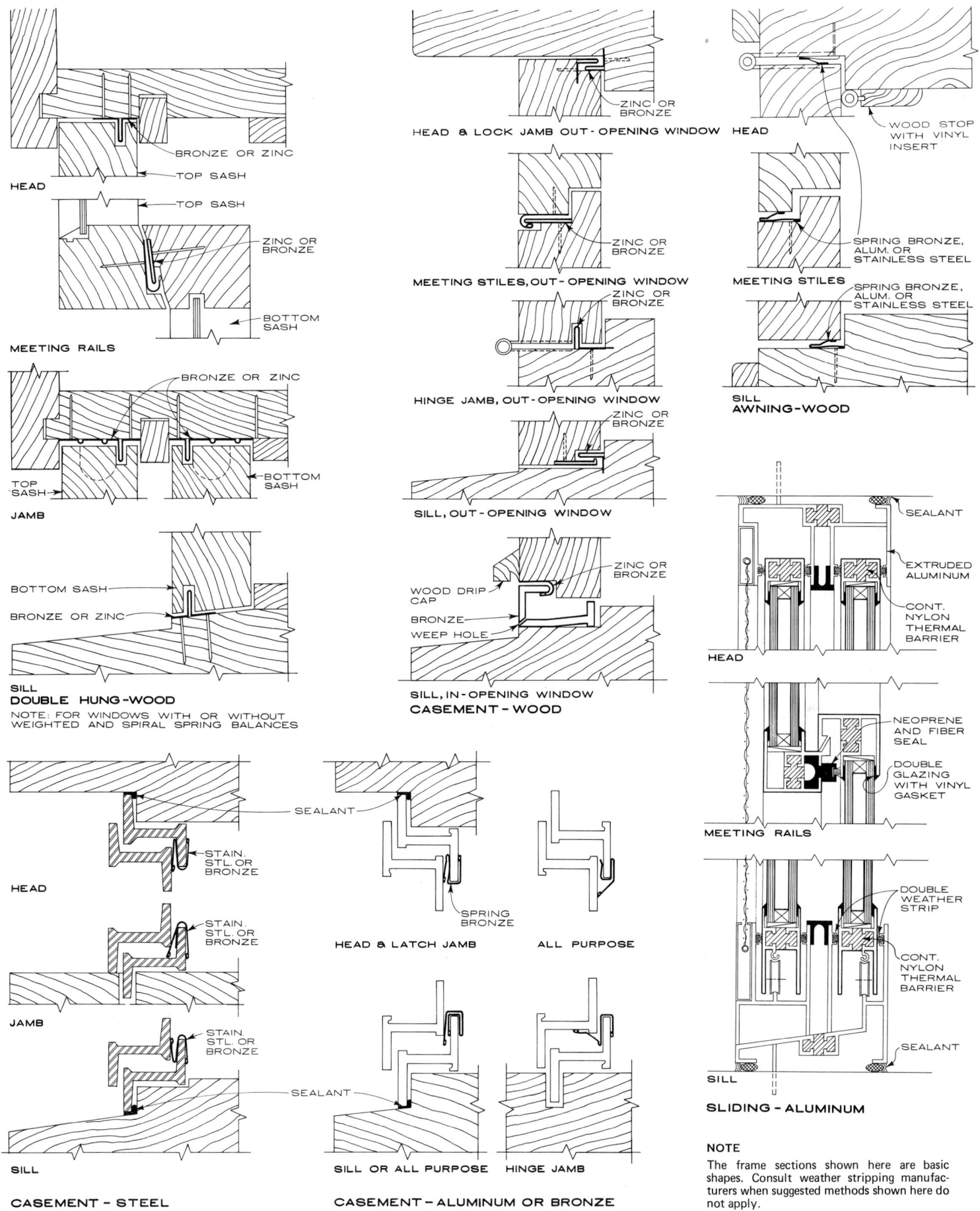

HEAD

BRONZE OR ZINC

TOP SASH

TOP SASH

ZINC OR BRONZE

BOTTOM SASH

MEETING RAILS

BRONZE OR ZINC

TOP SASH

BOTTOM SASH

JAMB

BOTTOM SASH

BRONZE OR ZINC

SILL
DOUBLE HUNG - WOOD
NOTE: FOR WINDOWS WITH OR WITHOUT WEIGHTED AND SPIRAL SPRING BALANCES

ZINC OR BRONZE

HEAD & LOCK JAMB OUT-OPENING WINDOW

ZINC OR BRONZE

MEETING STILES, OUT-OPENING WINDOW

ZINC OR BRONZE

HINGE JAMB, OUT-OPENING WINDOW

ZINC OR BRONZE

SILL, OUT-OPENING WINDOW

WOOD DRIP CAP

ZINC OR BRONZE

BRONZE

WEEP HOLE

SILL, IN-OPENING WINDOW
CASEMENT - WOOD

WOOD STOP WITH VINYL INSERT

HEAD

SPRING BRONZE, ALUM. OR STAINLESS STEEL

MEETING STILES

SPRING BRONZE, ALUM. OR STAINLESS STEEL

SILL
AWNING - WOOD

SEALANT

EXTRUDED ALUMINUM

CONT. NYLON THERMAL BARRIER

HEAD

NEOPRENE AND FIBER SEAL

DOUBLE GLAZING WITH VINYL GASKET

MEETING RAILS

DOUBLE WEATHER STRIP

CONT. NYLON THERMAL BARRIER

SEALANT

SILL
SLIDING - ALUMINUM

SEALANT

STAIN. STL. OR BRONZE

HEAD

STAIN. STL. OR BRONZE

JAMB

STAIN. STL. OR BRONZE

SEALANT

SILL

CASEMENT - STEEL

SPRING BRONZE

HEAD & LATCH JAMB

ALL PURPOSE

SEALANT

SILL OR ALL PURPOSE   **HINGE JAMB**

CASEMENT - ALUMINUM OR BRONZE

NOTE

The frame sections shown here are basic shapes. Consult weather stripping manufacturers when suggested methods shown here do not apply.

Dan Cowling & Associates, Inc.; Little Rock, Arkansas

HARDWARE 8

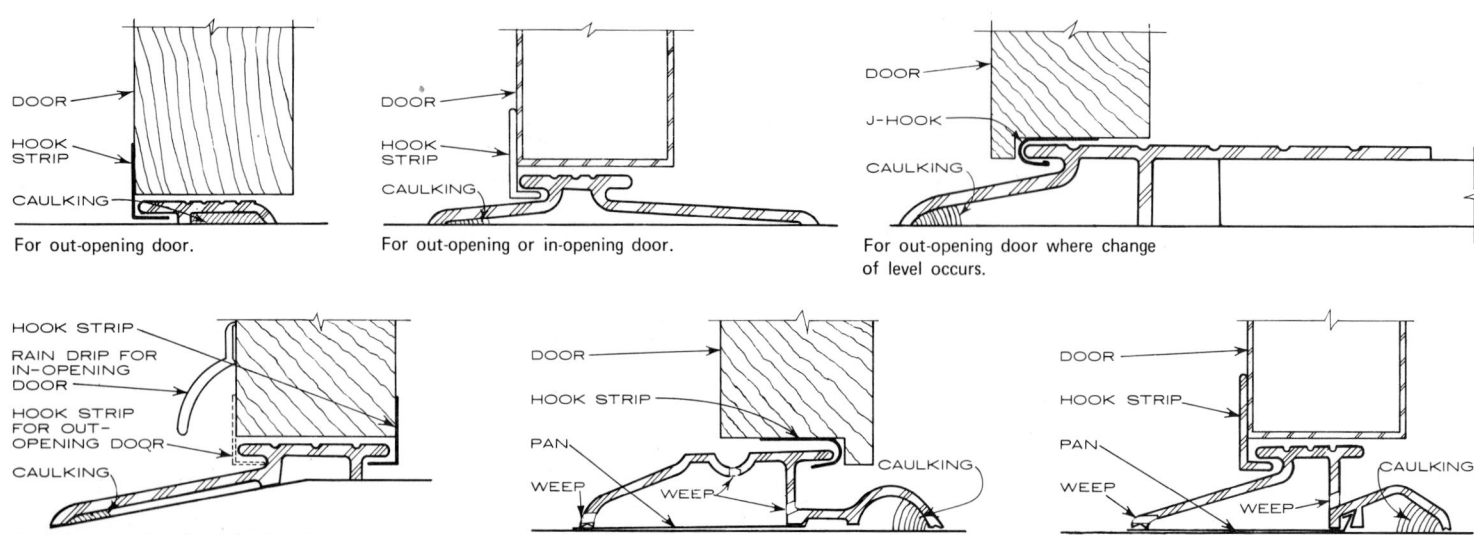

For out-opening door.

For out-opening or in-opening door.

For out-opening door where change of level occurs.

For in-opening door (as shown) and out-opening door where change of level occurs.

For in-opening door.

For out-opening door.

INTERLOCKING THRESHOLDS

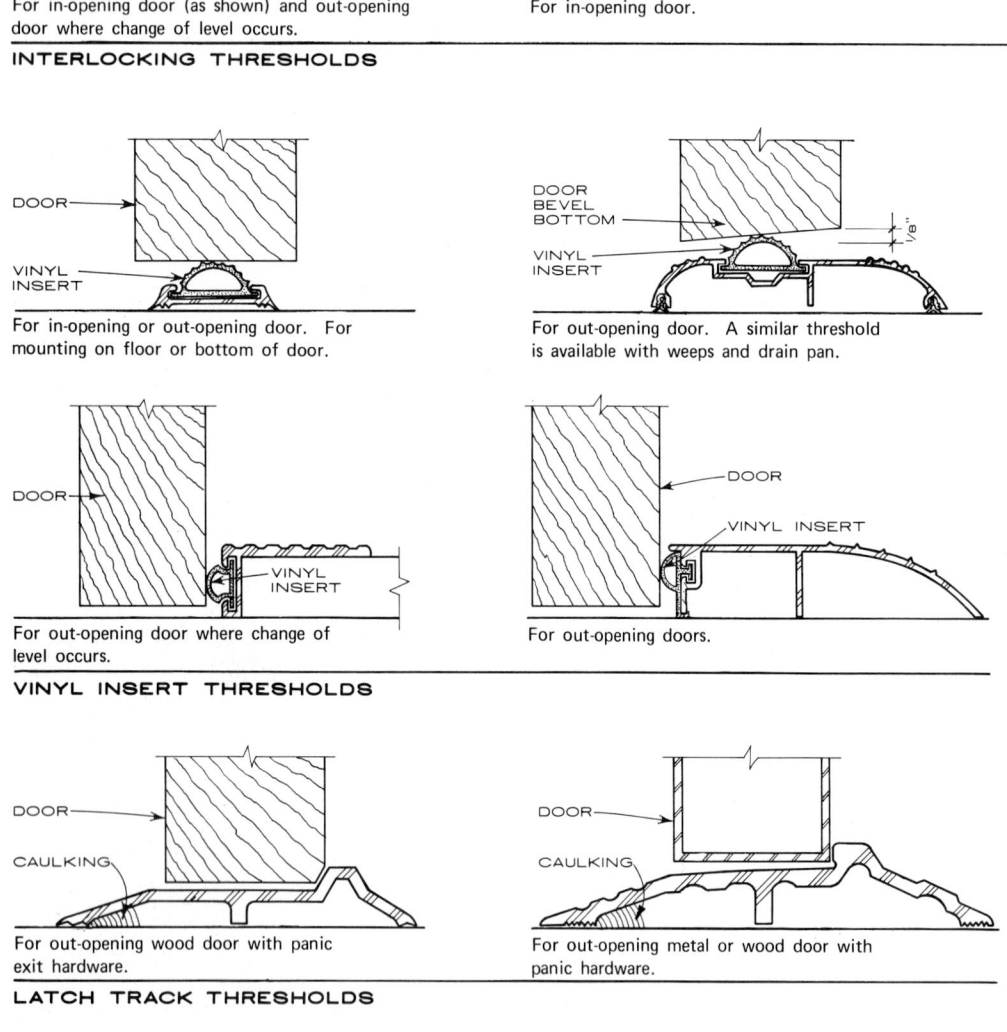

For in-opening or out-opening door. For mounting on floor or bottom of door.

For out-opening door. A similar threshold is available with weeps and drain pan.

SURFACE HOOKS

EXTRUDED METAL   ROLLED METAL

For out-opening door where change of level occurs.

For out-opening doors.

VINYL INSERT THRESHOLDS

EXTRUDED METAL

ROLLED METAL

CONCEALED HOOKS

INTERLOCKING HOOK STRIPS

NOTE
Hook strips are available in aluminum, brass, bronze, and zinc, and vary in thickness and dimensions. Consult manufacturers catalogs.

For out-opening wood door with panic exit hardware.

For out-opening metal or wood door with panic hardware.

LATCH TRACK THRESHOLDS

EXTRUDED METAL   EXTRUDED METAL

THRESHOLD ELEVATORS

NOTE
Available in alum. and bronze. Consult manufacturers' catalogs.

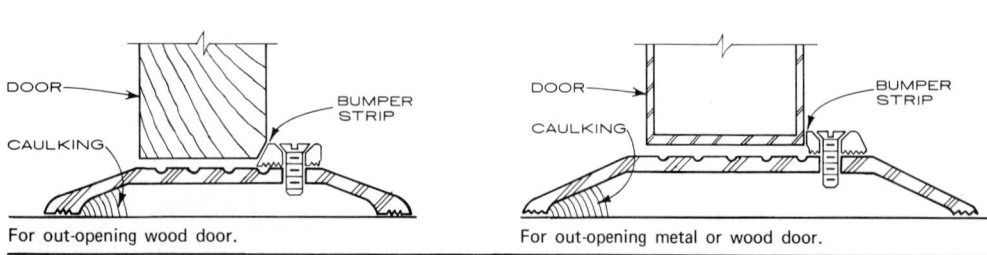

For out-opening wood door.

For out-opening metal or wood door.

FLAT SADDLE THRESHOLDS

GENERAL NOTE
Thresholds are available in bronze and aluminum with a wide selection of shapes and dimensions.

Dan Cowling and Associates, Inc.; Little Rock, Arkansas

 HARDWARE

INTRODUCTION:

The following is a selection of hollow metal details from various manufacturers. They are in no way intended to favor a manufacturer or a product. Details vary. Consult manufacturers literature.

Hollow metal is divided into a frame section and a door section. The frame section can be used with wood doors. Both sections are complete in themselves.

NOMENCLATURE

Active Leaf	The door leaf of a pair in which the lock is normally installed.
Astragal (overlapping)	A vertical molding attached to the meeting edge of one leaf of a pair of doors for protection against weather conditions and to retard passage of smoke, flame and gasses.
Astragal (split)	A vertical molding attached to both leaves at a pair of doors at the meeting edge for protection against weather conditions.
Barrier Screen	See Smoke Screen.
Beveled Edge	The edge at a door that is not at a 90° angle to the face of the door (std. bevel is 1/8" in 2").
Blank Jamb	Vertical member of frame without hardware preparation. Used when doors are furnished with push and pull hardware or surface mounted strikes and single active floor hinges.
Borrowed Light	Four-sided frame prepared for glass installation in field.
Bullnose Trim	The face & jamb width joined by a radius rather than a 90° break.
Cabinet Jamb	Frame in three or more pieces applied as the finished frame over rough buck.
Cap	See Soffit.
Cased Opening	Frame section which does not have any stops.
Covemold Frame	Frame having contour faces (exposed) simulating contour of wood frame.
Cut-Out	A preparation for hardware and/or accessories.
Double Acting Door	Type of door prepared for pivot or spring type hinge permitting the door to swing 90° in either direction.
Double Egress Frame	Double rabbeted double frame prepared to receive two single-acting doors swinging in opposite directions.
Dutch Door	Door having two separate leaves, one hung above the other. Shelf on lower leaf, optional.

Face	Exposed part of frame parallel to face of wall.
Filler Plate	A blank plate used to fill mortised cutouts.
Flat Frame	Frame having flat faces exposed.
Floor Clearance	Distance between bottom of door and finished floor.
Glass Stop	Fixed trim on a glass tight door against which glass is set.
Glazing Bead	A removable trim at glazing opening to hold glass securely in place.
Hand	Term used to designate direction in which door swings.
Handing	The swinging of the door e.g., right hand or left hand. To determine the hand of a door, view the door from the outside. The side that the hinges are on is the hand of the door. If the door swings away from the viewer, the hand is a regular hand, i.e. right or left hand. If the door swings to the viewer, the door is reverse swing, i.e. right hand reverse swing or left hand reverse swing.
Head	Horizontal frame member at top of door opening or top member of transom frames.
Header	See Head.
Hinge Backset	Distance from edge to hinge to stop on frame.
Hinge Filler Plate	Plate installed for a hinge cut-out when no hinge is required.
Inactive Leaf	The door leaf in a pair of doors which is normally held closed by top and bottom bolts.
Jamb	Vertical frame member; between door and glass or wall; between glass and door or wall. See also Mullion.
Jamb Depth	Over-all width of frame section.
Knock Down (KD) Frame	Door frame furnished by manufacturer in three or more basic parts for assembly in field.
Lock Backset	Distance from edge of door to centerline of cylinder or knob.
Masonry Box	See Plaster Guard.
Mortise Preparation	Reinforcing drilling and tapping for hardware which is to be mortised into door or frame.
Mullion	Vertical or horizontal frame member; between glass and glass, or door and door.
Muntin	Non-structural member used to subdivide an open area in frame or door.

Opening Size	Size of frame opening measured between rabbets and finished floor.
Plaster Guard	Metal shield attached behind hinge and strike reinforcement to prevent mortar or plaster from entering mounting holes.
Return	See Backband.
Reveal	That part of the backband which extends beyond finished wall.
Reveal	Distance from face of frame to surface of finished wall.
Reversing Channel	See End Channel.
Reverse Bevel	Refers to hand of door or lock when doors swing to outside.
Rough Opening	Size of wall opening into which frame is installed.
Rubber Silencer	A part attached to the stop of a frame to cushion the closing of door.
Section Width	See Jamb Depth.
Single Acting Door	Type of door prepared for a pivot type or spring-type single-acting hinge permitting the door to swing 90° in one direction only.
Smoke Screen	A door frame combined with sidelights on either or both sides of door openings, including transom opening when and if required.
Soffit	Underside of stop on frame.
Split Jambs	Frames with jamb width in two pieces.
Stilts	See Floor Struts.
Stop	Part of frame against which door closes or glass rests.
Strike Stile	Vertical member of an inactive door leaf which receives the strike.
Strut Guide	Metal piece attached inside throat of frame which guides and holds ceiling strut to frame (usually incorporated in clip).
Sub Buck	See Rough Buck.
Surface Hardware Preparation	Reinforcing or machining or both, for hardware which is applied to surface of door or frame in field.
Top & Bottom Cap	Horizontal channel used in doors which do not have a flush top or bottom.
Transom Bar	The part of a transom frame which separates the top of the door from the transom.
Trim	(1) See face. (2) An applied face.
Trimmed Opening	See Cased Opening.

James W. G. Watson, AIA; Ronald A. Spahn and Associates; Cleveland Heights, Ohio

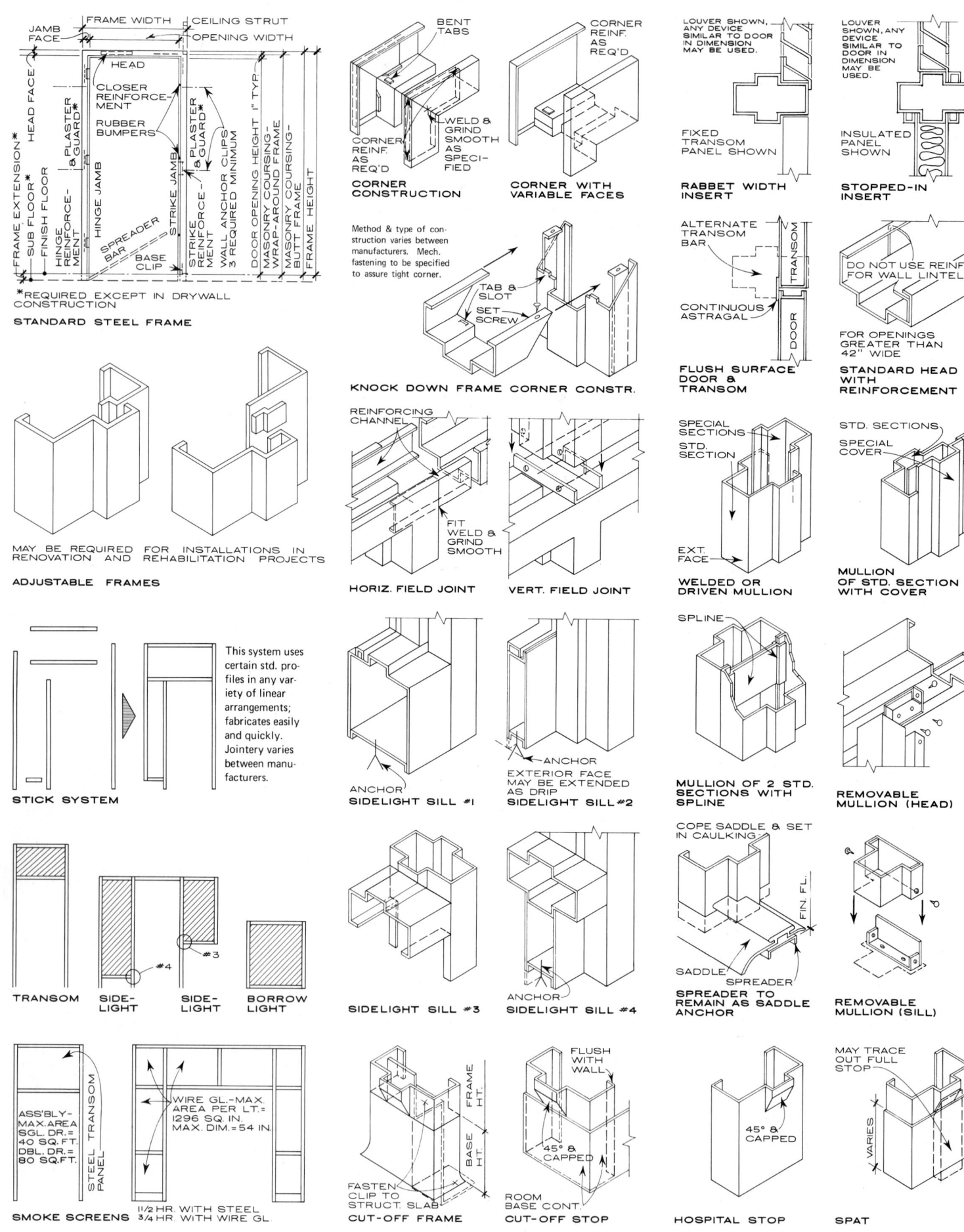

STANDARD STEEL FRAME

*REQUIRED EXCEPT IN DRYWALL CONSTRUCTION

ADJUSTABLE FRAMES

MAY BE REQUIRED FOR INSTALLATIONS IN RENOVATION AND REHABILITATION PROJECTS

STICK SYSTEM

This system uses certain std. profiles in any variety of linear arrangements; fabricates easily and quickly. Jointery varies between manufacturers.

TRANSOM   **SIDE-LIGHT**   **SIDE-LIGHT**   **BORROW LIGHT**

ASS'BLY-MAX.AREA SGL. DR.= 40 SQ. FT. DBL. DR.= 80 SQ. FT.

WIRE GL.-MAX. AREA PER LT.= 1296 SQ. IN. MAX. DIM.= 54 IN.

SMOKE SCREENS   1½ HR. WITH STEEL   ¾ HR. WITH WIRE GL.

CORNER CONSTRUCTION

BENT TABS

CORNER REINF. AS REQ'D

WELD & GRIND SMOOTH AS SPECIFIED

CORNER WITH VARIABLE FACES

CORNER REINF. AS REQ'D

KNOCK DOWN FRAME CORNER CONSTR.

Method & type of construction varies between manufacturers. Mech. fastening to be specified to assure tight corner.

TAB & SLOT

SET SCREW

HORIZ. FIELD JOINT

REINFORCING CHANNEL

FIT WELD & GRIND SMOOTH

VERT. FIELD JOINT

SIDELIGHT SILL #1

ANCHOR

SIDELIGHT SILL #2

ANCHOR

EXTERIOR FACE MAY BE EXTENDED AS DRIP

SIDELIGHT SILL #3

SIDELIGHT SILL #4

ANCHOR

CUT-OFF FRAME

FASTEN CLIP TO STRUCT. SLAB

CUT-OFF STOP

FLUSH WITH WALL

45° & CAPPED

ROOM BASE CONT.

RABBET WIDTH INSERT

LOUVER SHOWN, ANY DEVICE SIMILAR TO DOOR IN DIMENSION MAY BE USED.

FIXED TRANSOM PANEL SHOWN

STOPPED-IN INSERT

LOUVER SHOWN, ANY DEVICE SIMILAR TO DOOR IN DIMENSION MAY BE USED.

INSULATED PANEL SHOWN

FLUSH SURFACE DOOR & TRANSOM

ALTERNATE TRANSOM BAR

CONTINUOUS ASTRAGAL

STANDARD HEAD WITH REINFORCEMENT

DO NOT USE REINF. FOR WALL LINTEL.

FOR OPENINGS GREATER THAN 42" WIDE

WELDED OR DRIVEN MULLION

SPECIAL SECTIONS

STD. SECTION

EXT. FACE

MULLION OF STD. SECTION WITH COVER

STD. SECTIONS

SPECIAL COVER

MULLION OF 2 STD. SECTIONS WITH SPLINE

SPLINE

REMOVABLE MULLION (HEAD)

SPREADER TO REMAIN AS SADDLE ANCHOR

COPE SADDLE & SET IN CAULKING

FIN. FL.

SADDLE   SPREADER

REMOVABLE MULLION (SILL)

HOSPITAL STOP

45° CAPPED

SPAT

MAY TRACE OUT FULL STOP

VARIES

James W. G. Watson, AIA; Ronald A. Spahn and Associates; Cleveland Heights, Ohio

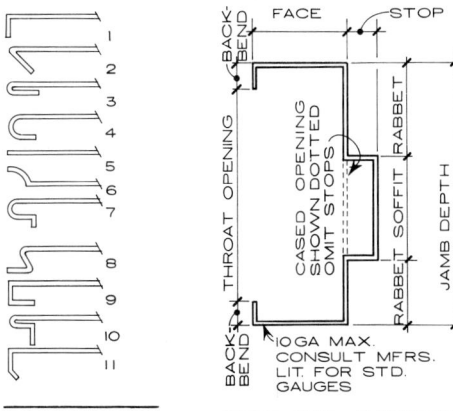

BACKBENDS **STD. DBL. RABBET**

(labels within: FACE, STOP, BACKBEND, THROAT OPENING, CASED OPENING SHOWN DOTTED OMIT STOPS, RABBET, SOFFIT, RABBET, JAMB DEPTH, 10 GA. MAX. CONSULT MFRS. LIT. FOR STD. GAUGES)

VARIOUS STANDARD PROFILES [1]

JAMB DEPTH	2¾	3	3¾	4¾	5½	5¾	6¾	7¾	8¾	12¾
RABBET [3]	SINGLE		1¹⁵⁄₁₆ STD. FOR 1¾" DOOR							
SOFFIT [3]	RABBET									
RABBET [3]	ONLY		1⁹⁄₁₆ STD. FOR 1⅜" DOOR							
BACKBEND	½	⁷⁄₁₆	½	½	¾	½	½	½	½	½
THROAT	1¾	2⅛	2	3¾	4	4¾	5¾	6¾	7¾	11¾

NOTES

1. Many others available. Consult mfrs. list for dimensions and options.
2. Depths vary in ⅛" increments to 12 ¾" max.
3. Omit stops for cased opening frames.
4. Std. stop ⅝", ½" min. + std. face 2", 1" min.

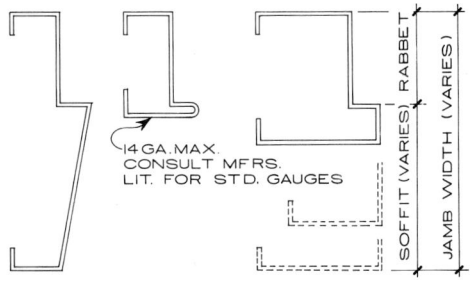

VARIOUS SINGLE RABBETS

(labels: 14 GA. MAX. CONSULT MFRS. LIT. FOR STD. GAUGES, SOFFIT (VARIES) RABBET, RABBET (VARIES), JAMB WIDTH (VARIES))

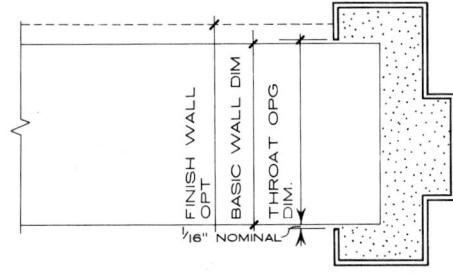

1. Basic wall dim. < throat opening dim. Fin wall mat'l (dotted may encroach on backbend).
2. Anchors appropriate for wall constr. Req'd min. 3 per jamb.
3. Fill frame w/mortar or plaster as used in wall.
4. Grout frame, backbend at masonry wall.
5. Backbend may vary as selected.

(labels: FINISH WALL OPT, BASIC WALL DIM, THROAT OPG DIM, 1/16" NOMINAL)

WRAP - AROUND FRAMES

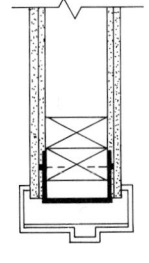 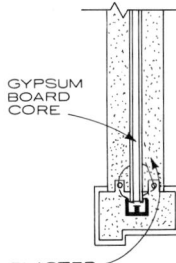

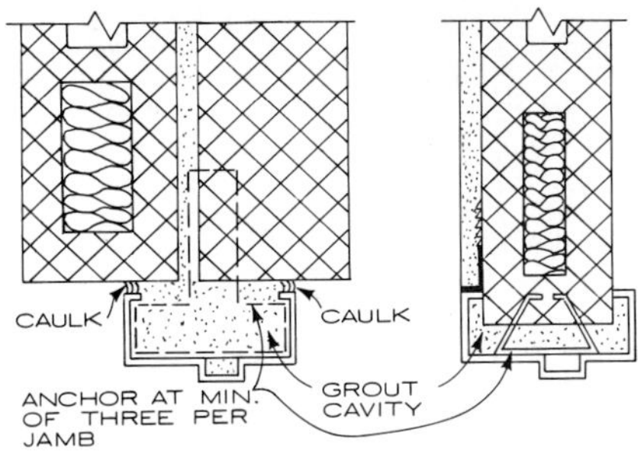

BUTTED TO MASONRY **CONCRETE MASONRY UNIT WITH PLASTER FINISH**

(labels: CAULK, CAULK, ANCHOR AT MIN. OF THREE PER JAMB, GROUT CAVITY)

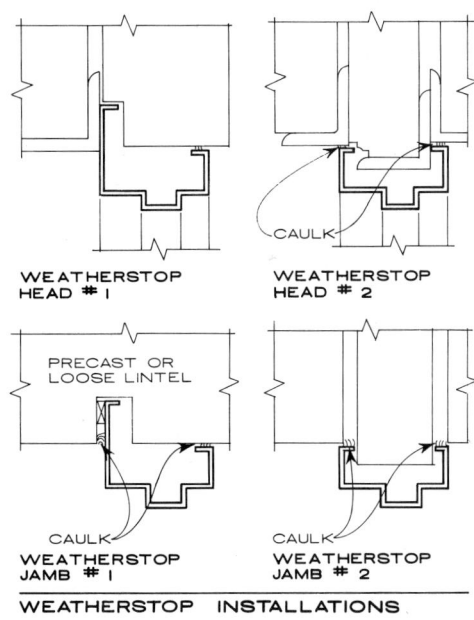

WOOD STUD WITH PLASTER ON PLASTER LATH **SOLID PLASTER**

(labels: GYPSUM BOARD CORE, PLASTER)

VARIOUS INSTALLATIONS

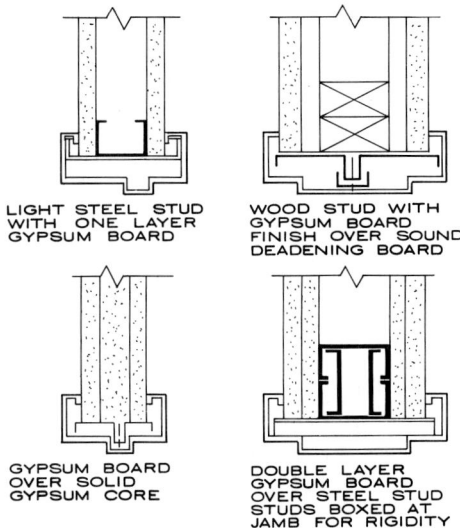

DRYWALL INSTALLATIONS

LIGHT STEEL STUD WITH ONE LAYER GYPSUM BOARD

WOOD STUD WITH GYPSUM BOARD FINISH OVER SOUND DEADENING BOARD

GYPSUM BOARD OVER SOLID GYPSUM CORE

DOUBLE LAYER GYPSUM BOARD OVER STEEL STUD STUDS BOXED AT JAMB FOR RIGIDITY

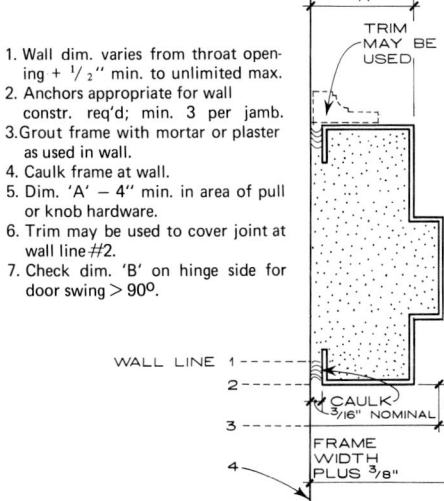

1. Wall dim. varies from throat opening + ½" min. to unlimited max.
2. Anchors appropriate for wall constr. req'd; min. 3 per jamb.
3. Grout frame with mortar or plaster as used in wall.
4. Caulk frame at wall.
5. Dim. 'A' − 4" min. in area of pull or knob hardware.
6. Trim may be used to cover joint at wall line #2.
7. Check dim. 'B' on hinge side for door swing > 90°.

(labels: A, TRIM MAY BE USED, WALL LINE 1, 2, 3, 4, CAULK 3/16" NOMINAL, FRAME WIDTH PLUS 3/8")

BUTT FRAME

(Weatherstop installation drawings)

WEATHERSTOP HEAD #1 **WEATHERSTOP HEAD #2**

WEATHERSTOP JAMB #1 **WEATHERSTOP JAMB #2**

(labels: CAULK, PRECAST OR LOOSE LINTEL, CAULK, CAULK)

WEATHERSTOP INSTALLATIONS

NOTES

1. Some details vary between manufacturers.

2. Stock frames stocked in warehouse prior to receipt of order. Certain profiles are warehoused locally.

3. Standard frames manufactured from existing jigs and tooling upon receipt of order. Certain profiles are readily available.

4. Custom frames manufactured in response to specific dimensional requirements of a particular customer. Custom profiles are available with relative delay.

5. Selection should reflect anticipated requirements of construction schedule.

6. Certain detail features will constitute a custom frame, verify with manufacturer.

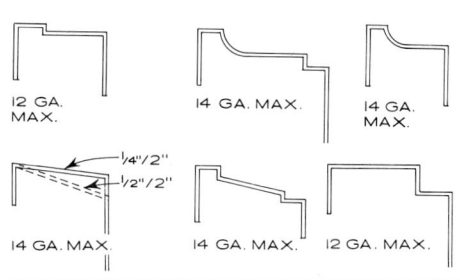

VARIOUS FACES

(labels: 12 GA. MAX., 14 GA. MAX., 14 GA. MAX., 1/4"/2", 1/2"/2", 14 GA. MAX., 14 GA. MAX., 12 GA. MAX.)

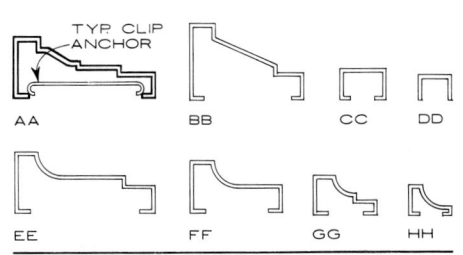

VARIOUS TRIM & SCRIBE MOLDING

(labels: TYP CLIP ANCHOR, AA, BB, CC, DD, EE, FF, GG, HH)

James W. G. Watson, AIA; Ronald A. Spahn and Associates; Cleveland Heights, Ohio

METAL DOORS 8

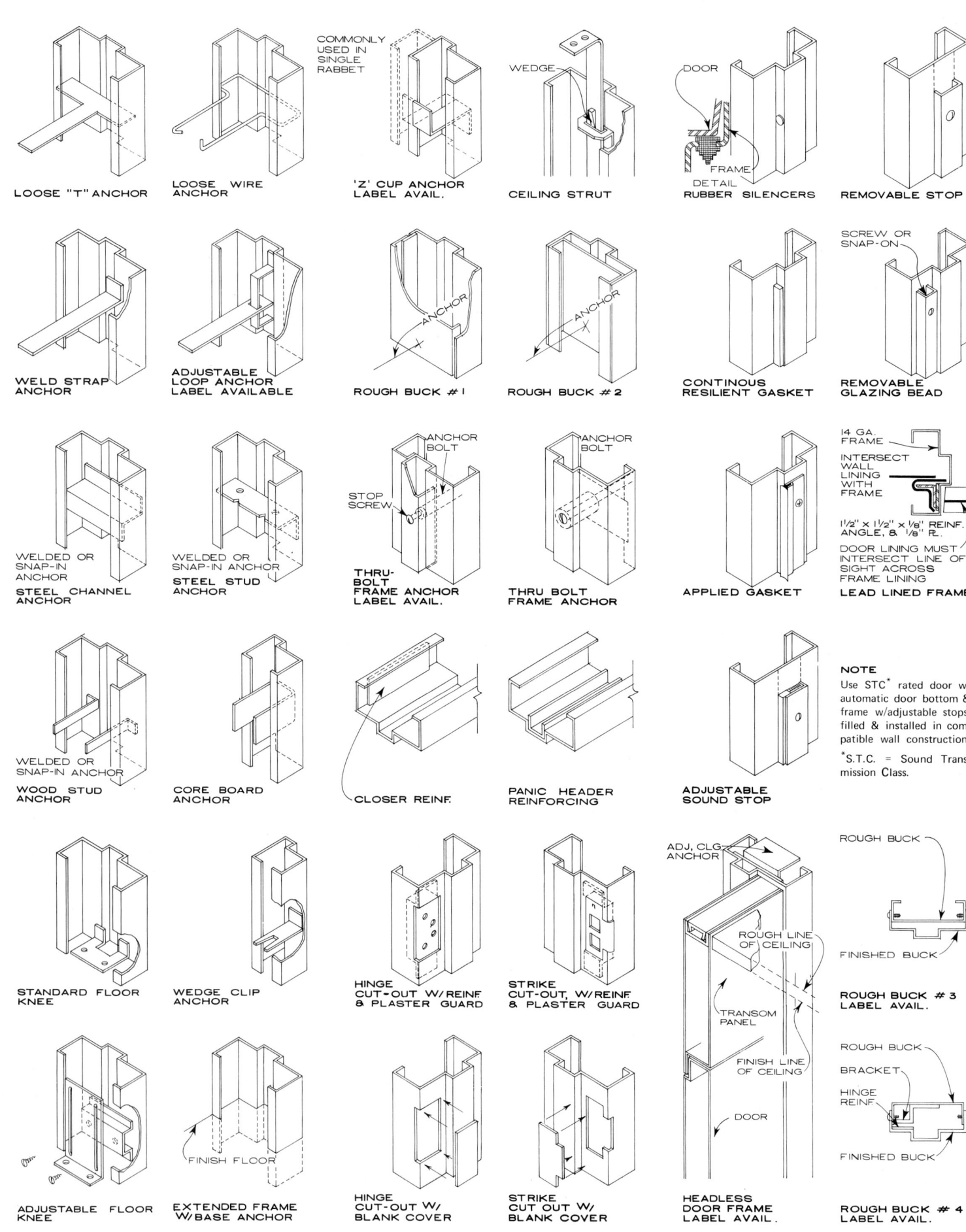

LOOSE "T" ANCHOR

LOOSE WIRE ANCHOR

'Z' CUP ANCHOR LABEL AVAIL.

COMMONLY USED IN SINGLE RABBET

CEILING STRUT

WEDGE

DOOR
FRAME DETAIL
RUBBER SILENCERS

REMOVABLE STOP

WELD STRAP ANCHOR

ADJUSTABLE LOOP ANCHOR LABEL AVAILABLE

ROUGH BUCK #1

ANCHOR

ROUGH BUCK #2

ANCHOR

CONTINOUS RESILIENT GASKET

SCREW OR SNAP-ON
REMOVABLE GLAZING BEAD

WELDED OR SNAP-IN ANCHOR
STEEL CHANNEL ANCHOR

WELDED OR SNAP-IN ANCHOR
STEEL STUD ANCHOR

ANCHOR BOLT
STOP SCREW
THRU-BOLT FRAME ANCHOR LABEL AVAIL.

ANCHOR BOLT
THRU BOLT FRAME ANCHOR

APPLIED GASKET

14 GA. FRAME
INTERSECT WALL LINING WITH FRAME
1½" x 1½" x ⅛" REINF. ANGLE, & ⅛" PL.
DOOR LINING MUST INTERSECT LINE OF SIGHT ACROSS FRAME LINING
LEAD LINED FRAME

WELDED OR SNAP-IN ANCHOR
WOOD STUD ANCHOR

CORE BOARD ANCHOR

CLOSER REINF.

PANIC HEADER REINFORCING

ADJUSTABLE SOUND STOP

NOTE
Use STC* rated door w/ automatic door bottom & frame w/adjustable stops; filled & installed in compatible wall construction.

*S.T.C. = Sound Transmission Class.

STANDARD FLOOR KNEE

WEDGE CLIP ANCHOR

HINGE CUT-OUT W/ REINF & PLASTER GUARD

STRIKE CUT-OUT, W/ REINF & PLASTER GUARD

ADJ, CLG. ANCHOR
ROUGH LINE OF CEILING
TRANSOM PANEL
FINISH LINE OF CEILING
DOOR

ROUGH BUCK
FINISHED BUCK
ROUGH BUCK #3 LABEL AVAIL.

ADJUSTABLE FLOOR KNEE

EXTENDED FRAME W/ BASE ANCHOR
FINISH FLOOR

HINGE CUT-OUT W/ BLANK COVER

STRIKE CUT OUT W/ BLANK COVER

HEADLESS DOOR FRAME LABEL AVAIL.

ROUGH BUCK
BRACKET
HINGE REINF
FINISHED BUCK
ROUGH BUCK #4 LABEL AVAIL.

James W. G. Watson, AIA; Ronald A. Spahn and Associates; Cleveland Heights, Ohio

GENERAL

Fire doors are the most widely used and accepted means for the protection of both vertical and horizontal openings. Suitability of fire doors is determined by test by nationally recognized testing laboratories. The doors are tested as they are installed in the field; that is, with the frame, hardware, wired glass panels, and other accessories necessary to complete the installation.

NFPA 80, Standard for the Installation of Fire Doors and Windows, classifies the various types of openings commonly encountered.

TYPES OF OPENINGS

1. CLASS A OPENINGS: These are in walls separating buildings or dividing a single building into fire areas. Doors for the protection of these openings have a fire protection rating of 3 hr.
2. CLASS B OPENINGS: These are in enclosures of vertical communication through buildings (stairs, elevators, etc.). Doors for the protection of these openings have a fire protection rating of 1 or 1 1/2 hr.
3. CLASS C OPENINGS: These are in corridor and room partitions. Doors for the protection of these openings have a fire protection rating of 3/4 hr.
4. CLASS D OPENINGS: These are in exterior walls, which are subject to severe fire exposure from outside of the building. Doors and shutters for the protection of these openings have a fire protection rating of 1 1/2 hr.
5. CLASS E OPENINGS: These are in exterior walls, which are subject to moderate or light fire exposure from outside of the building. Doors, shutters, or windows for the protection of these openings have a fire protection rating of 3/4 hr.

TYPES OF DOORS

There are several types of construction for fire doors; a few are as follows:

1. COMPOSITE DOORS: These are of the flush design and consist of a manufactured core material with chemically impregnated wood edge banding and untreated wood face veneers, or laminated plastic faces, or surrounded by and encased in steel.
2. HOLLOW METAL DOORS: These are of formed steel of the flush and paneled designs of #20 gauge or heavier steel.
3. METAL CLAD (KALAMEIN) DOORS: These are of flush and paneled design consisting of metal covered wood cores or stiles and rails and insulated panels covered with steel of 20 gauge or lighter.
4. SHEET METAL DOORS: These are of formed #22 gauge or lighter steel and of the corrugated, flush, and paneled designs.
5. ROLLING STEEL DOORS: These are of the interlocking steel slat design or plate steel construction.
6. TIN CLAD DOORS: These are of two- or three-ply wood core construction, covered with #30 gauge galvanized steel or terneplate (maximum size 14 by 20 in.); or #24 gauge galvanized steel sheets not more than 48 in. wide.
7. CURTAIN TYPE DOORS: These consist of interlocking steel blades or a continuous formed spring steel curtain in a steel frame.

DOOR LABELS

FRAME LABEL
UNDERWRITERS LABELS

Wm. G. Miner, AIA; Architect; Washington, D.C.

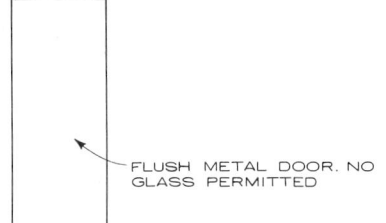

FLUSH METAL DOOR. NO GLASS PERMITTED

CLASS A AND D (3 AND 1 1/2 HR)

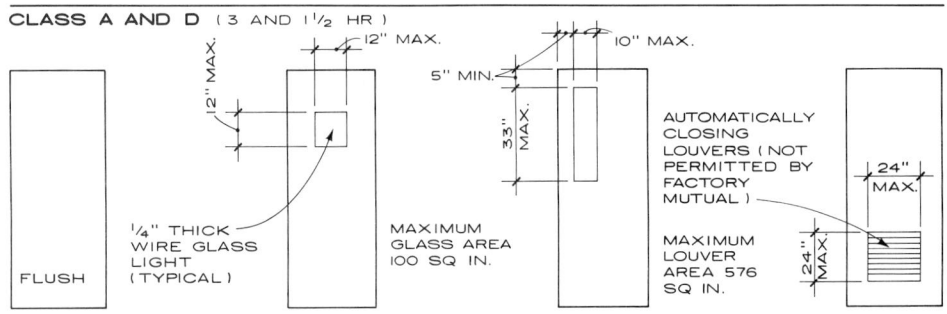

FLUSH — 1/4" THICK WIRE GLASS LIGHT (TYPICAL) — MAXIMUM GLASS AREA 100 SQ IN. — AUTOMATICALLY CLOSING LOUVERS (NOT PERMITTED BY FACTORY MUTUAL) — MAXIMUM LOUVER AREA 576 SQ IN.

CLASS B (1 OR 1 1/2 HR)

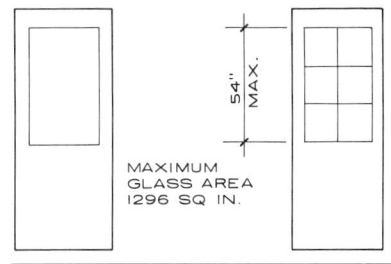

MAXIMUM GLASS AREA 1296 SQ IN.

MAXIMUM DOOR SIZES

Single door	4' x 10' with 3-point lock or approved single latch
	4' x 8' with fire exit hardware
Pair of doors	8' x 10' with 3-point lock
	8' x 8' with approved single latch
	8' x 7'2'' with fire exit hardware

NOTE: Three hinges (or pivots) are required on doors up to 7'6'' in height; 4 hinges (or pivots) on higher doors.

MAXIMUM DOOR SIZES

Single door	4' x 10' with 3-point lock
	4' x 9' with approved single latch
	4' x 8' with fire exit hardware
Pair of doors	8' x 10' with 3-point lock
	8' x 9' with approved single latch
	8' x 7'2'' with fire exit hardware

CLASS C AND E (3/4 HR)

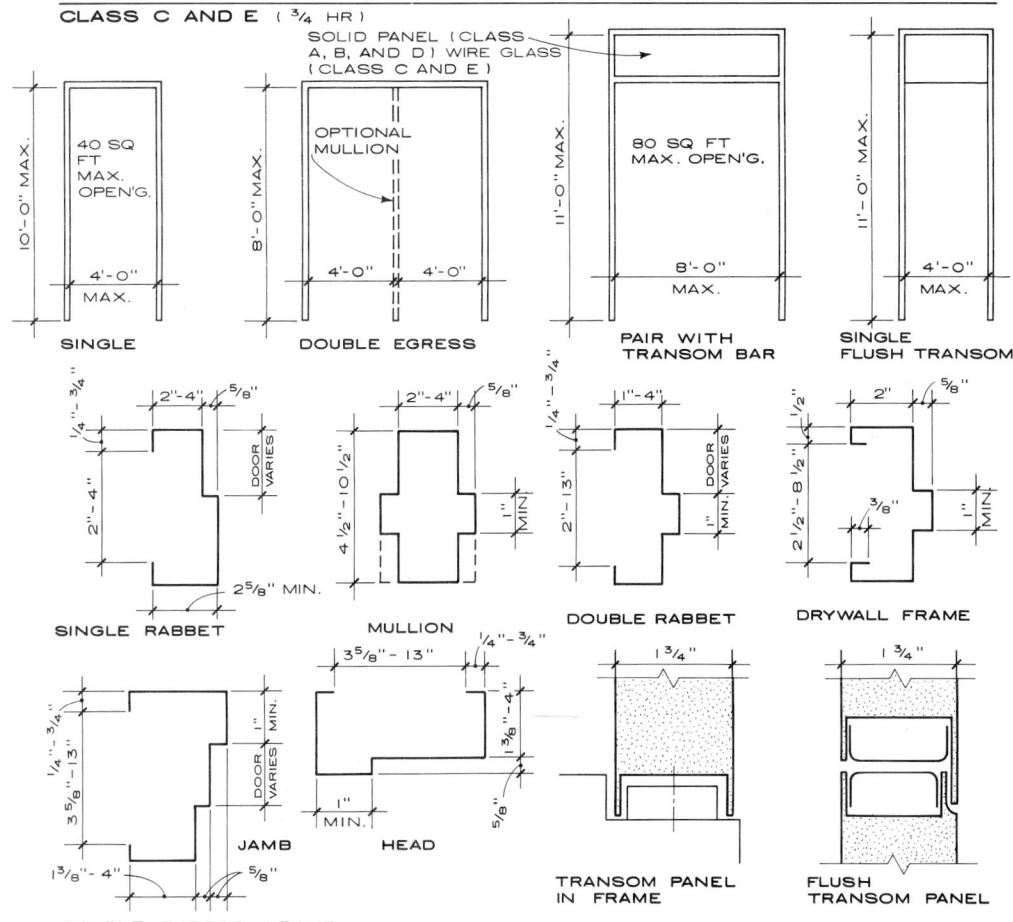

SOLID PANEL (CLASS A, B, AND D) WIRE GLASS (CLASS C AND E)

SINGLE — DOUBLE EGRESS — PAIR WITH TRANSOM BAR — SINGLE FLUSH TRANSOM

SINGLE RABBET — MULLION — DOUBLE RABBET — DRYWALL FRAME

JAMB — HEAD — TRANSOM PANEL IN FRAME — FLUSH TRANSOM PANEL

DOUBLE EGRESS FRAME
FIRE RATED FRAMES AND DETAILS

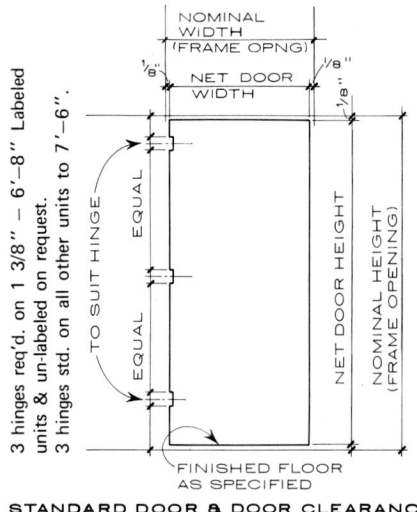

3 hinges req'd. on 1 3/8" — 6'-8" Labeled units & un-labeled on request. 3 hinges std. on all other units to 7'-6".

NOMINAL WIDTH (FRAME OPNG)
NET DOOR WIDTH
TO SUIT HINGE
EQUAL / EQUAL / EQUAL / EQUAL
NET DOOR HEIGHT
NOMINAL HEIGHT (FRAME OPENING)
FINISHED FLOOR AS SPECIFIED

STANDARD DOOR & DOOR CLEARANCE

Tubular stiles & rails compose structural elements.

Stiles and rails hold in place a flush or recessed panel.

A recessed panel door is generally considered an industrial type door. May be used for decorative purposes.

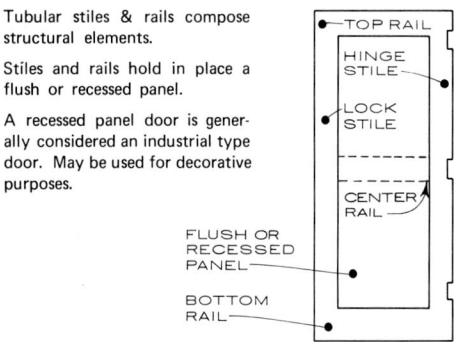

TOP RAIL
HINGE STILE
LOCK STILE
CENTER RAIL
FLUSH OR RECESSED PANEL
BOTTOM RAIL

STILE & RAIL CONSTRUCTION

Relatively wide center panel connected to hinge & lock stile by interlocking and/or welding—forming 2 exposed vertical seams on door face.

Inverted channel closes top & bottom.

Exterior door is furnished with cap.

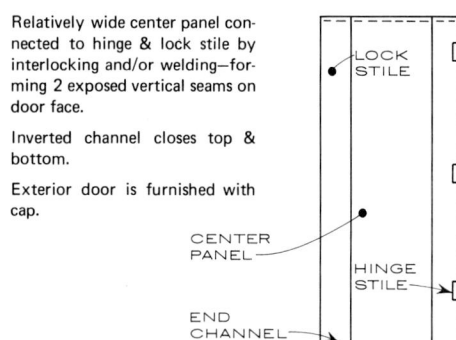

LOCK STILE
CENTER PANEL
HINGE STILE
END CHANNEL

STILE & PANEL CONSTRUCTION

Pan type or enclosed grid construction.

No seams visible on face.

Exposed seams may be on vertical edges where two pans join.

Top &/or bottom of door may be flush or recessed.

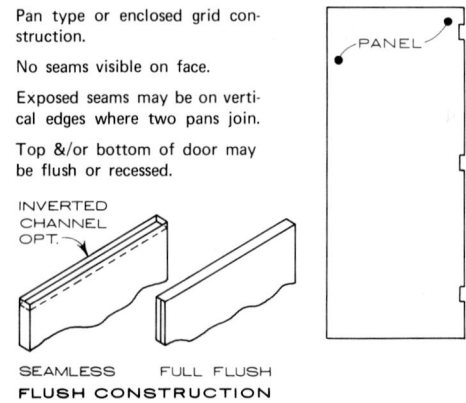

PANEL
INVERTED CHANNEL OPT.
SEAMLESS / FULL FLUSH

FLUSH CONSTRUCTION

DOOR TYPES

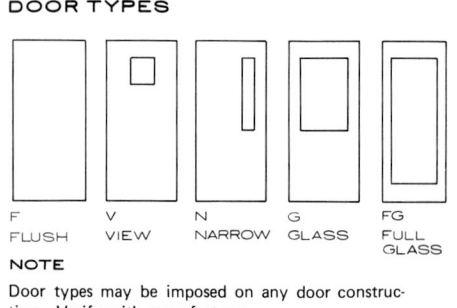

| F FLUSH | V VIEW | N NARROW | G GLASS | FG FULL GLASS |

NOTE

Door types may be imposed on any door construction. Verify with manufacturer.

Divisions are made of stiles and rails or muntins.

Areas defined are filled with glass, screening, louvers, recessed or flush panels.

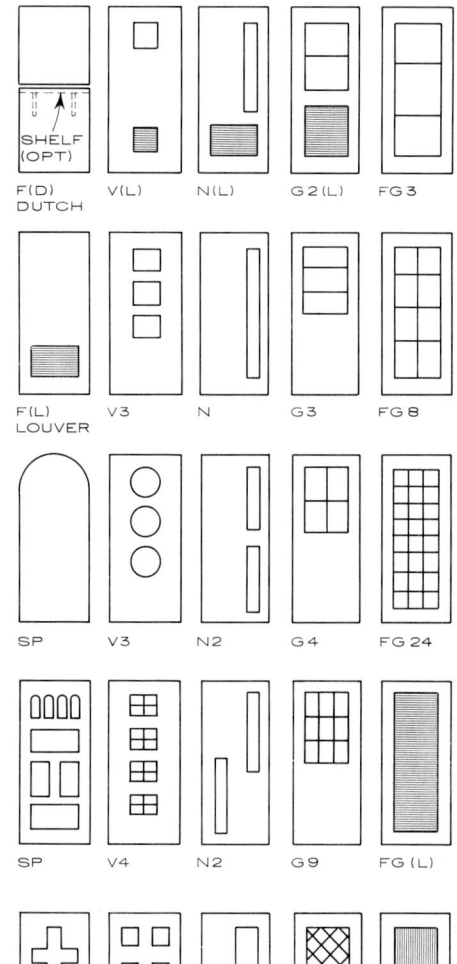

F(D) DUTCH / SHELF (OPT)	V(L)	N(L)	G2(L)	FG3
F(L) LOUVER	V3	N	G3	FG8
SP	V3	N2	G4	FG24
SP	V4	N2	G9	FG(L)
SP	V8	N	GX	FG(V)

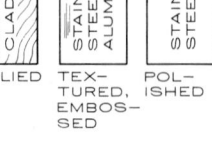

| STANDARD PRIMED AND/OR GALV. | FINISH PAINT BAKED ENAMEL | APPLIED VINYL CLAD | TEXTURED, EMBOSSED STAINLESS STEEL, ALUM. | POLISHED STAINLESS STEEL |

FINISHES

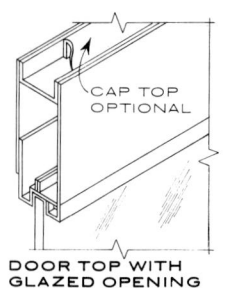

CAP TOP OPTIONAL

DOOR TOP WITH GLAZED OPENING

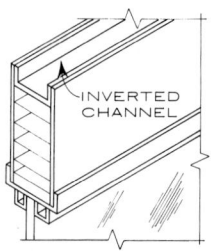

INVERTED CHANNEL

STILE & PANEL DOOR TOP WITH GLAZED OPENING

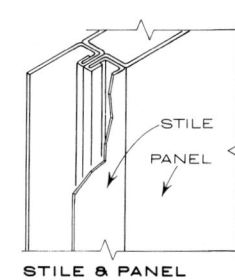

FLUSH DOOR CLOSER REINF.

STILE
PANEL

STILE & PANEL JOINT

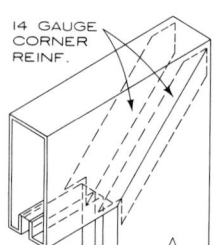
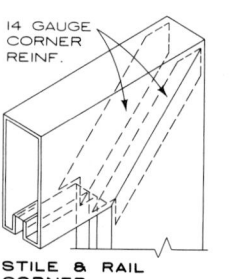

SPOT OR PROJECTION WELD TO DR.

HINGE REINFORCEMENT

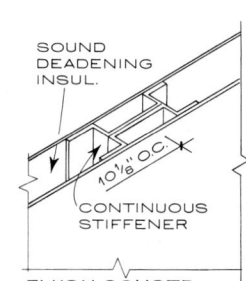

SHEET METAL

STILE & RAIL DOOR

14 GAUGE CORNER REINF.

STILE & RAIL CORNER

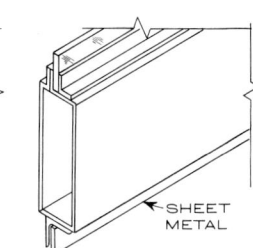

SOUND DEADENING INSUL.
10 1/2" O.C.
CONTINUOUS STIFFENER

FLUSH CONSTR.

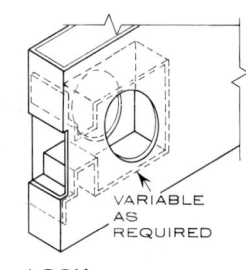

KRAFT HONEYCOMB CORE

FLUSH DOOR CORE

VARIABLE AS REQUIRED

LOCK REINFORCEMENT

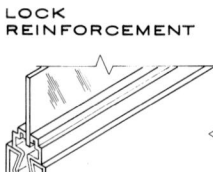

CONT. EDGE STIFFENER
CONT. WELD SEAM

FLUSH DOOR BOTTOM & EDGE CONSTR.

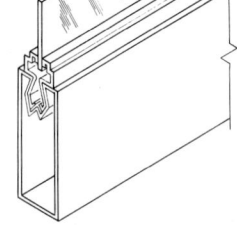

STILE & RAIL DOOR BOTTOM CONSTR.

James W. G. Watson, AIA; Ronald A. Spahn and Associates; Cleveland Heights, Ohio

MINIMUM GAUGES FOR COMMERCIAL STEEL DOORS

ITEM	GAUGE NO.	EQUIVALENT THICKNESS (IN.)
Door frames	16	0.0598
Surface applied hardware reinforcement	16	0.0598
Doors—hollow steel construction		
Panels and stile	18	0.0478
Doors—composite construction		
Perimeter channel	18	0.0478
Surface sheets	22	0.0299
Reinforcement		
Surface applied hardware	16	0.0598
Lock and strike	16	0.0598
Hinge	10	0.1345
Flush bolt	16	0.0598
Glass molding	20	0.0359
Glass muntins	22	0.0299

NOTES

1. The steel door tables represent minimum standards published by the U.S. Department of Commerce for standard stock commercial, 1 3/4 in. thick steel doors and frames, and flush type interior steel doors and frames (doors not more than 3 ft in width).

2. Specifications for custom hollow metal doors and frames are published by the National Association of Architectural Metal Manufacturers. Standards may also vary according to location or the agency—always consult with the local authorities and/or agencies to determine what they require. Doors must be selected according to the project requirements such as frequency of usage, type of traffic, conditions required by the enclosed space, and environmental conditions.

MINIMUM GAUGES FOR INTERIOR STEEL DOORS

ITEM	GAUGE NO.	EQUIVALENT THICKNESS (IN.)
Door frames, 1 3/8 in. thick	18	0.0478
Door frames, 1 3/4 in. thick	16	0.0598
Stiles and panels	20	0.0359
Reinforcement		
Lock and strike	16	0.0598
Hinge	11	0.1196
Closer	14	0.0747

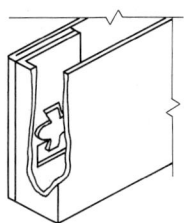

MECHANICAL INTERLOCKING

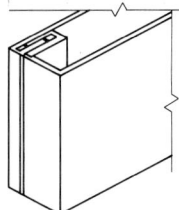

HEMMED

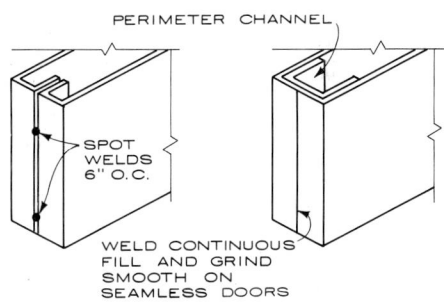

SPOT WELDED SEAM   **EXPOSED SEAM OR SEAMLESS**

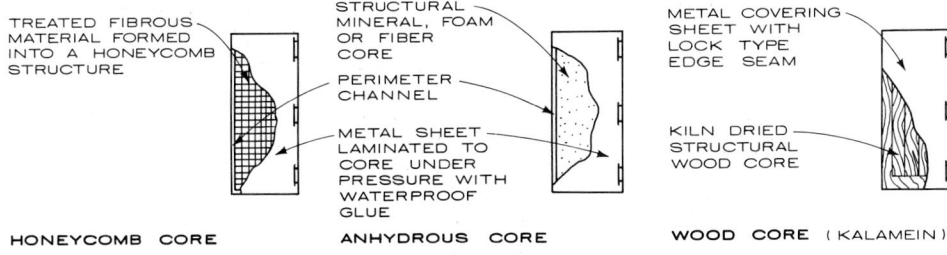

HONEYCOMB CORE   **ANHYDROUS CORE**   **WOOD CORE** (KALAMEIN)

NONMETALLIC CORE DOORS

DOOR EDGES

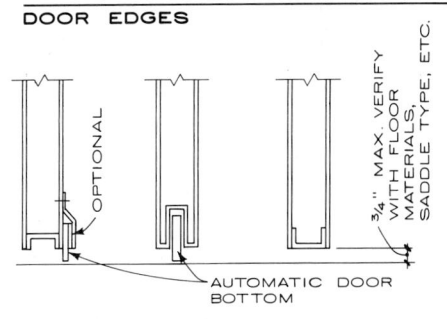

DOOR BOTTOMS

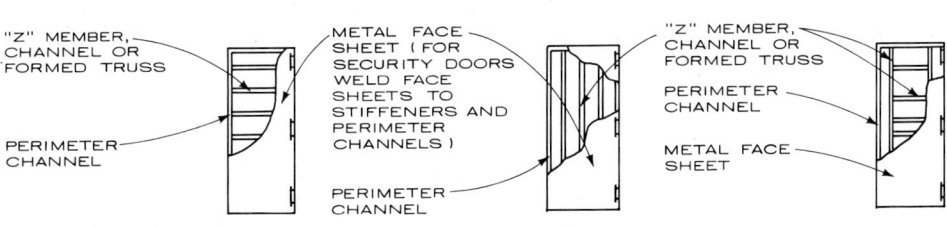

HORIZONTAL STIFFENERS   **VERTICAL STIFFENERS**   **GRID STIFFENERS**

STIFFENED CORE DOORS (HEAVY DOORS) **NORMALLY SOUND DEADENED OR INSULATED**

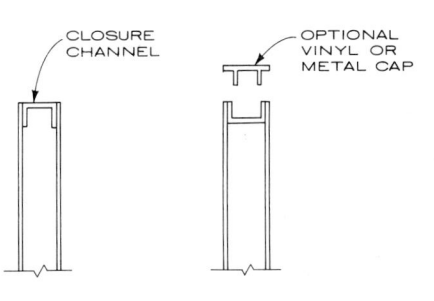

DOOR TOPS

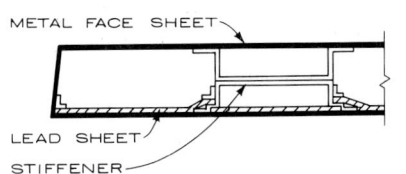

LEAD LINED CORE

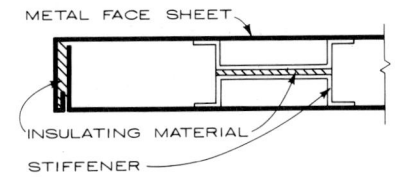

THERMAL BREAK CORE

SPECIAL CORE DOORS

Kelly Sacher & Associates; Architects Engineers Planners; N. Babylon, New York

METAL DOORS   **8**

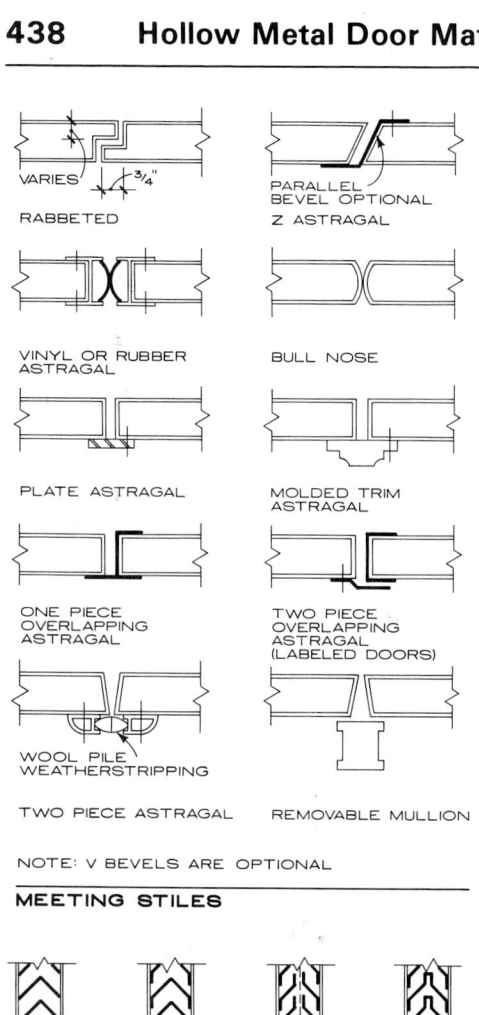

RABBETED

PARALLEL BEVEL OPTIONAL
Z ASTRAGAL

VINYL OR RUBBER ASTRAGAL

BULL NOSE

PLATE ASTRAGAL

MOLDED TRIM ASTRAGAL

ONE PIECE OVERLAPPING ASTRAGAL

TWO PIECE OVERLAPPING ASTRAGAL (LABELED DOORS)

WOOL PILE WEATHERSTRIPPING

TWO PIECE ASTRAGAL

REMOVABLE MULLION

NOTE: V BEVELS ARE OPTIONAL

MEETING STILES

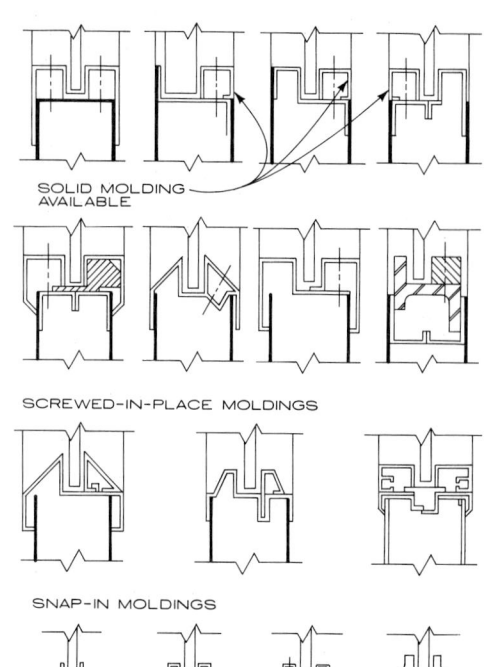

SOLID MOLDING AVAILABLE

SCREWED-IN-PLACE MOLDINGS

SNAP-IN MOLDINGS

MUNTINS

GLAZING DETAILS

INVERTED V LOUVERS

 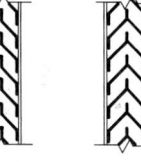 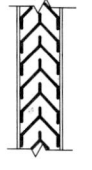

INVERTED Y LOUVERS

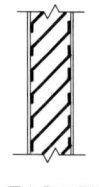

Z LOUVER

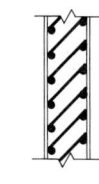

BAR GRILLES

LIGHTPROOF LOUVERS

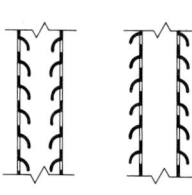

USED WITH AIR CONDITIONING (I.E. PRESSURE DROP)

AIR CONDITIONING LOUVER

PUNCHED GRILLE

STAMPED LOUVERS

DOOR LOUVER MOLDINGS

SPOT WELDS OR SCREWS

WEEP HOLES

INSECT OR BIRD SCREEN

INSECT SCREEN

BIRD SCREEN

DOOR LOUVER MOLDINGS

STANDARD FOLDED

EXTRUDED ALUMINUM REWIRABLE

EXTRUDED ALUMINUM REWIRABLE

DOOR SCREENS

LOUVERS AND VENTS

Kelly Sacher & Associates; Architects Engineers Planners; N. Babylon, New York

MATERIALS

Hollow metal doors are available in various steel gauges according to where and how they will be used. The following gradings should be used only as guidelines in selecting doors for a particular project. Local codes and governing authorities establish minimum gauges, which should always be consulted.

GRADE	GAUGE
Residential	20 gauge and lighter
Commercial	16 and 18 gauge
Institutional	12 and 14 gauge
High security	Steel plate

Some manufacturers will custom make moldings and muntins to meet a specific design, as long as there is sufficient quantity involved.

For security, the exterior moldings on exterior doors should be welded into the door and all exposed fasteners should be tamperproof.

For fire ratings of hollow metal doors and requirements for fire doors see other pages in this series.

FINISH

Hollow metal doors should receive at least one shop coat of rust inhibitive primer before they are delivered to the job site. In very corrosive atmospheres, such as saltwater beach locations, it is advisable to have the doors and frames hot dipped galvanized for additional protection.

Doors are available from several manufacturers, with factory applied paint finishes in various colors.

GLAZING

The size and type of glass permitted in fire rated doors is determined by local building codes and governing authorities having jurisdiction. The following table should only be used as a guide:

DOOR RATING	GLAZING REQUIREMENTS
*A—3 hr	No glazing permitted
*B—1½ hr	100 sq in. of glazing per door leaf
C—¾ hr	Max. 1296 sq in. of glazing per light. Max. dim. per light = 54 in. Min. dim. per light = 3 in.
*D—1½ hr	No glazing permitted
E—¾ hr	Max. 720 sq in. of glazing per light. Max. dim. per light = 54 in.

NOTE: Available on composite doors only. A, B, and D doors are available with Heat Transmission Ratings of 250°F or 650°F, or are not rated.

LOUVERS AND VENTS

Door louvers are available extruded, formed, and stamped in various metals and configurations; operable with or without a fusible link. Punched, stamped, and bar grilles are also available.

The percentage of free area for louvers depends on the louver blade thickness, spacing, and type. For this information consult the manufacturer's catalogs.

Door louvers and grilles are available prefinished, without moldings, and with moldings attached at the factory on one or both sides.

Insert screens are often used in conjunction with louvers or grilles; they may be used by themselves as well, however, in some applications. Screen material is available in various grid and wire sizes and materials.

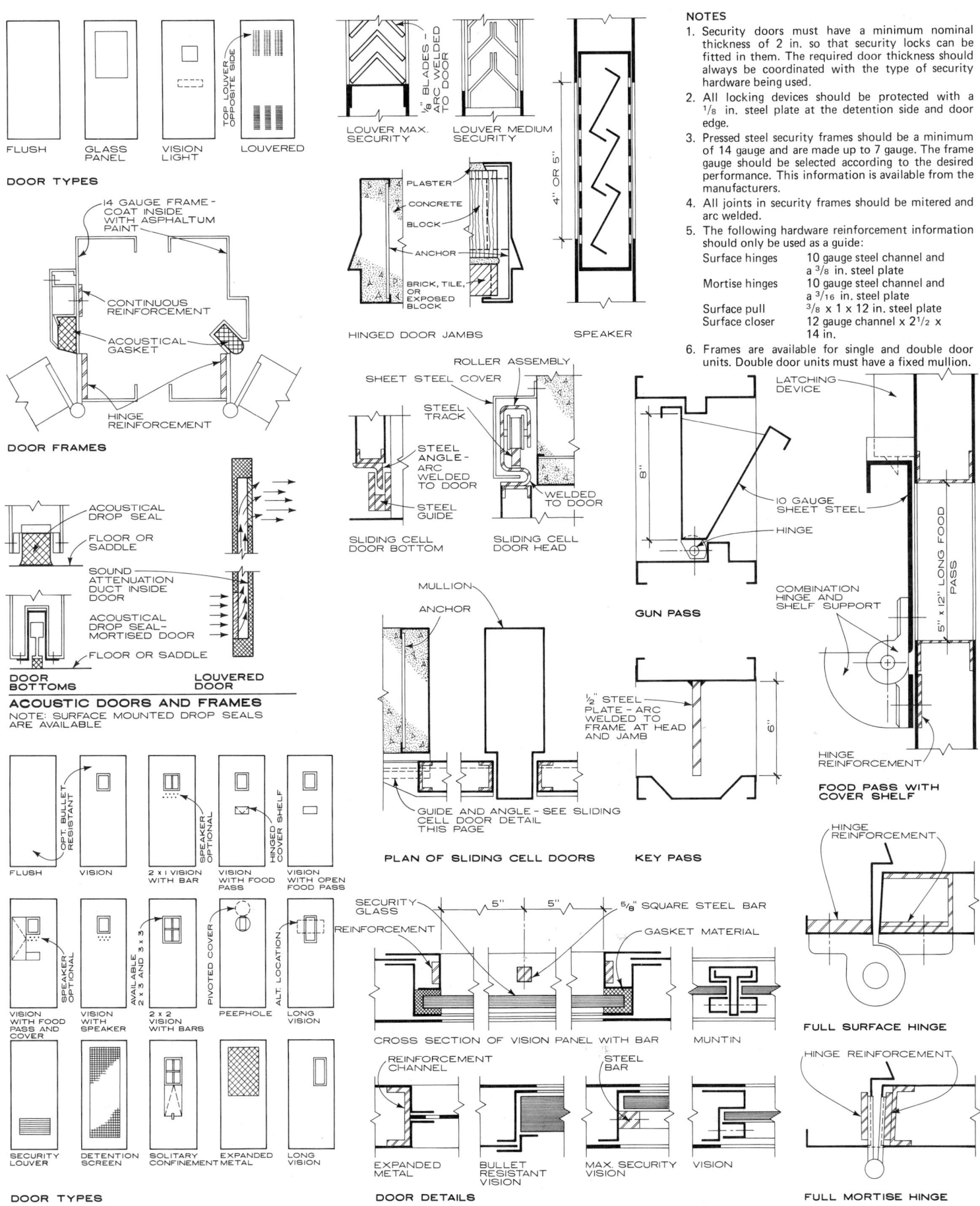

DOOR TYPES

FLUSH | GLASS PANEL | VISION LIGHT | LOUVERED

TOP LOUVER OPPOSITE SIDE

DOOR FRAMES

14 GAUGE FRAME - COAT INSIDE WITH ASPHALTUM PAINT
CONTINUOUS REINFORCEMENT
ACOUSTICAL GASKET
HINGE REINFORCEMENT

ACOUSTIC DOORS AND FRAMES

ACOUSTICAL DROP SEAL
FLOOR OR SADDLE
SOUND ATTENUATION DUCT INSIDE DOOR
ACOUSTICAL DROP SEAL - MORTISED DOOR
FLOOR OR SADDLE

DOOR BOTTOMS | LOUVERED DOOR

NOTE: SURFACE MOUNTED DROP SEALS ARE AVAILABLE

DOOR TYPES

FLUSH | VISION | 2 x 1 VISION WITH BAR | VISION WITH FOOD PASS | VISION WITH OPEN FOOD PASS

OPT. BULLET RESISTANT
SPEAKER OPTIONAL
HINGED COVER SHELF

VISION WITH FOOD PASS AND COVER | VISION WITH SPEAKER | 2 x 2 VISION WITH BARS | PEEPHOLE | LONG VISION

SPEAKER OPTIONAL
AVAILABLE 2 x 3 AND 3 x 3
PIVOTED COVER
ALT. LOCATION

SECURITY LOUVER | DETENTION SCREEN | SOLITARY CONFINEMENT | EXPANDED METAL | LONG VISION

DETENTION DOORS AND DETAILS

LOUVER MAX. SECURITY | LOUVER MEDIUM SECURITY

1/8" BLADES - ARC WELDED TO DOOR

PLASTER
CONCRETE
BLOCK
ANCHOR
BRICK, TILE, OR EXPOSED BLOCK

HINGED DOOR JAMBS | SPEAKER

4" OR 5"

ROLLER ASSEMBLY
SHEET STEEL COVER
STEEL TRACK
STEEL ANGLE - ARC WELDED TO DOOR
STEEL GUIDE
WELDED TO DOOR

SLIDING CELL DOOR BOTTOM | SLIDING CELL DOOR HEAD

MULLION
ANCHOR

GUIDE AND ANGLE - SEE SLIDING CELL DOOR DETAIL THIS PAGE

PLAN OF SLIDING CELL DOORS

1/2" STEEL PLATE - ARC WELDED TO FRAME AT HEAD AND JAMB

6"

KEY PASS

SECURITY GLASS
REINFORCEMENT
5" | 5" | 5/8" SQUARE STEEL BAR
GASKET MATERIAL

CROSS SECTION OF VISION PANEL WITH BAR | MUNTIN

REINFORCEMENT CHANNEL
STEEL BAR

EXPANDED METAL | BULLET RESISTANT VISION | MAX. SECURITY VISION | VISION

DOOR DETAILS

NOTES

1. Security doors must have a minimum nominal thickness of 2 in. so that security locks can be fitted in them. The required door thickness should always be coordinated with the type of security hardware being used.
2. All locking devices should be protected with a 1/8 in. steel plate at the detention side and door edge.
3. Pressed steel security frames should be a minimum of 14 gauge and are made up to 7 gauge. The frame gauge should be selected according to the desired performance. This information is available from the manufacturers.
4. All joints in security frames should be mitered and arc welded.
5. The following hardware reinforcement information should only be used as a guide:

Surface hinges — 10 gauge steel channel and a 3/8 in. steel plate
Mortise hinges — 10 gauge steel channel and a 3/16 in. steel plate
Surface pull — 3/8 x 1 x 12 in. steel plate
Surface closer — 12 gauge channel x 2 1/2 x 14 in.

6. Frames are available for single and double door units. Double door units must have a fixed mullion.

LATCHING DEVICE
8"
10 GAUGE SHEET STEEL
HINGE

GUN PASS

COMBINATION HINGE AND SHELF SUPPORT
5" x 12" LONG FOOD PASS
HINGE REINFORCEMENT

FOOD PASS WITH COVER SHELF

HINGE REINFORCEMENT

FULL SURFACE HINGE

HINGE REINFORCEMENT

FULL MORTISE HINGE

Kelly, Sacher & Associates; Architects, Engineers, Planners; N. Babylon, New York

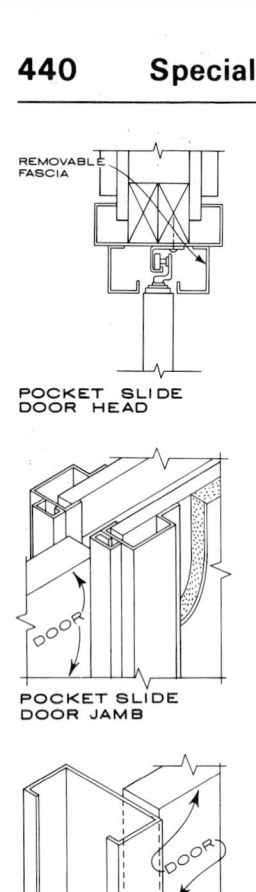

POCKET SLIDE
DOOR HEAD

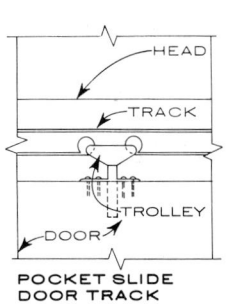

POCKET SLIDE
DOOR TRACK

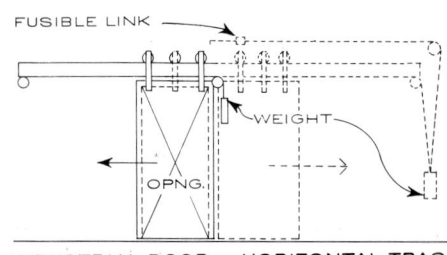
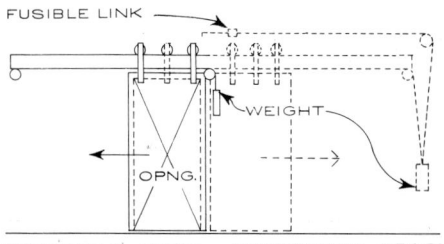

INDUSTRIAL DOOR--HORIZONTAL TRACK

ELEVATION

POCKET SLIDE
DOOR JAMB

POCKET SLIDE
DOOR ELEVATION

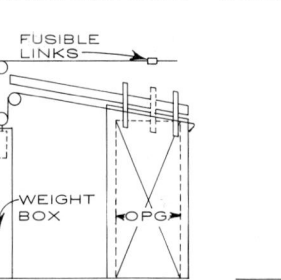

SLOPED TRACK

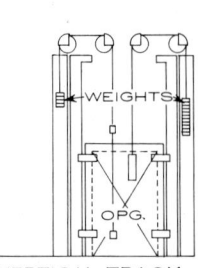

VERTICAL TRACK

PLAN THROUGH BUMPER

DOUBLE ACTING DOOR (POSTAL
SERVICE TYPE)

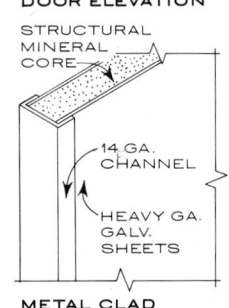

POCKET SLIDE
DOOR JAMB

METAL CLAD
CONSTRUCTION

FLUSH OR LAP
SWING DOOR

BINDER

TYPICAL CONSTRUCTION
WITH STIFFENERS
SECURITY DOOR DETAILS

VISION PANEL

METAL CLAD
CONSTRUCTION

VISION PANEL

INDUSTRIAL SLIDING DOOR--HEAD

FIRE RATED SLIDING DOOR HEAD

TIN CLAD
CONSTRUCTION

KALAMEIN
GLAZING

SWING LAP JAMB

U.L. APPROVED JAMB

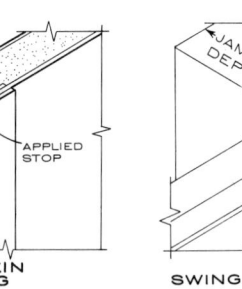

INSIDE
ELEVATION

OUTSIDE
ELEVATION

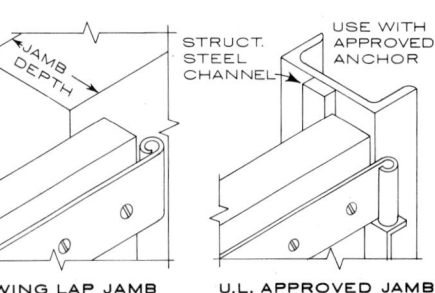

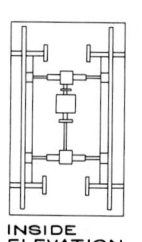

HEAD

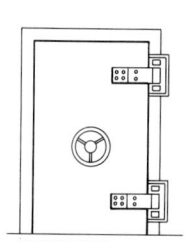

JAMB

FLOOR GUIDE #1

FLOOR GUIDE #2

UNDERWRITERS SPECIFICATIONS--FIRE DOOR

class	hourly rating	operation	maximum size		
			width	height	area
A	3	S/SW	6'-0''	12'-0''	72 sq ft
		PR/SW	10'-0''	12'-0''	120
		S/SW	12'-0''	12'-0''	120
		PR/SW	12'-0''	12'-0''	120
B	1 1/2	S/SL	10'-0''	10'-0''	80
C	3/4	S/SW	10'-0''	10'-0''	60
D	1 1/2	PR/SW	10'-0''	10'-0''	80
E	3/4	S/SL	10'-0''	10'-0''	80
		S/SW	16'-0''	10'-0''	60
		PR/SL	10'-0''	10'-0''	80

Note: for glass requirements see another page in this
series.

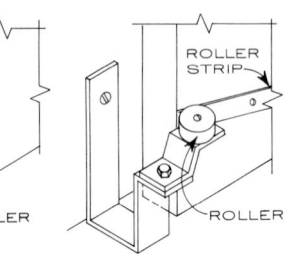

STIFFENER DETAIL

**BLAST DOOR - COMPOSITE
STEEL CONSTRUCTION**

BLAST DOORS ARE USED TO
ISOLATE HAZARDOUS
SECTIONS OF BUILDINGS TO
PROTECT HUMANS AND
PROPERTY. DOOR MUST BE
ABLE TO CONTAIN BLAST,
BUT REMAIN OPERABLE
AFTERWARD. SOLID PLATE
ALSO AVAILABLE

Darrel Rippeteau, Architect; Washington, D.C.

James W. G. Watson, AIA; Ronald A. Spahn and Associates, Cleveland Heights, Ohio

METAL DOORS

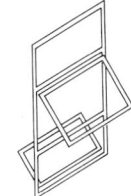

PROJECTED

NOTE

This is the workhorse of metal windows, available in many combinations of fixed and operating sash. Usually the lowest light will project in and the upper vents project out for maximum comfort and convenience. However, the flexibility of substituting fixed lights for vents and omitting muntins permits a variety of configurations.

Available in various weights, these windows are frequently used in institutional, commercial, and industrial projects. They will receive single or double glazing, from inside or outside. A wide assortment of hardware has been developed to meet almost every need, including special accessories for manual or mechanical operation of sash above normal reach.

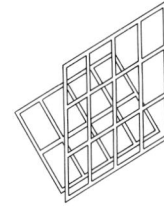

SECURITY

NOTE

Another variation of the projected sash, this window provides an integral grill permitting ventilation but restricting the size of an object that can pass through the window. Used in institutions requiring detention or tight security against outside entry, this sash minimizes the psychological, installation, and maintenance problems associated with a separate grill.

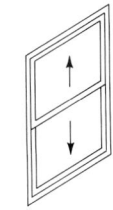

DOUBLE HUNG

NOTE

The traditional window of the United States wood window industry, metal double hung windows are finding wide application in projects where economy and flush window treatment are paramount. Single hung windows, which provide a fixed light in lieu of the top sash, are employed where economy is particularly critical. Triple hung windows are another variation, providing three operating sash for ease of operation in tall windows.

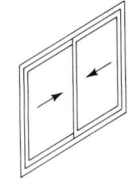

SLIDING

NOTE

Horizontally sliding or rolling sash provide flush interior and exterior wall surfaces without the need for counterbalancing hardware intrinsic in the double hung window. Initially they were popular as economical sash in residential applications; the sliding window industry has subsequently made substantial product improvements. Their inherent weatherproofing problems have been overcome with careful engineering and workmanship utilizing heavier members. Generally speaking, horizontally or squarely proportioned sash will operate more smoothly than tall, narrow sash. Most manufacturers apply full width insect screens on the exterior.

William A. Klene, AIA, Architect; Herndon, Virginia

COMBINATION

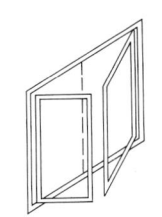

NOTE

An economical variation of the projected sash which is used where a larger amount of light than ventilation is desired. This sash was developed for suburban classroom use but has found wide application in other structures. Operating vents may be designed to project in or out. Insect screens pose different problems in both situations.

CASEMENT

NOTE

Consisting of vertically proportioned sash that swing outward, somewhat like a door, casement windows offer an aesthetic appeal not furnished by other window types. Insect screens are necessarily placed on the inside. Thus underscreen mechanical operators are usually provided. Otherwise the screen would have to be hinged or equipped with wickets for access to manual pulls.

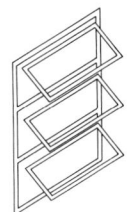

AWNING

NOTE

A window that has grown in popularity from its Southern residential origins, an awning window offers 100% ventilation combined with a degree of rain protection not attainable with casement sash. Awning sash can be fully weatherstripped and will readily receive double glazing or storm sash. Since their inherent horizontal proportions are not currently in vogue, their use has diminished recently. Insect screens are mounted in the interior, and rotary operators are standard.

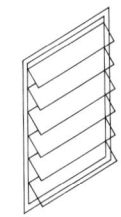

JALOUSIE

NOTE

When the individual sash depth of the awning window is reduced to the point where it becomes, in effect, an operating louver, horizontal sash members are unnecessary. This has a profound effect on appearance and the ability to provide weatherstripping. Most often found in residences and commercial work, particularly where ventilation is most desirable, jalousie windows are not as widely used as most other sash. Sash widths are limited to the free span capability of the blade materials (usually glass, wood, or metal). Storm sash are readily available and, in some instances, are an integral part of the jalousie. Insect screens are necessarily placed on the interior, with operating hardware usually placed at normal hand height.

PIVOTED

NOTE

Popular in multistory, air-conditioned commercial buildings, horizontally or vertically pivoting sash are used only for maintenance. Though they usually rotate 90°, some manufacturers produce a sash that rotates 180°. Effective weatherstripping is mandatory in both cases. Wind action on walls of highrise structures must be considered in sash design. Top or side hung sash are also produced by some manufacturers for occasional opening of fixed sash.

GENERAL NOTES

1. Most types are readily available in steel or aluminum. Steel sash tend to be more rigid and have thinner sight lines. They will be galvanized and/or bonderized and primed prior to finishing if so specified. While aluminum sash may be more economical and may offer greater inherent corrosion resistance, they have greater thermal expansion and conductance. Both are available in a variety of finishes.
2. All operating sash are regularly mulled to fixed sash, thus providing for economy, appearance, and a variety of functions.
3. Thoughtful selection of glazing material is as important as window type selection. Plastic glazing materials generally have greater coefficients of thermal expansion than glass, requiring deeper glazing legs and stops.
4. Effective thermal isolation requires double glazing (some manufacturers offer triple glazing or dual sash), continuous weatherstripping, and a "thermal break" in aluminum sash for colder climates.
5. Many manufacturers produce more than one quality window. SWI criteria for various weights of steel sash are useful in making comparisons. Current criteria for aluminum sash are based on performance of a tested specimen, hence require careful consideration unless the manufacturer has a well established reputation.
6. Many manufacturers have ceased using "stock sizes" and produce only custom work. Consequently, special shapes and configurations are easier to obtain, particularly in monumental or commercial grades. Some manufacturers also produce specialized windows that are sound resistant, contain venetian blinds, and so on. Since there is little correlation between the manufacturers' dimensioning systems, individual consultation is imperative where dimensions are critical.
7. Residential grades are somewhat more standardized, generally based on available dimensions of welded edge insulating glass.
8. Muntins, either simulating or forming small glass lights, are usually available for residential sash, if desired.
9. Installation details must take into account internal condensation in most climates. Hardware selection must consider insect screens as well as mounting heights, operating convenience, security, and so on.
10. Most codes have a minimum light and ventilation, minimum wind load resistance, and maximum thermal transmittance requirements, as well as minimum egress provisions from residential sleeping space. All these factors may affect window selection.
11. Prefinished window frames are generally installed after contiguous masonry rather than being built in.

METAL WINDOWS

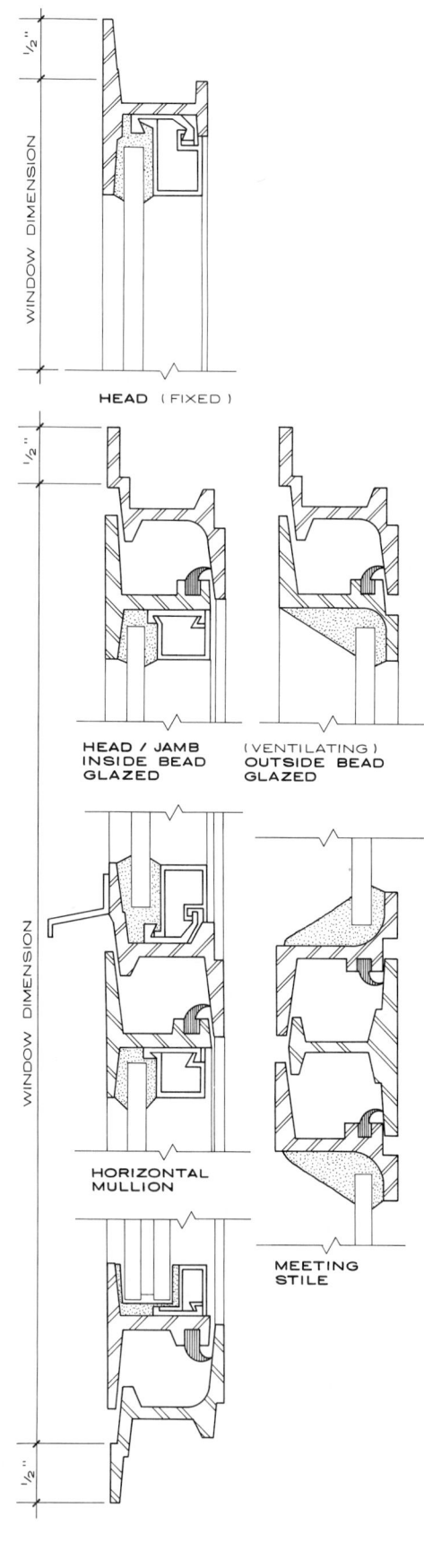

HEAD (FIXED)

HEAD / JAMB
INSIDE BEAD
GLAZED

(VENTILATING)
OUTSIDE BEAD
GLAZED

HORIZONTAL
MULLION

MEETING
STILE

STEEL SASH CONSTRUCTION

William A. Klene, AIA, Architect; Herndon, Virginia

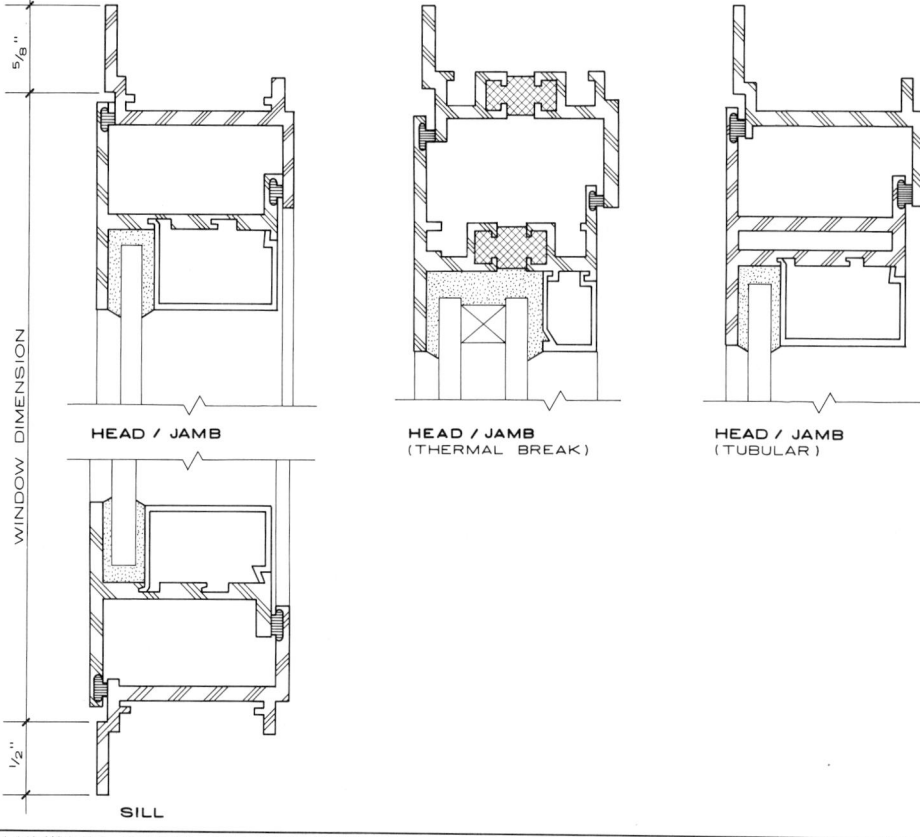

HEAD

MULLION

FIXED
GLASS

HORIZONTAL
MULLION

MEETING
STILE

CASEMENT
VENTILATING
SASH

JAMB

SILL

EXTERIOR

WINDOW NOMENCLATURE

HEAD / JAMB

HEAD / JAMB
(THERMAL BREAK)

HEAD / JAMB
(TUBULAR)

SILL

ALUMINUM SASH CONSTRUCTION

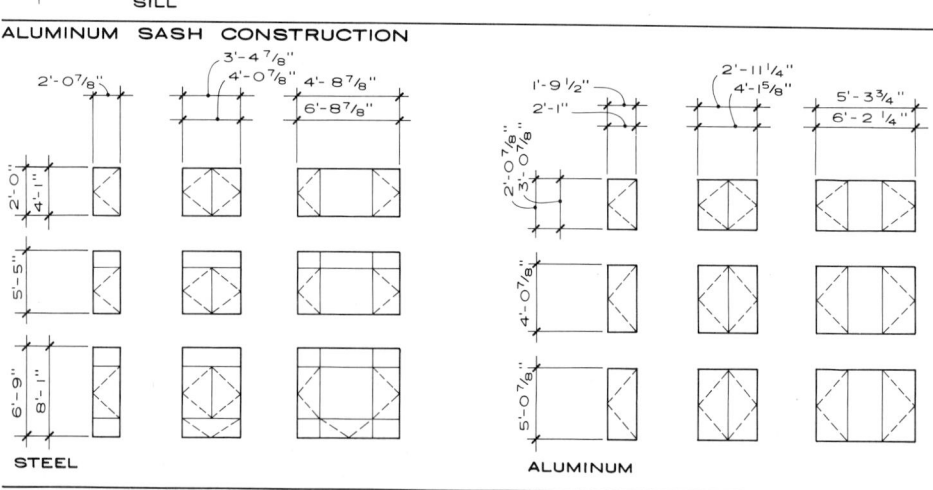

STEEL

ALUMINUM

WINDOW SIZES

NOTES

1. Window sizes and dimensioning methods, as listed, are not uniform for all manufacturers. Some manufacturers have no stock sizes, producing only custom work. Check with those who supply sash for each geographical area.

2. In general, heavier grades of windows offer greater configuration flexibility. Larger operating sash can be produced with heavier members than with lighter members. Thus the fixed lights shown for taller steel sash can be avoided, if desired.

3. Insect screens are necessarily installed on the interior and must be taken into account when selecting hardware.

4. The raindrip indicated on the horizontal mullion may be required at ventilating heads if sash is placed flush with exterior face of wall.

5. Drawings or specification must contain the following information: window size and location, installation details, sills, stools, flashing, sealing, and anchors; sash material and finish; glazing material; glazing method (tape, putty, or bead, inside or outside); weatherstripping, insect screen material, and hardware.

METAL WINDOWS

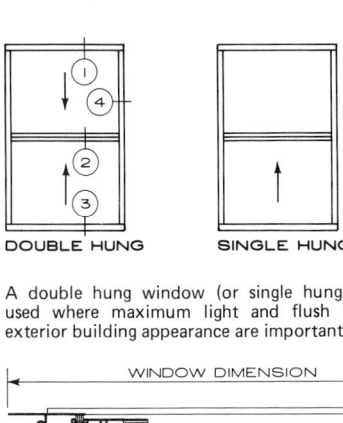

DOUBLE HUNG   **SINGLE HUNG**

A double hung window (or single hung window) is used where maximum light and flush interior and exterior building appearance are important factors.

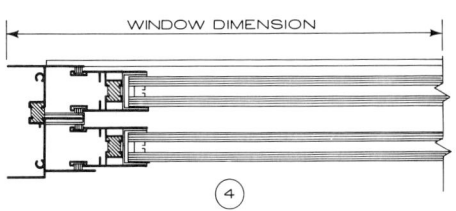

WINDOW DIMENSION

ALUMINUM

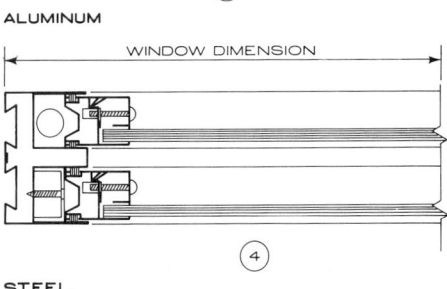

WINDOW DIMENSION

STEEL

JAMB SECTIONS

SINGLE AND DOUBLE HUNG WINDOWS

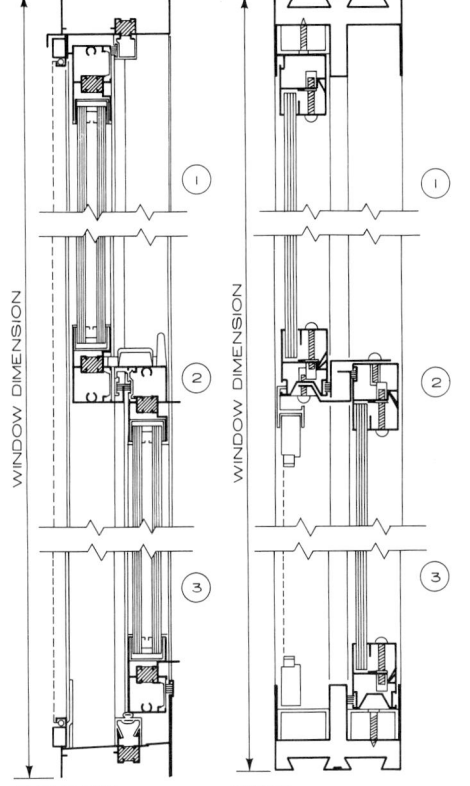

WINDOW DIMENSION

ALUMINUM   **STEEL**

VERTICAL SECTIONS

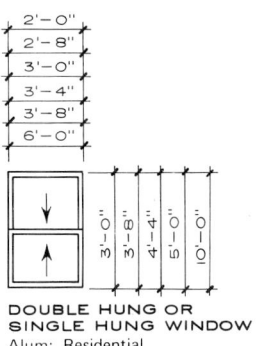

2'-0"
2'-8"
3'-0"
3'-4"
3'-8"
6'-0"

3'-0" 3'-8" 4'-4" 5'-0" 10'-0"

DOUBLE HUNG OR SINGLE HUNG WINDOW
Alum: Residential
Steel: No std. by SWI

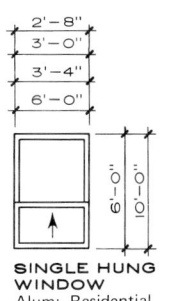

2'-8"
3'-0"
3'-4"
6'-0"

6'-0" 10'-0"

SINGLE HUNG WINDOW
Alum: Residential
Steel: No std. by SWI

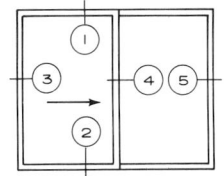

SLIDING

A horizontal sliding glass window (single or double) is used where maximum light, flush interior and exterior building appearance, simple manual operation, and accessibility are important factors.

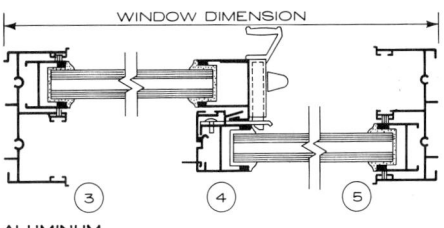

WINDOW DIMENSION

ALUMINUM

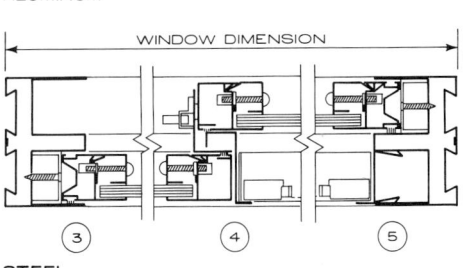

WINDOW DIMENSION

STEEL

JAMB SECTIONS

SLIDING WINDOWS

David W. Johnson; Washington, D.C.

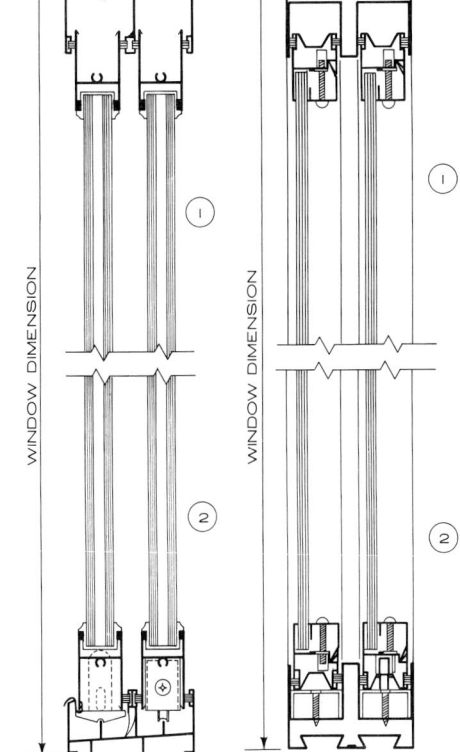

WINDOW DIMENSION

ALUMINUM   **STEEL**

VERTICAL SECTIONS

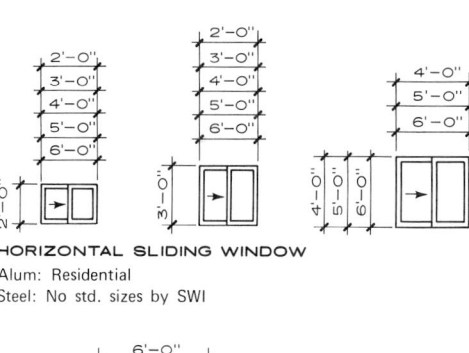

2'-0"
3'-0"
4'-0"
5'-0"
6'-0"

2'-0"
3'-0"
4'-0"
5'-0"
6'-0"

4'-0"
5'-0"
6'-0"

2'-0"   3'-0"   4'-0" 5'-0" 6'-0"

HORIZONTAL SLIDING WINDOW
Alum: Residential
Steel: No std. sizes by SWI

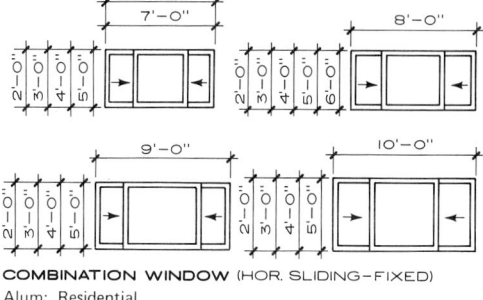

6'-0"
7'-0"

8'-0"

9'-0"

10'-0"

COMBINATION WINDOW (HOR. SLIDING–FIXED)
Alum: Residential
Steel: No std. sizes by SWI

METAL WINDOWS   8

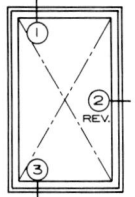

ELEVATION

NOTE

A reversible window is used mostly in multistory, air conditioned buildings where window washing from the interior is desired. It is normally opened for cleaning only; however, it may be combined with a hopper if ventilation is required.

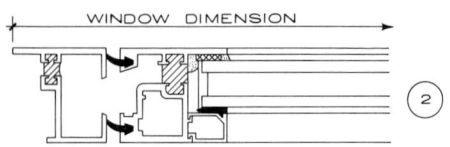

ALUMINUM

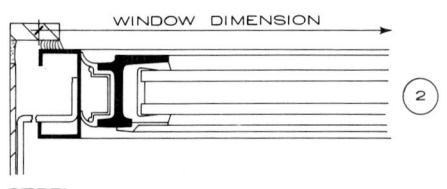

STEEL

JAMB SECTIONS

REVERSIBLE WINDOWS

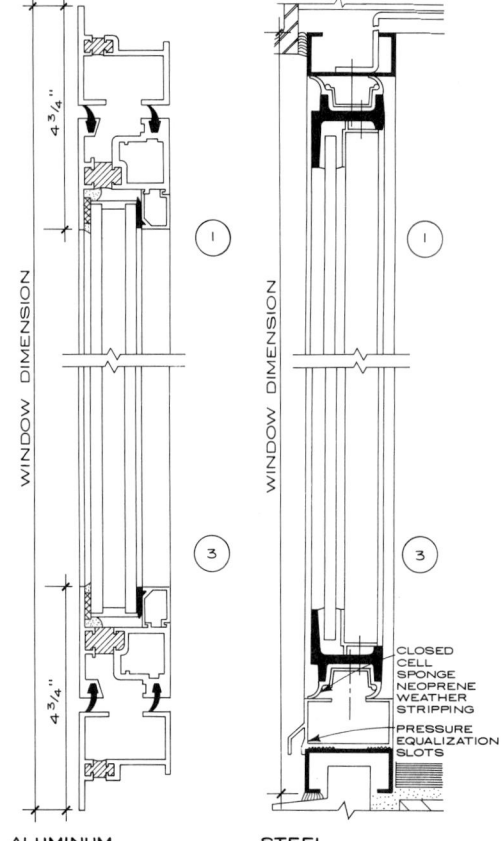

4 3/4"

4 3/4"

ALUMINUM   **STEEL**

CLOSED CELL SPONGE NEOPRENE WEATHER STRIPPING

PRESSURE EQUALIZATION SLOTS

VERTICAL SECTIONS

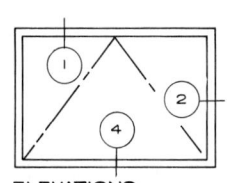

ELEVATIONS

NOTE

A projected (special) window is used mostly in multistory, air conditioned buildings where window washing from the interior is desired. It is normally opened for cleaning only; however, it may be combined with a hopper if ventilation is required. For such use see alternate above.

ALUMINUM

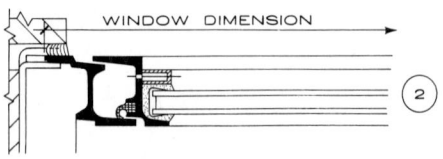

STEEL

JAMB SECTIONS

PROJECTED WINDOWS

David W. Johnson, Washington, D. C.

3 13/16"

5 5/16"

3 5/8"

ALUMINUM   **STEEL**

VERTICAL SECTIONS

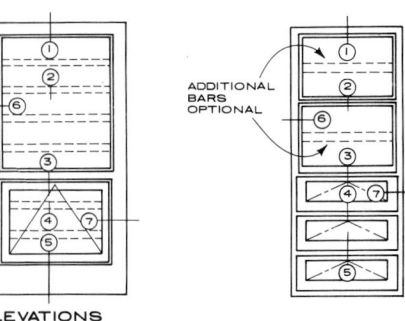

ADDITIONAL BARS OPTIONAL

ELEVATIONS

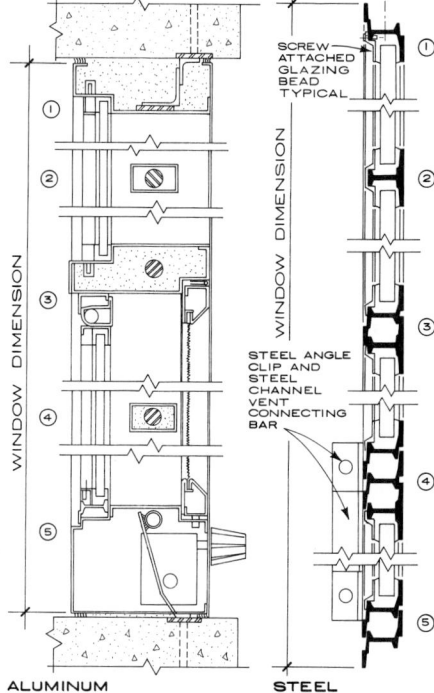

SCREW ATTACHED GLAZING BEAD TYPICAL

STEEL ANGLE CLIP AND STEEL CHANNEL VENT CONNECTING BAR

ALUMINUM   **STEEL**

VERTICAL SECTIONS

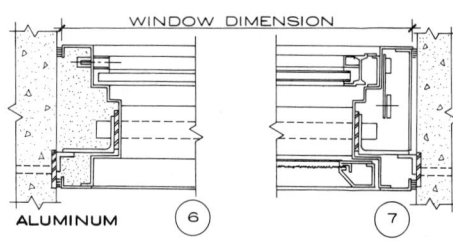

WINDOW DIMENSION

ALUMINUM

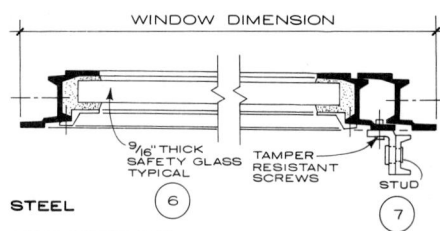

WINDOW DIMENSION

9/16" THICK SAFETY GLASS TYPICAL

TAMPER RESISTANT SCREWS

STUD

STEEL

JAMB SECTIONS

NOTES

1. Housing sill frame size varies with manufacturer of window operator.
2. Muntin and mullion tubes are 12 gauge maximum and 14 gauge medium security, grouted full, and contain a 7/8 in. diameter tamper resistant bar.
3. Tempered glass is 1/2 in. on exterior side.
4. Horizontal tube/bars to have maximum spacing of 5 in.

SECURITY WINDOWS

METAL WINDOWS

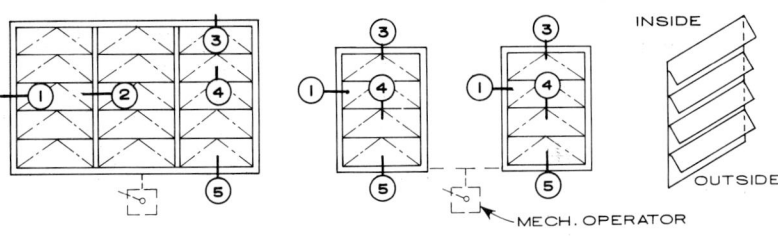

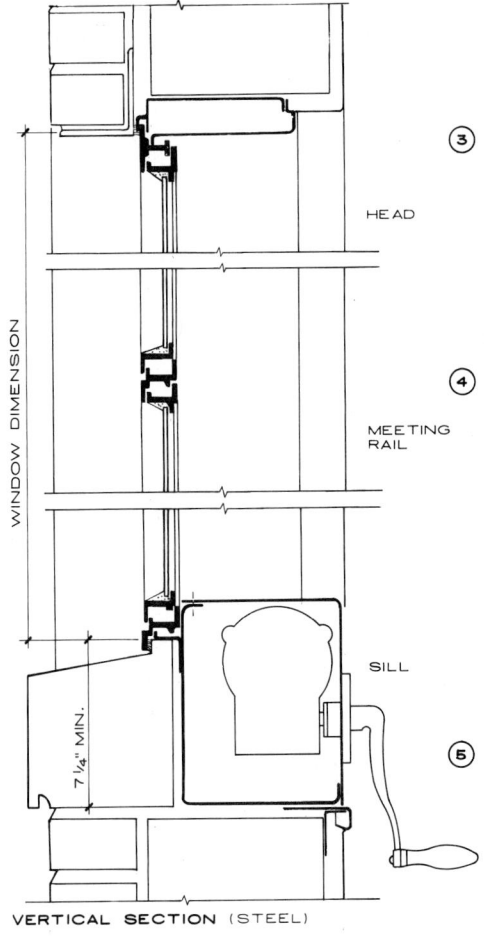

AWNING

AN AWNING WINDOW is one whose movable units consist of a group of hand operated or gear operated outward projecting ventilators, all of which move in unison. It is used where maximum height and ventilation is required in inaccessible areas such as upper parts of gymnasiums or auditoriums. Hand operation is limited to one window only, while a single gear operator may be connected to two or more awning windows, and may be motorized.

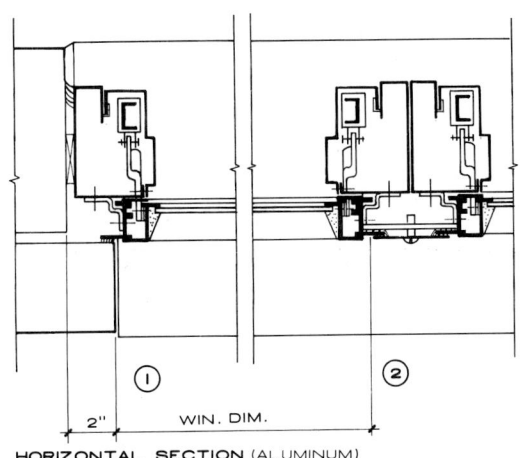

HORIZONTAL SECTION (ALUMINUM)

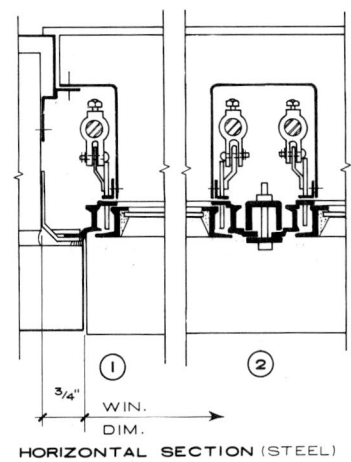

HORIZONTAL SECTION (STEEL)

VERTICAL SECTION (STEEL)

AWNING WINDOWS

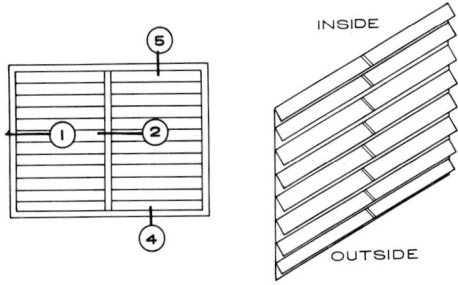

JALOUSIE

A JALOUSIE WINDOW (ALUMINUM) consists of a series of operable overlapping glass louvers which pivot in unison. It may be combined in the same frame with a series of operable opaque louvers for climate control. It is used mostly in residential type constructions in southern climates, where maximum ventilation and flush exterior and interior appearance is desired.

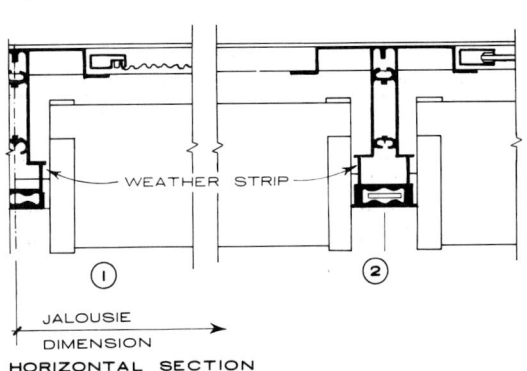

HORIZONTAL SECTION

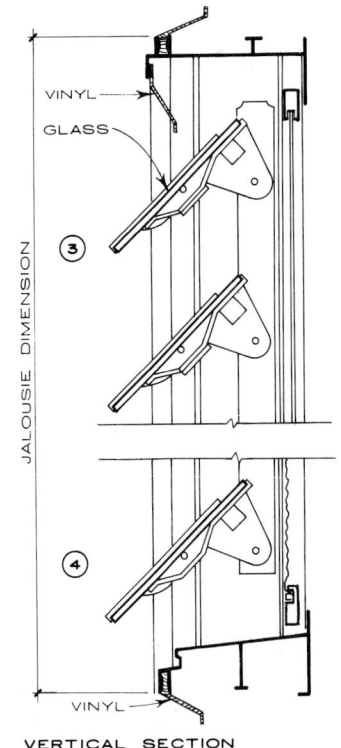

VERTICAL SECTION

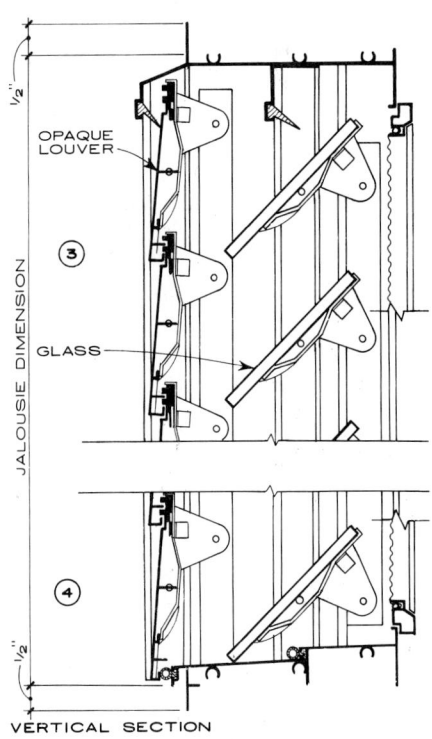

VERTICAL SECTION

JALOUSIE WINDOWS

METAL WINDOWS 8

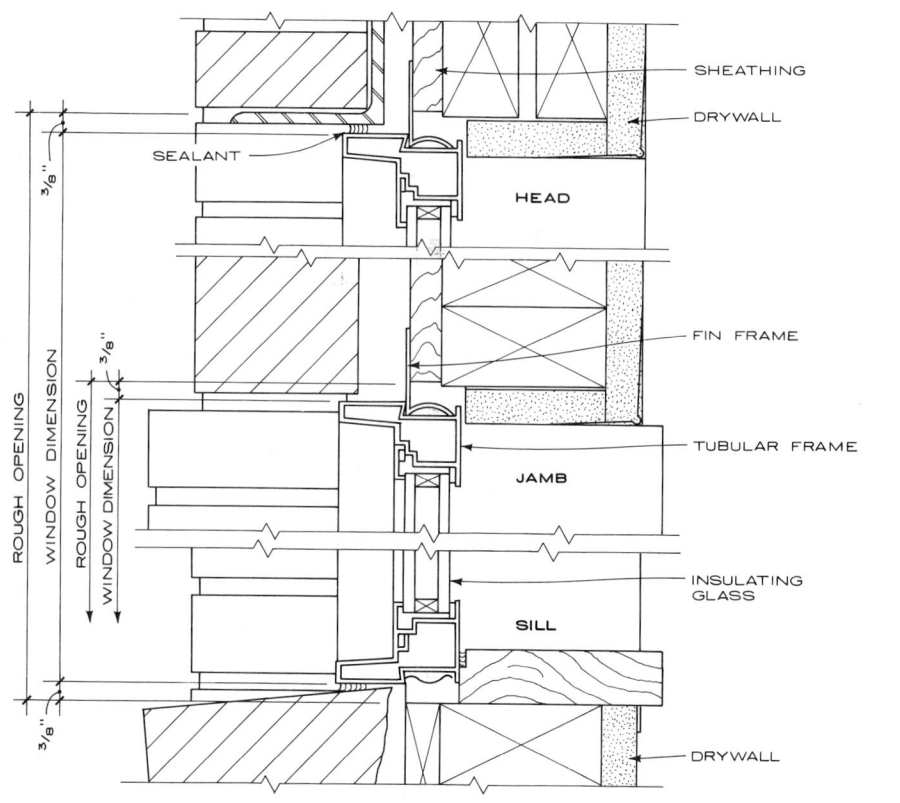

BRICK VENEER ON WOOD FRAME WALL

Labels: SHEATHING, DRYWALL, HEAD, FIN FRAME, TUBULAR FRAME, JAMB, INSULATING GLASS, SILL, SEALANT, DRYWALL, ROUGH OPENING, WINDOW DIMENSION, 3/8"

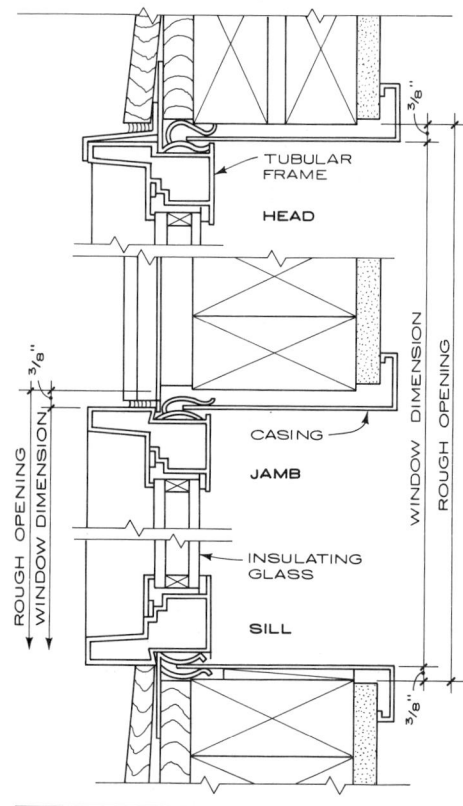

WOOD FRAME WALL

Labels: TUBULAR FRAME, HEAD, CASING, JAMB, INSULATING GLASS, SILL, WINDOW DIMENSION, ROUGH OPENING, 3/8"

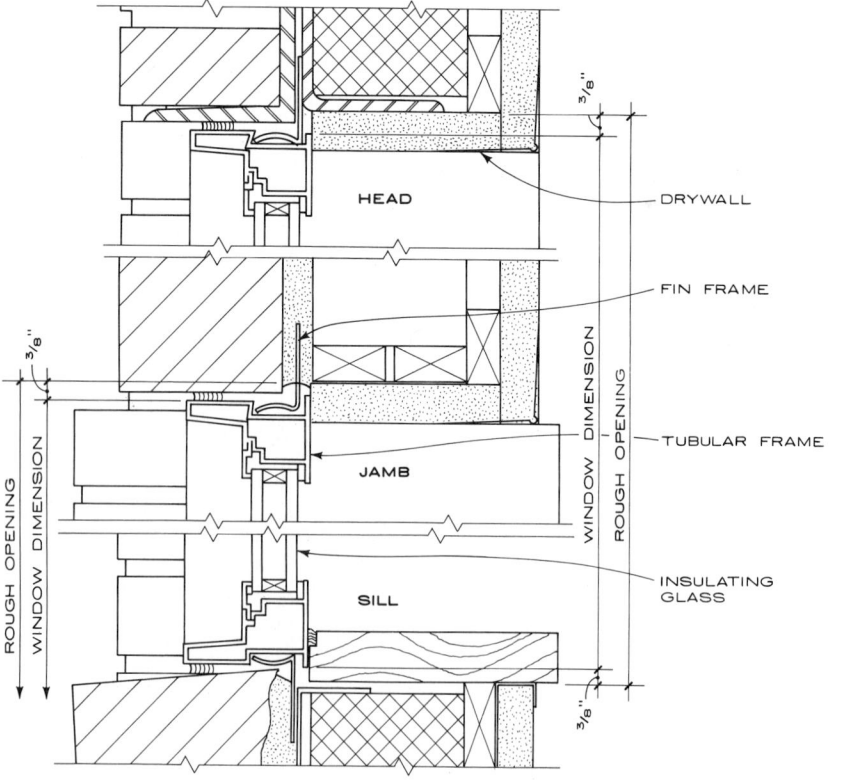

MASONRY WALL

Labels: DRYWALL, HEAD, FIN FRAME, TUBULAR FRAME, JAMB, INSULATING GLASS, SILL, ROUGH OPENING, WINDOW DIMENSION, 3/8"

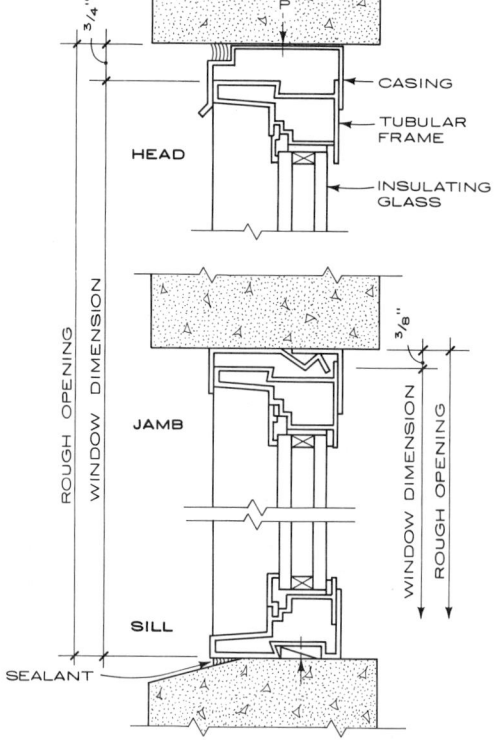

CONCRETE WALL

Labels: CASING, TUBULAR FRAME, INSULATING GLASS, HEAD, JAMB, SILL, SEALANT, ROUGH OPENING, WINDOW DIMENSION, 3/4", 3/8"

NOTES

1. Fins and interior casings are available to meet various installation requirements. Interior trims are available in depths of 2 to 10 in., in 1/2 in. increments.

2. Thermal-break type extrusions are available. Consult with manufacturers for sizes and shapes.

Nicanor A. Alano, Architect; Tacoma, Washington

 METAL WINDOWS

TYPICAL OPERATING HARDWARE FOR METAL WINDOWS

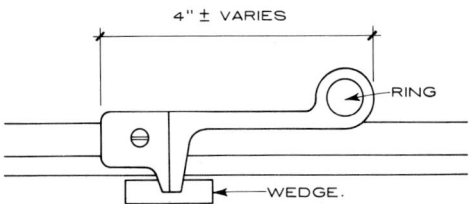

4" ± VARIES

RING

WEDGE.

TYPICAL (CAM) LOCKING HANDLE

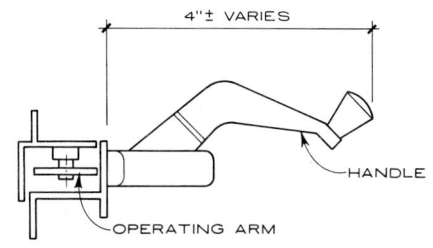

4" ± VARIES

HANDLE

OPERATING ARM

TYPICAL CRANK (ROTO) OPERATOR

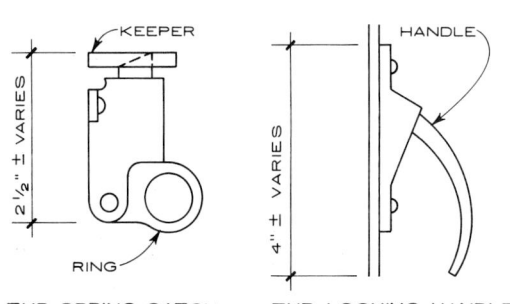

KEEPER

HANDLE

2½" ± VARIES

4" ± VARIES

RING

TYP. SPRING CATCH   **TYP. LOCKING HANDLE**

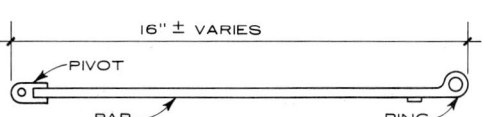

16" ± VARIES

PIVOT

BAR   RING

TYPICAL STAY BAR (PUSH BAR)

OTHER TYPES OF HARDWARE

1. Concealed cam hardware.
2. Hardware with removable handles for A.C. buildings. Also key locks.
3. Sliding window hardware.
4. D. H. window hardware (sweeplock).
5. Telescoping adjuster.
6. Chain, pole & cord operated hardware.
7. Hardware for security windows.
8. Heavy duty, electrical powered hardware for group window control.

FINISHES INCLUDE

1. Steel: diecast, lacquered & painted.
2. Aluminum: wide range of finishes and colors. Generally match window finish.
3. Bronze
4. White bronze & nickel bronze

Charles F. D. Egbert, AIA; Architect; Washington, D. C.

EXTRUDED ALUMINUM SILLS

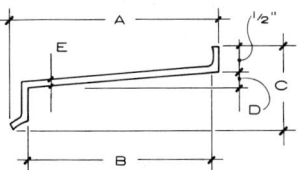

A	B	C	D	E	Std. No.*
3 7/16"	3"	1 9/16"	3/16"	3/32"	37734
3 29/32"		1 1/2"			P-3684
3 15/16"	3 1/2"	1 19/32"	7/32"	3/32"	37735
4 13/32"		1 17/32"			P-3683
4 7/16"	4"	1 5/8"	1/4"	3/32"	37736
4 7/8"		1 9/16"			3686
4 15/16"	4 1/2"	1 21/32"	9/32"	3/32"	37737
5 3/8"		1 9/16"			3687
5 7/16"	5"	1 11/16"	5/16"	3/32"	37738
5 7/8"		1 5/8"			3685
5 15/16"	5 1/2"	1 23/32"	11/32"	3/32"	37739
9 1/16"	8 1/2"	1 31/32"	7/32"	5/32"	37745

For Lug Sills
Extend into brick joints at window jambs and allow 1/4" space for expansion at ends.

For Continuous Sills
At joints allow 1/4" to 3/8" expansion and flash joints.

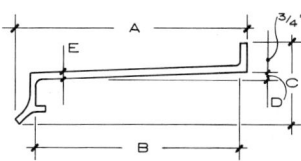

A	B	C	D	E	Std. No.*
3 1/2"	2 3/4"	1 13/16"	3/16"	1/8"	54684
4"	3 1/4"	1 27/32"	7/32"	1/8"	54685
4 1/2"	3 3/4"	1 7/8"	1/4"	1/8"	54686
					9558
5"	4 1/4"	1 29/32"	9/32"	1/8"	54687
					13008
5 1/2"	4 3/4"	1 15/16"	5/16"	1/8"	54688
					13009
6"	5 1/4"	1 31/32"	11/32"	1/8"	54689
6 9/16"	5 3/4"	2"	3/8"	5/32"	54690
7 9/16"	6 3/4	2 1/16"	7/16"	5/32"	54691
8 1/8"	7 1/4"	2 5/32"	15/32"	3/16"	54692
9 1/8"	8 1/4"	2 7/32"	17/32"	3/16"	54693

Used for continuous line of windows. Provide 1/4" to 3/8" expansion space at jamb or butt joints of continuous sills.

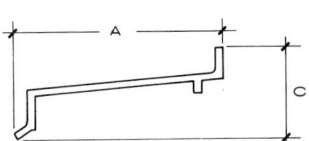

A	B	C	D	E	Std. No.*
3 1/2"		1 9/16"			P-3692
4"		1 19/32"			P-3691
4 1/2"		1 5/8"			P-3690
5"		1 21/32"			P-3126
5 1/2"		1 11/16"			P-3127
6"		1 23/32"			P-3128
9 1/16"		1 29/32"			P-3230

Sills may be made to fit posts or mullions, and may be mitered at corners. Sills over eight feet in length should have central anchorage to keep them in proper position.

* Non-warehouse items

Refer to aluminum manufacturers catalogs.

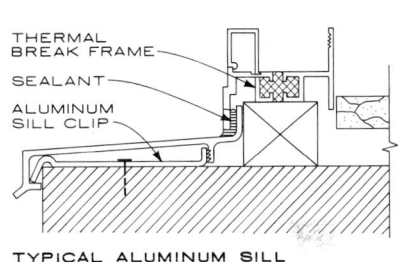

THERMAL BREAK FRAME

SEALANT

ALUMINUM SILL CLIP

TYPICAL ALUMINUM SILL

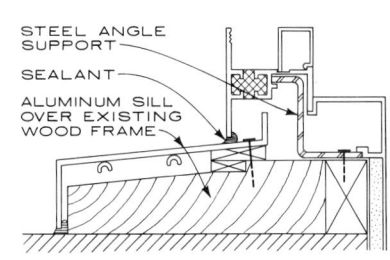

STEEL ANGLE SUPPORT

SEALANT

ALUMINUM SILL OVER EXISTING WOOD FRAME

REPLACEMENT SILL

INSTALLATION DETAILS

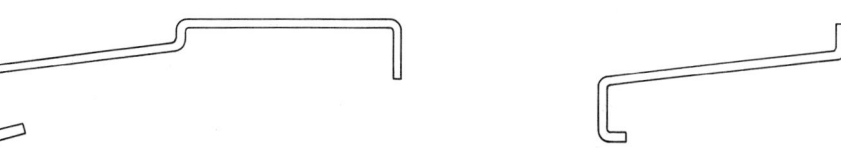

TYPICAL FORMED METAL SILLS
SHAPES MADE TO ORDER

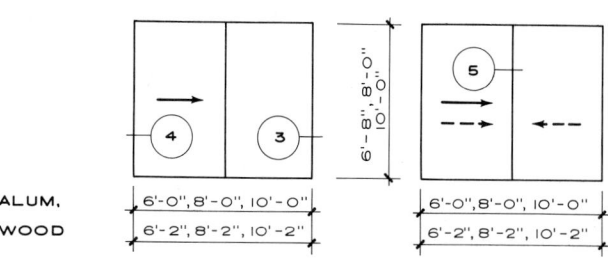
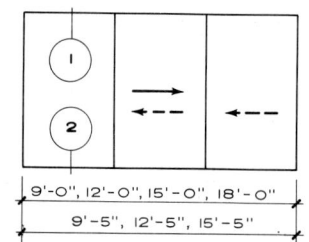
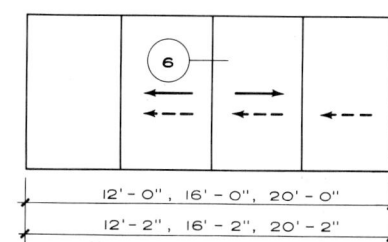

	ALUM.	WOOD
	6'-0", 8'-0", 10'-0"	6'-2", 8'-2", 10'-2"
	6'-0", 8'-0", 10'-0"	6'-2", 8'-2", 10'-2"
	9'-0", 12'-0", 15'-0", 18'-0"	9'-5", 12'-5", 15'-5"
	12'-0", 16'-0", 20'-0"	12'-2", 16'-2", 20'-2"

RESIDENTIAL SLIDING DOOR DIMENSIONS
DIMENSIONS SHOWN ARE NOMINAL STOCK SIZES

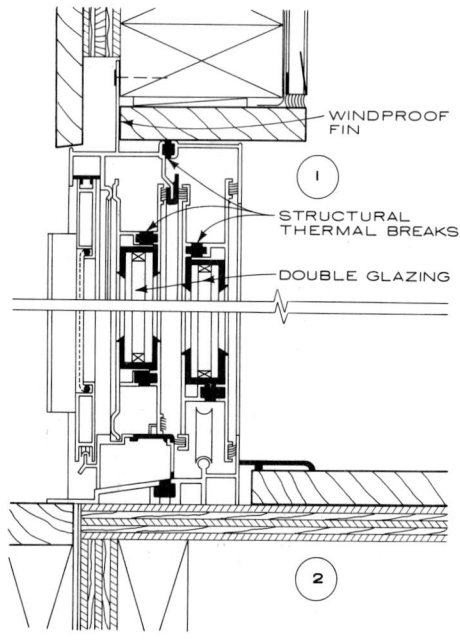

WINDPROOF FIN

STRUCTURAL THERMAL BREAKS

DOUBLE GLAZING

NOTES

1. Residential sliding door dimensions shown are nominal stock sizes. Custom sizes are available in accordance with individual manufacturing limitations and availability of glass sizes.
2. Details shown are for wood frame construction. Interior and exterior finishes and trim are optional. See manufacturer's data for typical installation details.
3. Tempered glass should always be used to reduce the chance of breakage and to avoid dangerous glass shards if breakage occurs.
4. Screens are available for all doors. Details show screens on the exterior for both the metal and wood doors. Consult individual manufacturer's literature to determine if screens are interior only, exterior only, or available either way.
5. Energy conservation is enhanced through the use of structural thermal breaks in aluminum sliding doors along with windproof mounting fins and double glazing. Standard aluminum sliding doors are also available.
6. See manufacturer's data for special sizes, locking devices, finishes, and specific limitations.

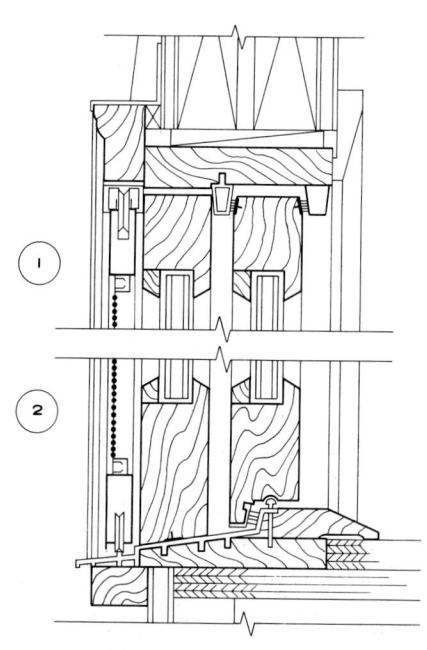

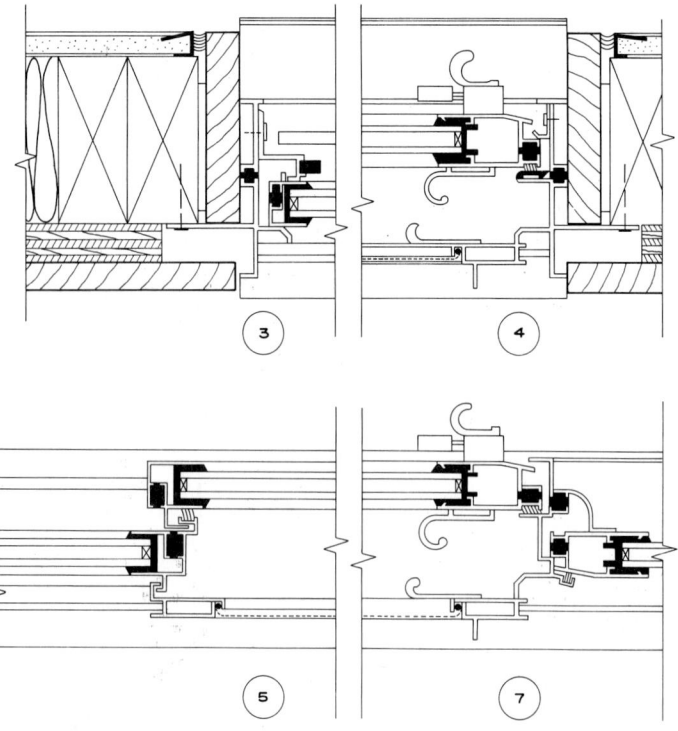

ALUMINUM SLIDING DOOR DETAILS WITH ENERGY CONSERVATION FEATURES

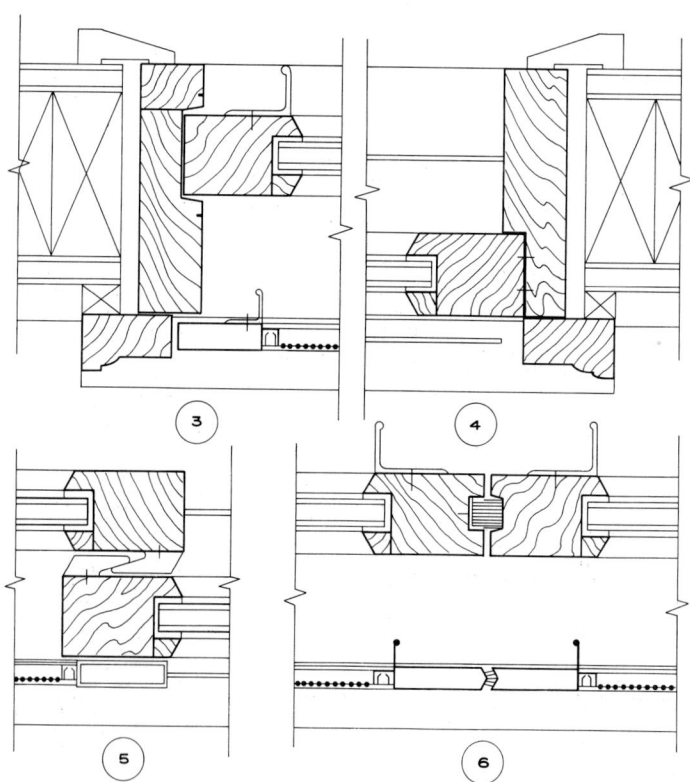

WOOD SLIDING DOOR DETAILS

Leo A. Daly; Architecture-Engineering-Planning; Omaha, Nebraska

SPECIAL DOORS

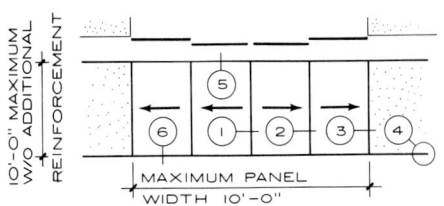

BYPASS DOOR ELEVATION

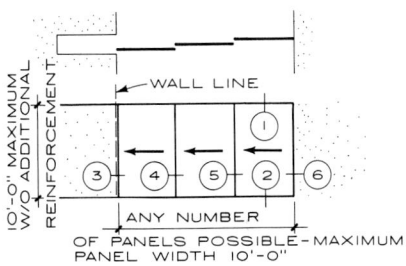

POCKET DOOR ELEVATION

MULTIPLE SLIDING DOOR ELEVATION

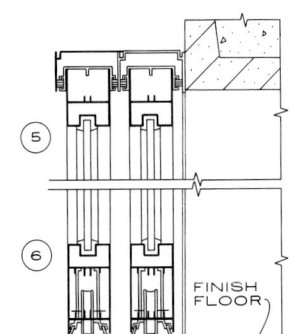

BYPASS DOOR DETAILS

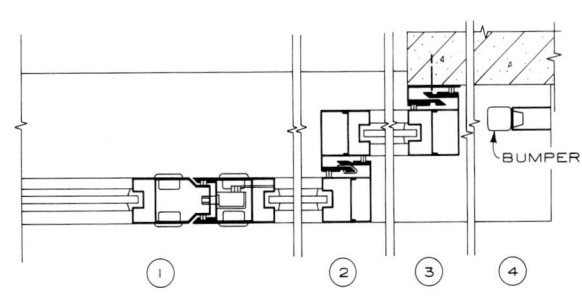

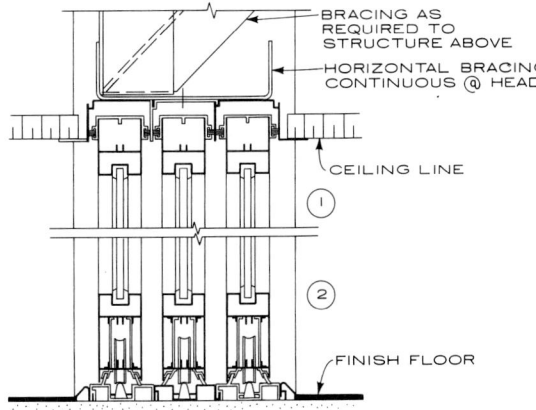

POCKET DOOR DETAILS

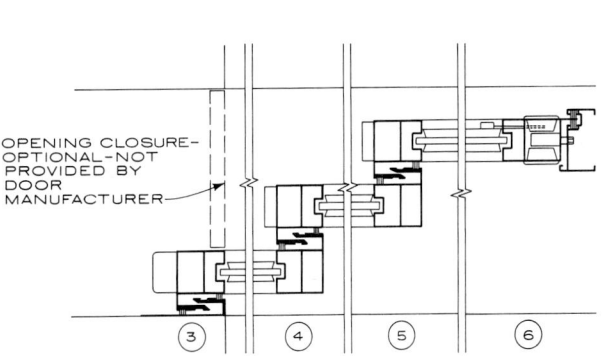

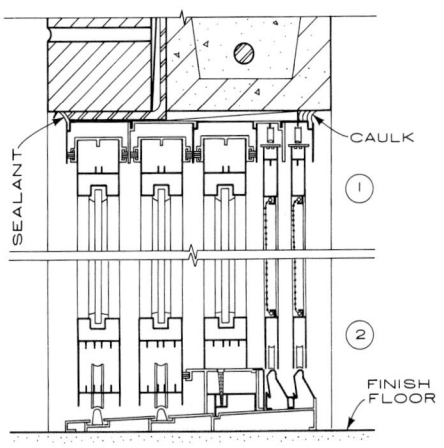

MULTIPLE SLIDING DOOR DETAILS

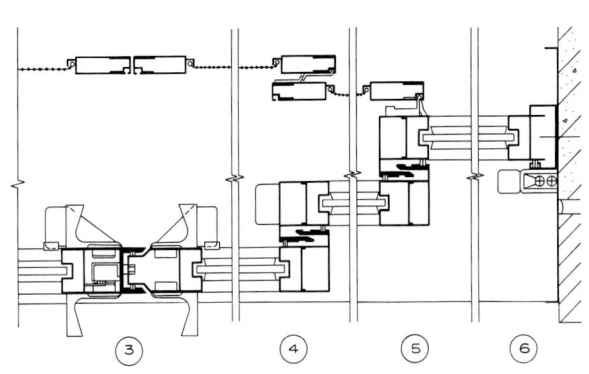

NOTES

1. Details shown are for masonry construction. Interior and exterior finishes are optional. Consult manufacturer's data for typical installation details.

2. Screens are available for all doors if required. Where shown, the details indicate screens on the interior. Consult specific manufacturer's literature to determine if screens are available for interior only, exterior only, or both. Glazing should be of safety glass, tempered, or insulating glass. Maximum manufacturable sizes of individual glass types will be the governing factor in determining maximum panel sizes. Consult industry standards for applicable data.

3. Consult manufacturer's data for available sizes, locking devices, and finishes.

Leo A. Daly; Architecture-Engineering-Planning; Omaha, Nebraska

SPECIAL DOORS 8

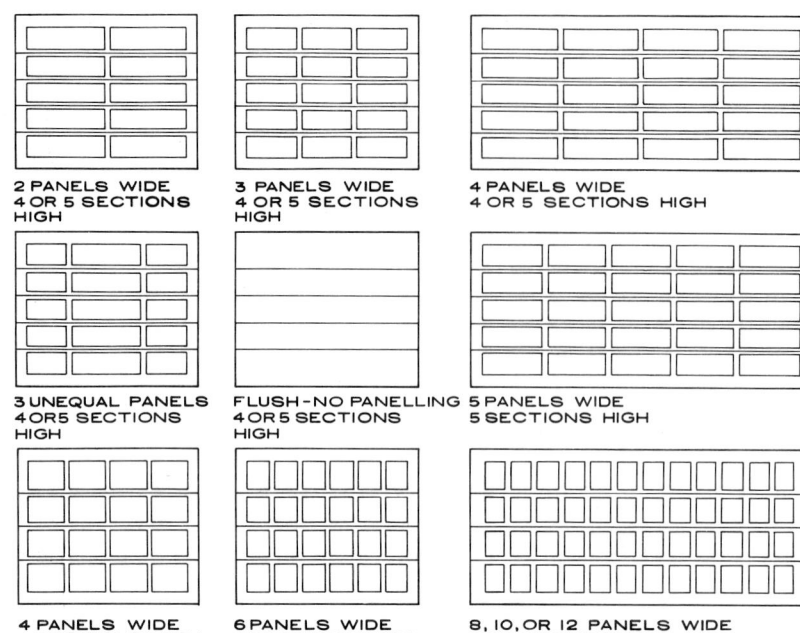

2 PANELS WIDE 4 OR 5 SECTIONS HIGH

3 PANELS WIDE 4 OR 5 SECTIONS HIGH

4 PANELS WIDE 4 OR 5 SECTIONS HIGH

3 UNEQUAL PANELS 4 OR 5 SECTIONS HIGH

FLUSH-NO PANELLING 4 OR 5 SECTIONS HIGH

5 PANELS WIDE 5 SECTIONS HIGH

4 PANELS WIDE 4 SECTIONS HIGH

6 PANELS WIDE 4 SECTIONS HIGH

8, 10, OR 12 PANELS WIDE 4 SECTIONS HIGH

Panel and section dimensions are set in the factory to provide overall door dimensions that meet the design requirements. Manufacturers will recommend the optimum number of panels and sections to best accommodate specific dimensional ranges. Heights range up to 20 ft, widths to 30 ft (approximate).

WOOD DOORS STANDARD STOCK DESIGNS

NOTE

Glazed panels may be located as desired. 3 section doors also available. Other stock designs and sizes available varying with manufacturers.

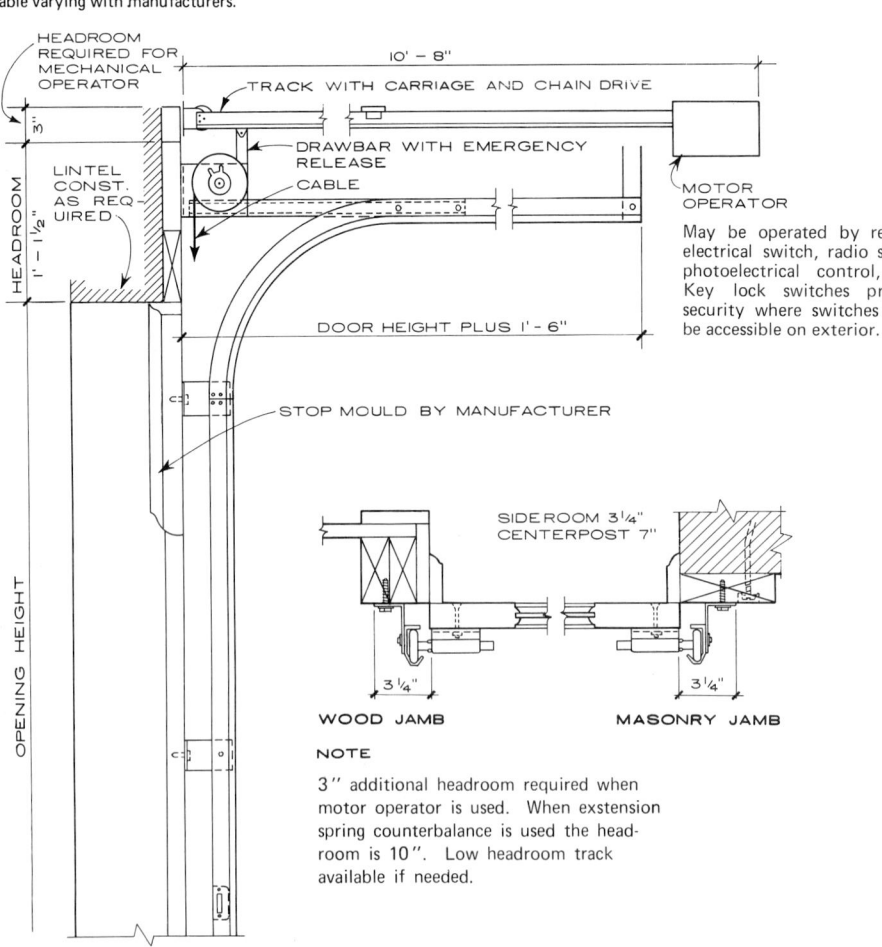

May be operated by remote electrical switch, radio signal, photoelectrical control, etc. Key lock switches provide security where switches must be accessible on exterior.

NOTE

3" additional headroom required when motor operator is used. When extension spring counterbalance is used the headroom is 10". Low headroom track available if needed.

SECTION

INSTALLATION DETAILS

Eugene Patrick Holden, AIA; Dale E. Selzer, AIA, Architect; Dallas, Texas

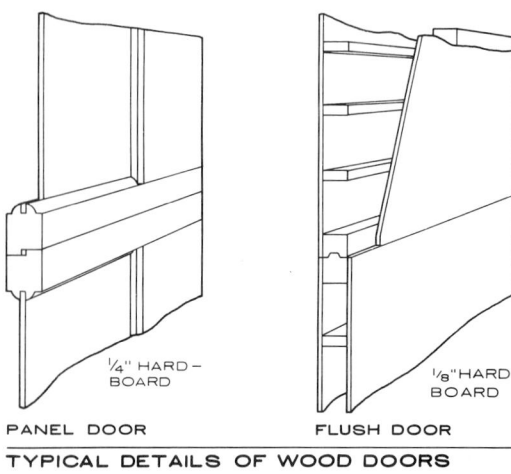

PANEL DOOR   **FLUSH DOOR**

TYPICAL DETAILS OF WOOD DOORS

All doors available with torsion or extension spring counterbalance.

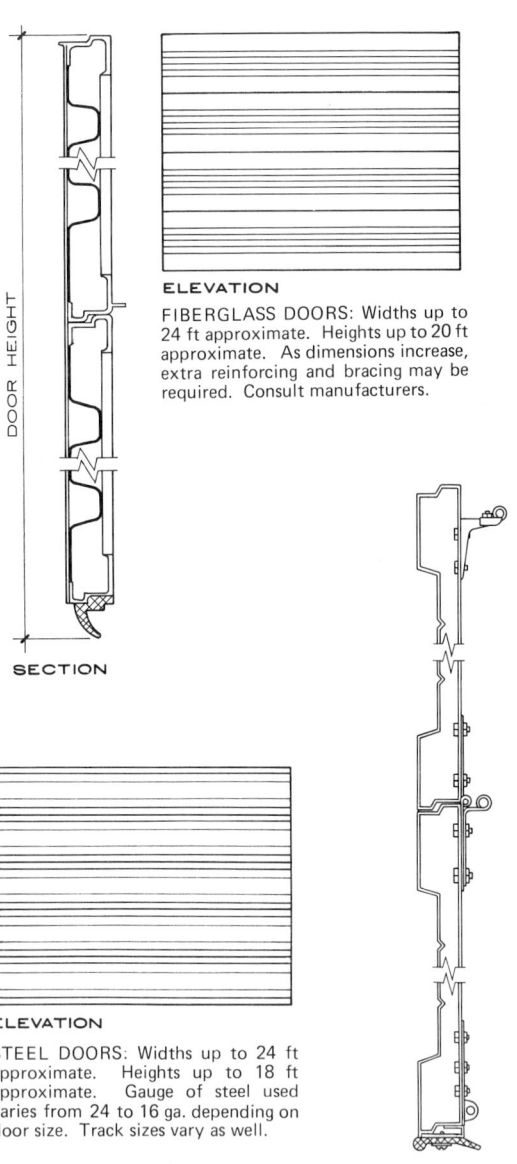

ELEVATION

FIBERGLASS DOORS: Widths up to 24 ft approximate. Heights up to 20 ft approximate. As dimensions increase, extra reinforcing and bracing may be required. Consult manufacturers.

SECTION

ELEVATION

STEEL DOORS: Widths up to 24 ft approximate. Heights up to 18 ft approximate. Gauge of steel used varies from 24 to 16 ga. depending on door size. Track sizes vary as well.

SECTION

FIBERGLASS AND STEEL DOORS

SPECIAL DOORS

WOOD PANEL DOOR

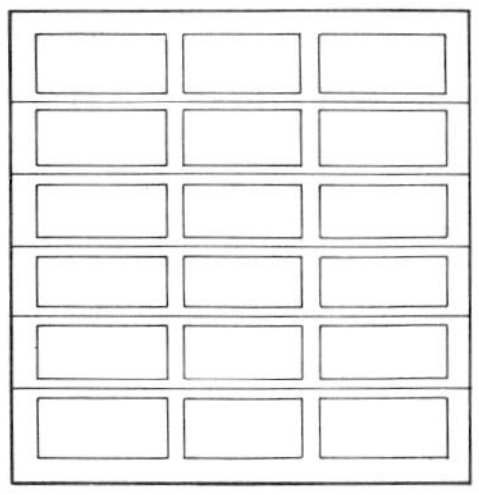

ELEVATION

SIZE LIMITATIONS:

2'' Track — not to exceed 240 sq. ft., 24'— 2'' wide or 16'— 1'' high.

3'' Track — not to exceed 600 sq. ft., 33'— 2'' wide or 25'— 1'' high.

Wood doors are easily repaired, but are more susceptible to moisture and heat damage than are metal and fiberglass doors.

NOTE

Number of panels varies from 2 for an 8'— 6'' wide door, through 14 for widths from 30'— 4'' to 33'— 3''; number of vertical sections varies from 4 for doors up to 8'— 6'' high through 13 sections for doors from 24'— 2'' to 25'— 1'' high. Number of panels and sections depend on increments in height and width established by manufacturer.

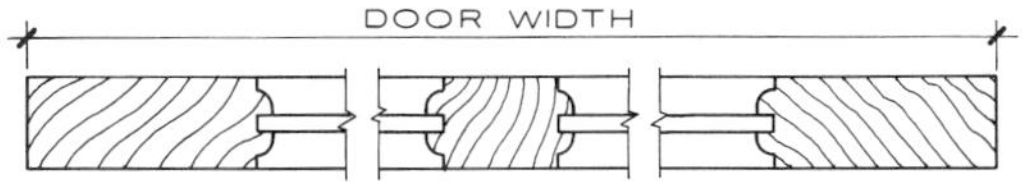

DOOR WIDTH

HORIZONTAL SECTION

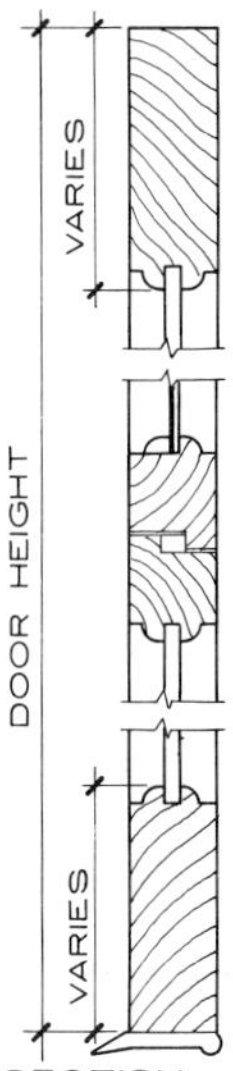

SECTION

FLUSH WOOD DOOR

ELEVATION

SIZE LIMITATIONS:

2'' Track — not to exceed 240 sq. ft., 24'— 2'' wide or 16'— 1'' high.

3'' Track — not to exceed 600 sq. ft., 33'— 2'' wide or 25'— 1'' high.

MATERIAL:

$1/8$'' hardboard secured with waterproof adhesive on both sides of $1 1/2$'' wood frame. Pressure bonded between the hardboard walls are thick, tough waterproof core strips of styrofoam.

NOTE

Number of vertical sections varies from 4 for doors up to 7'— 0'' high through 15 sections for doors from 24'— 7'' to 25'— 1'' high, depending on increments in height established by particular manufacturers.

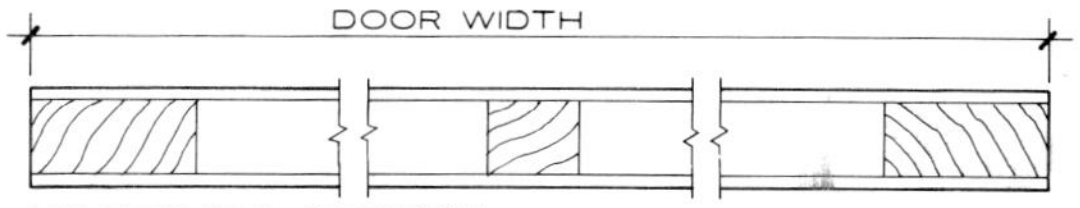

DOOR WIDTH

HORIZONTAL SECTION

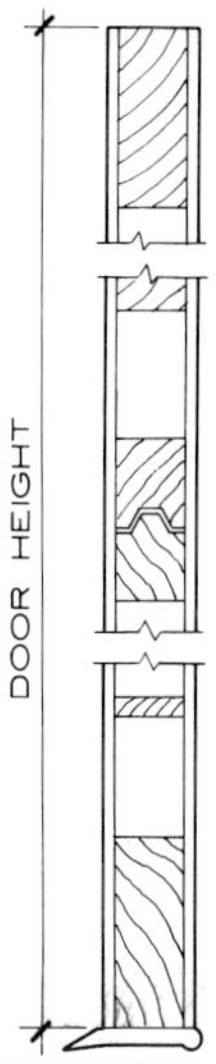

SECTION

PANORAMIC ALUMINUM

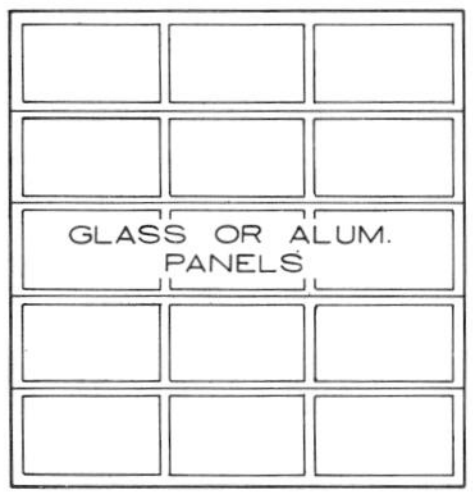

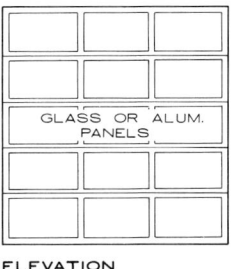

GLASS OR ALUM. PANELS

ELEVATION

SIZE LIMITATIONS:

2'' Track — not to exceed 240 sq. ft., 20'— 2'' wide or 16'— 1'' high.

Rails and stiles of extruded aluminum. Stiles and rails bolted with $1/4$'' rods the length of the stile.

NOTE

Number of panels varies from 2 for doors up to 8'— 11'' wide, through 6 for widths from 18'— 0'' to 20'— 2''; number of vertical sections varies from 4 for doors up to 8'— 6'' high, through 8 sections for doors from 14'— 2'' to 16'— 1'' high. Number of panels and sections depend on increments in height and width established by manufacturer.

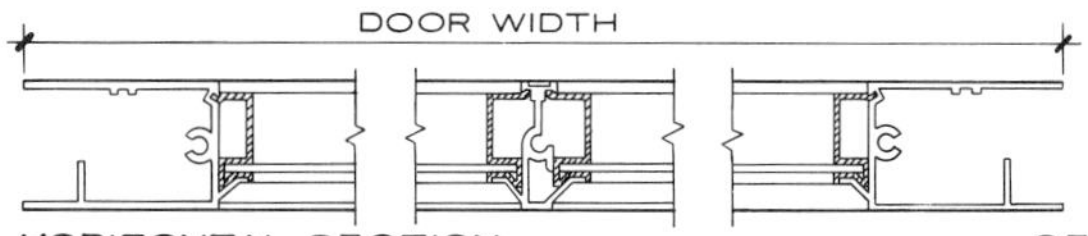

DOOR WIDTH

HORIZONTAL SECTION

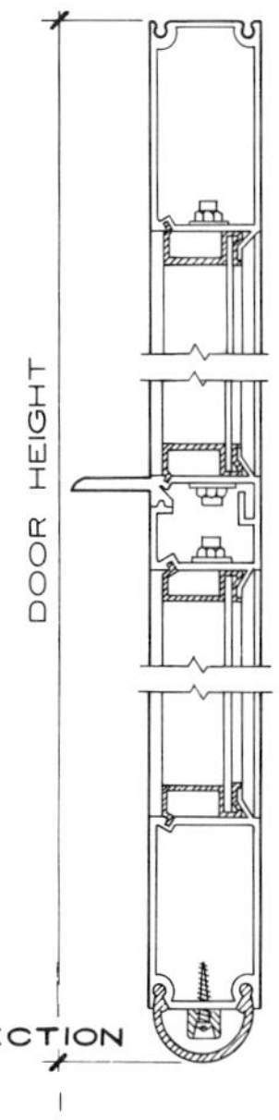

SECTION

HEAVY DUTY ALUMINUM

GLASS OR ALUM. PANELS

ELEVATION

SIZE LIMITATIONS:

2'' Track — not to exceed 336 sq. ft., 24'— 2'' wide or 16'— 1'' high.

3'' Track — not to exceed 384 sq. ft., 24'— 2'' wide or 16'— 1'' high.

Stiles and rails of extruded aluminum. Stiles are bolted to rails with $1/4$'' rods the length of the stile.

NOTE

Number of panels varies from 2 for doors up to 8'— 11'' wide through 8 for widths from 21'— 0'' to 23'— 11''; number of vertical sections varies from 4 for doors up to 8'— 6'' high, through 8 sections for doors from 14'— 2'' to 16'— 1'' high. Number of panels and sections depend on increments in height and width established by manufacturer.

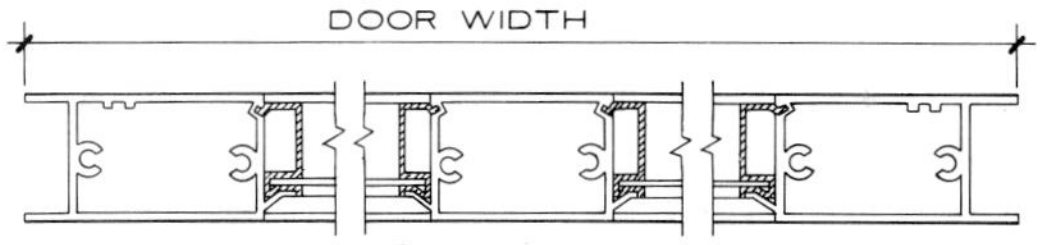

DOOR WIDTH

HORIZONTAL SECTION

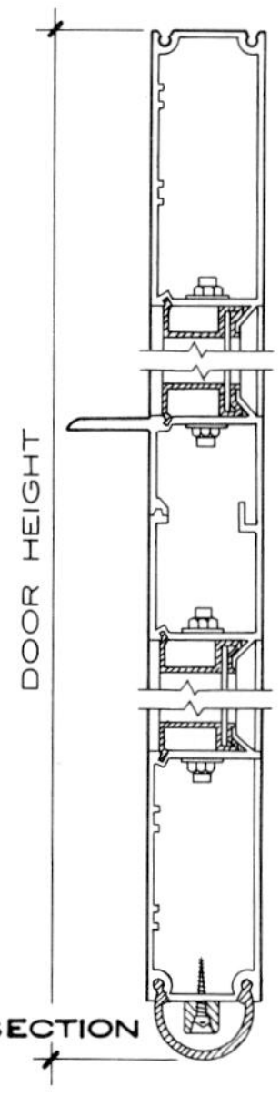

SECTION

16 GAUGE STEEL DOOR

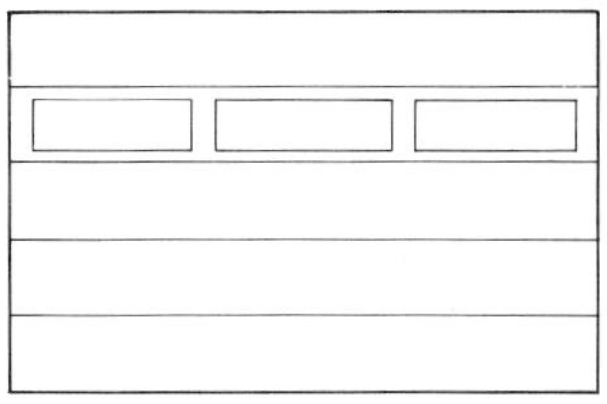

ELEVATION

SIZE LIMITATIONS:

2'' Track — not to exceed 180 sq. ft., 16'— 2'' wide or 14'— 1'' high.

3'' Track — not to exceed 450 sq. ft., 33'— 2'' wide or 22'— 1'' high.

NOTE

Number of panels varies from 2 for doors up to 9'— 11'' wide through 10 for widths from 31'— 11'' to 33'— 2''; number of vertical sections varies from 5 for doors up to 8'— 0'' high, through 14 sections for doors from 20'— 11'' to 22'— 1'' high. Number of panels and sections depends on increments in height and width established by particular manufacturers.

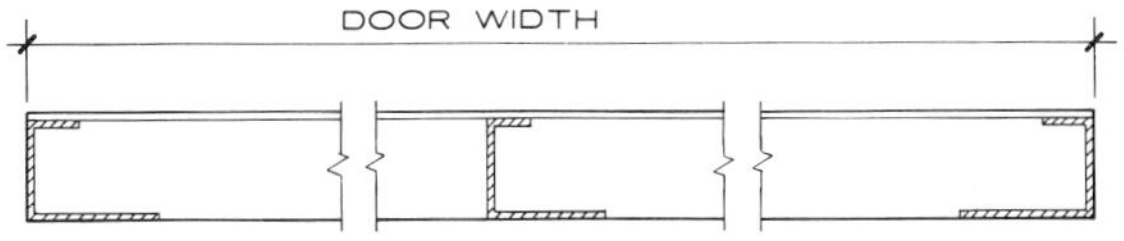

DOOR WIDTH

HORIZONTAL SECTION

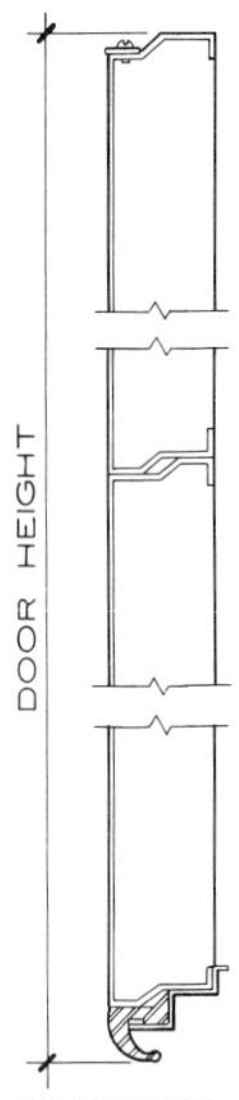

SECTION

FIBERGLASS

ELEVATION

SIZE LIMITATIONS:

2'' Track — not to exceed 340 sq. ft., 26'— 2'' wide or 16'— 1'' high.

3'' Track — optional.

Stiles and rails made of extruded aluminum.

Doors made of fiberglass fastened to both the rails and stiles.

NOTE

Number of stiles varies from 2 for doors up to 12'— 2'' wide, through 7 for widths from 22'— 3'' to 26'— 2''; number of vertical sections varies from 4 for doors up to 8'— 1'' high, through 8 sections for doors from 14'— 2'' to 16'— 1'' high. Number of stiles and sections depends on increments in height and width established by particular manufacturers.

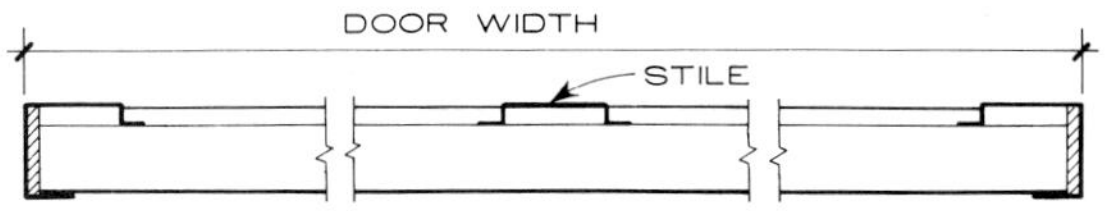

DOOR WIDTH
STILE

HORIZONTAL SECTION

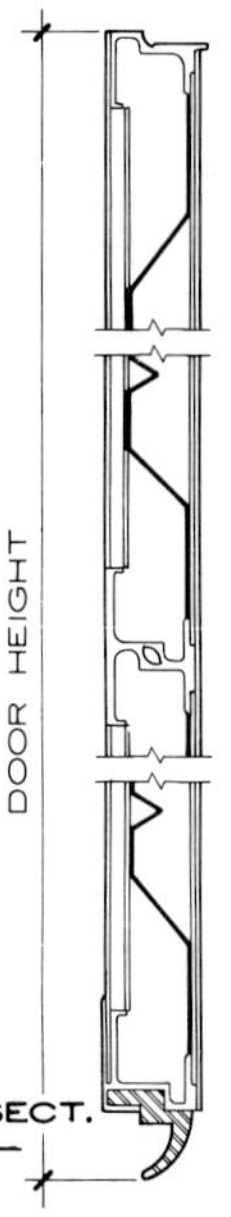

SECT.

Eugene Patrick Holden, AIA; Dale E. Selzer, AIA, Architect; Dallas, Texas

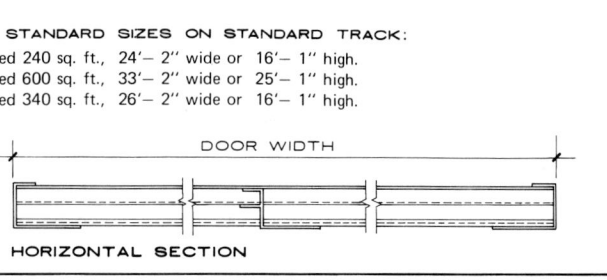

ELEVATION

CENTER STILE		SECTION	
DOOR WIDTH	NO. OF STILES	DOOR HEIGHT	NO. OF SECTIONS
to 12'-2''	2	to 8'-1''	4
12'-3'' to 16'-2''	3	8'-2'' to 10'-1''	5
16'-3'' to 19'-2''	4	10'-2'' to 12'-1''	6
19'-3'' to 22'-2''	5	12'-2'' to 14'-1''	7
22'-3'' to 26'-2''	7	14'-2'' to 16'-1''	8
26'-3'' to 33'-2''	9	16'-2'' to 18'-1''	9
		18'-2'' to 20'-1''	10
		20'-2'' to 22'-1''	11
		22'-2'' to 24'-1''	12
		24'-2'' to 25'-1''	13

SIZE LIMITATIONS FOR STANDARD SIZES ON STANDARD TRACK:

20 ga., 2'' track—not to exceed 240 sq. ft., 24'–2'' wide or 16'–1'' high.
     3'' track—not to exceed 600 sq. ft., 33'–2'' wide or 25'–1'' high.
24 ga., 2'' track—not to exceed 340 sq. ft., 26'–2'' wide or 16'–1'' high.

DOOR WIDTH

HORIZONTAL SECTION

DOOR HEIGHT

SECTION

COMBINED DOOR — 20 AND 24 GAUGE STEEL AND FIBERGLASS

GENERAL INFORMATION

1. Standard commercial doors are designed to 20 $\#$/ft.^{2} wind load.

2. All doors are available with sash sections or sash openings in standard section.

3. Doors are available using 20 or 24 gauge steel sections on the top and bottom and intermediate fiberglass sections.

4. Larger openings can be enclosed by using 2 or more doors with removable or swing up center posts. When the center posts are removed or raised, the entire opening is clear.

5. Doors of larger sizes can be manufactured with special engineering.

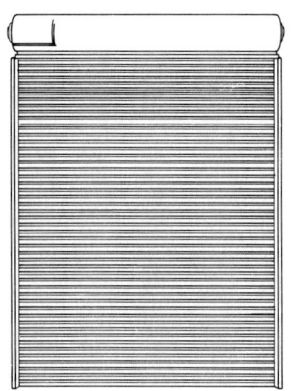

CURTAIN
Available in sizes listed below.

GRILLE
Available in sizes listed below: galvanized or stainless steel or aluminum.

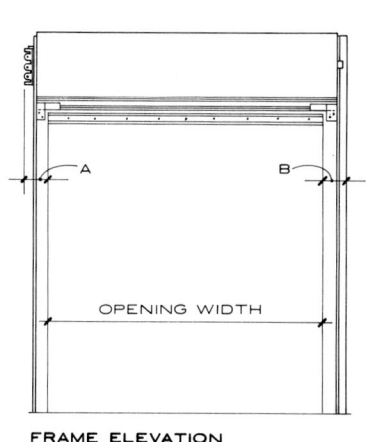

FRAME ELEVATION

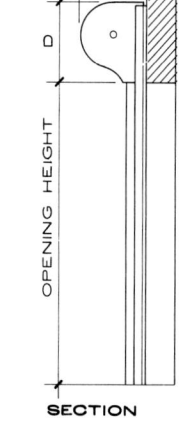

SECTION

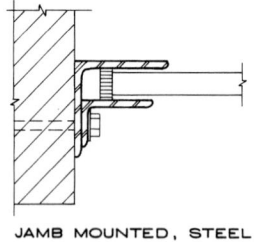

JAMB MOUNTED, STEEL

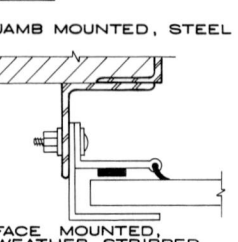

FACE MOUNTED, WEATHER STRIPPED

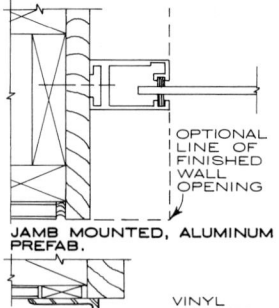

OPTIONAL LINE OF FINISHED WALL OPENING

VINYL INSERTS

JAMB MOUNTED, ALUMINUM PREFAB.

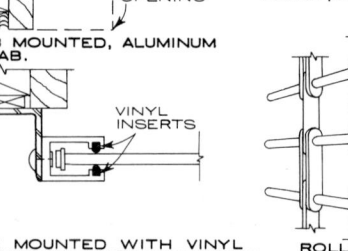

FACE MOUNTED WITH VINYL INSERTS TO EASE OPERATION

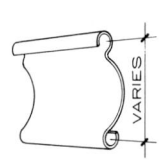

FLAT SLAT
Provides best weather protection.

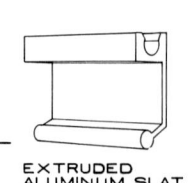

VARIES

ROLLED SLAT
Available in galvanized, stainless steel and aluminum.

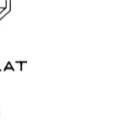

ROLLING GRILLE

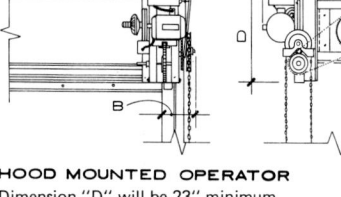

HOOD MOUNTED OPERATOR
Dimension "D" will be 23" minimum.
Dimension "C" will increase 15".

GUIDE DETAILS (THESE VARY AMONG MANUFACTURERS)

NOTE

Doors and grilles are manufactured in a wide range of sizes. Many makers provide standard products up to approximately 30 ft high and 33 ft wide. Larger items may require special engineering. Operator dimensions A, B, C, D, and E vary with size and type of rolling door. Small units may be obtained in preassembled form.

EXTRUDED ALUMINUM SLAT
For use with rolling counter doors.

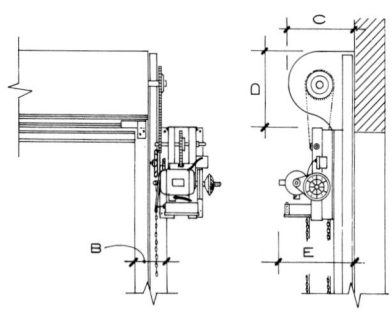

WALL MOUNTED OPERATOR
Dimension "B" will increase by 12".
Dimension "E" will be 20" for all doors.

ROLLING METAL DOORS & GRILLES

Eugene Patrick Holden, AIA; Dale E. Selzer, AIA, Architect; Dallas, Texas

SPECIAL DOORS

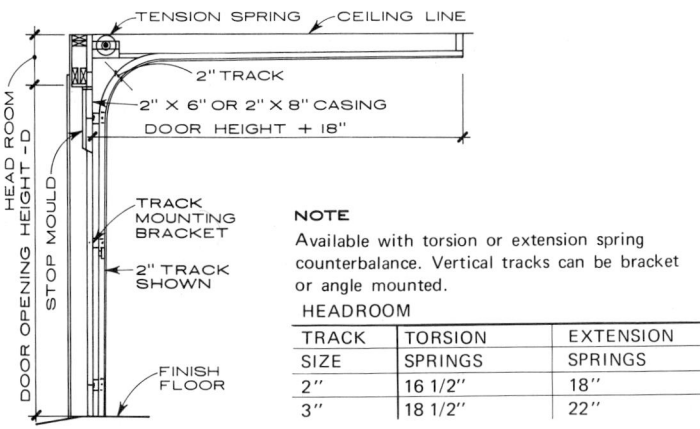

NOTE

Available with torsion or extension spring counterbalance. Vertical tracks can be bracket or angle mounted.

HEADROOM

TRACK SIZE	TORSION SPRINGS	EXTENSION SPRINGS
2″	16 1/2″	18″
3″	18 1/2″	22″

STANDARD HEADROOM TRACK – 2″ OR 3″

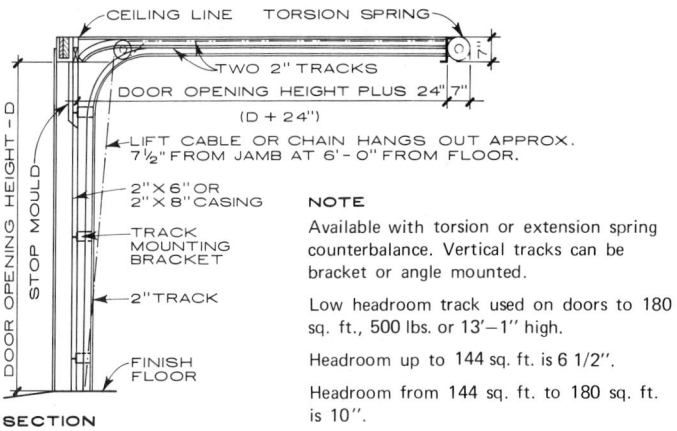

NOTE

Available with torsion or extension spring counterbalance. Vertical tracks can be bracket or angle mounted.

Low headroom track used on doors to 180 sq. ft., 500 lbs. or 13′–1″ high.

Headroom up to 144 sq. ft. is 6 1/2″.

Headroom from 144 sq. ft. to 180 sq. ft. is 10″.

SECTION

LOW HEADROOM TRACK – 2″

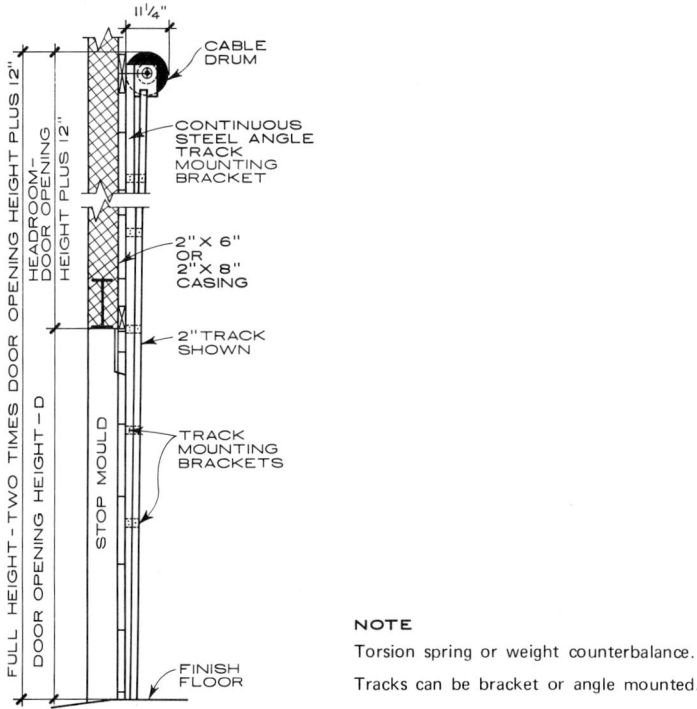

NOTE

Torsion spring or weight counterbalance.

Tracks can be bracket or angle mounted.

FULL VERTICAL TRACK – 2″ OR 3″

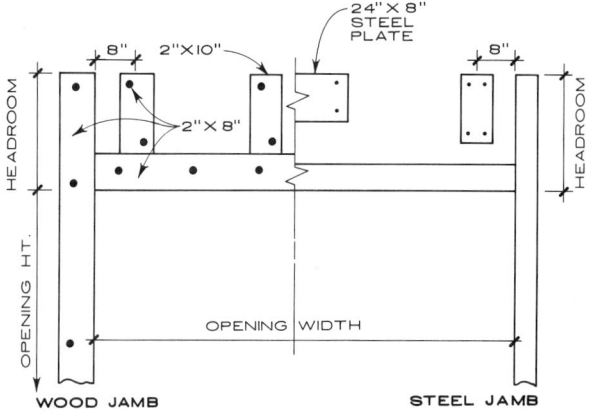

WOOD JAMB   **STEEL JAMB**

All pads and plates to be flush with wood or steel jambs.

Wide or heavy doors which require more than two springs will require pads additional to those shown in the above detail.

INTERIOR ELEVATION OF DOOR OPENING

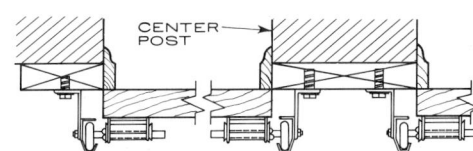

NOTE

For weight counterbalance doors, additional sideroom is required.

See note for asterisk at Table for Steel Jamb sideroom below.

WOOD JAMBS

SIDEROOM

TRACK SIZE	SIDEROOM	FOR DOORS		CENTER POST
2″	3″	to 12′–1″ high		6″
2″	3 1/2″	12′–2″ to 14′–1″	*	7″
2″	4 1/2″	14′–2″ to 16′–1″	*	9″
3″	5″	to 320 sq. ft.	*	10″
3″	5 1/2″	over 320 sq. ft.	*	11″

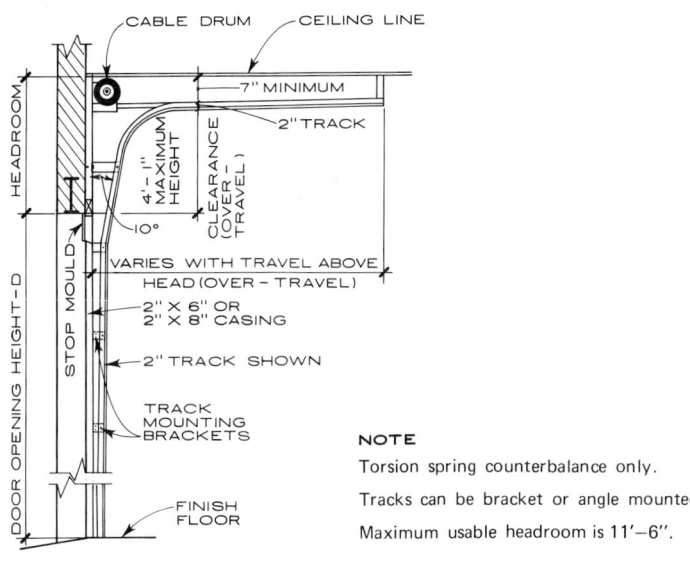

NOTE

Torsion spring counterbalance only.

Tracks can be bracket or angle mounted.

Maximum usable headroom is 11′–6″.

LIFT CLEARANCE TRACK – 2″ OR 3″

Eugene Patrick Holden, AIA; Dale E. Selzer, AIA, Architect; Dallas, Texas

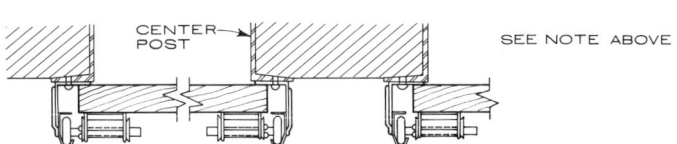

STEEL JAMBS

SIDEROOM

TRACK SIZE	SIDEROOM	FOR DOORS		CENTER POST
2″	4″	to 12′–1″ high		8″
2″	4 1/2″	12′–2″ to 14′–1″	*	9″
2″	5 1/2″	14′–2″ to 16′–1″	*	11″
3″	6″	to 320 sq. ft.	*	12″
3″	7″	over 320 sq. ft.	*	14″

* 16 ga. steel doors over 168 sq. ft. Use 3″ angle mounted track with 7″ sideroom, 14″ center post.

SPECIAL DOORS

NOTE

If door is not electric operated, a chain hoist is recommended for all doors exceeding 160 sq. ft. or 13'-0" high. For 16 ga. steel use chain hoist on doors exceeding 120 sq. ft. or 12'-0" high.

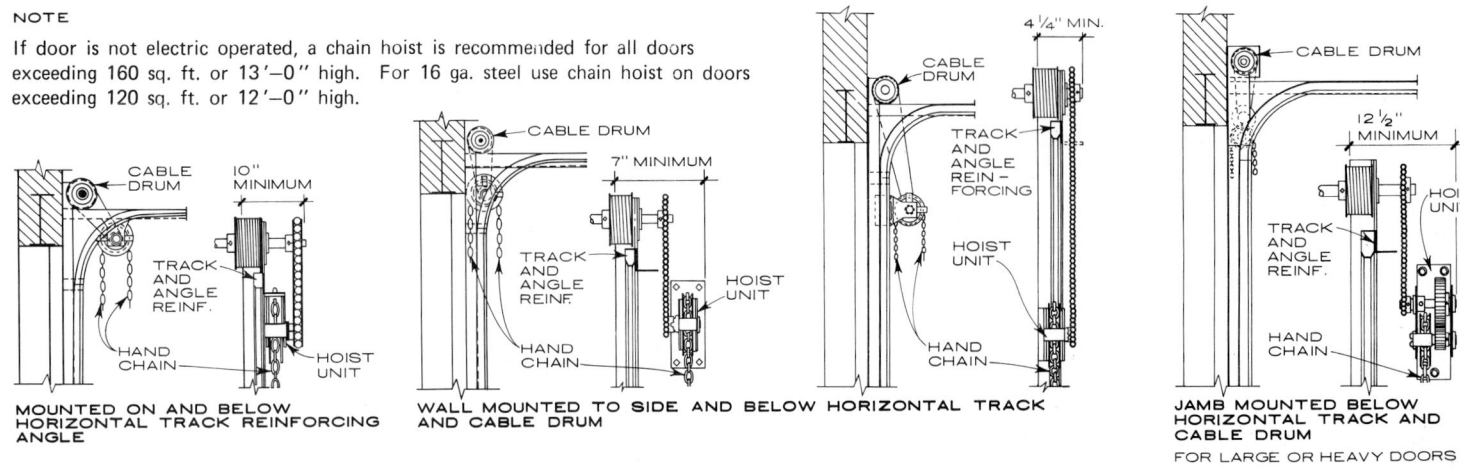

MOUNTED ON AND BELOW HORIZONTAL TRACK REINFORCING ANGLE

WALL MOUNTED TO SIDE AND BELOW HORIZONTAL TRACK AND CABLE DRUM

JAMB MOUNTED BELOW HORIZONTAL TRACK AND CABLE DRUM
FOR LARGE OR HEAVY DOORS

CHAIN HOIST OPERATORS - MINIMUM SIDE ROOM CLEARANCE

NOTE: All chain hoist operators require additional sideroom clearance. Operator may be mounted on left or right side as shown; on the left greater sideroom is required. Dimensions shown are from door jamb to projection of operator.

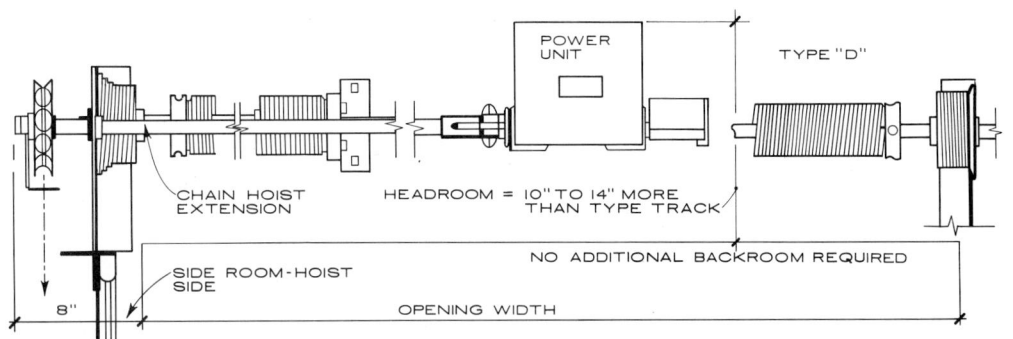

CENTER MOUNTED OPERATOR

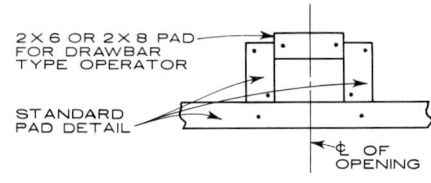

SIDE MOUNTED OPERATOR

SIDEROOM WIDTHS FOR HEAVY COMMER-CIAL USE - 20" FOR 2" TRACK AND 21" FOR 3" TRACK. FOR INDUSTRIAL USE, WIDTHS ARE 23" FOR 2" TRACK AND 24" FOR 3" TRACK.

NOTES
CENTER MOUNTED
Same principle as side mounted operator except power unit is located on front wall above door opening. No additional sideroom is needed. Needs from 10" to 14" additional headroom; 3" additional sideroom on chain hoist side.

NOTES
SIDE MOUNTED
Power unit is mounted on inside front wall to the right or left of the door and is connected to the crosshead shaft with a drive chain and sprockets or an adjustable coupling. Power is applied to the shaft to raise the door. The door closes by its own weight with the speed controlled by the operator.

No extra headroom required. Needs 20" to 24" of sideroom on mounting side.
Side mounted operators are available with direct coupled or chain drive, depending on installation condition.

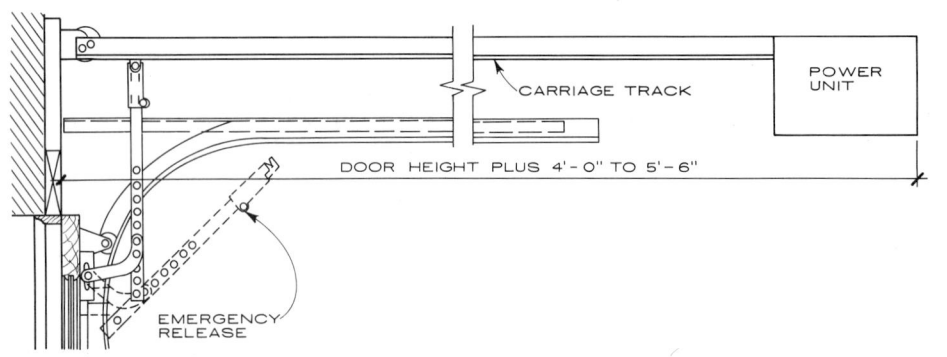

DRAWBAR TYPE OPERATOR
NOTE

PAD DETAIL FOR DRAWBAR TYPE OPERATORS

Power unit is mounted between, above and to the rear of horizontal tracks of door. A chain-driven carriage slides forward and back in its own tracks, which run from power unit to front wall above door. An arm linking the carriage and the door applies force to open and close the door as the carriage moves backward and forward. Door requires a minimum of 2" additional head room above tracks plus 1" to 3 1/2" more at power unit. No additional sideroom is required.

Drawbar type is not recommended for use on extra large doors nor with lift clearance track installations. Emergency chain hoists are not normally used on drawbar type operators.

ELECTRIC MOTOR OPERATORS

Available in all standard voltages, frequency and phase. Control can be by 2 or 3 button push button station, pull switches, photoelectric, radio control (single or multiple), time delay closing and/or reversing or stop only safety switch. For Operator Selector chart see manufacturers data.

Eugene Patrick Holden, AIA; Dale E. Selzer, AIA, Architect; Dallas, Texas

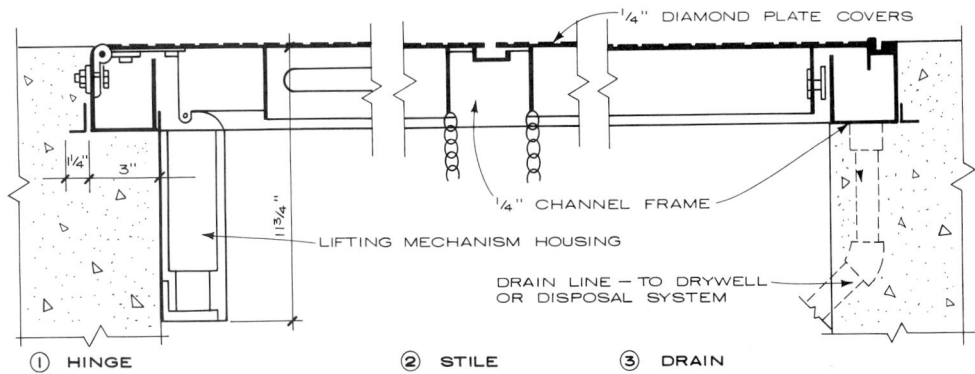

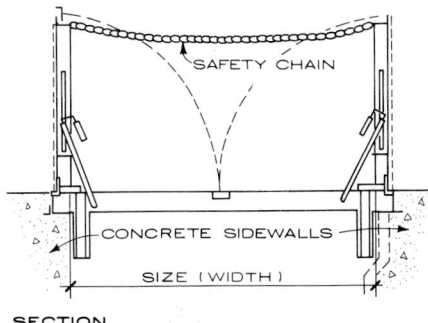

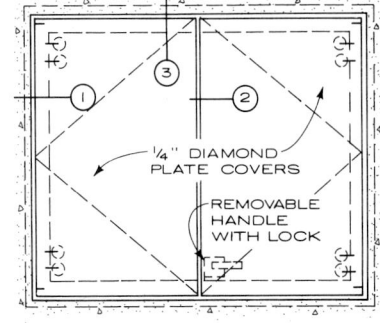

¼" DIAMOND PLATE COVERS

SAFETY CHAIN

¼" CHANNEL FRAME

LIFTING MECHANISM HOUSING

DRAIN LINE — TO DRYWELL OR DISPOSAL SYSTEM

① HINGE ② STILE ③ DRAIN

DETAILS

CONCRETE SIDEWALLS

SIZE (WIDTH)

SECTION

¼" DIAMOND PLATE COVERS

REMOVABLE HANDLE WITH LOCK

PLAN

SIDEWALK DOORS are available in single and double leaf openings. Single leaf doors range in size from 2 ft to 3 ft 6 in. in 6 in. increments. Double leaf doors range in size from 4 to 6 ft in 1 ft increments. Special sizes are available.

Units are constructed in steel or aluminum. The door leafs are made of ¼ in. diamond plate and are reinforced to withstand 300 psf of live load. Doors can be reinforced for greater loading conditions. The channel frames are made of ¼ in. steel or aluminum with an anchor flange around the perimeter. Each door leaf is equipped with forged brass hinges, stainless steel pins, spring operators, and an automatic hold-open arm with release handle and is locked with a concealed snap lock. A drain coupling is provided to drain the internal gutter system. Safety chains are required to protect the opening.

SIDEWALK DOOR

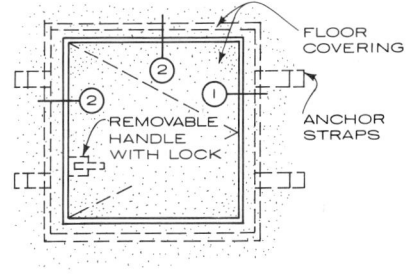

FLOOR COVERING

ANCHOR STRAPS

REMOVABLE HANDLE WITH LOCK

PLAN

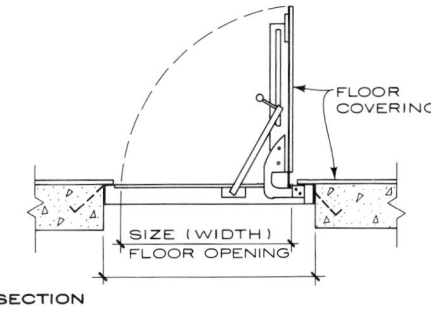

FLOOR COVERING

SIZE (WIDTH) FLOOR OPENING

SECTION

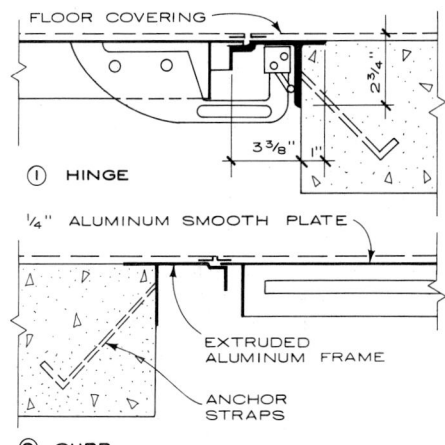

FLOOR COVERING

① HINGE

¼" ALUMINUM SMOOTH PLATE

EXTRUDED ALUMINUM FRAME

ANCHOR STRAPS

② CURB

FLOOR DOORS are available in single and double leaf openings. Single leaf doors range in size from 2 ft to 3 ft 6 in. in 6 in. increments. Double leaf doors range in size from 4 to 6 ft in 1 ft increments. Special sizes are available. Units are constructed in aluminum.

The door leafs are made of ¼ in. extruded aluminum. Doors are made to accept ⅛ or 3/16 in. flooring. Each leaf has cast steel hinges and torsion bars. Doors open by a removable handle and are locked with a concealed snap lock.

FLOOR DOOR

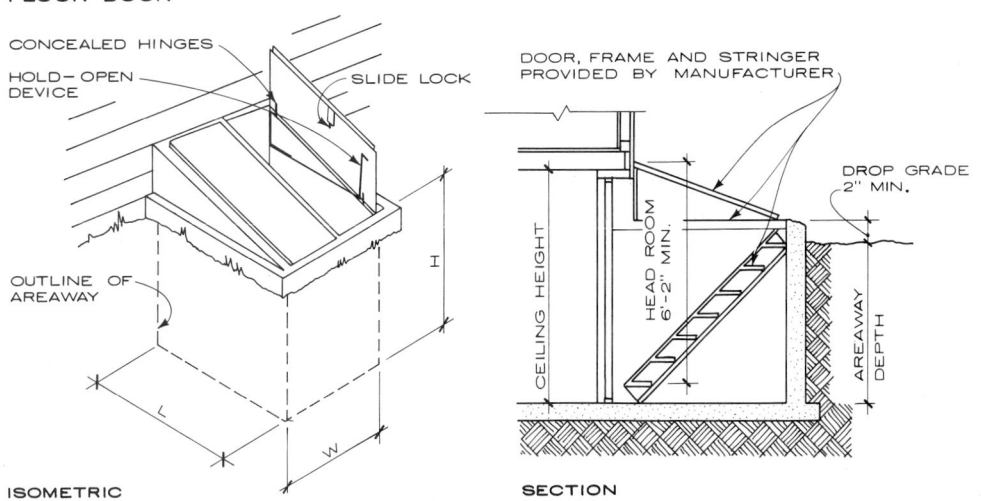

CONCEALED HINGES

HOLD-OPEN DEVICE

SLIDE LOCK

OUTLINE OF AREAWAY

ISOMETRIC

DOOR, FRAME AND STRINGER PROVIDED BY MANUFACTURER

DROP GRADE 2" MIN.

CEILING HEIGHT

HEAD ROOM 6'-2" MIN.

AREAWAY DEPTH

SECTION

CELLAR DOOR

CELLAR DOOR DIMENSIONS

TYPE	LENGTH	WIDTH	HEIGHT
S/L	3'-7¼"	4'-3"	4'-4"
O	4'-10"	3'-11"	2'-6"
B	5'-4"	4'-3"	1'-10"
C	6'-0"	4'-7"	1'-7½"

AREAWAY DIMENSIONS (INSIDE)

TYPE	LENGTH	WIDTH	HEIGHT
S/L	3'-4"	3'-8"	3'-5¼"
O	4'-6"	3'-4"	4'-9¾"
B	5'-0"	3'-8"	5'-6"
C*	5'-8"	4'-0"	6'-2¼"

*Type C door can have a deeper areaway dimension with the use of stringer extensions.

Ronald C. Olech; SRGF, Inc., Architects; Champaign, Illinois

SPECIAL DOORS 8

METAL CURTAIN WALLS

Exterior metal and glass enclosure walls require more careful development and skilled erection than traditional wall construction. Because metal and glass react differently to environmental conditions than do other wall materials, the technology is different from all other enclosure systems.

Errors in judgment can be avoided if behavior of the wall is understood. Some of the important considerations for successful curtain wall development are delineated below. (Further in-depth material on the following points is available from a variety of sources.)

FUNCTION OF THE WALL

The metal and glass curtain wall functions as an "enclosure system" which, when properly developed, can serve multiple functions: (1) withstand the action of the elements; (2) control the passage inward and outward of heat, light, air, and sound; (3) prevent or control access from outside.

NATURAL FORCES

Curtain wall development requirements are determined in part by the impact of natural forces. Natural forces that cause the most destruction and failures are (1) water, (2) wind, (3) sunlight, (4) temperature, (5) gravity, and (6) seismic forces. To understand the impact of these forces on the curtain wall development requirements, the effects of each should be separately examined.

WATER

The most frequent cause of problems with all enclosures is leakage from rain, snow, vapor, or condensate. Wind driven moisture can enter very small openings and may move within the wall, appearing far from its point of entry. Water vapor can penetrate microscopic pores and will condense on cool surfaces. Such moisture trapped within a wall can cause serious damage that is difficult to detect. Leaks are usually limited to joints and openings, which must be designed to provide a weathertight enclosure.

WIND

Structural design development of the wall must take into account both positive and negative pressures caused by wind action, increasing in effect with the height of the building. Increases in wind loading will occur in corner areas of the wall and must be included accordingly. Framing members, panels, and glass thicknesses should be determined by maximum wind load anticipated. Winds contribute to the movement of the wall, affecting joint seals and wall anchorage. The effect of positive or negative wind pressure can cause stress reversal on framing members and glass, and will cause water to travel in any direction (including upward) across the face of the wall. Wind is a major factor in potential water leakage.

SUNLIGHT

The ultraviolet spectrum of sunlight can cause breakdown of organic materials such as color pigments, plastics, and sealants. Fading and failure of these materials can cause serious problems with appearance and weathertightness of the curtain wall. All organic materials should be tested for resistance to ultraviolet radiation and ozone attack.

Sunlight passing through glass can cause excessive brightness and glare and will cause fading of interior furnishings and finishes. Shading devices and the use of glare reducing or reflective types of glass should be considered in development of the wall.

TEMPERATURE

Change in temperature causes the expansion and contraction of materials. Control of the passage of heat or cold through the wall is required. Thermal movement

Skidmore, Owings & Merrill

as a result of solar heat is one of the major problems in curtain wall development. Minimum outdoor temperatures vary about 80°F. Throughout the country, the maximum surface temperature of the darker colored metals on buildings can range as high as 170°F. This temperature fluctuation, both daily and seasonally, critically affects wall development. Thermal expansion and contraction is much greater in metals than in wood or masonry.

Heat passage through the wall causes heat gain in hot weather and heat loss in cold weather, the relative importance of the two varying with geographic location. Thermal insulation of opaque wall areas becomes an extremely important problem, especially whenever these areas constitute a large portion of the total wall area. When vision glass areas predominate, the use of insulating glass and the minimizing of through metal or "cold bridges" (usually by inserting continuous non-metallic breaks in the metal assembly) are more effective in lowering the heat transfer (U-valve) through the wall.

GRAVITY

Because gravity is constant and static rather than variable and dynamic, gravity is a less critical force affecting the development of a window wall design but is important in that it should be recognized. It causes deflection in horizontal load carrying members, particularly under the weight of large sheets of heavy glass. However, because the weight of the wall is transferred at frequent intervals to the building frame, the structural effect of gravity is small in comparison with that imposed by wind action. Far greater gravity forces, in the form of floor and roof loads, are acting on the building frame to which the wall is attached. As these loads may cause deflections and displacements of the frame, connections of the wall to this frame must be designed to provide sufficient relative movement to ensure that the displacements do not impose vertical loads on the wall itself.

SEISMIC

Seismic (earthquake) loadings will produce additional static and dynamic loadings to the window wall system. Seismic loadings will produce both vertical and horizontal deflections of the wall. This will necessitate special energy absorption considerations in the detail of all wall anchorages.

DESIGN DEVELOPMENT CONSIDERATIONS: STRUCTURAL INTEGRITY

Structural integrity of the curtain wall is a prime concern involving the same design procedures that are used in any other exterior wall. However, deficiencies of weathertightness and temperature movements are more prevalent than difference in strength which will be further elaborated upon.

The structural integrity of the window wall must be evaluated using two criteria: strength and deflection. Based on numerous window wall tests, it has been found that the ultimate performance of the system is usually dependent on the elastic and inelastic deflections of the system rather than just the strength of component parts.

Wall fabrication and erection tolerances must be carefully reviewed. Many window wall test failures have been caused by inadequate anchorage details.

WEATHERTIGHTNESS

Weathertightness ensures protection against the penetration of water and an excessive amount of air through the wall. This depends on adequate provision for movement and is closely related to proper joint design. A major share of the problems experienced over the years have been due to the lack of weathertightness.

PROVISION FOR MOVEMENT

Development of the wall must accommodate relative movements of the wall components and also differential movements between the wall assembly and the building structure. Relative movements of the wall components will primarily be affected by thermal movements of the wall elements and erection tolerances of the individual wall elements. Erection tolerances may exceed the tolerance for thermal movement. The differential movements between the wall components of the building structure will be a direct function of the dead and live load deflections of the structure and also the creep, shrinkage, thermal, wind, and seismic deformations of the building structure. These differential movements may be of considerable magnitude, and the effects of such differential movements must not be transferred from the structure directly to the window wall system. Usually provisions for such differential movement are provided at the head and jamb anchorage locations between the wall jointery and/or joints between wall and adjacent cladding. Behavior of sealants must be considered. Current recommendations from sealant manufacturer are to limit movement of the joint to prevent sealant failure. Temperature of metal parts at time of erection, as well as the anticipated design temperature range, will establish the extent of movement in a joint.

MOISTURE CONTROL

Control of condensation is essential because metal and glass are not only impermeable to moisture, but have low heat retention capacity. A vapor barrier should be provided on or near the room side wallface. Impervious surfaces within the wall should be insulated to keep them warmer than the dew point of the air contacting them. Provision should be made for the escape of water vapor to the outside. The wall should be detailed so that any condensation occurring within it will be collected and drained away via weeps as required.

THERMAL INSULATION

A low U-value of the wall is a good long term investment to minimize heat loss in cold weather or heat gain in hot weather. Such devices as minimizing the exposure of the framing members by using thermal breaks, employing insulating glass, and insulating opaque surfaces are recommended.

SOUND TRANSMISSION

By careful selection of details and materials, sound transmission characteristics of the metal and glass wall can be made equal to traditional construction.

Use of insulating glass improves behavior of the wall. Increased mass of the wall will reduce the transmission of sound.

FIRE STOPS

Prevention of the spread of fire will be implemented by continuous fire stopping between the curtain wall and the edge of each floor. Proper detailing with a quality insulation not subject to breakdown by fire and good field inspections will all help to avoid what can become an extremely dangerous condition.

CONCLUSION

The following items can be utilized to further refine the techniques of good curtain wall development and construction. It is necessary to work with the contractors or manufacturers who have specialized for a period of not less than five years in the fabrication and installation of a curtain wall. Visits to the various job sites and interviews with owner or managers will help give an overall view of their products. It is important at the start of design to work with basic metal, basic glass, and sealant producers' technical personnel when developing a metal curtain wall system. Before construction starts, wall testing should be done under both laboratory and field conditions. This is a highly desirable method and also leads to a greater success rate in construction of a good curtain wall.

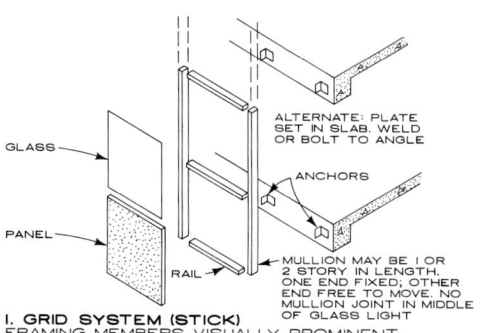

1. GRID SYSTEM (STICK)
FRAMING MEMBERS VISUALLY PROMINENT
COMPONENTS INSTALLED PIECE BY PIECE

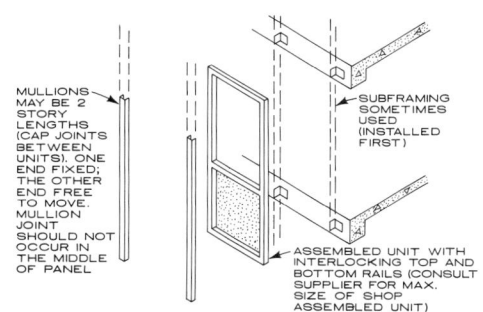

2. GRID SYSTEM (PANEL AND MULLION)
FRAMING MEMBERS VISUALLY PROMINENT
PANEL PREASSEMBLED AND INSTALLED AS SHOWN

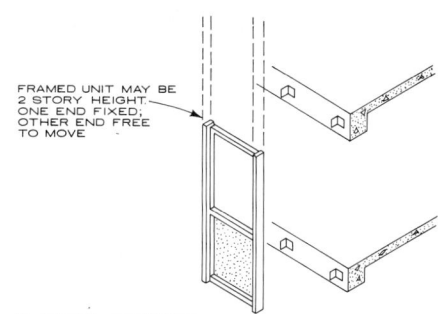

3. PANEL SYSTEM
COMPLETELY PREASSEMBLED UNITS; MAY OR MAY NOT
INCLUDE INTERIOR FINISH

CUSTOM TYPE

Walls designed specifically for one project, using specially designed parts and details. Such walls may be used on buildings of any height but are more typical of multistoried structures. Included in this category are the highly publicized (and often more expensive) walls that serve as design pacesetters.

COMMERCIAL TYPE

Walls made up principally of parts and details standardized by the manufacturer and assembled either in the manufacturer's stock patterns or in accord with the architect's design. This type is offered by many manufacturers and is commonly used on one and two story buildings, though it may be used on taller structures. Commercial walls cost less because of quantity production and also offer the advantages of proved performance.

INDUSTRIAL TYPE

Walls in which ribbed, fluted, or otherwise preformed metal sheets in stock sizes are used, along with standard metal sash, as the principal components. This type of metal curtain wall has a long history of satisfactory performance and, in its insulated form, finds wide use in many important buildings outside the industrial field.

CLASSIFICATION BY NATURE OF COMPONENTS AND BY USAGE

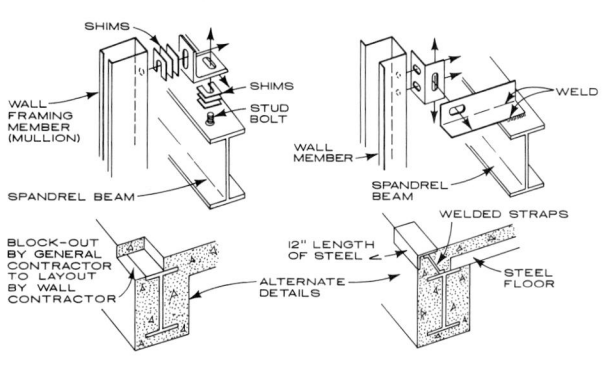

STEEL STRUCTURE

CONCRETE STRUCTURE

NOTES

1. Anchorage devices should permit three-dimensional adjustment. Use permanent lubricant at all metal-to-metal connections subject to intentional movement to eliminate noise caused by movement due to rapid temperature change.
2. Anchors must be designed to withstand wind loads acting outward as well as inward.
3. Anchors must be permanently secured in position after final assembly and adjustment of wall components.
4. All anchorage members must be protected against corrosion.

ATTACHMENT AND ANCHORAGE DETAILS

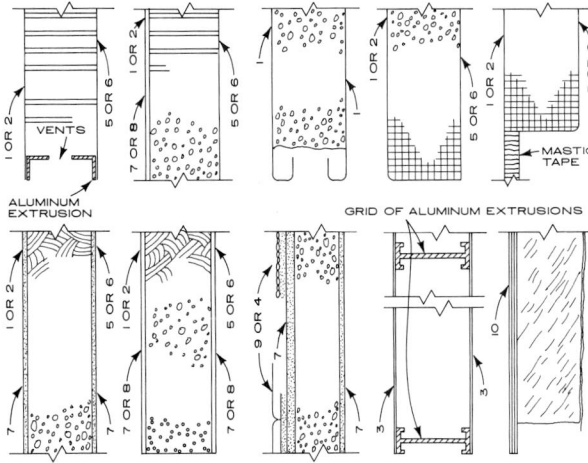

REPRESENTATIVE INSULATING PANEL TYPES
(EXTERIOR FACE ON LEFT)

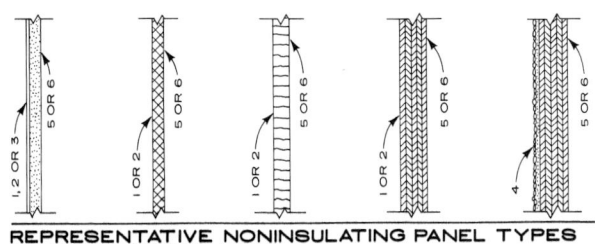

REPRESENTATIVE NONINSULATING PANEL TYPES
(EXTERIOR FACE ON LEFT)

Skidmore, Owings & Merrill

TYPICAL FACING MATERIALS

1. Aluminum or stainless steel sheet, textured or smooth.
2. Porcelain enameled metal.
3. Glass reinforced plastic sheet.
4. Stone chips in plastic matrix.
5. Galvanized bonderized steel sheet.
6. Aluminum sheet.
7. Cement-asbestos board.
8. Tempered hardboard.
9. Ceramic tile in plastic matrix.
10. Opaque colored glass.

TYPICAL CORE MATERIALS

- CEMENT ASBESTOS
- TEMPERED HARDWOOD
- ALUMINUM HONEYCOMB
- EXTERIOR PLYWOOD
- PAPER HONEYCOMB
- FOAMED PLASTIC
- CELLULAR GLASS
- IMPREGNATED WOOD FIBERBOARD
- PERLITE BEADS IN MINERAL BINDER
- FIBROUS GLASS
- ALUMINUM FOIL

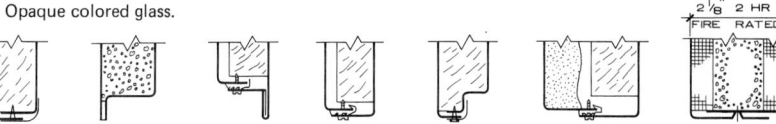

MECHANICALLY ASSEMBLED "ARCHITECTURAL" PANELS (EDGE DETAILS—OUTSIDE FACE IS TO LEFT)

PROPERTIES OF COMMON CORE MATERIALS

MATERIAL (METALLIC AND PAPER)	DENSITY (LB/CU FT)	APPROX. K-VALUE	SENSITIVITY TO MOISTURE	FIRE RESISTANCE
Paper honeycomb	2.5 to 7.0	0.45 to 0.55	Slight, if impregnated	Poor
Paper honeycomb, with foamed plastic fill	4.5 to 10.0	0.20 to 0.35	Slight	Poor
Paper honeycomb, with vermiculite fill	5 to 14	0.35 to 0.40	High	Fair, if faced with steel or cement asbestos
Polystyrene foam	1.7 to 2.3	0.23 to 0.27	None	Poor
Polyurethane foam	1.5 to 2.0	0.12 to 0.15	None	Poor
Impregnated wood fiberboard	20	0.36 to 0.38	Slight	UL rating—incombustible
Cellular glass	9	0.39	None	Excellent
Perlite beads in mineral binder	11	0.33	None	Good

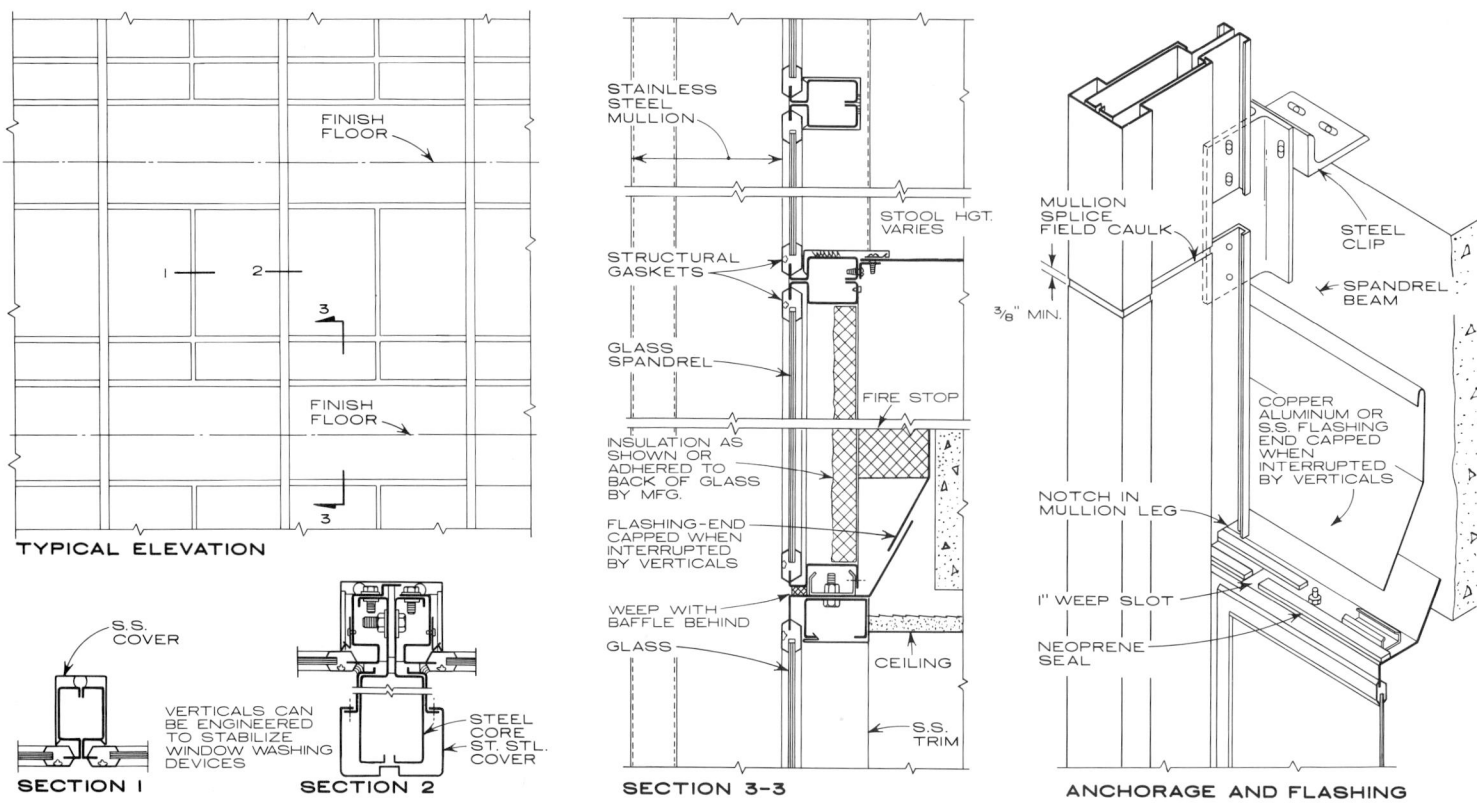

TYPICAL ELEVATION

S.S. COVER

SECTION I

VERTICALS CAN BE ENGINEERED TO STABILIZE WINDOW WASHING DEVICES

STEEL CORE ST. STL. COVER

SECTION 2

STAINLESS STEEL MULLION

STRUCTURAL GASKETS

GLASS SPANDREL

INSULATION AS SHOWN OR ADHERED TO BACK OF GLASS BY MFG.

FLASHING-END CAPPED WHEN INTERRUPTED BY VERTICALS

WEEP WITH BAFFLE BEHIND

GLASS

STOOL HGT. VARIES

FIRE STOP

CEILING

S.S. TRIM

SECTION 3-3

MULLION SPLICE FIELD CAULK

3/8" MIN.

NOTCH IN MULLION LEG

I" WEEP SLOT

NEOPRENE SEAL

STEEL CLIP

SPANDREL BEAM

COPPER ALUMINUM OR S.S. FLASHING END CAPPED WHEN INTERRUPTED BY VERTICALS

ANCHORAGE AND FLASHING

GRID SYSTEM (STICK)-CUSTOM TYPE-STAINLESS STEEL-GASKETED-MULTISTORY PANEL AND MULLION SYSTEM USING STRUCTURAL GASKETS

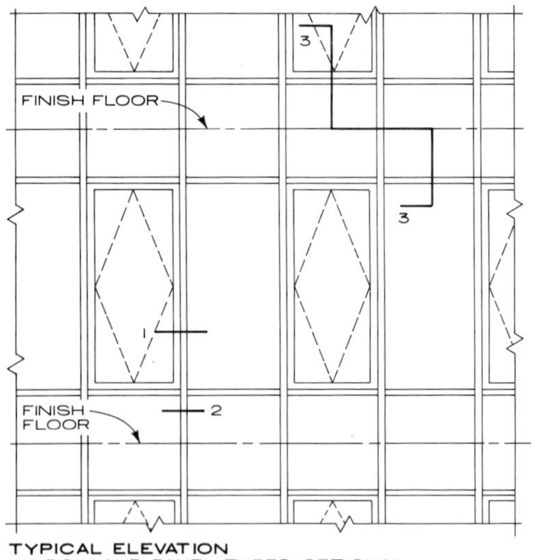

FINISH FLOOR

FINISH FLOOR

TYPICAL ELEVATION
WINDOW AND PANEL TYPES OPTIONAL

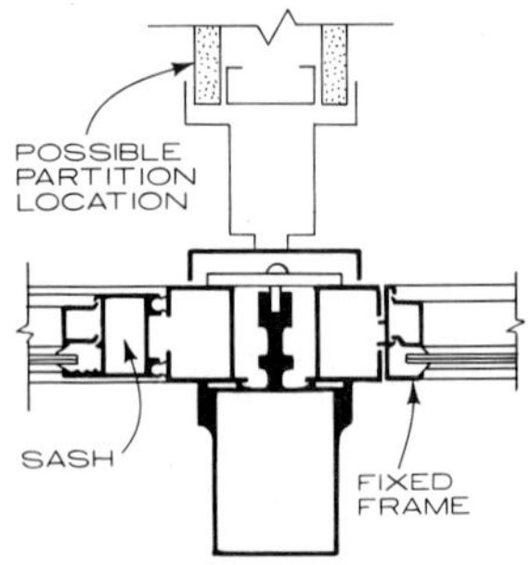

POSSIBLE PARTITION LOCATION

SASH

FIXED FRAME

SECTION I

VERTICALS CAN BE ENGINEERED TO STABILIZE WINDOW WASHING DEVICES

INSULATED PANEL

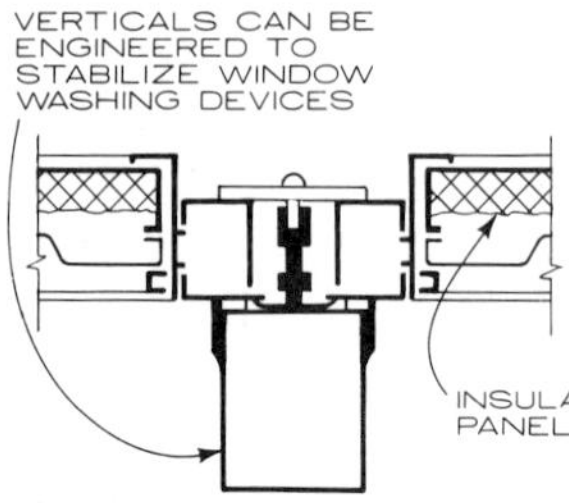

SECTION 2

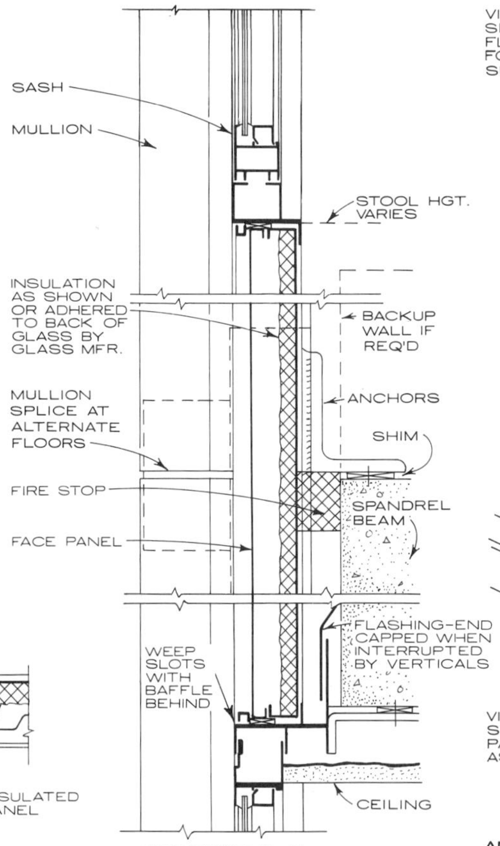

SASH

MULLION

INSULATION AS SHOWN OR ADHERED TO BACK OF GLASS BY GLASS MFR.

MULLION SPLICE AT ALTERNATE FLOORS

FIRE STOP

FACE PANEL

WEEP SLOTS WITH BAFFLE BEHIND

STOOL HGT. VARIES

BACKUP WALL IF REQ'D

ANCHORS

SHIM

SPANDREL BEAM

FLASHING-END CAPPED WHEN INTERRUPTED BY VERTICALS

CEILING

SECTION 3-3

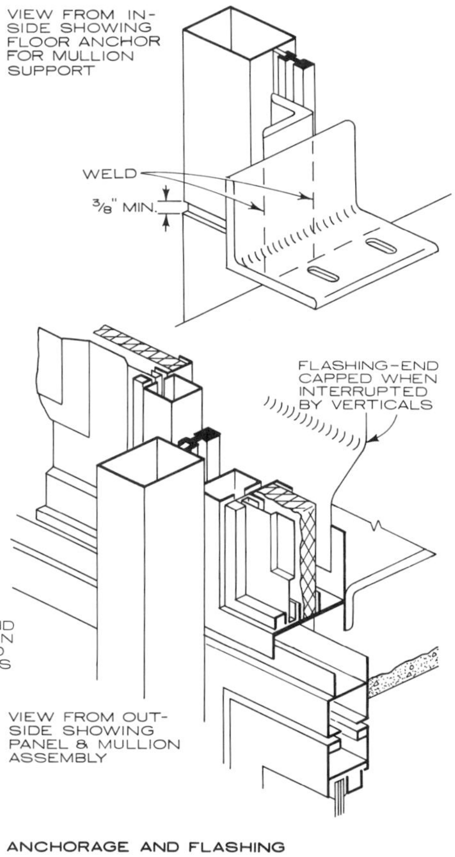

VIEW FROM INSIDE SHOWING FLOOR ANCHOR FOR MULLION SUPPORT

WELD

3/8" MIN.

FLASHING-END CAPPED WHEN INTERRUPTED BY VERTICALS

VIEW FROM OUTSIDE SHOWING PANEL & MULLION ASSEMBLY

ANCHORAGE AND FLASHING
MULLIONS INSTALLED FIRST; PANELS INSTALLED FROM BUILDING FLOORS

GRID SYSTEM (STICK)-COMMERCIAL TYPE-ALUMINUM-TYPICAL MULTISTORY PANEL-AND-MULLION DESIGN

Skidmore, Owings & Merrill

 WINDOW WALLS

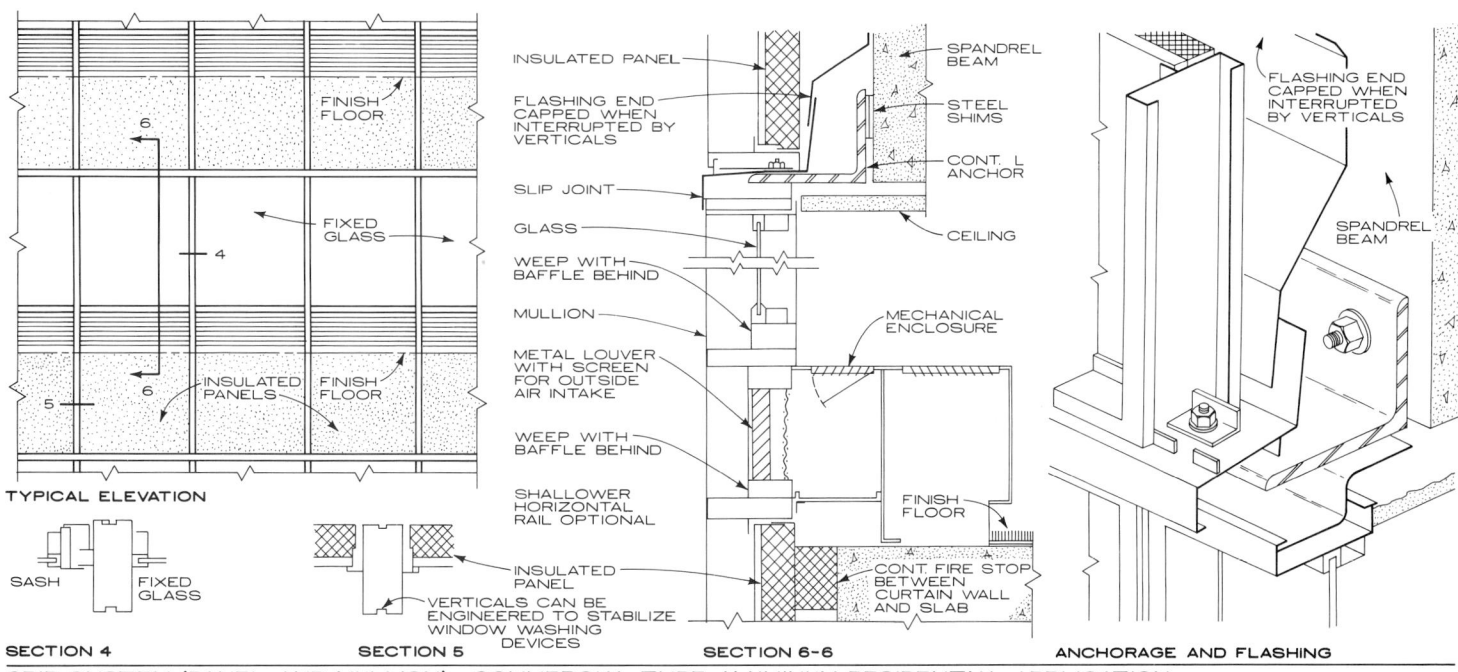

TYPICAL ELEVATION

SASH   FIXED GLASS

SECTION 4

SECTION 5

SECTION 6-6

ANCHORAGE AND FLASHING

GRID SYSTEM (PANEL AND MULLION) – COMMERCIAL TYPE-ALUMINUM-RESIDENTIAL APPLICATION

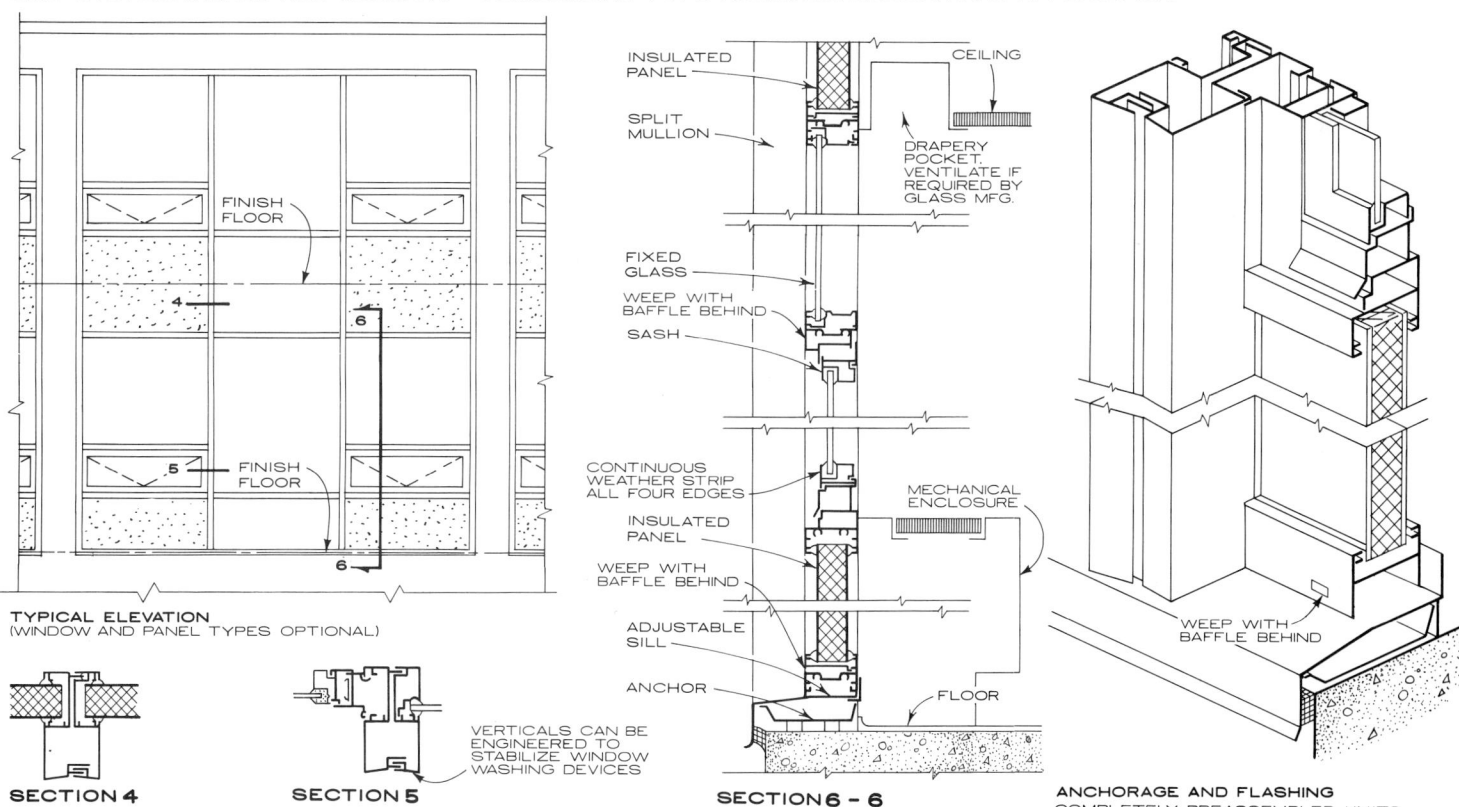

TYPICAL ELEVATION
(WINDOW AND PANEL TYPES OPTIONAL)

SECTION 4

SECTION 5

SECTION 6 - 6

ANCHORAGE AND FLASHING
COMPLETELY PREASSEMBLED UNITS
INSTALLED IN INTERLOCKING FASHION

PANEL SYSTEM–COMMERCIAL TYPE-ALUMINUM-RESIDENTIAL APPLICATION

GENERAL NOTES

1. All metal parts that extend through the wall and are exposed on both exterior and interior of the building should include a thermal break (especially if they are of aluminum).

2. When mullions serve as guide rails for roof mounted window washing platforms or "rigs," mullions should be designed as a track and reinforced against thrust, using information on loads from cleaning equipment manufacturers.

3. It is considered good practice when developing curtain walls construction to consult with a single firm that has specialized in fabrication and installation of all components of metal and glass wall assemblies.

4. Separate unlike metals or alloys with a heavy coating of bituminous paint or zinc chromate or by hot dipped galvanizing of ferrous metals to prevent destructive galvanic action in the presence of moisture.

5. To allow for building movement (caused by wind forces and normal temperature fluctuation) and erection tolerances and to avoid sudden noises (caused by thermal expansion or contraction), elongated or oversized holes for attaching wall assemblies should be provided but separated with nylon, teflon, or similar permanent lubricating materials.

6. Metal curtain wall systems shown here are only examples. Different composite systems can be made up from various components.

7. All buildings (both lowrise and highrise) that have sleeping facilities must be equipped with natural ventilation/operating sash. Check with local governing bodies for requirements.

8. Single glazing in metal curtain walls today would be considered energy consuming; however, large glass areas are still appropriate if insulating glass (both double and triple) and tinted/reflective glass glazing systems are used. Consult glass manufacturers for current information.

Skidmore, Owings & Merrill

WINDOW WALLS   8

GENERAL NOTES FOR ALL WOOD DOORS:
Kiln dried wood, moisture content @ 6–12%.

Type 1 doors: Fully waterproof bond ext. and int.
Type 11 doors: Water resistant bond. Interior only.

Tolerances: Height, width, thickness, squareness and warp per NWMA STANDARDS and vary with solid vs. built-up construction.

Prefit: Doors @ $3/16$" less in width and $1/8$" less in height than nominal size, $\pm 1/32$" tolerance, with vertical edges eased.

Premachining: Doors mortised for locks and cut out for hinges when so specified.
Grading:

Premium: For transparent finish. Good/custom: For paint or transparent finish. Sound: For paint, with 2 coats completely covering defects.

FLUSH WOOD DOORS:
CORE MATERIAL
SOLID CORES:
Wood block, single specie, @ $2^{1/2}$" max. width, surfaced two sides, without spaces or defects impairing strength or visible thru hdwd. veneer facing.

HOLLOW CORES:
Wood, wood derivative, or class A insulation board.

TYPES OF WOOD FACES:
Standard thickness face veneers @ $1/16$"–$1/32$", bonded to hardwood, crossband @ $1/10$"–$1/16$". Most economical and widely used, inhibits checking, difficult to refinish or repair face damage, for use on all cores.

$1/8$" Sawn veneers, bonded to crossband, easily refinished and repaired.

For use on staved block and stile and rail solid cores. $1/4$" Sawn veneers: same as $1/8$" but without crossband on stile and rail solid cores with horizontal blocks. Decorative grooves can be cut into faces.

LIGHT & LOUVER OPENINGS:
Custom made to specifications. Wood beads and slats to match face veneer. 5" min. between opening and edge of door.

Hollow core: Cut-out area max. $1/2$ height of door. Door not guaranteed with openings greater than 40%. Exterior doors: Weatherproofing required to prevent moisture from leaking into core.

FACTORY FINISHING:
Partial: Sealing coats applied, final job finish.
Complete: Requires prefit and premachining.

SPECIAL FACING:
High or medium-low density overlay faces of phenolic resins and cellulose fibers fused to inner faces of hardwood in lieu of final veneers as base for final opaque finish only.

$1/16$" min. laminated plastic bonded to $1/16$" min. wood back of two or more piles.

$1/8$" hardboard, smooth one or two sides.

SPECIAL CORES:
SOUND INSULATING DOORS:
Thicknesses $1^{3/4}$", $2^{1/4}$". Transmission loss rating C Stc 36 for $1^{3/4}$", 42 for $2^{1/4}$". Barrier faces separated by a void or damping compound to keep faces from vibrating in unison. Special stops, gaskets, and threshold devices required. Mfrs. requirements as to wd. frames and wall specs.

FIRE RATED DOORS:
$3/4$ hr "C" label and 1 hr "B" label-maximum size 4'0" x 10'0".
$1^{1/2}$ hr "B" label-maximum size 4'0" x 9'0". All doors $1^{3/4}$" minimum thickness.

LEAD LINED DOORS:
See U/L requirements. Optional location within door construction of $1/32$" to $1/2$" continuous lead sheet from edge to edge which may be reinforced with lead bolts or glued.

GROUNDED DOORS:
Wire mesh located at center of core, grounded with copper wire through hinges to frame.

TYPES OF HOLLOW CORE DOORS:

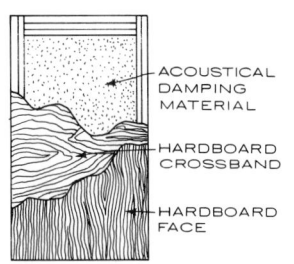

ACOUSTICAL DOOR:
Uses gasketed stops and neoprene bottom seals to cut sound transmission.

HONEYCOMB FIBER:
INSTITUTIONAL:
With cross rail.
INTERIOR:
Without cross rail. Uniform core of honeycomb fiber to form $1/2$" air cells.

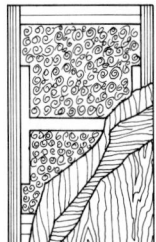

IMPLANTED BLANKS:
Spirals or other forms separated or joined, implanted between & supporting outer faces of door.

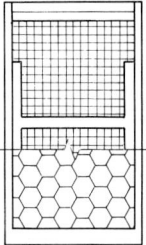

MESH:
Interlocked, horizontal & vertical strips, equally spaced, notched into stiles, or expandable cellular or honey-comb core.

TYPES OF SOLID CORES:

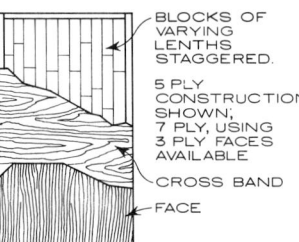

CONTINUOUS BLOCK STAVED CORE:
Bonded staggered blocks bonded to face panels. Most widely used & economical solid core.

FRAMED BLOCK STAVED CORE:
Non-bonded staggered blocks laid up within stile rail frame, bonded to face panels.

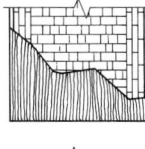

STILE AND RAIL:
Horizontal blocks when cross banding is not used. Vertical panel blocks when cross banding is used.

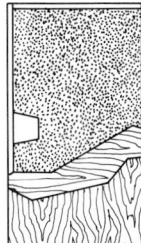

PARTICLE BOARD:
Extremely heavy, more soundproof, economical door, available in hardwood face veneer or high pressure laminate face.

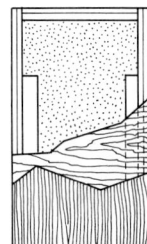

MINERAL COMPOSITION:
Lightest weight of all cores. Details, as cut-outs, difficult. Low screw holding strength.

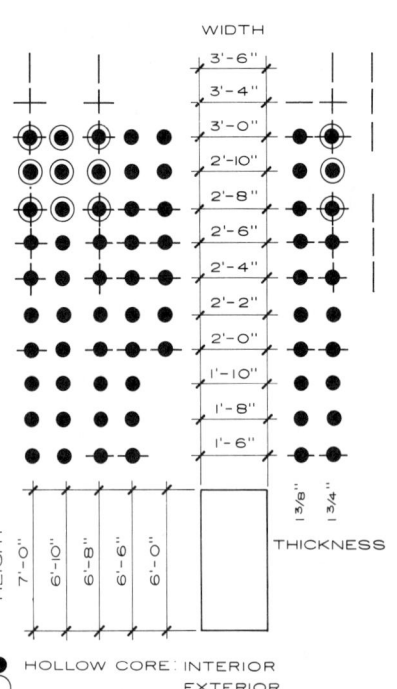

STANDARD SIZES

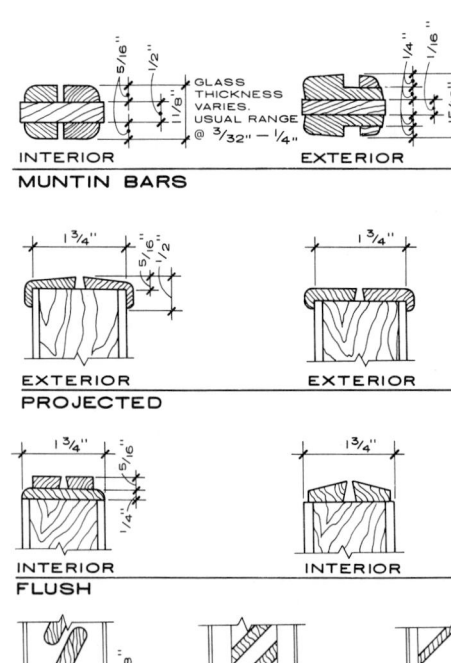

MUNTIN BARS

PROJECTED

FLUSH

LOUVERS· METAL LOUVERS ALSO AVAILABLE
STOCK OPENING AND LOUVER DETAIL

GLASS AND WOOD PANEL DOORS

CONSTRUCTION

Solid pine or built-up stiles, rails and vertical members or mullions, doweled as in NWMA std.

BUILT-UP MEMBERS

Core as in solid core of flush doors.
Edge and end strips as in flush doors.
Face veneers: Hdwd. @ $\frac{1}{8}$" min.

PANELS

Flat: 3 ply hdwd. or soft.
Raised—2 sides: Solid hdwd. or soft or built-up of 2 or more plies.

STICKING, GLASS STOPS, AND MUNTINS

Cove or bead or ovolo, solid, matching face.

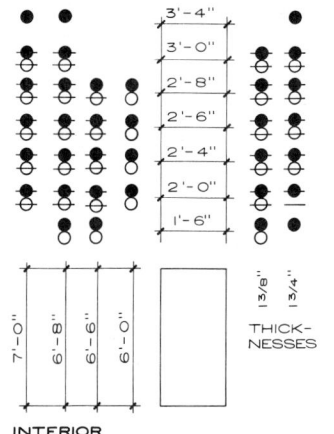

KEY TO SYMBOLS

● Hardwood veneer.
○ Ponderosa pine.
— 1 light & divided light.
Divided lights @
8: Lights @ 2 wide 4 high.
10: Lights @ 2 wide 5 high.
12: Lights @ 3 wide 4 high.
15: Lights @ 3 wide 5 high.
5 horizontal lights.
Interior:
Hdwd. veneer: Available in all sizes.
Pond. pine: 12 & 15 lights.
Not available @ 2'–0" wide.
Exterior:
Hdwd. veneer only.
Available in all sizes.

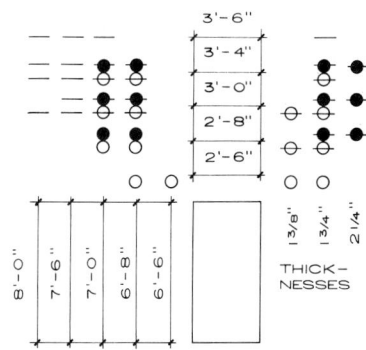

STANDARD SIZES

INTERIOR

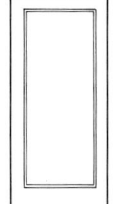 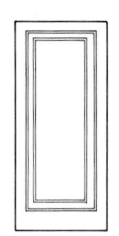  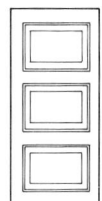 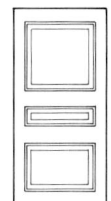 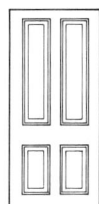 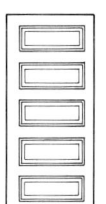   

EXTERIOR (AVAILABLE IN SINGLE & DIVIDED LIGHTS)

 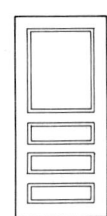 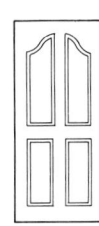  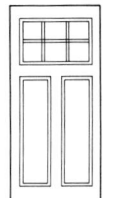 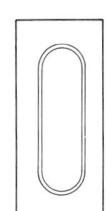 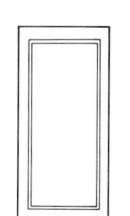 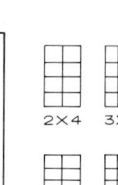 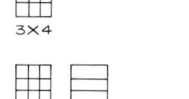

DIVIDED LIGHTS FOR INTERIOR AND EXTERIOR DOORS

2×4   3×4

2×5   3×5   5 HORIZ.

SELECTED STANDARD DOOR TYPES

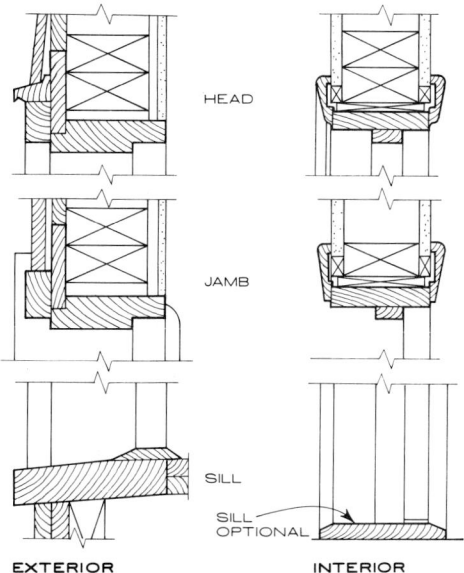

HEAD

JAMB

SILL

SILL OPTIONAL

EXTERIOR   **INTERIOR**

DOOR FRAMES

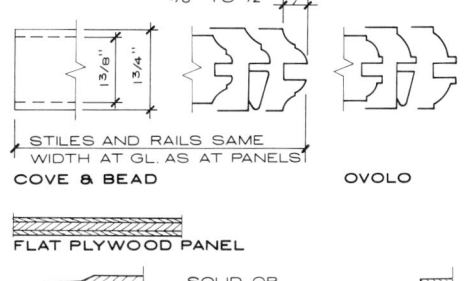

3/8" TO 1/2"

STILES AND RAILS SAME WIDTH AT GL. AS AT PANELS

COVE & BEAD   **OVOLO**

FLAT PLYWOOD PANEL

SOLID OR LAMINATED

BEVEL RAISED PANEL   **HIP RAISED PANEL**

STICKING AND PANEL DETAILS

DOOR HUNG HERE

1/16" MIN.

1/16" MIN. 3/8"

ADJUSTABLE DOOR FRAME

JALOUSIES

$1\frac{3}{4}$" rim type door as in panel door construction with square sticking and fitted with full or half alum. framed inserts housing 4" high clear or obscure glass louvers.
Usual widths @ 2'–6", 2'–8", and 3'–0".
Heights standard.

Simultaneous louver activation outward (similar to venetian blind) by roto operator.

Full frame with 17 louvers with double operators for top 9 and lower 8.

Half frame with 8 louvers—single operators.

Left or right side operation with jambs punched for both and metal plate to cover side not used.

Storm sash/screens on interior.

DUTCH DOORS

Divided door with top half independent of lower. Horiz. meeting rail w/ or w/o interior shelf. Provide WS, separate locking devices and joining hardware for both leaves to act in unison.

SCREEN/STORM DOORS

$1\frac{1}{8}$" screen, storm or combination doors. 1" greater height than nom. due to sill bevel. Combination: Interchange screen/glass inserts.

See index for garage doors and for hardware for doors.

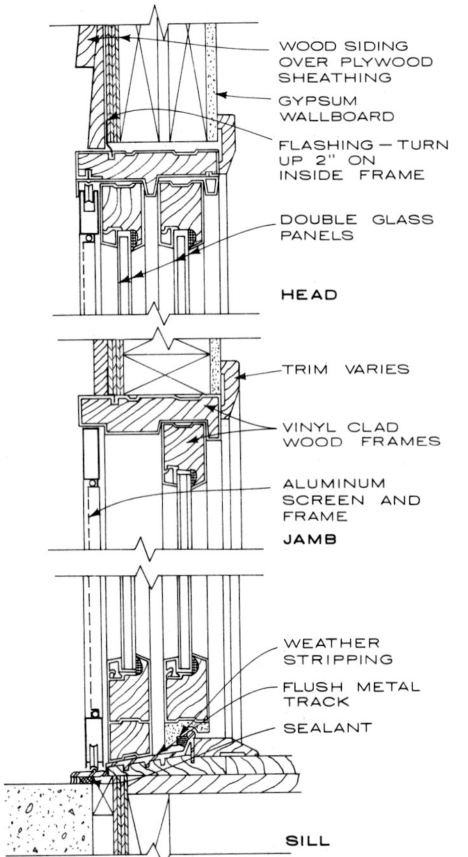

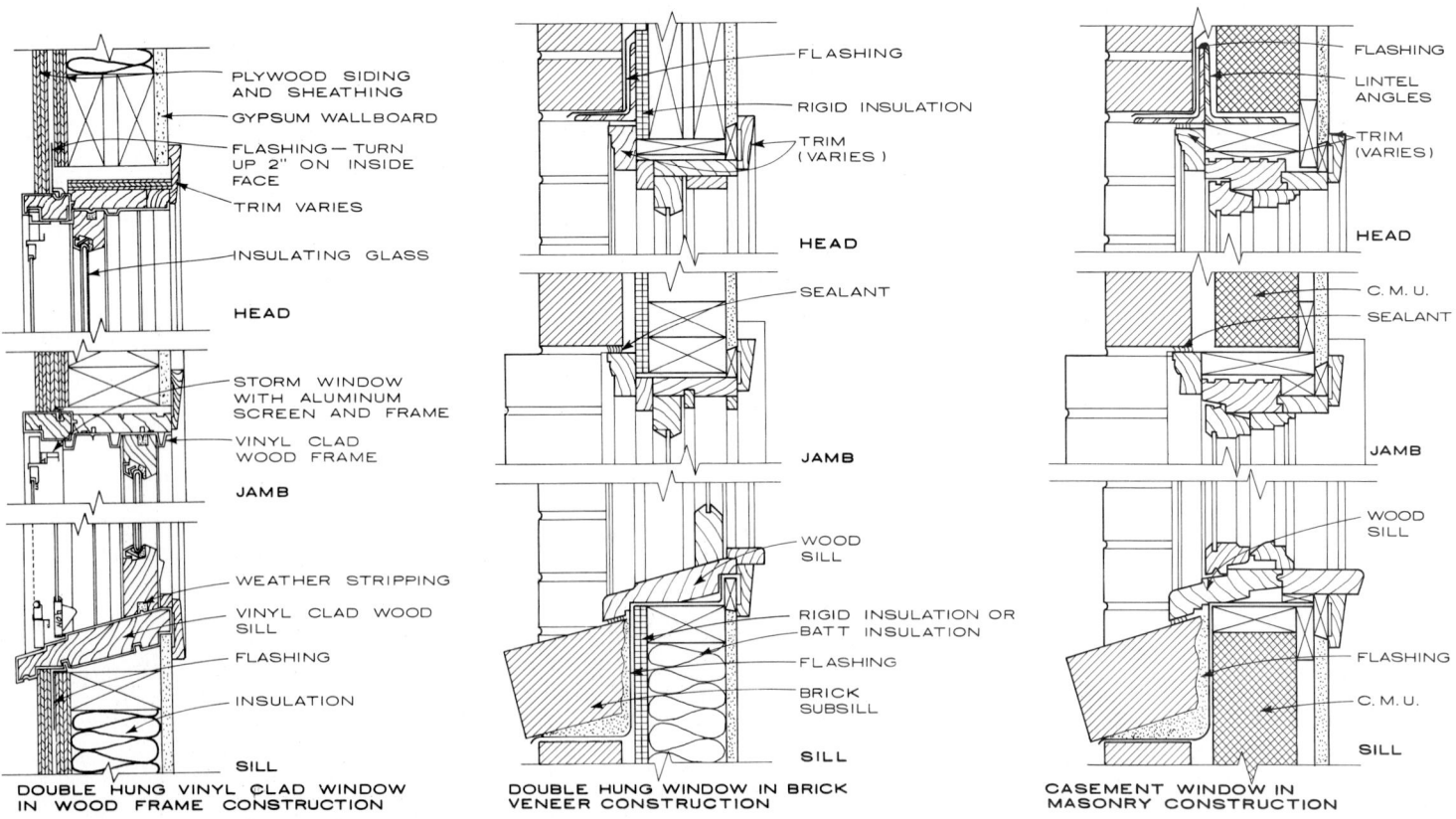

WOOD DOOR INSTALLATIONS

Sliding Vinyl Clad Door in Wood Frame Construction
- WOOD SIDING OVER PLYWOOD SHEATHING
- GYPSUM WALLBOARD
- FLASHING — TURN UP 2" ON INSIDE FRAME
- DOUBLE GLASS PANELS
- HEAD
- TRIM VARIES
- VINYL CLAD WOOD FRAMES
- ALUMINUM SCREEN AND FRAME
- JAMB
- WEATHER STRIPPING
- FLUSH METAL TRACK
- SEALANT
- SILL

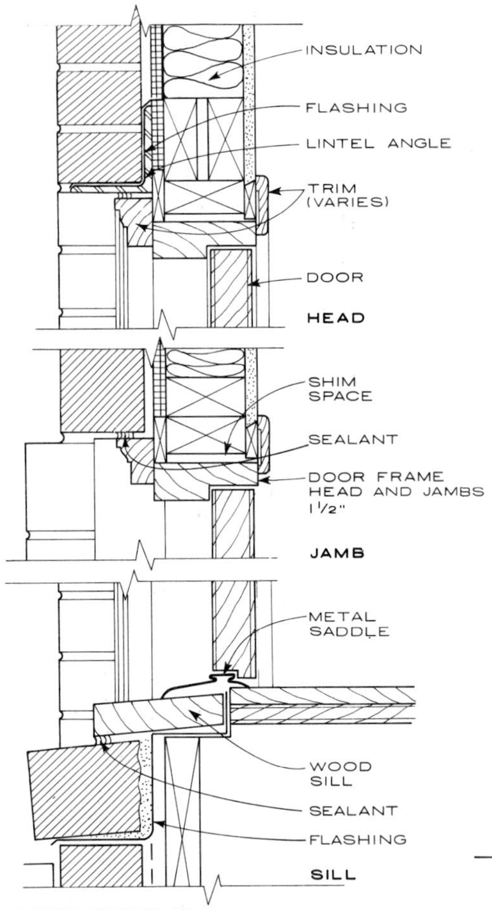

Door Frame in Brick Veneer Construction
- INSULATION
- FLASHING
- LINTEL ANGLE
- TRIM (VARIES)
- DOOR
- HEAD
- SHIM SPACE
- SEALANT
- DOOR FRAME HEAD AND JAMBS 1½"
- JAMB
- METAL SADDLE
- WOOD SILL
- SEALANT
- FLASHING
- SILL

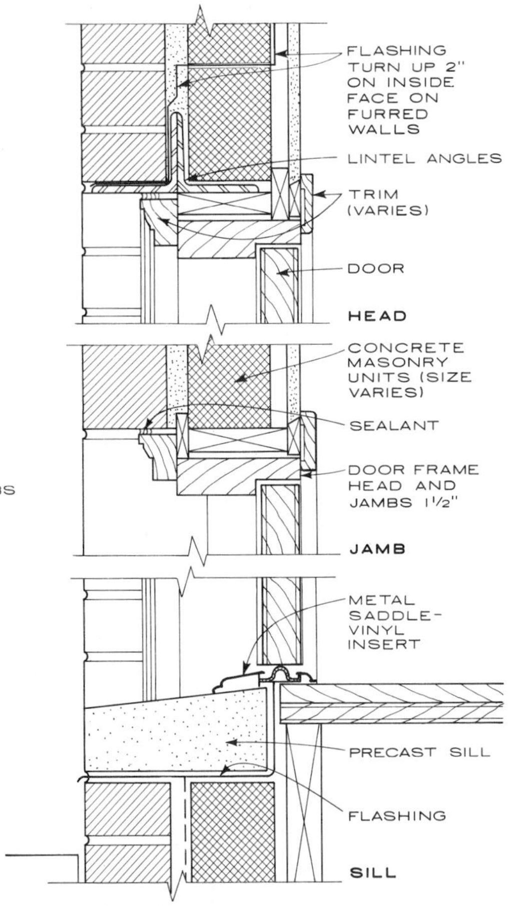

Door Frame in Masonry Construction
- FLASHING TURN UP 2" ON INSIDE FACE ON FURRED WALLS
- LINTEL ANGLES
- TRIM (VARIES)
- DOOR
- HEAD
- CONCRETE MASONRY UNITS (SIZE VARIES)
- SEALANT
- DOOR FRAME HEAD AND JAMBS 1½"
- JAMB
- METAL SADDLE-VINYL INSERT
- PRECAST SILL
- FLASHING
- SILL

NOTE: Flashing at masonry sills should make bond with waterproofing of basement wall (dashed lines above).

Double Hung Vinyl Clad Window in Wood Frame Construction
- PLYWOOD SIDING AND SHEATHING
- GYPSUM WALLBOARD
- FLASHING — TURN UP 2" ON INSIDE FACE
- TRIM VARIES
- INSULATING GLASS
- HEAD
- STORM WINDOW WITH ALUMINUM SCREEN AND FRAME
- VINYL CLAD WOOD FRAME
- JAMB
- WEATHER STRIPPING
- VINYL CLAD WOOD SILL
- FLASHING
- INSULATION
- SILL

Double Hung Window in Brick Veneer Construction
- FLASHING
- RIGID INSULATION
- TRIM (VARIES)
- HEAD
- SEALANT
- JAMB
- WOOD SILL
- RIGID INSULATION OR BATT INSULATION
- FLASHING
- BRICK SUBSILL
- SILL

Casement Window in Masonry Construction
- FLASHING
- LINTEL ANGLES
- TRIM (VARIES)
- HEAD
- C.M.U.
- SEALANT
- JAMB
- WOOD SILL
- FLASHING
- C.M.U.
- SILL

WOOD WINDOW INSTALLATIONS

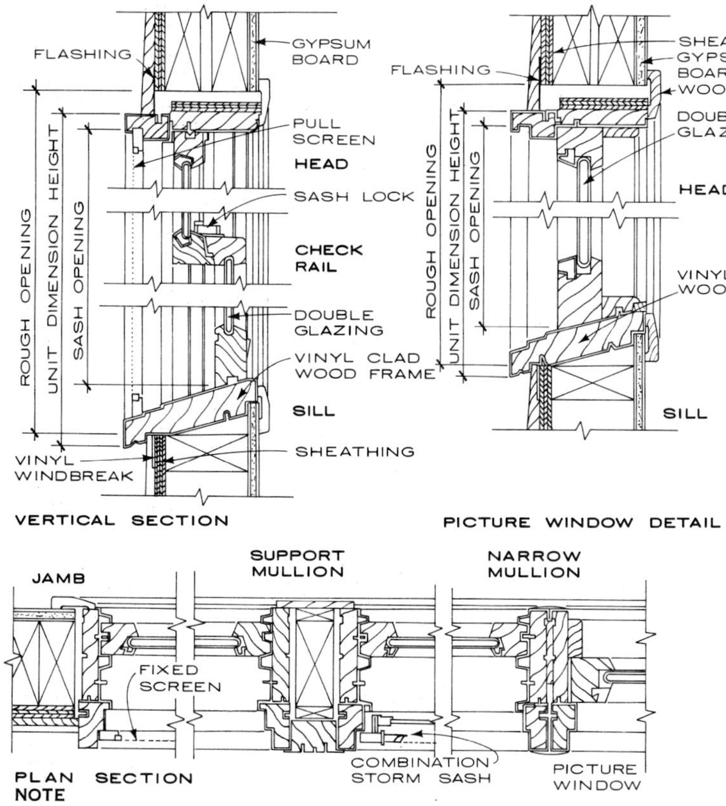

FLASHING — GYPSUM BOARD
PULL SCREEN
HEAD
SASH LOCK
CHECK RAIL
DOUBLE GLAZING
VINYL CLAD WOOD FRAME
SILL
SHEATHING
VINYL WINDBREAK
ROUGH OPENING — UNIT DIMENSION HEIGHT — SASH OPENING

VERTICAL SECTION

FLASHING — SHEATHING / GYPSUM BOARD / WOOD TRIM
DOUBLE GLAZING
HEAD
VINYL CLAD WOOD FRAME
SILL
ROUGH OPENING — UNIT DIMENSION HEIGHT — SASH OPENING

PICTURE WINDOW DETAIL

JAMB
SUPPORT MULLION
NARROW MULLION
FIXED SCREEN
COMBINATION STORM SASH
PICTURE WINDOW

PLAN SECTION

NOTE
Spiral or reel spring balances or pressure weatherstrip operation. Glass size 12 x 12 in. to 44 x 40 in. for 1-light sash.

PLAIN RAIL WINDOW: No parting stop; movable sash slides against fixed sash with hold-open jamb bolts.

DOUBLE HUNG WINDOWS

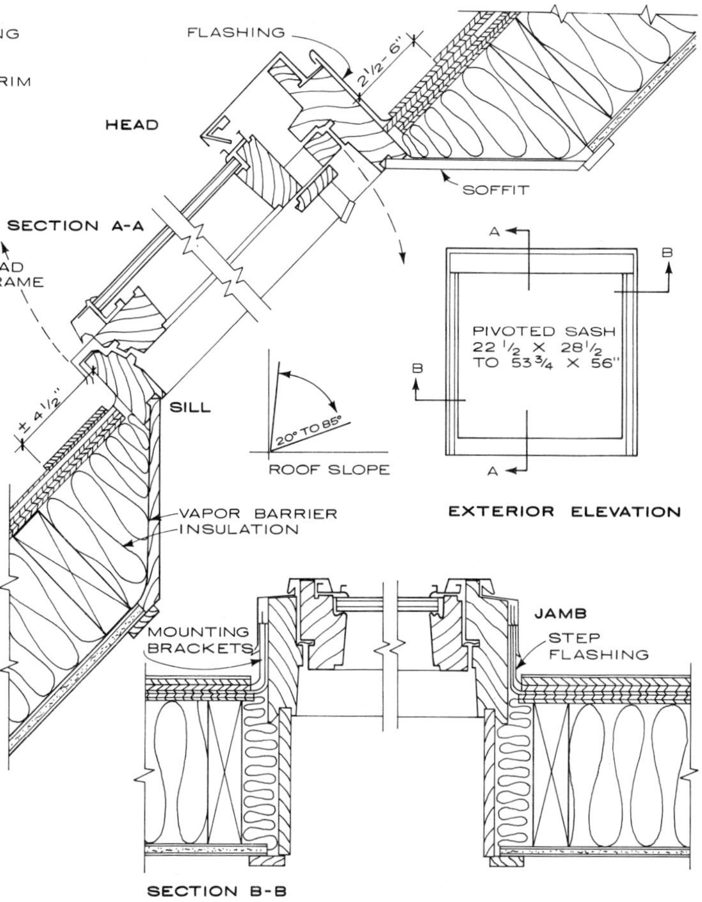

NOTE

CASEMENT WINDOWS: Stiles and top rail 1 to 2 in., bottom rail 3 in. nominal. Outswinging: screen inside, regular or self-storing flexible type with operation similar to window shade. Sash opening range for 1 sash per frame 1 ft 4 in. x 2 ft 2 in. to 2 x 6 ft. Extension hinges, friction arms, folding push bar or roto worm gear operator.

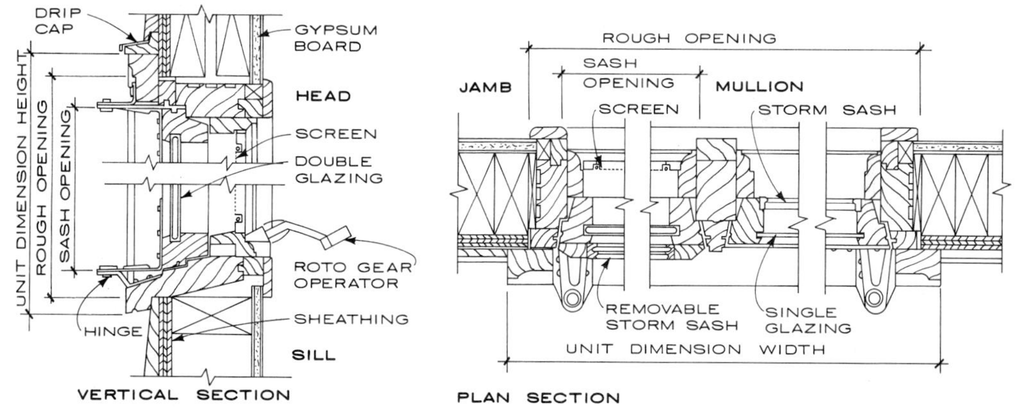

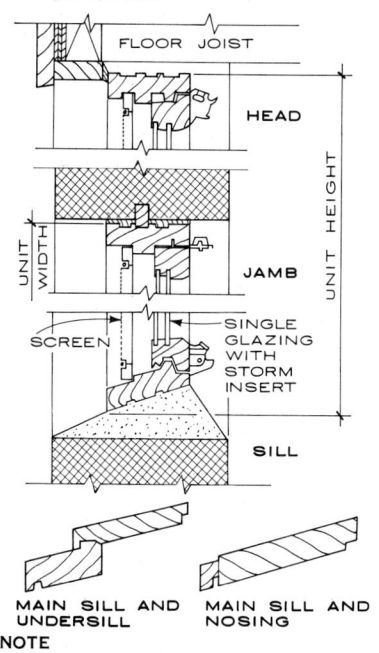

FLOOR JOIST
HEAD
JAMB
UNIT WIDTH — UNIT HEIGHT
SCREEN
SINGLE GLAZING WITH STORM INSERT
SILL

MAIN SILL AND UNDERSILL
MAIN SILL AND NOSING

NOTE
Removable sash and dual purpose hinges for opening from top or bottom.

BASEMENT WINDOWS

Carleton Granbery, FAIA; Guilford, Connecticut

FLASHING
HEAD
SECTION A-A
VINYL CLAD WOOD FRAME
SILL
± 4 1/2"
2 1/2 - 6"
SOFFIT
ROOF SLOPE
20° TO 85°
VAPOR BARRIER / INSULATION
MOUNTING BRACKETS
SECTION B-B

A — B
PIVOTED SASH 22 1/2 X 28 1/2 TO 53 3/4 X 56"
B — A
EXTERIOR ELEVATION

JAMB
STEP FLASHING

ROOF WINDOW

DRIP CAP
GYPSUM BOARD
HEAD
SCREEN
DOUBLE GLAZING
ROTO GEAR OPERATOR
HINGE
SHEATHING
SILL
UNIT DIMENSION HEIGHT — ROUGH OPENING — SASH OPENING

VERTICAL SECTION

CASEMENT WINDOWS

ROUGH OPENING
JAMB
SASH OPENING — MULLION
SCREEN — STORM SASH
REMOVABLE STORM SASH
SINGLE GLAZING
UNIT DIMENSION WIDTH

PLAN SECTION

ROUGH OPENING
MASONRY JAMB
CHECK STILE
FRAMED JAMB
4 1/2"
UNIT DIMENSION WIDTH

PLAN SECTION

NOTE
Sash opening for 2 sash per frame approximately 3 x 2 ft to 5 ft 6 in. x 6 ft. Plastic or metal weatherstrip track top and bottom, center lock with handle.

HORIZONTAL SLIDING WINDOWS

EXTRUDED ALUMINUM TRACK WITH SPRINGS FOR SASH REMOVAL
DOUBLE GLAZING
HEAD
EXTRUDED ALUMINUM TRACK WITH WEEP HOLE
WEATHER STRIPPING
SILL
UNIT DIMENSION HEIGHT — ROUGH OPENING — SASH OPENING

VERTICAL SECTION

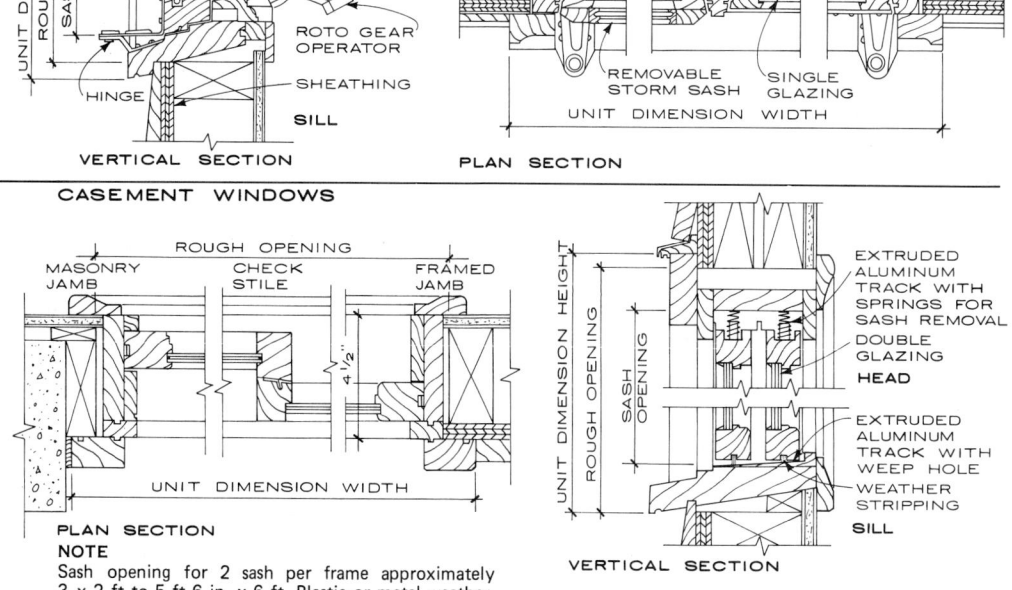

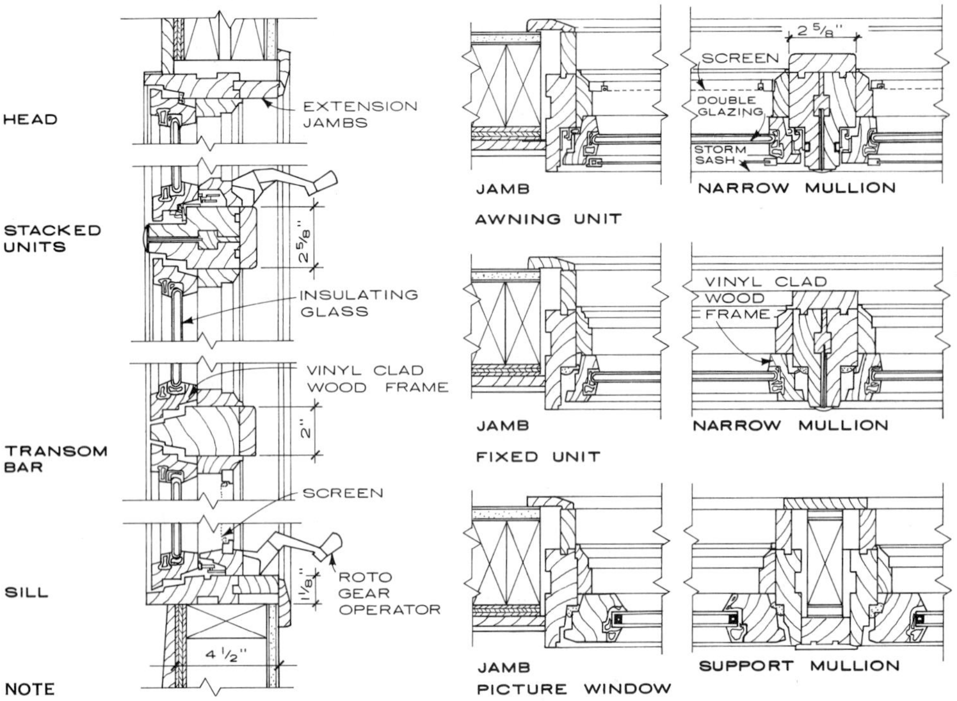

HEAD

EXTENSION JAMBS

STACKED UNITS

2 5/8"

INSULATING GLASS

VINYL CLAD WOOD FRAME

TRANSOM BAR

2"

SCREEN

SILL

1 1/8"

ROTO GEAR OPERATOR

4 1/2"

NOTE

Glass size: 1-light sash 27 x 14 in. to 48 x 32 in. Friction hinge on sliding tracks. Push bar with lock or roto operator. Multiple awning sash also available within single frame, operating in unison.

COMBINED UNITS — AWNING, FIXED, PICTURE WINDOW

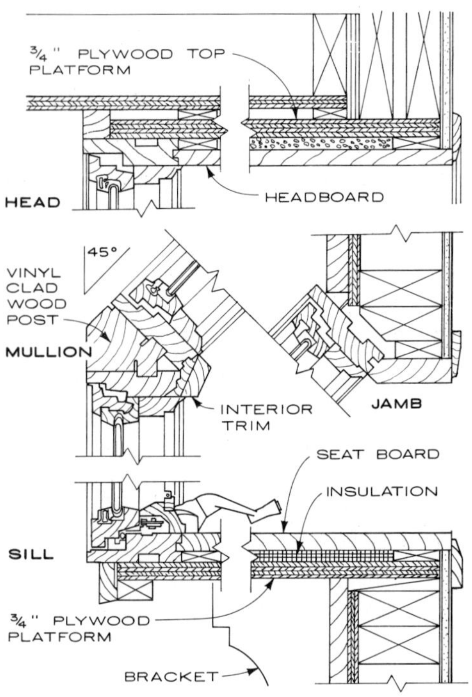

JAMB

AWNING UNIT

2 5/8"

SCREEN

DOUBLE GLAZING

STORM SASH

NARROW MULLION

JAMB

FIXED UNIT

VINYL CLAD WOOD FRAME

NARROW MULLION

JAMB

PICTURE WINDOW

SUPPORT MULLION

3/4" PLYWOOD TOP PLATFORM

HEAD

HEADBOARD

45°

VINYL CLAD WOOD POST

MULLION

INTERIOR TRIM

JAMB

SEAT BOARD

INSULATION

SILL

3/4" PLYWOOD PLATFORM

BRACKET

CASEMENT — 45° ANGLE BAY WINDOW

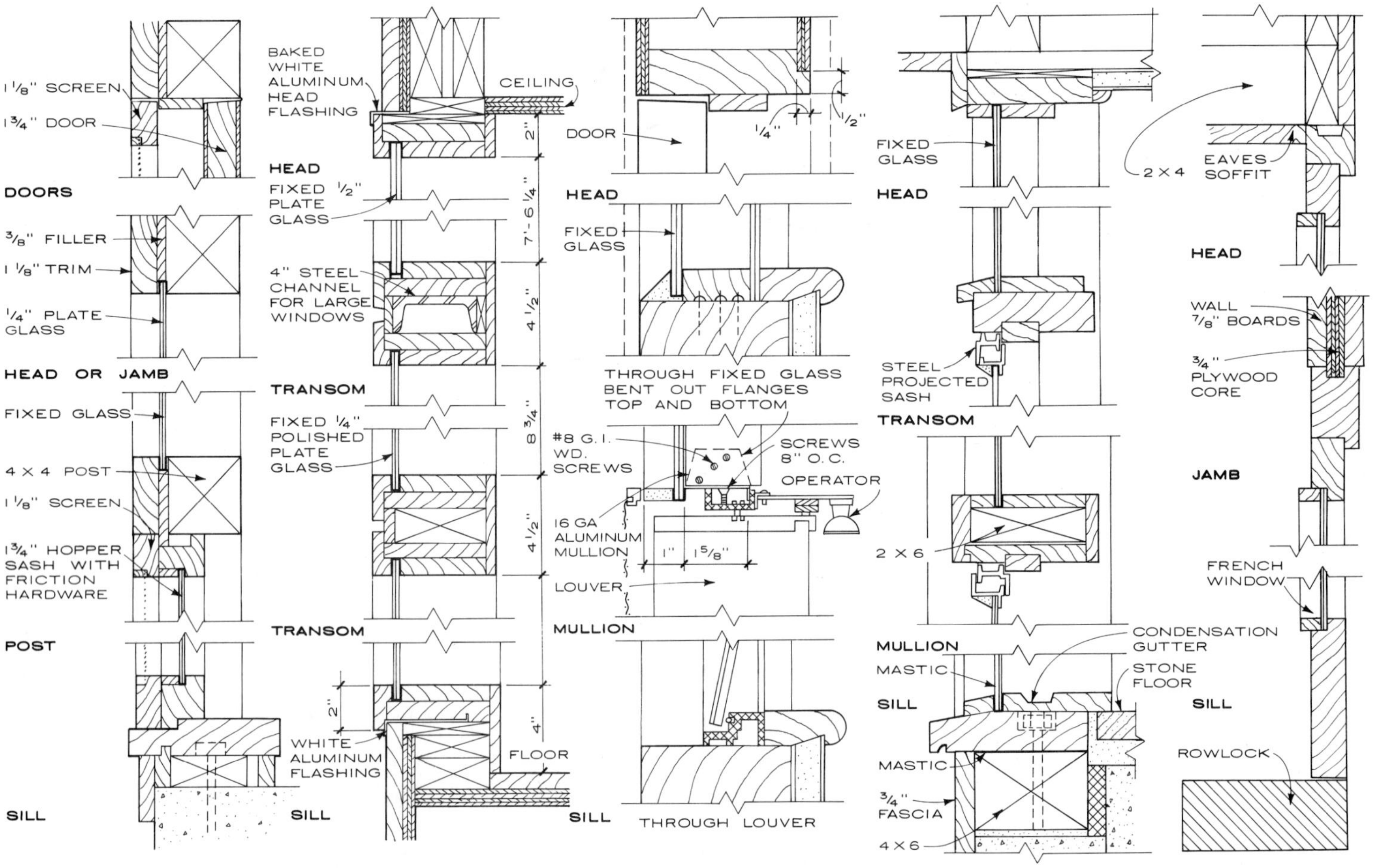

1 1/8" SCREEN

1 3/4" DOOR

DOORS

3/8" FILLER

1 1/8" TRIM

1/4" PLATE GLASS

HEAD OR JAMB

FIXED GLASS

4 x 4 POST

1 1/8" SCREEN

1 3/4" HOPPER SASH WITH FRICTION HARDWARE

POST

SILL

BAKED WHITE ALUMINUM HEAD FLASHING

HEAD

FIXED 1/2" PLATE GLASS

4" STEEL CHANNEL FOR LARGE WINDOWS

TRANSOM

FIXED 1/4" POLISHED PLATE GLASS

2"

TRANSOM

WHITE ALUMINUM FLASHING

SILL

CEILING

DOOR

2"

7'-6 1/4"

4 1/2"

8 3/4"

4 1/2"

4"

FLOOR

1/4"

1/2"

HEAD

FIXED GLASS

THROUGH FIXED GLASS BENT OUT FLANGES TOP AND BOTTOM

#8 G.I. WD. SCREWS

16 GA ALUMINUM MULLION

LOUVER

SCREWS 8" O.C.

OPERATOR

1"

5/8"

MULLION

SILL

THROUGH LOUVER

FIXED GLASS

HEAD

STEEL PROJECTED SASH

TRANSOM

2 x 6

MULLION

MASTIC

SILL

MASTIC

3/4" FASCIA

4 x 6

CONDENSATION GUTTER

STONE FLOOR

2 x 4

EAVES SOFFIT

HEAD

WALL 7/8" BOARDS

3/4" PLYWOOD CORE

JAMB

FRENCH WINDOW

SILL

ROWLOCK

PIETRO BELLUSCHI FAIA

RICHARD MEIER FAIA

RICHARD J. NEUTRA FAIA

HUGH A. STUBBINS, JR. FAIA

THE OFFICE OF FRANK LLOYD WRIGHT

NOTE

Selected examples indicating joinery to achieve weathertight narrow profiles. Adaptable to insulating glass for energy conservation where dictated by local conditions.

CUSTOM DETAILS — FIXED GLASS, HOPPER, CASEMENTS, JALOUSIE, AWNING, AND TRANSOM SASH

Carleton Granbery, FAIA; Guilford, Connecticut

WOOD DOORS AND WINDOWS

FRAMING ARRANGEMENTS

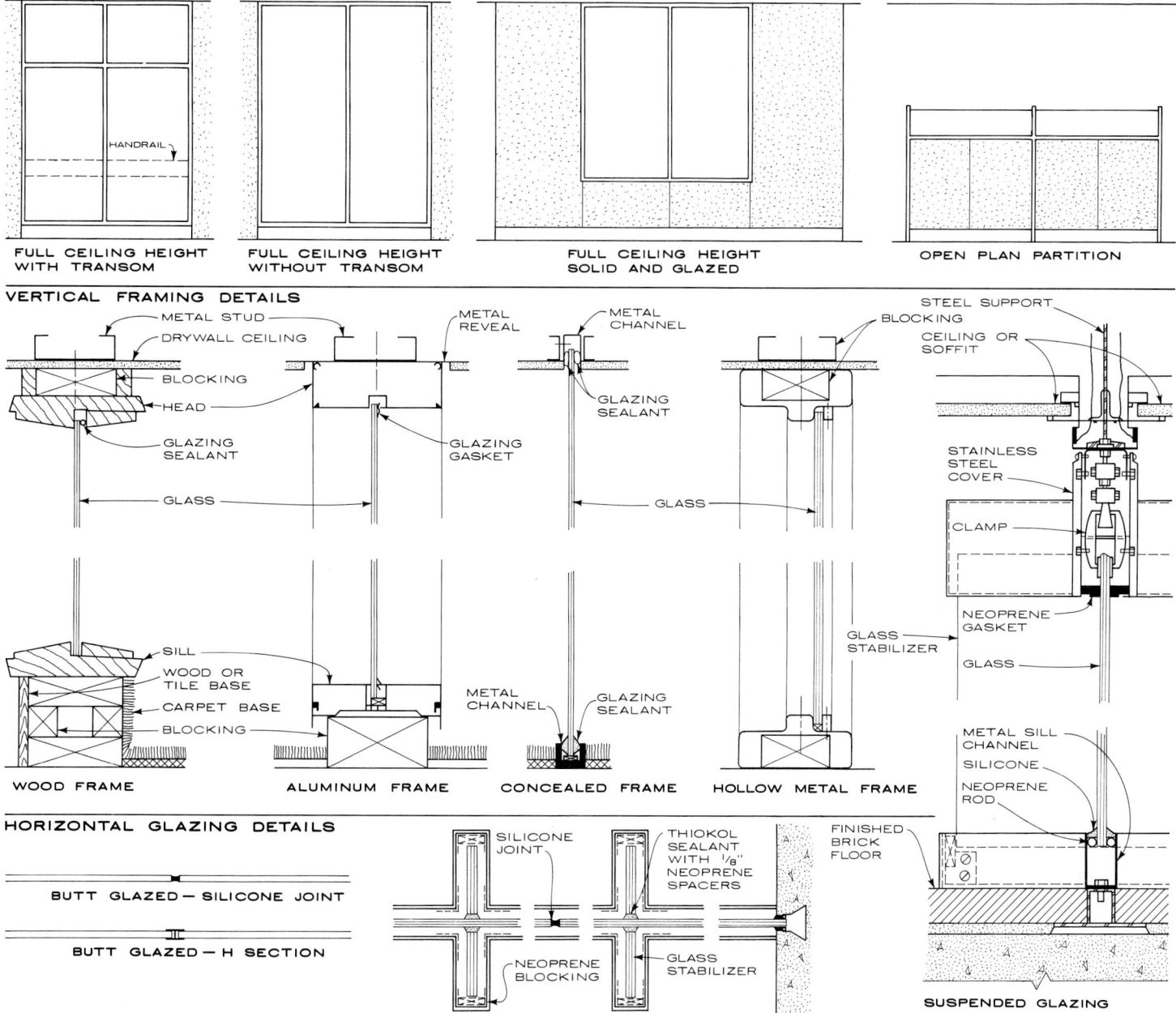

FULL CEILING HEIGHT WITH TRANSOM

FULL CEILING HEIGHT WITHOUT TRANSOM

FULL CEILING HEIGHT SOLID AND GLAZED

OPEN PLAN PARTITION

VERTICAL FRAMING DETAILS

WOOD FRAME
ALUMINUM FRAME
CONCEALED FRAME
HOLLOW METAL FRAME
SUSPENDED GLAZING

HORIZONTAL GLAZING DETAILS

BUTT GLAZED — SILICONE JOINT

BUTT GLAZED — H SECTION

SUSPENDED GLAZING

GLASS TYPES AND SIZES

TYPE	THICK-NESS (IN.)	MAXIMUM SIZE WIDTH (IN.)	MAXIMUM SIZE LENGTH (IN.)	WEIGHT (LB/SQ FT)
Standard	$1^3/_{16}$	48	80	2.5
Sound control 250–4000 cps	$9/_{32}$	48	154	3.5
	$7/_{16}$	48	154	5.1
	$1/_2$	48	154	6.3
	$3/_4$	48	154	9.6
Burglary resisting and bullet proof	$5/_{16}$	48	154	3.6
	$7/_{16}$	48	154	5.2
	$9/_{16}$	48	154	6.4
	$1^3/_{16}$	48	120	14.1
	$1^5/_8$	48	120	20.7
	$1^3/_4$	48	120	21.7
	$2^1/_4$	48	120	28.7
Security for prisons, mental institutions and zoos	$1^3/_{16}$	48	144	9.7
	$7/_8$	48	120	10.5

Walter H. Sobel, FAIA & Associates; Chicago, Illinois

NOTES

Interior glazed partitions are available in various standard hollow metal, aluminum, and wood framing systems. Many standard systems may not be suitable to the architect's design, however. For this reason most systems are custom-made to fit the application.

1. SIZES: Depending on the manufacturer, frames are available in any width or height. Check dimension limitations specified by glass manufacturer.

2. FRAME FINISH MATERIALS: Framing components are available in various finishes that can be matched to any texture or color.

3. PERFORMANCE: Interior partitions can be installed temporarily or permanently. Every form for corners and intersections is available. Check with manufacturer for data on fire ratings, sound transmission, deflection, and other requirements.

4. TYPES: Suspended plate glass panels make uninterrupted transparent walls. Each light is suspended from the structural system by specially designed clamps. For excessive heights, glass stabilizers are used to brace both sides of each panel, providing extra stability without interrupting the upward sweep of the glass.

Translucent or patterned glass partitions allow partial transmission of light while maintaining a reasonable degree of privacy. Primary applications include bathtub and shower enclosures, clerestories, and any area where obscured vision is desired.

One-way glass allows for one-way viewing in security areas where inconspicuous observation is desired.

Laminated safety glass and wire glass should be considered for use in corridors, stairwells, and security areas. Any glass adjacent to an opening is to be approved safety glass.

Laminated safety glass is manufactured by sandwiching sheets of polyvinyl butyral between two or more lights of plate, float, or sheet glass. Should the glass be broken, fragments adhere safely to the interlayer.

Pinstriped wire glass is primarily selected for its sophisticated modern appearance; it is also used in hazardous locations, as defined by applicable codes and state laws.

Tempered glass is four to five times stronger than regular annealed glass. Produced with a special heat treatment, this glass resists breakage. Should the glass be broken, it disintegrates into pebblelike particles.

CHAPTER 9 FINISHES

TYPES OF GYPSUM PANEL PRODUCTS

DESCRIPTION	THICKNESS (IN.)	WIDTH/EDGE (FT)	STOCK LENGTH (FT)
Regular gypsum wallboard used as a base layer for improving sound control; repair and remodeling	1/4	4, square or tapered	8-10
Regular gypsum wallboard used in a double wall system over wood framing; repair and remodeling	3/8	4, square or tapered	8-14
Regular gypsum wallboard for use in single layer construction	1/2, 5/8	4, square or tapered	8-16
Rounded taper edge system offers maximum joint strength and minimizes joint deformity problems	3/8 1/2, 5/8	4, rounded taper	8-16
Type X gypsum wallboard with core containing special additives to give increased fire resistance ratings. Consult manufacturer for approved assemblies	1/2, 5/8	4, tapered, rounded taper, or rounded	8-16
Aluminum foil backed board effective as a vapor barrier for exterior walls and ceilings and as a thermal insulator when foil faces 3/4" minimum air space. Not for use as a tile base or in air conditioned buildings in hot, humid climates (Southern Atlantic and Gulf Coasts)	3/8 1/2, 5/8	4, square or tapered	8-16
Water resistant board for use as a base for ceramic and other nonabsorbant wall tiles in bath and shower areas. Type X core is available	1/2, 5/8	4, tapered	8, 10, 12
Prefinished vinyl surface gypsum board in standard and special colors	1/2, 5/8	2, 2 1/2, 4, square and beveled	8, 9, 10
Prefinished board available in many colors and textures. See manufacturers' literature	5/16	4, square	8
Coreboard for use to enclose vent shafts and laminated gypsum partitions	1	2, tongue and groove or square	4-16
Shaft wall liner core board type X with gypsum core used to enclose elevator shafts and other vertical chases	1, 2	2, square or beveled	6-16
Sound underlayment gypsum wallboard attached to plywood subfloor acts as a base for any durable floor covering. When used with resiliently attached gypsum panel ceiling, the assembly meets HUD requirements for sound control in multifamily dwellings	3/4	4, square	6-8
Exterior ceiling/soffit panel for use on surfaces with indirect exposure to the weather	1/2	4, rounded taper	8, 12
Sheathing used as underlayment on exterior walls with type X or regular core	1/2	2, tongue and groove	8
	1/2, 5/8	4, square	8, 9, 10

NOTE: A large range of adhesives, sealants, joint treatments, and texture products are available from the manufacturers of most gypsum board products. Consult available literature for current recommendations and products.

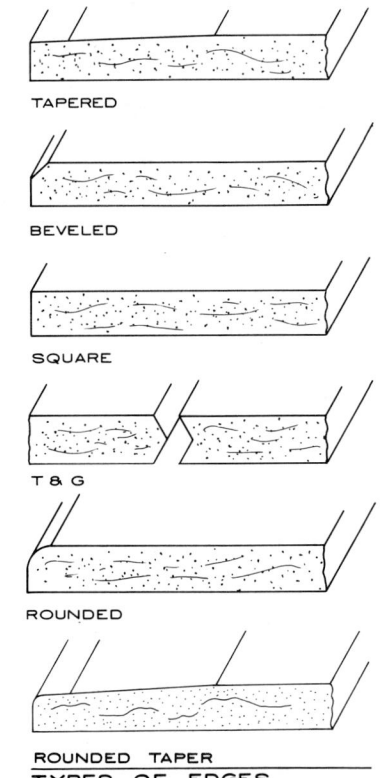

TAPERED

BEVELED

SQUARE

T & G

ROUNDED

ROUNDED TAPER
TYPES OF EDGES

MAX. BENDING FOR DRYWALL

	BENDING RADII	
THICKNESS	LENGTHWISE	WIDTH
1/4"	5'-0"	15'-0"
3/8"	7'-6"	25'-0"
1/2"	20'-0"	—

Shorter radii may be obtained by moistening face and back so that water will soak well into core of board.

MAXIMUM ALLOWABLE PARTITION HEIGHT

STUD SPACING (IN.) (FACING ON EACH SIDE)	STUD DEPTH (IN.)				
	1 5/8 *	2 1/2	3 1/4	3 5/8	4
	MAXIMUM ALLOWABLE HEIGHT				
16 (1/2 one-ply)	11'-0"	14'-8"	17'-10"	19'-5"	20'-8"
24 (1/2 one-ply)	10'-0"	13'-5"	16'-0"	17'-3"	18'-5"
24 (1/2 two-ply)	12'-4"	15'-10"	18'-3"	19'-5"	20'-8"

*1 5/8" stud with single layer of gypsum wallboard recommended for chase walls and closets only.

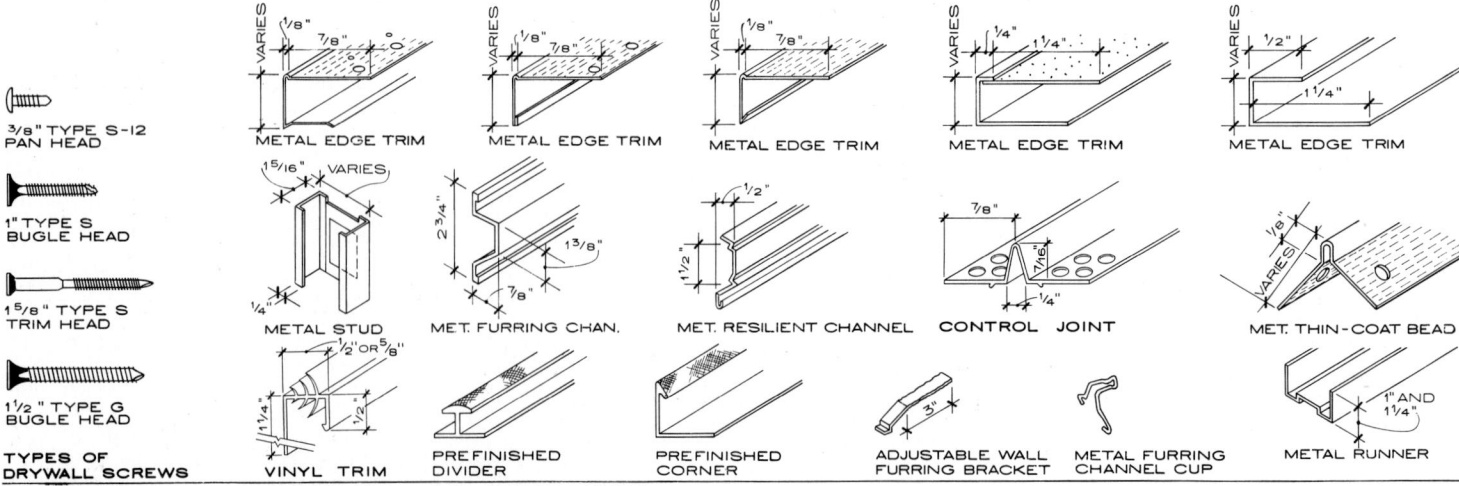

3/8" TYPE S-12 PAN HEAD	METAL EDGE TRIM
1" TYPE S BUGLE HEAD	METAL EDGE TRIM
1 5/8" TYPE S TRIM HEAD	METAL EDGE TRIM
1 1/2" TYPE G BUGLE HEAD	METAL EDGE TRIM

TYPES OF DRYWALL SCREWS

METAL STUD　MET. FURRING CHAN.　MET. RESILIENT CHANNEL　CONTROL JOINT　MET. THIN-COAT BEAD

VINYL TRIM　PREFINISHED DIVIDER　PREFINISHED CORNER　ADJUSTABLE WALL FURRING BRACKET　METAL FURRING CHANNEL CUP　METAL RUNNER

GYPSUM DRYWALL ACCESSORIES AND COMPONENTS

Ferdinand R. Scheeler, AIA; Skidmore, Owings and Merrill; Chicago, Illinois

James Lloyd; Kennett Square, Pennsylvania

 GYPSUM WALLBOARD

FIRE RATING	STC	WALL THICKNESS	CONSTRUCTION DESCRIPTION	WALL SECTIONS
1 HOUR	30 TO 34	4 7/8"	One layer 1/2 in. type X veneer base nailed to each side of 2 x 4 in. wood studs 16 in. o.c. with 5d coated nails 8 in. o.c. Minimum 3/32 in. gypsum veneer plaster. Joints staggered vertically 16 in. and horizontal joints each side at 12 in.	
		4 7/8"	One layer 5/8 in. type X gypsum wallboard or veneer base nailed to each side of 2 x 4 in. wood studs 16 in. o.c. with 6d coated nails 7 in. o.c. Stagger joints 24 in. on each side.	
	35 TO 39	5 1/8"	Two layers 3/8 in. regular gypsum wallboard or veneer base nailed to each side of 2 x 4 in. wood studs 16 in. o.c. First layer attached with 4d coated nails, second layer applied with laminating compound and nailed with 5d coated nails 8 in. o.c. Stagger joints 16 in. o.c. each side.	
	45 TO 49	5 3/8"	Base layer 3/8 in. regular gypsum wallboard or veneer base nailed to each side of 2 x 4 in. wood studs 16 in. o.c. Face layer 1/2 in. (same as base layer). Use 5d coated nails 24 in. o.c. for base layer and 8d coated nails 12 in. o.c. to edge and 24 in. o.c. to intermediate studs. Stagger joints 16 in. o.c. each layer and side.	
		5 7/8"	Base layer 1/2 in. wood fiberboard to each side of 2 x 4 in. wood studs 16 in. o.c. with 5d coated nails 24 in. o.c. on vertical joints and 16 in. o.c. to top and bottom plates. Face layer 5/8 in. type X gypsum wallboard or veneer base applied to each side with laminating compound and nailed with 8d coated nails 24 in. o.c. on vertical joints and 16 in. o.c. to top and bottom plates. Stagger joints 24 in. o.c. each layer and side.	
		5 7/8"	Both sides resilient channels 24 in. o.c. attached with GWB 54 drywall nails to each side of 2 x 4 in. wood studs 16 in. o.c. One layer 5/8 in. type X gypsum wallboard or veneer base attached with 1 in. type S drywall screws 12 in. o.c. to each side and vertical joints back-blocked. GWB filler strips along floor and ceiling both sides. Stagger joints 24 in. o.c. each side.	
	50 TO 54	5 3/8"	Base layer 1/4 in. proprietary gypsum wallboard applied to each side of 2 x 4 in. wood studs 16 in. o.c. with 4d coated nails 12 in. o.c. Face layer 5/8 in. type X gypsum wallboard or veneer base applied with laminating compound and nailed with 6d coated nails 16 in. o.c. to each side. 1 1/2 in. mineral fiber insulation in cavity. Stagger joints 24 in. o.c. each side.	
		5 3/8"	One side resilient channel 24 in. o.c. with 1 1/4 in. type S drywall screws to 2 x 4 in. wood studs 16 in. o.c. Both sides 5/8 in. gypsum wallboard or veneer base attached to resilient channel with 1 in. type S drywall screws 12 in. o.c. and GWB to stud with 1 1/4 in. type W drywall screws. 1 1/2 in. mineral fiber insulation in cavity. Stagger joints 48 in. o.c. each side.	
	60 TO 64	6 7/8"	One side resilient channels 24 in. o.c. attached with 1 in. type S drywall screws to 2 x 4 in. wood studs 16 in. o.c. Two layers of 5/8 in. type X gypsum wallboard or veneer base. First layer attached with 1 in. type S drywall screws, second layer applied with laminating compound. Other side one layer each of 5/8 in. and 1/2 in. gypsum wallboard or veneer base plus top 3/8 in. gypsum wallboard applied with laminating compound. Use 5d coated nails 32 in. o.c. for base, 8d for 1/2 in. center layer. 2 in. glass fiber insulation in cavity. Stagger all joints 16 in. o.c.	
2 HOUR	40 TO 44	6 1/8"	Two layers 5/8 in. type X gypsum wallboard or veneer base applied to each side of 2 x 4 in. wood studs 24 in. o.c. Use 6d coated nails 24 in. o.c. for base layer and 8d coated nails 8 in. o.c. for face layer. Stagger joints 24 in. o.c. each layer and side.	
	50 TO 54	8"	Two layers 5/8 in. type X gypsum wallboard or veneer base applied to each side of 2 x 4 in. wood studs 16 in. o.c. staggered 8 in. o.c. on 2 x 6 in. wood plates. Use 6d coated nails 24 in. o.c. for base layer and 8d coated nails 8 in. o.c. for face layer. Stagger vertical joints 16 in. o.c. each layer and side.	
	55 TO 59	10 3/4"	Two layers 5/8 in. type X gypsum wallboard or veneer base applied to each side of double row of 2 x 4 in. wood studs 16 in. o.c. on separate plates 1 in. apart. Use 6d coated nails 24 in. o.c. for base layer and 8d coated nails 8 in. o.c. for face layer. 3 1/2 in. glass fiber insulation in cavity. Stagger joints 16 in. o.c. each layer and side. GWB fire stop continuous in space between plates.	

CONSULT MANUFACTURER OR GYPSUM ASSOCIATION FOR ADDITIONAL INFORMATION

GYPSUM WALLBOARD   9

FIRE RATING	STC	WALL THICKNESS	CONSTRUCTION DESCRIPTION	WALL SECTIONS
	35 TO 39	2 7/8"	One layer 5/8 in. type X gypsum wallboard or veneer base applied to each side of 1 5/8 in. metal studs 24 in. o.c. with 1 in. type S drywall screws 8 in. o.c. to edges and 12 in. o.c. to intermediate studs. Stagger joints 24 in. o.c. each side.	
	40 TO 44	3 3/8"	Base layer 3/8 in. regular gypsum wallboard or veneer base applied to each side of 1 5/8 in. metal studs 24 in. o.c. with 1 in. type S drywall screws 27 in. o.c. to edges and 54 in. o.c. to intermediate studs. Face layer 1/2 in. attached on each side to studs with 1 5/8 in. type S drywall screws 12 in. o.c. to perimeter and 24 in. o.c. to intermediate studs. Stagger joints 24 in. o.c. each layer and side.	
		4 7/8"	One layer 5/8 in. type X gypsum wallboard or veneer base applied to each side of 3 5/8 in. metal studs 24 in. o.c. with 1 in. type S drywall screws 8 in. o.c. to vertical edges and 12 in. o.c. to intermediate studs. Stagger joints 24 in. o.c. each side.	
	45 TO 49	3 1/8"	Two layers 1/2 in. regular gypsum wallboard or veneer base applied to each side of 1 5/8 in. metal studs 24 in. o.c. Use 1 in. type S drywall screws 12 in. o.c. for base layer and 1 5/8 in. type S drywall screws 12 in. o.c. for face layer. Stagger joints 24 in. o.c. each layer and side.	
		3 1/8"	Base layer 1/4 in. gypsum wallboard applied to each side of 1 5/8 in. metal studs 24 in. o.c. with 1 in. type S drywall screws 24 in. o.c. to edges and 36 in. o.c. to intermediate studs. Face layer 1/2 in. type X gypsum wallboard or veneer base applied to each side of studs with 1 5/8 in. type S drywall screws 12 in. o.c. Stagger joints 24 in. o.c. each layer and side.	
1 HOUR		5 1/2"	One layer 5/8 in. type X gypsum wallboard or veneer base applied to each side of 3 5/8 in. metal studs 24 in. o.c. with 1 in. type S drywall screws 8 in. o.c. to edge and vertical joints and 12 in. o.c. to intermediate stud. Face layer 5/8 in. (same as other layer) applied on one side to stud with laminating compound and attached with 1 5/8 in. type S drywall screws 8 in. o.c. to edges and sides and 12 in. o.c. to intermediate studs. 3 1/2 in. glass fiber insulation in cavity. Stagger joints 24 in. o.c. each layer and side.	
	50 TO 54	4"	Base layer 1/4 in. regular gypsum wallboard applied to each side of 2 1/2 in. metal studs 24 in. o.c. with 1 in. type S drywall screws 12 in. o.c. Face layer 1/2 in. type X gypsum wallboard or veneer base applied to each side of studs with laminating compound and with 1 5/8 in. type S drywall screws in top and bottom runners 8 in. o.c. 2 in. glass fiber insulation in cavity. Stagger joints 24 in. o.c. each layer and side.	
		4"	Two layers 1/2 in. type X gypsum wallboard or veneer base applied to one side of 2 1/2 in. metal studs 24 in. o.c. Base layer 1 in. and face layer 1 5/8 in. type S drywall screws 8 in. o.c. to edge and adhesive beads to intermediate studs. Opposite side layer 1/2 in. type X gypsum wallboard or veneer base applied with 1 in. type S drywall screws 8 in. o.c. to vertical edges and 12 in. o.c. to intermediate studs. 3 in. glass fiber insulation in cavity. Stagger joints 24 in. o.c. each layer and face.	
	55 TO 59	4 1/4"	Base layer 1/4 in. gypsum wallboard applied to each side of 2 1/2 in. metal studs 24 in. o.c. with 7/8 in. type S drywall screws 12 in. o.c. Face layer 5/8 in. type X gypsum wallboard or veneer base applied on each side of studs with 1 5/16 in. type S drywall screws 12 in. o.c. 1 1/2 in. glass fiber insulation in cavity. Stagger joints 24 in. o.c. each layer and side.	
	40 TO 44	5"	Two layers 5/8 in. type X gypsum wallboard or veneer base applied to each side of 2 1/2 in. metal studs 16 in. o.c. braced laterally. Use 1 in. for base layer and 1 5/8 in. for facelayer type S-12 drywall screws 12 in. o.c. Stagger joints 16 in. o.c. each layer and side.	
2 HOUR	50 TO 54	3 5/8"	Base layer 1/2 in. type X gypsum wallboard or veneer base applied to each side of 1 5/8 in. metal studs 24 in. o.c. Use 1 in. type S drywall screws 12 in. o.c. for base layer and 1 5/8 in. type S drywall screws 12 in. o.c. for face layer. 1 1/2 in. glass fiber insulation in cavity. Stagger joints 24 in. o.c. each layer and side.	
	55 TO 59	6 1/4"	Two layers 5/8 in. type X gypsum wallboard or veneer base applied to each side of 3 5/8 in. metal studs 24 in. o.c. Use 1 in. type S drywall screws 32 in. o.c. for base layer and 1 5/8 in. type S drywall screws 12 in. o.c. to edge and 24 in. o.c. to intermediate studs. One side third layer 1/4 or 3/8 in. gypsum wallboard or veneer base applied with laminating compound. Stagger joints 24 in. o.c. each layer and side.	

CONSULT MANUFACTURER OR GYPSUM ASSOCIATION FOR ADDITIONAL INFORMATION

FIRE RATING	STC	WALL THICKNESS	CONSTRUCTION DESCRIPTION	WALL SECTIONS
1 HOUR	30 TO 34	2"	Two 1 x 24 in. wide gypsum coreboards with metal edges offset 2½ in. applied with 1⅝ in. type S drywall screws 24 in. o.c. to 1 x ¾ in. metal strips not over 5 ft o.c. attached with one ⅜ in. pan bead type S screw per channel. Secure to top and bottom tracks with three 2⅝ in. type S screws per panel through ¾ in. wide metal strapping.	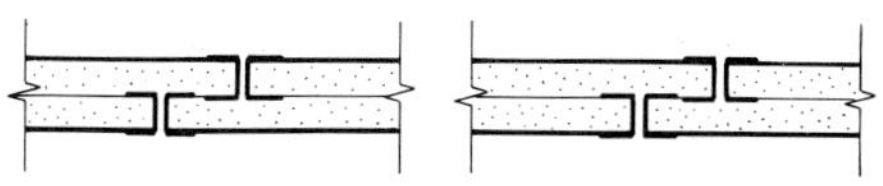
2 HOUR	35 TO 39	2"	One layer ½ in. regular gypsum wallboard or veneer base applied with laminating compound over entire surface to each side of 1 in. laminated, interlocking gypsum coreboard. Stagger joints 24 in. o.c. each layer and side.	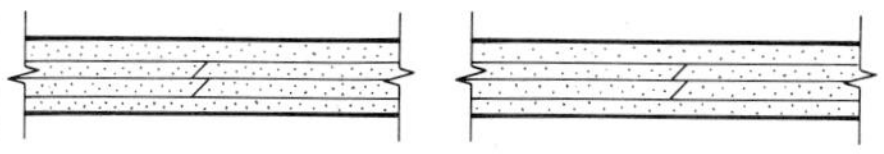
		2"	One layer ½ in. type X gypsum wallboard or veneer base applied parallel to each side of 1 in. tongue and groove gypsum coreboard with laminating compound over entire surface. Stagger joints 24 in. o.c. each layer and side.	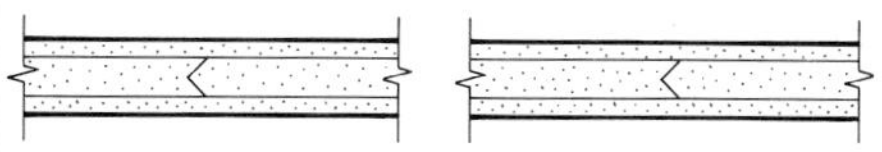
		4⅛"	Four layers ⅝ in. type X gypsum wallboard or veneer base applied to one side of 1⅝ in. metal studs 24 in. o.c. First three layers attached to metal studs with type S drywall screws; between third and face layer use steel strips 1½ in. wide vertically applied at stud lines and attached 12 in. o.c. to studs with 2⅝ in. type S drywall screws. Face layer is attached to steel strips. Stagger joints of each layer.	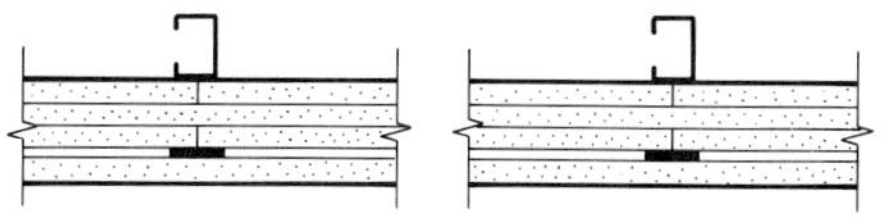
	40 TO 44	2⅞"	1⅝ x 24 in. laminated gypsum board panels attached to floor and ceiling L runners and to flanges of metal T spline between panels at vertical edges. 1½ in. wide x 22 in. gauge steel strips applied at top and bottom of panels to T spline and L runners. Two layers ⅝ in. type X gypsum wallboard applied parallel to T splines. Stagger joints 24 in. o.c. each layer.	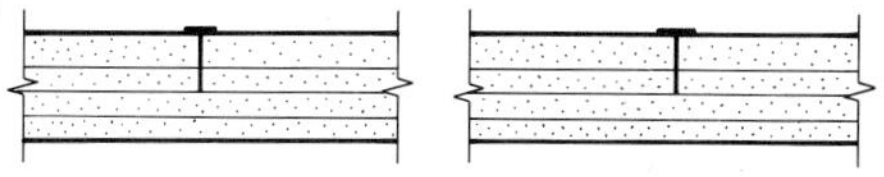
	45 TO 49	3½"	1 x 24 in. proprietary type X gypsum coreboard inserted between 2½ in. floor and ceiling J runners with T section of 2½ in. proprietary C-t metal studs between coreboards. One layer ½ in. type X gypsum wallboard applied vertically to each side of studs with 1 in. type S drywall screws 8 in. o.c. 1 in. glass fiber insulation stapled in cavity. Stagger joints each side.	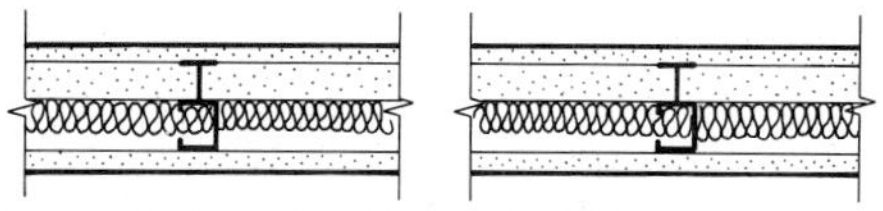
	50 TO 54	6¾"	Double row of proprietary hollow core tongue and groove gypsum panels set 3 in. apart. Panels made of one layer ⅝ in. type X gypsum wallboard or veneer base laminated to ⅝ x 6 in. wide type X gypsum board studs. Panels attached to floor and ceiling runners with 2¼ in. type S drywall screws 18 in. o.c. Joints reinforced with 1½ in. type G drywall screws at quarter points.	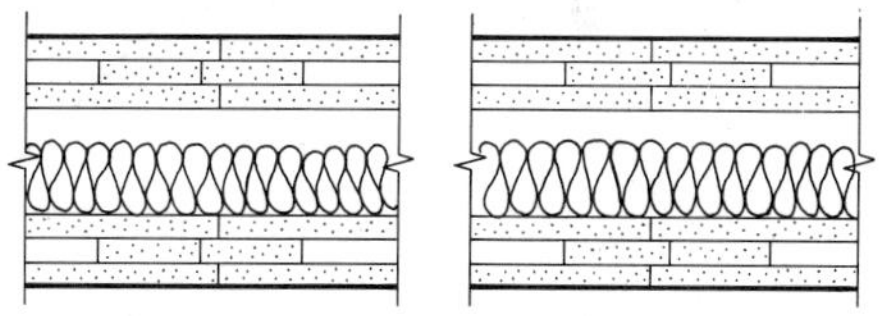
		4¼"	1 x 24 in. type X gypsum coreboard inserted between 2½ in. floor and ceiling track with tab-flange section of 2½ in. metal I studs between coreboards. One layer of ⅝ in. type X gypsum wallboard or veneer base applied over coreboard. Resilient channels spaced 24 in. o.c. horizontally, screw attached, top leg only, to opposite flanges of I studs. Face layer ⅝ in. type X gypsum wallboard or veneer base applied to resilient furring channels. 1½ in. glass fiber friction fir insulation in cavity.	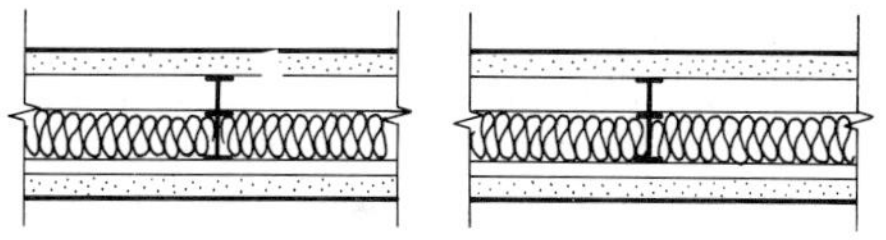
		4⅜"	1⅝ x 24 in. laminated gypsum board panels inserted in 2½ in. floor track and attached to ceiling L runner and to flanges of metal T splines between panels at vertical edges. Metal furring channel attached to panel centers at either flange and at top to L runner. Three layers ⅝ in. type X gypsum wallboard applied to furring. 1 in. glass fiber insulation stapled in cavity. Stagger joints 24 in. each layer.	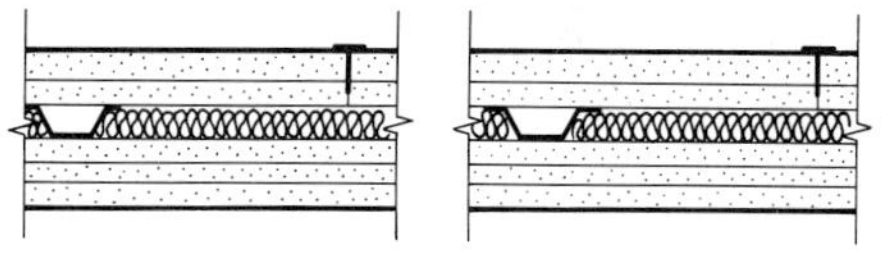
3 HOUR		3⅞"	1 x 24 in. gypsum coreboard panels attached to 2½ in. angle runners at floor and ceiling. Proprietary 2 in. shart studs fitted between panels. 1 x 6 in. gypsum coreboard ribs fitted in stud flange and attached to coreboard. Three layers of ⅝ in. type X gypsum board applied on room side. Face layer may be type X gypsum wallboard or veneer base applied vertically with stagger joints 24 in. relative to base layer. 1 in. glass fiber insulation friction fit in cavity.	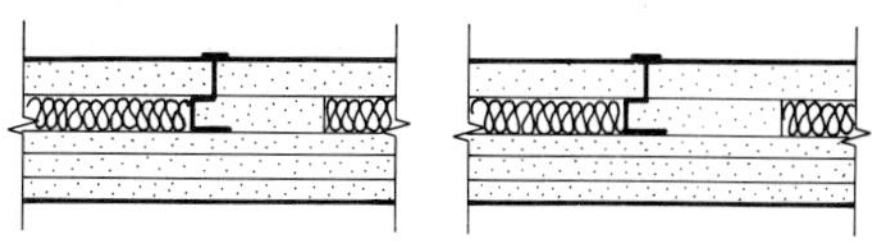
	40 TO 44	3¼"	Base layer ⅝ in. type X gypsum wallboard or veneer base attached to 2 in. shiplapped metal edged gypsum coreboard panels. Face layer ⅝ in. type X gypsum wallboard or veneer base attached over base layer into near side coreboard channels along vertical edges and intermediate channels. Coreboard panels consist of two 1 x 16 in. or 24 in. wide gypsum coreboards with metal channels on long edges mill laminated with 2½ in. offset and are secured to top and bottom tracks.	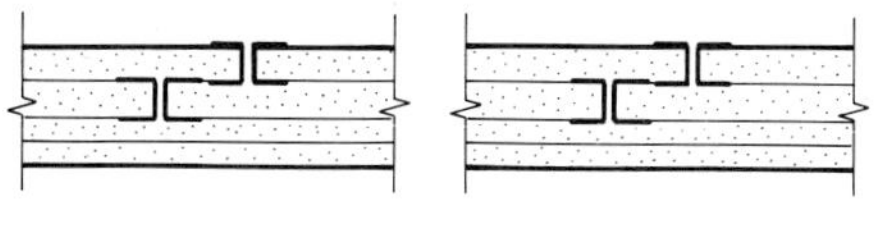
4 HOUR		6¼"	Base layer ⅝ in. type X gypsum wallboard or veneer base attached to both sides of 2 in. proprietary shiplapped metal edged gypsum coreboard panels. Drywall furring channels attached to both sides metal edges of gypsum coreboard panels. Face layer ⅝ in. type X gypsum wallboard or veneer base attached vertically to each side of furring channels. Two 1 x 24 in. wide gypsum coreboards with metal channels on long edges, mill laminated with 2½ in. offset and are attached to top and bottom tracks.	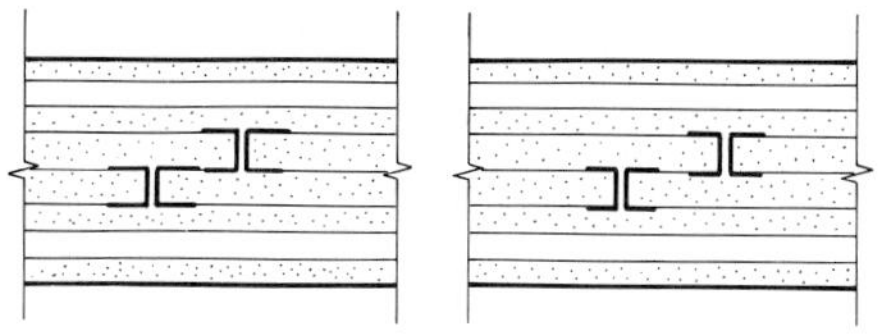

CONSULT MANUFACTURER OR GYPSUM ASSOCIATION FOR ADDITIONAL INFORMATION

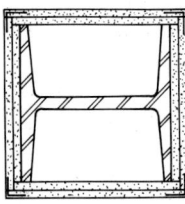

1 HR FIRE RATING

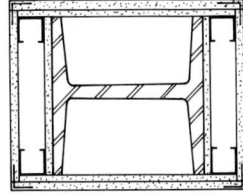

2 HR FIRE RATING

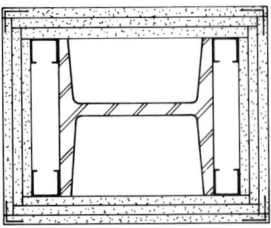

3 HR FIRE RATING

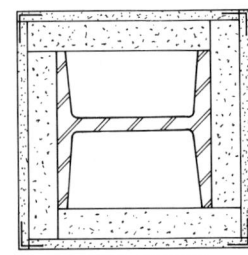

4 HR FIRE RATING

Base layer $\frac{1}{2}$ in. regular gypsum wallboard or veneer base tied to column with 18 gauge wire 15 in. o.c. Face layer $\frac{1}{2}$ in. regular gypsum wallboard or veneer base laminated over entire contact surface.

Base layer $\frac{1}{2}$ in. type X gypsum wallboard or veneer base against flanges and across web openings screwed 24 in. o.c. to $1\frac{5}{8}$ in. metal studs. Face layer $\frac{1}{2}$ in. type X gypsum wallboard or veneer base screwed to studs 12 in. o.c. to provide a cavity between boards on flange. Metal corner beads nailed 12 in. o.c.

Three layers $\frac{5}{8}$ in. type X gypsum wallboard or veneer base screwed to $1\frac{5}{8}$ in. metal studs at each corner. Base layer screwed 24 in. o.c. Middle layer screwed 12 in. o.c. and wire tied 24 in. o.c. with 18 gauge wire. Face layer screwed 12 in. o.c. $1\frac{1}{4}$ in. metal corner beads nailed 12 in. o.c.

$\frac{5}{8}$ in. type X gypsum wallboard or veneer base screwed 12 in. o.c. to 22 gauge, $1\frac{3}{8}$ x $\frac{7}{8}$ in., galvanized steel corner angles screwed along vertical edges of 2 in. solid gypsum block. Gypsum block secured with $\frac{3}{8}$ in. mortar bed and 26 ft gauge galvanized steel strapping 2 in. wide, 24 in. o.c. encasing column.

COLUMNS · FIRE RESISTIVE CONSTRUCTION

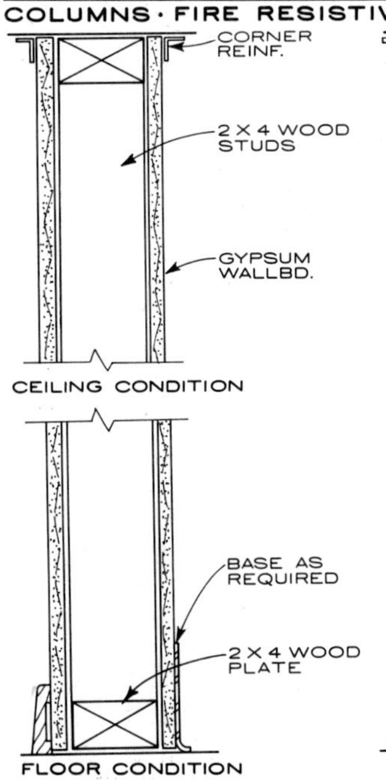

CORNER REINF.
2 × 4 WOOD STUDS
GYPSUM WALLBD.

CEILING CONDITION

BASE AS REQUIRED
2 × 4 WOOD PLATE

FLOOR CONDITION

FIRE RATING 1 HR STC 35 TO 39

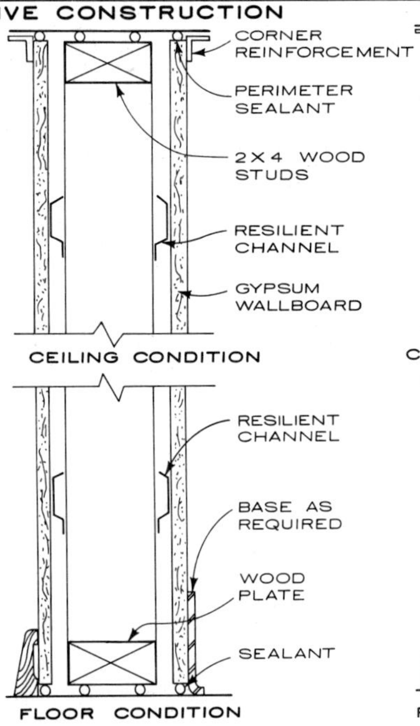

CORNER REINFORCEMENT
PERIMETER SEALANT
2 × 4 WOOD STUDS
RESILIENT CHANNEL
GYPSUM WALLBOARD

CEILING CONDITION

RESILIENT CHANNEL
BASE AS REQUIRED
WOOD PLATE
SEALANT

FLOOR CONDITION

FIRE RATING 1 HR STC 45 TO 49

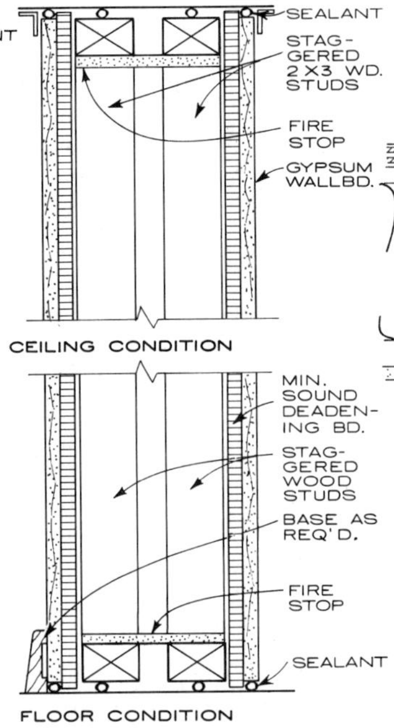

SEALANT
STAGGERED 2 × 3 WD. STUDS
FIRE STOP
GYPSUM WALLBD.

CEILING CONDITION

MIN. SOUND DEADENING BD.
STAGGERED WOOD STUDS
BASE AS REQ'D.
FIRE STOP
SEALANT

FLOOR CONDITION

FIRE RATING 2 HR STC 55 TO 59

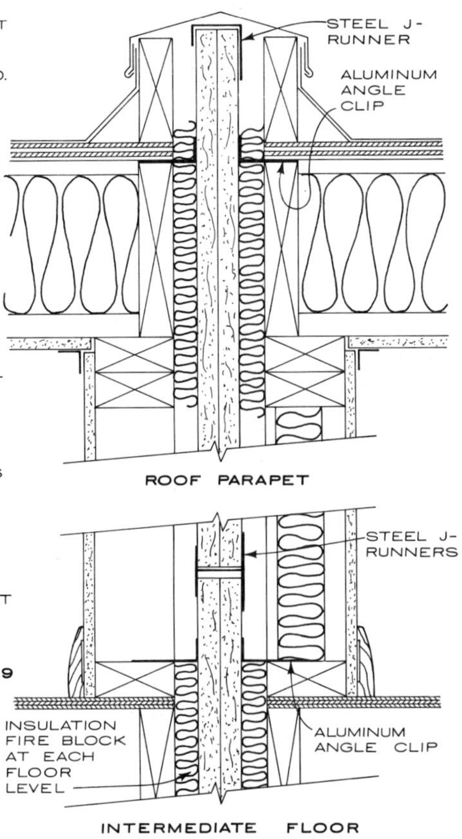

STEEL J-RUNNER
ALUMINUM ANGLE CLIP

ROOF PARAPET

METAL TRACK
GYPSUM WALLBD.
METAL DRYWALL STUD SIZE VARIES

CEILING CONDITION

METAL TRACK
BASE - AS REQUIRED

FLOOR CONDITION

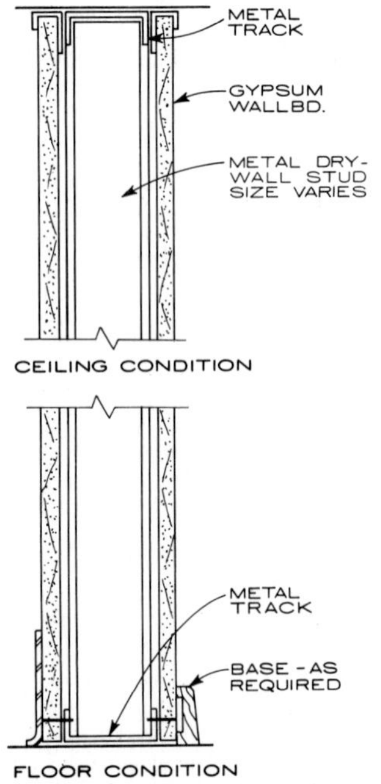

FIRE RATING 2 HR STC 35 TO 39

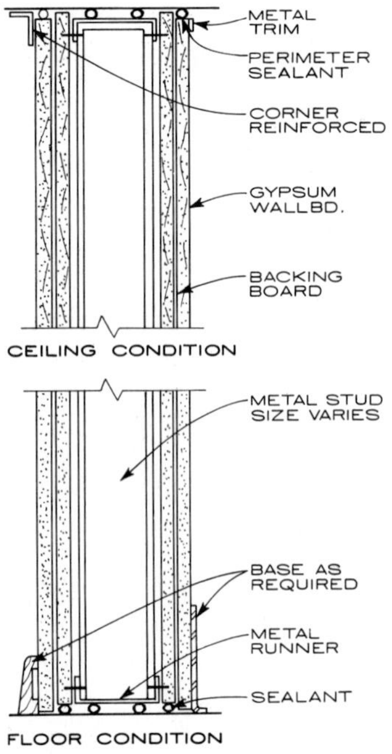

METAL TRIM
PERIMETER SEALANT
CORNER REINFORCED
GYPSUM WALLBD.
BACKING BOARD

CEILING CONDITION

METAL STUD SIZE VARIES
BASE AS REQUIRED
METAL RUNNER
SEALANT

FLOOR CONDITION

FIRE RATING 2 HR STC 45 TO 49

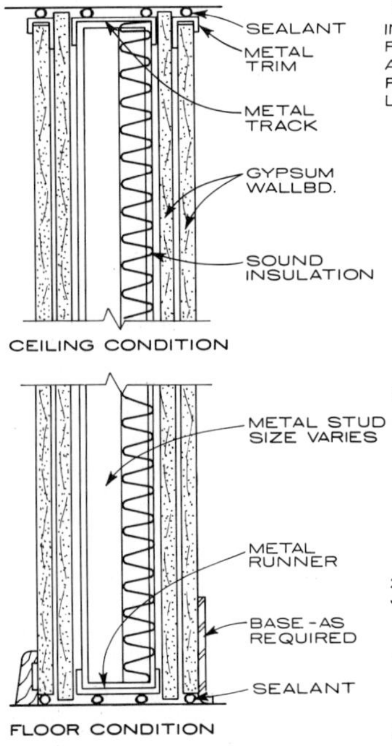

SEALANT
METAL TRIM
METAL TRACK
GYPSUM WALLBD.
SOUND INSULATION

CEILING CONDITION

METAL STUD SIZE VARIES
METAL RUNNER
BASE - AS REQUIRED
SEALANT

FLOOR CONDITION

FIRE RATING 2 HR STC 50 TO 54

STEEL J-RUNNERS
INSULATION FIRE BLOCK AT EACH FLOOR LEVEL
ALUMINUM ANGLE CLIP

INTERMEDIATE FLOOR

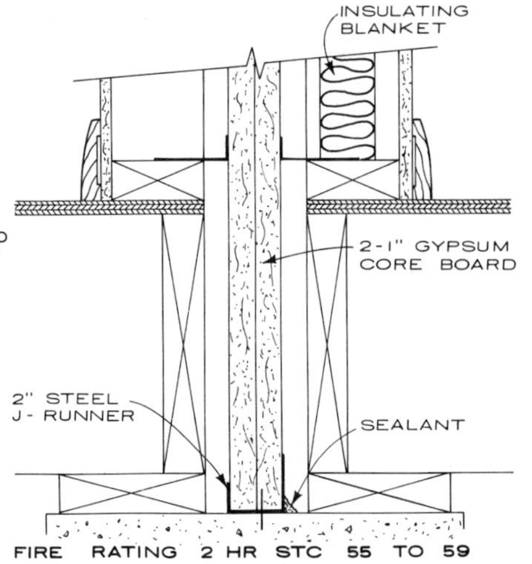

INSULATING BLANKET
2-1" GYPSUM CORE BOARD
2" STEEL J-RUNNER
SEALANT

FIRE RATING 2 HR STC 55 TO 59

AREA SEPARATION WALL

GYPSUM WOOD AND METAL FRAMED TYPE PARTITIONS

Ferdinand R. Scheeler, AIA; Skidmore, Owings and Merrill; Chicago, Illinois

James Lloyd; Kennett Square, Pennsylvania

GYPSUM WALLBOARD

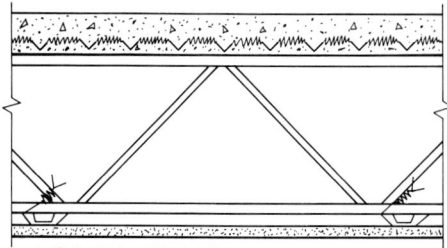

2 HR / STC 50 TO 54

1/2 in. type X gypsum wallboard or veneer base applied to drywall furring channels. Furring channels 24 in. o.c. attached with 18 gauge wire ties 48 in. o.c. to open web steel joists 24 in. o.c. supporting 3/8 in. rib metal lath or 9/16 in. deep, 28 gauge corrugated steel and 2 1/2 in. concrete slab measured from top of flute. Double channel at wallboard end joints.

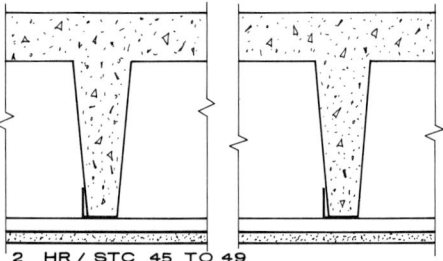

2 HR / STC 45 TO 49

5/8 in. type X gypsum wallboard or veneer base screw attached to drywall furring channels. Furring channels 24 in. o.c. suspended from 2 1/2 in. precast reinforced concrete joists 35 in. o.c. with 21 gauge galvanized steel hanger straps fastened to sides of joists. Joist leg depth, 10 in. Double channel at wallboard end joints.

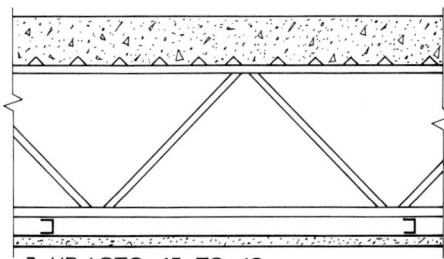

3 HR / STC 45 TO 49

5/8 in. proprietary type X gypsum wallboard or veneer base screw attached to furring channels 24 in. o.c. (double channels at end joints). Furring channel wire tied to open web steel joist 24 in. o.c. supporting 3 in. concrete slab over 3/8 in. rib metal lath. 5/8 x 2 3/4 in. type X gypsum wallboard strips over butt joints.

FLOOR/CEILING ASSEMBLIES, NONCOMBUSTIBLE

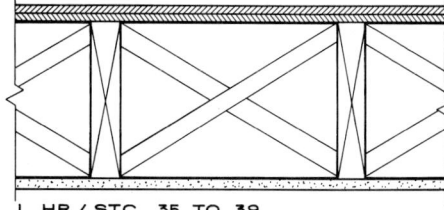

1 HR / STC 35 TO 39

5/8 in. type X gypsum wallboard or veneer base applied to wood joists 16 in. o.c. Joists supporting 1 in. nominal wood sub and finish floor, or 5/8 in. plywood finished floor with long edges T & G and 1/2 in. interior plywood with exterior glue subfloor perpendicular to joists with joints staggered.

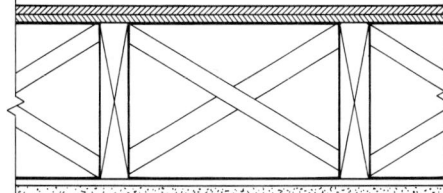

1 HR / STC 40 TO 44

1/2 in. type X gypsum wallboard or veneer base applied to drywall resilient furring channels 24 in. o.c. and nailed to wood joists 16 in. o.c. Wood joists supporting 1 in. nominal T & G wood sub and finish floor, or 5/8 in. plywood finished floor with long edges T & G and 1/2 in. interior plywood with exterior glue subfloor perpendicular to joists with joints staggered.

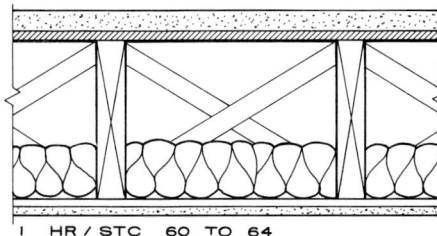

1 HR / STC 60 TO 64

1/2 in. type X gypsum wallboard or veneer base applied to resilient furring channels. Resilient channels applied 24 in. o.c. to wood joists 16 in. o.c. Wood joists support 1/2 in. plywood subfloor and 1 1/2 in. cellular or lightweight concrete over felt. 3 1/2 in. glass fiber batts in joist spaces. Sound tested with carpet and pad over 5/8 in. plywood subfloor.

FLOOR/CEILING ASSEMBLIES, WOOD FRAMED

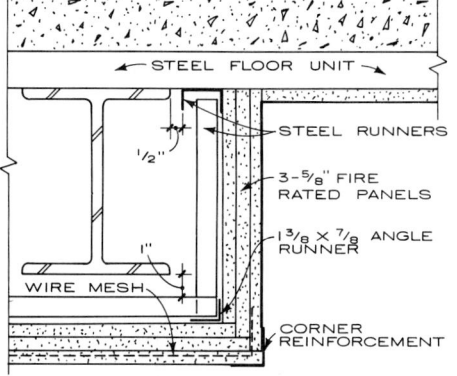

BEAM PROTECTION
3 HR. RESTRAINED   2 HR. UNRESTRAINED

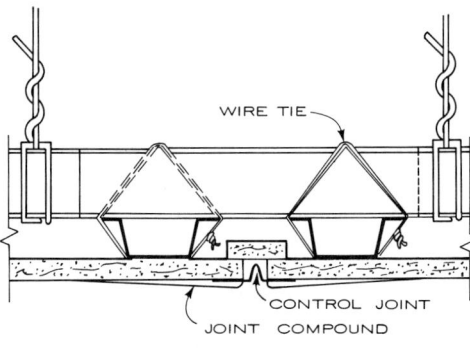

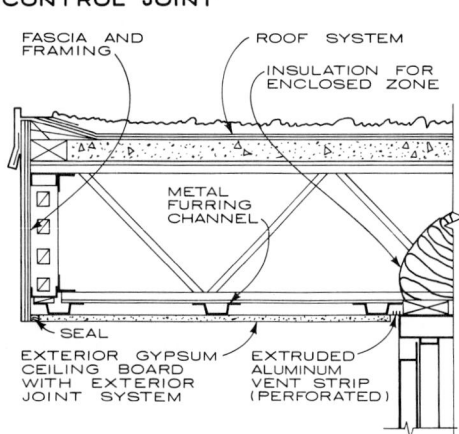

CONTROL JOINT

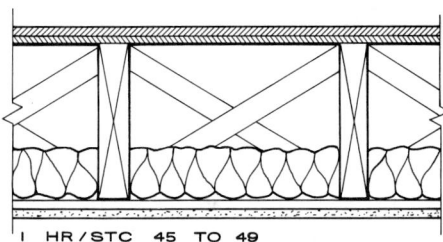

1 HR / STC 45 TO 49

5/8 in. proprietary type X gypsum board electrical radiant heating panels attached to resilient furring channels spaced 24 in. o.c. installed to 2 x 10 in. wood joists 16 in. o.c. 3/12 in. glass fiber insulation friction fit in joist space. Wood floor of nominal 1 in. T & G or 1/2 in. plywood subfloor and nominal 1 in. T & G or 5/8 in. plywood finish floor.

FLOOR/CEILING ASSEMBLIES, WOOD FRAMED

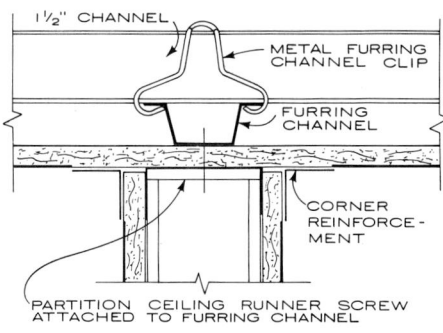

PARTITION ATTACHMENT
(SCREW ATTACHED)

EXTERIOR SOFFIT

CONTINUOUS CEILING

James Lloyd; Kennett Square, Pennsylvania

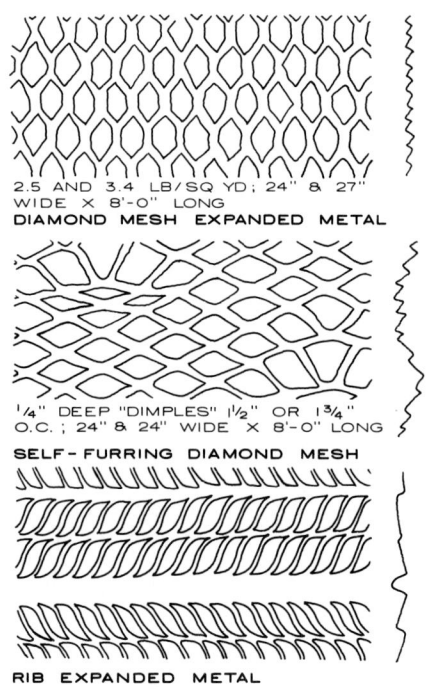

2.5 AND 3.4 LB/SQ YD; 24" & 27"
WIDE X 8'-0" LONG
DIAMOND MESH EXPANDED METAL

¼" DEEP "DIMPLES" 1½" OR 1¾"
O.C. ; 24" & 24" WIDE X 8'-0" LONG
SELF-FURRING DIAMOND MESH

RIB EXPANDED METAL

LATHING SYSTEMS

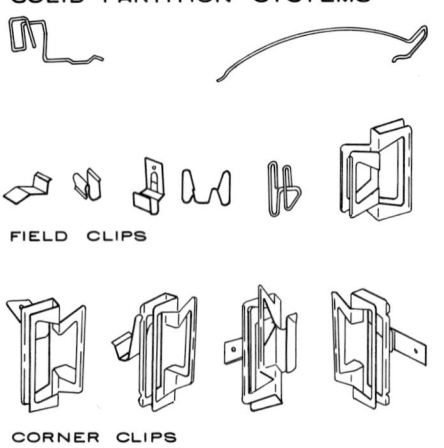

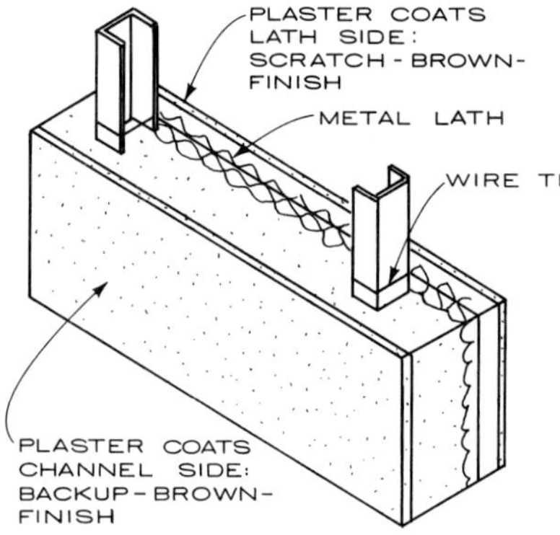

PLASTER COATS
LATH SIDE:
SCRATCH - BROWN-
FINISH

METAL LATH

WIRE TIE

PLASTER COATS
CHANNEL SIDE:
BACKUP - BROWN-
FINISH

SOLID PARTITION SYSTEMS

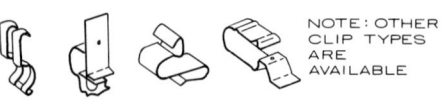

FIELD CLIPS

CORNER CLIPS

NOTE: OTHER
CLIP TYPES
ARE
AVAILABLE

MISCELLANEOUS

CLIPS FOR GYPSUM LATH SYSTEM

The Marmon Mok Partnership; San Antonio, Texas

LATH AND PLASTER

NOTES

Self-furring paperbacked reinforcing is available in diamond mesh, welded wire, and hexagonal woven wire. Paperbacks are available to conform to Federal Specifications UU-B-790, Type 1, Grade A, Style 2 for highly water-vapor resistant paper.

Metal lath is also manufactured in large diamond mesh 27 x 96 in., 2.5 or 3.4 lb/sq yd, painted steel or galvanized; ⅛ in. flat rib 27 x 96 in., 2.75 or 3.4 lb/sq yd painted or galvanized; ⅜ in. rib expanded 27 x 96 in., 3.4 lb/sq yd painted or galvanized and ¾ in. rib expanded 24 x 96 in., 5.4 lb/sq yd painted.

Other types of lath are available from some manufacturers.

GYPSUM LATH

Gypsum lath is composed of an air entrained gypsum core sandwiched between two sheets of fibrous absorbent paper and used as a basecoat for gypsum plaster.

1. PLAIN GYPSUM LATH: ⅜ and ½ in. thick, 48 in. long, and 16 in. wide (16⅕ in. in the Western U.S.).
2. PERFORATED GYPSUM LATH: Plain gypsum lath with ¾ in. diameter holes punches 4 in. o.c. in both directions to provide mechanical key to plaster.
3. INSULATING GYPSUM LATH: Plain gypsum lath with aluminum foil laminated to the backside as insulator or vapor barrier.
4. LONG LENGTH GYPSUM LATH: 16, and 24 in. wide, in lengths up to 12 ft, available insulated or plain with square or vee-jointed T & G edges or interlocking as ship-lap edge.

SOLID PLASTER PARTITION CONSTRUCTION

PARTITION CONSTRUCTION	THICKNESS	MAXIMUM HEIGHT
¾" cold-rolled channels Diamond mesh lath and plaster	2"	12'-0"
¾" cold-rolled channels Diamond mesh lath and plaster	2½"	16'-0"
1½" cold-rolled channels Diamond mesh lath and plaster	3"	20'-0"
1½" cold-rolled channels Diamond mesh lath and plaster	3½"	22'-0"

NOTE: Maximum partition length is unrestricted if less than 10 ft tall. Twice the height if over 10 ft tall; one and one half the height if over 14 ft tall and equal to the height if over 20 ft tall.

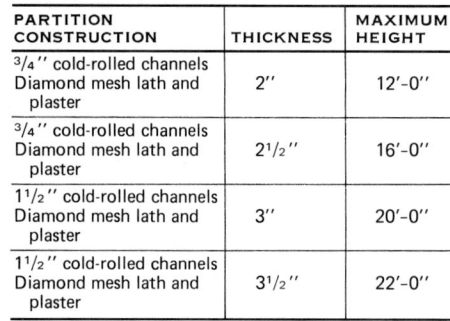

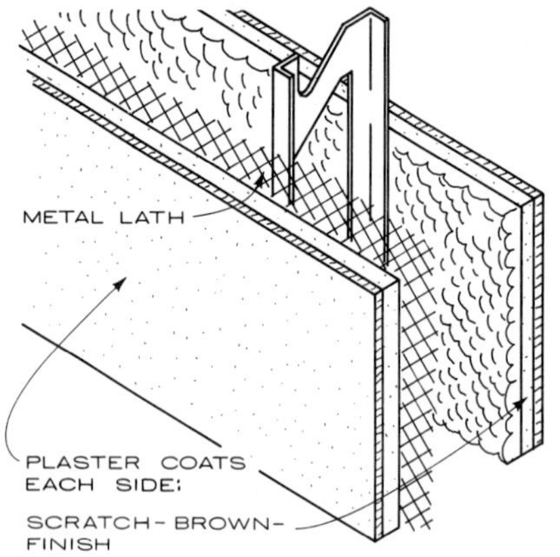

METAL LATH

PLASTER COATS
EACH SIDE:

SCRATCH- BROWN-
FINISH

NOTES

Prefabricated metal studs are used as the supporting elements of lath and plaster hollow partitions. They are available in 1⅝, 2, 2½, 3¼, 4, and 6 in. widths. Lengths are available in various increments up to 24 ft. Prefabricated studs are usually of the nonload bearing type, but load bearing metal studs also are manufactured. Designs vary with the manufacturer, and most manufacturers produce a line of related accessories, such as clips, runners, stud shoes, and similar articles.

HOLLOW PARTITION SYSTEMS

DEFINITIONS

AGGREGATE: Inert material used as filler with a cementitious material and water to produce plaster or concrete. Usually implies sand, perlite, or vermiculite.

BASECOAT: Any plaster coat applied before the finish coat.

BEAD: Light gauge metal strip with one or more expanded or short perforated flanges and variously shaped noses; used at the perimeter of plastered surfaces.

BROWN COAT: In three-coat plaster, the brown coat is the second coat; in two-coat plaster, the base coat.

CALCINED GYPSUM: Gypsum that has been partially dehydrated by heating.

CLIP: A device made of wire or sheet metal for attaching various types of lath to the substructure and lath sheets to one another.

FIBERED PLASTER: Gypsum plaster containing fibers of hair, glass, nylon, or sisal.

FINISH COAT: The final coat of plaster, which provides the decorative surface.

FURRING: Grillage for the attachment of gypsum or metal lath.

GAUGING: Cementitious material, usually calcined gypsum or portland cement combined with lime putty to control set.

GROUND: A formed metal shape or wood strip that acts as a combined edge and gauge for various thicknesses of plaster to be applied to a plaster base.

GYPSUM: Hydrous calcium sulphate, a natural mineral in crystalline form.

GYPSUM LATH: A base for plaster; a sheet having a gypsum core, faced with paper.

GYPSUM READY MIX PLASTER: Ground gypsum that has been calcined and then mixed with various additives to control its setting and working qualities; used, with the addition of aggregate and water, for basecoat plaster.

HYDRATED LIME: Quicklime mixed with water, on the job, to form a lime putty.

LIME: Obtained by burning various types of limestone, consisting of oxides or hydroxides of calcium and magnesium.

LIME PLASTER: Basecoat plaster of hydrated lime and an aggregate.

NEAT PLASTER: Basecoat plaster, fibered or unfibered, used for job mixing with aggregates.

PERLITE: Siliceous volcanic glass containing silica and alumina expanded by heat for use as a lightweight plaster aggregate.

PLASTER: Cementitious material or combination of cementitious materials and aggregate that, when mixed with water, forms a plastic mass that sets and hardens when applied to a surface.

PORTLAND CEMENT: Manufactured combination of limestone and an argillaceous substance.

SCRATCH COAT: In three-coat plastering, the first coat, which is then scratched to provide a bond for second or brown coat.

SCREED: A device secured to a surface which serves as a guide for subsequent applications of plaster. Thicknesses and widths vary with the thicknesses desired for each operation.

STUCCO PORTLAND CEMENT: Plaster used in exterior application.

VERMICULITE: Micaceous mineral of silica, magnesium, and alumina oxides made up in a series of parallel plates or laminae and expanded by heat for use as a lightweight plaster aggregate.

NOTES

Keene's cement plaster is a specialty finish coat of gypsum plaster primarily used where a smooth, dense, white finish is desired.

Thickness, proportions of mixes of various plastering materials, and finishes vary. Systems and methods of application vary widely depending on local traditions and innovations promoted by the industry.

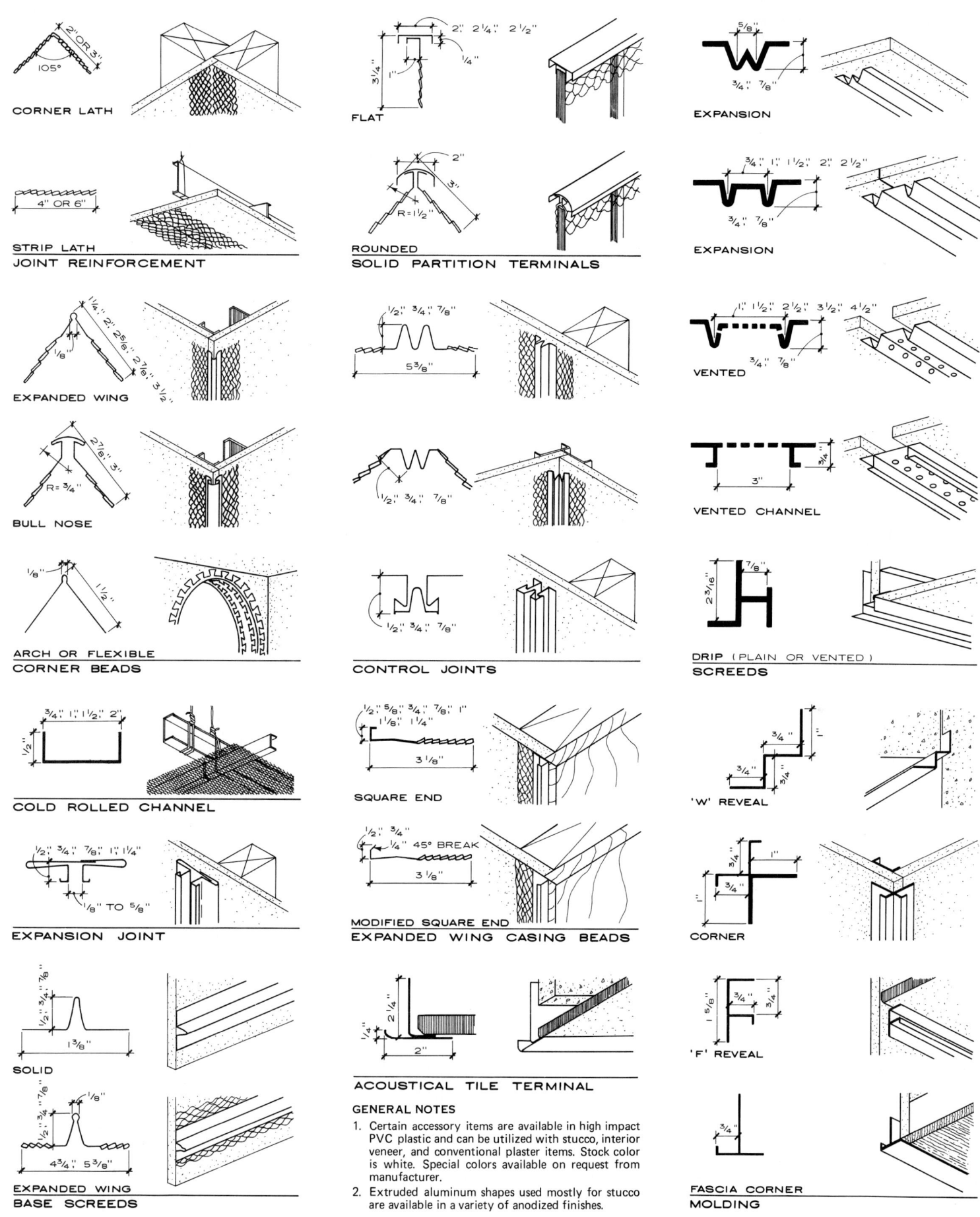

CORNER LATH

STRIP LATH
JOINT REINFORCEMENT

EXPANDED WING

BULL NOSE

ARCH OR FLEXIBLE
CORNER BEADS

COLD ROLLED CHANNEL

EXPANSION JOINT

SOLID

EXPANDED WING
BASE SCREEDS

FLAT

ROUNDED
SOLID PARTITION TERMINALS

CONTROL JOINTS

SQUARE END

MODIFIED SQUARE END
EXPANDED WING CASING BEADS

ACOUSTICAL TILE TERMINAL

GENERAL NOTES

1. Certain accessory items are available in high impact PVC plastic and can be utilized with stucco, interior veneer, and conventional plaster items. Stock color is white. Special colors available on request from manufacturer.

2. Extruded aluminum shapes used mostly for stucco are available in a variety of anodized finishes.

EXPANSION

EXPANSION

VENTED

VENTED CHANNEL

DRIP (PLAIN OR VENTED)
SCREEDS

'W' REVEAL

CORNER

'F' REVEAL

FASCIA CORNER
MOLDING

The Marmon Mok Partnership; San Antonio, Texas

LATH AND PLASTER

9

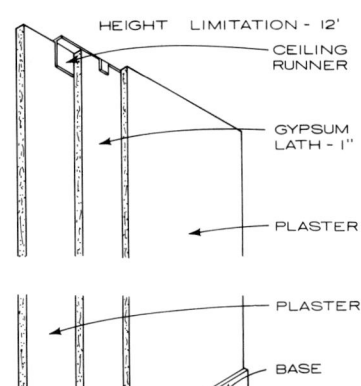

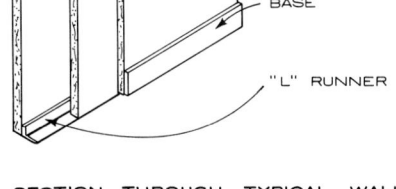

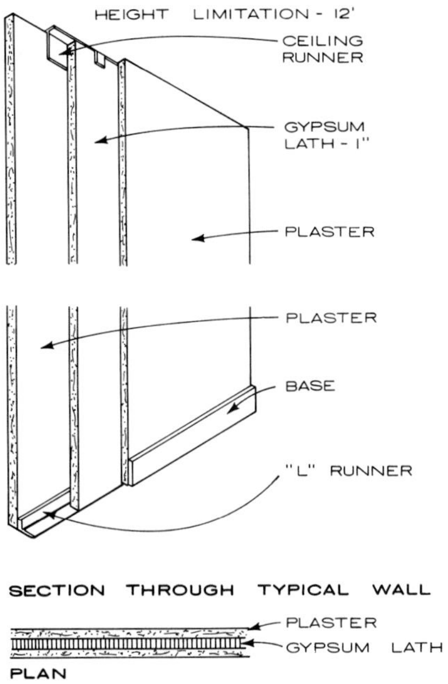

SECTION THROUGH TYPICAL WALL

PLAN

2 IN. SOLID GYPSUM LATH

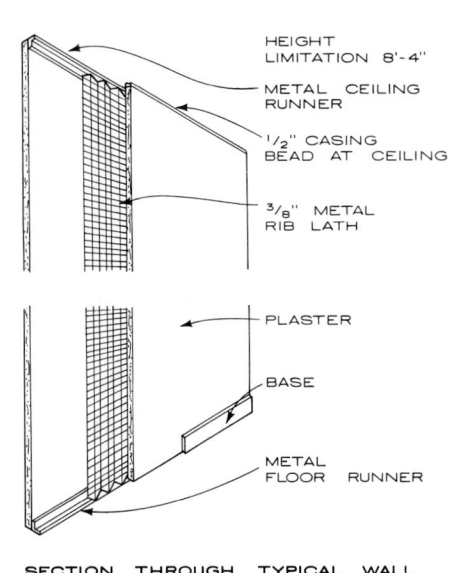

SECTION THROUGH TYPICAL WALL

PLAN

2 IN. SOLID METAL LATH AND PLASTER

CHANNEL STUD SPACING

TYPE OF LATH	WEIGHT #/SQ YD	SPACING OF SUPPORTS
Diamond mesh	2.5	16
	3.4	16
Flat rib	2.75	16
	3.4	24*

*Spacing for solid partitions not to exceed 16'-0" in height.

TABLE FOR CHANNEL STUD SIZE PARTITIONS THICKNESS HEIGHT

HEIGHT	THICK	CHANNEL
12'	2"	
14'	2¼"	¾ in. 300 lb per 1000 ft
16'	2½"	
18'	2¾"	1½ in. 475 lb per 1000 ft

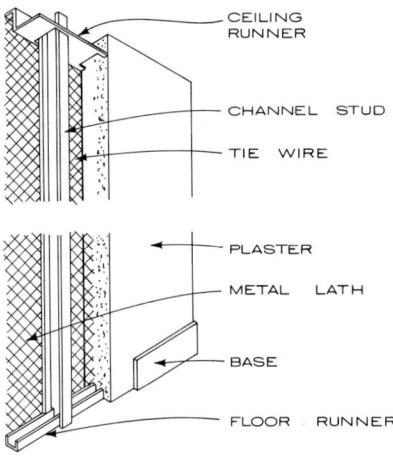

SECTION THROUGH TYPICAL WALL

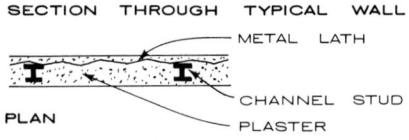

PLAN

METAL LATH-CHANNEL STUD-PLASTER

METAL STUD WITH METAL LATH STUD SPACING AND HEIGHT LIMITATION*

STUD WIDTH	THICKNESS	MAXIMUM HEIGHT		
		16" OC.	19" OC.	24" OC.
2½"	4"	15'	14'	9'
3¼"	4¾"	21'	18'	13'
4"	5½"	22'	20'	16'
6"	7½"	26'	24'	20'

*For length not exceeding 1½ times height; for lengths exceeding this, reduce 20%.

Walter H. Sobel, FAIA & Associates; Chicago, Illinois

METAL STUD WITH ⅜" GYPSUM LATH HEIGHT LIMITATIONS

STUD WIDTH	THICKNESS STANDARD SYSTEM	MAX. HEIGHT STUDS 16" OC.
2½"	4¼"	15'
3¼"	5"	21'
4"	5¾"	22'
6"	7¾"	26'

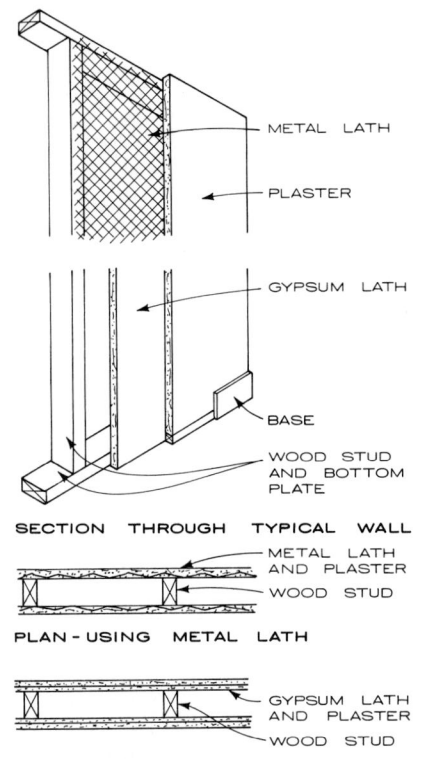

SECTION THROUGH TYPICAL WALL

PLAN - USING METAL LATH

PLAN - USING GYPSUM LATH

WOOD STUD AND LATH

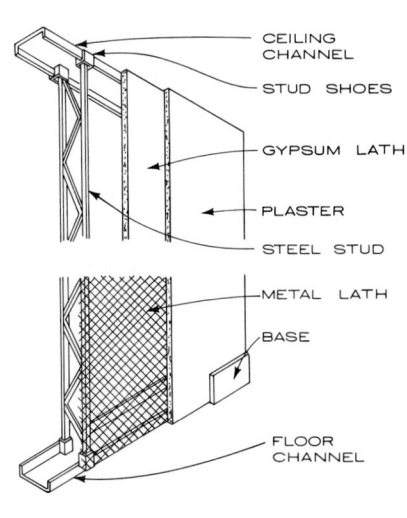

SECTION THROUGH TYPICAL WALL

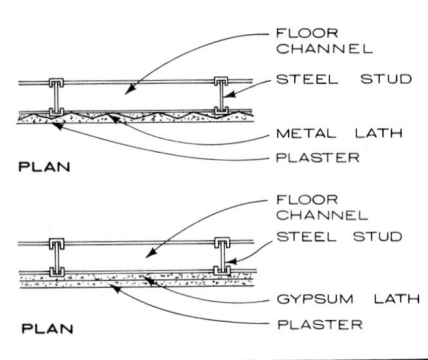

PLAN

PLAN

PREFABRICATED METAL STUD

 LATH AND PLASTER

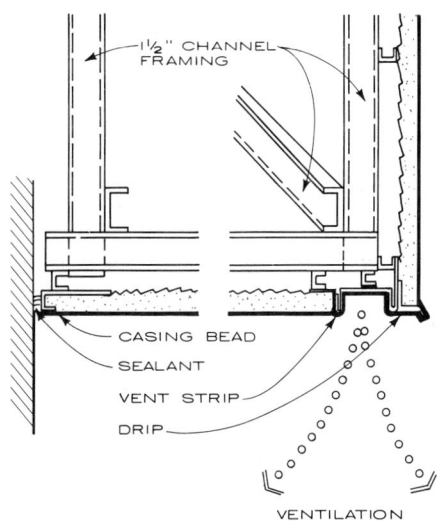

SOFFIT DETAIL

NOTE

Framing details for exterior cement plaster (stucco) are similar to details shown. Wind loads must be considered in designing framing systems for exterior stucco work. Galvanized mesh is available for exterior applications and use in humid areas. Ventilation strips should be used for ventilating all dead airspaces. Where plenum or attic spaces are closed off by ceiling installation, ventilation shall be provided with a minimum of $1/2$ sq in./sq ft of horizontal surface.

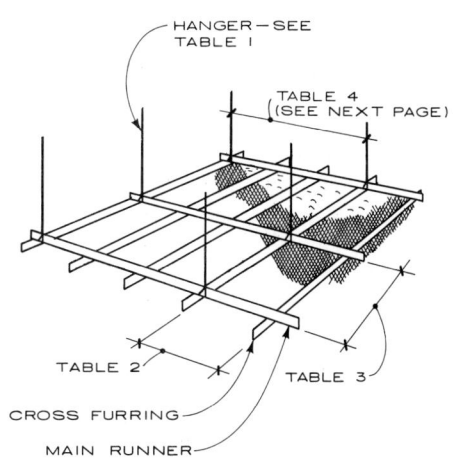

FURRED AND SUSPENSION SYSTEM COMPONENT SELECTION DETAIL

NOTE

Details shown are for furred (contact) ceilings that are attached directly to the structural members. The architect or ceiling designer should give consideration to the deflection and movement of the structure, since excessive movement and deflection of more than $1/360$ of the span will cause cracking of plaster ceilings. If spacing of structural members exceeds the maximum span of furring members shown in the span charts, the addition of suspended main runners between structural members will be required. Flat rib lath may be attached directly to wood framing members, but is subjected to stresses created by wood members.

DIRECTIONS FOR USE OF TABLES

1. Select lath and plaster system.
2. Determine spacing of cross furring channels from Table 1—Lath Span.
3. Determine spacing of main runners from Table 2—Maximum Spacing Between Runners.
4. Determine hanger support spacing for main runner from Table 3—Maximum Spacing Between Hangers (see next page).
5. Calculate area of ceiling supported per hanger.
6. Select hanger type from Table 4—Hanger Selection Table (see next page).
7. Select tie wire size from Table 5—Tie Wire Selection (see next page).

TABLE 1. LATH SPAN

	LATH TYPE	WEIGHT/SQ FT	SPAN (IN.)
Gypsum lath	$3/8''$ plain	1.5#	16
	$1/2''$ plain	2.0#	16
	$1/2''$ veneer	1.8#	16
	$5/8''$ veneer	2.25#	16
	$3/8''$ perforated	1.4#	16
Metal lath	Diamond mesh	0.27#	12
	Diamond mesh	0.38#	16
	$1/8''$ flat rib	0.31#	12
	$1/8''$ flat rib	0.38#	19
	$3/8''$ flat rib	0.38#	24

TABLE 2. MAXIMUM SPACING BETWEEN RUNNERS

CROSS FURRING TYPE	CROSS FURRING SPACING			
	12''	16''	19''	24''
$1/4''$ diam. pencil rod	2'-0''	—	—	—
$3/8''$ diam. pencil rod	2'-6''	—	2'-0''	—
$3/4''$ CRC, HRC (0.3 lb/ft)	—	4'-6''	3'-6''	3'-0''
1'' HRC (0.41 lb/ft)	5'-0''	—	4'-6''	4'-0''

CRC = Cold rolled channel
HRC = Hot rolled channel

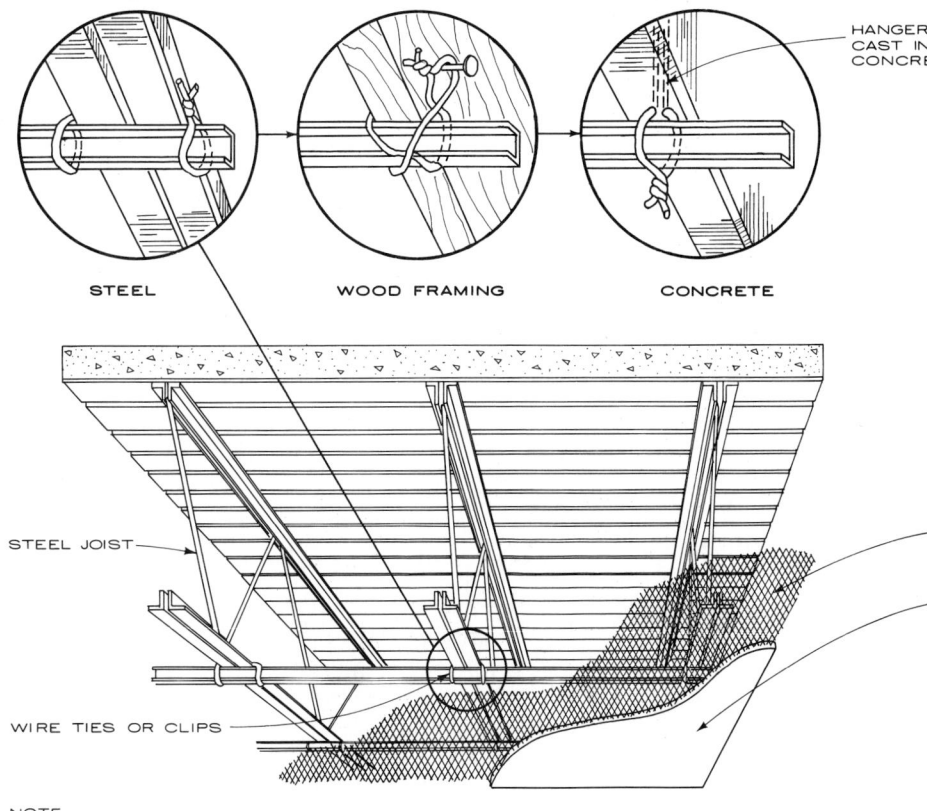

FURRED METAL LATH ON STEEL JOIST

NOTE
RIB METAL LATH MAY BE USED IN LIEU OF DIAMOND MESH LATH AND FURRING CHANNELS IF LATH SPANS DO NOT EXCEED ALLOWABLE MAXIMUM

James E. Phillips, AIA; Liles/Associates/Architects, Inc.; Greenville, South Carolina

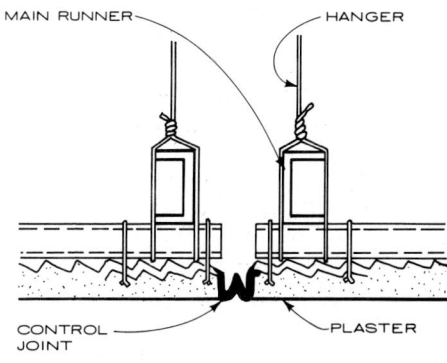

CONTROL JOINT DETAIL

DIAMOND MESH METAL LATH WIRED TO $3/4''$ METAL FURRING CHANNELS

PLASTER—THREE-COAT SYSTEM WITH EXPANSION JOINTS AT 30' ON CENTER EACH DIRECTION

NOTE

Control joints shall be spaced no further than 30 ft on center in each direction for large plastered ceiling areas. Area shall not exceed 900 sq ft without provision for expansion control. Exterior plaster soffits should have control joints spaced no further than 25 ft on center. For portland cement plaster (stucco) areas, interior or exterior, control joints should be placed at 10 ft on center and areas should not exceed 100 sq ft without provisions for expansion/contraction control. Control joints are spaced closer for cement plaster because of its inherent shrinkage during curing.

TABLE 3. MAXIMUM SPACING BETWEEN HANGERS

MAIN RUNNER TYPE	MAIN RUNNER SPACING				
	3'-0"	3'-6"	4'-0"	4'-6"	5'-0"
3/4" CRC (0.3 lb/ft)	2'-0"	—	—	—	—
1½" CRC (0.3 lb/ft)	3'-0"*	—	—	—	—
1½" CRC (0.875 lb/ft)	4'-0"	3'-6"	3'-0"	—	—
1½" HRC (1.12 lb/ft)	—	—	—	4'-0"	—
2" CRC (0.59 lb/ft)	—	—	5'-0"	—	—
2" HRC (1.26 lb/ft)	—	—	—	—	5'-0"
½" x ½" x 3/16" ST1	—	5'-0"	—	—	—

*For concrete construction only—a 10-gauge wire may be inserted in the joint before concrete is poured.

TABLE 4. HANGER SELECTION

MAX. CEILING AREA	MIN. HANGER SIZE
12 sq ft	9-gauge galvanized wire
16 sq ft	8-gauge galvanized wire
18 sq ft	3/16" mild steel rod*
25 sq ft	1/4" mild steel rod*
25 sq ft	3/16" x 1" steel flat*

*Rods galvanized or painted with rust inhibitive paint and galvanized straps are recommended under severe moisture conditions.

TABLE 5. TIE WIRE SELECTION

SUPPORT		MAX. CEILING AREA	MIN. HANGER SIZE
Cross furring		8 sq ft	14-gauge wire
		8 sq ft	16-gauge wire (two loops)
Main runners	Single hangers between beams	8 sq ft	12-gauge wire
		12 sq ft	10-gauge wire
		16 sq ft	8-gauge wire
	Double wire loops at supports	8 sq ft	14-gauge wire
		12 sq ft	12-gauge wire
		16 sq ft	11-gauge wire

ERECTION OF METAL LATH SUSPENSIONS

Metal lath suspensions are commonly made below all types of construction for fire rated plaster ceilings. The lath is supported by framing channels and furring channels suspended from the floor or roof structure above with wire hangers. Framing channels are normally spaced up to 4 ft o.c. perpendicular to joists and should be erected to conform with the contour of the finished ceiling. The framing channels are furred with 3/4 in. channels, which are spaced according to the requirements for types and weights of metal lath and erected at right angles to the framing channels. The lath should be lapped at both sides and ends and secured to the 3/4 in. channels with wire ties every 6 in. Where plaster on metal lath ceilings abuts masonry walls, partitions, or arch soffits, galvanized casing beads should be installed at the periphery.

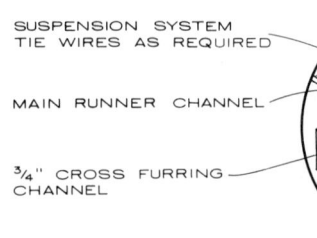

SUSPENSION SYSTEM TIE WIRES AS REQUIRED

MAIN RUNNER CHANNEL

3/4" CROSS FURRING CHANNEL

NOTE

Dimensional requirements for support spacing, runner spacing, hanger spacing, hanger type selection, and tie wire selection are given in tables on this and other page.

David H. Ross, AIA; Liles/Associates/Architects, Inc.; Greenville, South Carolina

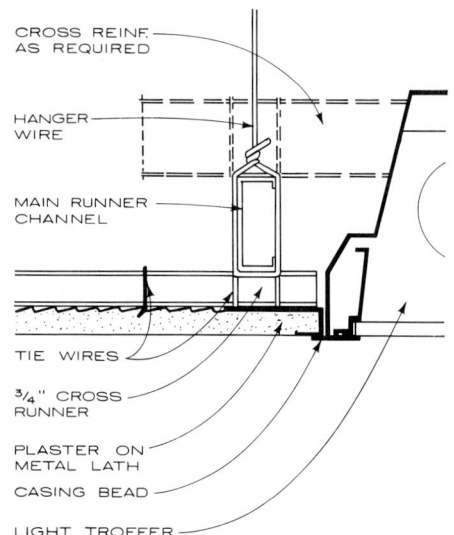

SUSPENDED PLASTER CEILING AT RECESSED LIGHT FIXTURE

NOTE

Penetrations of the lath and plaster ceiling—at borrowed light openings, vents, grilles, access panels, and light troffers, for example—require additional reinforcement to distribute concentrated stresses if a control joint is not used. Where a plaster surface is flush with metal, as at metal access panels, grilles, or light troffers, the plaster should be grooved between the two materials.

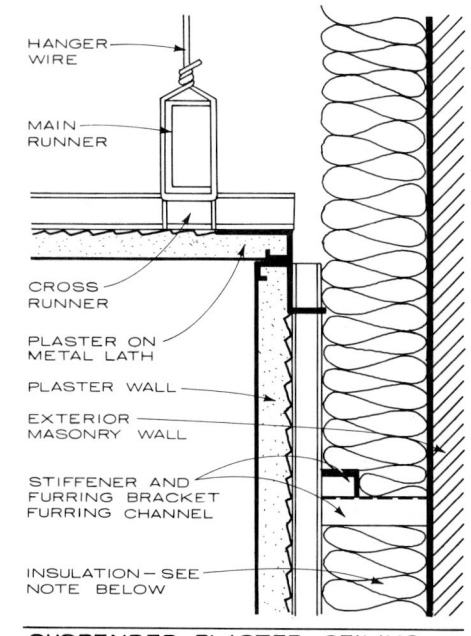

SUSPENDED PLASTER CEILING AT FURRED MASONRY WALL

NOTE

When interior walls are furred from an exterior masonry wall and insulated, the ceiling should stop short of the furred space. This allows wall insulation to continue above the ceiling line to ceiling or roof insulation, thus forming a complete insulation envelope. In a suspension system that abuts masonry wall, provide 1 in. clearance between ends of main runners or furring channels and wall face.

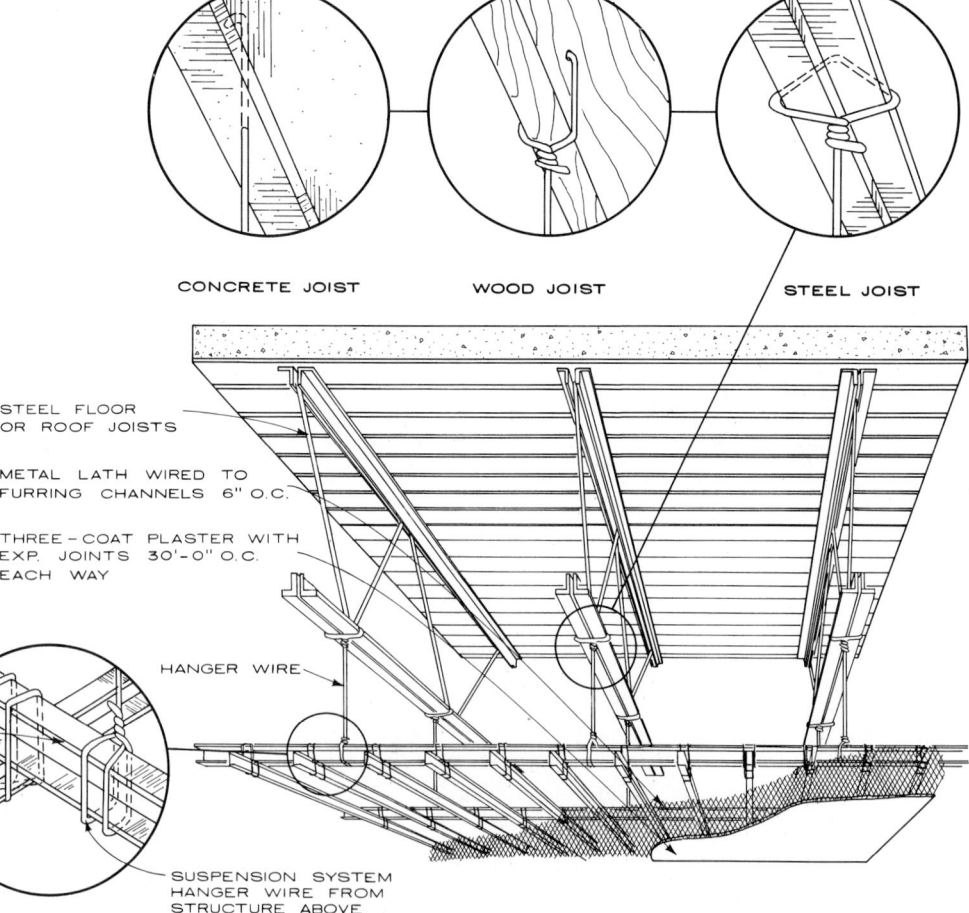

CONCRETE JOIST   WOOD JOIST   STEEL JOIST

STEEL FLOOR OR ROOF JOISTS

METAL LATH WIRED TO FURRING CHANNELS 6" O.C.

THREE-COAT PLASTER WITH EXP. JOINTS 30'-0" O.C. EACH WAY

HANGER WIRE

SUSPENSION SYSTEM HANGER WIRE FROM STRUCTURE ABOVE

METAL LATH SUSPENDED FROM STEEL JOISTS

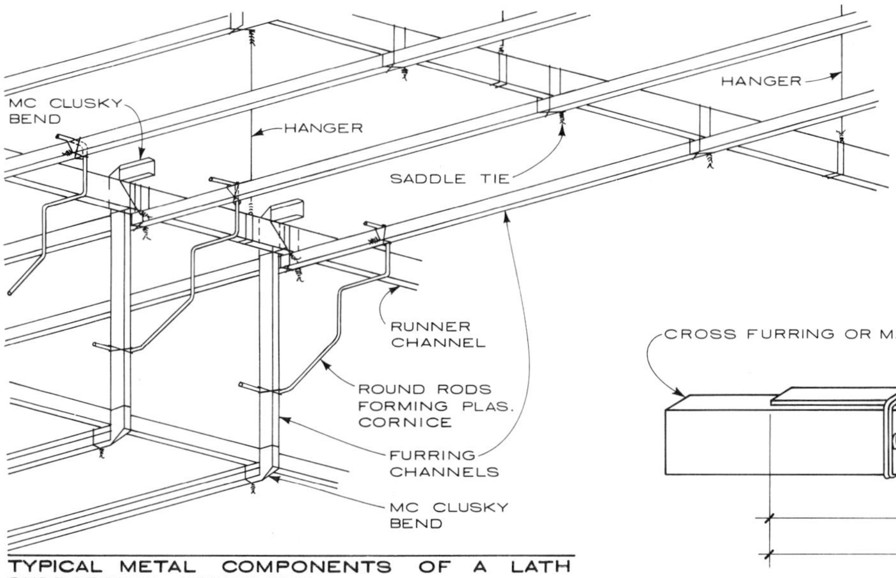

TYPICAL METAL COMPONENTS OF A LATH SUPPORTING STRUCTURE

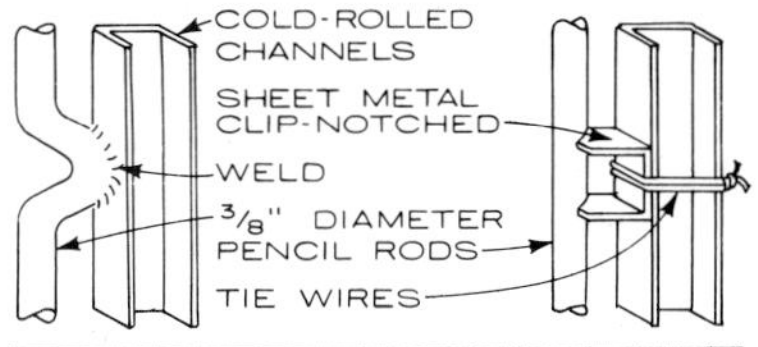

(labels: MC CLUSKY BEND, HANGER, HANGER, SADDLE TIE, RUNNER CHANNEL, ROUND RODS FORMING PLAS. CORNICE, FURRING CHANNELS, MC CLUSKY BEND)

SHIM DETAILS

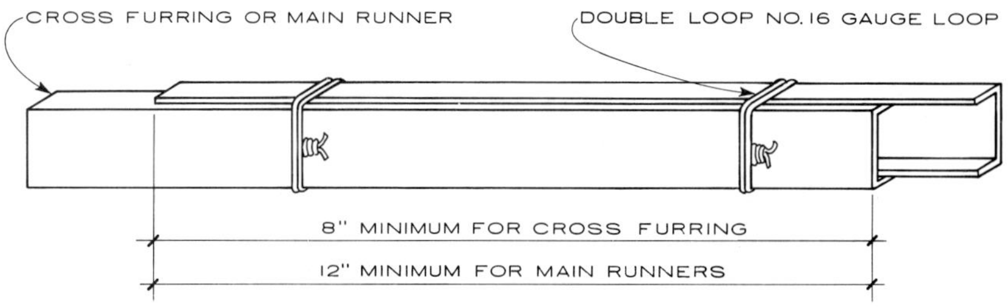

(labels: COLD-ROLLED CHANNELS, SHEET METAL CLIP-NOTCHED, WELD, 3/8" DIAMETER PENCIL RODS, TIE WIRES)

CHANNEL SPLICE

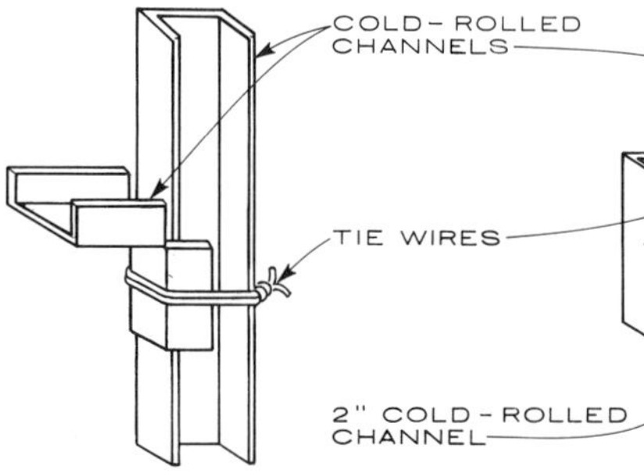

(labels: CROSS FURRING OR MAIN RUNNER, DOUBLE LOOP NO. 16 GAUGE LOOP, 8" MINIMUM FOR CROSS FURRING, 12" MINIMUM FOR MAIN RUNNERS)

TYPICAL METAL CHANNEL SUSPENSION AND FURRING DETAILS

SPACER DETAILS

(labels: COLD-ROLLED CHANNELS, TIE WIRES, 2" COLD-ROLLED CHANNEL)

SADDLE TIES

(labels: HANGER WIRE SIZE VARIES, MAIN RUNNER CHANNEL, TIE WIRES, CROSS FURRING CHANNEL)

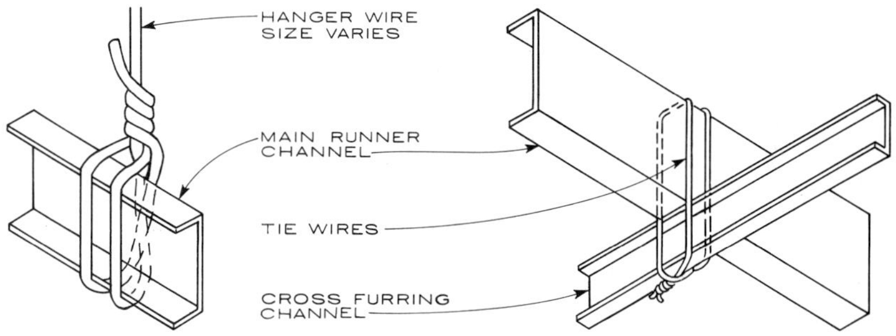

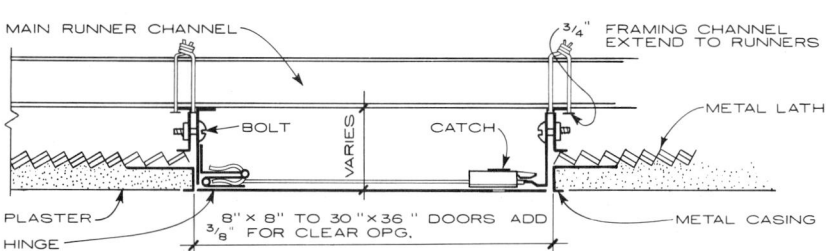

FLUSH METAL FACE

(labels: MAIN RUNNER CHANNEL, 3/4" FRAMING CHANNEL EXTEND TO RUNNERS, BOLT, CATCH, METAL LATH, VARIES, PLASTER, HINGE, 8"×8" TO 30"×36" DOORS ADD 3/8" FOR CLEAR OPG., METAL CASING)

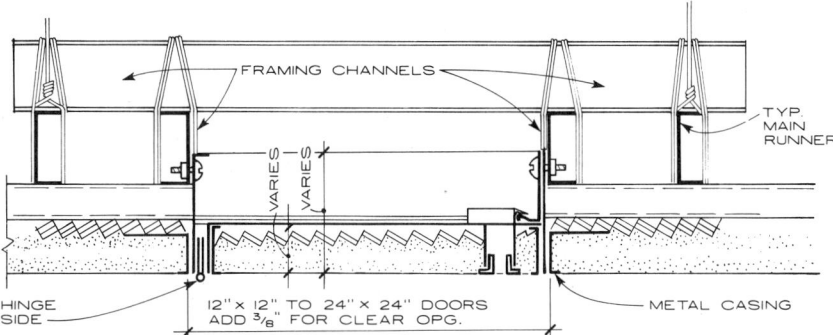

FLUSH PLASTER FACE

(labels: FRAMING CHANNELS, TYP. MAIN RUNNER, VARIES, VARIES, HINGE SIDE, 12"×12" TO 24"×24" DOORS ADD 3/8" FOR CLEAR OPG., METAL CASING)

METAL ACCESS DOORS AND FRAMES

NOTE
GAGE OF METAL, NO. OF LOCKS, HINGES VARY. FIRE-RATED DOORS AVAILABLE

Douglas S. Stenhouse, AIA; Los Angeles, California

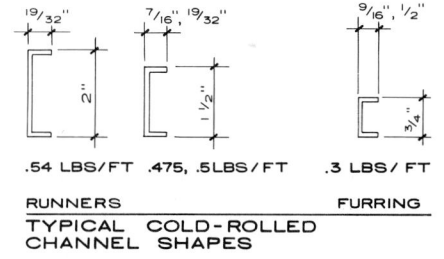

.54 LBS/FT   .475, .5 LBS/FT   .3 LBS/FT

RUNNERS   **FURRING**

TYPICAL COLD-ROLLED CHANNEL SHAPES

Heat-rolled channels (HRC) generally run heavier than cold-rolled channels (CRC). Shapes illustrated are available in 16 gauge, 16 and 20 ft standard lengths.

Galvanizing of all components is recommended where moisture is a factor, extra heavy galvanizing for swimming pools.

See Suspended Ceiling Systems for instructions for selection of components.

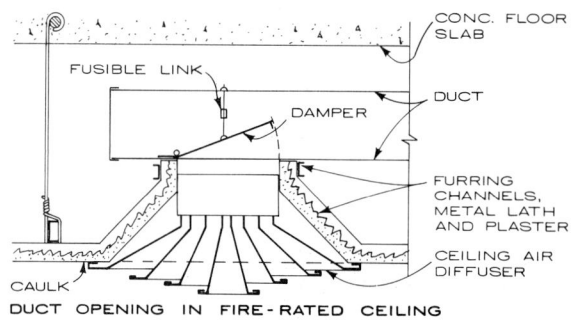

DUCT OPENING IN FIRE-RATED CEILING

(labels: CONC. FLOOR SLAB, FUSIBLE LINK, DAMPER, DUCT, FURRING CHANNELS, METAL LATH AND PLASTER, CEILING AIR DIFFUSER, CAULK)

LATH AND PLASTER

FLAT TILE

4¼ × 4¼ 6 × 4¼ 6 × 6

STANDARD SHAPES AND SIZES

Scored Tile: Consult manufacturer's literature for available sizes and shapes.

OCTAGON SPANISH HEXAGON

OTHER SHAPES AND SIZES

NOMINAL THICKNESS — 5/16 IN.

Other shapes and sizes of flat tile and trim shapes are available from some manufacturers. Glazes—bright, matte. Other special glazes are available from some manufacturers.

TRIM SHAPES

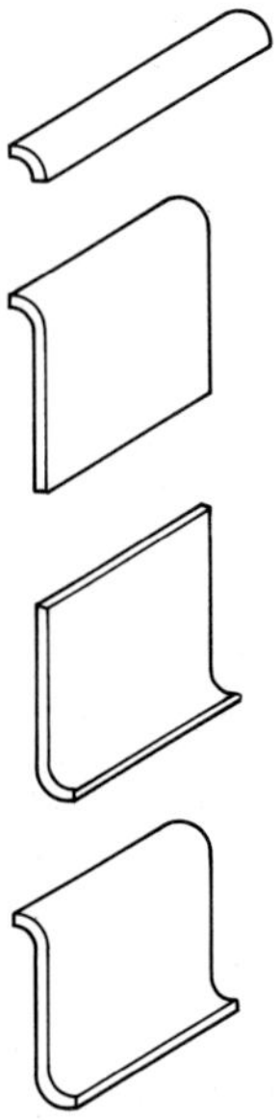

STANDARD SHAPES AND SIZES

NUMBER	SIZES (IN.)
A106	6 x 3/4
BEAD	
A1662	6 x 3 3/4
A3602	6 x 6
A4200	6 x 2
A4402	4 1/4 x 4 1/4
A4640	4 1/4 x 6
A4460	6 x 4 1/4
BULLNOSE	
A1663	6 x 3 3/8
A3401	4 1/4 x 3 7/8
A3461	6 x 3 7/8
A3601	6 x 5 5/8
A3641	4 1/4 x 5 5/8
COVE	
A3610	6 x 5 5/8
BASE	

MORTAR BED SHAPES

TRIM SHAPES

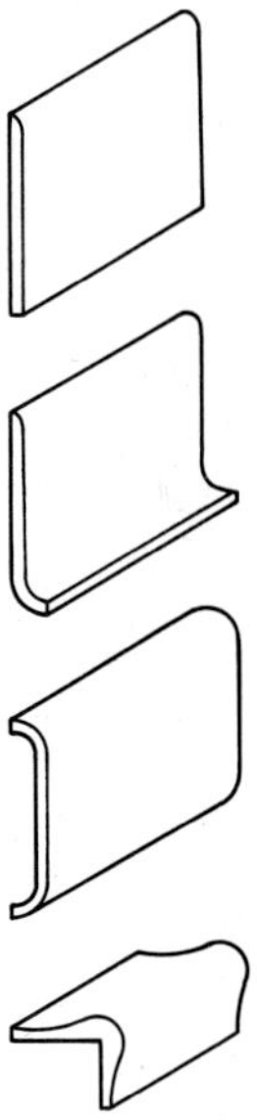

STANDARD SHAPES AND SIZES

NUMBER	SIZES (IN.)
S4269	6 x 2
S4449	4 1/4 x 4 1/4
S4469	6 x 4 1/4
S4649	4 1/4 x 6
SURFACE BULLNOSE	
S3419	4 1/4 x 3 7/8
S3619	6 x 5 5/8
SURFACE BASE	
A7510	6 x 5
TILE CURB	
A8262	6 x 2 1/4
COUNTER TOP TRIM	

GLAZED WALL TILE

FLAT TILE

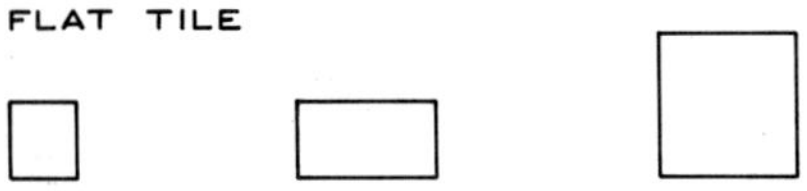

1 × 1 2 × 1 2 × 2

STANDARD SHAPES AND SIZES

1" HEX 2" HEX

OTHER SHAPES AND SIZES

TRIM SHAPES

STANDARD SHAPES AND SIZES

NUMBER	SIZES (IN.)
C812	1 x 1
C832	2 x 1
BEAD	
C813	1 x 1
C833	2 x 1
COVE	
MORTAR BED SHAPES	
S862	1 x 1
S866	1 x 2
S886	2 x 2
S882	2 x 1
SURFACE BULLNOSE	

NOMINAL THICKNESS—1/4 IN.

Other sizes and shapes of flat tile and trim are available from some manufacturers.

Ceramic mosaic tile may be either natural clay or porcelain in composition.

Abrasive or slip resistant surface available only in 1 x 1.

Conductive tile available only in 1 x 1.

CERAMIC MOSAIC TILE

FLAT TILE

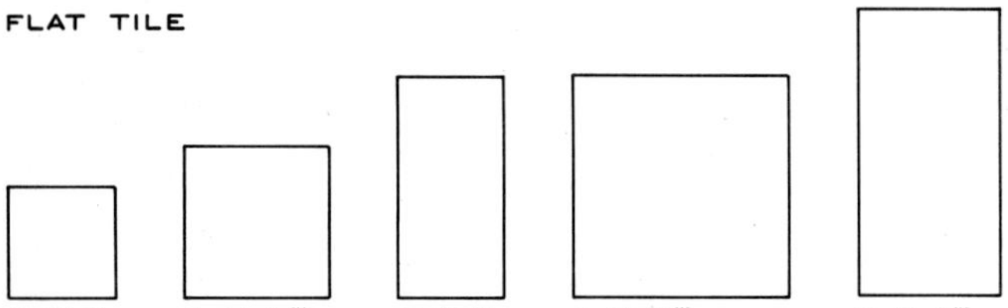

3 × 3 4 × 4* 6 × 3 6 × 6* 8 × 4*

STANDARD SHAPES AND SIZES

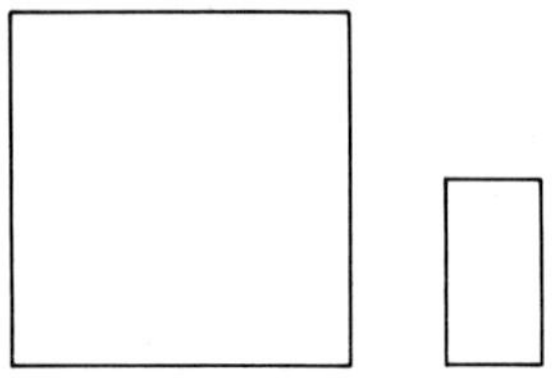

8 × 8 4 × 2†

OTHER SHAPES AND SIZES

NOMINAL THICKNESS:
QUARRY 1/2" AND 3/4"
6 × 6 AND 8 × 4 - ONLY SIZES AVAILABLE IN 3/4"
PAVER 3/8" AND 1/2"
* SIZES AVAILABLE IN BOTH QUARRY AND PAVER TILE. OTHERS — QUARRY ONLY
† PAVER ONLY

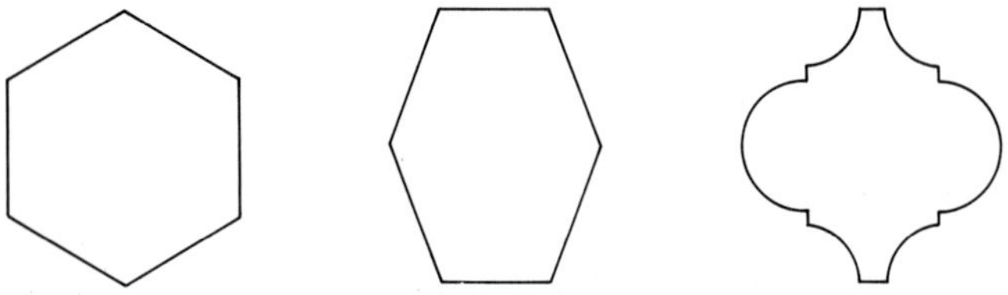

HEXAGON ELONGATED HEX SPANISH

OTHER SHAPES AND SIZES

TRIM SHAPES

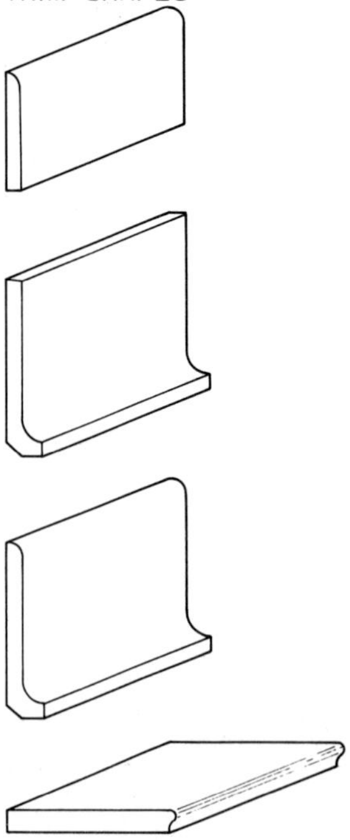

STANDARD SHAPES AND SIZES

NUMBER	SIZES (IN.)
Q1445	4 x 4 x 1/2
Q1465	6 x 4 x 1/2
Q1665	6 x 6 x 1/2
Q1485	8 x 4 x 1/2
Q1845	4 x 8 x 1/2
Q1660	6 x 6 x 3/4
BULLNOSE	
Q3266	6 x 2 x 1/2
Q3261	6 x 2 x 3/4
Q3566	6 x 5 x 1/2
Q3561	6 x 5 x 3/4
COVE	
Q3565	6 x 5 x 1/2
Q3560	6 x 6 x 3/4
COVE BASE	
Q6665	6 x 6 x 3/4
Q6666	6 x 6 x 3/4
WINDOWSILL/STEP NOSING	

QUARRY TILE AND PAVER TILE

Tile Council of America, Inc.

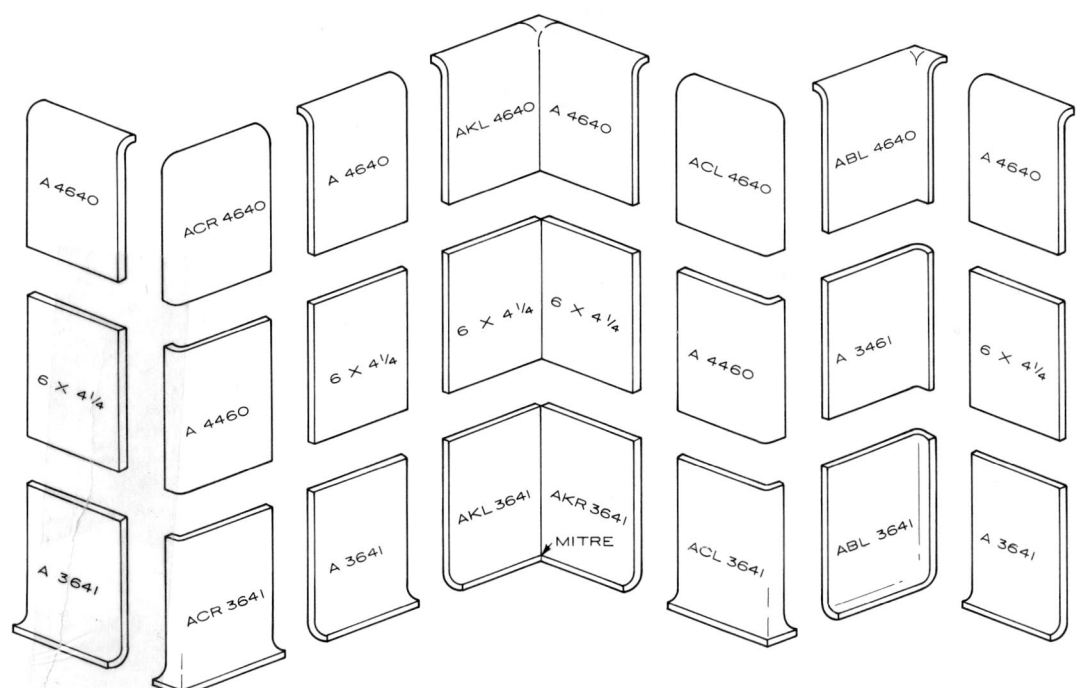

NOTE

This trim diagram shows typical shapes available for portland cement mortar installations of glazed wall tile. Similar types are available for thin-set installations and for ceramic mosaic tile, quarry tile, and paver tile. Not all shapes are available from every manufacturer. Check particular manufacturer's literature for exact shapes, colors, and type of glaze available.

PORTLAND CEMENT MORTAR TRIM SHAPES
VERTICAL INSTALLATION 6" X 4 1/4" GLAZED WALL TILE

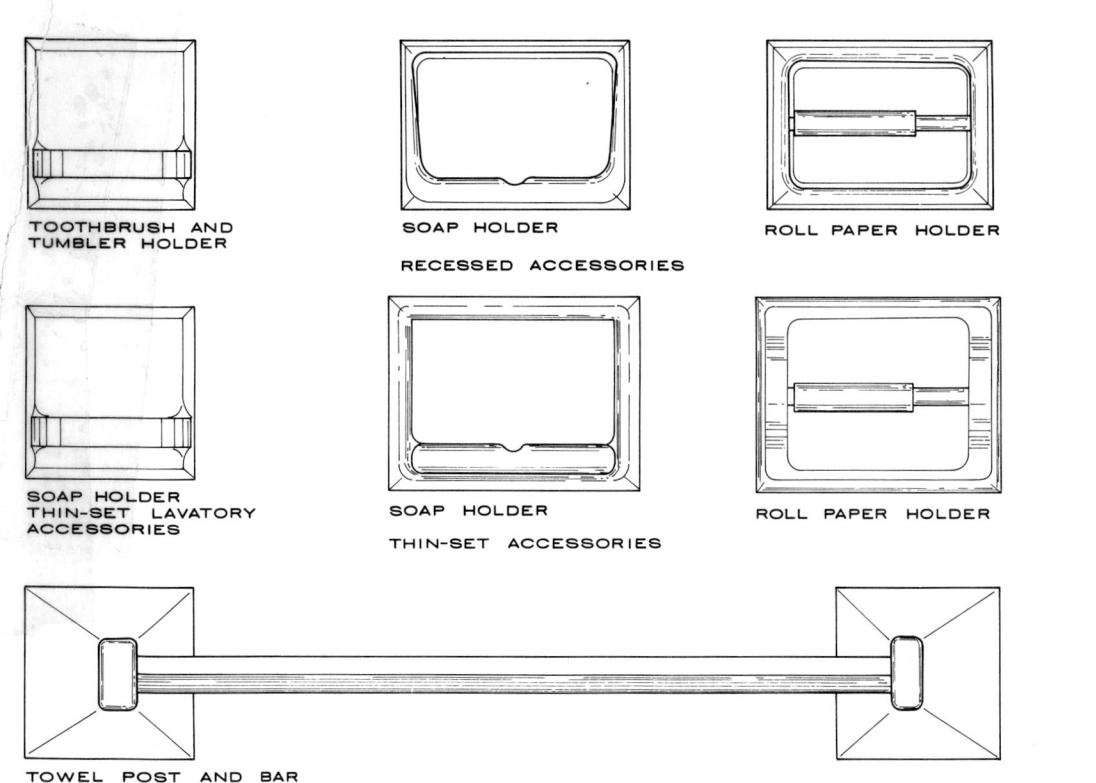

TOOTHBRUSH AND TUMBLER HOLDER

SOAP HOLDER

RECESSED ACCESSORIES

ROLL PAPER HOLDER

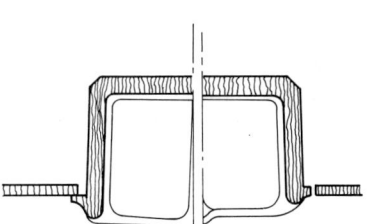

PLAN OF RECESSED ACCESSORY

SOAP HOLDER THIN-SET LAVATORY ACCESSORIES

SOAP HOLDER

THIN-SET ACCESSORIES

ROLL PAPER HOLDER

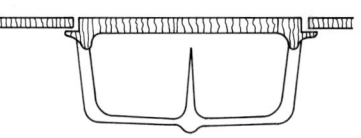

PLAN OF THIN-SET ACCESSORY

TOWEL POST AND BAR THIN-SET

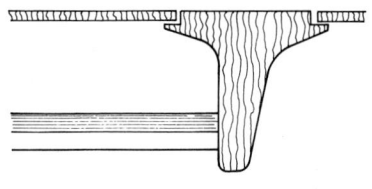

DETAIL OF THIN-SET TOWEL POST

NOTES

Accessories are normally supplied in sets which include toothbrush-tumbler holder and soap holder for lavatories, soap holder, roll paper holder, and towel posts. Designs include fully recessed models, fully recessed models with flanges to cover edges of surrounding tile (normally used with portland cement mortar installations); thin-set mounted models with flanges to cover surrounding wall tile. These are normally used with organic adhesives and dryset portland cement mortar.

Soap holder may include a rail. Where a grab bar is required, select a separate accessory which can be anchored into structural parts of a wall.

Accessories are available in glazes and colors to match most glazed wall tile. Check particular manufacturer for colors and glazes available.

CERAMIC BATHROOM ACCESSORIES

Tile Council of America, Inc.

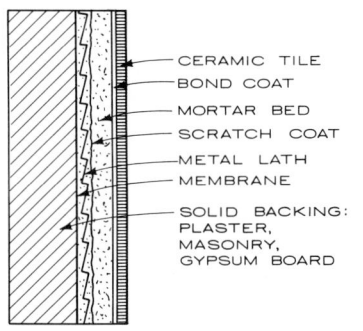

PORTLAND CEMENT MORTAR

Use over solid backing, over wood or metal studs. Preferred method for showers and tub enclosures. Ideal for remodeling.

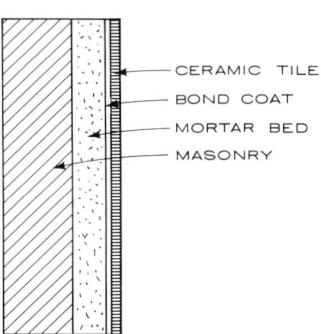

BONDED CEMENT MORTAR

Use over clean, sound, dimensionally stable masonry or concrete. Require a scratch coat over irregular surface if mortar bed exceeds 3/4''.

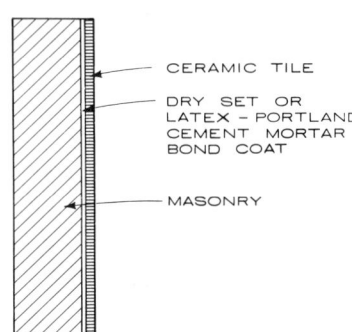

DRY-SET MORTAR

Use over clean, sound, dimensionally stable masonry, concrete, or concrete glass fiber reinforced backer board.

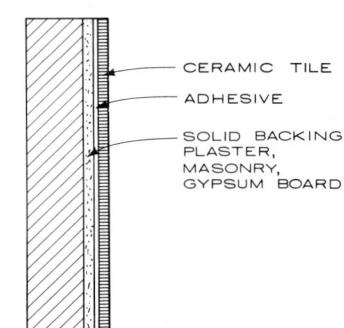

ORGANIC ADHESIVE

Use over gypsum board, plaster, exterior plywood, or other smooth, dimensionally stable surfaces. Use W-R gypsum board in wet areas.

CERAMIC TILE INSTALLATION DETAILS FOR INTERIOR WALLS

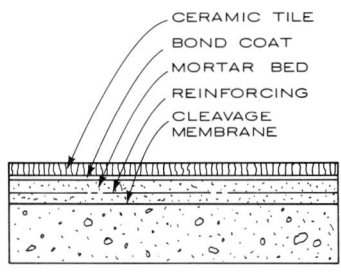

PORTLAND CEMENT MORTAR

Use over structural floors subject to bending and deflection. Mortar bed thickness to be uniform—nominal 1¼'' thick.

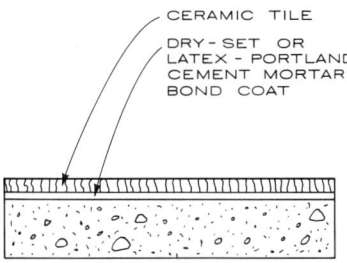

DRY-SET MORTAR

Use on plane clean concrete where no bending stresses occur, on properly cured structural slabs of limited area.

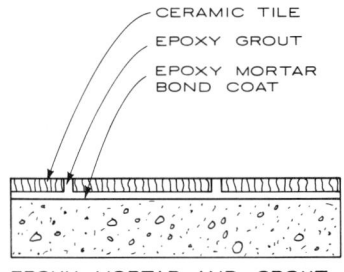

EPOXY MORTAR AND GROUT

Use where moderate chemical exposure and severe cleaning methods are used, such as in commercial kitchens, dairies, breweries, and food plants.

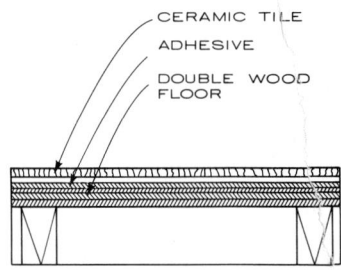

ORGANIC ADHESIVE

Use over wood or concrete floors in residential construction only. Not recommended in wet areas.

CERAMIC TILE INSTALLATION DETAILS FOR INTERIOR FLOORS

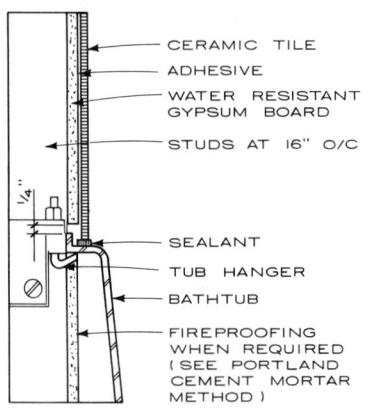

CERAMIC TILE TUB ENCLOSURE

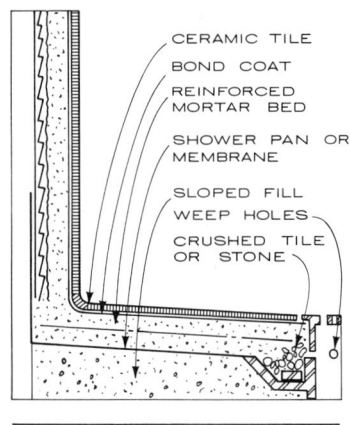

TILE SHOWER RECEPTOR

REMODELING WITH TILE OVER TILE

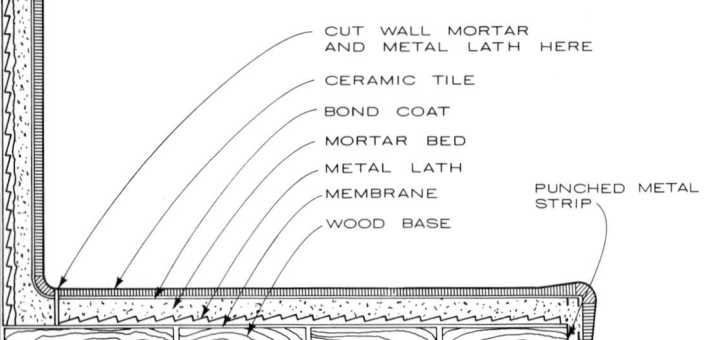

CERAMIC TILE COUNTERTOP

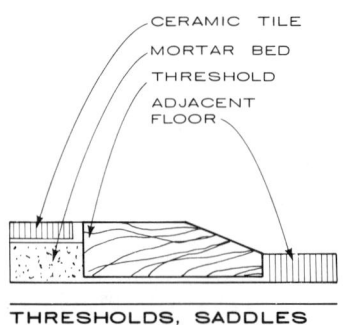

THRESHOLDS, SADDLES

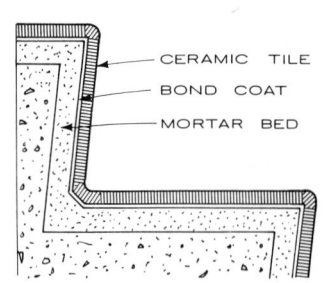

CERAMIC TILE STAIRS

Tile Council of America, Inc.

Terrazzo is a material composed of stone chips and cement matrix and is usually polished. There are four generally accepted types, classified by appearance:

1. STANDARD TERRAZZO: The most common type; relatively small chip sizes (#1 and #2 size chips).
2. VENETIAN TERRAZZO: Larger chips (size #3 through #8), with smaller chips filling the spaces between.
3. PALLADIANA: Random fractured slabs of marble up to approximately 15 in. greatest dimension, $3/8$ to 1 in. thick, with smaller chips filling spaces between.
4. RUSTIC TERRAZZO: Uniformly textured terrazzo in which matrix is depressed to expose chips, not ground or only slightly ground.

MATRIX DATA

Two basic types exist: portland cement and chemical binders. Color pigments are added to create special effects. Limeproof mineral pigments or synthetic mineral pigments compatible with portland cement are required. Both white and grey portland cement is used depending on final color.

CHEMICAL BINDERS

All five types of chemical binders provide excellent chemical and abrasion resistance, except for latex, which is rated good.

1. EPOXY MATRIX: Two component resinous matrix.
2. POLYESTER MATRIX: Two component resinous matrix.
3. POLYACRYLATE MATRIX: Composite resinous matrix.
4. LATEX MATRIX: Synthetic latex matrix.
5. CONDUCTIVE MATRIX: Special formulated matrix to conduct electricity with regulated resistance, use in surgical areas and where explosive gases are a hazard.

PRECAST TERRAZZO

Several units are routinely available and almost any shape can be produced. Examples include: straight, coved, and splayed bases; window sills; stair treads and risers; shower receptors; floor tiles; and wall facings.

STONE CHIPS

Stone used in terrazzo includes all calcareous serpentine and other rocks capable of taking a good polish. Marble and onyx are the preferred materials. Quartz, granite, quartzite, and silica pebbles are used for rustic terrazzo and textured mosaics not requiring polishing.

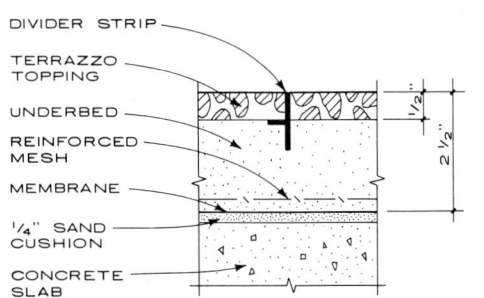

SAND CUSHION TERRAZZO

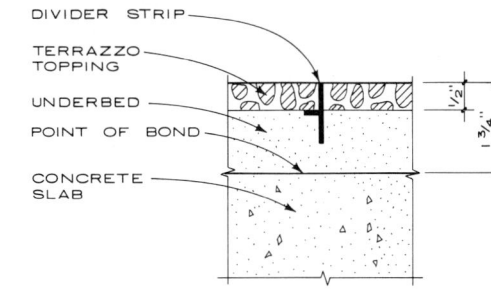

BONDED TERRAZZO

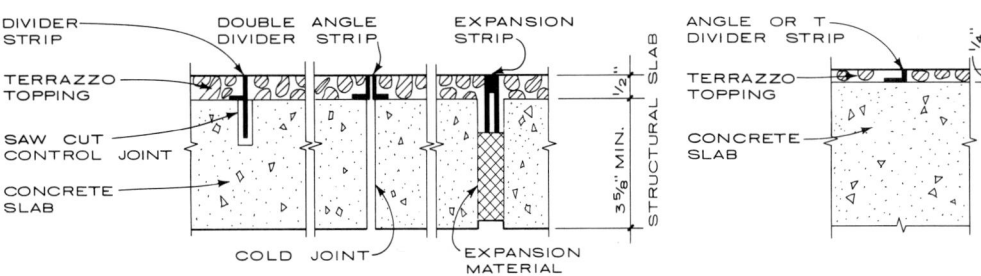

MONOLITHIC TERRAZZO

THIN-SET TERRAZZO

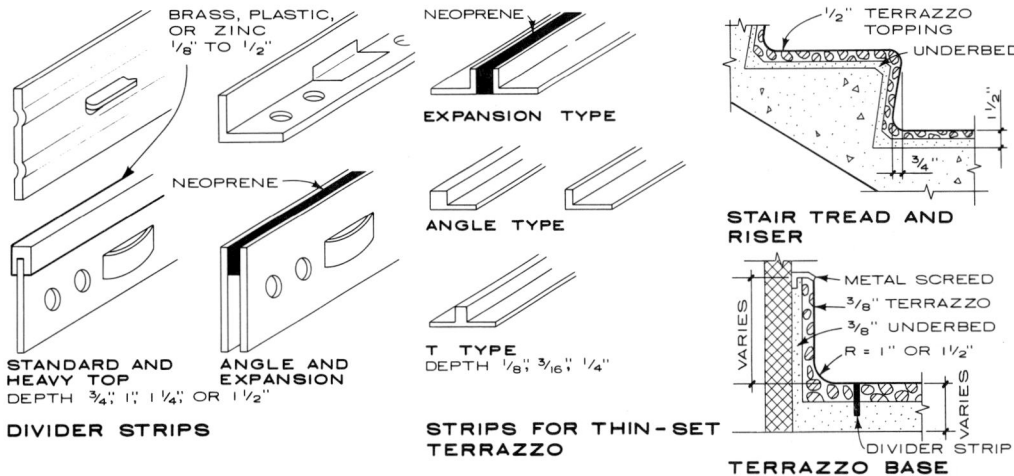

DIVIDER STRIPS

STRIPS FOR THIN-SET TERRAZZO

STAIR TREAD AND RISER

TERRAZZO BASE

TERRAZO SYSTEMS

TERRAZZO SYSTEM	MINIMUM ALLOWANCE FOR FINISH	MINIMUM WEIGHT/ SQ FT	CONTROL JOINT STRIP LOCATION	SUGGESTED PANEL SIZE AND DIVIDER STRIP LOCATION	COMMENTS
Sand cushion terrazzo	$2\frac{1}{2}''$	27 lb	At all control joints in structure	9 to 36 sq ft	Avoid narrow proportions (length no more than twice the width) and acute angles
Bonded underbed or strip terrazzo	$1\frac{3}{4}''$	18 lb	At all control joints in structure	16 to 36 sq ft	Avoid narrow proportions as in sand cushion
Monolithic terrazzo	$1/2''$	7 lb	At all control joints in structure and at column centers or over grade beams where spans are great	At column centers in sawn or recessed slots maximum 24 x 24 ft	T or L strips usually provide decorative feature only
Thin-set terrazzo (chemical binders)	$1/4''$	3 lb	At all control joints	Only where structural crack can be anticipated	
Modified thin-set terrazzo	$3/8''$	$4\frac{1}{2}$ lb	At all control joints	Only where structural crack can be anticipated	
Terrazzo over permanent metal forms	Varies, 3'' minimum	Varies	Directly over beam	Directly over joist centers and at 3 to 5 ft on center in the opposite direction	
Structural terrazzo	Varies, 4'' minimum	Varies	At all control joints at columns and at perimeter of floor	Deep strip ($1\frac{1}{2}$ in. min.) at all column centers and over grade beams	Use divider strip at any location where structural crack can be anticipated

NOTES

1. Venetian and Palladiana require greater depth due to larger chip size $2\frac{3}{4}$ in. minimum allowance for finish 28 lb/sq ft.
2. Divider and control joint strips are made of white alloy of zinc, brass, aluminum, or plastic. Aluminum is not satisfactory for portland cement matrix terrazzo; use brass and plastic in chemical binder matrix only with approval of binder manufacturer.
3. In exterior terrazzo, brass will tarnish and white alloy of zinc will deteriorate.

John C. Lunsford, AIA, Varney Sexton Sydnor Architects; Phoenix, Arizona

ACOUSTICAL CEILING SYSTEMS

CEILING TYPE	MAIN, CROSS T	ACCESS T's	Z CHANNEL	H CHANNEL	T SPLINE	FLAT SPLINE	SPACER	MODULAR T	METAL PAN T	SPECIAL	BENT STEEL	BENT STEEL ALUM. CAP	BENT ALUMINUM	EXTRUDED ALUMINUM	GALVANIZED	PAINTED	ANODIZED	EMBOSSED PATTERN	FIRE RATING AVAILABLE	12x12	12x24	24x24	24x48	24x60	20x60	30x60	60x60	48x48	NOTES
GYPSUM WALLBOARD																													
Suspended	●										●				●	●			●										
Exposed grid	●										●	●	●	●	●	●	●	●	●			●	●						
Semiconcealed grid	●			●	●						●				●	●			●			●	●						
Concealed H & T				●	●	●					●				●	●			●	●									
Concealed T & G			●								●				●	●			●	●									
Concealed Z			●			●					●				●	●			●	●									
Concealed access	●	●			●	●	●				●				●	●			●			●							
Modular	●				●	●		●			●					●			●					●	●	●	●	●	50 or 60" sq main grid
Metal pan									●		●		●		●		●		●	●	●								12" sq pattern
Linear metal										●	●					●													4" o.c. typical
Perforated metal	●			●							●					●													1 way grid 4'-8' o.c.
Luminous ceiling										●			●			●	●												1" to 4" sq grid

ACOUSTICAL CEILING MATERIALS

MATERIALS	12x12	12x24	24x24	24x48	24x60	20x60	30x60	60x60	48x48	CUSTOM SIZES	1/2	5/8	3/4	1	1 1/2	3	SQUARE	TEGULAR	T & G	KERFED AND RABETED	.45-.60	.60-.70	.70-.80	.80-.90	.90-.95	HIGH HUMIDITY	EXTERIOR SOFFIT	HIGH ABUSE/IMPACT	SCRUBBABLE	FIRE RATING AVAILABLE
Mineral fiber:																														
Painted	●	●	●	●	●	●				●	●	●	●				●	●			●	●	●	●						●
Plastic face		●	●									●					●					●						●	●	●
Aluminum face	●	●	●									●					●				●	●						●	●	
Ceramic face		●	●									●					●					●				●		●	●	
Mineral face	●	●	●		●							●	●				●	●		●		●							●	●
Glass fiber:																														
Painted		●	●	●										●			●							●			●			
Film face		●	●	●										●	●		●	●	●	●				●		●	●			
Glass cloth face		●	●	●	●	●	●							●	●	●	●	●	●					●			●		●	
Molded			●	●	●	●					Varies						●							●						
Gypsum		●	●								●						●				●					●			●	
Asbestos		●	●	●							3/16						●				●					●		●		
Tectum		●	●		●	●	●				1–3						●	●			●							●		

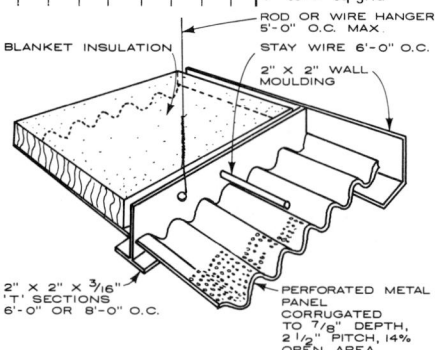

PERFORATED METAL CEILING

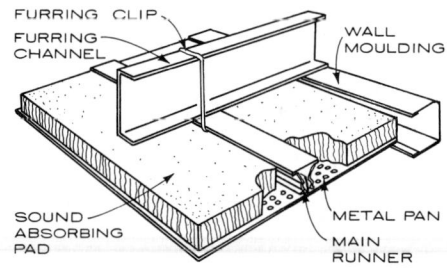

METAL PAN CEILING

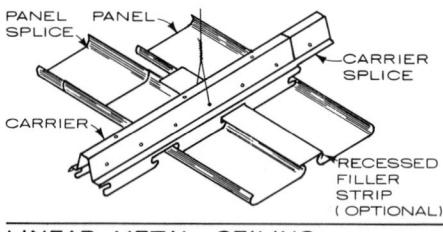

LINEAR METAL CEILING

METAL CEILINGS
USE: Sound absorption depends on batt insulation.
MATERIALS: Bent steel, aluminum, or stainless steel.
N.R.C.: 0.70 to 0.90.
FINISH: Painted, anodized, or stainless steel.

SPECIAL ACOUSTICAL SYSTEMS
SOUND ISOLATION: When it is necessary to isolate a high noise area from a building or a "quiet room" from a high surrounding noise level; floors, walls, and ceilings should be built free of rigid contact with the building structure to reduce sound and vibration transmission.

CUSTOM WALLS: Auditoriums, concert halls, and other special acoustically conditioned space may require both absorptive and reflective surfaces and in some cases surfaces that can be adjusted for varying absorption coefficients to "tune" the space.

LOOSE BATTS
USE: Reduce sound transmission through or over partitions; installed over suspended acoustical tile. Also used between gypsum wall partitions.
MATERIALS: Expanded fiberglass or mineral fiber.
S.T.C.: Based on total designed system, can range from 40 to 60.

Setter, Leach & Lindstrom, Inc.; Minneapolis, Minnesota

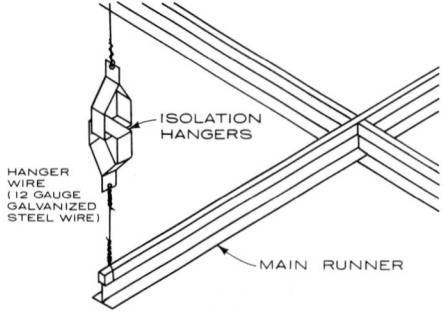

ISOLATION HANGER
CEILING ISOLATION HANGER
Isolates ceilings from noise traveling through the building structure. Hangers also available for isolating ceiling systems to shield spaces from mechanical equipment and/or aircraft noise.

ACOUSTICAL TREATMENT

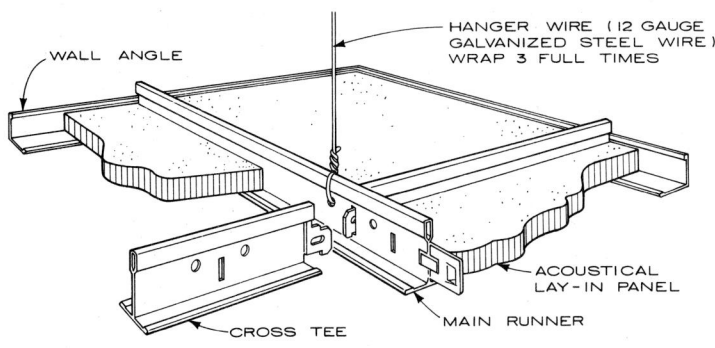

EXPOSED GRID

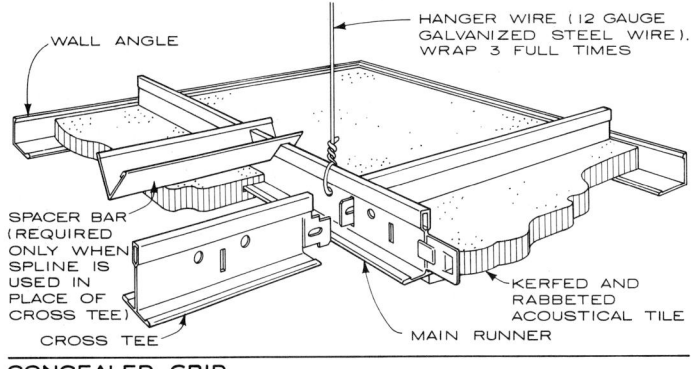

CONCEALED GRID

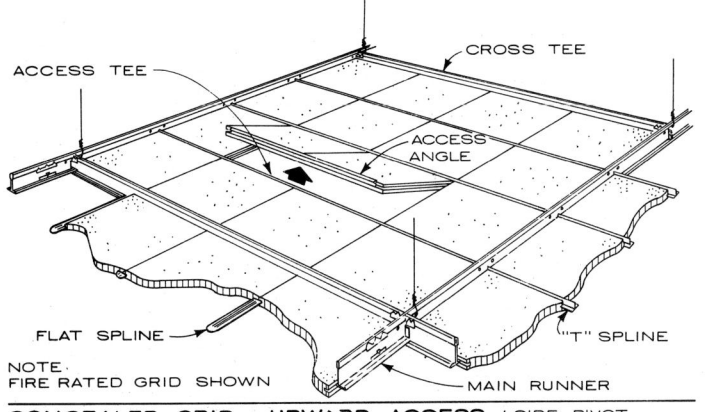

CONCEALED GRID – UPWARD ACCESS (SIDE PIVOT SHOWN – END PIVOT AVAILABLE)

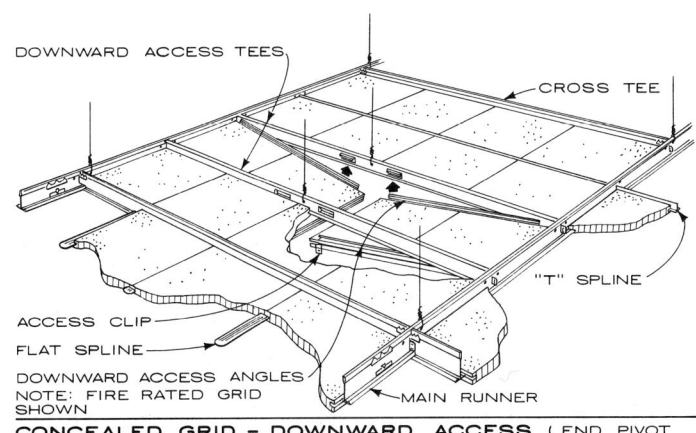

CONCEALED GRID – DOWNWARD ACCESS (END PIVOT SHOWN – SIDE PIVOT AVAILABLE)

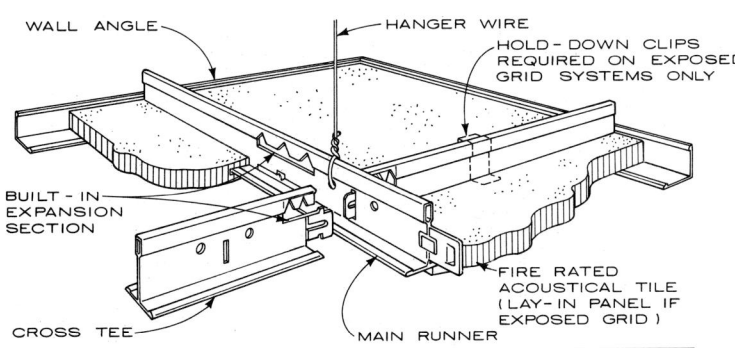

FIRE RATED GRID (CONCEALED GRID SHOWN)

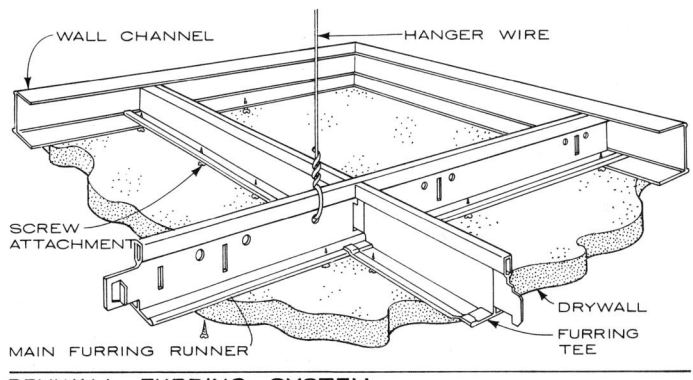

DRYWALL FURRING SYSTEM

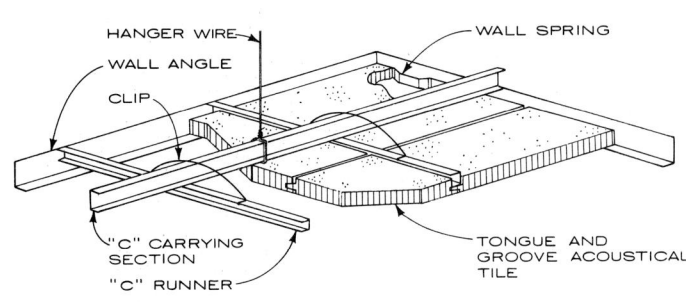

TONGUE AND GROOVE

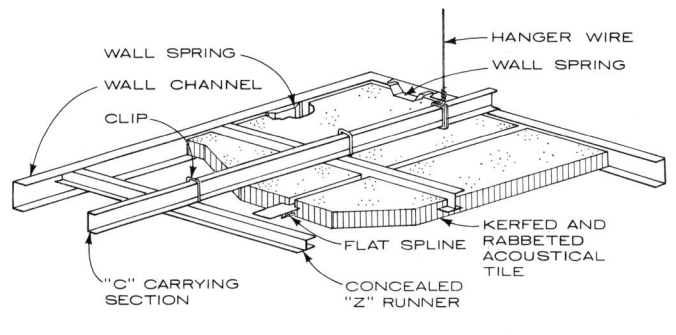

CONCEALED "Z" SYSTEM

Setter, Leach & Lindstrom, Inc.; Minneapolis, Minnesota

ACOUSTICAL TREATMENT

⑨

WALL PANELS

1. USE: Sound absorption.
2. MATERIALS: Fabric-wrapped glass, wood, or mineral fiber.
3. N.R.C.: 0.55–0.85.
4. NOTES: May be used as individual panels or entire wall surfaces. N.R.C. varies with material, thickness and "sound-transparency" of fabric facing. Maximum sizes vary with manufacturer up to 4 x 12 ft.

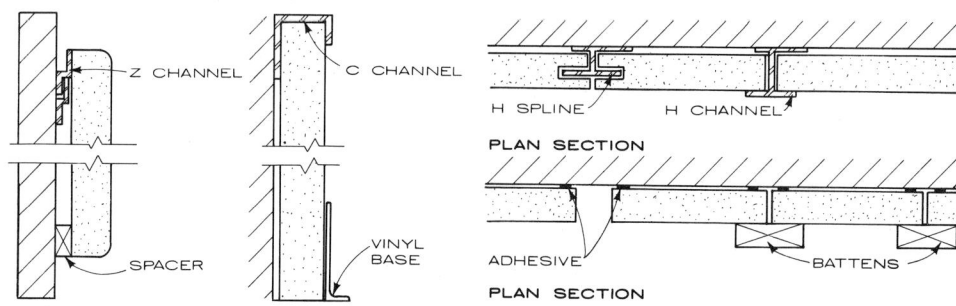

WALL PANELS

SUSPENDED PANELS

1. USE: Sound absorption.
2. MATERIALS: Vertical suspension—glass fiber blanket wrapped with perforated aluminum foil or fabric stretched over frame. Horizontal suspension—perforated steel or aluminum with glass fiber blanket, or similar to vertical.
3. S.A.C.: 1.2–1.5 sabins per square foot of ceiling.
4. NOTES: Panels may be suspended from structure or attached directly to ceiling grid. May be arranged in a variety of patterns including linear, square, zigzag vertical, or regular or random spaced horizontal panels.

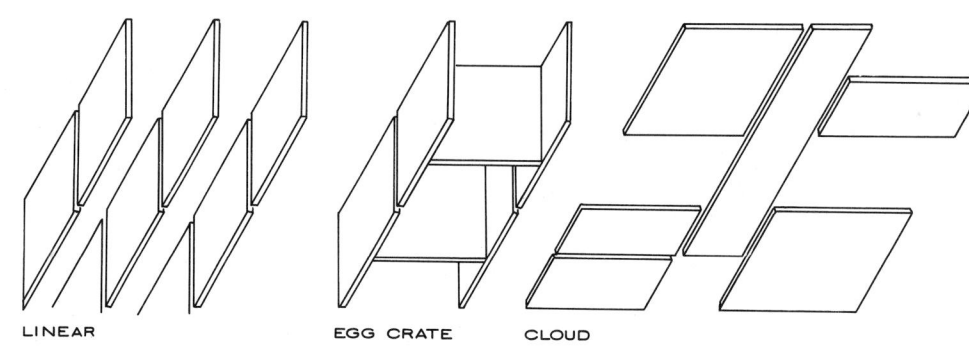

SUSPENDED PANELS

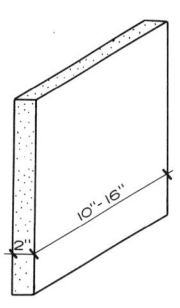
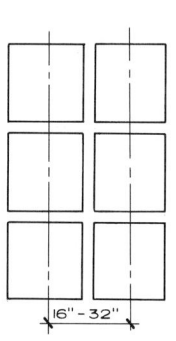
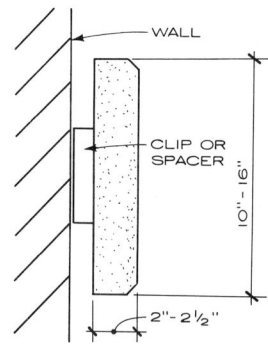

WALL UNITS

1. USE: Sound absorption.
2. MATERIALS: Wood or mineral fiber or cellular glass.
3. S.A.C.: 1.6–2.0 sabins/unit (average).
4. FINISH: Paint.
5. NOTES: Applied to walls or ceilings with adhesive or special clips.

WALL UNITS

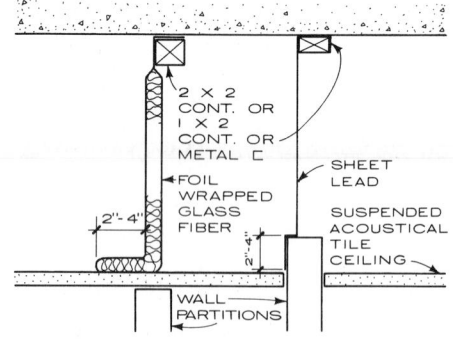

PLENUM BARRIER

1. USE: Reduce sound transmission through plenum above partitions.
2. MATERIALS: $1/64$ in. sheet lead, lead-loaded vinyl, perforated aluminum, or foil-wrapped glass fiber.
3. S.T.C.: 18–41 dB improvement.
4. NOTES: All openings through barrier for pipes, ducts, etc., must be sealed airtight for maximum effectiveness.

PLENUM BARRIERS

CONCRETE MASONRY UNITS

1. USE: Sound absorption.
2. MATERIALS: Modular concrete block, 4, 6, 8 in. thick, with metal baffle and/or fibrous filler in slotted cores.
3. N.R.C.: .45–.65.

CONCRETE MASONRY UNITS

SPRAY-ON ACOUSTICAL MATERIAL

1. USE: Sound absorption.
2. MATERIALS: Mineral or cellulose fibers spray applied to metal lath or directly to hard surfaces such as concrete, steel, masonry, or gypsum board.
3. N.R.C.: .50–.95.
4. NOTES: Application to metal lath provides slightly better sound absorption and permits irregular shapes. Available with a hard surface for wall applications. Available with fire protection rating.

SPRAY-ON ACOUSTICAL MATERIAL

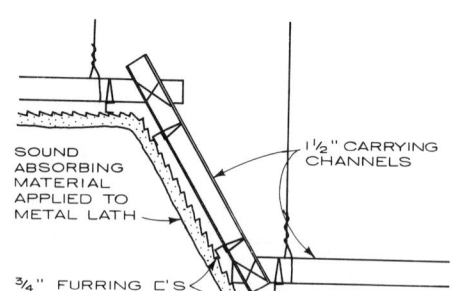

Setter, Leach & Lindstrom, Inc.; Minneapolis, Minnesota

ACOUSTICAL TREATMENT

TABLE OF RESILIENT FLOORING CHARACTERISTICS

TYPE OF RESILIENT FLOORING	BASIC COMPONENTS	SUBFLOOR APPLICATION*			RECOMMENDED LOAD LIMIT (PSI)	DURABILITY†	RESISTANCE TO HEEL DAMAGE	EASE OF MAINTENANCE	GREASE RESISTANCE	SURFACE ALKALI RESISTANCE	RESISTANCE TO STAINING	CIGARETTE BURN RESISTANCE	RESILIENCE	QUIETNESS
Vinyl sheet	Vinyl resins with fiber back	B	O	S	75-100	2-3	2-5	1-2	1	1-3	3-4	4	4	4
Homogeneous vinyl tile	Vinyl resins	B	O	S	150-200	1-3	1-4	2-4	1	1-2	1-5	2-5	2-5	2-5
Vinyl asbestos tile	Vinyl resins and asbestos fibers	B	O	S	25-50	2	4-5	2-3	2	4	2	6	6	6
Cork tile with vinyl coating	Raw cork and vinyl resins			S	150	4	3	2	1	1	5	3	3	3
Cork tile	Raw cork and resins			S	75	5	4	4	4	5	4	1	1	1
Rubber tile	Rubber compound	B	O	S	200	2	4	4	3	2	1	2	2	2
Linoleum	Cork, wood, floor, and oleoresins			S	75	3	4-5	4-5	1	4	2	4	4	4
Asphalt tile	Resins, asphalt compounds-asbestos	B	O	S	25	3-4	4	4	5	5	4	7	7	6

*B: below grade; O: on grade; S: suspended.
†Numerals indicate subjective ratings (relative rank of each floor to others listed above) "1" indicating highest.
 Bruce A. Kenan, AIA; Pederson, Hueber, Hares & Glavin; Syracuse, New York.

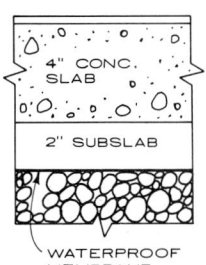
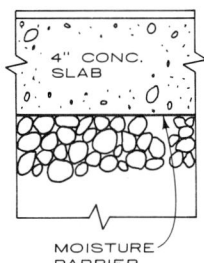

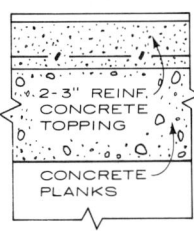
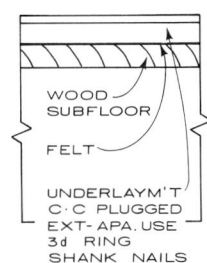
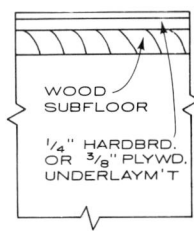

| SLAB BELOW GRADE | SLAB ON GRADE | SLAB ABOVE GRADE | SLAB OVER PRECAST | WOOD SUBFLOOR | WOOD SUBFLOOR |

RESILIENT FLOORING

PREPARING OLD WOOD FLOORS

TYPE OF SUBFLOOR		COVER WITH
Single wood floor	Tongue-&-groove not over 3"	Hardboard or plywood, 1/4" or heavier
	Not tongue-&-groove	Plywood 1/2" or heavier
Double wood floor	Strips 3" or more	Hardboard or plywood 1" or heavier
	Strips less than 3" tongue-&-groove	Renail or replace loose boards, remove surface irregularities

PREPARING OLD CONCRETE FLOORS

Check for dampness
Remove all existing surface coatings
Wirebrush and sweep dusty, porous surfaces. Apply primer

PREPARING LIFT SLABS

Remove curing compounds prior to resilient flooring installation
For installation of vinyl-asbestos tile, see manufacturer's instructions

CONCRETE SLABS BY DENSITY

Density			
Light		Medium	Heavy
Pounds per cubic foot			
20/40	60/90	90/120	120/150
Type of concrete			
Expanded perlite, vermiculite, and others		Expanded slag shale, and clay	Standard concrete of sand, gravel, or stone
Recommendations			
Top with 1" thickness of standard concrete mix		Approved for use of resilient flooring if troweled smooth and even	

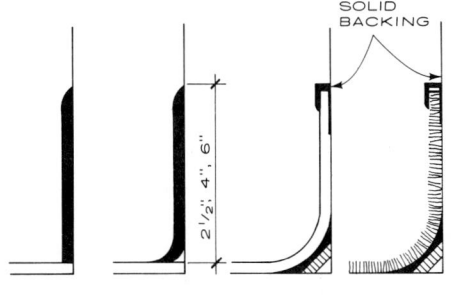

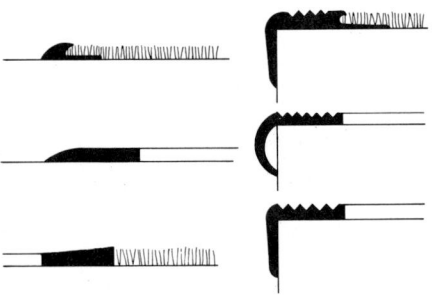
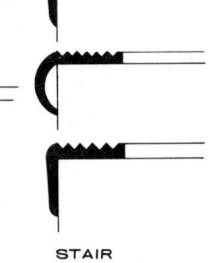
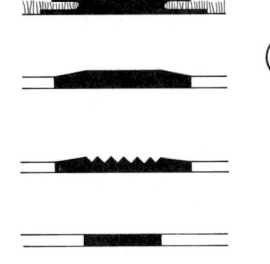
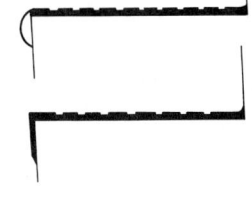

| BASES - STRAIGHT OR COVED | COVE STRIP AND CAP STRIP | REDUCERS | STAIR NOSINGS | THRESHOLDS, SADDLES FEATURE STRIP | STAIR TREAD |

RESILIENT FLOORING ACCESSORIES, CARPET ACCESSORIES

Broome, Oringdulph, O'Toole, Rudolf & Associates; Portland, Oregon

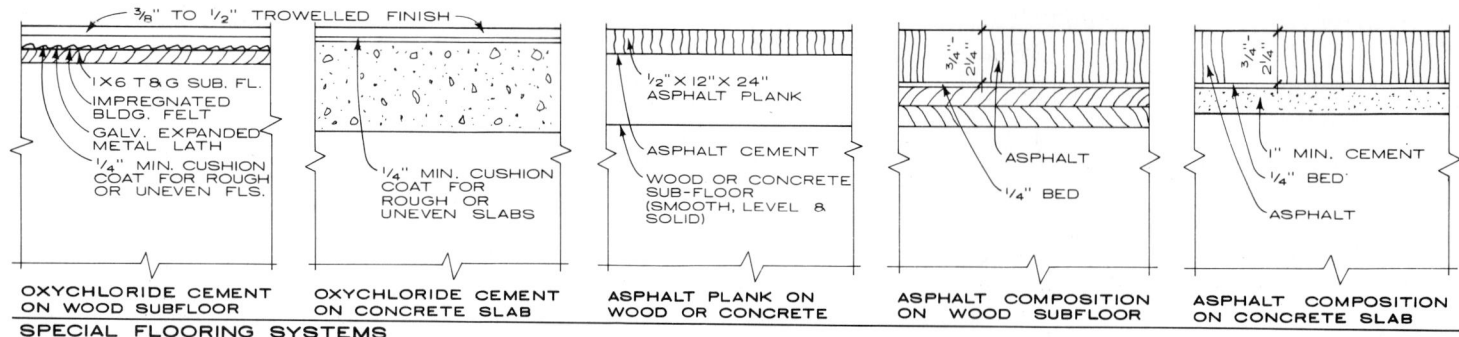

SPECIAL FLOORING SYSTEMS

OXYCHLORIDE CEMENT ON WOOD SUBFLOOR | OXYCHLORIDE CEMENT ON CONCRETE SLAB | ASPHALT PLANK ON WOOD OR CONCRETE | ASPHALT COMPOSITION ON WOOD SUBFLOOR | ASPHALT COMPOSITION ON CONCRETE SLAB

NOTE

Asphalt flooring is intended for heavy traffic industrial use.

NOTE

Oxychloride floors are especially suited to food preparation areas, locker rooms, and explosive hazard areas.

STYLE	SIZE	WEIGHT
Center tile	24″ x 24″ x 7/16″	10 lb
Beveled edge	6″ x 24″ x 7/16″	5 lb
Beveled corner	6″ x 12″ x 7/16″	2.5 lb

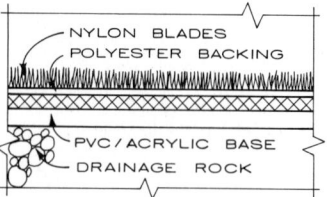

INTERLOCKING RUBBER FLOOR SYSTEMS

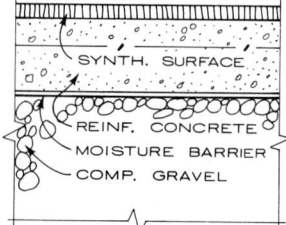

PREFABRICATED SYNTHETIC SPORTS SURFACE

PRODUCT DESCRIPTION

1. Solid cast or laminated polyvinyl chloride sheet goods.
2. Width: 4 to 5 ft.
3. Length: up to 90 ft.
4. Thickness: 3/16, 1/4, 3/8 in.
5. Surface texture: smooth, embossed, or tennis embossed.

SYNTHETIC TURF

FIELD TYPES	PILE HEIGHT	PAD THICKNESS
Stadium school	1/2″	3/16″–1/4″
Playground	3/8″	3/16″–1/4″
Tennis	1/4″	—
Golf	3/8″	1/8″–3/8″

SYNTHETIC TURF

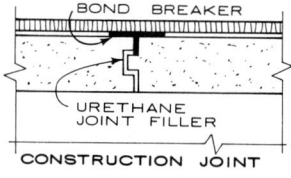

PRODUCT DESCRIPTION

1. Poured-in-place urethane, usually two lifts.
2. Thickness: 1/8, 1/4, 3/8, 1/2 in.
3. Shore hardness:
   a. Gyms, 50.
   b. Conditioning track, 35–40.
   c. Speed track, 50–60.

SEAMLESS SYNTHETIC FLOORING

Seamless synthetic floorings consist of a resin matrix (epoxy, urethane, polyester, etc.) by itself or with an aggregate such as stone or plastic chips for texture, color and design. They are applied by spraying, rolling or troweling. Thickness varies from 1/8″–3/8″. They may be applied to concrete, wood, asphalt and other ease materials depending on the type selected and its use. Special chemical resistant, slip-resistant, and conductive types are available. Due to the numerous types that are produced, a check with manufacturers of these types of flooring is suggested for the specific product and method of installation that is best for each specific application.

CONSTRUCTION JOINT | OVER EXISTING WOOD FLOOR

POURED-IN-PLACED SYNTHETIC SPORTS SURFACE

PROPERTIES

TESTS	PROPERTY	TEST METHOD
Impact resilience is the percentage that an object rebounds when dropped on the material. A high number indicates more energy returned to the object—therefore a livelier surface.	Impact resilience, %	ASTM D 2632
Shore hardness measures the force necessary to push a probe into the material. The higher the number, the harder the material. (This test is a static test, not using movement such as bouncing, pulling, or tearing.)	Hardness shore A-2	ASTM D 2240
Breaking strength measures the force necessary to pull the material apart.	Breaking strength, psi	ASTM D 412
Elongation measures how far the material stretches before breaking.	Elongation to break, %	ASTM D 412
Tear strength measures the force required to tear a V-shaped piece of the material, pulling the two legs of the V apart. The gouging, tearing action of track spikes involves all of these actions.	Tear strength, pli	ASTM D 624
Compression resistance measures the resistance to indentation caused by placing heavy objects on the material. This property can be observed by squeezing a sample between thumb and finger.	10% compression, psi	ASTM D 575
Compression recovery measures the material's ability to return to its original thickness after heavy objects are removed from it.	Compression recovery, %	ASTM D 395(A)
Thermal conductivity measures the heat transfer characteristics of the material.	Thermal conductivity, BTU/sq ft · hr · °F	ASTM C518
Linear coefficient of thermal expansion measures the material's dimensional changes in response to temperature variations.	Linear coefficient of thermal expansion, ft./ft./°F.	ASTM 696

Broome, Oringdulph, O'Toole, Rudolf & Associates; Portland, Oregon

FINISH FLOORING

RECOMMENDED GUIDELINES FOR CARPET SELECTION

1. Know the budget, including installation costs.
2. Be aware of the types of traffic load—moderate, heavy, or extra heavy. Be aware of potential pivot, funnel, and traffic flow areas.
3. Know the minimum life expectancy required.
4. Make certain that maintenance levels are appropriate for the required life expectancy.
5. Make certain that colors, textures, and patterns are appropriate for the expected types of soiling, staining, and wear.
6. Know what types of surface texture will be required.
7. Be assured that the right gauge or pitch has been selected.
8. Make sure that pile or face yarns are selected that can do the job.
9. Make certain that the carpet construction fits the needs of the job. Will it:
   a. Eliminate static shock?
   b. Have sufficient tuft bind strength?
   c. Meet local and Federal flame spread restrictions?
   d. Have pilling and fuzzing resistance?
   e. Be suitable if subjected to rolling traffic?
   f. Have enough bond strength between primary carpet structure and secondary backing to prevent delamination?
   g. Have crush and wear resistance?
   h. Have adequate resistance to sunlight?
   i. Have attached backings that are properly constructed?
   j. Meet sound absorption requirements?
10. Know that the carpet construction is not being overspecified, thus adding unneeded expense.
11. Be certain that the best methods of installation are being used. Are there any special requirements to be considered?

INSTALLATION REQUIREMENTS

Factors that must be considered before making a final decision include:

1. Traffic classification in terms of load and nature.
2. Acoustical requirements, heat transfer properties, and resilience.
3. Dimensional stability.
4. Condition and type of subfloor.
5. Budget.

STRETCH-IN TACKLESS

The conventional method of installing a carpet is by power stretching over a separate cushion. A padded carpet offers superior sound control, resilience, and added foot comfort. This method is not recommended for large open areas where shifting and buckling could present a problem or in areas where heavy, wheeled traffic is anticipated.

DIRECT GLUE DOWN

Recommended for large areas where heavy, wheeled traffic is anticipated and for maximum carpet stability. This method also significantly reduces seam splitting and delamination problems. The correct pile density will minimize loss of resilience and give thermal and acoustical control. The direct glue down method usually involves three basic types of carpet backing: jute or nonwoven synthetic secondary back; attached cushion back; or latex, polyvinyl chloride, or polyurethane compounds. This method has been used effectively on all types of subflooring ranging from below grade concrete to grade concrete, suspended concrete, suspended wood, and existing resilient floors. Preparation of the subfloor is of primary importance when specifying this method.

SEAMING

The three main methods of seaming are heat seams, sewn seams, and latex seams.

SOUND ABSORPTION

The carpet's texture, density, and weight determine its noise reduction coefficient (NRC). The greater the NRC rating the more absorbent the material. The combination of pad and carpet can vary the NRC rating.

Walter H. Sobel, FAIA & Associates; Chicago, Illinois

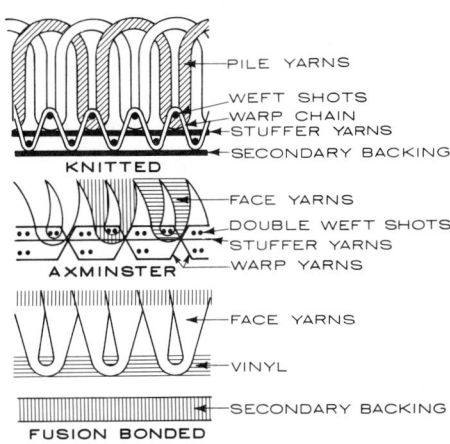

CONSTRUCTION MODES

TUFTED

A tufted carpet is made by inserting face yarn or tufts through premanufactured backing by use of needles (like a sewing machine). Yarns are held in place by coating the back with latex; a secondary back is applied to add body and stability. 87% of contract carpet used today is tufted.

VELVET WOVEN

The simplest of all carpet weaves. Pile is formed as loom loops warp yarns over wires inserted across loom. Pile height is determined by height of wire inserted. Velvets are traditionally known for smooth cut pile plush or loop pile textures, but can also create hi-lo loop or cut-uncut textures. 7% of contract carpet used today is velvet woven.

AXMINSTER WOVEN

The Axminster loom is highly specialized and nearly as versatile as hand weaving. Color combinations and designs are limited only by the number of tufts in the carpet. Almost all the yarn appears on the surface, and characteristic of this weave is a heavy ribbed back that allows the carpet to be rolled lengthwise only. 1% of contract carpet used today is Axminster woven.

FUSION BONDED

This process produces complete carpet by imbedding pile yarns and adhering backing to a viscous vinyl paste that hardens after curing carpet. Has superior tuft bind and practically eliminates backing delamination. Over 90% of yarn is in the face. Fusion bonded process produces very dense cut pile or level loop fabrics in solid or moresque colors. 1% of contract carpet used today is fusion bonded.

KNITTED

The knitted process resembles weaving in that the face and back are made simultaneously. Backing and pile yarns are looped together with a stitching yarn on machines that have three sets of needles. Knitted carpets usually have solid or tweed colors, with a level loop pile texture. 1% of contract carpet used today is knitted.

WILTON WOVEN

The Wilton loom operates basically like a velvet loom, except that it has the Jacquard mechanism with up to six colors or frames. Only one color at a time is utilized on the surface; other yarns therefore remain buried in the body of the carpet until needed. Wilton looms can produce cut pile, level loop, multilevel, or carved textures. 3% of contract carpet used today is Wilton woven.

CONSTRUCTION COMPONENTS

PITCH OR GAUGE

In woven carpet pitch is the number of ends of yarn in 27 in. of width. In tufted carpet gauge is the spacing of needles across the width of the tufting machine expressed in fractions of an inch.

STITCHES OR ROWS/WIRES

These are the number of per 1 in. of carpet tufts, counting lengthwise.

TUFTS PER SQUARE INCH

A calculation made by multiplying the number of ends across the width (gauge or pitch) by the number of tufts lengthwise (stitches or rows) per inch.

PILE HEIGHT

The height of the loop or tuft from the surface of the backing to the top of the pile is measured in fractions or decimals of an inch.

FACE WEIGHT

The total weight of pile yarns in the carpet measured in oz/yd^2. This excludes backing yarns or fabric.

DENSITY

A calculation used to measure the compactness of face yarns in a carpet. Increased density generally results in better performance.

YARN SIZE AND PLY

DENIER: The unit of weight for the size of a single filament yarn. The higher the denier number the heavier the yarn.

PLY: The number of single ends of yarn twisted together to form a heavier, larger yarn.

BACKING: The foundation construction that supports the pile yarns.

PRIMARY BACKING: In tufted carpet, a woven or nonwoven fabric into which pile yarns are attached; usually jute or polypropylene. In woven carpets backing yarns are usually kraftcord, cotton, polyester, jute, or rayon.

SECONDARY BACKING: An extra layer of material laminated to the underside of the carpet for additional dimensional stability and body. Usually latex, jute, H.D. foam, sponge rubber, or vinyl.

STANDARD CARPET AND RUG SIZES

CARPET	WIDTH
Synthetic fibers	4'-6'', 6'-0'', 7'-6'', 9'-0'', 12'-0'', 15'-0''
Wool fibers	9'-0'', 12'-0'', 15'-0''
Sponge bonded, Rubber backed	4'-6'', 12'-0''
PADS	
All hair, hair and fiber, and rubberized hair and fiber	2'-3'', 3'-0'', 4'-6'', 9'-0'', 12'-0''
Foam rubber	3'-0'', 6'-0''
Sponge rubber	3'-0'', 4'-6'', 9'-0''

RUGS: Rugs are bound pieces of carpet that are not attached to the floor. The sizes therefore vary.

NOTES

1. Flooring can be manufactured from practically every commercially available species of wood. In the United States wood flooring is grouped for marketing purposes roughly according to species and region. There are various grading systems used with various species, and often different specifications for different sized boards in a given species. For instance, nail size and spacing varies among the several board sizes typically available in oak.

2. Information given here should be used for preliminary decision making only. Precise specifications must be obtained from the supplier or from the appropriate industry organization named below.

3. Several considerations in wood flooring selection and installation are applicable industrywide. These are shown graphically at right.

4. The table below includes typical grades and sizes of boards for each species or regional group. Grade classifications vary, but in each case one can assume that the first grade listed is the highest quality, and that the quality decreases with each succeeding grade. The best grade will typically minimize or exclude features such as knots, streaks, spots, checks, and torn grain and will contain the highest percentage of longer boards. Grade standards have been reduced in recent years for practically all commercially produced flooring, hence a thorough review of exact grade specifications is in order when selecting wood flooring.

5. End matching gives a complete tongue and grooved joint all around each board. Board length is reduced as required to obtain the matched ends.

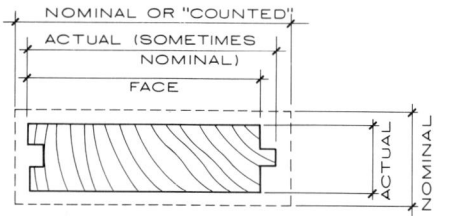

CROSS SECTIONAL DIMENSIONING SYSTEMS VARY AMONG SPECIES, PATTERNS, MANUFACTURERS. TRADE ORGANIZATIONS PROVIDE PERCENTAGE MULTIPLIERS FOR COMPUTING COVERAGE.

CROSS SECTIONAL DIMENSIONS

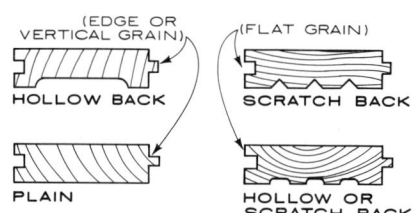

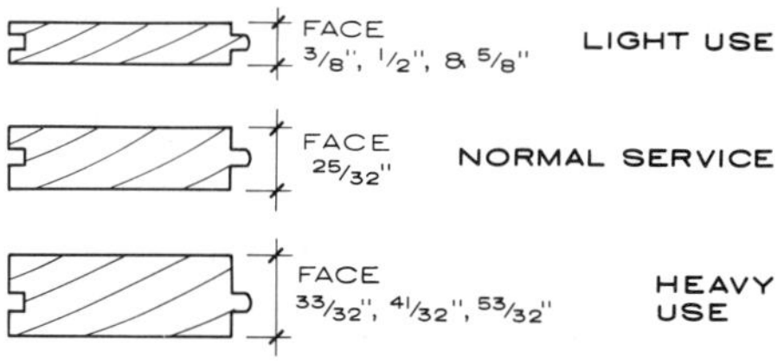

THE UNDERSIDE OF FLOORING BOARDS MAY BE PATTERNED AND OFTEN WILL CONTAIN MORE DEFECTS THAN ARE ALLOWED IN THE TOP FACE. GRAIN IS OFTEN MIXED IN ANY GIVEN RUN OF BOARDS.

BOARD CHARACTERISTICS

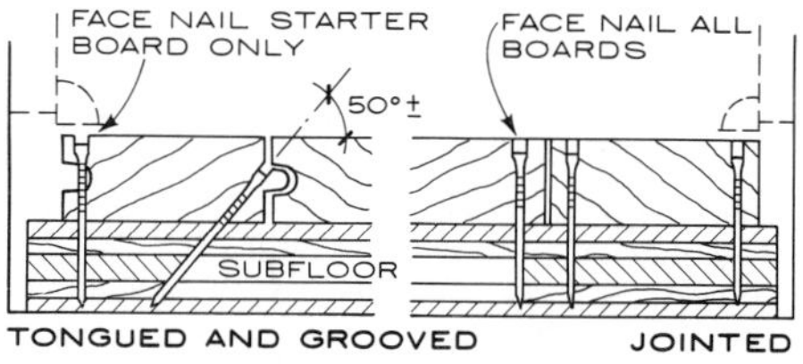

MOST FLOORING MAY BE HAD IN VARYING THICKNESSES TO SUIT WEAR REQUIREMENTS. ACTUAL DIMENSIONS SHOWN ARE AVAILABLE IN MAPLE.

VARIOUS THICKNESSES

JOINTED FLOORING MUST BE FACE NAILED, USUALLY WITH FULLY BARBED FLOORING BRADS.
TONGUE AND GROOVED BOARDS ARE BLIND NAILED WITH SPIRAL FLOOR SCREWS, CEMENT COATED NAILS, CUT NAILS, MACHINE DRIVEN FASTENERS, USE MANUFACTURER'S RECOMMENDATIONS.

FASTENING

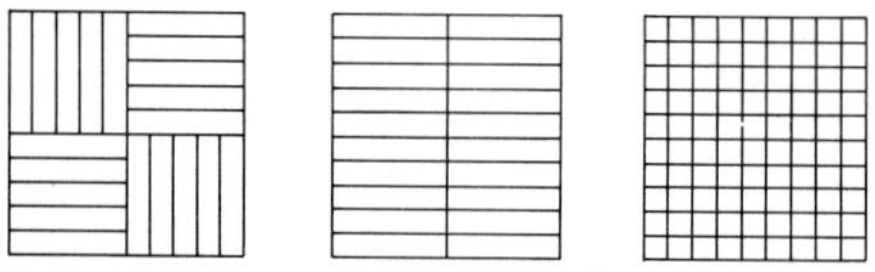

PARQUET FLOORING—SQUARE PANELS

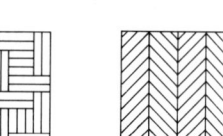

THICKNESS	FACE DIMENSIONS
5/16" (most common) 9/16", 11/16", 3/4"	6" x 6", 6¼" x 6½", 12" x 12", 19" x 19" Other sizes are available from certain manufacturers

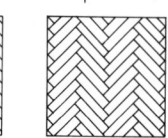 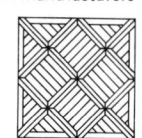

PARQUET FLOORING—INDIVIDUAL STRIPS

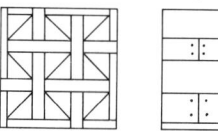

THICKNESS	FACE DIMENSIONS
5/16"	2" x 12" typical strips can be cut, mitered, etc., to obtain pieces required for special patterns

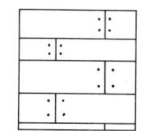 

TYPICAL GRADES AND SIZES OF BOARDS BY SPECIES OR REGIONAL GROUP

GROUP	INDUSTRY ORGANIZATION	GRADE	THICKNESS	WIDTH		NOTES
Oak (also beech, birch, pecan, and hard maple)	National Oak Flooring Manufacturers' Assoc.	Quarter Sawn: Clear Select Plain Sawn: Clear Select No. 1 Common No. 2 Common	3/4", 1/2" Standard; also 3/8" 5/16"	Face 1½" 2" 2¼"		This association grades birch, beech, and hard maple: First Grade, Second Grade, Third Grade, and "Special Grades." Pecan is graded: First Grade, First Grade Red, Second Grade, Second Grade Red, Third Grade
Hard maple (also beech and birch) (acer saccharum—not soft maple)	Maple Flooring Manufacturers' Assoc. Inc.	First Grade Second Grade Third Grade Fourth Grade Combinations	3/8", 12/32" 41/32", 1/2" 33/32", 53/32", 5/8"	Face 1½" 2" 2¼" 3¼"		Association states that beech and birch have physical properties that make them fully suitable as substitutes for hard maple. See manufacturer for available width and thickness combinations
Southern pine	Southern Pine Inspection Bureau	B & B C C & Btr D No. 2	3/8", 1/2" 5/8", 1" 1¼", 1½"	Nom. 2" 3" 4" 5" 6"	Face 1⅛" 2⅛" 3⅛" 4⅛" 5⅛"	Grain may be specified as edge (rift), near-rift, or flat. If not specified, manufacturer will ship flat or mixed grain boards. See manufacturer for available width and thickness combinations
Western woods (Douglas fir, hemlock, Englemann spruce, Idaho pine, incense cedar, lodgepole pine, Ponderosa pine, sugar pine, Western larch, Western red cedar)	Western Wood Products Association	Select: 1 & 2 clear- B & Btr C Select D Select Finish: Superior Prime E	2" and thinner	Nominal 3" 4" 6"		Flooring is machined tongue and groove and may be furnished in any grade agreeable to buyer and seller. Grain may be specified as vertical (VG), flat (FG), or mixed (MG). Basic size for flooring is 1" x 4" x 12'; standard lengths 4' and above
Eastern white pine Norway pine Jack pine Eastern spruce Balsam fir Eastern hemlock Tamarack	Northern Hardwood & Pine Manufacturers' Association	C & Btr Select D Select Stained Select	3/8", 1/2" 5/8", 1", 1¼", 1½"	Nom. 2" 3" 4" 5" 6"	Face 1⅛" 2⅛" 3⅛" 4⅛" 5⅛"	The various species included in this "Lake States Region" group provide different visual features. Consult manufacturer or local supplier to determine precisely what is available in terms of species and appearance

Darrel Rippeteau, Architect; Washington, D.C.

WOOD FLOORING

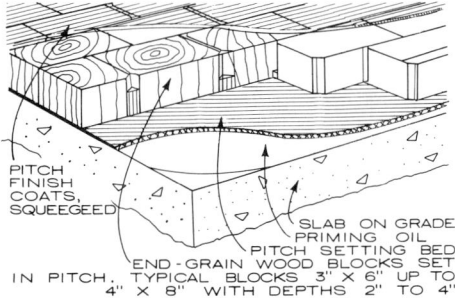

INDUSTRIAL WOOD BLOCK URETHANE FINISH COATS AVAILABLE FOR NONINDUSTRIAL USES

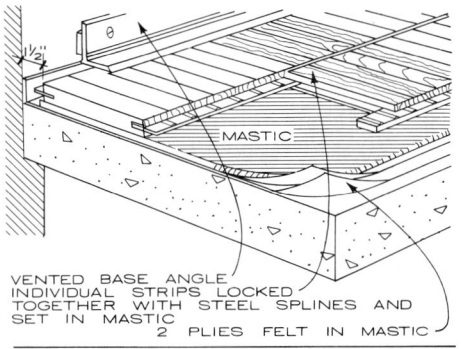

STEEL SPLINED ROWS OF STRIPS CORK UNDERLAYMENT ADDED FOR NON-INDUSTRIAL USE

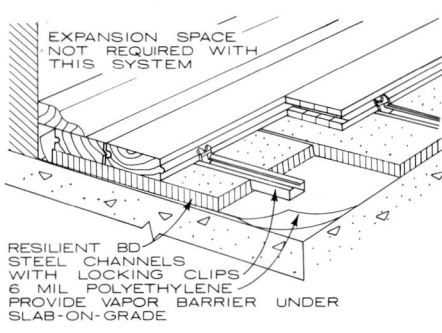

METAL CHANNEL RUNNERS WITH CLIPS

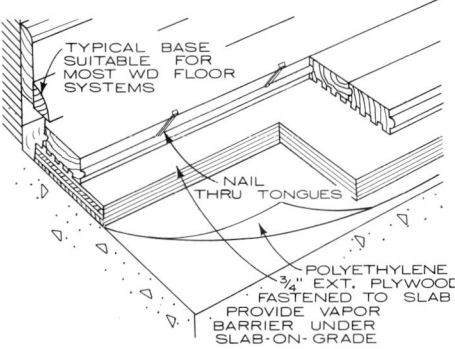

STRIPS OVER PLYWOOD UNDERLAYMENT A NOFMA STANDARD

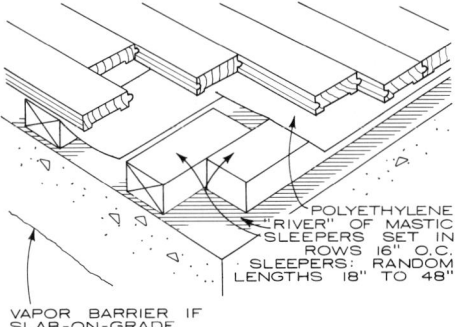

STRIPS OVER STAGGERED 2 X 4 SLEEPERS A NOFMA STANDARD

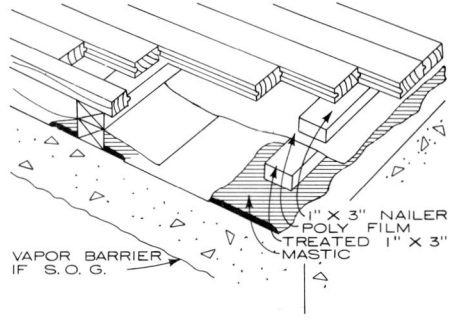

DOUBLE COURSE OF SLEEPER STRIPS A NOFMA STANDARD

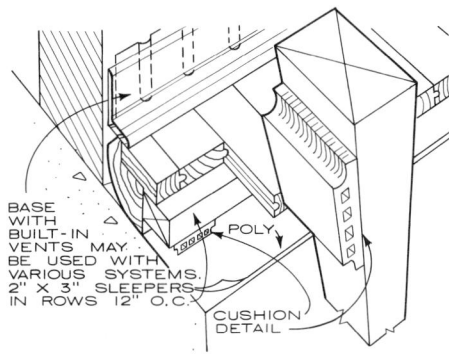

STRIPS OVER CUSHIONED SLEEPERS

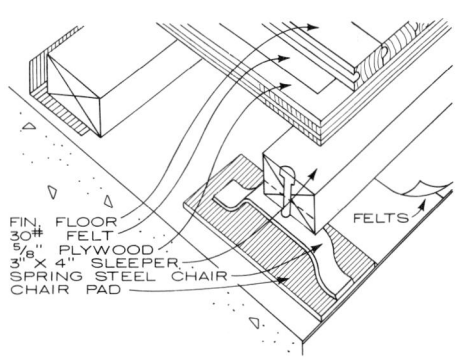

STRIPS OVER SLEEPERS MOUNTED ON SPRING-STEEL CHAIRS

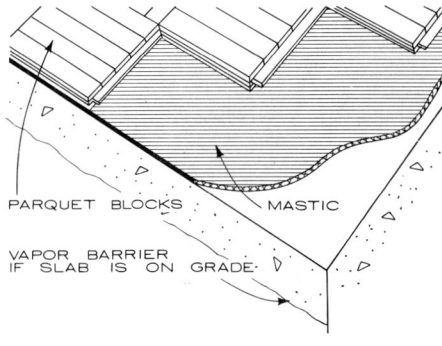

PARQUET BLOCKS SET IN MASTIC

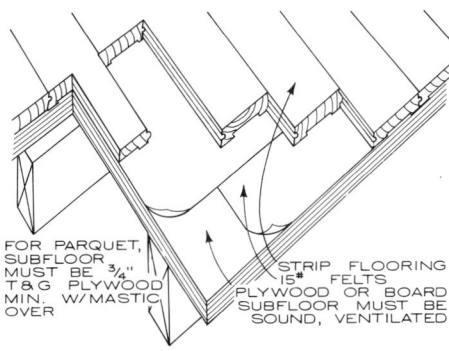

STRIPS OVER SUBFLOOR ON WOOD JOISTS

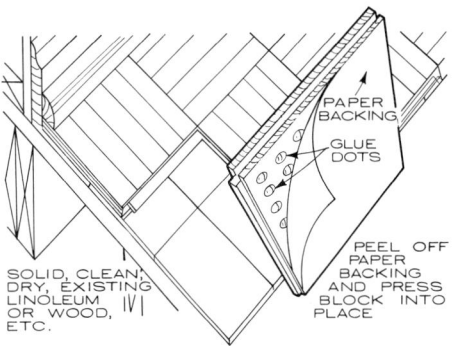

PRESSURE-SENSITIVE "DO-IT-YOURSELF" PANELS (PRE-FINISHED)

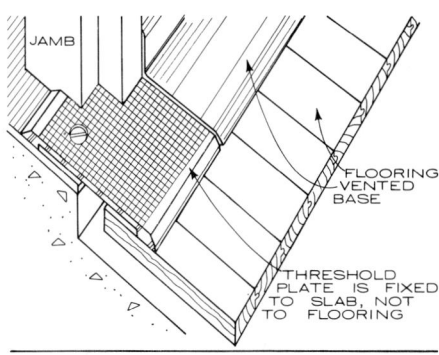

EXPANSION PLATE AT DOORWAY /JOINT WITH DISSIMILAR CONSTRUCTION

Wood flooring is visually attractive and provides an excellent wearing surface. However, wood requires particular care in handling and installation to prevent moisture attack. Minimize moisture attack on wood floors by avoiding proximity to wet areas. Installation should occur after all "wet" jobs are completed. All the permanent lighting and heating plant should be installed to ensure constant temperature and humidity.

Expansion and contraction is a fact of life with most wood flooring. Perimeter base details that allow for movement and ventilation are included in the details above. Moisture control is further enhanced by use of a vapor barrier under a slab on or below grade. This provision should be carefully considered for each installation. Wood structures require adequate ventilation in basement and crawl space.

Wearing properties vary from species to species in wood flooring and should be considered along with appearance. In addition, grain pattern will affect a given species wearability. For instance, industrial wood blocks are typically placed with the end grain exposed because it presents the toughest wearing surface. The thickness of the wood above tongues in T & G flooring may be increased for extra service.

Darrel Rippeteau, Architect; Washington, D.C.

TYPICAL COVERINGS AND AVAILABLE SIZES

DESCRIPTION	WIDTH	LENGTH PER SINGLE ROLL	MINIMUM[1] UNIT SOLD	FLAME SPREAD RATING	ADHESIVE USED[2]	GENERAL WEARABILITY
Burlap Vinyl backed Paper backed	30", 36"	4 yards	Single roll	Class A-25	Premixed vinyl adhesive	Durable
Canvas Paper backed	24", 27", 48"	5 yards	Single roll	Class A-25	Premixed vinyl adhesive	Durable
Cork Paper backed Cloth backed	30", 36"	4 yards 5 yards	Single roll	Class A-25 Class B-35	Nonstaining paste Wheat paste Premixed vinyl	Less durable
Fabric (wool, linen, cotton, rayon, jute, etc.) Paper backed Acrylic backed Polyfoam backed	36", 54"	4 yards Continuous rolls	Single roll	Class A-25, 15	Premixed vinyl adhesive	Variable
Felt Paper backed	20 1/2", 24", 30", 36", 54"	5 yards	Single roll	Class A-25	Premixed adhesive	Less durable
Grass cloth Paper backed	30", 36"	4 yards	Single roll	Class A-25	Wheat paste Cellulose paste	Less durable
Paper American	18" 20 1/2" 27"	8 yards 7 yards 5 yards	Single roll	Class A-25 Class B-35	Vinyl adhesive	Less durable
European	18" 20 1/2" 27"	12 1/2 yards 11 yards 8 1/2 yards	Single roll	Class A-25 Class B-35	Vinyl adhesive	Less durable
Flocked	27"	5 yards	Single roll	Class A-25 Class B-35	Vinyl adhesive	Less durable
Foil	27", 30"	5 yards	Single roll	Class A-25	Vinyl adhesive	Less durable
Handprinted sheets	30"	5 yards	Single roll	Class A-25	Vinyl adhesive	Less durable
Murals (variable)	28" Variations	Variable	Single panel	Class A-25	Vinyl adhesive	Less durable
Scenic (variable)	11', 28" Variations	5 yards	Single roll	Class A-25	Vinyl adhesive	Less durable
Silk Paper backed	30", 36"	5 yards	Single roll	Class A-25	Cellulose paste	Less durable
Textures (sand, etc.) Plastic coated Paper backed	3', 4'	5 yards	Single roll	Class A-25	Premixed vinyl nonstaining paste	Durable
Vinyl Cloth backed Paper backed Felt polyester Backed	27", 54"	Variable	Variable	Class A-25, 15 Class B-35	Vinyl adhesive	Durable
Wood veneer	Up to 24" flitch	12' flitch	Single flitch	Class A-25	Premixed adhesive	Durable
Substrate Indian/Bangladesh jute with a stainless jute backing	48"	5 yards	Single roll	Class A-15	Nonstaining and nonbleeding type that causes a crystallization and forms a bond	Very durable

NOTES
1. Large quantities are available in multiple rolls or continuous yardages.
2. Consult manufacturers concerning proper adhesive to be used for specific applications.

K. Shahid Rab, AIA; Friesen International; Washington, D.C.

FORMULA FOR COVERAGE

1. Determine number of panels required: total lineal feet of wall divided by width of fabric.
2. Find number of rolls required: number of full (floor to ceiling) panels per roll times number of panels required.
3. Window and door areas may be deducted, but only to the extent that no horizontal seaming occurs.

TYPICAL ROOM COVERAGE

ROOM SIZE (FT)	SINGLE ROLLS REQUIRED USING 30 SQ FT/ROLL			SINGLE ROLLS FOR CEILING
	8-FT CEILING	10-FT CEILING	12-FT CEILING	
9 x 12	11	14	17	4
12 x 14	14	17	21	6
14 x 16	16	20	24	8
16 x 18	18	22	27	10
18 x 20	21	25	30	12

NOTE: Deduct approximately two thirds of the roll for each door and window opening.

CLASSIFICATION OF VINYL WALL COVERINGS

Type I, Light Duty (7 oz/sq yd). For use on surfaces not subjected to abrasion or wear.

Type II, Medium Duty (13 oz/sq yd). For general use in areas of average traffic and scuffing.

TYPE III, Heavy Duty (22 oz/sq yd). For use as wainscot or wall protection for areas exposed to damage, or for decorative effect.

REGULAR FINISH (CLASS I) AND MILDEW RESISTANT FINISH (CLASS II)

Composition may be of three layers, the first being a supporting material of cotton cloth, nonwoven fiberglass, asbestos, or other suitable material. Supporting material for Class II must be mildew resistant. The second layer is a coating compound of specialized vinyl chloride resin which is laminated to the supporting material in a continuous film. This layer is embossed, color printed, or integrally pigmented. A clear coating may be added as a third layer if needed to meet the physical requirements noted in the specification.

AVAILABLE SIZES OF VINYL WALL COVERINGS

TYPE	PIECES PER ROLL	WIDTH PER ROLL	YARDAGE PER ROLL (3 YD LENGTH OR MULTIPLES)
Type I	1 piece	27", 54"	Not less than 72 sq ft plus 1 ft-tolerance
Type II	2 pieces	54"	Not less than 15 yd or more than 45 yd
Type III	4 pieces	54"	15 to 30 yd
	6 pieces		Over 30 yd

Manufacturers should be able to supply all information concerning specification requirements and test data on the covering's breaking strength, tear strength, hydrostatic resistance, abrasion resistance, flame resistance, char length, colorfastness to light, shrinkage, cold crack, blocking, heat aging, and crocking.

SUBSTRATE FABRICS

The material that lies between the wallcovering and the wall itself becomes a substrate which performs a wide variety of functions such as reducing noise, increasing flame retardancy, and allowing a smoother application of a wall covering over surfaces that are imperfect. Manufacturers can supply information on types of substrates they carry and the qualities of each.

THE GYPSUM SUBSTRATE consists of fabric impregnated with uncrystallized gypsum. The gypsum is formulated so that when it is applied to a substrate with an adhesive, it will crystallize and form a secure bond with the substrate. The fabric can be used in many cases as a finished surface over rough walls as well as a surface prepared for an additional covering.

PREFINISHED PANELS

MATERIAL TYPE	USE	THICKNESS									
		1/32	1/16	1/8	3/16	1/4	5/16	3/8	1/2	5/8	3/4
PLYWOOD											
Hardwood veneer	Cabinets, interior paneling, protective surfaces					●		●	●		●
Softwood veneer	Interior paneling					●		●	●	●	●
Printed/embossed	Interior paneling					●		●	●	●	●
Textured	Interior paneling, siding							●	●	●	●
Printed vinyl faced	Decorative interior finish							●	●	●	
HARDBOARD											
Standard	Interior use, cabinet liner			●	●	●	●	●	●		
Tempered	Interior and exterior use, underlayment where strength and wear count			●	●	●	●	●	●		
Plastic finished	Interior paneling, wearing surfaces			●		●		●		●	
Embossed factory finish	Interior decorative paneling				●	●					
FIBERBOARD											
Vinyl covered	Tackboard—interior decorative paneling								●		
Fabric covered	Acoustic, panels, tackboard								●		
LAMINATES											
Plastic laminates	Cabinets, countertops, protective wall finish	●	●	●							
Metal faced	Decorative paneling	●	●	●							
GYPSUM											
Vinyl covered	Interior walls					●		●	●	●	
Fabric covered	Interior walls					●			●	●	●

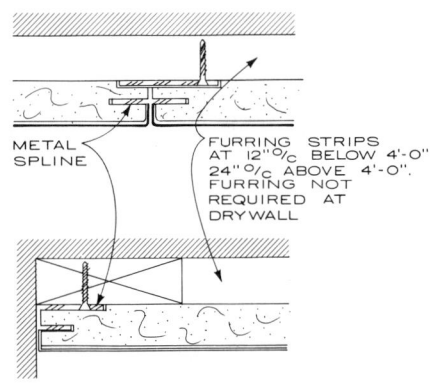

FABRIC COVERED FIBERBOARD

METAL SPLINE — FURRING STRIPS AT 12" O/C BELOW 4'-0" 24" O/C ABOVE 4'-0". FURRING NOT REQUIRED AT DRYWALL

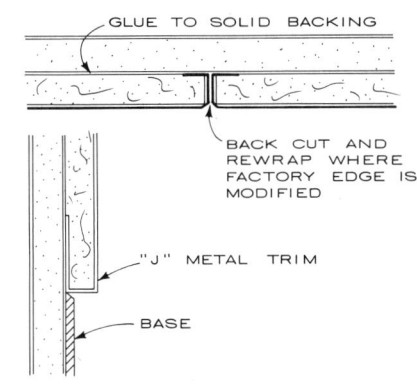

VINYL COVERED FIBERBOARD

GLUE TO SOLID BACKING — BACK CUT AND REWRAP WHERE FACTORY EDGE IS MODIFIED — "J" METAL TRIM — BASE

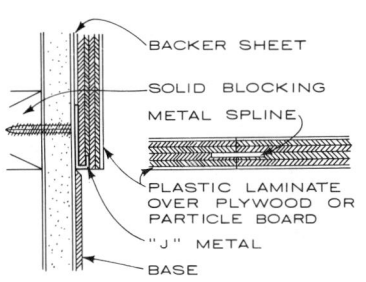

PLASTIC LAMINATE PANELS

BACKER SHEET — SOLID BLOCKING — METAL SPLINE — PLASTIC LAMINATE OVER PLYWOOD OR PARTICLE BOARD — "J" METAL — BASE

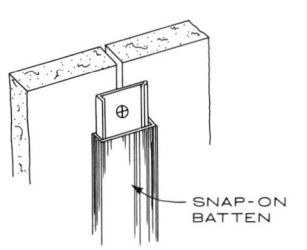

VINYL COVERED GYPSUM BOARD

SNAP-ON BATTEN

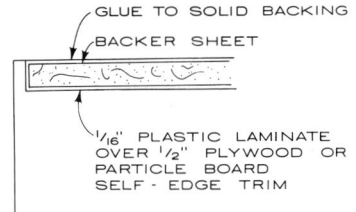

PLASTIC LAMINATE PANELS

GLUE TO SOLID BACKING — BACKER SHEET — 1/16" PLASTIC LAMINATE OVER 1/2" PLYWOOD OR PARTICLE BOARD SELF-EDGE TRIM

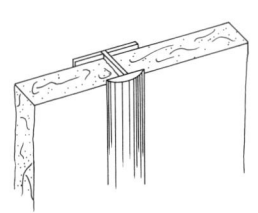

DIVIDER

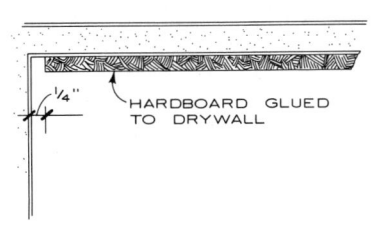

TEMPERED HARDBOARD

1/4" — HARDBOARD GLUED TO DRYWALL

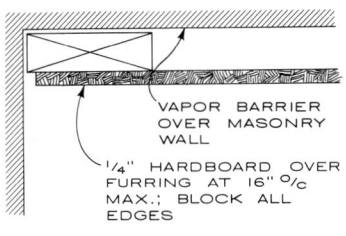

TEMPERED HARDBOARD

VAPOR BARRIER OVER MASONRY WALL — 1/4" HARDBOARD OVER FURRING AT 16" O/C MAX.; BLOCK ALL EDGES

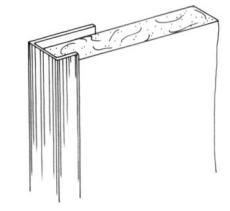

END CAP

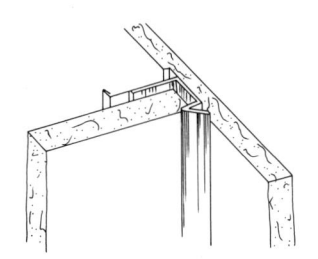

INSIDE CORNER TRIM

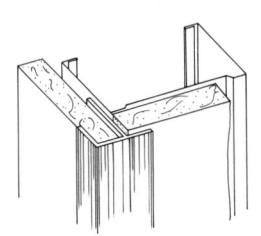

OUTSIDE CORNER TRIM

Broome, Oringdulph, O'Toole, Rudolf & Associates; Portland, Oregon

WALL COVERINGS

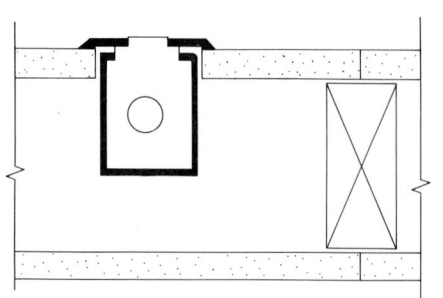

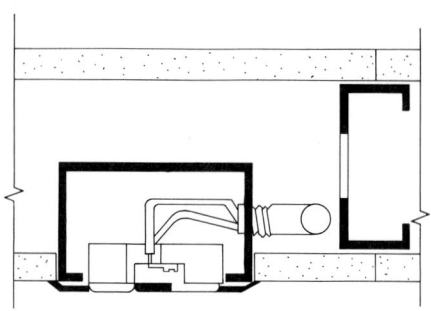

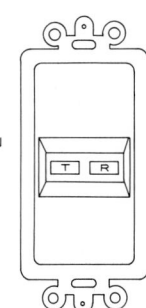

CAN REPLACE A DUPLEX RECEPTACLE IN ANY STANDARD OUTLET BOX. INSTALL AS FIRST RECEPTACLE FROM PANEL OR FUSE BOX TO PROVIDE GROUND FAULT PROTECTION TO CIRCUIT

ALTERNATE: USE GROUND FAULT CIRCUIT BREAKER IN PANEL

PLANS OF SWITCH BOXES

GROUP FAULT CIRCUIT INTERRUPTER

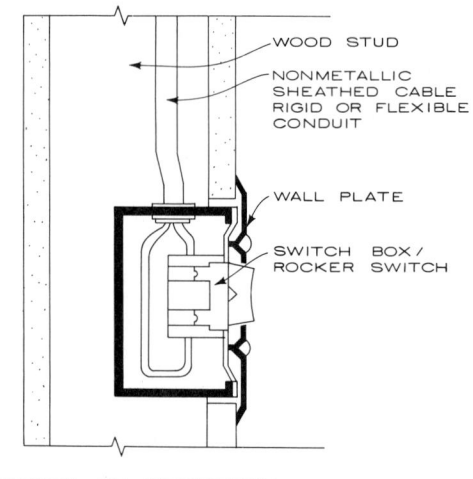

WOOD STUD

NONMETALLIC SHEATHED CABLE RIGID OR FLEXIBLE CONDUIT

WALL PLATE

SWITCH BOX / ROCKER SWITCH

SECTION OF SWITCHBOX

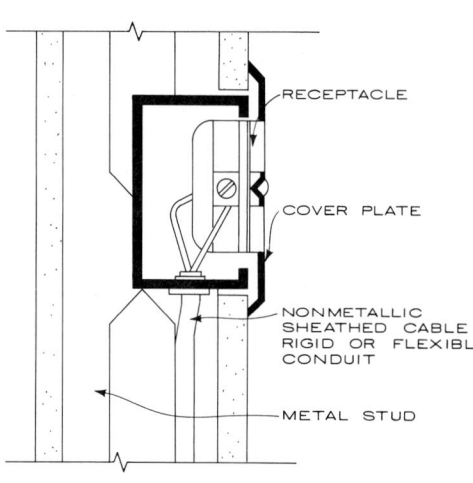

RECEPTACLE

COVER PLATE

NONMETALLIC SHEATHED CABLE RIGID OR FLEXIBLE CONDUIT

METAL STUD

SECTION OF RECEPTACLE

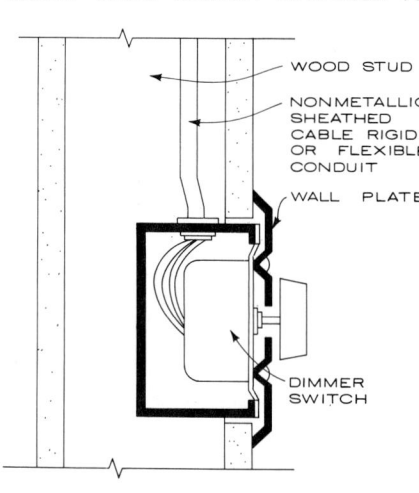

WOOD STUD

NONMETALLIC SHEATHED CABLE RIGID OR FLEXIBLE CONDUIT

WALL PLATE

DIMMER SWITCH

SECTION OF DIMMER SWITCH

ELECTRICAL WORK IN SINGLE LAYER DRYWALL-WOOD STUD AND METAL STUD PARTITIONS

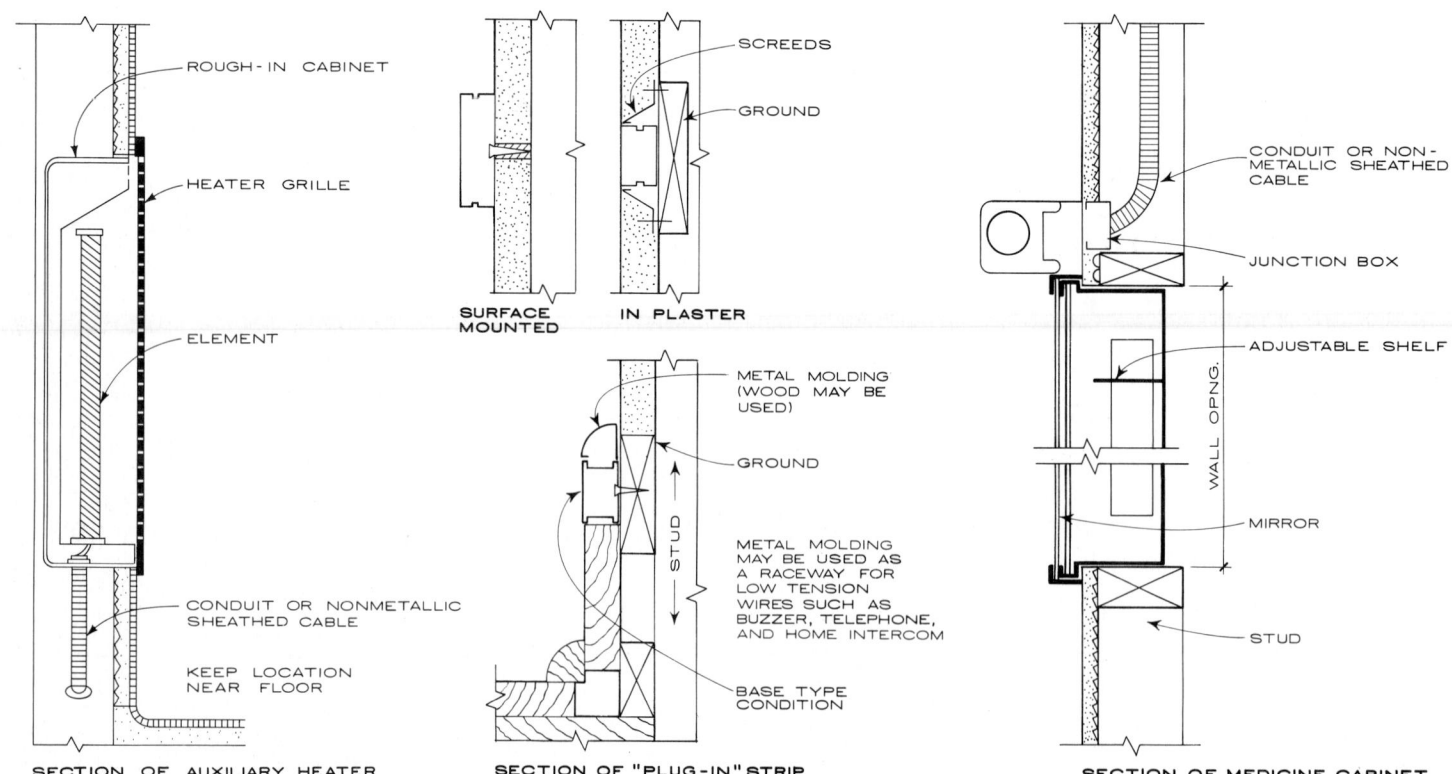

ROUGH-IN CABINET

HEATER GRILLE

ELEMENT

CONDUIT OR NONMETALLIC SHEATHED CABLE

KEEP LOCATION NEAR FLOOR

SECTION OF AUXILIARY HEATER

SCREEDS

GROUND

SURFACE MOUNTED   **IN PLASTER**

METAL MOLDING (WOOD MAY BE USED)

GROUND

STUD

METAL MOLDING MAY BE USED AS A RACEWAY FOR LOW TENSION WIRES SUCH AS BUZZER, TELEPHONE, AND HOME INTERCOM

BASE TYPE CONDITION

SECTION OF "PLUG-IN" STRIP

CONDUIT OR NON-METALLIC SHEATHED CABLE

JUNCTION BOX

ADJUSTABLE SHELF

WALL OPNG.

MIRROR

STUD

SECTION OF MEDICINE CABINET

ELECTRICAL WORK IN BUILT-IN EQUIPMENT

Walter H. Sobel, FAIA & Associates; Chicago, Illinois

B. J. Baldwin; Giffels & Rossetti, Inc.; Detroit, Michigan

 WALL COVERINGS

CHAPTER 10 SPECIALTIES

TACKBOARD TYPES AND SIZES

TYPE	VARIATIONS	BACKING	THICKNESS	MAXIMUM SIZE WITHOUT JOINTS	COLORS
Cork	Unfaced cork, plain or burlap backed	Unmounted	1/8″, 1/4″	4′ x 130′, 6′ x 90′	Natural, tan, brown, green, blue, gray, black
		Particle board	1/2″	4′ x 16′	
		Hardboard			
	Vinyl covered cork	Unmounted	1/4″	4′ x 100′	Many
		Particle board	1/2″	4′ x 16′	
		Hardboard		4′ x 12′ fire rated	
	Vinyl impregnated cork	Unmounted	1/8″, 1/4″	6′ x 90′	Tan, brown, green, blue, gray, black
		Hardboard	1/2″	4′ x 12′	
Fiberboard	Vinyl covered fiberboard		1/2″	4′ x 12′	Many
	Burlap covered fiberboard			4′ x 8′, 4′ x 14′ spec.	Natural

CHALKBOARD TYPES AND SIZES

TYPE	CORE	THICKNESS	MAXIMUM SIZE WITHOUT JOINTS	COLORS
Porcelain enamel steel (18-28 gauge)*	None	1/32″	4′ x 12′	12 chalkboard
	Plywood	1/4″-7/16″	4′ x 12′	7 liquid marker
	Hardboard	1/4″, 7/16″	5′ x 12′, 4′ x 16′	
	Fiberboard	7/16″, 1/2″	4′ x 12′	
	Particle board	3/8″-1/2″	4′ x 16′	
	Gypsum board	3/8″, 1/2″	4′ x 12′	
	Honeycomb	3/8″, 7/16″	4′ x 16′	
Painted-on composition*	Hardboard	1/4″, 1/2″	4′ x 16′	7
	Cement asbestos	3/16″, 1/4″	4′ x 8′	
	Gypsum board	1/4″, 1/2″	4′ x 12′	
Natural slate		1/4″-3/8″	4′ x 6′	Black only

*Available in either chalkboard or liquid marker board.

AVERAGE RECOMMENDED CHALKBOARD MOUNTING HEIGHT
(Chalkrail to Floor)

Nursery	20″
Kindergarten	24″
1st–3rd grade	30″
4th–6th grade	32″
Junior high	36″
Senior high	36″
Adult	36″

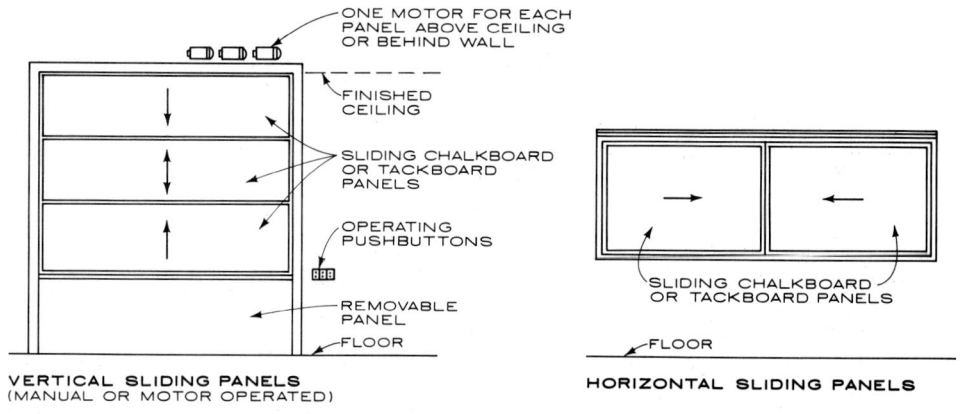

SLIDING CHALKBOARDS AND TACKBOARDS

ONE MOTOR FOR EACH PANEL ABOVE CEILING OR BEHIND WALL
FINISHED CEILING
SLIDING CHALKBOARD OR TACKBOARD PANELS
OPERATING PUSHBUTTONS
REMOVABLE PANEL
FLOOR
VERTICAL SLIDING PANELS
(MANUAL OR MOTOR OPERATED)

SLIDING CHALKBOARD OR TACKBOARD PANELS
FLOOR
HORIZONTAL SLIDING PANELS

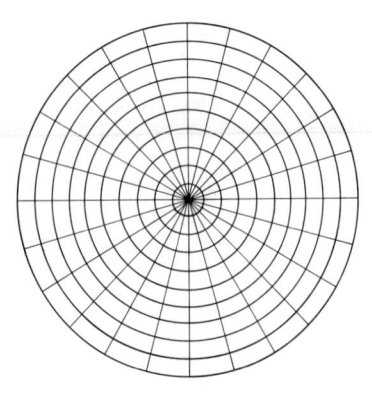

NOTE
Some of the special designs available are grids, polar coordinates, music staff, football field layout, basketball court layout, and ledger page.

SPECIAL PURPOSE CHALKBOARDS

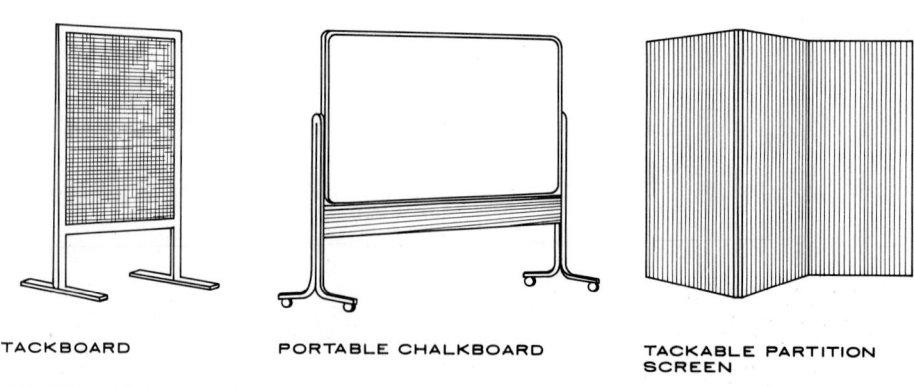

TACKBOARD   **PORTABLE CHALKBOARD**   **TACKABLE PARTITION SCREEN**

FREESTANDING CHALKBOARDS AND TACKING SURFACES

Broome, Oringdulph, O'Toole, Rudolf & Associates; Portland, Oregon

CHALKBOARDS AND TACKBOARDS

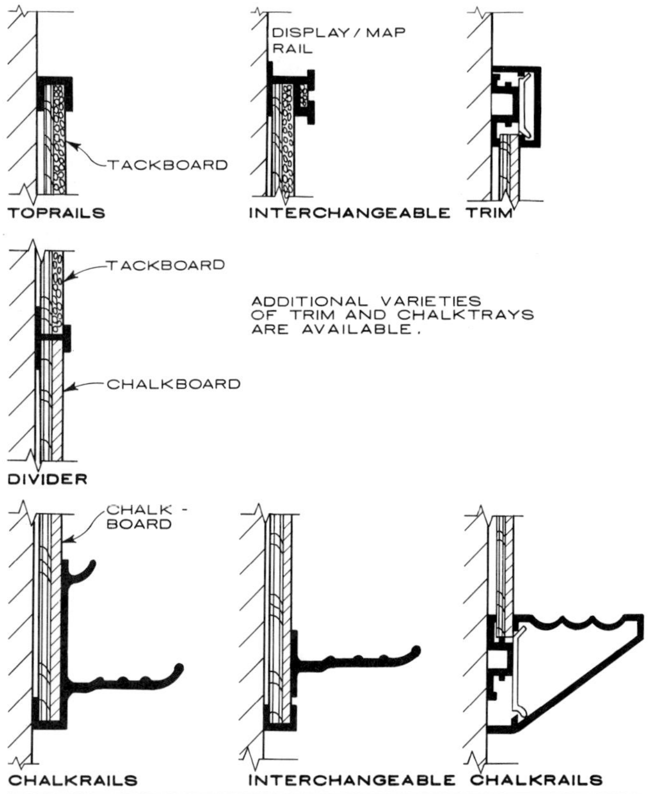

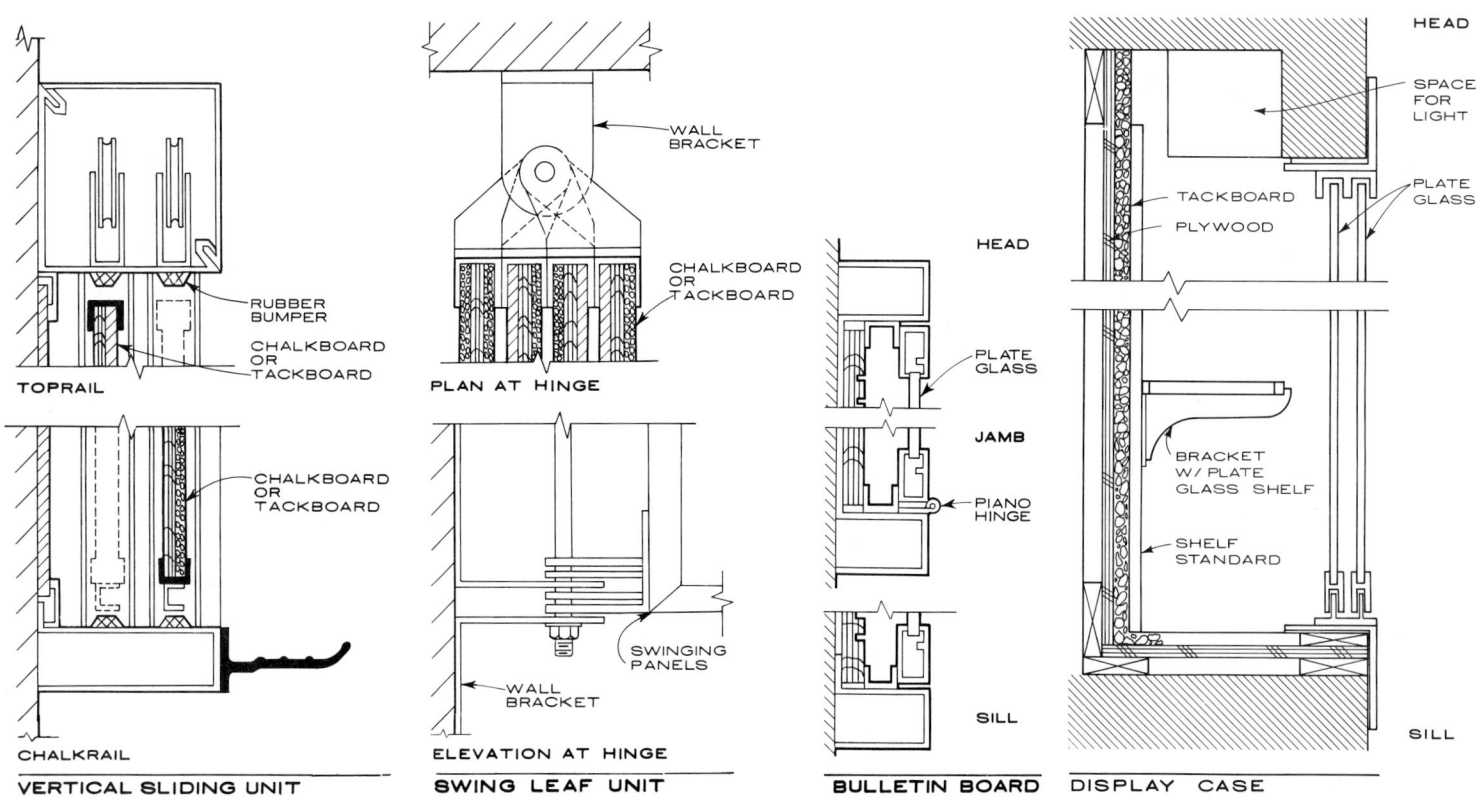

CHALKBOARDS WITH ALUMINUM FRAMING

Note: Additional types of trim and chalktrays available.

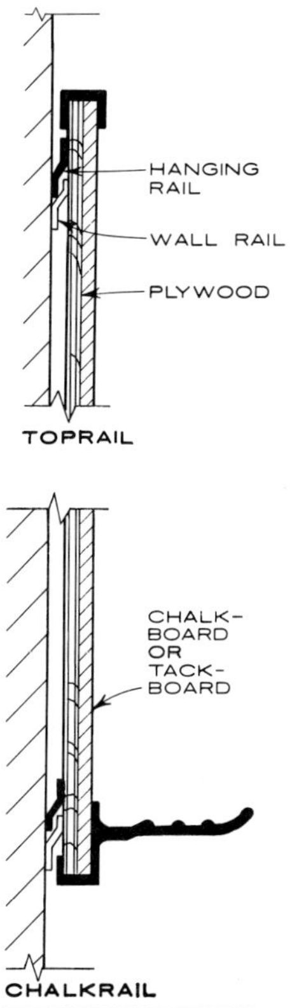

TOPRAILS — TACKBOARD

INTERCHANGEABLE TRIM — DISPLAY/MAP RAIL

DIVIDER — TACKBOARD — CHALKBOARD

ADDITIONAL VARIETIES OF TRIM AND CHALKTRAYS ARE AVAILABLE.

CHALKRAILS — CHALK-BOARD

INTERCHANGEABLE CHALKRAILS

TOPRAIL — HANGING RAIL — WALL RAIL — PLYWOOD

CHALKRAIL — CHALK-BOARD OR TACK-BOARD

PORTABLE CHALKBOARD PANELS

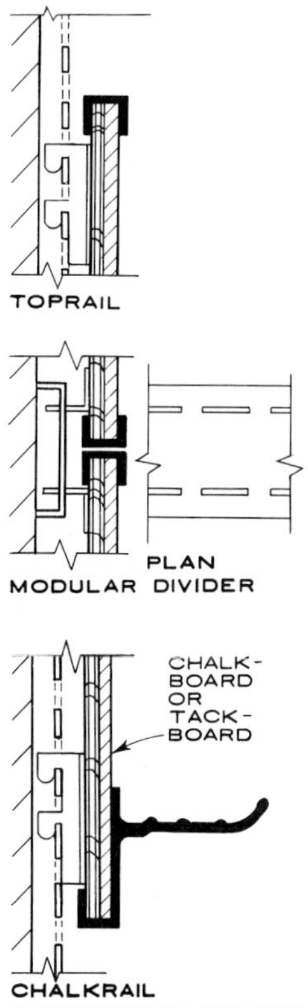

TOPRAIL

PLAN MODULAR DIVIDER

CHALKRAIL — CHALK-BOARD OR TACK-BOARD

MODULAR UNIT

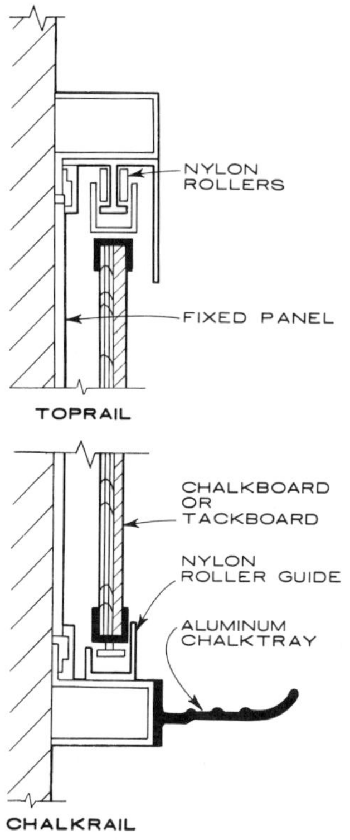

TOPRAIL — NYLON ROLLERS — FIXED PANEL

CHALKRAIL — CHALKBOARD OR TACKBOARD — NYLON ROLLER GUIDE — ALUMINUM CHALKTRAY

HORIZONTAL SLID'G UNIT

TOPRAIL — RUBBER BUMPER — CHALKBOARD OR TACKBOARD

CHALKRAIL — CHALKBOARD OR TACKBOARD

VERTICAL SLIDING UNIT

NOTE: May be motor operated.

PLAN AT HINGE — WALL BRACKET — CHALKBOARD OR TACKBOARD

ELEVATION AT HINGE — SWINGING PANELS — WALL BRACKET

SWING LEAF UNIT

HEAD — PLATE GLASS

JAMB — PIANO HINGE

SILL

BULLETIN BOARD

NOTE: May be recessed.

HEAD — SPACE FOR LIGHT — TACKBOARD — PLYWOOD — PLATE GLASS — BRACKET W/ PLATE GLASS SHELF — SHELF STANDARD

SILL

DISPLAY CASE

Rex Whitaker Allen and Associates, San Francisco, California

Broome, Oringdulph, O'Toole, Rudolf & Associates; Portland, Oregon

CHALKBOARDS AND TACKBOARDS **10**

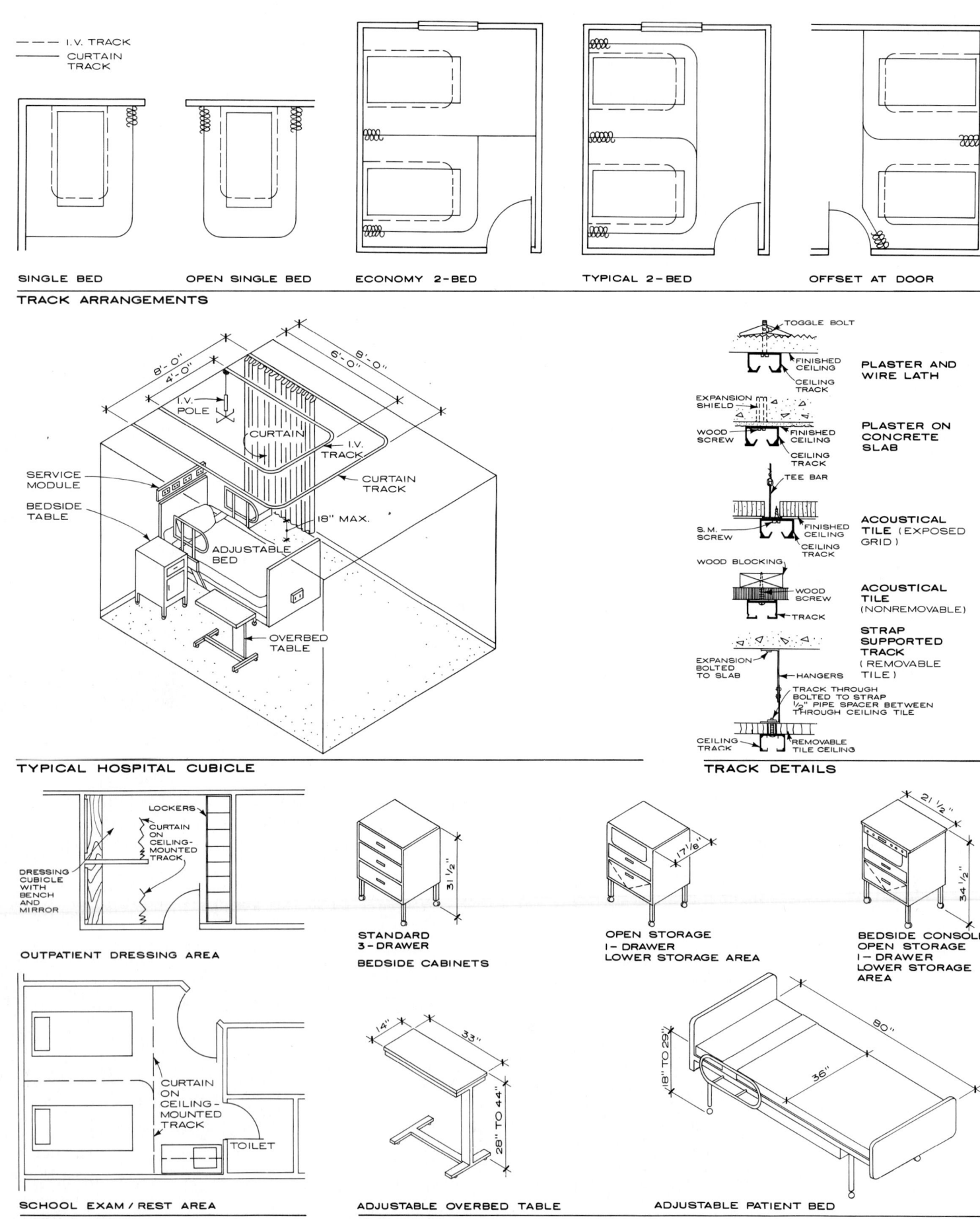

I.V. TRACK
CURTAIN TRACK

SINGLE BED   OPEN SINGLE BED   ECONOMY 2-BED   TYPICAL 2-BED   OFFSET AT DOOR

TRACK ARRANGEMENTS

8'-0"
4'-0"
6'-0"
8'-0"
I.V. POLE
CURTAIN
I.V. TRACK
SERVICE MODULE
BEDSIDE TABLE
CURTAIN TRACK
18" MAX.
ADJUSTABLE BED
OVERBED TABLE

TYPICAL HOSPITAL CUBICLE

TOGGLE BOLT
FINISHED CEILING
CEILING TRACK
PLASTER AND WIRE LATH

EXPANSION SHIELD
WOOD SCREW
FINISHED CEILING
CEILING TRACK
PLASTER ON CONCRETE SLAB

TEE BAR
S. M. SCREW
FINISHED CEILING
CEILING TRACK
ACOUSTICAL TILE (EXPOSED GRID)

WOOD BLOCKING
WOOD SCREW
TRACK
ACOUSTICAL TILE (NONREMOVABLE)

EXPANSION BOLTED TO SLAB
HANGERS
TRACK THROUGH BOLTED TO STRAP 1/2" PIPE SPACER BETWEEN THROUGH CEILING TILE
CEILING TRACK
REMOVABLE TILE CEILING
STRAP SUPPORTED TRACK (REMOVABLE TILE)

TRACK DETAILS

LOCKERS
CURTAIN ON CEILING-MOUNTED TRACK
DRESSING CUBICLE WITH BENCH AND MIRROR

OUTPATIENT DRESSING AREA

31 1/2"
STANDARD 3-DRAWER
BEDSIDE CABINETS

17 1/8"
OPEN STORAGE 1-DRAWER LOWER STORAGE AREA

21 1/2"
34 1/2"
BEDSIDE CONSOLE OPEN STORAGE 1-DRAWER LOWER STORAGE AREA

CURTAIN ON CEILING-MOUNTED TRACK
TOILET

SCHOOL EXAM / REST AREA

14"
33"
28" TO 44"
ADJUSTABLE OVERBED TABLE

80"
18" TO 29"
36"
ADJUSTABLE PATIENT BED

APPLICATIONS   **FURNITURE**

Liz Karp; The Architects Collaborative, Inc.; Cambridge, Massachusetts

10 **COMPARTMENTS AND CUBICLES**

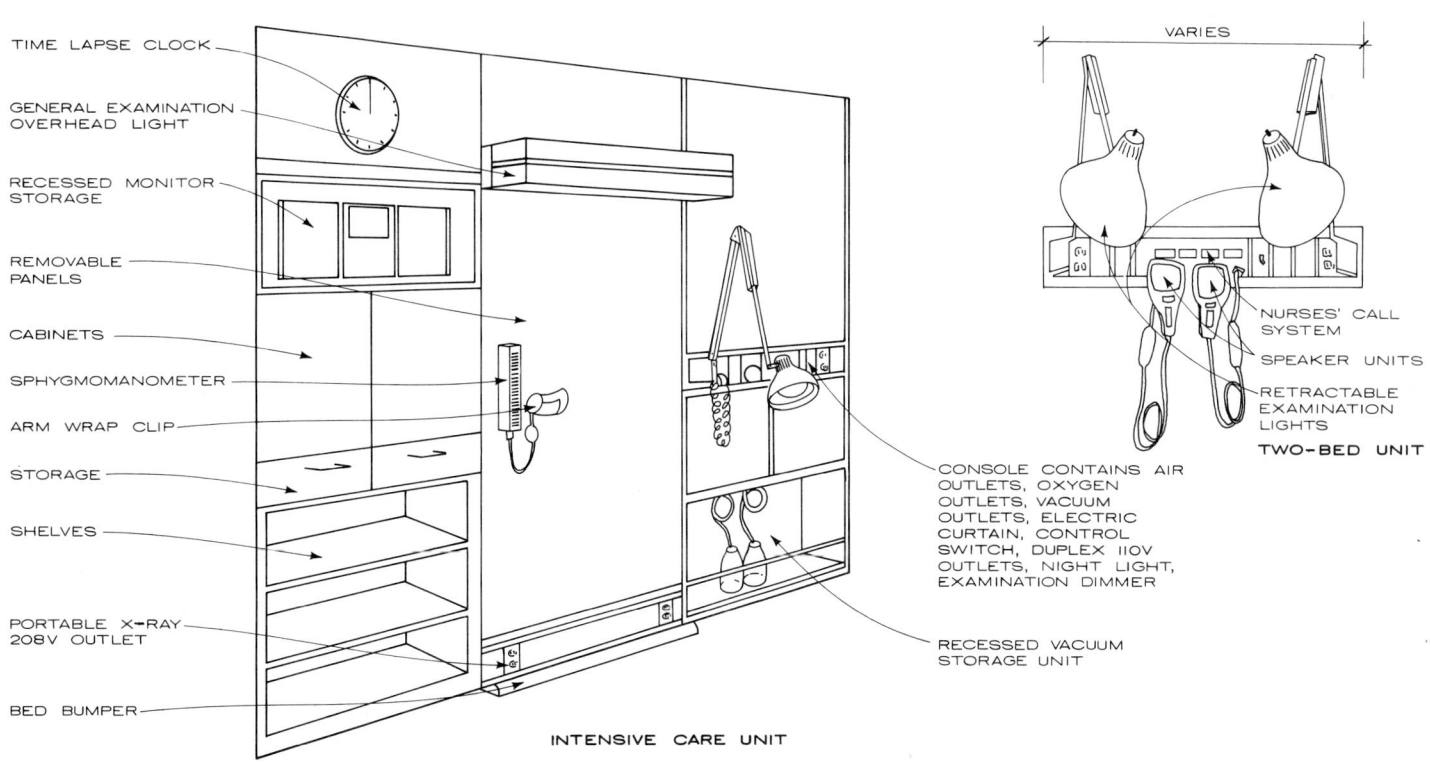

TIME LAPSE CLOCK

GENERAL EXAMINATION OVERHEAD LIGHT

RECESSED MONITOR STORAGE

REMOVABLE PANELS

CABINETS

SPHYGMOMANOMETER

ARM WRAP CLIP

STORAGE

SHELVES

PORTABLE X-RAY 208V OUTLET

BED BUMPER

CONSOLE CONTAINS AIR OUTLETS, OXYGEN OUTLETS, VACUUM OUTLETS, ELECTRIC CURTAIN, CONTROL SWITCH, DUPLEX 110V OUTLETS, NIGHT LIGHT, EXAMINATION DIMMER

RECESSED VACUUM STORAGE UNIT

INTENSIVE CARE UNIT

VARIES

NURSES' CALL SYSTEM

SPEAKER UNITS

RETRACTABLE EXAMINATION LIGHTS

TWO-BED UNIT

HOSPITAL SERVICE MODULES

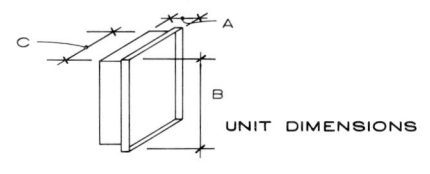

UNIT DIMENSIONS

UNIT	A	B	C
Fire hose cabinet	10″	30″	30″
Fire extinguisher	10″	30″	14″
Fountain	10″	30″	14″
Waste receptacle	7″	30″	14″
Louvers	11″	30″	14″
Speaker	3″	15″	15″
Clock	3″	15″	15″
Fire pull	7″	14″	6″
Electric outlet	3″	30″	6″

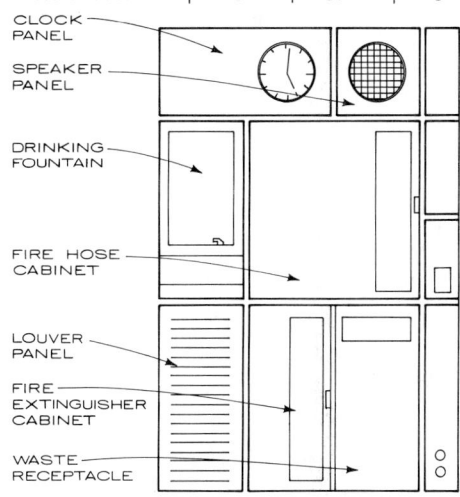

CLOCK PANEL

SPEAKER PANEL

DRINKING FOUNTAIN

FIRE HOSE CABINET

LOUVER PANEL

FIRE EXTINGUISHER CABINET

WASTE RECEPTACLE

CORRIDOR SERVICE MODULE

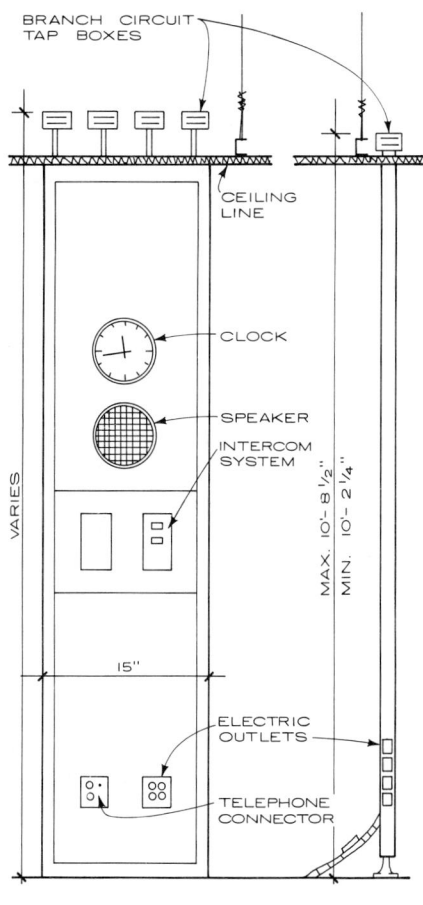

BRANCH CIRCUIT TAP BOXES

CEILING LINE

CLOCK

SPEAKER

INTERCOM SYSTEM

VARIES

MAX. 10′-8½″

MIN. 10′-2¼″

15″

ELECTRIC OUTLETS

TELEPHONE CONNECTOR

COMMUNICATION AND POWER COLUMNS

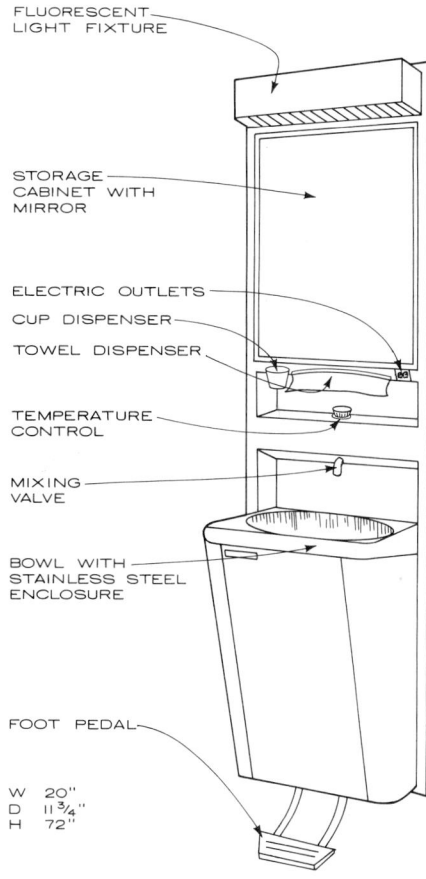

FLUORESCENT LIGHT FIXTURE

STORAGE CABINET WITH MIRROR

ELECTRIC OUTLETS

CUP DISPENSER

TOWEL DISPENSER

TEMPERATURE CONTROL

MIXING VALVE

BOWL WITH STAINLESS STEEL ENCLOSURE

FOOT PEDAL

W 20″
D 11¾″
H 72″

WASH CENTER

John Sava; The Architects Collaborative, Inc.; Cambridge, Massachusetts

COMPARTMENTS AND CUBICLES   **10**

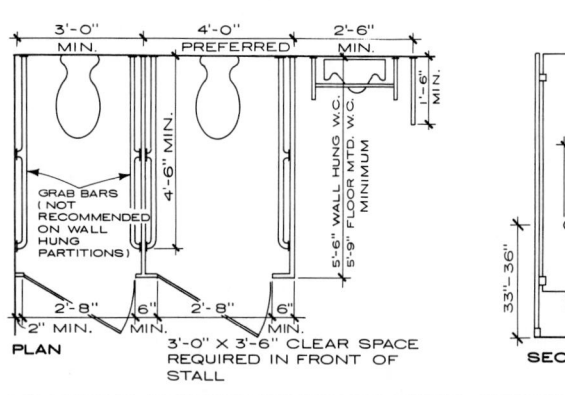
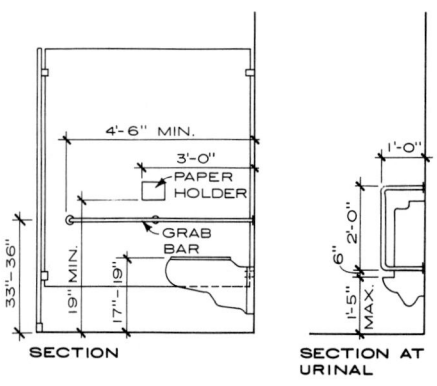
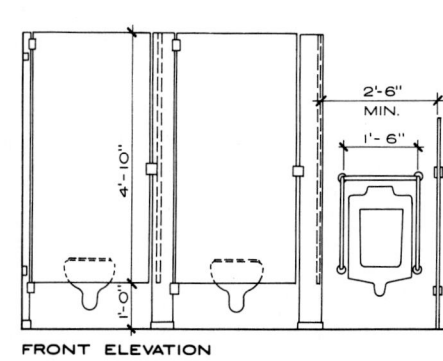

HANDICAPPED TOILET LAYOUT

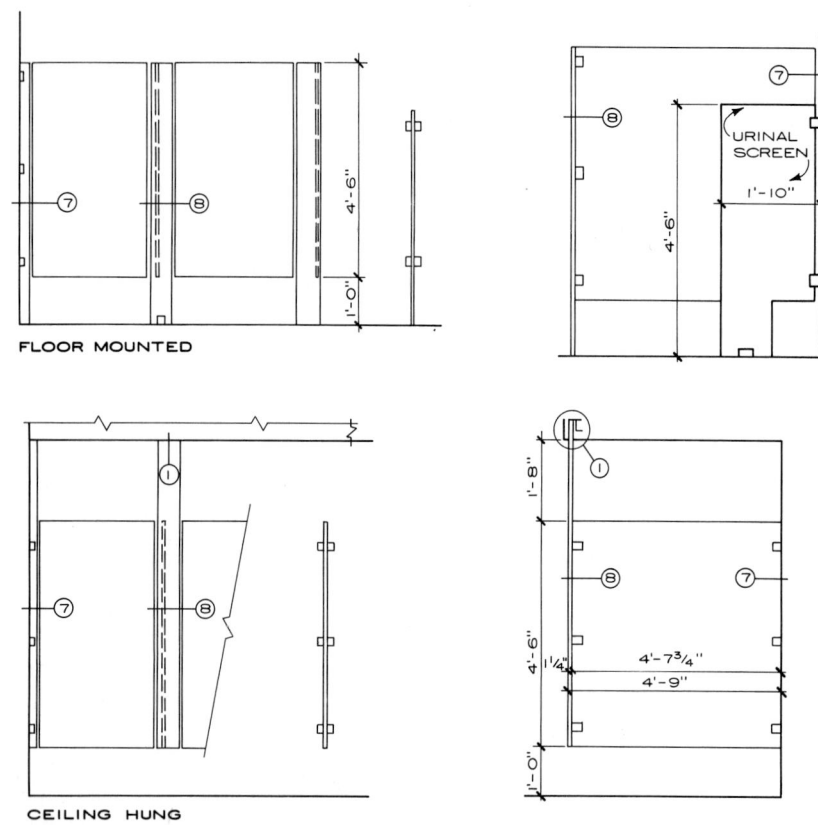

MARBLE TOILET PARTITIONS

MARBLE TOILET PARTITIONS

Marble toilet partitions are precast, predrilled, and prefinished and are delivered to the site ready to install. Partitions are available in floor mounted or ceiling hung styles. Floor mounted units are set on dowels cast into the finish floor. Ceiling hung units are bolted to overhead channel supports.

Marble toilet partitions are available in polished finish only. Panel thickness ranges from 7/8 to 1 1/4 in., height to 4 ft 6 in., and widths from 1 ft 10 in. to 3 ft. Black, buff, gray, green, pink, and white colors are standard. Marble partitions are provided with either solid core flush wood doors or 22 gauge hollow core steel doors.

Nonstaining, waterproof sealants are recommended for marble work.

Toilet partition hardware is usually made of brass and is chrome plated for exposed applications. Custom accessories such as shelves, coat hooks, and paper holders may be ordered with marble panels.

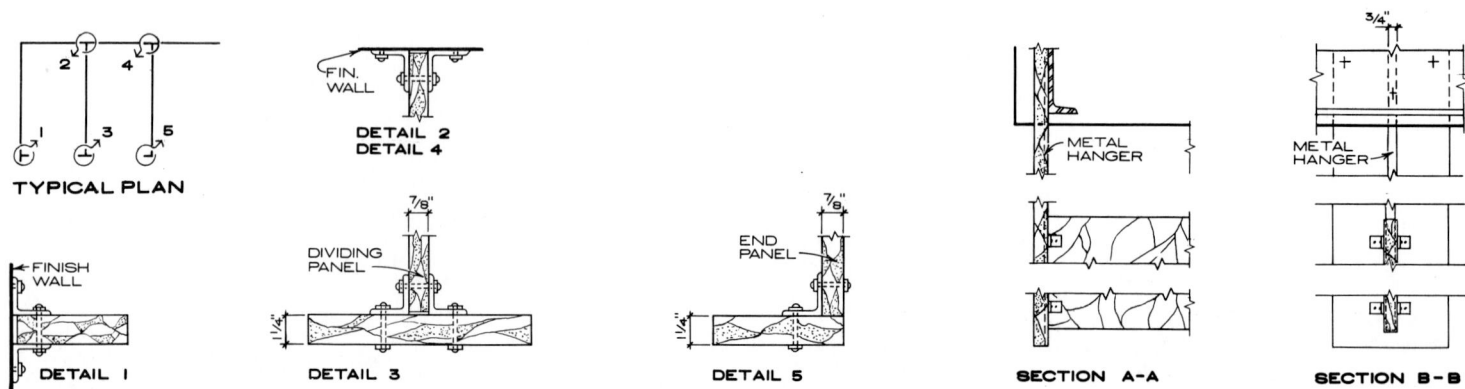

MARBLE PARTITION DETAILS

Pearce Corporation; St. Louis, Missouri

COMPARTMENTS AND CUBICLES

GENERAL NOTES

1. Compartment types: ceiling hung (marble or metal), overhead braced, wall hung (metal only).
2. Metal finishes: baked-on enamel, porcelain enamel, stainless steel.
3. A = standard compartment widths: 2'-6", 2'-8", 2'-10", 3'-0" (2'-10" is most frequently used).
4. B = standard door widths: 1'-8", 1'-10", 2'-0", 2'-2", 2'-4", 2'-6". (2'-0" metal doors are standard with marble compartments.) Nonstandard sizes that are sometimes used: 1'-11", 2'-3", 2'-5".
5. C = standard pilaster widths: 3", 4", 5", 6", 8", 10", 1'-0". Nonstandard sizes that are sometimes used: 2", 7", 1'-2".
6. D = standard panel widths: 18" to 57" in 1" increments. All panels are 58" high.

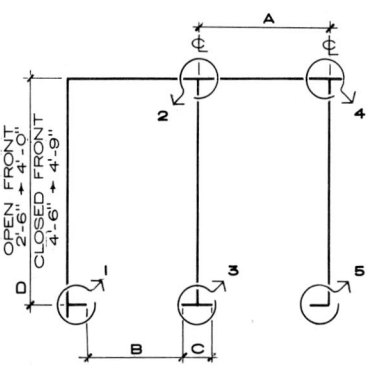

PLAN OF STANDARD W.C. COMPARTMENT
(TYPICAL FOR METAL OR PLASTIC LAMINATE)

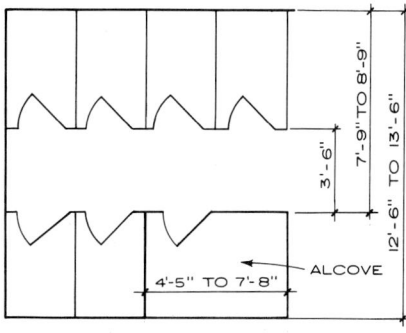

SPACE REQUIREMENTS

GENERAL PLANNING DATA

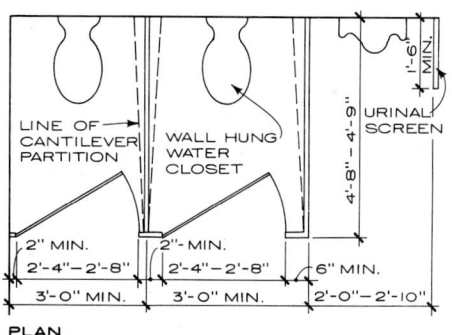

PLAN

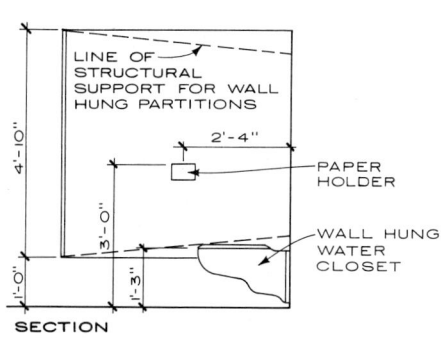

SECTION

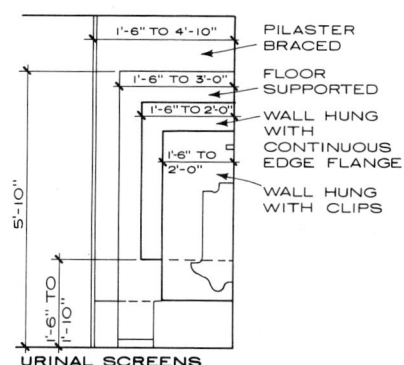

URINAL SCREENS

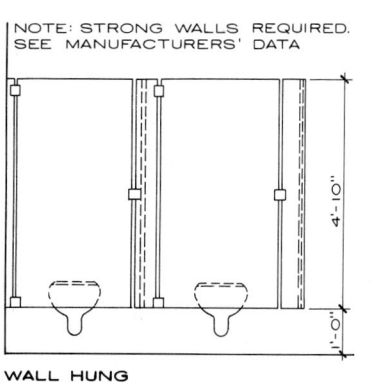

FLOOR MOUNTED

WALL HUNG

NOTE: STRONG WALLS REQUIRED. SEE MANUFACTURERS' DATA

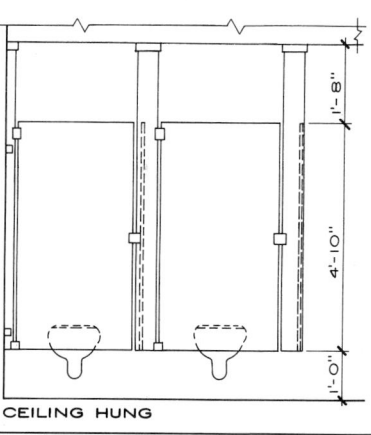

CEILING HUNG

METAL AND PLASTIC LAMINATE PARTITIONS

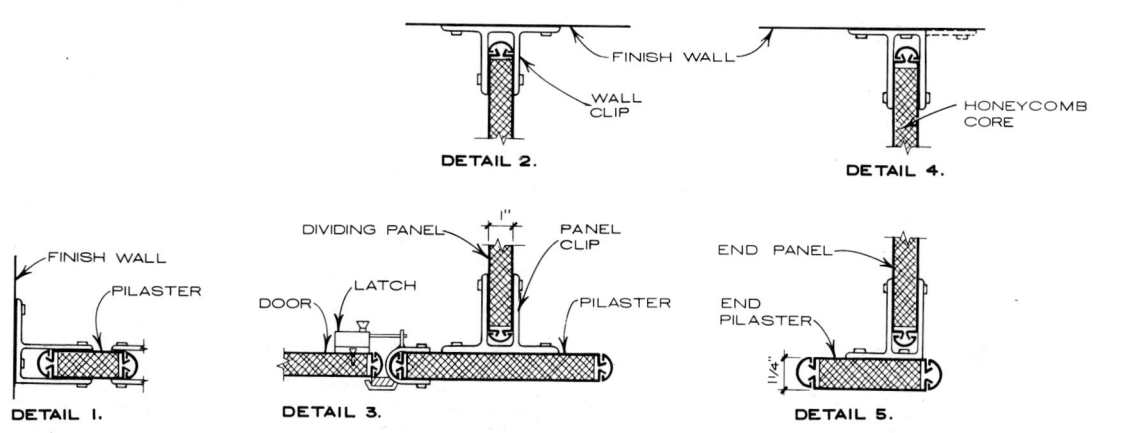

DETAIL 2.

DETAIL 4.

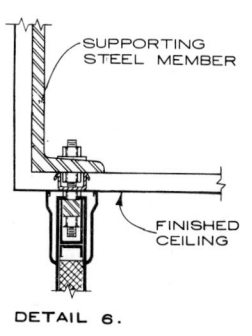

DETAIL 6.

SEE MANUFACTURERS' LITERATURE FOR ADDITIONAL CEILING HUNG ENCLOSURE DETAILS

DETAIL I.

DETAIL 3.

DETAIL 5.

METAL PARTITION DETAILS

Pearce Corporation; St. Louis, Missouri

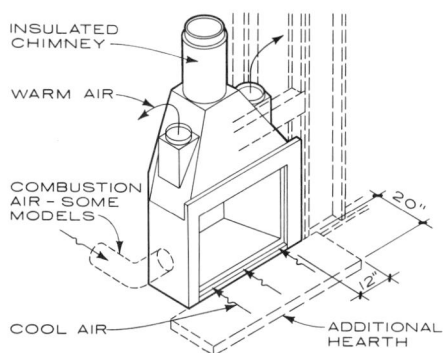

ZERO CLEARANCE FIREPLACE BUILT INTO COMBUSTIBLE WALL – OPTIONS

1. Outside combustion air ducts.
2. Warm air circulation.
3. Firebox size range 28 to 42 in.
4. Corner models (open side and end).

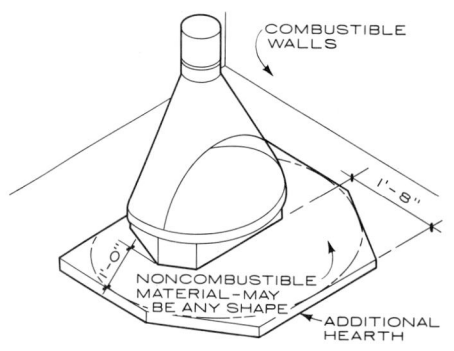

FREESTANDING, OPEN HEARTH – OPTIONS

1. Outside combustion air ducts (through base).
2. Warm air circulation.
3. Variety of shapes and sizes.
4. Decorative exposed chimney.

NOTE
All open hearth fireplaces require noncombustible hearth extending 20 in. forward from firebox, 12 in. each side.

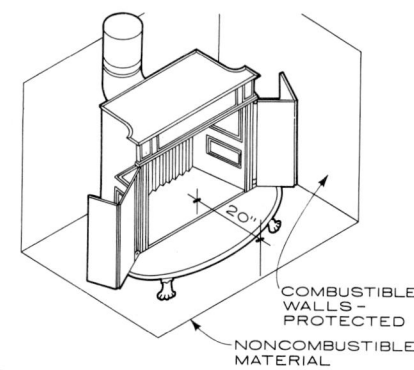

FRANKLIN STOVE – OPTIONS

1. Top or back flue thimble location.
2. Back shield for reduced wall clearance.
3. Decorative accessories.
4. Functional accessories.

OPEN HEARTH

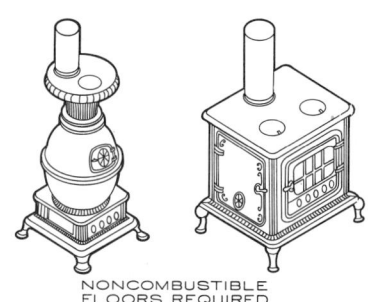

PARLOR STOVE – OPTIONS

1. Wide variety of shapes and sizes.
2. Most have functional tops.
3. Variety of fender shapes.

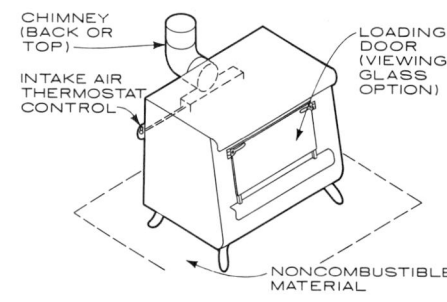

"AIRTIGHT" HEATER – OPTIONS

1. Wide variety of shapes.
2. Front or side loading.
3. Manual or thermostatic combustion air control.
4. Glass fronts.

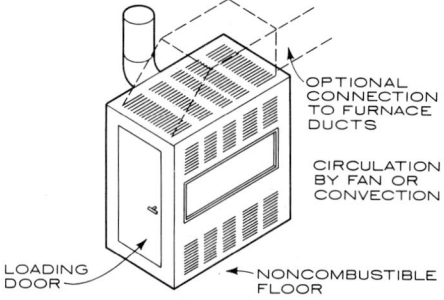

WOOD BURNING HEATER – OPTIONS

1. Manual or thermostatic combustion air control.
2. Limited variety in size.
3. Ducted models may be connected to forced air duct system from standard furnace.

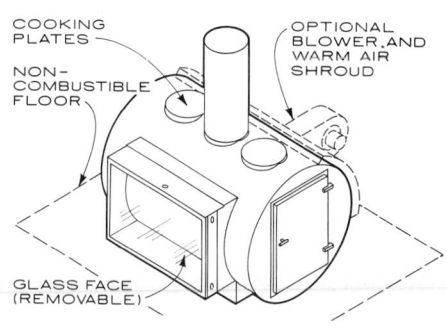

COOKING FIREPLACE

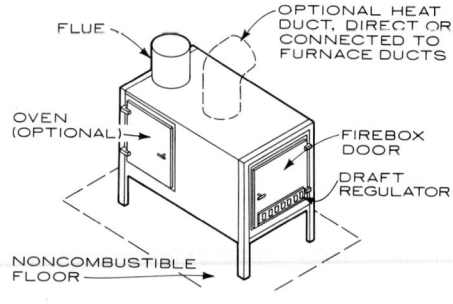

BARREL TYPE WOOD HEATER

BOX TYPE WOOD HEATER

STOVE

CHIMNEYS

1. Factory fabricated metal.
2. Double or triple wall.
3. Flue diameter 6 to 14 in.

CONSTRUCTION OPTIONS

1. Stainless steel flue.
2. Air chambered between walls.
3. Insulated between walls.

ACCESSORY OPTIONS

1. Decorator color chimneys.
2. Elbows, collars, caps, flanges.
3. Simulated brick roof jacks.

FLUE CLEARANCES AND INSTALLATION

All flues must extend through and above roof and must have 2 in. or more clearance to combustible material, according to manufacturer's listing. Flues may be connected to masonry chimneys suitable for solid fuel appliances. Flues passing through floors, ceiling, roof, or walls must have ventilated, noncombustible (metal) spacer fittings and must be anchored to structure at each passage. At least one passage must also support chimney.

REQUIRED CLEARANCES TO COMBUSTIBLE MATERIALS

These distances may be reduced, provided that heat baffles, insulation, noncombustible materials, or combinations of these are provided to protect combustible materials. Check local ordinances and manufacturer's listing for variations.

PREFABRICATED FIREPLACES

FIREPLACE	SIDES	BACK	FRONT	TOP	CONNECTOR
Zero clearance fireplace	0''–2''	0''–2''	44''	0''–2''	2''–18''
Freestanding fireplace	36''	36''	48''	36''	15''
Franklin stove	36''	36''	36''	36''	18''
Parlor stove	36''	36''	36''	36''	18''
"Airtight" heater	36''	36''	36''	36''	18''
Wood heater—radiant	36''	36''	36''	36''	18''
Wood heater—circulating	12''	12''	24''	36''	18''

Ralph D. Provencal, AIA; Olympia, Washington

FIREPLACES AND STOVES

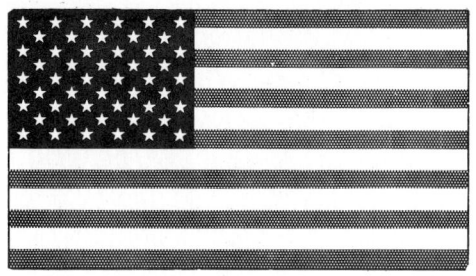

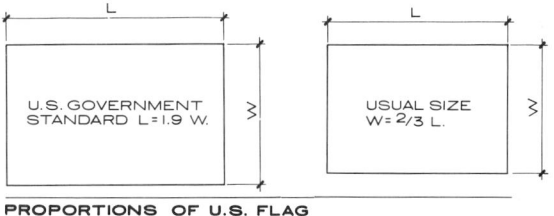

PROPORTIONS OF U.S. FLAG

U.S. GOVERNMENT STANDARD L = 1.9 W.

USUAL SIZE W = 2/3 L.

SIDE TYPE   CORNER TYPE

POLE   POLE

BRACES

POLE   POLE

PARAPET

BRACING PLAN FOR POLE ON ROOF

U.S. FLAG SIZES AS MANUFACTURED AND USED

WIDTH	LENGTH	WIDTH	LENGTH
3'–0''	5'–0''	10'–0''	18'–0''
4'–0''	6'–0''	10'–0''	19'–0''
4'–4''	5'–6''	12'–0''	20'–0''
5'–0''	8'–0''	15'–0''	25'–0''
5'–0''	9'–6''	20'–0''	30'–0''
6'–0''	10'–0''	20'–0''	38'–0''
8'–0''	12'–0''	26'–0''	45'–0''
10'–0''	15'–0''		

FROM 5'' DIAM. ON 20'–0'' POLE TO 14'' DIAM. ON 125'–0'' POLE

BALL

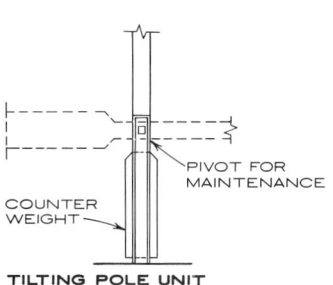

PIVOT FOR MAINTENANCE

COUNTER WEIGHT

TILTING POLE UNIT

* 1/4 LENGTH OF POLE

POLE ON GROUND

3/8 TO 1/2 LENGTH OF POLE

* 45° OR MORE

NOTE
Outrigger poles require bracing for lengths over 13'–0'', and are available in entasis tapered shapes of bronze, aluminum and stainless steel.

OUTRIGGER POLES FOR FLAGS ON BUILDING FRONTS

* 1/3 LENGTH OF POLE

FOR FLAGS ON ROOFS

SIZE OF FLAG IN RELATION TO POLE HEIGHT

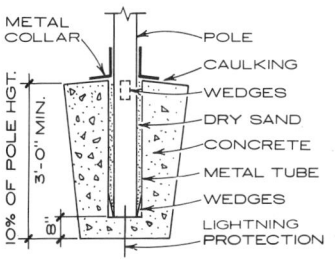

METAL COLLAR

POLE

CAULKING

WEDGES

DRY SAND

CONCRETE

METAL TUBE

WEDGES

LIGHTNING PROTECTION

10% OF POLE HGT. — 3'–0'' MIN.

8''

FOUNDATION FOR GROUND SET POLE

RECOMMENDED FLAG SIZES

POLE	FLAG SIZE	POLE	FLAG SIZE
15'–0''	3'–0'' x 5'–0''	50'–0''	8'–0'' x 12'–0''
20'–0''	4'–0'' x 6'–0''	60'–0''	8'–0'' x 12'–0''
25'–0''	4'–0'' x 6'–0''	65'–0''	9'–0'' x 15'–0''
30'–0''	5'–0'' x 8'–0''	70'–0''	9'–0'' x 15'–0''
35'–0''	5'–0'' x 8'–0''	80'–0''	10'–0'' x 15'–0''
40'–0''	6'–0'' x 10'–0''	90'–0''	10'–0'' x 15'–0''
45'–0''	6'–0'' x 10'–0''	100'–0''	12'–0'' x 18'–0''

*For windy weather, smaller flags than the above are generally used.

RELATION OF HEIGHT OF POLE TO HEIGHT OF BLDG.

HEIGHT OF POLE	HEIGHT OF BLDG.
20'–0''	1 to 2 stories
25'–0''	3 to 5 stories
33'–0'' to 35'–0''	6 to 10 stories
40'–0'' to 50'–0''	11 to 15 stories
60'–0'' to 75'–0''	over 15 stories

NOTE:

This rule serves for preliminary assumptions.

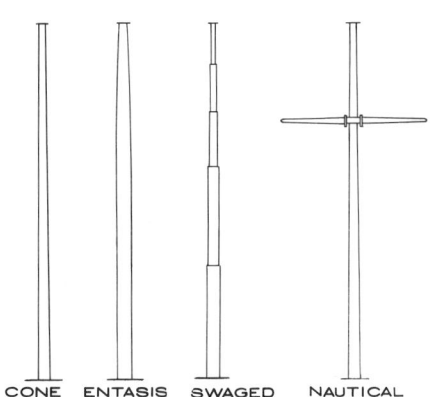

CONE   ENTASIS   SWAGED   NAUTICAL

Poles are manufactured in steel, aluminum, bronze, and fiberglass.

POLE STYLES

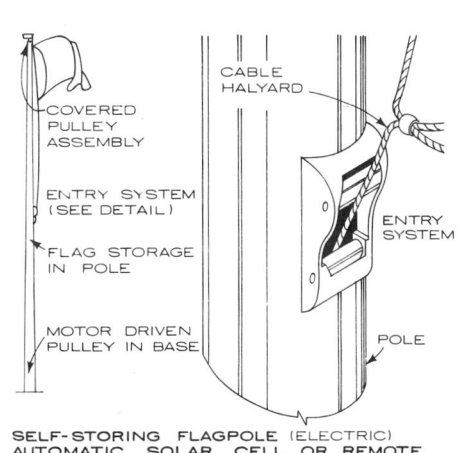

COVERED PULLEY ASSEMBLY

CABLE HALYARD

ENTRY SYSTEM (SEE DETAIL)

FLAG STORAGE IN POLE

ENTRY SYSTEM

MOTOR DRIVEN PULLEY IN BASE

POLE

SELF-STORING FLAGPOLE (ELECTRIC) AUTOMATIC SOLAR CELL OR REMOTE SWITCH OPERATION

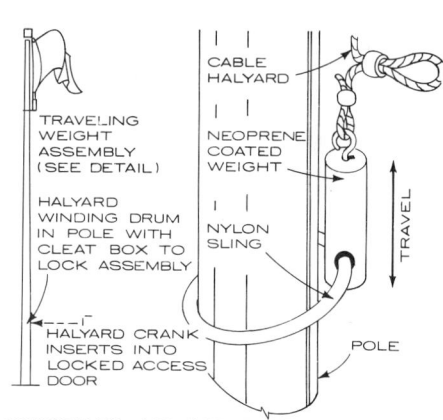

CABLE HALYARD

TRAVELING WEIGHT ASSEMBLY (SEE DETAIL)

HALYARD WINDING DRUM IN POLE WITH CLEAT BOX TO LOCK ASSEMBLY

NEOPRENE COATED WEIGHT

NYLON SLING

TRAVEL

HALYARD CRANK INSERTS INTO LOCKED ACCESS DOOR

POLE

CONCEALED HALYARD SYSTEM (HALYARD INACCESSIBLE WHEN STORED OR CARRYING FLAG)

SPECIAL MECHANISMS FOR REMOTE OR VANDAL – PROOF OPERATION

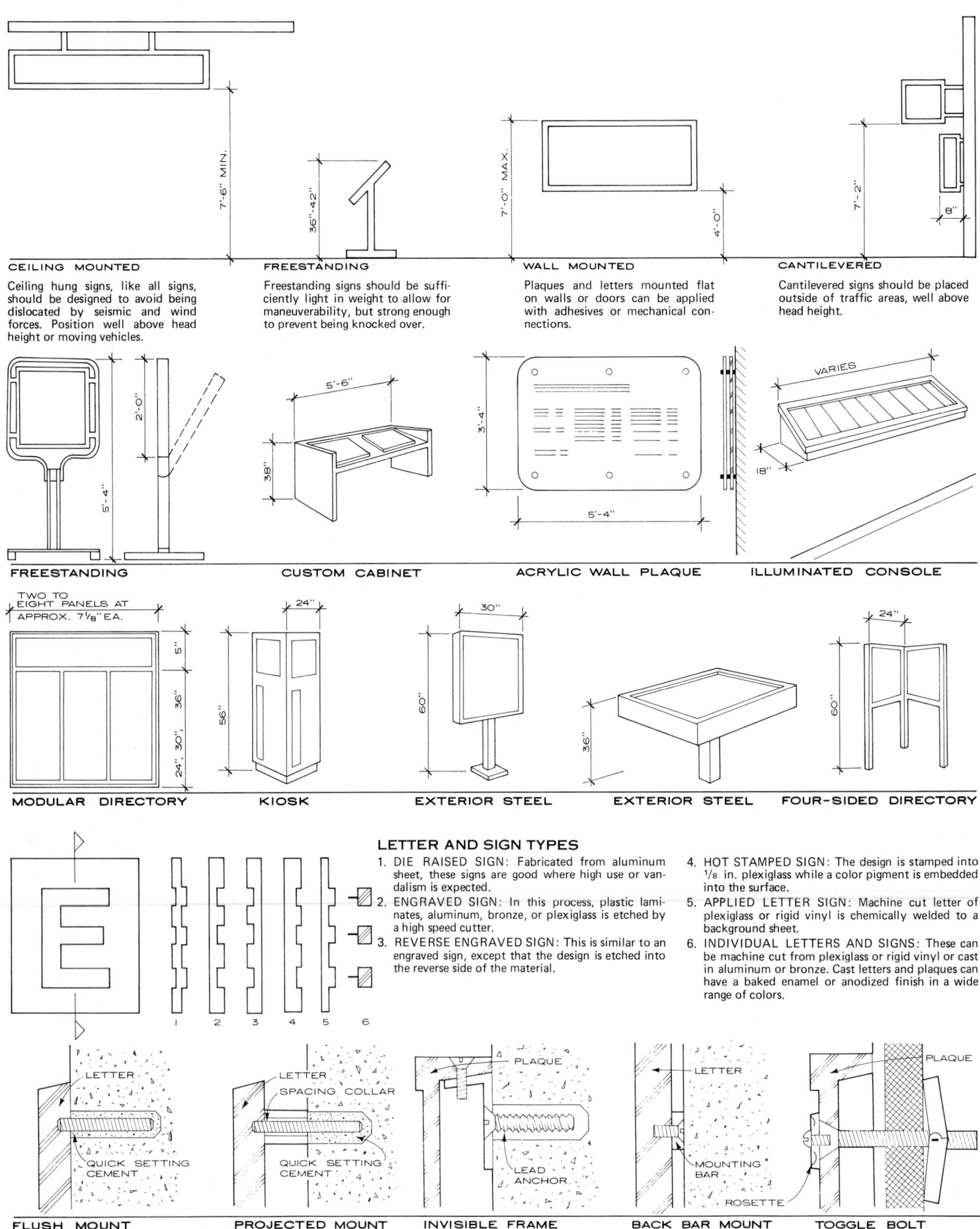

CEILING MOUNTED

Ceiling hung signs, like all signs, should be designed to avoid being dislocated by seismic and wind forces. Position well above head height or moving vehicles.

FREESTANDING

Freestanding signs should be sufficiently light in weight to allow for maneuverability, but strong enough to prevent being knocked over.

WALL MOUNTED

Plaques and letters mounted flat on walls or doors can be applied with adhesives or mechanical connections.

CANTILEVERED

Cantilevered signs should be placed outside of traffic areas, well above head height.

FREESTANDING   **CUSTOM CABINET**   **ACRYLIC WALL PLAQUE**   **ILLUMINATED CONSOLE**

MODULAR DIRECTORY   **KIOSK**   **EXTERIOR STEEL**   **EXTERIOR STEEL**   **FOUR-SIDED DIRECTORY**

LETTER AND SIGN TYPES

1. DIE RAISED SIGN: Fabricated from aluminum sheet, these signs are good where high use or vandalism is expected.

2. ENGRAVED SIGN: In this process, plastic laminates, aluminum, bronze, or plexiglass is etched by a high speed cutter.

3. REVERSE ENGRAVED SIGN: This is similar to an engraved sign, except that the design is etched into the reverse side of the material.

4. HOT STAMPED SIGN: The design is stamped into 1/8 in. plexiglass while a color pigment is embedded into the surface.

5. APPLIED LETTER SIGN: Machine cut letter of plexiglass or rigid vinyl is chemically welded to a background sheet.

6. INDIVIDUAL LETTERS AND SIGNS: These can be machine cut from plexiglass or rigid vinyl or cast in aluminum or bronze. Cast letters and plaques can have a baked enamel or anodized finish in a wide range of colors.

FLUSH MOUNT   **PROJECTED MOUNT**   **INVISIBLE FRAME**   **BACK BAR MOUNT**   **TOGGLE BOLT**

Brixen & Christopher, Architects; Salt Lake City, Utah

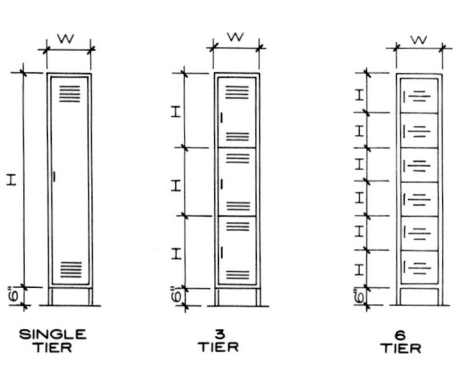

SINGLE TIER   3 TIER   6 TIER

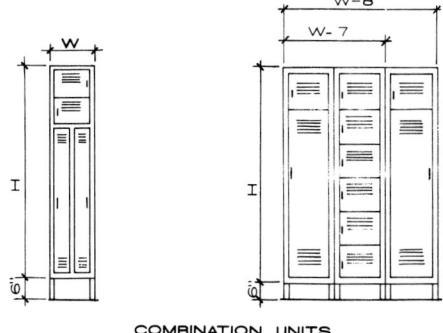

COMBINATION UNITS

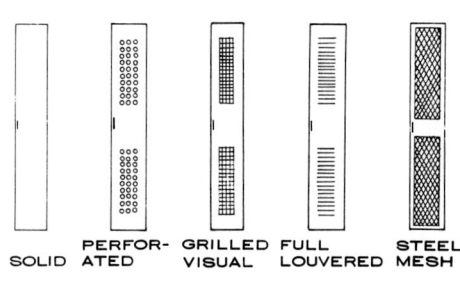

| SOLID | PERFORATED | GRILLED VISUAL | FULL LOUVERED | STEEL MESH |

DOOR VARIATIONS

SINGLE TIER

W	D	H
9"	1'-0" 1'-3" 1'-4" 1'-6"	
1'-0"	1'-0" 1'-3" 1'-6" 1'-9"	
1'-3"	1'-0" 1'-3" 1'-4" 1'-6" 1'-9"	5'-0" 6'-0"
1'-6"	1'-6" 1'-9" 1'-10" 2'-0"	
2'-0"	1'-6" 1'-9" 2'-0"	

3 TIER

W	D	H
9"	1'-0" 1'-3" 1'-6"	1'-8"
1'-0"		2'-0"

4 TIER

W	D	H
1'-0"	1'-0" 1'-3" 1'-6"	1'-3"
1'-3"	1'-3" 1'-6"	
1'-6"	1'-6"	

DOUBLE TIER

W	D	H
9"	1'-0" 1'-3" 1'-4" 1'-6"	2'-6" 3'-0"
1'-0"	1'-0" 1'-3" 1'-6" 1'-10"	2'-6" 3'-0" 3'-6"
1'-3"	1'-3" 1'-4" 1'-6" 1'-10"	
1'-6"	1'-0" 1'-4" 1'-10"	2'-6" 3'-0" 3'-6"

5 AND 6 TIER

W	D	H
1'-0"	1'-0" 1'-3" 1'-6"	1'-0"
1'-3"	1'-3" 1'-6" 1'-9"	1'-0" 1'-3"
1'-6"	1'-0" 1'-4" 1'-10"	1'-0"

2 UNIT

W	D	H
1'-3"	1'-3"	5'-0"
	1'-6"	6'-0"
1'-6"	1'-9"	6'-0"
	1'-9"	6'-0"

7 UNIT

W	D	H
3'-0"	1'-6" 1'-9"	6'-0"

8 UNIT

W	D	H
4'-6"	1'-9"	6'-0"

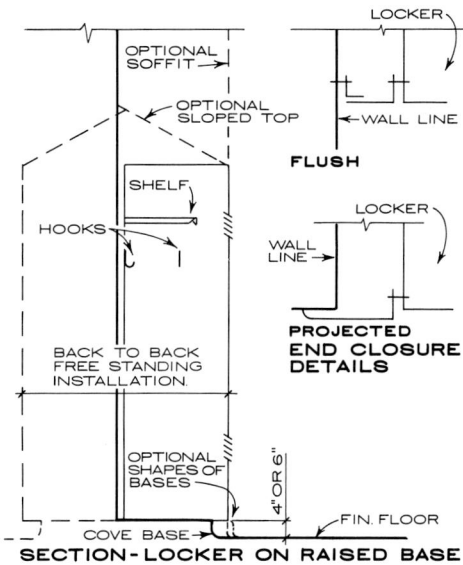

SECTION-LOCKER ON RAISED BASE

The shelf and 2 hooks shown are considered standard equipment.

FLUSH

PROJECTED
**END CLOSURE
DETAILS**

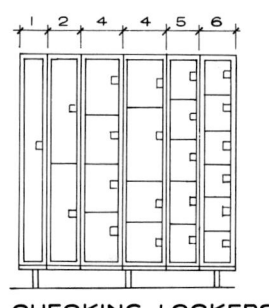

CHECKING LOCKERS

TYPES	W	D	H
1 Single tier	9" 1'-0"	1'-6"	6'-0"
2 Double tier	9" 1'-0"	1'-6"	1'-0"
4 Four tier	1'-3"	1'-6" 2'-0" 2'-7"	4 1'-3" 3 1'-1" 1 1'-10"
5 Five tier	1'-0"	1'-3" 1'-6" 1'-9"	1'-0" 1'-2"
6 Six tier	1'-0"	1'-3" 1'-6" 1'-9"	1'-0"

GENERAL NOTES

1. Locker frame and door are usually of No. 16 gauge steel; sides, back, top, and bottom of No. 20 to No. 24 gauge steel. Finishes vary.

2. The standard door type may be varied as follows:

a. Door type as shown.

b. Sides and backs of perforated sheet steel for expanded mesh metal specific ventilation requirements.

c. Optional equipment includes sloped top, closed base, 6 in. legs, and a variety of interior fittings such as hooks, shelves, and partitions.

d. Optional top hinged doors for box lockers.

NOTES

1. Checking lockers are available in enameled carbon steel, or stainless steel for heavy duty use, as in transportation terminals. Locks are provided with built in multiple coin selector, owner adjustable for coins, tokens, or "free" operations.

2. Lockers are available without legs for recessed installation. Overall height is 6 ft 0 in., some models, 5 ft 0 in. A variety of bases are available for freestanding or movable installation.

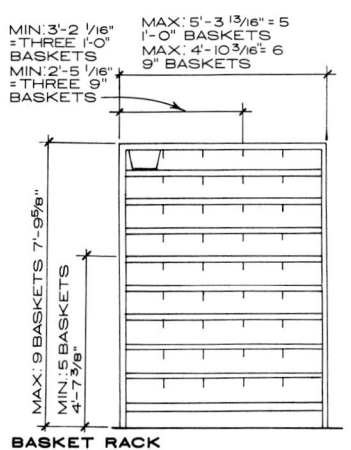

BASKET RACK

NOTE

Basket racks are arranged in single row or double (back to back) row. Single row depth is 1'-1 1/4".

Judith Plummer; Washington, D.C.

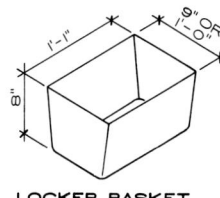

LOCKER BASKET

MATERIALS

1. Sides and bottom of perforated steel with louvered ends.

2. All surfaces of wire mesh with perforated steel ends.

3. All surfaces of wire mesh.

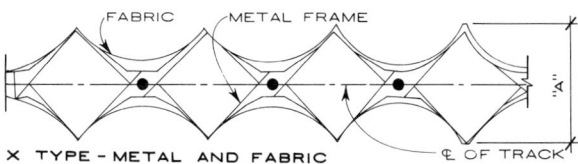

X TYPE - METAL AND FABRIC

"X" Type door is built of a metal frame with a vinyl fabric covering. Various insulation materials produce a wide range of acoustic properties. Dimensions given vary according to manufacturer. "A" Dimension varies from approximately 5" up to 12".

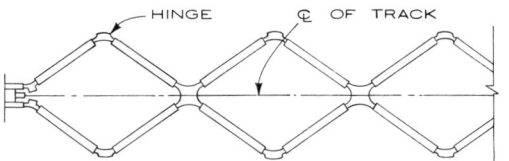

X TYPE - WOOD VENEER OR PLASTIC LAMINATE
HINGES ARE EXTRUDED VINYL

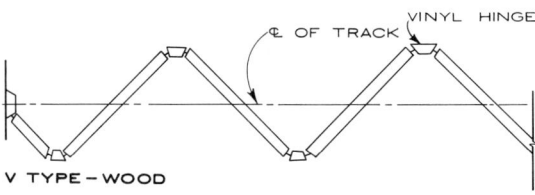

V TYPE - WOOD

"V" Type door is available in metal with fabric covering or in solid wood panels.

TYPICAL ACCORDION PARTITIONS

"X" and "V" Types may be installed on a curved track with a minimum radius of 3'-6".

All "X" and "V" partitions are ceiling supported and may be manually or power operated.

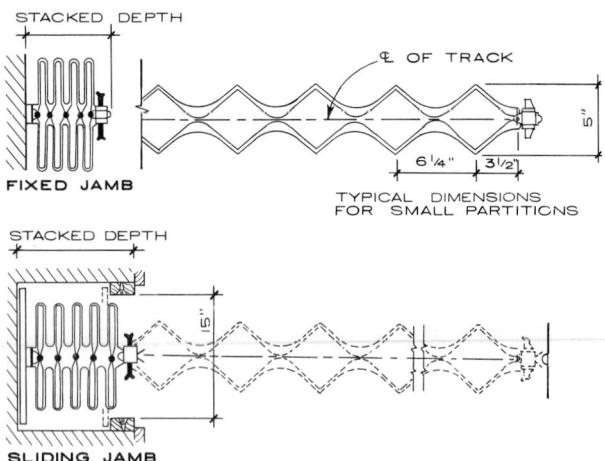

FIXED JAMB

TYPICAL DIMENSIONS FOR SMALL PARTITIONS

SLIDING JAMB

NOTE
Stacked depth usually equals about $1/6$ to $1/8$ the opened width.

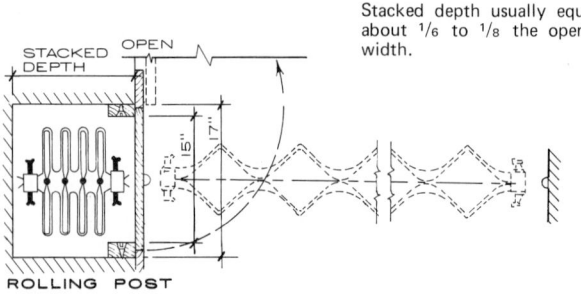

ROLLING POST

STACKING ARRANGEMENTS

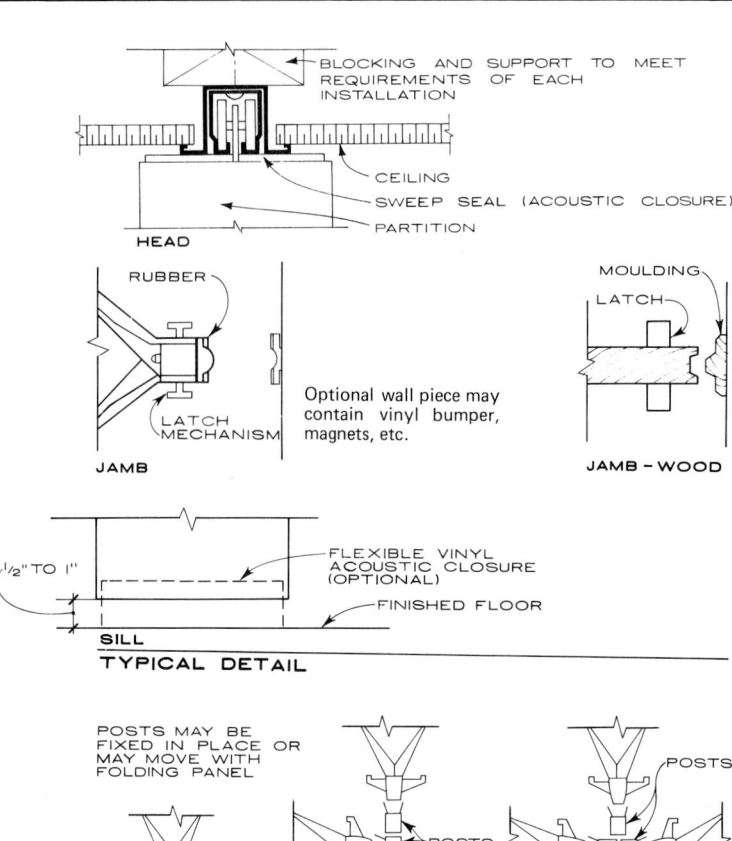

HEAD

Optional wall piece may contain vinyl bumper, magnets, etc.

JAMB

JAMB - WOOD

SILL

TYPICAL DETAIL

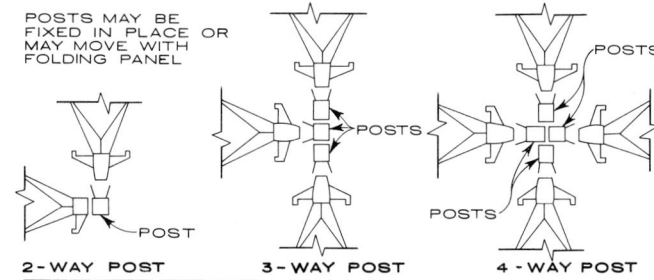

POSTS MAY BE FIXED IN PLACE OR MAY MOVE WITH FOLDING PANEL

2 - WAY POST   **3 - WAY POST**   **4 - WAY POST**

TYPES OF MEETING POSTS

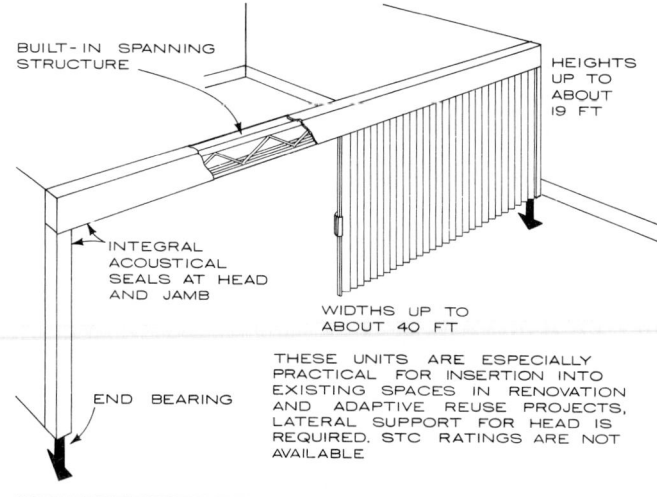

BUILT- IN SPANNING STRUCTURE

HEIGHTS UP TO ABOUT 19 FT

INTEGRAL ACOUSTICAL SEALS AT HEAD AND JAMB

WIDTHS UP TO ABOUT 40 FT

END BEARING

THESE UNITS ARE ESPECIALLY PRACTICAL FOR INSERTION INTO EXISTING SPACES IN RENOVATION AND ADAPTIVE REUSE PROJECTS. LATERAL SUPPORT FOR HEAD IS REQUIRED. STC RATINGS ARE NOT AVAILABLE.

SELF-CONTAINED, PREENGINEERED UNIT

GENERAL NOTES

1. Panel thickness, width, height, finish, and acoustic quality vary, dependent upon size of opening, usage, and manufacturer. Dimensions given vary according to manufacturer.
2. Enclosures for operable partitions vary. See manufacturer's literature for required clearances in pockets.
3. Overhead structure must be sufficient to support operable partition and must be properly anchored and braced.
4. The accordion type partition is recommended for small openings, which does not, however, preclude its use for large openings.
5. Track switches are available, which provide for various partitioning arrangements with one or more partition units.

CENTER TRACK

Center track—supported at either the floor or ceiling. Panels are connected to each other and are either manually or power operated.

NOTE: SOME SETS OF DOORS START WITH A HALF PANEL.

¢ OF TRACK

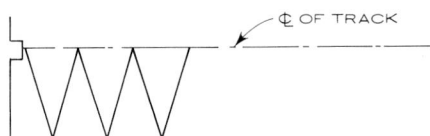

¢ OF TRACK

EDGE TRACK

Edge track—supported at either the floor or ceiling. Panels are connected to each other and are either manually or power operated.

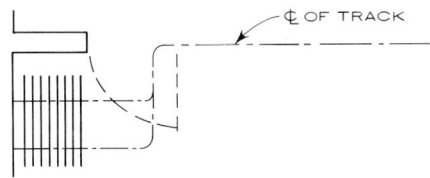

¢ OF TRACK

STACKING POCKET

Ceiling suspended, unconnected panels, manually operated only.

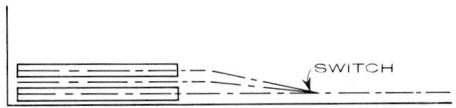

SWITCH

STACKING WITH SWITCHES

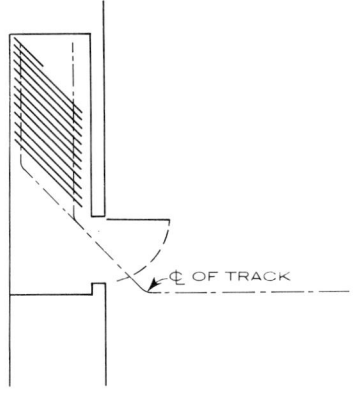

¢ OF TRACK

¢ OF TRACK

ANGULAR STACKING

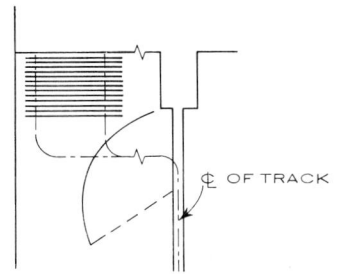

¢ OF TRACK

REMOTE STACK LOCATION WITH RIDE PANEL PASSAGE DOOR

VARIATIONS OF TYPE STACKING

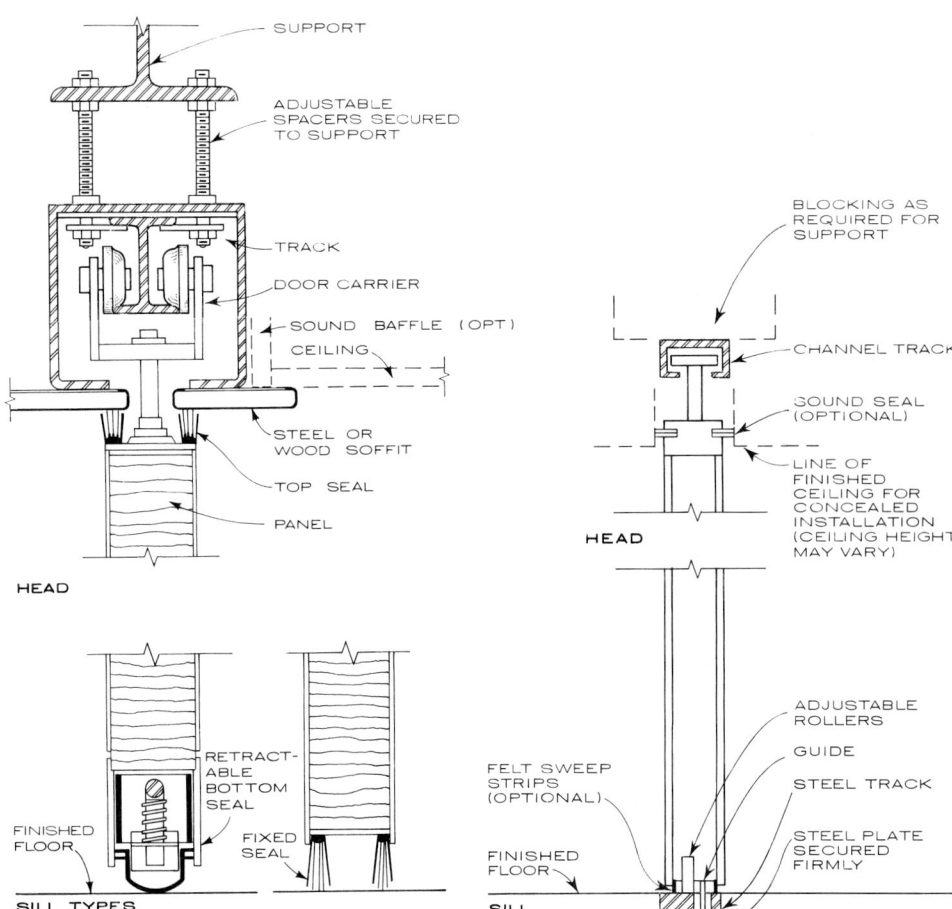

SUPPORT

ADJUSTABLE SPACERS SECURED TO SUPPORT

TRACK

DOOR CARRIER

SOUND BAFFLE (OPT)

CEILING

STEEL OR WOOD SOFFIT

TOP SEAL

PANEL

HEAD

RETRACTABLE BOTTOM SEAL

FINISHED FLOOR

FIXED SEAL

SILL TYPES

TOP HUNG

BLOCKING AS REQUIRED FOR SUPPORT

CHANNEL TRACK

SOUND SEAL (OPTIONAL)

LINE OF FINISHED CEILING FOR CONCEALED INSTALLATION (CEILING HEIGHT MAY VARY)

HEAD

ADJUSTABLE ROLLERS

GUIDE

STEEL TRACK

FELT SWEEP STRIPS (OPTIONAL)

STEEL PLATE SECURED FIRMLY

FINISHED FLOOR

SILL

FLOOR – SUPPORTED

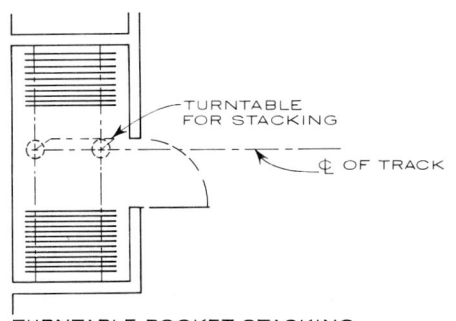

TURNTABLE FOR STACKING

¢ OF TRACK

TURNTABLE POCKET STACKING

Door panels are stacked on a pair of overhead tracks.

Manually operated track switches are provided to transfer panels to parallel stacking tracks as indicated.

Large panels are fabricated in similar fashion to typical doors, although in greater size and weight of construction. Many manufacturers offer wood frame panels faced with plywood, hardboard, or other thin skin and filled with honeycomb type of core, solid wood, sound absorbent material, etc. Steel framed panels with steel faces are also available.

Panel surfaces can be treated very much like regular wall surfaces. Various manufacturers provide vinyl, carpet, wood veneer, plastic laminate, and other coverings, while some additionally offer tackboard and chalkboard options with trays and other accessories.

Work closely with manufacturer to develop the correct combination of features for a given panel installation, and provide structural support based on the calculated weight of the actual panels specified.

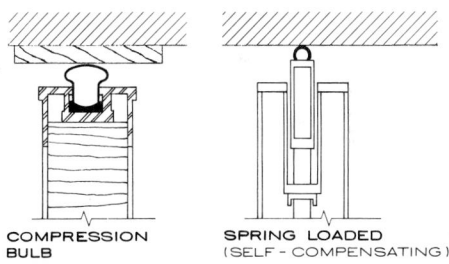

COMPRESSION BULB

SPRING LOADED (SELF – COMPENSATING)

LEAD JAMBS MAY BUTT DIRECTLY TO WALL, OR TO A TRIM STRIP FOR IMPROVED SEAL

LEAD JAMBS

NOTES

1. Panel thickness, width, height, finish and acoustic quality vary dependent upon size of opening, usage and manufacturer.

2. Enclosures for movable partitions vary. See manufacturers literature for required clearances in pockets.

3. Overhead structure must be sufficient to support movable partition and must be properly anchored and braced.

4. Leaf type partitions are recommended where rigidity and flat plane storage are important factors.

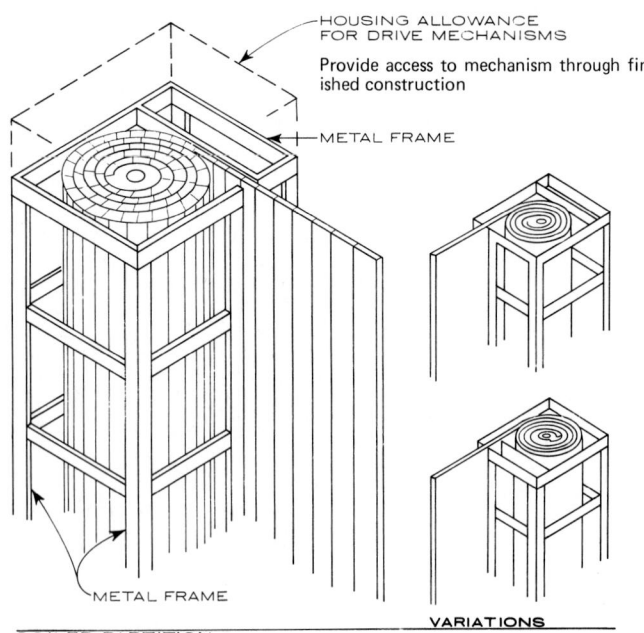

COILED PARTITION
METAL FRAME IS STANDARD MANU-
FACTURER'S EQUIPMENT WITH ALL
COILED PARTITIONS

- HOUSING ALLOWANCE FOR DRIVE MECHANISMS
- Provide access to mechanism through finished construction
- METAL FRAME
- METAL FRAME
- VARIATIONS

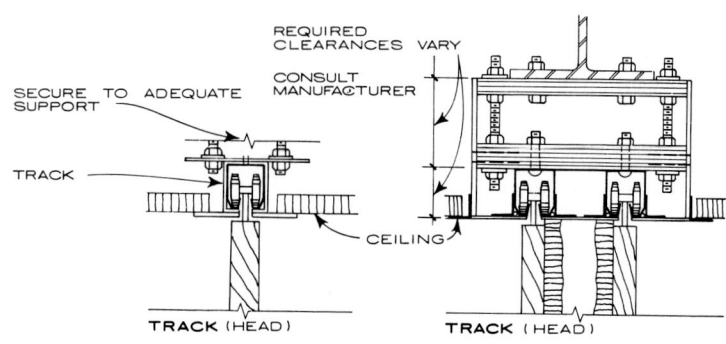

TRACK (HEAD)   **TRACK** (HEAD)

- REQUIRED CLEARANCES VARY
- CONSULT MANUFACTURER
- SECURE TO ADEQUATE SUPPORT
- TRACK
- CEILING

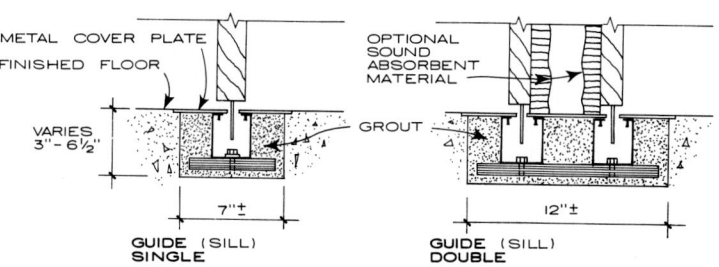

GUIDE (SILL) **SINGLE**   **GUIDE** (SILL) **DOUBLE**

- METAL COVER PLATE
- FINISHED FLOOR
- VARIES 3"–6½"
- 7"±
- OPTIONAL SOUND ABSORBENT MATERIAL
- GROUT
- 12"±

SECTIONS

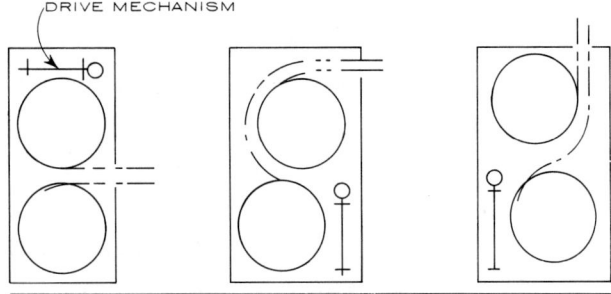

DOUBLE PARTITION COIL BOXES
(USED MOSTLY FOR ACOUSTIC PURPOSES)

- DRIVE MECHANISM

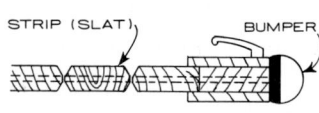

STRIP (SLAT)   BUMPER

LEAD STILE

NOTES

1. All coiled partitions are ceiling supported and may be operated by one of the four following methods:
   a. FULL MANUAL: Manually extended and manually retracted. Extended length should not exceed 10 ft 10 in.
   b. MANUAL MECHANICAL: Manually extended and retracted by hand crank. Extended length should not exceed 25 ft. Curves should be avoided.
   c. FULL MECHANICAL: Extended and retracted by hand crank. Limit length, avoid curves.
   d. ELECTRICAL: Extended and retracted by electric motor.
2. Required floor depression varies from about 3 in. up to about 6 in. Consult manufacturer to determine exact requirements.
3. Minimum radius for coiled partition track is 6 ft for mechanical and 4 ft for manual.
4. Standard material is wood strip, but metal strips, metal grilles, etc. may be substituted or used in conjunction with wood.

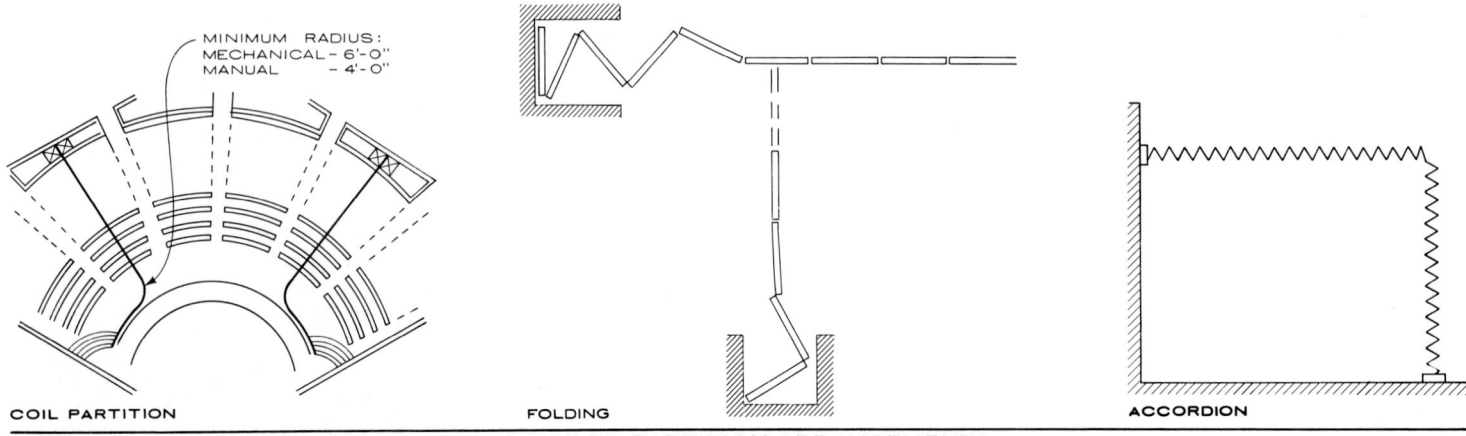

- MINIMUM RADIUS:
  MECHANICAL – 6'-0"
  MANUAL   – 4'-0"

COIL PARTITION   **FOLDING**   **ACCORDION**

TYPICAL FOLDING ACCORDION & SIDE COILED PARTITION ARRANGEMENTS

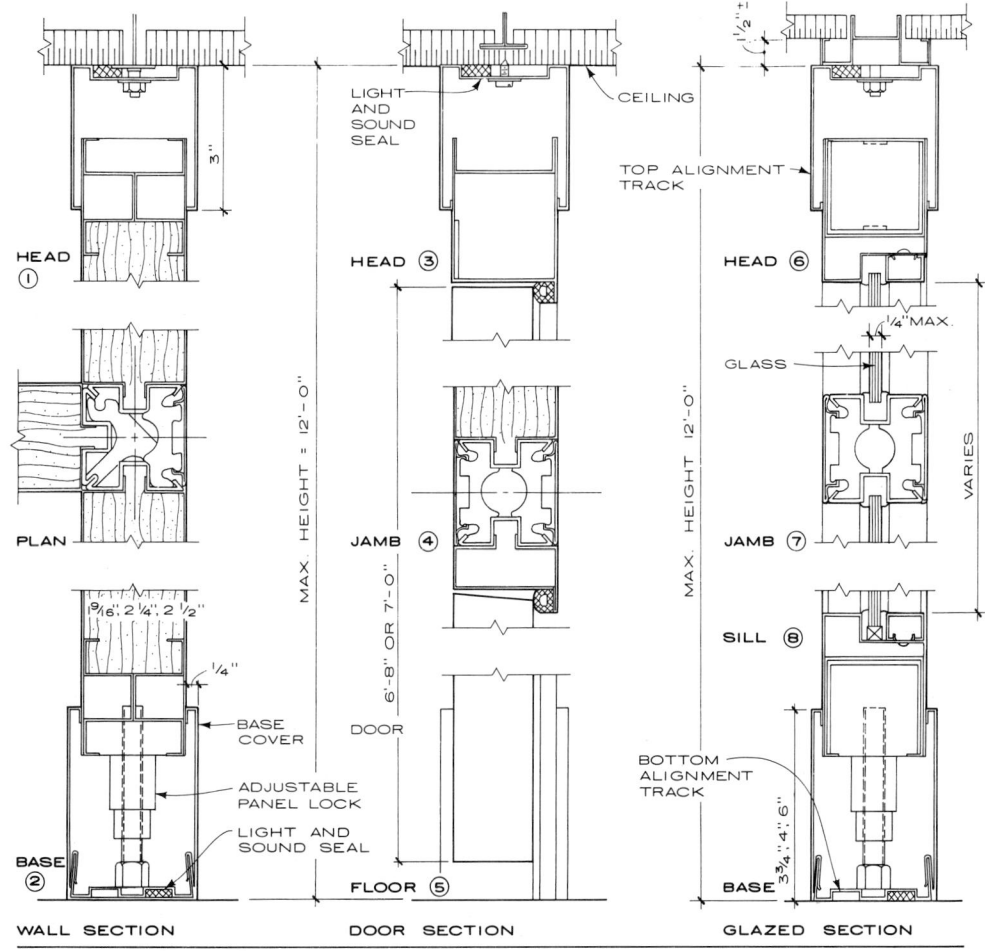

SOLID PANELS

WALL SECTION — DOOR SECTION — GLAZED SECTION

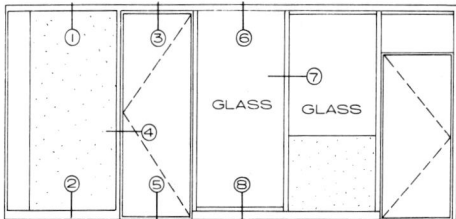

ELEVATION

SOLID PANEL PARTITIONS

Solid panel partition systems consist of prefabricated steel or aluminum panels with mineral wool core insulation. The unitized panels are held in place with an adjustable lock at floor and tracks at ceiling. Electrical runs are handled through floor or ceiling tracks horizontally and through posts vertically. There are also snap-in utility panels.

Solid panels provide substantial resistance to sound transmission (36 to 54 STC) with proper light and sound seals and have a 1 hr fire rating.

Standard panels are 24 to 60 in. wide (in 6 in. increments) and are prefinished in baked enamel, vinyl, or textured coverings. Available accessories include chalkboards, tackboards, shelves, and cabinets.

SOUND TRANSMISSION

	TOTAL PARTITION THICKNESS	VINYL COAT FACING	FIBERGLASS INSULATION BLANKET	SOUND TRANSMISSION CLASS (STC)
2½" wall cavity	3½"	½"	None	36
	3½"	½"	2½"	47
	3¾"	⅝"	None	41
	3¾"	⅝"	2½"	49
3⅝" wall cavity	4⅝"	½"	None	39
	4⅝"	½"	3½"	50
	4⅞"	⅝"	None	42
	4⅞"	⅝"	3½"	52

NOTES

1. Normally suspended ceilings are ineffective as a sound barrier. Consequently, when a series of sound-proofed offices are planned under such a ceiling, the chances of sound travel over the partitions should be considered. Baffles should be installed tightly above each run of partition, from the suspended ceiling to the bottom of the slab, to eliminate cracks through which sound can easily pass.
2. The perimeter of the partition installation—ceiling, floor, and sides—shall be gasketed with a factory applied sealant. All door frames shall be fitted with a factory applied rubber liner at the head and jambs that compress when the door is closed.
3. For extra sound control, all doors should have a continuous drop seal and threshold and all glazing in doors and partitions should be hermetically sealed double lights.

HOLLOW CORE PARTITIONS

Hollow partition systems consist of steel or aluminum heads, jambs, and sill members designed to receive standard gypsum board panels. Steel or porcelain panels may also be used.

Metal studs are spaced 24 in. on center and may be drilled to allow internal electrical runs.

Hollow partition systems are non-load-bearing. Sound and light seals should be used at floor and ceiling where privacy is desired. STC varies from 36 to 52. These systems normally have a 1 hr fire rating. Consult manufacturer's detail if additional protection is required.

Standard panels are available in 24 to 60 in. widths (in 6 in. increments) and are usually painted or covered in vinyl. A variety of accessories such as chalkboards, tackboard, shelves, and cabinets can be integrated into these systems.

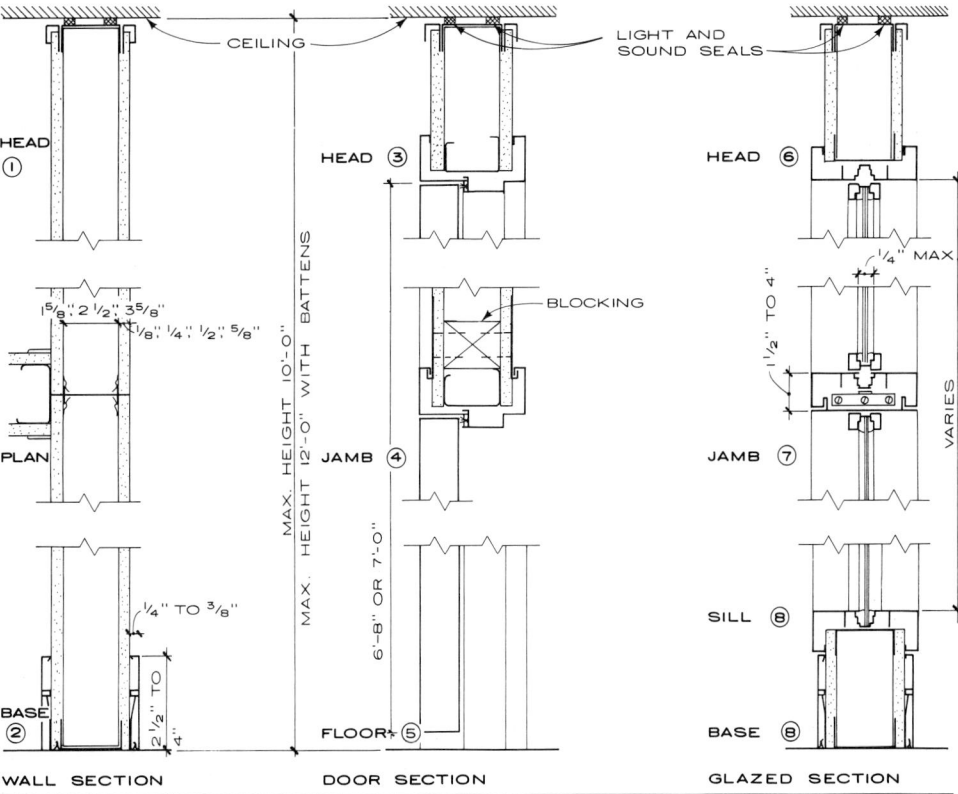

HOLLOW CORE PANELS

WALL SECTION — DOOR SECTION — GLAZED SECTION

Walter H. Sobel, FAIA & Associates; Chicago, Illinois

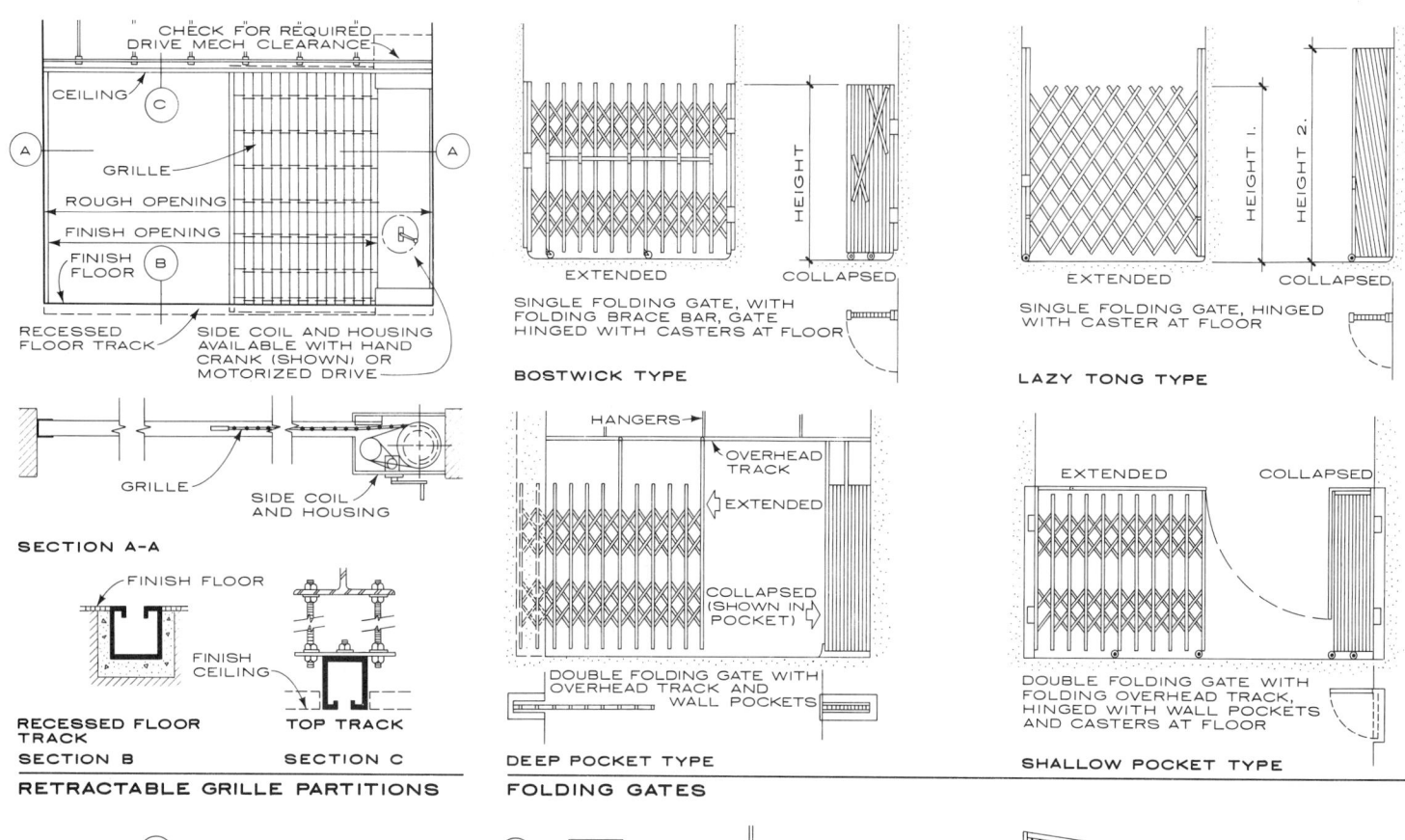

SECTION A-A

RECESSED FLOOR TRACK
SECTION B   SECTION C

RETRACTABLE GRILLE PARTITIONS

SINGLE FOLDING GATE, WITH FOLDING BRACE BAR, GATE HINGED WITH CASTERS AT FLOOR
BOSTWICK TYPE

DOUBLE FOLDING GATE WITH OVERHEAD TRACK AND WALL POCKETS
DEEP POCKET TYPE

FOLDING GATES

SINGLE FOLDING GATE, HINGED WITH CASTER AT FLOOR
LAZY TONG TYPE

DOUBLE FOLDING GATE WITH FOLDING OVERHEAD TRACK, HINGED WITH WALL POCKETS AND CASTERS AT FLOOR
SHALLOW POCKET TYPE

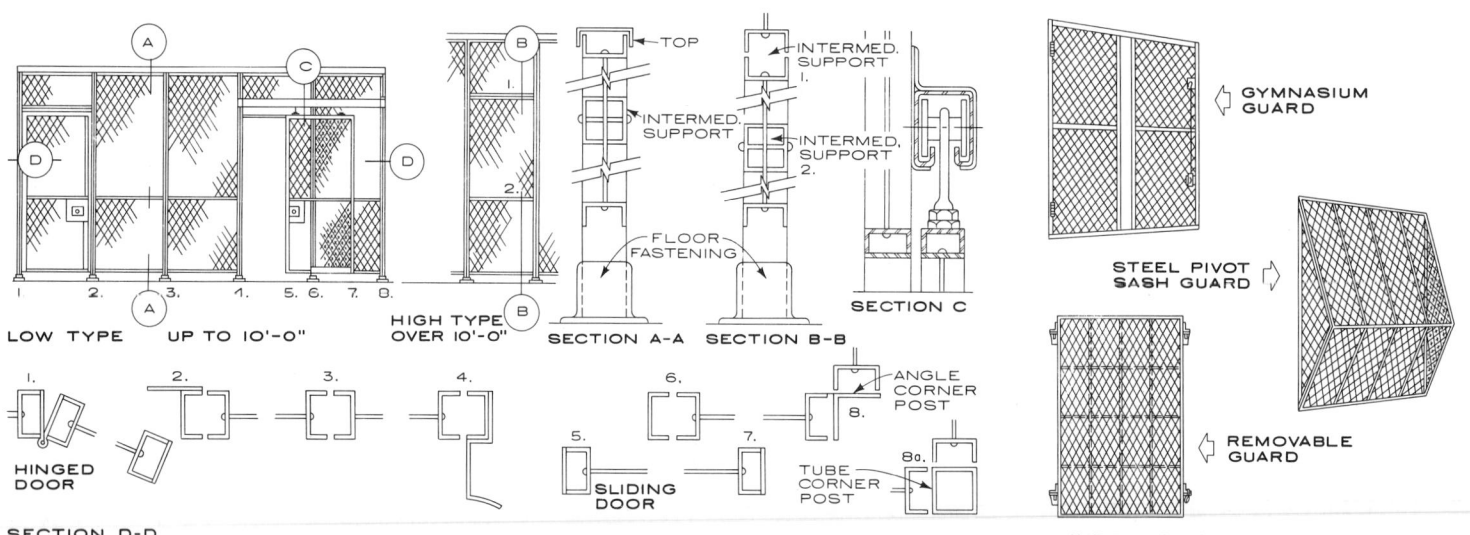

LOW TYPE   UP TO 10'-0"   HIGH TYPE OVER 10'-0"

SECTION A-A   SECTION B-B   SECTION C

GYMNASIUM GUARD
STEEL PIVOT SASH GUARD
REMOVABLE GUARD

HINGED DOOR   SLIDING DOOR   TUBE CORNER POST   ANGLE CORNER POST

SECTION D-D

WINDOW GUARDS

RECOMMENDED USES FOR WIRE MESH PARTITIONS

MESH	PATTERN	WIRE SIZE	FRAMES	USES
1¼"	◇ ▢	11	1" ⊏	Animal cages
1½"	◇	10	1" ⊏	Elevator shafts
1¾"	◇	9	1¼" ⊏	Fire escapes
2"	◇	8	1½" ⊏	Cashier cages
2"	◇	6	1¼" "C"	Runways
			Channel ¾" ⊏	Stair enclosures Locker rooms Departmental divisions Stock rooms Tool rooms

OTHER USES FOR WOVEN WIRE MESH

MESH	PATTERN	WIRE SIZE	FRAMES	USES
¾"	◇ ▢	12	5/16" ○ ¾" ⊏ 1" L	Air intake screens Bird screens
1"	◇ ▢	12	3/8" ○ 1" ⊏ 1" L	Basement window guards Shelves and trays Skylight guards
1½"	◇ ▢		3/8" ○ 1" ⊏	Door and window guards
2¼"	◇ ▢	7	7/16" ○	Wire roof signs
2½"	◇	6	1½" ⊏	Fencing gratings

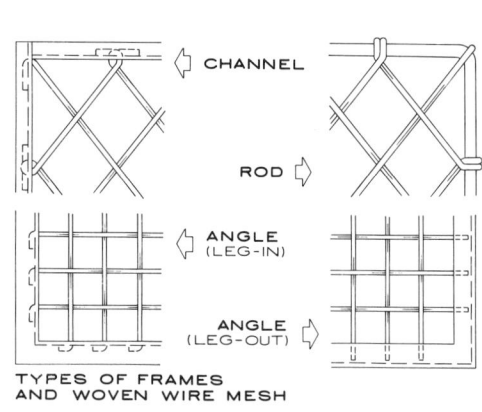

CHANNEL
ROD
ANGLE (LEG-IN)
ANGLE (LEG-OUT)

TYPES OF FRAMES AND WOVEN WIRE MESH

WIRE MESH PARTITIONS

Harnish, Morgan & Causey, Architects; Ontario, California

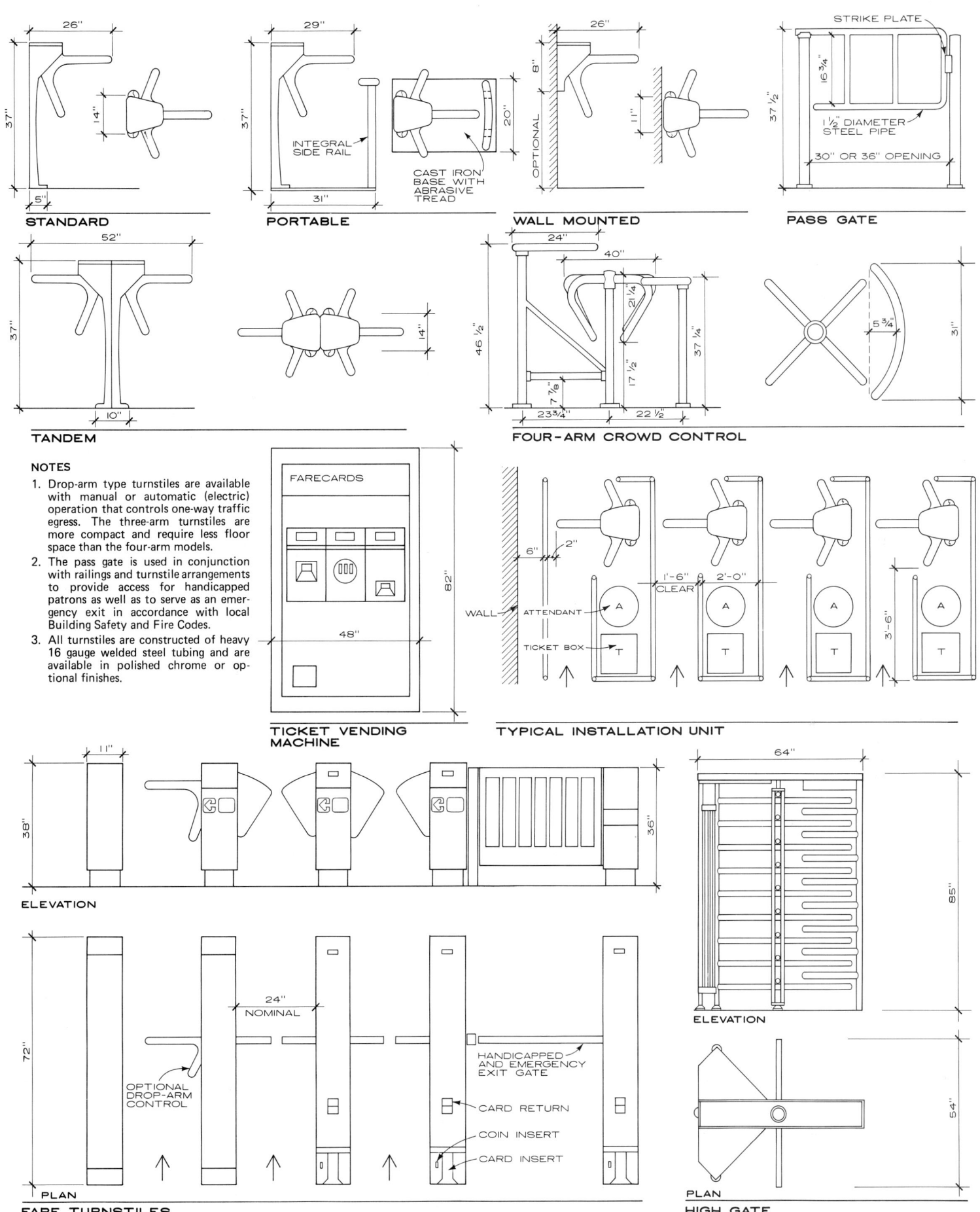

STANDARD

PORTABLE

WALL MOUNTED

PASS GATE

TANDEM

FOUR-ARM CROWD CONTROL

NOTES

1. Drop-arm type turnstiles are available with manual or automatic (electric) operation that controls one-way traffic egress. The three-arm turnstiles are more compact and require less floor space than the four-arm models.

2. The pass gate is used in conjunction with railings and turnstile arrangements to provide access for handicapped patrons as well as to serve as an emergency exit in accordance with local Building Safety and Fire Codes.

3. All turnstiles are constructed of heavy 16 gauge welded steel tubing and are available in polished chrome or optional finishes.

TICKET VENDING MACHINE

TYPICAL INSTALLATION UNIT

ELEVATION

PLAN

FARE TURNSTILES

ELEVATION

PLAN

HIGH GATE

William Cook; Lawrence Cook & Associates; Falls Church, Virginia

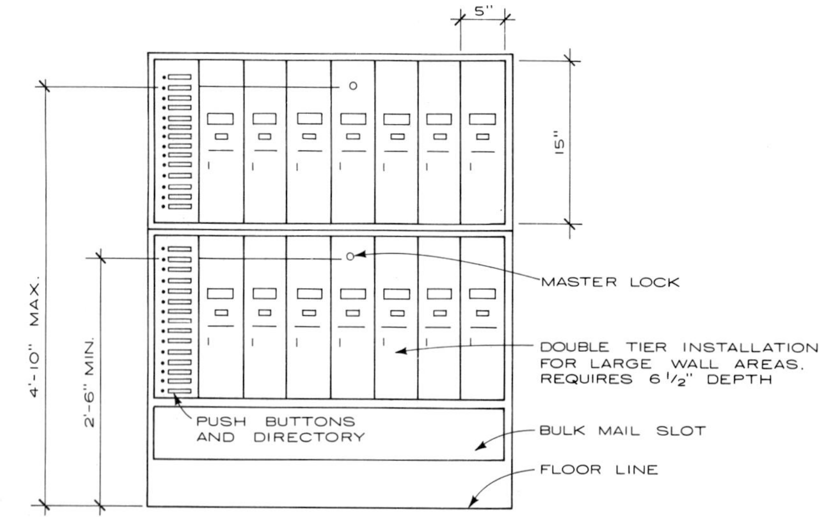

VERTICAL COMPARTMENT TYPE
FRONT LOADING

MASTER LOCK

DOUBLE TIER INSTALLATION FOR LARGE WALL AREAS. REQUIRES 6½" DEPTH

PUSH BUTTONS AND DIRECTORY

BULK MAIL SLOT

FLOOR LINE

ELEVATION

5"

15"

4'-10" MAX.

2'-6" MIN.

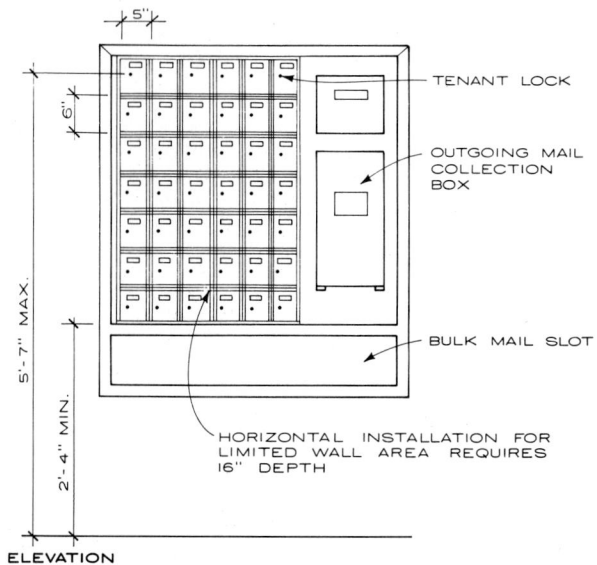

TENANT LOCK

OUTGOING MAIL COLLECTION BOX

BULK MAIL SLOT

HORIZONTAL INSTALLATION FOR LIMITED WALL AREA REQUIRES 16" DEPTH

ELEVATION

5"

6"

5'-7" MAX.

2'-4" MIN.

HORIZONTAL COMPARTMENT TYPE
FRONT OR REAR LOADING

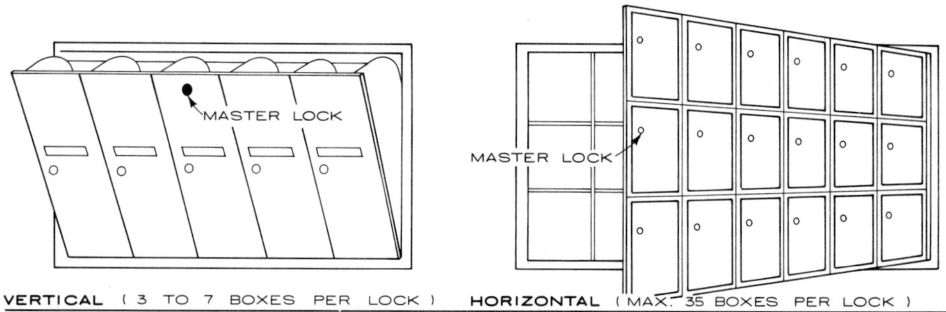

MASTER LOCK

VERTICAL (3 TO 7 BOXES PER LOCK)

MASTER LOCK

HORIZONTAL (MAX. 35 BOXES PER LOCK)

FRONT LOADING COMPARTMENTS WITH MASTER LOCK

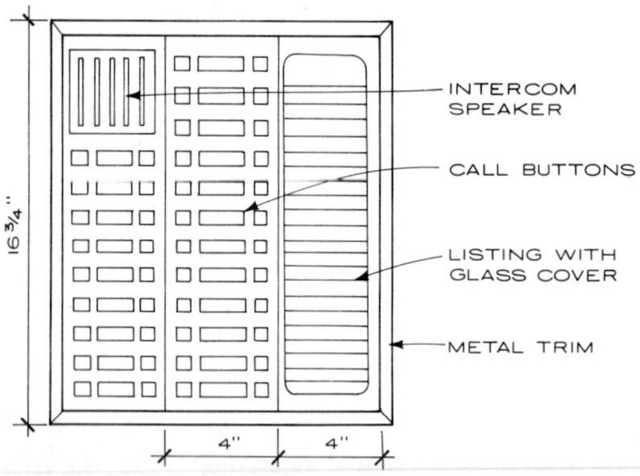

INTERCOM SPEAKER

CALL BUTTONS

LISTING WITH GLASS COVER

METAL TRIM

16¾"

4"   4"

DIRECTORY PANEL

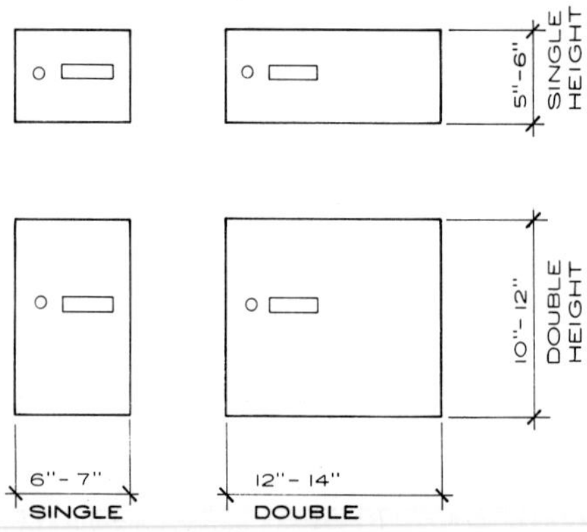

5"-6" SINGLE HEIGHT

10"-12" DOUBLE HEIGHT

6"-7"
SINGLE

12"-14"
DOUBLE

COMPARTMENT SIZES

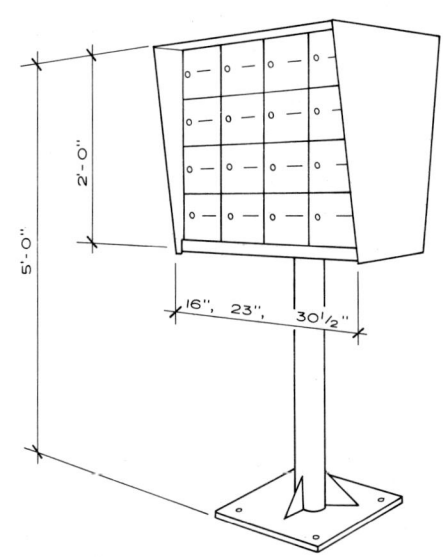

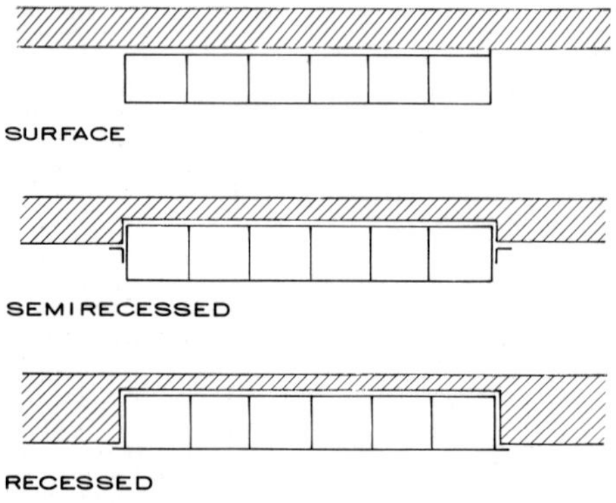

PEDESTAL MOUNTED TYPE

5'-0"

2'-0"

16", 23", 30½"

SURFACE

SEMIRECESSED

RECESSED

MOUNTING TYPES
FRONT LOADED COMPARTMENTS

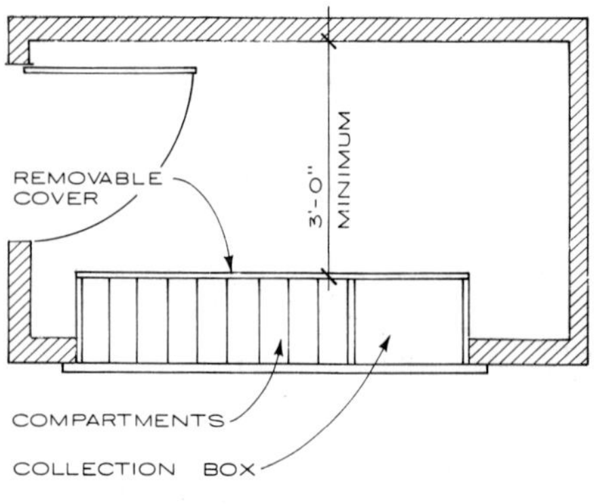

REMOVABLE COVER

3'-0" MINIMUM

COMPARTMENTS

COLLECTION BOX

MAILROOM PLAN
REAR LOADED COMPARTMENTS

GENERAL NOTES

1. Postal Service approved mail receptacles are required for apartment houses containing three or more apartments with a common building entrance and street number.

2. Individual compartments should be large enough to receive long letter mail 4½ in. wide and bulky magazines 14½ in. long and 3½ in. in diameter.

3. An outdoor installation should preferably be at least 15 ft from a street or public sidewalk, protected from driving rain, and visible from at least one apartment window.

4. All installations must be adequately lighted to afford better protection to the mail and enable carriers to read addresses on mail and names on boxes.

5. A directory, in alphabetical order, is required for installations with more than 15 compartments.

6. Each compartment group is supplied with mounting hardware for master lock.

7. Call buttons with telephone can be integrated into frame with mailboxes.

8. Depending on occupancy, a certain number of compartments shall be assigned to handicapped tenants. Key slots shall be no more than 48 in. from floor.

9. Use of collection boxes is subject to approval by local offices of the United States Postal Service.

Cohen, Karydas & Associates, Chartered; Washington, D.C.

GENERAL PLANNING NOTES

During the early stages of planning, consult with regional Postmaster General for regulations concerning postal facilities in office buildings.

PLATFORM

A dock area that provides off-the-street loading and unloading of mail.

MAILROOM

A security type room located at platform level, which has its own access door to the platform for off-hour service. Platform door should be 36 in. wide, security type. If window or lockbox service is provided, the mailroom should be located at the principal building entrance level. Standard interior treatment should apply in this space.

SERVICES

The size of mailroom and services provided by the post office vary with size and occupancy of the building. The U.S. Postal Service recognizes for its staffing and servicing two types of mailrooms for small, medium, and large office buildings.

1. LOCKBOX SERVICE: Buildings up to 200,000 sq ft of leasable space or with a maximum of 75 tenants. Provide one receptacle for each tenant and rear loading for 11 or more tenants. A building directory must be maintained.

   The vertical distance from floor to tenant locks on top tier of receptacles is 66 in. maximum; to bottom lowest tier 10 in. minimum, preferably 30 in. Install only at one entrance. Allow a minimum of 3 ft of clear working space behind units. Provide 80 sq ft of working space for each additional carrier. Allow 1 sq ft of working space for every 1000 sq ft of leasable office space. Specifications for construction of mail receptacles shall be identical to those for Type II, horizontal apartment house receptacles as prescribed in USPS Publication 17, except that the minimum inside dimensions shall be 5¾ in. high, 10½ in. wide, and 16 in. deep.

POSTAL SERVICES

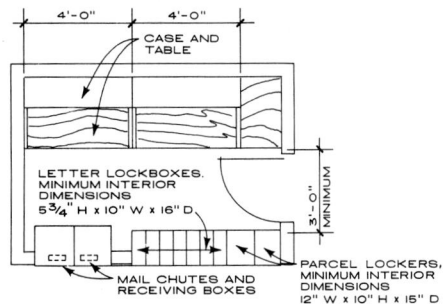

LOCKBOX

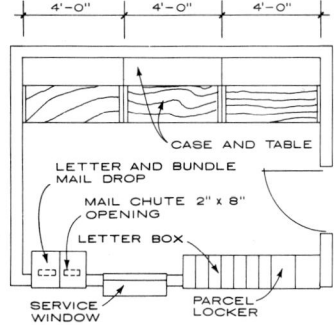

CALL WINDOW

2. CALL WINDOW SERVICE: Buildings with 75 or more tenants, one carrier for each 100,000 sq ft of leasable office space up to 500,000 sq ft, plus one carrier for each additional 200,000 sq ft of office building. Allow 1.5 sq ft for every 1000 sq ft of leasable space; the minimum call window service space is 100 sq ft.

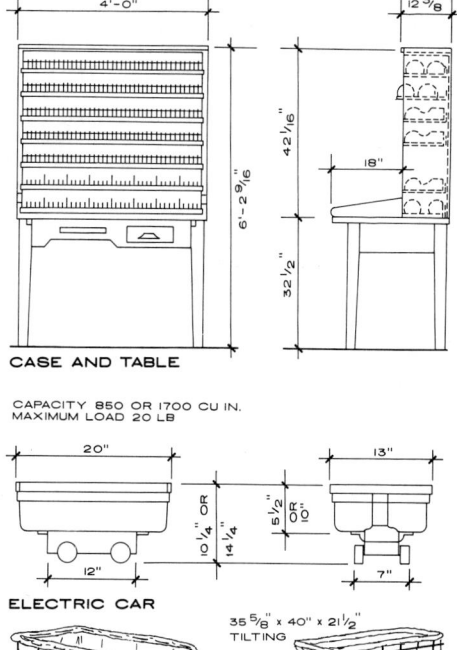

CASE AND TABLE

CAPACITY 850 OR 1700 CU IN.
MAXIMUM LOAD 20 LB

ELECTRIC CAR

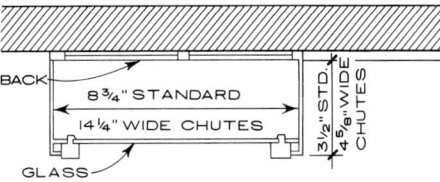

BASKET CARTS

EQUIPMENT

MAIL CHUTE—PLAN

1. May be recessed.
2. Use wide chutes for 8″ x 10″ envelopes.

MAIL CHUTES AND RECEIVING BOXES

1. CHUTES: Used in buildings of at least four stories. The chute must be approximately 2 x 8 in. in cross section and extend in a continuously vertical line from the beginning point to the receiving box or mailroom. The interior of the chute must be accessible throughout its entire length. Chutes installed in pairs are constructed with a divider and dual receiving boxes. Chutes are for first class mail only.

2. RECEIVING BOXES: Located within 100 ft of entrance used by collectors or in the loading-unloading area used by the post office for mail collection. Capacity of boxes is determined by postmaster. However, bottom of door of boxes must be 30 in. or more above floor and exterior bottom of boxes not less than 20 in. above floor and free of obstructions. All doors open to the right and range in sizes from 12 x 20 to 18 x 30 in. inclusive. Mail slot on box is not more than 5 ft 10 in. above floor. Receiving boxes are for first class mail only.

3. AUXILIARY BOXES: Used when receiving box is too small to accommodate deposit of first class mail. Located close to receiving box(es). Capacity is determined by postmaster. The mail openings must be large enough to receive first class mail tied in bundles.

4. COMBINATION LETTER AND BUNDLE BOX: May be attached to the chute in lieu of a regular receiving box. Its minimum dimensions are 6 in. high x 23 in. wide x 17 in. deep; with 3 ft 4 in. from the bottom of the box and not more than 5 ft above floor.

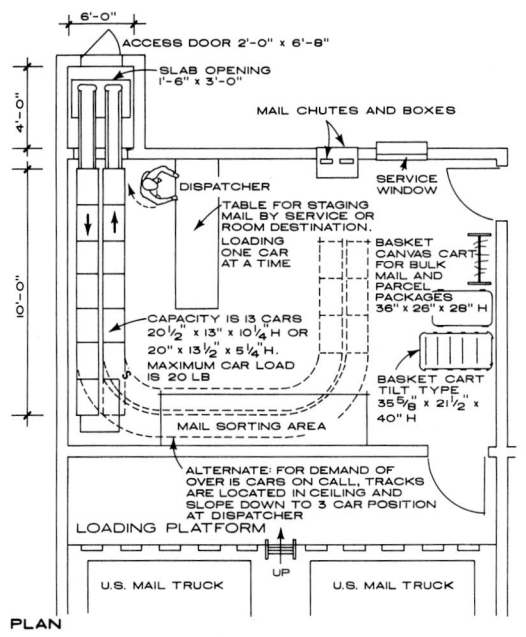

PLAN

CENTRAL MAILROOM

Buildings larger than 200,000 sq ft and with up to 2,000,000 sq ft of leasable space can be served on each floor from a central mailroom using a containerized mechanical system. Allow a minimum of 400 sq ft for first 50 tenants plus 135 sq ft for each additional 50 tenants, or 2 sq ft for each 1000 sq ft of leasable space.

SERVICE MAILROOMS shall be provided on each multitenant floor, unless containers are mechanically conveyed to tenant offices. Allow 5 x 7 ft minimum floor area for service mailroom. Mechanical systems accommodating 8 to 19 containers may require a

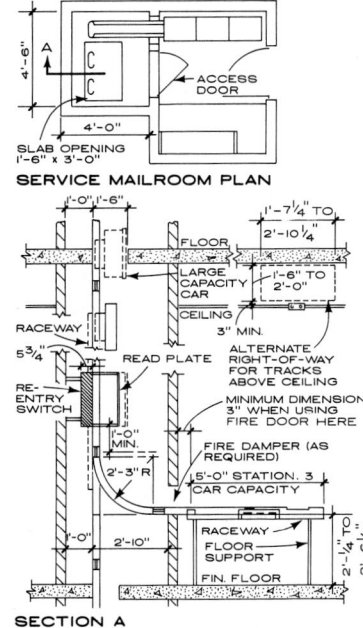

SERVICE MAILROOM PLAN

SECTION A

minimum area of 7 x 8 ft. Minimum inside dimensions of containers are 12 x 16 x 6 in.

There are two basic types of mechanical systems:

1. Selective vertical conveyor systems consisting of an endless chain carrying containers. When transportation is not purely vertical, horizontal capability must be added, such as conveyor belts.

2. Track and switch systems with self-propelled container cars. Systems permit inclines and declines and flexible routes. Destinations are actuated individually for each car.

CENTRAL MAILROOM

Walter Hart, AIA; North White Plains, New York

MAIL CHUTES AND BOXES

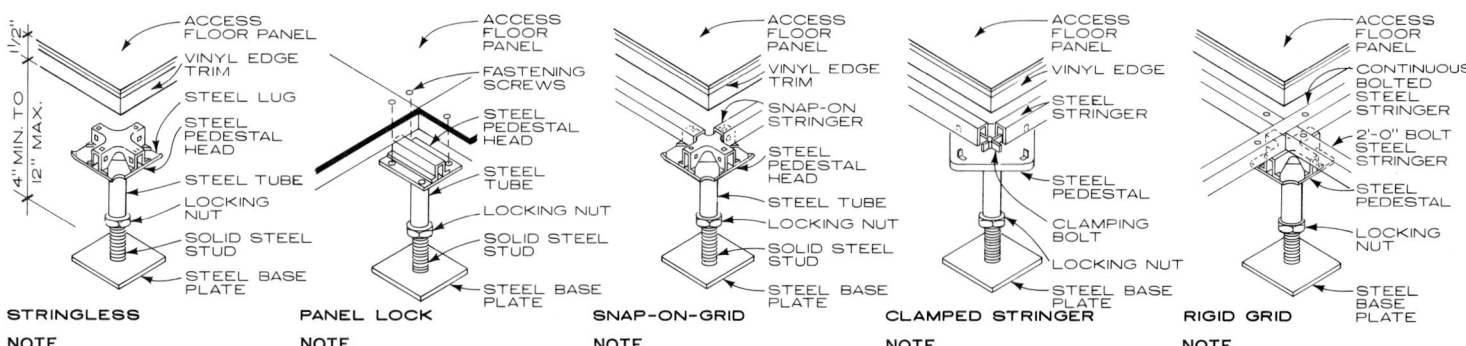

STRINGLESS

NOTE

This system is used in general construction or small computer rooms and provides maximum accessibility, optimum under-floor space, and electrical continuity. Note that it is dependent on panels being restrained by perimeter walls.

Maximum load: 150 psf.

Concentrated load: 400 lb.

PANEL LOCK

NOTE

This system is used in general construction and designed without a stringer connection at the edge. Bolted at the corner and at midpanel, it provides added rigidity over stringerless systems and maximum access and flexibility.

SNAP-ON-GRID

NOTE

This system is used in computer rooms and in general construction where frequent access is required. It provides improved lateral stability when compared to stringerless systems, electrical continuity, and plenum seal.

CLAMPED STRINGER

NOTE

This system is used in computer rooms and provides high lateral stability, complete access to below-floor cavity, electrical continuity for grounding, and static control. The system's contact between panel edge and stringer provides a plenum seal.

RIGID GRID

NOTE

This system is used in computer rooms and areas of heavy loading. It provides maximum rigidity for seismic or dynamic loading, electrical continuity for grounding or static control, and plenum seal.

Maximum load: 400 psf.

Concentrated load: 1250 lb.

TYPES OF SUPPORT SYSTEMS – LEAST STABLE TO MOST STABLE

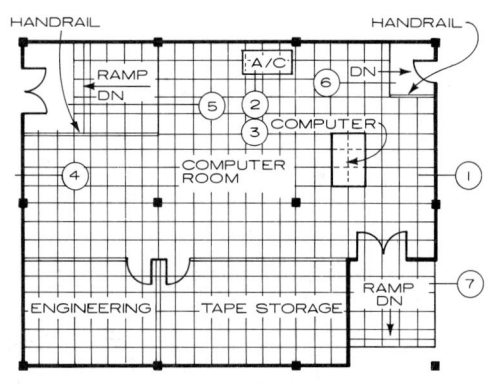

TYPICAL COMPUTER ROOM PLAN

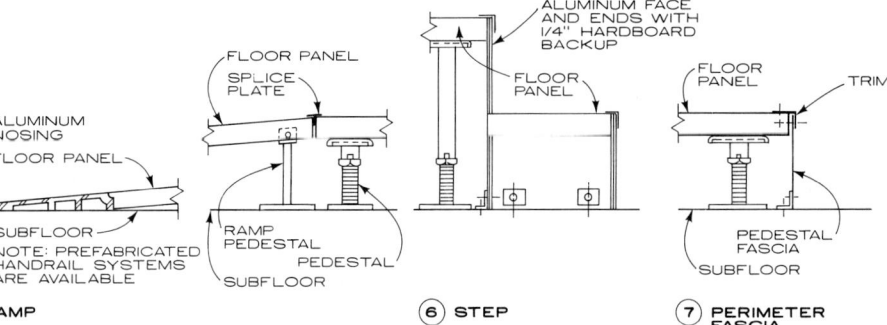

① CONDITION AT WALL OR COLUMN ② PLENUM ③ DUCT OR OTHER OBSTRUCTIONS ④ EDGE CONDITION

⑤ RAMP ⑥ STEP ⑦ PERIMETER FASCIA

TYPICAL ACCESS FLOOR CONDITIONS

COMPUTER ROOMS

Computers place high demands on electrical and mechanical as well as floor systems. The floor surface must be conductive, grounded to avoid accumulation of static electricity, and dustfree. Some floors are required to be nonmagnetic. An automatic fire detection system should be installed in plenums below floors. Plenums may not exceed 10,000 sq ft in areas and must be divided by noncombustible bulkheads. Computer rooms should be separated from all other occupancies within buildings by fire resistant rated walls, floors, and ceilings with a resistance of not less than 1 hr. Structural floors beneath access floors should incorporate provisions for water drainage to minimize damage to computer systems. All openings in access floors should be protected to minimize entrance of debris. Computer rooms require precision temperature and humidity control. Package air-conditioning units are available for computer room applications that supply air within tolerances of ±1.5° and ±5% relative humidity.

Computer room heat gains are often highly concentrated. For minimum room temperature gradients, supply air distribution should closely match load distribution. The distribution system should be sufficiently flexible to accommodate changes in the location and magnitude of the heat gains, with a minimum amount of change in the basic distribution system. Supply air systems usually require approximately 74 litres/sec per kilowatt of cooling to satisfy computer room conditions. This will provide a high enough air change rate to allow for even air temperature distribution. Packaged air-conditioning systems using the under-floor air supply plenum should adequately supply the large computer area. The area of the zoning is controlled by the various floor registers and perforated floor panels.

Setter, Leach and Lindstrom, Inc.; Minneapolis, Minnesota

ACCESS FLOORS

Access floors provide accessibility and flexibility to mechanical and electrical functions with added flexibility for placement of desks, telephone services, machines, and general office equipment. Equipment can be moved and reconnected to the floor quickly. Access floor systems are used in business offices, hospitals, laboratories, open area schools, television systems, computer rooms, and telephone-communication centers. Raised access floors in large areas offer maximum flexibility for future change, but can also be used in a recessed area of structural floor.

Panel types constructed of reinforced steel, aluminum, or steel encased wood core are available with finish surfaces of vinyl, vinyl asbestos tile, plastic laminate, and carpet. Basic panel sizes are 18 x 18 in., 24 x 24 in., and 30 x 30 in. Panel systems generally rely on gravity held connections, but can be mechanically held, increasing rigidity but reducing speed of removal. Wraparound, butt, and a protective plastic edge carpet

systems are available. Some are available with flame spread ratings of Class A. Aluminum panels are generally used to hold computers because metallic dust is eliminated. Steel panels are available in three structural grades: heavy duty, computer, and general construction.

The use of modular wiring increases installation speed and simplifies panel variation. Space beneath floors can be utilized as an air-conditioning plenum. Special panels provide perforation for air distribution, cable slots, and sound, and thermal insulation. Thermally insulated panels can reduce the possibility of condensation when under-floor space is used for air-conditioning. A variety of support systems can be provided in either steel or aluminum. Aluminum supports eliminate the possibility of rust and are nonmagnetic. Among the problems encountered with access floor systems are some difficulties in accommodating building angles, curves, and irregularities. Wet washing techniques cannot be used, and poor placement of exceedingly heavy loads can damage floor systems.

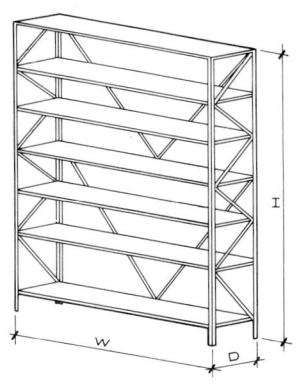

TYPICAL BASIC UNIT

AVAILABLE SIZES

W	D	H
24″	9″	3′-3″
30″	12″	6′-3″
36″	15″	7′-3″
42″	18″	8′-3″
48″	24″	10′-3″
	30″	
	36″	

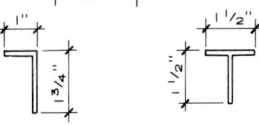

TYPICAL UPRIGHTS

CLASS 1 — STANDARD

CLASS 2 — REINFORCED

CLASS 3 — HEAVY DUTY

LOAD CAPACITY CLASSES

TYPICAL SHELF CAPACITIES

SHELF WIDTH	UNIFORM LOAD (LB)		
	CLASS 1	CLASS 2	CLASS 3
24″	900	1500	2000
30″	800	1300	1800
36″	700	1200	1500
42″	350	800	1200
48″	300	700	1000

NOTES
1. Shelving is available in two types. When bolted, the separate movable units are more permanent. When clipped, the shelving is continuous, but more easily set up and dismantled.
2. Shelves are adjustable at 1 in. increments.
3. Diagonal bracing may be eliminated when solid backs or ends are used.

SOLID SHELVING SYSTEM

UPRIGHTS — STANDARD OR REINFORCED — 12″, 18″, AND 24″ WIDE AND 53″, 63″, 73″, AND 88″ HIGH

SHELVES — 12″ AND 18″ DEEP AND 24″, 30″, 36″, 42″, 48″, AND 60″ LONG. USE TWO 12″ SHELVES WITH 24″ UPRIGHTS. SHELVES ADJUST ON 5″ CENTERS

NOTES
1. Approved by National Sanitation Foundation for food storage.
2. Available accessories include corner braces, dividers, bottle shelves, back, and side ledges.
3. Finishes may be nickel plated, chrome, stainless steel, and brass.

FLOOR MOUNTED — ERECTA SHELVING

WIRE SHELVING SYSTEM — FOR FOOD AND RESIDENTIAL STORAGE — METROPOLITAN WIRE CORPORATION

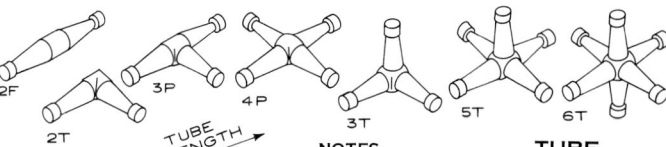

CONNECTIONS

2F 3P 4P 3T 5T 6T 2T

TUBE LENGTH

NOTES
1. Both connectors and tubes are available in chrome and matte black finishes.
2. Tubes are manufactured in heavy gauge stainless steel $\frac{1}{2}$ in. o.d.

TUBE LENGTHS

CM	IN.
65	2.09
130	4.68
275	10.39
395	15.08
460	17.68
530	20.27
595	22.87
805	31.18

FLOOR MOUNTED — ABSTRACTA SHELVING

TUBULAR STEEL SHELVING SYSTEM — FOR DISPLAYS AND EXHIBITS — ABSTRACTA STRUCTURES, INC.

VERTICAL MEMBERS ARE AVAILABLE IN 20″, 30″, 39″, AND 84″ HEIGHTS AND HAVE A DEPTH OF 11″

SHELVES AND OTHER COMPONENTS ARE 12″ DEEP AND 31″ WIDE. EACH SHELF CAN CARRY UP TO 200 LB OF DISTRIBUTED WEIGHT

OTHER COMPONENTS AVAILABLE INCLUDE DROP — LEAF CABINETS, MAGAZINE RACKS, AND RECORD STORAGE UNIT

NOTES
Shelves are hung from a steel truss; thus tension is transferred to metal members, increasing load capacity.

TYPICAL DIMENSIONS:
Height: 81$\frac{7}{8}$ in.
Depth: 15 in.
Length: 85, 119$\frac{1}{4}$, 121$\frac{5}{8}$ in.

METAL TRUSS
SHELF
TIE ROD
WOOD UPRIGHT
SLIDING PANELS

WALL MOUNTED — EUROWALL 73 STORAGE SYSTEM

METAL AND WOOD SHELVING SYSTEM ARCHITECTURAL SUPPLEMENTS INCORPORATED

FLOOR MOUNTED — BROOKLYN SHELVING SYSTEM

METAL AND WOOD SHELVING SYSTEM ACERBIS INTERNATIONAL

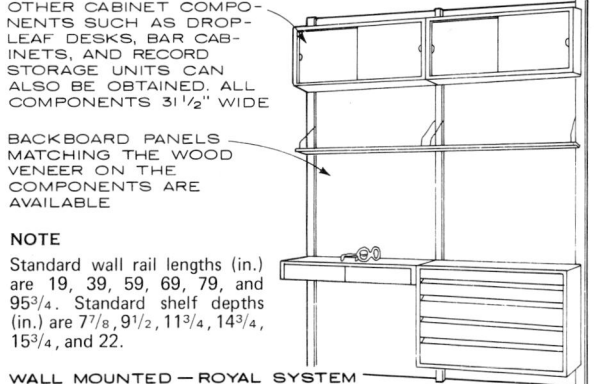

OTHER CABINET COMPONENTS SUCH AS DROP-LEAF DESKS, BAR CABINETS, AND RECORD STORAGE UNITS CAN ALSO BE OBTAINED. ALL COMPONENTS 31½″ WIDE

BACKBOARD PANELS MATCHING THE WOOD VENEER ON THE COMPONENTS ARE AVAILABLE

NOTE
Standard wall rail lengths (in.) are 19, 39, 59, 69, 79, and 95³/₄. Standard shelf depths (in.) are 7⁷/₈, 9¹/₂, 11³/₄, 14³/₄, 15³/₄, and 22.

NOTES
This storage system can be entirely assembled from the front. Available components include fold-down bar units, desk tops, drawer chests, and hideaway beds. Walk-in closets are also available. All units come in 15³/₄ and 24 in. depths.

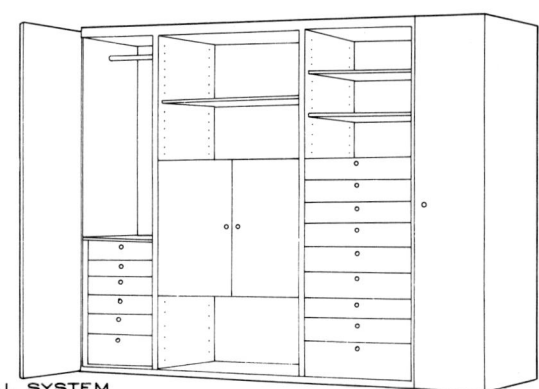

WALL MOUNTED — ROYAL SYSTEM

WOOD SHELVING SYSTEM ROYAL SYSTEM INC.

FLOOR MOUNTED — WALL SYSTEM

PANEL AND COMPONENT SHELVING SYSTEM INTERLUBKE - ICF

Charles Szoradi, AIA and F. Menendez; Washington, D.C.

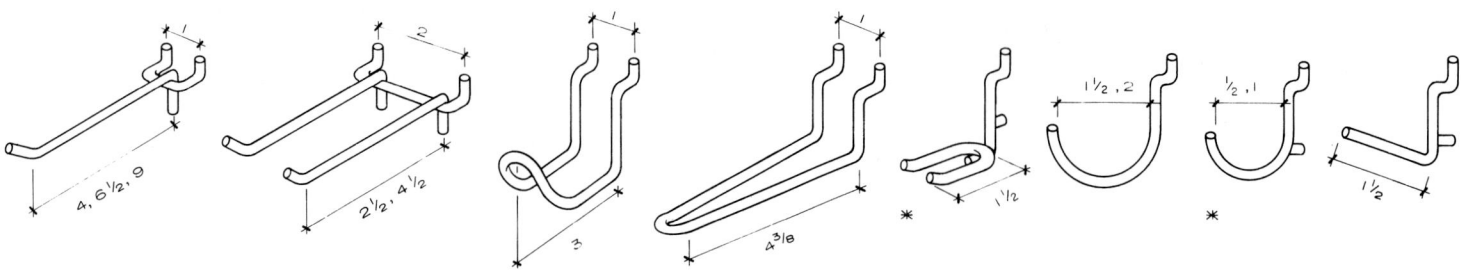

SINGLE AND DOUBLE HOOKS

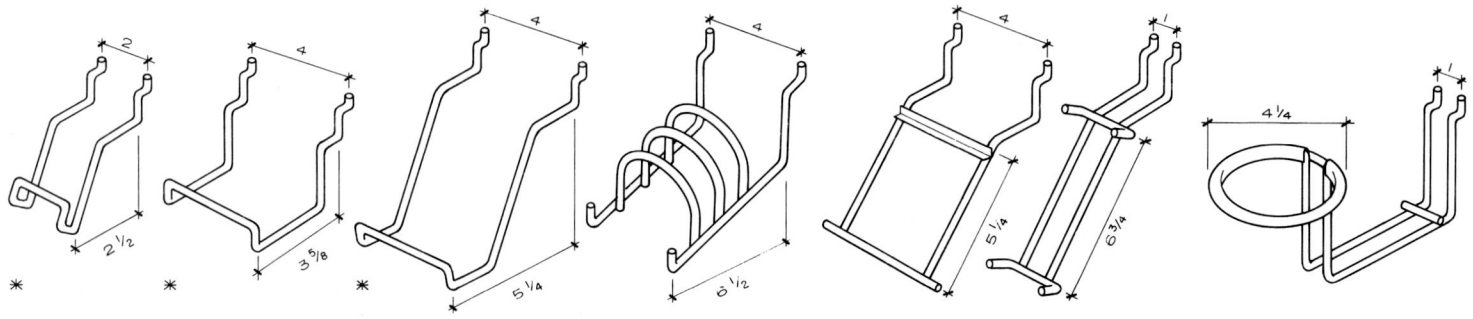

EASELS   SHOE BRACKETS   HAT BRACKET

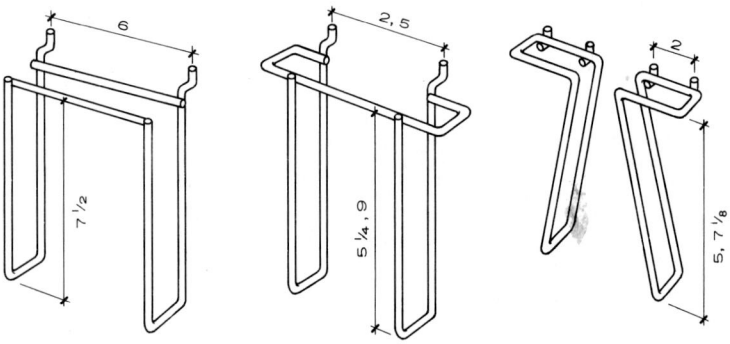

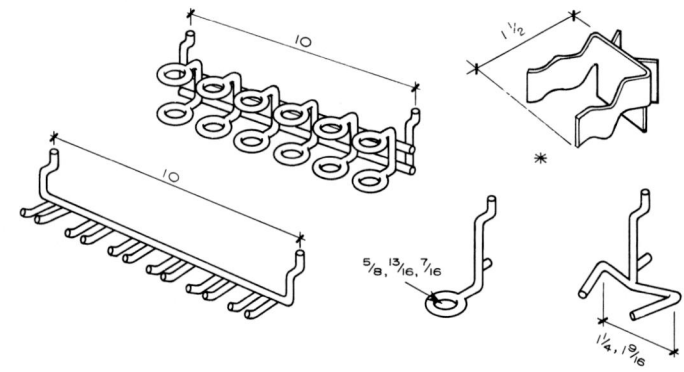

LITERATURE RACKS   TOOL HOLDERS

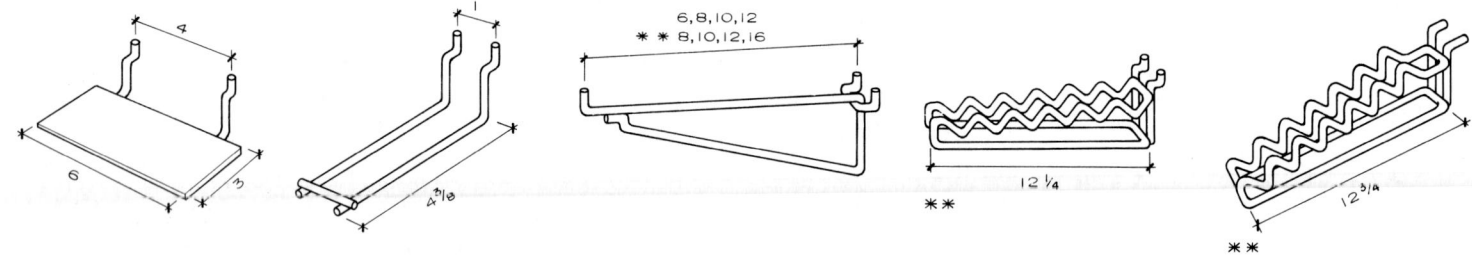

METAL SHELF   SHELF BRACKETS   GARDEN TOOL BRACKETS

PLASTIC HOUSEHOLD FIXTURES

NOTE

Perforated board fixtures are generally for use with $1/8''$ or $1/4''$ hardboard.

✳ To be used with $1/8''$ board only.

✳✳ To be used with $1/4''$ board only.

Above data is incomplete. Consult manufacturers' catalogs for a complete listing of fixtures and dimensions.

Geddes, Brecher, Qualls, Cunningham, Architects; Philadelphia, Pennsylvania

 STORAGE SHELVING

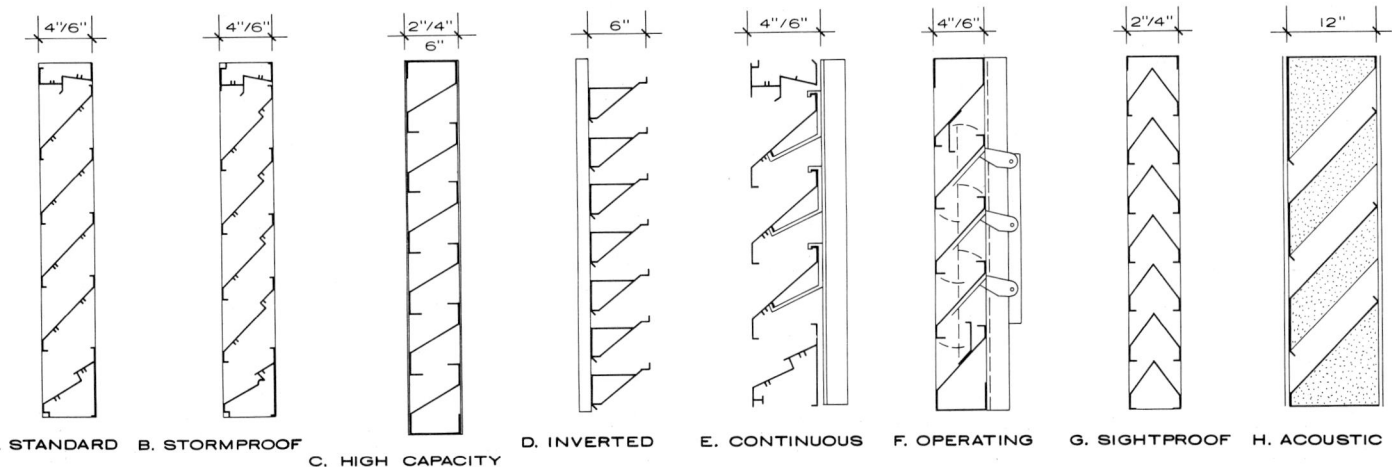

A. STANDARD   B. STORMPROOF

C. HIGH CAPACITY

D. INVERTED   E. CONTINUOUS   F. OPERATING   G. SIGHTPROOF   H. ACOUSTIC

TYPICAL LOUVER AND VENT PROFILES

A. For use in single louver application in small openings or in multiple louver applications where vertical mullion or horizontal joint appearance is desired.

B. Stormproof blades provide superior weather protection but reduce free area.
Maximum standard width is 6 ft; minimum width is 1 ft.

C. Used in situations where high velocity and maximum free area are of primary importance.

D. Used primarily as a cooling tower screen where water spray should be contained. They are field assembled and are available in unlimited widths.

E. Used for large openings where continuous horizontal line appearance is desired. Unlimited widths are available; they are field assembled.

F. This permits maximum ventilation capacity when open as well as resistance against weather penetration when closed. Airflow is easily controlled. Recommended maximum blade span is 5 ft; minimum width is 1 ft.

G. This is 100% sightproof from all angles with horizontal blade lines. Maximum recommended width is 7 ft.

H. Used to reduce ambient noise and noise transmission. Blades are backed with mineral fiber. Maximum recommended blade span is 7 ft.

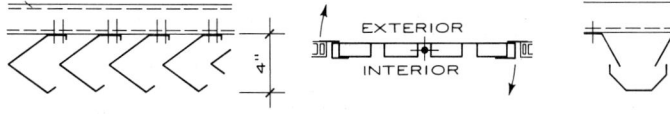

J. "V" BLADE   K. PIVOTED DOOR LOUVER   L. VERTICAL LINE

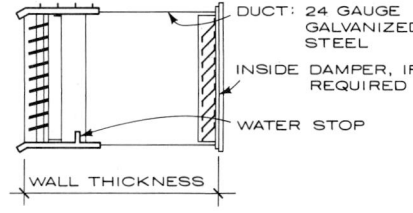

M. BRICK VENT

J. Used for soffit, vertical, continuous horizontal, or sightproof louvers. Blades are field assembled to any desired length or width. They must have horizontal supports at 5 ft maximum.

K. Vertically pivoted intake device provides large volumes of air. It may be individually or gang operated. Units are 24 in. wide and maximum height is 8 ft 5 in.

L. Vertical louver matches standard exterior metal building panel profiles. Maximum recommended blade width is 16 ft; additional length is lapped.

M. Vents for use in foundations, chimney flues, or crawl spaces are made from cast or extruded aluminum and are available with anodic, baked enamel, lacquer, or sandblasted finish. They are made to be compatible with standard, modular, speed, or fuel brick sizes in 4, 6, or 8 in. depths and in lengths to 20 ft.

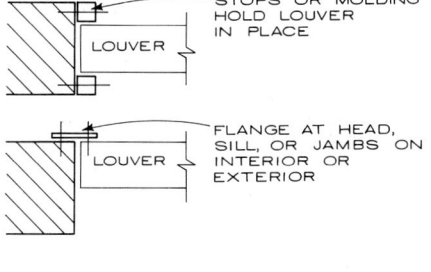

STOPS OR MOLDING HOLD LOUVER IN PLACE

FLANGE AT HEAD, SILL, OR JAMBS ON INTERIOR OR EXTERIOR

ANGLE AT HEAD, SILL, OR JAMBS ON INTERIOR OR EXTERIOR

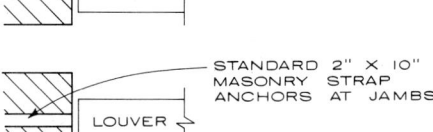

STANDARD 2" X 10" MASONRY STRAP ANCHORS AT JAMBS

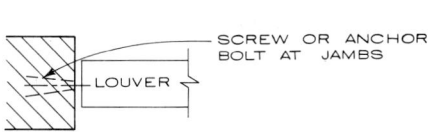

SCREW OR ANCHOR BOLT AT JAMBS

METHODS OF INSTALLATION

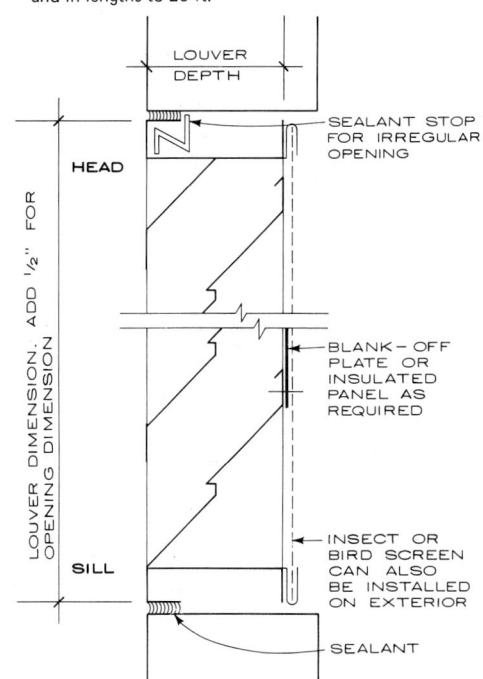

LOUVER ACCESSORIES

GENERAL NOTES

1. The dimensions shown are the most common; others are available.

2. Horizontal louvers can be of unlimited height. Larger louver depths provide more free area per square foot and better weather penetration resistance than smaller depths.

3. Standard materials are 16 gauge galvanized or cold rolled steel and 14 or 12 gauge extruded aluminum alloy. Other metals can be used for special applications. Translucent fiberglass is also a standard blade material where daylighting is desirable.

4. A welded assembly of louvers is preferred to mechanical assembly. This eliminates blade/frame loosening, wear, and vibration noise, as well as providing a better assembly for finishing.

5. Factory finishing is recommended for maximum control of color and durability. The finish for steel louvers is baked enamel in a variety of colors. Aluminum finishes include mill, clear lacquer, baked enamel, and anodic.

6. Screens may be used for protection from insects, birds, or vandalism. Supplied in frames, typical screening for insects is 16 x 18 mesh aluminum or fiberglass; for birds or vandalism 1/2 in. square mesh 14 or 16 gauge aluminum or 1/4 in. square mesh 16 or 18 gauge aluminum.

7. Other options available with louvers include mullions, blank-off plates or insulated panels, frame extensions, sill pieces, sealant stops, and fusible links.

Graham Davidson, Architect; Washington, D.C.

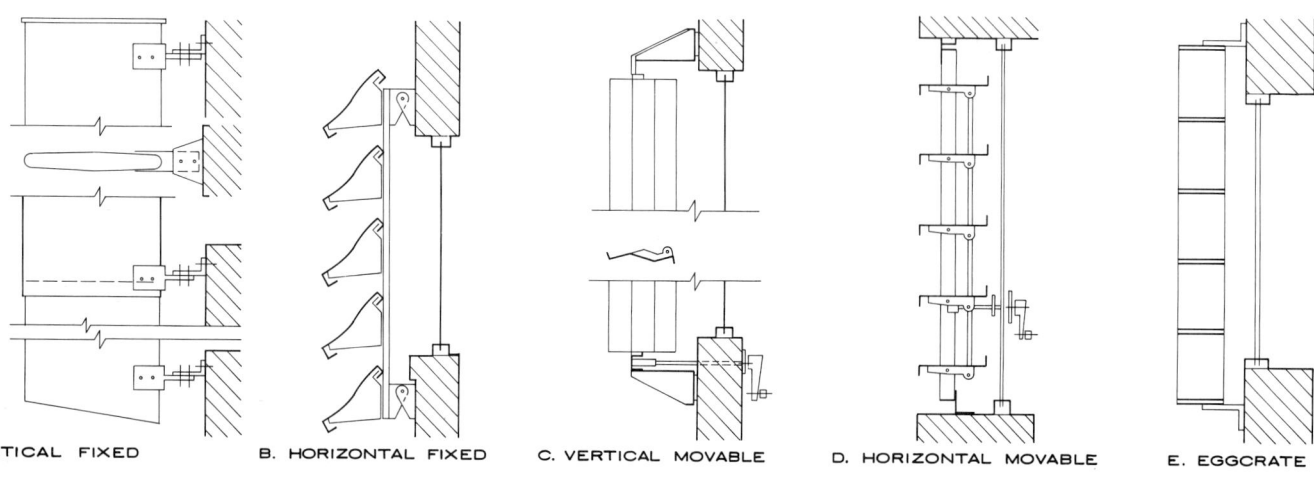

A. VERTICAL FIXED   B. HORIZONTAL FIXED   C. VERTICAL MOVABLE   D. HORIZONTAL MOVABLE   E. EGGCRATE

TYPICAL SUN SHADES AND CONTROLS

A. This device is effective on an east or west wall and can be attached at any degree of angle to facade. If slanted, it should incline to north. Fins are made in floor-to-floor lengths, capped at top and bottom, and telescoped top into bottom at intermediate levels.

B. This device is effective on any side of a building. Blades have a maximum length of 20 ft with supports of 6 ft on center.

C. Used on east or west side of building. This type may interfere with view. Many models are available up to 27 in. wide and 12 ft high.

D. Although this is effective on any side of a building, it is the least restrictive to view when used on the south side. It is usually hinged at the head for emergency exit and window washing. Blades are 9 in. deep; maximum width is 6 ft.

E. This type is very effective on southeast and southwest orientations. It is efficient in hot climates especially if bars can be tilted to more effective angles. All dimensions are variable according to desired function.

EXTERIOR SUN CONTROLS

The incidence of the sun's rays on a building transmits solar energy to the interior of the building. Since the heat gain through glass is particularly high, various forms of solar control for fenestration have been developed to reduce the use of mechanical equipment for cooling.

The most efficient of these is exterior shading, that is, avoiding the penetration of solar heat through the skin of the building. Exterior shading devices vary according to climate, orientation, and building function and are manufactured to suit specific conditions. They are strong design elements.

Sunshades (fixed horizontal or vertical fins, outriggers, and grills) shade glass completely or partially at critical times. Sun controls (movable horizontal or vertical fins) regulate the quantity of solar heat and light admitted through the glass, which is clear. Adjusting mechanisms can be manual or electric and can be automatically operated with time or photoelectric controls.

Aluminum, either sheet or extruded, is the standard material. Anodic and baked enamel coatings are available as finishes.

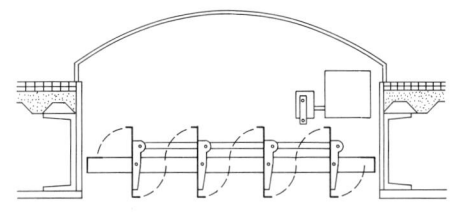

F. OUTRIGGER

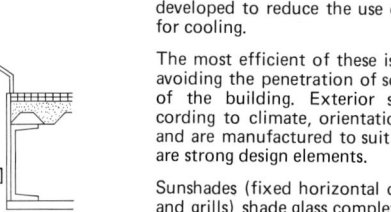

G. SKYLIGHT SHUTTER

F. Overhangs are most effectively used on the south side of a building. Wall brackets are made of cast aluminum. Projections greater than 6 ft require structural support or hangers.

G. Perimeter framing should be designed to suit mounting conditions. Electrically operated shutters are available. Maximum width is 10 ft; length is unlimited.

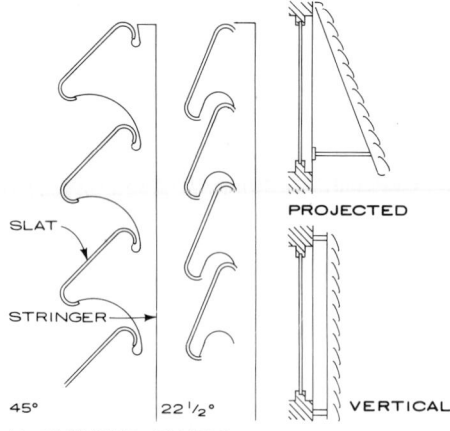

H. SHUTTER PANELS

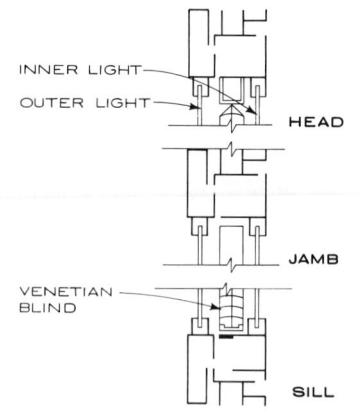

I. INTEGRAL VENETIAN BLINDS

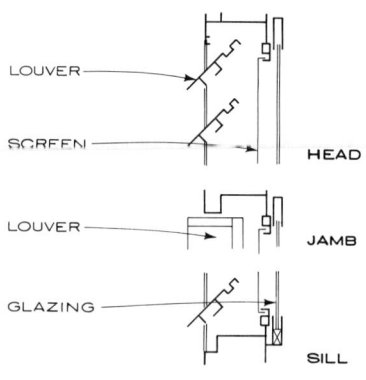

J. INTEGRAL HORIZONTAL SHADES

SPECIAL WINDOW TREATMENT

H. These panels are effective solar screens. The aluminum louvers are spaced to preserve the outside view and admit soft, diffused light while eliminating heat and glare. Horizontal slats snap onto stringer supports which can be easily attached to most structures.

I. This window type combines the thermal insulating values of dual glazing with the advantage of semi-external shading. An aluminum blind is provided between two pieces of glass, each in its own frame and each frame pivoted horizontally or vertically to make cleaning possible. The cavity between the two pieces of glass is ventilated to avoid condensation and to equalize air pressure.

The venetian blind can be tilted and, in some models, raised with controls on the interior window frame.

Window frames are constructed of aluminum, teak or pine.

J. A combination of exterior adjustable horizontal louvers and window frame, this window can be double hung, sliding, jalousie, or fixed. Louvers can be aluminum alloy extrusions, redwood, or glass.

Graham Davidson, Architect; Washington, D.C.

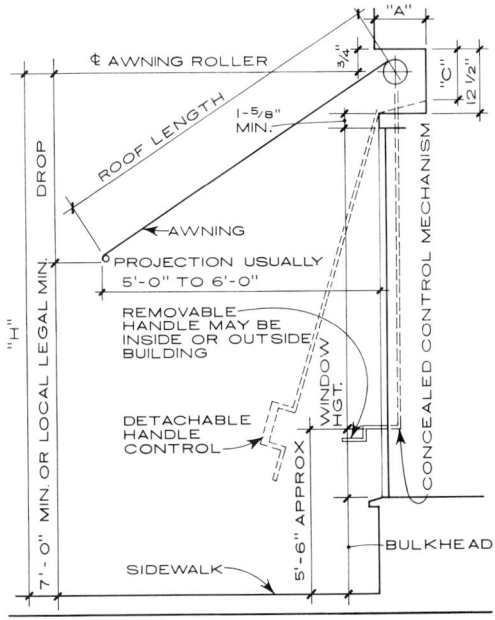

DIAGRAMATIC SECTION RECESSED BOX INSTALLATION

AWNING MATERIALS:
1. Canvas
2. Interlocking metal slats
   a. aluminum
   b. bronze
   c. stainless steel
3. Fiberglass

AWNING OPERATORS:
1. Detachable handle control
2. Gear box & shaft (concealed or exposed) with removable handle inside or outside of building
3. Electric control

AWNING BOX CLEARANCES:

Recessed box sizes	"H"	"A"	"B"	"C"
A. lateral arm type	9'-6" to 11'-0"	10"	10 1/2"	10"
	9'-6" to 12'-0"	10 1/2"	12"	10"
	9'-6" to 14'-0"	11"	13 1/2"	10"
B. outrigger arm type	varies	6'-2"	6'-2"	6'-2"

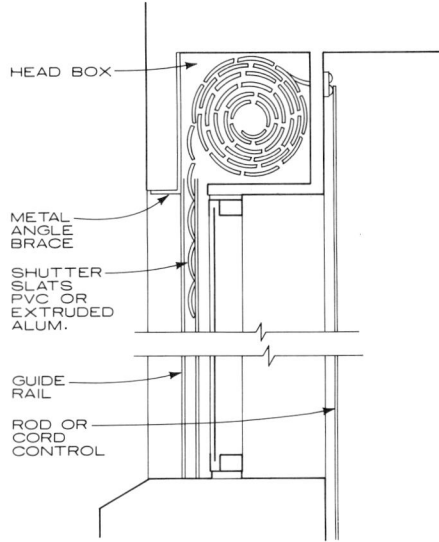

NOTE

Rolling shutters provide sun control not only by shading windows from direct sun rays but also by way of two dead airspaces—one between shutter and window, the other within the shutter extrusions to serve as insulation. The dead airspaces work as well in winter to prevent the escape of heat from the interior. In addition, shutters are useful as privacy and security measures. They can be installed in new or existing construction and are manufactured in standard window sizes.

ROLLING SHUTTERS

Graham Davidson, Architect; Washington, D.C.

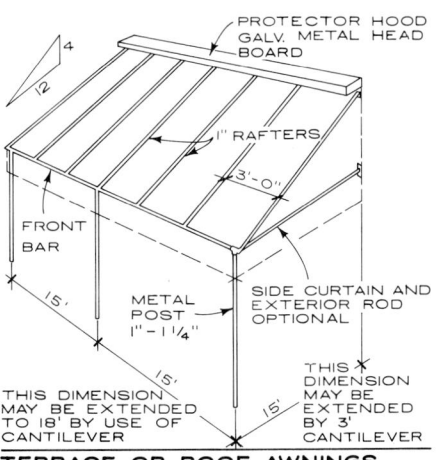

TERRACE OR ROOF AWNINGS

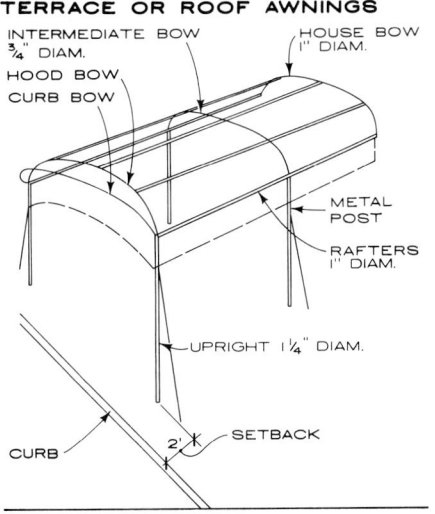

CANOPIES - LOW CURVED BOW SHOWN

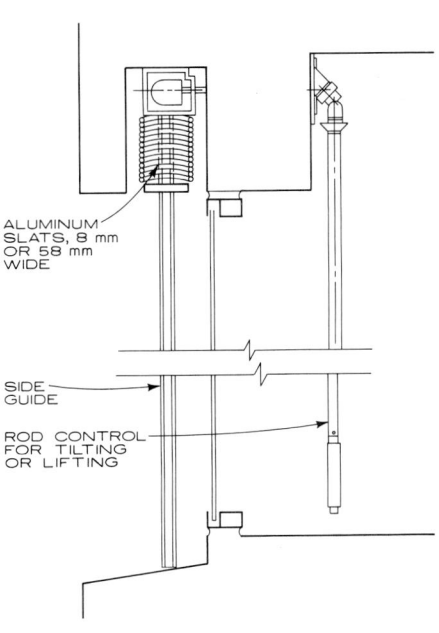

NOTE

External blinds protect the building interior from solar gain and glare, but can be raised partially or fully to the head when not needed. Manual or electric control is from inside the building.

EXTERNAL VENETIAN BLINDS

TERRACE OR ROOF AWNINGS

To provide complete sun protection and shade, the overall length of the awning bar should extend 3 in. past the glass line on both sides. For proper sunshade protection, awnings should project at least as far forward from the face of the window as the bottom of the window is below the front bar of the awning.

The wall measurement of an awning is the distance down the face of the building from the point where the awning attaches to the face of the building (or from the center of the roller in the case of the roller type awning).

The projection of an awning is the distance from the face of the building to the front bar of the awning in its correct projected position.

Right and left of an awning are your right and left as you are facing the awning looking into the building.

Framework consists of galvanized steel pipe, with non-rattling fittings. Awning is lace-on type canvas with rope reinforced eave. Protector hood is galvanized sheet metal or either bronze, copper, or aluminum.

Sizes of members should be checked by calculation for conditions not similar to those shown on this page.

Consult local building code for limitations on height and setback.

COVERED WALKWAYS

Covered walkways are available with aluminum fascia and soffit panels in a number of profiles. The fascia panels are supported with pipe columns and steel or aluminum structural members if necessary. Panels can cantilever up to 30% of span. Canopy designs can be supported from above.

Another method of providing covered exterior space is with stressed membrane structures. Using highly tensile synthetic fabric and cable in collaboration with compression members, usually metal, dynamic and versatile tentlike coverings can be created. Membrane structures are especially suited to temporary installations.

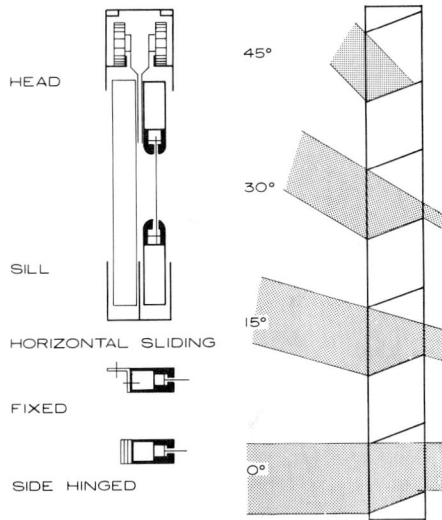

NOTE

These miniature external louvers shade windows from direct sunlight and glare while allowing a high degree of visibility, light, ventilation, insect protection, and daytime privacy. Much like a woven metal fabric, they are not strong architectural elements but present a uniform appearance in the areas covered. The solar screen is installed in aluminum frames and can be adapted to suit most applications.

SOLAR SCREEN SIZES

MATE-RIAL	LOUVERS	TILT	VERTICAL SPACING	SIZE (WIDTHS)
Aluminum	17"	17°	1" o.c.	18"–48"
Bronze	17", 23"	20°	1/2" o.c.	Up to 72 1/2"

Aluminum screens are available in black or light green. Bronze screens come in black only.

SOLAR SCREENS

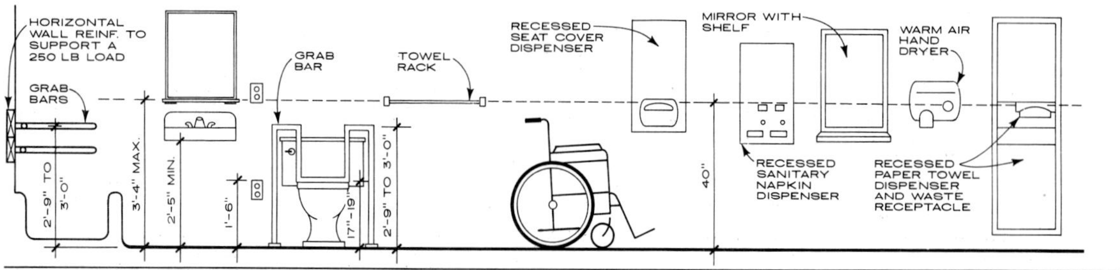

HEIGHT REQUIREMENTS FOR THE HANDICAPPED

NOTES ON GRAB BARS

1. SIZE: 1½ in. O.D. with 1½ in. clearance at wall.
2. MATERIAL: Stainless steel or chrome plated brass with knurled finish, standard.
3. INSTALLATION: Concealed or exposed fasteners; return all ends to wall, intermediate supports at 3 ft maximum. Use heavy duty type bars and methods of installation.

The provisions of the American National Standard, ANSI A117.1 must be consulted, as well as applicable local and federal regulations.

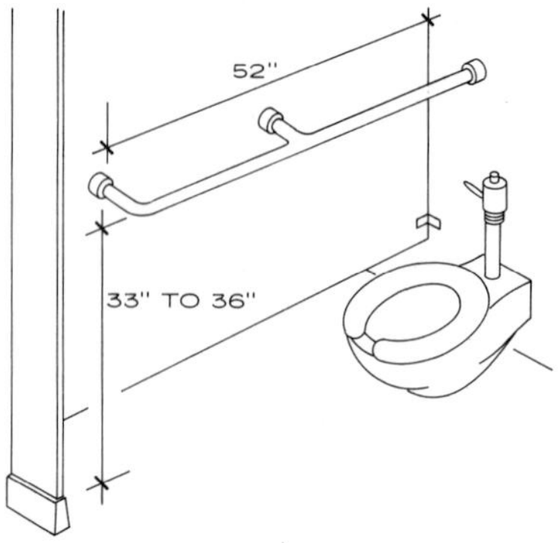

WHEELCHAIR COMPARTMENT

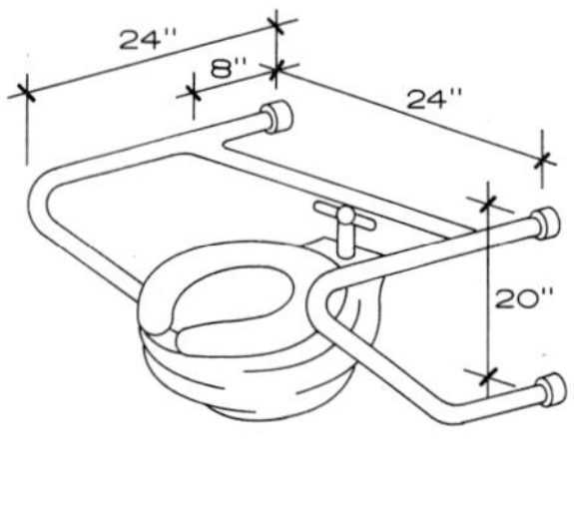

STRADDLE BAR

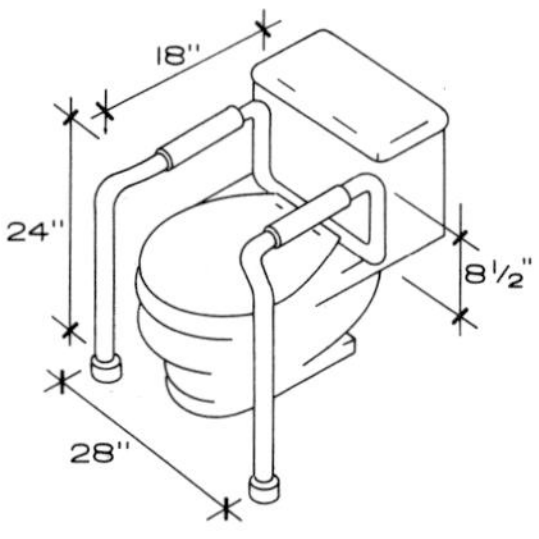

SAFETY ARM REST

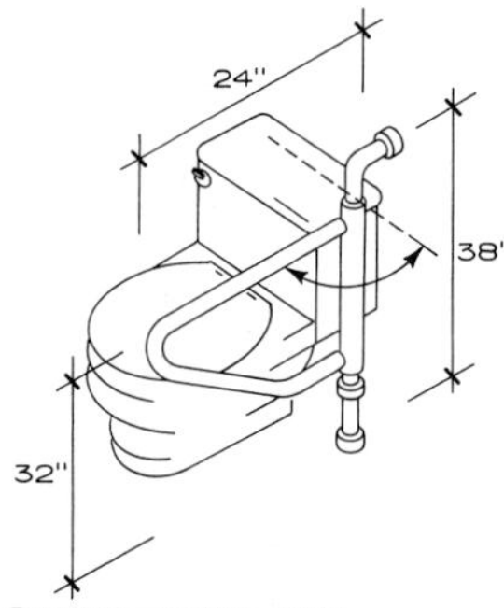

SWING—AWAY BAR

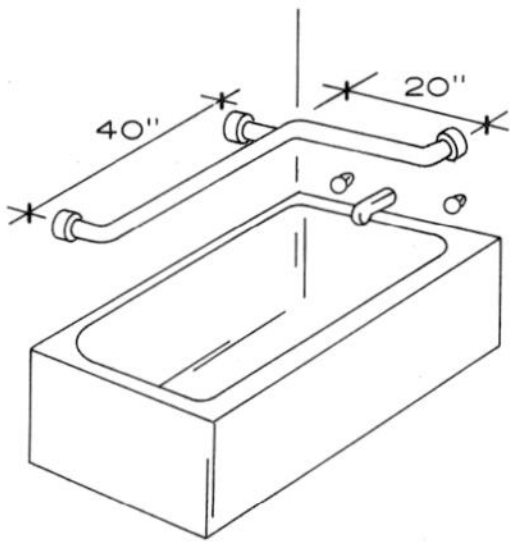

HORIZONTAL TUB BAR

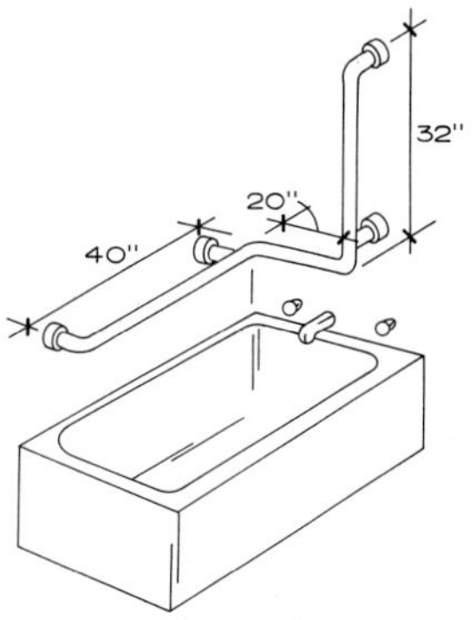

TUB WITH VERTICAL RAIL

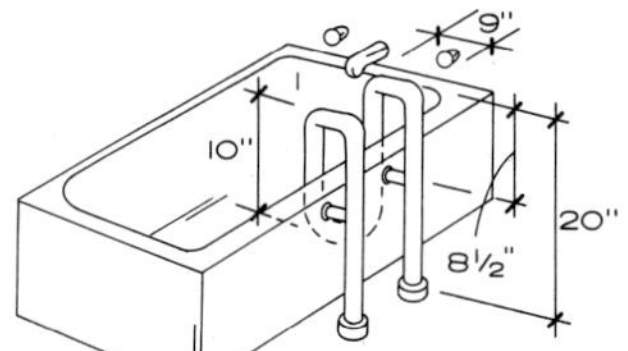

TUB ENTRY RAILS

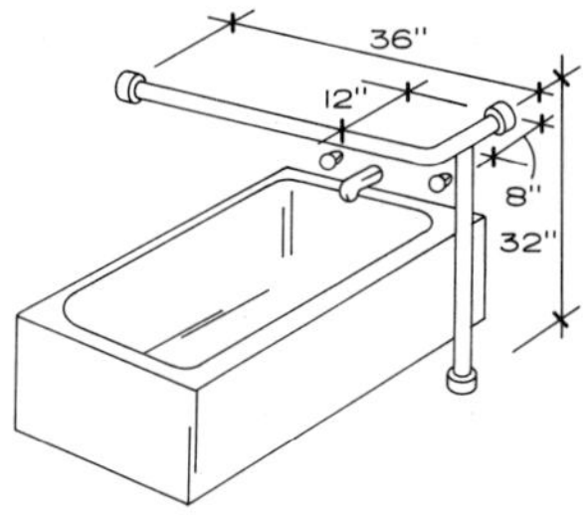

CORNER BAR

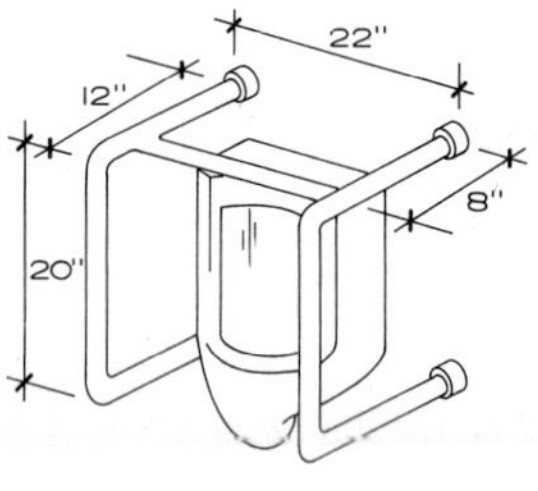

URINAL BAR

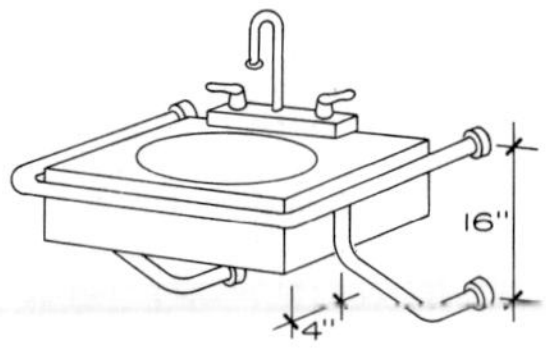

LAVATORY AID RAIL

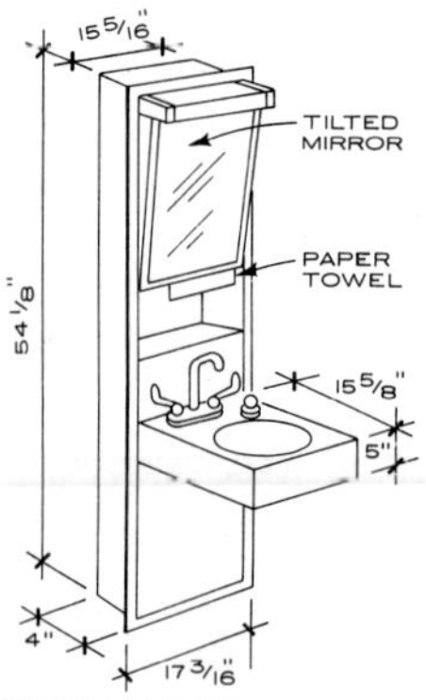

CONSOLE UNIT

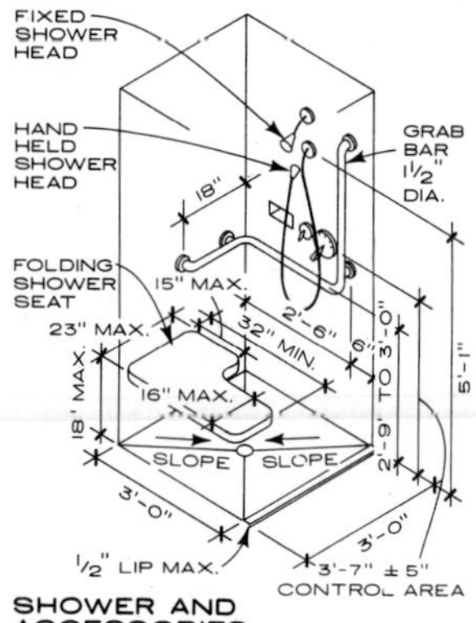

SHOWER AND ACCESSORIES

GRAB BAR CONFIGURATIONS

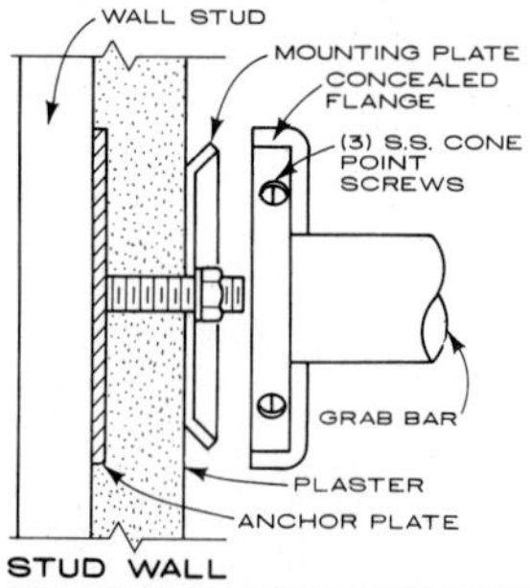

STUD WALL

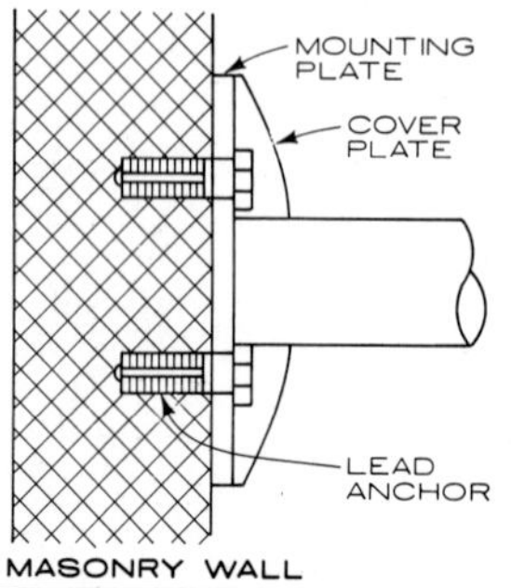

MASONRY WALL

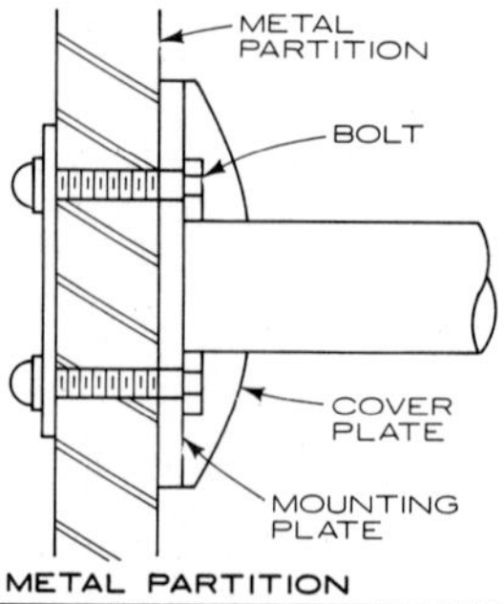

METAL PARTITION

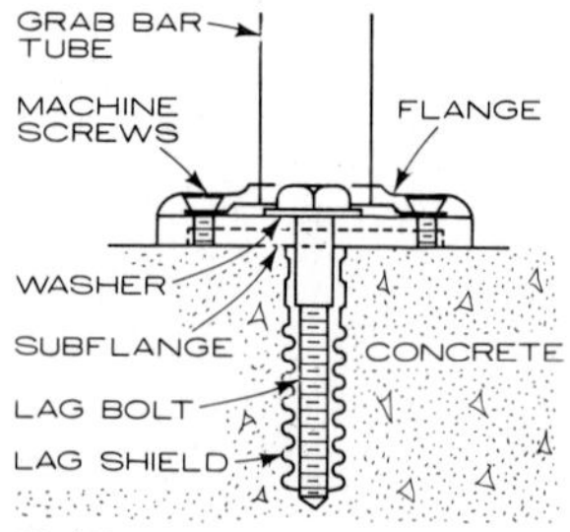

SLAB

ATTACHMENT DETAILS

A. Allen Hitchcock, AIA; Baltimore, Maryland

TOILET AND BATH ACCESSORIES

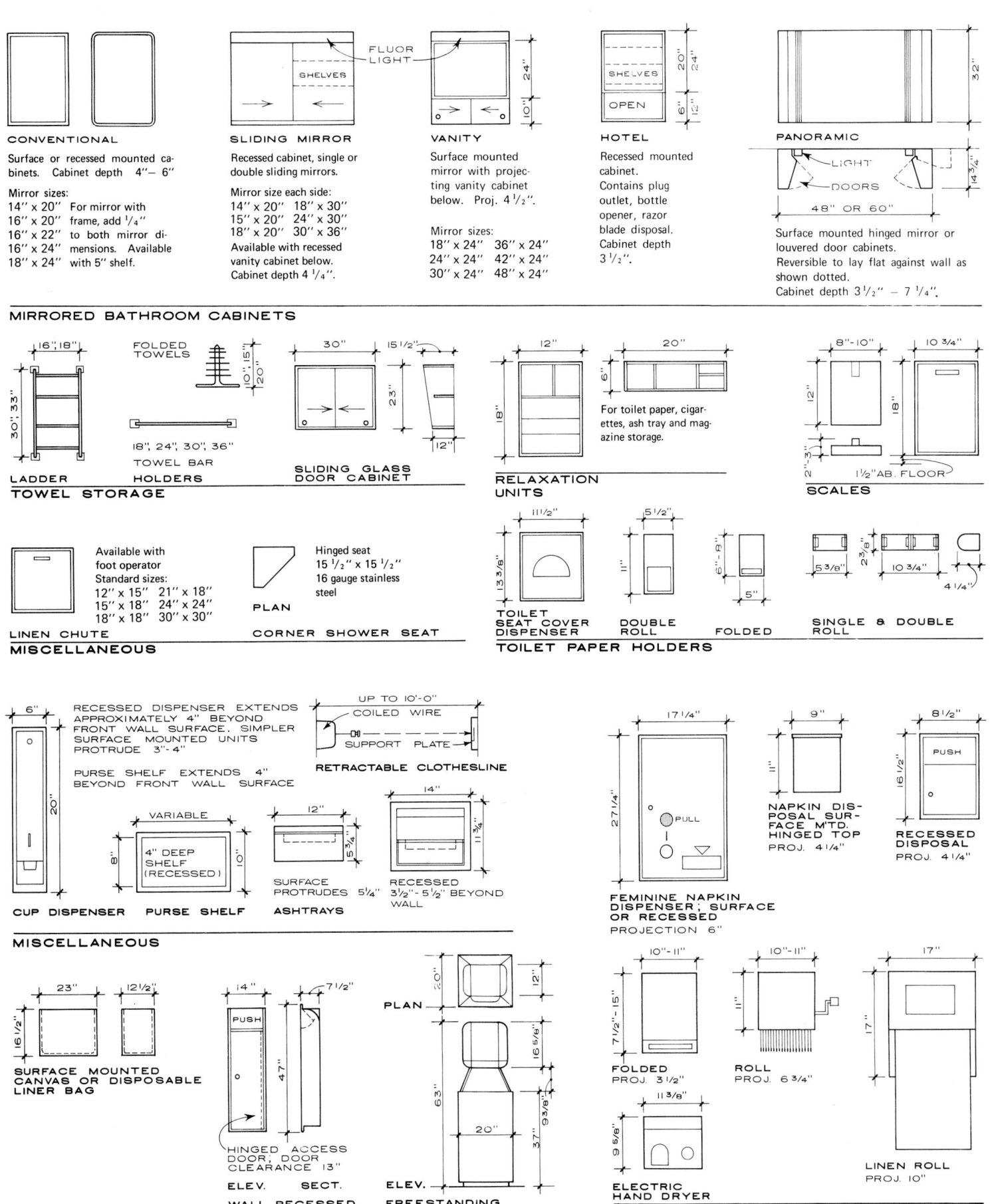

CONVENTIONAL

Surface or recessed mounted cabinets. Cabinet depth 4″– 6″

Mirror sizes:
14″ x 20″ For mirror with
16″ x 20″ frame, add 1/4″
16″ x 22″ to both mirror di-
16″ x 24″ mensions. Available
18″ x 24″ with 5″ shelf.

SLIDING MIRROR

Recessed cabinet, single or double sliding mirrors.

Mirror size each side:
14″ x 20″   18″ x 30″
15″ x 20″   24″ x 30″
18″ x 20″   30″ x 36″
Available with recessed vanity cabinet below.
Cabinet depth 4 1/4″.

VANITY

Surface mounted mirror with projecting vanity cabinet below. Proj. 4 1/2″.

Mirror sizes:
18″ x 24″   36″ x 24″
24″ x 24″   42″ x 24″
30″ x 24″   48″ x 24″

HOTEL

Recessed mounted cabinet. Contains plug outlet, bottle opener, razor blade disposal. Cabinet depth 3 1/2″.

PANORAMIC

Surface mounted hinged mirror or louvered door cabinets. Reversible to lay flat against wall as shown dotted.
Cabinet depth 3 1/2″ – 7 1/4″.

MIRRORED BATHROOM CABINETS

LADDER   **HOLDERS**   **SLIDING GLASS DOOR CABINET**

FOLDED TOWELS

18″, 24″, 30″, 36″ TOWEL BAR

TOWEL STORAGE

RELAXATION UNITS

For toilet paper, cigarettes, ash tray and magazine storage.

SCALES

1 1/2″ AB. FLOOR

LINEN CHUTE

Available with foot operator
Standard sizes:
12″ x 15″   21″ x 18″
15″ x 18″   24″ x 24″
18″ x 18″   30″ x 30″

CORNER SHOWER SEAT

Hinged seat 15 1/2″ x 15 1/2″ 16 gauge stainless steel

PLAN

MISCELLANEOUS

TOILET SEAT COVER DISPENSER   **DOUBLE ROLL**   **FOLDED**   **SINGLE & DOUBLE ROLL**

TOILET PAPER HOLDERS

RECESSED DISPENSER EXTENDS APPROXIMATELY 4″ BEYOND FRONT WALL SURFACE. SIMPLER SURFACE MOUNTED UNITS PROTRUDE 3″– 4″

PURSE SHELF EXTENDS 4″ BEYOND FRONT WALL SURFACE

UP TO 10′-0″
COILED WIRE
SUPPORT PLATE

RETRACTABLE CLOTHESLINE

VARIABLE

4″ DEEP SHELF (RECESSED)

CUP DISPENSER   **PURSE SHELF**   **ASHTRAYS**

SURFACE PROTRUDES 5 1/4″

RECESSED 3 1/2″ – 5 1/2″ BEYOND WALL

NAPKIN DISPOSAL SURFACE M'TD. HINGED TOP PROJ. 4 1/4″

RECESSED DISPOSAL PROJ. 4 1/4″

FEMININE NAPKIN DISPENSER; SURFACE OR RECESSED PROJECTION 6″

PULL

MISCELLANEOUS

SURFACE MOUNTED CANVAS OR DISPOSABLE LINER BAG

PUSH

HINGED ACCESS DOOR; DOOR CLEARANCE 13″

ELEV.   SECT.
WALL RECESSED

PLAN

ELEV. FREESTANDING

WASTE RECEPTACLES

FOLDED PROJ. 3 1/2″   **ROLL** PROJ. 6 3/4″

ELECTRIC HAND DRYER

LINEN ROLL PROJ. 10″

HAND TOWEL DISPENSERS AND DRYERS

H. E. Hallenbeck, Capuccilli-Bell Architects, AIA; Syracuse, New York

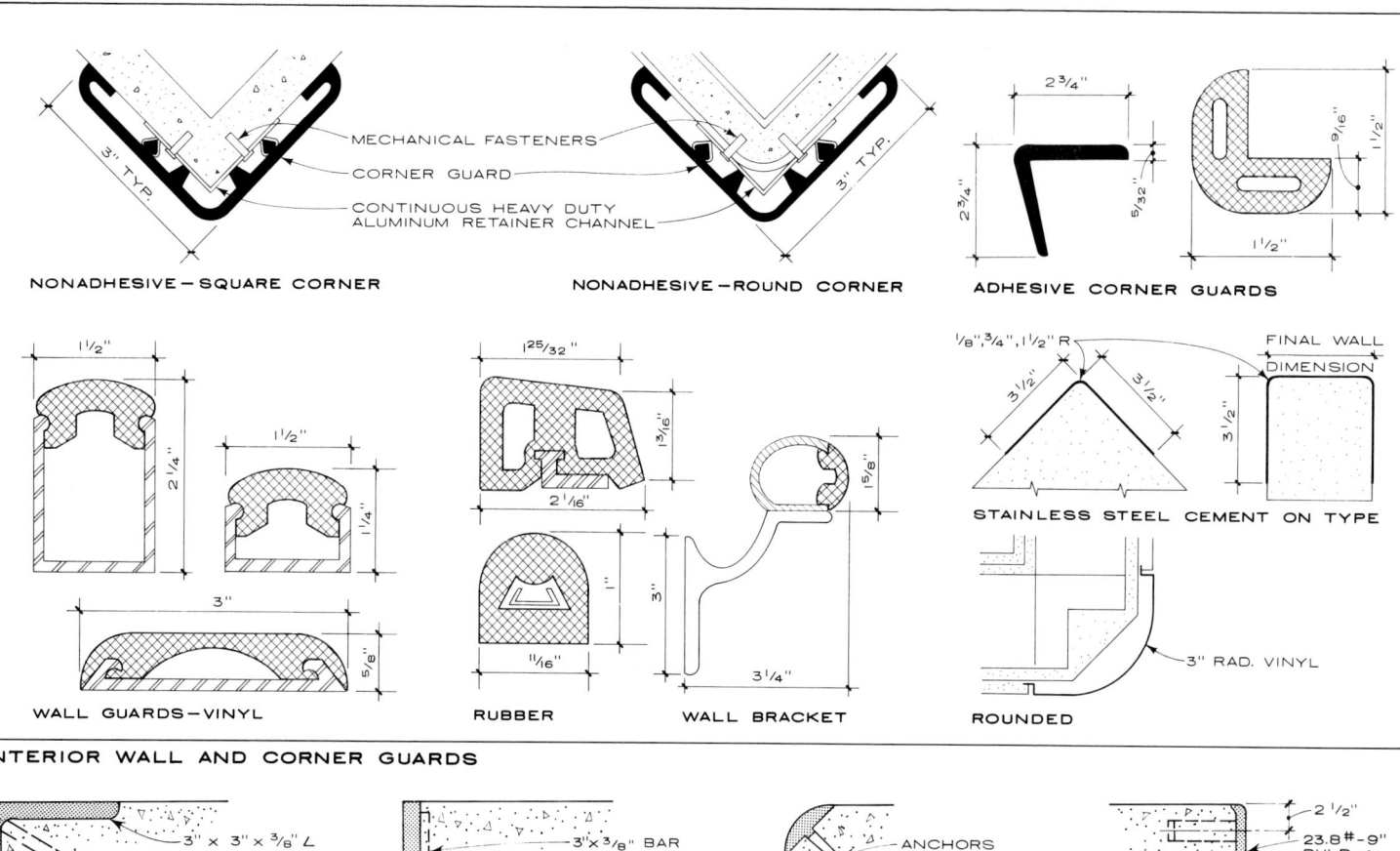

NONADHESIVE—SQUARE CORNER

NONADHESIVE—ROUND CORNER

ADHESIVE CORNER GUARDS

MECHANICAL FASTENERS

CORNER GUARD

CONTINUOUS HEAVY DUTY
ALUMINUM RETAINER CHANNEL

WALL GUARDS—VINYL

RUBBER

WALL BRACKET

ROUNDED

STAINLESS STEEL CEMENT ON TYPE

FINAL WALL DIMENSION

3" RAD. VINYL

INTERIOR WALL AND CORNER GUARDS

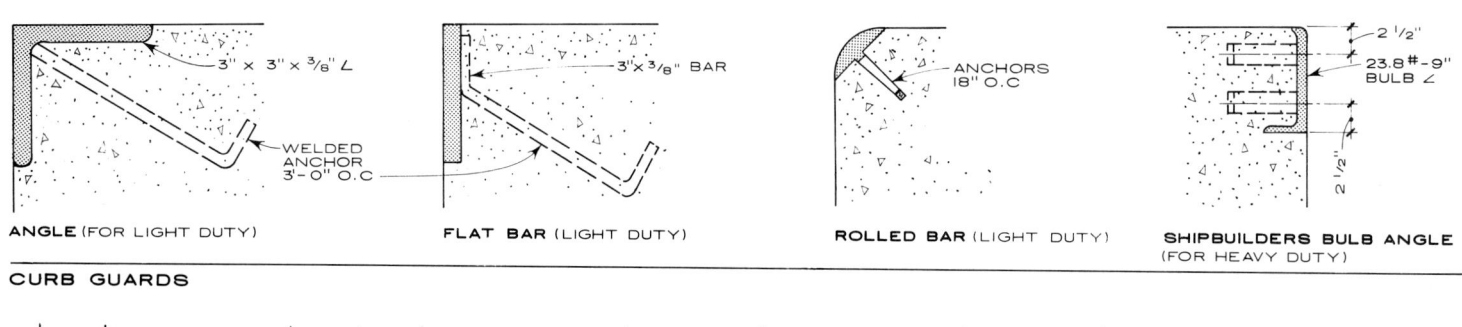

ANGLE (FOR LIGHT DUTY)

FLAT BAR (LIGHT DUTY)

ROLLED BAR (LIGHT DUTY)

SHIPBUILDERS BULB ANGLE
(FOR HEAVY DUTY)

3" × 3" × 3/8" ∟

WELDED ANCHOR 3'-0" O.C

3" × 3/8" BAR

ANCHORS 18" O.C

23.8#-9" BULB ∠

CURB GUARDS

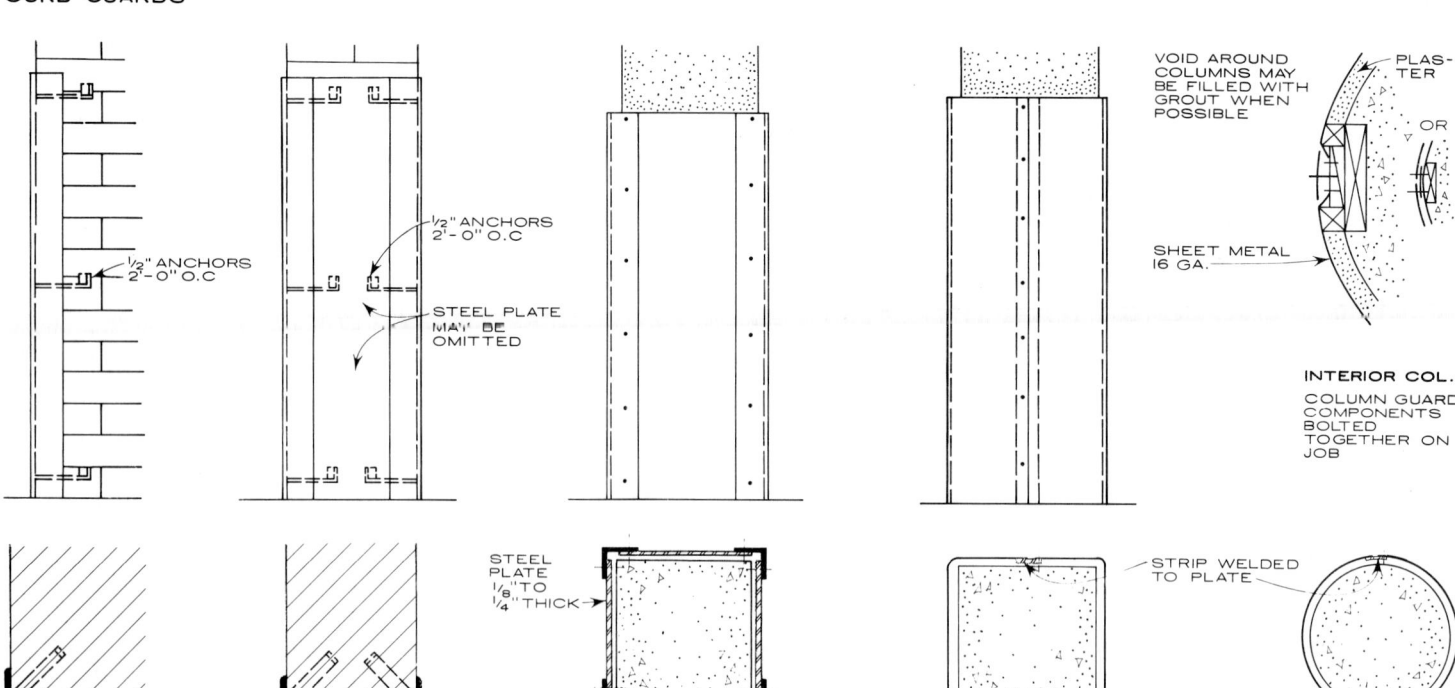

1/2" ANCHORS 2'-0" O.C

1/2" ANCHORS 2'-0" O.C

STEEL PLATE MAY BE OMITTED

VOID AROUND COLUMNS MAY BE FILLED WITH GROUT WHEN POSSIBLE

PLASTER

OR

SHEET METAL 16 GA.

INTERIOR COL.

COLUMN GUARD COMPONENTS BOLTED TOGETHER ON JOB

SINGLE CORNER

DOUBLE CORNER

COL. WITH ∠s & PLATES

COLUMNS WITH FORMED PLATE

4" × 4" × 1/4" ∠'s

STEEL PLATE

STEEL PLATE 1/8" TO 1/4" THICK

STRIP WELDED TO PLATE

CORNER AND COLUMN GUARDS

John Sava; The Architects Collaborative; Cambridge, Massachusetts

Vicente Cordero, AIA; Arlington, Virginia

10   WALL AND CORNER GUARDS

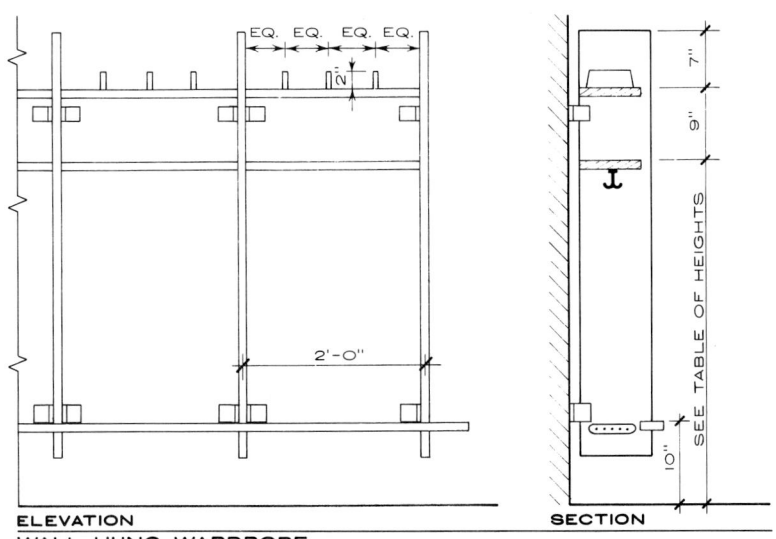

ELEVATION
SECTION
WALL HUNG WARDROBE

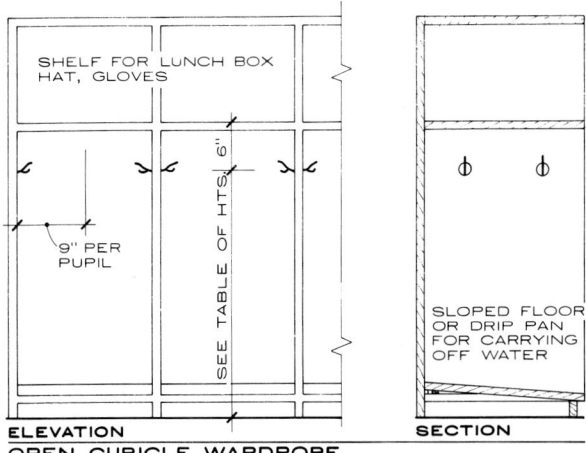

ELEVATION
SECTION
OPEN CUBICLE WARDROBE

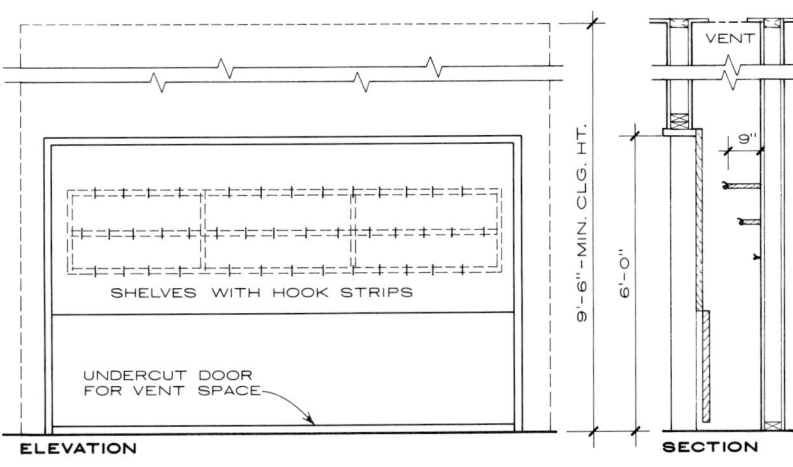

SHELVES WITH HOOK STRIPS

UNDERCUT DOOR
FOR VENT SPACE

ELEVATION
SECTION

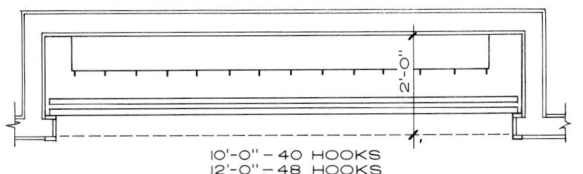

10'-0" — 40 HOOKS
12'-0" — 48 HOOKS

PLAN
VERTICAL-SLIDING DOOR WARDROBE

HANGING SPACE ON
PIVOTING DOOR

HANGING SPACE ON
REAR WALL

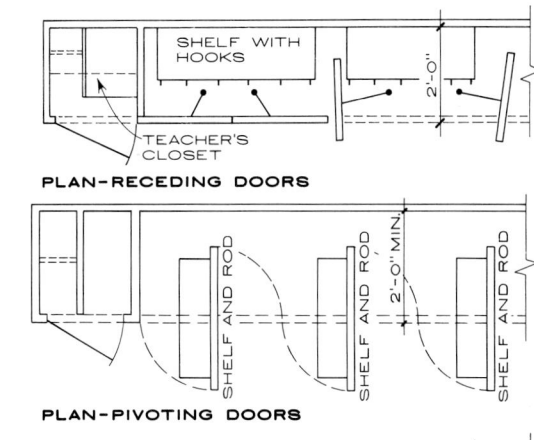

SHELF WITH
HOOKS

TEACHER'S
CLOSET

PLAN-RECEDING DOORS

SHELF AND ROD

PLAN-PIVOTING DOORS

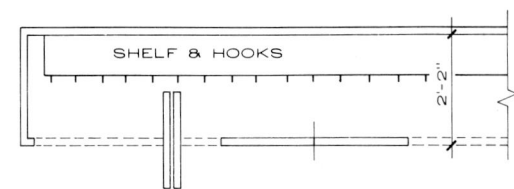

SHELF & HOOKS

PLAN-FOLDING OR PIVOTING DOORS

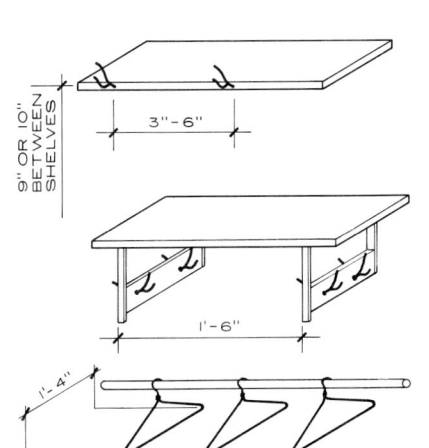

HANGING DEVICES

TABLE OF HEIGHTS

GRADE LEVEL	HEIGHT ABOVE FLOOR
Preschool and handicapped	4'-0''
Kindergarten through 3rd grade	4'-3''
4th through 6th grades	4'-7''
7th grade through high school	5'-1''

HOOKS ON SHELVING

3 tiers double-prong hooks—
4 hooks per foot.

2 tiers double-prong hooks—
3 hooks per foot.
8 hooks in 3'-0''

HANGING POLE

3 hangers per foot.

John Stetson; Palm Beach, Florida

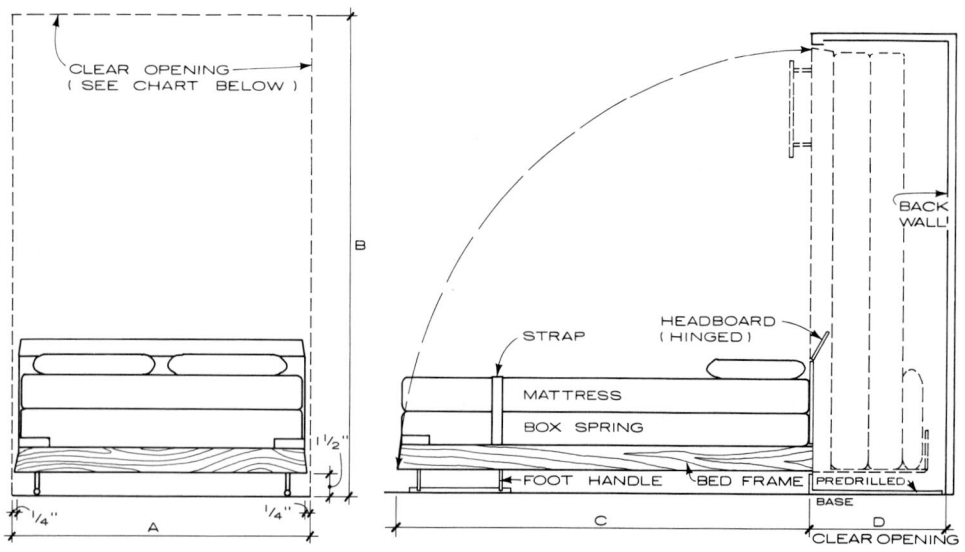

FOLDAWAY BED

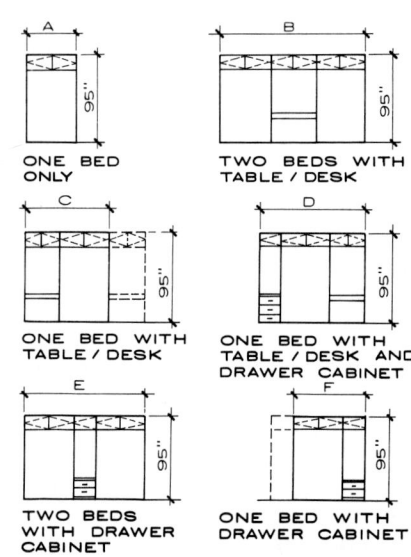

PREMANUFACTURED RECESSED BED CABINETS FOR FOLDAWAY BEDS

NOTE

A factory assembled bed frame includes anchors to fasten the hinge mechanism to the floor. This hinge may be attached to any type of floor. An optional predrilled base plate of 3/4 in. plywood is recommended to facilitate installation. The bed frame's base has a finished face which provides wall closure.

REQUIRED CLEARANCES FOR FOLD-AWAY BEDS

	A	B	C	D
Single bed	41″	83″	78″	24″
Double bed	56″	83″	78″	24″
Queen bed	63″	89″	84″	24″
Extra long bed	63″	89″	84″	24″

NOTE

Finished cabinet is made of 3/4 in. plywood with plastic laminated finish on all sides. The recessed unit includes bed face and predrilled base plate for the folding mechanism.

RECESSED CABINET DIMENSIONS

	A	B	C	D	E	F
Twin	43″	128″	85″	108″	108″	66″
Double	58″	158″	100″	123″	138″	102″
Queen	65″	152″	107″	130″	152″	109″

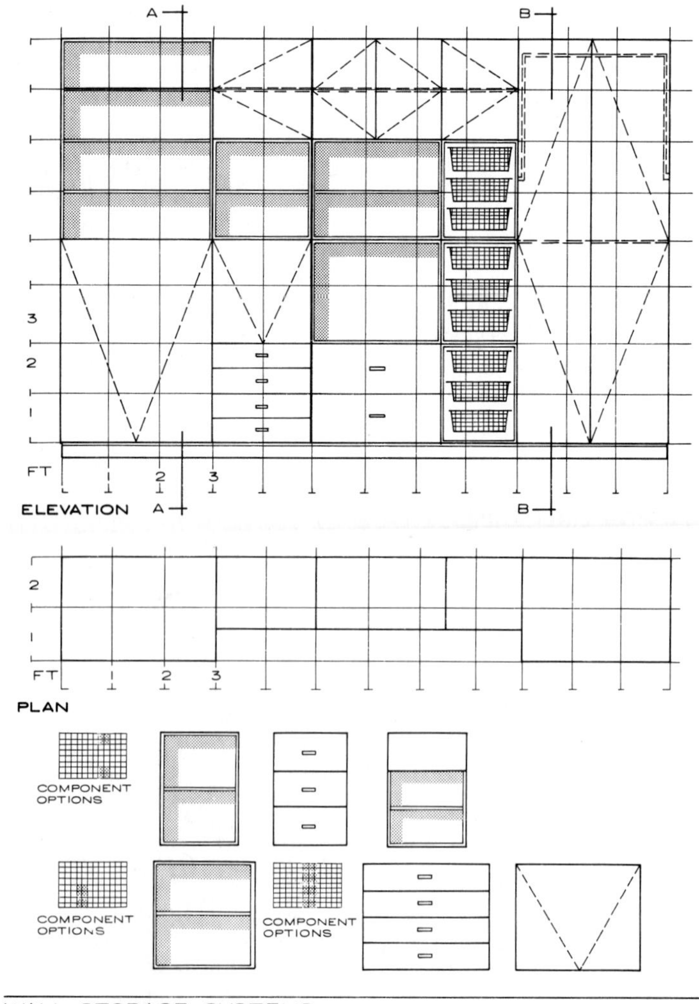

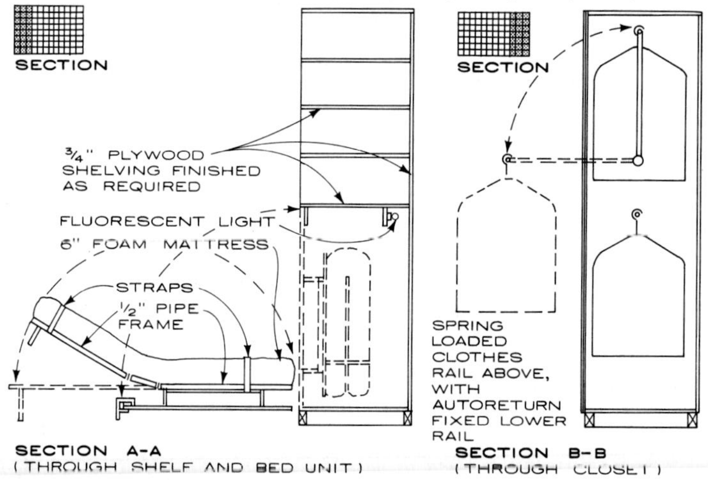

ELEVATION

PLAN

WALL STORAGE SYSTEMS

SECTION A-A
(THROUGH SHELF AND BED UNIT)

SECTION B-B
(THROUGH CLOSET)

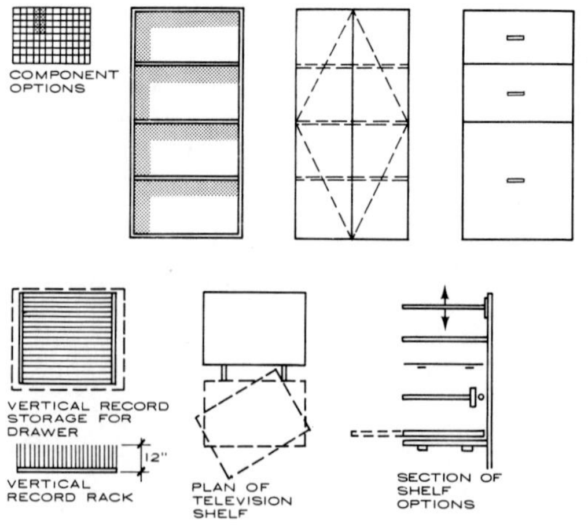

DOOR OPTIONS

Smoked glass
Clear glass
Solid core wood
Plastic laminate

SHELF OPTIONS

Adjustable shelf
Fixed shelf
Glass shelf
Concealed lighting shelf
Television shelf

Charles E. George; SHWC, Inc.; Dallas, Texas

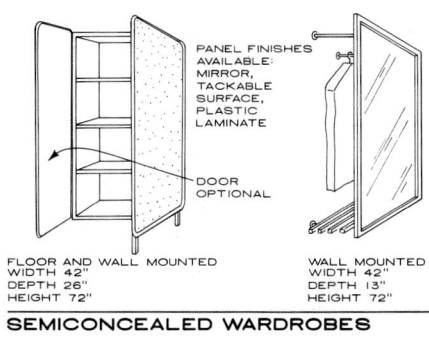

PANEL FINISHES
AVAILABLE:
MIRROR,
TACKABLE
SURFACE,
PLASTIC
LAMINATE

DOOR
OPTIONAL

FLOOR AND WALL MOUNTED
WIDTH 42"
DEPTH 26"
HEIGHT 72"

WALL MOUNTED
WIDTH 42"
DEPTH 13"
HEIGHT 72"

SEMICONCEALED WARDROBES

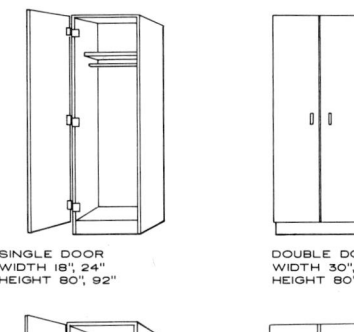
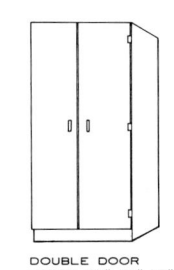

SINGLE DOOR
WIDTH 18", 24"
HEIGHT 80", 92"

DOUBLE DOOR
WIDTH 30", 36", 48"
HEIGHT 80", 92"

STANDARD FINISH IS PLASTIC LAMINATE.
ACCESSORIES INCLUDE: MIRRORS, TOWEL BARS, LOCKS,
AND ADJUSTABLE SHELVES

ENCLOSED FREESTANDING WARDROBES

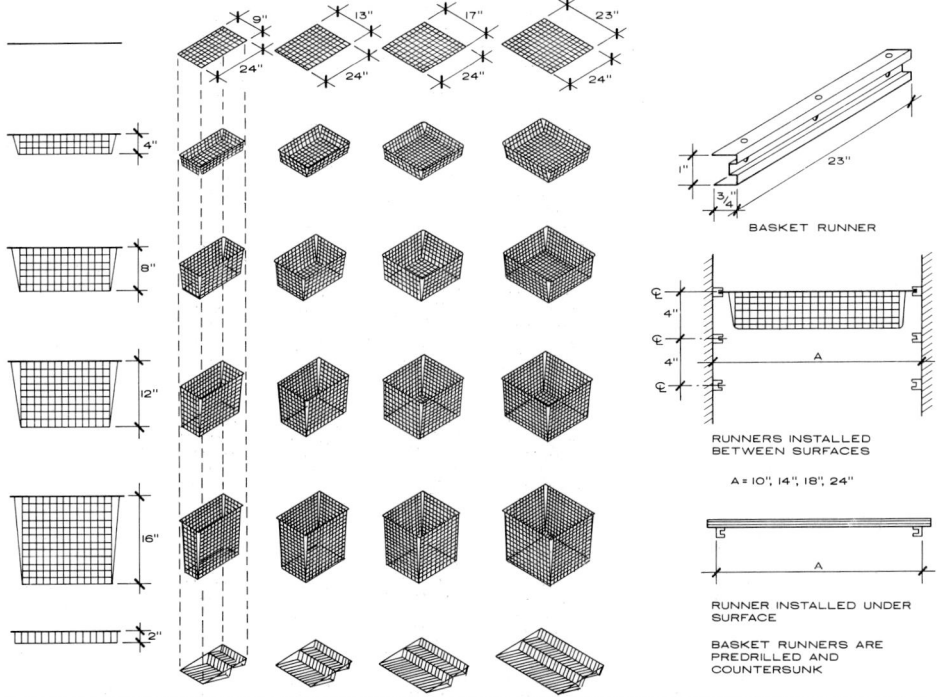

BASKET RUNNER

RUNNERS INSTALLED
BETWEEN SURFACES

A = 10", 14", 18", 24"

RUNNER INSTALLED UNDER
SURFACE

BASKET RUNNERS ARE
PREDRILLED AND
COUNTERSUNK

VINYL COATED DRAWERS, SHELVES, AND BOTTLE RACKS

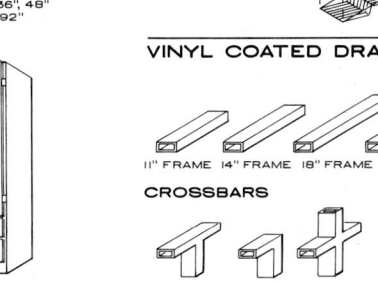

11" FRAME   14" FRAME   18" FRAME   24" FRAME

CROSSBARS

CONNECTORS

WHEEL
ASSEMBLY

RUNNER PARTS

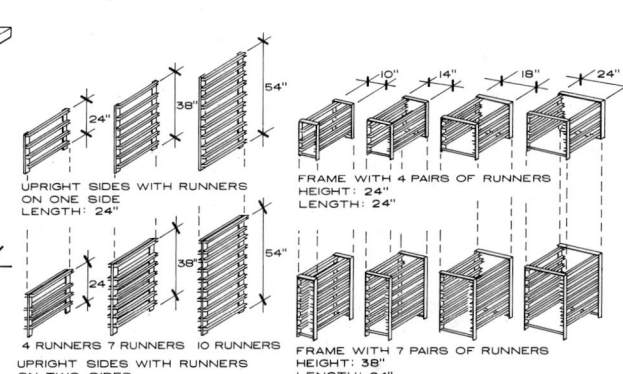

UPRIGHT SIDES WITH RUNNERS
ON ONE SIDE
LENGTH: 24"

4 RUNNERS 7 RUNNERS 10 RUNNERS
UPRIGHT SIDES WITH RUNNERS
ON TWO SIDES
LENGTH: 24"

FRAME WITH 4 PAIRS OF RUNNERS
HEIGHT: 24"
LENGTH: 24"

FRAME WITH 7 PAIRS OF RUNNERS
HEIGHT: 38"
LENGTH: 24"

RUNNER STACKS   ## PREPACKED FRAMES

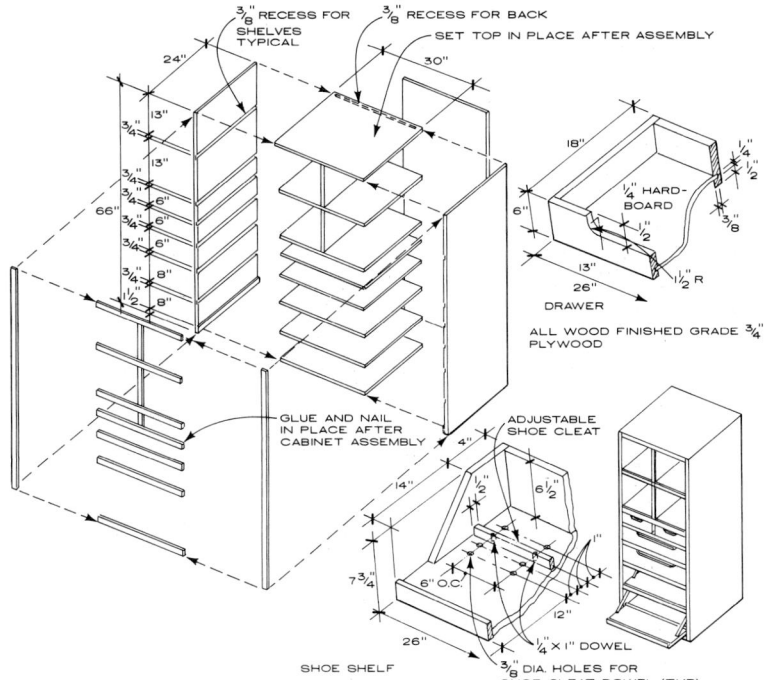

3/8" RECESS FOR
SHELVES
TYPICAL

3/8" RECESS FOR BACK

SET TOP IN PLACE AFTER ASSEMBLY

24"

30"

13"

13"

6"

6"

8"

8"

66"

18"

1/4" HARD-
BOARD

6"

13"

26"

1/2" R

DRAWER

ALL WOOD FINISHED GRADE 3/4"
PLYWOOD

GLUE AND NAIL
IN PLACE AFTER
CABINET ASSEMBLY

ADJUSTABLE
SHOE CLEAT

14"

6 1/2"

6 1/2"

7 3/4"

6" O.C.

26"

SHOE SHELF

1/4" X 1" DOWEL

3/8" DIA. HOLES FOR
SHOE CLEAT DOWEL (TYP)

BUILT-IN STORAGE CABINET

Charles E. George; SHWC, Inc.; Dallas, Texas

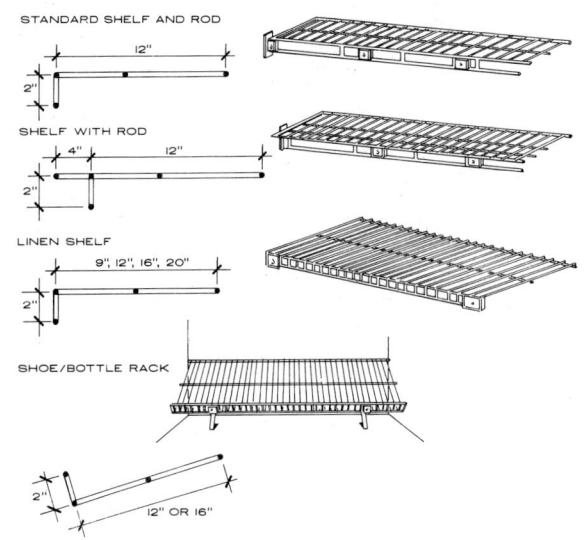

STANDARD SHELF AND ROD

12"

2"

SHELF WITH ROD

4"

12"

2"

LINEN SHELF

9", 12", 16", 20"

2"

SHOE/BOTTLE RACK

2"

12" OR 16"

VINYL COATED STEEL ROD SHELVING
NOTES

1. Available in brown or white vinyl coating.
2. All deck rods are welded on 1 in. centers.
3. Intermediate supports are needed every 3 ft 6 in.
4. Shelves are available in any length in 1 in. increments up to 8 ft.

CHAPTER 11 EQUIPMENT

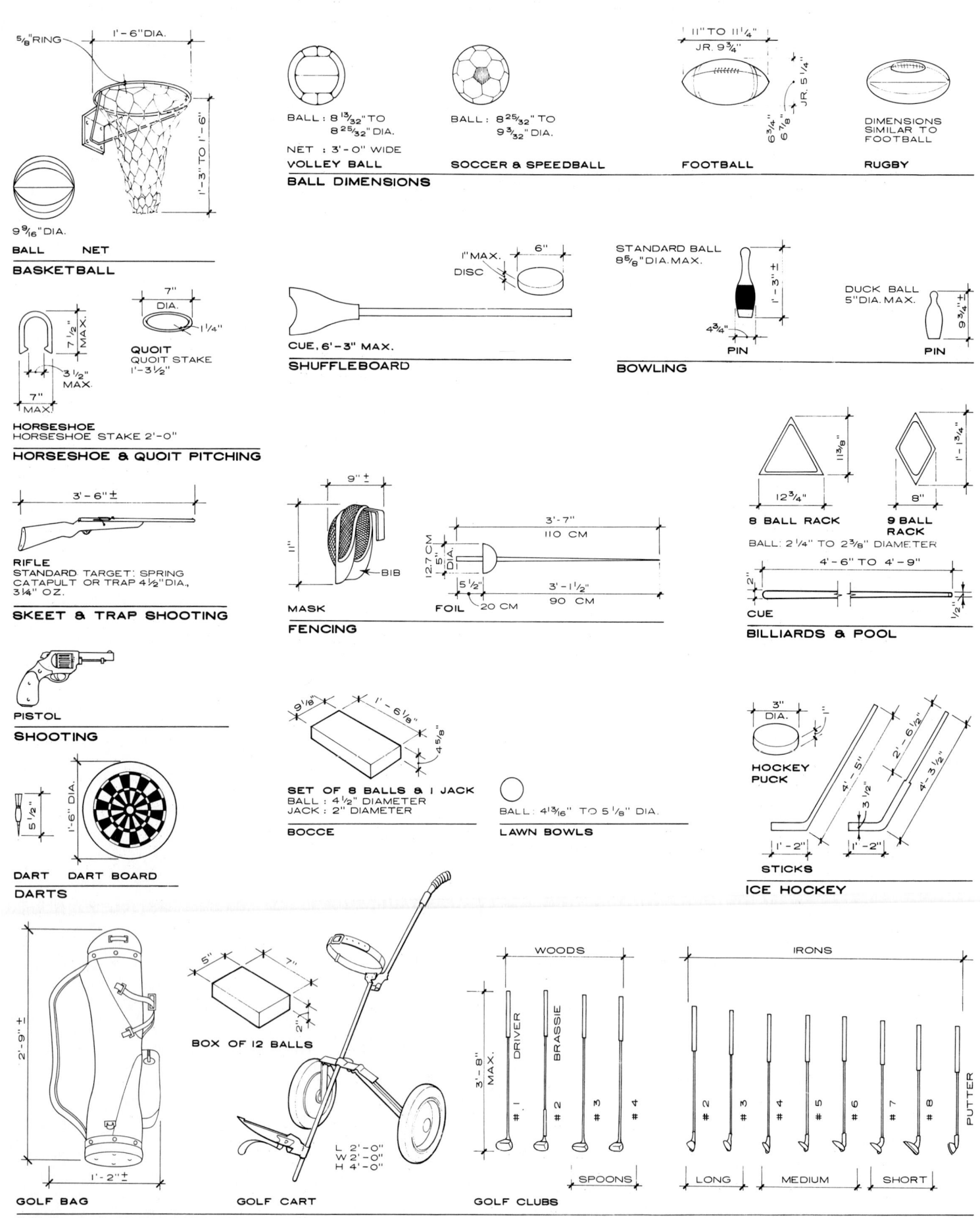

BASKETBALL

5/8" RING
1'-6" DIA.
1'-3" TO 1'-6"
9 9/16" DIA.
BALL   NET

BALL DIMENSIONS

VOLLEY BALL
BALL: 8 13/32" TO 8 25/32" DIA.
NET: 3'-0" WIDE

SOCCER & SPEEDBALL
BALL: 8 25/32" TO 9 3/32" DIA.

FOOTBALL
11" TO 11 1/4"
JR. 9 3/4"
6 3/4"
6 7/8"
JR. 5 1/4"

RUGBY
DIMENSIONS SIMILAR TO FOOTBALL

HORSESHOE & QUOIT PITCHING

HORSESHOE
HORSESHOE STAKE 2'-0"
7 1/2" MAX.
3 1/2" MAX.
7" MAX.

QUOIT
QUOIT STAKE 1'-3 1/2"
7" DIA.
1 1/4"

SHUFFLEBOARD

1" MAX.
DISC
6"
CUE, 6'-3" MAX.

BOWLING

STANDARD BALL 8 5/8" DIA. MAX.
1'-3" ±
PIN
4 3/4"

DUCK BALL 5" DIA. MAX.
9 3/4" ±
PIN

SKEET & TRAP SHOOTING

3'-6" ±
RIFLE
STANDARD TARGET: SPRING CATAPULT OR TRAP 4 1/2" DIA., 3 1/4" OZ.

FENCING

9" ±
11"
MASK
BIB

3'-7"
110 CM
12.7 CM
5" DIA.
5 1/2"
3'-1 1/2"
90 CM
FOIL
20 CM

BILLIARDS & POOL

11 3/8"
12 3/4"
8 BALL RACK

1'-3 3/4"
8"
9 BALL RACK

BALL: 2 1/4" TO 2 3/8" DIAMETER

4'-6" TO 4'-9"
2"
1/2"
CUE

SHOOTING

PISTOL

DARTS

1'-6" DIA.
5 1/2"
DART   DART BOARD

BOCCE

9 1/8"
1'-6 1/2"
4 5/8"
SET OF 8 BALLS & 1 JACK
BALL: 4 1/2" DIAMETER
JACK: 2" DIAMETER

LAWN BOWLS

BALL: 4 13/16" TO 5 1/8" DIA.

ICE HOCKEY

3" DIA.
1"
HOCKEY PUCK

4'-5"
2'-6 1/2"
4'-3 1/2"
3 1/2"
3"
1'-2"
1'-2"
STICKS

GOLF (FOR MOTORIZED GOLF CARTS FOR PASSENGERS, SEE MISCELLANEOUS VEHICLES)

GOLF BAG
2'-9" ±
1'-2" ±

GOLF CART
5"
7"
2"
BOX OF 12 BALLS
L 2'-0"
W 2'-0"
H 4'-0"

GOLF CLUBS
WOODS
IRONS
3'-8" MAX.
DRIVER #1
BRASSIE #2
#3
#4
SPOONS
#2
#3
#4
#5
#6
#7
#8
PUTTER
LONG
MEDIUM
SHORT

Jacques J. Amsellem, AIA; Silver Spring, Maryland

11 ATHLETIC EQUIPMENT

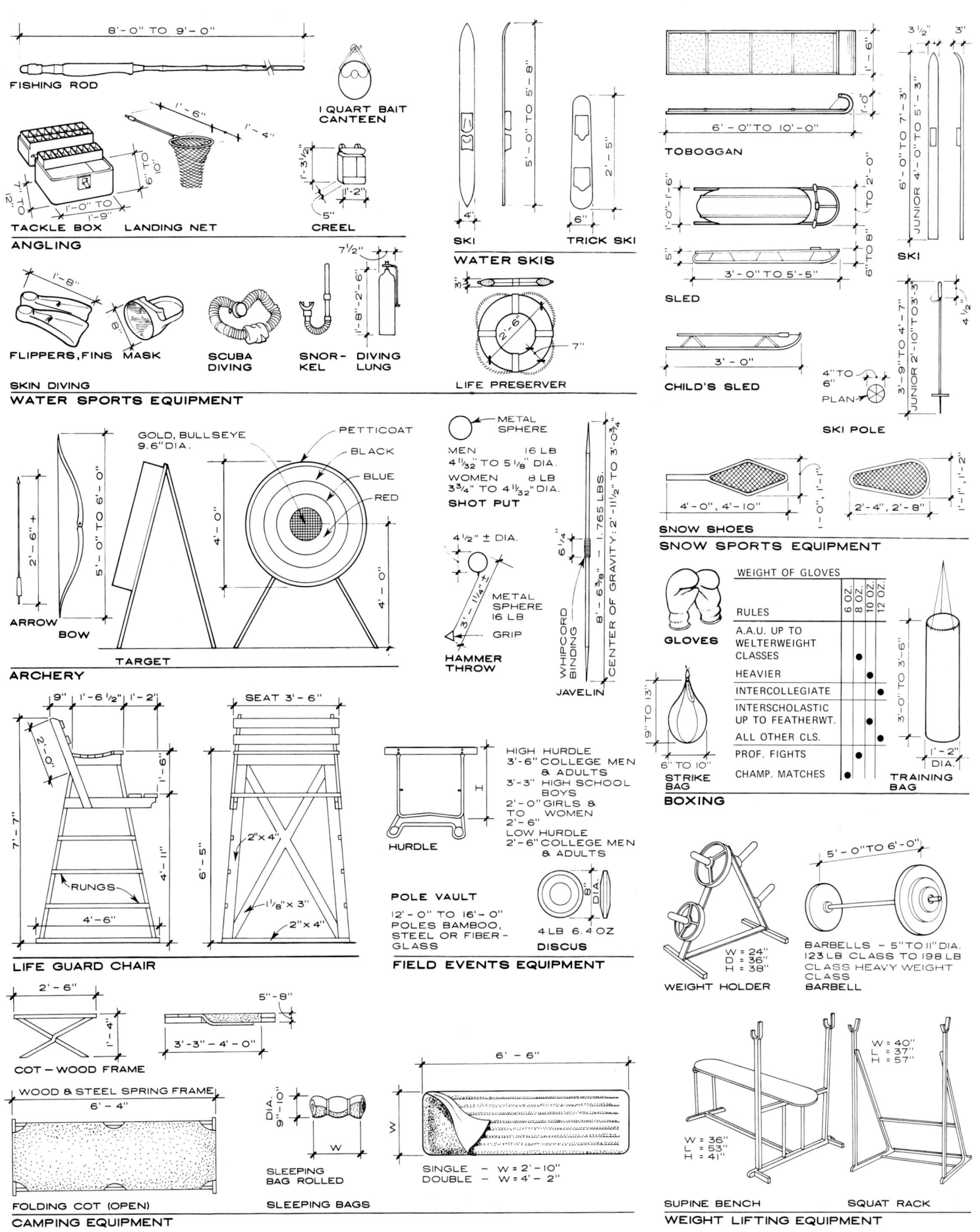

FISHING ROD

8'-0" TO 9'-0"

I QUART BAIT CANTEEN

TACKLE BOX   **LANDING NET**   **CREEL**

ANGLING

FLIPPERS, FINS   **MASK**   **SCUBA DIVING**   **SNOR-KEL**   **DIVING LUNG**

SKIN DIVING

WATER SPORTS EQUIPMENT

SKI   **TRICK SKI**

WATER SKIS

LIFE PRESERVER

TOBOGGAN

SLED

CHILD'S SLED

SKI

SKI POLE

SNOW SHOES

SNOW SPORTS EQUIPMENT

GOLD, BULLSEYE 9.6" DIA.

PETTICOAT

BLACK

BLUE

RED

ARROW   **BOW**

TARGET

ARCHERY

METAL SPHERE

MEN   16 LB
4 11/32 TO 5 1/8 DIA.

WOMEN   8 LB
3 3/4 TO 4 11/32 DIA.

SHOT PUT

4 1/2" ± DIA.

METAL SPHERE 16 LB

GRIP

HAMMER THROW

WHIPCORD BINDING

CENTER OF GRAVITY: 2'-11 1/2" TO 3'-0 3/4"

8'-6 3/8" — 1,765 LBS.

JAVELIN

GLOVES

WEIGHT OF GLOVES				
RULES	6 OZ.	8 OZ.	10 OZ.	12 OZ.
A.A.U. UP TO WELTERWEIGHT CLASSES		●		
HEAVIER			●	
INTERCOLLEGIATE			●	
INTERSCHOLASTIC UP TO FEATHERWT.			●	
ALL OTHER CLS.			●	
PROF. FIGHTS	●			
CHAMP. MATCHES	●			

STRIKE BAG

TRAINING BAG

BOXING

LIFE GUARD CHAIR

SEAT 3'-6"

HURDLE

HIGH HURDLE
3'-6" COLLEGE MEN & ADULTS
3'-3" HIGH SCHOOL BOYS
2'-0" GIRLS & TO WOMEN
2'-6"

LOW HURDLE
2'-6" COLLEGE MEN & ADULTS

POLE VAULT

12'-0" TO 16'-0"
POLES BAMBOO, STEEL OR FIBER-GLASS

4 LB 6.4 OZ

DISCUS

FIELD EVENTS EQUIPMENT

WEIGHT HOLDER
W = 24"
D = 36"
H = 38"

BARBELL
BARBELLS - 5" TO 11" DIA.
123 LB CLASS TO 198 LB CLASS HEAVY WEIGHT CLASS

COT — WOOD FRAME

FOLDING COT (OPEN)

WOOD & STEEL SPRING FRAME
6'-4"

CAMPING EQUIPMENT

SLEEPING BAG ROLLED

SINGLE — W = 2'-10"
DOUBLE — W = 4'-2"

SLEEPING BAGS

SUPINE BENCH
W = 36"
L = 53"
H = 41"

SQUAT RACK
W = 40"
L = 37"
H = 57"

WEIGHT LIFTING EQUIPMENT

Jacques J. Amsellem, AIA; Silver Spring, Maryland

ATHLETIC EQUIPMENT

11

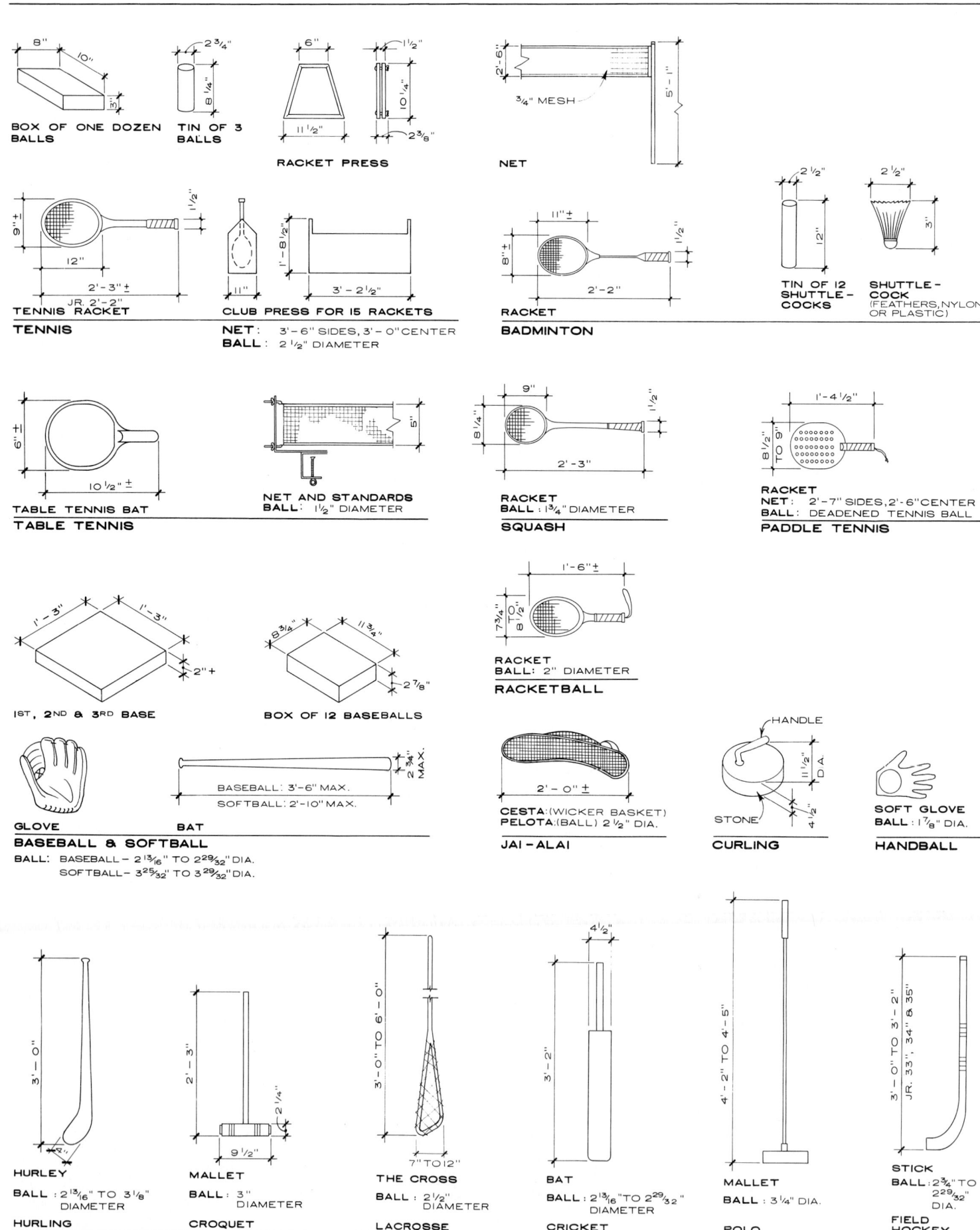

BOX OF ONE DOZEN BALLS

TIN OF 3 BALLS

RACKET PRESS

NET

TENNIS RACKET
JR. 2'-2"

CLUB PRESS FOR 15 RACKETS

RACKET

TIN OF 12 SHUTTLE-COCKS

SHUTTLE-COCK (FEATHERS, NYLON OR PLASTIC)

TENNIS
NET: 3'-6" SIDES, 3'-0" CENTER
BALL: 2 1/2" DIAMETER

BADMINTON

TABLE TENNIS BAT

NET AND STANDARDS
BALL: 1 1/2" DIAMETER

RACKET
BALL: 1 3/4" DIAMETER

RACKET
NET: 2'-7" SIDES, 2'-6" CENTER
BALL: DEADENED TENNIS BALL

TABLE TENNIS

SQUASH

PADDLE TENNIS

1ST, 2ND & 3RD BASE

BOX OF 12 BASEBALLS

RACKET
BALL: 2" DIAMETER

RACKETBALL

GLOVE

BAT
BASEBALL: 3'-6" MAX.
SOFTBALL: 2'-10" MAX.

BASEBALL & SOFTBALL
BALL: BASEBALL – 2 13/16" TO 2 29/32" DIA.
SOFTBALL – 3 25/32" TO 3 29/32" DIA.

CESTA: (WICKER BASKET)
PELOTA: (BALL) 2 1/2" DIA.

JAI-ALAI

HANDLE

STONE

CURLING

SOFT GLOVE
BALL: 1 7/8" DIA.

HANDBALL

HURLEY
BALL: 2 13/16" TO 3 1/8" DIAMETER

HURLING

MALLET
BALL: 3" DIAMETER

CROQUET

THE CROSS
BALL: 2 1/2" DIAMETER

LACROSSE

BAT
BALL: 2 13/16" TO 2 29/32" DIAMETER

CRICKET

MALLET
BALL: 3 1/4" DIA.

POLO

STICK
BALL: 2 3/4" TO 2 29/32" DIA.

FIELD HOCKEY

FIELD GAMES

Jacques J. Amsellem, AIA; Silver Spring, Maryland

11 ATHLETIC EQUIPMENT

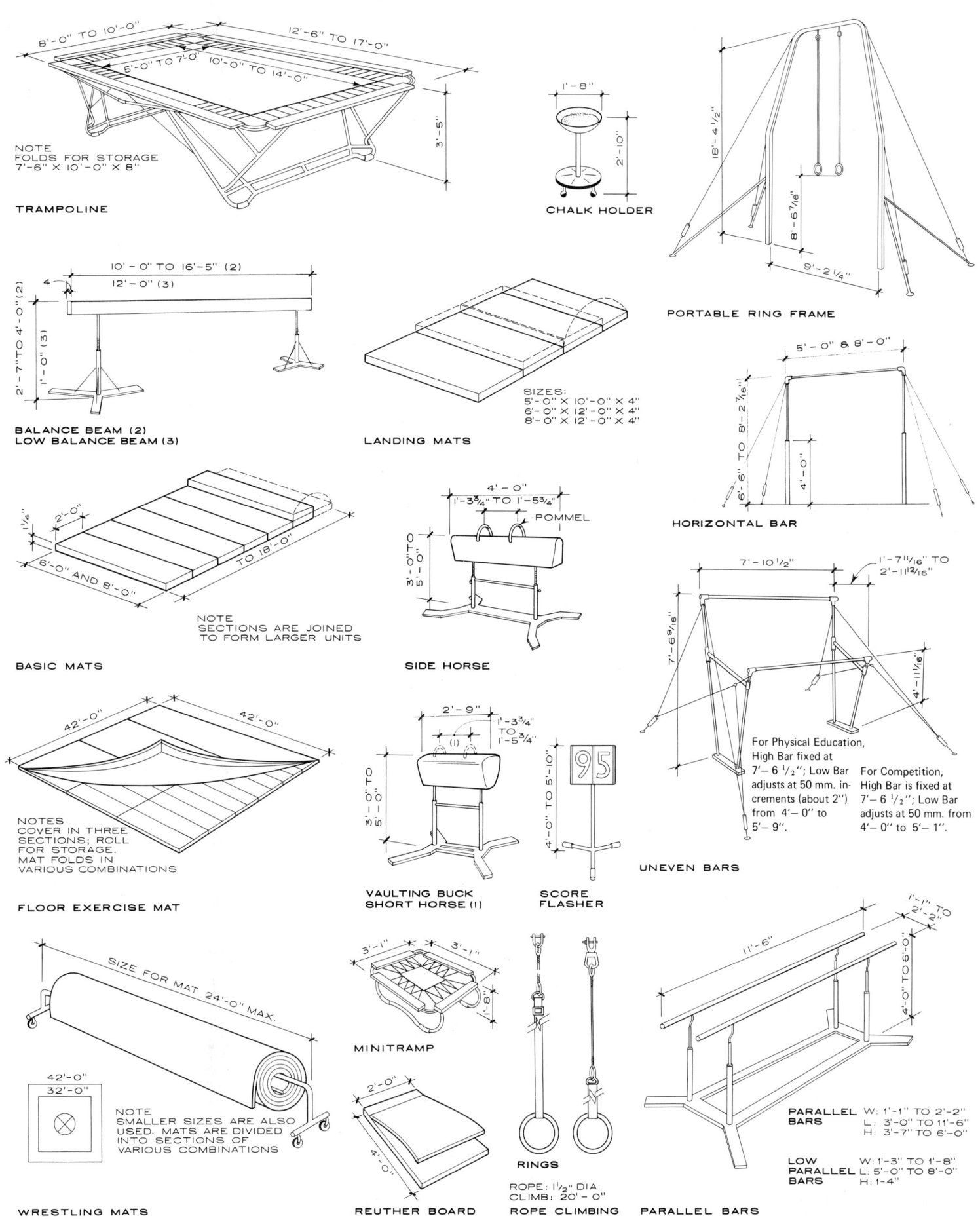

TRAMPOLINE

NOTE
FOLDS FOR STORAGE
7'-6" X 10'-0" X 8"

8'-0" TO 10'-0"
12'-6" TO 17'-0"
5'-0" TO 7'-0"
10'-0" TO 14'-0"
3'-5"

CHALK HOLDER
1'-8"
2'-0"

PORTABLE RING FRAME
18'-4 1/2"
8'-6 7/16"
9'-2 1/4"

BALANCE BEAM (2)
LOW BALANCE BEAM (3)
10'-0" TO 16'-5" (2)
12'-0" (3)
2'-7" TO 4'-0" (2)
1'-0" (3)
4

LANDING MATS
SIZES:
5'-0" X 10'-0" X 4"
6'-0" X 12'-0" X 4"
8'-0" X 12'-0" X 4"

HORIZONTAL BAR
5'-0" & 8'-0"
6'-6" TO 8'-2 7/16"
4'-0"

BASIC MATS
NOTE
SECTIONS ARE JOINED
TO FORM LARGER UNITS
2'-0"
1/4"
6'-0" AND 8'-0"
TO 18'-0"

SIDE HORSE
4'-0"
1'-3 3/4" TO 1'-5 3/4"
POMMEL
3'-0" TO 5'-0"

FLOOR EXERCISE MAT
NOTES
COVER IN THREE
SECTIONS; ROLL
FOR STORAGE.
MAT FOLDS IN
VARIOUS COMBINATIONS
42'-0"
42'-0"

VAULTING BUCK
SHORT HORSE (1)
2'-9"
1'-3 3/4" TO 1'-5 3/4" (1)
3'-0" TO 5'-0"

SCORE
FLASHER
95
4'-0" TO 5'-10"

UNEVEN BARS
7'-10 1/2"
1'-7 11/16" TO 2'-11 12/16"
7'-6 9/16"
4'-11 1/16"

For Physical Education, High Bar fixed at 7'-6 1/2"; Low Bar adjusts at 50 mm. increments (about 2") from 4'-0" to 5'-9".

For Competition, High Bar is fixed at 7'-6 1/2"; Low Bar adjusts at 50 mm. from 4'-0" to 5'-1".

WRESTLING MATS
SIZE FOR MAT 24'-0" MAX.
42'-0"
32'-0"
NOTE
SMALLER SIZES ARE ALSO
USED. MATS ARE DIVIDED
INTO SECTIONS OF
VARIOUS COMBINATIONS

MINITRAMP
3'-1"
3'-1"
1'-8"

REUTHER BOARD
2'-0"
4'-0"

RINGS
ROPE CLIMBING
ROPE: 1 1/2" DIA.
CLIMB: 20'-0"

PARALLEL BARS
11'-6"
1'-1" TO 2'-2"
4'-0" TO 6'-0"

PARALLEL   W: 1'-1" TO 2'-2"
BARS   L: 3'-0" TO 11'-6"
      H: 3'-7" TO 6'-0"

LOW   W: 1'-3" TO 1'-8"
PARALLEL L: 5'-0" TO 8'-0"
BARS   H: 1-4"

John C. Lunsford, AIA, Varney Sexton Sydnor Associates; Phoenix, Arizona

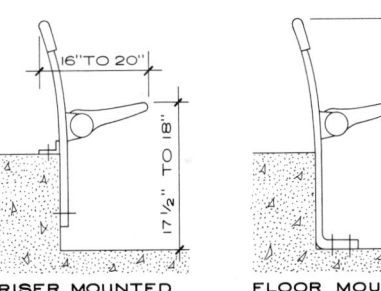

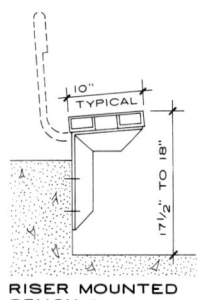

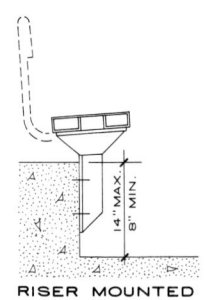

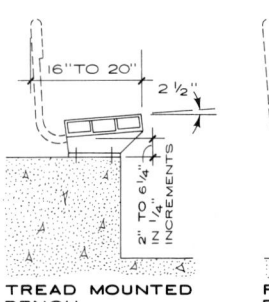

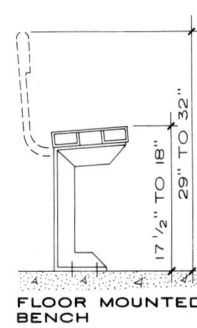

RISER MOUNTED CHAIR   FLOOR MOUNTED CHAIR   RISER MOUNTED BENCH L   RISER MOUNTED BENCH T   TREAD MOUNTED BENCH   FLOOR MOUNTED BENCH

STANDARD SEATS AND SEAT SUPPORTS

SEATING CAPACITY

Allow 18 in. of bleacher length per person per row. Normal aisle width of 36 in. reduces seating capacity by two seats per row x number of rows x number of aisles. See table below.

SAFETY AREAS

1. BASEBALL FIELDS: Minimum 60 ft from seating to foul line or baseline at each side of home plate.
2. SOFTBALL FIELDS: Minimum 25 ft from seating to foul line or baseline at each side of home plate.
3. BASKETBALL COURTS: Minimum 6 ft from seating to court sides, 8 in. minimum to court ends.
4. SWIMMING POOLS: Minimum 5 ft from seating to pool decks. Spectator area must be separate from pool area to avoid mixing dry and wet traffic.

STADIUM SEATING

Concrete risers and treads with seating attached. See typical seats and seat supports above.

FIXED GRANDSTAND

8 in. rise with 24 in. row spacing typical. Available options include front, end, and back rails, crosswalks, ramps, stairs, aisles, vomitories, closed risers, double foot plates, folding seat backs, and waterproof covers of metal or fiberglass for resurfacing existing wooden bleachers.

PORTABLE BLEACHERS

3, 4, or 5 row sections typical. Transportable options include wheels and trailer attachments. Bleachers of up to 25 rows may be assembled of portable, assemblable sections.

TELESCOPIC BLEACHERS

1. LOWRISE: $9^5/8$ in. normal rise for most uses. 22 in. minimum row spacing gives maximum seating capacity. 24 in. spacing gives greater leg room. 30 or 32 in. spacing provides extra passage and leg room space and space for optional folding back rests.
2. HIGHRISE: Models with $11^5/8$ or 16 in. risers are suggested for pools, balconies, hockey rinks, or similarly difficult viewing situations where seating must be banked more steeply than is normal.

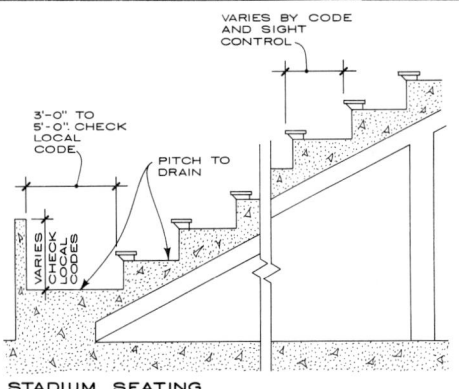

STADIUM SEATING

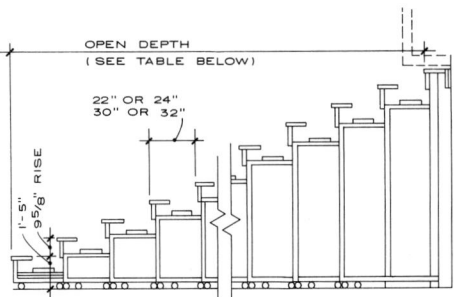

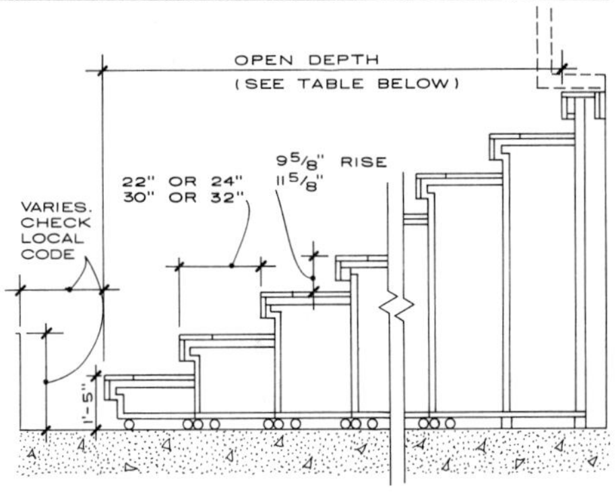

TELESCOPIC BLEACHERS (HIGHRISE)

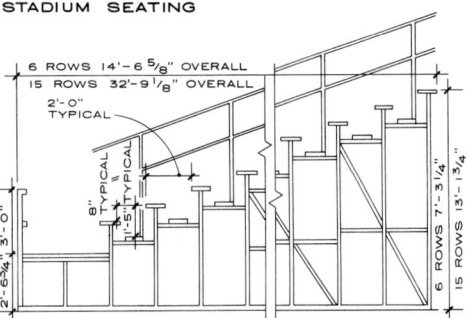

FIXED GRANDSTAND (ELEVATED)

TELESCOPIC BLEACHERS (LOWRISE)

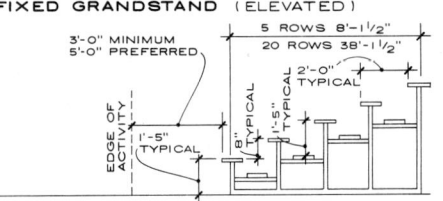

PORTABLE BLEACHERS

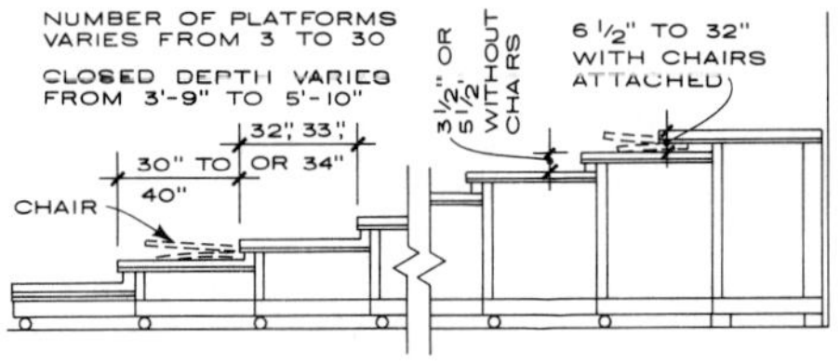

TELESCOPIC PLATFORM

SEATING CAPACITY

LENGTH (FT)									
ROW	8	12	16	20	24	28	32	36	40
3	16	24	32	40	48	56	64	72	80
4	21	32	42	53	64	74	85	96	106
5	26	40	53	66	80	93	106	120	133
6	32	48	64	80	96	112	128	144	160
7	37	56	74	93	112	130	149	168	186
8	42	64	85	106	128	149	170	192	213
9	48	72	96	120	144	168	192	216	240
10	53	80	106	133	160	186	213	240	266
12	64	96	128	160	192	224	256	288	320
14	74	112	149	186	224	261	298	336	373
16	85	128	170	213	256	298	341	384	426
18	96	144	192	240	288	336	384	432	480
20	106	160	213	266	320	373	426	480	533

NOTE: Consult manufacturers for additional information.

GRANDSTANDS AND BLEACHERS DIMENSIONS

ROW	OPEN DEPTH				$9^5/8$" RISE CLOSED DEPTH		$11^5/8$" AND 16" RISE CLOSED DEPTH	
	22"	24"	30"	32"	22" OR 24"	30" OR 32"	22" OR 24"	30" OR 32"
3	4'-11½"	5'-1½"	6'-3½"	6'-5½"	3'-1¹³/₁₆"	3'-9¹³/₁₆"	3'-1¹³/₁₆"	3'-9¹³/₁₆"
4	6'-9½"	7'-1½"	8'-9½"	9'-1½"	3'-2⅛"	3'-10⅛"	3'-2⅛"	3'-10⅛"
5	8'-7½"	9'-1½"	11'-3½"	11'-9½"	3'-2⁷/₁₆"	3'-10⁷/₁₆"	3'-2⁷/₁₆"	3'-10⁷/₁₆"
6	10'-5½"	11'-1½"	13'-9½"	14'-5½"	3'-2¾"	3'-10¾"	3'-2¾"	3'-10¾"
7	12'-3½"	13'-1½"	16'-3½"	17'-1½"	3'-3¹/₁₆"	3'-11¹/₁₆"	3'-3¹/₁₆"	3'-11¹/₁₆"
8	14'-1½"	15'-1½"	18'-9½"	19'-9½"	3'-3⅜"	3'-11⅜"	3'-3⅜"	3'-11⅜"
9	15'-11½"	17'-1½"	21'-3½"	22'-5½"	3'-3¹¹/₁₆"	3'-11¹¹/₁₆"	3'-3¹¹/₁₆"	3'-11¹¹/₁₆"
10	17'-9½"	19'-1½"	23'-9½"	25'-1½"	3'-4"	4'-0"	3'-4"	4'-0"
12	21'-5½"	23'-1½"	28'-9½"	30'-5½"	3'-4⅝"	4'-0⅝"	3'-4⅝"	4'-0⅝"
14	25'-1½"	27'-1½"	33'-9½"	35'-9½"	3'-5¼"	4'-1¼"	NOTE: For $11^5/8$" rise of 18 or more rows and 16" rise of 13 or more rows check with manufacturer for modified closed depth dimensions.	
16	28'-9½"	31'-1½"	38'-9½"	41'-1½"	3'-5⅞"	4'-1⅞"		
18	32'-5½"	35'-1½"	43'-9½"	46'-5½"	3'-6½"	4'-2½"		
20	36'-1½"	39'-1½"	48'-9½"	51'-9½"	3'-7⅛"	4'-3⅛"		

Erik Johnson; Lawrence Cook & Associates; Falls Church, Virginia

David W. Johnson; Washington, D.C.

11   ATHLETIC EQUIPMENT

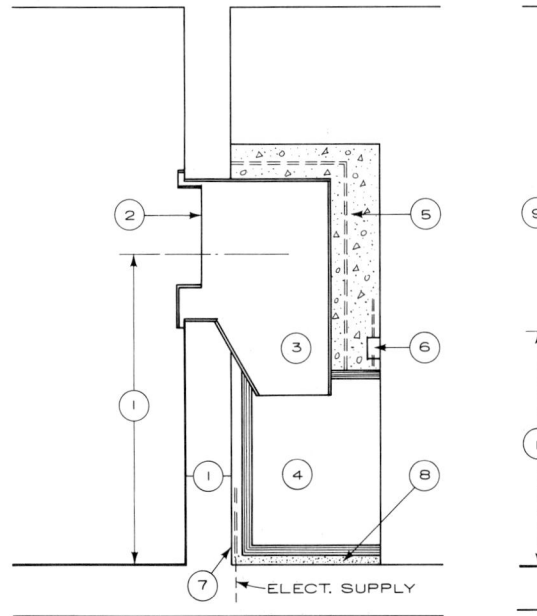

AFTER HOURS DEPOSITORY

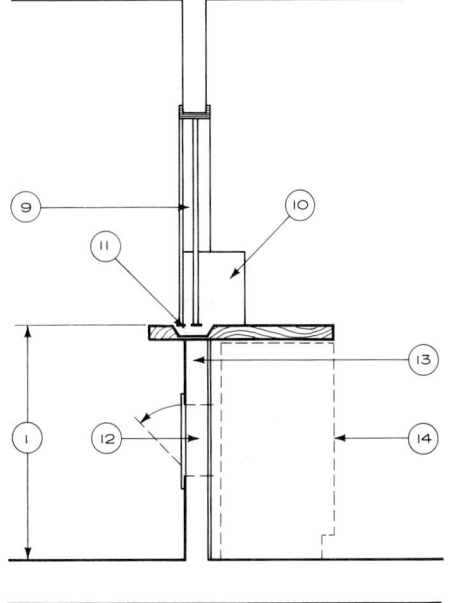

WALK-UP TELLER WICKET

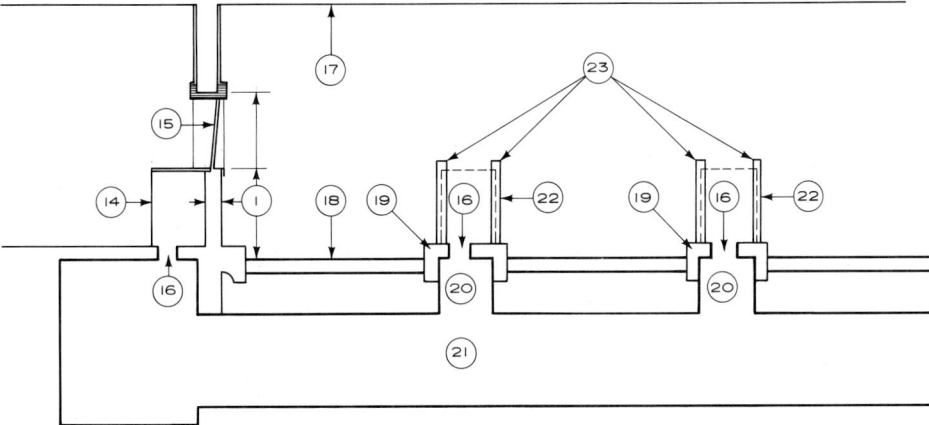

SECTION – AUTO BANK (CONTRACT OR EXPAND AS DESIRED)

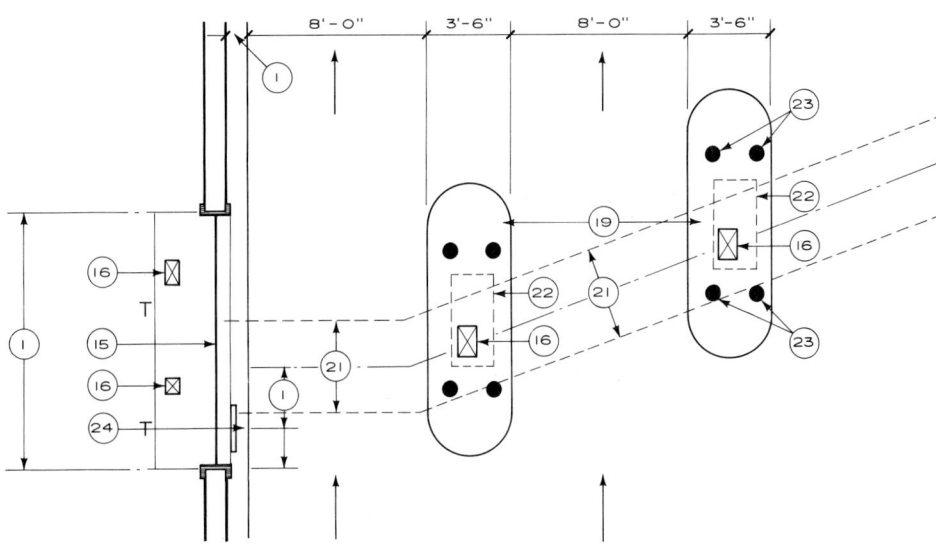

PLAN – AUTO BANK (CONTRACT OR EXPAND AS DESIRED)

BANK EQUIPMENT TO BE CONSIDERED

1. Vault equipment—see previous page.
2. Safe deposit boxes.
3. Cash storage equipment.
4. After hours depository head and chest.
5. Automatic teller machine.
6. Auto bank equipment (visual, T.V., through-wall, and remote units).
7. Walk-up and drive-up windows (bullet-resistant glass).
8. Walk-up teller wicket (bullet resistant glass).
9. Package receiver.
10. Tellers' fixtures.
11. Tellers' undercounter equipment.
12. Bandit barrier door (bullet resistive).
13. File vault door (fire rated).
14. Alarm system.
15. Camera/surveillance system.

KEY

(1) Manufacturers' recommended dimension.

(2) Depository head.

(3) Depository chute.

(4) Depository chest.

(5) Minimum 6 in. reinforced (#4's at 6 in. o.c. each way) concrete envelope around head housing, chute, and chest. Alarm wire wrapping around assembly must be completed prior to pouring envelope.

(6) Alarm terminal box.

(7) Electric supply (for light fixture and motor when specified).

(8) Grout space under chest.

(9) Bullet resistant window.

(10) Riser (parapet), as desired.

(11) Pass through tray.

(12) Package receiver equipment.

(13) Bullet resistive wall construction—provide space for electrical chases.

(14) Undercounter steel tellers' equipment.

(15) Auto bank vision window (bullet resistant glass).

(16) Opening for pneumatic tubes.

(17) Canopy, as desired.

(18) Driving surface.

(19) Concrete island.

(20) Pneumatic tube riser enclosure.

(21) Pneumatic tube tunnel enclosure (note that overhead pneumatic tube runs eliminate the need for riser and tunnel enclosures).

(22) Remote transaction unit equipment—stagger locations as per manufacturers' recommendation.

(23) Steel guard posts filled with concrete.

(24) Through wall transaction drawer.

Jon P. Thorstenson; Gene E. Hickey and Associates, Inc.; Edina, Minnesota

Vern Wilcox, First Bank System; Minneapolis, Minnesota

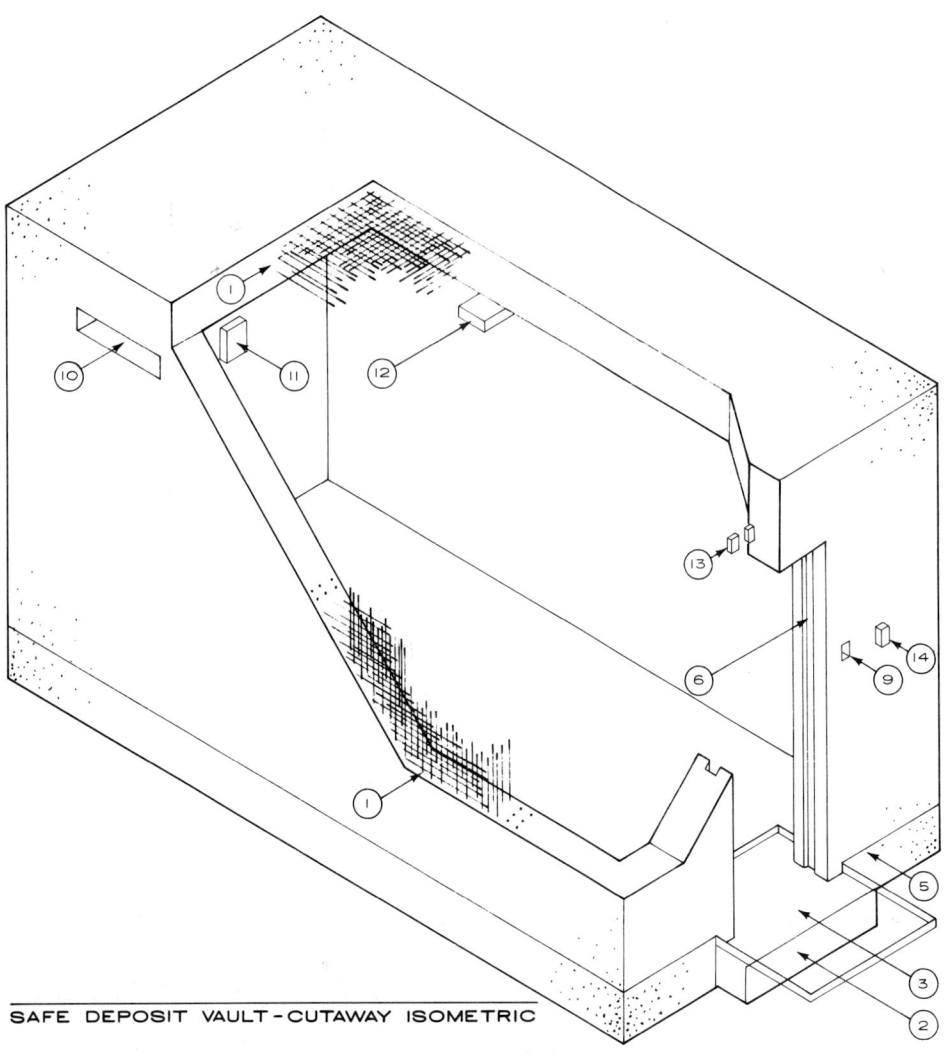

SAFE DEPOSIT VAULT – CUTAWAY ISOMETRIC

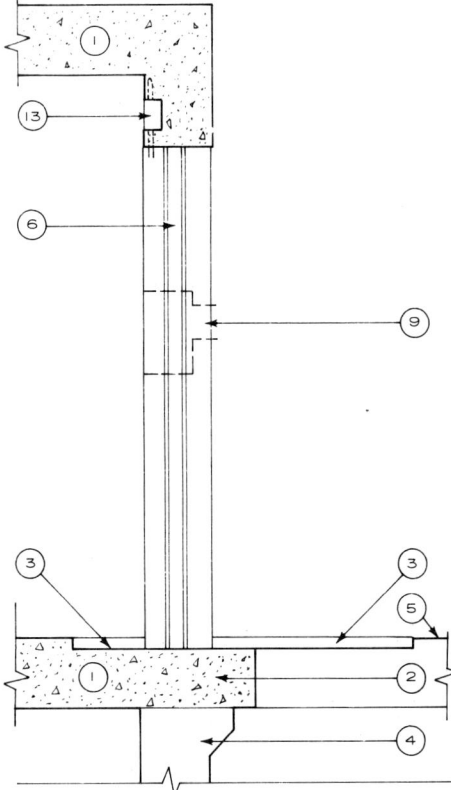

SECTION – VAULT DOOR OPENING

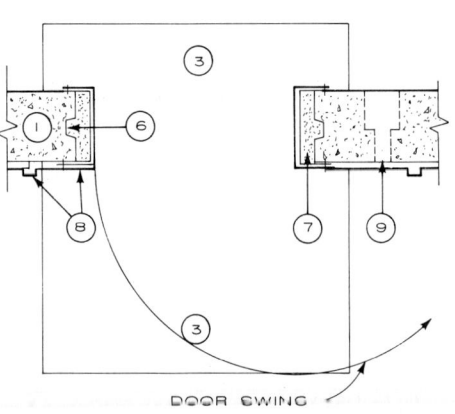

DOOR SWING

PLAN – VAULT DOOR OPENING

VAULT STRUCTURE

Concrete shall develop an ultimate compression strength of at least 3000 lb/in.^{2}.

REINFORCING

No. 5 ($^5/_8$ in. diameter) deformed steel reinforcing bars located on 4 in. centers in horizontal and vertical rows to form a grid, or expanded steel bank vault mesh weighing 6 lb/ft^2 per grid and having a diamond pattern of 3 x 8 in.

Grids are to be located not less than 4 in. apart and shall be staggered in each direction. The number of grids required depends on the thickness of the wall, floor and ceiling (and specific insurance requirements).

MINIMUM NUMBER OF GRIDS FOR DEFORMED BARS

12 in. concrete thickness	3 grids
18 in. concrete thickness	4 grids
27 in. concrete thickness or over	5 grids

MINIMUM NUMBER OF GRIDS FOR #6 EXPANDED STEEL

12 in. concrete thickness	2 grids
18 in. concrete thickness	3 grids
27 in. concrete thickness or over	4 grids

ELECTRICAL

All electrical conduit for the alarm system, security equipment, lighting, telephone, etc., shall be in accordance with the National Electric Code. All conduit entering the walls, ceiling, or floor shall have at least one offset within the vault structure. Arrangement of bends shall be so that drainage is to the exterior. Conduit shall not exceed 1$^1/_2$ in. diameter.

Jon P. Thorstenson; Gene E. Hickey and Associates, Inc.; Edina, Minnesota

Vern Wilcox, First Bank System; Minneapolis, Minnesota

KEY

1. Reinforced concrete walls, floor and ceiling.

2. Extend structural vault floor as necessary to support door during setting operation.

3. Pit for installing door must support imposed load (weight of door plus jack screw pressures). Grout-in to level floor after door is set in place.

4. Supporting foundation—corbel as necessary at door.

5. Finish floor line.

6. Tapered 2 x 4 in. key for grouting in door.

7. Grout-in frame after door is set in place.

8. Vault door frame and architrave.

9. Opening for emergency vault ventilator equipment.

10. Opening for approved device for air duct entry.

11. Alarm control cabinet.

12. Sound detector(s).

13. Alarm junction box (and electrical, as required).

14. Auxiliary alarm control box.

NOTE

The size, configuration, and specific requirements of all equipment and alarm systems that might be included in a bank will vary with different manufacturers and design considerations.

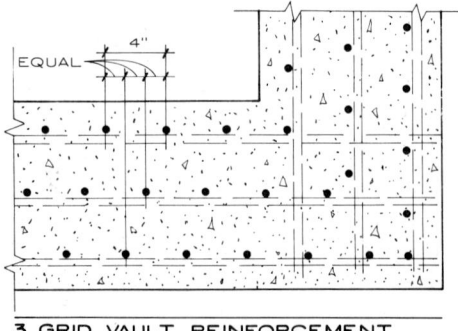

3 GRID VAULT REINFORCEMENT

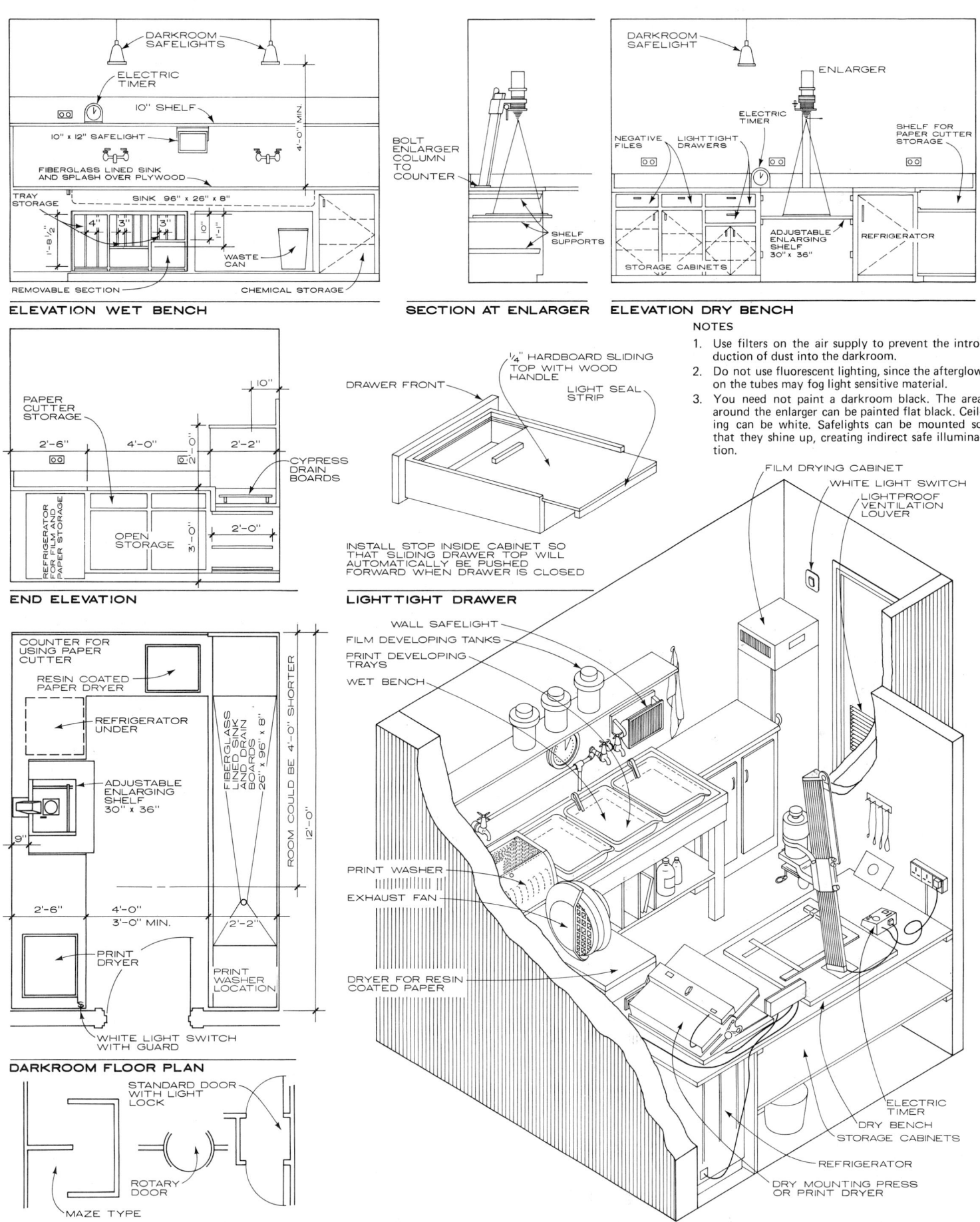

ELEVATION WET BENCH

SECTION AT ENLARGER

ELEVATION DRY BENCH

END ELEVATION

LIGHTTIGHT DRAWER

INSTALL STOP INSIDE CABINET SO THAT SLIDING DRAWER TOP WILL AUTOMATICALLY BE PUSHED FORWARD WHEN DRAWER IS CLOSED

DARKROOM FLOOR PLAN

DARKROOM ENTRANCES

DARKROOM WITH TYPICAL EQUIPMENT

NOTES

1. Use filters on the air supply to prevent the introduction of dust into the darkroom.
2. Do not use fluorescent lighting, since the afterglow on the tubes may fog light sensitive material.
3. You need not paint a darkroom black. The area around the enlarger can be painted flat black. Ceiling can be white. Safelights can be mounted so that they shine up, creating indirect safe illumination.

Robert E. Fehlberg, FAIA; CTA Architects Engineers; Billings, Montana

DARKROOM EQUIPMENT

11

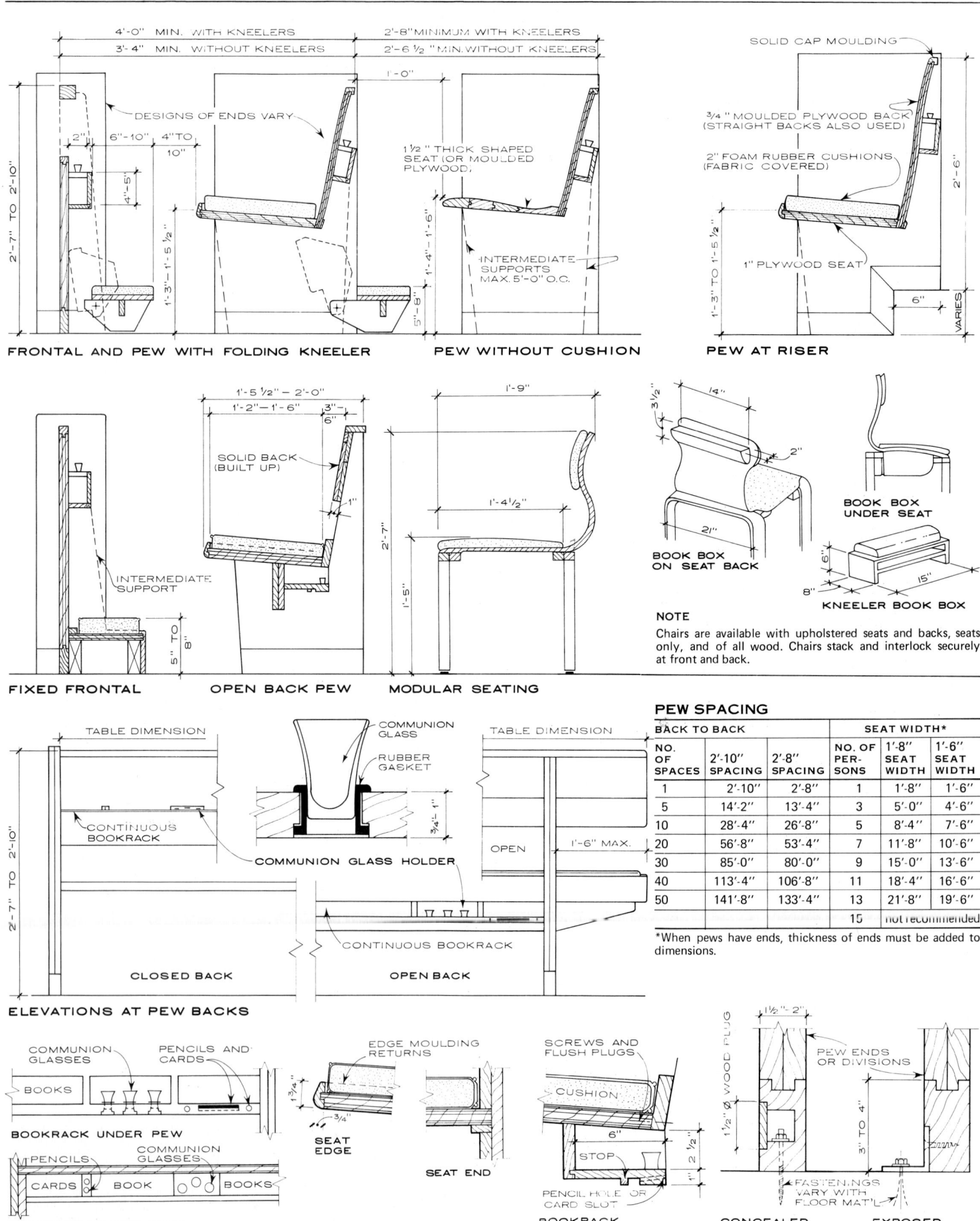

FRONTAL AND PEW WITH FOLDING KNEELER

PEW WITHOUT CUSHION

PEW AT RISER

FIXED FRONTAL

OPEN BACK PEW

MODULAR SEATING

BOOK BOX ON SEAT BACK

BOOK BOX UNDER SEAT

KNEELER BOOK BOX

NOTE

Chairs are available with upholstered seats and backs, seats only, and of all wood. Chairs stack and interlock securely at front and back.

ELEVATIONS AT PEW BACKS

COMMUNION GLASS HOLDER

CLOSED BACK

OPEN BACK

PEW SPACING

BACK TO BACK			SEAT WIDTH*		
NO. OF SPACES	2'-10" SPACING	2'-8" SPACING	NO. OF PERSONS	1'-8" SEAT WIDTH	1'-6" SEAT WIDTH
1	2'-10"	2'-8"	1	1'-8"	1'-6"
5	14'-2"	13'-4"	3	5'-0"	4'-6"
10	28'-4"	26'-8"	5	8'-4"	7'-6"
20	56'-8"	53'-4"	7	11'-8"	10'-6"
30	85'-0"	80'-0"	9	15'-0"	13'-6"
40	113'-4"	106'-8"	11	18'-4"	16'-6"
50	141'-8"	133'-4"	13	21'-8"	19'-6"
			15	not recommended	

*When pews have ends, thickness of ends must be added to dimensions.

BOOKRACK UNDER PEW

BOOKRACK ON PEW BACK

TYPICAL DETAILS

SEAT EDGE

SEAT END

BOOKRACK

CONCEALED

EXPOSED

PEW FASTENING DETAILS

Pecsok, Jelliffe & Randall, AIA, Architects; Indianapolis, Indiana

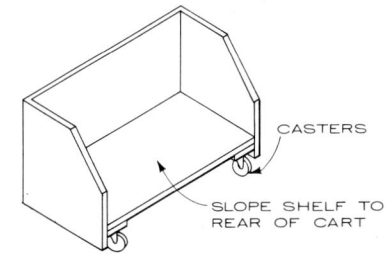

CASTERS

SLOPE SHELF TO REAR OF CART

24" W × 12" TO 18" D × 15" TO 18"H
BLOCK CART

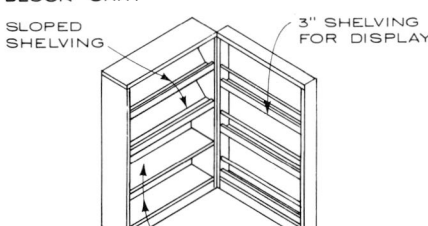

SLOPED SHELVING

3" SHELVING FOR DISPLAY

10"SHELVING

36" W × 52"H
FOLDING BOOKCASE

24" W × 3"D × 48"H SECTIONS
FOLDING BOOKSCREEN

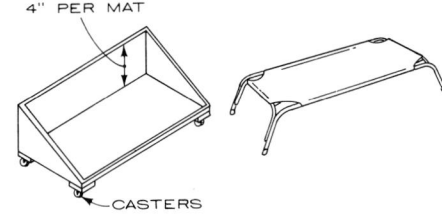

4" PER MAT

CASTERS

26"W × 14"D
REST MAT CART

22" TO 27"W × 54" TO 62"D × 12"H
STACKABLE REST COT

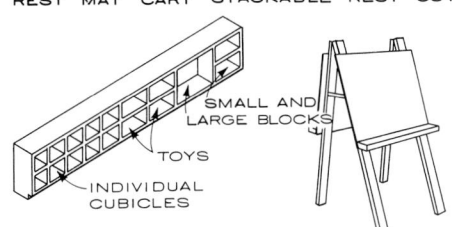

SMALL AND LARGE BLOCKS

TOYS

INDIVIDUAL CUBICLES

12" TO 18"D × 24"H
BUILT-IN STORAGE CUBICLES

FLOOR EASEL

BUMPER

CASTERS

24" SQUARE CARTS TO CARRY 50-100 LB
CLAY CART

UNDERCOUNTER CLAY CART

Kent Wong; Hewlett, Jamison, Atkinson & Luey; Portland, Oregon

60"L × 41"W × 42" H
EXERCISE LADDER

20"L × 22"W × 19"H SEAT
PLAY HORSE

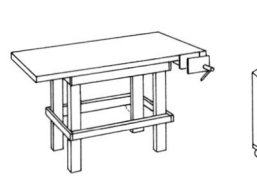

44"L × 20"W × 26"H
WORKBENCH

30"W × 24"D × 18" × 24"H
CARPENTRY TOOL CART

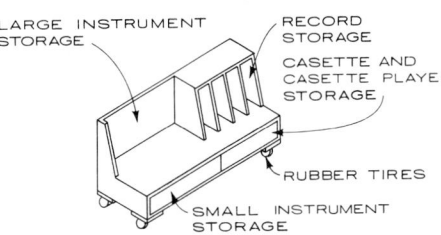

LARGE INSTRUMENT STORAGE

RECORD STORAGE

CASETTE AND CASETTE PLAYER STORAGE

RUBBER TIRES

SMALL INSTRUMENT STORAGE

54"W × 18"D × 28"H
MUSIC CART

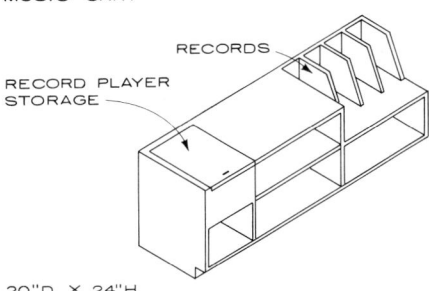

RECORDS

RECORD PLAYER STORAGE

20"D × 24"H
RECORD PLAYER AND STORAGE UNIT

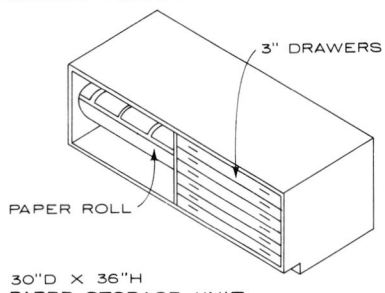

3" DRAWERS

PAPER ROLL

30"D × 36"H
PAPER STORAGE UNIT

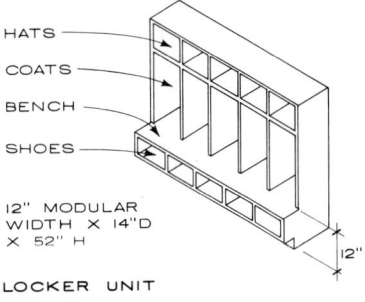

HATS

COATS

BENCH

SHOES

12" MODULAR WIDTH × 14"D × 52" H

12"

LOCKER UNIT

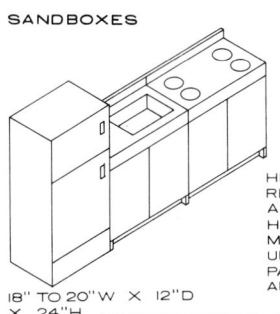

MOLDED PLASTIC LINER

TOY STORAGE UNDER HINGED 10" SEATS

24"W × 48"L × 24" H 6"-8" DEEP BOX FOR SAND OR WATER

96"SQ. × 18"H 96" × 72" × 18"H

SANDBOXES

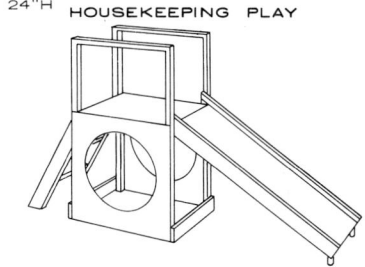

HEIGHT OF REFRIGERATOR AND OTHER FULL HEIGHT ITEMS MAX. 38". STORAGE UNITS FOR POTS, PANS, AND DISHES ARE RECOMMENDED

18" TO 20"W × 12"D × 24"H
HOUSEKEEPING PLAY

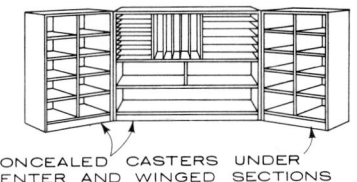

62"L × 24"W × 36"H
INDOOR SLIDE

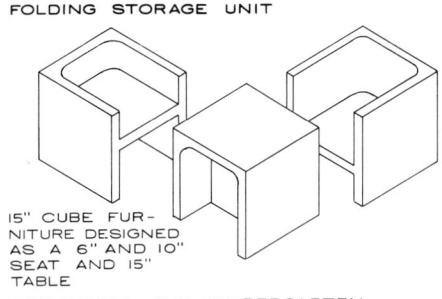

SHELVES MOVABLE IN 2" INTERVALS

CONCEALED CASTERS UNDER CENTER AND WINGED SECTIONS

46"W (CLOSED) × 14"D × 34"H
FOLDING STORAGE UNIT

15" CUBE FURNITURE DESIGNED AS A 6" AND 10" SEAT AND 15" TABLE

PRESCHOOL AND KINDERGARTEN SEATING

GENERAL CHAIR AND TABLE REQUIREMENTS

AGE OF CHILD	CHAIR SEAT HEIGHT				TABLE HEIGHT
	8"	10"	12"	14"	
2 years	80%	20%			—
3 years	40%	50%	10%		18"
4 years		25%	75%		20"
5 years			75%	25%	22"

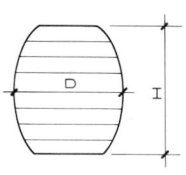

KEGS

KEGS	DIA.	H
1/2	17 1/2''	25''
1/4	14 1/2''	16 1/2''

KEG

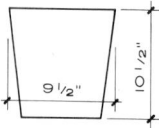

CHAMPAGNE BUCKET

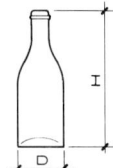

BOTTLE — MIX AND SOFT DRINK

MIX AND SOFT DRINK BOTTLES

OZ	ML	DIA.	H
32 (qt)	946	2 1/2''	11 3/4''
16 (pt)	473	2 1/2''	11''
12	355	2 1/2''	9 1/2''
10 (split)	296		8''

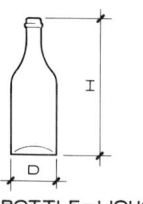

BOTTLE—LIQUOR

LIQUOR BOTTLES

TYPE	OZ	ML	DIA.	H
	7	207	2 3/4''	6''
Beer	12	355	2 3/4''	9''
	32	946	3 1/2''	9 3/4''
Wine	25.6	757	3''	14 1/2''
Whiskey	25.6	757	3 1/2''	11 1/2''
	64	1750	5 1/2''	11 1/2''
Champagne	25.6	757	3''	12''
Brandy	25.6	757	3''	12''
Fine champagne	25.6	757	3 1/2''	10 1/2''
Vermouth	25.6	757	3''	12 1/4''

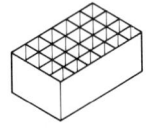

CASE

NOTES

Full kegs are no longer commonly used. Half-kegs are the most often used in beverage operations. Half-kegs = 248-8 oz glasses. Quarter-kegs = 124-8 oz glasses.

Can sizes: 2 5/8 in. diameter, 4 3/4 in. (12 oz) or 6 1/4 in. (16 oz) high. Packed in case or six-pack. Bottles and cans vary in size depending on manufacturer's specifications.

CONTAINER SIZES

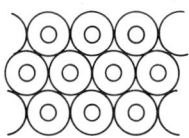

Bottle Size	Number per sq ft
2 1/2'' d.	20
2 3/4 d.	18
3'' d.	14
3 1/2'' d.	9

These figures also for standing bottles

STACKED BOTTLES

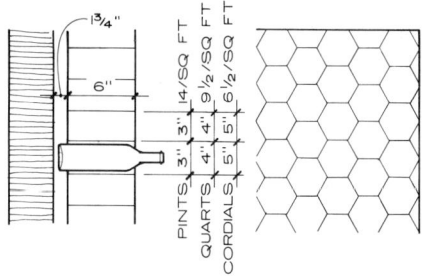

METAL HONEYCOMB RACK

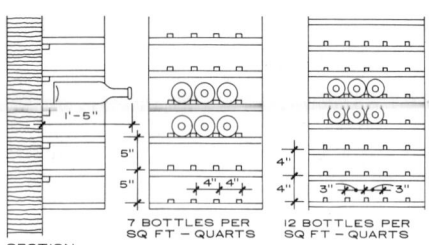

7 BOTTLES PER SQ FT — QUARTS
12 BOTTLES PER SQ FT — QUARTS
SECTION

WOOD BOARD SHELVES

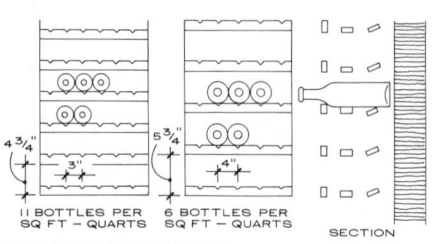

11 BOTTLES PER SQ FT — QUARTS
6 BOTTLES PER SQ FT — QUARTS
SECTION

WOOD SLAT SHELVES

BOTTLE STORAGE

Dimensions and connections vary slightly with supplier.

DIAMETER 10'' HEIGHT 26''

CARBON DIOXIDE

PRESSURIZED 5 GAL DIAMETER 9'' HEIGHT 24''

SYRUP

20 and 50 lb cylinders. Check with supplier for exact dimensions, regulators, and pressures.

POSTMIX SODA SYSTEMS: Available in capacities of 2 to 7-6 oz drinks per minute. Dispensing heads may be located a maximum of 250 ft from master unit. Mechanically refrigerated and ice plate systems are available. Both systems require syrup and carbon dioxide tanks, water supply, and electrical hookup. Used in connection with flexible dispensing head or stationary faucets.

BEER SYSTEMS: Maximum distance between keg and dispensing head is 150 ft. Kegs to be refrigerated at 35 to 38°F.

LIQUOR DISPENSING SYSTEMS: Available in mechanical, automatic, and computerized systems. Efficient control of portions, cost, and theft.

NOTE: All dispensing systems should be conveniently located near cocktail station.

PRESSURIZED DISPENSING SYSTEMS

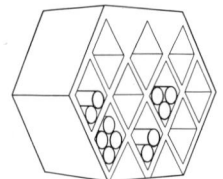

WIDTH 30'', DEPTH 10'', HEIGHT 27''

WINE BIN

WIDTH 8 1/2'' DEPTH 12 1/4'' HEIGHT 18''

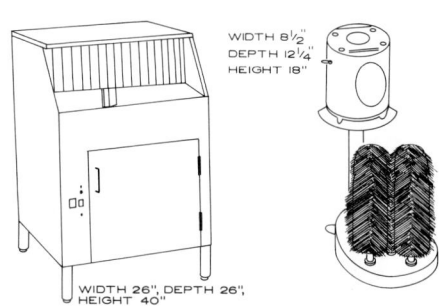

WIDTH 26'', DEPTH 26'', HEIGHT 40''

APPLIANCE TYPE

SINK TYPE

Automatic units available for underbar installation integral to workboard. Local codes require specific methods of glass washing and sanitation. Size and type used will depend on codes, type, and volume of operation.

GLASS WASHERS

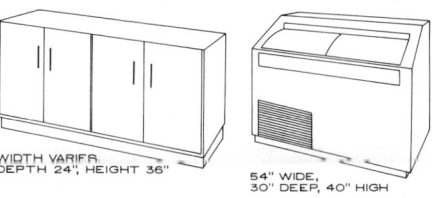

WIDTH VARIES. DEPTH 24'', HEIGHT 36''

UNDERCOUNTER REFRIGERATOR

54'' WIDE, 30'' DEEP, 40'' HIGH

BOTTLE COOLER

Various sizes and capacities. May be self-contained or have remote refrigeration compressor. Suggested options include locking doors, flat doors, flat door slide or roller lid, adjustable dividers, interior light, beer dispenser, and bottle opener with cap catcher. Check utility requirements.

REFRIGERATOR AND COOLER

GENERAL NOTES AND CONDITIONS

The most common surface material for carpentry is plastic laminate. It is very durable and easily cleaned. Wood is often used, but requires coating or sealer for greater protection, longer life, and good sanitation. Other materials are glass, plexiglass, mirrors, and metals. All must fill local code requirements for cleaning, safety, and fire resistance.

Cini-Grissom Associates; Food Service Consultants; Washington, D.C.

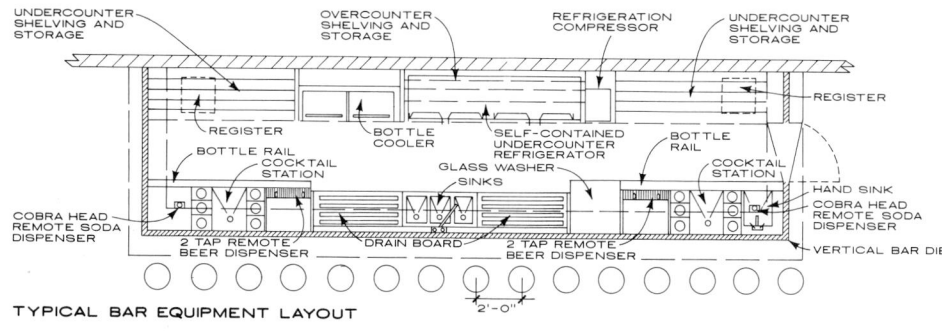

TYPICAL BAR EQUIPMENT LAYOUT

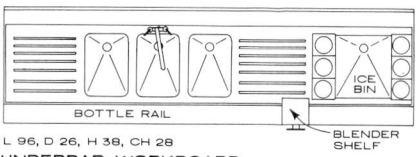

L 96, D 26, H 38, CH 28
UNDERBAR WORKBOARD

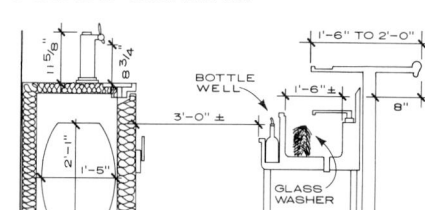

BEER DISPENSING UNIT WITH KEG

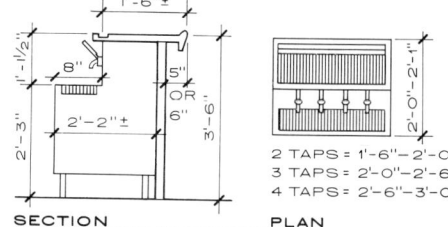

2 TAPS = 1'-6"–2'-0"
3 TAPS = 2'-0"–2'-6"
4 TAPS = 2'-6"–3'-0"

SECTION   PLAN
BUILT-IN BEER DISPENSING UNIT

NOTES

1. Other commonly found beverage service equipment includes glass froster, ice machine, automatic liquor dispensing system, blender, mixer, bottle disposal devices, condiment trays, and preparation tools. Service stations on outside of bar may include equipment such as ice bin, soda dispenser, water, cash register access, glass storage, glass washer access, coffee urn, condiments, and tabletop accessories.

2. BACK BAR: Above—space allocated for register, glass storage, beer keg dispenser, and wine and liquor storage and dispensing. Under—generally refrigerated cases for wine, beer, mixer, and condiment storage and shelving for glass and liquor storage and display.

3. WORKBOARD: Corrugated metal top, stainless steel preferred, for clean glass drainage and storage.

4. SINKS: Three compartments or as required by codes; includes glass washer if not located elsewhere.

5. COCKTAIL STATION: Contains ice bin with integral, but separate (for safety and sanitation) bottle rack compartments.

6. Underbar options include blender shelf, cutting board, condiment trays, and utility outlets, built in. Bottle and glass chillers are available; check utility requirements and space available. Drainage and waste disposal required. Check local codes for hand sink requirements.

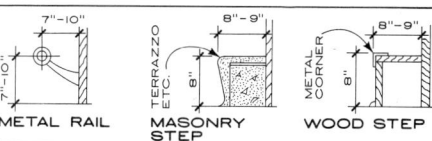

METAL RAIL   MASONRY   WOOD STEP
              STEP
FOOT RAIL AND STEP

BAR EQUIPMENT

SECTION
GLASS STORAGE

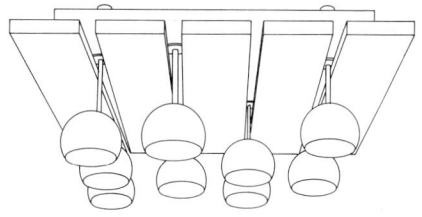

HANGING RACK
GLASSWARE

TYPE	HGT. (IN.)	DIA. (IN.)	NUMBER PER LINEAR FT OF SHELF	SIZE (OZ.)
BEER				
Tapered beer glass	$5\frac{1}{2}$	$2\frac{3}{4}$	4	8
Bulge top beer glass	$5\frac{3}{4}$	$2\frac{3}{4}$	4	9
Pilsner	$7\frac{1}{2}$	$3\frac{1}{4}$	3	10
Handled mug	5	3	4	10–12
Goblet	6	3	4	11
Tankard mug	$5\frac{1}{2}$	3	4	14
Pitcher	$9\frac{1}{4}$	$5\frac{3}{4}$	2	60
WHISKEY				
Cordial	$4\frac{1}{4}$	$1\frac{3}{4}$	6	$1-1\frac{1}{4}$
Cocktail	$5\frac{1}{2}$	3	4	$4\frac{1}{2}$
Whiskey sour	$5\frac{3}{4}$	$2\frac{1}{4}$	4	$4\frac{1}{2}$
Footed highball	$5\frac{3}{4}$	$2\frac{3}{4}$	4	8–10
Frosted Collins	$4\frac{3}{4}$	$2\frac{1}{2}$	4	10
Frosted tumbler	5	$2\frac{1}{2}$	4	10
Footed hurricane	10	$3\frac{1}{2}$	3	22
WINE				
Champagne	$4\frac{1}{2}$	$3\frac{3}{4}$	3	$4\frac{1}{2}$
All purpose wine	$5\frac{1}{2}$	3	4	6–8
White wine	8	3	4	12
Round wine	$6\frac{3}{4}$	$3\frac{1}{4}$	3	14
Half-liter carafe	$9\frac{1}{4}$	$3\frac{1}{4}$	3	$\frac{1}{2}$ liter
Full-liter carafe	11	4	3	1 liter

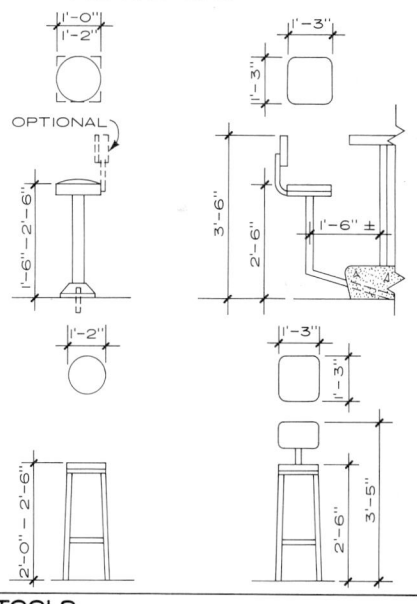

STOOLS
NOTE
Many styles are available. Shapes and sizes depend on the operation and type of service. Refer to section on seating for more details.

GENERAL DESIGN CRITERIA

1. In beverage service situations only, smaller tables may be used in comparison to food service size requirements. 1 ft 6 in. square minimum. Refer to section on counters and seating for additional dimensional requirements.

2. If beverage service from cocktail lounge to dining room is planned, convenient access between service areas should be provided.

3. Most health codes require a hand sink in the under-bar area.

4. Service bar should not interfere with regular bar service and seating.

Cini-Grissom Associates; Food Service Consultants; Washington, D.C.

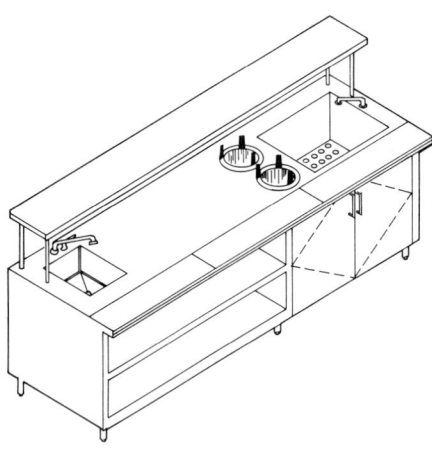

CHEF TABLE
DIMENSIONS AS SPECIFIED

NOTE

Size depends on individual operation. Illustrated with bain marie, self-leveling dish dispenser, overshelf, cutting board, heat lamp, and undercounter shelving; other options include a heated or refrigerated base. May be equipped as hot food table. For preparation and delivery of food to service personnel.

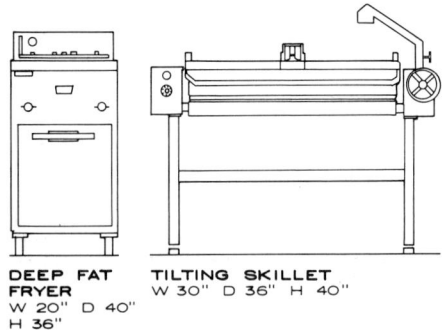

DEEP FAT FRYER
W 20" D 40" H 36"

TILTING SKILLET
W 30" D 36" H 40"

NOTE

Deep fat fryers are available in several capacities and counter top or floor model types. Fry basket lift may be automatic or manual. For fabricated equipment, drop-in units are available. Fat filter may be self-contained. Gas or electrically operated.

Tilting skillet capacities depend on operational requirements and manufacturer. Types available are counter top, cabinet base, and leg. Operate on gas or electricity.

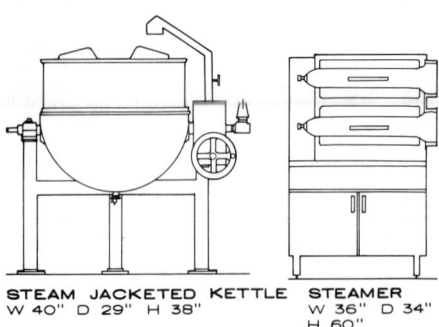

STEAM JACKETED KETTLE
W 40" D 29" H 38"

STEAMER
W 36" D 34" H 60"

NOTE

Steam jacketed kettle capacities are variable, tilting or stationary, tri-leg, pedestal, or wall hung. Wall hung units are expensive to install. Smaller capacity kettles are usually counter top. Units may be gas, electric, or steam.

Steamers are available with one, two, or three compartments. They are self-contained units that use gas, electric, or direct fired steam. Counter or floor models available.

HOT FOOD EQUIPMENT

Cini-Grissom Associates; Food Service Consultants; Washington, D.C.

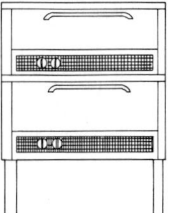

DECK OVEN
W 52" D 38" H 60"

CONVECTION OVEN
W 38" D 46" H 60"

NOTE

One, two, or three decks, depending on function. Used to bake or roast. Dimensions vary. Equipped with legs or cabinet base.

Convection ovens are available with one or two sections. Single section available with legs or stand, modular or cabinet base. Ovens contain adjustable racks. Gas or electrically operated.

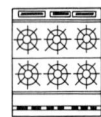

PLAN

GRIDDLE TOP
RANGE

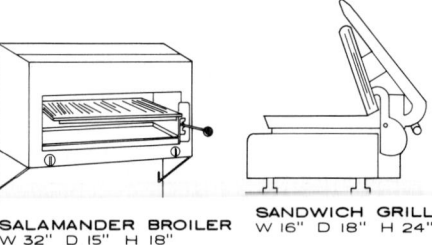

ELEVATION
RANGE
W 32" D 42" H 40"

NOTE

Ranges use gas or electricity and are available with various numbers of burners and cook tops. Fry top is equipped with grease trough, burner top with drip tray, griddle top with spillage channels. Ranges are installed in counter tops or mounted on a cabinet or oven base with flue riser and shelves. Install under vented hood and check local codes for fire and sanitary regulations.

SALAMANDER BROILER
W 32" D 15" H 18"

SANDWICH GRILL
W 16" D 18" H 24"

NOTE

Salamander broiler is installed in the shelf area above the range top. For light broiling and finishing with drip shield to protect range top. Gas or electrically operated.

Sandwich grill is an electric counter top unit. It is available in various capacities.

TOASTER
W 11" D 12" H 8"

NOTE

Electric pop-up, rotary model available.

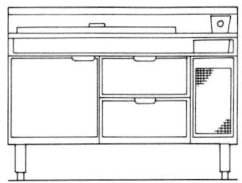

SANDWICH UNIT
W 60" D 32" H 42"

NOTE

Sandwich unit is used for the preparation of salads and sandwiches. Various capacities and combinations. Refrigerated pans are accessible from top. Base or cabinet is refrigerated. Refrigeration compressor is self-contained or remote.

REFRIGERATOR
W 52" D 56" H 84"

NOTE

Refrigerators are available in many types, such as roll-in, pass through, mobile, and undercounter. They come with sliding or hinged, glass or stainless steel, full or half doors. Units are available with dual temperature control for combination refrigerator/freezer units. Refrigeration compressor may be self-contained or remote.

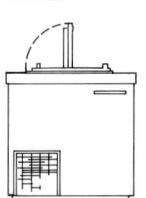

ICE CREAM CABINET
W 30" D 17" H 30"

NOTE

Electrically operated and available in various types and sizes. Accessories include syrup rail, dipper well, self-leveling dish dispenser, and sink. For door sizes and types consult manufacturer catalogs. Refrigeration compressor is remote or self-contained.

COLD FOOD EQUIPMENT

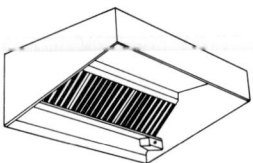

VIEW
W VARIES D 46" H 29"

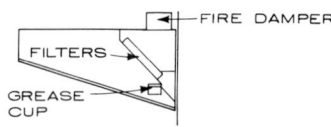

SECTION

NOTE

Exhaust ventilators are required over equipment producing grease ladened vapors. Hung from wall or ceiling, single depth for one line of equipment or double-sided for use with island equipment. Mesh or baffle washable and removable filters or an internal stationary baffle.

OVERHEAD VENTILATOR

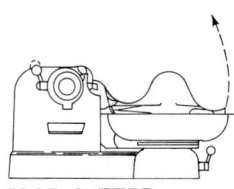
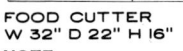
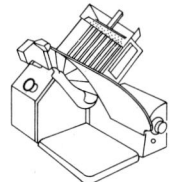

FOOD CUTTER
W 32" D 22" H 16"

FOOD SLICER
W 20" D 24" H 19"

NOTE

Food cutters vary in size and motor capacities. Counter top equipment. Optional attachment equipment available if offered by manufacturer. Safety, sanitary, and electrical codes must be complied with.

Food slicers are counter top equipment of various capacities. Optional feed carriages are available. Check sanitary, safety, and electrical codes.

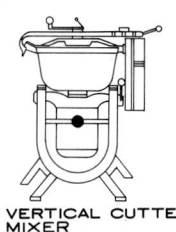

MEAT CHOPPER
W 12" D 18" H 24"

VERTICAL CUTTER MIXER
W 24" D 22" H 41"

NOTE

Meat choppers are counter top or floor type equipment of various sizes and capacities for chopping fresh and frozen meats. It should be easily accessible for cleaning. Check local electrical, sanitation, and safety codes.

Vertical cutter mixer comes in various sizes, and electrical capacities. For cutting, kneading, mixing, and similar purposes. It is usually a floor unit. Check local safety and sanitation codes.

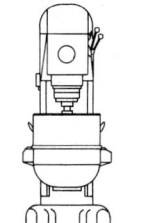
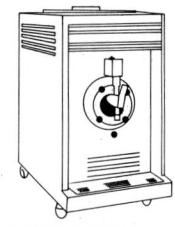

MIXER
W 21" D 20" H 45"

SOFT SERVE MACHINE
W 18" D 30" H 32"

NOTE

Mixer is either counter top or floor model and available in many sizes with many types of attachments. Check specifics with manufacturer. Consult local sanitary and electrical codes.

Soft serve machines are either counter or floor model. Accessibility of controls and components is important. Sizes and capacities vary, so consult manufacturer. Check safety and sanitary codes.

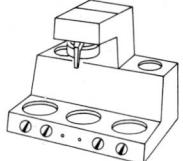
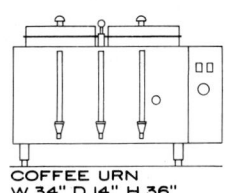

FIVE STATION COFFEE WARMER
W 24" D 18" H 24"

COFFEE URN
W 34" D 14" H 36"

NOTE

Coffee warmers are available with various station quantities and electrical capacities. They are used where large capacity is not usually needed. Water line is not required on some models. Warmer may be fully automatic or manually operated.

Coffee urns are usually automatic with twin coffee liners and unlimited water capacity for brewing. Suggested with swivel spray arm and heated coils for incoming water. Other options available. Check local sanitation and plumbing codes.

PREPARATION EQUIPMENT

Cini-Grissom Associates, Inc.; Food Service Consultants; Washington, D.C.

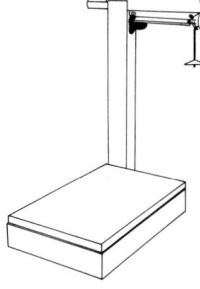
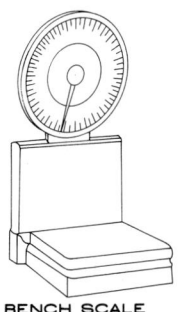

BEAM SCALE
W 20" D 36" H 50"

BENCH SCALE
W 24" D 30" H 51"

NOTE

Beam scales are accurate and easy to use, generally located at receiving area. Preferably on wheels. Accessories include ratio counting kit with scoops and balance indicator; others available. Capacities are variable.

Bench scales are available in many capacities, with beam and/or dial head. Accessories include platform or cabinet base, wheels, extra pans, and heater in head to protect from moisture and dust.

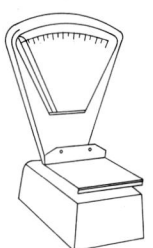

FAN SCALE
W 12" D 12" H 20"

NOTE

Fan scales are available in many weighing capacities, generally up to 6 lb. Usually automatic; should have well defined figures and graduations for accurate reading. May be supplied with platter (as shown), scoops, and round pans and equipped with a beam for more accurate and increased weight capacities.

Scales should be of durable, corrosion resistant, and easily cleaned material. Many varieties of scales are available depending on general use. For use in portion control situations, electronic models are very useful.

SCALES

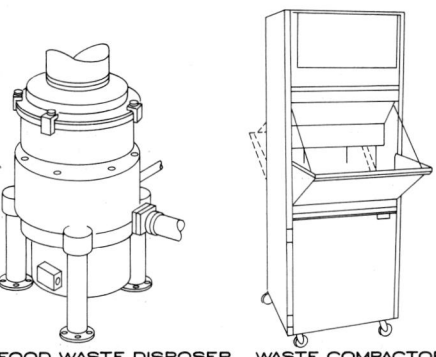

FOOD WASTE DISPOSER
W 17" D 17" H 27"

WASTE COMPACTOR
W 27" D 25" H 75"

NOTE

Food waste disposers are available in many sizes for specific operational requirements. Options include silver trap, sink stopper, spray rinser, cone with water swirl, sink, and vacuum breaker. Check local plumbing and sanitary codes.

Waste compactors are generally located at point of waste generation or in central accumulation area. Compacted into either bag or box. Reduce labor costs because of less waste handling. An efficient means of reducing volume of waste.

WASTE HANDLING EQUIPMENT

CONVEYOR DISHWASHER
W 64" D 30" H 60"

SINGLE TANK DISHWASHER
W 38" D 28" H 60"

NOTE

Conveyor dishwashers are available with single tank or two tanks, or with prewash tank, partially or fully automatic rack type. Accessories include inspection door, automatic temperature control with visible thermometers, splash shields, and others. Check local sanitary, safety, and electrical codes.

Single tank dishwashers are generally used in small operations. Manual operation for straight through or corner installations. Available with low temperature for use with sanitizing solution.

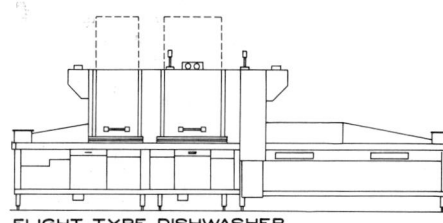

FLIGHT TYPE DISHWASHER
W 196" D 30" H 60"

NOTE

Flight type dishwasher is generally automatic with visible water temperature thermometers, inspection doors, and detergent dispensers. Optional equipment includes blow dryers, control sensors, energy saving connections, and other mechanical and electrical equipment. Electrically powered with gas, electrical or steam tank heats. Check electrical, sanitary plumbing, and safety codes.

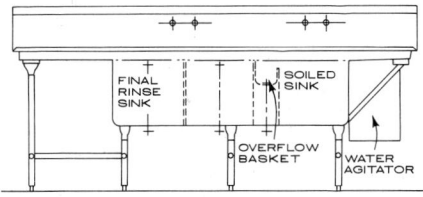

POT SINK WITH OVERFLOW BASKET. DIMENSIONS AS SPECIFIED

NOTE

Three compartment pot sink with integral drainboards, overflow compartment, and basket. It is suggested that drainboards shorter than 24 in. long require no legs or braces, drainboards 25 to 30 in. long require brace, and drainboards over 30 in. long require legs and channel framework. Drainboards and sink compartments should have sufficient pitch for complete drainage without pooling. Lever or rotary handle wastes recommended, strainer basket and plug also available. Recirculating water agitator may be installed on soiled compartment for ease in soil removal. Overflow basket may be installed next to soiled compartment with suggested perforated basket. Final rinse sink should be supplied with a sanitizing solution or heater to raise water temperature to required level. Check local codes.

WARE WASHING EQUIPMENT

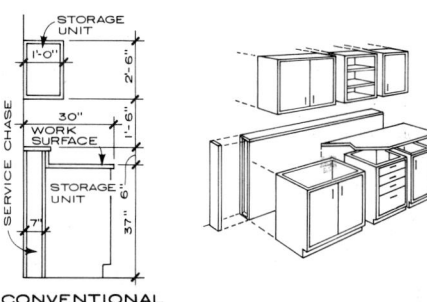

CONVENTIONAL

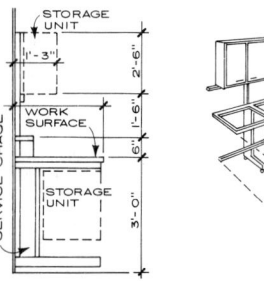

STRUCTURAL FRAME / SUSPENDED

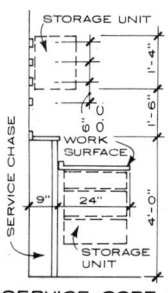
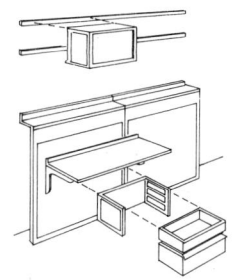

SERVICE CORE / SUSPENDED

CASEWORK SYSTEMS

Laboratory casework systems are an assembly of base storage units, work surfaces, and upper storage units. Regardless of the application, mechanical service spaces and waste systems are integral components. Typical systems, in order of increasing flexibility, are the following:

1. THE CONVENTIONAL FIXED SYSTEM: Consists of base cabinet units supporting a work surface and wall mounted upper cabinet units. The cabinets are available in a range of sizes and types. A plumb-

ing chase can be provided as shown or can be within the existing wall cavity. This system is applicable to a high storage situation.

2. THE STRUCTURAL FRAME/SUSPENDED CASE-WORK SYSTEM: Consists of a basic frame designed to support work surfaces, plumbing fixtures, base, and upper storage units. The storage units can be repositioned or removed independently of the countertops. Plumbing space is provided within the basic frame. This system is applicable where work surface space is needed but storage requirements are minimal.

3. THE SERVICE CORE/SUSPENDED CASEWORK SYSTEM: Consists of a basic service core and wall rails designed to support storage components and work surfaces. There is a wide range of sizes and types of storage components available and both the mounting heights and types are readily change-able. In addition, transport components are an interchangeable part of the system. Gas and plumbing lines are located within the service core, access-ible through removable panels.

All three types of systems are applicable to wall, peninsula, and island arrangements.

CASEWORK SYSTEMS

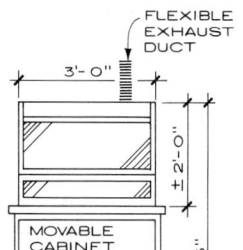

PORTABLE

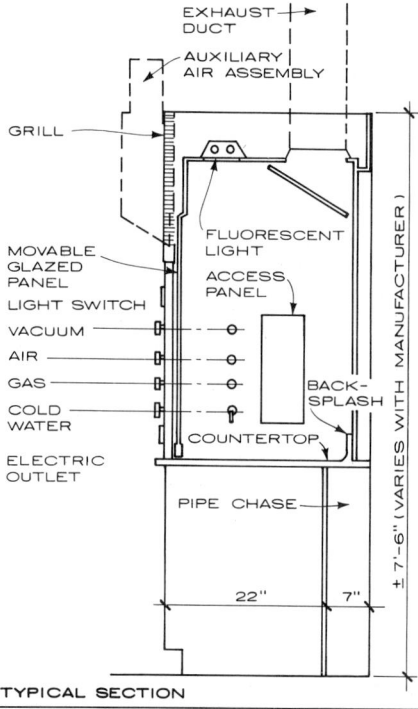

BENCH

WALK–IN

FUME HOODS

DEFINITION

Fume hoods collect and remove contaminants from the laboratory environment by maintaining a flow of air through the hood and exhausting it to the outside.

SELECTION

Factors to be considered:

1. Type of laboratory and materials to be handled.
2. Nature of work to be performed.
3. Frequency of usage.
4. Apparatus site.
5. Government codes and regulations.

CLASSIFICATION

1. CLASS A: Average face velocity 125-150 fpm with minimum at any point of 100-125 fpm.
2. CLASS B: Average face velocity 100 fpm with minimum at any point of 80 fpm.
3. CLASS C: Average face velocity 75-80 fpm with minimums at any point of 50-60 fpm.

Further classification groups these classes A, B, and C within Class I. Class II contains biological safety hoods. Class III includes totally enclosed hoods (with glove holes for performing the work).

These classifications are based on American Industrial Hygiene Association, The American Conference of Governmental Industrial Hygienists, and The National Fire Protection Association (Publication 45).

TYPICAL SECTION

FUME HOODS

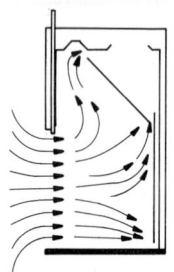

SASH OPEN STANDARD

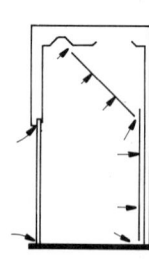

SASH CLOSED

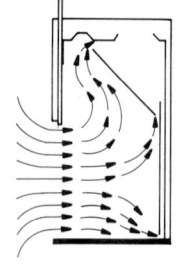

SASH OPEN BYPASS

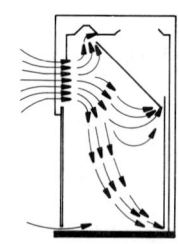

SASH CLOSED

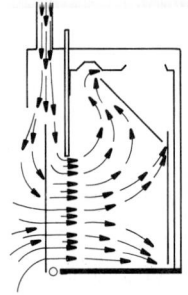

SASH OPEN AUXILIARY AIR

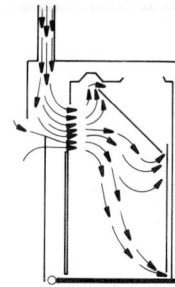

SASH CLOSED

AIR FLOW PATTERNS

1. STANDARD TYPE: Room air is used to exhaust contaminants.
2. BYPASS TYPE: An additional hood opening is used to maintain a constant volume exhaust from

the hood regardless of sash position, limiting high face velocity.

3. AUXILIARY AIR TYPE: Supplemental air is used to reduce room air consumption, either when the

quantity of room air is not adequate for hood operation or as an energy saving measure to reduce the quantity of conditioned air removal from the room.

AIRFLOW PATTERNS

Liz Karp; The Architects Collaborative, Inc.; Cambridge, Massachusetts

LABORATORY EQUIPMENT

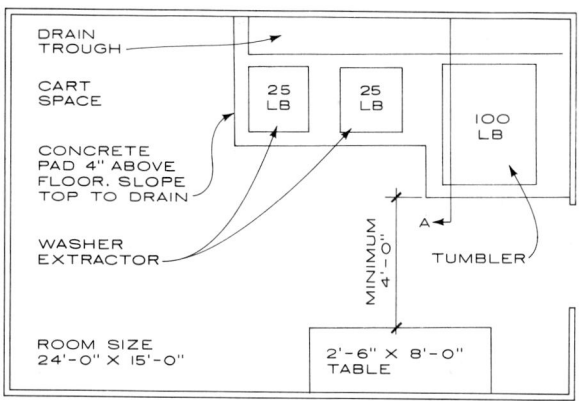

40-60 UNIT MOTEL

DRAIN TROUGH
CART SPACE
CONCRETE PAD 4" ABOVE FLOOR. SLOPE TOP TO DRAIN
WASHER EXTRACTOR
25 LB 25 LB 100 LB
MINIMUM 4'-0"
A
TUMBLER
ROOM SIZE 24'-0" X 15'-0"
2'-6" X 8'-0" TABLE

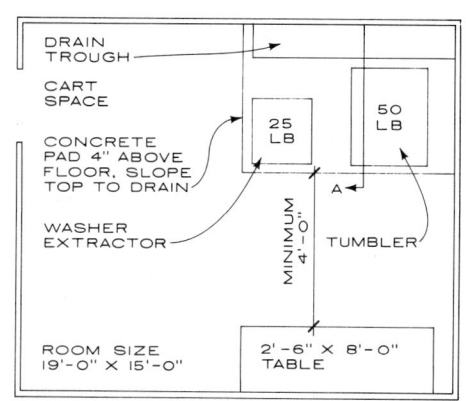

100-125 UNIT MOTEL

DRAIN TROUGH
CART SPACE
CONCRETE PAD 4" ABOVE FLOOR. SLOPE TOP TO DRAIN
WASHER EXTRACTOR
25 LB 50 LB 50 LB 100 LB
A
MINIMUM 4'-0"
TUMBLERS
ROOM SIZE 29'-0" X 16'-0"
2'-6" X 8'-0" TABLE

IF IRONER IS TO BE INCLUDED, INCREASE ROOM SIZE 8'-0". TUMBLER CAPACITY CAN BE DECREASED

TABLE
IRONER

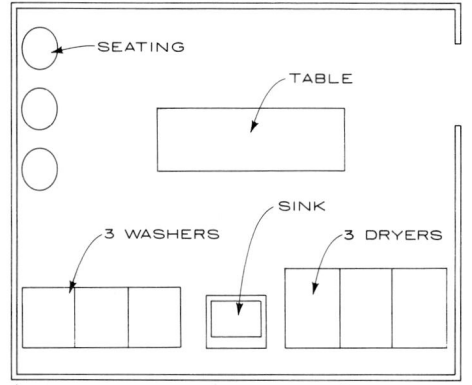

20 UNIT APARTMENT

SEATING
TABLE
3 WASHERS
SINK
3 DRYERS

EXHAUST, WATER AND ELECTRIC SUPPLY FROM ABOVE

8'-0" MINIMUM CEILING HEIGHT
4"
2'-0" MINIMUM
DRAIN TROUGH 8" DEEP, 15" WIDE 2" MINIMUM FLOOR DRAIN WITH LINT COVER
CONCRETE PAD 24" DEEP. VERIFY REINFORCING

SECTION A

NOTE

Drain trench underneath or behind washers is sized to contain one complete dump from all machines. Waste line 2 in. minimum with lint grating. Tumbler capacity is twice washer capacity for permanent press fabrics. Venting, electric, and gas lines should run overhead and drop down to machines. Apartment machines are the usual coin operated residential size.

DRAIN TROUGH
CART SPACE
CONCRETE PAD 4" ABOVE FLOOR. SLOPE TOP TO DRAIN
WASHER EXTRACTOR
25 LB 50 LB
A
MINIMUM 4'-0"
TUMBLER
ROOM SIZE 19'-0" X 15'-0"
2'-6" X 8'-0" TABLE

20-30 UNIT MOTEL

WASHER/EXTRACTOR SIZES

CAPACITY (LB)	WIDTH	DEPTH
20	28"	30"
20–30	30"	32"
30–40	34"	36"
40–50	36"	44"
50–60	46"	40"

Above 60 lb, sizes may vary with manufacturer. Minimum clearances: 18 in. sides, 24 in. behind, and 48 in. front.

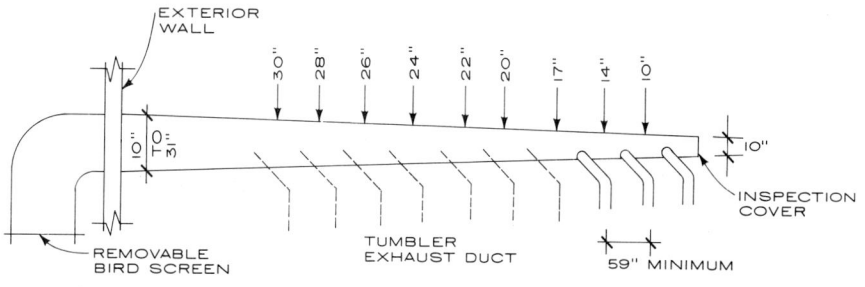

EXTERIOR WALL
30" 28" 26" 24" 22" 20" 17" 14" 10"
10" TO 31"
10"
INSPECTION COVER
REMOVABLE BIRD SCREEN
TUMBLER EXHAUST DUCT
59" MINIMUM

EXHAUST DUCT

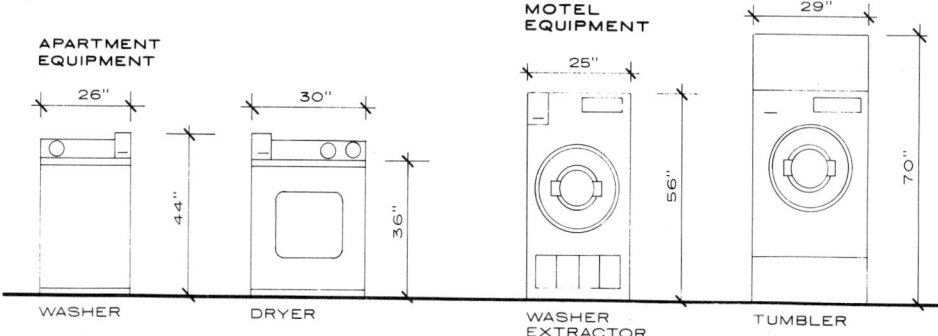

APARTMENT EQUIPMENT
MOTEL EQUIPMENT
26" 44" WASHER
30" 36" DRYER
25" 56" WASHER EXTRACTOR
29" 70" TUMBLER

TUMBLER SIZES

CAPACITY (LB)	WIDTH	DEPTH
30	32"	45"
50	39"	47"
65	39"	53"
100	47"	64"

Minimum clearances: 24 in. behind, none sides, 48 in. front.

Smiley-Glotter Associates-Architects Engineers Planners; Minneapolis, Minnesota

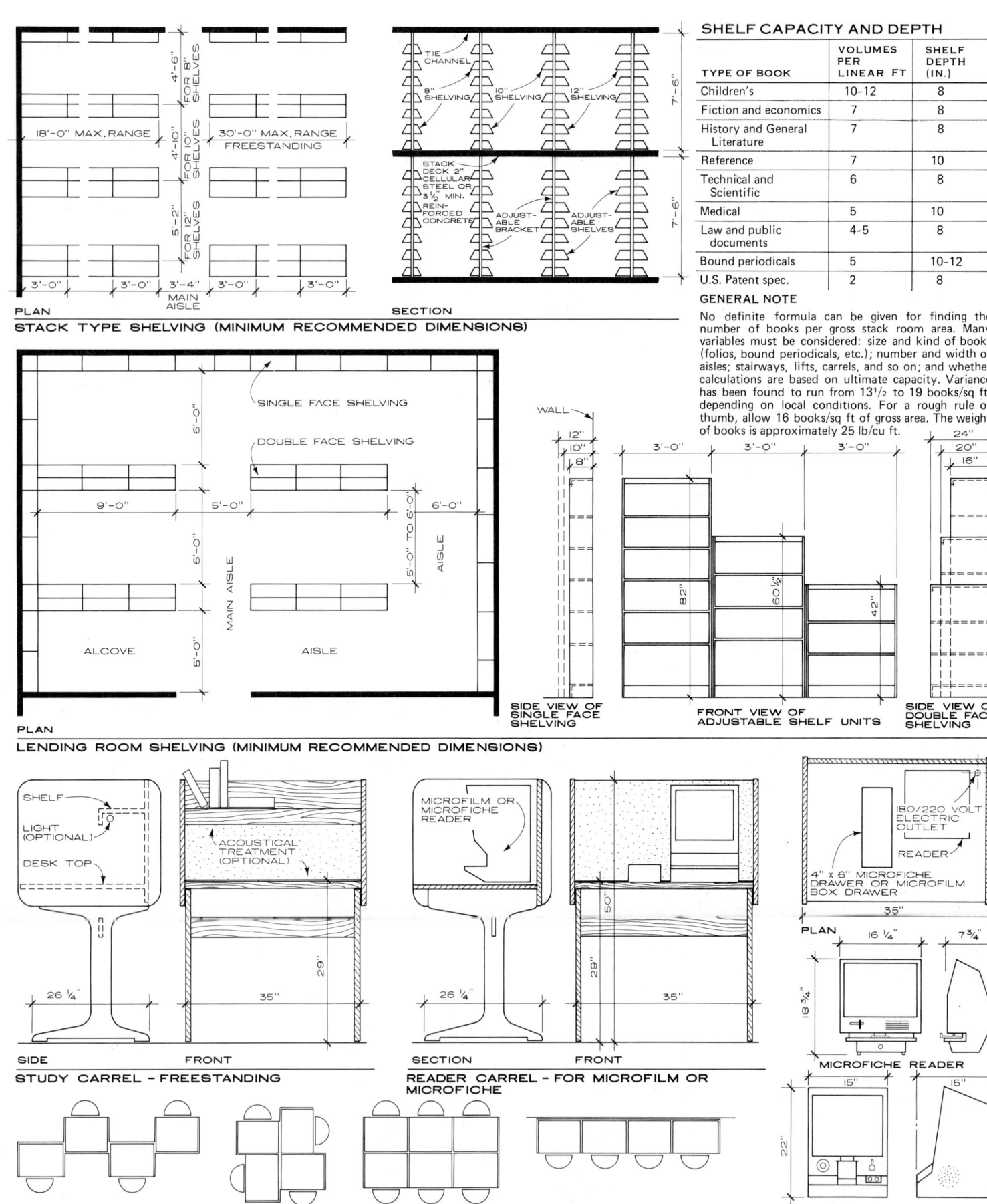

SHELF CAPACITY AND DEPTH

TYPE OF BOOK	VOLUMES PER LINEAR FT	SHELF DEPTH (IN.)
Children's	10-12	8
Fiction and economics	7	8
History and General Literature	7	8
Reference	7	10
Technical and Scientific	6	8
Medical	5	10
Law and public documents	4-5	8
Bound periodicals	5	10-12
U.S. Patent spec.	2	8

GENERAL NOTE

No definite formula can be given for finding the number of books per gross stack room area. Many variables must be considered: size and kind of books (folios, bound periodicals, etc.); number and width of aisles; stairways, lifts, carrels, and so on; and whether calculations are based on ultimate capacity. Variance has been found to run from 13½ to 19 books/sq ft, depending on local conditions. For a rough rule of thumb, allow 16 books/sq ft of gross area. The weight of books is approximately 25 lb/cu ft.

STACK TYPE SHELVING (MINIMUM RECOMMENDED DIMENSIONS)

LENDING ROOM SHELVING (MINIMUM RECOMMENDED DIMENSIONS)

STUDY CARREL – FREESTANDING

READER CARREL – FOR MICROFILM OR MICROFICHE

STUDY CARREL ARRANGEMENTS

FREESTANDING   PINWHEEL   DOUBLE SIDED   WALL HUNG

Walter Hart, AIA, and Frank Giersback, R.A.; North White Plains, New York

11 **LIBRARY EQUIPMENT**

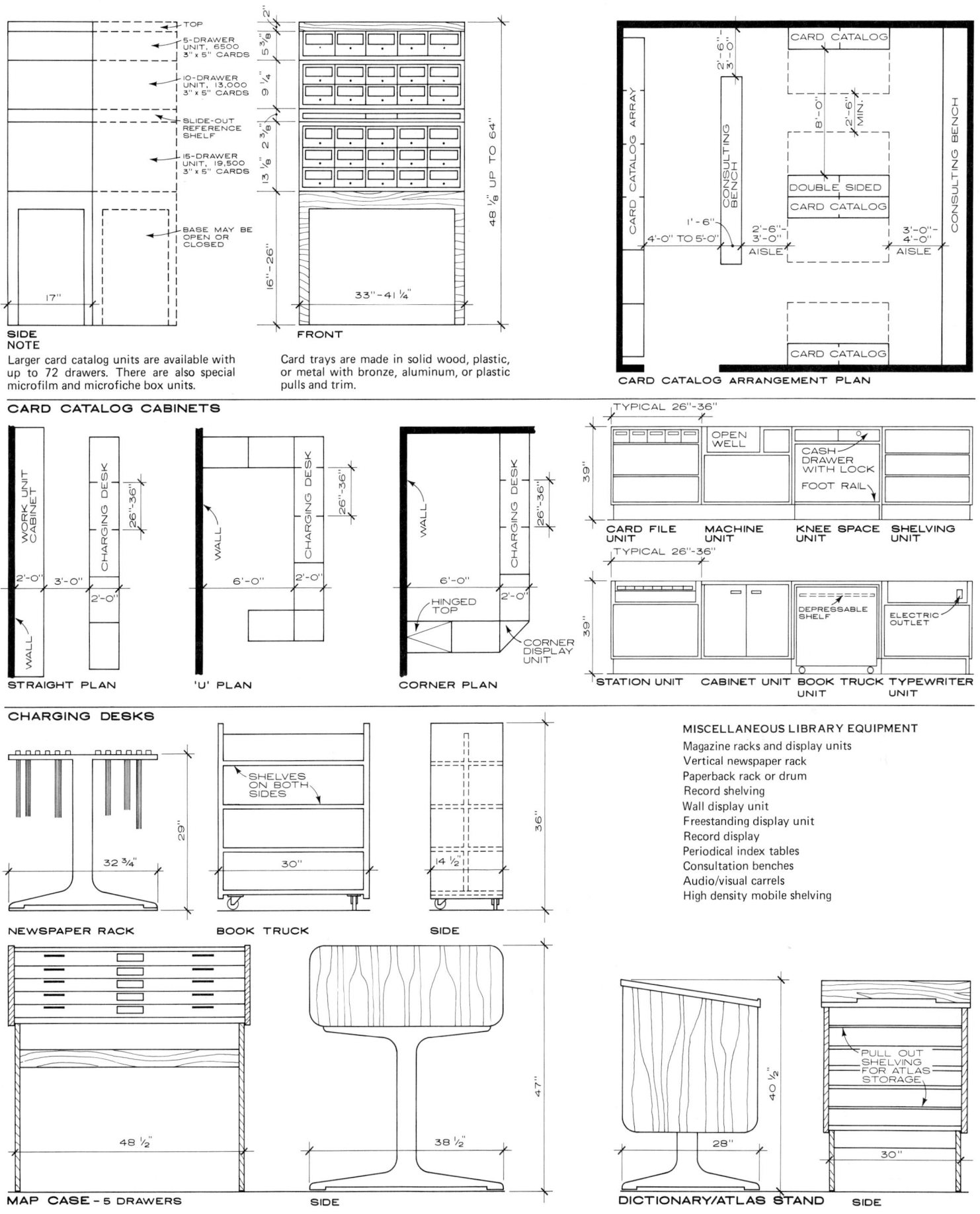

CARD CATALOG CABINETS

SIDE

NOTE
Larger card catalog units are available with up to 72 drawers. There are also special microfilm and microfiche box units.

Card trays are made in solid wood, plastic, or metal with bronze, aluminum, or plastic pulls and trim.

FRONT

TOP
5-DRAWER UNIT, 6500 3" x 5" CARDS
10-DRAWER UNIT, 13,000 3" x 5" CARDS
SLIDE-OUT REFERENCE SHELF
15-DRAWER UNIT, 19,500 3" x 5" CARDS
BASE MAY BE OPEN OR CLOSED

CARD CATALOG ARRANGEMENT PLAN

STRAIGHT PLAN · 'U' PLAN · CORNER PLAN

CARD FILE UNIT · MACHINE UNIT · KNEE SPACE UNIT · SHELVING UNIT

STATION UNIT · CABINET UNIT · BOOK TRUCK UNIT · TYPEWRITER UNIT

CHARGING DESKS

NEWSPAPER RACK · BOOK TRUCK · SIDE

MAP CASE - 5 DRAWERS · SIDE

DICTIONARY/ATLAS STAND · SIDE

MISCELLANEOUS LIBRARY EQUIPMENT
Magazine racks and display units
Vertical newspaper rack
Paperback rack or drum
Record shelving
Wall display unit
Freestanding display unit
Record display
Periodical index tables
Consultation benches
Audio/visual carrels
High density mobile shelving

Walter Hart, AIA, and Frank Giersback, R.A.; North White Plains, New York

LIBRARY EQUIPMENT

11

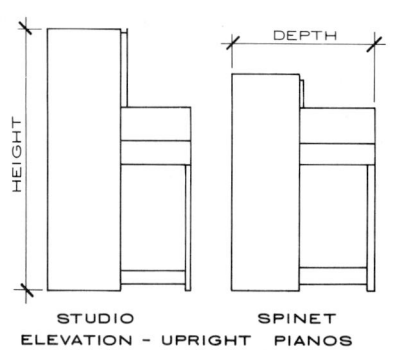

STUDIO   SPINET
ELEVATION - UPRIGHT PIANOS

	DEPTH	WIDTH	HEIGHT	HEIGHT WITH LID RAISED
Concert grand	9'-8''	5'-4''	3'-3''	6'-1''
Music room grand	7'	5'	3'-4''	6'-1''
Parlor grand	6'-3''	4'-10''	3'-4''	5'-10''
Baby grand	4'-5''	4'-7''	3'	4'-4''
Spinet	2'-1''	4'-10''	3'-4''	—
Studio	2'-1''	4'-9''	3'-10''	—

PIANOS

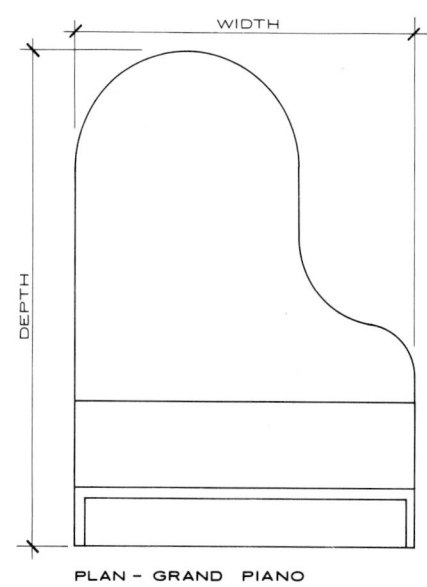

PLAN - GRAND PIANO

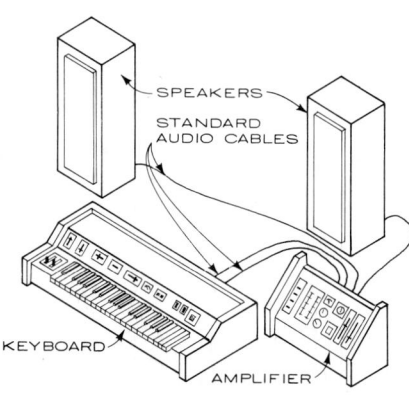

NOTE

Shown are the typical elements of synthesizers: keyboard, amplifier, and speakers. Many different models, combining two or more of the standard elements, are available as small portable or large sophisticated units.

ELECTRONIC SYNTHESIZERS

INSTRUMENTS

	CABINET SIZE (IN.)*		
	H	W	D
A. Clarinet, alto clarinet, bass clarinet, flute, oboe, piccolo, soprano saxophone, trumpet	12	12	30
B. Cornet, flugel horn, double trumpet	20	12	30
C. Bassoon, alto saxophone, tenor saxophone, brass trumpet, violin, viola, trombone	40	12	30
D. Alto horn, French horn, baritone horn, tenor horn	40	18	30
E. Valve trombone, parade drum, snare drum	20	24	30
F. Bass drum, concert drum, scotch drum	40	36	30
G. Tuba, sousaphone, baritone saxophone	40	48	30

*General sizes only. Actual instrument and case sizes may vary in size requirements. Commercially manufactured cabinets, which can be stacked together as units, are shown to the left.

MUSICAL INSTRUMENT STORAGE CABINETS

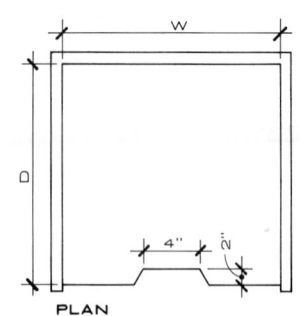

PLAN

FOLIO MUSIC STORAGE

	D	W
Choral folio music	14¼''	10½''
Band folio music	16''	14¾''
Orchestra folio music	16''	14¾''
Marching band folio music	8¼''	7''

Doors may be added for security and to keep out dust. Shelves should be adjustable to accommodate thicker material when required.

FOLIO MUSIC STORAGE

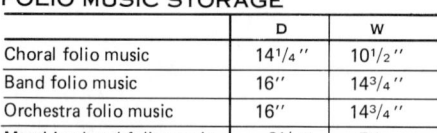

ELEVATION

NOTE

Music folio, uniform and choral robe, and other music storage components are available commercially. Consult manufacturer for additional information.

NOTE

Dimensions shown are for "adult" size; vary rod height according to size requirements. Allow 2½ in. of rod length for each choral robe, 3 to 5 in. of rod length for each uniform.

UNIFORM - ROBE STORAGE

Leland D. Blackledge, AIA; South St. Paul, Minnesota

MUSIC EQUIPMENT

Dimensions shown are maximum of several models.
If several styles exist, the longest, widest, and
highest dimension found in the group are given.

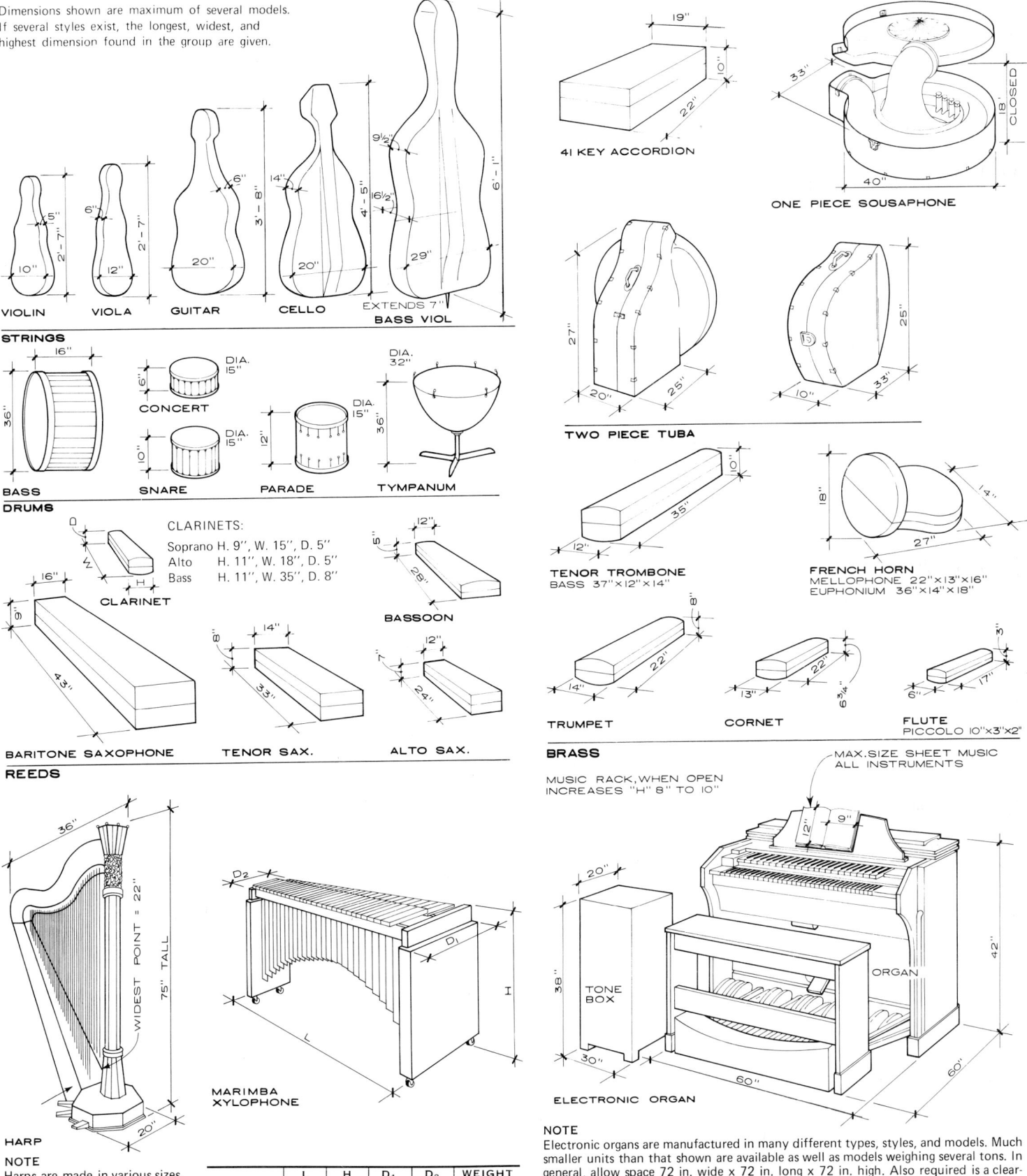

STRINGS

VIOLIN   VIOLA   GUITAR   CELLO   BASS VIOL

EXTENDS 7"

DRUMS

BASS   CONCERT   SNARE   PARADE   TYMPANUM

DIA. 15"   DIA. 15"   DIA. 15"   DIA. 32"

REEDS

CLARINETS:
Soprano H. 9", W. 15", D. 5"
Alto   H. 11", W. 18", D. 5"
Bass   H. 11", W. 35", D. 8"

CLARINET   BASSOON

BARITONE SAXOPHONE   TENOR SAX.   ALTO SAX.

HARP

NOTE
Harps are made in various sizes.
A typical larger model is shown.
The widest dimension is at the
"soundboard" and equals 22 in.
A harp case is 25 in. wide x 84
in. deep. Total weight, including harp and case, is approximately 200 lb.

WIDEST POINT = 22"   75" TALL

MARIMBA XYLOPHONE

	L	H	D₁	D₂	WEIGHT
Marimba	87	36	33	16	175 lb
Xylophone	54	34	32	13	70 lb

NOTE: All dimensions are in inches. Many sizes are
manufactured. The sizes given above are typical larger
size that are available.

Leland D. Blackledge, AIA; South St. Paul, Minnesota

John A. Lesire, AIA; Arlington, Virginia

41 KEY ACCORDION

ONE PIECE SOUSAPHONE

CLOSED

TWO PIECE TUBA

TENOR TROMBONE
BASS 37"x12"x14"

FRENCH HORN
MELLOPHONE 22"x13"x16"
EUPHONIUM 36"x14"x18"

TRUMPET   **CORNET**   **FLUTE**
PICCOLO 10"x3"x2"

BRASS

MUSIC RACK, WHEN OPEN
INCREASES "H" 8" TO 10"

MAX. SIZE SHEET MUSIC
ALL INSTRUMENTS

TONE BOX

ORGAN

ELECTRONIC ORGAN

NOTE
Electronic organs are manufactured in many different types, styles, and models. Much
smaller units than that shown are available as well as models weighing several tons. In
general, allow space 72 in. wide x 72 in. long x 72 in. high. Also required is a clearance of approximately 50 in. to rear of unit for servicing. Consult organ manufacturers
for exact details and models available.

Pipe organs are designed to fit the building in which they are to be used. After factory
assembly and testing, they are disassembled and shipped. Pipes may vary from less
than 1 in. to more than 30 ft in length. A single organ may have thousands of pipes.
Basic components are the pipes, wind chest, blower, valve mechanism, and keyboards.

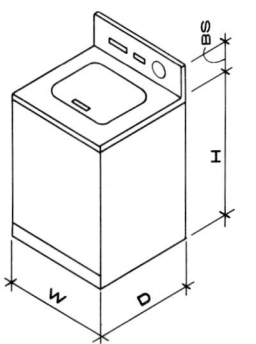

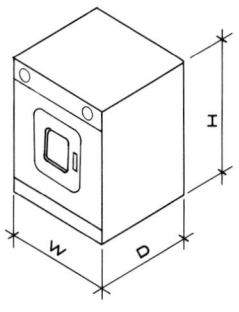

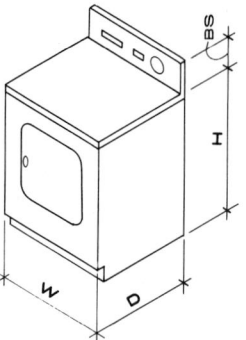

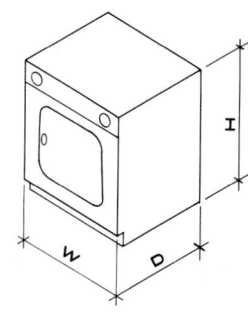

FREESTANDING-TOP OR FRONT LOADING

UNDER COUNTER

AUTOMATIC WASHERS (SOME HAVE KICK SPACES, SOME NOT)

	MIN.	MAX.	OTHER
W	25 1/2	27	25 5/8 - 26 3/4
D	24 7/8	28 23/32	25 - 28 5/16
H	36	36 1/2	36 1/8 - 36 1/4
BS	6 3/32	8 3/4	6 1/2 - 8 1/2

	MIN.	MAX.
W	26 3/4	30 1/4
D	24 7/8	24 7/8
H	34 1/2	

FREESTANDING FRONT LOADING

UNDER COUNTER

AUTOMATIC DRYERS (SOME HAVE KICK SPACES, SOME NOT)

	MIN.	MAX.	OTHER
W	26 3/4	31 1/2	27 - 31
D	24 7/8	28 23/32	25 - 28 5/16
H	36	36 1/2	36 1/8 - 36 1/4
BS	6 3/32	8 3/4	6 1/2 - 8 1/2

	MIN.	MAX.
W	26 3/4	
D	24 7/8	
H	34 1/2	

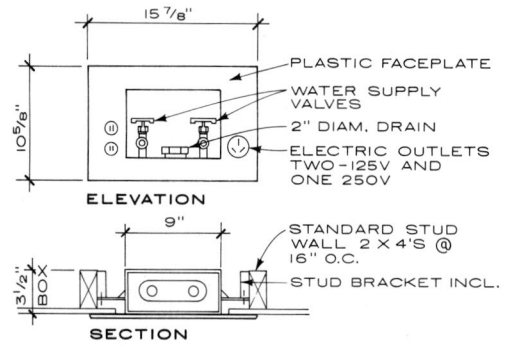

ELEVATION

SECTION

UTILITY CONNECTION BOX (RECESSED)

GENERAL NOTES

See kitchen & laundry layout pages for locations of washers & dryers and wall chases for pipes & vents and for dishwasher locations.

Where clearances of doors of machines (when open) may be a problem, check manufacturers catalog for "open-door" dimension.

All dimensions given are actual ones but certain variations in body design may affect actual depths of models. Check all units for exact voltage. Some units available with gas.

ELEVATION

PLAN

WASHER AND DRYER STACKED IN CLOSET

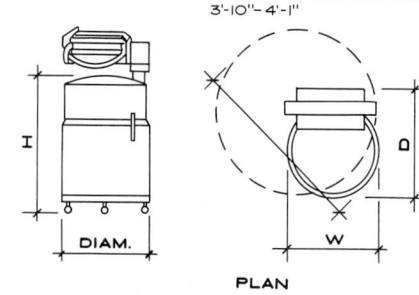

PLAN

WRINGER WASHERS

	MIN.	MAX.	OTHER
W	23 1/4	27 1/4	24 - 27
D	24	29 3/4	26 - 28
H	33	46	35 1/2 - 38 1/4
DIAM.	23	29	23 1/8 - 23 1/2

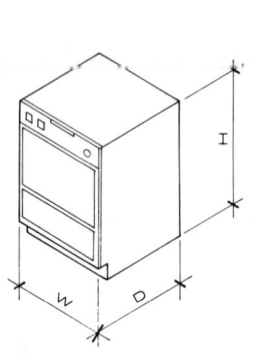

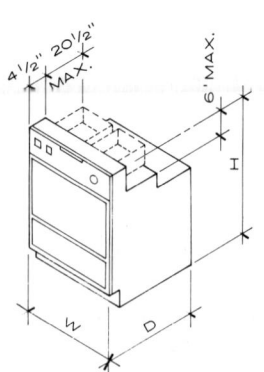

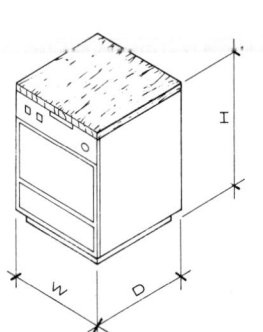

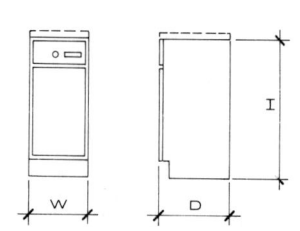

AUTOMATIC DISHWASHERS

UNDER COUNTER

	MIN.	MAX.	OTHER
W	23	24	23 7/8
D	23 11/16	26 1/4	25 1/2
H	33 1/2	34 1/2	34 1/8

UNDER SINK

	MIN.	MAX.	OTHER
W	24	24 1/4	24
D	24	25 1/2	25
H	34 1/2	34 1/2	34 1/2

MOBILE (WITH COUNTER TOP)

	MIN.	MAX.	OTHER
W	22 1/2	27	24 5/8
D	23 11/16	26 1/2	25
H	34 1/8	39	36

TRASH COMPACTOR: UNDER COUNTER OR FREESTANDING

	MIN.	MAX.	OTHER
W	11 7/8	17 3/4	14 7/8
D	18	24 3/16	18 1/4
H	33 1/2	35	34 1/2

Wm. G. Miner, AIA, Architect; Washington, D.C.

R. E. Powe, Jr., AIA; Hugh N. Jacobsen, FAIA; Washington, D.C.

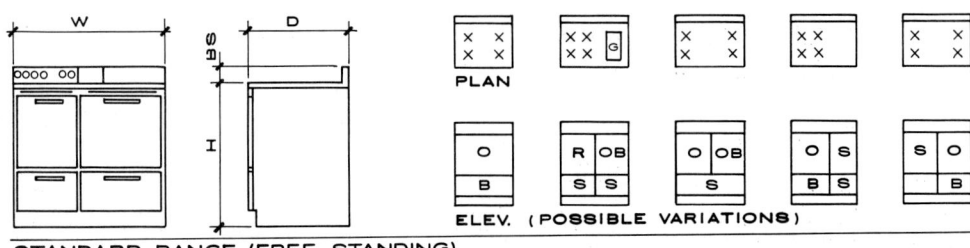

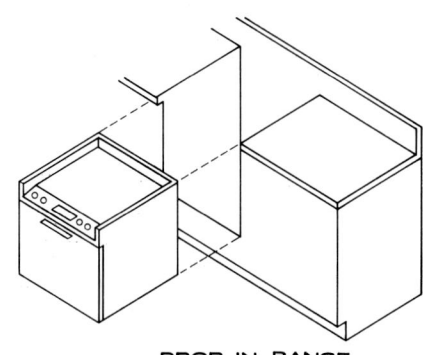

PLAN

ELEV. (POSSIBLE VARIATIONS)

STANDARD RANGE (FREE STANDING)

ONE OVEN - FOUR UNITS

	MIN.	MAX.	OTHER
W	19 1/2	40	21-30
D	24 1/4	27 1/2	25-26 1/4
H	35 1/8	36 1/8	35 1/4-36
BS	4 11/16	12 1/2	8 1/4-11 1/2

TWO OVENS FOUR UNITS

	MIN.	MAX.	OTHER
W		40	
D	25	27 1/2	25 1/2-26 1/4
H	35 1/8	36	35 1/4
BS	8 1/4	11 1/8	8 1/8-10 3/8

SYMBOLS
O - OVEN
B - BROILER
G - REVOLVING GRILL
X - BURNER, GAS OR ELECTRIC
W - WARMING OVEN
S - STORAGE
R - ROTISSERIE

DROP-IN RANGE

	MIN.	MAX.	OTHER
W	22 7/8	30	23 7/8
D	22 1/8	25	22 1/2 24
H	23	24 1/16	23 1/2

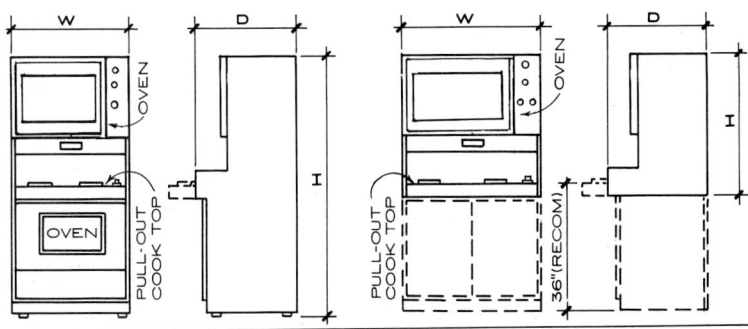

RANGES WITH EYE LEVEL OVENS

DOUBLE OVEN - 4 UNITS

	MIN.	MAX.	OTHER
W	29 7/8	30	
D	25 1/2	27 5/8	25 5/8-27 1/2
H	61 1/2	71 1/4	63 3/4-67 7/16

SINGLE OVEN TOP ONLY - 4 UNITS

	MIN.	MAX.	OTHER
W	29 13/16	38 7/8	29 7/8
D	25 1/2	27 5/8	27 1/4
H	33 1/2	41 1/16	36 3/4

DOUBLE OVEN TOP ONLY - 4 UNITS

	MIN.	MAX.	OTHER
W	39	40 1/4	40
D	25 1/2	27 5/8	26 3/4
H	34 7/8	36 3/4	

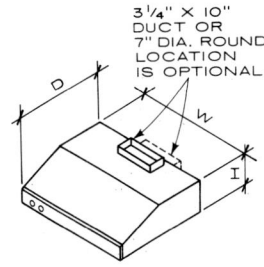

Range hoods are available with vents as shown or without vent. Manufacturers provide accessories such as fans, filters, and lights.

RANGE HOOD

	MIN.	MAX.	OTHER
W	24	72	30-66
D	12	27 1/2	17-26
H	5 1/2	8 5/8	5 5/8-7 1/2

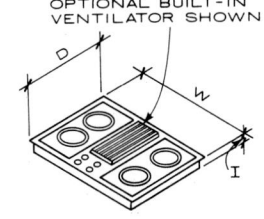

Cook tops are available with two to seven heating elements. Griddles, grills, and built-in ventilators are optional.

BUILT-IN COOK TOP ELECTRIC OR GAS

	MIN.	MAX.
W	12	48
D	18	22
H	2	3

NOTE
SELF CLEANING OVENS MUST VENT TO OUTSIDE

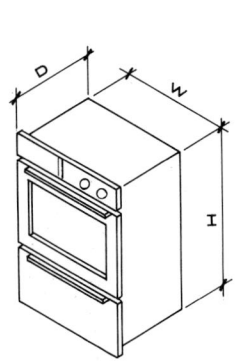

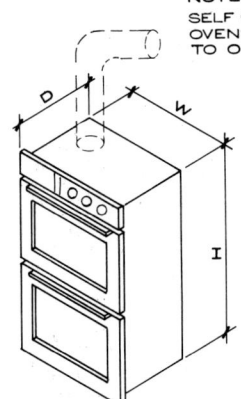

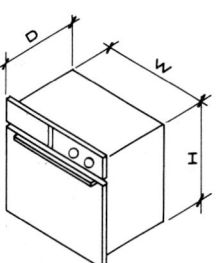

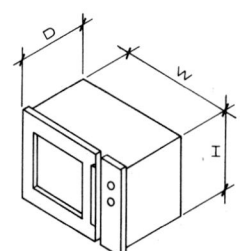

BUILT-IN WALL OVENS (GAS OR ELECTRIC)

OVEN & BROILER

	MIN.	MAX.	OTHER
W	21	24 1/4	22 1/2-24
D	21 1/8	24	22 1/2-22 11/16
H	38	40 7/16	40 3/16

DOUBLE OVEN

	MIN.	MAX.	OTHER
W	21	24 1/4	22 1/2-24
D	21 1/8	24	22 1/2-22 11/16
H	39 1/4	50 3/8	42-46 13/16

SINGLE OVEN

	MIN.	MAX.	OTHER
W	21	24 1/4	22 1/2-24
D	21 1/8	24	22 1/2-22 11/16
H	23 1/2	26 7/8	25

MICROWAVE OVEN

	MIN.	MAX.	OTHER
W	21 1/2	24 3/4	22 1/2
D	14 1/2	22	18 3/4
H	13 5/8	18	17

NOTES

1. Check manufacturers requirements for rough clearances.

2. Dimensions shown are in inches.

3. Optional equipment available for ranges or wall ovens are broilers and rotisseries.

Wm. G. Miner, AIA, Architect; Washington, D.C.

R. E. Powe, Jr., AIA; Hugh N. Jacobsen, FAIA; Washington. D.C.

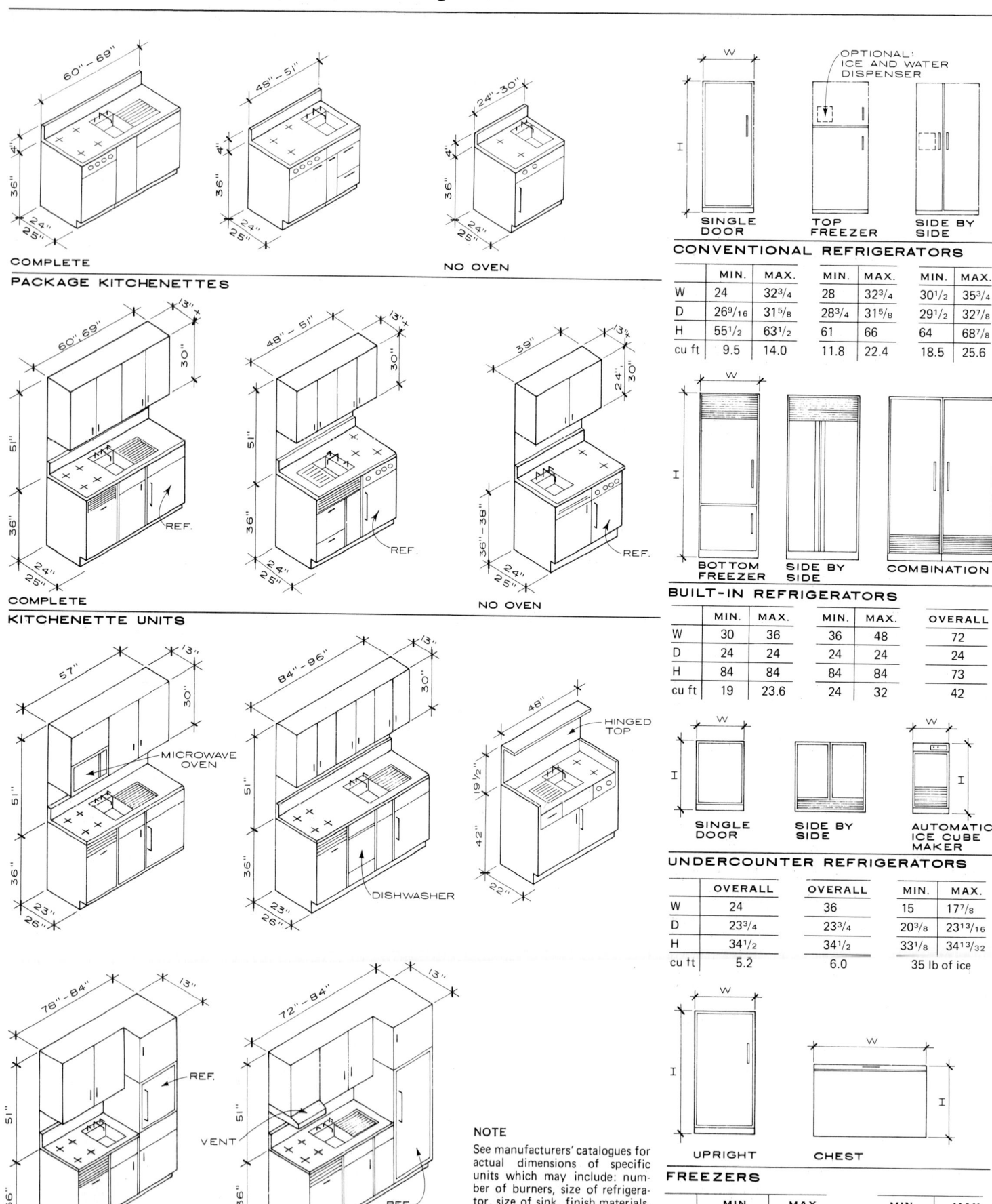

PACKAGE KITCHENETTES

COMPLETE   NO OVEN

KITCHENETTE UNITS

COMPLETE   NO OVEN

SPECIAL KITCHENETTE UNITS

Wm. G. Miner, AIA, Architect; Washington, D.C.

NOTE

See manufacturers' catalogues for actual dimensions of specific units which may include: number of burners, size of refrigerator, size of sink, finish materials, and options such as garbage disposer, range hood, microwave oven, ice maker, dishwasher, or freezer.

CONVENTIONAL REFRIGERATORS

	MIN.	MAX.	MIN.	MAX.	MIN.	MAX.
W	24	$32^3/_4$	28	$32^3/_4$	$30^1/_2$	$35^3/_4$
D	$26^9/_{16}$	$31^5/_8$	$28^3/_4$	$31^5/_8$	$29^1/_2$	$32^7/_8$
H	$55^1/_2$	$63^1/_2$	61	66	64	$68^7/_8$
cu ft	9.5	14.0	11.8	22.4	18.5	25.6

BUILT-IN REFRIGERATORS

	MIN.	MAX.	MIN.	MAX.	OVERALL
W	30	36	36	48	72
D	24	24	24	24	24
H	84	84	84	84	73
cu ft	19	23.6	24	32	42

UNDERCOUNTER REFRIGERATORS

	OVERALL	OVERALL	MIN.	MAX.
W	24	36	15	$17^7/_8$
D	$23^3/_4$	$23^3/_4$	$20^3/_8$	$23^{13}/_{16}$
H	$34^1/_2$	$34^1/_2$	$33^1/_8$	$34^{13}/_{32}$
cu ft	5.2	6.0	35 lb of ice	

FREEZERS

	MIN.	MAX.	MIN.	MAX.
W	28	32	25	$69^1/_2$
D	$28^7/_8$	$30^{11}/_{16}$	$23^1/_4$	31
H	$59^1/_8$	$70^1/_8$	$34^{11}/_{16}$	35
cu ft	11.6	21.1	5.3	25.3

2 5/8"
1"
10 5 0
TIMER
9"
10"
CANDY THERMOMETERS MEAT
8"
4 TRAYS AT 1 1/2" = 6"
SPROUTER
4"
8 3/4"
ESPRESSO MAKER
23 1/2"
23 1/2"
6 5/8" D.
WINE RACK
8"-12"
CRÊPE PAN
20"
5 1/4"
WOK
14"
14"
ORIENTAL STEAMER
16"
4"
FISH POACHER
1 1/2"
4 1/2"
PASTRY JAGGER
9 1/2"
4" D.
POTATO RICER
18"
9 1/4"
GRIDDLE

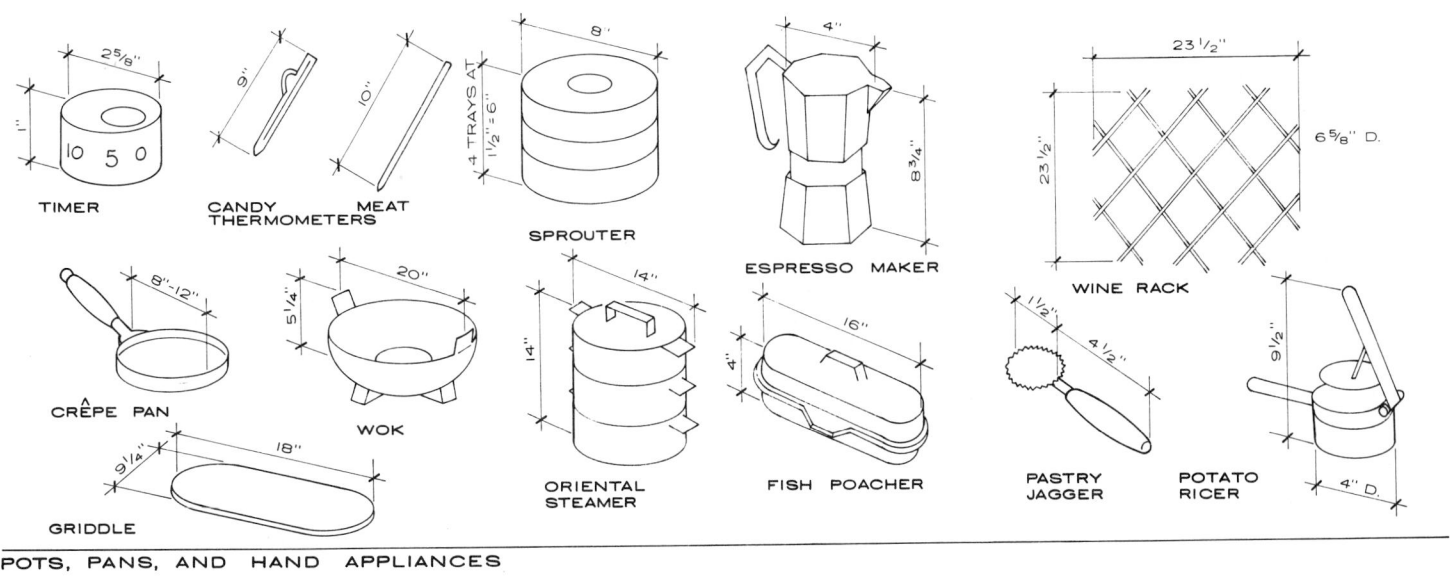

POTS, PANS, AND HAND APPLIANCES

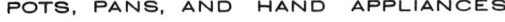

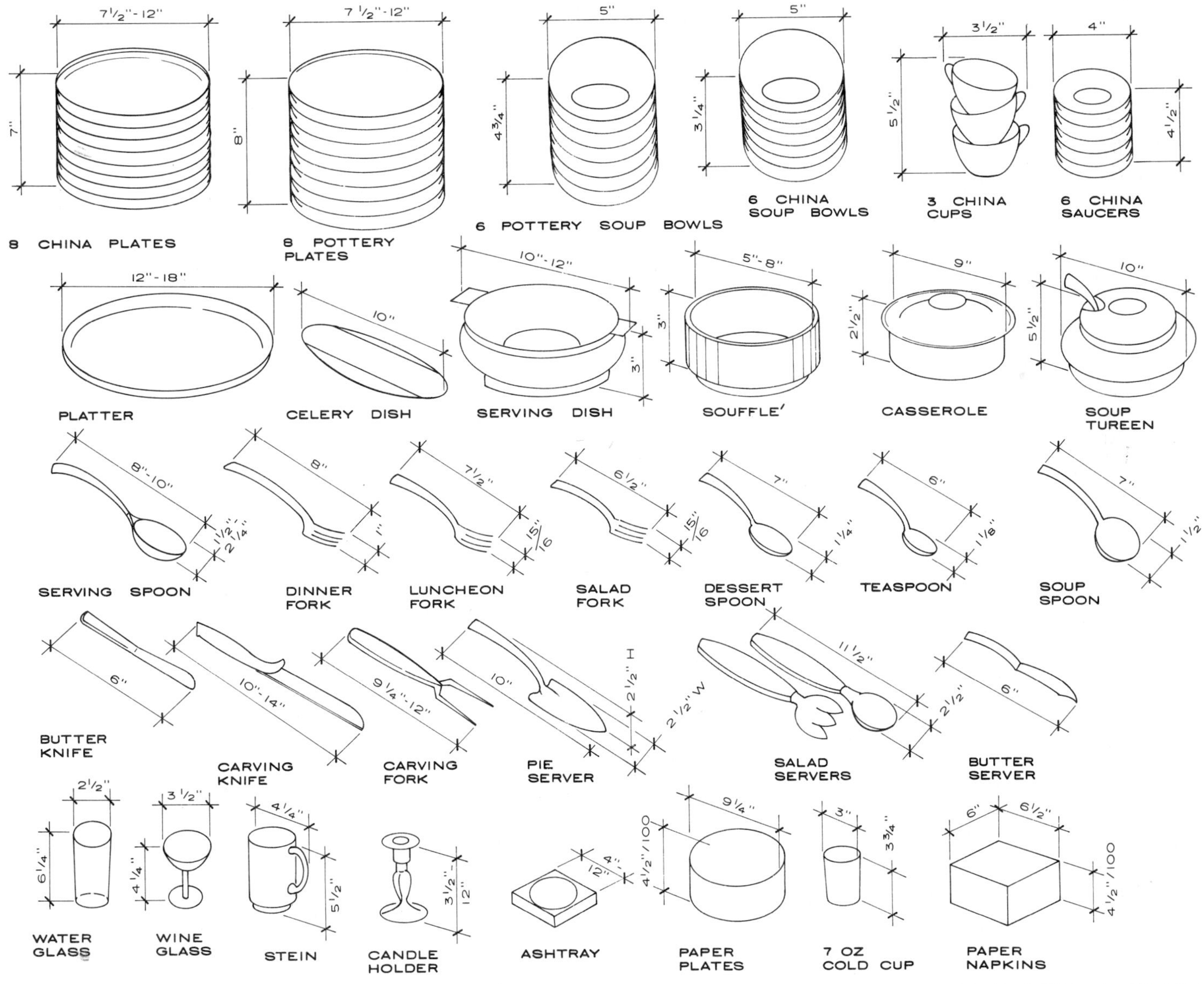

7 1/2"-12"
7"
8 CHINA PLATES
7 1/2"-12"
8"
8 POTTERY PLATES
5"
4 3/4"
6 POTTERY SOUP BOWLS
5"
3 1/4"
6 CHINA SOUP BOWLS
3 1/2"
5 1/2"
3 CHINA CUPS
4"
4 1/2"
6 CHINA SAUCERS
12"-18"
PLATTER
10"
CELERY DISH
10"-12"
3"
SERVING DISH
5"-8"
3"
SOUFFLE'
9"
2 1/2"
CASSEROLE
10"
5 1/2"
SOUP TUREEN
8"-10"
1 1/2"
2 1/4"
SERVING SPOON
8"
1"
DINNER FORK
7 1/2"
15/16"
LUNCHEON FORK
6 1/2"
15/16"
SALAD FORK
7"
1 1/4"
DESSERT SPOON
6"
1 1/8"
TEASPOON
7"
1 1/2"
SOUP SPOON
6"
BUTTER KNIFE
10"-14"
CARVING KNIFE
9 1/4"-12"
CARVING FORK
10"
2 1/2" H
2 1/2" W
PIE SERVER
11 1/2"
2 1/2"
SALAD SERVERS
6"
BUTTER SERVER
2 1/2"
6 1/4"
WATER GLASS
3 1/2"
4 1/4"
WINE GLASS
4 1/4"
5 1/2"
STEIN
3 1/2"
12"
CANDLE HOLDER
4"
12"
ASHTRAY
9 1/4"
4 1/2"/100
PAPER PLATES
3"
3 3/4"
7 OZ COLD CUP
6"
6 1/2"
4 1/2"/100
PAPER NAPKINS

DINING ROOM TABLEWARE

E. H. & M. K. Hunter, Architects; Raleigh, North Carolina

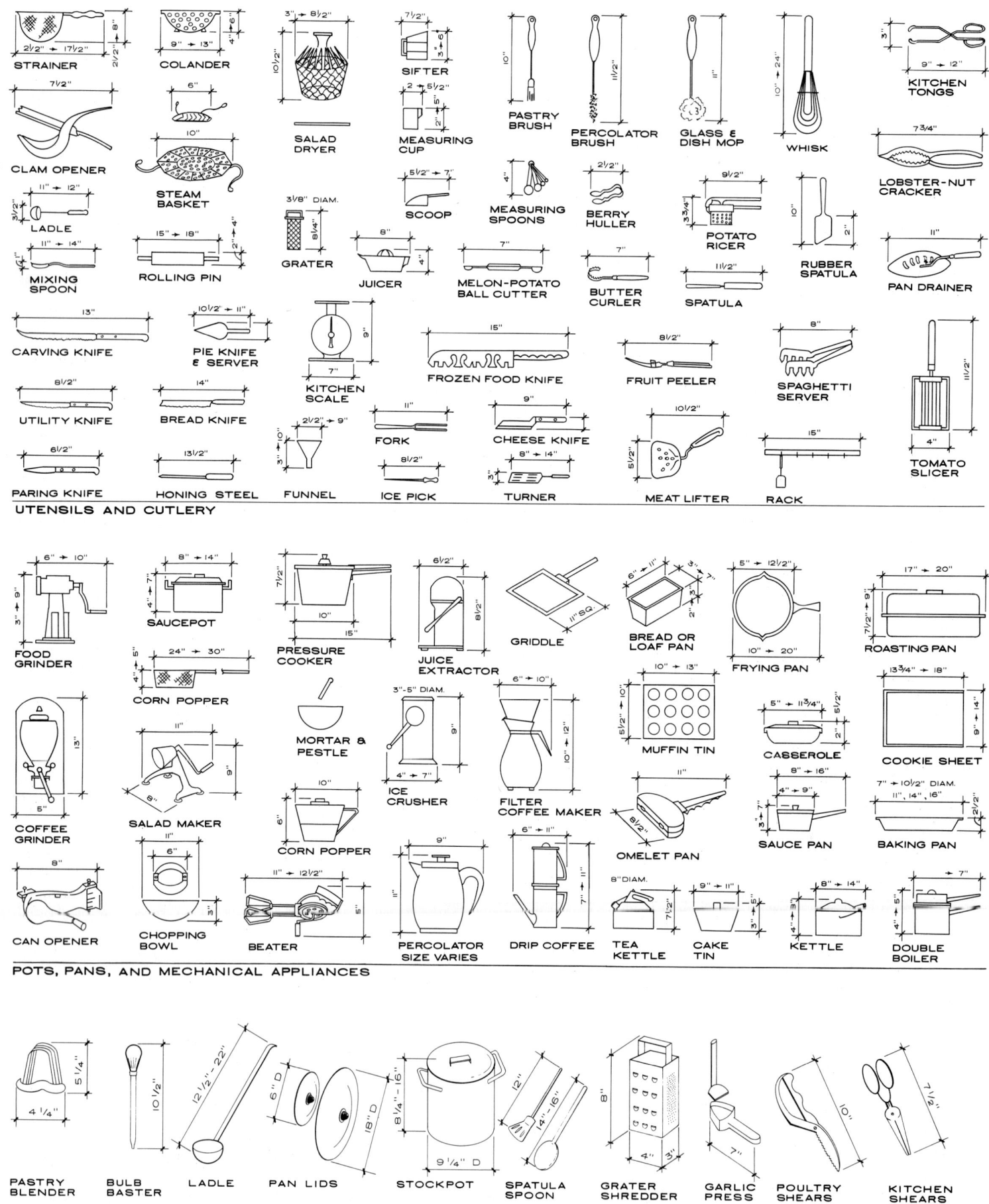

STRAINER • COLANDER • SIFTER • PASTRY BRUSH • PERCOLATOR BRUSH • GLASS & DISH MOP • WHISK • KITCHEN TONGS

CLAM OPENER • SALAD DRYER • MEASURING CUP • STEAM BASKET • SCOOP • MEASURING SPOONS • BERRY HULLER • POTATO RICER • LOBSTER-NUT CRACKER

LADLE • MIXING SPOON • ROLLING PIN • GRATER • JUICER • MELON-POTATO BALL CUTTER • BUTTER CURLER • SPATULA • RUBBER SPATULA • PAN DRAINER

CARVING KNIFE • PIE KNIFE & SERVER • KITCHEN SCALE • FROZEN FOOD KNIFE • FRUIT PEELER • SPAGHETTI SERVER

UTILITY KNIFE • BREAD KNIFE • FORK • CHEESE KNIFE • MEAT LIFTER • TOMATO SLICER

PARING KNIFE • HONING STEEL • FUNNEL • ICE PICK • TURNER • RACK

UTENSILS AND CUTLERY

FOOD GRINDER • SAUCEPOT • PRESSURE COOKER • JUICE EXTRACTOR • GRIDDLE • BREAD OR LOAF PAN • FRYING PAN • ROASTING PAN

CORN POPPER • MORTAR & PESTLE • ICE CRUSHER • MUFFIN TIN • CASSEROLE • COOKIE SHEET

COFFEE GRINDER • SALAD MAKER • CORN POPPER • FILTER COFFEE MAKER • OMELET PAN • SAUCE PAN • BAKING PAN

CAN OPENER • CHOPPING BOWL • BEATER • PERCOLATOR SIZE VARIES • DRIP COFFEE • TEA KETTLE • CAKE TIN • KETTLE • DOUBLE BOILER

POTS, PANS, AND MECHANICAL APPLIANCES

PASTRY BLENDER • BULB BASTER • LADLE • PAN LIDS • STOCKPOT • SPATULA SPOON • GRATER SHREDDER • GARLIC PRESS • POULTRY SHEARS • KITCHEN SHEARS

POTS, PANS, AND HAND APPLIANCES

E. H. & M. K. Hunter, Architects; Raleigh, North Carolina

11 RESIDENTIAL EQUIPMENT

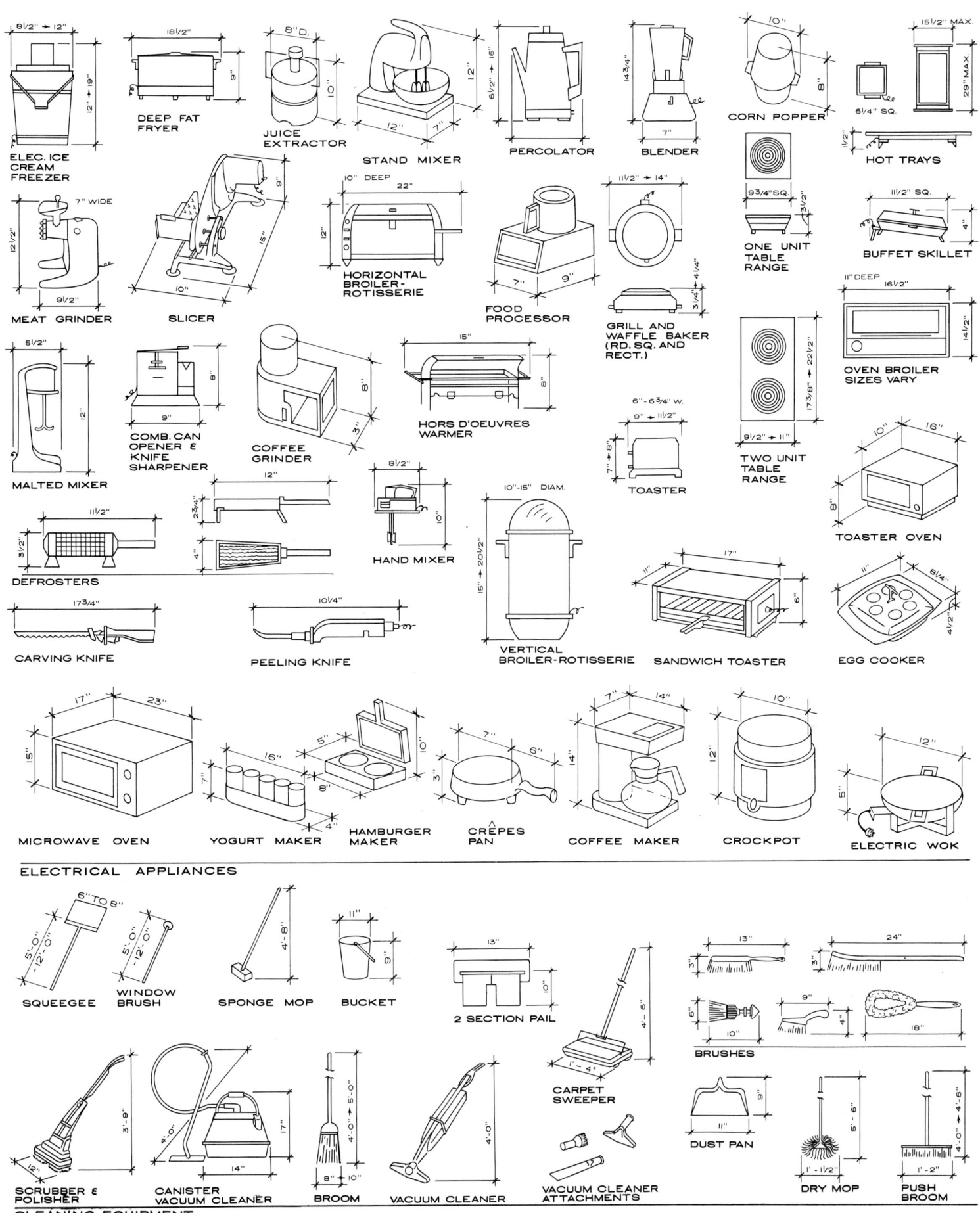

ELEC. ICE CREAM FREEZER

DEEP FAT FRYER

JUICE EXTRACTOR

STAND MIXER

PERCOLATOR

BLENDER

CORN POPPER

HOT TRAYS

MEAT GRINDER

SLICER

HORIZONTAL BROILER-ROTISSERIE

FOOD PROCESSOR

GRILL AND WAFFLE BAKER (RD. SQ. AND RECT.)

ONE UNIT TABLE RANGE

BUFFET SKILLET

MALTED MIXER

COMB. CAN OPENER & KNIFE SHARPENER

COFFEE GRINDER

HORS D'OEUVRES WARMER

TOASTER

TWO UNIT TABLE RANGE

OVEN BROILER SIZES VARY

DEFROSTERS

HAND MIXER

TOASTER OVEN

CARVING KNIFE

PEELING KNIFE

VERTICAL BROILER-ROTISSERIE

SANDWICH TOASTER

EGG COOKER

MICROWAVE OVEN

YOGURT MAKER

HAMBURGER MAKER

CREPES PAN

COFFEE MAKER

CROCKPOT

ELECTRIC WOK

ELECTRICAL APPLIANCES

SQUEEGEE

WINDOW BRUSH

SPONGE MOP

BUCKET

2 SECTION PAIL

CARPET SWEEPER

BRUSHES

DUST PAN

SCRUBBER & POLISHER

CANISTER VACUUM CLEANER

BROOM

VACUUM CLEANER

VACUUM CLEANER ATTACHMENTS

DRY MOP

PUSH BROOM

CLEANING EQUIPMENT

E. H. & M. K. Hunter, Architects; Raleigh, North Carolina

RESIDENTIAL EQUIPMENT

11

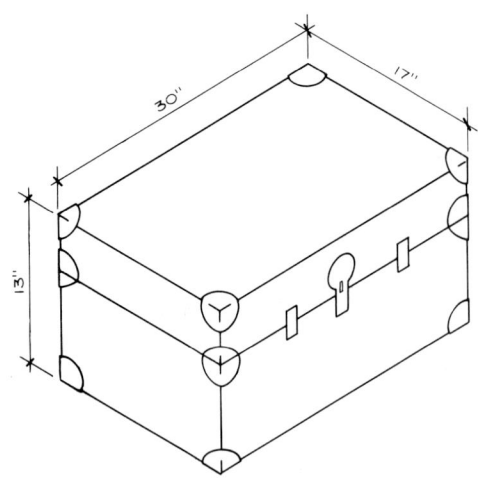

TRUNK

	W	H	D
End table trunk	18	18	20
Footlocker	30¼	12½	15¾
Car trunk	30¼	16¼	15¾
Camp trunk	33¼	21	18¾
Packing trunk	40¼	22¼	22½

TRUNKS

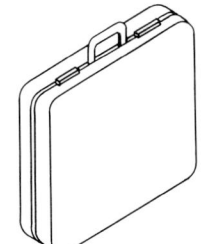

WOMEN'S LUGGAGE

	W	H	D
Carry-on	20	17	7
Junior Pullman	23¾	19½	8
Pullman	26¾	21½	9
Overseas	32	20	10

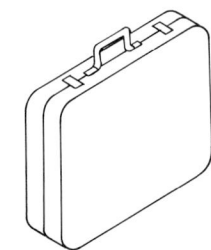

MEN'S LUGGAGE

	W	H	D
Carry-on	20	17	7
Two-suiter	26¾	18½	8
Three-suiter	26¾	21½	9
Overseas	32	20	10

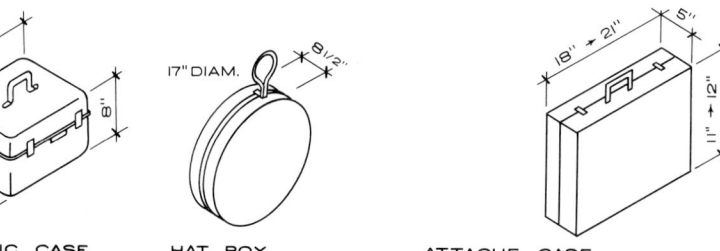

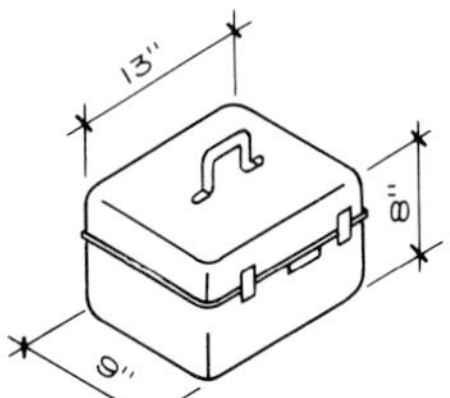

COSMETIC CASE   **HAT BOX**   **ATTACHE CASE**

CASES

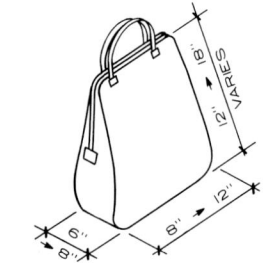

COSMETIC TOTE

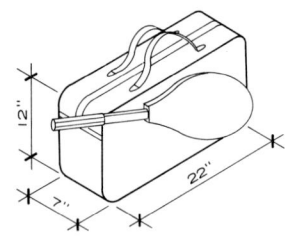

TENNIS PACK

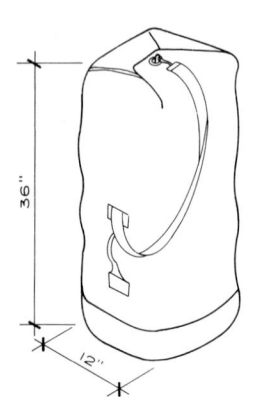

DUFFEL BAG

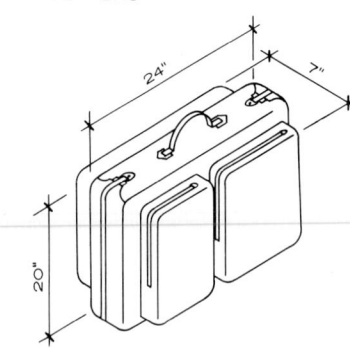

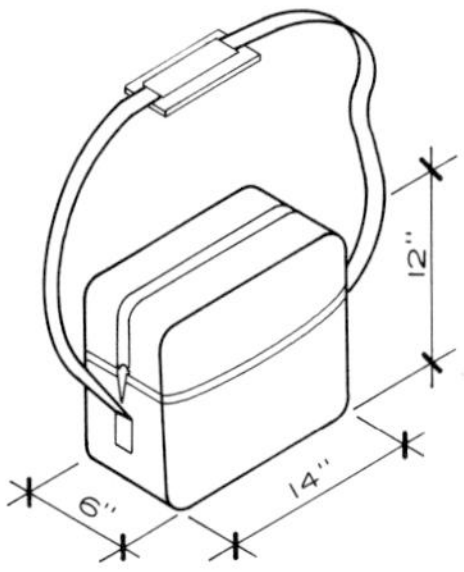

SHOULDER BAG

FLIGHT BAG

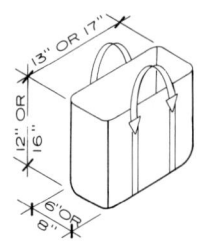

CARRY-ALL

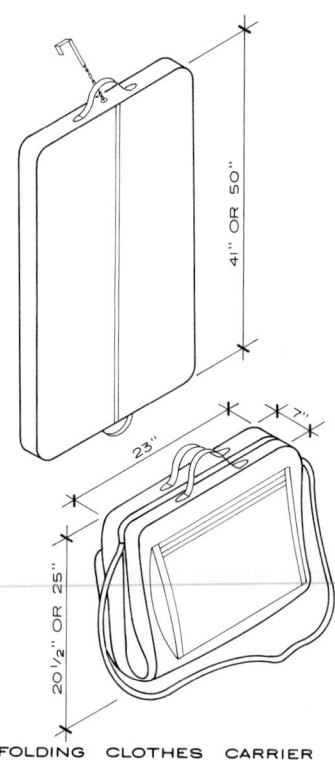

FOLDING CLOTHES CARRIER

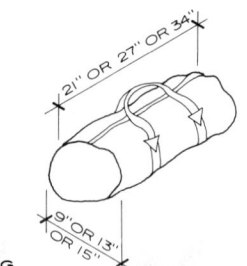

KIT BAG

BAGS

E. H. and M. K. Hunter, AIA; Raleigh, North Carolina

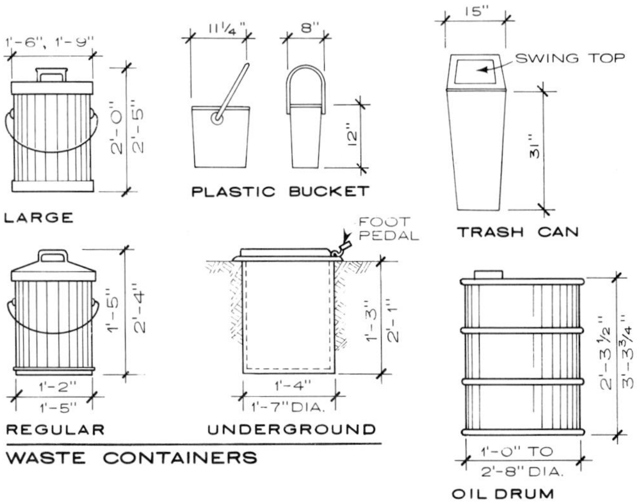

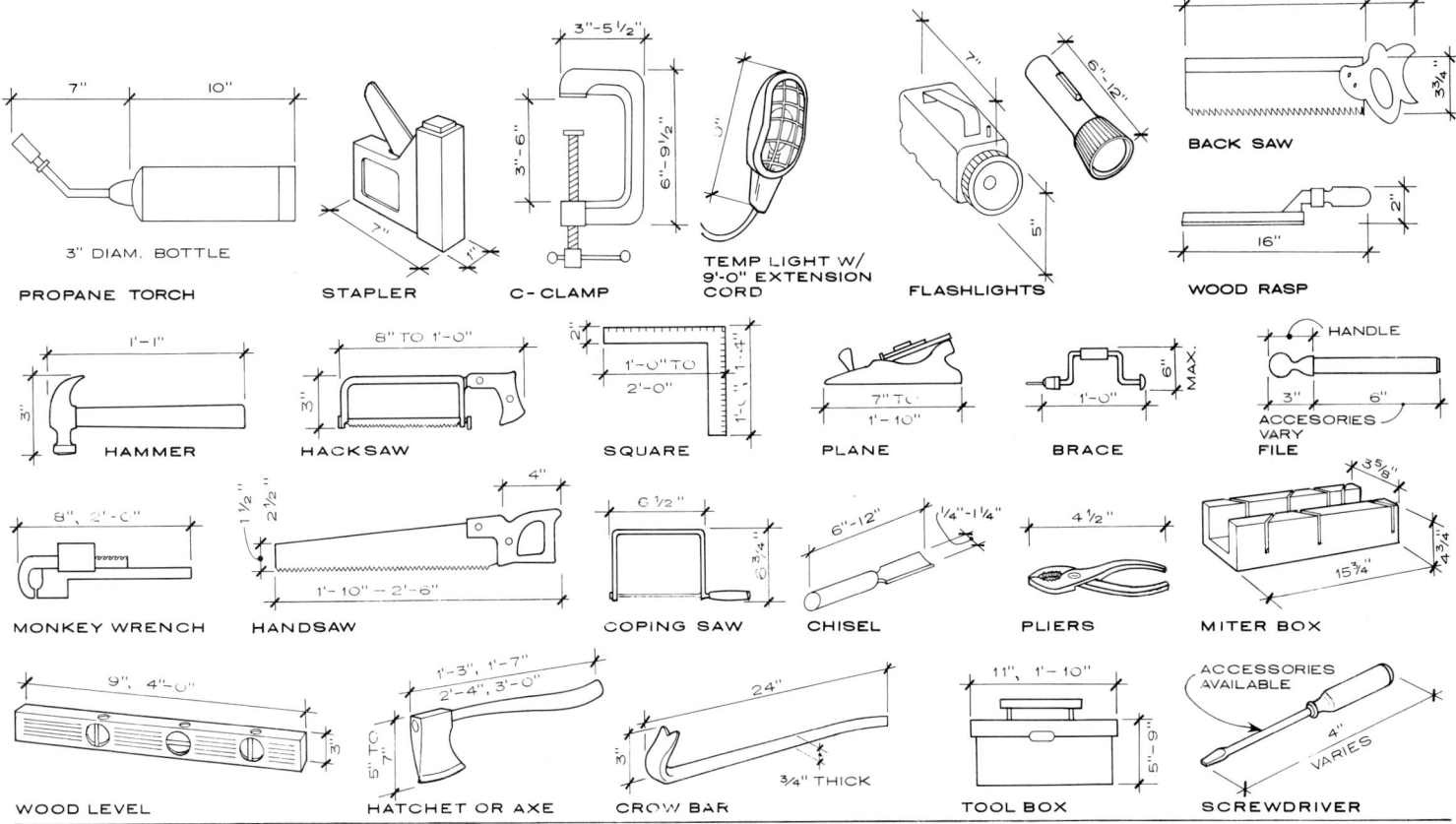

LARGE

PLASTIC BUCKET

SWING TOP

TRASH CAN

FOOT PEDAL

REGULAR

UNDERGROUND

WASTE CONTAINERS

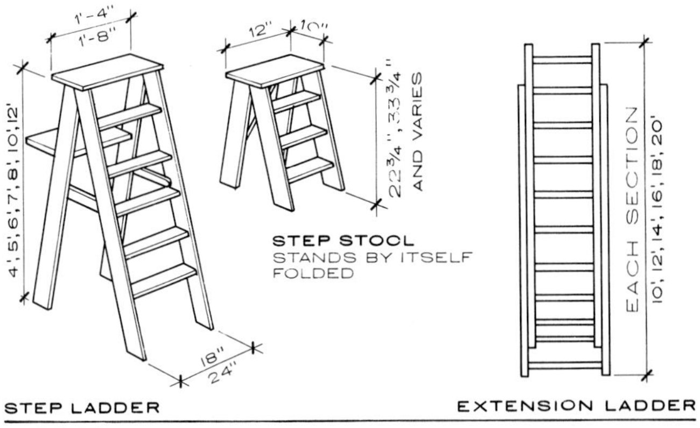

OIL DRUM

STEP STOOL
STANDS BY ITSELF FOLDED

STEP LADDER

EXTENSION LADDER

LADDERS

NOTE: MAGNESIUM LADDERS ARE ABOUT ONE-HALF THE WEIGHT OF COMPARABLE WOOD LADDERS

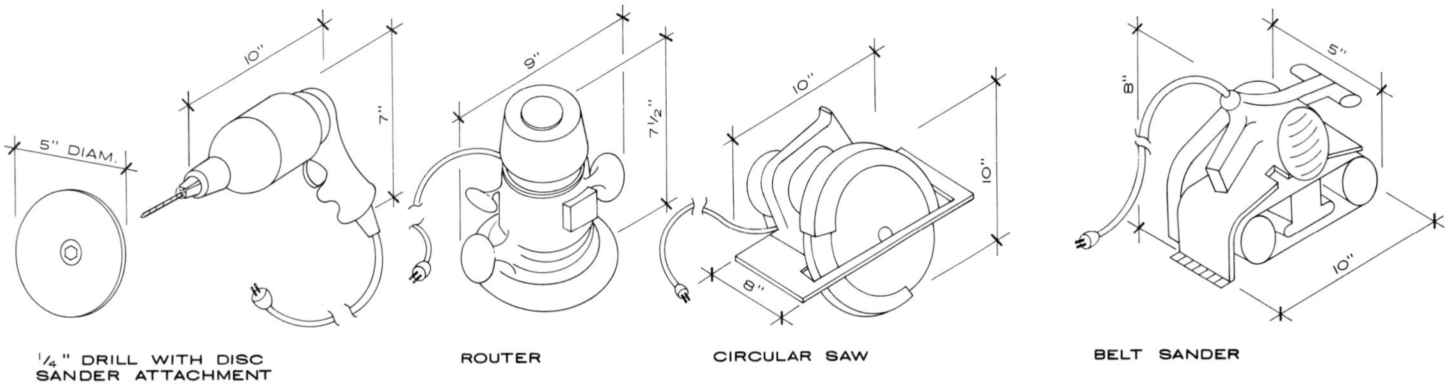

¼" DRILL WITH DISC SANDER ATTACHMENT

ROUTER

CIRCULAR SAW

BELT SANDER

ELECTRIC HAND TOOLS

PROPANE TORCH

3" DIAM. BOTTLE

STAPLER

C-CLAMP

TEMP LIGHT W/ 9'-0" EXTENSION CORD

FLASHLIGHTS

BACK SAW

WOOD RASP

HAMMER

HACKSAW

SQUARE

PLANE

BRACE

FILE

ACCESSORIES VARY

HANDLE

MONKEY WRENCH

HANDSAW

COPING SAW

CHISEL

PLIERS

MITER BOX

WOOD LEVEL

HATCHET OR AXE

CROW BAR

¾" THICK

TOOL BOX

SCREWDRIVER

ACCESSORIES AVAILABLE

VARIES

TYPICAL HOUSEHOLD HAND TOOLS

E. H. and M. K. Hunter, AIA; Raleigh, North Carolina

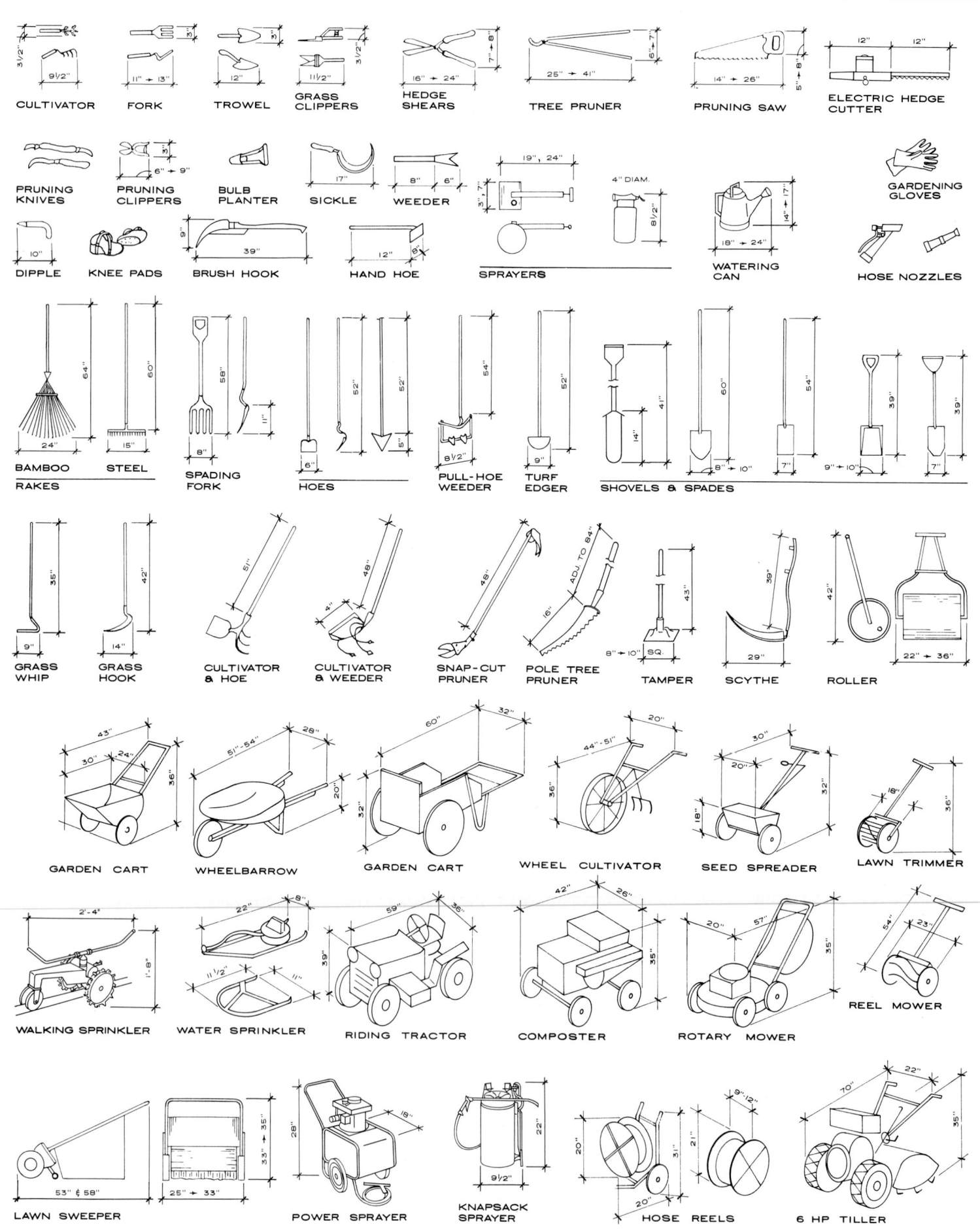

CULTIVATOR   FORK   TROWEL   GRASS CLIPPERS   HEDGE SHEARS   TREE PRUNER   PRUNING SAW   ELECTRIC HEDGE CUTTER

PRUNING KNIVES   PRUNING CLIPPERS   BULB PLANTER   SICKLE   WEEDER   SPRAYERS   WATERING CAN   GARDENING GLOVES

DIPPLE   KNEE PADS   BRUSH HOOK   HAND HOE   HOSE NOZZLES

BAMBOO   STEEL   RAKES   SPADING FORK   HOES   PULL-HOE WEEDER   TURF EDGER   SHOVELS & SPADES

GRASS WHIP   GRASS HOOK   CULTIVATOR & HOE   CULTIVATOR & WEEDER   SNAP-CUT PRUNER   POLE TREE PRUNER   TAMPER   SCYTHE   ROLLER

GARDEN CART   WHEELBARROW   GARDEN CART   WHEEL CULTIVATOR   SEED SPREADER   LAWN TRIMMER

WALKING SPRINKLER   WATER SPRINKLER   RIDING TRACTOR   COMPOSTER   ROTARY MOWER   REEL MOWER

LAWN SWEEPER   POWER SPRAYER   KNAPSACK SPRAYER   HOSE REELS   6 HP TILLER

E. H. & M. K. Hunter, Architects; Raleigh, North Carolina

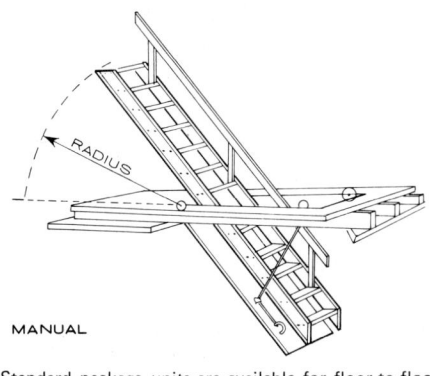

MANUAL

Standard package units are available for floor-to-floor heights from 7 ft up to 13 ft in 1 ft increments. Ladder is inclined at 52° above horizontal. Standard box frame is used for ceiling thickness up to 13 in. Special deep frame is specified for ceiling thicknesses ranging from 13 in. up to 48 in.

Typical rough opening in ceiling = 30 x 72 in.

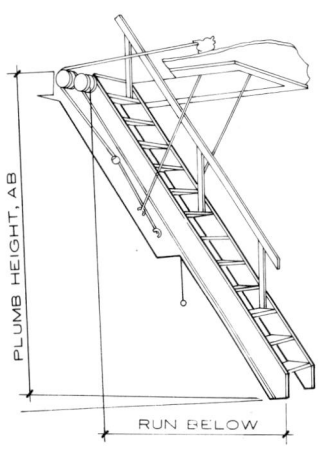

MANUAL

MOTORIZED

SLIDE UP PIVOT TYPE

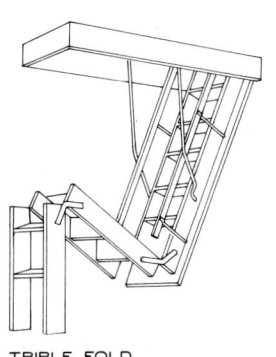

TRIPLE FOLD

STANDARD SIZES FOR DISAPPEARING STAIRS

ROUGH OPENING	FLOOR-TO-FLOOR	COIL PROJECTION	LANDING SPACE
22″ x 48″	8′-5″	60″	58½″
22″ x 54″	8′-9″	66″	65″
	10′-0″	79″	73″
25½″ x 48″	8′-5″	60″	58½″
25½″ x 54″ 25½″ x 60″ 30″ x 54″ 30″ x 60″	8′-9″ 10′-0″	66″ 79″	65″ 73″

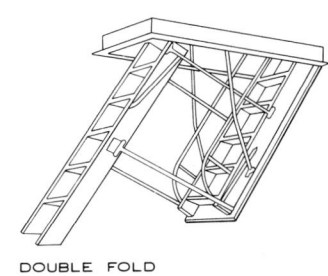

DOUBLE FOLD

FOLDING TYPE

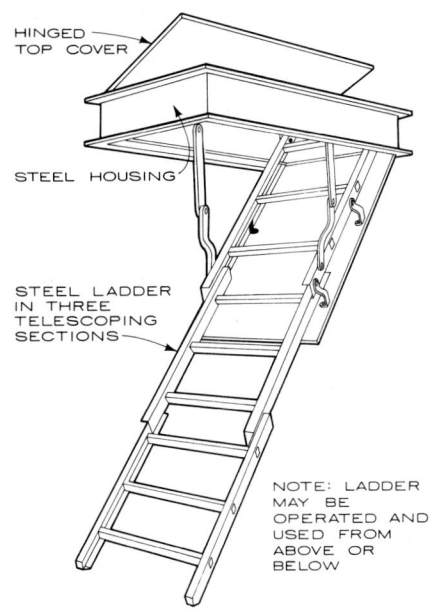

HINGED TOP COVER

STEEL HOUSING

STEEL LADDER IN THREE TELESCOPING SECTIONS

NOTE: LADDER MAY BE OPERATED AND USED FROM ABOVE OR BELOW

Several models are available using three or four telescoping sections.

Floor-to-floor heights ranging from 8 ft up to 13 ft 4 in. can be accommodated as the ladder angle varies from 53° above horizontal up to 74° above horizontal.

TYPICAL HEIGHTS FOR ONE STANDARD MODEL
(Rough Opening = 24″ x 48″)

FLOOR-TO-FLOOR	LAND SPACE	ABOVE HORIZONTAL
8′-0″	72″	53°
8′-3″	62″	61°
8′-6″	60″	62°
8′-9″	73″	56°
9′-0″	71″	57°
9′-3″	69″	58°
9′-6″	59″	64°
9′-10″	58″	65°
10′-2″	44″	72°

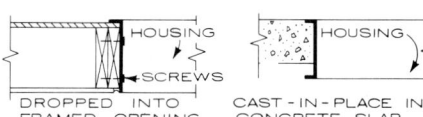

DROPPED INTO FRAMED OPENING

CAST-IN-PLACE IN CONCRETE SLAB

TYPICAL METAL HOUSING INSTALLATION DETAILS

TELESCOPING ACCESS LADDER

CAUTION SHOULD BE TAKEN IN LOADING ATTIC SPACE WHERE JOIST NOT DESIGNED FOR OCCUPANCY LOADS. IT IS PREFERRED TO INSULATE ENTIRE ROOF

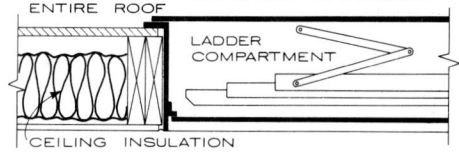

LADDER COMPARTMENT

CEILING INSULATION

TELESCOPING METAL LADDER

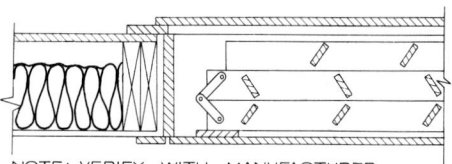

NOTE: VERIFY WITH MANUFACTURER WHETHER ADDED TOP CLOSURE IS COMPATIBLE WITH STAIR PACKAGE

FOLDING WOODEN STAIR

WHEN USED FOR ATTIC ACCESS, DISAPPEARING STAIRS MAY COMPROMISE A WELL-INSULATED CEILING. SELECT STAIR PACKAGE WITH TIGHT JOINTS AND DESIGN THAT ALLOWS INSULATION

INSULATION CONSIDERATIONS

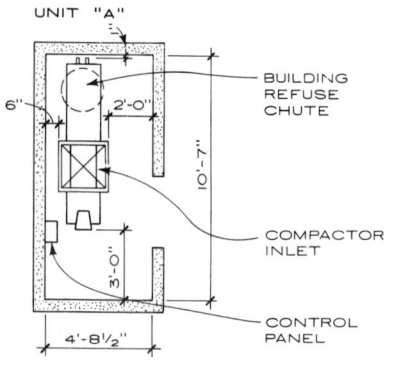

ROOM PLAN

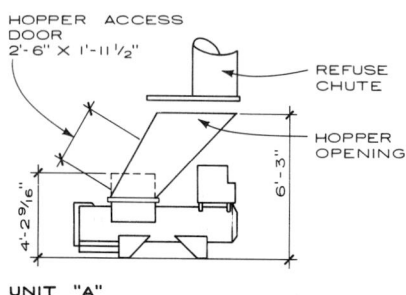

UNIT "A"
COMPACTOR UNIT WITHOUT
CONTAINERS

WASTE COMPACTORS AND CONTAINERS

UNIT TYPE	SIZE	CAPACITY OF CONTAINER
Average household compactor	12'' W, 24'' D, 33½''–34½'' H	1.3 cu ft
Small industrial	See units A, B, and C	4 cu ft per bag
Industrial	See unit D	2 cu yd per container
Schools, offices, restaurants	26'' W, 53'' H, 31'' D	6 cu ft
Apartment house stationary compactor with roll away containers	Units vary	2 to 8 cu yd
Industrial waste containers	95'' W, 36'' H, 62'' D to 95'' W, 102'' H, 92'' D	3 to 15 cu yd
Heavy duty industrial waste containers	8' ± W, 8'-10'' H, 23'-2'' L	Up to 43 cu yd
Combination shredder/compactor	45'' W, 29'' D, 78'' H See unit "E"	5.25 cu ft per bag

APARTMENT SELECTION GUIDE

The daily refuse output of 15 to 30 apartments in approximately ½ cu yd (13½ cu ft) weighing about 75 lb. At standard compaction ratios of 4 or 5 to 1, a compactor will reduce the refuse to an approximate volume of 3 cu ft.

If the apartments are large, averaging two or three bedrooms, use the figure of 15 apartments per bag. If apartments average one or two bedrooms, use 20 to 25 apartments per compacted bag, and if the units are small efficiency apartments or one-bedroom apartments occupied by young working people or the elderly, use the figure of 30 apartments per compacted bag per day.

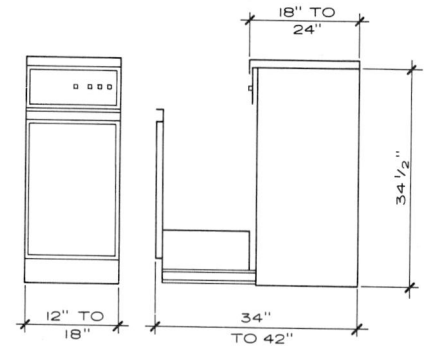

AVERAGE HOUSEHOLD COMPACTOR

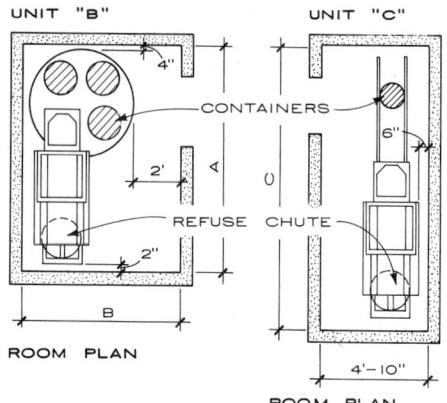

NO. OF CONTAINERS	A	B	C
3			11'-10''
4	9'-8''	7'-0''	13'-5''
5			17'-1''
6	10'-6''	8'-0''	
8	11'-6''	9'-1''	
10	12'-6''	10'-9''	

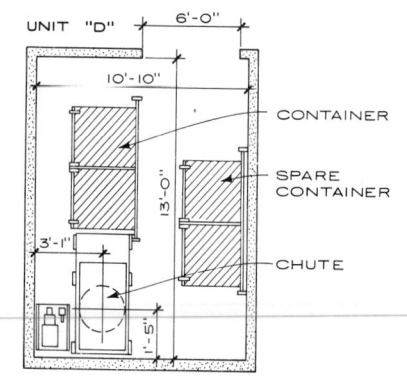

ROOM PLAN

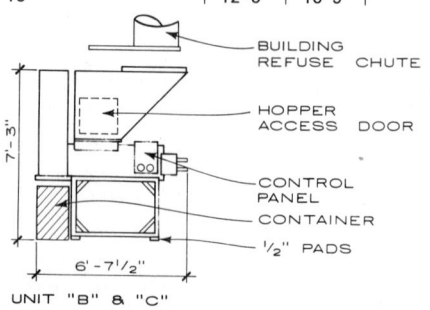

UNIT "B" & "C"
COMPACTOR WITH STORAGE
CONTAINERS

Walter H. Sobel, FAIA & Associates; Chicago, Illinois

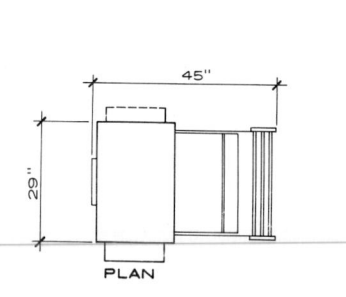

UNIT "D"
INDUSTRIAL COMPACTOR

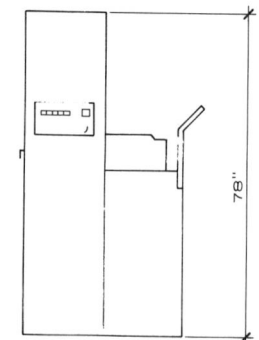

UNIT "E"
COMBINATION SHREDDER
COMPACTOR

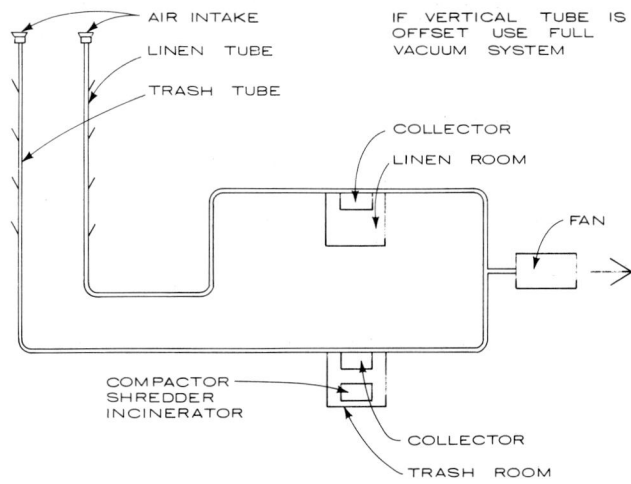

DUAL TUBE FULL VACUUM SYSTEM

DUAL TUBE FULL VACUUM

The two-tube fully pneumatic system offers flexibility in design and improved sanitation. A two-tube system eliminates the need to place trash and linen depositories at the same location. The vertical tubes can be offset, adding to the flexibility of the system. Horizontal tubes dispose at a central point, eliminating manually operated collections.

DUAL TUBE GRAVITY/VACUUM SYSTEM

The two-tube gravity/pneumatic system consists of gravity vertical chutes and pneumatic horizontal collection, leading to centralized collection point. The gravity/pneumatic system does not permit offsets in vertical tubes.

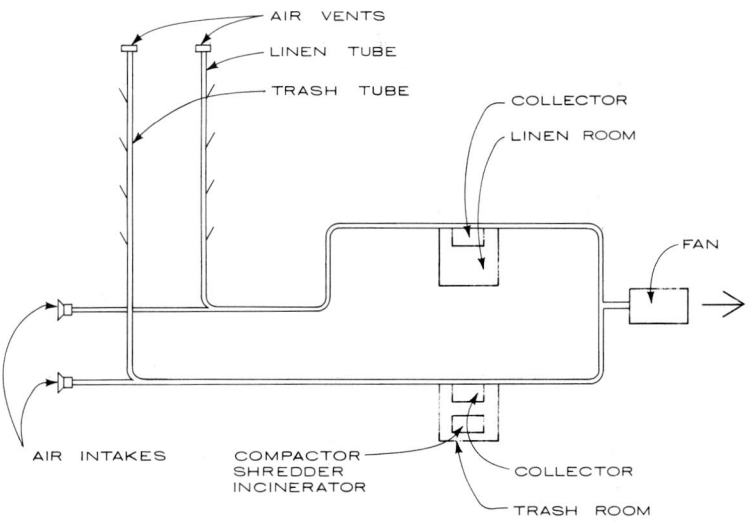

DUAL TUBE GRAVITY / VACUUM SYSTEM

SINGLE TUBE FULL VACUUM SYSTEM

The single tube fully pneumatic system offers the advantage of centralized collection of linen and trash. The system is limited in flexibility. Sanitation is somewhat compromised by having trash and linen using the same tubes. Manufacturers do not recommend this situation. A diverter valve controlled from loading station directs material to proper central receiving room.

SPECIFICS

GRAVITY TYPE VERTICAL CHUTES

Recommended 24 in. minimum diameter tube with air vent above roof and flushing spray and sprinkler head above top loading door.

PNEUMATIC TYPE VERTICAL CHUTES

Recommended 16 in. diameter tube with air intake above roof. Fire rated tube enclosure at each floor with electricity air and sprinkler at each enclosure.

CAPACITY

Uniform or variable size/regular or irregular in shape, a waste/linen handling system can accommodate a wide variety of materials. A standard 16 in. system can convey individual units weighing up to 50 lb.

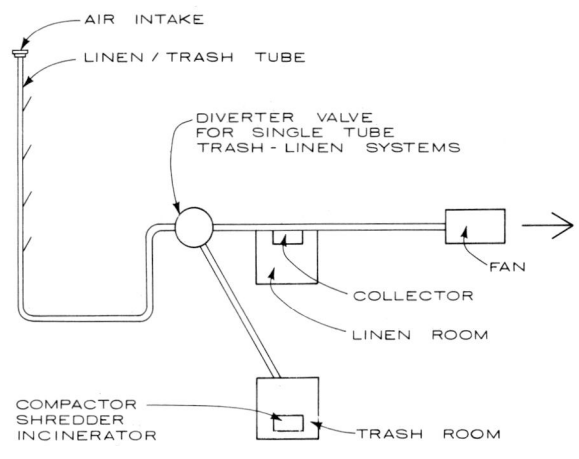

SINGLE TUBE FULL VACUUM SYSTEM

AVERAGE PER DAY WASTE QUANTITIES

BUILDING TYPE	WASTE IN POUNDS	LINEN IN POUNDS*
Apartments	5 per apartment	N/A
Hospitals	8 per bed	15 per room, double occupancy
Nurses' or interns' homes	3 per person	8 per person
Rest homes	3 per person	10–12 per person
Homes for the aged	6 per person	10–12 per person
Hotels	3 per room	15 per room
Motels	3 per room	15 per room
Schools	10 per room + ¼ per pupil	N/A
Office building	1 per 100 sq ft	N/A

*Pounds will vary per use of disposable linens.

Walter H. Sobel, FAIA & Associates; Chicago, Illinois

WASTE HANDLING EQUIPMENT **11**

STANDARD LINEN SIZES (IN.)

	SIZE	SUGGESTED FOLDED SIZE	MIN. DEPTH OF SHELF
Flat sheet			
Twin	66 x 104	88¼ x 13	
Double	81 x 104	10⅛ x 13	
Queen size	90 x 110	11¼ x 13¾	
King size	108 x 110	13½ x 13¾	
Fitted sheet			18″
Twin	39 x 80	7¼ x 9⅜	
Double	54 x 75	13⅓ x 9⅜	
Queen size	60 x 80	15 x 10	
King size	72 x 84	18 x 10½	
Pillowcase			
Standard	21 x 33	7 x 11	12″
King	21 x 33	7 x 15	
Pillows			
Standard	20 x 26	Not	
Queen	20 x 30	Applicable	
King	20 x 36		
Blanket			24″
Twin	66 x 90	16½ x 22½	
	72 x 90	18 x 22½	
Double	80 x 90	20 x 22½	
Queen/king	108 x 90	27 x 22½	
Hand towel	11 x 18	5½ x 9	12″
	12 x 20	6 x 10	
Face towel	15 x 26	7½ x 13	
	16 x 32	8 x 16	
	18 x 36	9 x 18	
Bath towel	22 x 44	11 x 11	18″
	24 x 48	12 x 12	
	26 x 50	13 x 12½	
	28 x 52	14 x 13	
Bath sheet	36 x 68	12 x 17	
	44 x 72	14¾ x 18	
Wash cloth	9 x 9	4½ x 9	
	12 x 12	6 x 12	
	14 x 14	7 x 14	
Bath mat	20 x 30	10 x 7½	12″
	20 x 34	10 x 8½	
	22 x 36	10 x 9	
Tablecloth			
Rectangular	52 x 52		
	52 x 70		
	62 x 85		
	62 x 104		18″
	70 x 90		to
	70 x 126		
Round	72″ diam.		24″
	90″ diam.		
Oval	52 x 70		
	64 x 84		
	72 x 90		
Napkin	14 x 14	4¾ x 7	
	18 x 18	6 x 9	12″
	22 x 22	7½ x 11	
Dish towel	16 x 30	8 x 15	
	18 x 36	9 x 18	
	20 x 32	10 x 16	18″
Sleeping bag	Varies	8 x 18	
		11 x 22	

MAIN LINEN STORAGE ROOM IN HOTELS AND MOTELS

Requires a room with minimum 20-24 in. wide shelving. Shelving less than 20 in. may not accommodate linen processed by professional linen service. Provisions for storage of dining linen and uniforms and a sewing/mending room are recommended in hotels. A clear space in the room for loading of carts (24″W x 60″L x 60″H) is required.

SECONDARY LINEN STORAGE ROOM IN HOTELS AND MOTELS

Requires a room with minimum 20-24 in. wide shelving. A clear space in the room for loading of two cleaning carts (24″W x 52″L) at one time is recommended. In most cases, the linen room is also used for storing some room service/nonlinen items.

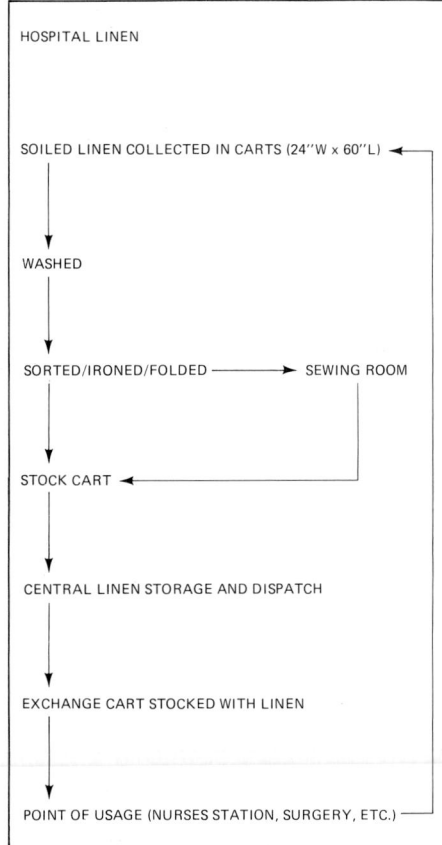

GENERAL NOTES

1. Rolled-up size (diam. x length). Manufacturer recommends storing bag(s) by hanging up unrolled.
2. Requires a room large enough to accommodate 24 in. wide shelving and circulation space for parking and storing of stock carts (24″W x 60″L) and loading of exchange carts (28″W x 52″L x 72″H).
3. Exchange cart may be stored in a closet near point of usage. An overhead shelf in closet for extra blankets and pillows is recommended.
4. Consult with Joint Commission on Accreditation of Hospitals and American Hospital Association for guidelines and standards.

Kent Wong; Hewlett, Jamison, Atkinson & Luey; Portland, Oregon

WASTE HANDLING EQUIPMENT

CHAPTER 12 FURNISHINGS

OVERFILE STORAGE

TYPE	W	H	D	WEIGHT*
Over 2-drawer letter	30	26 or 37	29	170
Over 2-drawer legal	36		29	308
Over 3-drawer letter	43		29	377
Over 3-drawer legal	54		29	445

VERTICAL FILES

TYPE	W	H	D	WEIGHT*
5-drawer letter	15	60	29	405
5-drawer legal	18	60	29	430
4-drawer letter	15	50	29	324
4-drawer legal	18	50	29	344
3-drawer letter	15	41	29	258
3-drawer legal	18	41	29	162
2-drawer letter	15	30	29	162
2-drawer legal	18	30	29	172

INSIDE DRAWER DIMENSIONS

TYPE	W	H	D
Letter	12¼	10½	26¾
Legal	15¼	10½	26¾

*Weights = fully loaded file.

VERTICAL FILE CABINETS

LATERAL FILES

TYPE	W	H	D	WEIGHT*
5-drawer	30, 36, 42	64	18	610-843
4-drawer	30-36-42	52	18	524-720
3-drawer	30, 36, 42	40	18	401-553
2-drawer	30, 36, 42	32	18	285-391

*Weights = fully loaded file.

LATERAL FILE CABINETS

SPECIAL FILES

TYPE	W	H	D
A. Ledger sheet file	21	52	27
B. Check file	15	52	27
C. Document file	18	52	27
D. Card record file	22	52	27
6-drawer (3 x 5, 4 x 6 cards)	22	52	27
5-drawer (3 x 5, 4 x 6, 5 x 8 cards)	22	52	27
E. Tabulation card file	19	52	30
F. 5 x 8 card file	20	52	27

SPECIAL FILING CABINETS

FIRE INSULATED FILES

TYPE	W	H	D	WEIGHT*
4-drawer letter	17	52	30	600
4-drawer legal	20	52	30	660
3-drawer letter	17	51	30	465
3-drawer legal	20	41	30	515
2-drawer letter	17	28	30	330
2-drawer legal	20	28	30	370
3-drawer lateral	39	56	24	1220
2-drawer lateral	39	39	24	875

*Weight = fully loaded.

FIRE INSULATED FILE CABINETS

Associated Space Design, Inc.; Atlanta, Georgia

PLANNING

1. Users' filing needs should be tabulated in inches and in turn converted into number of cabinets. Consult manufacturer for inches available in specific cabinets.
2. For open space planning, the following square footage allowances should be used:

TYPES	SPACE ALLOWANCE (FT²)
Vertical and 36 in. lateral files	10
Lateral file for computer printout	15

NOTE: All dimensions shown are approximate. Consult manufacturer for actual dimensions.

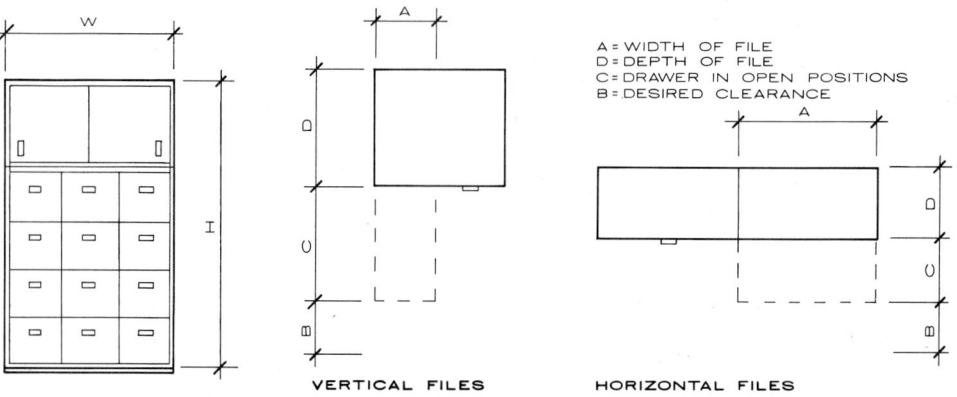

A = WIDTH OF FILE
D = DEPTH OF FILE
C = DRAWER IN OPEN POSITIONS
B = DESIRED CLEARANCE

VERTICAL FILES   **HORIZONTAL FILES**

DIMENSIONS FOR PLANNING

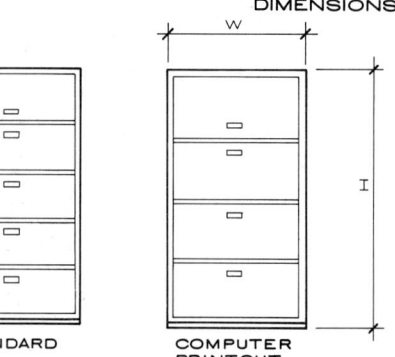

STANDARD   COMPUTER PRINTOUT

NOTES

1. Basic types accommodate multiple configurations of drawers, doors, and shelves.
2. 6 in. drawer accommodates cards and vouchers not exceeding 5 in. in one direction.
3. 12 in. drawer accommodates letter and legal files.
4. 15 in. drawer accommodates computer printouts.
5. Files are available to five-drawer height. Files more than five drawers high are not recommended.
6. Typical overfile storage is 26 or 37 in. high.

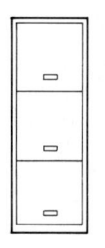 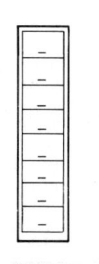 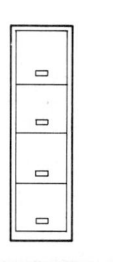 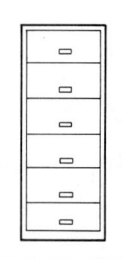 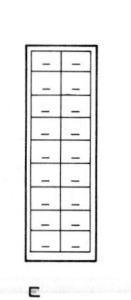 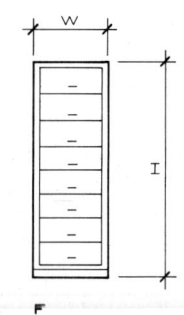

A   B   C   D   E   F

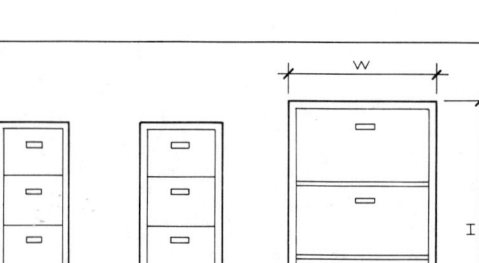

VERTICAL LETTER   VERTICAL LEGAL   LATERAL

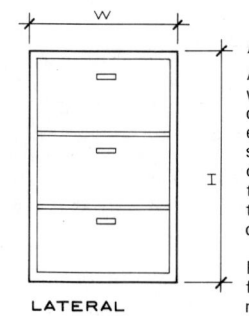

AUTOMATED RETRIEVAL SYSTEM

An automated system permits the retrieval of records within seconds. Records are stored in the unit on carriers. Each carrier is individually suspended and equally spaced on a conveyor system. The operator sits or stands at a posting board, and at the touch of a button the proper carrier moves into position so that a record may be pulled or filed. If there are card trays (there may be two to six trays per carrier), the correct tray slides forward.

Records that may be stored in these units include file folders, binders, reference books, ledgers, tape reels, microfilm, and cards.

WARDROBE AND STORAGE UNITS (IN.)

W	H	D
18, 24, 36	64½–80½	18
18, 24, 36	41¼–52¼	18
18, 24, 36	64½–80½	24
18, 24, 36	41¼–52¼	24

NOTE: Capacity depends on type of coats stored.

SHELVING UNITS (IN.)

	W	D	H
2 shelves	18, 24, 36	18	29
3 shelves	18, 24, 36	18	42
4 shelves	18, 24, 36	18	60
5 shelves	18, 24, 36	18	78
6 shelves	18, 24, 36	18	84

NOTE: Heights vary with manufacturer.

NOTES

1. Files, wardrobe, and storage shelving units if used together should be compatible in dimension and design. If possible, one manufacturer should be selected to furnish all items.

2. If storage units are used as space dividers in an open plan, some acoustical corrections can be gained by applying acoustical panels to the back of the units.

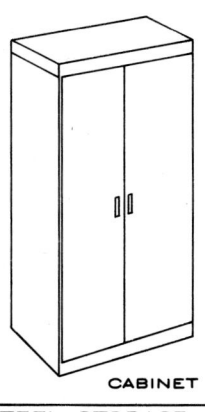
CABINET

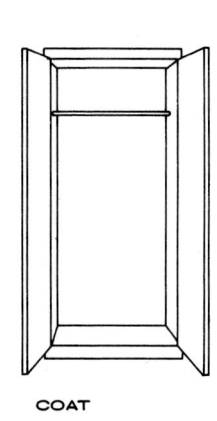
COAT

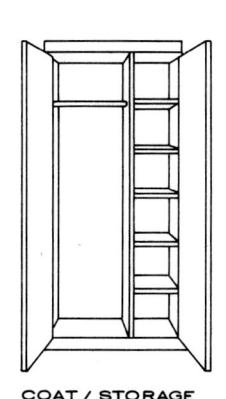
COAT / STORAGE

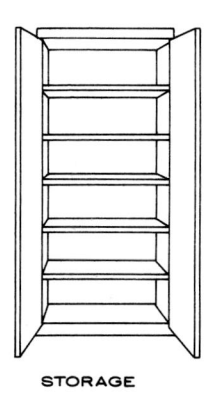
STORAGE

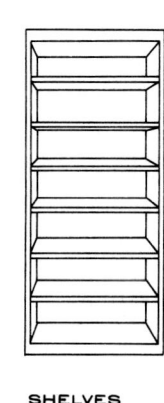
SHELVES

STEEL STORAGE CABINETS

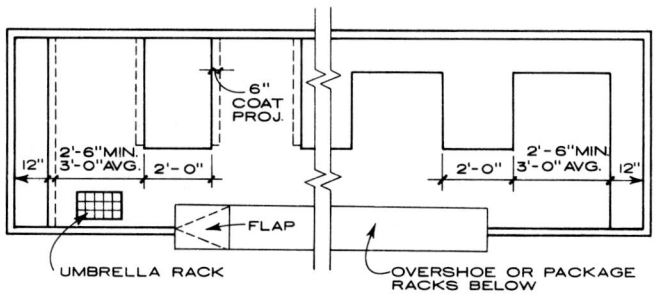

METAL RACKS

WOOD RACKS

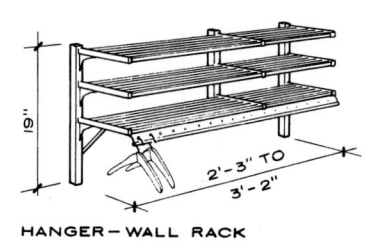
HANGER — WALL RACK

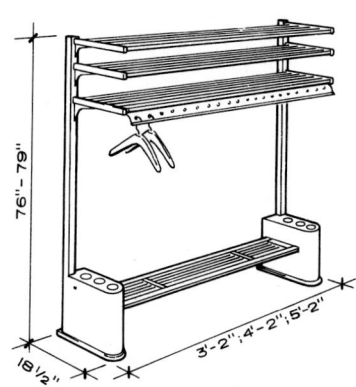

COMBINATION COAT, HAT, UMBRELLA, OVERSHOE RACK

Above model may be mounted back-to-back. Portable models are mounted on casters. Models available with or without umbrella and overshoe racks, and some are collapsible.

NOTE
Allow ¾ sq ft per person, which accommodates coat on hanger, hat, umbrella, and overshoes. Allow approximately 20% of hanger capacity for overshoe–umbrella racks. Standard hanger spacing is 3 in. o.c. (4 per lin. ft). Capacity may be increased 25% by spacing 2½ in. o.c. (5 per lin. ft). Use of hooks increases capacity to 8 per lin. ft.

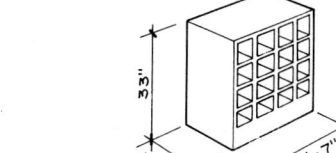
OVERSHOE RACK

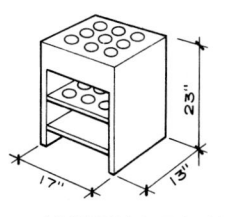
UMBRELLA RACK

CHECKROOM LAYOUT AND EQUIPMENT

CASEWORK UNITS (IN.)

	W	D
A. Single door base unit	12-24	18, 22, 25
B. Double door base unit	27-48	18, 22, 25
C. Drawer unit	15-48	18, 22, 25
D. File unit	15-48	18, 22, 25
E. Double door wall unit	27-48	13, 18
F. Glass door wall unit	27-48	13, 18
G. Open shelf unit	15-60	13, 18

NOTE: Consult manufacturers for exact dimensions.

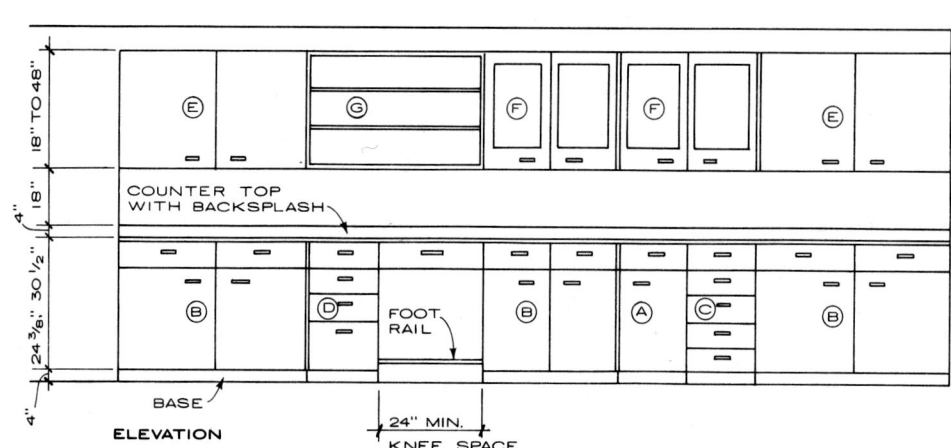
ELEVATION

STEEL CASEWORK

Associated Space Design, Inc; Atlanta, Georgia

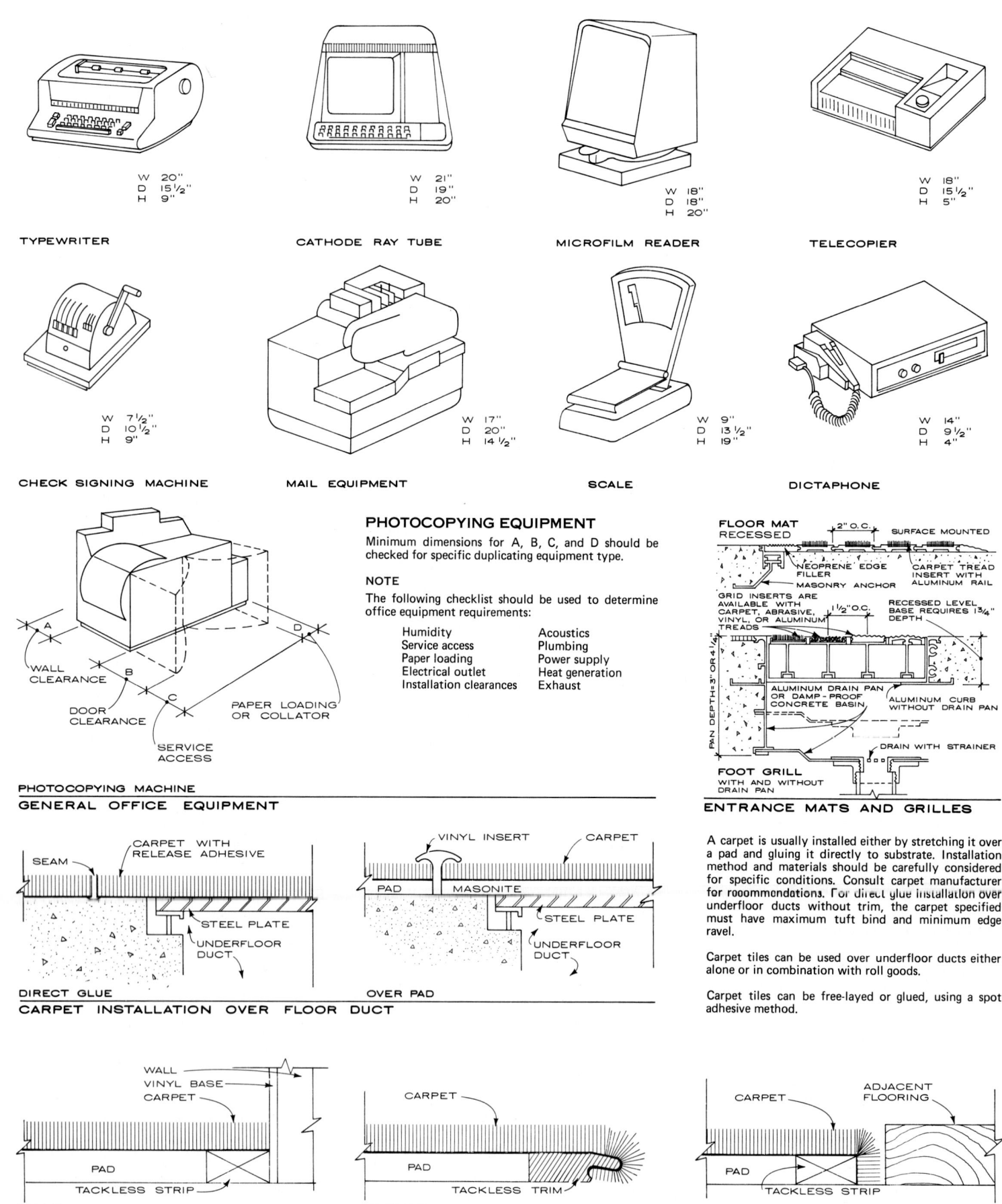

W 20"
D 15½"
H 9"

TYPEWRITER

W 21"
D 19"
H 20"

CATHODE RAY TUBE

W 18"
D 18"
H 20"

MICROFILM READER

W 18"
D 15½"
H 5"

TELECOPIER

W 7½"
D 10½"
H 9"

CHECK SIGNING MACHINE

W 17"
D 20"
H 14½"

MAIL EQUIPMENT

W 9"
D 13½"
H 19"

SCALE

W 14"
D 9½"
H 4"

DICTAPHONE

A
WALL
CLEARANCE
B
DOOR
CLEARANCE
C
SERVICE
ACCESS
D
PAPER LOADING
OR COLLATOR

PHOTOCOPYING MACHINE
GENERAL OFFICE EQUIPMENT

PHOTOCOPYING EQUIPMENT
Minimum dimensions for A, B, C, and D should be checked for specific duplicating equipment type.

NOTE
The following checklist should be used to determine office equipment requirements:

Humidity — Acoustics
Service access — Plumbing
Paper loading — Power supply
Electrical outlet — Heat generation
Installation clearances — Exhaust

FLOOR MAT
RECESSED
2" O.C.
SURFACE MOUNTED
NEOPRENE EDGE
FILLER
MASONRY ANCHOR
CARPET TREAD
INSERT WITH
ALUMINUM RAIL
GRID INSERTS ARE
AVAILABLE WITH
CARPET, ABRASIVE,
VINYL, OR ALUMINUM
TREADS
1½" O.C.
RECESSED LEVEL
BASE REQUIRES 1¾"
DEPTH
PAN DEPTH=3" OR 4¼"
ALUMINUM DRAIN PAN
OR DAMP-PROOF
CONCRETE BASIN
ALUMINUM CURB
WITHOUT DRAIN PAN
DRAIN WITH STRAINER
FOOT GRILL
WITH AND WITHOUT
DRAIN PAN

ENTRANCE MATS AND GRILLES

A carpet is usually installed either by stretching it over a pad and gluing it directly to substrate. Installation method and materials should be carefully considered for specific conditions. Consult carpet manufacturer for recommendations. For direct glue installation over underfloor ducts without trim, the carpet specified must have maximum tuft bind and minimum edge ravel.

Carpet tiles can be used over underfloor ducts either alone or in combination with roll goods.

Carpet tiles can be free-layed or glued, using a spot adhesive method.

SEAM
CARPET WITH
RELEASE ADHESIVE
STEEL PLATE
UNDERFLOOR
DUCT
DIRECT GLUE

VINYL INSERT
CARPET
PAD
MASONITE
STEEL PLATE
UNDERFLOOR
DUCT
OVER PAD

CARPET INSTALLATION OVER FLOOR DUCT

WALL
VINYL BASE
CARPET
PAD
TACKLESS STRIP
FLUSH

CARPET
PAD
TACKLESS TRIM
SURFACE

CARPET
ADJACENT
FLOORING
PAD
TACKLESS STRIP
RECESSED

CARPET INSTALLATION OVER PAD

Associated Space Design, Inc.; Atlanta, Georgia

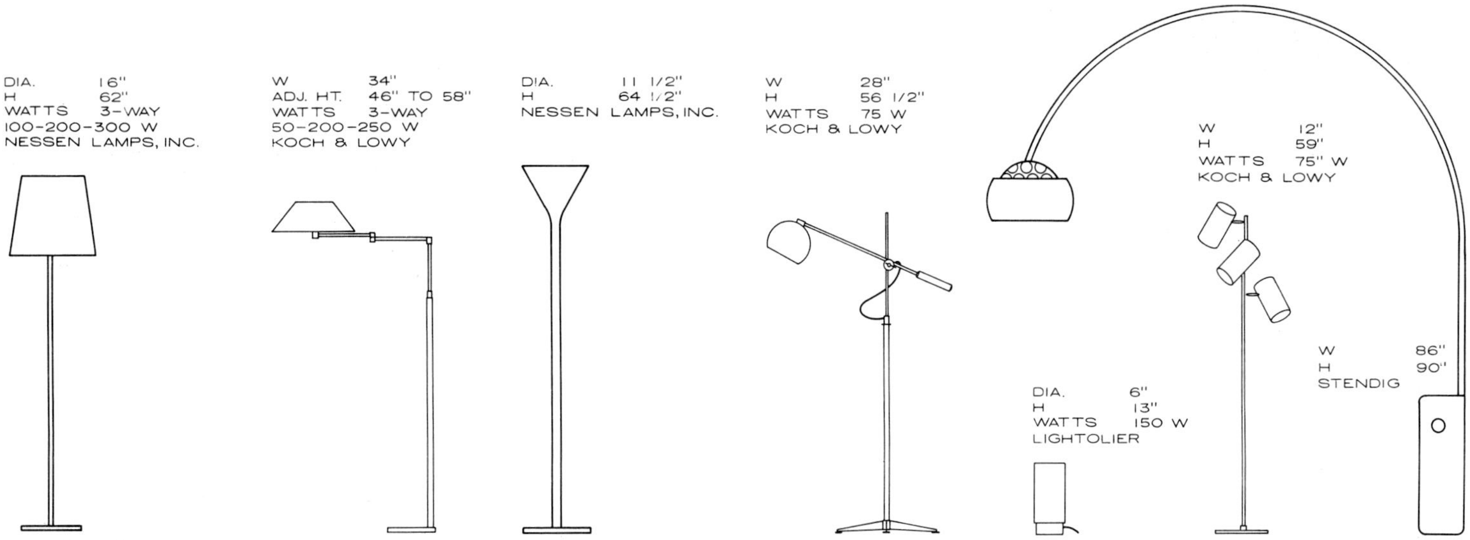

DIA.   16"
H   62"
WATTS   3-WAY
100-200-300 W
NESSEN LAMPS, INC.

W   34"
ADJ. HT.   46" TO 58"
WATTS   3-WAY
50-200-250 W
KOCH & LOWY

DIA.   11 1/2"
H   64 1/2"
NESSEN LAMPS, INC.

W   28"
H   56 1/2"
WATTS   75 W
KOCH & LOWY

W   12"
H   59"
WATTS   75" W
KOCH & LOWY

DIA.   6"
H   13"
WATTS   150 W
LIGHTOLIER

W   86"
H   90"
STENDIG

FLOOR LAMPS

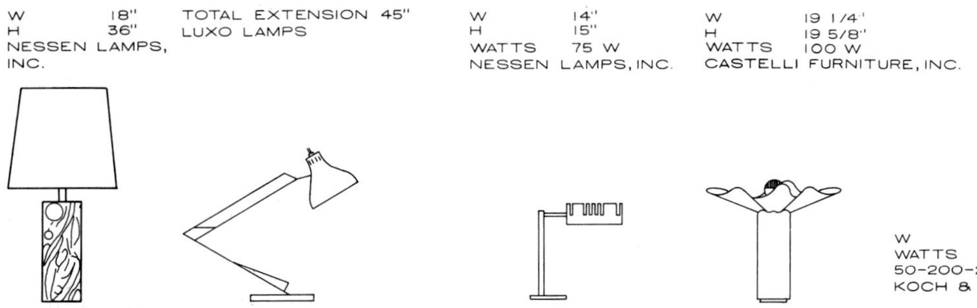

W   18"
H   36"
NESSEN LAMPS, INC.

TOTAL EXTENSION 45"
LUXO LAMPS

W   14"
H   15"
WATTS   75 W
NESSEN LAMPS, INC.

W   19 1/4'
H   19 5/8"
WATTS   100 W
CASTELLI FURNITURE, INC.

Lamps consist of three components:

1. Light source.
2. Reflector or diffuser.
3. Support structure.

Various combinations of these components create an unlimited variety of lamps for accent lighting, task lighting, ambient lighting, and general lighting. Each type of bulb creates different qualities and quantities of light; consult manufacturer for specific attributes. Light can be reflected in specific directions for accent, task, or ambient lighting or diffused for general lighting.

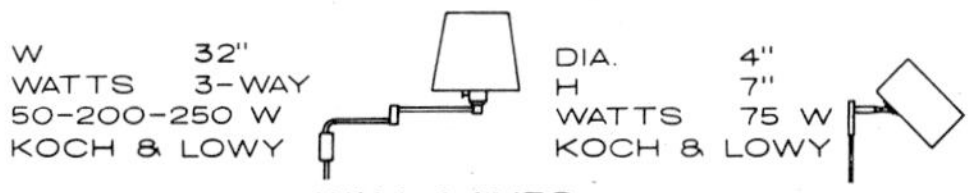

W   32"
WATTS   3-WAY
50-200-250 W
KOCH & LOWY

DIA.   4"
H   7"
WATTS   75 W
KOCH & LOWY

TABLE AND DESK LAMPS

WALL LAMPS

LAMPS

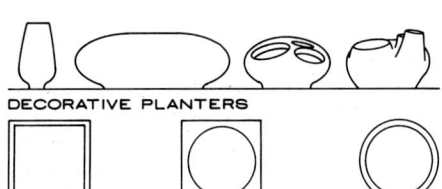

DECORATIVE PLANTERS

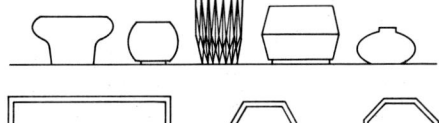

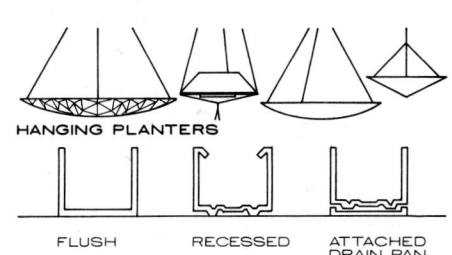

HANGING PLANTERS

PLANTER PLANS

SQUARE   CUBE   CYLINDER

W (IN.) 9, 11, 14, 16, 19, 20, 22, 24, 30, 36, 48, 60, 72, 96, 120, AND 144

RECTANGLE   HEXAGON   OCTAGON

W (IN.) 12, 15, 18, 24, 28, 34, 36, AND 48.
L (IN.) 18, 24, 30, 36, 48, 72, 78, 84, 96, 102, 108, AND 120.

FLUSH   RECESSED   ATTACHED DRAIN PAN

H (IN.) 9, 12, 15, 18, 20, 21, 25, 27, 30, 33, 48, AND 60.

PLANTER PROFILES

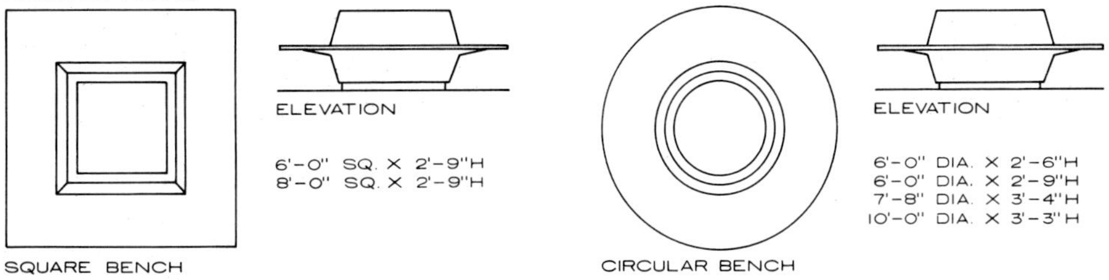

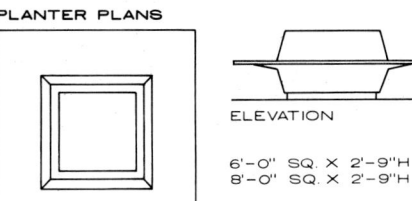

ELEVATION

6'-0" SQ. X 2'-9"H
8'-0" SQ. X 2'-9"H

ELEVATION

6'-0" DIA. X 2'-6"H
6'-0" DIA. X 2'-9"H
7'-8" DIA. X 3'-4"H
10'-0" DIA. X 3'-3"H

CIRCULAR SEAT

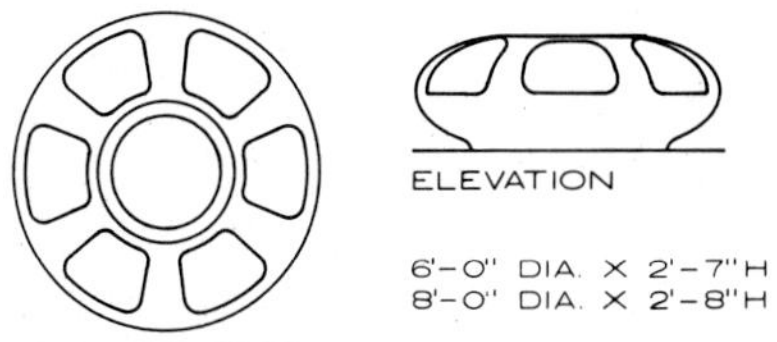

ELEVATION

6'-0" DIA. X 2'-7"H
8'-0" DIA. X 2'-8"H

SQUARE BENCH   CIRCULAR BENCH

BENCH AND SEAT PLANTERS

Planters are available in concrete, plastic, reinforced plastic, fiberglass, wood, and various metal finishes.

Planters are also available with casters, self-contained water reservoir, and self-contained regulatable water feeder systems.

Colors, shapes, textures, and sizes vary extensively; check with manufacturers for specifics.

When selecting planters consider:

1. Weight of planter plus plant.
2. Drainage provisions.
3. Ventilation provisions beneath planter.

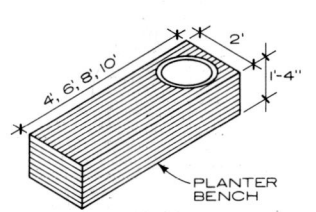

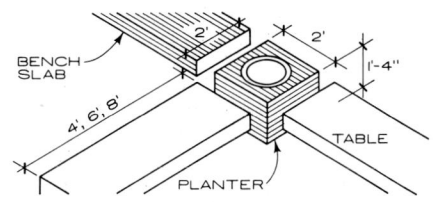

MODULAR PLANTER SYSTEM

PLANTERS AND BENCHES

Associated Space Design, Inc.; Atlanta, Georgia

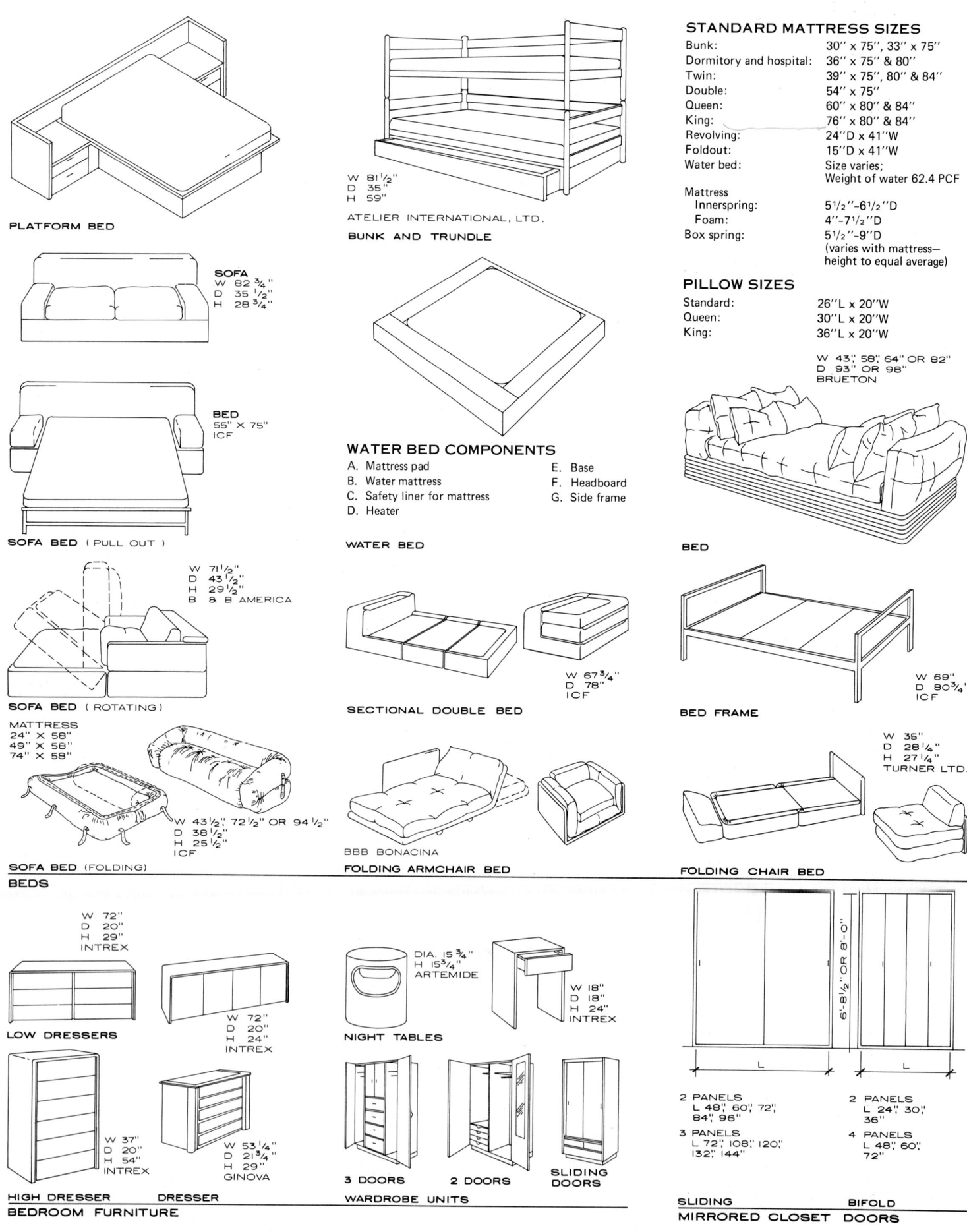

PLATFORM BED

SOFA
W 82¾"
D 35½"
H 28¾"

BED
55" X 75"
ICF

SOFA BED (PULL OUT)

W 71½"
D 43½"
H 29½"
B & B AMERICA

SOFA BED (ROTATING)

MATTRESS
24" X 58"
49" X 58"
74" X 58"

W 43½", 72½" OR 94½"
D 38½"
H 25½"
ICF

SOFA BED (FOLDING)

BEDS

W 81½"
D 35"
H 59"

ATELIER INTERNATIONAL, LTD.

BUNK AND TRUNDLE

WATER BED COMPONENTS

A. Mattress pad
B. Water mattress
C. Safety liner for mattress
D. Heater
E. Base
F. Headboard
G. Side frame

WATER BED

W 67¾"
D 78"
ICF

SECTIONAL DOUBLE BED

BBB BONACINA
FOLDING ARMCHAIR BED

STANDARD MATTRESS SIZES

Bunk:	30" x 75", 33" x 75"
Dormitory and hospital:	36" x 75" & 80"
Twin:	39" x 75", 80" & 84"
Double:	54" x 75"
Queen:	60" x 80" & 84"
King:	76" x 80" & 84"
Revolving:	24"D x 41"W
Foldout:	15"D x 41"W
Water bed:	Size varies; Weight of water 62.4 PCF
Mattress Innerspring:	5½"–6½"D
Foam:	4"–7½"D
Box spring:	5½"–9"D (varies with mattress— height to equal average)

PILLOW SIZES

Standard:	26"L x 20"W
Queen:	30"L x 20"W
King:	36"L x 20"W

W 43", 58", 64" OR 82"
D 93" OR 98"
BRUETON

BED

BED FRAME
W 69"
D 80¾"
ICF

W 35"
D 28¼"
H 27¼"
TURNER LTD.

FOLDING CHAIR BED

LOW DRESSERS
W 72"
D 20"
H 29"
INTREX

W 72"
D 20"
H 24"
INTREX

HIGH DRESSER
W 37"
D 20"
H 54"
INTREX

DRESSER
W 53¼"
D 21¾"
H 29"
GINOVA

BEDROOM FURNITURE

DIA. 15¾"
H 15¾"
ARTEMIDE

W 18"
D 18"
H 24"
INTREX

NIGHT TABLES

3 DOORS   2 DOORS   SLIDING DOORS
WARDROBE UNITS

6'-8½" OR 8'-0"

L   L

2 PANELS
L 48", 60", 72", 84", 96"

3 PANELS
L 72", 108", 120", 132", 144"

2 PANELS
L 24", 30", 36"

4 PANELS
L 48", 60", 72"

SLIDING   **BIFOLD**
MIRRORED CLOSET DOORS

Associated Space Design, Inc.; Atlanta, Georgia

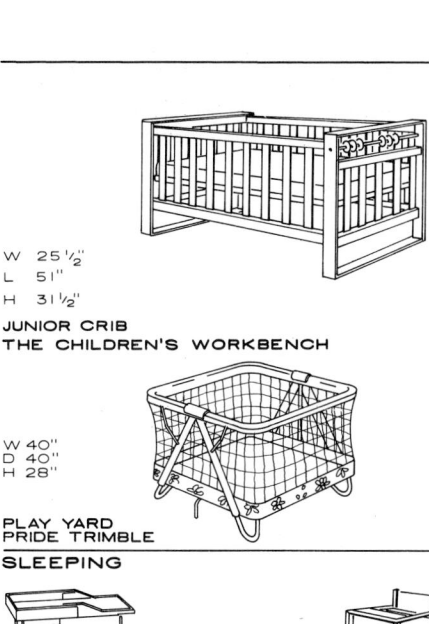

W 25½"
L 51"
H 31½"

**JUNIOR CRIB
THE CHILDREN'S WORKBENCH**

W 40"
D 40"
H 28"

**PLAY YARD
PRIDE TRIMBLE**

SLEEPING

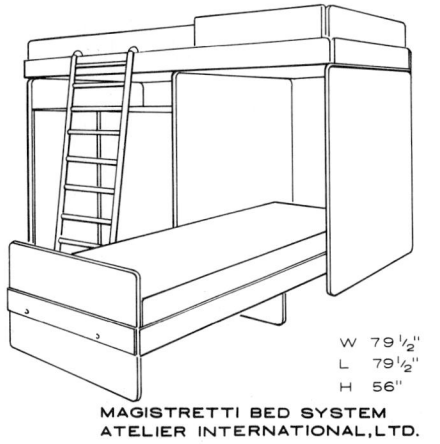

W 79½"
L 79½"
H 56"

**MAGISTRETTI BED SYSTEM
ATELIER INTERNATIONAL, LTD.**

W 37½"
L 79"
H 12" + 5" GUARD RAILS

**YOUTH BED WITH STORAGE
THE CHILDREN'S WORKBENCH**

STANDARD JUVENILE MATTRESS SIZES (IN.)

TYPE	LENGTH	WIDTH
Bassinet	36	18
Bassinet	38¾	22¼
Junior crib	46	23
Junior crib	50¾	25¼
6-year crib	51	27
6-year crib	56¾	31¼
Youth bed	66	33
Youth bed	76	36

SAFETY FACTORS

Correct spacing of bars or slats
Nontoxic materials
Flame retardant materials
Structural soundness
Tamperproof fastenings
Correct heights
Unbreakable
No sharp edges

W 36"
D 19"
H 36½"

**DIAPER CHANGER
HEDSTROM**

W 14"
D 12"
H 16"

TYPICAL UNIT
HAS HINGED
SEAT LID;
REMOVABLE
TRAY

POTTY CHAIR

W 23⅜"
D 23¾"
H 20½" – 28½"

**FEEDING TABLE
WELSH CO.**

SH 21"
H 28"

**HIGH CHAIR TRIO
COMFORTLINE**

INFANT CARE

DIA. 24"
H 12"

**FROG BOX
LITTLE TIKES**

W 16"
D 14"
H 27"

**MAILBOX
LITTLE TIKES**

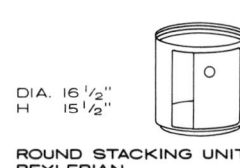

DIA. 16½"
H 15½"

**ROUND STACKING UNIT
BEYLERIAN**

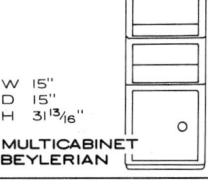

W 15"
D 15"
H 31¹³⁄₁₆"

**MULTICABINET
BEYLERIAN**

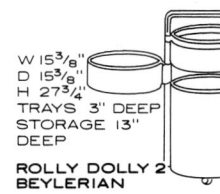

W 15⅜"
D 15⅜"
H 27¾"
TRAYS 3" DEEP
STORAGE 13"
DEEP

**ROLLY DOLLY 2
BEYLERIAN**

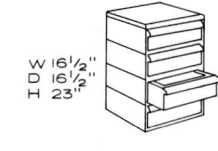

W 16½"
D 16½"
H 23"

**DRAWERS AND LID
BEYLERIAN**

STORAGE

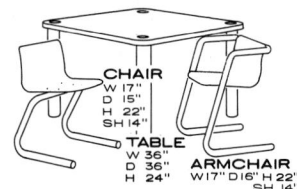

CHAIR
W 17"
D 15"
H 22"
SH 14"

TABLE
W 36"
D 36"
H 24"

ARMCHAIR
W17" D16" H 22"
SH 14"

**TABLE AND CHAIRS
KINETICS**

CHAIR
DIA. 14"
SH 10"

TABLE
DIA. 30"
H 20"

**TABLE AND CHAIR
LITTLE TIKES**

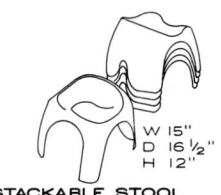

W 15"
D 16½"
H 12"

**STACKABLE STOOL
CASTELLI**

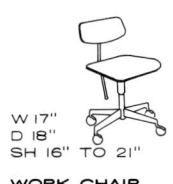

W 17"
D 18"
SH 16" TO 21"

**WORK CHAIR
STENDIG**

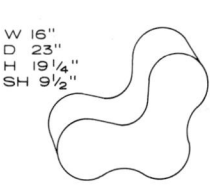

W 16"
D 23"
H 19¼"
SH 9½"

**CHILD'S CHAIR
STENDIG**

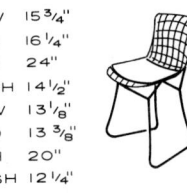

W 15¾"
D 16¼"
H 24"
SH 14½"
W 13⅛"
D 13⅜"
H 20"
SH 12¼"

**CHILD'S CHAIR
KNOLL**

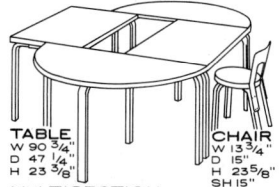

TABLE
W 90¾"
D 47¼"
H 23⅜"

CHAIR
W 13¾"
D 15"
H 23⅝"
SH 15"

**MULTISECTION
TABLE AND CHAIR ICF**

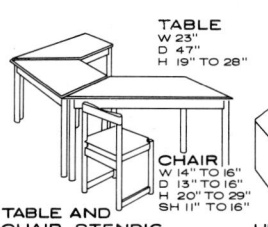

TABLE
W 23"
D 47"
H 19" TO 28"

CHAIR
W 14" TO 16"
D 13" TO 16"
H 20" TO 29"
SH 11" TO 16"

**TABLE AND
CHAIR STENDIG**

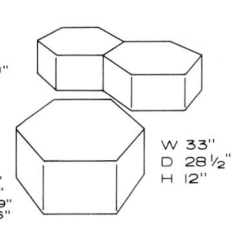

W 33"
D 28½"
H 12"

HEXAGONS STENDIG

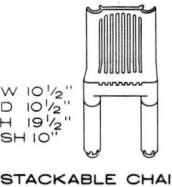

W 10½"
D 10½"
H 19½"
SH 10"

**STACKABLE CHAIR
BEYLERIAN**

STANDARD HEIGHTS

SEAT HEIGHT (IN.)	AGE GROUP	TABLE HEIGHT (IN.)
10–12	1–4	22
12–14	5, 6, 7	22–25
13–17	8, 9, 10	24–29
15–18	11, 12, 13	26–30

TABLES AND CHAIRS

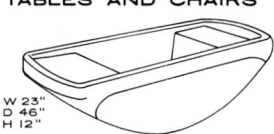

W 23"
D 46"
H 12"

**TEETER – TIKES
LITTLE TIKES**

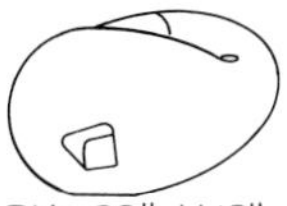

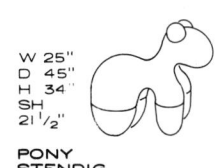

DIA. 20" H 12"

**WHIRLY CHAIR
LITTLE TIKES**

W 25"
D 45"
H 34"
SH 21½"

**PONY
STENDIG**

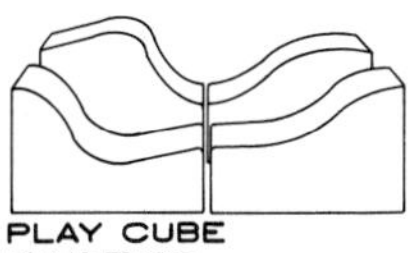

EACH
W 15"
D 30" H 20"

ASSEMBLED
W, D, AND H 30"

**PLAY CUBE
KINETICS**

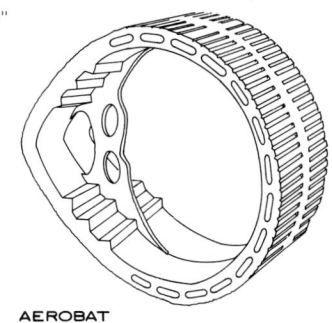

W 11"
L 34"
H 28"

**AEROBAT
LITTLE TIKES**

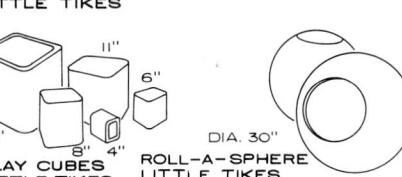

14"
11"
8"
6"
4"

**PLAY CUBES
LITTLE TIKES**

DIA. 30"

**ROLL-A-SPHERE
LITTLE TIKES**

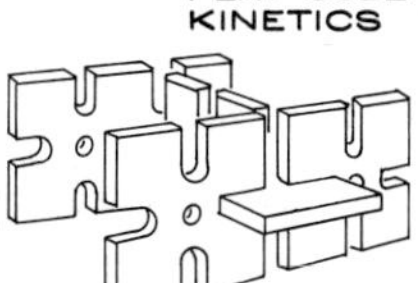

W 23"
L 23"
D 3"

**INTERLOCKING SQUARES
LITTLE TIKES**

PLAYTHINGS

Associated Space Design, Inc.; Atlanta, Georgia

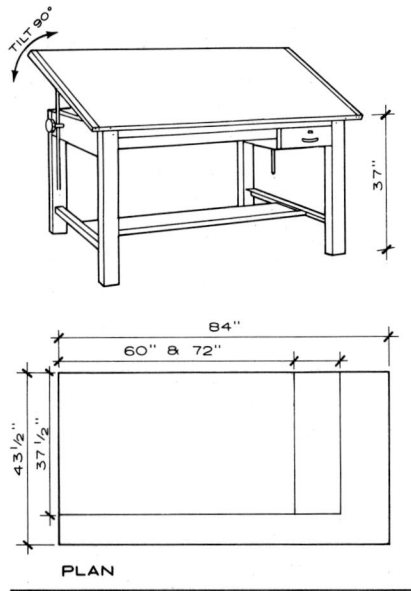

DRAFTING TABLE WITH ADJUSTABLE TOP

Drafting and/or engineering table is available in wood, in steel, or in combination. Various drawer and pedestal arrangements are available.

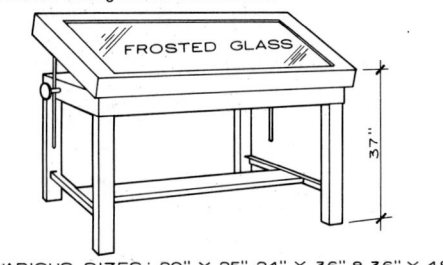

VARIOUS SIZES: 20" X 25", 24" X 36" & 36" X 48"

FLUORESCENT TRACING TABLE

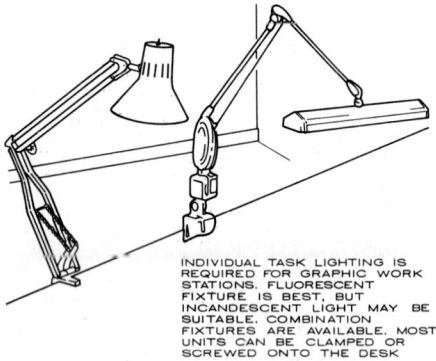

INDIVIDUAL TASK LIGHTING IS REQUIRED FOR GRAPHIC WORK STATIONS. FLUORESCENT FIXTURE IS BEST, BUT INCANDESCENT LIGHT MAY BE SUITABLE. COMBINATION FIXTURES ARE AVAILABLE. MOST UNITS CAN BE CLAMPED OR SCREWED ONTO THE DESK

DESK LAMPS

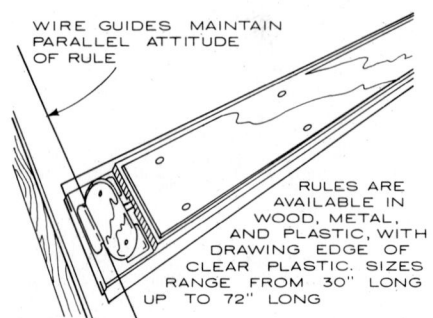

WIRE GUIDES MAINTAIN PARALLEL ATTITUDE OF RULE

RULES ARE AVAILABLE IN WOOD, METAL, AND PLASTIC, WITH DRAWING EDGE OF CLEAR PLASTIC. SIZES RANGE FROM 30" LONG UP TO 72" LONG

PARALLEL RULE

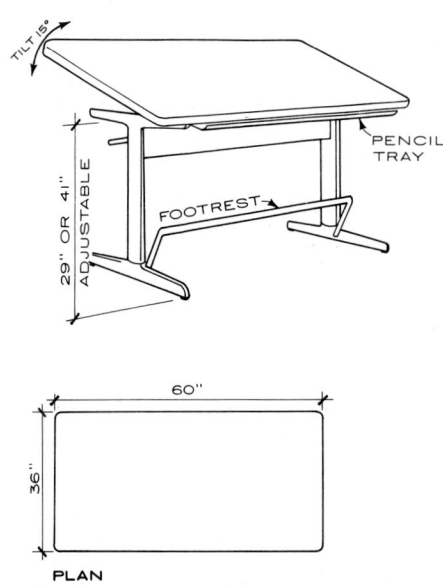

ADJUSTABLE WORKING SURFACE

Several manufacturers produce an array of drawing tables with adjustable tops, optional footrests, and pencil drawers.

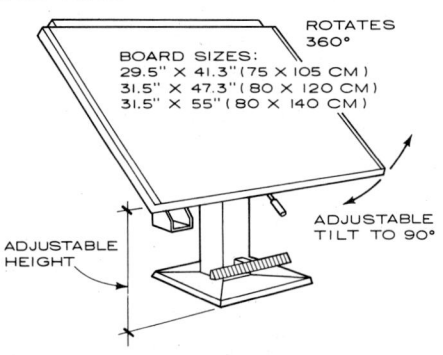

ROTATES 360°

BOARD SIZES:
29.5" X 41.3" (75 X 105 CM)
31.5" X 47.3" (80 X 120 CM)
31.5" X 55" (80 X 140 CM)

ADJUSTABLE TILT TO 90°

ADJUSTABLE HEIGHT

COUNTERBALANCED AUTOMATIC DRAFTING TABLE

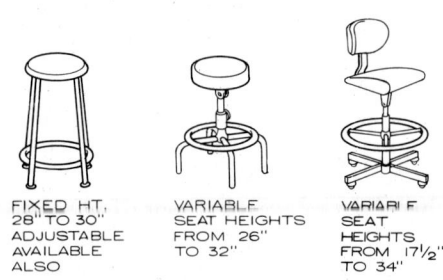

FIXED HT. 28" TO 30" ADJUSTABLE AVAILABLE ALSO

VARIABLE SEAT HEIGHTS FROM 26" TO 32"

VARIABLE SEAT HEIGHTS FROM 17½" TO 34"

STOOLS AND CHAIRS

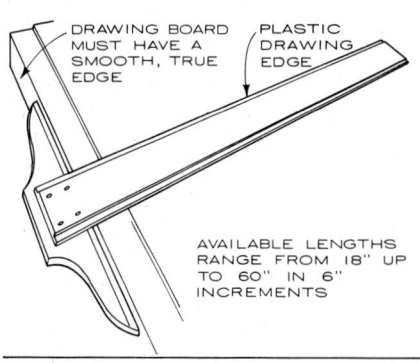

DRAWING BOARD MUST HAVE A SMOOTH, TRUE EDGE

PLASTIC DRAWING EDGE

AVAILABLE LENGTHS RANGE FROM 18" UP TO 60" IN 6" INCREMENTS

TRADITIONAL T SQUARE

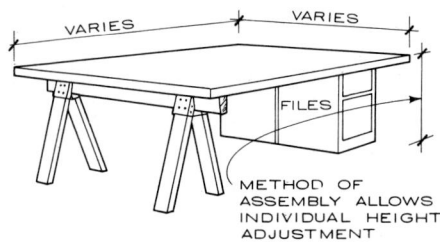

METHOD OF ASSEMBLY ALLOWS INDIVIDUAL HEIGHT ADJUSTMENT

HOLLOW CORE DOOR TABLE ON SAWHORSES

A serviceable drawing board can be inexpensively constructed with a flush door set on sawhorses, file cabinets, or blocks.

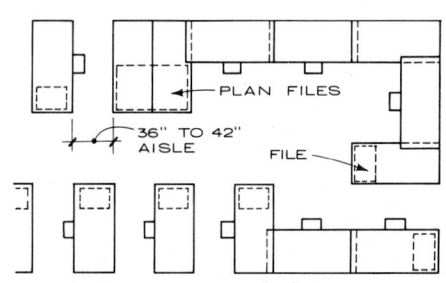

PLAN FILES

36" TO 42" AISLE

FILE

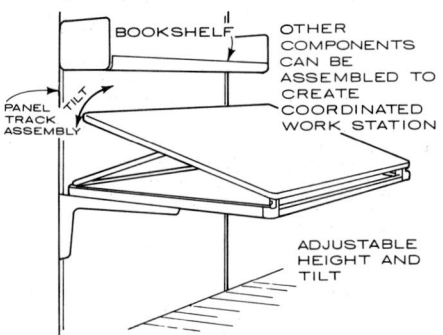

BOOKSHELF

OTHER COMPONENTS CAN BE ASSEMBLED TO CREATE COORDINATED WORK STATION

PANEL TRACK ASSEMBLY

TILT

ADJUSTABLE HEIGHT AND TILT

PANEL-HUNG DRAFTING BOARD

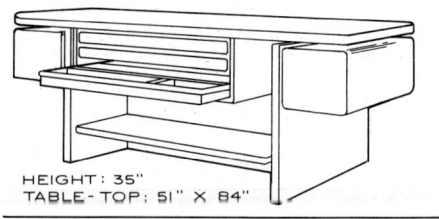

HEIGHT: 35"
TABLE-TOP: 51" X 84"

SERVICE TABLE

Service table provides a large worktop and integral storage compartments. Entire offices can be furnished with coordinated units.

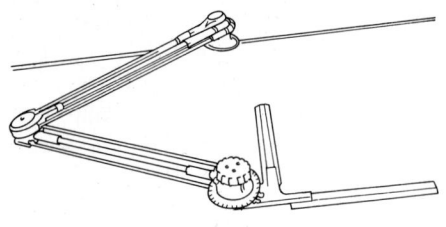

DRAFTING MACHINE

Clamp-on device combines parallel rule, triangles, protractor, and scales. Especially useful for technical drawing with few long lines. Straight edges can be had in several scales and are interchangeable.

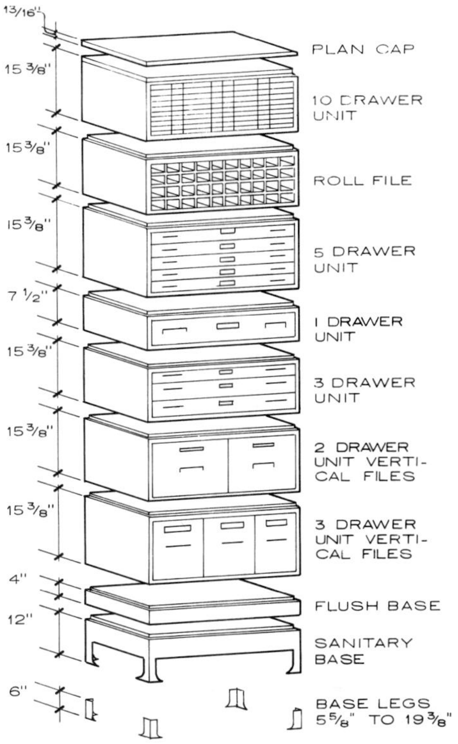

PLAN FILE SYSTEM

- PLAN CAP
- 10 DRAWER UNIT
- ROLL FILE
- 5 DRAWER UNIT
- 1 DRAWER UNIT
- 3 DRAWER UNIT
- 2 DRAWER UNIT VERTICAL FILES
- 3 DRAWER UNIT VERTICAL FILES
- FLUSH BASE
- SANITARY BASE
- BASE LEGS 5⅝" TO 19⅜"

STEEL SHOWN, WOOD SIMILAR; DEPTH 28½" TO 50½"; WIDTH 40¾" TO 79⁵⁄₁₆"; DRAWER EXTENDS 26" TO 42"

PIVOT FILING SYSTEM

WALL MOUNTED DATA FILES 1¾" X 8" X 11½" SHEET WIDTHS: 12" TO 48"

WALL MOUNTED RACK FILES FOR FRICTION TYPE BINDERS 18" TO 54" AT 6" INTERVALS

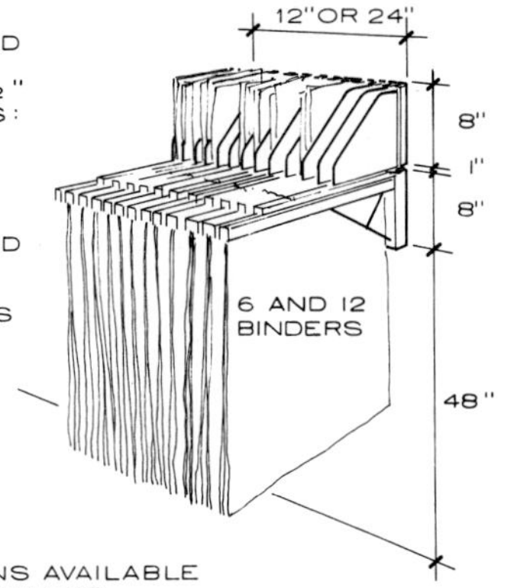

WALL RACK
FILE VARIATIONS AVAILABLE ON ROLLING STANDS

SHEET SIZES: LENGTH UP TO 52", WIDTH 18" TO 42"

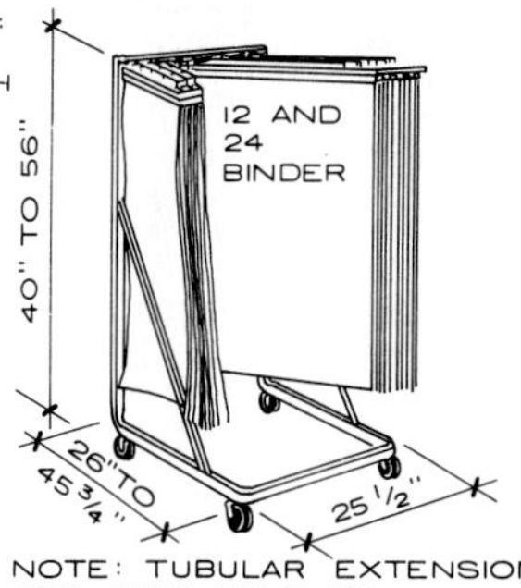

12 AND 24 BINDER

NOTE: TUBULAR EXTENSIONS ARE AVAILABLE TO ACCOMMODATE 72" SHEET LENGTHS

ROLLING STAND

CABINET FILES

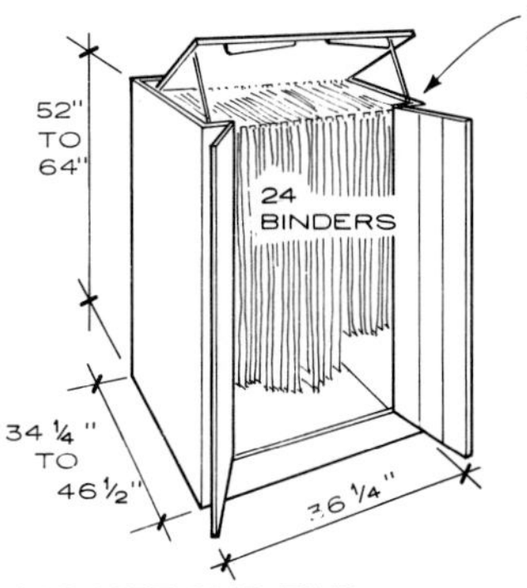

CABINET CLIP FILE
24 BINDERS
SHEET SIZES: 24" X 48", 30" X 48" 36" X 60", AND 42" X 60"

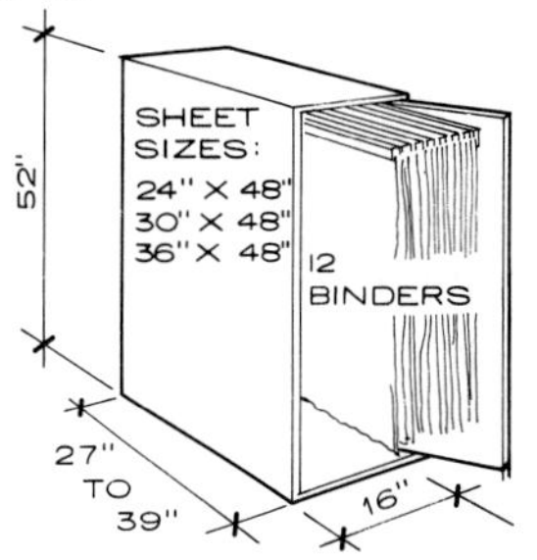

CABINET VERTICAL FILES
12 BINDERS
SHEET SIZES: 24" X 48" 30" X 48" 36" X 48"

CABINET ROLL FILE
NO. OF TUBES: 27, 48, AND 108 SQ. TUBE SIZES: 4½", 3⅜", AND 2⅛"

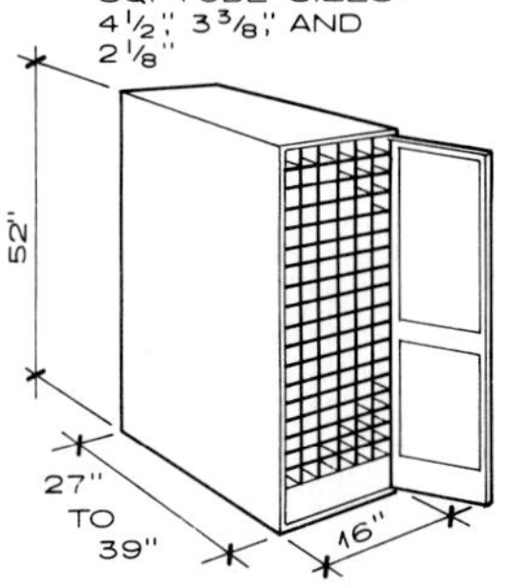

MODULAR FILE SYSTEMS

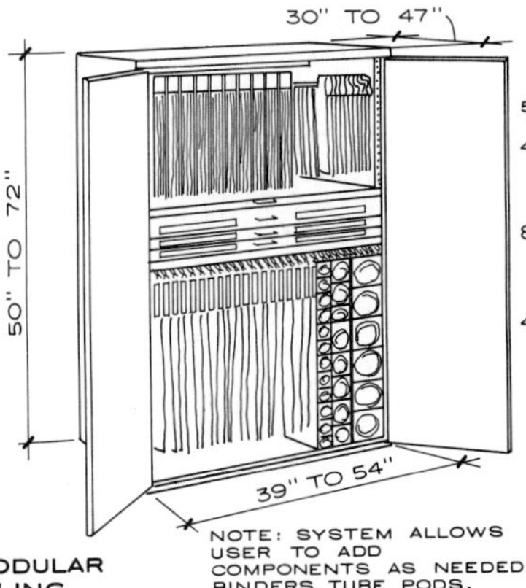

MODULAR FILING CABINET
NOTE: SYSTEM ALLOWS USER TO ADD COMPONENTS AS NEEDED. BINDERS, TUBE PODS, DRAWERS, ENVELOPES, AND BOX FOLDERS ARE ACCESSORIES

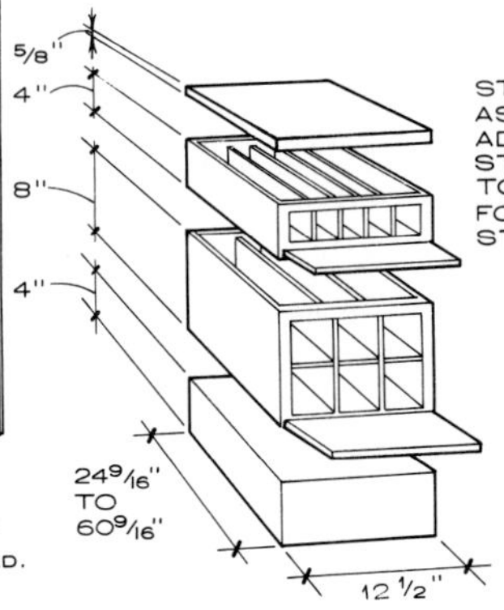

ROLL FILE UNITS
STACK HEIGHT AS REQUIRED. ADJACENT STACKS CLIP TOGETHER FOR LATERAL STABILITY

POCKET FILE

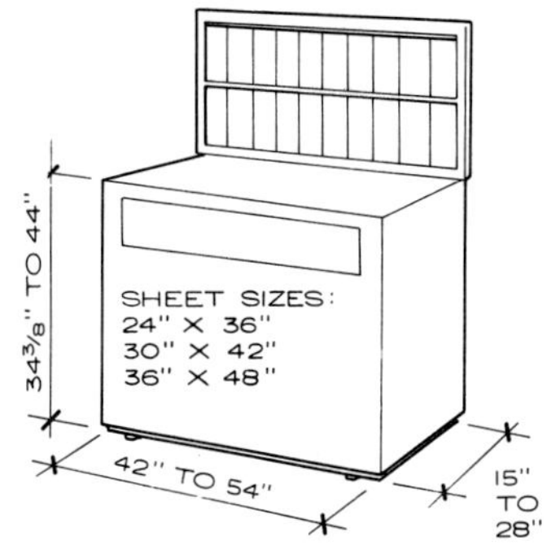

VERTICAL PLAN FILE
SHEET SIZES: 24" X 36" 30" X 42" 36" X 48"

STORAGE TUBES
TRANSPARENT PLASTIC STORAGE TUBE 2" DIAMETER 13" TO 55" LENGTHS

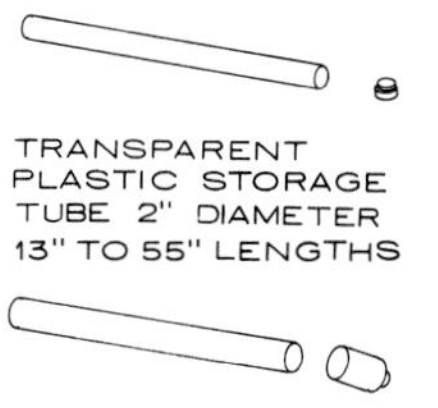

METAL STORAGE TUBE 2½" AND 4" DIAMETER 31" TO 55" LENGTHS

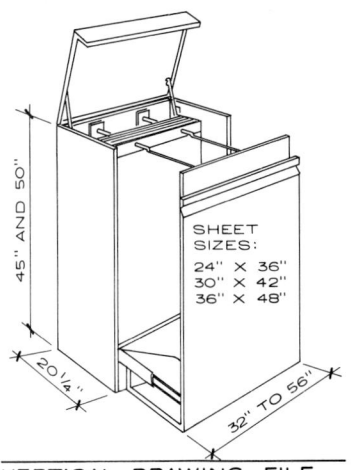

VERTICAL DRAWING FILE
SHEET SIZES: 24" X 36" 30" X 42" 36" X 48"

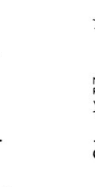

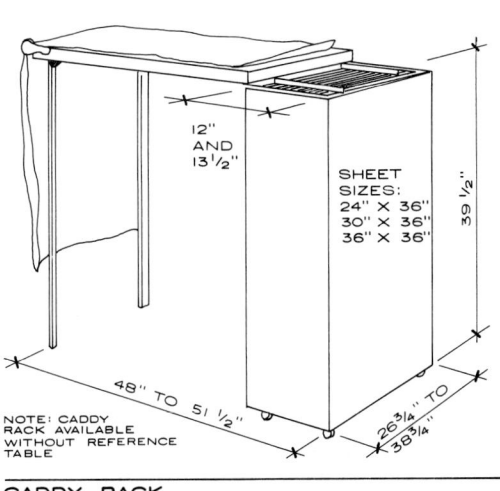

CADDY RACK
SHEET SIZES: 24" X 36" 30" X 36" 36" X 36"
NOTE: CADDY RACK AVAILABLE WITHOUT REFERENCE TABLE

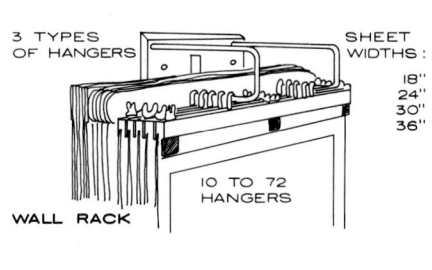

3 TYPES OF HANGERS

SHEET WIDTHS: 18" 24" 30" 36"

10 TO 72 HANGERS

WALL RACK

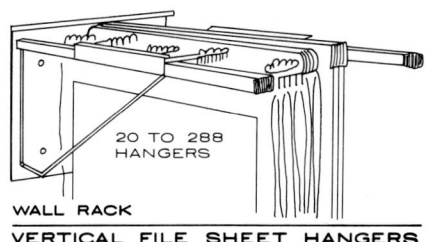

20 TO 288 HANGERS

WALL RACK

VERTICAL FILE SHEET HANGERS

John R. Hoke, Jr., AIA, Architect; Washington, D.C.

DESIGN RATIONALE

Systems furniture is designed primarily for utilization in an open office plan which uses few fixed floor-to-ceiling partitions as compared to conventional office layouts. Open office planning receives its impetus from its ability to respond to requirements for increased flexibility and lower long term expenses. Some of the major areas of response are the following:

1. FLEXIBILITY OF PLANNING: Systems furniture in an open plan maximizes the efficient use of net plannable space. This is the result of the use of more vertical space without fixed floor-to-ceiling partitions, thereby freeing floor area and reducing space planning inefficiencies.

2. FLEXIBILITY OF FUNCTION: Systems furniture allows individual workstation modification so that workstation design can reflect functional requirements of the task performed. In this way, changes in function can be accommodated without total furniture replacement.

3. FLEXIBILITY OF PLAN MODIFICATION: Systems furniture in open office planning allows institutions to respond more easily to organizational changes of size, structure, and function. Open planning allows institutions to respond to change at lower cost by reducing expenses related to partition relocation, HVAC modification, lighting relocation, construction, and moving time.

NOTES

1. Any open office plan as commonly applied will utilize some enclosed spaces having fixed, floor-to-ceiling partitions.

2. Systems furniture requires careful planning and engineering consultation to achieve the maximum functional advantage.

3. Systems furniture components are not compatible from one manufacturer to another regardless of generic type.

4. The generic types listed below are broad classifications for descriptive purposes only.

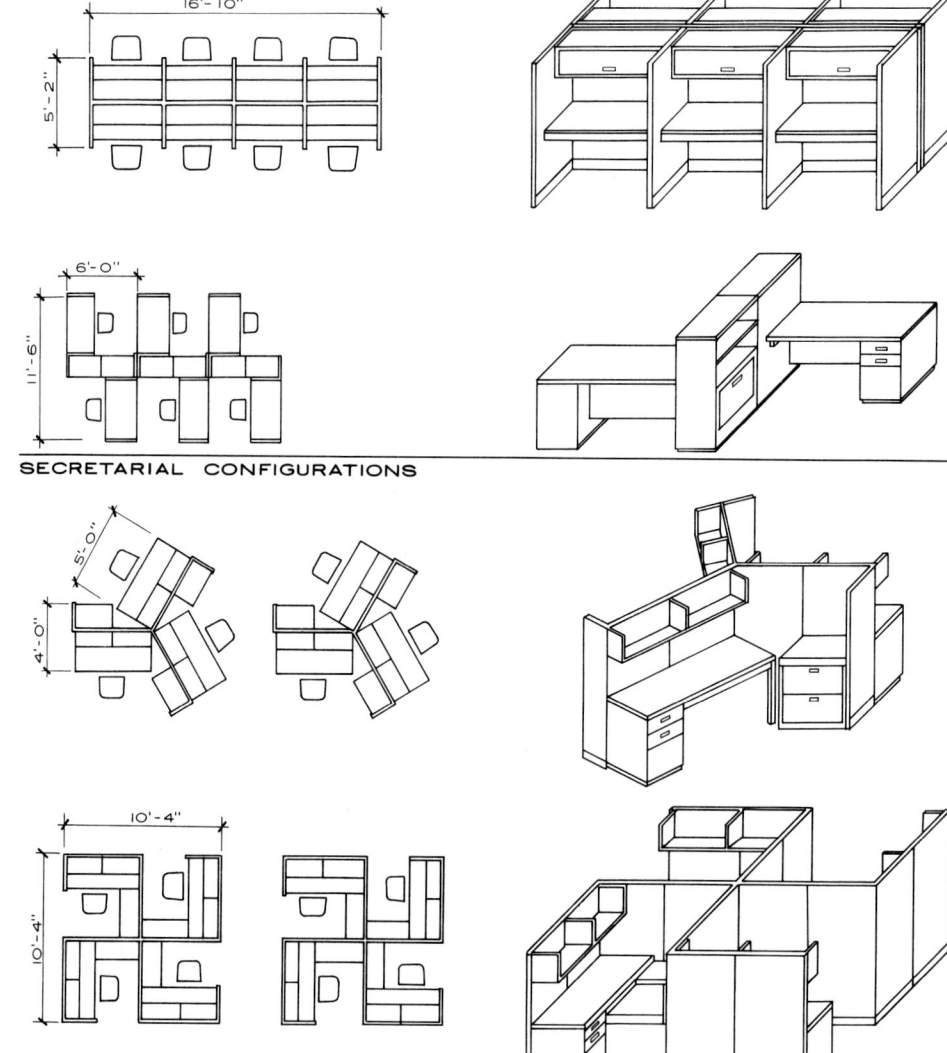

SECRETARIAL CONFIGURATIONS

CLERICAL CONFIGURATIONS

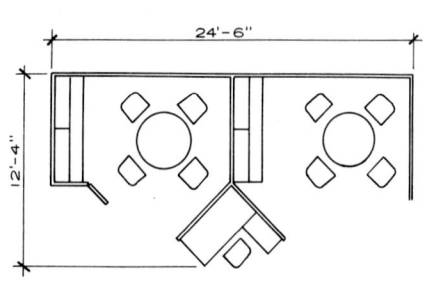

CONFERENCE

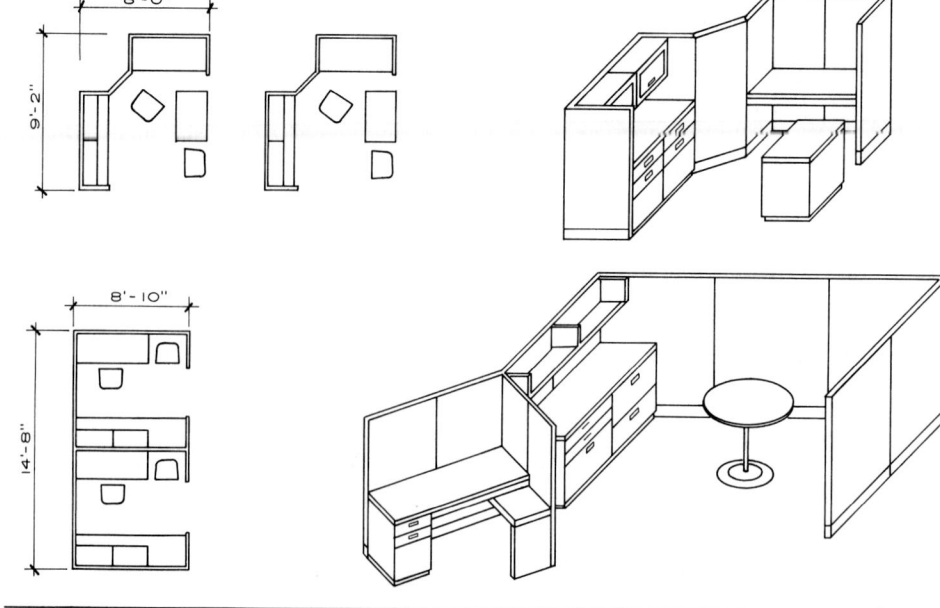

EXECUTIVE CONFIGURATIONS

Interspace Incorporated; Washington, D.C.

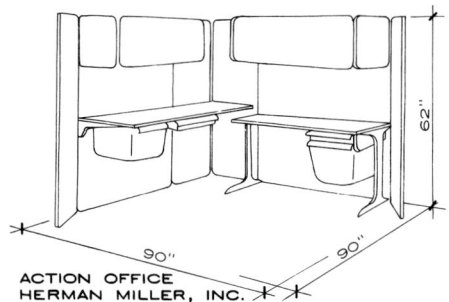

ACTION OFFICE
HERMAN MILLER, INC.

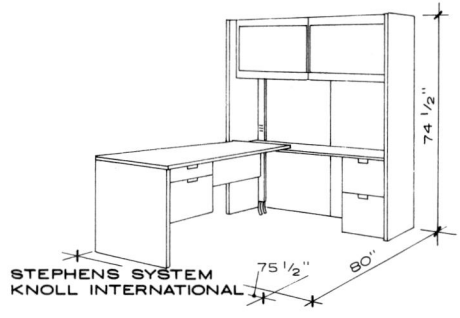

STEPHENS SYSTEM
KNOLL INTERNATIONAL

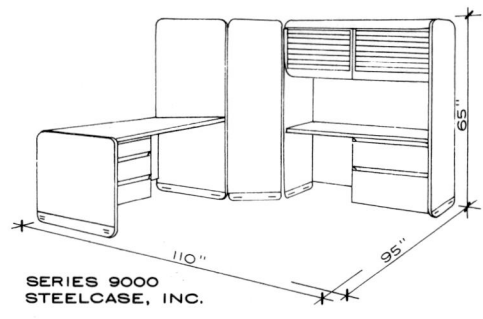

SERIES 9000
STEELCASE, INC.

PANEL HUNG TYPE

These systems are based on panels that can be connected at various angles (angle options depend on manufacturer). Panels achieve stability through configuration or by attached stabilizing feet. Components are hung on panels at desired heights (usually on 1 in. increments).

SYSTEM ADVANTAGES

Panel hung systems usually have a large variety of components. They offer the highest degree of planning flexibility. These systems are easily modified and are relatively light.

OPTIONS OFFERED (VARY WITH MANUFACTURER)

1. Ability to hang components on fixed, full height partitions.
2. Specialized use components (i.e., hospitals, schools, libraries).
3. Integrated wiring in panels with fast connect or wire manager components for horizontal raceways.
4. Integrated task/ambient lighting components.
5. Multiple standard panel heights (dimensions vary).
6. Fabric covered acoustical panels as structural panel option.
7. Integrated file storage components.

PANEL ENCLOSURE TYPE

These systems are based on building rectilinear enclosures with panel components. Panels achieve stability through right angle panel-to-panel configuration. Components are hung in panel enclosures (usually at several predetermined mounting heights) and are supported by end panels rather than back panels.

SYSTEM ADVANTAGES

Assembled systems have a somewhat unitized appearance. They are stable and, when assembled, are not easily moved. They have a relatively high level of flexibility with a more limited number of components and accessories than in most panel hung systems.

OPTIONS OFFERED (VARY WITH MANUFACTURER)

1. Multiple standard panel heights.
2. Full panel high closed storage units (i.e., wardrobes, shelf).
3. Vertical power poles with lighting outlets, convenience outlets, circuit breakers, telephone raceway.
4. Wire manager components for vertical and horizontal raceways.
5. Integrated task/ambient lighting components and freestanding ambient light units.
6. Fabric covered acoustical panels are structural panel option.
7. Integrated file storage components.

UNITIZED PANEL TYPE

These systems are based on ganging assembled units and panels to form workstations and workstation groupings. Units are individually stable and panels achieve stability by attachment to units and right angle panel-to-panel configuration. Some of these systems are more componentized than others (similar to panel enclosure type) but are marketed as assembled units. Components within assembled units are usually supported by end panels.

SYSTEM ADVANTAGES

Assembled systems have a unitized appearance more closely resembling conventional furniture. They are very stable and, when assembled, are not easily moved. They have a relatively high level of flexibility depending on the degree to which they are unitized. These systems simplify purchase, inventory management, and installation because of their unitized character.

OPTIONS OFFERED (VARY WITH MANUFACTURER)

1. Multiple standard panel heights (dimensions vary).
2. Full panel high closed storage units (i.e., wardrobes, shelf).
3. Wire raceways (horizontal and vertical), convenience outlets, and switches are an integral part of system.
4. Integrated task/ambient light units.
5. Fabric covered acoustical panels usually as hang on or finish panel option.
6. Integrated flexible branch wiring system.
7. Can be used in conventional configurations.

GENERIC TYPES OF SYSTEM FURNITURE

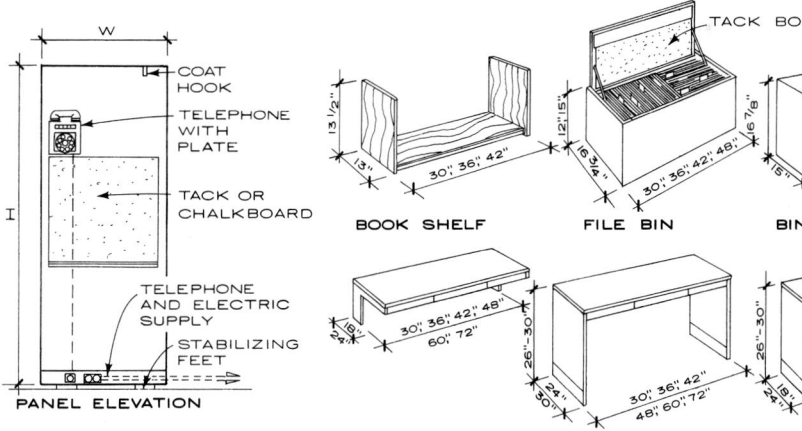

WORKSTATION SECTION

INTEGRATED LIGHTING

Artificial lighting is integrated into most open office furniture systems. The components consist of task oriented downlights located directly over work surfaces, which provide the user with control of intensity and direction of light. Uplights are mounted in the top of workstations to provide indirect light reflected off the ceiling to the ambient surroundings.

Task/ambient lighting provides more flexibility than do standard ceiling mounted fixtures. It can reduce energy consumption by decreasing general light levels and utilizing more efficient light sources. It can also improve acoustics, since fewer fixtures are installed in the acoustical ceiling.

PANEL ELEVATION

TYPICAL PANEL
HEIGHTS (H)
50", 62", 80"

TYPICAL PANEL
WIDTHS (W)
12", 24", 36", 48"

PANEL FINISH OPTIONS
Plastic laminate
Wood veneer
Tempered safety glass
Acoustical fabric

NOTE: Consult manufacturer for specific sizes and finishes available.

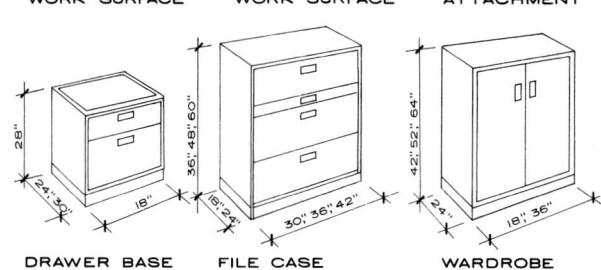

SYSTEMS FURNITURE COMPONENTS

Interspace Incorporated; Washington, D.C.

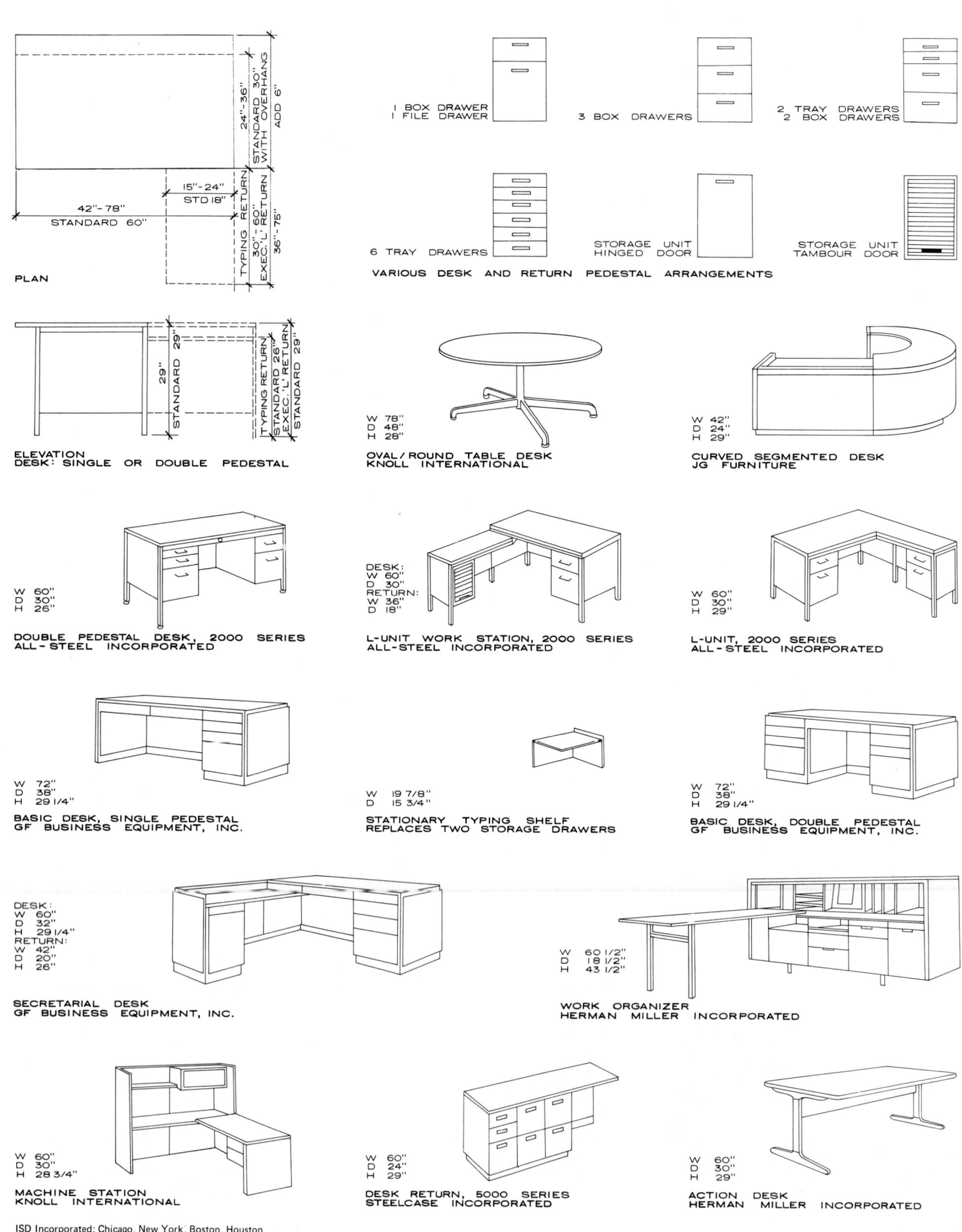

PLAN

1 BOX DRAWER
1 FILE DRAWER

3 BOX DRAWERS

2 TRAY DRAWERS
2 BOX DRAWERS

6 TRAY DRAWERS

STORAGE UNIT
HINGED DOOR

STORAGE UNIT
TAMBOUR DOOR

VARIOUS DESK AND RETURN PEDESTAL ARRANGEMENTS

ELEVATION
DESK: SINGLE OR DOUBLE PEDESTAL

W 78"
D 48"
H 28"

OVAL / ROUND TABLE DESK
KNOLL INTERNATIONAL

W 42"
D 24"
H 29"

CURVED SEGMENTED DESK
JG FURNITURE

W 60"
D 30"
H 26"

DOUBLE PEDESTAL DESK, 2000 SERIES
ALL-STEEL INCORPORATED

DESK:
W 60"
D 30"
RETURN:
W 36"
D 18"

L-UNIT WORK STATION, 2000 SERIES
ALL-STEEL INCORPORATED

W 60"
D 30"
H 29"

L-UNIT, 2000 SERIES
ALL-STEEL INCORPORATED

W 72"
D 38"
H 29 1/4"

BASIC DESK, SINGLE PEDESTAL
GF BUSINESS EQUIPMENT, INC.

W 19 7/8"
D 15 3/4"

STATIONARY TYPING SHELF
REPLACES TWO STORAGE DRAWERS

W 72"
D 38"
H 29 1/4"

BASIC DESK, DOUBLE PEDESTAL
GF BUSINESS EQUIPMENT, INC.

DESK:
W 60"
D 32"
H 29 1/4"
RETURN:
W 42"
D 20"
H 26"

SECRETARIAL DESK
GF BUSINESS EQUIPMENT, INC.

W 60 1/2"
D 18 1/2"
H 43 1/2"

WORK ORGANIZER
HERMAN MILLER INCORPORATED

W 60"
D 30"
H 28 3/4"

MACHINE STATION
KNOLL INTERNATIONAL

W 60"
D 24"
H 29"

DESK RETURN, 5000 SERIES
STEELCASE INCORPORATED

W 60"
D 30"
H 29"

ACTION DESK
HERMAN MILLER INCORPORATED

ISD Incorporated; Chicago, New York, Boston, Houston

12   **FURNITURE**

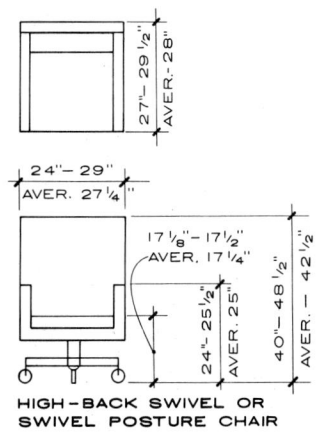

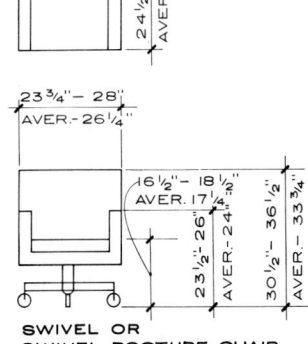

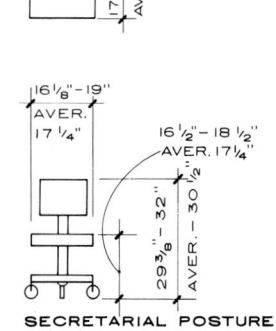

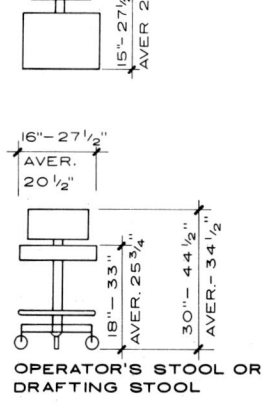

HIGH-BACK SWIVEL OR
SWIVEL POSTURE CHAIR

SWIVEL OR
SWIVEL POSTURE CHAIR

SECRETARIAL POSTURE
CHAIR

OPERATOR'S STOOL OR
DRAFTING STOOL

W 22½"
D 23¾"
H 41"
SH 19½"

HIGH BACK DESK CHAIR
DESIGNER: CHARLES EAMES
HERMAN MILLER, INC.

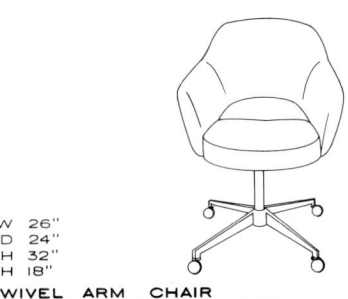

W 26"
D 24"
H 32"
SH 18"

SWIVEL ARM CHAIR
DESIGNER: EERO SAARINEN
KNOLL INTERNATIONAL, INC.

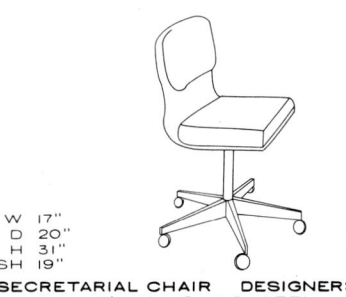

W 17"
D 20"
H 31"
SH 19"

SECRETARIAL CHAIR DESIGNER:
DE PAS, D'URBINO, LOMAZZI
ATELIER INTERNATIONAL, LTD.

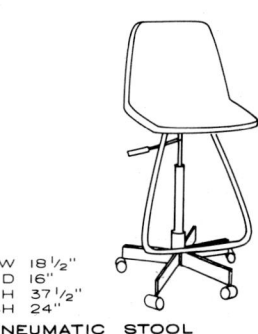

W 18½"
D 16"
H 37½"
SH 24"

PNEUMATIC STOOL
ARIES SERIES
KRUEGER, INC.

W 24"
D 32½"
H 39½"
SH 18"

EXECUTIVE HI BACK CHAIR
DESIGNER: ROBERT BERNARD
THONET INDUSTRIES, INC.

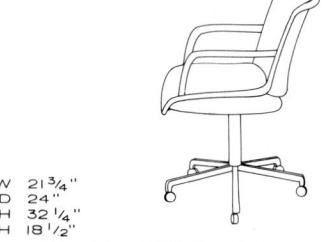

W 21¾"
D 24"
H 32¼"
SH 18½"

SWIVEL ARM CHAIR CAS
SERIES SUNAR LIMITED

W 18¾"
D 20"
H 30"
SH 18"

ERGON SECRETARIAL CHAIR
DESIGNER: BILL STUMPF
HERMAN MILLER, INC.

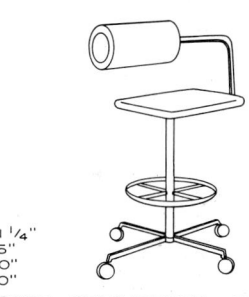

W 21¼"
D 25"
H 40"
SH 30"

ROLLBACK OPERATIONAL STOOL
DESIGNER: RAY WILKES
HERMAN MILLER, INC.

TYPICAL CREDENZA DIMENSIONS

	WIDTH	DEPTH	HEIGHT
One component	27" to 30"	17¾" to 21"	25½" to 29¾"
Two component	37¼" to 41½"	17¾" to 21"	25½" to 29¾"
Three component	44¾" to 60½"	17¾" to 21"	25½" to 29¾"
Four component	62¼" to 79¾"	17¾" to 21"	25½" to 29¾"
Five component	95¾" to 98½"	17¾" to 21"	25½" to 29¾"

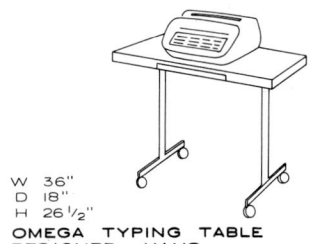

W 36"
D 18"
H 26½"

OMEGA TYPING TABLE
DESIGNER: HANS
EICHENBERGER; STENDIG, INC.

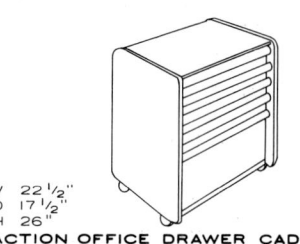

W 22½"
D 17½"
H 26"

ACTION OFFICE DRAWER CADDIE
DESIGNER: ROBERT L. PROPST
HERMAN MILLER, INC.

W 64"
D 19"
H 29"

FL SYSTEM CREDENZA
DESIGNER: DOUGLAS BALL
SUNAR LIMITED

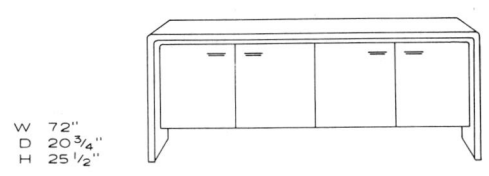

W 72"
D 20¾"
H 25½"

CABINET CREDENZA
DESIGNER: HANS W. WEITZ
DESIGN GROUP, INC.

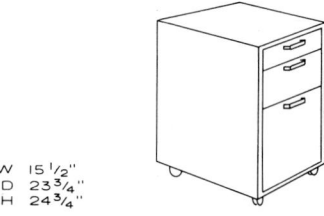

W 15½"
D 23¾"
H 24¾"

OMEGA 3 DRAWER PEDESTAL
DESIGNER: HANS
EICHENBERGER; STENDIG, INC.

Craig Mulford and Jeff Wirt; The Spitznagel Partners; Sioux Falls, South Dakota

TYPICAL SOFA DIMENSIONS

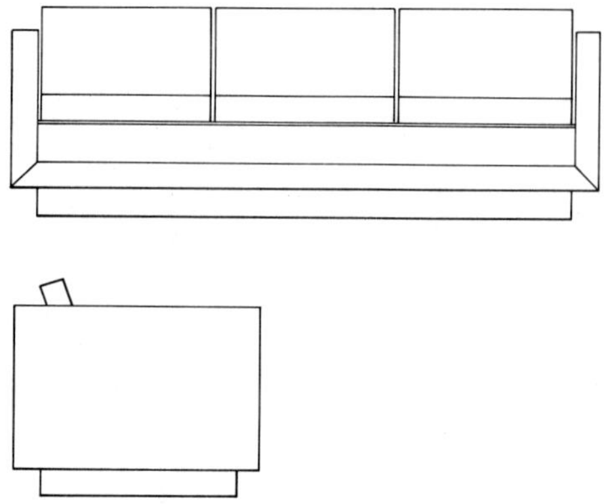

D = 28"-37" AVERAGE 30"

W = 48"-112"

H = 22"-35" AVERAGE 30"

H = 22"-35" AVERAGE 30"

SH = 14"-18" AVERAGE 16"

20"-29" AVERAGE 22"

A. LOOSE PILLOW BACK, TUXEDO ARMS, PLATFORM BASE

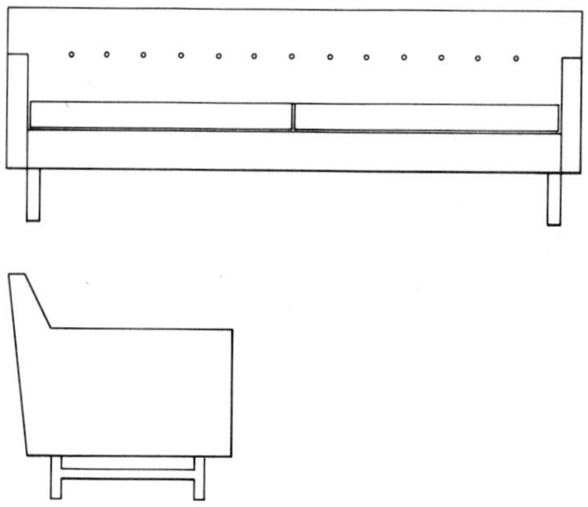

B. LAWSON ARM AND BACK, RUNNER LEGS

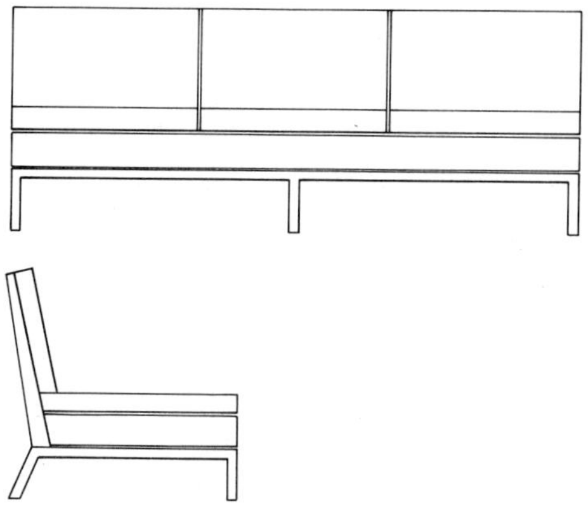

C. ARMLESS, STEEL BASE

SOFA TYPES

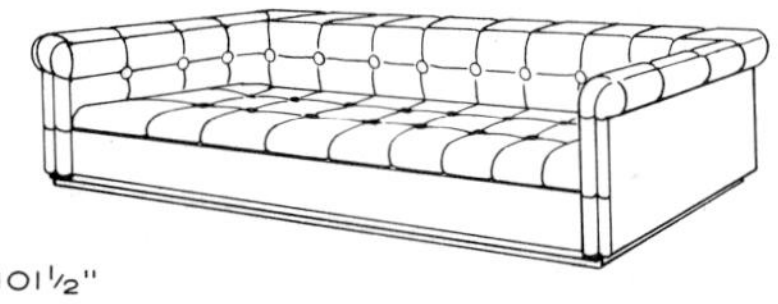

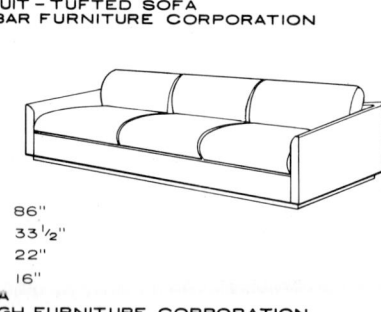

W   101½"
D   36"
H   24"
SH   14"

BISCUIT — TUFTED SOFA
DUNBAR FURNITURE CORPORATION

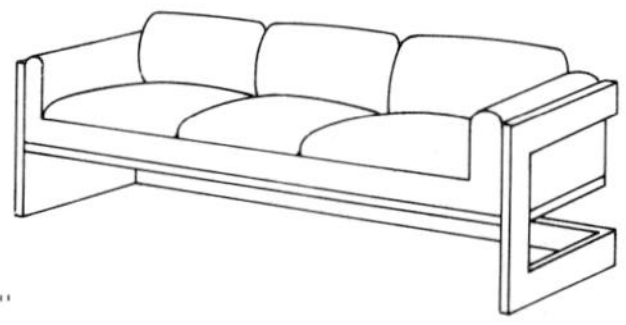

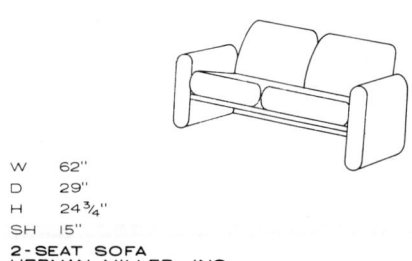

W   82½"
D   31¾"
H   26½"
SH   16½"

RAIMOND 3-SEAT SOFA
STENDIG, INC.

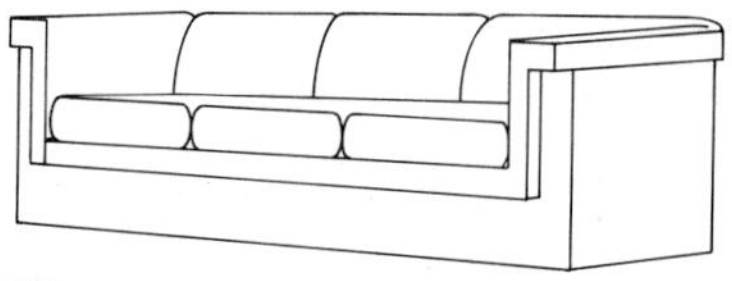

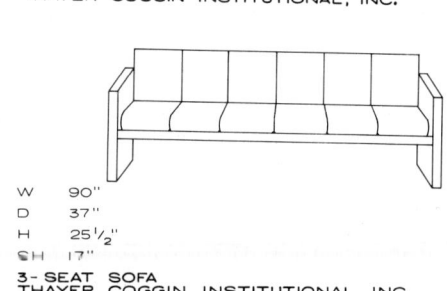

W   83"
D   32"
H   29"
SH   17"

SOFA
THAYER COGGIN INSTITUTIONAL, INC.

W   86"
D   33½"
H   22"
SH   16"

SOFA
LEHIGH FURNITURE CORPORATION

W   62"
D   29"
H   24¾"
SH   15"

2-SEAT SOFA
HERMAN MILLER, INC.

W   90"
D   37"
H   25½"
SH   17"

3-SEAT SOFA
THAYER COGGIN INSTITUTIONAL, INC.

AVAILABLE UNITS
7 TOTAL
2 TYPES SHOWN
SEATING HEIGHTS:
W/ BASE 18"
WITHOUT 16"

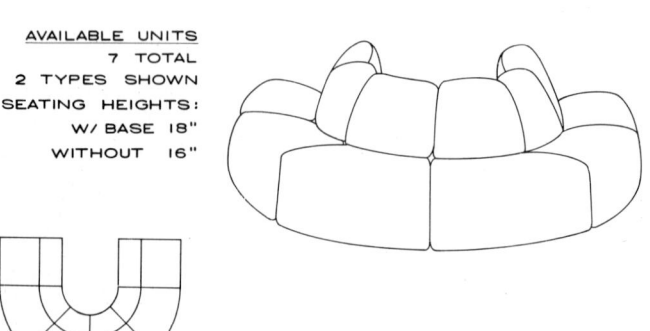

TAPPO SEATING SYSTEM
VECTA CONTRACT

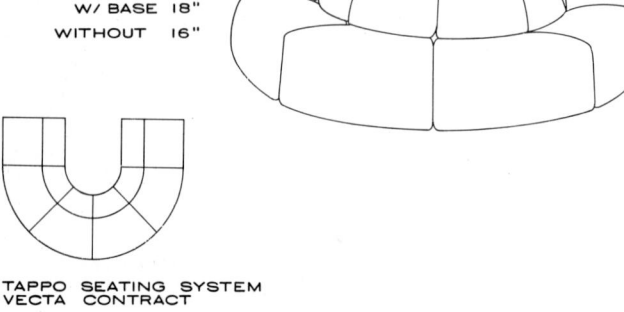

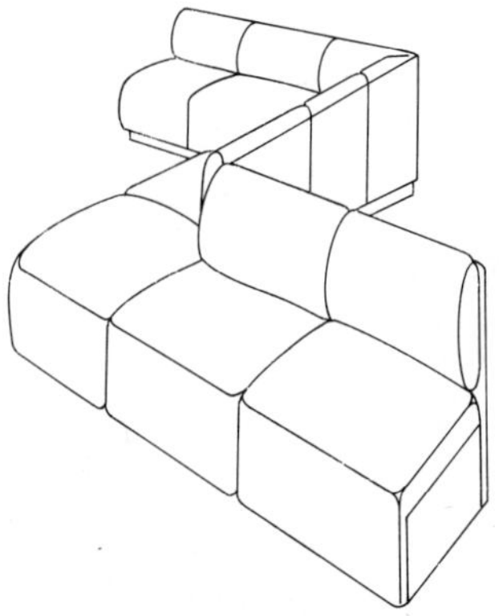

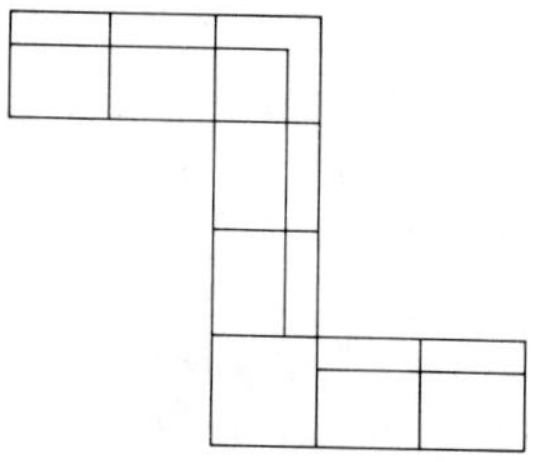

MODULAR LOUNGE SEATING SYSTEM
ATELIER INTERNATIONAL, LTD.

AVAILABLE UNITS
10 TOTAL
5 TYPES SHOWN
SEATING HEIGHT:
17¾"

Craig Mulford and Jeff Wirt; The Spitznagel Partners; Sioux Falls, South Dakota
ISD Incorporated; Chicago, New York, Boston, Houston

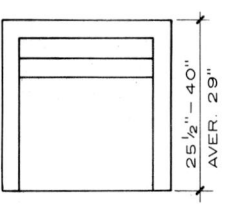
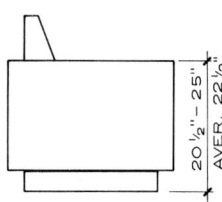
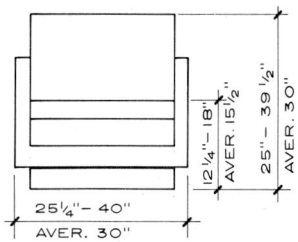

TYPICAL LOUNGE CHAIR DIMENSIONS

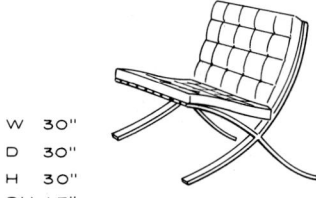

W 30"
D 30"
H 30"
SH 17"

BARCELONA CHAIR
DESIGNER: LUDWIG MIES VAN
DER ROHE
KNOLL INTERNATIONAL, INC.

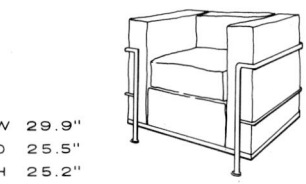

W 29.9"
D 25.5"
H 25.2"
SH 16.9"

GRAND CONFORT
DESIGNER: LE CORBUSIER
ATELIER INTERNATIONAL, LTD.

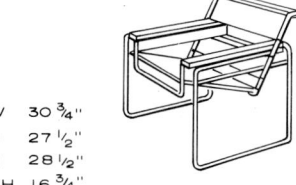

W 30¾"
D 27½"
H 28½"
SH 16¾"

WASSILY CHAIR
DESIGNER: MARCEL BREUER
THONET INDUSTRIES, INC.

W 25⅝"
D 33½"
H 25¼"
SH 13"

ARMCHAIR 41
DESIGNER: ALVAR AALTO
ICF, INC.

W 27"
D 30"
H 28"
SH 13½"

CLAVERDON LOUNGE CHAIR
DESIGNER: MAURICE BURKE
HANK LOEWENSTEIN, INC.

W 35½"
D 41⅜"
H 28"
SH 16½"

SORIANA ARMLESS CHAIR
DESIGNERS: AFRA & TOBIA SCARPA
ATELIER INTERNATIONAL, LTD.

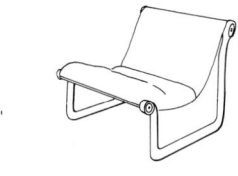

W 28½"
D 34"
H 26"
SH 16"

LOUNGE CHAIR
DESIGNERS: ANDREW MORRISON &
BRUCE HANNAH
KNOLL INTERNATIONAL, INC.

W 36¼"
D 34⅝"
H 31½"
SH 17"

CIPREA ARMCHAIR
DESIGNERS: AFRA &
TOBIA SCARPA
ATELIER INTERNATIONAL, LTD.

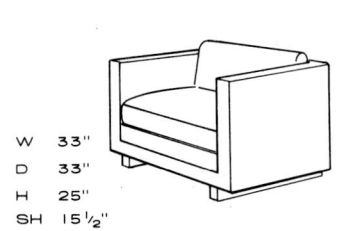

W 33"
D 33"
H 25"
SH 15½"

LOUNGE CHAIR
DESIGNER: WARD BENNETT
BRICKEL ASSOCIATES, INC.

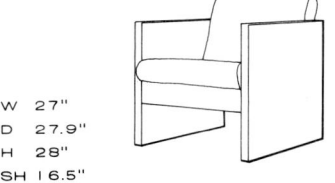

W 27"
D 27.9"
H 28"
SH 16.5"

BUTCHER BLOCK LOUNGE CHAIR
DESIGNER: THOUHY DESIGN STAFF
THOUHY FURNITURE CORPORATION

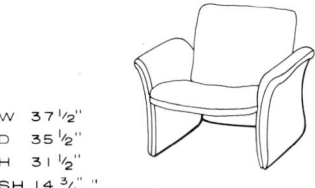

W 37½"
D 35½"
H 31½"
SH 14¾"

BYRON LOUNGE CHAIR
DESIGNERS: ERNST LUTHY &
URS FELBER
STENDIG, INC.

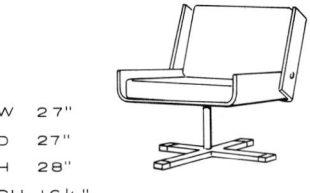

W 27"
D 27"
H 28"
SH 16½"

VARI-PULKKA LOUNGE CHAIR
DESIGNER: IIMARI LAPPALAINEN
STENDIG, INC.

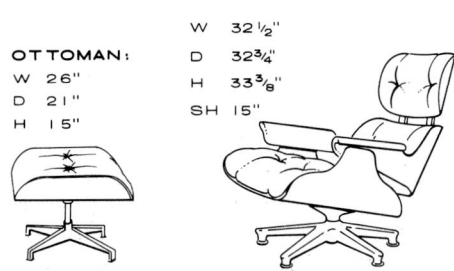

OTTOMAN:
W 26"
D 21"
H 15"

W 32½"
D 32¾"
H 33⅜"
SH 15"

EAMES LOUNGE CHAIR
DESIGNER: CHARLES EAMES
HERMAN MILLER, INC.

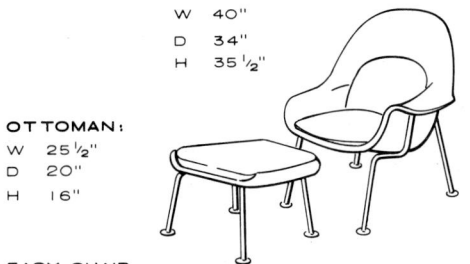

W 40"
D 34"
H 35½"

OTTOMAN:
W 25½"
D 20"
H 16"

EASY CHAIR
DESIGNER: EERO SAARINEN
KNOLL INTERNATIONAL, INC.

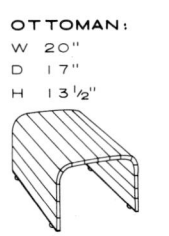

OTTOMAN:
W 20"
D 17"
H 13½"

W 24"
D 30"
H 42"
SH 19½"

IDG HIGH BACK CHAIR
DESIGNERS: JOE RUSSO AND
RIC SONDER
THONET INDUSTRIES, INC.

John R. Hoke, Jr., AIA, Architect; Washington, D.C.

Craig Mulford and Jeff Wirt; The Spitznagel Partners; Sioux Falls, South Dakota

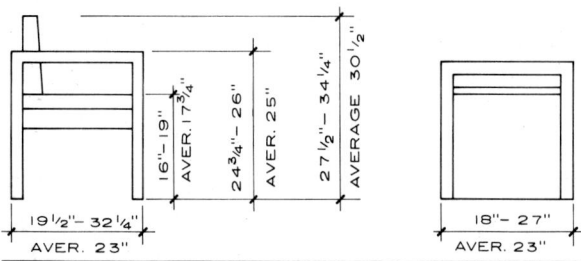

16"–19" AVER. 17¾"
24¾"–26" AVER. 25"
27½"–34¼" AVERAGE 30½"
19½"–32¼" AVER. 23"
18"–27" AVER. 23"

ARM CHAIR DIMENSIONS

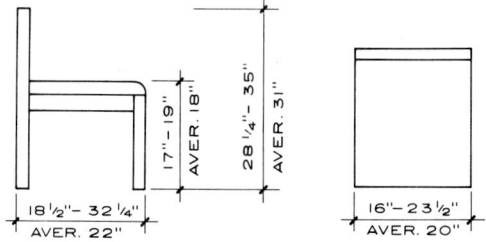

17"–19" AVER. 18"
28¼"–35" AVER. 31"
18½"–32¼" AVER. 22"
16"–23½" AVER. 20"

SIDE CHAIR DIMENSIONS

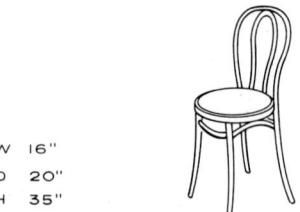

W 16"
D 20"
H 35"

VIENNA CHAIR
DESIGNER: MICHAEL THONET
THONET INDUSTRIES, INC.

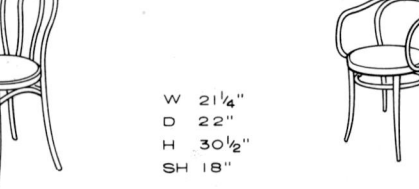

W 21¼"
D 22"
H 30½"
SH 18"

CORBUSIER ARM CHAIR
DESIGNER: MICHAEL THONET
THONET INDUSTRIES, INC.

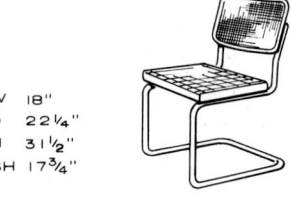

W 18"
D 22¼"
H 31½"
SH 17¾"

CESSA
DESIGNER: MARCEL BREUER
KNOLL INTERNATIONAL, INC.

W 26"
D 23½"
H 32"
SH 18½"

SAARINEN CHAIR
DESIGNER: EERO SAARINEN
KNOLL INTERNATIONAL, INC.

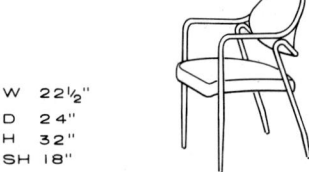

W 22½"
D 24"
H 32"
SH 18"

PETITT ARM CHAIR
DESIGNER: DON PETITT
KNOLL INTERNATIONAL, INC.

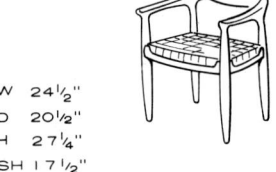

W 24½"
D 20½"
H 27¼"
SH 17½"

THE CHAIR
DESIGNER: HANS WAGNERS
KNOLL INTERNATIONAL, INC.

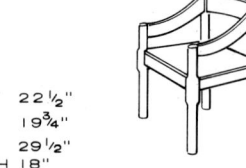

W 22½"
D 19¾"
H 29½"
SH 18"

MAGISTRETTI CHAIR
DESIGNER: VICO MAGISTRETTI
ATELIER INTERNATIONAL, LTD.

W 24"
D 24½"
H 31½"
SH 16"

ARMCHAIR 45
DESIGNER: ALVAR AALTO
ICF, INC.

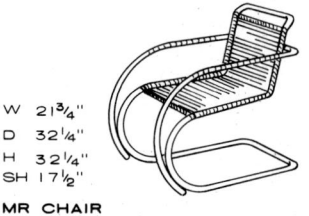

W 21¾"
D 32¼"
H 32¼"
SH 17½"

MR CHAIR
DESIGNER: MIES VAN DER ROHE
STENDIG, INC.

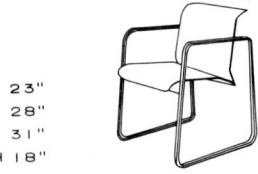

W 23"
D 28"
H 31"
SH 18"

TUBULAR CHAIR
DESIGNER: PETER PROTZMAN
HERMAN MILLER, INC.

W 22"
D 21¼"
H 33"
SH 18½"

EAMES ARM CHAIR
DESIGNER: CHARLES EAMES
HERMAN MILLER, INC.

W 23"
D 23"
H 31"
SH 17½"

BRNO CHAIR
DESIGNER: MIES VAN DER ROHE
KNOLL INTERNATIONAL, INC.

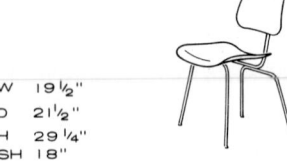

W 19½"
D 21½"
H 29¼"
SH 18"

LCM CHAIR
DESIGNER: CHARLES EAMES
HERMAN MILLER, INC.

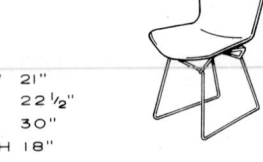

W 21"
D 22½"
H 30"
SH 18"

BERTOIA SIDE CHAIR
DESIGNER: HARRY BERTOIA
KNOLL INTERNATIONAL, INC.

W 21½"
D 22"
H 31½"
SH 17½"

ZETA ARM CHAIR
DESIGNER: ARTHUR UMANOFF
THONET INDUSTRIES, INC.

W 18½"
D 22"
H 32¼"
SH 18½"

SWIVEL CHAIR
DESIGNER: CHARLES EAMES
HERMAN MILLER, INC.

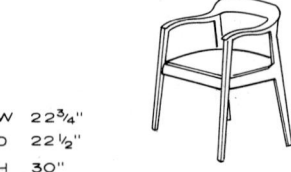

W 22¾"
D 22½"
H 30"
SH 18"

RIEMERSCHMID CHAIR
DESIGNER: RICHARD RIEMERSCHMID
DUNBAR FURNITURE CORPORATION

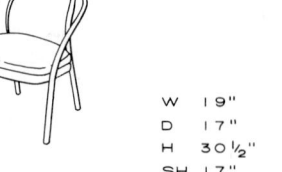

W 24½"
D 27"
H 30"
SH 22"

BENTWOOD CLUB CHAIR
DESIGNER: PAUL TUTTLE
THONET INDUSTRIES, INC.

W 19"
D 17"
H 30½"
SH 17"

PADOVA CHAIR
DESIGNER: STUDIO TIPI
HANK LOEWENSTEIN, INC.

W 17¾"
D 15¼"
H 41"
SH 16½"

WILLOW, 2 - DESIGNER:
CHARLES R. MACKINTOSH
ATELIER INTERNATIONAL, LTD.

John R. Hoke, Jr., AIA, Architect; Washington, D.C.

Craig Mulford and Jeff Wirt; The Spitznagel Partners; Sioux Falls, South Dakota

 12   **FURNITURE**

W 23"
D 28"
H 26½"

LOUNGE CHAIR
KNOLL INTERNATIONAL

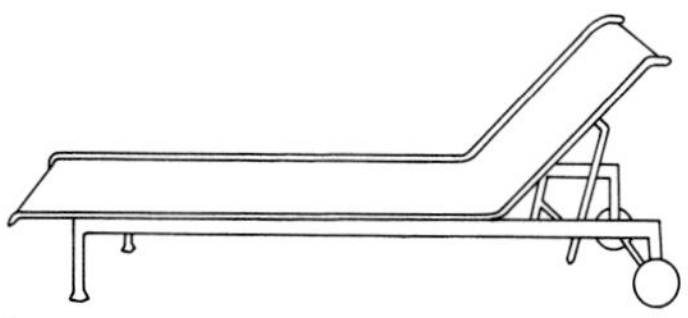

W 25½"
D 76"
H 14½" / 35½"

CHAISE LOUNGE
KNOLL INTERNATIONAL

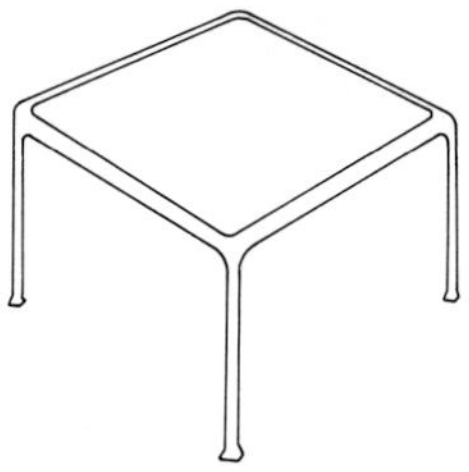

W 38"
D 38"
H 26¼"

DINING TABLE
KNOLL INTERNATIONAL

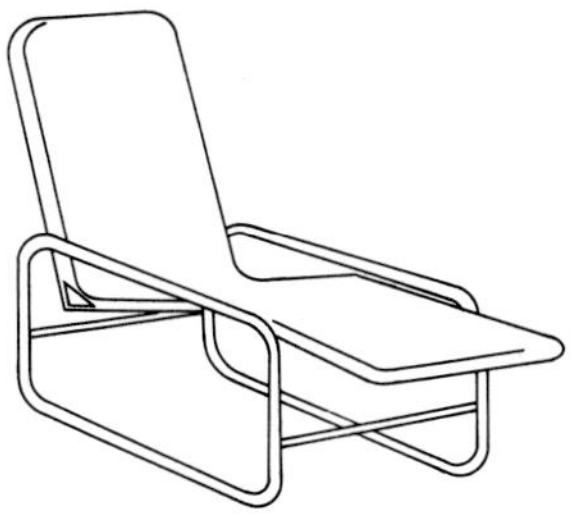

W 25"
D 80"
H 20⅝"

CHAISE LOUNGE
SAMSONITE CORPORATION

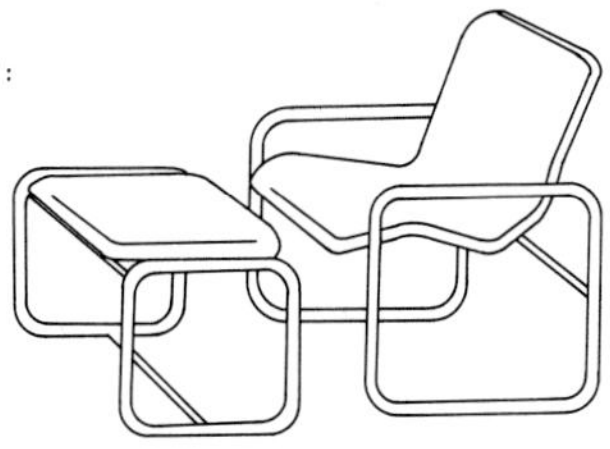

OTTOMAN:
W 25"
D 17"
H 17¾"

W 25"
D 31½"
H 35"

LOUNGE CHAIR
SAMSONITE CORPORATION

W 21"
D 22"
H 30"

SIDE CHAIR
KNOLL INTERNATIONAL

W 26"
L 74"

CHAISE LOUNGE
TELESCOPE FOLDING FURNITURE CO., INC.

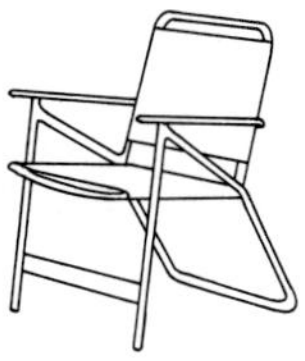

W 30⅛"
L 70"
H 28"

ARM CHAIR
TELESCOPE FOLDING FURNITURE CO., INC.

W 24"
D 18"
H 31"
SH 16½"

DIRECTOR'S CHAIR
GOLDMEDAL, INCORPORATED

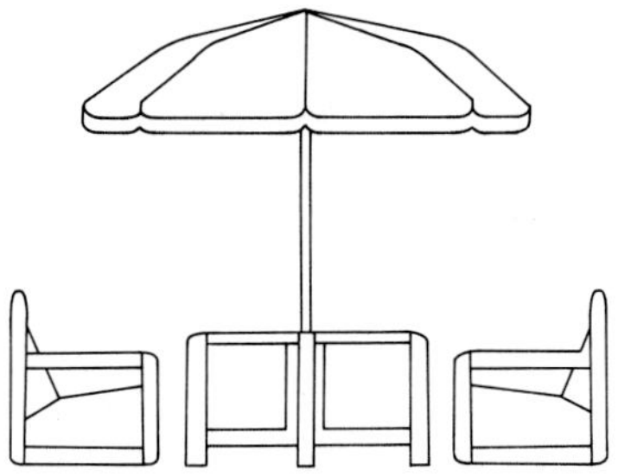

CHAIR:
W 21¾"
D 24"
H 34¼"

TABLE:
D 42"
H 27"

UMBRELLA:
D 84½"
H 96"

TABLE, UMBRELLA, AND CHAIRS
SAMSONITE CORPORATION

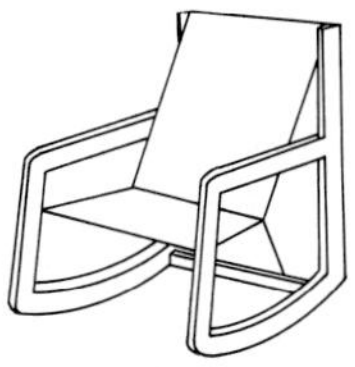

W 25½"
D 34½"
H 32"

ROCKER
SAMSONITE CORPORATION

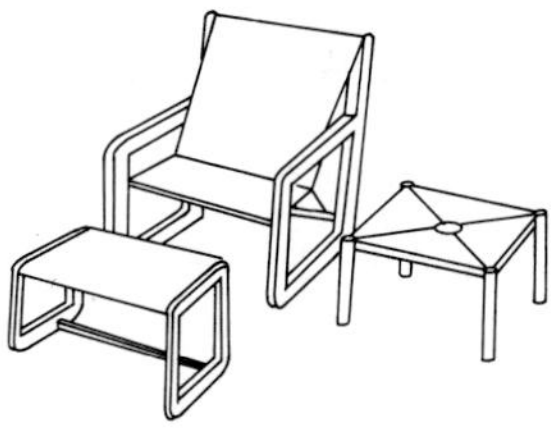

W 25½"
D 30"
H 34¼"

OTTOMAN:
W 25½"
D 30"
H 34¼"

TABLE:
W 27¾"
D 17¾"
H 15¼"

LOUNGE CHAIR
SAMSONITE CORPORATION

W 23"
L 70"
H 33½"

LAWN BENCH
VANDY-CRAFT INCORPORATED

W 48½"
D 28½"
H 32"

SANS SOUCI SETTEE
VANDY-CRAFT INCORPORATED

BENCH:
W 10⅛"
L 68"
H 16"

RUSTIC WIDE TABLE
LITTLE LAKE INDUSTRIES

ISD Incorporated; Chicago, New York, Boston, Houston

FURNITURE **12**

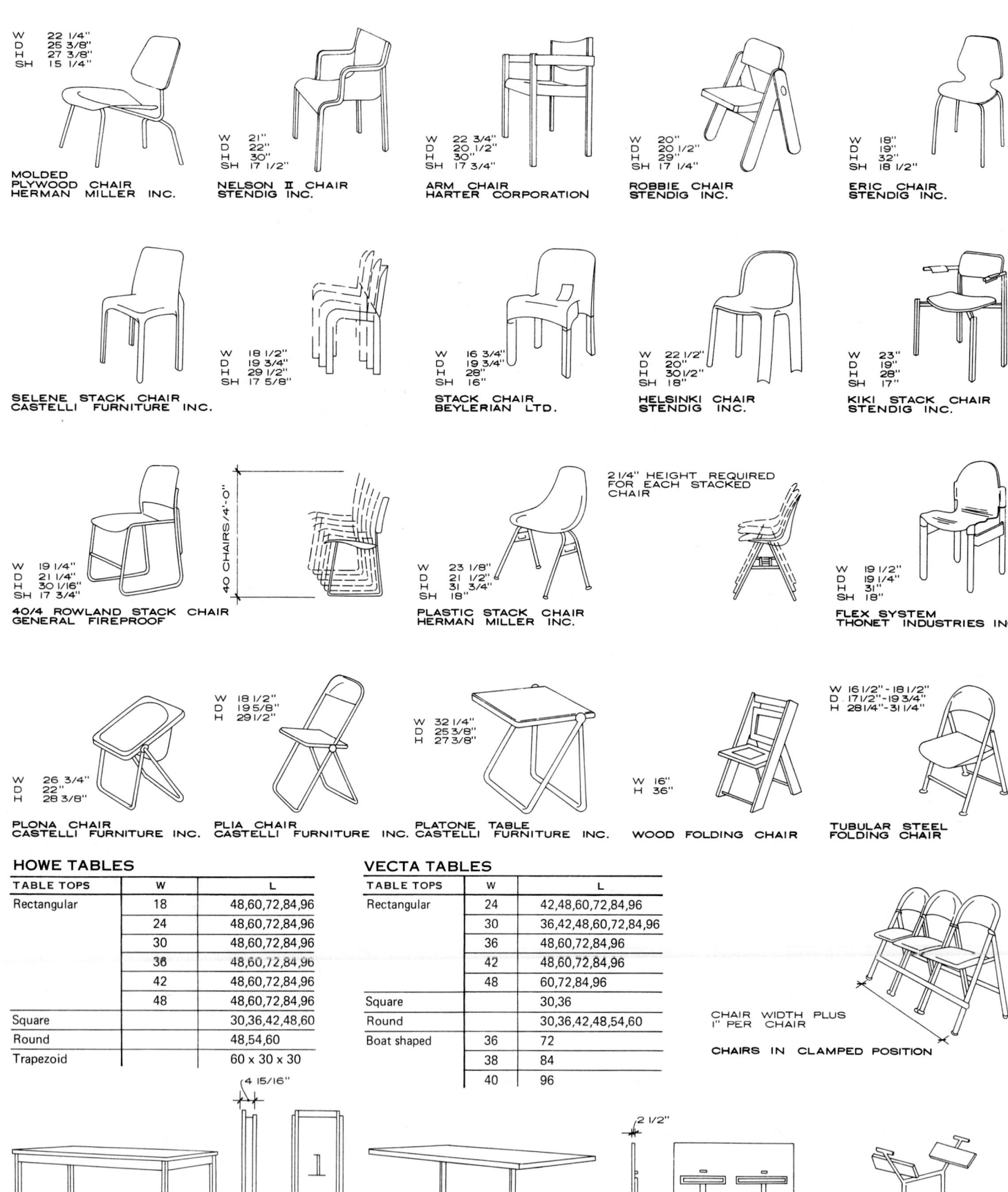

W 22 1/4"
D 25 3/8"
H 27 3/8"
SH 15 1/4"

MOLDED
PLYWOOD CHAIR
HERMAN MILLER INC.

W 21"
D 22"
H 30"
SH 17 1/2"

NELSON II CHAIR
STENDIG INC.

W 22 3/4"
D 20 1/2"
H 30"
SH 17 3/4"

ARM CHAIR
HARTER CORPORATION

W 20"
D 20 1/2"
H 29"
SH 17 1/4"

ROBBIE CHAIR
STENDIG INC.

W 18"
D 19"
H 32"
SH 18 1/2"

ERIC CHAIR
STENDIG INC.

W 18 1/2"
D 19 3/4"
H 29 1/2"
SH 17 5/8"

SELENE STACK CHAIR
CASTELLI FURNITURE INC.

W 16 3/4"
D 19 3/4"
H 28"
SH 16"

STACK CHAIR
BEYLERIAN LTD.

W 22 1/2"
D 20"
H 30 1/2"
SH 18"

HELSINKI CHAIR
STENDIG INC.

W 23"
D 19"
H 28"
SH 17"

KIKI STACK CHAIR
STENDIG INC.

W 19 1/4"
D 21 1/4"
H 30 1/16"
SH 17 3/4"

40/4 ROWLAND STACK CHAIR
GENERAL FIREPROOF

40 CHAIRS/4'-0"

2 1/4" HEIGHT REQUIRED
FOR EACH STACKED
CHAIR

W 23 1/8"
D 21 1/2"
H 31 3/4"
SH 18"

PLASTIC STACK CHAIR
HERMAN MILLER INC.

W 19 1/2"
D 19 1/4"
H 31"
SH 18"

FLEX SYSTEM
THONET INDUSTRIES INC.

W 26 3/4"
D 22"
H 28 3/8"

PLONA CHAIR
CASTELLI FURNITURE INC.

W 18 1/2"
D 19 5/8"
H 29 1/2"

PLIA CHAIR
CASTELLI FURNITURE INC.

W 32 1/4"
D 25 3/8"
H 27 3/8"

PLATONE TABLE
CASTELLI FURNITURE INC.

W 16"
H 36"

WOOD FOLDING CHAIR

W 16 1/2"-18 1/2"
D 17 1/2"-19 3/4"
H 28 1/4"-31 1/4"

TUBULAR STEEL
FOLDING CHAIR

HOWE TABLES

TABLE TOPS	W	L
Rectangular	18	48,60,72,84,96
	24	48,60,72,84,96
	30	48,60,72,84,96
	36	48,60,72,84,96
	42	48,60,72,84,96
	48	48,60,72,84,96
Square		30,36,42,48,60
Round		48,54,60
Trapezoid		60 x 30 x 30

VECTA TABLES

TABLE TOPS	W	L
Rectangular	24	42,48,60,72,84,96
	30	36,42,48,60,72,84,96
	36	48,60,72,84,96
	42	48,60,72,84,96
	48	60,72,84,96
Square		30,36
Round		30,36,42,48,54,60
Boat shaped	36	72
	38	84
	40	96

CHAIR WIDTH PLUS
1" PER CHAIR

CHAIRS IN CLAMPED POSITION

4 15/16"

FOLDING TABLE
HOWE FURNITURE CORP.

2 1/2"

TILT TOP TABLE
VECTA CONTRACT

W 31"
L 50 1/2"
H 37 1/2"

TABLE CART
VECTA CONTRACT

ISD Incorporated; Chicago, New York, Boston, Houston

TYPICAL END OR SIDE TABLE DIMENSIONS (IN.)

DESCRIPTION	DEPTH		WIDTH		HEIGHT	
	MIN.	MAX.	MIN.	MAX.	MIN.	MAX.
RECTANGULAR	19	28	21	48	17	28
SQUARE	15	32	15	32	17	28
ROUND	16	30	16	30	18	22½

TYPICAL LOW TABLE DIMENSIONS (IN.)

DESCRIPTION	DEPTH		WIDTH		HEIGHT	
	MIN.	MAX.	MIN.	MAX.	MIN.	MAX.
RECTANGULAR	15½	24	21	86	12	18
SQUARE	36	42	32	42	15	17
ROUND	30	42	20	42	15	16½

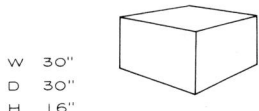

W 30"
D 30"
H 16"

CUBE TABLE
STENDIG INC.

W 39½"
D 39½"
H 12"

TABLE
ATELIER INTERNATIONAL, LTD.

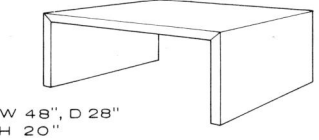

W 48", D 28"
H 20"

PANEL TABLE
INTREX INC.

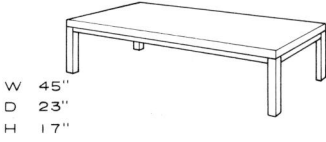

W 45"
D 23"
H 17"

COFFEE TABLE
KNOLL ASSOCIATES, INC.

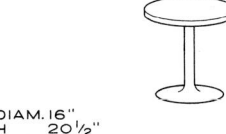

DIAM. 16"
H   20½"

SIDE TABLE
KNOLL ASSOCIATES

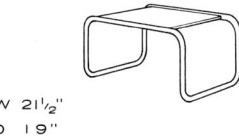

W 21½"
D 19"
H 17½"

BREUER TABLE
STENDIG INC.

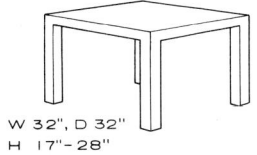

W 32", D 32"
H 17"-28"

PARSONS TABLE
DIRECTIONAL

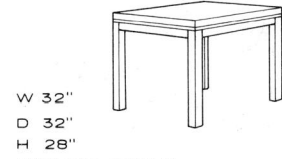

W 32"
D 32"
H 28"

SQUARE TABLE
JENS RISOM

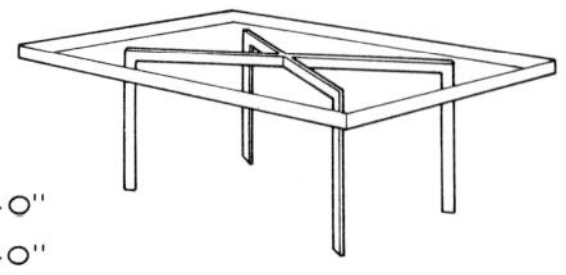

W 40"
D 40"
H 17"

BARCELONA TABLE
KNOLL ASSOCIATES, INC.

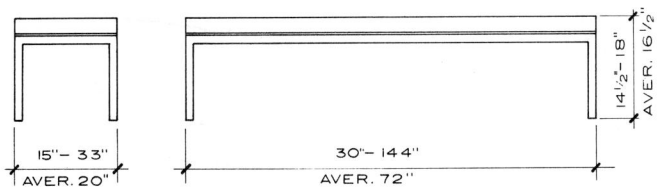

15"- 33"
AVER. 20"

30"- 144"
AVER. 72"

14½"-18"
AVER. 16½"

BENCH DIMENSIONS

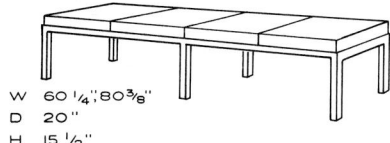

W 60¼", 80⅜"
D 20"
H 15½"

BENCH
KNOLL ASSOCIATES, INC.

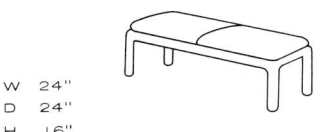

W 24"
D 24"
H 16"

TUBO BENCH
VECTA CONTRACT

W 54" TO 90"
D 20"
H 18"

BENCH
LEHIGH FURNITURE CORP.

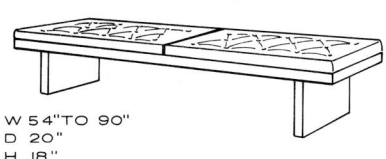

W 48⅜"
D 21⅜"
H 17¼"

BENCH
ALL-STEEL, INC.

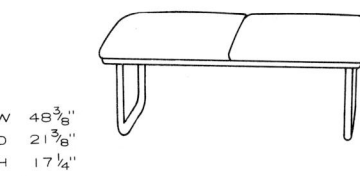

TYPICAL RUG SIZES

	WIDTH	LENGTH
AREA RUGS		
Rectangular	3'	5'
	4'	6'
	6'	8', 9'
	9'	12'
	12'	14', 15', 18'
Square and round	4'	4'
	6'	6'
	9'	9'
	12'	12'
HEMP RUGS	6'	9'
	8'	10'
	9'	12', 36' rolls
	12'	15'
HANDWOVEN RUGS (such as RYA)	2'	2'-4'', 4'
	3'-4''	4', 5'-10''
	4'	4'-5'', 5', 6'-8''
	5'	6'-8'', 8'-4''
	6'-8''	8'-4'', 10'
	9'-10''	13'
ORIENTAL		
Moroccan	4'	6'
	6'	9'
	9'	12'
	12'	15', 18'
Persian		
Dozar	4'-3''	6'-11''
Kellegi	5'-11''	16'-4''
Kenareh	3'	8' to 20'
Pushti	2'	3'
Qali	5'-11''	10'
Yastik	10'' to 1'-3''	1'-8'' to 2'-7''
Zarcherek	2'-4''	4'-7''
Zaronim	3'-5''	5'

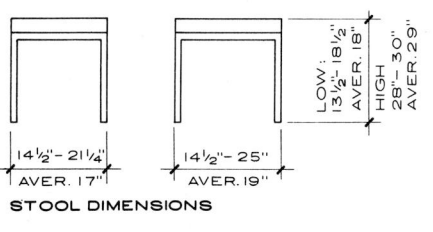

LOW: 13½"-18½" AVER. 18"
HIGH: 28"-30" AVER. 29"

14½"- 21¼"
AVER. 17"

14½"- 25"
AVER. 19"

STOOL DIMENSIONS

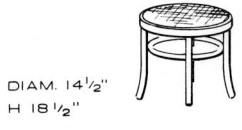

DIAM. 14½"
H 18½"

BENTWOOD STOOL
STENDIG INC.

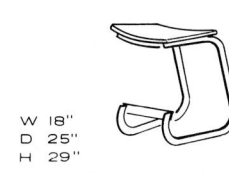

W 18"
D 25"
H 29"

BAR STOOL
STENDIG INC.

W 18½"
D 24"
H 41"
SH 30"

BAR STOOL
SHELBY WILLIAMS
INDUSTRIES, INC.

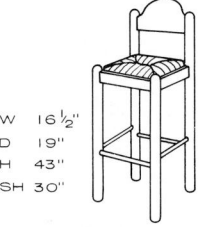

W 16½"
D 19"
H 43"
SH 30"

PADOVA BAR
STOOL. HANK
LOEWENSTEIN, INC.

Craig Mulford and Jeff Wirt; The Spitznagel Partners; Sioux Falls, South Dakota

ISD Incorporated; Chicago, New York, Boston, Houston

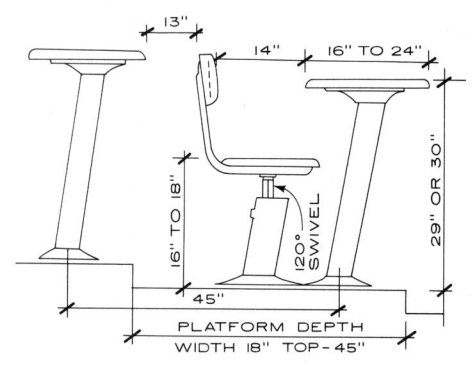

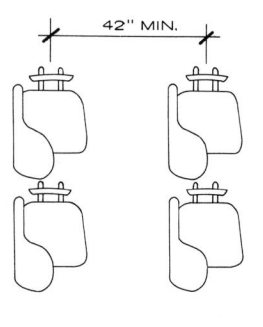

TYPICAL VERTICAL ARRANGEMENT

FIXED ARMS   **FOLDING ARMS**

TYPICAL HORIZONTAL ARRANGEMENTS

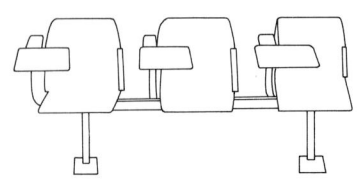

**PEDESTAL HORIZONTAL SEATING
AMERICAN SEATING CO.**

**ACTON STACKER
AMERICAN SEATING CO.**

**DOUBLE ENTRY STUDY
AMERICAN SEATING CO,**

**TABLET ARM CHAIR
AMERICAN SEATING CO,**

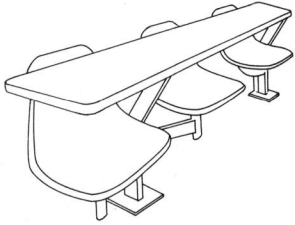

**SATELITE SEATING
HEYWOOD WAKEFIELD**

**LIFT LID TABLE AND CHAIR
AMERICAN SEATING CO.**

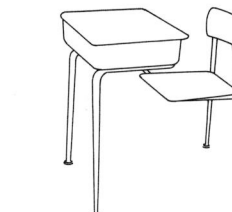

**CLASSROOM UNIT
HEYWOOD WAKEFIELD**

**DESK WITH CHAIR
HEYWOOD WAKEFIELD**

**AUDITORIUM SEATING UNIT
HEYWOOD WAKEFIELD**

**CLASSROOM TYPING TABLE
HEYWOOD WAKEFIELD**

**DESK
HEYWOOD WAKEFIELD**

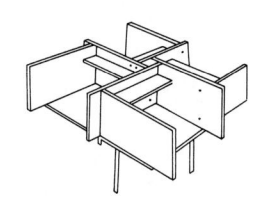

**STUDY CARRELS
HOWE FURNITURE CORP.**

Wall Pockets:

1. Fully recessed.
2. Partially recessed.
3. Surface mounted.

NOTE: When folded, five sets can be stored on a floor area 5 x 5 ft. When nesting tables without benches, allow storage depth of 12 in. per table.

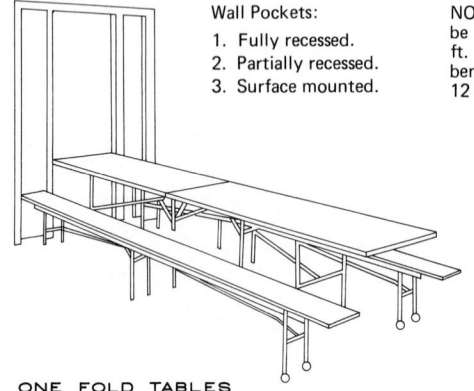

**ONE FOLD TABLES
WALL-FOL**

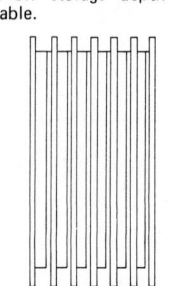

**COMPACT STORAGE
WALL-FOL**

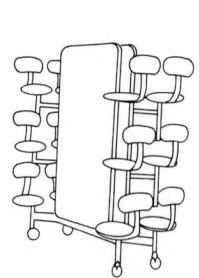

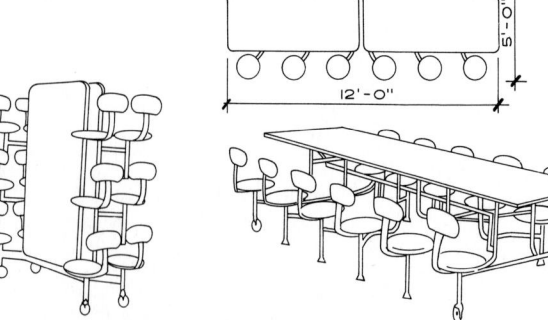

**FOLDING TABLE AND CHAIRS
SICO INCORPORATED**

ISD Incorporated; Chicago, New York, Boston, Houston

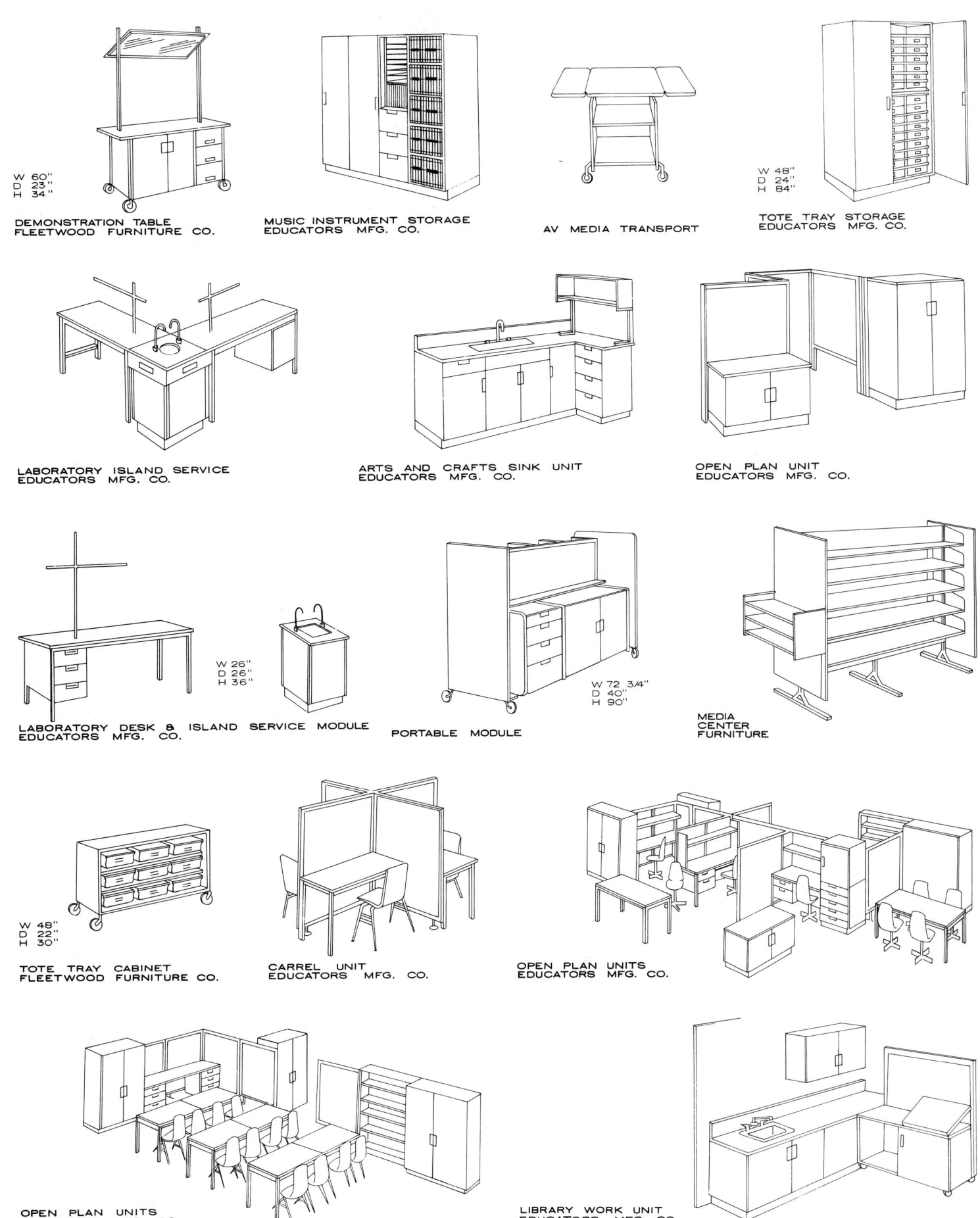

W 60"
D 23"
H 34"

DEMONSTRATION TABLE
FLEETWOOD FURNITURE CO.

MUSIC INSTRUMENT STORAGE
EDUCATORS MFG. CO.

AV MEDIA TRANSPORT

W 48"
D 24"
H 84"

TOTE TRAY STORAGE
EDUCATORS MFG. CO.

LABORATORY ISLAND SERVICE
EDUCATORS MFG. CO.

ARTS AND CRAFTS SINK UNIT
EDUCATORS MFG. CO.

OPEN PLAN UNIT
EDUCATORS MFG. CO.

W 26"
D 26"
H 36"

LABORATORY DESK & ISLAND SERVICE MODULE
EDUCATORS MFG. CO.

PORTABLE MODULE

W 72 3/4"
D 40"
H 90"

MEDIA
CENTER
FURNITURE

W 48"
D 22"
H 30"

TOTE TRAY CABINET
FLEETWOOD FURNITURE CO.

CARREL UNIT
EDUCATORS MFG. CO.

OPEN PLAN UNITS
EDUCATORS MFG. CO.

OPEN PLAN UNITS
EDUCATORS MFG. CO.

LIBRARY WORK UNIT
EDUCATORS MFG. CO.

ISD Incorporated; Chicago, New York, Boston, Houston

ROUND

DIAMETER	CIRCUM.	APPROXIMATE SEATING
8'-0''	25'-1''	10-12
7'-0''	21'-8''	8-10
6'-0''	18'-9''	7-8
5'-0''	15'-7''	6-7
4'-6''	14'-1''	5-6
4'-0''	12'-6''	5-6
3'-6''	11'-0''	4-5

BOAT SHAPED

WIDTH			
CENTER	END	LENGTH	APPROXIMATE SEATING
6'-0''	4'-0''	20'-0''	20-24
5'-6''	4'-0''	18'-0''	18-20
5'-6''	4'-0''	16'-0''	16-18
5'-0''	3'-6''	14'-0''	14-16
4'-6''	3'-6''	12'-0''	12-14
4'-0''	3'-2''	11'-0''	10-12
4'-0''	3'-2''	10'-0''	10-12
3'-6''	3'-0''	9'-0''	8-10
3'-6''	3'-0''	8'-0''	8-10
3'-0''	2'-10''	7'-0''	6-8
3'-0''	2'-10''	6'-0''	6-8

RECTANGULAR TABLE (TYPICAL)

BOAT SHAPED TABLE (TYPICAL)

RECTANGULAR

WIDTH	LENGTH	APPROXIMATE SEATING
5'-0''	20'-0''	20-22
4'-6''	18'-0''	18-20
4'-6''	16'-0''	16-18
4'-6''	14'-0''	14-16
4'-0''	12'-0''	12-14
4'-0''	11'-0''	10-12
4'-0''	10'-0''	10-12
4'-0''	9'-0''	8-10
4'-0''	8'-0''	8-10
3'-6''	9'-0''	8-10
3'-6''	8'-0''	8-10
3'-6''	7'-6''	6-8
3'-6''	7'-0''	6-8
3'-0''	7'-0''	6-8
3'-0''	6'-6''	6-8
2'-6''	5'-6''	4-6
2'-6''	5'-0''	4-6

SQUARE

WIDTH	LENGTH	APPROXIMATE SEATING
5'-0''	5'-0''	8-12
4'-6''	4'-6''	4-8
4'-0''	4'-0''	4-8
3'-6''	3'-6''	4
3'-0''	3'-0''	4

W 72''
D 38''
H 28 1/2''

EXECUTIVE TABLE DESK
KNOLL INTERNATIONAL

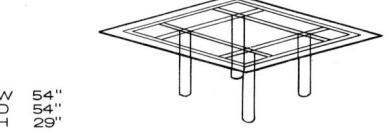

W 54''
D 54''
H 29''

ANDRE TABLE
KNOLL INTERNATIONAL

W 54''
D 30''
H 29 1/4''

OMEGA DESK TABLE
STENDIG INCORPORATED

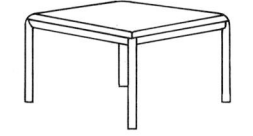

W 47 1/4''
D 47 1/4''
H 28 3/4''

DINING TABLE
KNOLL INTERNATIONAL

D 48''
H 28''

CONFERENCE/DINING TABLE
ZOGRAPHOS DESIGNS LTD.

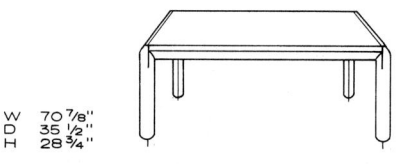

W 70 7/8''
D 35 1/2''
H 28 3/4''

MAGISTRETTI TABLE
ATELIER INTERNATIONAL LTD.

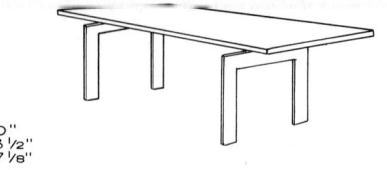

W 90''
D 33 1/2''
H 27 1/8''

CONFERENCE/DINING TABLE
ATELIER INTERNATIONAL LTD.

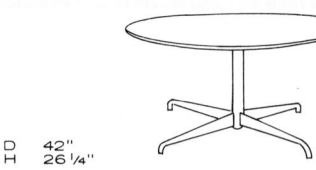

D 42''
H 26 1/4''

EXECUTIVE TABLE
HERMAN MILLER, INCORPORATED

ROUND/OVAL PEDESTAL TABLE
VECTA CONTRACT

D 18''-60''
H 29''

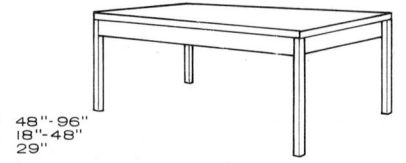

W 48''-96''
D 18''-48''
H 29''

CONFERENCE TABLE
HOWE FURNITURE CORP.

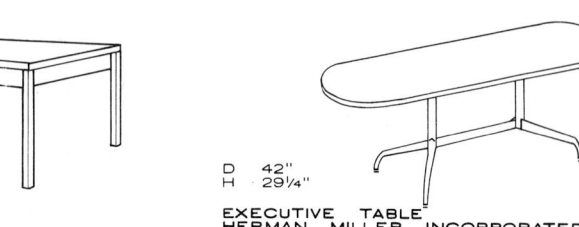

D 42''
H 29 1/4''

EXECUTIVE TABLE
HERMAN MILLER, INCORPORATED

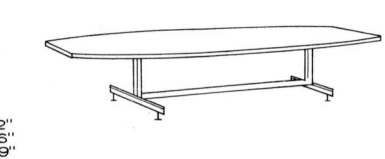

W 72''
D 36''
H 29''

CONFERENCE TABLE
VECTA CONTRACT

ISD Incorporated; Chicago, New York, Boston, Houston

12   FURNITURE

HORIZONTAL BLINDS

TYPE OF SLAT	SIZE		PULLEY OPERATED	OSCILLATING LIFT
1" aluminum	Blind	Maximum width	12'-0"	25'-0"
		Maximum length	10'-0"	25'-0"
		Maximum area	120 sq ft	180 sq ft
		Head box	$1\frac{1}{2}$ to $2\frac{1}{4}$ sq in.	4" × 4"
	Pocket	Width W	$2\frac{1}{2}$"	6"
		Height H	$1\frac{1}{2}$" to $2\frac{1}{4}$" + $\frac{1}{2}$" per linear foot of blind height	4" × $\frac{1}{2}$" per linear foot of blind height
2" aluminum	Blind	Maximum width	16'-0"	20'-0"
		Maximum length	20'-0"	16'-0"
		Maximum area	120 sq ft	245 sq ft
		Head box	2" H × $2\frac{3}{8}$" W	$5\frac{5}{8}$" × $4\frac{7}{8}$"
	Pocket	Width W	$4\frac{1}{2}$"	$7\frac{1}{4}$"
		Height H	$2\frac{1}{2}$" × $\frac{3}{4}$" per linear foot of blind height	$7\frac{3}{4}$" × $\frac{3}{4}$" per linear foot of blind height

NOTE: Pulley operated blinds up to $69\frac{7}{8}$"—single pull. Larger blinds—compound pull.

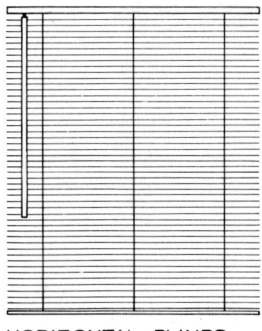
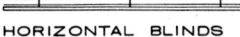
HORIZONTAL BLINDS

VERTICAL BLINDS

NOTES
1. Blinds available to fit most geometric shapes.
2. Use of light colored fabric or venetian blinds reduces solar heat gain.
3. Solid insulated shutters may be installed for control of heat loss.

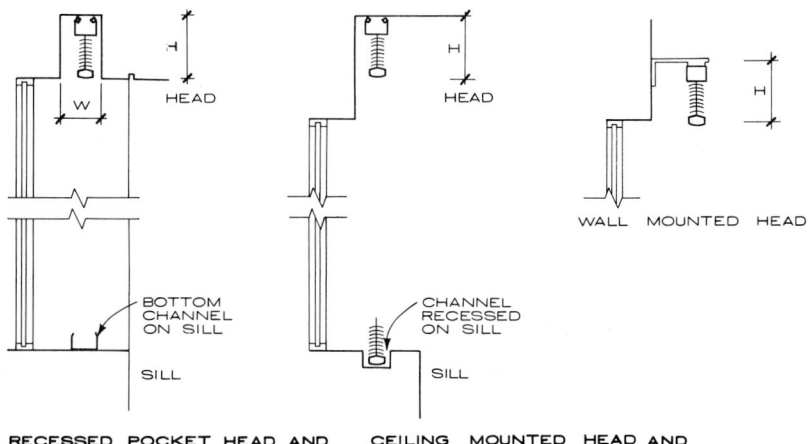

RECESSED POCKET HEAD AND SURFACE MOUNTED SILL

CEILING MOUNTED HEAD AND RECESSED SILL

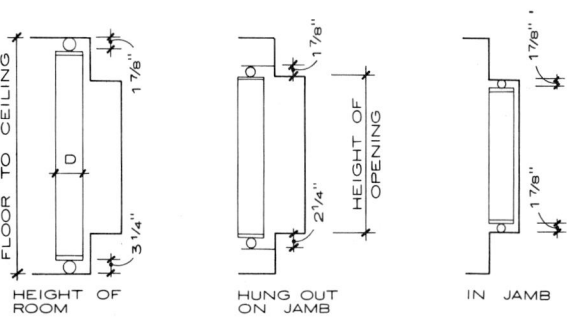

HEIGHT OF ROOM

HUNG OUT ON JAMB

IN JAMB

VERTICAL BLINDS

Single span width limit	16'-0"
Height	Up to 25'-0"
Depth of vane D	$3\frac{1}{2}$" to $7\frac{1}{2}$"; metal: 4" to 7"

DRAPERIES AND DRAPERY HARDWARE

TWO-CHANNEL EXTRUDED ALUMINUM TRACK; CORD PULL FLUSH, RECESSED, OR BRACKET MOUNTED

Maximum length—two-way draw	42'-0"
Maximum length—one-way draw	30'-0"
Maximum length—multiple draw	64'-0"
Maximum fabric weight—two-way	110 lb
Maximum farbic weight—one-way	80 lb
Maximum fabric weight—multiple	160 lb
Projection and brackets required	$\frac{3}{4}$" to "E" projection 48" o.c. typical; 24" o.c. at ends
Curve	12" radius
Pleat spacing	4" to 6"
Ceiling pocket for drapery only	5" front to back minimum

NOTE: Wand available for manual pull. Hand pull rarely used except for hospital cubicle curtains.

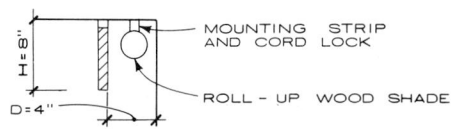

MOUNTING STRIP AND CORD LOCK

ROLL-UP WOOD SHADE

DEPTH OF POCKET REQUIRED = DIAM. + $\frac{1}{2}$"
HEIGHT OF POCKET REQUIRED = DIAM. + $2\frac{1}{2}$"

ROLL-UP WOOD SHADES

SHADE HEIGHT	DIAMETER ROLLED	SHADE HEIGHT	DIAMETER ROLLED
3'-0"	$3\frac{1}{2}$"	7'-0"	$4\frac{3}{4}$"
4'-0"	$3\frac{3}{4}$"	8'-0"	5"
5'-0"	4"	9'-0"	$5\frac{1}{8}$"
6'-0"	$4\frac{3}{8}$"	10'-0"	$5\frac{1}{2}$"

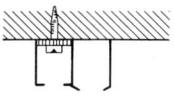

CEILING INSTALLATION

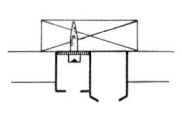

RECESSED PLASTER OR ACOUSTICAL TILE INSTALLATION

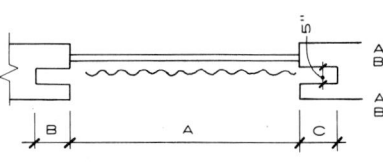

POCKET INSTALLATION

AT ONE-WAY DRAW
B OR C = $\frac{1}{2}$A

AT TWO-WAY DRAW
B + C = $\frac{1}{2}$A

Fullness of fabric lining and pleating determines exact width of gathering space (bunching). For 100% fullness (double width): basic allowance = $\frac{1}{3}$ of window width. For bunching this includes overlap and pulleys.

ISD Incorporated; Chicago, New York, Boston, Houston

FURNITURE 12

CHAPTER 13 SPECIAL CONSTRUCTION

FLOOR STRUCTURE ASSEMBLIES FOR ADDITIONAL INFORMATION CONSULT MANUFACTURERS' LITERATURE AND TRADE ASSOCIATIONS		DEPTH OF SYSTEM (IN.)	STANDARD MEMBER SIZES (IN.)	DEAD LOAD OF STRUCTURE (PSF)	SUITABLE LIVE LOAD RANGE (PSF)	SPAN RANGE (FT)	DIMENSIONAL STABILITY AFFECTED BY
WOOD JOIST	PLYWOOD SUBFLOOR / WOOD JOIST / CEILING	7–13	Nominal joist 2 x 6, 8, 10, and 12	5–8	30–40	Up to 18	Deflection
WOOD TRUSS OR PLYWOOD JOIST	PLYWOOD SUBFLOOR / PLYWOOD JOIST (OR WOOD TRUSS) / CEILING	13–21	Plywood joists 12, 14, 16, 18, and 20	6–12	30–40	12–30	Deflection
WOOD BEAM AND PLANK	WOOD PLANK / WOOD BEAM	10–22	Nominal plank 2, 3, and 4	6–16	30–40	10–22	—
LAMINATED WOOD BEAM AND PLANK	WOOD PLANK / GLUE LAMINATED WOOD BEAM	8–22	Nominal plank 2, 3, and 4	6–20	30–40	8–34	—
STEEL JOIST	PLYWOOD SUBFLOOR / WOOD NAILER / STEEL JOIST / CEILING	9–31	Steel joists 8–30	8–20	30–40	16–40	Deflection
STEEL JOIST	CONCRETE SLAB / STEEL CENTERING / STEEL JOIST / CEILING	11–75	Steel joists 8–72	30–110	30–100	16–60 (up to 130)	Deflection
LIGHT-WEIGHT STEEL FRAME	PLYWOOD SUBFLOOR / LIGHTWEIGHT STEEL FRAME / CEILING	7–12	Consult manufacturers' literature	6–20	30–60	10–22	—
STEEL FRAME	CONCRETE SLAB / STEEL CENTERING / STEEL BEAM / CEILING	9–15	—	35–60	30–100	16–35	Deflection
STEEL FRAME	CONCRETE TOPPING / PRECAST CONCRETE PLANK / STEEL BEAM / CEILING	8–16	Concrete plank 16–48 W 4–12 D	40–75	60–150	Up to 50 Generally below 35	Deflection and creep
PRECAST CONCRETE	CONCRETE TOPPING / PRECAST CONCRETE PLANK / CONCRETE BEAM	6–12	Concrete plank 16–48 W 4–12 D	40–75	60–150	Up to 60 Generally below 35	Deflection and creep
ONE–WAY CONCRETE SLAB	CONCRETE SLAB / CONCRETE BEAM	4–10	—	50–120	40–150	10–20 More with prestressing	—
TWO–WAY CONCRETE SLAB	CONCRETE SLAB / CONCRETE BEAM	4–10	—	50–120	40–250	10–30 More with prestressing	—
ONE–WAY RIBBED CONCRETE SLAB	CONCRETE SLAB / RIB (JOIST)	8–22	Standard pan forms 20 and 30 W 6–20 D	40–90	40–150	15–50 More with prestressing	Creep
TWO–WAY RIBBED CONCRETE SLAB	CONCRETE SLAB / RIB (JOIST)	8–22	Standard dome forms 19 x 19, 30 x 30 6–20 D	75–105	60–200	25–60 More with prestressing	Creep
CONCRETE FLAT SLAB	CONCRETE SLAB / DROP PANEL / CAPITAL / COLUMN	6–16	Min. slab thickness 5 without} Drop 4 with } panel	75–170	60–250	20–40 Up to 70 with prestressing	Creep
PRECAST DOUBLE TEE	CONCRETE TOPPING / PRECAST DOUBLE TEE	8–18	4′, 5′, 6′, 8′, and 10′ W 6–16 D	50–80	40–150	20–50	Creep
PRECAST TEE	CONCRETE TOPPING / PRECAST SINGLE TEE	18–38	16–36 D	50–90	40–150	25–65	Creep
COMPOSITE	CONCRETE SLAB / WELDED STUD (SHEAR CONNECTOR) / STEEL BEAM	4–6	—	35–70	60–200	Up to 35	Deflection
CONCRETE FLAT PLATE	COLUMN / CONCRETE FLAT PLATE	5–14	—	60–175	60–200	18–35 More with prestressing	Creep

Roger K. Lewis, AIA, and Mehmet T. Ergene, Architect; Roger K. Lewis, AIA, & Associates; Washington, D.C.

DESIGN ELEMENTS

Bay Size Charac-teristics	Requires Finished Floor Surface	Requires Finished Ceiling Surface	Service Plenum	Comparative Resistance to Sound Transmission		Fire Resistive Rating per Code and Underwriters		Construction Type Classi-fication	Remarks
				Impact	Airborne	Unprotected Hours	Maximum Protected Hours		
—	Yes	Visual or fire protection purposes	Between joists —one way	Poor	Fair	—	2 (combustible)	4B (A) 3C (B)	Economical, light, easy to construct. Limited to lowrise construction
—	Yes	Visual or fire protection purposes	Between trusses and joists —two ways	Poor	Fair	—	2 (combustible)	4B (A) 3C (B)	Close dimensional toler-ances; cutting holes through web permissible
Maximum beam spacing 8'-0"	Optional	No	Under structure —one way	Poor	Fair	—	2	3A 6" x 10" frame min. 4" planks min.	Most efficient with planks continuous over more than one span
—	Optional	No	Under structure —one way	Poor	Fair	—	2	3A 6" x 10" frame min. 4" planks min.	—
Light joists 16" to 30" o.c. Heavy joists 4'–12' o.c.	Yes	Visual or fire protection purposes	Between joists —two ways	Poor	Poor	—	1	3C (B)	—
Light joists 16" to 30" o.c. Heavy joists 4'–12' o.c.	No	Visual or fire protection purposes	Between joists —two ways	Poor	Fair	—	1–3	1, 2 and 3	Economical system, selective partition place-ment required. Canti-levers difficult
—	Yes	Visual or fire protection purposes	Under structure	Poor	Poor	—	1	3C (B)	—
—	No	Visual or fire protection purposes	Under structure	Poor	Fair	1–3	1–4	1, 2, and 3	—
—	Optional	Visual or fire protection purposes	Under structure	Fair	Fair	—	1–4	1, 2, and 3	—
—	Optional	No	Under structure	Fair	Fair	2–4	3–4	1 and 2	—
L ≤ ½ W	No	No	Under structure	Good	Good	1–4	3–4	1 and 2	Restricted to short spans because of exces-sive dead load
L ≥ 1.33 W	No	No	Under structure	Good	Good	1–4	3–4	1 and 2	Suitable for concen-trated loads, easy parti-tion placement
—	No	No	Between ribs —one way	Good	Good	1–4	3–4	1 and 2	Economy through re-use of forms, shear at supports controlling factor
L ≥ 1.33 W	No	No	Under structure	Good	Good	1–4	3–4	1 and 2	For heavy loads, columns should be equidistant. Not good for cantilevers
L ≥ 1.33 W	No	No	Under structure	Good	Good	1–4	3–4	1 and 2	Drop panels against shear required for spans above 12 ft
—	Optional	Visual purposes; differential camber	Between ribs —one way	Fair	Good	2–3	3–4	1 and 2	Most widely used pre-stressed concrete product in the medium span range
—	Optional	Visual purposes; differential camber	Between ribs —one way	Fair	Good	2–3	3–4	1 and 2	Easy construction, lack continuity, poor earth-quake resistance
—	No	Visual or fire protection purposes	Under structure	Good	Good	—	1–4	1, 2, and 3	—
L ≥ 1.33 W	No	No	Under structure	Good	Good	1–4	3–4	1 and 2	Uniform slab thickness, economical to form, easy to cantilever

Roger K. Lewis, AIA, and Mehmet T. Ergene, Architect; Roger K. Lewis, AIA, & Associates; Washington, D.C.

DESIGN ELEMENTS 13

ROOF STRUCTURE ASSEMBLIES FOR ADDITIONAL INFORMATION CONSULT MANUFACTURER'S LITERATURE AND TRADE ASSOCIATIONS		DEPTH OF SYSTEM (IN.)	STANDARD MEMBER SIZES (IN.)	DEAD LOAD OF STRUCTURE (PSF)	SUITABLE LIVE LOAD RANGE (PSF)	SPAN RANGE (FT)	BAY SIZE CHARAC-TERISTICS	DIMENSIONAL STABILITY AFFECTED BY
WOOD RAFTER	PLYWOOD SHEATHING / WOOD JOIST / CEILING	5–13	Nominal rafters 2 x 4, 6, 8, 10, and 12	4–8	10–50	Up to 22	—	Deflection
WOOD BEAM AND PLANK	WOOD PLANK / WOOD BEAM (OR LAMINATED BEAM)	8–22	Nominal planks 2, 3, and 4	5–12	10–50	8–34	Maximum beam spacing 8'-0''	—
PLYWOOD PANEL	PLYWOOD (STRESSED SKIN) PANELS	3¼ and 8¼	—	3–6	10–50	8–32	4'-0'' modules	—
WOOD TRUSS	SHEATHING / WOOD TRUSS / CEILING	Varies (1'–12')	—	5–15	10–50	30–50	2'–8' between trusses	Deflection
STEEL TRUSS	STEEL DECK / PURLIN / STEEL TRUSS	Varies	—	15–25	10–60	100–200	—	Deflection
STEEL JOIST	CONCRETE / STEEL CENTERING / STEEL JOIST / CEILING	11–75	Steel joists 8–72	10–28	10–50	Up to 96	Light joists 16''–30'' o.c. Heavy joists 4'–12' o.c.	Deflection
STEEL JOIST	PLYWOOD DECK / WOOD NAILER / STEEL JOIST / CEILING	10–32	Steel joists 8–30	8–20	10–50	Up to 96	Light joists 16''–30'' o.c. Heavy joists 4'–12' o.c.	Deflection
STEEL JOIST	INSULATION / STEEL DECK / STEEL JOIST / CEILING	11–75	Steel joists 8–72	6–24	10–50	Up to 96	—	Deflection
STEEL FRAME	PRECAST CONCRETE PLANK / STEEL BEAM / CEILING	4–12 plus beam depth	Concrete plank 16–48 W 4–12 D	40–75	30–70	20–60 Generally below 35	—	Deflection and creep
PRECAST CONCRETE	PRECAST CONCRETE PLANK / CONCRETE BEAM	4–12 plus beam depth	Concrete plank 16–48 W 4–12 D	40–75	30–70	20–60 Generally below 35	—	Deflection and creep
ONE-WAY CONCRETE SLAB	CONCRETE SLAB / CONCRETE BEAM	4–10 slab plus beam depth	—	50–120	Up to 100	10–25 More with prestressing	L ≤ ½ W	—
TWO-WAY CONCRETE SLAB	CONCRETE SLAB / CONCRETE BEAM	4–10 slab plus beam depth	—	50–120	Up to 100	10–30 More with prestressing	L ≥ 1.33 W	—
ONE-WAY RIBBED CONCRETE SLAB	CONCRETE SLAB / RIB (JOIST)	8–22	Standard pan forms 20 and 30 W 6–20 D	40–90	Up to 100	15–50 More with prestressing	—	Creep
TWO-WAY RIBBED CONCRETE SLAB	CONCRETE SLAB / RIB (JOIST)	8–24	Standard dome forms 19 x 19, 30 x 30 6–20 D	75–105	Up to 100	25–60 More with prestressing	L ≥ 1.33 W	Creep
PRECAST TEE		16–36	16–36 deep	65–85	20–80	30–100	—	Creep
PRECAST DOUBLE TEE		6–16	4', 5', 6', 8', and 10' wide 6''–16'' deep	35–55	25–60	20–75	—	Creep
CONCRETE FLAT PLATE	CONCRETE FLAT PLATE / COLUMN	4–14	—	50–160	Up to 100	Up to 35 More with prestressing	L ≥ 1.33 W	Creep
CONCRETE FLAT SLAB	CONCRETE SLAB / DROP PANEL / CAPITAL / COLUMN	5–16	Min. slab thickness 5 w/o ⎫ Drop 4 w/ ⎬ panel	50–200	Up to 100	Up to 40 More with prestressing	L ≥ 1.33 W Equal column spacing required	Creep
GYPSUM DECK	GYPSUM CONCRETE / FORM BOARD / SUBPURLIN / CEILING	3–6	—	5–20	Up to 50	Up to 10	Up to 8' between subpurlins	Deflection and creep

Roger K. Lewis, AIA, and Mehmet T. Ergene, Architect; Roger K. Lewis, AIA, & Associates; Washington, D.C.

DESIGN ELEMENTS

SUITABLE FOR INCLINED ROOFS	REQUIRES FINISHED CEILING SURFACE	SERVICE PLENUM	RELATIVE THERMAL CAPACITY	COMPARATIVE RESISTANCE TO SOUND TRANSMISSION		FIRE RESISTIVE RATING PER CODE AND UNDERWRITERS		CONSTRUCTION TYPE CLASSIFICATION	REMARKS
				IMPACT	AIRBORNE	UNPROTECTED HOURS	MAXIMUM PROTECTED HOURS		
Yes	For visual or fire protection purposes	Between rafters —one way	Low	Poor	Fair	–	2 (combustible)	4B (A) 3C (B)	
Yes	For fire protection purposes	Under structure —one way	Medium	Poor	Fair	–	2	3A 6″ x 10″ frame min. 4″ plank min.	
Yes	No	Under structure only	Low	Poor	Fair	–	2	4B (A) 3C (B)	
Yes	For visual or fire protection purposes	Between trusses	Low	Poor	Fair	–	2 (combustible)	4B (A) 3C (B)	Truss depth to span ratio 1:5 to 1:10
Yes Pitched trusses usually used for short spans	For visual or fire protection purposes	Between trusses	Low	Fair	Fair	–	1–4	1, 2, and 3	Truss depth to span ratio 1:5 to 1:15
No	For visual or fire protection purposes	Between joists	Medium	Fair	Fair	–	1–4	1, 2, and 3	
Yes	For visual or fire protection purposes	Between joists	Low	Poor	Fair	–	1	1, 2, and 3	
Yes	For visual or fire protection purposes	Between joists	High	Excellent	Good	–	2	1, 2, and 3	
Yes	For visual or fire protection purposes	Under structure	High	Fair	Fair	–	1–4	1, 2, and 3	Easy to design; quick erection
Yes	No	Under structure	High	Fair	Fair	2–4	3–4	1 and 2	Provides finished flush ceiling. May be used with any framing system
No	No	Under structure	High	Good	Good	1–4	3–4	1 and 2	
No	No	Under structure	High	Good	Good	1–4	3–4	1 and 2	
No	For visual purposes	Between ribs —one way	High	Good	Good	1–4	3–4	1 and 2	
No	No	Under structure	High	Good	Good	1–4	3–4	1 and 2	Economy in forming; suitable for two-way cantilevering
Yes	For visual or fire protection purposes	Between ribs —one way	High	Fair	Good	2–3	3–4	1 and 2	Generally used for long spans
Yes	For visual or fire protection purposes	Between ribs —one way	High	Fair	Good	2–3	3–4	1 and 2	Most widely used prestressed concrete element.
No	No	Under structure	High	Good	Good	1–4	3–4	1 and 2	Uniform slab thickness; easy to form; suitable for vertical expansion of building
No	No	Under structure	High	Good	Good	1–4	3–4	1 and 2	Suitable for heavy roof loads
No	For visual or fire protection purposes	Under structure	High	Good	Good	–	2	1, 2, and 3	Provides resistance to wind and seismic loads

Roger K. Lewis, AIA, and Mehmet T. Ergene, Architect; Roger K. Lewis, AIA, & Associates; Washington, D.C.

DESIGN ELEMENTS   13

EXTERIOR WALL ASSEMBLIES FOR ADDITIONAL INFORMATION CONSULT MANUFACTURERS' LITERATURE AND TRADE ASSOCIATIONS	WALL THICKNESS (NOMINAL) (IN.)	WEIGHT (PSF)	VERTICAL SPAN RANGE UNSUPPORTED HEIGHT) (FT)	WIND RESIST.	RACKING RESISTANCE	SERVICE PLENUM SPACE	HEAT TRANSMISSION COEFFICIENT (U-FACTOR) (BTU/HR·SQ FT·°F)
C.M.U. — C.M.U. (GRAVEL AGGREGATE)	8 12	55 85	Up to 13 Up to 20		Good	None	0.56 0.49
C.M.U. (INSULATED) — C.M.U. / INSULATION / INT. WALL FIN.	8 + 12 +	60 90	Up to 13 Up to 20		Good	Through insulation	0.21 0.20
C.M.U. AND BRICK VENEER (INSULATED) — BRICK VENEER / C.M.U. / INSULATION / INT. WALL FIN.	4 + 4 + 4 + 8 +	75 100	Up to 13 (w/filled cavity) Up to 20 (w/filled cavity)		Good	Through insulation	0.19 0.18
CAVITY — BRICK VENEER / CAVITY (MIN. 2") / INSULATION (WATER REPELLENT) / C.M.U. / INT. WALL FIN.	4 + 2 + 4 4 + 2 + 8	75 100	Up to 9 Up to 13		Fair	None	0.12 0.11
C.M.U. AND STUCCO (INSULATED) — STUCCO / C.M.U. / INSULATION / INT. WALL FIN.	8 +	67	Up to 13		Good	Through interior insulation	0.16
WOOD STUD — EXT. WALL FIN. / SHEATHING WITH MOISTURE BARRIER / WOOD STUD / INSULATION WITH VAPOR BARRIER / INT. WALL FIN.	4 6	12 16	Up to 14 Up to 20 (L/d ≤ 50)		Poor to fair	Between studs	0.06 0.04
BRICK VENEER — BRICK VENEER / SHEATHING WITH MOISTURE BARRIER / WOOD STUD / INSULATION WITH VAPOR BARRIER / INT. WALL FIN.	4 + 4	52	Up to 14		Poor to fair	Between studs	0.07
METAL STUD — EXT. WALL FIN. / METAL STUD AT 16" O.C. / INSULATION WITH VAPOR BARRIER / INT. WALL FIN.	4 5	14 18	Up to 13 Up to 17		Poor	Between studs	0.06 0.04
BRICK VENEER — BRICK VENEER / SHEATHING WITH MOISTURE BARRIER / METAL STUD AT 16" O.C. / INSULATION WITH VAPOR BARRIER / INT. WALL FIN.	4 + 4	54	Up to 15		Good	Between studs	0.07
INSULATED SANDWICH PANEL — METAL SKIN / AIRSPACE / INSULATING CORE / METAL SKIN	5	6	See manufacturers' literature		Fair to good	None	0.05 See manufacturers' literature
CONCRETE — CONCRETE	8 12	92 138	Up to 13 (w/reinf. 17) Up to 20 (w/reinf. 25)		Excellent	None	0.68 0.55
CONCRETE (INSULATED) — CONCRETE / INSULATION / INT. WALL FIN.	8 +	97	Up to 13 (w/reinf. 17)		Excellent	Through insulation	0.13
CONCRETE AND BRICK VENEER (INSULATED) — BRICK VENEER / CONCRETE / INSULATION / INT. WALL FIN.	4 + 8 +	112	Up to 13 (w/reinf. 17)		Excellent	Through insulation	0.13
PRECAST CONCRETE — CONCRETE (REINFORCED) / INSULATION / INT. WALL FINISH	2 + 4 +	23 46	Up to 6 Up to 12		Fair to good	Through insulation	0.00 0.85
PRECAST CONCRETE SANDWICH — CONCRETE / INSULATION	5	45	Up to 14		Fair to good	None	0.14

WIND RESIST. (vertical note): Wind resistance depends on geographical location and height of building; wind velocity; wall material thickness, strength; workmanship; axial loads; and horizontal span. Design walls for both inward and outward pressures.

GLASS SEE CHAPTER 8 FOR DETAILED INFORMATION ON GLASS			SIZE RANGE MAXIMUM ALLOWABLE GLASS AREA / WIND LOAD		SHADING COEFFICIENT S.C.	
SINGLE GLAZING — ¼" GLASS	¼	3.2	Four side supported 110 SF @ 10 PSF / 20 SF @ 60 PSF Two side supported 40 SF @ 10 PSF / 17 SF @ 60 PSF		Clear 0.94 Tinted 0.70 Reflective 0.44	Clear/tinted 1.1 Reflective 0.8–1.1
DOUBLE GLAZING — ¼" GLASS / ¼" CAVITY	¾	6.4	Four side supported 55 SF @ 30 PSF / 28 SF @ 60 PSF Heat strengthened 70 SF @ 80 PSF / 30 SF @ 200 PSF			Clear/tinted 0.5–0.6 Reflective 0.3–0.6
TRIPLE GLAZING — ¼" GLASS / ¼" CAVITY	1¼	9.6	—			Clear/tinted 0.3–0.4 Reflective 0.2–0.4

Roger K. Lewis, AIA, and Mehmet T. Ergene, Architect; Roger K. Lewis, AIA & Associates; Washington, D.C.

DESIGN ELEMENTS

Hazard Classification (Fire) — detail:

Classification provides data in regard to (1) flame spread, (2) fuel contributed, and (3) smoke developed during fire exposure of materials in comparison to asbestos-cement boards as zero and untreated red oak lumber as 100 when exposed to fire under similar conditions

	FLAME SPREAD	FUEL CONTRIBUTED	SMOKE DEVELOPED
Paint on CMU	5-25	0-5	0-10
Gypsum board surfaced on both sides with paper	15	15	0
Gypsum board surfaced on both sides with paper, vinyl faced	25-35	0-10	15-45
Untreated wood particle board	180	75	190
Treated wood particle board with untreated wood face veneer	25-180	10-160	10-250
Vermiculite acoustical plaster	10-20	10-20	0
Glass fiber batts and blankets (basic)	20	15	20
(foil kraft faced)	25	0	0
Treated lumber (Douglas fir)	15	10	0-5
(Hemlock)	10-15	5-15	0
Laminated plastic (fr)	20-30	0-15	5-30

NFPA CLASSIFICATION:

CLASS	FLAME SPREAD	SMOKE DEVELOPED
A	0-25	0-450
B	26-75	0-450
C	76-200	0-450

For lesser classifications, permitted in residential construction only, refer to regulating agency guidelines

RESISTANCE TO EXTERIOR AIRBORNE SOUND TRANSMISSION	FIRE RESISTIVE RATING PER CODE AND UNDERWRITERS (HRS)	CONSTRUCTION TYPE CLASSIFICATION	SUBCONTRACTORS REQUIRED FOR ERECTION (PLUS FINISHES)	EXTERIOR MAINTENANCE REQUIREMENTS	REMARKS
Fair to good	2-4 / 4	1, 2, and 3	Masonry	Washing, re-pointing joints, painting, sand blasting	Properties of non-engineered masonry are drastically reduced
Fair to good	2-4 / 4	1, 2, and 3	Masonry, Carpentry, Drywall	Washing, re-pointing joints, painting, sand blasting	
Excellent	3-4 / 4	1, 2, and 3	Masonry, Carpentry, Drywall	Washing, re-pointing joints, sand blasting	
Excellent	4	1, 2, and 3	Masonry, Drywall (Carpentry)	Washing, re-pointing joints, sand blasting	Cavity increases heat storage capacity and resistance to rain penetration
Good	2-4	1, 2, and 3	Masonry, Drywall, Lath and plaster (Carpentry)	Washing, painting, and re-stuccoing	The assembly is reversed for optimum energy conservation
Poor to fair	1 (combustible)	4	Carpentry, Drywall (Lath and plaster)	Washing, painting, and replacing exterior finish	Exterior wall finishes: • wood, plywood, • aluminum siding, • stucco
Good to excellent	1-2 (combustible)	3B, C	Masonry, Carpentry, Drywall	Washing, re-pointing joints, sand blasting	
Poor to fair	1-2	1 (nonbearing) 2 and 3	Carpentry, Drywall (Lath and plaster)	Washing, painting, and replacing exterior finish	Exterior wall finishes: • wood, plywood, • aluminum siding, • stucco
Good to excellent	1-2	1 (nonbearing) 2 and 3	Masonry, Carpentry, Drywall	Washing, re-pointing joints, sand blasting	
Poor to good; see manufacturers' literature	See manufacturers' literature	See manufacturers' literature	Curtain walls—erection	Washing, steam cleaning, painting, replacing joint sealers	Temperature change critical; Minimize metal through connections
Good	4 / 4	1, 2, and 3	Concrete work	Washing, sand blasting	Concrete walls have very high heat storage capacity
Good	4 / 4	1, 2, and 3	Concrete work, Drywall (Carpentry)	Washing, sand blasting	
Excellent	4	1, 2, and 3	Concrete work, Masonry, Drywall (Carpentry)	Washing, re-pointing joints, sand blasting	
Poor to fair	1-3 / —	1A (nonbearing) 1B, 2, and 3	Curtain walls—erection, Drywall (Carpentry)	Washing, sand blasting, replacing joint sealers	Large size economical (fewer joints) units available with various finishes
Fair	1-3	1A (nonbearing) 1B, 2, and 3	Curtain walls—erection	Washing, sand blasting, replacing joint sealers	8' x 20' max. size for concrete sandwich panels; Plant quality control is very essential
Poor	—	—	Curtain walls—erection (Glazing)	Washing, replacing joint sealers, gaskets	Anchorage to building is critical; Anchors must isolate wall to limit building movement transmitted to glass; Wall design must limit wall movement transmitted to glass
Fair	—	—	Curtain walls—erection (Glazing)	Washing, replacing joint sealers, gaskets	Mullions should accommodate movement through gaskets, sliding connections, etc.
Good	—	—	Curtain walls—erection (Glazing)	Washing, replacing joint sealers, gaskets	

Roger K. Lewis, AIA, and Mehmet T. Ergene, Architect; Roger K. Lewis, AIA, & Associates; Washington, D.C.

GENERAL INFORMATION

Most air structures are primarily designed to resist wind loads. Mechanical blowers must maintain 3 to 5 psf pressure inside the structure at all times. Architectural elements of the building must be detailed to avoid loss of air pressure. Normal entering and exiting should be through revolving doors, while emergency exiting is provided through pressure balanced doors, and vehicles pass through air locks. Avoid using interior furnishings that could possibly puncture the structural membrane. Automatic auxilliary fans should be activated in the event of a pressure drop due to primary power failure.

The structural membrane is usually a nylon, fiberglass, or polyester fabric coated with polyvinyl chloride. Such skins have a life span from 7 to 10 years, and provide fire retardation that passes NFPA 701. A urethane topcoat will reduce dirt adhesion and improve service life. New Teflon coated fiberglass membranes have a life expectancy of more than 25 years. This material is incombustible, passing NFPA 70, with flame spread rating = 10, smoke developed = 50, and fuel contributed = 10. An acoustical liner (NCR = 0.65) is also available.

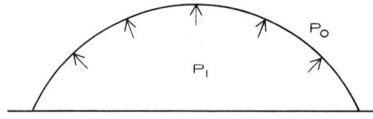

SINGLE MEMBRANE $P_I > P_O$

This is the most common type of air structure. The internal pressure (P_I) is kept approximately 0.03 psi above the external atmospheric pressure (P_O). It is this pressure difference that keeps the dome inflated.

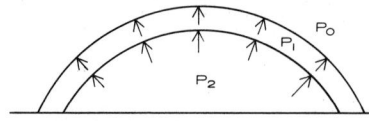
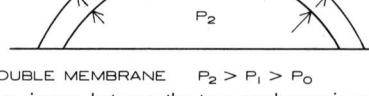

DOUBLE MEMBRANE $P_2 > P_I > P_O$

The airspace between the two membranes is used for insulation and security. If the outer skin is punctured the inner skin will remain standing. Both single and double membrane air structures require the constant use of blowers to keep them inflated.

AIR SUPPORTED

DUAL MEMBRANE $P_I > P_O$

Here the internal and external pressures are the same. Only the area between the skins is pressurized. The inflated area of a dual membrane structure can be sealed, thus eliminating the need for constant use of blowers.

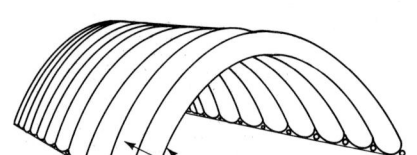

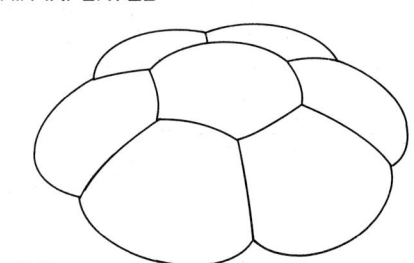

HIGH PRESSURE TUBE SUPPORTS

AIR INFLATED

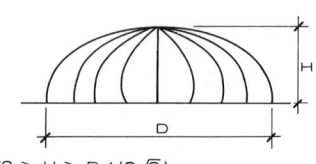

$D/2 > H > D/(2\sqrt{2})$

SPAN LIMITATIONS	VAULT	DOME
Without cables	D = 120' - 0''	D = 150' - 0''
With cables	D = 400' - 0''	D = 600' - 0''

VAULT

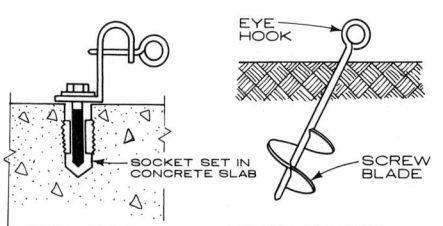
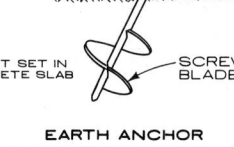

DOME

BASIC CONFIGURATIONS

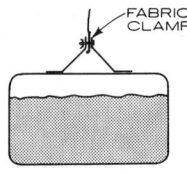

FABRIC CLAMP

WATER TANK   SAND BAGS

EYE HOOK

SCREW PLUG   EARTH ANCHOR

SOCKET SET IN CONCRETE SLAB

SCREW BLADE

C-PROFILE   MEMBRANE

STRADDLING DOWEL

CABLE

GRADE BEAM

ROD SET IN CONCRETE PIER

ANGLE CLAMP

ANCHORAGE DETAILS

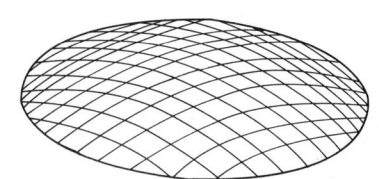

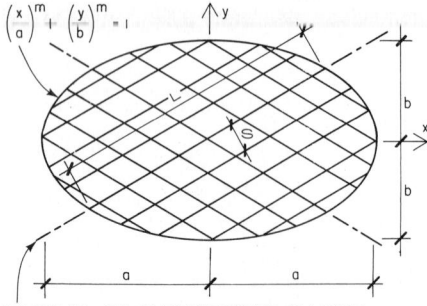

$$\left(\frac{x}{a}\right)^m + \left(\frac{y}{b}\right)^m = 1$$

DIAGONAL OF SUPERSCRIBED ELLIPSE MAXIMUM CABLE SPACING = 50'-0''

SUPERELLIPSE PLAN

KEY TO NOTATIONS
a/b—One half of major/minor axes of superellipse.
s—Cable spacing.
L—Length of cable along diagonal of superscribed rectangle of proportions 2a and 2b.
e/f—One half of major/minor axes of superscribed

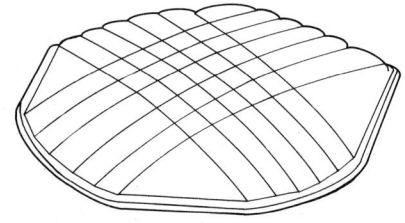

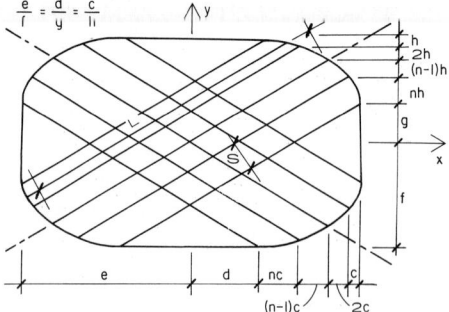

$$\frac{e}{f} = \frac{d}{g} = \frac{c}{li}$$

MAXIMUM STRAIGHT SIDE = 200'-0''
PROGRESSION PLAN

rectangle of plan progession.
d/g—One half of straight sides of and parallel to the major/minor axes of the plan progression.
c, 2c, (n-1)c, nc/h, 2h, (n-1)h, nh—The sequences of curve coordinates parallel to the major/minor axes of the plan progression.

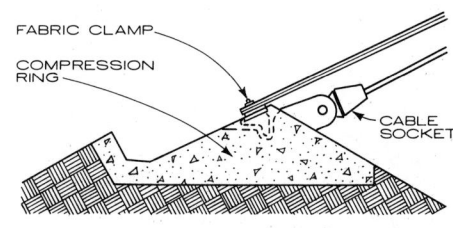

FABRIC CLAMP

COMPRESSION RING

CABLE SOCKET

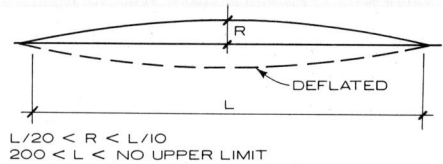

DEFLATED

$L/20 < R < L/10$
$200 < L <$ NO UPPER LIMIT

STRUCTURAL CONSIDERATIONS

Membrane strengths up to 1000 lb/in. are available; a safety factor of 4 for short term loading and 8 for long term loading is required. The membrane must be patterned to carry loads without wrinkling. Structural behavior is nonlinear with large displacements. The roof shape shall be established such that the horizontal components of the cable forces result in minimum bending moment in the compression ring under maximum loads. The skewed symmetry indicated permits this condition to be realized. Consult specialist in air structures to integrate structural and architectural requirements.

LONG SPAN STRUCTURES

Geiger-Berger Associates, P.C.; New York, New York

DESIGN ISSUES

The major design issues affecting underground and earth sheltered buildings are sun orientation, wind, topography and drainage, access to outside light and views, acoustics, landscaping, and thermal characteristics. Proper orientation can produce significant energy savings. Exterior views are an important aesthetic and psychological determinant of orientation.

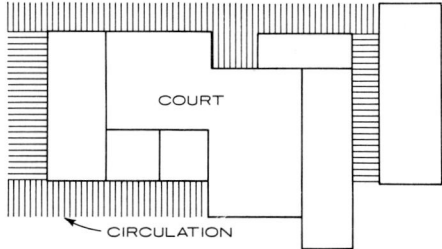

CIRCULATION AT PERIMETER

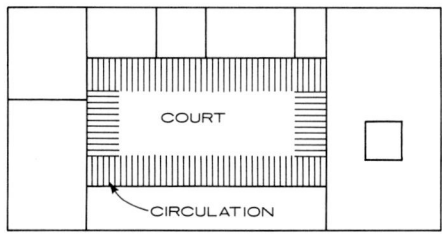

CIRCULATION AT INTERIOR

ATRIUM

NOTE

The atrium plan places spaces around a courtyard with orientation into the court.

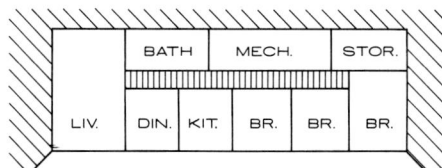

ELEVATIONAL

NOTE

The concept of the elevational plan is to maximize the earth cover by concentrating all openings on one side, preferably south. The arrangement of spaces requiring light and view, are on the exposed side.

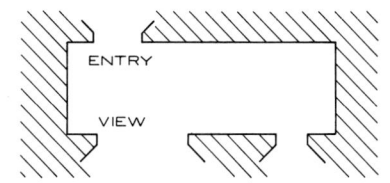

PENETRATIONAL

NOTE

Penetrational plans place openings around the structure for light and view on the perimeter.

MAJOR STRUCTURAL CONSIDERATIONS

Since earth sheltered structures have greater than normal loads on the roof and walls, additional structural analysis is required. Consult an engineer.

SUN

The radiant energy from the sun can be used for active and/or passive heating.

Myers & Bennett/BRW, Inc.; Minneapolis, Minnesota

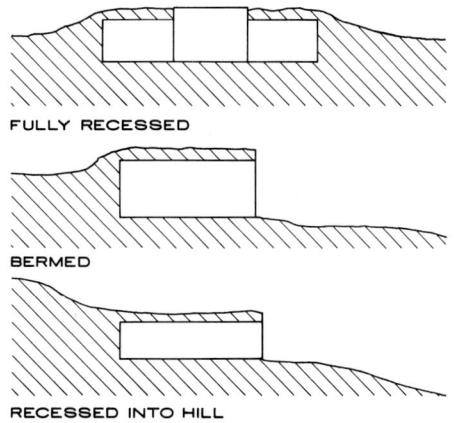

FULLY RECESSED

BERMED

RECESSED INTO HILL

TYPICAL SECTIONS

NOTE

Fully recessed structures with earth berms on flat sites and semirecessed structures on sloping sites are typical. The depth of the structure and surface relationships can influence the amount of earth placed on the roof and walls, as does the relationship between the earth mass and energy requirements for comfort conditioning.

WIND

Cold winter winds increase heat loss because of infiltration and wind chill factor. Protecting a building from exposure on the winter wind side will reduce heat loss. In the summer it is desirable to take advantage of prevailing breezes to provide natural ventilation. Cross-ventilation is desirable.

TOPOGRAPHY

The most important issue to topography is the degree and orientation of slope. A sloping site offers the opportunity to set an earth covered space into the hillside; it also limits the orientation of most openings to the direction of slope.

DRAINAGE

Correctly sloped sites, divert water away by creating a swale or a cutoff gravel trench. On sites with sunken courts, the ground should slope away on all sides, then only the rainfall that falls directly into the court has to be handled by a drainage system. French drains are commonly used.

ACOUSTICS

Earth sheltered construction greatly dampens outside sound. This acoustic insulation benefits sites that are close to undesirable noise sources.

LANDSCAPING

PERIMETER PLANTING

Where openings are exposed to sun and wind, plant material can contribute to significant energy savings. Deciduous plant material can shade the building when solar radiation is undesirable and let it in when desirable. Coniferous vegetation can provide protection in winter against prevailing winter winds.

ROOFTOP PLANTING

It is desirable to have plant growth on the roof for aesthetic, ecological, and energy saving reasons. The reflective nature of plants and their respiration considerably reduce solar heat gain as compared with conventional roofing systems.

THERMAL CHARACTERISTICS OF EARTH SHELTERED STRUCTURES

Heat loss (or gain) depends on two factors: the ventilation load for heating or cooling intake air and the heat transmission through the building envelope. The thermal mass of soil surrounding a building reduces the temperature variation of the structure. Maintaining a steady temperature will eventually (within about 1 to 3 yr depending on the size of the structure) create a "thermal envelope" that will maintain itself at an almost constant temperature approaching that of the interior space.

WALLS

The upper portions of the walls should be insulated to a depth of at least 7 ft below grade in very cold climate only. Below this the insulation may be eliminated or tapered, depending on the building's particular needs.

THERMAL BREAKS

Many earth sheltered structures are constructed of concrete, thus the loss by conduction is a major factor. Interruption of the roof or wall and insertion of an insulating barrier will have a significant impact on this heat transfer.

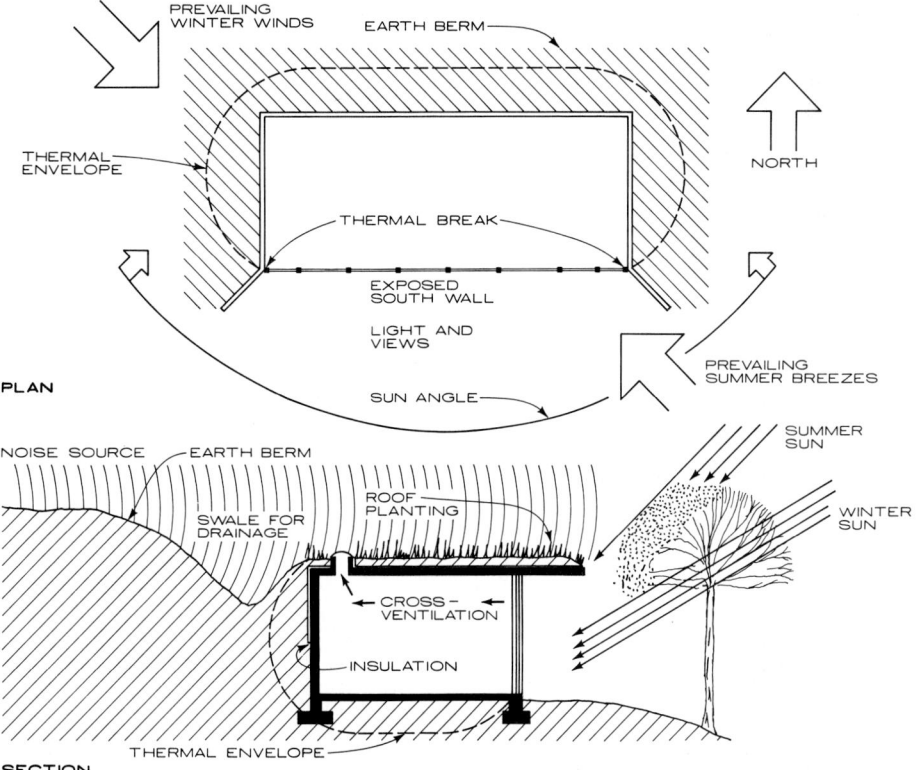

ENVIRONMENT CHARACTERISTICS OF EARTH SHELTERS

CEILING SYSTEMS	MANGER SPACING (o.c.)	WALL MOLDINGS			MAIN RUNNERS			SPACING	CROSS MEMBERS			SPACING (o.c.)	AIR BAR AIR BOOT			ACOUSTIC PANELS			LIGHT FIXTURES		
		L	W	H	L	W	H		L	W	H		L	W	H	L	W	H	L	W	H
Flat modular	2'-6"	10'	3/4"	3/4"	10'	3/4"	1 1/2"	5'	60"	3/4"	1 1/2"	20"	5'	3 1/8"	9 3/4"	5'	20"	5/8"	—	1.	—
Coffered lighting	30"	60"	1 1/4"	1 1/4"	5'	2 1/4"	1 1/4"	5'	60"	2 1/4"	1 1/4"	5'	5'	7 1/4"	8"	5'	15"	5/8"	48"	14 1/2"	5"
Luminair modular	5'	—	—	—	58 1/2"	3"	1 1/2"	5'	57"	15/16"	1 1/2"	5'	5'	7 1/4"	8"	5'	15"	5/8"	48"	14 1/2"	5"
Vertical screen	7' Max.	—	—	—	16'	1 1/2"	1 7/8"	7' Max.	16' Max.	5/8"	4"	2'-6"	—	2.	—	—	—	—	—	2.	—
Linear screen	5' Max.	—	—	—	16'	1 27/32"	1 1/4"	50"	3'-16'	3"	5/8"	2"	—	3.	—	—	4.	—	—	5.	—

NOTES

1. Size can vary.
2. No special type necessary.
3. Utilizes slots between panels for delivery and return.
4. Acoustic blanket.
5. Designed to fit panel width.

WALL MOUNTS

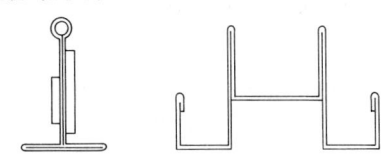

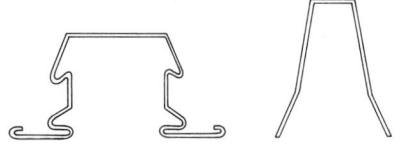

MAIN RUNNERS

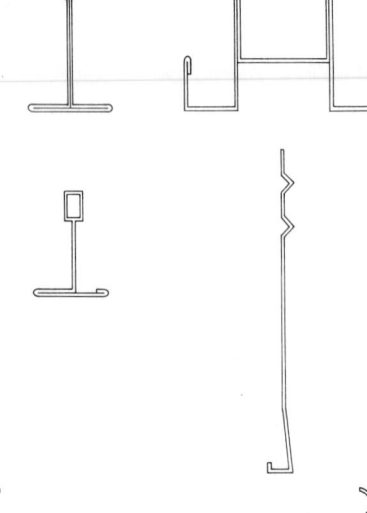

CROSS MEMBERS

INTEGRATED CEILINGS

Integrated ceilings combine lighting, air diffusion, fire protection, and acoustical control into a single, unified unit. Demountable partitions can be accommodated by the use of an adaptor attached on the modular grid lines. A 60 x 60 in. module is basic to most integrated ceiling systems. Custom sized modules are also available. Air diffusion is by two integral means: (1) supply air plenum/supply air bar; (2) ducted supply air boot/supply air bar in framing.

FLAT MODULAR CEILING SYSTEM

The 60 x 60 in. module is divided into three sections nominally 20 x 60 in. in size which can accommodate either a light fixture or an acoustical panel. Light fixtures are 20 x 60, 20 x 30, or 20 x 20 in. The lens frame provides a regress for handling air return.

Narrow grid members of the slide-lock type are easily installed and repositioned.

COFFERED LIGHTING CEILING SYSTEM

A 60 x 60 or a 60 x 30 in. module is standard. The coffered design permits a variety of lighting arrangements with either flat or coffered lighted modules. Maximum coffer depth is about 11 3/4 in. Air return is by return air lighted modules.

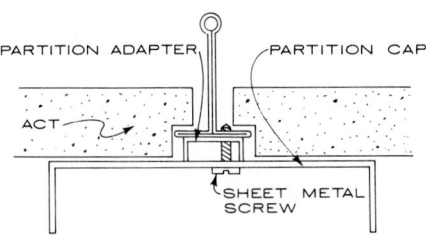

PARTITION ATTACHMENT

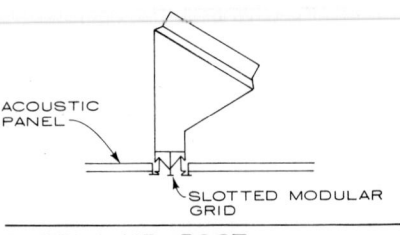

SUPPLY AIR—BOOT

LUMINAIR MODULAR CEILING

The basic configuration is a 60 x 60 in. module divided into four 15 x 60 in. modules.

A recess in the modular defining grid will accommodate demountable partitions, sprinkler heads, and slots for air diffusion.

The basic lighting unit is a 14 1/2 x 48 in. recessed troffer. Task lighting can be provided by a pendant lighting fixture suspended by rods from an electrified track that can be moved around the ceiling.

Air return is by return air light fixtures.

VERTICAL AND LINEAR SCREEN CEILINGS

These ceilings provide effective screening of the mechanical, wiring, and piping in the plenum area. A vertical screen does not achieve full enclosure, requiring extra costs for special air distribution, diffuser or lighting fixtures, and sprinkler heads. A linear screen requires specially designed air diffusers and lighting fixtures.

Acoustic control is accomplished by laying an acoustic insulating blanket across the top of the suspended ceiling panels.

The size of the system is unlimited, carriers and panels can run in any direction.

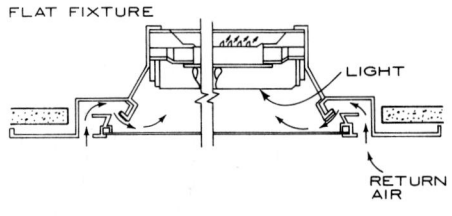

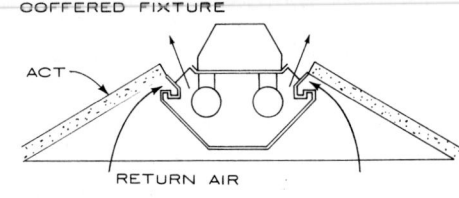

RETURN AIR—LIGHTING MODULE

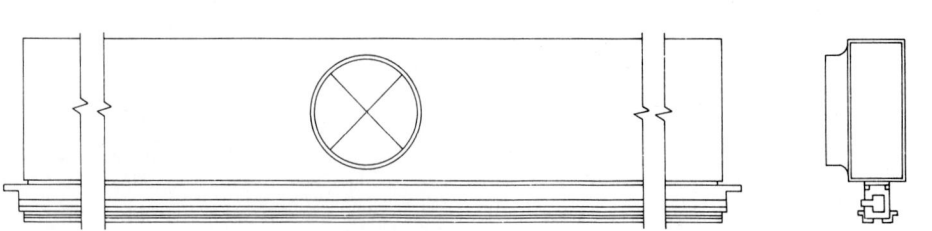

AIR BAR AND AIR BOOT

Walter H. Sobel, FAIA & Associates; Chicago, Illinois

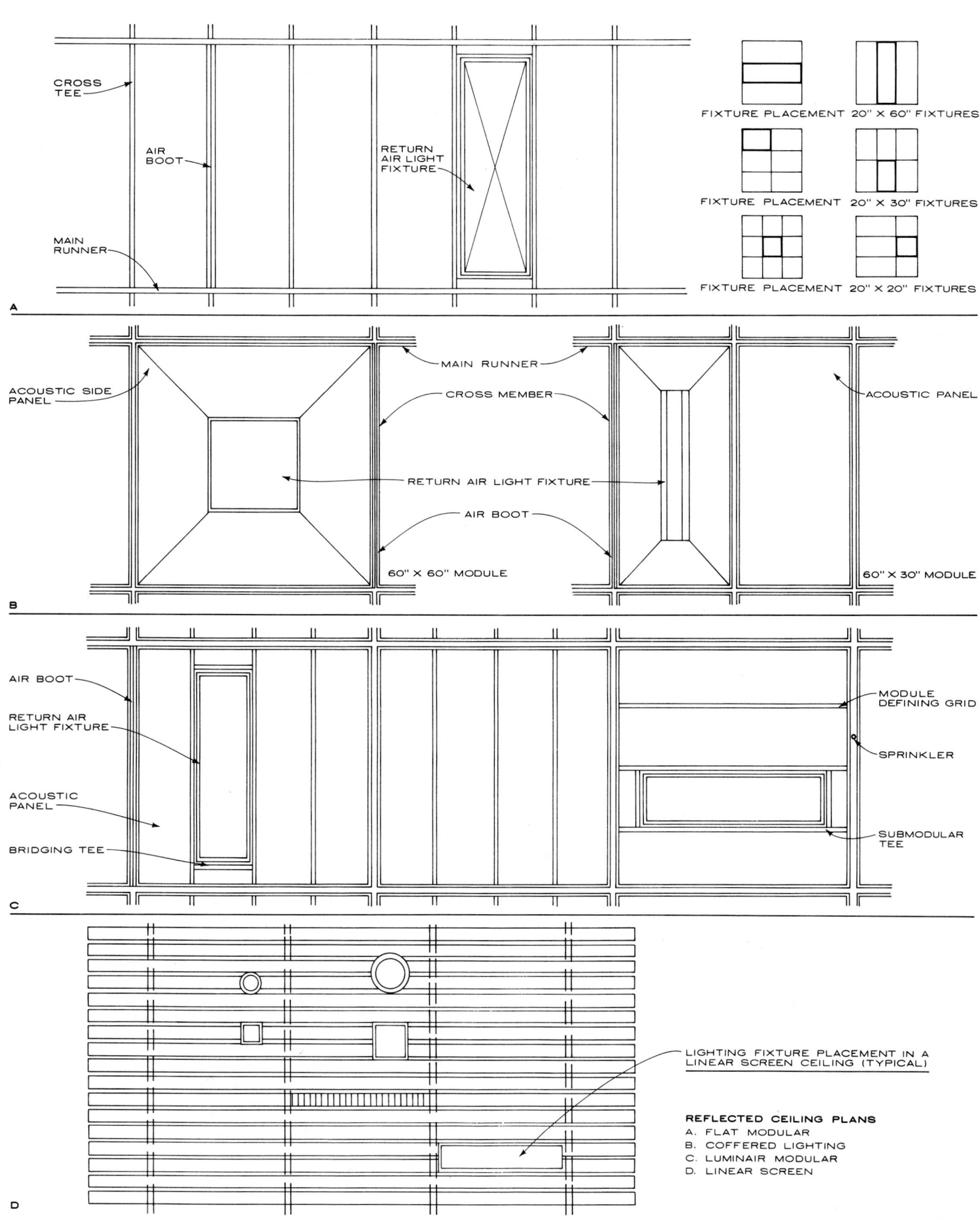

A

CROSS TEE

AIR BOOT

RETURN AIR LIGHT FIXTURE

MAIN RUNNER

FIXTURE PLACEMENT 20" X 60" FIXTURES

FIXTURE PLACEMENT 20" X 30" FIXTURES

FIXTURE PLACEMENT 20" X 20" FIXTURES

B

ACOUSTIC SIDE PANEL

MAIN RUNNER

CROSS MEMBER

ACOUSTIC PANEL

RETURN AIR LIGHT FIXTURE

AIR BOOT

60" X 60" MODULE

60" X 30" MODULE

C

AIR BOOT

RETURN AIR LIGHT FIXTURE

ACOUSTIC PANEL

BRIDGING TEE

MODULE DEFINING GRID

SPRINKLER

SUBMODULAR TEE

D

LIGHTING FIXTURE PLACEMENT IN A LINEAR SCREEN CEILING (TYPICAL)

REFLECTED CEILING PLANS
A. FLAT MODULAR
B. COFFERED LIGHTING
C. LUMINAIR MODULAR
D. LINEAR SCREEN

Walter H. Sobel, FAIA & Associates; Chicago, Illinois

INTEGRATED ASSEMBLIES **13**

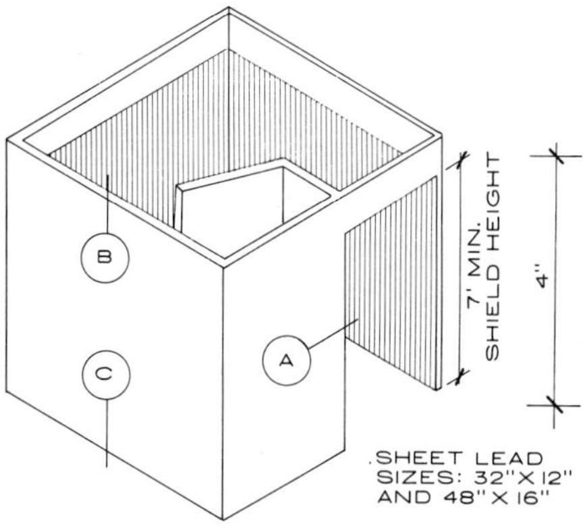

X-RAY ROOM

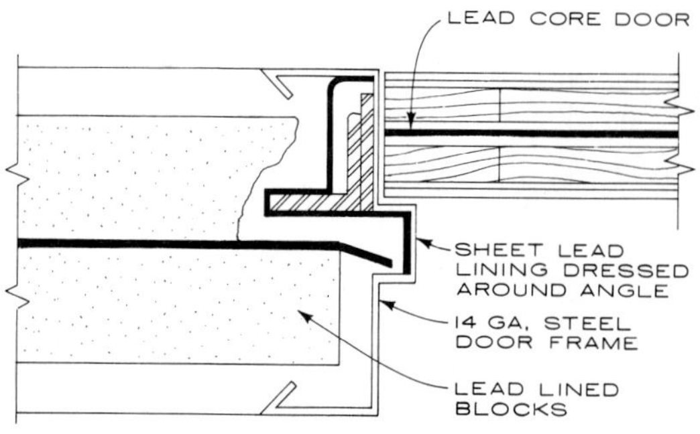

7' MIN. SHIELD HEIGHT

4"

.SHEET LEAD SIZES: 32"X 12" AND 48"X 16"

LEAD CORE DOOR

SHEET LEAD LINING DRESSED AROUND ANGLE

14 GA. STEEL DOOR FRAME

LEAD LINED BLOCKS

DETAIL "A"

REINFORCED STEEL DOOR FRAME

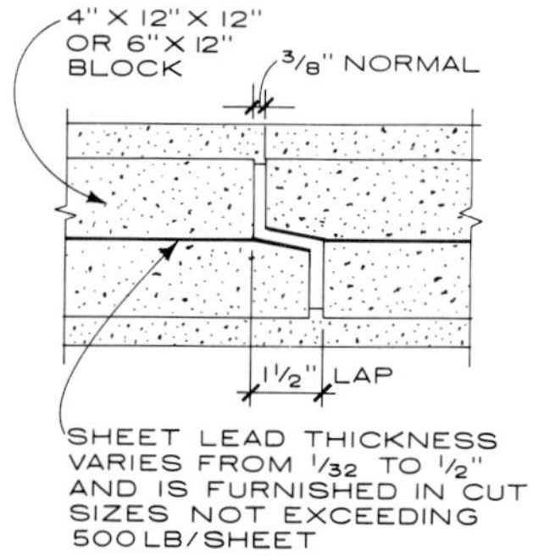

4" X 12" X 12" OR 6"X 12" BLOCK

3/8" NORMAL

1 1/2" LAP

SHEET LEAD THICKNESS VARIES FROM 1/32 TO 1/2" AND IS FURNISHED IN CUT SIZES NOT EXCEEDING 500 LB/SHEET

TYPICAL JOINT

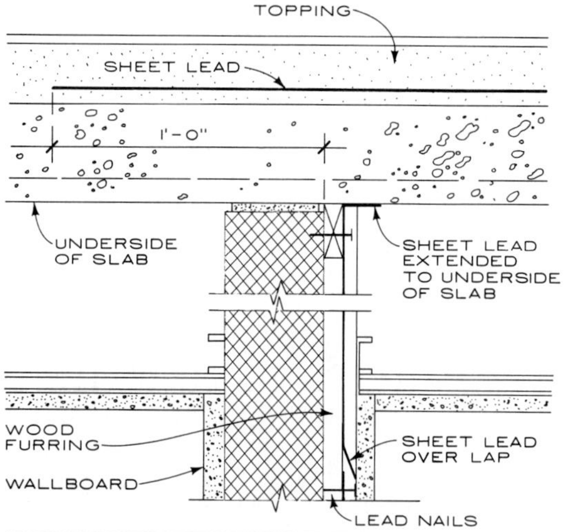

TOPPING

SHEET LEAD

1'-0"

UNDERSIDE OF SLAB

SHEET LEAD EXTENDED TO UNDERSIDE OF SLAB

WOOD FURRING

WALLBOARD

SHEET LEAD OVER LAP

LEAD NAILS

DETAIL WITH SHEET LEAD PLACED ON STRUCTURAL SLAB ABOVE X-RAY ROOM

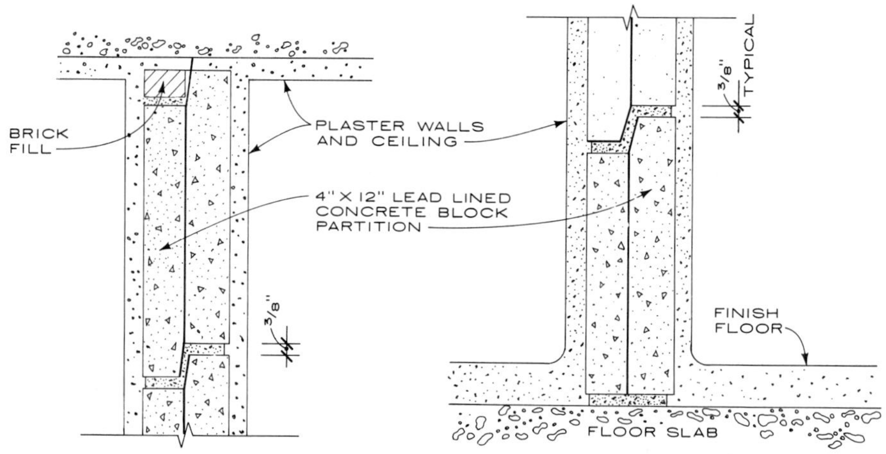

BRICK FILL

PLASTER WALLS AND CEILING

4" X 12" LEAD LINED CONCRETE BLOCK PARTITION

3/8"

DETAIL "B"

3/8" TYPICAL

FINISH FLOOR

FLOOR SLAB

DETAIL "C"

LEAD LINED CONCRETE PARTITIONS

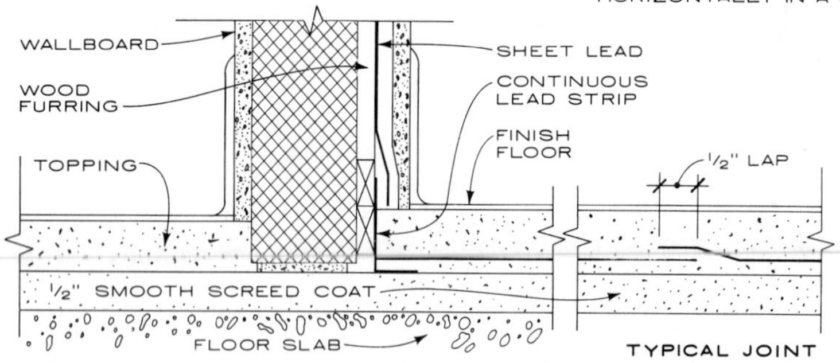

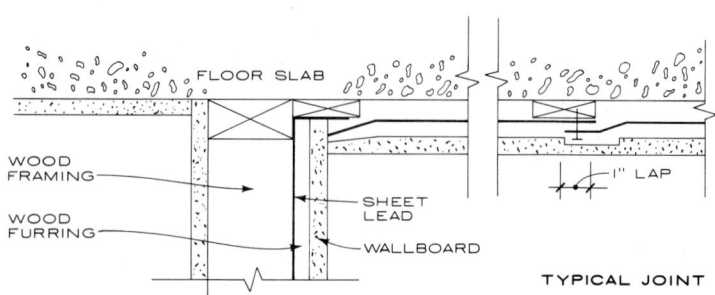

WALLBOARD

WOOD FURRING

TOPPING

SHEET LEAD

CONTINUOUS LEAD STRIP

FINISH FLOOR

1/2" LAP

1/2" SMOOTH SCREED COAT

FLOOR SLAB

TYPICAL JOINT

DETAIL OF SHEET LEAD ON FLOOR UNDER FILL

NOTE: WOOD FURRING STRIPS ARE APPLIED VERTICALLY AND HORIZONTALLY IN A GRID PATTERN

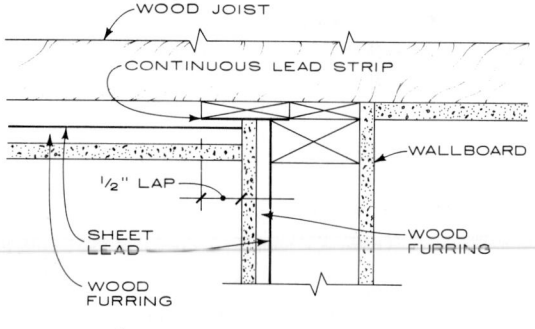

WOOD JOIST

CONTINUOUS LEAD STRIP

WALLBOARD

1/2" LAP

SHEET LEAD

WOOD FURRING

WOOD FURRING

WOOD CONSTRUCTION—CEILING

FLOOR SLAB

WOOD FRAMING

WOOD FURRING

SHEET LEAD

WALLBOARD

1" LAP

TYPICAL JOINT

DETAIL OF ATTACHED CEILING

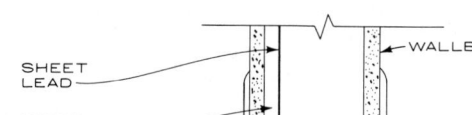
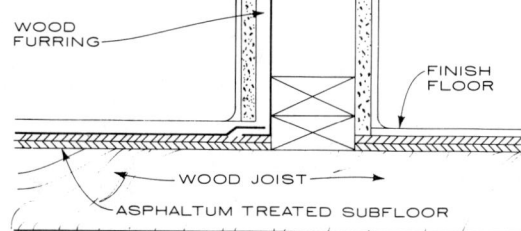

SHEET LEAD

WOOD FURRING

WALLBOARD

FINISH FLOOR

WOOD JOIST

ASPHALTUM TREATED SUBFLOOR

WOOD CONSTRUCTION—FLOOR

John Sava; The Architects Collaborative; Cambridge, Massachusetts

13   RADIATION PROTECTION

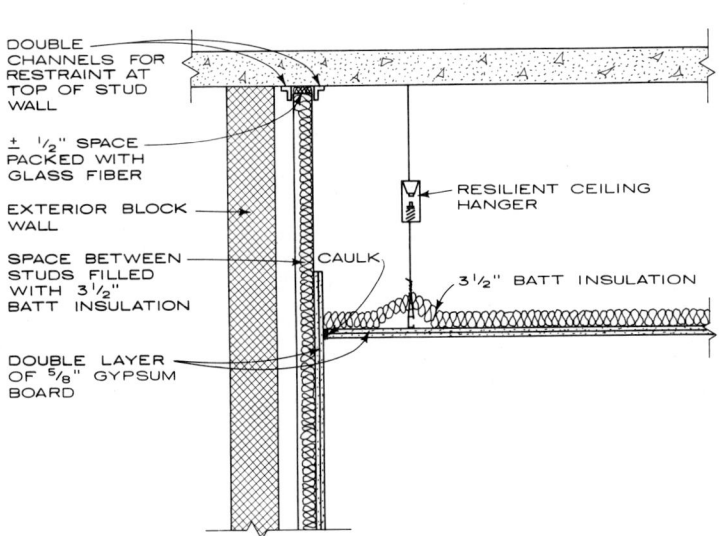

UPPER EXTERIOR WALL

DOUBLE CHANNELS FOR RESTRAINT AT TOP OF STUD WALL

± ¹/₂" SPACE PACKED WITH GLASS FIBER

EXTERIOR BLOCK WALL

SPACE BETWEEN STUDS FILLED WITH 3¹/₂" BATT INSULATION

DOUBLE LAYER OF ⁵/₈" GYPSUM BOARD

CAULK

RESILIENT CEILING HANGER

3¹/₂" BATT INSULATION

UPPER INTERIOR WALL
WITH HVAC AND ELECTRICAL PENETRATIONS

FLEXIBLE DUCT CONNECTION REQUIRED IF PENETRATION THROUGH STUD WALL IS RIGID

± ¹/₂" SPACE PACKED WITH GLASS FIBER

RESILIENT DUCT HANGER

DOUBLE CHANNELS FOR RESTRAINT

FLEXIBLE CONDUIT

CAULKING, TYPICAL

TYPICAL DUCT

CAULKING

3¹/₂" BATT INSULATION

INTERIOR BLOCK WALL

SURFACE MOUNTED LIGHTING FIXTURE

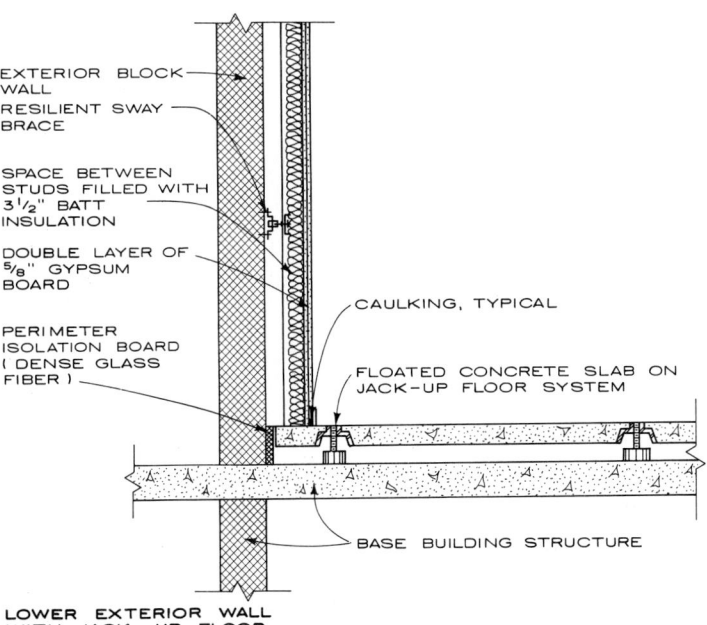

LOWER EXTERIOR WALL
WITH JACK-UP FLOOR

EXTERIOR BLOCK WALL
RESILIENT SWAY BRACE

SPACE BETWEEN STUDS FILLED WITH 3¹/₂" BATT INSULATION

DOUBLE LAYER OF ⁵/₈" GYPSUM BOARD

PERIMETER ISOLATION BOARD (DENSE GLASS FIBER)

CAULKING, TYPICAL

FLOATED CONCRETE SLAB ON JACK-UP FLOOR SYSTEM

BASE BUILDING STRUCTURE

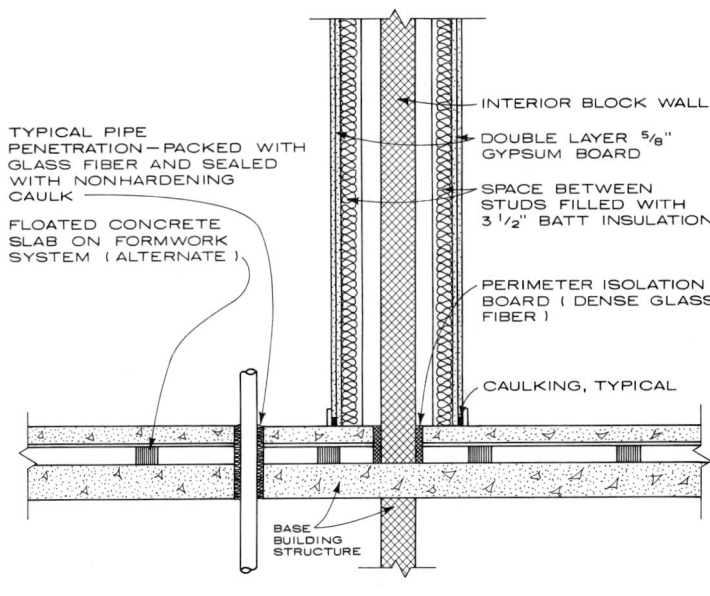

LOWER INTERIOR WALL

TYPICAL PIPE PENETRATION — PACKED WITH GLASS FIBER AND SEALED WITH NONHARDENING CAULK

FLOATED CONCRETE SLAB ON FORMWORK SYSTEM (ALTERNATE)

INTERIOR BLOCK WALL

DOUBLE LAYER ⁵/₈" GYPSUM BOARD

SPACE BETWEEN STUDS FILLED WITH 3¹/₂" BATT INSULATION

PERIMETER ISOLATION BOARD (DENSE GLASS FIBER)

CAULKING, TYPICAL

BASE BUILDING STRUCTURE

ISOLATED ROOM DETAILS
ISOLATED ROOMS

Isolated rooms incorporate special constructions to reduce intrusive noise and vibration from outside the room or to contain the sound and impact energy that is generated within the room. Typical applications include music practice rooms, sound studios, testing chambers, mechanical equipment rooms near sensitive areas, spaces exposed to nearby aircraft flyovers, and offices under gymnasiums. Isolated room construction can be very expensive; whenever possible, space planning and layout design should isolate high noise sources from acoustically critical uses so that the need for isolated rooms can be minimized.

The correct design of an isolated room is a "box-within-a-box." The inner box, which is the four walls, ceiling and floor of the isolated room, should be an airtight enclosure of dense impervious materials; this box must be isolated by resilient supports from the surrounding structure. It is also important that the base structure that supports the isolated room be as rigid and massive as possible.

The most effective floor construction is a "floated"

concrete pad, which is separated from the base building structure by steel springs, neoprene, or glass fiber isolation mounts. Inner walls can be supported from this slab. Any necessary structural bracing to the base building structure should be with a resilient nonrigid connection. The ceiling of the box can be suspended from resilient hangers, or it can be supported from the walls of the inner box. The diagram shows typical construction details.

It is necessary to avoid all flanking paths between an isolated room and the base building structure. Any penetrations through the walls or connections to outside services must be as well isolated as the room itself. Therefore, there should be flexible connections in ducts and conduit between the inner and outer box, and all piping must be resiliently supported.

Weatherstripped or sound rated doors and double glazed windows should be part of the continuous airtight enclosure that defines the inner box.

The degree of noise reduction that can be attained by an isolated room depends on the type of constructions, their resiliency, the elimination of flanking paths, and

the amount of dead airspace that surrounds the inner box. A well-built isolated room can achieve field performance ratings of STC 60 to 70 for airborne sound, and ratings of IIC 80 to 90 for impact noise. However, even minor flanking paths and short circuits can easily degrade these results by 10 points or more. The sound isolation between spaces will be only as great as the weakest sound path.

The advice and assistance of a qualified acoustical consultant should be sought in both the planning and design of isolated rooms and their related special constructions.

In addition to field erected isolated rooms as described above, several manufacturers make prefabricated units. These rooms are sold as self-contained music practice rooms, audiometric booths, and control booths for manufacturing plants. Although the detailing of their constructions is proprietary, one will find the same design approach as outlined here: a separate airtight box kept separate from the building structure. The degree of noise reduction that these prefabricated rooms can attain depends on the parameters used for field erected rooms.

Don Klabin, AIA; Bolt Beranek and Newman, Inc.; Cambridge, Massachusetts

STORAGE TEMPERATURES

PRODUCT	TEMPERATURES
Ice cream	-30°F (-34°C)
Frozen foods	-10°F (-23°C)
Produce	+35°F-40°F (2°C-4°C)
Meats	+34°F-36°F (1°C-2°C)
Dairy	+35°F-40°F (2°C-4°C)
Fish	+31°F-40°F (-0.5°C-4°C)

GENERAL NOTES

1. INSULATION: Insulation thicknesses vary with the box temperature, the type of insulation and conditions in surrounding areas and outside. In temperate climates cooler boxes at temperatures above 32°F (0°C) usually do not require floor insulation. Penetration of insulation by pipes, conduit, and hangers should be kept to an absolute minimum. Rods or pipes through ceiling insulation should be insulated 3'-0" above ceiling. Protection of insulation from damage from trucks and abrasion by stored goods is extremely important. Punctures in insulation finish allow moisture penetration with resulting drop in insulating efficiency and destruction of insulation structure.

2. DOORS: Refrigerator doors are available in a wide variety of types and finishes including sliding, overhead, and special vestibule doors to minimize refrigeration losses where long periods of opening will prevail. Consult manufacturers for door selection.

3. VENTILATION: All spaces above suspended ceilings must be well ventilated. Freezers on slab on grade must be vented or heated below the slab.

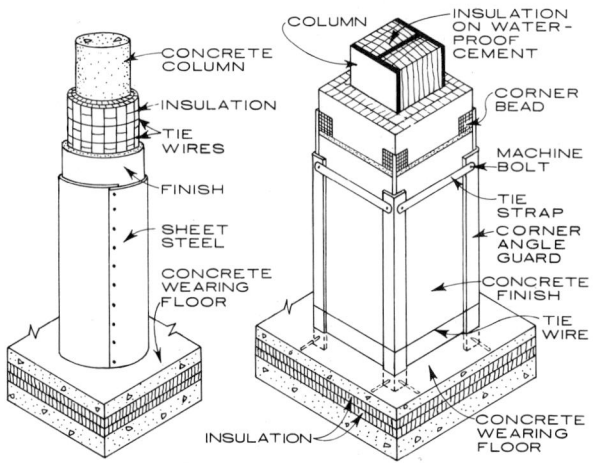

TYPICAL COLUMN GUARD DETAILS

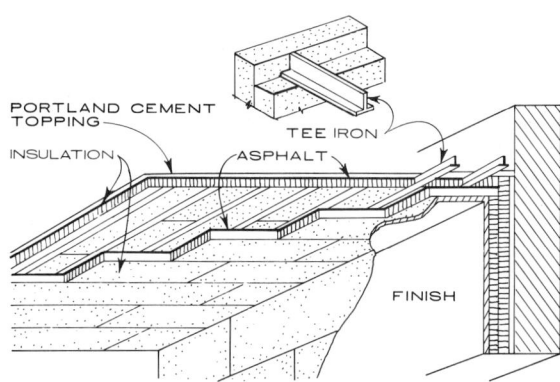

ON SUSPENDED STEEL CONSTRUCTION

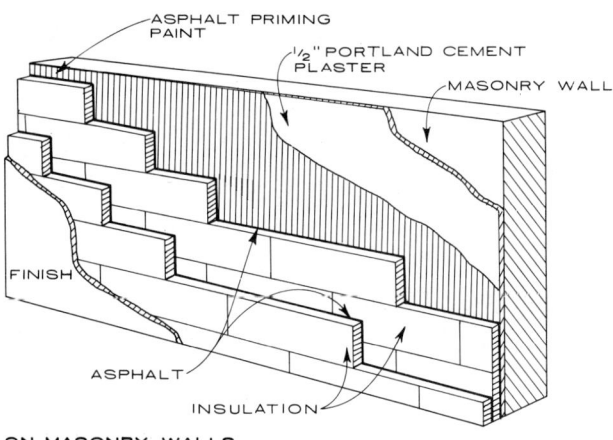

ON MASONRY WALLS

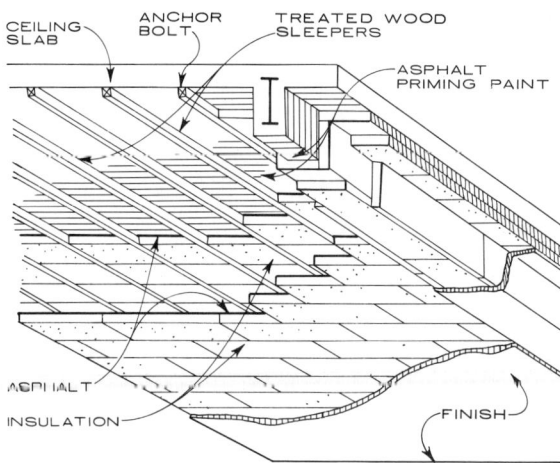

ON CONCRETE CONSTRUCTION

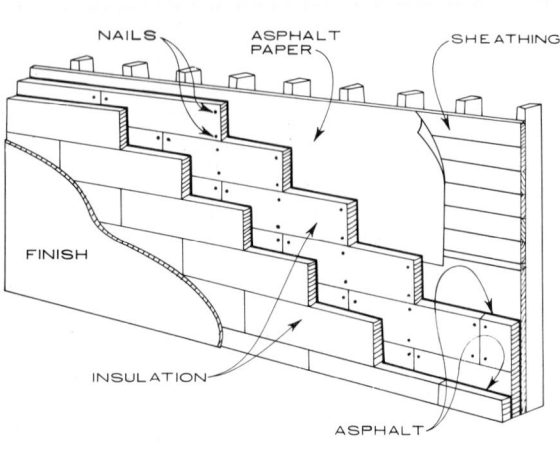

ON WOOD WALLS

TYPICAL WALL DETAILS

Elwood Taylor; The Ballinger Company; Philadelphia, Pennsylvania

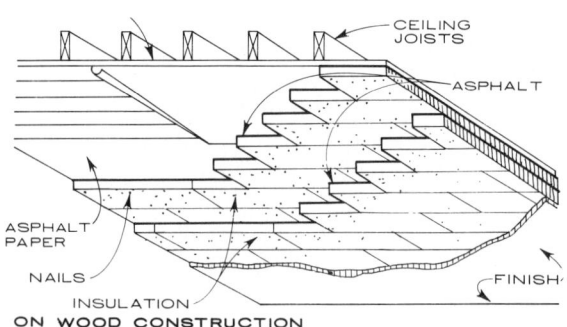

ON WOOD CONSTRUCTION

TYPICAL CEILING DETAILS

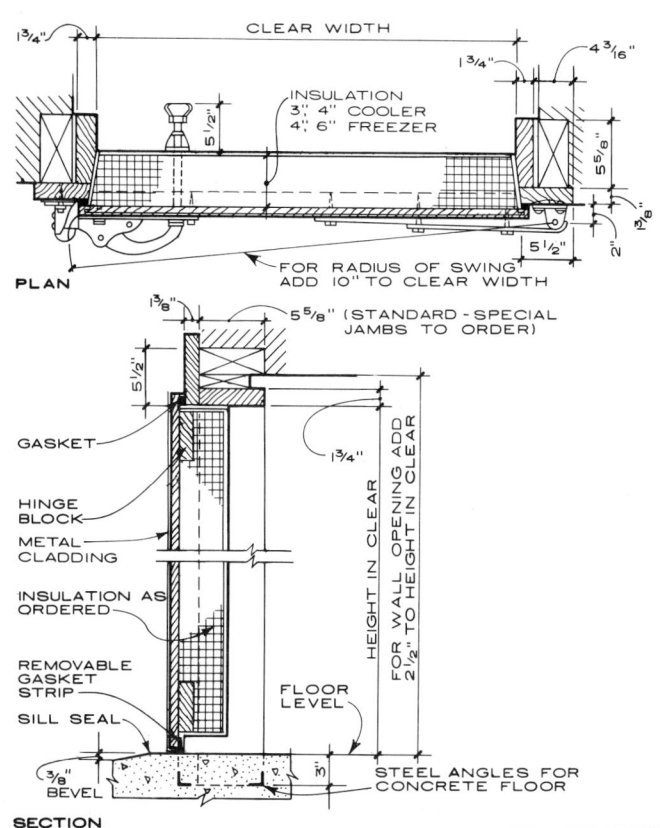

CLEAR WIDTH

INSULATION
3", 4" COOLER
4", 6" FREEZER

FOR RADIUS OF SWING
ADD 10" TO CLEAR WIDTH

PLAN

5⅝" (STANDARD - SPECIAL
JAMBS TO ORDER)

GASKET

HINGE BLOCK

METAL CLADDING

INSULATION AS ORDERED

REMOVABLE GASKET STRIP

SILL SEAL

⅜" BEVEL

STEEL ANGLES FOR CONCRETE FLOOR

FLOOR LEVEL

HEIGHT IN CLEAR

FOR WALL OPENING ADD 2½" TO HEIGHT IN CLEAR

SECTION
TYPICAL DOOR DETAILS

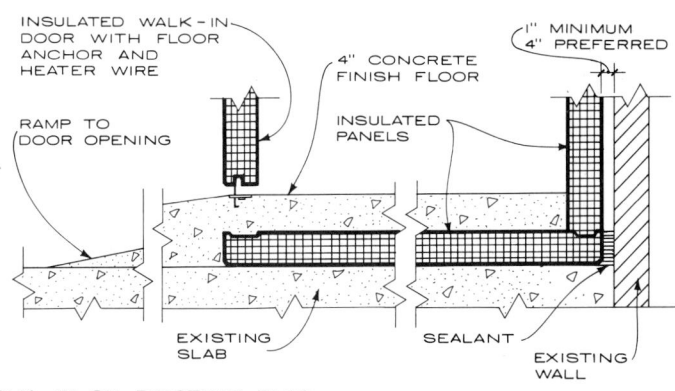

INSULATED WALK-IN DOOR WITH FLOOR ANCHOR AND HEATER WIRE

4" CONCRETE FINISH FLOOR

1" MINIMUM 4" PREFERRED

RAMP TO DOOR OPENING

INSULATED PANELS

EXISTING SLAB

SEALANT

EXISTING WALL

WALK-IN ON EXISTING SLAB

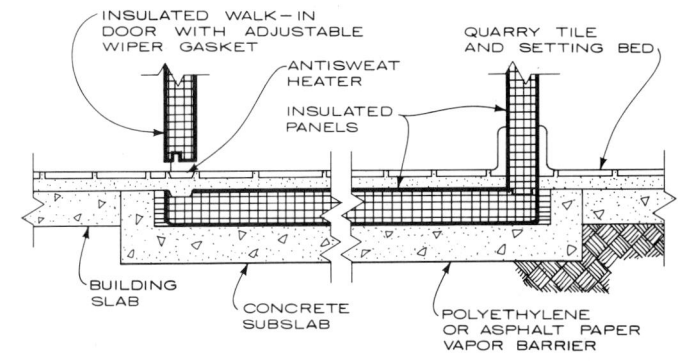

INSULATED WALK-IN DOOR WITH ADJUSTABLE WIPER GASKET

ANTISWEAT HEATER

INSULATED PANELS

QUARRY TILE AND SETTING BED

BUILDING SLAB

CONCRETE SUBSLAB

POLYETHYLENE OR ASPHALT PAPER VAPOR BARRIER

WALK-IN IN NEW CONSTRUCTION
WALK-IN FLOOR DETAILS

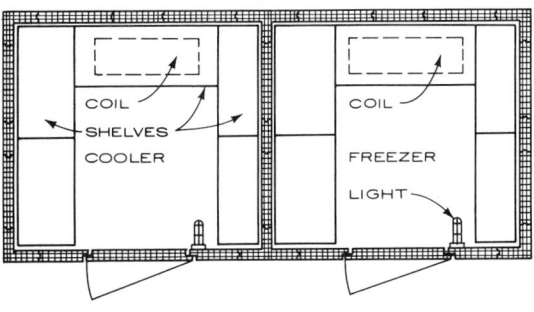

COIL
SHELVES
COOLER

COIL
FREEZER
LIGHT

SIDE-BY-SIDE PLAN

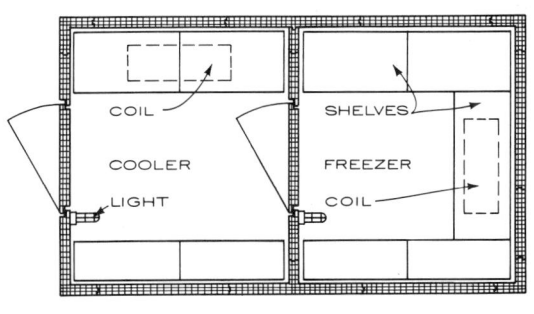

COIL
COOLER
LIGHT

SHELVES
FREEZER
COIL

WALK-THROUGH PLAN

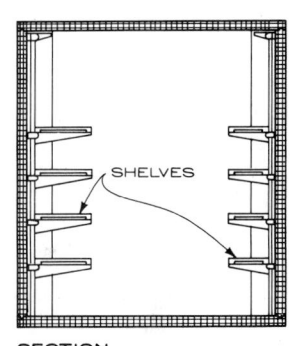

SHELVES

SECTION

WALK-IN TYPICAL PLANS AND SECTION

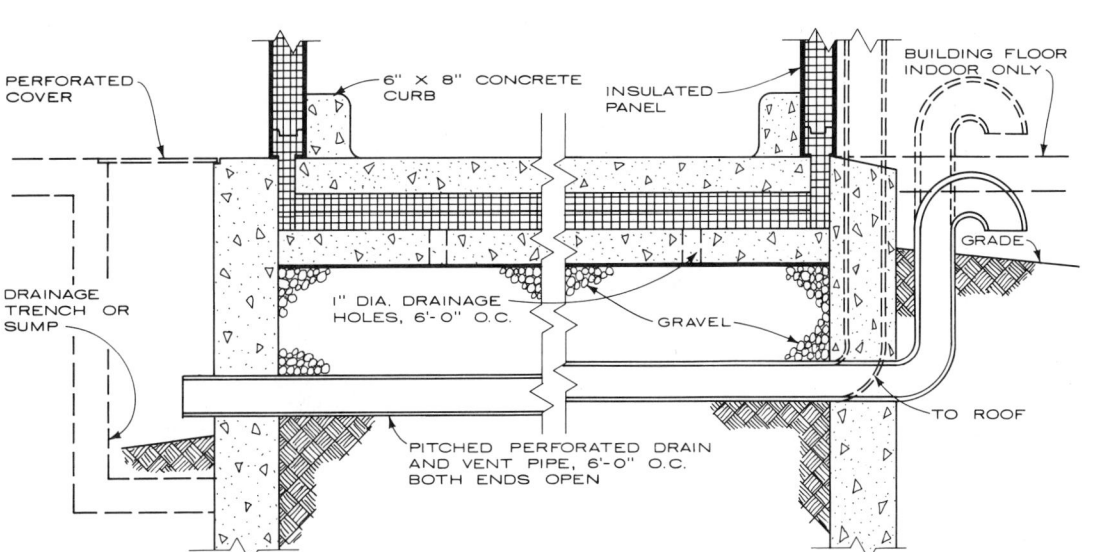

PERFORATED COVER

6" X 8" CONCRETE CURB

INSULATED PANEL

BUILDING FLOOR INDOOR ONLY

GRADE

DRAINAGE TRENCH OR SUMP

1" DIA. DRAINAGE HOLES, 6'-0" O.C.

GRAVEL

TO ROOF

PITCHED PERFORATED DRAIN AND VENT PIPE, 6'-0" O.C. BOTH ENDS OPEN

DRAIN AND VENT DETAIL

Cini-Grissom Associates, Inc.; Food Service Consultants; Washington, D.C.

GENERAL NOTES

1. DOORS

    Standard sizes: 2'-6'', 3'-2'', 3'-6'', 4'-0'', 5'-0'' wide x 6'-6'' high; 4'-0'', 5'-0'' wide x 7'-0'' high.

    Sliding, double action, and display doors are available.

    Manual or electrically operated.

2. PREFABRICATED INSULATED PANELS

    Standard sizes: 4'' thick.

    Width: 11½'', 23'', and 46''.

    Height: 7'-6'', 8'-6'', 10'-6'', and 11'-6''.

    Finish material usually aluminum, galvanized steel, or stainless steel.

3. WALK-IN UNIT SIZES

    Widths: 3'-11'', 5'-10'', 7'-9'', 9'-8'', and 11'-7''.

    Lengths: 5'-10'', 7'-9'', 11'-7'', 13'-6'', 15'-5'', 17'-4'', 19'-3''.

    Heights: 7'-6'', 8'-6'', 9'-6'', 10'-6'', 11'-6''.

    Available accessories: stationary or mobile shelf units and adjustable cantilevered shelves, windows, interior partitions, meat rails, floor racks, ramps, and walk-ins.

4. Check local codes for drainage requirements.

SPECIAL PURPOSE ROOMS **13**

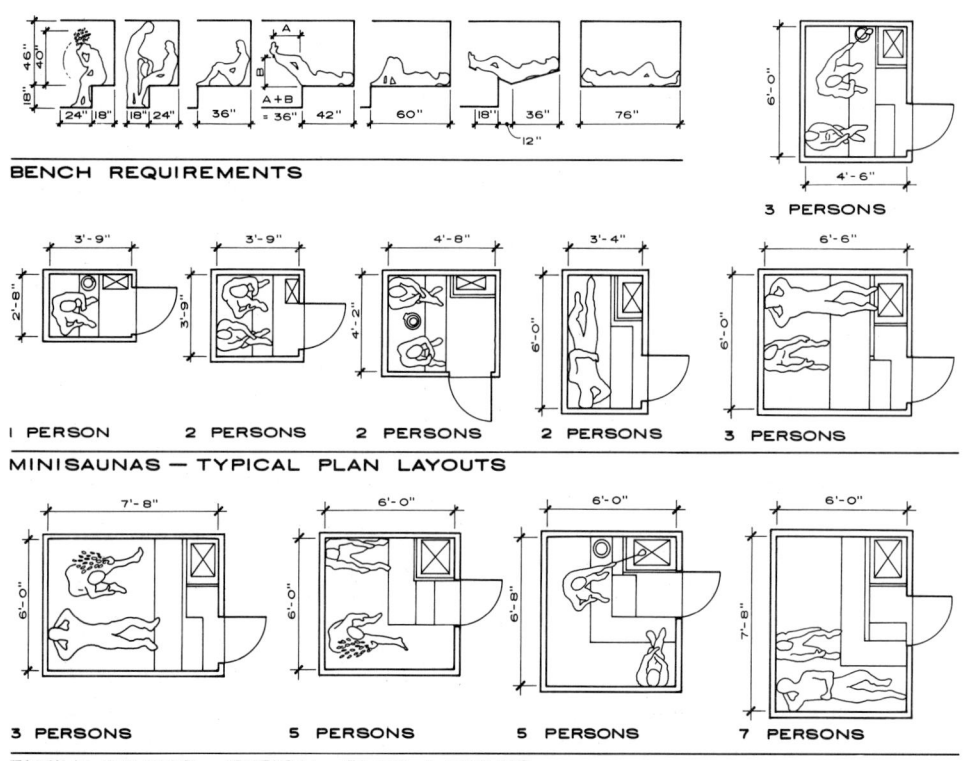

BENCH REQUIREMENTS

3 PERSONS

MINISAUNAS — TYPICAL PLAN LAYOUTS

I PERSON   2 PERSONS   2 PERSONS   2 PERSONS   3 PERSONS

FAMILY SAUNAS — TYPICAL PLAN LAYOUTS

3 PERSONS   5 PERSONS   5 PERSONS   7 PERSONS

PLANS
PUBLIC SAUNAS

PLAN

SECTION

SAUNA ROOM CONSTRUCTION

Jerry Graham; CTA Architects Engineers; Billings, Montana

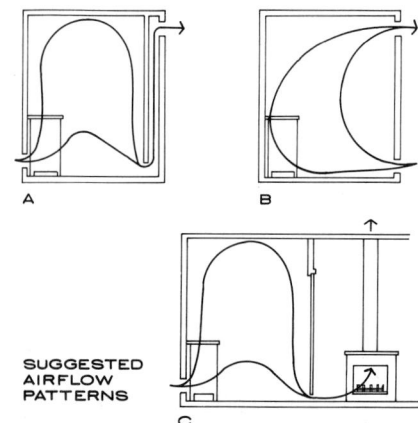

SUGGESTED AIRFLOW PATTERNS

PANEL SAUNA VENTILATION

DESIGN CONSIDERATIONS

The fundamental purpose of the sauna is to induce perspiration; the higher the temperature, the more quickly perspiration will begin.

The drier the air, the more heat one can stand. Temperatures on the platform can be as high as 212°F, 230°F, and 240°F. A little warm water thrown over the stove stones just before leaving the sauna produces a slightly humid wave of air that suddenly seems hotter and envelops the bather with an invisible glowing cloud, pleasantly stinging the skin. It is usually better to lie than to sit, for the temperature rises roughly 18°F for every 1 ft above the floor level; if one lies, heat is equally dispensed over the entire body. When lying down one may wish to raise one's feet against the wall or ceiling.

The expanded hot air in the sauna contains proportionately less oxygen than the denser atmosphere outside. Bathers sometimes experience faintness unless the air is changed regularly. An amount of fresh air enters each time the door is opened; this is insufficient, however. Normally two adjustable ventilators are built into the walls. One, the air inlet, is usually placed low near the stove. Fresh air should be drawn from outside and not from adjoining rooms where odors can be present.

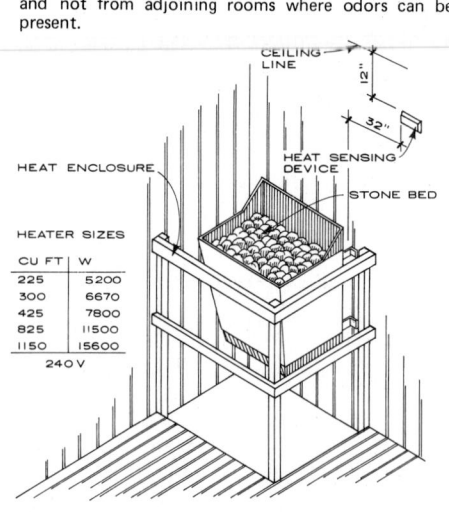

STOVE AND THERMOSTAT LOCATION

HEATER SIZES	
CU FT	W
225	5200
300	6670
425	7800
825	11500
1150	15600
240 V	

NATURAL VENTILATION

Air must flow freely into the room—inlet and outlet normally are on opposite walls and at approximately the same level. The inlet situated under the stove creates a strong updraft.

A. A flue or duct provides a chimney action that will pull air off the floor and out.

B. Inlet is low on the wall, with outlet high and directly above it. This ensures ventilation even if wind pressure exists on the wall containing the two ventilators because of the difference in air temperature at the two openings and the effect of normal convection.

C. Suggest fresh air from exterior with outlet through another room, fan, or fireplace.

HEATER: The heater depends on convection for air circulation. It is the preferred method, for the air in a sauna should be as static as possible to heat the sauna in 1 to 1½ hr.

INTERIOR PANELING: Tongue and grooved boards should be at least ⅝ in. thick, or thicker if possible because of the increased ability to absorb vapor and to retain the timber smell. Boards should not be wider than about six times their thickness. Blind nailing with galvanized or aluminum nails is common. Vapor barrier and insulation under the interior paneling must be completely vaporproof and heat resistant. Most conventional insulating materials are effective; mineral base is preferred; avoid using expanded polystyrene.

DOOR: The opening should be kept as small as possible to minimize loss of heat. Maximum height is 6 ft. Door must open outward as a safety measure. A close fitting rebate on all four sides is usually sufficient insurance against heat loss around the edges. The construction should approach the U value of the walls.

HARDWARE: Because of the weight of the door, a pair of 4 in. brass butt hinges with ball bearings are recommended. A heavy ball or roller catch keeps the door closed. Door handles are made of wood.

LIGHTING: The lighting must be indirect and the fitting unobtrusive. The best position for the light is above and slightly behind the bather's normal field of view. The switch is always outside the hot room.

TYPE OF WOOD: White or western red cedar and redwood are the materials suitable for sauna construction. They should be chosen based on their resistance to splitting and decay, color of the wood, and the thermal capacity of the wood. These woods stain badly by metal and perspiration.

CEILING HEIGHT: The bigger the volume the more heat required; hence, keep the ceiling as low as possible within the limits imposed by the benches.

The main platform or bench will be about 39 in. above floor in a family sauna or at least 60 in. in a large public sauna. The ceiling is about 43 in. above the highest bench. Average family sauna ceiling height is 82 in., public 110 in.

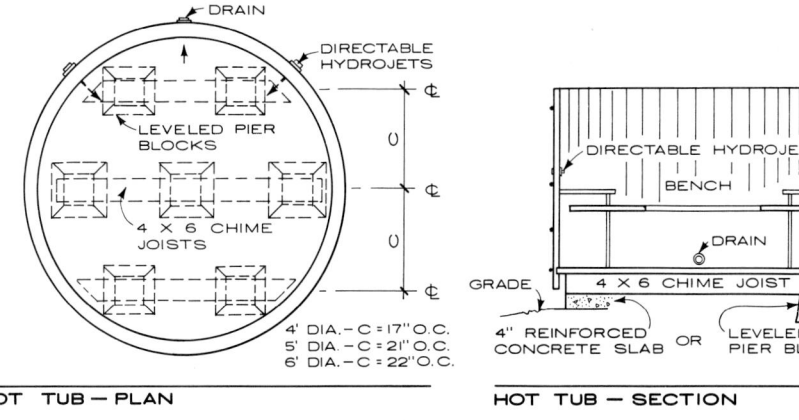

HOT TUB — PLAN

4' DIA. — C = 17" O.C.
5' DIA. — C = 21" O.C.
6' DIA. — C = 22" O.C.

HOT TUB — SECTION

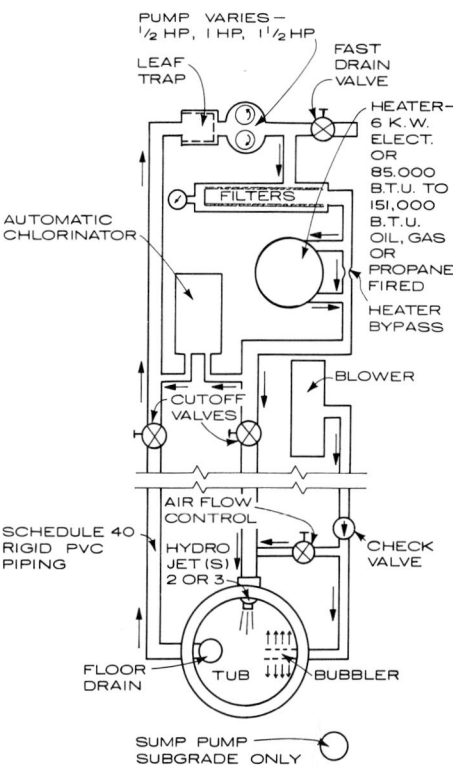

MECHANICAL SCHEMATIC

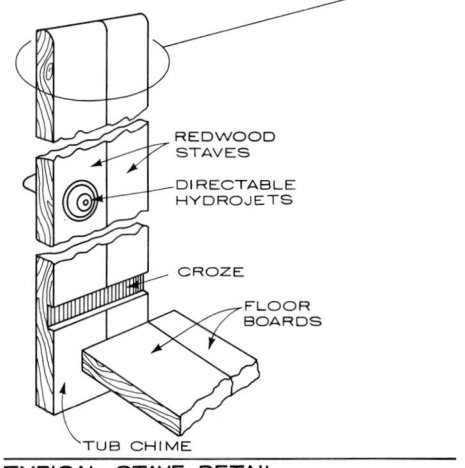

ALTERNATE INSTALLATIONS

TUB COVER. TO MINIMIZE HEAT LOSS A COVER IS RECOMMENDED. A PRIMARY FOAM BLANKET LIES ON THE SURFACE OF THE WATER. THE SECONDARY 1 X 6 T & G REDWOOD COVER IS FOR SECURITY AND HEAT RETENTION

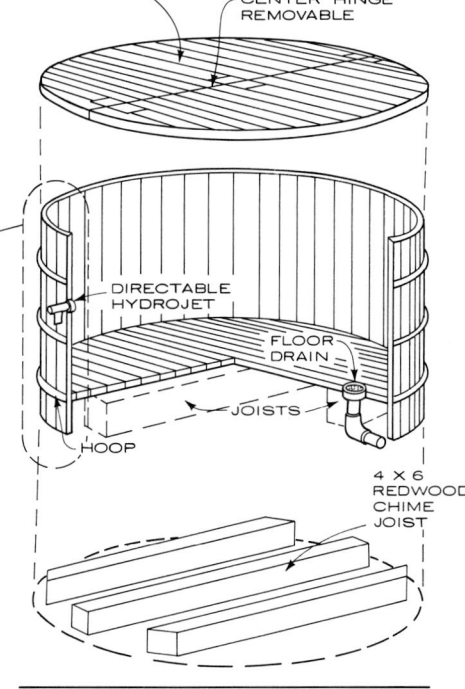

TYPICAL TUB

TYPICAL STAVE DETAIL

NOTES

Low profile tubs allow the bathers to sit directly on the floor with feet extended. Therapeutically, this style provides direct, close range hydromassage that comes from a floor bubbler. High profile tubs can accommodate more people per diameter foot and allows people to bath standing upright. Tub surfaces are normally left unsealed and will weather naturally to gray. Exterior can be stained or treated with silicone or oil resin to preserve the natural reddish finish. In high altitude, occasional repeated oil treatment is recommended. The size and sophistication of each tub is determined by capacity, budget, and preference for components. The most critical tub support components are the heater, filter system, chlorinator, and automatic cycling and temperature control system. Hydromassage jets are a significant part of every hot tub system. Many types of heaters are available: natural gas, electric, propane, and oil. Their sizes range from 50,000 to 175,000 Btu. All components should be approved and meet local codes and standards. Consult manufacturers for additional information. Tubs made of molded fiberglass with a smooth interior surface are generally referred to as SPAS. Their function and operation is similar to those of the hot tub.

HOT TUB DIMENSIONS

	STANDARD TUB						LOW PROFILE TUB					
NOM. DIA. (FT)	4	5	6	7	8	9	10	4 5 6 7 8 9 10					
INSIDE DIA. (IN.)	44	56	68	80	92	104	116	44 56 68 80 92 104 116					
NUMBER OF HOOPS	3	3	3	3	4	4		2 2 3 3 3 3					
HOOP INTERVAL (IN.)	19 ± 1 IN.							12 ± 1 IN.					
SEAT SECTIONS	2	3	4	5				SIT ON FLOOR					

LOW PROFILE TUB

STANDARD TUB

SEATING ARRANGEMENTS:

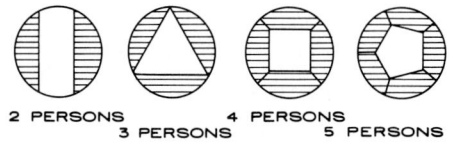

2 PERSONS   4 PERSONS
3 PERSONS   5 PERSONS

Jerry Graham; CTA Architects Engineers; Billings, Montana

ASEISMIC DESIGN

Earthquake forces result from random vertical and horizontal vibratory motions of the ground on which the structure rests. For the most part, the vertical forces are neglected by the building codes owing to the combination of safety factors inherent in the vertical framing members. Certain nonstructural elements, however, may require vertical considerations. The earthquake forces may vary in direction, intensity, and duration and are affected by geological conditions at and around the specific site.

Structural frames are composed of resisting elements that may be moment resisting, shear walls, or a combination. The configuration of a structure and its fundamental period (natural frequency) considerably affect the earthquake resistance of the structure. Symmetry in plan is generally very desirable. Unusually shaped plans result in high stress concentrations and must receive special attention during design. Structural elements must be tied together to make them respond to earthquake motions as a unit; otherwise structural separations may be required.

Most building materials are adaptable to use as resisting elements. Brittle materials must be avoided unless properly reinforced. Ductile materials are generally the most desirable. In high seismic risk areas, building codes commonly require all buildings higher than 160 ft to have "ductile" moment resisting frames.

Earthquake resistant buildings can be so designed that there will be minimal structural as well as nonstructural damage and maximum safety within reasonable economic limits. Nonstructural elements and building equipment often must be seismically considered to be an integral part of the building system. This is especially true for equipment found in essential facilities such as hospitals, etc. Equipment that generally must receive a seismic consideration includes emergency power supplies, other building utilities, critical or life support equipment, and general support equipment.

METHODS OF ASEISMIC DESIGN (OR QUALIFICATION)

DESIGN BY ANALYSIS

The static coefficient method of analysis is applicable to both the building structure and nonstructural elements such as partition walls and building equipment. The general formula for the static coefficient method is based on $F = CW$, where F is the seismic force, C the seismic coefficient (design acceleration value), and W the building or nonstructural element weight. Various modifiers can be included in the right hand portion of the equation (refer to the current Uniform Building Code—International Conference of Building Officials), such as zone values, frame characteristics, building importance, and soil structure interaction. The static coefficient method is applicable for simple building structures where a more complex method of analysis is not desirable or for nonstructural elements that only require anchorage to the main structure.

Dynamic analyses are a more complex form of aseismic design and generally yield more exact information. Two methods exist. The first and most common is the response spectrum technique. Various modes of vibration (and their associated periods) are determined with this technique. The second method is the most exact method of analysis, since it reviews the building systems with respect to the design earthquake time history (divided into small increments of time). This type of analysis results in predictions of building motion, building distortion, building forces, and absolute floor accelerations for every part of the building at every interval of the design earthquake motion. Dynamic analyses can be used to find resonance frequencies and determine seismic characteristics of fairly complex systems, in systems where the operation of nonstructural elements is required after but not during an earthquake, and in systems where the mode of failure of the building equipment is likely to be structural rather than operational.

The results of either type of dynamic analysis are only as good as the assumptions made in constructing the mathematical model for the analysis.

DESIGN BY SEISMIC TEST

Seismic simulation machines exist for the testing of structural systems and nonstructural elements. Seismic testing is the only viable method to test building equipment that must remain operational during and after an earthquake when the mode of failure is likely to be operational rather than structural. This includes equipment such as life support systems and communication equipment. Seismic shaking tables are generally designed to operate uniaxially, vector biaxially, or true independent biaxially.

DESIGN JUDGMENT

Great economic savings can be achieved by employing good design judgment. This method of seismic qualification is generally applicable to commodity types of nonstructural elements such as simple shelving. These items can generally be dealt with by adequate architectural detailing.

PRIOR EXPERIENCE

This method of seismic qualification is generally applicable to nonstructural elements. Once a particular element is qualified by any other method, that qualification will be applicable to subsequent installations that are similar in nature if adequate seismic qualification records are maintained.

COMBINED METHODS OF QUALIFICATION

This method of qualification is applicable to both structural systems and nonstructural elements. The common approach is to analyze portions of the system that are too large to test on existing seismic tables and to seismically test smaller portions of the system that are too complex to adequately model mathematically. Seismic tests can also be utilized to verify a previous analysis. Special seismic machines can be attached to existing structures to determine the system's natural period of vibration, which can then be compared with the previously calculated values. Combined methods of seismic qualification may often yield large economic advantages.

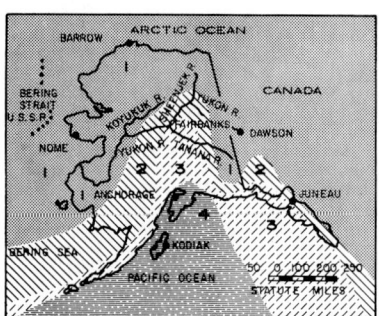

ALASKA

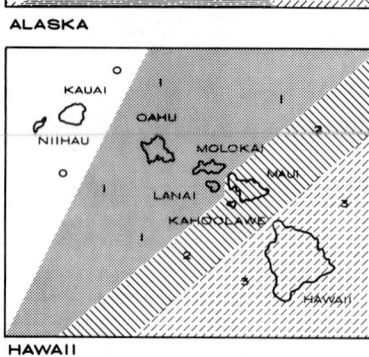

HAWAII

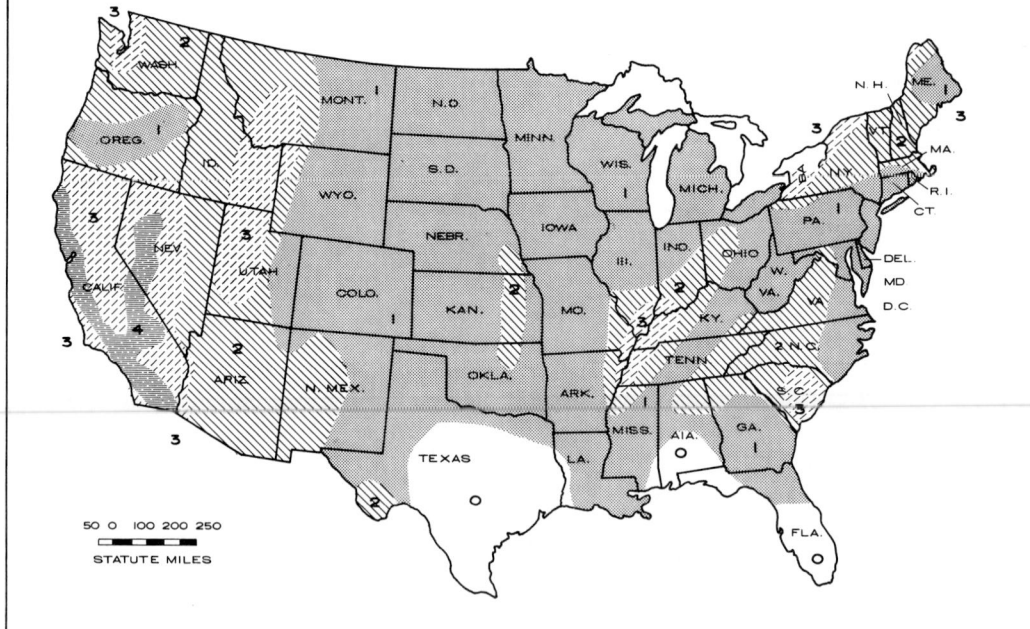

50 0 100 200 250
STATUTE MILES

KEY:

ZONE 1—Minor damage; distant earthquakes may cause damage to structures with fundamental periods greater than 1.0 second; corresponds to intensities V and VI of the M.M.* Scale.

ZONE 2—Moderate damage; corresponds to intensity VII of the M.M.* Scale.

ZONE 3—Major damage; corresponds to intensity VII and higher of the M.M.* Scale.

ZONE 4—Those areas within Zone No. 3 determined by the proximity to certain major fault systems.

*Modified Mercalli Intensity Scale of 1931

SOURCE: SEISMIC RISK MAP OF THE CONTERMINOUS UNITED STATES — AFTER S.T. ALGERMISSEN, "SEISMIC RISK STUDIES IN THE UNITED STATES," PROCEEDINGS OF THE FOURTH WORLD CONFERENCE ON EARTHQUAKE ENGINEERING (VOL.I, PP. 19-27), SANTIAGO, CHILE, 1969.

SEISMIC RISK MAP OF THE UNITED STATES

Gary L. McGavin; Wyle Laboratories; El Segundo, California
Alfred M. Kemper, AIA; Kemper & Associates; Los Angeles, California
Harold P. King, C.E.C.; King, Benioff, Steinmann, King; Sherman Oaks, California

13 **SEISMIC DESIGN**

THE EARTHQUAKE GENERATES GROUND MOTIONS THAT CAN BE EXPRESSED IN THREE MUTUALLY PERPENDICULAR AXES

GROUNDSHAKING, NOT GROUNDRUPTURE, GENERALLY CAUSES MOST BUILDING DAMAGE

GROUNDSHAKING

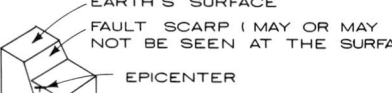
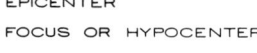

EARTH'S SURFACE
FAULT SCARP (MAY OR MAY NOT BE SEEN AT THE SURFACE)
EPICENTER
FOCUS OR HYPOCENTER
FAULT PLANE

STRIKE SLIP – LEFT LATERAL

STRIKE SLIP – RIGHT LATERAL

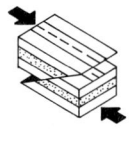
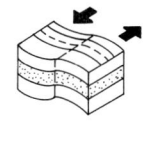

DIP SLIP NORMAL

DIP SLIP REVERSE

THRUST

CONTINUOUS FAULT CREEP

FAULT TERMINOLOGY AND TYPES

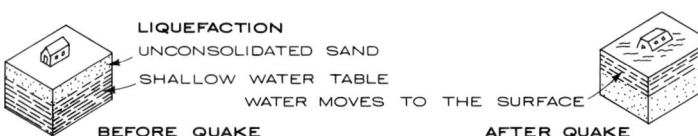

LIQUEFACTION
UNCONSOLIDATED SAND
SHALLOW WATER TABLE
WATER MOVES TO THE SURFACE

BEFORE QUAKE

AFTER QUAKE

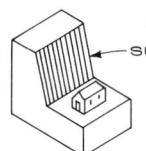

EARTHQUAKE INDUCED LANDSLIDE

SUSCEPTIBLE SLOPE

SLOPE FAILURE (ROCK FALL, AVALANCHE, SLUMP, OR EARTHFLOW) EXERCISE CARE WITH DIPPING SEDIMENTARY UNITS AND JOINTED ROCKS

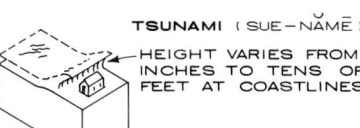

TSUNAMI (SUE–NĂMĒ)

SEICHE (SĀSH)

HEIGHT VARIES FROM INCHES TO TENS OF FEET AT COASTLINES

WAVE CREATED WITHIN AN ENCLOSED BASIN (DAM, LAKE, OR BAY) WAVES MAY BREECH OR TOP DAMS

SEISMIC SEA WAVES ARE MOST COMMON AT LOW LYING COAST LINES AND HARBORS

OTHER MAJOR EARTHQUAKE RELATED EVENTS

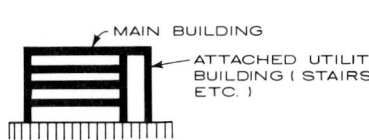

MAIN BUILDING
ATTACHED UTILITY BUILDING (STAIRS, ETC.)

SEVERE POUNDING OF THE TWO STRUCTURES

ANCHOR OR PROVIDE SEISMIC CRUSH JOINT

POSSIBLE COLLAPSE OF UTILITY BUILDING

REMEDY – ADEQUATELY ANCHOR OR PROVIDE "SEISMIC CRUSH JOINT" BETWEEN THE STRUCTURES

ATTACHED BUILDING CHARACTERISTICS

Gary L. McGavin; Wyle Laboratories; El Segundo, California

Alfred M. Kemper, AIA; Kemper & Associates; Los Angeles, California

TALL BUILDINGS

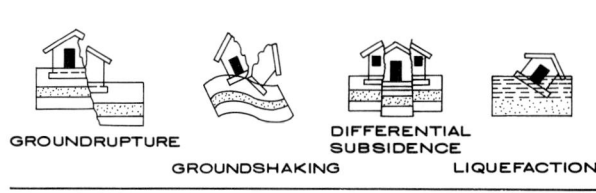

SWAY

STORY RACKING

COLLISION

TORSION

EARTHQUAKE EFFECTS ON BUILDINGS

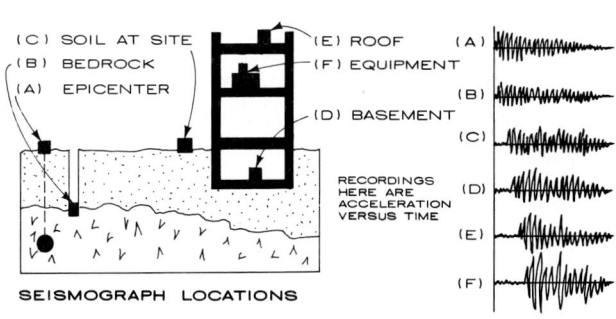

GROUNDRUPTURE

GROUNDSHAKING

DIFFERENTIAL SUBSIDENCE

LIQUEFACTION

FOUNDATION FAILURES — MAIN CAUSES

(C) SOIL AT SITE
(B) BEDROCK
(A) EPICENTER
(E) ROOF (A)
(F) EQUIPMENT
(D) BASEMENT

RECORDINGS HERE ARE ACCELERATION VERSUS TIME

(B)
(C)
(D)
(E)
(F)

SEISMOGRAPH LOCATIONS

VARIOUS SEISMOGRAPH RECORDINGS FROM A SINGLE EVENT

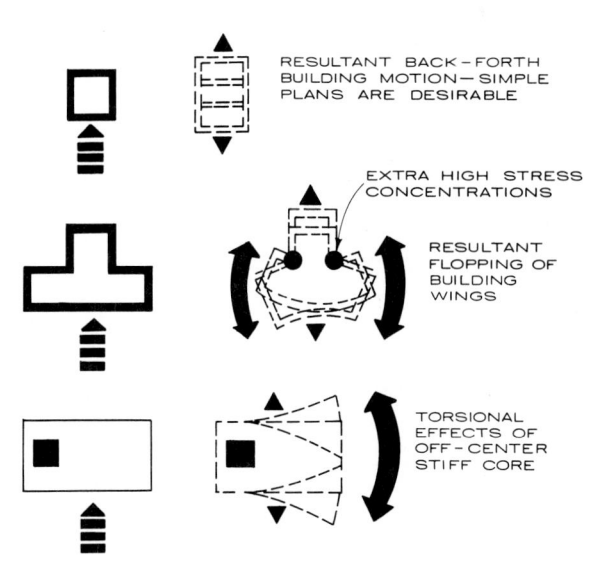

RESULTANT BACK–FORTH BUILDING MOTION—SIMPLE PLANS ARE DESIRABLE

EXTRA HIGH STRESS CONCENTRATIONS

RESULTANT FLOPPING OF BUILDING WINGS

TORSIONAL EFFECTS OF OFF–CENTER STIFF CORE

A GENERAL PHILOSOPHY OF EARTHQUAKE RESISTANT DESIGN MAY BE STATED AS: KEEP IT SIMPLE AND TIE IT TOGETHER

MOTIONS OF TYPICAL PLAN SHAPES

SEISMIC DESIGN **13**

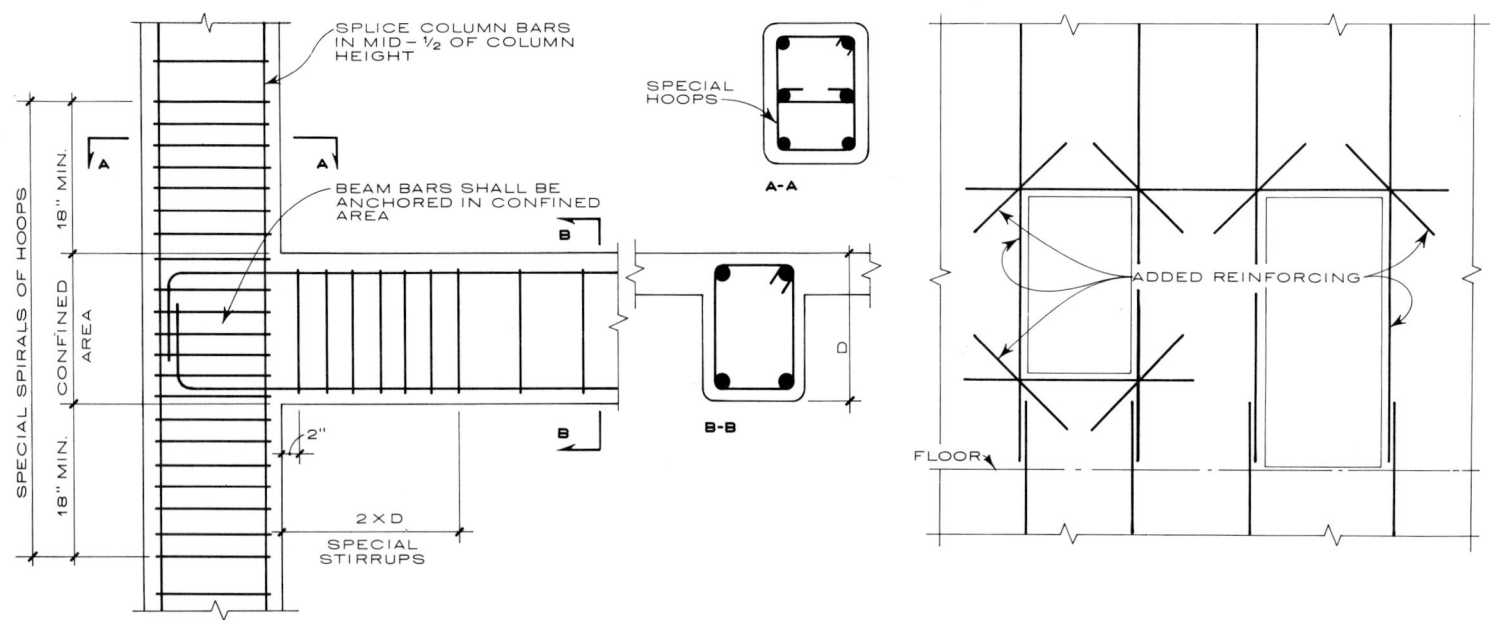

REINFORCING DETAIL FOR DUCTILE MOMENT RESISTING SPACE FRAME

OPENINGS IN MASONRY AND CONCRETE WALLS

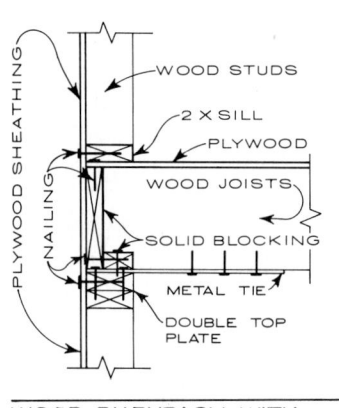

WOOD DIAPHRAGM WITH PLYWOOD SHEAR WALLS

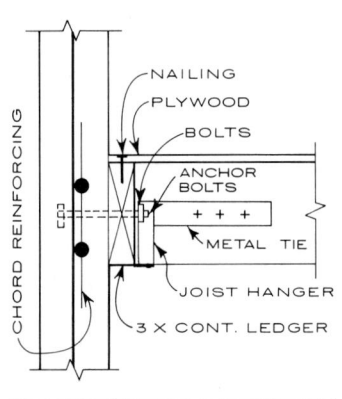

WOOD DIAPHRAGM WITH MASONRY OR CONCRETE SHEAR WALLS

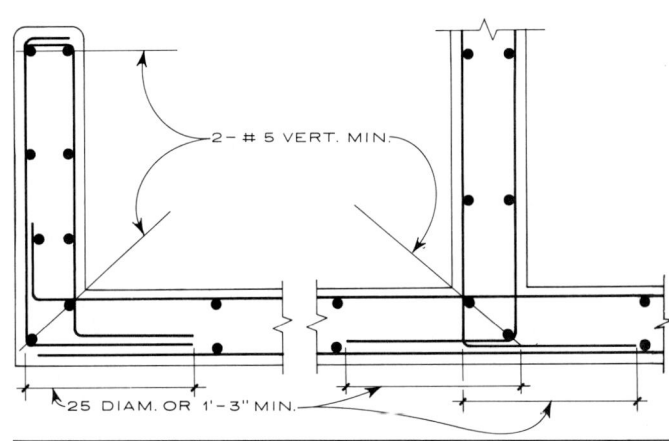

INTERSECTION OF CONCRETE OR REINFORCED MASONRY WALLS

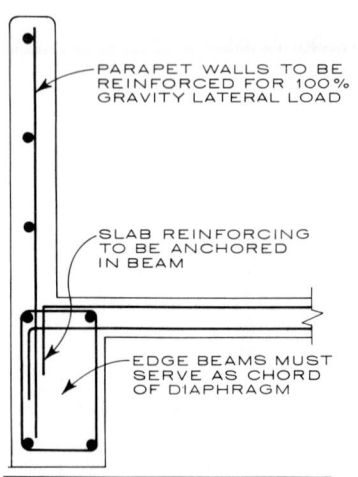

CONCRETE DIAPHRAGM WITH CONCRETE FRAME

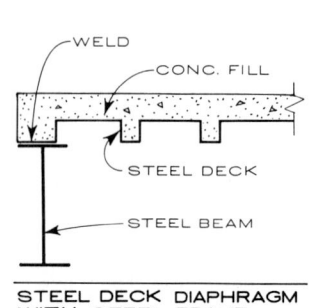

STEEL DECK DIAPHRAGM WITH STEEL FRAME

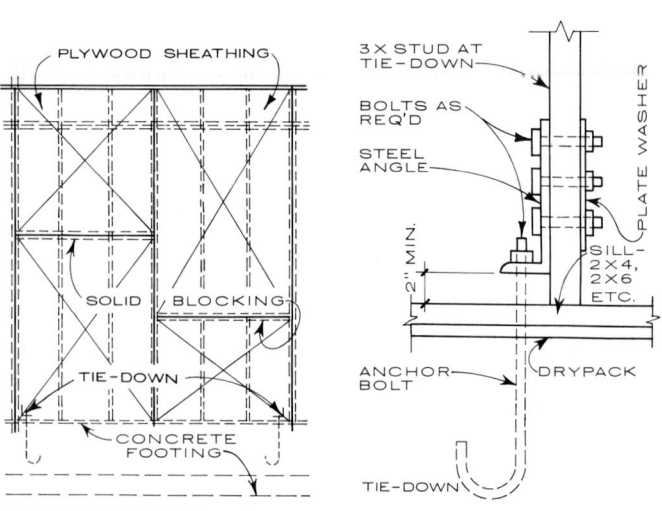

PLYWOOD SHEATHED SHEAR WALL WITH TIE-DOWNS

Harold P. King, CEC; King, Benioff, Steinmann, King; Sherman Oaks, California

SEISMIC DESIGN

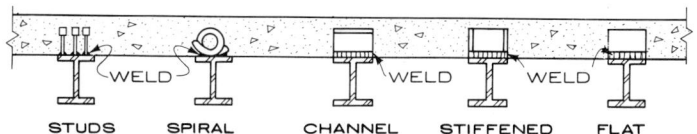

TYPICAL SHEAR CONNECTIONS OF STEEL BEAMS TO CONCRETE FLOORS (WELDED)

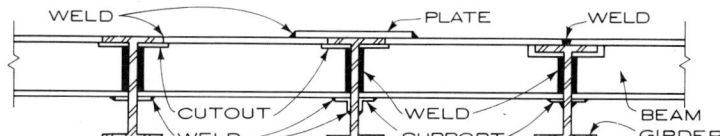

BEAM TO GIRDER—CONTINUOUS CONNECTIONS (WELDED)

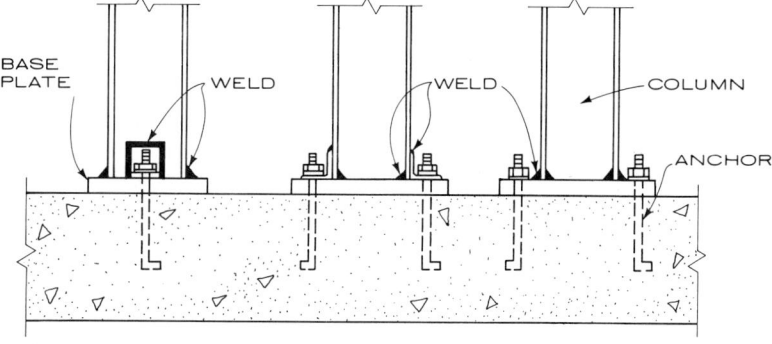

COLUMN CONNECTIONS TO CONCRETE FOUNDATION

MISCELLANEOUS DETAILS — STEEL FRAMING

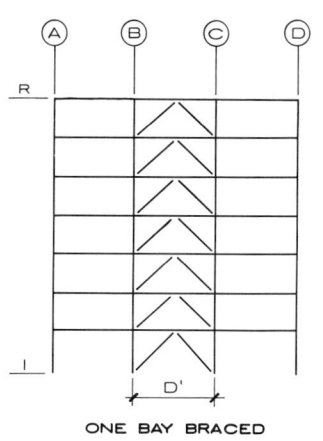

ONE BAY BRACED

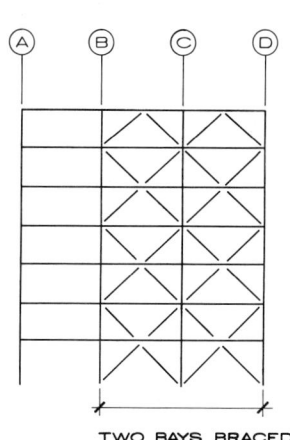

TWO BAYS BRACED

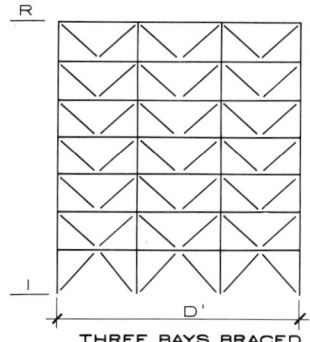

THREE BAYS BRACED

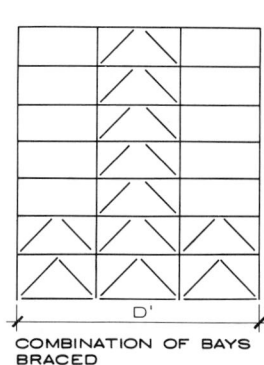

COMBINATION OF BAYS BRACED

NOTE: Avoid unbraced stories.

POSSIBLE BRACING SYSTEMS — STEEL BUILDINGS

Gary L. McGavin; Wyle Laboratories; El Segundo, California

Alfred M. Kemper, AIA; Kemper & Associates; Los Angeles, California

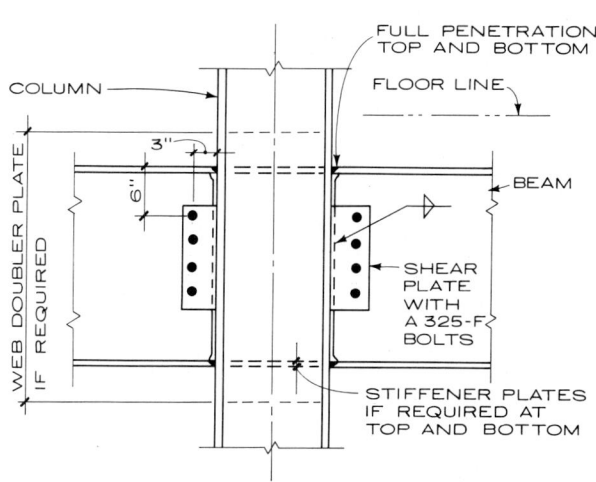

TYPICAL GIRDER AND COLUMN CONNECTION

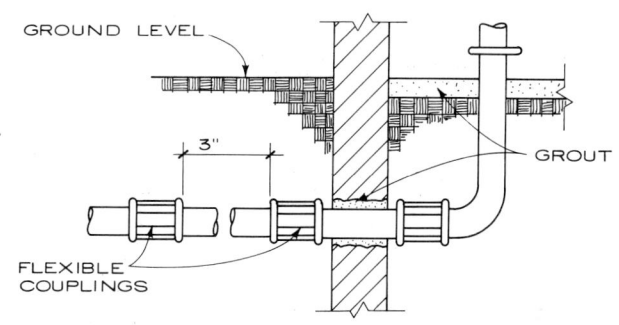

PIPE GROUTED IN WALL

PIPE ENTERING BUILDING

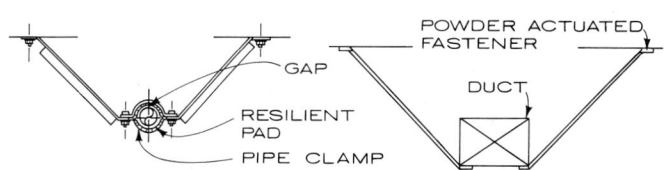

TRANSVERSE BRACING

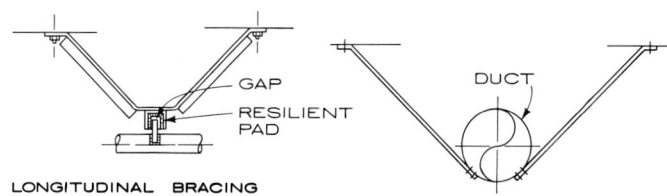

LONGITUDINAL BRACING

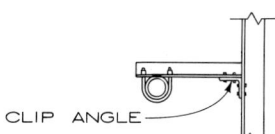

BRACING FOR PIPES AND DUCTS

NOTE

Details shown are representative of possible construction detailing. In addition to code defined structural requirements, safety considerations require nonstructural building elements and furnishings to be anchored in areas subjected to seismic movement. These pages show selected details as samples of recommended bracing and anchorage. Additional or variant details are developed as experience is gained.

SEISMIC DESIGN **13**

BUILDING TYPES AND WIDTHS

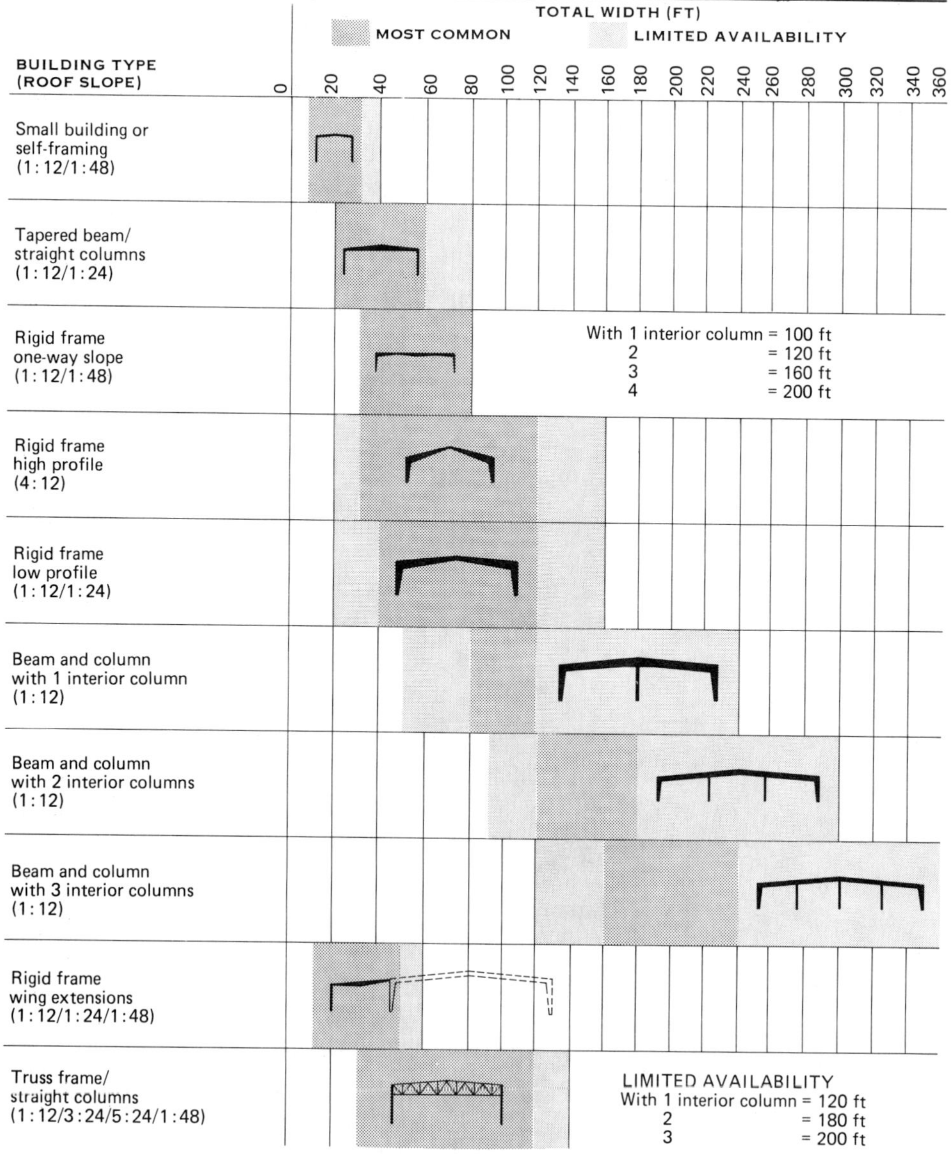

BUILDING TYPE (ROOF SLOPE)	TOTAL WIDTH (FT)
	MOST COMMON — LIMITED AVAILABILITY

Width scale: 0, 20, 40, 60, 80, 100, 120, 140, 160, 180, 200, 220, 240, 260, 280, 300, 320, 340, 360

Small building or self-framing (1:12/1:48)

Tapered beam/ straight columns (1:12/1:24)

Rigid frame one-way slope (1:12/1:48)

With 1 interior column = 100 ft
2 = 120 ft
3 = 160 ft
4 = 200 ft

Rigid frame high profile (4:12)

Rigid frame low profile (1:12/1:24)

Beam and column with 1 interior column (1:12)

Beam and column with 2 interior columns (1:12)

Beam and column with 3 interior columns (1:12)

Rigid frame wing extensions (1:12/1:24/1:48)

Truss frame/ straight columns (1:12/3:24/5:24/1:48)

LIMITED AVAILABILITY
With 1 interior column = 120 ft
2 = 180 ft
3 = 200 ft

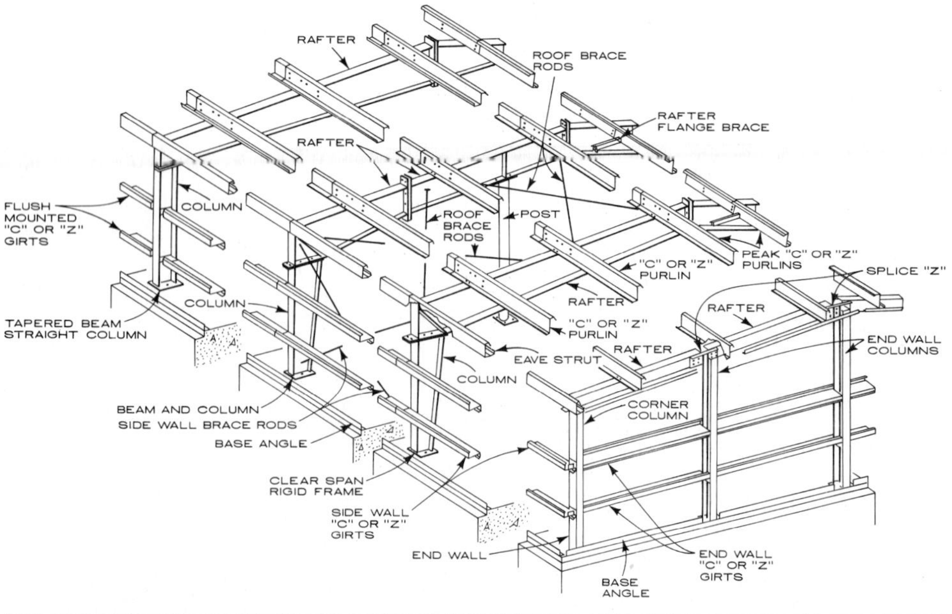

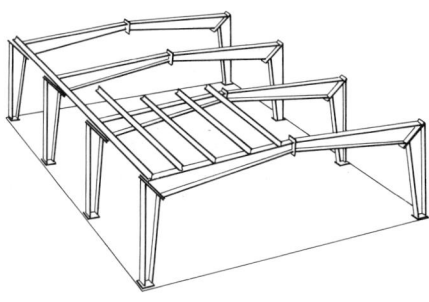

RIGID FRAME

NOTES

Preengineered metal buildings are available in standard framing sizes and types from a variety of manufacturers as proprietary products. The table illustrates the most commonly available systems. Many manufacturers offer these framing systems in widths greater than those shown, as well as offering other options aimed at filling the customer's needs. Regional availability should be checked. Use table for preliminary design only.

1. BAY SPACINGS: Range from 18 to 30 ft, with 20 to 25 being the most common. Wider bays, up to 60 ft, may be offered with joist systems.
2. WIDTH: Building dimension measured from outside surface of girts. Inside clearance varies.
3. EAVE HEIGHT: Distance from bottom to column to top of eave strut. Nominal 2 ft increments varying from 10 ft to 30 ft.
4. ROOF LIVE LOAD: Loads, including snow load, exerted on a roof except dead, wind, and lateral loads. Most systems commonly available in 12, 20, 30, or 40 psf.
5. DEAD LOAD: The weight of all permanent construction such as floor and roof framing and covering materials is building weight or dead load.
6. COLLATERAL LOADS: Additional dead loads other than the metal building framing, such as sprinklers, mechanical and electrical systems, and ceilings. Most systems commonly available in 15, 20, or 25 psf.
7. WIND LOAD: Load caused by the wind blowing from any horizontal direction. Most systems commonly available in 15, 20, or 25 psf.
8. SEISMIC LOAD: Assumed lateral load acting in any horizontal direction on the structural system because of the action of earthquakes. Individual design required.
9. AUXILIARY LOADS: Specified dynamic live loads other than the basic design loads which the building must safely withstand, such as cranes, materials handling systems, and impact loads. Individual design required.

The user should verify whether the manufacturer's standard practice meets or exceeds established engineering principles, local practice, or applicable building codes.

ISOMETRIC OF FRAMING SYSTEMS COMPONENTS

Labels: RAFTER, ROOF BRACE RODS, RAFTER FLANGE BRACE, RAFTER, FLUSH MOUNTED "C" OR "Z" GIRTS, COLUMN, ROOF BRACE RODS, POST, PEAK "C" OR "Z" PURLINS, SPLICE "Z", "C" OR "Z" PURLIN, TAPERED BEAM STRAIGHT COLUMN, COLUMN, RAFTER, "C" OR "Z" PURLIN, RAFTER, END WALL COLUMNS, BEAM AND COLUMN SIDE WALL BRACE RODS, BASE ANGLE, EAVE STRUT, RAFTER, CLEAR SPAN RIGID FRAME, COLUMN, CORNER COLUMN, SIDE WALL "C" OR "Z" GIRTS, END WALL, END WALL "C" OR "Z" GIRTS, BASE ANGLE

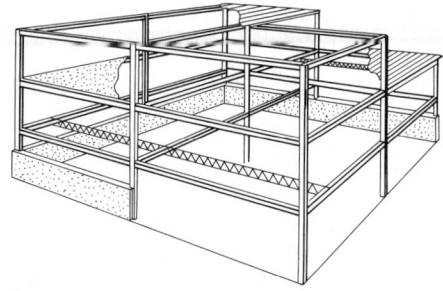

COLUMN SPACING

LENGTH	WIDTH
20'	20'
25'	25'
30'	30'
35'	35'
40'	40'

STANDARD HEIGHTS

FULL HEIGHT (BASE OF COLUMN TO FLOOR)
12', 13', 14'
Half-story (lower level in ground)
6', 7', 8', 9'

MULTISTORY LOWRISE
(LIMITED AVAILABILITY)

Robert P. Burns, AIA, David Hayes; Robert Burns & Associates; Riverside, Iowa

13 PREFABRICATED BUILDINGS

CHAPTER 14 CONVEYING SYSTEMS

GENERAL

An elevator system with its hoistway, machine room, and waiting lobbies is a major element in a building and requires special design consideration. Preengineered or custom-made elevator systems can be constructed to meet virtually all vertical transportation needs for passenger, freight, or service.

In all cases, design of an elevator system must be carefully considered throughout all stages of the building design process. During initial stages, the elevator handling capacity and quality of service desired determines the size, number, type, and location of elevator systems. Proper selection depends on type of tenancy, number of occupants, and the building design (number of floors, floor heights, building circulation, etc.). Elevator ARRANGEMENT locates the elevator within the building plan to provide efficient and accessible service. Each elevator system, once selected, requires OPERATIONAL SPACES, hoistway and machine room, and PASSENGER SPACES, lobby, and elevator car.

Proper planning and contact with representatives of the elevator industry and local code officials are essential to each of these design areas.

NOTE: WHERE A HOISTWAY EXTENDS INTO THE TOP FLOOR OF A BUILDING, FIRE RESISTIVE HOISTWAY OR MACHINERY SPACE ENCLOSURES, AS REQUIRED, SHALL BE CARRIED TO THE UNDERSIDE OF THE ROOF IF THE ROOF IS OF FIRE RESISTIVE CONSTRUCTION, AND AT LEAST 3 FT. ABOVE THE TOP SURFACE OF A FIRE NON-RESISTIVE ROOF

The two most common systems, the HYDRAULIC ELEVATOR and the ELECTRIC ELEVATOR, are shown in the two diagrams on this page. The systems are distinguished mainly by their hoisting mechanisms.

The HYDRAULIC ELEVATOR uses a hydraulic driving machine to raise and lower the elevator car and its load. A hydraulic driving machine is one in which the energy is applied by means of a liquid under pressure in a cylinder equipped with a plunger or piston. The car and driving machine are supported at the pit floor (hoistway base). Lower speeds and the piston length restrict the use of this system to approximately 60 ft. It generally requires the least initial installation expense, but more power is used during operation because of the greater loads imposed on the driving machine.

An ELECTRIC ELEVATOR is a power elevator where the energy is applied by means of an electric driving machine. In the electric driving machine the energy is applied by an electric motor. It includes the motor, brake, and the driving sheave or drum together with its connecting gearing, belt, or chain, if any. High speeds and virtually limitless rise allow this elevator to serve highrise, medium-rise, and lowrise buildings.

MACHINE ROOM (ELECTRIC ELEVATOR)

Normally located directly over the top of the hoistway —it could also be below at side or rear—the machine room is designed to contain elevator hoisting machine and control equipment. Adequate ventilation, soundproofing, and structural support for the elevator must be considered.

ELEVATOR CAR

Guided by vertical guide rails, the elevator car conveys passenger or freight between floors. It consists of a car constructed within a supporting platform and frame. Design of the car focuses on the finished ceiling, walls, floor, and doors with lighting, ventilation, and elevator signal equipment.

The car of a hydraulic and elevator system is supported by a piston or cylinder.

The car of an electric system is suspended by wire ropes.

HOISTWAY

The hoistway is a shaftway for the travel of one or more elevators. It includes the pit and terminates at the underside of the overhang machinery space floor or grating, or at the underside of the roof where the hoistway does not penetrate the roof. Access to the elevator car and hoistway is normally through hoistway doors located at each floor serviced by the elevator system. Hoistway design is determined by the characteristics of the elevator system selected and by requirements of the applicable code for fire separation, ventilation, soundproofing, or nonstructural elements.

LOBBY

Elevator waiting areas are designed to allow free circulation of passengers, rapid access to elevator cars, and clear visibility of elevator signals.

MACHINE ROOM (HYDRAULIC ELEVATOR)

Normally located near the base of the hoistway, the machine room contains hydraulic equipment and controls. Provisions of adequate ventilation and soundproofing must be considered.

HYDRAULIC ELEVATOR: FIRE RESISTIVE ROOF, 3' MIN., FIRE NON-RESISTIVE ROOF, HYDRAULIC PISTON, PIT LADDER, ELEVATOR PIT, HYDRAULIC PISTON WELL

HYDRAULIC ELEVATOR

Alexander Keyes; Darrel Rippeteau, Architect; Washington, D.C.

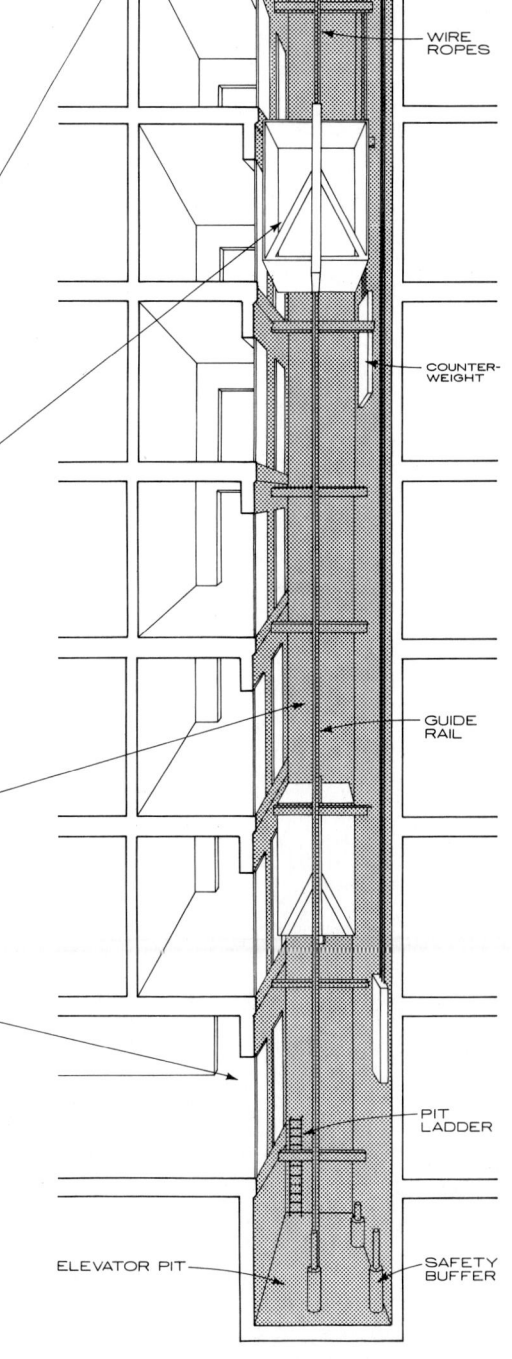

VENT, HOISTING MACHINE, MACHINE SUPPORT BEAMS, VENTILATION REQUIRED FOR HOISTWAY, WIRE ROPES, COUNTER-WEIGHT, GUIDE RAIL, PIT LADDER, ELEVATOR PIT, SAFETY BUFFER

ELECTRIC ELEVATOR

GENERAL NOTES

Lowrise buildings may use either the hydraulic or the electric elevator systems. Elevator selection, arrangement, and design of lobby and cars are similar in both cases. The primary differences between the two systems are in their operational requirements. The hydraulic elevator system is described below; the electric elevator system on the next page.

The major architectural considerations of the hydraulic elevator are the machine room, normally located at the base, and the hoistway serving as a fire protected, ventilated passageway for the elevator car. Adequate structure must be provided at the base of the hoistway to bear the load of the elevator car and its supporting piston or cylinder.

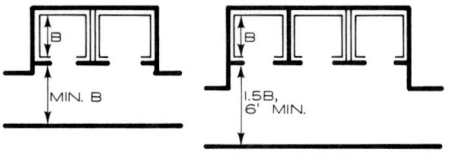

TWO CAR, SIDE BY SIDE

THREE CAR, SIDE BY SIDE

B = DEPTH OF CAR

NOTES

Certain guidelines lead to effective placement, grouping, and arrangement of elevators within a building. Elevators should be: (a) centrally located, (b) near the main entrance, and (c) easily accessible on all floors. If a building requires more than one elevator, they should be grouped, with possible exception of service elevators.

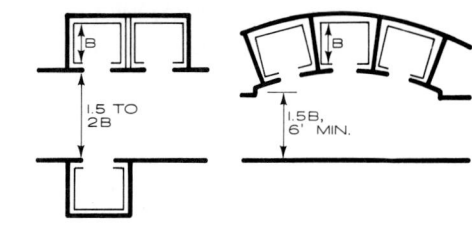

TWO OR THREE CAR, OPPOSITE

THREE CAR, SPECIAL ARRANGEMENT

Within each grouping, elevators should be arranged to minimize walking distance between cars. Sufficient lobby space must be provided to accommodate group movement.

ELEVATOR ARRANGEMENT, TWO AND THREE CARS (TYPICAL FOR LOWRISE APPLICATIONS)

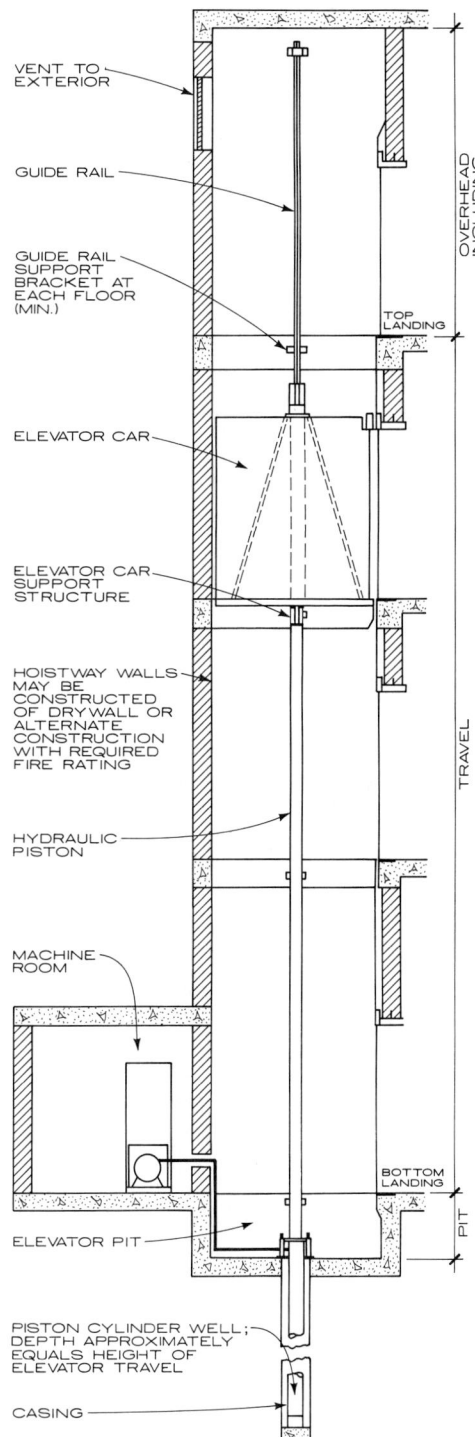

VENT TO EXTERIOR

GUIDE RAIL

GUIDE RAIL SUPPORT BRACKET AT EACH FLOOR (MIN.)

ELEVATOR CAR

ELEVATOR CAR SUPPORT STRUCTURE

HOISTWAY WALLS MAY BE CONSTRUCTED OF DRYWALL OR ALTERNATE CONSTRUCTION WITH REQUIRED FIRE RATING

HYDRAULIC PISTON

MACHINE ROOM

ELEVATOR PIT

PISTON CYLINDER WELL; DEPTH APPROXIMATELY EQUALS HEIGHT OF ELEVATOR TRAVEL

CASING

OVERHEAD INCLUDING CLEARANCE

TOP LANDING

TRAVEL

BOTTOM LANDING

PIT

HYDRAULIC ELEVATOR – SECTION

Alexander Keyes; Darrel Rippeteau, Architect; Washington, D.C.

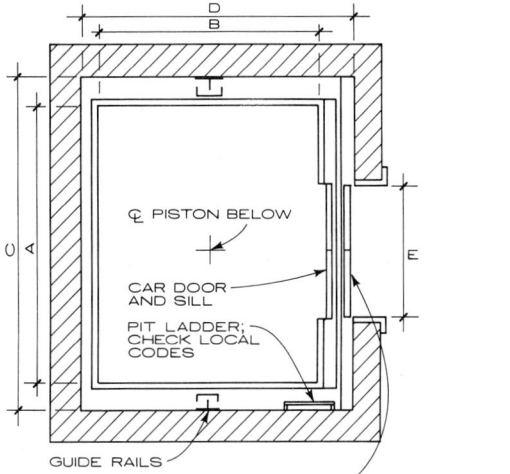

CL PISTON BELOW

CAR DOOR AND SILL

PIT LADDER; CHECK LOCAL CODES

GUIDE RAILS

HOISTWAY DOOR AND SILL

ELEVATOR CAR AND HOISTWAY

HYDRAULIC ELEVATOR DIMENSIONS

RATED LOAD (LB)	DIMENSIONS (FT-IN.)				
	A	B	C	D	E
1500	4-6	4-3	6-8	5-11	2-8
2000	5-8	4-3	7-4	5-11	3-0
2500	6-8	4-3	8-4	5-11	3-6
3000	6-8	4-7	8-4	6-3	3-6
3500	6-8	5-3	8-4	6-11	3-6
4000	7-8	5-3	9-4	6-11	4-0

Rated speeds are 75 to 200 fpm.

NOTES

Elevator car and hoistway dimensions of the preengineered units listed above are for reference purposes only. A broad selection of units is available. Representatives of the elevator industry should be contacted for the dimensions of specific systems.

Hoistway walls normally serve primarily as fireproof enclosures. Check local codes for required fire ratings. Guide rails extend from the pit floor to the underside of the overhead. When excessive floor heights are encountered consult the elevator supplier for special requirements.

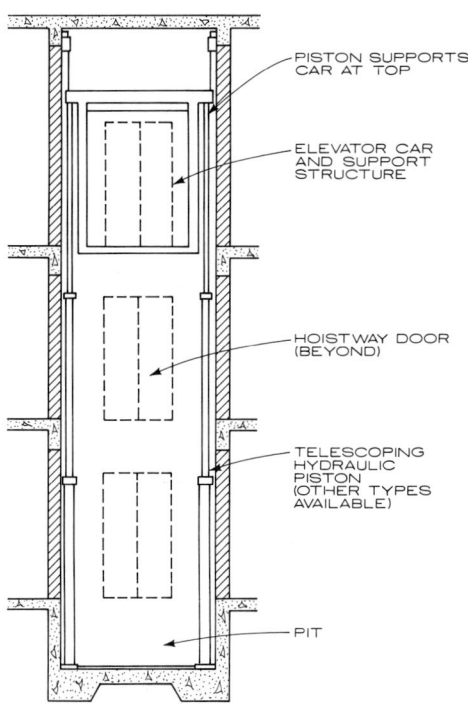

PISTON SUPPORTS CAR AT TOP

ELEVATOR CAR AND SUPPORT STRUCTURE

HOISTWAY DOOR (BEYOND)

TELESCOPING HYDRAULIC PISTON (OTHER TYPES AVAILABLE)

PIT

One type of holeless hydraulic elevator uses a telescoping hydraulic piston as the driving machine, eliminating the need for cylinder well excavation. This system is presently limited to a height of three stories or 21 ft 6 in. Other types of holeless hydraulic elevator units are also available using an inverted cylinder attached to the side of the elevator car.

HOLELESS HYDRAULIC ELEVATOR – SECTION

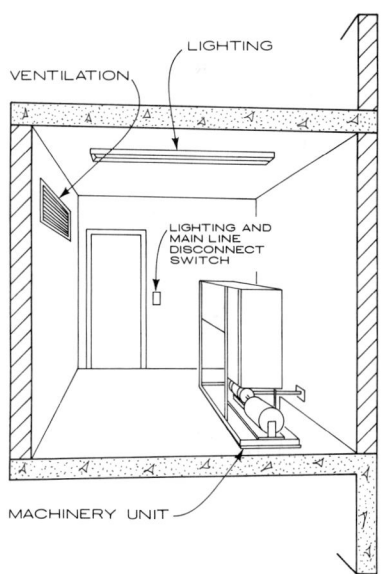

LIGHTING

VENTILATION

LIGHTING AND MAIN LINE DISCONNECT SWITCH

MACHINERY UNIT

The MACHINE ROOM of a hydraulic elevator system is usually located next to the hoistway at or near the bottom terminal landing. Consult with elevator manufacturers for required dimensions.

Machinery consists of a pump and motor drive unit, hydraulic fluid storage tank, and control panel. Adequate ventilation, lighting, and entrance access (usually 3 ft 6 in. x 7 ft) should be provided.

MACHINE ROOM

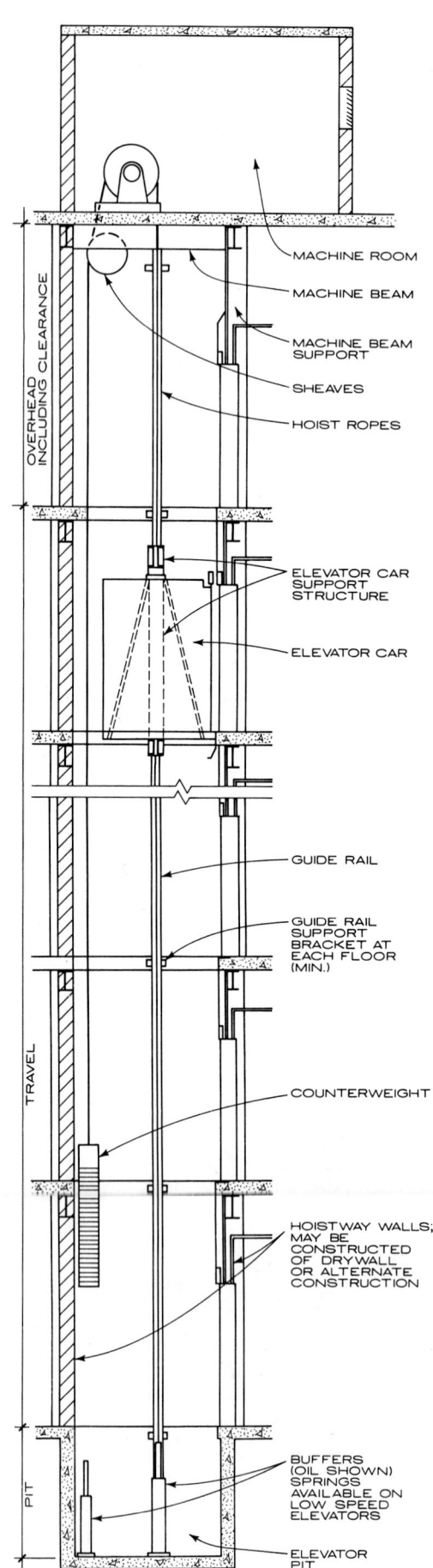

ELECTRIC ELEVATOR — SECTION

Labels on the section diagram:
- MACHINE ROOM
- MACHINE BEAM
- MACHINE BEAM SUPPORT
- SHEAVES
- HOIST ROPES
- ELEVATOR CAR SUPPORT STRUCTURE
- ELEVATOR CAR
- GUIDE RAIL
- GUIDE RAIL SUPPORT BRACKET AT EACH FLOOR (MIN.)
- COUNTERWEIGHT
- HOISTWAY WALLS; MAY BE CONSTRUCTED OF DRYWALL OR ALTERNATE CONSTRUCTION
- BUFFERS (OIL SHOWN) SPRINGS AVAILABLE ON LOW SPEED ELEVATORS
- ELEVATOR PIT
- OVERHEAD INCLUDING CLEARANCE
- TRAVEL
- PIT

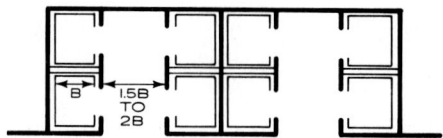

B = DEPTH OF CAR

B — 1.5B TO 2B

NOTES

The largest practical grouping of elevators in a building is eight cars. One row of more than four cars is generally unacceptable. With groupings of four or six cars, waiting lobbies may be alcoved (one end closed) or open at both ends. In case of several elevator groupings, one grouping may serve lower floors, while others are express elevators to upper floors.

ELEVATOR ARRANGEMENTS — FOUR, SIX, AND EIGHT CARS (TYPICAL FOR HIGHRISE APPLICATIONS)

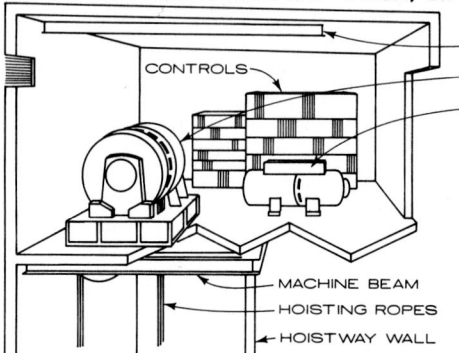

- CONTROLS
- MACHINE HOISTING BEAM
- GEARLESS HOISTING MACHINE
- MOTOR – GENERATOR SET
- MACHINE BEAM
- HOISTING ROPES
- HOISTWAY WALL

NOTES

The MACHINE ROOM for electric elevators is normally located directly above the hoistway. Space must be provided for the elevator drive, control equipment, and governor with sufficient clearance for equipment installation, repair, or removal. Space requirements vary substantially according to code capacity and speed of the system selected. Adequate lighting and ventilation are required by codes, and sound insulation should be provided.

MACHINE ROOM (GEARLESS ELEVATOR)

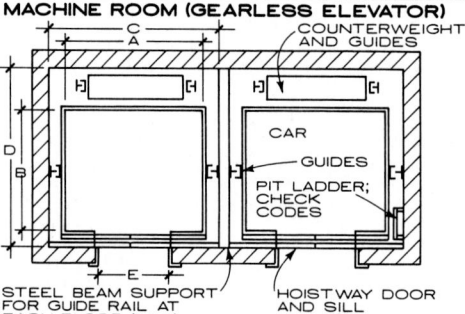

- COUNTERWEIGHT AND GUIDES
- CAR
- GUIDES
- PIT LADDER; CHECK CODES
- STEEL BEAM SUPPORT FOR GUIDE RAIL AT EACH FLOOR (MIN.)
- HOISTWAY DOOR AND SILL

ELEVATOR HOISTWAY AND CAR — ELECTRIC ELEVATOR

NOTES

Medium and highrise buildings utilize ELECTRIC GEARED TRACTION and ELECTRIC GEARLESS TRACTION elevator systems. The main difference between the two systems lies in the hoisting machinery. General design considerations involving hoistway, machine room, and elevator planning are similar.

ELECTRIC GEARLESS TRACTION ELEVATOR systems are available in preengineered units with speeds of 500 to 1200 fpm. Systems with greater speeds are also available. Gearless elevators, when used in conjunction with appropriate controls, offer the advantages of a long life and smoothness of ride.

ELECTRIC GEARED TRACTION ELEVATOR systems are designed to operate within the range of 100 to 350 fpm, which restricts their use to medium rise buildings.

Both geared and gearless drive units are governed by CONTROLS, which coordinate care leveling, passenger calls, collective operation of elevators, door operation, car acceleration and deceleration, and safety applications. A broad range of control systems are available to meet individual building requirements.

STRUCTURAL REQUIREMENTS call for the total weight of the elevator system to be supported by the MACHINE BEAMS and transmitted to the building (or hoistway) structure. Consult with elevator and structural engineers.

If the elevator machine is to be supported solely by the machine room floor slab, the floor slab shall be designed in accordance with the requirements of ANSI A17.1-1978 Rules 105.4 and 105.5.

Check local codes for required fire enclosures.

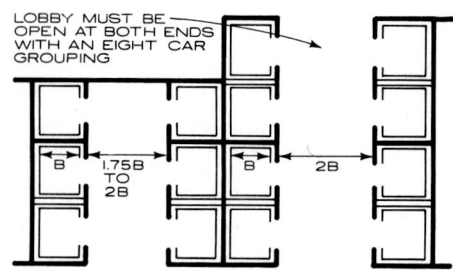

LOBBY MUST BE OPEN AT BOTH ENDS WITH AN EIGHT CAR GROUPING

B — 1.75B TO 2B — B — 2B

Where 4 or more elevators serve all or the same portion of a building, they shall be located in not less than 2 hoistways, but in no case shall more than 4 elevators be located in any one hoistway.

ELECTRIC ELEVATOR DIMENSIONS

RATED LOAD (LB)	DIMENSIONS (FT-IN.)				
	A	B	C	D	E
2000	5-8	4-3	7-4	6-10	3-0
2500	6-8	4-3	8-4	6-10	3-6
3000	6-8	4-3	8-4	7-2	3-6
3500	6-8	5-3	8-4	7-10	3-6
4000	7-8	5-3	9-4	7-10	4-0

NOTES

Dimensions of preengineered units, listed above, are for reference purposes only. Elevator manufacturers should be consulted for a complete selection.

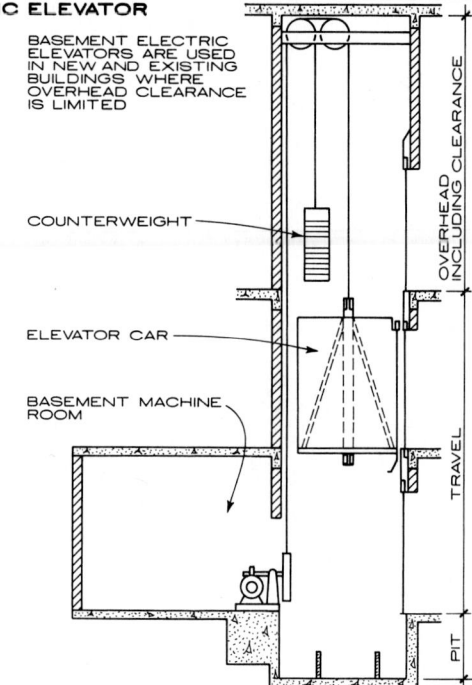

- BASEMENT ELECTRIC ELEVATORS ARE USED IN NEW AND EXISTING BUILDINGS WHERE OVERHEAD CLEARANCE IS LIMITED
- COUNTERWEIGHT
- ELEVATOR CAR
- BASEMENT MACHINE ROOM
- OVERHEAD INCLUDING CLEARANCE
- TRAVEL
- PIT

BASEMENT ELECTRIC ELEVATOR — SECTION

GENERAL

ELEVATOR SELECTION depends on several factors: the building's physical characteristics, available elevator systems, and code regulations. The functions that relate these selection parameters and indicate the number, size, and type of elevators are, in most cases, complex and are based on the performance of the elevator systems. Representatives of the elevator industry or consulting elevator engineers should be contacted during the selection process to ensure that the most suitable elevator system is chosen.

PRIVATE RESIDENCES

Elevator selection for private residences can be simplified to a few parameters. By code they are limited in size, capacity, rise, and speed and are installed only in a private residence or a multiple dwelling as a means of access to a single private dwelling.

AVAILABLE ELEVATOR SYSTEMS are outlined on another page. The speed, capacity type, and controls of preengineered systems are generally limited to only a few options.

BUILDING POPULATION analysis involves the identification of the needs of prospective users. Relevant information includes the number of passengers expected to occupy the elevator in one trip and elevator service in a given time period, as well as the number of passengers expected and the possible need for a wheelchair.

BUILDING CHARACTERISTICS affect elevator selection by establishing the building height (distance of elevator travel) and hoistway location. In private residences, the elevator may occupy a tier of closets, an exterior shaft, a room corner, or a stairwell.

ELEVATOR SELECTION

The accompanying diagram illustrates elevator selection parameters in the context of a hospital layout. Actual calculations relating these parameters are complex. Consultation with an elevator industry representative or consulting elevator engineer is recommended.

1. BUILDING HEIGHT: Floor-to-floor height and number of floors.
2. BUILDING POPULATION: Total number of building occupants and expected visitors and their expected distribution throughout the building.
3. BUILDING USE ANALYSIS: Location of offices, patient's rooms, service areas, and ancillary spaces conducive to mass assembly. Primary public circulation areas and primary staff circulation areas should be identified.
4. WAITING AREA: Peak loading and waiting time are two important concepts in providing the quality of elevator service expected by hospital visitors and staff. Different standards are applied according to building use. Consult an elevator engineer.
5. LOCATION OF MAJOR ENTRANCES
6. ELEVATOR SYSTEMS: A large selection of elevator capacities, speed, controls, and type are available. In this case, passenger and service elevators are shown. An elevator with a front and rear entrance serves as a passenger elevator during peak visiting hours. The wide variety of elevator alternatives should be discussed with an elevator engineer to select the system most suitable for each individual situation.

SERVICE REQUIREMENTS: Elevators must have sufficient capacity and speed to meet building service requirements. In this case, the elevator must accommodate a 24 x 76 in. ambulance type stretcher with attendants.

For patient service in hospitals, to accommodate beds with their attachments, use 5000 lb elevators; platforms 6 ft wide x 9 ft 6 in. deep, doors at least 4 ft wide (4 ft 6 in. width is preferred).

CODE AND REGULATIONS: Recommendations and code restrictions regarding handicapped access, fire safety, elevator controls, and so on, may affect elevator selection. Consult with an elevator industry representative or consulting elevator engineer. As a minimum the ANSI A17.1-1978 Safety Code for Elevators, Dumbwaiters, Escalators and Moving Walks should be complied with.

NOTE: Elevators should not be considered as emergency exits.

ELEVATOR SYSTEMS IN BUILDINGS OTHER THAN PRIVATE HOMES

Selection of elevator systems increases in complexity with the size and complexity of the project. Even though the vertical transportation needs of lowrise residential and commercial projects may be simply met, all the parameters listed below should be considered and analyzed with a consulting elevator engineer to ensure proper selection.

BUILDING POPULATION

The elevator selection process must begin with a thorough analysis of how people will occupy the building.

1. TOTAL POPULATION AND DENSITY: The total number of occupants and visitors and their distribution by floors within a building.
2. PEAK LOADING: Periods when elevators carry the highest traffic loads. For example, peak loading in office buildings coincides with rush hours and/or lunch periods, while peak loading in hospitals may occur during visiting hours.
3. WAITING TIME: The length of time a passenger is expected to wait for the next elevator to arrive. These demands vary according to building use and building occupant expectations. A person willing to wait 50–70 sec in an apartment building may be willing to wait only 20–35 sec in an office building.
4. DEMAND FOR QUALITY: Sophistication of controls and elevator capacity may be varied to cater to

the expected taste of passengers. Large elevator cars and the smooth, long life operation of a gearless elevator may convey an image of luxury even if a smaller elevator having a less sophisticated system would be technically sufficient.

BUILDING CHARACTERISTICS

Physical building characteristics are considered together with population characteristics to determine size, speed, type, and location of elevator systems.

1. HEIGHT: The distance of elevator travel (from lowest terminal to top terminal), number of floors, and floor height.
2. BUILDING USE ANALYSIS: Location of building entrance areas of heavy use such as cafeteria, restaurant, auditorium, and service areas must be identified. Typically, a building should be planned to ensure that no prospective passengers must walk more than 200 ft to reach an elevator.

ELEVATOR SYSTEMS AND REGULATIONS

The parameters previously described outline the environment in which the elevator operates. Local code regulations and ANSI A17.1-1978 requirements provide further elevator guidelines.

Available elevator systems are analyzed to ensure that suitable speed, capacity, controls, and number of cars are selected.

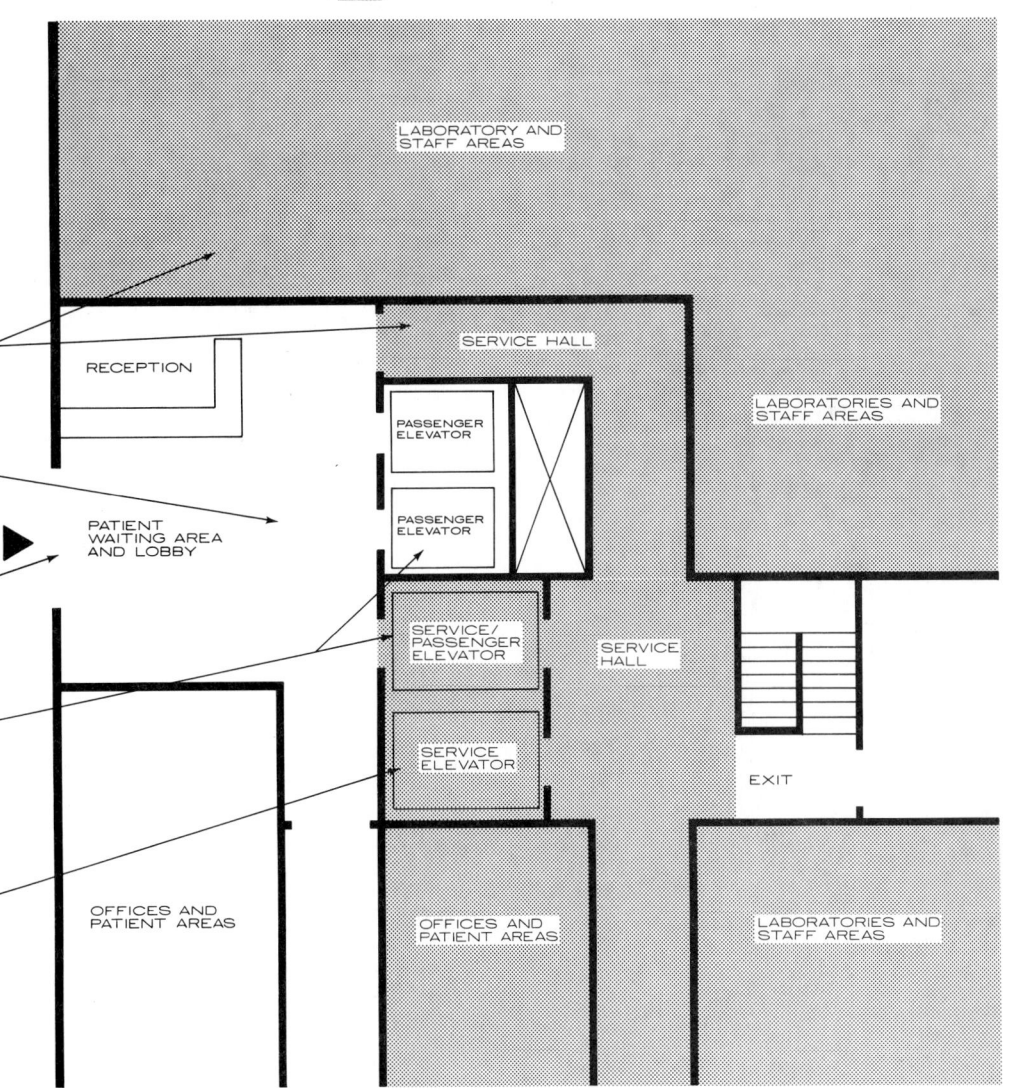

ELEVATOR SELECTION FACTORS – HOSPITAL

Alexander Keyes; Darrel Rippeteau, Architect; Washington, D.C.

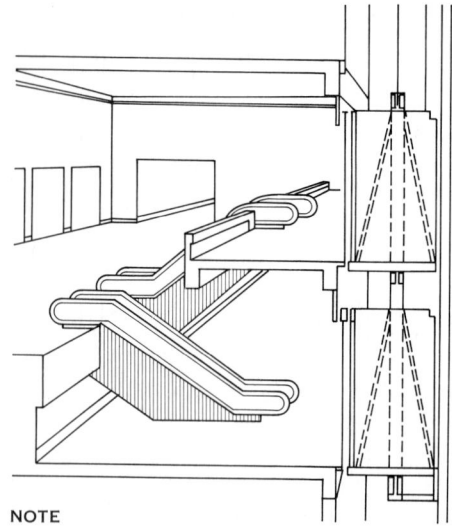

NOTE

In buildings with heavy populations double deck elevators permit an increase in handling capacity without increasing the number of elevators. Two cars in tandem operate simultaneously, one serving all floors. Escalators connect the two floors in 2-story lobbies.

DOUBLE DECK ELEVATOR

FIRE RATED HOISTWAY ENCLOSURE

CAR DOOR

HOISTWAY DOOR

HANDRAILS 32" ABOVE FLOOR

GUIDE RAILS IN HOISTWAY

NONSLIP FLOOR COVERING

CONTROL PANEL ACCESSIBLE FROM WHEELCHAIR

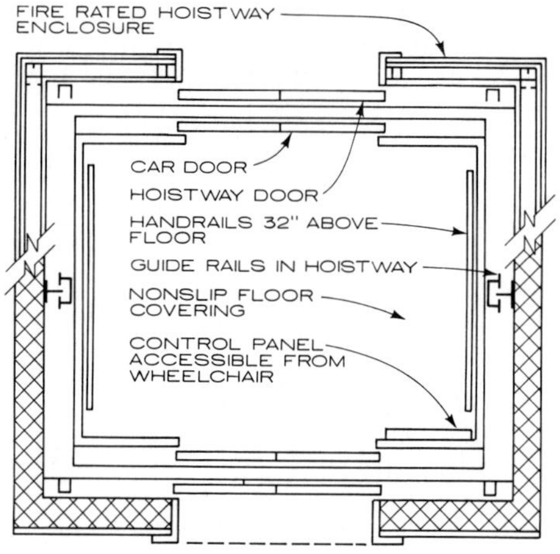

PLAN OF ELEVATOR CAR WITH REAR DOOR

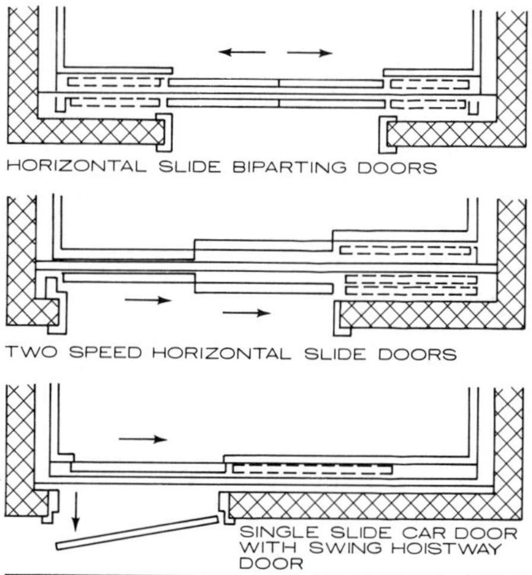

HORIZONTAL SLIDE BIPARTING DOORS

TWO SPEED HORIZONTAL SLIDE DOORS

SINGLE SLIDE CAR DOOR WITH SWING HOISTWAY DOOR

ELEVATOR DOOR TYPES

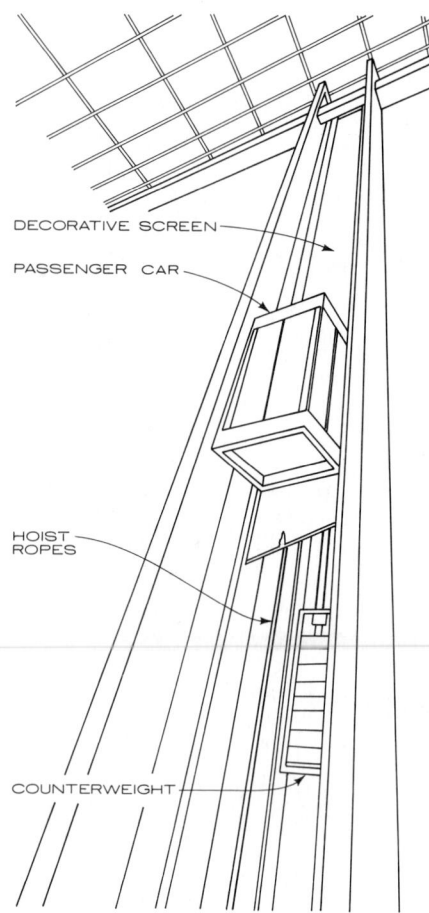

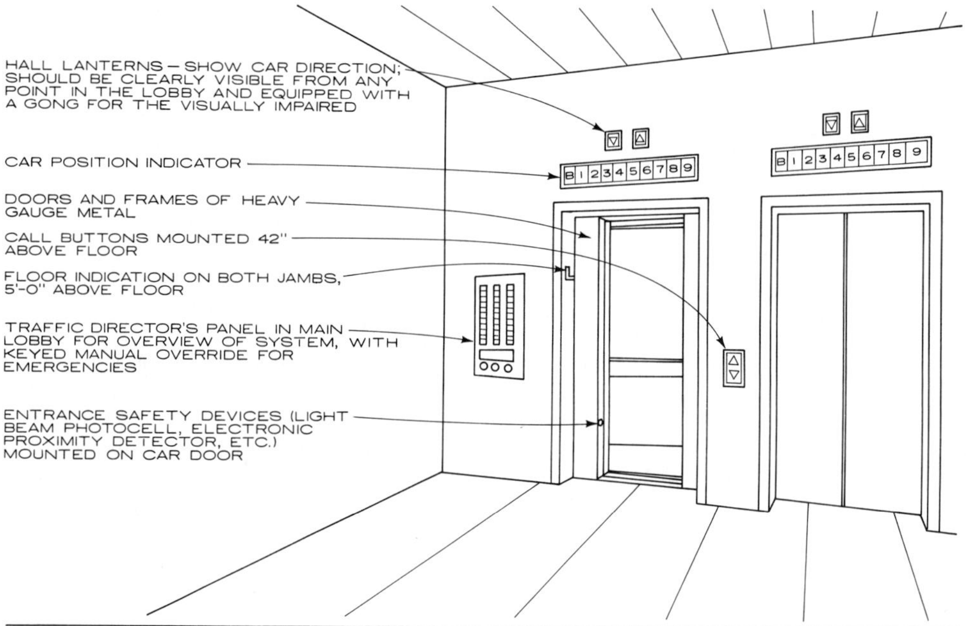

DECORATIVE SCREEN

PASSENGER CAR

HOIST ROPES

COUNTERWEIGHT

NOTE

Observation elevators travel outside of a hoistway or in a hoistway open on one side. Machinery is concealed or designed to be inconspicuous. These elevators serve as important visual elements, and specially designed glass cars make the ride a more significant experience.

OBSERVATION ELEVATOR

Alexander Keyes; Darrel Rippeteau, Architect; Washington, D.C.

HALL LANTERNS — SHOW CAR DIRECTION; SHOULD BE CLEARLY VISIBLE FROM ANY POINT IN THE LOBBY AND EQUIPPED WITH A GONG FOR THE VISUALLY IMPAIRED

CAR POSITION INDICATOR

DOORS AND FRAMES OF HEAVY GAUGE METAL

CALL BUTTONS MOUNTED 42" ABOVE FLOOR

FLOOR INDICATION ON BOTH JAMBS, 5'-0" ABOVE FLOOR

TRAFFIC DIRECTOR'S PANEL IN MAIN LOBBY FOR OVERVIEW OF SYSTEM, WITH KEYED MANUAL OVERRIDE FOR EMERGENCIES

ENTRANCE SAFETY DEVICES (LIGHT BEAM PHOTOCELL, ELECTRONIC PROXIMITY DETECTOR, ETC.) MOUNTED ON CAR DOOR

ELEVATOR LOBBY

VENTILATION — CHANGE AIR TWICE EVERY MINUTE

LIGHTING — GLAREFREE, MIN. 5 FT-C

CAR POSITION INDICATOR

SIGN PROHIBITING USE OF ELEVATOR DURING EMERGENCIES

CONTROL PANEL: CALL BUTTONS, DOOR OPEN, EMERGENCY STOP, FLOOR ALARM, INTERCOM TO TRAFFIC DIRECTOR'S PANEL

HANDRAIL, MOUNTED 32" ABOVE FLOOR

TELEPHONE FOR EMERGENCY USE

NONSLIP FLOOR FINISH

LOAD WEIGHING DEVICE BELOW CAR

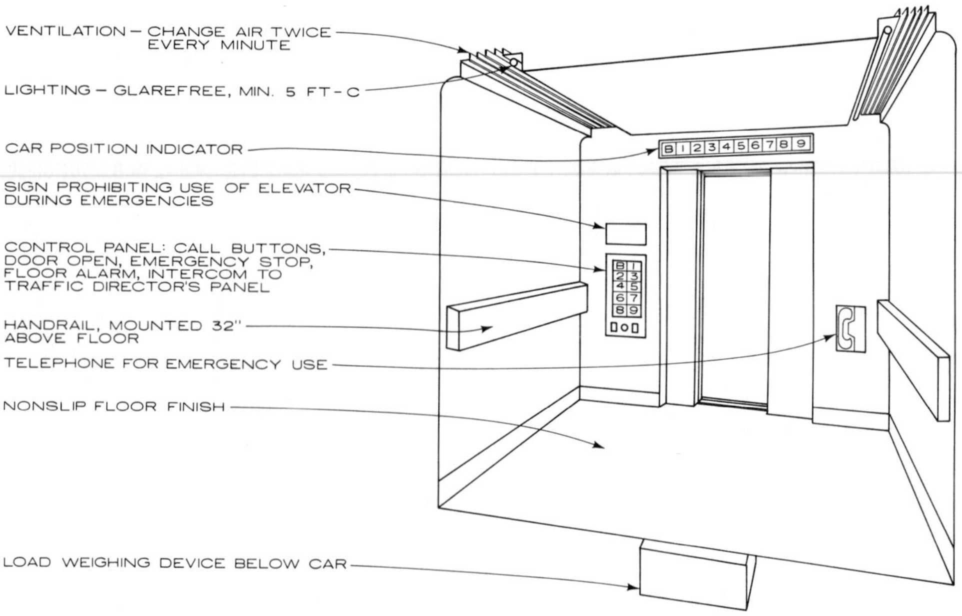

INTERIOR OF ELEVATOR CAR

ELEVATORS

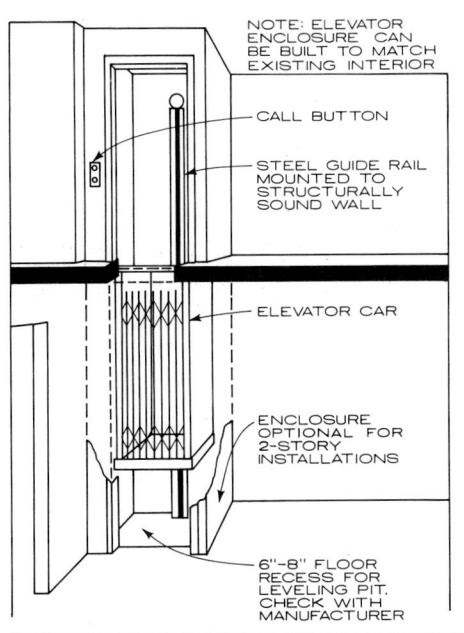

NOTE: ELEVATOR ENCLOSURE CAN BE BUILT TO MATCH EXISTING INTERIOR

CALL BUTTON

STEEL GUIDE RAIL MOUNTED TO STRUCTURALLY SOUND WALL

ELEVATOR CAR

ENCLOSURE OPTIONAL FOR 2-STORY INSTALLATIONS

6"-8" FLOOR RECESS FOR LEVELING PIT. CHECK WITH MANUFACTURER

RESIDENTIAL ELEVATOR

NOTE

Barrierfree residential elevators are typically package designed. Structures, both monorail cable driven types and twin screw drive systems, are self-supporting, anchored to the existing structure. Cars are assembled separately and mounted on platforms driven by remote power units. Open installations are permitted for 2-story applications. Recommended speed: 30 fpm.

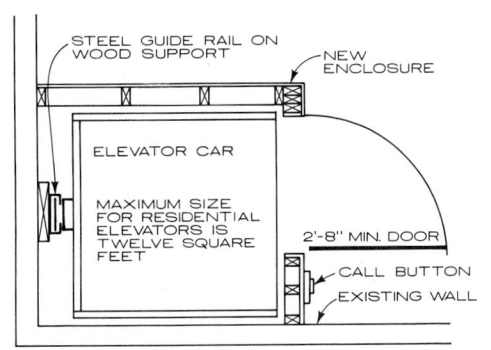

STEEL GUIDE RAIL ON WOOD SUPPORT

NEW ENCLOSURE

ELEVATOR CAR

MAXIMUM SIZE FOR RESIDENTIAL ELEVATORS IS TWELVE SQUARE FEET

2'-8" MIN. DOOR

CALL BUTTON

EXISTING WALL

PLAN — ACCOMMODATES STANDARD WHEELCHAIR

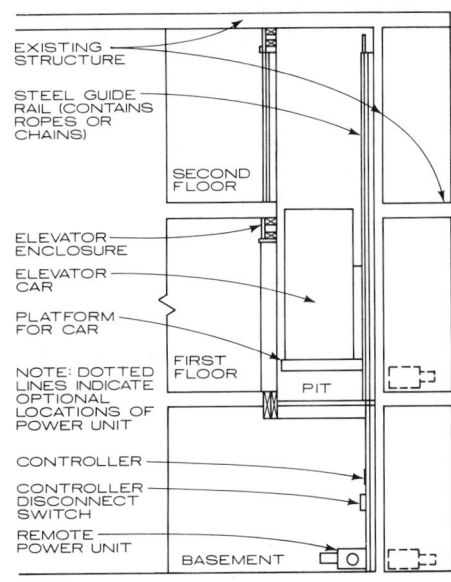

EXISTING STRUCTURE

STEEL GUIDE RAIL (CONTAINS ROPES OR CHAINS)

SECOND FLOOR

ELEVATOR ENCLOSURE

ELEVATOR CAR

PLATFORM FOR CAR

NOTE: DOTTED LINES INDICATE OPTIONAL LOCATIONS OF POWER UNIT

FIRST FLOOR

PIT

CONTROLLER

CONTROLLER DISCONNECT SWITCH

REMOTE POWER UNIT

BASEMENT

SECTION

NOTE

Wheelchair lifts are suitable for retrofits on nonbarrier-free buildings. Bridges are available from manufacturers for installation over chairs. Potential hazards, however, include slipping on platforms, jolting that might result in loss of balance, failure that causes the platform to drop, and entrapment under the platform.

Lifts operate on standard household current and are suitable for interior and exterior applications. Maximum lifting height: 7 ft 9 in.

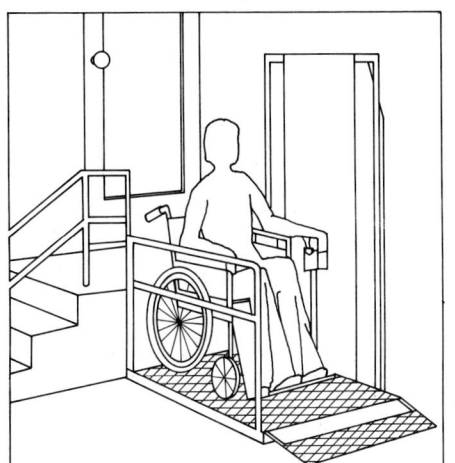

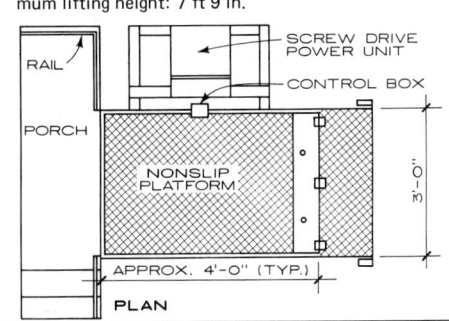

RAIL

PORCH

SCREW DRIVE POWER UNIT

CONTROL BOX

NONSLIP PLATFORM

3'-0"

APPROX. 4'-0" (TYP.)

PLAN

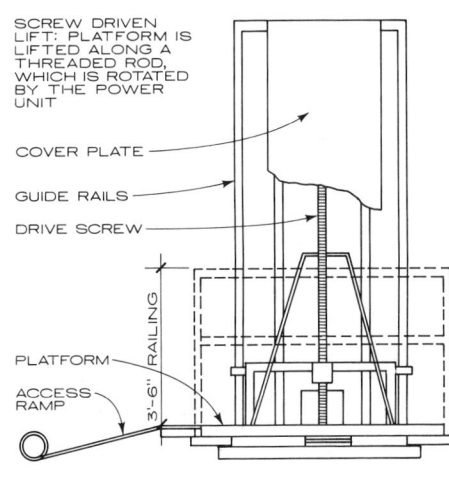

SCREW DRIVEN LIFT: PLATFORM IS LIFTED ALONG A THREADED ROD, WHICH IS ROTATED BY THE POWER UNIT

COVER PLATE

GUIDE RAILS

DRIVE SCREW

PLATFORM

ACCESS RAMP

3'-6" RAILING

SIDE VIEW

WHEELCHAIR LIFT

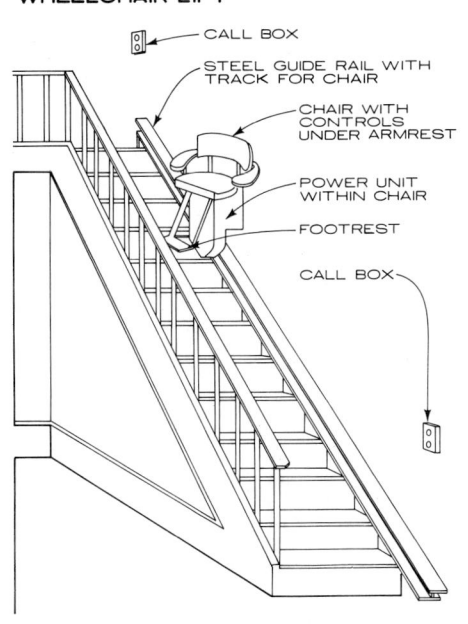

CALL BOX

STEEL GUIDE RAIL WITH TRACK FOR CHAIR

CHAIR WITH CONTROLS UNDER ARMREST

POWER UNIT WITHIN CHAIR

FOOTREST

CALL BOX

POWER UNIT IF REQUIRED

TRACK FOR CHAIR

6½" – 7½" FROM WALL

NOTE: SOME TYPES MAY REQUIRE SEPARATE POWER UNITS. THESE MAY BE LOCATED WHERE SHOWN IN DOTTED LINES IN PLAN AND SECTION, OR IN BASEMENT OR ATTIC

CHAIR

TRACK FOR CHAIR

PLAN

NOTE

Stair lifts can be adapted to straight run and spiral stairs. Standard types run along a track fastened to the steps. Power units, when not contained in a housing under the chair, can be located as shown in section, or in basement or attic. Similar inclined wheelchair lifts are also available for installations down stairs. Recommended speed: 25 fpm. Capacity: 250–350 lb.

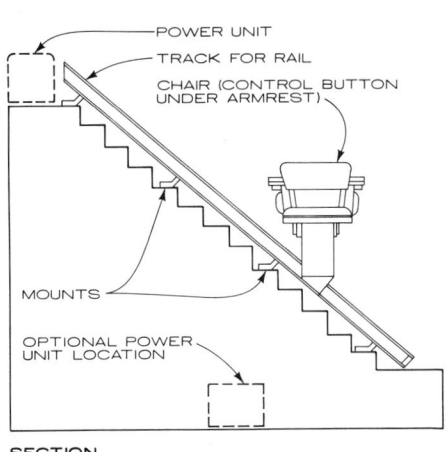

POWER UNIT

TRACK FOR RAIL

CHAIR (CONTROL BUTTON UNDER ARMREST)

MOUNTS

OPTIONAL POWER UNIT LOCATION

SECTION

STAIR LIFT

Olga Barmine; Darrel Rippeteau, Architect; Washington, D.C.

ELEVATORS

14

SERVICE ELEVATORS

Service elevators in industrial, residential, and commercial buildings are often standard passenger elevator packages modified for service use. These modified systems, when compared with custom made freight elevator systems, are generally more economical, are delivered in less time, and have more stringent load ratings related to the platform area. Special provisions include interior cab protection (steel or oak rubbing strips or suitable abuse resistant finish surface) and a door and cab of sufficient size to handle expected loads. Standard horizontal sliding doors can often meet service needs. If the full width of the car platform is needed for loading, vertical biparting doors can be used. If bulky loads are expected only occasionally, a removable car front with swinging hoistway door panels can be provided.

Vertically sliding doors and vertically sliding gates, where permitted by ANSI A17.1-1978 Rule 204.5b, shall conform to the following requirements:

1. At entrances used by passengers they shall be:
   a. Of the balanced counterweighted type which slide in the up direction to open.
   b. Power operated.
2. At entrances used exclusively for freight, they shall be:
   a. Of the balanced counterweighted type or the biparting counterbalanced type.
   b. Manually or power operated.

CAPACITY: Size to largest expected load, with the exception of single one piece loading, which is restricted to 25% of the rated capacity.

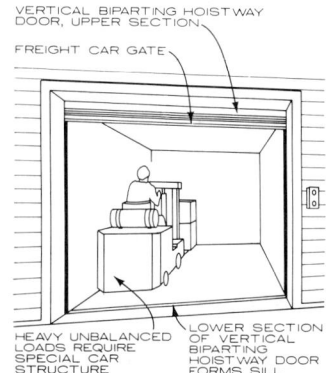

VERTICAL BIPARTING HOISTWAY DOOR, UPPER SECTION

FREIGHT CAR GATE

HEAVY UNBALANCED LOADS REQUIRE SPECIAL CAR STRUCTURE

LOWER SECTION OF VERTICAL BIPARTING HOISTWAY DOOR FORMS SILL

INTERIOR VIEW

FREIGHT ELEVATOR DIMENSIONS

CAPACITY (LB)	PLATFORM		HOISTWAY	
	WIDTH	DEPTH	WIDTH	DEPTH
2,500	5'-4"	7'-0"	7'-3"	7'-11"
5,000	8'-4"	10'-0"	10'-6"	10'-11"
10,000	8'-4"	12'-0"	11'-4"	12'-11"
16,000	8'-4"	16'-0"	11'-8"	17'-3"
20,000	12'-0"	20'-0"	15'-9"	21'-3"

FREIGHT ELEVATOR

FREIGHT ELEVATORS

Freight elevators are usually classed as general freight loading, motor vehicle loading, industrial truck or concentrated loading elevators. General freight loading elevators, described below, may be electric drum type or traction or hydraulic elevators.

General freight loading elevators satisfy a variety of material handling requirements with capacities of 2500 to 10,000 lb. Industrial truck loading freight elevators require special design considerations to handle truck loads of 10,000 to 20,000 lb or more.

General freight or industrial truck elevators may have either hydraulic or electric drive systems, similar to those described on previous pages. The units are usually custom designed with vertical biparting doors and special structural support to carry increased loads and eccentric loading conditions.

Freight elevators usually operate at slower speeds with simple control systems. Capacity must be sized for the largest expected load.

LIGHT DUTY FREIGHT ELEVATORS with capacities of 1000 to 2500 lb may utilize hydraulic or traction drives. Standard systems are illustrated on other pages of this section. Two special types of light freight elevators, with rises limited according to manufacturer, are the SIDEWALK ELEVATOR and the SELF-SUPPORTING ELEVATOR.

The SIDEWALK ELEVATOR, illustrated on this page with an electric winding drum type machine, rises to a top level through hatch doors. Note that local codes often forbid the raising of an elevator in a public sidewalk; elevators may have to be located within building lines.

The SELF-SUPPORTING FREIGHT ELEVATOR is similar to the sidewalk elevator illustrated and operates within a building up to three stories (rise varies with manufacturer). Weight of the car is transferred through the supporting guide rails to the elevator pit.

With the electric winding drum machine, machinery must lift the full weight of car and its load. The drum must be anchored to the floor to resist uplifting forces. Safety codes forbid use of electric winding drum machines for passenger elevators and restrict their use on freight elevators to a speed not exceeding 50 fpm and a travel not exceeding 40 ft; they shall not be provided with counterweights.

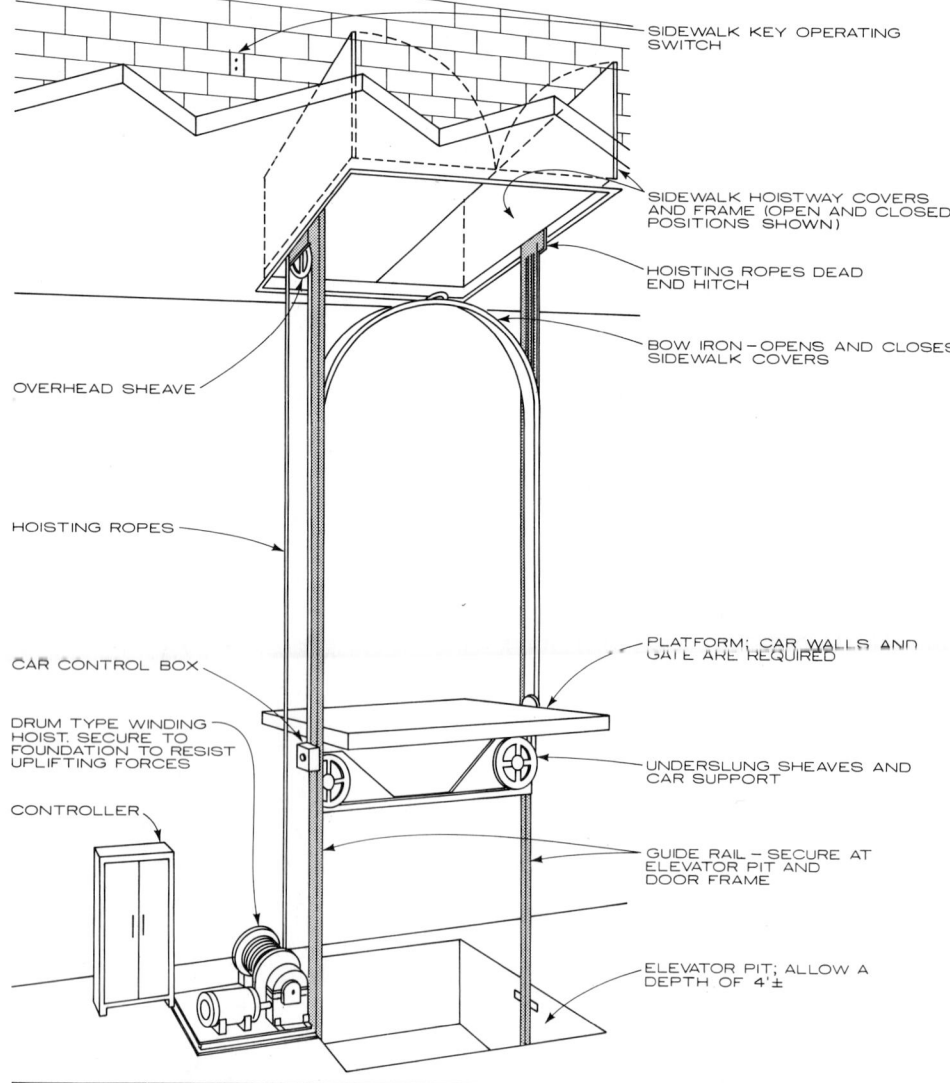

SIDEWALK KEY OPERATING SWITCH

SIDEWALK HOISTWAY COVERS AND FRAME (OPEN AND CLOSED POSITIONS SHOWN)

HOISTING ROPES DEAD END HITCH

BOW IRON—OPENS AND CLOSES SIDEWALK COVERS

OVERHEAD SHEAVE

HOISTING ROPES

CAR CONTROL BOX

DRUM TYPE WINDING HOIST. SECURE TO FOUNDATION TO RESIST UPLIFTING FORCES

CONTROLLER

PLATFORM; CAR WALLS AND GATE ARE REQUIRED

UNDERSLUNG SHEAVES AND CAR SUPPORT

GUIDE RAIL — SECURE AT ELEVATOR PIT AND DOOR FRAME

ELEVATOR PIT; ALLOW A DEPTH OF 4'±

SIDEWALK ELEVATOR

Alexander Keyes; Darrel Rippeteau, Architect; Washington, D.C.

SELF-SUPPORTING ELEVATOR DIMENSIONS

CAPACITY (LB)	PLATFORM		HOISTWAY	
	WIDTH	DEPTH	WIDTH	DEPTH
1,500	5'-4"	6'-1"	6'-11"	6'-9"
2,000	6'-4"	7'-0"	7'-11"	7'-8"
2,500	6'-4"	8'-0"	7'-11"	8'-8"

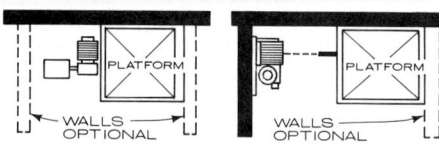

SIDE MOUNTED

WALL MOUNTED

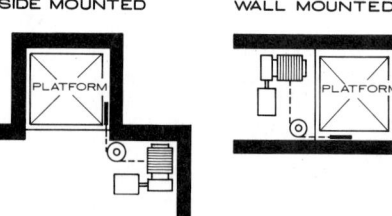

AROUND THE CORNER

MACHINE IN BACK

MACHINE LAYOUTS — WINDING DRUM TYPE

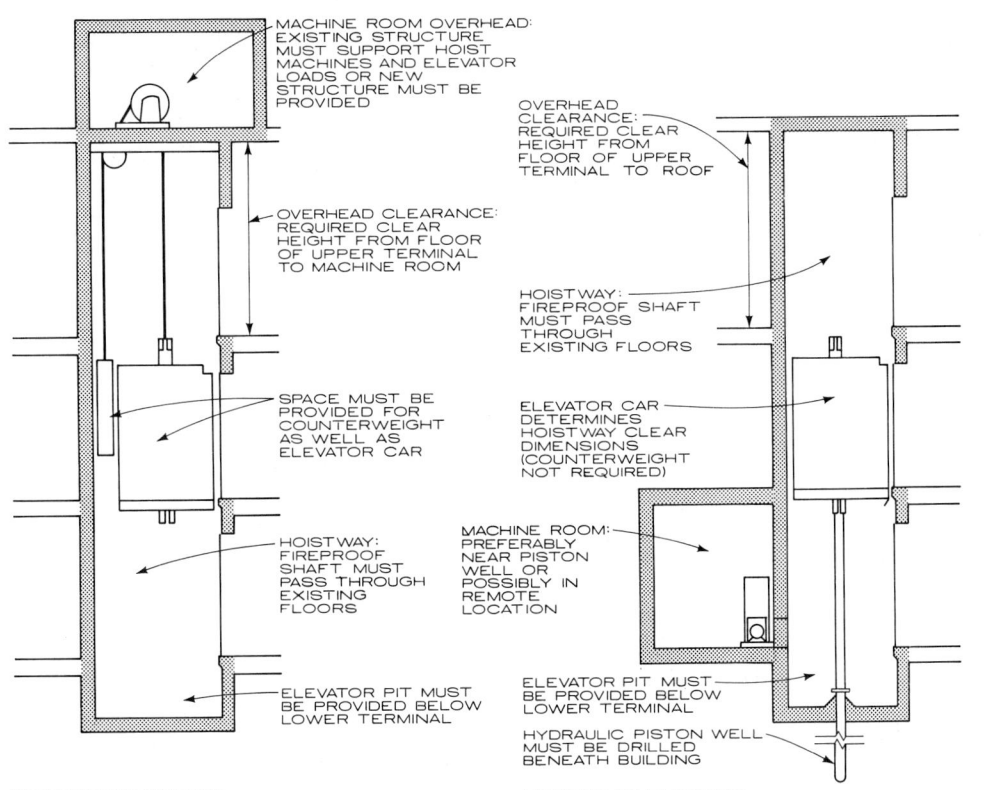

MACHINE ROOM OVERHEAD: EXISTING STRUCTURE MUST SUPPORT HOIST MACHINES AND ELEVATOR LOADS OR NEW STRUCTURE MUST BE PROVIDED

OVERHEAD CLEARANCE: REQUIRED CLEAR HEIGHT FROM FLOOR OF UPPER TERMINAL TO ROOF

OVERHEAD CLEARANCE: REQUIRED CLEAR HEIGHT FROM FLOOR OF UPPER TERMINAL TO MACHINE ROOM

HOISTWAY: FIREPROOF SHAFT MUST PASS THROUGH EXISTING FLOORS

SPACE MUST BE PROVIDED FOR COUNTERWEIGHT AS WELL AS ELEVATOR CAR

ELEVATOR CAR DETERMINES HOISTWAY CLEAR DIMENSIONS (COUNTERWEIGHT NOT REQUIRED)

HOISTWAY: FIREPROOF SHAFT MUST PASS THROUGH EXISTING FLOORS

MACHINE ROOM: PREFERABLY NEAR PISTON WELL OR POSSIBLY IN REMOTE LOCATION

ELEVATOR PIT MUST BE PROVIDED BELOW LOWER TERMINAL

ELEVATOR PIT MUST BE PROVIDED BELOW LOWER TERMINAL

HYDRAULIC PISTON WELL MUST BE DRILLED BENEATH BUILDING

TRACTION ELEVATOR   **HYDRAULIC ELEVATOR**

ELEVATOR RETROFIT

Existing buildings may be retrofitted with the elevator systems previously illustrated. General selection, location, and arrangement guidelines apply. Additional constraints imposed by existing building conditions must also be considered.

HYDRAULIC ELEVATORS generally require the least initial installation expense in buildings of 2 to 6 stories. The hoistway need only be a fireproof shaft, separating the elevator passageway from the rest of the building. Elevator car guide rails are attached from within the hoistway to the existing structural frame at each floor. A machine room is located near the lower terminal, often in an existing basement. The weight of the system bears upon a concrete pad at the base of the hoistway, beneath which a hole must be drilled to accommodate the hydraulic piston, approximately equal in length to the distance of elevator travel. A HOLELESS HYDRAULIC system eliminates the need for this hole but is limited to a rise of 3 stories.

ELECTRIC ELEVATORS can serve buildings of higher rises at greater speeds and generally lower operating costs. Hoisting machines are located above the hoistway and bear the weight of the elevator system. A structural frame must be designed to support these machines within the existing structural system. Sufficient space for a machine room must be provided, often on an existing roof. The hoistway is designed as a fireproof shaft with elevator guide rails attached to the building structure at each floor. An alternate elevator system permits the hoist machines to be located in the basement (see ELECTRIC ELEVATOR SYSTEMS) in situations where low overhead clearance is available. The weight of the system must still be supported at the top of the hoistway.

In all cases, representatives of the elevator industry must be contacted for proper elevator selection and design specifications.

ELEVATOR RETROFIT

MACHINE ROOM: HOISTING MACHINES MAY BE OVERHAULED OR MODERNIZED TO PROVIDE GREATER SPEED OR HOISTING CAPACITY. AGE OF MACHINERY AND PRESENT USAGE DEMANDS ARE DETERMINING FACTORS

MODERN CONTROLS ARE OFTEN INSTALLED TO SYNCHRONIZE GROUP ELEVATOR SERVICE AND REDUCE CAR STOPPING AND STARTING TIME

SOUNDPROOFING OR STRUCTURAL REINFORCEMENT MAY BE REQUIRED

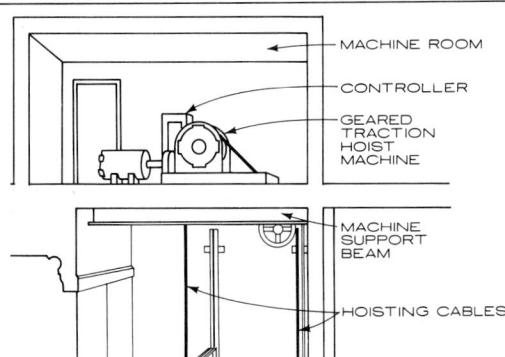

MACHINE ROOM

CONTROLLER

GEARED TRACTION HOIST MACHINE

MACHINE SUPPORT BEAM

HOISTING CABLES

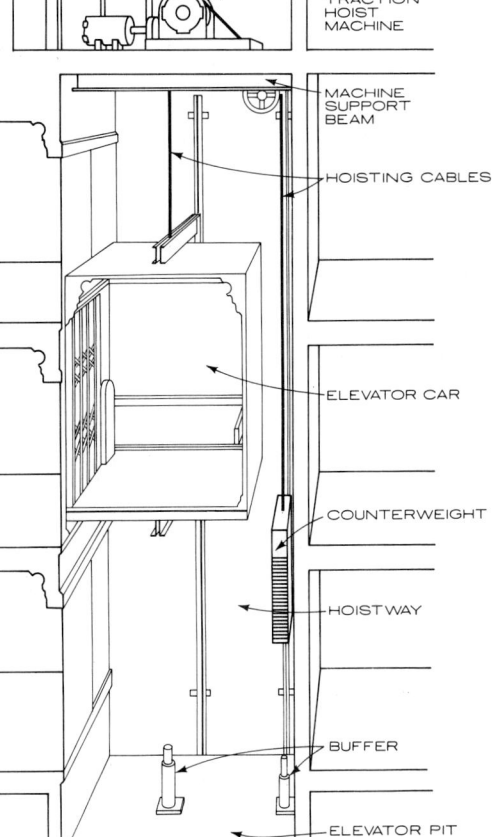

ELEVATOR CAR: EXISTING CAR MAY BE RENOVATED OR REPLACED

IF RENOVATED, CONTROLS AND DOORS MAY BE AUTOMATED TO PROVIDE SELF-SERVICE ELEVATORS, AND REDUCE DOOR OPERATING TIME. CENTER OPENING (HORIZONTAL BIPARTING) DOORS WITH ENTRANCE SAFETY DEVICES (SEE "ELEVATOR CAR DESIGN") REPLACE SINGLE SLIDE DOORS FOR INCREASED EFFICIENCY. THE CAR INTERIOR MAY BE RENOVATED OR RESTORED TO RETAIN ORIGINAL APPEARANCES

IF REPLACED, A FULLY AUTOMATED CAR WITH MODERN CONTROLS MAY BE INSERTED INTO AN EXISTING ELEVATOR HOISTWAY

CONSULT REPRESENTATIVES OF THE ELEVATOR INDUSTRY

ELEVATOR CAR

COUNTERWEIGHT

HOISTWAY

BUFFER

ELEVATOR PIT

HOISTWAY: ADDITIONAL FIREPROOFING OF HOISTWAY WALLS MAY BE REQUIRED. CHECK LOCAL CODES

HOISTWAY WALLS AND GUIDE RAILS MAY BE SOUNDPROOFED

ELEVATOR RENOVATION AND MODERNIZATION

Elevator systems in older buildings may be renovated and modernized to provide improved service. Certain service components (controls, hoist machines, door operators) may be overhauled or modernized, while visual components (elevator car, lobby) may be renovated or restored to original appearance. The extent of modernization will vary in each case; consult representatives of the elevator industry.

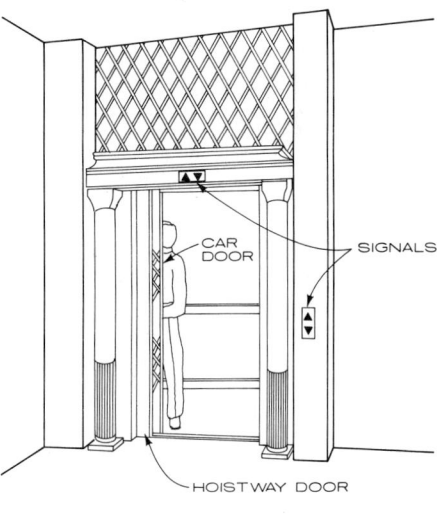

CAR DOOR

SIGNALS

HOISTWAY DOOR

ELEVATOR LOBBY: LOBBY MAY BE RESTORED TO RETAIN ORIGINAL APPEARANCES. NEW SIGNALS AND INDICATORS MAY BE INSERTED INTO AN EXISTING LOBBY WALL (SEE "ELEVATOR LOBBY DESIGN"). HOISTWAY DOORS MAY BE REPLACED FOR INCREASED EFFICIENCY

ELEVATOR RENOVATION

Olga Barmine; Darrel Rippeteau, Architect; Washington, D.C.

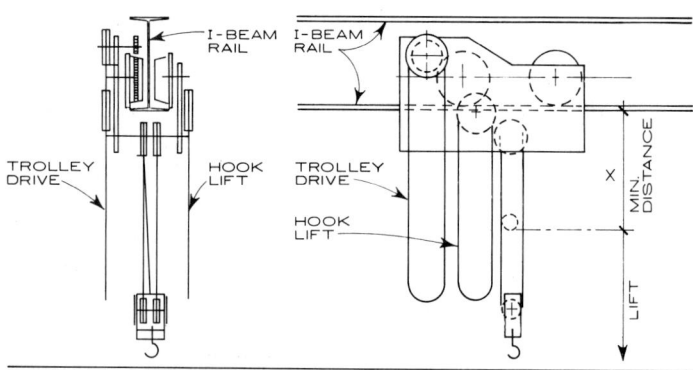

TROLLEY HOISTS

TROLLEY HOIST DATA

CAPACITY (TONS)	STANDARD LIFT (FT)	X	STANDARD I-BEAM	MIN. CURVE RADIUS
$1/4$	8	$8^{1/2}''$	5''	3'-6''
$1/2$	8	$8^{1/2}''$	5''	3'-6''
1	8	$11^{1/4}''$	6''	3'-6''
$1^{1/2}$	8	13''	7''	3'-6''
2	9	$15^{1/8}''$	8''	4'-6''
3	10	$18^{3/4}''$	10''	5'-0''
4	10	$21^{3/4}''$	10''	7'-6''
5	12	25''	12''	7'-6''
6	12	25''	12''	7'-6''
8	12	$31^{3/8}''$	15''	8'-0''
10	12	39''	15''	8'-0''

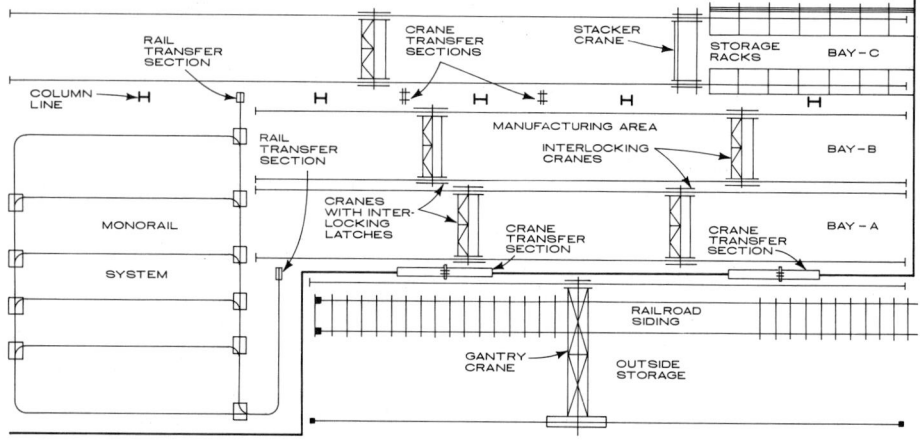

TYPICAL PLANT LAYOUT

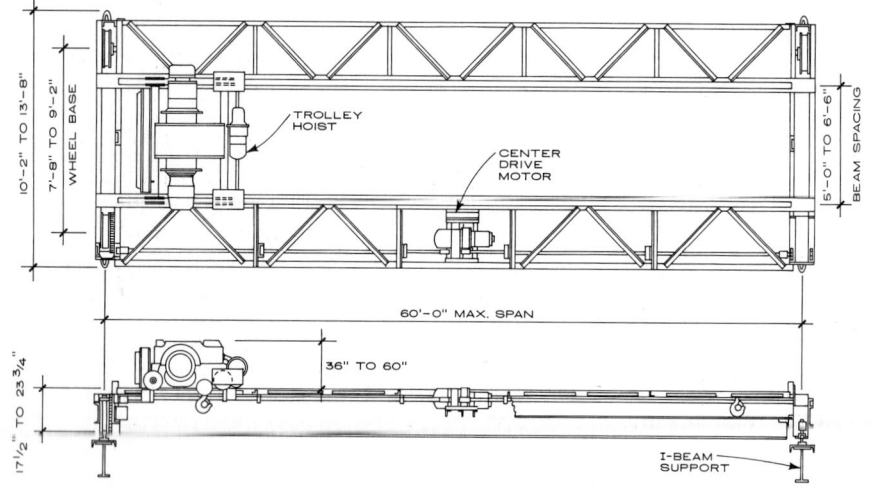

DOUBLE BEAM CRANE (CAPACITY 3 TO 10 TONS)

CRANES

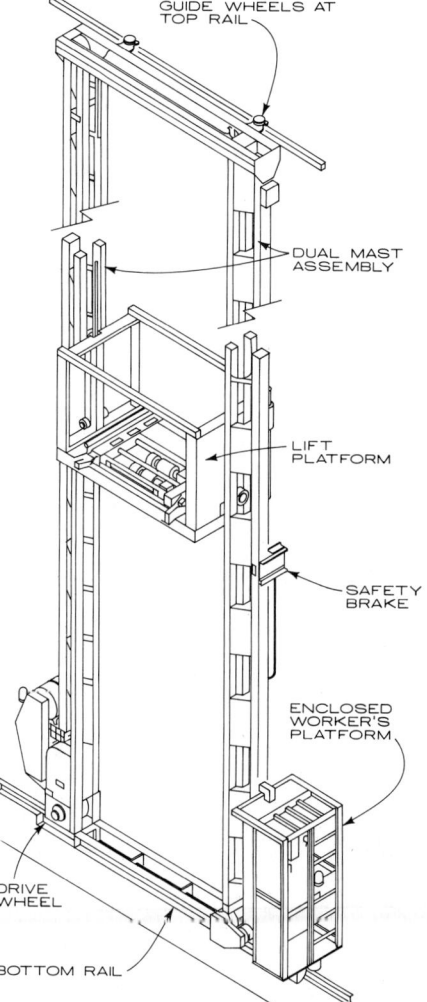

STACKER CRANE (CAPACITY 2 TONS)

CRANE LOCATION AND OPERATION

In the typical plant layout above there are three bays in the manufacturing area. The cranes in bays A and B may latch directly to each other, since there are no columns to block them. Due to the column line of the building between bays B and C cranes must be aligned and latched at transfer sections to move loads from the cranes in bay B to bay C without rehandling. A stacker crane is located in bay C to service the storage racks. A gantry crane is located outside the plant to load and unload railroad cars. This crane may interlock with the cranes in bay A through transfer sections located in the doorway.

St. Onge, Ruff & Associates; York, Pennsylvania

DOUBLE BEAM CRANE

Used to handle heavy loads in manufacturing and storage areas where aisle access and load clearances are limited. The beam crane allows two-directional horizontal travel plus vertical lift over the entire area serviced by the crane.

Load capacity: 6000 to 50,000 lb; span: 25 to 60 ft; crane weight: 4500 to 36,000 lb; wheel base: 7 to 13 ft; beam spacing: 5 to 9 ft; working span: 20 to 57 ft; hoist clearance above rail: 37 to 70 in.

STACKER CRANE

Stacker cranes allow storage/retrieval of loads above conventional fork lift truck heights. Also, multiple loads can be handled by manipulating load platform sizes. Cranes can be computer controlled to reduce manpower demands in S/R operations.

Load capacity: up to 4000 lb; overall height: 40 to 100 ft; working heights: 2 to 92 ft, depending on load heights; aisle width: 4 to 10 ft, depending on load configuration; aisle overrun: 15 to 20 ft, depending on crane structure; crane weight: up to 34,000 lb, depending on load and crane configuration; travel speeds: horizontal—up to 300 fpm; vertical—up to 75 fmp.

NOTE

Stacker cranes are typically built to customer specifications. Specific applications and details should be obtained from crane suppliers.

VERTICAL PALLET LIFT

Used to transport loads from level to level within a conveyor system or for manually loading/unloading at each level. Typically used where basement or second floor serves for storage of reserve or overstock.

Capacity: up to 6000 lb; lift height: up to 20 ft; platform sizes: 13 x 15 to 48 x 72 in.

Lift speed: 20 fpm; installation: floor to floor, with platform either flush with or above floor, depending on loading/unloading technique.

CIRCULAR CONVEYOR LIFT

Used to transport cartons between operating levels and between work stations within a level. Useful where vertical distance is great while horizontal distance is limited.

Lift height: 45 to 144 in. vertical lift per 360° unit. Lift height is relative to radius of unit. Load sizes: width—6 to 48 in.; length—relative to width and radius of conveyor.

Installation: dependent on height of feed and exit conveyors. System requires shaft through floor of O.D. of conveyor plus 12 in.

90° VERTICAL PALLET LIFT

Used to transport unit loads between operating levels in multiple level or multiple floor buildings. Typically used where vertical lift is great and a continuous conveyor system serves in loading/unloading the lift.

Capacity: up to 6000 lb; lift height: up to 80 ft; load sizes: typically 48 x 40 x 72 in.; however, other sizes can be specified; lift speed: 60 fpm; installation: typically installed floor to floor, with shaft through each floor.

NOTE

Lifts presented show various types with data and nomenclature to illustrate systems and equipment available to move loads vertically. Specific sizes and capacity should be obtained from lift manufacturers.

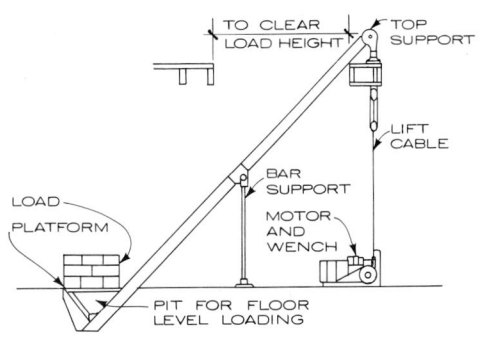

VERTICAL PALLET LIFT

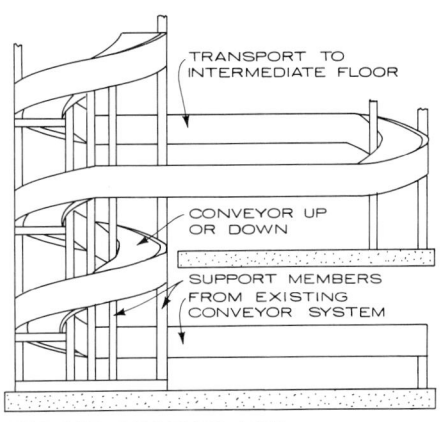

CIRCULAR CONVEYOR LIFT

90° VERTICAL PALLET LIFT

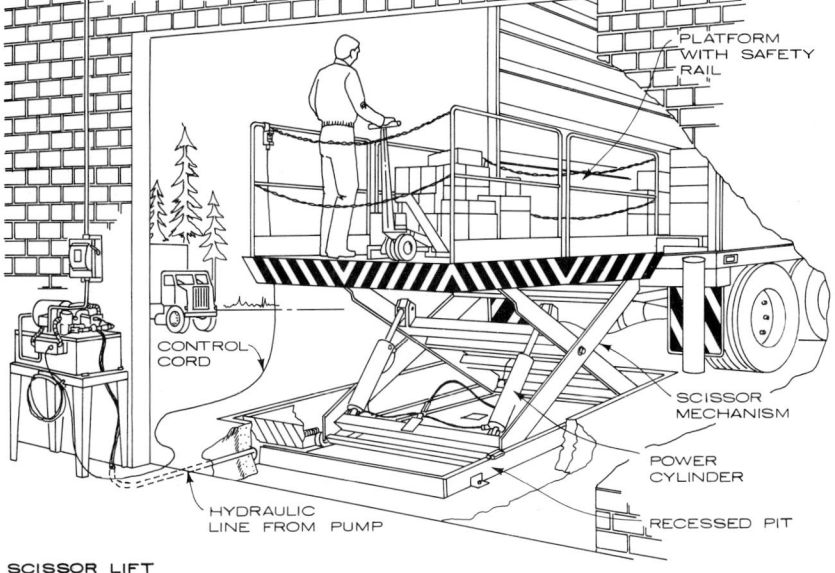

SCISSOR LIFT

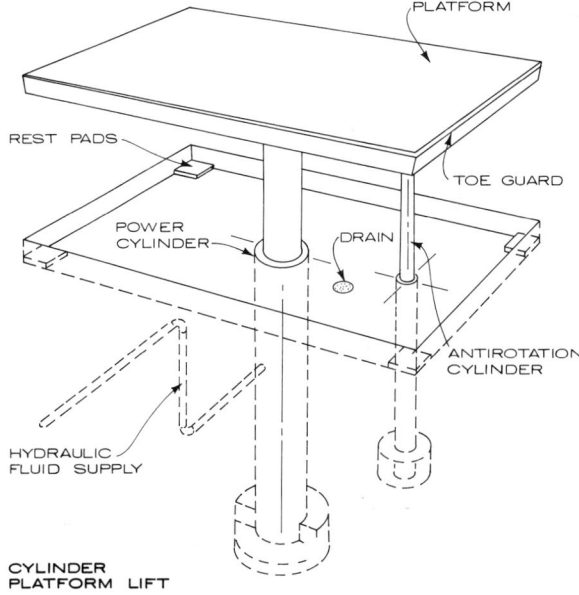

CYLINDER PLATFORM LIFT

MISCELLANEOUS LIFTS

SCISSOR LIFT

Used to raise/lower unit loads to delivery vehicles from ground or floor levels that do not align with vehicles.

Load capacity: 2500 to 30,000 lb; lifting height: up to 12 ft; platform sizes: typically 5 x 7 ft to 8 x 12 ft, but other sizes can be specified; lift rate: cycle rate is manually controlled by loading/unloading rate. Up cycle of lift ranges from 40 to 100 sec depending on lift size.

St. Onge, Ruff & Associates; York, Pennsylvania

Installation: lifts available in permanent pit installation or portable aboveground units. Limiting factor on installation is electric power source for hydraulic pump and reservoir.

CYLINDER PLATFORM LIFT

Used to move unitized loads from floor or ground to delivery vehicle level to facilitate loading/unloading operations. Used also for machine loading/unloading of heavy/bulky materials.

Load capacity: 2000 to 30,000 lb; lifting height: up to 5 ft; platform sizes: typically 5 x 5 ft to 8 x 15 ft, but other sizes can be specified.

Lift rate: cycle rate is manually controlled by loading/unloading rate. Up cycle of lift ranges up to 12 fpm. Installation: pit used to facilitate platform flush with floor or ground for loading/unloading. Cylinder shaft is centered under platform with antirotational shaft at one end. Both shafts recessed into ground.

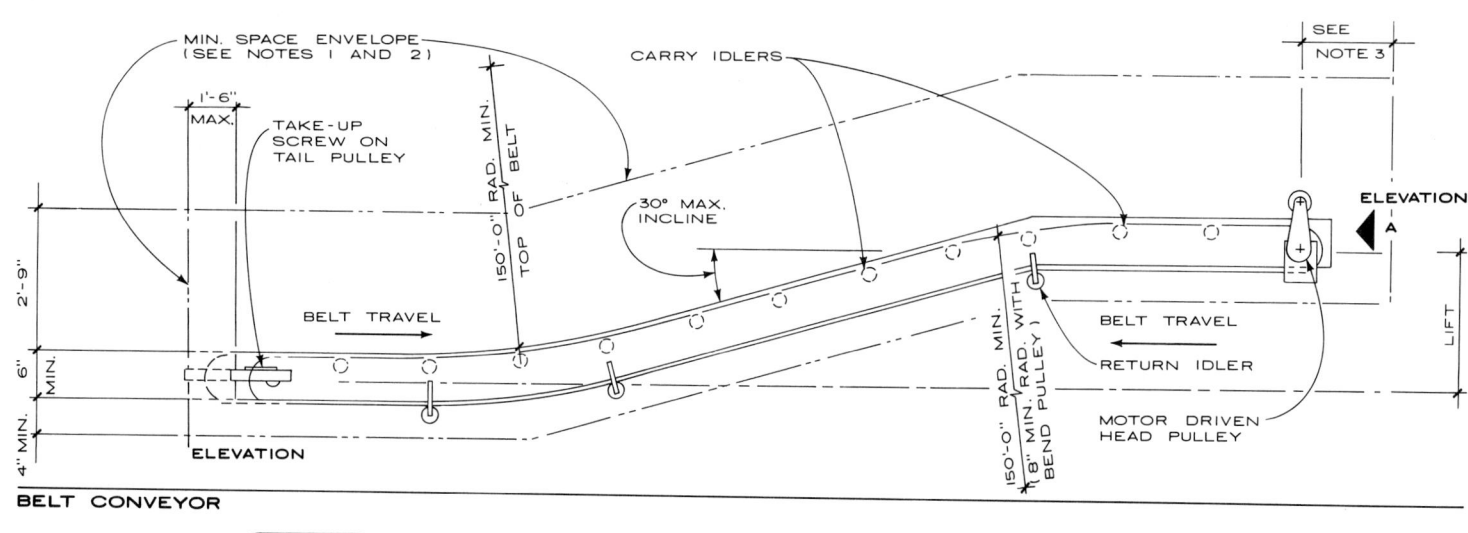

BELT CONVEYOR

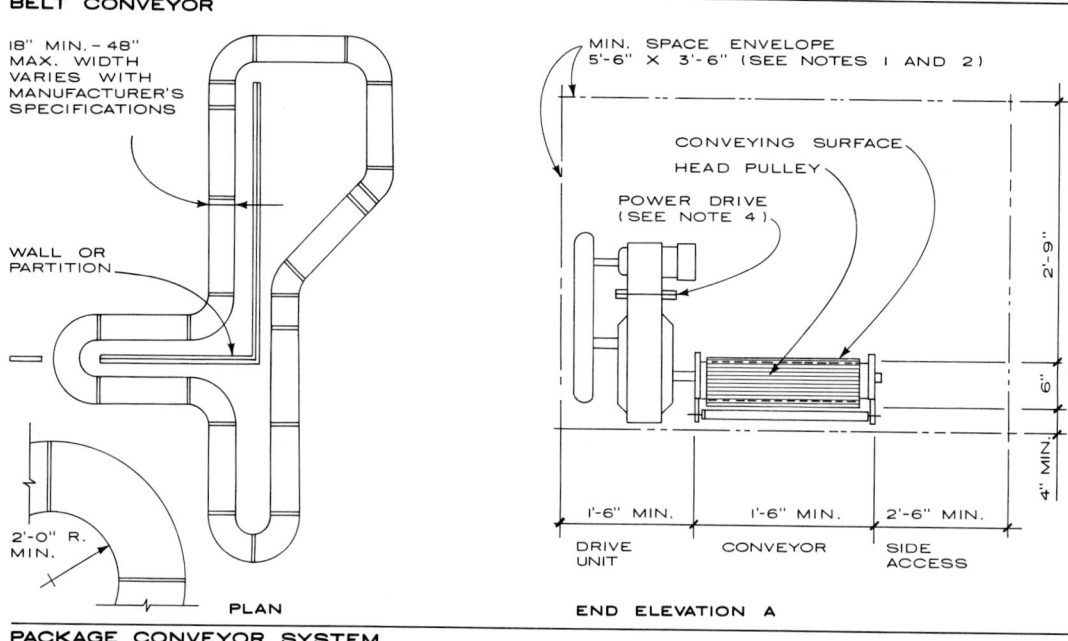

PLAN

PACKAGE CONVEYOR SYSTEM

END ELEVATION A

COMPARISON OF MATERIAL CONVEYORS

CONVEYOR	TYPE	APPLICATION	ADVANTAGES	LIMITATIONS
Belt	Flat (power drive)	Airport baggage Manufacturing, assembly, and inspection Packaged goods	Very common Many vendors Economical High capacity output Extensive speed range	Frequent maintenance required Friction drive pulley slips Belt replacement and realignment required Will not curve horizontally (powered belt curves are available)
	Troughed (power drive)	Bulk handling Dry granular materials Dry solid waste		
Roller	Skate wheel (gravity)	Light duty packages	Mobile units available Can turn in horizontal planes (see typical plan arrangement) Can accumulate loads	Poor for sacked items or resilient outer surfaces Light duty (skate wheel) Limited weight range for rollers Package or unit material Occasional noise problems Regularly inspect wheels or rollers for free rolling
	Gravity roller (unpowered) Live roller (power drive)	Medium to heavy duty handling Pallets or other flat bottom containers or items		
Segmented (articulated) moving surface	Pan Apron Slat (All power driven)	Airport baggage Loose waste handling Solid waste handling	Can handle heavy loads Durable carrying surface Can turn in horizontal planes (see typical plan arrangement) Good for steep inclines Handles hot or wet material	Very costly

Alpha Engineers, Inc.; Pocatello, Idaho

NOTES

1. Clearance dimensions shown are nominal. Exact dimensions should be determined after specific equipment has been designed.
2. Service access must be provided at tail pulley, drive area, and along at least one side.
3. Trajectory of material leaving the conveyor depends on the material's characteristics and the speed of its travel.
4. Drive unit does not necessarily protrude above belt surface and can be located below the frame and at locations other than at the head pulley.
5. Access safety rails, guards, etc., should comply with applicable codes and with manufacturers' recommendations.

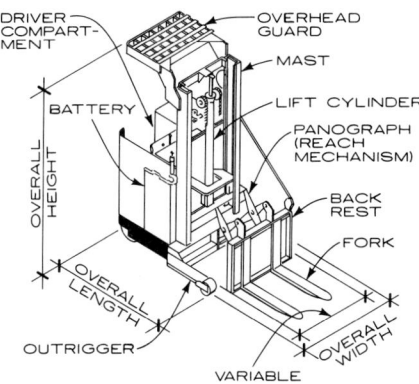

REACH TRUCK

APPLICATION

Narrow aisle operations without limiting pallet sizes and rack openings.

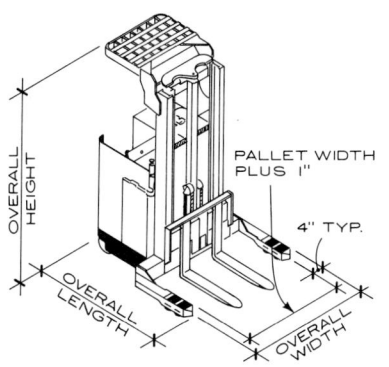

STRADDLE TRUCK

APPLICATION

Narrow aisle operations with a fixed pallet width (pallet must fit between outriggers). Clearances must be allowed between pallets and rack uprights for outriggers in rack operations unless a winged pallet is used.

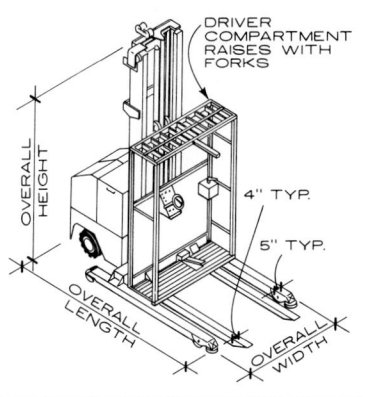

ORDER PICKER TRUCK

APPLICATION

Allows access to multiple level pick slots; an efficient technique with a large item base that has limited space for selection line.

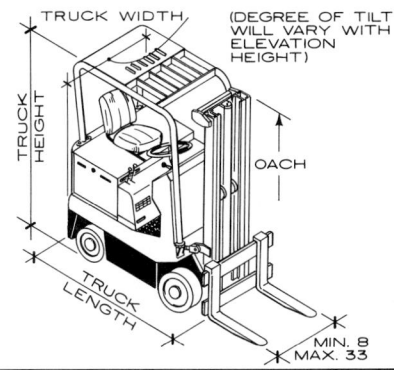

COUNTERBALANCE TRUCK

APPLICATION

Ideal for moving large volumes of material where maneuvering area is not limited.

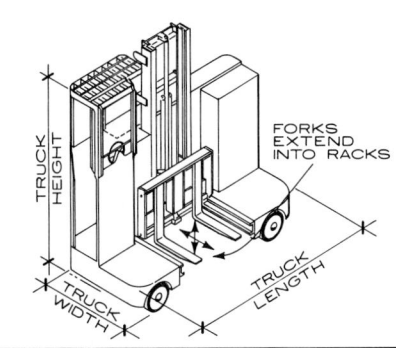

SIDELOADER TRUCK

APPLICATION

Allows lift capacity beyond conventional heights with narrow aisle operation plus flexibility to maneuver aisle to aisle.

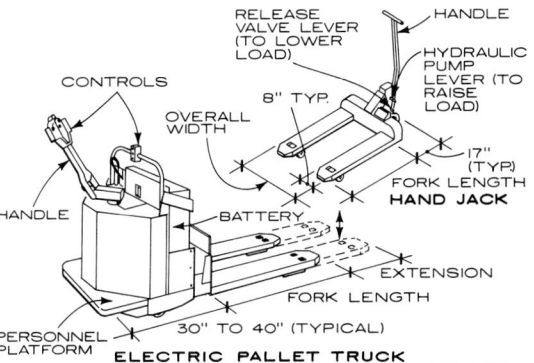

HAND PALLET TRUCKS

APPLICATION

Used to transport unitized loads when stacking of loads is not necessary. Ideal for dock work and production areas.

FORKLIFTS—DIMENSIONS AND CAPACITIES

	REACH TRUCK	STRADDLE TRUCK	ORDER PICKER TRUCK	COUNTER-BALANCE TRUCK	SIDE-LOADER TRUCK	ELECTRIC PALLET TRUCK	HAND JACK
Load capacity (lb)	2000 to 6000	2000 to 6000	1500 to 3000	2000 to 15,000	2000 to 10,000	1500 to 6000	2000 to 6500
Maximum lift height	20'-0''	19'-9''	30'-6''	17'-9''	30'-0''	6'' to 7''	4'' to 7³/₄''
Operating aisle width	6'-4'' to 7'-6''	6'-0'' to 8'-2''	4'-6'' to 5'-2''	10'-3'' to 10'-0''	Load length plus 20''-30''	Load or truck length plus 6''	Load or truck length plus 6''
Intersecting aisle requirement	—	—	5'-6'' to 17'-0''	—	10'-3'' to 12'-8''	—	6'-9'' to 10'-5''
Right angle stacking aisle requirement	6'-0'' to 10'-0''	5'-5'' to 9'-6''	—	10'-4'' to 14'-2''	—	Truck length plus 3'-0''	Truck length plus 3'-0''
Truck weight without load (lb)	4000 to 8000	3000 to 5000	5700 to 9500	5400 to 22,000	9000 to 12,000	1000 to 2000	250 to 300
Overall truck width	3'-1'' to 5'-4''	3'-0'' to 5'-1''	3'-10'' to 5'-10''	2'-11'' to 4'-10''	4'-0'' to 7'-6''	2'-7'' to 3'-2''	1'-6'' to 2'-6''
Overall truck height	6'-0'' to 11'-8''	6'-0'' to 11'-8''	7'-1'' to 12'-4''	5'-8'' to 7'-6''	7'-9'' to 12'-9''	4'-0'' to 5'-0''	4'-0''
Overall truck length without load	5'-2'' to 6'-0''	5'-4'' to 7'-1''	7'-4'' to 10'-6''	5'-6'' to 9'-7''	7'-0'' to 9'-8''	5'-7'' to 9'-7''	3'-9'' to 7'-5''
Fork length	2'-6'' to 4'-0''	2'-6'' to 4'-0''	3'-0'' to 8'-0''	2'-6'' to 4'-0''	2'-6'' to 4'-6''	2'-6'' to 7'-0''	2'-0'' to 6'-0''
Travel speeds	Up to 7 mph	Up to 6 mph	Up to 5 mph	Up to 11 mph	Up to 5.5 mph	Up to 5 mph	Manually operated
Load speeds (fpm) Lifting Lowering	27 to 68 67 to 40	50 to 104 88 to 61	31 to 62 77 to 44	30 to 70 110 to 40	30 to 70 70 to 40	2 to 4 sec 4 to 2 sec	Manually operated
Ramp slope	15 to 23%	10 to 16%	3 to 16%	10 to 37%	Up to 15%	Up to 10%	Manually operated

GENERAL NOTES

Data and figures given here represent the ranges of general specification available on forklift trucks. Aisle width is controlled by type of forklift and pallet size used in a warehouse. Specific data and applications should be obtained from material handling engineers. The trucks presented are electrically powered (excluding the hand jack) using industrial batteries as a source of energy. Industrial batteries typically must be charged after each 8-hr shift. Two batteries per truck are typical to allow back-to-back shift operation. The charging operation should take place in an area segregated from the warehouse or production area and must be designed to meet the various OSHA requirements.

St. Onge, Ruff & Associates; York, Pennsylvania

Escalators are a very efficient form of vertical transportation for very heavy traffic where the number of floors served is limited, normally a maximum of five to six floors. Escalators are not usually accepted as a required exit.

Dimensions shown are general and will vary somewhat with the manufacturer. Consult manufacturers for structural support, electrical supply, and specific dimensional requirements.

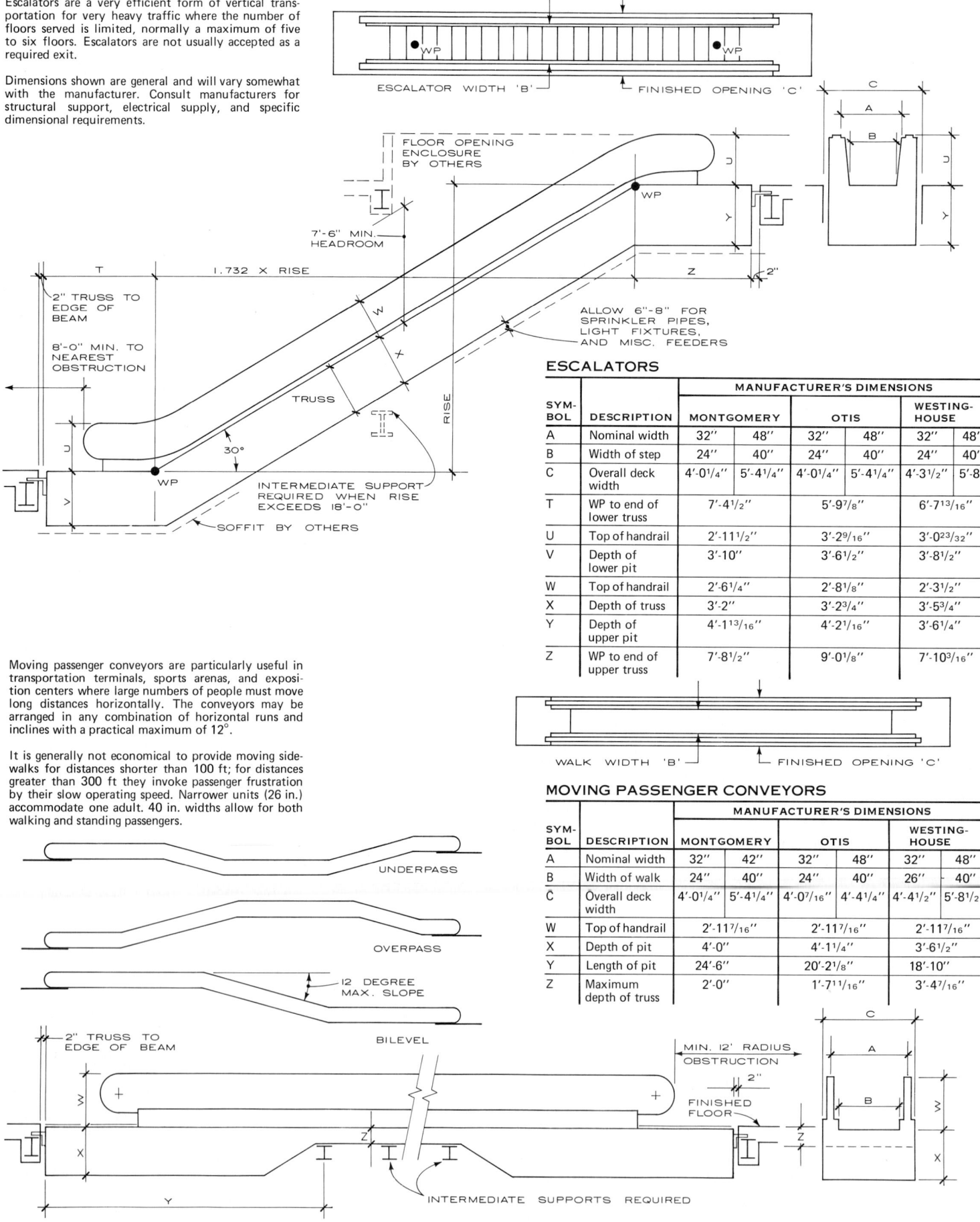

ESCALATORS

SYM-BOL	DESCRIPTION	MANUFACTURER'S DIMENSIONS					
		MONTGOMERY		OTIS		WESTING-HOUSE	
A	Nominal width	32''	48''	32''	48''	32''	48''
B	Width of step	24''	40''	24''	40''	24''	40''
C	Overall deck width	4'-0¼''	5'-4¼''	4'-0¼''	5'-4¼''	4'-3½''	5'-8''
T	WP to end of lower truss	7'-4½''		5'-9⅞''		6'-7¹³⁄₁₆''	
U	Top of handrail	2'-11½''		3'-2⁹⁄₁₆''		3'-0²³⁄₃₂''	
V	Depth of lower pit	3'-10''		3'-6½''		3'-8½''	
W	Top of handrail	2'-6¼''		2'-8⅛''		2'-3½''	
X	Depth of truss	3'-2''		3'-2¾''		3'-5¾''	
Y	Depth of upper pit	4'-1¹³⁄₁₆''		4'-2¹⁄₁₆''		3'-6¼''	
Z	WP to end of upper truss	7'-8½''		9'-0⅛''		7'-10³⁄₁₆''	

Moving passenger conveyors are particularly useful in transportation terminals, sports arenas, and exposition centers where large numbers of people must move long distances horizontally. The conveyors may be arranged in any combination of horizontal runs and inclines with a practical maximum of 12°.

It is generally not economical to provide moving sidewalks for distances shorter than 100 ft; for distances greater than 300 ft they invoke passenger frustration by their slow operating speed. Narrower units (26 in.) accommodate one adult. 40 in. widths allow for both walking and standing passengers.

MOVING PASSENGER CONVEYORS

SYM-BOL	DESCRIPTION	MANUFACTURER'S DIMENSIONS					
		MONTGOMERY		OTIS		WESTING-HOUSE	
A	Nominal width	32''	42''	32''	48''	32''	48''
B	Width of walk	24''	40''	24''	40''	26''	40''
C	Overall deck width	4'-0¼''	5'-4¼''	4'-0⁷⁄₁₆''	4'-4¼''	4'-4½''	5'-8½''
W	Top of handrail	2'-11⁷⁄₁₆''		2'-11⁷⁄₁₆''		2'-11⁷⁄₁₆''	
X	Depth of pit	4'-0''		4'-1¼''		3'-6½''	
Y	Length of pit	24'-6''		20'-2⅛''		18'-10''	
Z	Maximum depth of truss	2'-0''		1'-7¹¹⁄₁₆''		3'-4⁷⁄₁₆''	

Alan H. Rider, AIA; Daniel, Mann, Johnson & Mendenhall; Washington, D.C.

GENERAL NOTES

Pneumatic Tube Systems: Use of pneumatic tube systems, under vacuum or pressure, allows transmission of paper, small articles and liquids in "carrier" tubes to and from predetermined stations.

Applicable systems are commercial offices and stores; industrial plants, warehouses and air and rail stations; banks; hospitals and laboratories. Care should be taken in the latter instances to exclude services in areas where centrifuge action in transmitted liquids is undesirable.

Installation of Systems: Systems can be placed anywhere in or about the area served, exposed or furred in structure, outside or underground. Lines exposed to weather or through refrigerated spaces must be protected and insulated to prevent condensation in the system. Subsurface installations should be placed in corrugated pipe below the frost line, and tubing should be mill wrapped and joints welded and protected with mill wrap tape and pressure tested.

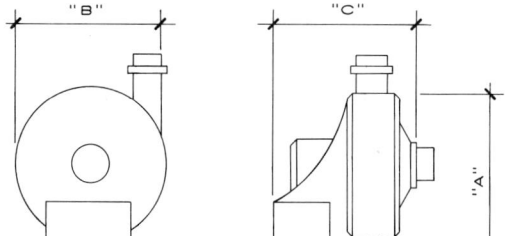

CENTRIFUGAL UNIT

CENTRIFUGAL EXHAUSTERS AND BLOWERS (This chart shows only extremes for each case.)

VACUUM	RPM	HP	A	B	C	VACUUM	RPM	HP	A	B	C
12 oz	3500	1 min.	30	29	20	20 oz	3500	1 1/2 min.	36	35	20
		5 max.	36	35	27			15 max.	46	41	42
	1750	7 1/2 min.	54	54	34		1750	7 1/2 min.	54	54	38
		50 max.	93	79	54			60 max.	80	67	60
16 oz	3500	1 min.	30	29	20	24 oz	3500	1 1/2 min.	36	35	22
		10 max.	42	42	31			25 max.	59	54	46
	1750	7 1/2 min.	54	54	30		1750	7 1/2 min.	54	54	36
		75 max.	92	80	60			75 max.	80	67	60

Used indoor or outside, centrifugal types operate on vacuum or vacuum and pressure combinations. Quieter than most types, they are recommended except where long lines are to be used or where reversible action is required. Sizes vary with horsepower of motor, vacuum and rpm.

POWER UNITS FOR VACUUM OR PRESSURE

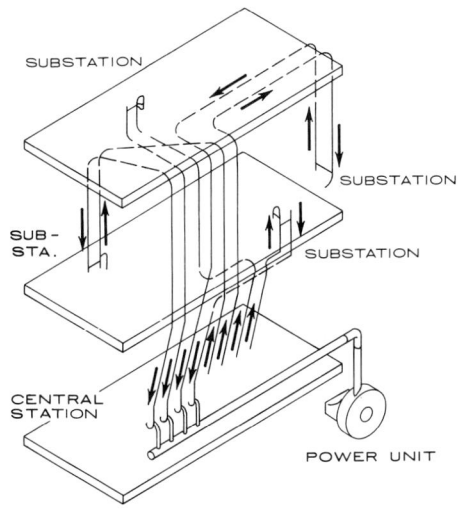

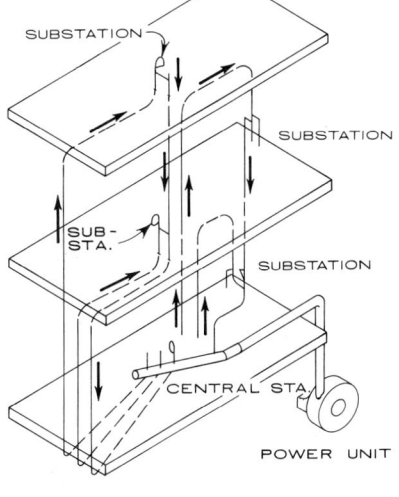

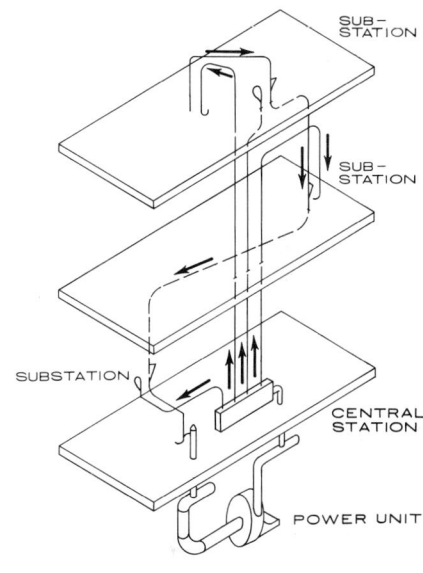

VACUUM TYPE INDEPENDENT TWIN LINE

This system may dispatch carriers from all stations simultaneously with continuous, nearly unlimited transaction. It may have any number of stations since independent lines run to and from all stations. It is considered to be most efficient, low in maintenance cost, and is the quietest system.

VACUUM TYPE COMBINATION LINE

This system may dispatch carriers from the central station to all substations via separate lines, but return lines are common. Where intermittent service is satisfactory, such as in mail order houses and industrial plants, this system may be used to advantage.

VACUUM-PRESSURE TYPE COMBINATION LINE

This system utilizes both vacuum and pressure. It is economical of power and of length of return lines. It is necessary that the number of open ends be the same for the vacuum as for the pressure lines. Provides quick service. Its use is restricted to mercantile houses, drug, grocery and meat packing plants, and similar types of buildings.

NOTES

Computer controlled systems consist of control center, stations, transfer units, blowers, transmission piping, and associated wiring. They can be single or multiple zone, utilizing 4-in. or 6-in. diameter carriers. Station attendant inserts carrier in dispatcher, selects station, and presses send button; computer checks address and rejects carrier if station is overloaded or out of service. If station is ready to receive, carrier is accepted as soon as route is clear. Traffic is two-way in all lines using pressure or vacuum. Switching occurs at transfer units, and temporary storage (until route is clear) occurs in interzone storage pipes between zones. Bends are minimum 48-in. radius. Control center is usually located in central area so it can be observed continuously.

COMPUTER CONTROLLED SYSTEM

Hills Gilbertson Fisher/Centrum Architects, Inc.; Minneapolis, Minnesota

LWH; King and King; Syracuse, New York

CARRIER STATISTICS

SIZE	TYPE	DESCRIPTION	BODY MATERIAL	CLEAR INSIDE LENGTH	CLEAR INSIDE DIMENSIONS	MINIMUM RADIUS BEND
1 1/2″	1	Message	Fiber	5 1/8″	15/16″	15″
	2	Cash	Brass	3 15/16″	1 5/8″	14″
	3	Telegram	Plastic	4 1/4″	1 3/8″	14″
	4	Message	Plastic	6″	1 3/8″	24″
2 1/4″ O.D.	4	Message	Plastic	9″	1 3/8″	42″
	4	Message	Plastic	10″	1 3/8″	42″
	6	Utility	Rubber	6″	1 3/8″	24″
	6	Utility	Rubber	9″	1 3/8″	42″
	6	Utility	Rubber	10″	1 3/8″	42″
	5	Message	Plastic	9″	2″	30″
	5	Message	Plastic	10″	2″	48″
	5	Message	Plastic	11″	2″	48″
3″ O.D.	6	Utility	Rubber	9″	1 15/16″	30″
	6	Utility	Rubber	10″	1 15/16″	48″
	6	Utility	Rubber	11″	1 15/16″	48″
	7	Test Piece	Steel	3 1/2″	2″	48″
	15	Message	Fiberglass	11″	1 3/4″	48″
	5	Message	Plastic	10″	2 3/4″	48″
	5	Message	Plastic	12″	2 3/4″	48″
	5	Message	Plastic	14″	2 3/4″	60″
	6	Message	Rubber	10″	2 11/16″	48″
	6	Message	Rubber	12″	2 11/16″	48″
	6	Message	Rubber	14″	2 11/16″	60″
4″ O.D.	7	Test Piece	Steel	Varies	Varies	48″
	8	Punch Card	Alum.	Varies	3 3/8″	48″
	9	Blueprint	Alum.	42″	2 3/8″	SPCL.
	13	Bottle	Leather	Varies	Varies	48″
	16	Message	Plastic	12″	2 13/16″	48″
	16	Message	Plastic	12 1/2″	2 13/16″	60″
	17	X-ray	Plastic	14 1/2″	2″	48″
6″ O.D.	11	Utility	Plastic	15 1/2″	4 5/8″	72″
	14	Message	Plastic	14 3/4″	4 1/2″	48″
4″ x 7″	12	Message	Plastic	14 5/16″	2 9/16″ x 5 9/16″	48″
	18	Message	Plastic	14 5/16″	2 1/2″ x 5 9/16″	48″
4″ x 12″	10	Utility	Alum.	15″	2 9/16″ x 10 7/16″	60″
5″ x 13″	10	Utility	Alum.	15 7/8″	3″ x 11″	60″

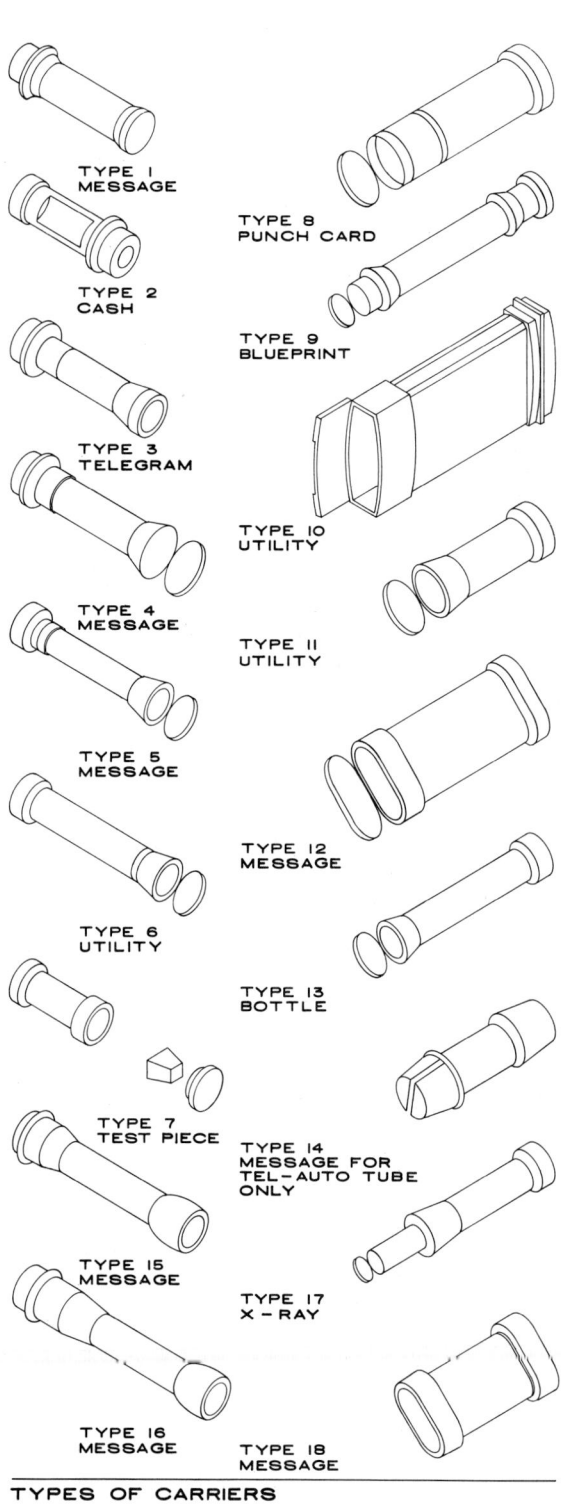

TYPE 1 MESSAGE
TYPE 2 CASH
TYPE 3 TELEGRAM
TYPE 4 MESSAGE
TYPE 5 MESSAGE
TYPE 6 UTILITY
TYPE 7 TEST PIECE
TYPE 8 PUNCH CARD
TYPE 9 BLUEPRINT
TYPE 10 UTILITY
TYPE 11 UTILITY
TYPE 12 MESSAGE
TYPE 13 BOTTLE
TYPE 14 MESSAGE FOR TEL-AUTO TUBE ONLY
TYPE 15 MESSAGE
TYPE 16 MESSAGE
TYPE 17 X-RAY
TYPE 18 MESSAGE

TYPES OF CARRIERS

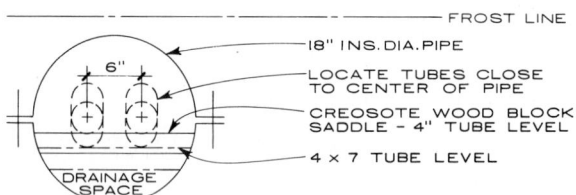

FROST LINE
18″ INS. DIA. PIPE
LOCATE TUBES CLOSE TO CENTER OF PIPE
CREOSOTE WOOD BLOCK SADDLE – 4″ TUBE LEVEL
4 x 7 TUBE LEVEL
6″
DRAINAGE SPACE

DETAIL OF PIPE BELOW GROUND

TUBE STANDARDS

SIZE TUBE O.D.	MATL.	NET WGT. PER FOOT LB	STAND LENGTH	WALL THICKNESS GA.	WALL THICKNESS DIM.
1 1/2″	Steel	.55	15′–0″	20	.035″
2 1/4″	Steel	.85	15′–0″	20	.035″
3″	Steel	1.36	15′–0″	19	.042″
4″	Steel	2.75	15′–0″	16	.065″
6″	Steel	4.00	15′–0″	16	.065″
4″ x 7″	Steel	4.54	15′–0″	16	.065″
4″ x 12″	Steel	9.00	10′–0″	14	.078″
5″ x 13″	Steel	13.15	10′–0″	12	.109″

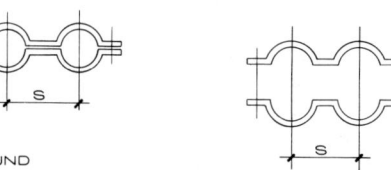

ROUND
S 1 1/2″ Size = 2 1/2″
2 1/4 Size = 3″ + 3 3/4″
3″ Size = 4-1/4″
4″ Size = 6″
6″ Size = 9″

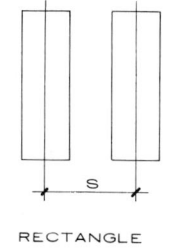

OVAL
S 4″ x 7″ Size = 6″

RECTANGLE
S 4″ x 12″ Size = 6″
5″ x 13″ Size = 9″

STANDARD TUBE SPACING

Hills Gilbertson Fisher/Centrum Architects, Inc.; Minneapolis, Minnesota

LWH & RWL; King and King; Syracuse, New York

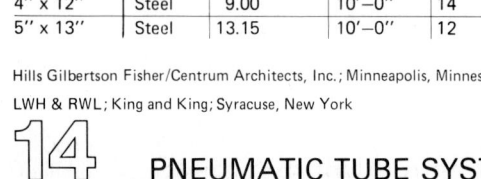

14   PNEUMATIC TUBE SYSTEMS

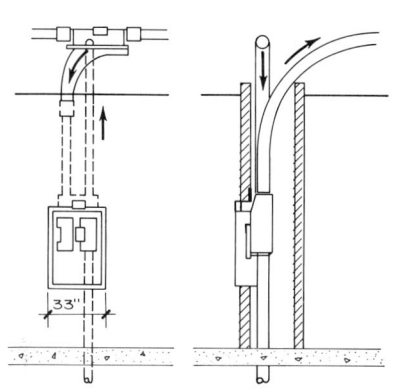

DOWN DISCHARGE TERMINALS

GENERAL NOTES

A carrier, placed in the sending side of the loop at any one of 16 sending-receiving stations shown at right, will be conveyed swiftly and directly to any one of the other 15. No human element enters to delay or impede the carrier's transit. An Automatic Monitor, in a matter of seconds, transfers the carrier to its correct receiving tube . . . then, an electrically controlled deflector in the receiving tube, delivers the carrier into its ordered station. Such a system has much to recommend it to any user. First, an Automatic System eliminates operating personnel at a Central Station. Not only does this automatic device speed carrier delivery but also permits 24 hour a day communications service, 7 days a week without supervision. Second, by grouping sending-receiving sub-stations along one or more twin-tube loops, 2 airtubes can service all 5 sub-stations as illustrated. The same 2 airtubes could service all 10 sub-stations if that maximum number were located on a given loop. This design effects a tangible saving in space, materials and labor. It also sharply reduces problems encountered when installing a system in existing structures.

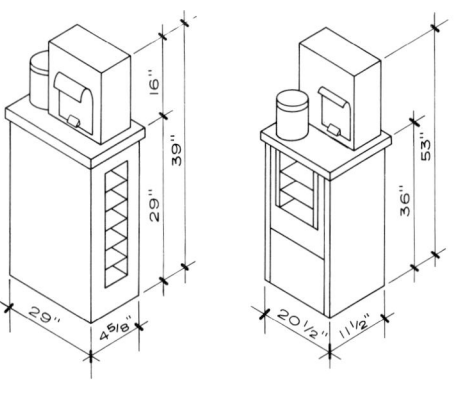

PEDESTALS FOR 2¼" PNEUMATIC TERMINALS

Down Discharge Terminals can be recessed in walls with only dispatching and receiving doors exposed. Can be used for all automatic selective systems.

Pedestal for 2¼" Pneumatic terminals have steel cabinet bases with carrier storage under top. Sending inlet on opposite end.

Pedestals for Down Discharge closed receiver terminals for conventional or automatic systems are supplied with base units 20½" wide, 11½" deep, 36" to countertop and an overall height of 53" on 2¼" and 3" systems or an overall height of 56" on 4" systems.

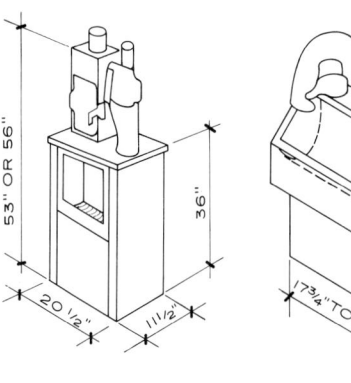

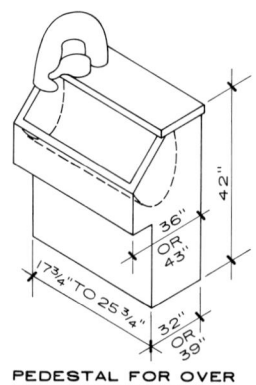

PEDESTAL FOR DOWN DISCHARGE CLOSED RECEIVER TERMINAL

PEDESTAL FOR OVER DELIVERY CARRIER RECEIVING STATION

Pedestal for Over delivery carrier receiving stations have belt sling type pocket sizes available for 2¼", 3" and 4" two station systems. 2¼" and 3" system pedestals are 18" wide and 36" deep; 4" system pedestals are 26" wide by 43" deep.

TUBE BENDS: CARRIER LENGTHS AND TYPES

SIZE	FIG.	R	A	B	MATERIAL	GAUGE	CARRIER LENGTH AND TYPE
1½"	A	15	21	21	Steel	20	5⅛" Type #1
2¼"	A	14	19	20	Steel	20	Varies, Types #2 and 3
	A	18	22	26	Steel	20	Varies, Types #2 and 3
	A	24	30	33	Steel	20	6" Type 4 and 6
	A	42	50	50	Steel	20	10" Type 4 and 6
	B	7½	8⅜	8⅜	Cast		Varies, Types #2 and 3
	B	15	17¾	17¾	Cast		9" Type 4 and 6
3"	A	30	36	36	Steel	19	9" Type 5 and 6
	A	48	54	56	Steel	19	11" Type 5, 6, and 15
	B	24	28	28	Cast		11" Type 5, 6, and 15
4"	A	48	54	86	Steel	16	10" and 12" Types 5, 6, and 13
	A	60	65	80	Steel	16	14" Type 5, 6, and 13
	B	24	28	28	Cast		14" Type 5, 6, 8, 13 and 16
	C	23	32½	32½	Weld		14" Type 5, 6, 8, 13 and 16
6"	A	48			Steel	16	14¾" Type 14
	A	72			Steel	16	15½" Type 11
4 x 7 Edge	D	60	72	74	Steel	16	14⁵⁄₁₆" Type 12 and 18
4 x 7 Flat	E	60	72	74	Steel	16	14⁵⁄₁₆" Type 12 and 18
4 x 7 Edge	H	24	29	29	Cast		14⁵⁄₁₆" Type 12 and 18
4 x 7 Flat	J	24	29	29	Cast		14⁵⁄₁₆" Type 12 and 18
4 x 7 Edge	H	24	32	32	Weld		14⁵⁄₁₆" Type 12 and 18
4 x 7 Flat	J	24	32	32	Weld		14⁵⁄₁₆" Type 12 and 18
4 x 12 Edge	F	60	60	60	Steel	14	15" Type 10
4 x 12 Flat	G	60	60	60	Steel	14	15" Type 10
5 x 13 Edge	K	60	66	66	Steel	12	15⅞" Type 10
5 x 13 Flat	L	60	66	66	Steel	12	15⅞" Type 10

Hills Gilbertson Fisher/Centrum Architects, Inc.; Minneapolis, Minnesota

LWH; King and King; Syracuse, New York

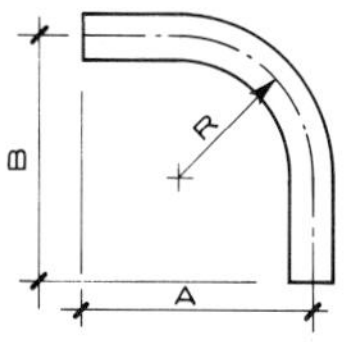

1½ x 2¼, 3, 4 & 6 TUBE
FIGURE A

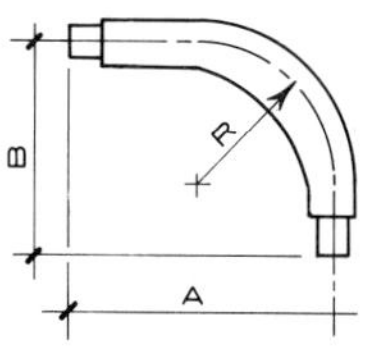

2¼, 3 & 4 CAST
FIGURE B

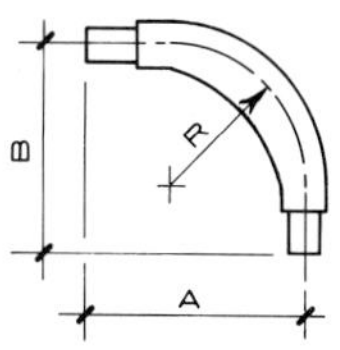

4" WELD
FIGURE C

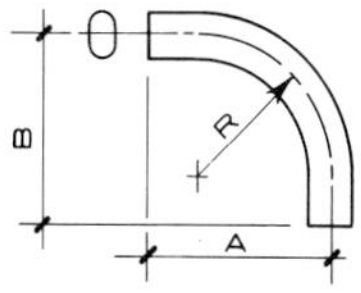

4 x 7 EDGE TUBE
FIGURE D

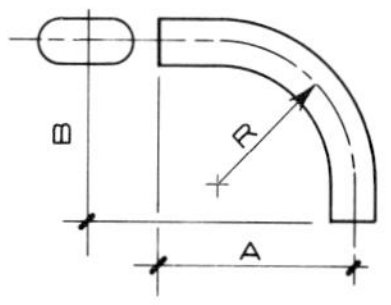

4 x 7 FLAT TUBE
FIGURE E

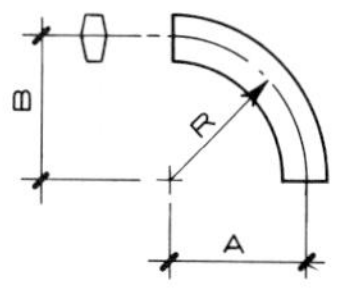

4 x 12 EDGE TUBE
FIGURE F

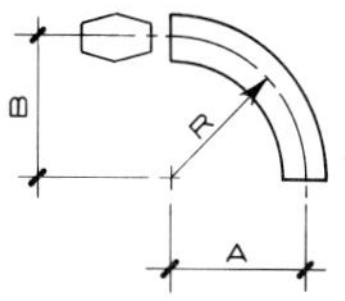

4 x 12 FLAT TUBE
FIGURE G

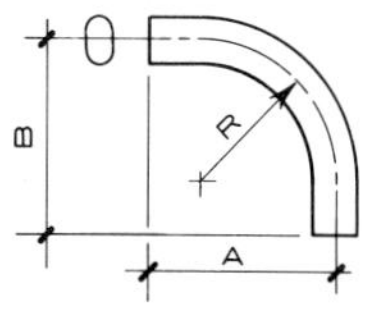

4 x 7 EDGE CAST OR WELD
FIGURE H

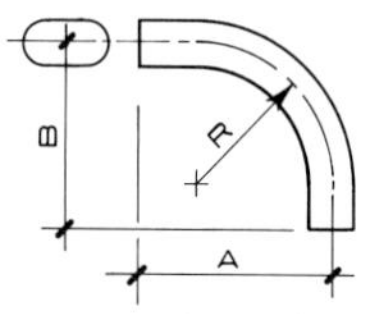

4 x 7 FLAT CAST OR WELD
FIGURE J

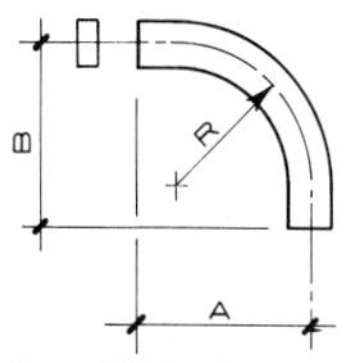

5 x 13 EDGE TUBE
FIGURE K

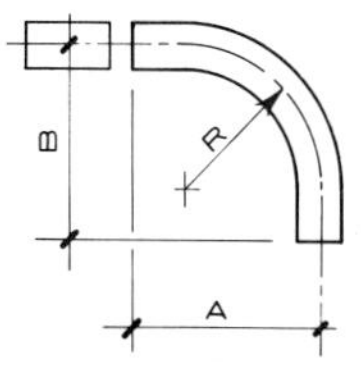

5 x 13 FLAT TUBE
FIGURE L

TUBE BENDS

NOTES

Automated people movers are a reliable and efficient means for moving varying numbers of people over a fixed route at distances from 1000 ft to several miles. Vehicles operate individually, in pairs, or in trains on a fixed guideway which may be designed in a continuous loop or in a two-way shuttle configuration. Guideways may be located at grade, on elevated structures, or in tunnels.

Vehicles are controlled automatically and may be programmed to operate in a scheduled mode or a demand mode. In scheduled mode operation, the vehicles operate continuously, stopping at each station for a predetermined dwell time before moving on to the next station. In the demand mode, the vehicle waits in a station until called by a passenger who may then direct the vehicle to proceed to a selected on-line station.

Successful applications now exist at several recreation centers, airport terminals, shopping complexes, and college campuses. Extensive studies are currently under way to demonstrate the feasibility of automated people moving systems in the urban commercial districts of major cities. All systems have individual provisions for switching and off-line parking of vehicles for storage and maintenance. Each installation must be individually designed to meet specific user requirements. Consultation with manufacturers of the various systems is essential during the earliest planning stages.

WEDWAY PEOPLE MOVER

SUSPENSION	ALUMINUM WHEELS ON STEEL TUBING
PROPULSION	LINEAR INDUCTION
MAX. SPEED	13.6 MPH
MAX. GRADE	15%
MIN. TURN RAD	20'
CAPACITY	4 SEATED / VEHICLE
	20 SEATED — TYPICAL 5 CAR TRAIN

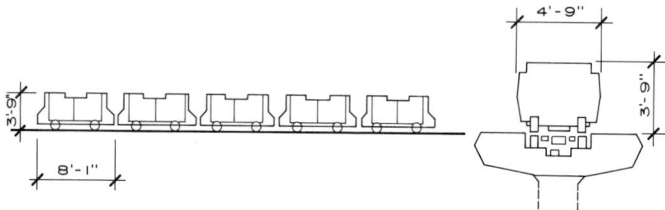

LTV AIRTRANS

SUSPENSION	FOAM FILLED RUBBER TIRES ON CONCRETE
PROPULSION	ROTARY ELECTRIC MOTORS
MAX. SPEED	19 MPH
MAX. GRADE	7.8%
MIN. TURN RAD	100'
CAPACITY	16 SEATED
	24-44 STANDING

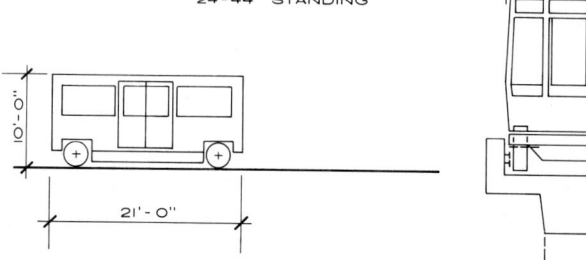

UNIMOBIL AGT SYSTEM

SUSPENSION	PNEUMATIC TIRES ON STEEL GUIDEWAY
PROPULSION	ROTARY ELECTRIC MOTORS
MAX. SPEED	12 MPH
MAX. GRADE	8%
MIN. TURN RAD	80'
CAPACITY	12 SEATED / VEHICLE
	90 SEATED — TYPICAL AND CAR TRAIN

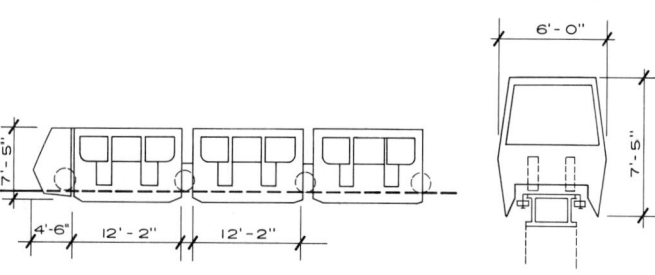

BOEING MPRT

SUSPENSION	PNEUMATIC TIRE ON CONCRETE
PROPULSION	ROTARY ELECTRIC MOTORS
MAX. SPEED	30 MPH
MAX. GRADE	10%
MIN. TURN RAD	30'
CAPACITY	15-21

OTIS-TTD PEOPLE MOVER

SUSPENSION	"HOVAIR" AIR SUSPENSION
PROPULSION	LINEAR INDUCTION
MAX. SPEED	25 MPH
MAX. GRADE	8%
MIN. TURN RAD	60'
CAPACITY	4 SEATED, 18 STANDING

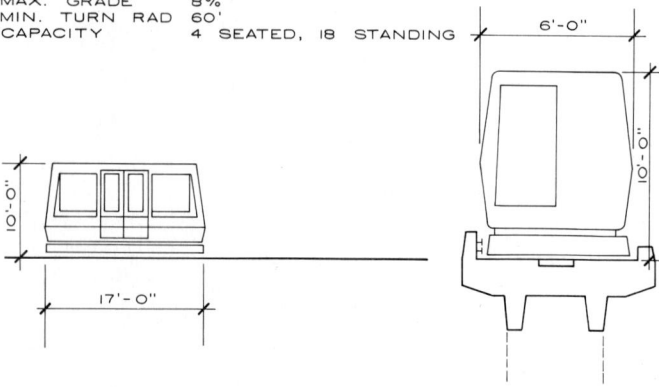

WESTINGHOUSE TRANSIT EXPRESSWAY

SUSPENSION	PNEUMATIC TIRES ON CONCRETE
PROPULSION	ROTARY ELECTRIC MOTORS
MAX. SPEED	70 MPH
MAX. GRADE	10%
MIN. TURN RAD	90'
CAPACITY	34 SEATED
	100 ALL STANDING

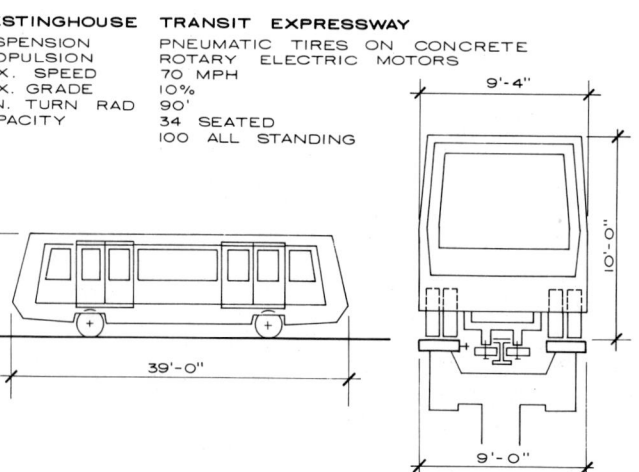

Alan H. Rider, AIA; Daniel, Mann, Johnson & Mendenhall; Washington, D.C.

CHAPTER 15 MECHANICAL

PLUMBING PIPING

SOIL, WASTE OR LEADER (ABOVE GRADE)	————————
SOIL, WASTE OR LEADER (BELOW GRADE)	— — — —
VENT	- - - - - - -
COMBINATION WASTE AND VENT	—— CWV ——
ACID WASTE	—— AW ——
ACID VENT	— — AV — —
INDIRECT DRAIN	—— D ——
STORM DRAIN	—— SD ——
COLD WATER	— - — - —
SOFT COLD WATER	—— SW ——
INDUSTRIALIZED COLD WATER	—— ICW ——
CHILLED DRINKING WATER SUPPLY	—— DWS ——
CHILLED DRINKING WATER RETURN	—— DWR ——
HOT WATER	— -- — -- —
HOT WATER RETURN	— --- — --- —
SANITIZING HOT WATER SUPPLY (180° F.)	⫢ -- ⫢ -- ⫢
SANITIZING HOT WATER RETURN (180° F.)	⫢ --- ⫢ --
INDUSTRIALIZED HOT WATER SUPPLY	—— IHW ——
INDUSTRIALIZED HOT WATER RETURN	—— IHR ——
TEMPERED WATER SUPPLY	—— TS ——
TEMPERED WATER RETURN	—— TR ——
FIRE LINE	—— F —— F ——
WET STANDPIPE	—— WSP ——

DRY STANDPIPE	—— DSP ——
COMBINATION STANDPIPE	—— CSP ——
MAIN SUPPLIES SPRINKLER	—— S ——
BRANCH AND HEAD SPRINKLER	——o——o——
GAS - LOW PRESSURE	—— G —— G ——
GAS - MEDIUM PRESSURE	—— MG ——
GAS - HIGH PRESSURE	—— HG ——
COMPRESSED AIR	—— A ——
VACUUM	—— V ——
VACUUM CLEANING	—— VC ——
OXYGEN	—— O ——
LIQUID OXYGEN	—— LOX ——
NITROGEN	—— N ——
LIQUID NITROGEN	—— LN ——
NITROUS OXIDE	—— NO ——
HYDROGEN	—— H ——
HELIUM	—— HE ——
ARGON	—— AR ——
LIQUID PETROLEUM GAS	—— LPG ——
INDUSTRIAL WASTE	—— INW ——
PNEUMATIC TUBES TUBE RUNS	—— PN ——
SEWER - CAST IRON	S-CI
SEWER - CLAY TILE BELL & SPIGOT	S-CT
DRAIN - CLAY TILE BELL & SPIGOT	————————
DRAIN - OPEN TILE OR AGRICULTURAL TILE	— — — -

HEATING PIPING

HIGH PRESSURE STEAM	—— HPS ——
MEDIUM PRESSURE STEAM	—— MPS ——
LOW PRESSURE STEAM	—— LPS ——
HIGH PRESSURE RETURN	—— HPR ——
MEDIUM PRESSURE RETURN	—— MPR ——
LOW PRESSURE RETURN	—— LPR ——
BOILER BLOW OFF	—— BD ——
CONDENSATE OR VACUUM PUMP DISCHARGE	—— VPD ——
FEEDWATER PUMP DISCHARGE	—— PPD ——
MAKE UP WATER	—— MU ——
AIR RELIEF LINE	—— V ——
FUEL OIL SUPPLY	—— FOS ——
FUEL OIL RETURN	—— FOR ——
FUEL OIL TANK VENT	—— FOV ——
COMPRESSED AIR	—— A ——
HOT WATER HEATING SUPPLY	—— HW ——
HOT WATER HEATING RETURN	—— HWR ——

AIR CONDITIONING PIPING

REFRIGERANT LIQUID	—— RL ——
REFRIGERANT DISCHARGE	—— RD ——
REFRIGERANT SUCTION	—— RS ——
CONDENSER WATER SUPPLY	—— C ——
CONDENSER WATER RETURN	—— CR ——
CHILLED WATER SUPPLY	—— CHWS ——
CHILLED WATER RETURN	—— CHWR ——
MAKE UP WATER	—— MU ——
HUMIDIFICATION LINE	—— H ——
DRAIN	—— D ——
BRINE SUPPLY	—— B ——
BRINE RETURN	—— BR ——

Amor Halperin, P.E.; Ayres, Cohen, and Hayakawa; Consulting Engineers; Los Angeles/San Francisco, California

MATERIALS AND METHODS

FITTINGS	VALVES	MISCELLANEOUS
ELBOW – 90°	GATE	FLANGED JOINT
ELBOW – 45°	GLOBE	SCREWED JOINT
ELBOW – TURNED UP	HOSE GATE	BELL AND SPIGOT JOINT
ELBOW – TURNED DOWN	HOSE GLOBE	WELD JOINT
ELBOW – LONG RAD.	ANGLE GATE – ELEV.	SOLDER JOINT
ELBOW – SIDE OUTLET DOWN	ANGLE GATE – PLAN	EXPANSION JOINT
ELBOW – SIDE OUTLET UP	ANGLE GLOBE – ELEV.	UNION
BASE ELBOW	ANGLE GLOBE – PLAN	SLEEVE
DOUBLE BRANCH ELBOW	CHECK	SCREWED BUSHING
REDUCING ELBOW	ANGLE CHECK	BELL AND SPIGOT BUSHING
SINGLE SWEEP TEE	SAFETY	SOLDER BUSHING
DOUBLE SWEEP TEE	COCK	WELD BUSHING
STRAIGHT TEE	QUICK OPEN	REDUCING FLANGE
TEE OUTLET UP	FLOAT	PIPE PLUGS
TEE OUTLET DOWN	MOTOR OPERATION GATE	BULL PLUGS
TEE – SIDE OUTLET UP	MOTOR OPERATION GLOBE	CAPS
TEE – SIDE OUTLET DOWN	DIAPHRAGM	CROSSOVER
STRAIGHT CROSS	AUTO BYPASS	CONCENTRIC REDUCER
LATERAL	AUTO GOVERNOR OPERATION	ECCENTRIC REDUCER

NOTE: FITTINGS AND VALVES ARE SHOWN WITH FLANGED CONNECTIONS

Sargent, Webster, Crenshaw & Folley, Architects Engineers Planners; Syracuse, New York

MATERIALS AND METHODS **15**

SEAMLESS STEEL PIPE

NOMINAL PIPE SIZE	DIMENSION (IN.) O.D.	WALL	CLASS	LB/FT P.E.	LB/FT T&C
2″	2.375	0.154	Std.	3.65	3.68
	2.375	0.218	X.S.	5.02	5.07
	2.375	0.436	XXS.	9.03	—
2½″	2.875	0.203	Std.	5.79	5.82
	2.875	0.276	X.S.	7.66	7.73
	2.875	0.552	XXS.	13.70	—
3″	3.500	0.216	Std.	7.58	7.62
	3.500	0.300	X.S.	10.25	10.33
	3.500	0.600	XXS.	18.58	—
3½″	4.000	0.226	Std.	9.11	9.20
	4.000	0.318	X.S.	12.51	12.63
	4.000	0.634	XXS.	22.85	—
4″	4.500	0.237	Std.	10.79	10.89
	4.500	0.337	X.S.	14.98	15.17
	4.500	0.674	XXS.	27.54	—
5″	5.563	0.258	Std.	14.62	14.81
	5.563	0.375	X.S.	20.78	21.09
	5.563	0.750	XXS.	38.55	—
6″	6.625	0.280	Std.	18.97	19.18
	6.625	0.432	X.S.	28.57	28.89
	6.625	0.864	XXS.	53.16	—
8″	8.625	0.277	—	24.70	25.55
	8.625	0.322	Std.	28.55	29.35
	8.625	0.500	X.S.	43.39	43.90
	8.625	0.875	XXS.	72.42	—
10″	10.750	0.307	—	34.34	35.75
	10.750	0.365	Std.	40.48	41.85
	10.750	0.500	X.S.	54.74	55.82
12″	12.750	0.330	—	43.77	45.45
	12.750	0.375	Std.	49.56	51.15
	12.750	0.406	—	53.53	—
	12.750	0.500	X.S.	65.42	66.71
	12.750	0.687	—	88.50	—
14″	14.000	0.312	—	45.68	—
	14.000	0.375	Std.	54.75	—
	14.000	0.500	X.S.	72.09	—
16″	16.000	0.312	—	52.36	—
	16.000	0.375	Std.	62.58	—
	16.000	0.500	X.S.	82.77	—
18″	18.000	0.312	—	59.03	—
	18.000	0.375	Std.	70.59	—
	18.000	0.500	X.S.	93.45	—
20″	20.000	0.312	—	68.71	—
	20.000	0.375	Std.	78.60	—
	20.000	0.500	X.S.	104.13	—
24″	24.000	0.312	—	79.06	—
	24.000	0.375	Std.	94.62	—
	24.000	0.500	X.S.	125.49	—

SEAMLESS STEEL PRESSURE TUBING

NOMINAL PIPE SIZE	DIMENSION (IN.) O.D.	WALL	CLASS	WEIGHT (LB/FT)
⅛″	0.405	0.068	Std.	0.240
		0.095	X.S.	0.310
¼″	0.540	0.088	Std.	0.420
		0.119	X.S.	0.540
⅜″	0.675	0.091	Std.	0.570
		0.126	X.S.	0.740
½″	0.840	0.109	Std.	0.850
		0.147	X.S.	1.087
		0.187	—	1.310
		0.294	XXS.	1.714
¾″	1.050	0.113	Std.	1.130
		0.154	X.S.	1.473
		0.218	—	1.940
		0.308	XXS.	2.440
1″	1.315	0.133	Std.	1.678
		0.179	X.S.	2.171
		0.250	—	2.850
		0.358	XXS.	3.659
1¼″	1.660	0.140	Std.	2.272
		0.191	X.S.	2.996
		0.250	—	3.764
		0.382	XXS.	5.214
1½″	1.900	0.145	Std.	2.717
		0.200	X.S.	3.631
		0.281	—	4.862
		0.400	XXS.	6.408

BUTTWELD STEEL PIPE

NOMINAL PIPE SIZE	DIMENSION (IN.) O.D.	STANDARD WEIGHT WALL (IN.)	LB/FT P.E.	LB/FT T&C	EXTRA STRONG WALL (IN.)	LB/FT P.E.	LB/FT T&C	DOUBLE EXTRA STRONG WALL (IN.)	LB/FT P.E.	LB/FT T&C
⅛″	0.405	0.068	0.24	0.24	0.095	0.31	0.32	—	—	—
¼″	0.540	0.088	0.42	0.42	0.119	0.54	0.54	—	—	—
⅜″	0.675	0.091	0.57	0.57	0.126	0.74	0.74	—	—	—
½″	0.840	0.109	0.85	0.85	0.147	1.09	1.09	—	—	—
¾″	1.050	0.113	1.13	1.13	0.154	1.47	1.48	0.308	2.441	—
1″	1.315	0.133	1.68	1.68	0.179	2.17	2.18	0.358	2.659	—
1¼″	1.660	0.140	2.27	2.28	0.191	3.00	3.02	0.382	5.214	—
1½″	1.900	0.145	2.72	2.73	0.200	3.63	3.66	0.400	6.408	—
2″	2.375	0.154	3.65	3.68	0.218	5.02	5.07	—	—	—
2½″	2.875	0.203	5.79	5.82	0.276	7.66	7.73	—	—	—
3″	3.500	0.216	7.58	7.62	0.300	10.25	10.33	—	—	—
3½″	4.000	0.226	9.11	9.20	0.318	12.51	12.63	—	—	—
4″	4.500	0.237	10.79	10.89	0.337	14.98	15.17	—	—	—

COPPER TUBING

NOMINAL PIPE SIZE	DIMENSION (IN.) O.D.	TYPE K WALL (IN.)	TYPE K LB/FT	TYPE L AND ACR WALL (IN.)	TYPE L AND ACR LB/FT	TYPE M WALL (IN.)	TYPE M LB/FT	REFRIGERATOR TUBE WALL (IN.)	REFRIGERATOR TUBE LB/COIL
	⅛	—	—	—	—	—	—	0.030	1.74
	3/16	—	—	—	—	—	—	0.030	2.88
	¼	—	—	—	—	—	—	0.030	4.02
	5/16	—	—	—	—	—	—	0.032	5.45
¼″	⅜	0.035	0.145	0.030	0.126	0.025	0.106	0.032	6.70
⅜″	½	0.049	0.269	0.035	0.198	0.025	0.145	0.032	9.10
½″	⅝	0.049	0.344	0.040	0.285	0.028	0.204	0.035	12.55
⅝″	¾	0.049	0.418	0.042	0.362	0.030	0.263	0.035	15.25
¾″	⅞	0.065	0.641	0.045	0.455	0.032	0.328	0.045	22.75
1″	1⅛	0.065	0.839	0.050	0.655	0.035	0.465	0.050	32.75
1¼″	1⅜	0.065	1.040	0.055	0.884	0.042	0.682	0.055	44.20
1½″	1⅝	0.072	1.360	0.060	1.140	0.049	0.940	—	—
2″	2⅛	0.083	2.060	0.070	1.750	0.058	1.460	—	—
2½″	2⅝	0.095	2.930	0.080	2.480	0.065	2.030	—	—
3″	3⅛	0.109	4.000	0.090	3.330	0.072	2.680	—	—
3½″	3⅝	0.120	5.120	0.100	4.290	0.083	3.580	—	—
4″	4⅛	0.134	6.510	0.110	5.380	0.095	4.660	—	—
5″	5⅛	0.160	9.670	0.125	7.610	0.109	6.666	—	—
6″	6⅛	0.192	13.900	0.140	10.200	0.122	8.920	—	—

RED BRASS PIPE

NOMINAL PIPE SIZE	DIMENSION (IN.) O.D.	STANDARD WEIGHT WALL (IN.)	STANDARD WEIGHT LB/FT	EXTRA STRONG WALL (IN.)	EXTRA STRONG LB/FT
⅛″	0.405	0.062	0.253	0.100	0.363
¼″	0.540	0.082	0.447	0.123	0.611
⅜″	0.675	0.090	0.627	0.127	0.829
½″	0.840	0.107	0.934	0.149	1.230
¾″	1.050	0.114	1.270	0.157	1.670
1″	1.315	0.126	1.780	0.182	2.460
1¼″	1.660	0.146	2.630	0.194	3.390
1½″	1.900	0.150	3.130	0.203	4.100
2″	2.375	0.156	3.650	0.221	5.670
2½″	2.875	0.187	5.990	0.280	8.660
3″	3.500	0.219	8.560	0.304	11.600
3½″	4.000	0.250	11.200	0.321	14.100
4″	4.500	0.250	12.700	0.341	16.900
5″	5.562	0.250	15.800	0.375	23.200
6″	6.625	0.250	19.000	0.437	32.200

PVC (POLYVINYLCHLORIDE) PIPE

NOMINAL PIPE SIZE	FOR CEMENTING ONLY WALL (IN.)	FOR CEMENTING ONLY PSI AT 73.4°F	FOR CEMENTING OR THREADING WALL (IN.)	PSI AT 73.4°F CEMENT	PSI AT 73.4°F THREAD
¼″	—	—	0.119	1130	565
⅜″	0.031	620	0.126	920	460
½″	0.109	600	0.147	425	425
¾″	0.113	480	0.154	690	345
1″	0.133	450	0.179	630	315
1¼″	0.140	370	0.191	520	260
1½″	0.145	330	0.200	470	235
2″	0.154	280	0.218	400	200
2½″	0.203	300	0.276	420	210
3″	0.216	260	0.300	370	185
4″	0.237	220	0.337	320	160
6″	0.280	180	0.432	280	140

YOLOY STEEL PIPE

NOMINAL PIPE SIZE	DIMENSION (IN.) O.D.	WALL	WEIGHT (LB/FT)	CLASS
½″	0.840	0.109	0.85	C.W.
	0.840	0.147	1.09	C.W.
¾″	1.050	0.113	1.13	C.W.
	1.050	0.154	1.47	C.W.
1″	1.315	0.133	1.68	C.W.
	1.315	0.179	2.17	C.W.
1¼″	1.660	0.140	2.27	C.W.
	1.660	0.191	3.00	C.W.
1½″	1.900	0.145	2.72	C.W.
	1.900	0.200	3.63	C.W.
2″	2.375	0.154	3.65	C.W.
	2.375	0.218	5.02	C.W.
	2.375	0.154	3.65	S1 Std.
	2.375	0.218	5.02	S1 XHvy.
2½″	2.875	0.203	5.79	C.W.
	2.875	0.276	7.66	C.W.
	2.875	0.203	5.79	S1 Std.
	2.875	0.276	7.66	S1 XHvy.
3″	3.500	0.216	7.58	C.W.
	3.500	0.300	10.25	C.W.
	3.500	0.216	77.58	S1 Std.
	3.500	0.300	10.25	S1 XHvy.
3½″	4.000	0.226	9.11	S1 Std.
	4.000	0.318	12.51	S1 XHvy.
4″	4.500	0.237	10.79	S1 Std.
	4.500	0.337	15.00	S1 XHvy.
5″	5.563	0.258	14.62	S1 Std.
	5.563	0.375	20.78	S1 XHvy.
6″	6.625	0.280	18.97	S1 Std.
	6.625	0.472	28.57	S1 XHvy.
8″	8.625	0.322	28.55	S1 Std.
	8.625	0.500	43.39	S1 XHvy.
10″	10.750	0.365	40.48	S1 Std.
	10.750	0.500	54.74	S1 XHvy.
12″	12.750	0.375	49.56	S1 Std.
	12.750	0.500	65.42	S1 XHvy.
14″	14.000	0.375	54.57	S1 Std.

Walter H. Sobel, FAIA & Associates; Chicago, Illinois

STAINLESS STEEL PIPE

NOMINAL PIPE SIZE	DIMENSION O.D. (IN.)	SCHEDULE 5·S		SCHEDULE 10·S		SCHEDULE 40·S	
		WALL (IN.)	LB/FT	WALL (IN.)	LB/FT	WALL (IN.)	LB/FT
1/8″	0.405	—	—	0.049	0.186	0.068	0.245
1/4″	0.540	—	—	0.065	0.330	0.088	0.425
3/8″	0.675	—	—	0.065	0.424	0.091	0.568
1/2″	0.840	0.065	0.538	0.083	0.671	0.109	0.851
3/4″	1.050	0.065	0.684	0.083	0.857	0.113	1.131
1″	1.315	0.065	0.868	0.109	1.404	0.133	1.679
1¼″	1.660	0.065	1.107	0.109	1.806	0.140	2.278
1½″	1.900	0.065	1.274	0.109	2.085	0.145	2.718
2″	2.375	0.065	1.604	0.109	2.638	0.154	3.653
2½″	2.875	0.083	2.475	0.120	3.531	0.203	5.793
3″	3.500	0.083	3.029	0.120	4.332	0.216	7.576
3½″	4.000	0.083	3.472	0.120	4.973	0.226	9.109
4″	4.500	0.083	3.915	0.120	5.613	0.237	10.790
5″	5.563	0.109	6.350	0.134	7.770	0.258	14.620
6″	6.625	0.109	7.585	0.134	9.290	0.280	18.970
8″	8.625	0.109	9.914	0.148	13.400	0.322	28.550
10″	10.750	0.134	15.190	0.165	18.700	0.365	40.480
12″	12.750	0.165	22.180	0.180	24.200	0.375	49.550

ALUMINUM PIPE AND SOFT ALUMINUM TUBING

NOMINAL PIPE SIZE	ALUMINUM PIPE (PLAIN END)			SOFT ALUMINUM TUBING		
	DIMENSION (IN.)		WEIGHT (LB/FT)	DIMENSION (IN.)		LB/50 FT COIL
	O.D.	WALL		O.D.	WALL	
1/2″	0.840	0.145	0.294	1/4	0.032	1.30
3/4″	1.050	0.113	0.391	3/8	0.035	2.22
1″	1.315	0.133	0.581	1/2	0.035	3.03
1¼″	1.660	0.140	0.786	5/8	0.035	3.84
1½″	1.900	0.145	0.940	—	—	—
2″	2.375	0.154	1.264	—	—	—
2½″	2.875	0.203	2.004	—	—	—
3″	3.500	0.216	2.621	—	—	—

COPPER TUBING

1. Type K is a water tube for underground and interior service.
2. Type L is a water tube for interior service only.
3. Type K and type L can be specially cleaned for oxygen service.
4. Type ACR is for air conditioning and refrigeration service.
5. Type M is a nonpressure water tube for aboveground application.

STAINLESS STEEL PIPE

This is an excellent material to be used whenever corrosion or contamination of process materials is a problem. The corrosion resistance depends greatly on a thin metal oxide layer, which forms a protective film on the surface of the metal. Air forms this film in time. Full or partial destruction of this film will very much affect the corrosion resistance of the alloy. For selection of the proper alloy consult manufacturer.

ALUMINUM PIPE

This is suitable for water piping and hand railings.

YOLOY STEEL PIPE

This pipe is used for high, low, and moderate temperature service. It features high ductility and better formability, easy bending, good welding, and fine cutting. This pipe is corrosion resistant in atmosphere, soils, saltwater, and chemical solutions. It has high tensile and great impact strength.

SEAMLESS STEEL PIPE

1. ASTM Spec. A-53: This is a general service pipe, suitable for bending, coiling, fusion welding, lapping or flanging. Grade B does not lend itself to close coiling, forge-welding, or cold bends.
2. ASTM Spec. A-106: Manufactured from carbon steel for high temperature, high pressure service. An open hearth steel that comes in Grades A and B. Grade A works well for all forming or welding operations. Grade B has somewhat higher carbon and manganese content, which gives it greater tensile strength, but less ductility.

BUTTWELD STEEL PIPE

This pipe is for ordinary use on steam, water, gas, or air. It is not intended for medium or high pressure or close coiling or bending. Specifications require only hydrostatic testing; there are no chemical requirements.

Walter H. Sobel, FAIA & Associates; Chicago, Illinois

CAST IRON, MALLEABLE, AND DUCTILE IRON PIPE FITTING MATERIALS

The material used in the manufacture of cast iron, malleable, and ductile iron pipe fittings should conform to specifications set by ASTM.

DESIGN: THREADED FITTINGS

Cast iron, malleable, and ductile iron pipe fittings are manufactured according to ANSI standards. Since cast iron has little or no ductility, excessive hammering or shock could cause fitting failure. The use of malleable or ductile fittings is suggested under these conditions.

DESIGN: DRAINAGE FITTINGS

Drainage fittings should be designed to give unobstructed flow. Fittings with openings at right angles should have pitched threads so that the horizontal line will pitch 1/4 in./ft, assuring positive drainage. Pressure-temperature ratings do not apply to drainage fittings.

DESIGN: PLUGS, BUSHINGS, AND LOCKNUTS

Common plug designs are square head, countersunk, and bar plug. Face bushings and hexagon head bushings are available in a wide range of sizes, and generally are furnished in cast iron or malleable iron. Some small sizes of plugs, bushings, and locknuts are furnished in steel.

Sprinkler lines, heating and air conditioning systems, and plumbing installations utilize cast iron fittings. There is a wide range of types and sizes of fittings available from various manufacturers. Common types of threaded and flanged fittings:

1. ELBOWS: 90°, 90° reducing, 90° side outlet, 45°-90° long radius, 45°, 11¼°, 22½°, three way and drop elbows.
2. TEES: Straight run, reducing outlet, reduced run, other end and outlet equal, reduced on run and outlet, side outlet.

Crosses	Laterals
Reducers	Couplings
Double 45° Y's	Increasers
60° Y's	Unions
P traps	Caps
Running traps	Plugs
Return bends	Locknuts

RATED WORKING PRESSURES

CLASSES 125 AND 250 CAST IRON THREADED FITTINGS
ANSI STANDARD B16.4

TEMPERATURE (°F)	WORKING PRESSURE, NONSHOCK PSIG	
	CLASS 125	CLASS 250
-20 to 150	175	400
200	165	370
250	150	340
300	140	310
350	125	280
400	—	250

CLASSES 125 AND 250 CAST IRON FLANGED FITTINGS
ANSI STANDARD B16.1

TEMPERATURE (°F)	WORKING PRESSURE, NONSHOCK PSIG				
	CLASS 125			CLASS 250	
	SIZE 1-12	SIZE 14-24	SIZE 30-48	SIZE 1-12	SIZE 14-24
-20 to 250	200	150	150	500	300
200	190	135	115	460	280
225	180	130	100	440	270
250	175	125	85	415	260
275	170	120	65	395	250
300	165	110	50	375	240
325	155	105		355	230
350	150	100		335	220
375	145			315	210
400	140			290	200
425	130			270	
450	125			250	

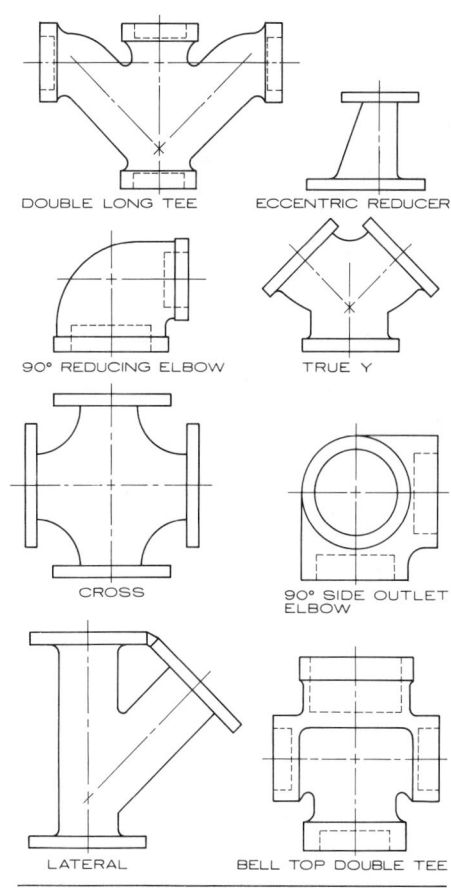

DOUBLE LONG TEE   ECCENTRIC REDUCER

90° REDUCING ELBOW   TRUE Y

CROSS   90° SIDE OUTLET ELBOW

LATERAL   BELL TOP DOUBLE TEE

VARIOUS PIPE FITTINGS

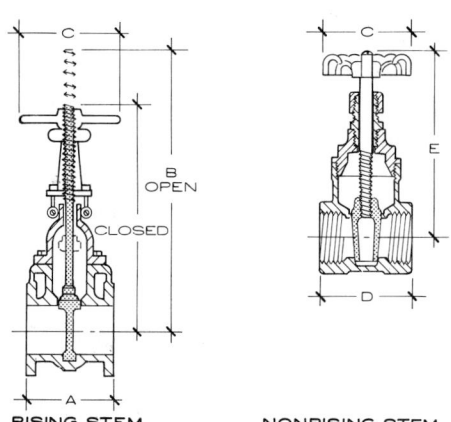

RISING STEM NONRISING STEM

GATE VALVES

GATE VALVES

Used for on-off service; offers practically no resistance to flow when fully open. Not recommended for throttling or flow modulation. Available in rising and nonrising stems. Suitable for hot and cold water, oil, and gas.

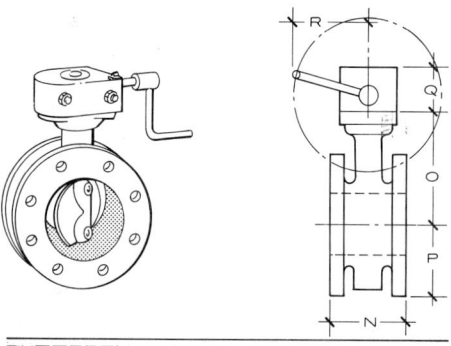

BUTTERFLY VALVE

BUTTERFLY

Feature quarter-turn, on-off operation for water, air, gas, or vacuum lines. Recommended for on-off service and some noncritical throttling applications.

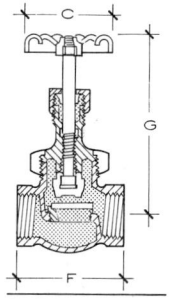

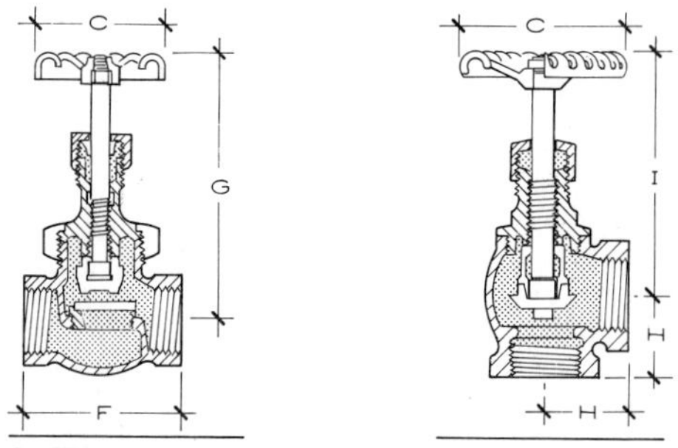

GLOBE VALVE ANGLE VALVE

GLOBE VALVES

Ideal for throttling service in hot and cold water, oil, and gas piping. Caution must be exercised, however, to avoid extremely close throttling. Vibration may cause valve damage or excessive noise. These valves are seldom used in sizes above 12 in.

ANGLE VALVES

Effectively utilize the globe valves throttling control while providing for a 90° turn in piping. Conditions regarding excessive throttling and size above 12 in., noted for globe valves, also apply to angle valves.

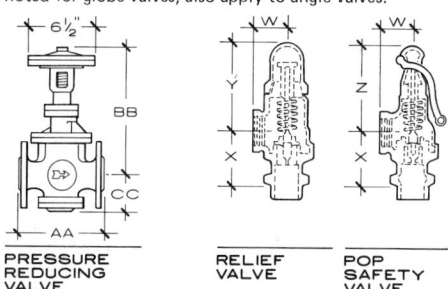

PRESSURE REDUCING VALVE RELIEF VALVE POP SAFETY VALVE

PRESSURE REDUCING VALVES

Used in steam, water, air, or gas lines where it is necessary to reduce incoming pressure to the required service pressure. They also maintain it at the point desired.

RELIEF VALVES AND SAFETY VALVES

Usually spring loaded valves that open automatically when pressure exceeds limit for which the valve is set. Should always be installed with the stem in a vertical position. Relief valves are usually used for liquids. Safety valves are generally used for steam, air, or other gases.

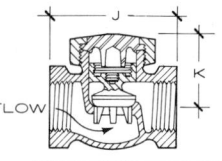

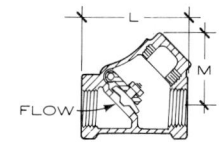

LIFT CHECK VALVE SWING CHECK VALVE

LIFT CHECK VALVES

Prevent reversal of flow. For use in horizontal lines only. Generally used in conjunction with globe valves.

SWING CHECK VALVES

Prevent reversal of flow and are particularly suited to low velocity service. Most swing check valves can be installed in horizontal or vertical upward flow piping. Generally used in conjunction with gate valves.

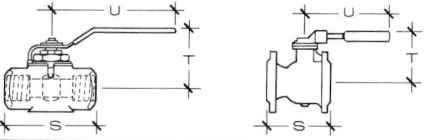

BALL VALVES

BALL VALVES

Feature quarter-turn, on-off operation, straight-through flow, minimum turbulance, low operating torque, tight closure, compact design, and light weight. Available with threaded, solder joint, or flanged ends.

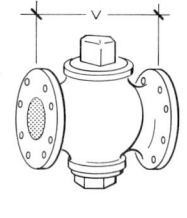

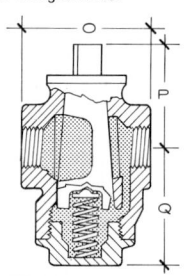

GAS COCK SPRING LOADED COCK

COCKS AND STOPS

Available in two-way, three-way, and four-way patterns with threaded or flanged ends. Suitable for cold water, oil, air, or gas.

VALVE DIMENSIONS

THREADED UNLESS OTHERWISE NOTED

SIZE (IN.)	GATE					GLOBE		ANGLE		LIFT CHECK		SWING CHECK		SPRING LOADED COCK			BALL			COCK	RELIEF AND SAFETY				PRESSURE REDUCING		
	A	B	C	D	E	F	G	H	I	J	K	L	M	O	P	Q	S	T	U	V	W	X	Y	Z	AA	BB	CC
1/4	1 3/4	4 1/2	1 3/4	1 7/8	3 3/4	1 3/4	2 3/4	7/8	3	1 7/8	1	2 1/8	1 1/2				3	1 1/4	4	1 5/8							
3/8	1 3/4	4 1/2	1 3/4	1 7/8	3 3/4	1 7/8	2 7/8	1	3 1/4	2	1 1/8	2 1/8	1 1/2				3	1 1/4	4	1 3/4	1 1/8	2 1/4	3 1/8	3 3/4	Flanged		
1/2	2 1/8	5 1/4	2 1/8	2 1/8	3 3/4	2 1/4	3 1/2	1 1/8	3 3/4	2 1/2	1 3/8	2 1/2	1 3/4	1 1/4	2 1/8	2 3/8	2 1/2	1 1/4	4	2 1/8	1 1/8	2 1/4	3 1/8	3 3/4	7 1/2	11 3/4	3 1/2
3/4	2 1/4	6 1/2	2 5/8	2 1/4	4 1/2	2 3/4	4	1 3/8	4 1/4	3	1 7/8	3	2 1/8	1 5/8	2 1/2	2 7/8	2 3/4	1 1/2	4 1/2	2 1/2	1 3/8	2 3/4	3 1/4	3 3/4	7 1/2	11 3/4	3 1/2
1	2 3/4	7 3/4	2 3/4	2 7/8	5 1/4	3 3/8	4 1/2	1 5/8	5	3 1/2	2	3 3/4	2 1/2	2	3 1/8	3 1/2	3 1/2	2 1/8	6	3	1 5/8	3 1/4	3 5/8	4 5/8	7 1/2	11 3/4	3 1/2
1 1/4	3	9 1/4	3 1/8	3	5 7/8	3 7/8	4 7/8	1 3/4	5 1/2	4 1/8	2 3/8	4 1/4	3				4	2 5/8	7	3 1/2	2 1/8	3 3/4	4 1/4	4 3/8	7 7/8	12	3 3/4
1 1/2	3 1/4	10 1/2	3 5/8	3 1/4	7 1/4	4 1/2	5 1/2	2 1/4	6 1/4	4 5/8	2 5/8	5	3 1/2				4 1/4	2 3/4	7	3 3/4	2 1/2	4 3/8	5 3/8	5 1/4	8 3/8	12 1/2	4 1/4
2	3 3/4	12 3/4	4 3/4	3 3/4	8 3/8	5 1/4	6	2 5/8	7 1/2	5 3/4	3 1/4	6	4 1/4				4 1/2	3 1/8	8	4 5/8	2 3/4	4 1/2	6 5/8	6 1/8	10 1/4	12	4 1/2

VALVE DIMENSIONS

FLANGED UNLESS OTHERWISE NOTED

SIZE (IN.)	GATE					GLOBE		ANGLE		LIFT CHECK		SWING CHECK		BUTTERFLY					BALL			COCK	RELIEF AND SAFETY				PRESSURE REDUCING		
	A	B	C	D	E	F	G	H	I	J	K	L	M	N	O	P	Q	R	S	T	U	V	W	X	Y	Z	AA	BB	CC
2	8 1/2	18	8	8 1/2	11	8	13 3/4	4	12 1/2	Threaded		8	5	1 3/4	5 1/2	2 1/2	2 7/8	5					Threaded						
2 1/2	9 1/2	19	9	9 1/2	13 1/4	8 1/2	14 1/2	4 1/4	13	6 7/8	3 7/8	8 1/2	5 1/2	1 7/8	6	2 3/4	2 7/8	5				8 5/8	3	4 7/8	7 5/8	7 3/4	11 5/8	13	6
3	11 1/8	19 7/8	10	11 1/8	14 3/4	9 1/2	16 1/2	4 3/4	15	8	4 1/2	9 1/2	6	5	6 1/4	3 1/2	2 7/8	5	8	7	12	9 5/8	3 1/2	5 1/4	8 1/2	9 1/2	12 1/2	13 3/4	6 3/4
4	12	23 3/4	12	12	17 1/2	11 1/2	19 3/4	5 3/4	17 3/4			11 1/2	7	5	7	4 1/4	2 7/8	5	9	7 1/2	15	12 1/8					14 1/4	14 3/4	7 5/8
6	15 7/8	32 1/2	16	15 7/8	23	16	24 1/2	8	21 3/4			14	9	5	8	5 3/4	2 7/8	5	10 1/2	9 1/4	30						17 3/4	19 1/8	10 1/4
8	16 1/2	40 3/4	20	16 1/2	30 3/4	19 1/2	26 1/2	9 3/4	24			19 1/2	10 1/4	6	9 1/4	7 1/2	2 7/8	5	11 1/2	10 3/4	37 1/2						21 1/4	43 1/4	14 1/4
10	18	49 1/2	22	18	36	24 1/2	31 5/8	12 1/4	31 3/4			24 1/2	13 5/8	8	10 1/2	9	2 7/8	5	13	12 3/4	50						26 1/2	45 3/4	16 1/2
12	19 3/4	57 1/4	24	19 3/4	39 3/4	27 1/2	42	13 3/4	55 1/8			27 1/2	15 5/8	8	12	10 1/2	3 5/8	6	14	14 5/8	50								
14	30	61 1/4	20	15	39 1/2							31	18 3/8	8	13 1/4	11 1/2	3 5/8	6											
16	33	71 1/2	22	16	48							30	20 5/8	8	14 3/4	13 1/4	5 3/4	18											

NOTE: Sizes are nominal, all dimensions are in inches.

Victor J. Saccaro; Hoyem-Basso Associates; Bloomfield Hills, Michigan

NOTES

The cleanout provides access to horizontal and vertical plumbing lines and stacks and a means to remove obstructions. Generally, cleanouts consist of an iron body and brass plug with neoprene seal. The outlet must be gas tight and watertight and must provide ample space for rodding tools. An adjustable housing will allow for variations in floor fill. Cleanout covers must be designed to support the weight of traffic directed over them. The inside caulk type outlet provides greater ease of installation while the wide flange type assures a waterproof bond between floor covering and cleanout.

Most codes require cleanouts located not more than 50 ft apart in horizontal drainage lines of 4 in. pipe or less and not more than 100 ft apart for larger pipe. Also, install cleanouts at each change of direction greater than 45° and at the base of each vertical waste stack. Access covers should be secured with vandal-proof screws or hinged where these units are likely to be removed.

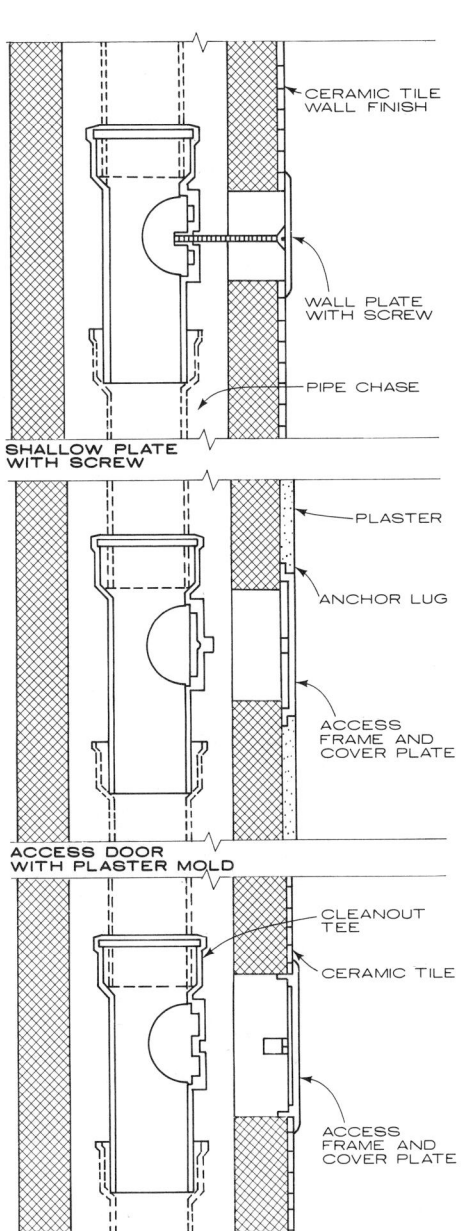

SHALLOW PLATE WITH SCREW

ACCESS DOOR WITH PLASTER MOLD

ACCESS DOOR WITH HINGE

WALL TYPE CLEANOUTS

Sargent, Webster, Crenshaw & Folley, Architects Engineers Planners; Syracuse, New York

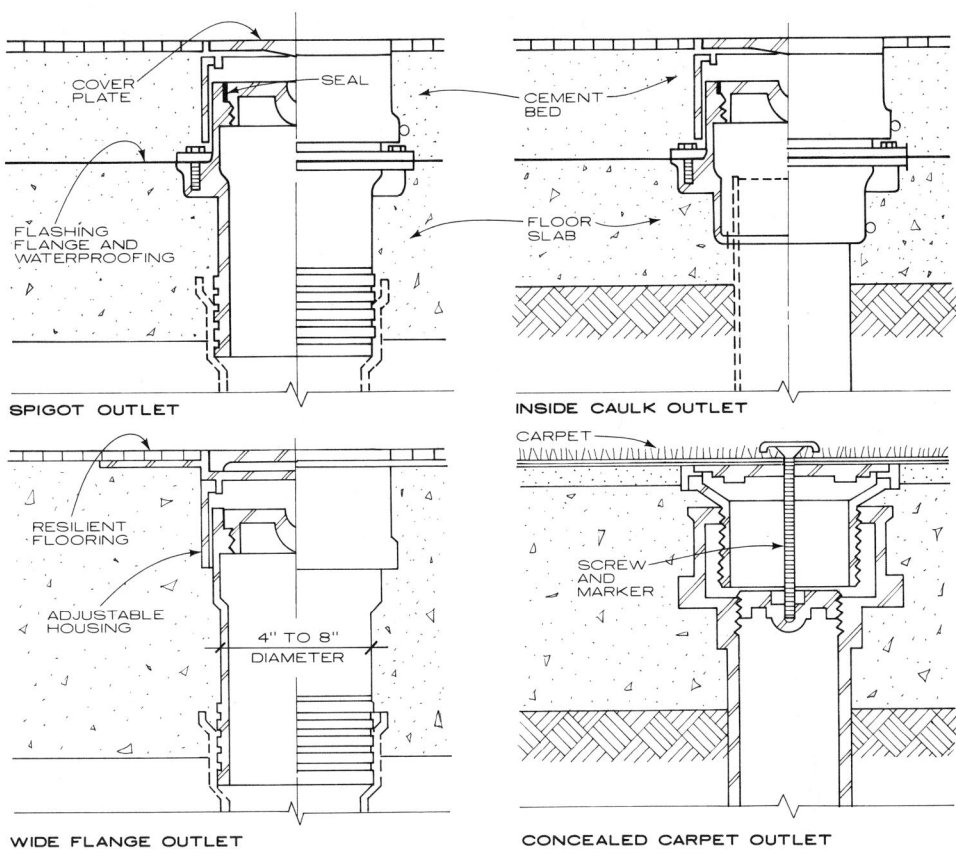

SPIGOT OUTLET

INSIDE CAULK OUTLET

WIDE FLANGE OUTLET

CONCEALED CARPET OUTLET

FLOOR TYPE CLEANOUTS

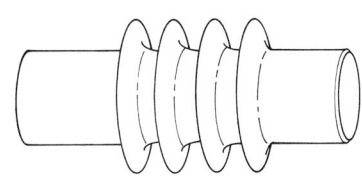

PACKLESS EXPANSION JOINT has stainless steel bellows and carbon steel weld-end nipples (shown) or flanged ends. Sizes 3 to 60 in. diameter may have 1 to 10 corrugations.

EXPANSION JOINT ASSEMBLIES

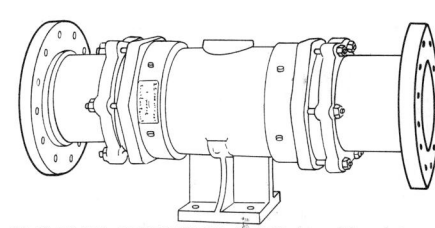

SLIP TYPE EXPANSION JOINT has either internal or external guides. Double joint type is shown with flanged end connections and base. Sizes 1¼ to 20 in. are fabricated or cast semisteel.

TOTAL THERMAL EXPANSION OF PIPING MATERIAL (IN.) PER 100 FT ABOVE 32°F

TEMPERATURE (°F)	CARBON AND CARBON MOLY STEEL	CAST IRON	COPPER	BRASS AND BRONZE	WROUGHT IRON	PLASTIC
32	0	0	0	0	0	0
100	0.5	0.5	0.8	0.8	0.5	2.0
150	0.8	0.8	1.4	1.4	0.9	4.25
200	1.2	1.2	2.0	2.0	1.3	6.25
250	1.7	1.5	2.7	2.6	1.7	—
300	2.0	1.9	3.3	3.2	2.2	—
350	2.5	2.3	4.0	3.9	2.6	—
400	2.9	2.7	4.7	4.6	3.1	—
450	3.4	3.1	5.3	5.2	3.6	—
500	3.8	3.5	6.0	5.9	4.1	—
550	4.3	3.9	6.7	6.5	4.6	—
600	4.8	4.0	7.4	7.2	5.2	—
650	5.3	4.7	8.2	7.9	5.6	—
700	5.9	5.3	9.0	8.5	6.1	—
750	6.4	5.8	—	—	6.7	—
800	7.0	6.3	—	—	7.2	—
850	7.4	—	—	—	—	—
900	8.0	—	—	—	—	—
950	8.5	—	—	—	—	—
1000	9.1	—	—	—	—	—

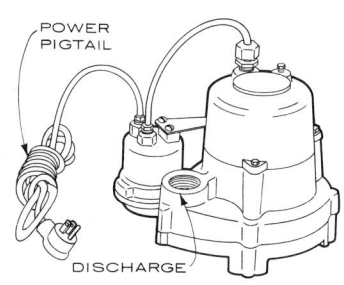

SUBMERSIBLE

Installed directly in pipe line and supported by pipe and structure. Gpm range to 130 gpm; heads to 50 ft.

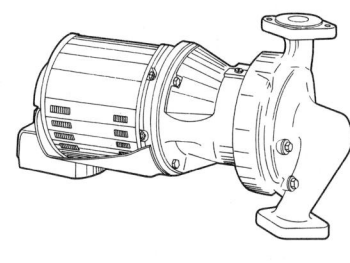

IN-LINE CENTRIFUGAL

Gpm range to 2000 gpm; heads to 360 ft. Required floor space approximately 24 x 48 in.

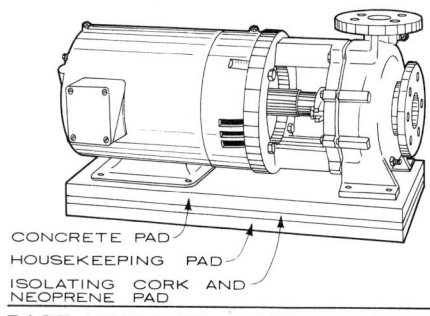

BASE MOUNTED CENTRIFUGAL CLOSED COUPLED

Gpm range to 3000 gpm; heads to 360 ft. Required floor space approximately 24 x 36 in. to 36 x 60 in.

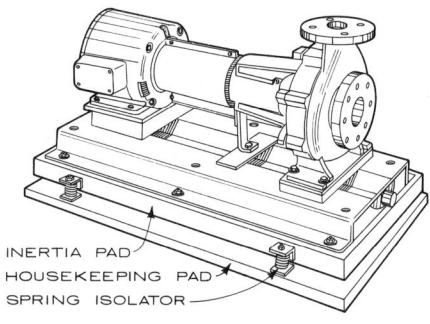

FRAME MOUNTED CENTRIFUGAL END SUCTION

Gpm range to 25,000 gpm; head range to 600 ft. Required floor space approximately 24 x 48 in. to 72 x 144 in.

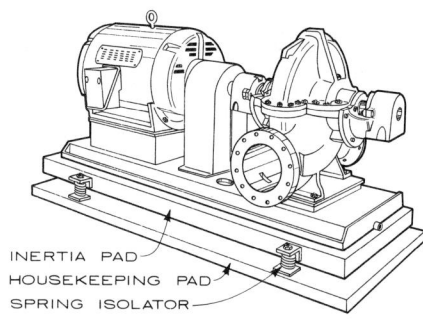

FRAME MOUNTED CENTRIFUGAL DOUBLE SUCTION

Gpm range to 14,000 gpm; head range to 1200 ft. Available with integral suction sump. Ideal for low NPSH applications. Floor space required less than for centrifugal pumps.

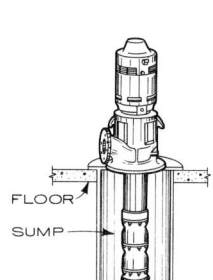

VERTICAL TURBINE

Sewage or sump pump for small installations up to 150 gpm to 40 ft total head. Will operate completely submerged in sump.

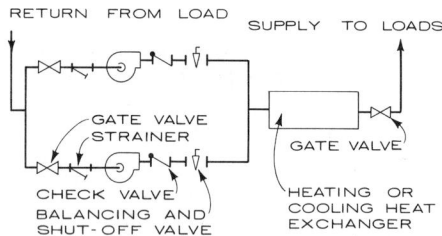

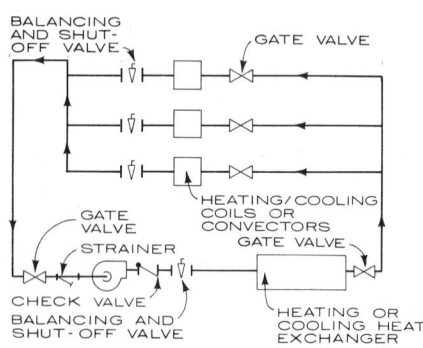

PARALLEL PUMPING

REVERSE RETURN

PARALLEL PUMPING

Provides a degree of standby. If one pump fails, approximately 70% of flow can be obtained with one pump. Too, it can be applied to variable flow rate system where one pump can be shut down under certain operative conditions; also if flow required is greater than capacity of a single standard pump, parallel pumps may be installed to achieve desired flow rate.

PRIMARY SECONDARY PUMP

Characteristics of secondary circuit are essentially unaffected by changes in primary circuit or by other secondary circuits. Can be used to provide a different water temperature to each secondary circuit by using mixing valves; also can be used for variable flow primary circuit and constant flow secondary circuits.

REVERSE RETURN

Provides an approximate equal pressure drop to each secondary heat transfer surface, thereby minimizing balancing requirements. Preferred on extensive piping loops for radiation, fan coil units, etc.

CONVENTIONAL PUMPING

Least costly and applicable to systems requiring only basic circulation, such as heat exchangers, chillers, and cooling towers. Also can be used for loops to radiation, fan coil units, etc., where runs are short and balancing can be easily achieved.

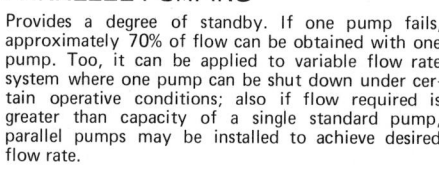

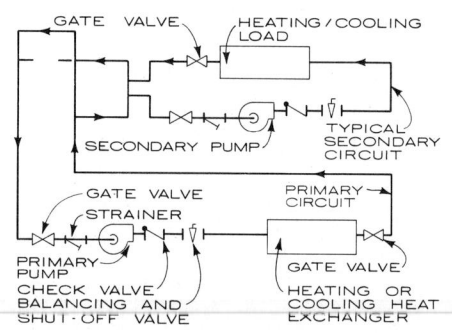

PRIMARY/SECONDARY CIRCUIT

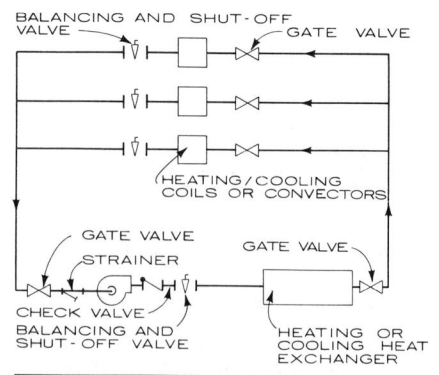

CONVENTIONAL PUMPING

William Tao & Associates, Inc., Consulting Engineers; St. Louis, Missouri

MATERIALS AND METHODS

GENERAL

Attention must be given to vibration of mechanical equipment to ensure that there is no transmission of objectionable vibration or structureborne noise to the building and occupied spaces. The following general procedure should be followed to avoid problems of vibration and structureborne noise transmission:

1. Evaluate the inherent quietness of the various types of equipment and try to select the types with the lowest sound and vibration levels, consistent with engineering and cost considerations.
2. Try to locate equipment rooms so they are not directly adjacent to, above, or below areas that are critical from a noise and vibration standpoint. Equipment with inherently large unbalance or vibratory forces should be installed at grade or remote basement locations whenever possible.
3. Try to locate pipe and duct shafts in utility or service cores near noncritical areas such as elevator shafts, stairwells, and toilets, rather than adjoining critical areas such as bedrooms or private offices.
4. Design supporting structures to be as stiff as possible. Although most equipment room floors are usually 10 or more times stiffer than equipment isolators, they are capable of deflections resulting in floor natural frequencies in the operating speed range of most HVAC equipment. Primary concern is with low speed equipment on long spans that have low natural frequencies and high speed equipment on short span or rigid floors that have high natural frequencies.
5. Specify maximum allowable equipment vibration levels.
6. Provide appropriate vibration isolation for equipment.

Many types of equipment require some support base to maintain alignment of driving and driven components such as fans or where equipment cannot be supported at individual isolator locations. Support bases may be constructed of structural steel members, concrete, or a combination of concrete and structural members, and should always be designed with ample rigidity to resist all starting and operating forces without supplemental hold-down devices. It is common practice to install many types of equipment on inertia blocks as shown below. Inertia blocks or mass of the system have no effect on the efficiency of isolators; however, they do affect the movement of the equipment itself and, as such, can affect the transmission to the building structure through connected piping and ducts.

Inertia blocks should be used for:

1. Equipment that has large unbalance or vibratory forces such as horizontal air compressors, and some reciprocating compressors and engines. For such equipment, the designer should obtain from the equipment manufacturer the magnitude and frequency of the unbalance forces to permit proper sizing of inertia block.
2. Equipment such as certain large fans, pumps, and compressors, where some type of structural base must be furnished to support driving and driven components and/or maintain alignment.
3. Equipment subject to external forces such as high pressure fans, where use of an inertia block will result in stiffer isolators and thereby limit movement resulting from reaction to pressure thrust.

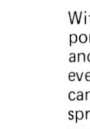

NOTE

Within earthquake zones, inertia blocks and other support bases must be designed to resist the horizontal and vertical thrusts that can occur during a seismic event. Heavy equipment mounted on a floating base can easily develop enough motion to fly free of its springs. Excessive lateral movement should be prevented through the use of angle iron stops, spring mounts with integral restraints or all-directional snubbers. All of these devices must be carefully installed so that they do not hinder the normal operation of the isolation system.

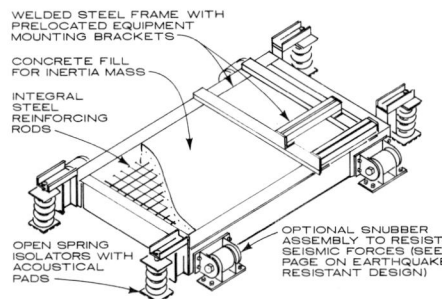

CONCRETE AND STEEL BASE

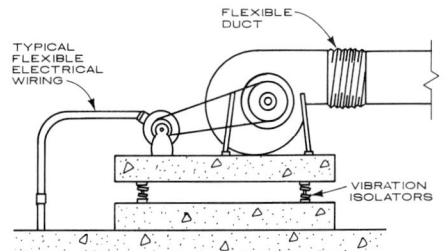

INERTIA BLOCKS

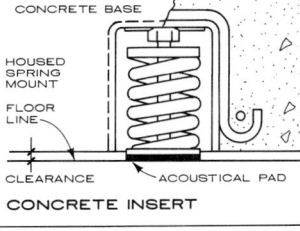

CONCRETE INSERT

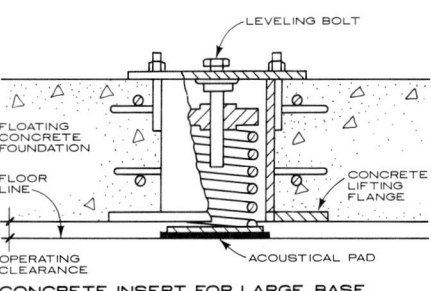

CONCRETE INSERT FOR LARGE BASE

EQUIPMENT SUPPORT BASES

The choice of isolators for any given application primarily depends on required deflection; however, consideration must also be given to life, cost, and suitability for specific application.

STEEL SPRINGS are the most popular and versatile isolators for HVAC application, since they are available for almost any desired deflection and have virtually unlimited lift. Steel springs, when installed outdoors or in corrosive environments, should be properly protected by the electroplating or other protective coatings. The two basic types of spring isolators are open spring mountings and housed spring mountings.

Open spring mountings consist of a steel spring between a bottom and top plate and usually incorporate an adjustment bolt for leveling. Open spring mounts have become popular, since they avoid the binding and "short circuiting" that can occur with housed mountings. However, misalignment (non-parallel condition of floor and base) should generally be avoided.

It is very important that open springs have proper stiffness in the vertical and horizontal directions so that the springs will be stable and equipment will move sideways.

Housed spring mountings consist of a spring element in a housing incorporating an adjustment bolt for leveling that can be internally located to permit installation of the mount under equipment without legs or holes for an adjustment bolt. The springs in housed mountings are not generally designed to meet stability requirements, since housings limit excessive lateral movement.

It should be noted that all spring mounts must incorporate an elastomeric acoustical and friction pad to prevent the transmission of audible high frequency vibration directly through the spring to the structure.

VIBRATION ISOLATORS

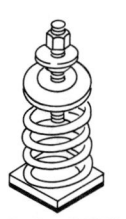

OPEN SPRING

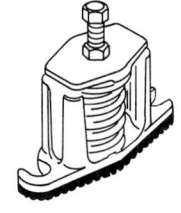

HOUSED SPRING

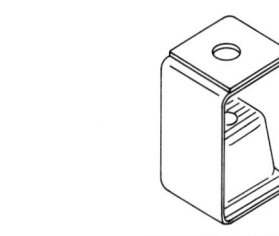

SPRING AND RUBBER

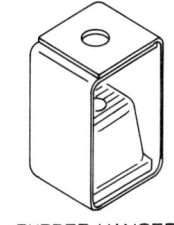

RUBBER HANGER

ISOLATION HANGERS are used for pipe and suspended equipment and usually incorporate rubber, spring, or combination spring and rubber isolator elements. Where spring elements are used, stable springs should be specified. Where isolation hangers are used for suspending piping, provision must be made to accommodate expansion and contraction of pipe due to thermal changes. For pipelines subject to significant thermal movement, this is best accomplished with an eye bolt or swivel arrangement for attachment to structure so that hanger box can swivel to avoid "cocking" of isolation element.

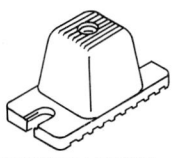

RUBBER MOUNT

NEOPRENE PAD

RUBBER ISOLATORS are available in mount and pad configuration and are generally molded of rubber or neoprene, although other materials such as fiberglass and cork can be used to meet specific service requirements.

Rubber isolators provide a very high resistance to the transmission of noise (high frequency vibration in the acoustical range). In general, their use should be restricted to minor equipment or basement locations.

COMPARISON TABLE

RANGE	RPM	SPRINGS	ELAS-TOMERS	CORK
Low	Up to 1200	Required	Unsuitable except for shock	Unsuitable except for shock
Medium	1200–1800	Excellent	Fair	Not recommended
High	Over 1800	Excellent for critical jobs	Good	Fair to good

PIPE INSULATION

PA GLASS FIBER: Available in both light and heavy density material and with factory applied jacket. Flame spread 25, smoke developed 50; k value 0.25; thickness 1/2 to 2 in. most commonly used. Use multiple layers for greater thickness. Suitable for −60 to +450°F temperature range.

PB PHENOLIC: Molded rigid insulation from neutral phenolic foam, medium density with factory applied jacket. Flame spread 25, smoke developed 50; k value 0.23; suitable for −40 to +250°F temperature range; available in 1, 1 1/2, and 2 in. thickness.

PC POLYURETHANE: Foamed polyurethane, medium density, available with factory applied jacket. Flame spread 25, smoke developed 50 when covered with jacket of 1 mil thick aluminum foil laminated to Kraft paper; available thickness 1 in.; k value 0.16. Polyurethane without proper jacket exceeds 25/50 flame spread/smoke developed rating. Temperature range −100 to +220°F.

PD FOAMED PLASTIC: Flexible foamed plastic insulation, requires no jacket but may be painted with alkyd paint. Fire retardant type available in 3/8 and 1/2 in. thickness with flame spread of 25, smoke developed 200; standard type available in 3/8, 1/2, 3/4 in. thickness with flame spread and smoke developed exceeding 25/200; k value 0.25; suitable for −40 to +220°F temperature range.

PE CALCIUM SILICATE: Rigid pipe insulation, k value 0.40, with factory jacket, for pipe up to 1200°F.

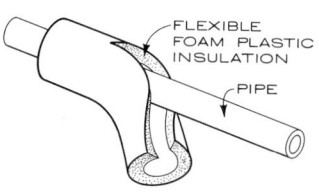

VALVE AND FITTING INSULATION AND JACKETS

VA Field mitered glass fiber or calcium silicate of same composition as adjacent pipe insulation with jacket of glass fiber reinforced cloth embedded in mastic. As an alternative fittings may be covered with factory fabricated weatherproof PVC or aluminum fitting covers arranged to fit over blanket type insulation inserts, overmitered pipe insulation or overmolded fitting insulators fabricated from calcium silicate, foam glass, urethane, polystyrene, and so on.

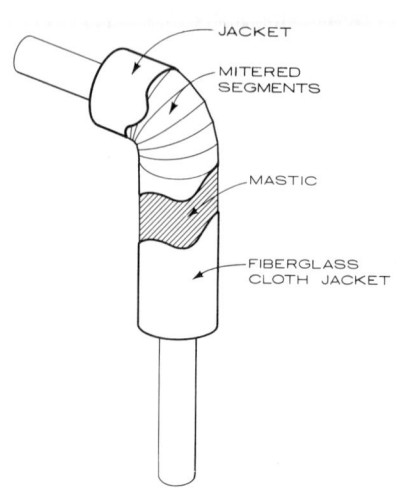

William Tao & Associates, Inc., Consulting Engineers; St. Louis, Missouri

PIPING JACKETS

JA HOT OR COLD PIPE: Glass fiber reinforced vinyl coated paper and aluminum foil laminate.

JB HOT PIPE: Presized glass cloth coated with lagging adhesive.

JC WEATHERPROOF: Same as above with additional aluminum jacket or additional roofing felt jacket.

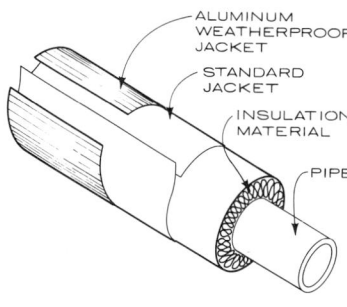

DUCT INSULATION

DA DUCT LINER: Glass fiber duct liner, most used densities 3/4, 1 1/2, and 2 lb/cu ft; thickness 1/2, 3/4, and 1 in. most common; coated with neoprene or similar material to limit erosion and reduce coefficient of friction. Serves as insulator and provides sound attenuation of approximately 1 dB/ft. Maximum allowable duct velocity to prevent erosion—4000 fpm or as recommended by manufacturer.

DB EXTERNAL DUCT INSULATION
Blanket type: Blanket type light density glass fiber insulation with reinforced aluminum foil vapor barrier facing. This type of duct covering is especially adaptable to round ducts.

Board type: Glass fiber board type duct insulation with factory applied vapor barrier jacket. This type of duct covering is especially applicable to rectangular ducts and is available in various densities. Heavy density (6 lb/cu ft) should be used where ducts are subject to potential damage.

DC KITCHEN EXHAUST DUCTS: Calcium silicate block insulation; k = 0.40; wired in place and troweled with insulating cement and finished with canvas jacket. Available in scored block to facilitate forming around large cylindrical shapes.

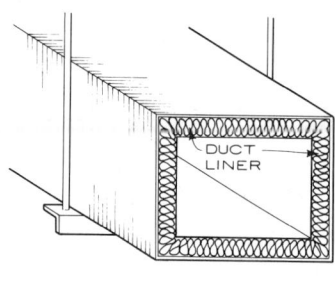

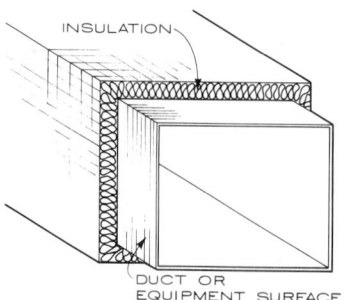

EQUIPMENT INSULATION

EA EQUIPMENT TO 220°F: Flexible foamed plastic; k = 0.24; available in sheet form.

EB EQUIPMENT TO 450°F: Glass fiber blanket type low density or rigid board type insulation with factory applied vapor barrier jacket; k = 0.25.

EC EQUIPMENT TO 850°F: Glass fiber board with high temperature binder finished with metal mesh, insulating cement and canvas or glass fabric jacket; k = 0.25.

ED EQUIPMENT AND BREECHING TO 1200°F: Calcium silicate block insulation; k = 0.40; wired in place and troweled with insulating cement and finished with canvas jacket. Available in scored block to facilitate forming around large cylindrical shapes. Mineral wool insulation with wire mesh cover and canvas jacket also applicable for high temperature applications.

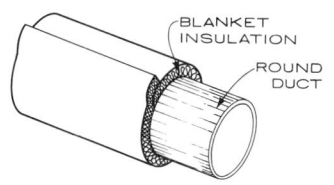

APPLICATIONS

EQUIPMENT

1. PUMPS (COLD FLUIDS): Use type EA for pumps handling cold fluids. Insulation can be fabricated into a boxlike enclosure and arranged for easy removal to facilitate servicing.

2. PUMPS (HIGH TEMPERATURE HOT WATER, ETC.): Use type EB for pumps handling hot fluids, fabricated same as indicated above for cold fluid pumps.

3. HEAT EXCHANGERS (TO 850°F SURFACE TEMPERATURE): Use type EB or EC depending on surface temperature of vessel.

4. HEAT EXCHANGERS (TO 1200°F SURFACE TEMPERATURES): Use type ED, either calcium silicate or mineral wool.

5. DOMESTIC WATER AND CHILLED WATER TANKS: Use type EA or EB. EB has 25/50 fire spread/smoke developed rating, whereas type EA exceeds these limits.

6. CHILLERS: Use type EA unless restricted by fire spread/smoke developed ratings, in which case use type EB.

GENERAL INFORMATION

The insulation and methods described on this page are typical of those used for HVAC work. There are other materials that are equally suitable for use on HVAC and similar systems. The designer should evaluate all available insulating materials and apply what is best suited to the situation with regard to both service and cost. One of the major considerations is the fuel contributed—fire spread—and smoke developed characteristics of various insulating materials. Insulating materials used where air is moved from one area to another such as return and supply air plenums should not exceed a 25/50 fire spread, smoke developed rating.

HOT PIPING OPERATING ABOVE AMBIENT DEW POINT

HEAT FLOW

Insulate with enough thickness to satisfy the engineering limits as specified or to maintain the exposed surface temperature below 60°C (140°F) for personnel protection.

VAPOR FLOW

Install with a permeable jacket to allow moisture and gas flow out of the system. Do not establish a vapor dam at the interface of multiple layer installations.

WEATHER PROOFING

Install weather resistant jackets with the laps in a rain shield position, sealing only the areas where rain might enter. Weather resistant mastics may be used in place of a jacket. The mastic should be applied in at least two coats, with an open weave glass fabric embedded in the first coat.

HANGERS

Clevis hangers may be installed directly on pipes operating up to 100°C (212°F). On higher temperature lines the hangers should be external and the pipe should be supported by a saddle and shield.

COLD PIPING OPERATING BELOW AMBIENT DEW POINT

HEAT FLOW

Insulate with enough thickness to satisfy the engineering limits as specified or to maintain the exposed service at a temperature higher than the ambient dew point temperature, whichever is greater. The condensation of atmospheric moisture on the insulation surface must be avoided.

VAPOR FLOW

Install with a vapor barrier jacket or use insulation of a low permeability, closed cell type. All joints and seams in the vapor barrier must be perfectly sealed and the insulation must be vapor sealed at all terminals, fittings, and valves.

WEATHER PROOFING

Install weather resistant jacket with the laps in a rain shield position, with all seams, joints, and terminals sealed.

HANGERS

Clevis hangers or similar devices may be used, but they should be outside the vapor barrier jacket, with a protective shield having enough area to support the load of the pipe and its contents without crushing or indenting the insulation. Some insulations require a load bearing material insert between the shield and the pipe. The load bearing material should be a high density insulation or a poor conductor of heat such as waterproofed wood. Preinsulated hangers are also available for low temperature pipe support.

INSULATION FOR BOILER BREECHING AND HIGH TEMPERATURE EQUIPMENT

INSULATION CHOICE

First consideration must be given to the operating temperature of the surfaces to be insulated, as each material has a maximum use temperature. A second consideration concerns the size and shape of the surfaces, as these factors will determine whether it is expedient to use blanket, block, or spray-on insulation.

HEAT FLOW

Insulate with a great enough thickness to satisfy the engineering limits or to provide personnel protection by limiting the exposed surface temperature to 60°C (140°F).

VAPOR FLOW

The choice and installation of the insulation and its finish must establish a system that allows free movement of vapor out of the system. Insulation and finishes that contain water or other volatile substances must be exposed to slowly rising temperatures at startup to provide time for vapor escape.

Charles F. Gilbo; Consultant; Lancaster, Pennsylvania

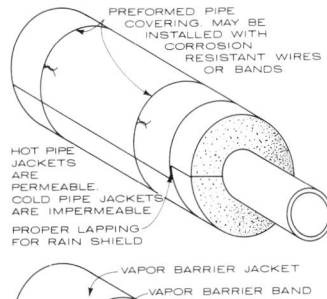

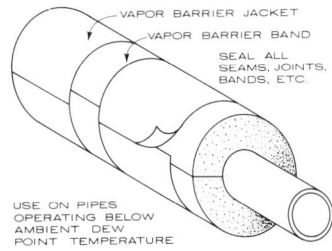

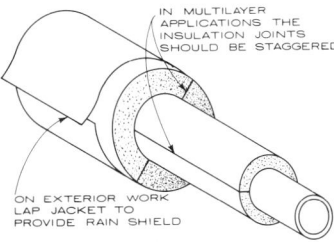

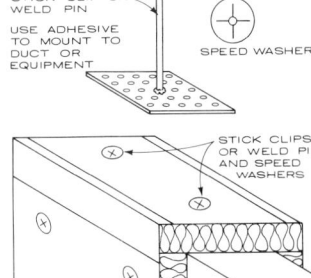

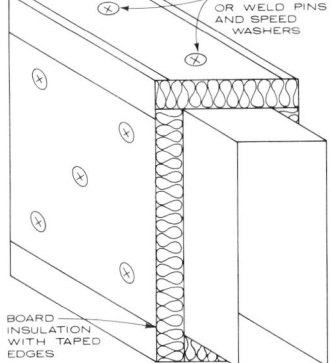

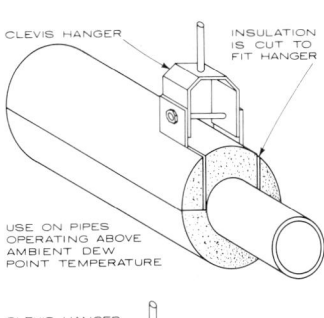

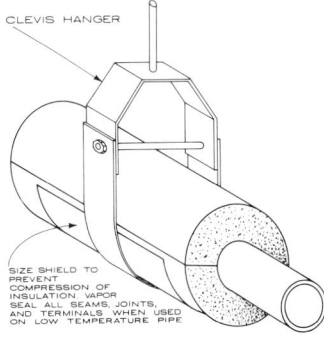

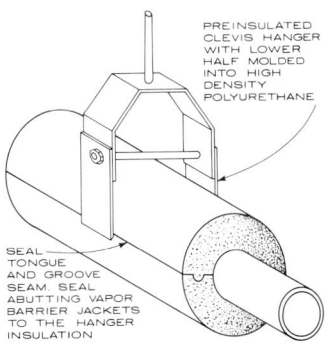

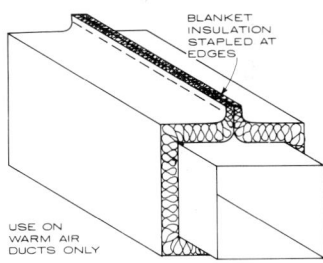

DUCTS FOR LOW TEMPERATURES

VAPOR FLOW

Ducts that operate at temperatures below the ambient dew point temperature must be covered with an insulation system that incorporates a near perfect vapor barrier on the warm side of the insulation. Such ducts may also be successfully insulated with flexible, closed celled, low permeability plastic insulation. If stick clips or weld pins are used to hold board type insulation in place, all penetrations of the vapor barrier must be sealed.

HEAT FLOW

Enough insulation must be used to maintain the temperature of the exposed surface at a level higher than the ambient dew point temperature to prevent the condensation of water. If the engineering specification limits heat flow to the duct, both the limits and condensation control must be considered and the insulation thickness chosen to satisfy the most severe condition.

DUCTS FOR KITCHEN EXHAUST AND HEATING

VAPOR FLOW

Ducts that operate at temperatures above ambient dew point temperature may be insulated without vapor sealing; therefore mechanical anchors and fasteners may be used.

HEAT FLOW

Enough insulation should be used to restrict heat flow to the engineered level. Due consideration must be given to the increased heat flow at the pins, anchors, stick clips, etc.; therefore greater insulation thicknesses are needed when such fasteners are used.

BUSINESS, MERCANTILE, INDUSTRIAL OTHER THAN FOUNDRY, AND STORAGE

WATER CLOSETS	EMPLOYEES	LAVATORIES	EMPLOYEES
1	1-15	1	1-20
2	16-35	2	21-40
3	36-55	3	41-60
4	56-80	4	61-80
5	81-110	5	81-100
6	111-150	6	101-125
7	151-190	7	126-150
		8	151-175
One additional water closet for each 40 in excess of 190		One additional lavatory for each 30 in excess of 175	

INDUSTRIAL, FOUNDRIES, AND STORAGE

WATER CLOSETS	EMPLOYEES	LAVATORIES	EMPLOYEES
1	1-10	1	1-8
2	11-25	2	9-16
3	26-50	3	17-30
4	51-80	4	31-45
5	81-125	5	46-65
One additional water closet for each 45 in excess of 125		One additional lavatory for each 25 in excess of 65	

ASSEMBLY, OTHER THAN RELIGIOUS, AND SCHOOLS

WATER CLOSETS	OCCUPANTS	URINALS	MALE OCCUPANTS	LAVATORIES	OCCUPANTS
1	1-100	1	1-100	1	1-100
2	101-200	2	101-200	2	101-200
3	201-400	3	201-400	3	201-400
4	401-700	4	401-700	4	401-700
5	701-1100	5	701-1100	5	701-1100
One additional water closet for each 600 in excess of 1100		One additional urinal for each 300 in excess of 1100		One additional lavatory for each 1500 in excess of 1100. Such lavatories need not be supplied with hot water	

ASSEMBLY, RELIGIOUS

One water closet and one lavatory.

ASSEMBLY, SCHOOL

For pupils' use:

1. Water closets for pupils; in elementary schools, 1 for each 100 males and 1 for each 35 females; in secondary schools, 1 for each 100 males and 1 for each 45 females.
2. One lavatory for each 50 pupils.
3. One urinal for each 30 male pupils.
4. One drinking fountain for each 150 pupils, but at least one on each floor having classrooms.

Where more than 5 persons are employed, provide fixtures as required for group C1 occupancy.

INSTITUTIONAL

(Persons whose movements are not limited.) Within each dwelling unit:

1. One kitchen sink.
2. One water closet.
3. One bathtub or shower.
4. One lavatory.

Where sleeping accommodations are arranged as individual rooms, provide the following for each six sleeping rooms:

1. One water closet.
2. One bathtub and shower.
3. One lavatory.

Where sleeping accommodations are arranged as a dormitory, provide the following for each 15 persons:

1. One water closet.
2. One bathtub or shower.
3. One lavatory.

INSTITUTIONAL, OTHER THAN HOSPITALS

(Persons whose movements are limited.) On each story:

1. Water closets: 1 for each 25 males and 1 for each 20 females.
2. One urinal for each 50 male occupants.
3. One lavatory for each 10 occupants.
4. One shower for each 10 occupants.
5. One drinking fountain for each 50 occupants.

Fixtures for employees the same as required for group C1 occupancy.

INSTITUTIONAL, HOSPITALS

For patients' use:

1. One water closet and one lavatory for each 10 patients.
2. One shower or bathtub for each 20 patients.
3. One drinking fountain or equivalent fixture for each 100 patients.

Fixtures for employees the same as required for group C1 occupancy.

INSTITUTIONAL, MENTAL HOSPITALS

For patients' use:

1. One water closet, one lavatory, and one shower or bathtub, for each 8 patients.
2. One drinking fountain or equivalent fixture for each 50 patients.

Fixtures for employees the same as required for group C1 occupancy.

INSTITUTIONAL, PENAL INSTITUTIONS

For inmate use:

1. One water closet and one lavatory in each cell.
2. One shower on each floor on which cells are located.
3. One water closet and one lavatory for inmate use available in each exercise area.

Lavatories for inmate use need not be supplied with hot water. Fixtures for employees the same as required for group C1 occupancy.

MISCELLANEOUS

Temporary toilet facilities shall be provided for employees engaged in the construction, alteration, repair, or demolition of buildings on the basis of 1 unit for each 30 persons.

PUBLIC BATHING OCCUPANCIES

Facilities for bathers at swimming pools shall consist of at least the following:

1. One water closet for each 40 females and 60 males.
2. One urinal for each 60 males.
3. One lavatory for each 40 females and 60 males.
4. One shower for each 40 females and 40 males. In schools such required showers shall equal one third the number of pupils in the largest class.

Sargent, Webster, Crenshaw & Folley, Architects, Engineers, Planners; Syracuse, New York

BUSINESS

Buildings used primarily for the transaction of business, with the handling of merchandise being incidental to the primary use.

MERCANTILE

Buildings used primarily for the display of merchandise and its sale to the public.

ADDITIONAL REQUIREMENTS

1. One drinking fountain or equivalent fixture for each 75 employees.
2. Urinals may be substituted for not more than one third of the required number of water closets when more than 35 males are employed.

INDUSTRIAL

Buildings used primarily for the manufacture or processing of products.

STORAGE

Buildings used primarily for the storage of or shelter for merchandise, vehicles, or animals.

ADDITIONAL REQUIREMENTS

1. One drinking fountain or equivalent fixture for each 75 employees.
2. Urinals provided where more than 10 males are employed: 1 for 11-29; 2 for 30-79; one additional urinal for each 80 in excess of 79.

ASSEMBLY

Buildings used primarily for the assembly for athletic, educational, religious, social, or similar purposes.

ADDITIONAL REQUIREMENT

One drinking fountain for each 1000 occupants, but at least one on each floor.

MULTIPLE DWELLINGS

Provide plumbing systems and furnish hot and cold water. Provide within each dwelling unit:

1. One kitchen sink.
2. One water closet.
3. One bathtub or shower.
4. One lavatory.

Sleeping accommodations—for each multiple of six sleeping room provide:

1. One water closet.
2. One bathtub or shower.
3. One lavatory.

Sleeping accommodations—dormitories for each multiple of 15 persons provide:

1. One water closet.
2. One bathtub or shower.
3. One lavatory.

Urinals may be substituted for not more than one third of the required number of water closets. Facilities for bathers at swimming pools shall consist of at least the following:

1. One water closet for each 40 females and 60 males.
2. One urinal for each 60 males.
3. One lavatory for each 60 females and 60 males.
4. One shower for each 40 females and 40 males.

GENERAL NOTES

1. Plumbing fixture requirements shown are based on New York State General Construction Code and Multiple Dwelling Code and can serve only as a guide. Consult codes in force in area of construction and state and federal agencies (Labor Department, General Services Administration, etc.) and comply with their requirements.
2. Plumbing fixture requirements are to be based on the maximum legal occupancy and not on the actual or anticipated occupancy.
3. Proportioning of toilet facilities between men and women is based on a 50-50 distribution. However, in certain cases conditions of occupancy may warrant additional facilities for men or women above the basic 50-50 distribution.

15 PLUMBING

DIMENSIONS OF STANDARD IRON SCREW PIPE (ASA SCHEDULE 40)

NOMINAL INTERNAL DIAMETER	1/8"	1/4"	3/8"	1/2"	3/4"	1"	1 1/4"	1 1/2"	2"	2 1/2"	3"	3 1/2"	4"	5"	6"	8"	10"	12"
ACTUAL INTERNAL DIAMETER	.269	.364	.493	.622	.824	1.049	1.38	1.61	2.067	2.469	3.068	3.548	4.026	5.047	6.065	7.981	10.02	12.00
ACTUAL EXTERNAL DIAMETER	.405	.540	.675	.840	1.05	1.315	1.66	1.90	2.375	2.875	3.50	4.00	4.50	5.563	6.625	8.625	10.75	12.75
INTERNAL AREA	.057	.104	.191	.304	.533	.864	1.496	2.036	3.355	4.788	7.393	9.886	12.73	20.00	28.89	50.02	78.85	113.09

DIAMETERS OF FITTINGS ACROSS OUTSIDE FACE

NOMINAL SIZE	1/8"	1/4"	3/8"	1/2"	3/4"	1"	1/4"	1/2"	2"	2 1/2"	3"	3 1/2"	4"	5"	6"	8"	10"	12"
MALLEABLE 150# SWP	11/16"	7/8"	1"	1 1/4"	1 1/2"	1 13/16"	2 3/16"	2 7/16"	3"	3 9/16"	4 5/16"	4 7/8"	5 7/16"	6 5/8"	7 13/16"			
MALLEABLE 300# SWP		15/16"	1 1/8"	1 3/8"	1 5/8"	1 15/16"	2 3/8"	2 11/16"	3 5/16"	3 7/8"	4 5/8"	5 1/4"	5 13/16"	7 1/16"	8 5/16"			
CAST IRON SCREW 125# SWP		15/16"	1 1/8"	1 3/8"	1 5/8"	1 15/16"	2 3/8"	2 11/16"	3 5/16"	3 7/8"	4 5/8"	5 1/4"	5 13/16"	7 1/16"	8 5/16"	10 5/8"	13 1/8"	15 1/2"
CAST IRON SCREW DRAINAGE							2 3/8"	2 11/16"	3 5/16"	3 7/8"	4 5/8"		5 13/16"	7 1/16"	8 5/16"	10 5/8"		
EXTERNAL DIAMETER OF SOIL PIPE XH							2 3/8"		3 1/2"		4 1/2"	5 1/2"	6 1/2"		8 5/8"	10 3/4"	12 3/4"	
EXT. DIA. OF BELL ON SOIL PIPE & FITTING XH							3 15/16"		5 3/16"		6 3/16"	7 3/16"	8 3/16"		10 7/8"	13 1/8"	15 1/4"	

Standard lengths of iron soil pipes = 5'-0" laying lengths

150# SWP malleable fittings are used on water and vent piping.

300# SWP malleable fittings are used for severe service.

125# SWP cast iron screw fittings are used for sprinkler and steam piping.

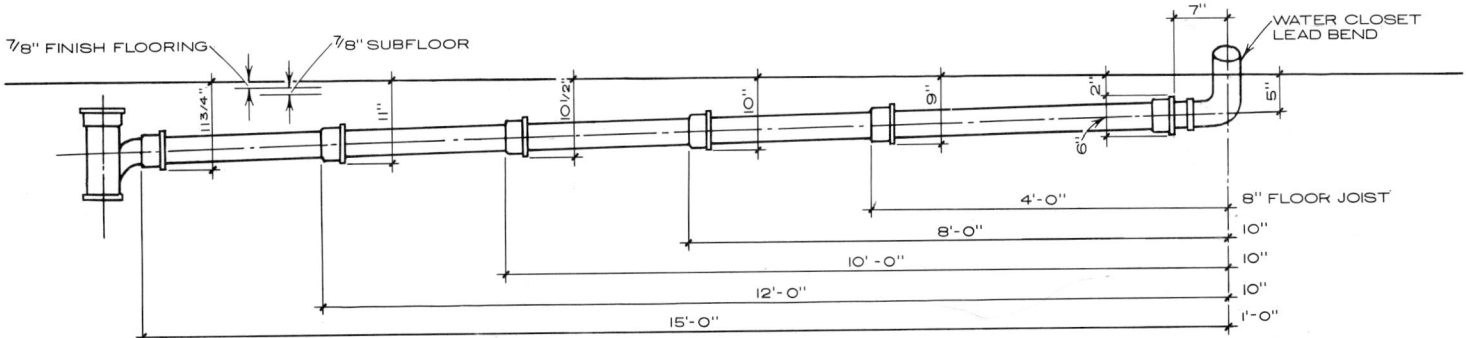

LENGTH OF RUN FROM WATER CLOSET FOR 4" C.I. SOIL LINE (INCLUDING BEND) IN DIFFERENT FLOOR THICKNESSES

DIMENSIONS OF INTERSECTIONS OF VENT WITH SOIL OR WASTE LINE

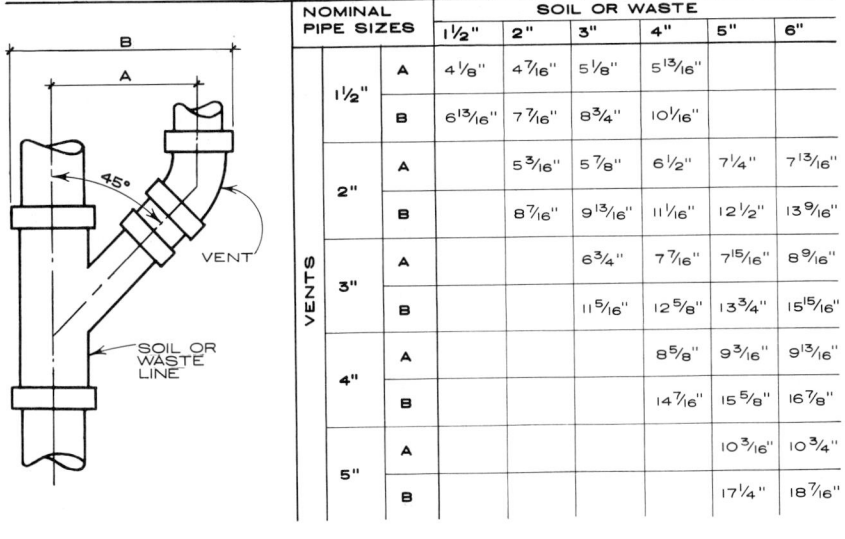

NOMINAL PIPE SIZES			SOIL OR WASTE 1 1/2"	2"	3"	4"	5"	6"
VENTS	1 1/2"	A	4 1/8"	4 7/16"	5 1/8"	5 13/16"		
		B	6 13/16"	7 7/16"	8 3/4"	10 1/16"		
	2"	A		5 3/16"	5 7/8"	6 1/2"	7 1/4"	7 13/16"
		B		8 7/16"	9 13/16"	11 1/16"	12 1/2"	13 9/16"
	3"	A			6 3/4"	7 7/16"	7 15/16"	8 9/16"
		B			11 5/16"	12 5/8"	13 3/4"	15 15/16"
	4"	A				8 5/8"	9 3/16"	9 13/16"
		B				14 7/16"	15 5/8"	16 7/8"
	5"	A					10 3/16"	10 3/4"
		B					17 1/4"	18 7/16"

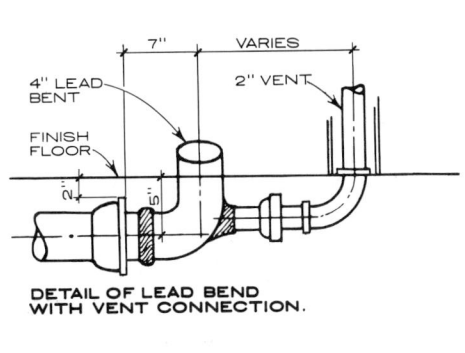

DETAIL OF LEAD BEND WITH VENT CONNECTION.

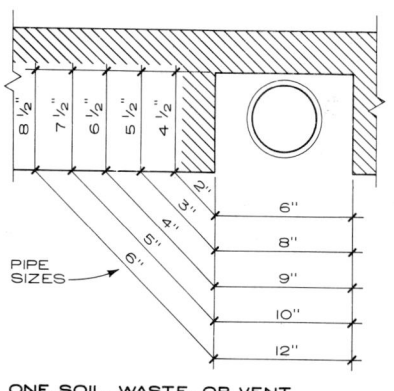

ONE SOIL, WASTE, OR VENT

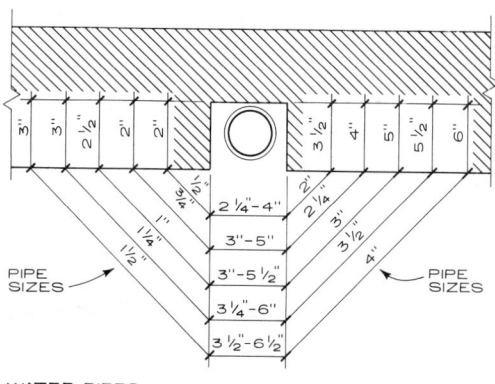

TWO SOILS, WASTES, OR VENTS

WATER PIPES

RECOMMENDED CHASE SIZES FOR VARIOUS PIPE SIZES

NOTE: SEE NOTES 2, 3, AND 4 ON THIS PAGE

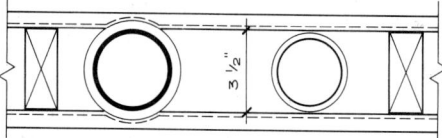

2" B & S WASTE PIPE
3" M.P. VENT OR
WATER PIPE

3" C., P., OR N.H. VENT
PIPE
3" C. WATER PIPE
2" M.P. VENT OR WATER
PIPE

4" STUD

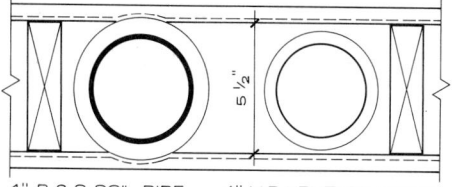

4" B & S SOIL PIPE
5" M.P. VENT PIPE

4" M.P. VENT OR WATER
PIPE
4" OR 5" N.H. OR P. SOIL
PIPE
4" OR 5" N.H., C., OR P.
VENT PIPE
4" OR 5" C. WATER PIPE

6" STUD

6" B & S SOIL PIPE

6" M.P., N.H., C., OR P.
VENT PIPE
6" N.H. OR P. SOIL PIPE
6" M.P. OR C. WATER PIPE

8" STUD

WOOD STUD PARTITIONS WITH 3/4" METAL LATH AND PLASTER

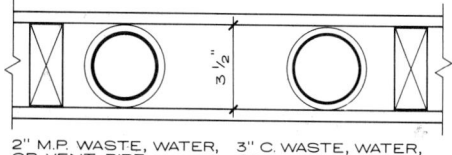

2" M.P. WASTE, WATER,
OR VENT PIPE
3" N.H. SOIL PIPE

3" C. WASTE, WATER,
OR VENT PIPE
3" P. WASTE OR VENT
PIPE

4" STUD

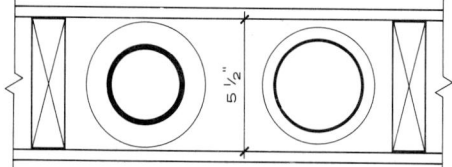

3" B & S SOIL OR
VENT PIPE

3 1/2" M.P. WASTE, VENT,
OR WATER PIPE
5" C. WATER OR VENT
PIPE
5" N.H. OR P. SOIL OR
VENT PIPE

6" STUD

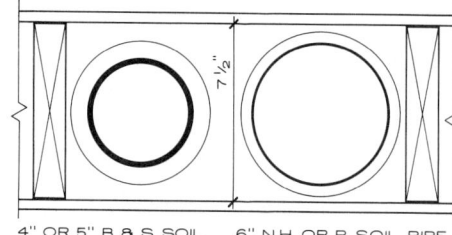

4" OR 5" B & S SOIL
OR VENT PIPE

6" N.H. OR P. SOIL PIPE
6" N.H., M.P., C., OR P.
VENT PIPE
5" M.P. OR 6" C. WATER
PIPE

8" STUD

WOOD STUD PARTITIONS WITH RIGID BOARD OR RIGID LATH

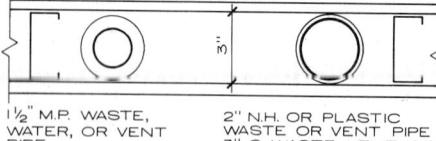

1 1/2" M.P. WASTE,
WATER, OR VENT
PIPE

2" N.H. OR PLASTIC
WASTE OR VENT PIPE
3" C. WASTE, VENT, OR
WATER PIPE

3" STUD

2" B & S WASTE OR
VENT PIPE
2 1/2" M.P. WASTE, VENT,
OR WATER PIPE

3" N.H. OR P. SOIL OR
VENT PIPE
4" C. WASTE, VENT, OR
WATER PIPE

4" STUD

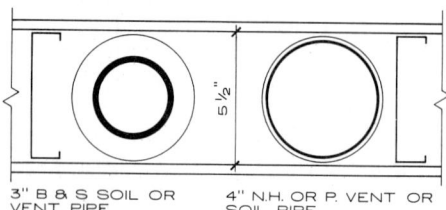

3" B & S SOIL OR
VENT PIPE
3" M.P. WASTE, VENT,
OR WATER PIPE

4" N.H. OR P. VENT OR
SOIL PIPE
5" C. WATER OR VENT
PIPE

5 1/2" STUD

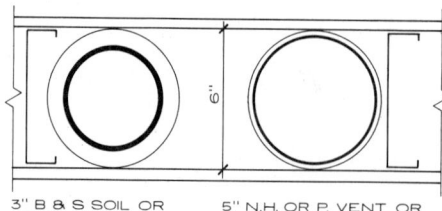

3" B & S SOIL OR
VENT PIPE
4" M.P. VENT OR
WATER PIPE

5" N.H. OR P. VENT OR
SOIL PIPE
6" C. WATER OR VENT
PIPE

6" STUD

STEEL STUD PARTITIONS WITH RIGID BOARD

Kelly Sacher & Associates; Architects Engineers Planners; N. Babylon, Long Island, New York

NOTES

1. Abbreviations:
   B&S: Extra heavy cast iron bell and spigot (push or caulked joints).
   C: Copper tubing.
   NH: Extra heavy cast iron no-hub pipe.
   MP: Malleable pattern (galvanized or nongalvanized).
   P: Plastic pipe.
2. Recommended chase sizes for various pipes include a 3/4 in. covering. For additional cover take the amount of cover required; subtract 3/4 in.; add the result to the dimension given for the pipe size desired.
3. Chases may be provided with or without access. Chases for several pipes, especially those containing main water supply pipes, should be provided with a means of access in case repair is necessary.
4. For the size of a chase with several pipes, add the widths required for each.
5. Partitions with 3/4 in. lath and plaster are shown with certain maximum pipe sizes encroaching on the lath and plaster. Encroaching portions of the pipes should be coated with asphaltic paint to prevent any staining of the plaster.
6. When rigid board or lath, such as gypsum board, plaster board, or gypsum lath, is used, the extreme diameter of the bead or bell of the pipe fitting should come within the actual clear dimension of the wall core.
7. Larger pipe spaces can be obtained by placing the piping between two partitions constructed back to back with the required clear space between them.

15 **PLUMBING**

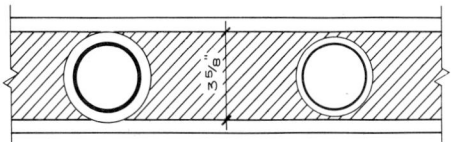

2 ½" M.P. WATER, WASTE, OR VENT PIPE
3" N.H. OR P. SOIL OR VENT PIPE

3" C. WATER OR VENT PIPE

4" BLOCK OR TILE

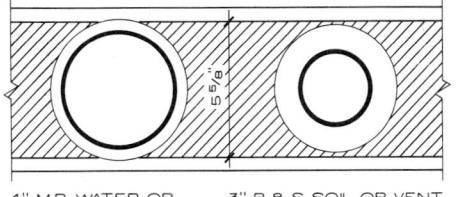

4" M.P. WATER OR VENT PIPE
5" P. OR N.H. SOIL OR VENT PIPE

3" B & S SOIL OR VENT PIPE
5" C. WATER OR VENT PIPE

6" BLOCK OR TILE

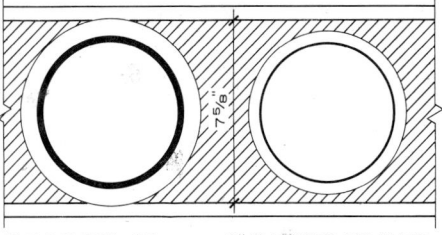

6" B & S SOIL OR VENT PIPE
6" M.P. WATER OR VENT PIPE

6" C. WATER OR VENT PIPE
6" P. OR N.H. SOIL OR VENT PIPE

8" BLOCK OR TILE

MASONRY PARTITIONS WITH 5/8" PLASTER
NOTE: SEE NOTES ON PRECEDING PAGE

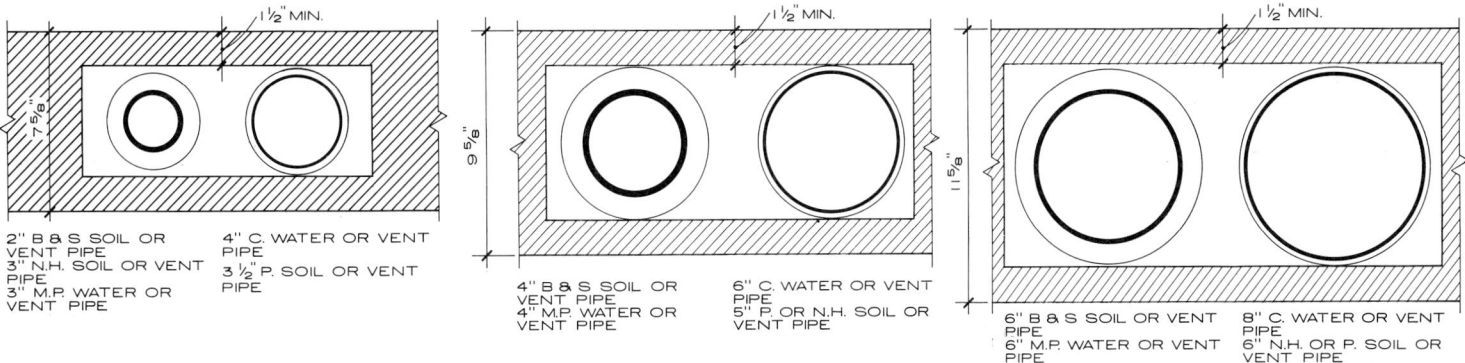

2" B & S SOIL OR VENT PIPE
3" N.H. SOIL OR VENT PIPE
3" M.P. WATER OR VENT PIPE

4" C. WATER OR VENT PIPE
3 ½" P. SOIL OR VENT PIPE

8" BLOCK OR TILE

4" B & S SOIL OR VENT PIPE
4" M.P. WATER OR VENT PIPE

6" C. WATER OR VENT PIPE
5" P. OR N.H. SOIL OR VENT PIPE

10" BLOCK OR TILE

6" B & S SOIL OR VENT PIPE
6" M.P. WATER OR VENT PIPE

8" C. WATER OR VENT PIPE
6" N.H. OR P. SOIL OR VENT PIPE

12" BLOCK OR TILE

EXPOSED MASONRY PARTITIONS
NOTE: SEE NOTES ON PRECEDING PAGE

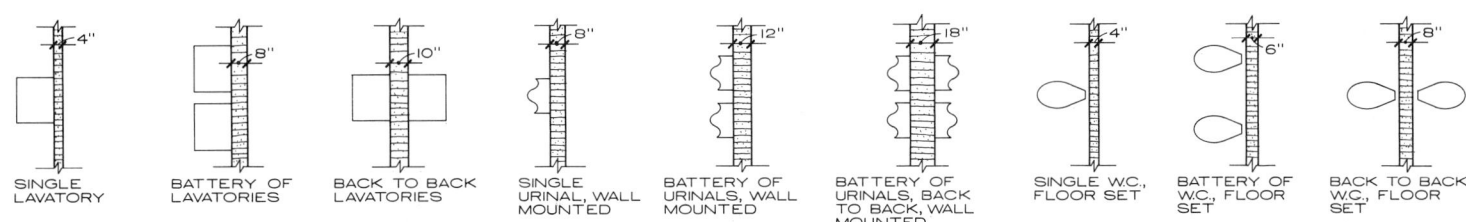

SINGLE LAVATORY — BATTERY OF LAVATORIES — BACK TO BACK LAVATORIES — SINGLE URINAL, WALL MOUNTED — BATTERY OF URINALS, WALL MOUNTED — BATTERY OF URINALS, BACK TO BACK, WALL MOUNTED — SINGLE W.C., FLOOR SET — BATTERY OF W.C., FLOOR SET — BACK TO BACK W.C., FLOOR SET

REQUIRED MINIMUM BLOCK OR FRAME WALL THICKNESS FOR VARIOUS FIXTURE COMBINATIONS
NOTE: DIMENSIONS SHOWN ARE FOR ROUGH WALLS ONLY AND DO NOT INCLUDE FINISH

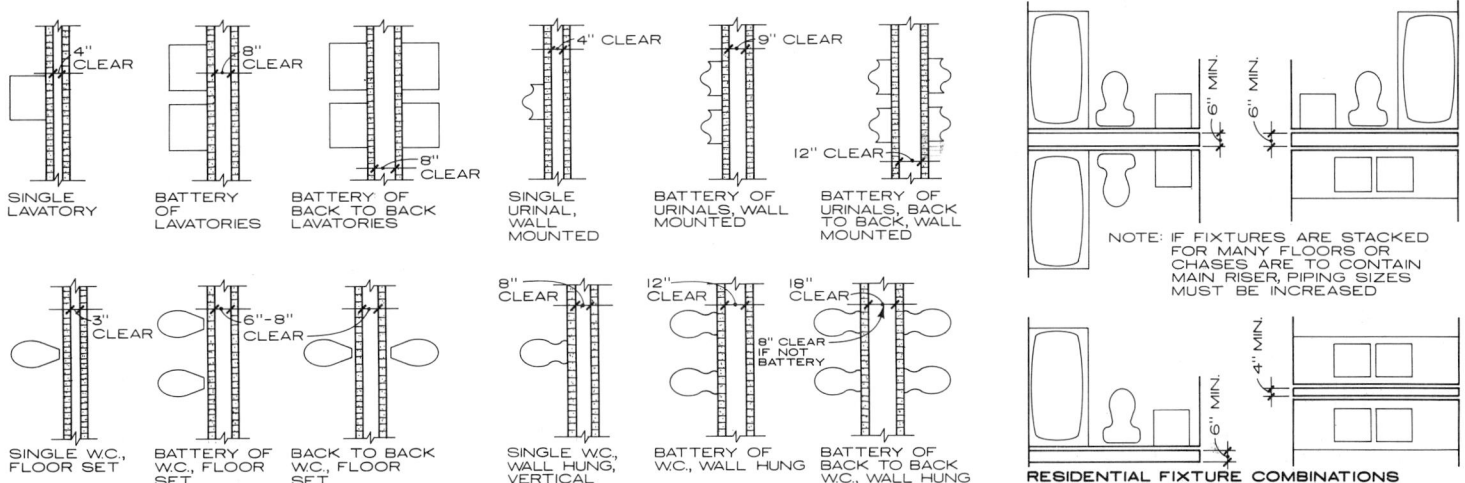

SINGLE LAVATORY — BATTERY OF LAVATORIES — BATTERY OF BACK TO BACK LAVATORIES — SINGLE URINAL, WALL MOUNTED — BATTERY OF URINALS, WALL MOUNTED — BATTERY OF URINALS, BACK TO BACK, WALL MOUNTED

SINGLE W.C., FLOOR SET — BATTERY OF W.C., FLOOR SET — BACK TO BACK W.C., FLOOR SET — SINGLE W.C., WALL HUNG, VERTICAL FITTING — BATTERY OF W.C., WALL HUNG — BATTERY OF BACK TO BACK W.C., WALL HUNG

NOTE: IF FIXTURES ARE STACKED FOR MANY FLOORS OR CHASES ARE TO CONTAIN MAIN RISER, PIPING SIZES MUST BE INCREASED

RESIDENTIAL FIXTURE COMBINATIONS

REQUIRED MINIMUM CLEAR CHASE DIMENSIONS FOR VARIOUS FIXTURE COMBINATIONS

NOTES
1. Dimensions are minimum and are based on the fixture chair carriers clear of the partition.
2. Partitions shown are based on 4 in. block (3⅝ in.), wood stud (3½ in.), or 4 in. steel stud and do not include the finish.
3. Dimensions are for branch piping for the fixture and do not in all cases provide for the main riser piping.
4. For conditions where main riser piping occurs in the fixture chase, dimensions must be altered to accommodate them.

Kelly Sacher & Associates; Architects Engineers Planners; N. Babylon, Long Island, New York

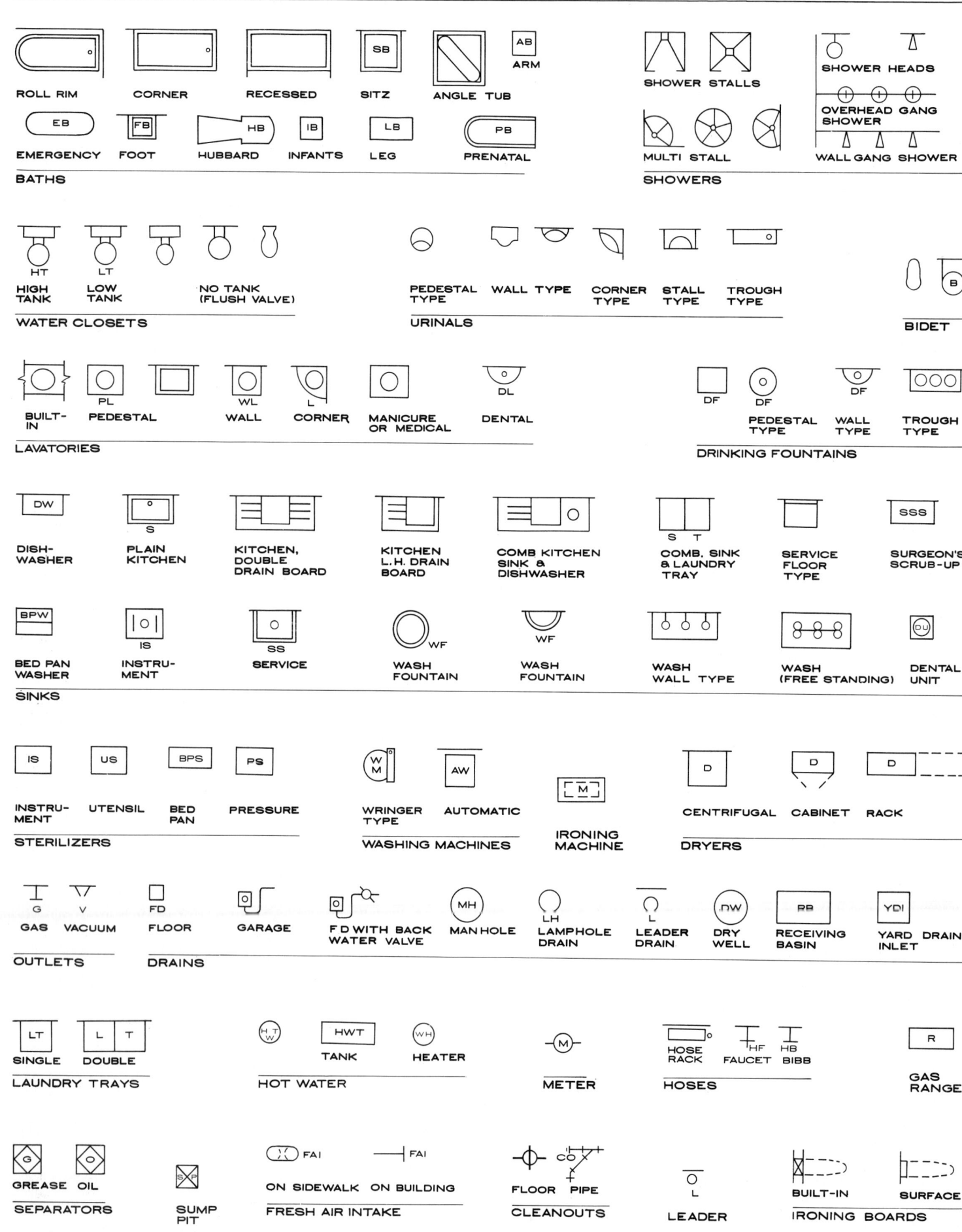

BATHS — ROLL RIM, CORNER, RECESSED, SITZ (SB), ANGLE TUB, ARM (AB), EMERGENCY (EB), FOOT (FB), HUBBARD (HB), INFANTS (IB), LEG (LB), PRENATAL (PB)

SHOWERS — SHOWER STALLS, MULTI STALL, SHOWER HEADS, OVERHEAD GANG SHOWER, WALL GANG SHOWER

WATER CLOSETS — HIGH TANK (HT), LOW TANK (LT), NO TANK (FLUSH VALVE)

URINALS — PEDESTAL TYPE, WALL TYPE, CORNER TYPE, STALL TYPE, TROUGH TYPE

BIDET

LAVATORIES — BUILT-IN, PEDESTAL (PL), WALL (WL), CORNER (L), MANICURE OR MEDICAL, DENTAL (DL)

DRINKING FOUNTAINS — PEDESTAL TYPE (DF), WALL TYPE (DF), TROUGH TYPE

SINKS — DISH-WASHER (DW), PLAIN KITCHEN (S), KITCHEN, DOUBLE DRAIN BOARD, KITCHEN L.H. DRAIN BOARD, COMB KITCHEN SINK & DISHWASHER, COMB. SINK & LAUNDRY TRAY (S T), SERVICE FLOOR TYPE, SURGEON'S SCRUB-UP (SSS), BED PAN WASHER (BPW), INSTRUMENT (IS), SERVICE (SS), WASH FOUNTAIN (WF), WASH FOUNTAIN (WF), WASH WALL TYPE, WASH (FREE STANDING), DENTAL UNIT (DU)

STERILIZERS — INSTRUMENT (IS), UTENSIL (US), BED PAN (BPS), PRESSURE (PS)

WASHING MACHINES — WRINGER TYPE (WM), AUTOMATIC (AW)

IRONING MACHINE (M)

DRYERS — CENTRIFUGAL (D), CABINET (D), RACK (D)

OUTLETS — GAS (G), VACUUM (V)

DRAINS — FLOOR (FD), GARAGE, F D WITH BACK WATER VALVE, MAN HOLE (MH), LAMPHOLE DRAIN (LH), LEADER DRAIN (L), DRY WELL (DW), RECEIVING BASIN (RB), YARD DRAIN INLET (YDI)

LAUNDRY TRAYS — SINGLE (LT), DOUBLE (L T)

HOT WATER — (HTW), TANK (HWT), HEATER (WH)

METER (M)

HOSES — HOSE RACK, FAUCET (HF), BIBB (HB)

GAS RANGE (R)

SEPARATORS — GREASE (G), OIL

SUMP PIT (SP)

FRESH AIR INTAKE — ON SIDEWALK (FAI), ON BUILDING (FAI)

CLEANOUTS — FLOOR (CO), PIPE

LEADER (L)

IRONING BOARDS — BUILT-IN, SURFACE

Amor Halperin, P. E.; Ayres, Cohen and Hayakawa; Consulting Engineers; Los Angeles/San Francisco, California

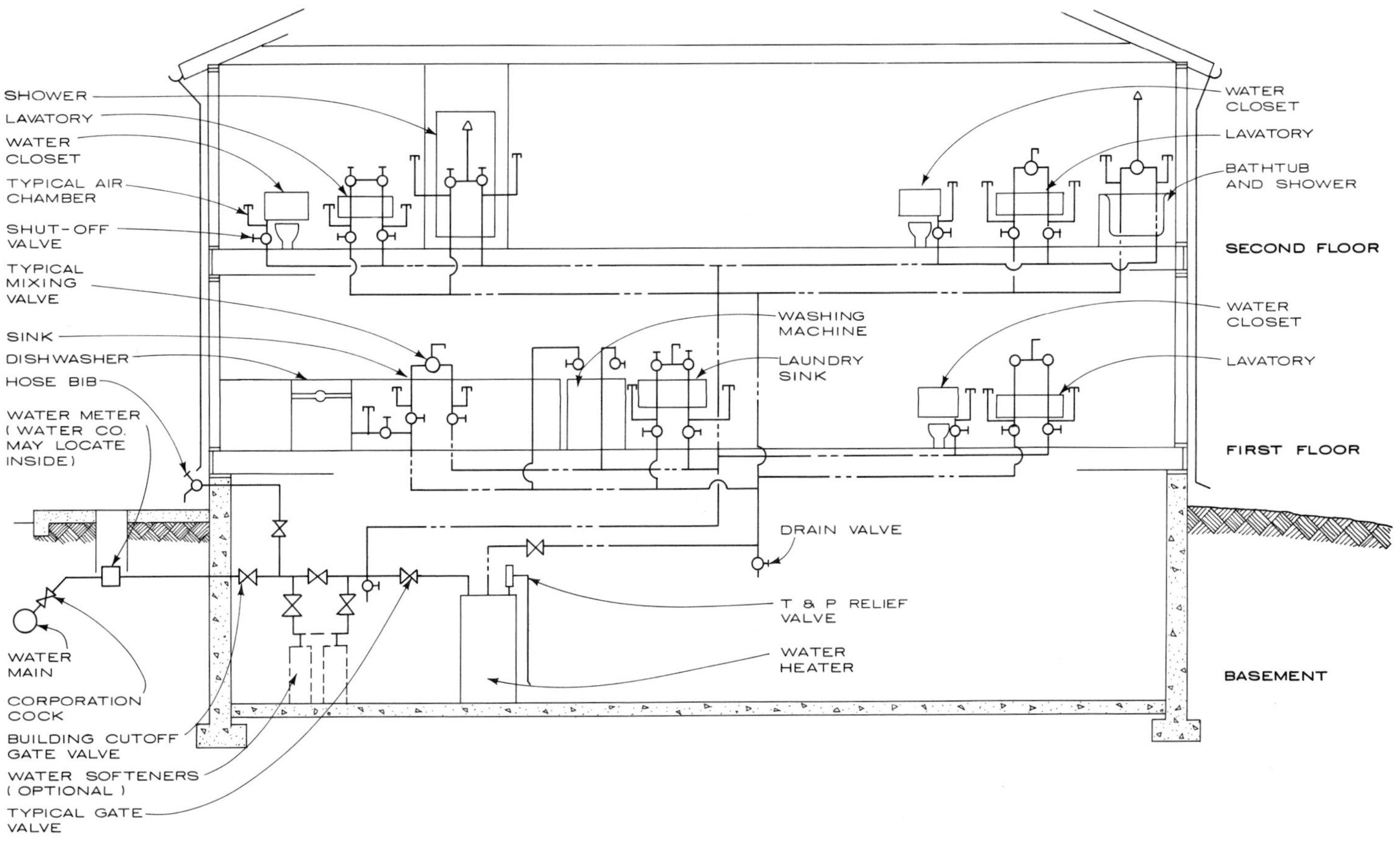

SHOWER
LAVATORY
WATER CLOSET
TYPICAL AIR CHAMBER
SHUT-OFF VALVE
TYPICAL MIXING VALVE
SINK
DISHWASHER
HOSE BIB
WATER METER (WATER CO. MAY LOCATE INSIDE)
WATER MAIN
CORPORATION COCK
BUILDING CUTOFF GATE VALVE
WATER SOFTENERS (OPTIONAL)
TYPICAL GATE VALVE

WASHING MACHINE
LAUNDRY SINK

WATER CLOSET
LAVATORY
BATHTUB AND SHOWER
SECOND FLOOR
WATER CLOSET
LAVATORY
FIRST FLOOR

DRAIN VALVE
T & P RELIEF VALVE
WATER HEATER
BASEMENT

WATER SUPPLY PIPING

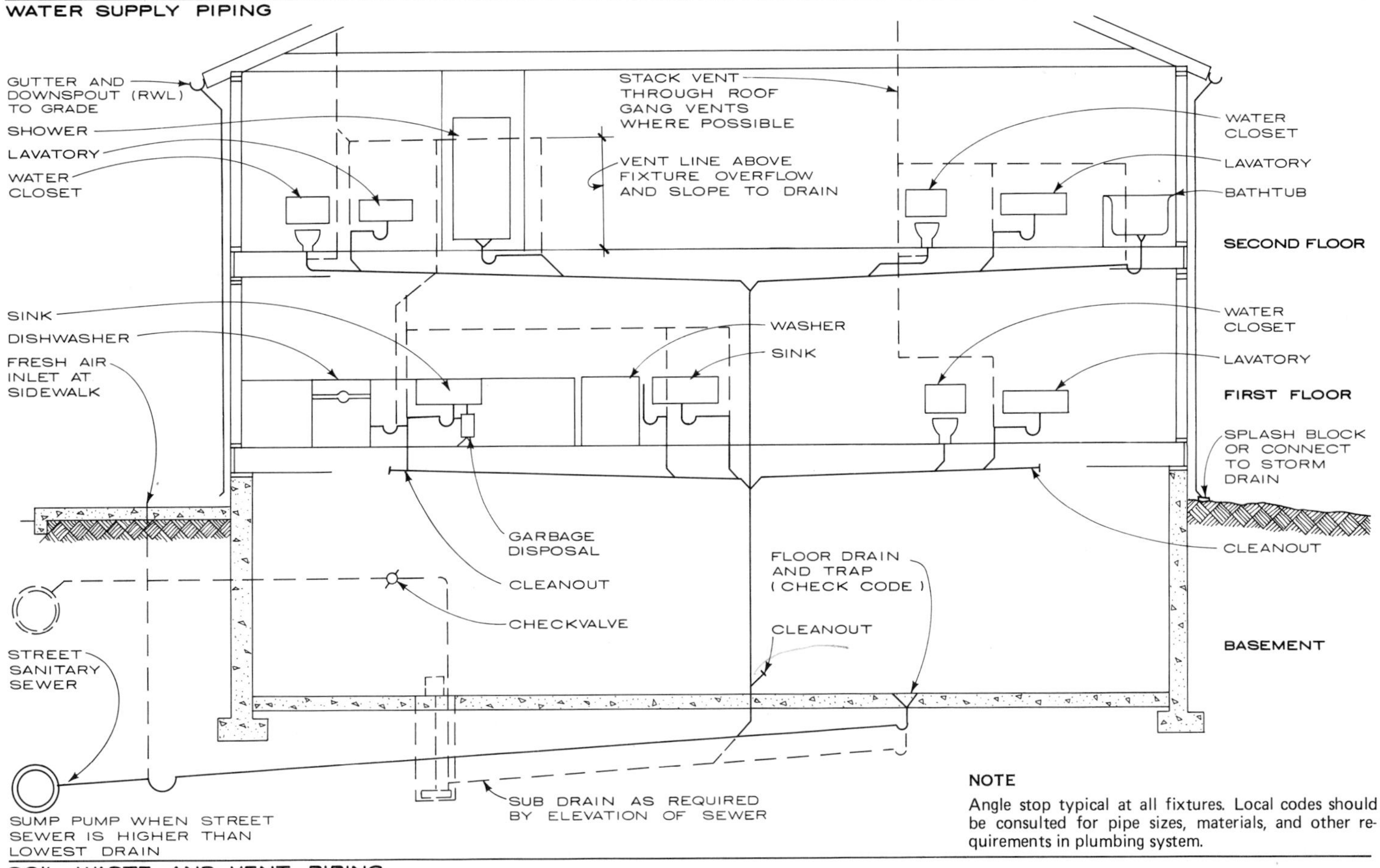

GUTTER AND DOWNSPOUT (RWL) TO GRADE
SHOWER
LAVATORY
WATER CLOSET
SINK
DISHWASHER
FRESH AIR INLET AT SIDEWALK
STREET SANITARY SEWER
SUMP PUMP WHEN STREET SEWER IS HIGHER THAN LOWEST DRAIN

STACK VENT THROUGH ROOF GANG VENTS WHERE POSSIBLE
VENT LINE ABOVE FIXTURE OVERFLOW AND SLOPE TO DRAIN

WASHER
SINK

GARBAGE DISPOSAL
CLEANOUT
CHECKVALVE

FLOOR DRAIN AND TRAP (CHECK CODE)
CLEANOUT

SUB DRAIN AS REQUIRED BY ELEVATION OF SEWER

WATER CLOSET
LAVATORY
BATHTUB
SECOND FLOOR
WATER CLOSET
LAVATORY
FIRST FLOOR
SPLASH BLOCK OR CONNECT TO STORM DRAIN
CLEANOUT
BASEMENT

NOTE

Angle stop typical at all fixtures. Local codes should be consulted for pipe sizes, materials, and other requirements in plumbing system.

SOIL, WASTE AND VENT PIPING

Brent Dickens, AIA, Architect; San Rafael, California

PLUMBING **15**

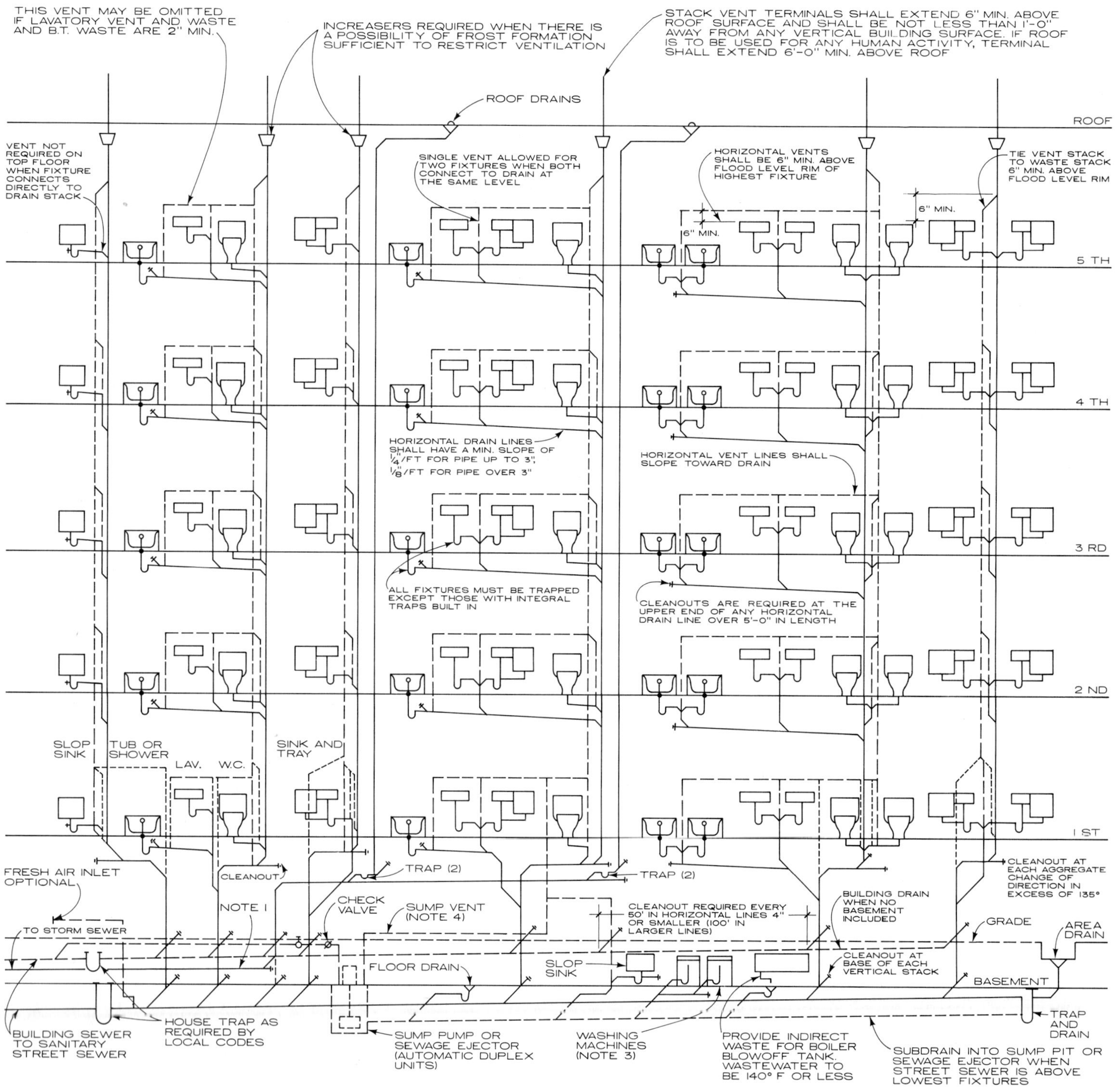

THIS VENT MAY BE OMITTED IF LAVATORY VENT AND WASTE AND B.T. WASTE ARE 2" MIN.

INCREASERS REQUIRED WHEN THERE IS A POSSIBILITY OF FROST FORMATION SUFFICIENT TO RESTRICT VENTILATION

STACK VENT TERMINALS SHALL EXTEND 6" MIN. ABOVE ROOF SURFACE AND SHALL BE NOT LESS THAN I'-0" AWAY FROM ANY VERTICAL BUILDING SURFACE. IF ROOF IS TO BE USED FOR ANY HUMAN ACTIVITY, TERMINAL SHALL EXTEND 6'-0" MIN. ABOVE ROOF

ROOF DRAINS

ROOF

VENT NOT REQUIRED ON TOP FLOOR WHEN FIXTURE CONNECTS DIRECTLY TO DRAIN STACK

SINGLE VENT ALLOWED FOR TWO FIXTURES WHEN BOTH CONNECT TO DRAIN AT THE SAME LEVEL

HORIZONTAL VENTS SHALL BE 6" MIN. ABOVE FLOOD LEVEL RIM OF HIGHEST FIXTURE

TIE VENT STACK TO WASTE STACK 6" MIN. ABOVE FLOOD LEVEL RIM

6" MIN.

6" MIN.

5 TH

4 TH

HORIZONTAL DRAIN LINES SHALL HAVE A MIN. SLOPE OF $\frac{1}{4}$/FT FOR PIPE UP TO 3", $\frac{1}{8}$/FT FOR PIPE OVER 3"

HORIZONTAL VENT LINES SHALL SLOPE TOWARD DRAIN

3 RD

ALL FIXTURES MUST BE TRAPPED EXCEPT THOSE WITH INTEGRAL TRAPS BUILT IN

CLEANOUTS ARE REQUIRED AT THE UPPER END OF ANY HORIZONTAL DRAIN LINE OVER 5'-0" IN LENGTH

2 ND

SLOP SINK

TUB OR SHOWER

LAV. W.C.

SINK AND TRAY

1 ST

FRESH AIR INLET OPTIONAL

CLEANOUT

TRAP (2)

TRAP (2)

CLEANOUT AT EACH AGGREGATE CHANGE OF DIRECTION IN EXCESS OF 135°

NOTE I

CHECK VALVE

SUMP VENT (NOTE 4)

CLEANOUT REQUIRED EVERY 50' IN HORIZONTAL LINES 4" OR SMALLER (100' IN LARGER LINES)

BUILDING DRAIN WHEN NO BASEMENT INCLUDED

GRADE

AREA DRAIN

TO STORM SEWER

FLOOR DRAIN

SLOP SINK

CLEANOUT AT BASE OF EACH VERTICAL STACK

BASEMENT

TRAP AND DRAIN

BUILDING SEWER TO SANITARY STREET SEWER

HOUSE TRAP AS REQUIRED BY LOCAL CODES

SUMP PUMP OR SEWAGE EJECTOR (AUTOMATIC DUPLEX UNITS)

WASHING MACHINES (NOTE 3)

PROVIDE INDIRECT WASTE FOR BOILER BLOWOFF TANK. WASTEWATER TO BE 140° F OR LESS

SUBDRAIN INTO SUMP PIT OR SEWAGE EJECTOR WHEN STREET SEWER IS ABOVE LOWEST FIXTURES

DIAGRAM NOTES

1. Roof drains and outside area drains must drain into storm drainage sewer where a separate system is available.

2. Traps are required on roof drain and area drain leaders when connected to a combined sanitary and storm sewer system.

3. Provide one washing machine connection for every eight living units (individual connections in each living unit are preferable if space permits). Provide standpipe type indirect waste pipes, 18 in. min. above trap weir. Special consideration must be given to suds pressure zones where washing machines discharge upstream from other fixtures; special venting to nonpressure zones should be provided.

4. Sump vent line shall run independently and unrestricted to the open air when pneumatic type sewage ejectors are used.

Killebrew/Rucker/Associates, Inc.; Wichita Falls, Texas

NOTE

The diagram generally indicates plumbing drainage solutions that constitute good plumbing practice. Because of variances between different local codes, some of the items shown may be prohibited in some areas, while other items may far exceed the minimum requirements of local codes. Always consult local codes for exact requirements and for such items as fixture unit allotments, pipe sizing, pipe materials, general regulations, and special conditions.

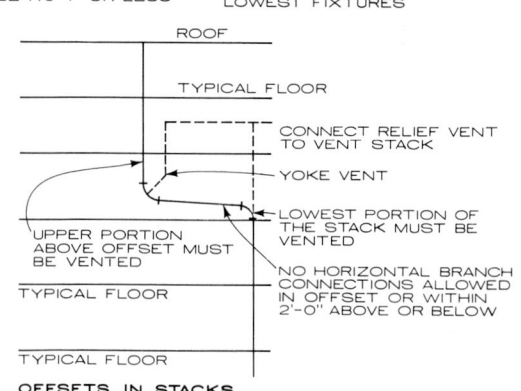

ROOF

TYPICAL FLOOR

CONNECT RELIEF VENT TO VENT STACK

YOKE VENT

LOWEST PORTION OF THE STACK MUST BE VENTED

NO HORIZONTAL BRANCH CONNECTIONS ALLOWED IN OFFSET OR WITHIN 2'-0" ABOVE OR BELOW

UPPER PORTION ABOVE OFFSET MUST BE VENTED

TYPICAL FLOOR

TYPICAL FLOOR

OFFSETS IN STACKS

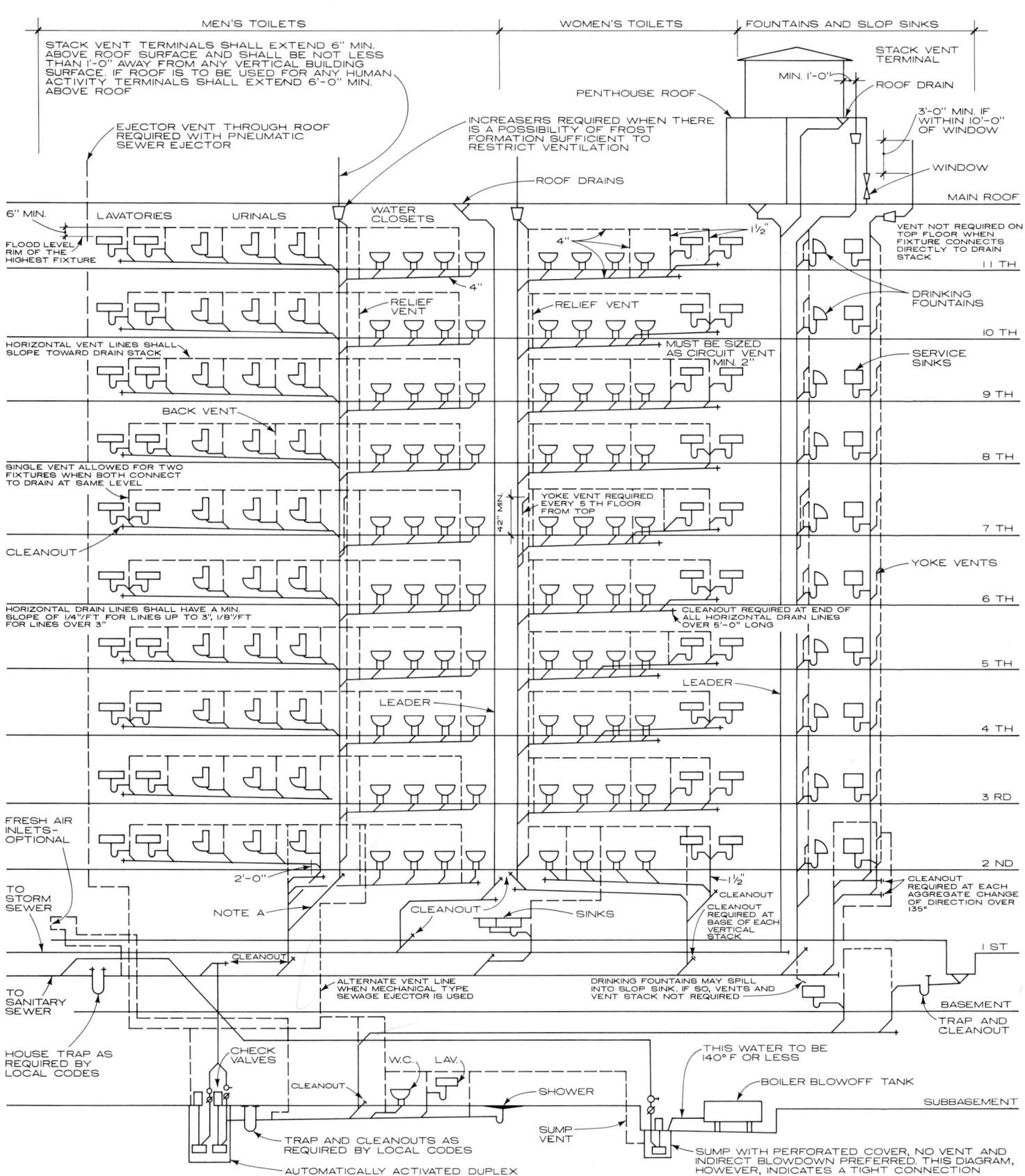

GENERAL NOTES

This diagram generally indicates plumbing drainage solutions that constitute good plumbing practice. Because of variances between different local codes, some of the items shown may be prohibited in some areas, while other items may far exceed the minimum requirements of local codes.

Always consult local codes for exact requirements and for such items as fixture unit allotments, pipe sizing, pipe materials, general regulations, and special conditions.

NOTE A

45° or less from vertical may be considered as straight stock in sizing, except that no fixtures or branches may be connected within 2 ft of offset.

Killebrew/Rucker/Associates, Inc.; Wichita Falls, Texas

GENERAL NOTES

Nonflammable medical gas piping systems carry oxygen, nitrous oxide, medical compressed air, carbon dioxide, helium, nitrogen, and other gases or mixtures of gases used for medical purposes in hospitals, laboratories, clinics, and other health related institutions. Nonflammable medical gas systems consist of three divisions: (1) source of supply; (2) safety warning systems; and (3) piping and distribution systems.

1. SOURCE OF SUPPLY: The three basic kinds of central supply systems for medical gases may be either of the cylinder or bulk type and may be installed permanently in a trailer. Generally, supply systems should be located in well ventilated, lockable, fireproofed areas of the building, away from all sources of heat, electrical equipment, or the possibility of physical damage. They should be equipped with pressure relief valves, check valves between tanks and manifolds, pressure regulators, and mechanical fittings to ensure the noninterchangeability of cylinders.

   a. Cylinder supply system without reserve supply (illustrated) is a system with two banks of cylinders that alternately supply the piping system. Each bank shall contain at least one day's operating supply and each bank shall have its own pressure regulator with cylinders connected to a common manifold header. When the primary bank cannot supply the system, the changeover switch shall automatically activate the secondary bank to supply the system.

   b. Cylinder supply system with reserve supply consists of the same primary and secondary banks of cylinders described above, with the addition of a reserve supply that consists of high pressure cylinders containing at least one day's operating supply, which is activated automatically when both the primary and secondary banks are unable to supply the system.

   c. A bulk supply system, containing more than 20,000 cu ft of oxygen or 28,000 cu ft of nitrous oxide (generally used only by larger facilities or institutions), usually consists of two sources of supply, one being a reserve supply for emergency use. The preferred system is an alternating type, containing a primary and secondary supply plus the emergency reserve. Because of the increased danger of storing large volumes of gases, bulk systems are generally located outdoors and must be at least 50 ft away from any structure.

2. WARNING SYSTEMS: Medical gas monitoring and alarm systems consist of the master alarm system, which monitors the entire system including the source of supply, and the area alarm system, which monitors the local supply line in patients' care areas.

   a. The master alarm system should consist of two or more master signal panels located in areas where they will be under continuous responsible observation, such as the maintenance director's

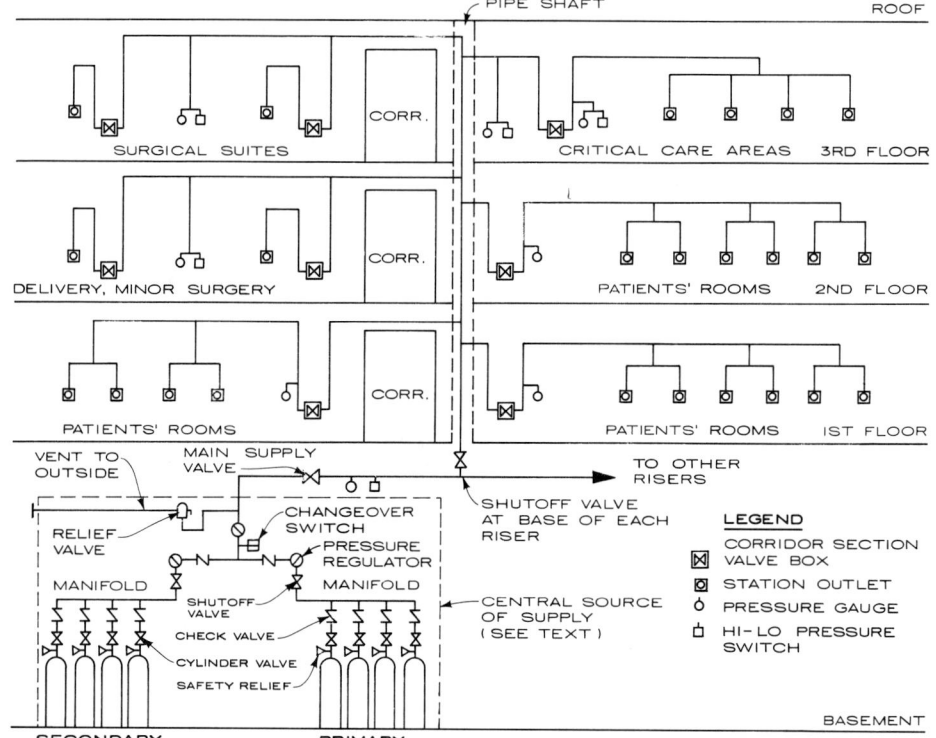

SCHEMATIC—TYPICAL MEDICAL GAS INSTALLATION

office, telephone switchboard, or security office. These panels should indicate by audible and visual means when changeovers from primary, secondary, or reserve supplies occur, when supplies fall below one day's operating supply, when line pressures fall below 20% of normal operating pressure, and so on.

   b. Area alarms shall be located in supervisory locations of surgical suites, recovery areas, intensive and coronary care units, and similar areas and shall monitor line pressures at each outlet to provide an audible and visual signal when line pressure falls below 20% of normal operating pressure.

3. PIPING SYSTEMS: Piping systems shall be designed to provide 50-55 psi pressure at each outlet and shall consist of seamless copper tubing or brass pipe with the appropriate fitting of the screw or brazed type in copper, brass, or bronze. Piping must

be protected from physical abuse, excessive heat, corrosion, contact with oil, and so on, and should be properly fireproofed and fire stopped between floors. Main supply line and each vertical riser shall be equipped with a manual shutoff valve, and each lateral branch from the main riser shall have a shutoff valve to stop the flow of gas to the area it serves. Operating rooms, recovery rooms, and so on, should be supplied directly from the main riser with a shutoff valve located in each such room. Shutoff valves should be in boxes with breakable glass fronts to prevent unauthorized use. Floors that contain oxygen therapy facilities should have dual main risers, so that the entire floor will not be without oxygen in case one riser is shutoff.

System design, pipe sizing, and routing should be done by a registered professional engineer in accordance with codes of the National Fire Protection, State and National Hospital Codes, and others.

MEDICAL GAS DISTRIBUTION SYSTEMS

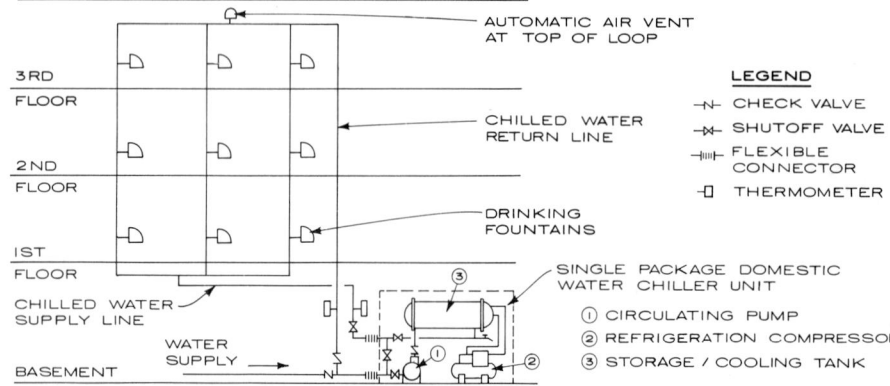

SCHEMATIC—CIRCULATING CHILLED WATER SYSTEM

DOMESTIC CHILLED WATER SYSTEMS

GENERAL

Automated central chilled water systems offer many advantages over individual water cooler arrangements. Principal among the advantages are savings of valuable floor space at each fountain location; greater flexibility in locating fountains; the greater attractiveness of fountains without attached cooling units. Central chilling plants generally are also more durable and use less energy than do smaller individual units, resulting in much lower operating and maintenance costs. System design, pipe sizing, and layout should be done by a registered professional engineer in accordance with applicable plumbing codes, with particular attention paid to such details as proper insulation of chilled water supply and return lines to meet the cooling requirements of refrigeration compressor units and the location and installation of check valves, pressure relief valves, air vents, thermometers, and flexible connections. The following formula provides an approximate chiller unit size (gph) for most applications:

$$\frac{\text{total floor space}}{135} = \text{number of persons served}$$

$$\text{number of persons served} \times 0.05 \text{ gph} = \text{net gph used}$$

$$\text{total feet in circulating line} \times 0.03 = \text{net gph loss}$$

$$\text{net gph used plus net gph loss} = \text{net gph required}$$

Killebrew/Rucker/Associates, Inc.; Wichita Falls, Texas

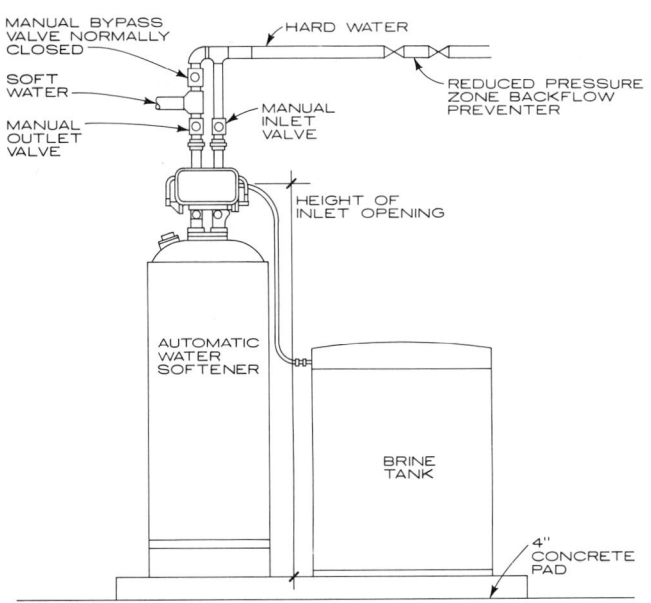

AUTOMATIC WATER SOFTENER PIPING DIAGRAM

GENERAL

Water hardness is caused by calcium and magnesium salts and is usually expressed in grains per gallon. For example: New York City 1-5 grains (low); Grand Rapids, Mich., 9 grains (5-9 moderate); Jacksonville, Fla., 18 grains (over 9 high); well water 0-50 grains.

A water softener is typically one tank for manual operation and two adjacent or concentric tanks with automatic controls. To determine the proper size softener for a residence, use this formula:

No. of people x 50 gal (75 if 3 or more baths) = gal water used/day

Gal water/day x no. of days of service = gal soft water needed

Gal soft water x hardness (grains/gal = capacity of softener needed

If the capacity found necessary by this formula is too large, reduce the number of days of service; the softener will need to be regenerated more often. The table lists data for residential size softeners. If a softener is needed for use in another building type, consult a manufacturer. Rental equipment with service plans is available in some areas, and responsibility for design adequacy should be assumed by the renting company.

When water supplies contain suspended matter, a filter should be placed at the hard water inlet. The softening process often removes any taste the water may have, but filters can also correct bad taste, acidity, or odor problems caused by other salts and minerals.

AUTOMATIC WATER SOFTENER SCHEDULE—FLOW RATE—17 TO 40 GPM

GRAIN CAPACITY AND SALT DOSAGE PER POUND	SERVICE FLOW RATE (GPM)		PIPE SIZE (IN.)	RESIN QUANTITY (CU FT)	TANK SIZE (IN.)	
	PEAK	CONTINUOUS			SOFTENER	BRINE
14,000 grains/5 lb	25	12	1½	1.5	12 x 40	18 x 38
28,000 grains/10 lb	17	13	1	3	16 x 48	24 x 38
43,000 grains/15 lb	17	13	1	4	16 x 60	24 x 38
45,000 grains/22 lb	25	12	1½	1.5	12 x 40	18 x 38
90,000 grains/45 lb	40	20	1½	3	16 x 48	24 x 38
120,000 grains/60 lb	40	20	1½	4	16 x 60	24 x 38

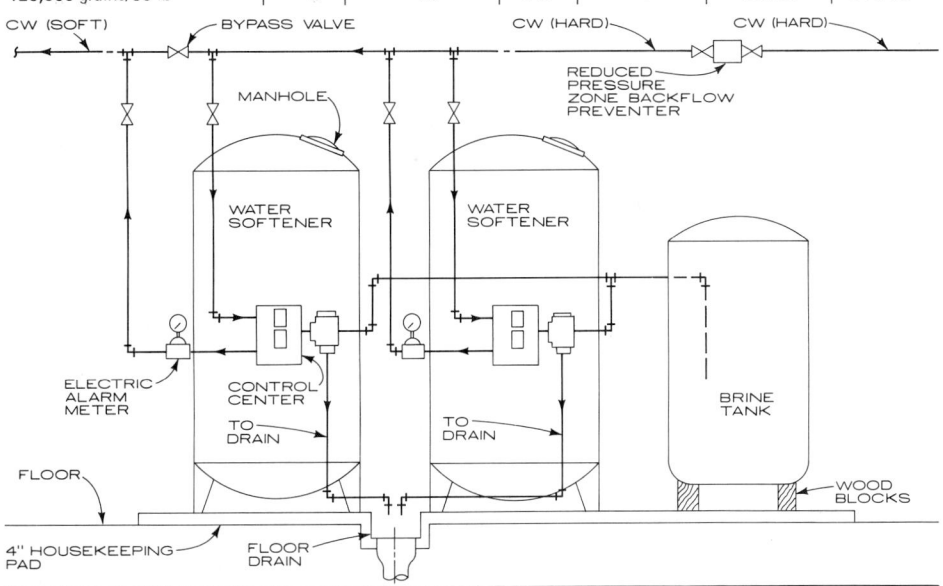

INDUSTRIAL WATER SOFTENER PIPING DIAGRAM

INDUSTRIAL WATER SOFTENER—FLOW RATE—60 TO 200 GPM

GRAIN CAPACITY AND SALT DOSAGE PER POUND	SERVICE FLOW RATE (GPM)		PIPE SIZE (IN.)	RESIN QUANTITY (CU FT)	TANK SIZE (IN.)	
	PEAK	CONTINUOUS			SOFTENER	BRINE
80,000 grains/20 lb	60	35	1½	5	24 x 54	24 x 48
116,000 grains/30 lb	75	50	1½	6.75	24 x 54	24 x 48
250,000 grains/125 lb	75	50	1½	8.5	24 x 54	24 x 48
300,000 grains/150 lb	110	80	2	10	30 x 60	30 x 48
450,000 grains/225 lb	110	80	2	15	30 x 60	30 x 48
600,000 grains/300 lb	150	110	2½	20	36 x 60	36 x 48
800,000 grains/405 lb	200	150	3	27	42 x 60	42 x 48

DiClemente-Siegel Engineering, Inc.; Southfield, Michigan

TYPICAL MANUFACTURERS' DATA

CHARAC- TERISTICS	MODELS		
REGEN- ERATION METHOD	FULLY AUTO- MATIC[1]	SEMI- AUTO- MATIC[2]	MANUAL[3]
Capacity (grains)	18,000	25,000	50,000
Service flow rate (gal)	10	7.5	8
Rinse flow rate (gal)	0.7	0.5	1.0
Ion exchanger (cu ft)	1.0	0.85	1.7
Salt per regen- eration (lb)	5.5	10	30
Regeneration time (min)	60	120	90
Service piping (in.)	1	¾	¾
Waste piping (in.)	⅜	¾	½
Pressure range (lb)	25-100	25-100	25-100
Electric current (V)	110-60 capacity	110-60 capacity	—
Resin tank diameter (in.)	9³/₁₆	9	12
Bed area (sq ft)	0.442	0.44	0.78
Shipping weight (lb)	100	116	197
Floor space (in.)	22 x 30	11 x 15	13 x 18
Overall height (in.)	43¾	44¾	54

1. Complete regeneration by time clock.
2. Manually operated switch to start regeneration.
3. Complete manual regeneration by adding dry pellet type salt directly to the softener.

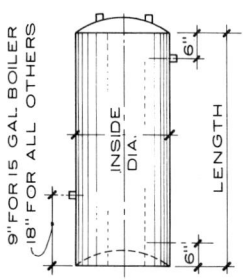

RANGE BOILER

Galvanized Standard
pressure = 85 psi
Extra heavy pressure = 150 psi
Double extra heavy = 150 psi
2'-0'' dia. tank—tapping is 1½'', others 1''

RANGE BOILERS

CAPACITY (GAL)	DIAMETER	LENGTH
15	1'-0''	2'-6''
30	1'-0''	5'-0''
40	1'-2''	5'-0''
66	1'-6''	5'-0''
82	1'-8''	5'-0''
120	2'-0''	5'-0''

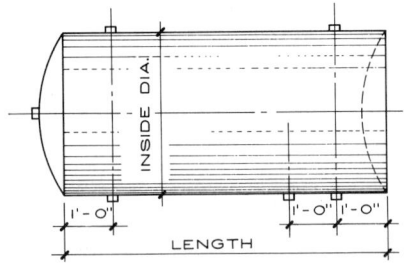

HOT WATER STORAGE TANK

Manhole 11'' x 15'' in shell or head
Standard pressure = 65 psi
Extra heavy pressure = 100 psi
Tanks used vertically or horizontally.
6 tappings in each tank of diameters listed

GENERAL WATER TANK DATA

PAINTED, ATTIC TYPE

GALVANIZED EXPANSION TANKS

Galvanized, tapping 1'' Φ
Max. pressure = 30 psi
Max. no. of tappings shown

EXPANSION TANKS

CAPACITY (GAL)	DIAMETER	LENGTH
10	1'-0''	1'-8''
15	1'-0''	2'-6''
20	1'-2''	2'-6''
30	1'-0''	5'-0''
40	1'-2''	5'-0''

HOT WATER STORAGE TANKS

CAPACITY (GAL)	DIAMETER	LENGTH
82	1'-8''	5'-0''
118	2'-0''	5'-0''
141	2'-0''	6'-0''
220	2'-6''	6'-0''
294	2'-6''	8'-0''
317	3'-0''	6'-0''
428	3'-0''	8'-0''
504	3'-6''	7'-0''
576	3'-6''	8'-0''
720	3'-6''	10'-0''
904	4'-0''	10'-0''
1008	3'-6''	14'-0''
1504	4'-0''	16'-0''
1880	4'-0''	20'-0''

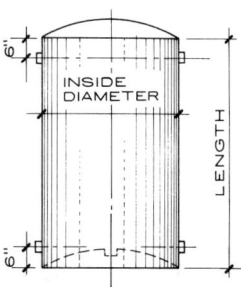

SOLAR TANK

Galvanized
Double extra heavy = 120 psi
Used vertically only 1'-8''
dia. tank, 1'' tapping, all
others 1½'' tapping

SOLAR TANKS

CAPACITY (GAL)	DIAMETER	LENGTH
66	1'-8''	4'-0''
100	2'-0''	4'-0''
150	2'-6''	4'-0''
210	3'-0''	4'-0''
270	3'-0''	5'-0''

TAP SIZES

TANK DIAMETER	TAP DIAMETER
1'-8''	1½''
2'-0''	1½''
2'-6''	2''
3'-0''	2''
3'-6''	2''
4'-0''	3''

FORMULAS FOR CAPACITY OF CYLINDRICAL TANKS:

$$DIA.^2 \times 0.7854 \times LENGTH = VOLUME$$

$$CU.FT. \times 7.4805 = \left.\begin{array}{c} \end{array}\right\} \begin{array}{c} CAPACITY \\ IN \ GALLONS \end{array}$$

$$\frac{CU.IN.}{1728} \times 7.4805 =$$

WATER DATA:
1 GALLON = 231 CU.IN.
1 CU. FT. WEIGHS 62.5 LBS.

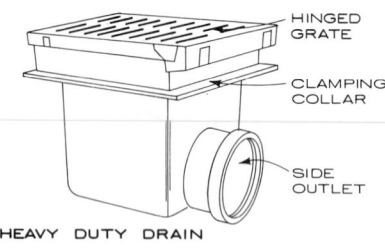

HEAVY DUTY DRAIN

HINGED GRATE
CLAMPING COLLAR
SIDE OUTLET

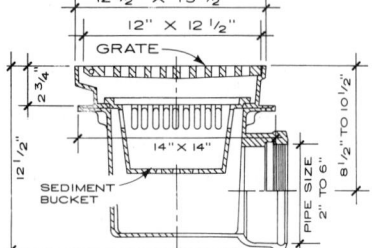

DETAIL

12½'' X 13½''
12'' X 12½''
GRATE
2¾''
12½''
14'' X 14''
SEDIMENT BUCKET
7¾''
8½'' TO 10½''
PIPE SIZE 2'' TO 6''

FLOOR AND SHOWER DRAINS

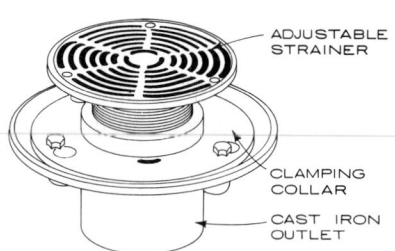

STANDARD DRAIN

ADJUSTABLE STRAINER
CLAMPING COLLAR
CAST IRON OUTLET

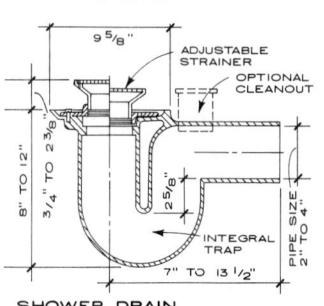

SHOWER DRAIN

9⅝''
ADJUSTABLE STRAINER
OPTIONAL CLEANOUT
3⅜''
2⅝''
8'' TO 12''
¾'' TO 2⅜''
INTEGRAL TRAP
7'' TO 13½''
PIPE SIZE 2'' TO 4''

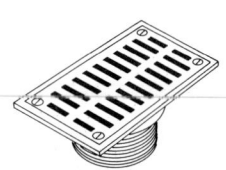

RECTANGULAR   **ANGLE**

DOME   **COVER AND LOCK**

NOTE

Strainers are constructed of nickel brass or cast iron for heavy duty. Sediment baskets and backwater valves are optional accessories. Vandalproof covers and locks are also available. In waste disposal areas, spray nozzles are installed for washdown of drains.

Wm. G. Miner, AIA, Architect; Washington, D.C.

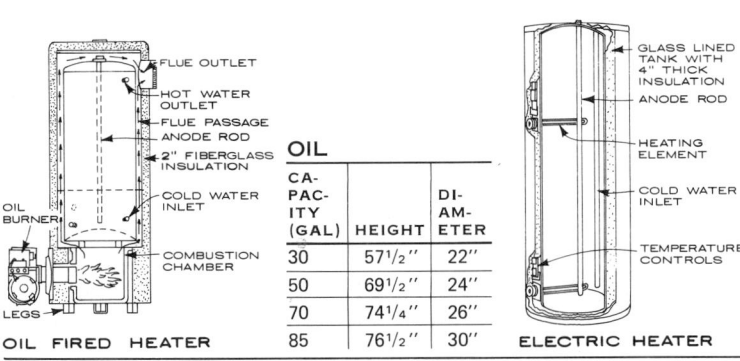

OIL

CA-PAC-ITY (GAL)	HEIGHT	DI-AM-ETER
30	57½''	22''
50	69½''	24''
70	74¼''	26''
85	76½''	30''

OIL FIRED HEATER

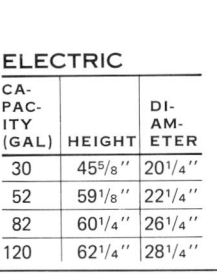

ELECTRIC

CA-PAC-ITY (GAL)	HEIGHT	DI-AM-ETER
30	45⅝''	20¼''
52	59⅛''	22¼''
82	60¼''	26¼''
120	62¼''	28¼''

ELECTRIC HEATER

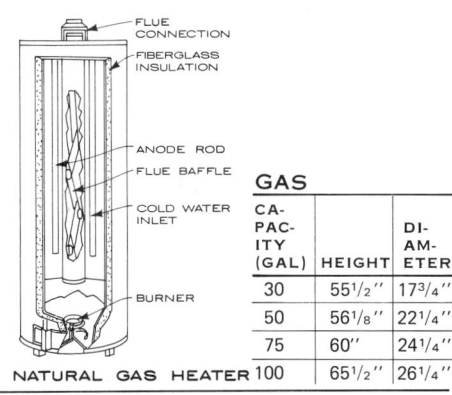

GAS

CA-PAC-ITY (GAL)	HEIGHT	DI-AM-ETER
30	55½''	17¾''
50	56⅛''	22¼''
75	60''	24¼''
100	65½''	26¼''

NATURAL GAS HEATER

RESIDENTIAL, STORAGE TYPE WATER HEATERS

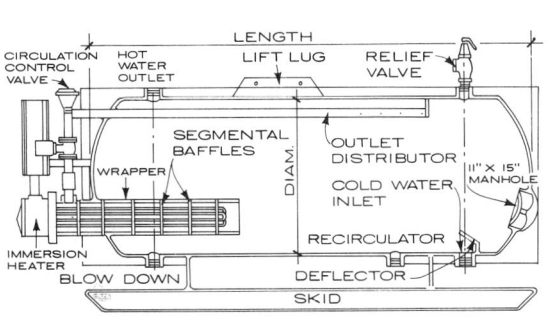

ELECTRIC OR STEAM HEATER

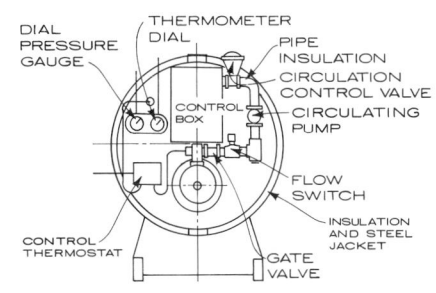

END VIEW

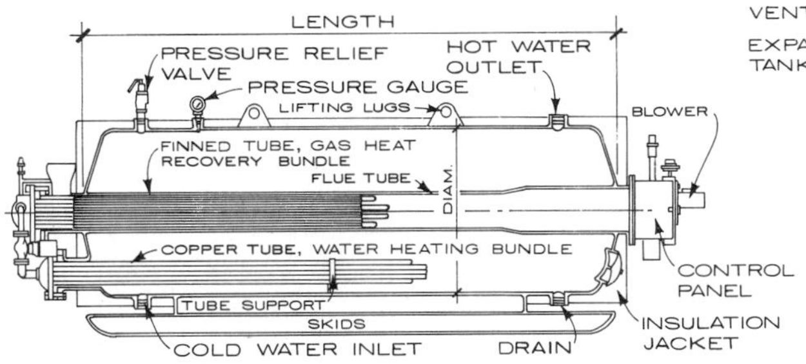

GAS OR OIL FIRED HEATER

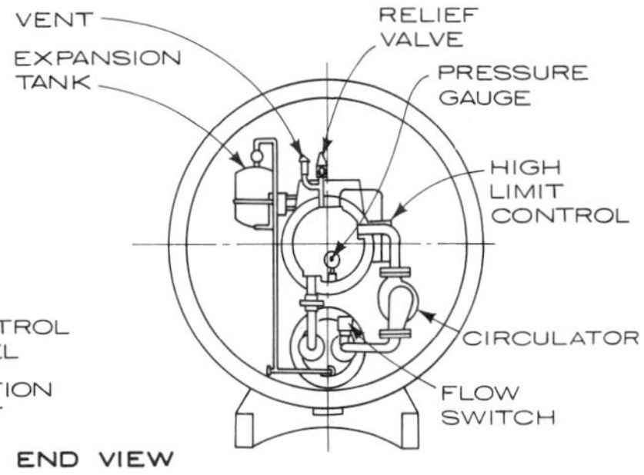

END VIEW

COMMERCIAL, STORAGE TYPE WATER HEATERS

ELECTRIC/STEAM HEATER DIMENSIONS

CAPACITY (GAL)	LENGTH	DIAM-ETER	SPACE TO REMOVE HEATING SECTION	
			ELECTRIC	STEAM
530	96''	42''	39''	12''
1034	96''	60''	39''	18''
1300	120''	60''	39''	24''
1980	120''	72''	79''	29''
2400	144''	72''	79''	29''
3150	144''	84''	79''	27''
4070	144''	96''	79''	27''

GAS/OIL HEATER DIMENSIONS

CAPACITY (GAL)	LENGTH	DIAMETER	SPACE TO REMOVE HEATING SECTION
560	108''	42''	85''
820	120''	48''	87''
1250	120''	60''	97''
1930	120''	72''	103''
2340	144''	72''	103''
3090	144''	84''	89''
4010	144''	96''	89''

GENERAL NOTE
These dimensions are for horizontal type heaters only. Space saving, vertical type heaters with same capacities are available from most manufacturers.

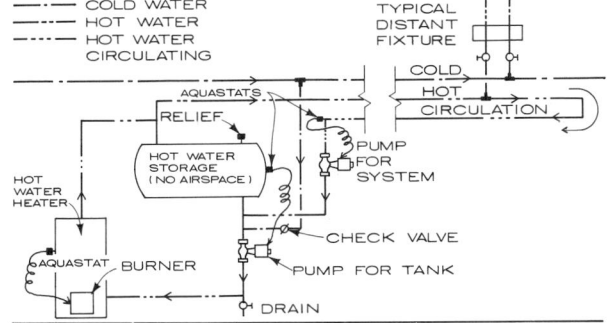

FORCED CIRCULATION SYSTEM

ESTIMATED HOT WATER DEMAND

BUILDING TYPE	HOT WATER[1] PER PERSON DAY'S USE	HOURLY DEMAND DAY'S USE	DURATION OF PEAK LOAD	STORAGE CAPACITY DAY'S USE	HEATING CAPACITY DAY'S USE
Residences, apartments, hotels[2]	20-40 gal/day	1/7	4 hr	1/5	1/7
Office buildings	2-3 gal/day	1/5	2 hr	1/5	1/6
Factory buildings	5 gal/day	1/3	1 hr	2/5	1/8

1. At 140°F.
2. Allow additional 15 gal per dishwasher and 40 gal per laundry washer.

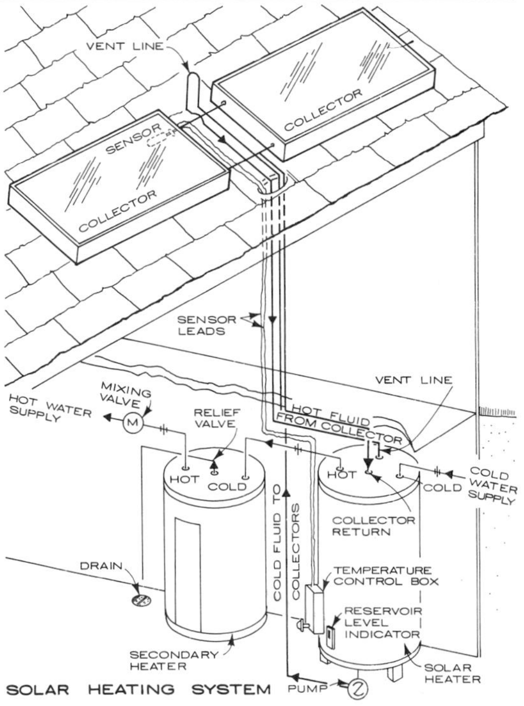

Syska & Hennessy, Consulting Engineers; New York, New York

SOLAR HEATING SYSTEM

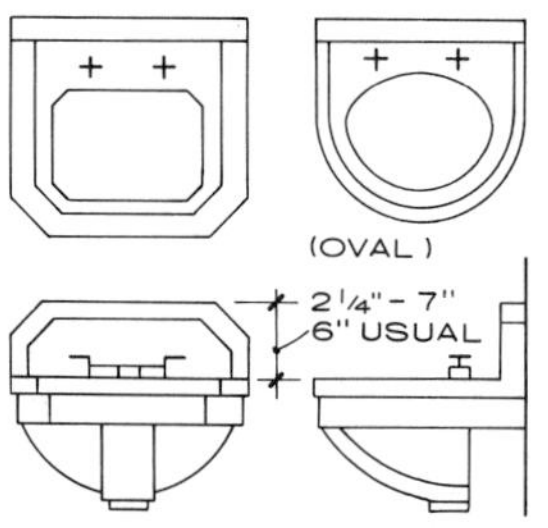
(OVAL)
2 1/4" - 7"
6" USUAL

FLAT BACK

VIT. CH.	EN. C. I.	EN. STEEL
Wall Hung	Wall Hung	Wall Hung, with Legs, or Pedestal
14"x14"*	19"x17"	
18"x15⅞"†	20"x18"tlp	
19"x17"	21"x18"†	
20"x18"†	22"x19"tlp	24"x20"
24"x21"		
Wall Hung or with legs		
20"x18"p		
24"x20"*		
24"x21"*		

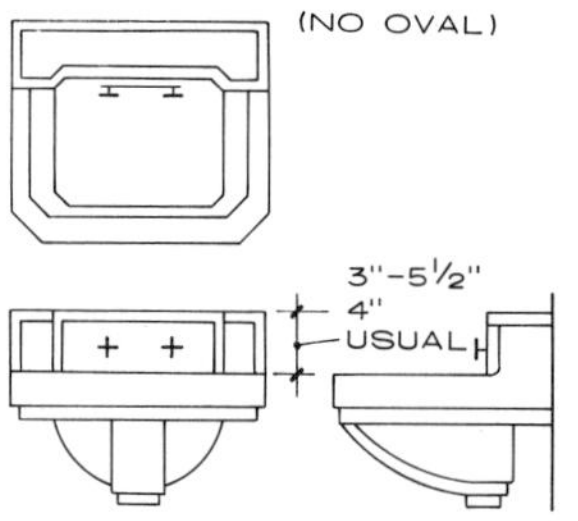
(NO OVAL)
3"-5 1/2"
4"
USUAL

SHELF BACK

VIT. CH.	EN. C. I.	EN. STEEL
Wall Hung or with legs	Wall Hung	Wall Hung
	13"x13"†	19"x17"
18"x14"†	16"x14"	20"x18"
19"x17"†	18"x15"	
20"x14"†	20"x14"	
22"x18"lp	Wall Hung or with legs	
24"x20"l		
With legs	19"x11"*	
27"x22"*p	22"x19"†	
26"x22"l		

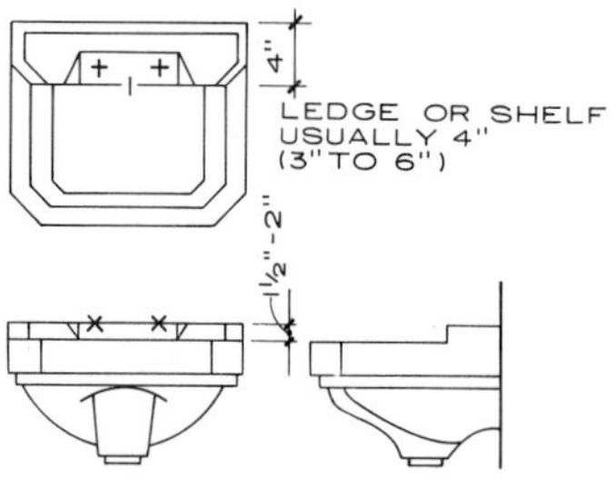
4"
LEDGE OR SHELF
USUALLY 4"
(3" TO 6")
1 1/2"-2"

LEDGE BACK

VIT. CH.	EN. C. I.	EN. STEEL
Wall Hung	Wall Hung	Wall Hung or with Legs
18"x15"	19"x17"	
Wall Hung or with legs		19"x17"p
19"x17"		24"x20"p
20"x18"†		20"x18"
24"x20"		
26"x22"		
With legs		
32"x18"		
36"x18"		

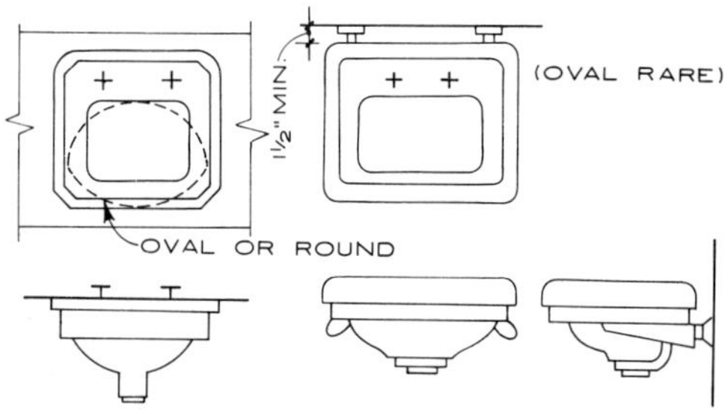
1 1/2" MIN.
(OVAL RARE)
OVAL OR ROUND

BUILT-IN

VIT. CH.	EN. C.I.	EN. STEEL
18"&19"rd	18"&19"rd	18"&19"rd
19"x14"	19"x16"	19½"x15¾"†
19"x16"	20"x12"†	20"x18"†
20"x18"†	20"x18"†	20½"x16¾"†
22"x18"	22"x19"†	20"x17"
21"x19"†	26"x18"	
24"x18"†		
24"x20¾"†		
27"x20"		

SLAB

VIT. CH.	EN. STEEL
Wall Hung or with Legs	Wall Hung or with Legs
20"x18"tlp	24"x20"p
24"x20"lp	
24"x21"tlp	
27"x22"p	
With legs	
30"x22"	
36"x22"†	

LAVATORIES—ALL DIMENSIONS IN INCHES

LEGEND & NOTES

Vit. Ch. = Vitreous China
En. C.I. = Enameled Cast Iron
En. Steel = Enameled Steel
p = may have vitreous china leg or pedestal in addition to wall brackets.

* Made in oval rim only
L = may have 2 chrome legs & wall brackets
C = Chair support
Sizes under "with legs" are supported by legs & brackets; they may not be used with bracket support alone.
† = made in rectangular rim only.
Height — finished floor to sink, 2′–6″ to 2′–8″ (Standard 2′–7″).

Lavatories shown with bevelled rect. rims; others have rounded corners or D-shaped (oval) rims. Basins—rectangular or oval, or other shapes (see mfr.). Flat back may have bevelled, rounded or D-shaped corners.

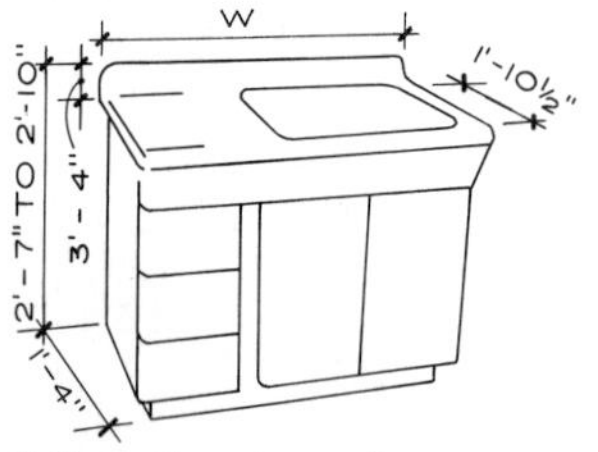
W
1'-10 1/2"
2'-7" TO 2'-10"
3'-4"
2'-7"
1'-4"

Units may have drawers, hampers, or combinations.

	1 BOWL	2 BOWL
W	2′, 2′–6″, 3′, 3′–6″, 4′, 4′–6″, 5′, 5′–6″, 6′	5′, 5′–6″, 6′

CABINET

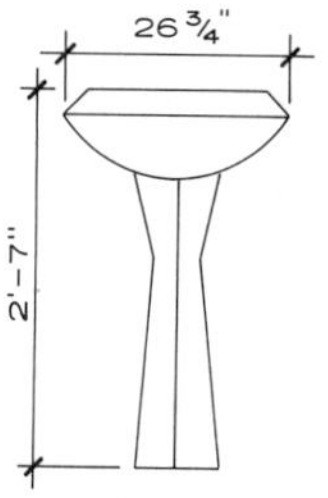
26 3/4"
2'-7"

VITREOUS CHINA
DEPTH = 22 1/2"

PEDESTAL

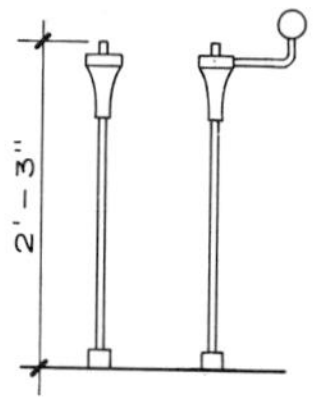
2'-3"

PAIRED LEGS WITH OR WITHOUT TOWEL BARS

CHROME LEGS

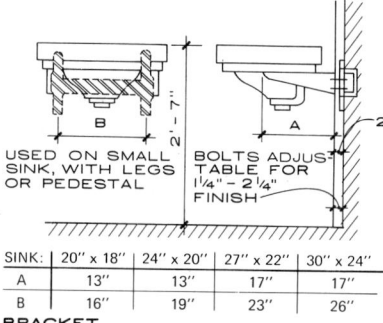

FLOOR SUPPORTED

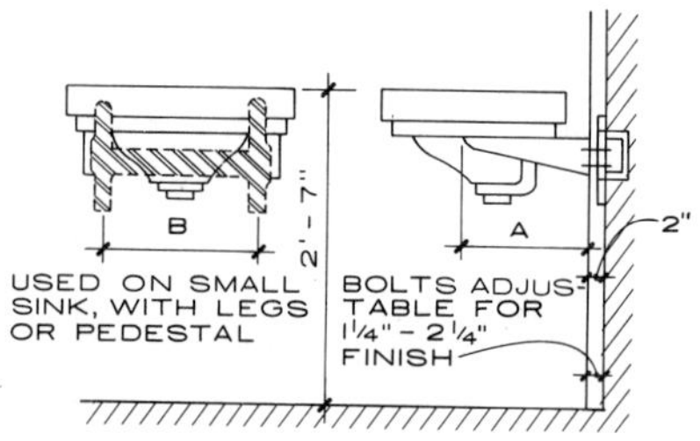
B
A
2'-7"
2"
USED ON SMALL SINK, WITH LEGS OR PEDESTAL
BOLTS ADJUST TABLE FOR 1 1/4" - 2 1/4" FINISH

SINK:	20" x 18"	24" x 20"	27" x 22"	30" x 24"
A	13"	13"	17"	17"
B	16"	19"	23"	26"

BRACKET

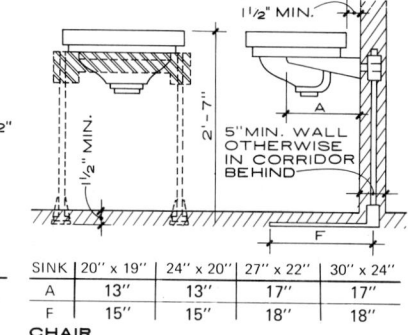

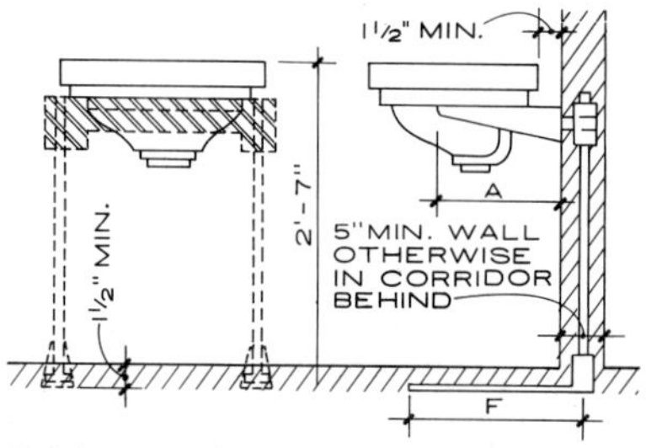
1 1/2" MIN.
A
2'-7"
1 1/2" MIN.
5" MIN. WALL OTHERWISE IN CORRIDOR BEHIND
F

SINK	20" x 19"	24" x 20"	27" x 22"	30" x 24"
A	13"	13"	17"	17"
F	15"	15"	18"	18"

CHAIR

WALL HUNG

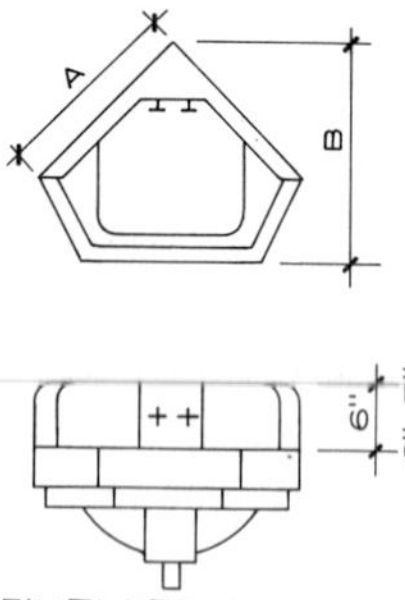
A
B
6"
2'-7"

VIT. CH.	
A	B
17"	19 1/2"
17"	20"
11"	16 1/4"
EN. C. I.	
16"	20 1/2"
11"	16"

In flat and shelf back.

FIXTURES ON PANEL OR ON BASIN RIM

CORNER LAVATORY

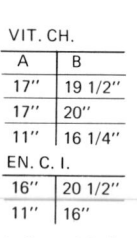

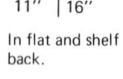

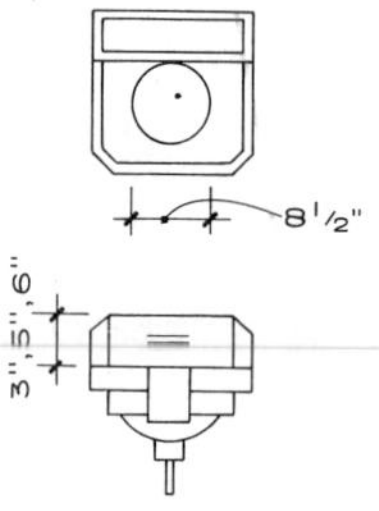
8 1/2"
3'-5 1/2"

VIT.CH.	14" x 14"

DENTAL

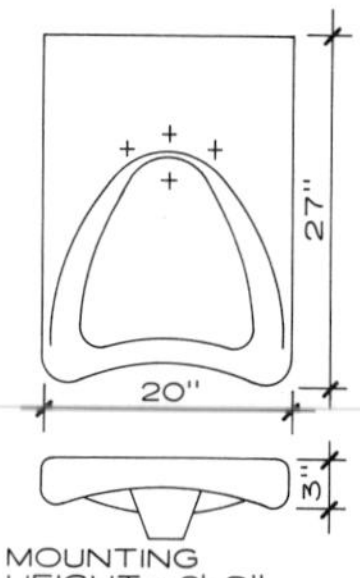
27"
20"
3"

MOUNTING HEIGHT = 2′-8″

WHEELCHAIR

	BACK				NO BACK		
	A	B	C	D	A	B	C
VIT. CH.	20"	16"	10"	8"	20"	22"	18"
	22"	19"	12"	10"	22"	24"	20"
	24"	22"	12"	12"			
C. I. EN.	20"	16"	12"	12"	16"	16"	10"
	22"	18"	12"	12"	20"	14"	12"
	22"	20"	12"	12"	20"	16"	12"
	24"	26"	12"	12"	22"	18"	12"
					24"	20"	12"
					30"	20"	12"
					36"	20"	12"
EARTHEN WARE	20"	18"	12"	8"			
	22"	20"	12"	8"			

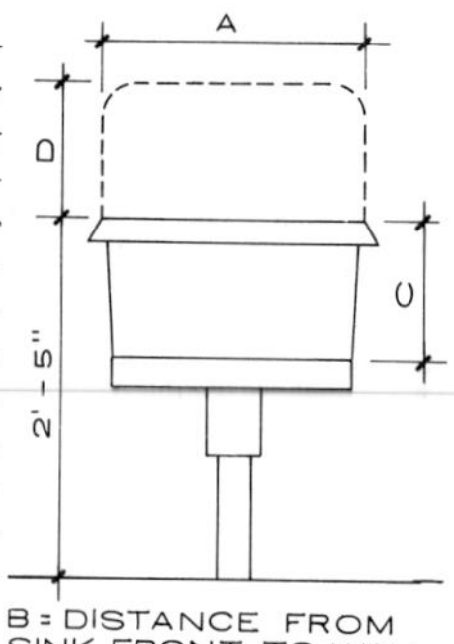
A
D
C
2'-5"

B = DISTANCE FROM SINK FRONT TO WALL

SERVICE SINKS

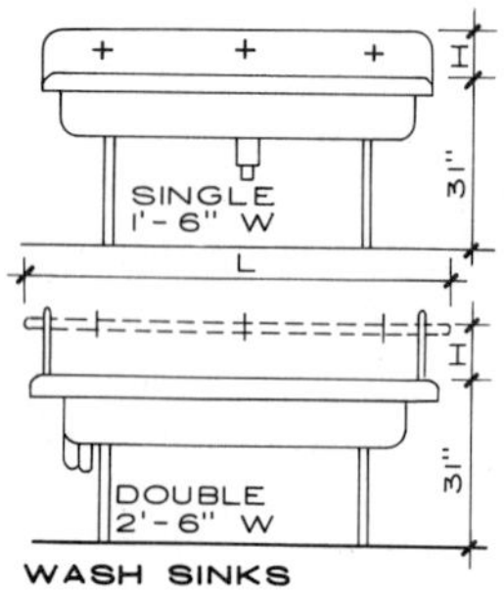
H
SINGLE
1'-6" W
31"
L
H
DOUBLE
2'-6" W
31"

L	FAUCETS SGL.	FAUCETS DBL.	H
4′ 0″	2	4	8″
5′ 0″	3	6	8″
6′ 0″	3	6	8″
8′ 0″	4	8	10″

Enameled C. I. only

WASH SINKS

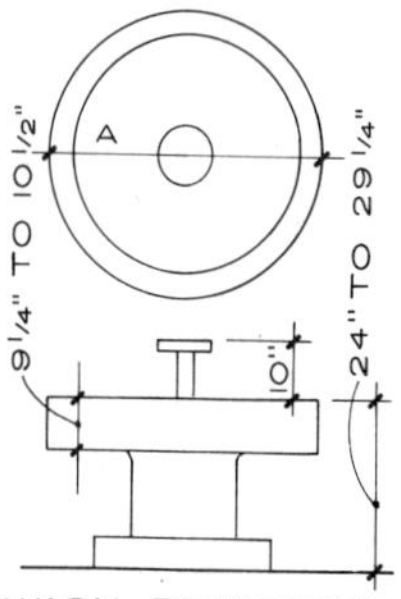
A
9 1/4" TO 10 1/2"
24" TO 29 1/4"
10"

A	SERVES
4′ 6″	8 to 10
4′ 0″*	8
3′ 0″	5 to 6

*Cast Iron only. Others in marble stone, stainless steel, also semicircular

WASH FOUNTAINS

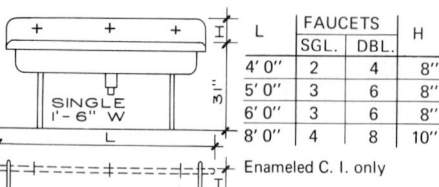

	20″ x 18″ VIT.CH.	24″ x 20″, 21″ VIT.CH.EN.C.I.
A	5′ 8″ or 6′ 2″	6′ 7″ or 7′ 2″
B	2′ 0″	2′ 4″
C	1′ 8″	1′ 10″ to 2′ 0″
D	3′ 2″ to 5′ 4″	3′ 6″ to 3′ 10″

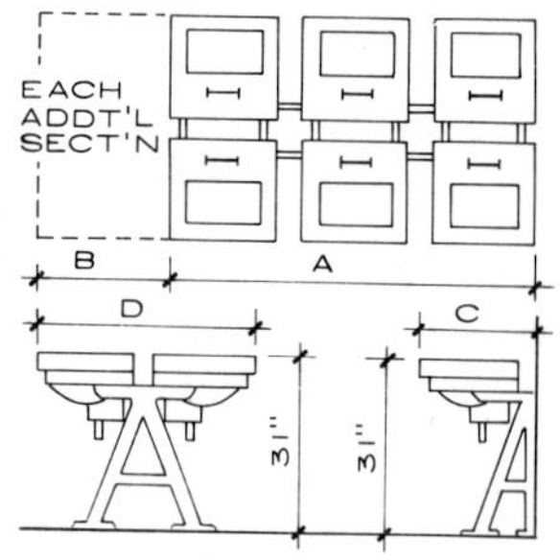
EACH ADDT'L SECT'N
B
A
D
C
31"
31"

BATTERY WASH SINKS

B. J. Baldwin; Giffels & Rossetti, Inc.; Detroit, Michigan

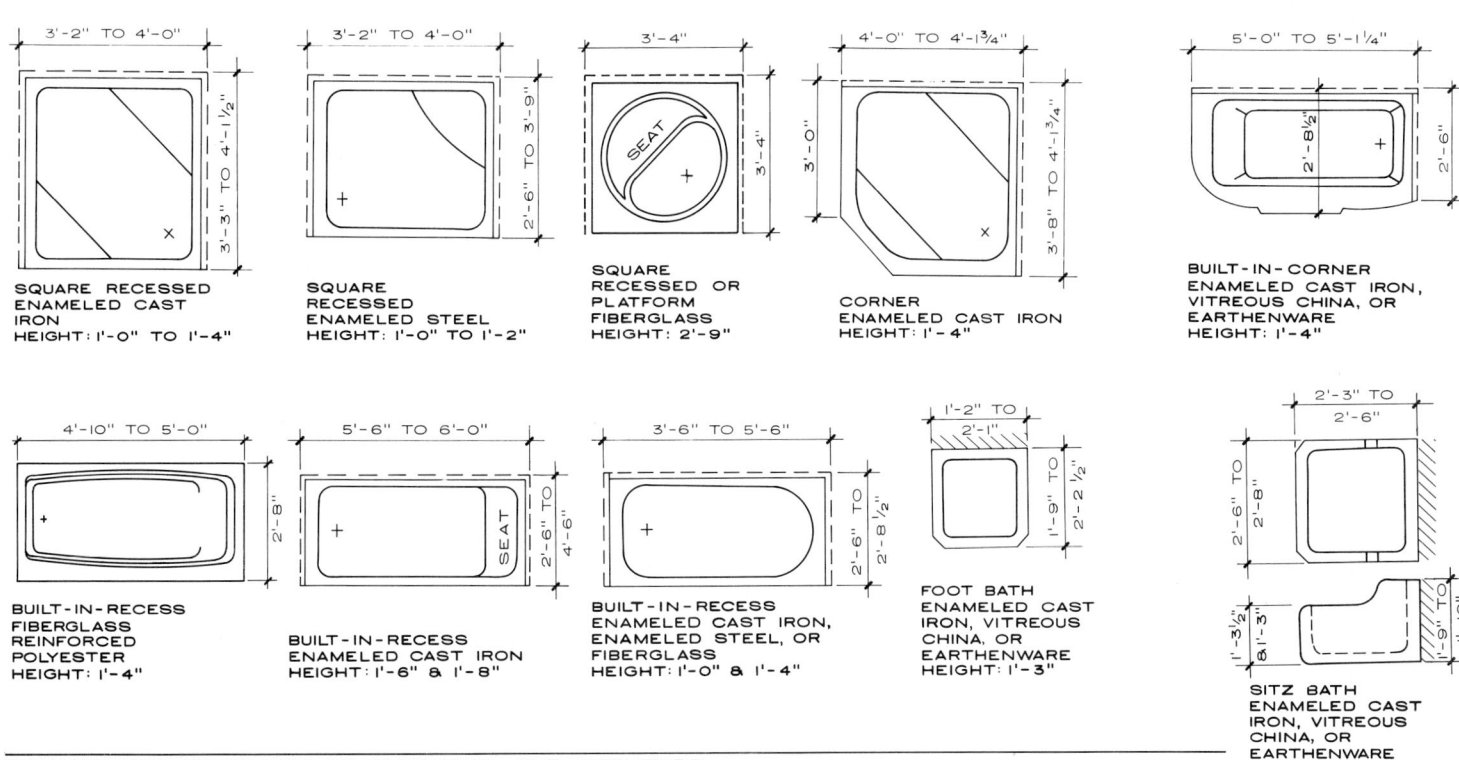

SQUARE RECESSED ENAMELED CAST IRON
HEIGHT: 1'-0" TO 1'-4"

SQUARE RECESSED ENAMELED STEEL
HEIGHT: 1'-0" TO 1'-2"

SQUARE RECESSED OR PLATFORM FIBERGLASS
HEIGHT: 2'-9"

CORNER ENAMELED CAST IRON
HEIGHT: 1'-4"

BUILT-IN-CORNER ENAMELED CAST IRON, VITREOUS CHINA, OR EARTHENWARE
HEIGHT: 1'-4"

BUILT-IN-RECESS FIBERGLASS REINFORCED POLYESTER
HEIGHT: 1'-4"

BUILT-IN-RECESS ENAMELED CAST IRON
HEIGHT: 1'-6" & 1'-8"

BUILT-IN-RECESS ENAMELED CAST IRON, ENAMELED STEEL, OR FIBERGLASS
HEIGHT: 1'-0" & 1'-4"

FOOT BATH ENAMELED CAST IRON, VITREOUS CHINA, OR EARTHENWARE
HEIGHT: 1'-3"

SITZ BATH ENAMELED CAST IRON, VITREOUS CHINA, OR EARTHENWARE

SQUARE AND RECTANGULAR SHOWERS AND BATHTUBS

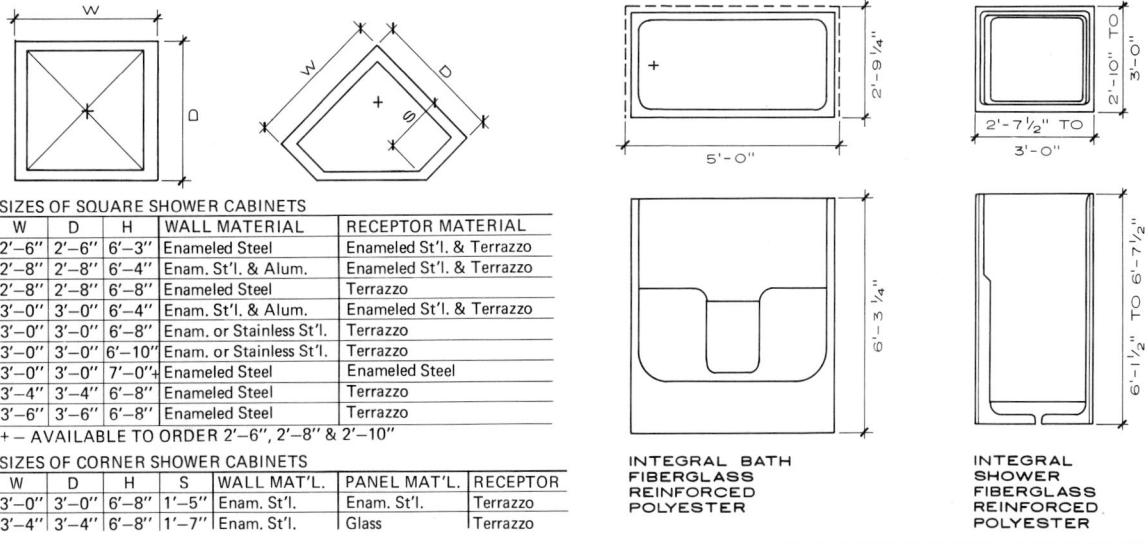

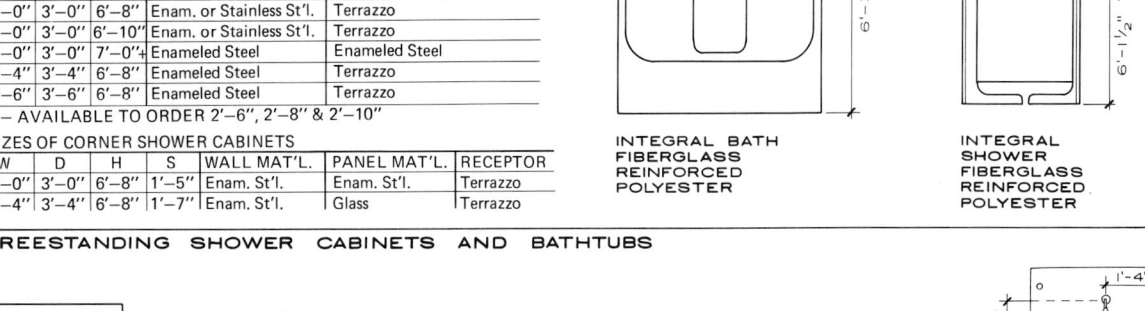

SIZES OF SQUARE SHOWER CABINETS

W	D	H	WALL MATERIAL	RECEPTOR MATERIAL
2'-6"	2'-6"	6'-3"	Enameled Steel	Enameled St'l. & Terrazzo
2'-8"	2'-8"	6'-4"	Enam. St'l. & Alum.	Enameled St'l. & Terrazzo
2'-8"	2'-8"	6'-8"	Enameled Steel	Terrazzo
3'-0"	3'-0"	6'-4"	Enam. St'l. & Alum.	Enameled St'l. & Terrazzo
3'-0"	3'-0"	6'-8"	Enam. or Stainless St'l.	Terrazzo
3'-0"	3'-0"	6'-10"	Enam. or Stainless St'l.	Terrazzo
3'-0"	3'-0"	7'-0"+	Enameled Steel	Enameled Steel
3'-4"	3'-4"	6'-8"	Enameled Steel	Terrazzo
3'-6"	3'-6"	6'-8"	Enameled Steel	Terrazzo

+ — AVAILABLE TO ORDER 2'-6", 2'-8" & 2'-10"

SIZES OF CORNER SHOWER CABINETS

W	D	H	S	WALL MAT'L.	PANEL MAT'L.	RECEPTOR
3'-0"	3'-0"	6'-8"	1'-5"	Enam. St'l.	Enam. St'l.	Terrazzo
3'-4"	3'-4"	6'-8"	1'-7"	Enam. St'l.	Glass	Terrazzo

INTEGRAL BATH FIBERGLASS REINFORCED POLYESTER

INTEGRAL SHOWER FIBERGLASS REINFORCED POLYESTER

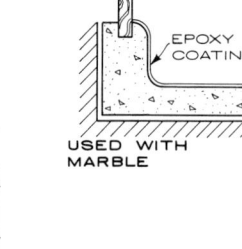

USED FOR HANDICAPPED

SECTION THRU THRESHOLD

EPOXY COATING

USED WITH MARBLE

FREESTANDING SHOWER CABINETS AND BATHTUBS

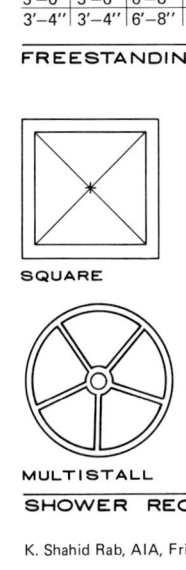

SQUARE

CORNER

MULTISTALL

Wedge Shaped Stalls Grouped in 2's, 3's, 4's, 5's & 6's, with 6'-0" Standard Ht., 5'-6" Intermediate Ht. & 5'-0" Junior Ht.

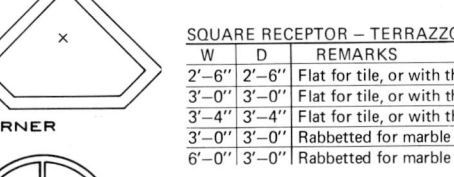

SQUARE RECEPTOR – TERRAZZO

W	D	REMARKS
2'-6"	2'-6"	Flat for tile, or with threshold
3'-0"	3'-0"	Flat for tile, or with threshold
3'-4"	3'-4"	Flat for tile, or with threshold
3'-0"	3'-0"	Rabbetted for marble wall
6'-0"	3'-0"	Rabbetted for marble wall

CORNER RECEPTOR – TERRAZZO

W	D	REMARKS
3'-0"	3'-0"	Flat for tile, or with threshold
3'-4"	3'-4"	Flat for tile, or with threshold

SHOWER RECEPTOR TYPES

PLAN SHOWING FOLDING SHOWER SEAT

ELEVATION OF PLUMBING WALL

FOLDING SEAT ON OPPOSITE WALL

SHOWER USED BY HANDICAPPED

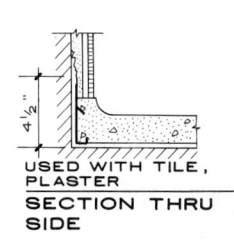

USED WITH TILE, PLASTER

SECTION THRU SIDE

NOTE
Adequate waterproofing should be added to each of the sections.

K. Shahid Rab, AIA, Friesen International; Washington, D.C.

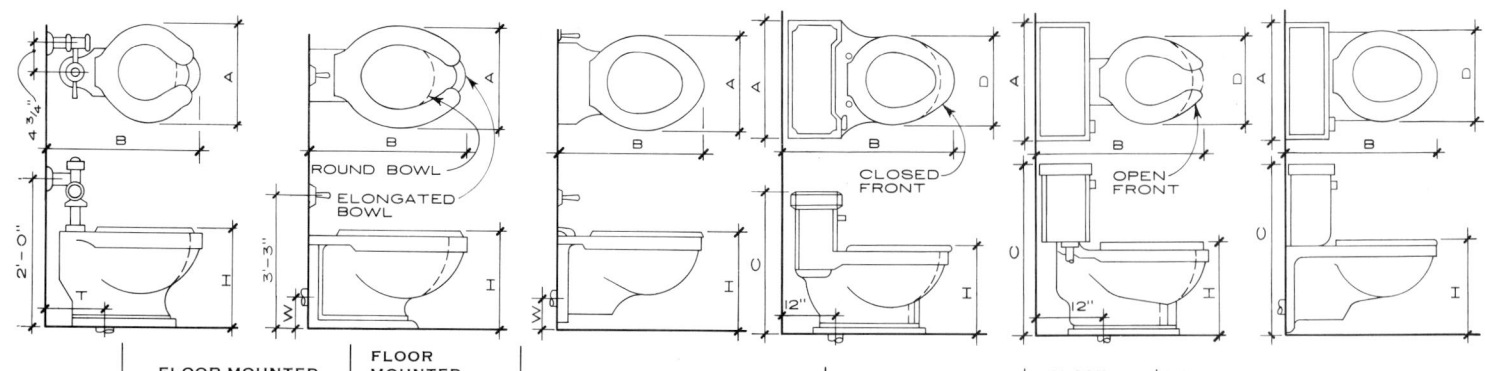

	FLOOR MOUNTED BOTTOM OUTLET			FLOOR MOUNTED BACK OUTLET		WALL HUNG	
	SJ	WD	BO	SJ	BO	SJ	BO
A	14″	14″	14″	14″	14″	14″	14″
Round B	24″	27″		20 1/8″			
Elongated	24 1/2″ or 26 1/2″		26 1/4″	25 1/2″ to 26″	21 1/2″	21 1/2″ to 25 3/4″	24 1/4″ to 26″
H	14″ to 14 3/4″ 10″* 17″† to 19″	15″	15″	14 1/2″ to 15″	15″	15″	15″ to 15 3/4″
W				4 1/4″ or 4 1/2″	10 1/4″	4″ to 5 1/2″	11 1/2″ to 12 1/4″
T	10″ or 12″	12″ to 14″	9″	9″ or 10″	9″ or 10″		

*For children.
†For handicapped.

	ONE PIECE			CLOSE COUPLED		WALL HUNG
	SV	SJ	SA	SJ	RT	SJ
A	20 3/4″ to 22″	20 5/8″ to 23 3/4″	20 3/4″ to 21″	20 7/8″ to 21 1/2″	17″ to 20 7/8″	20 7/8″ to 23 3/4″
Round B	27 3/4″	24 3/4″	27 3/4″	27 1/2″ to 29″	22″ to 27 5/8″	26 1/2″ to 29 3/4″
Elongated	29 1/4″	28 1/2″ to 29″	28 1/2″ to 29 3/4″	29 1/8″ to 29 7/8″		28 1/4″
C	20″ to 23 3/4″	18 3/4″ to 20 1/2″	18 3/4″ to 19 1/2″	26 1/8″ to 31 7/8″	28 1/4″ to 31″	29″ to 29 1/2″
D	14 3/4″ to 15 1/2″	14 3/4″ to 15 1/2″	14 3/4″ to 15 1/2″	14 3/4″ to 15 1/2″	14 3/4″ to 15 1/2″	14 3/4″ to 15 1/2″
H	14″	14″ to 15″	14 1/2″	14″ 17″† to 19″ 10″*	14 1/2″ to 15″	15″

NOTE: Dimensions include seat. For closed front seats, add 1 in. to B. With seat cover, add 3/4 in. to height. All fixtures are of vitreous china except where noted. For concealed carrier wall hung, allow 10 1/2 in. minimum from back of closet to outside edge of soil pipe.

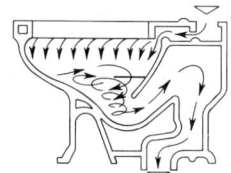

SIPHON - VORTEX (S-V) Quiet, extremely sanitary. Water directed through rim to create vortex. Scours bowl. Folds over into jet; siphon.

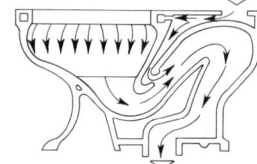

SIPHON - JET (S-J)
SIPHON - ACTION (S-A) Sanitary, efficient, very quiet. Water enters through rim and siphons in down leg.

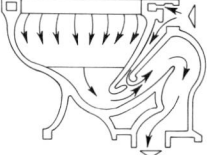

REVERSE - TRAP (R-T) Similar to siphon-jet except that trap passageway and water surface area are smaller, moderately noisy.

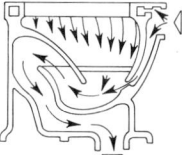

WASH - DOWN (W-D) Minimum cost. Least efficient, subject to clogging, noisy. Simple washout action through small irregular passageway.

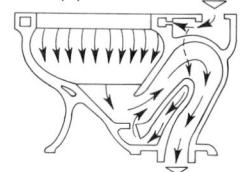

BLOWOUT (BO) Noisy but highly efficient. Strong jet into up leg forces contents out. Use with FV only. Higher pressure required.

WATER CLOSETS

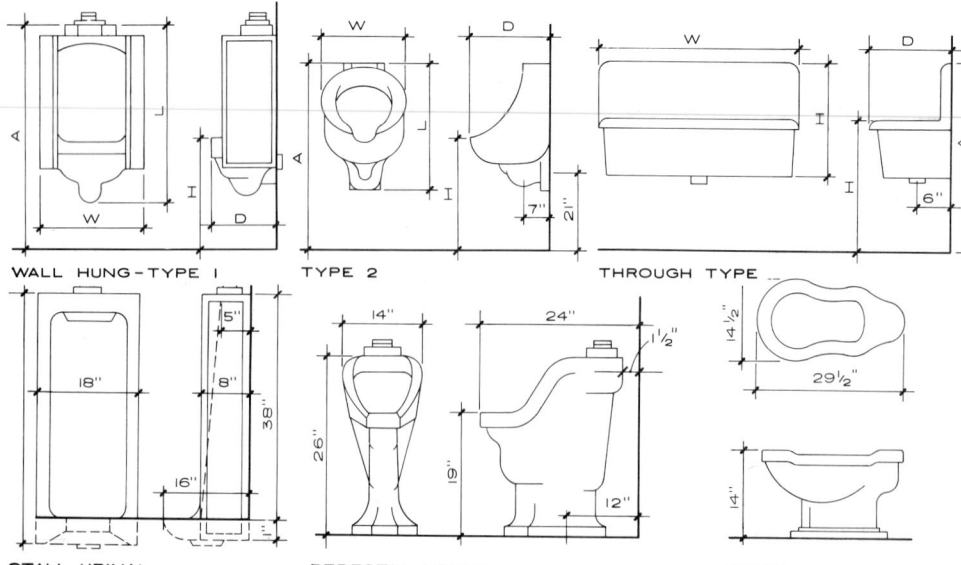

WALL HUNG - TYPE I   TYPE 2   THROUGH TYPE

STALL URINAL   PEDESTAL URINAL   BIDET

	TYPE 1 (SJ, WD, BO)	TYPE 2			THROUGH TYPE
		SJ	BO	WD	
A	35″, 42 1/2″	35 1/2″ to 37 1/8″	26 1/2″ to 27″	34 1/2″ to 37 1/8″	32″- 34″
W	13″, 18″	13″ to 14 1/4″	14″	12 3/4″ to 14 1/4″	36″, 48″, 60″, 72″
L	18″ to 30″	17″ to 20″	17″ to 20″	17″ to 20″	16″, 17 3/4″, 18 3/4″
D	11 3/4″ to 13 1/4″	11 1/4″ to 14″	11 1/2″ to 14″	12 7/8″ to 14″	14″, 18″
H	24″	24″, 17″*, 19″*			24″

*For handicapped.

NOTE: Provide minimum 4 in. clear pipe chase for urinal piping and support.

BATTERY STALLS
Stall urinals available with seam covers for battery installation on 1′- 9″ or 2′- 0″ centers.

URINALS AND BIDETS

K. Shahid Rab, AIA; Friesen International; Washington, D.C.

B. J. Baldwin; Giffels & Rossetti, Inc.; Detroit, Michigan

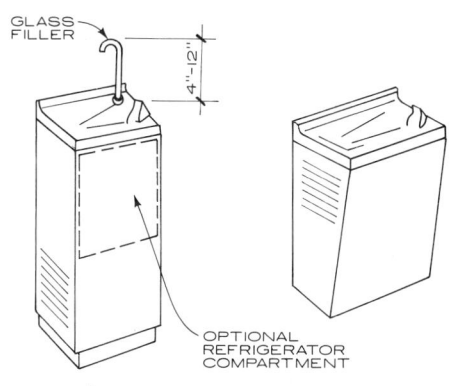
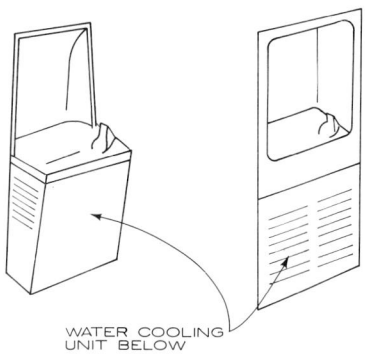
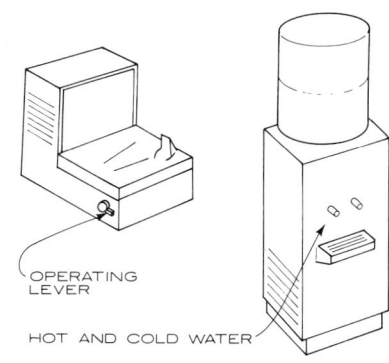

FLOOR MOUNTED (IN.) FLUSH TO WALL OR FREESTANDING				WALL MOUNTED (IN.)				SEMIRECESSED (IN.)				FULLY RECESSED (IN.)				HANDICAPPED (IN.)				BOTTLE TYPE (IN.)			
H	W	D	GPH	H	W	D	GPH	H	W	D	GPH	H	W	D	GPH	H	W	D	GPH	H	W	D	GPH
30½	15	15	7-12	16	17	13¼	2-5	35¾	17	13½	11-17	50¼	18	12	8-14	5	14	20	5-20	36	12	12	1
33½	18	14½	4-20	22	18	14½	4-14	37½	16½	14½	7-15	54¼	19	12¼	7-12	7	15	21	20-100	40	14	14	2
40	12	12	3-10	26	17	14	5-15	39¾	18	13½	7-12	55¼	21	13	5-10	25	18	18½	7-9	44	17	14	1
41½	18	14½	4-20	29½	18	14½	4-20	44¼	17¼	14	5-13					28	17¼	18½	7-10				

SELF-CONTAINED WATER COOLERS

Air cooled condensers are used for normal room temperatures; water cooled units for high room temperatures and larger capacities. Many fountain models are available with cold and hot water supply, a glass filler attachment, or refrigerated compartments. There is a wide selection of colors and finishes to choose from.

Floor and wall mounted fountains are made in lower heights for children's use and can be mounted low on the side of regular height models.

Recommended fountain rim heights, above the floor:

1. 40 in. adults.
2. 30 in. children.
3. 34-36 in. handicapped.

Special explosionproof fountains are recommended for use in hazardous atmospheres. Corrosion resistant fountains are available as well as a water cooled type for excessively hot and dusty atmospheres.

Power requirements are 110, 115, 230 V; 50 to 60 cycles, single phase AC; otherwise a transformer is used.

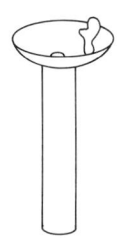
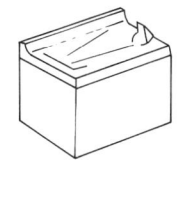
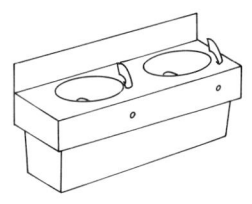
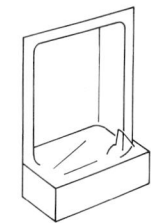
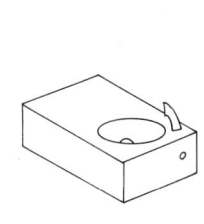
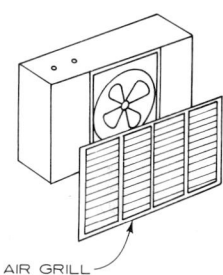

PEDESTAL DISH (IN.)			WALL MOUNTED (IN.)				TWO STATION (IN.)				SEMIRECESSED OR FULLY RECESSED (IN.)				HANDICAPPED (IN.)				REMOTE PACKAGE COOLER (IN.)			
H	D	SUPPLY/WASTE	H	W	D	SUPPLY/WASTE	H	W	D	SUPPLY/WASTE	H	W	D	SUPPLY/WASTE	H	W	D	SUPPLY/WASTE	H	W	D	GPH
38¼	4	¼, 1½	7¾	10	10	⅜, 1¼	6	39	11¼	½, 1½	27¾	17½	13	⅜, 1¼	6	12	20	½, 1¼	16¼	15¾	8	5-6
38¼	14¼	¼, 1½	16	17	13¼	⅜, 1¼	15	31	14	½, 1½	29	21	13	⅜, 1¼	7	15	21	⅜, 1¼	22¼	30	6½	6-10

DRINKING FOUNTAINS (FOR USE WITH REMOTE STORAGE COOLERS)

DRINKING WATER REQUIREMENTS

TYPE OF SERVICE	GPH PER PERSON	
	CUP	BUBBLER
Offices, schools, cafeterias, hotels (per room), hospitals (per bed and per attendant)	0.033	0.083
Restaurants	0.04	0.1
Light manufacturing	0.0573	0.143
Heavy manufacturing	0.08	0.20
Hot, heavy manufacturing	0.10	0.25
Theaters per 100 seats	0.4 gph/100 seats	1.0 gph/100 seats
Department stores, lobbies, hotel and office buildings	1.6-2.0 gph/fountain	4-5 gph/fountain

Wm. G. Miner, AIA, Architect, Washington, D.C.

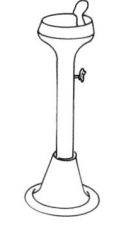
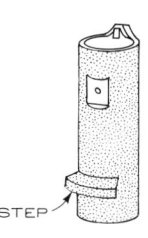
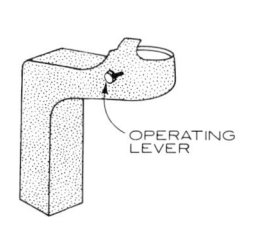
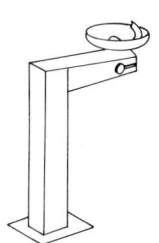

PEDESTAL (IN.)			CONCRETE CYLINDER (IN.)			CONCRETE HANDICAPPED (IN.)			PROJECTING PEDESTAL (IN.)		
H	DIA.	SUPPLY/WASTE	H	DIA.	SUPPLY/WASTE	H	L	SUPPLY/WASTE	H	L	SUPPLY/WASTE
36	12	⅜, 1	36	12	½, 1¼	33	30¾	½, 1¼	33	29¾	½, 1¼

OUTDOOR TYPE FOUNTAINS

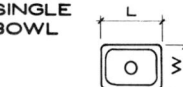

SINGLE BOWL

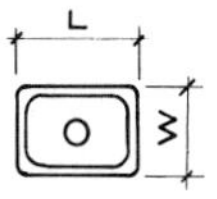

STAINLESS STEEL

	MIN.	MAX.	OTHER
L	11½	33	12½ → 31
W	13	22⅜	14 → 22¼
D	5½	12	6 → 7½

PORCELAIN ENAMELED STEEL

	MIN.	MAX.	OTHER
L	24	30	
W	21		
D	7⅜	8⅛	

ENAMELED CAST IRON

	MIN.	MAX.	OTHER
L	12	30	
W	12	21	18 → 20
D	6	8	6½ → 7½

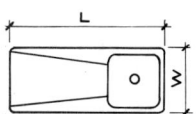

SINGLE BOWL & DRAINBOARD
(RIGHT OR LEFT)

STAINLESS STEEL

	MIN.	MAX.	OTHER
L	33	48	43
W	21	25	
D	7	7½	

ENAMELED CAST IRON

	MIN.	MAX.	OTHER
L	42	72	
W	20	25	24
D	6	8	6½ → 7½

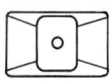

SINGLE BOWL DOUBLE DRAINBOARD

STAINLESS STEEL

	MIN.	MAX.	OTHER
L	54	72	60
W	22	25	
D	7	7½	

ENAMELED CAST IRON

	MIN.	MAX.	OTHER
L	54	72	
W	21	25	24
D	6	8	6½ → 7½

DOUBLE BOWL

STAINLESS STEEL

	MIN.	MAX.	OTHER
L	28	46	30 → 42
W	16	22	17 → 21¼
D	5	10	6½ → 7½

PORCELAIN ENAMELED

	MIN.	MAX.	OTHER
L	32		
W	21		
D	7	8⅛	

ENAMELED CAST IRON STEEL

	MIN.	MAX.	OTHER
L	32	42	
W	20	25	
D	6	8	6½ → 7½

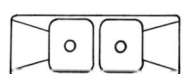

DOUBLE BOWL & DRAINBOARD

STAINLESS STEEL

	MIN.	MAX.	OTHER
L	60	72	66
W	21	25	
D	7	7½	

ENAMELED CAST IRON

	MIN.	MAX.	OTHER
L	54	72	60
W	24	25	
D	6	8	6½ → 7½

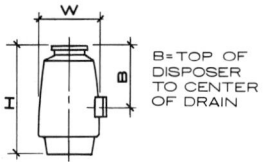

B=TOP OF DISPOSER TO CENTER OF DRAIN

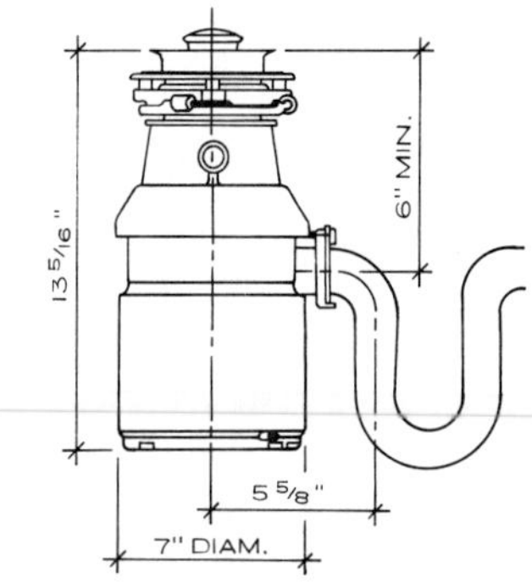

GARBAGE DISPOSER

	MIN.	MAX.	OTHER
W	6¼	10⅛	7⅜ → 9½
B	6	9⅜	6⅝ → 8¾
H	12¾	9 3/16	12⅝ → 16

GARBAGE DISPOSER UNITS

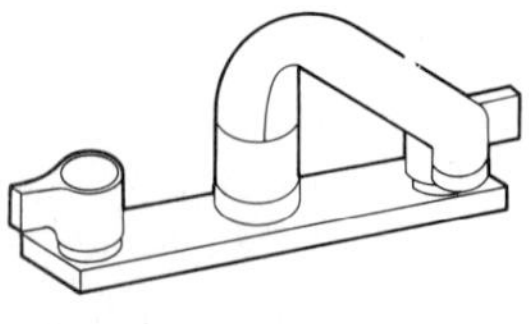

TRIPLE BOWL

STAINLESS STEEL

	MIN.	MAX.	OTHER
L	43	54	45
W	22		
D	5	7½	

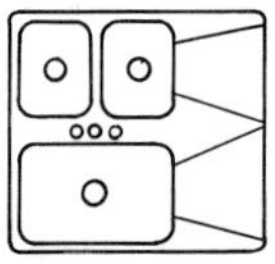

TRIPLE BOWL & DRAIN BOARD (ISLAND)

STAINLESS STEEL

	MIN.	MAX.	OTHER
L	54½	57	
W	40½		
D	4	7½	

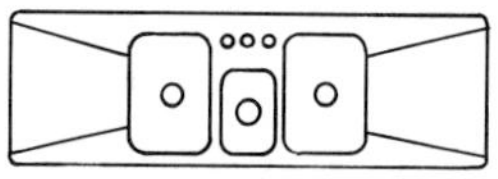

TRIPLE BOWL & DOUBLE DRAINBOARD

STAINLESS STEEL

	MIN.	MAX.	OTHER
L	84		
W	25		
D	7½		

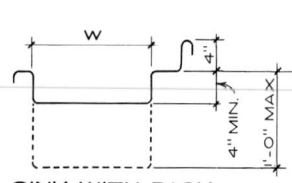

13 5/16"

6" MIN.

5 ⅝"

7" DIAM.

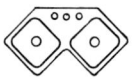

CORNER BOWL

STAINLESS STEEL

	MIN.	MAX.	OTHER
L	31⅞	32½	
W	31⅞	32½	
D	7	7½	

BAR SINK

STAINLESS STEEL

	MIN.	MAX.	OTHER
L	14	16¼	15
W	14	20¼	15
D	6	7⅜	6

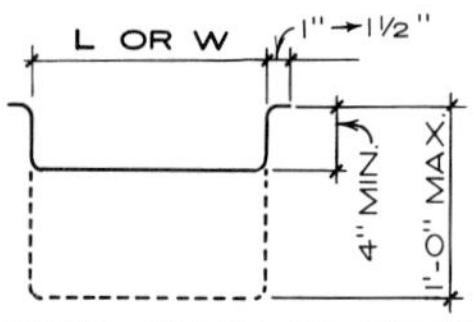

L OR W   1" → 1½"

4" MIN.

1'-0" MAX

SINK WITH FLAT RIM

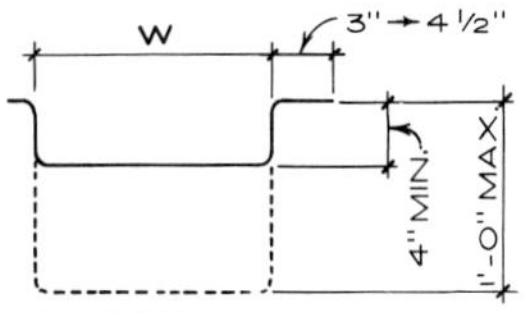

W   3" → 4½"

4" MIN.

1'-0" MAX

SINK WITH BACK LEDGE

W   4"

4" MIN.

1'-0" MAX

SINK WITH BACK LEDGE & BACKSPLASH

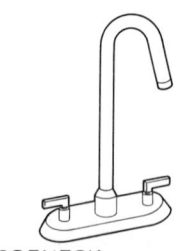

NOTES

All dimensions shown on this page are in inches.

Consult manufacturers' literature for variations in bowl finish and available accessories, such as cup strainer, spray head, cutting boards, and trim.

See pages on handicapped accessibility for suggested modifications to mounting height and cabinetry.

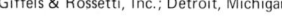

WASHER TYPE   WASHERLESS   GOOSENECK

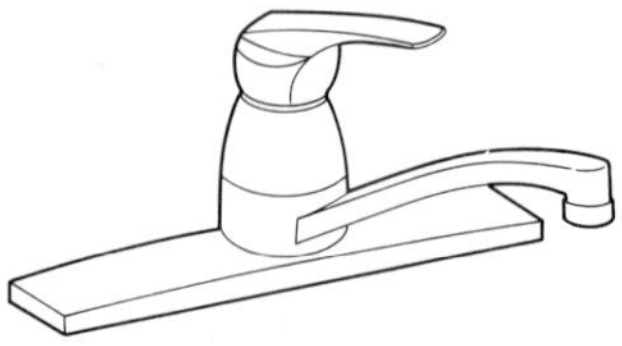

KITCHEN FAUCETS

Giffels & Rossetti, Inc.; Detroit, Michigan

15   PLUMBING FIXTURES

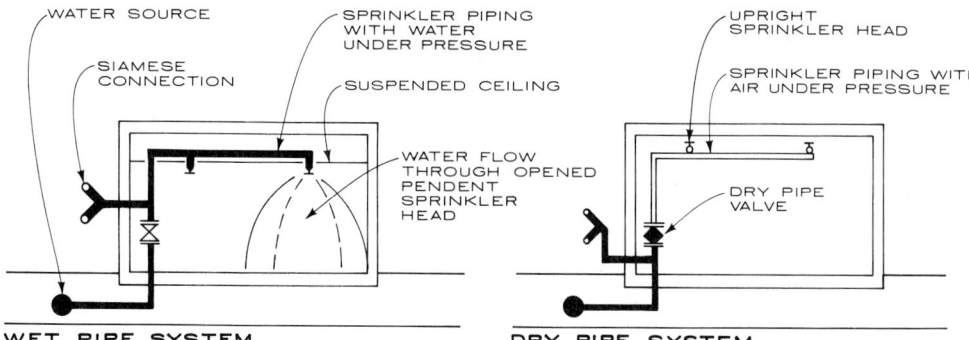

WET PIPE SYSTEM

DRY PIPE SYSTEM

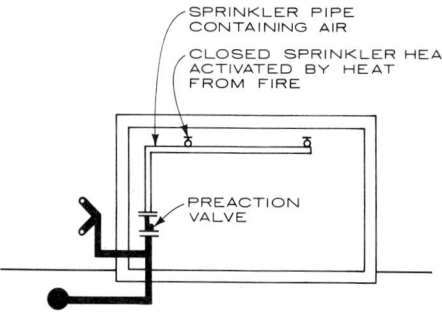

PREACTION SYSTEM

DELUGE SYSTEM

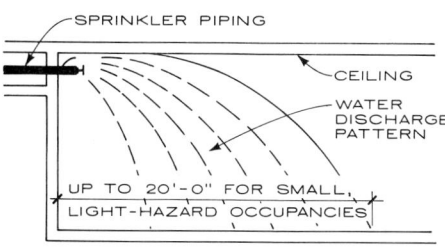

SIDEWALL SPRINKLER HEAD
(HORIZONTAL SIDEWALL SHOWN)

PENDENT SPRINKLER HEAD

Piping can be unobtrusively installed along sides of exposed ceiling beams or joists. In small rooms, sidewall heads provide water discharge coverage without overhead piping.

Can be recessed in ceiling (e.g., coffered, modeled) or hidden above flat metal cover plate. (Flush sprinkler heads are also available.)

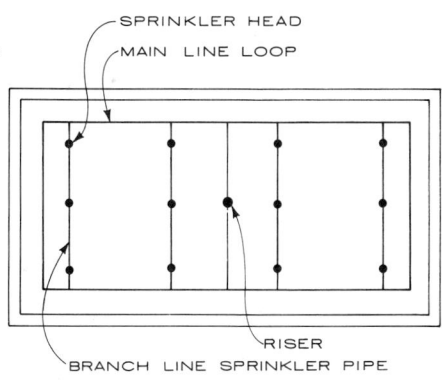

HYDRAULICALLY DESIGNED SPRINKLER SYSTEM LAYOUT

Loop provides water flow from two directions to operating sprinkler heads so pipe sizes will be small. Hydraulic calculations can assure delivery of adequate water flow and pressure throughout piping network to meet design requirements.

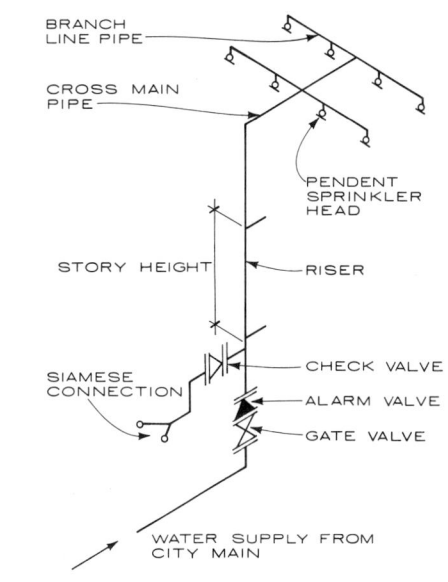

SPRINKLER SYSTEM RISER

M. David Egan, P.E.; College of Architecture; Clemson University; Clemson, South Carolina

TYPES OF SYSTEMS

WET PIPE: Piping network contains water under pressure at all times for immediate release through sprinkler heads as they are activated by heat from fire. Wet pipe system is the most widely used system, since water delivery here is faster than with a dry pipe system.

DRY PIPE: Piping network contains air (or nitrogen) under pressure. Following loss of air pressure through opened sprinkler head, dry pipe valve opens allowing water to enter piping network and to flow through opened sprinkler head (or heads). Used where piping is subject to freezing.

PREACTION: Closed head, dry system containing air in piping network. Preaction valve is activated by independent fire detection system more sensitive than sprinkler heads. The opened preaction valve allows water to fill piping network and to flow through sprinkler heads, as they are activated by heat from fire. Used where leakage or accidental discharge would cause serious damage.

DELUGE: Sprinkler heads (or spray nozzles) are open at all times and normally there is no water in piping network. Mechanical or hydraulic valves, operated by heat, smoke, or flame sensitive devices, are used to control water flow to heads by opening water control clapper. Deluge systems are special use systems, as water discharges from all heads (or nozzles) at the same time.

STANDPIPE AND HOSE: Dry standpipes are empty water pipes used by fire fighters to connect hoses in buildings to water sources such as ground level fire hydrants. Wet standpipes are water filled pipes permanently connected to public or private water mains for use by building occupants on small fires or by fire fighters.

FOAM: Used to suppress flammable liquid fires. Foam can be distributed by piping network to nozzles or other discharge outlets (e.g., tubes, troughs, chutes) depending on the hazard.

HALON (halogenated hydrocarbon): Can be used where water damage to building contents would be unacceptable. Piping network connects fixed supply of halon to nozzles that discharge uniform, low concentration throughout room. To avoid piping network, discharge cylinders may be installed throughout room or area. Though generally nontoxic, delayed discharge can cause problems by allowing decomposition of halon. Rapid detection is necessary.

CO_2 (carbon dioxide): Does not conduct electricity and leaves no residue after its use. Piping network connects fixed supply of CO_2 to nozzles that discharge CO_2 directly on burning materials where location of fire hazard is known (called "local application") or discharge CO_2 uniformly throughout room (called "total flooding"). In total flooding systems, safety requirements dictate advance alarm to allow occupants to evacuate area prior to discharge.

DRY CHEMICAL: Can be especially useful on electrical and flammable liquid fires. Powdered extinguishing agent, under pressure of dry air or nitrogen, commonly discharged over cooking surfaces (e.g., frying).

PREPARATION FOR SPRINKLER SYSTEMS

1. Begin planning sprinkler system at the very earliest design stages of project.
2. Determine hazard classification of building and type of system best suited for suppression needs.
3. Refer to national standards (NFPA), state and local codes.
4. Check with authority having jurisdiction:
   a. State and local fire marshals.
   b. Insurance Services Office (ISO).
   c. Insurance underwriting groups such as IRI, OIA, or FM (if they have jurisdiction).
5. Use qualified engineers to design system. Be sure water supply is adequate (e.g., by water flow tests). Integrate system with structural, mechanical, and other building services.
6. Check space requirements for sprinkler equipment. Sprinkler control room must be heated to prevent freezing of equipment.
7. Consider possible future alterations to building.

FIRE CLASSIFICATION

CLASS Ⓐ

Incipient fires on which quenching or the cooling effect of water is of primary importance. Fires of wood, paper, textile, and rubbish.

CLASS Ⓑ

Incipient fires on which blanketing or smothering effect of extinguishing is of primary importance. Fires of gasoline, oil, grease, and fat.

CLASS Ⓒ

Incipient fires in electrical equipment where a non-conducting extinguishing agent is needed.

OCCUPANCY CLASSIFICATION

Light hazard occupancies (schools, offices, and public buildings) require one unit of extinguishing capacity for every 3000 sq ft of floor area for use on Class A fires.

Ordinary hazard occupancies (dry goods shops and warehouses) require one unit of extinguishing capacity for every 1500 sq ft of floor space for use on Class A fires.

Extra hazard occupancies (paint shops, etc.) require one unit of extinguishing capacity for every 1000 sq ft of floor area for use on Class A fires.

Class A fire extinguishers, regardless of occupancy, shall be located so that maximum travel distance from any point to the nearest extinguisher is less than 75 ft.

The maximum travel distance to a Class B extinguisher is 50 ft (smaller rated extinguishers shall be placed no more than 30 ft from the hazard).

NOTES

1. These classifications are taken from the National Fire Protection Association, Publication #10, Portable Extinguishers, 1978.
2. In all cases check the requirements of local codes.

WATER BASE EXTINGUISHERS

	PRESSURIZED	CARTRIDGE	PUMP TANK		LOADED STREAM
	CLASS A ONLY	**CLASS A ONLY**	**CLASS A ONLY**		**CLASS A & B**
Capacity (gal)	2¹/₂	2¹/₂	2¹/₂	5	2¹/₂
Height	25″	25″	26″	28″	27″
Diameter	8″	8″	8″	11″	8″
Weight (lb)	28	26	36	55	42
Class	2A	2A	2A	4A	2A, ¹/₂B
Recharge	Weigh cylinder and check annually. In all cases, follow instructions on extinguisher label				
Effective range	45-55 ft		30-40 ft		35-40 ft
Pressure source	Compressed air	Gas cartridge	Hand pump		Pressure
Temperature effect	Will freeze	Will freeze	Will freeze		Will operate at –40°F
Method of extinguishing	Quenches, cools	Quenches, cools	Quenches, cools		Alkametal salt quenches, cools, and fireproofs

NOTE: All water base extinguishing agents are electrical conductors.

Dimensions below are for three makes of extinguisher to show relative sizes

CARBON DIOXIDE

CLASS B & C FIRES

CAPACITY (LB)	2¹/₂	5	10	15	20
Height	18″	17″	22″	26″	26″
Diameter	4″	6″	7″	7″	8″
Weight (lb)	10	18	35	44	55
Class	2 B, C	2 B, C	5 B, C	10 B, C	10 B, C
Height	16″	15″	26″	30″	37″
Diameter	7″	10″	13″	12″	11″
Weight (lb)	12	17	34	44	55
Class	2 B, C	5 B, C	10 B, C	10 B, C	10 B, C
Height	18″	17″	26″	33″	33″
Diameter	9″	9″	11″	11″	12″
Weight (lb)	9	17	34	42	55
Class	2 B, C	5 B, C	10 B, C	10 B, C	10 B, C

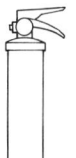

PRESSURIZED

HALOGENATED AGENT

CLASS B & C FIRES

CAPACITY (LB)	2¹/₂	5
Height	14″	15″
Diameter	3″	3¹/₂″
Weight (lb)	7¹/₂	9¹/₂
Class	5 B, C	10 B, C
Height	15″	15¹/₂″
Diameter	3″	4¹/₂″
Weight (lb)	5	10
Class	5 B, C	10 B, C

Dimensions below are for two makes of extinguisher to show relative sizes

DRY CHEMICAL

CLASS A, B, & C

CAPACITY (LB)	5	10	20	30
Height	19″	21″	22″	30″
Diameter	5″	6″	8″	8″
Weight (lb)	15	33	48	70
Class	2A,10B,C	2A,20B,C	2A,80B,C	2A,80B,C
Height	13″	22″	21″	25″
Diameter	5″	7″	9″	9″
Weight (lb)	12	21	35	50
Class	2A,10B,C	2A,20B,C	2A,80B,C	2A,80B,C

EFFECTIVE RANGE
3 to 8 ft
DISCHARGE TIME
2¹/₂ lb, 12 sec; 5 lb, 22 sec; 10 lb, 23 sec; 15 lb, 26 sec; 20 lb, 25 sec
RECHARGE
after use
PRESSURE SOURCE
compressed gas
TEMPERATURE EFFECT
will operate at minus 40°F
ELECTRICAL CONDUCTIVITY
will not conduct

EFFECTIVE RANGE
25 to 30 ft
DISCHARGE TIME
2¹/₂ lb, 11 sec; 5 lb, 11 sec
RECHARGE
after use
PRESSURE SOURCE
pump or pressurized
TEMPERATURE EFFECT
will operate at minus 40°F
ELECTRICAL CONDUCTIVITY
will not conduct

EFFECTIVE RANGE
10 to 20 ft
DISCHARGE TIME
5 lb, 10 sec; 10 lb, 11 sec; 20 lb, 15 sec; 30 lb, 34 sec
RECHARGE
after use
PRESSURE SOURCE
compressed gas
TEMPERATURE EFFECT
will operate at minus 40°F
ELECTRICAL CONDUCTIVITY
will not conduct

Wm. G. Miner, AIA, Architect; Washington, D.C.

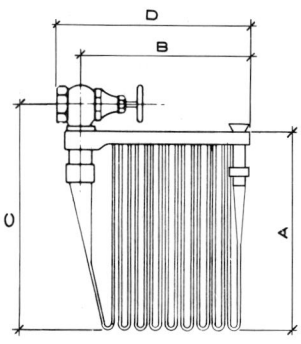

SWING RACK SEMIAUTOMATIC
1½" LINED HOSE

HOSE CAPACITY	25	50	75	100
A	10"	20"	24"	27"
B	15"	16"	19"	20"
C	14"	23"	27"	32"
D	17"	18"	20"	22"
WIDTH	4"	4"	4"	4"

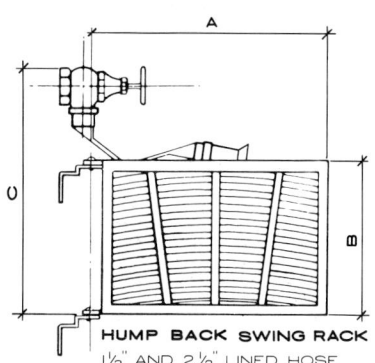

HUMP BACK SWING RACK
1½" AND 2½" LINED HOSE

HOSE CAPACITY	50	100	150	200
A	30"	30"	34"	40"
B	17"	21"	28"	39"
C	30"	33"	40"	50"
WIDTH 1½" HOSE	4"	4"	4"	4"
WIDTH 2½" HOSE	6"	6"	6"	6"

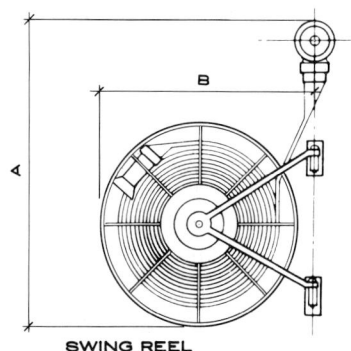

SWING REEL
1½" AND 2½" LINED HOSE

HOSE CAPACITY	50	100	150
A	38"	38"	36"
B	21"	27"	31"
WIDTH 1½" HOSE	4"	4"	4"
WIDTH 2½" HOSE	6"	6"	6"

FIRE HOSE RACK AND REELS

NOTE

Recommended hose size for use with building standpipes should not exceed 1½ in. in diameter and 100 ft in length. A larger hose used by amateurs is likely to tangle, cause excessive water damage, and create injuries.

A connection for 2½ in. hose should be available to each station for the use of firemen. Many codes require 2½ in. outlets at all standpipes.

By using a reducing coupling 1½ in. hose can be attached. When a 2½ in. stream is required the coupling may be removed. Industrial installations use 2½ in. hoses and train personnel in the use of the heavier equipment. Valves may be located 5 ft 6 in. above floor (check local code).

Lined synthetic fiber plastic hose is recommended for use on standpipe installations. Cotton rubber lined hose is standard for fire department and heavy equipment hose.

Tables show rack and reels for 1½ and 2½ in. lined hose only. Consult manufacturer's literature for rack and reel dimensions when other types and sizes of hose are used.

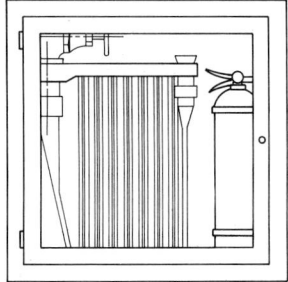

75' 1½" LINED HOSE, RACK, AND ANGLE VALVE; 2½ GAL EXTINGUISHER
2'-9" x 2'-9" x 8½" TO 2'-11" x 2'-11" x 9"

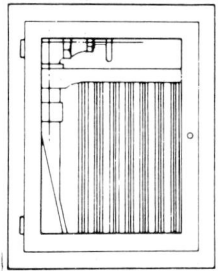

75' 1½" LINED HOSE, RACK, AND ANGLE VALVE
1'-9" x 2'-5" x 8" TO 1'-4" x 2'-7" x 8½"

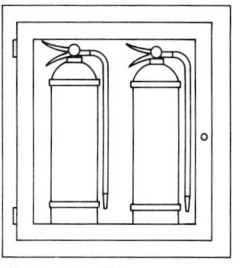

TWO 2½ GAL EXTINGUISHERS
1'-11"X2'-9"X7" TO 2'-2"X2'-11"X8"

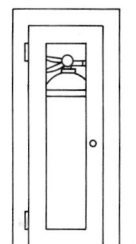

ONE 2½ GAL EXTINGUISHER
1'-0"X 2'-6"X8" TO 1'-4"X2'-7"X8½"
NOTE: RESIDENTIAL EXTINGUISHER CABINET 1'-5"X 7"X2"

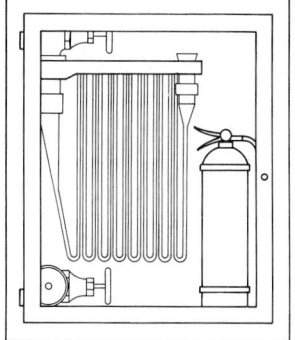

75' 1½" LINED HOSE AND RACK; 1½" AND 2½" ANGLE VALVE; 2½ GAL EXTINGUISHER
2'-9" x 3'-4" x 8½" TO 2'-10" x 3'-7" x 9"

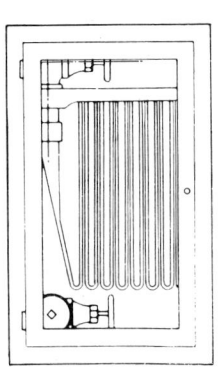

75' 1½" LINED HOSE AND RACK; 1½" AND 2½" ANGLE VALVE
1'-11" x 3'-3" x 8½" TO 2'-4" x 3'-4" x 9"

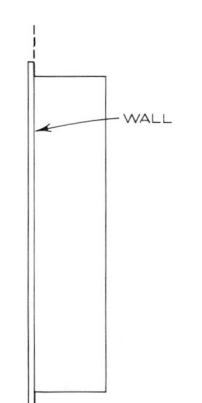

RECESSED

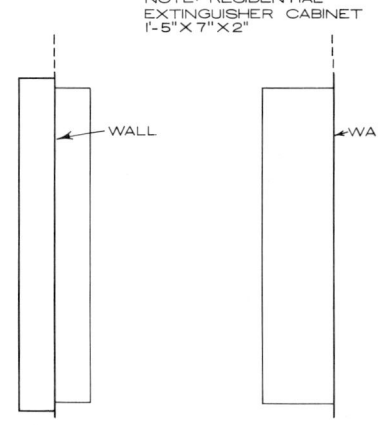

SEMIRECESSED   **SURFACE MOUNTED**

FIRE HOSE AND EXTINGUISHER CABINETS

NOTE

Cabinets are #18 gauge steel with glass doors as shown or with doors of metal, wood, mirror, and so on.

Consult manufacturer's literature for cabinets with special features such as revolving door, twin doors, pivoting door with attached extinguisher, and curved door.

Cabinets are obtainable for 25, 50, 75, and 100 ft hose racks. Rough dimensions are shown.

Wm. G. Miner, AIA, Architect; Washington, D.C.

FIRE PROTECTION   **15**

MAJOR CODES AND STANDARDS INVOLVING MECHANICAL WORK

General Industry Safety Orders (GISO)
National Electrical Code (NEC)
National Electrical Safety Code (NESC)
National Fire Protection Association (NFPA)
Occupational Safety and Health Act (OSHA)
Uniform Building Code (UBC)
Uniform Plumbing Code (UPC)
Uniform Mechanical Code (UMC)
Uniform Fire Code (UFC)
Applicable State and Local Codes

TECHNICAL SOCIETY STANDARDS AND HANDBOOKS

Acoustical Society of America (ASA)
American Gas Association (AGA)
American Society of Heating, Refrigeration and Air Conditioning Engineers (ASHRAE)
American Society of Mechanical Engineers (ASME)
American Society of Testing and Materials (ASTM)
American Water Works Association (AWWA)
American Welding Society (AWS)
Compressed Gas Association (CGA)
Instrument Society of America (ISA)
Mechanical Power Transmission Association (MPTA)
Air Diffusion Council (ADC)
Hydraulic Institute
Compressed Air and Gas Institute (CAGI)

INDUSTRY ASSOCIATIONS AND NATIONAL STANDARDS

U.S. Government Federal Specifications
National Bureau of Standards (NBS)
Underwriters Laboratories, Inc. (UL)
Anti-Friction Bearing Manufacturer's Association (AFBMA)
American Gear Manufacturer's Association (AGMA)
Air Moving and Conditioning Association (AMCA)
American Nuclear Society (ANS)
American National Standards Institute (ANSI)
American Petroleum Institute (API)
Air-Conditioning and Refrigeration Institute (ARI)
Cooling Tower Institute (CTI)
Sheet Metal and Air Conditioning Contractors National Association (SMACNA)
Institute of Boiler and Radiator Manufacturers (IBR)
Mechanical Contractors Association of America (MCAA)
Conveyor Equipment Manufacturers Association (CEMA)
Joint Industry Conferences of Hydraulic Manufacturers (JIC)
Manufacturers' Standardization Society of the Valve and Fittings Industry (MSS)
National Electrical Manufacturers Association (NEMA)

ENERGY NOTES

Energy conservation measures can be made when selecting and applying electric motors. Several motor manufacturers offer an improved efficiency motor line at a higher purchase price. Payback periods range from two years upward. By matching the motor size to the load and not putting on a larger motor than is necessary, some power will be saved. Power factor correction is another energy conservation method. Not only will this avoid some power losses in the motor, but it may also lower the utility rate.

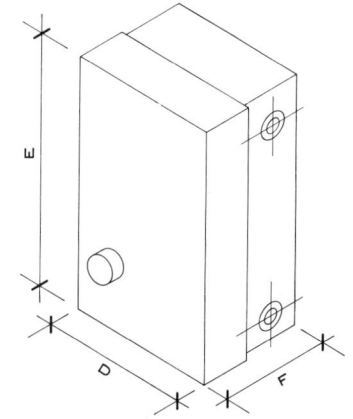

TYPICAL MOTOR STARTER

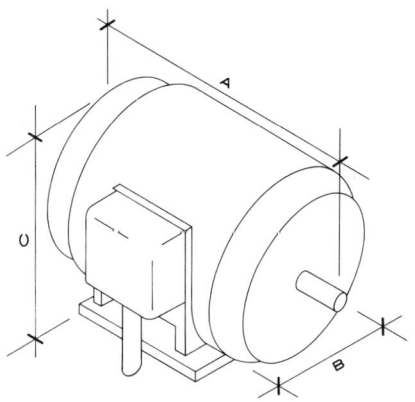

TYPICAL ELECTRIC MOTOR

CODES AND STANDARDS REFERENCES

MOTOR AND MOTOR STARTER DATA

	HP	TYPICAL NEMA FRAME SIZE	TYPICAL FRAME DIMENSIONS			STARTER SIZE*‡	TYPICAL STARTER DIMENSIONS†		
			A	B	C		D	E	F
115 V/230 V SINGLE-PHASE HORIZONTAL TOTALLY ENCLOSED, FAN COOLED§	1/4	L48Y	10 1/8 ''	6 1/4 ''	7 5/16 ''	00*	4 3/16 ''	7 1/4 ''	4 1/4 ''
	1/3	M48Y	10 3/4 ''						
	1/2	M56C	11 9/16 ''		8 1/4 ''	0	6''	10''	59/32 ''
	3/4	P56C	12 5/8 ''	7 5/16 ''	8 5/8 ''				
	1	T56C	14 1/16 ''						
	1 1/2	T56HC				1			
	2								
230 V/460 V THREE-PHASE HORIZONTAL, DRIP-PROOF§	3/4	143T	11 11/16 ''	6 7/8 ''	6 3/4 ''	0	6''	10''	59/32 ''
	1								
	1 1/2	145T	12 11/16 ''	6 7/8 ''					
	2								
	3	182T	12 9/16 ''	9 1/8 ''	9 1/16 ''	1			
	5	184T	13 9/16 ''	9 1/4 ''	9 1/8 ''				
	7 1/2	213T	15 11/16 ''	10 5/8 ''	10 9/16 ''				
	10	215T	17 3/16 ''						
	15	254T	20 1/2 ''	12 5/8 ''	12 9/16 ''	2	7 13/16 ''	12 11/16 ''	6 1/32 ''
	20	256T	22 1/4 ''						
	25	284T	23 3/8 ''	14 1/8 ''	14 1/16 ''				
	30	286T	24 7/8 ''			3	11 7/16 ''	21 13/16 ''	7 3/4 ''
	40	324T	26''	16 1/16 ''	16 1/8 ''				
	50	326T	27 1/2 ''						
	60	364T	28 5/8 ''	18 5/8 ''	18 5/16 ''	4			
	75	365T	29 5/8 ''						
	100	404T	32 3/8 ''	20 1/2 ''	20 1/4 ''				

*Starter size based on 120 V supply.
†Starter size based on 480 V supply.
‡Starter in NEMA 1 enclosure.
§Other dimensions apply to different enclosure types.

CH₂M Hill, Inc.; Corvallis, Oregon

15   HVAC

WASTE HEAT SOURCES FOR HEAT RECOVERY SYSTEMS

1. Flues of fuel burning heating boilers and furnaces.
2. Refrigeration systems hot gas and condenser water.
3. Exhaust gases from diesel engine and gas turbine driven electric power generating equipment.
4. Cooling water from diesel engine cooling jackets and air compressor aftercoolers.
5. Exhaust steam and condenser water from steam turbine driven electric generators and refrigeration units.
6. Exhaust air from toilet rooms, mechanical equipment rooms, transformer vaults, kitchen range hoods, laundries, laboratory hoods, hospital operating rooms, locker rooms, shower rooms, and swimming pools.
7. Wastewater from washing machines and dishwashers.
8. Internal heat gain from lights, people, and appliances.
9. Heat recovery systems may consist of a direct or indirect heat transfer from airstreams, liquids, refrigerants, water, or gases.

APPLICATIONS FOR WASTE HEAT RECOVERY SYSTEMS

1. Building space heating.
2. Preheating ventilation outdoor air intake.
3. Air conditioning systems supply air reheat.
4. Preheating domestic hot water and boiler feed water.

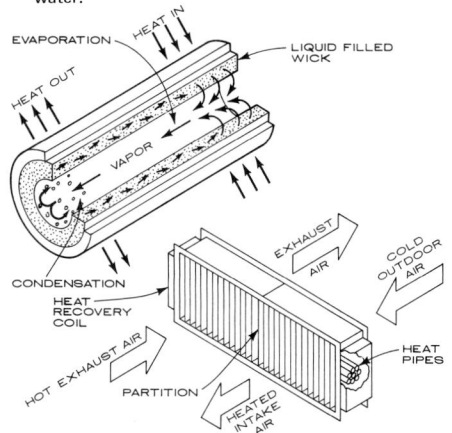

NOTE

Counterflow, indirect air-to-air sensible heat transfer. No leakage between airstreams. Alternate evaporation, condensation, and capillary migration of fluid in porous wick lining of tubes. Coil tilting or fact and bypass damper control. Efficiency 50-70%. Modular sizes to 54 in. x 138 in. x 8 rows deep.

HEAT PIPE

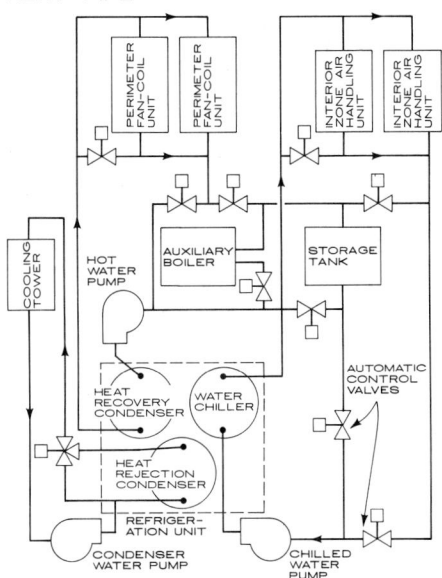

DUAL CONDENSER WATER CHILLING

Syska & Hennessy, Consulting Engineers; New York, New York

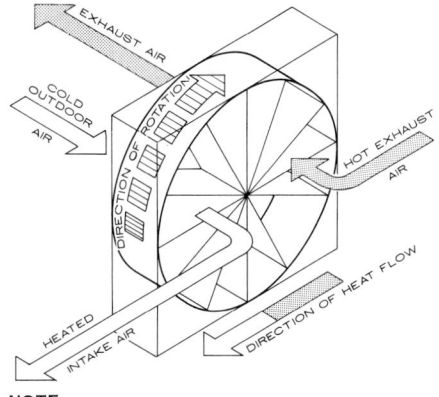

NOTE

Sensible heat absorbing aluminum or stainless steel mesh. Dessicant impregnated for latent heat transfer. Leakage 4-8% between opposing airstreams. Added purging section reduces cross-contamination to less than 1%. Speed variations or face and bypass damper capacity control. Efficiency 70-80%. Sizes to 144 in. diameter.

THERMAL WHEEL

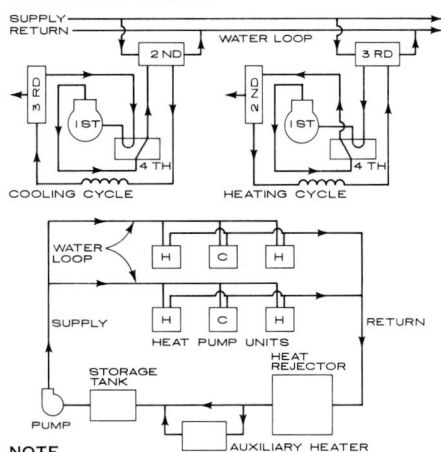

NOTE

Heat transfer from cooled to heated areas. Individually controlled heat pump terminal units with air and water coils. Auxiliary heater operation when heat loss exceeds heat gain. Heat rejector operation when heat gain exceeds heat loss. Tank stores excess capacity. Loop water 60-90°F.

WATER LOOP HEAT PUMPS

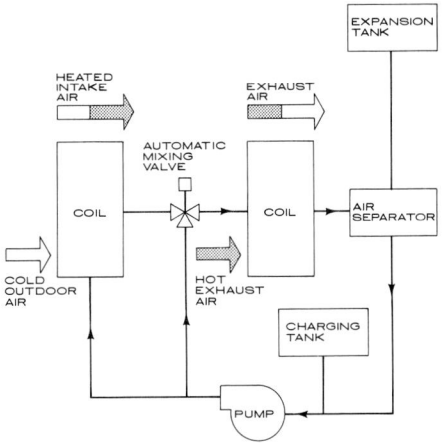

NOTE

Indirect sensible heat transfer between remote air streams with no cross-contamination. Exhaust airstream coil construction to suit application. Antifreeze fluid for low air temperatures. Bypass valve temperature control. Computerized equipment selection. Efficiency 50-70%. Modular coils to 20,000 cfm.

RUNAROUND COILS

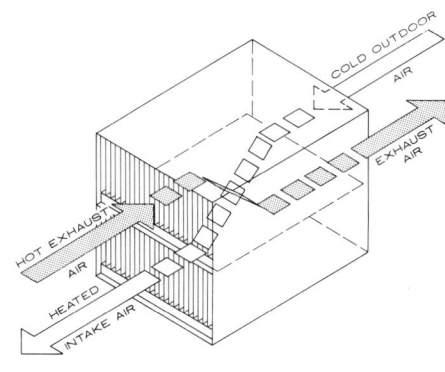

NOTE

Counterflow, direct air-to-air type heat exchanger. Sensible heat transfer only. No leakage between airstreams. Corrugated aluminum or stainless steel construction. Washdown spray manifold for dirty exhaust airstreams. Bypass damper temperature control. Modular sizes to 10,000 cfm. Efficiency 60-80%.

PLATE TYPE HEAT EXCHANGER

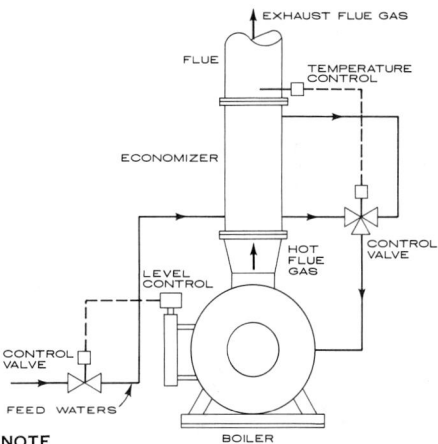

NOTE

Direct flue gas to feed water heat transfer for high pressure steam boilers. Boiler flue gas at 500°F leaving economizer at 325°F, heats feed water from 200 to 248°F. Mixing valve maintains minimum stack temperature leaving economizer to prevent moisture condensation in stack.

BOILER FLUE ECONOMIZER

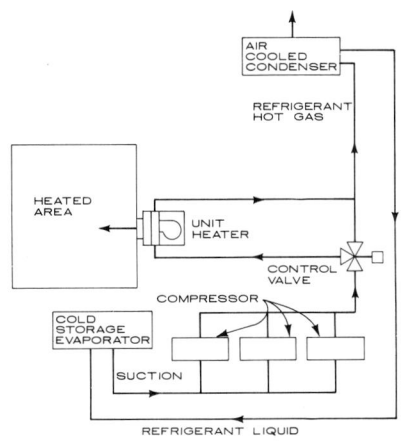

NOTE

Rejected heat from cold storage refrigeration system used to heat occupied areas. For heating, hot gas refrigerant from compressor discharge flows through space heating units to extract heat. When heating is not required, hot gas refrigerant flows directly to air cooled condenser for heat rejection to outdoor air.

REFRIGERANT HOT GAS

HVAC 15

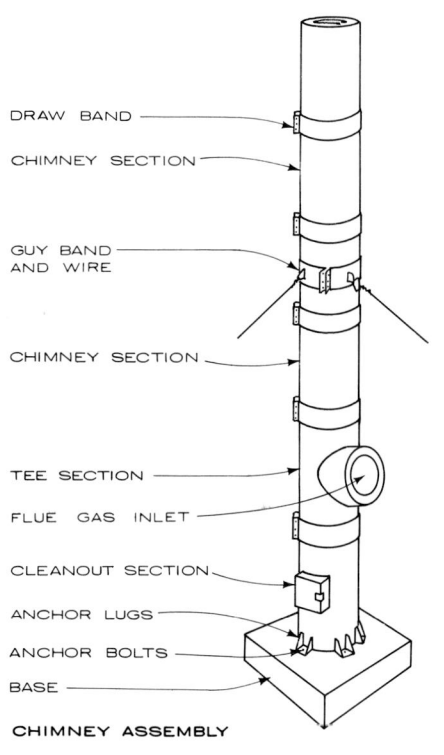

CHIMNEY ASSEMBLY

MEDIUM HEAT CHIMNEYS

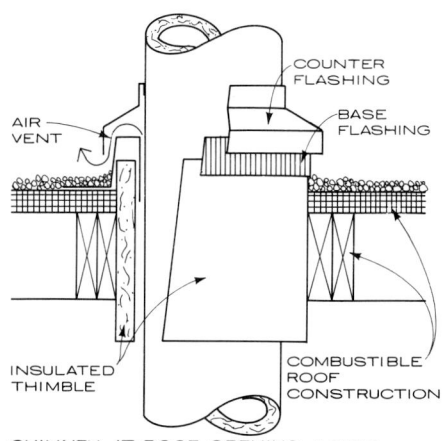

CHIMNEY AT ROOF OPENING (ZERO CLEARANCE)

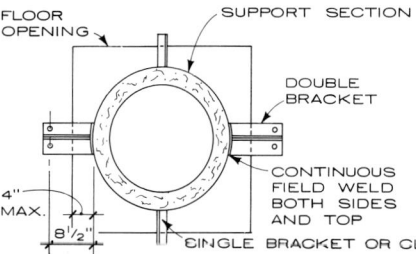

SUPPORT AT FLOOR OPENING

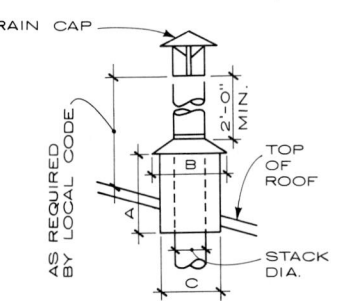

ROOF PENETRATION

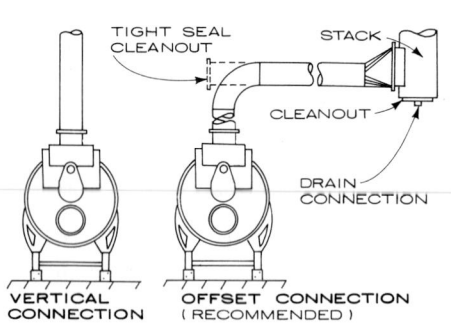

VERTICAL CONNECTION   **OFFSET CONNECTION** (RECOMMENDED)

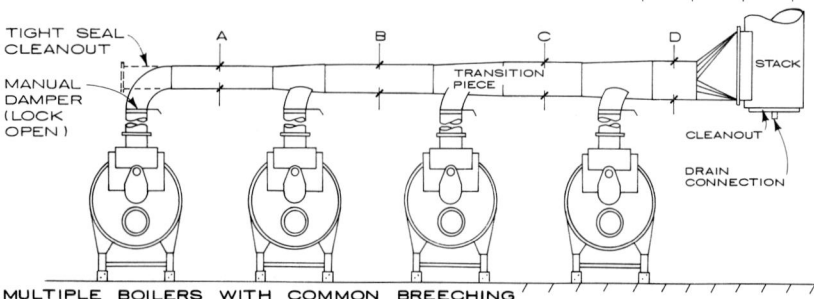

MULTIPLE BOILERS WITH COMMON BREECHING

VENT STACKS

Syska and Hennessey, Consulting Engineers; New York, New York

CHIMNEY CONSTRUCTION

The chimney should be supported on a foundation of masonry or reinforced concrete or other noncombustible material having a fire resistance rating of not less than 3 hr. When installed on an appliance, the chimney should be so supported as to not place excessive stress on the appliance. The base of the chimney should be secured to prevent movement of the chimney and anchor lugs should be used for this purpose whenever possible.

A cleanout section may be used in the chimney assembly but must not be used above the chimney inlet.

CLEARANCES

Chimneys of the medium heat appliance or commercial-industrial incinerator type are not intended to be enclosed in walls of combustible materials. These chimneys should be placed in fire resistive or noncombustible shafts where they extend through any story of a building above that in which the connected appliance is located.

An enclosed chimney may be placed adjacent to walls of combustible material with the following minimum clearances:

10 to 15 in. I.D. requires 16 in. clearance
15 to 21 in. I.D. requires 18 in. clearance
21 to 27 in. I.D. requires 20 in. clearance
27 to 36 in. I.D. requires 22 in. clearance

Where the chimney passes through a roof of combustible material it shall be installed with an insulated thimble and flashing. This insulated thimble may be installed at zero inch clearance to combustibles.

The chimney should extend at least 3 ft above the highest point where it passes through the roof and 2 ft higher than any ridge within 10 ft.

VENT STACKS

The purpose of a vent stack is to conduct the products of combustion to a point of safe discharge (atmosphere). Forced draft design eliminates the need for a stack designed to create a draft. An offset type of stack connection to the stub vent on the boiler is preferred. A direct vertical connection can also be made when boiler vent outlets can withstand the direct vertical load of the stack, including the effect of wind and guy wires.

STACK CONSTRUCTION

The stack can be terminated several feet above the top of the roof. (State and local codes may govern the stack height above the roof.) If down drafts are unavoidable, the stack outlet can be provided with a ventilator. Minimum 12 gauge steel is recommended for stack sections. If the stack will be inaccessible, the use of a noncorrosive material (e.g., glass lining) should be considered.

A rain cap or hood should be used at the top of the stack to minimize the entrance of rain or snow.

STACK DIAMETER—SINGLE BOILER VENT OR STACK

BOILER HORSE-POWER	STACK DIAMETER (IN.)	A (IN.)	B (IN.)	C (IN.)
15–20	6	15	15	12
25–40	8	20	20	16
50–60	10	25	25	20
70–100	12	30	30	24
125–200	16	40	40	32
250–350	20	50	50	40
400–800	24	60	60	48

STACK DIAMETER—MULTIPLE BOILERS: COMMON BREECHING AND STACK

BOILER HORSE-POWER	MINIMUM STACK DIAMETER (IN.) NUMBER OF BOILERS					
	2		3		4	
	100 FT	200 FT	100 FT	200 FT	100 FT	200 FT
25–40	11	12	13	14	14	16
50–60	13	14	15	16	17	18
70–100	16	17	19	20	21	23
125–200	21	22	24	26	28	30
250–350	26	28	32	34	34	40
400–600	32	34	38	40	42	46

BREECHING DIAMETER—
SINGLE AND MULTIPLE BOILERS

BOILER HORSE-POWER	MINIMUM BREECHING DIAMETER (IN. OD)			
	A (IN.) 1 BOIL-ER	B (IN.) 2 BOIL-ERS	C (IN.) 3 BOIL-ERS	D (IN.) 4 BOIL-ERS
15–20	6	8	9	9
25–40	8	10	11	12
50–60	10	12	14	15
70–100	12	15	17	18
125–200	16	20	22	24
250–350	20	25	28	30
400–600	24	30	33	36
700–800	24	34	38	42

Note: Stack diameter should be larger than breeching diameter.

HVAC

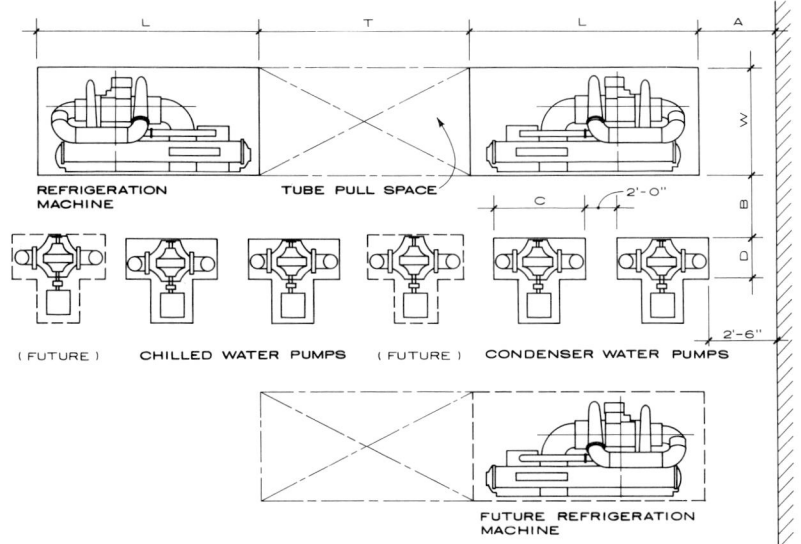

REFRIGERATION MACHINE   TUBE PULL SPACE

(FUTURE)   CHILLED WATER PUMPS   (FUTURE)   CONDENSER WATER PUMPS

FUTURE REFRIGERATION MACHINE

GENERAL

The capacity of each refrigeration machine is equal to 50% of the peak cooling load.

Each water pump provides the flow requirement of one refrigeration machine. Therefore, one pair of condenser and chilled water pumps is needed for each machine.

The cooling tower may be located on the roof of the refrigeration equipment room or on the ground adjacent to the equipment room. When located on ground, the condenser water outlet(s) on the cooling tower must be not less than 5 ft above the equipment room floor elevation for proper functioning of condenser water pumps.

EXPANSION OF EQUIPMENT

For operational flexibility of a refrigeration plant, the size of the future refrigeration machine is generally planned to be the same as of the present machines. It may be economically advantageous to oversize some portions of the chilled and condenser waterpipes to handle the future flow rates.

Provision must also be made for expansion of the cooling tower capacity when the future refrigeration machine is installed.

REFRIGERATION EQUIPMENT ROOM SPACE REQUIREMENTS

EQUIPMENT (TONS)	DIMENSIONS								MINIMUM ROOM HEIGHT
	L	W	HEIGHT	T	A	B	C	D	
RECIPROCATING MACHINES									
Up to 50	9'-0"	3'-0"	4'-0"	6'-0"	2'-6"	3'-6"	4'-0"	3'-0"	9'-0"
50 to 100	9'-6"	3'-0"	4'-6"	6'-0"	2'-6"	3'-6"	4'-0"	3'-6"	9'-0"
CENTRIFUGAL MACHINES									
Up to 120	14'-6"	6'-0"	6'-6"	14'-0"	2'-6"	5'-6"	4'-6"	4'-0"	10'-0"
120 to 225	15'-0"	6'-0"	6'-0"	14'-0"	2'-6"	5'-6"	4'-6"	4'-0"	10'-0"
225 to 350	15'-0"	6'-6"	7'-0"	14'-0"	2'-6"	5'-6"	5'-0"	5'-0"	11'-0"
350 to 550	15'-0"	8'-0"	7'-0"	14'-0"	2'-6"	5'-6"	6'-0"	5'-6"	11'-0"
550 to 750	15'-6"	11'-0"	8'-6"	14'-6"	2'-6"	5'-6"	6'-0"	5'-6"	12'-0"
750 to 1500	18'-6"	13'-6"	10'-0"	16'-0"	2'-6"	5'-6"	7'-6"	6'-0"	14'-0"
STEAM ABSORPTION MACHINES									
Up to 200	18'-0"	4'-0"	8'-0"	17'-0"	2'-6"	3'-6"	4'-6"	4'-0"	11'-0"
200 to 450	20'-0"	5'-6"	10'-0"	19'-0"	2'-6"	3'-6"	5'-0"	5'-0"	13'-0"
450 to 550	24'-0"	5'-6"	10'-0"	23'-0"	2'-6"	3'-6"	6'-0"	5'-6"	13'-0"
550 to 750	24'-0"	6'-6"	12'-0"	23'-0"	2'-6"	3'-6"	6'-0"	5'-6"	15'-0"
750 to 1000	27'-0"	7'-6"	12'-6"	26'-0"	2'-6"	3'-6"	7'-0"	6'-0"	16'-0"

REFRIGERATION ROOM LAYOUT

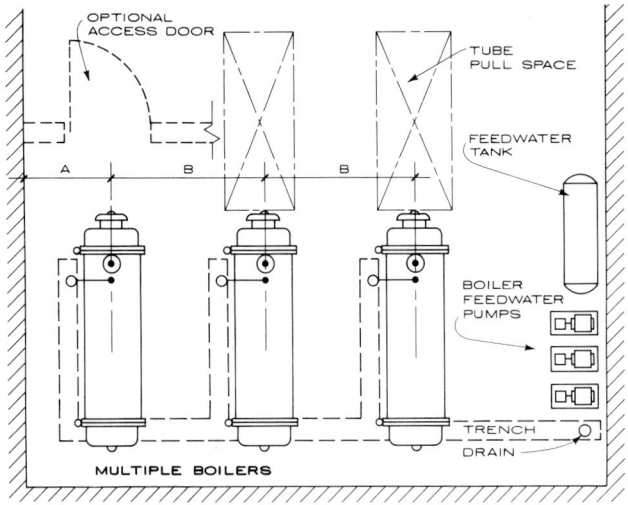

OPTIONAL ACCESS DOOR

TUBE PULL SPACE

FEEDWATER TANK

BOILER FEEDWATER PUMPS

TRENCH DRAIN

MULTIPLE BOILERS

ROOM DIMENSIONS

Dimension A allows for a minimum 3 ft 6 in. aisle between the water column on the boiler and the wall. Dimension B between boilers allows for a clear aisle of:

3'-6" — 15-200 hp
4'-0" — 250-350 hp
5'-0" — 400-800 hp

The shortest boiler room length is obtained by allowing for possible future tube replacement (from front or rear of boiler) through a window or doorway. Allowance is only made for minimum door swing at each end of the boiler.

AIR SUPPLY

Two permanent air supply openings on opposite walls of the boiler room are recommended. These openings should be located below a height of 7 ft with a total clear area of at least 1 sq ft. Air supply openings can be louvered for weather protection.

Size the openings by using the following formula:

$$\text{area (sq ft)} = \frac{CFM}{FPM}$$

Amount of air required (CFM):

Combustion air—max. boiler HP x 2 CMF/BHP

Ventilation air—max. boiler HP x 2 CFM/BHP

NOTE: a total of 10 CFM/BHP applies up to 1000 ft elevation. Add 3% more per 1000 ft of added elevation.

Air velocity required (FPM):

Up to 7 ft height— 250 FPM
Above 7 ft height— 500 FPM
Supply air duct to boiler—1000 FPM

BOILER ROOM SPACE REQUIREMENTS

BOILER HP	15-40	50-100	125-200	250-350	400-800
Dimension A	5'-9"	6'-6"	6'-10"	7'-9"	8'-6"
Dimension B	7'-5"	8'-9"	9'-7"	11'-9"	14'-3"

BOILER ROOM LAYOUT

Anilkumar V. Patel; Joseph R. Loring & Associates, Inc.; Consulting Engineers; New York, New York

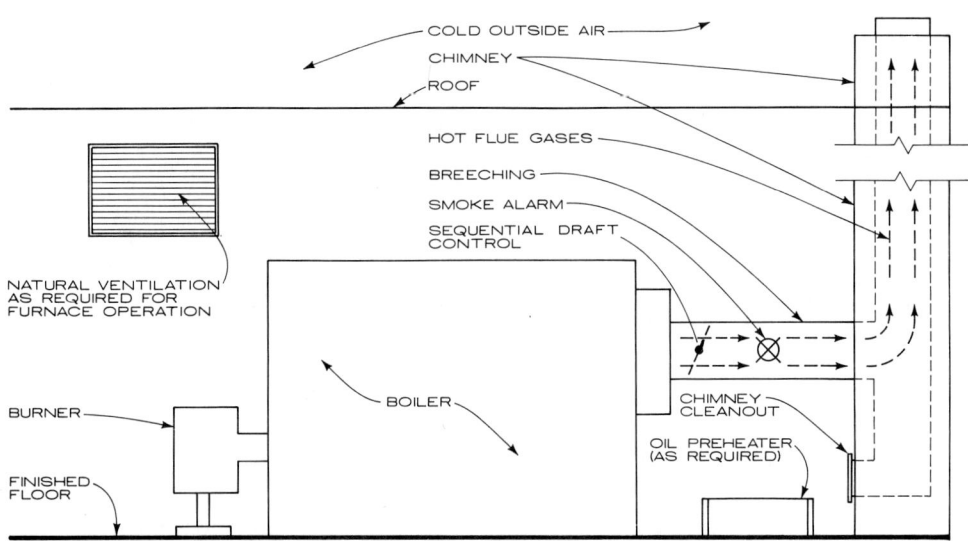

TYPICAL BOILER EQUIPMENT FOR NATURAL DRAFT INSTALLATION

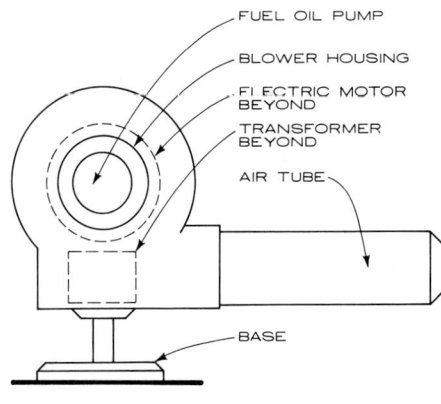

HIGH PRESSURE GUN TYPE BURNER (NO. 2 FUEL OIL)
NOTE: FOR DOMESTIC INSTALLATIONS UP TO 10 FAMILIES AND SINGLE STORY COMMERCIAL INSTALLATIONS UP TO 10,000 SQ FT

BOILERS AND BURNERS

In selecting a boiler, efficiency depends on the number of passes the hot gasses make. The greater the number of passes the greater the efficiency of the boiler. During operation, boiler efficiency depends on cleanliness of the tubes and the heat exchange surfaces.

Burner efficiency depends on the proper combustion of fuel (air-fuel ratio) and the maintenance (annual tune-up) of the burner. To handle a boiler properly and efficiently, the maintenance staff must be trained to operate the unit and to conduct efficiency tests, which include testing for CO_2, stack temperature, smoke, and draft.

NOTE: Air pollution regulations must be obtained from authorities having jurisdiction.

RATINGS

1. Gross rating = input in Btu/hr.
2. Net rating = output in Btu/hr. = gross rating x efficiency.
3. ## FUEL RATINGS

FUEL	HEAT VALUE	EFFICIENCY (%)
Anthracite coal	14,600 Btu/lb	65-75
No. 2 oil	140,000 Btu/gal	70-80
No. 4 oil	145,000 Btu/gal	70-80
No. 6 oil	150,000 Btu/gal	70-80
Natural gas	1052 Btu/cu ft	70-80
Electricity	1 W = 3.4 Btuh	95-100

4. Example: If boiler-burner combination is 80% efficient, No. 2 fuel oil is burned, and the total heat load is 168,000 Btu/hr, what is the required firing rate?

$$\text{Firing rate} = \frac{\text{gross rating}}{\text{fuel rating} \times \text{efficiency}}$$

$$\frac{168,000 \text{ (Btu/hr)}}{140,000 \text{ (Btu/gal)} \times 80\%} = 1.5 \text{ gal/hr}$$

NOTE: Gross and net ratings are found on equipment plates.

CONTROLS

Automatic fuel burning equipment requires a control system that will provide a prescribed sequence of operating events and will take proper corrective action if failure occurs in the equipment or its operation. The basic requirements for oil burners, gas burners, and coal burners (stokers) are the same. The controls can be classified as operating controls, limit controls, and interlocks.

Operating controls initiate the normal starting and stopping of the burner in response to the primary sensor acting through appropriate actuators.

Examples of primary sensors are: a room thermostat for a residential furnace; a pressure actuated switch for a steam boiler; a thermostat for a hot water heater. Since the heat output of a burner may be widely distributed, the location of the primary sensor is important.

An actuator is defined as a device that converts the control system signal into a useful function. Actuators generally consist of valves, dampers, or relays.

An automatic burner ignitor is necessary for safe operation and is, in most applications, an essential part of the automatic control system. The burner ignitor is an electric spark that directly ignites the main fuel supply. On small input, gas fired appliances, ignition of the main fuel is facilitated by a small standing gas pilot that burns continuously.

Limit controls and interlocks function only when the system exceeds prescribed unsafe operating conditions. They actuate electric switches that will close the fuel valve in the event of an unsafe condition, such as (1) excessive temperature in the combustion chamber or heat exchanger, (2) excessive pressure in a boiler or hot water heater, (3) low water level in a boiler and in larger commercial and industrial burners, (4) high or low gas pressure, (5) low oil pressure, (6) low atomizing media pressure, and (7) low oil temperature when firing residual fuel oil. Separate limit and operating controls are always recommended.

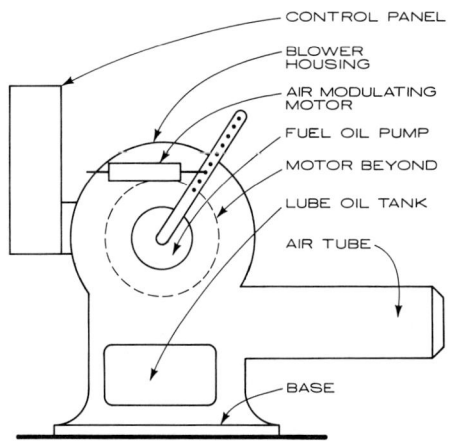

LOW PRESSURE GUN TYPE BURNER (NO. 4 FUEL OIL)
NOTE: FOR LARGE DOMESTIC, SEMICOMMERCIAL, AND COMMERCIAL INSTALLATIONS

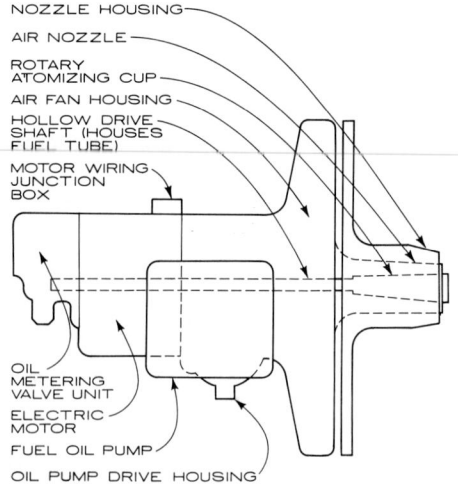

HORIZONTAL ROTARY TYPE BURNER DIRECT DRIVE (NO. 6 FUEL OIL)
NOTE: ALSO AVAILABLE WITH BELT DRIVE, USED IN DOMESTIC, SEMICOMMERCIAL, COMMERCIAL, AND HEAVY INDUSTRIAL.

BURNER TYPES

CAST IRON SECTIONAL TYPE BOILER

Kelly Sacher & Associates, Architects Engineers Planners; Seaford, Long Island, New York

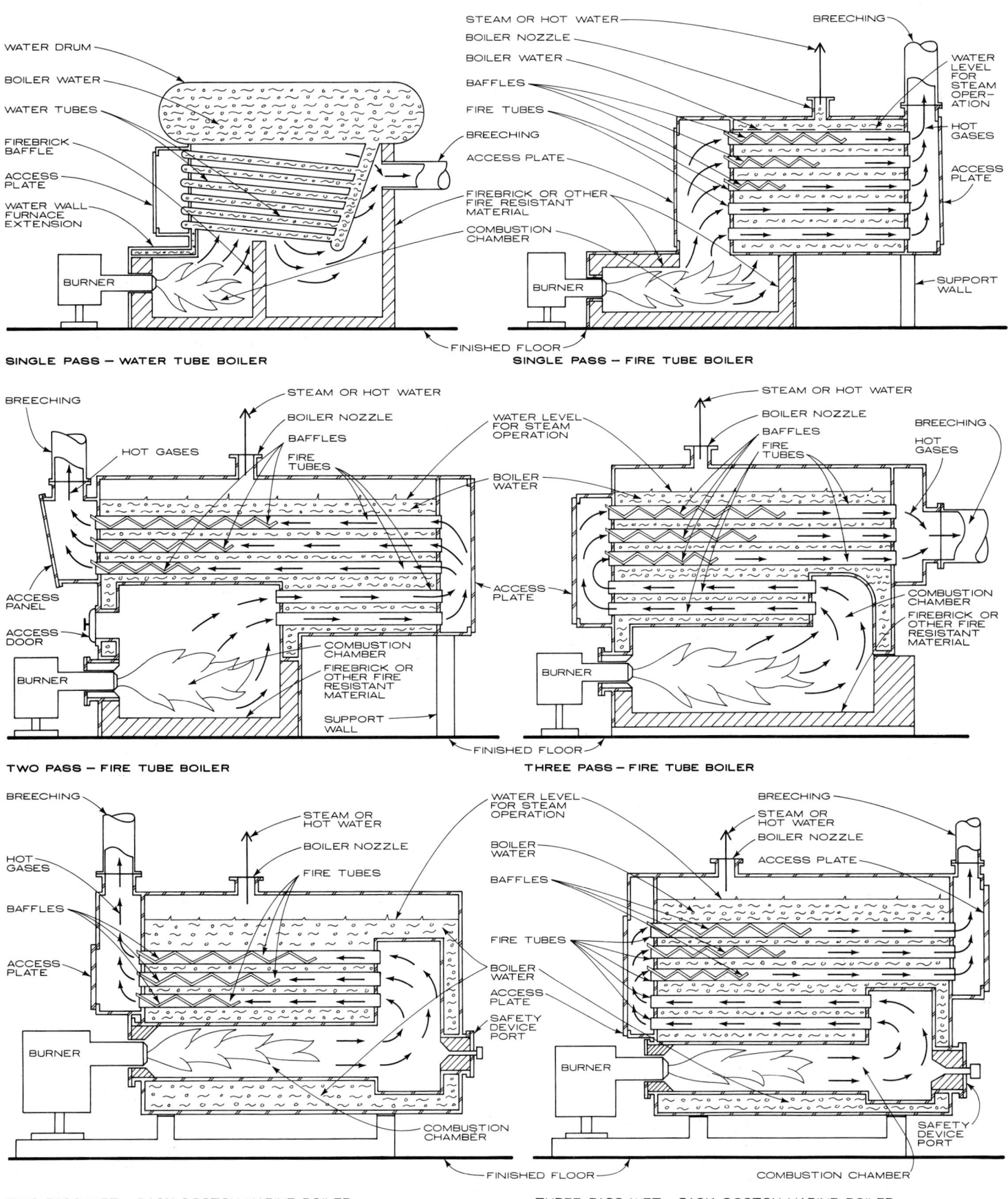

SINGLE PASS — WATER TUBE BOILER

SINGLE PASS — FIRE TUBE BOILER

TWO PASS — FIRE TUBE BOILER

THREE PASS — FIRE TUBE BOILER

TWO PASS WET — BACK SCOTCH MARINE BOILER

THREE PASS WET — BACK SCOTCH MARINE BOILER

TUBE TYPE BOILERS

Kelly Sacher & Associates, Architects Engineers Planners; Seaford, Long Island, New York

DECENTRALIZED HEATING SYSTEMS

Electric energy is ideally suited to space heating because it is simple to distribute and control. Complete electric heating systems are widely used in residences, schools, and commercial and industrial establishments.

A decentralized electric system applies heating units to individual rooms or spaces. Often the rooms are combined into zones with automatic temperature controls. In terms of heat output, electric in-space heating systems may be classified as natural convection, radiant, or forced air.

NATURAL CONVECTION UNITS

Heating units for wall mounting, recessed placement or surface placement are made with elements of incandescent bare wire or lower temperature bare wire or sheathed elements. An inner liner or reflector is usually placed between elements so that part of the heat is distributed by convection and part by radiation. Electric convectors should be located so that air movement across the elements is not impeded. Small units with ratings up to 1650 W operate at 120 V. Higher wattage units are made for 208 or higher voltages and require heavy duty receptacles.

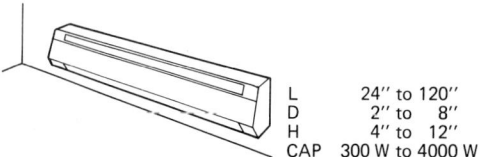

L	24″ to 120″
D	2″ to 8″
H	4″ to 12″
CAP	300 W to 4000 W

BASEBOARD HEATER (Wall Mounted)

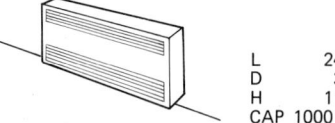

L	24″ to 96″
D	3″ to 8″
H	11″ to 32″
CAP	1000 W to 4000 W

CABINET CONVECTOR (Surface Mounted or Recessed)

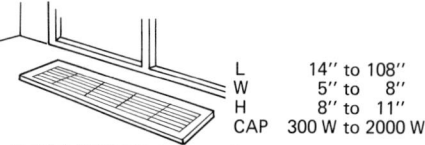

L	14″ to 108″
W	5″ to 8″
H	8″ to 11″
CAP	300 W to 2000 W

FLOOR HEATER (Recessed)

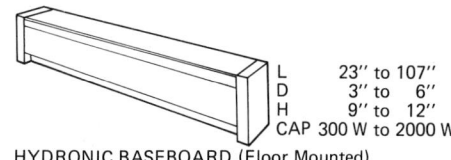

L	23″ to 107″
D	3″ to 6″
H	9″ to 12″
CAP	300 W to 2000 W

HYDRONIC BASEBOARD (Floor Mounted)

NATURAL CONVECTION UNITS

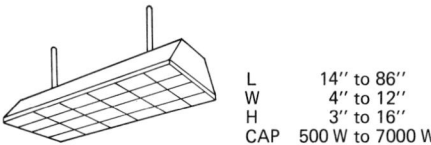

L	14″ to 86″
W	4″ to 12″
H	3″ to 16″
CAP	500 W to 7000 W

INFRARED HEATER (Pendant Mounted) Circular heat lamp is available

L	48″ to 144″
W	24″ to 48″
D	1″
CAP	500 W to 1000 W

RADIANT HEAT PANEL (Surface Mounted or Recessed) Decorative murals are available

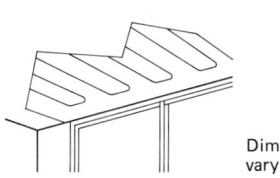

Dimensions and capacity vary with coverage

RADIANT CEILING WITH EMBEDDED CONDUCTORS

RADIANT HEATING UNITS

RADIANT HEATING

Heat is produced by a current that flows in a high resistance wire or ribbon and is then transferred by radiation to a heat absorbing body. Manufacturer's recommendations for clearance between a radiant fixture and combustible materials or occupants should be followed.

FORCED AIR UNITS

Unit ventilators and heaters combine common convective heating with controlled natural ventilation.

Unit ventilators are most often mounted on an outside wall for air intake and at windowsills to prevent the down draft of cold air.

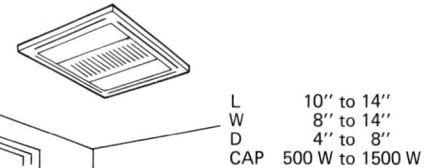

L	10″ to 14″
W	8″ to 14″
D	4″ to 8″
CAP	500 W to 1500 W

CEILING HEATER (Recessed) Circular unit with light is available

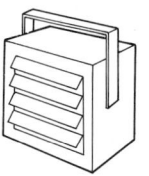

W	12″ to 52″
D	6″ to 22″
H	12″ to 26″
CAP	1.5 KW to 50 KW

UNIT HEATER (Bracket Mounted)

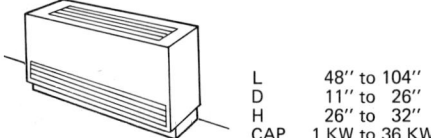

L	48″ to 104″
D	11″ to 26″
H	26″ to 32″
CAP	1 KW to 36 KW

UNIT VENTILATOR (Surface Mounted or Recessed)

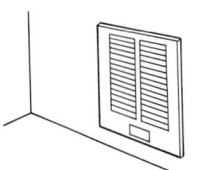

W	10″ to 18″
D	2″ to 6″
H	9″ to 24″
CAP	750 W to 4000 W

WALL HEATER (Recessed)

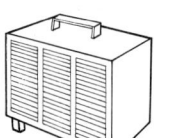

W	10″ to 72″
D	2″ to 12″
H	7″ to 24″
CAP	500 W to 5000 W

PORTABLE HEATER

FORCED AIR UNITS

CENTRALIZED HEATING SYSTEMS

A central hot water system with terminal radiators can be operated using an electric hot water boiler that contains immersion heating elements.

An electric furnace, consisting of resistance heating coils and a blower, can supply a ducted warm air system. Electric heating units are also installed in supply ducts to provide final temperatures and relative humidities in central air systems.

Integrated recovery systems make use of heat gains from electrical loads such as lights and motors. The excess heat accumulated from these sources can either be transferred or stored for later use.

L	25″
W	23″
H	35″
CAP	5 KW to 60 KW

ELECTRIC FURNACE

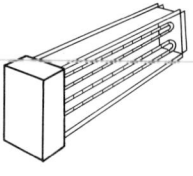

Size varies with duct dimensions
CAP 0.3 KW to 2000 KW

DUCT INSERT HEATER

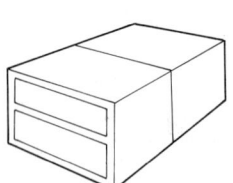

Size varies
CAP 2 KW to 100 KW

HEAT PUMP

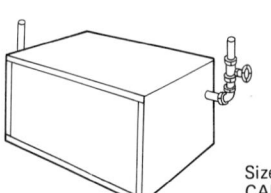

Size varies
CAP 6 KW to 40 KW

ELECTRIC BOILER

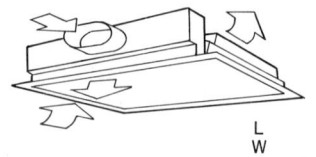

L	24″ to 72″
W	24″ to 72″

Capacity varies with air velocity

INTEGRATED HEAT RECOVERY Heat is gained from light fixtures

CENTRALIZED HEATING SYSTEMS

Tseng-Yao Sun, P.E. and Kyoung S. Park, P.E.; Ayres, Cohen and Hayakawa; Consulting Engineers; Los Angeles/San Francisco, California

HVAC

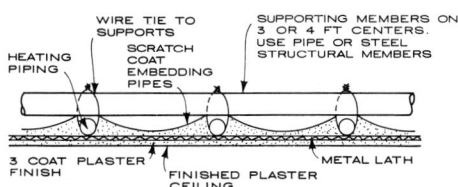

PIPES IN SUSPENDED PLASTER CEILING

In a suspended plaster ceiling both the lath and the heating coils are securely wired to the support members so that the lath is below but in good contact with the coils. Plaster is then applied to the lath to embed the tubes. Some local codes may prohibit this assembly.

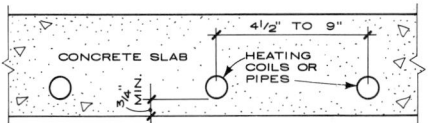

COILS IN STRUCTURAL CONCRETE SLAB

Heating pipes can be embedded in the lower portion of a concrete slab. If plaster is to be applied to the concrete, the piping may be placed directly on the wood forms. The minimum coverage for an exposed concrete slab is generally 3/4 in. but may vary with local codes.

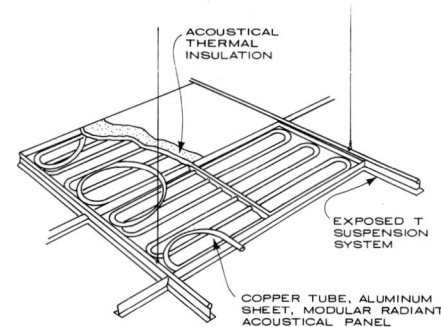

METAL CEILING PANELS

Metal panel ceiling systems use copper tubing bonded to an aluminum panel which can be mounted into a standard suspended ceiling grid. An insulating blanket is required to reduce the upward flow of heat from the metal panel. The heating pipes can be connected in either a sinuous or parallel flow welded system. A ceiling panel system can also be used for cooling purposes if chilled water is supplied through the tubes.

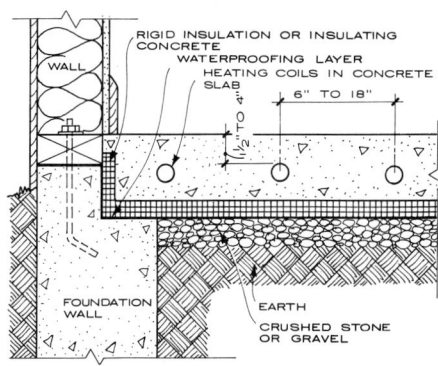

COILS IN FLOOR SLAB ON GRADE

Plastic, ferrous, or nonferrous heating pipes are used in floor slabs that rest on grade. It is recommended that perimeter insulation be used to reduce thermal losses at the edges. Coils should be embedded completely in the concrete slab and should not rest on an interface. Supports used to position the coils while pouring the slab should be nonabsorbent and inorganic. A layer of waterproofing should be placed above grade to protect insulation and piping.

LIQUID RADIANT HEATING SYSTEMS

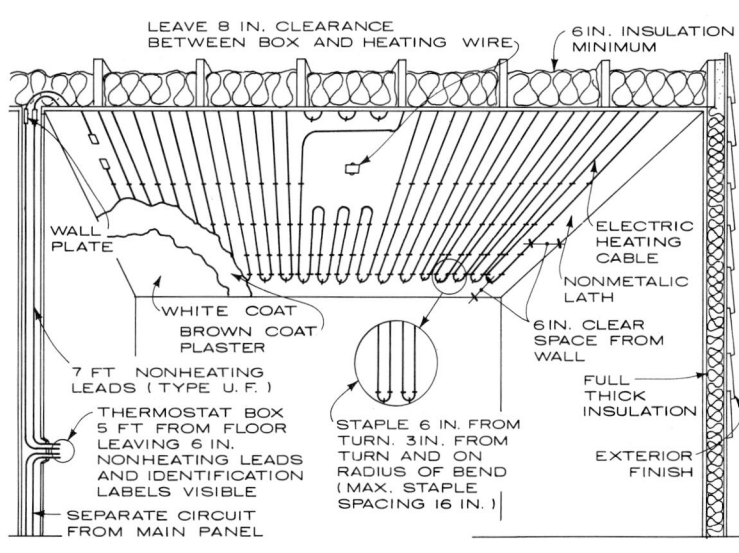

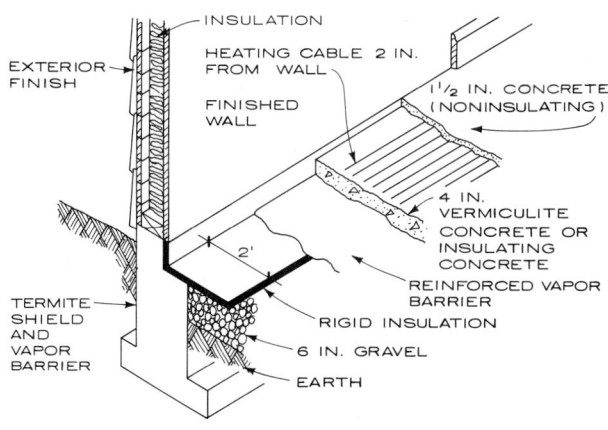

ELECTRIC HEATING CABLE IN CONCRETE SLAB

Electric heating cables embedded in plaster ceilings or concrete floors or laminated in gypsum board construction are factory-assembled units furnished in standard lengths from 75 to 1800 ft. Standard cable assemblies are normally rated at 2.75 W/linear ft and are available for 120,208 and 240 V.

ELECTRIC RADIANT HEATING SYSTEMS

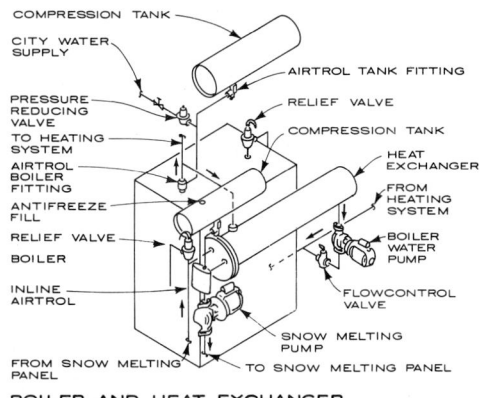

BOILER AND HEAT EXCHANGER

DRIVEWAY PIPING PLAN

HEATING CABLE IN ASPHALT

EXPANSION JOINT IN CONCRETE WALK OR DRIVEWAY

SNOW MELTING SYSTEMS

Snow melting systems for driveways and sidewalks can be of the ethylene-glycol type, hot oil or electric cables. The hot liquid types use a central hot water boiler with a heat exchanger that pumps the fluid through tubes embedded in the asphalt pavement.

Vents, drains, slab pitch, and expansion joints must be provided for in the initial design. A 3/4 in. pipe or tube on 12 in. centers is used as a standard coil. Header pipes are normally 1 1/2 in. in diameter. Piping should be supported with a minimum of 2 in. of concrete above and below the pipe.

If piping must pass through a concrete expansion joint, provision should be made to avoid any stresses on the tubing. By dipping the tube below the expansion joint any movement or heaving in the slab can be accommodated. All piping below the level of the concrete slab must be waterproofed and covered with insulation.

W. S. Fleming and Associates, Inc.; Fayetteville, New York

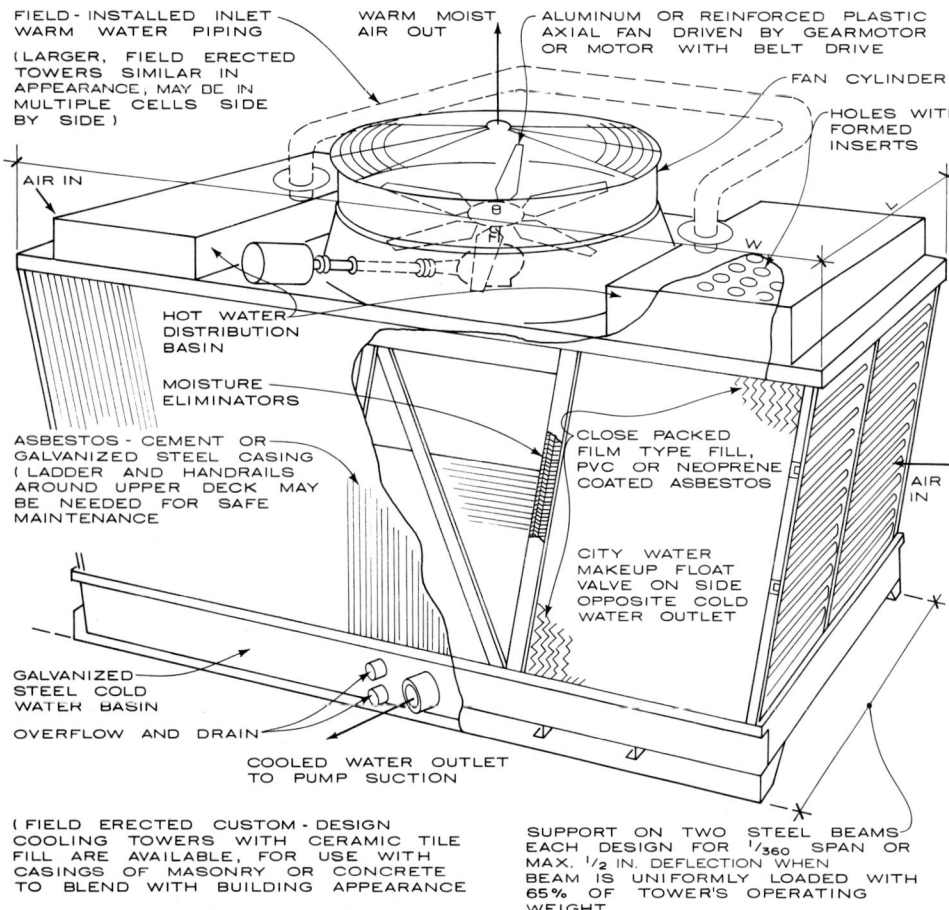

FIELD - INSTALLED INLET WARM WATER PIPING

(LARGER, FIELD ERECTED TOWERS SIMILAR IN APPEARANCE; MAY BE IN MULTIPLE CELLS SIDE BY SIDE)

AIR IN

WARM MOIST AIR OUT

ALUMINUM OR REINFORCED PLASTIC AXIAL FAN DRIVEN BY GEARMOTOR OR MOTOR WITH BELT DRIVE

FAN CYLINDER

HOLES WITH FORMED INSERTS

HOT WATER DISTRIBUTION BASIN

MOISTURE ELIMINATORS

ASBESTOS - CEMENT OR GALVANIZED STEEL CASING (LADDER AND HANDRAILS AROUND UPPER DECK MAY BE NEEDED FOR SAFE MAINTENANCE

CLOSE PACKED FILM TYPE FILL, PVC OR NEOPRENE COATED ASBESTOS

AIR IN

CITY WATER MAKEUP FLOAT VALVE ON SIDE OPPOSITE COLD WATER OUTLET

GALVANIZED STEEL COLD WATER BASIN

OVERFLOW AND DRAIN

COOLED WATER OUTLET TO PUMP SUCTION

(FIELD ERECTED CUSTOM - DESIGN COOLING TOWERS WITH CERAMIC TILE FILL ARE AVAILABLE, FOR USE WITH CASINGS OF MASONRY OR CONCRETE TO BLEND WITH BUILDING APPEARANCE

SUPPORT ON TWO STEEL BEAMS EACH DESIGN FOR 1/360 SPAN OR MAX. 1/2 IN. DEFLECTION WHEN BEAM IS UNIFORMLY LOADED WITH 65% OF TOWER'S OPERATING WEIGHT

CROSSFLOW INDUCED - DRAFT PACKAGED COOLING TOWER - 200 TO 500 TON CAPACITY

NOTES

1. Cooling towers cool water for reuse in refrigeration condensers or other heat exchangers. Standard ratings are in tons of refrigeration when cooling 3 gal/min per ton from 95 to 85°F with ambient air at 78°F wet bulb. Selection is based on performance at local outdoor design conditions. Frequently the local outdoor ambient wet bulb temperature used is equal to or exceeded by 1% of summer hours.

2. Fans move air horizontally (crossflow) or up (counterflow) against water falling and wetting the fill or packing, to expose maximum water surface to the air. Reduced air flow reduces tower performance. Architectural enclosures should minimize obstruction to air flow.

3. Warm water is distributed at the top of the cooling tower by spray nozzles or basins with multiple orifices, and cooled water is collected in a basin at the bottom and pumped to condensers. Water is cooled by evaporating a very small portion. Water droplets may also be carried out by the air stream. Minerals and impurities present in all water increase concentration as pure water evaporates, so a little water is "bled" and chemicals are added to minimize scaling, corrosion, or biological fouling of condenser tubes. Towers for critical or large systems should be multicell for maintenance without shutdown.

4. Fan, motor, and water splashing noise may be a nuisance. Fan noise is reduced by two speed motors (about 8 dB at half speed, 15% power, and 60% capacity) and by intake and discharge attenuators (about 12 dB) with 10% power increase. Tower noise is louder in line with fan discharge and intake than in other directions. Each doubling of distance decreases noise about 6 dB. Barriers can reflect some noise from critical directions. Locate towers for free air movement. Avoid hot air recirculation, long piping from pumps and condensers, and inadequate substructures. Cooling towers should be located so that noise and water droplet carryover and fog at air discharge in cold weather will not be a nuisance. Consider seismic and wind load in anchoring tower to supports; towers are usually designed to withstand 30 psf wind load. Basins may be heated for winter use.

ENCLOSURE CONSIDERATIONS

Provide liberal wall openings on air inlet sides and mount tower so that air outlet is at top of enclosure. Consider effect of wind on nearby structure and enclosure to minimize hot, moist discharge air from being recirculated into inlet.

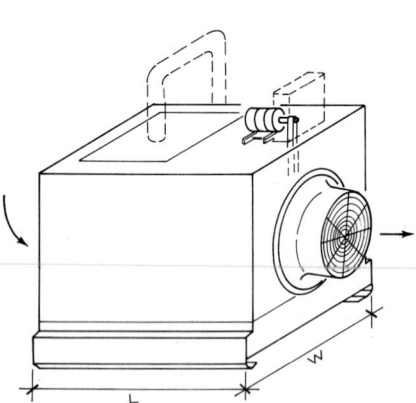

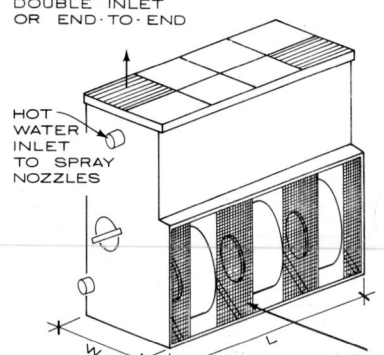

NOTE AVAILABLE IN SINGLE MODULES AS SKETCHED, OR BACK-TO-BACK DOUBLE INLET OR END-TO-END

HOT WATER INLET TO SPRAY NOZZLES

AIR IN

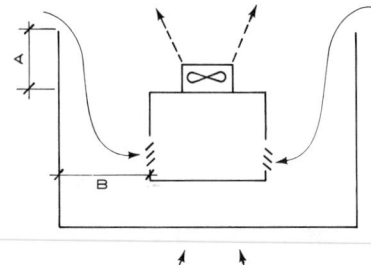

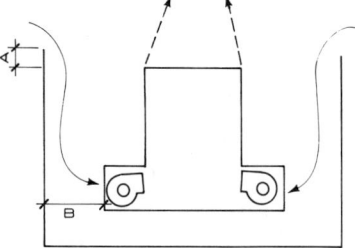

A = Height of enclosure above tower outlet. Minimize or extend shroud up from tower.

B = If enclosure walls have no opening, horizontal distance from tower inlet must increase greatly.

(Power for fan must be increased.)

Consult cooling tower manufacturer for minimum "B" dimension.

SMALL CROSSFLOW INDUCED DRAFT PACKAGE COOLING TOWER

TONS 3GPM/ TON 95-85-78	OVERALL DIMENSIONS (IN.)			OPERATING WEIGHT (LB)	MOTOR (HP)
	L	W	HT.		
5	62	34	49	750	1/3
25	70	48	78	1,200	3/4
50	82	76	92	2,400	1 1/2
100	100	95	100	5,600	5
200	83	164	117	8,300	10
500	113	232	160	19,300	25

COUNTERFLOW FORCED DRAFT PACKAGE COOLING TOWER

TONS 3GPM/ TON 95-85-78	OVERALL DIMENSIONS (IN.)			OPERATING WEIGHT (LB)	MOTOR (HP)
	L	W	HT.		
20	45	48	78	950	1 1/2
50	81	48	78	1,500	5
200	156	63	161	5,600	25
400	156	115	198	12,000	50
800	300	115	198	24,000	Two-50
1600	448	115	198	47,000	Four-50

Frederick H. Kohloss; Frederick H. Kohloss & Associates; Honolulu, Hawaii

15

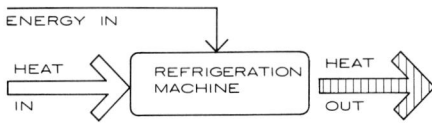

The basic refrigeration cycle performs one simple job; it moves heat from one place to another. Refrigerators move heat from the storage compartment to the surrounding room. Air-conditioners move heat from building rooms to the outside environment. Refrigeration equipment's efficiency is indicated by its Energy Efficiency Rating. EER is an index of the number of BTU's of heat movement accomplished per watt of electrical input energy. The higher the EER, the more efficient, and less costly it will be to operate a given piece of equipment.

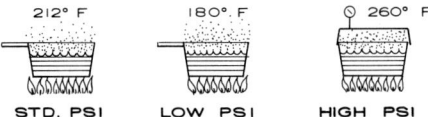

A large quantity of heat is required to boil or evaporate a liquid. This latent or hidden heat is the key to moving large quantities of heat with a small amount of refrigerant.

To move heat from an area of low temperature to an area of high temperature (e.g., a building at 75°F to its environment at 95°F) refrigeration equipment needs to change boiling temperature of the refrigerant. This is accomplished by changing the pressure on the refrigerant.

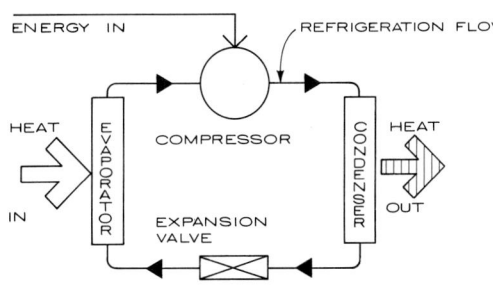

The basic refrigeration cycle includes an evaporator coil which absorbs heat from its surroundings as a refrigerant evaporates internally. The refrigerant vapor is then drawn into a compressor where its pressure and boiling (or condensing) temperature are increased. The refrigerant vapor is then discharged into a condenser coil where it gives up the latent heat absorbed in the evaporator and returns to a liquid state. Finally, liquid refrigerant circulates through an expansion valve where pressure and evaporation temperature are reduced, and the cycle is repeated.

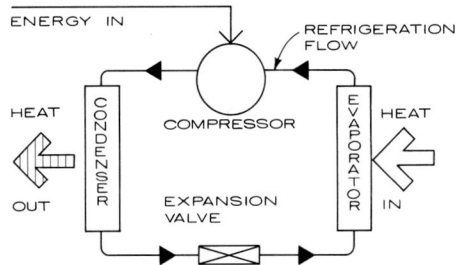

The compressive refrigeration cycle may be reversed to extract heat from a low temperature source (such as outside air) and reject that heat at higher temperature to heat a building. The basic equipment is unchanged with the exception of a four-way reversing valve and controls which permit the condensor and evaporator to exchange functions. The heat pump is more efficient than electrical resistance heat. Its efficiency, of course, is a function of heat source temperature.

F. J. Trost; Texas A & M University; College Station, Texas

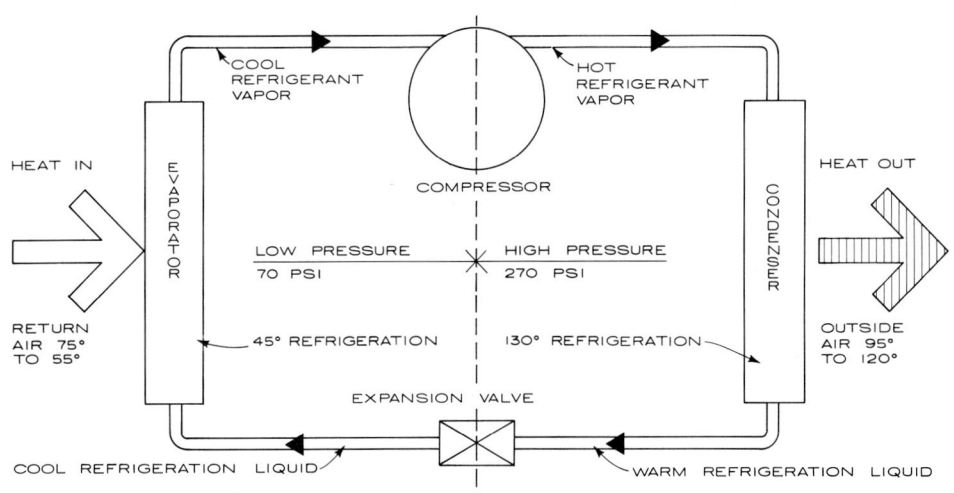

TYPICAL SYSTEM TEMPERATURES AND PRESSURES

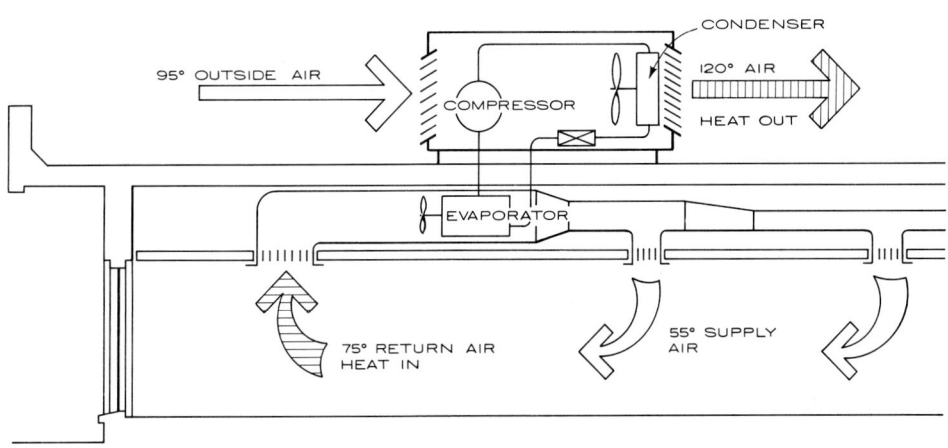

TYPICAL ROOM APPLICATION

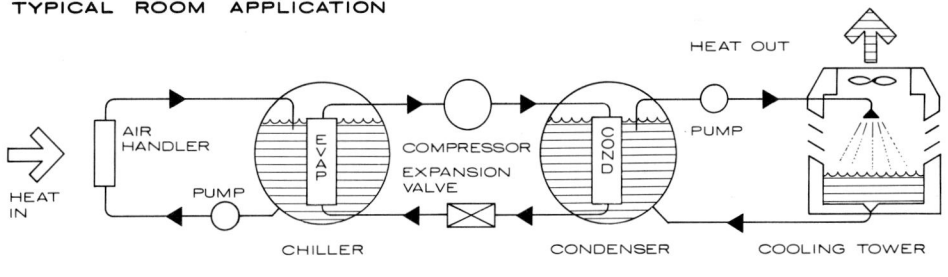

CHILLER AND COOLING TOWER

In large buildings it is impractical to move heat with air only, since duct size would be excessive. Therefore, a chiller (water tank) is added to the evaporator, and chilled water is circulated to air handling units throughout the building. Cooling towers are typically installed in such large systems to increase efficiency. Air-conditioning equipment rejecting heat to 80°F cooling tower water will require less input energy than the same equipment rejecting heat to 95°F outside air.

A second refrigeration cycle, the absorption cycle, uses a heat source and an absorbent to move heat.

The absorber and generator perform the same function as the compressor (see above); and the cycle operates under high vacuum. Generally speaking, absorption systems are less efficient than compressive systems and are a wise choice only when waste heat is available for input energy.

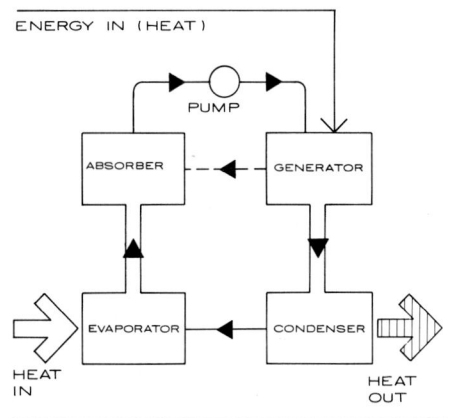

ABSORPTION CYCLE

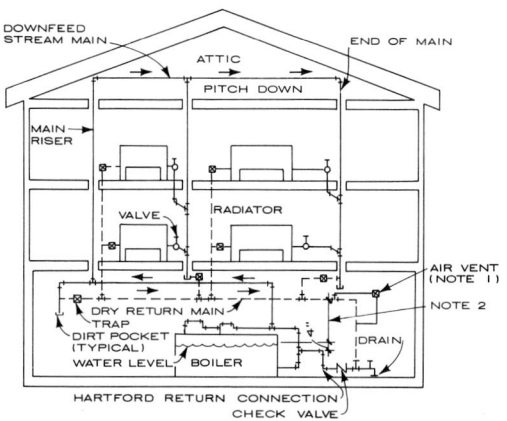

NOTES

1. AIR VENT: When used, boiler operating pressure must not exceed static head required for the return of condensate by gravity.
2. WATER COLUMN HEIGHT: From water line to end of dry main it determines maximum boiler operating pressure.

DOWNFEED TWO PIPE VAPOR SYSTEM

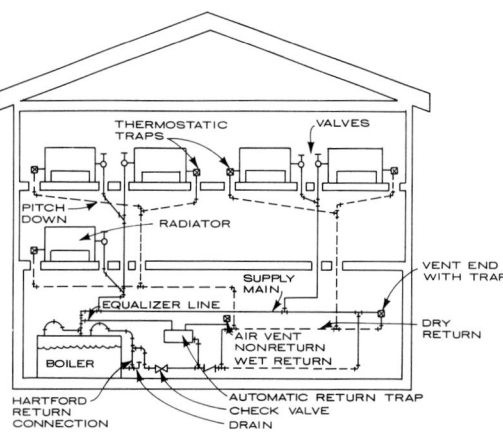

NOTES

1. Proper connections are critical for air venting and pressure equalization. Operating pressure ranges from 0 to 15 psig. Use of return trap permits operating at a vacuum.
2. Two pipe vacuum system distribution piping is the same as shown for upfeed or downfeed systems.

UPFEED TWO PIPE VAPOR SYSTEM WITH AUTOMATIC RETURN TRAP

PIPING DIMENSIONS

VACUUM RETURN PIPE DIAMETER	MAXIMUM LENGTH (A)
1″	7″
1 1/4″	8″
1 1/2″	9″
2″	10″
2 1/2″	14″
3″	13″
4″	16″
5″	21″
6″	24″

VACUUM SYSTEM—CONDENSATE LIFT

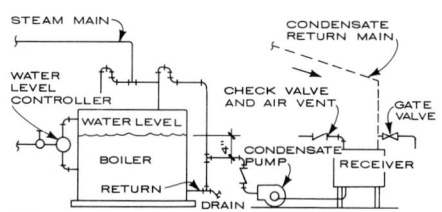

TWO PIPE SYSTEM WITH CONDENSATE RETURN PUMP
(SAME FOR GRAVITY OR VACUUM SYSTEMS)

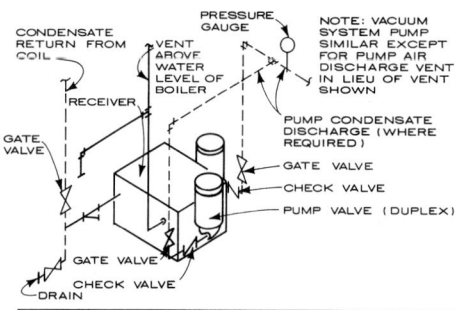

CONDENSATE PUMP PIPING DETAIL

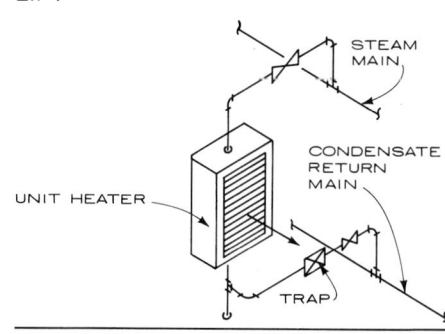

UNIT HEATER PIPING DETAIL

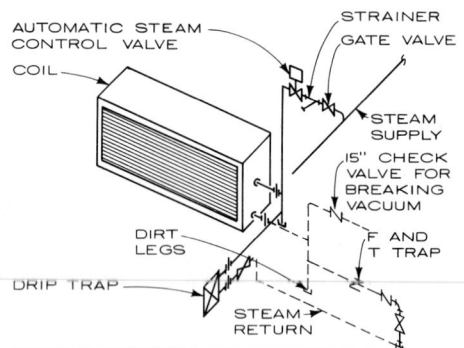

STEAM COIL DETAIL

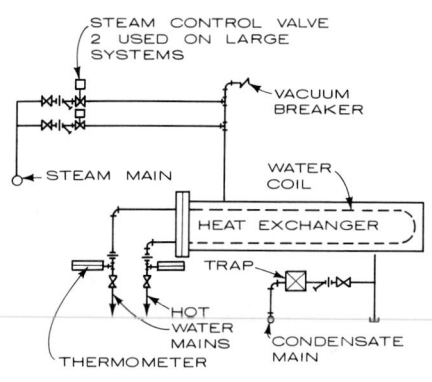

TYPICAL HEAT EXCHANGER DETAIL

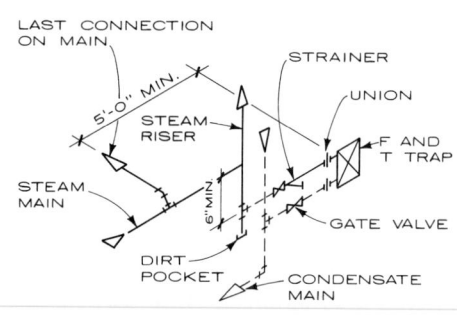

DRIP AT RISE OR END OF STEAM MAIN

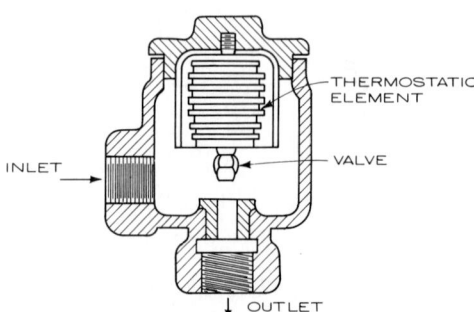

THERMOSTATIC TRAP — BELLOWS TYPE

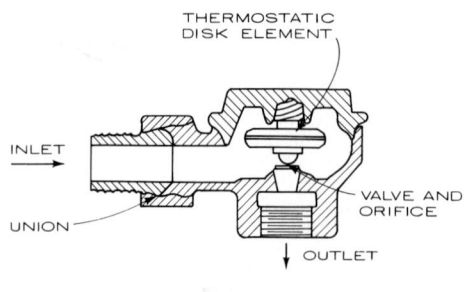

THERMOSTATIC TRAP—DISK DIAPHRAGM TYPE

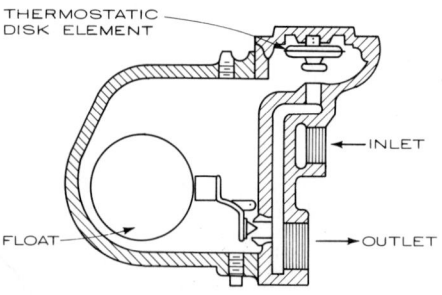

TYPICAL FLOAT AND THERMOSTATIC TRAP

TYPICAL STEAM TRAPS

Raymond G. Alvine and Associates, P.E.; Omaha, Nebraska

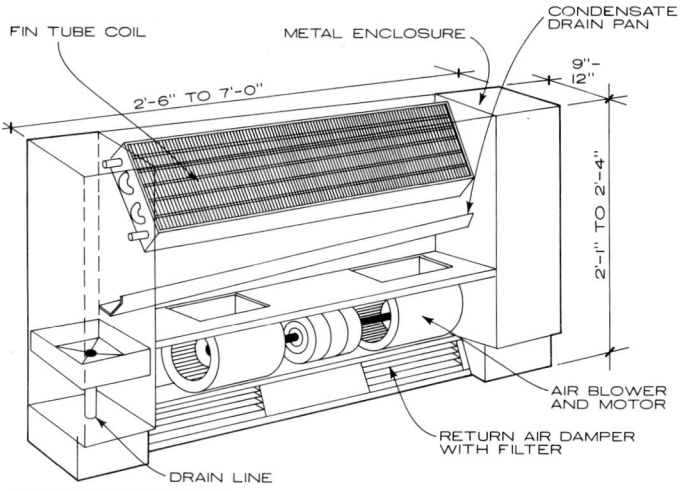

FIN TUBE COIL   METAL ENCLOSURE   CONDENSATE DRAIN PAN
2'-6" TO 7'-0"   9"-12"   2'-1" TO 2'-4"
AIR BLOWER AND MOTOR
RETURN AIR DAMPER WITH FILTER
DRAIN LINE

STANDARD FAN COIL UNIT

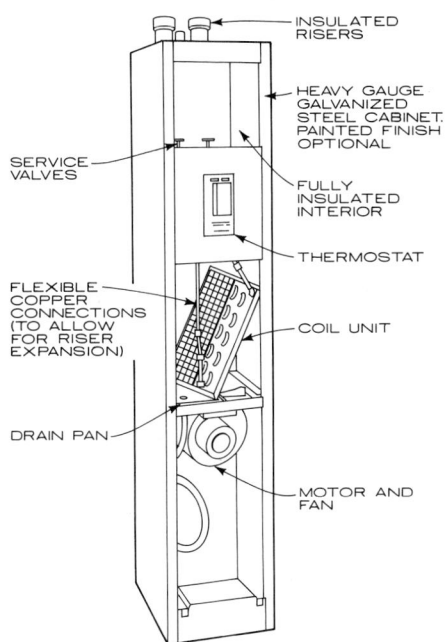

INSULATED RISERS
HEAVY GAUGE GALVANIZED STEEL CABINET. PAINTED FINISH OPTIONAL
SERVICE VALVES
FULLY INSULATED INTERIOR
THERMOSTAT
FLEXIBLE COPPER CONNECTIONS (TO ALLOW FOR RISER EXPANSION)
COIL UNIT
DRAIN PAN
MOTOR AND FAN

STANDARD HIGHRISE UNIT

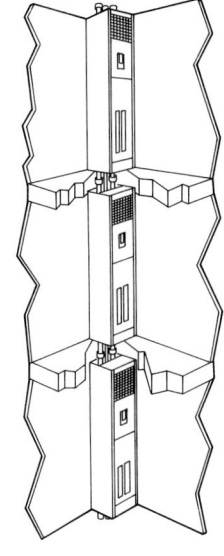

HIGHRISE APPLICATION

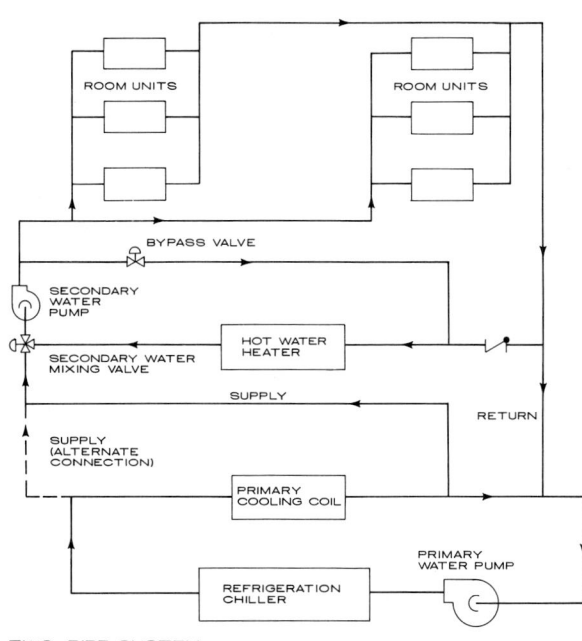

ROOM UNITS   ROOM UNITS
BYPASS VALVE
SECONDARY WATER PUMP
HOT WATER HEATER
SECONDARY WATER MIXING VALVE
SUPPLY
SUPPLY (ALTERNATE CONNECTION)
RETURN
PRIMARY COOLING COIL
PRIMARY WATER PUMP
REFRIGERATION CHILLER

TWO-PIPE SYSTEM

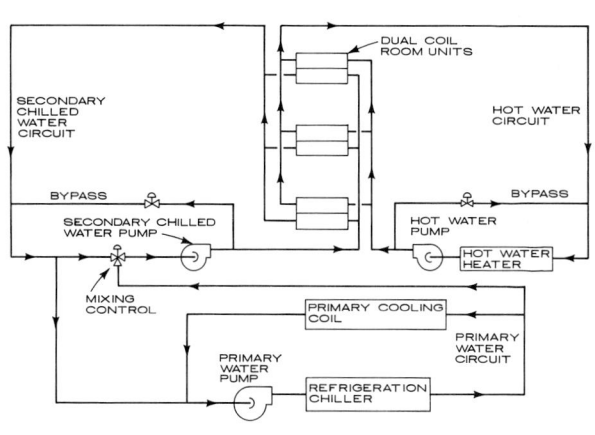

DUAL COIL ROOM UNITS
SECONDARY CHILLED WATER CIRCUIT
HOT WATER CIRCUIT
BYPASS   BYPASS
SECONDARY CHILLED WATER PUMP
HOT WATER PUMP
HOT WATER HEATER
MIXING CONTROL
PRIMARY COOLING COIL
PRIMARY WATER PUMP
PRIMARY WATER CIRCUIT
REFRIGERATION CHILLER

FOUR-PIPE SYSTEM

PIPING SYSTEMS

NOTES

Chilled water terminals are fan coil units used to dehumidify and cool the airstream injected into the conditioned space.

The typical fan coil unit consists of a finned tube chilled water coil, which is finned to increase its heat transfer surface, a fan used to circulate air over the coil and discharge cool air into the conditioned space, a drip pan to collect condensate from the dehumidified air and drain line to transport the condensate away from the fan coil unit.

Fan coil systems are classified into two major groups:

1. A TWO-PIPE SYSTEM uses a single supply pipe (hot or cold depending on the season) and a single return pipe, in a secondary water circuit. Chilled water is introduced into the secondary circuit directly through a mixing valve from the primary chilled water circuit. If the terminal unit is to provide heat, a hot water, steam, or electric heat exchanger is incorporated into the loop. Direct introduction of hot water from a primary circuit is also employed. The water coil output of each terminal unit is controlled by a local space thermostat.

2. The FOUR-PIPE SYSTEM provides independent sources of heating and cooling to each room unit through separate supply and return chilled water pipes and separate supply and return hot water pipes. The terminal units usually have two separate water coils as well. Local thermostats control the volume of secondary water supplied to each unit.

NOTE

Highrise corner units can be furred into the walls of the room. They minimize the piping from floor to floor since they are stacked and directly connected to the units above and below for water supply, returns, and drains.

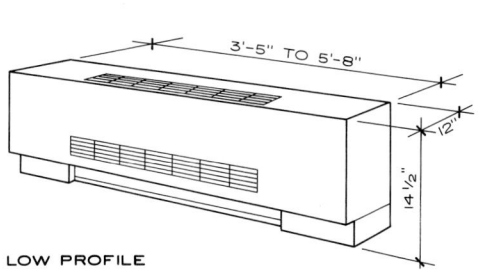

3'-5" TO 5'-8"
14 1/2"
12"

LOW PROFILE

NOTE

A low profile fan coil unit is available for installation along window walls, below chalkboards, or in lobbies and hallways where appearance is important. They normally stand free from the wall, with clearance behind the unit for draperies.

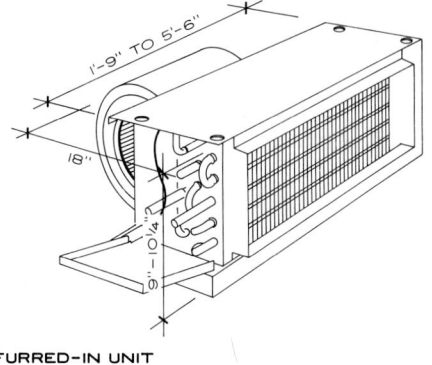

1'-9" TO 5'-6"
18"
9'-10 1/4"

FURRED-IN UNIT

NOTE

Furred-in units can be mounted where convenient in the room. They can use ducts to bring in outside air and can be mounted in wall alcoves or ceiling spaces. A removable front panel is needed to conceal the unit and provide complete access to internal components.

GENERAL NOTES

Chilled water is the most common medium for transferring heat from any type of cooling equipment, such as cooling coils and heat exchangers, to some source of refrigeration.

A chilled water system is a closed circuit system that recirculates water between a mechanical refrigeration water chilling unit and remote cooling equipment, usually operating with water temperatures in the range between 40 and 55°F. There are three types of refrigeration units used in chilled water systems.

1. Centrifugal chiller with electric motor or steam turbine drive.
2. Reciprocating chiller, with electric motor drive.
3. Steam absorption chiller.

When a chilled water system is also used to circulate hot water for winter heating, it is called a dual temperature water system. A heat pump may serve as a source for both hot water and chilled water in a dual temperature system. The design water temperature of chilled water systems usually falls in a rather narrow range because of limitations imposed by the necessity for dehumidification and by avoidance of the possibility of freeze-up in the chiller. Chilled water supply temperatures ranging from 42 to 60°F are normally employed in comfort applications.

Design flow rates depend on the type of terminal apparatus and the supply temperature. In general, a higher temperature rise (or a greater temperature difference between supply and return temperatures) reduces the initial cost and the operating cost of the distribution system and pumps required and increases the efficiency of the chillers. In a given chilled water system, the selection of the design flow rate and the supply temperature, therefore, are closely related.

Although lower chilled water temperatures permit higher rises (or larger temperature difference) lower chiller efficiencies result.

Water treatment may be required in chilled water systems to control corrosion rate, scaling, or algae growth.

Layout of piping systems for chilled water distribution vary greatly depending on system capacity, extent of distribution, type of terminals used, and control scheme to be employed.

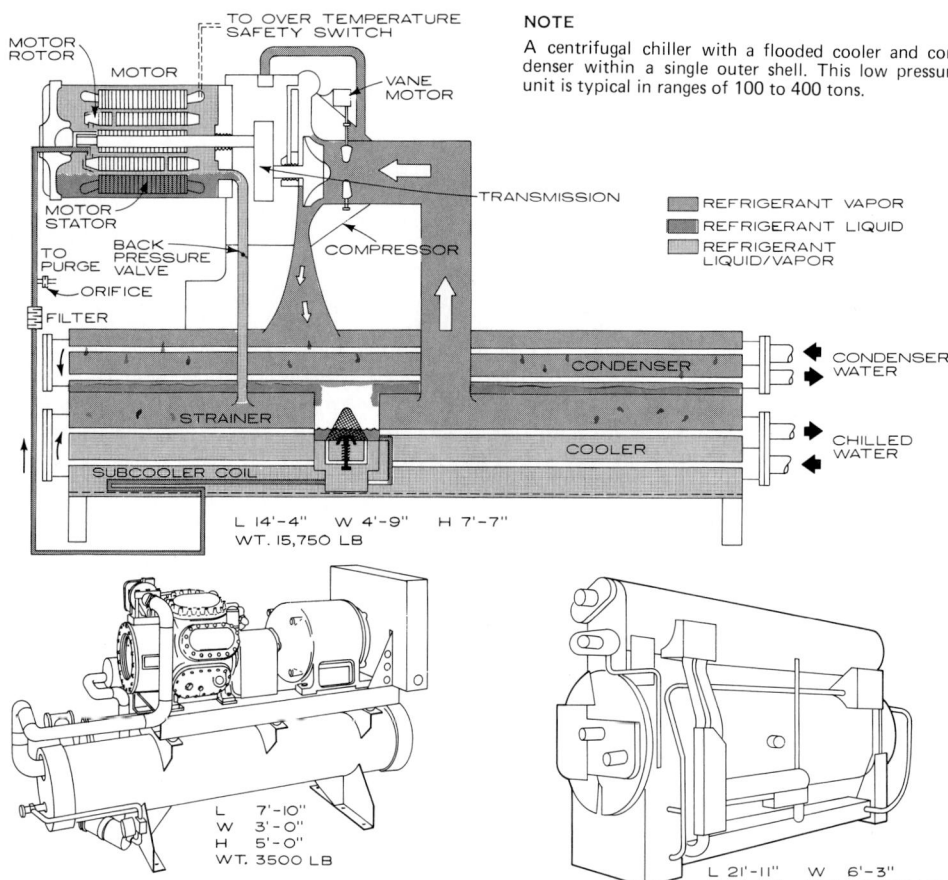

NOTE

A centrifugal chiller with a flooded cooler and condenser within a single outer shell. This low pressure unit is typical in ranges of 100 to 400 tons.

REFRIGERANT VAPOR
REFRIGERANT LIQUID
REFRIGERANT LIQUID/VAPOR

L 14'-4" W 4'-9" H 7'-7"
WT. 15,750 LB

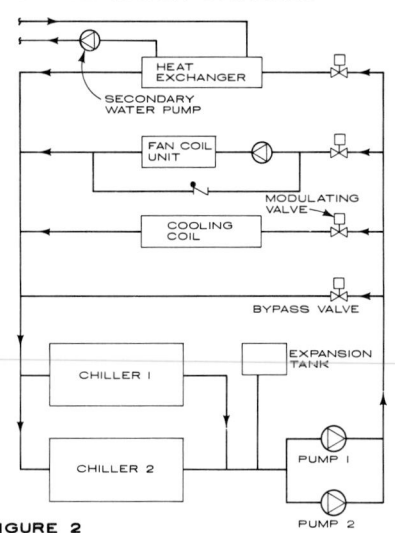

NOTE

A typical reciprocating package chiller, ideally suited to smaller jobs requiring less than 200 tons cooling.

L 7'-10"
W 3'-0"
H 5'-0"
WT. 3500 LB

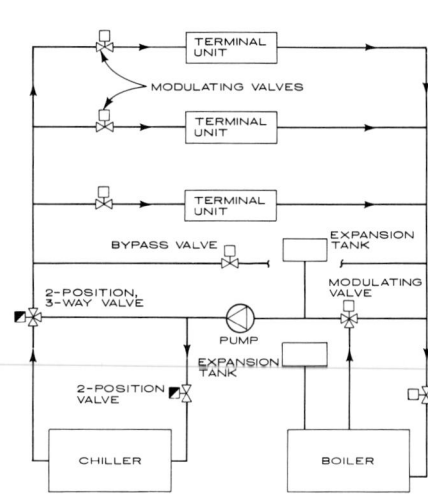

NOTE

A two-stage absorption chiller, steam powered for efficient production of 200 to 600 tons of cooling.

L 21'-11" W 6'-3"
H 11'-10" WT. 65,000 LB

PACKAGE WATER CHILLERS

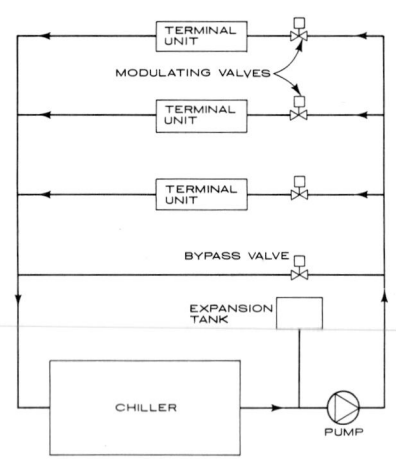

FIGURE I
ELEMENTARY CHILLED WATER SYSTEM

NOTE

A chilled water system basically consists of a refrigeration water chilling unit, a chilled water recirculating pump, terminal cooling equipment, and an expansion tank. A chilled water bypass valve may be required in systems with two-way modulating valve control at the terminal units. As the cooling load on the terminal equipment decreases, the modulating valve closes and reduces the flow through the terminal. When the water flow through the terminal units is significantly throttled, the bypass valve opens gradually to prevent system pressure buildup and to maintain the water flow required for the proper operation of the chiller.

FIGURE 2
MULTIPLE END USE CHILLED WATER SYSTEM

NOTE

In large commercial system applications, the chilled water system consists of multiple chillers and pumps and a differential pressure controlled bypass valve arrangement. The terminal cooling equipment may be chilled water cooling coil of a central station air-conditioning unit, direct injection secondary water pump of a terminal fan coil unit system, heat exchanger of a closed loop dual-temperature secondary water system, and so on.

The chilled water bypass valve operates as described under elementary chilled water system.

FIGURE 3
TWO-PIPE DUAL TEMPERATURE SYSTEM

NOTE

In a two-pipe dual temperature system hot water is circulated through the terminal units during cold weather and chilled water is circulated during the hot weather. The distribution system may be divided into zones, each of which is capable of changeover from heating to cooling, independent of the other zones.

When the hot and chilled water supply to each terminal unit is in two separate pipes, but the return is in a common pipe, the system is called a three-pipe system. In a four-pipe system, separate supply and return mains for both hot and chilled water are run to each terminal unit.

Anilkumar V. Patel; Joseph R. Loring & Associates, Inc., Consulting Engineers; New York, New York

GENERAL

The process of removing heat from a refrigerant is called condensing. It is during the condensing process, in a refrigerant cycle, that the refrigerant rejects heat absorbed during the evaporation and compression processes, is reconverted to a liquid state, and becomes ready to repeat the cycle.

To convert the refrigerant from gaseous to liquid state heat exchangers called condensers are used. Air cooled and water cooled condensers are the predominant types used in the building construction industry.

In the less than 50 ton capacity range, water cooled condensers are favored mostly where city water or other water sources such as lake, river, or well are available for once-through use without recirculation of water.

Where water is scarce, as well as in computer rooms and other special air-conditioning applications where year-round temperature and humidity control is required, dry coolers of up to 25 ton capacity are normally used. Where winter ambient is below the water freezing temperature, glycol is added to the condenser water. The heat rejection to the outdoor air is by sensible heat transfer, which is dependent on the dry bulb temperature of the air.

In refrigeration systems larger than 50 ton capacity, water cooled condensers are used to cool the recirculating condenser water. Both the closed circuit evaporative cooler and the cooling tower operate on the principle of evaporative cooling, which is dependent on the wet bulb temperature of the air. The closed circuit evaporative coolers are available in sizes up to 300 tons, and are used when contamination of the condenser water by its direct contact with the outdoor air cannot be tolerated.

Use of cooling tower is generally acceptable in most installations in the building construction industry. Temperature of the water leaving the cooling tower is approximately 7 to 10°F above the wet bulb temperature of the air flowing through the spray deck of the tower.

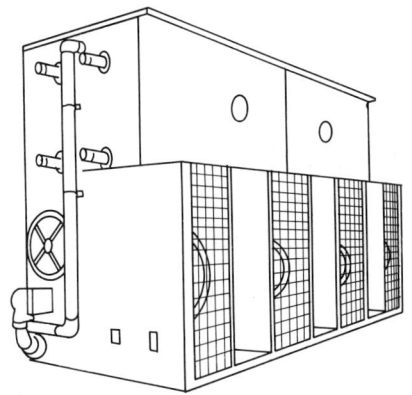

THE EVAPORATIVE CONDENSER combines the functions of a cooling tower and a water cooling condenser. Latent heat transfer is more effective as a means of heat dissipation. This permits a smaller sized unit than an equivalent tonnage air cooled unit, and considerable energy savings in fan horsepower.

Installations can be either indoors in an equipment room with appropriate ducts or outdoors ground mounted or mounted on a roof. When outdoors, adequate protection from freezing must be provided.

For sizing of condensing units, the manufacturers' rating is the only reliable method of determining the unit capacity.

Multiple evaporative condensers may be connected in parallel, or an evaporative condenser may be connected in parallel with a shell and tube condenser. Proper piping and traps must be installed in these cases to prevent unequal loading or overloading.

Two or more independent refrigeration circuits may be incorporated in a single evaporative condenser unit. With the proper circuiting arrangements, each may operate at a different suction and condensing temperature.

Anilkumar V. Patel; Joseph R. Loring & Associates, Inc., Consulting Engineers; New York, New York

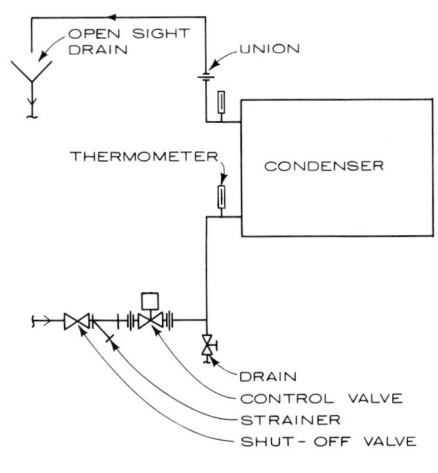

WATER COOLED CONDENSER

For water cooled condenser using city, well, or river water, the return is run higher than the condenser so that the condenser is always full of water. Water flow through the condenser is regulated by a supply line control valve, which is actuated from condenser head pressure control to maintain a constant condensing temperature with variations in load. City water systems usually require check valves and open sight drains, as shown.

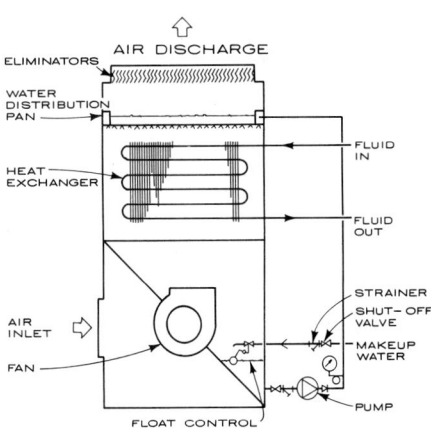

EVAPORATIVE COOLER

The condenser water is circulated inside the tubes of the unit's heat exchanger. Heat flows from the condenser water through the heat exchanger tubes to the spray water outside, which is cascading downward over the tubes. Air is forced upward through the heat exchanger, evaporating a small percentage of the spray water, absorbing the latent heat of vaporization, and discharging the heat to the atmosphere.

The remaining water falls to the sump to be recirculated by the pump. The water consumed is the amount evaporated plus a small amount that is bled off to limit the concentration of impurities in the pan.

The condenser water circulates through the clean, closed loop of the heat exchanger and is never exposed to the airstream or the spray water outside the heat exchanger tubes.

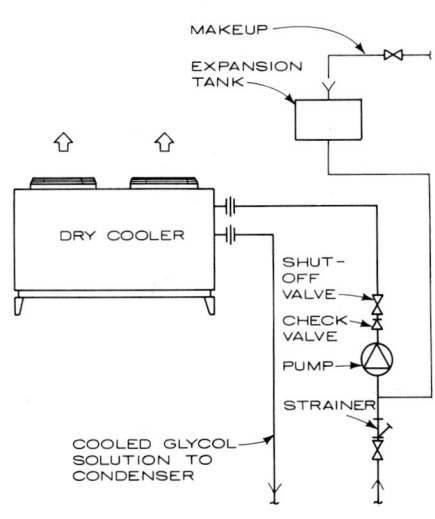

DRY COOLER

The condenser water-glycol solution is circulated inside the finned tubes of the dry cooler's heat exchanger. Heat flows from the condenser water-glycol solution through the heat exchanger tube walls to the fins. Propeller fans draw air over the fins, which transfer its heat to the air passing over it.

An aquastat sensing the temperature of the solution that leaves the dry cooler cycles the fan(s) to maintain the desired temperature.

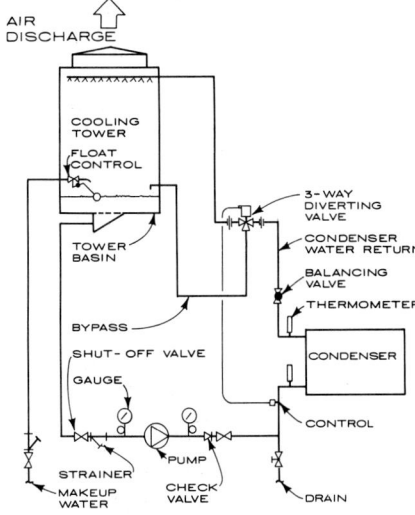

COOLING TOWER

Water flows to the pump from the tower basin and is discharged under pressure to the condenser and back to the tower where it is cooled through the spray deck. Since it is usually desirable to maintain condenser water temperature above a predetermined minimum, return water is partially bypassed around the tower through a control valve to maintain desired supply water temperature.

In this condenser water system, air is continuously in contact with the water. Special consideration for chemical treatment and allowance for impurities, scale, and corrosion in condenser and piping system designs is then required.

Water flow quantity required depends on the refrigeration system employed and the available temperature of the condenser water. Lower condenser water supply temperature results in increased refrigeration machine efficiency.

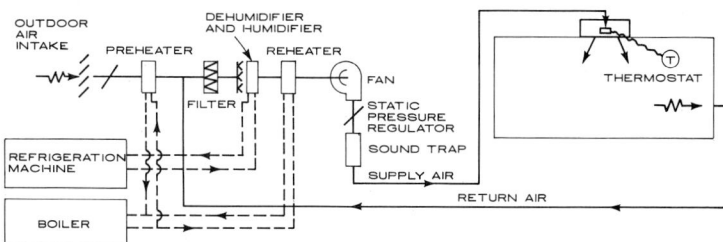

SINGLE DUCT, VARIABLE VOLUME

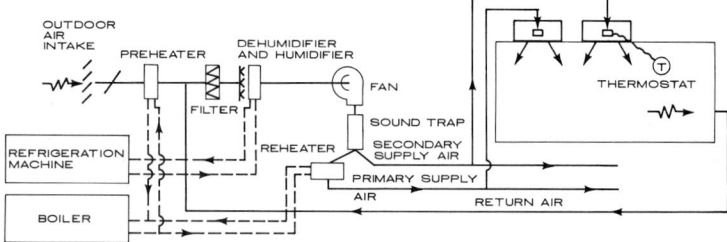

DUAL CONDUIT

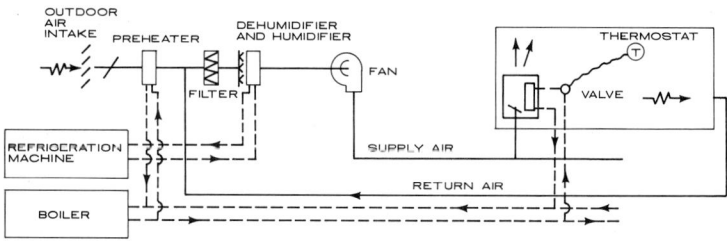

SINGLE DUCT WITH REHEAT

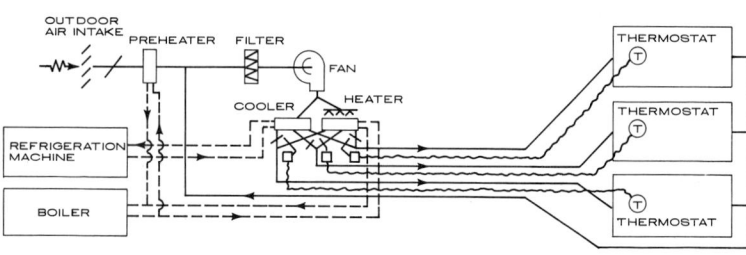

MULTIZONE

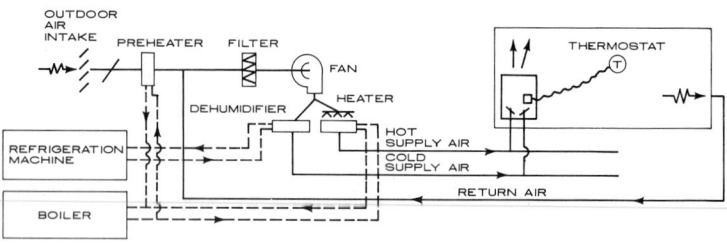

DOUBLE DUCT, CONSTANT VOLUME

ALL—AIR SYSTEMS

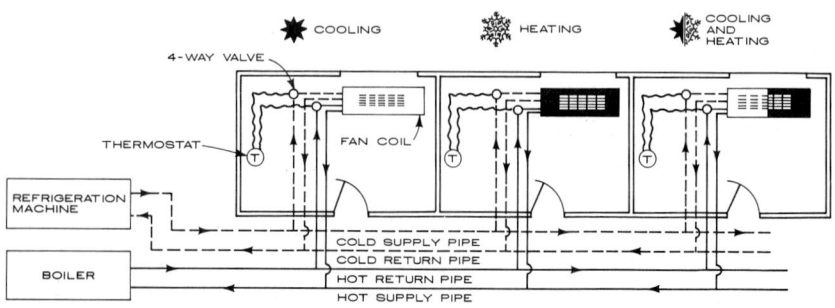

FOUR—PIPE DISTRIBUTION

ALL—WATER SYSTEMS

Carrier Corporation; Syracuse, New York

ALL-AIR SYSTEMS

With this type of system, the air treating and refrigeration plants may be located some distance from the conditioned space in a central mechanical room. The central treating station not only cleans the air, but also heats or cools, humidifies or dehumidifies. Only the final cooling-heating medium (air) is brought into the conditioned space through ducts and distributed within the space through outlets or mixing terminals.

The common names for some of the all-air types are:

Single duct, variable volume.
Dual conduit.
Single duct with reheat.
Multizone.
Double duct.

SINGLE DUCT, VARIABLE VOLUME

This central station system supplies a single stream of either hot or cold air at normal velocity. Capacity is adjusted to load by automatic volume control. Systems for exterior rooms would be zoned by exposure.

There are air terminal diffusers available that have self-contained, self-balancing, system operated controls, which are factory installed and calibrated.

DUAL CONDUIT

This high velocity system with central air treating plant supplies two air streams to each room. The constant volume, variable temperature primary air supply neutralizes transmission gains or losses throughout the year. The secondary stream is variable volume, constant temperature. Room terminals incorporate thermostatically controlled air volume regulators.

SINGLE DUCT WITH REHEAT

This system consolidates all major equipment in the machine room except the reheat element that is located at times near the room or in the module. Primary treated air is supplied at constant volume from this central point through a single duct to room units. Each room unit is equipped with a small steam or hot water reheat coil, which is located either in the supply air stream or in an induced air position. Supply air temperature can be as low as 38°F, thus conserving on duct size and fan horsepower.

MULTIZONE

This method distributes a single air stream to each room through finger ducts at normal velocity. Central air treating apparatus includes dampers that premix the cold and warm air supplies controlled by room thermostats.

DOUBLE DUCT, CONSTANT VOLUME

This central station system supplies treated air through a pair of ducts to room terminals of special design and function. These terminals mix air automatically to maintain proper temperatures as well as proper volume and air patterns.

ALL-WATER SYSTEMS

The all-water systems are those with fan coil types of room terminals to which may be connected one or two water circuits. The cooling medium (such as chilled water or brine) may be supplied from a remote source and circulated through the coils in the fan coil terminal, which is located in the conditioned space. These circuits may be either two-pipe or four-pipe distribution. Ventilation is obtained through an opening in the wall or from bleed-off from the interior zone system or by infiltration. Another variation, uses a unit ventilator.

TWO-PIPE

Either hot or chilled water is piped throughout the building to a number of fan coil units. One pipe supplies water and the other returns it.

FOUR-PIPE

Two separate piping circuits are used—one for hot and one for chilled water. The modified fan coil unit has a double or split coil. Part of this heats only and part cools only.

AIR-WATER SYSTEMS

Like the all-air system, the air apparatus and refrigeration plants are separate from the conditioned space; however, the cooling-heating of the conditioned space is affected in only a small part by air brought from the central apparatus. The major part of room thermal load is balanced by warm or cooled water circulated either through a coil in an induction unit or through a radiant panel.

The different air-water types are:

  Induction . . . either bypass air or water control.
  Fan coil with supplementary air.
  Radiant panels with supplementary air.

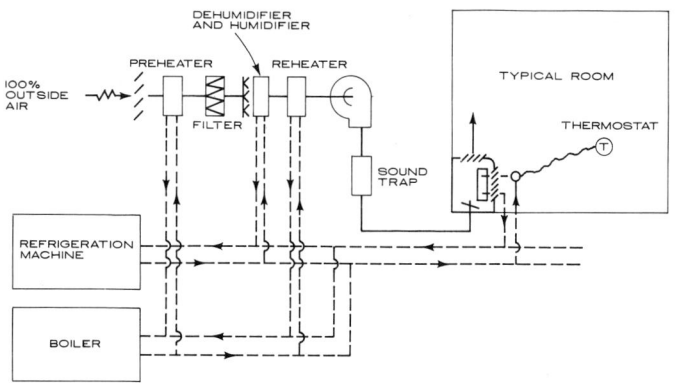

INDUCTION

INDUCTION

This system uses a high velocity, high pressure, constant volume air supply to a high induction type of terminal. Induced air from the room is either heated or cooled within the terminal as required. This capacity control is by flow of water or air bypass. This system may use two pipes (one water circuit) or four pipes (two water circuits) for heating and cooling.

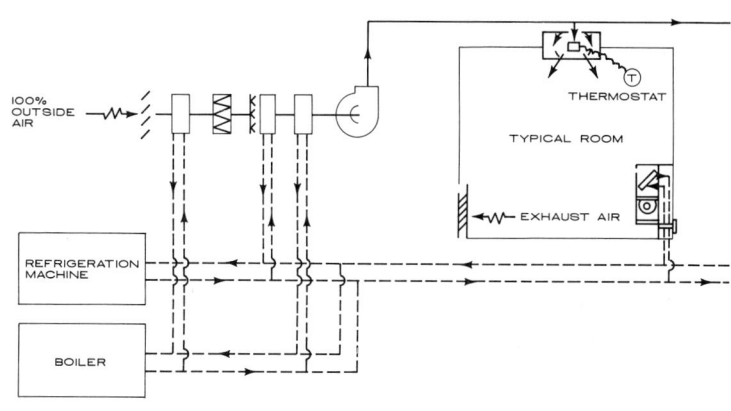

FAN COIL WITH SUPPLY AIR

THE FAN-COIL WITH SUPPLEMENTARY AIR

The fan-coil type of terminal provides direct heating or cooling of the room air. A supplementary constant volume air supply provides the necessary ventilation.

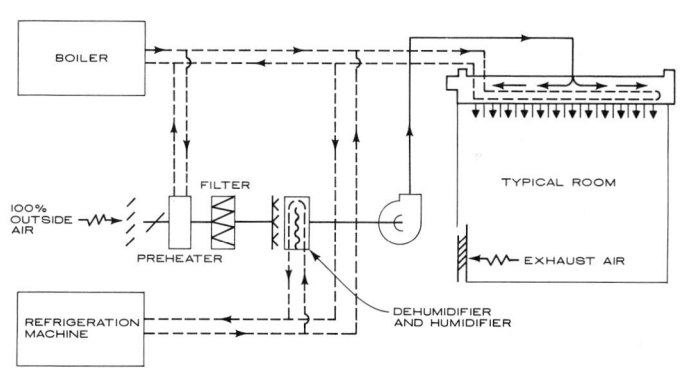

RADIANT PANELS WITH SUPPLY AIR

RADIANT PANELS WITH SUPPLEMENTARY AIR

The radiant panel terminal in ceiling or wall provides either radiant heating or cooling. A constant volume air stream is supplied for dehumidification and ventilation.

AIR — WATER SYSTEMS

DIRECT REFRIGERANT SYSTEMS

Refrigerant systems are those that utilize self-contained window, in-the-wall, roof, or floor mounted units for extracting or adding heat. The units are normally located within or next to the air conditioned space and consist of only the elements essential to producing the cooling or heating effect. Heating can be provided either by reverse cycle type, such as a heat pump, or by supplementary heating elements.

ROOFTOP

Uses gas or electricity to supply both heating and cooling.

THROUGH-THE-WALL

Cooling unit used with gas, electric, or central hot water heating for year-round air conditioning.

PACKAGED

Systems contained roof mounted, air cooled condensing units. A reverse cycle heat pump or supplementary heating is required for year-round operation.

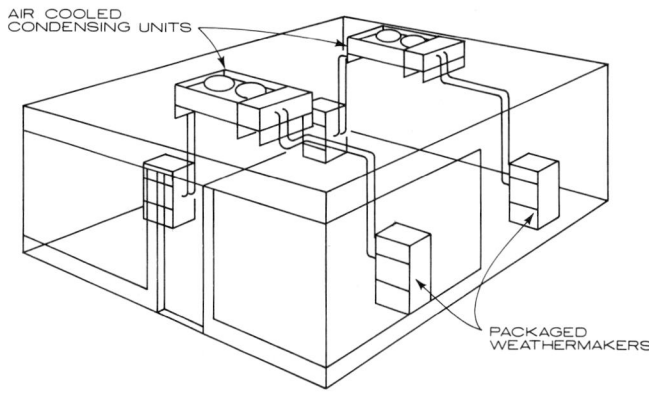

DIRECT REFRIGERANT SYSTEMS

Carrier Corporation; Syracuse, New York

GENERAL NOTES

The air handling equipment room should be centrally located to minimize the distance the air has to travel from equipment room to the farthest air-conditioned space. The fan noise transmission to the adjacent spaces must also be considered. If the equipment room is located near conference rooms, sleeping quarters, broadcasting studios, or other sound sensitive areas, special treatment of the equipment room area will be required to provide adequate sound and vibration isolation from the surrounding areas.

Adequate access space must be provided to maintain and replace heating coils, cooling coils, filters, damper motors and linkage, control valves, bearings, fan motors, fans, belts, pulleys, and so on.

The figure below shows plan of a typical equipment room with one floor mounted air-conditioning unit and one suspended return air fan. The air-conditioning unit shown is of the horizontal draw-through type and consists of fan head, reheat coil, cooling coil, preheat coil, filters, return air plenum, outdoor air intake plenum, and access sections on either side of coils.

Note that the outdoor air intake louver and the exhaust air louver are located on different walls. Where both the intake and the exhaust louver must be located on the same wall, they must be as far apart as possible, but not less than 10 ft in order to minimize the short circuiting between the exhaust and intake air. Baffles, of masonry or other suitable construction, may be used to achieve the separation between the exhaust and the intake air.

NOTES

1. Where a horizontal blow-through type of unit is used, the length of the unit will essentially be the same as shown for the draw-through unit.

2. Where higher headroom is available, a vertical unit, which can only be of the draw-through type, may be used to reduce the length of the unit. Depending on the size of the unit, this reduction in length will range from 2 ft to 3 ft 6 in.

3. The figure shows an axial fan for returning air from the space. The return air fan may not be required where the air-conditioning system is not designed to operate under economizer cycle (cooling by cold outdoor air) mode.

4. A floor mounted centrifugal fan, of single width, single inlet type or double width, double inlet type, may be used in place of the suspended axial fan shown. However, this will generally result in increased width of the equipment room.

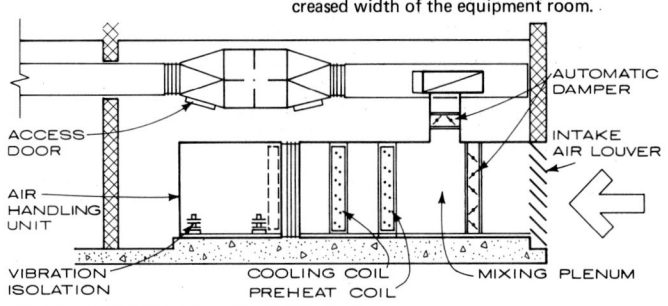

EQUIPMENT ROOM SECTION A-A

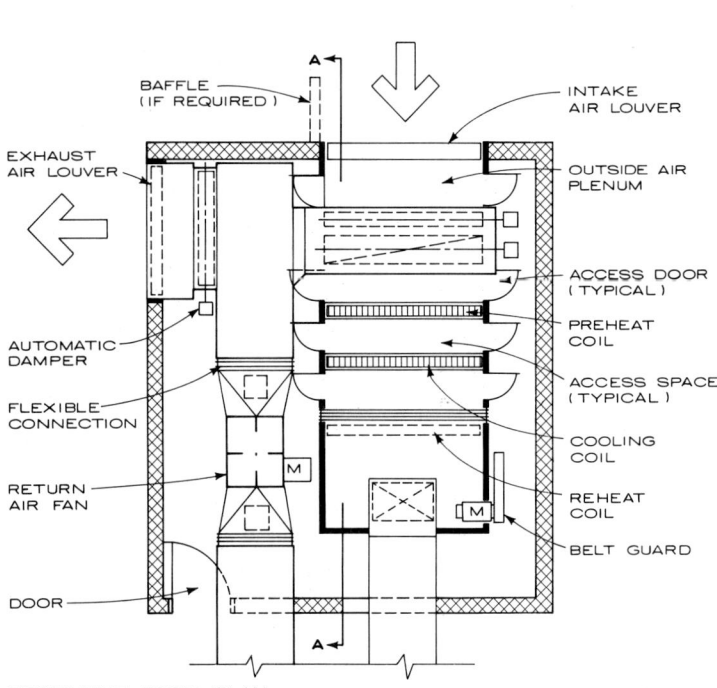

EQUIPMENT ROOM PLAN

AIR HANDLING EQUIPMENT ROOM REQUIREMENTS

EQUIPMENT ROOM SPACE REQUIREMENTS

CFM RANGE	APPROXIMATE OVERALL DIMENSION OF SUPPLY AIR UNITS			RECOMMENDED ROOM DIMENSIONS		
	W	H	L	W	H	L
1,000– 1,800	4'-9''	2'-9''	14'-9''	12'-6''	9'-0''	18'-9''
1,801– 3,000	5'-0''	3'-6''	16'-0''	13'-9''	9'-0''	20'-0''
3,001– 4,000	6'-9''	4'-6''	16'-0''	17'-6''	9'-0''	20'-0''
4,001– 6,000	7'-6''	4'-6''	16'-9''	18'-0''	9'-0''	20'-9''
6,001– 7,000	7'-6''	4'-9''	18'-3''	18'-6''	9'-6''	22'-3''
7,001– 9,000	8'-0''	5'-0''	18'-9''	19'-0''	10'-0''	22'-9''
9,001–12,000	10'-0''	5'-6''	21'-0''	23'-0''	11'-0''	25'-0''
12,001–16,000	10'-3''	6'-0''	22'-0''	23'-6''	12'-6''	26'-0''
16,001–19,000	10'-6''	6'-6''	23'-9''	24'-0''	13'-0''	27'-9''
19,001–22,000	11'-9''	7'-3''	25'-0''	26'-9''	15'-0''	29'-0''
22,001–27,000	11'-9''	8'-6''	26'-0''	27'-0''	16'-0''	30'-0''
27,001–32,000	13'-0''	9'-9''	27'-9''	29'-0''	18'-0''	31'-9''

AIR FILTRATION AND ODOR REMOVAL

Air filter selection is determined by the degree of cleanliness required. The initial cost, ease of maintenance, improvement of housekeeping, health benefits, and product quality are considerations. Size and quantity of dust and contaminants are also factors.

Filters most often are located at the air inlet of the heating, ventilating, and air-conditioning equipment, providing protection to the equipment and the area served. Filters are located at the equipment discharge and at entry of air into clean rooms, operating rooms, critical health care rooms, and various industrial process areas. Filters located in return air and exhaust air limit the contamination of other areas and the atmosphere.

AIR FILTER types are dry media, viscous (sticky) media, renewable media, and electronic. Filter performance tests and ratings have been established by ASHRAE, NBS, and AFI. The three operating characteristics that distinguish the various types of air cleaners are efficiency, air flow resistance, and dust holding capacity. Efficiency measures the ability of the air cleaner to remove particulate matter from an air stream. Average efficiency over the life of the filter is the most important consideration. Airflow resistance is the static pressure drop across the filter at a given airflow rate. Dust holding capacity defines the amount of a particular type of dust that an air cleaner can hold when operated at a specified airflow rate to some

maximum resistance value, or before its efficiency is seriously reduced as a result of the collected dust. Filter efficiency comparisons should always be based on the same test conditions.

PREFILTERS are required to extend the life of costlier high efficiency filters. High efficiency particulate filters (HEPA), and their integral frames, should be tested and certified in place. Filter pressure

drop gauges are recommended as an aid to economical replacement scheduling for all types of filters.

ODOR REMOVAL is best controlled by limiting the source. Dilution of odors by direct exhaust ventilation is the most common control method. Air washer and carbon filters are usually used for reclaiming odorous air. Ozone treatment and aerosol masking of odors are sometimes used.

AIR FILTER CHARACTERISTICS

MEDIA AND TYPE	PERCENT EFFICIENCY RANGE		DUST HOLDING CAPACITY	AIRFLOW RESISTANCE (IN. WATER)
	ATMOSPHERIC DUST	SMALL PARTICLES		
Dry panel throwaway	15–30	NA	Excellent	0.1–0.5
Viscous panel throwaway	20–35	NA	Good	0.1–0.5
Dry panel cleanable	15–20	NA	Superior	0.08–0.5
Viscous panel cleanable	15–25	NA	Superior	0.08–0.5
Mat panel renewable	10–90	0–60	Good to superior	0.15–1.0
Roll mat renewable	10–90	0–55	Good to superior	0.15–0.65
Roll oil bath	15–25	NA	Superior	0.3–0.5
Close pleat mat panel	NA	85–95	Varies	0.4–1.0
High efficiency particulate	NA	95–99.9	Varies	1.0–3.0
Membrane	NA	to 100	NA	NA
Electrostatic with mat	80–98	NA	Varies	0.15–1.25

Anilkmar V. Patel; Joseph R. Loring & Associates, Inc., Consulting Engineers; New York, New York

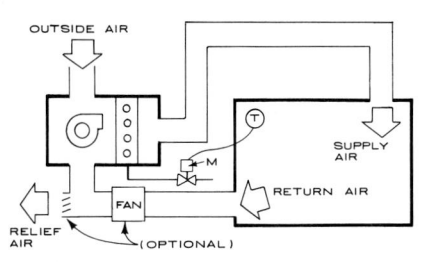

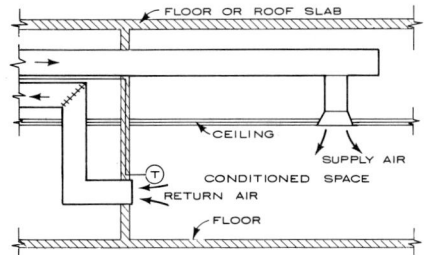

Low pressure system suitable for serving areas requiring only one zone of control. May be used in multiple where more than one zone of control is required. Relatively low first cost. Air handling unit may be blow through or draw through type.

SINGLE ZONE SYSTEM

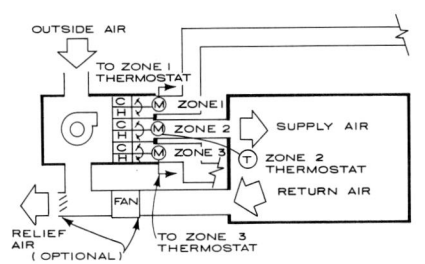

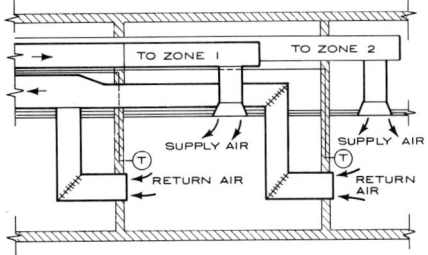

Low pressure system for serving areas requiring more than one zone of control. Practical limit of approximately eight zones per air handling unit. Can be used for simultaneously heating some areas while cooling others; however, control is relatively poor because of leakage at unit dampers and coil wiping. Relatively low first cost.

MULTIZONE SYSTEM

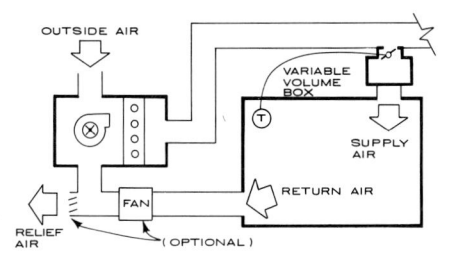

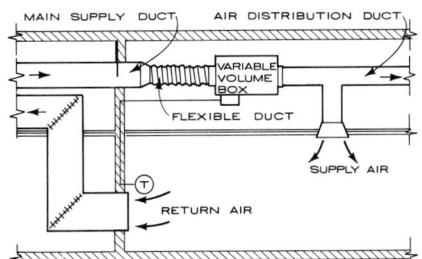

Low, medium, or high pressure system capable of providing a control zone for each box. Can be used for cooling only or for heating and cooling. Changeover from heating to cooling should be zoned by exposure. Provides variable air change rate and not applicable to areas requiring fixed air change rates such as certain hospital and laboratory applications. Relatively low first cost. Air handling system may be blow through or draw through type.

SINGLE DUCT VARIABLE VOLUME SYSTEM

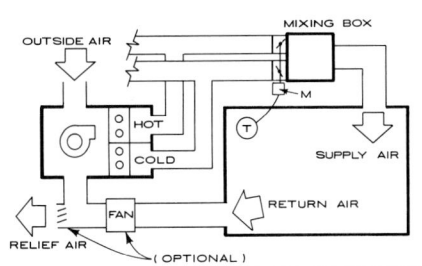

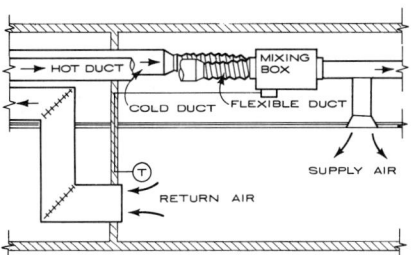

Low, medium, or high pressure system capable of providing a control zone for each box. Provides complete heating and cooling capability with no need for changeover. Available for both constant and variable volume systems (normally does not reduce air flow below 50% of maximum). Provides excellent year-round control. Relatively high first cost.

DOUBLE DUCT SYSTEM

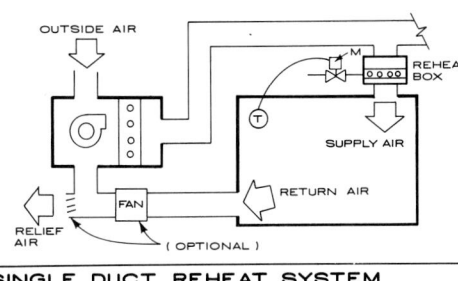

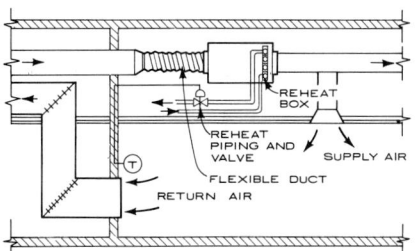

Low, medium, or high pressure system capable of providing a control zone per box. Provides heating and cooling capability (no changeover required). Available for constant and variable volume systems that normally do not reduce airflow below 50% of maximum. Excellent control, high first cost, high energy consumption; use generally limited to laboratory and hospital applications where constant volume and excellent control is required. Air handling system may be blow through or draw through type.

SINGLE DUCT REHEAT SYSTEM

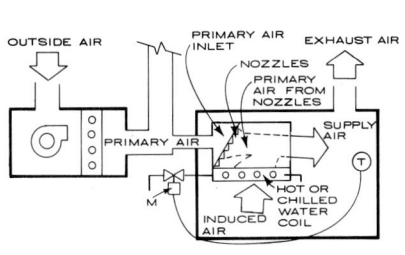

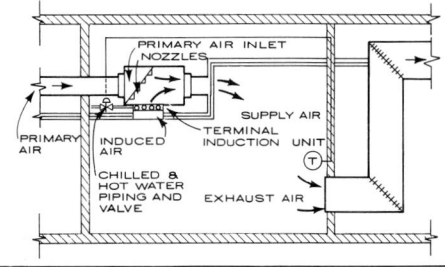

Medium or high pressure system capable of providing a control zone per induction unit. Can be used for cooling or heating and cooling. Changeover accomplished by providing hot or chilled water to coil. Primary air (approximately 20 to 40% of air circulated) passes through unit and is usually exhausted. Provides excellent control. Complies with requirements of hospital patient rooms where air cannot be recirculated to main unit. Relatively high first cost. Air handling unit may be blow through or draw through type.

INDUCTION SYSTEM

William Tao & Associates, Inc., Consulting Engineers; St. Louis, Missouri

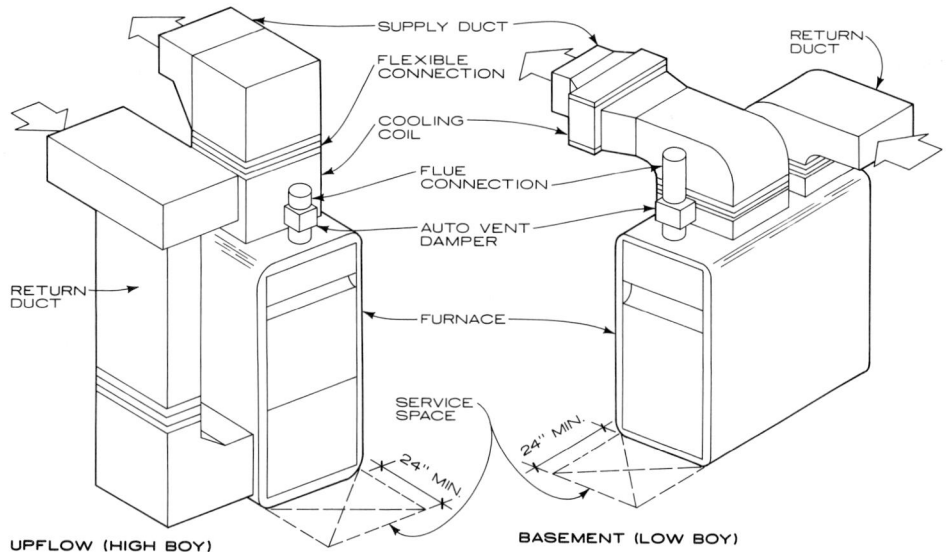

UPFLOW (HIGH BOY)

BASEMENT (LOW BOY)

Labels: SUPPLY DUCT, FLEXIBLE CONNECTION, COOLING COIL, FLUE CONNECTION, AUTO VENT DAMPER, FURNACE, RETURN DUCT, RETURN DUCT, SERVICE SPACE, 24" MIN., 24" MIN., 24" MIN.

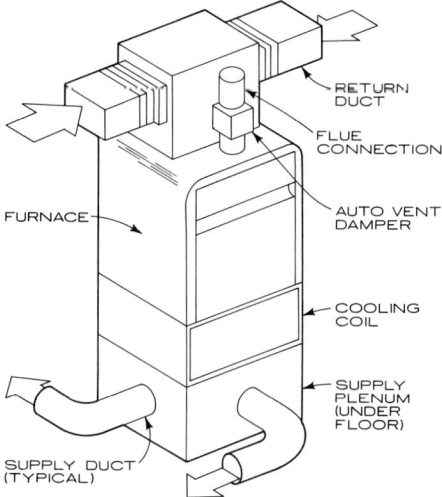

DOWNFLOW (COUNTER FLOW)

Labels: RETURN DUCT, FLUE CONNECTION, FURNACE, AUTO VENT DAMPER, COOLING COIL, SUPPLY PLENUM (UNDER FLOOR), SUPPLY DUCT (TYPICAL)

WARM AIR FURNACES

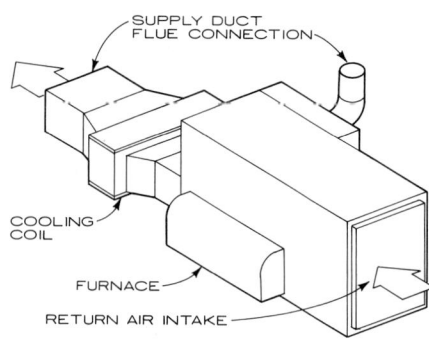
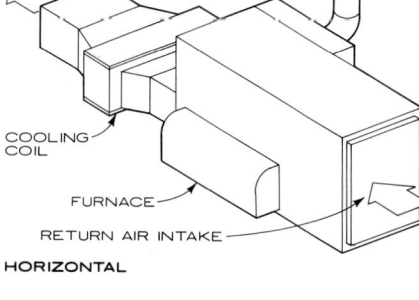

HORIZONTAL

Labels: SUPPLY DUCT FLUE CONNECTION, COOLING COIL, FURNACE, RETURN AIR INTAKE

FLOOR AREA REQUIRED BY WARM AIR FURNACE

OUTPUT CAPACITY (BTU/HR)	FURNACE FLOOR AREA (SQ FT)*
Up to 52,000	2.4
52,000–84,000	4.2
84,000–120,000	6.6
120,000–200,000	13.1

*Based on net floor area occupied by the upflow or downflow furnace. Low boy unit requires 50% more floor area. Space for combustion air should be added as required by local codes. Adequate space should be provided for service.

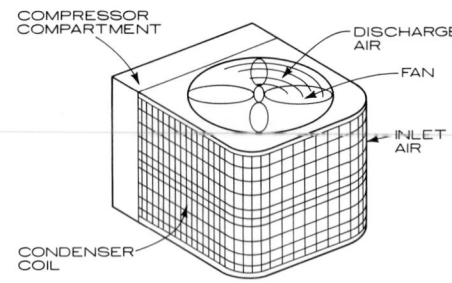

CONDENSING UNIT

Labels: COMPRESSOR COMPARTMENT, DISCHARGE AIR, FAN, INLET AIR, CONDENSER COIL

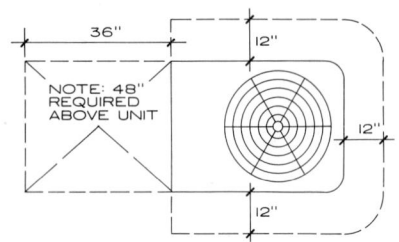

INSTALLATION CLEARANCES
CONDENSING UNIT

Labels: 36", 12", NOTE: 48" REQUIRED ABOVE UNIT, 12", 12"

NOTES

1. Warm air furnace units are designed primarily for residential, small commercial, or classroom heating. Cooling can be added to these units by installing a cooling coil downstream from the furnace, with refrigerant compressor and condenser remotely located outside of the building.

2. Duct system from the furnace unit can be either above the ceiling or in the floor slab. Above ceiling distribution systems are usually the radial type with high wall registers. Perimeter loop and extended plenum systems in floor slabs provide good air distribution. There are smaller temperature variations across the floor with perimeter loop systems than with radial or extended plenum systems.

3. Duct systems may also be installed below the living spaces in a crawl space or basement.

DiClemente-Siegel Engineering, Inc.; Southfield, Michigan

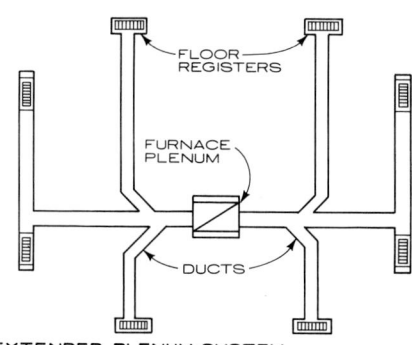

EXTENDED PLENUM SYSTEM

Labels: FLOOR REGISTERS, FURNACE PLENUM, DUCTS

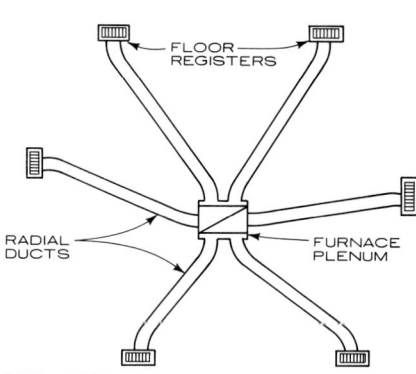

PERIMETER RADIAL SYSTEM

Labels: FLOOR REGISTERS, RADIAL DUCTS, FURNACE PLENUM

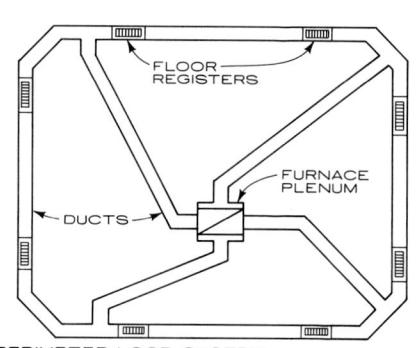

PERIMETER LOOP SYSTEM
DUCT SYSTEMS

Labels: FLOOR REGISTERS, DUCTS, FURNACE PLENUM

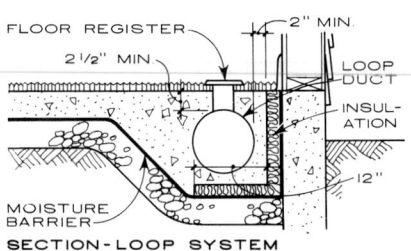

SECTION-LOOP SYSTEM

Labels: FLOOR REGISTER, 2" MIN., 2½" MIN, LOOP DUCT, INSULATION, 12", MOISTURE BARRIER

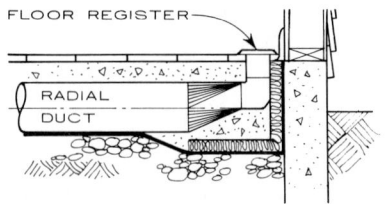

SECTION-RADIAL SYSTEM
AIR OUTLETS

Labels: FLOOR REGISTER, RADIAL DUCT

DUCT CONSTRUCTION

Ductwork must be permanent, rigid, nonbuckling, and nonrattling. Joints in ductwork should be airtight. Galvanized iron or aluminum sheets are usually used in the construction of ducts. The ducts may be either round or rectangular in cross section.

In general, supply ducts should be constructed entirely of noncombustible material. Supply ducts serving a single family dwelling need not meet this requirement, except for the first 3 ft from the unit, provided they are used in conjunction with listed heating units, are properly constructed from a base material of metal or mineral, and are properly applied. Warm air ducts passing through cold spaces or located in exposed walls should have 1 to 2 in. of insulation.

Supply ducts must be securely supported by metal hangers, straps, lugs, or brackets. No nails should be driven through duct walls, and no unnecessary holes should be cut in them.

Supply ducts should be equipped with an adjustable locking type damper for air volume control. The damper should be installed in the branch duct as far from the outlet as possible, where it is accessible.

Automatic smoke dampers are required wherever ductwork passes through a rated smoke barrier partition.

Return systems having more than one return intake may be equipped with balancing dampers.

Attention should be given to the elimination of noise. Metal ducts should be connected to the unit by strips of flexible fire resistant fabric. Electrical conduit and piping, if directly connected to the unit, may increase noise transmission. Return air intakes immediately adjacent to the unit may also increase noise transmission. Installation of a fan directly under a return air grille should be avoided.

DUCT MATERIAL THICKNESS

ROUND DUCT DIA. OR RECTANGULAR DUCT WIDTH (IN.)	GALVANIZED IRON U.S. GAUGE	ALUMINUM B & S GAUGE
	Ducts enclosed in partitions	
14 or less	30	24
Over 14	28	24
	Ducts not enclosed in partitions	
14 or less	28	24
Over 14	26	23

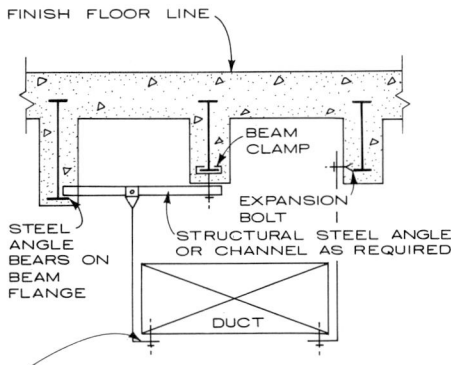

FINISH FLOOR LINE

BEAM CLAMP

EXPANSION BOLT

STRUCTURAL STEEL ANGLE OR CHANNEL AS REQUIRED

STEEL ANGLE BEARS ON BEAM FLANGE

DUCT

DUCT LESS THAN 60" WIDE USE 1/8" X 1" GALVANIZED IRON HANGER. DUCT OVER 60" WIDE USE 1/8" X 1 3/8" GALVANIZED IRON HANGER

NOTE

On ducts over 48 in. wide hangers shall turn under and fasten to bottom of duct. When cross-sectional area exceeds 8 sq ft duct will be braced by angles on all four sides.

DUCT SUPPORT DETAIL

Wm. G. Miner, AIA, Architect, Washington, D.C.

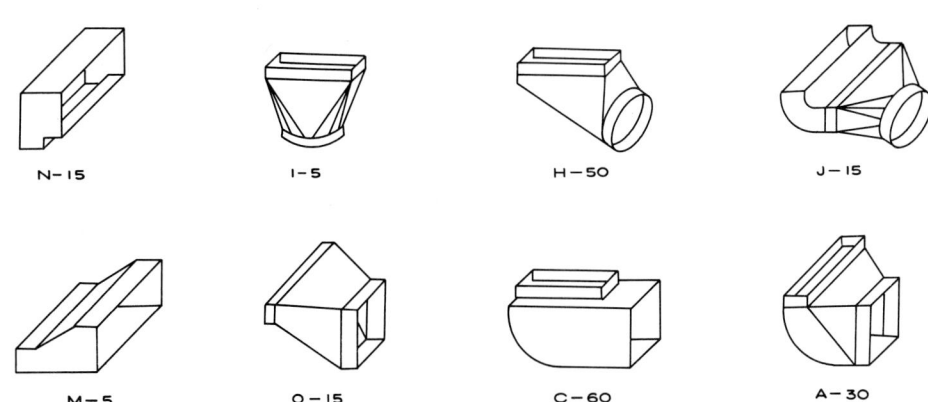

N-15   I-5   H-50   J-15

M-5   O-15   C-60   A-30

AIR BOOT FITTINGS

NOTE: N-15 ← NUMBER = EQUIVALENT LENGTH (FT)
↑ LETTER = SHAPE DESIGNATION

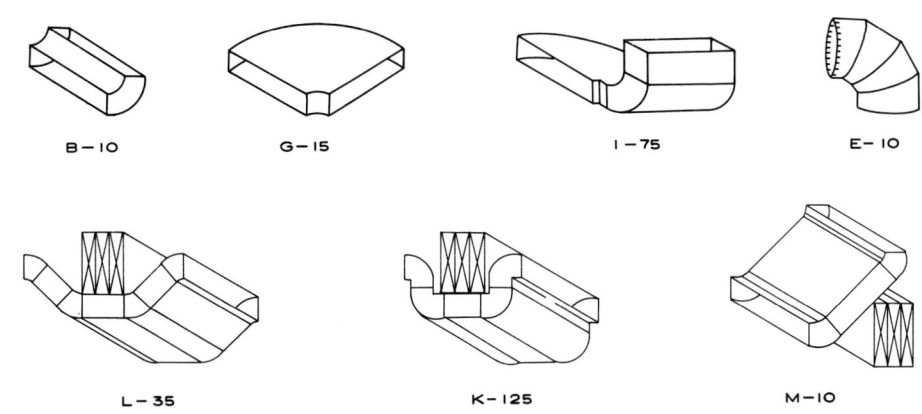

B-10   G-15   I-75   E-10

L-35   K-125   M-10

ANGLES AND ELBOWS FOR BRANCH DUCTS

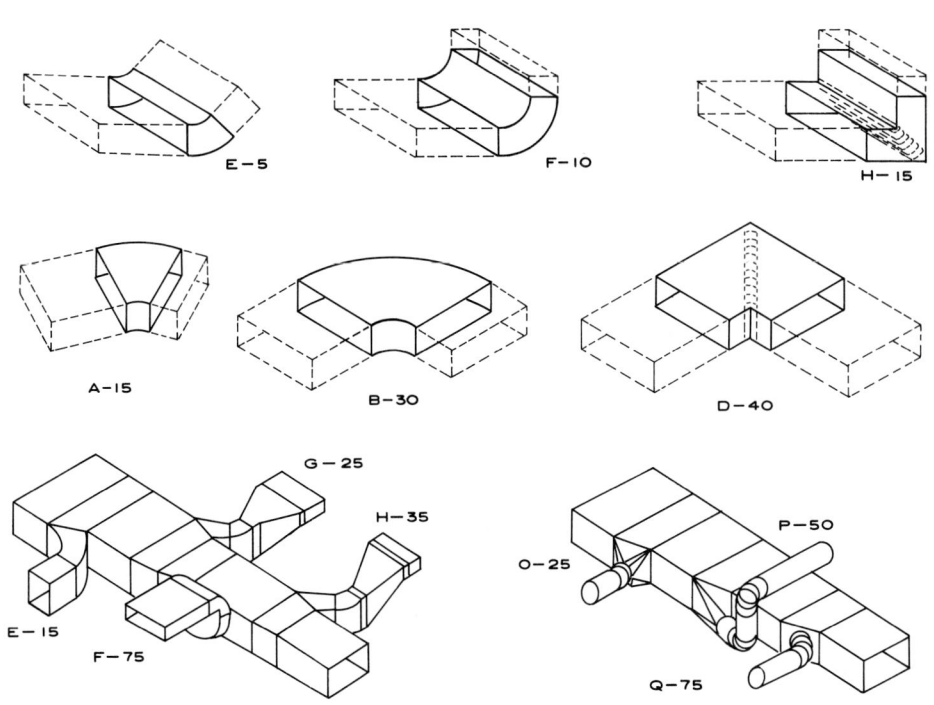

E-5   F-10   H-15

A-15   B-30   D-40

G-25   H-35   P-50

E-15   F-75   O-25   Q-75

TRUNK DUCTS AND FITTINGS

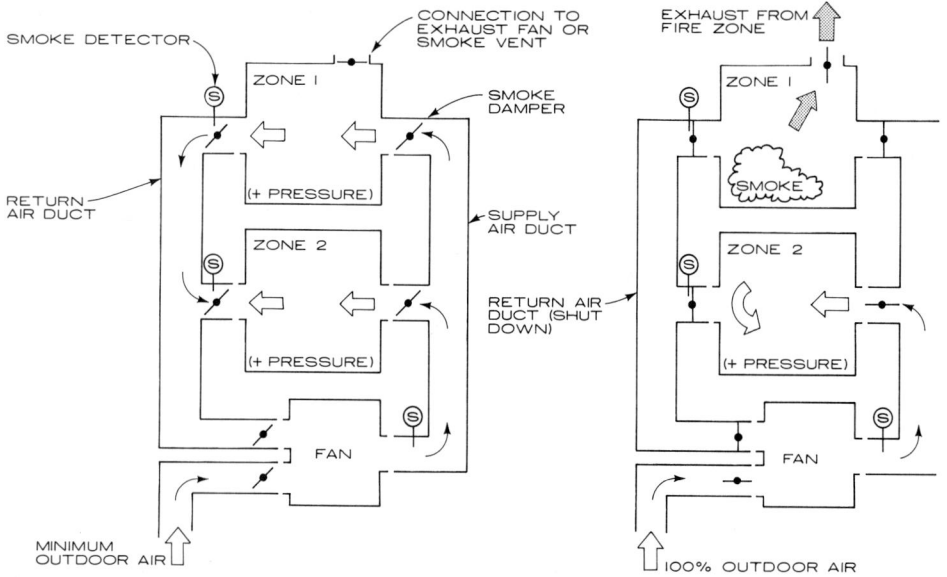

SMOKE CONTROL SYSTEM DIAGRAM

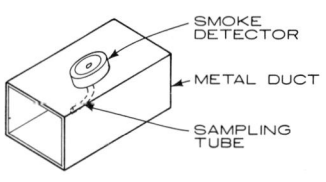

IN-DUCT SMOKE DETECTOR

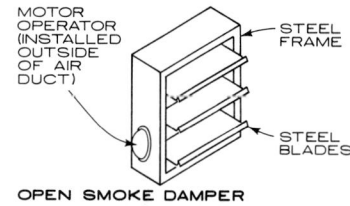

OPEN SMOKE DAMPER

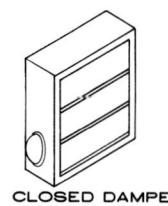

CLOSED DAMPER

SMOKE CONTROL SYSTEMS

SMOKE CONTROL SYSTEM DIAGRAM

Diagram at far left shows normal conditions with positive air pressure in each zone. During a fire, significant positive pressure is established in zones adjacent to fire zones (which is under negative pressure because of exhaust airflow as shown in right hand drawing).

CHECKLIST FOR SMOKE CONTROL SYSTEMS

1. Use mechanical air distribution systems to control smoke spread in buildings. For example, positive air pressure in exit corridors, stairwells, and service shafts can prevent smoke migration.
2. In cold climate regions, outside air intakes should be well below building's neutral plane.
3. Specify air duct materials that can withstand both additional pressure from supply and exhaust fans and elevated temperatures of smoke and hot gases.
4. Fire dampers (with 1½ hr UL label) used to restrict heat flow through air ducts also may prevent smoke spread if there is sufficient air pressure difference on opposite sides of damper. Smoke dampers must restrict passage of smoke when closed, operate automatically so they can be periodically tested, and be controlled by smoke detection devices.
5. In-duct detectors are usually not responsive to small fires. Room smoke detectors, located on ceilings and upper walls, will give earliest response.
6. Use automatic or self-closing hardware on doors in smoke partitions and on doors to smokeproof stairwells.
7. Coordinate energy conservation features (e.g., variable air volume, night or weekend fan shutdown for office occupancies) with smoke control airflow requirements.
8. Provide protected central facility to monitor operation of mechanical system and remote smoke control equipment such as smoke detectors, doors, dampers, and fans.

MECHANICAL EQUIPMENT NOISE CONTROL

1. Do not attach vibrating equipment directly to building structure. Support vibrating equipment with properly selected resilient mounts such as unhoused steel springs, ribbed neoprene, or pre-compressed glass fiber.
2. Use pads or continuous layers of soft, resilient material under structurally isolated slab (i.e., "floated floor") to isolate especially high levels of mechanical equipment room noise and vibration. In addition, use heavy wall and flooring-ceiling constructions surrounding mechanical equipment room. In critical applications, both floated floor and resiliently suspended ceiling underneath structural floor may be required.
3. Isolate all duct, pipe, and conduit connections to vibration isolated equipment for considerable distances from equipment. Use flexible duct connectors, resilient electrical conduit, and special reinforced flexible pipe connections.
4. Check to see if duct borne fan or downstream air control valves create noise requiring lining of supply and return air ducts with glass fiber or installation of prefabricated sound attenuators.
5. Where ducts and pipes penetrate walls, floors, or ceilings of mechanical rooms or other critical barriers, pack openings with mineral fiber or glass fiber and caulk perimeters to assure airtight seal.
6. Pipes carrying water at high velocities should be isolated from building structure and wrapped with dense material (e.g., lead sheet, vinyl covered glass fiber) to isolate water flow noise.
7. Roof mounted mechanical equipment subject to wind loading (e.g., cooling towers, packaged air conditioning units, etc.) and all mechanical equipment subject to earthquake forces may require special vibration isolation mounts. These well anchored lateral and vertical restraints must be carefully selected and installed to avoid short circuiting vibration isolation system.

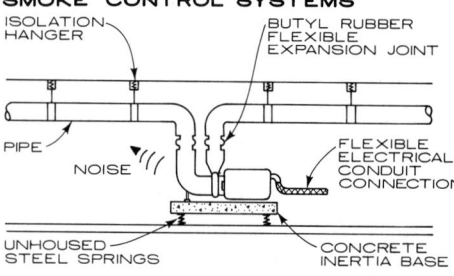

VIBRATION ISOLATION OF PUMPS
Pump motor assembly is supported by concrete inertia base sized at about one to two times fluid-filled pump weight plus all piping to first isolation hanger. Steel springs in turn support inertia base to isolate pump vibrations. Isolation hangers give resilient support to piping for distance of at least 150 times pipe diameter (or preferably complete length of pipeline). Butyl rubber or nylon tire cord-neoprene expansion joints can reduce noise and vibration transmission along pipe walls.

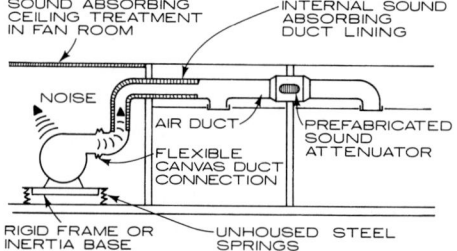

VIBRATION ISOLATION OF FANS (AND AIR DUCT NOISE CONTROL)
Unhoused, laterally stable steel springs, attached to rigid frame or inertia base, will isolate fan vibrations. Buildup of noise in fan room is reduced by sound absorbing room surface treatment (e.g., acoustical tiles or boards) and contained by heavy wall and floor-ceiling constructions. In some situations, floated floor and resiliently suspended ceiling underneath fan room floor slab may be required. Internal duct linings and prefabricated sound attenuators are used to control noise transmission through supply and return air ducts.

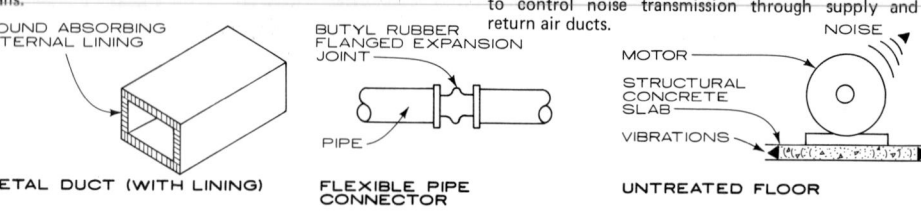

METAL DUCT (WITH LINING)

FLEXIBLE PIPE CONNECTOR

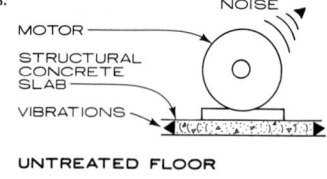

UNTREATED FLOOR

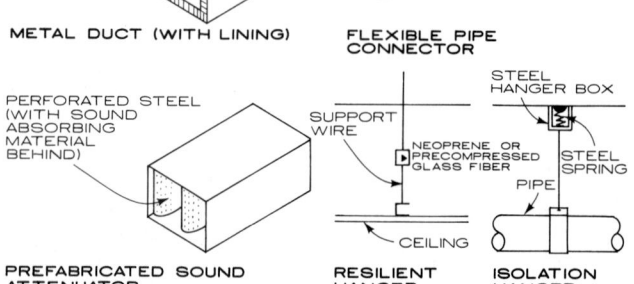

PREFABRICATED SOUND ATTENUATOR

RESILIENT HANGER

ISOLATION HANGER

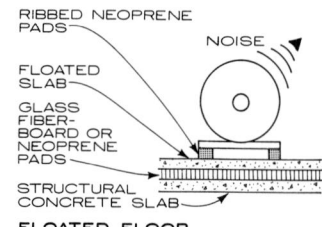

FLOATED FLOOR

NOISE CONTROL METHODS AND EQUIPMENT

M. David Egan, P.E.; Consultant in Acoustics; Anderson, South Carolina

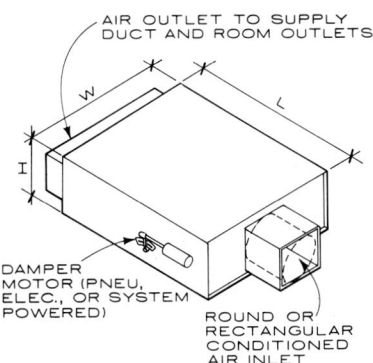

High, medium, or low velocity systems. Inlet pressure required ¼ to 1½ in. W.C. Capacity range 200 to 3200 cfm per box. Box serves as converter from high to low velocity air system, noise attenuator, and control device by modulating air quantity.

RANGE OF DIMENSIONS

CFM	HEIGHT	LENGTH	WIDTH
400	8"- 9"	24"-39"	14"-30"
800	10"-11"	24"-53"	18"-42"
1600	14"	30"-48"	22"-44"
2400	16"	42"-60"	26"-54"
3200	18"	42"-67"	33"-54"

VARIABLE VOLUME PINCH BACK BOX

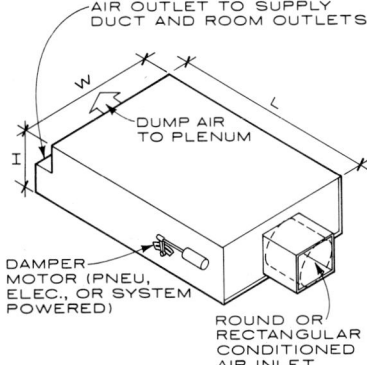

High, medium, or low velocity systems. Inlet pressure required ¼ to 1 in. W.C. Capacity range 200 to 3200 cfm per box. Available with or without reheat coil. Box serves as converter from high to low velocity air system, noise attenuator, and control device by modulating air quantity to space and/or by reheat.

RANGE OF DIMENSIONS

CFM	HEIGHT	LENGTH	WIDTH
200	8"- 9"	24"-39"	12"-19"
400	9"-11"	25"-51"	12"-24"
800	9"-11"	25"-51"	22"-31"
1600	10"-16"	25"-51"	22"-47"
2400	10"-16"	25"-51"	42"-47"
3200	10"-16"	25"-51"	42"-47"

VARIABLE VOLUME DUMP TYPE BOX

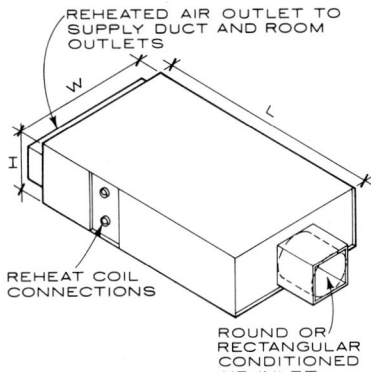

High, medium, or low velocity systems. Inlet pressures ½ to 1½ in. W.C. Capacity range 200 to 5000 cfm. Box serves as converter from high to low velocity air system, noise attenuator, and control device by reheat of conditioned air.

RANGE OF DIMENSIONS

CFM	HEIGHT	LENGTH	WIDTH
200	9"-11"	30"-50"	16"-22"
400	9"-11"	30"-51"	18"-30"
800	9"-11"	30"-51"	22"-42"
1600	14"-16"	48"-51"	40"-44"
2400	16"-18"	60"-55"	40"-54"
3200	16"-18"	60"-55"	16"-66"
5000	20"-18"	60"-55"	20"-80"

REHEAT CONSTANT VOLUME BOX

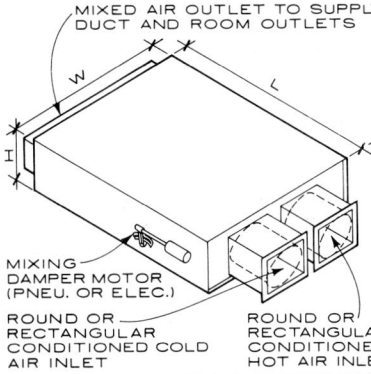

High, medium, or low velocity systems. Inlet pressure ¼ to 1½ in. W.C. Capacity range from 150 to 2000 cfm per box (low velocity) to 5000 cfm (high velocity). Box serves as converter from high to low velocity air system, noise attenuator, and control device by mixing hot and cold air streams.

RANGE OF DIMENSIONS

CFM	HEIGHT	LENGTH	WIDTH
400	6"-10"	40"-51"	30"-19"
800	8"-11"	50"-51"	42"-24"
1600	12"-14"	48"-51"	44"-40"
2400	14"-18"	60"-55"	54"-44"
3200	14"-18"	60"-55"	54"-44"
5000	16"-18"	60"-55"	54"-66"

DUAL DUCT MIXING BOX

William Tao & Associates, Inc., Consulting Engineers; St. Louis, Missouri

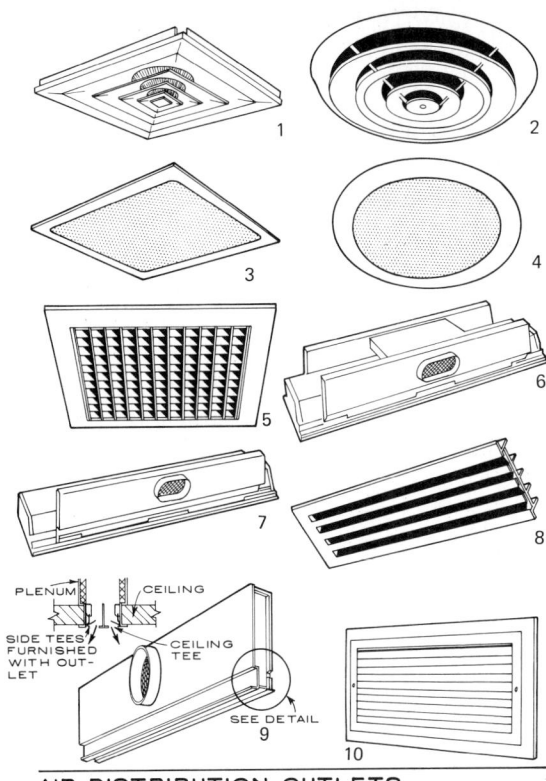

AIR DISTRIBUTION OUTLETS

KEY

1 RECTANGULAR LOUVERED FACE DIFFUSER: Available in 1, 2, 3, or 4-way pattern, steel or aluminum. Flanged overlap frame or inserted in 2 × 2 ft or 2 × 4 ft baked enamel steel panel to fit tile modules of lay-in ceilings. Supply or return.

2 ROUND LOUVERED FACE DIFFUSER: Normal 360° air pattern with blank-off plate for other air patterns. Surface mounting for all type ceilings. Normally of steel with baked enamel finish. Supply or return.

3 RECTANGULAR PERFORATED FACE DIFFUSER: Available in 1, 2, 3, or 4-way pattern, steel or aluminum. Flanged overlap frame or 2 × 2 ft and 2 × 4 ft for replacing tile of lay-in ceiling can be used for supply or return air.

4 ROUND PERFORATED FACE DIFFUSER: Normal 360° air pattern with blank-off plate for other air patterns. Steel or aluminum. Flanged overlap frame for all type ceilings. Can be used for supply or return air.

5 LATTICE TYPE RETURN: All aluminum square grid type return grille for ceiling installation with flanged overlap frame or of correct size to replace tile.

6 SADDLE TYPE LUMINAIRE AIR BOOT: Provides air supply from both sides of standard size luminaires. Maximum air delivery (total both sides) approximately 150 to 170 cfm for 4 ft long luminaire.

7 SINGLE SIDE TYPE LUMINAIRE AIR BOOT: Provides air supply from one side of standard size luminaires. Maximum air delivery approximately 75 cfm for 4 ft long luminaire.

8 LINEAR DIFFUSER: Extruded aluminum, anodized, duranodic, or special finishes, one way or opposite direction or vertical down air pattern. Any length with one to eight slots. Can be used for supply or return and for ceiling, sidewall, or cabinet top application.

9 INTEGRATED PLENUM TYPE OUTLET FOR "T" BAR CEILINGS: Slot type outlet, one way or two way opposite direction air pattern. Available in 24, 36, 48, and 60 in. lengths. Replaces or integrates with "T" bar. Approximately 150 to 175 cfm for 4 ft long, two-slot unit.

10 SIDEWALL OR DUCT MOUNTED REGISTER: Steel or aluminum for supply or return. Adjustable horizontal and vertical deflection. Plaster frame available. Suitable for long throw and high air volume.

FUNDAMENTALS

Conditioning of air requires the use of equipment to change conditions in a space: temperature, humidity, air movement, and air cleaning. Automatic controls applied to this equipment accomplish one or more of the following:

1. Ensure desired or required conditions.
2. Serve as a safety function by limiting and overriding mechanical equipment.
3. Yield economic results.
4. Eliminate human error.

Properly designed controls must consider:

1. Effects of exterior: prevailing winds, solar radiation (hot and cold spots), humidity.
2. Varying occupancy requirements: offices, storage space, and so on.

MECHANICAL SYSTEM CHARACTERISTICS

1. AIR CIRCULATION: The distribution of air in a space never achieves complete uniformity. High

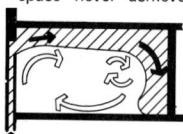 

COOLING   **HEATING**

ceilings, stairways, elevator shafts, doors, and walls are major factors.

2. LAG: Lag is one of the negative aspects of any mechanical system. It is the time between a controller's indication that a change is required and the time that the effective correction action is felt by the controller.
3. ZONE CONTROL: As the size of the building increases, more than one thermostat becomes necessary for proper air regulation. Temperature differences of greater than 5°F may cause temporary discomfort, thus creating various "zones."
4. CONTROL DIFFERENTIAL: It is not practical to maintain a single thermal condition. Controls must operate between minimum and maximum points that govern the operation or shutdown of mechanical systems.

HUMIDITY CONTROL

A 10 to 20% change in relative humidity is equivalent to a 1°F change in temperature. It is not often economically justifiable, however, to control humidity within this range by mechanical systems. Humidity can be maintained within certain broader comfort limits (see graph). Outside air can sometimes be used for humidity control.

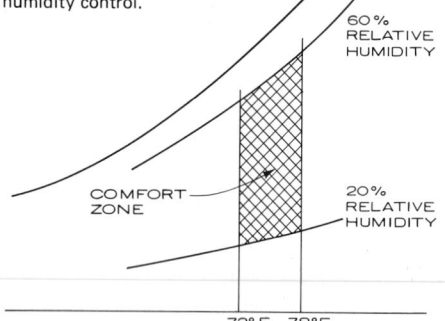

PSYCHROMETRIC CHART

EQUIPMENT

Control equipment is gaining new responsibilities and sophistication as energy becomes costlier. Controls falls into three categories:

1. CONTROLLERS: Measure changes and initiate corrective action.
2. ACTUATORS: Regulate mechanical systems in response to controller.
3. LIMIT AND SAFETY CONTROLS: Take command of actuators when there is a hazard or undesirable parameter or condition.
4. ACCESSORIES.

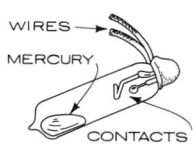 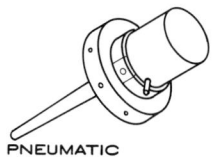

MERCURY SWITCH   **PNEUMATIC THERMOSTAT**

Mercury switch that, when tipped by contraction of coil sensing element, creates an electrical connection.

Pneumatic thermostats for controlling air or water temperatures (electric are similar).

THERMOSTATS

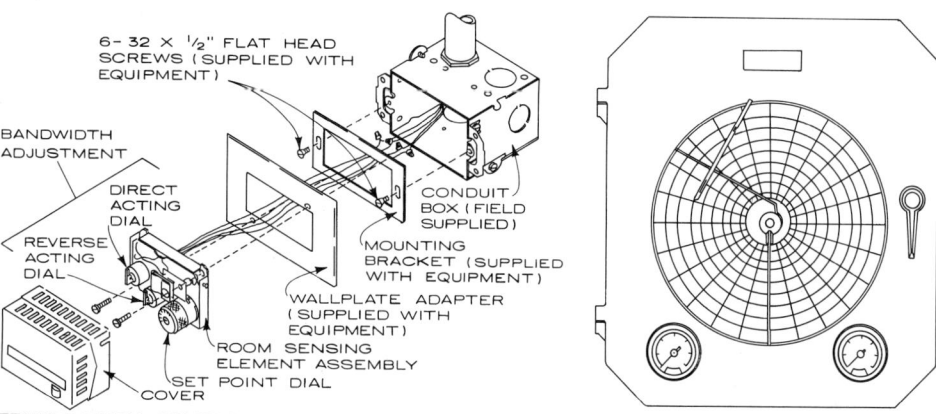

TEMPERATURE CONTROLLER   **RECORDING CONTROLLER**

CONTROLLERS

Conditioned air recording and control devices, often used in central/main plant operations, also are useful in analysis of a building.

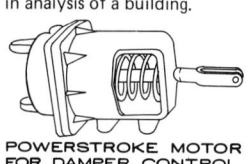

POWERSTROKE MOTOR FOR DAMPER CONTROL

ACTUATOR

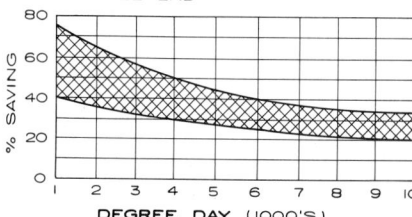

APPROXIMATE NIGHT SETBACK SAVING 10° SETBACK FOR 12 HR/DAY 42 HR/WEEKEND

% SAVING / DEGREE DAY (1000'S)

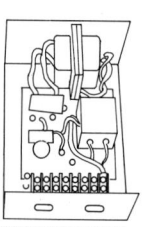 

DIFFERENTIAL   **DAY-NIGHT ROOM TYPE**

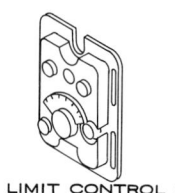 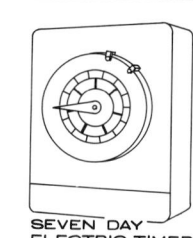

LIMIT CONTROL STOPS EQUIPMENT IN CASE OF TEMPERATURE OVERRUN   **SEVEN DAY ELECTRIC TIMER**

ACCESSORIES

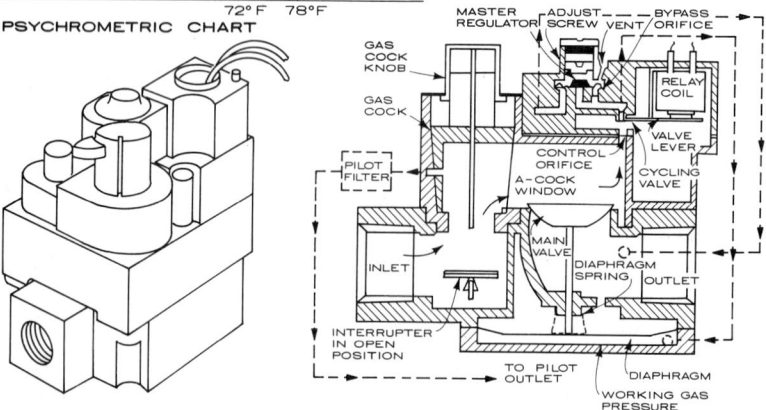

MAIN GAS VALVE

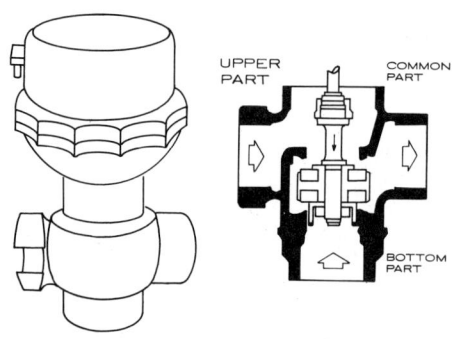

3 WAY VALVE (WATER OR STEAM)

Rex Beasley, III; Energy Management Consultants Inc.; Los Angeles, California

CONTROLS

GENERAL NOTES

Control systems vary, each having its own strengths and applications. They are grouped by:

1. SOURCE OF POWER: Pneumatic, electric, electronic, and self-contained.
2. MOTION OF CONTROLLER EQUIPMENT:
   a. Two position (on-off).
   b. Multiposition control—a combination of two or more stages of on-off (i.e., ability to operate one or more compressors).
   c. Floating control—actuators can assume any position between minimum and maximum.
   d. Logic control—central control systems through software programs control equipment to provide demand monitoring, load control, load scheduling, and load cycling.
3. DIVISION OF SPACE UNDER CONTROL:
   a. Single unit control—single thermostat.
   b. Zone control—larger buildings using two or more thermostats.
   c. Individual room control—locates thermostats in each room.

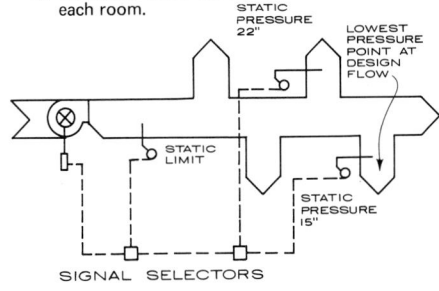

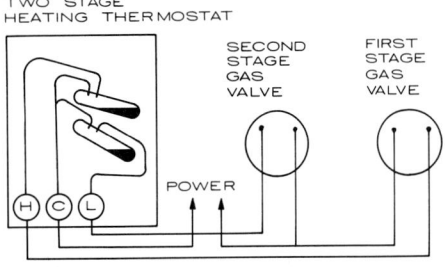

CIRCUIT FOR TWO STAGES OF ON-OFF CONTROL

MULTIPOSITION CONTROL

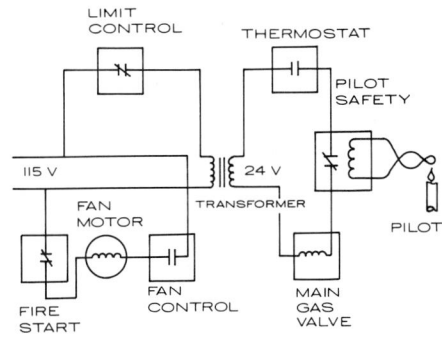

RESIDENTIAL GAS FURNACE CONTROL

DOUBLE DUCT SYSTEM

SINGLE DUCT VARIABLE AIR VOLUME SYSTEMS
NOTE
Variable air volume systems increase the operating economy of a system.

NOTE
Double duct systems have had wide use in large buildings because of their proved ability to control conditions with minimum operation complications but they are not energy efficient.

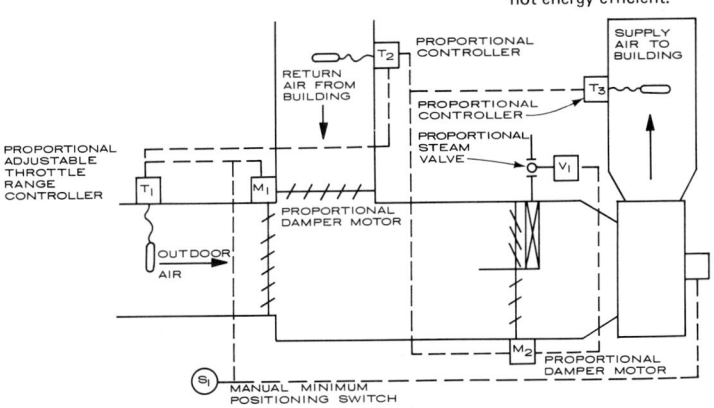

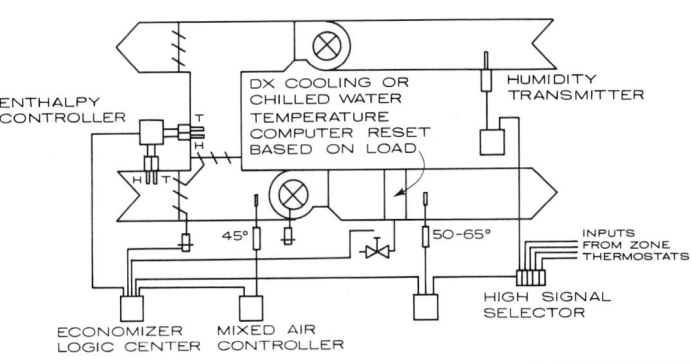

ECONOMIZER CONTROL
NOTE
Economizers use outside air for cooling when practical.

MAXIMUM ECONOMY CONTROL SYSTEM
(TEMPERATURE RESET FROM ZONE DEMAND)

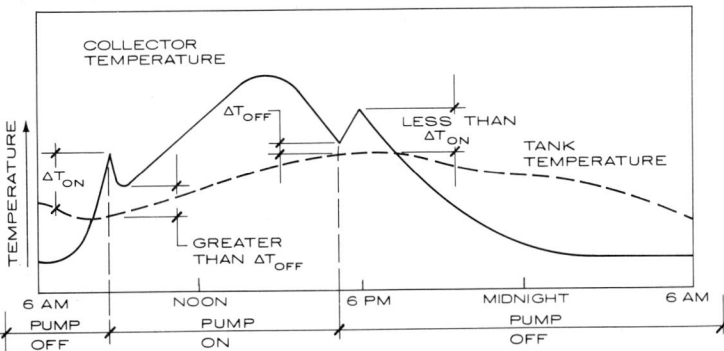

SOLAR SYSTEM OPERATING CYCLE
NOTE
Solar energy systems rely heavily on well designed control systems.

SOLAR HEATING SYSTEM WITH SENSORS

Rex Beasley, III; Energy Management Consultants Inc.; Los Angeles, California

CONTROLS **15**

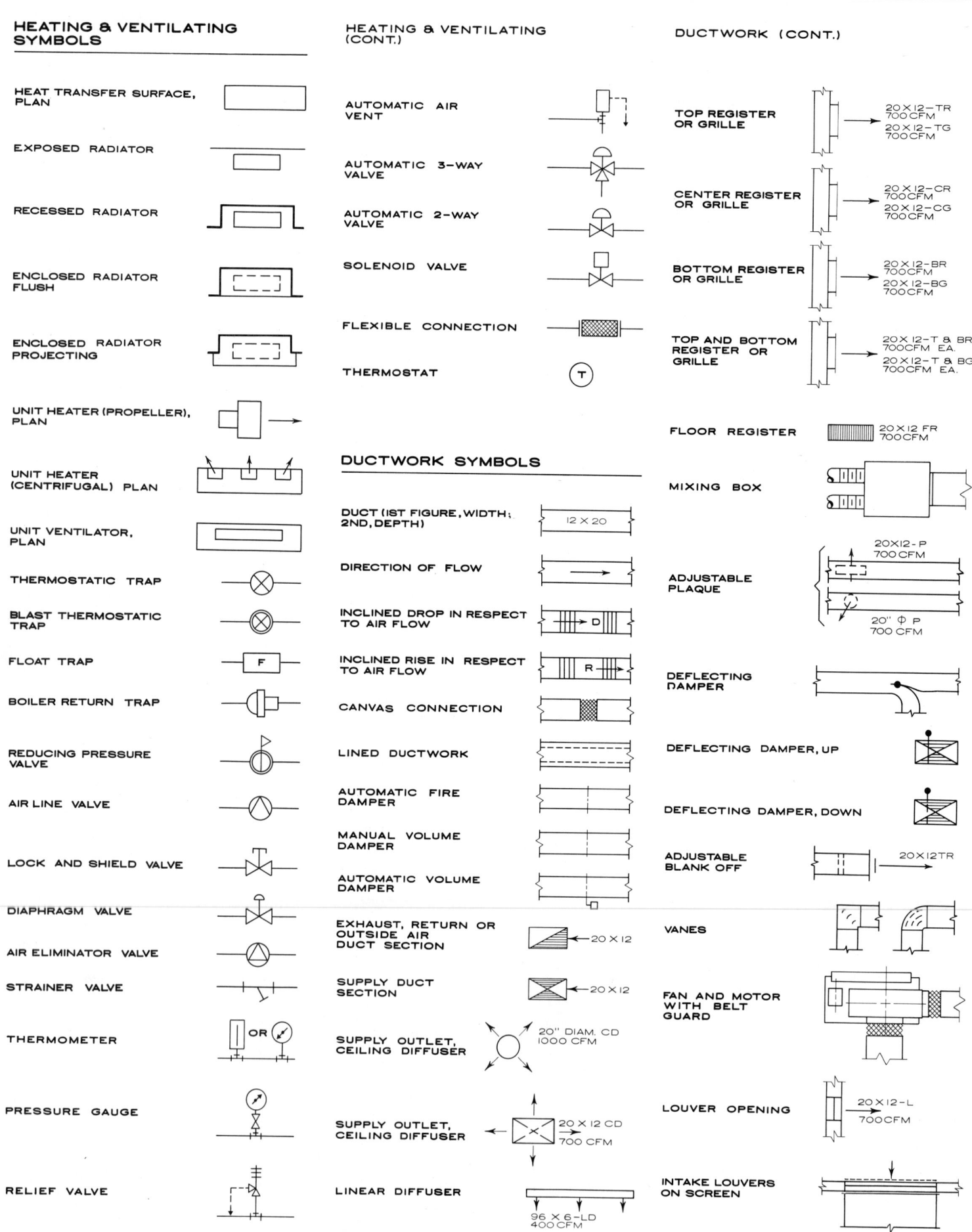

HEATING & VENTILATING SYMBOLS

HEAT TRANSFER SURFACE, PLAN

EXPOSED RADIATOR

RECESSED RADIATOR

ENCLOSED RADIATOR FLUSH

ENCLOSED RADIATOR PROJECTING

UNIT HEATER (PROPELLER), PLAN

UNIT HEATER (CENTRIFUGAL) PLAN

UNIT VENTILATOR, PLAN

THERMOSTATIC TRAP

BLAST THERMOSTATIC TRAP

FLOAT TRAP

BOILER RETURN TRAP

REDUCING PRESSURE VALVE

AIR LINE VALVE

LOCK AND SHIELD VALVE

DIAPHRAGM VALVE

AIR ELIMINATOR VALVE

STRAINER VALVE

THERMOMETER

PRESSURE GAUGE

RELIEF VALVE

HEATING & VENTILATING (CONT.)

AUTOMATIC AIR VENT

AUTOMATIC 3-WAY VALVE

AUTOMATIC 2-WAY VALVE

SOLENOID VALVE

FLEXIBLE CONNECTION

THERMOSTAT

DUCTWORK SYMBOLS

DUCT (IST FIGURE, WIDTH; 2ND, DEPTH)   12 X 20

DIRECTION OF FLOW

INCLINED DROP IN RESPECT TO AIR FLOW   D

INCLINED RISE IN RESPECT TO AIR FLOW   R

CANVAS CONNECTION

LINED DUCTWORK

AUTOMATIC FIRE DAMPER

MANUAL VOLUME DAMPER

AUTOMATIC VOLUME DAMPER

EXHAUST, RETURN OR OUTSIDE AIR DUCT SECTION   20 X 12

SUPPLY DUCT SECTION   20 X 12

SUPPLY OUTLET, CEILING DIFFUSER   20" DIAM. CD 1000 CFM

SUPPLY OUTLET, CEILING DIFFUSER   20 X 12 CD 700 CFM

LINEAR DIFFUSER   96 X 6-LD 400 CFM

DUCTWORK (CONT.)

TOP REGISTER OR GRILLE   20 X 12-TR 700 CFM / 20 X 12-TG 700 CFM

CENTER REGISTER OR GRILLE   20 X 12-CR 700 CFM / 20 X 12-CG 700 CFM

BOTTOM REGISTER OR GRILLE   20 X 12-BR 700 CFM / 20 X 12-BG 700 CFM

TOP AND BOTTOM REGISTER OR GRILLE   20 X 12-T & BR 700 CFM EA. / 20 X 12-T & BG 700 CFM EA.

FLOOR REGISTER   20 X 12 FR 700 CFM

MIXING BOX

ADJUSTABLE PLAQUE   20 X 12-P 700 CFM / 20" Φ P 700 CFM

DEFLECTING DAMPER

DEFLECTING DAMPER, UP

DEFLECTING DAMPER, DOWN

ADJUSTABLE BLANK OFF   20 X 12 TR

VANES

FAN AND MOTOR WITH BELT GUARD

LOUVER OPENING   20 X 12-L 700 CFM

INTAKE LOUVERS ON SCREEN

Amor Halperin, P. E.; Ayres, Cohen and Hayakawa; Consulting Engineers; Los Angeles/San Francisco, California

HEAT-POWER APPARATUS

STEAM GENERATOR (BOILER) .....

FLUE GAS REHEATER
(INTERMEDIATE SUPERHEATER) ..

LIVE STEAM SUPERHEATER ......
OR REHEATER

FEED HEATER WITH
AIR OUTLET ....

CONDENSER, SURFACE ....

STEAM TURBINE ....

CONDENSING TURBINE ....

OPEN TANK ....

CLOSED TANK ....

AUTOMATIC REDUCING VALVE ....

AUTOMATIC BYPASS VALVE .....

AUTOMATIC VALVE
OPERATED BY GOVERNOR ......

BOILER FEED PUMP ....

SERVICE PUMP ....

CONDENSATE PUMP ....

CIRCULATING WATER PUMP .....

AIR PUMP ....

OIL PUMP ....

RECIPROCATING PUMP ....

AIR EJECTOR
(DYNAMIC PUMP)

VACUUM TRAP ....

REFRIGERATION

THERMOSTAT, SELF-CONTAINED

THERMOSTAT, REMOTE BULB ...

PRESSURE SWITCH ....

EXPANSION VALVE, HAND ....

EXPANSION VALVE, AUTOMATIC .

EXPANSION VALVE,
THERMOSTATIC ....

EVAPORATOR PRESSURE
REGULATING VALVE,
THROTTLING TYPE
(EVAPORATOR SIDE)

EVAPORATOR PRESSURE
REGULATING VALVE,
THERMOSTATIC, THROTTLING
TYPE

EVAPORATOR PRESSURE
REGULATING VALVE
SNAP-ACTION

COMPRESSOR SUCTION VALVE,
PRESSURE LIMITING,
THROTTLING TYPE
(COMPRESSOR SIDE)

CONSTANT PRESSURE VALVE,
SUCTION

THERMAL BULB ....

SCALE TRAP ....

DRYER ....

FILTER AND STRAINER ....

COMBINATION STRAINER
AND DRYER

SIGHT GLASS ....

FLOAT VALVE
HIGH SIDE

FLOAT VALVE
LOW SIDE

GAUGE ....

COOLING TOWER ....

EVAPORATOR,
FINNED TYPE, NATURAL
CONVECTION

EVAPORATOR,
FORCED CONVECTION ....

IMMERSION COOLING UNIT ....

CONDENSER,
AIR-COOLED,
FINNED, FORCED AIR

CONDENSER,
WATER-COOLED,
SHELL AND TUBE

CONDENSER
EVAPORATIVE

HEAT EXCHANGER

CONDENSING UNIT
AIR COOLED

CONDENSING UNIT
WATER COOLED

PRESSURE SWITCH WITH
HIGH PRESSURE CUT-OUT

COMPRESSOR

COMPRESSOR
OPEN CRANKCASE
RECIPROCATING, DIRECT
DRIVE

COMPRESSOR
OPEN CRANKCASE
RECIPROCATING BELTED

COMPRESSOR
ENCLOSED CRANKCASE,
ROTARY, BELTED

Amor Halperin, P. E.; Ayres, Cohen and Hayakawa; Consulting Engineers; Los Angeles/San Francisco, California

CONTROLS **15**

CHAPTER 16 ELECTRICAL

LIGHTING OUTLETS

CEILING, WALL

○ —○	SURFACE INCANDESCENT
ⓇR —Ⓡ	RECESS INCANDESCENT
Ⓑ —Ⓑ	BLANKED OUTLET
Ⓓ	DROP CORD
Ⓔ —Ⓔ	ELECTRICAL OUTLET
Ⓕ —Ⓕ	FAN OUTLET
Ⓙ —Ⓙ	JUNCTION BOX
Ⓛ PS —Ⓛ PS	LAMP HOLDER WITH PULL SWITCH
Ⓥ —Ⓥ	OUTLET FOR VAPOR DISCHARGE LAMP
Ⓧ —Ⓧ	EXIT LIGHT OUTLET
ⓍR —ⓍR	RECESSED EXIT LIGHT OUTLET
Ⓛ —Ⓛ	OUTLET CONTROLLED BY LOW VOLTAGE SWITCHING WHEN RELAY IS INSTALLED IN OUTLET BOX
▭O▭	SURFACE OR PENDANT INDIVIDUAL FLUORESCENT FIXTURE
▭OR▭	RECESSED INDIVIDUAL FLUORESCENT FIXTURE
▭O▭▭	SURFACE OR PENDANT CONTINUOUS ROW FLUORESCENT FIXTURE
▭OR▭▭	RECESSED CONTINUOUS ROW FLUORESCENT FIXTURE

RECEPTACLE OUTLETS

—⊖	SINGLE RECEPTACLE OUTLET
⊜	DUPLEX RECEPTACLE OUTLET
⊕	TRIPLEX RECEPTACLE OUTLET
⊕	QUADRUPLEX RECEPTACLE OUTLET
⊖	DUPLEX RECEPTACLE OUTLET-SPLIT WIRED
⊕	TRIPLEX RECEPTACLE OUTLET-SPLIT WIRED
—△	SINGLE SPECIAL PURPOSE RECEPTACLE OUTLET
▱△	DUPLEX SPECIAL PURPOSE RECEPTACLE OUTLET
⊜ R	RANGE OUTLET
▶ DW	SPECIAL PURPOSE CONNECTION
⊕↑ X"	MULTI OUTLET ASSEMBLY
Ⓒ	CLOCK HANGER RECEPTACLE
Ⓕ	FAN HANGER RECEPTACLE
⊡	FLOOR SINGLE RECEPTACLE OUTLET
⊟	FLOOR DUPLEX RECEPTACLE OUTLET
△	FLOOR SPECIAL PURPOSE OUTLET
◀	FLOOR TELEPHONE OUTLET-PUBLIC
◁	FLOOR TELEPHONE OUTLET-PRIVATE
⊞	UNDERFLOOR DUCT AND JUNCTION BOX FOR TRIPLE, DOUBLE, OR SINGLE DUCT SYSTEM AS INDICATED BY NUMBER OF PARALLEL LINES
⊞⊞	CELLULAR FLOOR HEADER DUCT

SWITCH OUTLETS

S	SINGLE POLE SWITCH
S$_2$	DOUBLE POLE SWITCH
S$_3$	THREE-WAY SWITCH
S$_4$	FOUR-WAY SWITCH
S$_D$	AUTOMATIC DOOR SWITCH
S$_K$	KEY OPERATED SWITCH
S$_P$	SWITCH AND PILOT LAMP
S$_{CB}$	CIRCUIT BREAKER
S$_{WCB}$	WEATHERPROOF CIRCUIT BREAKER
S$_{MC}$	MOMENTARY CONTACT SWITCH
S$_{RC}$	REMOTE CONTROL SWITCH
S$_{WP}$	WEATHERPROOF SWITCH
S$_F$	FUSED SWITCH
S$_{WF}$	WEATHERPROOF FUSED SWITCH
S$_L$	SWITCH FOR LOW VOLTAGE SWITCHING SYSTEM
S$_{LM}$	MASTER SWITCH FOR LOW VOLTAGE SWITCHING SYSTEM
S$_T$	TIME SWITCH
Ⓢ	CEILING PULL SWITCH
⊖$_S$	SWITCH AND SINGLE RECEPTACLE
⊜$_S$	SWITCH AND DOUBLE RECEPTACLE

○ A,B,C ETC.
⊜ A,B,C ETC. } SPECIAL OUTLETS
S A,B,C ETC.

Any standard symbol is given above with the addition of lowercase subscript lettering may be used to designate some special variation of standard equipment of particular interest in specific set of architectural plans.

When used they must be listed in the schedule of symbols on each drawing and if necessary further described in the specifications.

Frederick R. Brown, P. E.; Ayres, Cohen and Hayakawa; Consulting Engineers; Los Angeles/San Francisco, California

MATERIALS AND METHODS

INSTITUTIONAL COMMERCIAL & INDUSTRIAL OCCUPANCIES

+○	NURSES CALL SYSTEM DEVICES. (ANY TYPE)
+◇	PAGING SYSTEM DEVICES (ANY TYPE)
+□	FIRE ALARM SYSTEM DEVICES (ANY TYPE)
+◇	STAFF REGISTER, SYSTEM (ANY TYPE)
+⬡	ELECTRICAL CLOCK SYSTEM DEVICES (ANY TYPE)
+◀	PUBLIC TELEPHONE SYSTEM DEVICES
+◁	PRIVATE TELEPHONE SYSTEM DEVICES
+⌂	WATCHMAN SYSTEM DEVICES
+◁	SOUND SYSTEM
+◻	OTHER SIGNAL SYSTEM DEVICES
[SC]	SIGNAL CENTRAL STATION
▭	INTERCONNECTION BOX
– – – – –	AUXILIARY SYSTEM CIRCUITS

Any line without further designation indicates two-wire system. For a greater number of wires designate with numerals in manner similar to: 12- no. 18W - 3/4" C. Designate by numbers corresponding to listing in schedule.

| □ A, B, C, ETC. | SPECIAL AUXILIARY OUTLETS |

Subscript lettering refers to notes on drawings or detailed description in specifications.

PANELBOARDS

▭	FLUSH MOUNTED PANELBOARD & CABINET
▭	SURFACE MOUNTED PANELBOARD & CABINET

BUSDUCTS & WIREWAYS

[T][T][T]	TROLLEY DUCT
[B][B][B]	BUSWAY (SERVICE, FEEDER OR PLUG-IN)
[C][C][C]	CABLE THROUGH LADDER OR CHANNEL
[W][W][W]	WIREWAY

SIGNALING SYSTEM OUTLETS RESIDENTIAL OCCUPANCIES

⊡	PUSH BUTTON
◻	BUZZER
◻	BELL
◻	BELL & BUZZER COMBINATION
◇	ANNUNCIATOR
◀	OUTSIDE TELEPHONE
◁	INTERCONNECTING TELEPHONE
◀	TELEPHONE SWITCHBOARD
[BT]	BELL RINGING TRANSFORMER
[D]	ELECTRIC DOOR OPENER
[M]	MAID'S SIGNAL PLUG
[R]	RADIO OUTLET
[CH]	CHIME
[TV]	TELEVISION OUTLET
(T)	THERMOSTAT

ELECTRICAL DISTRIBUTION OR LIGHTING SYSTEM, UNDERGROUND

[M]	MANHOLE
[H]	HANDHOLE
[TM]	TRANSFORMER- MANHOLE OR VAULT
[TP]	TRANSFORMER PAD
– – – – –	UNDERGROUND DIRECT BURIAL CABLE
⊢→	UNDERGROUND DUCT LINE
⊗	STREET LIGHT STANDARD FED FROM UNDERGROUND CIRCUIT

ELECTRICAL DISTRIBUTION OR LIGHTING SYSTEM, AERIAL

○	POLE
⊗	STREET LIGHT & BRACKET
△	TRANSFORMER
———	PRIMARY CIRCUIT
– – – –	SECONDARY CIRCUIT
——→	DOWN GUY
——●—	HEAD GUY
——○→	SIDEWALK GUY
⊢	SERVICE WEATHER

PANELS CIRCUITS & MISCELLANEOUS

▰	LIGHTING PANEL
▨	POWER PANEL
———	WIRING, CONCEALED IN CEILING OR WALL
– – – –	WIRING, CONCEALED IN FLOOR
- - - - -	WIRING EXPOSED
——→	HOME RUN TO PANEL BOARD.

Indicate number of circuits by number of arrows. Any circuit without such designation indicates a two-wire circuit. For a greater number of wires indicate as follows: ⫫ (3 wires) ⫫ (4 wires), etc.

| ▬▬▬ | FEEDERS |

Use heavy lines and designate by number corresponding to listing in feeder schedule.

▬—○	WIRING TURNED UP
▬—●	WIRING TURNED DOWN
(G)	GENERATOR
(M)	MOTOR
(I)	INSTRUMENT (SPECIFY)
[T]	TRANSFORMER (OR DRAW TO SCALE)
⊠	CONTROLLER
▭	EXTERNALLY OPERATED DISCONNECT SWITCH

Frederick R. Brown, P. E.; Ayres, Cohen and Hayakawa; Consulting Engineers; Los Angeles/San Francisco, California

MATERIALS AND METHODS 16

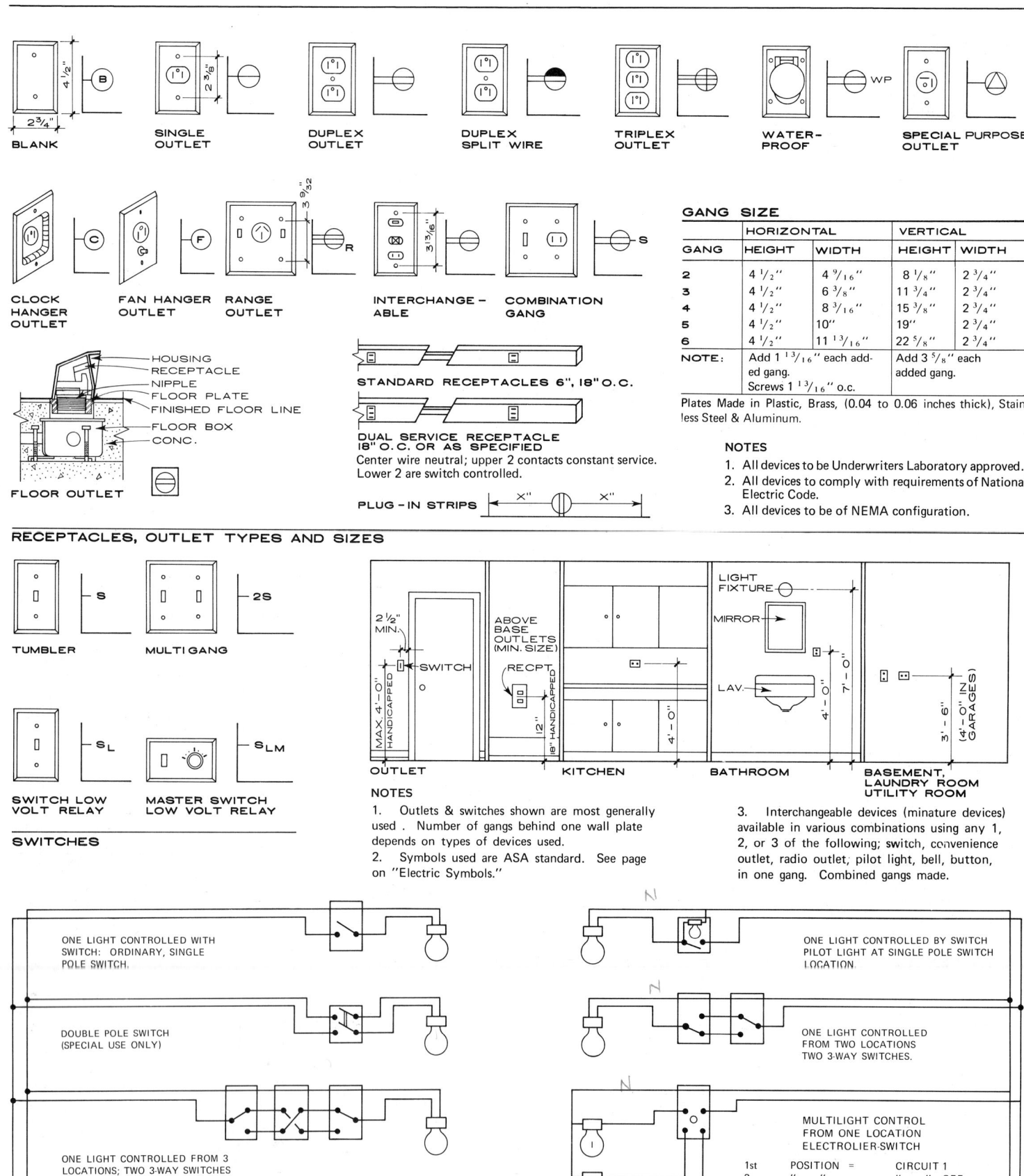

BLANK | **SINGLE OUTLET** | **DUPLEX OUTLET** | **DUPLEX SPLIT WIRE** | **TRIPLEX OUTLET** | **WATER-PROOF** | **SPECIAL PURPOSE OUTLET**

CLOCK HANGER OUTLET | **FAN HANGER OUTLET** | **RANGE OUTLET** | **INTERCHANGE-ABLE** | **COMBINATION GANG**

FLOOR OUTLET
- HOUSING
- RECEPTACLE
- NIPPLE
- FLOOR PLATE
- FINISHED FLOOR LINE
- FLOOR BOX
- CONC.

STANDARD RECEPTACLES 6", 18" O.C.

DUAL SERVICE RECEPTACLE 18" O.C. OR AS SPECIFIED
Center wire neutral; upper 2 contacts constant service. Lower 2 are switch controlled.

PLUG-IN STRIPS

GANG SIZE

GANG	HORIZONTAL		VERTICAL	
	HEIGHT	WIDTH	HEIGHT	WIDTH
2	4 1/2"	4 9/16"	8 1/8"	2 3/4"
3	4 1/2"	6 3/8"	11 3/4"	2 3/4"
4	4 1/2"	8 3/16"	15 3/8"	2 3/4"
5	4 1/2"	10"	19"	2 3/4"
6	4 1/2"	11 13/16"	22 5/8"	2 3/4"
NOTE:	Add 1 13/16" each added gang. Screws 1 13/16" o.c.		Add 3 5/8" each added gang.	

Plates Made in Plastic, Brass, (0.04 to 0.06 inches thick), Stainless Steel & Aluminum.

NOTES
1. All devices to be Underwriters Laboratory approved.
2. All devices to comply with requirements of National Electric Code.
3. All devices to be of NEMA configuration.

RECEPTACLES, OUTLET TYPES AND SIZES

TUMBLER | **MULTI GANG**

SWITCH LOW VOLT RELAY | **MASTER SWITCH LOW VOLT RELAY**

SWITCHES

OUTLET | **KITCHEN** | **BATHROOM** | **BASEMENT, LAUNDRY ROOM UTILITY ROOM**

NOTES
1. Outlets & switches shown are most generally used. Number of gangs behind one wall plate depends on types of devices used.
2. Symbols used are ASA standard. See page on "Electric Symbols."
3. Interchangeable devices (minature devices) available in various combinations using any 1, 2, or 3 of the following; switch, convenience outlet, radio outlet, pilot light, bell, button, in one gang. Combined gangs made.

ONE LIGHT CONTROLLED WITH SWITCH: ORDINARY, SINGLE POLE SWITCH.

DOUBLE POLE SWITCH (SPECIAL USE ONLY)

ONE LIGHT CONTROLLED FROM 3 LOCATIONS; TWO 3-WAY SWITCHES & ONE 4-WAY SWITCH

ONE LIGHT CONTROLLED BY SWITCH PILOT LIGHT AT SINGLE POLE SWITCH LOCATION.

ONE LIGHT CONTROLLED FROM TWO LOCATIONS TWO 3-WAY SWITCHES.

MULTILIGHT CONTROL FROM ONE LOCATION ELECTROLIER-SWITCH

	POSITION	=	CIRCUIT 1
1st	POSITION	=	CIRCUIT 1 OFF
2	" "	=	" " 1 & 2
3	" "	=	" " OFF
4	" "	=	" " 1, 2 & 3
5	" "	=	" " OFF
6			

NEUTRAL

PHASE

SWITCH WIRING DIAGRAMS

B. J. Baldwin; Giffels & Rossetti, Inc.; Detroit, Michigan

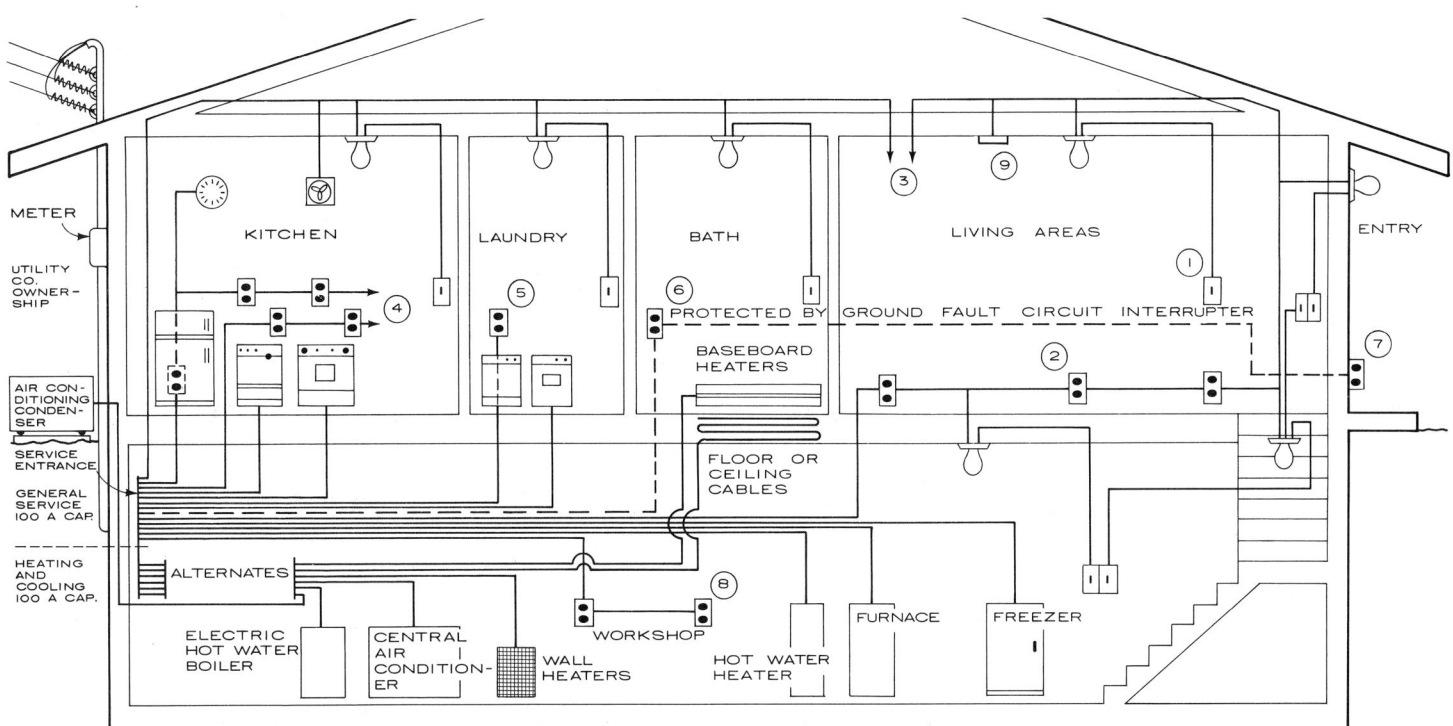

SCHEMATIC DIAGRAM OF TYPICAL RESIDENTIAL ELECTRICAL LAYOUT

GENERAL REQUIREMENTS

1. A minimum of one wall switch controlled lighting outlet is required in every habitable room, in hallways, stairways, and attached garages, and at outdoor entrances. Exception: in habitable rooms other than kitchens and bathrooms one or more receptacles controlled by a wall switch are permitted in lieu of lighting outlets.

2. In every kitchen, family room, dining room, den, breakfast room, living room, parlor, sunroom, bedroom, recreation room, and similar rooms, receptacle outlets are required such that no point along the floor line in any space is greater than 12 ft, measured horizontally, from an outlet in that space, including any wall space 2 ft or more wide and the wall space occupied by sliding panels in exterior walls.

3. A minimum of two #12 wire 20 A small appliance circuits are required to serve only small appliance

outlets, including refrigeration equipment, in kitchen, pantry, dining room, breakfast room, and family room. Both circuits must extend to kitchen; the other rooms may be served by either one or both of them. No other outlets may be connected to these circuits, other than a receptacle installed solely for the supply to and support of an electric clock. In kitchen and dining areas receptacle outlets must be installed at each and every counter space wider than 12 in.

4. A minimum of one #12 wire 20 A circuit must be provided to supply the laundry receptacle(s), and it may have no other outlets.

5. A minimum of one receptacle outlet must be installed in bathroom near the basin and must be provided with ground fault circuit interrupter protection.

6. The code requires sufficient lighting circuits to supply 3 W of power for every square foot of

floor space, not including garage and open porch areas. Minimum code suggestion is one circuit per 600 sq ft; one circuit per 500 sq ft is desirable.

7. A minimum of one exterior receptacle outlet is required (two are desirable) and must be provided with ground fault circuit interrupter protection.

8. A minimum of one receptacle outlet is required in basement and garage, in addition to that in the laundry. In attached garages it must be provided with ground fault circuit interrupter protection.

9. Many building codes require a smoke detector in the hallway outside bedrooms or above the stairway leading to upper floor bedrooms.

NOTE

Refer to the National Electrical Code (NEC) for further information on residential requirements.

INDIVIDUAL APPLIANCE CIRCUITS

TYPE	VOLTS	TYPE	VOLTS
Range	240	Dishwasher	120
Separate oven or countertop cooking unit	240	Freezer	120
Water heater	240	Oil furnace motor	120
Automatic washer	240	Furnace blower motor	120
Clothes dryer	240	Water pump	240
Garbage disposal	240	Permanently connected appliances > 1000 W	Varies

BRANCH CIRCUIT PROTECTION

Lighting (general purpose)	#12 wires	20 A
Small appliance	#12 wires	20 A
Individual appliances	#12 wires	20 A
	#10 wires	30 A
	#8 wires	40 A
	#6 wires	50 A

AVERAGE WATTAGES OF COMMON RESIDENTIAL ELECTRICAL DEVICES

TYPE	WATTS	TYPE	WATTS	TYPE	WATTS
Air conditioner, central	2500-6000	Heating pad	50-75	Range oven (separate)	4000-5000
Air conditioner, room type	800-2500	Heat lamp (infrared)	250	Razor	8-12
Blanket, electric	150-200	Iron, hand	600-1200	Refrigerator	150-300
Clock	2-3	Knife, electric	100	Refrigerator, frostless	400-600
Clothes dryer	4000-6000	Lamp, incandescent	10 upward	Roaster	1200-1650
Deep fat fryer	1200-1650	Lamp, fluorescent	15-60	Rotisserie (broiler)	1200-1650
Dishwasher	1000-1500	Lights, Christmas tree	30-150	Sewing machine	60-90
Fan, portable	50-200	Microwave oven	1000-1500	Stereo (solid state)	30-100
Food blender	500-1000	Mixer	120-250	Sunlamp (ultraviolet)	275-400
Freezer	300-500	Percolator	500-1000	Television	50-450
Frying pan, electric	1000-1200	Power tools	Up to 1000	Toaster	500-1200
Furnace blower	380-670	Projector, slide or movie	300-500	Vacuum cleaner	250-1200
Garbage disposal	500-900	Radio	40-150	Waffle iron	600-1000
Hair dryer	350-1200	Range (all burners and oven "on")	8000-14000	Washer, automatic	500-800
Heater, portable	1000-1500	Range top (separate)	4000-8000	Water heater	2000-5000

Ed Hesner; Rasmussen & Hobbs Architects, AIA; Tacoma, Washington

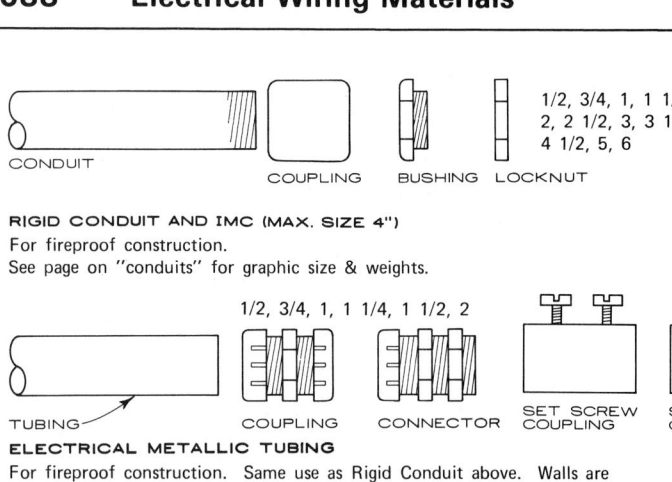

1/2, 3/4, 1, 1 1/4, 1 1/2,
2, 2 1/2, 3, 3 1/2, 4,
4 1/2, 5, 6

CONDUIT   COUPLING   BUSHING   LOCKNUT

RIGID CONDUIT AND IMC (MAX. SIZE 4")
For fireproof construction.
See page on "conduits" for graphic size & weights.

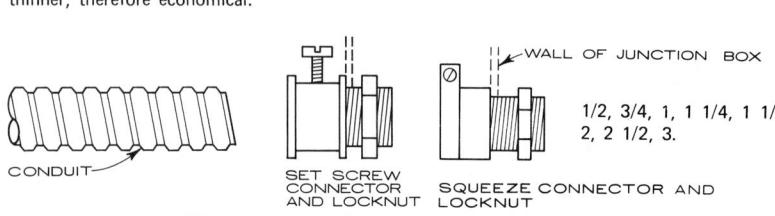

1/2, 3/4, 1, 1 1/4, 1 1/2, 2

TUBING   COUPLING   CONNECTOR   SET SCREW COUPLING   SET SCREW CONNECTOR

ELECTRICAL METALLIC TUBING
For fireproof construction. Same use as Rigid Conduit above. Walls are thinner, therefore economical.

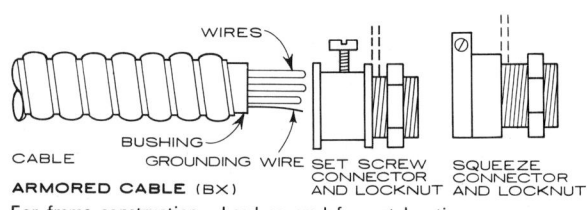

WALL OF JUNCTION BOX

1/2, 3/4, 1, 1 1/4, 1 1/2, 2, 2 1/2, 3.

CONDUIT

SET SCREW CONNECTOR AND LOCKNUT   SQUEEZE CONNECTOR AND LOCKNUT

FLEXIBLE CONDUIT
For fireproof construction.

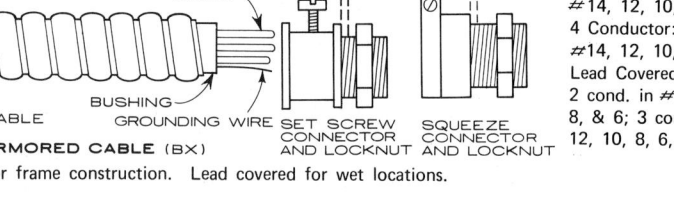

WIRES

2 & 3 Conductor:
#14, 12, 10, 8, 6, 4, 2.
4 Conductor:
#14, 12, 10, 8, 6, 4.
Lead Covered—
2 cond. in #14, 12, 10, 8, & 6; 3 cond. in #14, 12, 10, 8, 6, & 4.

CABLE   BUSHING   GROUNDING WIRE   SET SCREW CONNECTOR AND LOCKNUT   SQUEEZE CONNECTOR AND LOCKNUT

ARMORED CABLE (BX)
For frame construction. Lead covered for wet locations.

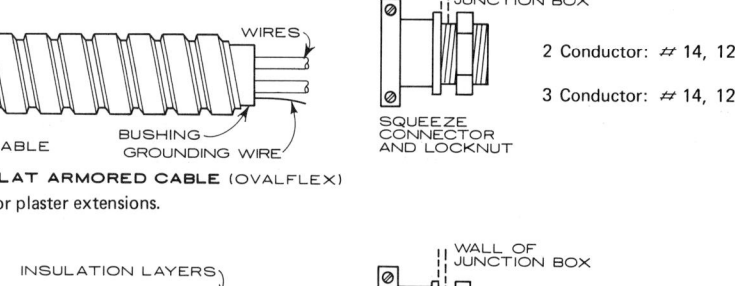

WALL OF JUNCTION BOX

WIRES

2 Conductor: # 14, 12, 10

3 Conductor: # 14, 12

CABLE   BUSHING   GROUNDING WIRE   SQUEEZE CONNECTOR AND LOCKNUT

FLAT ARMORED CABLE (OVALFLEX)
For plaster extensions.

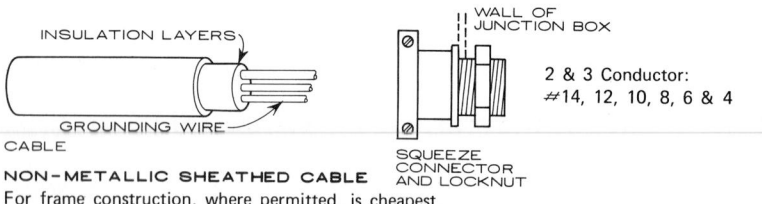

WALL OF JUNCTION BOX

INSULATION LAYERS

2 & 3 Conductor:
#14, 12, 10, 8, 6 & 4

CABLE   GROUNDING WIRE   SQUEEZE CONNECTOR AND LOCKNUT

NON-METALLIC SHEATHED CABLE
For frame construction, where permitted, is cheapest.

CABLES, CONDUITS AND TUBING
STANDARD NOMINAL SIZES IN INCHES

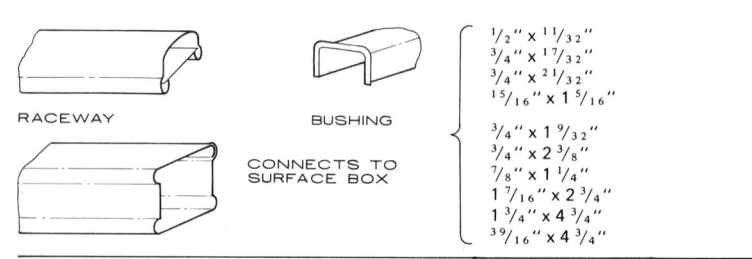

RACEWAY   BUSHING

CONNECTS TO SURFACE BOX

1/2" x 11/32"
3/4" x 17/32"
3/4" x 21/32"
15/16" x 1 5/16"

3/4" x 1 9/32"
3/4" x 2 3/8"
7/8" x 1 1/4"
1 7/16" x 2 3/4"
1 3/4" x 4 3/4"
3 9/16" x 4 3/4"

SURFACE METAL RACEWAYS

Syska & Hennessy; New York, New York

Smith, Hinchman & Grylls Associates, Inc.; Detroit, Michigan

MATERIALS AND METHODS

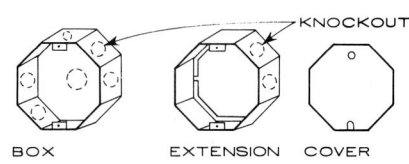

KNOCKOUTS

WIDTH & DEPTH
3 1/4 x 1 1/2
3 1/2 x 1 1/2
4 x 1 1/2
4 x 2 1/8

BOX   EXTENSION   COVER

OCTAGONAL
Used in ceilings and walls.

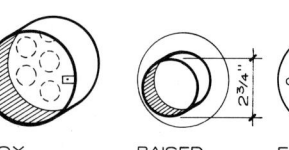

WIDTH & DEPTH
3 1/4 x 3/4, 1 1/2
3 1/2 x 1/2, 1 1/2
4 x 1/2
*4 x 5/8

* Raised Cover

BOX   RAISED COVER   FLAT COVER

ROUND
Used in ceilings.

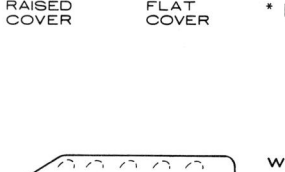

WIDTH & DEPTH
Square box:
4 x 1 1/2, 2 1/8
4 11/16 x 1 1/2, 2 1/8
2 Gang Box
4 1/2 x 1 3/4 x 6 13/16 long

SQUARE   RECTANGULAR

RECTANGULAR
Used in ceilings and walls.

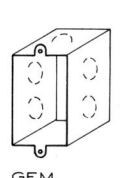
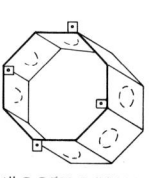
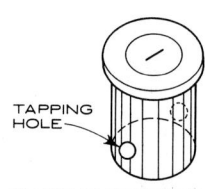

TAPPING HOLE

GEM
for switch or receptacle in narrow location
2" wide x 3" long x 2" or 2 1/2" deep

4" OCTAGONAL
for concrete 1 1/2, 2, 2 1/2, 3, 3 1/2, 4, 5, 6 deep

FLUSH FLOOR BOX
for masonry sizes vary

IN MASONRY

SIZES VARY

ADJUSTABLE JUNCTION BOX   UTILITY BOX   OUTLET & DEVICE BOX

EXPOSED
See manufacturers catalogs for other fittings.

OUTLET AND JUNCTION BOXES
SIZES IN INCHES

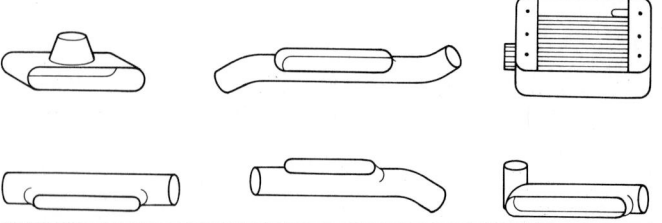

CONDULETS (FOR EXPOSED WORK)
Condulets made in a great many shapes & sizes; consult manufacturers.

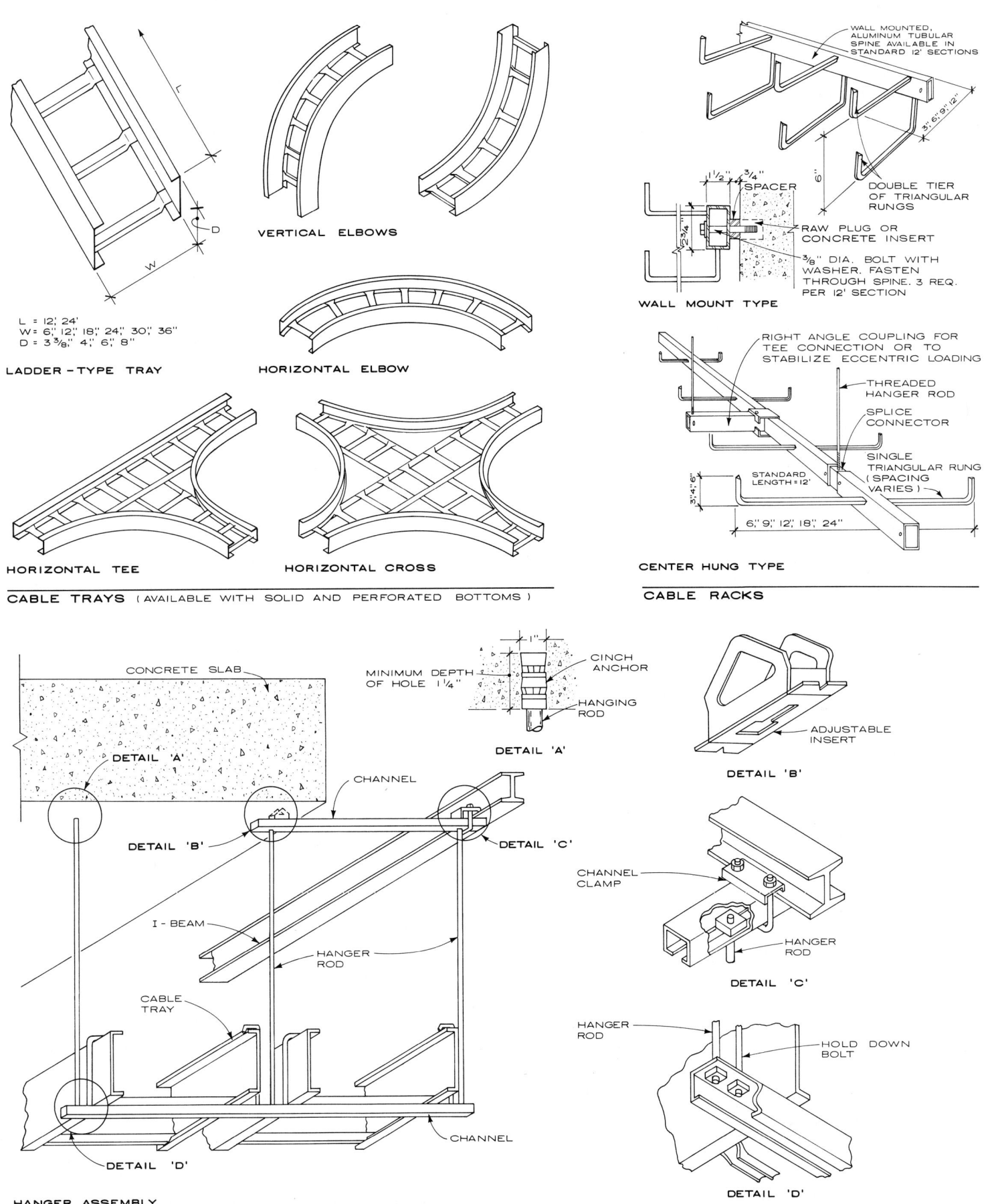

VERTICAL ELBOWS

L = 12; 24'
W = 6; 12; 18; 24; 30; 36"
D = 3⅜; 4; 6; 8"

LADDER – TYPE TRAY

HORIZONTAL ELBOW

HORIZONTAL TEE

HORIZONTAL CROSS

CABLE TRAYS (AVAILABLE WITH SOLID AND PERFORATED BOTTOMS)

WALL MOUNTED, ALUMINUM TUBULAR SPINE AVAILABLE IN STANDARD 12' SECTIONS

DOUBLE TIER OF TRIANGULAR RUNGS

SPACER

RAW PLUG OR CONCRETE INSERT

⅜" DIA. BOLT WITH WASHER. FASTEN THROUGH SPINE. 3 REQ. PER 12' SECTION

WALL MOUNT TYPE

RIGHT ANGLE COUPLING FOR TEE CONNECTION OR TO STABILIZE ECCENTRIC LOADING

THREADED HANGER ROD

SPLICE CONNECTOR

SINGLE TRIANGULAR RUNG (SPACING VARIES)

STANDARD LENGTH = 12'

6; 9; 12; 18; 24"

CENTER HUNG TYPE

CABLE RACKS

CONCRETE SLAB

DETAIL 'A'

DETAIL 'B'

CHANNEL

DETAIL 'C'

I - BEAM

HANGER ROD

CABLE TRAY

DETAIL 'D'

CHANNEL

HANGER ASSEMBLY

MINIMUM DEPTH OF HOLE 1¼"

CINCH ANCHOR

HANGING ROD

DETAIL 'A'

ADJUSTABLE INSERT

DETAIL 'B'

CHANNEL CLAMP

HANGER ROD

DETAIL 'C'

HANGER ROD

HOLD DOWN BOLT

DETAIL 'D'

CABLE TRAY INSTALLATION DETAILS

CH₂M Hill, Inc; Corvallis, Oregon

SERVICE AND DISTRIBUTION   16

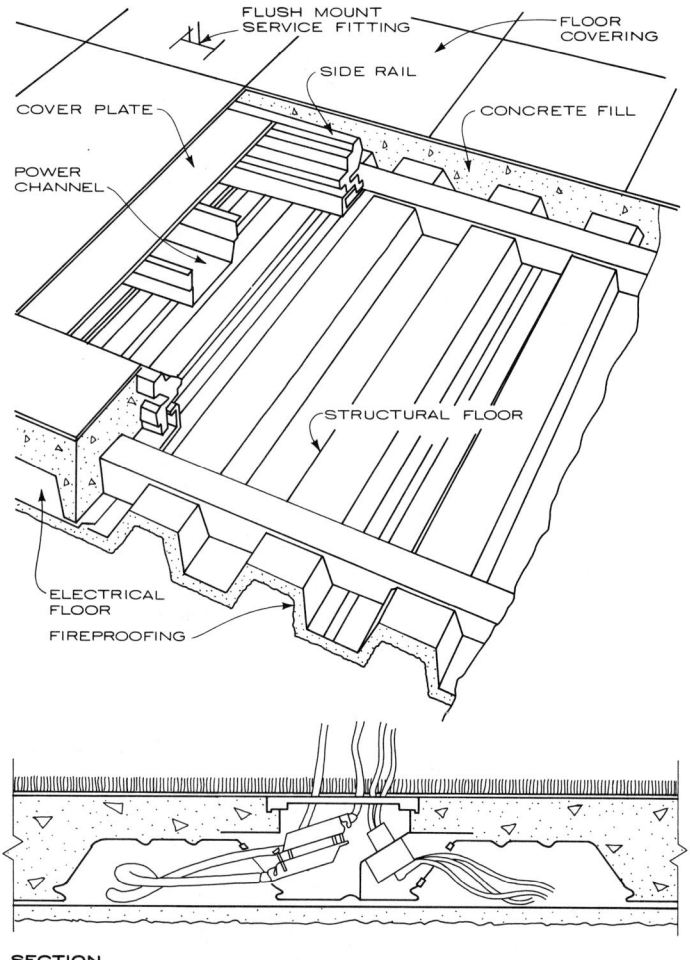

SECTION

BOTTOMLESS TRENCH DUCT FOR STRUCTURAL DECK

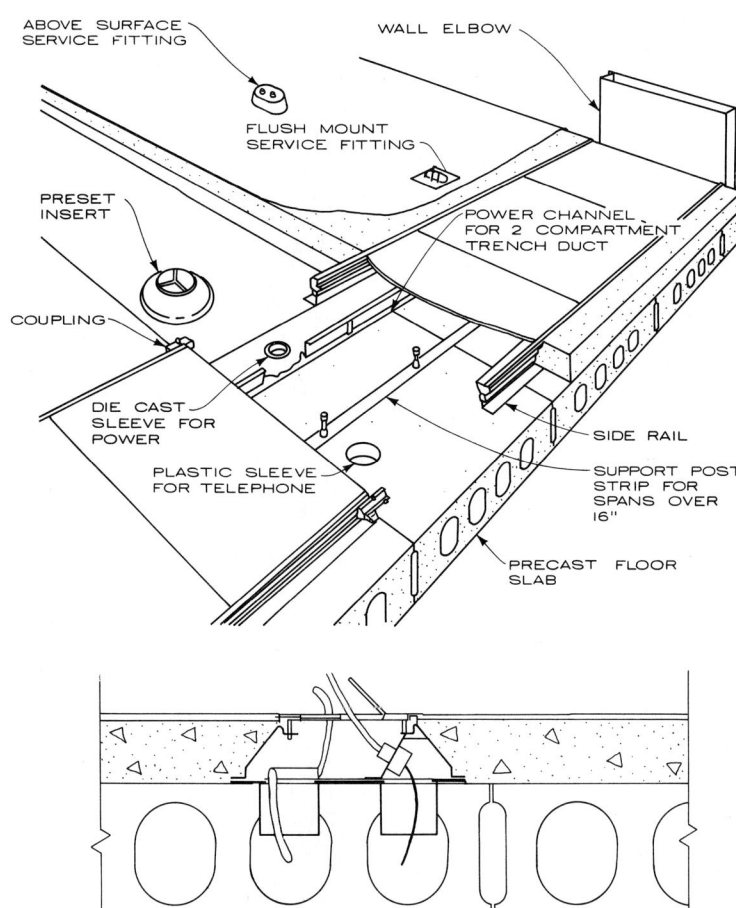

SECTION

BOTTOMLESS TRENCH DUCT FOR PRECAST CONCRETE RACEWAY

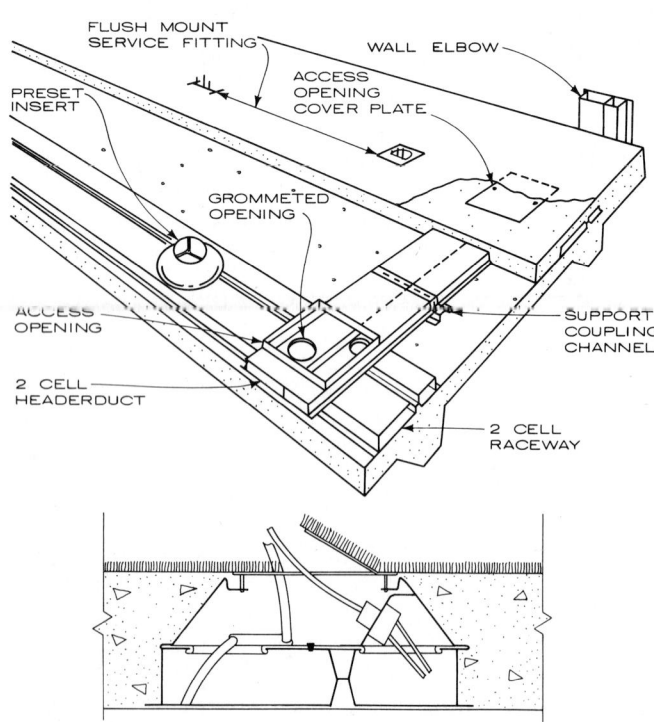

SECTION

HEADER DUCT SYSTEM WITH TWO-CELL METAL RACEWAY AND PRESET INSERT

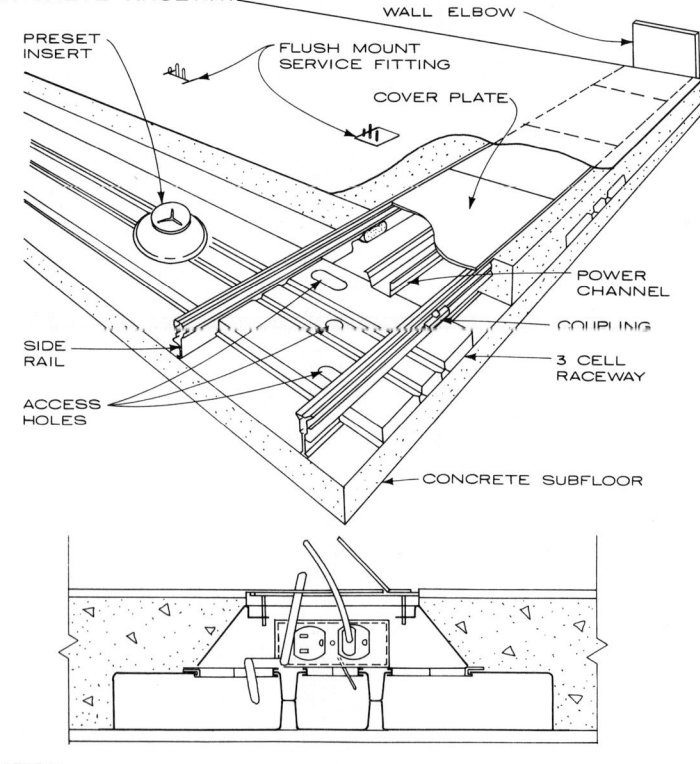

SECTION

BOTTOMLESS TRENCH DUCT WITH THREE-CELL METAL RACEWAY AND PRESET INSERT

Walter H. Sobel, FAIA & Associates; Chicago, Illinois

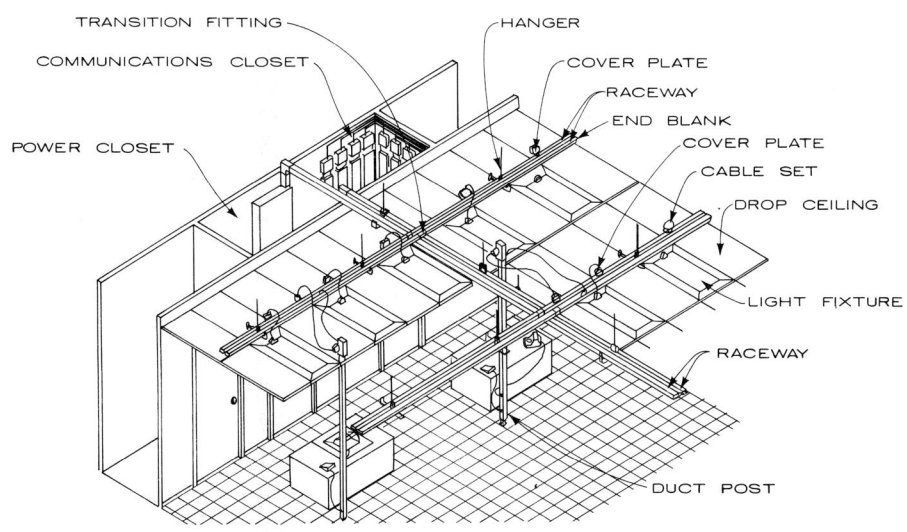

CEILING RACEWAY SYSTEM

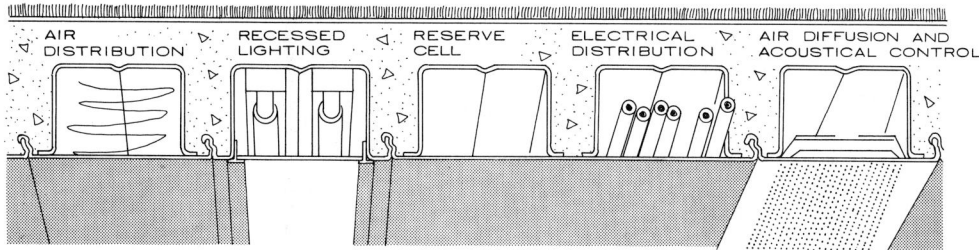

ARCHITECTURAL FLOOR / CEILING SYSTEM

Raceway systems and underfloor ducts are available to match virtually any architectural design. Cost analysis and field experience have made it possible in composite beam design to reduce steel costs by 15 to 20%. This permits shallower beams, lighter beam sections, or both. Total building height can be reduced when power and electrical cables run through the open cells. In older buildings that have no underfloor electrical and telephone systems surface and overhead or ceiling raceway systems may be effectively utilized. Most raceway and underfloor duct systems can be adapted to carrying any capacity necessary to make a work station usable. Major building codes require that all floors in a building have fire rated construction. Underwriters Laboratories approves a 2 in. minimum cover over the top of floor cells. In addition to the UL fire rating, all components of the system must have an approved UL electrical rating.

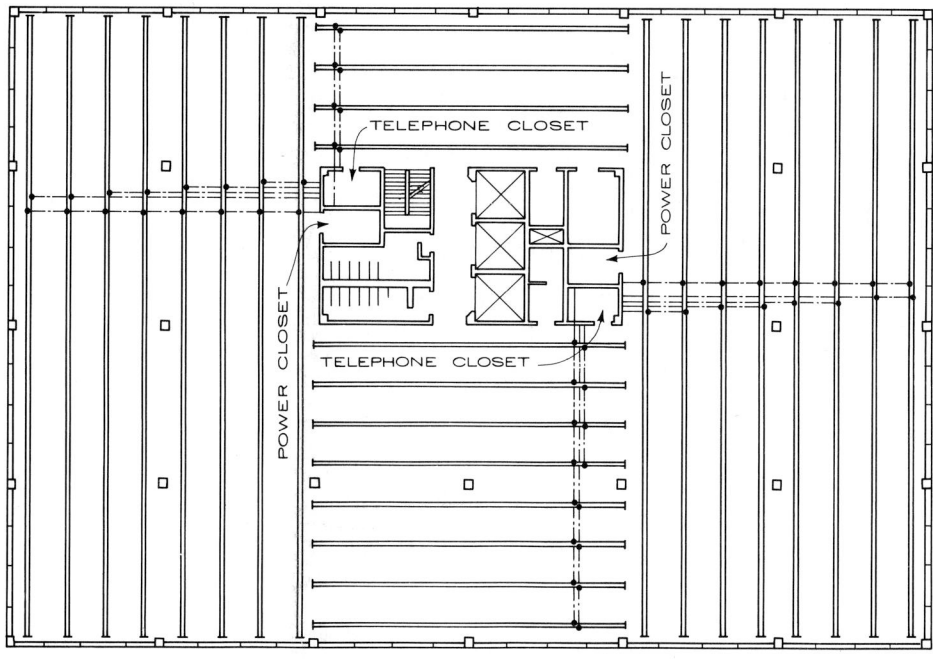

TYPICAL FLOOR DUCT PLAN

Walter H. Sobel, FAIA & Associates; Chicago, Illinois

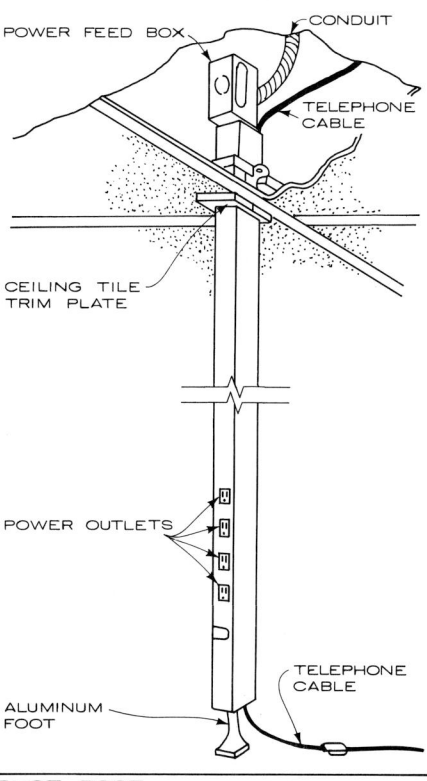

DUCT POST

WEIGHTS AND DIMENSIONS FOR RIGID STEEL CONDUIT

SIZE (IN.)	LB/ 100 FT	I.D.	O.D.	THICK-NESS	THREADS/ IN.
$1/2$	80	0.622	0.840	0.109	14
$3/4$	109	0.824	1.050	0.113	14
1	165	1.049	1.315	0.133	$11 1/2$
$1 1/4$	215	1.380	1.660	0.140	$11 1/2$
$1 1/2$	258	1.610	1.900	0.145	$11 1/2$
2	352	2.067	2.375	0.154	$11 1/2$
$2 1/2$	567	2.469	2.875	0.203	8
3	714	3.068	3.500	0.216	8
$3 1/2$	860	3.548	4.000	0.226	8
4	1000	4.026	4.500	0.237	8
5	1320	5.047	5.563	0.258	8
6	1785	6.065	6.625	0.280	8

WEIGHTS AND DIMENSIONS FOR IN-TERMEDIATE METAL CONDUIT (IMC)

SIZE (IN.)	NOMINAL	LENGTH OF CONDUIT WITHOUT COUPLING	WALL THICK-NESS	LB/100 FT
$1/2$	0.815	$119 1/4$	0.070	60
$3/4$	1.029	$119 1/4$	0.075	82
1	1.290	119	0.085	116
$1 1/4$	1.638	119	0.085	150
$1 1/2$	1.883	119	0.090	182
2	2.360	119	0.095	242
$2 1/2$	2.857	$118 1/2$	0.130	428
3	3.476	$118 1/2$	0.130	526
$3 1/2$	3.971	$118 1/4$	0.130	612
4	4.466	$118 1/4$	0.130	682

WEIGHTS AND DIMENSIONS FOR ELECTRICAL METALIC TUBING (EMT)

SIZE (IN.)	LB/100 FT	I.D.	O.D.
$1/2$	29	0.622	0.706
$3/4$	45	0.824	0.922
1	65	1.049	1.163
$1 1/4$	96	1.380	1.510
$1 1/2$	111	1.610	1.740
2	141	2.067	2.197
$2 1/2$	215	2.731	2.875
3	260	3.356	3.500
$3 1/2$	325	3.834	4.000
4	390	4.334	4.500

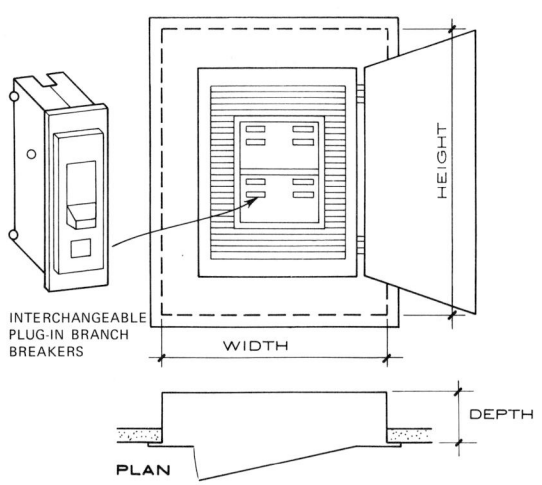

INTERCHANGEABLE
PLUG-IN BRANCH
BREAKERS

WIDTH

HEIGHT

DEPTH

PLAN

PLUG-IN CIRCUIT BREAKER

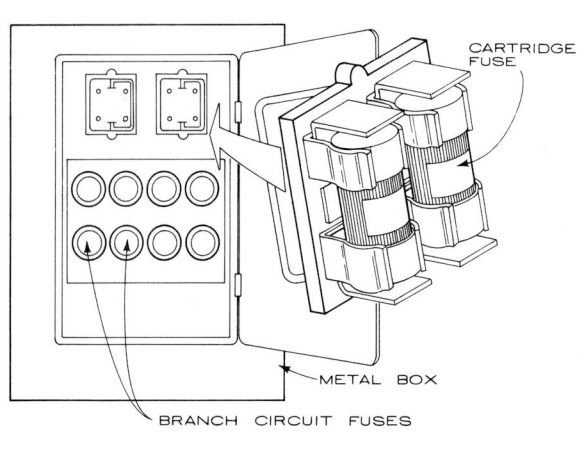

CARTRIDGE
FUSE

METAL BOX

BRANCH CIRCUIT FUSES

FUSE BOX WITH FUSED MAIN DISCONNECTS

RESIDENTIAL AND SMALL COMMERCIAL PANEL BOARDS

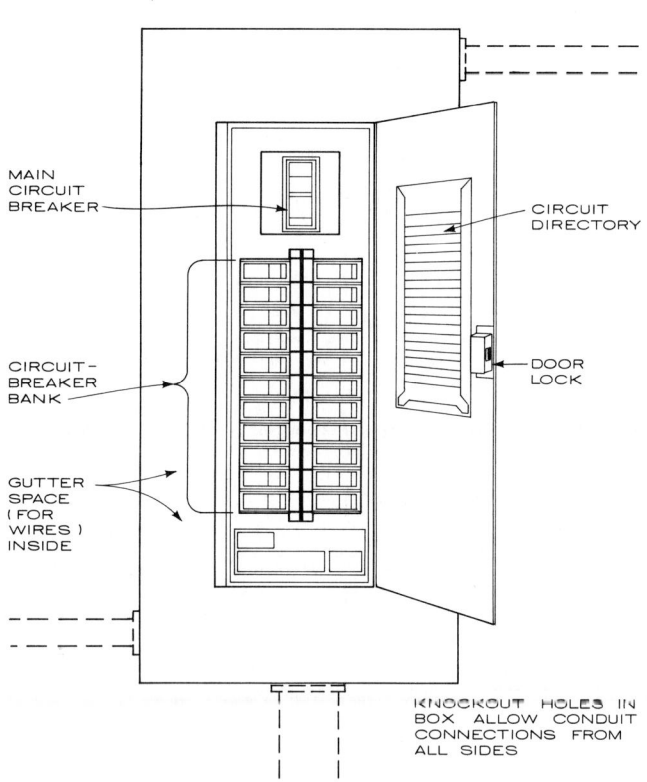

MAIN
CIRCUIT
BREAKER

CIRCUIT
DIRECTORY

CIRCUIT-
BREAKER
BANK

DOOR
LOCK

GUTTER
SPACE
(FOR
WIRES)
INSIDE

KNOCKOUT HOLES IN
BOX ALLOW CONDUIT
CONNECTIONS FROM
ALL SIDES

LARGE RESIDENTIAL PANELBOARD

PANELBOARD DIMENSIONS

MAXIMUM NUMBER OF CIRCUITS	BOX DIMENSIONS (IN.)		
	WIDTH	HEIGHT	DEPTH
12	9-15	16-20	$3^3/_4$-$4^5/_8$
20	9-15	$20^1/_4$-24	$3^3/_4$-$4^5/_8$
30	12-15	30-33	$3^3/_4$-$4^5/_8$
40	14-15	34-39	4-$4^5/_8$

Darrel Rippeteau, Architect; Washington, D.C.

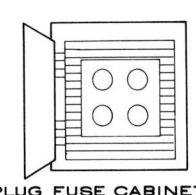

Box dimensions below.
For outside dimension
add 1 1/4" to height &
width.

PLUG FUSE CABINET

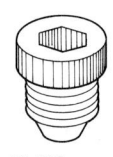

PLUG
FUSE

BOX DIMENSIONS (IN.)

BRANCHES	HEIGHT	WIDTH	DEPTH
2	6 5/8	6 5/8	2 3/4
4	6 5/8	6 5/8	2 3/4
6	11 1/8	7 3/8	3 1/8
8	14 1/8	7 3/8	3 1/8

Up to 12 branches same as 8 branches

PLUG FUSE AND PLUG FUSE CABINET
FOR APARTMENTS AND SMALL HOUSES

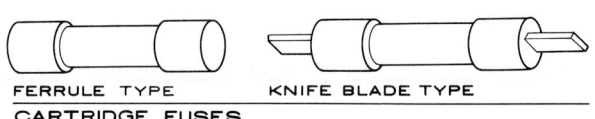

FERRULE TYPE

KNIFE BLADE TYPE

CARTRIDGE FUSES

Ferrule contact 1 to 60 amps.
Knife blade contact 70 to 600 amps and larger.
Ferrule type non-renewable. Knife blade type non-renewable and renewable link.

STANDARD FUSE SIZES

Plug Fuse: 1, 3, 5, 6, 8, 10, 15, 20, 25 and 30 amperes.
Cartridge: 1, 3, 6, 10, 15, 20, 25, 30, 35, 40, 50, 60, 70, 80, 90, 100, 110, 125, 150, 175, 200, 225, 250, 275, 300, 325, 350, 400, 450, 500, 600 amperes, and larger.

Standard knife switches are rated at 30, 60, 100, 200, 400 & 600 amps, and take cartridge fuses up to and including their rating.

Circuit breakers at 50 (trip at 15, 20, 30, 40, 50); 100 (trip at 15, 20, 30, 40, 50, 70, 100); 225 (70 – 225, increment 25); 600 (125 – 350, increment 25 & 400, 500, 600 amp.)

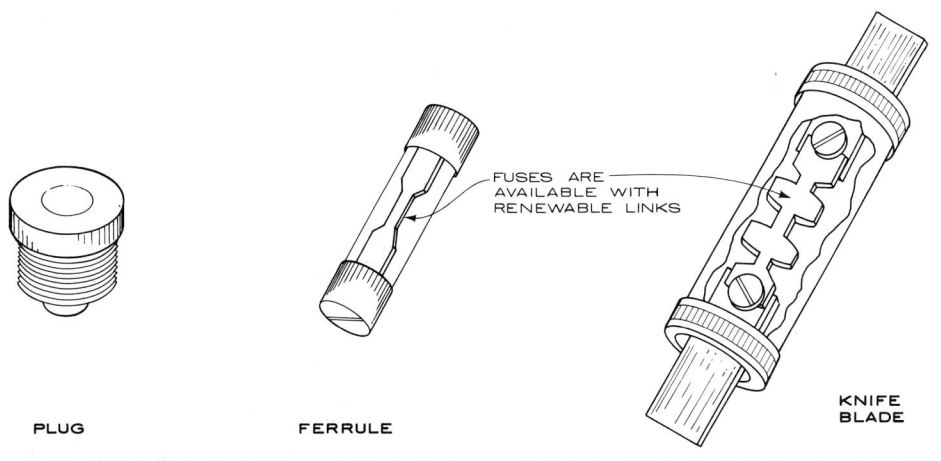

PLUG   FERRULE   KNIFE BLADE

STANDARD FUSES

PLUG FUSES

1. MAXIMUM VOLTAGE: 125.
2. AMPERE RATING: 1-30 A.
3. FUSE TYPE: S.

CARTRIDGE FUSES

1. MAXIMUM VOLTAGE: 250 and 600.
2. AMPERE RATINGS: $1/10$-60 A.
3. FUSE TYPES: K1, K1R, K5, K5R, T, J, H, and G.

KNIFE FUSES

1. MAXIMUM VOLTAGE: 250 and 600.
2. AMPERE RATINGS: 70 -6000 A.
3. FUSE TYPES: K1, K1R, K5, K5R, T, J, H, G, and L.

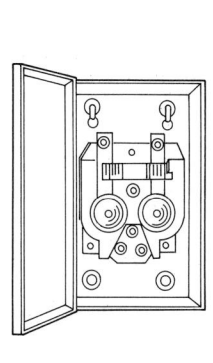
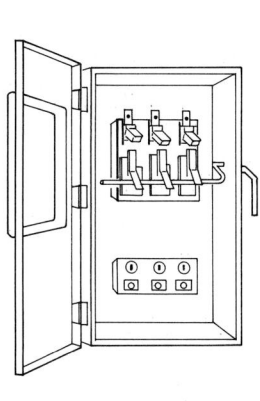
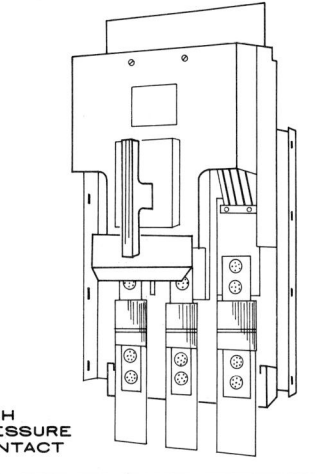

TOGGLE   KNIFE BLADE   HIGH PRESSURE CONTACT

DISCONNECT SWITCHES

TOGGLE SWITCHES

1. MAXIMUM VOLTAGES: 125 VAC/DC, 125 or 250 VAC/DC, or 240 VAC.
2. RATING: 30 A max.

SAFETY SWITCHES

1. MAXIMUM VOLTAGES: 240 VAC, 125-250 VDC, 600 VAC.
2. POLES: 2, 3, or 4 plus S/N and/or GRD Lug.
3. TYPES: TG, TH, or TC fusible and no fuse.
4. RATING: 30-1200 A.

HIGH PRESSURE CONTACT SWITCHES

1. MAXIMUM VOLTAGES: 240 VAC or 480 VAC.
2. POLES: 3.
3. RATINGS: 800-4000 A.

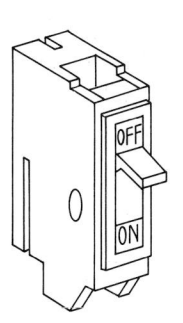

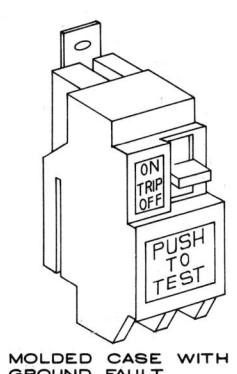

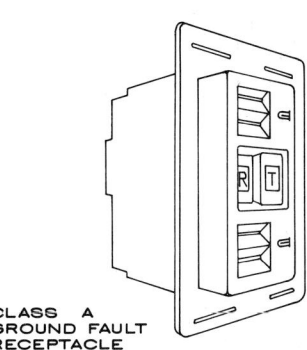

MOLDED CASE   MOLDED CASE WITH GROUND FAULT   CLASS A GROUND FAULT RECEPTACLE

CIRCUIT BREAKERS

STANDARD MOLDED CASE CIRCUIT BREAKERS

1. MAXIMUM VOLTAGES: 120 VAC, 240 VAC, 600 VAC, 125 VDC, and 250 VDC.
2. FRAME SIZES: 100 A, 225 A, 400 A, 600 A, 800 A, 1200 A Poles—2 or 3.

MOLDED CASE CIRCUIT BREAKERS INCORPORATING GROUND FAULT CIRCUIT INTERRUPTION

1. MAXIMUM VOLTAGES: 120 VAC or 120/240 VAC.
2. FRAME SIZE: 100 A ratings, 15-30 A poles—1 or 2.

CLASS A GROUND FAULT CIRCUIT INTERRUPTION RECEPTACLES

1. MAXIMUM VOLTAGE: 125 VAC.
2. RATINGS: 15 or 20 A NEMA configuration single outlet.

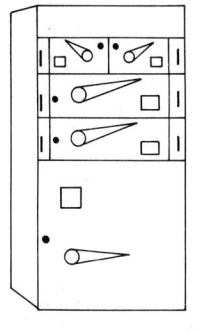

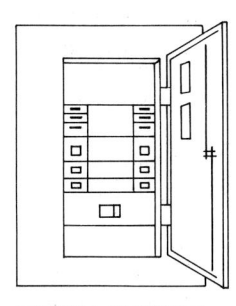

SWITCH AND FUSE   CIRCUIT BREAKER

DISTRIBUTION PANEL BOARDS

CIRCUIT BREAKER PANELS

MANUFACTURER	MAX. NO. OF CIRCUITS	BOX SIZES (IN.)		
		WIDTH	HEIGHT	DEPTH
Square D	12	14	$20^{1}/_{4}$	4
	20	14	$24^{1}/_{4}$	4
	42	14	$32^{1}/_{2}$	4
General Electric Co.	12	14	$21^{1}/_{2}$	$4^{1}/_{2}$
	20	14	$27^{1}/_{2}$	$4^{1}/_{2}$
	30	14	$33^{1}/_{2}$	$4^{1}/_{2}$
	42	14	$36^{1}/_{2}$	$4^{1}/_{2}$
Westinghouse	12	15	20	$4^{1}/_{4}$
	18	15	23	$4^{1}/_{4}$
	30	15	29	$4^{1}/_{4}$
	40	15	35	$4^{1}/_{4}$

NOTE: Other manufacturers' panels are available in similar sizes.

A. A. Erdman; Sargent, Webster, Crenshaw & Folley; Architects Engineers Planners; Syracuse, New York

SERVICE AND DISTRIBUTION   **16**

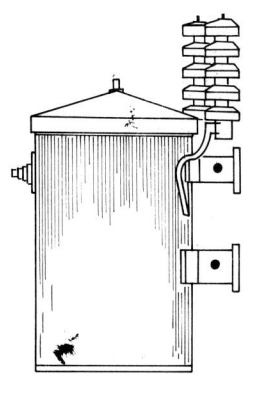 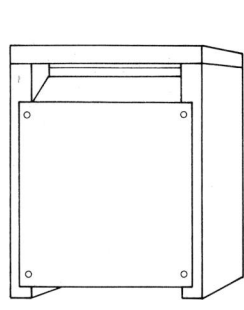 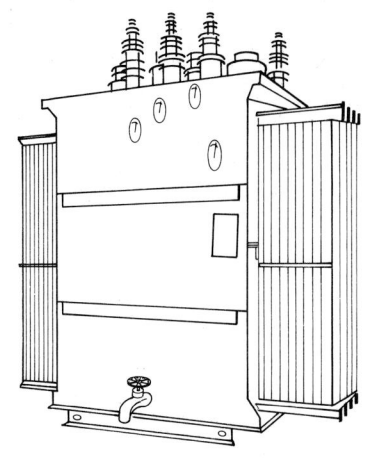 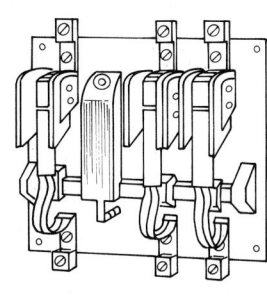

DISTRIBUTION   DRY TYPE   LIQUID FILLED   LOAD CIRCUITS

DISTRIBUTION: High to low voltage. Immersed in oil. Self-cooled. Primarily mounted on outdoor poles.
DRY: Maximum voltage 600 VAC. Primarily mounted on indoor floors and walls.
LIQUID: Secondary substation transformer with high to low voltage. Primarily a commercial type transformer for the outdoors.

Maximum voltage: 600 VAC. For load circuits that are closed and opened repeatedly various design combinations are allowed. Used for all classes of magnetically held loads, open or closed.

TRANSFORMERS   **CONTACTOR**

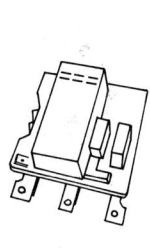 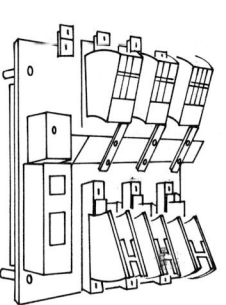 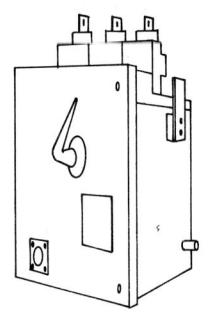 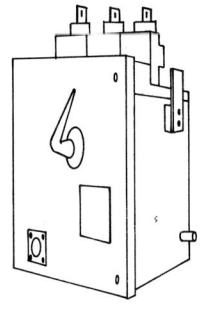

REMOTE CONTROL   AUTOTRANSFER   NETWORK TYPE   MAIN CIRCUIT BREAKER

REMOTE CONTROL: Provides convenient control of lighting and power circuits from control stations.
AUTOTRANSFER: Automatically transfers loads from a normal source to the emergency source.

Maximum voltage: 125/216 VAC or 277/480 VAC. Interrupting capacity 30,000 and 60,000 A. RMS. SYM. A fault on primary cable or network transformer will open protector to isolate fault from system.

Maximum voltage ratings: 120/240, 3 wire, single phase or 208V/120, 4 wire three phase. Either indoor or outdoor construction. Number of sockets as required by application.

SWITCHES   **PROTECTOR**   **METER BANK**

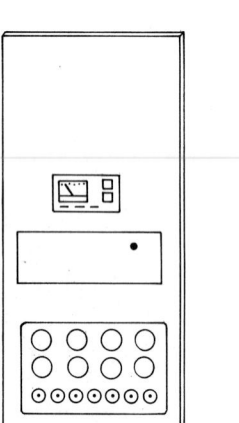 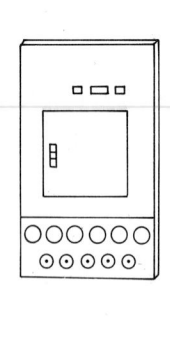 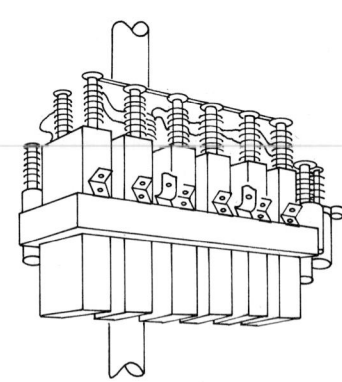 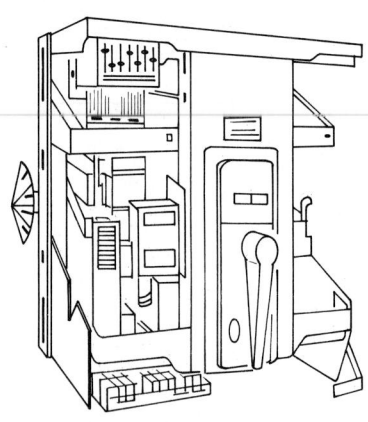

LARGE   SMALL   POLE RACK   LOW VOLTAGE

PRIMARY VOLTAGES: 120, 208, 240, or 277.
SECONDARY VOLTAGE: 120.
APPLICATION: Power and lighting panels, special panels for hospitals (operating, coronary, and X-ray).

Application: Power factor correction on either low or high voltage systems. Types, indoor or outdoor. Size and voltage as required. Switched or floating.

Maximum voltages: 240 VAC, 480 VAC, 600 VAC, and 250 VDC. Operation is manual or electric. Breaker trip devices: Electromechanical or solid state. Type: stationary or drawout.

ISOLATED POWER CENTER   **CAPACITOR**   **CIRCUIT BREAKER**

A. A. Erdman; Sargent, Webster, Crenshaw & Folley; Architects Engineers Planners; Syracuse, New York

 SERVICE AND DISTRIBUTION

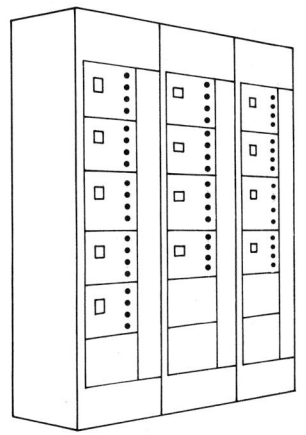

MOTOR CONTROL CENTER

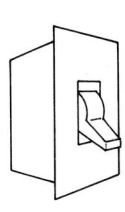

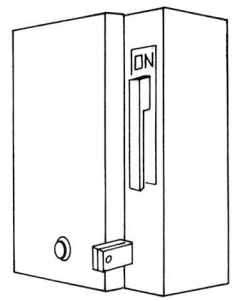

MANUAL   MAGNETIC   COMBINATION

MANUAL: Maximum voltage—240 VAC. Maximum horsepower—1.

MAGNETIC: Maximum voltage—600 VAC. Maximum horsepower—200.

COMBINATION: A magnetic motor starter with a variety of fusible disconnects or circuit breakers.

MOTOR STARTERS

UNIT SUBSTATION: Primary entrance cubicle, air interrupter switch, transformer section, and low voltage distribution sections. See manufacturer's literature for type, size, and arrangements. See National Electric Code for required aisle space, ventilation, servicing area, and special building condition requirements.

UNIT SUBSTATION

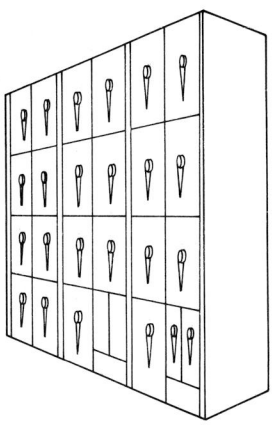

SECONDARY   WITH MAIN

SWITCHBOARD: Metering compartment, main disconnect, check meters, and low voltage distribution section. See manufacturer's literature for type, size, and arrangements. See National Electric Code for required aisle space, servicing area, and room layout.

SWITCHBOARDS

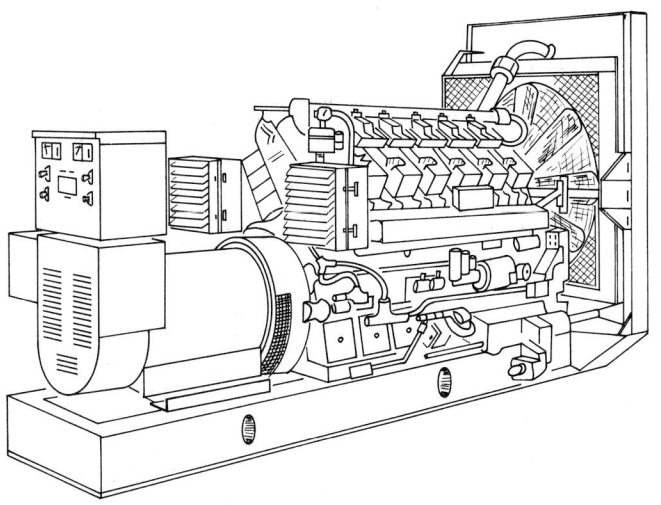

EMERGENCY GENERATOR: Engine driven prime mover, alternator, and controls. Application: to provide emergency power during power outages. See manufacturer's literature for ratings, dimensions, weight, ventilation, and fuel consumption. See National Electric Code for working space requirements and proper application.

**EMERGENCY GENERATOR WITH CONTROL PANEL
(800 KW)**

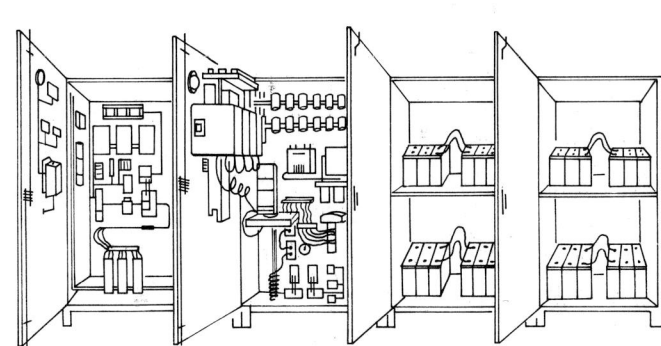

UNINTERRUPTIBLE POWER SUPPLY: D.C. batteries, battery charger, rectifier, and static inverter. Application: to provide continuous power during outage or abnormal transient power conditions. See manufacturer's literature for ratings, dimensions, weight, and ventilation requirements. See National Electric Code for working space requirements.

UNINTERRUPTIBLE POWER SUPPLY

A. A. Erdman; Sargent, Webster, Crenshaw & Folley; Architects Engineers Planners; Syracuse, New York

SERVICE AND DISTRIBUTION   **16**

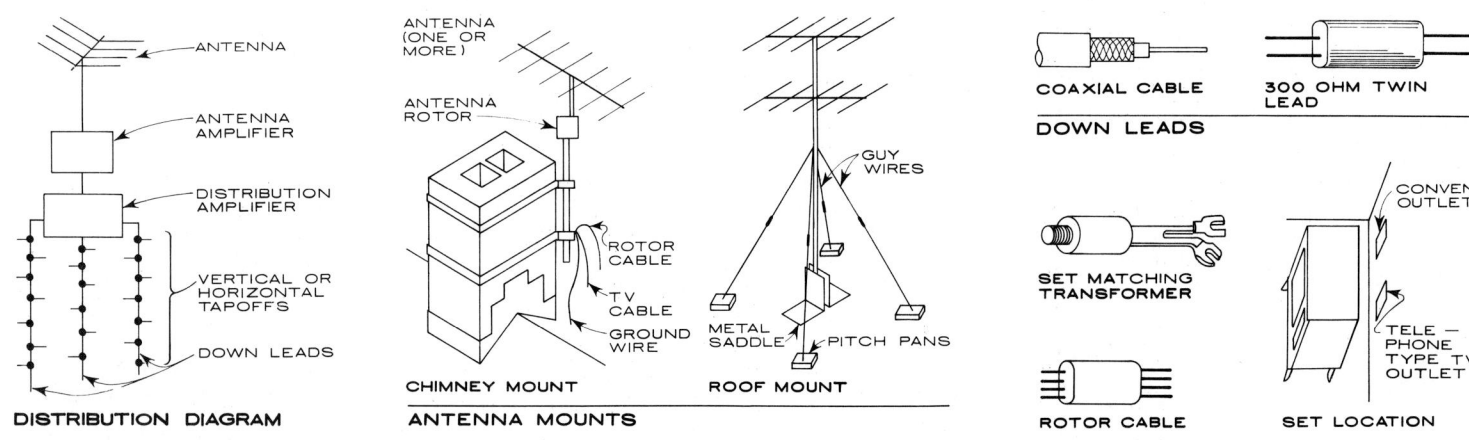

DISTRIBUTION DIAGRAM   ANTENNA MOUNTS

ANTENNA SYSTEMS FOR TELEVISION AND FM RADIO

NOTES

Television and FM radio distribution systems are the same for horizontal "motel type" and for vertical "hotel type" installations. Summary information shown can be used as a guide for small residential as well as for large systems. TV signals in apartment houses, hotels, institutions, and other large buildings go directly from the antenna installation to the amplification and distribution point at roof level or, after a short cable run, to the basement. Locate the amplifiers, power supplies, mixers, filters, and related equipment as close to antenna as project conditions permit. Distribution line amplifiers, if necessary may be located in closets, shafts, or similar areas accessible for service.

Broadband TV/FM distribution systems are extremely vulnerable to intermodulation interference problems from nearby radio transmitters. If the presence of a nearby, powerful transmitter is known, consult the manufacturer of the distribution equipment. Grounding should be provided as required by the National Electric Code.

The number of antennas depends on the number of broadcast stations that can be received. A small tower or guyed mast may be used for either residential or commercial antenna installations. Locate towers, mast, and mounts to assure a signal path free of obstructions and of sufficient size to support the antennas required. If on a rooftop, a base or saddle must be provided to prevent damage to the roof. For details of Master Antenna Television (MATV) systems, consult a local MATV installer.

Runs to TV tapoffs are usually 75 ohm coaxial cable and should be in conduit if possibility of stress or accidental cutting exists. If a rotor is used (for residential installation only) on the antenna, the down lead is a low voltage cable and may be routed in a manner to comply with wiring of low voltage. The down lead from the antenna or from the rotor may be terminated in an outlet box at the TV set location. A power outlet should be installed near the TV set. The same power outlet may provide power to the antenna rotor if used. If a coaxial cable is used from the TV antenna to the outlet box, a set matching transformer (illustrated above) will be required at the TV set. Consult TV set manufacturer for specific antenna, power supply, and ventilation requirements.

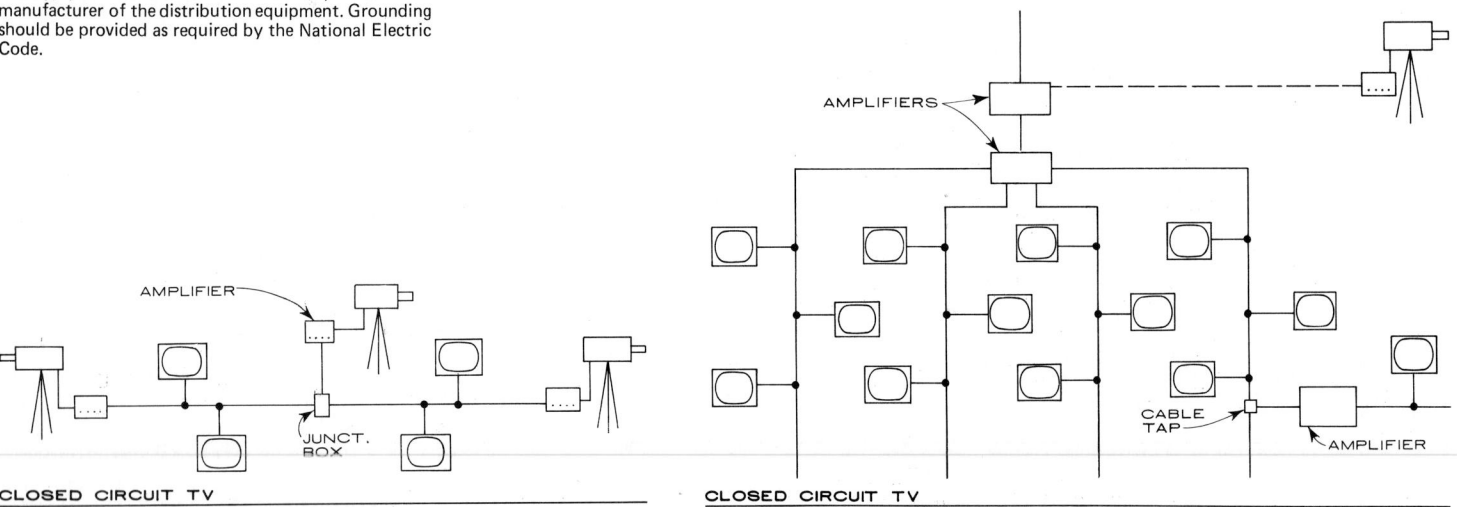

CLOSED CIRCUIT TV
CAMERA / MONITOR ARRANGEMENT

CLOSED CIRCUIT TV
CAMERA AND DISTRIBUTION SYSTEM

NOTES

Closed circuit television cameras are used for observing remote or inaccessible locations, for security viewing of restricted areas, or for viewing a hazardous environment. In this TV system, a live pickup camera signal is fed to a standard television set or a video monitor used as a picture monitor. One closed circuit television camera can be called to feed several TV set picture monitors or several closed circuit television cameras may feed one TV set picture monitor by a switching arrangement. The pickup camera signal can be transmitted over coaxial cable by either direct video signal or by modulated (AM) radio frequency signals.

Closed circuit television cameras may be added to any Master Antenna system (MATV) or to any Community Antenna Television system. This may be done by considering the camera signal as an additional channel antenna. The closed circuit television camera modulated radio frequency signal is fed into the television distribution system on any unused TV channel. Any number of TV cameras may be fed into a TV distribution system, depending on the number of TV channels the TV distribution system can accommodate. Video signals from a closed circuit television camera may be fed to a TV picture monitor by coaxial cable up to 2500 ft; consult your local installer or manufacturer.

Adequate lighting must be provided for closed circuit television camera pickup locations. The audio or sound associated with the closed circuit television system must be treated in the same manner as the television signal when cabled separately, otherwise the audio or sound is transmitted as a part of the television signal.

Videotape (VTR) and film/slide systems may be operated in addition to closed circuit television cameras. The video signal from videotape recorders or from film/slide systems is distributed in the same manner as for closed circuit television. If videotape recorders and film/slide equipment are to be operated in conjunction with live closed circuit television cameras, adequate space must be provided for equipment and operators. Power must be supplied for the operating equipment and numerous small pieces of associated equipment. For videotape operation, it is desirable to control the dust and humidity, both in the operating and the storage areas.

Virgil D. Duncan, P.E.; Raleigh, North Carolina

 COMMUNICATIONS

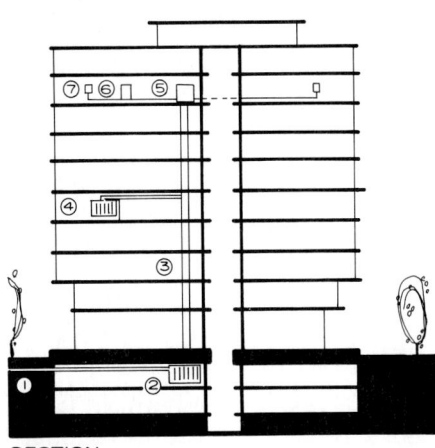

SECTION

BASIC ELEMENTS OF IN—BUILDING COMMUNICATIONS FACILITIES

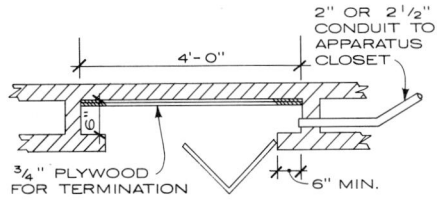

2" OR 2½" CONDUIT TO APPARATUS CLOSET

4'-0"

¾" PLYWOOD FOR TERMINATION

6" MIN.

NOTE: A MINIMUM 3'-0" WORKING SPACE AND ADEQUATE LIGHTING ARE REQUIRED IN FRONT OF CLOSET. TYPICAL FOR 5000 SQ FT OF USABLE FLOOR AREA

SATELLITE TERMINAL CLOSET

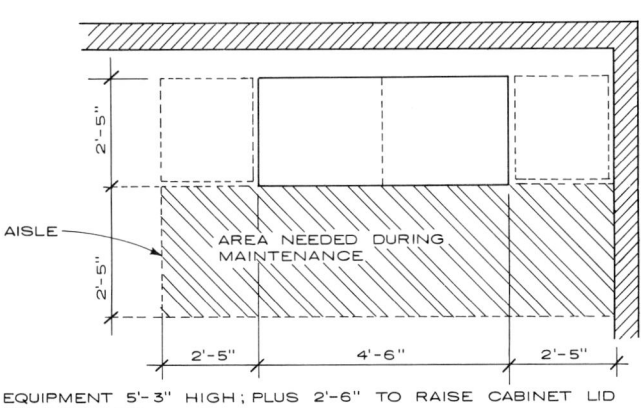

AISLE

2'-5"

2'-5"

AREA NEEDED DURING MAINTENANCE

2'-5"   4'-6"   2'-5"

EQUIPMENT 5'-3" HIGH; PLUS 2'-6" TO RAISE CABINET LID
WT 1500 ± LB

FLOOR SPACE NEEDED FOR PBX EQUIPMENT

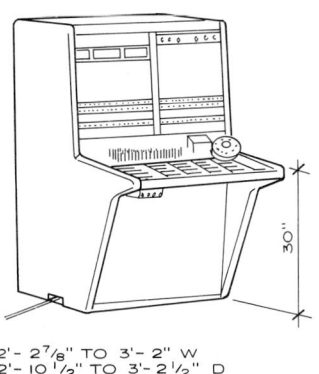

2'- 2⅞" TO 3'- 2" W
2'- 10½" TO 3'- 2½" D
3'- 10 1/16" TO 5'- 0" H
WT 400 TO 500 LB

SWITCHBOARD

NOTES: STEEL CASING — VARIOUS COLORS AND FINISHES. THERE ARE MANY TYPES OF SWITCHBOARDS

Charles Szoradi, AIA and F. Menendez; Washington, D.C.

NOTES

This diagram illustrates the interrelationship of the basic part of an in-building communications system. When consulted early in the planning of a structure, your Telephone Company Building Industry Consultant will be able to suggest alternatives to the in-building communication needs.

The elements depicted above are:

1. SERVICE ENTRANCE: This is the point where telephone lines cross the property line and enter the building.
2. MAIN TERMINAL ROOM: Incoming cables meet the building's system here.
3. RISER SYSTEM: In multistory buildings such a system provides vertical distribution from the main terminal room to the floors above.
4. EQUIPMENT ROOM: Many buildings, particularly those with PBX or contrex services, require special space for its switching equipment.
5. APPARATUS CLOSET: A typical closet usually contains cable terminals as well as relay circuitry and power equipment.
6. SATELLITE TERMINAL CLOSET: Serves as a subdistribution center of each serviced area.
7. DISTRIBUTION METHOD: From apparatus closets or satellite locations, cables extend above ceilings or under floors and terminate in appropriately spaced service fittings.

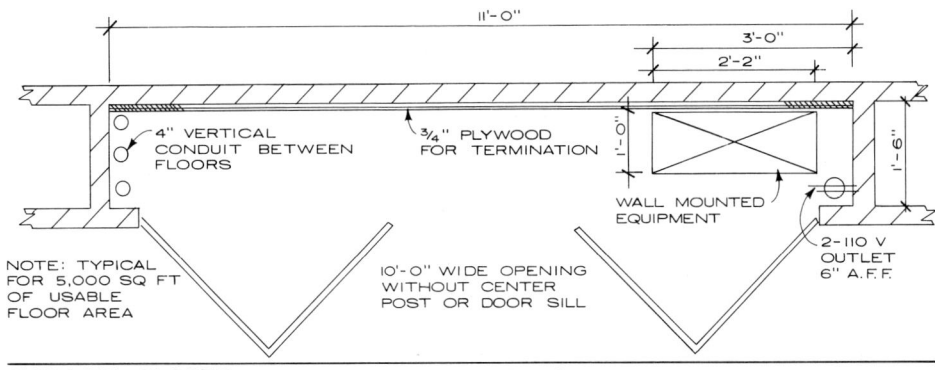

4" VERTICAL CONDUIT BETWEEN FLOORS

¾" PLYWOOD FOR TERMINATION

WALL MOUNTED EQUIPMENT

11'-0"

3'-0"

2'-2"

1'-0"

1'-6"

2-110 V OUTLET 6" A.F.F.

NOTE: TYPICAL FOR 5,000 SQ FT OF USABLE FLOOR AREA

10'-0" WIDE OPENING WITHOUT CENTER POST OR DOOR SILL

SHALLOW CLOSET (WALL MOUNTED EQUIPMENT)

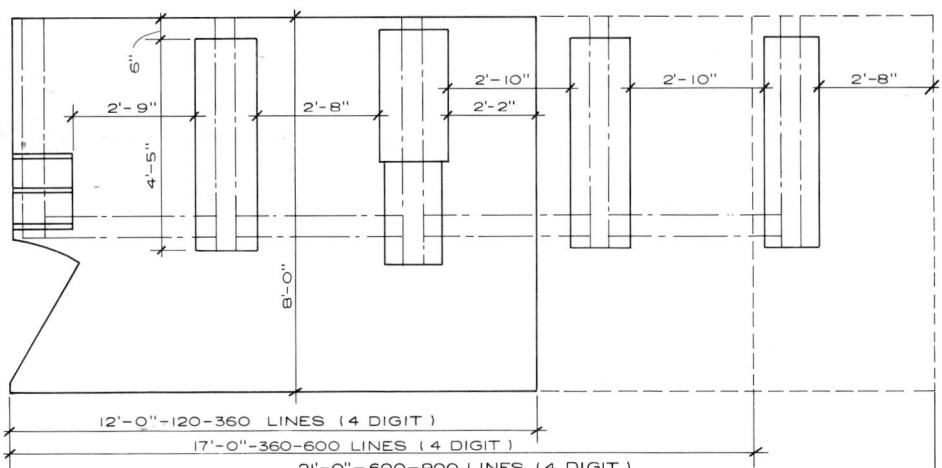

7'-0"

¾" PLYWOOD FOR TERMINATIONS

4" VERTICAL CONDUIT BETWEEN FLOORS

CENTER LINE OF OVERHEAD LIGHT

FLOOR MOUNTED EQUIPMENT

2-110 V OUTLET

4'-0"

6"   2'-6"

NOTE: TYPICAL FOR 9,000–10,000 SQ FT OF USABLE FLOOR AREA

WALK—IN CLOSET (FLOOR MOUNTED)

6"

2'-9"   2'-8"   2'-10"   2'-10"   2'-8"

2'-2"

4'-5"

8'-0"

12'-0"—120-360 LINES (4 DIGIT)
17'-0"—360-600 LINES (4 DIGIT)
21'-0"—600-900 LINES (4 DIGIT)

EQUIPMENT ROOM REQUIREMENTS

GENERAL NOTES

Telephone equipment as shown is typical. A large variety of special equipment is available, and its use is determined by the requirements of the telephone service desired. Telephone companies provide design and engineering assistance without charge. The local telephone company should be consulted in advance for any type of telephone installation. Large installations are custom designed to meet many diversified types of service requirements, with space and facilities provided as needed for housing equipment.

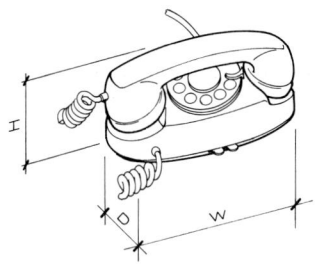
8 ½"W × 5 ½"D × 4"H
PRINCESS ®

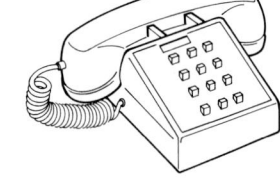
5 ½"W × 8 ½"D × 5"H
PUSH BUTTON

8 ½"W × 9 ¼"D × 5 ⅜"H
1 OR 6 BUTTON KEY SET

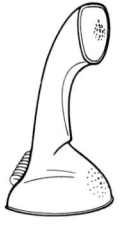
4" × 4 ½" BASE - 9"H
ERICOFON DIAL

8 ½" W × 8 ½" D ×15"H ©
MICKEY MOUSE

DESK / TABLE TELEPHONE SETS (ALL MODELS AVAILABLE WITH PUSH BUTTONS)
PLASTIC CASING : IN VARIOUS COLORS

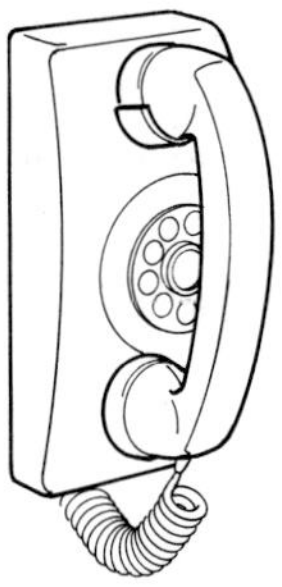

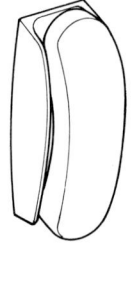
4 ½"W × 4 ½"D × 8 ¾"H
STANDARD
PLASTIC CASING: IN VARIOUS COLORS

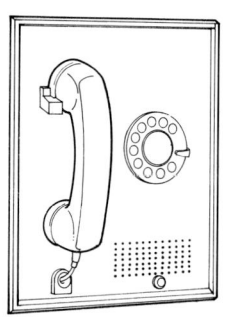
3 ½"W × 3 ½"D × 8 ½"H
TRIMLINE ®
DESK TYPE ALSO

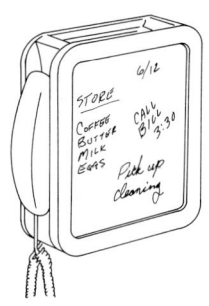
8 ⅜"W × 1 ⅝"D × 11 ¹¹⁄₁₆"H (OPENING)
RECESSED PANEL
S.S. COVER PLATE

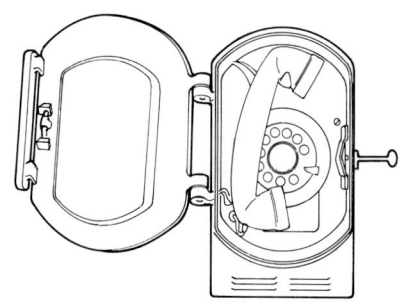
11 ¼" W × 4 ⅜"D × 12 ¼"H
NOTEWORTHY ®

8 ⅜"W × 6 ¼"D × 12 ⅞" H
OUTDOOR / INDOOR PHONE
WEATHERPROOF, STEEL CASING AND COVER

HANGING OR WALL TELEPHONE SETS (ALL MODELS AVAILABLE WITH PUSH BUTTONS)

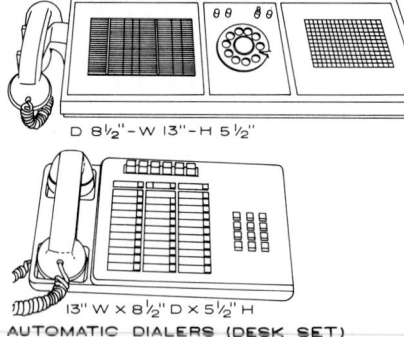
D 8 ½" - W 13" - H 5 ½"

13"W × 8 ½"D × 5 ½"H
AUTOMATIC DIALERS (DESK SET)

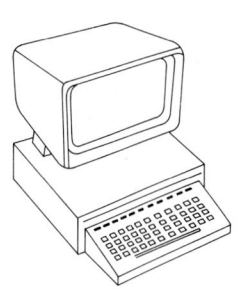
17" W × 25"D × 19"H
DATASPEED ®

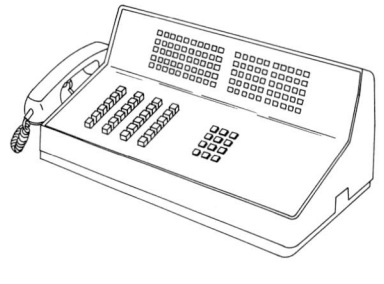
22" W × 12" D × 9 ½" H
ATTENDANT CONSOLE

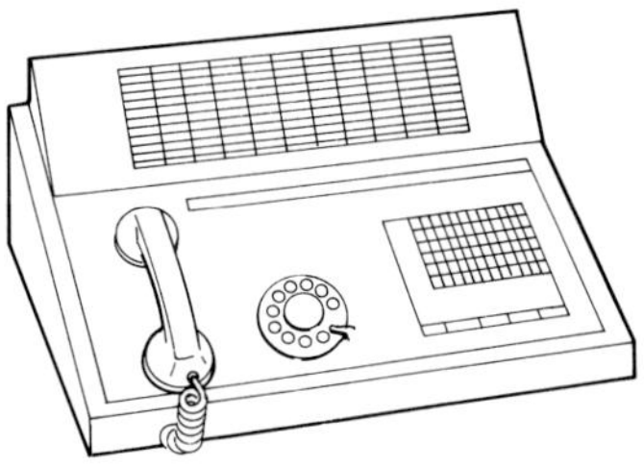

D 12" - W 22" - H 9 ½"
MOTEL ATTENDANT CONSOLE

CONSOLE — DESK TYPE (ALL MODELS AVAILABLE WITH PUSH BUTTONS)
MANY TYPES OF CONSOLES ARE AVAILABLE

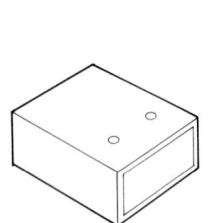
7 ⅛"W × 8"D × 3 ⅛"H
SUBSTATION

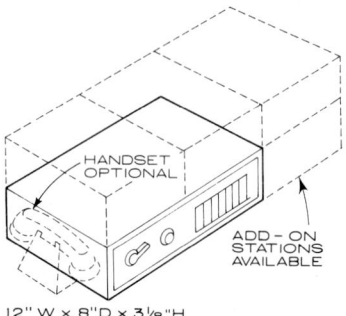
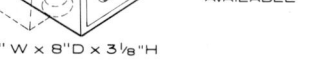
HANDSET OPTIONAL
ADD - ON STATIONS AVAILABLE
12" W × 8"D × 3 ⅛"H
MASTER CONTROL (12 STATIONS)

OFFICE INTERCOM

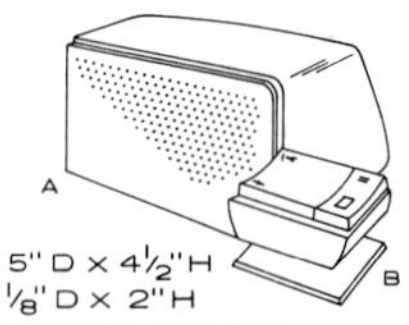

A. 6 ½" W × 5"D × 4 ½"H
B. 3" W × 2 ⅛"D × 2"H
SPEAKERPHONE SETUP

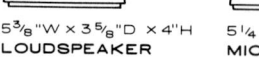
5 ⅜"W × 3 ⅝"D × 4"H
LOUDSPEAKER

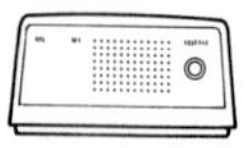

5 ¼"W × 3 ⅛"D × 2 ⅝"H
MICROPHONE

SPEAKERPHONE

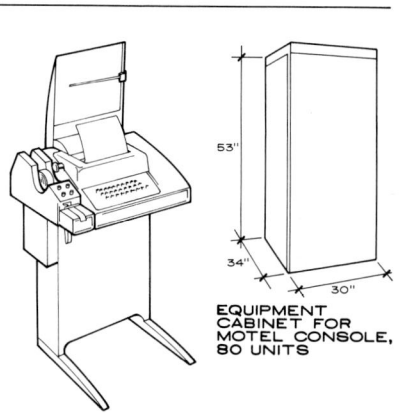
53"
34"
30"
EQUIPMENT CABINET FOR MOTEL CONSOLE, 80 UNITS

21 ½" W × 18 ½"D × 33"H WT = 136 LB
TELETYPEWRITER ®
AUTOMATIC SEND-RECEIVE SET

Charles Szoradi, AIA and F. Menéndez; Washington, D.C.

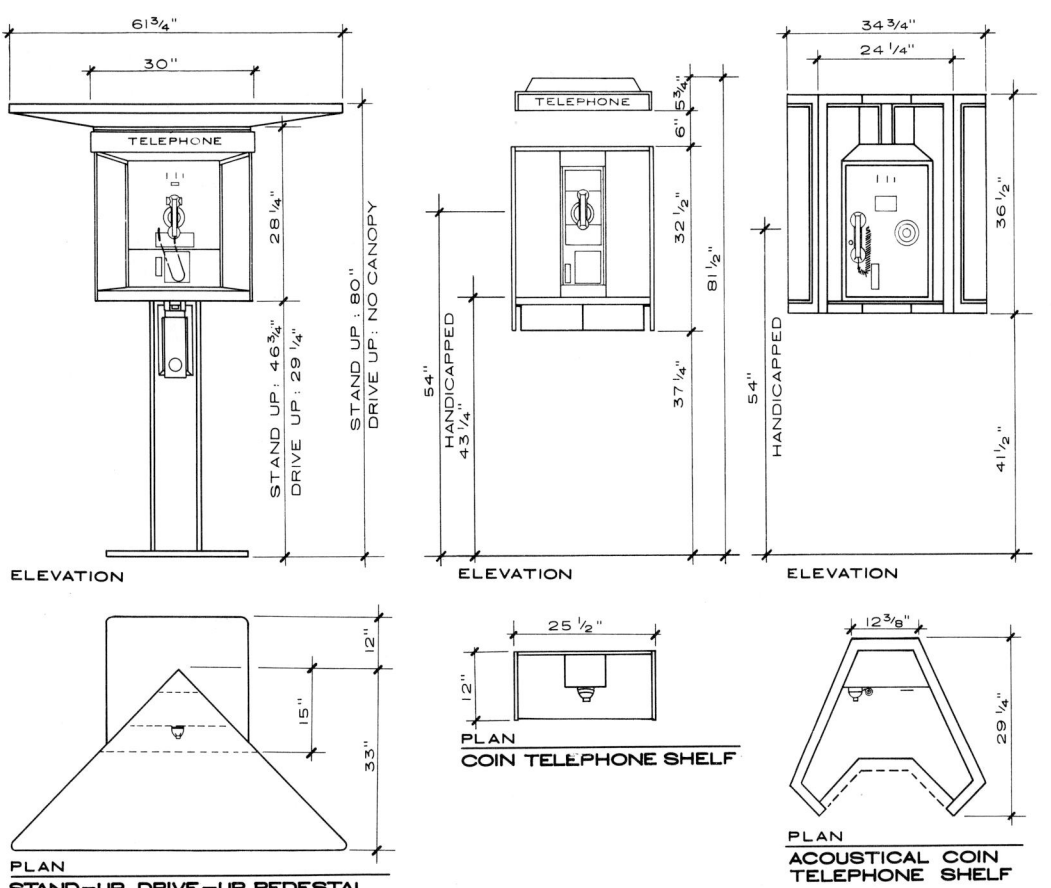

ELEVATION

PLAN
STAND-UP, DRIVE-UP PEDESTAL TYPE COIN TELEPHONE STATION

ELEVATION

PLAN
COIN TELEPHONE SHELF

ELEVATION

PLAN
ACOUSTICAL COIN TELEPHONE SHELF

PEDESTAL TYPE COIN TELEPHONE

Panel type coin telephone set. Steel weather hood and side panels. Built-in fluorescent lighting with sign. S.S. writing ledge. S.S. pedestal with directory holder.

Interior/exterior finishes: Porcelain enamel, various colors.

COIN TELEPHONE SHELF

Wall mounted unit. Surface mounted coin telephone set. Steel side and back panels. Fluorescent lighting with sign. S.S. writing ledge with directory holder.

Interior/exterior finishes: Porcelain enamel, various colors or wood finishes.

ACOUSTICAL COIN TELEPHONE SHELF

With any standard surface mount or panel type coin telephone set.

Fabricated with legs, or accessories available for back or side wall mount, shelf mount or pedestal installation.

With built-in fluorescent lighting.

Exterior finish: Steel with porcelain baked enamel finish. Standard color: blue. Other colors available.

Interior finish: Perforated S.S. encasing high-density sound-absorbing fiberglass insulation.

Adaptable to various combinations of multiple assemblies.

Accessories available: Illuminated telephone sign. Directory holder.

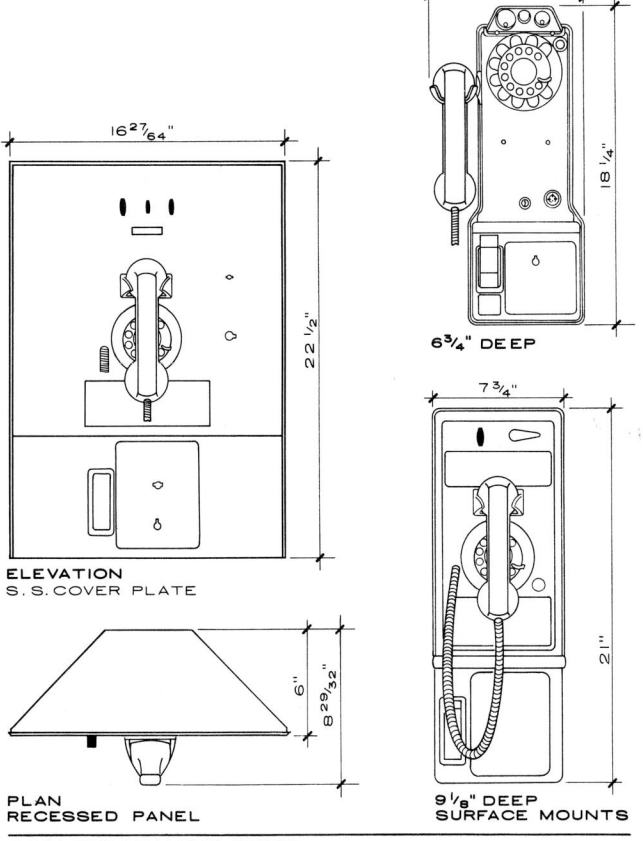

ELEVATION
S.S. COVER PLATE

PLAN
RECESSED PANEL
COIN TELEPHONE SETS

6¾" DEEP

9⅛" DEEP
SURFACE MOUNTS

ELEVATION

PLAN
AIRLIGHT BOOTH

COIN TELEPHONE BOOTHS

Glass lights = plain tempered glass.

Wooden Booths: Stock woods: Birch, oak, walnut, mahogany. Special woods available for Custom order.

Universal and Airtight booths: Standard indoor/outdoor booths. Metal frame: aluminum, plain or anodized, with bright or matte finish.

Side and back panels: Full or $\frac{1}{2}$ glass, or red, green, or blue porcelain baked enamel or aluminum. Airtight booths available for outdoor installation with panels cut short for easier cleaning.

Other similar standard booths are available.

For multiple installations, booths are fabricated with common panels.

SIX PHONE STATION

60" DIA. STAND-UP

SEATS ALSO AVAILABLE

Robert L. Plumley; Medford, Oregon

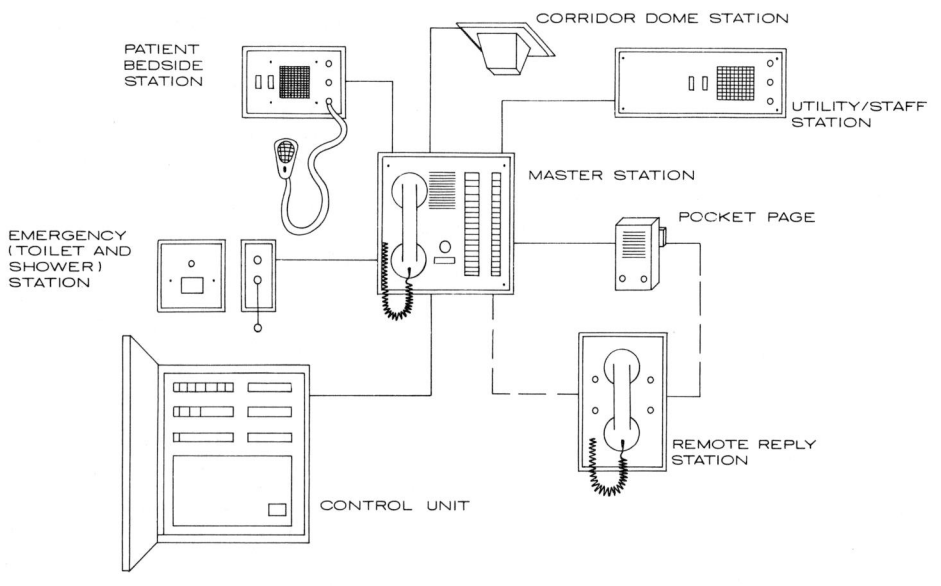

NURSE CALL SYSTEM

The nurse call system provides immediate two-way communication between patient/staff and staff/staff within a given patient unit through a combination of voice, visual, and audio signals.

1. MASTER STATION: The master station provides the nursing staff with two-way communication to patient and staff stations, giving audiovisual indications when a call is placed or connecting to a closed loop pocket pager system. In either case, the indicators distinguish between routine and emergency calls.

2. PATIENT BEDSIDE STATION: The basic bedside station includes one calling cord jack, a reset button to clear the call from the bedside, a call-placed indicator that lights when a patient places a call, and a monitor indicator that lights when the patient's area is being monitored or a call is being answered. Additional features include a pillow speaker with radio/TV control and a privacy indicator when the intercom line is ''open.''

Types of cordsets: The available cordsets, interchangeable within the same multipurpose receptacle on all patient stations, include the following: pillow speaker units with nurse call buttons and TV/radio controls for general use, explosion-proof pull cord action type for use in an oxygen tent, low pressure geriatric type.

3. EMERGENCY STATIONS: The toilet emergency station consists of a nurse call button and reset button. The shower/bath emergency station is similar but with a cord and ball for call origination. A call from these stations actuates an emergency audio signal and flashing light at the nurse's station and changes the corridor dome light to intermittent flashing.

4. DUTY/STAFF STATIONS: The duty station provides audio and visual indication that a patient is requesting assistance and two-way conversation with the nurse's station. The features include speaker/microphone, combination privacy lamp/cancel button, patient call lamp, nurse call button.

The staff station is similar to the duty station, except that it does not have the patient call lamp. Patient calls are not signaled through staff stations.

5. CORRIDOR DOME STATIONS: Corridor dome lights indicate calls placed from stations within the room and alert all staff members in the corridor that a call has been placed.

6. CONTROL UNIT: The control unit serves as a central system check point during system installation and maintenance. It houses the speech amplifier for the system, a motor flasher for the buzzers and lights, the power system supply, and necessary terminal boards.

7. RESET PROCEDURE: After normal conversations, the patient station can be reset from either the nurse's station or at the patient's console. If the toilet or shower stations originate a call, reset procedure can only be carried out at the emergency station. Any reset procedure will automatically and simultaneously extinguish all call signals in the system corresponding to that call.

NURSE CALL SYSTEM

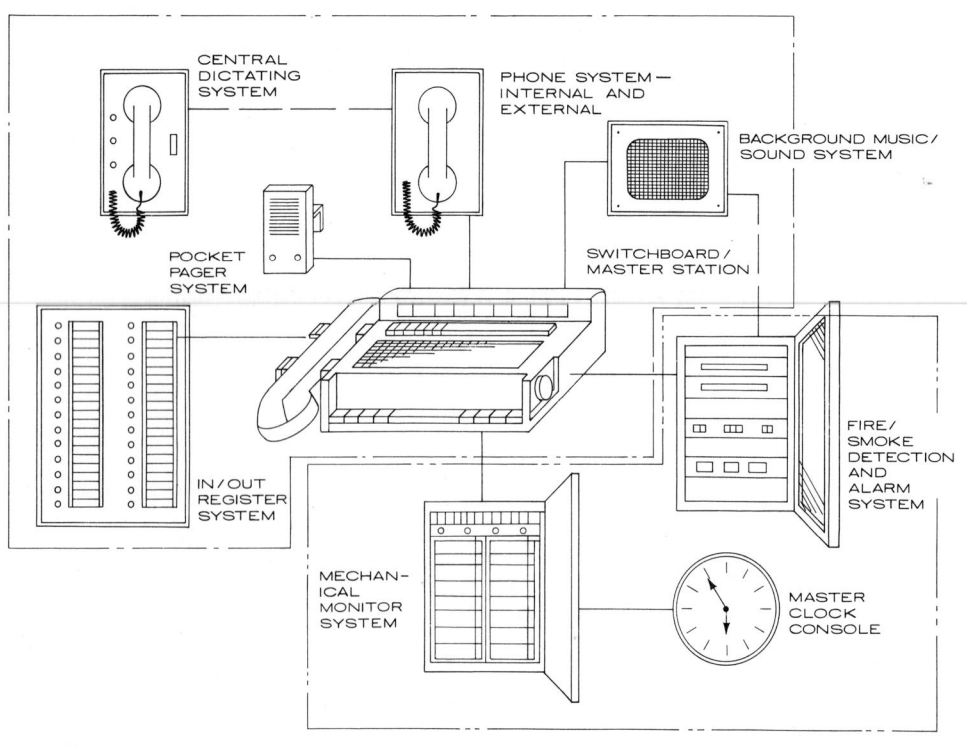

HOSPITALWIDE CENTRAL SYSTEM

1. Staff and personnel intercommunication is provided by a central phone system and public address/sound system. The phone system consists of an internal network interfaced with the public utility phone company for external calling. The public address/sound system provides background music, in appropriate areas, and voice paging-Code Blue interface and, secondarily, routine paging taking precedence over background music.

2. Monitoring of mechanical services and equipment is coordinated within a central control panel, incorporating also a master clock console. The panel provides instantaneous audiovisual alarms of emergency conditions. The fire alarm system consists of a control panel, manual fire boxes, alarm signals, door holders, and ionization detector units, with monitors at the central switchboard station and the nurse master stations.

All equipment and installation must meet the requirements of the National Electric Code and applicable local codes which frequently stipulate UL approval. With the wide variety of system components and optional features, understanding of the specific facility and administration is essential to satisfy both present and projected future needs.

HOSPITALWIDE CENTRAL SYSTEM

Liz Karp; The Architects Collaborative, Inc.; Cambridge, Massachusetts

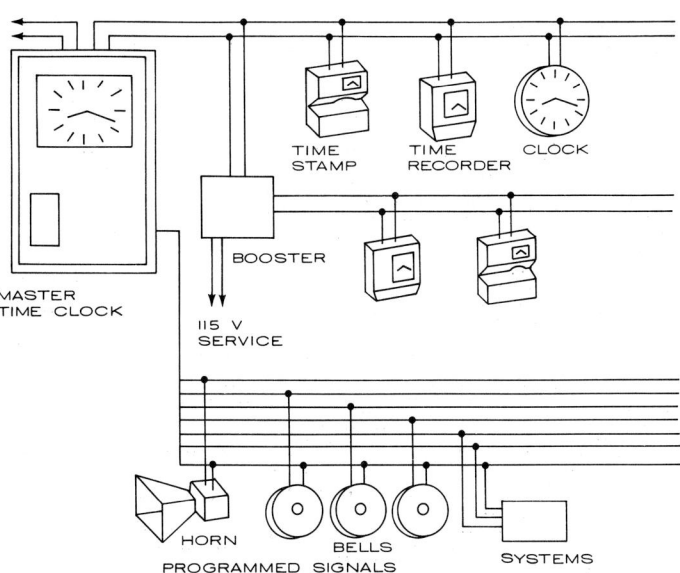

MASTER
TIME CLOCK

TIME
STAMP

TIME
RECORDER

CLOCK

BOOSTER

115 V
SERVICE

HORN

BELLS

SYSTEMS

PROGRAMMED SIGNALS

SYNCHRONOUS WIRED CLOCK SYSTEM DIAGRAM

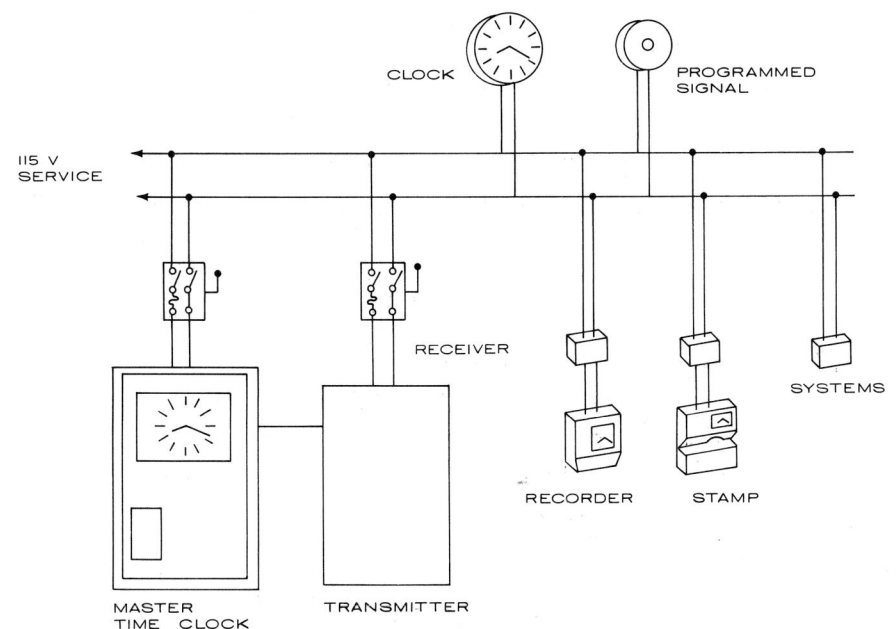

CLOCK

PROGRAMMED
SIGNAL

115 V
SERVICE

RECEIVER

SYSTEMS

MASTER
TIME CLOCK

TRANSMITTER

RECORDER

STAMP

ELECTRONIC CLOCK SYSTEM DIAGRAM

MASTER CLOCK SYSTEMS

Master clock systems, consisting primarily of accurate clock and signaling mechanisms, are used to coordinate separated operations and activities that depend on time. These master systems control the accuracy of indicating clocks, time recorders, and time stamps.

Master clock systems are also used for program and system control, such as daily program activity signaling, day-night heating and air-conditioning, and after-hours lighting control.

The electronic and the synchronous wired systems are the most commonly used ones.

The electronic master clock system transmits high frequency signals over lighting circuits to receivers in the controlled unit. This system is generally used for large numbers of controlled devices because there is no requirement for control wire distribution. Units with their receivers can be added or moved, wherever lighting circuits are available, without regard to control wiring, thus making it particularly useful in renovation work or in multiple building schools.

The synchronous master clock system operates in a similar manner to the electronic system, except the signals are carried over assigned 3-wire clock circuits to the secondary clocks that are driven by synchronous motors. This system can be used for both small and large installations, free from possible circuit interference from other electronic devices.

Booster panels are available to expand either system for highrise buildings or large industrial plants where loads exceed the capacity of the master clock or excessively long runs are required.

The minute impulse system also utilizes master and secondary units, the latter being driven by a DC signal from the master, transmitted at minute intervals, rather than by individual synchronous motors. A correcting signal is also normally transmitted hourly. This system uses a 2-wire connection between units and master.

The dual motor system does not employ a master clock. Instead it utilizes clocks with dual motors; one synchronous for normal drive and one high-speed motor for correction. These clocks depend on their synchronous motors and the constancy of the 60-cycle power supply for accuracy. The high-speed correcting motors merely speed up the clock hands to correct for loss of time because of power interruption. This resetting is centrally controlled, either manually or automatically. The system is separately wired, thus allowing for ease of intentional corrections, such as is required for daylight-saving time.

GENERAL USES

1. Clock correction.
2. Operations program signaling.
3. After-hours building lighting control.
4. Parking lot lighting control.
5. Day-night utilities control.
6. Sign lighting control.

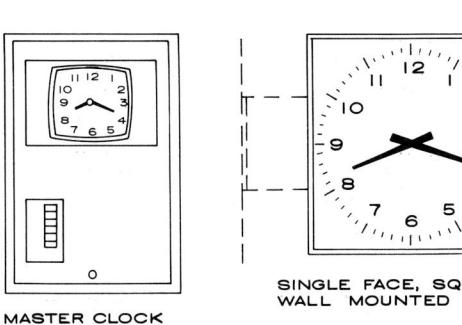

MASTER CLOCK
AND CONTROLS

SINGLE FACE, SQUARE
WALL MOUNTED

DOUBLE FACE ROUND
CEILING MOUNTED

ELAPSED TIME
CLOCK

DIGITAL CLOCK
WITH DAY AND
DATE

TYPICAL CLOCK FACES

Albert Kahn Associates, Inc., Architects & Engineers; Detroit, Michigan

SYSTEM	FUNCTION	TIME BASE	DESCRIPTION
A. Card reader	Controlled access	Real After	An electronic system identifies precoded card. Performs real time function when reporting to authority in the immediate area The card reader system will provide after-the-fact reporting when used in conjunction with outside reporting authority—Police Department, etc.
B. Combination doors and locks	Controlled access	Real	Mechanical combination lock, access can only be achieved by selecting the correct push buttons in the correct numerical sequence
C. Patrol tour system	Intrusion fire	Real and after	A system of key actuated switches in particular locations. Patrolman will visually survey the area along a predetermined route. The patrolman must activate switches along the route in a predetermined time or the system will sound alarm. The most simple system is a watch clock that indicates each location activated and inspected at a later date to determine if the patrolman completed the route. The more sophisticated system is electronic reporting to a central console each time a particular location switch is activated, allowing the security supervisor to track the patrolman through the complete route
D. Door and window burglar alarm	Intrusion	After or real	Door switches on doors and conducting tape on windows, any interruption of continuity causes alarm. When used with outside law enforcement agency may or may not provide real time base reporting depending upon the response of the law enforcement agency
E. Photoelectric or infrared detection system	Intrusion	Real	Photocell receives light beam from sender. Any interruption of beam sends alarm. The system is flexible for indoor or outdoor use and can be a single set of devices or many devices reporting to a central annunciator. Infrared detection is similar except that infrared is not visible light, which may have advantages in some instances
F. Capacitance detection system	Intrusion	Real	Balanced electronic circuit becomes unbalanced by the capacitance of an organic body in the immediate area
G. & H. Ultrasonic system Microwave system	Intrusion (broad coverage) Intrusion (narrow coverage)	Real	A transmitter emitting high frequency sound to a receiver. Intruder unbalances system and indicated alarm. A real time base system when reporting to an authority in the immediate area. Similar to ultrasonic except that it uses microwaves instead of high frequency sound. Microwave will travel long distances (150–200 ft); ideal for long corridors, etc.
I. Vibration detection system	Intrusion	Real	Contact microphone system attached to particular object such as a safe. Any vibration or noise initiates alarm
J. Closed circuit television	Visual surveillance	Real	Video camera is connected to monitors. Design considerations include lighting levels, lens selection, switcher networks, special enclosures, and ambient temperature range
K. Audio communication and detection	Controlled access area monitoring	Real and after	A system of microphones, speakers, and amplifiers, such as intercom, public address—audio level sensing
L. Building control system (includes any desired security system monitoring, fire alarm, and HVAC monitoring)	Monitoring system for all building functions	Real and after	Provides complete status report of all building functions by use of a minicomputer and annunciators. Allows building engineer to handle building systems and security systems from the same console. Building security systems can be procured with printout to establish record of security violations for after-the-fact investigation. Software programs for the computer are available from all building control system manufacturers to establish almost any degree of sophistication desired or different degrees of security for different hours of the day. The additional advantage is that one person has control of the entire system and can thus better direct such corrective action as calling the police, the fire department, or local security, as well as advise the building occupants about what action to take for protection. Depending on the software program, the building engineer can also control the security access or emergency evacuation routes in case of emergency to protect property or life

SECURITY SYSTEMS

Security systems can only perform the functions of controlled access, intrusion alarm, personnel or intruder identification, or fire watch. Some security systems perform one function, while other systems are multifunctioning. In most cases, security systems are provided to improve the capability of a security guard system. The most effective is a trained security personnel system. Any other system is usually merely an aid and has been established as a compromise measure to limit the need for trained personnel.

The design of a security system must be based on certain factors:

1. Type of security needed is based on the type of facility, the company's public image, location, environment, personnel safety, manufacturing proprietary secret security, number of work shifts, the type of people employed, internal security requirements, need for security from external sources, and in some instances even political ramifications or use of secret or classified materials that may be subject to espionage or sabotage.

2. The degree of security needed depends on numerous factors, including the location of the facility in high risk or low risk area, which could well affect the degree of security needed from external sources, and the need for internal security safeguards against theft, rape, and sabotage. The acceptance of the facility in the neighborhood can have a great bearing on the degree of security needed. Employment of union labor with the possibility of lockouts and strikes would also have a bearing on the degree of security.

3. A building designed with security in mind will reduce the cost of an effective security system. The building area-to-site ratio is also a definite factor in security. Building access, type of building construction, the proximity of local law enforcement agencies, parking access, and control of planned expansion are all prime factors to be considered.

4. The extent and degree of sophistication built into a security system is normally controlled by the cost of the security system versus expected losses. A complete system of trained security guards is expensive and, in many cases, cannot be justified; therefore, other means of extending the guards' capability are necessary compromises to keep the system's cost in perspective with expected losses. Cost may not always be the major factor in selecting security systems, but in most instances a compromise results in the desire for system sophistication and cost.

5. The availability of personnel to service and maintain the selected equipment should be thoroughly investigated. Companies that have several years of successful maintenance and service records and are recommended by their customers should be given the greatest consideration.

6. A prime consideration is the response of the local law enforcement agency to a security alarm. When the local law enforcement agency cannot perform adequately, other alternatives must be considered, such as private investigation companies or in-house security personnel.

7. The time base of the security system, that is, real time or after-the-fact time, has a bearing. Real time is the capability of notifying the enforcement authority in charge in time to control the event. After-the-fact time is notification that an incident is occurring, but that, because of the time required to respond, it cannot be controlled immediately. Selection of a system must be based on the functions desired. Only one type of system may be required or a combination of many systems for large installations. If desired, all systems can be connected to an off-premises monitoring company or law enforcement agency.

8. If a large security system is contemplated, the local law enforcement agency and the local outside reporting agency should be consulted to determine what services they can provide. These agencies can also advise the designer about the equipment and type of system that will best fit their particular method of operation. The manufacturers of the particular equipment must also be contacted, and each type of equipment should be discussed. In special cases, mockups should be required to determine whether the particular equipment will, in fact, perform as stated by the manufacturer, and will perform the desired function.

Victor D. Langhart, AIA; RNL/Interplan; Denver, Colorado

COMMUNICATIONS

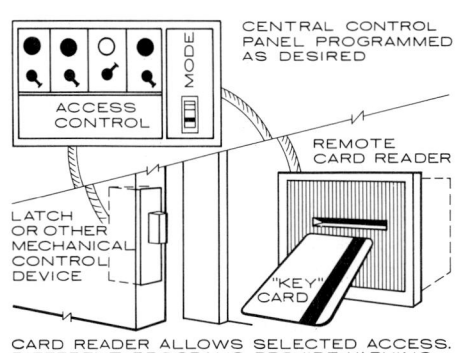

CENTRAL CONTROL PANEL PROGRAMMED AS DESIRED

REMOTE CARD READER

LATCH OR OTHER MECHANICAL CONTROL DEVICE

"KEY" CARD

CARD READER ALLOWS SELECTED ACCESS. DIFFERENT PROGRAMS PROVIDE VARYING MODES OF ACCESSIBILITY

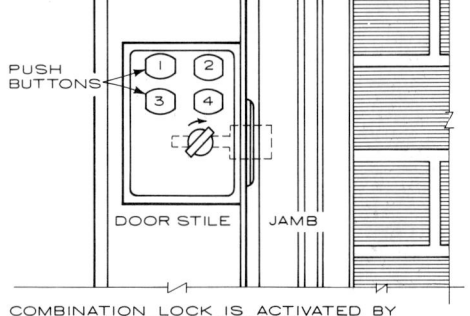

PUSH BUTTONS

DOOR STILE   JAMB

COMBINATION LOCK IS ACTIVATED BY PUNCHING IN CORRECT NUMERICAL SEQUENCE

ACCESS CONTROL

KEY ACTION IN PATROL STATION SIGNALS CENTRAL CONTROL PANEL, GIVING INSTANT DATA ON GUARD'S LOCATION AND MAKING PRINTED RECORD OF PATROL TOUR SEQUENCE

PATROL STATION

BUILDING PLAN WITH PATROL STATIONS

PATROL TOUR MONITORING SYSTEM ENSURES THAT HUMAN GUARDS COMPLETE REGULAR TOURS PER PROGRAM, IF SOMETHING HAPPENS TO GUARD BETWEEN STATIONS, MONITOR CAN SUMMON AID

SYSTEMATIC PATROL

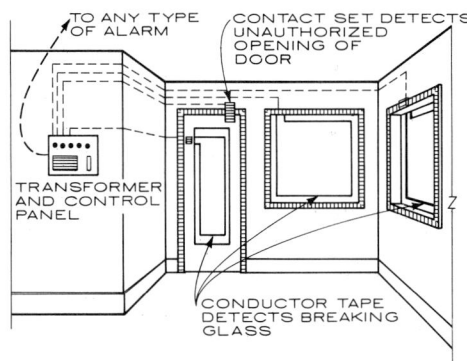

TO ANY TYPE OF ALARM

CONTACT SET DETECTS UNAUTHORIZED OPENING OF DOOR

TRANSFORMER AND CONTROL PANEL

CONDUCTOR TAPE DETECTS BREAKING GLASS

ELECTRICAL SENSORS AT WINDOWS AND DOORS PROVIDE PERIMETER SECURITY

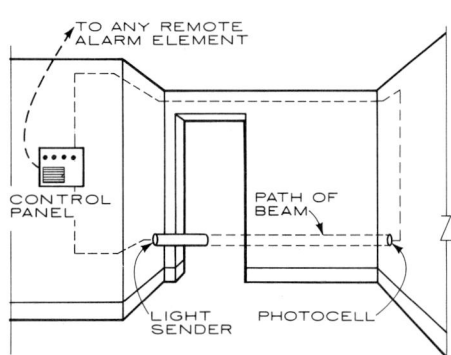

TO ANY REMOTE ALARM ELEMENT

CONTROL PANEL

PATH OF BEAM

LIGHT SENDER   PHOTOCELL

PHOTOCELL SENSOR ACTIVATES ALARM WHEN PERSON, ANIMAL, OR OBJECT INTERRUPTS LIGHT BEAM

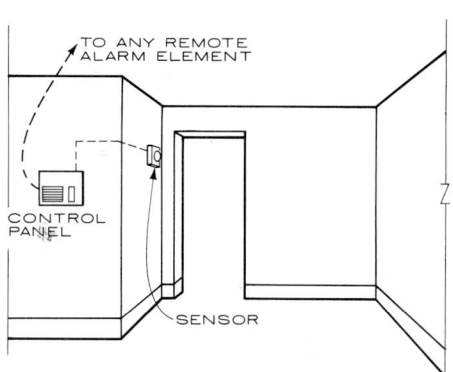

TO ANY REMOTE ALARM ELEMENT

CONTROL PANEL

SENSOR

CAPACITANCE SENSOR ACTIVATES ALARM BY DETECTING NATURAL ELECTRICAL PHENOMENON OF HUMAN BODY

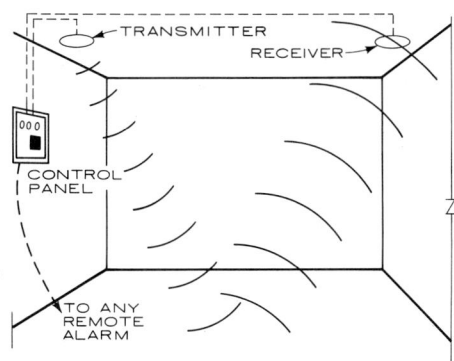

TRANSMITTER

RECEIVER

CONTROL PANEL

TO ANY REMOTE ALARM

ULTRASONIC SENSOR DETECTS MOVING HUMAN OR OBJECTS OVER A BROAD COVERAGE AREA

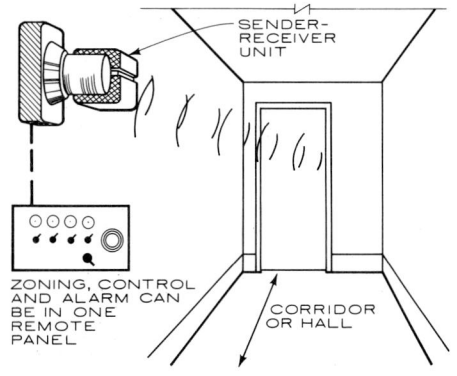

SENDER-RECEIVER UNIT

ZONING, CONTROL AND ALARM CAN BE IN ONE REMOTE PANEL

CORRIDOR OR HALL

MICROWAVE SENSOR IS BEST SUITED FOR USE IN LONG, NARROW SPACES

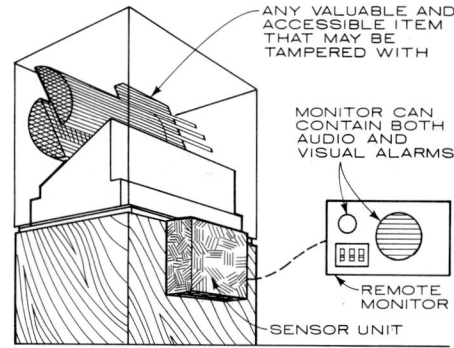

ANY VALUABLE AND ACCESSIBLE ITEM THAT MAY BE TAMPERED WITH

MONITOR CAN CONTAIN BOTH AUDIO AND VISUAL ALARMS

REMOTE MONITOR

SENSOR UNIT

VIBRATION DETECTOR, MOUNTED ON ITEM TO BE MONITORED, PICKS UP MINUTE VIBRATIONS AND SOUNDS CAUSED BY TAMPERING

INTRUDER DETECTION

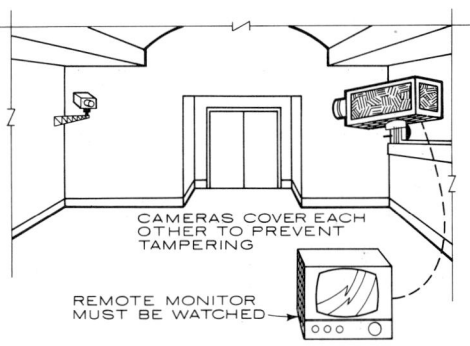

CAMERAS COVER EACH OTHER TO PREVENT TAMPERING

REMOTE MONITOR MUST BE WATCHED

CLOSED CIRCUIT TELEVISION PROVIDES CONSTANT VISUAL SURVEILLANCE OF LARGE SPACES. MONITORING PERSON CAN IDENTIFY PERSONNEL, OBSERVE CRIMES, FIRE OUTBREAK, RODENT INFESTATION

CLOSED CIRCUIT TELEVISION MONITORS

INTEGRATED SECURITY CONSOLE CAN BE ASSEMBLED FROM COMPONENTS REQUIRED FOR INDIVIDUAL BUILDING OR MULTIBUILDING SECURITY PROGRAM. MECHANICAL AND ELECTRICAL EQUIPMENT CAN ALSO BE MONITORED IN CONJUNCTION WITH SECURITY EQUIPMENT

THE CENTRAL CONSOLE, WHEN STAFFED PROPERLY, HELPS ENSURE THAT ALARMS AND WARNINGS FROM FAR FLUNG DETECTION DEVICES WILL BE QUICKLY (HENCE EFFECTIVELY) HEEDED

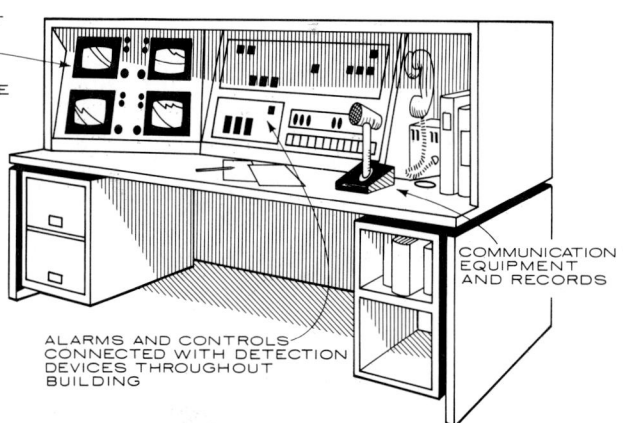

COMMUNICATION EQUIPMENT AND RECORDS

ALARMS AND CONTROLS CONNECTED WITH DETECTION DEVICES THROUGHOUT BUILDING

GENERAL SURVEILLANCE

Darrel Rippeteau, Architect; Washington, D.C.

Victor D. Langhart, AIA; Rnl/Interplan; Denver, Colorado

COMMUNICATIONS 16

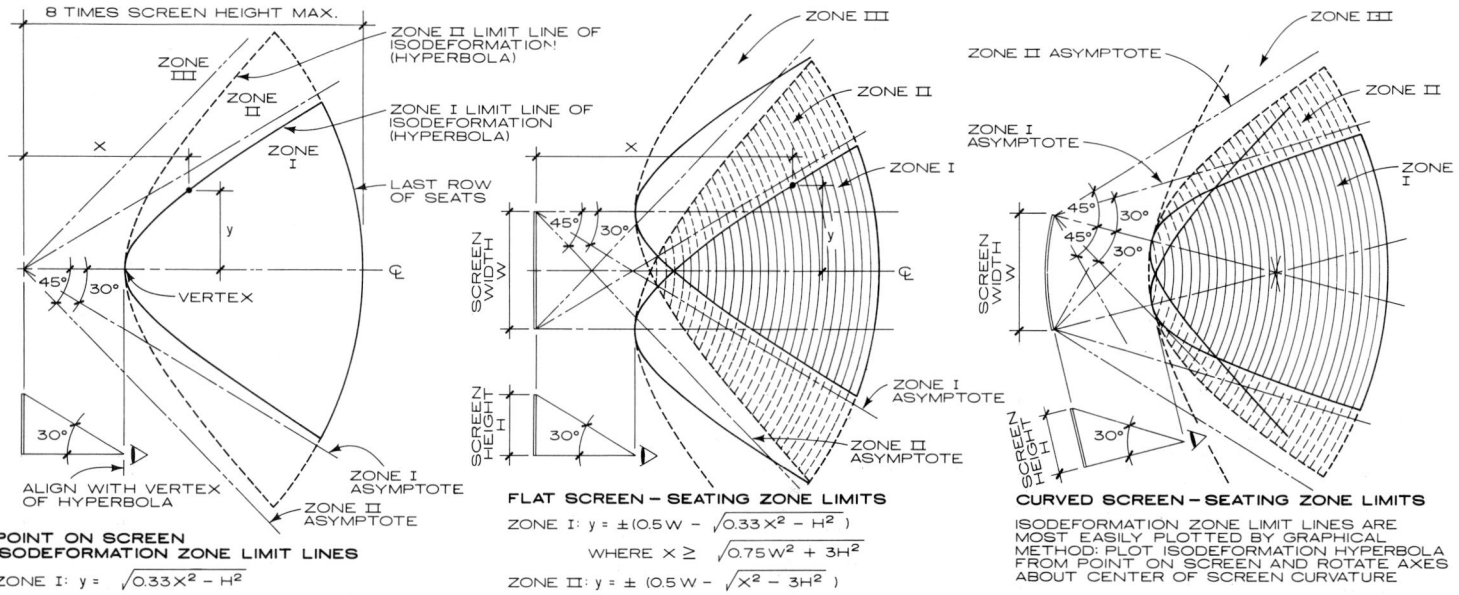

POINT ON SCREEN ISODEFORMATION ZONE LIMIT LINES

ZONE I: $y = \sqrt{0.33X^2 - H^2}$

ZONE II: $y = \sqrt{X^2 - 3H^2}$

WHERE H = SCREEN HEIGHT

FLAT SCREEN – SEATING ZONE LIMITS

ZONE I: $y = \pm(0.5W - \sqrt{0.33X^2 - H^2})$

WHERE $X \geq \sqrt{0.75W^2 + 3H^2}$

ZONE II: $y = \pm(0.5W - \sqrt{X^2 - 3H^2})$

WHERE $X \geq \sqrt{0.25W^2 + 3H^2}$

CURVED SCREEN – SEATING ZONE LIMITS

ISODEFORMATION ZONE LIMIT LINES ARE MOST EASILY PLOTTED BY GRAPHICAL METHOD: PLOT ISODEFORMATION HYPERBOLA FROM POINT ON SCREEN AND ROTATE AXES ABOUT CENTER OF SCREEN CURVATURE

VIEWING OF A POINT ON A SCREEN

A projected image on a screen will have an apparent distortion when viewed from an angle beyond the perpendicular to a point on the screen in plan and section. The boundary of the seating area for which spectators will see the same apparent distortion is called the line of isodeformation. This shape in plan is a hyperbola, which is defined in plan by asymptotes from the point on the screen.

1. SEATING ZONE I: Distortion of a projected image exists but will not be noticed from seats falling within the hyperbola which is bounded by the asymptotes drawn from a point on the screen at an angle of no greater than 30° from the perpendicular at that point on the screen. The minimum horizontal distance from the vertex of the hyperbola to the screen is determined by the limitation of the

vertical angle from the eye of the first row to the top of the screen to a maximum of 30 to 35°.

2. SEATING ZONE II: Distortions of the projected image will be noticed but tolerated from the seats falling outside of Zone I but within the hyperbola bounded by the asymptotes drawn from a point on the screen at an angle no greater than 45° from the perpendicular at that point.

3. SEATING ZONE III (seating placed beyond the limits of Zone II): Distortions of the projected image will not be tolerated and the viewer will refuse to use the seats placed here.

VIEWING OF A FLAT SCREEN

A projected image occupies a space on a screen rather than a point. The seating area, defined by the isode-

formation lines, for which the entire width of the projected image is considered, is represented by the area common to the space within the two hyperbolas which are drawn within asymptotes from both sides of the projected image. The area in Zone I for a wide, projected image is less than the Zone I seating area for a point on the screen. The seating area in Zone II for a wide image on a flat screen may approximately correspond to the Zone I area for a point on the screen.

VIEWING OF A CURVED SCREEN

Zone I seating area for a given screen width can be increased by curving the screen. An appropriate screen curve will cause an overlap of the hyperbolas drawn from the sides of the projected image in such a way that they define a greater common seating area.

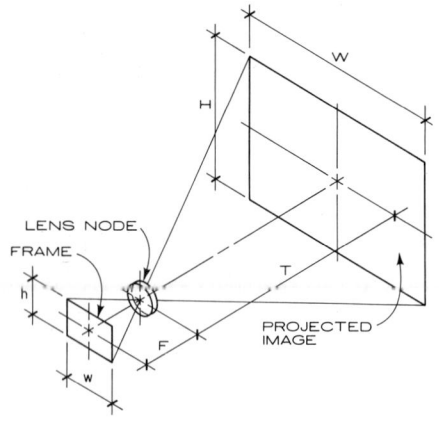

BASIC PROJECTION GEOMETRY

PROJECTION FORMULAS

$T = F(W/w) = F(H/h)$
$F = T(w/W) = T(h/H)$
$W = w(T/F)$
$H = h(T/F)$

where

W = picture width
H = picture height
w = frame width
h = frame height
T = throw distance
F = focal length

Peter H. Frink; Frink and Beuchat: Architects; Philadelphia, Pennsylvania

ASPECT RATIOS AND FRAME DIMENSIONS FOR PROJECTED MEDIA

PROJECTION MEDIUM	FRAME (mm) h x w	ASPECT RATIO	FRAME (IN.) h	FRAME (IN.) w
8 mm motion picture	(3.28 x 4.37)	1:1.33	0.129	0.172
Super 8 motion picture	(4.01 x 5.36)	1.33	0.158	0.211
16 mm motion picture	(7.21 x 9.65)	1.34	0.284	0.380
16 mm CinemaScope	(7.21 x 9.65)	2.68	0.284	2 x 0.380
35 mm motion picture	(15.2 x 20.9)	1.375	0.600	0.825
35 mm CinemaScope	(18.2 x 42.6)	2.34	0.715	2 x 0.839
70 mm motion picture	(22.1 x 49.0)	2.21	0.868	1.913
70 mm IMAX	(51.0 x 71.0)	1.39	2.00	2.80
35 mm filmstrip	(17.0 x 22.5)	1.32	0.668	0.885
2 x 2 35 mm double frame slides	(22.9 x 34.2)	1.493	0.902	1.346
2 x 2 35 mm half frame slides	(15.9 x 22.9)	1.44	0.626	0.902
2 x 2 35 mm square slides	(22.9 x 22.9)	1.00	0.902	0.902
126 Insta-Load slides	(12.7 x 17.0)	1.34	0.500	0.669
2 x 2 Instamatic slides	(26.5 x 26.5)	1.00	1.043	1.043
2 x 2 superslides	(38.0 x 38.0)	1.00	1.496	1.496
2¼ x 2¼ slides	(51.6 x 51.6)	1.00	2.030	2.030
2¾ x 2¾ slides	(55.5 x 55.5)	1.00	2.187	2.187
3½ x 4 lantern slides	(69.9 x 76.2)	1.09	2.75	3.00
3½ x 4 Polaroid slides	(61.0 x 82.8)	1.36	2.40	3.26
4 x 5 lantern slides	(88.9 x 114.3)	1.28	3.50	4.50
Overhead projector	—	1.26	7.50	9.50
Overhead projector	—	1.00	10.00	10.00
Television projector	—	1.33	—	—

PROJECTION ROOM DETAILS

1. DIMENSIONS: 14 ft deep by 21 ft wide minimum for two projectors. Add 5 ft width for each additional piece of projection apparatus. Ceiling height should never be less than 8 ft; 9 ft is preferred.
2. WALL CONSTRUCTION: Wall separating projection room and auditorium should be made of brick, concrete, or concrete block to minimize sound transmission.
3. FLOOR CONSTRUCTION: Provide for a live load of 200 psf minimum. Recommend 4 in.

reinforced concrete slab, 4 in. tamped cinder fill (to accommodate concealed conduit), and 2 in. topping slab.
4. FLOOR FINISH: Recommend heavy battleship linoleum. A good grade of vinyl tile is also acceptable.
5. PORTS: Projection ports should be glazed with $\frac{1}{4}$ in. optical quality or select water white glass. Observation ports may be glazed with $\frac{1}{4}$ in. select plate glass that is free from distortion.

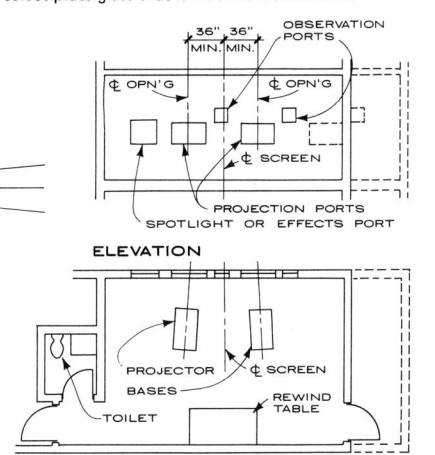

TYPICAL 35 MM MOVIE PROJECTOR

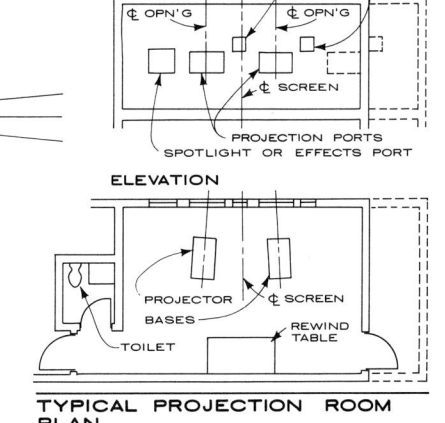

TYPICAL PROJECTION ROOM PLAN

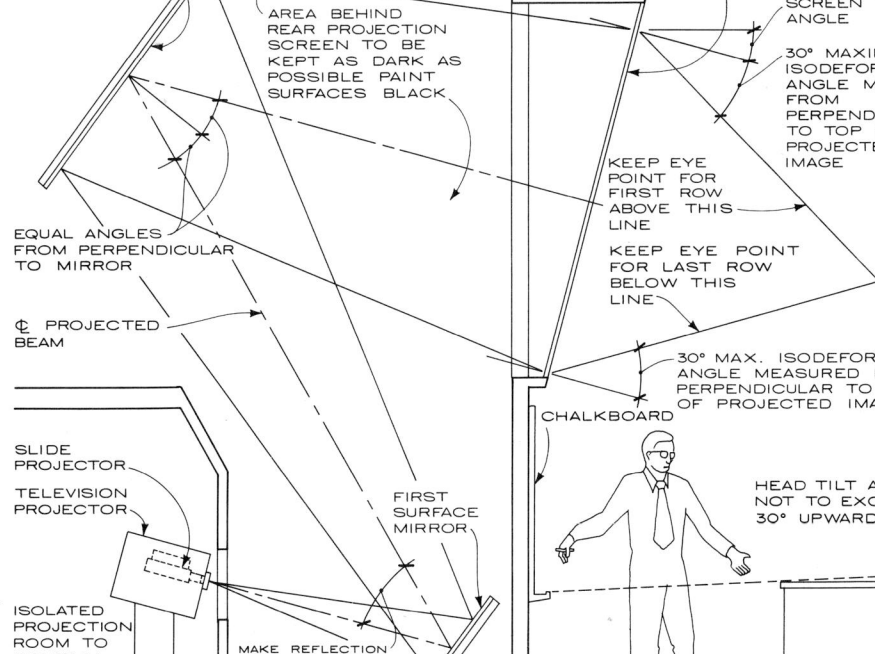

REAR PROJECTION

SCREEN TYPES

An ideal screen would be one that would diffuse all the light from the projector into the audience spaces with uniform brightness for every viewer and simultaneously reject any stray light falling on the screen, reflecting it away from the audience. Most common screen materials possess characteristics that fall short of the ideal.

MATTE WHITE SCREEN

Uniform brightness from all viewing angles. Good resolution and color fidelity. Because much of the light reflected from a matte white screen falls outside of the viewing area, the picture will be less bright than a picture from the same source on a gain screen. Rejects less stray light than gain screens.

GAIN SCREENS

Mechanical or chemical treatment of screen surface increases the amount of light reflected in the direction of the audience and decreases the amount reflected in other directions. Because brightness from all viewing angles is not uniform, gain screens dictate a narrower viewing area. For high gain screens, viewing area should be restricted to zone I as described on other pages. While the picture on a gain screen will be brighter than on a matte screen, resolution and color fidelity may suffer somewhat depending on the type of gain screen used. Gain screen types include: beaded, silver, pearl, and lenticular.

AVAILABLE SCREEN SIZES

1. Tripod screens: 30 x 40 to 72 x 86 in., bottom of screen usually 3 to 4 ft above floor (adjustable).
2. Table or wall hung screens: 18 x 24 to 36 x 36 in.
3. Wall or ceiling mounted, manually operated spring loaded roll-up: 50 x 50 in. to 12 x 12 ft.
4. Wall or ceiling mounted, electrically operated roll-up: 50 x 50 in. to 20 x 20 or 12 x 24 ft. Custom sizes: up to 40 ft wide.
5. Bottom roller, rope controlled: 5 ft 6 in. x 14 to 30 x 30 ft. Winch controlled: up to 40 ft wide.
6. Framed screen (lace and grommet): custom made to any size. Economical for larger sizes. Frames made of 2 x 6 in. lumber or steel tubing or angle. Wood frames usually 2 ft wider than screen size. Metal frames usually 1 ft wider than screen size.
7. Rear projection screens: 3 x 4 to 7 x 14 ft. Custom sizes, acrylic: up to 10 x 12 or 8 x 14 ft. Custom sizes, glass: up to 10 x 25 ft.

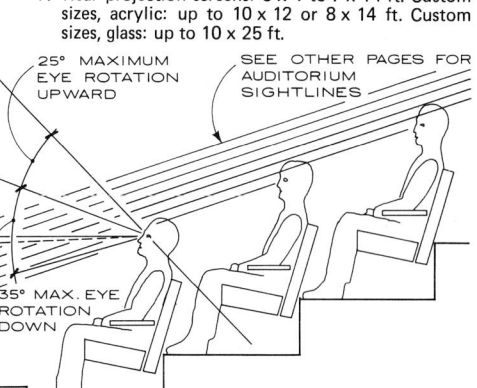

NOTES

1. The average rear projection screen is usually smaller than a possible front projection screen because of physical and/or economic reasons. Front projection, therefore, is usually preferable for larger audiences. The size of a rear projection screen may be restricted by its greater cost and by limitations of projection geometry for lack of space.
2. Projection equipment and projection formulas are the same for both front and rear projection. Front

projection usually permits an adequate throw distance over the heads of an audience in order to fill a larger screen. An equivalent depth is not typically available for rear projection. Larger images for rear projection can be achieved through the use of shorter focal length lenses which allow a shorter throw distance. Mirrors can also be used to bend or fold a projected beam into a shallower space behind the screen.

3. Front projection usually results in better resolution,

better color fidelity, and better contrast ratios.
4. The principal advantage of rear projection over front projection is the ability of the rear projection screen to reject stray ambient light in the auditorium. This ability may allow a higher light level within a learning space for, for example, taking notes while viewing a projected image.
5. Rear projection will also allow a speaker or a spectator to stand in front of a screen without casting a shadow.

Peter H. Frink; Frink and Beuchat: Architects; Philadelphia, Pennsylvania

COMMUNICATIONS **16**

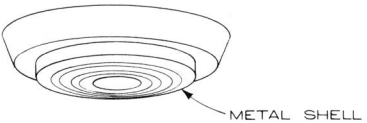

HEAT DETECTOR

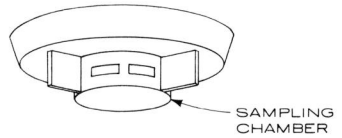

IONIZATION SMOKE DETECTOR

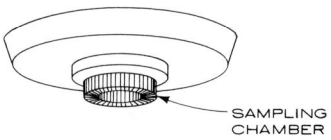

PHOTOELECTRIC SMOKE DETECTOR

FIRE AND SMOKE DETECTORS

INFRARED FLAME DETECTOR

HEAT DETECTOR

Fixed temperature heat detectors (e.g., those rated at 135 to 197°F) use low melting point solder or metals that expand when exposed to heat to detect fire. Rate-of-rise heat detectors alarm when rate of temperature change exceeds about 15°F/min. Expansion of air in chamber with calibrated vent is used to detect rapidly developing fires. Devices are available with both rate-of-rise and fixed temperature detection features.

IONIZATION SMOKE DETECTOR

Ionization detectors use the interruption of small current flow between electrodes by smoke in ionized sampling chamber to detect fire. Dual chamber (with reference chamber exposed only to air temperature, pressure, and humidity) and single chamber detectors are available. Ionization detectors can be used in rooms and in air ducts to detect smoke in air distribution systems.

PHOTOELECTRIC SMOKE DETECTOR

Photoelectric smoke detectors use the scattering of light by smoke into view of photocell. Sources of light may be either incandescent lamp or light emitting diode (LED). Photoelectric detectors can be used in rooms and in air ducts to detect smoke in air distribution systems.

INFRARED FLAME DETECTOR

Infrared flame detectors respond to the high-frequency (IR) radiant energy from flames. Alarm is only triggered when IR energy flickers at rate which is characteristic of flames. Infrared detectors can be used in large open areas where rapid development of flaming conditions could occur (e.g., flammable liquids fire hazards).

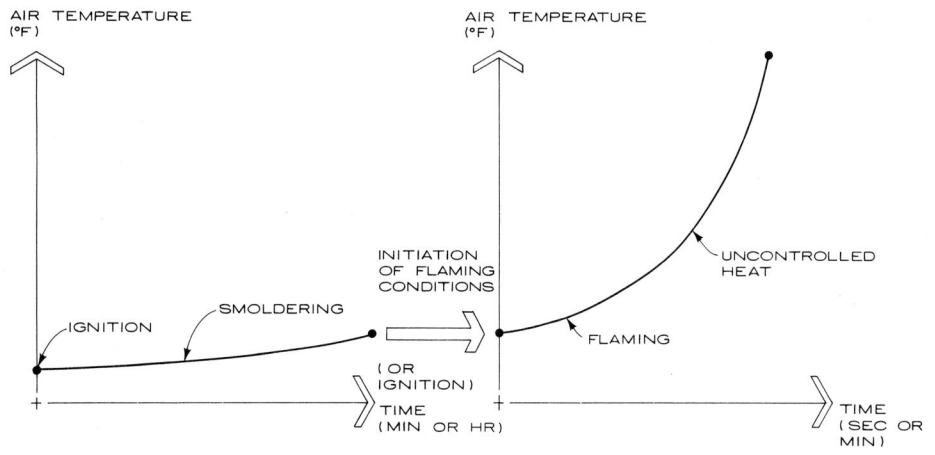

STAGES OF FIRE

STAGES OF FIRE

Carefully match fire detectors to anticipated fire hazard (e.g., photoelectric smoke detectors for smoldering fires, ionization smoke detectors for flaming fires, infrared flame detectors for flash fires). The time-temperature curves show growth to hazardous conditions for smoldering, flaming, and uncontrolled heat stages of fire.

CHECKLIST FOR RESIDENTIAL FIRE DETECTION

1. Use smoke detectors to protect the following (in decreasing order of importance):
   a. Every occupied floor and basement.
   b. Sleeping areas and basement near stairs.
   c. Sleeping areas only.
2. Use heat detectors to protect remote areas (e.g., basement shops, attics) where serious fires could develop before smoke would reach smoke detector or in areas such as garages or kitchens where smoke detectors would be exposed to high smoke levels during normal conditions.
3. Locate smoke detectors on ceilings near center of rooms (or on the upper walls 6 to 12 in. from ceiling) where smoke can collect. In long corridors, consider using two or more detectors.
4. Use closer spacing between detectors where ceiling beams, joists, and the like will interrupt flow of smoke to detector.
5. Do not place smoke detectors near supply air registers or diffusers, or near return air grilles where return air could remove smoke from the area before it reaches detector.
6. For guidelines on fire detection for residences, refer to "Household Fire Warning Equipment," NFPA No. 74, available from the National Fire Protection Association.

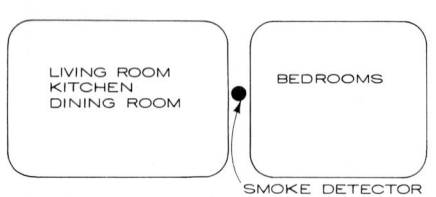

RESIDENTIAL OCCUPANCY (WITH SINGLE SLEEPING AREA)

RESIDENTIAL OCCUPANCY (WITH SPLIT SLEEPING AREAS)

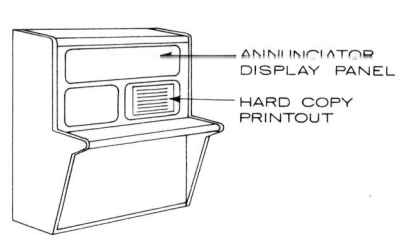

AUTOMATED CONTROL CONSOLE

NOTE

When fire is detected (e.g., by smoke, heat, infrared detectors, or water flow indicators in sprinkler system piping), automated control systems immediately summon the fire department. Floor plans of fire area can be projected on annunciator display panel to pinpoint trouble spots. Controls can be designed to automatically shut down fan systems or activate fans and dampers for smoke removal and control. In addition, remote firefighter control panel, with telephone communication to control console and to each floor in building, can be used to control and monitor status of elevators, pumps and emergency generators, fans, dampers, and the like.

M. David Egan, P.E.; College of Architecture, Clemson University; Clemson, South Carolina

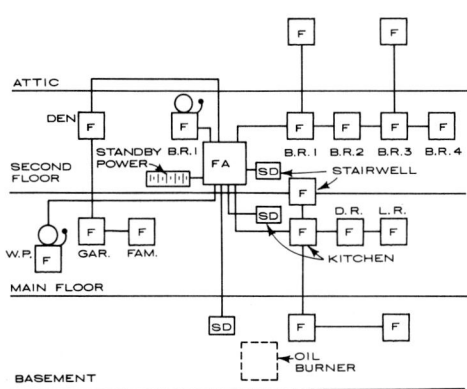

TYPICAL FIRE ALARM LAYOUT

Residential fire alarm systems, if properly designed and functioning normally, should provide sufficient time for the evacuation of the residents and for the initiation of appropriate countermeasures. The elements of the system are the various alarm initiating devices, the wiring and control panel, and the audible alarm devices. Since the purpose of a residential system is evacuation, manual systems with hand pulled stations are rarely used. Instead, automatic smoke and heat sensing equipment that sounds a continuous alarm is preferred. Automatic alarm systems may include some form of system "supervision" that will trigger a trouble bell or light signal indicating a broken wire or other equipment failure. If the system becomes extensive it may be desirable to arrange the circuiting so that the alarm devices are grouped by zones or floor levels, allowing the resident to trace the source of the alarm.

For multiple dwelling units such as dormitories, a supervised, zoned, noncoded system with continuously ringing bells is commonly used. Since dormitories are designed with soundproofing in mind for ideal study and sleeping conditions, bells and horns of high sound intensity must be selected. A hotel normally uses a supervised, presignal, selectively coded system with automatic stations in storerooms, boiler rooms, kitchens, and other unsupervised areas. Apartment houses, being a collection of individual residences, rarely have a common fire alarm system.

Requirements for residential fire alarm systems vary according to local fire code regulations. Details for the design of these systems are best left to a fire alarm expert.

RESIDENTIAL ALARM SYSTEM

NONCODED SYSTEM

The actuation of a manual or automatic alarm initiating device causes a continuous general alarm throughout the building until the initiating device is returned to normal and the system is reset manually. This system is used in moderately sized industrial, commercial, and educational buildings where a continuous general alarm is required.

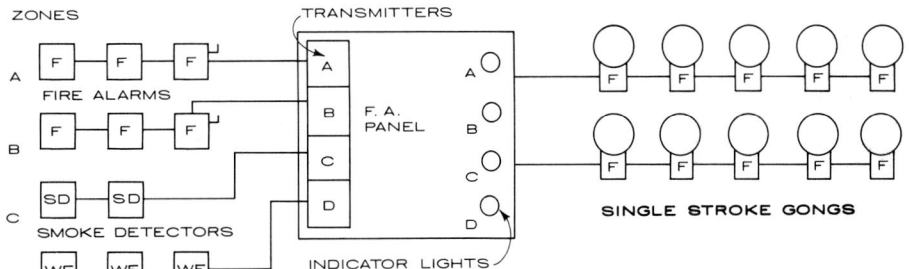

NONCODED ALARM SYSTEM

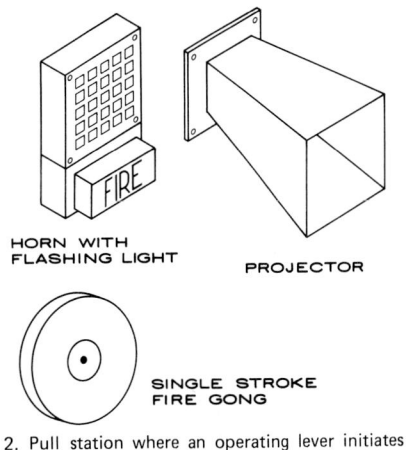

MASTER CODED SYSTEM

The actuation of a noncoded manual or automatic initiating device sounds four rounds of general alarm signal throughout the building for orderly evacuation. This system may be used in small hospitals, nursing homes, or office buildings.

SELECTIVE CODED SYSTEM

Activation of a manual coded station in a selective coded system sounds four rounds on all alarm sounding devices identifying the initiating station by numerical code. The alarm stops after four rounds. This system is used for installations requiring selective coding to indicate the location of the fire and notify the occupants to evacuate.

PRESIGNAL SYSTEMS

In the presignal systems, the actuation of an initiating device sounds four rounds of an identifying code on presignal devices at selected locations. The presignal indicates to key personnel the specific location of the manual station for which the alarm was initiated.

Authorized personnel then investigate the fire, evaluate the danger, and, if conditions warrant, sound a master coded general evacuation alarm by inserting and turning a special key in any manual station. The signal sounds until the key is removed. For presignal fire alarm systems it is vital to locate the fire immediately and to alert key personnel without unnecessarily alarming the occupants.

Any one of the abovementioned systems may be tied in with smoke detection and sprinkler alarm systems. The result of the activation of these alarm systems is a general alarm throughout the building for a noncoded system and a predetermined code sound throughout the building for a coded system. In case of a presignal system, the alarm will be actuated at a predetermined selective location similar to the operation described above.

CODED ALARM SYSTEMS

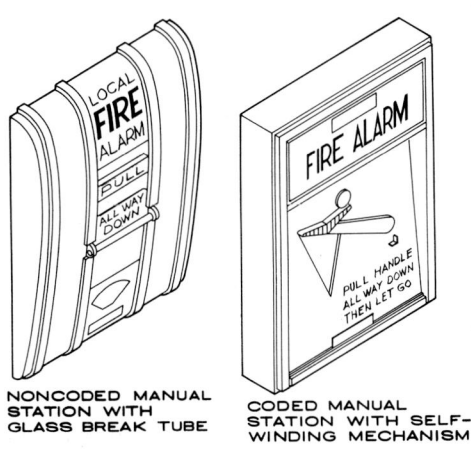

NONCODED MANUAL STATION WITH GLASS BREAK TUBE

CODED MANUAL STATION WITH SELF-WINDING MECHANISM

EQUIPMENT

All fire alarm systems consist of a control panel, alarm initiation, and alarm sounding devices.

MANUAL FIRE ALARM STATIONS are wall mounted devices that initiate an alarm signal. There are two types of manual stations:

1. Break glass station.

FIRE ALARM SYSTEM EQUIPMENT

Syska & Hennessey, Consulting Engineers; New York, New York

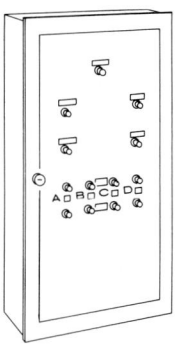

HORN WITH FLASHING LIGHT

PROJECTOR

SINGLE STROKE FIRE GONG

2. Pull station where an operating lever initiates the alarm.

ALARM SIGNALING DEVICES are of three basic types: gongs, horns, and chimes. Gongs come in three standard sizes; 4, 6, and 10 in. in diameter. Horns are especially suitable for use in high ambient noise areas. Chimes are used in areas where a lower sound is necessary than that normally available from a fire alarm gong, for use in hospitals, rest homes, and similar places. All signaling devices may be surface or recess mounted in suitable enclosures.

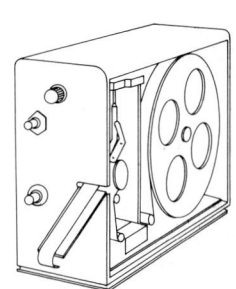

CONTROL PANEL WITH ZONE ANNUNCIATOR

REMOTE TAPE REGISTER

CONTROL PANELS serve as the central logic unit with the required relays, annunciators, electronics, power supplies, and so on, for proper systems operation.

Annunciators provide a visual indication of station or zone from which a fire alarm signal was initiated.

Remote printout units are used to provide a permanent record of station or zone from which a fire alarm was initiated.

The input voltage to the control panel is usually 120/208 V.

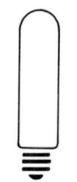
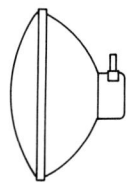

| A-19 | PS-52 | PAR-38 | R-40 | T-6 | PAR-56 |

GENERAL SERVICE

BULB	DIA. (IN.)	LENGTH (IN.)	BASE	WATTS
A-15	$1^7/_8$	$3^1/_2$	Med.	15
A-19	$2^3/_8$	$4^7/_{16}$	Med.	60
A-21	$2^5/_8$	$5^5/_{16}$	Med.	100
PS-25	$3^1/_8$	$6^{15}/_{16}$	Med.	150
PS-30	$3^3/_4$	$8^1/_{16}$	Med.	300
PS-40	5	$9^3/_4$	Mogul	500
PS-52	$6^1/_2$	$13^1/_{16}$	Mogul	1000

The efficacy of light production by incandescent filament lamps depends on the temperature of the filament—the higher the temperature, the greater the portion of radiated energy that falls in the visible region. Tungsten filaments have a high melting point (3655°K) and low-vapor pressure, which permit higher operating temperatures and, as a result, high efficacies. Past improvements in incandescent lamps have involved changes in filament shape. Recent improvement, however, are primarily a result of changes in the atmosphere inside the glass bulb that encloses the filament. The discovery that inert gases retard evaporation of the filament made it possible to design lamps for higher filament temperatures. Today, most incandescent lamps use a fill mixture of argon and nitrogen.

PARABOLIC REFLECTORS

BULB	DIA. (IN.)	LENGTH (IN.)	BASE	WATTS
R-20	$2^1/_2$	$3^{15}/_{16}$	Med.	30
R-30	$3^3/_4$	$5^3/_{16}$	Med.	75
PAR-38	$4^3/_4$	$5^5/_{16}$	Med. skt.	150
PAR-38	$4^3/_4$	$5^5/_{16}$	Med. skt.	150
R-40	5	$6^1/_2$	Med.	150
R-40	5	$6^1/_2$	Med.	300
R-40	5	$7^1/_4$	Mogul	500

The most popular incandescent lamps are general service (GS) ones, which range from the 15-W A-15 to the 1500-W PS-52 types and are designed for 120-, 125-, and 130-V circuits. The letter prefix refers to the lamp shape—for example, PS has a pear straight neck; A is of the standard incandescent shape. Other common designations are G for globe and PAR for parabolic aluminizer reflector. The number following the letter prefix is the bulb diameter in eighths of an inch. For the same wattage, GS lamps (750 to 1000 hr of life) are more efficient than extended service (ES) lamps (2500 hr of life). ES lamps—for use where replacement costs are relatively high, such as hard-to-reach locations—achieve long life by use of a filament that is stronger, but less efficacious.

TUNGSTEN HALOGEN

BULB	DIA. (IN.)	LENGTH (IN.)	BASE	WATTS
T-4	$1/_2$	$3^1/_8$	Minicam	250
T-4	$1/_2$	$3^1/_8$	Rec. S.C.	400
PAR-56	7	5	End prong	500
T-3	$3/_8$	$4^{11}/_{16}$	Rec. S.C.	500
T-4	$1/_2$	$3^5/_8$	Minicam	500
T-6	$3/_4$	$5^5/_8$	Rec. S.C.	1000
T-3	$3/_8$	$10^1/_{16}$	Rec. S.C.	1500

TUNGSTEN HALOGEN lamps are a variation of incandescent filament sources. A halogen additive in the bulb reacts chemically with the tungsten, removing deposited tungsten from the bulb and redepositing it on the filament. This results in a lumen maintenance factor of close to 100%. (Lumen maintenance refers to the ability of a lamp to maintain a constant light output.) However, such a lamp does have a definite life, usually a maximum of 3000 hr. The smaller size, good optical control, and high color temperatures of tungsten-halogen lamps, as well as a continuous spectrum, particularly fit theatrical lighting needs.

INCANDESCENT LAMPS

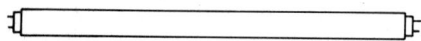

T-12

T-12

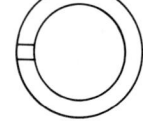

U-BENT   CIRCLINE

STANDARD TUBE

BULB	DIA. (IN.)	LENGTH (IN.)	BASE	WATTS
T-8	1	18	Med. bipin	15
T-12	$1^1/_2$	24	Med. bipin	20
T-12	$1^1/_2$	36	Med. bipin	30
T-12	$1^1/_2$	48	Med. bipin	40
T-12	$1^1/_2$	96	Single pin	75

NOTE: Dimensions are similar for preheat, rapid start, and extended service lamps.

FLUORESCENT lamps offer three to five times the efficacy of incandescent sources and compare favorably with most high intensity discharge sources. Efficacies vary with lamp length, lamp loading, and lamp phosphor coating.

Both geometric design and operating conditions of a fluorescent lamp affect the efficacy with which electrical energy is converted into visible radiation. For example, as lamp diameter increases, efficacy increases, passes through a maximum, then decreases. The length of the lamp also influences its efficacy: the longer it is, the higher the efficacy.

This lamp uses an electric discharge source, in which light is produced predominantly by fluorescent powders activated by ultraviolet energy generated by a mercury arc. The fluorescent lamp cannot be operated directly from the nominal 120-V ac source because the arc discharge would not be established. As a result, it must be operated in series with a ballast that limits the current and provides the starting and operating lamp voltages.

HIGH OUTPUT (800 mA)

BULB	DIA. (IN.)	LENGTH (IN.)	BASE	WATTS
T-12	$1^1/_2$	48	Rec. D.C.	60
T-12	$1^1/_2$	72	Rec. D.C.	85
T-12	$1^1/_2$	96	Rec. D.C.	110
T-12*	$1^1/_2$	72	Rec. D.C.	160
T-12*	$1^1/_2$	96	Rec. D.C.	215

*Requires 1500 milli amps.

The starting process occurs in two stages. Once a sufficient voltage exists between an electrode and ground, ionization of the gas (mercury plus an inert gas) in the lamp occurs. Then a sufficient voltage must exist across the lamp to extend the ionization throughout the lamp and to develop an arc. Three basic types of ballasts—preheat, instant start, and rapid start—provide means of starting.

For the preheat variety, the electrodes are heated before the application of high voltage across the lamp. Arc initiation in instant start lamps depends entirely on the application of a high voltage (400 to 1000 V) across the lamp, which ejects electrons by field emission. These electrons ionize the gas and initiate arc discharge. The rapid start principle makes use of electrodes that are heated continuously by means of low voltage windings built into the ballast. A power saving feature of rapid start circuits is that the lamps show little change in rated life as a result of frequent on/off/on cycles.

SPECIAL SHAPES

BULB	DIA. (IN.)	LENGTH (IN.)	BASE	WATTS
U-Bent	$1^1/_2$	$22^1/_2$	Med. bipin	40
Circle	$1^1/_8$	$8^1/_4$ dia.	Four pin	22
Circle	$1^1/_4$	12 dia.	Four pin	32
Circle	$1^1/_4$	16 dia.	Four pin	40

NOTE: Fluorescent lamps are available in cool white, warm white, and daylight tints.

BASES

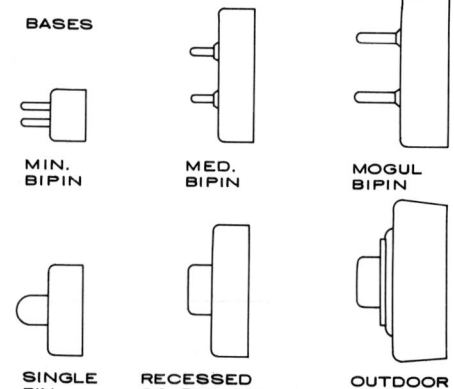

MIN. BIPIN   MED. BIPIN   MOGUL BIPIN

SINGLE PIN   RECESSED DOUBLE CONTACT   OUTDOOR R.D.C.

FLUORESCENT LAMPS

Wm G. Miner, AIA, Architect; Washington, D.C.

16 **LIGHTING**

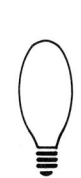
B-21

R-60

BT-28

BT-37

BT-25

E-18

MERCURY VAPOR

BULB	DIA. (IN.)	LENGTH (IN.)	BASE	WATTS
B-17	2 1/8	5 1/8	Med.	40
B-21	2 5/8	6 1/2	Med.	75
BT-25	3 1/8	7 1/2	Mogul	100
BT-28	3 1/2	8 5/16	Mogul	250
BT-37	4 5/8	11 1/2	Mogul	400
R-60	7 1/2	10 7/8	Mogul	400
BT-56	7	15 3/8	Mogul	1000

METAL-HALIDE

BULB	DIA. (IN.)	LENGTH (IN.)	BASE	WATTS
BT-28	3 1/2	8 5/16	Mogul	175
BT-37	4 5/8	11 1/2	Mogul	400
BT-56	7	15 3/8	Mogul	1000
BT-56	7	15 3/8	Mogul	1500

HIGH PRESSURE SODIUM

BULB	DIA. (IN.)	LENGTH (IN.)	BASE	WATTS
BT-25	3 1/8	7 5/8	Mogul	70
BT-25	3 1/8	7 5/8	Mogul	150
BT-28	3 1/2	8 5/16	Mogul	150
E-18	2 1/4	9 3/4	Mogul	250
E-18	2 1/4	9 3/4	Mogul	400
BT-37	4 5/8	11 1/2	Mogul	400
E-25	3 1/8	15 1/16	Mogul	1000

MERCURY lamps, which are now popular for lighting commercial interiors, use argon gas to ease starting because mercury has a low vapor pressure at room temperature. When the lighting circuit is energized, the starting voltage is impressed across the gap between the main electrode and the starting electrode, which creates an argon arc that causes the mercury to vaporize. The lamp warmup process takes 5 to 7 min, depending on ambient temperature conditions. Most mercury lamps are constructed with two envelopes—an inner one that contains the arc and an outer one that shields the arc tube from outside drafts and changes in temperature. The outer envelope usually contains an inert gas.

The mercury spectrum results in greenish-blue light at efficacies of 30 to 65 lm/W, which ranks it between incandescent and fluorescent lamps. Economics favor mercury where burning hours are long, service is difficult, and replacement labor is high. Many mercury lamps lose as much as 50% of their initial output during their rated life of 24,000 hr or more.

METAL-HALIDE lamps are similar in construction to the mercury lamp, except that the arc tube contains various metal halides in addition to mercury. When the halide vapor approaches the high temperature, central core of the discharge, it disassociates into the halogen and the metal, with the metal radiating its appropriate spectrum. As the halogen and metal move near the cooler arc tube wall by diffusion and convection, they recombine, and the cycle repeats itself.

These lamps generate light with more than half the efficacy of the mercury arc, offer a small light source size for optical control, and provide good color rendition as compared with clear mercury. They have been applied in nearly every type of interior and exterior lighting application because they offer an efficient "white," light source. The average rated life of this lamp is 15,000 hr.

In both low pressure and high pressure sodium sources, light is produced by electricity passing through sodium vapor. In the LPS lamp, a starting gas of neon produces

a red glow when the lamp is initially ignited. As heat is generated, the sodium metal vaporizes, and the emitted light turns into the characteristic yellow color.

HIGH PRESSURE SODIUM (HPS) lamps are used for roadway and sidewalk illumination and offer more suitable color rendition characteristics. Sodium is a particularly suitable gas because most of its radiation is concentrated in a wavelength interval where the sensitivity of the human eye is high. It also has a relatively low excitation energy.

The HPS lamp is constructed with two envelopes—the inner being polycrystalline alumina, which is resistant to sodium attack. The arc tube contains xenon as a starting gas and a small amount of sodium-mercury amalgam. The outer glass envelope is evacuated and protects against chemical attack of the arc tube and maintains the arc tube temperature.

HPS sources are compact, yet have high efficacies (up to 140 lm/W) and high lumen maintenance characteristics. They radiate energy across the visible spectrum and produce a golden-white color. They are available in sizes from 70 to 1000 W, with the low wattage sources finding application in residential street lighting and shopping mall illumination.

HPS lamps have five times the efficacy of incandescent sources, more than twice that of mercury, and 50% more than metal-halide.

HIGH INTENSITY DISCHARGE LAMPS

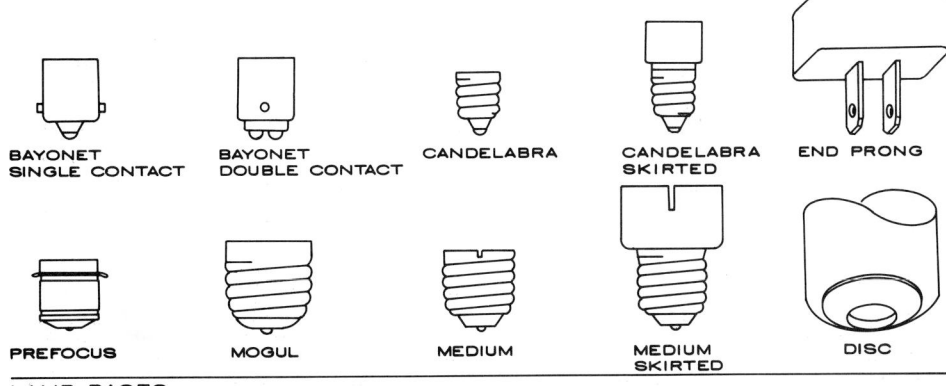

BAYONET SINGLE CONTACT

BAYONET DOUBLE CONTACT

CANDELABRA

CANDELABRA SKIRTED

END PRONG

PREFOCUS

MOGUL

MEDIUM

MEDIUM SKIRTED

DISC

LAMP BASES

CHARACTERISTICS OF BASIC LAMP TYPES

CHARACTERISTICS	INCANDESCENT (INCLUDING TUNGSTEN HALOGEN)	FLUORESCENT	HIGH INTENSITY DISCHARGE (HID)		
			MERCURY-VAPOR	METAL-HALIDE	HIGH PRESSURE SODIUM
Wattages (lamp only)	15-1500	40-1000	40-1000	400, 100, 1500	75, 150, 250, 400, 1000
Life (hr)	750-12,000	9000-30,000	16,000-24,000	1500-15,000	10,000-20,000
Efficacy (lm/W, lamp only)	15-25	55-88	20-63	80-100	100-130
Color rendition	Very good to excellent	Good to excellent	Poor to very good	Good to very good	Fair
Light direction control	Very good to excellent	Fair	Very good	Very good	Very good
Source size	Compact	Extended	Compact	Compact	Compact
Relight time	Immediate	Immediate	3-5 min	10-20 min	Less than 1 min

Wm. G. Miner, AIA, Architect; Washington, D.C.

COEFFICIENTS OF UTILIZATION

TYPICAL LUMINAIRE	MAINT. CAT.	MAXIMUM S/MH GUIDE[4]	RCR[3] ↓	ρcc[1] → 80 ρw[2] → 50	80 30	80 10	70 50	70 30	70 10	50 50	50 30	50 10	30 50	30 30	30 10	10 50	10 30	10 10	0 0
Pendant diffusing sphere with incandescent lamp (35½%↑ 45%↓)	V	1.5	0	.87	.87	.87	.81	.81	.81	.69	.69	.69	.59	.59	.59	.49	.49	.49	.44
			1	.71	.67	.63	.66	.62	.59	.56	.53	.50	.47	.45	.43	.39	.37	.35	.31
			2	.61	.54	.49	.56	.50	.46	.47	.43	.39	.39	.36	.33	.32	.29	.27	.23
			3	.52	.45	.39	.48	.42	.37	.41	.36	.31	.34	.30	.26	.27	.24	.22	.18
			4	.46	.38	.33	.42	.36	.30	.36	.30	.26	.30	.26	.22	.24	.21	.18	.15
			5	.40	.33	.27	.37	.30	.25	.32	.26	.22	.26	.22	.19	.21	.18	.15	.12
			6	.36	.28	.23	.33	.26	.21	.28	.23	.19	.23	.19	.16	.19	.15	.13	.10
			7	.32	.25	.20	.29	.23	.18	.25	.20	.16	.21	.16	.13	.17	.13	.11	.09
			8	.29	.22	.17	.27	.20	.16	.23	.17	.14	.19	.15	.12	.15	.12	.09	.07
			9	.26	.19	.15	.24	.18	.14	.20	.15	.12	.17	.13	.10	.14	.11	.08	.06
			10	.23	.17	.13	.22	.16	.12	.19	.14	.10	.16	.12	.09	.13	.09	.07	.05
Porcelain enameled ventilated standard dome with incandescent lamp (0%↑ 83½%↓)	IV	1.3	0	.99	.99	.99	.97	.97	.97	.92	.92	.92	.88	.88	.88	.85	.85	.85	.83
			1	.88	.85	.82	.86	.83	.81	.83	.80	.78	.79	.78	.76	.77	.75	.73	.72
			2	.78	.73	.68	.76	.72	.67	.73	.69	.66	.71	.67	.64	.68	.65	.63	.61
			3	.69	.62	.57	.67	.61	.57	.65	.60	.56	.63	.58	.55	.61	.57	.54	.52
			4	.61	.54	.49	.60	.53	.48	.58	.52	.48	.56	.51	.47	.54	.50	.46	.45
			5	.54	.47	.41	.53	.46	.41	.51	.45	.41	.50	.44	.40	.48	.43	.40	.38
			6	.48	.41	.35	.47	.40	.35	.46	.39	.35	.44	.39	.34	.43	.38	.34	.32
			7	.43	.35	.30	.42	.35	.30	.41	.34	.30	.39	.34	.30	.38	.33	.29	.28
			8	.38	.31	.26	.38	.31	.26	.37	.30	.26	.36	.30	.26	.35	.30	.26	.24
			9	.35	.28	.23	.34	.27	.23	.33	.27	.23	.32	.27	.23	.31	.26	.22	.21
			10	.31	.25	.20	.31	.24	.20	.30	.24	.20	.29	.24	.20	.29	.23	.20	.18
Prismatic square surface drum (18½%↑ 60½%↓)	V	1.3	0	.89	.89	.89	.85	.85	.85	.77	.77	.77	.70	.70	.70	.63	.63	.63	.60
			1	.78	.75	.72	.74	.72	.69	.68	.66	.64	.62	.60	.58	.56	.55	.54	.51
			2	.69	.65	.61	.66	.62	.58	.61	.57	.54	.56	.53	.50	.51	.49	.47	.44
			3	.62	.57	.52	.60	.55	.50	.55	.51	.47	.50	.47	.44	.46	.44	.41	.39
			4	.56	.50	.46	.54	.49	.44	.50	.45	.42	.46	.42	.39	.42	.39	.37	.35
			5	.51	.45	.40	.49	.43	.39	.45	.41	.37	.42	.38	.35	.39	.36	.33	.31
			6	.46	.40	.36	.45	.39	.35	.42	.37	.33	.39	.35	.31	.36	.32	.30	.28
			7	.42	.36	.32	.41	.35	.31	.38	.33	.29	.35	.31	.28	.33	.29	.27	.25
			8	.39	.32	.28	.37	.32	.28	.35	.30	.26	.32	.28	.25	.30	.27	.24	.22
			9	.35	.29	.25	.34	.29	.25	.32	.27	.24	.30	.26	.23	.28	.24	.22	.20
			10	.32	.27	.23	.31	.26	.22	.29	.25	.21	.27	.23	.20	.26	.22	.20	.18
Medium distribution unit with lens plate and inside frost lamp (0%↑ 54½%↓)	V	1.0	0	.64	.64	.64	.63	.63	.63	.60	.60	.60	.57	.57	.57	.55	.55	.55	.54
			1	.60	.58	.57	.58	.57	.56	.56	.55	.54	.54	.53	.52	.52	.52	.51	.50
			2	.55	.53	.51	.54	.52	.50	.52	.50	.49	.51	.49	.48	.49	.48	.47	.46
			3	.51	.48	.46	.50	.47	.45	.49	.46	.44	.47	.45	.44	.46	.44	.43	.42
			4	.47	.44	.41	.47	.44	.41	.45	.43	.41	.44	.42	.40	.43	.41	.40	.39
			5	.44	.40	.38	.43	.40	.38	.42	.39	.37	.41	.39	.37	.40	.38	.37	.36
			6	.41	.37	.35	.40	.37	.35	.39	.36	.34	.39	.36	.34	.38	.36	.34	.33
			7	.38	.34	.32	.37	.34	.32	.37	.34	.31	.36	.33	.31	.35	.33	.31	.30
			8	.35	.32	.29	.35	.31	.29	.34	.31	.29	.34	.31	.29	.33	.30	.29	.28
			9	.33	.29	.27	.32	.29	.27	.32	.29	.26	.31	.28	.26	.31	.28	.26	.25
			10	.30	.27	.25	.30	.27	.24	.30	.27	.24	.29	.26	.24	.29	.26	.24	.23
Reflector downlight with baffles and inside frosted lamp (0%↑ 44½%↓)	IV	0.7	0	.53	.53	.53	.52	.52	.52	.49	.49	.49	.47	.47	.47	.45	.45	.45	.44
			1	.51	.50	.49	.50	.49	.48	.48	.47	.47	.46	.46	.45	.45	.44	.44	.43
			2	.48	.47	.46	.48	.46	.45	.46	.45	.44	.45	.44	.44	.44	.43	.43	.42
			3	.47	.45	.44	.46	.45	.43	.45	.44	.43	.44	.43	.42	.43	.42	.41	.41
			4	.45	.43	.42	.44	.43	.42	.43	.42	.41	.43	.41	.41	.42	.41	.40	.40
			5	.43	.41	.40	.43	.41	.40	.42	.40	.39	.41	.40	.39	.41	.40	.39	.38
			6	.42	.40	.39	.41	.40	.38	.41	.39	.38	.40	.39	.38	.40	.39	.38	.37
			7	.40	.38	.37	.40	.38	.37	.39	.38	.37	.39	.38	.37	.38	.37	.37	.36
			8	.39	.37	.36	.38	.37	.36	.38	.37	.35	.38	.36	.35	.37	.36	.35	.35
			9	.37	.36	.34	.37	.35	.34	.37	.35	.34	.36	.35	.34	.36	.35	.34	.33
			10	.36	.34	.33	.36	.34	.33	.36	.34	.33	.35	.34	.33	.35	.34	.33	.32

COEFFICIENTS OF UTILIZATION FOR 20% EFFECTIVE FLOOR CAVITY REFLECTANCE (ρFC = 20)

GENERAL NOTES

Luminaire data in this table are based on a composite of generic luminaire types. The polar intensity sketch (candlepower distribution curve) and the corresponding spacing to mounting height guide are representative of many luminaires of each type shown.

SYMBOLS

1. pcc = percent effective ceiling cavity reflectance.
2. pw = percent wall reflectance.
3. RCR = room cavity ratio.
4. Maximum S/MH guide = ratio of maximum luminaire spacing to mounting or ceiling height above work plane.

Maintenance categories (maint. cat.):

Cat. I	Bare lamps and strips
Cat. II	15% or more uplight, open or louvered / Large louvered, 1 in. or more
Cat. III	Less than 15% uplight, open or louvered / Small louvered, less than 1 in.
Cat. IV	Recessed with closed top only / Lighted ceiling with louvers
Cat. V	Recessed with total enclosure / Surface suspended and enclosed
Cat. VI	Totally direct / Totally indirect lighting / Lighted ceiling with solid diffuser

Illuminating Engineering Society; New York, New York

COEFFICIENTS OF UTILIZATION

TYPICAL LUMINAIRE	MAINT. CAT.	MAX. S/MH GUIDE[4]	RCR[3]	ρCC 80			ρCC 70			ρCC 50			ρCC 30			ρCC 10			ρCC 0
			ρW →	50	30	10	50	30	10	50	30	10	50	30	10	50	30	10	0
R-40 flood without shielding (0% ↑ / 100% ↓)	IV	0.8	0	1.18	1.18	1.18	1.16	1.16	1.16	1.11	1.11	1.11	1.06	1.06	1.06	1.01	1.01	1.01	.99
			1	1.09	1.07	1.04	1.07	1.05	1.02	1.03	1.01	.99	.99	.98	.96	.96	.95	.94	.92
			2	1.01	.97	.93	.99	.95	.92	.96	.93	.90	.93	.90	.88	.90	.88	.86	.84
			3	.93	.88	.84	.92	.87	.83	.89	.85	.81	.87	.83	.80	.84	.82	.79	.77
			4	.87	.81	.76	.85	.80	.75	.83	.78	.75	.81	.77	.74	.79	.76	.73	.71
			5	.80	.74	.69	.79	.73	.69	.77	.72	.68	.76	.71	.67	.74	.70	.67	.65
			6	.74	.68	.63	.73	.67	.63	.72	.66	.62	.70	.66	.62	.69	.65	.61	.60
			7	.69	.62	.57	.68	.62	.57	.67	.61	.57	.65	.60	.56	.64	.60	.56	.55
			8	.64	.57	.53	.63	.57	.52	.62	.56	.52	.61	.56	.52	.60	.55	.52	.50
			9	.59	.52	.48	.59	.52	.48	.58	.52	.48	.57	.51	.48	.56	.51	.47	.46
			10	.55	.49	.44	.55	.48	.44	.54	.48	.44	.53	.48	.44	.52	.47	.44	.42
R-40 flood with specular anodized reflector skirt; 45° cutoff (0% ↑ / 85% ↓)	IV	0.7	0	1.00	1.00	1.00	.98	.98	.98	.94	.94	.94	.90	.90	.90	.86	.86	.86	.84
			1	.96	.94	.92	.94	.92	.91	.90	.89	.88	.87	.86	.85	.84	.84	.83	.82
			2	.91	.88	.86	.90	.87	.85	.87	.85	.83	.84	.83	.82	.82	.81	.80	.79
			3	.87	.84	.81	.86	.83	.81	.84	.81	.79	.82	.80	.78	.80	.78	.77	.76
			4	.83	.80	.77	.82	.79	.77	.81	.78	.76	.79	.77	.75	.78	.76	.74	.73
			5	.79	.76	.73	.79	.75	.73	.77	.74	.72	.76	.73	.71	.75	.73	.71	.70
			6	.76	.73	.70	.76	.72	.70	.75	.72	.69	.74	.71	.69	.73	.70	.68	.67
			7	.73	.69	.66	.73	.69	.66	.72	.68	.66	.71	.68	.66	.70	.67	.65	.64
			8	.70	.66	.63	.70	.66	.63	.69	.65	.63	.68	.65	.63	.67	.65	.63	.62
			9	.67	.63	.60	.67	.63	.60	.66	.62	.60	.65	.62	.60	.65	.62	.60	.59
			10	.64	.60	.58	.64	.60	.58	.63	.60	.58	.63	.60	.57	.62	.59	.57	.56
Intermediate distribution ventilated reflector with clear HID lamp (1% ↑ / 76% ↓)	III	1.0	0	.91	.91	.91	.89	.89	.89	.84	.84	.84	.81	.81	.81	.77	.77	.77	.75
			1	.84	.81	.79	.82	.80	.78	.79	.77	.76	.76	.74	.73	.73	.72	.71	.69
			2	.77	.73	.70	.76	.72	.70	.73	.70	.68	.70	.68	.66	.68	.66	.65	.63
			3	.71	.66	.63	.69	.65	.62	.67	.64	.61	.65	.62	.60	.63	.61	.59	.57
			4	.65	.60	.56	.64	.59	.56	.62	.58	.55	.60	.57	.54	.59	.56	.54	.52
			5	.59	.54	.50	.59	.54	.50	.57	.53	.50	.56	.52	.49	.54	.51	.48	.47
			6	.54	.49	.45	.54	.49	.45	.52	.48	.45	.51	.47	.44	.50	.47	.44	.42
			7	.50	.44	.40	.49	.44	.40	.48	.43	.40	.47	.43	.39	.46	.42	.39	.38
			8	.45	.40	.36	.45	.40	.36	.44	.39	.36	.43	.39	.35	.42	.38	.35	.34
			9	.41	.36	.32	.41	.36	.32	.40	.35	.32	.39	.35	.32	.38	.35	.32	.30
			10	.38	.33	.29	.37	.32	.29	.37	.32	.29	.36	.32	.29	.35	.31	.28	.27
Intermediate distribution ventilated reflector with phosphor coated HID lamp (6½% ↑ / 75½% ↓)	III	1.0	0	.96	.96	.96	.93	.93	.93	.87	.87	.87	.82	.82	.82	.77	.77	.77	.75
			1	.89	.87	.84	.86	.84	.83	.82	.80	.79	.78	.76	.75	.74	.73	.72	.70
			2	.82	.79	.76	.80	.77	.74	.76	.74	.72	.73	.71	.69	.70	.68	.67	.65
			3	.76	.72	.68	.74	.70	.67	.71	.68	.65	.68	.66	.63	.66	.63	.61	.60
			4	.70	.66	.62	.69	.65	.61	.66	.63	.60	.64	.61	.58	.62	.59	.57	.55
			5	.65	.60	.56	.64	.59	.56	.62	.58	.54	.60	.56	.53	.58	.55	.52	.51
			6	.60	.55	.51	.59	.55	.51	.57	.53	.50	.56	.52	.49	.54	.51	.48	.47
			7	.56	.51	.47	.55	.50	.46	.53	.49	.46	.52	.48	.45	.50	.47	.44	.43
			8	.52	.47	.43	.51	.46	.43	.50	.45	.42	.48	.44	.41	.47	.43	.41	.40
			9	.48	.43	.39	.47	.42	.39	.46	.42	.39	.45	.41	.38	.44	.40	.38	.36
			10	.45	.40	.36	.44	.39	.36	.43	.39	.36	.42	.38	.35	.41	.37	.35	.34
Porcelain-enameled reflector with 30°CW x 30°LW shielding (23½% ↑ / 57% ↓)	II	1.0	0	.90	.90	.90	.85	.85	.85	.76	.76	.76	.68	.68	.68	.60	.60	.60	.57
			1	.81	.78	.76	.77	.74	.72	.69	.67	.66	.62	.61	.60	.56	.55	.54	.57
			2	.72	.68	.64	.69	.65	.62	.62	.59	.57	.56	.54	.52	.51	.49	.47	.45
			3	.65	.59	.55	.62	.57	.53	.56	.52	.49	.51	.48	.46	.46	.44	.42	.39
			4	.58	.52	.48	.56	.50	.46	.51	.46	.43	.46	.43	.40	.42	.39	.37	.35
			5	.52	.46	.41	.50	.44	.40	.46	.41	.38	.42	.38	.35	.38	.35	.33	.30
			6	.47	.41	.36	.45	.39	.35	.41	.37	.33	.38	.34	.31	.35	.31	.29	.27
			7	.43	.36	.32	.41	.35	.31	.38	.33	.29	.34	.30	.27	.32	.28	.26	.24
			8	.38	.32	.28	.37	.31	.27	.34	.29	.26	.31	.27	.24	.29	.25	.23	.21
			9	.35	.29	.24	.33	.28	.24	.31	.26	.22	.28	.24	.21	.26	.22	.20	.18
			10	.32	.26	.22	.30	.25	.21	.28	.23	.20	.26	.22	.19	.24	.20	.18	.16
2 lamp prismatic wraparound—multiply by 0.95 for 4 lamps (11½% ↑ / 58½% ↓)	V	1.5/1.2	0	.80	.80	.80	.77	.77	.77	.71	.71	.71	.66	.66	.66	.60	.60	.60	.58
			1	.71	.69	.66	.69	.66	.64	.64	.62	.60	.59	.58	.56	.55	.54	.53	.50
			2	.64	.59	.56	.61	.58	.54	.57	.54	.51	.53	.51	.49	.49	.48	.46	.44
			3	.57	.52	.48	.55	.50	.47	.51	.48	.45	.48	.45	.42	.45	.42	.40	.38
			4	.51	.46	.41	.49	.44	.40	.46	.42	.39	.43	.40	.37	.41	.38	.35	.34
			5	.46	.40	.36	.44	.39	.35	.41	.37	.34	.39	.35	.32	.37	.33	.31	.29
			6	.41	.35	.31	.40	.35	.31	.38	.33	.30	.35	.31	.28	.33	.30	.27	.26
			7	.37	.31	.27	.36	.31	.27	.34	.29	.26	.32	.28	.25	.30	.27	.24	.23
			8	.33	.28	.24	.32	.27	.23	.30	.26	.22	.29	.25	.22	.27	.24	.21	.19
			9	.30	.24	.20	.29	.24	.20	.27	.23	.19	.26	.22	.19	.24	.21	.18	.17
			10	.27	.22	.18	.26	.21	.18	.25	.20	.17	.23	.19	.16	.22	.18	.16	.15

Notes: ρCC[1] → ; ρW[2] → ; COEFFICIENTS OF UTILIZATION FOR 20% EFFECTIVE FLOOR CAVITY REFLECTANCE (ρFC = 20)

Illuminating Engineering Society; New York, New York

COEFFICIENTS OF UTILIZATION

TYPICAL LUMINAIRE	MAINT. CAT.	MAXIMUM S/MH GUIDE(4)	RCR(3) ↓	80			70			50			30			10			0
				50	30	10	50	30	10	50	30	10	50	30	10	50	30	10	0
2 lamp 1 ft wide troffer with 45° plastic louver—multiply by 0.90 for 3 lamps (0% up, 46% down)	IV	1.0	0	.54	.54	.54	.53	.53	.53	.51	.51	.51	.48	.48	.48	.46	.46	.46	.45
			1	.49	.48	.46	.48	.47	.46	.46	.45	.44	.45	.44	.43	.43	.42	.42	.41
			2	.44	.42	.40	.43	.41	.39	.42	.40	.38	.40	.39	.37	.39	.38	.37	.36
			3	.40	.37	.34	.39	.36	.34	.38	.36	.34	.37	.35	.33	.36	.34	.33	.32
			4	.36	.33	.30	.36	.32	.30	.35	.32	.30	.34	.31	.29	.33	.31	.29	.28
			5	.33	.29	.26	.32	.29	.26	.31	.28	.26	.30	.28	.26	.30	.27	.26	.25
			6	.30	.26	.24	.29	.26	.24	.29	.26	.23	.28	.25	.23	.27	.25	.23	.22
			7	.27	.24	.21	.27	.23	.21	.26	.23	.21	.26	.23	.21	.25	.22	.21	.20
			8	.25	.21	.19	.24	.21	.19	.24	.21	.19	.23	.21	.18	.23	.20	.18	.18
			9	.22	.19	.17	.22	.19	.17	.22	.19	.17	.21	.18	.16	.21	.18	.16	.16
			10	.21	.17	.15	.20	.17	.15	.20	.17	.15	.20	.17	.15	.19	.17	.15	.14
Fluorescent unit with flat prismatic lens, 2 lamp 1 ft wide (0% up, 56% down, 60°)	V	1.4/1.2	0	.66	.66	.66	.65	.65	.65	.62	.62	.62	.59	.59	.59	.57	.57	.57	.56
			1	.61	.59	.57	.59	.58	.56	.57	.56	.54	.55	.54	.53	.53	.52	.51	.50
			2	.55	.52	.50	.54	.51	.49	.52	.50	.48	.50	.48	.47	.49	.47	.46	.45
			3	.50	.46	.43	.49	.46	.43	.47	.45	.42	.46	.44	.42	.45	.43	.41	.40
			4	.45	.41	.38	.45	.41	.38	.43	.40	.38	.42	.39	.37	.41	.39	.37	.36
			5	.41	.37	.34	.40	.36	.34	.39	.36	.33	.38	.35	.33	.37	.35	.33	.32
			6	.37	.33	.30	.37	.33	.30	.36	.32	.30	.35	.32	.29	.34	.31	.29	.28
			7	.34	.30	.27	.34	.29	.27	.33	.29	.26	.32	.29	.26	.31	.28	.26	.25
			8	.31	.26	.24	.30	.26	.23	.30	.26	.23	.29	.26	.23	.28	.25	.23	.22
			9	.28	.23	.21	.27	.23	.21	.27	.23	.20	.26	.23	.20	.26	.23	.20	.19
			10	.25	.21	.18	.25	.21	.18	.24	.21	.18	.24	.21	.18	.23	.20	.18	.17
1 ft wide aluminum troffer with 40°CW x 45°LW shielding and single extrahigh-output lamp (0% up, 42½% down)	IV	1.1/0.8	0	.50	.50	.50	.49	.49	.49	.47	.47	.47	.45	.45	.45	.43	.43	.43	.42
			1	.46	.45	.44	.45	.44	.43	.44	.43	.42	.42	.41	.41	.41	.40	.40	.39
			2	.43	.41	.39	.42	.40	.38	.40	.39	.38	.39	.38	.37	.38	.37	.36	.35
			3	.39	.37	.35	.39	.36	.34	.37	.35	.34	.36	.35	.33	.35	.34	.33	.32
			4	.36	.33	.31	.35	.33	.31	.35	.32	.31	.34	.32	.30	.33	.31	.30	.29
			5	.33	.30	.28	.33	.30	.28	.32	.29	.28	.31	.29	.27	.30	.29	.27	.26
			6	.31	.28	.26	.30	.28	.26	.30	.27	.25	.29	.27	.25	.28	.26	.25	.24
			7	.28	.25	.23	.28	.25	.23	.27	.25	.23	.27	.25	.23	.26	.24	.23	.22
			8	.26	.23	.21	.26	.23	.21	.25	.23	.21	.25	.23	.21	.24	.22	.21	.20
			9	.24	.21	.19	.24	.21	.19	.23	.21	.19	.23	.20	.19	.22	.20	.19	.18
			10	.22	.19	.17	.22	.19	.17	.21	.19	.17	.21	.19	.17	.21	.19	.17	.16
Luminous bottom suspended unit with extrahigh-output lamp (66% up, 12% down)	VI	1.5	0	.77	.77	.77	.67	.67	.67	.49	.49	.49	.33	.33	.33	.18	.18	.18	.11
			1	.67	.64	.62	.59	.57	.54	.44	.42	.41	.30	.29	.28	.17	.16	.16	.10
			2	.59	.54	.50	.51	.48	.45	.38	.36	.34	.26	.25	.23	.15	.14	.13	.09
			3	.51	.46	.42	.45	.41	.37	.34	.31	.28	.23	.21	.20	.13	.12	.12	.07
			4	.45	.40	.35	.40	.35	.31	.30	.27	.24	.20	.18	.17	.12	.11	.10	.06
			5	.40	.34	.30	.35	.30	.27	.26	.23	.20	.18	.16	.14	.10	.09	.08	.05
			6	.36	.30	.26	.32	.27	.23	.24	.20	.18	.16	.14	.12	.09	.08	.07	.05
			7	.32	.26	.22	.28	.23	.20	.21	.18	.15	.15	.12	.11	.08	.07	.06	.04
			8	.29	.23	.19	.25	.21	.17	.19	.16	.13	.13	.11	.09	.08	.06	.06	.03
			9	.26	.20	.17	.23	.18	.15	.17	.14	.12	.12	.10	.08	.07	.06	.05	.03
			10	.24	.18	.15	.21	.16	.13	.16	.12	.10	.11	.09	.07	.06	.05	.04	.03
Diffusing plastic or glass		ρcc from below ~65%	1				.60	.58	.56	.58	.56	.54							
			2				.53	.49	.45	.51	.47	.43							
			3				.47	.42	.37	.45	.41	.36							
			4				.41	.36	.32	.39	.35	.31							
			5				.37	.31	.27	.35	.30	.26							
			6				.33	.27	.23	.31	.26	.23							
			7				.29	.24	.20	.28	.23	.20							
			8				.26	.21	.18	.25	.20	.17							
			9				.23	.19	.15	.23	.18	.15							
			10				.21	.17	.13	.21	.16	.13							
Louvered ceiling		ρcc from below ~45%	1							.51	.49	.48				.47	.46	.45	
			2							.46	.44	.42				.43	.42	.40	
			3							.42	.39	.37				.39	.38	.36	
			4							.38	.35	.33				.36	.34	.32	
			5							.35	.32	.29				.33	.31	.29	
			6							.32	.29	.26				.30	.28	.26	
			7							.29	.26	.23				.28	.25	.23	
			8							.27	.23	.21				.26	.23	.21	
			9							.24	.21	.19				.24	.21	.19	
			10							.22	.19	.17				.22	.19	.17	

COEFFICIENTS OF UTILIZATION FOR 20% EFFECTIVE FLOOR CAVITY REFLECTANCE (ρFC = 20)

Diffusing plastic or glass
1. Ceiling efficiency ~60%; diffuser transmittance ~50%; diffuser reflectance ~40%. Cavity with minimum obstructions and painted with 80% reflectance paint—use ρc = 70
2. For lower reflectance paint or obstructions—use ρc = 50

Louvered ceiling
1. Ceiling efficiency ~50%; 45° shielding opaque louvers of 80% reflectance. Cavity with minimum obstructions and painted with 80% reflectance paint—use ρc = 50

Illuminating Engineering Society; New York, New York

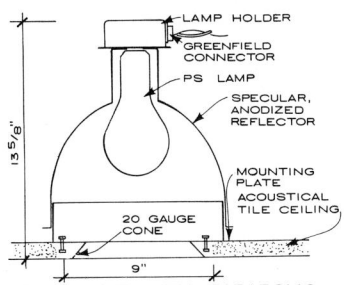

DOWNLIGHT WITH PARABOLIC REFLECTOR

The open reflector downlight uses general service lamps in a polished parabolic reflector to produce controlled light without a lens. The reflector efficiently redirects the upward component of the light source down through the aperture.

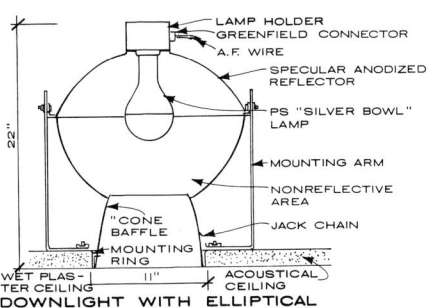

DOWNLIGHT WITH ELLIPTICAL REFLECTOR

A more sophisticated downlight uses a silver bowl lamp to project light up into an elliptical reflector. When the light source is located at one focal point the output light converges and can be redirected through a constricted aperture at the other focal point.

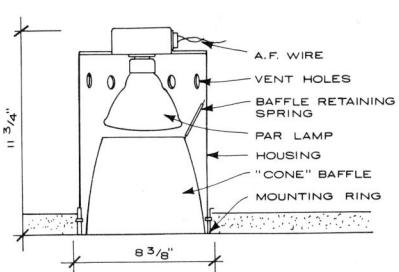

DOWNLIGHT WITH REFLECTOR LAMP

Downlights without reflectors or lenses are commonly called "cans." They have cylindrical housings and rely on a PAR or R lamp for optical control. Cones, annular rings, or lower type baffles will shield an observer from glare in the normal field of view.

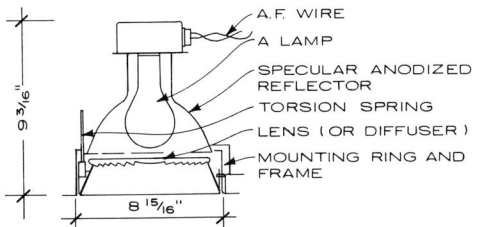

DOWNLIGHT WITH FRESNEL LENS

One downlight type combines a general service lamp with a reflector housing and a diffusing lens. The lens provides directional control of the light as it leaves the luminaire. The lens covers the ceiling aperture, thus keeping dust from the reflector and providing a heat shield.

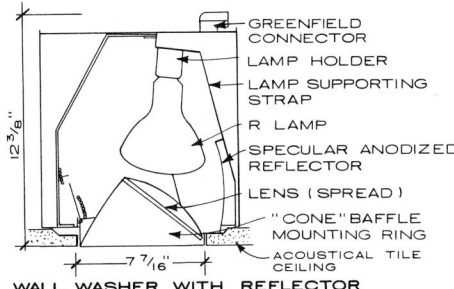

WALL WASHER WITH REFLECTOR LAMP AND LENS

Wall washers provide shadowless coverage of vertical surfaces with an even "wash" of light. They are used to set a mood within a space, to accent surrounding walls, or to obscure undesirable unevenness of the surface.

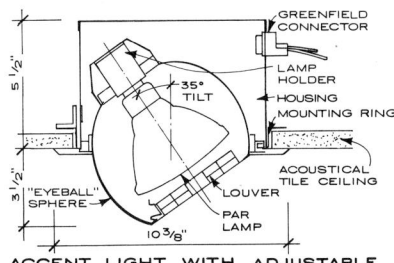

ACCENT LIGHT WITH ADJUSTABLE REFLECTOR LAMP

The accent light produces an asymmetrical distribution of light and normally allows for adjustments in the lamp position. It is used for gallery lighting to emphasize objects or small wall areas.

INCANDESCENT FIXTURES

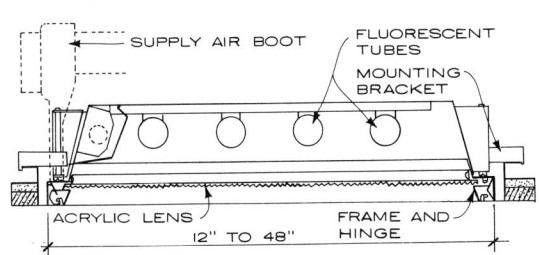

RECESSED UNIT WITH PRISMATIC LENS

The recessed fluorescent luminaire is usually designed to fit into a standard ceiling grid. A transparent, prismatic lens usually encloses the fixture and directs useful light to the work surface.

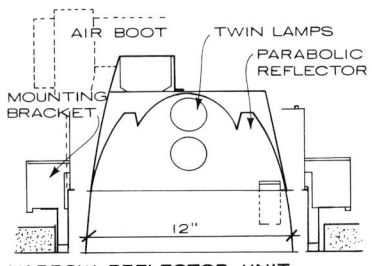

NARROW REFLECTOR UNIT

Parabolic reflectors are used in narrow profile fixtures to redirect the upward component of the light source down to the task area. The fluorescent lamps are stacked so that one may be switched off without sacrificing the even distribution of light.

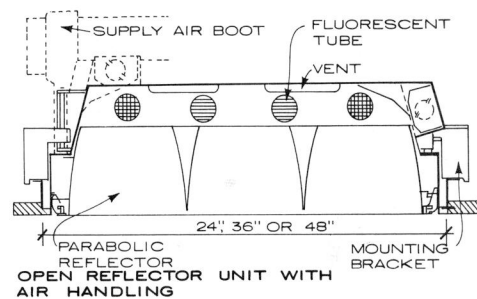

OPEN REFLECTOR UNIT WITH AIR HANDLING

Some open reflector units are fitted with parabola shaped louver blades to better control glare and veiling reflections. Air fittings are also integrated into the lamp housing for ducted air supply or return.

FLUORESCENT FIXTURES

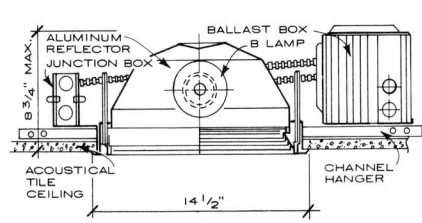

SQUARE LENS AND REFLECTOR UNIT

HID fixtures are usually preassembled and wired for fast installation. A recessed reflector with a fresnel or prismatic lens will maximize the utilization and control of the high lamp output.

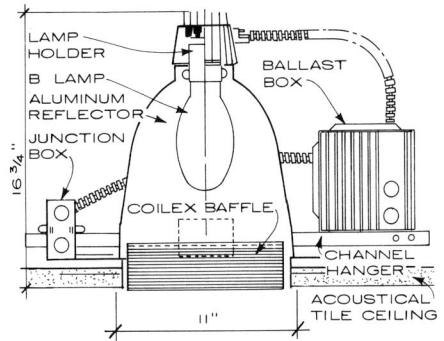

OPEN REFLECTOR DOWNLIGHT

HID luminaires require a deep ceiling space to fully recess the large lamp housing. Open reflector downlights often use elliptical reflectors that focus the lamp light through a small aperture. Coil or cone baffles help reduce fixture surface brightness.

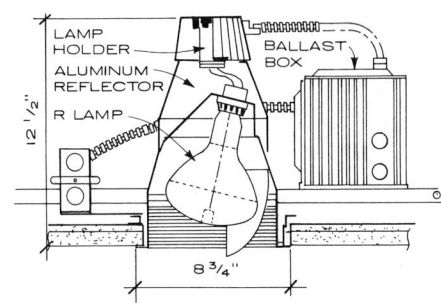

ADJUSTABLE WALL WASHER

A special scoop insert can be added to a standard downlight fixture to create a HID wall washer unit. The reflector and lamp socket can be rotated for desired positioning of light throw.

HIGH INTENSITY DISCHARGE FIXTURES

Wm. G. Miner, AIA, Architect; Washington, D.C.

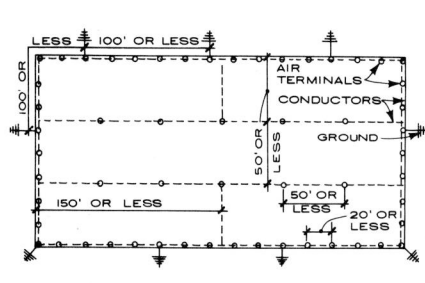

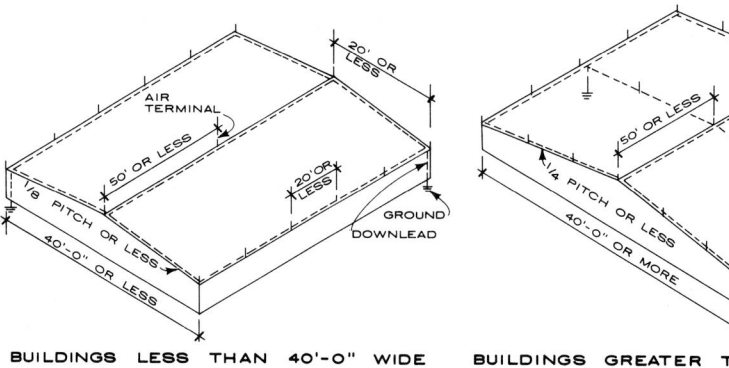

FLAT ROOF PLAN

ROOF LAYOUT PLANS

BUILDINGS LESS THAN 40'-0" WIDE

BUILDINGS GREATER THAN 40'-0" WIDE

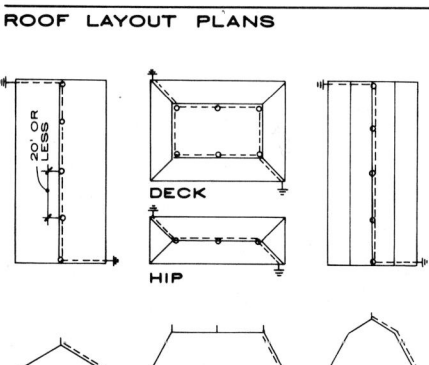

DECK

HIP

GABLE   HIP OR DECK   GAMBREL

PITCH ROOF TYPES

OVERALL SYSTEMS DESIGN

1. Air terminals shall be located around the perimeter of flat roof buildings and along the ridge of pitched roof buildings spaced at 20 ft on center maximum and located not more than 2 ft from ridge ends, outside corners, and edges of building walls.

2. Full size main conductors shall interconnect all air terminals.

3. Additional air terminals shall be located in the center of large open flat roofs at spacings not to exceed 50 ft maximum.

4. Cable runs connecting these center roof air terminals shall not exceed 150 ft in length without a lead back to the perimeter cable.

5. Gently sloping roofs are classed as flat under the rules shown above and are protected in the same fashion as flat roof.

6. Download cables to ground shall be connected to the roof perimeter cable at a maximum spacing of 100 ft on center. Buildings having a perimeter of 250 to 300 ft shall have three downleads. For each additional 100 ft or fraction thereof add one downlead.

7. No building or structure shall have less than two downleads.

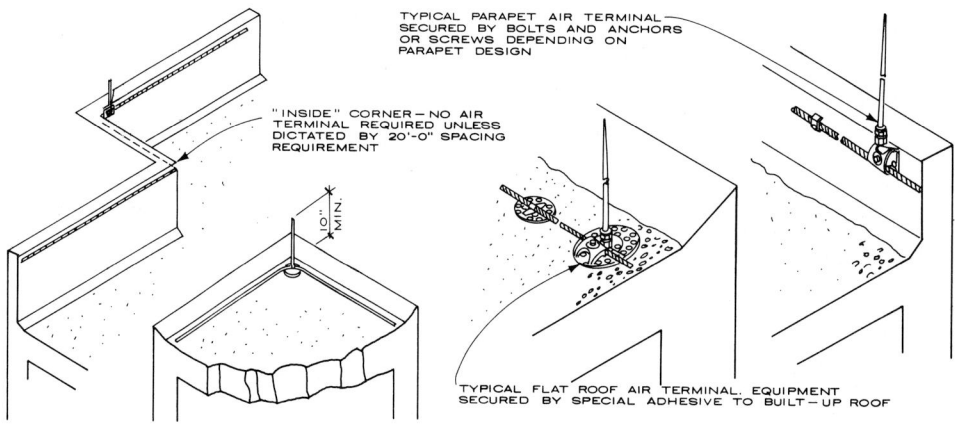

AIR TERMINALS

GENERAL NOTES

A lightning protection system is an integrated arrangement of air terminals, bonding connections, arrestors, splicers, and other fittings installed on a structure in order to safely conduct to ground any lightning discharge to the structure.

Lightning protection systems and components are grouped into three categories (U.L. classes) based on building height and intended applications. Class I equipment and systems are for ordinary buildings under 75 ft in height, Class II is for those over 75 ft in height, and Class II Modified is a specialty area covering only large, heavy duty stacks and chimneys similar to those used at power plants, for example. Each of these types of systems consists of five or six major groups of components:

1. Air terminals (lightning rods) located on the roof and building projections.

2. Main conductors that tie the air terminals together and interconnect with the grounding system.

3. Bonds to metal roof structures and equipment.

4. Arrestors to prevent powerline surge damage.

5. Ground terminals, typically rods or plates driven or buried in the earth.

6. Tree protection (usually applicable only to residential work).

Each of these types of equipment and the methods for their installation are covered in the following drawings.

Beyond these material requirements, other factors to be considered relative to lightning protection systems include (a) selection of codes for compliance, (b) inspection criteria (again based on code), (c) criteria to evaluate competency of installing personnel, and (d) requirement for annual inspection and maintenance.

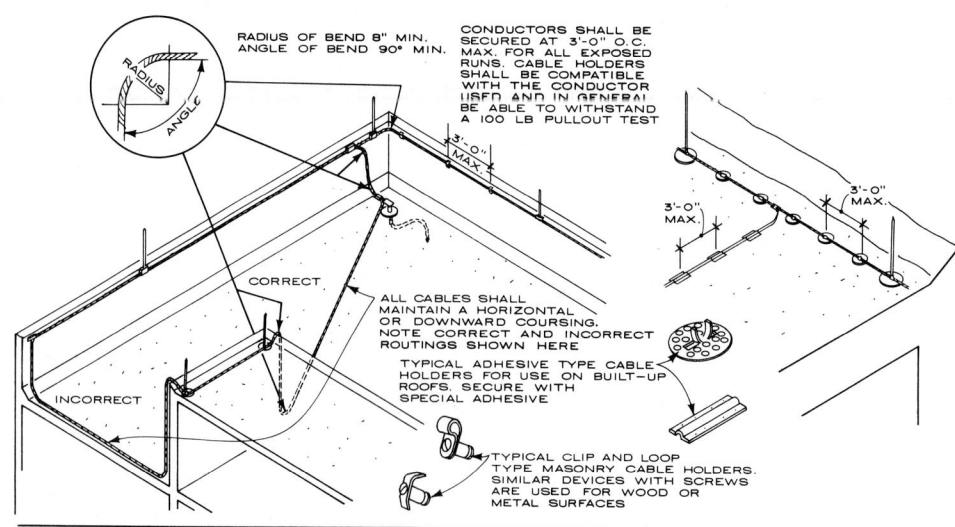

CONDUCTORS

Robert W. Lindquist and Douglas J. Franklin; Thompson Lightning Protection, Inc.; St. Paul, Minnesota

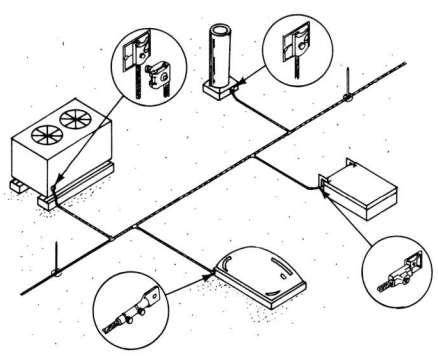
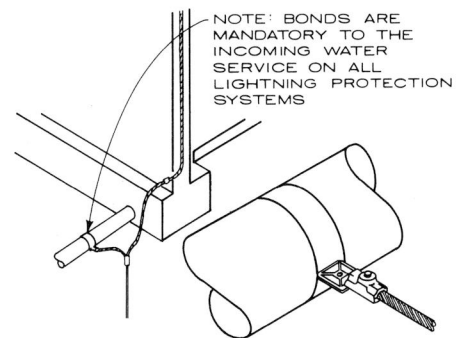

NOTE: BONDS ARE MANDATORY TO THE INCOMING WATER SERVICE ON ALL LIGHTNING PROTECTION SYSTEMS

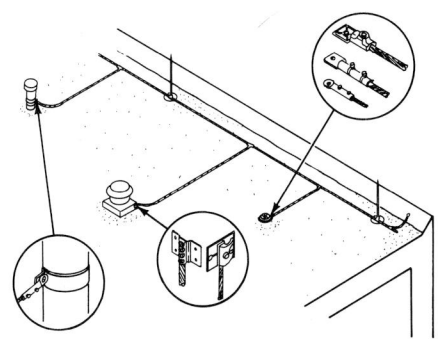

BONDING

NOTES

There are two classes of equipment that require bonding to the lightning protection systems.

1. METAL BODIES OF CONDUCTANCE: Larger metal objects located on the roof and subject to direct lightning strike. These objects must be bonded using full size conductor and fittings regardless of their location on the roof. Typical examples as shown include plumbing vents, exhaust fans, air-conditioning units, metal stacks, skylite frames, and roof hatches. Television and radio antennas must also be bonded.

2. METAL BODIES OF INDUCTANCE: Smaller objects such as roof drains, gutters, downspouts, flashings, coping, and expansion joint caps. These require bonding only if within 6 ft of the system.

I" SIZE P.V.C. OR METAL CONDUIT. BOND CABLE TO METAL CONDUIT AT TOP AND BOTTOM

THROUGH ROOF TRANSITION

THROUGH ROOF CONNECTOR

FLASHING OR PITCH POCKET

NOTE: IN NO CASE SHOULD CONDUIT BE ROUTED DIRECTLY THROUGH A ROOF

CONDUIT IS OPTIONAL — CABLE MAY BE CONCEALED DIRECTLY IN CONSTRUCTION

TYPICAL CONCEALED DOWNLEAD CABLE

TYPICAL GROUND ROD INSTALLATION

CONSULT CODES FOR ALTERNATE GROUNDING METHODS WHERE SOIL CONDUCTIVITY IS POOR OR ROD CANNOT BE DRIVEN

1'-0" MIN.

2'-0" MIN.

10'-0" MIN. DEPTH

DOWNLEADS AND GROUNDS

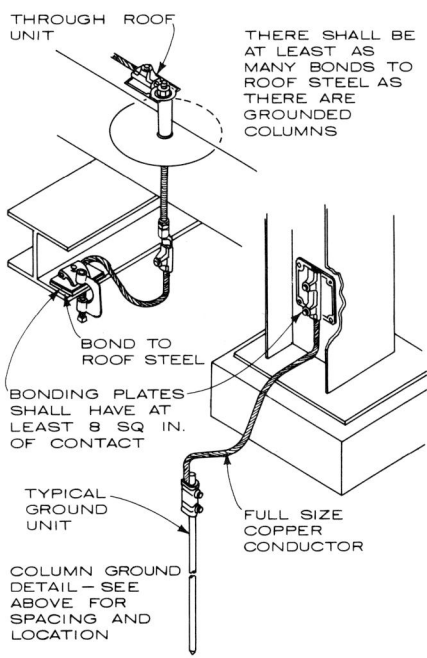

THROUGH ROOF UNIT

THERE SHALL BE AT LEAST AS MANY BONDS TO ROOF STEEL AS THERE ARE GROUNDED COLUMNS

BOND TO ROOF STEEL

BONDING PLATES SHALL HAVE AT LEAST 8 SQ. IN. OF CONTACT

TYPICAL GROUND UNIT

FULL SIZE COPPER CONDUCTOR

COLUMN GROUND DETAIL — SEE ABOVE FOR SPACING AND LOCATION

STEEL FRAME AS CONDUCTOR

NOTE

In some cases, especially on tall structures, it may be advantageous to substitute the steel frame of a structure for portions of the usual conductor system, normally the downleads. Connections are made to cleaned areas of the building steel, at grade and roof level, and the columns serve to connect the roof and ground systems.

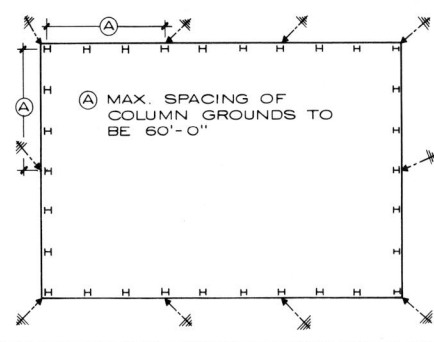

(A) MAX. SPACING OF COLUMN GROUNDS TO BE 60'-0"

COLUMN GROUND LOCATION

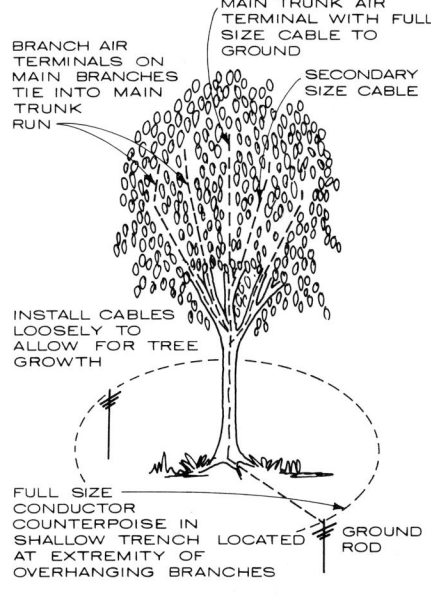

MAIN TRUNK AIR TERMINAL WITH FULL SIZE CABLE TO GROUND

BRANCH AIR TERMINALS ON MAIN BRANCHES TIE INTO MAIN TRUNK RUN

SECONDARY SIZE CABLE

INSTALL CABLES LOOSELY TO ALLOW FOR TREE GROWTH

FULL SIZE CONDUCTOR COUNTERPOISE IN SHALLOW TRENCH LOCATED AT EXTREMITY OF OVERHANGING BRANCHES

GROUND ROD

TREE INSTALLATION
OTHER CONSIDERATIONS

1. Arresters should be installed on the electric and telephone services and on all radio and television lead-ins to a structure. Responsibility and jurisdiction for the installation of these devices can vary with locality so that special consideration may have to be given to these items.

2. Trees adjacent to residences pose another special hazard. It is recommended that all trees taller than an adjacent structure that are within 10 ft be fully protected. Consult codes or manufacturer for recommendations on materials and installation requirements.

3. On-site inspections and certification of completed systems, installer competency certification, and guaranteed inspection/maintenance options are all available under existing standards. Consult codes and standards for specifics.

REFERENCES

The following codes, technical sources, and quality control procedures are standards for lightning protection systems.

1. CONSTRUCTION SPECIFICATION INSTITUTE: C.S.I. "Spec Data."
2. LIGHTNING PROTECTION INSTITUTE: "Installation Code L.P.I.—175."
3. UNDERWRITERS LABORATORIES: Master Labeled program under "U.L. Installation Requirements 96A."
4. NATIONAL FIRE PROTECTION ASSOCIATION: "Lightning Protection Code N.F.P.A. 78."
5. U.S. BUREAU OF STANDARDS: Handbook 46.

Robert W. Lindquist and Douglas J. Franklin; Thompson Lightning Protection, Inc.; St. Paul, Minnesota

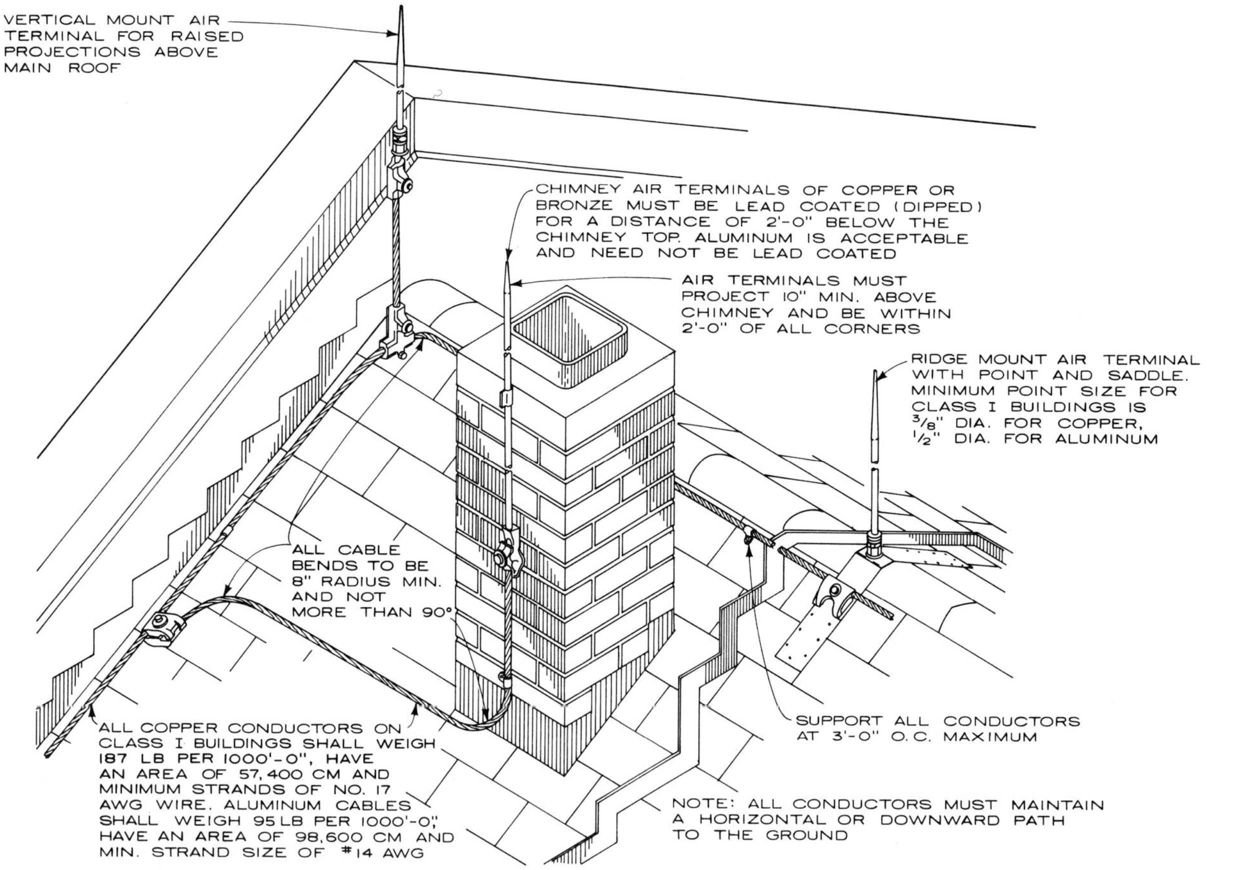

VERTICAL MOUNT AIR TERMINAL FOR RAISED PROJECTIONS ABOVE MAIN ROOF

CHIMNEY AIR TERMINALS OF COPPER OR BRONZE MUST BE LEAD COATED (DIPPED) FOR A DISTANCE OF 2'-0" BELOW THE CHIMNEY TOP. ALUMINUM IS ACCEPTABLE AND NEED NOT BE LEAD COATED

AIR TERMINALS MUST PROJECT 10" MIN. ABOVE CHIMNEY AND BE WITHIN 2'-0" OF ALL CORNERS

RIDGE MOUNT AIR TERMINAL WITH POINT AND SADDLE. MINIMUM POINT SIZE FOR CLASS I BUILDINGS IS 3/8" DIA. FOR COPPER, 1/2" DIA. FOR ALUMINUM

ALL CABLE BENDS TO BE 8" RADIUS MIN. AND NOT MORE THAN 90°

ALL COPPER CONDUCTORS ON CLASS I BUILDINGS SHALL WEIGH 187 LB PER 1000'-0", HAVE AN AREA OF 57,400 CM AND MINIMUM STRANDS OF NO. 17 AWG WIRE. ALUMINUM CABLES SHALL WEIGH 95 LB PER 1000'-0", HAVE AN AREA OF 98,600 CM AND MIN. STRAND SIZE OF #14 AWG

SUPPORT ALL CONDUCTORS AT 3'-0" O.C. MAXIMUM

NOTE: ALL CONDUCTORS MUST MAINTAIN A HORIZONTAL OR DOWNWARD PATH TO THE GROUND

CLASS I SYSTEMS — TYPICAL DETAILS

ON HEAVY DUTY STACKS (OVER 75'-0" HIGH WITH FLUE OPENING OVER 500 SQ IN.) ALL EQUIPMENT SHALL BE CLASS II MODIFIED. ALL POINTS MUST BE 5/8" DIA. OF COPPER OR STAINLESS STEEL. ALL COPPER/BRONZE FITTINGS AND CABLE MUST BE 1/16" LEAD COVERED WITHIN 25'-0" OF STACK TOP

CONFIGURATION SAME AS OTHER SIDE. ALL STACK POINTS MUST PROJECT A MINIMUM OF 18" ABOVE STACK, BE WITHIN 2'-0" OF ALL CORNERS, AND BE SPACED NOT MORE THAN 8'-0" APART. MOST LARGER STACKS REQUIRE FOUR OR MORE AIR TERMINALS. ALL STACKS MUST HAVE TWO DOWNLEADS TO GROUND

TOP MOUNT PARAPET AIR TERMINAL FOR CLASS II STRUCTURES. COPPER POINTS MUST BE 1/2" DIA. MIN. ALUMINUM POINTS MUST BE 5/8" DIA. MIN.

PARALLEL CABLE SPLICER. ALL CONNECTORS MUST CONTACT CABLE FOR 1 1/2" LENGTH

SUPPORT ALL CABLES ON STACKS AT 2'-0" O.C. HORIZONTALLY AND 4'-0" O.C. VERTICALLY

ALL CABLE BENDS TO BE 8" RADIUS MIN. AND NOT MORE THAN 90°

FOR CLASS II STRUCTURES, COPPER CONDUCTORS SHALL WEIGH 375 LB PER 1000'-0", HAVE AN AREA OF 115,000 CM AND STRANDS OF NOT LESS THAN #16 AWG. ALUMINUM CONDUCTORS SHALL WEIGH 190 LB PER 1000'-0", HAVE AN AREA OF 192,000 CM AND STRANDS OF NOT LESS THAN #13 AWG

CONDUCTOR ON THE TOP 25'-0" OF A STACK OR TO ROOF LEVEL SHALL MEET CLASS II COPPER CRITERIA AND MUST BE COVERED WITH LEAD 1/16" THICK

STRAIGHT SPLICE TRANSITION FROM LEAD COVERED TO BARE CONDUCTOR

SUPPORT CABLES ON BUILDING AT 3'-0" O.C. MAX.

FOR EXPOSED DOWNLEADS LOCATED IN SCHOOL YARDS, DRIVEWAYS, WALK AREAS, ETC., WHERE SUBJECT TO DAMAGE OR DISPLACEMENT, PROPER GUARDS SHALL BE PROVIDED. TUBULAR METAL GUARDS MUST BE BONDED TO THE CABLE AT BOTH ENDS

SEE GROUNDING REQUIREMENTS ON OTHER PAGE

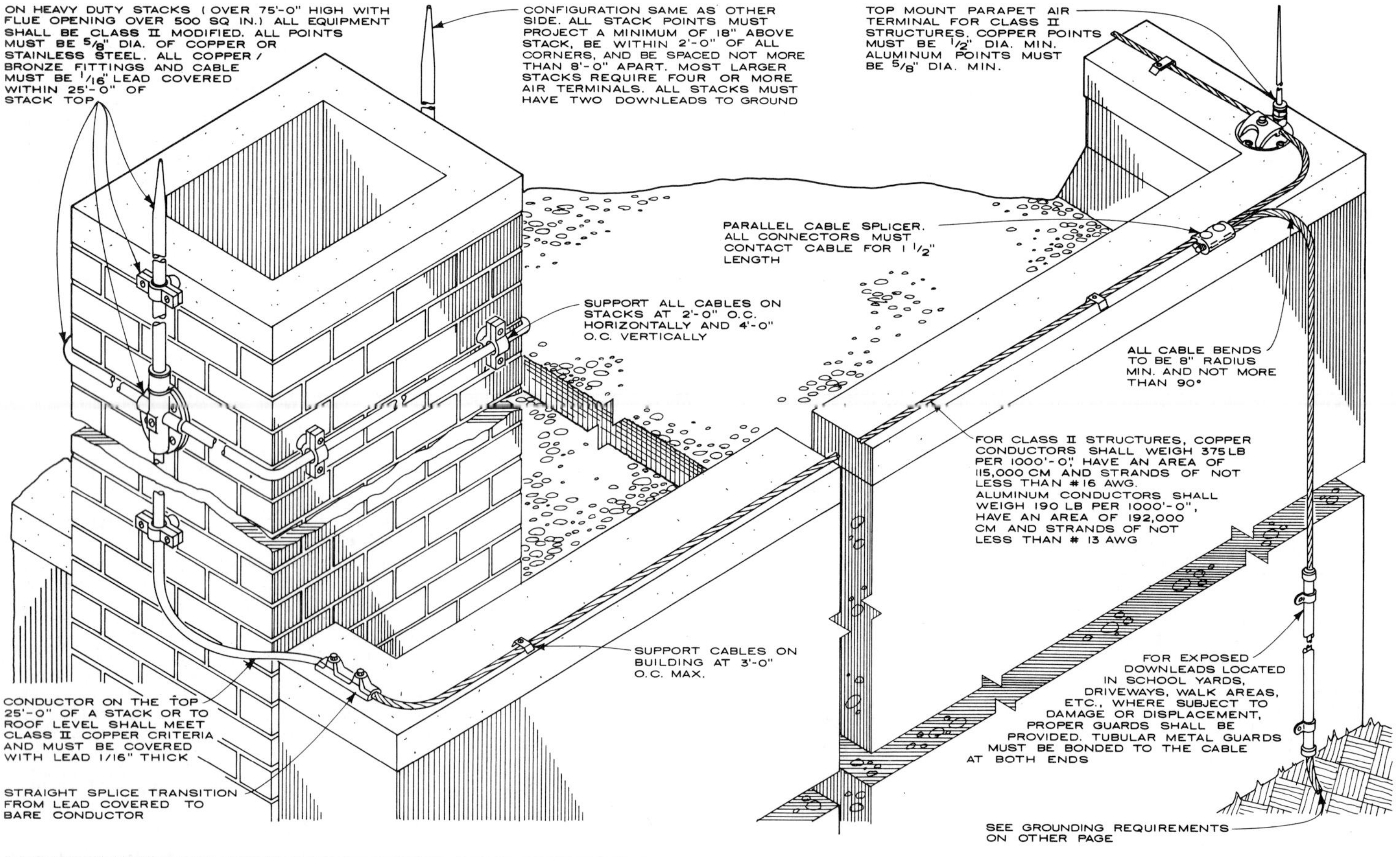

CLASS II SYSTEMS — TYPICAL DETAILS

Robert W. Lindquist and Douglas J. Franklin; Thompson Lightning Protection, Inc.; St. Paul, Minnesota

BATTERY PACKS AND INVERTORS

Battery powered lighting equipment is utilized to provide minimal emergency illumination required for personnel safety and evacuation purposes in buildings not requiring standby generator power. This equipment is also utilized in buildings requiring standby generator power at central control room, telephone switchboard room, generator room, and electrical switchgear rooms to provide lighting for continuity of critical operations and troubleshooting if the generator fails to start. The batteries require frequent inspection, tests, and maintenance if they are to perform their intended function.

BATTERY PACK   **BATTERIES AND INVERTER**

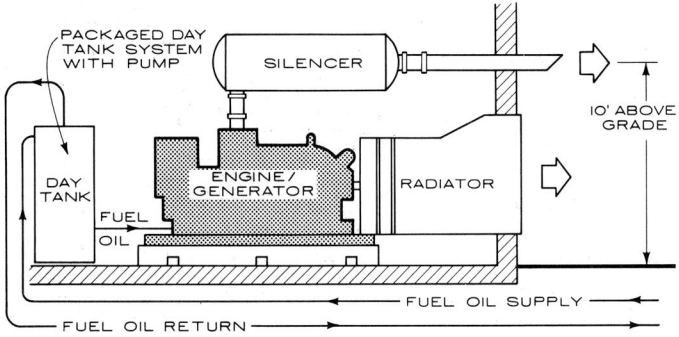

UNIT MOUNTED RADIATOR

STANDBY GENERATORS

Standby generators are utilized where the life safety lighting requirements and/or the requirements to drive critical equipment are beyond the capacity of battery units. Engines are cooled by methods illustrated, and should be located in rooms separate from main electrical switchgear. Engine rooms must have adequate ventilation for engine and generator radiated heat and must be protected against extreme environments under all conditions of airflow. Room size and space at sides of power generating unit(s) must be adequate for service. Access to room must allow for removal of generation unit. Standby generators require frequent inspections, tests under load conditions, and maintenance if they are to perform their intended function. Vibration isolation provisions are required to prevent vibration transmission to surrounding occupied areas. In addition to the cooling methods illustrated, cooling by heat exchanger, submerged pipe, cooling tower, and evaporative cooler should be considered.

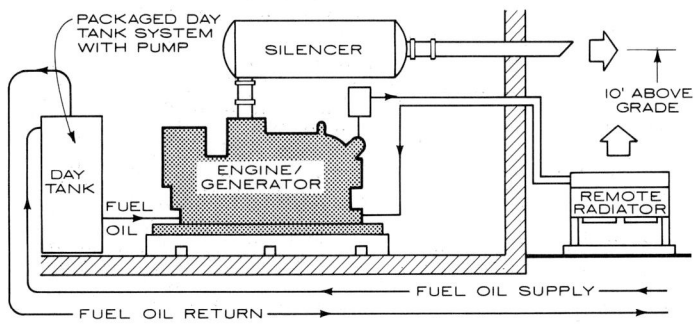

REMOTE RADIATOR

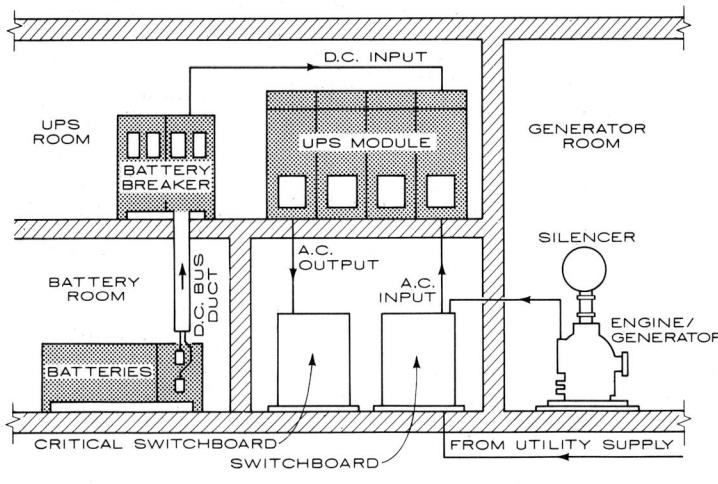

UNINTERRUPTIBLE POWER SUPPLY SYSTEM

Uninterruptible power supply (UPS) systems closely control the power supply voltage and frequency to critical equipment such as computers, communications systems, medical instrumentation, and similar sophisticated loads. Such UPS installations often are served from both utility and standby generator sources and provide "buffering" or complete isolation between the service and the critical load. The UPS batteries supply power through the UPS inverter to the critical AC loads until normal or generator power is restored or until the batteries reach end-of-discharge voltage. UPS systems require frequent inspections, tests, and maintenance if they are to perform their intended function.

UNINTERRUPTIBLE POWER SUPPLY SYSTEM

William Tao & Associates, Inc., Consulting Engineers; St. Louis, Missouri

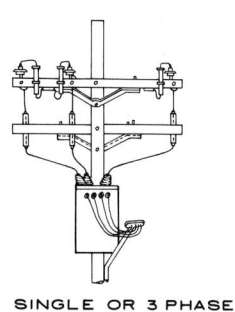

SINGLE OR 3 PHASE

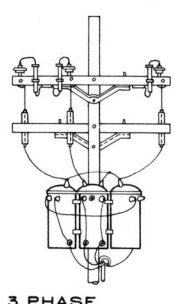

3 PHASE

OVERHEAD TRANSFORMER

OVERHEAD TRANSFORMER: Three phase transformers are available up to 500 kVA in a single unit. Three single phase units can total to 1500 kVA with adequate platform support. Service lateral to building can be either overhead or underground.

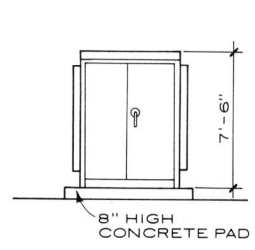

8" HIGH CONCRETE PAD

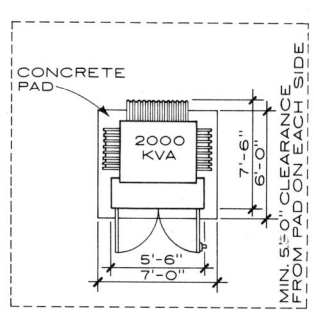

CONCRETE PAD

2000 KVA

5'-6"
7'-0"

7'-6"
6'-0"

MIN. 5'-0" CLEARANCE FROM PAD ON EACH SIDE

PAD MOUNTED TRANSFORMER

PAD MOUNTED TRANSFORMER: Pad mounted transformers with weatherproof tamperproof enclosure permits installation at ground level without danger from exposed live parts. Three phase units up to 2500 kVA are available and are normally used with underground primary and secondary feeders.

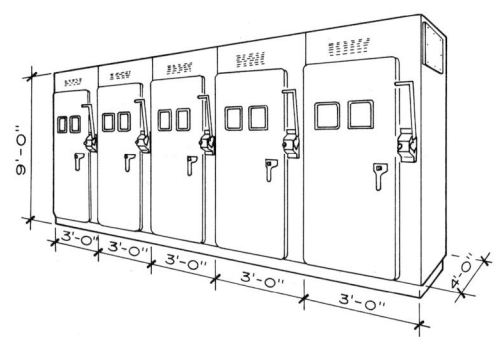

9'-0"

3'-0" 3'-0" 3'-0" 3'-0" 3'-0"

PRIMARY SWITCHGEAR

PRIMARY SWITCHGEAR: Where the owner's buildings cover a large area such as a college campus or medical center, the application usually requires the use of medium voltages of 5 kV to 15 kV for distribution feeders. Therefore, the utility company will terminate their primary feeders on the owner's metal clad or metal enclosed switchgear. This switchgear may be interior or exterior weatherproof construction. Code clearance in front and back of board must be provided in accordance with 1978 National Electric Code, Table 110-34(a); clearances range from 4 to 9 ft.

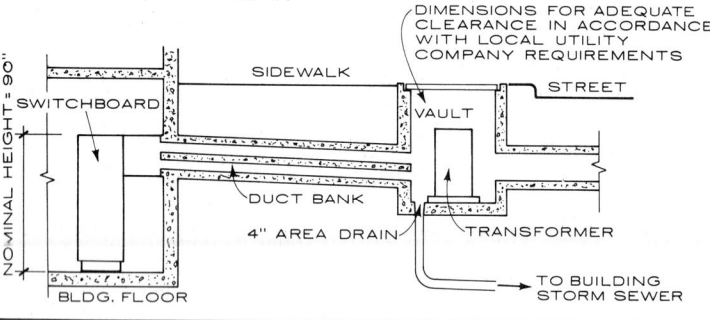

NOMINAL HEIGHT = 90"

SWITCHBOARD

BLDG. FLOOR

DUCT BANK

4" AREA DRAIN

SIDEWALK

DIMENSIONS FOR ADEQUATE CLEARANCE IN ACCORDANCE WITH LOCAL UTILITY COMPANY REQUIREMENTS

VAULT

STREET

TRANSFORMER

TO BUILDING STORM SEWER

UNDERGROUND VAULT

UNDERGROUND VAULT: Underground vaults are generally used for utility company transformers where all distribution feeders are underground. These systems usually constitute a network or spot network. Vaults often are located below the sidewalks and have grating tops.

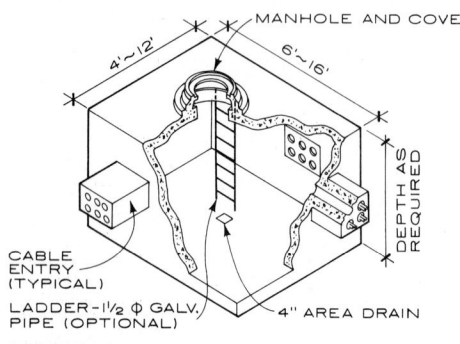

MANHOLE AND COVER

4'~12'
6'~16'

DEPTH AS REQUIRED

CABLE ENTRY (TYPICAL)

LADDER-1½" Ø GALV. PIPE (OPTIONAL)

4" AREA DRAIN

MANHOLE

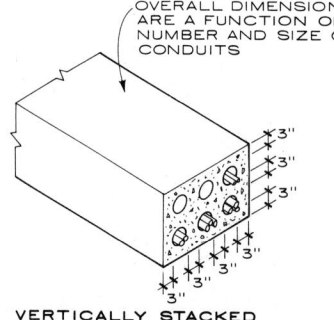

OVERALL DIMENSIONS ARE A FUNCTION OF NUMBER AND SIZE OF CONDUITS

3"
3"
3"
3"
3"

VERTICALLY STACKED

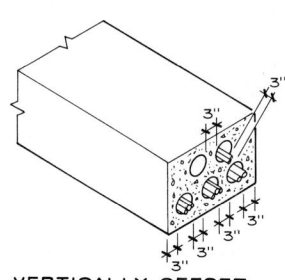

3"
3"
3"
3"
3"

VERTICALLY OFFSET

UNDERGROUND DUCT BANK

William Tao & Associates, Inc., Consulting Engineers; St. Louis, Missouri

SPECIAL SYSTEMS

CHAPTER 17 METRIC (SI) UNITS IN DESIGN AND CONSTRUCTION

SI METRIC BACKGROUND DATA

The metric system originated in France as a product of the French Revolution, and gained gradual acceptance in Europe and in the French and Spanish colonies. In 1875 the United States joined 16 other countries in signing the Treaty of the Meter. The work of the General Conference of Weights and Measures resulted in a revised metric system in 1960, named Système International d'Unités (SI). It is this SI metric system that is referenced in the US Metric Act of 1975, and is presented in this chapter.

The Metric Conversion Act, Public Law 94-168, calls for a voluntary conversion process, and established the US Metric Board. In 1972 the American National Metric Council (ANMC) was formed under the sponsorship of the American National Standards Institute (ANSI). Involving more than 300 trade, professional, labor, consumer, and government organizations and more than 400 major corporations, the American National Metric Council has organized the voluntary conversion process. The ANMC Construction Industries Coordinating Committee (CICC) has prepared a conversion plan for adoption by the industry.

ANSI/ASTM Metric Standards are developed under the jurisdiction of ASTM Committee E-6 on Performance of Building Constructions. Subcommittee E 06.62 on Coordination of Dimensions for Building Materials and Systems has responsibility for such ANSI/ASTM Standards as E621-78 "Metric (SI) Units in Building Design and Construction." In addition, the Center for Building Technology of the National Bureau of Standards has published a number of Technical Notes and other special publications concerning metric conversion and dimensional coordination. The American Institute of Architects, with the cooperation of the ANMC, and the Center for Building Technology, has produced the "AIA Metric Building and Construction Guide." This chapter is based on information contained in that publication.

THE SI SYSTEM

Although the metric (SI) system applies to all measurement related systems, this chapter concerns the application of the SI System to construction. Concepts of dimensional coordination, although not restricted to the metric system, are seen as an essential part of a smooth transition of the construction industry to the use of the metric (SI) system.

MATERIALS AND COMPONENTS FOR METRIC BUILDING IN THE TRANSITIONAL PERIOD—SUGGESTED ADAPTATION IN DESIGN AND CONSTRUCTION FOR VARIOUS PRODUCT CATEGORIES*

CATEGORY	COMPLEXITY OF ADAPTATION	TYPICAL EXAMPLES OF MATERIALS AND COMPONENTS	ADAPTIVE ACTION IN DESIGN	ADAPTIVE ACTION IN CONSTRUCTION
A. DIMENSIONAL COORDINATION NOT REQUIRED				
A.1	No change in materials—no problems foreseen	Formless or plastic materials: water, paint, mastics, tar; sand, cement, lime, dry mortar mix, loose-fill insulation; read-mixed concrete, premixed masonry mortar	Specify in metric units. Develop necessary site guidelines	Weigh or measure in metric quantities. Use metric data on coverage, mix ratios, etc.
A.2	Customary sizes usable—interim "soft conversion"	Structural steel sections, reinforcing bars, pipes, tubes, hardware, fixtures, fittings	Specify metric equivalents or show permissible substitutions. Select preferred "free" dimensions such as length or centerlines	Order or cut to metric length; set out to coordinated centerlines
B. MINOR SITE ADJUSTMENTS TO COORDINATE WITH PREFERRED DIMENSIONS				
B.1	Modification in one direction to fit in with preferred dimensions	a. Adjustment by trimming: lumber studs and joists, laminates, roofing, gutters b. Adjustment by lapping: shingles, tar felt, underlay, sheathing, waterproof membranes c. Adjustment by change in joint width: bricks, blocks, ceramic tiles	Specify preferred metric dimensions to expedite the transition. Indicate construction adjustments in drawings or instructions	Set out project in preferred building dimensions and adjust products accordingly
C. DIMENSIONAL COORDINATION REQUIRED				
C.1	Purpose-made items—no difficulties foreseen	Precast panels and slabs, door assemblies, window assemblies, fabricated metalwork, built-in units	Specify rationalized metric sizes	Order or fabricate components in rationalized metric sizes
C.2	Reshaping of customary dimensions possible	Glazing, plywood, gypsum wallboard, sheathing, lath, rigid insulation materials	Investigate supply in rationalized metric sizes and specify	Order rationalized metric sizes. Cut off site or on site
C.3	Reshaping of customary dimensions difficult, costly, or impossible	Windows, doors, metal partitions, metal roof decking, fluorescent fixture, metal cladding panels, stainless steel sections and sinks, large ceramic panels, distribution boards and panels, fixed appliances and cabinets, lockers	Preorder preferred sizes before job commencement. Discuss trial batches with manufacturers. Use adaptive design and detailing	Adapt during the interim period until preferred metric sizes emerge. Construct suitable openings or spaces for non-coordinated components and assemblies

*The list may be expanded or modified to suit particular market conditions.

LINEAR MEASURE—EQUIVALENTS

MILLIMETERS	CENTIMETERS	DECIMETERS	METERS	DECAMETERS	HECTOMETERS	KILOMETERS	YARDS
1	0.1	0.01	0.001	0.0001	0.00001	0.000001	
10	1	0.1	0.01	0.001	0.0001	0.00001	
100	10	1	0.1	0.01	0.001	0.0001	
1,000	100	10	1	0.1	0.01	0.001	1.0936
10,000	1,000	100	10	1	0.1	0.01	
100,000	10,000	1,000	100	10	1	0.1	
1,000,000	100,000	10,000	1,000	100	10	1	
			.9144				1

AREA MEASURE—EQUIVALENTS

SQUARE MILLIMETERS	SQUARE CENTIMETERS	SQUARE DECIMETERS	SQUARE METERS	ARES	HECTARES	SQUARE KILOMETERS	ACRES
1	0.01	0.0001	0.000001				
100	1	0.01	0.0001	0.000001			
10,000	100	1	0.01	0.0001	0.000001		
1,000,000	10,000	100	1	0.01	0.0001	0.000001	
	1,000,000	10,000	100	1	0.01	0.0001	
		1,000,000	10,000	100	1	0.01	2.471
			1,000,000	10,000	100	1	247.1
				40.47	.4047		1

SI UNITS AND RULES FOR USE

Specific rules for use, type style, and punctuation have been established by the General Conference on Weights and Measures (CGPM); the National Bureau of Standards (NBS) is responsible for determining preferred usage in the United States.

Standard, lowercase type is used for unit names and symbols, except when the symbols are derived from proper names, such as newton (N) or pascal (Pa). There is one exception to this in the use of the capital letter L as the symbol for liter. This is because the lowercase "l" was thought by the U.S. Department of Commerce to be easily confused with the numeral "1." Symbols are not followed by a period or a full stop, except at the end of a sentence. The symbols for all quantities, such as length, mass, and time, are printed in italic ($l, k, s, . . .$). In typewriting and longhand, underlining is an acceptable substitute for italic letters. Unit names are used in the plural to express numerical values greater than 1, equal to 0, or less than -1. All other values take the singular form of the unit name, thus 100 meters, 1.1 meters, 0 degrees Celsius, -4 degrees Celsius, 0.5 meter, $1/2$ liter, -0.2 degree Celsius, -1 degree Celsius. The plural of unit names is formed by adding an "s." Exceptions are hertz, lux, and siemens, which remain unchanged, and henry, which becomes henries. Symbols are the same in both singular and plural.

Prefixes denoting decimal multiples and submultiples (allowing SI units to express magnitudes from the sub-atomic to the astronomic) are governed by the same rules concerning capitalization and punctuation.

It is important to note that mega, giga, and tera (M, G, T) are capitalized in symbol form to avoid confusion with established unit symbols, but they maintain the lowercase form when spelled out in full. No space is left between the prefix and the letter for the unit name, thus mL (milliliter), mm (millimeter), kA (kiloampere).

Preference is given to the use of decimal multiples that are related to the basic units by multiples of 1000. As far as possible, prefixes denoting magnitudes of 100, 10, 0.1, and 0.01 should be limited. Certain multiples of SI units, not likely to be extensively used, have been given special names (Table 4).

The prefix symbol is considered to be part of the unit symbol and is attached to it without a space or dot, thus km not k m, k-m, or k.m.

A space is left between a numeral and the unit name or symbol to which it refers, thus 20 mm, 10^6 N. In angle measure no space is left between the numeral and the degree symbol, thus $27°$. The symbol for degree Celsius $°C$ is an inseparable symbol with no space between the two parts; it is also preferable to leave no space between the numeral and the unit, thus $20°C$.

When a quantity is used as an adjective, it is preferable to use a hyphen instead of a space between the number and the unit name or between the number and the symbol; thus a 3-meter pole, a 35-mm film.

In the United States and Canada, the decimal point is a dot on the line, but in some other countries a comma or a raised dot is used.

Decimal notation is preferred with metric measurements, but simple fractions are acceptable (except on engineering drawings), such as those where the denominator is 2, 3, 4, 5, 8, and 10.

Examples: 0.5 g, 1.75 kg, and 0.7 L are preferred; $1/2$ g, $1^3/4$ kg, and $7/10$ L are acceptable (except on engineering drawings).

A zero before the decimal point should be used in numbers between 1 and -1 to prevent the possibility that a faint decimal point will be overlooked.

Example: The oral expression "point seven five" is written 0.75.

Since the comma is used as the decimal marker in many countries, a comma should not be used to separate groups of digits. Instead, the digits should be separated into groups of three, counting both to the left and to the right from the decimal point, and a space used to separate the groups of three digits. The space should be of fixed width, equal to that formerly occupied by the comma.

Examples: 4 720 525   0. 528 75

If there are only four digits to the left or right of the decimal point, the space is acceptable but is not preferred.

Examples: 6875 or 6 875
0.1234 or 0.123 4

However, in a column with other numbers that show the space and are aligned on the decimal point, the space is necessary.

Example: 14.8
            3 780
          $+$12 100
          15 894.8

Compound units are those formed by combining simple units by means of the mathematical signs for multiplication and division and by the use of exponents.

When writing symbols for units such as square centimeter or cubic meter, the symbol for the unit should be written followed by the superscript ^{2} or ^{3}, respectively, thus 26 cm^2 and 14 m^3.

For a compound unit that is a quotient, "per" should be used to form the name (kilometer per hour) and a slash (/) to form the symbol (km/h). There is no space before or after the slash. Compound units that are quotients may also be written by using negative exponents (km $\cdot$ h^{-1}).

For everyday rounding of metric values obtained by converting untoleranced customary values, the following simplified rules are suggested:

1. If the customary value is expressed by a combination of units such as feet and inches, or pounds and ounces, first express it in terms of the smaller unit.
   Example: 14 ft 5 in. = 173 in.
2. When the digits to be discarded begin with a 5 or more, increase by one unit the last digit retained.
   Example: 8.3745, if rounded to three digits, would be 8.37; if rounded to four digits, 8.375.
3. Multiply the customary value by the conversion factor. If the first significant digit of the metric value is equal to or larger than the first significant digit of the customary value, round the metric value to the same number of significant digits as there are in the customary value.
   Examples: 11 mi x 1.609 km/mi = 17.699 km, which rounds to 18 km

   61 mi x 1.609 km/mi = 98.149 km, which rounds to 98 km
4. If smaller, round to one more significant digit.
   Examples: 66 mi x 1.609 km/mi = 106.194 km, which rounds to 106 km

   8 ft x 0.3048 m/ft = 2.4384 m, which rounds to 2.4 m
   Exceptions: It is sometimes better to round to one less digit than specified above. For example, according to the foregoing, 26 pounds per square inch air pressure in an automobile tire would be converted as follows:

   26 psi* x 6.895 kPa/psi = 179.27 kPa

   which rounds to 179 kPa

   but kPa, where the zero is not a significant digit, would usually be better because tire pressures are not expected to be very precise. The rules do not apply to conversion of $°F$ to $°C$.
5. Where a customary value represents a maximum or minimum limit that must be respected, the rounding must be in the direction that does not violate the original limit.

TABLE 1.   SI BASE UNITS

PHYSICAL QUANTITY	UNIT	SYMBOL
Length	Meter	m
Mass	Kilogram	k
Time	Second	s
Electric current	Ampere	A
Thermodynamic temperature	Kelvin	K
Luminous intensity	Candela	cd
Amount of substance	Mole	mol

TABLE 2.   SI SUPPLEMENTARY UNITS

PHYSICAL QUANTITY	UNIT	SYMBOL
Plane angle	Radian	rad
Solid angle	Steradian	sr

TABLE 3.   DERIVED UNITS WITH COMPOUND NAMES

PHYSICAL QUANTITY	UNIT	SYMBOL
Area	Square meter	m^2
Volume	Cubic meter	m^3
Density	Kilogram per cubic meter	kg/m^3
Velocity	Meter per second	m/s
Angular velocity	Radian per second	rad/s
Acceleration	Meter per second squared	m/s^2
Angular acceleration	Radian per second squared	rad/s^2
Volume rate of flow	Cubic meter per second	m^3/s
Moment of inertia	Kilogram meter squared	kg $\cdot$ m^2
Moment of force	Newton meter	N $\cdot$ m
Intensity of heat flow	Watt per square meter	W/m^2
Thermal conductivity	Watt per meter Kelvin	W/m $\cdot$ K
Luminance	Candela per square meter	cd/m^2

TABLE 4.   MULTIPLES OF SI UNITS WITH SPECIAL NAMES

PHYSICAL QUANTITY	NAME	SYMBOL	MAGNITUDE
Volume	Liter	L	10^{-3} m^3 = 0.0001 m^3
Mass	Megagram (metric ton)	Mg(t)	10^3 kg = 1000 kg
Area	Hectare	ha	10^4 m^2 = 10 000 m^2
Pressure	Millibar*	mbar*	10^2 Pa = 100 Pa

*Used for meteorological purposes only.

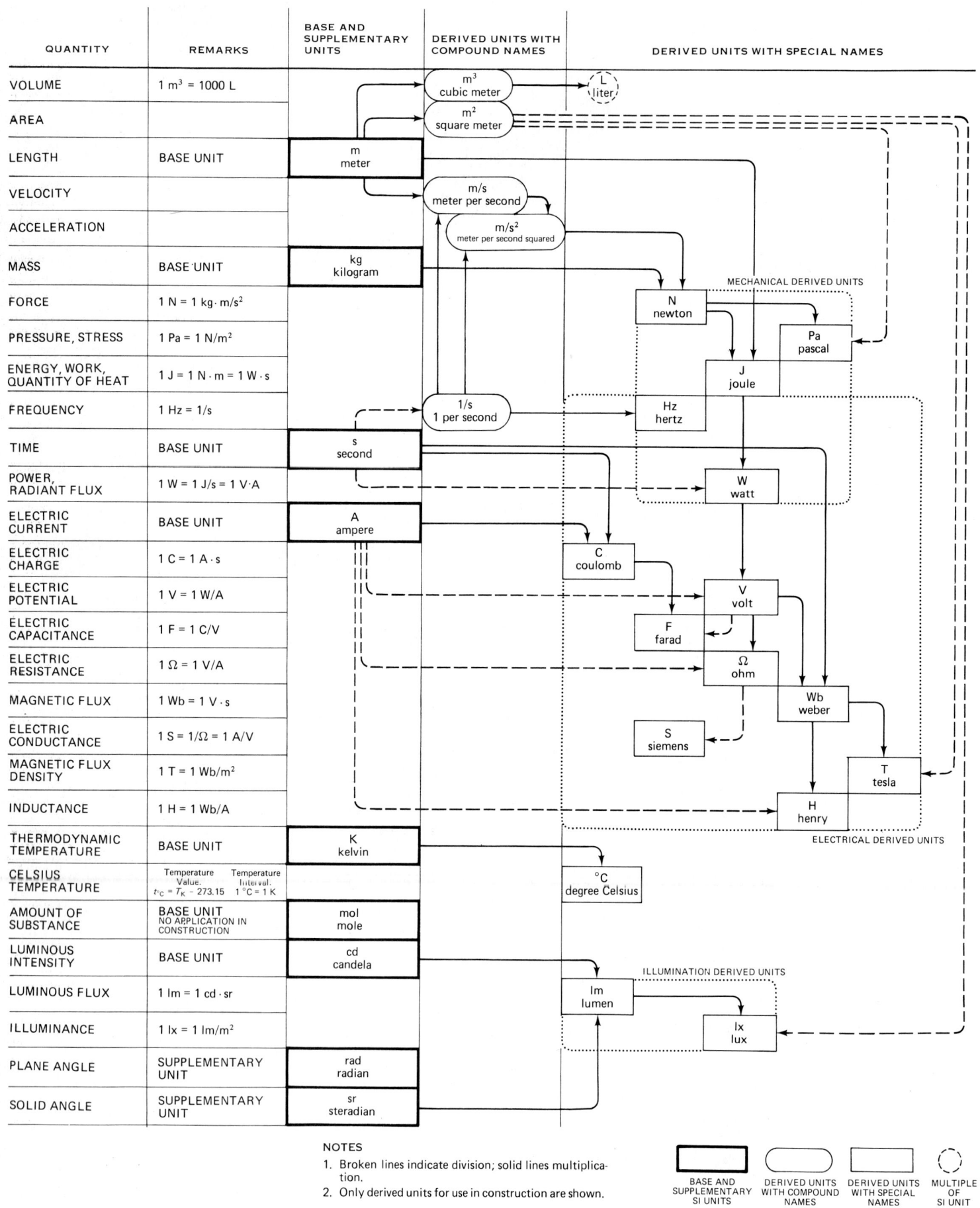

QUANTITY	REMARKS	BASE AND SUPPLEMENTARY UNITS	DERIVED UNITS WITH COMPOUND NAMES	DERIVED UNITS WITH SPECIAL NAMES
VOLUME	1 m³ = 1000 L		m³ cubic meter	L liter
AREA			m² square meter	
LENGTH	BASE UNIT	m meter		
VELOCITY			m/s meter per second	
ACCELERATION			m/s² meter per second squared	
MASS	BASE UNIT	kg kilogram		
FORCE	1 N = 1 kg·m/s²			N newton
PRESSURE, STRESS	1 Pa = 1 N/m²			Pa pascal
ENERGY, WORK, QUANTITY OF HEAT	1 J = 1 N·m = 1 W·s			J joule
FREQUENCY	1 Hz = 1/s		1/s 1 per second	Hz hertz
TIME	BASE UNIT	s second		
POWER, RADIANT FLUX	1 W = 1 J/s = 1 V·A			W watt
ELECTRIC CURRENT	BASE UNIT	A ampere		
ELECTRIC CHARGE	1 C = 1 A·s			C coulomb
ELECTRIC POTENTIAL	1 V = 1 W/A			V volt
ELECTRIC CAPACITANCE	1 F = 1 C/V			F farad
ELECTRIC RESISTANCE	1 Ω = 1 V/A			Ω ohm
MAGNETIC FLUX	1 Wb = 1 V·s			Wb weber
ELECTRIC CONDUCTANCE	1 S = 1/Ω = 1 A/V			S siemens
MAGNETIC FLUX DENSITY	1 T = 1 Wb/m²			T tesla
INDUCTANCE	1 H = 1 Wb/A			H henry
THERMODYNAMIC TEMPERATURE	BASE UNIT	K kelvin		
CELSIUS TEMPERATURE	Temperature Value. $t_C = T_K - 273.15$ Temperature Interval. $1\,°C = 1\,K$			°C degree Celsius
AMOUNT OF SUBSTANCE	BASE UNIT NO APPLICATION IN CONSTRUCTION	mol mole		
LUMINOUS INTENSITY	BASE UNIT	cd candela		
LUMINOUS FLUX	1 lm = 1 cd·sr			lm lumen
ILLUMINANCE	1 lx = 1 lm/m²			lx lux
PLANE ANGLE	SUPPLEMENTARY UNIT	rad radian		
SOLID ANGLE	SUPPLEMENTARY UNIT	sr steradian		

MECHANICAL DERIVED UNITS

ELECTRICAL DERIVED UNITS

ILLUMINATION DERIVED UNITS

NOTES

1. Broken lines indicate division; solid lines multiplication.
2. Only derived units for use in construction are shown.

| BASE AND SUPPLEMENTARY SI UNITS | DERIVED UNITS WITH COMPOUND NAMES | DERIVED UNITS WITH SPECIAL NAMES | MULTIPLE OF SI UNIT |

Hans J. Milton, FRAIA, Technical Consultant, National Bureau of Standards; Gaithersburg, Maryland

17

GENERAL INFORMATION

MEASUREMENT OF LENGTH

The basic SI unit of length is the meter. Fractions or multiples of the base unit are expressed with prefixes, only some of which are recommended for construction. In order to be clear, avoid those prefixes that are not specifically recommended for construction.

Common SI units for length as used in construction are:

UNIT NAME	SYMBOL	COMMENT	COMPUTER SYMBOL
Meter	m	Also spelled metre	M
Millimeter	mm	0.001 meter	MM
Kilometer	km	1000 meters	KM
Micrometer	um	0.000 001 meter	UM

Note: Centimeter is not recommended for construction.

The recommended unit for dimensioning buildings is the millimeter. The use of the meter would be limited to large dimensions, such as levels, overall dimensions, and engineering computations. Meters are also used for estimating and land surveying. On architectural drawings, dimensions require no symbol if millimeters are consistently used.

Kilometers are used for transportation and surveying. Micrometers would be used for thicknesses of materials, such as coatings.

Conversion factors for length are shown below:

METRIC	CUSTOMARY
1 meter	3.280 84 feet or 1.093 61 yards
1 millimeter	0.039 370 1 inch
1 kilometer	0.621 371 mile or 49.709 6 chains
1 micrometer	0.000 393 7 inch or 0.3937 mils

CUSTOMARY	METRIC
1 mile	1.609 344 km
1 chain	20.1168 m
1 yard	0.9144 m
1 foot	0.3048 m / 304.8 mm
1 inch	25.4 mm

(1 U.S. survey foot = 0.304 800 6 m.)

The recommended linear basic module for construction is 100 mm in the United States. See page on dimensional coordination for application of this basic module. This is very close to the 4 in. module in general use for light construction. Scales of drawing relate to units of length. Use meters on all drawings with scale ratios between 1:200 and 1:2000. Use millimeters on drawings with scale ratios between 1:1 and 1:200.

MEASUREMENT OF AREA

There are no basic SI metric units for area. Rather, area units are derived from units for length, as follows:

UNIT NAME	SYMBOL	COMMENT
Square meter	m^2	$1\ m^2 = 10^6\ mm^2$
Square millimeter	mm^2	
Square kilometer	km^2	Land area
Hectare	ha	$1\ ha = 10\ 000\ m^2$

Note that the hectare, although not an SI unit, is acceptable as a supplemental unit. It is used for surface measurement of land and water only.

At times, area is expressed by linear dimensions such as 40 mm x 90 mm; 300 x 600. Normally the width is written first and depth or height second.

The square centimeter is not recommended for construction. Such measurements may be converted to millimeters (1 cm² = 100 mm²) or to meters (1 cm² = 10^{-4} m² = 0.0001 m²).

Conversion factors for area are shown below.

METRIC	CUSTOMARY
1 km²	0.386 101 mile² (U.S. Survey)
1 ha	2.471 04 acre (U.S. Survey)
1 m²	10.7639 ft² / 1.195 99 yd²
1 mm²	0.001 550 in.²

CUSTOMARY	METRIC
1 mile² (U.S. Survey)	2.590 00 km²
1 acre (U.S. Survey)	0.404 687 ha / 4046.87 m²
1 yd²	0.836 127 m²
1 ft²	0.092 903 m²
1 in.²	645.16 mm²

MEASUREMENT OF VOLUME AND SECTION MODULUS

There are no basic SI metric units for volume, but these are derived from units for length as well as non-SI units that are acceptable for use.

UNIT NAME	SYMBOL	COMMENT
Cubic meter	m^3	$1\ m^3 = 1000\ L$
Cubic millimeter	mm^3	
Liter	L	Volume of fluids
Milliliter	mL	$1\ mL = 1\ cm^3$
Cubic centimeter	cm^3	$1\ cm^3 = 1000\ mm^3$

In construction, the cubic meter is used for volume and capacity of large quantities of earth, concrete, sand, and so on. It is preferred for all engineering purposes.

The section modulus is also expressed as unit of length to the third power (m^3 and mm^3).

Conversion factors are listed below.

VOLUME, MODULUS OF SECTION

METRIC	CUSTOMARY
1 m³	$0.810\ 709 \times 10^3$ acre ft / 1.307 95 yd³ / 35.3147 ft³ / 423.776 board ft
1 mm³	61.0237×10^{-6} in.³

CUSTOMARY	METRIC
1 acre ft	1233.49 m³
1 yd³	0.764 555 m³
100 board ft	0.028 316 8 m³
1 ft³	16.387 1 mm³ / 28 3168 1 (cm³)
1 in.³	16.3871 mL(cm³)

LIQUID, CAPACITY

METRIC	CUSTOMARY
1 L	0.035 3147 ft³ / 0.264 172 gal (U.S.) / 1.056 69 qt (U.S.)
1 mL	0.061 023 7 in.³

CUSTOMARY	METRIC
1 gal (U.S. liquid)	3.785 41 L
1 qt (U.S. liquid)	946.353 mL
1 pt (U.S. liquid)	473.177 mL
1 fl oz (U.S.)	29.5735 mL

NOTE: 1 gal (U.K.) = approximately 1.2 gal (U.S.).

MEASUREMENT OF MASS

The SI metric system recommends the use of the word mass in place of the more common word weight, because weight refers specifically to the pull of gravity, which can vary in different locations. The SI system also separates the concept of mass from that of force.

SI metric units and other acceptable units for mass are:

UNIT NAME	SYMBOL	COMMENT
Kilogram	kg	Most used
Gram	g	
Metric ton	t	1 t = 1000 kg

The kilogram is based on a prototype, and unlike other SI units cannot be derived without reference to the international prototype kilogram maintained under specified conditions at the International Bureau of Weights and Measures (BIPM) near Paris, France.

Conversion factors are listed below.

METRIC	CUSTOMARY
1 kg	2.204 62 lb (avoirdupois) / 35.2740 02 oz (avoirdupois)
1 metric ton	1.102 31 ton (short, 2000 lb) / 2204.62 lb
1 g	0.035 274 oz / 0.643 015 pennyweight

CUSTOMARY	METRIC
1 ton (short)	0.907 185 metric ton (megagram) / 907.185 kg
1 lb	0.453 592 kg
1 oz	28.3495 9 g
1 pennyweight	1.555 17 g

NOTE: A long ton (2240 lb) = 1016.05 kg or 1.016 05 metric ton.

TIME

The SI unit for time is the second, from which other units of time are derived. In construction measurements, such as flow rates, the use of minutes is not recommended, so that cubic meters per second, liters per second, or cubic meters per hour would be normally used. Time symbols are as follows:

Second	s
Minute	min
Hour	h
Day	d
Month	—
Year	a (365 days or 31 536 000 seconds)

For clarity, international recommendations for writing time and dates are as follows:

Time   Express by hour/minute/second on a 24 hour day:

03:20:30
16:45

Dates   Express by year/month/day:

1978-06-30
1978 06 30 (second preference)
19780630 (computer entry)

MEASUREMENT OF TEMPERATURE

The SI base unit of temperature is the Kelvin, which is a scale based on absolute zero. The allowable unit Celsius is equal to the Kelvin unit except that 0° Celsius is the freezing point of water. Thus a temperature listed in degrees Celsius plus 275.15 degrees is the temperature in degrees Kelvin. Celsius is in common use for construction, not Kelvin.

CUSTOMARY	METRIC
1°F	0.555 556°C / $^5/_9$ ° C or $^5/_9$ K

METRIC	CUSTOMARY
1°C	1 K / 1.8°F

NOTE: Centigrade is not recognized as part of the SI system.

PLANE ANGLE

While the SI unit for plane angle is the radian, the customary units degree (°), minute ('), and second ('') of arc will be retained in most applications in construction, engineering, and land surveying.

CUSTOMARY	METRIC
1°	$(\pi/180)$ rad

ENERGY RELATIONSHIP

SI metric units provide a direct, coherent relationship between mechanical, thermal, and electrical energy.

The ampere (A) (SI base unit) is that constant current which, if maintained in two straight, parallel conductors of infinite length and of negligible cross section, placed 1 meter apart in a vacuum, would produce between these conductors a force equal to 2×10^{-7} newton per meter of length.

One newton (N) is that force which gives to a mass of 1 kilogram (kg) an acceleration of 1 meter per second squared (m/s^2). Hence 1.0 N = 1.0 kg · m/s^2.

One joule (J) is the work done when the point of application of a force of 1 newton moves a distance of 1 meter along the line of action of the force. Hence 1.0 J = 1.0 N · m.

A watt (W) is the power which in 1 second gives rise to the energy of 1 joule. Conversely, a joule is a watt-second.

Since the customary coherent relationships with other electrical quantities will still prevail, the observations made above in respect to work, energy, quantity of heat, and power may be summarized, from a "units" point of view as follows:

N · m = J   J/s = W   J = W · s   W = A · V   J = A · V · s

MASS

The preferred unit multiples of mass are milligram, gram, kilogram, and megagram (or metric ton), which are written respectively as:

mg   g   kg   Mg   (or t)

Weight is predominantly a concept of the customary "gravitational" system. Since SI is an absolute system dealing with mass and with the forces related to the acceleration of a mass, there is no special name for a unit of weight in SI.

Weight in a particular force due solely to gravitational attraction on a mass.

FORCE

Since SI is a coherent system and since the fundamental law of physics (F α ma) states that force is dependent solely on mass and on acceleration,

1.0 kg accelerated at 1.0 m/s^2

$\longrightarrow$ 1.0 force unit

$\longrightarrow$ 1.0 newton (1.0 N)

The use of the name "newton" for the unit of force should fix in the mind the full significance of the distinctions between mass and force.

Normally a mass to be supported or moved will be specified or labeled in terms of kilograms (kg), but all forces acting on structure, either gravitationally or laterally (including wind, sway, and impact), should be specified or determined ultimately in terms of newtons (N).

Based on customary gravitational usage:

Mass: 1.0 slug   32.17 lb   14.59 kg

1.488 kgf/(m/s^2)

Force: 1.0 lbf   32.17 pdl   4.448 N

0.4536 kgf

Based on SI usage:

Mass: 1.0 kg   2.205 lb   0.068 52 slug

0.1020 kgf/(m/s^2)

Force: 1.0 N   7.233 pdl   0.2248 lbf

0.1020 kgf

The force definitions are as follows:

The "newton" is the force required to accelerate 1 kilogram mass at the rate of 1.0 m/s^2.

The "poundal" is the force required to accelerate 1 pound of mass at the rate of 1.0 ft/s^2.

The "pound force" is the force required to accelerate 1 pound of mass at the rate of 32.1740 ft/s^2.

The related definitions for the derived mass units are:

The "slug" is that mass which, when acted upon by 1 pound-force, will be accelerated at the rate of 1.0 ft/s^2.

The gravitational metric unit of mass is that unit of mass which, when acted upon by 1 kilogram-force, will be accelerated at 1.0 m/s^2. There seems to be no generally accepted name or symbol for this gravitational unit of mass, except the inference to the kilogram.

The "kilogram" and the "pound" are base units, not derived units as are the slug and the gravitational metric unit of mass. The kilogram and the pound relate directly to an artifact of mass which, by convention, is regarded as dimensionally independent—thus the name "base unit."

DERIVED UNITS WITH SPECIAL NAMES

PHYSICAL QUANTITY	UNIT	SYMBOL	DERIVATION
Frequency	Hertz	Hz	s^{-1}
Force	Newton	N	kg · m/s^2
Pressure, stress	Pascal	Pa	N/m^2
Work, energy, quantity of heat	Joule	J	N · m
Power	Watt	W	J/s
Electric charge	Coulomb	C	A · s
Electric potential	Volt	V	W/A
Electric capacitance	Farad	F	C/V
Electric resistance	Ohm	O	V/A
Electric conductance	Siemens	S	Ω^{-1}
Magnetic flux	Weber	Wb	V · s
Magnetic flux density	Tesla	T	Wb/m^2
Inductance	Henry	H	Wb/A
Celsius temperature	Degree Celsius	°C	K
Luminous flux	Lumen	lm	cd · sr
Illumination	Lux	lx	lm/m^2
Activity	Becquerel	Bq	s^{-1}
Absorbed dose	Gray	Gy	J/kg

COMPARISON OF UNIT SYSTEMS

QUANTITY	MASS LENGTH, TIME (ABSOLUTE)		FORCE, LENGTH, TIME (GRAVITATIONAL)		CUSTOMARY COMBINED SYSTEM
	SI	ENGLISH	METRIC	ENGLISH	
Mass	kg	lb	kgf/(m/s^2)	lbf/(ft/s^2) (slug)	lb (alt: lbm)
Force	kg m/s^2 N (newton)	lb ft/s^2 1 dp (poundal)	kgf (alt:kp)	lbf	lbf
Coherence factor	1.0	1.0	1.0	1.0	1/32.17

COMPARATIVE ANALYSIS OF SOME APPROXIMATE PHYSICAL PROPERTIES[a] FOR REPRESENTATIVE ENGINEERING MATERIALS

IN TERMS OF U.S. CUSTOMARY UNITS								IN TERMS OF PREFERRED SI UNITS						
COEFFICIENT OF LINEAR EXPANSION α (10^6 IN./IN °F)	ALLOWABLE STRESSES (LBF/IN.^{2} x 10^3)			ELASTIC MODULUS (LBF/IN.^{2} x 10^6)		WEIGHT DENSITY W (LB/FT^3)	MATERIAL	MASS DENSITY ρ (KG/M^3)	ELASTIC MODULUS (GPA = GN/M^2)		ALLOWABLE STRESSES (MPA = MN/M^2)			COEFFICIENT OF LINEAR EXPANSION α µM/(M · K)
	σ_f^b	σ_c^c	τ_s	E	G				E	G	σ_f^b	σ_c^c	τ_s	
6.5	20	20	10	30	12	490	Mild steel	7850	200	80	140	140	70	11.7
6.9	24	24	15	30	12	490	High-strength steel	7850	200	80	165	165	100	12.4
6.0	3	10	2	15	6	450	Cast iron	7200	100	40	20	70	15	10.8
9.3	8	8	5	17	6.4	560	Copper	8960	120	45	55	55	35	16.7
10.4	12	8	6	13	5	520	Brass	8300	90	35	80	55	40	18.7
13.0	16	15	8	10.3	4	170	Aluminum	2700	70	27	110	100	55	23.4
							Timber							
1.7	1.3	0.8	0.05	1.2	—	27	Softwood	430	9	—	9.6	5.5	0.3	3.1
2.5	1.8	1.2	0.10	1.6	—	48	Hardwood	770	12	—	12.4	8.3	0.7	4.5
6.2	1.2	1.0	0.15	2.5	—	150	Concrete (reinf.)	2400	17	—	8.3	6.9	1.0	11.2
—	—	0.03	—	—	—	105	Soil	1680	—	—	—	0.2	—	—
4.4	—	0.3	—	—	—	165	Rock	2640	—	—	—	2.0	—	7.9
	—	—	—	—	—	62.4	Water	1000	—	—	—	—	—	—

NOTE: Values given are rounded in each system and are not direct conversions.
[a] For use only for comparing representative values in the respective unit systems; not intended for design. For design purposes see other standard references such as ANSI, AISC, ACI, and IFI.
[b] Extreme fiber bending.
[c] Short compression block; in timber, parallel to grain.

UNITS FOR USE IN HEAT TRANSFER CALCULATIONS

QUANTITY NAME	SI UNIT	UNIT NAME	CONVERSION FACTOR	
Energy, quantity of heat (E, Q)	J(W · s)	joule	1 Btu (int.) 1 kWh 1 therm 1 Btu/h 1 Btu/s	= 1.055 056 kJ = 3.6 MJ = 105.5056 MJ = 0.293 071 W = 1.055 056 kW
Heat flow rate (P, q)	W(J/s)	watt	1 ton (refrig.)	= 3.516 800 kW
Specific energy, calorific value (mass basis) Irradiation, intensity of heat flow, heat loss from surfaces	J/kg W/m²	joule per kilogram watt per square meter	1 Btu/lb 1 Btu/ft ² · h 1 W/ft² 1 Btu/ft² · s	= 2.326 kJ/kg = 3.152 481 W/m² = 10.763 91 W/m² = 11.348 93 kW/m²
Specific heat capacity (mass basis) Thermal conductivity (k-value)	J/(kg · K) W/(m · K)	joule per kilogram kelvin watt per meter kelvin	1 Btu/lb · °F 1 Btu · in/h · ft² · °F 1 Btu · in/s · ft² · °F 1 Btu/h · ft · °F	= 4.1868 kJ/(kg · K) = 0.144 228 W/(m · K) = 519.2204 W/(m · K) = 1.730 73 W/(m · K)
Thermal conductance, coefficient of heat transfer (c, U-value) Thermal resistance, thermal insulance (R)	W/(m² · K) m² · K/W	watt per square meter kelvin square meter kelvin per watt	1 Btu/h · ft² · °F 1 °F · h · ft²/Btu	= 5.678 26 W/(m² · K) = 0.176 110 m² · K/W

HEAT TRANSFER IN BUILDINGS

Heat transfer calculations, involving heat loss, heat gain, or thermal insulating properties of materials, will be simplified in SI because of the coherent relationships between units used. Heat transfer units are generally derived from the unit for temperature (kelvin or degree Celsius), the unit for energy and quantity of heat (joule), the unit for heat transfer rate (watt), and the units for time (second), length (meter), areas (square meter), and mass (kilogram).

TEMPERATURE

The Celsius temperature scale, for which the zero reference is the freezing point of water, will also be used for ambient temperatures.

TIME

Use of the hour (h), as in 5 km/h, and the day (d), as in m³/d, will occur in special cases, but the use of the minute (min) will be deemphasized in favor of the second (s).

HEATING DEGREE-DAYS

For heating design purposes and the determination of suitable insulation, the concept of heating degree-days, founded on a base temperature of 65°F (18.33°C), will possibly be revised to use a base temperature of 18°C (64.4°F).

In heat transfer through a composite element, such as a building wall, a sequence of conduction and convection coefficients may be involved. As in other "series type" problems the approach to determining the combined or "overall" coefficient U is based on the sum of the resistances, which is the sum of the reciprocals of the conductances in the path of the heat transfer.

The following definitions can be used to identify the coefficients:

K = thermal conductance;

$$K = \frac{kA}{L} \frac{W}{m \cdot K} \times \frac{m^2}{m} = W/K$$

R = thermal resistance;

$$R = \frac{L}{kA} \frac{m \cdot K}{W} \times \frac{m}{m^2} = K/W$$

Frequently, these factors may be stated in terms of unit areas. Any data taken from reference tables should be checked carefully.

The overall heat transfer relationship can be stated as:

$$q = U \cdot A \cdot \Delta T$$

where q = heat transfer rate
A = cross-sectional area of heat, W(=J/s) transfer path, m²
ΔT = overall temperature differential, K
U = overall heat transfer coefficient, W/(m · K)

To determine U is often necessary to use the relationship:

$$\frac{1}{U} = R_1 + R_2 + R_3, \text{ etc.}; \quad \frac{1}{U} = R_1$$

Alternatively, this may be stated as:

$$R_1 = \frac{1}{h_i} + \frac{L_2}{k_2} + \frac{L_3}{k_3} + \frac{1}{h_c}$$

EXAMPLE CALCULATION OF HEAT LOSS THROUGH A WALL

An exterior building wall consists of 100 mm of brick, 200 mm of dense concrete, and 20 mm of gypsum plaster, for which the thermal conductivities are, respectively, k = 0.50, 1.50, and 1.20 W/(m · K). The surface heat transfer (film) coefficients are as follows: (interior) h_i = 8.1 and (exterior) h_c = 19.0 W/(m² · K). What is the heat loss through a 2400 mm (2.4 m) by 6000 mm (6.0 m) panel of this wall when there is a temperature difference of 30°C (30°K)?

THERMAL CONDUCTIVITY

The thermal conductivity, or k-value, of a material is defined as the amount of heat energy conducted through a unit area of unit thickness in unit time with unit temperature difference between the two faces. In SI the unit W/(m · K) replaces Btu · in/h · ft² · °F, but if unit time is considered useful, the alternative expression is J/(s · m · K), because 1 W = 1 J/s. Unit thickness has been canceled out against unit area; otherwise the expression should be J · m/(s · m² · K), which directly resembles the customary expression in terms of constituent units.

OVERALL HEAT TRANSFER

Conductivity generally increases with the level of absolute temperature. Some typical thermal conductivities (k-values) at 300 K are:

MATERIAL OR SUBSTANCE	K = W/(m · K)
Copper	386
Aluminum	202
Steel	55
Concrete	0.9-1.4
Glass	0.8-1.1
Brick	0.4-0.7
Water	0.614
Mineral wool	0.04
Air	0.0262

Computation of thermal resistance:

$$R_T = \frac{1}{8.1} + \frac{0.100}{0.50} + \frac{0.200}{1.50} + \frac{0.020}{1.20} + \frac{1}{19.0}$$

$$= 0.5261 \text{ m}^2 \cdot \text{K/W}$$

$$U = \frac{1}{R_T}; \quad U = 1.901 \text{ W/(m}^2 \cdot \text{K)}$$

$$q = U \cdot A \cdot \Delta T$$

$$q = 1.901(2.4 \times 6.0)30$$

$$= 821 \text{ W} = 821 \text{ J/s}$$

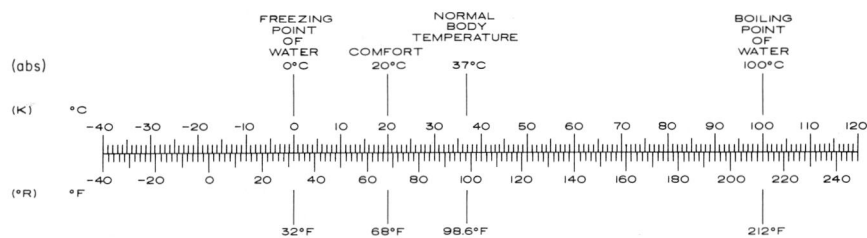

TEMPERATURE CONVERSION

ENERGY VALUES FOR ALTERNATIVE ENERGY SOURCES

ENERGY SOURCE AND QUANTITY	VALUE (MEGAJOULES, MJ)
1 kg of dry wood (8600 Btu/lb)	20
1 kg of bituminous coal (25 800 000 Btu/ton)	30
1 L of kerosene (135 000 Btu/gal)	37.6
1 L of crude oil (5 800 000 Btu/barrel)	38.5
1 m³ of natural gas (1050 Btu/ft³)	39
1 kWh of electricity	3.6
1 therm (100,000 Btu)	105.5

MOMENT BENDING, TORSIONAL

Bending moment and torsional moment are concepts of statics. Both involve the production of a force and a perpendicular distance, the latter being termed the moment arm. Thus the primary SI unit is the newton-meter, which may be symbolized as N · m, kN · m, and so on.

TORQUE

When rotation occurs as a result of an applied moment the condition is one requiring the application of the principles of dynamics. In such cases the key factor is torque, which is based on a product of force and distance moved along the line of action of the force. This product is expressed in newton-meters per radian (N · m/rad), which is equal to joules per radian (J/rad). The radian may be omitted where only complete revolutions are of concern or where dynamic conditions are equated instantaneously with static conditions.

PRESSURE, STRESS, ELASTIC MODULUS

These may be stated directly either in pascals (Pa) or in newtons per square meter (N/m²). Common multiples are kPa, MPa, GPa or kN/m², MN/m², GN/m². Occasionally stress is expressed in newtons per square millimeter (N/mm²).

MOMENT OF INERTIA

The mass moment of inertia of any body relating to rotation about a given axis is the second moment of the particles of that mass about the given axis and as such is given generally in kilogram-square meters per radian squared (kg · m²/rad²). The radius of gyration is normally given in meters per radian (m/rad). The radian may be omitted where only complete revolutions are of concern or where dynamic conditions are equated instantaneously with static conditions.

Second moment of area (1) and section modulus (S) of the cross-section of structural sections or machine parts are usually preferred in terms of 10^6 mm⁴ and 10^3 mm³, respectively, for consistency with other dimensions of sections, which usually will be given in millimeters.

ANGULAR MEASURE

The "radian" (rad), although not a base unit, is specifically identified as a "supplementary unit" and as such is the preferred unit for measurement of plane angles. The customary units of degrees, minutes, and seconds of angular measure are considered to be outside SI, but are acceptable where there is a specific practical reason to use them, as in cartography. If degrees are to be used, a statement of parts of degrees in decimals is preferred. The SI unit of solid angle is the "steradian" (sr).

FLUID MECHANICS

Fluid mechanics utilizes the physical concepts of density (mass per unit volume), dynamic viscosity, kinematic viscosity, surface tension, potential energy, and pressure in dealing with the flow of relatively incompressible fluids at constant temperatures. There is a proper SI expression for each of these quantities, derived from base units in accordance with applicable physical relationships. Metric considerations in fluid mechanics are discussed in other engineering metric reference sources.

UNITS OUTSIDE SI NOT RECOMMENDED FOR USE

UNIT NAME	SYMBOL	VALUE IN SI UNITS	
dyne	dyn	10^{-5} N	(or 10 uN)
bar	bar	10^5 Pa	(or 100 kPa)
erg	erg	10^{-7} J	(or 100 nJ)
poise	P	10^{-1} Pa · s	(or 100 mPa · s)
stokes	St	10^{-4} m²/s	(or 100 mm²/s)
gauss	Gs, (G)	10^{-4} T	(or 100 uT)
maxwell	Mx	10^{-8} Wb	(or 10 nWb)
stilb	sb	10^4 cd/m²	(or 10 kcd/m²)
phot	ph	10^4 lx	(or 10 klx)
kilogram-force	kgf	9.806 65 N	
calorie (int.)	cal	4.1868 J	
kilocalorie (int.)	kcal	4.1868 kJ	
torr	torr	133.322 Pa	
oersted	Oe	79.5775 A/m	

ROUNDING OF NUMBERS

Conversion from one measuring system to another requires rounding of numbers. For example, a quantity rounded to the nearest meter has an implied precision of ±0.5 m, while a quantity rounded to the nearest foot has an implied precision of ±0.5 ft. The two are quite different. If a quantity in feet (to the nearest foot) is to be converted to meters, any rounding should be to the nearest 0.3 m.

In making the changeover to SI, critical decisions about new rounded values will be required for many factors widely used in technical work.

SIGNIFICANT DIGITS

In general, the result of any multiplication, division, addition, or subtraction cannot be given in more significant digits than are present in any one component of the original data. This condition pertains regardless of the number of decimal places in which a conversion factor is given.

In reference tables conversion factors should be stated to a substantial number of decimal places to cover a wide range of uses. It is the responsibility of the user to interpret the resultant decimal number to the extent applicable.

Example: What is the equivalent of 3 miles in terms of kilometers?

CONVERSION FACTOR	DIRECT MULTIPLICATION		SIGNIFICANT EQUIVALENT	
miles to kilometers = 1.609	3 mi = 4.827 km		3 mi	5 km
Or, in reverse form: kilometers to miles = 0.6214	5 km = 3.107 mi		5 km	3 mi

SINGLE LINE, DUAL SCALE CHARTS

Conversions also can be interpreted on a single line, dual scale, graphical representation.

METERS TO FEET (CONVERSION FACTORS I M = 3.281 FT, I FT = 0.3048 M)

ACOUSTICS

SI units have been applied in acoustics to define frequency (hertz), sound power (watt), sound intensity (watt per square meter), and sound pressure level (pascal).

The reference quantities for the dimensionless logarithmic unit decibel (dB) are also expressed in SI units.

1. Sound power reference quantity: 1 pW = 10^{-12} W; therefore

$$\text{sound power level (dB)} = 10 \log_{10} \frac{\text{actual power (W)}}{10^{-12}}$$

2. Sound intensity reference quantity: 1 pW/m² = 10^{-12} W/m2; therefore

$$\text{sound intensity level (dB)} = 10 \log_{10} \frac{\text{actual intensity (W/m}^2\text{)}}{10^{-12}}$$

3. Sound pressure reference quantity: 20 Pa = 2 x 20 x 10^6 Pa; therefore

$$\text{sound pressure level (dB)} = 20 \log_{10} \frac{\text{actual pressure (Pa)}}{20 \times 10^6}$$

ELECTRICITY AND MAGNETISM

Electrical engineering, for many years, has used metric (SI) units as practical electrical units. These units are all coherent in that they are formed directly from SI base and derived units on a unity (one-to-one) basis.

The only changes involved the use of the term "siemens" (S) for electrical conductance, instead of the previous name "mho," and the replacement of the cycle per second with the SI unit hertz (Hz).

The kilowatt-hour (kWh) is not an SI unit but will probably be retained for the measurement of electrical energy consumption because of its long history and extensive use. The recalibration of existing electricity meters from kilowatt-hours to megajoules (MJ), on the basis of 1 kWh = 3.6 MJ, hardly seems justified at this time. However, the kilowatt-hour should not be introduced into new areas.

ILLUMINATION ENGINEERING

The SI units for luminous intensity, the candela (cd), and for luminous flux, the lumen (lm), are already in general use in the United States.

Illuminance (luminous flux per unit area) will be expressed in the derived SI unit lux (lx), which is a special name for the lumen per square meter (lm/m²). The lux (lx) and kilolux (klx) replace the footcandle, which is also known as the lumen per square foot.

Similarly, the SI unit of luminance, the candela per square meter (cd/m²), replaces the candela per square foot, the lambert, and the footlambert.

Conversion factors are:

1 lx =	0.092 footcandle
1 footcandle =	10.7639 lx
1 klx =	92.903 footcandles
1 cd/m² =	0.092 903 cd/ft²
	0.291 964 footlambert
1 cd/ft² =	10.7639 cd/m²
1 footlambert =	3.426 259 cd/m²

UNITS FOR ELECTRICITY AND MAGNETISM

QUANTITY	UNIT NAME	SYMBOL	DERIVATION	REMARKS
Electric current	ampere	A		SI base unit
Current density	ampere per square meter	A/m²		
Magnetic field strength	ampere per meter	A/m		
Electric charge quantity of electricity	coulomb	C	(A · s)	
Electric charge density	coulomb per cubic meter	C/m³		
Electric potential, electromotive force	volt	V	(W/A)	
Electric field strength	volt per meter	V/m		1 V/m = 1 N/C
Electric capacitance	farad	F	(C/V)	
Permittivity	farad per meter	F/m		
Electric resistance	ohm	Ω	(V/A)	
Electric conductance	siemens	S	(A/V)	Replaces "mho"; also equals 1/Ω
Electric power	watt	W	(V · A)	Also equals J/s
Magnetic flux	weber	Wb	(V · s)	
Magnetic flux density	tesla	T	(Wb/m²)	1 T = 1 V · s/m²
Inductance	henry	H	(Wb/A)	1 H = 1 V · s/A
Permeability	henry per meter	H/m		

METRIC DRAWINGS

Metric drawing sizes are those set by the International Standards Organization (ISO), "A" Series, with a $1:\sqrt{2}$ aspect ratio. These sizes are suitable for reduction using a 35 mm microfilm frame. Metric drawing scales are comparable to U.S. customary scales, as shown in the table. The metric system favors the use of ratios to define slopes, and a table comparing this with pitches and percentages is shown. Other recommended metric drawing practices are similar to customary standard drawing practices.

DRAWING SHEET DIMENSIONS (MM)

SIZE	SHEET SIZE	TOP AND BOT-TOM	BIND-ING MAR-GIN	RIGHT BOR-DER	NET SIZE
A0	1189 x 841	20	40	16	1133 x 801
A1	841 x 594	14	28	12	801 x 566
A2	594 x 420	10	20	8	566 x 400
A3	420 x 297	7	20	6	394 x 283
A4*	210 x 297	7	20	6	184 x 283
B1	1000 x 707	14	28	12	960 x 679

*The filing edge of A4 size sheets is the long edge.

COMPARISON OF DRAWING SCALES

METRIC SCALES	CUSTOMARY RATIO	CUSTOMARY SCALES
1:5	1:4	3″ = 1′0″
1:10	1:18	1½″ = 1′0″
	1:12	1″ = 1′0″
1:20	1:16	¾″ = 1′0″
	1:24	½″ = 1′0″
1:50	1:48	¼″ = 1′0″
1:100	1:96	⅛″ = 1′0″
1:200	1:92	1/16″ = 1′0″
1:500	1:384	1/32″ = 1′0″
	1:480	1″ = 40′0″
	1:600	1″ = 50′0″
1:1000	1:960	1″ = 80′0″
	1:1200	1″ = 100′0″
1:2000	1:2400	1″ = 200′0″
1:5000	1:4800	1″ = 400′0″
	1:6000	1″ = 500′0″
1:10 000	1:10 560	6″ = 1 mi
	1:12 000	1″ = 1000′0″
1:25 000	1:21 120	3″ = 1 mi
	1:24 000	1″ = 2000′0″
1:50 000	1:63 360	1″ = 1 mi
1:100 000	1:126 720	½″ = 1 mi

EXPRESSION OF SLOPE

RATIO Y/X	ANGLE	ANGLE (RAD)	PERCENTAGE (%)
Shallow slopes			
1:100	0°34′	0.0100	1
1:67	0°52′	0.0150	1.5
1:57	1°	0.0175	1.75
1:50	1°09′	0.0200	2
1:40	1°26′	0.0250	2.5
1:33	1°43′	0.0300	3
1:29	2°	0.0349	3.5
1:25	2°17′	0.0399	4
1:20	2°52′	0.0499	5
1:19	3°	0.0524	5.25
Slight slopes			
1:17	3°26′	0.0599	6
1:15	3°48′	0.0664	6.7
1:14.3	4°	0.0698	7
1:12	4°46′	0.0832	8.3
1:11.4	5°	0.0873	8.75
1:10	5°43′	0.0998	10
1:9.5	6°	0.1047	10.5
1:8	7°07′	0.1245	12.5
1:7.1	8°	0.1396	14
1:6.7	8°32′	0.1490	15
1:6	9°28′	0.1652	16.7
1:5.7	10°	0.1745	17.6
1:5	11°19′	0.1975	20
1:4.5	12°30′	0.2182	22.2
1:4	14°02′	0.2450	25
Medium slopes			
1:3.7	15°	0.2618	25.8
1:3.3	16°42′	0.2915	30
1:3	18°26′	0.3217	33.3
1:2.75	20°	0.3491	36.4
1:2.5	21°48′	0.3805	40
1:2.4	22°30′	0.3927	41.4
1:2.15	25°	0.4363	46.6
1:2	26°34′	0.4537	50
1:1.73	30°	0.5326	57.5
1:1.67	30°58′	0.5405	60
1:1.5	33°42′	0.5880	67
1:1.33	36°52′	0.6434	75
1:1.2	40°	0.6981	84
1:1	45°	0.7854	100
Steep slopes			
1.19:1	50°	0.8727	119
1.43:1	55°	0.9599	143
1.5:1	56°19′	0.9827	150
1.73:1	60°	1.0472	173
2:1	63°26′	1.1071	200
2.15:1	65°	1.1345	215
2.5:1	68°12′	1.1903	250
2.75:1	70°	1.2217	275
3:1	71°34′	1.2491	300
3.73:1	75°	1.3090	373
4:1	75°58′	1.3253	400
5:1	78°42′	1.3735	500
5.67:1	80°	1.3963	567
6:1	80°32′	1.4056	600
11.43:1	85°	1.4835	1143
∞	90°	1.5708	∞

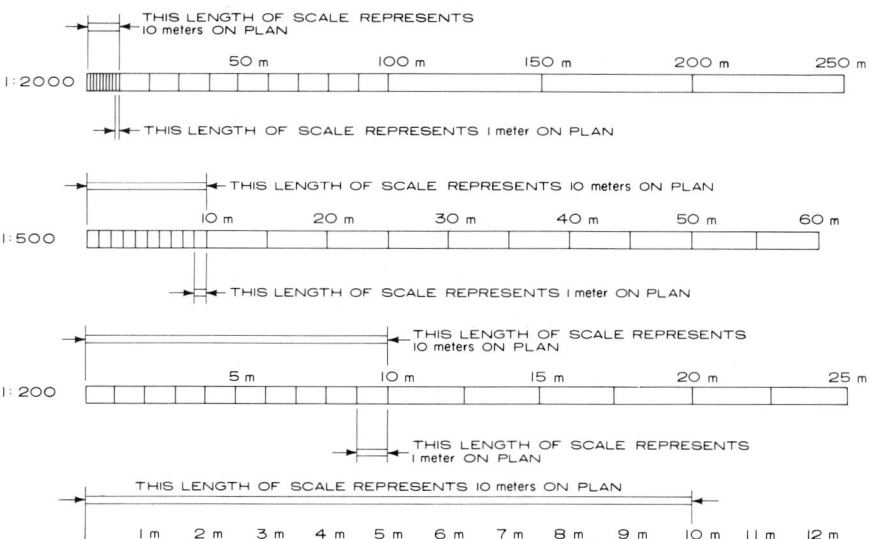

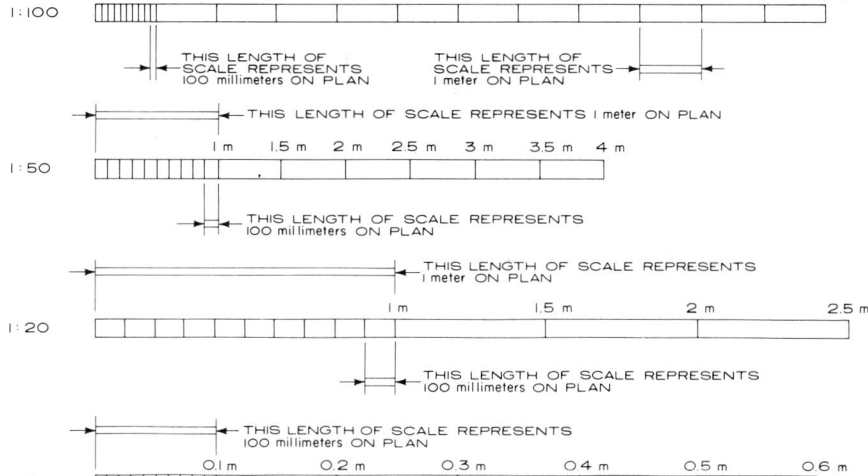

METRIC LENGTHS TO SCALE

METRIC DIMENSIONS **17**

The Basic Module for the construction industry is 100 mm. This is an internationally accepted value. The basic module should apply to building components as well as entire buildings.

Multimodules, if carefully selected, can be coordinated with the controlling dimensions for a building, thus minimizing component sizes.

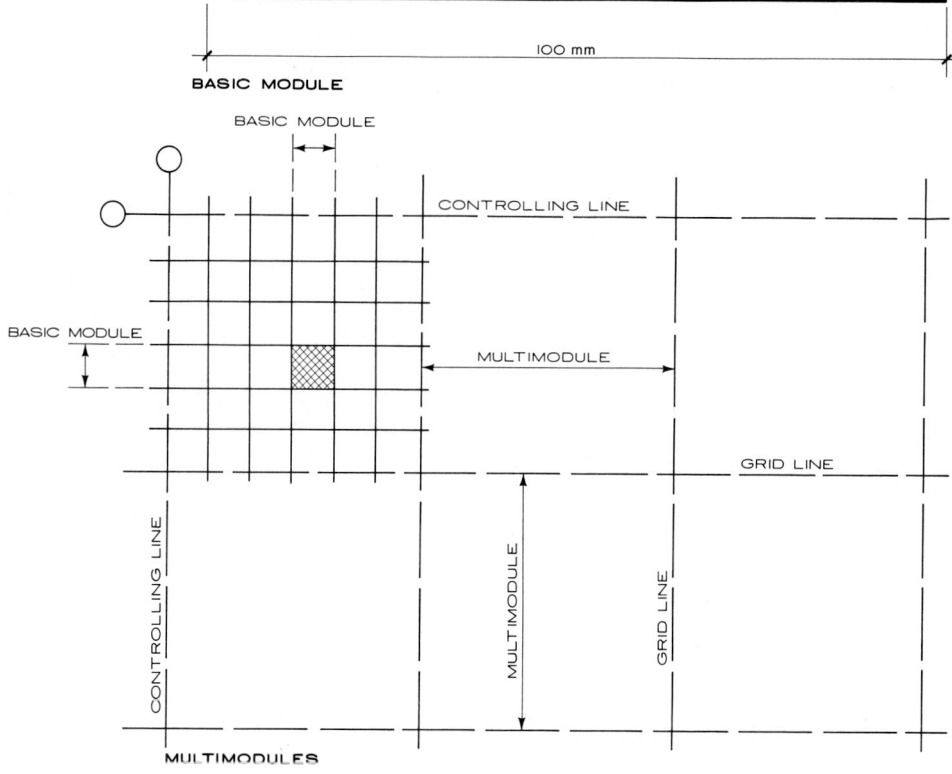

BASIC MODULE

100 mm

BASIC MODULE

BASIC MODULE

MULTIMODULE

CONTROLLING LINE

GRID LINE

CONTROLLING LINE

MULTIMODULE

GRID LINE

CONTROLLING LINE

MULTIMODULES

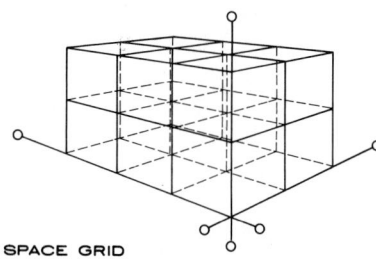

SPACE GRID

In a dimensional reference system the reference space grid is made up of the horizontal and vertical planes used to define the locations of points, lines, or surfaces in space.

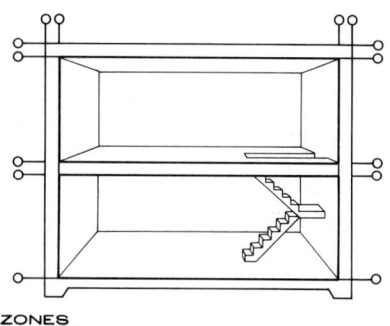

ZONES

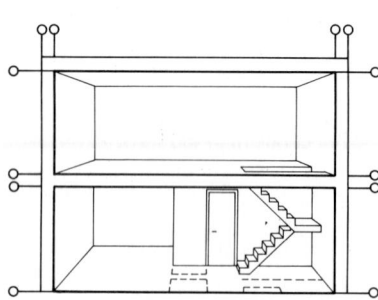

ACTIVITY SPACES

Zones and usable spaces: Zones are the spaces between controlling planes. They may be occupied but not always filled by one or more components. Finishes should be contained within the zone, although on occasion they may be placed outside as long as this does not inhibit the use of other coordinated components.

The space between zones can be referred to as an activity space. This is the space in which human or mechanical activities take place. In turn it may contain components such as partitions or stairs.

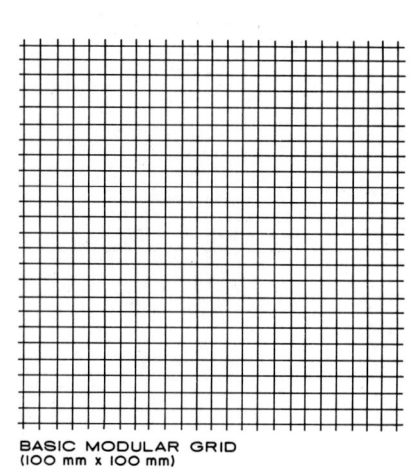

BASIC MODULAR GRID
(100 mm x 100 mm)

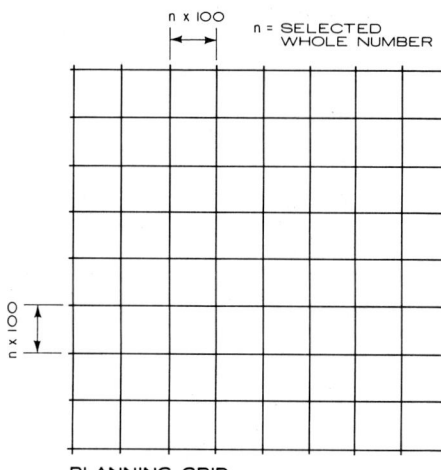

n x 100

n = SELECTED WHOLE NUMBER

n x 100

PLANNING GRID

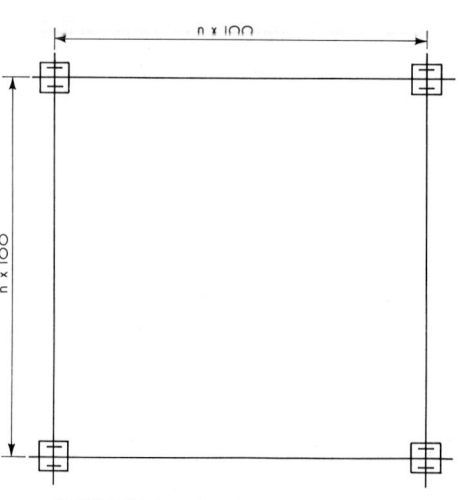

n x 100

n x 100

STRUCTURAL GRID

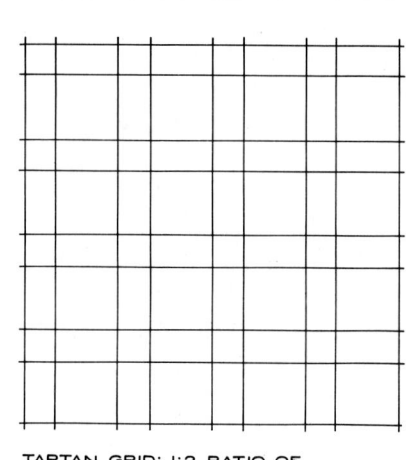

TARTAN GRID: 1:2 RATIO OF BANDWIDTHS

17 METRIC DIMENSIONS

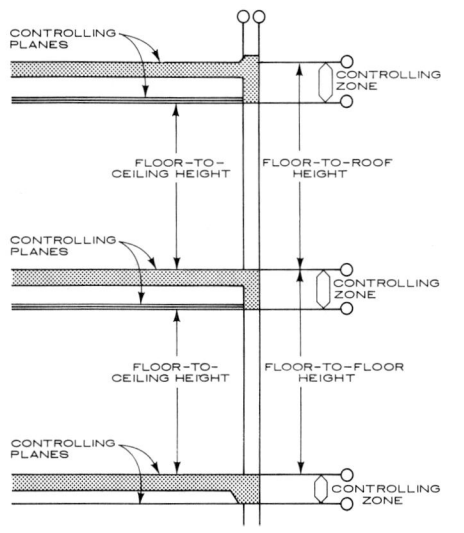

VERTICAL CONTROLLING DIMENSIONS

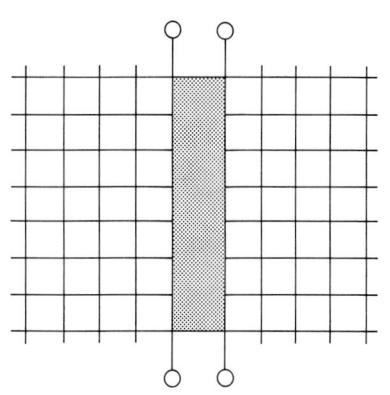

PARALLEL REFERENCE PLANES

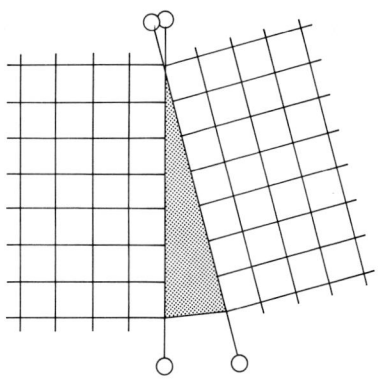

OBLIQUE REFERENCE PLANES

Neutral zones are nonmodular interruptions of a modular reference grid to accommodate intermediate building elements, such as walls or floors, or parts of a building placed at an angle with a separate grid for each portion.

NEUTRAL ZONES

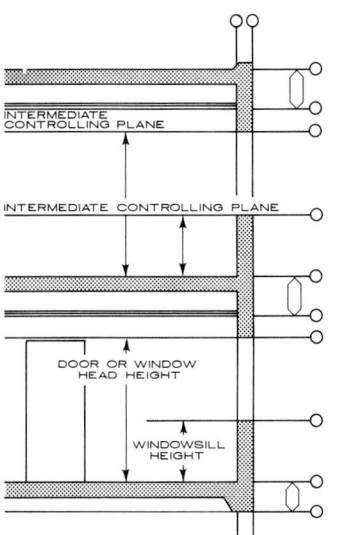

INTERMEDIATE CONTROLLING PLANES

CONTROLLING DIMENSIONS IN BUILDING DESIGN

The application of dimensional coordination in building design involves the use of horizontal and vertical controlling dimensions, either axial or face-to-face, between the major reference planes for structural elements. Enclosing elements, or "solids," are assigned controlling zones, such as floors, roofs, structural walls, or columns. Controlling lines normally coincide with the space reference system. To permit maximum flexibility and interchangeability of building components, controlling dimensions should bear a direct relationship to the coordinating sizes of building products.

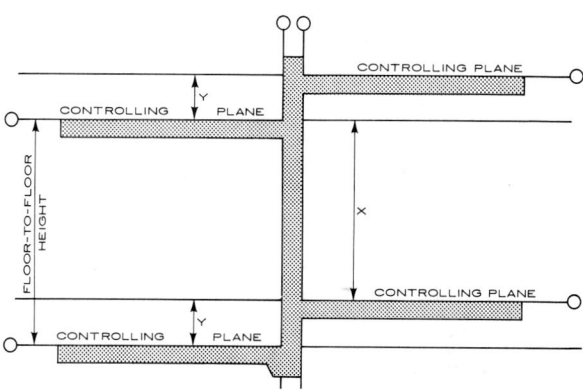

CHANGE OF LEVEL FOR FLOORS AND ROOFS

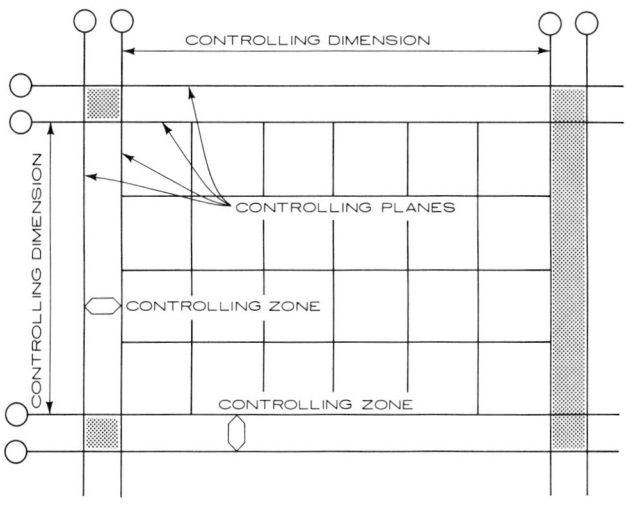

BOUNDARY CONTROLLING PLANES

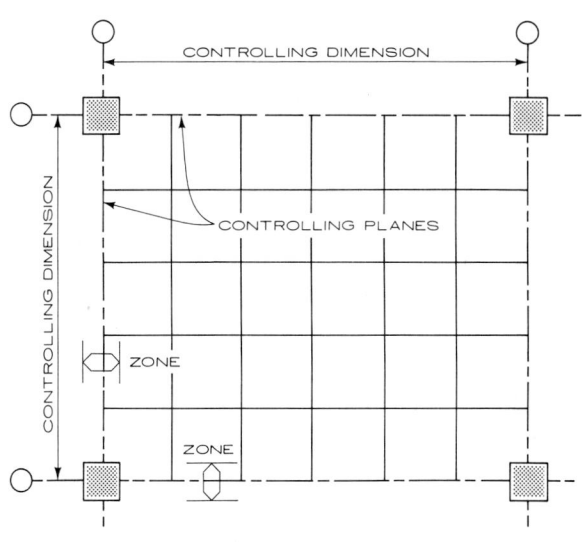

AXIAL CONTROLLING PLANES

METRIC DIMENSIONS 17

HORIZONTAL CONTROLLING DIMENSIONS (mm)

DIMENSIONS	MULTIPLES OF MULTIMODULES					MOST PRE-FERRED VALUES
	300	600	1200	3000	6000	
300	x					
600	x	x				x
900	x					
1 200	x	x	x			x
1 500	x					
1 800	x	x				x
2 100	x					
2 400	x	x	x			x
2 700	x					
3 000	x	x		x		x
3 300	x					
3 600	x	x	x			x
4 200		x				
4 800		x	x			x
5 400		x				
6 000		x	x	x	x	x
6 600		x				
7 200		x	x			x
7 800		x				
8 400		x	x			x
9 000		x		x		x
9 600		x	x			x
10 800			x			
12 000			x	x	x	x
13 200			x			
14 000			x			
15 000				x		
15 600			x			
16 800			x			
18 000			x	x	x	x
19 200			x			
20 400			x			
21 000				x		
21 600			x			
22 800			x			
24 000			x	x	x	x
25 200			x			
26 400			x			
27 000				x		
27 600			x			
30 000			x	x	x	x

NOMINAL AND COORDINATING DIMENSIONS FOR CLAY MASONRY: FULL SIZE UNITS

NOMINAL HEIGHT (mm)	COORDINATING HEIGHT (mm)	COORDINATING LENGTH (mm)
50	2 courses to 100	300
67	3 courses to 200	200 300
75	4 courses to 300	200 300
80	5 courses to 400	200 300
100	100	200 300 400
133	3 courses to 400	200 300 400
150	2 courses to 300	300 400
200	200	200 300 400
300	300	300

Note: For horizontal flexibility and/or to maintain bond patterns, the following supplementary lengths may be required:

NOMINAL LENGTH (mm)	SUPPLEMENTARY LENGTHS (mm)
200	100
300	100, 150, 200, 250
400	100, 200, 300

PREFERRED SIZES FOR BUILDING COMPONENTS AND ASSEMBLIES

CATE-GORY	EXAM-PLES	PREFERRED SIZES (mm)		
		1ST	2ND	
Small (under 500 mm)	Brick block, tile, paving units	100 200 300 400	25 50 75 150 250	
Medium (under 1 500 mm)	Panels, parti-tions, doorsets, windows, slabs	600 800 900 1 200	500 700 1 000 1 400 See Note 1	
Large (under 3 600 mm)	Precast floor and wall units, panels, doors, windows, stairs	1 800 2 400 3 000 3 600	(n x 300) 1 500 2 100 2 700 3 300 See Note 2	(n x 200) 1 600 2 000 2 200 2 600 2 800 3 200 3 400
Very Large (over 3 600 mm)	Prefabri-cated building elements, precast floor and roof sections	4 800 6 000 7 200 8 400 9 500 10 800 12 000	(n x 600) 4 200 6 600 7 800 9 000 10 200 11 400 See Note 3	(n x 1 500) 4 500 7 500 10 500

NOTES

1. For the purposes of rationalization, those multiples of 100 mm, above 1 000 mm, that are prime numbers (e.g., 1 100, 1 300) constitute a lower order of preferences when special requirements exist.
2. Alternative second preferences are shown; for vertical dimensions the use of multiples of 200 mm may sometimes be more appropriate than the use of multiples of 300 mm, as with masonry materials.
3. Alternative second preferences are shown; for some projects it will be more appropriate to size large components or assemblies in multiples of 1 500 mm.

PRODUCTS FOR USE IN THE VERTICAL PLANE: MASONRY PANELS

VERTICAL (mm)	HORIZONTAL (mm)		
	600 x n	300 x n	200 x n
600 x n	1	2	3
220 x n	2	3	3
100 x n	3	3	

GENERAL NOTES

Preferred sizes and dimensions allow better coordination between manufactured components, design, and construction operations. The tables are presented to allow an open system of selection compatible with dimensional coordination concepts presented on the preceding pages. Preferred dimensions in building are selected multimodules for horizontal and vertical applications derived from the basic 100 mm module.

The preferred dimension concept is similar to the customary 4 in. module concept presently in use in the construction industry. As an example, preferred horizontal controlling dimensions similar to the customary 1, 2, or 4 ft multimodule in metric terms may be stated this way:

up to 3600 mm : 300 mm

up to 9600 mm : 600 mm

above 9600 mm : 1200 mm

For large dimensions, 6000 mm may be more useful or, as a second preference, 3000 mm.

Certain numbers are preferred because they are divisible by 2 or 3. Such numbers are 600, 1200, 1800, 2400 mm, as indicated in the table. The long history of using such multimodules is incorporated in the conversion plans to SI metric.

Refer to standards and manufacturer's data for application of the preferred SI metric sizes and dimensions.

PREFERRED DIMENSIONS FOR PANELS AND PLANKS

TYPE	PREFERENCE	WIDTH (mm)	LENGTH (mm)
Panels	First	1 200	2 400
	Second	600	2 400 3 000
		1 200	1 200 1 800 3 000 3 600
	Third	1 200	2 100 2 700
Planks	First	400	2 400
	Second	400	3 000 3 600

PREFERRED DOOR SIZES

HEIGHT (mm)	SINGLE WIDTH				DOUBLE WIDTH		
	700*	800	900	1 000	1 200	1 500	1 800
2 100	2	2	1	2	1	1	1
2 200	2	2	2	1	2	2	1
2 400	2	1	1	1	2	2	1

*Too narrow for wheelchair use.

PREFERRED SIZES FOR WINDOWS

HEIGHT (mm) 1ST PREFER-ENCE / 1ST 2ND	WIDTH (mm)								
	600	900	1200	1500	1800	2100	2400	2700	3000
600	1	2	1	2	1	2	1	2	1
800	2	3	2	3	2	3	2	3	2
900	2	3	2	3	2	3	2	3	2
1000	2	3	2	3	2	3	2	3	2
1200	1	2	1	2	1	2	1	2	1
1400	2	3	2	3	2	3	2	3	2
1500	2	3	2	3	2	3	2	3	2
1600	2	3	2	3	2	3	2	3	2
1800	1	2	1	2	1	2	1	2	1
2000	2	3	2	3	2	3	2	3	2
2100	2	3	2	3	2	3	2	3	2
2400	1	2	1	2	1	2	1	2	1
2700	2	3	2	3	2	3	2	3	2
3000	1	2	1	2	1	2	1	2	1

Note: In some construction, widths of 1000, 1400, 1600, and 2000 mm may be required for brick or block sizes and, combined with first preference heights, may be substituted as a third preference series of sizes.

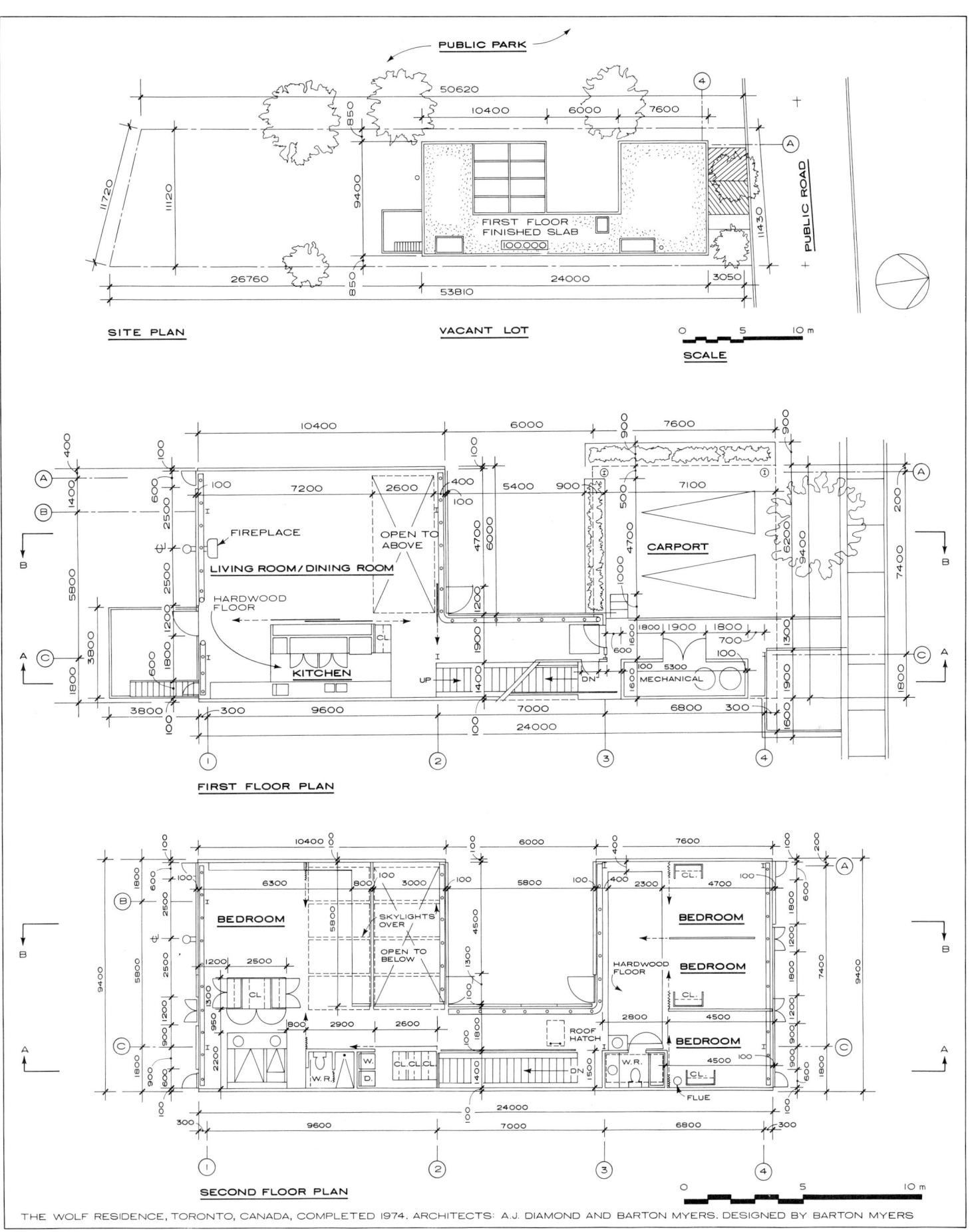

PUBLIC PARK

PUBLIC ROAD

FIRST FLOOR
FINISHED SLAB
100.000

SITE PLAN   VACANT LOT

O   5   10 m
SCALE

FIREPLACE

OPEN TO
ABOVE

CARPORT

LIVING ROOM/DINING ROOM

HARDWOOD
FLOOR

KITCHEN   MECHANICAL

UP   DN

FIRST FLOOR PLAN

BEDROOM

SKYLIGHTS
OVER

OPEN TO
BELOW

CL   CL

BEDROOM

HARDWOOD
FLOOR

BEDROOM

ROOF
HATCH

W.R.

W.
D.

CL.CL.CL.

DN

W.R.

BEDROOM

FLUE

SECOND FLOOR PLAN

O   5   10 m

THE WOLF RESIDENCE, TORONTO, CANADA, COMPLETED 1974. ARCHITECTS: A.J. DIAMOND AND BARTON MYERS. DESIGNED BY BARTON MYERS.

Robert Hill, Barton Myers Associates; Toronto, Canada

METRIC BUILDING 17

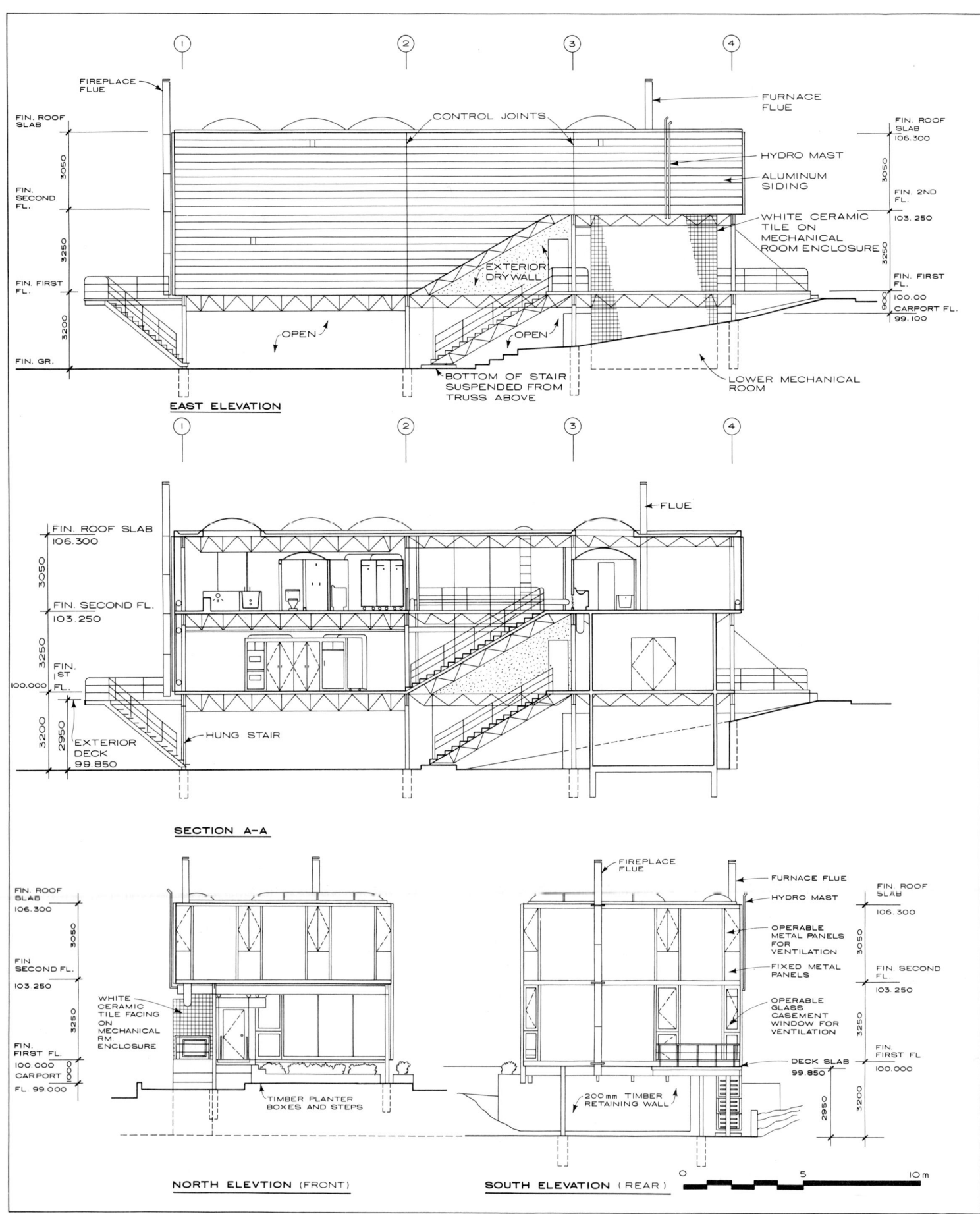

EAST ELEVATION

FIREPLACE FLUE

FIN. ROOF SLAB

3050

FIN. SECOND FL.

3250

FIN. FIRST FL.

3200

FIN. GR.

CONTROL JOINTS

FURNACE FLUE

FIN. ROOF SLAB 106.300

3050

HYDRO MAST

ALUMINUM SIDING

FIN. 2ND FL. 103.250

WHITE CERAMIC TILE ON MECHANICAL ROOM ENCLOSURE

3250

EXTERIOR DRYWALL

FIN. FIRST FL. 100.00

900

OPEN

OPEN

CARPORT FL. 99.100

BOTTOM OF STAIR SUSPENDED FROM TRUSS ABOVE

LOWER MECHANICAL ROOM

SECTION A-A

FIN. ROOF SLAB 106.300

3050

FIN. SECOND FL. 103.250

3250

100.000 FIN. 1ST FL.

3200

2950

EXTERIOR DECK 99.850

HUNG STAIR

FLUE

NORTH ELEVTION (FRONT)

FIN. ROOF SLAB 106.300

3050

FIN SECOND FL. 103.250

3250

FIN. FIRST FL. 100.000 CARPORT FL. 99.000

WHITE CERAMIC TILE FACING ON MECHANICAL RM. ENCLOSURE

TIMBER PLANTER BOXES AND STEPS

SOUTH ELEVATION (REAR)

FIREPLACE FLUE

FURNACE FLUE

FIN. ROOF SLAB 106.300

HYDRO MAST

OPERABLE METAL PANELS FOR VENTILATION

3050

FIN SECOND FL. 103.250

FIXED METAL PANELS

OPERABLE GLASS CASEMENT WINDOW FOR VENTILATION

3250

FIN. FIRST FL. 100.000

DECK SLAB 99.850

200 mm TIMBER RETAINING WALL

2950

3200

0   5   10 m

Robert Hill, Barton Myers Associates; Toronto, Canada

17 METRIC BUILDING

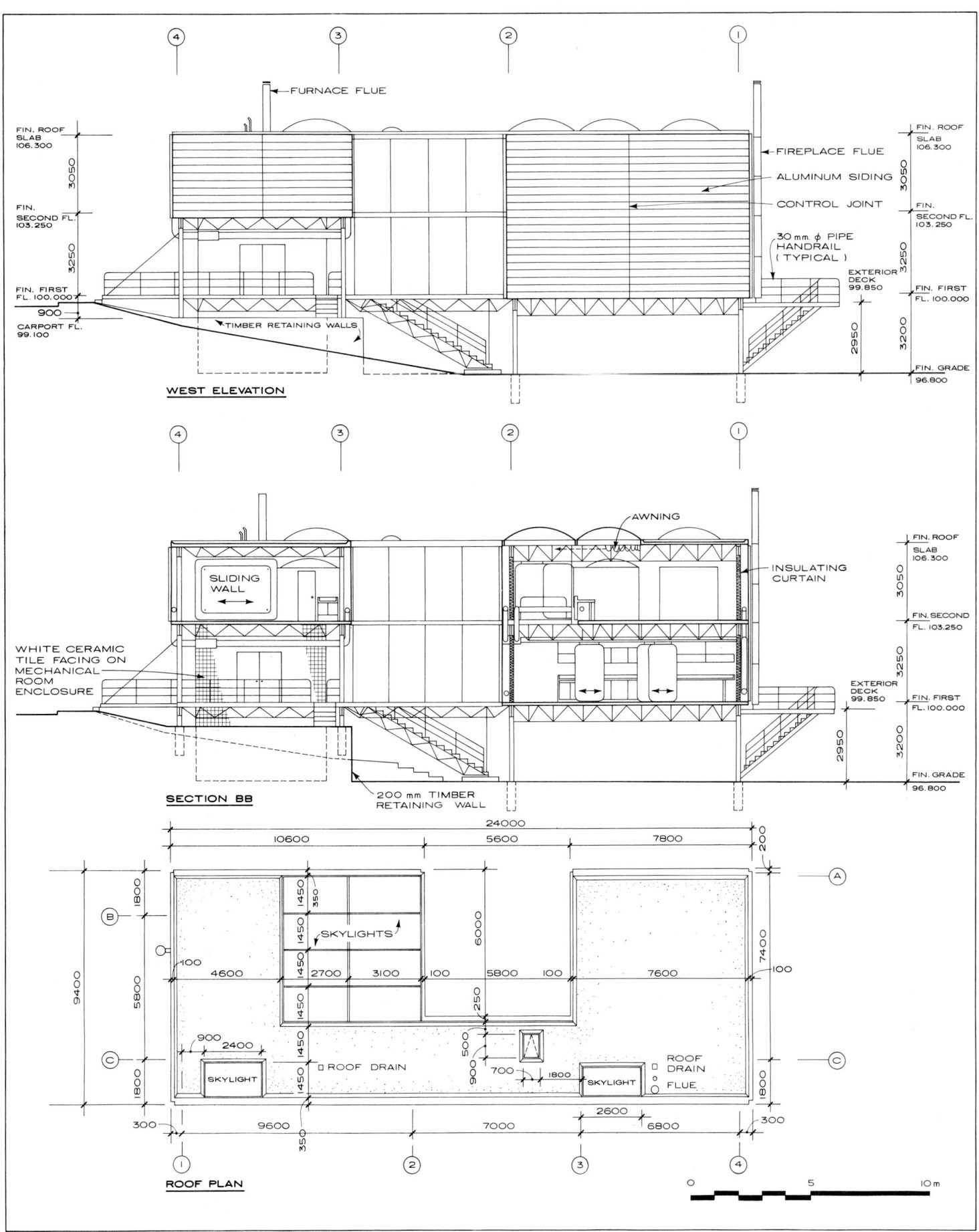

WEST ELEVATION

FURNACE FLUE

FIN. ROOF SLAB 106.300

3050

FIN. SECOND FL. 103.250

3250

FIN. FIRST FL. 100.000

900

CARPORT FL. 99.100

TIMBER RETAINING WALLS

FIREPLACE FLUE

ALUMINUM SIDING

CONTROL JOINT

FIN. ROOF SLAB 106.300

3050

FIN. SECOND FL. 103.250

30 mm. ⌀ PIPE HANDRAIL (TYPICAL)

3250

EXTERIOR DECK 99.850

FIN. FIRST FL. 100.000

2950

3200

FIN. GRADE 96.800

SECTION BB

AWNING

SLIDING WALL

WHITE CERAMIC TILE FACING ON MECHANICAL ROOM ENCLOSURE

INSULATING CURTAIN

FIN. ROOF SLAB 106.300

3050

FIN. SECOND FL. 103.250

3250

EXTERIOR DECK 99.850

FIN. FIRST FL. 100.000

2950

3200

FIN. GRADE 96.800

200 mm TIMBER RETAINING WALL

ROOF PLAN

24000

10600   5600   7800   200

1800

B

100

9400   5800

4600   2700   3100   100   5800   100   7600

1450   1450   1450   1450   1450

350

SKYLIGHTS

6000

250

A

7400

100

900   2400

SKYLIGHT

1450

ROOF DRAIN

500   900

700   1800

SKYLIGHT

ROOF DRAIN

FLUE

C

1800

1800

300   9600   7000   2600   6800   300

350

1   2   3   4

0   5   10 m

Robert Hill, Barton Myers Associates; Toronto, Canada

METRIC BUILDING

17

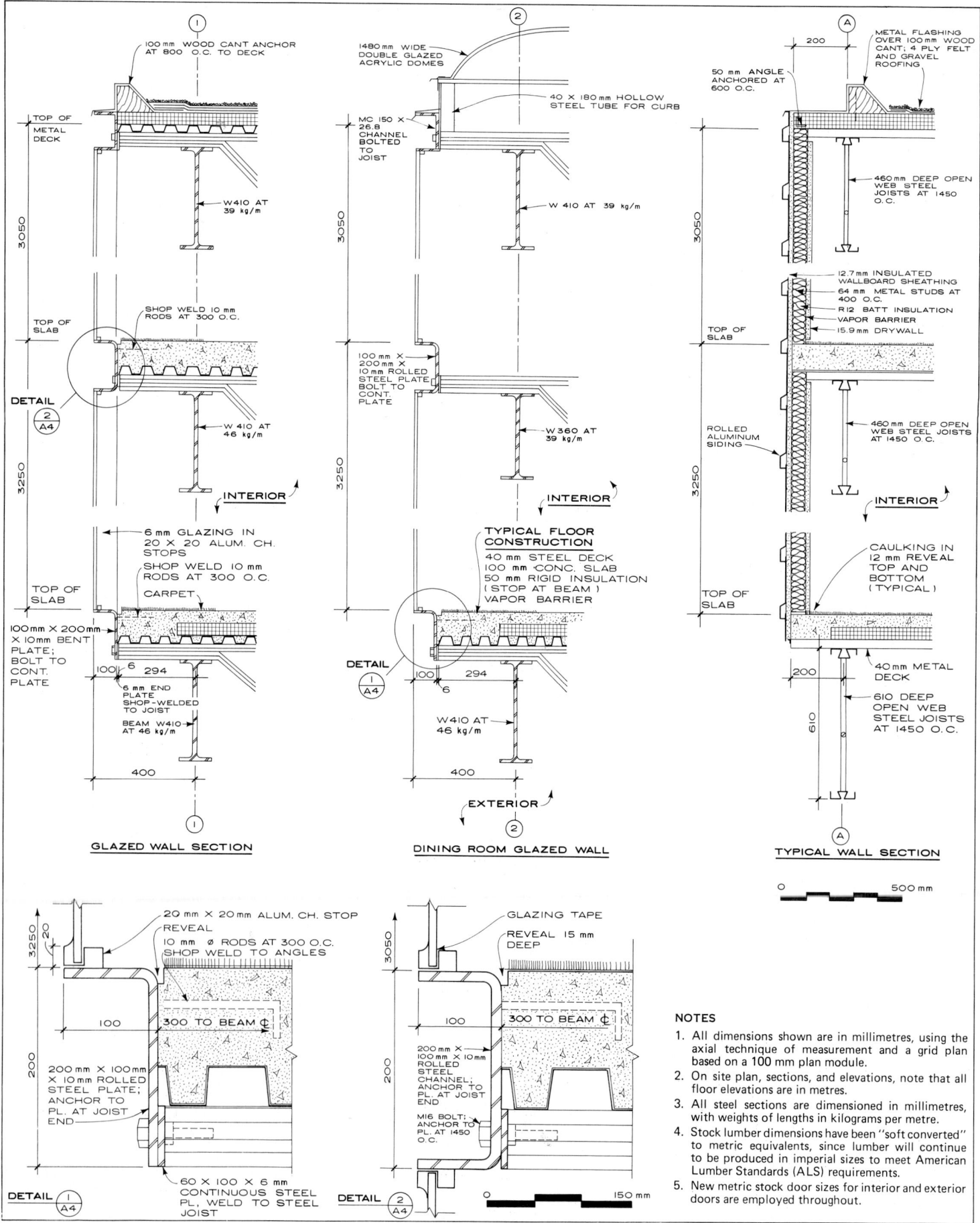

GLAZED WALL SECTION

100 mm WOOD CANT ANCHOR AT 800 O.C. TO DECK

TOP OF METAL DECK

W410 AT 39 kg/m

3050

TOP OF SLAB

SHOP WELD 10 mm RODS AT 300 O.C.

DETAIL 2 A4

W 410 AT 46 kg/m

3250

INTERIOR

6 mm GLAZING IN 20 X 20 ALUM. CH. STOPS

SHOP WELD 10 mm RODS AT 300 O.C.

CARPET

TOP OF SLAB

100 mm X 200 mm X 10 mm BENT PLATE; BOLT TO CONT. PLATE

100 | 6 | 294

6 mm END PLATE SHOP-WELDED TO JOIST

BEAM W410 AT 46 kg/m

400

DINING ROOM GLAZED WALL

1480 mm WIDE DOUBLE GLAZED ACRYLIC DOMES

40 X 180 mm HOLLOW STEEL TUBE FOR CURB

MC 150 X 26.8 CHANNEL BOLTED TO JOIST

W 410 AT 39 kg/m

3050

100 mm X 200 mm X 10 mm ROLLED STEEL PLATE BOLT TO CONT. PLATE

W 360 AT 39 kg/m

3250

INTERIOR

TYPICAL FLOOR CONSTRUCTION
40 mm STEEL DECK
100 mm CONC. SLAB
50 mm RIGID INSULATION (STOP AT BEAM)
VAPOR BARRIER

DETAIL 1 A4

100 | 294 | 6

W 410 AT 46 kg/m

400

EXTERIOR

2

TYPICAL WALL SECTION

200

METAL FLASHING OVER 100 mm WOOD CANT; 4 PLY FELT AND GRAVEL ROOFING

50 mm ANGLE ANCHORED AT 600 O.C.

A

460 mm DEEP OPEN WEB STEEL JOISTS O.C.

3050

TOP OF SLAB

12.7 mm INSULATED WALLBOARD SHEATHING
64 mm METAL STUDS AT 400 O.C.
R12 BATT INSULATION
VAPOR BARRIER
15.9 mm DRYWALL

460 mm DEEP OPEN WEB STEEL JOISTS AT 1450 O.C.

ROLLED ALUMINUM SIDING

3250

TOP OF SLAB

INTERIOR

CAULKING IN 12 mm REVEAL TOP AND BOTTOM (TYPICAL)

200

40 mm METAL DECK

610 DEEP OPEN WEB STEEL JOISTS AT 1450 O.C.

610

A

0 ——— 500 mm

DETAIL 1 A4

3250 | 20

20 mm X 20 mm ALUM. CH. STOP

REVEAL

10 mm ⌀ RODS AT 300 O.C. SHOP WELD TO ANGLES

100

300 TO BEAM ₵

200

200 mm X 100 mm X 10 mm ROLLED STEEL PLATE; ANCHOR TO PL. AT JOIST END

60 X 100 X 6 mm CONTINUOUS STEEL PL, WELD TO STEEL JOIST

DETAIL 2 A4

3050

GLAZING TAPE

REVEAL 15 mm DEEP

100

300 TO BEAM ₵

200

200 mm X 100 mm X 10 mm ROLLED STEEL CHANNEL; ANCHOR TO PL. AT JOIST END

M16 BOLT; ANCHOR TO PL. AT 1450 O.C.

0 ——— 150 mm

NOTES

1. All dimensions shown are in millimetres, using the axial technique of measurement and a grid plan based on a 100 mm plan module.
2. On site plan, sections, and elevations, note that all floor elevations are in metres.
3. All steel sections are dimensioned in millimetres, with weights of lengths in kilograms per metre.
4. Stock lumber dimensions have been "soft converted" to metric equivalents, since lumber will continue to be produced in imperial sizes to meet American Lumber Standards (ALS) requirements.
5. New metric stock door sizes for interior and exterior doors are employed throughout.

Robert Hill, Barton Myers Associates; Toronto, Canada

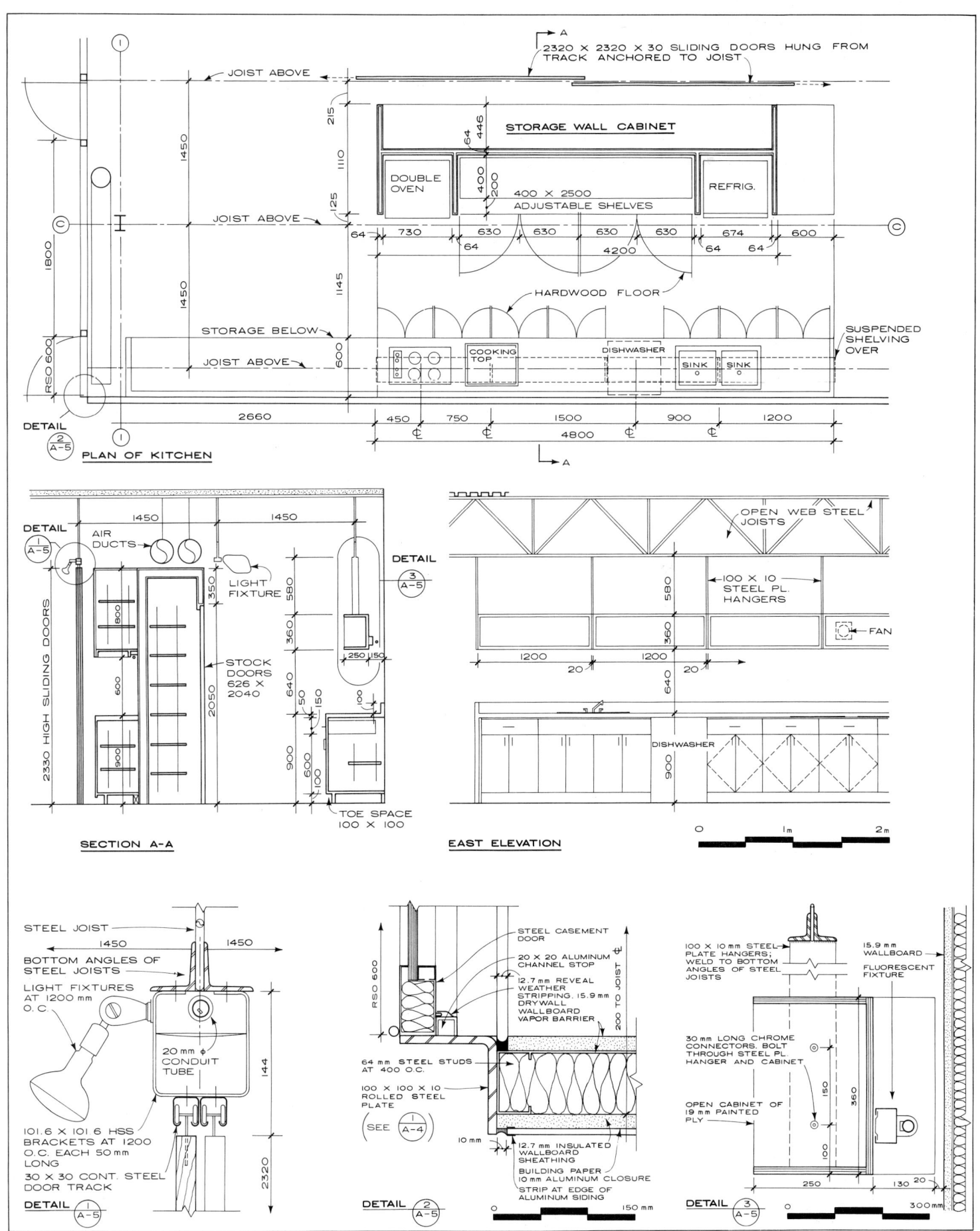

A → A

2320 X 2320 X 30 SLIDING DOORS HUNG FROM
TRACK ANCHORED TO JOIST

JOIST ABOVE

215

STORAGE WALL CABINET

64
446

1110
400 200

DOUBLE
OVEN

400 X 2500
ADJUSTABLE SHELVES

REFRIG.

JOIST ABOVE

125

64 | 730 | 630 | 630 | 630 | 630 | 674 | 600

64

4200

64 64

1450

1800

1145

HARDWOOD FLOOR

SUSPENDED
SHELVING
OVER

RSO 600

1450

STORAGE BELOW

JOIST ABOVE

600

COOKING
TOP

DISHWASHER

SINK SINK

DETAIL
2
A-5

PLAN OF KITCHEN

2660 | 450 | 750 | 1500 | 900 | 1200

4800

A

SECTION A-A

DETAIL
1
A-5

AIR
DUCTS

1450 | 1450

LIGHT
FIXTURE

350

580

360

250 150

DETAIL
3
A-5

2330 HIGH SLIDING DOORS

800

600

STOCK
DOORS
626 X
2040

2050

640

50 150

900

600 100

900

TOE SPACE
100 X 100

EAST ELEVATION

OPEN WEB STEEL
JOISTS

100 X 10
STEEL PL.
HANGERS

580

360

640

FAN

1200 | 1200

20 | 20

DISHWASHER

900

0   1m   2m

DETAIL 1 / A-5

STEEL JOIST

BOTTOM ANGLES OF
STEEL JOISTS

LIGHT FIXTURES
AT 1200 mm
O.C.

20 mm φ
CONDUIT
TUBE

1450 | 1450

144

2320

101.6 X 101.6 HSS
BRACKETS AT 1200
O.C. EACH 50 mm
LONG

30 X 30 CONT. STEEL
DOOR TRACK

DETAIL 2 / A-5

STEEL CASEMENT
DOOR

20 X 20 ALUMINUM
CHANNEL STOP

12.7 mm REVEAL
WEATHER
STRIPPING. 15.9 mm
DRYWALL
WALLBOARD
VAPOR BARRIER

RSO 600

200 TO JOIST

64 mm STEEL STUDS
AT 400 O.C.

100 X 100 X 10
ROLLED STEEL
PLATE

(SEE 1 / A-4)

10 mm

12.7 mm INSULATED
WALLBOARD
SHEATHING

BUILDING PAPER
10 mm ALUMINUM CLOSURE
STRIP AT EDGE OF
ALUMINUM SIDING

150 mm

DETAIL 3 / A-5

100 X 10 mm STEEL
PLATE HANGERS;
WELD TO BOTTOM
ANGLES OF STEEL
JOISTS

15.9 mm
WALLBOARD

FLUORESCENT
FIXTURE

30 mm LONG CHROME
CONNECTORS. BOLT
THROUGH STEEL PL.
HANGER AND CABINET

OPEN CABINET OF
19 mm PAINTED
PLY

150

360

100

250 | 130 | 20

0   300mm

Robert Hill, Barton Myers Associates; Toronto, Canada

METRIC BUILDING   **17**

INCHES AND FRACTIONS TO MILLIMETERS (1 IN. = 25.4 mm)

INCHES	0	1	2	3	4	5	6	7	8	9	10	11
						MILLIMETERS (mm)						
0	. . .	25.40	50.80	76.20	101.60	127.00	152.40	177.80	203.20	228.60	254.00	279.40
1/16	1.59	26.99	52.39	77.79	103.19	128.59	153.99	179.39	204.79	230.19	255.59	280.99
1/8	3.18	28.58	53.98	79.38	104.78	130.18	155.58	180.98	206.38	231.78	257.18	282.58
3/16	4.76	30.16	55.56	80.96	106.36	131.76	157.16	182.56	207.96	233.36	258.76	284.16
1/4	6.35	31.75	57.15	82.55	107.95	133.35	158.75	184.15	209.55	234.95	260.35	285.75
5/16	7.94	33.34	58.74	84.14	109.54	134.94	160.34	185.74	211.14	236.54	261.94	287.34
3/8	9.53	34.93	60.33	85.73	111.13	136.53	161.93	187.33	212.73	238.13	263.53	288.93
7/16	11.11	36.51	61.91	87.31	112.71	138.11	163.51	188.91	214.31	239.71	265.11	290.51
1/2	12.70	38.10	63.50	88.90	114.30	139.70	165.10	190.50	215.90	241.30	266.70	292.10
9/16	14.29	39.69	65.09	90.49	115.89	141.29	166.69	192.09	217.49	242.89	268.29	293.69
5/8	15.88	41.28	66.68	92.08	117.48	142.88	168.28	193.68	219.08	244.48	269.88	295.28
11/16	17.46	42.86	68.26	93.66	119.06	144.46	169.86	195.26	220.66	246.06	271.46	296.86
3/4	19.05	44.45	69.85	95.25	120.65	146.05	171.45	196.85	222.25	247.65	273.05	298.45
13/16	20.64	46.04	71.44	96.84	122.24	147.64	173.04	198.44	223.84	249.24	274.64	300.04
7/8	22.23	47.63	73.03	98.43	123.83	149.23	174.63	200.03	225.43	250.83	276.23	301.63
15/16	23.81	49.21	74.61	100.01	125.41	150.81	176.21	201.61	227.01	252.41	277.81	303.21

FEET AND INCHES TO MILLIMETERS (1 FT = 304.8 mm; 1 IN. = 25.4 mm)

INCHES	0	1	2	3	4	5	6	7	8	9	10	11
MILLIMETERS	. . .	25	51	76	102	127	152	178	203	229	254	279
	0	1	2	3	4	5	6	7	8	9		
FEET						MILLIMETERS (mm)						
0	. . .	305	610	914	1 219	1 524	1 829	2 134	2 438	2 743		
10	3 048	3 353	3 658	3 962	4 267	4 572	4 877	5 182	5 486	5 791		
20	6 096	6 401	6 706	7 010	7 315	7 620	7 925	8 230	8 534	8 839		
30	9 144	9 449	9 754	10 058	10 363	10 668	10 973	11 278	11 582	11 887		
40	12 192	12 497	12 802	13 106	13 411	13 716	14 021	14 326	14 630	14 935		
50	15 240	15 545	15 850	16 154	16 459	16 764	17 069	17 374	17 678	17 983		
60	18 288	18 593	18 898	19 202	19 507	19 812	20 117	20 422	20 726	21 031		
70	21 336	21 641	21 946	22 250	22 555	22 860	23 165	23 470	23 774	24 079		
80	24 384	24 689	24 994	25 298	25 603	25 908	26 213	26 518	26 882	27 127		
90	27 432	27 737	28 042	28 346	28 651	28 956	29 261	29 566	29 870	30 175		
100	30 480	30 785	31 090	31 394	31 699	32 004	32 309	32 614	32 918	33 223		
110	33 528	33 833	34 138	34 442	34 747	35 052	35 357	35 662	35 966	36 271		
120	36 576	36 881	37 186	37 490	37 795	38 100	38 405	38 710	39 014	39 319		
130	39 624	39 929	40 234	40 538	40 843	41 148	41 453	41 758	42 062	42 367		
140	42 672	42 977	43 282	43 586	43 891	44 196	44 501	44 806	45 110	45 415		
150	45 720											

FEET TO METERS (1 FT = 0.304 8 m)

FEET	0	1	2	3	4	5	6	7	8	9
						METERS (m)				
0	. . .	0.305	0.610	0.914	1.219	1.524	1.829	2.134	2.438	2.743
10	3.048	3.353	3.658	3.962	4.267	4.572	4.877	5.182	5.486	5.791
20	6.096	6.401	6.706	7.010	7.315	7.620	7.925	8.230	8.534	8.839
30	9.144	9.449	9.754	10.058	10.363	10.668	10.973	11.278	11.582	11.887
40	12.192	12.497	12.802	13.106	13.411	13.716	14.021	14.326	14.630	14.935
50	15.240	15.545	15.850	16.154	16.459	16.764	17.069	17.374	17.678	17.983
60	18.288	18.593	18.898	19.202	19.507	19.812	20.117	20.422	20.726	21.031
70	21.336	21.641	21.946	22.250	22.555	22.860	23.165	23.470	23.774	24.079
80	24.384	24.689	24.994	25.298	25.603	25.908	26.213	26.518	26.822	27.127
90	27.432	27.737	28.042	28.346	28.651	28.956	29.261	29.566	29.870	30.175
100	30.480	30.785	31.090	31.394	31.699	32.004	32.309	32.614	32.918	33.223
110	33.528	33.833	34.138	34.442	34.747	35.052	35.357	35.662	35.966	36.271
120	36.576	36.881	37.186	37.490	37.795	38.100	38.405	38.710	39.014	39.319
130	39.624	39.929	40.234	40.538	40.843	41.148	41.453	41.758	42.062	42.367
140	42.672	42.977	43.282	43.586	43.891	44.196	44.501	44.806	45.110	45.415
150	45.720	46.025	46.330	46.634	46.939	47.244	47.549	47.854	48.158	48.463
160	48.768	49.073	49.378	49.682	49.987	50.292	50.597	50.902	51.206	51.511
170	51.816	52.121	52.426	52.730	53.035	53.340	53.645	53.950	54.254	54.559
180	54.864	55.169	55.474	55.778	56.083	56.388	56.693	56.998	57.302	57.607
190	57.912	58.217	58.522	58.826	59.131	59.436	59.741	60.046	60.350	60.655
200	60.960									

MILES TO KILOMETERS (1 MI = 1.609 344 km)

MILES	0	1	2	3	4	5	6	7	8	9
					KILOMETERS (km)					
0	. . .	1.609	3.219	4.828	6.437	8.047	9.656	11.265	12.875	14.484
10	16.093	17.703	19.312	20.921	22.531	24.140	25.750	27.359	28.968	30.578
20	32.187	33.796	35.406	37.015	38.624	40.234	41.843	43.452	45.062	46.671
30	48.280	49.890	51.499	53.108	54.718	56.327	57.936	59.546	61.155	62.764
40	64.374	65.983	67.592	69.202	70.811	72.420	74.030	75.639	77.249	78.858
50	80.467	82.077	83.686	85.295	86.905	88.514	90.123	91.733	93.342	94.951
60	96.561	98.170	99.779	101.389	102.998	104.607	106.217	107.826	109.435	111.045
70	112.654	114.263	115.873	117.482	119.091	120.701	122.310	123.919	125.529	127.138
80	128.748	130.357	131.966	133.576	135.185	136.794	138.404	140.013	141.622	143.232
90	144.841	146.450	148.060	149.669	151.278	152.888	154.497	156.106	157.716	159.325
100	160.934	162.544	164.153	165.762	167.372	168.981	170.590	172.200	173.809	175.418
110	177.028	178.637	180.247	181.856	183.465	185.075	186.684	188.293	189.903	191.512
120	193.121	194.731	196.340	197.949	199.559	201.168	202.777	204.387	205.996	207.605
130	209.215	210.824	212.433	214.043	215.652	217.261	218.871	220.480	222.089	223.699
140	225.308	226.918	228.527	230.136	231.746	233.355	234.964	236.574	238.183	239.792
150	241.402	243.011	244.620	246.230	247.839	249.448	251.058	252.667	254.276	255.866
160	257.495	259.104	260.714	262.323	263.932	265.542	267.151	268.760	270.370	271.979
170	273.588	275.198	276.807	278.417	280.026	281.635	283.245	284.854	286.463	288.073
180	289.682	291.291	292.901	294.510	296.119	297.729	299.338	300.947	302.557	304.166
190	305.775	307.385	308.994	310.603	312.213	313.822	315.431	317.041	318.650	320.259
200	321.869									

SQUARE INCHES TO SQUARE MILLIMETERS (1 IN.^{2} = 645.16 mm^2)

SQUARE INCHES	0	1	2	3	4	5	6	7	8	9
					SQUARE MILLIMETERS (mm^2)					
0	. . .	0.645	1.290	1.935	2.581	3.226	3.781	4.516	5.161	5.806
10	6.452	7.097	7.742	8.387	9.032	9.677	10.323	10.968	11.613	12.258
20	12.903	13.548	14.194	14.839	15.484	16.129	16.774	17.419	18.064	18.710
30	19.355	20.000	20.645	21.290	21.935	22.581	23.226	23.871	24.516	25.161
40	25.806	26.452	27.097	27.742	28.387	29.032	29.677	30.323	30.968	31.613
50	32.258	32.903	33.548	34.193	34.839	35.484	36.129	36.774	37.419	38.064
60	38.710	39.355	40.000	40.645	41.290	41.935	42.581	43.226	43.871	44.516
70	45.161	45.806	46.452	47.097	47.742	48.387	49.032	49.677	50.322	50.968
80	51.613	52.258	52.903	53.548	54.193	54.839	55.484	56.129	56.774	57.419
90	58.064	58.710	59.355	60.000	60.645	61.290	61.935	62.581	63.226	63.871
100	64.516	65.161	65.806	66.451	67.097	67.742	68.387	69.032	69.677	70.322
110	70.968	71.613	72.258	72.903	73.548	74.193	74.839	75.484	76.129	76.774
120	77.419	78.064	78.710	79.355	80.000	80.645	81.290	81.935	82.580	83.226
130	83.871	84.516	85.161	85.806	86.451	87.097	87.742	88.387	89.032	89.677
140	90.322	90.968	91.613	92.258	92.903					

SQUARE FEET TO SQUARE METERS (1 FT^2 = 0.0929 m^2)

SQUARE FEET	0	1	2	3	4	5	6	7	8	9
SQUARE METER	. . .	0.09	0.19	0.28	0.37	0.46	0.56	0.65	0.74	0.84

SQUARE FEET	0	10	20	30	40	50	60	70	80	90
					SQUARE METERS (m^2)					
0	. . .	0.93	1.86	2.79	3.72	4.65	5.57	6.50	7.43	8.36
100	9.29	10.22	11.15	12.08	13.01	13.94	14.86	15.79	16.72	17.65
200	18.58	19.51	20.44	21.37	22.30	23.23	24.15	25.08	26.01	26.94
300	27.87	28.80	29.73	30.66	31.59	32.52	33.45	34.37	35.30	36.23
400	37.16	38.09	39.02	39.95	40.88	41.81	42.74	43.66	44.59	45.52
500	46.45	47.38	48.31	49.24	50.17	51.10	52.03	52.95	53.88	54.81
600	55.74	56.67	57.60	58.53	59.46	60.39	61.32	62.25	63.17	64.10
700	65.03	65.96	66.89	67.82	68.75	69.68	70.61	71.54	72.46	73.39
800	74.32	75.25	76.18	77.11	78.04	78.97	79.90	80.83	81.75	82.68
900	83.61	84.54	85.47	86.40	87.33	88.26	89.19	90.12	91.04	91.97
1000	92.90	93.83	94.76	95.69	96.62	97.55	98.48	99.41	100.34	101.26
1100	102.19	103.12	104.05	104.98	105.91	106.84	107.77	108.70	109.63	110.55
1200	111.48	112.41	113.34	114.27	115.20	116.13	117.06	117.99	118.92	119.84
1300	120.77	121.70	122.63	123.56	124.49	125.42	126.35	127.28	128.21	129.14
1400	130.06	130.99	131.92	132.85	133.78	134.71	135.64	136.57	137.50	138.43
1500	139.35									

METRIC CONVERSION TABLES

17

ACRES TO HECTARES (1 ACRE = 0.404 685 6 ha)

ACRES	0	1	2	3	4	5	6	7	8	9
HECTARES	...	0.40	0.81	1.21	1.62	2.02	2.43	2.83	3.24	3.64

	0	10	20	30	40	50	60	70	80	90
ACRES					HECTARES (ha)					
0	...	4.05	8.09	12.14	16.19	20.23	24.28	28.33	32.37	36.42
100	40.47	44.52	48.56	52.61	56.66	60.70	64.75	68.80	72.84	76.89
200	80.94	84.98	89.03	93.08	97.12	101.17	105.22	109.27	113.31	117.36
300	121.41	125.45	129.50	133.55	137.59	141.64	145.69	149.73	153.78	157.83
400	161.87	165.92	169.97	174.01	178.06	182.11	186.16	190.20	194.25	198.30
500	202.34	206.39	210.44	214.48	218.53	222.58	226.62	230.67	234.72	238.76
600	242.81	246.86	250.91	254.95	259.00	263.05	267.09	271.14	275.19	279.23
700	283.28	287.33	291.37	295.42	299.47	303.51	307.56	311.61	315.65	319.70
800	323.75	327.80	331.84	335.89	339.94	343.98	348.03	352.08	356.12	360.17
900	364.22	368.26	372.31	376.36	380.40	384.45	388.50	392.55	396.59	400.64
1000	404.69									

CUBIC FEET TO CUBIC METERS (1 FT^3 = 0.0283 m^3)

CUBIC FEET	0	1	2	3	4	5	6	7	8	9
					CUBIC METERS (m^3)					
0	...	0.028	0.057	0.085	0.113	0.142	0.170	0.198	0.227	0.255
10	0.283	0.311	0.340	0.368	0.396	0.425	0.453	0.481	0.510	0.538
20	0.566	0.595	0.623	0.651	0.680	0.708	0.736	0.765	0.793	0.821
30	0.850	0.878	0.906	0.934	0.963	0.991	0.019	1.048	1.076	1.104
40	1.133	1.161	1.189	1.218	1.246	1.274	1.303	1.331	1.359	1.386
50	1.416	1.444	1.472	1.501	1.529	1.557	1.586	1.614	1.642	1.671
60	1.699	1.727	1.756	1.784	1.812	1.841	1.869	1.897	1.926	1.954
70	1.982	2.010	2.034	2.067	2.095	2.124	2.152	2.180	2.209	2.237
80	2.265	2.293	2.322	2.350	2.379	2.407	2.435	2.464	2.492	2.520
90	2.549	2.577	2.605	2.633	2.662	2.690	2.718	2.747	2.775	2.803
100	2.832	2.860	2.888	2.917	2.945	2.973	3.002	3.030	3.058	3.087
110	3.115	3.143	3.171	3.200	3.228	3.256	3.285	3.313	3.341	3.370
120	3.398	3.426	3.455	3.483	3.511	3.540	3.568	3.596	3.625	3.653
130	3.681	3.710	3.738	3.766	3.794	3.823	3.851	3.879	3.908	3.936
140	3.964	3.993	4.021	4.049	4.078	4.106	4.134	4.163	4.191	4.219
150	4.248	4.276	4.304	4.332	4.361	4.389	4.417	4.446	4.474	4.502
160	4.531	4.559	4.587	4.616	4.644	4.672	4.701	4.729	4.757	4.786
170	4.814	4.482	4.870	4.899	4.927	4.955	4.984	5.012	5.040	5.069
180	5.097	5.125	5.154	5.182	5.210	5.239	5.267	5.295	5.234	5.352
190	5.380	5.409	5.437	5.465	5.493	5.522	5.550	5.578	5.606	5.635
200	5.663									

NOTE: 1 cubic meter (m^3) equals 1000 liters (L). Cubic feet can be converted to liters by shifting the decimal point three places to the right; for example, 125 cubic feet = 3.540 m^3 = 3540 L.

GALLONS TO LITERS (1 GAL [U.S.] = 3.785 41L)

GALLONS	0	1	2	3	4	5	6	7	8	9
					LITERS (L)					
0	...	3.79	7.57	11.36	15.14	18.93	22.71	26.50	30.28	34.07
10	37.85	41.64	45.42	49.21	53.00	56.78	60.57	64.35	68.14	71.92
20	75.71	79.49	83.28	87.06	90.85	94.64	98.42	102.21	105.99	109.78
30	113.56	117.35	121.13	124.92	128.70	132.49	136.27	140.06	143.85	147.63
40	151.42	155.20	158.99	162.77	166.56	170.34	174.13	177.91	181.70	185.49
50	189.27	193.06	196.84	200.63	204.41	208.20	211.98	215.77	219.55	223.34
60	227.12	230.91	234.70	238.48	242.27	246.05	249.84	253.62	257.41	261.19
70	264.98	268.76	272.55	276.34	280.12	283.91	287.69	291.48	295.26	299.05
80	302.83	306.62	310.40	314.19	317.97	321.76	325.55	329.33	333.12	336.90
90	340.69	344.47	348.26	352.04	355.83	359.61	363.40	367.18	370.97	374.76

	0	10	20	30	40	50	60	70	80	90
100	378.5	416.4	454.2	492.1	530.0	567.8	605.7	643.5	681.4	719.2
200	757.1	794.9	832.8	870.6	908.5	946.4	984.2	1022.1	1059.9	1097.8
300	1135.6	1173.5	1211.3	1249.2	1287.0	1324.9	1362.7	1400.6	1438.5	1476.3
400	1514.2	1552.0	1589.9	1627.7	1665.6	1703.4	1741.3	1779.1	1817.0	1854.9
500	1892.7	1930.6	1968.4	2006.3	2044.1	2082.0	2119.8	2157.7	2195.5	2233.4
600	2271.2	2309.1	2347.0	2384.8	2422.7	2460.5	2498.4	2536.2	2574.1	2611.9
700	2649.8	2687.6	2725.5	2763.4	2801.2	2839.1	2876.9	2914.8	2952.6	2990.5
800	3028.3	3066.3	3104.0	3141.9	3179.7	3217.6	3255.5	3293.3	3331.2	3369.0
900	3406.9	3444.7	3482.6	3520.4	3558.3	3596.1	3634.0	3671.8	3709.7	3747.6
1000	3785.4									

POUNDS TO KILOGRAMS (1 LB = 0.453 592 kg)

POUNDS	0	1	2	3	4	5	6	7	8	9
					KILOGRAMS (kg)					
0	...	0.45	0.91	1.36	1.81	2.27	2.72	3.18	3.63	4.08
10	4.54	4.99	5.44	5.90	6.35	6.80	7.26	7.71	8.16	8.62
20	9.07	9.53	9.98	10.43	10.89	11.34	11.79	12.25	12.70	13.15
30	13.61	14.06	14.52	14.97	15.42	15.88	16.33	16.78	17.24	17.69
40	18.14	18.60	19.05	19.50	19.96	20.41	20.87	21.32	21.77	22.23
50	22.68	23.13	23.59	24.04	24.49	24.95	25.40	25.85	26.31	26.76
60	27.22	27.67	28.12	28.58	29.03	29.48	29.94	30.39	30.84	31.30
70	31.75	32.21	32.66	33.11	33.57	34.02	34.47	34.93	35.38	35.83
80	36.29	36.74	37.19	37.65	38.10	38.56	39.01	39.46	39.92	40.37
90	40.82	41.28	41.73	42.18	42.64	43.09	43.54	44.00	44.45	44.91
100	45.36	45.81	46.27	46.72	47.17	47.63	48.08	48.53	48.99	49.44
110	49.90	50.35	50.80	51.26	51.71	52.16	52.62	53.07	53.52	53.98
120	54.43	54.88	55.34	55.79	56.25	56.70	57.15	57.61	58.06	58.51
130	58.97	59.42	59.87	60.33	60.78	61.24	61.69	62.14	62.60	63.05
140	63.50	63.96	64.41	64.86	65.32	65.77	66.22	66.68	67.13	67.59
150	68.04	68.49	68.95	69.40	69.85	70.31	70.76	71.21	71.67	72.12
160	72.57	73.03	73.48	73.94	74.39	74.84	75.30	75.75	76.20	76.66
170	77.11	77.56	78.02	78.47	78.93	79.38	79.83	80.29	80.74	81.19
180	81.65	82.10	82.55	83.01	83.46	83.91	84.37	84.82	85.28	85.73
190	86.18	86.64	87.09	87.54	88.00	88.45	88.90	89.36	89.81	90.26
200	90.72									

U.S. SHORT TONS (2000 LB) TO METRIC TONS (1 TON = 0.907 185 t)

SHORT TONS	0	1	2	3	4	5	6	7	8	9
					METRIC TONS (t)					
0	. . .	0.907	1.814	2.722	3.629	4.536	5.443	6.350	7.257	8.165
10	9.072	9.979	10.886	11.793	12.701	13.608	14.515	15.422	16.329	17.237
20	18.144	19.051	19.958	20.865	21.772	22.680	23.587	24.494	25.401	26.308
30	27.216	28.123	29.030	29.937	30.844	31.751	32.659	33.566	34.473	35.380
40	36.287	37.195	38.102	39.009	39.916	40.823	41.731	42.638	43.545	44.452
50	45.359	46.266	47.174	48.081	48.988	49.895	50.802	51.710	52.617	53.524
60	54.431	55.338	56.245	57.153	58.060	58.967	59.874	60.781	61.689	62.596
70	63.503	64.410	65.317	66.225	67.132	68.039	68.946	69.853	70.760	71.668
80	72.575	73.482	74.389	75.296	76.204	77.111	78.018	78.925	79.832	80.739
90	81.647	82.554	83.461	84.368	85.275	86.183	87.090	87.997	88.904	89.811
100	90.718									

NOTE: 1 metric ton (t) equals 1000 kilograms (kg). U.S. short tons can be converted to kilograms by shifting the decimal point three places to the right; for example, 48 short tons = 43.545 t = 43.545 kg (rounded to the nearest kilogram).

POUNDS PER CUBIC FOOT TO KILOGRAMS PER CUBIC METER (1 LB/FT³ = 16.018 46 kg/m³)

POUNDS PER CUBIC FOOT	0	1	2	3	4	5	6	7	8	9
					KILOGRAMS PER CUBIC METER (kg/m³)					
0	. . .	16.0	32.0	48.1	64.1	80.1	96.1	112.1	128.1	144.2
10	160.2	176.2	192.2	208.2	224.3	240.3	256.3	272.3	288.3	304.4
20	320.4	336.4	352.4	368.4	384.4	400.5	416.5	432.5	448.5	464.5
30	480.6	496.6	512.6	528.6	544.6	560.6	576.7	592.7	608.7	624.7
40	640.7	656.8	672.8	688.8	704.8	720.8	736.8	752.9	768.9	784.9
50	800.9	816.9	833.0	849.0	865.0	881.0	897.0	913.1	929.1	945.1
60	961.1	977.1	993.1	1009.2	1025.2	1041.2	1057.2	1073.2	1089.3	1105.3
70	1121.3	1137.3	1153.3	1169.3	1185.4	1201.4	1217.4	1233.4	1249.4	1265.5
80	1281.5	1297.5	1313.5	1329.5	1345.6	1361.6	1377.6	1393.6	1409.6	1425.6
90	1441.7	1457.7	1473.7	1489.7	1505.7	1521.8	1537.8	1553.8	1569.8	1585.8
100	1601.8	1617.9	1633.9	1649.9	1665.9	1681.9	1698.0	1714.0	1730.0	1746.0
110	1762.0	1778.0	1794.1	1810.1	1826.1	1842.1	1858.1	1874.2	1890.2	1906.2
120	1922.2	1938.2	1954.3	1970.3	1986.3	2002.3	2018.3	2034.3	2050.4	2066.4
130	2082.4	2098.4	2114.4	2130.5	2146.5	2162.5	2178.5	2194.5	2210.5	2226.6
140	2242.6	2258.6	2274.6	2290.6	2306.7	2322.7	2338.7	2354.7	2370.7	2386.8
150	2402.8	2418.8	2434.8	2450.8	2466.8	2482.9	2498.9	2514.9	2590.9	2546.9
160	2563.0	2579.0	2595.0	2611.0	2627.0	2643.0	2659.1	2675.1	2691.1	2707.1
170	2723.1	2739.2	2755.2	2771.2	2787.2	2803.2	2819.2	2835.3	2851.3	2867.3
180	2883.3	2899.3	2915.4	2931.4	2947.4	2963.4	2979.4	2995.4	3011.5	3027.5
190	3043.5	3059.5	3075.5	3091.6	3107.6	3123.6	3139.6	3155.6	3171.7	3187.7
200	3203.7									

POUNDS-FORCE PER SQUARE INCH (PSI) TO MEGAPASCALS (MPa) (1 PSI = 0.006 895 MPa)

POUNDS-FORCE PER SQUARE INCH	0	10	20	30	40	50	60	70	80	90
					MEGAPASCALS (MPa)					
0	. . .	0.069	0.138	0.207	0.276	0.345	0.414	0.483	0.552	0.621
100	0.689	0.758	0.827	0.896	0.965	1.034	1.103	1.172	1.241	1.310
200	1.379	1.448	1.517	1.586	1.655	1.724	1.793	1.862	1.931	1.999
300	2.068	2.137	2.206	2.275	2.344	2.413	2.482	2.551	2.620	2.689
400	2.758	2.827	2.896	2.965	3.034	3.103	3.172	3.241	3.309	3.378
500	3.447	3.516	3.585	3.654	3.723	3.792	3.861	3.903	3.999	4.068
600	4.137	4.206	4.275	4.344	4.413	4.482	4.551	4.619	4.688	4.757
700	4.826	4.895	4.964	5.033	5.102	5.171	5.240	5.309	5.378	5.447
800	5.516	5.585	5.654	5.723	5.792	5.861	5.929	5.998	6.067	6.136
900	6.205	6.274	6.343	6.412	6.481	6.550	6.619	6.688	6.757	6.826

	0	100	200	300	400	500	600	700	800	900
1000	6.895	7.584	8.274	8.963	9.653	10.342	11.032	11.721	12.411	13.100
2000	13.790	14.479	15.168	15.858	16.547	17.237	17.926	18.616	19.305	19.995
3000	20.684	21.374	22.063	22.753	23.442	24.132	24.821	25.511	26.200	26.890
4000	27.579	28.269	28.958	29.647	30.337	31.026	31.716	32.405	33.095	33.784
5000	34.474	35.163	35.853	36.542	37.232	37.921	38.611	39.300	39.990	40.679
6000	41.369	42.058	42.747	43.437	44.126	44.816	45.505	46.195	46.884	47.574
7000	48.263	48.953	49.642	50.332	51.021	51.711	52.400	53.090	53.779	54.469
8000	55.158	55.848	56.537	57.226	57.916	58.605	59.295	59.984	60.674	61.363
9000	62.053	64.742	63.432	64.121	64.811	65.500	66.190	66.879	67.569	68.258
10 000	68.948									

NOTE: 1 megapascal (MPa) is equal to 1 meganewton per square meter (MN/m²) and to 1 newton per square millimeter (N/mm²).

POUNDS-FORCE PER SQUARE FOOT TO KILOPASCALS (kPa) = 0.047 88 kN/m²

POUNDS-FORCE PER SQUARE FOOT	0	10	20	30	40	50	60	70	80	90
					KILOPASCALS (kPa = kN/m²)					
0	—	0.479	0.958	1.436	1.915	2.394	2.873	3.352	3.830	4.309
100	4.788	5.267	5.746	6.224	6.703	7.182	7.661	8.140	8.618	9.097
200	9.576	10.055	10.534	11.013	11.491	11.970	12.449	12.928	13.406	13.886
300	14.364	14.843	15.322	15.800	16.279	16.758	17.237	17.716	18.195	18.673
400	19.152	19.631	20.110	20.589	21.067	21.546	22.025	22.504	22.983	23.461
500	23.910	24.419	24.898	25.377	25.855	26.334	26.813	27.292	27.771	28.249
600	28.728	29.207	29.686	31.165	30.643	31.122	31.601	32.080	32.559	33.037
700	33.516	33.995	34.474	34.953	35.431	35.910	36.389	36.868	37.347	37.825
800	38.304	38.783	39.262	39.741	40.219	40.698	41.177	41.656	42.135	42.613
900	43.092	43.571	44.050	44.529	45.007	45.486	45.965	46.444	46.923	47.401
1000	47.880									

NOTE: 1 kilopascal (kPa) is equal to 1 kilonewton per square meter (kN/m²).

LUMENS PER SQUARE FOOT TO LUX (lm/m²) AND KILOLUX (1 lm/FT² = 10.7639 lx)

LUMENS PER SQUARE FOOT	0	1	2	3	4	5	6	7	8	9
					LUX (lm/m²)					
0	. . .	10.8	21.5	32.3	43.1	53.8	64.6	75.3	86.1	96.9
10	107.6	118.4	129.2	139.9	150.7	161.5	172.2	183.0	193.8	204.5
20	215.3	226.0	236.8	247.6	258.3	269.1	279.9	290.6	301.4	312.2
30	322.9	333.7	344.4	355.2	366.0	376.7	387.5	398.3	409.0	419.8
40	430.6	441.3	452.1	462.8	473.6	484.4	495.1	505.9	516.7	527.4
50	538.2	549.0	559.7	570.5	581.3	592.0	602.8	613.5	624.3	635.1
60	645.8	656.6	667.4	678.1	688.9	699.7	710.4	721.2	731.9	742.7
70	753.5	764.2	775.0	785.8	796.5	807.3	818.1	828.8	839.6	850.3
80	861.1	871.9	882.6	893.4	904.2	914.9	925.7	936.5	947.2	958.0
90	968.8	979.5	990.3	1001.0	1011.8	1022.6	1033.3	1044.1	1054.9	1065.6

	0	10	20	30	40	50	60	70	80	90
					KILOLUX (1000 lux)					
100	1.076	1.184	1.292	1.399	1.507	1.615	1.722	1.830	1.938	2.045
200	2.153	2.260	2.368	2.476	2.583	2.691	2.799	2.906	3.014	3.122
300	3.229	3.337	3.444	3.552	3.660	3.767	3.875	3.983	4.090	4.198
400	4.306	4.413	4.521	4.628	4.736	4.844	4.951	5.059	5.167	5.274
500	5.382	5.490	5.597	5.705	5.813	5.920	6.028	6.135	6.243	6.351
600	6.458	6.566	6.674	6.781	6.889	6.997	7.104	7.212	7.319	7.427
700	7.535	7.642	7.750	7.858	7.965	8.073	8.181	8.288	8.396	8.503
800	8.611	8.719	8.826	8.934	9.042	9.149	9.257	9.365	9.472	9.580
900	9.688	9.795	9.903	10.010	10.118	10.226	10.333	10.441	10.549	10.656
1000	10.764									

17 **METRIC CONVERSION TABLES**

POUND-FORCE TO NEWTONS (1 lbf = 4.448 22 N)

POUND-FORCE	0	1	2	3	4	5	6	7	8	9
	NEWTONS (N)									
0	. . .	4.45	8.90	13.34	17.79	22.24	26.69	31.14	35.59	40.03
10	44.48	48.93	53.38	57.83	62.28	66.72	71.17	75.62	80.07	84.52
20	88.96	93.41	97.86	102.31	106.76	111.21	115.65	120.10	124.55	129.00
30	133.45	137.89	142.34	146.79	151.24	155.69	160.14	164.58	169.03	173.48
40	177.93	182.38	186.83	191.27	195.72	200.17	204.62	209.07	213.51	217.96
50	222.41	226.86	231.31	235.76	240.20	244.65	249.10	253.55	258.00	262.45
60	266.89	271.34	275.79	280.24	284.69	289.13	293.58	298.03	302.48	306.93
70	311.38	315.82	320.27	324.72	329.17	333.62	338.06	342.51	346.96	351.41
80	355.86	360.31	364.75	369.20	373.65	378.10	382.55	387.00	391.44	395.89
90	400.34	404.79	409.24	413.68	418.13	422.58	427.03	431.48	435.93	440.37

POUND-FORCE	0	10	20	30	40	50	60	70	80	90
100	444.8	489.3	533.8	578.3	622.8	667.2	711.7	756.2	800.7	845.2
200	889.6	934.1	978.6	1023.1	1067.6	1112.1	1156.5	1201.0	1245.5	1290.0
300	1334.5	1378.9	1423.4	1467.9	1512.4	1556.9	1601.4	1645.8	1690.3	1734.8
400	1779.3	1823.8	1868.3	1912.7	1957.2	2001.7	2046.2	2090.7	2135.1	2179.6
500	2224.1	2268.6	2313.1	2357.6	2402.0	2446.5	2491.0	2535.5	2580.0	2624.5
600	2668.9	2713.4	2757.9	2802.4	2846.9	2891.3	2935.8	2980.3	3024.8	3069.3
700	3113.8	3158.2	3202.7	3247.2	3291.7	3336.2	3380.6	3425.1	3469.6	3514.1
800	3558.6	3603.1	3647.5	3692.0	3736.5	3781.0	3835.5	3870.0	3914.4	3958.9
900	4003.4	4047.9	4092.4	4136.8	4181.3	4225.8	4270.3	4314.8	4359.3	4403.7
1000	4448.2	4492.7	4537.2	4581.7	4626.1	4670.6	4715.1	4759.6	4804.1	4848.6
1100	4893.0	4937.5	4982.0	5026.5	5071.0	5115.5	5159.9	5204.4	5248.9	5293.4
1200	5337.9	5382.3	5426.8	5471.3	5515.8	5560.3	5604.8	5649.2	5693.7	5738.2
1300	5782.7	5827.2	5871.7	5916.1	5960.6	6005.1	6049.6	6094.1	6138.5	6183.0
1400	6227.5	6272.0	6316.5	6361.0	6405.4	6449.9	6494.4	6538.9	6583.4	6627.8
1500	6672.3	6716.8	6761.3	6805.8	6850.3	6894.7	6939.2	6983.7	7028.2	7072.7
1600	7117.2	7161.6	7206.1	7250.6	7295.1	7339.6	7384.0	7428.5	7473.0	7517.5
1700	7562.0	7606.5	7650.9	7695.4	7739.9	7784.4	7828.9	7873.3	7917.8	7962.3
1800	8006.0	8051.3	8095.8	8140.2	8184.7	8229.2	8273.7	8318.2	8362.7	8407.1
1900	8451.6	8496.1	8540.6	8585.1	8629.5	8674.0	8718.5	8763.0	8807.5	8852.0
2000	8896.4									

NOTE: 1000 newtons (N) equal 1 kilonewton (1kN). The lower portion of the table could also have been shown in kilonewtons; for example, 4893.0 N = 4.8930 kN. The table can also be used for the conversion of kips (1000 lbf) to kilonewtons (kN), since a multiplier of 1000 applies to both measurements units.

APPENDIX

GENERAL

Life cycle costing (LCC) is a method for evaluating all relevant costs over time of alternative building designs, systems, components, materials, or practices. The LCC method takes into account first costs, including the costs of planning, design, purchase, and installation; future costs, including costs of fuel, operation, maintenance, repair, and replacement; and any salvage value recovered during or at the end of the time period examined. These costs are displayed in the adjacent charts.

TIME ADJUSTMENTS

Adjustments to place all dollar values on a comparable time basis are necessary for valid assessment of a project's life cycle costs. The time adjustment is necessary because receiving or expending a dollar in the future is not the same as receiving or expending a dollar today. One reason for this "time value of money" is that the purchasing power of money may fall over time because of inflation. To ensure that all of a building's costs are expressed in dollars of equal purchasing power, they should be stated in "constant dollars," that is, with purely inflationary effects not included. Another reason for the "time value of money" is that money in hand may be invested productively to earn a return over time. Both inflation and the productive earning potential of resources in hand cause an investor usually to prefer to delay payments of costs or debts and to hasten receipts. The adjustment for time related earning potential can be accomplished by converting all costs to "present values," as though they were all to be incurred today, or to "annual values," as though they were all spread out over a given time in even, annual installments including the cost of money. This time adjustment, often called "discounting cash flows," is accomplished by using "discount formulas" or by multiplying dollar amounts by special "discount factors" calculated from the formulas. The most frequently used discount formulas for evaluating building projects are described below, where the following notation is used:

P = present value
F = future value
A = annual value
D = discount rate
N = number of periods
E = price escalation rate

SINGLE PRESENT WORTH

The single present worth (SPW) formula is used to find the present value of a future amount, such as the value today of a future replacement cost.

SPW (single present worth) $\qquad P = F(1 + D)^{-N}$

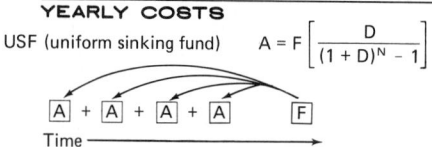

UNIFORM PRESENT WORTH

The uniform present worth (UPW) formula is used to find the present value of a series of uniform annual amounts, such as the value today of the costs of future yearly routine maintenance.

UPW (uniform present worth) $\quad P = A\left[\dfrac{(1 + D)^N - 1}{D(1 + D)^N}\right]$

UNIFORM PRESENT WORTH—MODIFIED

A modified version of the uniform present worth formula (here designated UPW*) is used to find the present value of an initial amount escalating at a constant annual rate, such as the value today of future yearly energy costs, when energy prices are expected to escalate at a given rate.

UPW* (uniform present worth—modified)

$$P = A\left[\left[\dfrac{1 + E}{D - E}\right]\left[1 - \left[\dfrac{1 + E}{1 + D}\right]^N\right]\right]$$

UNIFORM SINKING FUND

The uniform sinking fund (USF) formula is used to find the annual amount that must be accumulated to yield a given future amount, such as how much money must be set aside each year at interest in order to cover expected future replacement costs.

USF (uniform sinking fund) $\quad A = F\left[\dfrac{D}{(1 + D)^N - 1}\right]$

UNIFORM CAPITAL RECOVERY

The uniform capital recovery (UCR) formula is used to find the annual value of a present value amount, such as how much it would be necessary to pay each year in order to pay off a loan made today at a given rate of interest for a given period of time.

UCR (uniform capital recovery) $\quad A = P\left[\dfrac{D(1 + D)^N}{(1 + D)^N - 1}\right]$

NOTE

The discount factors for each of these discounting formulas have been precalculated for a range of discount rates and time periods and put into tables to facilitate their use. These tables can be found in most engineering economics textbooks. A table of discount factors for a 10% discount rate is shown opposite.

LIFE CYCLE COST FORMULA

To find the total life cycle cost of a project, sum the present values (or, alternatively, the annual values) of each kind of cost and subtract the present values (or annual values) of any positive cash flows such as salvage values. Thus, where all dollar amounts are adjusted by discounting either present values or annual values, the following formula applies:

LCC (life cycle cost formula)

Life cycle cost = first costs + maintenance and repair
+ energy + replacement − salvage value

APPLICATIONS

Alternative projects may be compared by computing the life cycle costs for each project using the formula above and seeing which is lower.

The LCC method can be applied to many different kinds of building problems. For example, it can be used to compare the long run costs of one building design to another; to determine the expected dollar savings of retrofitting a building for energy conservation or the least expensive way of reaching a targeted energy budget for a building; to select the most economical floor coverings and furnishings; and to determine the optimal size of a solar energy system.

In addition to the life cycle formula shown above, there are other closely related ways of combining present or annual values to measure a project's economic performance over time, such as the net savings technique, savings-to-investment ratio technique, internal rate of return technique, and discounted time to payback technique.

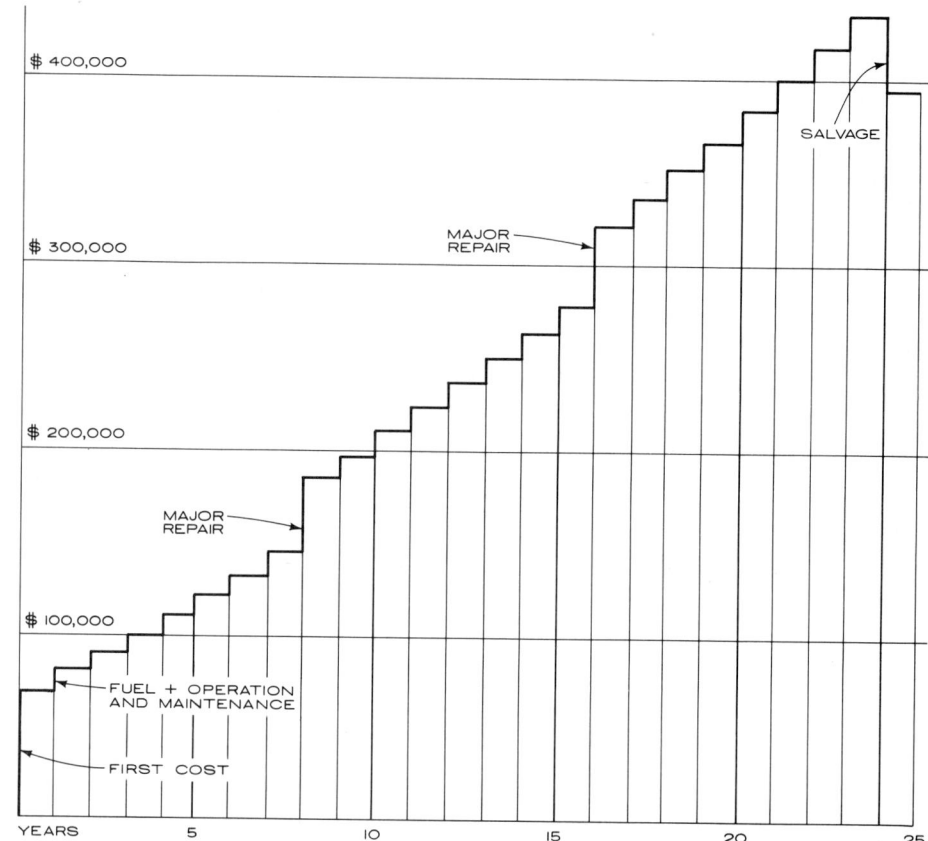

CUMULATIVE COSTS

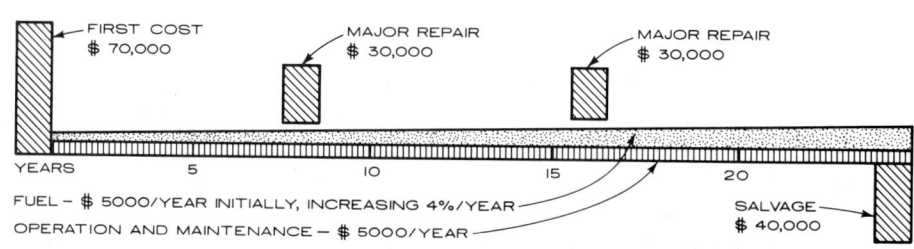

YEARLY COSTS

Harold E. Marshall and Rosalie Ruegg, Economists; Porter Driscoll, AIA, Architect; Center for Building Technology, National Bureau of Standards; United States of America

 ECONOMIC FACTORS

SAMPLE LCC PROBLEM

Determine present value of costs occurring during the life of a component so that they can be compared with the costs of an alternative component to serve the same purpose. Cumulative and yearly costs are indicated on the charts of the preceding page.

ASSUMPTIONS

Time horizon	25 years
Discount rate	10%
Fuel price increases in excess of inflation	4%
First cost of component	$70,000
Repairs to component at 8th and 16th years	$30,000/repair
Operations and maintenance (constant dollars)	$ 5,000/year
Annual cost of fuel at onset	$ 5,000

NOTE: When financing costs and tax effects are relevant they should be incorporated into LCC analysis.

SOLUTION

1. Establish present value of equipment. Convert all equipment costs (first cost, two major repair costs, and salvage value) to present value. Since the first cost occurs in the present, no change is made to the $70,000 sum.

   The first major repair, estimated to occur 8 years in the future, is discounted at the rate of 10% back to the present using the SPW factor (see Discount Factor Chart, column 2) for 8 years at 10%, 0.4665. Therefore, PV = $30,000 x 0.4665 = $13,995. This present value is added to the $70,000 first cost as shown in the Present Value of Equipment Chart.

   The second major repair is discounted 16 years back to the present in a similar manner. The SPW factor for 16 years at 10% = 0.2176. Therefore, PV = $30,000 x 0.2176 = $6528. This amount is also added to the present value in the chart.

   The $40,000 to be realized from salvage at the end of the 25 year period is discounted back to the present in the same manner. The SPW factor for 25 years, at 10% = 0.0923. Therefore, PV = $40,000 x 0.0923 = $3692. Since this sum is income, not expense, it must be subtracted from the sum of the other present values as indicated.

   Thus the present value of equipment is determined to be $86,832.

2. Establish present value of operation and maintenance costs and fuel costs. Operation and maintenance costs are estimated to be equal amounts that occur yearly during the period and are converted to present value using the UPW factor (column 3) for 25 years at 10%, 9.0770. Therefore, PV = $5000 x 9.0770 = $45,385. This amount is added to the present value of equipment as shown in the Total Present Value Chart.

   Annual fuel costs are estimated to be $5000 based on the initial price of fuel which is projected to increase at the rate of 4% per year. These costs are converted to present value using the modified UPW* factor (column 4) for 25 years at 10%, 13.0686. Therefore, PV = $5000 x 13.0686 = $65,343.

   This amount is also added to the present values of equipment and operation and maintenance costs as shown in the Total Present Value Chart.

3. Total life cycle cost in present value is the sum of the present value of equipment, operation, and maintenance and fuel costs which equals $197,559. The equipment, operation, and maintenance and fuel costs of other components to serve the same purpose can be compared to these figures to determine the best economic value.

REFERENCES

1. Gerald W. Smith, Engineering Economy: Analysis of Capital Expenditures, Iowa State University Press, Ames, Iowa, 1973.
2. Donald Watson, ed., Energy Conservation through Building Design, "Life-cycle Costing Guide for Energy Conservation in Buildings" chapter by Harold E. Marshall and Rosalie T. Ruegg, McGraw-Hill, New York, 1979.
3. Simplified Energy Design Economics, NBS special publication 544, Center for Building Technology, National Bureau of Standards, Washington, D.C., 1980.

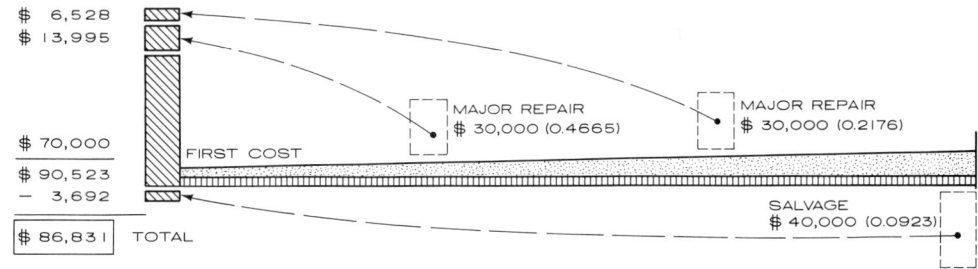

$ 6,528
$ 13,995

$ 70,000
$ 90,523
− 3,692

$ 86,831   TOTAL

FIRST COST

MAJOR REPAIR $ 30,000 (0.4665)

MAJOR REPAIR $ 30,000 (0.2176)

SALVAGE $ 40,000 (0.0923)

PRESENT VALUE OF EQUIPMENT

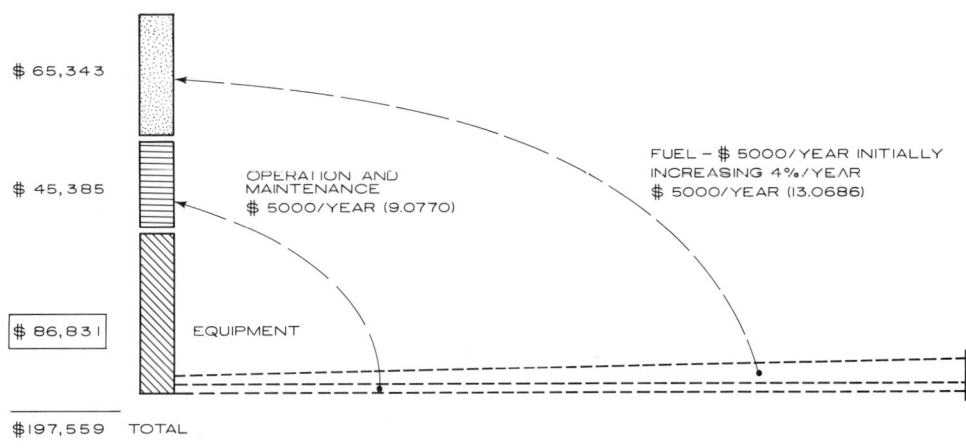

$ 65,343

$ 45,385

$ 86,831

OPERATION AND MAINTENANCE $ 5000/YEAR (9.0770)

FUEL − $ 5000/YEAR INITIALLY INCREASING 4%/YEAR $ 5000/YEAR (13.0686)

EQUIPMENT

$197,559   TOTAL

TOTAL PRESENT VALUE

DISCOUNT FACTORS

BASED ON 10% DISCOUNT RATE

1. YEARS	2. SPW	3. UPW	4. UPW* (4% PRICE ESCALATION)	5. USF	6. UCR
1	0.9091	0.909	0.9455	1.000 00	1.100 00
2	0.8264	1.736	1.8393	0.476 19	0.576 19
3	0.7513	2.487	2.6844	0.302 11	0.402 11
4	0.6830	3.170	3.4834	0.215 47	0.315 47
5	0.6209	3.791	4.2388	0.163 80	0.263 80
6	0.5645	4.355	4.9531	0.129 61	0.229 61
7	0.5132	4.868	5.6284	0.105 41	0.205 41
8	0.4665	5.335	6.2669	0.087 44	0.187 44
9	0.4241	5.759	6.8705	0.073 64	0.173 64
10	0.3855	6.144	7.4411	0.062 75	0.162 75
11	0.3505	6.495	7.9807	0.053 96	0.153 96
12	0.3186	6.814	8.4909	0.046 76	0.146 76
13	0.2897	7.103	8.9733	0.040 78	0.140 78
14	0.2633	7.367	9.4293	0.035 75	0.135 75
15	0.2394	7.606	9.8604	0.031 47	0.131 47
16	0.2176	7.824	10.2680	0.027 82	0.127 82
17	0.1978	8.022	10.6535	0.024 66	0.124 66
18	0.1799	8.201	11.0177	0.021 93	0.121 93
19	0.1635	8.365	11.3622	0.019 55	0.119 55
20	0.1486	8.514	11.6878	0.017 46	0.117 46
21	0.1351	8.649	11.9957	0.015 62	0.115 62
22	0.1228	8.772	12.2870	0.014 01	0.144 01
23	0.1117	8.883	12.5623	0.012 57	0.112 57
24	0.1015	8.985	12.8225	0.011 30	0.111 30
25	0.0923	9.077	13.0686	0.010 17	0.110 17

Harold E. Marshall and Rosalie Ruegg, Economists; Porter Driscoll, AIA, Architect; Center for Building Technology; National Bureau of Standards; United States of America

ECONOMIC FACTORS

MINIMUM UNIFORMLY DISTRIBUTED LIVE LOADS

OCCUPANCY OR USE	LIVE LOAD (PSF)
Armories and drill rooms	150
Assembly halls and other places of assembly	
Fixed seats	60
Movable seats	100
Platforms (assembly)	100
Attics	
Nonstorage	25
Storage	80*
Bakeries	150
Balconies	
Exterior	100
Interior (fixed seats)	60
Interior (movable seats)	100
Bowling alleys, poolrooms, and similar recreational areas	75
Broadcasting studios	100
Catwalks	25
Cold storage rooms	
Floor	150
Roof	250
Corridors	
First floor	100
Other floors, same as occupancy served except as indicated	
Dance halls and ballrooms	100
Dining rooms and restaurants	100
Dormitories	
Nonpartitioned	80
Partitioned	40
File rooms	
Card	125*
Letter	80*
Fire escapes on multifamily or single family residential buildings only	100
Foundries	600†
Fuel rooms, framed	400†
Garages (passenger cars only). For trucks and buses use AASHO‡ lane load	50
Grandstands	100
Greenhouses	150
Gymnasiums, main floors and balconies	100
Hospitals	
Operating rooms, laboratories	60
Private rooms	40
Wards	40
Corridors, above first floor	80
Hotels (see Residential)	–
Kitchens, other than domestic	150†
Laboratories, scientific	100
Laundries	150†
Libraries	
Reading rooms	60
Stack rooms (books and shelving at 65 pcf) but not less than	150
Corridors, above first floor	80
Manufacturing	
Light	125
Heavy	250
Ice	300
Marquees	75
Morgues	125
Office buildings	
Office	50
Business machine equipment	100†
Lobbies	100
Corridors, above the first floor	80
File and computer rooms require heavier loads based on anticipated occupancy	
Penal institutions	
Cell blocks	40
Corridors	100
Printing plants	
Composing rooms	100
Linotype rooms	100

David H. Holbert; Hansen Lind Meyer, P.C.; Iowa City, Iowa

Paper storage rooms	§
Pressrooms	150†
Public rooms	100
Residential	
Multifamily houses	
Private apartments	40
Public rooms	100
Corridors	80
Dwellings	
First floor	40
Second floor and habitable attics	30
Uninhabitable attics	20
Hotels	
Guest rooms	40
Public rooms	100
Corridors serving public rooms	100
Rest rooms and toilet rooms	60
Schools	
Classrooms	40
Corridors	80
Sidewalks, vehicular driveways, and yards subject to trucking	250
Skating rinks	100
Stairs and exitways	100
Storage warehouses	
Light	125
Heavy	250
Hay or grain	300
Stores	
Retail	
First floor, rooms	100
Upper floors	75
Wholesale	125
Telephone exchange rooms	150†
Theaters	
Aisles, corridors, and lobbies	100
Orchestra floors	60
Balconies	60
Stage floors	
Dressing rooms	40
Grid iron floor or fly gallery grating	60
Projection room	100
Transformer rooms	200†
Vaults, in offices	250*
Yards and terraces, pedestrians	100

*Increase when occupancy exceeds this amount.
†Use weight of actual equipment when greater.
‡American Association of State Highway Officials.
§Paper storage 50 lb/ft of clear story height.

LIVE LOAD

Live load is the weight superimposed by the use and occupancy of the building or other structure, not including the wind load, snow load, earthquake load, or dead load.

The live loads to be assumed in the design of buildings and other structures shall be the greatest loads that probably will be produced by the intended use or occupancy, but in no case less than the minimum uniformly distributed unit load.

THRUSTS AND HANDRAILS

Stairway and balcony railings, both exterior and interior, shall be designed to resist a vertical and a horizontal thrust of 50 lb/linear ft applied at the top of the railing.

CONCENTRATED LOADS

Floors shall be designed to support safely the uniformly distributed live load or the concentrated load in pounds given, whichever produces the greater stresses. Unless otherwise specified, the indicated concentration shall be assumed to occupy an area of $2\frac{1}{2}$ sq ft and shall be so located as to produce the maximum stress conditions in the structural members.

PARTIAL LOADING

The full intensity of the appropriately reduced live loads applied only to a portion of the length of a structure or member shall be considered if it produces a more unfavorable effect than the same intensity applied over the full length of the structure or member.

IMPACT LOADS

The live loads shall be assumed to include adequate allowance for ordinary impact conditions. Provision shall be made in structural design for uses and loads that involve unusual vibration and impact forces.

1. ELEVATORS: All moving elevator loads shall be increased 100% for impact, and the structural supports shall be designed within limits of deflection prescribed by American National Standard Safety Code for Elevators, Dumbwaiters, Escalators, and Moving Walks, A17.1-1971, and American National Standard Practice for the Inspection of Elevators (Inspector's Manual) A17.2-1960.
2. MACHINERY: For the purpose of design, the weight of machinery and moving loads shall be increased as follows to allow for impact: (a) elevator machinery, 100%; (b) light machinery, shaft or motor driven, 20%; (c) reciprocating machinery or power driven units, 50%; (d) hangers for floor or balconies, 33%. All percentages to be increased if so recommended by the manufacturer.
3. CRANEWAYS: All craneways shall have their design loads increased for impact as follows: (a) a vertical force equal to 25% of the maximum wheel load; (b) a lateral force equal to 20% of the weight of trolley and lifted load only, applied one-half at the top of each rail; and (c) a longitudinal force of 10% of the maximum wheel loads of the crane applied at top of rail.

MINIMUM ROOF LOADS

1. FLAT, PITCHED, OR CURVED ROOFS: Ordinary roofs—flat, pitched, or curved—shall be designed for the live loads or the snow load, whichever produces the greater stresses.
2. PONDING: For roofs, care shall be taken to provide drainage or the load shall be increased to represent all likely accumulations of water. Deflection of roof members will permit ponding of water accompanied by increased deflection and additional ponding.
3. SPECIAL PURPOSE ROOFS: When used for incidental promenade purposes, roofs shall be designed for a minimum live load of 60 psf; 100 psf when designed for roof garden or assembly uses. Roofs to be used for other special purposes shall be designed for appropriate loads, as directed or approved by the building official.

LIVE LOAD REDUCTION

In general, design live loads not in excess of 100 psf on any member supporting an area of 150 sq ft or more, except for places of public assembly, repair garages, parking structures, and roofs; may be reduced at a rate of 0.08%/sq ft supported by that member. The reduction shall not exceed the value of R from the following formula:

$$R = 23\left(\frac{1 + D}{L}\right)$$

where R = reduction (%)
  D = dead load per square foot of area supported by the member
  L = live load per square foot of area supported by the member

In no case should the reduction exceed 60% for vertical members, nor 40 to 60% for horizontal members.

For live loads in excess of 100 psf, some codes allow a live load reduction of 20% for columns only.

CODES AND STANDARDS

The applicable building code should be referred to for specific uniformly distributed live load, movable partition load, special, and concentrated load requirements.

In addition to the specific code requirements, the designer must consider the effects of special loading conditions, such as moving loads, construction loads, roof top planting loads, and concentrated loads from supported or hanging equipment (radiology, computer, heavy filing, or mechanical equipment).

The live loads given in this table are obtained by reference to ANSI A58.1-1972.

STANDARDS

ARCHITECTURAL AREA OF BUILDINGS

The architectural area of a building is the sum of the areas of the floors, measured horizontally in plan to the exterior faces of perimeter walls or to the centerline of walls separating buildings. Included are areas occupied by partitions, columns, stairwells, elevator shafts, duct shafts, elevator rooms, pipe spaces, mechanical penthouses, and similar spaces having a headroom of 6 ft and over. Areas of sloping surfaces, such as staircases, bleachers, and tiered terraces, should be measured horizontally in plan. Auditoriums, swimming pools, gymnasiums, foyers, and similar spaces extending through two or more floors should be measured once only, taking the largest area in plan at any level.

Mechanical penthouse rooms, pipe spaces, bulkheads, and similar spaces having a headroom less than 6 ft and balconies projecting beyond exterior walls, covered terraces and walkways, porches, and similar spaces shall have the architectural area multiplied by 0.50 in calculating the building gross area.

Exterior staircases and fire escapes, exterior steps, patios, terraces, open courtyards and lightwells, roof overhangs, cornices and chimneys, unfinished roof and attic areas, pipe trenches, and similar spaces are excluded from the architectural area calculations. Interstitial space in health care facilities is also excluded.

ARCHITECTURAL VOLUME OF BUILDINGS

The architectural volume of a building is the sum of the products of the areas defined in the architectural area times the height from the underside of the lowest floor construction to the average height of the surface of the finished roof above, for the various parts of the building. Included in the architectural volume is the actual space enclosed within the outer surfaces of the exterior or outer walls and contained between the outside of the roof and the bottom of the lowest floor, taken in full: bays, oriels, dormers; penthouses, chimneys; walk tunnels; enclosed porches and balconies, including screened areas.

The following volumes are multiplied by 0.50 in calculating the architectural volume of a building; nonenclosed porches, if recessed into the building and without enclosing sash or screens; nonenclosed porches built as an extension to the building and without sash or screen; areaways and pipe tunnels; and patio areas that have building walls extended on two sides, roof over, and paved surfacing.

Excluded from the architectural volume are outside steps, terraces, courts, garden walls; light shafts, parapets, cornices, roof overhangs; footings, deep foundations, piling cassions, special foundations, and similar features.

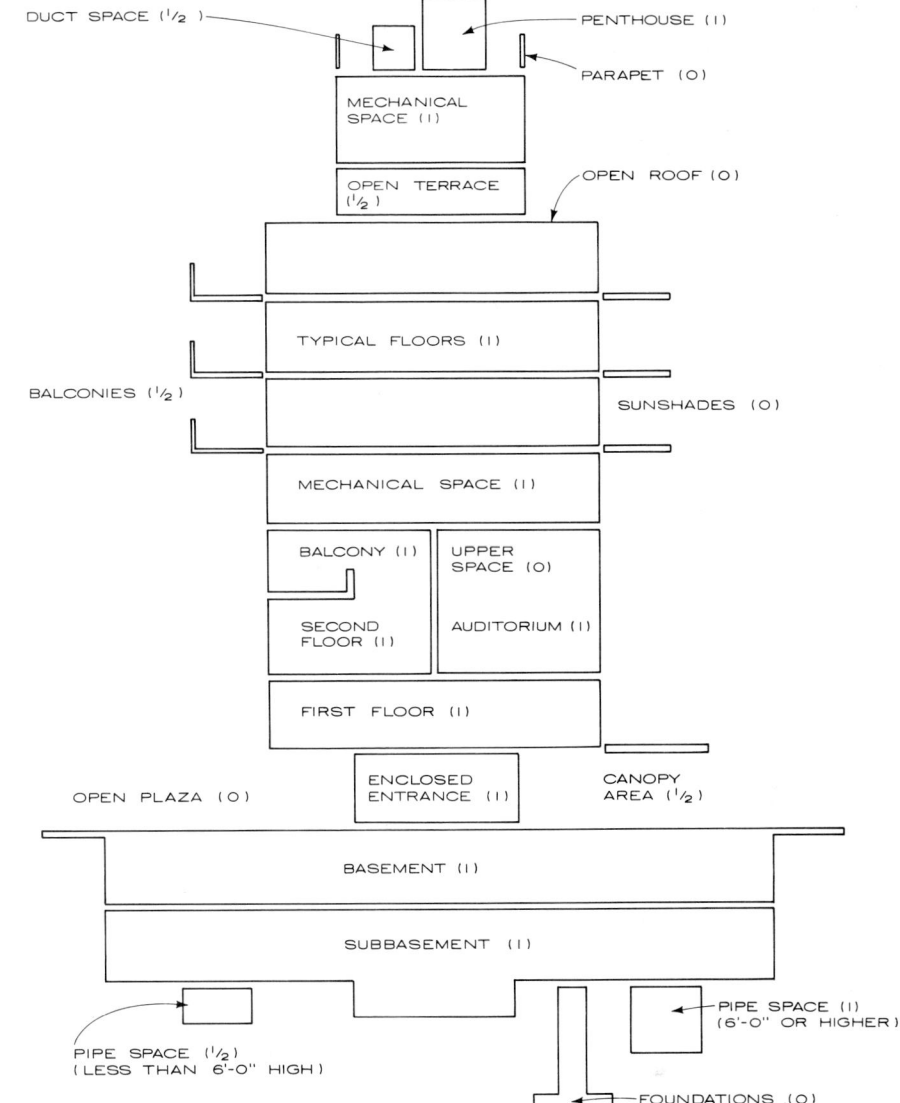

ARCHITECTURAL AREA DIAGRAM

NET ASSIGNABLE AREA

The net assignable area is that portion of the area which is available for assignment to an occupant, including every type of space usable by the occupant.

The net assignable area should be measured from the predominant inside finish of enclosing walls in the categories defined below. Areas occupied by exterior walls, partitions, internal structural, or party walls are to be excluded from the groups and are to be included under "construction area."

1. "NET ASSIGNABLE AREA": Total area of all enclosed spaces fulfilling the main functional requirements of the building for occupant use, including custodial and service areas such as guard rooms, workshops, locker rooms, janitors' closets, storerooms, and the total area of all toilet and washroom facilities.
2. "CIRCULATION AREA": Total area of all enclosed spaces which is required for physical access to subdivisions of space such as corridors, elevator shafts, escalators, fire towers or stairs, stairwells,

T. Edward Thomas; Hansen Lind Meyers, P.C.; Iowa City, Iowa

elevator entrances, public lobbies, and public vestibules.
3. "MECHANICAL AREA": Total area of all enclosed spaces designed to house mechanical and electrical equipment and utility services such as mechanical and electrical equipment rooms, duct shafts, boiler rooms, fuel rooms, and mechanical service shafts.
4. "CONSTRUCTION AREA": The area occupied by exterior walls, partitions, structure, and so on.
5. "GROSS FLOOR OR ARCHITECTURAL AREA": The sum of areas 1, 2, 3, and 4 plus the area of all factored non- and semienclosed areas equal the gross floor area or architectural area of a building.

In commercial buildings constructed for leasing, net areas are to be measured in accordance with the "Standard Method of Floor Measurement," as set by the Building Owners and Managers Association (BOMA).

The net rentable area for offices is to be measured from the inside finish of permanent outer building walls, to the office or occupancy side of corridors and/or other permanent partitions, and to the center of partitions that separate the premises from adjoining rentable areas. No deductions are to be made for columns and projections necessary to the building.

The net rentable area for stores is to be measured from the building line in case of street frontages and from the inside finish of other outer building walls, corridor, and permanent partitions and to the center of partitions that separate the premises from adjoining rentable areas. No deductions are to be made for vestibules inside the building line or for columns and projections necessary to the building. No addition is to be made for projecting bay windows.

If a single occupant is to occupy the total floor in either the office or store categories, the net rentable area would include the accessory area for that floor of corridors, elevator lobbies, toilets, janitors' closets, electrical and telephone closets, air-conditioning rooms and fan rooms, and similar spaces.

The net rentable area for apartments is to be measured from the inside face of exterior walls, and all enclosing walls of the unit.

NOTE

Various governmental agencies have their own methods of calculating the net assignable area of buildings. They should be investigated if federal authority or funding apply to a project. Also, various building codes provide their own definitions of net and gross areas of building for use in quantifying requirements.

BRICK AND BLOCK MASONRY	PSF
4" brickwork	40
4" concrete block, stone or gravel	34
4" concrete block, lightweight	22
4" concrete brick, stone or gravel	46
4" concrete brick, lightweight	33
6" concrete block, stone or gravel	50
6" concrete block, lightweight	31
8" concrete block, stone or gravel	55
8" concrete block, lightweight	35
12" concrete block, stone or gravel	85
12" concrete block, lightweight	55

CONCRETE		PCF
Plain	Cinder	108
	Expanded slag aggregate	100
	Expanded clay	90
	Slag	132
	Stone and cast stone	144
Reinforced	Cinder	111
	Slag	138
	Stone	150

FINISH MATERIALS	PSF
Acoustical tile unsupported per 1/2"	0.8
Building board, 1/2"	0.8
Cement finish, 1"	12
Fiberboard, 1/2"	0.75
Gypsum wallboard, 1/2"	2
Marble and setting bed	25-30
Plaster, 1/2"	4.5
Plaster on wood lath	8
Plaster suspended with lath	10
Plywood, 1/2"	1.5
Tile, glazed wall 3/8"	3
Tile, ceramic mosaic, 1/4"	2.5
Quarry tile, 1/2"	5.8
Quarry tile, 3/4"	8.6
Terrazzo 1", 2" in stone concrete	25
Vinyl asbestos tile, 1/8"	1.33
Hardwood flooring, 25/32"	4
Wood block flooring, 3" on mastic	15

FLOOR AND ROOF (CONCRETE)		PSF
Flexicore, 6" precast lightweight concrete		30
Flexicore, 6" precast stone concrete		40
Plank, cinder concrete, 2"		15
Plank, gypsum, 2"		12
Concrete, reinforced, 1"	Stone	12.5
	Slag	11.5
	Lightweight	6-10
Concrete, plain, 1"	Stone	12
	Slag	11
	Lightweight	3-9

FUELS AND LIQUIDS	PCF
Coal, piled anthracite	47-58
Coal, piled bituminous	40-54
Ice	57.2
Gasoline	75
Snow	8
Water, fresh	62.4
Water, sea	64

GLASS	PSF
Polished plate, 1/4"	3.28
Polished plate, 1/2"	6.56
Double strength, 1/8"	26 oz
Sheet A, B, 1/32"	45 oz
Sheet A, B, 1/4"	52 oz

Insulating glass 5/8" plate with airspace	3.25
1/4" wire glass	3.5
Glass block	18

INSULATION AND WATERPROOFING	PSF
Batt, blankets per 1" thickness	0.1-0.4
Corkboard per 1" thickness	0.58
Foamed board insulation per 1" thickness	2.6 oz
Five-ply membrane	5
Rigid insulation	0.75

LIGHTWEIGHT CONCRETE	PSF
Concrete, aerocrete	50-80
Concrete, cinder fill	60
Concrete, expanded clay	85-100
Concrete, expanded shale-sand	105-120
Concrete, perlite	35-50
Concrete, pumice	60-90
Concrete, vermiculite	25-60

METALS	PCF
Aluminum, cast	165
Brass, cast, rolled	534
Bronze, commercial	552
Bronze, statuary	509
Copper, cast or rolled	556
Gold, cast, solid	1205
Gold coin in bags	509
Iron, cast gray, pig	450
Iron, wrought	480
Lead	710
Nickel	565
Silver, cast, solid	656
Silver coin in bags	590
Tin	459
Stainless steel, rolled	492-510
Steel, rolled, cold drawn	490
Zinc, rolled, cast or sheet	449

MORTAR AND PLASTER	PCF
Mortar, masonry	116
Plaster, gypsum, sand	104-120
Plaster, gypsum, perlite, vermiculite	50-55

PARTITIONS	PSF
2 x 4 wood stud, GWB, two sides	8
4" metal stud, GWB, two sides	6
4" concrete block, lightweight, GWB	26
6" concrete block, lightweight, GWB	35
2" solid plaster	20
4" solid plaster	32

ROOFING MATERIALS	PSF
Built up	6.5
Concrete roof tile	9.5
Copper	1.5-2.5
Corrugated iron	2
Deck, steel without roofing or insulation	2.2-3.6
Fiberglass panels (2 1/2" corrugated)	5-8 oz
Galvanized iron	1.2-1.7
Lead, 1/8"	6-8
Plastic sandwich panel, 2 1/2" thick	2.6
Shingles, asphalt	1.7-2.8
Shingles, wood	2-3
Slate, 3/16" to 1/4"	7-9.5
Slate, 3/8" to 1/2"	14-18
Stainless steel	2.5
Tile, cement flat	13
Tile, cement ribbed	16
Tile, clay shingle type	8-16
Tile, clay flat with setting bed	15-20

Wood sheathing per inch	3

SOIL, SAND, AND GRAVEL	PCF
Ashes or cinder	40-50
Clay, damp and plastic	110
Clay, dry	63
Clay and gravel, dry	100
Earth, dry and loose	76
Earth, dry and packed	95
Earth, moist and loose	78
Earth, moist and packed	96
Earth, mud, packed	115
Sand or gravel, dry and loose	90-105
Sand or gravel, dry and packed	100-120
Sand or gravel, dry and wet	118-120
Silt, moist, loose	78
Silt, moist, packed	96

STONE (ASHLAR)	PCF
Granite, limestone, crystalline	165
Limestone, oolitic	135
Marble	173
Sandstone, bluestone	144
Slate	172

STONE VENEER	PSF
2" granite, 1/2" parging	30
4" granite, 1/2" parging	59
6" limestone facing, 1/2" parging	55
4" sandstone or bluestone, 1/2" parging	49
1" marble	13
1" slate	14

STRUCTURAL CLAY TILE	PSF
4" hollow	23
6" hollow	38
8" hollow	45

STRUCTURAL FACING TILE	PSF
2" facing tile	14
4" facing tile	24
6" facing tile	34
8" facing tile	44

SUSPENDED CEILINGS	PSF
Mineral fiber tile 3/4", 12" x 12"	1.2-1.57
Mineral fiberboard 5/8", 24" x 24"	1.4
Acoustic plaster on gypsum lath base	10-11

WOOD	PCF
Ash, commercial white	40.5
Birch, red oak, sweet and yellow	44
Cedar, northern white	22.2
Cedar, western red	24.2
Cypress, southern	33.5
Douglas fir (coast region)	32.7
Fir, commercial white; Idaho white pine	27
Hemlock	28-29
Maple, hard (black and sugar)	44.5
Oak, white and red	47.3
Pine, northern white sugar	25
Pine, southern yellow	37.3
Pine, ponderosa, spruce: eastern and sitka	28.6
Poplar, yellow	29.4
Redwood	26
Walnut, black	38

NOTE

To establish uniform practice among designers, it is desirable to present a list of materials generally used in building construction, together with their proper weights. Many building codes prescribe the minimum weights of only a few building materials. It should be noted that there is a difference of more than 25% in some cases.

STANDARDS

DECIMALS OF A FOOT

FRACTION	DECIMAL	FRACTION	DECIMAL	FRACTION	DECIMAL
1/16	0.0052	4-1/16	0.3385	8-1/16	0.6719
1/8	0.0104	4-1/8	0.3438	8-1/8	0.6771
3/16	0.0156	4-3/16	0.3490	8-3/16	0.6823
1/4	0.0208	4-1/4	0.3542	8-1/4	0.6875
5/16	0.0260	4-5/16	0.3594	8-5/16	0.6927
3/8	0.0313	4-3/8	0.3646	8-3/8	0.6979
7/16	0.0365	4-7/16	0.3698	8-7/16	0.7031
1/2	0.0417	4-1/2	0.3750	8-1/2	0.7083
9/16	0.0469	4-9/16	0.3802	8-9/16	0.7135
5/8	0.0521	4-5/8	0.3854	8-5/8	0.7188
11/16	0.0573	4-11/16	0.3906	8-11/16	0.7240
3/4	0.0625	4-3/4	0.3958	8-3/4	0.7292
13/16	0.0677	4-13/16	0.4010	8-13/16	0.7344
7/8	0.0729	4-7/8	0.4063	8-7/8	0.7396
15/16	0.0781	4-15/16	0.4115	8-15/16	0.7448
1-	0.0833	5-	0.4167	9-	0.7500
1-1/16	0.0885	5-1/16	0.4219	9-1/16	0.7552
1-1/8	0.0938	5-1/8	0.4271	9-1/8	0.7604
1-3/16	0.0990	5-3/16	0.4323	9-3/16	0.7656
1-1/4	0.1042	5-1/4	0.4375	9-1/4	0.7708
1-5/16	0.1094	5-5/16	0.4427	9-5/16	0.7760
1-3/8	0.1146	5-3/8	0.4479	9-3/8	0.7813
1-7/16	0.1198	5-7/16	0.4531	9-7/16	0.7865
1-1/2	0.1250	5-1/2	0.4583	9-1/2	0.7917
1-9/16	0.1302	5-9/16	0.4635	9-9/16	0.7969
1-5/8	0.1354	5-5/8	0.4688	9-5/8	0.8021
1-11/16	0.1406	5-11/16	0.4740	9-11/16	0.8073
1-3/4	0.1458	5-3/4	0.4792	9-3/4	0.8125
1-13/16	0.1510	5-13/16	0.4844	9-13/16	0.8177
1-7/8	0.1563	5-7/8	0.4896	9-7/8	0.8229
1-15/16	0.1615	5-15/16	0.4948	9-15/16	0.8281
2-	0.1667	6-	0.5000	10-	0.8333
2-1/16	0.1719	6-1/16	0.5052	10-1/16	0.8385
2-1/8	0.1771	6-1/8	0.5104	10-1/8	0.8438
2-3/16	0.1823	6-3/16	0.5156	10-3/16	0.8490
2-1/4	0.1875	6-1/4	0.5208	10-1/4	0.8542
2-5/16	0.1927	6-5/16	0.5260	10-5/16	0.8594
2-3/8	0.1979	6-3/8	0.5313	10-3/8	0.8646
2-7/16	0.2031	6-7/16	0.5365	10-7/16	0.8698
2-1/2	0.2083	6-1/2	0.5417	10-1/2	0.8750
2-9/16	0.2135	6-9/16	0.5469	10-9/16	0.8802
2-5/8	0.2188	6-5/8	0.5521	10-5/8	0.8854
2-11/16	0.2240	6-11/16	0.5573	10-11/16	0.8906
2-3/4	0.2292	6-3/4	0.5625	10-3/4	0.8958
2-13/16	0.2344	6-13/16	0.5677	10-13/16	0.9010
2-7/8	0.2396	6-7/8	0.5729	10-7/8	0.9063
2-15/16	0.2448	6-15/16	0.5781	10-15/16	0.9115
3-	0.2500	7-	0.5833	11-	0.9167
3-1/16	0.2552	7-1/16	0.5885	11-1/16	0.9219
3-1/8	0.2604	7-1/8	0.5938	11-1/8	0.9271
3-3/16	0.2656	7-3/16	0.5990	11-3/16	0.9323
3-1/4	0.2708	7-1/4	0.6042	11-1/4	0.9375
3-5/16	0.2760	7-5/16	0.6094	11-5/16	0.9427
3-3/8	0.2813	7-3/8	0.6146	11-3/8	0.9479
3-7/16	0.2865	7-7/16	0.6198	11-7/16	0.9531
3-1/2	0.2917	7-1/2	0.6250	11-1/2	0.9583
3-9/16	0.2969	7-9/16	0.6302	11-9/16	0.9635
3-5/8	0.3021	7-5/8	0.6354	11-5/8	0.9688
3-11/16	0.3073	7-11/16	0.6406	11-11/16	0.9740
3-3/4	0.3125	7-3/4	0.6458	11-3/4	0.9792
3-13/16	0.3177	7-13/16	0.6510	11-13/16	0.9844
3-7/8	**0.3229**	7-7/8	0.6563	11-7/8	0.9896
3-15/16	**0.3281**	7-15/16	0.6615	11-15/16	0.9948
4-	0.3333	8-	0.6667	12-	1.0000

DECIMALS OF AN INCH

FRACTION	DECIMAL
1/64	0.015625
1/32	0.03125
3/64	0.046875
1/16	0.0625
5/64	0.078125
3/32	0.09375
7/64	0.109375
1/8	0.125
9/64	0.140625
5/32	0.15625
11/64	0.171875
3/16	0.1875
13/64	0.203125
7/32	0.21875
15/64	0.234375
1/4	0.250
17/64	0.265625
9/32	0.28125
19/64	0.296875
5/16	0.3125
21/64	0.328125
11/32	0.34375
23/64	0.359375
3/8	0.375
25/64	0.390625
13/32	0.40625
27/64	0.421875
7/16	0.4375
29/64	0.453125
15/32	0.46875
31/64	0.484375
1/2	0.500
33/64	0.515625
17/32	0.53125
35/64	0.546875
9/16	0.5625
37/64	0.578125
19/32	0.59375
39/64	0.609375
5/8	0.625
41/64	0.640625
21/32	0.65625
43/64	0.671875
11/16	0.6875
45/64	0.703125
23/32	0.71875
47/64	0.734375
3/4	0.750
49/64	0.765625
25/32	0.78125
51/64	0.796875
13/16	0.8125
53/64	0.828125
27/32	0.84375
55/64	0.859375
7/8	0.875
57/64	0.890625
29/32	0.90625
59/64	0.921875
15/16	0.9375
61/64	0.953125
31/32	0.96875
63/64	0.984375
1"	1.000

STANDARDS

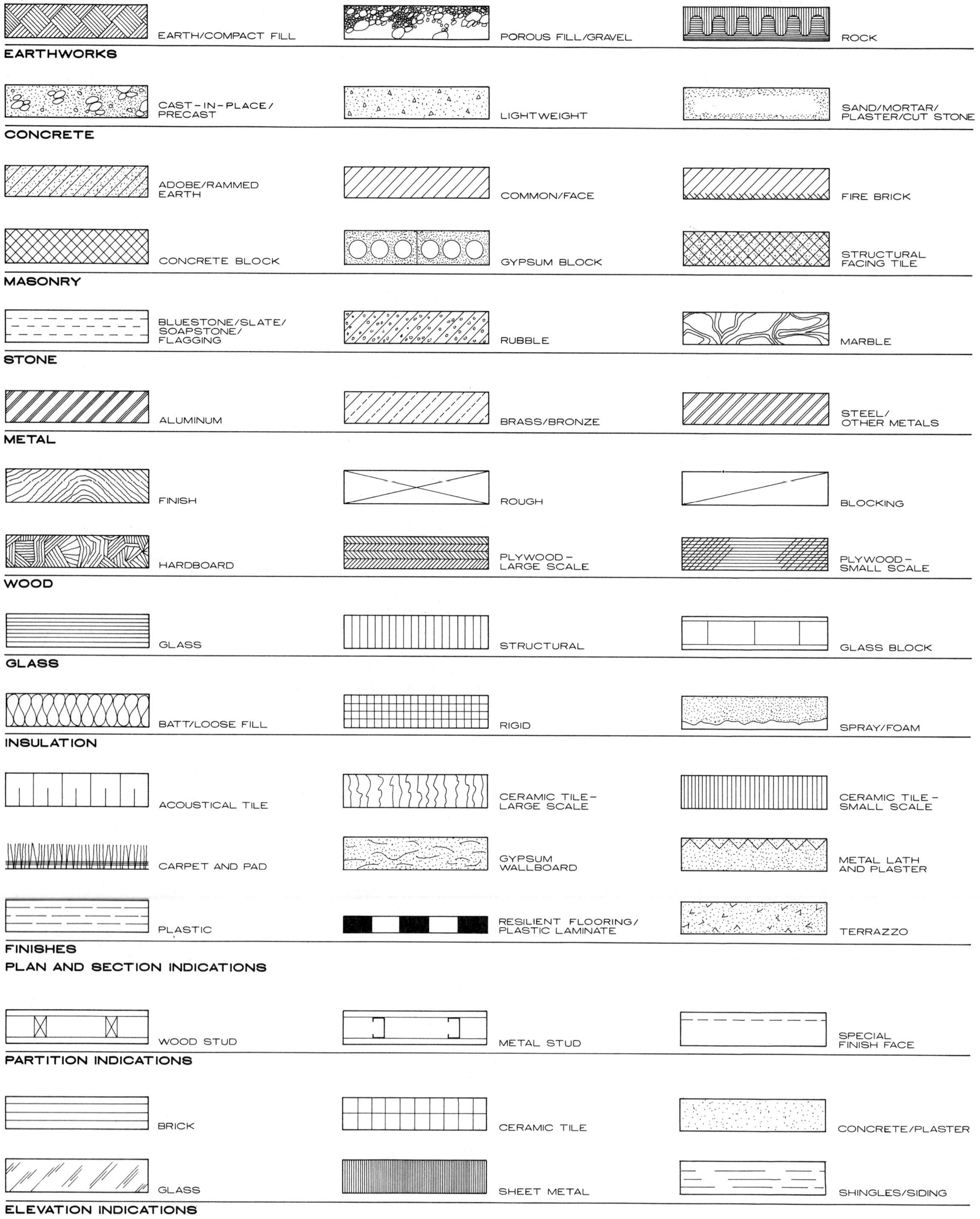

EARTH/COMPACT FILL   POROUS FILL/GRAVEL   ROCK

EARTHWORKS

CAST-IN-PLACE/PRECAST   LIGHTWEIGHT   SAND/MORTAR/PLASTER/CUT STONE

CONCRETE

ADOBE/RAMMED EARTH   COMMON/FACE   FIRE BRICK

CONCRETE BLOCK   GYPSUM BLOCK   STRUCTURAL FACING TILE

MASONRY

BLUESTONE/SLATE/SOAPSTONE/FLAGGING   RUBBLE   MARBLE

STONE

ALUMINUM   BRASS/BRONZE   STEEL/OTHER METALS

METAL

FINISH   ROUGH   BLOCKING

HARDBOARD   PLYWOOD – LARGE SCALE   PLYWOOD – SMALL SCALE

WOOD

GLASS   STRUCTURAL   GLASS BLOCK

GLASS

BATT/LOOSE FILL   RIGID   SPRAY/FOAM

INSULATION

ACOUSTICAL TILE   CERAMIC TILE – LARGE SCALE   CERAMIC TILE – SMALL SCALE

CARPET AND PAD   GYPSUM WALLBOARD   METAL LATH AND PLASTER

PLASTIC   RESILIENT FLOORING/PLASTIC LAMINATE   TERRAZZO

FINISHES

PLAN AND SECTION INDICATIONS

WOOD STUD   METAL STUD   SPECIAL FINISH FACE

PARTITION INDICATIONS

BRICK   CERAMIC TILE   CONCRETE/PLASTER

GLASS   SHEET METAL   SHINGLES/SIDING

ELEVATION INDICATIONS

John R. Hoke, Jr., AIA, Architect; Washington, D.C.

DRAFTING TECHNIQUES

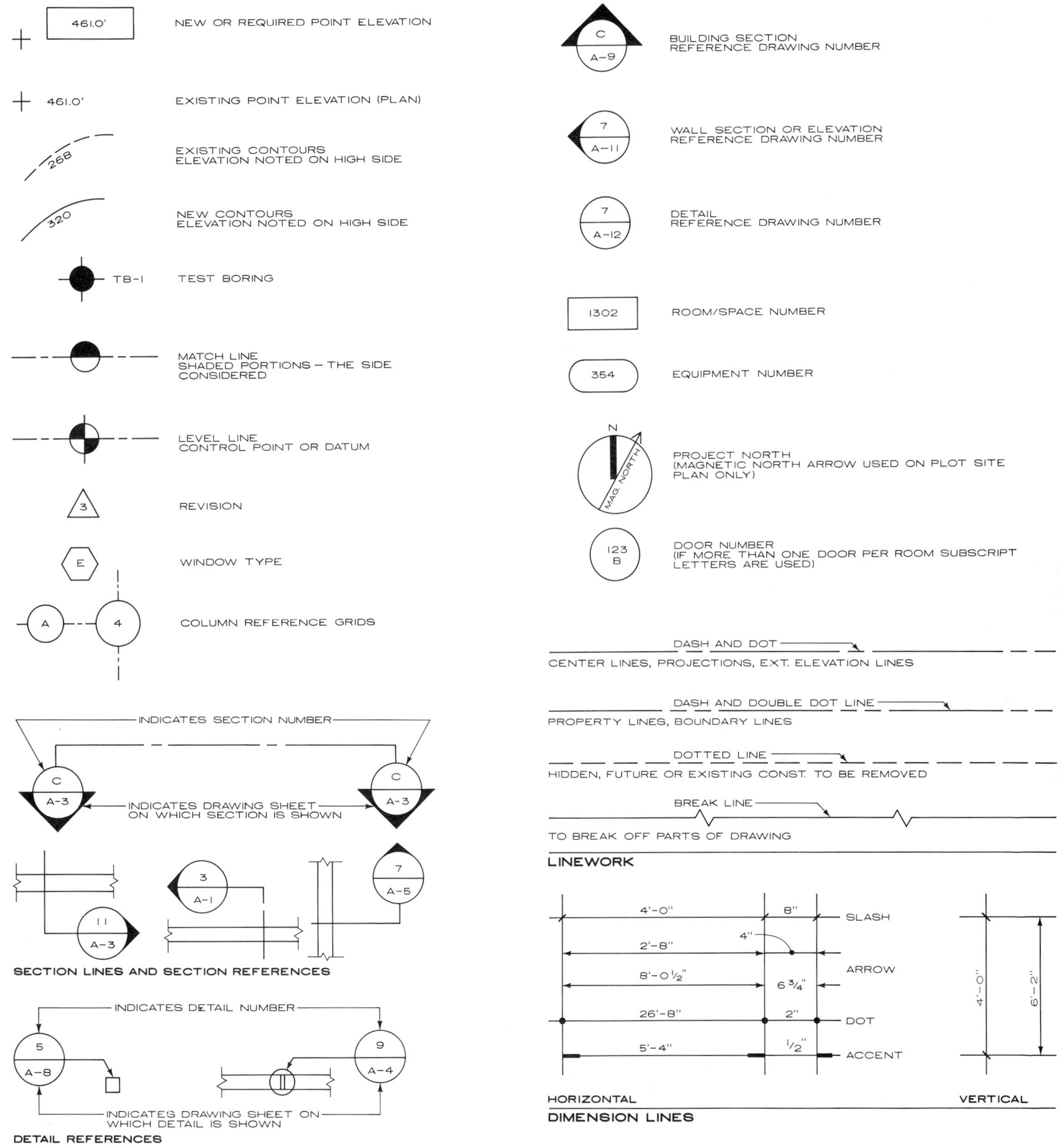

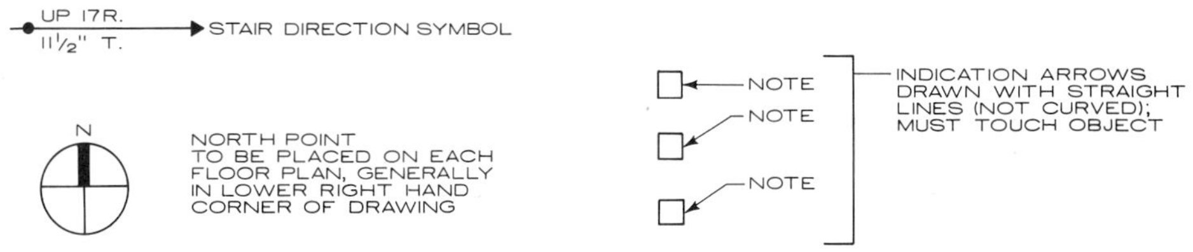

+ [461.0']	NEW OR REQUIRED POINT ELEVATION
+ 461.0'	EXISTING POINT ELEVATION (PLAN)
268	EXISTING CONTOURS ELEVATION NOTED ON HIGH SIDE
320	NEW CONTOURS ELEVATION NOTED ON HIGH SIDE
● TB-1	TEST BORING
◐	MATCH LINE SHADED PORTIONS – THE SIDE CONSIDERED
◕	LEVEL LINE CONTROL POINT OR DATUM
△3	REVISION
⬡E	WINDOW TYPE
Ⓐ --- Ⓐ	COLUMN REFERENCE GRIDS

SECTION LINES AND SECTION REFERENCES

INDICATES SECTION NUMBER

INDICATES DRAWING SHEET ON WHICH SECTION IS SHOWN

DETAIL REFERENCES

INDICATES DETAIL NUMBER

INDICATES DRAWING SHEET ON WHICH DETAIL IS SHOWN

GRAPHIC SYMBOLS

The symbols shown are those that seem to be the most common and acceptable, judged by the frequency of use by the architectural offices surveyed. This list can and should be expanded by each office to include symbols generally used by it, but not indicated here. Adoption of these symbols as standard practice is desirable to improve communication in the industry.

John R. Hoke, Jr., AIA, Architect; Washington, D.C.

▲ C / A-9	BUILDING SECTION REFERENCE DRAWING NUMBER
◖7 / A-11	WALL SECTION OR ELEVATION REFERENCE DRAWING NUMBER
7 / A-12	DETAIL REFERENCE DRAWING NUMBER
[1302]	ROOM/SPACE NUMBER
(354)	EQUIPMENT NUMBER
N / MAG. NORTH	PROJECT NORTH (MAGNETIC NORTH ARROW USED ON PLOT SITE PLAN ONLY)
123 / B	DOOR NUMBER (IF MORE THAN ONE DOOR PER ROOM SUBSCRIPT LETTERS ARE USED)

DASH AND DOT
CENTER LINES, PROJECTIONS, EXT. ELEVATION LINES

DASH AND DOUBLE DOT LINE
PROPERTY LINES, BOUNDARY LINES

DOTTED LINE
HIDDEN, FUTURE OR EXISTING CONST. TO BE REMOVED

BREAK LINE
TO BREAK OFF PARTS OF DRAWING

LINEWORK

HORIZONTAL		VERTICAL
4'-0"	8"	SLASH
2'-8"	4"	
8'-0 1/2"	6 3/4"	ARROW
26'-8"	2"	DOT
5'-4"	1/2"	ACCENT

DIMENSION LINES

UP 17R. / 11 1/2" T. → STAIR DIRECTION SYMBOL

N — NORTH POINT TO BE PLACED ON EACH FLOOR PLAN, GENERALLY IN LOWER RIGHT HAND CORNER OF DRAWING

□← NOTE
□← NOTE
□← NOTE

INDICATION ARROWS DRAWN WITH STRAIGHT LINES (NOT CURVED); MUST TOUCH OBJECT

DRAFTING TECHNIQUES

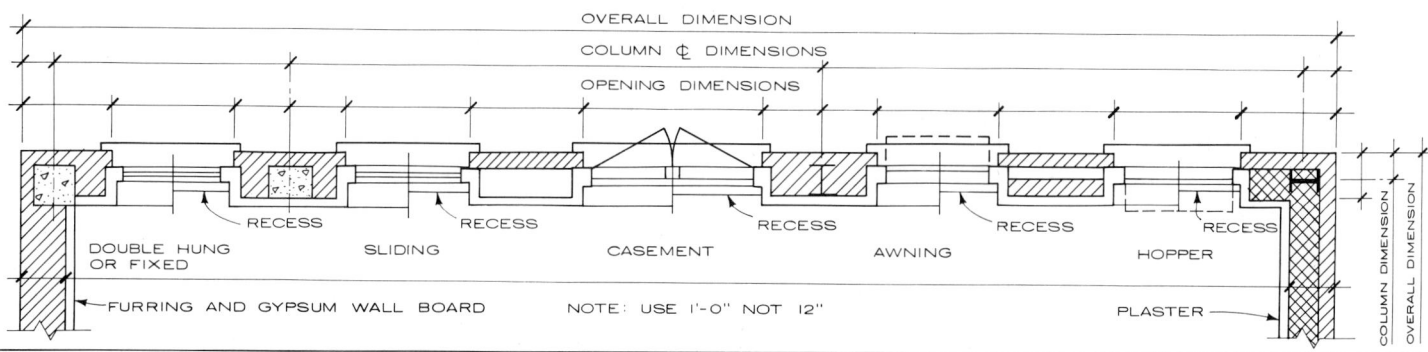

OVERALL DIMENSION
COLUMN ₡ DIMENSIONS
OPENING DIMENSIONS

RECESS — RECESS — RECESS — RECESS — RECESS

DOUBLE HUNG OR FIXED | SLIDING | CASEMENT | AWNING | HOPPER

FURRING AND GYPSUM WALL BOARD | NOTE: USE 1'-0" NOT 12" | PLASTER

COLUMN DIMENSION / OVERALL DIMENSION

METHOD FOR DIMENSIONING EXTERIOR WINDOW OPENINGS IN MASONRY WALLS (DOORS SIMILAR)

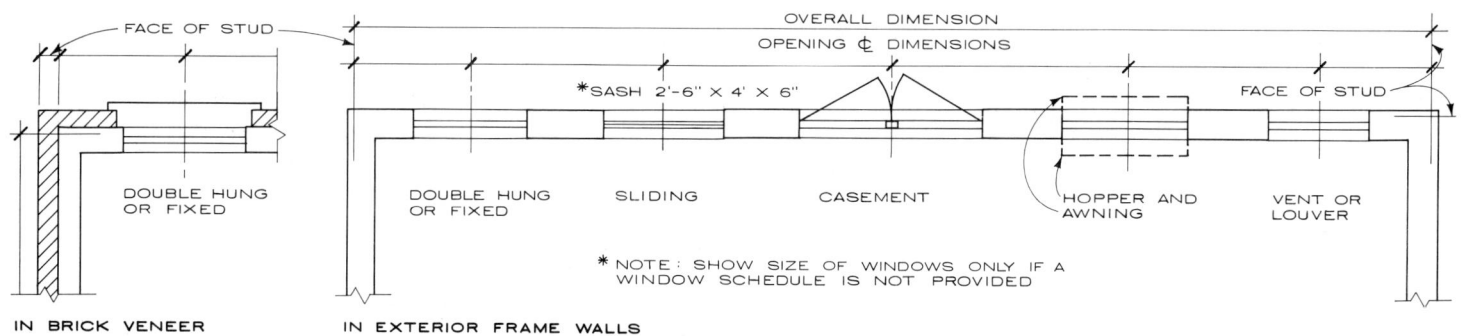

FACE OF STUD

OVERALL DIMENSION
OPENING ₡ DIMENSIONS

*SASH 2'-6" X 4' X 6"

FACE OF STUD

DOUBLE HUNG OR FIXED | DOUBLE HUNG OR FIXED | SLIDING | CASEMENT | HOPPER AND AWNING | VENT OR LOUVER

* NOTE: SHOW SIZE OF WINDOWS ONLY IF A WINDOW SCHEDULE IS NOT PROVIDED

IN BRICK VENEER | IN EXTERIOR FRAME WALLS

METHOD FOR DIMENSIONING EXTERIOR WINDOW OPENINGS IN FRAME WALLS (DOORS SIMILAR)

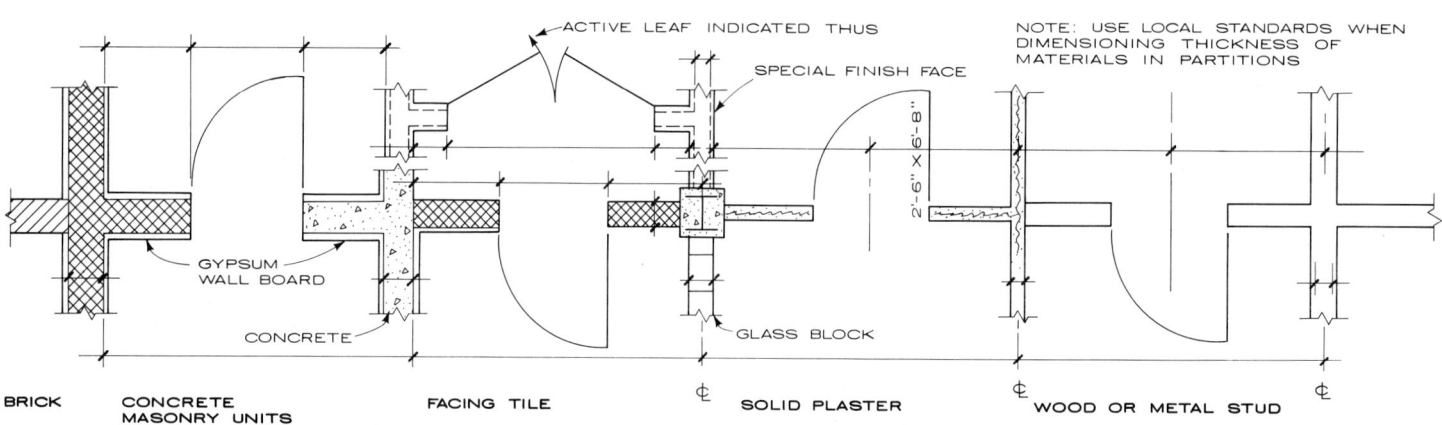

ACTIVE LEAF INDICATED THUS
SPECIAL FINISH FACE
NOTE: USE LOCAL STANDARDS WHEN DIMENSIONING THICKNESS OF MATERIALS IN PARTITIONS

2'-6" X 6'-8"

GYPSUM WALL BOARD
CONCRETE
GLASS BLOCK

BRICK | CONCRETE MASONRY UNITS | FACING TILE | ₡ SOLID PLASTER | ₡ WOOD OR METAL STUD ₡

METHOD FOR DIMENSIONING AND INDICATIONS OF INTERIOR PARTITIONS AND DOORS

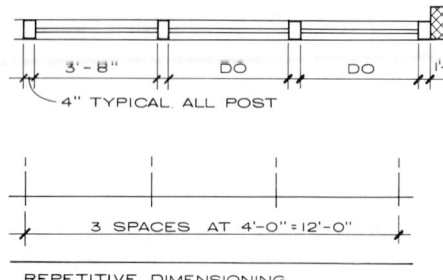

3'-8" | DO | DO | 1'-0"
4" TYPICAL ALL POST

3 SPACES AT 4'-0" = 12'-0"

REPETITIVE DIMENSIONING

EXTERIOR DOOR | SWINGING DOOR

INTERIOR DOOR | FRENCH DOOR

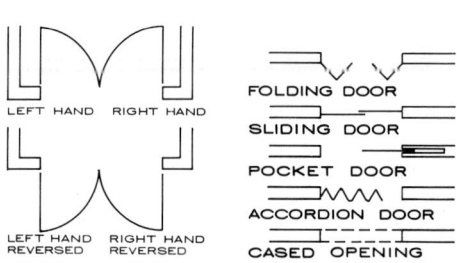

LEFT HAND | RIGHT HAND

LEFT HAND REVERSED | RIGHT HAND REVERSED

FOLDING DOOR
SLIDING DOOR
POCKET DOOR
ACCORDION DOOR
CASED OPENING

GENERAL NOTES

Dimensioning should start with critical dimensions and should be kept to a minimum. Consideration must be given to the trades using them and the sequencing adjusted to their respective work. It is also necessary to bear in mind that tolerances in actual construction will be varied. This means that as-built dimensions do not always coincide with design dimensions. Dimensioning from established grids or structural elements, such as columns and structural walls, assists the trades that must locate their work prior to that of others.

John R. Hoke, Jr., AIA; Architect; Washington, D.C.

RECOMMENDATIONS

1. Dimensions under 1 ft shall be noted in inches. Dimensions 1 ft and over shall be expressed in feet.
2. Fractions under 1 in. shall NOT be preceded by a zero. Fractions must have a diagonal dividing line between numerator and denominator.
3. Dimension points to be noted with a short blunt 45° line. Dash to be oriented differently for vertical (✻) and horizontal (✱) runs of dimensions. Modular dimension points may be designated with an arrow or a dot.
4. Dimension all items from an established grid or reference point and do not close the string of dimensions to the next grid or reference point.
5. Dimension: to face of concrete or masonry work; to centerlines of columns or other grid points; to centerlines of partitions. In nonmodular wood construction dimension to critical face of studs. When a clear dimension is required, dimension to the finish faces and note as such. Do not use the word "clear."
6. Dimension as much as possible from structural elements.
7. Overall readability, conciseness, completeness, and accuracy must be foremost in any dimensional system. It takes experience to determine how to use dimensions to the best advantage.

A **DRAFTING TECHNIQUES**

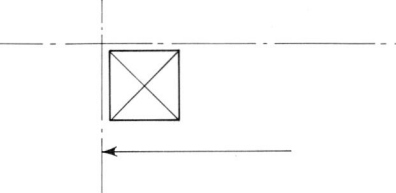

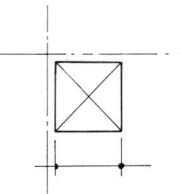

GRID LINES:

Are used to establish reference planes four inches apart in all three dimensions. Grid lines are imaginary and can be thought of as dimensional egg-crates running throughout the structure. The grid lines are partially or entirely shown on large-scale details but will not be shown at all on small scale plans.

ARROW HEADS:

Indicate all dimensions referenced to grid-line locations. This feature of modular drafting is the key to the efficiencies resulting from the use of the system. Preliminary drawings can be fully dimensioned as small scale working drawings knowing that the materials will fit when fully detailed. A number of personnel can proceed with the detailing using the single small scale plan reference without the necessity of frequent checking with each other for dimensional reference points.

DOTS:

Are used to indicate off-grid locations for dimensions. (Half-dots may be used whenever drawing space is limited.) Generally, such dimensional reference points occur when it is critical to show the measured distance to the actual face of a material. Dots are also used for joint centerlines if those points occur off the grid-lines. Column centerlines frequently are located between grid-lines to accommodate more dimensionally critical enclosure and finish materials.

MODULAR DIMENSIONING

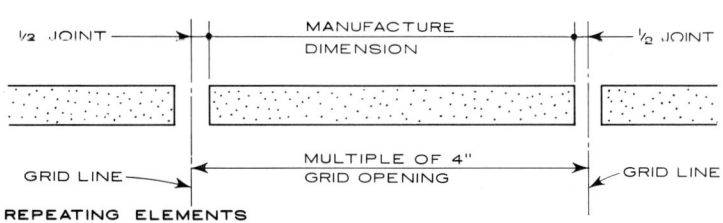

REPEATING ELEMENTS

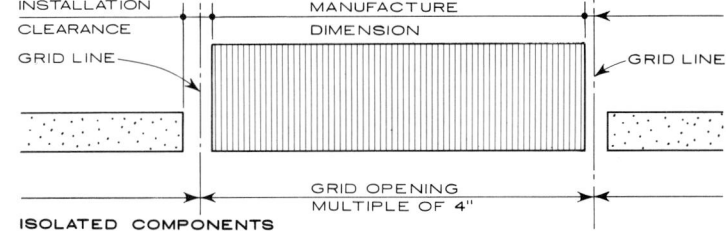

ISOLATED COMPONENTS

DIMENSIONAL CHARACTERISTICS OF MODULAR BUILDING PRODUCTS

NOTES

Modular Construction results from architectural planning based on the use of modular sized building materials and products. The joint-centerline concept of modular products permits accommodation of those materials into buildings designed with planning modules of some multiple of 4" (e.g. 3'−0", 40", 5'−4", etc.)

Small-scale assembly drawings such as plans, sections and elevations diagram the relationship of components. Since modular products are normally 4" multiples to joint centerlines, most dimensions are in multiples of 4". Arrowheads indicate dimensions are to grid-lines.

Large-scale details show the relationship of the components to the grid. Some architects prefer not to draw the entire grid on such details but include only those used as dimensional reference points on the small-scale drawings.

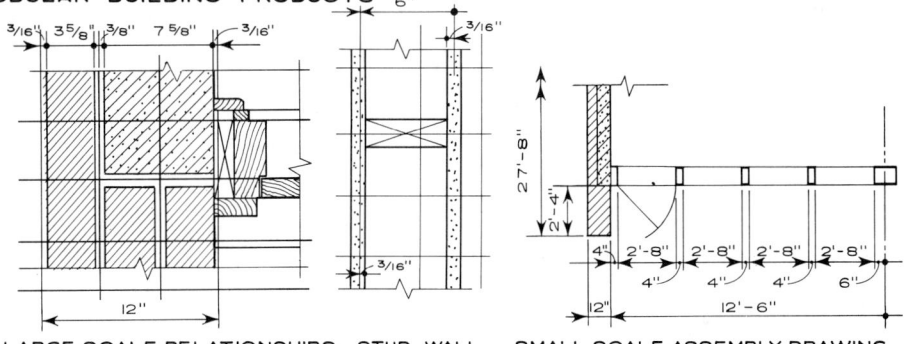

LARGE SCALE RELATIONSHIPS   STUD WALL   SMALL SCALE ASSEMBLY DRAWING

MODULAR DIMENSIONED WORKING DRAWINGS

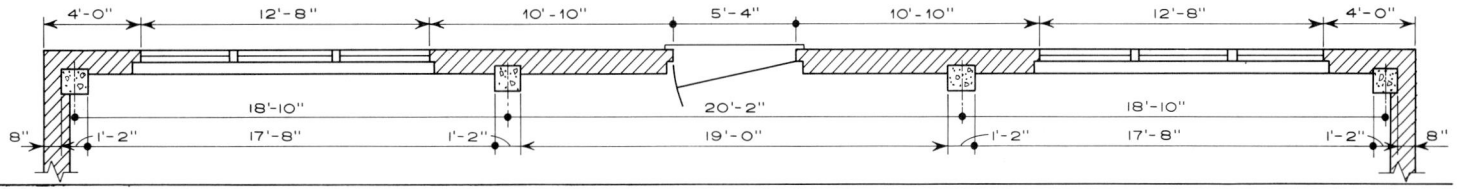

COLUMN LAYOUTS

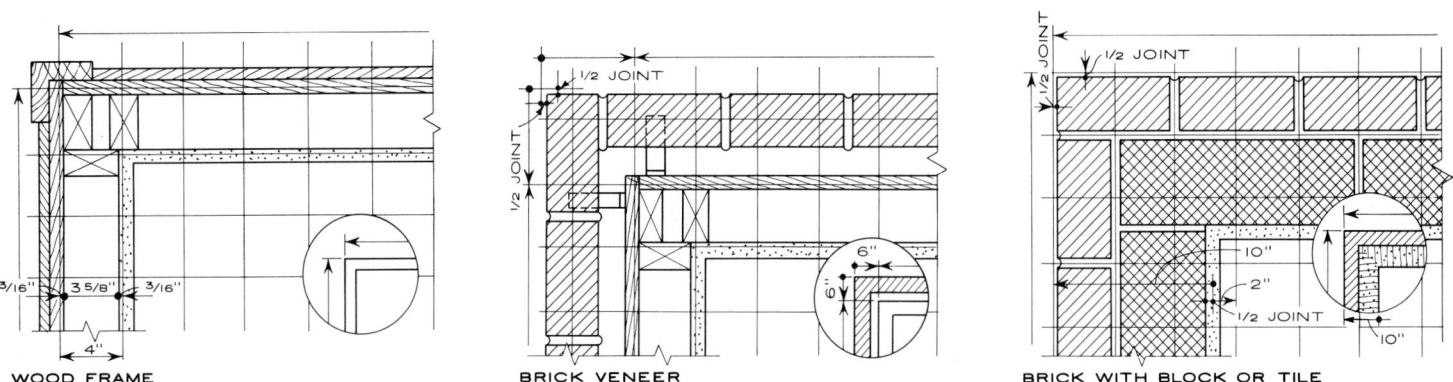

WOOD FRAME   **BRICK VENEER**   **BRICK WITH BLOCK OR TILE**

LARGE SCALE DETAILS

Byron C. Bloomfield; Madison, Wisconsin

DRAFTING TECHNIQUES   A

GRAPHIC REPRODUCTION SYSTEMS

PROCESS	EQUIPMENT	APPROXIMATE SIZE	COPY SIZE	COPY MEDIUM	ORIGINALS	SPACE REQUIRED	REMARKS
Diazo moist	Print machine Paper (specified) Solution	64"H 74"W 53"D	Up to 42" x any	Alkaline solution	Up to 42" x any	30 sq ft + 45 sq ft circ.	Sheets become wet and are dried in machine
Diazo dry	Print machine Paper (specified) Solution	64"H 74"W 84"D	Up to 42" x any	Ammonia solution	Up to 42" x any	42 sq ft + 45 sq ft circ.	Ventilation needed for ammonia vapor
PD diazo	Print machine Paper (specified) Activator	14"H 64"W 16"D	Up to 42" x any	Toner activator	Up to 42" x any	10 sq ft + 15 sq ft circ.	No vapors, seals, heat, or drying
Electrostatic	Print machine Paper (bond or translucent) Toner	20"H 48"W 36"D	8½" x 11" Up to 11" x 17"	Dry toner	8½" x 11" Up to 11" x 17"	12 sq ft + 10 sq ft circ.	Can reduce original size
Image drafting system	Print machine Paper		8½" x 11"	Photography	8½" x 11"		Rarely used
Diffusion (photocopy)	Machine Paper (special)	8"H 20"W 15"D	8½" x 11" Up to 11" x 17"	Photography	8½" x 11" Up to 11" x 17"	2 sq ft + 6 sq ft circ.	Rarely used. Replaced by electro-static machine
Dye transfer (photocopy)	Machine Paper (special) Gelatin	30"H 18"W 27"D	8½" x 11" Up to 11" x 17"	Gelatin dye	8½" x 11" Up to 11" x 17"	3 sq ft + 9 sq ft circ.	Rarely used. Replaced by electro-static machine
Thermal	Print machine Paper (bond)	13"H 24"W 19"D	8½" x 10½" Up to 11" x 14"	Only strong heat	8½" x 10½" Up to 11" x 14" One to one	2½ sq ft + 8 sq ft circ.	Totally dry heat process, no ventilation required. Rarely used
Offset	Offset printer Ink	Manual 40"H, 60"W, 36"D Auto 40"H, 60"W, 60"D	3" x 5" Up to 11" x 17"	Ink transfer	3" x 5" Up to 11" x 17"	Manual 15 sq ft Auto 25 sq ft	Camera takes picture of typed page. Colors, two sides, envelopes
Stencil	Machine Stencil Ink	19"H 38"W 20"D	3" x 5" Up to 7¾" x 14"	Ink transfer	Master (variable)	6 sq ft + 9 sq ft circ.	Postcards and regular prints. Type-writer or stylus type cut
Spirit process	Machine Ink	24"H 24"W 30"D	9" x 14" 14" x 18"	Ink transfer	Master (variable)	6 sq ft + 9 sq ft circ.	Ink transfer by pressure. Colors available
Stencil cutting	Machine Ink	9"H 16"W 25"D	9" x 15"	Ink transfer	Master (variable)	1½ sq ft + 6 sq ft circ.	Electronic stencil cutting from line originals
Microfilm	Processor Reader Film	111"H 119"W 81"D	7½" x 3¼"	Photo	Up to 63" x 45"	70 sq ft + 70 sq ft circ.	Rarely done in-house
Spirit master maker	Machine Ink	6"H 18"W 12"D	9" x any	Ink transfer		1½ sq ft + 6 sq ft circ.	Spirit masters from line originals

NOTE

This is a brief sampling of processes, sizes, and capacities. Many of the machines have optional equipment to be used with them. Consult manufacturers for location and quantity of electric service.

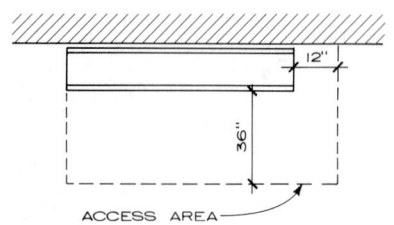

PD DIAZO MACHINE

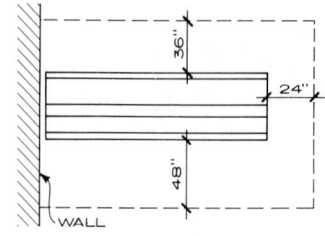

DIAZO MACHINE (MOIST OR DRY)

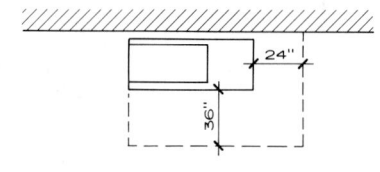

FLOOR OR TABLE PRINTER

SPACE REQUIREMENTS OF GRAPHIC REPRODUCTION SYSTEMS

K. Shahid Rab, AIA; Friesen International; Washington, D.C.

 DRAFTING TECHNIQUES

PARALINE DRAWINGS

Paraline drawings are sometimes referred to as AXONOMETRIC (Greek) or AXIOMETRIC (English) drawings. These drawings are projected pictorial representations of an object which give a three-dimensional quality. They can be classified as orthographic projections inasmuch as the plan view is rotated and the side view is tilted. The resulting "front" view is projected at a 90° angle to the picture plane (as illustrated in the projected method). These drawings differ from perspective drawings, since the projection lines remain parallel instead of converging to a point on the horizon.

Drawings prepared by using the projection method require three views of the object, which tends to be more time-consuming and complex than drawing by the direct measuring method. The following drawings utilize this method; they are simple to draw and represent reasonably accurate proportions.

OBLIQUE

In an oblique drawing one face (either plan or elevation) of the object is drawn directly on the picture plane. Projected lines are drawn at a 30 or 45° angle to the picture plane. The length of the projecting lines is determined as illustrated and varies according to the angle chosen.

DIMETRIC

A dimetric drawing is similar to oblique, with one exception—the object is rotated so that only one of its corners touches the picture plane. The most frequently used angle for the projecting lines is an equal division of 45° on either side of the leading edge. A 15° angle is sometimes used when it is less important to show the "roof view" of the object.

ISOMETRIC

The isometric, a special type of dimetric drawing, is the easiest and most popular paraline drawing. All axis of the object are simultaneously rotated away from the picture plane and kept at the same angle of projection (30° from the picture plane). All legs are equally distorted in length at a given scale and therefore maintain an exact proportion of 1:1:1.

TRIMETRIC

The trimetric drawing is similar to the dimetric, except that the plan of the object is rotated so that the two exposed sides of the object are not at equal angles to the picture plane. The plan is usually positioned at 30/60° angle to the ground plane. The height of the object is reduced proportionately as illustrated (similar to the 45° dimetric).

SHADES AND SHADOWS

Shades and shadows are easily constructed and can be very effective in paraline drawings. The location of the light source will determine the direction of the shadows cast by the object. The shade line is the line (or the edge) that separates the light area from the shaded areas of the object. Shadows are constructed by drawing a line, representing a light ray, from a corner of the lighted surface at a 45° angle to the ground plane. Shadows cast by a vertical edge of the object will be drawn midway in the angle created by the intersection of the projected line of the object and the ground, or baseline (the baseline represents the intersection of the picture plane). The 45° light ray is extended until it meets the shadow line (as illustrated), and this point determines the length of the shadow for any given vertical height of the object. Shadow lines of all vertical edges of the object are drawn parallel to one another.

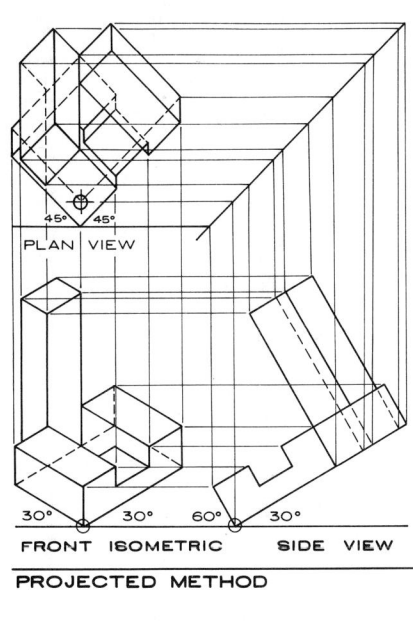

PLAN VIEW
45° 45°

30°   30°   60°   30°
FRONT ISOMETRIC   SIDE VIEW

PROJECTED METHOD

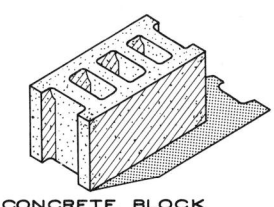

CONCRETE BLOCK

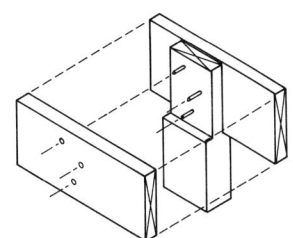

EXPLODED VIEW OF DETAIL

ISOMETRIC

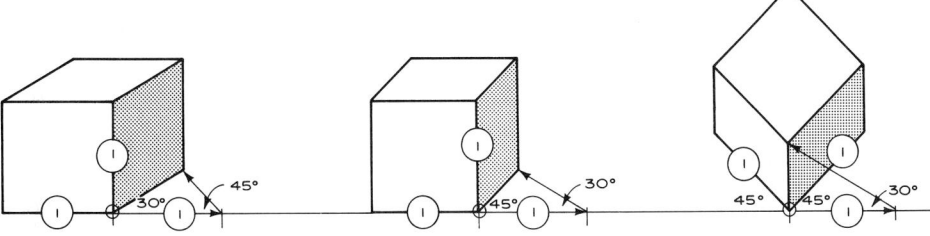

45°
30° OBLIQUE

30°   45°
45° OBLIQUE

45°   45°   30°
45° DIMETRIC
(ROTATED PLAN)

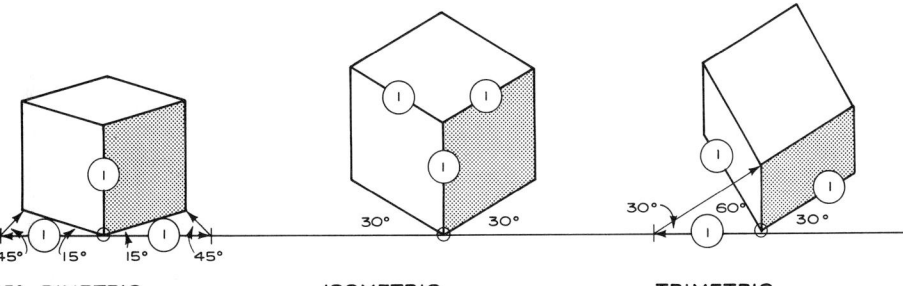

45°   15°   15°   45°
15° DIMETRIC

30°   30°
ISOMETRIC
(30° DIMETRIC)

30°   60°   30°
TRIMETRIC
(ROTATED PLAN)

AXIOMETRIC — MEASURED METHOD

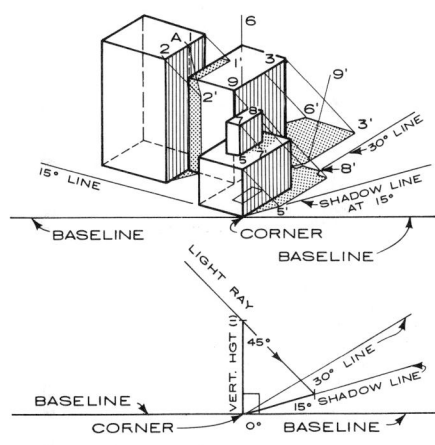

A
2   6
3
9   9'
2'   6'
5   3'
15° LINE   30° LINE
8'
SHADOW LINE
AT 15°
BASELINE   CORNER
BASELINE

LIGHT RAY
VERT. HGT (1)
45°
30° LINE
SHADOW LINE
15°
BASELINE
CORNER   0°   BASELINE

15 / 30° TRIMETRIC SHADOW

SHADES AND SHADOWS

Jim Maeda; Samuel J. De Santo and Associates; New York, New York

GRAPHIC METHODS

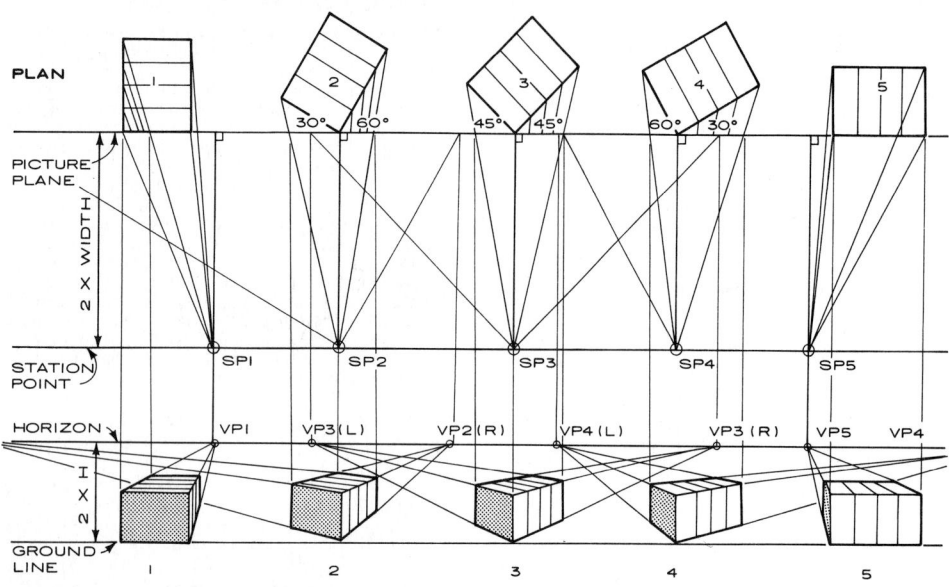

PERSPECTIVE — PROJECTION METHOD

GENERAL NOTES

Before the drawing can be laid out, the following information must be obtained:

1. An approximation of the overall dimensions of the building.
2. The location of the building in relation to the picture plane.
3. The orientation of the building, either in front of or behind the picture plane.

While the building can be located anywhere in the drawing—in front of, behind, or at any angle to the picture plane—the simplest approach is to place the building at the picture plane. The horizontal lines of the building would be parallel to the picture plane in a one-point perspective or placed at an angle to the picture plane. Usually this will be a 30/60 or 45° angle in a two-point perspective.

TERMS AND CONCEPTS

1. THE OBJECT: Called a building in this example.
2. THE PICTURE PLANE: An imaginary, transparent plane, onto or through which the object is perceived in a perspective rendering. It is:
   a. Parallel to one face of the drawing paper, if it is a one-point perspective.
   b. Perpendicular to the ground line and at any angle to the building if it is a two-point perspective.
   c. Tilted and placed at any angle to the building if it is a three-point perspective.
   d. A curved plane if it is a wide angle perspective view.
3. HORIZON LINE: A line drawn on the picture plane to represent the horizon. It is usually located at the point where all parallel lines recede away from the viewer and finally converge. This point is aptly designed as the vanishing point. Not that although the horizon is generally thought of as a horizontal line, in certain applications it could be vertical, or even at an angle, to the picture plane. For example, in drawing shades and shadows it appears to be at a 90° angle and in a three-point perspective it appears to be slanted.
4. STATION POINT: The point from which the object is being viewed or, in other words the point from which the viewer is seeing the building. The location of this point will be the factor that determines the width of the drawing. A 30° cone of vision is drawn from the station point, as the viewer moves away from the object, the cone widens, the object becomes smaller, and more material is included in the area surrounding the object. A common way of determining the distance between the station point and the picture plane is by referring to the following parameters:
   Minimum—1.73 times the width of the drawing.
   Average—2.00 times the width of the drawing.
   Maximum—2.50 times the width of the drawing.
5. VANISHING POINT(S): A specific point or points located on the horizon line, where all parallel lines, drawn in perspective, converge or terminate. The location of the vanishing point varies with the type of perspective drawing. In a two-point perspective, the distance between the vanishing point left and the vanishing point right is estimated as being approximately four times the overall size of the building.
6. VISUAL RAY: An imaginary line drawn from the station point to any specific point lying within the designated scope of the plan layout of the object. The point at which this projected line passes through the picture plane will determine the location of that point in the perspective drawing.
7. GROUND PLANE: The ground on which the viewer is standing. In plan, this is determined at the station point. In perspective, it is the primary plane on which the building is sited. When the lines of this plane are extended to infinity, it becomes the horizon line. The intersection formed when the picture plane and the ground plane come together is called the ground line. In this way the horizontal dimension of the drawing is determined. The vertical dimension is determined by the vertical distance from the ground line to the horizon line. This should be approximately twice the height of object, in perspective, or a 30° cone in elevation.
8. ONE-POINT INTERIOR PERSPECTIVE: The most frequently used application of a one-point perspective. This is the same method as that used in setting up a one-point exterior perspective, except for the limitations that the confinement of space places on the location of the vanishing points. The vanishing point is usually located at the sitting or standing height of an average person within the space (eye level can be considered to be at 5 ft 4 in. from the floor). In most cases, the vanishing point is located within the confines of the enclosed space being represented in the drawing.
9. TWO-POINT PERSPECTIVE USING THE MEASURING POINT METHOD: This is a simplified alternative to the conventional method of laying out the plan picture plane and projecting the vanishing lines. The measuring point method of drawing a two-point perspective eliminates the necessity of the preliminary layout of the plan. One of the obvious advantages of this method is the ease with which the size of the drawing can be adjusted. A perspective can be made larger by simply increasing the scale of the drawing.

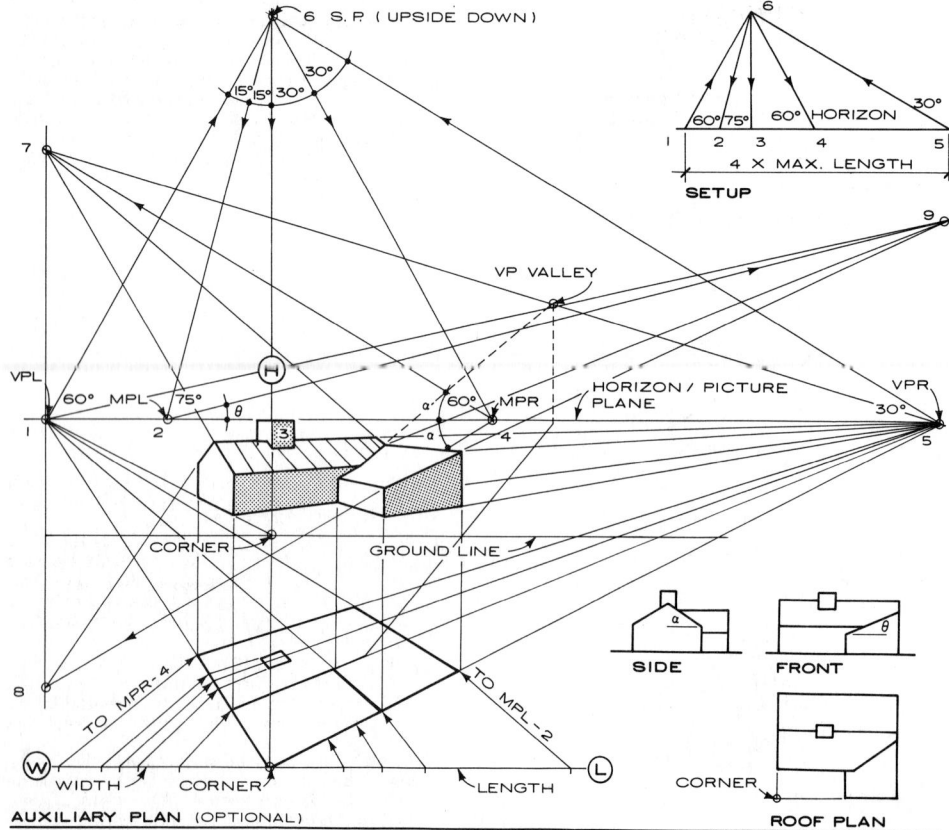

PERSPECTIVE — TWO-POINT CONVENTIONAL METHOD

Jim Maeda; Samuel J. De Santo and Associates; New York, New York

GRAPHIC METHODS

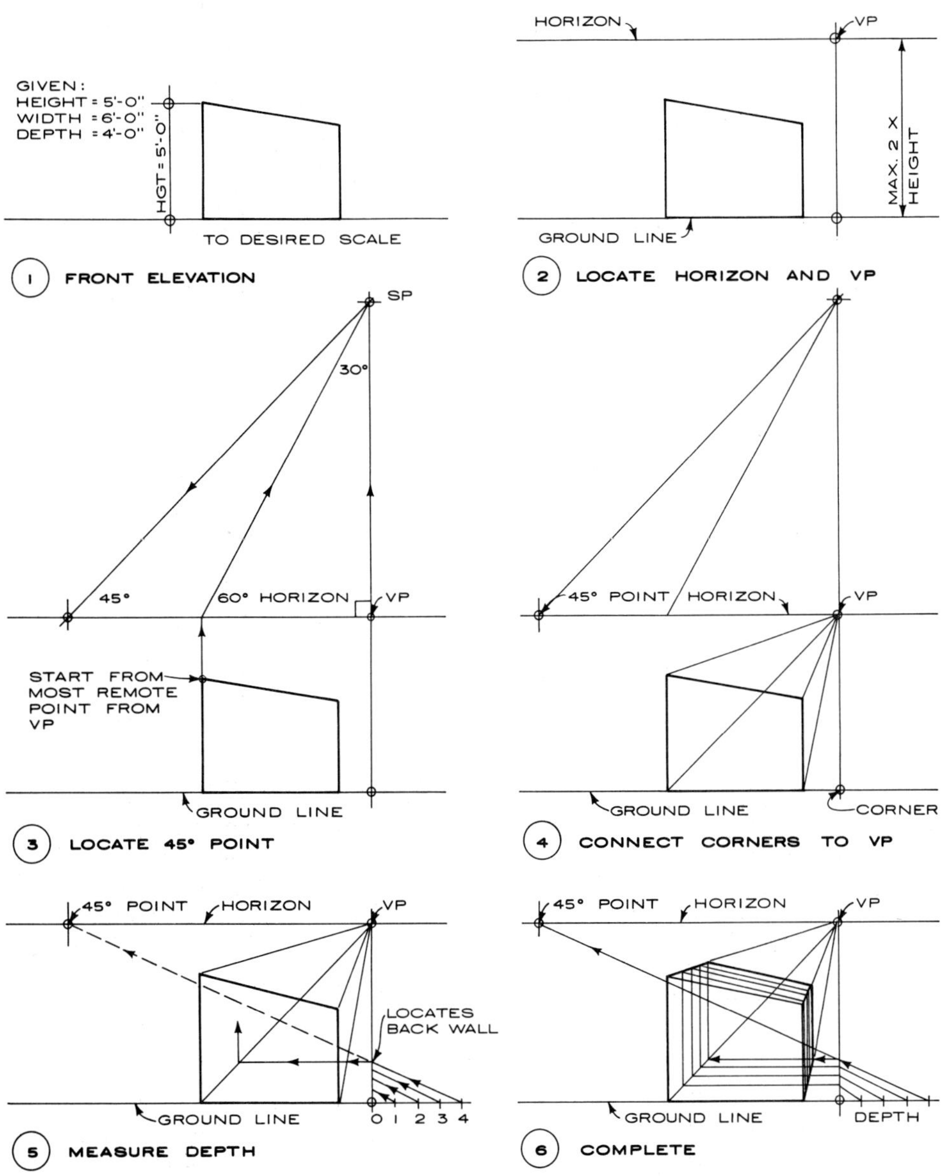

ONE-POINT PERSPECTIVE BY 45° MEASURING POINT

GIVEN:
HEIGHT = 5'-0"
WIDTH = 6'-0"
DEPTH = 4'-0"

HGT = 5'-0"

TO DESIRED SCALE

1 **FRONT ELEVATION**

2 **LOCATE HORIZON AND VP**

HORIZON — VP
MAX. 2 X HEIGHT
GROUND LINE

SP
30°
45°   60° HORIZON   VP
START FROM MOST REMOTE POINT FROM VP
GROUND LINE

3 **LOCATE 45° POINT**

45° POINT / HORIZON   VP
GROUND LINE   CORNER

4 **CONNECT CORNERS TO VP**

45° POINT   HORIZON   VP
LOCATES BACK WALL
GROUND LINE   0 1 2 3 4

5 **MEASURE DEPTH**

45° POINT   HORIZON   VP
GROUND LINE   DEPTH

6 **COMPLETE**

ONE-POINT PERSPECTIVE BY 45° MEASURING POINT

GIVEN:
FRONT ELEVATION
DEPTH = 4'

VP   HORIZON
TO DESIRED SCALE

1 **FRONT ELEVATION**

SP
45° 30°
45°   VP 60°   HORIZON
GROUND LINE

2 **LOCATE 45° POINT**

45° POINT   VP   HORIZON
START 0 1 2 3 4

3 **LOCATE BACK WALL**

45° POINT   HORIZON

4 **COMPLETE**

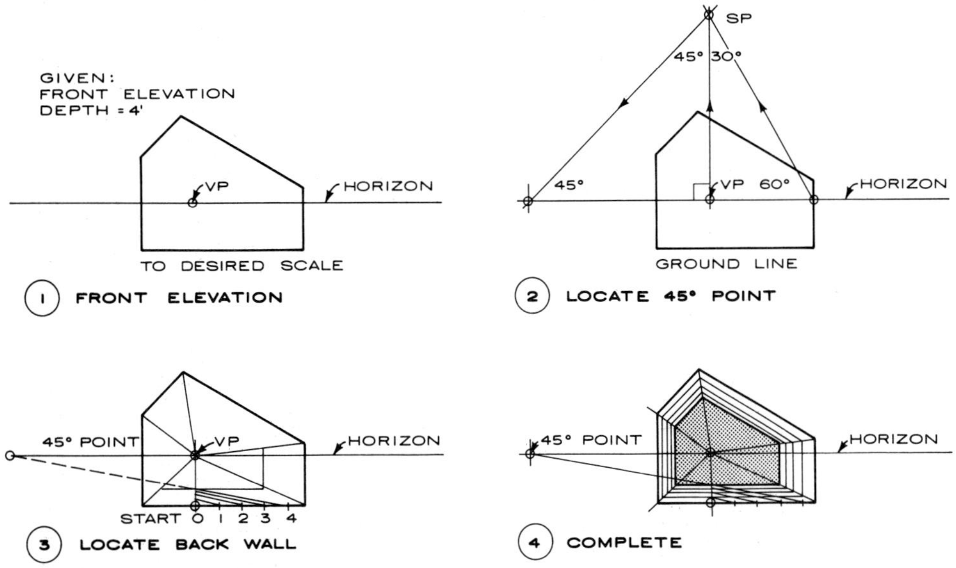

ONE-POINT MEASURED INTERIOR PERSPECTIVE

Jim Maeda; Samuel J. De Santo and Associates; New York, New York

ONE-POINT PERSPECTIVE

The one-point perspective is probably the least complicated of the projected perspective methods. The primary face of the building or object is placed directly on the picture plane. The adjacent planes, generally connected to the primary plane at right angles, converge to the vanishing point—which can be either in front of or behind the picture plane. The vanishing point, located on the horizon line, also determines the height from which the building is viewed.

The conventional method of laying out a one-point exterior perspective is illustrated on the preceding page. A plan view, roof view, and elevation are required for the layout. The size of the object, and therefore the drawing, can be increased or decreased by moving the plan further in front of or behind the picture plane. This method is more flexible but much more complicated and time-consuming than the method that follows.

EXTERIOR ONE-POINT PERSPECTIVE

1. Draw the primary elevation of the building to scale.
2. Locate the horizon above the ground line at the desired level (eye level is at approximately 5 ft 4 in.). To ensure that the final perspective will fall within the 60° cone vision, the height should not exceed 2X the height of the building. The VP is located left or right arbitrarily depending on the view desired.
3. A 45° vanishing point can be graphically located by starting at the most remote point of the roof and extending a vertical line to the horizon line. From this point, draw a line upward, at a 60° angle. Another line should be drawn vertically upward from the vanishing point. The station point (upside down) is located at the point where these two lines intersect. From the station point, draw a line at a 45° angle to meet the horizon line. This point will be the vanishing point for all lines that are positioned at 45° angle and parallel to the picture plane.
4. From each corner of the primary elevation, draw a line to the vanishing point.
5. The correct building depth (drawn at 6 ft in the illustration) is measured along the ground line—on the picture plane—starting at point 0. Draw a line connecting this point to the 45° point on the horizon line. The point at which this line intersects the line extended between the lower corner of the elevation to the vanishing point will determine the location of the back wall of the building.
6. The perspective is completed by constructing the back wall at the location established in step 5 and connecting it to the front wall. Note that the lines that are drawn at a 45° angle in the drawing remain parallel to each other as they are extended in perspective.

ONE-POINT INTERIOR AND SECTIONAL PERSPECTIVE

1. Draw the primary elevation, or section, to scale. Locate the horizon line and vanishing point within the confines of the interior space.
2. A 45° point is located in a similar manner to the one-point exterior perspective. The station point is established by drawing a line, at a 60° angle, from the most remote point in the elevation to intersect another line extended upward at a perpendicular from the vanishing point.
3. The room depth is determined by starting at point 0 on the ground line and measuring the appropriate distance to the 45° point on the horizon line. The back wall is located where these two lines come together.
4. Complete the back wall as illustrated. Note that all lines occurring at a 45° angle in the elevation remain parallel in perspective. All surfaces that are parallel to the picture plane will remain parallel in perspective.

GRAPHIC METHODS

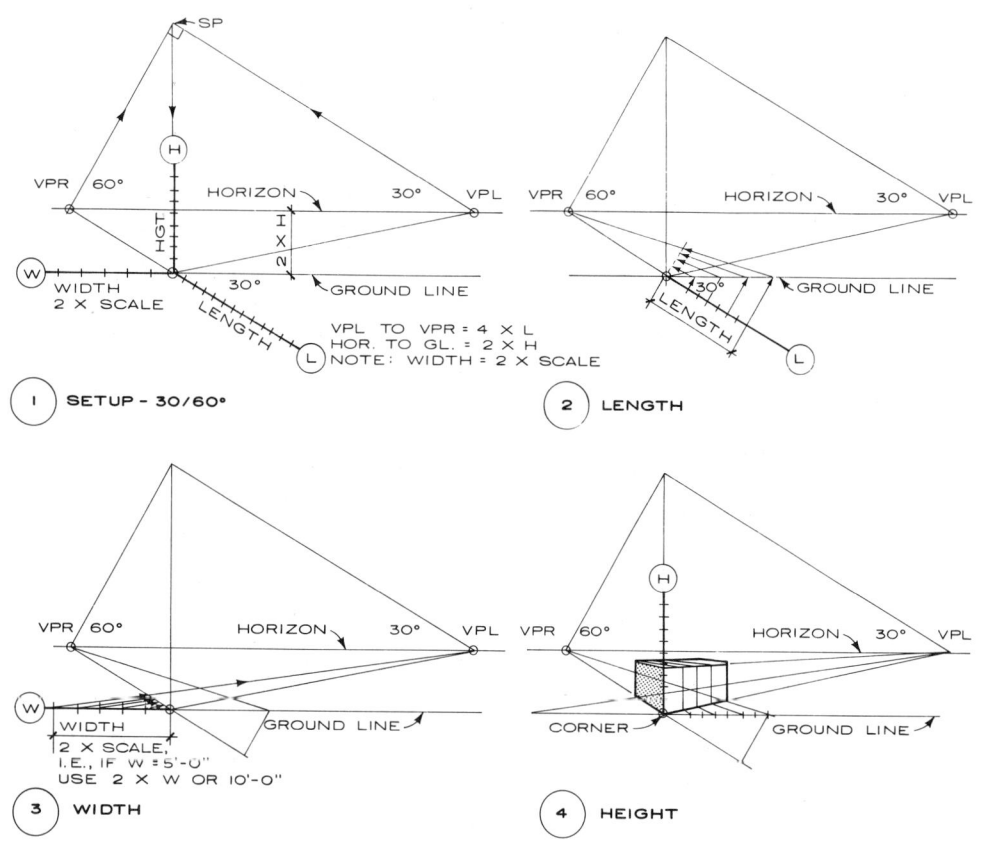

TWO—POINT PERSPECTIVE — 30/60° MEASURED SYSTEM

TWO-POINT PERSPECTIVE

The projection method of constructing a two-point perspective is illustrated on the preceding page. This is the most widely used and most flexible method of drawing a two-point perspective. It can be taken from any viewpoint by simply turning the plan to the desired position in the preliminary layout. The size of the perspective can also be adjusted by moving the plan in front of the picture plane for a larger drawing and behind the picture plane for a smaller drawing. As in all projected methods, an inordinate amount of time and energy is devoted to the layout. The measured method is equally accurate, less time-consuming, and much easier to construct, since it eliminates the need to lay out the drawing in plan. The desired size of the drawing is determined by drawing the primary elevation at the desired scale.

30/60° MEASURED SYSTEM

① SET-UP: Draw a horizon line and locate VPR and VPL separated at a distance that is approximately four to four and a half times the maximum width of the building. Follow the illustration to locate the station point and leading corner of the building.

② LENGTH: Measure, to scale, the length of the building along length line L. A perpendicular line is drawn from these designated points to the ground line. The vanishing perspective lines are then drawn directly from these points to the appropriate vanishing point (VPL). In this way the correct length of the line can be determined. Note what happens when equally spaced points are projected from the ground line to the vanishing point. The visual distance (length) between them, as they get closer to the vanishing point, is progressively foreshortened.

③ WIDTH: The width is measured along the width line (see illustration) at double the scale. That is, if the perspective is drawn at a scale of 1/8 in. = 1 ft and a particular line is to be drawn at 5 ft, measure 5 ft at 1/4-in. scale starting at the corner and measure to the left of the corner horizontally. A line is drawn from each point on the width line to the appropriate vanishing point (VPR). The intersections of the length and width vanishing lines will define the "plan" in perspective.

④ HEIGHT: Since the leading corner of the building is placed directly on the picture plane, the height is measured, to scale, directly on the H line. It is then carried to VPL and VPR as illustrated.

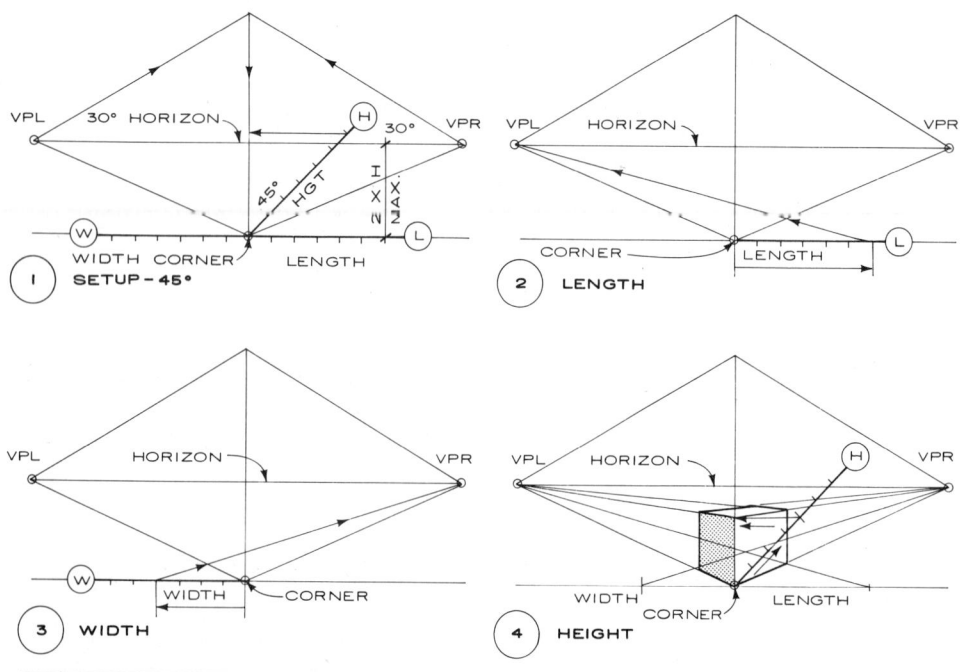

TWO—POINT PERSPECTIVE — 45° MEASURED SYSTEM

45° METHOD SYSTEM

① SETUP: Similar to the method used in the 30/60° setup, the vanishing points are placed on the horizon line and separated by four to four and a half times the maximum width of the building. Complete the setup as illustrated.

② LENGTH: Measure, to scale, the length of the building along the length line L. Connect the points directly to VPL.

③ WIDTH: In this setup, the width is the same as the length scale. Measure the width of the building along the width line W. The length and width lines will form an outline of the "plan" in perspective.

④ HEIGHT: The height line is positioned at a 45° angle and marked off to scale. A line representing the leading corner of the building is drawn perpendicular to the ground line. Connect or draw a line from the measurement points along the height line to the vertical corner line. As in the 30/60° setup, these points are then carried to VPR and VPL.

Jim Maeda; Samuel J. De Santo and Associates; New York, New York

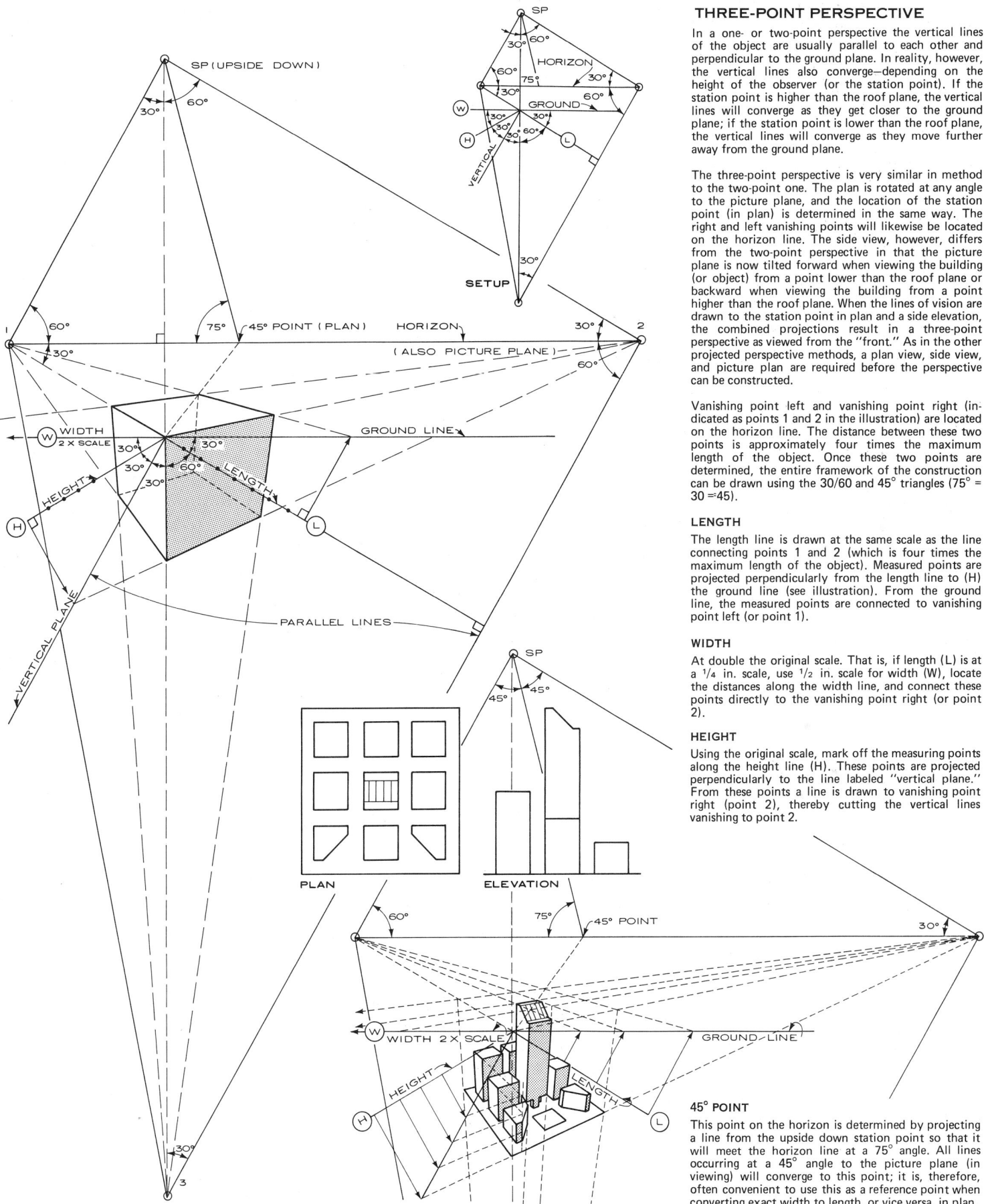

SP (UPSIDE DOWN)

SETUP

1   75° 45° POINT (PLAN)   HORIZON   2
(ALSO PICTURE PLANE)

GROUND LINE

WIDTH 2 X SCALE

HEIGHT   LENGTH

VERTICAL PLANE

PARALLEL LINES

PLAN   ELEVATION

3

PROJECTING THE PERSPECTIVE

WIDTH 2 X SCALE   GROUND LINE

HEIGHT   LENGTH

Jim Maeda; Samuel J. De Santo and Associates; New York, New York

THREE-POINT PERSPECTIVE

In a one- or two-point perspective the vertical lines of the object are usually parallel to each other and perpendicular to the ground plane. In reality, however, the vertical lines also converge—depending on the height of the observer (or the station point). If the station point is higher than the roof plane, the vertical lines will converge as they get closer to the ground plane; if the station point is lower than the roof plane, the vertical lines will converge as they move further away from the ground plane.

The three-point perspective is very similar in method to the two-point one. The plan is rotated at any angle to the picture plane, and the location of the station point (in plan) is determined in the same way. The right and left vanishing points will likewise be located on the horizon line. The side view, however, differs from the two-point perspective in that the picture plane is now tilted forward when viewing the building (or object) from a point lower than the roof plane or backward when viewing the building from a point higher than the roof plane. When the lines of vision are drawn to the station point in plan and a side elevation, the combined projections result in a three-point perspective as viewed from the "front." As in the other projected perspective methods, a plan view, side view, and picture plan are required before the perspective can be constructed.

Vanishing point left and vanishing point right (indicated as points 1 and 2 in the illustration) are located on the horizon line. The distance between these two points is approximately four times the maximum length of the object. Once these two points are determined, the entire framework of the construction can be drawn using the 30/60 and 45° triangles (75° = 30 =45).

LENGTH

The length line is drawn at the same scale as the line connecting points 1 and 2 (which is four times the maximum length of the object). Measured points are projected perpendicularly from the length line to (H) the ground line (see illustration). From the ground line, the measured points are connected to vanishing point left (or point 1).

WIDTH

At double the original scale. That is, if length (L) is at a 1/4 in. scale, use 1/2 in. scale for width (W), locate the distances along the width line, and connect these points directly to the vanishing point right (or point 2).

HEIGHT

Using the original scale, mark off the measuring points along the height line (H). These points are projected perpendicularly to the line labeled "vertical plane." From these points a line is drawn to vanishing point right (point 2), thereby cutting the vertical lines vanishing to point 2.

45° POINT

This point on the horizon is determined by projecting a line from the upside down station point so that it will meet the horizon line at a 75° angle. All lines occurring at a 45° angle to the picture plane (in viewing) will converge to this point; it is, therefore, often convenient to use this as a reference point when converting exact width to length, or vice versa, in plan.

GRAPHIC METHODS   **A**

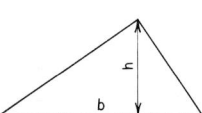

TRIANGLE
AREA = ½ ANY ALTITUDE × ITS BASE (ALTITUDE IS PERPENDICULAR DISTANCE TO OPPOSITE VERTEX OR CORNER.)
$A = \frac{1}{2} b \times h$

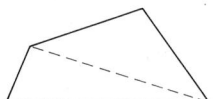

TRAPEZUM (IRREGULAR QUADRILATERAL)
AREA = DIVIDE FIGURE INTO TWO TRIANGLES AND FIND AREAS AS ABOVE

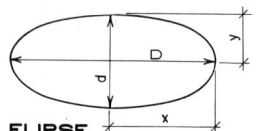

ELIPSE
AREA = .7854 Dd
APPROX. PERIMETER = $\pi \sqrt{2(x^2+y^2)}$

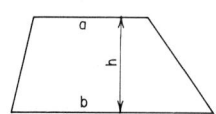

TRAPEZOID
AREA = ½ SUM OF PARALLEL SIDES × ALTITUDE
$A = h\frac{(a+b)}{2}$

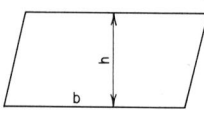

PARALLELOGRAM
AREA = EITHER SIDE × ALTITUDE

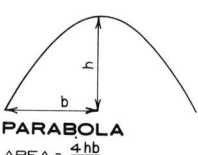

PARABOLA
AREA = $\frac{4hb}{3}$

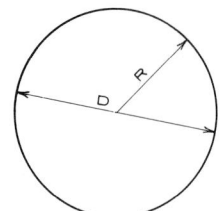

CIRCLE
AREA = $\frac{\pi D^2}{4} = \pi R^2$
CIRCUMFERENCE = $2\pi R = \pi D$
(π = 3.14159265359)

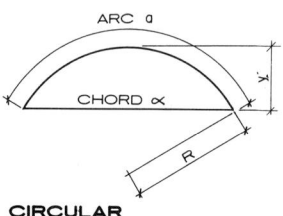

CIRCULAR SEGMENT
AREA = $\frac{(\text{LENGTH OF ARC } a \times R - a(R-y))}{2}$
CHORD $a = 2\sqrt{2yR - y^2}$
= $2R \sin \frac{A°}{2}$

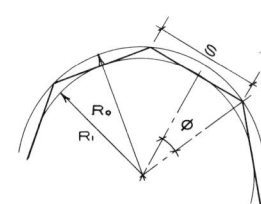

REGULAR POLYGON
AREA = $\frac{nSR_i}{2}$
(n = NUMBER OF SIDES)
ANY SIDE S = $2\sqrt{R_o^2 - R_i^2}$
$R_i = \frac{S}{2 \tan \emptyset}$ $R_o = \frac{S}{2 \sin \emptyset}$

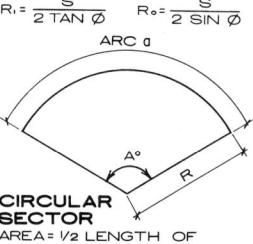

CIRCULAR SECTOR
AREA = ½ LENGTH OF ARC $a \times R$
= AREA OF CIRCLE × $\frac{A°}{360}$
= $0.0087 R^2 A°$
ARC $a = \frac{\pi R A°}{180°} = 0.0175 R A°$

GEOMETRIC PROPERTIES OF PLANE FIGURES

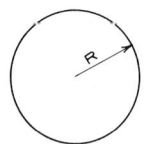

SPHERE
VOLUME = $\frac{4\pi R^3}{3}$
= $0.5236 D^3$
SURFACE = $4\pi R^2$
= πD^2

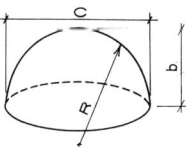

SEGMENT OF SPHERE
VOLUME = $\frac{\pi b^2(3R-b)}{3}$
(OR SECTOR - CONE)
SURFACE = $2\pi Rb$
(NOT INCLUDING SURFACE OF CIRCULAR BASE)

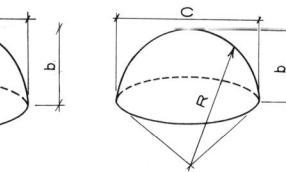

SECTOR OF SPHERE
VOLUME = $\frac{2\pi R^2 b}{3}$
SURFACE = $\frac{\pi R(4b+c)}{2}$
(OR: SEGMENT + CONE)

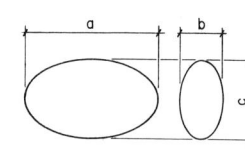

ELIPSOID
VOLUME = $\frac{\pi abc}{6}$
SURFACE: NO SIMPLE RULE

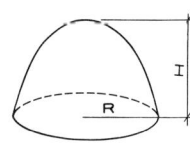

PARABOLOID OF REVOLUTION
VOLUME = AREA OF CIRCULAR BASE × ½ ALTITUDE.
SURFACE: NO SIMPLE RULE

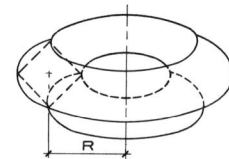

CIRCULAR RING OF ANY SECTION
R = DISTANCE FROM AXIS OF RING TO TRUE CENTER OF SECTION
VOLUME = AREA OF SECTION × $2\pi R$
SURFACE = PERIMETER OF SECTION × $2\pi R$ (CONSIDER THE SECTION ON ONE SIDE OF AXIS ONLY)

VOLUMES AND SURFACES OF DOUBLE - CURVED SOLIDS

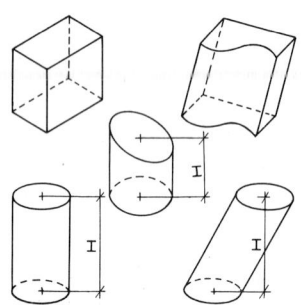

ANY PRISM OR CYLINDER, RIGHT OR OBLIQUE, REGULAR OR IRREGULAR.

Volume = area of base x altitude

Altitude = distance between parallel bases, measured perpendicular to the bases. When bases are not parallel, then Altitude = perpendicular distance from one base to the center of the other.

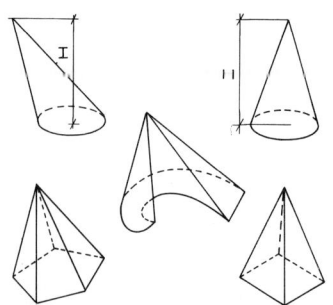

ANY PYRAMID OR CONE, RIGHT OR OBLIQUE, REGULAR OR IRREGULAR.

Volume = area of base x 1/3 altitude

Altitude = distance from base to apex, measured perpendicular to base.

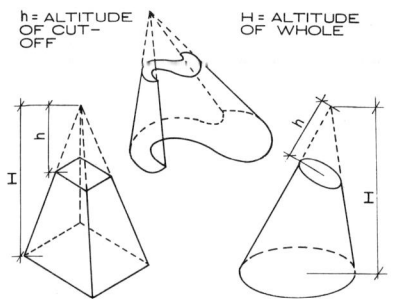

ANY FRUSTUM OR TRUNCATED PORTION OF THE SOLIDS SHOWN

Volume: From the volume of the whole solid, if complete, subtract the volume of the portion cut off.

The altitude of the cut-off part must be measured perpendicular to its own base.

SURFACES OF SOLIDS

The area of the surface is best found by adding together the areas of all the faces.

The area of a right cylindrical surface = perimeter of base x length of elements (average length if other base is oblique).

The area of a right conical surface = perimeter of base x 1/2 length of elements.

There is no simple rule for the area of an oblique conical surface, or for a cylindrical one where neither base is perpendicular to the elements. The best method is to construct a development, as if making a paper model, and measure its area by one of the methods given on the next page.

VOLUMES AND SURFACES OF TYPICAL SOLIDS

GRAPHIC METHODS

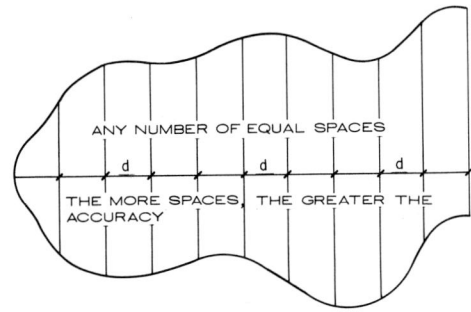

TO FIND THE AREA OF AN IRREGULAR PLANE FIGURE

1. Divide the figure into parallel strips by equally spaced parallel lines.

2. Measure the length of each of the parallel lines.

3. Obtain a summation of the unit areas by one of these 3 "rules".

TRAPEZOID RULE

Add together the length of the parallels, taking the first and last at $1/2$ value, and multiply by the width of the internal "d". This rule is sufficiently accurate for estimating and other ordinary purposes.

SIMPSON'S RULE

Add the parallels, taking the first and last at full value, second the, fourth, sixth, etc. from each end at 4 times full value, and the third, fifth, seventh, etc. from each end at 2 times the value, then multiply by $1/3$ d. This rule works only for an even number of spaces and is accurate for areas bounded by smooth curves.

DURAND'S RULE

Add the parallels taking the first and last at $5/12$ value, the second from each end at $13/12$ value, and all others at full value, then multiply by d. This rule is the most accurate for very irregular shapes.

NOTE

Irregular areas may be directly read off by means of a simple instrument called a Planimeter.

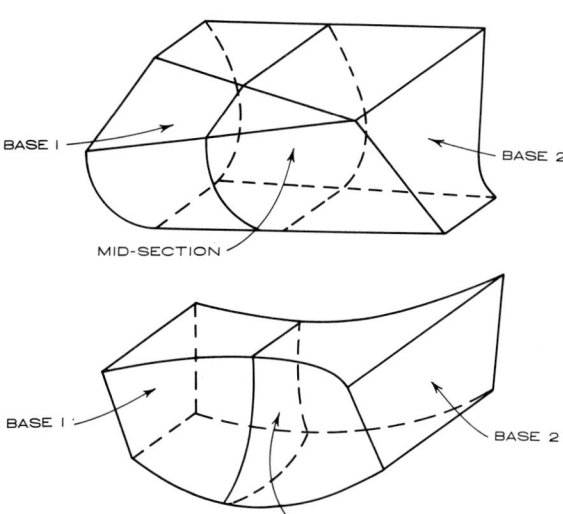

TO FIND THE VOLUME OF AN IRREGULAR FIGURE BY THE PRISMATOID FORMULA

Construct a section midway between the bases. Add 4 to the sum of the areas of the 2 bases and multiply the quantity by the area of the mid-section. Then multiply the total by $1/6$ the perpendicular distance between the bases.

V = [(area of base$_1$ + area of base$_2$ + 4) (area of midsection) x $1/6$ perpendicular distance between bases.

This formula is quite accurate for any solid with two parallel bases connected by a surface of straight line elements (upper figure), or smooth simple curves (lower figure).

TO FIND THE VOLUME OF A VERY IRREGULAR FIGURE BY THE SECTIONING METHOD

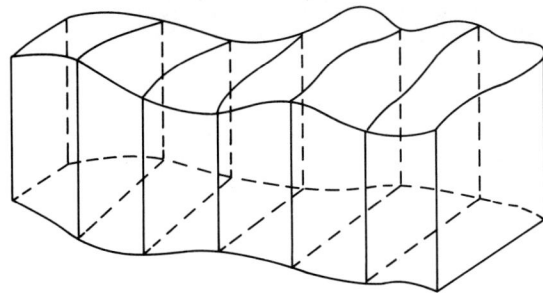

1. Construct a series of equally spaced sections or profiles.

2. Determine the area of each section by any of the methods shown at left (preferably with a Planimeter).

3. Apply any one of the 3 summation "rules" given at left, to determine the total volume.

This method is in general use for estimating quantities of earthwork, etc.

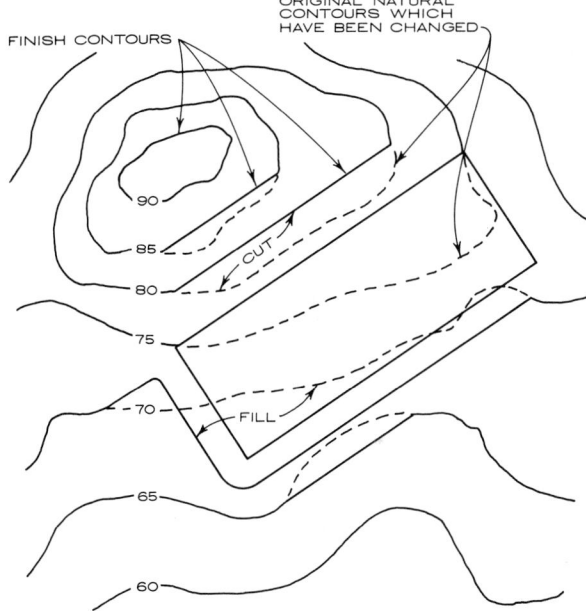

TO FIND THE VOLUME OF CUT AND FILL DIRECTLY FROM THE CONTOUR PLAN

1. Draw "finish" and "original" contours on same contour map.

2. Measure the differential areas between new and old contours of each contour and enter in columns according to whether cut or fill.

3. Add up each column and multiply by the contour interval to determine the volume in cubic feet.

EXAMPLE

CONTOUR	CUT		FILL	
85		300		
80		960		
75	2,460 − 2 =	1,230	3,800 − 2 =	1,900
70		20		2,200
		9,200		6,800
		x5		x5
TOTALS		46,000 cu. ft.		34,000 cu. ft.

NOTE

1. Where a cut or fill ends directly on a contour level use $1/2$ value.

2. The closer the contour interval, the greater the accuracy.

This method is more rapid than the sectioning method, and is sufficiently accurate for simple estimating purposes and for balancing of cut and fill.

GRAPHIC METHODS

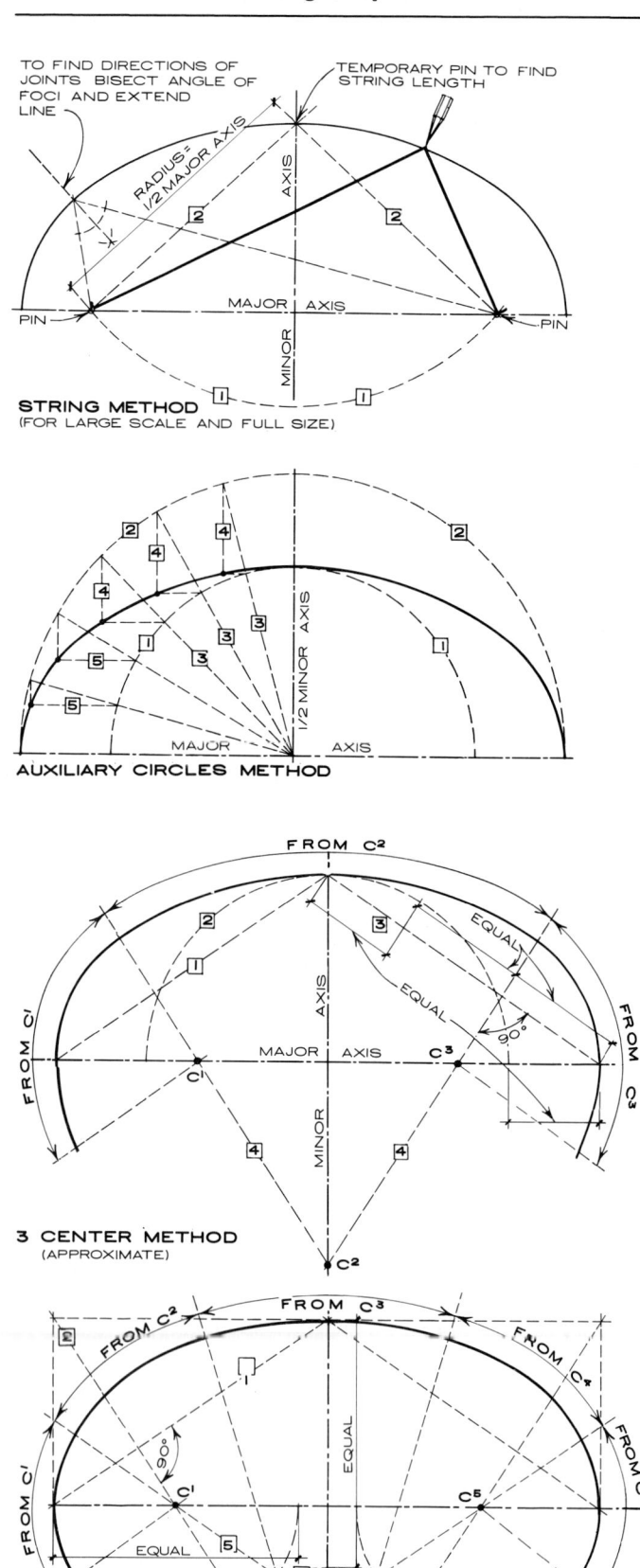

TO FIND DIRECTIONS OF JOINTS BISECT ANGLE OF FOCI AND EXTEND LINE

TEMPORARY PIN TO FIND STRING LENGTH

RADIUS = 1/2 MAJOR AXIS

AXIS

PIN   MAJOR AXIS   PIN

MINOR AXIS

STRING METHOD
(FOR LARGE SCALE AND FULL SIZE)

AUXILIARY CIRCLES METHOD

1/2 MINOR AXIS

MAJOR AXIS

3 CENTER METHOD
(APPROXIMATE)

FROM C²

AXIS

MAJOR AXIS   C³

EQUAL

EQUAL

90°

FROM C¹

FROM C³

MINOR

C²

5 CENTER METHOD

FROM C³

FROM C²   FROM C⁴

FROM C¹   FROM C⁵

90°

C¹   C⁵

EQUAL

C²   C⁴

C³

3 and 5 center methods are not true ellipses, but only approximations which are useful for small scale drawings.

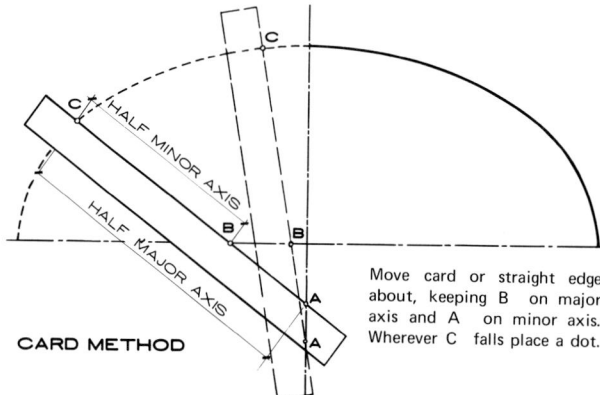

C

C   HALF MINOR AXIS

B   B

HALF MAJOR AXIS

A

A

CARD METHOD

Move card or straight edge about, keeping B on major axis and A on minor axis. Wherever C falls place a dot.

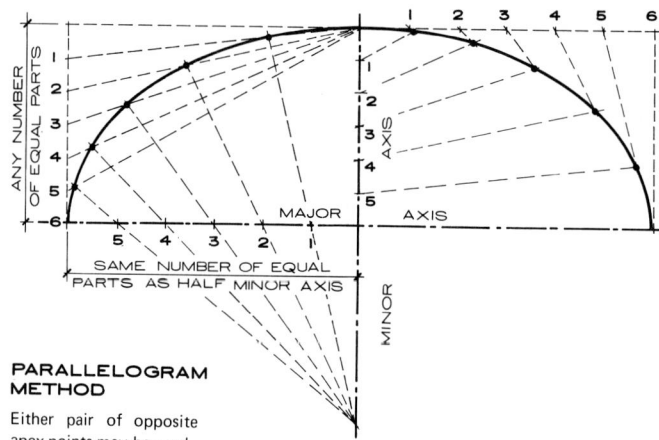

ANY NUMBER   OF EQUAL PARTS

1   2   3   4   5   6

C

1
2
3
4
5

AXIS

MAJOR   AXIS

5   4   3   2

SAME NUMBER OF EQUAL
PARTS AS HALF MINOR AXIS

MINOR

PARALLELOGRAM METHOD

Either pair of opposite apex points may be used.

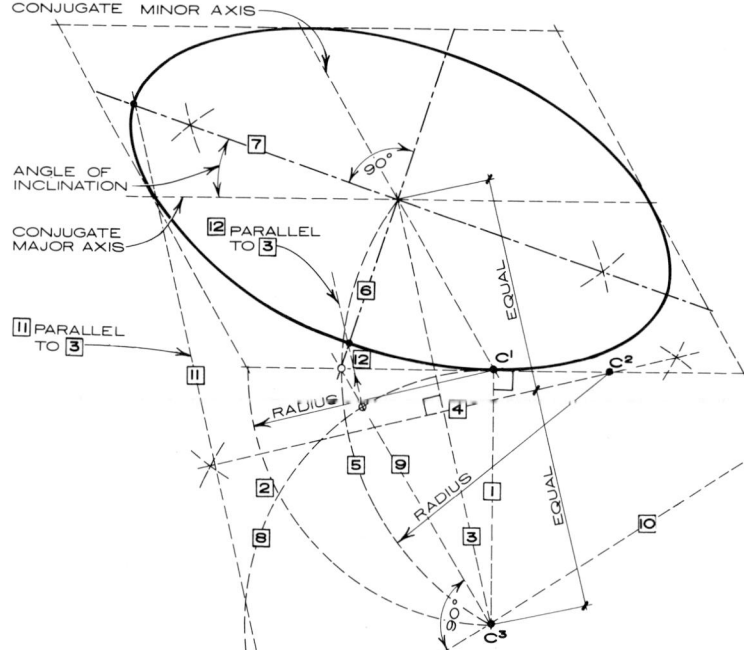

CONJUGATE MINOR AXIS

ANGLE OF INCLINATION

CONJUGATE MAJOR AXIS

90°

7

12 PARALLEL TO 3

6

11 PARALLEL TO 3

12

RADIUS

C¹   C²

EQUAL

4

5   9

2   RADIUS   1

8   3   10

90°

C³

METHOD FOR FINDING THE ANGLE OF INCLINATION AND THEN THE TRUE LENGTHS OF THE MAJOR & MINOR AXES OF AN ELLIPSE TO BE INSCRIBED WITHIN A PARALLELOGRAM

NOTE

1. Using the conjugate axes, the ellipse can be drawn directly by using the parallelogram method.

2. Using the true lengths of the axes, the ellipse may be drawn with any one of the methods illustrated on this page.

 GRAPHIC METHODS

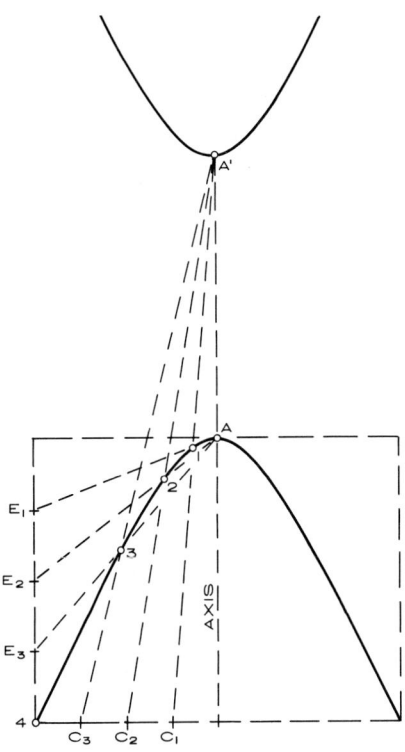

HYPERBOLA
PARALLELOGRAM METHOD
GIVEN:

Axis, two apexes (A and A') and a chord.

1. Draw surrounding parallelogram.
2. Divide chord in whole number of equal spaces (C_1, C_2, C_3, etc.).
3. Divide edge of parallelogram into same integral number of equal spaces (E_1, E_2, E_3, etc.).
4. Join A to points E on edge; join A' to points C on chord. Intersection of these rays are points on curve.

This method can be used equally well for any type of orthogonal or perspective projection, as shown by example of ellipse.

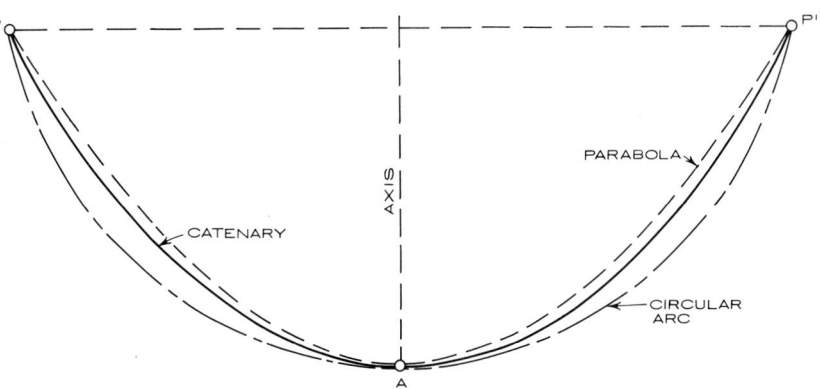

CATENARY

A catenary curve lies between a parabola and a circular arc drawn through the same three points, but is closer to the parabola. The catenary is not a conic section. The easiest method of drawing it is to tilt the drafting board and hang a very fine chain on it, and then prick guide points through the links of the chain.

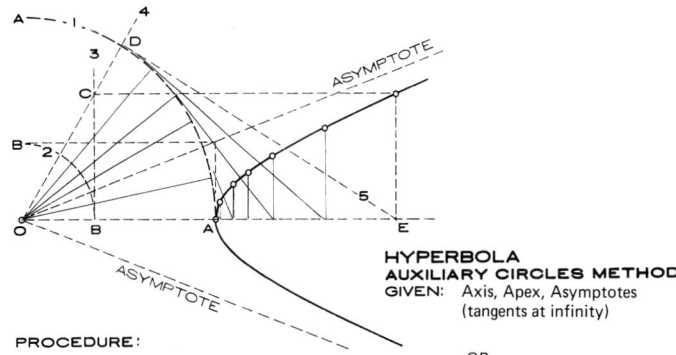

HYPERBOLA
AUXILIARY CIRCLES METHOD
GIVEN: Axis, Apex, Asymptotes
(tangents at infinity)

PROCEDURE:

1. Draw auxiliary circles with OB and OA as radii: note $\dfrac{OB}{OA}$ = slope of asymptote.
2. Erect perpendicular 3 where circle 2 intersects axis.
3. Draw any line 4 through 0, intersecting circle 1 at B and line 3 at C.
4. Draw line 5 through C parallel to axis.
5. Draw tangent 6 at D, intersecting axis at E.
6. Erect perpendicular 7 at E, intersecting 5 at P, a point on hyperbola.

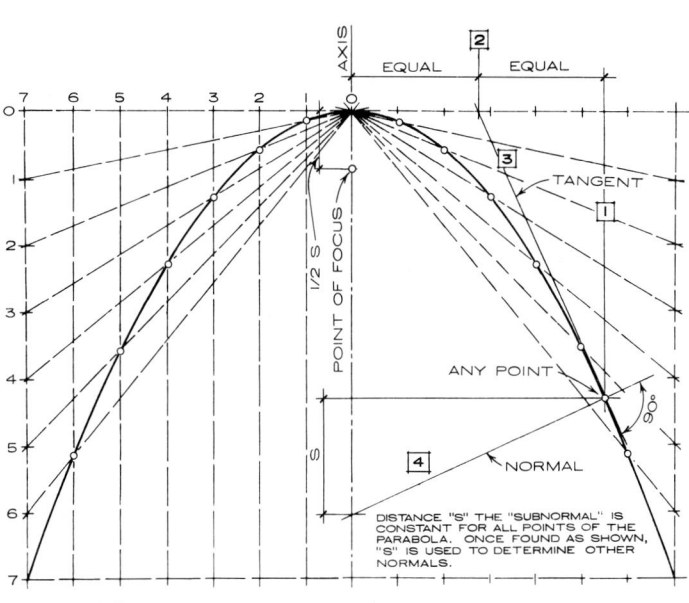

PARABOLA
PARALLELOGRAM METHOD

This method is comparable to the "Parallelogram Method" shown for the hyperbola above and the ellipse on previous page. The other apex 'A' is at infinity.

H. Seymour Howard, Jr.; Oyster Bay, New York

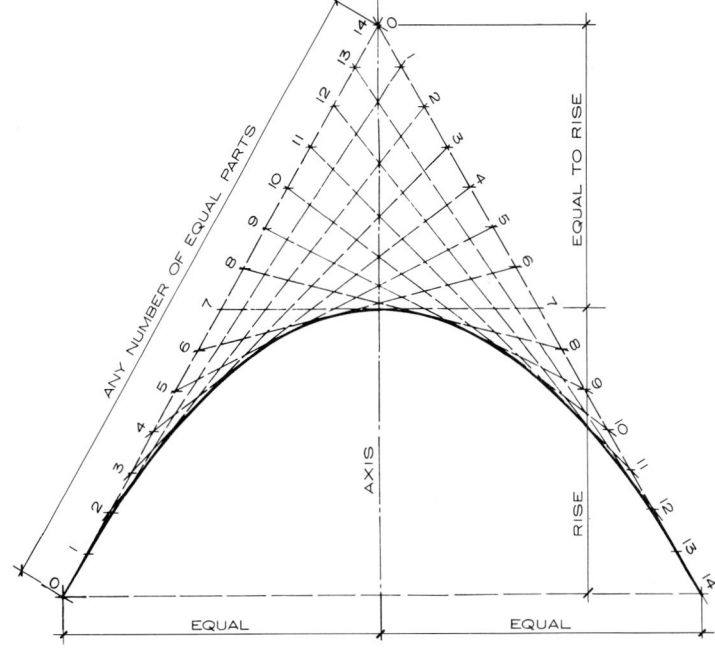

PARABOLA
ENVELOPE OF TANGENTS

This method does not give points on the curve, but a series of tangents within which the parabola can be drawn.

GRAPHIC METHODS

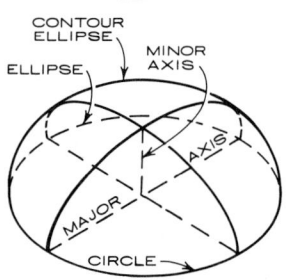

OBLATE SPHEROID

An ellipse rotated about its minor axis.

NOTES

1. The dome shapes shown above are SURFACES OF POSITIVE CUR-VATURE, that is, the centers of both principal radii of curvature are on the same side of the surface.

2. SURFACES OF NEGATIVE CURVATURE (saddle shapes) such as those shown below, are surfaces in which the centers of the two principal radii of curvature are on opposite sides of the surface.

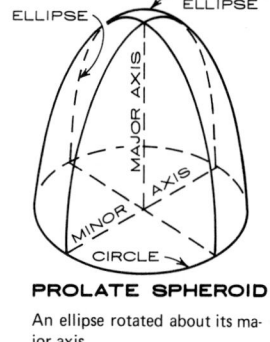

PROLATE SPHEROID

An ellipse rotated about its major axis.

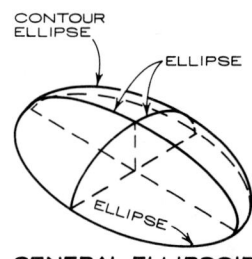

PARABOLOID OF REVOLUTION

A parabola rotated about its axis.

The elliptic paraboloid is similar, but its plan is an ellipse instead of circle, and vertical sections are varying parabolas.

GENERAL ELLIPSOID

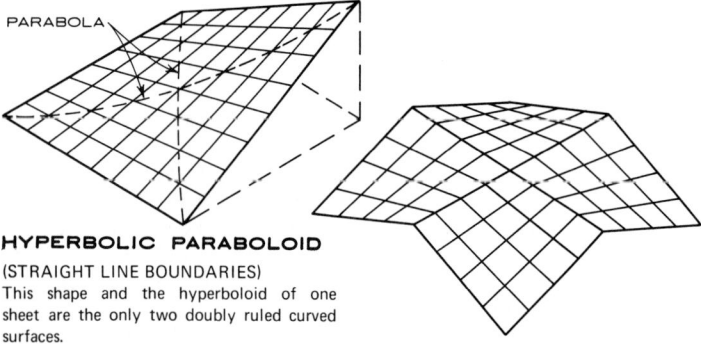

HYPERBOLIC PARABOLOID

(STRAIGHT LINE BOUNDARIES)

This shape and the hyperboloid of one sheet are the only two doubly ruled curved surfaces.

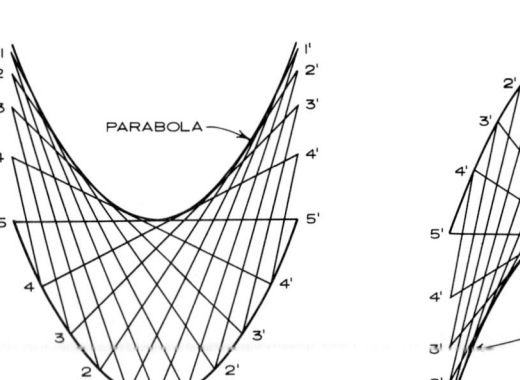

SECTION A-A

SECTION B-B

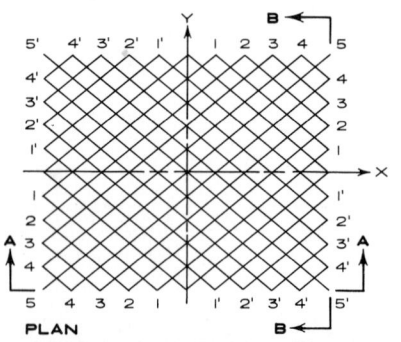

PLAN

HYPERBOLIC PARABOLOID

(PARABOLA BOUNDATIONS)

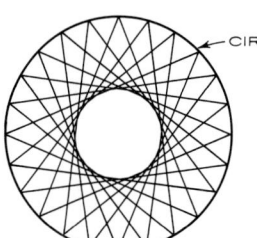

PROJECTION

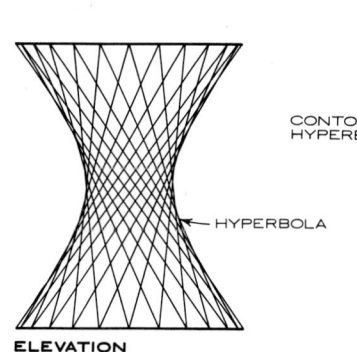

ELEVATION

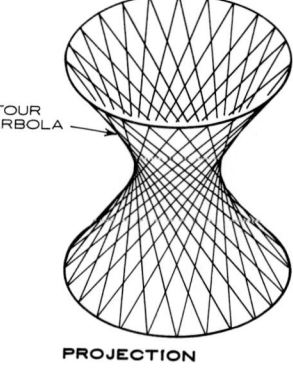

PROJECTION

PLAN

HYPERBOLOID OF REVOLUTION

(OR HYPERBOLOID OF ONE SHEET)

NOTE

This shape is a doubly ruled surface, which can also be drawn with ellipses as plan sections instead of the circles shown.

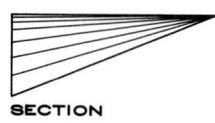

SECTION

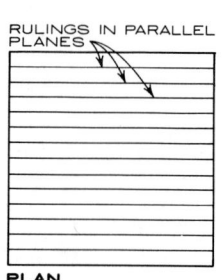

PLAN

CONOID

(SINGLY RULED SURFACE)

ELEVATION

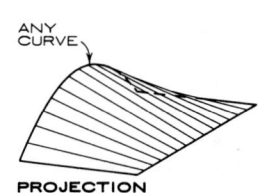

PROJECTION

 GRAPHIC METHODS

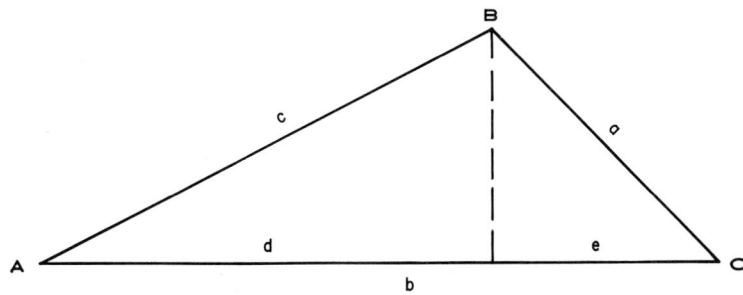

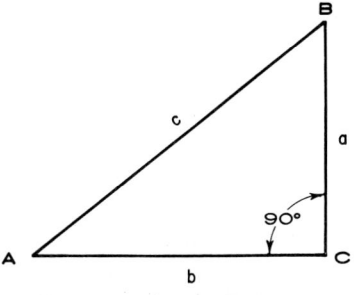

OBLIQUE TRIANGLES

FIND	GIVEN	SOLUTION	FIND	GIVEN	SOLUTION
a	A B b	$b \sin A \div \sin B$	A	a b c s	$\sin \frac{1}{2} A = \sqrt{(s-b)(s-c) \div bc}$
	A B c	$c \sin A \div \sin (A+B)$			$\cos \frac{1}{2} A = \sqrt{s(s-a) \div bc}$
	A C b	$b \sin A \div \sin (A+C)$			$\tan \frac{1}{2} A = \sqrt{(s-b)(s-c) \div s(s-a)}$
	A C c	$c \sin A \div \sin C$		B a b	$\sin A = a \sin B \div b$
	B C b	$b \sin (B+C) \div \sin B$		B a c	$\frac{1}{2}(A+C) + \frac{1}{2}(A-C)$
	B C c	$c \sin (B+C) \div \sin C$		C a b	$\frac{1}{2}(A+B) + \frac{1}{2}(A-B)$
	A b c	$\sqrt{b^2 + c^2 - 2bc \cdot \cos A}$		C a c	$\sin A = a \sin C \div c$
b	A B a	$a \sin B \div \sin A$	B	a b c s	$\sin \frac{1}{2} B = \sqrt{(s-a)(s-c) \div ac}$
	A B c	$c \sin B \div \sin (A+B)$			$\cos \frac{1}{2} B = \sqrt{s(s-b) \div ac}$
	A C a	$a \sin (A+C) \div \sin A$			$\tan \frac{1}{2} B = \sqrt{(s-a)(s-c) \div s(s-b)}$
	A C c	$c \sin (A+C) \div \sin C$		A a b	$\sin B = b \sin A \div a$
	B C a	$a \sin B \div \sin (B+C)$		A b c	$\frac{1}{2}(B+C) + \frac{1}{2}(B-C)$
	B C c	$c \sin B \div \sin C$		C a b	$\frac{1}{2}(A+B) - \frac{1}{2}(A-B)$
	B a c	$\sqrt{a^2 + c^2 - 2ac \cdot \cos B}$		C a c	$\sin B = b \sin C \div c$
c	A B a	$a \sin (A+B) \div \sin A$	C	a b c s	$\sin \frac{1}{2} C = \sqrt{(s-a)(s-b) \div ab}$
	A B b	$b \sin (A+B) \div \sin B$			$\cos \frac{1}{2} C = \sqrt{s(s-c) \div ab}$
	A C a	$a \sin C \div \sin A$			$\tan \frac{1}{2} C = \sqrt{(s-a)(s-b) \div s(s-c)}$
	A C b	$b \sin C \div \sin (A+C)$		A a c	$\sin C = c \sin A \div a$
	B C a	$a \sin C \div \sin (B+C)$		A b c	$\frac{1}{2}(B+C) - \frac{1}{2}(B-C)$
	B C b	$b \sin C \div \sin B$		B a c	$\frac{1}{2}(A+C) - \frac{1}{2}(A-C)$
	C a b	$\sqrt{a^2 + b^2 - 2ab \cdot \cos C}$		B b c	$\sin C = c \sin B \div b$
$\frac{1}{2}(B+C)$	A b c	$90° - \frac{1}{2} A$	AREA	a b c	$\sqrt{s(s-a)(s-b)(s-c)}$
$\frac{1}{2}(B-C)$		$\tan = [(b-c)\tan(90°-\frac{1}{2}A)] \div (b+c)$		C a b	$\frac{1}{2} ab \sin C$
$\frac{1}{2}(A+C)$	B a c	$90° - \frac{1}{2} B$	s	a b c	$(a+b+c) \div 2$
$\frac{1}{2}(A-C)$		$\tan = [(a-c)\tan(90°-\frac{1}{2}B)] \div (a+c)$	d	a b c s	$(b^2 + c^2 - a^2) \div 2b$
$\frac{1}{2}(A+B)$	C a b	$90° - \frac{1}{2} C$	e	a b c s	$(a^2 + b^2 - c^2) \div 2b$
$\frac{1}{2}(A-B)$		$\tan = [(a-b)\tan(90°-\frac{1}{2}C)] \div (a+b)$			

RIGHT TRIANGLES

FIND	GIVEN	SOLUTION
A	a b	$\tan A = a \div b$
	a c	$\sin A = a \div c$
	b c	$\cos A = b \div c$
B	a b	$\tan B = b \div a$
	a c	$\cos B = a \div c$
	b c	$\sin B = b \div c$
a	A b	$b \tan A$
	A c	$c \sin A$
b	A a	$a \div \tan A$
	A c	$c \cos A$
c	A a	$a \div \sin A$
	A b	$b \div \cos A$
AREA	a b	$ab \div 2$

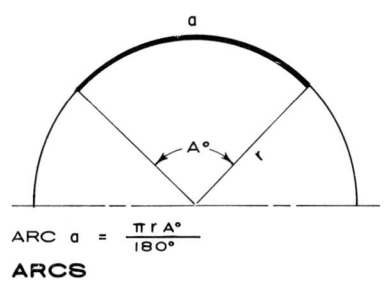

$$\text{ARC } a = \frac{\pi r A°}{180°}$$

ARCS

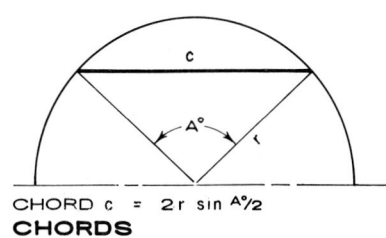

$$\text{CHORD } c = 2r \sin \frac{A°}{2}$$

CHORDS

MATHEMATICAL DATA   A

NATURAL SINES

ANGLE	0′	10′	20′	30′	40′	50′	60′	
0°	0.00000	0.00291	0.00582	0.00873	0.01164	0.01454	0.01745	89°
1	0.01745	0.02036	0.02327	0.02618	0.02908	0.03199	0.03490	88
2	0.03490	0.03781	0.04071	0.04362	0.04653	0.04943	0.05234	87
3	0.05234	0.05524	0.05814	0.06105	0.06395	0.06685	0.06976	86
4	0.06976	0.07266	0.07556	0.07846	0.08136	0.08426	0.08716	85
5	0.08716	0.09005	0.09295	0.09585	0.09874	0.10164	0.10453	84
6	0.10453	0.10742	0.11031	0.11320	0.11609	0.11898	0.12187	83
7	0.12187	0.12476	0.12764	0.13053	0.13341	0.13629	0.13917	82
8	0.13917	0.14205	0.14493	0.14781	0.15069	0.15356	0.15643	81
9	0.15643	0.15931	0.16218	0.16505	0.16792	0.17078	0.17365	80
10	0.17365	0.17651	0.17937	0.18224	0.18509	0.18795	0.19081	79
11	0.19081	0.19366	0.19652	0.19937	0.20222	0.20507	0.20791	78
12	0.20791	0.21076	0.21360	0.21644	0.21928	0.22212	0.22495	77
13	0.22495	0.22778	0.23062	0.23345	0.23627	0.23910	0.24192	76
14	0.24192	0.24474	0.24756	0.25038	0.25320	0.25601	0.25882	75
15	0.25882	0.26163	0.26443	0.26724	0.27004	0.27284	0.27564	74
16	0.27564	0.27843	0.28123	0.28402	0.28680	0.28959	0.29237	73
17	0.29237	0.29515	0.29793	0.30071	0.30348	0.30625	0.30902	72
18	0.30902	0.31178	0.31454	0.31730	0.32006	0.32282	0.32557	71
19	0.32557	0.32832	0.33106	0.33381	0.33655	0.33929	0.34202	70
20	0.34202	0.34475	0.34748	0.35021	0.35293	0.35565	0.35837	69
21	0.35837	0.36108	0.36379	0.36650	0.36921	0.37191	0.37461	68
22	0.37461	0.37730	0.37999	0.38268	0.38537	0.38805	0.39073	67
23	0.39073	0.39341	0.39608	0.39875	0.40141	0.40408	0.40674	66
24	0.40674	0.40939	0.41204	0.41469	0.41734	0.41998	0.42262	65
25	0.42262	0.42525	0.42788	0.43051	0.43313	0.43575	0.43837	64
26	0.43837	0.44098	0.44359	0.44620	0.44880	0.45140	0.45399	63
27	0.45399	0.45658	0.45917	0.46175	0.46433	0.46690	0.46947	62
28	0.46947	0.47204	0.47460	0.47716	0.47971	0.48226	0.48481	61
29	0.48481	0.48735	0.48989	0.49242	0.49495	0.49748	0.50000	60
30	0.50000	0.50252	0.50503	0.50754	0.51004	0.51254	0.51504	59
31	0.51504	0.51753	0.52002	0.52250	0.52498	0.52745	0.52992	58
32	0.52992	0.53238	0.53484	0.53730	0.53975	0.54220	0.54464	57
33	0.54464	0.54708	0.54951	0.55194	0.55436	0.55678	0.55919	56
34	0.55919	0.56160	0.56401	0.56641	0.56880	0.57119	0.57358	55
35	0.57358	0.57596	0.57833	0.58070	0.58307	0.58543	0.58779	54
36	0.58779	0.59014	0.59248	0.59482	0.59716	0.59949	0.60182	53
37	0.60182	0.60414	0.60645	0.60876	0.61107	0.61337	0.61566	52
38	0.61566	0.61795	0.62024	0.62251	0.62479	0.62706	0.62932	51
39	0.62932	0.63158	0.63383	0.63608	0.63832	0.64056	0.64279	50
40	0.64279	0.64501	0.64723	0.64945	0.65166	0.65386	0.65606	49
41	0.65606	0.65825	0.66044	0.66262	0.66480	0.66697	0.66913	48
42	0.66913	0.67129	0.67344	0.67559	0.67773	0.67987	0.68200	47
43	0.68200	0.68412	0.68624	0.68835	0.69046	0.69256	0.69466	46
44°	0.69466	0.69675	0.69883	0.70091	0.70298	0.70505	0.70711	45°
	60′	50′	40′	30′	20′	10′	0′	ANGLE

NATURAL COSINES

NATURAL TANGENTS

ANGLE	0′	10′	20′	30′	40′	50′	60′	
0°	0.00000	0.00291	0.00582	0.00873	0.01164	0.01455	0.01746	89°
1	0.01746	0.02036	0.02328	0.02619	0.02910	0.03201	0.03492	88
2	0.03492	0.03783	0.04075	0.04366	0.04658	0.04949	0.05241	87
3	0.05241	0.05533	0.05824	0.06116	0.06408	0.06700	0.06993	86
4	0.06993	0.07285	0.07578	0.07870	0.08163	0.08456	0.08749	85
5	0.08749	0.09042	0.09335	0.09629	0.09923	0.10216	0.10510	84
6	0.10510	0.10805	0.11099	0.11394	0.11688	0.11983	0.12278	83
7	0.12278	0.12574	0.12869	0.13165	0.13461	0.13758	0.14054	82
8	0.14054	0.14351	0.14648	0.14945	0.15243	0.15540	0.15838	81
9	0.15838	0.16137	0.16435	0.16734	0.17033	0.17333	0.17633	80
10	0.17633	0.17933	0.18233	0.18534	0.18835	0.19136	0.19438	79
11	0.19438	0.19740	0.20042	0.20345	0.20648	0.20952	0.21256	78
12	0.21256	0.21560	0.21864	0.22169	0.22475	0.22781	0.23087	77
13	0.23087	0.23393	0.23700	0.24008	0.24316	0.24624	0.24933	76
14	0.24933	0.25242	0.25552	0.25862	0.26172	0.26483	0.26795	75
15	0.26795	0.27107	0.27419	0.27732	0.28046	0.28360	0.28675	74
16	0.28675	0.28990	0.29305	0.29621	0.29938	0.30255	0.30573	73
17	0.30573	0.30891	0.31210	0.31530	0.31850	0.32171	0.32492	72
18	0.32492	0.32814	0.33136	0.33460	0.33783	0.34108	0.34433	71
19	0.34433	0.34758	0.35085	0.35412	0.35740	0.36068	0.36397	70
20	0.36397	0.36727	0.37057	0.37388	0.37720	0.38053	0.38386	69
21	0.38386	0.38721	0.39055	0.39391	0.39727	0.40065	0.40403	68
22	0.40403	0.40741	0.41081	0.41421	0.41763	0.42105	0.42447	67
23	0.42447	0.42791	0.43136	0.43481	0.43828	0.44175	0.44523	66
24	0.44523	0.44872	0.45222	0.45573	0.45924	0.46277	0.46631	65
25	0.46631	0.46985	0.47341	0.47698	0.48055	0.48414	0.48773	64
26	0.48773	0.49134	0.49495	0.49858	0.50222	0.50587	0.50953	63
27	0.50953	0.51320	0.51688	0.52057	0.52427	0.52798	0.53171	62
28	0.53171	0.53545	0.53920	0.54296	0.54673	0.55051	0.55431	61
29	0.55431	0.55812	0.56194	0.56577	0.56962	0.57348	0.57735	60
30	0.57735	0.58124	0.58513	0.58905	0.59297	0.59691	0.60086	59
31	0.60086	0.60483	0.60881	0.61280	0.61681	0.62083	0.62487	58
32	0.62487	0.62892	0.63299	0.63707	0.64117	0.64528	0.64941	57
33	0.64941	0.65355	0.65771	0.66189	0.66608	0.67028	0.67451	56
34	0.67451	0.67875	0.68301	0.68728	0.69157	0.69588	0.70021	55
35	0.70021	0.70455	0.70891	0.71329	0.71769	0.72211	0.72654	54
36	0.72654	0.73100	0.73547	0.73996	0.74447	0.74900	0.75355	53
37	0.75355	0.75812	0.76272	0.76733	0.77196	0.77661	0.78129	52
38	0.78129	0.78598	0.79070	0.79544	0.80020	0.80498	0.80978	51
39	0.80978	0.81461	0.81946	0.82434	0.82923	0.83415	0.83910	50
40	0.83910	0.84407	0.84906	0.85408	0.85912	0.86419	0.86929	49
41	0.86929	0.87441	0.87955	0.88473	0.88992	0.89515	0.90040	48
42	0.90040	0.90569	0.91099	0.91633	0.92170	0.92709	0.93252	47
43	0.93252	0.93797	0.94345	0.94896	0.95451	0.96008	0.96569	46
44°	0.96569	0.97133	0.97700	0.98270	0.98843	0.99420	1.00000	45°
	60′	50′	40′	30′	20′	10′	0′	ANGLE

NATURAL COTANGENTS

NATURAL SINES

ANGLE	0′	10′	20′	30′	40′	50′	60′	
45°	0.70711	0.70916	0.71121	0.71325	0.71529	0.71732	0.71934	44°
46	0.71934	0.72136	0.72337	0.72537	0.72737	0.72937	0.73135	43
47	0.73135	0.73333	0.73531	0.73728	0.73924	0.74120	0.74314	42
48	0.74314	0.74509	0.74703	0.74896	0.75088	0.75280	0.75471	41
49	0.75471	0.75661	0.75851	0.76041	0.76229	0.76417	0.76604	40
50	0.76604	0.76791	0.76977	0.77162	0.77347	0.77531	0.77715	39
51	0.77715	0.77897	0.78079	0.78261	0.78442	0.78622	0.78801	38
52	0.78801	0.78980	0.79158	0.79335	0.79512	0.79688	0.79864	37
53	0.79864	0.80038	0.80212	0.80386	0.80558	0.80730	0.80902	36
54	0.80902	0.81072	0.81242	0.81412	0.81580	0.81748	0.81915	35
55	0.81915	0.82082	0.82248	0.82413	0.82577	0.82741	0.82904	34
56	0.82904	0.83066	0.83228	0.83389	0.83549	0.83708	0.83867	33
57	0.83867	0.84025	0.84182	0.84339	0.84495	0.84650	0.84805	32
58	0.84805	0.84959	0.85112	0.85264	0.85416	0.85567	0.85717	31
59	0.85717	0.85866	0.86015	0.86163	0.86310	0.86457	0.86603	30
60	0.86603	0.86748	0.86892	0.87036	0.87178	0.87321	0.87462	29
61	0.87462	0.87603	0.87743	0.87882	0.88020	0.88158	0.88295	28
62	0.88295	0.88431	0.88566	0.88701	0.88835	0.88968	0.89101	27
63	0.89101	0.89232	0.89363	0.89493	0.89623	0.89752	0.89879	26
64	0.89879	0.90007	0.90133	0.90259	0.90383	0.90507	0.90631	25
65	0.90631	0.90753	0.90875	0.90996	0.91116	0.91236	0.91355	24
66	0.91355	0.91472	0.91590	0.91706	0.91822	0.91936	0.92050	23
67	0.92050	0.92164	0.92276	0.92388	0.92499	0.92609	0.92718	22
68	0.92718	0.92827	0.92935	0.93042	0.93148	0.93253	0.93358	21
69	0.93358	0.93462	0.93565	0.93667	0.93769	0.93869	0.93969	20
70	0.93969	0.94068	0.94167	0.94264	0.94361	0.94457	0.94552	19
71	0.94552	0.94646	0.94740	0.94832	0.94924	0.95015	0.95106	18
72	0.95106	0.95195	0.95284	0.95372	0.95459	0.95545	0.95630	17
73	0.95630	0.95715	0.95799	0.95882	0.95964	0.96046	0.96126	16
74	0.96126	0.96206	0.96285	0.96363	0.96440	0.96517	0.96593	15
75	0.96593	0.96667	0.96742	0.96815	0.96887	0.96959	0.97030	14
76	0.97030	0.97100	0.97169	0.97237	0.97304	0.97371	0.97437	13
77	0.97437	0.97502	0.97566	0.97630	0.97692	0.97754	0.97815	12
78	0.97815	0.97875	0.97934	0.97992	0.98050	0.98107	0.98163	11
79	0.98163	0.98218	0.98272	0.98325	0.98378	0.98430	0.98481	10
80	0.98481	0.98531	0.98580	0.98629	0.98676	0.98723	0.98769	9
81	0.98769	0.98814	0.98858	0.98902	0.98944	0.98986	0.99027	8
82	0.99027	0.99067	0.99106	0.99144	0.99182	0.99219	0.99255	7
83	0.99255	0.99290	0.99324	0.99357	0.99390	0.99421	0.99452	6
84	0.99452	0.99482	0.99511	0.99540	0.99567	0.99594	0.99619	5
85	0.99619	0.99644	0.99668	0.99692	0.99714	0.99736	0.99756	4
86	0.99756	0.99776	0.99795	0.99813	0.99831	0.99847	0.99863	3
87	0.99863	0.99878	0.99892	0.99905	0.99917	0.99929	0.99939	2
88	0.99939	0.99949	0.99958	0.99966	0.99973	0.99979	0.99985	1
89°	0.99985	0.99989	0.99993	0.99996	0.99998	1.00000	1.00000	0°
	60′	50′	40′	30′	20′	10′	0′	ANGLE

NATURAL COSINES

NATURAL TANGENTS

ANGLE	0′	10′	20′	30′	40′	50′	60′	
45°	1.00000	1.00583	1.01170	1.01761	1.02355	1.02952	1.03553	44°
46	1.03553	1.04158	1.04766	1.05378	1.05994	1.06613	1.07237	43
47	1.07237	1.07864	1.08496	1.09131	1.09770	1.10414	1.11061	42
48	1.11061	1.11713	1.12369	1.13029	1.13694	1.14363	1.15037	41
49	1.15037	1.15715	1.16398	1.17085	1.17777	1.18474	1.19175	40
50	1.19175	1.19882	1.20593	1.21310	1.22031	1.22758	1.23490	39
51	1.23490	1.24227	1.24969	1.25717	1.26471	1.27230	1.27994	38
52	1.27994	1.28764	1.29541	1.30323	1.31110	1.31904	1.32704	37
53	1.32704	1.33511	1.34323	1.35142	1.35968	1.36800	1.37638	36
54	1.37638	1.38484	1.39336	1.40195	1.41061	1.41934	1.42815	35
55	1.42815	1.43703	1.44598	1.45501	1.46411	1.47330	1.48256	34
56	1.48256	1.49190	1.50133	1.51084	1.52043	1.53010	1.53987	33
57	1.53987	1.54972	1.55966	1.56969	1.57981	1.59002	1.60033	32
58	1.60033	1.61074	1.62125	1.63185	1.64256	1.65337	1.66428	31
59	1.66428	1.67530	1.68643	1.69766	1.70901	1.72047	1.73205	30
60	1.73205	1.74375	1.75556	1.76749	1.77955	1.79174	1.80405	29
61	1.80405	1.81649	1.82906	1.84177	1.85462	1.86760	1.88073	28
62	1.88073	1.89400	1.90741	1.92098	1.93470	1.94858	1.96261	27
63	1.96261	1.97681	1.99116	2.00569	2.02039	2.03526	2.05030	26
64	2.05030	2.06553	2.08094	2.09654	2.11233	2.12832	2.14451	25
65	2.14451	2.16090	2.17749	2.19430	2.21132	2.22857	2.24604	24
66	2.24604	2.26374	2.28167	2.29984	2.31826	2.33693	2.35585	23
67	2.35585	2.37504	2.39449	2.41421	2.43422	2.45451	2.47509	22
68	2.47509	2.49597	2.51715	2.53865	2.56046	2.58261	2.60509	21
69	2.60509	2.62791	2.65109	2.67462	2.69853	2.72281	2.74748	20
70	2.74748	2.77254	2.79802	2.82391	2.85023	2.87700	2.90421	19
71	2.90421	2.93189	2.96004	2.98869	3.01783	3.04749	3.07768	18
72	3.07768	3.10842	3.13972	3.17159	3.20406	3.23714	3.27085	17
73	3.27085	3.30521	3.34023	3.37594	3.41236	3.44951	3.48741	16
74	3.48741	3.52609	3.56557	3.60588	3.64705	3.68909	3.73205	15
75	3.73205	3.77595	3.82083	3.86671	3.91364	3.96165	4.01078	14
76	4.01078	4.06107	4.11256	4.16530	4.21933	4.27471	4.33148	13
77	4.33148	4.38969	4.44942	4.51071	4.57363	4.63825	4.70463	12
78	4.70463	4.77286	4.84300	4.91516	4.98940	5.06584	5.14455	11
79	5.14455	5.22566	5.30928	5.39552	5.48451	5.57638	5.67128	10
80	5.67128	5.76937	5.87080	5.97576	6.08444	6.19703	6.31375	9
81	6.31375	6.43484	6.56055	6.69116	6.82694	6.96823	7.11537	8
82	7.11537	7.26873	7.42871	7.59575	7.77035	7.95302	8.14435	7
83	8.14435	8.34496	8.55555	8.77689	9.00983	9.25530	9.51436	6
84	9.51436	9.78817	10.07803	10.38540	10.71191	11.05943	11.43005	5
85	11.43005	11.82617	12.25051	12.70621	13.19688	13.72674	14.30067	4
86	14.30067	14.92442	15.60478	16.34986	17.16934	18.07498	19.08114	3
87	19.08114	20.20555	21.47040	22.90377	24.54176	26.43160	28.63625	2
88	28.63625	31.24158	34.36777	38.18846	42.96408	49.10388	57.28996	1
89°	57.28996	68.75009	85.93979	114.58865	171.88540	343.77371	Infinite	0°
	60′	50′	40′	30′	20′	10′	0′	ANGLE

NATURAL COTANGENTS

A MATHEMATICAL DATA

NATURAL SECANTS

ANGLE	0′	10′	20′	30′	40′	50′	60′	
0°	1.00000	1.00001	1.00002	1.00004	1.00007	1.00011	1.00015	89°
1	1.00015	1.00021	1.00027	1.00034	1.00042	1.00051	1.00061	88
2	1.00061	1.00072	1.00083	1.00095	1.00108	1.00122	1.00137	87
3	1.00137	1.00153	1.00169	1.00187	1.00205	1.00224	1.00244	86
4	1.00244	1.00265	1.00287	1.00309	1.00333	1.00357	1.00382	85
5	1.00382	1.00408	1.00435	1.00463	1.00491	1.00521	1.00551	84
6	1.00551	1.00582	1.00614	1.00647	1.00681	1.00715	1.00751	83
7	1.00751	1.00787	1.00825	1.00863	1.00902	1.00942	1.00983	82
8	1.00983	1.01024	1.01067	1.01111	1.01155	1.01200	1.01247	81
9	1.01247	1.01294	1.01342	1.01391	1.01440	1.10491	1.01543	80
10	1.01543	1.01595	1.01649	1.01703	1.01758	1.01815	1.01872	79
11	1.01872	1.01930	1.01989	1.02049	1.02110	1.02171	1.02234	78
12	1.02234	1.02298	1.02362	1.02428	1.02494	1.02562	1.02630	77
13	1.02630	1.02700	1.02770	1.02842	1.02914	1.02987	1.03061	76
14	1.03061	1.03137	1.03213	1.03290	1.03368	1.03447	1.03528	75
15	1.03528	1.03609	1.03691	1.03774	1.03858	1.03944	1.04030	74
16	1.04030	1.04117	1.04206	1.04295	1.04385	1.04477	1.04569	73
17	1.04569	1.04663	1.04757	1.04853	1.04950	1.05047	1.05146	72
18	1.05146	1.05246	1.05347	1.05449	1.05552	1.05657	1.05762	71
19	1.05762	1.05869	1.05976	1.06085	1.06195	1.06306	1.06418	70
20	1.06418	1.06531	1.06645	1.06761	1.06878	1.06995	1.07115	69
21	1.07115	1.07235	1.07356	1.07479	1.07602	1.07727	1.07853	68
22	1.07853	1.07981	1.08109	1.08239	1.08370	1.08503	1.08636	67
23	1.08636	1.08771	1.08907	1.09044	1.09183	1.09323	1.09464	66
24	1.09464	1.09606	1.09750	1.09895	1.10041	1.10189	1.10338	65
25	1.10338	1.10488	1.10640	1.10793	1.10947	1.11103	1.11260	64
26	1.11260	1.11419	1.11579	1.11740	1.11903	1.12067	1.12233	63
27	1.12233	1.12400	1.12568	1.12738	1.12910	1.13083	1.13257	62
28	1.13257	1.13433	1.13610	1.13789	1.13970	1.14152	1.14335	61
29	1.14335	1.14521	1.14707	1.14896	1.15085	1.15277	1.15470	60
30	1.15470	1.15665	1.15861	1.16059	1.16259	1.16460	1.16663	59
31	1.16663	1.16868	1.17075	1.17283	1.17493	1.17704	1.17918	58
32	1.17918	1.18133	1.18350	1.18569	1.18790	1.19012	1.19236	57
33	1.19236	1.19463	1.19691	1.19920	1.20152	1.20386	1.20622	56
34	1.20622	1.20859	1.21099	1.21341	1.21584	1.21830	1.22077	55
35	1.22077	1.22327	1.22579	1.22833	1.23089	1.23347	1.23607	54
36	1.23607	1.23869	1.24134	1.24400	1.24669	1.24940	1.25214	53
37	1.25214	1.25489	1.25767	1.26047	1.26330	1.26615	1.26902	52
38	1.26902	1.27191	1.27483	1.27778	1.28075	1.28374	1.28676	51
39	1.28676	1.28980	1.29287	1.29597	1.29909	1.30223	1.30541	50
40	1.30541	1.30861	1.31183	1.31509	1.31837	1.32168	1.32501	49
41	1.32501	1.32838	1.33177	1.33519	1.33864	1.34212	1.34563	48
42	1.34563	1.34917	1.35274	1.35634	1.35997	1.36363	1.36733	47
43	1.36733	1.37105	1.37481	1.37860	1.38242	1.38628	1.39016	46
44°	1.39016	1.39409	1.39804	1.40203	1.40606	1.41012	1.41421	45°
	60′	50′	40′	30′	20′	10′	0′	ANGLE

NATURAL COSECANTS

NATURAL SECANTS

ANGLE	0′	10′	20′	30′	40′	50′	60′	
45°	1.41421	1.41835	1.42251	1.42672	1.43096	1.43524	1.43956	44°
46	1.43956	1.44391	1.44831	1.45274	1.45721	1.46173	1.46628	43
47	1.46628	1.47087	1.47551	1.48019	1.48491	1.48967	1.49448	42
48	1.49448	1.49933	1.50422	1.50916	1.51415	1.51918	1.52425	41
49	1.52425	1.52938	1.53455	1.53977	1.54504	1.55036	1.55572	40
50	1.55572	1.56114	1.56661	1.57213	1.57771	1.58333	1.58902	39
51	1.58902	1.59475	1.60054	1.60639	1.61229	1.61825	1.62427	38
52	1.62427	1.63035	1.63648	1.64268	1.64894	1.65526	1.66164	37
53	1.66164	1.66809	1.67460	1.68117	1.68782	1.69452	1.70130	36
54	1.70130	1.70815	1.71506	1.72205	1.72911	1.73624	1.74345	35
55	1.74345	1.75073	1.75808	1.76552	1.77303	1.78062	1.78829	34
56	1.78829	1.79604	1.80388	1.81180	1.81981	1.82790	1.83608	33
57	1.83608	1.84435	1.85271	1.86116	1.86970	1.87834	1.88708	32
58	1.88708	1.89591	1.90485	1.91388	1.92302	1.93226	1.94160	31
59	1.94160	1.95106	1.96062	1.97029	1.98008	1.98998	2.00000	30
60	2.00000	2.01014	2.02039	2.03077	2.04128	2.05191	2.06267	29
61	2.06267	2.07356	2.08458	2.09574	2.10704	2.11847	2.13005	28
62	2.13005	2.14178	2.15366	2.16568	2.17786	2.19019	2.20269	27
63	2.20269	2.21535	2.22817	2.24116	2.25432	2.26766	2.28117	26
64	2.28117	2.29487	2.30875	2.32282	2.33708	2.35154	2.36620	25
65	2.36620	2.38107	2.39614	2.41142	2.42692	2.44264	2.45859	24
66	2.45859	2.47477	2.49119	2.50784	2.52474	2.54190	2.55930	23
67	2.55930	2.57698	2.59491	2.61313	2.63162	2.65040	2.66947	22
68	2.66947	2.68884	2.70851	2.72850	2.74881	2.76945	2.79043	21
69	2.79043	2.81175	2.83342	2.85545	2.87785	2.90063	2.92380	20
70	2.92380	2.94737	2.97135	2.99574	3.02057	3.04584	3.07155	19
71	3.07155	3.09774	3.12440	3.15155	3.17920	3.20737	3.23607	18
72	3.23607	3.26531	3.29512	3.32551	3.35649	3.38808	3.42030	17
73	3.42030	3.45317	3.48671	3.52094	3.55587	3.59154	3.62796	16
74	3.62796	3.66515	3.70315	3.74198	3.78166	3.82223	3.86370	15
75	3.86370	3.90613	3.94952	3.99393	4.03938	4.08591	4.13357	14
76	4.13357	4.18238	4.23239	4.28366	4.33622	4.39012	4.44541	13
77	4.44541	4.50216	4.56041	4.62023	4.68167	4.74482	4.80973	12
78	4.80973	4.87649	4.94517	5.01585	5.08863	5.16359	5.24084	11
79	5.24084	5.32049	5.40263	5.48740	5.57493	5.66533	5.75877	10
80	5.75877	5.85539	5.95536	6.05886	6.16607	6.27719	6.39245	9
81	6.39245	6.51208	6.63633	6.76547	6.89979	7.03962	7.18530	8
82	7.18530	7.33719	7.49571	7.66130	7.83443	8.01565	8.20551	7
83	8.20551	8.40466	8.61379	8.83367	9.06515	9.30917	9.56677	6
84	9.56677	9.83912	10.12752	10.43343	10.75849	11.10455	11.47371	5
85	11.47371	11.86837	12.29125	12.74550	13.23472	13.76312	14.33559	4
86	14.33559	14.95788	15.63679	16.38041	17.19843	18.10262	19.10732	3
87	19.10732	20.23028	21.49368	22.92559	24.56212	26.45051	28.65371	2
88	28.65371	31.25758	34.38232	38.20155	42.97571	49.11406	57.29869	1
89°	57.29869	68.75736	85.94561	114.59301	171.88831	343.77516	Infinite	0°
	60′	50′	40′	30′	20′	10′	0′	ANGLE

NATURAL COSECANTS

FUNCTIONS OF NUMBERS

NO.	SQUARE	CUBE	SQUARE ROOT	CUBE ROOT	LOGARITHM	1000 x RECIPROCAL	NO. = DIAMETER CIRCUM.	AREA
1	1	1	1.0000	1.0000	0.00000	1000.000	3.142	0.7854
2	4	8	1.4142	1.2599	0.30103	500.000	6.283	3.1416
3	9	27	1.7321	1.4422	0.47712	333.333	9.425	7.0686
4	16	64	2.0000	1.5874	0.60206	250.000	12.566	12.5664
5	25	125	2.2361	1.7100	0.69897	200.000	15.708	19.6350
6	36	216	2.4495	1.8171	0.77815	166.667	18.850	28.2743
7	49	343	2.6458	1.9129	0.84510	142.857	21.991	38.4845
8	64	512	2.8284	2.0000	0.90309	125.000	25.133	50.2655
9	81	729	3.0000	2.0801	0.95424	111.111	28.274	63.6173
10	100	1000	3.1623	2.1544	1.00000	100.000	31.416	78.5398
11	121	1331	3.3166	2.2240	1.04139	90.9091	34.558	95.0332
12	144	1728	3.4641	2.2894	1.07918	83.3333	37.699	113.097
13	169	2197	3.6056	2.3513	1.11394	76.9231	40.841	132.732
14	196	2744	3.7417	2.4101	1.14613	71.4286	43.982	153.938
15	225	3375	3.8730	2.4662	1.17609	66.6667	47.124	176.715
16	256	4096	4.0000	2.5198	1.20412	62.5000	50.265	201.062
17	289	4913	4.1231	2.5713	1.23045	58.8235	53.407	226.980
18	324	5832	4.2426	2.6207	1.25527	55.5556	56.549	254.469
19	361	6859	4.3589	2.6684	1.27875	52.6316	59.690	283.529
20	400	8000	4.4721	2.7144	1.30103	50.0000	62.832	314.159
21	441	9261	4.5826	2.7589	1.32222	47.6190	65.973	346.361
22	484	10648	4.6904	2.8020	1.34242	45.4545	69.115	380.133
23	529	12167	4.7958	2.8439	1.36173	43.4783	72.257	415.476
24	576	13824	4.8990	2.8845	1.38021	41.6667	75.398	452.389
25	625	15625	5.0000	2.9240	1.39794	40.0000	78.540	490.874
26	676	17576	5.0990	2.9625	1.41497	38.4615	81.681	530.929
27	729	19683	5.1962	3.0000	1.43136	37.0370	84.823	572.555
28	784	21952	5.2915	3.0366	1.44716	35.7143	87.965	615.752
29	841	24389	5.3852	3.0723	1.46240	34.4828	91.106	660.520
30	900	27000	5.4772	3.1072	1.47712	33.3333	94.248	706.858
31	961	29791	5.5678	3.1414	1.49136	32.2581	97.389	754.768
32	1024	32768	5.6569	3.1748	1.50515	31.2500	100.531	804.248
33	1089	35937	5.7446	3.2075	1.51851	30.3030	103.673	855.299
34	1156	39304	5.8310	3.2396	1.53148	29.4118	106.814	907.920
35	1225	42875	5.9161	3.2711	1.54407	28.5714	109.956	962.113
36	1296	46656	6.0000	3.3019	1.55630	27.7778	113.097	1017.88
37	1369	50653	6.0828	3.3322	1.56820	27.0270	116.239	1075.21
38	1444	54872	6.1644	3.3620	1.57978	26.3158	119.381	1134.11
39	1521	59319	6.2450	3.3912	1.59106	25.6410	122.522	1194.59
40	1600	64000	6.3246	3.4200	1.60206	25.0000	125.66	1256.64
41	1681	68921	6.4031	3.4482	1.61278	24.3902	128.81	1320.25
42	1764	74088	6.4807	3.4760	1.62325	23.8095	131.95	1385.44
43	1849	79507	6.5574	3.5034	1.63347	23.2558	135.09	1452.20
44	1936	85184	6.6332	3.5303	1.64345	22.7273	138.23	1520.53
45	2025	91125	6.7082	3.5569	1.65321	22.2222	141.37	1590.43

FUNCTIONS OF NUMBERS

NO.	SQUARE	CUBE	SQUARE ROOT	CUBE ROOT	LOGARITHM	1000 x RECIPROCAL	NO. = DIAMETER CIRCUM.	AREA
46	2116	97336	6.7823	3.5830	1.66276	21.7391	144.51	1661.90
47	2209	103823	6.8557	3.6088	1.67210	21.2766	147.65	1734.94
48	2304	110592	6.9282	3.6342	1.68124	20.8333	150.80	1809.56
49	2401	117649	7.0000	3.6593	1.69020	20.4082	153.94	1885.74
50	2500	125000	7.0711	3.6840	1.69897	20.0000	157.08	1963.50
51	2601	132651	7.1414	3.7084	1.70757	19.6078	160.22	2042.82
52	2704	140608	7.2111	3.7325	1.71600	19.2308	163.36	2123.72
53	2809	148877	7.2801	3.7563	1.72428	18.8679	166.50	2206.18
54	2916	157464	7.3485	3.7798	1.73239	18.5185	169.65	2290.22
55	3025	166375	7.4162	3.8030	1.74036	18.1818	172.79	2375.83
56	3136	175616	7.4833	3.8259	1.74819	17.8571	175.93	2463.01
57	3249	185193	7.5498	3.8485	1.75587	17.5439	179.07	2551.76
58	3364	195112	7.6158	3.8709	1.76343	17.2414	182.21	2642.08
59	3481	205379	7.6811	3.8930	1.77085	16.9492	185.35	2733.97
60	3600	216000	7.7460	3.9149	1.77815	16.6667	188.50	2827.43
61	3721	226981	7.8102	3.9365	1.78533	16.3934	191.64	2922.47
62	3844	238328	7.8740	3.9579	1.79239	16.1290	194.78	3019.07
63	3969	250047	7.9373	3.9791	1.79934	15.8730	197.92	3117.25
64	4096	262144	8.0000	4.0000	1.80618	15.6250	201.06	3216.99
65	4225	274625	8.0623	4.0207	1.81291	15.3846	204.20	3318.31
66	4356	287496	8.1240	4.0412	1.81954	15.1515	207.35	3421.19
67	4489	300763	8.1854	4.0615	1.82607	14.9254	210.49	3525.65
68	4624	314432	8.2462	4.0817	1.83251	14.7059	213.63	3631.68
69	4761	328509	8.3066	4.1016	1.83885	14.4928	216.77	3739.28
70	4900	343000	8.3666	4.1213	1.84510	14.2857	219.91	3848.45
71	5041	357911	8.4261	4.1408	1.85126	14.0845	223.05	3959.19
72	5184	373248	8.4853	4.1602	1.85733	13.8889	226.19	4071.50
73	5329	389017	8.5440	4.1793	1.86332	13.6986	229.34	4185.39
74	5476	405224	8.6023	4.1983	1.86923	13.5135	232.48	4300.84
75	5625	421875	8.6603	4.2172	1.87506	13.3333	235.62	4417.86
76	5776	438976	8.7178	4.2358	1.88081	13.1579	238.76	4536.46
77	5929	456533	8.7750	4.2543	1.88649	12.9870	241.90	4656.63
78	6084	474552	8.8318	4.2727	1.89209	12.8205	245.04	4778.36
79	6241	493039	8.8882	4.2908	1.89763	12.6582	248.19	4901.67
80	6400	512000	8.9443	4.3089	1.90309	12.5000	251.33	5026.55
81	6561	531441	9.0000	4.3267	1.90849	12.3457	254.47	5153.00
82	6724	551368	9.0554	4.3445	1.91381	12.1951	257.61	5281.02
83	6889	571787	9.1104	4.3621	1.91908	12.0482	260.75	5410.61
84	7056	592704	9.1652	4.3795	1.92428	11.9048	263.89	5541.77
85	7225	614125	9.2195	4.3968	1.92942	11.7647	267.04	5674.50
86	7396	636056	9.2736	4.4140	1.93450	11.6279	270.18	5808.80
87	7569	658503	9.3274	4.4310	1.93952	11.4943	273.32	5944.68
88	7744	681472	9.3808	4.4480	1.94448	11.3636	276.46	6082.12
89	7921	704969	9.4340	4.4647	1.94939	11.2360	279.60	6221.14
90	8100	729000	9.4868	4.4814	1.95424	11.1111	282.74	6361.73

MATHEMATICAL DATA A

DATA SOURCES

INDEX